Patterns of Economic Change by State and Area

INCOME, EMPLOYMENT, AND GROSS DOMESTIC PRODUCT

Eighth Edition

2021

Patterns of Economic Change by State and Area

INCOME, EMPLOYMENT, AND GROSS DOMESTIC PRODUCT

Eighth Edition

2021

EDITED BY HANNAH ANDERSON KROG

Lanham • Boulder • New York • London

Published by Bernan Press
An imprint of The Rowman & Littlefield Publishing Group, Inc.
4501 Forbes Boulevard, Suite 200, Lanham, Maryland 20706
www.rowman.com

86-90 Paul Street, London EC2A 4NE

ISBN 978-1-63671-038-9 (paperback)
ISBN 978-1-63671-039-6 (ebook)

♾™ The paper used in this publication meets the minimum requirements
of American National Standard for Information Sciences—Permanence of
Paper for Printed Library Materials, ANSI/NISO Z39.48-1992.

Contents

PREFACE

Bernan Press is pleased to present the eighth edition of *Patterns of Economic Change by State and Area*. It is a special edition of *Business Statistics of the United States: Patterns of Economic Change*, bringing together measurements for regions, states, and metropolitan areas of some of the time trends that are displayed at the national level in *Business Statistics*. The title was added to the Bernan Press library of reference books in 2013. It includes some state indicators that were formerly shown in earlier editions of *Business Statistics*, which have been expanded to cover many more geographical entities including 384 metropolitan statistical areas (MSAs).

This volume also complements such titles as *State and Metropolitan Area Data Book* and *County and City Extra*. In contrast to their predominantly current and detailed cross-section data on states and metropolitan areas, this book contributes historical time-series measurements of key aggregates that show how the economies of regions, states, and metropolitan areas have responded over time to cyclical currents and long-term trends.

All these data are compiled and published by U.S. government professional statistical agencies—the Bureau of Economic Analysis and the Census Bureau. Specific references to publications and web sites, along with definitions of terms and other essential information, are detailed before each data series. With this information, the user can properly interpret and use the data and can update it, if desired, as the source agencies release new information over the course of the year.

The largest body of data included is "Personal Income and Employment by Region, State, and Metropolitan Area." These tables provide annual data, going as far back as 1960, for farm and nonfarm earnings of persons;

payments to persons of dividends, interest, and rent; personal current transfer receipts, which are income sources such as Social Security; total personal income; population; per capita personal income and disposable (after income taxes) personal income (that is, total income divided by the size of the population); and the total number of jobs in the state or area. Using these data, the performance of any given state or area, whether at one moment in time or over a span of years, can be studied, and compared and contrasted with that of the nation and other states or areas.

Even more comprehensive than personal income is gross domestic product (GDP), the measure of total U.S. economic activity, available and published here at the state level both in current dollar values and in the form of an index of quantities produced (that is to say, change in real output, corrected to remove the effects of inflation).

Moving from indicators of aggregate economic trends to effects on individuals and households, the third section shows data on the poverty rate and median household incomes (the income of the "typical" household in the exact middle of the income distribution), corrected for inflation.

This edition includes the reintroduction of the Poughkeepsie–Newburgh–Middletown, NY, statistical area, which from 2013 to 2018 was included in the New York-Newark-Jersey City, NY-NJ-PA, statistical area.

Hannah Anderson Krog edited the past five editions of *Patterns of Economic Change by State and Area*. Mary Meghan Ryan edited previous editions, and Cornelia J. Strawser provided assistance in planning the first edition.

PART A

PERSONAL INCOME AND EMPLOYMENT BY REGION, STATE, AND AREA

PART A. PERSONAL INCOME AND EMPLOYMENT BY REGION, STATE, AND METROPOLITAN AREA

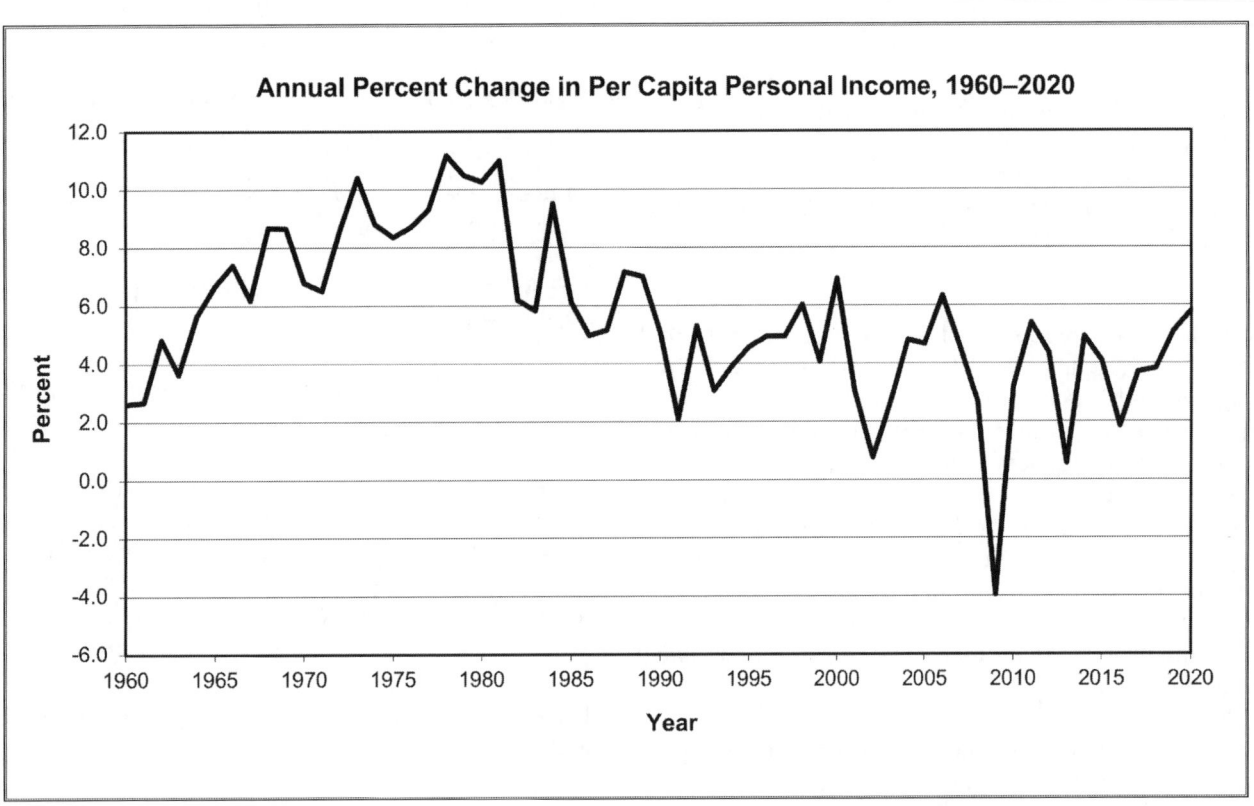

HIGHLIGHTS:

- In 2020, nationwide per capita personal income increased 5.8 percent after increasing 5.1 percent in 2019 and 3.8 percent in 2018. From 1960 through 2020, per capita personal income only declined once, dropping from $40,904 in 2008 to $39,284 in 2009.

- Per capita personal income provides one measure of the affluence of the states and regions, and it varies widely. The District of Columbia had the highest per capita personal income in 2020, at $87,064, followed by Connecticut ($79,771) and Massachusetts ($79,721). Mississippi had the lowest per capita income at $41,745. The per capita personal income nationally was $59,729.

- Employment growth also differs significantly by state and metropolitan area. Total employment increased 1.8 percent nationwide in 2019, but it declined by -0.1 percent or more in 34 MSAs. The areas with the largest growth in employment between 2018 and 2019 were: The Villages, FL (5.0 percent), Boise, ID (3.8 percent), and Austin-Round Rock-Georgetown, TX (3.7 percent).

- The value of total earnings by place of work in the United States increased just 0.4 percent in 2020. These earnings include wages and salaries, supplements, and proprietors' income.

3

PART A NOTES AND DEFINITIONS: PERSONAL INCOME AND EMPLOYMENT BY REGION, STATE, AND METROPOLITAN AREA

Source: U.S. Department of Commerce, Bureau of Economic Analysis (BEA), <http://www.bea.gov>

The personal income data set presented here provides a comprehensive, though not complete, measure of economic activity and purchasing power for individual states and smaller areas, with historical records that enable users to observe developments over extensive periods of time.

These data are stated in current-dollar terms not corrected for inflation, so that changes over time represent changes in both quantity and price. And they do not completely represent corporate economic activity: compensation of corporate employees is covered, as are corporate dividends received by individuals, but the remaining undistributed corporate profits—difficult to allocate to small geographical units—are not. See Part B that follows for measures of Gross Domestic Product by state, which provide a complete allocation to states of GDP in current dollars and include inflation-corrected indexes of growth in quantity terms.

The summary definitions of personal income and its components in the next section are taken from a BEA press release. In a following section, further detail and explanation of the concepts is provided.

BEA definitions

Personal income is the income received by persons from all sources. Personal income is the sum of net earnings by place of residence, property income, and personal current transfer receipts. **Property income** is rental income of persons, personal dividend income, and personal interest income. **Net earnings** is earnings by place of work (the sum of wage and salary disbursements, supplements to wages and salaries, and proprietors' income) less contributions for government social insurance, plus an adjustment to convert earnings by place of work to a place-of-residence basis. Personal income is measured before the deduction of personal income taxes and other personal taxes and is reported in current dollars (no adjustment is made for price changes).

The estimate of personal income in the United States is derived as the sum of the state estimates and the estimate for the District of Columbia; it differs from the estimate of personal income in the national income and product accounts (NIPAs) because of differences in coverage, in the methodologies used to prepare the estimates, and in the timing of the availability of source data.

BEA groups all 50 states and the District of Columbia into eight distinct regions for purposes of data collecting and analyses:

New England (Connecticut, Maine, Massachusetts, New Hampshire, Rhode Island, and Vermont);

Mideast (Delaware, District of Columbia, Maryland, New Jersey, New York, and Pennsylvania);

Great Lakes (Illinois, Indiana, Michigan, Ohio, and Wisconsin);

Plains (Iowa, Kansas, Minnesota, Missouri, Nebraska, North Dakota, and South Dakota);

Southeast (Alabama, Arkansas, Florida, Georgia, Kentucky, Louisiana, Mississippi, North Carolina, South Carolina, Tennessee, Virginia, and West Virginia);

Southwest (Arizona, New Mexico, Oklahoma, and Texas);

Rocky Mountain (Colorado, Idaho, Montana, Utah, and Wyoming); and

Far West (Alaska, California, Hawaii, Nevada, Oregon, and Washington).

State personal income statistics provide a framework for analyzing current economic conditions in each state and can serve as a basis for decision-making.

For example:

- Federal government agencies use the statistics as a basis for allocating funds and determining matching grants to states. The statistics are also used in forecasting models to project energy and water use.

- State governments use the statistics to project tax revenues and the need for public services.

- Academic regional economists use the statistics for applied research.

- Businesses, trade associations, and labor organizations use the statistics for market research.

BEA's national, international, regional, and industry estimates; the Survey of Current Business; and BEA news releases are available without charge on BEA's Web site at www.bea.gov. By visiting the site, you can also subscribe to receive free e-mail summaries of BEA releases and announcements.

More about income concepts

For the sake of simplicity, the following definitions and clarifications are written in terms of states, but all statements about "states" apply equally to regions and metropolitan areas.

The sum of state personal incomes for the United States (50 states and the District of Columbia) is somewhat smaller than U.S. personal income as shown in the national income and product accounts (NIPAs), due to slightly different definitions. The national total of the state estimates consists only of the income earned by persons who live in the United States and of foreign residents who work in the United States. The measure of personal income in the NIPAs is broader. It includes the earnings of federal civilian and military personnel stationed abroad and of U.S. residents on foreign assignment for less than a year. It also includes the investment income received by federal retirement plans for federal workers stationed abroad. NIPA personal income includes all income earned by U.S. citizens living abroad for less than a year; state personal income excludes the portion earned while the individual lives abroad. Earnings of foreign residents are included in the NIPAs only if they live and work in the United States for a year or more; state personal income, on the other hand, includes income paid to foreign nationals working in the United States regardless of length of residency. There are also statistical differences that reflect different timing of the availability of source data.

As in the NIPAs, personal income is defined to exclude capital gains.

Earnings by place of work consists of payments, to persons who work in the state, of wages and salaries; all supplements to wages and salaries (including employer contributions for government social insurance and all other benefits); and farm and nonfarm proprietors' income. Proprietor's income includes inventory valuation and capital consumption adjustments.

Contributions for government social insurance, which is subtracted from total earnings, includes both the employer and the employee contributions, on behalf of persons working in the state, for Social Security, Medicare, unemployment insurance, and other government social insurance, but does not include contributions to government employee retirement plans. Hence, personal income is defined as net of all contributions for government social insurance, which are commonly referred to as "Social Security taxes." Personal income is not net of other taxes on wages or other income such as Federal and state income taxes. These taxes are subtracted, however, to yield *"disposable personal income."*

Adjustment for residence. BEA adjusts earnings by place of work to a place-of-residence basis, to account for interstate and international commuting. The difference between earnings by place of residence and earnings by place of work is shown in the "Adjustment for residence" column. This adjustment is a net figure, equaling income received by state residents from employment outside the state minus income paid to persons residing outside the state but working in the state.

The effect of interstate commuting can be seen in its most extreme form in the District of Columbia. Its large negative adjustment for residence says that roughly half of total earnings by people working there are paid to persons living outside D.C. Compare with Maryland and Virginia, which have substantial positive adjustments, representing income flowing from the District of Columbia and other employment sources outside the state. There is also a large negative adjustment for New York, associated with positive adjustments for New Jersey and Connecticut.

Dividends, interest, and rent. The rental income component of personal income, like that in the NIPAs, includes imputed rent on owner-occupied homes, net of capital consumption with capital consumption adjustment.

Personal current transfer receipts are aggregates for state residents of benefits from Social Security, Medicare, Medicaid, unemployment insurance, veterans' benefits, and other government benefits including the earned income credit. It does not include payments from government employee retirement plans, which are accounted for in supplements to wages and salaries.

It should be noted that in both the personal income and the NIPA accounts, the value of Medicare and Medicaid spending, even though in practice it is usually paid directly from the government to the health care provider, is treated as if it were cash income to the consumer, which is then expended in personal consumption expenditures.

Population is the U.S. Census Bureau estimate for the middle of the year. Note that because Hurricane Katrina occurred in August 2005, the population decline in Louisiana caused by that event does not appear until the entry for 2006.

Total employment is the total number of jobs, full-time plus part-time; each job that any person holds is counted at full weight. The employment estimates are on a place-of-work basis. Both wage and salary employment and self-employment are included. The main source for the wage and salary employment estimates is Bureau of Labor Statistics (BLS) estimates from unemployment insurance data (the ES-202 data), which also provides benchmarks for the widely-followed BLS payroll employment measures. Self-employment is estimated mainly from individual and partnership federal income tax returns. Therefore, this definition of employment is broader than BLS "total nonfarm payroll employment."

This concept of employment also differs from the concept of employment in the Current Population Survey (CPS), another BLS monthly survey, which is derived from a monthly count of persons employed; any individual will appear only once in the CPS in a given month, no matter how many different jobs he or she might hold. In addition, a self-employed individual who files more than one Schedule C income-tax filing will be counted more than once in the state figures. Finally, the state figures include members of the armed forces, who are not covered in the CPS. Due to these differences and other possible reporting inconsistencies, the BEA employment estimates are different from, and usually larger than, state employment estimates from the CPS.

The employment estimates correspond closely in coverage to the earnings estimates by place of work. However, the earnings estimates include the income of limited partnerships and of tax-exempt cooperatives, for which there are no corresponding employment estimates.

Per capita income is total income divided by the state's midyear population. This is an important tool for "scaling" income data to the size of the state, so that meaningful comparisons of economic performance among states can be made. Per capita income provides a useful gauge of economic strength, purchasing power, and fiscal capacity.

Users should not, however, assume that per capita income well represents the income of a typical state resident. Per capita incomes are averages—"means" in the technical language of statistics. Income of a typical person is better represented by the "median," which is the income of a person at the middle of the income distribution; half the population has higher income and half has lower. Where income is distributed so unequally that a relatively small number of persons have extremely high incomes, the mean will be higher than the median; and if the income distribution is becoming more unequal, the mean will rise faster than the median. Both of these conditions have been present for the U.S. economy as a whole in recent decades. Median household (not personal) incomes by state are presented in Part C.

UNITED STATES

Personal Income and Employment by Region and State: United States

(Millions of dollars, except as noted.)

Year	Personal income, total	Earnings by place of work			Less: Contributions for government social insurance	Plus: Adjustment for residence	Equals: Net earnings by place of residence	Plus: Dividends, interest, and rent	Plus: Personal current transfer receipts	Per capita (dollars)		Population (thousands)	Total employment (thousands)
		Nonfarm	Farm	Total						Personal income	Disposable personal income		
1960	417,700	334,492	13,734	348,226	16,358	-260	331,608	60,352	25,740	2,321	2,066	179,972	...
1961	436,047	345,444	14,467	359,911	16,916	-250	342,745	63,852	29,450	2,383	2,126	182,976	...
1962	464,000	368,896	14,526	383,422	19,023	-202	364,197	69,411	30,392	2,498	2,221	185,739	...
1963	487,780	388,214	14,414	402,628	21,559	-173	380,896	74,675	32,209	2,589	2,300	188,434	...
1964	522,633	417,196	13,227	430,423	22,258	-170	407,995	81,134	33,504	2,735	2,463	191,085	...
1965	564,444	448,173	15,576	463,749	23,278	-111	440,360	87,906	36,178	2,918	2,620	193,460	...
1966	612,713	493,890	16,631	510,521	31,136	-99	479,286	93,810	39,617	3,134	2,796	195,499	...
1967	656,828	528,209	15,259	543,468	34,600	-96	508,772	100,042	48,014	3,328	2,959	197,375	...
1968	720,877	580,338	15,420	595,758	38,392	-119	557,247	107,536	56,094	3,617	3,183	199,312	...
1969	791,229	636,235	17,430	653,665	43,791	-107	609,767	119,140	62,322	3,931	3,415	201,298	91,053
1970	855,525	675,692	17,660	693,352	46,012	-112	647,228	133,564	74,733	4,198	3,695	203,799	91,278
1971	924,613	723,952	18,142	742,094	50,859	-122	691,113	145,252	88,248	4,471	3,981	206,818	91,581
1972	1,016,408	797,699	21,947	819,646	58,897	-145	760,604	157,674	98,130	4,857	4,269	209,275	94,312
1973	1,133,468	884,089	34,875	918,964	75,183	-153	843,628	176,992	112,848	5,363	4,739	211,349	98,428
1974	1,244,912	963,812	30,097	993,909	84,872	-163	908,874	202,399	133,639	5,836	5,130	213,334	100,112
1975	1,362,505	1,030,360	29,132	1,059,492	88,974	-199	970,319	221,762	170,424	6,324	5,641	215,457	98,901
1976	1,495,704	1,148,053	25,218	1,173,271	100,987	-211	1,072,073	238,786	184,845	6,875	6,083	217,554	101,591
1977	1,651,632	1,279,276	24,491	1,303,767	112,699	-235	1,190,833	265,688	195,111	7,516	6,618	219,761	105,042
1978	1,855,849	1,447,696	28,384	1,476,080	130,827	-257	1,344,996	300,292	210,561	8,356	7,324	222,098	109,687
1979	2,073,257	1,618,142	30,221	1,648,363	152,273	-231	1,495,859	341,022	236,376	9,232	8,038	224,569	113,147
1980	2,313,160	1,763,859	20,738	1,784,597	165,670	-255	1,618,672	413,614	280,874	10,180	8,865	227,225	113,983
1981	2,592,915	1,933,697	27,476	1,961,173	195,066	-208	1,765,899	507,254	319,762	11,300	9,797	229,466	114,914
1982	2,779,794	2,028,963	24,766	2,053,729	208,173	-255	1,845,301	578,352	356,141	11,999	10,472	231,664	114,163
1983	2,968,676	2,170,568	17,450	2,188,018	225,143	-212	1,962,663	621,342	384,671	12,698	11,192	233,792	115,646
1984	3,279,488	2,400,243	32,159	2,432,402	256,550	-254	2,175,598	702,658	401,232	13,906	12,308	235,825	120,528
1985	3,510,471	2,583,536	32,255	2,615,791	280,379	-257	2,335,155	749,555	425,761	14,755	13,003	237,924	123,797
1986	3,719,647	2,753,507	33,394	2,786,901	302,389	228	2,484,740	783,196	451,711	15,490	13,671	240,133	126,232
1987	3,946,593	2,956,412	39,588	2,996,000	322,006	259	2,674,253	804,246	468,094	16,289	14,273	242,289	129,548
1988	4,267,813	3,220,748	39,231	3,259,979	360,285	226	2,899,920	870,483	497,410	17,455	15,391	244,499	133,564
1989	4,609,667	3,420,858	46,169	3,467,027	384,001	236	3,083,262	982,219	544,186	18,676	16,381	246,819	136,178
1990	4,897,821	3,631,845	47,615	3,679,460	408,676	313	3,271,097	1,029,493	597,231	19,621	17,244	249,623	138,331
1991	5,067,291	3,746,947	42,481	3,789,428	428,555	367	3,361,240	1,038,003	668,048	20,030	17,708	252,981	137,613
1992	5,409,920	4,008,307	50,716	4,059,023	453,768	478	3,605,733	1,056,248	747,939	21,090	18,705	256,514	138,166
1993	5,648,732	4,189,837	47,600	4,237,437	476,331	493	3,761,599	1,094,227	792,906	21,733	19,240	259,919	140,774
1994	5,940,128	4,405,940	51,008	4,456,948	507,188	533	3,950,293	1,160,955	828,880	22,575	19,945	263,126	144,197
1995	6,286,143	4,635,040	39,809	4,674,849	531,874	703	4,143,678	1,259,091	883,374	23,607	20,800	266,278	147,916
1996	6,673,186	4,900,819	55,361	4,956,180	554,150	675	4,402,705	1,341,353	929,128	24,771	21,667	269,394	151,056
1997	7,086,935	5,236,736	51,311	5,288,047	586,295	672	4,702,424	1,429,714	954,797	25,993	22,579	272,647	154,541
1998	7,601,594	5,658,042	48,972	5,707,014	623,685	755	5,084,084	1,533,632	983,878	27,557	23,818	275,854	158,481
1999	8,001,563	6,048,481	49,561	6,098,042	660,310	2,515	5,440,247	1,535,172	1,026,144	28,675	24,694	279,040	161,531
2000	8,650,325	6,546,103	52,640	6,598,743	704,849	2,587	5,896,481	1,666,564	1,087,280	30,657	26,279	282,162	165,371
2001	9,001,839	6,810,126	55,165	6,865,291	732,117	2,692	6,135,866	1,673,408	1,192,565	31,589	27,245	284,969	165,522
2002	9,155,663	6,957,749	43,381	7,001,130	750,339	2,657	6,253,448	1,617,025	1,285,190	31,832	28,177	287,625	165,095
2003	9,480,901	7,184,365	59,300	7,243,665	777,956	2,679	6,468,388	1,665,285	1,347,228	32,681	29,225	290,108	165,922
2004	10,028,781	7,598,827	76,306	7,675,133	827,824	2,659	6,849,968	1,757,607	1,421,206	34,251	30,673	292,805	168,840
2005	10,593,946	7,967,309	72,339	8,039,648	871,945	2,614	7,170,317	1,906,918	1,516,711	35,849	31,750	295,517	172,338
2006	11,372,589	8,463,962	55,815	8,519,777	921,128	2,617	7,601,266	2,157,509	1,613,814	38,114	33,572	298,380	175,869
2007	12,002,204	8,798,362	68,422	8,866,784	960,003	2,596	7,909,377	2,364,762	1,728,065	39,844	34,895	301,231	179,544
2008	12,438,527	8,943,677	69,781	9,013,458	986,875	2,649	8,029,232	2,454,213	1,955,082	40,904	35,952	304,094	179,214
2009	12,051,307	8,630,392	58,054	8,688,446	962,827	3,019	7,728,638	2,175,976	2,146,693	39,284	35,533	306,772	173,637
2010	12,541,995	8,955,253	67,945	9,023,198	982,045	3,068	8,044,221	2,172,657	2,325,117	40,546	36,550	309,326	172,902
2011	13,315,478	9,349,989	93,539	9,443,528	915,062	3,201	8,531,667	2,425,157	2,358,654	42,735	38,076	311,580	176,092
2012	13,998,383	9,808,544	93,338	9,901,882	948,953	3,411	8,956,340	2,679,055	2,362,988	44,599	39,796	313,874	178,980
2013	14,175,503	10,105,775	125,703	10,231,478	1,102,460	3,651	9,132,669	2,618,537	2,424,297	44,851	39,554	316,058	182,325
2014	14,983,140	10,582,190	104,416	10,686,606	1,151,948	3,438	9,538,096	2,904,750	2,540,294	47,060	41,457	318,386	186,236
2015	15,711,634	11,021,411	88,700	11,110,111	1,203,451	3,403	9,910,063	3,118,571	2,683,000	48,985	42,957	320,743	190,318
2016	16,115,630	11,295,798	69,933	11,365,731	1,237,916	3,198	10,131,013	3,206,592	2,778,025	49,883	43,839	323,071	193,369
2017	16,820,250	11,826,339	71,071	11,897,410	1,296,599	2,935	10,603,746	3,356,872	2,859,632	51,731	45,480	325,147	196,132
2018	17,572,929	12,353,737	73,490	12,427,227	1,359,022	2,849	11,071,054	3,520,984	2,980,891	53,712	47,451	327,167	200,284
2019	18,542,262	18,458,931	83,331	13,080,565	1,416,666	3,113	11,667,012	3,750,076	3,125,174	56,474	49,774	328,330	203,810
2020	19,679,715	19,580,677	99,039	13,132,608	1,433,939	3,106	11,701,774	3,709,407	4,268,534	59,729	53,080	329,484	...

... = Not available.

REGION

Personal Income and Employment by Region and State: Far West

(Millions of dollars, except as noted.)

Year	Personal income, total	Derivation of personal income								Per capita (dollars)		Population (thousands)	Total employment (thousands)
		Earnings by place of work			Less: Contributions for government social insurance	Plus: Adjustment for residence	Equals: Net earnings by place of residence	Plus: Dividends, interest, and rent	Plus: Personal current transfer receipts	Personal income	Disposable personal income		
		Nonfarm	Farm	Total									
1960	61,279	48,132	1,965	50,097	2,357	-1	47,739	10,027	3,513	2,829	2,513	21,659	...
1961	64,770	50,820	1,866	52,687	2,496	-1	50,189	10,531	4,049	2,894	2,574	22,378	...
1962	69,808	55,159	1,975	57,134	2,978	-3	54,153	11,406	4,250	3,020	2,683	23,114	...
1963	74,242	58,967	1,914	60,881	3,461	-5	57,415	12,187	4,640	3,118	2,768	23,811	...
1964	80,068	63,360	2,018	65,379	3,582	-6	61,791	13,285	4,992	3,283	2,962	24,389	...
1965	85,799	67,585	2,009	69,594	3,732	-7	65,855	14,470	5,474	3,445	3,109	24,908	...
1966	93,565	74,686	2,259	76,945	4,926	-8	72,010	15,559	5,996	3,697	3,315	25,311	...
1967	100,755	80,087	2,125	82,211	5,452	-10	76,750	16,635	7,370	3,908	3,493	25,779	...
1968	110,716	88,310	2,383	90,692	6,123	-12	84,558	17,662	8,496	4,234	3,744	26,151	...
1969	121,725	96,417	2,481	98,898	6,626	-149	92,124	19,909	9,693	4,570	4,006	26,635	12,295
1970	131,576	101,828	2,440	104,267	6,894	-178	97,195	22,413	11,967	4,855	4,327	27,101	12,313
1971	140,637	107,701	2,470	110,171	7,515	-203	102,453	24,340	13,844	5,101	4,596	27,570	12,300
1972	154,353	118,742	3,114	121,855	8,729	-211	112,916	26,464	14,973	5,529	4,905	27,918	12,742
1973	170,589	131,079	4,254	135,333	11,058	-212	124,063	29,675	16,852	6,022	5,377	28,328	13,405
1974	191,194	144,766	5,389	150,155	12,600	-293	137,262	34,000	19,933	6,638	5,906	28,801	13,865
1975	212,899	159,546	4,811	164,358	13,656	-482	150,220	37,624	25,054	7,255	6,529	29,346	14,103
1976	236,675	179,946	4,813	184,759	15,727	-594	168,438	40,593	27,644	7,908	7,050	29,929	14,625
1977	262,401	201,508	4,684	206,192	17,862	-399	187,931	45,093	29,377	8,588	7,607	30,553	15,287
1978	298,986	231,858	4,757	236,615	21,059	-318	215,237	51,947	31,801	9,557	8,410	31,285	16,248
1979	339,286	263,608	5,909	269,516	25,060	-37	244,419	59,781	35,087	10,614	9,275	31,965	17,133
1980	385,032	291,682	7,355	299,037	27,354	-123	271,560	72,341	41,131	11,746	10,266	32,780	17,523
1981	430,716	320,814	5,852	326,665	32,526	-175	293,964	88,466	48,287	12,883	11,271	33,434	17,693
1982	460,617	338,206	5,929	344,136	34,875	-211	309,050	97,938	53,628	13,513	11,931	34,086	17,564
1983	496,483	364,642	5,969	370,611	38,249	-236	332,125	107,130	57,228	14,301	12,681	34,716	17,989
1984	547,058	403,662	6,614	410,276	43,877	-307	366,091	121,175	59,792	15,488	13,740	35,321	18,767
1985	588,982	437,078	6,383	443,461	48,006	-365	395,091	129,313	64,578	16,344	14,425	36,037	19,392
1986	630,292	471,785	7,290	479,075	52,251	-379	426,446	134,801	69,046	17,120	15,122	36,815	19,959
1987	675,313	513,537	8,487	522,024	56,781	-450	464,793	138,414	72,106	17,941	15,688	37,641	20,793
1988	734,929	563,551	8,996	572,547	64,107	-540	507,900	149,654	77,375	19,068	16,808	38,542	21,790
1989	796,500	602,481	9,003	611,484	69,060	-636	541,789	169,761	84,950	20,147	17,581	39,534	22,453
1990	857,643	649,865	9,490	659,355	74,731	-748	583,876	180,256	93,511	21,119	18,462	40,610	23,122
1991	894,209	677,754	8,641	686,395	78,399	-745	607,251	182,718	104,240	21,585	19,044	41,428	23,124
1992	948,870	716,768	9,397	726,165	82,247	-732	643,186	186,390	119,293	22,471	19,960	42,226	22,825
1993	980,448	735,050	10,709	745,759	84,534	-724	660,501	193,461	126,487	22,909	20,356	42,798	22,934
1994	1,018,477	762,545	10,055	772,600	88,381	-750	683,468	204,678	130,331	23,537	20,882	43,271	23,380
1995	1,073,913	797,148	9,667	806,815	91,651	-782	714,382	221,734	137,797	24,549	21,689	43,745	23,938
1996	1,143,491	846,798	11,191	857,989	95,355	-851	761,782	236,934	144,775	25,804	22,567	44,314	24,580
1997	1,218,605	910,066	11,489	921,555	101,059	-928	819,568	252,213	146,824	27,048	23,448	45,054	25,149
1998	1,324,509	995,053	11,103	1,006,155	108,701	-1,017	896,437	273,565	154,506	28,920	24,922	45,798	26,089
1999	1,411,649	1,078,866	11,608	1,090,475	116,479	-1,087	972,909	275,743	162,998	30,354	25,801	46,506	26,659
2000	1,547,744	1,193,146	11,786	1,204,932	127,413	-1,188	1,076,331	300,563	170,850	32,799	27,479	47,188	27,241
2001	1,601,433	1,230,263	11,209	1,241,472	132,590	-1,266	1,107,616	303,904	189,913	33,439	28,563	47,891	27,369
2002	1,629,697	1,254,999	11,821	1,266,821	136,542	-1,341	1,128,937	296,416	204,343	33,607	29,637	48,493	27,369
2003	1,704,840	1,308,013	13,796	1,321,809	143,078	-1,503	1,177,228	312,715	214,897	34,755	30,947	49,053	27,604
2004	1,818,036	1,396,614	16,102	1,412,717	155,412	-1,716	1,255,589	338,483	223,964	36,653	32,677	49,602	28,155
2005	1,927,913	1,471,392	15,914	1,487,307	163,406	-1,889	1,322,012	370,125	235,776	38,489	33,845	50,090	28,787
2006	2,081,151	1,566,031	13,881	1,579,913	170,460	-1,958	1,407,495	420,489	253,167	41,153	36,033	50,571	29,438
2007	2,183,212	1,618,839	16,883	1,635,723	174,771	-2,092	1,458,860	454,108	270,244	42,782	37,265	51,031	30,069
2008	2,230,240	1,614,974	15,000	1,629,974	177,537	-2,233	1,450,204	471,417	308,618	43,214	37,835	51,609	29,819
2009	2,154,405	1,551,506	16,124	1,567,630	172,567	-2,097	1,392,966	419,556	341,883	41,298	37,239	52,168	28,628
2010	2,246,369	1,612,040	17,137	1,629,177	174,538	-2,014	1,452,625	415,926	377,817	42,640	38,249	52,682	28,335
2011	2,391,122	1,689,935	20,218	1,710,152	164,053	-1,917	1,544,182	466,559	380,381	44,989	39,882	53,149	28,789
2012	2,547,187	1,791,267	22,574	1,813,842	170,690	-1,973	1,641,178	523,091	382,917	47,502	42,100	53,623	29,624
2013	2,589,966	1,855,098	25,706	1,880,804	199,269	-1,827	1,679,708	513,701	396,557	47,883	41,825	54,089	30,462
2014	2,777,826	1,953,699	27,478	1,981,177	210,452	-1,997	1,768,728	584,243	424,855	50,865	44,342	54,612	31,370
2015	2,978,517	2,076,315	28,476	2,104,791	222,685	-2,100	1,880,006	644,080	454,432	53,996	46,762	55,162	32,304
2016	3,098,159	2,165,138	24,545	2,189,683	231,811	-2,364	1,955,508	671,055	471,596	55,638	48,182	55,685	33,021
2017	3,248,359	2,291,365	28,150	2,319,515	244,381	-2,565	2,072,569	703,030	472,760	57,895	50,094	56,108	33,639
2018	3,410,750	2,412,734	25,850	2,438,585	258,482	-2,772	2,177,331	743,605	489,814	60,393	52,491	56,476	34,429
2019	3,634,009	3,607,255	26,754	2,580,361	273,420	-3,131	2,303,810	799,520	530,679	64,310	55,950	56,508	35,163
2020	3,881,554	3,849,739	31,815	2,610,999	279,202	-3,166	2,328,631	791,887	761,036	68,603	60,183	56,580	...

... = Not available.

Personal Income and Employment by Area: Great Lakes

(Millions of dollars, except as noted.)

Year	Personal income, total	Earnings by place of work			Less: Contributions for government social insurance	Plus: Adjustment for residence	Equals: Net earnings by place of residence	Plus: Dividends, interest, and rent	Plus: Personal current transfer receipts	Per capita (dollars)		Population (thousands)	Total employment (thousands)
		Nonfarm	Farm	Total						Personal income	Disposable personal income		
1960	88,934	73,742	2,014	75,757	3,657	-123	71,977	11,699	5,257	2,451	2,173	36,290	...
1961	91,139	73,915	2,446	76,361	3,618	-111	72,632	12,377	6,130	2,489	2,220	36,616	...
1962	96,685	78,906	2,352	81,259	4,044	-116	77,099	13,432	6,154	2,618	2,323	36,927	...
1963	101,231	82,828	2,365	85,193	4,562	-114	80,516	14,371	6,343	2,710	2,401	37,357	...
1964	108,770	89,549	2,045	91,594	4,763	-122	86,710	15,586	6,474	2,872	2,578	37,868	...
1965	118,706	97,360	2,631	99,992	4,947	-133	94,912	16,859	6,935	3,091	2,763	38,405	...
1966	129,096	107,454	2,972	110,426	6,742	-146	103,538	18,028	7,529	3,314	2,943	38,951	...
1967	135,847	112,657	2,535	115,192	7,274	-134	107,784	19,054	9,009	3,453	3,056	39,347	...
1968	148,258	123,088	2,431	125,519	7,989	-144	117,386	20,459	10,413	3,740	3,272	39,645	...
1969	162,017	134,868	2,870	137,737	9,311	262	128,688	21,994	11,334	4,060	3,495	39,904	17,785
1970	170,705	139,623	2,518	142,141	9,503	246	132,884	24,274	13,548	4,234	3,688	40,320	17,630
1971	183,695	148,678	2,899	151,577	10,424	319	141,472	26,120	16,102	4,522	3,992	40,622	17,549
1972	200,708	163,199	3,168	166,367	12,095	366	154,638	28,097	17,972	4,916	4,279	40,824	17,933
1973	224,429	182,057	5,213	187,271	15,631	417	172,057	31,434	20,938	5,481	4,794	40,947	18,710
1974	243,766	195,283	4,661	199,944	17,400	512	183,056	35,778	24,932	5,940	5,177	41,037	18,911
1975	263,253	203,397	5,818	209,215	17,669	587	192,134	39,088	32,031	6,404	5,658	41,105	18,399
1976	289,628	228,236	4,816	233,052	20,242	719	213,529	41,851	34,248	7,032	6,149	41,187	18,891
1977	321,434	256,353	4,818	261,171	22,758	899	239,311	46,353	35,769	7,773	6,760	41,353	19,508
1978	356,578	287,356	4,506	291,861	26,286	1,105	266,680	51,456	38,442	8,590	7,432	41,510	20,190
1979	392,788	314,968	5,223	320,191	29,932	1,269	291,528	57,795	43,465	9,440	8,131	41,611	20,491
1980	425,781	327,614	3,317	330,931	30,928	1,532	301,535	69,642	54,603	10,212	8,856	41,694	19,978
1981	464,804	349,522	3,683	353,205	35,439	1,340	319,107	84,994	60,703	11,160	9,639	41,648	19,795
1982	486,801	353,935	2,926	356,861	36,377	1,215	321,698	96,990	68,113	11,732	10,270	41,492	19,248
1983	512,203	374,045	-119	373,926	38,845	1,209	336,290	103,144	72,769	12,382	10,880	41,366	19,265
1984	565,478	413,823	4,409	418,232	44,260	1,335	375,307	115,639	74,532	13,661	12,059	41,393	20,028
1985	600,324	442,954	4,964	447,918	48,192	1,397	401,123	120,947	78,253	14,494	12,746	41,418	20,492
1986	632,500	470,521	4,488	475,008	51,647	1,472	424,833	125,733	81,934	15,257	13,439	41,455	20,934
1987	664,886	500,363	5,012	505,375	54,318	1,528	452,585	128,117	84,183	15,987	13,986	41,590	21,516
1988	712,816	543,351	3,363	546,714	60,614	1,647	487,747	137,155	87,914	17,085	15,014	41,721	22,070
1989	767,370	576,171	7,032	583,202	64,605	1,665	520,262	152,796	94,311	18,326	16,028	41,873	22,556
1990	810,354	608,229	6,005	614,234	68,950	1,923	547,206	160,090	103,058	19,252	16,866	42,091	22,928
1991	830,741	625,096	3,606	628,702	72,225	1,908	558,385	160,089	112,267	19,549	17,197	42,496	22,845
1992	890,729	670,955	6,123	677,078	76,663	2,021	602,436	164,296	123,996	20,762	18,346	42,903	22,971
1993	930,988	704,234	5,204	709,438	81,158	2,094	630,373	170,302	130,313	21,513	18,930	43,275	23,359
1994	987,886	748,980	6,083	755,063	87,642	2,271	669,692	183,830	134,363	22,663	19,879	43,590	24,060
1995	1,041,549	786,952	3,336	790,289	92,242	2,430	700,477	199,416	141,656	23,713	20,743	43,924	24,713
1996	1,099,479	824,326	6,936	831,263	95,305	2,677	738,635	212,662	148,182	24,853	21,609	44,239	25,105
1997	1,161,499	872,470	6,589	879,059	99,864	2,981	782,176	226,237	153,085	26,105	22,582	44,494	25,513
1998	1,233,781	933,009	5,575	938,584	104,854	3,020	836,750	241,492	155,539	27,584	23,750	44,728	25,953
1999	1,285,994	988,745	4,553	993,298	110,196	3,449	886,550	237,785	161,659	28,597	24,630	44,969	26,333
2000	1,371,399	1,049,572	5,392	1,054,964	114,559	3,792	944,197	255,973	171,229	30,330	26,164	45,216	26,830
2001	1,412,374	1,078,110	5,655	1,083,765	116,267	4,089	971,587	252,912	187,876	31,108	26,977	45,402	26,554
2002	1,429,734	1,097,558	3,755	1,101,314	117,883	4,145	987,576	242,507	199,651	31,388	27,770	45,550	26,272
2003	1,463,584	1,121,525	6,221	1,127,746	121,240	4,423	1,010,929	244,311	208,344	32,020	28,630	45,708	26,220
2004	1,519,487	1,164,163	10,226	1,174,389	127,570	4,927	1,051,745	250,605	217,137	33,144	29,728	45,844	26,440
2005	1,567,601	1,194,815	6,921	1,201,736	132,744	5,347	1,074,339	259,745	233,517	34,116	30,365	45,949	26,682
2006	1,651,102	1,242,517	6,617	1,249,134	138,350	5,657	1,116,441	289,199	245,462	35,838	31,748	46,072	26,875
2007	1,723,602	1,275,325	9,397	1,284,722	142,423	5,774	1,148,073	310,086	265,444	37,317	32,888	46,188	27,135
2008	1,774,339	1,283,795	11,190	1,294,985	145,147	6,360	1,156,197	319,350	298,791	38,343	33,877	46,275	26,872
2009	1,708,116	1,220,625	7,466	1,228,092	138,919	5,479	1,094,651	280,982	332,483	36,848	33,445	46,356	25,773
2010	1,763,572	1,257,773	8,900	1,266,673	140,960	5,352	1,131,065	276,511	355,996	37,976	34,340	46,439	25,659
2011	1,869,361	1,317,224	16,536	1,333,760	132,004	5,314	1,207,071	309,342	352,948	40,190	35,879	46,513	26,128
2012	1,950,541	1,378,179	11,656	1,389,835	137,137	5,636	1,258,335	339,155	353,052	41,869	37,390	46,587	26,417
2013	1,980,332	1,417,512	21,585	1,439,097	157,360	5,410	1,287,147	331,765	361,420	42,411	37,549	46,694	26,732
2014	2,069,389	1,470,727	13,019	1,483,746	162,492	5,844	1,327,099	366,502	375,788	44,248	39,220	46,768	27,125
2015	2,159,301	1,529,656	6,156	1,535,812	168,415	6,413	1,373,809	391,135	394,357	46,154	40,749	46,784	27,533
2016	2,206,069	1,561,648	7,814	1,569,462	172,496	6,416	1,403,382	400,811	401,877	47,118	41,631	46,820	27,813
2017	2,283,656	1,621,526	4,685	1,626,211	179,605	6,714	1,453,320	418,470	411,867	48,714	43,047	46,879	28,091
2018	2,372,170	1,679,983	4,894	1,684,878	186,766	6,987	1,505,098	437,104	429,967	50,545	44,883	46,932	28,342
2019	2,460,678	2,452,847	7,831	1,745,126	192,921	7,928	1,560,134	453,522	447,023	52,462	46,644	46,904	28,638
2020	2,614,465	2,603,092	11,373	1,737,980	193,162	7,939	1,552,757	448,748	612,960	55,823	50087	46,835	...

... = Not available.

Personal Income and Employment by Region and State: Mideast

(Millions of dollars, except as noted.)

Year	Personal income, total	Earnings by place of work			Less: Contributions for government social insurance	Plus: Adjustment for residence	Equals: Net earnings by place of residence	Plus: Dividends, interest, and rent	Plus: Personal current transfer receipts	Per capita (dollars)		Population (thousands)	Total employment (thousands)
		Nonfarm	Farm	Total						Personal income	Disposable personal income		
1960	102,030	85,593	901	86,495	4,355	-761	81,378	14,533	6,119	2,643	2,319	38,597	...
1961	106,262	88,420	906	89,326	4,582	-791	83,953	15,316	6,994	2,715	2,383	39,133	...
1962	112,437	93,612	733	94,345	5,118	-804	88,423	16,864	7,150	2,843	2,488	39,552	...
1963	117,654	97,361	799	98,160	5,644	-841	91,675	18,386	7,593	2,935	2,569	40,083	...
1964	126,000	103,790	802	104,592	5,693	-902	97,997	20,142	7,861	3,107	2,758	40,555	...
1965	134,825	110,543	896	111,439	5,940	-933	104,567	21,854	8,405	3,286	2,906	41,025	...
1966	145,317	120,725	917	121,642	7,891	-1,011	112,740	23,176	9,401	3,513	3,088	41,360	...
1967	156,524	129,069	972	130,040	8,614	-1,183	120,243	24,679	11,602	3,761	3,290	41,617	...
1968	171,747	140,938	920	141,859	9,400	-1,301	131,157	26,718	13,872	4,097	3,550	41,924	...
1969	184,917	153,081	1,105	154,186	11,072	-1,782	141,332	28,328	15,257	4,391	3,753	42,111	19,432
1970	199,975	163,311	1,063	164,374	11,658	-1,703	151,013	30,857	18,105	4,703	4,078	42,517	19,465
1971	214,652	173,493	970	174,464	12,772	-1,779	159,912	33,002	21,738	5,007	4,399	42,870	19,299
1972	232,153	188,066	966	189,032	14,535	-1,950	172,546	35,188	24,419	5,400	4,679	42,992	19,521
1973	251,007	203,906	1,387	205,293	18,195	-2,082	185,016	38,689	27,301	5,860	5,104	42,837	19,968
1974	272,562	218,491	1,292	219,783	20,160	-2,296	197,327	43,426	31,808	6,382	5,535	42,709	19,954
1975	295,272	230,686	1,198	231,884	20,837	-2,641	208,405	46,400	40,467	6,911	6,085	42,728	19,480
1976	317,632	249,080	1,278	250,359	22,890	-2,964	224,504	49,380	43,748	7,444	6,518	42,667	19,563
1977	345,171	271,848	1,097	272,946	24,858	-3,354	244,734	54,358	46,080	8,113	7,062	42,547	19,848
1978	378,978	301,100	1,311	302,412	28,208	-3,971	270,233	59,882	48,863	8,934	7,747	42,421	20,411
1979	416,696	331,582	1,523	333,105	32,254	-4,760	296,091	66,982	53,623	9,837	8,468	42,358	20,871
1980	462,775	360,298	1,140	361,438	35,164	-5,615	320,660	80,371	61,744	10,947	9,412	42,272	20,911
1981	514,658	392,584	1,499	394,083	40,993	-5,943	347,147	97,890	69,621	12,159	10,371	42,329	20,978
1982	555,921	415,170	1,458	416,628	43,999	-6,123	366,506	112,109	77,306	13,117	11,217	42,382	20,858
1983	594,414	445,111	1,092	446,202	47,849	-6,182	392,171	118,668	83,575	13,972	12,117	42,544	21,045
1984	653,790	490,129	1,904	492,033	54,383	-6,584	431,066	135,759	86,965	15,316	13,310	42,687	21,766
1985	699,171	528,536	2,016	530,552	59,564	-6,967	464,021	143,756	91,394	16,338	14,132	42,794	22,333
1986	744,959	567,698	2,200	569,898	64,798	-6,872	498,227	150,152	96,579	17,328	14,987	42,991	22,837
1987	795,876	616,451	2,286	618,737	69,479	-7,221	542,037	154,624	99,214	18,427	15,795	43,190	23,321
1988	870,727	679,111	2,187	681,298	77,653	-7,991	595,653	169,705	105,368	20,046	17,350	43,435	23,927
1989	940,367	719,726	2,579	722,305	81,572	-8,372	632,361	194,009	113,997	21,576	18,599	43,585	24,201
1990	998,459	761,626	2,519	764,145	84,116	-8,635	671,394	202,182	124,884	22,816	19,778	43,762	24,260
1991	1,017,674	767,150	2,052	769,202	86,917	-9,023	673,262	203,031	141,381	23,092	20,132	44,071	23,703
1992	1,077,695	816,603	2,646	819,250	91,293	-10,687	717,270	203,621	156,803	24,277	21,201	44,392	23,597
1993	1,113,459	842,950	2,516	845,467	94,558	-10,451	740,457	207,452	165,549	24,900	21,699	44,717	23,714
1994	1,152,220	871,502	2,305	873,807	99,384	-10,167	764,256	216,473	171,491	25,622	22,281	44,970	23,879
1995	1,211,698	908,644	1,759	910,403	102,991	-10,953	796,458	233,909	181,331	26,816	23,278	45,186	24,157
1996	1,275,883	952,756	2,698	955,454	106,056	-11,404	837,993	247,571	190,318	28,113	24,225	45,384	24,387
1997	1,347,506	1,012,597	1,845	1,014,442	110,906	-11,756	891,780	263,308	192,419	29,564	25,267	45,580	24,763
1998	1,430,577	1,079,778	2,312	1,082,090	116,433	-13,004	952,652	278,927	198,998	31,220	26,519	45,822	25,170
1999	1,507,263	1,154,584	2,304	1,156,888	122,348	-13,274	1,021,266	279,400	206,597	32,691	27,657	46,106	25,710
2000	1,630,951	1,249,144	2,767	1,251,910	130,693	-11,982	1,109,236	303,761	217,955	35,160	29,658	46,386	26,409
2001	1,694,998	1,306,543	2,840	1,309,383	136,829	-12,805	1,159,749	300,806	234,444	36,358	30,586	46,619	26,496
2002	1,714,313	1,329,037	1,958	1,330,994	140,474	-14,570	1,175,951	285,540	252,822	36,598	31,786	46,841	26,442
2003	1,758,017	1,360,983	2,897	1,363,880	144,547	-15,729	1,203,605	291,671	262,801	37,378	32,789	47,035	26,529
2004	1,851,770	1,434,166	3,664	1,437,829	152,321	-17,734	1,267,774	307,351	276,644	39,264	34,426	47,162	26,904
2005	1,933,919	1,488,293	3,439	1,491,732	159,755	-19,406	1,312,571	335,087	286,261	40,939	35,451	47,239	27,309
2006	2,064,808	1,569,368	2,971	1,572,339	168,347	-22,335	1,381,657	380,499	302,652	43,622	37,458	47,334	27,713
2007	2,197,595	1,652,887	3,557	1,656,444	177,048	-25,134	1,454,262	423,688	319,645	46,291	39,339	47,474	28,252
2008	2,256,752	1,678,568	3,906	1,682,474	183,282	-28,269	1,470,924	431,156	354,672	47,326	40,343	47,685	28,371
2009	2,216,263	1,643,572	2,991	1,646,563	179,777	-24,955	1,441,831	386,184	388,249	46,226	40,804	47,944	27,759
2010	2,304,343	1,714,487	3,842	1,718,329	184,384	-28,623	1,505,322	383,077	415,945	47,804	42,069	48,204	27,763
2011	2,432,782	1,781,875	4,671	1,786,546	170,225	-31,443	1,584,878	425,720	422,184	50,226	43,650	48,437	28,282
2012	2,542,298	1,850,360	5,221	1,855,581	174,527	-32,977	1,648,076	473,922	420,300	52,285	45,656	48,624	28,579
2013	2,568,074	1,899,800	6,125	1,905,924	203,074	-31,492	1,671,358	470,313	426,402	52,667	45,279	48,761	28,990
2014	2,678,628	1,967,344	6,340	1,973,683	211,549	-34,224	1,727,911	510,545	440,173	54,816	47,027	48,865	29,466
2015	2,794,994	2,042,395	4,336	2,046,731	220,423	-35,076	1,791,232	541,604	462,158	57,132	48,756	48,921	29,961
2016	2,874,152	2,098,319	3,042	2,101,361	226,025	-35,999	1,839,337	554,461	480,354	58,728	50,364	48,940	30,375
2017	3,016,365	2,201,972	3,661	2,205,632	237,342	-40,246	1,928,044	582,813	505,509	61,625	52,956	48,947	30,773
2018	3,140,523	2,290,006	3,152	2,293,157	247,770	-41,870	2,003,517	610,657	526,349	64,131	55,432	48,970	31,229
2019	3,266,721	3,262,471	4,250	2,387,000	253,133	-43,237	2,090,630	642,646	533,446	66,813	57,515	48,893	31,717
2020	3,455,746	3,451,065	4,681	2,357,426	252,180	-43,032	2,062,214	634,431	759,101	70,876	61,707	48,758	...

... = Not available.

Personal Income and Employment by Region and State: New England

(Millions of dollars, except as noted.)

Year	Personal income, total	Earnings by place of work			Less: Contributions for government social insurance	Plus: Adjustment for residence	Equals: Net earnings by place of residence	Plus: Dividends, interest, and rent	Plus: Personal current transfer receipts	Per capita (dollars)		Population (thousands)	Total employment (thousands)
		Nonfarm	Farm	Total						Personal income	Disposable personal income		
1960	26,543	21,356	318	21,674	1,025	27	20,676	4,106	1,761	2,520	2,219	10,532	...
1961	27,858	22,281	269	22,550	1,073	28	21,504	4,377	1,977	2,612	2,311	10,666	...
1962	29,543	23,651	259	23,910	1,216	32	22,725	4,810	2,007	2,735	2,414	10,800	...
1963	30,881	24,585	251	24,837	1,358	36	23,515	5,239	2,126	2,811	2,476	10,986	...
1964	33,063	26,134	289	26,423	1,400	42	25,064	5,792	2,207	2,956	2,646	11,186	...
1965	35,462	27,879	340	28,220	1,451	44	26,813	6,319	2,330	3,130	2,794	11,329	...
1966	38,500	30,746	345	31,090	1,937	51	29,204	6,785	2,512	3,368	2,982	11,430	...
1967	41,842	33,161	239	33,401	2,135	58	31,324	7,436	3,082	3,619	3,192	11,562	...
1968	45,291	35,993	266	36,260	2,370	71	33,961	7,649	3,682	3,892	3,382	11,637	...
1969	50,009	39,196	294	39,490	2,639	835	37,686	8,213	4,111	4,262	3,656	11,735	5,516
1970	53,915	41,706	306	42,012	2,775	842	40,080	8,932	4,903	4,539	3,961	11,878	5,518
1971	57,438	43,877	283	44,161	3,015	885	42,031	9,532	5,876	4,788	4,237	11,996	5,454
1972	62,243	47,830	288	48,118	3,456	951	45,613	10,223	6,408	5,149	4,491	12,088	5,573
1973	67,916	52,504	398	52,903	4,364	997	49,536	11,183	7,197	5,591	4,904	12,148	5,783
1974	73,639	55,983	430	56,413	4,833	1,083	52,663	12,445	8,531	6,058	5,303	12,157	5,843
1975	79,316	58,456	313	58,769	4,922	1,183	55,030	13,150	11,136	6,514	5,791	12,176	5,685
1976	86,257	64,298	428	64,727	5,524	1,286	60,488	14,078	11,690	7,066	6,227	12,207	5,811
1977	94,470	71,062	385	71,447	6,136	1,435	66,746	15,593	12,131	7,707	6,776	12,257	6,007
1978	104,955	79,969	397	80,366	7,102	1,626	74,890	17,244	12,821	8,531	7,451	12,303	6,276
1979	117,375	89,790	380	90,169	8,296	1,840	83,714	19,381	14,279	9,508	8,237	12,345	6,503
1980	132,710	99,350	368	99,718	9,177	2,158	92,700	23,571	16,439	10,727	9,260	12,372	6,623
1981	148,438	108,669	471	109,140	10,790	2,345	100,696	28,938	18,804	11,936	10,240	12,436	6,666
1982	161,734	116,202	513	116,715	11,780	2,514	107,449	33,733	20,552	12,972	11,194	12,468	6,667
1983	174,683	127,158	480	127,637	13,047	2,665	117,256	35,484	21,944	13,925	12,145	12,544	6,799
1984	195,850	143,581	568	144,149	15,176	2,859	131,832	41,025	22,992	15,492	13,575	12,642	7,159
1985	211,532	157,286	558	157,844	16,770	3,119	144,193	43,153	24,186	16,603	14,452	12,741	7,400
1986	228,359	171,426	576	172,002	18,495	3,237	156,744	46,218	25,396	17,795	15,409	12,833	7,638
1987	248,105	189,165	638	189,803	20,166	3,427	173,064	48,930	26,112	19,157	16,468	12,951	7,771
1988	273,207	208,760	653	209,413	22,629	3,693	190,477	54,645	28,085	20,880	18,157	13,085	8,018
1989	293,086	219,160	609	219,770	23,628	3,745	199,886	61,837	31,362	22,234	19,305	13,182	8,005
1990	301,735	223,211	702	223,912	24,142	3,436	203,207	63,459	35,069	22,808	19,840	13,230	7,853
1991	306,345	223,851	645	224,497	24,627	3,434	203,304	62,483	40,558	23,125	20,217	13,248	7,526
1992	323,879	236,864	794	237,658	25,840	4,688	216,507	63,392	43,980	24,405	21,318	13,271	7,566
1993	335,792	246,571	731	247,302	27,034	4,116	224,384	65,853	45,555	25,182	21,934	13,334	7,689
1994	350,230	257,843	678	258,521	28,609	3,910	233,821	68,542	47,866	26,144	22,729	13,396	7,782
1995	369,981	270,399	602	271,001	30,150	4,674	245,525	73,536	50,920	27,462	23,753	13,473	7,875
1996	390,679	285,779	688	286,468	31,550	5,430	260,348	77,905	52,426	28,822	24,642	13,555	8,004
1997	415,533	306,363	593	306,957	33,589	5,059	278,426	82,726	54,380	30,459	25,766	13,642	8,165
1998	444,784	330,053	656	330,708	35,668	6,550	301,591	88,097	55,096	32,386	27,145	13,734	8,361
1999	472,603	357,524	700	358,224	37,882	6,507	326,849	88,866	56,888	34,153	28,526	13,838	8,513
2000	521,118	396,459	774	397,233	41,129	6,760	362,864	98,207	60,046	37,357	30,766	13,950	8,740
2001	546,221	415,327	713	416,040	42,479	6,808	380,370	100,645	65,206	38,902	32,472	14,041	8,766
2002	549,227	418,659	658	419,317	43,106	6,900	383,110	95,927	70,190	38,890	33,681	14,122	8,712
2003	562,164	426,773	700	427,473	44,051	6,969	390,391	98,381	73,392	39,638	34,685	14,182	8,697
2004	592,718	450,422	800	451,222	47,107	8,000	412,115	103,271	77,332	41,721	36,532	14,207	8,809
2005	618,499	465,579	757	466,335	49,067	8,821	426,090	110,372	82,037	43,505	37,643	14,217	8,901
2006	665,189	490,664	660	491,324	51,069	9,945	450,199	128,593	86,397	46,695	40,236	14,246	8,998
2007	701,987	511,831	804	512,635	53,392	11,517	470,759	139,699	91,528	49,161	41,853	14,279	9,168
2008	731,512	526,193	910	527,103	55,036	12,570	484,637	142,443	104,433	51,012	43,821	14,340	9,173
2009	722,458	524,775	742	525,518	54,101	9,806	481,223	126,868	114,367	50,158	44,640	14,404	8,936
2010	754,552	549,291	909	550,201	55,130	11,707	506,777	127,215	120,560	52,147	46,182	14,470	8,892
2011	786,564	562,225	909	563,134	51,191	12,183	524,126	140,974	121,465	54,135	47,201	14,530	9,003
2012	814,598	574,116	1,116	575,232	52,764	13,874	536,343	156,002	122,253	55,833	48,839	14,590	9,113
2013	813,492	582,291	1,156	583,446	61,078	12,989	535,357	154,161	123,973	55,548	47,713	14,645	9,266
2014	851,831	602,679	1,040	603,718	63,585	13,382	553,515	169,920	128,396	57,933	49,652	14,704	9,413
2015	892,863	628,450	922	629,372	65,971	13,614	577,015	180,106	135,741	60,617	51,789	14,730	9,658
2016	915,453	644,794	756	645,549	67,848	13,024	590,725	184,047	140,681	62,026	53,182	14,759	9,778
2017	952,331	670,000	710	670,710	70,743	16,179	616,146	192,551	143,634	64,334	55,223	14,803	9,887
2018	989,116	694,043	574	694,618	73,457	17,064	638,225	201,542	149,349	66,592	57,531	14,853	9,994
2019	1,035,507	1,034,720	787	727,409	76,490	19,262	670,181	210,869	154,457	69,733	60,042	14,850	10,127
2020	1,098,141	1,097,118	1,023	720,608	76,692	18,813	662,729	208,439	226,973	73,961	64,398	14,847	...

... = Not available.

Personal Income and Employment by Region and State: Plains

(Millions of dollars, except as noted.)

Year	Personal income, total	Derivation of personal income								Per capita (dollars)		Population (thousands)	Total employment (thousands)
		Earnings by place of work			Less: Contributions for government social insurance	Plus: Adjustment for residence	Equals: Net earnings by place of residence	Plus: Dividends, interest, and rent	Plus: Personal current transfer receipts	Personal income	Disposable personal income		
		Nonfarm	Farm	Total									
1960	33,349	24,119	3,122	27,240	1,157	8	26,091	5,040	2,218	2,162	1,942	15,424	...
1961	34,589	25,031	3,042	28,073	1,212	6	26,867	5,257	2,464	2,221	1,996	15,570	...
1962	36,922	26,543	3,542	30,084	1,317	7	28,774	5,589	2,560	2,358	2,117	15,657	...
1963	38,403	27,780	3,487	31,267	1,493	4	29,778	5,929	2,696	2,444	2,190	15,715	...
1964	40,038	29,687	2,795	32,482	1,555	5	30,932	6,317	2,788	2,536	2,303	15,787	...
1965	43,929	31,633	4,110	35,743	1,632	4	34,114	6,794	3,021	2,777	2,515	15,819	...
1966	47,250	34,720	4,310	39,030	2,197	-0	36,833	7,154	3,263	2,974	2,673	15,888	...
1967	49,583	37,182	3,678	40,860	2,551	-5	38,304	7,385	3,894	3,110	2,788	15,942	...
1968	54,099	40,694	3,670	44,364	2,839	-14	41,510	8,084	4,505	3,371	3,000	16,047	...
1969	59,316	44,699	4,220	48,918	3,160	-402	45,356	9,020	4,940	3,661	3,210	16,202	7,506
1970	64,334	47,663	4,443	52,106	3,338	-340	48,429	10,114	5,792	3,935	3,489	16,350	7,516
1971	69,267	51,030	4,611	55,640	3,693	-338	51,610	11,004	6,653	4,204	3,772	16,475	7,544
1972	76,510	55,663	6,161	61,823	4,221	-343	57,259	11,999	7,252	4,619	4,092	16,563	7,731
1973	89,249	61,651	11,294	72,944	5,396	-379	67,169	13,630	8,450	5,367	4,789	16,628	8,065
1974	94,449	67,832	7,686	75,518	6,185	-415	68,918	15,681	9,850	5,665	4,973	16,672	8,219
1975	103,645	73,512	7,499	81,012	6,595	-411	74,006	17,517	12,122	6,191	5,505	16,743	8,181
1976	111,098	82,629	4,408	87,036	7,513	-502	79,022	18,882	13,194	6,588	5,818	16,864	8,438
1977	122,799	91,373	5,192	96,565	8,271	-634	87,659	21,197	13,943	7,245	6,385	16,950	8,657
1978	138,981	102,717	7,837	110,554	9,610	-787	100,157	23,647	15,177	8,162	7,171	17,028	8,953
1979	153,329	115,180	6,613	121,793	11,215	-974	109,604	26,729	16,996	8,968	7,813	17,097	9,232
1980	165,726	124,093	1,879	125,973	12,037	-1,126	112,809	32,596	20,321	9,631	8,386	17,208	9,227
1981	187,486	133,902	5,447	139,348	13,885	-1,299	124,164	40,165	23,157	10,860	9,435	17,264	9,180
1982	199,706	138,806	4,004	142,811	14,670	-1,295	126,846	47,064	25,797	11,549	10,053	17,292	9,050
1983	209,174	147,580	1,577	149,157	15,668	-1,380	132,109	49,321	27,745	12,073	10,663	17,325	9,163
1984	233,264	162,450	6,545	168,995	17,707	-1,544	149,743	54,614	28,906	13,420	11,963	17,382	9,470
1985	246,146	171,852	7,464	179,317	19,108	-1,660	158,549	56,988	30,609	14,145	12,585	17,402	9,612
1986	257,591	180,991	8,061	189,052	20,469	-1,784	166,799	58,702	32,090	14,810	13,214	17,393	9,701
1987	271,386	193,085	9,777	202,861	21,690	-1,894	179,277	59,097	33,012	15,572	13,807	17,428	9,949
1988	284,961	206,938	7,383	214,321	24,079	-2,057	188,184	62,118	34,659	16,253	14,421	17,533	10,156
1989	307,374	220,563	9,207	229,771	25,698	-2,138	201,935	67,836	37,604	17,469	15,442	17,595	10,357
1990	325,179	233,385	10,544	243,929	27,917	-2,413	213,599	70,926	40,655	18,374	16,225	17,698	10,544
1991	336,324	243,055	8,117	251,171	29,420	-2,433	219,319	72,214	44,792	18,849	16,721	17,843	10,597
1992	360,431	261,004	10,635	271,639	31,222	-2,549	237,868	74,034	48,529	19,995	17,776	18,026	10,708
1993	372,543	273,681	6,237	279,918	32,831	-2,645	244,443	76,616	51,484	20,459	18,140	18,210	10,934
1994	397,796	290,478	10,482	300,960	35,227	-2,806	262,928	81,090	53,778	21,642	19,175	18,381	11,230
1995	417,276	306,991	5,742	312,733	37,055	-3,038	272,640	87,600	57,037	22,495	19,845	18,550	11,537
1996	448,955	324,702	13,572	338,274	38,591	-3,300	296,383	92,878	59,694	24,002	21,075	18,705	11,761
1997	471,677	345,600	9,882	355,482	41,154	-3,691	310,637	99,426	61,614	25,021	21,839	18,851	11,980
1998	503,068	371,105	9,199	380,303	43,759	-3,930	332,615	106,887	63,566	26,494	23,069	18,988	12,240
1999	523,408	393,034	7,938	400,972	46,129	-4,237	350,607	106,290	66,511	27,359	23,860	19,131	12,411
2000	560,204	418,180	9,609	427,788	48,646	-4,537	374,605	114,429	71,169	29,063	25,299	19,275	12,604
2001	579,594	432,831	9,072	441,903	50,180	-4,637	387,085	114,263	78,246	29,915	26,123	19,375	12,601
2002	591,497	446,157	6,248	452,404	51,454	-4,689	396,261	111,068	84,167	30,383	27,058	19,468	12,519
2003	616,061	460,358	12,507	472,865	53,396	-4,853	414,616	114,155	87,291	31,481	28,346	19,569	12,521
2004	648,958	486,059	16,761	502,820	56,026	-5,119	441,674	115,874	91,409	32,962	29,775	19,688	12,674
2005	672,762	504,101	16,020	520,121	58,723	-5,409	455,989	119,836	96,937	33,973	30,386	19,803	12,863
2006	715,362	532,789	10,882	543,672	62,088	-5,672	475,912	134,533	104,917	35,845	31,879	19,957	13,061
2007	762,388	556,398	15,958	572,357	64,930	-5,689	501,738	147,900	112,750	37,919	33,542	20,106	13,280
2008	807,194	576,901	20,428	597,329	67,568	-6,219	523,632	156,183	127,379	39,864	35,315	20,249	13,298
2009	784,028	563,635	14,882	578,517	66,212	-5,252	507,053	139,339	137,636	38,447	34,932	20,393	12,991
2010	812,922	581,757	17,580	599,337	67,455	-5,108	526,773	138,850	147,299	39,585	35,861	20,536	12,918
2011	872,003	607,439	29,372	636,811	62,813	-5,333	568,665	153,697	149,640	42,249	37,887	20,640	13,099
2012	921,647	642,047	27,675	669,722	65,079	-5,908	598,735	172,946	149,966	44,417	39,829	20,750	13,262
2013	931,393	660,871	33,939	694,810	75,793	-6,335	612,682	165,197	153,514	44,627	39,635	20,871	13,446
2014	971,530	690,980	24,310	715,291	78,669	-7,065	629,556	182,444	159,529	46,298	41,090	20,984	13,619
2015	1,003,740	715,937	17,925	733,862	81,634	-7,280	644,948	192,046	166,746	47,605	42,096	21,085	13,788
2016	1,016,405	724,081	12,944	737,026	83,076	-6,987	646,964	197,284	172,157	47,996	42,446	21,177	13,876
2017	1,047,115	747,957	9,990	757,946	86,002	-7,183	664,761	206,144	176,210	49,213	43,509	21,277	13,984
2018	1,088,197	775,407	10,701	786,108	89,347	-7,438	689,322	214,736	184,138	50,905	45,221	21,377	14,072
2019	1,146,515	1,127,286	19,229	825,804	93,059	-7,901	724,845	225,863	195,807	53,485	47,586	21,436	14,227
2020	1,209,885	1,185,151	24,734	833,832	94,480	-7,929	731,423	223,199	255,263	56,321	50,442	21,482	...

... = Not available.

Personal Income and Employment by Region and State: Rocky Mountain

(Millions of dollars, except as noted.)

| Year | Personal income, total | Earnings by place of work | | | Less: Contributions for government social insurance | Plus: Adjustment for residence | Equals: Net earnings by place of residence | Plus: Dividends, interest, and rent | Plus: Personal current transfer receipts | Per capita (dollars) | | Population (thousands) | Total employment (thousands) |
		Nonfarm	Farm	Total						Personal income	Disposable personal income		
1960	9,819	7,372	590	7,962	354	-2	7,605	1,591	624	2,257	2,021	4,350	...
1961	10,407	7,883	536	8,420	382	-3	8,035	1,682	690	2,314	2,072	4,497	...
1962	11,218	8,366	721	9,087	412	-3	8,673	1,825	721	2,449	2,201	4,580	...
1963	11,583	8,759	636	9,395	478	-2	8,915	1,911	758	2,501	2,241	4,632	...
1964	12,120	9,267	520	9,786	491	-2	9,293	2,049	777	2,594	2,364	4,673	...
1965	13,010	9,747	736	10,483	499	-2	9,982	2,187	840	2,766	2,518	4,703	...
1966	13,792	10,506	706	11,212	646	-1	10,565	2,326	902	2,913	2,637	4,735	...
1967	14,653	11,125	717	11,842	722	-1	11,119	2,465	1,069	3,064	2,762	4,783	...
1968	15,901	12,166	754	12,920	805	-1	12,115	2,572	1,215	3,267	2,921	4,868	...
1969	17,806	13,437	889	14,326	881	18	13,463	2,998	1,345	3,602	3,177	4,943	2,216
1970	19,931	14,797	1,003	15,799	962	20	14,858	3,472	1,601	3,956	3,530	5,038	2,271
1971	22,182	16,543	966	17,510	1,102	20	16,428	3,883	1,871	4,271	3,834	5,194	2,343
1972	25,137	18,788	1,269	20,056	1,320	23	18,759	4,288	2,090	4,682	4,174	5,368	2,482
1973	28,740	21,327	1,751	23,078	1,728	22	21,372	4,926	2,442	5,200	4,630	5,527	2,646
1974	32,390	23,981	1,836	25,818	2,002	24	23,840	5,712	2,838	5,733	5,079	5,650	2,740
1975	35,793	26,573	1,385	27,958	2,179	36	25,815	6,449	3,530	6,191	5,551	5,782	2,778
1976	39,578	30,110	1,026	31,136	2,512	40	28,665	7,024	3,889	6,690	5,957	5,916	2,912
1977	44,131	34,200	685	34,885	2,870	42	32,057	7,919	4,154	7,260	6,429	6,079	3,060
1978	51,079	39,772	956	40,728	3,411	52	37,370	9,168	4,542	8,164	7,217	6,257	3,257
1979	57,686	45,355	748	46,103	4,090	45	42,058	10,471	5,157	8,959	7,860	6,439	3,402
1980	65,483	50,410	964	51,374	4,596	68	46,846	12,580	6,056	9,933	8,723	6,592	3,474
1981	74,507	56,598	1,053	57,651	5,564	51	52,138	15,295	7,074	11,050	9,651	6,743	3,559
1982	80,525	60,191	824	61,015	6,033	52	55,034	17,443	8,048	11,664	10,215	6,904	3,596
1983	86,074	63,433	1,144	64,577	6,397	54	58,234	18,995	8,845	12,235	10,905	7,035	3,642
1984	93,219	69,070	1,042	70,113	7,175	75	63,012	20,975	9,231	13,113	11,733	7,109	3,801
1985	98,385	72,878	844	73,722	7,730	92	66,084	22,512	9,789	13,726	12,257	7,168	3,861
1986	101,921	74,974	1,242	76,216	8,019	113	68,309	23,104	10,508	14,156	12,693	7,200	3,854
1987	105,381	77,291	1,578	78,869	8,209	135	70,795	23,439	11,147	14,625	13,061	7,206	3,885
1988	111,343	82,283	1,625	83,908	9,123	174	74,959	24,629	11,755	15,459	13,819	7,203	4,021
1989	120,543	87,594	2,216	89,811	9,870	209	80,150	27,416	12,976	16,663	14,809	7,234	4,114
1990	128,616	94,193	2,514	96,707	10,976	245	85,976	28,608	14,032	17,606	15,580	7,305	4,230
1991	136,495	100,831	2,466	103,297	12,004	274	91,567	29,458	15,470	18,255	16,206	7,477	4,335
1992	147,774	110,190	2,543	112,733	12,992	306	100,047	30,506	17,221	19,200	17,036	7,696	4,434
1993	159,847	119,354	3,220	122,574	14,206	341	108,709	32,599	18,539	20,135	17,838	7,939	4,626
1994	171,008	128,625	2,094	130,719	15,410	393	115,701	35,814	19,492	20,928	18,480	8,171	4,886
1995	184,801	137,320	1,995	139,315	16,397	452	123,370	39,970	21,461	22,053	19,457	8,380	5,046
1996	198,591	147,253	2,190	149,442	17,263	524	132,704	43,423	22,464	23,185	20,325	8,565	5,249
1997	212,577	158,556	2,053	160,609	18,380	601	142,829	46,716	23,032	24,306	21,175	8,746	5,440
1998	231,347	173,756	2,393	176,148	19,327	699	157,520	50,076	23,750	25,941	22,522	8,918	5,621
1999	246,924	188,205	2,740	190,945	20,642	798	171,100	50,851	24,972	27,151	23,494	9,094	5,752
2000	270,373	206,935	2,383	209,318	22,510	857	187,664	55,910	26,798	29,170	25,117	9,269	5,953
2001	282,986	215,810	3,060	218,870	23,609	843	196,104	57,345	29,536	30,006	26,083	9,431	6,007
2002	287,142	219,913	2,319	222,231	24,377	834	198,689	56,197	32,256	30,013	26,715	9,567	6,002
2003	295,768	225,148	2,378	227,527	25,131	850	203,246	58,451	34,071	30,569	27,494	9,675	6,023
2004	311,688	236,940	3,387	240,327	26,919	880	214,289	61,491	35,908	31,781	28,606	9,808	6,166
2005	335,449	252,872	3,399	256,271	28,876	884	228,278	68,408	38,763	33,639	29,891	9,972	6,371
2006	367,141	275,817	2,328	278,145	31,435	858	247,568	77,757	41,817	36,030	31,748	10,190	6,589
2007	393,281	290,970	3,436	294,407	33,418	871	261,860	86,411	45,011	37,793	33,122	10,406	6,848
2008	409,182	297,173	3,355	300,528	34,540	929	266,917	89,964	52,301	38,567	34,045	10,610	6,895
2009	391,529	283,932	2,348	286,280	33,450	1,047	253,877	79,947	57,705	36,273	32,886	10,794	6,686
2010	405,708	290,997	3,325	294,321	34,008	1,225	261,538	79,860	64,310	37,052	33,498	10,950	6,635
2011	438,404	306,509	4,753	311,262	32,096	1,628	280,793	91,898	65,713	39,552	35,390	11,084	6,761
2012	467,422	324,898	4,519	329,417	33,558	2,254	298,114	103,226	66,083	41,650	37,232	11,223	6,882
2013	485,386	345,907	5,470	351,377	39,025	2,553	314,905	102,102	68,379	42,669	37,873	11,376	7,055
2014	521,693	369,275	5,576	374,851	41,472	2,827	336,205	113,372	72,116	45,268	40,115	11,525	7,250
2015	550,009	384,215	5,529	389,743	43,333	2,631	349,042	123,936	77,031	47,000	41,500	11,702	7,453
2016	564,265	392,709	4,379	397,088	44,640	2,424	354,872	128,539	80,853	47,451	41,811	11,892	7,639
2017	593,926	415,966	4,277	420,244	47,322	2,646	375,567	134,636	83,723	49,207	43,359	12,070	7,807
2018	627,568	439,748	4,367	444,115	50,140	2,797	396,773	141,966	88,829	51,226	45,358	12,251	8,052
2019	680,390	675,447	4,943	479,823	53,189	2,986	429,621	155,007	95,763	54,865	48,638	12,401	8,256
2020	722,012	715,871	6,142	491,796	55,101	2,935	439,631	153,286	129,096	57,543	51271	12,547	...

... = Not available.

Personal Income and Employment by Region and State: Southeast

(Millions of dollars, except as noted.)

Year	Personal income, total	Earnings by place of work			Less: Contributions for government social insurance	Plus: Adjustment for residence	Equals: Net earnings by place of residence	Plus: Dividends, interest, and rent	Plus: Personal current transfer receipts	Per capita (dollars)		Population (thousands)	Total employment (thousands)
		Nonfarm	Farm	Total						Personal income	Disposable personal income		
1960	66,930	51,896	3,350	55,246	2,447	589	53,388	8,939	4,603	1,721	1,565	38,885	...
1961	70,593	53,773	3,773	57,546	2,513	616	55,650	9,648	5,295	1,785	1,626	39,544	...
1962	75,390	57,877	3,533	61,410	2,806	676	59,281	10,553	5,556	1,876	1,700	40,179	...
1963	80,425	61,902	3,765	65,667	3,287	738	63,117	11,406	5,901	1,974	1,787	40,742	...
1964	86,835	67,360	3,625	70,985	3,444	801	68,343	12,335	6,157	2,100	1,920	41,349	...
1965	94,368	73,503	3,505	77,007	3,677	899	74,229	13,416	6,723	2,255	2,054	41,857	...
1966	103,487	81,959	3,714	85,673	4,914	1,000	81,759	14,388	7,340	2,449	2,214	42,257	...
1967	112,234	88,700	3,700	92,400	5,668	1,160	87,892	15,596	8,746	2,634	2,381	42,611	...
1968	124,348	98,752	3,572	102,324	6,410	1,258	97,173	17,075	10,100	2,889	2,585	43,042	...
1969	138,939	109,456	4,060	113,516	7,214	1,173	107,475	20,075	11,390	3,198	2,826	43,440	19,085
1970	152,550	117,976	4,050	122,026	7,779	1,084	115,332	23,440	13,778	3,469	3,095	43,974	19,254
1971	168,335	129,403	4,262	133,664	8,837	1,064	125,891	26,165	16,279	3,740	3,362	45,013	19,635
1972	189,159	146,065	4,964	151,029	10,454	1,127	141,702	29,037	18,420	4,110	3,653	46,019	20,523
1973	214,956	164,853	7,279	172,132	13,506	1,205	159,831	33,295	21,829	4,574	4,084	46,992	21,636
1974	239,478	181,787	6,663	188,450	15,479	1,305	174,276	38,811	26,391	4,994	4,439	47,955	22,069
1975	262,258	193,771	5,996	199,767	16,286	1,575	185,055	42,950	34,253	5,376	4,864	48,788	21,642
1976	291,460	217,654	6,366	224,020	18,675	1,779	207,124	46,883	37,453	5,886	5,281	49,514	22,351
1977	323,485	243,985	5,766	249,751	20,914	1,996	230,833	52,777	39,876	6,430	5,750	50,312	23,208
1978	367,595	278,118	6,931	285,048	24,375	2,393	263,066	60,877	43,652	7,192	6,399	51,113	24,305
1979	412,930	311,625	6,844	318,469	28,418	2,748	292,799	69,795	50,337	7,945	7,024	51,977	24,987
1980	465,434	343,617	4,173	347,790	31,420	3,314	319,685	85,651	60,098	8,802	7,771	52,881	25,324
1981	526,762	379,323	6,634	385,957	37,261	3,641	352,337	105,694	68,731	9,823	8,643	53,627	25,594
1982	564,551	399,041	6,759	405,799	39,941	3,822	369,680	118,617	76,254	10,407	9,201	54,249	25,499
1983	607,945	431,608	4,899	436,507	43,698	3,815	396,625	128,271	83,049	11,083	9,876	54,856	26,030
1984	675,543	479,757	8,400	488,156	49,934	4,070	442,293	145,742	87,508	12,169	10,910	55,515	27,280
1985	726,369	518,345	7,444	525,789	54,899	4,250	475,139	157,809	93,421	12,925	11,519	56,199	28,090
1986	773,946	555,092	6,952	562,043	59,997	4,449	506,496	167,839	99,611	13,611	12,139	56,861	28,826
1987	826,506	599,058	8,292	607,350	64,249	4,649	547,750	175,037	103,718	14,365	12,753	57,536	29,529
1988	898,850	651,929	10,868	662,797	72,102	5,120	595,815	191,737	111,298	15,465	13,800	58,120	30,527
1989	977,273	693,926	11,406	705,332	77,510	5,499	633,321	220,220	123,732	16,639	14,784	58,733	31,251
1990	1,039,866	737,578	10,875	748,453	83,396	6,148	671,205	232,836	135,825	17,472	15,561	59,516	31,840
1991	1,089,343	768,150	12,420	780,569	87,898	6,635	699,307	236,439	153,597	18,005	16,125	60,501	31,724
1992	1,169,367	829,036	13,206	842,242	94,074	7,073	755,241	240,780	173,347	19,012	17,058	61,508	32,180
1993	1,235,141	877,705	12,804	890,509	100,058	7,353	797,804	251,649	185,688	19,753	17,695	62,531	33,186
1994	1,309,965	931,123	14,006	945,129	107,408	7,255	844,975	267,727	197,262	20,605	18,410	63,574	34,135
1995	1,395,633	985,443	12,430	997,873	113,546	7,511	891,838	291,102	212,692	21,604	19,258	64,602	35,254
1996	1,481,272	1,042,682	14,181	1,056,863	118,968	7,178	945,073	310,847	225,352	22,576	20,002	65,611	36,087
1997	1,571,741	1,110,100	13,860	1,123,960	126,228	7,989	1,005,721	332,117	233,903	23,580	20,772	66,655	37,050
1998	1,688,395	1,203,741	12,928	1,216,669	135,202	8,011	1,089,478	358,327	240,590	24,966	21,902	67,627	38,014
1999	1,771,679	1,281,763	13,076	1,294,839	143,365	9,821	1,161,295	359,271	251,113	25,838	22,640	68,569	38,802
2000	1,898,390	1,371,739	14,403	1,386,143	151,844	8,281	1,242,580	387,613	268,197	27,316	23,914	69,497	39,694
2001	1,984,447	1,428,773	16,278	1,445,051	158,517	8,981	1,295,514	393,164	295,769	28,221	24,769	70,318	39,630
2002	2,038,474	1,477,937	10,354	1,488,292	163,459	10,636	1,335,469	383,789	319,216	28,650	25,677	71,152	39,667
2003	2,126,430	1,543,439	13,258	1,556,696	170,390	11,636	1,397,942	393,550	334,938	29,550	26,759	71,962	40,062
2004	2,276,134	1,648,067	16,863	1,664,930	181,838	12,366	1,495,458	421,671	359,005	31,172	28,242	73,019	41,037
2005	2,435,707	1,747,755	17,718	1,765,474	193,106	13,173	1,585,541	460,753	389,414	32,849	29,476	74,148	42,110
2006	2,615,658	1,857,901	13,192	1,871,093	206,547	15,098	1,679,644	522,561	413,453	34,845	31,125	75,066	43,151
2007	2,756,629	1,923,455	12,354	1,935,809	215,107	16,374	1,737,076	577,384	442,169	36,213	32,257	76,123	44,065
2008	2,841,012	1,939,932	11,621	1,951,552	220,562	18,547	1,749,537	589,479	501,995	36,869	32,992	77,058	43,725
2009	2,753,800	1,873,626	11,632	1,885,258	216,160	18,413	1,687,510	519,328	546,962	35,389	32,415	77,815	42,223
2010	2,866,027	1,934,702	10,636	1,945,338	220,605	20,186	1,744,919	527,985	593,124	36,477	33,344	78,571	42,066
2011	3,020,755	1,996,837	10,694	2,007,531	203,951	22,817	1,826,397	584,166	610,191	38,122	34,511	79,239	42,886
2012	3,151,613	2,086,275	14,315	2,100,590	211,144	22,825	1,912,271	627,149	612,193	39,432	35,742	79,926	43,433
2013	3,164,660	2,128,908	22,462	2,151,370	244,534	22,974	1,929,809	605,314	629,537	39,287	35,263	80,553	44,149
2014	3,350,203	2,231,912	17,213	2,249,125	254,988	25,270	2,019,407	670,993	659,803	41,234	36,981	81,249	45,189
2015	3,526,433	2,335,206	15,091	2,350,297	266,711	25,769	2,109,355	720,715	696,363	42,986	38,367	82,038	46,284
2016	3,626,161	2,401,963	10,757	2,412,720	274,746	26,825	2,164,799	740,283	721,080	43,743	39,124	82,896	47,168
2017	3,783,717	2,508,524	12,511	2,521,035	286,850	27,262	2,261,448	774,114	748,156	45,224	40,463	83,665	47,861
2018	3,952,330	2,616,808	16,337	2,633,145	300,167	28,024	2,361,002	809,644	781,684	46,830	42,085	84,397	49,285
2019	4,173,677	4,161,389	12,288	2,767,741	314,891	27,277	2,480,127	874,631	818,919	49,103	43,872	84,999	50,219
2020	4,431,929	4,420,445	11,484	2,811,154	321,595	27,652	2,517,211	864,930	1,049,787	51,796	46590	85,566	...

... = Not available.

Personal Income and Employment by Region and State: Southwest

(Millions of dollars, except as noted.)

| Year | Personal income, total | Derivation of personal income | | | | | | | | Per capita (dollars) | | Population (thousands) | Total employment (thousands) |
| | | Earnings by place of work | | | Less: Contributions for government social insurance | Plus: Adjustment for residence | Equals: Net earnings by place of residence | Plus: Dividends, interest, and rent | Plus: Personal current transfer receipts | Personal income | Disposable personal income | | |
		Nonfarm	Farm	Total									
1960	28,817	22,282	1,474	23,756	1,006	5	22,755	4,417	1,645	2,024	1,826	14,235	...
1961	30,430	23,321	1,628	24,949	1,040	6	23,915	4,664	1,851	2,088	1,883	14,572	...
1962	31,996	24,782	1,411	26,192	1,132	9	25,069	4,932	1,995	2,143	1,928	14,930	...
1963	33,362	26,032	1,197	27,229	1,277	12	25,964	5,246	2,152	2,208	1,985	15,108	...
1964	35,741	28,050	1,132	29,182	1,330	14	27,865	5,629	2,247	2,339	2,134	15,278	...
1965	38,346	29,923	1,349	31,272	1,400	16	29,888	6,007	2,451	2,488	2,264	15,414	...
1966	41,706	33,093	1,409	34,503	1,882	17	32,638	6,394	2,674	2,679	2,420	15,567	...
1967	45,390	36,228	1,294	37,522	2,185	19	35,356	6,792	3,242	2,885	2,600	15,734	...
1968	50,518	40,397	1,423	41,820	2,456	24	39,388	7,318	3,812	3,158	2,817	15,998	...
1969	56,501	45,081	1,513	46,594	2,887	-62	43,644	8,604	4,252	3,460	3,052	16,328	7,219
1970	62,539	48,789	1,837	50,626	3,104	-84	47,438	10,062	5,038	3,763	3,356	16,621	7,311
1971	68,408	53,227	1,681	54,907	3,501	-90	51,317	11,206	5,885	4,006	3,615	17,077	7,457
1972	76,145	59,347	2,017	61,364	4,085	-107	57,171	12,379	6,594	4,350	3,884	17,503	7,807
1973	86,582	66,711	3,298	70,009	5,306	-121	64,583	14,160	7,839	4,825	4,325	17,943	8,215
1974	97,435	75,688	2,139	77,828	6,213	-82	71,532	16,546	9,357	5,309	4,712	18,354	8,511
1975	110,068	84,419	2,112	86,530	6,831	-46	79,653	18,584	11,831	5,858	5,276	18,789	8,633
1976	123,377	96,099	2,083	98,182	7,904	25	90,303	20,095	12,980	6,403	5,723	19,270	9,001
1977	137,741	108,947	1,864	110,811	9,030	-220	101,562	22,399	13,781	6,988	6,199	19,710	9,466
1978	158,697	126,806	1,689	128,496	10,776	-357	117,363	26,071	15,263	7,864	6,960	20,180	10,046
1979	183,167	146,035	2,982	149,017	13,007	-363	135,647	30,087	17,433	8,816	7,726	20,777	10,528
1980	210,220	166,795	1,542	168,336	14,995	-463	152,877	36,862	20,480	9,811	8,563	21,426	10,923
1981	245,544	192,286	2,837	195,123	18,608	-168	176,347	45,812	23,385	11,169	9,641	21,985	11,449
1982	269,939	207,412	2,353	209,765	20,499	-229	189,038	54,458	26,443	11,844	10,301	22,791	11,682
1983	287,700	216,992	2,409	219,401	21,389	-159	197,854	60,329	29,517	12,292	10,909	23,405	11,712
1984	315,288	237,772	2,677	240,449	24,038	-157	216,254	67,729	31,305	13,260	11,829	23,776	12,259
1985	339,561	254,606	2,582	257,188	26,109	-124	230,954	75,077	33,530	14,051	12,531	24,166	12,617
1986	350,080	261,020	2,586	263,606	26,713	-7	236,885	76,647	36,548	14,240	12,835	24,585	12,483
1987	359,140	267,461	3,519	270,980	27,114	84	243,951	76,587	38,602	14,512	13,014	24,748	12,785
1988	380,981	284,825	4,156	288,981	29,977	180	259,185	80,840	40,956	15,325	13,806	24,860	13,055
1989	407,156	301,237	4,117	305,354	32,059	264	273,559	88,344	45,253	16,232	14,541	25,083	13,241
1990	435,970	323,758	4,967	328,725	34,447	357	294,635	91,137	50,198	17,157	15,341	25,411	13,553
1991	456,160	341,059	4,535	345,594	37,064	316	308,845	91,570	55,744	17,601	15,816	25,917	13,759
1992	491,175	366,887	5,371	372,258	39,437	357	333,177	93,228	64,769	18,541	16,737	26,491	13,885
1993	520,514	390,291	6,179	396,470	41,953	409	354,927	96,295	69,292	19,196	17,310	27,116	14,332
1994	552,548	414,846	5,304	420,149	45,127	428	375,450	102,801	74,297	19,896	17,915	27,772	14,845
1995	591,292	442,143	4,279	446,422	47,841	408	398,988	111,824	80,480	20,806	18,706	28,420	15,396
1996	634,837	476,523	3,905	480,428	51,061	421	429,787	119,132	85,918	21,876	19,533	29,020	15,883
1997	687,796	520,983	5,000	525,984	55,115	417	471,285	126,972	89,539	23,217	20,599	29,625	16,482
1998	745,133	571,548	4,808	576,356	59,742	427	517,040	136,260	91,833	24,641	21,774	30,240	17,034
1999	782,043	605,760	6,642	612,403	63,268	537	549,671	136,966	95,406	25,369	22,407	30,827	17,353
2000	850,147	660,929	5,526	666,455	68,054	603	599,004	150,108	101,035	27,091	23,837	31,381	17,900
2001	899,787	702,469	6,338	708,808	71,645	678	637,841	150,371	111,575	28,214	24,944	31,892	18,099
2002	915,581	713,489	6,268	719,757	73,044	742	647,455	145,581	122,545	28,232	25,548	32,431	18,111
2003	953,978	738,126	7,542	745,668	76,122	887	670,433	152,051	131,494	28,975	26,464	32,924	18,266
2004	1,009,992	782,396	8,503	790,899	80,630	1,055	711,324	158,861	139,807	30,171	27,613	33,475	18,655
2005	1,102,095	842,502	8,171	850,672	86,268	1,092	765,497	182,592	154,006	32,321	29,238	34,098	19,317
2006	1,212,178	928,875	5,284	934,158	92,832	1,024	842,351	203,878	165,949	34,688	31,188	34,945	20,044
2007	1,283,510	968,656	6,032	974,688	98,913	975	876,750	225,485	181,274	36,029	32,308	35,624	20,726
2008	1,388,297	1,026,141	3,372	1,029,514	103,204	875	927,185	254,221	206,892	38,278	34,236	36,269	21,061
2009	1,320,708	968,720	1,869	970,590	101,641	578	869,528	223,773	227,408	35,792	33,020	36,899	20,640
2010	1,388,502	1,014,206	5,616	1,019,823	104,964	344	915,203	223,233	250,067	37,052	34,078	37,475	20,634
2011	1,504,486	1,087,946	6,386	1,094,332	98,730	-48	995,554	252,801	256,132	39,604	35,967	37,988	21,144
2012	1,603,076	1,161,401	6,262	1,167,662	104,055	-320	1,063,288	283,565	256,224	41,582	37,819	38,552	21,670
2013	1,642,200	1,215,389	9,262	1,224,651	122,327	-620	1,101,704	275,983	264,513	42,032	37,897	39,070	22,225
2014	1,762,041	1,295,574	9,441	1,305,015	128,742	-598	1,175,675	306,731	279,634	44,407	39,976	39,680	22,803
2015	1,805,776	1,309,238	10,266	1,319,503	134,278	-569	1,184,657	324,948	296,172	44,786	40,263	40,320	23,336
2016	1,814,967	1,307,146	5,696	1,312,843	137,274	-141	1,175,427	330,111	309,429	44,373	40,145	40,903	23,698
2017	1,894,780	1,369,030	7,087	1,376,117	144,354	128	1,231,891	345,115	317,774	45,770	41,428	41,398	24,091
2018	1,992,276	1,445,008	7,614	1,452,622	152,893	57	1,299,787	361,730	330,759	47,535	43,192	41,912	24,880
2019	2,144,764	2,137,515	7,249	1,567,300	159,564	-70	1,407,666	388,018	349,080	50,657	45,745	42,339	25,461
2020	2,265,983	2,258,196	7,787	1,568,812	161,527	-108	1,407,177	384,487	474,319	52,858	48,053	42,869	...

... = Not available.

STATE

Personal Income and Employment by Region and State: Alabama

(Millions of dollars, except as noted.)

Year	Personal income, total	Earnings by place of work			Less: Contributions for government social insurance	Plus: Adjustment for residence	Equals: Net earnings by place of residence	Plus: Dividends, interest, and rent	Plus: Personal current transfer receipts	Per capita (dollars)		Population (thousands)	Total employment (thousands)
		Nonfarm	Farm	Total						Personal income	Disposable personal income		
1960	5,188	4,170	257	4,427	187	2	4,242	561	385	1,585	1,448	3,274	...
1961	5,360	4,279	247	4,526	194	3	4,335	596	429	1,616	1,484	3,316	...
1962	5,634	4,512	227	4,738	219	4	4,523	643	468	1,695	1,545	3,323	...
1963	5,984	4,779	275	5,054	260	7	4,801	687	496	1,782	1,625	3,358	...
1964	6,498	5,244	247	5,492	265	8	5,234	750	513	1,914	1,755	3,395	...
1965	7,052	5,704	257	5,961	273	11	5,699	803	551	2,048	1,874	3,443	...
1966	7,564	6,246	244	6,491	376	17	6,132	834	599	2,184	1,981	3,464	...
1967	7,992	6,613	209	6,822	429	23	6,415	886	691	2,311	2,096	3,458	...
1968	8,738	7,184	229	7,413	473	27	6,967	970	801	2,536	2,282	3,446	...
1969	9,738	7,833	280	8,112	550	130	7,692	1,154	892	2,831	2,515	3,440	1,411
1970	10,628	8,378	250	8,629	590	127	8,166	1,366	1,097	3,081	2,781	3,450	1,413
1971	11,699	9,124	279	9,403	655	133	8,881	1,534	1,285	3,345	3,032	3,497	1,423
1972	12,999	10,148	348	10,496	765	165	9,896	1,672	1,431	3,672	3,303	3,540	1,471
1973	14,639	11,327	535	11,862	983	183	11,062	1,896	1,681	4,088	3,677	3,581	1,526
1974	16,241	12,621	340	12,961	1,136	194	12,019	2,211	2,011	4,477	4,019	3,628	1,552
1975	18,100	13,631	414	14,045	1,222	200	13,024	2,476	2,601	4,918	4,460	3,681	1,543
1976	20,324	15,499	479	15,978	1,422	214	14,770	2,706	2,849	5,438	4,896	3,737	1,594
1977	22,395	17,332	383	17,716	1,596	246	16,365	3,024	3,005	5,920	5,324	3,783	1,651
1978	25,340	19,656	509	20,165	1,840	266	18,591	3,480	3,269	6,609	5,928	3,834	1,713
1979	28,151	21,682	521	22,204	2,103	291	20,392	3,951	3,809	7,275	6,491	3,869	1,736
1980	31,037	23,498	211	23,709	2,277	324	21,755	4,803	4,479	7,957	7,082	3,900	1,732
1981	34,466	25,323	490	25,813	2,644	421	23,589	5,851	5,025	8,796	7,811	3,919	1,719
1982	36,396	26,219	411	26,629	2,783	444	24,291	6,552	5,553	9,272	8,315	3,925	1,687
1983	38,971	28,289	293	28,582	3,053	436	25,965	6,994	6,012	9,906	8,884	3,934	1,717
1984	42,870	31,153	482	31,634	3,427	465	28,672	7,847	6,352	10,848	9,772	3,952	1,780
1985	46,099	33,713	467	34,180	3,739	473	30,914	8,477	6,708	11,604	10,388	3,973	1,822
1986	48,790	35,877	458	36,336	3,972	503	32,866	8,945	6,980	12,223	10,944	3,992	1,858
1987	51,652	38,286	541	38,827	4,194	513	35,145	9,373	7,133	12,864	11,454	4,015	1,912
1988	55,559	41,170	802	41,973	4,668	517	37,821	10,287	7,451	13,807	12,391	4,024	1,970
1989	60,396	43,679	941	44,619	4,970	539	40,188	11,785	8,422	14,986	13,377	4,030	2,006
1990	64,240	46,584	849	47,433	5,366	532	42,599	12,366	9,275	15,861	14,175	4,050	2,048
1991	67,930	48,981	1,124	50,105	5,681	563	44,987	12,686	10,257	16,572	14,867	4,099	2,060
1992	73,040	52,806	1,003	53,809	6,062	614	48,361	13,027	11,652	17,583	15,821	4,154	2,097
1993	76,398	55,246	1,018	56,263	6,419	665	50,509	13,522	12,366	18,129	16,294	4,214	2,159
1994	80,848	58,196	1,069	59,265	6,849	758	53,174	14,554	13,120	18,977	16,995	4,260	2,180
1995	85,474	60,931	788	61,720	7,217	839	55,342	15,938	14,194	19,892	17,772	4,297	2,242
1996	89,350	63,517	917	64,434	7,464	845	57,815	16,534	15,000	20,630	18,364	4,331	2,275
1997	93,981	66,557	954	67,511	7,830	949	60,630	17,674	15,678	21,516	19,087	4,368	2,321
1998	100,081	71,089	1,076	72,165	8,228	1,065	65,001	19,093	15,987	22,721	20,173	4,405	2,362
1999	103,536	74,185	1,244	75,429	8,593	1,131	67,968	18,916	16,653	23,371	20,723	4,430	2,378
2000	108,506	77,019	960	77,979	8,886	1,257	70,349	20,408	17,750	24,372	21,640	4,452	2,392
2001	112,312	78,918	1,391	80,309	9,189	1,315	72,435	20,670	19,207	25,139	22,337	4,468	2,376
2002	115,166	81,659	987	82,646	9,484	1,374	74,536	20,076	20,554	25,706	23,228	4,480	2,365
2003	120,210	84,600	1,308	85,908	9,831	1,455	77,533	20,865	21,812	26,693	24,323	4,503	2,371
2004	128,670	89,760	1,806	91,566	10,332	1,489	82,723	22,840	23,107	28,399	25,976	4,531	2,426
2005	136,215	95,148	1,680	96,828	10,989	1,555	87,393	23,971	24,851	29,808	26,989	4,570	2,487
2006	144,914	101,211	1,011	102,223	11,667	1,611	92,166	25,984	26,764	31,306	28,128	4,629	2,546
2007	152,211	104,734	830	105,564	12,224	1,726	95,066	28,333	28,812	32,573	29,205	4,673	2,604
2008	157,480	105,357	858	106,215	12,606	1,834	95,443	29,858	32,179	33,377	29,996	4,718	2,583
2009	155,255	103,271	914	104,185	12,336	1,804	93,653	26,925	34,677	32,631	30,017	4,758	2,480
2010	161,966	106,276	772	107,048	12,710	1,888	96,226	27,761	37,978	33,845	31,086	4,785	2,460
2011	167,676	109,425	378	109,803	11,646	2,033	100,189	28,766	38,720	34,941	31,805	4,799	2,498
2012	172,428	111,972	689	112,661	11,885	2,294	103,069	30,497	38,862	35,806	32,727	4,816	2,504
2013	174,119	113,965	2,013	115,978	13,696	2,378	104,660	29,749	39,709	36,046	32,708	4,830	2,523
2014	180,220	117,747	1,380	119,127	14,073	2,370	107,423	31,442	41,355	37,217	33,805	4,842	2,553
2015	187,302	121,717	1,417	123,134	14,550	2,311	110,895	33,364	43,042	38,594	34,902	4,853	2,588
2016	190,991	124,437	782	125,219	14,807	2,421	112,833	34,070	44,088	39,260	35,425	4,865	2,621
2017	198,916	129,549	1,241	130,790	15,394	2,437	117,834	35,489	45,594	40,802	36,831	4,875	2,652
2018	206,924	134,404	1,790	136,193	16,023	2,546	122,716	36,733	47,475	42,334	38,369	4,888	2,691
2019	216,449	215,863	586	141,193	16,848	2,548	126,893	39,056	50,500	44,102	39,956	4,908	2,736
2020	230,861	230,666	195	143,417	17,210	2,541	128,748	38,687	63,426	46,908	42742	4922	...

... = Not available.

Personal Income and Employment by Region and State: Alaska

(Millions of dollars, except as noted.)

Year	Personal income, total	Earnings by place of work			Less: Contributions for government social insurance	Plus: Adjustment for residence	Equals: Net earnings by place of residence	Plus: Dividends, interest, and rent	Plus: Personal current transfer receipts	Per capita (dollars)		Population (thousands)	Total employment (thousands)
		Nonfarm	Farm	Total						Personal income	Disposable personal income		
1960	806	721	2	723	28	-2	694	91	22	3,521	3,162	229	...
1961	797	707	2	709	28	-3	678	92	27	3,347	3,026	238	...
1962	831	739	1	741	29	-5	707	98	26	3,378	3,030	246	...
1963	901	804	1	805	33	-9	763	110	27	3,518	3,146	256	...
1964	1,009	903	1	904	37	-13	854	126	29	3,835	3,497	263	...
1965	1,089	980	1	981	41	-18	922	135	31	4,016	3,612	271	...
1966	1,159	1,050	1	1,051	48	-23	980	145	34	4,276	3,853	271	...
1967	1,264	1,151	1	1,152	54	-31	1,067	158	39	4,545	4,091	278	...
1968	1,365	1,256	2	1,258	67	-39	1,152	166	48	4,790	4,293	285	...
1969	1,575	1,434	1	1,436	94	-25	1,317	206	53	5,322	4,624	296	144
1970	1,799	1,622	2	1,624	105	-46	1,472	255	72	5,911	5,222	304	149
1971	1,984	1,786	2	1,787	118	-60	1,609	284	91	6,269	5,569	316	153
1972	2,167	1,955	2	1,957	134	-75	1,748	314	104	6,636	5,822	326	158
1973	2,508	2,159	2	2,161	165	-93	1,902	359	246	7,525	6,681	333	167
1974	3,043	2,863	2	2,865	241	-209	2,415	419	208	8,827	7,643	345	189
1975	4,157	4,428	4	4,432	408	-610	3,414	506	237	11,205	9,577	371	227
1976	4,893	5,490	4	5,494	526	-879	4,088	571	234	12,447	10,600	393	243
1977	5,082	5,079	5	5,084	463	-452	4,169	635	278	12,789	10,937	397	237
1978	5,236	4,964	5	4,969	435	-324	4,210	727	299	13,018	11,335	402	238
1979	5,547	5,183	4	5,186	468	-274	4,445	809	293	13,745	11,817	404	241
1980	6,285	5,857	3	5,860	511	-329	5,021	920	344	15,507	13,586	405	244
1981	7,152	6,775	2	6,777	653	-457	5,667	1,078	407	17,091	14,647	418	252
1982	8,733	7,842	3	7,844	766	-548	6,530	1,339	864	19,424	16,935	450	277
1983	9,514	8,772	2	8,774	852	-606	7,316	1,564	633	19,478	17,172	488	297
1984	10,121	9,284	2	9,287	952	-620	7,714	1,724	683	19,701	17,573	514	309
1985	10,966	9,767	2	9,769	976	-616	8,177	1,902	887	20,593	18,455	532	316
1986	11,066	9,597	7	9,603	925	-561	8,118	1,950	998	20,331	18,461	544	310
1987	10,618	9,031	9	9,040	871	-526	7,643	1,935	1,039	19,688	17,703	539	310
1988	11,068	9,443	11	9,454	949	-552	7,953	1,997	1,118	20,420	18,483	542	317
1989	12,111	10,312	6	10,318	1,048	-618	8,652	2,220	1,239	22,133	19,732	547	329
1990	12,843	10,927	8	10,936	1,169	-625	9,142	2,331	1,371	23,213	20,549	553	339
1991	13,405	11,449	9	11,458	1,239	-669	9,551	2,382	1,473	23,510	21,008	570	347
1992	14,271	12,110	9	12,119	1,307	-705	10,107	2,529	1,635	24,240	21,767	589	351
1993	15,007	12,557	11	12,569	1,387	-726	10,455	2,731	1,821	25,036	22,515	599	358
1994	15,513	12,877	12	12,889	1,442	-741	10,706	2,942	1,866	25,713	23,059	603	363
1995	15,956	13,067	13	13,080	1,455	-746	10,880	3,120	1,956	26,399	23,705	604	365
1996	16,403	13,276	14	13,290	1,459	-769	11,062	3,236	2,105	26,953	24,138	609	369
1997	17,277	13,869	16	13,885	1,505	-777	11,604	3,400	2,273	28,185	25,176	613	374
1998	18,046	14,510	17	14,527	1,548	-822	12,157	3,419	2,471	29,110	25,935	620	382
1999	18,603	14,863	19	14,882	1,570	-827	12,485	3,402	2,716	29,776	26,594	625	381
2000	20,020	15,846	21	15,867	1,644	-878	13,345	3,598	3,077	31,881	28,443	628	390
2001	21,182	17,010	20	17,030	1,738	-863	14,429	3,534	3,220	33,425	29,766	634	395
2002	22,202	18,003	20	18,023	1,828	-792	15,404	3,491	3,307	34,564	31,391	642	402
2003	23,191	18,940	12	18,952	1,891	-700	16,361	3,584	3,246	35,765	32,801	648	406
2004	24,270	19,916	15	19,930	2,015	-608	17,308	3,755	3,208	36,813	33,953	659	414
2005	25,889	21,147	14	21,161	2,156	-513	18,492	3,992	3,405	38,817	35,590	667	421
2006	27,607	22,320	10	22,330	2,363	-420	19,547	4,444	3,616	40,881	37,298	675	431
2007	29,713	23,384	9	23,393	2,462	-308	20,624	5,005	4,084	43,676	39,576	680	440
2008	32,702	24,430	0	24,430	2,543	-173	21,714	5,527	5,461	47,569	42,962	687	444
2009	32,749	25,466	5	25,471	2,587	-179	22,705	5,297	4,748	46,858	43,332	699	442
2010	35,163	26,974	6	26,980	2,677	-180	24,124	5,703	5,336	49,254	45,514	714	444
2011	37,581	28,469	6	28,475	2,546	-194	25,735	6,307	5,539	52,048	47,780	722	450
2012	38,823	29,645	11	29,656	2,698	-205	26,753	6,668	5,402	53,153	48,974	730	459
2013	38,503	29,863	10	29,873	3,120	-206	26,547	6,542	5,414	52,239	47,658	737	461
2014	40,935	30,716	12	30,728	3,123	-220	27,385	7,022	6,529	55,595	50,753	736	461
2015	42,291	31,563	12	31,575	3,162	-224	28,190	7,425	6,677	57,340	52,146	738	461
2016	41,461	30,501	15	30,516	3,063	-197	27,256	7,555	6,650	55,915	51,101	742	457
2017	42,301	30,773	8	30,781	3,092	-185	27,504	7,839	6,958	57,180	52,384	740	454
2018	44,015	31,686	5	31,691	3,198	-189	28,305	8,103	7,608	59,687	54,951	737	455
2019	45,945	45,929	16	32,694	3,233	-199	29,262	8,745	7,939	62,629	57,774	734	460
2020	47,365	47,340	25	32,205	3,187	-192	28,826	8,680	9,859	64,780	60,098	731	...

... = Not available.

Personal Income and Employment by Region and State: Arizona

(Millions of dollars, except as noted.)

Year	Personal income, total	Earnings by place of work			Less: Contributions for government social insurance	Plus: Adjustment for residence	Equals: Net earnings by place of residence	Plus: Dividends, interest, and rent	Plus: Personal current transfer receipts	Per capita (dollars)		Population (thousands)	Total employment (thousands)
		Nonfarm	Farm	Total						Personal income	Disposable personal income		
1960	2,856	2,205	128	2,333	118	-2	2,213	477	166	2,162	1,940	1,321	...
1961	3,110	2,370	135	2,505	125	-2	2,378	538	194	2,210	1,994	1,407	...
1962	3,350	2,567	138	2,705	139	-2	2,564	574	212	2,277	2,046	1,471	...
1963	3,522	2,724	113	2,837	162	-1	2,675	616	231	2,315	2,082	1,521	...
1964	3,777	2,898	130	3,029	167	L	2,861	666	250	2,427	2,219	1,556	...
1965	4,004	3,060	128	3,188	174	1	3,015	707	282	2,528	2,310	1,584	...
1966	4,360	3,425	121	3,547	232	0	3,315	740	305	2,701	2,456	1,614	...
1967	4,739	3,680	149	3,829	266	0	3,564	799	377	2,879	2,604	1,646	...
1968	5,437	4,161	192	4,353	313	3	4,043	959	435	3,233	2,902	1,682	...
1969	6,327	4,775	203	4,979	322	-26	4,631	1,204	492	3,643	3,218	1,737	711
1970	7,216	5,379	180	5,559	362	-30	5,168	1,456	592	4,020	3,570	1,795	747
1971	8,256	6,140	201	6,341	430	-29	5,882	1,664	710	4,354	3,912	1,896	786
1972	9,465	7,126	205	7,332	525	-32	6,775	1,874	816	4,711	4,192	2,009	850
1973	10,934	8,273	240	8,512	695	-31	7,786	2,165	983	5,145	4,624	2,125	925
1974	12,336	9,075	384	9,458	791	-41	8,627	2,522	1,188	5,546	4,956	2,224	955
1975	13,318	9,462	217	9,680	816	-47	8,816	2,841	1,660	5,825	5,324	2,286	935
1976	14,813	10,558	330	10,888	916	-48	9,924	3,061	1,828	6,309	5,723	2,348	976
1977	16,647	12,112	267	12,378	1,061	-57	11,261	3,459	1,928	6,858	6,175	2,427	1,048
1978	19,560	14,371	318	14,689	1,292	-70	13,328	4,059	2,173	7,768	6,935	2,518	1,150
1979	22,987	17,050	399	17,449	1,606	-72	15,771	4,743	2,472	8,712	7,722	2,639	1,240
1980	26,478	19,104	477	19,580	1,822	-81	17,678	5,824	2,976	9,671	8,602	2,738	1,283
1981	30,247	21,357	414	21,771	2,191	-16	19,564	7,187	3,496	10,764	9,489	2,810	1,313
1982	32,197	22,187	396	22,583	2,315	-9	20,259	8,037	3,902	11,141	9,872	2,890	1,315
1983	35,453	24,367	328	24,695	2,580	2	22,117	9,065	4,271	11,941	10,678	2,969	1,379
1984	40,056	27,746	526	28,272	3,018	5	25,259	10,218	4,578	13,060	11,696	3,067	1,504
1985	44,570	31,023	492	31,515	3,435	18	28,098	11,504	4,968	14,000	12,479	3,184	1,622
1986	48,739	34,175	472	34,646	3,805	38	30,880	12,409	5,450	14,733	13,153	3,308	1,701
1987	52,518	36,899	634	37,533	4,075	64	33,522	13,042	5,954	15,280	13,615	3,437	1,765
1988	56,718	39,995	760	40,755	4,563	106	36,298	13,885	6,536	16,044	14,382	3,535	1,833
1989	60,863	41,532	690	42,222	4,873	164	37,513	15,770	7,580	16,803	14,990	3,622	1,865
1990	63,821	43,722	642	44,364	5,269	223	39,319	16,099	8,403	17,323	15,440	3,684	1,894
1991	67,175	46,430	739	47,169	5,627	220	41,761	16,030	9,383	17,731	15,840	3,789	1,903
1992	71,692	50,011	673	50,683	6,016	247	44,914	16,094	10,684	18,309	16,429	3,916	1,925
1993	77,041	53,898	789	54,687	6,488	264	48,463	17,054	11,525	18,950	16,974	4,065	2,011
1994	84,344	59,449	577	60,026	7,169	275	53,131	18,906	12,306	19,869	17,750	4,245	2,141
1995	91,989	64,517	824	65,341	7,483	292	58,150	20,723	13,117	20,753	18,526	4,432	2,258
1996	99,708	70,756	737	71,493	8,373	322	63,442	22,296	13,969	21,737	19,202	4,587	2,388
1997	108,023	77,028	740	77,768	8,976	358	69,150	24,296	14,578	22,804	20,080	4,737	2,497
1998	117,364	85,265	870	86,136	9,786	406	76,756	25,478	15,130	24,033	21,050	4,883	2,616
1999	124,100	91,374	847	92,222	10,488	466	82,200	25,784	16,116	24,702	21,597	5,024	2,696
2000	134,952	99,984	807	100,790	11,419	525	89,896	28,028	17,028	26,151	22,811	5,161	2,802
2001	140,806	104,198	747	104,945	11,946	638	93,637	27,856	19,313	26,701	23,424	5,273	2,829
2002	145,930	107,767	765	108,532	12,346	696	96,882	27,535	21,514	27,043	24,289	5,396	2,847
2003	154,811	113,571	724	114,295	12,824	796	102,267	29,068	23,475	28,094	25,449	5,510	2,917
2004	169,310	123,952	1,024	124,976	13,892	947	112,031	31,504	25,775	29,954	27,100	5,652	3,041
2005	188,149	136,543	986	137,529	15,248	1,058	123,339	36,323	28,487	32,222	28,799	5,839	3,220
2006	209,010	151,863	714	152,576	16,722	1,092	136,946	40,932	31,132	34,667	30,881	6,029	3,375
2007	220,652	158,413	851	159,265	17,693	1,175	142,747	44,122	33,784	35,776	31,892	6,168	3,465
2008	223,222	156,224	632	156,856	17,904	1,214	140,167	43,695	39,360	35,543	31,993	6,280	3,403
2009	211,398	145,068	489	145,557	17,068	1,224	129,714	37,674	44,011	33,327	30,753	6,343	3,228
2010	215,012	145,606	669	146,275	17,246	1,249	130,279	36,848	47,886	33,555	30,838	6,408	3,182
2011	225,853	151,127	1,165	152,292	15,979	1,248	137,561	40,469	47,823	34,889	31,633	6,473	3,239
2012	236,456	158,590	880	159,470	16,523	1,349	144,296	44,308	47,852	36,064	32,774	6,557	3,296
2013	242,572	165,559	1,288	166,847	19,314	1,345	148,879	44,156	49,537	36,559	32,962	6,635	3,371
2014	257,067	172,900	1,063	173,964	19,989	1,452	155,426	48,997	52,644	38,175	34,449	6,734	3,449
2015	270,807	180,805	1,361	182,166	21,034	1,515	162,647	53,233	54,927	39,629	35,552	6,834	3,549
2016	280,988	188,587	1,520	190,107	21,960	1,566	169,713	54,870	56,405	40,456	36,284	6,945	3,647
2017	296,649	200,131	1,885	202,016	23,306	1,592	180,302	57,465	58,882	42,085	37,804	7,049	3,728
2018	313,040	212,295	1,755	214,050	24,868	1,660	190,842	60,340	61,859	43,650	39,345	7,172	3,854
2019	335,243	333,774	1,469	227,140	26,323	1,834	202,650	66,140	66,453	45,975	41,266	7,292	3,969
2020	363,274	361,617	1,657	235,544	27,565	1,771	209,749	65,521	88,004	48,950	44,191	7,421	...

... = Not available.
L = Less than $50,000

Personal Income and Employment by Region and State: Arkansas

(Millions of dollars, except as noted.)

Year	Personal income, total	Earnings by place of work			Less: Contributions for government social insurance	Plus: Adjustment for residence	Equals: Net earnings by place of residence	Plus: Dividends, interest, and rent	Plus: Personal current transfer receipts	Per capita (dollars)		Population (thousands)	Total employment (thousands)
		Nonfarm	Farm	Total						Personal income	Disposable personal income		
1960	2,548	1,805	313	2,118	92	-2	2,025	283	240	1,424	1,314	1,789	...
1961	2,772	1,919	368	2,287	95	-2	2,190	313	269	1,535	1,418	1,806	...
1962	2,966	2,112	324	2,436	109	-3	2,324	354	288	1,600	1,464	1,853	...
1963	3,142	2,254	322	2,577	127	-4	2,446	386	310	1,676	1,533	1,875	...
1964	3,412	2,441	360	2,802	137	-4	2,661	425	326	1,799	1,668	1,897	...
1965	3,602	2,621	288	2,909	147	-6	2,756	488	357	1,902	1,755	1,894	...
1966	4,005	2,876	393	3,269	191	-4	3,074	540	391	2,109	1,925	1,899	...
1967	4,254	3,123	301	3,424	221	-5	3,198	588	468	2,238	2,043	1,901	...
1968	4,601	3,437	337	3,774	252	-7	3,516	560	525	2,419	2,184	1,902	...
1969	5,129	3,775	346	4,121	278	32	3,875	670	584	2,681	2,399	1,913	800
1970	5,627	4,026	415	4,441	296	24	4,168	775	684	2,915	2,623	1,930	805
1971	6,263	4,503	407	4,911	340	22	4,593	869	802	3,176	2,893	1,972	831
1972	7,071	5,123	482	5,605	405	22	5,222	956	893	3,504	3,178	2,018	867
1973	8,376	5,773	914	6,687	524	18	6,180	1,113	1,083	4,069	3,676	2,058	902
1974	9,354	6,468	833	7,301	609	11	6,704	1,335	1,315	4,453	3,993	2,100	927
1975	10,292	6,938	795	7,732	638	9	7,103	1,520	1,669	4,769	4,355	2,158	905
1976	11,379	7,991	641	8,632	745	-1	7,886	1,664	1,829	5,247	4,726	2,169	941
1977	12,662	8,968	725	9,693	847	-7	8,839	1,881	1,942	5,736	5,183	2,207	981
1978	14,669	10,203	1,176	11,379	987	-12	10,380	2,157	2,132	6,546	5,912	2,241	1,021
1979	16,088	11,320	995	12,315	1,134	-15	11,166	2,478	2,444	7,090	6,355	2,269	1,031
1980	17,388	12,275	372	12,647	1,220	-5	11,422	3,067	2,900	7,597	6,773	2,289	1,032
1981	19,703	13,193	851	14,044	1,422	-23	12,598	3,824	3,280	8,592	7,669	2,293	1,026
1982	20,702	13,647	642	14,289	1,498	-21	12,770	4,366	3,567	9,024	8,006	2,294	1,011
1983	21,935	14,819	417	15,237	1,638	-50	13,548	4,528	3,859	9,513	8,538	2,306	1,039
1984	24,458	16,424	883	17,307	1,869	-69	15,369	5,046	4,044	10,543	9,533	2,320	1,079
1985	25,982	17,435	865	18,300	2,005	-75	16,219	5,482	4,282	11,165	10,065	2,327	1,098
1986	27,304	18,534	805	19,338	2,141	-101	17,097	5,695	4,512	11,708	10,588	2,332	1,110
1987	28,435	19,594	935	20,529	2,251	-124	18,154	5,638	4,644	12,139	10,933	2,342	1,137
1988	30,506	20,919	1,344	22,264	2,507	-158	19,599	6,022	4,885	13,022	11,754	2,343	1,170
1989	32,721	22,240	1,238	23,477	2,675	-161	20,641	6,681	5,399	13,946	12,550	2,346	1,189
1990	34,458	23,756	1,048	24,803	2,965	-220	21,618	6,993	5,847	14,622	13,137	2,357	1,204
1991	36,459	25,240	1,128	26,368	3,149	-248	22,971	7,005	6,483	15,299	13,787	2,383	1,230
1992	39,714	27,564	1,430	28,994	3,409	-271	25,314	7,212	7,189	16,438	14,838	2,416	1,255
1993	41,648	29,115	1,336	30,450	3,619	-308	26,524	7,538	7,587	16,956	15,301	2,456	1,301
1994	44,289	31,067	1,466	32,533	3,908	-334	28,291	8,035	7,963	17,758	15,957	2,494	1,329
1995	47,165	32,823	1,481	34,305	4,110	-304	29,891	8,684	8,590	18,602	16,674	2,535	1,382
1996	50,048	34,261	1,922	36,183	4,251	-301	31,631	9,315	9,102	19,458	17,424	2,572	1,405
1997	52,508	36,076	1,811	37,887	4,460	-305	33,122	9,884	9,502	20,187	17,992	2,601	1,427
1998	55,917	38,815	1,596	40,410	4,734	-306	35,370	10,729	9,818	21,291	18,924	2,626	1,446
1999	58,130	40,849	1,807	42,655	4,962	-322	37,372	10,637	10,121	21,920	19,512	2,652	1,460
2000	61,137	43,005	1,704	44,709	5,196	-360	39,153	11,242	10,741	22,824	20,261	2,679	1,482
2001	64,375	44,768	2,010	46,778	5,350	-374	41,054	11,411	11,910	23,917	21,278	2,692	1,483
2002	65,878	46,555	1,275	47,830	5,517	-373	41,940	11,113	12,825	24,346	22,016	2,706	1,479
2003	69,722	48,609	2,411	51,019	5,719	-351	44,949	11,382	13,391	25,588	23,385	2,725	1,482
2004	74,159	51,512	2,772	54,285	6,005	-319	47,961	11,848	14,350	26,970	24,691	2,750	1,505
2005	78,139	54,262	1,874	56,136	6,357	-288	49,492	13,252	15,395	28,096	25,523	2,781	1,538
2006	83,021	56,821	1,514	58,336	6,817	-249	51,270	14,941	16,810	29,422	26,645	2,822	1,568
2007	88,485	58,692	1,921	60,613	7,102	-182	53,330	16,979	18,176	31,062	27,946	2,849	1,583
2008	91,798	59,189	1,597	60,787	7,393	-139	53,254	18,277	20,267	31,935	28,694	2,875	1,579
2009	90,243	58,443	933	59,376	7,393	-120	51,863	16,383	21,997	31,152	28,543	2,897	1,543
2010	93,103	60,514	661	61,175	7,603	-129	53,443	16,048	23,612	31,863	29,214	2,922	1,541
2011	99,329	62,848	702	63,551	7,116	-112	56,322	18,919	24,087	33,781	30,705	2,940	1,562
2012	106,537	65,849	1,114	66,963	7,258	-156	59,548	22,652	24,337	36,088	32,887	2,952	1,565
2013	106,430	67,122	2,496	69,618	8,263	-215	61,139	20,533	24,758	35,961	32,476	2,960	1,569
2014	112,619	69,367	2,013	71,380	8,601	-225	62,554	23,825	26,240	37,948	34,305	2,968	1,587
2015	116,249	70,955	1,148	72,103	8,872	-234	62,997	25,835	27,417	39,030	35,209	2,978	1,610
2016	118,770	72,274	854	73,129	8,952	-206	63,971	26,346	28,453	39,717	35,757	2,990	1,629
2017	123,313	74,655	1,288	75,943	9,233	-246	66,464	27,787	29,062	41,063	37,000	3,003	1,641
2018	128,286	76,826	2,199	79,024	9,521	-226	69,278	29,260	29,748	42,566	38,540	3,014	1,658
2019	134,683	133,509	1,174	80,928	9,980	-370	70,578	32,547	31,559	44,582	40,278	3,021	1,674
2020	142,765	142,018	747	82,380	10,325	-417	71,638	32,022	39,104	47,109	42,746	3,031	...

... = Not available.

Personal Income and Employment by Region and State: California

(Millions of dollars, except as noted.)

Year	Personal income, total	Derivation of personal income								Per capita (dollars)		Population (thousands)	Total employment (thousands)
		Earnings by place of work			Less: Contributions for government social insurance	Plus: Adjustment for residence	Equals: Net earnings by place of residence	Plus: Dividends, interest, and rent	Plus: Personal current transfer receipts	Personal income	Disposable personal income		
		Nonfarm	Farm	Total									
1960	46,521	36,478	1,437	37,915	1,720	-5	36,190	7,747	2,585	2,931	2,602	15,870	...
1961	49,267	38,626	1,369	39,995	1,832	-5	38,158	8,109	2,999	2,986	2,654	16,497	...
1962	53,086	41,937	1,433	43,370	2,249	-6	41,116	8,791	3,179	3,110	2,759	17,072	...
1963	56,740	45,049	1,367	46,416	2,625	-6	43,786	9,437	3,517	3,211	2,850	17,668	...
1964	61,405	48,481	1,517	49,997	2,731	-7	47,260	10,332	3,813	3,383	3,053	18,151	...
1965	65,618	51,529	1,464	52,993	2,846	-8	50,138	11,267	4,213	3,531	3,187	18,585	...
1966	71,356	56,763	1,583	58,346	3,740	-11	54,595	12,108	4,653	3,784	3,397	18,858	...
1967	76,732	60,732	1,496	62,227	4,100	-12	58,115	12,862	5,755	4,001	3,578	19,176	...
1968	84,056	66,766	1,720	68,486	4,587	-14	63,885	13,528	6,643	4,334	3,832	19,394	...
1969	92,160	72,625	1,705	74,329	4,827	-98	69,405	15,139	7,616	4,676	4,105	19,711	9,033
1970	99,418	76,644	1,709	78,352	5,018	-94	73,241	16,876	9,301	4,965	4,430	20,023	9,057
1971	105,987	80,876	1,707	82,583	5,449	-111	77,023	18,269	10,696	5,209	4,701	20,346	9,036
1972	116,351	89,229	2,173	91,402	6,333	-118	84,951	19,878	11,522	5,652	5,013	20,585	9,368
1973	127,777	97,953	2,931	100,884	7,973	-103	92,808	22,211	12,758	6,123	5,477	20,868	9,844
1974	142,507	107,472	3,645	111,117	9,013	-100	102,004	25,386	15,118	6,731	5,998	21,173	10,163
1975	157,640	117,020	3,273	120,293	9,600	17	110,710	27,936	18,994	7,320	6,602	21,537	10,286
1976	174,925	131,249	3,477	134,726	10,978	120	123,868	30,045	21,012	7,975	7,121	21,935	10,633
1977	194,033	147,538	3,543	151,081	12,560	-21	138,500	33,226	22,307	8,681	7,699	22,350	11,119
1978	220,640	169,787	3,489	173,277	14,806	-22	158,449	38,085	24,106	9,661	8,509	22,839	11,816
1979	250,174	192,947	4,573	197,520	17,663	62	179,919	43,770	26,486	10,758	9,410	23,255	12,461
1980	284,308	214,018	5,582	219,600	19,262	7	200,344	53,180	30,784	11,945	10,434	23,801	12,762
1981	319,557	236,420	4,354	240,774	23,093	286	217,967	65,379	36,211	13,158	11,518	24,286	12,935
1982	342,343	250,604	4,600	255,203	24,994	296	230,504	72,151	39,688	13,793	12,165	24,820	12,863
1983	369,809	271,683	4,235	275,917	27,641	300	248,577	78,857	42,376	14,582	12,896	25,360	13,182
1984	410,796	303,540	4,910	308,450	32,061	245	276,634	89,947	44,216	15,895	14,046	25,844	13,797
1985	444,067	330,520	4,950	335,470	35,323	195	300,342	95,922	47,803	16,795	14,755	26,441	14,285
1986	476,682	358,456	5,390	363,846	38,688	154	325,313	100,017	51,353	17,588	15,467	27,102	14,710
1987	513,377	392,750	6,591	399,341	42,355	76	357,062	102,736	53,579	18,482	16,073	27,777	15,300
1988	558,041	430,149	6,936	437,086	47,729	38	389,394	111,296	57,351	19,605	17,205	28,464	16,022
1989	600,755	456,298	6,839	463,137	51,065	25	412,098	125,843	62,814	20,561	17,869	29,218	16,426
1990	643,685	488,244	7,216	495,460	54,273	-47	441,140	133,372	69,173	21,485	18,711	29,960	16,835
1991	665,993	505,398	6,316	511,714	56,411	-38	455,264	134,003	76,725	21,857	19,253	30,471	16,750
1992	702,449	529,964	6,825	536,789	58,517	-43	478,229	135,584	88,636	22,678	20,135	30,975	16,391
1993	719,731	538,594	7,769	546,363	59,531	25	486,856	139,271	93,604	23,013	20,437	31,275	16,367
1994	742,429	554,983	7,547	562,530	61,692	36	500,874	145,732	95,824	23,581	20,913	31,484	16,541
1995	780,643	579,282	7,227	586,509	63,539	25	522,995	157,304	100,343	24,629	21,714	31,697	16,940
1996	829,667	614,255	8,129	622,384	65,645	14	556,752	167,650	105,264	25,912	22,592	32,019	17,342
1997	882,677	659,334	8,693	668,027	69,728	-68	598,231	178,621	105,825	27,171	23,454	32,486	17,667
1998	962,746	721,879	8,186	730,065	75,085	-74	654,906	196,114	111,725	29,185	25,047	32,988	18,433
1999	1,028,383	785,504	8,940	794,444	81,356	-79	713,009	197,989	117,386	30,699	25,940	33,499	18,852
2000	1,135,315	878,689	8,860	887,549	90,070	-254	797,226	215,911	122,178	33,403	27,653	33,988	19,229
2001	1,175,178	906,336	8,429	914,764	94,915	-314	819,536	219,958	135,685	34,083	28,846	34,479	19,341
2002	1,193,779	923,182	8,969	932,151	97,840	-428	833,883	213,852	146,045	34,233	30,030	34,872	19,358
2003	1,249,800	963,387	10,119	973,506	102,893	-594	870,019	225,539	154,242	35,452	31,409	35,253	19,479
2004	1,329,225	1,029,140	12,314	1,041,454	112,470	-788	928,197	239,577	161,452	37,364	33,127	35,575	19,784
2005	1,408,965	1,078,900	12,392	1,091,292	117,547	-977	972,768	266,896	169,301	39,326	34,360	35,828	20,127
2006	1,517,898	1,144,294	10,341	1,154,635	120,870	-1,232	1,032,534	303,511	181,853	42,139	36,651	36,021	20,505
2007	1,583,030	1,176,705	12,906	1,189,611	122,701	-1,504	1,065,406	324,828	192,795	43,669	37,730	36,250	20,888
2008	1,606,765	1,168,747	11,106	1,179,853	125,000	-1,754	1,053,099	335,598	218,067	43,895	38,105	36,604	20,654
2009	1,554,230	1,124,230	12,354	1,136,584	121,063	-1,514	1,014,006	299,173	241,051	42,050	37,680	36,961	19,838
2010	1,627,839	1,172,948	13,158	1,186,106	121,824	-1,453	1,062,830	298,102	266,907	43,617	38,843	37,321	19,642
2011	1,738,413	1,233,632	15,198	1,248,830	114,605	-1,400	1,132,825	337,084	268,504	46,183	40,636	37,642	19,986
2012	1,853,467	1,308,356	17,357	1,325,713	119,274	-1,306	1,205,133	377,234	271,101	48,826	42,918	37,961	20,667
2013	1,885,672	1,354,086	20,049	1,374,135	139,628	-1,158	1,233,349	370,313	282,011	49,259	42,633	38,281	21,320
2014	2,021,640	1,427,483	22,059	1,449,542	147,601	-1,248	1,300,694	421,309	299,638	52,340	45,186	38,625	21,998
2015	2,173,300	1,520,845	21,372	1,542,218	156,422	-1,460	1,384,335	465,242	323,722	55,793	47,848	38,953	22,689
2016	2,259,414	1,585,199	18,531	1,603,729	162,969	-1,626	1,439,134	485,233	335,046	57,625	49,498	39,209	23,169
2017	2,364,129	1,674,798	22,524	1,697,321	171,163	-1,853	1,524,305	508,393	331,432	60,004	51,481	39,399	23,585
2018	2,475,728	1,757,935	20,370	1,778,305	180,174	-1,948	1,596,182	538,325	341,220	62,586	53,944	39,557	24,086
2019	2,632,280	2,610,581	21,699	1,876,840	191,666	-2,089	1,683,085	576,065	373,130	66,745	57,497	39,438	24,602
2020	2,814,011	2,788,530	25,481	1,903,151	196,374	-2,216	1,704,562	570,562	538,887	71,480	62,096	39,368	...

... = Not available.

Personal Income and Employment by Region and State: Colorado

(Millions of dollars, except as noted.)

Year	Personal income, total	Earnings by place of work			Less: Contributions for government social insurance	Plus: Adjustment for residence	Equals: Net earnings by place of residence	Plus: Dividends, interest, and rent	Plus: Personal current transfer receipts	Per capita (dollars)		Population (thousands)	Total employment (thousands)
		Nonfarm	Farm	Total						Personal income	Disposable personal income		
1960	4,353	3,287	174	3,461	133	1	3,330	748	276	2,461	2,184	1,769	...
1961	4,684	3,557	176	3,733	150	1	3,584	799	302	2,540	2,255	1,844	...
1962	4,942	3,755	156	3,911	163	1	3,748	875	319	2,602	2,314	1,899	...
1963	5,174	3,960	140	4,100	191	0	3,909	926	339	2,673	2,377	1,936	...
1964	5,474	4,206	137	4,343	197	L	4,146	985	344	2,779	2,520	1,970	...
1965	5,841	4,408	213	4,621	198	-0	4,423	1,043	375	2,942	2,664	1,985	...
1966	6,276	4,831	192	5,023	263	-1	4,759	1,110	407	3,127	2,812	2,007	...
1967	6,764	5,189	186	5,375	295	-1	5,079	1,201	483	3,294	2,951	2,053	...
1968	7,503	5,768	244	6,012	334	-2	5,676	1,278	549	3,539	3,137	2,120	...
1969	8,439	6,455	251	6,706	387	1	6,319	1,514	605	3,896	3,409	2,166	1,001
1970	9,540	7,184	289	7,473	427	3	7,049	1,761	730	4,290	3,800	2,224	1,032
1971	10,760	8,147	301	8,449	499	4	7,954	1,956	850	4,671	4,160	2,304	1,072
1972	12,176	9,340	333	9,673	606	5	9,072	2,162	943	5,064	4,452	2,405	1,149
1973	13,923	10,680	440	11,120	798	3	10,326	2,490	1,108	5,579	4,923	2,496	1,243
1974	15,609	11,815	535	12,350	905	4	11,449	2,877	1,283	6,142	5,396	2,541	1,276
1975	17,250	12,904	464	13,368	967	9	12,409	3,230	1,610	6,670	5,939	2,586	1,285
1976	18,981	14,483	336	14,820	1,105	9	13,723	3,496	1,762	7,211	6,385	2,632	1,340
1977	21,174	16,379	266	16,645	1,261	11	15,395	3,911	1,869	7,854	6,904	2,696	1,411
1978	24,414	19,130	209	19,339	1,507	19	17,852	4,529	2,033	8,824	7,733	2,767	1,506
1979	27,979	22,126	218	22,343	1,839	13	20,518	5,178	2,284	9,820	8,549	2,849	1,593
1980	32,051	24,945	290	25,235	2,106	20	23,149	6,250	2,653	11,019	9,589	2,909	1,651
1981	36,883	28,429	306	28,735	2,598	3	26,140	7,629	3,114	12,386	10,714	2,978	1,717
1982	40,506	31,059	185	31,244	2,908	0	28,336	8,641	3,529	13,230	11,429	3,062	1,760
1983	43,694	32,980	361	33,341	3,130	-2	30,209	9,582	3,903	13,944	12,353	3,134	1,788
1984	47,645	36,070	426	36,496	3,539	7	32,964	10,567	4,113	15,030	13,361	3,170	1,883
1985	50,484	38,164	396	38,559	3,835	16	34,741	11,438	4,305	15,733	13,954	3,209	1,915
1986	52,446	39,583	398	39,981	4,021	21	35,981	11,844	4,621	16,200	14,421	3,237	1,914
1987	54,400	40,935	477	41,413	4,121	32	37,323	12,096	4,981	16,685	14,800	3,260	1,903
1988	57,557	43,443	578	44,020	4,530	46	39,536	12,771	5,249	17,643	15,693	3,262	1,968
1989	62,010	45,962	621	46,582	4,888	63	41,757	14,403	5,850	18,930	16,715	3,276	2,003
1990	65,667	49,007	713	49,719	5,334	86	44,471	14,928	6,269	19,853	17,471	3,308	2,040
1991	69,602	52,468	640	53,107	5,856	97	47,348	15,291	6,963	20,549	18,121	3,387	2,087
1992	75,599	57,556	679	58,235	6,359	112	51,989	15,791	7,819	21,625	19,077	3,496	2,135
1993	81,812	62,492	815	63,307	6,987	124	56,444	16,986	8,382	22,639	19,922	3,614	2,234
1994	87,984	67,131	584	67,714	7,557	142	60,299	18,792	8,893	23,625	20,733	3,724	2,345
1995	95,649	72,072	544	72,616	8,075	163	64,704	20,970	9,975	24,995	21,930	3,827	2,425
1996	103,236	77,860	671	78,531	8,626	182	70,088	22,814	10,335	26,336	22,924	3,920	2,519
1997	111,208	84,530	676	85,206	9,300	205	76,111	24,597	10,501	27,675	23,881	4,018	2,629
1998	122,315	94,416	806	95,222	9,710	231	85,743	25,853	10,719	29,712	25,476	4,117	2,732
1999	132,205	103,813	937	104,750	10,549	261	94,462	26,340	11,404	31,284	26,726	4,226	2,808
2000	147,234	116,473	777	117,250	11,704	288	105,835	29,351	12,049	34,027	28,895	4,327	2,918
2001	154,410	121,840	1,074	122,915	12,314	309	110,910	30,146	13,355	34,889	30,022	4,426	2,942
2002	154,766	122,448	714	123,162	12,725	339	110,776	29,148	14,841	34,466	30,383	4,490	2,917
2003	157,543	123,990	755	124,745	12,955	363	112,154	29,806	15,583	34,787	31,045	4,529	2,909
2004	163,427	128,797	959	129,756	13,827	398	116,328	30,858	16,241	35,722	31,878	4,575	2,958
2005	174,772	136,332	1,117	137,450	14,684	429	123,195	34,028	17,549	37,732	33,300	4,632	3,037
2006	188,803	145,616	813	146,429	15,587	476	131,318	38,633	18,853	39,997	34,999	4,720	3,109
2007	201,227	152,466	1,106	153,572	16,420	505	137,657	43,378	20,193	41,889	36,404	4,804	3,218
2008	207,773	155,239	904	156,143	17,113	523	139,553	44,696	23,524	42,492	37,111	4,890	3,251
2009	198,147	146,735	763	147,498	16,490	563	131,571	40,446	26,130	39,851	35,830	4,972	3,164
2010	204,692	150,240	1,014	151,254	16,668	663	135,250	39,849	29,593	40,547	36,242	5,048	3,144
2011	222,572	159,116	1,321	160,437	15,796	827	145,467	46,554	30,551	43,456	38,371	5,122	3,204
2012	236,687	168,505	1,248	169,753	16,572	1,027	154,208	51,779	30,701	45,572	40,333	5,194	3,263
2013	248,959	182,350	1,335	183,685	19,223	1,183	165,645	51,453	31,861	47,236	41,517	5,270	3,356
2014	271,101	197,428	1,398	198,827	20,682	1,232	179,377	57,530	34,194	50,662	44,455	5,351	3,466
2015	284,143	203,533	1,587	205,120	21,829	1,230	184,521	62,634	36,988	52,116	45,517	5,452	3,572
2016	289,621	205,939	1,270	207,209	22,473	1,203	185,940	65,128	38,553	52,269	45,508	5,541	3,665
2017	306,411	219,726	1,436	221,162	23,780	1,309	198,692	68,190	39,530	54,561	47,524	5,616	3,743
2018	323,767	232,085	1,385	233,470	25,093	1,367	209,744	71,880	42,143	56,846	49,801	5,696	3,855
2019	352,185	350,873	1,312	254,320	26,867	1,382	228,835	77,891	45,459	61,159	53,704	5,758	3,950
2020	368,920	367,441	1,479	256,718	27,446	1,365	230,636	77,151	61,133	63,522	56,083	5,808	...

... = Not available.
L = Less than $50,000.

Personal Income and Employment by Region and State: Connecticut

(Millions of dollars, except as noted.)

Year	Personal income, total	Earnings by place of work			Less: Contributions for government social insurance	Plus: Adjustment for residence	Equals: Net earnings by place of residence	Plus: Dividends, interest, and rent	Plus: Personal current transfer receipts	Per capita (dollars)		Population (thousands)	Total employment (thousands)
		Nonfarm	Farm	Total						Personal income	Disposable personal income		
1960	7,276	5,829	63	5,892	278	3	5,617	1,270	389	2,860	2,499	2,544	...
1961	7,702	6,094	58	6,152	290	3	5,864	1,389	448	2,978	2,612	2,586	...
1962	8,227	6,517	59	6,576	320	3	6,259	1,528	441	3,108	2,722	2,647	...
1963	8,691	6,865	64	6,929	369	4	6,564	1,658	469	3,187	2,777	2,727	...
1964	9,335	7,337	62	7,399	379	5	7,025	1,815	495	3,336	2,963	2,798	...
1965	10,039	7,858	71	7,929	395	2	7,535	1,980	523	3,514	3,100	2,857	...
1966	11,024	8,795	73	8,868	553	-1	8,315	2,145	564	3,797	3,323	2,903	...
1967	12,086	9,505	58	9,562	602	1	8,961	2,424	702	4,118	3,575	2,935	...
1968	12,829	10,213	68	10,281	671	7	9,617	2,358	854	4,328	3,689	2,964	...
1969	14,693	11,149	67	11,216	753	723	11,187	2,559	948	4,898	4,144	3,000	1,417
1970	15,674	11,734	72	11,805	784	717	11,738	2,790	1,146	5,158	4,485	3,039	1,414
1971	16,514	12,145	69	12,215	841	749	12,122	2,968	1,424	5,394	4,764	3,061	1,388
1972	17,805	13,216	68	13,284	969	793	13,108	3,191	1,505	5,800	5,050	3,070	1,416
1973	19,393	14,633	81	14,714	1,236	804	14,283	3,481	1,630	6,319	5,537	3,069	1,480
1974	21,157	15,832	84	15,916	1,397	838	15,357	3,882	1,918	6,879	6,024	3,076	1,511
1975	22,726	16,487	75	16,563	1,424	929	16,068	4,112	2,546	7,367	6,547	3,085	1,468
1976	24,536	17,946	83	18,028	1,578	1,000	17,450	4,373	2,714	7,951	6,974	3,086	1,493
1977	27,033	19,979	84	20,062	1,779	1,105	19,389	4,807	2,837	8,752	7,678	3,089	1,546
1978	30,081	22,509	80	22,590	2,061	1,264	21,793	5,364	2,924	9,720	8,441	3,095	1,615
1979	33,814	25,390	79	25,469	2,421	1,439	24,487	6,073	3,254	10,908	9,397	3,100	1,673
1980	38,494	28,231	84	28,315	2,680	1,689	27,324	7,425	3,745	12,365	10,593	3,113	1,705
1981	43,243	30,953	82	31,035	3,155	1,893	29,772	9,151	4,320	13,821	11,788	3,129	1,727
1982	46,701	33,014	108	33,122	3,431	2,040	31,732	10,167	4,802	14,878	12,672	3,139	1,726
1983	49,958	35,629	106	35,735	3,737	2,178	34,176	10,598	5,185	15,798	13,799	3,162	1,743
1984	55,881	40,098	129	40,228	4,306	2,339	38,261	12,199	5,421	17,572	15,436	3,180	1,823
1985	60,000	43,677	128	43,805	4,742	2,577	41,640	12,612	5,748	18,743	16,319	3,201	1,879
1986	64,553	47,450	140	47,590	5,165	2,674	45,098	13,375	6,080	20,024	17,335	3,224	1,937
1987	70,443	52,742	142	52,884	5,653	2,823	50,054	14,105	6,284	21,693	18,593	3,247	1,984
1988	77,668	58,304	155	58,459	6,356	3,072	55,175	15,712	6,781	23,738	20,612	3,272	2,039
1989	84,249	61,502	141	61,642	6,676	3,087	58,053	18,594	7,602	25,659	22,300	3,283	2,032
1990	86,889	63,319	186	63,504	6,798	2,745	59,451	18,938	8,500	26,394	23,007	3,292	2,003
1991	87,816	64,201	165	64,366	7,011	2,709	60,065	18,230	9,521	26,588	23,198	3,303	1,923
1992	94,269	67,580	188	67,768	7,251	3,939	64,456	18,614	11,200	28,560	24,665	3,301	1,904
1993	97,348	70,246	210	70,456	7,515	3,346	66,286	19,379	11,683	29,417	25,298	3,309	1,925
1994	100,108	72,569	186	72,755	7,873	3,102	67,984	20,026	12,099	30,188	25,958	3,316	1,906
1995	105,643	75,853	173	76,026	8,269	3,827	71,584	21,105	12,954	31,780	27,144	3,324	1,944
1996	110,746	79,352	161	79,513	8,622	4,537	75,428	22,016	13,303	33,191	27,863	3,337	1,975
1997	117,992	86,018	158	86,175	9,146	4,072	81,102	23,222	13,668	35,228	29,192	3,349	2,000
1998	126,867	92,714	179	92,893	9,592	5,482	88,782	24,244	13,840	37,698	30,929	3,365	2,037
1999	134,176	99,841	192	100,033	10,054	5,362	95,341	24,664	14,171	39,622	32,428	3,386	2,070
2000	147,015	109,656	225	109,881	10,680	5,526	104,728	27,368	14,920	43,091	35,000	3,412	2,118
2001	155,327	116,759	200	116,959	11,047	5,563	111,474	28,016	15,836	45,247	36,875	3,433	2,125
2002	155,241	117,549	189	117,738	11,506	5,728	111,961	26,301	16,980	44,884	38,177	3,459	2,118
2003	157,488	118,824	189	119,013	11,752	5,830	113,091	27,072	17,325	45,199	38,869	3,484	2,112
2004	166,423	123,788	199	123,987	12,345	6,843	118,485	29,563	18,376	47,603	40,858	3,496	2,144
2005	175,733	129,022	189	129,211	12,768	7,652	124,095	32,680	18,958	50,110	42,321	3,507	2,172
2006	190,586	135,627	174	135,801	13,240	8,814	131,375	38,980	20,231	54,183	45,580	3,517	2,202
2007	205,013	143,090	200	143,291	13,837	10,336	139,790	43,756	21,466	58,122	48,317	3,527	2,246
2008	217,023	150,694	210	150,904	14,286	11,467	148,084	44,376	24,563	61,209	51,611	3,546	2,256
2009	213,687	152,772	204	152,976	13,919	8,859	147,915	38,528	27,244	59,994	52,746	3,562	2,196
2010	222,632	157,166	207	157,373	14,026	10,852	154,199	39,367	29,066	62,203	54,421	3,579	2,172
2011	229,055	158,628	192	158,820	12,981	11,364	157,203	42,699	29,153	63,839	54,944	3,588	2,206
2012	233,699	156,966	251	157,218	13,324	13,194	157,087	47,112	29,499	65,018	55,895	3,594	2,223
2013	229,252	155,691	260	155,951	15,440	12,507	153,017	46,406	29,829	63,771	53,574	3,595	2,247
2014	239,857	160,451	190	160,642	15,921	12,927	157,648	51,589	30,620	66,724	56,149	3,595	2,266
2015	246,012	163,602	204	163,805	16,424	13,215	160,596	53,681	31,735	68,575	57,591	3,588	2,288
2016	249,513	166,086	173	166,259	16,726	12,705	162,239	54,540	32,735	69,722	59,089	3,579	2,301
2017	257,714	168,142	167	168,309	17,102	15,890	167,097	57,328	33,289	72,110	61,267	3,574	2,314
2018	266,382	172,038	151	172,189	17,509	16,812	171,492	60,116	34,774	74,561	63,893	3,573	2,317
2019	275,557	275,351	206	177,410	18,071	18,983	178,323	61,031	36,204	77,273	65,906	3,566	2,332
2020	283,747	283,480	267	174,555	17,962	18,587	175,181	60,161	48,405	79,771	68,622	3,557	...

... = Not available.

Personal Income and Employment by Region and State: Delaware

(Millions of dollars, except as noted.)

Year	Personal income, total	Derivation of personal income								Per capita (dollars)		Population (thousands)	Total employment (thousands)
		Earnings by place of work			Less: Contributions for government social insurance	Plus: Adjustment for residence	Equals: Net earnings by place of residence	Plus: Dividends, interest, and rent	Plus: Personal current transfer receipts	Personal income	Disposable personal income		
		Nonfarm	Farm	Total									
1960	1,290	1,035	34	1,069	53	-51	966	270	54	2,873	2,414	449	...
1961	1,331	1,062	30	1,092	51	-51	990	277	65	2,888	2,441	461	...
1962	1,414	1,127	33	1,160	58	-52	1,050	297	67	3,014	2,518	469	...
1963	1,517	1,223	26	1,249	69	-56	1,124	323	70	3,140	2,647	483	...
1964	1,641	1,322	26	1,348	68	-58	1,221	346	74	3,302	2,789	497	...
1965	1,806	1,459	35	1,494	69	-65	1,360	366	80	3,561	3,004	507	...
1966	1,903	1,599	26	1,625	99	-69	1,457	357	88	3,687	3,122	516	...
1967	2,031	1,701	32	1,733	117	-68	1,548	374	108	3,868	3,289	525	...
1968	2,215	1,860	29	1,889	119	-70	1,700	388	127	4,148	3,503	534	...
1969	2,441	2,000	55	2,055	139	-29	1,887	415	139	4,521	3,753	540	271
1970	2,600	2,136	35	2,171	147	-31	1,993	443	165	4,724	3,949	550	275
1971	2,844	2,360	38	2,398	168	-46	2,184	466	194	5,032	4,248	565	280
1972	3,125	2,616	49	2,665	196	-54	2,415	495	215	5,446	4,584	574	293
1973	3,462	2,912	96	3,007	253	-76	2,679	535	248	5,979	5,020	579	305
1974	3,747	3,129	82	3,211	282	-80	2,850	594	303	6,426	5,412	583	302
1975	4,029	3,316	92	3,408	293	-90	3,025	596	408	6,844	5,848	589	292
1976	4,404	3,643	84	3,727	325	-99	3,303	662	439	7,430	6,258	593	296
1977	4,741	3,934	56	3,990	351	-114	3,525	739	478	7,971	6,721	595	296
1978	5,202	4,368	61	4,429	401	-138	3,890	812	500	8,696	7,335	598	304
1979	5,717	4,798	54	4,853	460	-156	4,236	907	573	9,547	7,983	599	312
1980	6,431	5,318	13	5,331	510	-193	4,627	1,108	695	10,809	9,028	595	312
1981	7,094	5,714	43	5,756	591	-211	4,955	1,357	782	11,903	9,868	596	314
1982	7,634	6,145	65	6,211	647	-243	5,320	1,483	831	12,742	10,710	599	317
1983	8,132	6,622	79	6,700	703	-289	5,707	1,539	886	13,431	11,430	605	325
1984	8,973	7,280	96	7,376	779	-328	6,268	1,755	949	14,671	12,569	612	340
1985	9,734	7,963	104	8,068	865	-370	6,833	1,903	998	15,743	13,489	618	357
1986	10,357	8,434	144	8,578	933	-398	7,247	2,030	1,080	16,503	14,113	628	370
1987	11,194	9,270	114	9,384	1,016	-466	7,901	2,168	1,125	17,575	15,106	637	387
1988	12,256	10,126	181	10,307	1,149	-525	8,633	2,386	1,237	18,925	16,359	648	403
1989	13,631	11,092	192	11,284	1,262	-618	9,404	2,885	1,342	20,707	17,869	658	415
1990	14,367	11,762	141	11,903	1,312	-688	9,903	3,023	1,441	21,457	18,503	670	420
1991	15,196	12,294	133	12,427	1,378	-681	10,367	3,155	1,674	22,247	19,373	683	414
1992	15,854	12,884	117	13,001	1,421	-725	10,855	3,177	1,822	22,814	19,905	695	413
1993	16,467	13,255	108	13,363	1,476	-681	11,207	3,312	1,948	23,312	20,310	706	421
1994	17,165	13,863	121	13,985	1,571	-722	11,692	3,404	2,070	23,922	20,726	718	424
1995	18,172	14,617	87	14,704	1,656	-848	12,200	3,710	2,262	24,902	21,585	730	442
1996	19,434	15,554	120	15,675	1,735	-1,049	12,891	4,036	2,507	26,227	22,555	741	453
1997	20,342	16,633	95	16,728	1,843	-1,346	13,540	4,268	2,535	27,069	23,004	751	464
1998	22,495	18,456	142	18,597	1,997	-1,456	15,145	4,651	2,700	29,470	25,135	763	476
1999	24,140	20,474	140	20,613	2,134	-1,696	16,784	4,542	2,814	31,149	26,701	775	491
2000	26,629	22,371	147	22,519	2,237	-1,790	18,492	5,066	3,071	33,862	29,270	786	503
2001	29,340	24,863	212	25,074	2,295	-1,809	20,970	5,003	3,368	36,874	32,069	796	503
2002	30,329	25,689	88	25,777	2,399	-1,761	21,617	5,083	3,628	37,621	33,473	806	501
2003	31,031	26,094	175	26,270	2,500	-1,800	21,969	5,166	3,896	37,935	34,010	818	504
2004	32,296	26,896	254	27,151	2,690	-1,940	22,521	5,581	4,194	38,873	34,739	831	518
2005	33,166	27,494	291	27,785	2,820	-2,089	22,877	5,767	4,522	39,243	34,516	845	529
2006	35,226	28,903	207	29,111	3,001	-2,321	23,789	6,541	4,896	40,995	36,053	859	537
2007	36,336	29,161	210	29,371	3,084	-2,166	24,121	6,907	5,307	41,681	36,595	872	545
2008	36,034	27,996	228	28,225	3,192	-2,216	22,817	7,100	6,118	40,768	35,793	884	545
2009	36,291	27,669	295	27,964	3,122	-1,541	23,302	6,358	6,632	40,697	36,831	892	526
2010	36,707	27,994	262	28,256	3,144	-1,734	23,378	6,170	7,158	40,804	36,848	900	522
2011	39,797	30,298	231	30,528	2,847	-2,154	25,528	6,797	7,473	43,862	39,117	907	530
2012	40,309	30,312	290	30,602	2,980	-2,165	25,456	7,205	7,648	44,045	39,370	915	534
2013	40,898	30,783	440	31,223	3,483	-2,101	25,639	7,222	8,038	44,279	39,322	924	545
2014	42,751	32,155	518	32,673	3,677	-2,472	26,524	7,817	8,411	45,841	40,760	933	557
2015	45,012	33,881	385	34,266	3,828	-2,630	27,809	8,242	8,961	47,813	42,343	941	569
2016	45,917	33,981	341	34,323	3,855	-2,293	28,176	8,395	9,346	48,374	42,817	949	579
2017	47,782	35,100	413	35,513	3,983	-2,504	29,026	8,816	9,941	49,925	44,172	957	584
2018	49,760	36,195	494	36,689	4,106	-2,572	30,012	9,191	10,558	51,449	45,786	967	597
2019	53,055	52,629	427	39,113	4,386	-2,502	32,225	9,760	11,071	54,323	47,978	977	607
2020	56,019	55,710	309	38,985	4,411	-2,498	32,076	9,629	14,314	56,768	50517	987	...

... = Not available.

Personal Income and Employment by Region and State: District of Columbia

(Millions of dollars, except as noted.)

Year	Personal income, total	Derivation of personal income								Per capita (dollars)		Population (thousands)	Total employment (thousands)
		Earnings by place of work			Less: Contributions for government social insurance	Plus: Adjustment for residence	Equals: Net earnings by place of residence	Plus: Dividends, interest, and rent	Plus: Personal current transfer receipts	Personal income	Disposable personal income		
		Nonfarm	Farm	Total									
1960	2,390	3,255	0	3,255	102	-1,391	1,762	516	112	3,125	2,702	765	...
1961	2,517	3,454	0	3,454	108	-1,483	1,863	531	123	3,236	2,838	778	...
1962	2,709	3,718	0	3,718	115	-1,578	2,026	557	127	3,438	3,003	788	...
1963	2,877	4,005	0	4,005	139	-1,704	2,163	580	135	3,605	3,174	798	...
1964	3,054	4,294	0	4,294	136	-1,848	2,311	603	140	3,827	3,417	798	...
1965	3,291	4,631	0	4,631	141	-1,992	2,499	641	151	4,129	3,706	797	...
1966	3,436	4,995	0	4,995	186	-2,188	2,621	655	160	4,344	3,860	791	...
1967	3,682	5,651	0	5,651	215	-2,617	2,819	671	192	4,655	4,159	791	...
1968	3,865	6,079	0	6,079	237	-2,891	2,951	685	230	4,968	4,429	778	...
1969	3,764	6,459	0	6,459	254	-3,366	2,839	690	235	4,939	4,289	762	676
1970	4,174	7,066	0	7,066	276	-3,707	3,083	790	302	5,528	4,832	755	672
1971	4,647	7,747	0	7,747	301	-4,082	3,364	909	375	6,191	5,482	751	666
1972	5,044	8,391	0	8,391	346	-4,441	3,605	992	447	6,781	5,973	744	668
1973	5,316	8,916	0	8,916	417	-4,744	3,755	1,049	512	7,246	6,362	734	662
1974	5,769	9,625	0	9,625	475	-5,119	4,031	1,142	595	8,004	7,040	721	673
1975	6,275	10,598	0	10,598	524	-5,737	4,337	1,197	741	8,834	7,803	710	677
1976	6,648	11,463	0	11,463	576	-6,286	4,601	1,277	771	9,548	8,307	696	674
1977	7,138	12,407	0	12,407	612	-6,843	4,952	1,396	790	10,469	9,191	682	680
1978	7,604	13,579	0	13,579	674	-7,700	5,205	1,588	812	11,349	9,880	670	693
1979	8,003	14,711	0	14,711	777	-8,592	5,342	1,755	906	12,207	10,481	656	704
1980	8,447	16,000	0	16,000	866	-9,709	5,425	1,991	1,031	13,235	11,389	638	701
1981	9,094	17,115	0	17,115	1,010	-10,406	5,699	2,256	1,139	14,279	12,103	637	689
1982	9,694	18,049	0	18,049	1,077	-10,935	6,037	2,386	1,271	15,286	12,987	634	673
1983	10,193	18,929	0	18,929	1,298	-11,234	6,396	2,468	1,328	16,117	13,829	632	667
1984	11,126	20,642	0	20,642	1,472	-12,165	7,005	2,705	1,416	17,566	15,063	633	689
1985	11,782	22,068	0	22,068	1,687	-12,899	7,481	2,882	1,418	18,567	15,891	635	703
1986	12,399	23,269	0	23,269	1,867	-13,474	7,927	3,000	1,472	19,426	16,657	638	721
1987	13,079	24,768	0	24,768	2,031	-14,246	8,491	3,072	1,516	20,534	17,459	637	733
1988	14,310	27,404	0	27,404	2,320	-15,744	9,339	3,340	1,630	22,698	19,483	630	756
1989	15,153	29,005	0	29,005	2,556	-16,821	9,629	3,890	1,634	24,276	20,805	624	763
1990	15,818	30,998	0	30,998	2,759	-17,983	10,256	3,819	1,744	26,132	22,509	605	773
1991	16,537	32,678	0	32,678	2,940	-18,918	10,820	3,771	1,945	27,521	23,972	601	759
1992	17,369	34,522	0	34,522	3,124	-20,092	11,306	3,879	2,184	29,067	25,455	598	752
1993	18,067	35,643	0	35,643	3,273	-20,649	11,720	3,949	2,398	30,349	26,699	595	750
1994	18,485	36,434	0	36,434	3,414	-21,021	11,998	4,048	2,439	31,370	27,398	589	730
1995	18,621	36,700	0	36,700	3,484	-21,063	12,152	4,100	2,368	32,077	28,033	581	718
1996	19,387	37,294	0	37,294	3,521	-21,057	12,716	4,096	2,576	33,872	29,338	572	704
1997	20,291	38,590	0	38,590	3,666	-21,682	13,242	4,479	2,570	35,739	30,608	568	699
1998	21,526	40,635	0	40,635	3,742	-22,791	14,102	4,685	2,739	38,083	32,288	565	698
1999	22,512	44,067	0	44,067	4,084	-24,874	15,109	4,667	2,736	39,480	33,193	570	711
2000	24,787	46,750	0	46,750	4,310	-25,486	16,954	5,016	2,817	43,329	36,293	572	735
2001	25,671	50,026	0	50,026	4,922	-27,225	17,879	4,877	2,915	44,684	37,524	575	742
2002	25,838	52,652	0	52,652	5,233	-29,486	17,933	4,697	3,209	45,080	38,962	573	757
2003	26,174	55,165	0	55,165	5,453	-31,609	18,103	4,808	3,263	46,040	39,897	569	755
2004	28,509	59,956	0	59,956	5,836	-34,103	20,017	5,197	3,296	50,214	43,494	568	763
2005	30,276	63,302	0	63,302	6,161	-36,176	20,966	5,741	3,569	53,383	45,688	567	770
2006	32,037	65,685	0	65,685	6,524	-37,315	21,847	6,568	3,622	56,138	47,905	571	778
2007	34,497	69,568	0	69,568	6,877	-39,186	23,506	7,113	3,879	60,058	50,611	574	788
2008	35,534	71,891	0	71,891	7,403	-40,872	23,616	7,644	4,274	61,240	52,007	580	795
2009	35,803	73,246	0	73,246	7,631	-41,095	24,520	6,538	4,746	60,455	52,752	592	796
2010	38,514	78,016	0	78,016	8,047	-43,311	26,658	6,435	5,421	63,650	55,909	605	809
2011	41,969	81,593	0	81,593	7,369	-45,567	28,657	7,547	5,765	67,735	58,728	620	827
2012	43,621	82,524	0	82,524	7,611	-45,344	29,569	8,395	5,658	68,724	59,149	635	834
2013	44,370	83,741	0	83,741	8,863	-44,926	29,951	8,442	5,977	68,216	58,185	650	848
2014	47,302	88,031	0	88,031	9,303	-46,285	32,443	8,963	5,896	71,398	60,781	663	860
2015	50,947	92,749	0	92,749	9,668	-47,736	35,346	9,486	6,116	75,448	63,840	675	873
2016	53,041	96,449	0	96,449	9,994	-49,536	36,918	9,568	6,554	77,254	65,612	687	891
2017	55,510	100,647	0	100,647	10,408	-51,390	38,848	10,004	6,659	79,792	67,850	696	899
2018	57,518	104,230	0	104,230	10,793	-53,111	40,326	10,422	6,771	81,882	70,045	702	914
2019	58,864	58,864	0	105,843	11,078	-53,568	41,196	10,606	7,062	83,111	71,078	708	923
2020	62,061	62,061	0	107,612	11,371	-54,379	41,862	10,478	9,720	87,064	75,000	713	...

... = Not available.

Personal Income and Employment by Region and State: Florida

(Millions of dollars, except as noted.)

Year	Personal income, total	Earnings by place of work — Nonfarm	Farm	Total	Less: Contributions for government social insurance	Plus: Adjustment for residence	Equals: Net earnings by place of residence	Plus: Dividends, interest, and rent	Plus: Personal current transfer receipts	Per capita (dollars) — Personal income	Disposable personal income	Population (thousands)	Total employment (thousands)
1960	10,532	7,667	381	8,048	329	-1	7,718	2,099	715	2,105	1,911	5,004	...
1961	11,165	7,958	440	8,398	344	-1	8,053	2,284	829	2,130	1,934	5,243	...
1962	12,056	8,583	454	9,037	389	-1	8,647	2,481	929	2,209	2,004	5,458	...
1963	12,939	9,261	436	9,697	449	-1	9,247	2,681	1,011	2,299	2,087	5,628	...
1964	14,155	10,196	492	10,689	481	-1	10,206	2,895	1,055	2,449	2,238	5,781	...
1965	15,473	11,173	466	11,639	516	-1	11,122	3,180	1,171	2,599	2,369	5,954	...
1966	16,976	12,423	476	12,899	680	-2	12,217	3,453	1,306	2,781	2,530	6,104	...
1967	18,772	13,625	515	14,140	809	-3	13,327	3,816	1,628	3,007	2,711	6,242	...
1968	21,581	15,533	528	16,061	966	-5	15,091	4,555	1,936	3,355	2,989	6,433	...
1969	25,005	17,876	636	18,513	1,132	-19	17,361	5,450	2,195	3,765	3,326	6,641	2,857
1970	28,276	19,936	546	20,482	1,272	-22	19,188	6,443	2,646	4,131	3,692	6,845	2,966
1971	31,756	22,121	639	22,759	1,473	-17	21,270	7,299	3,188	4,433	3,987	7,163	3,082
1972	36,550	25,645	738	26,384	1,798	-14	24,572	8,223	3,755	4,860	4,302	7,520	3,338
1973	42,578	30,022	837	30,859	2,422	-12	28,425	9,593	4,561	5,371	4,778	7,927	3,666
1974	47,883	32,994	908	33,902	2,782	-3	31,117	11,268	5,498	5,757	5,139	8,317	3,766
1975	52,168	34,450	998	35,448	2,860	-11	32,577	12,408	7,183	6,107	5,558	8,542	3,676
1976	57,012	37,531	1,035	38,566	3,170	8	35,405	13,630	7,978	6,557	5,924	8,695	3,730
1977	63,844	42,079	1,033	43,112	3,572	19	39,560	15,555	8,730	7,182	6,471	8,889	3,929
1978	73,633	48,719	1,234	49,952	4,251	22	45,723	18,212	9,698	8,064	7,216	9,132	4,239
1979	84,660	55,770	1,312	57,082	5,112	13	51,982	21,441	11,237	8,939	7,942	9,471	4,454
1980	99,827	63,915	1,667	65,583	5,909	6	59,680	26,768	13,379	10,145	8,972	9,840	4,688
1981	115,731	72,211	1,402	73,613	7,183	117	66,547	33,555	15,630	11,354	10,023	10,193	4,865
1982	125,053	77,085	1,777	78,862	7,887	140	71,116	36,249	17,689	11,942	10,461	10,471	4,954
1983	138,093	85,333	2,465	87,798	8,778	166	79,187	39,565	19,341	12,846	11,520	10,750	5,167
1984	153,888	95,966	1,828	97,794	10,141	208	87,861	45,430	20,597	13,939	12,610	11,040	5,502
1985	168,327	105,471	1,835	107,306	11,348	254	96,212	49,892	22,224	14,829	13,259	11,351	5,772
1986	182,124	114,881	1,972	116,853	12,681	317	104,489	53,690	23,945	15,610	13,909	11,668	6,015
1987	197,185	126,439	2,135	128,573	13,789	378	115,162	56,637	25,387	16,436	14,620	11,997	6,094
1988	216,605	138,988	2,687	141,675	15,631	454	126,498	62,302	27,805	17,601	15,724	12,306	6,390
1989	241,143	148,914	2,484	151,397	16,945	534	134,986	74,787	31,370	19,081	17,028	12,638	6,596
1990	257,571	159,051	2,084	161,136	17,936	633	143,832	79,357	34,382	19,763	17,714	13,033	6,740
1991	268,375	165,646	2,458	168,104	18,806	677	149,975	79,765	38,635	20,073	18,125	13,370	6,718
1992	284,266	177,651	2,460	180,111	20,071	743	160,783	79,138	44,345	20,825	18,808	13,651	6,763
1993	301,393	189,871	2,535	192,406	21,337	793	171,862	82,049	47,482	21,641	19,522	13,927	7,002
1994	317,675	200,976	2,165	203,141	22,867	854	181,129	85,928	50,619	22,310	20,082	14,239	7,234
1995	341,584	214,077	2,211	216,287	24,235	922	192,974	93,937	54,673	23,496	21,107	14,538	7,494
1996	363,907	228,542	1,953	230,496	25,571	994	205,919	100,141	57,847	24,500	21,784	14,853	7,740
1997	385,402	242,218	2,167	244,384	27,135	1,095	218,344	107,053	60,005	25,378	22,365	15,186	8,005
1998	415,547	263,272	2,644	265,915	29,130	1,221	238,007	116,171	61,369	26,833	23,549	15,487	8,317
1999	435,726	282,203	2,703	284,906	30,996	1,353	255,264	116,666	63,797	27,649	24,243	15,759	8,578
2000	471,082	306,169	2,582	308,752	33,262	1,516	277,006	126,067	68,010	29,355	25,648	16,048	8,881
2001	495,620	324,422	2,582	327,004	35,634	1,618	292,988	128,493	74,139	30,300	26,621	16,357	8,939
2002	512,580	340,530	2,513	343,043	37,184	1,676	307,535	125,177	79,868	30,713	27,583	16,689	9,056
2003	538,104	359,791	2,199	361,990	39,193	1,773	324,569	128,269	85,265	31,646	28,835	17,004	9,283
2004	587,659	389,697	2,275	391,972	42,579	1,918	351,310	144,637	91,712	33,744	30,571	17,415	9,644
2005	641,627	422,431	2,687	425,117	46,457	2,080	380,740	162,401	98,486	35,962	32,065	17,842	10,067
2006	697,871	449,862	2,636	452,499	50,370	2,298	404,426	188,368	105,077	38,414	34,236	18,167	10,384
2007	726,357	457,268	2,264	459,533	51,861	2,597	410,268	204,283	111,807	39,545	35,246	18,368	10,531
2008	727,016	443,315	2,068	445,382	51,692	2,786	396,477	203,550	126,989	39,240	35,262	18,527	10,269
2009	682,320	418,121	2,191	420,312	49,961	2,644	372,995	170,841	138,483	36,580	33,683	18,653	9,842
2010	725,801	436,509	2,482	438,991	50,688	2,726	391,030	183,085	151,686	38,513	35,407	18,846	9,805
2011	766,186	448,314	2,188	450,502	46,682	2,932	406,752	201,676	157,758	40,128	36,472	19,093	10,037
2012	791,919	465,630	2,783	468,413	48,814	3,017	422,616	213,189	156,113	40,976	37,166	19,326	10,249
2013	794,797	480,064	2,836	482,900	56,725	3,052	429,227	204,650	160,921	40,627	36,433	19,563	10,539
2014	858,499	509,482	2,849	512,331	59,786	3,216	455,761	231,516	171,221	43,227	38,663	19,860	10,938
2015	919,227	541,522	3,600	545,122	62,969	3,344	485,497	253,171	180,559	45,452	40,389	20,224	11,367
2016	953,261	565,044	2,669	567,712	65,957	3,400	505,155	259,841	188,265	46,208	41,512	20,630	11,673
2017	1,000,624	593,743	2,417	596,160	69,122	3,510	530,548	272,474	197,602	47,701	42,869	20,977	11,913
2018	1,052,550	625,826	2,311	628,137	73,056	3,625	558,707	285,971	207,872	49,417	44,609	21,299	12,548
2019	1,125,984	1,122,432	3,552	672,455	78,332	3,755	597,877	311,365	216,742	52,391	46,339	21,492	12,857
2020	1,202,648	1,198,310	4,338	695,289	80,674	3,693	618,309	307,480	276,859	55,337	49,345	21,733	...

... = Not available.

Personal Income and Employment by Region and State: Georgia

(Millions of dollars, except as noted.)

Year	Personal income, total	Earnings by place of work			Less: Contributions for government social insurance	Plus: Adjustment for residence	Equals: Net earnings by place of residence	Plus: Dividends, interest, and rent	Plus: Personal current transfer receipts	Per capita (dollars)		Population (thousands)	Total employment (thousands)
		Nonfarm	Farm	Total						Personal income	Disposable personal income		
1960	6,918	5,602	326	5,928	262	-15	5,651	849	418	1,749	1,587	3,956	...
1961	7,221	5,764	347	6,111	266	-17	5,828	920	473	1,799	1,636	4,015	...
1962	7,768	6,279	312	6,591	298	-21	6,272	1,008	488	1,901	1,719	4,086	...
1963	8,445	6,797	400	7,196	349	-25	6,822	1,101	522	2,024	1,829	4,172	...
1964	9,145	7,457	334	7,791	377	-30	7,385	1,213	547	2,148	1,954	4,258	...
1965	10,099	8,214	377	8,591	408	-36	8,148	1,351	601	2,331	2,116	4,332	...
1966	11,144	9,210	389	9,599	546	-45	9,008	1,479	656	2,545	2,296	4,379	...
1967	12,120	10,017	386	10,403	626	-54	9,723	1,616	781	2,750	2,490	4,408	...
1968	13,381	11,201	343	11,544	684	-64	10,796	1,655	930	2,986	2,671	4,482	...
1969	14,980	12,475	420	12,895	786	-93	12,015	1,902	1,063	3,292	2,889	4,551	2,119
1970	16,310	13,324	398	13,722	837	-78	12,807	2,204	1,299	3,542	3,153	4,605	2,121
1971	18,010	14,590	456	15,047	952	-78	14,017	2,447	1,546	3,823	3,439	4,710	2,167
1972	20,206	16,489	471	16,960	1,128	-71	15,761	2,705	1,741	4,203	3,730	4,807	2,253
1973	22,848	18,461	788	19,249	1,445	-70	17,734	3,104	2,010	4,656	4,159	4,907	2,356
1974	25,068	20,011	672	20,684	1,628	-70	18,986	3,570	2,511	5,019	4,479	4,995	2,374
1975	27,084	20,982	638	21,620	1,680	-58	19,883	3,874	3,327	5,354	4,869	5,059	2,313
1976	30,147	23,786	629	24,415	1,946	-88	22,381	4,204	3,562	5,881	5,297	5,126	2,400
1977	33,332	26,898	365	27,263	2,190	-105	24,968	4,670	3,694	6,396	5,726	5,212	2,503
1978	37,819	30,533	568	31,101	2,552	-86	28,463	5,343	4,013	7,154	6,365	5,286	2,621
1979	42,321	34,176	598	34,774	2,974	-106	31,693	6,057	4,571	7,850	6,900	5,391	2,700
1980	47,193	37,709	40	37,749	3,302	-115	34,332	7,380	5,481	8,602	7,587	5,486	2,741
1981	53,459	41,622	523	42,145	3,919	-36	38,190	9,025	6,243	9,600	8,432	5,568	2,776
1982	57,867	44,454	683	45,137	4,272	-77	40,788	10,262	6,817	10,242	9,051	5,650	2,793
1983	63,380	49,088	476	49,563	4,793	-120	44,651	11,331	7,398	11,064	9,761	5,728	2,877
1984	71,863	55,825	956	56,782	5,611	-155	51,015	12,947	7,901	12,316	10,918	5,835	3,068
1985	78,686	61,833	787	62,620	6,361	-169	56,090	14,124	8,472	13,196	11,617	5,963	3,207
1986	85,846	68,004	828	68,832	7,085	-218	61,529	15,291	9,026	14,109	12,440	6,085	3,335
1987	92,434	73,645	895	74,540	7,617	-227	66,696	16,271	9,467	14,888	13,059	6,208	3,433
1988	100,797	80,114	1,151	81,266	8,521	-229	72,516	18,063	10,218	15,959	14,076	6,316	3,545
1989	108,619	84,605	1,357	85,961	9,070	-192	76,699	20,566	11,354	16,942	14,881	6,411	3,608
1990	116,150	90,194	1,261	91,455	9,696	-113	81,646	21,873	12,631	17,835	15,686	6,513	3,664
1991	121,895	93,591	1,565	95,156	10,179	-132	84,845	22,424	14,626	18,322	16,225	6,653	3,622
1992	131,979	102,091	1,640	103,731	10,960	-178	92,594	23,062	16,323	19,360	17,182	6,817	3,698
1993	140,173	108,698	1,475	110,172	11,712	-182	98,279	24,435	17,460	20,087	17,759	6,978	3,866
1994	150,942	116,328	1,941	118,269	12,670	-237	105,362	26,758	18,823	21,090	18,618	7,157	4,020
1995	162,948	125,360	1,764	127,125	13,607	-340	113,178	29,427	20,344	22,235	19,580	7,328	4,188
1996	176,086	135,472	1,857	137,329	14,539	-375	122,415	32,016	21,655	23,475	20,535	7,501	4,333
1997	187,548	144,937	1,813	146,750	15,463	-448	130,839	34,551	22,158	24,404	21,213	7,685	4,449
1998	205,109	161,028	1,803	162,832	16,839	-585	145,408	37,041	22,661	26,084	22,574	7,864	4,608
1999	218,793	174,671	1,945	176,616	18,151	-600	157,865	37,020	23,909	27,193	23,510	8,046	4,729
2000	236,810	188,470	1,845	190,315	19,382	-732	170,201	40,686	25,924	28,783	24,839	8,227	4,861
2001	248,728	196,991	2,218	199,209	20,151	-777	178,282	41,948	28,499	29,692	25,744	8,377	4,872
2002	255,618	201,889	1,645	203,534	20,555	-821	182,159	41,209	32,250	30,044	26,703	8,508	4,858
2003	264,926	209,005	2,051	211,056	21,154	-840	189,062	43,022	32,841	30,724	27,590	8,623	4,895
2004	279,469	221,459	2,163	223,623	23,015	-799	199,809	44,267	35,393	31,869	28,699	8,769	5,022
2005	296,727	231,981	2,480	234,461	23,999	-782	209,681	48,425	38,622	33,243	29,655	8,926	5,196
2006	316,878	245,752	1,581	247,333	25,477	-786	221,069	54,328	41,480	34,609	30,677	9,156	5,358
2007	331,391	252,085	1,881	253,966	26,200	-777	226,989	59,748	44,654	35,443	31,302	9,350	5,491
2008	333,747	247,721	2,184	249,906	27,303	-697	221,906	60,415	51,427	35,113	31,170	9,505	5,451
2009	327,375	241,418	1,934	243,352	26,537	-925	215,890	54,955	56,531	34,028	30,975	9,621	5,247
2010	335,318	245,949	1,383	247,332	27,011	-948	219,373	53,970	61,975	34,527	31,322	9,712	5,211
2011	359,575	256,199	1,612	257,811	24,828	-1,183	231,800	62,861	64,914	36,685	33,016	9,802	5,326
2012	367,804	264,003	2,460	266,464	25,731	-1,339	239,393	64,119	64,291	37,146	33,452	9,901	5,385
2013	373,356	273,354	2,611	275,964	30,209	-1,514	244,241	62,486	66,629	37,435	33,361	9,973	5,497
2014	398,882	290,000	1,984	291,984	31,698	-1,610	258,676	70,264	69,942	39,615	35,292	10,069	5,670
2015	422,845	306,717	2,354	309,071	33,366	-1,561	274,144	75,612	73,089	41,532	36,851	10,181	5,831
2016	439,574	321,047	1,641	322,689	34,788	-1,807	286,094	77,740	75,741	42,657	37,926	10,305	5,970
2017	460,403	337,761	1,946	339,707	36,479	-1,828	301,401	80,570	78,432	44,214	39,319	10,413	6,084
2018	481,213	351,919	2,649	354,567	38,125	-1,897	314,546	84,204	82,463	45,745	40,870	10,519	6,285
2019	512,138	510,185	1,953	373,233	39,974	-1,592	331,667	94,341	86,130	48,188	42,863	10,628	6,419
2020	1,202,648	1,198,310	4,338	695,289	80,674	3,693	618,309	307,480	276,859	55,337	49,345	21,733	...

... = Not available.

Personal Income and Employment by Region and State: Hawaii

(Millions of dollars, except as noted.)

Year	Personal income, total	Earnings by place of work			Less: Contributions for government social insurance	Plus: Adjustment for residence	Equals: Net earnings by place of residence	Plus: Dividends, interest, and rent	Plus: Personal current transfer receipts	Per capita (dollars)		Population (thousands)	Total employment (thousands)
		Nonfarm	Farm	Total						Personal income	Disposable personal income		
1960	1,615	1,278	82	1,360	52	0	1,307	260	48	2,516	2,191	642	...
1961	1,754	1,383	75	1,458	57	0	1,401	294	59	2,661	2,316	659	...
1962	1,881	1,471	79	1,550	61	0	1,489	325	67	2,750	2,434	684	...
1963	2,011	1,579	88	1,667	76	0	1,591	350	70	2,949	2,614	682	...
1964	2,188	1,725	89	1,814	82	0	1,731	386	70	3,125	2,805	700	...
1965	2,402	1,887	91	1,978	85	0	1,893	428	81	3,412	3,076	704	...
1966	2,608	2,077	95	2,172	114	0	2,058	455	95	3,674	3,262	710	...
1967	2,831	2,239	98	2,338	131	0	2,206	504	121	3,915	3,468	723	...
1968	3,184	2,540	117	2,658	153	0	2,505	539	140	4,338	3,814	734	...
1969	3,643	2,922	119	3,041	182	0	2,859	624	160	4,903	4,254	743	416
1970	4,225	3,338	133	3,471	211	0	3,260	759	207	5,538	4,833	763	434
1971	4,584	3,579	131	3,709	236	0	3,474	840	270	5,791	5,131	792	437
1972	5,048	3,944	131	4,076	274	0	3,802	923	323	6,170	5,401	818	453
1973	5,593	4,378	138	4,517	348	0	4,168	1,055	370	6,643	5,828	842	473
1974	6,361	4,783	340	5,123	400	0	4,723	1,194	444	7,412	6,525	858	485
1975	6,919	5,288	202	5,489	442	0	5,047	1,295	577	7,907	7,111	875	499
1976	7,466	5,731	173	5,904	484	0	5,420	1,371	675	8,367	7,465	892	505
1977	8,084	6,219	184	6,403	522	0	5,881	1,495	708	8,828	7,840	916	509
1978	8,954	6,897	168	7,065	597	0	6,467	1,726	761	9,640	8,501	929	528
1979	10,043	7,752	193	7,945	700	0	7,245	1,958	840	10,571	9,281	950	556
1980	11,484	8,624	374	8,998	777	0	8,221	2,298	965	11,867	10,429	968	575
1981	12,434	9,318	199	9,517	896	0	8,620	2,680	1,134	12,711	11,174	978	568
1982	13,166	9,913	234	10,147	946	0	9,201	2,736	1,229	13,249	11,860	994	567
1983	14,443	10,665	338	11,003	1,036	0	9,967	3,125	1,351	14,262	12,762	1,013	577
1984	15,473	11,448	239	11,687	1,135	0	10,552	3,496	1,425	15,052	13,490	1,028	582
1985	16,453	12,245	222	12,467	1,237	0	11,230	3,712	1,511	15,824	14,124	1,040	598
1986	17,458	13,099	256	13,355	1,351	0	12,004	3,880	1,574	16,599	14,788	1,052	612
1987	18,619	14,206	239	14,445	1,477	0	12,969	4,021	1,629	17,435	15,321	1,068	643
1988	20,478	15,815	262	16,077	1,696	0	14,381	4,350	1,746	18,964	16,647	1,080	669
1989	22,874	17,595	248	17,843	1,887	0	15,956	4,981	1,937	20,897	18,160	1,095	696
1990	24,979	19,526	260	19,786	2,178	0	17,608	5,273	2,098	22,433	19,510	1,113	724
1991	26,433	20,771	232	21,003	2,345	0	18,658	5,471	2,304	23,253	20,119	1,137	745
1992	28,435	22,194	219	22,412	2,494	0	19,918	5,841	2,676	24,542	21,669	1,159	746
1993	29,477	22,716	216	22,932	2,543	0	20,389	6,157	2,930	25,133	22,226	1,173	742
1994	30,164	22,921	210	23,131	2,588	0	20,543	6,449	3,172	25,400	22,485	1,188	737
1995	30,864	22,936	199	23,136	2,586	0	20,550	6,727	3,587	25,788	22,962	1,197	734
1996	30,895	22,905	195	23,100	2,590	0	20,511	6,705	3,680	25,665	22,714	1,204	733
1997	31,908	23,537	205	23,742	2,630	0	21,112	7,102	3,694	26,334	23,298	1,212	734
1998	32,703	23,901	218	24,119	2,671	0	21,448	7,489	3,766	26,911	23,731	1,215	738
1999	33,864	24,831	245	25,076	2,740	0	22,336	7,606	3,922	27,980	24,646	1,210	738
2000	35,852	26,352	240	26,593	2,889	0	23,704	8,018	4,130	29,544	25,963	1,214	749
2001	37,355	27,826	237	28,063	3,048	0	25,015	7,889	4,450	30,470	26,824	1,226	753
2002	39,012	29,586	251	29,837	3,244	0	26,593	7,612	4,807	31,471	28,207	1,240	758
2003	40,852	31,511	250	31,761	3,491	0	28,270	7,620	4,963	32,652	29,454	1,251	774
2004	44,055	33,798	251	34,049	3,667	0	30,381	8,382	5,292	34,592	31,202	1,274	797
2005	47,360	36,263	260	36,523	3,934	0	32,588	9,044	5,727	36,635	32,677	1,293	820
2006	50,774	38,330	260	38,590	4,247	0	34,343	10,389	6,042	38,766	34,511	1,310	842
2007	53,520	39,641	247	39,888	4,442	0	35,445	11,439	6,637	40,679	36,187	1,316	865
2008	56,166	40,428	253	40,681	4,532	0	36,149	12,291	7,727	42,160	37,713	1,332	858
2009	56,013	39,873	294	40,167	4,476	0	35,691	12,028	8,294	41,593	38,048	1,347	830
2010	57,101	40,674	279	40,953	4,707	0	36,246	11,568	9,287	41,864	38,367	1,364	824
2011	59,922	42,147	306	42,453	4,477	0	37,976	12,293	9,653	43,446	39,500	1,379	835
2012	62,435	44,150	345	44,496	4,633	0	39,863	13,058	9,515	44,759	40,691	1,395	849
2013	63,355	45,503	318	45,821	5,412	0	40,409	13,083	9,864	44,982	40,461	1,408	868
2014	66,899	47,361	297	47,658	5,456	0	42,203	14,151	10,545	47,283	42,500	1,415	883
2015	70,323	49,735	325	50,060	5,700	0	44,360	15,062	10,902	49,437	44,120	1,422	901
2016	72,650	51,177	265	51,442	5,834	0	45,609	15,735	11,307	50,872	45,343	1,428	913
2017	75,355	53,003	285	53,287	6,061	0	47,226	16,379	11,749	52,910	47,215	1,424	922
2018	77,509	54,314	290	54,604	6,238	0	48,367	17,029	12,113	54,565	48,905	1,420	927
2019	80,727	80,518	208	57,466	6,581	0	50,886	17,168	12,673	57,026	50,762	1,416	932
2020	85,446	85,172	273	53,711	6,161	0	47,550	17,092	20,804	60,729	54,923	1,407	...

... = Not available.

Personal Income and Employment by Region and State: Idaho

(Millions of dollars, except as noted.)

Year	Personal income, total	Earnings by place of work			Less: Contributions for government social insurance	Plus: Adjustment for residence	Equals: Net earnings by place of residence	Plus: Dividends, interest, and rent	Plus: Personal current transfer receipts	Per capita (dollars)		Population (thousands)	Total employment (thousands)
		Nonfarm	Farm	Total						Personal income	Disposable personal income		
1960	1,316	925	159	1,084	50	-3	1,031	195	90	1,961	1,762	671	...
1961	1,392	984	159	1,143	56	-3	1,084	206	102	2,035	1,841	684	...
1962	1,488	1,059	167	1,226	62	-3	1,161	221	106	2,150	1,949	692	...
1963	1,523	1,076	175	1,251	69	-2	1,180	234	109	2,230	2,013	683	...
1964	1,575	1,155	135	1,290	70	-2	1,218	245	112	2,316	2,117	680	...
1965	1,794	1,259	232	1,491	76	-2	1,414	260	120	2,615	2,392	686	...
1966	1,817	1,331	180	1,511	93	-1	1,417	271	129	2,638	2,401	689	...
1967	1,932	1,395	207	1,601	107	-1	1,494	283	155	2,808	2,547	688	...
1968	2,065	1,522	186	1,707	122	-0	1,586	305	174	2,971	2,682	695	...
1969	2,391	1,688	253	1,941	126	14	1,828	369	194	3,382	3,030	707	315
1970	2,648	1,843	267	2,110	136	15	1,988	431	229	3,691	3,336	717	324
1971	2,894	2,021	249	2,270	154	16	2,132	493	269	3,918	3,541	739	332
1972	3,304	2,302	320	2,622	182	17	2,457	541	306	4,329	3,938	763	347
1973	3,821	2,602	453	3,055	239	19	2,835	635	351	4,885	4,408	782	365
1974	4,497	2,966	628	3,594	281	23	3,336	740	422	5,566	4,983	808	381
1975	4,867	3,369	387	3,756	314	28	3,469	874	524	5,850	5,288	832	393
1976	5,436	3,895	343	4,237	368	35	3,904	940	593	6,343	5,719	857	419
1977	5,942	4,381	240	4,621	416	35	4,240	1,074	628	6,726	6,048	883	435
1978	6,830	5,069	308	5,377	485	42	4,935	1,225	670	7,497	6,722	911	460
1979	7,469	5,595	233	5,828	564	47	5,311	1,376	783	8,009	7,161	933	469
1980	8,395	5,969	408	6,376	606	60	5,830	1,627	937	8,856	7,924	948	464
1981	9,238	6,435	427	6,862	703	53	6,212	1,951	1,074	9,600	8,508	962	462
1982	9,700	6,450	393	6,844	720	62	6,186	2,282	1,233	9,961	8,928	974	452
1983	10,600	6,960	584	7,543	779	63	6,827	2,469	1,304	10,795	9,755	982	463
1984	11,294	7,546	501	8,046	870	76	7,253	2,692	1,349	11,399	10,324	991	472
1985	11,933	7,931	458	8,389	929	85	7,545	2,943	1,445	12,004	10,851	994	474
1986	12,177	8,066	479	8,545	955	100	7,690	2,962	1,525	12,297	11,172	990	474
1987	12,724	8,509	594	9,103	988	108	8,223	2,932	1,570	12,918	11,709	985	487
1988	13,766	9,340	670	10,010	1,128	126	9,008	3,072	1,686	13,966	12,640	986	508
1989	15,147	10,122	881	11,003	1,243	142	9,902	3,411	1,834	15,232	13,637	994	525
1990	16,352	11,071	1,000	12,071	1,435	157	10,794	3,580	1,979	16,152	14,407	1,012	548
1991	17,191	11,836	829	12,664	1,564	178	11,278	3,698	2,214	16,509	14,748	1,041	566
1992	18,905	13,141	875	14,016	1,701	196	12,510	3,917	2,478	17,640	15,673	1,072	586
1993	20,721	14,340	1,085	15,424	1,863	217	13,778	4,276	2,667	18,688	16,641	1,109	612
1994	22,179	15,699	779	16,478	2,051	246	14,673	4,678	2,829	19,368	17,244	1,145	647
1995	23,843	16,559	844	17,403	2,180	285	15,508	5,221	3,114	20,252	18,013	1,177	667
1996	25,335	17,375	952	18,327	2,242	331	16,416	5,590	3,330	21,058	18,687	1,203	689
1997	26,420	18,242	756	18,998	2,337	378	17,039	5,926	3,455	21,506	19,009	1,229	708
1998	28,286	19,713	956	20,669	2,483	446	18,632	6,056	3,599	22,587	19,971	1,252	733
1999	30,123	21,302	1,006	22,307	2,616	510	20,202	6,099	3,823	23,614	20,798	1,276	747
2000	32,601	23,290	1,013	24,304	2,847	524	21,981	6,476	4,145	25,089	21,965	1,299	777
2001	33,980	23,893	1,126	25,020	2,894	516	22,642	6,707	4,631	25,743	22,678	1,320	783
2002	35,112	24,863	1,102	25,964	2,979	501	23,486	6,601	5,026	26,196	23,713	1,340	791
2003	36,322	25,599	864	26,463	3,101	512	23,874	7,111	5,337	26,641	24,277	1,363	801
2004	39,252	27,142	1,377	28,519	3,310	520	25,729	7,806	5,718	28,202	25,706	1,392	825
2005	41,761	28,963	1,188	30,151	3,589	513	27,075	8,508	6,178	29,239	26,212	1,428	862
2006	46,002	32,014	1,099	33,114	3,997	489	29,605	9,691	6,707	31,322	27,863	1,469	900
2007	48,997	33,280	1,655	34,935	4,194	511	31,252	10,463	7,282	32,554	28,949	1,505	929
2008	50,089	33,026	1,641	34,667	4,225	562	31,004	10,608	8,477	32,646	29,304	1,534	921
2009	48,409	32,166	1,000	33,165	4,135	655	29,686	9,399	9,324	31,142	28,655	1,554	880
2010	50,145	32,618	1,420	34,038	4,317	724	30,445	9,450	10,249	31,923	29,378	1,571	869
2011	53,041	33,126	2,041	35,166	3,945	870	32,091	10,656	10,294	33,489	30,541	1,584	879
2012	56,112	34,321	2,061	36,382	4,045	1,098	33,435	12,246	10,431	35,170	32,073	1,595	883
2013	58,236	36,600	2,357	38,957	4,668	1,131	35,420	12,043	10,774	36,137	32,734	1,612	903
2014	61,616	38,408	2,449	40,856	4,857	1,236	37,235	13,138	11,243	37,767	34,188	1,631	925
2015	65,611	40,853	2,272	43,126	5,072	1,198	39,252	14,499	11,860	39,727	35,805	1,652	949
2016	68,055	42,671	2,007	44,678	5,319	1,251	40,610	15,072	12,373	40,438	36,307	1,683	976
2017	71,813	45,256	2,059	47,315	5,646	1,325	42,994	15,887	12,932	41,778	37,473	1,719	1,002
2018	75,703	47,998	1,868	49,865	6,002	1,426	45,289	16,767	13,647	43,155	38,826	1,754	1,040
2019	82,148	79,884	2,264	53,699	6,366	1,502	48,835	18,343	14,970	45,917	41,632	1,789	1,072
2020	88,817	86,180	2,636	56,425	6,798	1,501	51,128	18,093	19,595	48,616	44,213	1,827	...

... = Not available.

Personal Income and Employment by Region and State: Illinois

(Millions of dollars, except as noted.)

Year	Personal income, total	Derivation of personal income								Per capita (dollars)		Population (thousands)	Total employment (thousands)
		Earnings by place of work			Less: Contributions for government social insurance	Plus: Adjustment for residence	Equals: Net earnings by place of residence	Plus: Dividends, interest, and rent	Plus: Personal current transfer receipts	Personal income	Disposable personal income		
		Nonfarm	Farm	Total									
1960	27,210	22,630	647	23,277	1,073	-133	22,071	3,666	1,472	2,698	2,378	10,086	...
1961	28,282	23,063	814	23,877	1,089	-138	22,650	3,933	1,699	2,792	2,470	10,130	...
1962	29,885	24,344	798	25,142	1,196	-154	23,792	4,330	1,763	2,907	2,563	10,280	...
1963	31,096	25,257	821	26,078	1,329	-159	24,590	4,690	1,816	2,989	2,642	10,402	...
1964	33,241	27,105	665	27,770	1,337	-175	26,259	5,136	1,847	3,142	2,816	10,580	...
1965	36,068	29,103	903	30,006	1,356	-194	28,456	5,631	1,981	3,373	3,015	10,693	...
1966	39,099	32,041	976	33,017	1,821	-222	30,975	5,979	2,145	3,608	3,200	10,836	...
1967	41,606	34,021	936	34,957	1,988	-239	32,731	6,320	2,555	3,801	3,358	10,947	...
1968	44,582	36,706	691	37,397	2,193	-264	34,939	6,649	2,993	4,055	3,542	10,995	...
1969	48,485	40,069	913	40,982	2,715	64	38,330	6,918	3,236	4,392	3,765	11,039	5,179
1970	51,524	42,215	723	42,937	2,810	-16	40,111	7,576	3,837	4,632	3,992	11,125	5,144
1971	55,317	44,907	885	45,792	3,074	-59	42,659	8,068	4,590	4,936	4,321	11,206	5,104
1972	60,030	48,752	1,000	49,752	3,517	-83	46,152	8,711	5,167	5,332	4,608	11,258	5,155
1973	66,968	53,736	1,841	55,577	4,490	-100	50,987	9,833	6,147	5,947	5,172	11,260	5,351
1974	73,216	58,539	1,673	60,212	5,078	-117	55,016	11,192	7,009	6,494	5,622	11,274	5,441
1975	79,866	61,631	2,463	64,093	5,194	-141	58,758	12,125	8,984	7,064	6,202	11,306	5,342
1976	86,832	68,269	1,713	69,981	5,881	-132	63,969	12,936	9,927	7,644	6,642	11,360	5,458
1977	95,460	75,690	1,716	77,406	6,516	-70	70,819	14,256	10,384	8,369	7,252	11,406	5,587
1978	105,342	84,402	1,510	85,912	7,466	7	78,453	15,841	11,048	9,213	7,958	11,434	5,748
1979	115,570	92,288	1,838	94,126	8,484	74	85,716	17,822	12,032	10,117	8,674	11,423	5,803
1980	125,211	97,471	381	97,852	8,931	177	89,097	21,504	14,610	10,950	9,407	11,435	5,675
1981	138,877	104,307	1,522	105,829	10,249	116	95,696	26,399	16,782	12,136	10,408	11,443	5,664
1982	147,012	107,173	914	108,087	10,690	32	97,429	31,156	18,426	12,869	11,230	11,423	5,563
1983	153,020	112,268	-485	111,782	11,259	17	100,540	32,755	19,725	13,412	11,781	11,409	5,520
1984	168,717	123,383	1,227	124,610	12,810	-47	111,754	36,872	20,091	14,784	13,059	11,412	5,718
1985	177,210	130,498	1,718	132,215	13,763	-92	118,361	37,884	20,965	15,545	13,684	11,400	5,780
1986	186,406	138,918	1,426	140,344	14,681	-131	125,533	39,146	21,727	16,370	14,431	11,387	5,892
1987	197,183	149,490	1,431	150,921	15,562	-202	135,157	39,851	22,175	17,310	15,107	11,391	6,031
1988	212,643	163,793	856	164,649	17,396	-303	146,950	42,739	22,953	18,669	16,399	11,390	6,187
1989	226,917	172,648	2,174	174,822	18,513	-324	155,985	46,547	24,385	19,888	17,360	11,410	6,294
1990	240,801	183,408	1,763	185,172	19,273	-272	165,627	48,552	26,622	21,025	18,363	11,453	6,390
1991	245,872	187,719	977	188,696	20,215	-322	168,159	49,029	28,684	21,253	18,665	11,569	6,369
1992	265,737	201,962	2,056	204,018	21,320	-410	182,289	50,624	32,824	22,724	20,072	11,694	6,351
1993	275,363	210,352	1,712	212,063	22,492	-591	188,980	51,959	34,424	23,317	20,511	11,810	6,441
1994	290,055	221,487	2,306	223,794	24,002	-685	199,107	55,272	35,676	24,349	21,336	11,913	6,611
1995	307,809	234,255	604	234,860	25,277	-928	208,654	61,101	38,054	25,633	22,416	12,008	6,773
1996	327,553	246,538	2,501	249,039	26,332	-935	221,773	65,756	40,024	27,066	23,527	12,102	6,875
1997	346,339	261,993	2,135	264,128	27,787	-952	235,389	70,183	40,768	28,422	24,525	12,186	6,981
1998	368,119	279,080	1,537	280,617	29,384	-1,034	250,199	76,361	41,559	29,997	25,740	12,272	7,139
1999	384,036	297,355	1,083	298,437	30,782	-1,146	266,510	75,317	42,210	31,073	26,612	12,359	7,219
2000	413,443	317,609	1,810	319,419	32,338	-1,380	285,701	82,852	44,890	33,251	28,478	12,434	7,357
2001	428,742	331,258	1,691	332,949	33,140	-1,562	298,248	82,058	48,436	34,331	29,635	12,488	7,310
2002	434,250	337,841	997	338,837	33,648	-1,669	303,521	78,630	52,099	34,669	30,600	12,526	7,218
2003	441,946	343,273	1,891	345,164	34,518	-1,593	309,053	78,595	54,298	35,198	31,444	12,556	7,191
2004	459,074	356,072	3,668	359,740	36,574	-1,632	321,535	81,281	56,259	36,464	32,654	12,590	7,245
2005	477,013	368,408	1,780	370,187	38,658	-1,770	329,759	85,487	61,767	37,828	33,519	12,610	7,335
2006	509,272	388,814	1,977	390,791	40,457	-1,833	348,502	97,959	62,812	40,278	35,445	12,644	7,449
2007	538,588	404,621	3,238	407,859	42,265	-2,307	363,287	105,950	69,351	42,422	37,053	12,696	7,578
2008	552,022	406,969	4,482	411,450	43,039	-1,771	366,640	109,097	76,286	43,306	37,875	12,747	7,553
2009	525,582	386,056	2,565	388,621	41,145	-2,093	345,384	94,492	85,707	41,071	37,050	12,797	7,304
2010	540,464	396,181	2,558	398,740	41,808	-2,140	354,792	92,418	93,254	42,090	37,798	12,841	7,251
2011	568,154	412,361	5,362	417,723	39,296	-2,570	375,857	103,027	89,270	44,155	38,944	12,867	7,376
2012	593,271	431,195	3,061	434,255	41,008	-2,412	390,835	113,066	89,370	46,047	40,554	12,884	7,435
2013	607,910	445,747	7,958	453,705	47,040	-2,678	403,987	110,737	93,186	47,131	41,120	12,898	7,503
2014	638,061	465,094	3,566	468,659	48,545	-2,340	417,775	125,416	94,871	49,504	43,240	12,889	7,613
2015	664,296	483,431	324	483,755	50,049	-2,589	431,118	132,964	100,215	51,639	44,937	12,864	7,748
2016	673,529	487,943	2,676	490,619	50,838	-2,798	436,984	135,632	100,913	52,509	45,961	12,827	7,799
2017	693,914	502,399	1,510	503,909	52,348	-3,158	448,403	141,541	103,970	54,271	47,532	12,786	7,865
2018	725,394	522,334	1,463	523,797	54,538	-3,317	465,942	148,573	110,880	56,933	50,157	12,741	7,881
2019	744,641	742,534	2,106	542,219	56,703	-3,520	481,996	150,488	112,157	58,786	51,706	12,667	7,963
2020	792,729	788,779	3,950	541,056	56,607	-3,245	481,205	148,704	162,820	62,977	55,981	12,588	...

... = Not available.

Personal Income and Employment by Region and State: Indiana

(Millions of dollars, except as noted.)

Year	Personal income, total	Earnings by place of work			Less: Contributions for government social insurance	Plus: Adjustment for residence	Equals: Net earnings by place of residence	Plus: Dividends, interest, and rent	Plus: Personal current transfer receipts	Per capita (dollars)		Population (thousands)	Total employment (thousands)
		Nonfarm	Farm	Total						Personal income	Disposable personal income		
1960	10,390	8,573	366	8,939	415	41	8,564	1,222	604	2,223	1,986	4,674	...
1961	10,707	8,628	464	9,092	411	44	8,724	1,291	693	2,264	2,035	4,730	...
1962	11,464	9,328	452	9,779	461	49	9,367	1,400	697	2,421	2,163	4,736	...
1963	12,043	9,814	470	10,284	526	49	9,807	1,512	724	2,509	2,229	4,799	...
1964	12,817	10,637	301	10,938	545	47	10,440	1,629	749	2,639	2,368	4,856	...
1965	14,162	11,587	553	12,140	581	49	11,608	1,748	806	2,877	2,578	4,922	...
1966	15,288	12,835	480	13,315	818	56	12,553	1,869	866	3,058	2,715	4,999	...
1967	16,017	13,443	431	13,874	916	59	13,017	1,989	1,011	3,170	2,806	5,053	...
1968	17,413	14,645	379	15,024	993	69	14,100	2,133	1,180	3,419	3,001	5,093	...
1969	19,238	16,009	550	16,559	1,097	43	15,506	2,453	1,280	3,741	3,241	5,143	2,327
1970	20,029	16,441	381	16,821	1,115	78	15,785	2,744	1,501	3,849	3,377	5,204	2,291
1971	21,794	17,475	596	18,071	1,227	139	16,984	3,020	1,790	4,151	3,681	5,250	2,290
1972	23,847	19,381	507	19,888	1,440	178	18,625	3,252	1,970	4,503	3,950	5,296	2,367
1973	27,368	21,745	1,228	22,973	1,863	220	21,330	3,704	2,335	5,136	4,547	5,329	2,483
1974	29,274	23,332	735	24,066	2,089	280	22,258	4,260	2,757	5,472	4,769	5,350	2,493
1975	31,608	24,024	1,097	25,121	2,120	328	23,329	4,767	3,512	5,907	5,245	5,351	2,405
1976	35,132	27,285	1,076	28,362	2,438	385	26,309	5,149	3,674	6,540	5,742	5,372	2,489
1977	38,901	30,856	724	31,579	2,754	443	29,269	5,775	3,857	7,197	6,295	5,405	2,578
1978	43,398	34,726	731	35,457	3,190	498	32,765	6,392	4,242	7,968	6,938	5,446	2,670
1979	47,806	38,177	672	38,849	3,630	570	35,788	7,146	4,872	8,732	7,568	5,475	2,708
1980	51,419	39,292	379	39,671	3,714	682	36,639	8,680	6,099	9,365	8,176	5,491	2,626
1981	56,407	42,198	306	42,504	4,296	748	38,956	10,638	6,813	10,292	8,944	5,480	2,603
1982	58,429	42,247	307	42,555	4,390	811	38,975	11,863	7,592	10,686	9,370	5,468	2,522
1983	61,277	44,685	-260	44,425	4,660	839	40,603	12,501	8,172	11,243	9,928	5,450	2,542
1984	68,009	49,217	753	49,970	5,258	984	45,696	13,744	8,569	12,460	11,050	5,458	2,642
1985	71,813	52,223	682	52,905	5,686	1,058	48,277	14,517	9,019	13,154	11,625	5,459	2,695
1986	75,637	55,367	578	55,945	6,056	1,135	51,024	15,088	9,525	13,868	12,288	5,454	2,755
1987	80,258	59,677	763	60,440	6,434	1,185	55,191	15,358	9,709	14,664	12,945	5,473	2,849
1988	85,926	64,771	284	65,055	7,215	1,283	59,123	16,513	10,290	15,646	13,824	5,492	2,935
1989	93,581	69,194	965	70,158	7,737	1,349	63,770	18,623	11,188	16,942	14,897	5,524	3,010
1990	98,749	73,007	863	73,870	8,408	1,487	66,949	19,642	12,158	17,768	15,638	5,558	3,070
1991	101,775	76,121	242	76,363	8,884	1,495	68,973	19,423	13,378	18,121	15,996	5,616	3,072
1992	110,148	81,916	849	82,766	9,455	1,646	74,957	19,905	15,287	19,411	17,210	5,675	3,121
1993	116,112	86,578	866	87,444	10,062	1,866	79,247	20,727	16,138	20,232	17,892	5,739	3,197
1994	123,384	92,445	828	93,273	10,900	1,997	84,369	22,178	16,837	21,297	18,753	5,794	3,287
1995	129,006	96,459	349	96,808	11,416	2,278	87,671	24,184	17,151	22,047	19,381	5,851	3,379
1996	136,364	100,767	1,196	101,962	11,792	2,418	92,588	25,667	18,108	23,089	20,232	5,906	3,418
1997	143,496	106,429	1,161	107,590	12,409	2,547	97,728	27,178	18,590	24,096	21,018	5,955	3,476
1998	154,514	115,626	769	116,395	13,176	2,574	105,793	29,416	19,305	25,757	22,418	5,999	3,543
1999	160,747	122,398	473	122,871	13,815	2,826	111,882	28,663	20,202	26,592	23,170	6,045	3,597
2000	171,415	129,173	873	130,046	14,396	3,115	118,764	30,915	21,736	28,138	24,650	6,092	3,648
2001	175,498	130,784	1,068	131,852	14,582	3,360	120,629	30,840	24,028	28,640	25,108	6,128	3,589
2002	178,018	133,914	475	134,388	14,954	3,431	122,865	29,650	25,503	28,918	25,757	6,156	3,553
2003	182,142	136,958	1,257	138,215	15,463	3,515	126,267	29,362	26,513	29,394	26,416	6,197	3,552
2004	190,719	143,308	2,069	145,378	16,260	3,801	132,919	29,727	28,073	30,598	27,608	6,233	3,593
2005	196,767	147,892	1,348	149,241	16,990	4,105	136,355	29,844	30,568	31,339	28,090	6,279	3,635
2006	208,809	154,967	1,141	156,108	17,854	4,322	142,576	33,236	32,997	32,973	29,439	6,333	3,674
2007	216,351	158,183	1,589	159,772	18,368	4,696	146,100	35,639	34,612	33,913	30,096	6,380	3,720
2008	225,843	160,723	2,282	163,005	18,787	4,686	148,903	36,897	40,042	35,152	31,360	6,425	3,683
2009	219,713	154,097	1,544	155,641	18,024	4,601	142,218	33,244	44,251	34,015	31,056	6,459	3,523
2010	229,477	161,921	1,603	163,524	18,441	4,465	149,548	32,614	47,315	35,356	32,193	6,490	3,525
2011	244,551	170,806	2,774	173,580	17,084	4,722	161,218	35,974	47,359	37,531	33,841	6,516	3,590
2012	256,258	179,196	2,267	181,463	17,787	4,729	168,406	38,994	48,858	39,197	35,512	6,538	3,642
2013	259,525	182,049	5,319	187,368	20,662	5,231	171,938	38,352	49,236	39,511	35,534	6,568	3,684
2014	269,593	189,423	3,018	192,440	21,419	5,173	176,195	41,139	52,259	40,887	36,794	6,594	3,741
2015	279,705	196,358	1,233	197,591	22,325	5,888	181,154	43,863	54,688	42,326	37,897	6,608	3,796
2016	289,164	203,491	1,562	205,053	22,808	5,860	188,105	45,033	56,027	43,593	39,015	6,633	3,847
2017	301,008	212,830	913	213,743	23,713	6,006	196,036	47,283	57,689	45,196	40,437	6,660	3,893
2018	312,151	219,850	1,087	220,937	24,558	6,217	202,596	49,240	60,314	46,646	41,915	6,692	3,961
2019	327,713	326,316	1,396	229,896	25,828	7,355	211,423	53,008	63,282	48,687	43,960	6,731	4,007
2020	346,802	344,914	1,888	230,939	26,191	7,214	211,962	52,446	82,394	51,340	46,656	6,755	...

... = Not available.

Personal Income and Employment by Region and State: Iowa

(Millions of dollars, except as noted.)

Year	Personal income, total	Earnings by place of work			Less: Contributions for government social insurance	Plus: Adjustment for residence	Equals: Net earnings by place of residence	Plus: Dividends, interest, and rent	Plus: Personal current transfer receipts	Per capita (dollars)		Population (thousands)	Total employment (thousands)
		Nonfarm	Farm	Total						Personal income	Disposable personal income		
1960	5,745	3,908	732	4,640	186	35	4,489	872	385	2,085	1,876	2,756	...
1961	6,084	4,022	852	4,874	189	38	4,723	937	424	2,207	1,997	2,756	...
1962	6,345	4,203	883	5,086	203	41	4,924	977	444	2,307	2,086	2,750	...
1963	6,744	4,425	1,001	5,425	233	43	5,236	1,044	464	2,455	2,222	2,747	...
1964	7,059	4,742	921	5,663	247	47	5,463	1,117	479	2,571	2,346	2,746	...
1965	7,818	5,070	1,247	6,318	261	50	6,108	1,189	522	2,851	2,596	2,742	...
1966	8,513	5,640	1,346	6,986	352	55	6,689	1,258	566	3,082	2,777	2,762	...
1967	8,672	6,028	1,080	7,109	418	59	6,750	1,247	675	3,105	2,790	2,793	...
1968	9,347	6,490	1,021	7,511	457	63	7,117	1,448	782	3,335	2,974	2,803	...
1969	10,374	7,116	1,238	8,354	543	89	7,900	1,619	856	3,698	3,267	2,805	1,289
1970	11,095	7,540	1,215	8,756	567	97	8,285	1,818	992	3,923	3,493	2,829	1,295
1971	11,642	8,048	1,012	9,060	626	97	8,531	1,984	1,127	4,082	3,676	2,852	1,297
1972	13,040	8,770	1,485	10,255	719	103	9,640	2,185	1,216	4,559	4,039	2,861	1,316
1973	15,655	9,825	2,732	12,557	930	98	11,725	2,526	1,404	5,466	4,881	2,864	1,374
1974	16,225	11,001	1,721	12,722	1,092	91	11,721	2,878	1,626	5,657	4,920	2,868	1,407
1975	18,134	11,982	1,970	13,951	1,167	107	12,892	3,225	2,017	6,293	5,562	2,881	1,407
1976	19,280	13,552	1,227	14,779	1,322	100	13,557	3,504	2,219	6,640	5,815	2,904	1,455
1977	21,275	15,107	1,226	16,333	1,459	74	14,948	3,982	2,345	7,300	6,395	2,914	1,488
1978	24,537	16,681	2,441	19,122	1,671	73	17,524	4,430	2,584	8,406	7,387	2,919	1,513
1979	26,298	18,685	1,575	20,260	1,955	79	18,384	5,020	2,895	9,016	7,842	2,917	1,554
1980	27,994	19,755	717	20,473	2,058	98	18,513	6,068	3,412	9,607	8,340	2,914	1,537
1981	31,681	20,927	1,639	22,566	2,315	127	20,378	7,420	3,882	10,894	9,466	2,908	1,507
1982	32,544	20,949	816	21,765	2,344	200	19,621	8,497	4,426	11,268	9,892	2,888	1,471
1983	33,150	21,840	6	21,846	2,426	213	19,633	8,773	4,743	11,548	10,223	2,871	1,474
1984	36,944	23,534	1,463	24,997	2,684	242	22,555	9,530	4,859	12,924	11,616	2,859	1,499
1985	38,216	24,197	1,752	25,949	2,810	279	23,418	9,642	5,156	13,505	12,137	2,830	1,495
1986	39,480	24,982	2,128	27,110	2,966	274	24,418	9,711	5,351	14,141	12,738	2,792	1,494
1987	41,377	26,817	2,459	29,277	3,174	268	26,371	9,541	5,466	14,954	13,344	2,767	1,514
1988	42,760	28,845	1,646	30,491	3,527	311	27,276	9,771	5,714	15,446	13,756	2,768	1,557
1989	46,555	30,867	2,400	33,267	3,765	321	29,823	10,631	6,101	16,803	14,909	2,771	1,600
1990	49,023	32,666	2,504	35,170	4,079	319	31,410	10,983	6,630	17,628	15,602	2,781	1,635
1991	50,145	34,141	1,780	35,921	4,285	373	32,009	11,008	7,127	17,924	15,897	2,798	1,654
1992	53,792	36,441	2,700	39,141	4,529	411	35,023	11,070	7,698	19,086	17,013	2,818	1,669
1993	54,053	38,235	889	39,124	4,773	401	34,752	11,243	8,058	19,053	16,919	2,837	1,692
1994	58,946	40,747	2,861	43,608	5,142	423	38,889	11,682	8,376	20,677	18,410	2,851	1,725
1995	61,329	42,772	1,818	44,589	5,400	484	39,673	12,832	8,824	21,388	19,004	2,867	1,785
1996	66,841	44,925	3,724	48,649	5,382	529	43,796	13,776	9,269	23,209	20,634	2,880	1,815
1997	69,956	47,570	3,397	50,966	5,908	604	45,663	14,763	9,530	24,197	21,351	2,891	1,841
1998	73,576	51,278	2,161	53,438	6,289	695	47,844	15,963	9,769	25,346	22,354	2,903	1,877
1999	75,468	54,018	1,601	55,619	6,558	796	49,857	15,479	10,133	25,866	22,812	2,918	1,896
2000	80,651	56,758	2,462	59,219	6,806	881	53,295	16,504	10,853	27,535	24,367	2,929	1,915
2001	82,942	58,305	2,273	60,578	6,967	905	54,516	16,681	11,746	28,289	25,087	2,932	1,902
2002	84,927	59,792	2,146	61,938	7,118	943	55,763	16,232	12,932	28,944	26,141	2,934	1,880
2003	86,665	61,937	2,287	64,224	7,442	972	57,754	16,034	12,877	29,458	26,796	2,942	1,873
2004	93,570	65,916	4,835	70,751	7,833	989	63,907	16,322	13,341	31,680	28,936	2,954	1,902
2005	96,376	69,147	3,931	73,078	8,243	907	65,741	16,380	14,254	32,510	29,452	2,964	1,934
2006	102,448	73,669	2,916	76,585	8,684	841	68,742	17,986	15,720	34,348	30,942	2,983	1,966
2007	109,906	77,112	3,997	81,109	9,120	1,079	73,068	20,113	16,726	36,645	32,772	2,999	1,994
2008	116,372	79,752	4,726	84,477	9,546	1,149	76,081	21,238	19,054	38,576	34,597	3,017	1,998
2009	112,829	77,744	3,173	80,916	9,426	1,150	72,640	19,805	20,384	37,202	33,992	3,033	1,959
2010	116,353	80,001	3,560	83,561	9,739	1,187	75,010	19,623	21,721	38,139	34,759	3,051	1,950
2011	125,586	81,967	7,276	89,243	9,092	1,306	81,458	22,069	22,060	40,960	36,971	3,066	1,976
2012	131,982	87,000	6,675	93,676	9,384	1,230	85,521	24,478	21,984	42,906	38,660	3,076	1,993
2013	134,398	89,457	8,479	97,936	10,787	1,211	88,359	23,570	22,468	43,451	38,946	3,093	2,019
2014	139,149	94,521	5,788	100,309	11,116	1,048	90,242	25,432	23,476	44,749	40,133	3,110	2,039
2015	144,183	97,617	5,216	102,832	11,380	993	92,445	27,056	24,681	46,191	41,283	3,121	2,060
2016	145,157	100,055	2,668	102,723	11,852	1,046	91,916	27,930	25,311	46,350	41,388	3,132	2,067
2017	148,043	102,495	2,089	104,584	12,198	1,328	93,714	29,108	25,221	47,093	42,020	3,144	2,070
2018	154,091	106,041	2,591	108,632	12,637	1,381	97,376	30,286	26,430	48,823	43,770	3,156	2,076
2019	163,639	157,573	6,065	114,731	13,089	1,421	103,063	31,476	29,100	51,791	46,508	3,160	2,094
2020	174,685	167,224	7,461	116,947	13,391	1,417	104,972	31,108	38,605	55,218	49,913	3,164	...

... = Not available.

Personal Income and Employment by Region and State: Kansas

(Millions of dollars, except as noted.)

Year	Personal income, total	Earnings by place of work			Less: Contributions for government social insurance	Plus: Adjustment for residence	Equals: Net earnings by place of residence	Plus: Dividends, interest, and rent	Plus: Personal current transfer receipts	Per capita (dollars)		Population (thousands)	Total employment (thousands)
		Nonfarm	Farm	Total						Personal income	Disposable personal income		
1960	4,827	3,295	443	3,737	161	175	3,752	773	302	2,211	1,991	2,183	...
1961	5,039	3,453	451	3,904	177	178	3,906	799	335	2,275	2,051	2,215	...
1962	5,244	3,635	422	4,057	183	194	4,068	831	345	2,351	2,110	2,231	...
1963	5,364	3,735	404	4,138	206	214	4,147	852	366	2,420	2,162	2,217	...
1964	5,650	3,980	368	4,349	213	236	4,371	900	379	2,558	2,330	2,209	...
1965	6,024	4,155	462	4,617	222	259	4,655	957	413	2,731	2,486	2,206	...
1966	6,452	4,550	478	5,029	293	294	5,030	979	444	2,933	2,633	2,200	...
1967	6,756	4,840	407	5,247	340	325	5,232	992	532	3,075	2,755	2,197	...
1968	7,360	5,311	400	5,711	377	355	5,689	1,055	616	3,321	2,948	2,216	...
1969	8,195	5,780	465	6,245	421	445	6,269	1,237	689	3,665	3,226	2,236	1,029
1970	8,893	6,084	606	6,690	442	445	6,693	1,396	803	3,956	3,510	2,248	1,017
1971	9,654	6,558	706	7,264	492	439	7,211	1,527	916	4,298	3,867	2,246	1,022
1972	10,763	7,252	963	8,215	573	458	8,101	1,678	985	4,772	4,252	2,256	1,048
1973	12,266	8,095	1,386	9,480	734	472	9,218	1,897	1,151	5,417	4,814	2,264	1,090
1974	13,262	9,028	1,060	10,088	853	485	9,720	2,219	1,324	5,848	5,138	2,268	1,122
1975	14,488	10,011	807	10,817	936	500	10,381	2,494	1,613	6,358	5,656	2,279	1,133
1976	15,746	11,265	584	11,848	1,069	510	11,290	2,673	1,784	6,850	6,082	2,299	1,169
1977	17,182	12,400	498	12,898	1,175	553	12,276	2,977	1,930	7,413	6,537	2,318	1,208
1978	19,014	14,055	285	14,340	1,374	599	13,565	3,345	2,104	8,151	7,161	2,333	1,252
1979	21,715	15,868	706	16,574	1,615	642	15,601	3,794	2,321	9,251	8,047	2,347	1,296
1980	23,869	17,382	101	17,483	1,757	716	16,442	4,666	2,761	10,075	8,750	2,369	1,309
1981	27,049	19,035	345	19,380	2,055	742	18,066	5,802	3,181	11,342	9,756	2,385	1,322
1982	29,327	19,733	577	20,310	2,180	764	18,893	6,865	3,569	12,213	10,552	2,401	1,306
1983	30,540	20,767	384	21,151	2,288	741	19,604	7,131	3,804	12,643	11,148	2,416	1,323
1984	33,518	22,750	751	23,500	2,567	800	21,734	7,862	3,922	13,827	12,314	2,424	1,365
1985	35,255	23,846	811	24,657	2,732	853	22,778	8,342	4,136	14,524	12,882	2,427	1,368
1986	36,959	25,183	938	26,121	2,885	843	24,079	8,540	4,340	15,193	13,586	2,433	1,368
1987	38,648	26,490	1,173	27,663	3,003	914	25,574	8,612	4,462	15,805	14,021	2,445	1,421
1988	40,704	28,096	1,141	29,237	3,318	918	26,838	9,184	4,682	16,533	14,675	2,462	1,432
1989	43,110	29,937	831	30,768	3,510	975	28,233	9,736	5,142	17,433	15,368	2,473	1,454
1990	45,751	31,587	1,383	32,970	3,887	968	30,051	10,119	5,582	18,438	16,317	2,481	1,474
1991	47,310	32,967	1,035	34,001	4,119	947	30,829	10,417	6,064	18,934	16,817	2,499	1,489
1992	50,940	35,562	1,408	36,970	4,382	1,027	33,614	10,603	6,723	20,115	17,970	2,532	1,502
1993	53,312	37,361	1,346	38,707	4,591	1,115	35,231	10,959	7,122	20,853	18,584	2,557	1,525
1994	55,736	39,217	1,436	40,653	4,897	1,066	36,822	11,558	7,357	21,599	19,210	2,581	1,551
1995	58,129	41,202	794	41,996	5,091	1,157	38,063	12,314	7,752	22,349	19,771	2,601	1,600
1996	61,934	43,512	1,508	45,020	5,327	1,147	40,840	13,080	8,015	23,688	20,863	2,615	1,632
1997	65,771	46,643	1,421	48,064	5,697	1,044	43,411	13,950	8,410	24,958	21,823	2,635	1,677
1998	69,987	49,938	1,309	51,247	6,068	1,065	46,244	15,200	8,544	26,305	22,977	2,661	1,724
1999	72,284	52,375	1,403	53,778	6,343	1,018	48,453	14,929	8,902	26,988	23,556	2,678	1,740
2000	76,243	55,059	1,014	56,073	6,656	1,121	50,538	16,054	9,651	28,304	24,658	2,694	1,760
2001	78,695	56,918	1,164	58,081	6,870	1,133	52,345	15,802	10,549	29,123	25,475	2,702	1,768
2002	79,379	58,363	498	58,860	7,008	1,198	53,050	15,120	11,209	29,253	26,106	2,714	1,746
2003	81,547	59,165	1,662	60,827	7,173	1,169	54,824	15,014	11,709	29,947	27,000	2,723	1,734
2004	83,860	61,348	1,578	62,926	7,557	1,118	56,487	15,332	12,041	30,669	27,686	2,734	1,751
2005	88,492	64,190	1,976	66,166	7,911	1,260	59,515	16,281	12,697	32,234	28,801	2,745	1,766
2006	97,830	70,755	1,148	71,903	8,407	1,368	64,864	19,323	13,643	35,408	31,481	2,763	1,796
2007	105,159	74,901	1,666	76,567	8,807	1,254	69,013	21,459	14,687	37,776	33,362	2,784	1,844
2008	114,395	80,038	2,062	82,101	9,207	1,414	74,307	23,535	16,553	40,738	36,150	2,808	1,858
2009	110,482	77,530	1,982	79,513	9,003	1,694	72,204	20,252	18,026	39,002	35,496	2,833	1,813
2010	112,682	79,213	2,516	81,728	9,236	1,674	74,167	19,326	19,190	39,424	35,737	2,858	1,802
2011	122,295	84,164	3,634	87,798	8,516	1,239	80,520	22,149	19,626	42,626	38,337	2,869	1,819
2012	129,854	90,029	3,033	93,062	8,816	1,640	85,886	24,614	19,355	45,004	40,624	2,885	1,841
2013	132,570	93,431	4,921	98,352	10,225	1,367	89,494	23,437	19,639	45,816	41,091	2,894	1,869
2014	135,414	95,602	2,780	98,381	10,610	1,183	88,954	26,136	20,324	46,680	41,873	2,901	1,896
2015	137,238	97,968	1,757	99,725	11,031	1,160	89,854	26,114	21,271	47,169	42,283	2,910	1,911
2016	138,106	96,812	2,189	99,001	10,865	1,147	89,283	26,824	21,998	47,438	42,574	2,911	1,917
2017	141,459	99,050	1,864	100,914	11,152	1,313	91,075	27,885	22,499	48,600	43,615	2,911	1,923
2018	146,028	102,867	1,206	104,073	11,629	1,362	93,806	28,813	23,409	50,155	45,171	2,912	1,926
2019	155,648	151,859	3,788	111,130	12,145	1,661	100,646	30,278	24,724	53,439	47,909	2,913	1,946
2020	163,385	159,249	4,137	112,354	12,426	1,630	101,558	29,983	31,844	56,073	50,507	2,914	...

... = Not available.

Personal Income and Employment by Region and State: Kentucky

(Millions of dollars, except as noted.)

Year	Personal income, total	Earnings by place of work			Less: Contributions for government social insurance	Plus: Adjustment for residence	Equals: Net earnings by place of residence	Plus: Dividends, interest, and rent	Plus: Personal current transfer receipts	Per capita (dollars)		Population (thousands)	Total employment (thousands)
		Nonfarm	Farm	Total						Personal income	Disposable personal income		
1960	5,022	3,739	323	4,062	184	89	3,967	626	429	1,651	1,494	3,041	...
1961	5,346	3,838	396	4,234	185	81	4,131	661	555	1,750	1,593	3,054	...
1962	5,678	4,177	396	4,573	209	84	4,448	726	504	1,844	1,666	3,079	...
1963	5,968	4,445	405	4,850	240	84	4,693	771	504	1,928	1,745	3,096	...
1964	6,226	4,735	297	5,033	245	91	4,879	817	530	1,990	1,811	3,129	...
1965	6,750	5,119	366	5,485	258	96	5,323	848	579	2,150	1,953	3,140	...
1966	7,379	5,706	382	6,088	339	104	5,853	899	627	2,345	2,107	3,147	...
1967	7,988	6,206	383	6,589	400	79	6,268	974	746	2,518	2,274	3,172	...
1968	8,731	6,858	372	7,231	446	86	6,871	1,018	843	2,733	2,444	3,195	...
1969	9,712	7,494	428	7,922	509	162	7,575	1,193	944	3,037	2,669	3,198	1,332
1970	10,535	8,058	393	8,451	547	153	8,057	1,373	1,105	3,261	2,896	3,231	1,336
1971	11,466	8,773	408	9,180	615	97	8,662	1,506	1,298	3,476	3,116	3,298	1,360
1972	12,680	9,708	507	10,215	713	90	9,591	1,647	1,441	3,801	3,361	3,336	1,392
1973	14,253	10,966	579	11,545	919	45	10,670	1,863	1,720	4,227	3,780	3,372	1,461
1974	16,052	12,203	665	12,868	1,060	17	11,825	2,176	2,051	4,698	4,121	3,417	1,496
1975	17,479	13,107	482	13,589	1,122	10	12,478	2,418	2,584	5,039	4,517	3,469	1,465
1976	19,544	14,815	557	15,372	1,291	-18	14,063	2,650	2,831	5,536	4,938	3,530	1,523
1977	21,934	16,748	683	17,430	1,451	6	15,985	2,982	2,968	6,135	5,425	3,575	1,579
1978	24,444	18,942	605	19,547	1,686	28	17,890	3,377	3,178	6,769	5,962	3,611	1,645
1979	27,455	21,161	679	21,839	1,944	21	19,916	3,835	3,704	7,535	6,631	3,644	1,665
1980	29,872	22,189	561	22,750	2,059	52	20,743	4,661	4,469	8,152	7,209	3,664	1,642
1981	33,238	23,920	939	24,858	2,392	16	22,483	5,716	5,039	9,056	7,961	3,670	1,634
1982	35,402	24,786	902	25,689	2,526	10	23,173	6,730	5,499	9,611	8,475	3,683	1,616
1983	36,755	26,062	232	26,294	2,653	33	23,674	7,128	5,953	9,949	8,827	3,694	1,624
1984	41,062	28,742	1,121	29,863	3,000	3	26,866	7,968	6,229	11,111	9,954	3,695	1,676
1985	42,816	30,249	876	31,125	3,218	-4	27,903	8,396	6,517	11,588	10,334	3,695	1,698
1986	44,019	31,229	648	31,877	3,453	21	28,445	8,750	6,824	11,936	10,644	3,688	1,733
1987	46,497	33,475	731	34,207	3,682	4	30,529	8,911	7,057	12,624	11,202	3,683	1,765
1988	50,573	36,827	778	37,605	4,098	-7	33,500	9,578	7,495	13,743	12,246	3,680	1,816
1989	54,364	38,940	1,142	40,082	4,407	-43	35,632	10,497	8,235	14,784	13,084	3,677	1,865
1990	57,673	41,267	1,123	42,390	4,818	-32	37,540	11,124	9,010	15,613	13,788	3,694	1,906
1991	60,843	43,165	1,123	44,288	5,093	-38	39,157	11,441	10,245	16,345	14,521	3,722	1,903
1992	65,547	46,962	1,309	48,271	5,520	-255	42,496	11,803	11,248	17,407	15,474	3,765	1,949
1993	68,128	49,271	1,115	50,386	5,886	-245	44,255	12,170	11,702	17,871	15,868	3,812	1,993
1994	71,608	51,944	1,166	53,111	6,331	-328	46,452	12,883	12,274	18,604	16,478	3,849	2,035
1995	75,054	54,219	708	54,927	6,635	-330	47,963	13,890	13,202	19,307	17,035	3,887	2,110
1996	79,621	56,870	1,138	58,008	6,898	-314	50,796	14,843	13,982	20,314	17,882	3,920	2,141
1997	84,542	60,547	1,139	61,687	7,299	-315	54,073	15,693	14,777	21,388	18,729	3,953	2,189
1998	89,738	64,414	1,011	65,425	7,748	-188	57,490	17,077	15,171	22,517	19,671	3,985	2,224
1999	93,539	68,675	784	69,459	8,257	-272	60,930	16,873	15,736	23,280	20,334	4,018	2,264
2000	100,894	72,859	1,493	74,352	8,525	-295	65,533	18,454	16,908	24,918	21,842	4,049	2,306
2001	104,269	75,371	1,082	76,453	8,743	-444	67,267	18,576	18,427	25,631	22,446	4,068	2,284
2002	106,642	77,861	680	78,541	9,022	-510	69,009	17,900	19,733	26,075	23,246	4,090	2,263
2003	109,563	80,896	714	81,610	9,278	-736	71,596	17,621	20,347	26,611	23,889	4,117	2,273
2004	115,894	85,576	1,257	86,833	9,669	-928	76,236	17,758	21,900	27,953	25,242	4,146	2,301
2005	121,520	89,680	1,558	91,238	10,147	-1,313	79,778	18,535	23,207	29,053	26,059	4,183	2,338
2006	128,718	93,656	1,274	94,930	10,681	-1,360	82,890	20,827	25,001	30,507	27,347	4,219	2,375
2007	134,506	96,954	828	97,783	11,164	-1,502	85,117	22,492	26,897	31,599	28,181	4,257	2,415
2008	140,472	99,663	344	100,007	11,636	-1,793	86,579	23,564	30,329	32,745	29,224	4,290	2,403
2009	138,838	96,533	670	97,203	11,506	-1,855	83,842	21,530	33,466	32,160	29,323	4,317	2,325
2010	144,009	100,897	340	101,237	11,822	-2,141	87,274	21,281	35,454	33,119	30,139	4,348	2,326
2011	151,070	104,479	833	105,312	10,928	-2,344	92,040	23,099	35,930	34,574	31,206	4,369	2,368
2012	156,512	107,969	921	108,890	11,284	-2,397	95,209	25,327	35,976	35,681	32,301	4,386	2,389
2013	157,851	109,091	2,710	111,801	12,899	-2,041	96,861	24,148	36,842	35,836	32,197	4,405	2,408
2014	165,369	113,008	1,732	114,740	13,455	-1,984	99,302	26,004	40,063	37,461	33,621	4,414	2,440
2015	172,361	117,378	1,409	118,787	14,047	-2,073	102,667	27,478	42,217	38,943	34,777	4,426	2,473
2016	175,013	119,692	892	120,585	14,383	-1,931	104,271	28,269	42,473	39,433	35,160	4,438	2,498
2017	180,827	123,501	1,049	124,550	14,805	-2,108	107,638	29,449	43,740	40,600	36,219	4,454	2,521
2018	186,685	126,762	1,043	127,804	15,226	-2,082	110,497	30,599	45,589	41,779	37,441	4,468	2,545
2019	195,549	194,483	1,066	133,679	15,762	-2,440	115,476	33,037	47,036	43,724	39,238	4,472	2,572
2020	208,222	207,040	1,182	133,609	15,843	-2,410	115,356	32,749	60,116	46,507	42,051	4,477	...

... = Not available.

Personal Income and Employment by Region and State: Louisiana

(Millions of dollars, except as noted.)

Year	Personal income, total	Derivation of personal income								Per capita (dollars)		Population (thousands)	Total employment (thousands)
		Earnings by place of work			Less: Contributions for government social insurance	Plus: Adjustment for residence	Equals: Net earnings by place of residence	Plus: Dividends, interest, and rent	Plus: Personal current transfer receipts	Personal income	Disposable personal income		
		Nonfarm	Farm	Total									
1960	5,591	4,382	186	4,567	185	-1	4,381	775	436	1,715	1,566	3,260	...
1961	5,819	4,499	218	4,717	187	-1	4,529	804	486	1,770	1,616	3,287	...
1962	6,158	4,790	204	4,994	208	-0	4,786	867	504	1,841	1,677	3,345	...
1963	6,564	5,086	261	5,347	246	-0	5,101	928	535	1,944	1,762	3,377	...
1964	7,016	5,530	226	5,756	262	-1	5,494	968	554	2,036	1,865	3,446	...
1965	7,602	6,052	198	6,250	286	-0	5,964	1,039	598	2,174	1,994	3,496	...
1966	8,410	6,812	239	7,051	389	3	6,665	1,103	642	2,369	2,140	3,550	...
1967	9,225	7,454	267	7,721	432	5	7,294	1,179	752	2,576	2,334	3,581	...
1968	10,106	8,199	299	8,498	489	4	8,012	1,243	850	2,805	2,521	3,603	...
1969	10,766	8,703	241	8,944	569	8	8,384	1,421	961	2,975	2,655	3,619	1,440
1970	11,663	9,199	283	9,482	592	6	8,897	1,612	1,154	3,195	2,893	3,650	1,429
1971	12,715	9,970	320	10,290	658	-7	9,625	1,772	1,318	3,427	3,107	3,711	1,445
1972	13,912	10,959	349	11,308	757	-20	10,531	1,931	1,450	3,698	3,330	3,762	1,488
1973	15,529	12,105	579	12,684	960	-37	11,687	2,156	1,686	4,098	3,701	3,789	1,550
1974	17,652	13,654	614	14,268	1,118	-54	13,096	2,581	1,975	4,620	4,135	3,821	1,598
1975	19,875	15,433	419	15,852	1,243	-83	14,526	2,909	2,440	5,113	4,627	3,887	1,641
1976	22,416	17,701	455	18,157	1,454	-112	16,591	3,126	2,698	5,672	5,077	3,952	1,702
1977	25,031	19,962	454	20,416	1,627	-138	18,651	3,477	2,903	6,234	5,563	4,016	1,756
1978	28,631	23,191	373	23,565	1,933	-184	21,448	4,026	3,157	7,029	6,227	4,073	1,849
1979	32,478	26,312	503	26,815	2,277	-234	24,304	4,582	3,592	7,846	6,896	4,139	1,897
1980	37,369	30,111	175	30,286	2,594	-337	27,356	5,721	4,292	8,849	7,747	4,223	1,964
1981	43,084	34,383	266	34,650	3,177	-352	31,121	7,173	4,790	10,059	8,735	4,283	2,030
1982	46,380	35,925	263	36,188	3,376	-331	32,481	8,374	5,525	10,656	9,399	4,353	2,023
1983	48,423	36,383	232	36,614	3,378	-312	32,924	9,213	6,285	11,017	9,834	4,395	1,984
1984	51,505	38,469	323	38,792	3,663	-302	34,827	10,133	6,544	11,704	10,499	4,400	2,023
1985	53,630	39,411	231	39,642	3,775	-273	35,594	10,988	7,048	12,166	10,902	4,408	2,009
1986	53,695	38,636	235	38,871	3,646	-219	35,006	10,953	7,737	12,184	11,063	4,407	1,928
1987	53,932	38,778	396	39,174	3,609	-185	35,380	10,717	7,834	12,415	11,253	4,344	1,904
1988	56,881	41,049	629	41,678	4,014	-166	37,498	11,162	8,221	13,263	12,068	4,289	1,935
1989	60,326	43,148	469	43,616	4,273	-133	39,210	12,125	8,991	14,185	12,821	4,253	1,953
1990	64,881	46,811	404	47,216	4,760	-111	42,345	12,630	9,905	15,369	13,875	4,222	2,005
1991	68,408	49,195	469	49,664	5,135	-127	44,403	12,680	11,325	16,084	14,554	4,253	2,030
1992	73,264	52,243	577	52,821	5,381	-125	47,315	12,954	12,995	17,066	15,517	4,293	2,038
1993	76,873	54,349	590	54,939	5,634	-129	49,176	13,389	14,307	17,809	16,174	4,316	2,086
1994	81,906	57,537	679	58,216	6,083	-148	51,984	14,097	15,824	18,840	17,083	4,347	2,126
1995	85,953	60,393	673	61,066	6,384	-176	54,505	15,443	16,005	19,630	17,758	4,379	2,194
1996	89,777	63,217	884	64,101	6,696	-204	57,202	16,283	16,292	20,409	18,287	4,399	2,239
1997	94,401	67,211	643	67,855	7,088	-219	60,549	17,265	16,587	21,352	19,017	4,421	2,290
1998	98,924	71,061	464	71,525	7,530	-236	63,759	18,352	16,813	22,278	19,868	4,440	2,336
1999	101,340	73,312	636	73,947	7,651	-217	66,080	18,008	17,251	22,718	20,334	4,461	2,353
2000	107,072	77,536	622	78,158	7,906	-230	70,022	19,361	17,688	23,943	21,428	4,472	2,389
2001	114,378	82,970	659	83,630	8,345	-272	75,013	19,082	20,284	25,543	22,846	4,478	2,398
2002	117,657	86,236	430	86,666	8,644	-299	77,723	18,561	21,373	26,162	23,809	4,497	2,399
2003	121,062	89,330	794	90,123	8,885	-349	80,890	18,751	21,422	26,778	24,608	4,521	2,419
2004	126,175	92,217	794	93,010	9,167	-383	83,461	19,065	23,650	27,717	25,569	4,552	2,434
2005	135,725	96,408	674	97,082	9,387	-361	87,335	20,671	27,720	29,656	27,293	4,577	2,397
2006	143,751	103,301	727	104,029	10,064	-424	93,541	24,650	25,560	33,410	30,352	4,303	2,414
2007	156,785	108,992	765	109,757	10,739	-452	98,567	31,625	26,594	35,832	32,239	4,376	2,501
2008	167,983	117,282	541	117,823	11,405	-497	105,922	31,774	30,287	37,872	33,983	4,436	2,551
2009	163,382	114,980	741	115,721	11,366	-484	103,872	27,399	32,111	36,375	33,438	4,492	2,530
2010	170,477	120,783	798	121,581	11,721	-514	109,346	26,641	34,490	37,513	34,566	4,545	2,537
2011	176,175	122,618	846	123,464	10,832	-414	112,218	29,011	34,947	38,507	35,277	4,575	2,565
2012	186,004	127,520	1,182	128,701	11,164	-348	117,190	33,102	35,713	40,429	36,859	4,601	2,601
2013	188,377	131,984	1,502	133,486	13,014	-411	120,062	31,357	36,958	40,734	36,875	4,625	2,642
2014	197,686	140,424	882	141,306	13,559	-559	127,187	33,382	37,116	42,566	38,532	4,644	2,684
2015	200,078	138,894	542	139,436	13,812	-597	125,027	33,923	41,128	42,890	38,966	4,665	2,695
2016	199,543	134,927	551	135,479	13,629	-749	121,101	34,627	43,816	42,654	38,682	4,678	2,690
2017	204,517	137,310	612	137,922	13,963	-967	122,991	35,866	45,659	43,786	39,734	4,671	2,697
2018	212,223	142,543	677	143,220	14,540	-987	127,693	37,169	47,361	45,542	41,487	4,660	2,728
2019	220,630	220,019	611	148,628	15,047	-703	132,879	39,389	48,362	47,363	43,157	4,658	2,745
2020	232,437	231,635	802	145,692	14,668	-597	130,427	39,079	62,931	50,037	45,988	4,645	...

... = Not available.

Personal Income and Employment by Region and State: Maine

(Millions of dollars, except as noted.)

Year	Personal income, total	Earnings by place of work			Less: Contributions for government social insurance	Plus: Adjustment for residence	Equals: Net earnings by place of residence	Plus: Dividends, interest, and rent	Plus: Personal current transfer receipts	Per capita (dollars)		Population (thousands)	Total employment (thousands)
		Nonfarm	Farm	Total						Personal income	Disposable personal income		
1960	1,952	1,507	103	1,610	70	-32	1,508	292	152	2,002	1,825	975	...
1961	1,977	1,548	67	1,615	73	-33	1,509	301	167	1,987	1,812	995	...
1962	2,054	1,609	66	1,675	78	-34	1,563	319	172	2,067	1,878	994	...
1963	2,122	1,660	59	1,719	87	-34	1,598	344	181	2,137	1,952	993	...
1964	2,293	1,766	90	1,856	92	-34	1,730	379	184	2,309	2,125	993	...
1965	2,474	1,864	126	1,989	93	-32	1,865	417	192	2,482	2,286	997	...
1966	2,630	2,031	107	2,138	119	-36	1,984	436	210	2,632	2,420	999	...
1967	2,761	2,175	55	2,230	138	-38	2,055	458	248	2,750	2,515	1,004	...
1968	2,940	2,352	55	2,407	157	-41	2,209	452	279	2,958	2,673	994	...
1969	3,236	2,534	74	2,608	181	-25	2,402	522	312	3,262	2,913	992	443
1970	3,557	2,733	78	2,810	193	-20	2,596	590	371	3,569	3,225	997	446
1971	3,823	2,903	66	2,969	211	-19	2,739	645	438	3,764	3,450	1,016	443
1972	4,188	3,190	65	3,255	242	-22	2,992	706	490	4,047	3,690	1,035	453
1973	4,707	3,513	148	3,661	302	-13	3,347	776	584	4,498	4,064	1,046	470
1974	5,229	3,795	195	3,991	338	-8	3,645	881	703	4,933	4,462	1,060	478
1975	5,652	4,076	82	4,157	357	-21	3,779	974	899	5,266	4,815	1,073	475
1976	6,447	4,705	163	4,869	422	-24	4,422	1,048	977	5,915	5,381	1,090	498
1977	7,008	5,144	129	5,273	461	-26	4,786	1,181	1,041	6,340	5,773	1,105	513
1978	7,741	5,772	90	5,862	531	-25	5,306	1,318	1,117	6,939	6,282	1,115	531
1979	8,590	6,412	76	6,488	607	-18	5,863	1,465	1,262	7,636	6,870	1,125	545
1980	9,654	7,073	49	7,122	668	-15	6,439	1,739	1,475	8,567	7,680	1,127	553
1981	10,652	7,583	118	7,701	771	-48	6,882	2,089	1,681	9,401	8,359	1,133	551
1982	11,581	8,044	104	8,148	831	-46	7,271	2,467	1,843	10,188	9,000	1,137	553
1983	12,473	8,737	72	8,809	910	-33	7,866	2,614	1,992	10,896	9,749	1,145	565
1984	13,787	9,668	118	9,786	1,043	-26	8,717	2,969	2,101	11,930	10,722	1,156	587
1985	14,893	10,525	103	10,628	1,132	-5	9,492	3,179	2,223	12,807	11,458	1,163	606
1986	16,123	11,477	93	11,570	1,239	35	10,366	3,450	2,306	13,779	12,259	1,170	630
1987	17,491	12,596	135	12,731	1,356	59	11,434	3,697	2,360	14,766	13,007	1,185	653
1988	19,277	14,036	117	14,153	1,543	73	12,683	4,088	2,507	16,013	14,150	1,204	686
1989	21,011	15,133	126	15,258	1,650	72	13,681	4,631	2,700	17,223	15,240	1,220	702
1990	21,870	15,631	173	15,804	1,788	71	14,086	4,770	3,014	17,756	15,759	1,232	701
1991	22,250	15,598	127	15,725	1,803	88	14,010	4,769	3,470	17,986	16,077	1,237	678
1992	23,325	16,247	178	16,424	1,905	132	14,651	4,841	3,832	18,833	16,914	1,239	681
1993	24,095	16,785	156	16,942	2,016	191	15,117	4,936	4,042	19,395	17,435	1,242	692
1994	25,086	17,450	148	17,598	2,130	251	15,719	5,137	4,229	20,187	18,081	1,243	703
1995	26,179	17,924	123	18,047	2,208	318	16,157	5,561	4,461	21,053	18,859	1,243	705
1996	27,653	18,705	151	18,856	2,273	371	16,954	5,927	4,772	22,139	19,716	1,249	714
1997	29,170	19,794	105	19,898	2,399	445	17,945	6,232	4,993	23,247	20,555	1,255	727
1998	30,941	21,291	178	21,468	2,544	519	19,443	6,357	5,141	24,574	21,533	1,259	749
1999	32,546	22,861	194	23,055	2,683	584	20,956	6,298	5,291	25,691	22,533	1,267	763
2000	35,056	24,454	207	24,662	2,815	701	22,548	6,886	5,622	27,450	23,965	1,277	784
2001	37,000	25,921	193	26,115	2,949	712	23,878	7,066	6,056	28,778	25,229	1,286	788
2002	38,471	27,010	157	27,167	2,974	677	24,870	7,140	6,461	29,685	26,587	1,296	791
2003	40,117	28,099	163	28,262	3,059	657	25,859	7,228	7,029	30,705	27,777	1,307	795
2004	42,162	29,560	178	29,738	3,218	682	27,202	7,470	7,489	32,094	29,096	1,314	808
2005	43,170	30,128	172	30,300	3,322	689	27,667	7,360	8,143	32,735	29,412	1,319	809
2006	45,529	31,683	170	31,853	3,540	723	29,035	8,155	8,339	34,397	30,824	1,324	818
2007	47,262	32,332	184	32,516	3,697	723	29,542	8,772	8,949	35,614	31,813	1,327	828
2008	49,164	32,799	192	32,992	3,802	706	29,895	8,945	10,324	36,951	33,063	1,331	824
2009	49,085	32,493	184	32,677	3,723	688	29,641	8,234	11,209	36,917	33,727	1,330	801
2010	50,254	33,486	264	33,750	3,830	729	30,649	8,273	11,331	37,852	34,568	1,328	791
2011	52,256	33,952	219	34,171	3,510	796	31,458	8,981	11,817	39,345	35,583	1,328	794
2012	53,370	34,643	268	34,911	3,610	832	32,132	9,485	11,753	40,198	36,409	1,328	797
2013	53,316	35,093	275	35,368	4,183	870	32,055	9,265	11,996	40,142	36,063	1,328	804
2014	55,667	36,249	241	36,490	4,271	928	33,147	10,201	12,318	41,831	37,660	1,331	811
2015	57,978	37,701	246	37,947	4,499	988	34,436	10,694	12,848	43,642	39,095	1,328	817
2016	59,577	38,783	173	38,956	4,597	999	35,358	11,048	13,171	44,749	39,940	1,331	827
2017	62,060	40,471	162	40,633	4,796	1,012	36,849	11,578	13,633	46,485	41,541	1,335	836
2018	64,566	42,017	137	42,154	5,006	1,052	38,200	12,051	14,315	48,241	43,291	1,338	845
2019	68,062	67,857	206	44,511	5,266	1,097	40,343	12,651	15,069	50,575	45,455	1,346	856
2020	73,212	72,952	259	45,118	5,390	1,094	40,823	12,515	19,874	54,225	49,072	1,350	...

... = Not available.

Personal Income and Employment by Region and State: Maryland

(Millions of dollars, except as noted.)

Year	Personal income, total	Derivation of personal income								Per capita (dollars)		Population (thousands)	Total employment (thousands)
		Earnings by place of work			Less: Contributions for government social insurance	Plus: Adjustment for residence	Equals: Net earnings by place of residence	Plus: Dividends, interest, and rent	Plus: Personal current transfer receipts	Personal income	Disposable personal income		
		Nonfarm	Farm	Total									
1960	7,739	5,743	94	5,837	289	627	6,176	1,222	341	2,486	2,178	3,113	...
1961	8,234	6,077	90	6,167	312	690	6,545	1,298	392	2,593	2,287	3,176	...
1962	8,897	6,552	85	6,638	351	774	7,061	1,420	416	2,727	2,377	3,263	...
1963	9,532	6,995	67	7,062	381	865	7,547	1,550	436	2,815	2,445	3,386	...
1964	10,386	7,593	86	7,679	397	953	8,235	1,692	460	2,974	2,622	3,492	...
1965	11,317	8,199	98	8,297	399	1,066	8,964	1,849	504	3,144	2,762	3,600	...
1966	12,477	9,210	79	9,289	526	1,187	9,950	1,970	557	3,377	2,926	3,695	...
1967	13,580	9,797	95	9,891	587	1,451	10,756	2,133	691	3,615	3,125	3,757	...
1968	15,000	10,868	87	10,955	643	1,619	11,930	2,244	826	3,932	3,310	3,815	...
1969	17,236	12,123	133	12,256	751	2,321	13,827	2,465	944	4,456	3,742	3,868	1,679
1970	19,167	13,216	122	13,338	815	2,717	15,240	2,801	1,126	4,867	4,165	3,938	1,702
1971	21,126	14,414	94	14,508	917	3,028	16,620	3,133	1,373	5,252	4,559	4,023	1,729
1972	23,176	15,835	128	15,964	1,060	3,285	18,189	3,414	1,574	5,679	4,854	4,081	1,781
1973	25,561	17,561	209	17,770	1,354	3,485	19,901	3,844	1,816	6,221	5,343	4,109	1,846
1974	27,903	19,131	165	19,295	1,533	3,687	21,450	4,348	2,105	6,751	5,749	4,133	1,868
1975	30,204	20,257	204	20,461	1,624	4,065	22,903	4,655	2,647	7,265	6,290	4,157	1,846
1976	32,907	22,268	175	22,443	1,808	4,359	24,995	5,057	2,855	7,887	6,823	4,172	1,866
1977	35,676	24,203	130	24,332	1,974	4,701	27,059	5,574	3,042	8,505	7,290	4,195	1,919
1978	39,617	26,948	184	27,132	2,262	5,074	29,944	6,319	3,354	9,407	8,050	4,212	2,004
1979	43,546	29,721	160	29,881	2,611	5,401	32,671	7,070	3,805	10,311	8,762	4,223	2,059
1980	48,503	32,476	58	32,534	2,866	5,863	35,531	8,437	4,535	11,473	9,794	4,228	2,070
1981	54,043	35,670	129	35,800	3,381	6,253	38,671	10,177	5,195	12,680	10,706	4,262	2,095
1982	58,611	37,520	144	37,664	3,617	6,771	40,819	12,009	5,783	13,685	11,633	4,283	2,084
1983	62,787	40,823	90	40,913	4,071	7,143	43,986	12,498	6,303	14,557	12,531	4,313	2,151
1984	69,665	45,375	266	45,641	4,672	7,820	48,789	14,233	6,644	15,959	13,712	4,365	2,243
1985	75,503	49,797	278	50,075	5,284	8,423	53,213	15,267	7,023	17,109	14,759	4,413	2,342
1986	81,545	54,136	288	54,424	5,837	9,033	57,620	16,431	7,494	18,174	15,697	4,487	2,428
1987	88,008	59,251	300	59,550	6,331	9,663	62,883	17,345	7,780	19,276	16,446	4,566	2,553
1988	96,740	65,472	365	65,837	7,214	10,709	69,331	19,104	8,304	20,769	17,948	4,658	2,647
1989	104,601	69,951	366	70,316	7,758	11,515	74,073	21,482	9,046	22,127	18,945	4,727	2,704
1990	110,894	74,155	357	74,512	8,395	12,115	78,232	22,753	9,910	23,104	19,835	4,800	2,737
1991	114,899	75,897	310	76,207	8,671	12,660	80,196	23,541	11,162	23,605	20,428	4,868	2,662
1992	120,637	79,300	343	79,643	9,016	13,419	84,045	24,078	12,514	24,503	21,306	4,923	2,636
1993	125,486	82,522	320	82,842	9,364	13,639	87,117	25,314	13,056	25,239	21,916	4,972	2,659
1994	131,410	86,487	308	86,796	9,916	14,036	90,915	26,853	13,642	26,161	22,650	5,023	2,706
1995	137,245	90,139	215	90,354	10,287	14,003	94,069	28,874	14,302	27,070	23,337	5,070	2,765
1996	143,742	93,888	395	94,283	10,645	14,376	98,014	30,433	15,296	28,119	24,104	5,112	2,806
1997	151,792	100,296	280	100,576	11,307	14,308	103,577	32,605	15,610	29,432	24,837	5,157	2,870
1998	163,366	108,959	325	109,284	11,980	15,668	112,972	34,106	16,288	31,389	26,664	5,204	2,935
1999	173,600	116,908	350	117,258	12,721	16,747	121,284	35,054	17,262	33,038	28,041	5,255	3,008
2000	188,926	126,761	416	127,177	13,591	18,990	132,576	38,104	18,246	35,572	30,111	5,311	3,092
2001	199,093	134,797	417	135,214	14,646	19,868	140,436	38,781	19,877	37,043	31,420	5,375	3,120
2002	206,990	142,124	226	142,350	15,366	20,233	147,217	38,424	21,350	38,047	33,008	5,440	3,157
2003	216,519	148,946	311	149,257	16,068	21,098	154,287	39,249	22,983	39,394	34,498	5,496	3,191
2004	231,482	159,351	445	159,796	17,263	22,546	165,079	42,409	23,995	41,732	36,619	5,547	3,248
2005	244,347	167,942	385	168,327	18,189	23,607	173,745	44,617	25,984	43,693	37,987	5,592	3,311
2006	257,712	176,191	317	176,508	19,379	22,949	180,077	50,597	27,037	45,796	39,604	5,627	3,378
2007	268,336	181,199	310	181,510	20,236	23,615	184,888	54,095	29,354	47,465	40,733	5,653	3,441
2008	280,309	188,007	427	188,434	21,009	23,077	190,502	56,375	33,432	49,307	42,674	5,685	3,431
2009	278,547	188,565	437	189,002	20,985	23,232	191,249	51,282	36,016	48,609	43,055	5,730	3,359
2010	288,607	196,115	385	196,500	21,768	23,631	198,363	51,050	39,194	49,857	44,172	5,789	3,345
2011	305,178	205,473	476	205,949	20,183	23,278	209,044	55,780	40,355	52,266	45,780	5,839	3,395
2012	314,141	211,641	627	212,268	20,764	22,941	214,444	58,929	40,768	53,361	46,828	5,887	3,439
2013	313,195	213,421	785	214,206	23,557	22,902	213,551	57,429	42,215	52,871	45,878	5,924	3,494
2014	324,968	219,561	628	220,188	24,153	22,065	218,100	61,894	44,974	54,542	47,275	5,958	3,538
2015	341,295	230,944	453	231,398	25,395	22,846	228,848	65,607	46,841	57,009	49,291	5,987	3,603
2016	353,880	240,786	382	241,167	26,177	22,802	237,793	66,716	49,371	58,934	51,011	6,005	3,657
2017	368,258	250,750	438	251,188	27,176	23,654	247,666	70,024	50,569	61,123	52,939	6,025	3,697
2018	380,172	257,960	462	258,422	28,072	24,608	254,957	72,691	52,523	62,914	54,780	6,043	3,751
2019	390,793	390,289	504	262,586	28,828	25,808	259,566	76,429	54,797	64,541	56,041	6,055	3,804
2020	413,359	412,933	427	266,205	29,450	26,138	262,893	75,879	74,588	68,258	59,680	6,056	...

... = Not available.

Personal Income and Employment by Region and State: Massachusetts

(Millions of dollars, except as noted.)

Year	Personal income, total	Earnings by place of work			Less: Contributions for government social insurance	Plus: Adjustment for residence	Equals: Net earnings by place of residence	Plus: Dividends, interest, and rent	Plus: Personal current transfer receipts	Per capita (dollars)		Population (thousands)	Total employment (thousands)
		Nonfarm	Farm	Total						Personal income	Disposable personal income		
1960	13,147	10,795	68	10,864	499	-75	10,290	1,937	921	2,548	2,229	5,160	...
1961	13,814	11,303	60	11,363	528	-82	10,753	2,035	1,027	2,647	2,335	5,219	...
1962	14,597	11,957	61	12,017	617	-92	11,309	2,237	1,051	2,773	2,435	5,263	...
1963	15,203	12,363	61	12,424	680	-98	11,646	2,448	1,110	2,845	2,498	5,344	...
1964	16,233	13,084	63	13,147	698	-108	12,341	2,742	1,151	2,980	2,658	5,448	...
1965	17,320	13,887	69	13,956	714	-122	13,121	2,987	1,212	3,148	2,804	5,502	...
1966	18,650	15,162	72	15,234	942	-141	14,151	3,199	1,301	3,369	2,974	5,535	...
1967	20,261	16,325	56	16,381	1,033	-157	15,191	3,465	1,605	3,622	3,190	5,594	...
1968	22,127	17,783	65	17,847	1,139	-175	16,534	3,657	1,936	3,938	3,416	5,618	...
1969	24,042	19,391	66	19,458	1,262	-133	18,062	3,823	2,157	4,255	3,627	5,650	2,679
1970	25,961	20,692	69	20,761	1,327	-111	19,323	4,088	2,551	4,552	3,941	5,704	2,679
1971	27,742	21,885	63	21,948	1,448	-108	20,393	4,329	3,020	4,834	4,243	5,739	2,644
1972	29,978	23,764	63	23,826	1,651	-105	22,071	4,593	3,314	5,203	4,492	5,762	2,697
1973	32,574	25,968	71	26,039	2,075	-124	23,840	5,018	3,716	5,632	4,897	5,784	2,787
1974	35,182	27,560	70	27,630	2,275	-141	25,213	5,564	4,405	6,090	5,279	5,777	2,811
1975	37,802	28,677	69	28,746	2,295	-152	26,298	5,772	5,732	6,560	5,779	5,762	2,728
1976	40,689	31,218	76	31,295	2,556	-172	28,567	6,176	5,946	7,078	6,185	5,749	2,756
1977	44,298	34,335	79	34,414	2,817	-218	31,379	6,811	6,108	7,712	6,710	5,744	2,833
1978	48,939	38,438	104	38,542	3,248	-278	35,016	7,447	6,476	8,522	7,388	5,743	2,958
1979	54,481	43,061	91	43,152	3,796	-373	38,983	8,330	7,169	9,481	8,146	5,746	3,074
1980	61,389	47,684	106	47,789	4,215	-493	43,082	10,119	8,189	10,684	9,133	5,746	3,134
1981	68,493	52,262	116	52,378	4,981	-621	46,776	12,413	9,304	11,873	10,061	5,769	3,142
1982	75,099	56,170	132	56,301	5,484	-747	50,070	14,972	10,056	13,013	11,153	5,771	3,143
1983	81,446	61,918	164	62,082	6,141	-918	55,023	15,768	10,655	14,044	12,090	5,799	3,215
1984	91,928	70,529	183	70,711	7,225	-1,176	62,311	18,413	11,204	15,739	13,618	5,841	3,402
1985	99,342	77,403	160	77,564	8,002	-1,371	68,191	19,429	11,722	16,893	14,526	5,881	3,510
1986	107,147	84,175	175	84,350	8,883	-1,494	73,973	20,841	12,332	18,152	15,535	5,903	3,605
1987	116,044	92,452	153	92,605	9,651	-1,665	81,290	22,076	12,679	19,552	16,636	5,935	3,632
1988	127,723	101,838	172	102,010	10,787	-1,881	89,342	24,721	13,661	21,358	18,427	5,980	3,739
1989	135,209	106,030	153	106,183	11,166	-2,031	92,987	26,817	15,406	22,477	19,309	6,015	3,710
1990	139,233	107,297	153	107,450	11,186	-2,074	94,190	27,779	17,264	23,118	19,865	6,023	3,615
1991	141,352	107,264	173	107,436	11,384	-2,237	93,815	27,741	19,796	23,486	20,321	6,018	3,451
1992	148,478	113,789	171	113,960	11,985	-2,346	99,630	28,190	20,658	24,628	21,367	6,029	3,482
1993	154,367	118,617	164	118,781	12,586	-2,561	103,634	29,477	21,256	25,471	22,035	6,061	3,548
1994	162,175	124,844	150	124,994	13,379	-2,764	108,850	30,839	22,486	26,607	22,937	6,095	3,616
1995	171,742	131,467	146	131,613	14,168	-2,826	114,619	33,299	23,824	27,964	23,955	6,141	3,649
1996	182,580	140,289	166	140,455	14,935	-3,094	122,427	35,587	24,567	29,545	25,041	6,180	3,713
1997	194,131	149,916	168	150,084	15,992	-3,402	130,690	38,013	25,428	31,180	26,170	6,226	3,802
1998	206,746	160,461	108	160,568	17,060	-3,602	139,907	41,287	25,552	32,964	27,340	6,272	3,896
1999	220,851	175,059	108	175,167	18,308	-4,185	152,673	41,720	26,458	34,959	28,848	6,317	3,962
2000	245,392	196,523	131	196,654	20,253	-5,050	171,351	46,157	27,884	38,577	31,142	6,361	4,070
2001	255,190	203,031	110	203,141	20,769	-5,197	177,175	47,532	30,483	39,888	32,932	6,398	4,076
2002	254,258	201,858	131	201,989	20,729	-5,088	176,172	45,004	33,082	39,621	34,064	6,417	4,022
2003	259,815	204,748	130	204,879	20,951	-5,091	178,837	46,030	34,948	40,453	35,118	6,423	3,992
2004	273,401	217,930	146	218,076	22,741	-5,588	189,747	47,290	36,364	42,637	37,056	6,412	4,029
2005	285,647	224,359	125	224,483	23,801	-5,426	195,256	51,332	39,060	44,609	38,351	6,403	4,071
2006	307,761	236,941	132	237,073	24,663	-5,697	206,712	60,116	40,933	48,012	41,113	6,410	4,110
2007	323,215	248,480	132	248,612	25,846	-6,111	216,655	63,932	42,627	50,254	42,362	6,432	4,203
2008	335,476	254,266	193	254,460	26,683	-6,078	221,698	65,106	48,671	51,859	44,131	6,469	4,216
2009	332,152	252,246	164	252,410	26,302	-5,472	220,636	58,199	53,318	50,962	45,013	6,518	4,116
2010	348,419	267,013	166	267,178	26,859	-5,997	234,323	57,951	56,145	53,061	46,562	6,566	4,116
2011	365,527	275,703	165	275,868	25,046	-6,649	244,173	64,947	56,406	55,273	47,666	6,613	4,175
2012	381,950	285,713	231	285,943	25,914	-7,380	252,650	72,529	56,771	57,323	49,700	6,663	4,253
2013	385,338	293,084	208	293,292	30,058	-7,342	255,893	72,120	57,326	57,394	48,787	6,714	4,354
2014	405,090	304,295	153	304,448	31,542	-6,949	265,958	80,047	59,085	59,892	50,676	6,764	4,449
2015	431,572	322,254	139	322,393	32,699	-7,822	281,872	86,328	63,372	63,505	53,558	6,796	4,632
2016	444,813	332,768	136	332,904	33,850	-8,644	290,409	88,253	66,151	65,164	55,158	6,826	4,710
2017	463,931	349,827	119	349,945	35,590	-9,625	304,730	92,100	67,100	67,596	57,223	6,863	4,778
2018	483,657	365,087	102	365,189	37,236	-10,212	317,740	96,446	69,471	70,073	59,681	6,902	4,854
2019	511,334	511,243	91	385,169	39,009	-10,945	335,214	104,700	71,419	74,161	62,942	6,895	4,937
2020	549,565	549,417	148	380,501	39,033	-10,785	330,684	103,544	115,337	79,721	68,641	6,894	...

... = Not available.

Personal Income and Employment by Region and State: Michigan

(Millions of dollars, except as noted.)

Year	Personal income, total	Earnings by place of work			Less: Contributions for government social insurance	Plus: Adjustment for residence	Equals: Net earnings by place of residence	Plus: Dividends, interest, and rent	Plus: Personal current transfer receipts	Per capita (dollars)		Population (thousands)	Total employment (thousands)
		Nonfarm	Farm	Total						Personal income	Disposable personal income		
1960	18,884	15,838	240	16,078	824	37	15,290	2,482	1,112	2,411	2,148	7,834	...
1961	18,957	15,471	300	15,771	786	38	15,023	2,602	1,332	2,402	2,158	7,893	...
1962	20,319	16,771	275	17,047	888	42	16,200	2,815	1,304	2,561	2,280	7,933	...
1963	21,692	18,060	300	18,360	1,038	44	17,366	2,998	1,327	2,692	2,388	8,058	...
1964	23,774	19,843	295	20,138	1,077	49	19,111	3,298	1,366	2,904	2,608	8,187	...
1965	26,375	22,126	274	22,399	1,122	54	21,332	3,568	1,476	3,156	2,823	8,357	...
1966	28,764	24,429	349	24,778	1,572	63	23,270	3,877	1,617	3,379	3,006	8,512	...
1967	29,992	25,177	276	25,453	1,652	68	23,869	4,122	2,002	3,475	3,086	8,630	...
1968	33,161	27,965	304	28,269	1,854	76	26,491	4,357	2,312	3,813	3,325	8,696	...
1969	36,068	30,702	351	31,054	2,206	105	28,952	4,557	2,559	4,107	3,519	8,781	3,640
1970	37,362	30,875	341	31,216	2,196	113	29,132	5,014	3,216	4,200	3,656	8,897	3,558
1971	40,644	33,471	310	33,781	2,450	106	31,437	5,369	3,838	4,530	3,982	8,972	3,571
1972	45,132	37,389	427	37,816	2,905	114	35,024	5,790	4,318	5,001	4,319	9,025	3,687
1973	50,383	42,183	561	42,745	3,800	140	39,085	6,373	4,925	5,554	4,828	9,072	3,858
1974	53,913	43,801	649	44,450	4,082	140	40,507	7,253	6,153	5,918	5,170	9,109	3,854
1975	57,745	45,051	578	45,629	4,091	149	41,687	7,983	8,075	6,340	5,629	9,108	3,695
1976	64,458	51,691	478	52,169	4,794	191	47,566	8,569	8,323	7,070	6,176	9,117	3,844
1977	72,466	59,122	559	59,681	5,491	217	54,406	9,514	8,545	7,913	6,848	9,157	4,016
1978	80,773	66,736	510	67,245	6,391	260	61,115	10,575	9,083	8,778	7,527	9,202	4,186
1979	88,479	72,515	545	73,060	7,194	292	66,158	11,848	10,473	9,566	8,200	9,249	4,228
1980	94,684	73,189	536	73,725	7,174	337	66,888	13,970	13,826	10,230	8,898	9,256	4,030
1981	101,254	77,169	515	77,684	8,186	378	69,876	16,733	14,646	10,995	9,528	9,209	3,978
1982	104,817	76,677	410	77,087	8,241	381	69,227	19,241	16,349	11,499	10,105	9,115	3,823
1983	111,577	81,930	222	82,152	8,954	413	73,612	20,665	17,300	12,332	10,808	9,048	3,866
1984	123,177	91,555	551	92,106	10,356	479	82,229	23,458	17,491	13,612	11,958	9,049	4,040
1985	133,599	100,998	663	101,661	11,666	501	90,497	25,052	18,051	14,720	12,841	9,076	4,233
1986	142,048	108,387	493	108,879	12,551	488	96,817	26,301	18,930	15,562	13,596	9,128	4,349
1987	147,561	112,807	665	113,472	12,896	507	101,083	27,015	19,464	16,061	13,991	9,187	4,483
1988	157,523	121,619	585	122,204	14,305	515	108,413	28,808	20,302	17,089	14,959	9,218	4,582
1989	169,629	128,976	981	129,956	15,142	512	115,326	32,337	21,966	18,332	15,981	9,253	4,709
1990	177,393	134,521	776	135,297	16,053	458	119,702	33,888	23,803	19,051	16,695	9,311	4,791
1991	181,414	136,787	667	137,453	16,559	488	121,382	33,551	26,481	19,298	16,996	9,400	4,721
1992	192,235	146,116	757	146,873	17,547	552	129,879	34,306	28,051	20,280	17,975	9,479	4,751
1993	202,433	154,077	737	154,813	18,603	628	136,837	35,613	29,982	21,219	18,650	9,540	4,812
1994	217,745	165,969	563	166,532	20,421	754	146,865	40,605	30,276	22,687	19,874	9,598	4,985
1995	230,306	175,290	695	175,985	21,539	797	155,242	43,108	31,955	23,801	20,768	9,676	5,142
1996	242,219	183,671	618	184,289	22,020	823	163,092	45,570	33,557	24,821	21,542	9,759	5,247
1997	254,939	192,907	608	193,515	23,099	909	171,326	48,128	35,486	25,990	22,466	9,809	5,330
1998	269,062	206,810	628	207,438	24,260	993	184,171	49,645	35,247	27,322	23,464	9,848	5,384
1999	282,876	219,980	821	220,801	25,631	1,081	196,250	48,854	37,772	28,582	24,573	9,897	5,486
2000	301,662	235,341	607	235,949	26,849	1,098	210,197	52,421	39,043	30,310	26,191	9,952	5,621
2001	306,610	237,231	564	237,795	26,634	1,189	212,350	50,785	43,475	30,688	26,693	9,991	5,526
2002	306,385	237,599	602	238,201	26,922	1,217	212,496	48,827	45,063	30,590	27,168	10,016	5,466
2003	313,830	241,419	715	242,134	27,308	1,272	216,098	50,431	47,301	31,254	28,041	10,041	5,442
2004	322,532	246,940	1,155	248,095	28,277	1,369	221,187	52,028	49,317	32,076	28,923	10,055	5,468
2005	329,226	250,130	1,048	251,178	29,162	1,445	223,461	53,316	52,449	32,755	29,371	10,051	5,492
2006	337,456	252,219	1,150	253,369	29,854	1,631	225,145	56,318	55,993	33,624	30,073	10,036	5,457
2007	347,081	253,634	1,243	254,877	30,219	1,677	226,335	59,505	61,242	34,704	30,873	10,001	5,457
2008	354,064	250,525	1,368	251,893	30,253	1,682	223,323	61,029	69,712	35,595	31,712	9,947	5,338
2009	336,044	231,825	855	232,680	28,274	1,517	205,923	52,699	77,422	33,938	31,079	9,902	5,047
2010	348,673	239,307	1,405	240,711	28,641	1,579	213,650	52,339	82,685	35,300	32,162	9,878	5,038
2011	370,180	250,209	2,627	252,836	26,598	1,727	227,966	59,673	82,542	37,462	33,729	9,882	5,165
2012	385,408	262,301	1,644	263,945	27,730	1,911	238,126	65,154	82,129	38,942	34,993	9,897	5,234
2013	389,320	269,036	2,175	271,211	32,215	1,919	240,915	65,022	83,383	39,272	34,940	9,913	5,324
2014	407,649	278,772	1,369	280,141	33,293	2,076	248,924	71,954	86,771	41,050	36,548	9,931	5,413
2015	431,157	293,427	1,090	294,516	34,711	2,077	261,882	77,436	91,839	43,408	38,492	9,933	5,502
2016	444,532	303,561	897	304,458	35,659	2,245	271,044	79,341	94,148	44,668	39,455	9,952	5,577
2017	460,270	317,373	312	317,685	37,100	2,500	283,086	82,505	94,679	46,136	40,730	9,976	5,646
2018	475,626	327,974	260	328,234	38,460	2,597	292,371	85,946	97,309	47,582	42,202	9,996	5,713
2019	491,632	490,499	1,133	337,325	39,731	2,425	300,019	87,940	103,673	49,238	43,787	9,985	5,773
2020	528,093	526,536	1,557	330,458	38,949	2,481	293,989	87,338	146,766	52,987	47,706	9,967	...

... = Not available.

Personal Income and Employment by Region and State: Minnesota

(Millions of dollars, except as noted.)

Year	Personal income, total	Earnings by place of work			Less: Contributions for government social insurance	Plus: Adjustment for residence	Equals: Net earnings by place of residence	Plus: Dividends, interest, and rent	Plus: Personal current transfer receipts	Per capita (dollars)		Population (thousands)	Total employment (thousands)
		Nonfarm	Farm	Total						Personal income	Disposable personal income		
1960	7,472	5,596	514	6,111	260	-1	5,849	1,116	507	2,182	1,948	3,425	...
1961	7,853	5,842	540	6,382	269	-3	6,110	1,172	571	2,263	2,023	3,470	...
1962	8,278	6,282	467	6,748	303	-3	6,443	1,245	590	2,356	2,096	3,513	...
1963	8,779	6,540	621	7,162	339	-4	6,819	1,336	625	2,486	2,220	3,531	...
1964	9,132	6,997	402	7,399	348	-4	7,048	1,433	651	2,566	2,317	3,558	...
1965	10,088	7,547	652	8,199	372	-7	7,821	1,559	708	2,808	2,526	3,592	...
1966	10,934	8,323	733	9,056	522	-13	8,521	1,652	761	3,023	2,701	3,617	...
1967	11,750	9,035	643	9,678	602	-17	9,059	1,766	925	3,211	2,859	3,659	...
1968	12,934	9,982	680	10,662	683	-24	9,955	1,921	1,058	3,493	3,092	3,703	...
1969	14,388	11,172	720	11,892	781	-33	11,079	2,147	1,162	3,829	3,331	3,758	1,691
1970	15,709	11,935	876	12,811	825	-26	11,959	2,376	1,373	4,117	3,632	3,815	1,699
1971	16,766	12,725	796	13,521	910	-27	12,585	2,588	1,594	4,353	3,880	3,852	1,706
1972	18,229	13,797	959	14,756	1,036	-29	13,691	2,776	1,762	4,714	4,139	3,867	1,780
1973	21,370	15,357	2,179	17,536	1,333	-35	16,168	3,137	2,066	5,500	4,891	3,885	1,878
1974	23,012	16,889	1,644	18,533	1,525	-31	16,977	3,611	2,424	5,903	5,146	3,898	1,921
1975	24,891	18,306	1,264	19,571	1,613	-32	17,925	4,042	2,924	6,340	5,571	3,926	1,920
1976	26,907	20,452	782	21,235	1,845	-40	19,350	4,343	3,214	6,801	5,936	3,957	1,977
1977	30,293	22,648	1,501	24,150	2,043	-54	22,052	4,860	3,380	7,612	6,630	3,980	2,034
1978	33,989	25,807	1,625	27,432	2,409	-69	24,954	5,407	3,628	8,487	7,354	4,005	2,122
1979	37,795	29,364	1,245	30,609	2,855	-94	27,661	6,079	4,056	9,360	8,030	4,038	2,218
1980	42,002	32,001	959	32,960	3,107	-101	29,752	7,384	4,866	10,282	8,862	4,085	2,248
1981	46,548	34,622	1,040	35,662	3,604	-132	31,926	9,039	5,583	11,321	9,725	4,112	2,233
1982	49,868	36,143	819	36,962	3,838	-155	32,969	10,622	6,277	12,070	10,433	4,131	2,192
1983	52,578	38,691	119	38,810	4,161	-183	34,465	11,347	6,766	12,696	11,020	4,141	2,219
1984	59,667	43,444	1,444	44,889	4,796	-240	39,852	12,719	7,097	14,351	12,586	4,158	2,324
1985	63,361	46,561	1,343	47,903	5,234	-288	42,382	13,439	7,540	15,143	13,282	4,184	2,385
1986	67,018	49,447	1,641	51,088	5,701	-326	45,061	14,078	7,879	15,937	14,026	4,205	2,417
1987	71,480	53,311	2,138	55,450	6,107	-376	48,967	14,385	8,128	16,878	14,728	4,235	2,509
1988	75,425	57,661	1,253	58,914	6,828	-452	51,633	15,204	8,588	17,556	15,353	4,296	2,580
1989	82,388	61,745	2,051	63,796	7,303	-439	56,054	16,984	9,351	18,992	16,584	4,338	2,634
1990	87,514	65,807	1,956	67,763	7,829	-471	59,463	18,001	10,051	19,935	17,342	4,390	2,692
1991	90,246	68,763	1,207	69,970	8,278	-476	61,216	18,225	10,805	20,322	17,777	4,441	2,717
1992	97,019	74,587	1,401	75,987	8,869	-509	66,609	18,661	11,748	21,581	18,838	4,496	2,762
1993	99,990	77,969	187	78,156	9,313	-515	68,328	19,267	12,395	21,947	19,094	4,556	2,817
1994	107,155	82,615	1,340	83,954	9,990	-561	73,403	20,715	13,037	23,242	20,214	4,610	2,904
1995	113,338	87,329	519	87,848	10,530	-610	76,708	22,812	13,817	24,320	21,044	4,660	2,995
1996	122,211	93,303	1,921	95,224	11,136	-685	83,403	24,343	14,464	25,932	22,188	4,713	3,056
1997	129,028	99,731	898	100,629	11,836	-767	88,026	26,310	14,692	27,087	23,114	4,763	3,109
1998	139,859	108,801	1,397	110,198	12,712	-847	96,639	28,013	15,206	29,056	24,698	4,813	3,189
1999	146,942	115,841	1,261	117,103	13,569	-951	102,582	28,372	15,988	30,151	25,817	4,873	3,257
2000	159,119	125,396	1,453	126,849	14,525	-1,037	111,288	30,704	17,128	32,252	27,424	4,934	3,331
2001	165,716	130,650	1,029	131,679	15,034	-1,084	115,561	30,932	19,222	33,258	28,475	4,983	3,347
2002	169,900	134,110	1,018	135,128	15,409	-1,112	118,607	30,423	20,870	33,852	29,527	5,019	3,338
2003	177,860	139,299	1,847	141,147	16,100	-1,180	123,866	32,110	21,884	35,195	31,083	5,054	3,347
2004	188,385	148,517	2,471	150,988	17,010	-1,258	132,719	32,658	23,009	37,027	32,846	5,088	3,390
2005	193,841	152,028	2,942	154,970	17,754	-1,321	135,895	33,834	24,112	37,862	33,187	5,120	3,448
2006	204,123	157,035	2,553	159,589	18,564	-1,276	139,749	37,820	26,553	39,531	34,490	5,164	3,496
2007	216,240	164,544	2,632	167,176	19,330	-1,393	146,452	40,709	29,078	41,527	36,069	5,207	3,540
2008	225,276	167,952	3,970	171,922	19,934	-1,422	150,567	41,749	32,960	42,934	37,292	5,247	3,526
2009	215,788	160,670	2,121	162,791	19,269	-1,148	142,374	37,230	36,183	40,860	36,538	5,281	3,424
2010	225,594	166,543	3,140	169,683	19,580	-1,106	148,997	37,571	39,027	42,478	37,824	5,311	3,409
2011	241,435	175,384	4,300	179,684	18,318	-1,143	160,223	41,872	39,340	45,165	39,719	5,346	3,469
2012	256,332	184,204	5,977	190,181	19,060	-928	170,194	46,783	39,356	47,676	41,974	5,377	3,506
2013	258,320	189,648	5,613	195,261	22,415	-890	171,956	45,597	40,767	47,716	41,381	5,414	3,556
2014	272,292	199,066	3,658	202,724	23,115	-921	178,688	50,767	42,836	49,948	43,316	5,452	3,606
2015	284,740	207,856	3,179	211,035	23,953	-1,019	186,063	54,327	44,350	51,936	44,729	5,483	3,665
2016	291,362	213,885	1,339	215,223	24,577	-1,215	189,432	56,012	45,918	52,750	45,439	5,523	3,702
2017	303,141	223,745	493	224,237	25,628	-1,356	197,253	58,508	47,380	54,442	46,895	5,568	3,752
2018	316,327	232,039	1,154	233,194	26,613	-1,394	205,187	61,128	50,013	56,374	48,858	5,611	3,776
2019	331,802	329,048	2,754	243,143	27,871	-1,382	213,891	65,074	52,837	58,830	51,079	5,640	3,819
2020	348,152	344,449	3,704	242,041	27,901	-1,408	212,733	64,224	71,196	61,540	53,899	5,657	...

... = Not available.

Personal Income and Employment by Region and State: Mississippi

(Millions of dollars, except as noted.)

Year	Personal income, total	Earnings by place of work Nonfarm	Farm	Total	Less: Contributions for government social insurance	Plus: Adjustment for residence	Equals: Net earnings by place of residence	Plus: Dividends, interest, and rent	Plus: Personal current transfer receipts	Per capita (dollars) Personal income	Disposable personal income	Population (thousands)	Total employment (thousands)
1960	2,764	2,031	281	2,312	101	12	2,224	308	233	1,267	1,174	2,182	...
1961	2,997	2,122	353	2,475	104	13	2,384	351	262	1,359	1,270	2,206	...
1962	3,133	2,277	297	2,574	115	15	2,474	385	273	1,397	1,294	2,243	...
1963	3,442	2,422	432	2,854	136	17	2,735	418	290	1,534	1,419	2,244	...
1964	3,563	2,588	370	2,958	143	20	2,834	427	303	1,590	1,482	2,241	...
1965	3,869	2,874	352	3,226	152	22	3,096	445	328	1,722	1,601	2,246	...
1966	4,217	3,219	347	3,566	197	23	3,392	465	360	1,879	1,732	2,245	...
1967	4,563	3,441	386	3,826	226	25	3,625	507	432	2,048	1,890	2,228	...
1968	4,993	3,823	364	4,187	253	31	3,966	539	489	2,250	2,065	2,219	...
1969	5,541	4,222	349	4,571	291	36	4,316	673	552	2,496	2,279	2,220	909
1970	6,077	4,487	394	4,881	310	37	4,608	780	689	2,736	2,488	2,221	917
1971	6,737	4,918	436	5,354	351	59	5,062	861	814	2,974	2,746	2,266	939
1972	7,677	5,655	494	6,148	421	74	5,801	958	918	3,327	3,029	2,307	979
1973	8,779	6,358	692	7,050	538	94	6,606	1,109	1,065	3,736	3,421	2,350	1,019
1974	9,648	7,017	515	7,532	615	123	7,039	1,297	1,312	4,056	3,677	2,379	1,031
1975	10,463	7,519	377	7,895	653	149	7,391	1,441	1,631	4,360	4,015	2,400	1,001
1976	11,878	8,537	576	9,112	757	179	8,535	1,557	1,786	4,887	4,461	2,430	1,039
1977	13,222	9,598	609	10,208	850	218	9,575	1,738	1,910	5,375	4,919	2,460	1,071
1978	14,722	10,879	455	11,334	982	272	10,624	1,998	2,100	5,917	5,355	2,488	1,101
1979	16,637	12,059	704	12,763	1,129	325	11,960	2,280	2,396	6,633	5,981	2,508	1,114
1980	18,098	13,012	185	13,198	1,210	410	12,398	2,821	2,879	7,166	6,458	2,525	1,111
1981	20,332	14,215	334	14,548	1,421	440	13,566	3,502	3,263	8,008	7,164	2,539	1,107
1982	21,465	14,610	425	15,035	1,497	457	13,995	3,883	3,588	8,395	7,645	2,557	1,079
1983	22,452	15,392	102	15,494	1,594	513	14,413	4,088	3,951	8,744	7,931	2,568	1,088
1984	24,528	16,655	480	17,135	1,773	572	15,934	4,509	4,086	9,514	8,673	2,578	1,117
1985	25,819	17,582	438	18,020	1,914	603	16,709	4,830	4,280	9,976	9,089	2,588	1,124
1986	26,781	18,498	204	18,702	2,032	592	17,261	4,985	4,535	10,326	9,450	2,594	1,131
1987	28,324	19,421	587	20,008	2,125	630	18,512	5,091	4,721	10,942	9,982	2,589	1,141
1988	30,303	20,790	733	21,523	2,374	672	19,821	5,453	5,029	11,744	10,753	2,580	1,169
1989	32,736	22,229	569	22,798	2,542	715	20,971	6,269	5,495	12,717	11,587	2,574	1,189
1990	34,443	23,665	493	24,157	2,803	749	22,103	6,377	5,962	13,356	12,165	2,579	1,203
1991	36,288	24,732	588	25,320	2,989	804	23,136	6,444	6,708	13,964	12,773	2,599	1,211
1992	39,063	26,698	671	27,369	3,192	823	25,000	6,548	7,515	14,888	13,634	2,624	1,234
1993	41,597	28,775	584	29,359	3,453	840	26,746	6,839	8,012	15,667	14,304	2,655	1,287
1994	45,005	31,222	844	32,066	3,779	838	29,125	7,381	8,500	16,737	15,231	2,689	1,335
1995	47,613	32,721	679	33,400	3,946	920	30,374	7,949	9,291	17,488	15,888	2,723	1,365
1996	50,526	34,139	1,078	35,217	4,069	962	32,110	8,457	9,959	18,386	16,655	2,748	1,389
1997	53,378	36,134	991	37,125	4,284	1,112	33,954	9,090	10,334	19,221	17,369	2,777	1,415
1998	56,804	38,719	967	39,686	4,579	1,188	36,294	10,091	10,419	20,252	18,275	2,805	1,445
1999	58,633	40,448	946	41,394	4,783	1,287	37,898	10,004	10,731	20,730	18,691	2,828	1,470
2000	61,799	42,172	792	42,964	4,926	1,478	39,516	10,757	11,526	21,696	19,609	2,848	1,476
2001	65,234	43,147	1,583	44,730	5,013	1,541	41,258	11,108	12,867	22,865	20,684	2,853	1,456
2002	66,372	44,724	642	45,366	5,214	1,583	41,736	10,822	13,815	23,218	21,320	2,859	1,455
2003	68,980	46,392	1,187	47,579	5,375	1,667	43,870	10,670	14,440	24,049	22,211	2,868	1,453
2004	72,896	48,860	1,807	50,667	5,698	1,778	46,747	10,626	15,523	25,232	23,506	2,889	1,464
2005	77,774	51,006	1,762	52,768	5,914	1,895	48,749	11,566	17,460	26,764	24,776	2,906	1,474
2006	81,069	53,796	824	54,620	6,399	2,113	50,334	13,152	17,583	27,907	25,580	2,905	1,508
2007	86,110	55,411	1,164	56,575	6,671	2,268	52,173	15,569	18,368	29,406	26,978	2,928	1,539
2008	90,038	57,604	733	58,336	6,889	2,409	53,856	15,391	20,791	30,544	27,908	2,948	1,537
2009	88,580	55,446	841	56,287	6,799	2,366	51,853	14,499	22,228	29,938	27,871	2,959	1,492
2010	91,929	57,481	879	58,360	6,891	2,428	53,897	13,942	24,090	30,947	28,636	2,971	1,491
2011	95,844	59,114	567	59,681	6,404	2,649	55,926	14,984	24,935	32,179	29,794	2,978	1,510
2012	99,410	61,595	808	62,403	6,617	2,850	58,636	15,860	24,915	33,317	30,801	2,984	1,520
2013	101,137	62,706	2,297	65,003	7,551	2,990	60,442	15,228	25,468	33,839	31,105	2,989	1,533
2014	103,505	64,330	1,326	65,655	7,743	3,050	60,963	16,162	26,380	34,610	31,836	2,991	1,557
2015	104,893	64,584	677	65,261	7,949	3,197	60,509	16,940	27,444	35,097	32,175	2,989	1,569
2016	106,915	65,419	556	65,975	8,074	3,261	61,163	17,390	28,362	35,778	32,778	2,988	1,580
2017	109,324	66,869	722	67,591	8,302	3,358	62,647	18,045	28,632	36,567	33,504	2,990	1,591
2018	113,469	68,811	1,638	70,450	8,573	3,532	65,409	18,672	29,388	37,994	34,949	2,987	1,602
2019	115,814	114,822	992	71,806	8,870	3,605	66,541	18,591	30,683	38,887	35,791	2,978	1,617
2020	123,850	123,096	754	72,719	9,054	3,593	67,257	18,452	38,141	41,745	38,630	2,967	...

... = Not available.

Personal Income and Employment by Region and State: Missouri

(Millions of dollars, except as noted.)

Year	Personal income, total	Derivation of personal income									Per capita (dollars)		Population (thousands)	Total employment (thousands)
		Earnings by place of work			Less: Contributions for government social insurance	Plus: Adjustment for residence	Equals: Net earnings by place of residence	Plus: Dividends, interest, and rent	Plus: Personal current transfer receipts		Personal income	Disposable personal income		
		Nonfarm	Farm	Total										
1960	9,630	7,698	443	8,141	358	-180	7,603	1,356		671	2,226	1,984	4,326	...
1961	9,955	7,877	484	8,361	375	-185	7,801	1,409		745	2,289	2,040	4,349	...
1962	10,489	8,346	486	8,832	408	-202	8,222	1,496		771	2,407	2,138	4,357	...
1963	11,002	8,855	440	9,295	469	-227	8,599	1,595		808	2,505	2,219	4,392	...
1964	11,620	9,486	335	9,820	491	-250	9,079	1,710		830	2,616	2,354	4,442	...
1965	12,635	10,171	533	10,704	517	-275	9,911	1,835		888	2,828	2,528	4,467	...
1966	13,536	11,194	417	11,611	695	-314	10,602	1,974		960	2,993	2,666	4,523	...
1967	14,407	11,953	404	12,356	797	-351	11,209	2,078		1,120	3,174	2,825	4,539	...
1968	15,950	13,133	478	13,612	898	-387	12,326	2,310		1,313	3,492	3,086	4,568	...
1969	16,913	14,263	450	14,713	954	-752	13,006	2,478		1,428	3,645	3,163	4,640	2,216
1970	18,480	15,173	525	15,698	1,005	-694	13,999	2,788		1,692	3,945	3,471	4,685	2,203
1971	19,939	16,187	571	16,758	1,109	-680	14,970	3,018		1,951	4,222	3,750	4,723	2,200
1972	21,682	17,549	714	18,263	1,261	-698	16,304	3,266		2,112	4,562	4,003	4,753	2,242
1973	24,090	19,085	1,215	20,301	1,584	-729	17,987	3,653		2,450	5,045	4,473	4,775	2,325
1974	25,775	20,574	640	21,214	1,767	-756	18,691	4,192		2,892	5,386	4,737	4,785	2,341
1975	28,213	21,854	698	22,552	1,842	-771	19,939	4,618		3,655	5,883	5,248	4,795	2,291
1976	30,912	24,496	471	24,967	2,097	-839	22,032	4,976		3,904	6,409	5,667	4,824	2,365
1977	34,252	27,206	717	27,924	2,332	-969	24,623	5,555		4,075	7,070	6,250	4,845	2,424
1978	38,130	30,397	920	31,317	2,697	-1,121	27,499	6,202		4,428	7,828	6,869	4,871	2,512
1979	42,514	33,687	1,179	34,866	3,090	-1,287	30,489	7,016		5,008	8,695	7,592	4,889	2,576
1980	46,120	35,990	242	36,232	3,279	-1,495	31,458	8,564		6,099	9,370	8,186	4,922	2,549
1981	51,517	38,771	773	39,543	3,789	-1,629	34,125	10,539		6,852	10,445	9,083	4,932	2,540
1982	55,084	40,570	347	40,917	4,044	-1,685	35,189	12,445		7,470	11,174	9,672	4,929	2,516
1983	58,758	43,678	-103	43,575	4,389	-1,709	37,477	13,259		8,022	11,885	10,511	4,944	2,562
1984	65,189	48,321	426	48,746	4,997	-1,858	41,892	14,926		8,372	13,103	11,645	4,975	2,667
1985	69,744	51,821	798	52,619	5,479	-1,988	45,153	15,762		8,830	13,948	12,348	5,000	2,738
1986	73,417	55,042	584	55,626	5,879	-2,053	47,694	16,424		9,298	14,616	12,956	5,023	2,801
1987	77,346	58,668	739	59,407	6,196	-2,170	51,042	16,730		9,574	15,296	13,520	5,057	2,836
1988	82,132	62,711	658	63,368	6,836	-2,253	54,280	17,742		10,109	16,162	14,331	5,082	2,885
1989	88,040	66,534	912	67,446	7,299	-2,386	57,761	19,307		10,972	17,277	15,257	5,096	2,938
1990	91,909	69,600	708	70,308	7,872	-2,600	59,837	20,182		11,890	17,920	15,821	5,129	2,972
1991	95,964	71,629	589	72,218	8,214	-2,592	61,413	20,656		13,895	18,559	16,509	5,171	2,942
1992	102,139	76,312	862	77,173	8,666	-2,716	65,792	21,511		14,836	19,578	17,460	5,217	2,957
1993	106,821	79,824	500	80,324	9,093	-2,834	68,397	22,496		15,928	20,265	18,048	5,271	3,041
1994	113,391	84,809	725	85,534	9,774	-2,860	72,900	23,791		16,701	21,296	18,904	5,324	3,113
1995	119,590	90,015	219	90,234	10,357	-3,110	76,766	25,021		17,803	22,236	19,673	5,378	3,196
1996	126,668	94,801	1,052	95,854	10,779	-3,210	81,865	26,198		18,605	23,321	20,531	5,432	3,255
1997	134,328	100,826	1,059	101,886	11,410	-3,388	87,087	27,933		19,308	24,507	21,472	5,481	3,328
1998	141,142	106,686	545	107,230	12,010	-3,551	91,670	29,535		19,937	25,561	22,302	5,522	3,385
1999	147,025	113,122	241	113,363	12,637	-3,680	97,046	29,104		20,875	26,434	23,066	5,562	3,423
2000	157,163	120,047	788	120,835	13,301	-3,964	103,571	31,294		22,298	28,028	24,459	5,607	3,471
2001	162,072	123,503	836	124,340	13,689	-4,019	106,632	30,842		24,598	28,730	25,075	5,641	3,452
2002	165,773	127,628	406	128,034	14,020	-4,131	109,884	29,632		26,257	29,212	26,075	5,675	3,437
2003	171,790	131,172	1,048	132,220	14,448	-4,182	113,591	30,784		27,416	30,089	27,160	5,709	3,445
2004	180,586	137,267	2,281	139,548	14,983	-4,282	120,282	31,379		28,924	31,419	28,488	5,748	3,479
2005	186,878	142,569	1,442	144,010	15,738	-4,572	123,700	32,252		30,926	32,274	28,974	5,790	3,533
2006	198,448	149,820	1,268	151,088	16,725	-4,974	129,390	36,185		32,873	33,965	30,330	5,843	3,586
2007	208,185	154,567	1,429	155,996	17,499	-4,838	133,660	39,399		35,125	35,360	31,384	5,888	3,636
2008	219,412	160,269	2,016	162,285	18,254	-5,426	138,605	41,328		39,479	37,038	32,877	5,924	3,626
2009	215,541	157,486	1,622	159,108	17,721	-5,119	136,268	36,460		42,812	36,158	32,979	5,961	3,523
2010	220,547	160,003	1,456	161,459	17,701	-4,927	138,831	36,144		45,572	36,782	33,518	5,996	3,475
2011	229,644	163,161	2,158	165,319	16,304	-4,337	144,678	38,564		46,402	38,213	34,449	6,010	3,507
2012	240,973	169,903	1,384	171,287	16,747	-4,878	149,662	44,390		46,921	40,002	36,118	6,024	3,528
2013	242,565	175,077	2,865	177,942	19,443	-4,723	153,776	40,945		47,844	40,155	35,921	6,041	3,566
2014	251,640	178,835	3,113	181,947	20,020	-4,782	157,145	45,326		49,168	41,550	37,114	6,056	3,597
2015	260,145	186,143	621	186,764	21,086	-4,991	160,687	47,881		51,576	42,845	38,045	6,072	3,656
2016	265,495	188,903	946	189,848	21,572	-4,863	163,413	49,029		53,054	43,615	38,708	6,087	3,702
2017	274,976	195,377	1,062	196,439	22,234	-5,118	169,088	51,507		54,381	45,014	39,963	6,109	3,738
2018	285,704	202,673	1,358	204,031	23,091	-5,309	175,631	53,676		56,397	46,635	41,589	6,126	3,776
2019	298,620	297,359	1,261	212,767	24,011	-5,952	182,804	56,866		58,951	48,631	43,529	6,140	3,822
2020	314,818	313,291	1,527	214,837	24,462	-5,972	184,404	56,240		74,175	51,177	46,077	6,152	...

... = Not available.

Personal Income and Employment by Region and State: Montana

(Millions of dollars, except as noted.)

Year	Personal income, total	Earnings by place of work			Less: Contributions for government social insurance	Plus: Adjustment for residence	Equals: Net earnings by place of residence	Plus: Dividends, interest, and rent	Plus: Personal current transfer receipts	Per capita (dollars)		Population (thousands)	Total employment (thousands)
		Nonfarm	Farm	Total						Personal income	Disposable personal income		
1960	1,451	1,011	162	1,173	62	0	1,111	233	108	2,137	1,933	679	...
1961	1,455	1,059	110	1,169	63	L	1,106	231	117	2,090	1,878	696	...
1962	1,701	1,121	277	1,398	64	-0	1,334	248	119	2,437	2,223	698	...
1963	1,692	1,172	213	1,385	72	-0	1,313	258	121	2,406	2,181	703	...
1964	1,728	1,226	169	1,395	74	-0	1,321	281	126	2,447	2,245	706	...
1965	1,856	1,303	190	1,493	76	-0	1,417	305	134	2,629	2,398	706	...
1966	1,990	1,390	227	1,616	99	-0	1,517	330	143	2,814	2,556	707	...
1967	2,029	1,429	191	1,620	108	-0	1,511	349	169	2,895	2,620	701	...
1968	2,128	1,505	196	1,701	115	-1	1,585	352	191	3,040	2,750	700	...
1969	2,351	1,632	242	1,874	127	-1	1,747	394	210	3,387	2,980	694	298
1970	2,604	1,754	291	2,046	137	-1	1,908	455	241	3,735	3,339	697	301
1971	2,787	1,919	251	2,170	151	-1	2,018	489	280	3,920	3,549	711	307
1972	3,230	2,156	401	2,557	177	-0	2,380	541	310	4,492	4,022	719	319
1973	3,745	2,404	575	2,980	227	0	2,753	632	360	5,149	4,594	727	333
1974	4,070	2,705	466	3,171	262	1	2,909	738	423	5,521	4,909	737	344
1975	4,479	3,010	400	3,410	283	2	3,129	836	514	5,978	5,365	749	344
1976	4,807	3,419	225	3,644	324	3	3,323	913	570	6,337	5,639	759	359
1977	5,198	3,839	71	3,910	369	4	3,545	1,038	615	6,739	5,956	771	372
1978	6,091	4,361	303	4,664	433	3	4,235	1,182	675	7,768	6,908	784	390
1979	6,549	4,806	119	4,925	496	6	4,434	1,355	760	8,298	7,275	789	396
1980	7,211	5,108	120	5,228	542	13	4,699	1,617	895	9,142	8,037	789	393
1981	8,194	5,562	227	5,789	632	25	5,181	1,979	1,034	10,303	9,093	795	395
1982	8,636	5,714	172	5,886	664	17	5,239	2,239	1,158	10,741	9,586	804	391
1983	9,077	6,039	127	6,166	700	9	5,476	2,333	1,268	11,151	9,993	814	398
1984	9,603	6,392	44	6,436	758	6	5,684	2,566	1,353	11,698	10,519	821	408
1985	9,738	6,525	-84	6,441	790	3	5,655	2,653	1,431	11,843	10,650	822	406
1986	10,126	6,529	238	6,767	805	-2	5,960	2,638	1,528	12,443	11,302	814	402
1987	10,398	6,713	317	7,030	827	-3	6,200	2,598	1,601	12,916	11,635	805	406
1988	10,688	7,148	110	7,258	927	-1	6,331	2,664	1,693	13,356	11,972	800	416
1989	11,776	7,565	420	7,985	997	-3	6,985	2,935	1,856	14,726	13,121	800	424
1990	12,378	8,033	396	8,429	1,118	-4	7,306	3,040	2,033	15,469	13,806	800	433
1991	13,196	8,627	551	9,179	1,219	-11	7,948	3,109	2,140	16,298	14,625	810	444
1992	14,014	9,338	489	9,827	1,324	-2	8,501	3,192	2,321	16,971	15,208	826	456
1993	15,163	10,048	773	10,821	1,462	1	9,360	3,311	2,493	17,950	16,108	845	470
1994	15,585	10,634	390	11,024	1,547	5	9,482	3,515	2,589	18,095	16,162	861	494
1995	16,416	11,009	339	11,347	1,564	9	9,792	3,851	2,774	18,728	16,760	877	504
1996	17,203	11,496	310	11,806	1,563	11	10,255	4,069	2,880	19,411	17,326	886	519
1997	17,939	11,963	239	12,202	1,585	13	10,630	4,369	2,940	20,159	17,918	890	526
1998	19,269	12,772	299	13,071	1,643	18	11,446	4,771	3,052	21,592	19,178	892	536
1999	19,676	13,180	389	13,569	1,692	21	11,898	4,747	3,031	21,923	19,406	898	543
2000	20,963	13,996	261	14,256	1,793	26	12,490	5,084	3,390	23,195	20,490	904	553
2001	21,862	14,472	350	14,823	1,908	28	12,943	5,249	3,671	24,105	21,303	907	560
2002	22,491	15,313	199	15,512	2,019	26	13,519	5,163	3,808	24,670	22,206	912	565
2003	24,082	16,259	363	16,622	2,121	24	14,525	5,577	3,981	26,187	23,791	920	571
2004	25,995	17,548	561	18,109	2,257	23	15,875	5,876	4,243	27,951	25,444	930	586
2005	27,956	19,029	596	19,626	2,455	20	17,191	6,223	4,542	29,737	26,790	940	601
2006	30,323	20,729	168	20,897	2,655	15	18,257	7,149	4,917	31,828	28,509	953	617
2007	32,670	21,869	439	22,308	2,858	17	19,467	7,956	5,247	33,865	30,111	965	636
2008	34,419	22,476	512	22,988	2,930	27	20,085	8,369	5,965	35,250	31,492	976	636
2009	33,730	22,189	387	22,576	2,876	37	19,737	7,528	6,465	34,279	31,275	984	619
2010	35,558	23,195	554	23,749	2,943	74	20,880	7,619	7,059	35,891	32,838	991	616
2011	38,052	24,452	663	25,115	2,788	180	22,506	8,556	6,990	38,158	34,557	997	623
2012	40,443	25,717	745	26,461	2,871	358	23,949	9,307	7,187	40,292	36,360	1,004	633
2013	40,666	26,227	998	27,225	3,337	447	24,336	8,961	7,370	40,112	35,921	1,014	642
2014	42,726	27,298	738	28,036	3,486	548	25,098	9,922	7,706	41,811	37,247	1,022	649
2015	44,865	28,262	785	29,047	3,585	428	25,891	10,885	8,089	43,537	38,768	1,031	660
2016	45,747	28,488	607	29,095	3,544	273	25,824	11,195	8,729	43,951	39,225	1,041	668
2017	47,677	29,764	293	30,057	3,711	316	26,663	11,678	9,336	45,274	40,448	1,053	676
2018	50,055	30,821	558	31,378	3,857	331	27,852	12,229	9,974	47,120	42,341	1,062	684
2019	53,168	52,491	677	33,174	4,189	414	29,399	13,358	10,411	49,684	44,457	1,070	695
2020	57,626	56,485	1,141	34,560	4,367	390	30,583	13,214	13,829	53,329	48,008	1,081	...

... = Not available.
L = Less than $50,000.

Personal Income and Employment by Region and State: Nebraska

(Millions of dollars, except as noted.)

| Year | Personal income, total | Earnings by place of work | | | Less: Contributions for government social insurance | Plus: Adjustment for residence | Equals: Net earnings by place of residence | Plus: Dividends, interest, and rent | Plus: Personal current transfer receipts | Per capita (dollars) | | Population (thousands) | Total employment (thousands) |
		Nonfarm	Farm	Total						Personal income	Disposable personal income		
1960	3,140	2,154	392	2,546	116	-11	2,419	536	185	2,216	2,005	1,417	...
1961	3,214	2,263	319	2,583	119	-11	2,452	557	205	2,223	1,996	1,446	...
1962	3,494	2,388	437	2,825	128	-10	2,687	591	216	2,386	2,165	1,464	...
1963	3,591	2,471	394	2,865	140	-10	2,716	646	229	2,433	2,201	1,476	...
1964	3,691	2,618	312	2,930	146	-9	2,775	680	236	2,491	2,282	1,482	...
1965	4,061	2,732	497	3,229	148	-8	3,074	730	258	2,761	2,537	1,471	...
1966	4,360	2,935	592	3,527	196	-8	3,323	757	280	2,995	2,729	1,456	...
1967	4,513	3,166	488	3,654	228	-8	3,418	754	341	3,097	2,809	1,457	...
1968	4,815	3,457	444	3,901	245	-8	3,648	774	394	3,282	2,952	1,467	...
1969	5,379	3,830	604	4,434	269	-103	4,062	888	429	3,649	3,220	1,474	704
1970	5,798	4,151	542	4,693	289	-110	4,294	1,007	498	3,897	3,468	1,488	715
1971	6,369	4,468	688	5,156	321	-113	4,722	1,084	562	4,234	3,833	1,504	728
1972	7,053	4,905	808	5,713	364	-122	5,227	1,206	620	4,645	4,131	1,518	748
1973	8,226	5,471	1,227	6,698	468	-125	6,105	1,379	741	5,382	4,798	1,529	775
1974	8,565	6,061	771	6,832	541	-133	6,158	1,561	847	5,570	4,906	1,538	793
1975	9,766	6,605	1,109	7,713	580	-142	6,992	1,739	1,036	6,336	5,693	1,541	790
1976	10,217	7,468	588	8,056	662	-149	7,246	1,867	1,105	6,597	5,901	1,549	811
1977	11,073	8,140	532	8,672	722	-148	7,801	2,095	1,177	7,123	6,291	1,554	831
1978	12,811	9,100	1,085	10,185	831	-171	9,184	2,323	1,305	8,208	7,287	1,561	854
1979	13,834	10,164	754	10,919	966	-199	9,753	2,628	1,453	8,843	7,750	1,564	876
1980	14,758	11,014	107	11,121	1,044	-216	9,861	3,200	1,697	9,386	8,239	1,572	877
1981	17,141	11,868	834	12,702	1,201	-254	11,247	3,938	1,956	10,859	9,615	1,579	871
1982	18,421	12,340	767	13,107	1,279	-262	11,566	4,700	2,154	11,646	10,162	1,582	861
1983	19,047	12,961	550	13,511	1,351	-276	11,884	4,832	2,331	12,022	10,760	1,584	867
1984	21,215	14,166	1,161	15,327	1,520	-316	13,491	5,279	2,444	13,354	12,089	1,589	886
1985	22,348	14,896	1,450	16,346	1,645	-342	14,359	5,393	2,596	14,103	12,759	1,585	898
1986	23,000	15,506	1,414	16,920	1,766	-344	14,810	5,475	2,715	14,609	13,216	1,574	898
1987	24,066	16,415	1,636	18,051	1,867	-343	15,841	5,448	2,777	15,362	13,848	1,567	925
1988	25,727	17,530	2,031	19,560	2,086	-379	17,095	5,736	2,896	16,371	14,753	1,571	947
1989	27,306	18,699	1,847	20,546	2,231	-392	17,924	6,262	3,119	17,338	15,529	1,575	965
1990	29,240	19,999	2,199	22,198	2,466	-391	19,341	6,516	3,383	18,487	16,527	1,582	988
1991	30,305	20,980	1,997	22,977	2,606	-427	19,945	6,720	3,640	18,989	17,022	1,596	992
1992	32,208	22,441	2,117	24,558	2,735	-471	21,352	6,905	3,952	19,984	17,956	1,612	999
1993	33,289	23,559	1,746	25,305	2,880	-487	21,938	7,131	4,220	20,478	18,375	1,626	1,021
1994	35,431	25,213	1,851	27,064	3,086	-502	23,476	7,554	4,401	21,617	19,372	1,639	1,061
1995	37,436	26,903	1,324	28,227	3,235	-548	24,444	8,304	4,688	22,593	20,137	1,657	1,071
1996	40,790	28,434	2,596	31,030	3,415	-599	27,016	8,787	4,988	24,371	21,703	1,674	1,097
1997	42,018	30,040	1,757	31,797	3,637	-677	27,484	9,363	5,171	24,915	21,968	1,686	1,111
1998	45,067	32,115	1,647	33,762	3,856	-714	29,192	10,364	5,511	26,576	23,409	1,696	1,138
1999	47,166	34,145	1,575	35,721	4,061	-800	30,860	10,480	5,826	27,667	24,364	1,705	1,157
2000	49,898	36,088	1,450	37,538	4,242	-868	32,428	11,360	6,110	29,115	25,576	1,714	1,174
2001	52,060	37,631	1,815	39,446	4,412	-875	34,159	11,181	6,720	30,270	26,743	1,720	1,175
2002	52,987	39,231	1,070	40,301	4,574	-902	34,824	11,017	7,146	30,658	27,616	1,728	1,166
2003	56,258	40,432	2,689	43,122	4,742	-938	37,442	11,363	7,454	32,358	29,487	1,739	1,169
2004	58,622	42,734	2,783	45,517	4,957	-944	39,616	11,196	7,810	33,510	30,541	1,749	1,180
2005	60,705	43,939	3,005	46,944	5,221	-941	40,782	11,654	8,268	34,462	31,145	1,761	1,192
2006	63,575	46,712	1,618	48,330	5,617	-856	41,857	12,785	8,933	35,863	32,134	1,773	1,208
2007	68,559	48,745	2,784	51,529	5,847	-947	44,735	14,404	9,421	38,442	34,298	1,783	1,231
2008	72,397	50,482	3,019	53,501	6,044	-980	46,478	15,337	10,582	40,302	36,106	1,796	1,237
2009	71,200	50,873	2,685	53,557	6,055	-957	46,545	13,601	11,053	39,279	35,980	1,813	1,223
2010	74,787	53,303	3,115	56,418	6,269	-898	49,252	13,667	11,868	40,878	37,311	1,830	1,220
2011	83,474	56,725	6,400	63,126	5,733	-963	56,430	14,951	12,093	45,353	41,231	1,841	1,232
2012	86,118	59,515	4,562	64,077	5,899	-999	57,180	16,754	12,184	46,467	42,020	1,853	1,251
2013	86,683	59,509	6,746	66,255	6,761	-969	58,525	15,823	12,334	46,468	41,717	1,865	1,266
2014	91,845	64,078	5,748	69,826	7,099	-937	61,790	17,230	12,825	48,866	43,789	1,880	1,283
2015	95,455	66,721	5,208	71,929	7,389	-1,008	63,533	18,463	13,459	50,465	45,273	1,892	1,303
2016	94,731	66,445	3,887	70,332	7,510	-1,062	61,760	18,969	14,002	49,703	44,530	1,906	1,312
2017	97,557	68,728	3,518	72,246	7,865	-1,145	63,236	19,771	14,550	50,875	45,591	1,918	1,319
2018	100,534	70,981	3,088	74,069	8,157	-1,173	64,739	20,599	15,195	52,110	46,879	1,929	1,330
2019	105,454	102,657	2,797	77,432	8,507	-1,137	67,788	21,283	16,383	54,567	49,082	1,933	1,342
2020	112,266	108,280	3,987	79,933	8,801	-1,179	69,954	21,048	21,264	57,942	52,364	1,938	...

... = Not available.

Personal Income and Employment by Region and State: Nevada

(Millions of dollars, except as noted.)

Year	Personal income, total	Earnings by place of work			Less: Contributions for government social insurance	Plus: Adjustment for residence	Equals: Net earnings by place of residence	Plus: Dividends, interest, and rent	Plus: Personal current transfer receipts	Per capita (dollars)		Population (thousands)	Total employment (thousands)
		Nonfarm	Farm	Total						Personal income	Disposable personal income		
1960	896	746	15	760	36	-2	722	134	41	3,079	2,730	291	...
1961	993	822	13	835	40	-3	792	152	49	3,153	2,771	315	...
1962	1,186	1,002	19	1,021	50	-4	966	168	51	3,369	2,975	352	...
1963	1,330	1,146	20	1,166	66	-6	1,094	178	58	3,350	2,941	397	...
1964	1,443	1,241	12	1,252	67	-6	1,180	198	65	3,388	3,040	426	...
1965	1,545	1,306	14	1,319	66	-5	1,249	225	72	3,480	3,130	444	...
1966	1,630	1,381	18	1,399	80	-4	1,316	237	78	3,656	3,279	446	...
1967	1,732	1,452	17	1,469	87	-3	1,379	258	95	3,857	3,451	449	...
1968	2,014	1,670	20	1,689	101	-4	1,585	316	113	4,340	3,802	464	...
1969	2,279	1,924	32	1,956	132	-33	1,791	363	125	4,747	4,068	480	244
1970	2,560	2,135	34	2,169	144	-39	1,986	427	148	5,191	4,615	493	256
1971	2,860	2,366	35	2,401	165	-41	2,195	481	184	5,501	4,945	520	267
1972	3,197	2,634	42	2,677	194	-44	2,439	540	218	5,847	5,225	547	280
1973	3,630	3,010	56	3,066	256	-54	2,756	621	254	6,381	5,703	569	304
1974	4,025	3,300	35	3,335	288	-56	2,992	718	315	6,746	6,006	597	317
1975	4,544	3,646	33	3,679	313	-58	3,308	798	438	7,331	6,692	620	326
1976	5,171	4,178	36	4,214	368	-68	3,778	902	490	7,994	7,184	647	349
1977	5,978	4,909	27	4,936	439	-84	4,413	1,030	535	8,815	7,873	678	384
1978	7,226	5,994	23	6,017	555	-116	5,346	1,276	604	10,045	8,883	719	432
1979	8,375	6,950	9	6,959	681	-132	6,147	1,516	713	10,945	9,597	765	468
1980	9,683	7,877	57	7,934	778	-160	6,996	1,822	866	11,951	10,547	810	489
1981	11,012	8,829	28	8,857	931	-167	7,759	2,197	1,055	12,991	11,428	848	500
1982	11,762	9,116	33	9,148	953	-168	8,027	2,560	1,175	13,343	11,839	882	494
1983	12,530	9,656	26	9,683	1,049	-177	8,457	2,788	1,285	13,892	12,425	902	499
1984	13,652	10,514	36	10,549	1,191	-190	9,168	3,107	1,376	14,760	13,219	925	523
1985	14,799	11,352	29	11,381	1,313	-200	9,868	3,420	1,512	15,561	13,853	951	545
1986	15,989	12,283	28	12,311	1,452	-217	10,642	3,661	1,685	16,305	14,478	981	570
1987	17,474	13,601	48	13,649	1,615	-240	11,794	3,881	1,798	17,075	15,087	1,023	616
1988	19,843	15,637	65	15,701	1,873	-281	13,547	4,321	1,975	18,458	16,250	1,075	662
1989	22,353	17,406	79	17,485	2,119	-326	15,040	5,032	2,280	19,653	17,297	1,137	710
1990	25,043	19,593	82	19,675	2,497	-377	16,802	5,633	2,609	20,516	18,027	1,221	756
1991	27,515	21,109	76	21,185	2,660	-346	18,179	6,116	3,221	21,228	18,841	1,296	769
1992	30,479	23,280	73	23,353	2,890	-305	20,158	6,677	3,645	22,554	19,987	1,351	776
1993	32,966	25,264	119	25,383	3,163	-344	21,876	7,241	3,849	23,360	20,627	1,411	819
1994	36,486	27,991	82	28,073	3,534	-354	24,186	8,263	4,037	24,335	21,570	1,499	898
1995	40,138	30,668	70	30,738	3,879	-349	26,510	9,249	4,379	25,379	22,487	1,582	953
1996	44,435	33,947	70	34,017	4,196	-368	29,453	10,267	4,714	26,667	23,367	1,666	1,024
1997	48,573	37,158	70	37,228	4,477	-328	32,423	11,124	5,025	27,534	24,183	1,764	1,089
1998	54,525	41,713	93	41,806	4,785	-350	36,671	12,503	5,352	29,422	25,721	1,853	1,131
1999	58,886	45,777	85	45,862	5,086	-382	40,395	12,908	5,583	30,436	26,588	1,935	1,189
2000	64,576	49,569	104	49,673	4,986	-338	44,348	14,227	6,001	31,988	27,874	2,019	1,254
2001	68,036	52,424	118	52,542	5,292	-354	46,896	14,351	6,789	32,423	28,445	2,098	1,285
2002	69,976	53,742	90	53,832	5,482	-364	47,987	14,338	7,651	32,191	28,768	2,174	1,300
2003	74,570	56,548	93	56,641	5,568	-410	50,664	15,688	8,219	33,159	29,876	2,249	1,353
2004	83,003	62,741	127	62,868	6,093	-494	56,281	17,846	8,876	35,377	31,690	2,346	1,441
2005	93,329	69,646	135	69,781	6,696	-549	62,537	21,215	9,577	38,373	34,006	2,432	1,534
2006	100,381	75,438	129	75,567	7,751	-474	67,342	22,690	10,349	39,792	35,296	2,523	1,604
2007	104,455	77,497	98	77,595	8,179	-400	69,016	24,125	11,314	40,159	35,650	2,601	1,644
2008	102,763	73,626	150	73,776	7,699	-321	65,757	23,645	13,362	38,725	34,769	2,654	1,619
2009	97,544	68,983	126	69,109	7,419	-308	61,383	20,896	15,265	36,334	33,301	2,685	1,513
2010	101,205	71,373	144	71,517	7,311	-252	63,954	20,425	16,827	37,449	34,355	2,702	1,478
2011	105,185	72,853	206	73,058	6,915	-145	65,998	22,137	17,051	38,774	35,365	2,713	1,502
2012	109,446	74,011	114	74,125	7,274	-157	66,695	25,556	17,195	39,877	36,261	2,745	1,519
2013	109,901	75,970	118	76,088	8,006	-136	67,946	24,380	17,576	39,576	35,479	2,777	1,561
2014	117,423	79,287	233	79,520	8,816	-174	70,530	27,873	19,020	41,654	37,541	2,819	1,610
2015	126,930	84,363	169	84,532	9,398	-122	75,012	31,084	20,834	44,247	39,719	2,869	1,665
2016	130,757	86,442	89	86,531	9,753	-155	76,623	32,181	21,954	44,783	39,788	2,920	1,725
2017	138,386	91,857	100	91,956	10,125	-99	81,733	33,725	22,929	46,557	41,418	2,972	1,776
2018	146,334	97,308	77	97,385	10,784	-122	86,479	35,615	24,240	48,225	43,102	3,034	1,848
2019	157,584	157,414	169	104,920	11,953	-192	92,776	38,545	26,263	50,985	45,956	3,091	1,902
2020	168,319	168,111	208	102,017	11,650	-77	90,290	38,022	40,006	53,635	48,951	3,138	...

... = Not available.

Personal Income and Employment by Region and State: New Hampshire

(Millions of dollars, except as noted.)

Year	Personal income, total	Earnings by place of work			Less: Contributions for government social insurance	Plus: Adjustment for residence	Equals: Net earnings by place of residence	Plus: Dividends, interest, and rent	Plus: Personal current transfer receipts	Per capita (dollars)		Population (thousands)	Total employment (thousands)
		Nonfarm	Farm	Total						Personal income	Disposable personal income		
1960	1,383	1,037	20	1,056	55	82	1,083	210	90	2,271	2,036	609	...
1961	1,456	1,081	21	1,101	56	89	1,134	221	102	2,356	2,119	618	...
1962	1,557	1,153	19	1,172	62	98	1,208	244	105	2,464	2,210	632	...
1963	1,625	1,197	18	1,215	68	103	1,250	262	113	2,503	2,235	649	...
1964	1,747	1,283	18	1,301	71	112	1,342	290	116	2,635	2,401	663	...
1965	1,884	1,377	21	1,399	75	122	1,446	315	123	2,787	2,527	676	...
1966	2,064	1,528	24	1,552	103	142	1,591	341	132	3,031	2,716	681	...
1967	2,255	1,677	17	1,695	116	157	1,735	365	155	3,235	2,897	697	...
1968	2,491	1,846	20	1,866	128	175	1,913	399	180	3,513	3,124	709	...
1969	2,781	2,003	21	2,024	129	234	2,129	450	203	3,842	3,401	724	334
1970	2,966	2,125	17	2,141	136	220	2,226	499	241	3,997	3,520	742	334
1971	3,220	2,283	15	2,297	151	229	2,376	552	292	4,225	3,789	762	336
1972	3,562	2,536	16	2,552	177	252	2,628	611	322	4,557	4,025	782	350
1973	4,013	2,882	21	2,903	230	280	2,954	679	380	5,005	4,475	802	374
1974	4,417	3,114	14	3,128	258	323	3,193	769	456	5,406	4,812	817	381
1975	4,802	3,278	17	3,295	267	356	3,384	833	586	5,786	5,227	830	370
1976	5,436	3,779	19	3,798	310	400	3,888	922	626	6,418	5,748	847	394
1977	6,146	4,295	18	4,313	354	473	4,431	1,054	661	7,050	6,284	872	418
1978	7,091	5,008	19	5,027	421	564	5,170	1,196	725	7,932	7,008	894	446
1979	8,112	5,725	22	5,746	504	678	5,921	1,363	829	8,896	7,848	912	468
1980	9,278	6,347	14	6,361	559	840	6,642	1,664	972	10,039	8,884	924	482
1981	10,517	7,018	23	7,041	667	950	7,324	2,055	1,138	11,229	9,909	937	492
1982	11,580	7,573	19	7,592	740	1,036	7,889	2,443	1,248	12,219	10,904	948	498
1983	12,713	8,496	17	8,514	841	1,153	8,826	2,555	1,333	13,269	11,834	958	518
1984	14,376	9,593	22	9,614	977	1,362	9,999	2,967	1,410	14,717	13,166	977	553
1985	15,842	10,764	24	10,788	1,126	1,496	11,159	3,208	1,476	15,894	14,096	997	586
1986	17,509	12,099	25	12,124	1,276	1,571	12,419	3,541	1,548	17,081	15,055	1,025	617
1987	19,362	13,663	43	13,706	1,420	1,683	13,968	3,813	1,581	18,365	16,169	1,054	635
1988	21,322	15,081	45	15,126	1,606	1,823	15,343	4,266	1,713	19,696	17,464	1,083	660
1989	22,847	15,717	35	15,752	1,677	1,941	16,016	4,912	1,919	20,685	18,361	1,105	660
1990	23,007	15,582	44	15,626	1,710	1,972	15,889	4,968	2,150	20,682	18,456	1,112	643
1991	23,792	15,565	45	15,610	1,730	2,118	15,998	4,913	2,882	21,436	19,271	1,110	616
1992	24,968	16,677	51	16,728	1,839	2,177	17,067	4,832	3,070	22,337	20,105	1,118	629
1993	25,787	17,425	42	17,467	1,919	2,303	17,851	4,963	2,973	22,831	20,463	1,129	642
1994	27,522	18,583	40	18,623	2,074	2,399	18,947	5,199	3,376	24,088	21,614	1,143	666
1995	29,203	19,714	35	19,749	2,224	2,391	19,916	5,645	3,641	25,228	22,560	1,158	679
1996	30,942	21,039	41	21,079	2,347	2,566	21,298	6,044	3,599	26,339	23,331	1,175	696
1997	33,274	22,802	38	22,840	2,521	2,803	23,121	6,412	3,741	27,975	24,472	1,189	717
1998	36,646	25,535	40	25,575	2,734	2,904	25,745	7,022	3,880	30,388	26,628	1,206	743
1999	39,088	27,627	44	27,672	2,904	3,376	28,143	6,986	3,958	31,986	27,872	1,222	761
2000	44,074	31,066	44	31,111	3,190	4,021	31,941	7,871	4,261	35,547	30,720	1,240	784
2001	46,376	33,033	42	33,075	3,324	4,064	33,815	7,908	4,654	36,938	32,420	1,256	788
2002	47,156	33,922	43	33,965	3,385	3,935	34,515	7,574	5,067	37,157	33,457	1,269	788
2003	48,122	34,887	49	34,936	3,550	3,949	35,335	7,592	5,196	37,600	34,195	1,280	798
2004	51,035	36,828	58	36,886	3,809	4,229	37,306	8,047	5,682	39,559	36,103	1,290	813
2005	52,920	38,492	49	38,541	3,977	4,220	38,784	8,208	5,927	40,755	36,878	1,298	826
2006	56,713	40,909	41	40,950	4,150	4,375	41,175	9,210	6,329	43,346	39,057	1,308	836
2007	58,904	41,470	43	41,513	4,321	4,747	41,939	10,096	6,869	44,878	40,179	1,313	848
2008	60,396	41,580	60	41,639	4,459	4,878	42,058	10,385	7,953	45,897	41,211	1,316	845
2009	59,597	41,571	37	41,608	4,432	4,162	41,338	9,685	8,575	45,283	41,757	1,316	821
2010	62,306	43,425	52	43,478	4,558	4,768	43,688	9,482	9,136	47,317	43,472	1,317	814
2011	65,443	44,428	48	44,476	4,225	5,086	45,337	11,032	9,074	49,585	45,059	1,320	819
2012	68,558	45,470	85	45,554	4,330	5,493	46,718	12,624	9,216	51,782	47,301	1,324	824
2013	68,117	46,030	91	46,121	4,954	5,202	46,370	12,350	9,397	51,354	46,412	1,326	835
2014	70,507	47,757	77	47,834	5,131	4,947	47,651	12,845	10,010	52,884	47,580	1,333	845
2015	73,430	49,221	83	49,304	5,333	5,448	49,419	13,260	10,751	54,950	49,162	1,336	861
2016	76,247	50,600	51	50,651	5,520	6,046	51,177	13,657	11,413	56,800	50,662	1,342	874
2017	80,122	53,133	47	53,180	5,844	6,661	53,997	14,281	11,844	59,360	53,049	1,350	883
2018	83,293	55,108	34	55,142	6,105	6,961	55,998	14,953	12,342	61,405	55,165	1,356	892
2019	86,345	86,306	39	57,879	6,288	6,951	58,543	14,834	12,968	63,452	56,978	1,361	905
2020	90,745	90,692	53	58,359	6,450	6,772	58,681	14,707	17,357	66,418	59,966	1,366	...

... = Not available.

Personal Income and Employment by Region and State: New Jersey

(Millions of dollars, except as noted.)

Year	Personal income, total	Derivation of personal income								Per capita (dollars)		Population (thousands)	Total employment (thousands)
		Earnings by place of work			Less: Contributions for government social insurance	Plus: Adjustment for residence	Equals: Net earnings by place of residence	Plus: Dividends, interest, and rent	Plus: Personal current transfer receipts	Personal income	Disposable personal income		
		Nonfarm	Farm	Total									
1960	16,553	13,148	121	13,269	660	863	13,472	2,185	896	2,712	2,400	6,103	…
1961	17,396	13,698	120	13,818	695	920	14,044	2,328	1,024	2,777	2,457	6,265	…
1962	18,719	14,646	110	14,755	771	1,021	15,006	2,634	1,079	2,936	2,594	6,376	…
1963	19,647	15,280	108	15,388	869	1,097	15,615	2,873	1,159	3,008	2,655	6,531	…
1964	21,064	16,215	103	16,319	881	1,213	16,651	3,208	1,205	3,163	2,843	6,660	…
1965	22,629	17,351	119	17,471	935	1,324	17,860	3,484	1,286	3,344	2,983	6,767	…
1966	24,503	18,937	120	19,056	1,212	1,522	19,366	3,752	1,385	3,577	3,188	6,851	…
1967	26,394	20,281	105	20,386	1,346	1,687	20,726	4,025	1,642	3,810	3,372	6,928	…
1968	28,967	22,134	102	22,236	1,535	1,894	22,595	4,408	1,964	4,135	3,627	7,005	…
1969	32,504	24,069	105	24,174	1,829	3,165	25,510	4,782	2,213	4,581	3,982	7,095	3,061
1970	35,295	26,002	100	26,102	1,958	3,117	27,261	5,344	2,689	4,909	4,313	7,190	3,125
1971	38,078	27,808	93	27,902	2,170	3,213	28,944	5,857	3,277	5,229	4,658	7,282	3,119
1972	41,395	30,359	89	30,448	2,484	3,418	31,381	6,351	3,663	5,642	4,959	7,337	3,184
1973	45,063	33,412	127	33,538	3,131	3,513	33,921	7,011	4,131	6,143	5,442	7,335	3,288
1974	48,945	35,871	138	36,009	3,461	3,683	36,231	7,867	4,848	6,673	5,886	7,335	3,301
1975	52,878	37,649	97	37,746	3,544	3,887	38,090	8,451	6,338	7,203	6,445	7,341	3,191
1976	57,409	41,278	102	41,380	3,933	4,061	41,509	9,047	6,853	7,817	6,921	7,344	3,248
1977	62,802	45,429	112	45,541	4,316	4,420	45,645	9,929	7,229	8,554	7,490	7,342	3,325
1978	69,699	50,935	127	51,062	4,987	4,992	51,067	10,944	7,689	9,475	8,274	7,356	3,465
1979	77,363	56,448	127	56,575	5,748	5,707	56,534	12,279	8,550	10,493	9,068	7,373	3,552
1980	87,047	61,774	116	61,890	6,317	6,658	62,230	15,035	9,782	11,801	10,176	7,376	3,601
1981	97,265	67,613	150	67,763	7,368	7,275	67,669	18,615	10,980	13,131	11,292	7,407	3,631
1982	105,090	72,175	166	72,341	7,997	7,760	72,104	20,951	12,035	14,142	12,173	7,431	3,639
1983	113,439	78,787	192	78,979	8,983	8,101	78,097	22,350	12,992	15,190	13,221	7,468	3,739
1984	125,567	87,803	200	88,003	10,427	8,526	86,102	25,918	13,548	16,708	14,609	7,515	3,914
1985	134,574	95,257	227	95,484	11,395	8,952	93,040	27,334	14,199	17,788	15,407	7,566	4,026
1986	144,070	103,092	229	103,321	12,408	9,537	100,450	28,753	14,868	18,902	16,349	7,622	4,122
1987	155,341	113,024	258	113,281	13,525	10,071	109,828	30,154	15,360	20,251	17,353	7,671	4,220
1988	170,598	125,277	253	125,530	15,224	10,488	120,795	33,448	16,355	22,120	19,170	7,712	4,317
1989	183,043	132,044	246	132,290	15,871	10,338	126,757	38,759	17,527	23,692	20,554	7,726	4,351
1990	192,164	137,883	243	138,126	16,024	10,354	132,456	40,376	19,331	24,754	21,556	7,763	4,310
1991	195,933	139,450	228	139,678	16,533	10,312	133,457	40,228	22,249	25,072	21,919	7,815	4,172
1992	210,510	149,174	237	149,411	17,491	12,066	143,986	40,760	25,764	26,713	23,410	7,881	4,170
1993	217,596	155,154	265	155,419	18,116	12,251	149,554	41,120	26,922	27,374	23,904	7,949	4,197
1994	225,285	161,704	282	161,986	19,138	12,234	155,082	42,899	27,303	28,110	24,445	8,014	4,232
1995	239,165	169,469	277	169,746	19,894	13,366	163,218	46,776	29,170	29,588	25,794	8,083	4,296
1996	253,062	178,047	297	178,344	20,745	15,322	172,921	50,039	30,102	31,052	26,870	8,150	4,352
1997	269,606	188,565	247	188,812	21,524	18,082	185,369	53,372	30,865	32,804	28,153	8,219	4,412
1998	286,990	201,534	264	201,798	22,685	19,596	198,709	56,566	31,715	34,630	29,415	8,287	4,501
1999	300,848	213,127	230	213,357	23,766	21,496	211,088	56,721	33,039	35,988	30,364	8,360	4,571
2000	331,307	233,831	322	234,154	25,555	24,547	233,146	62,900	35,262	39,298	32,954	8,431	4,749
2001	342,293	241,842	269	242,111	26,593	25,181	240,700	62,395	39,198	40,305	33,923	8,493	4,777
2002	347,248	249,498	289	249,787	27,299	22,806	245,294	59,552	42,402	40,601	35,258	8,553	4,792
2003	356,003	256,930	307	257,237	27,736	23,053	252,554	60,571	42,878	41,389	36,368	8,601	4,825
2004	372,882	267,971	330	268,301	29,106	26,123	265,317	64,110	43,455	43,185	38,027	8,635	4,910
2005	386,943	276,971	337	277,308	30,543	28,566	275,331	65,852	45,760	44,723	38,832	8,652	4,991
2006	415,979	289,727	382	290,109	31,792	33,853	292,171	74,120	49,687	48,025	41,564	8,662	5,057
2007	440,855	300,007	396	300,403	33,660	40,276	307,019	81,781	52,055	50,802	43,443	8,678	5,130
2008	453,339	305,139	351	305,490	34,557	39,545	310,478	84,133	58,728	52,042	44,600	8,711	5,124
2009	439,322	300,446	358	300,804	33,747	31,111	298,168	75,890	65,264	50,176	44,559	8,756	4,992
2010	452,323	306,593	337	306,930	34,243	35,034	307,721	73,884	70,718	51,402	45,528	8,800	4,961
2011	473,913	312,683	358	313,041	31,436	39,097	320,702	81,758	71,454	53,684	46,900	8,828	5,019
2012	491,657	324,625	433	325,057	32,108	39,742	332,691	88,642	70,323	55,583	48,848	8,845	5,054
2013	496,306	334,895	405	335,300	37,384	40,740	338,657	86,668	70,981	56,027	48,452	8,858	5,133
2014	519,815	346,722	358	347,080	38,485	43,651	352,246	93,721	73,847	58,625	50,745	8,867	5,207
2015	542,405	357,848	433	358,281	39,809	46,336	364,808	100,612	76,984	61,144	52,641	8,871	5,303
2016	555,805	365,246	373	365,619	40,445	47,702	372,876	102,843	80,085	62,629	53,978	8,875	5,391
2017	581,199	380,680	350	381,030	42,159	53,229	392,101	107,193	81,905	65,387	56,462	8,889	5,471
2018	602,297	393,378	279	393,657	43,697	56,112	406,072	111,623	84,601	67,609	58,760	8,909	5,549
2019	625,938	625,550	388	412,159	44,834	59,126	426,451	112,465	87,021	70,399	61,023	8,891	5,636
2020	668,354	667,823	531	408,975	44,896	57,397	421,476	111,354	135,524	75,245	66,001	8,882	…

… = Not available.

Personal Income and Employment by Region and State: New Mexico

(Millions of dollars, except as noted.)

Year	Personal income, total	Earnings by place of work			Less: Contributions for government social insurance	Plus: Adjustment for residence	Equals: Net earnings by place of residence	Plus: Dividends, interest, and rent	Plus: Personal current transfer receipts	Per capita (dollars)		Population (thousands)	Total employment (thousands)
		Nonfarm	Farm	Total						Personal income	Disposable personal income		
1960	1,912	1,535	86	1,622	61	-16	1,545	264	102	2,004	1,829	954	...
1961	2,000	1,573	102	1,675	61	-16	1,598	284	118	2,073	1,892	965	...
1962	2,079	1,662	83	1,745	66	-17	1,662	297	120	2,124	1,932	979	...
1963	2,150	1,714	87	1,801	74	-18	1,708	313	129	2,174	1,979	989	...
1964	2,273	1,828	66	1,894	78	-19	1,797	342	135	2,260	2,083	1,006	...
1965	2,412	1,924	78	2,002	81	-21	1,901	366	145	2,383	2,180	1,012	...
1966	2,535	2,014	100	2,114	104	-21	1,990	388	156	2,517	2,302	1,007	...
1967	2,620	2,084	90	2,174	121	-21	2,032	393	195	2,620	2,395	1,000	...
1968	2,837	2,228	102	2,330	125	-23	2,183	426	228	2,854	2,597	994	...
1969	3,144	2,456	107	2,563	152	-21	2,391	493	261	3,109	2,787	1,011	395
1970	3,500	2,653	131	2,784	163	-23	2,598	576	325	3,420	3,081	1,023	399
1971	3,872	2,926	130	3,055	188	-24	2,844	651	378	3,677	3,363	1,053	416
1972	4,353	3,302	137	3,439	220	-22	3,197	734	422	4,039	3,668	1,078	440
1973	4,882	3,673	180	3,853	282	-19	3,552	830	500	4,421	4,016	1,104	461
1974	5,487	4,119	147	4,266	328	-17	3,921	965	601	4,858	4,391	1,130	478
1975	6,268	4,626	177	4,803	366	-14	4,423	1,107	738	5,391	4,955	1,163	491
1976	6,987	5,255	124	5,379	420	-14	4,944	1,215	828	5,846	5,323	1,195	512
1977	7,820	5,942	135	6,076	481	-12	5,583	1,364	872	6,382	5,802	1,225	539
1978	8,948	6,813	168	6,980	565	-12	6,403	1,589	956	7,148	6,435	1,252	568
1979	10,088	7,655	207	7,862	667	-11	7,184	1,801	1,103	7,878	7,078	1,281	592
1980	11,323	8,418	180	8,598	736	-6	7,856	2,153	1,315	8,647	7,779	1,309	597
1981	12,800	9,461	129	9,590	888	-16	8,686	2,612	1,502	9,604	8,540	1,333	611
1982	14,023	10,094	116	10,210	966	-19	9,225	3,146	1,651	10,282	9,125	1,364	619
1983	15,086	10,729	127	10,856	1,035	-14	9,808	3,475	1,804	10,819	9,825	1,394	631
1984	16,471	11,720	147	11,867	1,164	-6	10,697	3,847	1,927	11,626	10,594	1,417	655
1985	17,824	12,558	208	12,766	1,271	1	11,496	4,263	2,064	12,392	11,266	1,438	674
1986	18,525	12,962	194	13,156	1,327	8	11,837	4,466	2,223	12,665	11,572	1,463	680
1987	19,309	13,505	241	13,746	1,371	22	12,398	4,561	2,350	13,059	11,805	1,479	699
1988	20,402	14,296	319	14,616	1,530	33	13,119	4,763	2,520	13,689	12,383	1,490	733
1989	21,855	15,180	383	15,563	1,648	42	13,956	5,104	2,796	14,532	13,082	1,504	749
1990	23,301	16,339	417	16,756	1,872	49	14,934	5,320	3,048	15,314	13,793	1,522	761
1991	24,937	17,558	403	17,961	2,032	61	15,990	5,530	3,417	16,034	14,484	1,555	784
1992	26,803	18,875	484	19,359	2,166	77	17,271	5,733	3,799	16,800	15,202	1,595	797
1993	28,827	20,373	530	20,903	2,341	96	18,658	6,051	4,118	17,616	15,899	1,636	825
1994	30,772	21,761	457	22,218	2,547	111	19,782	6,560	4,430	18,291	16,479	1,682	857
1995	33,071	23,209	391	23,600	2,718	122	21,004	7,188	4,878	19,223	17,341	1,720	898
1996	34,741	23,984	402	24,386	2,808	142	21,720	7,699	5,323	19,826	17,805	1,752	909
1997	36,520	25,169	543	25,713	2,931	163	22,945	8,138	5,437	20,576	18,381	1,775	923
1998	38,229	26,412	585	26,996	3,083	187	24,099	8,410	5,719	21,315	19,019	1,793	938
1999	39,182	27,183	679	27,862	3,203	215	24,874	8,258	6,051	21,671	19,290	1,808	942
2000	42,213	29,687	542	30,229	3,386	240	27,083	8,707	6,423	23,178	20,694	1,821	965
2001	45,276	31,502	789	32,291	3,624	212	28,878	9,228	7,169	24,718	22,005	1,832	977
2002	46,932	33,268	549	33,817	3,806	194	30,206	8,853	7,873	25,296	22,952	1,855	984
2003	49,042	34,975	572	35,546	3,994	182	31,735	8,877	8,430	26,120	23,895	1,878	1,003
2004	52,094	37,042	877	37,919	4,205	136	33,850	9,252	8,992	27,363	25,087	1,904	1,027
2005	55,782	39,326	880	40,205	4,469	70	35,807	10,272	9,704	28,869	26,242	1,932	1,050
2006	59,702	42,281	610	42,891	4,874	82	38,099	11,017	10,585	30,427	27,443	1,962	1,079
2007	63,189	43,892	875	44,767	5,136	73	39,704	11,964	11,521	31,752	28,551	1,990	1,103
2008	67,065	45,812	732	46,544	5,414	58	41,188	12,632	13,245	33,355	30,234	2,011	1,105
2009	66,679	45,121	412	45,533	5,359	69	40,242	11,770	14,667	32,737	30,131	2,037	1,072
2010	69,262	46,229	887	47,117	5,452	8	41,673	11,711	15,879	33,548	31,022	2,065	1,060
2011	72,821	47,679	1,130	48,809	5,032	-21	43,756	13,002	16,063	35,003	32,108	2,080	1,064
2012	74,584	48,413	1,023	49,436	5,142	-16	44,278	14,288	16,018	35,728	32,836	2,088	1,067
2013	73,406	48,446	995	49,442	5,919	-67	43,456	13,771	16,179	35,076	31,910	2,093	1,075
2014	77,747	49,929	1,259	51,188	6,122	-77	44,989	15,053	17,705	37,194	33,865	2,090	1,083
2015	79,953	51,030	852	51,882	6,447	-56	45,379	15,497	19,077	38,251	34,803	2,090	1,092
2016	81,185	51,355	908	52,263	6,454	-17	45,792	15,858	19,535	38,793	35,326	2,093	1,092
2017	83,127	52,704	954	53,658	6,558	59	47,159	16,422	19,547	39,709	36,187	2,093	1,098
2018	86,328	55,026	849	55,875	6,857	74	49,092	16,961	20,276	41,198	37,655	2,095	1,111
2019	90,847	89,808	1,039	58,992	7,160	82	51,915	17,335	21,597	43,268	39,441	2,100	1,131
2020	96,476	95,383	1,094	58,310	7,137	106	51,278	17,268	27,930	45,803	42,062	2,106	...

... = Not available.

Personal Income and Employment by Region and State: New York

(Millions of dollars, except as noted.)

Year	Personal income, total	Earnings by place of work			Less: Contributions for government social insurance	Plus: Adjustment for residence	Equals: Net earnings by place of residence	Plus: Dividends, interest, and rent	Plus: Personal current transfer receipts	Per capita (dollars)		Population (thousands)	Total employment (thousands)
		Nonfarm	Farm	Total						Personal income	Disposable personal income		
1960	47,939	40,466	353	40,819	2,041	-729	38,050	7,096	2,794	2,847	2,478	16,838	...
1961	50,098	41,996	364	42,360	2,191	-781	39,387	7,504	3,207	2,936	2,543	17,061	...
1962	52,853	44,321	287	44,607	2,490	-866	41,251	8,307	3,295	3,055	2,649	17,301	...
1963	55,174	45,815	336	46,152	2,712	-930	42,509	9,116	3,549	3,160	2,742	17,461	...
1964	58,939	48,567	318	48,885	2,681	-1,026	45,177	10,039	3,723	3,351	2,948	17,589	...
1965	62,625	51,252	366	51,618	2,803	-1,110	47,705	10,904	4,016	3,531	3,097	17,734	...
1966	67,240	55,598	427	56,025	3,720	-1,263	51,042	11,563	4,636	3,768	3,284	17,843	...
1967	72,538	59,464	380	59,844	4,032	-1,404	54,407	12,231	5,900	4,044	3,496	17,935	...
1968	80,062	65,209	388	65,597	4,446	-1,584	59,568	13,281	7,213	4,435	3,807	18,051	...
1969	83,626	70,364	440	70,804	5,291	-3,437	62,076	13,815	7,735	4,619	3,896	18,105	8,494
1970	89,895	74,760	420	75,179	5,534	-3,395	66,251	14,736	8,909	4,920	4,228	18,272	8,466
1971	96,121	79,088	410	79,497	6,030	-3,518	69,949	15,428	10,744	5,234	4,564	18,365	8,345
1972	102,834	84,861	353	85,214	6,796	-3,786	74,633	16,208	11,994	5,603	4,833	18,352	8,348
1973	109,572	90,472	470	90,943	8,413	-3,919	78,611	17,672	13,289	6,022	5,217	18,195	8,465
1974	118,065	95,731	444	96,175	9,188	-4,120	82,867	19,780	15,418	6,533	5,640	18,073	8,392
1975	127,414	100,445	379	100,824	9,452	-4,406	86,966	20,942	19,506	7,066	6,194	18,032	8,172
1976	134,981	106,699	401	107,100	10,248	-4,663	92,189	21,992	20,800	7,510	6,550	17,975	8,125
1977	145,640	115,644	331	115,975	11,010	-5,198	99,767	24,115	21,759	8,158	7,088	17,852	8,199
1978	158,584	127,304	433	127,737	12,375	-5,879	109,483	26,314	22,786	8,949	7,741	17,720	8,384
1979	173,362	139,951	539	140,490	14,082	-6,758	119,649	29,376	24,337	9,831	8,442	17,634	8,581
1980	193,259	153,334	530	153,864	15,430	-7,854	130,580	34,688	27,991	11,001	9,409	17,567	8,602
1981	215,681	168,282	543	168,825	18,083	-8,521	142,221	41,872	31,588	12,277	10,400	17,568	8,666
1982	234,418	180,684	518	181,203	19,681	-9,315	152,207	47,656	34,555	13,327	11,268	17,590	8,673
1983	252,683	195,069	371	195,440	21,224	-9,879	164,337	50,969	37,377	14,286	12,290	17,687	8,730
1984	279,484	215,022	494	215,517	23,937	-10,582	180,997	58,927	39,559	15,749	13,587	17,746	9,003
1985	299,164	232,681	561	233,242	26,272	-11,352	195,618	61,790	41,755	16,815	14,409	17,792	9,227
1986	319,479	251,553	654	252,207	28,844	-11,969	211,394	63,839	44,246	17,915	15,338	17,833	9,424
1987	340,643	272,882	732	273,613	30,680	-12,771	230,163	65,093	45,387	19,064	16,160	17,869	9,472
1988	373,665	300,763	645	301,408	34,031	-13,698	253,679	71,692	48,295	20,827	17,865	17,941	9,684
1989	403,910	317,544	777	318,320	35,481	-13,758	269,082	81,805	53,023	22,461	19,156	17,983	9,752
1990	432,318	337,820	775	338,594	35,787	-13,471	289,337	84,816	58,165	23,990	20,644	18,021	9,727
1991	432,543	332,725	647	333,372	36,733	-13,448	283,190	84,609	64,744	23,868	20,645	18,123	9,483
1992	457,271	355,360	749	356,109	38,353	-16,580	301,176	83,732	72,364	25,061	21,711	18,247	9,410
1993	470,054	363,633	793	364,427	39,223	-16,351	308,852	84,348	76,854	25,581	22,080	18,375	9,431
1994	484,731	372,726	672	373,398	40,889	-16,345	316,164	87,966	80,601	26,259	22,662	18,459	9,465
1995	510,818	390,103	538	390,641	42,381	-18,578	329,683	95,361	85,775	27,576	23,746	18,524	9,511
1996	537,882	412,086	767	412,853	43,658	-21,430	347,765	100,682	89,435	28,936	24,705	18,588	9,595
1997	567,956	440,716	456	441,172	45,606	-23,990	371,576	107,042	89,338	30,443	25,810	18,657	9,732
1998	600,536	469,005	688	469,693	47,880	-27,293	394,521	112,688	93,328	32,019	26,900	18,756	9,901
1999	636,315	504,751	769	505,520	50,242	-28,503	426,775	113,373	96,167	33,698	28,157	18,883	10,165
2000	684,898	547,861	778	548,639	54,137	-32,299	462,203	122,049	100,646	36,044	30,019	19,002	10,425
2001	709,931	571,260	930	572,190	56,439	-33,137	482,615	120,104	107,213	37,203	30,625	19,083	10,439
2002	707,720	568,084	713	568,797	57,356	-30,952	480,489	110,645	116,586	36,980	31,712	19,138	10,348
2003	718,702	573,248	876	574,125	59,158	-31,551	483,415	113,783	121,503	37,479	32,460	19,176	10,378
2004	753,191	599,326	1,090	600,415	62,073	-36,228	502,115	120,202	130,874	39,287	33,857	19,172	10,513
2005	787,298	619,185	1,061	620,245	64,894	-40,207	515,145	141,828	130,326	41,150	34,977	19,133	10,655
2006	847,002	663,219	925	664,144	68,629	-46,842	548,673	160,836	137,493	44,335	37,164	19,105	10,810
2007	911,071	711,219	1,316	712,535	72,625	-55,898	584,012	183,377	143,683	47,619	39,419	19,132	11,083
2008	927,177	717,130	1,526	718,656	75,327	-56,378	586,952	183,154	157,071	48,259	40,026	19,212	11,198
2009	914,586	695,374	949	696,323	73,029	-43,993	579,300	163,224	172,062	47,371	41,096	19,307	10,984
2010	954,365	731,563	1,516	733,079	74,823	-50,246	608,010	163,883	182,471	49,194	42,472	19,400	11,006
2011	1,009,303	761,148	1,827	762,975	68,971	-53,964	640,041	183,630	185,633	51,763	44,085	19,499	11,294
2012	1,065,474	796,498	1,817	798,315	70,738	-56,380	671,198	209,988	184,288	54,432	46,673	19,575	11,433
2013	1,081,133	817,167	2,190	819,357	83,125	-56,260	679,972	215,285	185,876	55,081	46,264	19,628	11,619
2014	1,125,897	847,607	2,217	849,823	87,691	-60,142	701,990	233,822	190,085	57,279	47,900	19,656	11,867
2015	1,172,713	877,288	1,399	878,686	91,611	-62,757	724,318	247,741	200,654	59,645	49,564	19,661	12,100
2016	1,208,346	905,046	1,133	906,179	94,440	-64,221	747,518	254,950	205,878	61,520	51,645	19,642	12,260
2017	1,281,082	957,411	1,235	958,647	99,814	-73,448	785,385	268,993	226,705	65,392	55,114	19,591	12,436
2018	1,341,915	1,001,978	898	1,002,876	104,871	-77,352	820,652	283,754	237,509	68,667	58,256	19,542	12,651
2019	1,395,148	1,393,633	1,514	1,052,941	106,619	-82,910	863,411	302,178	229,559	71,682	60,329	19,463	12,874
2020	1,460,860	1,459,004	1,856	1,029,235	104,896	-80,591	843,748	297,123	319,989	75,548	64,398	19,337	...

... = Not available.

Personal Income and Employment by Region and State: North Carolina

(Millions of dollars, except as noted.)

Year	Personal income, total	Earnings by place of work			Less: Contributions for government social insurance	Plus: Adjustment for residence	Equals: Net earnings by place of residence	Plus: Dividends, interest, and rent	Plus: Personal current transfer receipts	Per capita (dollars)		Population (thousands)	Total employment (thousands)
		Nonfarm	Farm	Total						Personal income	Disposable personal income		
1960	7,618	5,979	604	6,583	307	10	6,287	874	457	1,666	1,517	4,573	...
1961	8,064	6,250	645	6,895	314	10	6,591	950	524	1,729	1,576	4,663	...
1962	8,661	6,763	627	7,391	347	11	7,055	1,054	552	1,840	1,668	4,707	...
1963	9,110	7,182	606	7,788	412	11	7,387	1,128	595	1,921	1,737	4,742	...
1964	9,868	7,796	634	8,431	435	12	8,007	1,238	623	2,055	1,880	4,802	...
1965	10,671	8,580	532	9,113	467	11	8,656	1,336	679	2,194	1,989	4,863	...
1966	11,855	9,662	618	10,280	617	11	9,673	1,444	738	2,421	2,182	4,896	...
1967	12,817	10,510	607	11,117	716	10	10,412	1,546	859	2,588	2,335	4,952	...
1968	14,136	11,783	518	12,301	826	13	11,487	1,667	981	2,825	2,516	5,004	...
1969	15,858	13,023	673	13,695	900	19	12,814	1,937	1,107	3,152	2,772	5,031	2,458
1970	17,320	13,993	672	14,665	971	20	13,713	2,270	1,338	3,397	3,008	5,099	2,469
1971	18,857	15,279	627	15,906	1,102	15	14,819	2,469	1,569	3,626	3,238	5,201	2,490
1972	21,319	17,367	750	18,117	1,309	9	16,817	2,745	1,757	4,025	3,550	5,296	2,602
1973	24,175	19,497	1,162	20,658	1,678	7	18,988	3,148	2,038	4,491	3,986	5,382	2,720
1974	26,654	21,242	1,110	22,351	1,901	13	20,463	3,658	2,533	4,881	4,306	5,461	2,743
1975	28,943	22,287	1,066	23,353	1,978	15	21,390	4,030	3,523	5,229	4,723	5,535	2,647
1976	32,132	25,041	1,148	26,189	2,272	14	23,931	4,403	3,798	5,745	5,128	5,593	2,754
1977	35,208	27,878	857	28,734	2,513	19	26,240	4,961	4,007	6,211	5,520	5,668	2,851
1978	39,736	31,523	1,142	32,665	2,920	18	29,763	5,659	4,315	6,922	6,125	5,740	2,946
1979	43,908	35,226	757	35,982	3,390	8	32,601	6,375	4,933	7,568	6,638	5,802	3,046
1980	49,247	38,582	651	39,233	3,717	11	35,528	7,822	5,898	8,348	7,320	5,899	3,052
1981	55,497	42,422	1,049	43,472	4,380	-29	39,062	9,637	6,798	9,317	8,154	5,957	3,072
1982	59,420	44,527	1,064	45,591	4,635	-41	40,916	10,936	7,568	9,872	8,762	6,019	3,042
1983	64,645	49,212	635	49,847	5,173	-59	44,615	11,875	8,155	10,637	9,411	6,077	3,129
1984	73,126	55,475	1,292	56,767	5,969	-95	50,703	13,808	8,615	11,863	10,535	6,164	3,292
1985	79,020	60,390	1,161	61,550	6,589	-157	54,804	14,979	9,237	12,635	11,179	6,254	3,392
1986	85,195	65,521	1,145	66,666	7,294	-219	59,153	16,214	9,827	13,477	11,920	6,322	3,494
1987	91,885	71,603	1,141	72,744	7,869	-301	64,574	17,091	10,220	14,349	12,591	6,404	3,610
1988	100,590	78,140	1,477	79,617	8,838	-363	70,416	19,097	11,077	15,522	13,707	6,481	3,751
1989	109,693	83,798	1,722	85,519	9,490	-418	75,611	21,715	12,367	16,708	14,661	6,565	3,838
1990	116,523	88,317	2,135	90,452	10,257	-458	79,738	23,111	13,674	17,485	15,425	6,664	3,902
1991	121,893	91,320	2,394	93,715	10,747	-440	82,527	23,642	15,724	17,967	15,926	6,784	3,866
1992	132,675	100,252	2,340	102,592	11,649	-465	90,479	24,787	17,409	19,236	17,103	6,897	3,964
1993	141,458	106,326	2,613	108,939	12,435	-481	96,022	26,302	19,134	20,085	17,824	7,043	4,087
1994	150,583	113,462	2,826	116,288	13,399	-546	102,343	28,332	19,908	20,951	18,521	7,187	4,201
1995	161,487	120,481	2,710	123,191	14,228	-618	108,345	30,837	22,305	21,987	19,386	7,345	4,355
1996	172,817	127,553	2,996	130,549	14,926	-682	114,941	33,660	24,216	23,040	20,244	7,501	4,459
1997	185,688	137,434	3,064	140,498	15,978	-760	123,760	36,510	25,418	24,251	21,205	7,657	4,603
1998	198,160	148,217	2,409	150,625	17,207	-738	132,681	39,054	26,425	25,375	22,012	7,809	4,708
1999	208,306	157,709	2,240	159,949	18,335	-807	140,807	39,438	28,062	26,204	22,763	7,949	4,802
2000	221,868	167,496	2,965	170,462	19,428	-921	150,113	41,729	30,026	27,453	23,778	8,082	4,892
2001	228,432	170,991	3,122	174,113	20,100	-930	153,083	41,845	33,504	27,823	24,153	8,210	4,855
2002	231,806	174,692	1,515	176,207	20,369	-899	154,938	40,604	36,264	27,841	24,674	8,326	4,842
2003	241,165	181,782	1,595	183,377	21,376	-756	161,245	41,781	38,139	28,633	25,645	8,423	4,852
2004	261,528	195,607	2,374	197,981	22,463	-757	174,762	45,649	41,117	30,577	27,525	8,553	4,962
2005	281,073	208,311	3,208	211,519	24,022	-826	186,671	49,771	44,631	32,287	28,801	8,705	5,093
2006	305,337	226,964	2,607	229,571	25,771	-1,010	202,790	53,889	48,659	34,241	30,407	8,917	5,252
2007	328,910	243,046	2,293	245,340	27,518	-1,240	216,582	59,985	52,344	36,072	31,889	9,118	5,431
2008	350,373	255,263	2,243	257,505	28,279	-1,272	227,956	62,967	59,450	37,636	33,578	9,309	5,414
2009	337,787	240,899	2,269	243,168	27,493	-1,046	214,630	56,659	66,498	35,746	32,613	9,450	5,216
2010	340,764	241,363	2,399	243,762	27,813	-962	214,988	55,132	70,644	35,592	32,354	9,574	5,178
2011	354,294	245,402	2,063	247,464	25,927	-891	220,647	61,270	72,378	36,689	32,951	9,657	5,293
2012	379,031	264,182	2,890	267,072	26,956	-939	239,177	65,877	73,977	38,878	35,102	9,749	5,356
2013	375,057	263,347	3,413	266,760	31,308	-847	234,605	65,062	75,390	38,102	34,002	9,844	5,437
2014	397,411	276,321	3,707	280,028	32,874	-903	246,251	72,736	78,423	40,005	35,720	9,934	5,561
2015	419,889	290,879	3,127	294,005	34,556	-1,124	258,325	78,718	82,845	41,850	37,098	10,033	5,696
2016	433,766	301,251	2,544	303,795	35,607	-1,313	266,875	81,287	85,605	42,707	37,796	10,157	5,829
2017	454,307	315,719	3,035	318,754	36,977	-1,375	280,402	84,973	88,932	44,233	39,181	10,271	5,920
2018	475,927	330,184	3,366	333,549	38,720	-1,491	293,338	89,327	93,262	45,834	40,779	10,384	6,057
2019	500,974	498,930	2,043	351,656	40,230	-1,506	309,920	93,303	97,751	47,706	42,513	10,501	6,189
2020	530,956	529,528	1,428	357,382	41,509	-1,620	314,253	92,508	124,195	50,086	44,863	10,601	...

... = Not available.

Personal Income and Employment by Region and State: North Dakota

(Millions of dollars, except as noted.)

Year	Personal income, total	Derivation of personal income								Per capita (dollars)		Population (thousands)	Total employment (thousands)
		Earnings by place of work			Less: Contributions for government social insurance	Plus: Adjustment for residence	Equals: Net earnings by place of residence	Plus: Dividends, interest, and rent	Plus: Personal current transfer receipts	Personal income	Disposable personal income		
		Nonfarm	Farm	Total									
1960	1,210	716	273	989	41	-12	937	190	83	1,909	1,764	634	...
1961	1,109	750	145	894	43	-12	840	179	90	1,730	1,593	641	...
1962	1,555	812	478	1,290	47	-14	1,229	232	94	2,441	2,268	637	...
1963	1,448	865	328	1,193	56	-14	1,123	228	98	2,249	2,072	644	...
1964	1,441	932	241	1,173	59	-17	1,097	239	104	2,220	2,051	649	...
1965	1,677	995	382	1,377	62	-17	1,298	265	114	2,584	2,402	649	...
1966	1,697	1,048	349	1,397	74	-16	1,307	267	123	2,623	2,422	647	...
1967	1,699	1,077	310	1,388	89	-16	1,282	270	147	2,714	2,489	626	...
1968	1,778	1,147	285	1,431	95	-16	1,320	294	164	2,864	2,624	621	...
1969	1,991	1,251	385	1,635	102	-55	1,478	330	183	3,205	2,889	621	274
1970	2,102	1,392	306	1,698	115	-58	1,525	365	212	3,397	3,088	619	281
1971	2,424	1,526	434	1,959	129	-60	1,770	406	248	3,868	3,573	627	284
1972	2,887	1,706	668	2,373	147	-64	2,162	449	276	4,576	4,215	631	288
1973	4,037	1,921	1,529	3,449	189	-68	3,193	534	310	6,383	5,880	632	300
1974	3,998	2,163	1,164	3,327	224	-79	3,024	619	356	6,304	5,635	634	308
1975	4,182	2,439	945	3,384	256	-83	3,045	716	420	6,549	5,881	638	314
1976	4,102	2,773	478	3,250	294	-97	2,860	777	465	6,357	5,704	645	326
1977	4,261	3,004	274	3,278	303	-103	2,873	882	507	6,564	5,918	649	331
1978	5,358	3,419	865	4,284	354	-113	3,818	987	553	8,235	7,398	651	345
1979	5,507	3,822	502	4,324	412	-130	3,783	1,112	613	8,445	7,565	652	353
1980	5,270	4,149	-383	3,766	450	-145	3,170	1,375	725	8,053	7,077	654	355
1981	6,899	4,637	372	5,009	533	-166	4,310	1,758	831	10,462	9,218	660	359
1982	7,453	4,903	306	5,209	576	-168	4,465	2,057	932	11,141	10,032	669	360
1983	7,831	5,163	366	5,529	613	-171	4,745	2,050	1,036	11,573	10,503	677	365
1984	8,458	5,361	612	5,973	652	-170	5,151	2,197	1,111	12,429	11,322	680	366
1985	8,741	5,453	699	6,152	678	-170	5,304	2,256	1,180	12,912	11,775	677	364
1986	8,870	5,510	693	6,203	698	-168	5,337	2,246	1,287	13,248	12,141	670	357
1987	9,133	5,736	789	6,525	727	-168	5,629	2,158	1,346	13,814	12,601	661	363
1988	8,467	5,984	-61	5,924	794	-175	4,954	2,159	1,353	12,920	11,669	655	366
1989	9,483	6,233	442	6,675	840	-180	5,655	2,353	1,474	14,671	13,292	646	370
1990	10,257	6,591	773	7,363	933	-184	6,246	2,432	1,578	16,084	14,590	638	374
1991	10,388	6,936	614	7,550	1,002	-191	6,357	2,426	1,605	16,340	14,795	636	382
1992	11,392	7,373	1,074	8,447	1,064	-206	7,176	2,444	1,772	17,849	16,256	638	388
1993	11,548	7,876	624	8,500	1,146	-225	7,129	2,552	1,867	18,009	16,303	641	397
1994	12,548	8,363	1,059	9,422	1,221	-241	7,961	2,686	1,901	19,460	17,688	645	411
1995	12,571	8,787	429	9,215	1,270	-262	7,684	2,877	2,010	19,404	17,530	648	418
1996	14,066	9,280	1,308	10,588	1,327	-294	8,967	3,006	2,093	21,627	19,626	650	426
1997	13,771	9,766	304	10,070	1,374	-321	8,375	3,215	2,182	21,196	19,052	650	430
1998	15,196	10,323	972	11,295	1,439	-344	9,513	3,474	2,209	23,467	21,198	648	435
1999	15,429	10,862	692	11,554	1,478	-370	9,705	3,419	2,304	23,948	21,617	644	436
2000	16,805	11,500	1,100	12,600	1,550	-404	10,646	3,686	2,472	26,175	23,662	642	441
2001	17,127	12,056	801	12,857	1,591	-432	10,833	3,757	2,537	26,800	24,131	639	445
2002	17,528	12,614	603	13,218	1,648	-447	11,123	3,717	2,689	27,466	25,150	638	443
2003	19,022	13,273	1,480	14,753	1,737	-469	12,546	3,689	2,788	29,777	27,524	639	444
2004	19,341	14,153	958	15,111	1,840	-522	12,750	3,644	2,948	30,000	27,700	645	453
2005	20,416	14,896	1,157	16,053	1,919	-570	13,564	3,745	3,107	31,599	28,968	646	462
2006	21,434	15,947	750	16,696	2,011	-635	14,051	4,069	3,314	33,005	29,971	649	471
2007	23,799	16,792	1,678	18,470	2,114	-704	15,653	4,594	3,552	36,455	32,930	653	483
2008	26,710	18,012	2,375	20,387	2,262	-762	17,364	5,329	4,018	40,620	36,498	658	492
2009	26,507	18,946	1,525	20,471	2,420	-803	17,249	5,059	4,200	39,863	36,555	665	492
2010	29,446	20,841	2,090	22,930	2,504	-967	19,460	5,443	4,543	43,643	39,820	675	504
2011	32,934	23,830	1,956	25,786	2,625	-1,322	21,839	6,445	4,650	48,068	43,057	685	530
2012	38,866	27,822	3,538	31,359	2,844	-1,901	26,614	7,560	4,692	55,435	49,471	701	567
2013	38,867	29,961	1,897	31,858	3,477	-2,292	26,090	7,921	4,857	53,833	47,472	722	587
2014	41,368	33,188	860	34,048	3,867	-2,635	27,546	8,763	5,059	56,101	49,483	737	608
2015	40,430	32,402	280	32,682	3,849	-2,393	26,440	8,666	5,324	53,619	47,788	754	599
2016	39,766	30,354	820	31,173	3,665	-1,982	25,527	8,709	5,531	52,716	47,512	754	579
2017	39,484	30,589	70	30,659	3,801	-2,080	24,778	9,063	5,642	52,284	47,006	755	578
2018	41,277	31,805	262	32,067	3,979	-2,173	25,915	9,467	5,895	54,306	49,056	760	578
2019	43,614	42,548	1,067	34,209	3,955	-2,393	27,861	9,446	6,308	57,108	51,669	764	587
2020	45,450	43,708	1,742	33,628	3,828	-2,268	27,532	9,375	8,544	59,388	54,236	765	...

... = Not available.

Personal Income and Employment by Region and State: Ohio

(Millions of dollars, except as noted.)

Year	Personal income, total	Earnings by place of work			Less: Contributions for government social insurance	Plus: Adjustment for residence	Equals: Net earnings by place of residence	Plus: Dividends, interest, and rent	Plus: Personal current transfer receipts	Per capita (dollars)		Population (thousands)	Total employment (thousands)
		Nonfarm	Farm	Total						Personal income	Disposable personal income		
1960	23,455	19,684	334	20,018	1,003	-131	18,884	3,060	1,512	2,410	2,139	9,734	...
1961	23,910	19,655	373	20,028	984	-122	18,922	3,227	1,760	2,426	2,167	9,854	...
1962	25,207	20,898	336	21,234	1,125	-126	19,983	3,493	1,731	2,539	2,258	9,929	...
1963	26,265	21,806	334	22,140	1,236	-129	20,775	3,708	1,782	2,630	2,336	9,986	...
1964	28,028	23,456	305	23,761	1,355	-134	22,272	3,967	1,789	2,781	2,505	10,080	...
1965	30,302	25,392	358	25,750	1,409	-147	24,195	4,214	1,893	2,970	2,659	10,201	...
1966	33,057	28,058	496	28,554	1,864	-166	26,524	4,495	2,039	3,200	2,850	10,330	...
1967	34,630	29,319	329	29,648	1,958	-160	27,529	4,722	2,379	3,325	2,959	10,414	...
1968	38,207	32,237	412	32,649	2,134	-183	30,332	5,186	2,690	3,633	3,194	10,516	...
1969	41,801	35,425	417	35,843	2,360	-200	33,284	5,617	2,900	3,957	3,432	10,563	4,695
1970	44,142	36,735	435	37,170	2,408	-183	34,579	6,168	3,396	4,137	3,640	10,669	4,683
1971	46,980	38,635	415	39,050	2,603	-134	36,313	6,654	4,014	4,376	3,911	10,735	4,627
1972	50,968	42,041	506	42,547	2,985	-133	39,429	7,101	4,438	4,743	4,173	10,747	4,710
1973	56,552	46,849	667	47,516	3,864	-158	43,494	7,893	5,166	5,252	4,626	10,767	4,902
1974	61,925	50,430	798	51,228	4,310	-134	46,784	8,939	6,203	5,752	5,051	10,766	4,964
1975	66,162	52,187	814	53,001	4,336	-93	48,572	9,658	7,933	6,143	5,444	10,770	4,809
1976	72,598	58,033	787	58,820	4,942	-108	53,770	10,325	8,502	6,752	5,945	10,753	4,889
1977	80,397	65,044	675	65,718	5,554	-114	60,050	11,417	8,930	7,464	6,530	10,771	5,034
1978	88,855	72,503	628	73,130	6,397	-136	66,598	12,662	9,594	8,231	7,180	10,795	5,206
1979	98,136	79,674	762	80,435	7,322	-172	72,942	14,241	10,953	9,088	7,871	10,799	5,291
1980	107,185	83,320	575	83,895	7,612	-194	76,089	17,285	13,811	9,924	8,646	10,801	5,204
1981	116,652	89,154	167	89,321	8,708	-483	80,130	21,175	15,348	10,813	9,365	10,788	5,135
1982	122,082	90,048	270	90,318	8,900	-609	80,810	23,462	17,810	11,349	9,952	10,757	4,967
1983	129,133	95,299	-69	95,230	9,613	-711	84,906	25,181	19,045	12,026	10,560	10,738	4,960
1984	142,661	105,804	874	106,678	10,932	-842	94,904	28,108	19,649	13,286	11,737	10,738	5,160
1985	151,426	113,033	870	113,904	11,870	-919	101,115	29,366	20,944	14,106	12,423	10,735	5,287
1986	158,493	118,945	684	119,629	12,856	-952	105,821	30,487	22,185	14,771	13,034	10,730	5,401
1987	166,090	125,890	734	126,624	13,614	-995	112,015	31,024	23,052	15,436	13,511	10,760	5,548
1988	178,268	136,113	783	136,896	15,149	-1,042	120,705	33,330	24,233	16,508	14,519	10,799	5,682
1989	191,708	144,483	1,171	145,654	16,209	-1,105	128,340	37,537	25,831	17,703	15,494	10,829	5,803
1990	202,980	152,071	1,205	153,276	17,415	-1,093	134,767	39,473	28,740	18,683	16,380	10,864	5,863
1991	207,677	156,084	702	156,786	18,308	-1,115	137,363	39,326	30,988	18,973	16,690	10,946	5,842
1992	221,201	166,674	1,184	167,858	19,470	-1,230	147,158	40,009	34,034	20,056	17,695	11,029	5,854
1993	230,366	174,334	933	175,267	20,592	-1,327	153,348	41,629	35,389	20,752	18,259	11,101	5,960
1994	243,307	185,104	1,162	186,265	22,172	-1,450	162,643	43,920	36,744	21,816	19,163	11,152	6,136
1995	255,101	192,988	891	193,879	23,353	-1,491	169,036	47,291	38,774	22,771	19,937	11,203	6,300
1996	267,147	201,099	1,250	202,348	24,062	-1,546	176,741	50,197	40,209	23,762	20,641	11,243	6,395
1997	282,809	212,537	1,684	214,221	24,790	-1,644	187,788	53,598	41,423	25,078	21,713	11,277	6,500
1998	299,076	226,220	1,270	227,491	25,558	-1,819	200,113	56,780	42,183	26,440	22,811	11,312	6,599
1999	309,266	237,388	851	238,238	26,717	-1,789	209,733	56,012	43,521	27,283	23,574	11,335	6,681
2000	325,952	248,750	1,208	249,958	27,074	-1,749	221,135	58,550	46,267	28,684	24,735	11,364	6,789
2001	334,714	254,539	1,139	255,679	27,710	-1,737	226,232	58,075	50,407	29,393	25,422	11,387	6,726
2002	339,908	259,456	584	260,040	27,770	-1,758	230,512	55,575	53,820	29,796	26,237	11,408	6,640
2003	349,796	267,397	796	268,193	28,879	-1,771	237,543	55,874	56,380	30,591	27,235	11,435	6,621
2004	363,250	278,685	1,421	280,107	30,585	-1,716	247,806	56,510	58,934	31,719	28,292	11,452	6,667
2005	374,068	284,831	1,076	285,907	31,413	-1,731	252,762	58,881	62,424	32,632	28,923	11,463	6,709
2006	393,111	296,182	946	297,128	32,780	-1,885	262,463	64,900	65,749	34,240	30,244	11,481	6,747
2007	409,696	304,152	1,197	305,349	33,588	-1,974	269,787	69,912	69,998	35,624	31,367	11,500	6,795
2008	422,895	307,648	1,260	308,908	34,516	-1,965	272,427	71,583	78,885	36,724	32,501	11,515	6,725
2009	410,864	295,081	1,574	296,656	33,450	-1,837	261,369	63,568	85,927	35,638	32,326	11,529	6,455
2010	423,062	303,736	1,579	305,316	33,656	-1,795	269,864	62,505	90,693	36,663	33,124	11,539	6,418
2011	451,901	319,958	2,860	322,818	31,791	-1,923	289,104	69,672	93,125	39,148	35,018	11,543	6,522
2012	469,904	334,603	1,927	336,530	32,846	-1,888	301,796	76,831	91,277	40,690	36,443	11,548	6,606
2013	476,450	345,355	3,042	348,397	36,901	-2,316	309,180	74,025	93,245	41,156	36,632	11,577	6,681
2014	496,514	356,348	1,955	358,302	38,059	-2,552	317,692	81,066	97,755	42,792	38,131	11,603	6,771
2015	515,905	369,139	659	369,798	39,416	-2,614	327,767	86,475	101,663	44,406	39,476	11,618	6,860
2016	525,057	374,829	680	375,508	40,868	-2,649	331,992	88,821	104,244	45,127	40,131	11,635	6,929
2017	544,829	390,432	191	390,623	43,196	-2,577	344,851	93,109	106,869	46,710	41,541	11,664	6,995
2018	563,926	403,744	321	404,065	44,937	-2,607	356,521	97,239	110,166	48,242	43,093	11,689	7,066
2019	586,784	585,965	819	418,505	45,681	-2,429	370,395	102,341	114,048	50,167	44,838	11,697	7,142
2020	623,207	622,125	1,082	418,549	46,195	-2,535	369,818	101,040	152,349	53,296	47,996	11,693	...

... = Not available.

Personal Income and Employment by Region and State: Oklahoma

(Millions of dollars, except as noted.)

Year	Personal income, total	Earnings by place of work			Less: Contributions for government social insurance	Plus: Adjustment for residence	Equals: Net earnings by place of residence	Plus: Dividends, interest, and rent	Plus: Personal current transfer receipts	Per capita (dollars)		Population (thousands)	Total employment (thousands)
		Nonfarm	Farm	Total						Personal income	Disposable personal income		
1960	4,612	3,359	335	3,694	150	7	3,550	684	378	1,974	1,789	2,336	...
1961	4,774	3,492	301	3,793	159	9	3,643	715	416	2,006	1,811	2,380	...
1962	4,985	3,723	240	3,963	178	11	3,796	749	441	2,054	1,853	2,427	...
1963	5,151	3,889	214	4,104	208	12	3,908	773	471	2,112	1,907	2,439	...
1964	5,519	4,180	208	4,388	208	14	4,195	833	491	2,256	2,056	2,446	...
1965	5,913	4,415	278	4,693	216	17	4,494	894	526	2,424	2,209	2,440	...
1966	6,343	4,812	267	5,079	286	21	4,814	946	584	2,585	2,343	2,454	...
1967	6,929	5,274	276	5,550	337	25	5,239	991	700	2,784	2,519	2,489	...
1968	7,589	5,856	219	6,076	385	31	5,721	1,080	789	3,032	2,726	2,503	...
1969	8,455	6,400	275	6,676	401	64	6,338	1,261	856	3,335	2,954	2,535	1,107
1970	9,326	6,897	359	7,256	431	65	6,890	1,454	981	3,634	3,257	2,566	1,120
1971	10,164	7,484	335	7,819	484	64	7,400	1,633	1,131	3,882	3,522	2,618	1,132
1972	11,153	8,246	417	8,664	558	73	8,179	1,735	1,240	4,197	3,754	2,657	1,183
1973	12,653	9,142	734	9,875	720	83	9,238	2,009	1,406	4,696	4,237	2,694	1,221
1974	14,080	10,379	452	10,831	845	106	10,092	2,324	1,664	5,153	4,576	2,732	1,256
1975	15,736	11,485	404	11,889	928	142	11,103	2,581	2,052	5,677	5,116	2,772	1,269
1976	17,349	12,810	338	13,148	1,054	177	12,270	2,828	2,251	6,145	5,503	2,823	1,305
1977	19,296	14,590	183	14,773	1,198	152	13,728	3,176	2,393	6,733	5,993	2,866	1,359
1978	21,896	16,739	174	16,913	1,418	149	15,644	3,678	2,575	7,517	6,623	2,913	1,428
1979	25,415	19,128	634	19,762	1,688	162	18,236	4,224	2,955	8,557	7,517	2,970	1,481
1980	29,279	22,149	265	22,413	1,971	170	20,612	5,248	3,419	9,629	8,399	3,041	1,547
1981	34,204	25,621	330	25,952	2,450	198	23,699	6,623	3,882	11,047	9,492	3,096	1,625
1982	38,176	28,022	487	28,509	2,748	204	25,965	7,835	4,376	11,907	10,157	3,206	1,673
1983	39,077	28,143	214	28,357	2,739	241	25,858	8,417	4,801	11,876	10,470	3,290	1,638
1984	41,927	29,974	376	30,351	2,969	289	27,671	9,275	4,982	12,761	11,354	3,286	1,665
1985	43,606	30,826	382	31,208	3,109	331	28,430	9,854	5,322	13,330	11,869	3,271	1,648
1986	43,882	30,715	645	31,360	3,161	382	28,580	9,644	5,658	13,491	12,279	3,253	1,588
1987	43,754	30,681	564	31,245	3,181	429	28,493	9,375	5,886	13,630	12,241	3,210	1,599
1988	45,620	31,950	765	32,715	3,498	478	29,694	9,695	6,231	14,405	12,936	3,167	1,608
1989	48,521	33,778	802	34,580	3,731	505	31,354	10,539	6,629	15,402	13,754	3,150	1,623
1990	51,121	35,735	862	36,597	4,066	568	33,099	10,889	7,133	16,235	14,319	3,149	1,655
1991	52,678	37,115	623	37,738	4,324	597	34,011	10,862	7,804	16,589	14,774	3,175	1,668
1992	56,034	39,331	844	40,175	4,550	618	36,244	11,060	8,730	17,399	15,567	3,221	1,680
1993	58,247	41,115	867	41,982	4,798	657	37,841	11,226	9,180	17,910	16,032	3,252	1,716
1994	60,818	42,739	826	43,565	5,058	714	39,221	11,845	9,753	18,537	16,561	3,281	1,748
1995	63,427	44,418	286	44,704	5,276	747	40,175	12,719	10,533	19,173	17,118	3,308	1,800
1996	67,223	47,018	359	47,377	5,474	780	42,682	13,486	11,055	20,126	17,883	3,340	1,850
1997	71,075	49,951	662	50,613	5,734	859	45,738	13,978	11,359	21,072	18,590	3,373	1,897
1998	75,062	52,879	518	53,397	6,033	893	48,257	15,216	11,589	22,043	19,417	3,405	1,939
1999	77,068	54,004	839	54,843	6,218	939	49,564	15,399	12,105	22,422	19,723	3,437	1,953
2000	83,364	58,212	831	59,044	6,600	1,019	53,463	17,104	12,797	24,133	21,233	3,454	1,994
2001	88,354	62,083	815	62,899	7,047	1,014	56,865	17,357	14,132	25,484	22,427	3,467	2,009
2002	90,233	63,593	979	64,572	7,256	987	58,302	16,833	15,098	25,862	23,262	3,489	1,987
2003	94,303	66,895	961	67,856	7,473	968	61,351	16,861	16,091	26,906	24,434	3,505	1,971
2004	101,714	72,789	1,265	74,054	7,998	950	67,006	17,710	16,999	28,853	26,283	3,525	1,998
2005	111,052	79,876	1,306	81,183	8,476	912	73,619	19,173	18,261	31,295	28,262	3,549	2,043
2006	123,412	88,925	688	89,613	9,116	884	81,382	22,027	20,004	34,337	30,838	3,594	2,096
2007	127,819	89,778	676	90,453	9,593	848	81,708	24,663	21,447	35,170	31,415	3,634	2,150
2008	141,464	99,901	793	100,694	10,044	793	91,443	25,963	24,058	38,557	34,572	3,669	2,187
2009	131,405	91,165	52	91,217	9,852	682	82,046	23,414	25,945	35,347	32,494	3,718	2,137
2010	137,328	94,771	809	95,579	10,092	615	86,102	23,538	27,688	36,527	33,580	3,760	2,130
2011	147,778	101,109	1,342	102,452	9,730	564	93,286	26,469	28,023	39,014	35,385	3,788	2,159
2012	158,236	108,510	1,756	110,267	10,320	555	100,501	29,093	28,642	41,438	37,649	3,819	2,212
2013	165,860	118,040	1,785	119,825	11,897	475	108,402	28,200	29,258	43,045	38,989	3,853	2,248
2014	176,377	125,002	2,657	127,659	12,223	465	115,902	30,207	30,269	45,477	41,217	3,878	2,273
2015	172,636	120,361	1,925	122,287	12,288	425	110,423	30,850	31,363	44,154	39,907	3,910	2,286
2016	165,107	112,277	985	113,263	12,193	455	101,525	31,162	32,421	42,047	38,073	3,927	2,285
2017	174,435	120,047	1,005	121,053	12,745	410	108,718	32,423	33,295	44,356	40,264	3,933	2,302
2018	181,886	126,243	845	127,087	13,388	421	114,120	33,506	34,260	46,128	42,011	3,943	2,311
2019	187,328	186,048	1,280	129,187	13,696	452	115,942	34,941	36,445	47,297	42,991	3,961	2,337
2020	196,051	194,613	1,438	126,464	13,561	494	113,398	34,707	47,947	49,249	45,070	3,981	...

... = Not available.

Personal Income and Employment by Region and State: Oregon

(Millions of dollars, except as noted.)

Year	Personal income, total	Derivation of personal income								Per capita (dollars)		Population (thousands)	Total employment (thousands)
		Earnings by place of work			Less: Contributions for government social insurance	Plus: Adjustment for residence	Equals: Net earnings by place of residence	Plus: Dividends, interest, and rent	Plus: Personal current transfer receipts	Personal income	Disposable personal income		
		Nonfarm	Farm	Total									
1960	4,192	3,290	174	3,463	207	-18	3,238	650	304	2,366	2,083	1,772	...
1961	4,351	3,378	161	3,539	211	-19	3,309	690	352	2,435	2,163	1,787	...
1962	4,622	3,606	172	3,778	232	-23	3,524	739	359	2,542	2,249	1,818	...
1963	4,867	3,849	163	4,012	266	-27	3,718	778	371	2,626	2,304	1,853	...
1964	5,236	4,178	150	4,328	271	-33	4,025	828	384	2,773	2,451	1,888	...
1965	5,681	4,540	168	4,708	276	-39	4,394	872	414	2,933	2,610	1,937	...
1966	6,118	4,942	195	5,137	352	-42	4,742	929	447	3,107	2,747	1,969	...
1967	6,487	5,198	185	5,383	392	-47	4,945	1,010	533	3,278	2,899	1,979	...
1968	7,063	5,693	183	5,876	444	-54	5,378	1,085	601	3,524	3,085	2,004	...
1969	7,832	6,225	226	6,451	482	-82	5,887	1,283	662	3,798	3,273	2,062	920
1970	8,537	6,605	216	6,821	505	-63	6,254	1,479	805	4,065	3,564	2,100	926
1971	9,383	7,232	204	7,437	569	-52	6,817	1,634	932	4,364	3,861	2,150	951
1972	10,511	8,165	259	8,424	679	-45	7,700	1,789	1,022	4,788	4,197	2,195	1,001
1973	11,845	9,177	371	9,548	880	-50	8,618	2,015	1,213	5,291	4,653	2,239	1,058
1974	13,432	10,174	477	10,651	1,002	-58	9,590	2,346	1,496	5,889	5,144	2,281	1,089
1975	14,920	11,053	394	11,447	1,056	-31	10,359	2,660	1,901	6,418	5,699	2,325	1,105
1976	16,822	12,730	370	13,099	1,234	-15	11,850	2,901	2,071	7,091	6,233	2,372	1,156
1977	18,812	14,459	320	14,778	1,420	-74	13,284	3,290	2,239	7,712	6,683	2,439	1,223
1978	21,563	16,791	317	17,108	1,693	-128	15,288	3,831	2,444	8,592	7,418	2,510	1,296
1979	24,392	18,994	390	19,384	1,987	-178	17,220	4,432	2,740	9,461	8,135	2,578	1,350
1980	27,030	20,316	477	20,793	2,127	-218	18,449	5,326	3,256	10,234	8,850	2,641	1,350
1981	29,170	21,172	406	21,578	2,369	-269	18,941	6,461	3,767	10,933	9,494	2,668	1,319
1982	30,006	21,075	293	21,369	2,403	-258	18,708	7,052	4,247	11,260	9,809	2,665	1,270
1983	31,906	22,242	301	22,543	2,558	-246	19,739	7,603	4,564	12,026	10,585	2,653	1,295
1984	34,585	24,305	402	24,707	2,890	-286	21,532	8,340	4,713	12,970	11,467	2,667	1,342
1985	36,321	25,609	428	26,037	3,070	-315	22,652	8,737	4,931	13,590	11,967	2,673	1,370
1986	38,222	27,194	550	27,744	3,251	-371	24,123	9,079	5,020	14,243	12,479	2,684	1,406
1987	40,195	29,134	515	29,649	3,438	-433	25,778	9,220	5,197	14,881	13,036	2,701	1,455
1988	43,776	32,115	702	32,817	3,931	-501	28,385	9,859	5,531	15,969	14,160	2,741	1,522
1989	48,095	34,896	675	35,571	4,272	-562	30,738	11,274	6,083	17,235	15,011	2,791	1,574
1990	51,941	38,183	713	38,896	4,791	-618	33,487	11,839	6,615	18,159	15,965	2,860	1,626
1991	54,674	40,258	727	40,985	5,106	-683	35,196	12,153	7,325	18,670	16,349	2,929	1,636
1992	58,477	43,359	730	44,089	5,459	-780	37,850	12,476	8,151	19,546	17,116	2,992	1,654
1993	62,591	46,361	850	47,211	5,830	-875	40,506	13,381	8,704	20,452	17,869	3,060	1,698
1994	67,030	49,956	776	50,732	6,322	-941	43,469	14,525	9,037	21,475	18,691	3,121	1,781
1995	72,166	53,273	688	53,961	6,789	-1,119	46,053	16,102	10,011	22,663	19,747	3,184	1,845
1996	77,845	57,824	840	58,665	7,452	-1,355	49,858	17,335	10,652	23,974	20,791	3,247	1,920
1997	82,657	62,090	956	63,046	7,910	-1,540	53,596	18,099	10,963	25,015	21,514	3,304	1,986
1998	86,863	66,141	859	67,000	8,366	-1,664	56,971	18,493	11,399	25,910	22,302	3,352	2,022
1999	90,548	69,695	821	70,516	8,726	-1,757	60,033	18,109	12,406	26,679	22,841	3,394	2,051
2000	97,773	75,653	823	76,476	9,417	-1,999	65,060	19,664	13,049	28,508	24,312	3,430	2,092
2001	100,607	77,069	833	77,902	9,449	-2,111	66,342	19,613	14,652	29,011	25,067	3,468	2,079
2002	101,865	78,057	838	78,895	9,605	-2,190	67,100	18,945	15,821	28,993	25,561	3,513	2,062
2003	105,562	80,639	1,118	81,757	9,914	-2,368	69,475	19,828	16,259	29,758	26,438	3,547	2,077
2004	111,488	85,573	1,257	86,829	10,617	-2,594	73,618	21,140	16,730	31,234	27,760	3,569	2,133
2005	117,145	90,281	1,238	91,519	11,208	-2,885	77,426	22,050	17,669	32,421	28,388	3,613	2,197
2006	127,974	97,409	1,336	98,745	12,042	-3,274	83,429	25,541	19,004	34,862	30,448	3,671	2,256
2007	133,839	100,946	1,337	102,284	12,549	-3,546	86,189	27,228	20,421	35,955	31,576	3,722	2,307
2008	139,500	101,918	1,306	103,224	12,717	-3,667	86,841	28,948	23,711	37,015	32,445	3,769	2,289
2009	134,831	96,519	1,113	97,633	12,204	-3,490	81,939	25,811	27,081	35,402	31,899	3,809	2,189
2010	138,328	98,505	1,042	99,548	12,551	-3,371	83,626	25,421	29,282	36,046	32,357	3,838	2,174
2011	146,082	102,331	1,267	103,598	11,569	-3,703	88,326	28,069	29,687	37,730	33,445	3,872	2,202
2012	154,067	108,492	1,402	109,894	12,112	-3,914	93,868	30,540	29,659	39,513	35,108	3,899	2,220
2013	156,644	112,129	1,640	113,769	14,201	-3,909	95,659	30,236	30,749	39,931	34,972	3,923	2,260
2014	167,978	118,125	1,583	119,708	15,051	-3,892	100,765	33,715	33,498	42,375	37,110	3,964	2,322
2015	181,022	126,625	1,754	128,379	15,906	-4,182	108,291	37,051	35,681	45,065	39,196	4,017	2,389
2016	189,644	133,769	1,584	135,353	16,684	-4,575	114,094	38,800	36,751	46,352	40,196	4,091	2,447
2017	199,422	142,389	1,427	143,816	17,933	-4,729	121,154	40,569	37,700	48,093	41,687	4,147	2,501
2018	209,148	149,390	1,439	150,829	18,961	-4,902	126,966	42,609	39,573	49,908	43,460	4,191	2,570
2019	224,346	223,144	1,202	159,615	19,601	-5,320	134,693	47,226	42,427	53,212	46,386	4,216	2,620
2020	240,771	239,134	1,637	160,909	19,975	-5,273	135,661	46,840	58,270	56,765	49,942	4,242	...

... = Not available.

Personal Income and Employment by Region and State: Pennsylvania

(Millions of dollars, except as noted.)

Year	Personal income, total	Earnings by place of work			Less: Contributions for government social insurance	Plus: Adjustment for residence	Equals: Net earnings by place of residence	Plus: Dividends, interest, and rent	Plus: Personal current transfer receipts	Per capita (dollars)		Population (thousands)	Total employment (thousands)
		Nonfarm	Farm	Total						Personal income	Disposable personal income		
1960	26,119	21,947	298	22,245	1,211	-81	20,954	3,243	1,922	2,305	2,049	11,329	...
1961	26,686	22,134	302	22,436	1,225	-86	21,125	3,378	2,183	2,342	2,095	11,392	...
1962	27,845	23,248	219	23,467	1,334	-104	22,029	3,650	2,167	2,452	2,180	11,355	...
1963	28,908	24,044	261	24,305	1,474	-113	22,719	3,945	2,245	2,530	2,246	11,424	...
1964	30,915	25,799	269	26,068	1,530	-136	24,401	4,255	2,259	2,684	2,412	11,519	...
1965	33,159	27,650	278	27,928	1,594	-155	26,180	4,609	2,370	2,854	2,556	11,620	...
1966	35,757	30,386	266	30,652	2,148	-201	28,303	4,879	2,575	3,066	2,726	11,664	...
1967	38,299	32,176	359	32,535	2,317	-231	29,987	5,244	3,068	3,279	2,918	11,681	...
1968	41,638	34,789	314	35,102	2,421	-268	32,413	5,713	3,512	3,546	3,132	11,741	...
1969	45,346	38,065	372	38,437	2,809	-436	35,192	6,162	3,992	3,862	3,364	11,741	5,250
1970	48,844	40,132	387	40,519	2,928	-405	37,187	6,743	4,914	4,135	3,630	11,812	5,226
1971	51,836	42,076	335	42,411	3,186	-373	38,851	7,209	5,775	4,362	3,872	11,884	5,159
1972	56,580	46,003	347	46,350	3,654	-373	42,323	7,730	6,527	4,753	4,132	11,905	5,247
1973	62,033	50,635	485	51,119	4,627	-342	46,150	8,578	7,305	5,219	4,565	11,885	5,402
1974	68,133	55,005	463	55,468	5,222	-348	49,898	9,695	8,539	5,743	4,996	11,864	5,419
1975	74,473	58,422	425	58,847	5,400	-361	53,085	10,560	10,828	6,259	5,535	11,898	5,302
1976	81,283	63,729	517	64,245	6,000	-337	57,908	11,345	12,030	6,838	6,021	11,887	5,353
1977	89,174	70,233	469	70,701	6,595	-321	63,786	12,606	12,783	7,505	6,571	11,882	5,429
1978	98,272	77,966	506	78,472	7,508	-320	70,644	13,906	13,722	8,283	7,224	11,865	5,562
1979	108,706	85,953	642	86,595	8,576	-360	77,659	15,595	15,452	9,155	7,942	11,874	5,664
1980	119,088	91,396	424	91,820	9,175	-380	82,266	19,112	17,711	10,034	8,717	11,868	5,624
1981	131,482	98,190	635	98,825	10,559	-333	87,932	23,613	19,937	11,088	9,566	11,859	5,584
1982	140,474	100,597	564	101,160	10,980	-162	90,019	27,624	22,831	11,859	10,323	11,845	5,474
1983	147,181	104,882	361	105,242	11,570	-23	93,648	28,844	24,688	12,433	10,957	11,838	5,433
1984	158,975	114,007	848	114,855	13,095	145	101,905	32,221	24,849	13,455	11,861	11,815	5,577
1985	168,416	120,770	846	121,616	14,060	280	107,836	34,579	26,001	14,308	12,598	11,771	5,679
1986	177,108	127,213	886	128,098	14,908	399	113,589	36,100	27,420	15,031	13,261	11,783	5,772
1987	187,611	137,257	883	138,140	15,896	528	122,772	36,793	28,046	15,885	13,928	11,811	5,957
1988	203,158	150,069	743	150,812	17,715	779	133,876	39,734	29,547	17,150	15,089	11,846	6,120
1989	220,030	160,091	998	161,089	18,645	971	143,415	45,188	31,426	18,543	16,269	11,866	6,216
1990	232,899	169,009	1,002	170,011	19,839	1,039	151,211	47,395	34,293	19,566	17,218	11,903	6,293
1991	242,566	174,106	734	174,841	20,662	1,053	155,231	47,728	39,607	20,244	17,920	11,982	6,212
1992	256,052	185,362	1,202	186,565	21,889	1,226	165,902	47,995	42,155	21,250	18,804	12,049	6,216
1993	265,789	192,744	1,030	193,773	23,105	1,340	172,008	49,410	44,371	21,930	19,421	12,120	6,256
1994	275,145	200,288	921	201,209	24,456	1,652	178,405	51,304	45,436	22,616	19,970	12,166	6,323
1995	287,676	207,617	642	208,259	25,290	2,167	185,136	55,087	47,453	23,583	20,751	12,198	6,423
1996	302,376	215,888	1,118	217,006	25,752	2,433	193,687	58,286	50,402	24,743	21,643	12,220	6,477
1997	317,520	227,798	767	228,564	26,960	2,873	204,477	61,543	51,501	25,967	22,571	12,228	6,585
1998	335,664	241,189	893	242,082	28,148	3,271	217,204	66,231	52,229	27,411	23,735	12,246	6,658
1999	349,848	255,257	815	256,072	29,402	3,556	230,227	65,043	54,579	28,527	24,679	12,264	6,764
2000	374,405	271,569	1,103	272,672	30,864	4,056	245,865	70,626	57,914	30,479	26,356	12,284	6,905
2001	388,669	283,756	1,011	284,767	31,934	4,317	257,150	69,646	61,874	31,602	27,438	12,299	6,915
2002	396,188	290,990	641	291,631	32,821	4,591	263,401	67,140	65,647	32,129	28,509	12,331	6,887
2003	409,649	300,600	1,228	301,827	33,631	5,080	273,276	68,094	68,278	33,104	29,647	12,375	6,876
2004	433,410	320,665	1,544	322,210	35,353	5,869	292,725	69,853	70,831	34,922	31,384	12,411	6,952
2005	451,890	333,399	1,365	334,764	37,149	6,892	304,507	71,282	76,101	36,296	32,290	12,450	7,054
2006	476,853	345,643	1,139	346,782	39,023	7,341	315,100	81,837	79,916	38,115	33,718	12,511	7,153
2007	506,499	361,732	1,324	363,056	40,566	8,225	330,716	90,416	85,367	40,314	35,429	12,564	7,265
2008	524,360	368,405	1,373	369,777	41,794	8,576	336,559	92,751	95,049	41,575	36,618	12,612	7,279
2009	511,714	358,271	952	359,223	41,263	7,332	325,292	82,893	103,529	40,398	36,466	12,667	7,102
2010	533,828	374,206	1,342	375,548	42,359	8,003	341,191	81,656	110,982	41,997	37,812	12,711	7,120
2011	562,622	390,681	1,779	392,460	39,419	7,867	360,908	90,208	111,506	44,146	39,348	12,745	7,217
2012	587,096	404,760	2,055	406,815	40,325	8,229	374,718	100,763	111,615	45,986	41,126	12,767	7,285
2013	592,172	419,793	2,305	422,098	46,661	8,152	383,589	95,269	113,315	46,348	41,060	12,777	7,351
2014	617,896	433,269	2,619	435,888	48,239	8,959	396,608	104,328	116,959	48,314	42,737	12,789	7,437
2015	642,623	449,685	1,665	451,351	50,113	8,865	410,103	109,917	122,603	50,261	44,242	12,786	7,513
2016	657,165	456,811	813	457,624	51,114	9,547	416,057	111,989	129,119	51,407	45,326	12,784	7,597
2017	682,534	477,383	1,224	478,607	53,802	10,214	435,019	117,784	129,731	53,363	47,069	12,790	7,685
2018	708,862	496,265	1,019	497,284	56,231	10,445	451,497	122,977	134,388	55,349	49,042	12,807	7,766
2019	742,924	741,507	1,418	514,359	57,388	10,809	467,780	131,208	143,936	58,046	51,473	12,799	7,874
2020	795,093	793,534	1,559	506,415	57,157	10,901	460,159	129,968	204,966	62,198	55,736	12,783	...

... = Not available.

Personal Income and Employment by Region and State: Rhode Island

(Millions of dollars, except as noted.)

Year	Personal income, total	Earnings by place of work			Less: Contributions for government social insurance	Plus: Adjustment for residence	Equals: Net earnings by place of residence	Plus: Dividends, interest, and rent	Plus: Personal current transfer receipts	Per capita (dollars)		Population (thousands)	Total employment (thousands)
		Nonfarm	Farm	Total						Personal income	Disposable personal income		
1960	2,016	1,615	8	1,622	96	54	1,580	285	151	2,358	2,107	855	...
1961	2,108	1,669	7	1,676	98	57	1,635	307	166	2,457	2,189	858	...
1962	2,267	1,788	7	1,796	108	62	1,750	348	169	2,603	2,328	871	...
1963	2,368	1,845	7	1,852	118	67	1,801	388	179	2,703	2,416	876	...
1964	2,522	1,969	8	1,977	122	73	1,928	410	184	2,849	2,580	885	...
1965	2,723	2,122	8	2,130	133	82	2,079	446	198	3,049	2,755	893	...
1966	2,973	2,344	9	2,353	162	95	2,286	469	218	3,307	2,966	899	...
1967	3,223	2,516	7	2,523	175	105	2,452	506	265	3,546	3,193	909	...
1968	3,522	2,748	8	2,757	200	115	2,672	543	308	3,820	3,403	922	...
1969	3,742	2,949	8	2,957	231	62	2,789	606	347	4,015	3,554	932	440
1970	4,093	3,164	9	3,174	245	63	2,992	678	423	4,306	3,854	951	440
1971	4,337	3,323	8	3,331	267	58	3,123	718	497	4,499	4,030	964	436
1972	4,722	3,656	8	3,664	307	53	3,410	766	546	4,836	4,283	976	447
1973	5,045	3,888	6	3,895	381	69	3,582	838	625	5,158	4,569	978	452
1974	5,289	3,956	9	3,965	410	88	3,642	913	734	5,547	4,898	954	439
1975	5,742	4,115	9	4,124	416	82	3,790	980	972	6,068	5,468	946	424
1976	6,272	4,606	9	4,615	473	88	4,229	1,049	995	6,600	5,890	950	442
1977	6,865	5,066	8	5,074	521	103	4,656	1,167	1,042	7,187	6,427	955	459
1978	7,531	5,628	9	5,637	597	101	5,141	1,278	1,112	7,868	6,937	957	474
1979	8,363	6,268	8	6,276	685	108	5,699	1,428	1,236	8,742	7,633	957	483
1980	9,391	6,823	8	6,831	745	122	6,208	1,752	1,431	9,898	8,696	949	484
1981	10,464	7,350	9	7,359	851	153	6,661	2,167	1,636	10,980	9,650	953	484
1982	11,271	7,701	27	7,728	902	207	7,034	2,442	1,796	11,812	10,441	954	475
1983	12,185	8,339	37	8,376	988	263	7,651	2,620	1,914	12,741	11,306	956	480
1984	13,381	9,223	32	9,256	1,136	331	8,451	2,963	1,967	13,911	12,388	962	504
1985	14,414	10,012	42	10,054	1,220	391	9,225	3,101	2,088	14,876	13,228	969	519
1986	15,453	10,873	43	10,917	1,330	417	10,003	3,277	2,172	15,811	13,981	977	537
1987	16,547	11,788	41	11,829	1,430	484	10,883	3,427	2,237	16,721	14,631	990	546
1988	18,239	12,997	42	13,039	1,595	559	12,003	3,838	2,398	18,305	16,122	996	560
1989	19,853	13,734	32	13,766	1,661	625	12,730	4,510	2,613	19,839	17,474	1,001	560
1990	20,438	14,076	31	14,107	1,790	671	12,987	4,561	2,890	20,316	17,943	1,006	550
1991	20,636	13,825	32	13,857	1,809	697	12,745	4,381	3,511	20,419	18,105	1,011	524
1992	21,597	14,684	29	14,713	1,923	718	13,508	4,428	3,661	21,329	18,997	1,013	529
1993	22,515	15,214	30	15,244	2,011	761	13,993	4,548	3,973	22,180	19,728	1,015	533
1994	23,091	15,747	25	15,772	2,109	830	14,492	4,648	3,951	22,728	20,177	1,016	533
1995	24,324	16,467	25	16,492	2,182	859	15,168	4,986	4,170	23,918	21,224	1,017	536
1996	25,172	16,958	23	16,981	2,229	929	15,681	5,238	4,253	24,657	21,751	1,021	540
1997	26,634	17,884	16	17,899	2,334	995	16,560	5,557	4,516	25,975	22,700	1,025	546
1998	28,280	19,354	15	19,369	2,472	1,074	17,971	5,743	4,566	27,425	23,852	1,031	555
1999	29,640	20,593	15	20,608	2,589	1,175	19,194	5,701	4,746	28,489	24,775	1,040	567
2000	31,954	22,225	16	22,241	2,756	1,335	20,820	6,212	4,922	30,424	26,267	1,050	583
2001	33,635	23,226	18	23,244	2,866	1,429	21,807	6,323	5,505	31,817	27,519	1,057	585
2002	35,028	24,464	22	24,486	2,961	1,414	22,939	6,345	5,744	32,859	29,118	1,066	588
2003	36,809	25,891	23	25,914	3,119	1,373	24,168	6,736	5,905	34,358	30,739	1,071	594
2004	38,732	27,193	25	27,218	3,286	1,598	25,530	6,904	6,298	36,044	32,299	1,075	602
2005	39,562	27,985	24	28,009	3,403	1,437	26,043	6,971	6,549	37,046	32,974	1,068	606
2006	41,659	29,346	23	29,369	3,592	1,449	27,226	7,646	6,786	39,186	34,742	1,063	611
2007	43,401	29,848	24	29,871	3,700	1,530	27,701	8,264	7,436	41,049	36,225	1,057	618
2008	44,086	29,720	27	29,747	3,750	1,311	27,308	8,516	8,262	41,787	37,011	1,055	609
2009	42,947	28,686	27	28,713	3,692	1,239	26,261	7,723	8,963	40,760	37,029	1,054	588
2010	45,155	30,577	27	30,604	3,791	1,024	27,836	7,785	9,534	42,844	38,860	1,054	586
2011	46,933	31,170	22	31,193	3,498	1,280	28,974	8,341	9,618	44,548	39,842	1,054	592
2012	48,718	32,469	26	32,495	3,581	1,423	30,337	8,891	9,490	46,196	41,541	1,055	593
2013	48,777	33,157	26	33,183	4,116	1,413	30,481	8,667	9,629	46,229	41,059	1,055	602
2014	50,903	34,430	22	34,452	4,292	1,156	31,317	9,269	10,318	48,203	42,757	1,056	613
2015	53,006	35,548	33	35,580	4,492	1,413	32,502	9,819	10,686	50,187	44,462	1,056	627
2016	53,731	35,920	22	35,942	4,568	1,574	32,948	10,046	10,737	50,830	44,940	1,057	633
2017	55,934	37,019	22	37,041	4,710	1,886	34,217	10,512	11,206	52,943	46,872	1,056	639
2018	57,648	37,726	19	37,745	4,802	2,076	35,019	10,951	11,678	54,523	48,577	1,057	648
2019	59,707	59,685	22	39,600	5,073	2,720	37,247	10,692	11,768	56,426	50,081	1,058	657
2020	64,313	64,285	28	39,606	5,102	2,668	37,172	10,610	16,532	60,837	54,548	1,057	...

... = Not available.

Personal Income and Employment by Region and State: South Carolina

(Millions of dollars, except as noted.)

Year	Personal income, total	Earnings by place of work			Less: Contributions for government social insurance	Plus: Adjustment for residence	Equals: Net earnings by place of residence	Plus: Dividends, interest, and rent	Plus: Personal current transfer receipts	Per capita (dollars)		Population (thousands)	Total employment (thousands)
		Nonfarm	Farm	Total						Personal income	Disposable personal income		
1960	3,570	2,898	169	3,068	135	18	2,950	410	210	1,493	1,371	2,392	...
1961	3,748	2,990	196	3,186	138	19	3,067	443	238	1,556	1,427	2,409	...
1962	4,018	3,227	185	3,412	153	23	3,282	484	253	1,658	1,512	2,423	...
1963	4,252	3,433	189	3,621	189	26	3,458	522	272	1,728	1,577	2,460	...
1964	4,567	3,721	180	3,902	203	30	3,729	554	284	1,845	1,697	2,475	...
1965	5,048	4,125	182	4,307	221	35	4,122	616	310	2,024	1,853	2,494	...
1966	5,672	4,720	196	4,916	290	44	4,670	660	342	2,251	2,043	2,520	...
1967	6,121	5,099	197	5,296	342	50	5,004	715	401	2,416	2,193	2,533	...
1968	6,796	5,728	155	5,884	387	58	5,554	771	471	2,656	2,391	2,559	...
1969	7,604	6,260	188	6,448	417	128	6,159	909	537	2,959	2,641	2,570	1,170
1970	8,380	6,753	189	6,942	449	128	6,621	1,090	669	3,225	2,912	2,598	1,196
1971	9,181	7,360	204	7,564	509	138	7,193	1,209	779	3,449	3,120	2,662	1,215
1972	10,309	8,311	214	8,525	600	154	8,080	1,353	876	3,792	3,368	2,718	1,262
1973	11,692	9,405	303	9,708	773	167	9,101	1,547	1,044	4,213	3,758	2,775	1,328
1974	13,235	10,506	342	10,849	898	180	10,131	1,786	1,318	4,655	4,144	2,843	1,365
1975	14,394	11,040	277	11,317	928	191	10,580	2,000	1,814	4,963	4,529	2,900	1,326
1976	16,096	12,610	234	12,844	1,089	225	11,980	2,189	1,927	5,472	4,926	2,941	1,376
1977	17,593	13,900	188	14,088	1,199	247	13,135	2,444	2,013	5,886	5,280	2,989	1,411
1978	19,879	15,746	246	15,993	1,389	264	14,868	2,801	2,210	6,537	5,848	3,041	1,466
1979	22,284	17,625	260	17,885	1,608	286	16,563	3,171	2,549	7,219	6,387	3,087	1,507
1980	24,967	19,452	36	19,488	1,774	318	18,032	3,833	3,103	7,965	7,064	3,135	1,523
1981	28,120	21,429	172	21,601	2,091	348	19,857	4,679	3,584	8,845	7,805	3,179	1,536
1982	29,894	22,212	195	22,406	2,196	381	20,591	5,368	3,935	9,320	8,307	3,208	1,514
1983	32,447	24,358	51	24,408	2,470	392	22,330	5,921	4,196	10,033	8,940	3,234	1,547
1984	36,183	27,185	270	27,455	2,850	425	25,030	6,728	4,425	11,059	9,900	3,272	1,625
1985	38,710	29,037	197	29,233	3,096	477	26,614	7,301	4,794	11,719	10,457	3,303	1,655
1986	41,372	31,238	91	31,329	3,425	543	28,446	7,868	5,058	12,377	11,053	3,343	1,697
1987	44,372	33,735	250	33,985	3,665	586	30,906	8,267	5,199	13,126	11,672	3,381	1,738
1988	48,237	36,871	348	37,219	4,151	610	33,678	9,010	5,549	14,137	12,646	3,412	1,809
1989	52,509	39,458	367	39,825	4,513	571	35,883	10,204	6,423	15,190	13,489	3,457	1,858
1990	56,400	42,562	300	42,862	4,974	507	38,395	10,888	7,116	16,109	14,299	3,501	1,913
1991	58,893	43,801	399	44,200	5,192	494	39,502	11,232	8,159	16,495	14,764	3,570	1,886
1992	62,694	46,512	377	46,889	5,480	504	41,913	11,604	9,177	17,316	15,538	3,620	1,897
1993	65,908	48,866	337	49,203	5,824	520	43,900	12,174	9,835	17,991	16,130	3,663	1,931
1994	69,909	51,258	491	51,749	6,195	636	46,190	13,032	10,688	18,867	16,874	3,705	1,979
1995	74,092	54,047	384	54,431	6,555	767	48,644	14,019	11,430	19,765	17,600	3,749	2,038
1996	78,792	56,777	463	57,241	6,771	878	51,347	15,141	12,303	20,755	18,396	3,796	2,080
1997	83,865	60,342	472	60,814	7,187	1,036	54,663	16,315	12,888	21,728	19,187	3,860	2,141
1998	89,797	65,002	334	65,336	7,734	1,115	58,717	17,532	13,548	22,912	20,169	3,919	2,191
1999	94,408	69,147	403	69,550	8,169	1,203	62,585	17,449	14,374	23,752	20,896	3,975	2,241
2000	101,161	73,288	526	73,814	8,623	1,429	66,621	19,089	15,452	25,138	22,205	4,024	2,280
2001	104,652	74,810	650	75,460	8,877	1,519	68,102	19,305	17,245	25,745	22,790	4,065	2,257
2002	107,527	77,106	231	77,336	9,138	1,557	69,756	19,046	18,726	26,176	23,618	4,108	2,248
2003	111,166	80,021	525	80,546	9,524	1,592	72,613	18,871	19,682	26,785	24,352	4,150	2,264
2004	117,507	83,865	644	84,509	10,010	1,675	76,174	20,047	21,287	27,905	25,407	4,211	2,306
2005	124,489	88,065	642	88,706	10,494	1,869	80,081	21,523	22,885	29,153	26,288	4,270	2,356
2006	134,579	93,883	464	94,347	11,432	2,143	85,058	24,763	24,758	30,882	27,713	4,358	2,419
2007	143,317	98,715	308	99,022	11,953	2,515	89,584	27,380	26,354	32,249	28,864	4,444	2,482
2008	149,236	100,154	443	100,597	12,282	2,598	90,914	27,939	30,383	32,951	29,719	4,529	2,472
2009	145,609	95,769	489	96,258	11,923	2,586	86,921	25,111	33,578	31,724	29,211	4,590	2,368
2010	150,452	98,689	485	99,174	12,136	2,527	89,565	24,529	36,357	32,455	29,840	4,636	2,358
2011	159,091	103,574	364	103,938	11,406	2,564	95,096	27,246	36,749	34,056	31,017	4,671	2,427
2012	167,539	109,874	476	110,350	11,739	2,853	101,463	29,159	36,917	35,517	32,393	4,717	2,453
2013	169,974	112,968	741	113,709	13,581	2,956	103,085	28,964	37,926	35,678	32,218	4,764	2,501
2014	181,108	119,538	241	119,779	14,251	3,105	108,633	32,251	40,224	37,545	33,979	4,824	2,564
2015	192,880	126,798	152	126,949	15,011	3,443	115,382	34,742	42,756	39,425	35,467	4,892	2,636
2016	199,942	130,983	171	131,154	15,523	3,904	119,535	36,138	44,268	40,325	36,148	4,958	2,700
2017	209,180	137,463	174	137,638	16,363	4,144	125,418	38,116	45,646	41,659	37,341	5,021	2,749
2018	217,276	141,724	319	142,043	16,953	4,377	129,466	40,061	47,749	42,736	38,487	5,084	2,846
2019	233,948	233,838	110	152,018	18,130	4,461	138,349	44,552	51,047	45,359	40,874	5,158	2,902
2020	247,869	247,833	35	153,319	18,409	4,577	139,486	44,053	64,329	47,502	43,068	5,218	...

... = Not available.

Personal Income and Employment by Region and State: South Dakota

(Millions of dollars, except as noted.)

Year	Personal income, total	Earnings by place of work			Less: Contributions for government social insurance	Plus: Adjustment for residence	Equals: Net earnings by place of residence	Plus: Dividends, interest, and rent	Plus: Personal current transfer receipts	Per capita (dollars)		Population (thousands)	Total employment (thousands)
		Nonfarm	Farm	Total						Personal income	Disposable personal income		
1960	1,325	752	324	1,076	35	1	1,042	198	86	1,940	1,803	683	...
1961	1,333	823	251	1,074	39	0	1,035	203	94	1,924	1,774	693	...
1962	1,519	877	368	1,246	45	1	1,201	218	100	2,154	1,993	705	...
1963	1,473	889	299	1,188	51	1	1,138	229	106	2,081	1,916	708	...
1964	1,445	932	216	1,148	50	1	1,099	238	109	2,062	1,922	701	...
1965	1,626	963	334	1,298	51	2	1,248	259	119	2,350	2,198	692	...
1966	1,758	1,030	393	1,424	64	2	1,362	267	129	2,574	2,394	683	...
1967	1,786	1,084	344	1,429	77	3	1,354	278	154	2,662	2,472	671	...
1968	1,914	1,174	362	1,536	84	3	1,456	281	177	2,861	2,633	669	...
1969	2,076	1,288	357	1,645	90	6	1,561	321	194	3,108	2,838	668	303
1970	2,257	1,388	373	1,762	95	6	1,672	363	222	3,386	3,126	667	305
1971	2,473	1,518	404	1,921	106	6	1,821	396	255	3,684	3,441	671	306
1972	2,855	1,684	564	2,248	121	7	2,134	439	282	4,215	3,940	677	309
1973	3,605	1,897	1,027	2,924	158	7	2,773	505	327	5,310	4,928	679	323
1974	3,612	2,115	688	2,803	183	8	2,628	602	383	5,313	4,861	680	326
1975	3,972	2,315	707	3,022	200	10	2,832	684	456	5,829	5,411	681	326
1976	3,933	2,624	277	2,901	225	12	2,688	742	503	5,726	5,246	687	336
1977	4,463	2,867	445	3,312	238	13	3,087	846	530	6,477	6,011	689	342
1978	5,143	3,258	616	3,874	274	14	3,614	953	575	7,460	6,880	689	355
1979	5,665	3,590	652	4,242	322	15	3,935	1,081	649	8,222	7,560	689	359
1980	5,713	3,801	137	3,938	342	16	3,612	1,340	761	8,269	7,511	691	353
1981	6,652	4,042	444	4,486	388	13	4,111	1,669	872	9,646	8,789	690	348
1982	7,010	4,167	373	4,540	408	10	4,143	1,899	969	10,151	9,198	691	344
1983	7,271	4,480	255	4,736	440	4	4,299	1,930	1,042	10,491	9,670	693	353
1984	8,272	4,874	689	5,563	491	-2	5,069	2,101	1,102	11,864	11,048	697	362
1985	8,481	5,078	612	5,690	530	-5	5,155	2,154	1,171	12,143	11,284	698	365
1986	8,848	5,322	663	5,985	574	-12	5,400	2,228	1,220	12,711	11,822	696	366
1987	9,336	5,646	843	6,489	618	-19	5,852	2,224	1,260	13,413	12,410	696	381
1988	9,748	6,112	715	6,826	692	-27	6,108	2,322	1,318	13,962	12,909	698	388
1989	10,492	6,549	724	7,273	750	-37	6,485	2,563	1,445	15,060	13,863	697	396
1990	11,485	7,136	1,021	8,157	851	-54	7,252	2,693	1,540	16,475	15,115	697	409
1991	11,967	7,639	894	8,533	916	-68	7,549	2,761	1,656	17,006	15,618	704	420
1992	12,942	8,289	1,074	9,363	976	-85	8,301	2,840	1,800	18,156	16,676	713	431
1993	13,531	8,858	945	9,803	1,035	-100	8,668	2,969	1,895	18,737	17,120	722	442
1994	14,588	9,514	1,211	10,725	1,117	-130	9,477	3,106	2,005	19,962	18,334	731	464
1995	14,884	9,983	640	10,623	1,171	-150	9,302	3,440	2,142	20,169	18,426	738	472
1996	16,445	10,446	1,462	11,908	1,224	-189	10,494	3,689	2,262	22,157	20,310	742	479
1997	16,806	11,025	1,046	12,070	1,292	-186	10,593	3,892	2,321	22,582	20,460	744	485
1998	18,241	11,964	1,167	13,132	1,385	-233	11,514	4,338	2,389	24,449	22,194	746	491
1999	19,094	12,670	1,165	13,835	1,482	-249	12,104	4,507	2,483	25,445	22,973	750	502
2000	20,325	13,332	1,342	14,674	1,568	-267	12,840	4,828	2,658	26,890	24,331	756	512
2001	20,983	13,768	1,153	14,922	1,617	-265	13,040	5,069	2,874	27,682	25,053	758	512
2002	21,004	14,420	506	14,925	1,677	-237	13,011	4,927	3,065	27,635	25,375	760	510
2003	22,920	15,079	1,493	16,572	1,754	-225	14,593	5,162	3,165	30,010	27,946	764	510
2004	24,593	16,124	1,856	17,981	1,847	-221	15,912	5,343	3,338	31,923	29,725	770	518
2005	26,055	17,332	1,568	18,900	1,937	-171	16,791	5,691	3,573	33,598	31,066	775	528
2006	27,504	18,851	629	19,480	2,081	-141	17,258	6,364	3,882	35,125	32,187	783	539
2007	30,540	19,738	1,772	21,510	2,214	-140	19,157	7,222	4,161	38,579	35,323	792	552
2008	32,633	20,397	2,259	22,656	2,322	-104	20,231	7,668	4,735	40,836	37,439	799	561
2009	31,682	20,386	1,773	22,160	2,318	-69	19,773	6,931	4,978	39,255	36,705	807	556
2010	33,512	21,853	1,703	23,557	2,427	-71	21,058	7,076	5,378	41,061	38,320	816	558
2011	36,636	22,209	3,647	25,856	2,225	-113	23,518	7,648	5,470	44,489	41,145	823	566
2012	37,522	23,574	2,505	26,080	2,328	-72	23,679	8,367	5,476	45,018	41,393	833	575
2013	37,991	23,789	3,416	27,205	2,685	-39	24,482	7,903	5,606	45,105	41,238	842	581
2014	39,823	25,691	2,364	28,055	2,842	-22	25,191	8,791	5,842	46,901	42,723	849	590
2015	41,550	27,230	1,665	28,895	2,947	-22	25,926	9,538	6,086	48,658	44,274	854	593
2016	41,789	27,629	1,097	28,725	3,034	-58	25,633	9,812	6,343	48,429	44,028	863	598
2017	42,455	27,972	894	28,866	3,124	-125	25,617	10,302	6,536	48,616	44,131	873	603
2018	44,236	29,000	1,042	30,042	3,242	-132	26,668	10,768	6,801	50,141	45,731	882	610
2019	47,738	46,242	1,496	32,392	3,481	-119	28,792	11,442	7,504	53,812	49,462	887	617
2020	51,128	48,951	2,178	34,093	3,673	-150	30,271	11,222	9,636	57,273	52,849	893	...

... = Not available.

Personal Income and Employment by Region and State: Tennessee

(Millions of dollars, except as noted.)

Year	Personal income, total	Earnings by place of work			Less: Contributions for government social insurance	Plus: Adjustment for residence	Equals: Net earnings by place of residence	Plus: Dividends, interest, and rent	Plus: Personal current transfer receipts	Per capita (dollars)		Population (thousands)	Total employment (thousands)
		Nonfarm	Farm	Total						Personal income	Disposable personal income		
1960	5,931	4,826	246	5,072	243	31	4,861	666	404	1,659	1,512	3,575	...
1961	6,278	5,025	294	5,319	247	31	5,103	716	459	1,733	1,584	3,622	...
1962	6,668	5,395	254	5,649	273	31	5,406	784	477	1,815	1,633	3,673	...
1963	7,072	5,748	278	6,026	323	31	5,733	836	502	1,902	1,730	3,718	...
1964	7,604	6,251	238	6,490	339	30	6,181	899	525	2,016	1,853	3,771	...
1965	8,287	6,821	254	7,075	363	32	6,744	965	578	2,182	1,996	3,798	...
1966	9,123	7,675	258	7,933	502	34	7,465	1,023	636	2,387	2,164	3,822	...
1967	9,770	8,209	219	8,428	564	51	7,914	1,093	763	2,532	2,302	3,859	...
1968	10,894	9,124	225	9,349	635	50	8,764	1,255	875	2,809	2,523	3,878	...
1969	11,816	9,978	256	10,233	659	-146	9,428	1,410	978	3,032	2,692	3,897	1,789
1970	12,849	10,605	269	10,875	696	-144	10,035	1,618	1,197	3,264	2,920	3,937	1,785
1971	14,188	11,668	267	11,935	789	-155	10,990	1,801	1,397	3,538	3,190	4,010	1,817
1972	15,971	13,224	326	13,550	938	-183	12,429	2,003	1,539	3,906	3,518	4,088	1,924
1973	18,142	14,917	493	15,409	1,211	-166	14,032	2,293	1,817	4,384	3,946	4,138	2,025
1974	20,074	16,415	318	16,733	1,384	-176	15,173	2,680	2,221	4,778	4,299	4,202	2,055
1975	21,894	17,316	250	17,566	1,431	-180	15,955	3,005	2,934	5,138	4,671	4,261	1,983
1976	24,520	19,499	371	19,871	1,640	-173	18,057	3,256	3,207	5,664	5,123	4,329	2,052
1977	27,176	21,943	300	22,242	1,847	-230	20,165	3,644	3,367	6,174	5,586	4,402	2,135
1978	30,979	25,254	319	25,573	2,152	-294	23,127	4,179	3,673	6,943	6,248	4,462	2,227
1979	34,544	27,996	342	28,337	2,482	-348	25,508	4,761	4,276	7,620	6,843	4,533	2,279
1980	38,078	30,027	197	30,224	2,668	-416	27,139	5,780	5,159	8,277	7,420	4,600	2,259
1981	42,383	32,695	360	33,055	3,136	-446	29,473	7,064	5,846	9,159	8,207	4,628	2,255
1982	45,046	33,928	302	34,230	3,331	-404	30,495	8,137	6,415	9,696	8,732	4,646	2,217
1983	48,057	36,658	-33	36,625	3,652	-417	32,555	8,614	6,888	10,313	9,312	4,660	2,239
1984	53,481	40,665	412	41,078	4,190	-443	36,444	9,826	7,211	11,411	10,362	4,687	2,344
1985	57,208	43,854	335	44,190	4,589	-469	39,132	10,412	7,664	12,132	10,972	4,715	2,399
1986	61,216	47,325	241	47,567	5,066	-505	41,996	10,992	8,228	12,918	11,699	4,739	2,477
1987	65,941	51,556	305	51,861	5,474	-534	45,853	11,420	8,667	13,787	12,430	4,783	2,578
1988	71,646	56,016	389	56,405	6,108	-546	49,751	12,578	9,317	14,857	13,460	4,822	2,663
1989	76,928	59,415	443	59,858	6,569	-571	52,719	13,952	10,257	15,847	14,304	4,854	2,735
1990	81,784	62,856	443	63,299	7,002	-629	55,668	14,762	11,354	16,709	15,129	4,894	2,777
1991	86,009	65,826	510	66,336	7,455	-622	58,258	14,837	12,914	17,318	15,736	4,967	2,778
1992	94,053	72,205	665	72,871	8,067	-483	64,321	15,202	14,529	18,625	16,930	5,050	2,837
1993	100,092	77,302	593	77,895	8,654	-596	68,646	15,864	15,582	19,482	17,691	5,138	2,943
1994	106,497	82,665	655	83,320	9,401	-687	73,232	16,917	16,348	20,357	18,430	5,231	3,061
1995	114,365	88,262	441	88,703	10,015	-767	77,920	18,518	17,926	21,469	19,406	5,327	3,145
1996	120,799	93,021	393	93,414	10,377	-785	82,252	19,671	18,876	22,301	20,051	5,417	3,195
1997	127,953	99,351	381	99,732	11,008	-1,031	87,694	20,636	19,624	23,267	20,856	5,499	3,269
1998	141,381	110,098	205	110,304	11,708	-1,175	97,421	23,467	20,492	25,382	22,823	5,570	3,340
1999	147,004	115,549	57	115,607	12,361	-1,359	101,887	23,740	21,377	26,070	23,445	5,639	3,397
2000	155,574	121,594	328	121,922	12,928	-1,550	107,445	24,935	23,195	27,276	24,577	5,704	3,459
2001	159,460	123,577	461	124,038	13,337	-1,563	109,138	25,032	25,290	27,728	24,959	5,751	3,421
2002	164,013	128,463	90	128,553	13,952	-1,548	113,053	23,833	27,126	28,298	25,942	5,796	3,409
2003	170,680	133,344	202	133,546	14,455	-1,555	117,535	24,354	28,791	29,187	26,956	5,848	3,433
2004	180,733	141,709	389	142,098	15,257	-1,639	125,202	24,908	30,624	30,577	28,324	5,911	3,508
2005	188,858	147,085	549	147,635	15,889	-1,454	130,292	25,802	32,764	31,523	29,003	5,991	3,572
2006	201,171	155,875	281	156,156	16,748	-1,382	138,026	28,546	34,598	33,040	30,158	6,089	3,644
2007	211,071	160,680	-105	160,575	17,529	-1,482	141,564	31,467	38,040	34,178	31,114	6,176	3,702
2008	218,783	161,821	242	162,063	17,986	-1,383	142,694	33,317	42,772	35,020	32,088	6,247	3,677
2009	217,319	158,807	316	159,123	17,639	-968	140,516	30,783	46,020	34,462	32,277	6,306	3,524
2010	227,763	164,455	113	164,568	17,983	-747	145,838	31,515	50,411	35,838	33,485	6,355	3,516
2011	241,769	173,088	513	173,601	16,678	-760	156,164	34,219	51,386	37,792	35,025	6,397	3,589
2012	254,406	183,524	339	183,863	17,199	-1,073	165,592	36,926	51,889	39,435	36,575	6,451	3,635
2013	256,706	187,617	1,021	188,639	19,853	-1,241	167,544	35,734	53,428	39,533	36,392	6,493	3,689
2014	267,989	196,477	393	196,869	20,603	-1,200	175,066	38,594	54,329	40,972	37,629	6,541	3,771
2015	282,150	206,553	237	206,790	21,656	-1,323	183,812	41,158	57,180	42,810	39,150	6,591	3,856
2016	292,120	215,138	-108	215,031	22,462	-1,765	190,804	42,755	58,562	43,961	40,092	6,645	3,947
2017	305,691	226,165	-82	226,082	23,734	-1,914	200,435	45,010	60,246	45,566	41,581	6,709	4,004
2018	319,401	236,517	185	236,702	24,970	-2,085	209,647	47,077	62,677	47,179	43,218	6,770	4,118
2019	332,473	332,585	-112	244,991	25,956	-2,151	216,885	49,331	66,256	48,676	44,724	6,830	4,206
2020	348,109	348,044	65	244,986	26,586	-2,215	216,184	48,772	83,153	50,547	46,644	6,887	...

... = Not available.

Personal Income and Employment by Region and State: Texas

(Millions of dollars, except as noted.)

Year	Personal income, total	Earnings by place of work			Less: Contributions for government social insurance	Plus: Adjustment for residence	Equals: Net earnings by place of residence	Plus: Dividends, interest, and rent	Plus: Personal current transfer receipts	Per capita (dollars)		Population (thousands)	Total employment (thousands)
		Nonfarm	Farm	Total						Personal income	Disposable personal income		
1960	19,438	15,184	924	16,108	677	16	15,447	2,993	998	2,020	1,819	9,624	...
1961	20,546	15,886	1,090	16,976	696	16	16,296	3,127	1,122	2,092	1,884	9,820	...
1962	21,582	16,829	950	17,779	749	17	17,047	3,314	1,222	2,147	1,928	10,053	...
1963	22,539	17,705	783	18,488	832	18	17,674	3,544	1,321	2,219	1,990	10,159	...
1964	24,171	19,143	728	19,871	877	18	19,012	3,788	1,371	2,354	2,144	10,270	...
1965	26,017	20,524	865	21,389	930	19	20,478	4,040	1,498	2,507	2,278	10,378	...
1966	28,469	22,842	920	23,762	1,259	17	22,519	4,320	1,630	2,713	2,444	10,492	...
1967	31,101	25,190	778	25,969	1,461	15	24,522	4,610	1,969	2,934	2,637	10,599	...
1968	34,654	28,151	910	29,061	1,634	14	27,441	4,853	2,360	3,203	2,845	10,819	...
1969	38,575	31,449	927	32,376	2,012	-79	30,285	5,646	2,644	3,493	3,073	11,045	5,005
1970	42,497	33,860	1,168	35,027	2,149	-96	32,782	6,575	3,139	3,782	3,370	11,237	5,045
1971	46,116	36,677	1,015	37,692	2,399	-101	35,192	7,258	3,667	4,007	3,611	11,510	5,123
1972	51,173	40,672	1,257	41,929	2,783	-126	39,020	8,037	4,116	4,352	3,880	11,759	5,334
1973	58,113	45,624	2,145	47,768	3,608	-154	44,007	9,156	4,950	4,835	4,320	12,019	5,608
1974	65,532	52,116	1,157	53,272	4,249	-131	48,893	10,735	5,904	5,342	4,728	12,268	5,822
1975	74,747	58,845	1,314	60,159	4,721	-127	55,311	12,055	7,380	5,947	5,332	12,568	5,938
1976	84,228	67,476	1,292	68,768	5,513	-91	63,164	12,991	8,073	6,528	5,809	12,903	6,207
1977	93,979	76,304	1,280	77,583	6,290	-303	70,990	14,401	8,588	7,124	6,285	13,192	6,521
1978	108,293	88,884	1,030	89,914	7,501	-424	81,989	16,745	9,560	8,023	7,086	13,498	6,900
1979	124,678	102,202	1,741	103,943	9,047	-442	94,455	19,319	10,903	8,978	7,831	13,887	7,215
1980	143,140	117,125	620	117,744	10,466	-546	106,732	23,638	12,770	9,983	8,662	14,338	7,496
1981	168,292	135,846	1,963	137,810	13,078	-334	124,398	29,390	14,505	11,413	9,800	14,746	7,900
1982	185,543	147,110	1,354	148,463	14,470	-405	133,589	35,441	16,514	12,102	10,517	15,331	8,074
1983	198,084	153,753	1,741	155,493	15,035	-388	140,071	39,372	18,640	12,575	11,141	15,752	8,064
1984	216,834	168,331	1,628	169,959	16,887	-445	152,627	44,389	19,818	13,546	12,061	16,007	8,434
1985	233,562	180,199	1,500	181,698	18,295	-474	162,930	49,456	21,176	14,353	12,786	16,273	8,674
1986	238,934	183,168	1,275	184,443	18,420	-435	165,588	50,129	23,217	14,427	12,993	16,561	8,514
1987	243,559	186,375	2,081	188,456	18,487	-431	169,538	49,609	24,412	14,653	13,146	16,622	8,723
1988	258,240	198,583	2,312	200,896	20,385	-437	180,074	52,497	25,669	15,494	13,976	16,667	8,880
1989	275,917	210,747	2,242	212,989	21,806	-446	190,737	56,931	28,248	16,417	14,722	16,807	9,005
1990	297,726	227,961	3,047	231,008	23,239	-485	207,284	58,829	31,613	17,455	15,646	17,057	9,243
1991	311,370	239,956	2,770	242,726	25,081	-563	217,083	59,148	35,140	17,897	16,120	17,398	9,404
1992	336,646	258,670	3,370	262,040	26,705	-586	234,749	60,341	41,556	18,956	17,156	17,760	9,483
1993	356,399	274,904	3,993	278,898	28,325	-607	249,966	61,965	44,468	19,624	17,741	18,162	9,781
1994	376,614	290,896	3,444	294,340	30,353	-671	263,316	65,490	47,808	20,287	18,322	18,564	10,098
1995	402,805	309,999	2,778	312,777	32,365	-753	279,659	71,194	51,952	21,246	19,149	18,959	10,440
1996	433,165	334,765	2,408	337,172	34,406	-823	301,943	75,651	55,571	22,397	20,052	19,340	10,738
1997	472,178	368,835	3,055	371,890	37,474	-963	333,453	80,560	58,166	23,919	21,266	19,740	11,165
1998	514,480	406,992	2,835	409,827	40,840	-1,058	367,928	87,156	59,396	25,523	22,593	20,158	11,542
1999	541,694	433,199	4,277	437,477	43,360	-1,083	393,034	87,525	61,135	26,349	23,328	20,558	11,761
2000	589,618	473,046	3,347	476,393	46,650	-1,180	428,562	96,269	64,787	28,151	24,793	20,944	12,139
2001	625,352	504,687	3,987	508,674	49,028	-1,185	458,461	95,930	70,962	29,332	25,982	21,320	12,285
2002	632,486	508,861	3,975	512,836	49,636	-1,135	462,065	92,360	78,060	29,160	26,451	21,690	12,292
2003	655,822	522,686	5,285	527,971	51,832	-1,060	475,080	97,244	83,498	29,768	27,260	22,031	12,375
2004	686,873	548,613	5,337	553,950	54,535	-978	498,438	100,395	88,041	30,672	28,167	22,394	12,588
2005	747,111	586,757	4,999	591,756	58,075	-948	532,733	116,824	97,554	32,799	29,756	22,778	13,004
2006	820,055	645,806	3,272	649,078	62,120	-1,034	585,925	129,902	104,228	35,106	31,636	23,360	13,493
2007	871,850	676,574	3,630	680,204	66,492	-1,121	612,591	144,737	114,522	36,583	32,865	23,832	14,008
2008	956,546	724,203	1,216	725,420	69,843	-1,190	654,387	171,931	130,228	39,349	35,095	24,309	14,366
2009	911,227	687,367	916	688,282	69,361	-1,396	617,526	150,915	142,786	36,740	33,916	24,802	14,203
2010	966,900	727,600	3,251	730,851	72,174	-1,528	657,149	151,137	158,615	38,304	35,224	25,243	14,263
2011	1,058,034	788,031	2,749	790,779	67,989	-1,840	720,950	172,862	164,222	41,255	37,459	25,646	14,681
2012	1,133,801	845,888	2,602	848,490	72,069	-2,208	774,213	195,877	163,712	43,458	39,511	26,090	15,096
2013	1,160,362	883,344	5,194	888,537	85,197	-2,373	800,967	189,856	169,539	43,805	39,447	26,489	15,530
2014	1,250,850	947,743	4,461	952,204	90,407	-2,439	859,359	212,474	179,017	46,367	41,651	26,977	15,998
2015	1,282,380	957,042	6,127	963,169	94,508	-2,453	866,208	225,367	190,805	46,654	41,900	27,487	16,409
2016	1,287,687	954,927	2,283	957,209	96,667	-2,146	858,397	228,221	201,069	46,092	41,758	27,937	16,674
2017	1,340,568	996,148	3,243	999,391	101,745	-1,933	895,713	238,805	206,050	47,332	42,879	28,323	16,963
2018	1,411,021	1,051,445	4,166	1,055,611	107,779	-2,098	945,734	250,924	214,364	49,161	44,720	28,702	17,605
2019	1,531,347	1,527,885	3,462	1,151,983	112,385	-2,439	1,037,159	269,602	224,585	52,829	47,705	28,987	18,024
2020	1,610,182	1,606,583	3,599	1,148,495	113,264	-2,479	1,032,752	266,992	310,438	54,841	49,863	29,361	...

... = Not available.

Personal Income and Employment by Region and State: Utah

(Millions of dollars, except as noted.)

| Year | Personal income, total | Derivation of personal income | | | | | | | | Per capita (dollars) | | Population (thousands) | Total employment (thousands) |
| | | Earnings by place of work | | | Less: Contributions for government social insurance | Plus: Adjustment for residence | Equals: Net earnings by place of residence | Plus: Dividends, interest, and rent | Plus: Personal current transfer receipts | Personal income | Disposable personal income | | |
		Nonfarm	Farm	Total									
1960	1,910	1,545	44	1,589	75	1	1,515	289	105	2,122	1,917	900	…
1961	2,047	1,665	35	1,700	79	1	1,621	309	117	2,187	1,972	936	…
1962	2,228	1,805	54	1,858	87	1	1,772	334	122	2,326	2,103	958	…
1963	2,315	1,904	41	1,945	105	1	1,841	343	132	2,377	2,146	974	…
1964	2,437	1,990	30	2,020	106	1	1,915	382	141	2,492	2,280	978	…
1965	2,583	2,079	47	2,127	109	1	2,019	412	152	2,599	2,381	994	…
1966	2,751	2,241	49	2,290	144	1	2,147	442	162	2,727	2,487	1,009	…
1967	2,904	2,356	63	2,419	159	1	2,262	451	191	2,849	2,592	1,019	…
1968	3,112	2,541	67	2,608	175	1	2,434	457	220	3,024	2,720	1,029	…
1969	3,407	2,751	74	2,825	175	4	2,654	505	248	3,254	2,895	1,047	444
1970	3,791	3,024	78	3,101	190	2	2,913	580	299	3,558	3,201	1,066	455
1971	4,243	3,363	77	3,440	218	2	3,224	666	352	3,855	3,495	1,101	467
1972	4,741	3,764	88	3,852	260	4	3,597	743	402	4,179	3,768	1,135	494
1973	5,283	4,198	130	4,328	338	7	3,997	814	472	4,520	4,070	1,169	523
1974	5,910	4,724	97	4,820	395	10	4,435	937	538	4,930	4,430	1,199	545
1975	6,591	5,232	67	5,299	432	13	4,880	1,037	673	5,341	4,854	1,234	553
1976	7,464	5,992	74	6,066	502	16	5,580	1,152	732	5,866	5,262	1,272	580
1977	8,441	6,842	64	6,906	575	21	6,351	1,301	788	6,412	5,733	1,316	613
1978	9,712	7,880	72	7,952	678	25	7,299	1,535	878	7,119	6,354	1,364	651
1979	10,972	8,911	82	8,993	810	33	8,216	1,757	999	7,748	6,877	1,416	678
1980	12,319	9,851	60	9,911	902	49	9,059	2,082	1,179	8,366	7,446	1,473	687
1981	13,893	11,026	42	11,067	1,088	53	10,032	2,480	1,381	9,167	8,116	1,515	697
1982	15,067	11,725	46	11,771	1,176	53	10,648	2,833	1,587	9,669	8,545	1,558	707
1983	16,135	12,479	36	12,515	1,267	43	11,291	3,115	1,729	10,116	9,048	1,595	719
1984	17,820	13,871	57	13,928	1,448	39	12,519	3,519	1,783	10,984	9,875	1,622	761
1985	19,070	14,844	57	14,901	1,578	41	13,364	3,771	1,936	11,607	10,406	1,643	789
1986	20,042	15,517	87	15,604	1,658	35	13,982	3,966	2,094	12,053	10,800	1,663	801
1987	20,995	16,182	130	16,313	1,723	26	14,616	4,135	2,244	12,511	11,172	1,678	830
1988	22,330	17,307	208	17,516	1,936	24	15,604	4,382	2,344	13,218	11,824	1,689	865
1989	23,967	18,536	205	18,741	2,115	22	16,648	4,731	2,588	14,050	12,584	1,706	897
1990	25,985	20,280	252	20,533	2,390	17	18,160	4,985	2,840	15,010	13,286	1,731	938
1991	27,864	21,905	233	22,138	2,619	12	19,530	5,197	3,137	15,656	13,941	1,780	961
1992	30,126	23,826	279	24,106	2,832	7	21,281	5,365	3,480	16,401	14,609	1,837	979
1993	32,491	25,763	300	26,063	3,077	7	22,993	5,723	3,775	17,115	15,208	1,898	1,026
1994	35,157	28,088	219	28,307	3,388	7	24,927	6,341	3,889	17,933	15,841	1,960	1,102
1995	38,308	30,417	166	30,583	3,687	0	26,896	7,193	4,219	19,019	16,738	2,014	1,150
1996	41,739	32,992	173	33,164	3,920	0	29,245	8,028	4,467	20,183	17,724	2,068	1,218
1997	45,125	35,831	198	36,029	4,202	-0	31,827	8,655	4,644	21,288	18,649	2,120	1,270
1998	48,821	38,426	232	38,658	4,484	-4	34,170	9,804	4,847	22,540	19,755	2,166	1,310
1999	51,414	40,937	240	41,176	4,730	-1	36,445	9,850	5,119	23,333	20,416	2,203	1,338
2000	55,060	43,537	207	43,744	5,046	5	38,703	10,858	5,499	24,531	21,458	2,245	1,381
2001	57,414	45,270	317	45,587	5,292	-0	40,295	11,088	6,031	25,141	22,115	2,284	1,392
2002	59,049	46,406	201	46,607	5,427	-2	41,178	11,270	6,601	25,399	22,807	2,325	1,395
2003	61,153	47,944	215	48,158	5,651	1	42,508	11,619	7,025	25,911	23,435	2,360	1,406
2004	65,207	51,568	308	51,876	6,128	2	45,750	12,018	7,439	27,152	24,601	2,402	1,453
2005	71,387	55,763	270	56,033	6,639	15	49,409	13,868	8,110	29,046	25,926	2,458	1,518
2006	79,438	62,511	149	62,660	7,282	19	55,397	15,230	8,811	31,454	27,879	2,526	1,593
2007	86,369	67,087	188	67,275	7,829	16	59,461	17,306	9,602	33,247	29,341	2,598	1,676
2008	90,567	68,359	192	68,550	8,022	33	60,562	18,791	11,214	34,009	30,364	2,663	1,688
2009	86,897	65,471	109	65,580	7,768	7	57,818	16,669	12,410	31,907	29,067	2,723	1,634
2010	89,346	66,726	216	66,942	7,863	1	59,080	16,500	13,767	32,193	29,374	2,775	1,621
2011	96,312	70,697	363	71,060	7,464	-1	63,594	18,498	14,220	34,223	30,960	2,814	1,664
2012	103,228	76,135	329	76,464	7,854	16	68,627	20,490	14,111	36,176	32,628	2,853	1,706
2013	106,613	79,862	535	80,397	9,302	27	71,123	20,900	14,591	36,789	32,904	2,898	1,753
2014	113,230	84,211	615	84,827	9,795	33	75,065	23,124	15,041	38,548	34,433	2,937	1,804
2015	121,876	89,745	598	90,343	10,238	10	80,114	25,837	15,925	40,864	36,343	2,982	1,866
2016	128,407	95,068	338	95,407	10,796	-31	84,579	26,991	16,837	42,203	37,396	3,043	1,933
2017	134,804	100,352	343	100,695	11,601	-38	89,055	28,356	17,392	43,441	38,469	3,103	1,988
2018	143,324	107,120	373	107,492	12,491	-51	94,951	30,045	18,329	45,340	40,291	3,161	2,068
2019	156,896	156,424	472	115,174	13,021	-43	102,111	34,906	19,880	48,978	43,533	3,203	2,127
2020	169,810	169,236	573	121,350	13,842	-83	107,425	34,431	27,954	52,251	46,616	3,250	…

… = Not available.

Personal Income and Employment by Region and State: Vermont

(Millions of dollars, except as noted.)

Year	Personal income, total	Earnings by place of work			Less: Contributions for government social insurance	Plus: Adjustment for residence	Equals: Net earnings by place of residence	Plus: Dividends, interest, and rent	Plus: Personal current transfer receipts	Per capita (dollars)		Population (thousands)	Total employment (thousands)
		Nonfarm	Farm	Total						Personal income	Disposable personal income		
1960	768	574	56	630	27	-6	597	112	59	1,975	1,781	389	...
1961	801	587	56	643	28	-5	609	124	67	2,053	1,855	390	...
1962	841	627	46	673	31	-5	637	134	70	2,139	1,933	393	...
1963	871	655	43	698	36	-5	657	140	75	2,195	1,963	397	...
1964	934	694	49	744	38	-5	700	156	77	2,340	2,110	399	...
1965	1,022	771	45	816	41	-8	767	174	81	2,530	2,297	404	...
1966	1,160	886	59	945	58	-10	877	196	87	2,808	2,513	413	...
1967	1,256	964	46	1,010	71	-10	929	219	107	2,969	2,654	423	...
1968	1,382	1,050	51	1,101	74	-11	1,016	240	126	3,215	2,844	430	...
1969	1,515	1,170	58	1,228	83	-27	1,118	254	144	3,468	3,019	437	203
1970	1,664	1,259	62	1,321	89	-26	1,205	287	172	3,728	3,265	446	205
1971	1,802	1,339	61	1,400	98	-24	1,278	319	205	3,967	3,570	454	206
1972	1,989	1,467	68	1,536	111	-21	1,404	355	230	4,294	3,797	463	211
1973	2,184	1,619	72	1,691	141	-20	1,531	391	262	4,661	4,168	469	220
1974	2,364	1,725	59	1,784	155	-16	1,613	436	315	4,996	4,469	473	222
1975	2,592	1,823	61	1,884	162	-11	1,711	479	401	5,401	4,857	480	220
1976	2,876	2,044	78	2,122	184	-5	1,933	511	432	5,928	5,356	485	228
1977	3,120	2,244	66	2,310	203	-1	2,105	572	442	6,339	5,679	492	236
1978	3,573	2,614	95	2,709	244	-1	2,464	642	467	7,171	6,417	498	252
1979	4,015	2,934	105	3,039	284	6	2,761	724	530	7,940	7,057	506	261
1980	4,505	3,191	108	3,299	309	15	3,005	872	629	8,790	7,782	513	266
1981	5,069	3,503	123	3,627	364	18	3,281	1,064	725	9,832	8,670	516	270
1982	5,502	3,699	123	3,822	392	24	3,454	1,242	807	10,600	9,448	519	271
1983	5,908	4,039	83	4,122	430	23	3,714	1,329	864	11,289	10,092	523	277
1984	6,496	4,469	84	4,553	489	29	4,092	1,514	890	12,335	11,053	527	289
1985	7,041	4,905	101	5,006	548	30	4,488	1,625	929	13,284	11,842	530	300
1986	7,574	5,352	99	5,452	602	34	4,884	1,733	957	14,182	12,584	534	311
1987	8,218	5,924	124	6,048	656	42	5,434	1,812	971	15,210	13,386	540	320
1988	8,977	6,505	121	6,626	742	47	5,931	2,021	1,025	16,328	14,441	550	334
1989	9,917	7,045	123	7,168	798	51	6,420	2,375	1,121	17,782	15,677	558	341
1990	10,298	7,306	115	7,421	870	52	6,603	2,444	1,251	18,233	16,108	565	341
1991	10,499	7,399	104	7,503	890	60	6,672	2,449	1,379	18,465	16,422	569	334
1992	11,242	7,887	177	8,064	937	68	7,195	2,487	1,560	19,627	17,517	573	342
1993	11,681	8,284	128	8,412	986	78	7,503	2,549	1,629	20,218	18,034	578	349
1994	12,247	8,650	129	8,780	1,043	93	7,829	2,693	1,725	20,977	18,739	584	359
1995	12,890	8,974	100	9,074	1,100	106	8,081	2,940	1,870	21,885	19,561	589	362
1996	13,586	9,436	147	9,583	1,144	122	8,561	3,093	1,932	22,883	20,318	594	367
1997	14,333	9,950	110	10,060	1,197	146	9,009	3,290	2,034	23,999	21,136	597	373
1998	15,304	10,699	136	10,835	1,266	174	9,743	3,444	2,117	25,488	22,354	600	381
1999	16,303	11,544	146	11,690	1,343	196	10,542	3,497	2,264	26,961	23,640	605	390
2000	17,627	12,534	150	12,685	1,435	227	11,477	3,714	2,437	28,915	25,239	610	401
2001	18,693	13,357	149	13,507	1,523	237	12,221	3,800	2,673	30,533	26,833	612	404
2002	19,073	13,856	115	13,971	1,552	235	12,654	3,564	2,856	30,991	27,716	615	406
2003	19,813	14,323	146	14,469	1,620	251	13,100	3,724	2,989	32,067	29,061	618	406
2004	20,965	15,123	194	15,317	1,709	238	13,846	3,997	3,123	33,818	30,718	620	413
2005	21,467	15,593	198	15,791	1,795	250	14,246	3,821	3,401	34,557	31,029	621	417
2006	22,941	16,157	121	16,278	1,884	281	14,675	4,486	3,780	36,830	32,898	623	421
2007	24,192	16,611	221	16,832	1,991	291	15,132	4,880	4,181	38,802	34,480	623	425
2008	25,369	17,133	228	17,362	2,054	286	15,593	5,116	4,661	40,645	36,305	624	424
2009	24,990	17,008	125	17,133	2,032	332	15,433	4,499	5,058	39,996	36,679	625	414
2010	25,787	17,625	193	17,818	2,065	330	16,083	4,357	5,348	41,201	37,750	626	413
2011	27,350	18,343	262	18,605	1,931	305	16,980	4,974	5,397	43,622	39,480	627	417
2012	28,304	18,856	255	19,111	2,005	313	17,419	5,361	5,525	45,209	41,069	626	422
2013	28,692	19,236	295	19,531	2,326	338	17,542	5,354	5,796	45,818	41,223	626	425
2014	29,808	19,496	356	19,851	2,429	371	17,794	5,969	6,045	47,676	42,814	625	429
2015	30,866	20,125	217	20,342	2,524	372	18,191	6,326	6,349	49,369	44,242	625	433
2016	31,572	20,637	200	20,837	2,588	346	18,594	6,503	6,474	50,625	45,317	624	434
2017	32,570	21,407	194	21,601	2,701	356	19,256	6,752	6,563	52,152	46,716	625	437
2018	33,569	22,067	131	22,198	2,799	377	19,776	7,023	6,769	53,598	48,206	626	438
2019	34,502	34,279	223	22,840	2,784	456	20,511	6,961	7,030	55,288	49,507	624	441
2020	36,560	36,292	267	22,469	2,756	477	20,190	6,902	9,467	58,650	52,979	623	...

... = Not available.

Personal Income and Employment by Region and State: Virginia

(Millions of dollars, except as noted.)

Year	Personal income, total	Earnings by place of work			Less: Contributions for government social insurance	Plus: Adjustment for residence	Equals: Net earnings by place of residence	Plus: Dividends, interest, and rent	Plus: Personal current transfer receipts	Per capita (dollars)		Population (thousands)	Total employment (thousands)
		Nonfarm	Farm	Total						Personal income	Disposable personal income		
1960	8,173	6,217	214	6,432	268	467	6,631	1,170	373	2,050	1,837	3,986	...
1961	8,706	6,557	225	6,782	284	500	6,998	1,280	428	2,126	1,911	4,095	...
1962	9,396	7,075	222	7,297	318	553	7,532	1,411	452	2,248	2,010	4,180	...
1963	10,107	7,687	136	7,823	370	611	8,064	1,558	485	2,364	2,097	4,276	...
1964	11,151	8,410	222	8,632	384	664	8,912	1,728	512	2,559	2,312	4,357	...
1965	12,038	9,029	208	9,237	403	748	9,581	1,896	560	2,729	2,453	4,411	...
1966	13,027	9,948	156	10,104	544	827	10,387	2,029	610	2,923	2,608	4,456	...
1967	14,251	10,760	201	10,961	633	988	11,316	2,201	734	3,161	2,815	4,508	...
1968	15,768	12,027	178	12,205	700	1,064	12,569	2,344	855	3,459	3,057	4,558	...
1969	17,848	13,676	213	13,889	799	991	14,080	2,789	979	3,868	3,361	4,614	2,148
1970	19,372	14,675	213	14,889	869	909	14,928	3,264	1,180	4,157	3,633	4,660	2,158
1971	21,411	16,168	193	16,362	999	947	16,310	3,688	1,413	4,505	3,975	4,753	2,196
1972	23,764	17,994	254	18,248	1,166	1,003	18,085	4,058	1,622	4,922	4,286	4,828	2,263
1973	26,613	20,139	355	20,494	1,483	1,081	20,092	4,584	1,938	5,424	4,752	4,907	2,384
1974	29,490	22,172	316	22,488	1,701	1,189	21,976	5,212	2,302	5,924	5,150	4,978	2,451
1975	32,380	23,842	266	24,108	1,822	1,457	23,743	5,689	2,948	6,404	5,688	5,056	2,425
1976	35,771	26,494	237	26,731	2,071	1,684	26,344	6,198	3,229	6,969	6,147	5,133	2,501
1977	39,631	29,463	169	29,633	2,302	1,907	29,238	6,931	3,463	7,613	6,675	5,206	2,585
1978	44,990	33,182	291	33,473	2,624	2,313	33,162	8,005	3,824	8,514	7,427	5,284	2,698
1979	50,182	36,945	157	37,102	3,054	2,734	36,783	9,012	4,388	9,425	8,203	5,325	2,767
1980	56,727	40,771	69	40,840	3,380	3,317	40,776	10,726	5,224	10,567	9,189	5,368	2,797
1981	63,698	45,128	271	45,399	4,013	3,413	44,799	12,870	6,029	11,700	10,106	5,444	2,812
1982	68,855	48,523	122	48,645	4,369	3,433	47,709	14,559	6,586	12,535	10,900	5,493	2,824
1983	74,239	53,033	45	53,078	4,945	3,378	51,511	15,607	7,120	13,341	11,712	5,565	2,897
1984	82,638	59,187	328	59,515	5,702	3,575	57,388	17,719	7,531	14,642	12,932	5,644	3,041
1985	89,308	64,824	231	65,055	6,436	3,698	62,316	18,945	8,048	15,627	13,717	5,715	3,181
1986	96,342	70,638	277	70,915	7,279	3,821	67,457	20,353	8,531	16,577	14,558	5,812	3,316
1987	104,064	77,372	371	77,743	7,981	3,935	73,697	21,507	8,860	17,542	15,282	5,932	3,480
1988	113,917	84,771	523	85,293	9,002	4,328	80,620	23,823	9,474	18,870	16,542	6,037	3,558
1989	123,237	90,578	643	91,221	9,746	4,562	86,037	26,824	10,376	20,136	17,574	6,120	3,655
1990	129,558	94,416	687	95,103	10,317	5,196	89,982	28,313	11,263	20,840	18,255	6,217	3,700
1991	135,042	97,909	622	98,531	10,808	5,629	93,352	29,248	12,442	21,431	18,873	6,301	3,642
1992	143,669	104,131	672	104,803	11,444	6,032	99,391	30,284	13,994	22,398	19,780	6,414	3,657
1993	150,973	109,183	544	109,727	12,027	6,344	104,045	32,129	14,800	23,192	20,440	6,510	3,730
1994	158,883	114,674	644	115,318	12,719	6,269	108,867	34,343	15,673	24,098	21,173	6,593	3,813
1995	167,003	119,719	567	120,286	13,264	6,376	113,398	36,631	16,975	25,035	21,972	6,671	3,903
1996	175,342	126,233	570	126,802	13,952	5,925	118,776	38,627	17,940	25,973	22,684	6,751	3,983
1997	186,846	135,316	425	135,742	14,948	6,482	127,276	41,006	18,564	27,360	23,782	6,829	4,082
1998	199,656	147,092	419	147,511	16,045	6,211	137,677	42,765	19,213	28,932	24,796	6,901	4,168
1999	213,982	159,093	326	159,419	17,282	7,922	150,058	43,674	20,249	30,568	25,992	7,000	4,261
2000	232,034	174,742	568	175,310	18,641	6,063	162,731	47,612	21,690	32,654	27,783	7,106	4,399
2001	244,137	184,178	488	184,666	19,664	6,575	171,577	48,422	24,137	33,916	28,921	7,198	4,417
2002	250,928	188,769	378	189,147	20,320	8,079	176,907	48,426	25,596	34,436	30,140	7,287	4,422
2003	265,980	199,635	286	199,921	21,346	8,775	187,350	51,184	27,447	36,104	31,913	7,367	4,467
2004	284,957	216,281	551	216,832	23,262	9,241	202,811	53,164	28,983	38,118	33,789	7,476	4,587
2005	304,721	230,067	593	230,660	24,881	9,508	215,288	57,834	31,599	40,216	35,289	7,577	4,701
2006	326,172	241,488	296	241,783	26,494	10,809	226,098	65,512	34,561	42,505	37,143	7,674	4,782
2007	343,288	251,271	262	251,533	27,640	11,417	235,310	71,184	36,794	44,289	38,599	7,751	4,869
2008	356,434	255,377	398	255,775	28,546	13,258	240,487	73,614	42,334	45,501	39,685	7,833	4,870
2009	348,944	252,926	370	253,295	28,610	13,084	237,769	65,766	45,409	44,026	39,401	7,926	4,758
2010	364,383	263,616	353	263,969	29,525	14,598	249,042	65,757	49,584	45,413	40,530	8,024	4,743
2011	386,298	271,491	621	272,112	27,123	16,876	261,865	73,017	51,416	47,688	42,058	8,100	4,803
2012	404,773	282,615	658	283,273	27,998	16,848	272,124	80,743	51,906	49,452	43,851	8,185	4,857
2013	402,065	285,074	792	285,866	32,386	16,613	270,092	78,101	53,872	48,717	42,710	8,253	4,899
2014	420,236	293,064	690	293,754	33,145	18,536	279,144	85,007	56,085	50,557	44,302	8,312	4,954
2015	440,824	307,046	437	307,483	34,667	18,847	291,662	89,605	59,557	52,712	45,986	8,363	5,061
2016	448,684	310,452	234	310,685	35,291	19,930	295,324	91,453	61,906	53,345	46,494	8,411	5,144
2017	466,743	322,845	186	323,031	36,904	20,520	306,647	95,567	64,529	55,137	48,048	8,465	5,200
2018	485,098	335,302	211	335,513	38,462	21,056	318,107	99,350	67,641	56,952	49,886	8,518	5,311
2019	509,201	508,855	346	350,117	39,895	20,077	330,298	107,610	71,293	59,509	52,015	8,557	5,407
2020	535,727	535,383	345	354,970	40,884	20,319	334,405	106,293	95,030	62,362	54,826	8,591	...

... = Not available.

Personal Income and Employment by Region and State: Washington

(Millions of dollars, except as noted.)

Year	Personal income, total	Earnings by place of work			Less: Contributions for government social insurance	Plus: Adjustment for residence	Equals: Net earnings by place of residence	Plus: Dividends, interest, and rent	Plus: Personal current transfer receipts	Per capita (dollars)		Population (thousands)	Total employment (thousands)
		Nonfarm	Farm	Total						Personal income	Disposable personal income		
1960	7,248	5,620	256	5,876	313	26	5,588	1,146	514	2,539	2,285	2,855	...
1961	7,609	5,904	247	6,150	327	29	5,852	1,194	563	2,640	2,374	2,882	...
1962	8,203	6,404	271	6,675	358	35	6,352	1,285	567	2,788	2,501	2,942	...
1963	8,394	6,541	275	6,815	395	42	6,463	1,333	598	2,841	2,544	2,955	...
1964	8,787	6,833	251	7,084	394	52	6,742	1,415	631	2,968	2,711	2,961	...
1965	9,465	7,343	271	7,614	418	63	7,259	1,543	663	3,190	2,905	2,967	...
1966	10,693	8,475	366	8,840	593	72	8,319	1,686	689	3,498	3,149	3,057	...
1967	11,710	9,314	327	9,642	688	83	9,037	1,845	829	3,689	3,307	3,174	...
1968	13,035	10,385	341	10,725	770	99	10,054	2,030	951	3,986	3,549	3,270	...
1969	14,236	11,287	398	11,685	909	89	10,865	2,294	1,077	4,258	3,755	3,343	1,539
1970	15,037	11,485	346	11,831	911	63	10,983	2,618	1,435	4,400	3,957	3,417	1,491
1971	15,839	11,863	391	12,254	979	61	11,336	2,831	1,671	4,595	4,171	3,447	1,457
1972	17,079	12,813	507	13,320	1,115	71	12,276	3,019	1,785	4,955	4,452	3,447	1,481
1973	19,236	14,402	756	15,158	1,435	87	13,810	3,415	2,011	5,532	4,953	3,477	1,558
1974	21,827	16,174	891	17,064	1,656	130	15,539	3,936	2,352	6,152	5,512	3,548	1,622
1975	24,720	18,112	906	19,018	1,837	200	17,381	4,431	2,907	6,831	6,145	3,619	1,659
1976	27,399	20,569	754	21,322	2,137	249	19,434	4,803	3,162	7,424	6,655	3,691	1,739
1977	30,412	23,305	604	23,909	2,457	232	21,684	5,418	3,310	8,062	7,206	3,772	1,815
1978	35,367	27,425	754	28,179	2,973	272	25,477	6,302	3,588	9,101	8,052	3,886	1,939
1979	40,756	31,782	740	32,521	3,561	484	29,444	7,296	4,015	10,156	8,909	4,013	2,058
1980	46,242	34,990	861	35,851	3,898	577	32,530	8,796	4,917	11,130	9,782	4,155	2,105
1981	51,391	38,301	863	39,163	4,585	431	35,009	10,670	5,712	12,133	10,630	4,236	2,119
1982	54,606	39,658	767	40,424	4,812	468	36,080	12,101	6,425	12,769	11,403	4,277	2,094
1983	58,282	41,624	1,066	42,690	5,114	494	38,070	13,193	7,019	13,553	12,233	4,300	2,140
1984	62,431	44,571	1,024	45,595	5,647	544	40,492	14,561	7,378	14,373	13,028	4,344	2,214
1985	66,376	47,585	753	48,337	6,087	572	42,823	15,619	7,935	15,085	13,645	4,400	2,277
1986	70,876	51,156	1,060	52,216	6,585	616	46,247	16,213	8,416	15,917	14,426	4,453	2,351
1987	75,031	54,816	1,084	55,899	7,025	672	49,547	16,622	8,862	16,556	14,890	4,532	2,470
1988	81,724	60,393	1,020	61,412	7,929	757	54,240	17,830	9,654	17,613	15,906	4,640	2,600
1989	90,313	65,974	1,156	67,129	8,669	845	59,305	20,412	10,596	19,028	17,006	4,746	2,718
1990	99,151	73,392	1,210	74,602	9,823	918	65,698	21,808	11,646	20,222	18,027	4,903	2,842
1991	106,189	78,770	1,281	80,051	10,637	990	70,404	22,593	13,192	21,129	18,935	5,026	2,877
1992	114,759	85,861	1,542	87,403	11,580	1,101	76,924	23,284	14,552	22,237	19,962	5,161	2,907
1993	120,677	89,558	1,744	91,302	12,079	1,196	80,419	24,680	15,578	22,860	20,585	5,279	2,951
1994	126,855	93,816	1,429	95,245	12,804	1,250	83,691	26,768	16,396	23,600	21,183	5,375	3,060
1995	134,146	97,921	1,468	99,389	13,404	1,407	87,393	29,232	17,521	24,475	21,935	5,481	3,101
1996	144,246	104,590	1,943	106,533	14,014	1,627	94,146	31,741	18,360	25,898	23,014	5,570	3,192
1997	155,514	114,078	1,549	115,627	14,810	1,786	102,602	33,867	19,044	27,405	24,160	5,675	3,298
1998	169,626	126,908	1,730	128,638	16,245	1,892	114,285	35,547	19,794	29,400	25,615	5,770	3,383
1999	181,365	138,196	1,498	139,694	17,002	1,958	124,651	35,728	20,986	31,042	26,621	5,843	3,447
2000	194,207	147,036	1,737	148,774	18,407	2,281	132,648	39,145	22,415	32,858	28,392	5,911	3,527
2001	199,075	149,599	1,573	151,171	18,149	2,376	135,399	38,560	25,117	33,258	29,234	5,986	3,516
2002	202,862	152,429	1,654	154,082	18,543	2,432	137,972	38,178	26,712	33,518	30,157	6,052	3,489
2003	210,864	156,988	2,205	159,192	19,320	2,568	142,440	40,456	27,968	34,545	31,407	6,104	3,516
2004	225,994	165,447	2,139	167,586	20,550	2,767	149,804	47,784	28,407	36,577	33,472	6,179	3,585
2005	235,227	175,155	1,876	177,031	21,864	3,035	158,201	46,928	30,097	37,592	34,042	6,257	3,688
2006	256,517	188,241	1,804	190,046	23,187	3,442	170,300	53,914	32,303	40,265	36,222	6,371	3,798
2007	278,656	200,667	2,285	202,952	24,438	3,665	182,179	61,483	34,994	43,125	38,556	6,462	3,925
2008	292,344	205,825	2,185	208,010	25,047	3,682	186,645	65,409	40,291	44,550	40,154	6,562	3,955
2009	279,038	196,435	2,232	198,666	24,818	3,394	177,242	56,351	45,445	41,851	38,630	6,667	3,816
2010	286,732	201,566	2,507	204,073	25,468	3,241	181,846	54,708	50,179	42,524	39,083	6,743	3,771
2011	303,939	210,503	3,235	213,738	23,940	3,525	193,322	60,670	49,948	44,555	40,414	6,822	3,814
2012	328,949	226,613	3,345	229,958	24,700	3,609	208,868	70,036	50,046	47,723	43,426	6,893	3,909
2013	335,891	237,548	3,570	241,118	28,901	3,582	215,798	69,147	50,945	48,240	43,430	6,963	3,992
2014	362,952	250,726	3,295	254,020	30,405	3,537	227,152	80,174	55,626	51,465	46,206	7,052	4,095
2015	384,651	263,184	4,844	268,028	32,098	3,888	239,817	88,216	56,617	53,696	47,891	7,164	4,199
2016	404,232	278,050	4,062	282,112	33,509	4,190	252,792	91,551	59,888	55,415	49,202	7,295	4,310
2017	428,765	298,546	3,807	302,354	36,007	4,301	270,648	96,125	61,992	57,743	51,222	7,425	4,401
2018	458,017	322,101	3,669	325,771	39,127	4,389	291,033	101,924	65,061	60,781	54,103	7,536	4,543
2019	493,128	489,669	3,459	348,827	40,387	4,668	313,109	111,772	68,247	64,766	58,077	7,614	4,647
2020	525,643	521,453	4,191	359,006	41,856	4,592	321,742	110,690	93,211	68,322	61,588	7,694	...

... = Not available.

Personal Income and Employment by Region and State: West Virginia

(Millions of dollars, except as noted.)

Year	Personal income, total	Derivation of personal income								Per capita (dollars)		Population (thousands)	Total employment (thousands)
		Earnings by place of work			Less: Contributions for government social insurance	Plus: Adjustment for residence	Equals: Net earnings by place of residence	Plus: Dividends, interest, and rent	Plus: Personal current transfer receipts	Personal income	Disposable personal income		
		Nonfarm	Farm	Total									
1960	3,076	2,579	50	2,629	155	-20	2,454	318	304	1,660	1,491	1,853	...
1961	3,117	2,572	43	2,615	153	-20	2,442	331	344	1,705	1,533	1,828	...
1962	3,256	2,687	32	2,719	168	-19	2,532	357	368	1,800	1,619	1,809	...
1963	3,400	2,809	25	2,834	186	-18	2,630	391	379	1,893	1,697	1,796	...
1964	3,628	2,988	23	3,011	173	-17	2,821	422	385	2,019	1,831	1,797	...
1965	3,878	3,190	25	3,215	184	-13	3,018	449	411	2,171	1,973	1,786	...
1966	4,115	3,463	15	3,477	244	-10	3,223	459	434	2,318	2,092	1,775	...
1967	4,361	3,642	29	3,671	268	-8	3,395	473	492	2,465	2,227	1,769	...
1968	4,623	3,855	23	3,877	298	2	3,581	498	544	2,622	2,344	1,763	...
1969	4,944	4,142	31	4,173	323	-73	3,777	569	599	2,832	2,487	1,746	652
1970	5,512	4,542	26	4,568	350	-75	4,143	647	722	3,156	2,800	1,747	660
1971	6,052	4,929	26	4,954	395	-90	4,469	712	871	3,418	3,049	1,770	670
1972	6,701	5,443	31	5,474	455	-103	4,917	786	998	3,729	3,312	1,797	684
1973	7,333	5,883	45	5,928	568	-105	5,255	892	1,186	4,062	3,631	1,805	700
1974	8,129	6,485	29	6,514	648	-120	5,747	1,038	1,344	4,481	3,959	1,814	711
1975	9,186	7,226	15	7,240	711	-124	6,405	1,180	1,601	4,991	4,423	1,841	717
1976	10,241	8,150	4	8,154	819	-153	7,183	1,300	1,758	5,455	4,805	1,877	739
1977	11,457	9,217	-1	9,215	918	-185	8,113	1,469	1,875	6,012	5,306	1,906	758
1978	12,753	10,288	13	10,301	1,058	-215	9,029	1,641	2,083	6,641	5,879	1,920	781
1979	14,223	11,352	18	11,370	1,212	-227	9,931	1,853	2,438	7,335	6,450	1,939	790
1980	15,633	12,076	9	12,085	1,311	-250	10,525	2,272	2,836	8,011	7,019	1,951	782
1981	17,051	12,783	-22	12,761	1,484	-227	11,051	2,798	3,203	8,726	7,661	1,954	762
1982	18,069	13,126	-28	13,098	1,572	-170	11,357	3,201	3,512	9,268	8,184	1,950	740
1983	18,550	12,983	-15	12,968	1,571	-145	11,252	3,407	3,891	9,537	8,475	1,945	722
1984	19,941	14,010	24	14,034	1,737	-112	12,185	3,781	3,975	10,344	9,237	1,928	732
1985	20,766	14,546	22	14,569	1,828	-107	12,633	3,984	4,149	10,890	9,721	1,907	732
1986	21,261	14,710	48	14,758	1,921	-86	12,751	4,104	4,406	11,295	10,122	1,882	731
1987	21,785	15,153	7	15,160	1,992	-26	13,142	4,114	4,528	11,728	10,500	1,858	738
1988	23,238	16,273	6	16,278	2,190	8	14,096	4,362	4,779	12,697	11,451	1,830	751
1989	24,601	16,923	34	16,957	2,310	95	14,743	4,815	5,043	13,618	12,191	1,807	757
1990	26,186	18,101	47	18,148	2,502	92	15,738	5,042	5,407	14,608	13,073	1,793	778
1991	27,308	18,745	37	18,782	2,663	74	16,194	5,035	6,079	15,182	13,632	1,799	779
1992	29,404	19,919	62	19,982	2,840	134	17,276	5,159	6,970	16,277	14,701	1,806	789
1993	30,499	20,703	65	20,767	3,059	132	17,840	5,238	7,420	16,780	15,160	1,818	801
1994	31,821	21,792	61	21,853	3,205	181	18,829	5,468	7,524	17,480	15,740	1,820	822
1995	32,895	22,410	24	22,434	3,352	224	19,306	5,829	7,759	18,037	16,219	1,824	838
1996	34,209	23,081	9	23,090	3,454	234	19,870	6,158	8,182	18,767	16,844	1,823	847
1997	35,630	23,976	-0	23,976	3,548	393	20,820	6,442	8,368	19,587	17,524	1,819	858
1998	37,282	24,934	1	24,934	3,721	439	21,653	6,956	8,673	20,534	18,359	1,816	868
1999	38,283	25,920	-13	25,907	3,826	501	22,582	6,848	8,853	21,130	18,895	1,812	868
2000	40,453	27,387	19	27,406	4,141	625	23,891	7,275	9,287	22,386	20,014	1,807	876
2001	42,850	28,630	30	28,660	4,115	772	25,317	7,271	10,261	23,786	21,237	1,801	873
2002	44,287	29,453	-33	29,421	4,061	817	26,176	7,023	11,087	24,530	22,278	1,805	871
2003	44,871	30,035	-14	30,021	4,253	961	26,729	6,781	11,361	24,759	22,636	1,812	868
2004	46,486	31,525	31	31,556	4,381	1,090	28,265	6,862	11,359	25,592	23,486	1,816	879
2005	48,840	33,311	12	33,323	4,571	1,289	30,042	7,004	11,795	26,828	24,400	1,820	891
2006	52,179	35,291	-24	35,268	4,627	1,336	31,977	7,601	12,601	28,546	25,909	1,828	903
2007	54,199	35,606	-57	35,549	4,508	1,486	32,527	8,341	13,331	29,551	26,689	1,834	916
2008	57,652	37,186	-30	37,156	4,546	1,441	34,051	8,813	14,789	31,328	28,139	1,840	918
2009	58,150	37,014	-36	36,979	4,598	1,328	33,709	8,476	15,965	31,470	28,810	1,848	899
2010	60,062	38,170	-29	38,141	4,702	1,459	34,898	8,323	16,841	32,392	29,640	1,854	899
2011	63,449	40,287	6	40,293	4,381	1,468	37,379	9,098	16,972	34,184	30,915	1,856	909
2012	65,252	41,543	-5	41,538	4,499	1,215	38,254	9,699	17,299	35,143	32,009	1,857	919
2013	64,793	41,616	30	41,645	5,049	1,256	37,852	9,302	17,638	34,950	31,621	1,854	914
2014	66,680	42,154	17	42,171	5,198	1,474	38,447	9,809	18,424	36,053	32,557	1,849	910
2015	67,737	42,165	-9	42,156	5,255	1,538	38,438	10,169	19,130	36,774	33,165	1,842	902
2016	67,583	41,298	-31	41,267	5,273	1,680	37,674	10,367	19,542	36,912	33,422	1,831	887
2017	69,873	42,944	-77	42,867	5,575	1,732	39,023	10,769	20,081	38,454	34,829	1,817	889
2018	73,278	45,992	-50	45,942	5,999	1,657	41,600	11,219	20,458	40,578	36,805	1,806	897
2019	75,835	75,866	-32	47,040	5,868	1,593	42,765	11,509	21,561	42,242	38,399	1,795	895
2020	80,510	80,552	-42	45,750	5,738	1,778	41,790	11,461	27,260	45,109	41,400	1,785	...

... = Not available.

Personal Income and Employment by Region and State: Wisconsin

(Millions of dollars, except as noted.)

Year	Personal income, total	Earnings by place of work			Less: Contributions for government social insurance	Plus: Adjustment for residence	Equals: Net earnings by place of residence	Plus: Dividends, interest, and rent	Plus: Personal current transfer receipts	Per capita (dollars)		Population (thousands)	Total employment (thousands)
		Nonfarm	Farm	Total						Personal income	Disposable personal income		
1960	8,994	7,017	428	7,445	341	64	7,167	1,269	558	2,270	2,003	3,962	...
1961	9,282	7,098	496	7,593	348	67	7,312	1,324	646	2,315	2,061	4,009	...
1962	9,810	7,565	492	8,056	374	75	7,757	1,395	658	2,423	2,146	4,049	...
1963	10,135	7,890	439	8,329	433	81	7,978	1,462	695	2,465	2,174	4,112	...
1964	10,909	8,508	478	8,986	449	92	8,628	1,557	724	2,619	2,336	4,165	...
1965	11,798	9,151	545	9,696	479	104	9,321	1,698	779	2,788	2,477	4,232	...
1966	12,888	10,092	670	10,762	668	124	10,217	1,809	863	3,016	2,654	4,274	...
1967	13,602	10,696	564	11,260	760	137	10,637	1,902	1,063	3,161	2,759	4,303	...
1968	14,896	11,536	645	12,181	815	158	11,524	2,135	1,237	3,428	2,991	4,345	...
1969	16,425	12,662	638	13,300	934	250	12,616	2,450	1,359	3,752	3,218	4,378	1,944
1970	17,649	13,357	639	13,997	974	255	13,277	2,773	1,599	3,988	3,469	4,426	1,954
1971	18,959	14,190	693	14,883	1,070	267	14,080	3,010	1,870	4,251	3,748	4,460	1,957
1972	20,732	15,635	729	16,365	1,248	291	15,408	3,244	2,079	4,609	4,019	4,498	2,014
1973	23,158	17,544	916	18,460	1,614	316	17,162	3,631	2,365	5,125	4,478	4,518	2,116
1974	25,437	19,183	806	19,988	1,840	343	18,491	4,135	2,811	5,605	4,870	4,538	2,159
1975	27,872	20,504	867	21,371	1,927	345	19,789	4,556	3,528	6,099	5,358	4,570	2,148
1976	30,609	22,957	762	23,720	2,188	383	21,915	4,872	3,823	6,676	5,828	4,585	2,211
1977	34,210	25,642	1,144	26,787	2,443	423	24,767	5,390	4,054	7,416	6,452	4,613	2,293
1978	38,210	28,989	1,128	30,117	2,843	475	27,749	5,986	4,475	8,249	7,117	4,632	2,380
1979	42,798	32,314	1,407	33,721	3,302	506	30,925	6,740	5,134	9,172	7,931	4,666	2,460
1980	47,282	34,342	1,446	35,788	3,497	530	32,822	8,203	6,257	10,034	8,712	4,712	2,443
1981	51,613	36,695	1,172	37,867	3,999	581	34,449	10,050	7,115	10,920	9,424	4,726	2,415
1982	54,462	37,789	1,024	38,814	4,156	601	35,258	11,268	7,936	11,517	10,034	4,729	2,373
1983	57,197	39,863	473	40,336	4,359	651	36,628	12,041	8,527	12,114	10,671	4,721	2,376
1984	62,913	43,864	1,003	44,868	4,904	761	40,725	13,457	8,732	13,285	11,739	4,736	2,467
1985	66,277	46,202	1,031	47,233	5,208	849	42,874	14,128	9,275	13,960	12,337	4,748	2,495
1986	69,917	48,904	1,307	50,211	5,503	930	45,638	14,711	9,568	14,702	12,995	4,756	2,537
1987	73,794	52,499	1,418	53,917	5,811	1,033	49,139	14,871	9,784	15,445	13,569	4,778	2,605
1988	78,456	57,055	855	57,910	6,549	1,194	52,555	15,766	10,136	16,269	14,312	4,822	2,684
1989	85,534	60,870	1,741	62,611	7,004	1,233	56,840	17,752	10,942	17,612	15,464	4,857	2,740
1990	90,431	65,223	1,397	66,620	7,801	1,343	60,161	18,535	11,735	18,438	16,162	4,905	2,814
1991	94,002	68,386	1,018	69,404	8,259	1,363	62,507	18,760	12,735	18,936	16,632	4,964	2,840
1992	101,408	74,287	1,276	75,563	8,872	1,462	68,153	19,453	13,802	20,179	17,742	5,025	2,894
1993	106,714	78,894	956	79,850	9,408	1,519	71,961	20,373	14,381	20,986	18,418	5,085	2,950
1994	113,394	83,975	1,224	85,199	10,146	1,656	76,709	21,855	14,830	22,088	19,334	5,134	3,040
1995	119,327	87,960	797	88,757	10,657	1,775	79,875	23,731	15,722	23,015	20,097	5,185	3,120
1996	126,197	92,251	1,372	93,623	11,100	1,918	84,442	25,472	16,283	24,129	20,934	5,230	3,171
1997	133,915	98,605	1,000	99,605	11,780	2,121	89,946	27,151	16,818	25,429	21,934	5,266	3,226
1998	143,011	105,273	1,370	106,643	12,476	2,306	96,473	29,290	17,247	26,995	23,187	5,298	3,288
1999	149,070	111,625	1,325	112,950	13,251	2,477	102,176	28,940	17,954	27,954	24,044	5,333	3,350
2000	158,928	118,698	894	119,592	13,901	2,707	108,399	31,234	19,294	29,573	25,502	5,374	3,414
2001	166,810	124,298	1,192	125,491	14,202	2,839	114,128	31,153	21,529	30,852	26,752	5,407	3,404
2002	171,174	128,749	1,098	129,847	14,589	2,924	118,182	29,825	23,166	31,436	27,852	5,445	3,395
2003	175,870	132,479	1,562	134,041	15,072	2,999	121,968	30,049	23,853	32,098	28,673	5,479	3,413
2004	183,913	139,157	1,913	141,069	15,875	3,105	128,299	31,060	24,554	33,354	29,897	5,514	3,468
2005	190,528	143,554	1,669	145,223	16,520	3,299	132,002	32,217	26,309	34,353	30,555	5,546	3,511
2006	202,454	150,336	1,403	151,739	17,406	3,423	137,755	36,787	27,912	36,297	32,098	5,578	3,547
2007	211,887	154,734	2,130	156,864	17,984	3,683	142,564	39,081	30,241	37,764	33,348	5,611	3,585
2008	219,515	157,930	1,799	159,728	18,552	3,728	144,904	40,743	33,867	38,914	34,337	5,641	3,573
2009	215,913	153,566	927	154,493	18,027	3,291	139,757	36,980	39,176	38,085	34,433	5,669	3,445
2010	221,895	156,627	1,754	158,382	18,413	3,243	143,211	36,635	42,049	38,994	35,231	5,690	3,426
2011	234,575	163,890	2,913	166,803	17,234	3,357	152,926	40,996	40,653	41,119	36,759	5,705	3,474
2012	245,700	170,884	2,758	173,642	17,766	3,296	159,172	45,111	41,418	42,956	38,469	5,720	3,499
2013	247,127	175,325	3,091	178,416	20,543	3,254	161,127	43,629	42,371	43,076	38,185	5,737	3,540
2014	257,572	181,091	3,112	184,203	21,176	3,486	166,513	46,927	44,132	44,780	39,801	5,752	3,587
2015	268,238	187,302	2,850	190,153	21,915	3,651	171,888	50,397	45,953	46,558	41,124	5,761	3,626
2016	273,788	191,825	1,999	193,824	22,324	3,757	175,258	51,984	46,546	47,426	41,795	5,773	3,660
2017	283,636	198,492	1,758	200,250	23,248	3,942	180,944	54,032	48,659	48,970	43,169	5,792	3,692
2018	295,073	206,082	1,763	207,845	24,273	4,097	187,669	56,106	51,299	50,756	44,953	5,814	3,721
2019	309,909	307,532	2,377	217,181	24,978	4,097	196,301	59,745	53,864	53,207	47,264	5,825	3,753
2020	323,635	320,739	2,896	216,979	25,221	4,024	195,782	59,221	68,631	55,487	49,601	5,833	...

... = Not available.

Personal Income and Employment by Region and State: Wyoming

(Millions of dollars, except as noted.)

| Year | Personal income, total | Earnings by place of work | | | Less: Contributions for government social insurance | Plus: Adjustment for residence | Equals: Net earnings by place of residence | Plus: Dividends, interest, and rent | Plus: Personal current transfer receipts | Per capita (dollars) | | Population (thousands) | Total employment (thousands) |
		Nonfarm	Farm	Total						Personal income	Disposable personal income		
1960	789	603	51	654	34	-2	618	125	45	2,382	2,138	331	...
1961	829	618	57	675	34	-1	640	137	53	2,461	2,223	337	...
1962	859	627	67	694	35	-1	658	147	55	2,580	2,319	333	...
1963	879	646	67	713	40	-1	672	151	56	2,616	2,327	336	...
1964	906	690	47	738	43	-1	694	158	55	2,673	2,445	339	...
1965	936	698	53	751	41	-1	710	168	58	2,818	2,574	332	...
1966	958	714	58	772	48	-0	724	173	62	2,967	2,692	323	...
1967	1,025	756	70	827	53	-0	773	181	72	3,184	2,871	322	...
1968	1,094	830	62	892	59	0	833	180	81	3,375	3,030	324	...
1969	1,219	911	70	981	66	L	915	215	89	3,704	3,285	329	158
1970	1,348	991	79	1,070	71	0	999	246	103	4,038	3,600	334	159
1971	1,498	1,093	88	1,181	81	-1	1,100	279	119	4,404	3,954	340	165
1972	1,685	1,226	126	1,352	95	-3	1,254	301	129	4,856	4,408	347	172
1973	1,969	1,443	153	1,596	127	-7	1,461	355	152	5,571	4,987	353	182
1974	2,303	1,771	111	1,882	158	-14	1,710	421	172	6,317	5,554	365	194
1975	2,607	2,058	67	2,125	181	-16	1,928	472	208	6,853	6,118	380	203
1976	2,890	2,322	48	2,369	213	-22	2,135	524	232	7,309	6,466	395	214
1977	3,376	2,759	45	2,804	249	-29	2,526	595	254	8,203	7,254	412	231
1978	4,034	3,331	65	3,396	309	-38	3,050	698	286	9,361	8,254	431	250
1979	4,716	3,917	96	4,014	380	-54	3,579	806	331	10,437	9,055	452	266
1980	5,506	4,538	86	4,623	441	-74	4,109	1,005	393	11,612	10,109	474	279
1981	6,300	5,146	51	5,197	541	-83	4,573	1,256	471	12,812	11,087	492	289
1982	6,617	5,242	29	5,271	565	-80	4,626	1,449	542	13,066	11,479	506	287
1983	6,568	4,976	36	5,012	522	-59	4,431	1,496	641	12,870	11,486	510	274
1984	6,857	5,193	14	5,207	560	-53	4,593	1,631	633	13,581	12,212	505	276
1985	7,160	5,414	18	5,432	599	-52	4,780	1,708	672	14,330	12,882	500	277
1986	7,131	5,279	40	5,319	581	-42	4,696	1,694	741	14,387	13,075	496	264
1987	6,864	4,951	59	5,010	550	-27	4,434	1,679	752	14,392	13,014	477	258
1988	7,003	5,045	59	5,104	602	-22	4,480	1,740	783	15,056	13,597	465	264
1989	7,643	5,410	90	5,500	628	-15	4,858	1,936	849	16,673	14,956	458	265
1990	8,233	5,802	153	5,955	699	-11	5,246	2,075	913	18,147	16,286	454	271
1991	8,642	5,996	213	6,209	745	-1	5,463	2,164	1,015	18,818	16,945	459	277
1992	9,131	6,328	221	6,549	777	-6	5,766	2,242	1,123	19,583	17,659	466	280
1993	9,660	6,712	247	6,959	817	-8	6,134	2,303	1,223	20,419	18,359	473	285
1994	10,103	7,073	122	7,195	866	-8	6,321	2,488	1,293	21,034	18,891	480	298
1995	10,585	7,263	102	7,365	891	-5	6,469	2,736	1,380	21,818	19,611	485	301
1996	11,078	7,530	83	7,614	913	0	6,702	2,923	1,453	22,693	19,960	488	304
1997	11,885	7,990	184	8,174	957	5	7,223	3,170	1,492	24,282	21,265	489	307
1998	12,656	8,429	99	8,528	1,007	8	7,529	3,593	1,534	25,788	22,546	491	310
1999	13,505	8,974	168	9,142	1,055	7	8,093	3,816	1,596	27,461	23,955	492	315
2000	14,514	9,639	124	9,764	1,121	14	8,656	4,142	1,716	29,363	25,402	494	325
2001	15,320	10,334	192	10,526	1,202	-9	9,315	4,157	1,849	30,971	27,008	495	330
2002	15,725	10,884	102	10,986	1,227	-29	9,729	4,015	1,980	31,448	28,216	500	334
2003	16,669	11,357	182	11,539	1,303	-50	10,186	4,338	2,145	33,109	30,059	503	337
2004	17,807	11,885	182	12,067	1,397	-63	10,607	4,933	2,267	34,977	31,800	509	344
2005	19,575	12,784	228	13,012	1,510	-93	11,409	5,781	2,385	38,071	34,023	514	354
2006	22,575	14,947	98	15,045	1,914	-141	12,990	7,055	2,530	43,192	37,894	523	370
2007	24,019	16,269	49	16,317	2,117	-177	14,023	7,308	2,687	44,905	39,196	535	388
2008	26,334	18,073	106	18,179	2,250	-216	15,713	7,500	3,121	48,227	42,428	546	399
2009	24,347	17,371	90	17,461	2,181	-216	15,065	5,905	3,377	43,488	39,903	560	387
2010	25,967	18,218	120	18,338	2,218	-238	15,883	6,442	3,642	46,002	41,861	564	385
2011	28,426	19,118	366	19,484	2,102	-247	17,135	7,633	3,658	50,115	45,460	567	390
2012	30,953	20,220	136	20,357	2,215	-246	17,896	9,403	3,654	53,712	47,874	576	397
2013	30,912	20,868	245	21,113	2,496	-235	18,382	8,745	3,784	53,102	47,236	582	400
2014	33,020	21,929	376	22,305	2,653	-222	19,430	9,658	3,933	56,682	50,522	583	406
2015	33,515	21,821	286	22,107	2,609	-234	19,265	10,081	4,169	57,225	51,226	586	406
2016	32,435	20,543	156	20,698	2,507	-272	17,919	10,154	4,361	55,511	50,207	584	398
2017	33,221	20,868	146	21,014	2,584	-267	18,163	10,525	4,533	57,384	51,944	579	398
2018	34,719	21,724	184	21,908	2,696	-276	18,936	11,046	4,737	60,095	54,657	578	404
2019	35,993	35,775	218	23,456	2,746	-270	20,441	10,508	5,043	62,044	55,858	580	413
2020	36,840	36,528	312	22,744	2,648	-239	19,858	10,397	6,585	63,263	57,451	582	...

... = Not available.

METROPOLITAN STATISTICAL AREA

Personal Income and Employment by Area: Abilene, TX

(Thousands of dollars, except as noted.)

Year	Personal income, total	Earnings by place of work			Less: Contributions for government social insurance	Plus: Adjustment for residence	Equals: Net earnings by place of residence	Plus: Dividends, interest, and rent	Plus: Personal current transfer receipts	Per capita personal income (dollars)	Population (persons)	Total employment
		Nonfarm	Farm	Total								
1970	445,225	322,395	23,059	345,454	19,934	1,887	327,407	76,169	41,649	3,634	122,505	56,215
1971	476,061	346,964	20,798	367,762	22,303	2,011	347,470	81,400	47,191	3,813	124,841	56,614
1972	541,293	392,737	28,946	421,683	26,147	2,370	397,906	91,107	52,280	4,212	128,517	59,092
1973	581,519	418,998	27,728	446,726	31,846	2,456	417,336	101,206	62,977	4,560	127,533	60,359
1974	655,804	487,544	8,813	496,357	38,282	1,621	459,696	122,291	73,817	5,099	128,625	63,366
1975	771,668	561,861	21,367	583,228	44,278	1,693	540,643	142,335	88,690	5,889	131,031	65,822
1976	852,803	632,663	17,641	650,304	50,603	2,088	601,789	154,059	96,955	6,394	133,379	68,298
1977	926,754	695,027	12,946	707,973	55,793	2,168	654,348	169,472	102,934	6,965	133,052	69,994
1978	1,062,407	805,455	9,999	815,454	65,480	1,508	751,482	196,762	114,163	7,901	134,462	72,932
1979	1,210,051	915,614	20,602	936,216	78,599	1,030	858,647	224,550	126,854	8,858	136,601	75,773
1980	1,396,724	1,053,472	10,764	1,064,236	91,347	350	973,239	278,688	144,797	9,970	140,098	78,280
1981	1,681,889	1,246,899	46,280	1,293,179	116,795	-3,110	1,173,274	345,886	162,729	11,736	143,310	84,737
1982	1,805,340	1,317,942	23,155	1,341,097	125,452	-1,682	1,213,963	410,323	181,054	12,125	148,899	86,685
1983	1,890,446	1,371,204	8,428	1,379,632	129,737	-2,173	1,247,722	445,261	197,463	12,361	152,939	86,693
1984	2,010,700	1,447,398	10,327	1,457,725	140,379	-2,598	1,314,748	485,357	210,595	13,092	153,587	87,720
1985	2,138,884	1,530,638	308	1,530,946	150,084	-2,406	1,378,456	535,274	225,154	13,937	153,470	88,722
1986	2,128,927	1,495,841	10,951	1,506,792	144,782	-323	1,361,687	520,671	246,569	13,732	155,031	83,720
1987	2,097,573	1,429,973	28,279	1,458,252	138,648	1,501	1,321,105	516,185	260,283	13,651	153,655	82,965
1988	2,189,009	1,520,668	15,165	1,535,833	152,195	3,296	1,386,934	530,510	271,565	14,589	150,042	83,645
1989	2,274,917	1,521,562	18,571	1,540,133	154,717	7,412	1,392,828	591,738	290,351	15,235	149,324	82,367
1990	2,324,820	1,556,932	38,433	1,595,365	156,668	10,185	1,448,882	554,967	320,971	15,726	147,834	80,942
1991	2,382,790	1,624,567	14,310	1,638,877	168,263	4,971	1,475,585	549,345	357,860	16,165	147,400	82,259
1992	2,541,971	1,720,134	36,748	1,756,882	176,728	6,095	1,586,249	547,480	408,242	16,956	149,917	82,277
1993	2,668,070	1,800,905	30,802	1,831,707	184,214	6,165	1,653,658	585,307	429,105	17,449	152,909	84,362
1994	2,724,394	1,872,355	19,614	1,891,969	193,362	4,548	1,703,155	561,550	459,689	17,716	153,779	85,682
1995	2,915,506	1,974,194	17,649	1,991,843	203,788	3,487	1,791,542	622,815	501,149	18,678	156,097	88,181
1996	3,105,725	2,120,190	6,377	2,126,567	214,106	3,104	1,915,565	654,785	535,375	19,864	156,351	89,587
1997	3,322,907	2,298,130	22,943	2,321,073	227,051	4,368	2,098,390	663,437	561,080	21,111	157,405	91,934
1998	3,468,509	2,405,758	8,463	2,414,221	232,366	6,340	2,188,195	713,582	566,732	21,916	158,264	92,577
1999	3,592,824	2,511,768	30,364	2,542,132	240,232	7,570	2,309,470	697,372	585,982	22,490	159,755	91,417
2000	3,677,809	2,540,158	7,822	2,547,980	244,234	10,116	2,313,862	756,728	607,219	22,945	160,288	91,027
2001	3,752,372	2,555,473	37,105	2,592,578	251,060	10,981	2,352,499	743,687	656,186	23,612	158,917	89,511
2002	3,901,140	2,715,045	15,672	2,730,717	266,877	5,496	2,469,336	724,889	706,915	24,534	159,012	90,338
2003	4,136,447	2,874,746	32,648	2,907,394	283,998	3,834	2,627,230	755,709	753,508	26,047	158,810	91,132
2004	4,322,852	3,045,136	36,871	3,082,007	301,298	2,716	2,783,425	745,012	794,415	26,992	160,156	91,998
2005	4,559,728	3,188,812	31,044	3,219,856	315,039	1,887	2,906,704	790,318	862,706	28,363	160,761	92,937
2006	4,846,348	3,456,489	8,509	3,464,998	334,553	358	3,130,803	807,369	908,176	30,029	161,389	94,097
2007	5,111,770	3,543,192	30,348	3,573,540	355,078	-4,346	3,214,116	906,578	991,076	31,550	162,023	96,484
2008	5,643,420	3,864,811	-15,415	3,849,396	377,471	-4,085	3,467,840	1,089,965	1,085,615	34,727	162,508	99,264
2009	5,419,806	3,675,427	-12,692	3,662,735	377,132	-6,820	3,278,783	975,912	1,165,111	33,070	163,888	97,269
2010	5,709,482	3,836,098	22,248	3,858,346	386,173	-2,870	3,469,303	968,923	1,271,256	34,481	165,583	96,809
2011	6,054,457	3,993,859	10,948	4,004,807	357,559	5,658	3,652,906	1,098,653	1,302,898	36,334	166,633	98,193
2012	6,364,885	4,231,415	-7,320	4,224,095	376,026	16,274	3,864,343	1,199,127	1,301,415	38,010	167,452	99,843
2013	6,565,759	4,434,433	53,120	4,487,553	434,726	20,991	4,073,818	1,141,984	1,349,957	39,216	167,426	101,199
2014	7,063,516	4,768,129	39,936	4,808,065	458,069	28,262	4,378,258	1,263,499	1,421,759	42,009	168,143	102,291
2015	6,929,282	4,492,084	50,650	4,542,734	455,285	19,914	4,107,363	1,317,267	1,504,652	40,886	169,478	102,511
2016	6,883,971	4,343,123	30,052	4,373,175	455,066	8,888	3,926,997	1,380,413	1,576,561	40,558	169,733	102,467
2017	7,034,503	4,399,283	44,430	4,443,713	477,244	20,356	3,986,825	1,443,377	1,604,301	41,326	170,219	103,969
2018	7,459,618	7,478,980	-19,362	4,754,501	509,982	39,901	4,284,420	1,476,572	1,698,626	43,585	171,150	104,536
2019	7,837,655	7,854,670	-17,015	5,057,005	540,147	45,636	4,562,494	1,505,268	1,769,893	45,552	172,060	107,405

Personal Income and Employment by Metropolitan Statistical Area: Akron, OH

(Thousands of dollars, except as noted.)

Year	Personal income, total	Earnings by place of work			Less: Contributions for government social insurance	Plus: Adjustment for residence	Equals: Net earnings by place of residence	Plus: Dividends, interest, and rent	Plus: Personal current transfer receipts	Per capita personal income (dollars)	Population (persons)	Total employment
		Nonfarm	Farm	Total								
1970	2,838,776	2,326,281	6,504	2,332,785	158,576	98,246	2,272,455	358,765	207,556	4,180	679,077	279,931
1971	2,990,538	2,419,744	8,998	2,428,742	169,666	102,133	2,361,209	386,161	243,168	4,403	679,231	274,958
1972	3,263,561	2,662,679	9,046	2,671,725	197,372	105,272	2,579,625	412,531	271,405	4,820	677,046	283,207
1973	3,568,727	2,911,961	11,556	2,923,517	250,765	126,857	2,799,609	450,759	318,359	5,278	676,196	292,971
1974	3,882,656	3,113,113	14,191	3,127,304	276,803	144,555	2,995,056	508,902	378,698	5,793	670,284	296,332
1975	4,114,360	3,167,018	12,512	3,179,530	270,258	165,235	3,074,507	544,606	495,247	6,115	672,844	285,325
1976	4,425,010	3,391,701	11,154	3,402,855	295,638	209,112	3,316,329	578,749	529,932	6,625	667,910	284,907
1977	4,944,761	3,856,406	8,387	3,864,793	337,775	239,996	3,767,014	633,699	544,048	7,467	662,233	297,537
1978	5,471,768	4,283,010	2,354	4,285,364	387,518	290,804	4,188,650	702,735	580,383	8,309	658,517	305,459
1979	6,012,395	4,663,360	2,036	4,665,396	438,962	339,628	4,566,062	788,014	658,319	9,105	660,364	307,763
1980	6,607,832	4,904,761	136	4,904,897	458,075	379,799	4,826,621	954,523	826,688	10,007	660,334	300,754
1981	7,243,539	5,261,838	885	5,262,723	526,076	407,217	5,143,864	1,180,459	919,216	10,994	658,870	297,681
1982	7,575,849	5,343,818	3,026	5,346,844	538,767	396,010	5,204,087	1,327,335	1,044,427	11,546	656,126	289,691
1983	7,987,788	5,627,447	608	5,628,055	579,166	394,467	5,443,356	1,420,927	1,123,505	12,214	653,968	285,981
1984	8,702,211	6,154,095	10,113	6,164,208	647,822	435,915	5,952,301	1,593,526	1,156,384	13,349	651,917	296,150
1985	9,210,231	6,512,011	5,841	6,517,852	693,342	464,893	6,289,403	1,683,929	1,236,899	14,203	648,457	303,855
1986	9,636,333	6,863,252	5,499	6,868,751	748,895	462,711	6,582,567	1,746,516	1,307,250	14,902	646,647	308,919
1987	10,095,804	7,236,430	5,481	7,241,911	787,366	485,340	6,939,885	1,781,192	1,374,727	15,585	647,810	316,920
1988	10,770,981	7,723,140	3,746	7,726,886	868,903	530,037	7,388,020	1,929,623	1,453,338	16,499	652,814	325,266
1989	11,738,137	8,307,340	6,396	8,313,736	941,016	566,540	7,939,260	2,230,918	1,567,959	17,904	655,626	333,052
1990	12,392,974	8,699,694	5,510	8,705,204	1,005,923	627,937	8,327,218	2,303,426	1,762,330	18,816	658,654	337,124
1991	12,698,519	8,976,304	4,478	8,980,782	1,062,749	614,157	8,532,190	2,298,720	1,867,609	19,111	664,478	337,813
1992	13,573,246	9,637,314	9,294	9,646,608	1,140,106	644,341	9,150,843	2,374,952	2,047,451	20,266	669,752	341,070
1993	14,178,987	10,194,639	9,975	10,204,614	1,217,357	600,562	9,587,819	2,433,830	2,157,338	21,034	674,114	350,680
1994	15,065,195	10,847,749	12,657	10,860,406	1,316,336	662,179	10,206,249	2,593,450	2,265,496	22,218	678,063	364,299
1995	15,997,336	11,348,459	8,600	11,357,059	1,390,837	687,325	10,653,547	2,930,695	2,413,094	23,451	682,146	374,193
1996	16,821,909	11,972,235	14,035	11,986,270	1,454,194	734,339	11,266,415	3,056,427	2,499,067	24,477	687,264	380,965
1997	17,779,727	12,528,610	15,526	12,544,136	1,480,989	883,240	11,946,387	3,249,541	2,583,799	25,788	689,461	387,561
1998	18,903,284	13,369,513	11,111	13,380,624	1,527,802	973,513	12,826,335	3,481,804	2,595,145	27,355	691,039	385,717
1999	19,579,156	13,807,667	9,566	13,817,233	1,567,162	1,245,555	13,495,626	3,414,890	2,668,640	28,248	693,125	393,612
2000	20,760,268	14,486,445	7,362	14,493,807	1,585,455	1,355,831	14,264,183	3,644,735	2,851,350	29,830	695,946	397,340
2001	21,110,868	14,807,041	7,183	14,814,224	1,592,013	1,329,140	14,551,351	3,480,575	3,078,942	30,240	698,108	396,954
2002	21,432,298	15,333,043	6,923	15,339,966	1,622,718	1,142,381	14,859,629	3,273,145	3,299,524	30,638	699,533	396,663
2003	22,263,292	16,021,843	6,624	16,028,467	1,709,171	1,056,407	15,375,703	3,427,513	3,460,076	31,753	701,139	396,391
2004	23,115,637	16,886,806	7,574	16,894,380	1,839,142	1,133,274	16,188,512	3,327,511	3,599,614	32,937	701,811	404,591
2005	23,765,677	17,421,590	8,863	17,430,453	1,911,879	895,639	16,414,213	3,581,986	3,769,478	33,830	702,498	412,097
2006	24,723,817	17,967,925	5,600	17,973,525	1,988,461	826,992	16,812,056	3,954,000	3,957,761	35,197	702,433	417,595
2007	26,023,479	18,817,678	8,933	18,826,611	2,068,324	688,328	17,446,615	4,376,065	4,200,799	36,995	703,423	424,012
2008	27,100,631	19,588,143	5,130	19,593,273	2,166,590	445,820	17,872,503	4,481,469	4,746,659	38,534	703,300	424,079
2009	26,255,692	18,662,479	7,856	18,670,335	2,077,838	508,311	17,100,808	3,966,194	5,188,690	37,329	703,361	404,521
2010	26,953,138	19,109,700	6,568	19,116,268	2,090,236	512,733	17,538,765	3,903,394	5,510,979	38,338	703,037	402,554
2011	28,080,311	19,537,969	17,839	19,555,808	1,931,753	596,466	18,220,521	4,247,963	5,611,827	39,935	703,152	407,811
2012	28,902,230	19,935,528	12,358	19,947,886	1,979,829	801,551	18,769,608	4,673,781	5,458,841	41,167	702,066	412,049
2013	29,455,134	20,545,913	12,823	20,558,736	2,204,963	983,989	19,337,762	4,557,160	5,560,212	41,894	703,085	414,493
2014	30,843,920	21,462,978	9,382	21,472,360	2,293,164	853,880	20,033,076	5,008,706	5,802,138	43,793	704,311	421,207
2015	31,734,742	22,168,794	7,324	22,176,118	2,382,510	646,505	20,440,113	5,262,896	6,031,733	45,108	703,530	425,946
2016	32,109,727	22,315,415	8,357	22,323,772	2,455,934	638,314	20,506,152	5,417,361	6,186,214	45,704	702,556	427,256
2017	33,424,171	23,039,455	4,298	23,043,753	2,572,233	942,460	21,413,980	5,676,148	6,334,043	47,511	703,505	429,591
2018	34,880,215	34,882,599	-2,384	23,817,805	2,619,834	957,704	22,155,675	6,253,278	6,471,262	49,556	703,855	430,261
2019	35,944,121	35,949,055	-4,934	24,389,450	2,686,671	1,180,336	22,883,115	6,314,627	6,746,379	51,095	703,479	433,800

Personal Income and Employment by Metropolitan Statistical Area: Albany, GA

(Thousands of dollars, except as noted.)

Year	Personal income, total	Earnings by place of work			Less: Contributions for government social insurance	Plus: Adjustment for residence	Equals: Net earnings by place of residence	Plus: Dividends, interest, and rent	Plus: Personal current transfer receipts	Per capita personal income (dollars)	Population (persons)	Total employment
		Nonfarm	Farm	Total								
1970	380,798	300,020	19,201	319,221	18,064	-11,335	289,822	55,539	35,437	2,989	127,420	55,527
1971	434,484	336,405	25,573	361,978	21,332	-11,882	328,764	63,147	42,573	3,315	131,064	57,139
1972	490,511	390,164	22,936	413,100	26,092	-14,535	372,473	69,852	48,186	3,621	135,481	60,656
1973	568,382	444,423	40,135	484,558	33,919	-17,256	433,383	80,797	54,202	4,126	137,763	64,136
1974	589,429	451,538	40,403	491,941	36,260	-17,412	438,269	83,856	67,304	4,395	134,109	61,360
1975	618,246	468,861	30,736	499,597	37,272	-18,414	443,911	88,420	85,915	4,560	135,587	59,212
1976	686,380	528,528	30,246	558,774	42,341	-20,655	495,778	96,473	94,129	4,969	138,131	59,886
1977	747,257	600,450	15,785	616,235	47,827	-24,558	543,850	107,874	95,533	5,288	141,309	61,621
1978	862,964	696,783	24,946	721,729	57,001	-29,480	635,248	123,715	104,001	6,074	142,070	64,454
1979	968,065	795,922	20,042	815,964	68,376	-34,591	712,997	138,273	116,795	6,700	144,480	66,510
1980	1,074,212	876,912	-8,766	868,146	75,763	-30,405	761,978	170,529	141,705	7,318	146,793	66,284
1981	1,230,188	962,046	28,242	990,288	89,744	-37,381	863,163	205,009	162,016	8,280	148,567	67,040
1982	1,300,003	1,002,000	24,404	1,026,404	94,880	-39,758	891,766	232,639	175,598	8,686	149,660	66,060
1983	1,383,439	1,066,869	20,128	1,086,997	102,460	-42,004	942,533	249,140	191,766	9,240	149,716	66,278
1984	1,550,524	1,171,682	61,678	1,233,360	115,267	-45,720	1,072,373	275,110	203,041	10,315	150,313	69,522
1985	1,625,321	1,246,634	44,877	1,291,511	125,679	-46,971	1,118,861	290,475	215,985	10,759	151,062	71,096
1986	1,694,029	1,280,578	45,601	1,326,179	130,292	-44,523	1,151,364	309,313	233,352	11,263	150,405	70,814
1987	1,752,164	1,312,476	49,300	1,361,776	132,851	-43,934	1,184,991	323,042	244,131	11,711	149,611	71,010
1988	1,883,454	1,400,869	67,038	1,467,907	146,217	-44,332	1,277,358	342,532	263,564	12,670	148,651	70,486
1989	2,012,897	1,472,070	53,026	1,525,096	155,229	-44,279	1,325,588	395,706	291,603	13,628	147,705	70,955
1990	2,141,335	1,579,018	49,756	1,628,774	166,216	-47,881	1,414,677	406,102	320,556	14,602	146,642	72,212
1991	2,285,168	1,658,907	72,623	1,731,530	177,460	-57,610	1,496,460	420,482	368,226	15,450	147,910	71,684
1992	2,398,393	1,727,307	78,943	1,806,250	183,592	-57,739	1,564,919	422,257	411,217	15,982	150,065	71,406
1993	2,511,560	1,820,880	65,440	1,886,320	195,110	-61,413	1,629,797	443,699	438,064	16,524	151,993	73,056
1994	2,747,228	1,984,527	106,393	2,090,920	214,939	-71,193	1,804,788	473,465	468,975	17,929	153,232	76,059
1995	2,901,057	2,111,421	99,771	2,211,192	227,328	-75,204	1,908,660	499,624	492,773	18,827	154,087	78,366
1996	3,082,004	2,255,348	91,318	2,346,666	240,644	-83,905	2,022,117	537,657	522,230	19,810	155,576	80,407
1997	3,171,774	2,310,699	89,293	2,399,992	245,035	-85,876	2,069,081	562,936	539,757	20,235	156,748	80,915
1998	3,291,668	2,419,183	76,546	2,495,729	251,957	-87,587	2,156,185	586,832	548,651	20,906	157,452	80,496
1999	3,385,759	2,483,000	88,316	2,571,316	255,648	-87,089	2,228,579	581,781	575,399	21,477	157,644	79,840
2000	3,522,864	2,571,995	90,825	2,662,820	263,459	-95,834	2,303,527	597,096	622,241	22,352	157,610	80,592
2001	3,629,130	2,591,695	100,383	2,692,078	271,140	-95,431	2,325,507	630,289	673,334	23,008	157,735	79,058
2002	3,781,417	2,669,094	106,096	2,775,190	279,147	-95,862	2,400,181	627,929	753,307	24,094	156,947	78,174
2003	3,922,923	2,768,262	118,351	2,886,613	288,113	-97,713	2,500,787	664,970	757,166	25,000	156,914	79,336
2004	4,015,036	2,856,619	90,452	2,947,071	306,960	-96,392	2,543,719	663,446	807,871	25,588	156,911	79,185
2005	4,158,663	2,959,719	119,707	3,079,426	317,017	-96,212	2,666,197	643,057	849,409	26,508	156,886	81,208
2006	4,246,468	3,003,861	101,888	3,105,749	325,318	-91,182	2,689,249	657,896	899,323	26,977	157,412	81,572
2007	4,408,031	3,035,320	104,538	3,139,858	328,537	-91,581	2,719,740	741,221	947,070	28,011	157,367	82,142
2008	4,590,511	3,075,628	109,259	3,184,887	350,576	-90,138	2,744,173	782,914	1,063,424	29,137	157,551	81,647
2009	4,687,210	3,111,958	101,460	3,213,418	350,424	-91,879	2,771,115	750,639	1,165,456	29,672	157,969	79,710
2010	4,833,416	3,173,609	71,959	3,245,568	357,539	-88,544	2,799,485	773,270	1,260,661	30,670	157,596	78,729
2011	5,213,285	3,211,961	131,416	3,343,377	320,978	-83,567	2,938,832	954,486	1,319,967	33,022	157,875	80,150
2012	5,219,553	3,285,595	149,605	3,435,200	327,871	-69,491	3,037,838	891,360	1,290,355	33,168	157,369	80,378
2013	5,163,430	3,325,414	130,351	3,455,765	374,505	-74,422	3,006,838	836,635	1,319,957	33,094	156,025	80,662
2014	5,274,146	3,382,253	38,847	3,421,100	379,068	-62,399	2,979,633	912,823	1,381,690	33,963	155,293	81,627
2015	5,343,625	3,358,063	58,276	3,416,339	380,149	-48,698	2,987,492	945,834	1,410,299	34,770	153,686	82,340
2016	5,431,330	3,451,698	63,290	3,514,988	393,047	-77,696	3,044,245	945,303	1,441,782	35,629	152,440	82,742
2017	5,573,563	3,540,859	51,114	3,591,973	405,879	-79,738	3,106,356	980,369	1,486,838	36,805	151,434	83,727
2018	5,622,985	5,573,263	49,722	3,638,074	415,152	-111,907	3,111,015	1,020,754	1,491,216	38,034	147,840	82,431
2019	5,857,583	5,736,040	121,543	3,805,345	428,064	-105,565	3,271,716	1,036,135	1,549,732	39,922	146,726	83,286

Personal Income and Employment by Metropolitan Statistical Area: Albany-Lebanon, OR

(Thousands of dollars, except as noted.)

Year	Personal income, total	Earnings by place of work			Less: Contributions for government social insurance	Plus: Adjustment for residence	Equals: Net earnings by place of residence	Plus: Dividends, interest, and rent	Plus: Personal current transfer receipts	Per capita personal income (dollars)	Population (persons)	Total employment
		Nonfarm	Farm	Total								
1970	242,957	197,621	9,156	206,777	16,044	-10,338	180,395	37,828	24,734	3,347	72,587	29,190
1971	268,934	219,603	9,305	228,908	18,472	-12,424	198,012	41,960	28,962	3,560	75,547	30,345
1972	298,356	246,218	9,966	256,184	21,770	-14,580	219,834	46,454	32,068	3,902	76,467	31,600
1973	345,781	279,172	20,904	300,076	28,275	-18,157	253,644	52,795	39,342	4,425	78,150	33,577
1974	396,139	315,326	24,904	340,230	32,806	-22,752	284,672	61,574	49,893	5,014	79,006	34,924
1975	430,189	345,304	10,517	355,821	34,806	-26,928	294,087	71,346	64,756	5,315	80,942	35,650
1976	496,928	405,812	18,081	423,893	41,288	-33,236	349,369	78,143	69,416	6,029	82,420	37,031
1977	561,977	464,701	17,381	482,082	47,606	-38,499	395,977	90,402	75,598	6,633	84,723	38,988
1978	626,200	530,514	8,533	539,047	55,649	-43,790	439,608	104,119	82,473	7,253	86,334	40,485
1979	692,242	580,794	7,402	588,196	62,649	-48,051	477,496	121,851	92,895	7,778	88,999	41,045
1980	763,418	621,534	8,106	629,640	67,047	-55,267	507,326	145,813	110,279	8,514	89,668	40,737
1981	833,933	639,605	21,633	661,238	73,921	-54,930	532,387	173,251	128,295	9,248	90,173	39,457
1982	858,057	626,513	17,560	644,073	73,527	-47,246	523,300	190,338	144,419	9,561	89,748	37,614
1983	904,395	665,038	11,243	676,281	79,247	-47,055	549,979	200,561	153,855	10,115	89,415	38,353
1984	971,595	712,679	13,701	726,380	88,384	-46,157	591,839	218,467	161,289	10,886	89,253	39,132
1985	1,012,785	732,336	20,176	752,512	91,647	-44,134	616,731	224,687	171,367	11,506	88,019	39,314
1986	1,055,672	749,081	27,446	776,527	93,033	-35,988	647,506	231,464	176,702	11,993	88,026	39,908
1987	1,120,327	801,795	35,590	837,385	98,036	-33,211	706,138	231,740	182,449	12,721	88,069	40,842
1988	1,247,940	886,310	65,344	951,654	111,697	-32,172	807,785	246,678	193,477	13,987	89,223	42,853
1989	1,344,041	949,388	46,701	996,089	119,410	-25,567	851,112	280,232	212,697	14,952	89,890	44,288
1990	1,415,677	994,709	47,858	1,042,567	128,354	-18,516	895,697	289,975	230,005	15,440	91,690	44,792
1991	1,493,662	1,040,462	49,302	1,089,764	136,171	-21,853	931,740	299,834	262,088	16,036	93,145	44,656
1992	1,589,035	1,103,699	56,730	1,160,429	143,269	-21,005	996,155	299,124	293,756	16,885	94,112	44,762
1993	1,700,272	1,169,018	60,085	1,229,103	153,941	-12,765	1,062,397	321,360	316,515	17,805	95,496	46,076
1994	1,799,553	1,277,105	57,032	1,334,137	168,314	-13,676	1,152,147	330,041	317,365	18,568	96,919	48,997
1995	1,920,465	1,381,992	31,183	1,413,175	183,023	-17,804	1,212,348	360,770	347,347	19,427	98,853	51,874
1996	2,092,053	1,494,822	60,586	1,555,408	200,735	-17,113	1,337,560	390,223	364,270	20,799	100,582	54,263
1997	2,163,857	1,583,734	35,554	1,619,288	209,543	-12,888	1,396,857	393,465	373,535	21,203	102,054	55,265
1998	2,219,301	1,609,166	28,929	1,638,095	212,715	-8,802	1,416,578	397,830	404,893	21,595	102,770	54,813
1999	2,279,547	1,633,202	35,709	1,668,911	214,179	-2,896	1,451,836	379,444	448,267	22,033	103,462	53,186
2000	2,372,370	1,678,360	24,495	1,702,855	218,515	14,037	1,498,377	405,842	468,151	23,028	103,020	52,649
2001	2,591,744	1,802,278	45,245	1,847,523	228,218	22,171	1,641,476	426,684	523,584	25,030	103,544	54,749
2002	2,669,017	1,838,219	57,071	1,895,290	231,758	37,475	1,701,007	410,077	557,933	25,526	104,561	54,136
2003	2,730,350	1,859,988	62,811	1,922,799	234,705	55,212	1,743,306	412,949	574,095	25,750	106,035	53,710
2004	2,914,114	1,951,478	85,944	2,037,422	248,687	77,753	1,866,488	443,055	604,571	27,286	106,799	54,697
2005	3,024,442	2,045,418	72,149	2,117,567	264,965	88,471	1,941,073	434,162	649,207	27,970	108,132	57,088
2006	3,279,559	2,188,736	92,926	2,281,662	284,227	103,791	2,101,226	475,148	703,185	29,609	110,764	58,162
2007	3,443,272	2,273,114	72,212	2,345,326	296,296	116,852	2,165,882	524,935	752,455	30,490	112,932	59,546
2008	3,558,241	2,293,938	45,165	2,339,103	303,652	100,844	2,136,295	578,351	843,595	30,950	114,967	59,473
2009	3,559,045	2,148,749	40,119	2,188,868	284,153	112,394	2,017,109	556,895	985,041	30,681	116,001	56,122
2010	3,692,148	2,203,879	34,916	2,238,795	291,232	120,856	2,068,419	551,010	1,072,719	31,590	116,878	55,562
2011	3,819,160	2,238,941	32,329	2,271,270	264,515	127,094	2,133,849	586,207	1,099,104	32,335	118,112	55,341
2012	3,958,412	2,362,091	41,506	2,403,597	276,312	129,160	2,256,445	596,947	1,105,020	33,477	118,242	55,676
2013	4,017,450	2,366,949	47,414	2,414,363	316,208	151,469	2,249,624	623,847	1,143,979	33,935	118,388	56,155
2014	4,262,761	2,444,778	43,149	2,487,927	332,506	150,612	2,306,033	696,030	1,260,698	35,814	119,025	57,585
2015	4,562,539	2,602,714	41,600	2,644,314	348,490	155,203	2,451,027	752,305	1,359,207	37,955	120,210	58,815
2016	4,792,800	2,781,044	44,761	2,825,805	370,748	177,235	2,632,292	759,185	1,401,323	39,061	122,700	59,324
2017	5,049,370	2,917,378	45,214	2,962,592	393,652	249,981	2,818,921	796,145	1,434,304	40,380	125,047	60,760
2018	5,522,081	5,462,940	59,141	3,242,489	418,755	267,866	3,091,600	886,778	1,543,703	43,327	127,451	63,422
2019	5,816,653	5,767,449	49,204	3,359,580	441,734	360,865	3,278,711	904,324	1,633,618	44,830	129,749	64,277

Personal Income and Employment by Metropolitan Statistical Area: Albany-Schenectady-Troy, NY

(Thousands of dollars, except as noted.)

Year	Personal income, total	Derivation of personal income			Less: Contributions for government social insurance	Plus: Adjustment for residence	Equals: Net earnings by place of residence	Plus: Dividends, interest, and rent	Plus: Personal current transfer receipts	Per capita personal income (dollars)	Population (persons)	Total employment
		Earnings by place of work										
		Nonfarm	Farm	Total								
1970	3,299,252	2,800,707	18,008	2,818,715	218,154	-99,150	2,501,411	499,322	298,519	4,401	749,695	338,712
1971	3,648,157	3,097,958	17,331	3,115,289	248,053	-110,976	2,756,260	540,963	350,934	4,792	761,289	347,216
1972	3,926,002	3,331,968	16,643	3,348,611	278,178	-112,208	2,958,225	581,267	386,510	5,082	772,468	350,334
1973	4,229,899	3,586,099	19,914	3,606,013	345,098	-118,024	3,142,891	645,339	441,669	5,462	774,486	358,789
1974	4,588,365	3,834,657	18,043	3,852,700	380,223	-134,734	3,337,743	731,934	518,688	5,938	772,691	359,694
1975	4,962,911	3,999,876	16,565	4,016,441	390,931	-146,276	3,479,234	798,212	685,465	6,409	774,345	354,340
1976	5,302,714	4,294,760	19,204	4,313,964	432,721	-179,480	3,701,763	843,484	757,467	6,861	772,927	357,485
1977	5,731,221	4,641,126	14,406	4,655,532	466,785	-208,916	3,979,831	929,932	821,458	7,399	774,635	366,349
1978	6,268,119	5,157,580	17,638	5,175,218	532,454	-244,120	4,398,644	1,002,078	867,397	8,071	776,648	378,544
1979	6,893,883	5,657,652	22,512	5,680,164	604,006	-272,498	4,803,660	1,139,504	950,719	8,882	776,196	385,189
1980	7,704,596	6,118,178	22,965	6,141,143	639,168	-301,060	5,200,915	1,383,816	1,119,865	9,982	771,823	385,427
1981	8,548,119	6,637,413	22,763	6,660,176	733,697	-309,278	5,617,201	1,675,633	1,255,285	11,065	772,505	383,685
1982	9,367,569	7,134,458	22,347	7,156,805	787,805	-323,217	6,045,783	1,946,226	1,375,560	12,108	773,678	384,637
1983	10,089,285	7,659,313	17,273	7,676,586	848,981	-329,004	6,498,601	2,111,501	1,479,183	12,974	777,649	387,575
1984	11,168,909	8,560,738	20,518	8,581,256	966,547	-347,090	7,267,619	2,383,836	1,517,454	14,323	779,804	404,423
1985	11,991,143	9,303,284	21,973	9,325,257	1,069,592	-365,545	7,890,120	2,493,139	1,607,884	15,300	783,736	419,617
1986	12,906,310	10,094,951	26,337	10,121,288	1,174,343	-372,515	8,574,430	2,656,461	1,675,419	16,363	788,761	435,382
1987	13,699,039	10,838,435	26,652	10,865,087	1,244,257	-377,748	9,243,082	2,756,466	1,699,491	17,308	791,466	442,103
1988	14,869,767	11,884,885	23,341	11,908,226	1,399,086	-390,105	10,119,035	2,949,809	1,800,923	18,631	798,121	457,684
1989	16,410,897	12,842,634	28,838	12,871,472	1,481,657	-419,754	10,970,061	3,498,994	1,941,842	20,414	803,919	468,296
1990	17,345,125	13,640,429	27,860	13,668,289	1,509,964	-436,492	11,721,833	3,525,352	2,097,940	21,378	811,352	477,904
1991	17,921,053	14,006,763	22,539	14,029,302	1,595,895	-439,648	11,993,759	3,584,296	2,342,998	21,901	818,272	474,065
1992	18,991,395	14,855,342	27,212	14,882,554	1,662,870	-476,352	12,743,332	3,588,601	2,659,462	23,040	824,285	476,931
1993	19,596,837	15,378,083	27,362	15,405,445	1,725,843	-515,846	13,163,756	3,629,321	2,803,760	23,673	827,812	483,377
1994	20,238,686	15,887,306	22,765	15,910,071	1,809,582	-528,409	13,572,080	3,756,949	2,909,657	24,360	830,817	491,282
1995	20,895,200	16,098,700	19,459	16,118,159	1,830,759	-528,421	13,758,979	4,060,792	3,075,429	25,162	830,439	484,903
1996	21,549,433	16,572,119	27,042	16,599,161	1,844,696	-576,687	14,177,778	4,171,237	3,200,418	26,026	828,007	482,555
1997	22,681,039	17,552,800	6,249	17,559,049	1,923,586	-624,309	15,011,154	4,421,576	3,248,309	27,502	824,711	487,706
1998	23,786,693	18,413,682	21,201	18,434,883	2,013,354	-689,778	15,731,751	4,579,052	3,475,890	28,877	823,712	500,443
1999	24,978,277	19,682,457	25,279	19,707,736	2,098,294	-719,347	16,890,095	4,502,199	3,585,983	30,309	824,119	512,344
2000	26,811,270	21,461,551	28,751	21,490,302	2,271,840	-852,548	18,365,914	4,787,726	3,657,630	32,404	827,399	524,195
2001	28,105,225	22,599,727	33,873	22,633,600	2,404,546	-906,198	19,322,856	4,824,117	3,958,252	33,820	831,034	516,432
2002	28,343,254	23,179,258	25,213	23,204,471	2,489,727	-895,883	19,818,861	4,263,332	4,261,061	33,873	836,753	514,437
2003	29,368,343	23,932,420	30,964	23,963,384	2,599,227	-914,138	20,450,019	4,520,988	4,397,336	34,771	844,619	518,106
2004	30,718,292	24,796,920	35,158	24,832,078	2,695,080	-901,596	21,235,402	4,851,038	4,631,852	36,123	850,384	524,002
2005	31,831,006	25,256,370	31,129	25,287,499	2,780,069	-864,883	21,642,547	5,365,523	4,822,936	37,246	854,604	530,740
2006	33,523,960	26,455,175	25,222	26,480,397	2,900,003	-927,565	22,652,829	5,767,160	5,103,971	38,965	860,365	534,257
2007	34,987,895	27,195,447	33,407	27,228,854	2,963,700	-816,364	23,448,790	6,247,277	5,291,828	40,539	863,068	540,904
2008	36,855,437	28,219,064	48,707	28,267,771	3,113,054	-772,146	24,382,571	6,481,287	5,991,579	42,544	866,282	543,929
2009	37,269,541	28,736,891	36,029	28,772,920	3,127,237	-850,233	24,795,450	5,889,680	6,584,411	42,870	869,361	535,314
2010	38,807,064	29,562,584	60,157	29,622,741	3,155,582	-776,609	25,690,550	6,079,813	7,036,701	44,546	871,159	528,095
2011	40,244,976	30,075,638	71,877	30,147,515	2,895,080	-805,798	26,446,637	6,444,014	7,354,325	46,089	873,206	531,541
2012	41,809,445	30,941,184	80,316	31,021,500	2,957,624	-763,928	27,299,948	7,274,275	7,235,222	47,750	875,586	537,634
2013	42,715,116	32,225,263	89,850	32,315,113	3,476,985	-923,186	27,914,942	7,450,797	7,349,377	48,616	878,628	543,163
2014	44,445,668	32,900,601	84,258	32,984,859	3,622,895	-838,818	28,523,146	8,318,578	7,603,944	50,498	880,140	548,435
2015	46,413,011	34,107,461	56,720	34,164,181	3,797,320	-836,388	29,530,473	8,918,904	7,963,634	52,649	881,551	556,339
2016	47,351,445	34,917,078	43,695	34,960,773	3,899,850	-903,732	30,157,191	8,889,681	8,304,573	53,638	882,801	563,130
2017	49,492,260	36,209,718	49,185	36,258,903	4,058,894	-902,293	31,297,716	9,349,454	8,845,090	55,848	886,188	569,738
2018	51,561,974	51,511,361	50,613	37,471,964	4,116,250	-1,029,750	32,325,964	10,546,001	8,690,009	58,443	882,263	575,772
2019	53,498,359	53,416,641	81,718	38,789,029	4,232,339	-1,089,324	33,467,366	10,726,091	9,304,902	60,767	880,381	579,135

Personal Income and Employment by Metropolitan Statistical Area: Albuquerque, NM

(Thousands of dollars, except as noted.)

Year	Personal income, total	Earnings by place of work			Less: Contributions for government social insurance	Plus: Adjustment for residence	Equals: Net earnings by place of residence	Plus: Dividends, interest, and rent	Plus: Personal current transfer receipts	Per capita personal income (dollars)	Population (persons)	Total employment
		Nonfarm	Farm	Total								
1970	1,414,627	1,099,938	8,526	1,108,464	69,248	14,663	1,053,879	237,800	122,948	3,702	382,076	152,994
1971	1,598,397	1,239,222	7,925	1,247,147	81,837	16,932	1,182,242	273,730	142,425	4,021	397,496	164,049
1972	1,834,590	1,433,302	9,518	1,442,820	98,796	19,045	1,363,069	311,896	159,625	4,499	407,732	177,980
1973	2,045,489	1,598,491	10,994	1,609,485	126,791	22,122	1,504,816	350,520	190,153	4,795	426,583	187,854
1974	2,292,455	1,754,689	11,608	1,766,297	142,552	32,265	1,656,010	408,348	228,097	5,203	440,633	193,502
1975	2,593,217	1,939,587	10,450	1,950,037	156,325	48,104	1,841,816	466,004	285,397	5,754	450,712	198,943
1976	2,935,369	2,205,178	8,613	2,213,791	180,604	66,231	2,099,418	514,117	321,834	6,318	464,570	210,271
1977	3,288,372	2,489,152	10,504	2,499,656	206,193	85,768	2,379,231	572,801	336,340	6,832	481,349	221,559
1978	3,809,512	2,895,245	16,512	2,911,757	247,261	107,888	2,772,384	672,595	364,533	7,729	492,914	237,762
1979	4,332,145	3,290,949	22,012	3,312,961	295,139	129,817	3,147,639	762,190	422,316	8,518	508,581	247,977
1980	4,859,365	3,607,732	25,181	3,632,913	322,760	127,562	3,437,715	908,977	512,673	9,245	525,593	248,765
1981	5,413,999	3,960,840	23,779	3,984,619	378,663	119,337	3,725,293	1,099,964	588,742	10,131	534,415	250,776
1982	5,724,635	4,126,812	21,598	4,148,410	400,925	60,614	3,808,099	1,299,080	617,456	11,199	511,169	248,041
1983	6,289,945	4,597,074	16,765	4,613,839	454,754	32,285	4,191,370	1,434,540	664,035	12,041	522,356	259,621
1984	6,990,630	5,122,781	22,804	5,145,585	522,520	33,113	4,656,178	1,609,844	724,608	13,102	533,544	275,851
1985	7,673,240	5,622,921	19,816	5,642,737	585,624	26,631	5,083,744	1,808,321	781,175	14,090	544,603	290,100
1986	8,175,036	5,990,074	17,588	6,007,662	631,203	27,506	5,403,965	1,930,577	840,494	14,628	558,859	300,497
1987	8,672,045	6,388,377	16,156	6,404,533	667,865	31,985	5,768,653	2,001,942	901,450	15,100	574,324	314,235
1988	9,220,626	6,832,863	22,915	6,855,778	739,904	31,959	6,147,833	2,100,605	972,188	15,789	583,976	330,259
1989	9,794,205	7,222,455	32,012	7,254,467	790,733	40,280	6,504,014	2,201,248	1,088,943	16,488	594,036	336,572
1990	10,482,512	7,735,466	31,253	7,766,719	899,468	49,046	6,916,297	2,371,975	1,194,240	17,396	602,588	341,067
1991	11,204,303	8,293,771	33,167	8,326,938	973,861	46,750	7,399,827	2,458,050	1,346,426	18,179	616,345	348,198
1992	12,036,684	8,977,563	26,268	9,003,831	1,045,197	41,967	8,000,601	2,548,515	1,487,568	19,014	633,032	355,488
1993	13,000,443	9,777,523	29,723	9,807,246	1,138,606	30,337	8,698,977	2,689,433	1,612,033	20,001	649,987	370,109
1994	14,131,170	10,695,020	23,835	10,718,855	1,270,717	30,222	9,478,360	2,953,717	1,699,093	21,100	669,734	389,822
1995	15,220,016	11,492,294	18,021	11,510,315	1,369,032	23,339	10,164,622	3,180,458	1,874,936	22,125	687,901	411,302
1996	16,044,180	11,983,379	24,087	12,007,466	1,425,874	9,135	10,590,727	3,413,153	2,040,300	22,915	700,161	418,022
1997	16,881,644	12,610,490	27,038	12,637,528	1,494,644	233	11,143,117	3,640,701	2,097,826	23,788	709,661	425,091
1998	17,569,993	13,235,479	27,424	13,262,903	1,568,638	3,629	11,697,894	3,729,089	2,143,010	24,491	717,406	431,253
1999	18,043,781	13,715,891	31,829	13,747,720	1,634,401	-6,493	12,106,826	3,648,628	2,288,327	24,967	722,692	433,808
2000	19,581,412	15,025,978	27,248	15,053,226	1,742,775	-16,452	13,293,999	3,839,574	2,447,839	26,743	732,220	446,700
2001	20,600,176	15,702,720	37,056	15,739,776	1,838,468	-27,041	13,874,267	3,973,736	2,752,173	27,766	741,932	448,753
2002	21,332,628	16,331,479	22,235	16,353,714	1,904,883	78	14,448,909	3,858,428	3,025,291	28,154	757,716	448,871
2003	22,332,039	17,161,008	35,371	17,196,379	1,992,807	24,911	15,228,483	3,841,968	3,261,588	28,923	772,128	454,370
2004	23,764,389	18,242,070	53,152	18,295,222	2,091,917	100,091	16,303,396	3,961,392	3,499,601	30,111	789,237	466,415
2005	25,389,162	19,200,183	43,409	19,243,592	2,207,354	174,409	17,210,647	4,390,265	3,788,250	31,362	809,551	476,212
2006	27,415,140	20,627,767	26,227	20,653,994	2,393,414	153,967	18,414,547	4,833,068	4,167,525	32,981	831,252	494,456
2007	28,709,814	21,244,419	46,420	21,290,839	2,491,506	194,118	18,993,451	5,183,375	4,532,988	33,791	849,641	503,901
2008	30,159,202	21,774,235	39,633	21,813,868	2,584,071	221,492	19,451,289	5,441,145	5,266,768	34,931	863,383	503,242
2009	30,105,452	21,634,214	16,755	21,650,969	2,572,182	168,099	19,246,886	5,045,143	5,813,423	34,349	876,448	486,519
2010	30,639,866	21,637,703	24,914	21,662,617	2,581,414	165,554	19,246,757	5,038,398	6,354,711	34,443	889,570	477,820
2011	31,977,918	22,105,548	49,688	22,155,236	2,361,015	173,240	19,967,461	5,557,911	6,452,546	35,656	896,838	476,883
2012	32,426,918	22,246,380	43,380	22,289,760	2,407,248	134,592	20,017,104	5,945,152	6,464,662	36,015	900,368	476,646
2013	31,992,795	22,079,236	41,008	22,120,244	2,763,231	149,689	19,506,702	5,909,312	6,576,781	35,465	902,083	479,153
2014	33,889,912	22,958,022	44,171	23,002,193	2,853,900	117,413	20,265,706	6,438,793	7,185,413	37,569	902,069	483,086
2015	35,225,227	23,758,595	24,806	23,783,401	3,054,896	130,460	20,858,965	6,636,541	7,729,721	38,988	903,489	489,291
2016	36,535,483	24,898,184	23,625	24,921,809	3,137,058	-5,519	21,779,232	6,811,832	7,944,419	40,287	906,877	497,115
2017	37,208,656	25,355,502	18,559	25,374,061	3,155,774	-38,283	22,180,004	7,053,619	7,975,033	40,856	910,726	501,552
2018	38,856,657	38,816,470	40,187	26,365,601	3,257,427	-22,977	23,085,197	7,357,314	8,414,146	42,469	914,947	509,209
2019	40,379,815	40,334,759	45,056	27,556,756	3,400,878	-8,101	24,147,777	7,427,389	8,804,649	43,986	918,018	518,672

Personal Income and Employment by Metropolitan Statistical Area: Alexandria, LA

(Thousands of dollars, except as noted.)

Year	Personal income, total	Earnings by place of work			Less: Contributions for government social insurance	Plus: Adjustment for residence	Equals: Net earnings by place of residence	Plus: Dividends, interest, and rent	Plus: Personal current transfer receipts	Per capita personal income (dollars)	Population (persons)	Total employment
		Nonfarm	Farm	Total								
1970	398,474	293,678	7,270	300,948	17,442	2,398	285,904	62,613	49,957	3,012	132,287	50,427
1971	452,673	332,276	9,715	341,991	20,344	2,819	324,466	72,441	55,766	3,310	136,756	52,411
1972	494,074	363,553	10,548	374,101	22,986	2,898	354,013	79,113	60,948	3,595	137,425	52,809
1973	549,564	400,679	13,353	414,032	28,429	5,206	390,809	88,749	70,006	3,926	139,971	55,643
1974	596,522	430,241	9,874	440,115	31,787	4,381	412,709	100,669	83,144	4,256	140,176	55,277
1975	667,030	469,271	7,520	476,791	34,510	5,242	447,523	112,767	106,740	4,726	141,141	55,321
1976	750,300	526,745	15,920	542,665	39,761	7,174	510,078	122,768	117,454	5,218	143,786	57,332
1977	821,170	579,625	10,656	590,281	43,249	10,160	557,192	137,858	126,120	5,614	146,270	58,249
1978	932,091	654,535	14,608	669,143	49,095	15,216	635,264	159,792	137,035	6,314	147,614	60,432
1979	1,032,092	713,720	16,103	729,823	55,037	20,727	695,513	179,210	157,369	6,886	149,880	60,097
1980	1,177,286	809,564	3,030	812,594	62,753	24,091	773,932	217,606	185,748	7,735	152,197	61,010
1981	1,310,750	887,640	3,317	890,957	73,153	30,391	848,195	260,169	202,386	8,580	152,773	61,163
1982	1,410,470	926,121	2,289	928,410	76,196	25,654	877,868	295,086	237,516	9,226	152,877	61,401
1983	1,522,769	991,698	16,209	1,007,907	82,131	23,013	948,789	318,767	255,213	9,887	154,017	62,122
1984	1,614,010	1,059,657	8,389	1,068,046	90,312	19,160	996,894	343,864	273,252	10,446	154,515	63,636
1985	1,711,522	1,102,838	9,225	1,112,063	95,519	16,072	1,032,616	378,282	300,624	11,115	153,989	63,606
1986	1,775,833	1,144,184	8,769	1,152,953	99,624	7,976	1,061,305	391,871	322,657	11,506	154,335	63,566
1987	1,832,036	1,189,757	14,161	1,203,918	102,962	3,153	1,104,109	395,216	332,711	11,959	153,188	64,188
1988	1,932,716	1,257,149	22,823	1,279,972	113,970	1,237	1,167,239	415,464	350,013	12,768	151,377	64,413
1989	2,080,986	1,349,066	14,966	1,364,032	126,114	-8,031	1,229,887	464,875	386,224	13,857	150,180	65,261
1990	2,207,846	1,442,368	14,302	1,456,670	137,338	-8,714	1,310,618	465,430	431,798	14,820	148,982	65,706
1991	2,285,734	1,494,613	6,633	1,501,246	147,455	-7,307	1,346,484	457,961	481,289	15,336	149,046	65,863
1992	2,374,547	1,529,044	20,480	1,549,524	149,629	-3,450	1,396,445	445,039	533,063	16,085	147,621	64,337
1993	2,509,158	1,582,398	20,678	1,603,076	156,108	-5,674	1,441,294	454,154	613,710	17,642	142,225	65,441
1994	2,692,139	1,654,611	24,939	1,679,550	167,106	-6,194	1,506,250	486,405	699,484	18,815	143,086	66,500
1995	2,790,875	1,733,426	22,071	1,755,497	176,030	-5,574	1,573,893	529,209	687,773	19,359	144,162	69,293
1996	2,868,955	1,796,210	26,878	1,823,088	184,216	-5,173	1,633,699	553,232	682,024	19,927	143,970	69,670
1997	2,972,718	1,839,380	19,408	1,858,788	190,137	-3,261	1,665,390	596,833	710,495	20,646	143,986	70,362
1998	3,145,538	1,980,148	13,743	1,993,891	206,167	-7,698	1,780,026	638,669	726,843	21,794	144,330	72,287
1999	3,261,468	2,115,717	22,035	2,137,752	216,492	-12,790	1,908,470	627,687	725,311	22,523	144,803	74,507
2000	3,397,423	2,200,674	23,985	2,224,659	222,383	-12,528	1,989,748	666,829	740,846	23,402	145,179	75,003
2001	3,699,755	2,358,499	21,860	2,380,359	232,946	-16,286	2,131,127	667,879	900,749	25,498	145,102	74,686
2002	3,827,296	2,494,642	16,430	2,511,072	245,216	-25,238	2,240,618	654,919	931,759	26,320	145,416	75,251
2003	3,871,767	2,558,818	28,804	2,587,622	251,283	-30,182	2,306,157	660,499	905,111	26,516	146,017	75,320
2004	4,144,409	2,709,789	21,563	2,731,352	267,943	-45,428	2,417,981	687,078	1,039,350	28,198	146,973	77,127
2005	4,519,869	2,928,839	21,442	2,950,281	284,521	-53,959	2,611,801	765,467	1,142,601	30,554	147,930	79,635
2006	4,782,351	3,189,155	28,672	3,217,827	312,783	-73,189	2,831,855	777,868	1,172,628	31,641	151,142	83,038
2007	4,960,398	3,294,064	31,903	3,325,967	329,214	-79,586	2,917,167	816,637	1,226,594	32,741	151,506	84,415
2008	5,299,767	3,401,233	23,763	3,424,996	343,634	-87,858	2,993,504	966,600	1,339,663	34,766	152,442	84,931
2009	5,246,999	3,394,914	38,337	3,433,251	344,861	-96,874	2,991,516	854,126	1,401,357	34,257	153,164	82,896
2010	5,344,597	3,489,606	47,609	3,537,215	348,434	-90,891	3,097,890	794,124	1,452,583	34,681	154,107	81,419
2011	5,638,892	3,576,356	55,060	3,631,416	323,078	-94,742	3,213,596	951,743	1,473,553	36,527	154,374	81,795
2012	5,906,612	3,688,071	68,836	3,756,907	329,425	-102,455	3,325,027	1,047,904	1,533,681	38,246	154,436	81,062
2013	5,931,968	3,783,896	67,791	3,851,687	377,807	-116,318	3,357,562	972,188	1,602,218	38,360	154,639	80,881
2014	6,042,168	3,952,136	36,544	3,988,680	385,865	-112,871	3,489,944	989,342	1,562,882	39,074	154,633	81,596
2015	6,242,235	3,962,465	26,993	3,989,458	393,266	-115,208	3,480,984	991,971	1,769,280	40,463	154,272	81,852
2016	6,402,018	4,020,690	24,909	4,045,599	401,320	-129,407	3,514,872	1,001,616	1,885,530	41,465	154,394	81,602
2017	6,561,682	4,030,828	28,250	4,059,078	402,378	-131,373	3,525,327	1,038,220	1,998,135	42,613	153,984	80,606
2018	6,570,992	6,520,944	50,048	4,221,902	422,591	-130,980	3,668,331	1,080,642	1,822,019	43,015	152,762	80,975
2019	6,757,395	6,703,843	53,552	4,333,115	430,193	-132,499	3,770,423	1,087,461	1,899,511	44,446	152,037	81,324

Personal Income and Employment by Metropolitan Statistical Area: Allentown-Bethlehem-Easton, PA-NJ

(Thousands of dollars, except as noted.)

Year	Personal income, total	Earnings by place of work			Less: Contributions for government social insurance	Plus: Adjustment for residence	Equals: Net earnings by place of residence	Plus: Dividends, interest, and rent	Plus: Personal current transfer receipts	Per capita personal income (dollars)	Population (persons)	Total employment
		Nonfarm	Farm	Total								
1970	2,470,715	2,045,622	15,931	2,061,553	156,077	22,192	1,927,668	326,336	216,711	4,148	595,577	272,973
1971	2,634,493	2,150,247	12,596	2,162,843	170,660	31,656	2,023,839	356,311	254,343	4,377	601,892	271,090
1972	2,921,986	2,392,436	13,758	2,406,194	199,397	39,217	2,246,014	388,667	287,305	4,828	605,156	277,879
1973	3,293,107	2,712,131	19,656	2,731,787	260,516	49,597	2,520,868	447,230	325,009	5,390	610,947	292,047
1974	3,695,845	3,016,404	21,975	3,038,379	300,799	56,673	2,794,253	517,312	384,280	5,983	617,690	297,119
1975	4,063,395	3,204,702	19,496	3,224,198	312,338	67,694	2,979,554	574,912	508,929	6,532	622,114	290,754
1976	4,421,259	3,450,069	21,927	3,471,996	339,840	92,278	3,224,434	615,702	581,123	7,076	624,814	291,781
1977	4,886,917	3,822,661	21,206	3,843,867	371,422	120,689	3,593,134	686,515	607,268	7,787	627,598	296,393
1978	5,432,118	4,270,480	23,713	4,294,193	426,495	152,251	4,019,949	756,715	655,454	8,626	629,719	304,849
1979	6,060,391	4,755,921	31,467	4,787,388	490,392	183,177	4,480,173	851,049	729,169	9,573	633,073	310,781
1980	6,686,058	5,061,136	16,665	5,077,801	527,711	227,997	4,778,087	1,054,915	853,056	10,506	636,389	310,670
1981	7,404,955	5,420,311	23,287	5,443,598	604,656	272,717	5,111,659	1,311,487	981,809	11,593	638,748	310,155
1982	7,937,732	5,533,041	20,473	5,553,514	626,695	325,890	5,252,709	1,548,087	1,136,936	12,387	640,790	302,259
1983	8,299,386	5,696,938	3,954	5,700,892	651,169	392,006	5,441,729	1,609,685	1,247,972	12,935	641,637	298,035
1984	9,105,802	6,311,417	26,639	6,338,056	750,312	454,017	6,041,761	1,815,859	1,248,182	14,121	644,843	309,576
1985	9,740,893	6,687,998	27,471	6,715,469	801,788	527,228	6,440,909	1,976,079	1,323,905	15,026	648,256	314,763
1986	10,260,641	6,957,755	22,123	6,979,878	829,533	614,509	6,764,854	2,077,696	1,418,091	15,680	654,365	317,329
1987	10,969,909	7,548,433	21,949	7,570,382	889,895	690,163	7,370,650	2,149,521	1,449,738	16,536	663,413	329,686
1988	11,895,780	8,212,969	26,781	8,239,750	988,633	800,418	8,051,535	2,299,876	1,544,369	17,629	674,767	339,830
1989	12,979,588	8,760,090	36,413	8,796,503	1,042,536	889,927	8,643,894	2,681,958	1,653,736	19,013	682,657	345,404
1990	13,678,791	9,185,091	33,673	9,218,764	1,088,667	984,129	9,114,226	2,731,010	1,833,555	19,859	688,801	349,846
1991	14,337,995	9,461,336	20,150	9,481,486	1,135,891	998,553	9,344,148	2,859,111	2,134,736	20,596	696,168	345,339
1992	15,192,704	10,179,798	35,527	10,215,325	1,211,040	1,077,087	10,081,372	2,821,100	2,290,232	21,613	702,948	345,658
1993	15,755,236	10,631,079	26,975	10,658,054	1,286,552	1,162,902	10,534,404	2,823,488	2,397,344	22,229	708,776	347,081
1994	16,334,381	11,053,320	21,304	11,074,624	1,360,581	1,207,430	10,921,473	2,948,811	2,464,097	22,877	714,019	351,274
1995	17,021,853	11,459,478	15,864	11,475,342	1,405,503	1,271,053	11,340,892	3,088,119	2,592,842	23,718	717,685	355,394
1996	17,945,703	11,906,128	33,545	11,939,673	1,420,267	1,395,872	11,915,278	3,262,070	2,768,355	24,853	722,063	357,386
1997	18,899,145	12,476,805	14,314	12,491,119	1,481,970	1,533,501	12,542,650	3,492,511	2,863,984	26,015	726,464	365,995
1998	19,868,216	13,062,238	16,069	13,078,307	1,539,031	1,712,513	13,251,789	3,704,670	2,911,757	27,188	730,779	369,703
1999	20,976,008	14,065,385	7,909	14,073,294	1,626,634	1,827,739	14,274,399	3,628,283	3,073,326	28,487	736,327	377,848
2000	22,622,089	14,900,759	27,725	14,928,484	1,702,769	2,172,147	15,397,862	3,949,758	3,274,469	30,496	741,817	388,803
2001	24,268,650	16,368,345	17,931	16,386,276	1,828,447	2,231,074	16,788,903	3,907,370	3,572,377	32,414	748,705	396,203
2002	25,048,046	16,928,003	11,050	16,939,053	1,889,748	2,304,666	17,353,971	3,853,034	3,841,041	33,105	756,628	395,667
2003	25,945,994	17,474,757	28,521	17,503,278	1,935,981	2,435,514	18,002,811	4,000,113	3,943,070	33,831	766,938	400,604
2004	27,400,510	18,568,532	38,695	18,607,227	2,031,865	2,808,519	19,383,881	3,910,400	4,106,229	35,252	777,277	408,168
2005	29,304,359	20,008,951	25,051	20,034,002	2,177,665	3,077,685	20,934,022	3,917,949	4,452,388	37,201	787,738	418,886
2006	30,852,532	20,590,733	22,608	20,613,341	2,294,300	3,432,685	21,751,726	4,380,603	4,720,203	38,634	798,586	428,104
2007	33,394,231	21,926,785	36,967	21,963,752	2,395,702	3,869,608	23,437,658	4,887,435	5,069,138	41,351	807,578	435,473
2008	34,506,025	22,241,740	36,312	22,278,052	2,443,427	3,716,281	23,550,906	5,213,265	5,741,854	42,388	814,050	435,265
2009	33,262,691	21,359,312	27,135	21,386,447	2,397,558	3,158,722	22,147,611	4,799,930	6,315,150	40,674	817,779	424,470
2010	34,533,052	22,072,425	33,198	22,105,623	2,457,007	3,423,484	23,072,100	4,646,284	6,814,668	42,013	821,963	425,825
2011	35,813,934	22,812,197	43,597	22,855,794	2,293,351	3,311,032	23,873,475	5,113,584	6,826,875	43,412	824,980	432,726
2012	36,461,196	23,329,145	56,713	23,385,858	2,343,780	3,078,446	24,120,524	5,472,376	6,868,296	44,108	826,634	438,772
2013	36,910,743	24,023,037	54,981	24,078,018	2,718,682	3,143,902	24,503,238	5,466,433	6,941,072	44,657	826,533	445,550
2014	38,460,497	24,913,440	48,907	24,962,347	2,820,439	3,173,980	25,315,888	5,954,532	7,190,077	46,359	829,625	452,961
2015	40,285,158	26,142,994	46,427	26,189,421	2,941,724	3,196,135	26,443,832	6,264,328	7,576,998	48,419	832,011	459,181
2016	41,431,141	26,726,865	18,890	26,745,755	3,041,175	3,350,041	27,054,621	6,398,355	7,978,165	49,604	835,233	467,029
2017	43,266,780	27,875,479	23,700	27,899,179	3,191,763	3,781,261	28,488,677	6,707,229	8,070,874	51,474	840,550	474,077
2018	45,112,429	45,083,471	28,958	28,608,392	3,268,939	3,722,311	29,061,764	7,326,499	8,724,166	53,538	842,626	480,595
2019	46,992,336	46,941,834	50,502	30,079,898	3,421,492	3,739,576	30,397,982	7,482,019	9,112,335	55,675	844,052	489,934

Personal Income and Employment by Metropolitan Statistical Area: Altoona, PA

(Thousands of dollars, except as noted.)

Year	Personal income, total	Earnings by place of work			Less: Contributions for government social insurance	Plus: Adjustment for residence	Equals: Net earnings by place of residence	Plus: Dividends, interest, and rent	Plus: Personal current transfer receipts	Per capita personal income (dollars)	Population (persons)	Total employment
		Nonfarm	Farm	Total								
1970	470,275	399,460	5,984	405,444	34,429	-18,697	352,318	49,266	68,691	3,470	135,538	57,438
1971	499,206	420,062	4,239	424,301	37,056	-19,261	367,984	52,867	78,355	3,644	136,999	56,621
1972	535,727	450,677	4,049	454,726	41,151	-21,087	392,488	56,584	86,655	3,891	137,687	57,144
1973	589,763	500,165	4,690	504,855	50,902	-24,338	429,615	63,530	96,618	4,319	136,556	59,254
1974	647,183	542,510	3,915	546,425	57,822	-26,668	461,935	72,020	113,228	4,725	136,956	58,969
1975	713,117	575,826	4,079	579,905	59,813	-27,735	492,357	79,630	141,130	5,220	136,611	57,981
1976	795,308	653,745	5,067	658,812	69,525	-33,229	556,058	86,372	152,878	5,847	136,023	59,523
1977	877,132	733,477	4,591	738,068	79,292	-39,330	619,446	96,830	160,856	6,402	137,015	60,379
1978	965,705	810,012	5,878	815,890	87,981	-45,210	682,699	106,910	176,096	7,013	137,705	61,616
1979	1,066,392	890,750	7,240	897,990	99,294	-50,634	748,062	119,180	199,150	7,729	137,966	61,945
1980	1,139,914	910,505	4,455	914,960	100,441	-53,620	760,899	151,205	227,810	8,355	136,443	60,840
1981	1,230,999	946,422	5,475	951,897	111,386	-53,458	787,053	187,643	256,303	9,088	135,457	59,371
1982	1,283,897	925,693	5,733	931,426	110,192	-46,927	774,307	219,944	289,646	9,468	135,600	56,566
1983	1,331,897	934,576	4,292	938,868	109,361	-44,964	784,543	231,797	315,557	9,910	134,397	55,220
1984	1,414,118	1,006,311	9,577	1,015,888	123,518	-48,291	844,079	257,706	312,333	10,638	132,925	56,874
1985	1,511,644	1,090,909	10,326	1,101,235	137,017	-57,124	907,094	276,574	327,976	11,430	132,253	58,346
1986	1,597,220	1,165,110	10,854	1,175,964	148,647	-62,355	964,962	293,776	338,482	12,141	131,556	59,616
1987	1,658,933	1,227,636	12,261	1,239,897	154,461	-63,570	1,021,866	295,697	341,370	12,595	131,712	60,857
1988	1,743,086	1,285,413	11,739	1,297,152	166,697	-60,752	1,069,703	314,600	358,783	13,265	131,408	62,323
1989	1,888,384	1,372,373	13,450	1,385,823	174,681	-61,465	1,149,677	362,271	376,436	14,465	130,546	63,201
1990	1,999,299	1,456,984	10,361	1,467,345	183,815	-65,532	1,217,998	364,998	416,303	15,309	130,593	64,824
1991	2,092,950	1,498,771	8,733	1,507,504	190,791	-68,366	1,248,347	370,500	474,103	15,957	131,160	63,975
1992	2,237,068	1,640,139	12,423	1,652,562	207,353	-80,663	1,364,546	374,825	497,697	17,042	131,270	65,472
1993	2,350,285	1,751,662	8,334	1,759,996	223,632	-91,553	1,444,811	386,003	519,471	17,851	131,661	67,208
1994	2,456,062	1,845,493	10,107	1,855,600	238,564	-99,031	1,518,005	405,807	532,250	18,589	132,124	68,011
1995	2,549,386	1,901,075	10,105	1,911,180	242,941	-103,166	1,565,073	433,097	551,216	19,343	131,802	69,263
1996	2,689,142	2,004,060	12,725	2,016,785	246,893	-112,103	1,657,789	447,730	583,623	20,515	131,080	70,018
1997	2,832,129	2,123,957	12,656	2,136,613	257,659	-118,624	1,760,330	473,618	598,181	21,631	130,931	70,970
1998	2,981,779	2,238,940	23,528	2,262,468	268,336	-132,051	1,862,081	499,944	619,754	22,847	130,509	71,039
1999	3,093,036	2,361,790	23,487	2,385,277	281,060	-144,847	1,959,370	489,899	643,767	23,837	129,757	72,406
2000	3,223,226	2,434,056	19,218	2,453,274	284,690	-151,027	2,017,557	523,917	681,752	24,990	128,981	72,331
2001	3,259,716	2,441,574	22,366	2,463,940	291,311	-152,562	2,020,067	508,676	730,973	25,373	128,471	72,750
2002	3,352,571	2,505,730	14,112	2,519,842	296,054	-154,328	2,069,460	507,182	775,929	26,268	127,631	72,974
2003	3,478,929	2,613,251	19,771	2,633,022	303,436	-165,657	2,163,929	513,669	801,331	27,317	127,353	73,403
2004	3,649,631	2,766,849	35,632	2,802,481	318,006	-175,153	2,309,322	499,276	841,033	28,693	127,194	74,357
2005	3,779,708	2,857,792	32,243	2,890,035	338,114	-186,337	2,365,584	520,029	894,095	29,825	126,730	75,271
2006	3,912,104	2,914,333	21,579	2,935,912	348,162	-179,555	2,408,195	564,915	938,994	30,803	127,002	75,417
2007	4,100,209	2,999,297	35,916	3,035,213	360,554	-189,511	2,485,148	618,957	996,104	32,273	127,048	76,076
2008	4,245,511	3,018,725	30,544	3,049,269	367,348	-183,925	2,497,996	649,104	1,098,411	33,400	127,112	75,332
2009	4,288,969	3,030,605	17,650	3,048,255	371,060	-186,218	2,490,977	622,426	1,175,566	33,729	127,161	74,055
2010	4,435,367	3,135,125	33,036	3,168,161	379,559	-179,120	2,609,482	609,848	1,216,037	34,916	127,030	73,707
2011	4,679,092	3,261,317	41,155	3,302,472	356,819	-186,725	2,758,928	678,083	1,242,081	36,846	126,989	74,408
2012	4,805,714	3,294,228	35,469	3,329,697	358,199	-192,466	2,779,032	766,791	1,259,891	37,962	126,593	74,542
2013	4,795,533	3,385,298	42,098	3,427,396	409,877	-196,621	2,820,898	702,470	1,272,165	38,067	125,977	75,189
2014	4,994,056	3,492,753	49,739	3,542,492	423,344	-199,945	2,919,203	765,619	1,309,234	39,793	125,502	75,242
2015	5,218,095	3,657,140	22,250	3,679,390	440,069	-209,879	3,029,442	817,466	1,371,187	41,806	124,818	75,583
2016	5,263,760	3,648,727	13,752	3,662,479	442,129	-201,961	3,018,389	812,055	1,433,316	42,475	123,927	75,308
2017	5,406,592	3,771,599	20,983	3,792,582	462,388	-213,279	3,116,915	850,632	1,439,045	43,793	123,457	75,554
2018	5,701,223	5,687,075	14,148	3,918,497	474,727	-217,808	3,225,962	919,363	1,555,898	46,539	122,503	75,542
2019	5,881,562	5,856,927	24,635	4,047,789	486,423	-226,394	3,334,972	938,837	1,607,753	48,277	121,829	75,728

Personal Income and Employment by Metropolitan Statistical Area: Amarillo, TX

(Thousands of dollars, except as noted.)

Year	Personal income, total	Earnings by place of work			Less: Contributions for government social insurance	Plus: Adjustment for residence	Equals: Net earnings by place of residence	Plus: Dividends, interest, and rent	Plus: Personal current transfer receipts	Per capita personal income (dollars)	Population (persons)	Total employment
		Nonfarm	Farm	Total								
1970	603,484	462,240	34,855	497,095	30,161	-4,164	462,770	98,008	42,706	3,887	155,258	73,776
1971	657,441	503,098	35,705	538,803	33,600	-3,889	501,314	107,091	49,036	4,156	158,182	74,731
1972	702,455	545,465	26,606	572,071	38,300	-3,550	530,221	116,881	55,353	4,375	160,557	76,674
1973	819,510	610,516	61,278	671,794	49,703	-608	621,483	132,086	65,941	5,070	161,637	80,252
1974	891,605	718,026	5,605	723,631	60,173	-3,125	660,333	156,031	75,241	5,457	163,395	85,601
1975	1,100,596	847,704	57,335	905,039	69,359	-1,596	834,084	175,231	91,281	6,633	165,916	89,728
1976	1,204,978	969,914	30,894	1,000,808	80,048	-4,906	915,854	190,633	98,491	7,115	169,368	92,626
1977	1,330,264	1,072,517	33,243	1,105,760	89,765	-6,346	1,009,649	214,116	106,499	7,688	173,027	95,339
1978	1,505,057	1,221,268	28,581	1,249,849	104,114	-2,644	1,143,091	243,353	118,613	8,568	175,670	98,271
1979	1,692,963	1,366,620	38,566	1,405,186	122,572	-1,899	1,280,715	276,162	136,086	9,347	181,120	101,304
1980	1,855,393	1,501,915	-2,565	1,499,350	135,124	-1,471	1,362,755	335,400	157,238	10,000	185,546	102,188
1981	2,142,554	1,667,196	34,200	1,701,396	162,641	-795	1,537,960	424,110	180,484	11,360	188,598	104,700
1982	2,356,454	1,794,509	28,833	1,823,342	178,863	5,419	1,649,898	504,219	202,337	12,238	192,559	106,682
1983	2,628,888	1,943,123	113,847	2,056,970	192,822	-1,697	1,862,451	541,268	225,169	13,432	195,720	109,796
1984	2,792,319	2,083,090	74,321	2,157,411	213,771	2,274	1,945,914	602,063	244,342	14,038	198,910	113,248
1985	2,926,895	2,177,776	54,116	2,231,892	227,019	2,440	2,007,313	654,295	265,287	14,678	199,407	115,109
1986	2,961,570	2,192,953	62,145	2,255,098	226,562	-1,186	2,027,350	644,687	289,533	14,762	200,618	111,050
1987	3,012,867	2,248,365	39,110	2,287,475	227,335	-1,011	2,059,129	644,258	309,480	15,037	200,360	113,749
1988	3,054,730	2,216,356	49,748	2,266,104	234,504	27,341	2,058,941	661,353	334,436	15,192	201,069	112,617
1989	3,201,986	2,284,958	53,257	2,338,215	242,026	12,809	2,108,998	733,911	359,077	16,032	199,721	109,387
1990	3,338,739	2,388,468	81,987	2,470,455	246,417	17,061	2,241,099	706,847	390,793	16,821	198,488	110,406
1991	3,419,313	2,438,745	84,189	2,522,934	259,945	14,419	2,277,408	706,587	435,318	17,043	200,626	112,231
1992	3,678,063	2,650,568	90,477	2,741,045	277,660	7,537	2,470,922	701,062	506,079	18,085	203,371	113,046
1993	3,920,092	2,860,015	100,772	2,960,787	298,737	3,461	2,665,511	719,208	535,373	18,912	207,282	117,950
1994	4,150,926	3,078,651	58,101	3,136,752	325,510	-2,381	2,808,861	773,082	568,983	19,644	211,306	122,956
1995	4,399,764	3,289,609	49,618	3,339,227	346,914	-3,259	2,989,054	794,151	616,559	20,238	217,400	126,957
1996	4,598,530	3,421,890	49,137	3,471,027	355,720	-2,258	3,113,049	828,542	656,939	20,921	219,808	128,079
1997	4,902,690	3,644,809	63,534	3,708,343	374,066	-146	3,334,131	881,598	686,961	22,079	222,054	130,252
1998	5,135,473	3,803,670	67,524	3,871,194	390,246	2,469	3,483,417	957,006	695,050	22,973	223,545	141,013
1999	5,258,772	3,936,421	88,984	4,025,405	406,433	-3,044	3,615,928	926,897	715,947	23,205	226,621	141,705
2000	5,502,114	4,095,874	72,046	4,167,920	418,071	-4,561	3,745,288	1,003,390	753,436	24,004	229,215	144,574
2001	6,031,035	4,571,814	101,522	4,673,336	448,820	-9,830	4,214,686	992,636	823,713	26,182	230,351	136,232
2002	6,217,027	4,794,380	85,207	4,879,587	468,321	-15,321	4,395,945	937,626	883,456	26,760	232,326	137,018
2003	6,456,751	4,928,967	112,063	5,041,030	496,339	-21,125	4,523,566	992,536	940,649	27,459	235,138	139,781
2004	6,548,244	5,024,425	100,923	5,125,348	517,784	-18,600	4,588,964	966,331	992,949	27,564	237,566	142,937
2005	6,992,016	5,250,911	96,638	5,347,549	538,059	-9,760	4,799,730	1,116,019	1,076,267	29,087	240,380	144,955
2006	7,480,946	5,697,638	77,743	5,775,381	571,200	-6,598	5,197,583	1,141,200	1,142,163	30,829	242,656	148,345
2007	7,993,534	5,929,745	115,864	6,045,609	602,197	9,419	5,452,831	1,294,757	1,245,946	32,679	244,608	151,879
2008	8,879,082	6,507,325	78,450	6,585,775	642,427	49,315	5,992,663	1,492,303	1,394,116	36,027	246,458	154,926
2009	8,675,186	6,463,357	65,300	6,528,657	656,650	69,474	5,941,481	1,249,813	1,483,892	34,788	249,373	154,258
2010	9,457,393	6,918,446	158,581	7,077,027	679,257	90,795	6,488,565	1,331,253	1,637,575	37,429	252,674	152,820
2011	10,091,071	7,275,009	171,644	7,446,653	620,720	98,302	6,924,235	1,467,459	1,699,377	39,419	255,992	155,100
2012	10,412,418	7,530,122	125,447	7,655,569	638,544	112,456	7,129,481	1,602,945	1,679,992	40,393	257,777	156,747
2013	10,541,283	7,744,271	137,582	7,881,853	740,764	103,593	7,244,682	1,568,829	1,727,772	40,724	258,847	159,562
2014	11,168,685	8,056,541	193,237	8,249,778	765,836	119,747	7,603,689	1,740,749	1,824,247	42,847	260,662	160,627
2015	11,352,194	8,031,489	267,396	8,298,885	795,733	142,475	7,645,627	1,781,335	1,925,232	43,411	261,508	162,621
2016	11,431,741	8,053,810	144,565	8,198,375	820,788	152,938	7,530,525	1,885,602	2,015,614	43,461	263,036	164,510
2017	11,609,076	8,143,497	142,836	8,286,333	841,710	139,974	7,584,597	1,970,061	2,054,418	43,820	264,925	164,941
2018	12,261,607	12,086,171	175,436	8,775,091	878,924	132,591	8,028,758	2,098,273	2,134,576	46,374	264,406	165,351
2019	12,739,902	12,564,527	175,375	9,142,584	908,636	119,172	8,353,120	2,139,455	2,247,327	48,065	265,053	167,327

Personal Income and Employment by Metropolitan Statistical Area: Ames, IA

(Thousands of dollars, except as noted.)

Year	Personal income, total	Earnings by place of work			Less: Contributions for government social insurance	Plus: Adjustment for residence	Equals: Net earnings by place of residence	Plus: Dividends, interest, and rent	Plus: Personal current transfer receipts	Per capita personal income (dollars)	Population (persons)	Total employment
		Nonfarm	Farm	Total								
1970	222,847	160,836	15,700	176,536	11,447	-78	165,011	42,638	15,198	3,544	62,885	28,559
1971	240,660	178,348	10,914	189,262	13,161	-383	175,718	47,764	17,178	3,781	63,651	29,140
1972	266,529	194,310	16,979	211,289	15,190	-1,578	194,521	53,319	18,689	4,125	64,612	30,331
1973	315,555	221,386	34,059	255,445	20,092	-3,109	232,244	61,477	21,834	4,754	66,375	32,103
1974	337,848	248,923	20,755	269,678	23,826	-4,195	241,657	70,808	25,383	4,993	67,669	33,140
1975	377,054	277,968	19,247	297,215	26,318	-5,693	265,204	80,496	31,354	5,544	68,014	33,849
1976	415,960	318,241	12,761	331,002	30,197	-8,081	292,724	88,585	34,651	6,022	69,071	35,772
1977	458,102	368,955	-3,110	365,845	34,371	-11,734	319,740	101,714	36,648	6,554	69,899	37,579
1978	542,013	418,642	24,041	442,683	40,785	-14,675	387,223	113,384	41,406	7,601	71,311	39,155
1979	592,743	466,761	13,252	480,013	47,392	-16,408	416,213	129,302	47,228	8,297	71,442	40,186
1980	655,592	499,319	15,415	514,734	50,488	-19,523	444,723	155,010	55,859	9,047	72,468	40,763
1981	722,576	527,073	20,826	547,899	56,844	-17,461	473,594	185,621	63,361	9,917	72,864	39,295
1982	769,717	550,255	14,919	565,174	59,804	-18,135	487,235	213,072	69,410	10,647	72,292	39,073
1983	817,399	583,464	11,120	594,584	62,991	-18,784	512,809	226,180	78,410	11,149	73,316	39,812
1984	901,569	646,359	20,908	667,267	71,024	-20,358	575,885	244,812	80,872	12,282	73,408	41,501
1985	958,563	691,232	22,178	713,410	77,553	-21,203	614,654	255,317	88,592	12,945	74,050	42,726
1986	993,869	715,035	28,768	743,803	82,313	-18,780	642,710	260,135	91,024	13,427	74,022	42,744
1987	1,042,047	757,142	30,112	787,254	87,119	-17,124	683,011	262,423	96,613	14,214	73,312	43,166
1988	1,082,342	813,510	13,091	826,601	98,163	-17,702	710,736	271,757	99,849	14,650	73,881	45,013
1989	1,189,917	885,539	31,276	916,815	105,469	-18,839	792,507	288,187	109,223	16,143	73,711	46,420
1990	1,257,769	937,448	22,564	960,012	113,310	-17,861	828,841	310,601	118,327	16,910	74,382	47,526
1991	1,316,042	981,271	19,915	1,001,186	117,896	-19,022	864,268	326,228	125,546	17,666	74,497	47,846
1992	1,385,475	1,039,401	32,604	1,072,005	123,238	-21,111	927,656	325,681	132,138	18,441	75,130	47,929
1993	1,431,363	1,104,388	6,480	1,110,868	129,803	-26,970	954,095	334,552	142,716	18,832	76,008	48,460
1994	1,544,758	1,166,301	33,163	1,199,464	138,000	-30,198	1,031,266	365,308	148,184	20,353	75,899	48,857
1995	1,628,002	1,214,911	30,095	1,245,006	143,315	-32,996	1,068,695	403,214	156,093	21,347	76,265	50,377
1996	1,746,967	1,288,223	42,044	1,330,267	146,287	-37,015	1,146,965	434,074	165,928	22,706	76,937	50,625
1997	1,858,513	1,380,235	40,002	1,420,237	161,806	-42,097	1,216,334	467,157	175,022	23,878	77,833	51,103
1998	1,960,526	1,488,299	26,140	1,514,439	172,170	-44,569	1,297,700	479,750	183,076	25,064	78,221	51,929
1999	2,039,511	1,592,551	20,814	1,613,365	183,388	-50,435	1,379,542	467,852	192,117	25,696	79,372	53,186
2000	2,134,838	1,661,910	26,537	1,688,447	189,616	-53,086	1,445,745	490,026	199,067	26,635	80,152	53,560
2001	2,184,345	1,712,981	22,095	1,735,076	193,241	-60,064	1,481,771	479,446	223,128	27,216	80,260	55,908
2002	2,260,293	1,778,639	30,078	1,808,717	199,854	-68,956	1,539,907	475,102	245,284	27,603	81,885	56,225
2003	2,348,435	1,868,700	28,426	1,897,126	211,115	-82,913	1,603,098	503,161	242,176	28,616	82,068	56,667
2004	2,469,835	1,963,855	54,435	2,018,290	220,293	-113,470	1,684,527	537,391	247,917	29,846	82,754	57,879
2005	2,553,133	2,040,455	48,542	2,088,997	227,745	-127,258	1,733,994	556,033	263,106	30,804	82,884	58,150
2006	2,755,240	2,190,856	39,709	2,230,565	241,212	-158,452	1,830,901	630,980	293,359	32,514	84,739	58,948
2007	2,948,077	2,298,779	59,089	2,357,868	254,046	-153,534	1,950,288	673,812	323,977	34,066	86,540	59,668
2008	3,166,314	2,513,714	40,387	2,554,101	274,875	-176,097	2,103,129	684,511	378,674	36,050	87,831	59,915
2009	2,958,388	2,398,625	36,720	2,435,345	267,221	-240,903	1,927,221	637,954	393,213	33,134	89,285	59,256
2010	2,936,531	2,404,136	21,110	2,425,246	270,938	-299,767	1,854,541	642,284	439,706	32,764	89,627	59,012
2011	3,177,771	2,458,104	54,342	2,512,446	247,157	-271,927	1,993,362	734,114	450,295	34,999	90,797	59,701
2012	3,629,944	2,840,378	57,694	2,898,072	270,088	-244,397	2,383,587	806,605	439,752	39,572	91,730	59,850
2013	3,416,180	2,810,762	34,298	2,845,060	305,958	-353,983	2,185,119	778,676	452,385	36,552	93,462	61,199
2014	3,587,844	2,991,985	15,885	3,007,870	324,907	-410,313	2,272,650	839,840	475,354	37,644	95,310	62,119
2015	3,738,159	3,162,865	7,213	3,170,078	337,207	-461,284	2,371,587	867,051	499,521	38,799	96,348	63,522
2016	3,786,410	3,153,184	-2,617	3,150,567	340,188	-435,736	2,374,643	898,270	513,497	39,109	96,816	63,165
2017	3,885,307	3,290,762	-10,578	3,280,184	357,380	-491,544	2,431,260	938,026	516,021	39,848	97,502	63,919
2018	5,389,612	5,351,277	38,335	4,056,229	450,085	-292,739	3,313,405	1,251,452	824,755	43,785	123,093	77,923
2019	5,544,823	5,472,458	72,365	4,186,660	463,481	-301,658	3,421,521	1,254,093	869,209	44,952	123,351	77,923

Personal Income and Employment by Area: Anchorage, AK

(Thousands of dollars, except as noted.)

Year	Personal income, total	Earnings by place of work			Less: Contributions for government social insurance	Plus: Adjustment for residence	Equals: Net earnings by place of residence	Plus: Dividends, interest, and rent	Plus: Personal current transfer receipts	Per capita personal income (dollars)	Population (persons)	Total employment
		Nonfarm	Farm	Total								
1970	910,435	782,862	1,403	784,265	49,609	14,764	749,420	136,228	24,787	6,783	134,230	70,329
1971	1,004,489	870,955	1,236	872,191	56,795	4,983	820,379	152,187	31,923	7,080	141,875	73,124
1972	1,110,361	966,339	1,442	967,781	65,427	-3,500	898,854	172,734	38,773	7,353	151,010	77,502
1973	1,225,781	1,055,467	1,218	1,056,685	79,061	-10,972	966,652	199,536	59,593	7,871	155,729	81,822
1974	1,510,511	1,340,109	1,222	1,341,331	108,671	-16,019	1,216,641	232,101	61,769	9,361	161,355	92,715
1975	2,016,802	1,801,557	2,448	1,804,005	156,755	22,151	1,669,401	274,147	73,254	11,509	175,236	106,942
1976	2,407,760	2,155,068	2,892	2,157,960	195,289	55,863	2,018,534	306,719	82,507	12,936	186,127	113,300
1977	2,679,418	2,420,912	3,230	2,424,142	219,220	20,708	2,225,630	347,935	105,853	14,126	189,680	117,650
1978	2,727,115	2,416,737	3,226	2,419,963	213,574	4,834	2,211,223	400,681	115,211	14,052	194,074	119,090
1979	2,861,807	2,506,877	3,340	2,510,217	228,100	45,162	2,327,279	421,011	113,517	14,674	195,031	119,439
1980	3,211,582	2,795,046	3,111	2,798,157	246,621	54,739	2,606,275	471,532	133,775	16,568	193,839	119,735
1981	3,723,866	3,235,962	1,537	3,237,499	313,005	85,836	3,010,330	549,503	164,033	18,635	199,831	123,606
1982	4,632,735	3,836,987	2,413	3,839,400	380,164	94,389	3,553,625	683,393	395,717	21,363	216,861	139,054
1983	5,128,428	4,342,077	2,824	4,344,901	440,388	135,723	4,040,236	808,410	279,782	21,611	237,309	150,798
1984	5,583,720	4,781,737	4,136	4,785,873	510,278	107,272	4,382,867	897,154	303,699	22,134	252,265	158,830
1985	5,961,447	5,032,259	5,421	5,037,680	527,826	58,487	4,568,341	998,867	394,239	22,570	264,128	163,306
1986	5,979,180	5,009,371	8,802	5,018,173	505,305	-8,021	4,504,847	1,023,134	451,199	22,139	270,074	158,789
1987	5,660,841	4,688,726	10,913	4,699,639	466,304	-45,950	4,187,385	994,833	478,623	21,345	265,211	157,016
1988	5,718,140	4,714,736	11,517	4,726,253	486,333	-57,780	4,182,140	1,015,875	520,125	21,689	263,645	156,200
1989	6,221,162	5,048,301	8,453	5,056,754	524,312	-1,616	4,530,826	1,114,987	575,349	23,569	263,958	159,968
1990	6,668,663	5,512,466	8,855	5,521,321	605,982	-94,744	4,820,595	1,198,847	649,221	24,905	267,762	166,968
1991	7,008,195	5,826,891	8,567	5,835,458	646,249	-110,827	5,078,382	1,230,365	699,448	25,263	277,407	172,470
1992	7,527,293	6,197,631	6,855	6,204,486	680,640	-106,026	5,417,820	1,330,013	779,460	25,929	290,307	173,979
1993	7,962,980	6,507,768	8,900	6,516,668	728,971	-123,144	5,664,553	1,434,413	864,014	26,855	296,514	177,780
1994	8,283,282	6,707,187	10,960	6,718,147	763,899	-121,120	5,833,128	1,566,387	883,767	27,594	300,188	181,242
1995	8,443,275	6,718,610	11,250	6,729,860	759,813	-113,140	5,856,907	1,647,212	939,156	27,969	301,878	182,105
1996	8,710,468	6,836,109	11,873	6,847,982	762,965	-111,168	5,973,849	1,724,079	1,012,540	28,785	302,606	183,521
1997	9,293,914	7,278,480	13,771	7,292,251	801,936	-119,187	6,371,128	1,820,748	1,102,038	30,325	306,480	187,454
1998	9,817,156	7,698,396	11,040	7,709,436	834,620	-108,225	6,766,591	1,846,040	1,204,525	31,375	312,895	193,548
1999	10,168,900	7,952,096	11,946	7,964,042	855,896	-123,196	6,984,950	1,850,735	1,333,215	32,061	317,172	193,959
2000	10,890,673	8,402,434	11,862	8,414,296	890,910	-117,364	7,406,022	1,963,653	1,520,998	33,968	320,618	197,879
2001	11,748,096	9,201,434	11,047	9,212,481	962,532	-53,594	8,196,355	1,950,223	1,601,518	36,028	326,081	203,258
2002	12,427,554	9,830,668	11,620	9,842,288	1,024,380	-6,052	8,811,856	1,974,597	1,641,101	37,367	332,582	207,654
2003	12,964,248	10,384,677	8,857	10,393,534	1,065,156	26,397	9,354,775	2,003,701	1,605,772	38,386	337,730	211,659
2004	13,701,661	11,036,263	10,456	11,046,719	1,142,603	89,738	9,993,854	2,106,229	1,601,578	39,687	345,245	215,930
2005	14,647,687	11,718,482	9,860	11,728,342	1,218,735	170,283	10,679,890	2,274,166	1,693,631	41,743	350,903	220,731
2006	15,748,276	12,318,498	8,322	12,326,820	1,324,071	334,211	11,336,960	2,598,658	1,812,658	43,902	358,718	226,471
2007	17,053,283	12,937,145	7,438	12,944,583	1,378,202	524,844	12,091,225	2,895,551	2,066,507	47,345	360,194	231,097
2008	18,860,835	13,526,519	5,092	13,531,611	1,426,081	738,650	12,844,180	3,184,770	2,831,885	51,584	365,633	233,394
2009	18,811,302	14,130,539	6,651	14,137,190	1,451,533	725,155	13,410,812	2,979,584	2,420,906	50,222	374,562	233,589
2010	20,130,054	14,902,944	5,457	14,908,401	1,500,924	692,240	14,099,717	3,301,354	2,728,983	52,544	383,108	233,963
2011	21,249,925	15,565,246	4,069	15,569,315	1,412,652	725,344	14,882,007	3,538,846	2,829,072	54,766	388,012	236,733
2012	21,718,790	16,060,987	6,027	16,067,014	1,500,542	723,087	15,289,559	3,691,753	2,737,478	55,377	392,201	242,955
2013	21,443,646	16,099,987	5,362	16,105,349	1,734,283	683,781	15,054,847	3,624,832	2,763,967	54,023	396,934	244,407
2014	22,777,808	16,483,645	6,361	16,490,006	1,734,581	783,500	15,538,925	3,886,778	3,352,105	57,173	398,400	244,089
2015	23,646,379	17,022,275	6,544	17,028,819	1,757,648	776,309	16,047,480	4,142,916	3,455,983	59,252	399,082	245,061
2016	23,053,380	16,476,948	6,001	16,482,949	1,705,767	670,157	15,447,339	4,210,432	3,395,609	57,418	401,499	242,783
2017	23,474,159	16,647,392	5,726	16,653,118	1,721,733	626,622	15,558,007	4,355,018	3,561,134	58,555	400,888	240,964
2018	24,583,919	24,576,027	7,892	16,927,471	1,747,441	625,837	15,805,867	4,892,720	3,885,332	61,825	397,636	242,122
2019	25,503,163	25,493,665	9,498	17,534,898	1,796,215	673,783	16,412,466	4,987,968	4,102,729	64,350	396,317	244,971

Personal Income and Employment by Area: Ann Arbor, MI

(Thousands of dollars, except as noted.)

Year	Personal income, total	Earnings by place of work			Less: Contributions for government social insurance	Plus: Adjustment for residence	Equals: Net earnings by place of residence	Plus: Dividends, interest, and rent	Plus: Personal current transfer receipts	Per capita personal income (dollars)	Population (persons)	Total employment
		Nonfarm	Farm	Total								
1970	1,095,725	933,143	6,117	939,260	64,093	3,652	878,819	157,250	59,656	4,678	234,226	105,059
1971	1,212,039	1,060,056	5,067	1,065,123	74,950	-20,983	969,190	172,550	70,299	5,131	236,222	109,389
1972	1,349,916	1,186,555	9,904	1,196,459	89,223	-28,705	1,078,531	191,146	80,239	5,590	241,470	114,647
1973	1,518,740	1,373,322	12,572	1,385,894	120,110	-53,405	1,212,379	211,846	94,515	6,154	246,780	124,307
1974	1,638,400	1,431,938	6,577	1,438,515	129,203	-37,088	1,272,224	242,031	124,145	6,389	256,447	128,003
1975	1,805,963	1,518,701	12,638	1,531,339	133,228	-37,224	1,360,887	272,102	172,974	7,194	251,024	126,982
1976	2,038,347	1,835,426	7,804	1,843,230	164,904	-113,380	1,564,946	298,801	174,600	8,027	253,934	136,907
1977	2,297,921	2,151,919	9,577	2,161,496	192,960	-181,580	1,786,956	334,914	176,051	8,927	257,407	146,330
1978	2,616,066	2,545,115	4,964	2,550,079	236,617	-258,238	2,055,224	376,997	183,845	10,071	259,775	157,722
1979	2,903,669	2,852,435	5,136	2,857,571	272,261	-324,480	2,260,830	426,173	216,666	11,046	262,859	165,863
1980	3,191,960	2,989,418	3,921	2,993,339	277,809	-332,044	2,383,486	503,045	305,429	12,072	264,400	164,425
1981	3,436,150	3,203,486	7,135	3,210,621	322,787	-362,705	2,525,129	604,278	306,743	13,092	262,466	165,139
1982	3,640,222	3,267,964	3,102	3,271,066	334,386	-343,456	2,593,224	708,419	338,579	13,988	260,239	163,116
1983	3,925,847	3,567,477	-339	3,567,138	373,401	-397,982	2,795,755	772,537	357,555	15,087	260,212	167,452
1984	4,311,669	4,027,371	4,921	4,032,292	438,596	-498,030	3,095,666	863,011	352,992	16,536	260,737	174,759
1985	4,700,285	4,458,840	9,576	4,468,416	495,653	-567,117	3,405,646	932,851	361,788	17,901	262,568	181,371
1986	5,019,182	4,719,198	4,022	4,723,220	525,235	-543,793	3,654,192	995,962	369,028	18,863	266,087	187,119
1987	5,279,965	4,931,560	4,932	4,936,492	543,160	-546,194	3,847,138	1,052,271	380,556	19,576	269,717	195,094
1988	5,775,220	5,459,398	3,421	5,462,819	622,017	-627,286	4,213,516	1,164,577	397,127	21,128	273,346	202,667
1989	6,274,868	5,801,327	8,223	5,809,550	658,594	-659,477	4,491,479	1,347,625	435,764	22,464	279,329	207,606
1990	6,667,023	6,199,718	7,757	6,207,475	713,841	-697,952	4,795,682	1,393,647	477,694	23,477	283,987	213,654
1991	6,758,413	6,232,810	3,050	6,235,860	726,643	-689,658	4,819,559	1,408,849	530,005	23,538	287,126	210,795
1992	7,223,539	6,661,953	6,866	6,668,819	768,751	-707,095	5,192,973	1,468,894	561,672	24,881	290,323	213,642
1993	7,623,930	6,912,845	3,227	6,916,072	800,545	-663,691	5,451,836	1,568,472	603,622	26,144	291,617	217,534
1994	8,170,770	7,310,896	2,302	7,313,198	865,568	-667,420	5,780,210	1,771,894	618,666	27,823	293,671	220,460
1995	8,731,492	7,458,630	1,933	7,460,563	883,360	-439,452	6,137,751	1,895,789	697,952	29,308	297,926	221,177
1996	9,139,407	7,797,612	1,301	7,798,913	903,407	-457,241	6,438,265	1,945,605	755,537	30,150	303,133	224,214
1997	9,635,229	8,432,516	1,284	8,433,800	975,250	-659,409	6,799,141	2,088,637	747,451	31,243	308,398	228,650
1998	10,206,368	9,071,528	3,088	9,074,616	1,042,070	-730,986	7,301,560	2,162,531	742,277	32,650	312,601	230,049
1999	10,928,014	10,052,448	6,636	10,059,084	1,141,127	-1,008,574	7,909,383	2,186,424	832,207	34,336	318,270	238,824
2000	11,758,614	10,778,116	1,878	10,779,994	1,201,623	-1,027,237	8,551,134	2,337,290	870,190	36,250	324,372	244,514
2001	12,251,049	11,159,108	853	11,159,961	1,208,371	-967,782	8,983,808	2,303,737	963,504	37,266	328,749	244,933
2002	12,706,995	11,651,753	1,499	11,653,252	1,265,834	-1,022,842	9,364,576	2,318,149	1,024,270	38,186	332,763	245,437
2003	13,286,962	11,860,308	6,272	11,866,580	1,279,997	-890,242	9,696,341	2,491,151	1,099,470	39,526	336,154	243,666
2004	13,430,373	12,031,394	12,789	12,044,183	1,317,704	-1,095,059	9,631,420	2,658,328	1,140,625	39,568	339,422	245,401
2005	13,682,260	12,256,129	11,083	12,267,212	1,350,284	-1,095,072	9,821,856	2,635,570	1,224,834	39,979	342,234	247,846
2006	14,192,205	12,455,279	12,166	12,467,445	1,382,634	-1,171,097	9,913,714	2,962,960	1,315,531	41,254	344,018	247,735
2007	14,625,196	12,764,942	11,690	12,776,632	1,417,960	-1,160,970	10,197,702	2,978,298	1,449,196	42,354	345,310	247,748
2008	15,125,024	12,535,687	7,933	12,543,620	1,402,995	-695,399	10,445,226	2,963,511	1,716,287	44,278	341,595	242,983
2009	14,182,070	12,077,070	8,792	12,085,862	1,358,983	-1,028,420	9,698,459	2,608,531	1,875,080	41,285	343,520	238,387
2010	15,646,384	12,569,194	13,206	12,582,400	1,381,305	-310,579	10,890,516	2,697,785	2,058,083	45,284	345,515	241,984
2011	15,734,011	12,812,297	36,435	12,848,732	1,235,317	-938,146	10,675,269	2,974,540	2,084,202	45,070	349,102	245,292
2012	16,780,028	13,444,530	12,319	13,456,849	1,287,629	-827,407	11,341,813	3,377,165	2,061,050	47,761	351,333	246,785
2013	16,942,563	13,780,552	33,544	13,814,096	1,506,425	-957,173	11,350,498	3,446,043	2,146,022	47,764	354,714	250,522
2014	17,803,229	14,020,260	14,125	14,034,385	1,551,202	-735,474	11,747,709	3,798,217	2,257,303	49,642	358,635	252,677
2015	18,923,904	15,017,275	13,161	15,030,436	1,634,898	-970,704	12,424,834	4,110,090	2,388,980	52,303	361,815	258,281
2016	19,814,019	15,556,651	9,364	15,566,015	1,681,668	-839,265	13,045,082	4,294,654	2,474,283	54,322	364,752	261,993
2017	20,715,047	16,415,738	-2,087	16,413,651	1,769,202	-919,174	13,725,275	4,492,508	2,497,264	56,348	367,627	266,789
2018	21,734,133	21,731,415	2,718	17,019,319	1,875,255	-929,900	14,214,164	4,890,081	2,629,888	58,823	369,483	272,013
2019	22,365,853	22,359,697	6,156	17,888,161	1,956,764	-1,324,945	14,606,452	4,963,332	2,796,069	60,843	367,601	278,183

Personal Income and Employment by Area: Anniston-Oxford-Jacksonville, AL

(Thousands of dollars, except as noted.)

Year	Personal income, total	Earnings by place of work			Less: Contributions for government social insurance	Plus: Adjustment for residence	Equals: Net earnings by place of residence	Plus: Dividends, interest, and rent	Plus: Personal current transfer receipts	Per capita personal income (dollars)	Population (persons)	Total employment
		Nonfarm	Farm	Total								
1970	313,931	278,760	2,076	280,836	17,144	-27,477	236,215	46,648	31,068	3,044	103,125	46,650
1971	353,608	313,482	2,099	315,581	19,851	-31,130	264,600	52,488	36,520	3,412	103,622	47,036
1972	396,486	351,388	2,782	354,170	23,011	-33,457	297,702	58,462	40,322	3,818	103,846	48,347
1973	433,646	376,675	5,683	382,358	28,220	-33,219	320,919	65,440	47,287	4,129	105,027	49,305
1974	485,455	413,937	2,398	416,335	32,063	-35,241	349,031	78,368	58,056	4,583	105,917	50,224
1975	557,197	458,904	5,713	464,617	35,225	-39,070	390,322	90,919	75,956	5,207	107,005	50,663
1976	624,434	522,276	4,806	527,082	42,063	-41,648	443,371	100,489	80,574	5,537	112,768	53,001
1977	702,104	589,344	4,940	594,284	47,028	-45,335	501,921	115,115	85,068	6,224	112,801	55,396
1978	776,570	642,831	5,394	648,225	51,477	-44,892	551,856	132,970	91,744	6,667	116,474	56,359
1979	849,706	693,419	5,118	698,537	58,357	-43,210	596,970	147,289	105,447	7,278	116,742	56,639
1980	972,898	786,063	4,448	790,511	64,801	-52,911	672,799	174,878	125,221	8,106	120,016	57,453
1981	1,069,632	854,152	3,916	858,068	75,747	-58,267	724,054	204,053	141,525	8,854	120,814	55,980
1982	1,144,879	899,287	4,605	903,892	78,953	-66,489	758,450	230,256	156,173	9,376	122,109	55,531
1983	1,219,116	960,897	2,359	963,256	90,000	-70,040	803,216	247,822	168,078	10,055	121,249	56,216
1984	1,341,222	1,066,173	2,759	1,068,932	101,985	-78,926	888,021	276,290	176,911	11,017	121,739	58,552
1985	1,403,278	1,118,946	2,982	1,121,928	109,495	-86,890	925,543	290,218	187,517	11,828	118,644	58,483
1986	1,470,316	1,170,716	3,899	1,174,615	114,975	-90,548	969,092	306,800	194,424	12,492	117,700	59,039
1987	1,525,463	1,223,249	360	1,223,609	120,758	-93,560	1,009,291	318,469	197,703	12,918	118,092	59,851
1988	1,607,503	1,290,433	3,502	1,293,935	133,515	-97,178	1,063,242	337,277	206,984	13,709	117,260	61,561
1989	1,703,924	1,326,583	14,589	1,341,172	139,597	-102,966	1,098,609	369,331	235,984	14,641	116,381	61,654
1990	1,759,063	1,356,847	17,407	1,374,254	146,927	-103,935	1,123,392	377,465	258,206	15,149	116,118	61,400
1991	1,851,118	1,425,250	22,715	1,447,965	155,902	-112,350	1,179,713	383,174	288,231	16,062	115,247	60,775
1992	1,951,649	1,489,528	12,187	1,501,715	163,387	-108,720	1,229,608	397,322	324,719	16,853	115,804	61,360
1993	2,005,237	1,510,253	15,986	1,526,239	170,059	-105,947	1,250,233	410,768	344,236	17,238	116,324	61,935
1994	2,073,014	1,546,583	12,121	1,558,704	175,668	-98,566	1,284,470	427,452	361,092	17,846	116,161	60,986
1995	2,183,521	1,597,298	12,631	1,609,929	183,008	-99,088	1,327,833	463,964	391,724	18,696	116,790	61,993
1996	2,248,460	1,609,612	15,864	1,625,476	185,003	-92,483	1,347,990	483,621	416,849	19,270	116,684	62,273
1997	2,324,902	1,677,526	17,029	1,694,555	193,510	-90,749	1,410,296	480,632	433,974	19,828	117,254	63,984
1998	2,466,291	1,765,235	14,078	1,779,313	201,956	-98,262	1,479,095	536,041	451,155	21,047	117,179	64,336
1999	2,471,999	1,782,332	7,744	1,790,076	205,216	-93,841	1,491,019	507,006	473,974	21,512	114,910	63,078
2000	2,461,380	1,709,381	4,909	1,714,290	198,768	-68,390	1,447,132	508,229	506,019	22,158	111,081	60,846
2001	2,585,157	1,770,120	10,174	1,780,294	206,787	-77,911	1,495,596	536,625	552,936	23,234	111,266	59,639
2002	2,695,935	1,871,325	5,883	1,877,208	217,398	-88,491	1,571,319	528,062	596,554	24,152	111,625	60,124
2003	2,834,944	1,977,208	7,463	1,984,671	229,871	-106,783	1,648,017	553,269	633,658	25,154	112,705	60,521
2004	3,012,640	2,136,035	10,820	2,146,855	245,599	-132,143	1,769,113	588,743	654,784	26,552	113,462	62,604
2005	3,141,469	2,251,084	16,159	2,267,243	260,128	-142,634	1,864,481	577,880	699,108	27,442	114,477	63,108
2006	3,292,546	2,368,483	7,357	2,375,840	273,744	-169,138	1,932,958	614,221	745,367	28,535	115,388	63,816
2007	3,494,723	2,544,497	7,322	2,551,819	297,131	-220,981	2,033,707	668,134	792,882	30,072	116,211	65,674
2008	3,621,797	2,591,948	8,258	2,600,206	308,810	-254,694	2,036,702	701,690	883,405	30,883	117,274	64,696
2009	3,575,446	2,529,596	13,360	2,542,956	300,767	-257,600	1,984,589	633,346	957,511	30,207	118,363	61,551
2010	3,669,749	2,539,537	13,243	2,552,780	305,756	-237,625	2,009,399	626,770	1,033,580	30,977	118,466	60,194
2011	3,754,285	2,560,128	5,158	2,565,286	277,251	-232,474	2,055,561	654,323	1,044,401	31,874	117,785	60,613
2012	3,791,206	2,493,885	13,647	2,507,532	270,995	-178,078	2,058,459	682,340	1,050,407	32,343	117,219	59,998
2013	3,729,885	2,382,847	29,635	2,412,482	293,613	-107,889	2,010,980	658,569	1,060,336	32,021	116,482	58,415
2014	3,836,182	2,429,940	24,036	2,453,976	295,512	-91,109	2,067,355	690,695	1,078,132	33,087	115,941	58,101
2015	3,948,903	2,427,166	25,813	2,452,979	294,625	-64,606	2,093,748	722,438	1,132,717	34,188	115,505	58,070
2016	4,009,249	2,474,629	14,419	2,489,048	300,792	-69,066	2,119,190	720,734	1,169,325	34,869	114,980	57,709
2017	4,159,490	2,573,101	21,030	2,594,131	314,654	-84,357	2,195,120	752,377	1,211,993	36,255	114,728	58,336
2018	4,228,930	4,216,213	12,717	2,626,838	325,055	-78,197	2,223,586	764,804	1,240,540	36,988	114,331	58,787
2019	4,361,788	4,357,276	4,512	2,734,113	336,008	-95,694	2,302,411	775,233	1,284,144	38,394	113,605	59,132

Personal Income and Employment by Area: Appleton, WI

(Thousands of dollars, except as noted.)

Year	Personal income, total	Earnings by place of work			Less: Contributions for government social insurance	Plus: Adjustment for residence	Equals: Net earnings by place of residence	Plus: Dividends, interest, and rent	Plus: Personal current transfer receipts	Per capita personal income (dollars)	Population (persons)	Total employment
		Nonfarm	Farm	Total								
1970	550,635	431,402	21,585	452,987	31,605	3,446	424,828	85,862	39,945	3,738	147,307	65,092
1971	581,862	450,163	24,127	474,290	34,056	2,602	442,836	92,757	46,269	3,923	148,324	64,945
1972	638,012	497,053	27,064	524,117	39,697	1,950	486,370	99,714	51,928	4,275	149,228	66,928
1973	723,046	573,426	31,917	605,343	53,011	-2,312	550,020	111,983	61,043	4,853	148,989	71,600
1974	800,861	642,544	27,607	670,151	61,582	-8,097	600,472	127,717	72,672	5,319	150,556	74,056
1975	877,279	676,090	32,698	708,788	63,425	-6,324	639,039	142,515	95,725	5,715	153,496	72,298
1976	977,626	777,488	30,329	807,817	74,164	-10,485	723,168	152,292	102,166	6,419	152,296	74,840
1977	1,092,940	865,519	48,117	913,636	82,671	-13,759	817,206	168,805	106,929	7,084	154,282	77,570
1978	1,211,224	975,152	42,134	1,017,286	95,932	-19,606	901,748	190,094	119,382	7,785	155,590	80,387
1979	1,398,104	1,146,008	59,161	1,205,169	117,583	-40,430	1,047,156	214,968	135,980	8,917	156,784	86,376
1980	1,543,317	1,232,348	57,885	1,290,233	126,106	-48,489	1,115,638	260,883	166,796	9,652	159,892	86,329
1981	1,685,126	1,325,034	40,137	1,365,171	144,820	-43,284	1,177,067	322,032	186,027	10,487	160,685	86,079
1982	1,781,003	1,377,941	30,510	1,408,451	152,278	-38,845	1,217,328	350,668	213,007	11,031	161,454	84,927
1983	1,907,996	1,471,855	19,134	1,490,989	162,367	-33,729	1,294,893	385,223	227,880	11,771	162,093	85,443
1984	2,132,295	1,646,098	36,915	1,683,013	185,940	-28,565	1,468,508	433,796	229,991	13,058	163,293	89,336
1985	2,283,300	1,768,288	39,811	1,808,099	201,469	-23,510	1,583,120	457,301	242,879	13,866	164,668	91,393
1986	2,448,636	1,899,329	50,700	1,950,029	215,930	-17,527	1,716,572	476,486	255,578	14,710	166,459	94,148
1987	2,607,322	2,063,562	57,328	2,120,890	230,837	-20,938	1,869,115	477,243	260,964	15,471	168,530	98,260
1988	2,776,949	2,246,891	33,449	2,280,340	259,451	-20,411	2,000,478	506,808	269,663	16,198	171,443	100,937
1989	3,026,601	2,393,085	64,510	2,457,595	274,877	-16,439	2,166,279	567,434	292,888	17,467	173,276	102,137
1990	3,206,585	2,533,011	51,740	2,584,751	303,945	10,546	2,291,352	600,674	314,559	18,289	175,333	105,276
1991	3,368,949	2,700,986	41,255	2,742,241	328,248	11,114	2,425,107	606,307	337,535	19,029	177,039	107,722
1992	3,694,968	2,957,411	62,295	3,019,706	354,871	18,120	2,682,955	648,170	363,843	20,581	179,533	109,626
1993	3,897,358	3,128,853	45,837	3,174,690	374,975	57,290	2,857,005	665,113	375,240	21,377	182,315	112,232
1994	4,188,266	3,361,225	66,530	3,427,755	407,322	62,392	3,082,825	716,003	389,438	22,540	185,813	116,611
1995	4,432,852	3,503,484	42,794	3,546,278	424,531	101,396	3,223,143	789,455	420,254	23,497	188,656	120,299
1996	4,715,137	3,725,578	61,312	3,786,890	448,721	87,188	3,425,357	847,473	442,307	24,611	191,586	124,832
1997	4,937,783	3,877,099	43,848	3,920,947	465,284	121,879	3,577,542	899,513	460,728	25,446	194,050	126,560
1998	5,216,358	3,988,543	64,275	4,052,818	475,235	188,751	3,766,334	974,936	475,088	26,509	196,776	125,341
1999	5,594,899	4,308,500	64,876	4,373,376	513,024	259,060	4,119,412	972,054	503,433	28,045	199,495	128,535
2000	6,055,117	4,637,123	43,974	4,681,097	545,383	303,560	4,439,274	1,069,771	546,072	29,884	202,618	132,249
2001	6,445,965	5,032,357	48,602	5,080,959	582,870	286,140	4,784,229	1,063,534	598,202	31,340	205,676	135,693
2002	6,693,544	5,193,223	43,999	5,237,222	592,111	347,645	4,992,756	1,036,052	664,736	32,065	208,747	136,552
2003	6,873,919	5,335,924	71,978	5,407,902	613,675	356,143	5,150,370	1,034,446	689,103	32,524	211,350	138,629
2004	7,138,151	5,667,843	74,098	5,741,941	654,962	285,842	5,372,821	1,050,627	714,703	33,420	213,592	142,535
2005	7,428,075	5,831,115	74,799	5,905,914	682,436	310,092	5,533,570	1,122,580	771,925	34,401	215,925	143,877
2006	7,827,548	6,037,098	56,017	6,093,115	712,776	325,748	5,706,087	1,283,205	838,256	35,834	218,441	145,286
2007	8,238,444	6,296,769	93,240	6,390,009	742,746	344,374	5,991,637	1,328,655	918,152	37,385	220,368	147,868
2008	8,583,355	6,381,609	79,876	6,461,485	760,132	402,322	6,103,675	1,421,748	1,057,932	38,594	222,402	146,873
2009	8,427,395	6,222,410	25,359	6,247,769	741,643	436,427	5,942,553	1,283,945	1,200,897	37,516	224,632	142,760
2010	8,669,419	6,325,323	59,191	6,384,514	759,551	469,005	6,093,968	1,275,563	1,299,888	38,370	225,940	141,901
2011	9,249,148	6,668,449	111,350	6,779,799	717,105	537,182	6,599,876	1,375,755	1,273,517	40,646	227,552	144,429
2012	9,645,986	6,985,940	119,876	7,105,816	743,427	526,978	6,889,367	1,482,970	1,273,649	42,182	228,676	146,010
2013	9,783,312	7,060,208	123,162	7,183,370	847,075	644,581	6,980,876	1,499,601	1,302,835	42,541	229,973	147,002
2014	10,313,823	7,379,045	155,480	7,534,525	879,136	622,469	7,277,858	1,654,580	1,381,385	44,534	231,595	150,035
2015	10,764,741	7,712,581	158,104	7,870,685	914,393	608,378	7,564,670	1,748,901	1,451,170	46,175	233,131	151,936
2016	11,161,272	8,031,335	112,321	8,143,656	943,979	647,406	7,847,083	1,831,924	1,482,265	47,636	234,302	154,803
2017	11,551,630	8,300,521	97,208	8,397,729	976,677	678,001	8,099,053	1,903,031	1,549,546	48,921	236,126	155,329
2018	12,097,566	12,016,083	81,483	8,706,185	1,006,495	654,175	8,353,865	2,088,292	1,655,409	51,042	237,011	157,181
2019	12,537,901	12,413,226	124,675	9,086,651	1,051,441	649,825	8,685,035	2,103,915	1,748,951	52,686	237,974	159,644

Personal Income and Employment by Area: Asheville, NC

(Thousands of dollars, except as noted.)

Year	Personal income, total	Earnings by place of work			Less: Contributions for government social insurance	Plus: Adjustment for residence	Equals: Net earnings by place of residence	Plus: Dividends, interest, and rent	Plus: Personal current transfer receipts	Per capita personal income (dollars)	Population (persons)	Total employment
		Nonfarm	Farm	Total								
1970	785,483	604,225	19,802	624,027	41,768	1,294	583,553	122,752	79,178	3,190	246,263	107,391
1971	861,652	664,748	17,192	681,940	47,442	916	635,414	135,111	91,127	3,431	251,104	108,988
1972	973,755	757,294	21,447	778,741	56,878	2,319	724,182	148,794	100,779	3,844	253,306	115,239
1973	1,111,269	875,051	20,034	895,085	75,821	2,068	821,332	171,493	118,444	4,319	257,291	122,493
1974	1,218,978	934,189	18,913	953,102	84,149	4,569	873,522	199,581	145,875	4,671	260,984	121,406
1975	1,318,910	950,469	23,361	973,830	84,222	8,332	897,940	219,298	201,672	4,981	264,807	115,701
1976	1,474,607	1,077,829	26,738	1,104,567	96,895	12,349	1,020,021	240,976	213,610	5,523	266,999	120,996
1977	1,653,861	1,210,375	37,511	1,247,886	108,165	15,775	1,155,496	273,240	225,125	6,108	270,770	126,497
1978	1,859,539	1,376,336	38,342	1,414,678	126,742	19,089	1,307,025	309,450	243,064	6,746	275,655	131,939
1979	2,064,325	1,516,845	38,992	1,555,837	144,801	25,828	1,436,864	350,370	277,091	7,382	279,654	134,546
1980	2,349,553	1,668,929	33,427	1,702,356	160,220	34,717	1,576,853	443,387	329,313	8,284	283,635	135,100
1981	2,649,227	1,810,736	49,471	1,860,207	186,898	38,174	1,711,483	553,853	383,891	9,263	285,988	136,135
1982	2,822,797	1,881,821	46,631	1,928,452	198,322	40,233	1,770,363	627,060	425,374	9,765	289,085	134,442
1983	3,096,007	2,063,902	54,479	2,118,381	219,368	41,075	1,940,088	692,203	463,716	10,682	289,822	138,779
1984	3,450,320	2,319,438	50,544	2,369,982	251,548	42,564	2,160,998	794,410	494,912	11,756	293,506	145,445
1985	3,685,999	2,486,906	41,163	2,528,069	274,382	39,411	2,293,098	861,067	531,834	12,428	296,586	149,776
1986	3,931,739	2,656,077	27,646	2,683,723	299,078	35,552	2,420,197	940,204	571,338	13,147	299,050	153,313
1987	4,225,639	2,873,920	36,167	2,910,087	319,888	37,108	2,627,307	995,122	603,210	14,075	300,229	156,232
1988	4,605,228	3,141,647	51,225	3,192,872	360,711	35,881	2,868,042	1,094,120	643,066	15,212	302,741	163,112
1989	5,040,778	3,339,472	38,993	3,378,465	386,395	34,969	3,027,039	1,298,345	715,394	16,501	305,480	167,964
1990	5,377,067	3,538,322	71,916	3,610,238	417,886	35,576	3,227,928	1,359,290	789,849	17,373	309,502	171,956
1991	5,661,789	3,714,616	70,075	3,784,691	443,852	32,881	3,373,720	1,385,991	902,078	17,965	315,160	172,486
1992	6,102,912	4,031,916	94,323	4,126,239	475,354	30,054	3,680,939	1,429,106	992,867	18,998	321,240	176,331
1993	6,523,774	4,299,374	112,821	4,412,195	510,769	22,600	3,924,026	1,511,364	1,088,384	19,876	328,220	181,752
1994	6,861,121	4,535,966	119,581	4,655,547	545,982	18,892	4,128,457	1,607,169	1,125,495	20,488	334,878	186,248
1995	7,389,530	4,772,356	123,208	4,895,564	576,466	16,742	4,335,840	1,795,521	1,258,169	21,623	341,739	191,577
1996	7,799,315	5,021,019	99,626	5,120,645	600,150	15,536	4,536,031	1,907,124	1,356,160	22,417	347,921	196,267
1997	8,430,196	5,440,362	96,290	5,536,652	642,957	14,820	4,908,515	2,098,868	1,422,813	23,811	354,052	203,879
1998	8,945,058	5,790,643	109,394	5,900,037	682,594	17,644	5,235,087	2,240,959	1,469,012	24,854	359,909	208,191
1999	9,271,704	6,081,178	129,993	6,211,171	718,055	15,146	5,508,262	2,199,037	1,564,405	25,391	365,159	211,901
2000	9,759,059	6,333,301	117,976	6,451,277	748,289	13,182	5,716,170	2,365,869	1,677,020	26,332	370,615	215,601
2001	10,178,826	6,709,701	94,007	6,803,708	782,811	-1,833	6,019,064	2,309,162	1,850,600	27,150	374,904	214,044
2002	10,295,615	6,842,908	57,898	6,900,806	795,106	-13,505	6,092,195	2,221,514	1,981,906	27,107	379,818	214,661
2003	10,534,038	7,102,009	66,616	7,168,625	840,127	-42,995	6,285,503	2,178,766	2,069,769	27,348	385,178	218,080
2004	11,372,560	7,526,612	75,240	7,601,852	880,685	-62,604	6,658,563	2,474,411	2,239,586	29,107	390,713	223,209
2005	12,060,823	7,890,658	116,353	8,007,011	935,048	-79,898	6,992,065	2,666,452	2,402,306	30,425	396,408	229,213
2006	13,087,634	8,514,868	112,652	8,627,520	1,000,668	-94,532	7,532,320	2,940,435	2,614,879	32,351	404,546	236,531
2007	13,928,707	8,922,819	56,378	8,979,197	1,060,696	-110,655	7,807,846	3,333,981	2,786,880	33,821	411,842	246,173
2008	14,318,867	8,991,775	70,910	9,062,685	1,071,356	-123,570	7,867,759	3,349,778	3,101,330	34,300	417,457	244,313
2009	13,880,506	8,543,399	75,425	8,618,824	1,040,010	-106,742	7,472,072	2,971,883	3,436,551	32,891	422,014	234,371
2010	14,164,352	8,777,903	64,622	8,842,525	1,056,950	-98,497	7,687,078	2,868,256	3,609,018	33,301	425,340	233,877
2011	14,778,383	8,897,799	64,980	8,962,779	986,200	-99,301	7,877,278	3,187,171	3,713,934	34,510	428,230	238,793
2012	15,710,045	9,411,895	59,455	9,471,350	1,019,399	-82,220	8,369,731	3,520,663	3,819,651	36,438	431,145	241,450
2013	15,758,099	9,651,852	52,508	9,704,360	1,194,773	-62,187	8,447,400	3,422,252	3,888,447	36,136	436,077	246,183
2014	16,917,366	10,278,192	64,149	10,342,341	1,264,479	-72,049	9,005,813	3,868,225	4,043,328	38,445	440,039	252,569
2015	18,061,212	10,851,435	74,396	10,925,831	1,335,050	-76,562	9,514,219	4,295,625	4,251,368	40,591	444,952	260,025
2016	18,838,663	11,434,324	69,958	11,504,282	1,397,589	-81,836	10,024,857	4,440,579	4,373,227	41,779	450,914	267,776
2017	19,721,229	11,994,904	69,568	12,064,472	1,450,541	-86,727	10,527,204	4,651,902	4,542,123	43,235	456,145	271,972
2018	21,017,694	20,979,315	38,379	12,758,746	1,518,413	-87,931	11,152,402	5,207,075	4,658,217	45,759	459,314	281,092
2019	21,945,716	21,893,669	52,047	13,441,022	1,599,986	-83,612	11,757,424	5,288,144	4,900,148	47,432	462,680	287,879

Personal Income and Employment by Area: Athens-Clarke County, GA

(Thousands of dollars, except as noted.)

Year	Personal income, total	Earnings by place of work Nonfarm	Earnings by place of work Farm	Earnings by place of work Total	Less: Contributions for government social insurance	Plus: Adjustment for residence	Equals: Net earnings by place of residence	Plus: Dividends, interest, and rent	Plus: Personal current transfer receipts	Per capita personal income (dollars)	Population (persons)	Total employment
1970	287,152	243,816	4,596	248,412	14,503	-10,546	223,363	42,106	21,683	3,033	94,672	42,435
1971	321,923	274,050	3,976	278,026	16,774	-11,825	249,427	47,055	25,441	3,311	97,214	44,721
1972	363,661	310,458	4,906	315,364	20,077	-13,930	281,357	53,011	29,293	3,601	100,987	47,189
1973	415,511	349,981	11,328	361,309	25,915	-16,563	318,831	61,879	34,801	3,936	105,560	48,552
1974	470,958	399,911	6,262	406,173	30,536	-20,689	354,948	72,985	43,025	4,374	107,666	50,427
1975	520,622	417,929	13,538	431,467	31,436	-18,723	381,308	81,556	57,758	4,811	108,211	49,988
1976	579,382	475,100	12,846	487,946	36,710	-23,136	428,100	89,810	61,472	5,460	106,120	51,555
1977	641,865	532,485	14,142	546,627	41,017	-28,419	477,191	100,468	64,206	5,981	107,309	54,049
1978	719,753	603,796	16,686	620,482	47,935	-35,789	536,758	112,296	70,699	6,637	108,452	56,422
1979	790,245	658,558	18,183	676,741	54,760	-36,548	585,433	124,390	80,422	7,240	109,148	57,722
1980	871,547	714,172	2,511	716,683	59,414	-38,926	618,343	155,667	97,537	7,623	114,324	57,313
1981	998,482	792,156	12,091	804,247	70,904	-39,355	693,988	193,001	111,493	8,533	117,011	58,812
1982	1,081,243	825,577	22,803	848,380	75,119	-38,765	734,496	223,636	123,111	9,141	118,289	58,163
1983	1,209,146	930,147	22,242	952,389	85,981	-42,326	824,082	249,831	135,233	10,046	120,365	60,122
1984	1,326,414	1,004,553	37,211	1,041,764	95,629	-41,377	904,758	276,775	144,881	10,830	122,473	63,350
1985	1,435,020	1,095,499	30,358	1,125,857	107,113	-42,511	976,233	301,187	157,600	11,542	124,327	65,645
1986	1,576,707	1,200,748	44,593	1,245,341	118,968	-44,402	1,081,971	325,516	169,220	12,570	125,434	68,018
1987	1,680,289	1,300,064	28,113	1,328,177	127,801	-44,317	1,156,059	345,018	179,212	13,127	128,002	70,290
1988	1,845,495	1,426,064	43,576	1,469,640	146,013	-44,020	1,279,607	375,189	190,699	14,132	130,586	72,042
1989	2,051,027	1,539,424	61,980	1,601,404	158,330	-45,100	1,397,974	442,681	210,372	15,318	133,894	73,601
1990	2,202,783	1,659,584	57,138	1,716,722	170,741	-46,416	1,499,565	465,377	237,841	16,089	136,914	74,955
1991	2,289,739	1,700,838	59,358	1,760,196	177,351	-45,552	1,537,293	479,297	273,149	16,431	139,359	73,882
1992	2,414,496	1,794,059	59,742	1,853,801	186,659	-38,696	1,628,446	482,763	303,287	17,016	141,899	74,262
1993	2,575,471	1,906,970	61,475	1,968,445	198,815	-32,637	1,736,993	517,037	321,441	17,772	144,916	78,030
1994	2,747,204	2,038,143	66,849	2,104,992	213,691	-39,481	1,851,820	555,623	339,761	18,443	148,953	80,774
1995	2,968,596	2,191,628	58,360	2,249,988	229,113	-37,209	1,983,666	615,268	369,662	19,567	151,718	85,085
1996	3,188,396	2,348,219	66,352	2,414,571	242,468	-38,754	2,133,349	661,575	393,472	20,573	154,977	88,923
1997	3,347,496	2,470,050	68,759	2,538,809	250,368	-49,553	2,238,888	712,505	396,103	21,148	158,291	90,120
1998	3,580,896	2,668,278	82,975	2,751,253	267,867	-49,059	2,434,327	744,274	402,295	22,335	160,330	92,124
1999	3,746,662	2,827,933	82,917	2,910,850	281,958	-58,411	2,570,481	747,076	429,105	22,922	163,456	93,748
2000	3,937,622	2,940,142	74,919	3,015,061	291,795	-62,125	2,661,141	801,735	474,746	23,612	166,763	95,550
2001	4,158,159	3,107,434	102,078	3,209,512	310,959	-81,430	2,817,123	820,540	520,496	24,608	168,973	95,547
2002	4,293,601	3,254,463	62,578	3,317,041	324,936	-97,788	2,894,317	816,178	583,106	25,133	170,838	96,128
2003	4,522,790	3,464,118	65,982	3,530,100	341,405	-139,016	3,049,679	884,731	588,380	26,016	173,847	97,807
2004	4,722,080	3,620,825	97,085	3,717,910	366,561	-142,074	3,209,275	879,743	633,062	26,513	178,106	99,793
2005	4,961,574	3,802,279	103,496	3,905,775	380,914	-171,113	3,353,748	911,143	696,683	27,722	178,974	103,703
2006	5,203,238	4,023,488	48,665	4,072,153	408,052	-225,718	3,438,383	1,027,461	737,394	28,406	183,171	107,249
2007	5,455,210	4,147,524	75,360	4,222,884	410,986	-286,005	3,525,893	1,128,881	800,436	29,206	186,781	111,049
2008	5,629,282	4,282,145	114,768	4,396,913	455,761	-398,848	3,542,304	1,155,425	931,553	29,636	189,948	111,948
2009	5,583,422	4,232,033	100,433	4,332,466	443,561	-463,858	3,425,047	1,144,865	1,013,510	29,077	192,021	109,067
2010	5,694,081	4,326,879	74,142	4,401,021	447,925	-516,735	3,436,361	1,136,230	1,121,490	29,435	193,446	108,282
2011	6,006,340	4,409,883	63,507	4,473,390	403,613	-516,773	3,553,004	1,257,318	1,196,018	30,880	194,508	108,818
2012	6,252,721	4,571,656	148,177	4,719,833	416,226	-517,869	3,785,738	1,288,107	1,178,876	31,874	196,169	110,126
2013	6,422,983	4,730,720	183,500	4,914,220	484,583	-502,949	3,926,688	1,276,876	1,219,419	32,483	197,731	112,556
2014	6,894,728	4,949,098	171,889	5,120,987	506,378	-424,850	4,189,759	1,428,247	1,276,722	34,708	198,650	114,037
2015	7,410,634	5,303,768	194,150	5,497,918	540,493	-478,278	4,479,147	1,583,190	1,348,297	36,537	202,824	117,317
2016	7,677,052	5,576,931	145,322	5,722,253	572,133	-516,098	4,634,022	1,648,387	1,394,643	37,372	205,421	121,956
2017	8,041,845	5,810,238	166,177	5,976,415	598,412	-490,549	4,887,454	1,715,846	1,438,545	38,428	209,271	125,546
2018	8,605,032	8,468,335	136,697	6,237,271	630,040	-506,898	5,100,333	1,988,868	1,515,831	40,692	211,468	128,858
2019	8,869,497	8,791,510	77,987	6,298,969	645,886	-380,315	5,272,768	2,003,425	1,593,304	41,495	213,750	130,064

Personal Income and Employment by Area: Atlanta-Sandy Springs-Alpharetta, GA

(Thousands of dollars, except as noted.)

Year	Personal income, total	Earnings by place of work			Less: Contributions for government social insurance	Plus: Adjustment for residence	Equals: Net earnings by place of residence	Plus: Dividends, interest, and rent	Plus: Personal current transfer receipts	Per capita personal income (dollars)	Population (persons)	Total employment
		Nonfarm	Farm	Total								
1970	7,695,760	6,697,987	32,676	6,730,663	424,490	-79,274	6,226,899	997,013	471,848	4,133	1,862,083	924,492
1971	8,534,310	7,385,975	28,231	7,414,206	485,358	-85,378	6,843,470	1,125,779	565,061	4,436	1,923,687	956,707
1972	9,754,566	8,498,897	36,008	8,534,905	587,731	-103,187	7,843,987	1,268,080	642,499	4,910	1,986,477	1,013,051
1973	11,042,213	9,652,707	67,946	9,720,653	767,896	-122,909	8,829,848	1,460,906	751,459	5,373	2,055,233	1,078,478
1974	12,157,534	10,475,353	33,695	10,509,048	862,290	-133,408	9,513,350	1,696,160	948,024	5,764	2,109,395	1,089,091
1975	13,096,935	10,934,479	63,265	10,997,744	880,136	-138,055	9,979,553	1,801,246	1,316,136	6,155	2,127,779	1,049,087
1976	14,504,859	12,264,616	71,420	12,336,036	1,009,289	-149,629	11,177,118	1,931,061	1,396,680	6,737	2,152,893	1,087,337
1977	16,314,364	14,013,062	63,099	14,076,161	1,148,484	-164,028	12,763,649	2,115,323	1,435,392	7,435	2,194,331	1,147,650
1978	18,510,403	16,006,272	68,900	16,075,172	1,351,575	-177,354	14,546,243	2,410,476	1,553,684	8,282	2,234,980	1,217,960
1979	20,856,158	18,059,329	72,610	18,131,939	1,586,598	-212,299	16,333,042	2,751,871	1,771,245	9,085	2,295,738	1,273,760
1980	23,755,858	20,259,773	27,771	20,287,544	1,788,440	-247,838	18,251,266	3,381,544	2,123,048	10,100	2,352,155	1,312,418
1981	26,827,948	22,567,671	57,878	22,625,549	2,148,708	-277,588	20,199,253	4,224,701	2,403,994	11,162	2,403,406	1,337,201
1982	29,069,283	24,236,859	95,879	24,332,738	2,366,061	-297,200	21,669,477	4,769,841	2,629,965	11,848	2,453,618	1,357,118
1983	32,382,541	27,101,118	69,657	27,170,775	2,681,241	-334,130	24,155,404	5,364,658	2,862,479	12,868	2,516,569	1,418,357
1984	37,264,505	31,372,930	106,421	31,479,351	3,192,267	-374,976	27,912,108	6,292,401	3,059,996	14,366	2,593,856	1,541,244
1985	41,718,654	35,461,380	84,875	35,546,255	3,691,992	-410,793	31,443,470	6,998,262	3,276,922	15,512	2,689,442	1,644,282
1986	46,111,602	39,467,364	101,677	39,569,041	4,155,215	-429,017	34,984,809	7,626,337	3,500,456	16,558	2,784,902	1,737,089
1987	50,350,752	43,416,808	57,437	43,474,245	4,528,976	-500,831	38,444,438	8,250,662	3,655,652	17,472	2,881,787	1,799,907
1988	55,371,110	47,539,042	100,323	47,639,365	5,075,484	-518,129	42,045,752	9,373,447	3,951,911	18,673	2,965,367	1,869,917
1989	59,512,828	50,102,768	153,761	50,256,529	5,379,911	-511,292	44,365,326	10,726,546	4,420,956	19,621	3,033,139	1,902,034
1990	64,033,797	53,655,678	144,832	53,800,510	5,790,472	-526,809	47,483,229	11,563,196	4,987,372	20,628	3,104,221	1,936,224
1991	66,969,658	55,810,627	160,299	55,970,926	6,085,729	-540,550	49,344,647	11,804,654	5,820,357	20,958	3,195,398	1,917,337
1992	72,962,981	61,307,423	172,661	61,480,084	6,580,558	-607,507	54,292,019	12,106,935	6,564,027	22,164	3,291,991	1,962,091
1993	78,347,953	65,856,736	167,381	66,024,117	7,086,996	-663,795	58,273,326	12,987,330	7,087,297	23,028	3,402,250	2,072,915
1994	84,778,242	70,877,072	192,293	71,069,365	7,724,387	-723,448	62,621,530	14,431,218	7,725,494	24,059	3,523,718	2,172,516
1995	92,783,942	77,202,240	156,150	77,358,390	8,385,323	-802,384	68,170,683	16,153,984	8,459,275	25,457	3,644,699	2,273,047
1996	101,611,806	84,644,509	175,481	84,819,990	9,078,334	-914,641	74,827,015	17,774,560	9,010,231	26,983	3,765,817	2,380,579
1997	109,575,090	91,523,953	178,862	91,702,815	9,784,315	-1,025,407	80,893,093	19,474,418	9,207,579	28,180	3,888,398	2,460,237
1998	122,130,244	103,542,136	213,859	103,755,995	10,810,080	-1,198,021	91,747,894	20,943,228	9,439,122	30,370	4,021,410	2,584,632
1999	131,887,678	113,892,335	203,708	114,096,043	11,840,565	-1,358,877	100,896,601	21,052,112	9,938,965	31,720	4,157,862	2,676,550
2000	145,422,465	125,267,913	164,511	125,432,424	12,836,545	-1,554,455	111,041,424	23,491,392	10,889,649	33,871	4,293,475	2,770,951
2001	153,394,685	131,982,805	228,703	132,211,508	13,367,097	-1,524,749	117,319,662	23,929,162	12,145,861	34,843	4,402,455	2,809,261
2002	156,694,544	134,031,669	135,262	134,166,931	13,489,090	-1,412,092	119,265,749	23,614,456	13,814,339	34,904	4,489,288	2,795,141
2003	161,624,010	137,548,536	146,546	137,695,082	13,785,907	-1,268,535	122,640,640	24,731,333	14,252,037	35,347	4,572,541	2,813,569
2004	171,176,199	146,174,959	229,046	146,404,005	14,994,851	-1,237,973	130,171,181	25,619,655	15,385,363	36,736	4,659,574	2,896,329
2005	183,116,142	153,303,562	234,094	153,537,656	15,640,385	-1,002,389	136,894,882	29,086,278	17,134,982	38,382	4,770,870	3,014,860
2006	197,820,146	163,145,705	112,560	163,258,265	16,619,894	-846,088	145,792,283	33,507,274	18,520,589	40,111	4,931,848	3,134,434
2007	206,845,931	167,969,314	168,306	168,137,620	17,218,155	-850,098	150,069,367	36,648,227	20,128,337	40,827	5,066,356	3,232,964
2008	205,167,164	162,656,494	225,345	162,881,839	17,708,073	-107,513	145,066,253	36,418,864	23,682,047	39,683	5,170,099	3,206,861
2009	199,360,961	157,520,889	193,257	157,714,146	17,109,971	279,788	140,883,963	32,169,876	26,307,122	38,040	5,240,828	3,087,160
2010	203,544,267	159,566,734	144,966	159,711,700	17,338,719	417,145	142,790,126	31,574,831	29,179,310	38,380	5,303,327	3,070,701
2011	219,715,009	167,473,923	107,684	167,581,607	15,945,728	321,380	151,957,259	37,113,232	30,644,518	40,892	5,373,016	3,151,193
2012	225,955,783	172,627,394	274,020	172,901,414	16,562,510	287,225	156,626,129	38,979,377	30,350,277	41,448	5,451,561	3,199,601
2013	229,730,494	179,660,888	334,867	179,995,755	19,666,589	277,972	160,607,138	37,519,753	31,603,603	41,640	5,517,034	3,285,224
2014	248,849,883	192,465,912	328,805	192,794,717	20,794,391	78,293	172,078,619	43,358,204	33,413,060	44,397	5,605,117	3,420,778
2015	264,837,762	204,756,980	363,826	205,120,806	21,995,513	101,536	183,226,829	46,497,360	35,113,573	46,444	5,702,331	3,540,124
2016	277,732,186	216,738,907	234,518	216,973,425	23,124,765	-518,023	193,330,637	47,909,478	36,492,071	47,920	5,795,723	3,652,170
2017	292,220,786	229,243,915	285,534	229,529,449	24,308,694	-374,291	204,846,464	49,609,318	37,765,004	49,657	5,884,736	3,732,877
2018	316,220,617	316,056,855	163,762	242,857,900	25,529,979	-383,472	216,944,449	59,502,504	39,773,664	53,188	5,945,303	3,878,093
2019	328,450,133	328,373,381	76,752	254,156,137	26,772,763	-535,968	226,847,406	59,746,670	41,856,057	54,557	6,020,364	3,976,488

Personal Income and Employment by Area: Atlantic City-Hammonton, NJ

(Thousands of dollars, except as noted.)

		Derivation of personal income										
		Earnings by place of work			Less: Contributions for government social insurance	Plus: Adjustment for residence	Equals: Net earnings by place of residence	Plus: Dividends, interest, and rent	Plus: Personal current transfer receipts	Per capita personal income (dollars)	Population (persons)	Total employment
Year	Personal income, total	Nonfarm	Farm	Total								
1970	782,866	555,691	6,342	562,033	39,518	35,867	558,382	124,240	100,244	4,450	175,908	79,885
1971	871,879	593,872	6,399	600,271	43,642	57,677	614,306	137,345	120,228	4,849	179,824	79,392
1972	964,555	651,292	5,316	656,608	50,285	74,206	680,529	149,736	134,290	5,214	184,987	82,297
1973	1,081,593	728,853	8,073	736,926	63,329	88,957	762,554	166,721	152,318	5,778	187,199	85,385
1974	1,173,626	763,744	8,991	772,735	68,812	104,358	808,281	186,919	178,426	6,206	189,113	84,867
1975	1,283,784	803,960	8,100	812,060	70,323	117,849	859,586	200,118	224,080	6,773	189,544	82,280
1976	1,421,862	901,015	8,936	909,951	77,981	129,498	961,468	213,516	246,878	7,499	189,613	84,161
1977	1,575,347	1,008,725	11,534	1,020,259	85,279	144,519	1,079,499	235,029	260,819	8,321	189,311	85,095
1978	1,779,776	1,180,610	11,718	1,192,328	103,083	149,616	1,238,861	265,544	275,371	9,312	191,121	90,253
1979	2,069,787	1,486,929	9,673	1,496,602	143,412	114,209	1,467,399	300,119	302,269	10,720	193,082	99,716
1980	2,386,106	1,792,440	11,740	1,804,180	180,700	65,015	1,688,495	366,979	330,632	12,264	194,566	109,410
1981	2,735,574	2,159,658	10,799	2,170,457	239,169	-2,231	1,929,057	450,004	356,513	13,958	195,984	118,656
1982	2,921,164	2,304,397	14,457	2,318,854	256,363	-34,785	2,027,706	517,231	376,227	14,862	196,548	119,783
1983	3,177,478	2,599,353	20,497	2,619,850	296,657	-86,287	2,236,906	540,568	400,004	15,954	199,168	124,824
1984	3,586,003	3,022,968	15,085	3,038,053	354,970	-143,070	2,540,013	633,745	412,245	17,687	202,752	133,475
1985	3,831,249	3,295,773	20,107	3,315,880	392,565	-198,372	2,724,943	669,942	436,364	18,594	206,045	139,336
1986	4,099,040	3,608,819	21,519	3,630,338	429,653	-269,689	2,930,996	708,854	459,190	19,576	209,388	141,884
1987	4,343,758	3,925,341	18,435	3,943,776	469,836	-349,855	3,124,085	743,494	476,179	20,433	212,581	148,142
1988	4,747,699	4,365,864	18,427	4,384,291	525,747	-450,998	3,407,546	827,597	512,556	21,834	217,445	152,703
1989	4,945,472	4,511,522	18,262	4,529,784	544,251	-548,976	3,436,557	955,801	553,114	22,318	221,589	155,641
1990	5,065,020	4,701,103	17,135	4,718,238	553,501	-679,996	3,484,741	973,839	606,440	22,468	225,431	159,479
1991	4,796,490	4,302,985	20,486	4,323,471	531,003	-647,708	3,144,760	938,737	712,993	20,967	228,763	152,342
1992	5,394,249	4,845,531	22,501	4,868,032	576,430	-672,976	3,618,626	934,693	840,930	23,290	231,612	152,205
1993	5,662,193	5,126,534	26,421	5,152,955	598,218	-705,633	3,849,104	929,720	883,369	24,168	234,288	153,047
1994	5,805,053	5,262,155	26,756	5,288,911	629,876	-704,206	3,954,829	972,187	878,037	24,536	236,589	154,444
1995	6,268,051	5,617,638	28,932	5,646,570	659,802	-708,400	4,278,368	1,043,188	946,495	26,203	239,212	157,855
1996	6,682,656	5,976,437	31,538	6,007,975	692,844	-713,318	4,601,813	1,103,413	977,430	27,597	242,152	159,704
1997	7,028,062	6,292,371	30,222	6,322,593	707,823	-746,039	4,868,731	1,157,117	1,002,214	28,713	244,771	162,668
1998	7,333,173	6,588,140	26,903	6,615,043	729,056	-780,184	5,105,803	1,200,233	1,027,137	29,586	247,863	167,700
1999	7,562,690	6,820,454	22,442	6,842,896	739,954	-781,138	5,321,804	1,190,511	1,050,375	30,199	250,432	170,052
2000	8,024,070	7,148,384	31,255	7,179,639	765,413	-793,178	5,621,048	1,278,948	1,124,074	31,631	253,674	173,765
2001	7,486,116	6,476,388	29,657	6,506,045	759,301	-839,103	4,907,641	1,317,818	1,260,657	29,273	255,737	171,600
2002	7,774,252	6,701,016	36,869	6,737,885	785,707	-811,716	5,140,462	1,252,336	1,381,454	29,986	259,263	171,667
2003	8,093,131	6,946,922	35,164	6,982,086	812,256	-789,408	5,380,422	1,282,228	1,430,481	30,739	263,285	174,184
2004	8,646,897	7,436,315	34,842	7,471,157	854,218	-784,864	5,832,075	1,390,131	1,424,691	32,298	267,723	177,412
2005	9,120,736	7,907,787	45,623	7,953,410	918,806	-792,152	6,242,452	1,319,334	1,558,950	33,739	270,332	183,113
2006	9,992,710	8,584,788	67,078	8,651,866	969,782	-740,365	6,941,719	1,344,403	1,706,588	36,770	271,759	184,525
2007	10,455,085	8,766,567	71,664	8,838,231	1,006,112	-697,377	7,134,742	1,507,006	1,813,337	38,395	272,303	183,099
2008	10,743,547	8,657,435	58,928	8,716,363	1,022,528	-692,251	7,001,584	1,687,819	2,054,144	39,352	273,014	181,292
2009	10,523,558	8,056,167	60,503	8,116,670	963,570	-592,771	6,560,329	1,667,896	2,295,333	38,400	274,049	172,715
2010	10,705,833	8,131,673	50,667	8,182,340	972,952	-631,937	6,577,451	1,637,328	2,491,054	38,964	274,761	171,005
2011	11,208,828	8,234,494	60,055	8,294,549	895,568	-537,587	6,861,394	1,814,906	2,532,528	40,744	275,107	170,762
2012	11,487,970	8,490,418	71,375	8,561,793	905,782	-585,813	7,070,198	1,919,666	2,498,106	41,664	275,732	171,854
2013	11,645,552	8,699,261	56,328	8,755,589	1,025,544	-528,540	7,201,505	1,906,492	2,537,555	42,201	275,954	171,402
2014	11,885,274	8,800,503	55,313	8,855,816	1,033,168	-590,908	7,231,740	2,008,131	2,645,403	43,244	274,842	168,459
2015	12,030,464	8,609,939	60,855	8,670,794	1,025,222	-473,489	7,172,083	2,093,619	2,764,762	44,053	273,088	164,827
2016	12,125,264	8,607,490	55,069	8,662,559	1,027,396	-439,922	7,195,241	2,087,562	2,842,461	44,771	270,830	165,204
2017	12,566,489	8,828,979	56,378	8,885,357	1,052,236	-347,081	7,486,040	2,173,474	2,906,975	46,557	269,918	164,558
2018	12,816,209	12,773,951	42,258	9,299,003	1,100,677	-464,740	7,733,586	2,123,796	2,958,827	48,548	263,989	168,101
2019	13,349,834	13,299,780	50,054	9,699,737	1,158,754	-468,143	8,072,840	2,153,057	3,123,937	50,631	263,670	171,340

Personal Income and Employment by Area: Auburn-Opelika, AL

(Thousands of dollars, except as noted.)

Year	Personal income, total	Earnings by place of work			Less: Contributions for government social insurance	Plus: Adjustment for residence	Equals: Net earnings by place of residence	Plus: Dividends, interest, and rent	Plus: Personal current transfer receipts	Per capita personal income (dollars)	Population (persons)	Total employment
		Nonfarm	Farm	Total								
1970	169,722	135,029	2,208	137,237	10,502	7,656	134,391	22,021	13,310	2,770	61,262	25,031
1971	189,457	147,579	2,833	150,412	11,785	10,370	148,997	25,207	15,253	3,061	61,896	24,952
1972	214,225	168,266	3,307	171,573	14,043	11,540	169,070	28,048	17,107	3,446	62,158	26,173
1973	243,444	191,905	4,206	196,111	18,356	13,257	191,012	32,093	20,339	3,769	64,588	27,551
1974	273,005	212,386	1,937	214,323	20,983	16,472	209,812	37,967	25,226	3,967	68,823	27,763
1975	303,672	227,786	1,641	229,427	22,485	19,230	226,172	43,349	34,151	4,377	69,373	27,700
1976	344,275	257,209	3,543	260,752	25,931	23,778	258,599	49,023	36,653	4,920	69,980	28,875
1977	397,165	301,124	4,294	305,418	30,201	25,493	300,710	56,963	39,492	5,527	71,861	30,460
1978	457,487	346,744	6,677	353,421	35,224	29,437	347,634	66,941	42,912	6,176	74,069	32,087
1979	505,368	377,118	7,184	384,302	39,536	34,245	379,011	75,520	50,837	6,650	75,990	32,315
1980	571,438	421,296	6,441	427,737	44,769	36,674	419,642	90,078	61,718	7,459	76,610	32,917
1981	627,182	458,987	6,436	465,423	52,590	37,801	450,634	109,037	67,511	8,064	77,777	32,811
1982	665,335	473,717	6,100	479,817	54,906	41,196	466,107	125,400	73,828	8,422	79,001	32,816
1983	737,201	536,226	4,844	541,070	61,814	41,271	520,527	136,379	80,295	9,317	79,121	34,028
1984	818,528	609,253	3,601	612,854	71,016	41,928	583,766	151,300	83,462	10,195	80,289	36,719
1985	879,390	646,777	4,710	651,487	74,525	48,195	625,157	164,147	90,086	10,833	81,176	37,024
1986	932,599	678,665	3,796	682,461	77,162	54,313	659,612	177,517	95,470	11,267	82,776	37,444
1987	993,407	725,045	4,876	729,921	81,299	58,920	707,542	187,571	98,294	12,015	82,681	38,845
1988	1,074,858	794,060	5,176	799,236	92,555	58,536	765,217	205,417	104,224	12,705	84,601	40,675
1989	1,199,799	881,891	5,290	887,181	101,734	54,220	839,667	239,541	120,591	13,975	85,851	43,158
1990	1,263,716	923,878	6,036	929,914	107,168	61,294	884,040	244,449	135,227	14,404	87,735	43,140
1991	1,337,279	945,484	9,466	954,950	109,328	80,735	926,357	258,654	152,268	14,940	89,508	43,300
1992	1,461,242	1,031,334	6,649	1,037,983	117,463	98,903	1,019,423	270,048	171,771	15,957	91,572	44,434
1993	1,552,650	1,070,623	17,090	1,087,713	122,334	120,990	1,086,369	281,609	184,672	16,466	94,295	45,513
1994	1,657,056	1,133,461	8,893	1,142,354	130,330	143,858	1,155,882	301,330	199,844	17,251	96,057	46,095
1995	1,784,325	1,188,482	8,524	1,197,006	137,146	167,338	1,227,198	340,558	216,569	17,953	99,386	48,314
1996	1,872,181	1,225,957	5,676	1,231,633	140,354	196,688	1,287,967	354,190	230,024	18,321	102,185	49,880
1997	2,018,792	1,304,017	6,079	1,310,096	149,463	228,032	1,388,665	383,494	246,633	18,942	106,578	51,253
1998	2,171,732	1,383,142	5,148	1,388,290	154,724	266,300	1,499,866	415,134	256,732	19,755	109,936	51,944
1999	2,304,664	1,471,067	4,228	1,475,295	163,671	294,251	1,605,875	424,594	274,195	20,414	112,898	52,880
2000	2,429,660	1,515,212	3,701	1,518,913	169,746	322,128	1,671,295	461,627	296,738	21,049	115,430	54,697
2001	2,499,889	1,507,898	5,273	1,513,171	174,007	343,829	1,682,993	479,309	337,587	21,400	116,819	54,497
2002	2,617,974	1,604,699	7,266	1,611,965	184,752	350,472	1,777,685	481,534	358,755	22,113	118,392	56,381
2003	2,795,712	1,724,439	7,313	1,731,752	197,842	355,150	1,889,060	523,142	383,510	23,284	120,071	57,402
2004	3,049,014	1,937,175	9,601	1,946,776	218,977	344,791	2,072,590	564,834	411,590	24,936	122,274	61,407
2005	3,241,980	2,058,127	6,620	2,064,747	232,622	364,839	2,196,964	596,542	448,474	25,703	126,133	63,934
2006	3,491,726	2,207,729	8,010	2,215,739	250,336	375,641	2,341,044	659,793	490,889	27,016	129,247	67,109
2007	3,728,552	2,312,488	7,889	2,320,377	265,002	409,105	2,464,480	714,683	549,389	28,261	131,934	69,314
2008	3,978,936	2,334,832	4,350	2,339,182	274,996	464,420	2,528,606	814,205	636,125	29,578	134,524	68,626
2009	3,962,088	2,307,070	5,901	2,312,971	269,746	463,872	2,507,097	775,285	679,706	28,594	138,566	66,847
2010	4,142,199	2,331,483	4,122	2,335,605	273,748	527,730	2,589,587	781,390	771,222	29,418	140,806	66,719
2011	4,430,367	2,434,279	4,727	2,439,006	254,037	596,185	2,781,154	844,154	805,059	30,741	144,117	69,655
2012	4,725,114	2,563,562	14,316	2,577,878	264,422	675,895	2,989,351	918,588	817,175	31,858	148,318	71,770
2013	4,846,318	2,686,060	16,230	2,702,290	311,297	696,888	3,087,881	915,173	843,264	32,001	151,445	73,933
2014	5,122,639	2,863,917	7,418	2,871,335	330,458	693,718	3,234,595	985,380	902,664	33,218	154,211	76,545
2015	5,360,144	3,028,355	9,678	3,038,033	347,943	679,508	3,369,598	1,030,440	960,106	34,198	156,740	78,200
2016	5,684,946	3,179,694	13,972	3,193,666	363,677	770,429	3,600,418	1,083,375	1,001,153	35,758	158,983	80,742
2017	5,969,782	3,425,467	10,321	3,435,788	390,897	749,924	3,794,815	1,132,533	1,042,434	36,941	161,604	83,017
2018	6,280,809	6,268,389	12,420	3,504,723	409,537	800,591	3,895,777	1,245,821	1,139,211	38,378	163,656	85,561
2019	6,545,660	6,533,608	12,052	3,698,621	431,376	793,469	4,060,714	1,269,346	1,215,600	39,781	164,542	87,625

Personal Income and Employment by Area: Augusta-Richmond County, GA-SC

(Thousands of dollars, except as noted.)

Year	Personal income, total	Earnings by place of work			Less: Contributions for government social insurance	Plus: Adjustment for residence	Equals: Net earnings by place of residence	Plus: Dividends, interest, and rent	Plus: Personal current transfer receipts	Per capita personal income (dollars)	Population (persons)	Total employment
		Nonfarm	Farm	Total								
1970	1,151,713	947,281	12,844	960,125	59,380	-17,736	883,009	176,536	92,168	3,489	330,105	149,954
1971	1,243,591	1,019,335	17,231	1,036,566	67,016	-28,026	941,524	188,779	113,288	3,765	330,340	149,885
1972	1,347,080	1,104,590	16,681	1,121,271	75,514	-27,996	1,017,761	199,876	129,443	4,102	328,410	151,635
1973	1,500,532	1,213,557	34,737	1,248,294	94,054	-27,946	1,126,294	224,582	149,656	4,513	332,508	157,074
1974	1,683,378	1,353,556	22,469	1,376,025	109,140	-30,503	1,236,382	260,168	186,828	4,940	340,794	160,613
1975	1,813,963	1,419,381	20,486	1,439,867	114,385	-30,688	1,294,794	281,439	237,730	5,199	348,901	157,238
1976	2,080,859	1,663,727	24,825	1,688,552	136,281	-43,537	1,508,734	314,989	257,136	5,795	359,074	165,293
1977	2,283,948	1,844,119	22,400	1,866,519	150,578	-47,837	1,668,104	348,734	267,110	6,261	364,786	172,285
1978	2,550,572	2,059,940	20,102	2,080,042	171,732	-53,344	1,854,966	402,686	292,920	6,815	374,244	178,197
1979	2,884,567	2,309,983	41,217	2,351,200	199,677	-63,263	2,088,260	461,793	334,514	7,524	383,370	184,512
1980	3,191,499	2,534,164	5,825	2,539,989	219,943	-72,927	2,247,119	543,920	400,460	8,173	390,476	186,358
1981	3,573,855	2,777,968	25,099	2,803,067	259,245	-64,820	2,479,002	631,300	463,553	9,084	393,411	187,332
1982	3,989,271	3,126,131	22,811	3,148,942	297,024	-82,576	2,769,342	717,542	502,387	10,020	398,117	191,980
1983	4,319,593	3,400,961	-1,782	3,399,179	330,052	-85,013	2,984,114	791,994	543,485	10,716	403,081	192,244
1984	4,897,233	3,880,023	26,619	3,906,642	388,635	-91,864	3,426,143	892,625	578,465	11,948	409,893	205,007
1985	5,387,174	4,315,114	28,328	4,343,442	440,626	-102,968	3,799,848	961,956	625,370	12,865	418,761	214,148
1986	5,841,699	4,686,708	21,646	4,708,354	487,627	-102,569	4,118,158	1,052,806	670,735	13,661	427,630	221,104
1987	6,047,138	4,809,401	28,808	4,838,209	495,899	-95,359	4,246,951	1,085,084	715,103	14,083	429,399	221,744
1988	6,491,268	5,143,292	44,131	5,187,423	549,924	-97,053	4,540,446	1,176,105	774,717	15,024	432,054	227,226
1989	7,142,251	5,608,818	47,243	5,656,061	608,662	-111,217	4,936,182	1,332,848	873,221	16,372	436,235	235,072
1990	7,801,627	6,210,727	28,140	6,238,867	683,729	-133,955	5,421,183	1,414,940	965,504	17,485	446,200	247,348
1991	8,156,486	6,372,144	45,798	6,417,942	712,568	-122,362	5,583,012	1,454,063	1,119,411	17,740	459,773	243,584
1992	8,750,900	6,823,478	43,057	6,866,535	756,502	-117,741	5,992,292	1,524,473	1,234,135	18,446	474,398	243,360
1993	9,017,776	6,996,807	26,637	7,023,444	782,284	-111,450	6,129,710	1,565,621	1,322,445	18,912	476,818	247,474
1994	9,417,837	7,172,991	46,644	7,219,635	810,718	-93,362	6,315,555	1,707,522	1,394,760	19,485	483,333	251,197
1995	9,798,542	7,347,772	38,406	7,386,178	828,559	-75,545	6,482,074	1,807,134	1,509,334	20,034	489,089	253,558
1996	10,231,097	7,471,391	36,765	7,508,156	830,913	-46,035	6,631,208	1,983,943	1,615,946	20,846	490,788	254,613
1997	10,683,901	7,773,394	37,575	7,810,969	857,519	-25,107	6,928,343	2,092,689	1,662,869	21,539	496,030	260,000
1998	11,393,751	8,313,140	34,545	8,347,685	908,746	5,770	7,444,709	2,237,545	1,711,497	22,759	500,636	264,879
1999	11,889,691	8,768,146	38,979	8,807,125	957,095	8,189	7,858,219	2,221,442	1,810,030	23,549	504,895	270,712
2000	12,533,534	9,120,444	48,318	9,168,762	993,415	15,467	8,190,814	2,396,620	1,946,100	24,629	508,896	274,209
2001	12,920,823	9,277,824	72,270	9,350,094	1,021,886	-10,958	8,317,250	2,471,180	2,132,393	25,205	512,626	269,418
2002	13,491,291	9,668,968	54,707	9,723,675	1,069,564	-24,470	8,629,641	2,473,705	2,387,945	26,105	516,818	269,277
2003	14,124,172	10,288,488	62,502	10,350,990	1,117,525	-32,767	9,200,698	2,472,956	2,450,518	27,156	520,120	273,401
2004	14,884,904	10,903,716	86,716	10,990,432	1,200,423	-31,334	9,758,675	2,510,870	2,615,359	28,256	526,789	279,068
2005	15,468,902	11,249,179	97,368	11,346,547	1,234,223	-35,729	10,076,595	2,600,343	2,791,964	29,116	531,294	282,917
2006	16,309,389	11,671,736	71,257	11,742,993	1,295,240	-28,788	10,418,965	2,892,399	2,998,025	30,279	538,643	284,058
2007	17,080,481	12,025,847	56,452	12,082,299	1,324,056	-39,411	10,718,832	3,167,785	3,193,864	31,310	545,524	289,914
2008	17,801,433	12,438,401	54,674	12,493,075	1,423,640	-44,945	11,024,490	3,141,523	3,635,420	32,212	552,627	289,736
2009	18,014,089	12,510,474	64,342	12,574,816	1,426,701	-103,165	11,044,950	3,013,566	3,955,573	32,278	558,096	284,308
2010	18,733,514	13,043,462	59,325	13,102,787	1,481,910	-153,910	11,466,967	2,988,623	4,277,924	33,069	566,492	284,786
2011	19,885,574	13,545,499	37,549	13,583,048	1,376,175	-207,820	11,999,053	3,395,937	4,490,584	34,839	570,777	288,575
2012	20,072,729	13,863,773	53,867	13,917,640	1,408,379	-232,340	12,276,921	3,339,958	4,455,850	34,839	576,149	289,106
2013	20,228,468	13,985,059	88,844	14,073,903	1,591,151	-253,081	12,229,671	3,409,761	4,589,036	34,897	579,670	292,207
2014	21,265,932	14,637,349	54,360	14,691,709	1,656,900	-257,518	12,777,291	3,693,948	4,794,693	36,464	583,198	299,593
2015	22,563,045	15,485,779	65,963	15,551,742	1,746,797	-276,113	13,528,832	3,996,541	5,037,672	38,263	589,688	307,203
2016	23,174,707	15,921,758	49,597	15,971,355	1,793,455	-277,048	13,900,852	4,043,169	5,230,686	38,956	594,889	310,973
2017	24,187,342	16,644,146	46,905	16,691,051	1,880,969	-274,952	14,535,130	4,219,895	5,432,317	40,302	600,151	315,675
2018	25,422,701	25,386,318	36,383	17,355,224	1,947,544	-284,161	15,123,519	4,569,109	5,730,073	42,075	604,221	325,789
2019	26,574,937	26,521,713	53,224	18,255,378	2,054,149	-316,559	15,884,670	4,657,261	6,033,006	43,638	608,980	331,227

Personal Income and Employment by Area: Austin-Round Rock-Georgetown, TX

(Thousands of dollars, except as noted.)

Year	Personal income, total	Earnings by place of work			Less: Contributions for government social insurance	Plus: Adjustment for residence	Equals: Net earnings by place of residence	Plus: Dividends, interest, and rent	Plus: Personal current transfer receipts	Per capita personal income (dollars)	Population (persons)	Total employment
		Nonfarm	Farm	Total								
1970	1,475,763	1,154,458	13,108	1,167,566	69,396	-1,049	1,097,121	273,548	105,094	3,672	401,871	184,371
1971	1,672,669	1,310,024	11,680	1,321,704	82,025	-126	1,239,553	311,934	121,182	3,990	419,249	195,537
1972	1,931,675	1,508,104	25,787	1,533,891	98,461	834	1,436,264	359,114	136,297	4,312	447,971	210,710
1973	2,213,246	1,716,806	45,885	1,762,691	128,968	1,944	1,635,667	408,966	168,613	4,676	473,351	226,304
1974	2,498,475	1,932,352	25,287	1,957,639	149,877	1,682	1,809,444	482,501	206,530	5,141	485,969	235,030
1975	2,874,184	2,192,861	18,666	2,211,527	167,560	3,940	2,047,907	560,196	266,081	5,779	497,356	240,694
1976	3,295,435	2,548,061	30,898	2,578,959	195,426	2,245	2,385,778	616,244	293,413	6,366	517,680	255,068
1977	3,657,562	2,880,709	6,674	2,887,383	224,831	-462	2,662,090	689,610	305,862	6,874	532,052	272,296
1978	4,258,129	3,352,895	15,778	3,368,673	269,208	-4,328	3,095,137	820,471	342,521	7,905	538,668	290,687
1979	4,928,128	3,869,012	28,186	3,897,198	326,104	-2,239	3,568,855	964,007	395,266	8,623	571,520	308,207
1980	5,676,806	4,419,614	2,256	4,421,870	373,621	382	4,048,631	1,160,715	467,460	9,629	589,582	322,221
1981	6,636,769	5,102,203	25,653	5,127,856	467,038	5,812	4,666,630	1,433,286	536,853	10,952	605,961	342,388
1982	7,620,658	5,760,113	28,665	5,788,778	532,851	6,331	5,262,258	1,753,626	604,774	12,030	633,452	362,756
1983	8,803,015	6,731,140	12,928	6,744,068	616,451	-8,127	6,119,490	2,016,247	667,278	13,172	668,303	388,622
1984	10,311,423	8,030,625	13,370	8,043,995	758,728	-23,084	7,262,183	2,328,810	720,430	14,571	707,646	431,932
1985	11,666,538	9,146,128	-6,662	9,139,466	877,555	-34,193	8,227,718	2,647,563	791,257	15,381	758,510	468,315
1986	12,187,544	9,532,708	-2,221	9,530,487	911,319	-34,431	8,584,737	2,717,941	884,866	15,367	793,109	471,436
1987	12,383,763	9,653,165	2,914	9,656,079	901,106	-22,248	8,732,725	2,695,303	955,735	15,338	807,392	481,326
1988	13,117,712	10,178,244	807	10,179,051	988,494	-11,237	9,179,320	2,914,725	1,023,667	16,053	817,153	484,629
1989	14,083,859	10,667,283	11,448	10,678,731	1,052,806	-1,386	9,624,539	3,316,151	1,143,169	16,931	831,848	490,138
1990	15,544,953	11,869,880	7,443	11,877,323	1,162,435	2,892	10,717,780	3,555,155	1,272,018	18,247	851,898	512,913
1991	16,505,681	12,992,033	12,737	13,004,770	1,301,884	-19,991	11,682,895	3,407,472	1,415,314	18,742	880,678	536,269
1992	18,131,918	14,340,745	19,923	14,360,668	1,432,140	-42,128	12,886,400	3,585,686	1,659,832	19,863	912,833	554,727
1993	19,850,908	15,873,548	30,278	15,903,826	1,589,251	-76,034	14,238,541	3,844,612	1,767,755	20,900	949,788	591,053
1994	21,711,558	17,465,266	20,938	17,486,204	1,777,162	-109,402	15,599,640	4,214,335	1,897,583	21,955	988,925	624,671
1995	23,996,690	19,454,834	21,924	19,476,758	1,994,940	-157,841	17,323,977	4,616,188	2,056,525	23,263	1,031,557	663,975
1996	26,309,157	21,522,017	-12,971	21,509,046	2,197,103	-212,794	19,099,149	5,000,228	2,209,780	24,518	1,073,037	692,327
1997	29,242,714	24,084,404	15,227	24,099,631	2,457,286	-280,329	21,362,016	5,538,089	2,342,609	26,315	1,111,264	725,886
1998	34,017,871	28,738,440	-5,486	28,732,954	2,884,186	-410,722	25,438,046	6,141,670	2,438,155	29,438	1,155,579	766,659
1999	38,195,146	32,838,693	28,249	32,866,942	3,276,563	-561,025	29,029,354	6,538,998	2,626,794	31,674	1,205,898	805,105
2000	41,809,616	36,152,559	13,534	36,166,093	3,638,499	-666,685	31,860,909	7,124,296	2,824,411	33,052	1,264,950	849,746
2001	46,276,740	40,358,290	14,131	40,372,421	3,785,399	-613,349	35,973,673	7,136,609	3,166,458	35,023	1,321,316	863,762
2002	45,913,014	39,585,787	15,602	39,601,389	3,686,463	-514,239	35,400,687	6,967,416	3,544,911	34,065	1,347,822	856,715
2003	46,630,893	39,768,561	42,956	39,811,517	3,826,655	-491,258	35,493,604	7,323,785	3,813,504	33,888	1,376,030	864,159
2004	47,627,677	39,965,238	67,756	40,032,994	3,965,472	-481,908	35,585,614	7,966,646	4,075,417	33,777	1,410,058	886,034
2005	52,450,246	43,095,008	49,570	43,144,578	4,256,605	-494,209	38,393,764	9,552,892	4,503,590	36,089	1,453,358	934,981
2006	58,616,894	47,795,297	43,728	47,839,025	4,565,360	-484,969	42,788,696	10,958,238	4,869,960	38,679	1,515,485	981,793
2007	62,478,465	50,582,289	44,145	50,626,434	4,905,324	-478,074	45,243,036	11,831,034	5,404,395	39,597	1,577,856	1,042,215
2008	67,995,405	52,205,817	-10,698	52,195,119	5,043,718	-416,707	46,734,694	14,846,701	6,414,010	41,616	1,633,870	1,072,058
2009	65,955,221	51,025,814	-12,538	51,013,276	5,068,719	-306,014	45,638,543	13,133,942	7,182,736	39,205	1,682,338	1,068,447
2010	70,428,496	54,517,840	238	54,518,078	5,340,082	-232,944	48,945,052	13,286,766	8,196,678	40,769	1,727,495	1,082,191
2011	77,908,118	59,487,729	-9,446	59,478,283	5,074,987	-117,203	54,286,093	15,031,082	8,590,943	43,754	1,780,610	1,116,595
2012	85,798,754	63,792,917	11,634	63,804,551	5,399,512	6,821	58,411,860	18,734,983	8,651,911	46,768	1,834,566	1,154,689
2013	89,014,789	68,163,151	42,975	68,206,126	6,507,476	114,219	61,812,869	18,084,590	9,117,330	47,260	1,883,528	1,211,230
2014	97,444,469	74,192,179	17,602	74,209,781	6,987,601	190,450	67,412,630	20,262,367	9,769,472	50,171	1,942,255	1,265,320
2015	103,473,836	78,815,833	40,226	78,856,059	7,623,508	156,155	71,388,706	21,565,543	10,519,587	51,717	2,000,784	1,325,983
2016	109,057,050	82,715,935	1,201	82,717,136	8,165,678	59,886	74,611,344	23,357,900	11,087,806	52,926	2,060,558	1,383,213
2017	115,982,256	88,920,586	6,081	88,926,667	8,851,955	-2,713	80,071,999	24,510,181	11,400,076	54,817	2,115,827	1,422,990
2018	129,146,253	129,158,927	-12,674	99,604,337	9,555,044	-57,124	89,992,169	26,891,242	12,262,842	59,638	2,165,497	1,509,526
2019	138,028,065	138,046,658	-18,593	107,894,766	10,292,649	-129,169	97,472,948	27,432,211	13,122,906	61,977	2,227,083	1,566,091

Personal Income and Employment by Area: Bakersfield, CA

(Thousands of dollars, except as noted.)

					Derivation of personal income								
		Earnings by place of work			Less: Contributions for government social insurance	Plus: Adjustment for residence	Equals: Net earnings by place of residence	Plus: Dividends, interest, and rent	Plus: Personal current transfer receipts	Per capita personal income (dollars)	Population (persons)	Total employment
Year	Personal income, total	Nonfarm	Farm	Total								
1970	1,357,079	1,005,293	118,613	1,123,906	62,497	-43,180	1,018,229	188,910	149,940	4,102	330,868	138,871
1971	1,464,866	1,078,629	130,600	1,209,229	69,145	-46,629	1,093,455	205,956	165,455	4,357	336,227	142,153
1972	1,593,327	1,166,044	149,304	1,315,348	77,970	-49,631	1,187,747	226,230	179,350	4,730	336,833	145,354
1973	1,818,667	1,307,130	203,198	1,510,328	99,741	-54,822	1,355,765	262,251	200,651	5,302	343,007	153,762
1974	2,156,400	1,485,631	316,347	1,801,978	118,147	-66,163	1,617,668	297,492	241,240	6,253	344,840	163,320
1975	2,343,300	1,671,625	255,472	1,927,097	130,242	-85,738	1,711,117	335,080	297,103	6,566	356,866	170,339
1976	2,763,966	1,890,159	418,562	2,308,721	150,213	-94,369	2,064,139	358,999	340,828	7,533	366,932	173,782
1977	2,921,259	2,097,594	334,713	2,432,307	170,352	-103,900	2,158,055	398,684	364,520	7,848	372,217	179,070
1978	3,216,417	2,384,974	276,117	2,661,091	196,120	-109,405	2,355,566	462,091	398,760	8,509	377,990	185,586
1979	3,830,294	2,728,872	473,541	3,202,413	233,331	-121,331	2,847,751	537,921	444,622	9,741	393,198	197,044
1980	4,498,790	3,072,783	641,573	3,714,356	260,094	-142,610	3,311,652	663,895	523,243	11,070	406,407	202,903
1981	4,819,966	3,457,147	398,604	3,855,751	321,575	-140,209	3,393,967	806,282	619,717	11,507	418,877	207,514
1982	5,253,132	3,730,040	447,822	4,177,862	358,328	-145,264	3,674,270	899,249	679,613	12,112	433,698	205,351
1983	5,467,802	3,922,694	346,178	4,268,872	388,348	-141,093	3,739,431	982,457	745,914	12,233	446,961	211,093
1984	6,028,100	4,347,523	367,679	4,715,202	447,857	-151,227	4,116,118	1,113,135	798,847	13,121	459,411	217,562
1985	6,466,455	4,731,854	335,570	5,067,424	495,995	-152,613	4,418,816	1,185,385	862,254	13,635	474,243	223,569
1986	6,902,908	4,975,803	428,057	5,403,860	528,616	-145,814	4,729,430	1,233,419	940,059	14,197	486,217	227,198
1987	7,159,440	5,140,302	464,962	5,605,264	547,258	-125,235	4,932,771	1,244,219	982,450	14,379	497,910	231,475
1988	7,851,244	5,707,273	503,156	6,210,429	629,888	-133,969	5,446,572	1,338,760	1,065,912	15,365	510,980	243,334
1989	8,365,507	5,987,471	483,707	6,471,178	667,124	-129,372	5,674,682	1,507,975	1,182,850	15,846	527,922	245,816
1990	9,089,058	6,519,468	567,906	7,087,374	724,774	-146,082	6,216,518	1,566,242	1,306,298	16,540	549,535	253,759
1991	9,706,159	7,128,741	440,670	7,569,411	796,668	-167,838	6,604,905	1,620,493	1,480,761	17,048	569,346	267,697
1992	10,190,092	7,301,971	502,880	7,804,851	810,003	-150,334	6,844,514	1,610,723	1,734,855	17,274	589,897	262,789
1993	10,682,018	7,465,810	695,604	8,161,414	832,911	-147,121	7,181,382	1,644,384	1,856,252	17,808	599,843	262,890
1994	10,926,342	7,607,304	650,492	8,257,796	846,041	-138,549	7,273,206	1,747,976	1,905,160	17,775	614,707	266,806
1995	11,322,808	7,931,250	566,500	8,497,750	871,572	-141,365	7,484,813	1,828,497	2,009,498	18,257	620,201	278,216
1996	11,936,703	8,247,029	647,960	8,894,989	875,197	-129,687	7,890,105	1,932,286	2,114,312	19,046	626,719	288,670
1997	12,276,732	8,594,613	560,139	9,154,752	900,356	-124,396	8,130,000	2,037,629	2,109,103	19,343	634,695	289,487
1998	13,059,821	9,332,739	425,385	9,758,124	958,485	-122,151	8,677,488	2,182,204	2,200,129	20,310	643,016	303,568
1999	13,426,338	9,554,119	402,941	9,957,060	980,461	-92,364	8,884,235	2,203,778	2,338,325	20,485	655,428	309,279
2000	14,255,711	10,219,431	503,584	10,723,015	1,049,406	-82,897	9,590,712	2,261,150	2,403,849	21,476	663,803	310,380
2001	15,273,385	10,919,007	510,950	11,429,957	1,194,181	-78,422	10,157,354	2,453,897	2,662,134	22,575	676,574	308,719
2002	16,215,677	11,533,511	726,072	12,259,583	1,280,172	-64,580	10,914,831	2,425,550	2,875,296	23,364	694,059	314,541
2003	17,362,969	12,405,001	635,498	13,040,499	1,387,820	-71,276	11,581,403	2,678,174	3,103,392	24,309	714,272	321,579
2004	18,724,744	13,167,709	1,077,843	14,245,552	1,518,863	-45,992	12,680,697	2,757,158	3,286,889	25,431	736,296	325,067
2005	20,188,632	14,393,242	1,167,957	15,561,199	1,653,897	-38,334	13,868,968	2,858,445	3,461,219	26,539	760,726	341,791
2006	21,770,225	15,966,371	889,120	16,855,491	1,756,593	-29,780	15,069,118	2,959,789	3,741,318	27,750	784,511	354,866
2007	23,446,859	16,716,607	1,262,077	17,978,684	1,812,222	-13,017	16,153,445	3,262,437	4,030,977	29,189	803,281	363,988
2008	24,162,021	17,273,406	769,854	18,043,260	1,895,186	-3,705	16,144,369	3,465,881	4,551,771	29,526	818,327	364,533
2009	24,005,085	16,748,027	898,279	17,646,306	1,866,619	-86,512	15,693,175	3,303,731	5,008,179	28,917	830,137	349,093
2010	26,093,086	18,088,817	1,242,493	19,331,310	1,904,122	-151,754	17,275,434	3,312,904	5,504,748	31,022	841,116	348,449
2011	27,746,031	19,230,642	1,350,865	20,581,507	1,846,502	-219,839	18,515,166	3,711,818	5,519,047	32,690	848,767	361,933
2012	29,474,858	20,465,160	1,599,882	22,065,042	1,960,969	-304,834	19,799,239	4,130,789	5,544,830	34,464	855,237	381,650
2013	30,373,033	21,117,965	1,877,478	22,995,443	2,258,032	-339,371	20,398,040	4,212,703	5,762,290	35,153	864,014	393,900
2014	32,548,645	22,250,061	2,054,961	24,305,022	2,362,480	-355,983	21,586,559	4,883,556	6,078,530	37,331	871,895	404,248
2015	33,397,327	22,166,717	1,991,050	24,157,767	2,345,219	-326,582	21,485,966	5,307,111	6,604,250	37,968	879,607	404,981
2016	33,494,783	21,839,218	2,123,122	23,962,340	2,355,713	-315,433	21,291,194	5,320,051	6,883,538	37,844	885,086	406,813
2017	34,438,280	22,286,578	2,492,139	24,778,717	2,419,499	-352,336	22,006,882	5,589,540	6,841,858	38,560	893,119	410,161
2018	35,566,558	33,828,690	1,737,868	25,531,511	2,575,769	-393,321	22,562,421	5,866,920	7,137,217	39,794	893,758	422,747
2019	37,666,752	35,511,887	2,154,865	27,263,157	2,759,600	-434,558	24,068,999	5,992,469	7,605,284	41,843	900,202	432,982

Personal Income and Employment by Area: Baltimore-Columbia-Towson, MD

(Thousands of dollars, except as noted.)

Year	Personal income, total	Earnings by place of work			Less: Contributions for government social insurance	Plus: Adjustment for residence	Equals: Net earnings by place of residence	Plus: Dividends, interest, and rent	Plus: Personal current transfer receipts	Per capita personal income (dollars)	Population (persons)	Total employment
		Nonfarm	Farm	Total								
1970	9,420,898	7,783,621	31,091	7,814,712	496,727	65,121	7,383,106	1,329,181	708,611	4,497	2,094,838	991,821
1971	10,314,326	8,380,680	23,419	8,404,099	552,062	144,280	7,996,317	1,454,228	863,781	4,838	2,132,113	994,410
1972	11,336,168	9,114,000	32,179	9,146,179	629,686	236,439	8,752,932	1,586,680	996,556	5,267	2,152,232	1,011,325
1973	12,535,270	10,041,060	47,689	10,088,749	797,680	318,125	9,609,194	1,784,358	1,141,718	5,782	2,167,899	1,041,876
1974	13,835,894	10,987,901	44,100	11,032,001	907,009	393,552	10,518,544	2,014,321	1,303,029	6,349	2,179,392	1,056,134
1975	14,987,764	11,626,158	50,531	11,676,689	956,010	485,063	11,205,742	2,149,559	1,632,463	6,861	2,184,332	1,038,096
1976	16,344,005	12,660,144	42,381	12,702,525	1,058,328	611,567	12,255,764	2,329,451	1,758,790	7,467	2,188,964	1,040,323
1977	17,827,450	13,748,804	32,102	13,780,906	1,154,071	753,890	13,380,725	2,571,031	1,875,694	8,096	2,201,877	1,068,371
1978	19,889,912	15,288,294	47,166	15,335,460	1,319,784	910,339	14,926,015	2,895,953	2,067,944	9,023	2,204,362	1,108,082
1979	21,951,910	16,746,277	44,409	16,790,686	1,515,579	1,103,496	16,378,603	3,235,802	2,337,505	9,937	2,209,160	1,139,209
1980	24,628,751	18,238,156	25,118	18,263,274	1,651,213	1,320,361	17,932,422	3,896,476	2,799,853	11,178	2,203,385	1,139,485
1981	27,264,037	19,959,348	36,098	19,995,446	1,938,378	1,310,455	19,367,523	4,737,286	3,159,228	12,312	2,214,413	1,146,005
1982	29,340,768	20,849,242	36,616	20,885,858	2,050,386	1,384,754	20,220,226	5,620,302	3,500,240	13,212	2,220,748	1,137,050
1983	31,328,742	22,518,185	29,743	22,547,928	2,279,282	1,452,291	21,720,937	5,811,316	3,796,489	14,059	2,228,439	1,164,025
1984	34,416,475	24,765,818	69,673	24,835,491	2,588,034	1,613,921	23,861,378	6,590,357	3,964,740	15,332	2,244,735	1,202,935
1985	37,069,457	26,919,116	68,515	26,987,631	2,895,298	1,773,196	25,865,529	7,032,713	4,171,215	16,432	2,255,970	1,243,523
1986	39,775,035	28,898,196	55,037	28,953,233	3,148,149	1,927,138	27,732,222	7,537,656	4,505,157	17,402	2,285,633	1,276,452
1987	42,482,919	31,231,004	67,075	31,298,079	3,371,142	2,092,435	30,019,372	7,894,530	4,569,017	18,393	2,309,719	1,332,191
1988	46,438,466	34,334,191	78,740	34,412,931	3,819,265	2,264,376	32,858,042	8,731,007	4,849,417	19,838	2,340,870	1,366,737
1989	49,698,479	36,436,528	78,618	36,515,146	4,076,345	2,397,515	34,836,316	9,618,980	5,243,183	21,053	2,360,610	1,393,176
1990	52,649,611	38,575,462	90,099	38,665,561	4,397,515	2,495,792	36,763,838	10,182,738	5,703,035	22,024	2,390,543	1,404,128
1991	54,612,636	39,562,706	77,117	39,639,823	4,548,857	2,581,863	37,672,829	10,524,209	6,415,598	22,585	2,418,136	1,358,484
1992	57,198,936	41,152,714	94,402	41,247,116	4,706,278	2,767,040	39,307,878	10,735,526	7,155,532	23,441	2,440,078	1,339,950
1993	59,178,785	42,528,842	96,257	42,625,099	4,858,716	2,908,926	40,675,309	11,081,488	7,421,988	24,076	2,458,038	1,347,488
1994	61,769,826	44,198,785	88,186	44,286,971	5,092,663	3,072,885	42,267,193	11,739,173	7,763,460	24,954	2,475,364	1,371,332
1995	64,703,504	46,019,964	78,522	46,098,486	5,271,529	3,169,341	43,996,298	12,636,306	8,070,900	25,981	2,490,370	1,394,314
1996	67,881,395	47,942,214	112,173	48,054,387	5,437,437	3,334,711	45,951,661	13,271,534	8,658,200	27,137	2,501,453	1,409,343
1997	71,926,659	50,712,845	91,119	50,803,964	5,714,623	3,594,943	48,684,284	14,448,920	8,793,455	28,616	2,513,492	1,436,116
1998	77,002,114	54,763,917	106,533	54,870,450	6,024,788	3,866,286	52,711,948	15,224,823	9,065,343	30,493	2,525,266	1,466,512
1999	82,064,366	59,216,255	106,605	59,322,860	6,433,162	4,204,385	57,094,083	15,404,521	9,565,762	32,305	2,540,307	1,509,853
2000	88,348,925	63,612,480	131,510	63,743,990	6,818,698	4,661,709	61,587,001	16,741,639	10,020,285	34,539	2,557,958	1,543,762
2001	92,278,129	66,769,920	110,311	66,880,231	7,351,630	4,695,480	64,224,081	17,250,666	10,803,382	35,830	2,575,471	1,547,690
2002	95,902,303	70,335,292	89,855	70,425,147	7,720,452	4,606,875	67,311,570	17,088,544	11,502,189	36,935	2,596,501	1,558,796
2003	99,771,142	73,070,163	74,672	73,144,835	8,021,749	4,767,419	69,890,505	17,559,098	12,321,539	38,165	2,614,232	1,566,963
2004	105,705,982	77,482,066	94,697	77,576,763	8,593,992	4,842,740	73,825,511	19,047,100	12,833,371	40,178	2,630,946	1,593,882
2005	111,780,420	82,198,090	77,345	82,275,435	9,076,807	5,117,153	78,315,781	19,566,211	13,898,428	42,273	2,644,231	1,623,895
2006	118,899,949	87,173,388	66,356	87,239,744	9,727,534	4,634,214	82,146,424	22,348,958	14,404,567	44,730	2,658,162	1,658,564
2007	124,594,991	90,476,473	61,051	90,537,524	10,183,135	4,680,071	85,034,460	23,954,894	15,605,637	46,706	2,667,619	1,689,183
2008	129,205,715	93,095,897	92,517	93,188,414	10,541,624	3,971,803	86,618,593	25,029,188	17,557,934	48,214	2,679,819	1,686,091
2009	127,845,670	92,928,614	122,991	93,051,605	10,480,108	3,533,102	86,104,599	22,770,234	18,970,837	47,420	2,696,018	1,649,432
2010	131,921,648	96,126,711	107,819	96,234,530	10,865,805	3,507,335	88,876,060	22,600,546	20,445,042	48,581	2,715,503	1,645,096
2011	138,962,462	100,185,082	116,430	100,301,512	10,081,866	2,879,000	93,098,646	24,868,421	20,995,395	50,810	2,734,969	1,677,182
2012	143,229,739	104,457,121	159,016	104,616,137	10,495,986	1,794,723	95,914,874	26,087,977	21,226,888	51,965	2,756,285	1,707,280
2013	144,080,289	106,895,319	175,948	107,071,267	12,007,281	1,471,276	96,535,262	25,647,147	21,897,880	51,985	2,771,586	1,734,243
2014	150,423,223	110,613,658	130,155	110,743,813	12,338,741	921,297	99,326,369	27,777,424	23,319,430	54,023	2,784,424	1,755,487
2015	156,914,843	115,414,212	91,933	115,506,145	12,962,814	754,434	103,297,765	29,432,125	24,184,953	56,141	2,795,036	1,788,669
2016	161,769,953	119,633,128	93,855	119,726,983	13,317,370	176,692	106,586,305	29,723,858	25,459,790	57,754	2,801,028	1,813,889
2017	167,920,899	124,385,674	86,834	124,472,508	13,810,575	36,511	110,698,444	31,182,148	26,040,307	59,797	2,808,175	1,833,008
2018	173,683,854	173,618,881	64,973	127,576,176	14,291,832	-101,548	113,182,796	33,685,638	26,815,420	62,013	2,800,743	1,865,227
2019	179,169,101	179,050,784	118,317	132,361,848	14,804,104	-351,546	117,206,198	34,102,630	27,860,273	63,988	2,800,053	1,889,243

Personal Income and Employment by Area: Bangor, ME

(Thousands of dollars, except as noted.)

Year	Personal income, total	Earnings by place of work			Less: Contributions for government social insurance	Plus: Adjustment for residence	Equals: Net earnings by place of residence	Plus: Dividends, interest, and rent	Plus: Personal current transfer receipts	Per capita personal income (dollars)	Population (persons)	Total employment
		Nonfarm	Farm	Total								
1970	412,911	334,644	4,999	339,643	24,136	-2,996	312,511	57,990	42,410	3,282	125,812	53,058
1971	446,233	360,661	4,725	365,386	26,637	-5,384	333,365	62,468	50,400	3,488	127,935	53,213
1972	493,117	403,087	5,027	408,114	31,014	-8,233	368,867	67,583	56,667	3,822	129,035	54,697
1973	547,346	443,745	9,235	452,980	38,652	-9,060	405,268	75,253	66,825	4,185	130,797	57,117
1974	609,213	479,220	10,276	489,496	43,214	-4,829	441,453	86,528	81,232	4,614	132,038	58,222
1975	676,072	526,793	5,129	531,922	47,314	-8,272	476,336	96,199	103,537	5,067	133,434	59,000
1976	768,008	607,507	12,834	620,341	56,185	-10,571	553,585	102,596	111,827	5,666	135,542	61,770
1977	825,136	661,538	5,670	667,208	60,903	-14,938	591,367	114,349	119,420	6,061	136,134	63,665
1978	906,943	731,169	6,218	737,387	68,841	-18,780	649,766	128,697	128,480	6,624	136,912	65,596
1979	1,012,641	823,157	4,827	827,984	79,837	-23,430	724,717	143,154	144,770	7,383	137,157	67,939
1980	1,130,404	900,280	2,486	902,766	86,748	-27,548	788,470	170,437	171,497	8,237	137,228	68,884
1981	1,233,592	961,500	8,985	970,485	99,796	-34,106	836,583	202,560	194,449	8,942	137,952	68,180
1982	1,318,547	1,004,640	7,172	1,011,812	106,957	-35,775	869,080	237,689	211,778	9,553	138,020	67,853
1983	1,423,485	1,097,490	5,266	1,102,756	117,253	-41,548	943,955	251,046	228,484	10,308	138,101	69,290
1984	1,571,009	1,217,415	8,837	1,226,252	134,109	-45,212	1,046,931	282,832	241,246	11,344	138,488	71,880
1985	1,663,854	1,291,851	6,847	1,298,698	142,720	-46,503	1,109,475	300,757	253,622	12,000	138,654	73,522
1986	1,763,093	1,363,505	7,908	1,371,413	149,155	-46,070	1,176,188	323,722	263,183	12,669	139,169	74,368
1987	1,924,212	1,511,111	9,727	1,520,838	162,172	-53,500	1,305,166	348,930	270,116	13,724	140,207	76,675
1988	2,126,846	1,686,494	8,582	1,695,076	184,350	-61,776	1,448,950	390,771	287,125	14,911	142,639	80,867
1989	2,296,550	1,840,411	8,983	1,849,394	197,205	-66,925	1,585,264	400,874	310,412	15,794	145,402	82,915
1990	2,369,319	1,868,941	11,056	1,879,997	210,934	-62,442	1,606,621	413,943	348,755	16,113	147,046	82,886
1991	2,427,871	1,860,744	7,187	1,867,931	211,944	-65,701	1,590,286	438,679	398,906	16,481	147,315	80,019
1992	2,537,917	1,951,744	10,722	1,962,466	224,740	-70,779	1,666,947	433,708	437,262	17,331	146,435	80,228
1993	2,641,980	2,034,549	9,406	2,043,955	240,364	-74,733	1,728,858	442,826	470,296	18,003	146,752	82,174
1994	2,748,288	2,103,393	7,486	2,110,879	251,418	-77,337	1,782,124	474,259	491,905	18,696	147,000	82,635
1995	2,813,406	2,136,625	6,318	2,142,943	257,778	-79,564	1,805,601	489,826	517,979	19,306	145,724	82,741
1996	2,933,552	2,196,852	8,227	2,205,079	261,809	-79,117	1,864,153	516,616	552,783	20,182	145,356	83,203
1997	3,069,151	2,301,036	4,537	2,305,573	273,134	-83,599	1,948,840	541,360	578,951	21,180	144,910	83,642
1998	3,221,737	2,457,212	7,392	2,464,604	288,033	-92,875	2,083,696	538,631	599,410	22,284	144,574	85,931
1999	3,360,146	2,606,726	8,026	2,614,752	301,186	-101,797	2,211,769	530,141	618,236	23,189	144,902	86,803
2000	3,605,136	2,773,485	7,803	2,781,288	313,688	-107,485	2,360,115	591,897	653,124	24,874	144,937	89,410
2001	3,754,533	2,920,462	6,979	2,927,441	331,092	-127,140	2,469,209	587,886	697,438	25,697	146,110	90,067
2002	3,938,706	3,033,876	4,226	3,038,102	333,046	-134,626	2,570,430	625,516	742,760	26,740	147,298	90,467
2003	4,049,050	3,059,633	4,899	3,064,532	332,860	-128,404	2,603,268	629,682	816,100	27,219	148,759	89,799
2004	4,205,160	3,193,533	7,794	3,201,327	347,899	-139,083	2,714,345	611,877	878,938	28,258	148,814	90,971
2005	4,370,689	3,334,782	6,350	3,341,132	367,549	-151,206	2,822,377	596,116	952,196	29,191	149,726	92,341
2006	4,549,950	3,470,098	3,334	3,473,432	387,431	-160,563	2,925,438	645,775	978,737	30,043	151,446	93,316
2007	4,726,866	3,522,488	6,717	3,529,205	402,648	-167,580	2,958,977	712,484	1,055,405	31,050	152,232	94,140
2008	4,969,125	3,577,604	6,916	3,584,520	415,280	-172,471	2,996,769	756,934	1,215,422	32,399	153,372	93,709
2009	5,101,812	3,663,166	5,577	3,668,743	414,430	-178,119	3,076,194	710,431	1,315,187	33,178	153,770	91,487
2010	5,128,607	3,649,197	18,942	3,668,139	417,860	-162,207	3,088,072	712,250	1,328,285	33,337	153,841	89,458
2011	5,313,807	3,684,463	10,937	3,695,400	380,232	-158,162	3,157,006	770,105	1,386,696	34,570	153,713	89,529
2012	5,379,496	3,727,743	15,255	3,742,998	388,407	-152,396	3,202,195	798,467	1,378,834	35,075	153,372	89,690
2013	5,389,140	3,790,969	14,696	3,805,665	448,950	-142,295	3,214,420	768,567	1,406,153	35,206	153,075	90,227
2014	5,583,460	3,883,203	14,620	3,897,823	453,636	-141,195	3,302,992	846,584	1,433,884	36,507	152,941	90,551
2015	5,759,313	4,015,551	10,778	4,026,329	476,802	-154,408	3,395,119	873,073	1,491,121	37,907	151,934	90,494
2016	5,853,366	4,066,725	6,765	4,073,490	479,823	-156,681	3,436,986	889,011	1,527,369	38,632	151,515	90,434
2017	6,060,742	4,203,237	6,800	4,210,037	497,755	-160,053	3,552,229	928,689	1,579,824	39,885	151,957	90,686
2018	6,317,871	6,314,816	3,055	4,409,944	527,345	-179,223	3,703,376	968,234	1,646,261	41,615	151,817	91,895
2019	6,563,124	6,557,295	5,829	4,616,386	547,351	-204,986	3,864,049	981,405	1,717,670	43,136	152,148	93,239

Personal Income and Employment by Area: Barnstable Town, MA

(Thousands of dollars, except as noted.)

Year	Personal income, total	Earnings by place of work			Less: Contributions for government social insurance	Plus: Adjustment for residence	Equals: Net earnings by place of residence	Plus: Dividends, interest, and rent	Plus: Personal current transfer receipts	Per capita personal income (dollars)	Population (persons)	Total employment
		Nonfarm	Farm	Total								
1970	467,126	295,491	1,016	296,507	17,483	-10,716	268,308	143,900	54,918	4,785	97,632	47,104
1971	537,720	331,593	942	332,535	20,635	-4,014	307,886	160,261	69,573	5,418	99,244	49,746
1972	614,361	371,515	1,042	372,557	24,040	3,759	352,276	178,694	83,391	6,191	99,237	52,776
1973	686,560	409,426	1,303	410,729	30,244	17,073	397,558	190,705	98,297	6,180	111,093	57,102
1974	756,444	429,015	1,271	430,286	32,765	29,222	426,743	210,591	119,110	6,109	123,816	57,828
1975	852,195	459,968	1,063	461,031	34,194	42,233	469,070	225,775	157,350	6,584	129,437	58,475
1976	966,532	529,904	1,205	531,109	39,344	54,757	546,522	251,143	168,867	7,259	133,142	61,244
1977	1,092,583	597,808	1,215	599,023	44,795	70,656	624,884	285,392	182,307	7,913	138,071	65,095
1978	1,240,807	685,664	1,853	687,517	52,316	90,647	725,848	315,846	199,113	8,802	140,966	69,572
1979	1,423,153	766,689	1,531	768,220	61,720	116,878	823,378	367,301	232,474	9,730	146,265	73,652
1980	1,650,105	846,968	2,161	849,129	69,045	147,756	927,840	448,494	273,771	11,086	148,847	76,419
1981	1,884,653	932,662	2,144	934,806	82,871	154,505	1,006,440	556,074	322,139	12,384	152,189	78,745
1982	2,110,736	996,095	2,902	998,997	91,500	165,848	1,073,345	680,874	356,517	13,665	154,460	81,237
1983	2,322,750	1,131,883	5,211	1,137,094	105,359	180,737	1,212,472	730,700	379,578	14,764	157,320	86,481
1984	2,673,043	1,334,972	4,481	1,339,453	128,140	202,418	1,413,731	849,937	409,375	16,487	162,135	92,174
1985	2,952,928	1,530,626	4,296	1,534,922	150,310	225,312	1,609,924	900,287	442,717	17,727	166,578	96,878
1986	3,250,014	1,718,921	4,405	1,723,326	174,084	248,003	1,797,245	975,310	477,459	18,936	171,633	101,045
1987	3,609,563	1,978,263	3,632	1,981,895	198,958	288,392	2,071,329	1,032,887	505,347	20,484	176,215	100,196
1988	3,929,722	2,162,931	4,838	2,167,769	221,023	321,312	2,268,058	1,127,201	534,463	21,695	181,137	104,357
1989	4,047,024	2,188,168	4,793	2,192,961	224,702	335,110	2,303,369	1,156,722	586,933	21,918	184,642	102,008
1990	4,324,877	2,167,716	4,460	2,172,176	219,873	390,739	2,343,042	1,314,076	667,759	23,086	187,335	100,006
1991	4,390,932	2,169,782	6,354	2,176,136	224,243	399,445	2,351,338	1,289,663	749,931	23,212	189,165	96,477
1992	4,695,441	2,324,864	6,365	2,331,229	237,615	424,900	2,518,514	1,365,042	811,885	24,507	191,595	99,683
1993	5,029,717	2,469,225	6,266	2,475,491	253,387	474,134	2,696,238	1,472,894	860,585	25,816	194,830	103,453
1994	5,348,810	2,641,858	5,500	2,647,358	273,854	528,302	2,901,806	1,543,369	903,635	26,942	198,533	107,427
1995	5,724,396	2,807,648	5,627	2,813,275	294,442	588,562	3,107,395	1,650,756	966,245	28,217	202,874	109,482
1996	6,153,648	2,998,292	9,896	3,008,188	308,868	625,068	3,324,388	1,802,918	1,026,342	29,749	206,852	112,108
1997	6,543,178	3,144,317	12,317	3,156,634	327,633	718,551	3,547,552	1,922,336	1,073,290	31,102	210,380	116,668
1998	7,128,494	3,452,014	3,014	3,455,028	355,236	806,527	3,906,319	2,119,306	1,102,869	33,234	214,497	121,308
1999	7,719,485	3,917,060	2,184	3,919,244	392,936	888,760	4,415,068	2,148,102	1,156,315	35,255	218,960	126,407
2000	8,144,107	4,058,090	3,581	4,061,671	408,383	1,011,313	4,664,601	2,248,503	1,231,003	36,516	223,031	131,099
2001	8,946,679	4,679,467	2,317	4,681,784	455,093	1,008,118	5,234,809	2,361,984	1,349,886	39,925	224,087	131,337
2002	9,020,108	4,955,001	3,140	4,958,141	486,791	963,643	5,434,993	2,155,600	1,429,515	40,014	225,421	133,340
2003	9,330,613	5,209,559	3,252	5,212,811	512,783	915,424	5,615,452	2,212,733	1,502,428	41,284	226,011	135,968
2004	9,992,597	5,561,252	4,232	5,565,484	563,635	930,044	5,931,893	2,498,761	1,561,943	44,557	224,264	138,761
2005	10,019,956	5,613,309	4,413	5,617,722	591,811	909,422	5,935,333	2,441,564	1,643,059	45,136	221,995	139,159
2006	10,440,666	5,727,897	4,638	5,732,535	601,490	900,600	6,031,645	2,658,559	1,750,462	47,450	220,037	138,664
2007	10,670,649	5,722,367	6,415	5,728,782	617,215	943,627	6,055,194	2,784,414	1,831,041	48,863	218,380	141,003
2008	10,915,216	5,694,363	8,763	5,703,126	621,997	861,288	5,942,417	2,940,752	2,032,047	50,285	217,066	139,828
2009	10,913,532	5,627,470	5,905	5,633,375	611,471	902,713	5,924,617	2,762,771	2,226,144	50,527	215,994	136,753
2010	11,311,833	5,857,906	7,066	5,864,972	613,201	893,863	6,145,634	2,834,184	2,332,015	52,399	215,877	136,163
2011	11,892,929	6,020,425	6,643	6,027,068	580,869	1,014,905	6,461,104	3,090,605	2,341,220	55,229	215,340	136,699
2012	12,493,156	6,339,662	8,452	6,348,114	603,006	1,043,356	6,788,464	3,333,995	2,370,697	58,165	214,787	139,344
2013	12,674,353	6,535,965	6,989	6,542,954	683,728	969,912	6,829,138	3,419,880	2,425,335	59,070	214,566	142,564
2014	13,280,825	6,768,135	2,853	6,770,988	715,591	869,956	6,925,353	3,856,747	2,498,725	61,979	214,279	145,011
2015	13,953,378	7,040,158	2,687	7,042,845	734,860	915,889	7,223,874	4,080,294	2,649,210	65,272	213,773	150,111
2016	14,409,840	7,247,808	943	7,248,751	767,361	1,039,461	7,520,851	4,136,488	2,752,501	67,512	213,440	151,448
2017	15,032,780	7,557,335	1,682	7,559,017	801,366	1,116,958	7,874,609	4,336,190	2,821,981	70,430	213,444	153,285
2018	15,949,290	15,946,433	2,857	7,840,037	840,604	1,128,144	8,127,577	4,834,810	2,986,903	74,714	213,471	153,760
2019	16,492,955	16,489,952	3,003	8,168,628	874,664	1,170,675	8,464,639	4,889,712	3,138,604	77,435	212,990	155,594

Personal Income and Employment by Area: Baton Rouge, LA

(Thousands of dollars, except as noted.)

| Year | Personal income, total | Earnings by place of work | | | Less: Contributions for government social insurance | Plus: Adjustment for residence | Equals: Net earnings by place of residence | Plus: Dividends, interest, and rent | Plus: Personal current transfer receipts | Per capita personal income (dollars) | Population (persons) | Total employment |
		Nonfarm	Farm	Total								
1970	1,530,009	1,231,543	27,926	1,259,469	77,644	20,555	1,202,380	199,176	128,453	3,275	467,187	175,083
1971	1,672,394	1,339,322	29,516	1,368,838	86,480	22,044	1,304,402	221,700	146,292	3,511	476,302	179,120
1972	1,848,151	1,478,494	34,997	1,513,491	100,089	27,326	1,440,728	244,817	162,606	3,780	488,967	187,519
1973	2,056,364	1,641,385	51,347	1,692,732	128,175	25,441	1,589,998	274,215	192,151	4,133	497,516	197,959
1974	2,415,768	1,930,598	58,585	1,989,183	156,257	26,961	1,859,887	329,288	226,593	4,758	507,687	210,762
1975	2,769,705	2,219,675	32,065	2,251,740	175,628	31,374	2,107,486	377,418	284,801	5,347	517,996	221,963
1976	3,258,211	2,667,239	50,527	2,717,766	216,961	27,664	2,528,469	414,341	315,401	6,116	532,769	238,072
1977	3,675,283	3,037,902	39,029	3,076,931	242,233	30,162	2,864,860	461,872	348,551	6,693	549,090	244,790
1978	4,179,496	3,482,653	34,979	3,517,632	285,513	36,322	3,268,441	534,731	376,324	7,448	561,187	260,518
1979	4,750,479	3,945,844	37,084	3,982,928	333,758	52,376	3,701,546	615,267	433,666	8,224	577,630	268,260
1980	5,619,785	4,631,816	20,204	4,652,020	389,604	44,655	4,307,071	796,375	516,339	9,450	594,659	281,511
1981	6,337,334	5,162,258	24,461	5,186,719	465,610	39,707	4,760,816	995,163	581,355	10,445	606,705	289,146
1982	6,802,548	5,429,538	22,044	5,451,582	492,704	14,966	4,973,844	1,162,688	666,016	11,000	618,386	291,462
1983	7,195,140	5,588,938	26,311	5,615,249	498,738	25,987	5,142,498	1,285,403	767,239	11,451	628,340	291,172
1984	7,708,483	5,969,320	13,358	5,982,678	545,584	20,074	5,457,168	1,444,748	806,567	12,169	633,436	302,207
1985	8,077,467	6,171,344	18,578	6,189,922	564,852	7,824	5,632,894	1,574,817	869,756	12,681	636,971	302,128
1986	8,056,846	6,050,010	27,665	6,077,675	542,967	-4,534	5,530,174	1,565,439	961,233	12,653	636,761	295,628
1987	8,135,858	6,159,239	20,017	6,179,256	545,242	-17,458	5,616,556	1,544,544	974,758	12,934	629,017	296,915
1988	8,717,878	6,722,630	46,644	6,769,274	631,749	-33,134	6,104,391	1,584,689	1,028,798	13,946	625,135	303,980
1989	9,435,874	7,192,807	31,248	7,224,055	688,189	-29,593	6,506,273	1,815,615	1,113,986	15,137	623,372	309,087
1990	10,229,877	7,901,442	32,403	7,933,845	779,814	-27,732	7,126,299	1,868,401	1,235,177	16,360	625,305	321,133
1991	10,877,066	8,460,602	19,804	8,480,406	857,415	-62,896	7,560,095	1,908,690	1,408,281	17,124	635,197	329,966
1992	11,924,123	9,312,910	42,460	9,355,370	935,409	-98,133	8,321,828	1,973,116	1,629,179	18,425	647,179	340,665
1993	12,405,170	9,600,844	35,260	9,636,104	971,506	-90,162	8,574,436	2,040,200	1,790,534	18,875	657,226	347,916
1994	13,307,240	10,177,906	33,531	10,211,437	1,057,987	-101,278	9,052,172	2,242,024	2,013,044	20,027	664,462	356,542
1995	13,976,531	10,652,950	39,919	10,692,869	1,108,555	-99,635	9,484,679	2,430,704	2,061,148	20,822	671,247	368,168
1996	14,649,770	11,213,890	53,083	11,266,973	1,179,826	-109,332	9,977,815	2,566,908	2,105,047	21,591	678,500	377,415
1997	15,210,031	11,707,567	48,323	11,755,890	1,226,628	-102,504	10,426,758	2,645,670	2,137,603	22,171	686,021	381,499
1998	16,162,051	12,556,379	35,245	12,591,624	1,328,979	-128,220	11,134,425	2,866,097	2,161,529	23,319	693,072	395,582
1999	16,765,292	13,212,223	52,071	13,264,294	1,379,340	-155,553	11,729,401	2,823,551	2,212,340	23,924	700,767	405,694
2000	17,778,280	14,010,648	53,686	14,064,334	1,433,939	-171,934	12,458,461	3,018,630	2,301,189	25,125	707,589	415,793
2001	18,542,989	14,544,917	52,136	14,597,053	1,450,546	-171,395	12,975,112	2,930,777	2,637,100	26,090	710,731	412,224
2002	19,167,855	15,126,405	42,774	15,169,179	1,507,568	-191,709	13,469,902	2,870,832	2,827,121	26,794	715,379	413,336
2003	19,922,280	15,856,198	48,632	15,904,830	1,557,110	-217,811	14,129,909	2,933,137	2,859,234	27,583	722,274	419,513
2004	21,436,071	16,847,256	50,530	16,897,786	1,613,740	-195,115	15,088,931	3,143,426	3,203,714	29,374	729,774	423,462
2005	23,430,785	17,814,506	44,569	17,859,075	1,686,842	-258,603	15,913,630	3,359,497	4,157,658	31,857	735,507	440,225
2006	25,771,930	19,426,188	60,009	19,486,197	1,863,968	200,382	17,822,611	3,951,166	3,998,153	33,386	771,940	461,283
2007	27,738,900	20,788,944	52,480	20,841,424	2,009,044	241,921	19,074,301	4,533,557	4,131,042	35,572	779,796	472,427
2008	29,779,881	22,125,578	42,007	22,167,585	2,129,332	228,954	20,267,207	4,745,059	4,767,615	37,803	787,767	480,073
2009	29,529,233	22,466,446	45,588	22,512,034	2,163,639	-190,847	20,157,548	4,361,931	5,009,754	37,102	795,897	479,053
2010	30,404,470	22,773,554	53,995	22,827,549	2,173,749	14,883	20,668,683	4,354,809	5,380,978	37,800	804,359	474,796
2011	32,176,487	23,484,619	59,414	23,544,033	2,020,378	213,251	21,736,906	4,959,032	5,480,549	39,817	808,105	480,210
2012	33,406,812	24,761,787	75,695	24,837,482	2,120,092	-141,844	22,575,546	5,225,723	5,605,543	41,067	813,476	487,276
2013	33,952,370	25,936,585	87,818	26,024,403	2,532,529	-527,223	22,964,651	5,202,560	5,785,159	41,441	819,304	499,689
2014	35,332,370	27,109,834	51,224	27,161,058	2,629,286	-655,797	23,875,975	5,601,862	5,854,533	42,831	824,923	511,690
2015	36,252,727	28,087,394	27,031	28,114,425	2,772,156	-1,085,906	24,256,363	5,498,573	6,497,791	43,693	829,719	516,419
2016	37,179,476	28,223,455	12,555	28,236,010	2,810,935	-1,186,669	24,238,406	6,086,499	6,854,571	44,495	835,596	518,759
2017	38,183,872	29,035,295	15,320	29,050,615	2,897,656	-1,394,246	24,758,713	6,286,137	7,139,022	45,775	834,159	522,027
2018	41,153,342	41,125,264	28,078	30,915,463	3,119,169	-1,141,894	26,654,400	7,027,193	7,471,749	48,159	854,526	539,596
2019	42,264,278	42,238,043	26,235	31,460,131	3,154,339	-926,526	27,379,266	7,067,422	7,817,590	49,439	854,884	541,538

Personal Income and Employment by Area: Battle Creek, MI

(Thousands of dollars, except as noted.)

Year	Personal income, total	Earnings by place of work			Less: Contributions for government social insurance	Plus: Adjustment for residence	Equals: Net earnings by place of residence	Plus: Dividends, interest, and rent	Plus: Personal current transfer receipts	Per capita personal income (dollars)	Population (persons)	Total employment
		Nonfarm	Farm	Total								
1970	576,982	500,248	7,173	507,421	36,214	-26,553	444,654	74,283	58,045	4,076	141,561	62,407
1971	628,950	546,341	6,267	552,608	40,854	-33,271	478,483	81,254	69,213	4,472	140,647	63,123
1972	692,203	604,719	9,419	614,138	47,211	-40,066	526,861	88,679	76,663	4,876	141,963	64,437
1973	761,421	672,120	15,821	687,941	60,903	-47,757	579,281	95,994	86,146	5,349	142,349	66,077
1974	806,447	708,617	7,321	715,938	66,185	-53,975	595,778	107,386	103,283	5,639	143,021	66,005
1975	895,883	762,360	12,747	775,107	69,442	-64,100	641,565	118,972	135,346	6,281	142,640	64,320
1976	980,447	857,529	9,566	867,095	80,024	-77,455	709,616	128,389	142,442	6,887	142,359	66,464
1977	1,061,283	943,955	8,157	952,112	88,510	-89,130	774,472	143,440	143,371	7,433	142,772	67,485
1978	1,163,902	1,047,678	6,575	1,054,253	100,211	-103,802	850,240	157,899	155,763	8,113	143,463	68,846
1979	1,263,112	1,130,988	6,581	1,137,569	112,584	-117,738	907,247	177,802	178,063	8,874	142,341	69,077
1980	1,339,901	1,142,470	4,081	1,146,551	112,244	-124,667	909,640	207,655	222,606	9,456	141,701	65,129
1981	1,452,074	1,202,812	10,190	1,213,002	127,255	-126,719	959,028	247,021	246,025	10,235	141,880	62,898
1982	1,516,735	1,199,419	2,563	1,201,982	127,081	-125,214	949,687	286,898	280,150	10,843	139,886	59,788
1983	1,553,984	1,221,002	-5,022	1,215,980	133,201	-121,649	961,130	300,344	292,510	11,291	137,629	59,063
1984	1,638,441	1,275,636	7,011	1,282,647	143,995	-122,003	1,016,649	330,076	291,716	12,076	135,682	59,859
1985	1,757,818	1,399,947	7,368	1,407,315	162,003	-134,740	1,110,572	348,784	298,462	13,067	134,523	61,694
1986	1,850,392	1,473,452	8,658	1,482,110	172,267	-139,362	1,170,481	366,901	313,010	13,776	134,316	62,869
1987	1,979,736	1,620,896	9,943	1,630,839	186,783	-159,302	1,284,754	374,848	320,134	14,681	134,849	66,233
1988	2,065,989	1,731,766	6,745	1,738,511	207,464	-169,553	1,361,494	372,780	331,715	15,365	134,459	66,844
1989	2,213,983	1,821,811	16,229	1,838,040	216,946	-171,425	1,449,669	409,717	354,597	16,345	135,457	67,838
1990	2,323,434	1,932,491	13,863	1,946,354	232,873	-180,538	1,532,943	412,890	377,601	17,056	136,226	69,258
1991	2,438,165	2,039,389	9,803	2,049,192	248,912	-197,954	1,602,326	419,162	416,677	17,821	136,814	71,364
1992	2,590,929	2,199,098	10,524	2,209,622	266,635	-221,296	1,721,691	429,004	440,234	18,871	137,298	72,964
1993	2,677,654	2,253,999	11,144	2,265,143	276,241	-221,768	1,767,134	440,602	469,918	19,435	137,775	73,362
1994	2,839,825	2,400,182	10,077	2,410,259	299,050	-238,393	1,872,816	489,993	477,016	20,592	137,910	75,666
1995	2,937,277	2,506,336	8,068	2,514,404	313,032	-250,736	1,950,636	487,756	498,885	21,379	137,393	78,757
1996	3,039,351	2,577,393	7,857	2,585,250	314,813	-252,279	2,018,158	502,976	518,217	22,245	136,630	77,972
1997	3,245,454	2,766,412	10,019	2,776,431	334,717	-274,919	2,166,795	526,252	552,407	23,718	136,834	80,495
1998	3,345,870	2,873,916	9,059	2,882,975	340,302	-278,926	2,263,747	537,550	544,573	24,284	137,783	78,310
1999	3,407,041	2,861,055	8,029	2,869,084	337,500	-259,013	2,272,571	552,051	582,419	24,685	138,021	75,611
2000	3,476,144	2,898,094	10,171	2,908,265	340,899	-265,474	2,301,892	570,246	604,006	25,187	138,014	75,174
2001	3,559,879	2,890,670	14,323	2,904,993	341,903	-257,764	2,305,326	577,267	677,286	25,767	138,158	77,978
2002	3,686,891	3,049,584	7,484	3,057,068	360,308	-285,682	2,411,078	576,068	699,745	26,605	138,580	77,978
2003	3,769,086	3,067,704	9,592	3,077,296	361,260	-270,404	2,445,632	584,962	738,492	27,123	138,962	76,411
2004	3,864,291	3,172,498	22,251	3,194,749	375,721	-306,826	2,512,202	585,190	766,899	27,712	139,443	76,704
2005	3,947,196	3,214,968	15,350	3,230,318	383,032	-317,470	2,529,816	606,095	811,285	28,408	138,946	75,646
2006	4,007,084	3,267,488	7,338	3,274,826	395,553	-325,781	2,553,492	582,638	870,954	28,976	138,291	74,704
2007	4,131,746	3,313,062	12,795	3,325,857	400,063	-347,056	2,578,738	607,564	945,444	30,031	137,582	74,215
2008	4,300,586	3,390,532	8,732	3,399,264	414,113	-402,884	2,582,267	655,684	1,062,635	31,320	137,313	72,227
2009	4,217,653	3,295,694	15,486	3,311,180	406,088	-439,641	2,465,451	595,899	1,156,303	30,944	136,301	68,941
2010	4,329,539	3,377,731	27,543	3,405,274	411,884	-495,236	2,498,154	587,650	1,243,735	31,849	135,941	68,650
2011	4,442,622	3,365,365	49,573	3,414,938	369,765	-487,982	2,557,191	649,671	1,235,760	32,899	135,039	69,084
2012	4,556,028	3,536,915	12,711	3,549,626	387,164	-529,015	2,633,447	698,152	1,224,429	33,847	134,605	68,495
2013	4,624,336	3,603,863	53,684	3,657,547	444,623	-539,079	2,673,845	703,850	1,246,641	34,363	134,572	69,548
2014	4,751,990	3,712,186	25,870	3,738,056	456,929	-584,025	2,697,102	756,522	1,298,366	35,304	134,602	70,366
2015	4,983,124	3,867,775	19,219	3,886,994	472,820	-613,846	2,800,328	803,258	1,379,538	37,145	134,154	71,346
2016	5,091,672	3,999,844	17,879	4,017,723	483,745	-655,021	2,878,957	802,284	1,410,431	37,947	134,178	71,273
2017	5,188,474	4,046,834	5,468	4,052,302	493,934	-615,582	2,942,786	831,550	1,414,138	38,683	134,128	70,742
2018	5,249,396	5,243,408	5,988	4,074,685	503,135	-638,111	2,933,439	860,462	1,455,495	39,160	134,049	69,915
2019	5,400,823	5,395,341	5,482	4,067,582	500,228	-570,294	2,997,060	866,980	1,536,783	40,257	134,159	69,503

Personal Income and Employment by Area: Bay City, MI

(Thousands of dollars, except as noted.)

		Derivation of personal income										
		Earnings by place of work			Less: Contributions for government social insurance	Plus: Adjustment for residence	Equals: Net earnings by place of residence	Plus: Dividends, interest, and rent	Plus: Personal current transfer receipts	Per capita personal income (dollars)	Population (persons)	Total employment
Year	Personal income, total	Nonfarm	Farm	Total								
1970	420,933	293,171	5,220	298,391	20,928	44,339	321,802	58,218	40,913	3,582	117,502	39,729
1971	464,555	319,945	4,167	324,112	23,426	52,885	353,571	62,993	47,991	3,920	118,513	39,422
1972	499,669	342,221	4,894	347,115	26,568	58,462	379,009	68,296	52,364	4,196	119,094	39,885
1973	561,721	385,948	11,092	397,040	34,621	65,470	427,889	75,372	58,460	4,688	119,824	41,851
1974	621,936	413,451	23,624	437,075	38,401	64,229	462,903	85,811	73,222	5,159	120,548	41,896
1975	662,994	428,891	10,222	439,113	39,024	70,387	470,476	97,405	95,113	5,505	120,441	40,211
1976	755,195	490,642	10,673	501,315	45,513	98,700	554,502	103,975	96,718	6,264	120,560	41,485
1977	862,681	562,104	10,968	573,072	52,335	124,738	645,475	116,510	100,696	7,100	121,500	43,222
1978	949,558	611,899	13,745	625,644	58,492	148,382	715,534	126,272	107,752	7,780	122,057	43,662
1979	1,037,742	653,386	17,957	671,343	64,790	164,777	771,330	141,809	124,603	8,571	121,074	43,509
1980	1,133,350	665,840	26,055	691,895	65,510	157,780	784,165	173,209	175,976	9,442	120,037	41,737
1981	1,220,646	734,563	4,991	739,554	78,205	170,925	832,274	210,158	178,214	10,138	120,401	42,279
1982	1,263,933	727,939	6,508	734,447	78,800	160,042	815,689	244,618	203,626	10,639	118,804	40,466
1983	1,328,915	753,758	5,011	758,769	82,139	174,651	851,281	259,663	217,971	11,326	117,330	40,371
1984	1,423,673	804,884	7,458	812,342	90,753	189,716	911,305	288,686	223,682	12,202	116,677	40,939
1985	1,499,357	847,921	13,314	861,235	98,160	207,748	970,823	299,657	228,877	13,036	115,017	41,442
1986	1,564,800	906,430	1,131	907,561	103,782	210,496	1,014,275	310,784	239,741	13,694	114,267	42,479
1987	1,621,964	935,297	10,654	945,951	105,920	220,599	1,060,630	311,138	250,196	14,233	113,959	43,197
1988	1,719,331	1,009,826	8,551	1,018,377	119,000	235,241	1,134,618	325,479	259,234	15,229	112,898	44,027
1989	1,800,018	1,028,296	16,004	1,044,300	121,084	252,792	1,176,008	340,953	283,057	16,063	112,061	44,282
1990	1,911,834	1,100,123	13,106	1,113,229	131,061	253,075	1,235,243	368,622	307,969	17,100	111,804	45,908
1991	1,975,535	1,132,904	11,929	1,144,833	137,290	264,235	1,271,778	368,833	334,924	17,670	111,803	45,846
1992	2,096,904	1,202,448	17,461	1,219,909	144,951	286,599	1,361,557	378,973	356,374	18,692	112,182	46,227
1993	2,183,299	1,280,894	14,293	1,295,187	155,429	273,025	1,412,783	390,230	380,286	19,425	112,397	46,432
1994	2,305,243	1,354,690	6,640	1,361,330	167,355	289,541	1,483,516	431,311	390,416	20,578	112,025	47,608
1995	2,388,194	1,432,599	17,518	1,450,117	177,855	274,341	1,546,603	436,858	404,733	21,384	111,680	49,673
1996	2,481,873	1,545,725	5,539	1,551,264	187,407	242,475	1,606,332	459,100	416,441	22,313	111,231	51,133
1997	2,598,926	1,608,401	7,438	1,615,839	194,336	249,806	1,671,309	488,747	438,870	23,405	111,040	52,171
1998	2,657,417	1,684,544	2,486	1,687,030	199,719	230,193	1,717,504	500,412	439,501	24,005	110,704	51,665
1999	2,769,089	1,741,541	8,506	1,750,047	204,049	270,226	1,816,224	479,612	473,253	25,106	110,295	52,077
2000	2,917,640	1,813,676	938	1,814,614	211,997	303,785	1,906,402	515,421	495,817	26,478	110,192	53,512
2001	2,973,500	1,812,489	-7,251	1,805,238	209,834	320,334	1,915,738	507,222	550,540	27,072	109,836	52,307
2002	2,965,198	1,823,264	8,409	1,831,673	212,588	292,773	1,911,858	485,154	568,186	26,990	109,861	51,737
2003	3,033,078	1,834,155	4,359	1,838,514	213,637	300,729	1,925,606	505,884	601,588	27,684	109,559	51,158
2004	3,096,114	1,855,888	12,291	1,868,179	219,614	326,478	1,975,043	490,195	630,876	28,287	109,453	51,482
2005	3,125,206	1,875,900	12,968	1,888,868	225,469	308,508	1,971,907	489,490	663,809	28,628	109,165	50,662
2006	3,235,602	1,940,076	15,408	1,955,484	236,407	315,391	2,034,468	489,099	712,035	29,763	108,711	50,201
2007	3,334,248	1,959,538	12,511	1,972,049	241,864	294,677	2,024,862	531,284	778,102	30,835	108,132	50,347
2008	3,476,231	1,983,745	20,994	2,004,739	248,127	259,395	2,016,007	583,611	876,613	32,092	108,320	49,858
2009	3,441,725	1,953,248	5,202	1,958,450	245,488	238,237	1,951,199	531,829	958,697	31,894	107,913	47,922
2010	3,582,108	1,978,754	12,501	1,991,255	244,673	273,825	2,020,407	520,986	1,040,715	33,267	107,676	47,473
2011	3,709,449	2,011,635	26,356	2,037,991	222,666	290,970	2,106,295	559,636	1,043,518	34,544	107,382	47,644
2012	3,754,083	2,066,829	18,766	2,085,595	229,709	277,163	2,133,049	587,500	1,033,534	35,108	106,930	48,000
2013	3,743,638	2,108,233	9,891	2,118,124	264,332	257,398	2,111,190	569,140	1,063,308	35,066	106,761	48,196
2014	3,870,561	2,112,971	-7,045	2,105,926	266,696	281,308	2,120,538	628,079	1,121,944	36,506	106,025	48,058
2015	4,039,427	2,171,887	-6,392	2,165,495	271,132	291,745	2,186,108	668,163	1,185,156	38,382	105,244	47,400
2016	4,114,650	2,188,680	-10,543	2,178,137	272,281	332,159	2,238,015	664,177	1,212,458	39,382	104,481	47,557
2017	4,276,348	2,184,894	-20,937	2,163,957	272,875	474,531	2,365,613	695,165	1,215,570	41,024	104,239	46,870
2018	4,393,535	4,393,783	-248	2,212,758	284,892	491,809	2,419,675	714,566	1,259,294	42,367	103,702	46,538
2019	4,502,212	4,504,915	-2,703	2,261,307	289,940	470,460	2,441,827	720,742	1,339,643	43,657	103,126	47,440

Personal Income and Employment by Area: Beaumont-Port Arthur, TX

(Thousands of dollars, except as noted.)

Year	Personal income, total	Earnings by place of work			Less: Contributions for government social insurance	Plus: Adjustment for residence	Equals: Net earnings by place of residence	Plus: Dividends, interest, and rent	Plus: Personal current transfer receipts	Per capita personal income (dollars)	Population (persons)	Total employment
		Nonfarm	Farm	Total								
1970	1,295,373	1,109,643	2,176	1,111,819	72,923	-13,221	1,025,675	164,327	105,371	3,605	359,291	139,079
1971	1,390,512	1,176,508	3,751	1,180,259	79,889	-11,883	1,088,487	178,747	123,278	3,849	361,233	140,072
1972	1,499,073	1,262,933	4,717	1,267,650	90,461	-11,049	1,166,140	194,382	138,551	4,133	362,681	141,566
1973	1,632,850	1,372,941	6,352	1,379,293	114,895	-10,271	1,254,127	214,685	164,038	4,567	357,512	146,460
1974	1,911,191	1,614,597	12,000	1,626,597	139,034	-17,393	1,470,170	250,169	190,852	5,331	358,506	153,311
1975	2,150,975	1,776,184	15,416	1,791,600	147,808	-12,083	1,631,709	282,382	236,884	5,916	363,590	153,637
1976	2,490,332	2,144,103	3,153	2,147,256	182,614	-36,485	1,928,157	307,191	254,984	6,744	369,268	163,590
1977	2,795,101	2,425,989	10,809	2,436,798	206,723	-47,854	2,182,221	341,543	271,337	7,446	375,363	169,957
1978	3,100,074	2,687,181	2,880	2,690,061	234,638	-47,528	2,407,895	390,325	301,854	8,217	377,286	173,977
1979	3,478,948	2,997,474	9,394	3,006,868	271,907	-49,393	2,685,568	449,425	343,955	9,064	383,832	179,197
1980	3,894,545	3,274,630	6,220	3,280,850	298,249	-43,981	2,938,620	556,039	399,886	10,036	388,072	177,396
1981	4,448,323	3,723,642	-1,830	3,721,812	363,444	-52,809	3,305,559	691,883	450,881	11,309	393,359	186,607
1982	4,709,723	3,795,119	-2,306	3,792,813	383,646	-56,376	3,352,791	829,860	527,072	11,795	399,300	179,648
1983	4,894,733	3,821,755	-21	3,821,734	380,754	-62,559	3,378,421	899,839	616,473	12,217	400,634	172,840
1984	5,073,713	3,868,056	-3,947	3,864,109	395,358	-61,382	3,407,369	1,010,339	656,005	12,732	398,516	172,570
1985	5,155,380	3,808,963	3,305	3,812,268	392,355	-57,437	3,362,476	1,108,820	684,084	13,092	393,786	168,736
1986	5,096,859	3,691,691	751	3,692,442	375,743	-54,775	3,261,924	1,092,988	741,947	13,363	381,420	160,923
1987	5,072,629	3,670,374	-2,137	3,668,237	371,899	-53,310	3,243,028	1,056,990	772,611	13,380	379,118	165,149
1988	5,358,455	3,920,221	13,434	3,933,655	414,438	-58,823	3,460,394	1,099,590	798,471	14,280	375,245	167,774
1989	5,682,550	4,050,356	11,139	4,061,495	432,120	-67,347	3,562,028	1,249,517	871,005	15,193	374,021	168,178
1990	5,985,015	4,388,768	10,633	4,399,401	460,790	-85,841	3,852,770	1,171,337	960,908	15,958	375,055	174,023
1991	6,464,237	4,853,887	15,972	4,869,859	519,315	-112,614	4,237,930	1,181,618	1,044,689	17,008	380,069	183,546
1992	6,947,521	5,180,624	12,654	5,193,278	550,141	-123,194	4,519,943	1,204,819	1,222,759	18,055	384,799	183,011
1993	6,959,068	5,175,625	12,148	5,187,773	549,863	-104,160	4,533,750	1,136,938	1,288,380	17,847	389,937	183,297
1994	7,248,211	5,371,328	8,869	5,380,197	579,146	-97,227	4,703,824	1,165,321	1,379,066	18,498	391,836	183,107
1995	7,566,027	5,489,225	8,961	5,498,186	599,028	-98,486	4,800,672	1,273,432	1,491,923	19,120	395,704	186,653
1996	7,764,317	5,576,851	4,727	5,581,578	603,707	-109,484	4,868,387	1,309,393	1,586,537	19,649	395,151	187,334
1997	8,425,327	6,207,265	6,022	6,213,287	661,351	-140,293	5,411,643	1,363,251	1,650,433	21,242	396,639	194,273
1998	8,941,611	6,719,976	5,801	6,725,777	704,919	-161,960	5,858,898	1,439,503	1,643,210	22,483	397,703	198,335
1999	8,885,710	6,706,951	6,563	6,713,514	699,971	-150,495	5,863,048	1,378,360	1,644,302	22,210	400,075	197,025
2000	9,356,989	7,059,915	3,110	7,063,025	716,963	-165,473	6,180,589	1,466,969	1,709,431	23,404	399,797	199,849
2001	9,709,564	7,308,543	2,636	7,311,179	733,154	-172,047	6,405,978	1,457,230	1,846,356	24,412	397,731	197,248
2002	9,869,371	7,423,560	3,528	7,427,088	750,181	-170,818	6,506,089	1,377,925	1,985,357	24,801	397,949	196,209
2003	10,253,118	7,683,431	15,580	7,699,011	790,183	-190,605	6,718,223	1,429,832	2,105,063	25,752	398,146	197,114
2004	10,410,837	7,841,151	21,702	7,862,853	805,489	-182,114	6,875,250	1,354,247	2,181,340	26,092	398,998	194,734
2005	11,079,675	8,197,653	26,744	8,224,397	854,177	-195,427	7,174,793	1,371,386	2,533,496	27,691	400,115	198,505
2006	11,809,938	9,041,402	33,019	9,074,421	931,593	-257,302	7,885,526	1,462,912	2,461,500	30,015	393,468	206,488
2007	12,449,527	9,385,589	30,603	9,416,192	985,493	-274,704	8,155,995	1,640,671	2,652,861	31,385	396,665	209,966
2008	13,441,736	10,004,507	-3,216	10,001,291	1,041,207	-358,844	8,601,240	1,916,471	2,924,025	33,635	399,641	212,387
2009	13,329,534	9,809,709	-2,697	9,807,012	1,032,126	-362,742	8,412,144	1,776,093	3,141,297	33,192	401,592	207,904
2010	14,003,063	10,210,085	-7,034	10,203,051	1,081,550	-404,010	8,717,491	1,876,129	3,409,443	34,687	403,697	206,310
2011	14,631,279	10,640,779	-12,600	10,628,179	1,005,522	-457,320	9,165,337	1,970,592	3,495,350	36,095	405,356	210,996
2012	15,367,722	11,114,430	-11,812	11,102,618	1,038,974	-473,492	9,590,152	2,301,827	3,475,743	38,049	403,895	210,827
2013	15,052,590	10,995,331	-1,231	10,994,100	1,160,089	-443,775	9,390,236	2,077,279	3,585,075	37,124	405,471	207,952
2014	16,347,956	11,906,551	-4,810	11,901,741	1,240,949	-347,575	10,313,217	2,296,759	3,737,980	40,290	405,754	213,510
2015	17,034,661	12,459,403	-5,284	12,454,119	1,303,804	-336,704	10,813,611	2,287,092	3,933,958	41,676	408,744	215,916
2016	17,132,876	12,355,624	-9,411	12,346,213	1,318,704	-221,594	10,805,915	2,202,005	4,124,956	41,695	410,909	212,195
2017	17,520,309	12,474,374	-13,503	12,460,871	1,352,607	-109,771	10,998,493	2,301,926	4,219,890	42,480	412,437	211,554
2018	17,382,152	17,394,626	-12,474	12,642,397	1,366,590	-325,888	10,949,919	2,368,673	4,063,560	44,138	393,815	213,442
2019	17,751,250	17,762,831	-11,581	13,029,982	1,389,932	-474,894	11,165,156	2,407,229	4,178,865	45,219	392,563	215,386

Personal Income and Employment by Area: Beckley, WV

(Thousands of dollars, except as noted.)

Year	Personal income, total	Earnings by place of work			Less: Contributions for government social insurance	Plus: Adjustment for residence	Equals: Net earnings by place of residence	Plus: Dividends, interest, and rent	Plus: Personal current transfer receipts	Per capita personal income (dollars)	Population (persons)	Total employment
		Nonfarm	Farm	Total								
1970	342,410	251,677	140	251,817	18,662	10,841	243,996	35,075	63,339	2,858	119,794	34,722
1971	383,565	272,329	278	272,607	21,177	11,565	262,995	39,343	81,227	3,134	122,399	35,712
1972	443,014	313,974	381	314,355	25,404	13,130	302,081	44,455	96,478	3,502	126,518	38,148
1973	494,158	337,210	651	337,861	31,511	13,764	320,114	51,802	122,242	3,839	128,707	39,217
1974	546,723	375,669	526	376,195	36,347	13,024	352,872	60,924	132,927	4,226	129,362	40,310
1975	645,359	451,517	488	452,005	43,395	16,415	425,025	70,688	149,646	4,867	132,602	43,351
1976	746,571	542,705	276	542,981	54,034	14,793	503,740	79,183	163,648	5,395	138,390	46,063
1977	810,403	592,080	288	592,368	57,770	15,216	549,814	88,826	171,763	5,697	142,246	46,317
1978	912,215	667,242	372	667,614	66,952	13,628	614,290	98,920	199,005	6,329	144,129	47,908
1979	1,002,767	695,943	837	696,780	72,995	23,404	647,189	112,357	243,221	6,913	145,047	46,987
1980	1,093,976	732,080	789	732,869	78,397	26,479	680,951	137,728	275,297	7,563	144,639	46,598
1981	1,191,482	790,176	-344	789,832	91,020	25,742	724,554	168,960	297,968	8,256	144,324	46,263
1982	1,276,557	820,539	-259	820,280	97,721	36,213	758,772	195,998	321,787	8,844	144,345	45,744
1983	1,281,513	781,388	-333	781,055	93,195	32,657	720,517	205,124	355,872	8,894	144,081	43,320
1984	1,375,395	862,166	100	862,266	105,675	36,121	792,712	228,573	354,110	9,674	142,180	44,190
1985	1,419,473	897,714	-292	897,422	112,018	35,997	821,401	239,733	358,339	10,123	140,228	44,214
1986	1,440,289	891,188	-411	890,777	114,608	44,867	821,036	239,565	379,688	10,450	137,822	43,044
1987	1,461,495	904,011	-346	903,665	117,441	54,278	840,502	237,663	383,330	10,929	133,725	42,517
1988	1,512,726	935,417	-553	934,864	124,629	52,249	862,484	248,310	401,932	11,658	129,757	42,630
1989	1,579,755	946,290	274	946,564	129,105	61,442	878,901	276,777	424,077	12,552	125,854	42,806
1990	1,664,276	999,207	-85	999,122	138,156	77,382	938,348	275,876	450,052	13,348	124,685	43,965
1991	1,766,203	1,051,158	-406	1,050,752	150,790	79,169	979,131	282,902	504,170	14,134	124,959	44,633
1992	1,881,320	1,101,416	53	1,101,469	160,399	86,581	1,027,651	283,448	570,221	15,024	125,222	45,282
1993	1,958,201	1,163,043	-51	1,162,992	176,515	71,683	1,058,160	291,049	608,992	15,499	126,345	46,344
1994	2,069,106	1,236,678	-316	1,236,362	187,441	83,729	1,132,650	307,723	628,733	16,347	126,577	48,415
1995	2,183,086	1,327,110	-576	1,326,534	205,287	86,741	1,207,988	331,913	643,185	17,113	127,571	50,747
1996	2,290,661	1,394,318	-958	1,393,360	215,541	89,176	1,266,995	350,680	672,986	17,837	128,425	52,378
1997	2,377,498	1,446,899	-635	1,446,264	220,495	93,424	1,319,193	372,604	685,701	18,534	128,275	53,304
1998	2,506,303	1,515,487	-917	1,514,570	232,045	96,184	1,378,709	404,548	723,046	19,597	127,892	54,760
1999	2,545,428	1,557,327	-1,396	1,555,931	236,771	99,162	1,418,322	397,370	729,736	19,975	127,431	54,481
2000	2,641,181	1,605,364	-978	1,604,386	250,295	107,593	1,461,684	424,027	755,470	20,875	126,525	54,322
2001	2,822,585	1,735,352	-1,087	1,734,265	253,180	95,904	1,576,989	423,589	822,007	22,523	125,318	54,716
2002	2,921,919	1,795,878	-1,839	1,794,039	251,145	85,016	1,627,910	411,566	882,443	23,250	125,672	54,883
2003	2,920,919	1,790,233	-1,963	1,788,270	257,247	79,065	1,610,088	398,174	912,657	23,271	125,519	54,029
2004	2,998,716	1,884,686	-1,456	1,883,230	267,977	67,772	1,683,025	395,629	920,062	23,962	125,145	55,171
2005	3,145,829	2,036,995	-1,947	2,035,048	285,315	57,103	1,806,836	389,043	949,950	25,254	124,570	56,027
2006	3,344,727	2,157,406	-2,081	2,155,325	290,006	56,066	1,921,385	417,746	1,005,596	26,892	124,378	56,871
2007	3,334,714	2,036,829	-2,593	2,034,236	283,284	41,224	1,792,176	475,576	1,066,962	26,771	124,566	57,277
2008	3,565,832	2,159,720	-1,432	2,158,288	287,698	27,809	1,898,399	509,303	1,158,130	28,630	124,550	57,762
2009	3,679,188	2,177,831	-1,374	2,176,457	297,863	33,791	1,912,385	536,631	1,230,172	29,477	124,816	56,337
2010	3,839,270	2,337,523	-1,202	2,336,321	305,862	43,252	2,073,711	486,958	1,278,601	30,724	124,959	56,736
2011	4,211,003	2,608,972	-919	2,608,053	291,637	72,517	2,388,933	542,422	1,279,648	33,639	125,183	58,011
2012	4,276,301	2,547,687	-565	2,547,122	294,292	86,839	2,339,669	623,121	1,313,511	34,207	125,014	58,220
2013	4,168,073	2,528,415	-525	2,527,890	318,237	87,018	2,296,671	546,523	1,324,879	33,539	124,277	56,915
2014	4,212,799	2,487,027	-953	2,486,074	318,701	85,521	2,252,894	561,550	1,398,355	34,170	123,291	56,218
2015	4,245,035	2,418,051	-632	2,417,419	312,797	88,578	2,193,200	610,019	1,441,816	34,789	122,022	55,199
2016	4,107,109	2,282,198	-902	2,281,296	304,754	67,674	2,044,216	590,738	1,472,155	34,123	120,361	53,261
2017	4,261,353	2,404,825	-1,837	2,402,988	325,499	53,754	2,131,243	613,561	1,516,549	35,948	118,543	53,634
2018	4,605,556	4,606,336	-780	2,652,394	342,969	67,702	2,377,127	639,698	1,588,731	39,312	117,154	53,860
2019	4,761,221	4,761,304	-83	2,788,632	356,709	52,049	2,483,972	647,145	1,630,104	41,128	115,767	54,761

Personal Income and Employment by Area: Bellingham, WA

(Thousands of dollars, except as noted.)

		Derivation of personal income										
		Earnings by place of work			Less: Contributions for government social insurance	Plus: Adjustment for residence	Equals: Net earnings by place of residence	Plus: Dividends, interest, and rent	Plus: Personal current transfer receipts	Per capita personal income (dollars)	Population (persons)	Total employment
Year	Personal income, total	Nonfarm	Farm	Total								
1970	321,153	236,478	15,801	252,279	19,139	-308	232,832	54,573	33,748	3,888	82,606	34,551
1971	369,028	278,308	17,662	295,970	23,859	-2,177	269,934	60,405	38,689	4,307	85,688	37,206
1972	389,183	287,246	20,011	307,257	25,342	-1,094	280,821	64,962	43,400	4,351	89,443	36,628
1973	434,564	318,446	24,205	342,651	32,310	-335	310,006	74,733	49,825	4,845	89,700	38,054
1974	490,746	355,963	25,038	381,001	37,079	-809	343,113	86,801	60,832	5,390	91,043	39,342
1975	557,944	402,445	25,466	427,911	41,778	-1,713	384,420	98,390	75,134	5,978	93,332	41,368
1976	635,961	464,202	32,419	496,621	48,448	-1,343	446,830	109,080	80,051	6,620	96,070	44,257
1977	703,824	522,154	29,485	551,639	55,259	-2,917	493,463	126,738	83,623	7,149	98,453	46,132
1978	799,446	603,850	26,584	630,434	65,007	-3,348	562,079	146,787	90,580	7,878	101,482	48,497
1979	911,802	683,912	32,817	716,729	76,119	-1,289	639,321	169,702	102,779	8,735	104,380	50,544
1980	996,713	722,336	24,518	746,854	80,749	312	666,417	204,118	126,178	9,296	107,222	50,074
1981	1,078,348	751,920	28,200	780,120	91,221	45	688,944	245,248	144,156	9,884	109,096	50,010
1982	1,133,041	773,910	26,531	800,441	96,332	951	705,060	267,887	160,094	10,311	109,885	49,658
1983	1,242,287	831,766	36,157	867,923	103,961	2,039	766,001	300,287	175,999	11,229	110,630	51,784
1984	1,327,116	881,058	35,699	916,757	113,542	2,930	806,145	333,471	187,500	11,924	111,294	52,881
1985	1,418,833	932,529	42,527	975,056	120,523	5,457	859,990	358,377	200,466	12,618	112,441	53,901
1986	1,522,449	1,013,620	53,521	1,067,141	131,482	6,433	942,092	369,034	211,323	13,442	113,262	56,022
1987	1,620,055	1,091,865	60,023	1,151,888	142,081	5,644	1,015,451	380,760	223,844	14,043	115,361	58,864
1988	1,754,371	1,186,058	57,470	1,243,528	157,061	11,123	1,097,590	415,969	240,812	14,742	119,002	62,798
1989	1,979,145	1,343,093	66,655	1,409,748	178,574	14,233	1,245,407	475,803	257,935	16,052	123,294	67,307
1990	2,262,361	1,591,920	75,914	1,667,834	213,535	14,172	1,468,471	508,597	285,293	17,523	129,111	73,036
1991	2,452,464	1,702,544	69,168	1,771,712	231,296	21,865	1,562,281	564,118	326,065	18,326	133,823	74,567
1992	2,607,648	1,815,695	89,406	1,905,101	246,567	29,336	1,687,870	564,799	354,979	18,766	138,957	77,046
1993	2,718,753	1,892,642	76,300	1,968,942	259,140	35,131	1,744,933	591,482	382,338	18,924	143,669	78,697
1994	2,901,284	2,013,979	75,184	2,089,163	277,226	41,244	1,853,181	635,651	412,452	19,657	147,593	82,327
1995	3,067,945	2,116,062	67,442	2,183,504	290,765	49,817	1,942,556	675,917	449,472	20,268	151,369	83,655
1996	3,318,052	2,241,436	95,281	2,336,717	300,369	57,166	2,093,514	745,932	478,606	21,388	155,134	86,113
1997	3,505,782	2,363,529	77,362	2,440,891	303,396	70,900	2,208,395	793,098	504,289	22,170	158,133	88,181
1998	3,761,650	2,520,536	104,978	2,625,514	320,373	85,804	2,390,945	840,662	530,043	23,366	160,988	89,503
1999	3,952,839	2,642,184	108,236	2,750,420	327,986	105,017	2,527,451	849,700	575,688	24,020	164,566	91,585
2000	4,185,988	2,751,660	89,497	2,841,157	347,087	122,266	2,616,336	939,417	630,235	24,962	167,696	93,409
2001	4,515,496	2,998,977	109,552	3,108,529	373,447	107,673	2,842,755	956,404	716,337	26,380	171,172	94,252
2002	4,597,906	3,152,746	91,205	3,243,951	392,261	108,943	2,960,633	879,096	758,177	26,288	174,904	96,470
2003	4,948,459	3,375,375	119,288	3,494,663	422,875	105,460	3,177,248	968,182	803,029	27,824	177,851	99,418
2004	5,347,459	3,677,652	124,911	3,802,563	459,408	102,545	3,445,700	1,066,386	835,373	29,421	181,756	102,987
2005	5,689,347	3,992,107	124,185	4,116,292	505,863	104,645	3,715,074	1,089,487	884,786	30,679	185,450	107,985
2006	6,165,908	4,236,005	85,875	4,321,880	528,570	124,971	3,918,281	1,296,636	950,991	32,637	188,926	110,385
2007	6,776,543	4,454,241	113,952	4,568,193	555,608	145,733	4,158,318	1,583,673	1,034,552	35,141	192,837	114,493
2008	7,254,016	4,644,222	85,889	4,730,111	579,312	151,152	4,301,951	1,751,396	1,200,669	36,877	196,708	114,978
2009	7,109,167	4,615,824	65,930	4,681,754	590,504	144,137	4,235,387	1,528,896	1,344,884	35,570	199,865	110,709
2010	7,385,960	4,760,000	103,836	4,863,836	602,292	141,244	4,402,788	1,491,729	1,491,443	36,651	201,520	109,057
2011	7,788,202	4,885,951	149,785	5,035,736	566,004	153,604	4,623,336	1,673,316	1,491,550	38,281	203,447	110,303
2012	8,300,511	5,241,209	145,283	5,386,492	582,202	161,948	4,966,238	1,842,601	1,491,672	40,514	204,878	112,790
2013	8,324,160	5,390,629	161,420	5,552,049	667,333	154,670	5,039,386	1,760,654	1,524,120	40,372	206,189	115,118
2014	8,770,077	5,449,349	200,171	5,649,520	682,137	176,471	5,143,854	1,964,515	1,661,708	42,141	208,112	117,180
2015	9,278,633	5,727,920	201,145	5,929,065	721,362	187,106	5,394,809	2,180,255	1,703,569	43,826	211,713	119,692
2016	9,663,378	6,009,482	176,865	6,186,347	751,543	200,733	5,635,537	2,219,781	1,808,060	44,681	216,274	123,400
2017	10,190,741	6,415,713	175,889	6,591,602	810,435	208,725	5,989,892	2,331,589	1,869,260	46,028	221,404	125,148
2018	11,139,242	11,012,764	126,478	7,092,443	861,198	206,563	6,437,808	2,707,431	1,994,003	49,464	225,197	129,134
2019	11,672,154	11,519,308	152,846	7,466,753	891,219	221,983	6,797,517	2,758,207	2,116,430	50,915	229,247	131,309

Personal Income and Employment by Area: Bend, OR

(Thousands of dollars, except as noted.)

Year	Personal income, total	Earnings by place of work			Less: Contributions for government social insurance	Plus: Adjustment for residence	Equals: Net earnings by place of residence	Plus: Dividends, interest, and rent	Plus: Personal current transfer receipts	Per capita personal income (dollars)	Population (persons)	Total employment
		Nonfarm	Farm	Total								
1970	124,676	90,412	1,419	91,831	6,623	2,318	87,526	24,821	12,329	4,037	30,882	13,667
1971	143,502	104,384	1,428	105,812	7,921	2,597	100,488	28,617	14,397	4,370	32,835	15,106
1972	168,880	123,271	3,740	127,011	9,891	2,933	120,053	32,392	16,435	4,852	34,804	16,767
1973	196,159	143,736	4,286	148,022	13,282	3,074	137,814	38,445	19,900	5,206	37,682	18,403
1974	221,209	156,821	3,468	160,289	14,878	3,635	149,046	46,476	25,687	5,509	40,155	18,902
1975	256,795	176,577	3,663	180,240	16,127	5,689	169,802	53,575	33,418	6,053	42,422	19,706
1976	308,998	221,349	3,277	224,626	20,214	4,372	208,784	62,484	37,730	6,915	44,686	22,354
1977	369,658	269,303	2,384	271,687	25,185	4,443	250,945	75,067	43,646	7,706	47,969	25,288
1978	443,826	328,928	132	329,060	31,690	4,307	301,677	92,920	49,229	8,319	53,349	28,444
1979	525,431	390,196	894	391,090	39,375	3,542	355,257	111,315	58,859	8,989	58,452	30,620
1980	573,952	402,570	1,159	403,729	40,276	4,173	367,626	132,643	73,683	9,203	62,365	30,066
1981	618,235	406,905	1,658	408,563	43,436	6,080	371,207	158,554	88,474	9,793	63,130	29,334
1982	640,723	400,660	901	401,561	43,503	6,727	364,785	173,134	102,804	10,165	63,031	27,771
1983	709,259	447,402	6,098	453,500	49,112	7,800	412,188	187,773	109,298	11,345	62,516	29,659
1984	791,075	508,790	6,702	515,492	57,380	9,011	467,123	208,760	115,192	12,392	63,839	31,566
1985	857,434	555,920	5,061	560,981	63,842	10,390	507,529	225,691	124,214	13,200	64,959	33,037
1986	914,324	596,503	1,660	598,163	68,210	12,448	542,401	244,005	127,918	13,820	66,160	34,685
1987	978,932	643,989	373	644,362	72,643	14,371	586,090	260,317	132,525	14,641	66,862	35,621
1988	1,091,408	728,980	2,340	731,320	85,024	17,310	663,606	281,964	145,838	15,845	68,882	38,234
1989	1,226,870	795,948	3,178	799,126	95,276	18,830	722,680	343,589	160,601	17,179	71,415	41,660
1990	1,392,418	940,480	1,483	941,963	114,536	17,956	845,383	372,005	175,030	18,309	76,053	45,455
1991	1,539,726	1,052,685	743	1,053,428	128,482	18,193	943,139	398,612	197,975	19,137	80,456	46,995
1992	1,680,779	1,145,013	-1,148	1,143,865	137,688	24,217	1,030,394	424,820	225,565	19,962	84,199	48,397
1993	1,848,330	1,264,066	-2,400	1,261,666	150,783	23,328	1,134,211	470,506	243,613	20,989	88,061	51,071
1994	1,982,640	1,359,337	-2,878	1,356,459	164,055	25,445	1,217,849	502,631	262,160	21,694	91,393	54,760
1995	2,150,396	1,426,925	-2,694	1,424,231	174,057	25,928	1,276,102	579,271	295,023	22,519	95,491	57,626
1996	2,353,833	1,555,263	-2,979	1,552,284	190,652	26,913	1,388,545	643,641	321,647	23,689	99,362	60,831
1997	2,516,282	1,653,885	-2,219	1,651,666	201,419	27,687	1,477,934	694,318	344,030	24,530	102,581	64,237
1998	2,737,302	1,807,304	176	1,807,480	219,272	27,725	1,615,933	760,762	360,607	25,625	106,820	66,592
1999	2,934,104	1,990,949	-4,365	1,986,584	240,501	26,447	1,772,530	758,463	403,111	26,213	111,933	70,590
2000	3,231,051	2,202,270	-5,976	2,196,294	266,207	26,246	1,956,333	841,202	433,516	27,719	116,566	74,782
2001	3,514,985	2,434,227	-4,569	2,429,658	284,014	19,196	2,164,840	854,746	495,399	29,164	120,526	76,099
2002	3,643,238	2,570,256	-4,695	2,565,561	301,903	13,600	2,277,258	812,379	553,601	29,088	125,247	77,415
2003	3,867,707	2,751,150	-3,080	2,748,070	324,572	3,942	2,427,440	859,836	580,431	29,960	129,094	80,405
2004	4,177,031	2,956,642	1,294	2,957,936	359,270	6,595	2,605,261	970,117	601,653	31,229	133,756	86,200
2005	4,653,431	3,325,222	-3,831	3,321,391	407,288	-796	2,913,307	1,088,379	651,745	33,105	140,567	92,848
2006	5,336,981	3,804,561	-5,009	3,799,552	462,651	-21,732	3,315,169	1,302,723	719,089	36,024	148,149	98,924
2007	5,660,392	3,915,527	-11,841	3,903,686	480,300	-18,993	3,404,393	1,465,317	790,682	37,085	152,633	102,267
2008	5,873,644	3,774,769	-13,808	3,760,961	467,725	-9,916	3,283,320	1,614,185	976,139	37,455	156,820	98,956
2009	5,421,446	3,332,177	-13,197	3,318,980	426,762	22,555	2,914,773	1,335,052	1,171,621	34,456	157,345	92,268
2010	5,474,282	3,261,827	-12,692	3,249,135	425,807	41,279	2,864,607	1,324,639	1,285,036	34,704	157,740	90,538
2011	5,845,658	3,373,770	-11,024	3,362,746	393,165	64,026	3,033,607	1,495,494	1,316,557	36,626	159,605	91,525
2012	6,330,821	3,717,463	-8,940	3,708,523	417,901	101,454	3,392,076	1,614,107	1,324,638	39,238	161,343	92,973
2013	6,778,393	4,077,638	-6,887	4,070,751	510,191	110,661	3,671,221	1,717,658	1,389,514	41,014	165,270	96,990
2014	7,314,206	4,572,966	-8,035	4,564,931	570,299	91,860	4,086,492	1,711,477	1,516,237	43,152	169,497	102,651
2015	8,240,978	5,122,265	-7,406	5,114,859	627,864	83,552	4,570,547	2,035,728	1,634,703	47,284	174,288	109,051
2016	9,012,257	5,757,737	-6,864	5,750,873	687,699	57,599	5,120,773	2,195,562	1,695,922	49,881	180,675	119,096
2017	9,522,219	6,191,292	-9,121	6,182,171	752,142	62,077	5,492,106	2,283,787	1,746,326	50,955	186,875	118,159
2018	10,672,155	10,683,424	-11,269	6,665,825	791,826	18,596	5,892,595	2,877,348	1,902,212	55,612	191,905	124,441
2019	11,159,204	11,173,478	-14,274	7,054,493	843,438	12,901	6,223,956	2,907,112	2,028,136	56,447	197,692	127,797

Personal Income and Employment by Area: Billings, MT

(Thousands of dollars, except as noted.)

Year	Personal income, total	Earnings by place of work			Less: Contributions for government social insurance	Plus: Adjustment for residence	Equals: Net earnings by place of residence	Plus: Dividends, interest, and rent	Plus: Personal current transfer receipts	Per capita personal income (dollars)	Population (persons)	Total employment
		Nonfarm	Farm	Total								
1970	372,929	278,723	21,119	299,842	21,611	-574	277,657	64,402	30,870	3,892	95,810	43,329
1971	411,959	310,999	19,473	330,472	24,478	-419	305,575	70,217	36,167	4,193	98,257	44,885
1972	474,208	351,753	33,796	385,549	29,206	-414	355,929	77,702	40,577	4,730	100,254	47,205
1973	526,066	394,204	32,842	427,046	37,863	-563	388,620	89,991	47,455	5,158	101,991	50,349
1974	597,877	450,760	29,474	480,234	44,203	-445	435,586	106,032	56,259	5,683	105,198	52,867
1975	668,970	509,450	13,919	523,369	48,184	1,845	477,030	123,217	68,723	6,214	107,654	53,779
1976	753,100	594,302	4,887	599,189	57,135	919	542,973	134,754	75,373	6,824	110,368	57,467
1977	856,148	682,848	3,628	686,476	66,290	1,292	621,478	153,049	81,621	7,592	112,764	60,302
1978	976,887	781,896	8,724	790,620	78,780	1,316	713,156	173,031	90,700	8,402	116,271	64,090
1979	1,090,579	877,427	3,293	880,720	92,405	949	789,264	199,825	101,490	9,290	117,391	65,442
1980	1,210,179	931,516	5,962	937,478	99,612	10,690	848,556	240,654	120,969	10,279	117,733	64,651
1981	1,372,329	1,033,149	3,939	1,037,088	118,482	8,037	926,643	306,367	139,319	11,470	119,645	66,183
1982	1,488,457	1,100,423	4,625	1,105,048	129,309	7,948	983,687	347,540	157,230	12,153	122,475	67,078
1983	1,577,691	1,170,300	5,439	1,175,739	137,993	4,800	1,042,546	359,987	175,158	12,558	125,635	68,542
1984	1,696,577	1,245,484	9,641	1,255,125	151,242	-948	1,102,935	404,143	189,499	13,223	128,301	70,868
1985	1,747,917	1,276,336	10,451	1,286,787	157,990	-1,828	1,126,969	418,539	202,409	13,550	128,999	70,516
1986	1,751,728	1,273,186	10,786	1,283,972	160,248	-2,254	1,121,470	412,806	217,452	13,681	128,041	69,709
1987	1,786,188	1,282,402	20,444	1,302,846	159,795	53	1,143,104	412,192	230,892	14,216	125,649	69,468
1988	1,850,342	1,338,384	18,826	1,357,210	174,565	1,287	1,183,932	417,785	248,625	14,973	123,581	71,737
1989	2,003,884	1,417,718	23,378	1,441,096	186,021	3,059	1,258,134	472,928	272,822	16,323	122,761	73,107
1990	2,102,123	1,503,603	22,084	1,525,687	209,623	4,817	1,320,881	477,649	303,593	17,154	122,545	73,868
1991	2,244,596	1,637,179	28,195	1,665,374	232,241	5,818	1,438,951	485,610	320,035	18,059	124,295	75,939
1992	2,396,044	1,768,367	33,817	1,802,184	252,659	2,620	1,552,145	499,808	344,091	18,782	127,568	78,363
1993	2,545,266	1,904,867	37,464	1,942,331	278,600	1,372	1,665,103	507,792	372,371	19,468	130,744	80,093
1994	2,688,980	2,015,001	25,776	2,040,777	295,285	1,610	1,747,102	549,453	392,425	20,182	133,239	83,702
1995	2,829,423	2,086,990	13,238	2,100,228	298,040	1,732	1,803,920	605,949	419,554	20,909	135,318	84,768
1996	2,954,768	2,165,649	14,053	2,179,702	296,114	1,188	1,884,776	636,064	433,928	21,596	136,818	87,037
1997	3,101,003	2,259,630	10,961	2,270,591	299,256	1,415	1,972,750	683,307	444,946	22,524	137,674	87,651
1998	3,324,176	2,405,696	13,594	2,419,290	310,782	2,472	2,110,980	750,234	462,962	24,077	138,062	90,242
1999	3,408,747	2,507,434	16,682	2,524,116	322,727	6,498	2,207,887	741,984	458,876	24,467	139,319	91,860
2000	3,643,153	2,658,182	15,159	2,673,341	341,094	12,895	2,345,142	786,808	511,203	25,995	140,150	93,441
2001	3,800,879	2,786,569	26,888	2,813,457	367,681	4,964	2,450,740	793,842	556,297	26,869	141,458	95,185
2002	3,899,972	2,939,921	10,045	2,949,966	393,155	-1,785	2,555,026	770,228	574,718	27,293	142,891	96,302
2003	4,121,043	3,109,054	24,630	3,133,684	411,955	-7,224	2,714,505	806,204	600,334	28,531	144,443	97,266
2004	4,479,396	3,361,524	43,746	3,405,270	440,367	-9,231	2,955,672	878,158	645,566	30,631	146,238	99,877
2005	4,814,527	3,637,845	38,691	3,676,536	476,540	-17,839	3,182,157	940,038	692,332	32,408	148,558	102,373
2006	5,196,844	3,899,243	2,827	3,902,070	507,812	-27,267	3,366,991	1,071,197	758,656	34,537	150,471	104,211
2007	5,627,033	4,208,546	6,880	4,215,426	555,707	-37,992	3,621,727	1,191,352	813,954	36,909	152,455	107,874
2008	5,981,473	4,356,384	10,157	4,366,541	568,995	-45,222	3,752,324	1,303,544	925,605	38,563	155,110	108,839
2009	5,872,230	4,349,383	6,355	4,355,738	564,482	-19,167	3,772,089	1,114,596	985,545	37,309	157,395	106,775
2010	6,167,315	4,469,786	13,160	4,482,946	572,650	858	3,911,154	1,169,515	1,086,646	38,716	159,297	106,233
2011	6,606,312	4,723,210	25,940	4,749,150	543,589	38,293	4,243,854	1,289,997	1,072,461	41,130	160,622	108,079
2012	7,219,468	5,087,390	31,795	5,119,185	567,938	104,093	4,655,340	1,458,374	1,105,754	44,409	162,568	110,095
2013	7,277,731	5,302,066	42,543	5,344,609	663,632	160,502	4,841,479	1,308,910	1,127,342	44,166	164,783	110,178
2014	7,757,875	5,584,064	40,065	5,624,129	695,063	185,120	5,114,186	1,457,903	1,185,786	46,633	166,360	111,519
2015	8,048,652	5,800,567	47,208	5,847,775	723,249	129,194	5,253,720	1,554,488	1,240,444	48,043	167,531	114,231
2016	8,082,460	5,731,221	37,351	5,768,572	700,871	60,275	5,127,976	1,607,686	1,346,798	47,836	168,961	115,150
2017	8,484,064	5,996,721	28,939	6,025,660	728,999	71,300	5,367,961	1,675,553	1,440,550	49,760	170,498	116,182
2018	9,461,062	9,406,227	54,835	6,495,396	821,568	109,284	5,783,112	2,076,601	1,601,349	52,502	180,203	121,330
2019	9,802,775	9,739,578	63,197	6,748,602	848,715	116,515	6,016,402	2,096,954	1,689,419	53,960	181,667	122,698

Personal Income and Employment by Area: Binghamton, NY

(Thousands of dollars, except as noted.)

Year	Personal income, total	Earnings by place of work			Less: Contributions for government social insurance	Plus: Adjustment for residence	Equals: Net earnings by place of residence	Plus: Dividends, interest, and rent	Plus: Personal current transfer receipts	Per capita personal income (dollars)	Population (persons)	Total employment
		Nonfarm	Farm	Total								
1970	1,096,008	947,976	8,644	956,620	71,901	-32,537	852,182	139,431	104,395	4,077	268,851	117,119
1971	1,169,453	995,597	8,709	1,004,306	78,160	-35,921	890,225	150,584	128,644	4,319	270,746	116,349
1972	1,235,754	1,053,517	8,840	1,062,357	87,343	-36,472	938,542	162,556	134,656	4,619	267,509	117,444
1973	1,332,843	1,135,541	10,063	1,145,604	108,690	-37,418	999,496	181,261	152,086	4,982	267,518	120,927
1974	1,441,396	1,210,104	7,005	1,217,109	119,004	-38,143	1,059,962	204,081	177,353	5,426	265,630	121,541
1975	1,582,300	1,290,938	6,632	1,297,570	124,685	-44,596	1,128,289	224,056	229,955	5,890	268,656	119,091
1976	1,693,251	1,388,506	8,396	1,396,902	137,684	-48,956	1,210,262	238,667	244,322	6,293	269,063	120,675
1977	1,846,831	1,529,082	4,869	1,533,951	151,332	-59,543	1,323,076	263,691	260,064	6,874	268,668	124,414
1978	2,028,177	1,699,925	7,722	1,707,647	172,170	-67,866	1,467,611	280,747	279,819	7,576	267,705	128,940
1979	2,224,229	1,866,116	9,421	1,875,537	194,532	-76,784	1,604,221	317,638	302,370	8,331	266,989	130,555
1980	2,454,074	2,015,721	9,728	2,025,449	209,227	-85,762	1,730,460	378,136	345,478	9,308	263,639	129,633
1981	2,732,896	2,209,511	7,811	2,217,322	243,390	-96,836	1,877,096	460,720	395,080	10,357	263,859	129,925
1982	3,013,449	2,397,588	14,097	2,411,685	266,749	-110,602	2,034,334	535,359	443,756	11,414	264,005	129,662
1983	3,222,929	2,554,158	7,900	2,562,058	287,485	-113,789	2,160,784	587,019	475,126	12,232	263,473	128,801
1984	3,580,021	2,855,913	8,857	2,864,770	328,436	-125,157	2,411,177	674,795	494,049	13,603	263,182	135,188
1985	3,788,498	3,064,351	9,830	3,074,181	355,797	-136,692	2,581,692	689,421	517,385	14,311	264,719	139,580
1986	3,961,533	3,177,263	10,358	3,187,621	375,398	-133,264	2,678,959	730,908	551,666	15,026	263,651	140,401
1987	4,170,309	3,382,819	10,639	3,393,458	390,613	-136,720	2,866,125	740,626	563,558	15,901	262,266	140,900
1988	4,420,720	3,597,159	7,672	3,604,831	424,415	-138,516	3,041,900	781,024	597,796	16,758	263,797	145,553
1989	4,747,737	3,753,003	12,087	3,765,090	437,573	-135,423	3,192,094	908,290	647,353	17,957	264,388	143,469
1990	4,923,618	3,842,113	13,620	3,855,733	429,025	-137,304	3,289,404	929,666	704,548	18,599	264,731	142,457
1991	5,086,610	3,964,362	9,602	3,973,964	452,179	-142,050	3,379,735	938,328	768,547	19,149	265,632	139,936
1992	5,278,830	4,071,105	13,779	4,084,884	457,065	-148,880	3,478,939	936,282	863,609	19,803	266,571	138,396
1993	5,271,085	4,067,779	14,745	4,082,524	463,676	-152,952	3,465,896	889,898	915,291	19,817	265,993	137,687
1994	5,307,142	4,047,652	13,015	4,060,667	464,806	-145,663	3,450,198	903,330	953,614	20,097	264,082	136,661
1995	5,426,728	4,075,874	9,727	4,085,601	463,522	-145,195	3,476,884	946,333	1,003,511	20,866	260,079	134,001
1996	5,583,950	4,161,812	16,315	4,178,127	465,062	-139,323	3,573,742	968,095	1,042,113	21,753	256,702	132,577
1997	5,785,985	4,325,356	5,366	4,330,722	479,294	-135,514	3,715,914	1,032,736	1,037,335	22,760	254,213	134,726
1998	5,898,568	4,402,992	8,881	4,411,873	486,807	-141,432	3,783,634	1,037,632	1,077,302	23,293	253,235	134,427
1999	6,178,205	4,697,560	6,443	4,704,003	505,997	-152,591	4,045,415	1,027,416	1,105,374	24,442	252,773	138,052
2000	6,550,960	5,044,966	4,267	5,049,233	540,277	-172,029	4,336,927	1,080,073	1,133,960	25,976	252,189	141,139
2001	6,648,396	5,069,982	4,485	5,074,467	558,884	-153,972	4,361,611	1,072,289	1,214,496	26,322	252,580	139,580
2002	6,752,395	5,117,374	288	5,117,662	565,640	-137,345	4,414,677	1,017,350	1,320,368	26,644	253,430	136,479
2003	6,797,408	5,073,915	7,185	5,081,100	560,893	-109,166	4,411,041	1,019,997	1,366,370	26,874	252,932	134,838
2004	7,096,497	5,221,159	15,401	5,236,560	577,492	-99,309	4,559,759	1,104,610	1,432,128	28,093	252,605	134,828
2005	7,215,308	5,388,745	18,923	5,407,668	606,328	-100,057	4,701,283	1,015,258	1,498,767	28,622	252,088	135,172
2006	7,654,798	5,726,703	17,488	5,744,191	643,237	-100,481	5,000,473	1,060,803	1,593,522	30,323	252,441	136,660
2007	8,127,536	5,996,956	16,665	6,013,621	665,459	-97,136	5,251,026	1,191,159	1,685,351	32,196	252,442	139,310
2008	8,582,159	6,184,028	15,128	6,199,156	695,629	-84,883	5,418,644	1,287,186	1,876,329	33,985	252,527	139,391
2009	8,742,134	6,162,102	6,906	6,169,008	685,578	-72,346	5,411,084	1,244,847	2,086,203	34,667	252,171	135,666
2010	8,966,940	6,225,391	12,561	6,237,952	683,220	-11,531	5,543,201	1,198,271	2,225,468	35,651	251,519	133,187
2011	9,206,319	6,222,093	17,404	6,239,497	619,363	39,591	5,659,725	1,297,984	2,248,610	36,778	250,321	132,381
2012	9,495,277	6,347,743	13,505	6,361,248	619,900	87,899	5,829,247	1,432,188	2,233,842	38,124	249,064	131,868
2013	9,529,429	6,398,006	18,819	6,416,825	701,720	115,483	5,830,588	1,443,376	2,255,465	38,375	248,323	130,485
2014	9,675,074	6,427,754	20,141	6,447,895	715,593	132,804	5,865,106	1,516,167	2,293,801	39,096	247,469	129,550
2015	9,873,505	6,439,763	7,269	6,447,032	728,072	145,875	5,864,835	1,592,760	2,415,910	40,199	245,615	128,353
2016	9,971,880	6,500,351	6,691	6,507,042	742,968	118,331	5,882,405	1,630,980	2,458,495	40,934	243,608	128,166
2017	10,426,604	6,697,126	9,846	6,706,972	770,327	131,664	6,068,309	1,710,435	2,647,860	43,047	242,217	128,369
2018	10,678,703	10,668,893	9,810	7,000,825	792,770	131,689	6,339,744	1,792,141	2,546,818	44,427	240,366	127,507
2019	11,095,201	11,075,896	19,305	7,246,419	814,853	132,786	6,564,352	1,825,283	2,705,566	46,484	238,691	127,623

Personal Income and Employment by Area: Birmingham-Hoover, AL

(Thousands of dollars, except as noted.)

Year	Personal income, total	Earnings by place of work			Less: Contributions for government social insurance	Plus: Adjustment for residence	Equals: Net earnings by place of residence	Plus: Dividends, interest, and rent	Plus: Personal current transfer receipts	Per capita personal income (dollars)	Population (persons)	Total employment
		Nonfarm	Farm	Total								
1970	2,851,440	2,379,405	17,346	2,396,751	173,881	-7,814	2,215,056	345,407	290,977	3,418	834,280	356,195
1971	3,131,911	2,588,676	19,381	2,608,057	192,855	-18,466	2,396,736	383,812	351,363	3,704	845,548	360,430
1972	3,483,840	2,902,582	25,868	2,928,450	227,028	-33,633	2,667,789	419,336	396,715	4,086	852,711	373,689
1973	3,921,783	3,259,867	43,422	3,303,289	294,270	-39,533	2,969,486	473,734	478,563	4,539	864,085	388,783
1974	4,415,944	3,681,181	18,811	3,699,992	342,915	-44,767	3,312,310	551,487	552,147	5,074	870,341	398,688
1975	4,949,600	4,022,722	36,095	4,058,817	369,872	-47,010	3,641,935	614,471	693,194	5,604	883,172	399,287
1976	5,502,353	4,491,330	36,100	4,527,430	421,711	-43,119	4,062,600	669,101	770,652	6,144	895,598	407,393
1977	6,076,351	5,001,680	40,289	5,041,969	470,750	-43,865	4,527,354	740,870	808,127	6,687	908,642	421,750
1978	6,835,177	5,662,734	35,593	5,698,327	543,275	-42,711	5,112,341	839,834	883,002	7,436	919,252	435,995
1979	7,643,332	6,287,066	42,940	6,330,006	624,929	-43,845	5,661,232	956,529	1,025,571	8,239	927,712	445,633
1980	8,400,830	6,705,487	28,813	6,734,300	664,678	-37,030	6,032,592	1,164,174	1,204,064	9,027	930,680	438,371
1981	9,130,207	7,120,792	29,113	7,149,905	761,575	-50,109	6,338,221	1,449,101	1,342,885	9,815	930,227	430,843
1982	9,656,392	7,392,455	33,312	7,425,767	805,577	-50,958	6,569,232	1,619,688	1,467,472	10,426	926,197	423,068
1983	10,253,529	7,844,071	28,481	7,872,552	863,791	-59,130	6,949,631	1,719,865	1,584,033	11,060	927,062	425,578
1984	11,255,663	8,632,338	36,137	8,668,475	968,769	-58,180	7,641,526	1,946,000	1,668,137	12,085	931,399	442,199
1985	12,146,097	9,392,640	40,217	9,432,857	1,063,034	-67,817	8,302,006	2,115,559	1,728,532	12,964	936,926	457,464
1986	12,842,801	9,999,584	25,798	10,025,382	1,130,344	-76,208	8,818,830	2,235,552	1,788,419	13,641	941,503	471,914
1987	13,619,661	10,640,407	37,999	10,678,406	1,188,957	-89,757	9,399,692	2,388,498	1,831,471	14,360	948,471	485,505
1988	14,769,020	11,548,036	62,445	11,610,481	1,327,575	-113,454	10,169,452	2,711,701	1,887,867	15,529	951,042	500,481
1989	16,089,171	12,264,688	88,893	12,353,581	1,408,117	-121,245	10,824,219	3,144,970	2,119,982	16,858	954,416	507,055
1990	17,264,731	13,205,865	86,432	13,292,297	1,532,421	-129,295	11,630,581	3,322,939	2,311,211	18,008	958,709	518,079
1991	18,149,374	13,837,557	109,684	13,947,241	1,617,459	-137,408	12,192,374	3,434,545	2,522,455	18,721	969,491	519,983
1992	19,417,458	14,888,185	96,330	14,984,515	1,717,648	-150,989	13,115,878	3,452,047	2,849,533	19,813	980,037	528,501
1993	20,328,105	15,528,498	111,156	15,639,654	1,809,070	-146,386	13,684,198	3,645,006	2,998,901	20,494	991,884	542,304
1994	21,673,590	16,500,447	84,611	16,585,058	1,947,552	-153,763	14,483,743	4,021,275	3,168,572	21,605	1,003,186	549,975
1995	23,137,991	17,528,347	83,420	17,611,767	2,080,194	-162,430	15,369,143	4,354,069	3,414,779	22,827	1,013,634	566,345
1996	24,409,346	18,593,810	76,686	18,670,496	2,182,003	-174,643	16,313,850	4,501,961	3,593,535	23,874	1,022,434	578,023
1997	25,743,326	19,460,501	88,902	19,549,403	2,287,543	-179,664	17,082,196	4,932,116	3,729,014	24,983	1,030,425	590,779
1998	27,528,108	20,953,346	107,910	21,061,256	2,416,592	-181,992	18,462,672	5,339,783	3,725,653	26,481	1,039,523	603,585
1999	28,695,850	22,203,011	94,274	22,297,285	2,557,190	-196,131	19,543,964	5,287,360	3,864,526	27,396	1,047,440	612,234
2000	30,635,338	23,603,165	65,432	23,668,597	2,684,534	-212,008	20,772,055	5,756,980	4,106,303	29,085	1,053,306	618,709
2001	31,467,083	24,225,914	104,870	24,330,784	2,783,306	-227,734	21,319,744	5,802,369	4,344,970	29,712	1,059,082	615,843
2002	32,391,496	25,156,508	73,664	25,230,172	2,887,996	-228,607	22,113,569	5,622,271	4,655,656	30,473	1,062,966	613,752
2003	33,669,237	25,865,413	99,205	25,964,618	2,973,328	-201,608	22,789,682	5,951,920	4,927,635	31,441	1,070,886	614,462
2004	36,316,177	27,420,635	119,331	27,539,966	3,109,284	-221,600	24,209,082	6,919,742	5,187,353	33,682	1,078,204	625,578
2005	38,519,541	28,791,181	98,137	28,889,318	3,263,519	-136,014	25,489,785	7,483,083	5,546,673	35,459	1,086,318	639,606
2006	41,139,546	30,313,974	46,501	30,360,475	3,417,685	-74,951	26,867,839	8,274,308	5,997,399	37,440	1,098,818	653,022
2007	42,979,902	31,479,077	35,893	31,514,970	3,587,929	-53,600	27,873,441	8,680,337	6,426,124	38,817	1,107,256	667,249
2008	44,115,990	31,541,400	32,779	31,574,179	3,687,210	1,022	27,887,991	8,988,982	7,239,017	39,491	1,117,101	661,379
2009	42,282,553	30,568,770	45,952	30,614,722	3,557,008	-10,970	27,046,744	7,555,574	7,680,235	37,575	1,125,271	632,372
2010	44,041,654	31,155,851	41,461	31,197,312	3,604,039	54,328	27,647,601	7,973,219	8,420,834	39,017	1,128,791	625,721
2011	45,652,611	32,213,102	2,194	32,215,296	3,296,324	11,956	28,930,928	8,005,248	8,716,435	40,384	1,130,457	633,688
2012	47,871,357	33,753,042	25,316	33,778,358	3,436,266	-29,730	30,312,362	8,816,865	8,742,130	42,237	1,133,409	642,479
2013	47,759,550	34,312,179	104,407	34,416,586	3,972,338	-33,973	30,410,275	8,395,344	8,953,931	41,962	1,138,173	648,538
2014	49,813,478	35,454,776	77,820	35,532,596	4,086,135	29,468	31,475,929	8,996,927	9,340,622	43,654	1,141,099	656,925
2015	52,084,376	36,668,296	83,768	36,752,064	4,241,227	91,215	32,602,052	9,810,078	9,672,246	45,508	1,144,518	665,250
2016	52,903,455	37,176,205	37,422	37,213,627	4,276,258	32,762	32,970,131	10,053,765	9,879,559	46,128	1,146,888	674,678
2017	55,311,901	39,009,390	68,184	39,077,574	4,457,810	-6,381	34,613,383	10,488,003	10,210,515	48,105	1,149,807	682,034
2018	56,272,785	56,213,890	58,895	39,995,013	4,594,359	-434,665	34,965,989	11,350,546	9,956,250	51,723	1,087,967	671,189
2019	58,200,404	58,181,464	18,940	41,506,672	4,740,792	-392,783	36,373,097	11,448,089	10,379,218	53,374	1,090,435	681,778

Personal Income and Employment by Area: Bismarck, ND

(Thousands of dollars, except as noted.)

Year	Personal income, total	Derivation of personal income								Per capita personal income (dollars)	Population (persons)	Total employment
		Earnings by place of work			Less: Contributions for government social insurance	Plus: Adjustment for residence	Equals: Net earnings by place of residence	Plus: Dividends, interest, and rent	Plus: Personal current transfer receipts			
		Nonfarm	Farm	Total								
1970	236,408	174,435	19,530	193,965	14,005	-1,542	178,418	37,303	20,687	3,522	67,114	30,677
1971	266,948	190,710	26,517	217,227	15,628	-1,292	200,307	41,748	24,893	3,924	68,027	30,842
1972	310,645	214,880	40,442	255,322	18,163	-941	236,218	46,426	28,001	4,499	69,047	31,964
1973	371,001	246,597	63,093	309,690	24,380	-769	284,541	54,474	31,986	5,210	71,215	33,892
1974	403,772	286,062	43,830	329,892	29,821	1,920	301,991	64,548	37,233	5,525	73,082	35,517
1975	455,966	332,615	35,926	368,541	34,764	4,453	338,230	72,743	44,993	6,027	75,660	37,555
1976	508,456	397,230	21,483	418,713	41,802	-215	376,696	81,538	50,222	6,510	78,103	40,157
1977	572,017	446,356	17,503	463,859	44,847	3,982	422,994	94,217	54,806	7,140	80,117	42,079
1978	671,227	499,758	39,405	539,163	51,417	13,120	500,866	109,709	60,652	8,216	81,696	44,053
1979	749,997	572,610	26,722	599,332	61,512	16,516	554,336	127,350	68,311	8,904	84,232	46,483
1980	805,123	630,631	-12,474	618,157	68,504	16,519	566,172	155,553	83,398	9,326	86,328	46,997
1981	945,350	672,320	37,449	709,769	76,741	18,749	651,777	197,062	96,511	10,861	87,039	46,555
1982	1,023,070	714,573	21,043	735,616	82,943	29,921	682,594	233,319	107,157	11,596	88,228	46,654
1983	1,090,262	754,093	15,437	769,530	87,850	55,557	737,237	231,691	121,334	12,119	89,961	47,560
1984	1,138,657	797,672	20,450	818,122	95,770	35,064	757,416	246,891	134,350	12,462	91,367	48,441
1985	1,163,848	825,104	18,564	843,668	102,064	20,797	762,401	257,469	143,978	12,702	91,624	48,697
1986	1,210,015	845,821	34,382	880,203	106,830	14,198	787,571	261,379	161,065	13,239	91,397	48,760
1987	1,260,964	890,215	42,197	932,412	112,261	15,470	835,621	255,658	169,685	13,949	90,400	50,050
1988	1,257,530	937,002	362	937,364	123,481	12,612	826,495	257,147	173,888	13,971	90,011	50,981
1989	1,372,266	992,200	18,557	1,010,757	132,065	11,856	890,548	285,693	196,025	15,249	89,992	52,751
1990	1,457,206	1,064,500	18,746	1,083,246	149,758	11,621	945,109	300,366	211,731	16,172	90,106	54,138
1991	1,515,753	1,128,410	18,326	1,146,736	161,543	9,946	995,139	302,090	218,524	16,675	90,902	55,794
1992	1,660,810	1,222,249	39,129	1,261,378	174,664	10,021	1,096,735	316,566	247,509	17,962	92,461	57,107
1993	1,766,425	1,311,011	38,413	1,349,424	188,636	9,615	1,170,403	333,195	262,827	18,791	94,002	58,940
1994	1,850,810	1,397,572	24,811	1,422,383	203,405	8,960	1,227,938	356,222	266,650	19,484	94,993	61,673
1995	1,942,568	1,469,915	5,617	1,475,532	213,375	10,650	1,272,807	384,702	285,059	20,161	96,355	62,530
1996	2,063,310	1,529,007	23,807	1,552,814	220,010	16,211	1,349,015	410,551	303,744	21,107	97,755	63,482
1997	2,143,129	1,614,210	-12,555	1,601,655	229,789	9,150	1,381,016	439,759	322,354	21,721	98,667	64,878
1998	2,322,827	1,724,782	24,895	1,749,677	243,630	8,141	1,514,188	477,802	330,837	23,282	99,769	66,877
1999	2,423,966	1,827,483	23,972	1,851,455	252,368	9,039	1,608,126	474,099	341,741	24,166	100,303	68,547
2000	2,628,503	1,942,719	52,224	1,994,943	265,938	7,742	1,736,747	517,006	374,750	26,020	101,020	69,724
2001	2,823,035	2,135,300	43,284	2,178,584	280,211	10,260	1,908,633	526,686	387,716	27,871	101,289	70,153
2002	2,884,889	2,227,787	7,877	2,235,664	289,564	12,568	1,958,668	514,293	411,928	28,189	102,340	70,554
2003	3,082,878	2,361,053	46,976	2,408,029	309,270	12,929	2,111,688	537,571	433,619	29,873	103,201	71,670
2004	3,260,078	2,484,963	46,733	2,531,696	324,375	19,214	2,226,535	567,764	465,779	31,283	104,211	73,586
2005	3,460,633	2,630,668	71,028	2,701,696	339,039	21,260	2,383,917	579,584	497,132	32,665	105,942	75,628
2006	3,677,740	2,800,545	25,923	2,826,468	355,818	30,336	2,500,986	645,223	531,531	34,097	107,861	78,181
2007	3,993,149	2,965,022	62,684	3,027,706	373,228	35,816	2,690,294	724,977	577,878	36,387	109,742	80,260
2008	4,299,435	3,122,934	57,148	3,180,082	391,021	44,903	2,833,964	803,801	661,670	38,635	111,282	81,962
2009	4,491,179	3,325,375	51,418	3,376,793	425,273	70,146	3,021,666	776,354	693,159	39,695	113,143	82,854
2010	4,892,074	3,582,500	64,940	3,647,440	430,810	81,318	3,297,948	829,267	764,859	42,446	115,253	84,374
2011	5,425,400	3,869,418	70,138	3,939,556	428,191	121,691	3,633,056	1,002,681	789,663	46,245	117,318	86,741
2012	6,073,513	4,190,836	173,678	4,364,514	433,351	187,289	4,118,452	1,152,143	802,918	50,515	120,233	90,196
2013	6,368,096	4,504,222	88,306	4,592,528	530,899	250,770	4,312,399	1,220,045	835,652	51,403	123,885	93,287
2014	6,906,293	4,898,179	52,495	4,950,674	580,860	298,317	4,668,131	1,360,843	877,319	54,507	126,704	95,651
2015	7,092,385	5,112,639	32,786	5,145,425	615,377	273,477	4,803,525	1,359,133	929,727	54,732	129,583	97,251
2016	7,146,452	5,113,136	17,843	5,130,979	617,022	231,388	4,745,345	1,429,256	971,851	54,388	131,397	97,163
2017	7,215,805	5,134,151	-1,614	5,132,537	635,190	233,902	4,731,249	1,486,696	997,860	54,606	132,142	96,460
2018	7,278,884	7,246,476	32,408	5,130,246	623,411	280,587	4,787,422	1,479,511	1,011,951	56,743	128,279	92,989
2019	7,511,736	7,484,291	27,445	5,266,826	629,853	306,069	4,943,042	1,496,445	1,072,249	58,254	128,949	94,128

Personal Income and Employment by Area: Blacksburg-Christiansburg, VA

(Thousands of dollars, except as noted.)

Year	Personal income, total	Derivation of personal income									Per capita personal income (dollars)	Population (persons)	Total employment
		Earnings by place of work			Less: Contributions for government social insurance	Plus: Adjustment for residence	Equals: Net earnings by place of residence	Plus: Dividends, interest, and rent	Plus: Personal current transfer receipts				
		Nonfarm	Farm	Total									
1970	335,464	291,005	3,517	294,522	18,674	-9,625	266,223	39,245	29,996		2,916	115,045	49,602
1971	359,393	303,774	3,480	307,254	20,368	-7,283	279,603	43,842	35,948		3,045	118,015	49,332
1972	405,115	342,380	5,497	347,877	24,187	-7,696	315,994	48,764	40,357		3,348	120,995	51,367
1973	463,509	389,006	5,989	394,995	31,566	-6,493	356,936	57,254	49,319		3,719	124,637	54,208
1974	513,456	423,545	3,673	427,218	35,812	-4,008	387,398	66,691	59,367		3,969	129,374	55,589
1975	566,031	445,318	2,466	447,784	36,957	-778	410,049	75,832	80,150		4,270	132,569	54,664
1976	632,223	497,462	4,474	501,936	41,894	265	460,307	83,946	87,970		4,704	134,388	56,066
1977	708,570	564,943	3,143	568,086	47,710	48	520,424	94,772	93,374		5,168	137,116	58,455
1978	808,838	646,087	5,140	651,227	55,965	671	595,933	109,632	103,273		5,779	139,973	61,737
1979	906,550	715,446	7,963	723,409	64,393	-520	658,496	127,474	120,580		6,413	141,368	63,660
1980	1,017,435	773,887	7,021	780,908	70,302	3,425	714,031	159,380	144,024		7,174	141,822	64,487
1981	1,118,359	832,596	4,556	837,152	81,279	4,407	760,280	191,801	166,278		7,794	143,481	63,247
1982	1,205,480	880,845	2,145	882,990	87,722	2,377	797,645	226,947	180,888		8,379	143,876	62,976
1983	1,319,131	975,062	5,436	980,498	98,504	-4,187	877,807	245,167	196,157		9,164	143,941	64,508
1984	1,473,420	1,111,926	6,653	1,118,579	115,917	-11,647	991,015	277,943	204,462		10,148	145,187	68,180
1985	1,575,086	1,198,865	5,447	1,204,312	126,974	-15,989	1,061,349	296,623	217,114		10,794	145,916	70,289
1986	1,674,747	1,280,380	7,149	1,287,529	139,607	-20,034	1,127,888	318,316	228,543		11,389	147,046	71,382
1987	1,788,695	1,388,395	16,600	1,404,995	149,787	-26,304	1,228,904	327,677	232,114		12,076	148,117	73,880
1988	1,932,312	1,519,525	18,940	1,538,465	168,842	-36,753	1,332,870	353,035	246,407		12,852	150,354	76,291
1989	2,070,289	1,599,220	21,935	1,621,155	177,761	-42,234	1,401,160	402,513	266,616		13,666	151,489	77,183
1990	2,149,409	1,649,935	22,893	1,672,828	183,297	-41,182	1,448,349	408,743	292,317		14,033	153,166	77,391
1991	2,180,806	1,634,178	18,421	1,652,599	183,662	-32,522	1,436,415	427,883	316,508		14,167	153,932	75,259
1992	2,298,730	1,725,405	16,396	1,741,801	192,718	-33,564	1,515,519	433,065	350,146		14,813	155,188	75,068
1993	2,390,952	1,795,786	13,579	1,809,365	200,436	-31,574	1,577,355	446,600	366,997		15,317	156,096	76,456
1994	2,529,809	1,911,175	13,357	1,924,532	211,220	-32,275	1,681,037	464,067	384,705		16,051	157,612	78,109
1995	2,662,916	1,972,832	11,046	1,983,878	217,257	-26,548	1,740,073	508,267	414,576		16,813	158,380	80,647
1996	2,754,298	2,029,878	9,239	2,039,117	221,187	-24,673	1,793,257	526,125	434,916		17,305	159,164	81,325
1997	2,948,493	2,180,732	7,357	2,188,089	235,847	-27,568	1,924,674	572,699	451,120		18,403	160,219	82,437
1998	3,101,442	2,311,681	9,794	2,321,475	245,429	-24,442	2,051,604	581,851	467,987		19,092	162,444	82,885
1999	3,299,235	2,513,452	8,746	2,522,198	265,571	-34,325	2,222,302	589,014	487,919		20,071	164,379	86,761
2000	3,498,252	2,617,483	18,701	2,636,184	274,594	-25,047	2,336,543	642,934	518,775		21,142	165,462	87,727
2001	3,662,525	2,707,093	14,554	2,721,647	297,147	-23,122	2,401,378	683,849	577,298		21,874	167,434	86,106
2002	3,780,627	2,841,197	16,952	2,858,149	312,288	-24,386	2,521,475	655,943	603,209		22,571	167,498	86,700
2003	3,974,906	2,985,333	10,162	2,995,495	324,783	-35,036	2,635,676	682,729	656,501		23,622	168,270	87,440
2004	4,181,758	3,136,738	14,157	3,150,895	344,615	-36,531	2,769,749	715,208	696,801		24,741	169,018	88,203
2005	4,410,377	3,294,735	14,256	3,308,991	369,836	-40,162	2,898,993	754,206	757,178		25,793	170,990	89,674
2006	4,673,417	3,432,423	2,770	3,435,193	390,677	-44,994	2,999,522	849,268	824,627		27,008	173,039	90,426
2007	4,924,683	3,548,695	-1,103	3,547,592	404,103	-30,690	3,112,799	930,289	881,595		28,156	174,908	91,426
2008	5,095,079	3,518,344	1,364	3,519,708	408,400	-8,200	3,103,108	986,955	1,005,016		28,892	176,348	91,433
2009	5,125,939	3,438,224	3,756	3,441,980	401,061	6,355	3,047,274	1,006,742	1,071,923		28,873	177,535	88,748
2010	5,156,565	3,461,054	3,513	3,464,567	402,191	5,051	3,067,427	935,306	1,153,832		28,883	178,530	86,912
2011	5,415,787	3,555,887	10,460	3,566,347	372,088	-3,968	3,190,291	1,058,048	1,167,448		30,264	178,949	88,420
2012	5,673,530	3,740,875	12,061	3,752,936	388,499	-11,806	3,352,631	1,149,139	1,171,760		31,595	179,572	89,793
2013	5,730,837	3,866,763	14,022	3,880,785	448,412	-18,647	3,413,726	1,116,026	1,201,085		31,686	180,862	90,815
2014	6,040,268	4,048,582	15,244	4,063,826	467,314	-35,155	3,561,357	1,226,560	1,252,351		33,306	181,357	91,832
2015	6,352,381	4,271,272	13,408	4,284,680	486,905	-26,661	3,771,114	1,283,257	1,298,010		35,006	181,464	93,435
2016	6,456,231	4,299,936	-281	4,299,655	492,676	-35,889	3,771,090	1,340,409	1,344,732		35,350	182,635	93,808
2017	6,698,251	4,447,626	-8,170	4,439,456	510,483	-43,168	3,885,805	1,407,698	1,404,748		36,604	182,993	94,031
2018	6,435,256	6,435,075	181	4,498,483	517,712	-249,230	3,731,541	1,414,601	1,289,114		38,421	167,492	88,949
2019	6,620,300	6,617,122	3,178	4,642,485	535,034	-265,772	3,841,679	1,432,200	1,346,421		39,517	167,531	90,266

Personal Income and Employment by Area: Bloomington, IL

(Thousands of dollars, except as noted.)

					Derivation of personal income							
		Earnings by place of work			Less: Contributions for government social insurance	Plus: Adjustment for residence	Equals: Net earnings by place of residence	Plus: Dividends, interest, and rent	Plus: Personal current transfer receipts	Per capita personal income (dollars)	Population (persons)	Total employment
Year	Personal income, total	Nonfarm	Farm	Total								
1970	490,812	365,452	29,630	395,082	23,520	5,779	377,341	77,444	36,027	4,022	122,030	55,784
1971	546,799	403,982	39,221	443,203	26,753	5,818	422,268	83,591	40,940	4,376	124,949	57,171
1972	592,522	448,834	28,618	477,452	31,363	5,640	451,729	94,830	45,963	4,544	130,387	59,551
1973	703,300	497,947	71,492	569,439	40,161	6,581	535,859	113,892	53,549	5,336	131,804	62,641
1974	783,554	552,977	79,086	632,063	46,806	8,346	593,603	128,182	61,769	5,921	132,331	64,356
1975	917,951	617,865	115,397	733,262	50,512	9,068	691,818	146,152	79,981	6,973	131,642	64,245
1976	980,657	693,636	92,531	786,167	57,886	7,121	735,402	157,438	87,817	7,366	133,130	65,859
1977	1,075,006	785,019	85,863	870,882	66,262	651	805,271	177,414	92,321	7,977	134,758	68,361
1978	1,146,883	877,551	50,209	927,760	75,943	1,522	853,339	194,106	99,438	8,453	135,673	71,369
1979	1,288,875	990,143	67,792	1,057,935	90,113	-9,409	958,413	220,170	110,292	9,459	136,266	73,714
1980	1,369,395	1,064,989	13,240	1,078,229	96,731	-10,836	970,662	261,852	136,881	9,961	137,480	72,290
1981	1,567,817	1,175,991	53,382	1,229,373	115,975	-19,426	1,093,972	315,649	158,196	11,350	138,131	73,541
1982	1,676,607	1,239,559	31,970	1,271,529	123,132	-31,853	1,116,544	384,083	175,980	12,128	138,240	73,521
1983	1,711,983	1,338,115	-28,814	1,309,301	133,345	-52,032	1,123,924	398,659	189,400	12,290	139,295	74,776
1984	1,930,840	1,517,486	48,744	1,566,230	158,542	-111,947	1,295,741	440,778	194,321	13,804	139,879	77,336
1985	2,015,095	1,616,241	63,185	1,679,426	171,195	-137,555	1,370,676	437,083	207,336	14,357	140,360	76,738
1986	2,041,708	1,506,603	56,875	1,563,478	156,364	-36,109	1,371,005	455,741	214,962	14,607	139,774	74,708
1987	2,125,397	1,596,971	44,850	1,641,821	163,611	-20,234	1,457,976	445,108	222,313	15,068	141,058	76,745
1988	2,270,890	1,799,682	21,887	1,821,569	188,934	-53,085	1,579,550	456,768	234,572	15,920	142,641	81,146
1989	2,556,281	2,005,130	60,313	2,065,443	213,136	-78,657	1,773,650	535,988	246,643	17,731	144,167	85,475
1990	2,733,280	2,225,880	58,264	2,284,144	231,699	-100,422	1,952,023	514,462	266,795	18,687	146,269	87,860
1991	2,805,644	2,332,476	19,548	2,352,024	249,665	-110,159	1,992,200	528,180	285,264	18,853	148,813	89,538
1992	3,085,816	2,565,217	55,349	2,620,566	270,416	-129,074	2,221,076	546,041	318,699	20,453	150,875	92,071
1993	3,195,007	2,686,839	33,397	2,720,236	284,835	-135,751	2,299,650	561,296	334,061	20,807	153,557	93,063
1994	3,465,374	2,938,231	74,024	3,012,255	313,951	-155,033	2,543,271	580,502	341,601	22,290	155,467	96,956
1995	3,635,438	3,137,017	-3,723	3,133,294	332,327	-175,429	2,625,538	642,522	367,378	23,043	157,769	99,502
1996	3,912,016	3,266,741	91,253	3,357,994	340,464	-182,512	2,835,018	686,924	390,074	24,589	159,099	101,224
1997	4,118,727	3,441,494	77,821	3,519,315	354,331	-191,447	2,973,537	741,837	403,353	25,566	161,099	104,868
1998	4,375,484	3,744,740	24,845	3,769,585	380,179	-224,694	3,164,712	789,429	421,343	26,793	163,307	110,008
1999	4,709,538	4,134,758	28,115	4,162,873	410,346	-260,554	3,491,973	783,481	434,084	28,388	165,899	115,151
2000	4,996,358	4,341,858	65,645	4,407,503	425,687	-278,939	3,702,877	833,855	459,626	29,803	167,644	116,701
2001	5,391,800	4,751,762	68,513	4,820,275	470,155	-303,397	4,046,723	850,453	494,624	31,809	169,505	116,888
2002	5,549,622	5,021,185	57,573	5,078,758	496,306	-328,218	4,254,234	766,527	528,861	32,161	172,555	117,842
2003	5,732,674	5,178,551	70,346	5,248,897	513,413	-348,122	4,387,362	794,038	551,274	32,856	174,481	117,309
2004	5,935,689	5,254,004	136,982	5,390,986	532,659	-359,346	4,498,981	855,350	581,358	33,770	175,767	116,344
2005	5,997,681	5,362,733	64,896	5,427,629	543,150	-340,966	4,543,513	811,035	643,133	33,882	177,015	117,209
2006	6,483,024	5,722,159	89,331	5,811,490	575,677	-355,378	4,880,435	932,490	670,099	36,074	179,717	118,096
2007	6,792,230	5,840,742	156,329	5,997,071	592,212	-337,547	5,067,312	991,569	733,349	37,327	181,965	120,009
2008	7,183,664	6,086,487	212,768	6,299,255	622,307	-363,757	5,313,191	1,041,602	828,871	39,136	183,558	121,304
2009	7,190,220	6,128,550	125,100	6,253,650	624,703	-395,315	5,233,632	1,038,600	917,988	38,810	185,265	119,571
2010	7,451,670	6,353,012	129,202	6,482,214	638,567	-433,487	5,410,160	1,026,334	1,015,176	39,977	186,398	118,982
2011	7,918,148	6,556,088	258,715	6,814,803	588,160	-440,083	5,786,560	1,133,458	998,130	42,270	187,325	119,595
2012	8,067,360	6,743,256	166,606	6,909,862	610,386	-448,317	5,851,159	1,220,959	995,242	42,681	189,016	120,570
2013	8,443,321	6,963,716	372,269	7,335,985	708,982	-457,024	6,169,979	1,240,230	1,033,112	44,180	191,110	118,916
2014	8,395,873	6,901,364	183,649	7,085,013	699,229	-404,228	5,981,556	1,351,925	1,062,392	44,202	189,944	118,092
2015	8,664,937	7,079,757	59,998	7,139,755	708,905	-304,021	6,126,829	1,410,963	1,127,145	45,869	188,905	120,004
2016	8,858,867	7,097,970	171,614	7,269,584	711,928	-313,424	6,244,232	1,462,613	1,152,022	46,910	188,847	118,795
2017	8,912,850	7,141,299	82,646	7,223,945	712,581	-302,525	6,208,839	1,522,056	1,181,955	47,350	188,232	119,011
2018	8,488,859	8,378,529	110,330	7,052,598	695,881	-379,065	5,977,652	1,407,361	1,103,846	49,236	172,410	111,568
2019	8,507,653	8,444,608	63,045	6,944,331	691,317	-334,431	5,918,583	1,422,255	1,166,815	49,602	171,517	111,472

Personal Income and Employment by Area: Bloomington, IN

(Thousands of dollars, except as noted.)

Year	Personal income, total	Earnings by place of work			Less: Contributions for government social insurance	Plus: Adjustment for residence	Equals: Net earnings by place of residence	Plus: Dividends, interest, and rent	Plus: Personal current transfer receipts	Per capita personal income (dollars)	Population (persons)	Total employment
		Nonfarm	Farm	Total								
1970	295,962	245,530	1,772	247,302	16,732	-2,338	228,232	46,647	21,083	3,031	97,656	40,115
1971	339,662	284,719	2,718	287,437	20,166	-4,207	263,064	52,579	24,019	3,406	99,712	43,719
1972	372,513	307,737	3,263	311,000	23,115	-682	287,203	57,952	27,358	3,597	103,553	45,422
1973	417,304	339,642	6,908	346,550	29,379	1,126	318,297	65,496	33,511	4,001	104,311	47,027
1974	449,449	357,808	4,027	361,835	32,425	4,273	333,683	75,322	40,444	4,231	106,218	46,825
1975	486,091	360,750	3,663	364,413	32,416	12,169	344,166	86,349	55,576	4,676	103,965	44,564
1976	551,508	419,148	5,377	424,525	37,758	13,308	400,075	95,585	55,848	5,206	105,944	47,509
1977	620,179	471,357	3,593	474,950	42,021	18,067	450,996	108,966	60,217	5,647	109,821	48,817
1978	707,249	535,610	3,150	538,760	49,020	24,014	513,754	125,161	68,334	6,302	112,226	50,475
1979	778,383	578,870	2,958	581,828	54,893	33,960	560,895	138,787	78,701	6,886	113,041	51,520
1980	875,590	634,954	-424	634,530	59,704	37,379	612,205	171,123	92,262	7,610	115,057	53,462
1981	983,597	700,631	3	700,634	71,211	38,864	668,287	210,018	105,292	8,440	116,537	54,013
1982	1,049,632	737,043	27	737,070	76,225	36,206	697,051	235,380	117,201	8,932	117,520	54,716
1983	1,124,867	802,262	-6,533	795,729	82,352	31,933	745,310	253,534	126,023	9,530	118,037	55,528
1984	1,235,117	880,014	-150	879,864	91,264	36,295	824,895	277,300	132,922	10,472	117,945	57,620
1985	1,322,254	947,634	-1,712	945,922	99,460	38,674	885,136	295,799	141,319	11,192	118,146	59,678
1986	1,432,339	1,045,555	-2,662	1,042,893	110,086	35,283	968,090	317,806	146,443	12,032	119,043	61,907
1987	1,539,923	1,151,256	-1,707	1,149,549	118,969	28,128	1,058,708	326,946	154,269	12,780	120,497	65,078
1988	1,662,395	1,251,405	-4,104	1,247,301	135,487	25,857	1,137,671	358,003	166,721	13,614	122,111	67,474
1989	1,831,845	1,353,762	1,960	1,355,722	146,849	26,440	1,235,313	412,209	184,323	14,672	124,856	68,835
1990	1,963,426	1,450,795	6	1,450,801	161,910	28,689	1,317,580	443,718	202,128	15,488	126,773	70,276
1991	2,070,731	1,543,240	-1,831	1,541,409	173,933	27,578	1,395,054	450,575	225,102	16,180	127,983	70,628
1992	2,233,800	1,674,679	2,602	1,677,281	187,554	19,265	1,508,992	472,388	252,420	17,166	130,131	72,264
1993	2,333,948	1,762,577	2,007	1,764,584	198,452	7,109	1,573,241	492,607	268,100	17,629	132,395	74,141
1994	2,448,178	1,856,263	2,090	1,858,353	213,630	-9,161	1,635,562	534,252	278,364	18,178	134,678	75,988
1995	2,579,856	1,950,252	50	1,950,302	224,497	-13,051	1,712,754	578,573	288,529	18,931	136,275	78,167
1996	2,741,973	2,061,017	2,885	2,063,902	235,628	-23,395	1,804,879	621,432	315,662	19,899	137,794	80,732
1997	2,919,063	2,208,500	2,638	2,211,138	251,722	-36,313	1,923,103	666,265	329,695	20,960	139,271	82,095
1998	3,106,356	2,343,880	-566	2,343,314	262,697	-43,185	2,037,432	706,910	362,014	22,105	140,527	82,583
1999	3,253,156	2,480,930	-1,511	2,479,419	275,245	-51,496	2,152,678	712,212	388,266	22,947	141,770	84,309
2000	3,464,743	2,633,042	792	2,633,834	289,429	-61,788	2,282,617	765,083	417,043	24,278	142,709	85,477
2001	3,530,915	2,639,104	1,579	2,640,683	285,517	-67,074	2,288,092	784,809	458,014	24,580	143,650	86,472
2002	3,587,320	2,744,548	-297	2,744,251	296,646	-73,285	2,374,320	729,377	483,623	24,790	144,707	86,455
2003	3,753,068	2,890,934	3,576	2,894,510	314,116	-90,637	2,489,757	758,042	505,269	25,560	146,835	88,861
2004	3,967,165	3,004,633	7,804	3,012,437	327,716	-98,686	2,586,035	846,693	534,437	26,706	148,549	90,050
2005	4,096,747	3,113,808	5,395	3,119,203	345,004	-100,176	2,674,023	837,656	585,068	27,294	150,096	90,907
2006	4,363,935	3,230,539	2,820	3,233,359	361,448	-103,980	2,767,931	958,653	637,351	28,607	152,548	92,092
2007	4,538,828	3,339,134	4,774	3,343,908	377,803	-113,037	2,853,068	1,013,043	672,717	29,406	154,352	94,409
2008	4,837,887	3,445,614	7,726	3,453,340	391,779	-121,911	2,939,650	1,111,744	786,493	30,980	156,164	94,475
2009	4,776,665	3,470,103	8,139	3,478,242	395,412	-116,596	2,966,234	960,770	849,661	30,263	157,840	94,200
2010	4,896,312	3,514,359	10,354	3,524,713	395,372	-104,375	3,024,966	942,130	929,216	30,586	160,086	93,020
2011	5,169,331	3,648,620	12,846	3,661,466	358,388	-93,581	3,209,497	1,027,021	932,813	31,988	161,603	93,309
2012	5,423,551	3,807,294	2,925	3,810,219	370,821	-77,599	3,361,799	1,099,949	961,803	33,344	162,653	92,926
2013	5,432,266	3,818,366	23,134	3,841,500	428,201	-74,061	3,339,238	1,129,718	963,310	33,319	163,039	92,762
2014	5,681,931	3,973,291	6,913	3,980,204	443,331	-81,035	3,455,838	1,187,972	1,038,121	34,554	164,434	93,834
2015	5,998,235	4,189,350	11,481	4,200,831	467,349	-95,720	3,637,762	1,262,550	1,097,923	36,341	165,056	94,433
2016	6,304,604	4,410,252	17,673	4,427,925	481,331	-85,600	3,860,994	1,309,763	1,133,847	37,840	166,614	95,304
2017	6,655,664	4,694,018	5,047	4,699,065	506,673	-89,047	4,103,345	1,381,492	1,170,827	39,658	167,825	96,462
2018	7,041,016	7,038,443	2,573	4,871,417	526,788	-80,051	4,264,578	1,559,034	1,217,404	41,888	168,092	98,930
2019	7,346,430	7,345,589	841	5,108,257	554,907	-84,849	4,468,501	1,585,739	1,292,190	43,411	169,230	101,124

Personal Income and Employment by Area: Bloomsberg-Berwick, PA

(Thousands of dollars, except as noted.)

Year	Personal income, total	Earnings by place of work — Nonfarm	Farm	Total	Less: Contributions for government social insurance	Plus: Adjustment for residence	Equals: Net earnings by place of residence	Plus: Dividends, interest, and rent	Plus: Personal current transfer receipts	Per capita personal income (dollars)	Population (persons)	Total employment
1970	250,744	206,101	6,163	212,264	15,627	-11,192	185,445	30,231	35,068	3,488	71,882	33,766
1971	267,673	218,976	4,975	223,951	17,361	-8,829	197,761	32,696	37,216	3,655	73,233	33,943
1972	303,979	249,270	4,873	254,143	20,463	-9,182	224,498	36,461	43,020	4,080	74,511	35,339
1973	344,214	282,155	7,632	289,787	26,299	-9,585	253,903	42,002	48,309	4,577	75,213	37,183
1974	382,390	313,792	7,241	321,033	30,729	-14,991	275,313	48,051	59,026	5,021	76,162	37,830
1975	412,614	309,436	7,075	316,511	28,978	-5,749	281,784	52,710	78,120	5,364	76,926	35,596
1976	450,624	332,725	8,236	340,961	31,763	-3,376	305,822	56,924	87,878	5,847	77,069	35,569
1977	489,756	369,040	7,012	376,052	35,346	-5,216	335,490	64,086	90,180	6,323	77,452	36,182
1978	546,098	421,502	7,769	429,271	41,398	-8,244	379,629	70,805	95,664	7,020	77,789	37,911
1979	611,134	476,008	10,442	486,450	48,245	-14,956	423,249	78,668	109,217	7,796	78,394	38,953
1980	659,398	502,503	5,215	507,718	51,415	-19,705	436,598	96,977	125,823	8,369	78,787	38,905
1981	734,265	542,114	9,826	551,940	59,321	-20,012	472,607	118,682	142,976	9,270	79,211	38,916
1982	785,807	559,300	8,196	567,496	61,708	-20,217	485,571	138,316	161,920	9,919	79,223	37,763
1983	836,923	607,619	-1,411	606,208	67,718	-28,282	510,208	153,426	173,289	10,504	79,674	38,203
1984	902,402	663,927	7,281	671,208	76,996	-37,327	556,885	169,843	175,674	11,403	79,135	39,057
1985	965,954	725,646	8,420	734,066	85,560	-48,209	600,297	183,880	181,777	12,277	78,679	40,396
1986	1,015,938	758,597	6,188	764,785	89,567	-46,058	629,160	195,094	191,684	12,904	78,729	40,797
1987	1,072,407	814,135	7,788	821,923	94,966	-49,643	677,314	200,317	194,776	13,623	78,718	41,605
1988	1,156,290	887,567	9,295	896,862	106,285	-51,226	739,351	211,158	205,781	14,554	79,446	43,282
1989	1,262,724	952,530	12,390	964,920	112,265	-57,291	795,364	241,108	226,252	15,740	80,226	44,433
1990	1,318,551	1,018,861	11,032	1,029,893	120,234	-68,356	841,303	242,909	234,339	16,256	81,113	45,090
1991	1,386,457	1,063,339	3,361	1,066,700	126,958	-77,757	861,985	251,012	273,460	16,977	81,669	44,976
1992	1,474,922	1,154,012	18,069	1,172,081	137,573	-100,202	934,306	253,821	286,795	17,904	82,381	45,346
1993	1,527,400	1,211,594	15,083	1,226,677	146,651	-111,035	968,991	261,758	296,651	18,446	82,802	45,742
1994	1,566,890	1,291,421	15,604	1,307,025	159,541	-134,793	1,012,691	264,464	289,735	18,924	82,801	46,889
1995	1,618,697	1,256,991	5,784	1,262,775	154,393	-83,180	1,025,202	290,669	302,826	19,500	83,012	46,421
1996	1,676,366	1,263,296	15,878	1,279,174	151,946	-66,384	1,060,844	294,246	321,276	20,194	83,013	45,448
1997	1,731,032	1,347,040	14,226	1,361,266	161,202	-108,159	1,091,905	311,796	327,331	20,877	82,914	45,712
1998	1,812,804	1,480,203	12,366	1,492,569	173,093	-163,352	1,156,124	331,400	325,280	21,941	82,623	47,654
1999	1,855,526	1,546,587	8,392	1,554,979	177,329	-174,267	1,203,383	314,289	337,854	22,505	82,449	47,905
2000	1,981,026	1,593,669	15,455	1,609,124	180,255	-141,578	1,287,291	332,524	361,211	24,097	82,211	48,593
2001	2,056,483	1,596,968	10,948	1,607,916	180,680	-102,868	1,324,368	343,378	388,737	24,899	82,592	46,782
2002	2,180,503	1,707,785	5,972	1,713,757	190,816	-105,420	1,417,521	344,456	418,526	26,322	82,838	47,456
2003	2,273,226	1,743,993	15,519	1,759,512	192,731	-76,591	1,490,190	342,225	440,811	27,309	83,240	47,107
2004	2,351,485	1,865,083	23,529	1,888,612	205,739	-124,750	1,558,123	333,442	459,920	28,158	83,511	48,150
2005	2,419,649	1,955,460	17,690	1,973,150	218,402	-147,109	1,607,639	317,250	494,760	28,902	83,718	49,459
2006	2,540,335	2,065,598	16,228	2,081,826	230,710	-167,148	1,683,968	340,825	515,542	30,244	83,996	50,639
2007	2,718,368	2,206,108	14,810	2,220,918	247,073	-193,478	1,780,367	384,271	553,730	32,245	84,303	51,636
2008	2,854,662	2,280,346	10,388	2,290,734	258,398	-230,911	1,801,425	429,896	623,341	33,689	84,735	52,004
2009	2,831,995	2,285,844	8,307	2,294,151	261,015	-302,000	1,731,136	414,210	686,649	33,167	85,385	51,230
2010	2,976,368	2,401,698	16,281	2,417,979	271,973	-288,590	1,857,416	411,354	707,598	34,748	85,655	51,591
2011	3,135,605	2,540,737	14,592	2,555,329	254,857	-335,772	1,964,700	448,971	721,934	36,710	85,415	52,582
2012	3,221,575	2,623,778	22,042	2,645,820	260,633	-354,612	2,030,575	473,283	717,717	37,698	85,458	53,550
2013	3,277,300	2,781,205	19,131	2,800,336	307,652	-418,324	2,074,360	473,041	729,899	38,303	85,563	54,480
2014	3,342,277	2,726,967	14,771	2,741,738	308,678	-354,915	2,078,145	503,313	760,819	39,098	85,484	53,134
2015	3,455,353	2,824,203	4,651	2,828,854	319,360	-371,263	2,138,231	527,229	789,893	40,675	84,950	52,787
2016	3,545,038	2,877,499	-6,996	2,870,503	326,038	-347,698	2,196,767	529,246	819,025	42,012	84,382	52,777
2017	3,663,705	2,984,458	-2,505	2,981,953	344,072	-354,079	2,283,802	553,636	826,267	43,510	84,204	53,192
2018	3,807,656	3,799,900	7,756	3,073,199	348,321	-374,044	2,350,834	587,956	868,866	45,625	83,455	52,833
2019	3,918,174	3,902,908	15,266	3,178,641	358,100	-411,316	2,409,225	600,050	908,899	47,097	83,194	53,417

Personal Income and Employment by Area: Boise City, ID

(Thousands of dollars, except as noted.)

Year	Personal income, total	Earnings by place of work			Less: Contributions for government social insurance	Plus: Adjustment for residence	Equals: Net earnings by place of residence	Plus: Dividends, interest, and rent	Plus: Personal current transfer receipts	Per capita personal income (dollars)	Population (persons)	Total employment
		Nonfarm	Farm	Total								
1970	779,735	574,503	42,703	617,206	40,945	4,147	580,408	133,624	65,703	4,042	192,885	93,530
1971	875,459	645,302	42,222	687,524	47,174	4,019	644,369	153,300	77,790	4,322	202,549	97,869
1972	996,230	744,039	49,919	793,958	57,213	3,496	740,241	167,099	88,890	4,709	211,579	103,513
1973	1,146,673	849,734	74,955	924,689	76,192	3,112	851,609	192,729	102,335	5,214	219,916	110,066
1974	1,319,146	965,328	87,151	1,052,479	88,942	3,533	967,070	226,367	125,709	5,733	230,081	114,790
1975	1,511,201	1,118,116	64,001	1,182,117	101,179	6,646	1,087,584	269,165	154,452	6,382	236,798	119,885
1976	1,703,255	1,302,391	52,111	1,354,502	120,033	7,997	1,242,466	292,150	168,639	6,915	246,322	128,647
1977	1,919,604	1,490,477	39,297	1,529,774	138,147	10,256	1,401,883	337,244	180,477	7,499	255,984	136,175
1978	2,225,440	1,746,071	47,195	1,793,266	163,952	12,028	1,641,342	384,840	199,258	8,330	267,147	146,795
1979	2,448,845	1,913,838	42,590	1,956,428	190,026	15,110	1,781,512	430,112	237,221	8,874	275,953	150,083
1980	2,715,190	2,045,709	62,521	2,108,230	205,087	15,438	1,918,581	508,015	288,594	9,650	281,376	148,453
1981	2,992,865	2,207,009	64,806	2,271,815	239,179	18,793	2,051,429	611,326	330,110	10,468	285,918	146,355
1982	3,202,197	2,280,504	66,400	2,346,904	252,351	15,708	2,110,261	716,249	375,687	11,066	289,363	145,330
1983	3,471,725	2,449,761	93,734	2,543,495	271,882	16,562	2,288,175	781,503	402,047	11,874	292,391	148,415
1984	3,767,611	2,701,653	84,064	2,785,717	307,614	14,476	2,492,579	859,873	415,159	12,683	297,051	154,103
1985	4,037,683	2,886,607	76,445	2,963,052	334,317	12,063	2,640,798	950,209	446,676	13,408	301,145	156,609
1986	4,163,993	2,979,838	77,450	3,057,288	347,902	12,836	2,722,222	969,845	471,926	13,754	302,755	158,446
1987	4,380,898	3,175,513	89,486	3,264,999	361,845	12,405	2,915,559	977,973	487,366	14,424	303,727	163,218
1988	4,809,880	3,561,184	100,905	3,662,089	422,204	9,423	3,249,308	1,039,163	521,409	15,695	306,455	172,597
1989	5,292,858	3,897,915	135,821	4,033,736	468,796	6,977	3,571,917	1,155,656	565,285	16,912	312,962	181,032
1990	5,757,151	4,272,798	145,370	4,418,168	543,905	11,592	3,885,855	1,263,559	607,737	17,862	322,316	190,433
1991	6,186,865	4,654,453	149,546	4,803,999	605,818	9,628	4,207,809	1,294,068	684,988	18,447	335,378	198,902
1992	6,934,761	5,296,795	143,780	5,440,575	674,563	9,581	4,775,593	1,390,227	768,941	19,948	347,646	207,984
1993	7,750,940	5,953,007	192,678	6,145,685	758,923	5,427	5,392,189	1,530,575	828,176	21,287	364,123	220,250
1994	8,604,211	6,676,807	134,865	6,811,672	855,552	10,394	5,966,514	1,756,729	880,968	22,633	380,160	236,337
1995	9,363,965	7,217,877	132,566	7,350,443	931,138	15,141	6,434,446	1,956,699	972,820	23,683	395,382	245,882
1996	9,900,474	7,562,474	135,754	7,698,228	957,172	15,618	6,756,674	2,095,081	1,048,719	24,179	409,471	255,743
1997	10,425,733	7,949,378	121,237	8,070,615	999,287	19,051	7,090,379	2,245,210	1,090,144	24,659	422,797	266,539
1998	11,314,032	8,679,243	155,169	8,834,412	1,075,034	20,059	7,779,437	2,356,852	1,177,743	25,806	438,421	279,851
1999	12,339,719	9,626,878	150,283	9,777,161	1,159,224	23,671	8,641,608	2,435,942	1,262,169	27,250	452,837	287,846
2000	13,819,448	10,991,436	147,349	11,138,785	1,317,635	25,516	9,846,666	2,604,725	1,368,057	29,465	469,017	304,508
2001	14,126,089	11,030,879	181,107	11,211,986	1,326,071	30,618	9,916,533	2,683,865	1,525,691	29,061	486,078	311,229
2002	14,727,711	11,404,835	168,315	11,573,150	1,343,255	42,516	10,272,411	2,764,581	1,690,719	29,456	499,994	313,222
2003	15,234,262	11,692,889	139,926	11,832,815	1,388,577	45,796	10,490,034	2,933,693	1,810,535	29,726	512,491	317,239
2004	16,434,569	12,452,373	215,675	12,668,048	1,490,680	46,305	11,223,673	3,273,935	1,936,961	31,246	525,975	328,238
2005	17,598,167	13,348,298	191,298	13,539,596	1,626,095	64,235	11,977,736	3,495,643	2,124,788	32,173	546,980	346,498
2006	19,775,574	14,889,873	166,057	15,055,930	1,833,479	33,384	13,255,835	4,211,657	2,308,082	34,659	570,583	367,714
2007	20,753,722	15,367,463	242,992	15,610,455	1,897,889	57,237	13,769,803	4,437,593	2,546,326	35,156	590,330	379,138
2008	20,796,244	15,057,639	226,996	15,284,635	1,876,568	84,701	13,492,768	4,245,925	3,057,551	34,476	603,218	373,367
2009	20,111,379	14,589,960	102,349	14,692,309	1,820,750	159,454	13,031,013	3,632,453	3,447,913	32,897	611,341	353,830
2010	20,717,211	14,672,680	220,819	14,893,499	1,898,951	193,696	13,188,244	3,704,539	3,824,428	33,524	617,980	350,361
2011	21,836,207	15,069,427	297,563	15,366,990	1,746,172	238,752	13,859,570	4,143,844	3,832,793	34,807	627,349	356,775
2012	23,253,973	15,599,652	317,653	15,917,305	1,794,041	290,823	14,414,087	4,915,631	3,924,255	36,485	637,354	361,944
2013	24,359,160	16,948,481	323,942	17,272,423	2,106,846	326,072	15,491,649	4,774,069	4,093,442	37,525	649,140	372,424
2014	26,118,012	18,115,845	354,739	18,470,584	2,218,747	343,844	16,595,681	5,239,427	4,282,904	39,416	662,625	383,079
2015	27,893,531	19,259,004	335,252	19,594,256	2,333,782	312,357	17,572,831	5,794,399	4,526,301	41,366	674,310	395,687
2016	29,158,941	20,222,433	292,125	20,514,558	2,460,196	317,255	18,371,617	6,038,596	4,748,728	42,210	690,810	410,905
2017	30,953,634	21,648,106	297,917	21,946,023	2,627,270	303,161	19,621,914	6,371,091	4,960,629	43,606	709,845	424,199
2018	34,014,138	33,757,748	256,390	23,722,281	2,852,265	312,915	21,182,931	7,421,071	5,410,136	46,664	728,911	448,734
2019	35,872,855	35,564,612	308,243	25,338,164	3,045,547	305,648	22,598,265	7,483,457	5,791,133	47,881	749,202	465,949

Personal Income and Employment by Area: Boston-Cambridge-Newton, MA-NH

(Thousands of dollars, except as noted.)

Year	Personal income, total	Earnings by place of work			Less: Contributions for government social insurance	Plus: Adjustment for residence	Equals: Net earnings by place of residence	Plus: Dividends, interest, and rent	Plus: Personal current transfer receipts	Per capita personal income (dollars)	Population (persons)	Total employment
		Nonfarm	Farm	Total								
1970	18,740,176	15,238,914	28,963	15,267,877	969,109	-250,943	14,047,825	2,956,834	1,735,517	4,770	3,928,508	1,906,572
1971	20,020,412	16,180,918	27,487	16,208,405	1,061,528	-306,074	14,840,803	3,132,887	2,046,722	5,064	3,953,760	1,880,515
1972	21,594,282	17,579,606	29,773	17,609,379	1,211,526	-373,090	16,024,763	3,322,375	2,247,144	5,425	3,980,347	1,918,584
1973	23,369,418	19,146,754	32,016	19,178,770	1,515,854	-461,314	17,201,602	3,645,133	2,522,683	5,867	3,982,918	1,976,758
1974	25,216,971	20,325,075	30,843	20,355,918	1,663,210	-547,831	18,144,877	4,065,765	3,006,329	6,352	3,969,705	1,995,376
1975	26,958,682	21,255,778	32,501	21,288,279	1,692,392	-632,845	18,963,042	4,199,728	3,795,912	6,819	3,953,504	1,943,843
1976	28,988,024	23,089,919	36,941	23,126,860	1,878,742	-743,612	20,504,506	4,507,373	3,976,145	7,345	3,946,719	1,961,507
1977	31,575,637	25,498,977	39,821	25,538,798	2,078,220	-930,894	22,529,684	4,980,850	4,065,103	7,999	3,947,472	2,021,580
1978	34,874,102	28,644,337	50,711	28,695,048	2,404,024	-1,179,412	25,111,612	5,467,860	4,294,630	8,842	3,944,294	2,118,025
1979	38,842,908	32,274,276	49,871	32,324,147	2,826,669	-1,457,149	28,040,329	6,105,362	4,697,217	9,852	3,942,625	2,213,716
1980	43,921,452	36,087,528	59,301	36,146,829	3,172,323	-1,787,547	31,186,959	7,390,134	5,344,359	11,130	3,946,114	2,271,006
1981	49,271,786	39,821,372	61,881	39,883,253	3,786,086	-1,980,790	34,116,377	9,085,353	6,070,056	12,421	3,966,836	2,288,684
1982	54,290,274	43,175,506	71,846	43,247,352	4,217,874	-2,182,492	36,846,986	10,939,512	6,503,776	13,650	3,977,211	2,304,308
1983	59,199,900	47,930,787	93,378	48,024,165	4,762,616	-2,450,105	40,811,444	11,498,679	6,889,777	14,775	4,006,648	2,364,109
1984	67,016,058	54,621,754	96,576	54,718,330	5,601,867	-2,806,856	46,309,607	13,457,036	7,249,415	16,594	4,038,686	2,509,018
1985	72,686,413	60,146,142	83,269	60,229,411	6,241,202	-3,102,538	50,885,671	14,253,445	7,547,297	17,851	4,071,845	2,591,649
1986	78,488,998	65,421,072	88,426	65,509,498	6,932,105	-3,314,520	55,262,873	15,327,121	7,899,004	19,197	4,088,650	2,660,368
1987	85,049,895	71,704,507	79,340	71,783,847	7,518,153	-3,591,271	60,674,423	16,304,135	8,071,337	20,720	4,104,797	2,682,717
1988	93,972,761	79,054,496	94,044	79,148,540	8,407,372	-3,948,663	66,792,505	18,450,528	8,729,728	22,780	4,125,293	2,758,108
1989	99,301,380	82,231,809	80,238	82,312,047	8,689,863	-4,062,384	69,559,800	19,918,697	9,822,883	23,989	4,139,484	2,735,161
1990	102,262,812	83,295,942	78,374	83,374,316	8,743,141	-4,220,117	70,411,058	20,838,524	11,013,230	24,717	4,137,302	2,665,144
1991	103,975,559	83,460,145	95,748	83,555,893	8,918,557	-4,176,836	70,460,500	20,862,492	12,652,567	25,187	4,128,150	2,541,026
1992	109,710,065	88,716,165	97,012	88,813,177	9,416,088	-4,306,428	75,090,661	21,379,516	13,239,888	26,515	4,137,692	2,555,157
1993	114,095,209	92,389,532	96,751	92,486,283	9,866,980	-4,450,400	78,168,903	22,325,382	13,600,924	27,402	4,163,698	2,603,207
1994	119,824,758	97,285,822	85,358	97,371,180	10,519,475	-4,828,291	82,023,414	23,388,679	14,412,665	28,603	4,189,180	2,655,650
1995	127,433,681	103,307,414	89,064	103,396,478	11,225,962	-5,320,083	86,850,433	25,264,463	15,318,785	30,121	4,230,795	2,685,848
1996	135,889,771	110,564,610	93,865	110,658,475	11,888,420	-5,660,085	93,109,970	27,008,492	15,771,309	31,857	4,265,564	2,740,663
1997	144,739,232	118,842,425	91,918	118,934,343	12,809,869	-6,630,096	99,494,378	28,930,630	16,314,224	33,639	4,302,696	2,813,151
1998	155,167,731	128,057,917	60,552	128,118,469	13,741,716	-7,301,778	107,074,975	31,703,222	16,389,534	35,771	4,337,751	2,889,492
1999	166,536,681	140,634,220	53,847	140,688,067	14,842,772	-8,453,737	117,391,558	32,210,664	16,934,459	38,111	4,369,743	2,941,149
2000	187,233,258	159,789,607	64,743	159,854,350	16,565,380	-10,018,985	133,269,985	36,108,516	17,854,757	42,541	4,401,256	3,027,183
2001	193,272,094	163,740,905	54,833	163,795,738	16,817,846	-10,386,385	136,591,507	37,159,831	19,520,756	43,607	4,432,132	3,031,090
2002	191,365,014	161,255,578	69,170	161,324,748	16,637,668	-10,070,715	134,616,365	35,600,187	21,148,462	43,100	4,440,034	2,977,857
2003	194,631,533	162,754,544	72,521	162,827,065	16,743,174	-10,033,899	136,049,992	36,334,064	22,247,477	43,888	4,434,723	2,947,152
2004	205,169,918	173,999,551	78,644	174,078,195	18,186,655	-11,009,869	144,881,671	37,097,258	23,190,989	46,367	4,424,956	2,973,111
2005	215,326,188	179,531,093	63,321	179,594,414	18,995,745	-11,303,716	149,294,953	41,236,216	24,795,019	48,738	4,418,046	3,013,744
2006	233,536,171	190,564,613	75,875	190,640,488	19,749,913	-12,122,554	158,768,021	48,784,714	25,983,436	52,748	4,427,356	3,051,211
2007	245,839,022	200,660,820	78,378	200,739,198	20,798,237	-12,797,170	167,143,791	51,547,036	27,148,195	55,272	4,447,838	3,131,667
2008	254,419,273	204,951,342	122,972	205,074,314	21,500,151	-12,582,828	170,991,335	52,285,559	31,142,379	56,750	4,483,141	3,150,417
2009	251,626,954	204,527,338	100,607	204,627,945	21,258,788	-11,843,658	171,525,499	46,114,863	33,986,592	55,581	4,527,220	3,081,345
2010	265,318,729	217,480,223	98,704	217,578,927	21,814,477	-12,445,003	183,319,447	46,128,184	35,871,098	58,117	4,565,220	3,085,620
2011	278,659,698	224,057,599	120,941	224,178,540	20,238,088	-13,025,749	190,914,703	51,732,256	36,012,739	60,469	4,608,303	3,132,923
2012	291,263,344	231,788,634	174,686	231,963,320	20,969,245	-14,120,513	196,873,562	58,288,744	36,101,038	62,597	4,653,023	3,190,639
2013	293,875,912	238,021,621	164,959	238,186,580	24,425,192	-13,884,077	199,877,311	57,523,599	36,475,002	62,528	4,699,912	3,268,006
2014	309,894,737	247,740,069	136,039	247,876,108	25,671,210	-13,827,176	208,377,722	63,829,756	37,687,259	65,357	4,741,544	3,345,252
2015	331,394,291	263,242,216	125,368	263,367,584	26,742,072	-14,808,333	221,817,179	69,154,261	40,422,851	69,391	4,775,755	3,491,040
2016	342,456,856	272,517,018	135,799	272,652,817	27,703,837	-15,958,800	228,990,180	71,155,406	42,311,270	71,257	4,805,942	3,557,298
2017	358,021,093	287,142,052	124,866	287,266,918	29,187,080	-17,310,564	240,769,274	74,246,826	43,004,993	74,024	4,836,531	3,610,562
2018	383,529,173	383,437,105	92,068	302,818,604	30,687,282	-17,323,409	254,807,913	83,987,489	44,733,771	78,923	4,859,536	3,673,566
2019	397,139,161	397,061,221	77,940	317,967,542	32,112,265	-19,149,214	266,706,063	84,632,333	45,800,765	81,498	4,873,019	3,743,187

Personal Income and Employment by Area: Boulder, CO

(Thousands of dollars, except as noted.)

| Year | Personal income, total | Derivation of personal income | | | | | | | | Per capita personal income (dollars) | Population (persons) | Total employment |
| | | Earnings by place of work | | | Less: Contributions for government social insurance | Plus: Adjustment for residence | Equals: Net earnings by place of residence | Plus: Dividends, interest, and rent | Plus: Personal current transfer receipts | | | |
		Nonfarm	Farm	Total								
1970	600,343	394,155	5,052	399,207	21,172	78,885	456,920	110,838	32,585	4,502	133,342	55,395
1971	680,907	452,090	474	452,564	24,881	88,777	516,460	125,725	38,722	4,836	140,808	59,121
1972	768,819	512,284	4,041	516,325	30,157	100,009	586,177	138,854	43,788	5,081	151,309	64,116
1973	864,808	574,054	2,914	576,968	39,837	115,077	652,208	157,983	54,617	5,422	159,509	69,942
1974	979,831	660,914	2,695	663,609	46,970	115,564	732,203	184,486	63,142	5,887	166,449	75,635
1975	1,109,846	749,498	6,510	756,008	52,425	114,065	817,648	211,485	80,713	6,659	166,670	78,961
1976	1,245,164	859,746	7,921	867,667	61,907	116,065	921,825	234,964	88,375	7,363	169,117	85,236
1977	1,434,420	1,020,741	7,292	1,028,033	74,657	119,529	1,072,905	265,788	95,727	8,053	178,121	92,627
1978	1,683,852	1,223,210	6,797	1,230,007	92,236	130,401	1,268,172	310,863	104,817	9,180	183,432	102,720
1979	1,959,091	1,429,615	5,149	1,434,764	114,316	162,073	1,482,521	357,574	118,996	10,469	187,125	110,002
1980	2,217,801	1,557,263	9,224	1,566,487	127,270	209,267	1,648,484	432,280	137,037	11,615	190,935	112,861
1981	2,556,325	1,774,431	12,943	1,787,374	156,444	227,322	1,858,252	537,969	160,104	13,062	195,705	117,528
1982	2,822,610	1,988,313	8,662	1,996,975	181,654	226,234	2,041,555	603,751	177,304	14,055	200,827	121,300
1983	3,095,368	2,223,219	9,338	2,232,557	208,132	212,014	2,236,439	665,206	193,723	14,994	206,440	128,223
1984	3,452,403	2,530,218	10,185	2,540,403	247,455	202,813	2,495,761	755,428	201,214	16,346	211,206	141,199
1985	3,621,559	2,597,339	5,064	2,602,403	258,111	241,883	2,586,175	821,066	214,318	16,928	213,942	140,650
1986	3,793,647	2,725,919	4,846	2,730,765	273,381	244,942	2,702,326	858,542	232,779	17,566	215,971	141,908
1987	4,022,785	2,957,351	5,572	2,962,923	294,035	210,790	2,879,678	891,281	251,826	18,451	218,024	143,586
1988	4,339,346	3,217,085	8,427	3,225,512	332,840	224,968	3,117,640	955,442	266,264	19,732	219,915	152,086
1989	4,740,937	3,423,711	10,222	3,433,933	361,914	224,851	3,296,870	1,136,975	307,092	21,212	223,507	155,495
1990	5,074,432	3,724,890	11,309	3,736,199	403,647	217,693	3,550,245	1,199,966	324,221	22,416	226,374	160,076
1991	5,390,167	4,074,399	12,648	4,087,047	452,876	166,419	3,800,590	1,237,454	352,123	23,149	232,846	164,862
1992	5,960,244	4,587,347	7,319	4,594,666	503,546	142,533	4,233,653	1,336,427	390,164	24,790	240,430	169,291
1993	6,429,321	5,016,126	9,237	5,025,363	555,170	93,209	4,563,402	1,448,771	417,148	25,987	247,405	178,775
1994	6,968,605	5,446,358	9,281	5,455,639	609,705	-20,036	4,825,898	1,701,357	441,350	27,401	254,324	186,270
1995	7,546,846	5,868,502	9,403	5,877,905	658,239	-72,238	5,147,428	1,915,835	483,583	29,080	259,520	192,888
1996	8,159,812	6,352,059	11,385	6,363,444	707,621	-78,666	5,577,157	2,074,447	508,208	30,835	264,630	198,754
1997	8,878,042	6,998,726	11,363	7,010,089	779,674	-133,779	6,096,636	2,271,159	510,247	32,791	270,744	207,295
1998	9,692,349	8,176,368	10,361	8,186,729	867,531	-516,243	6,802,955	2,381,160	508,234	34,920	277,562	213,453
1999	10,621,526	8,983,948	9,179	8,993,127	944,613	-451,240	7,597,274	2,486,802	537,450	37,151	285,901	221,120
2000	12,197,752	11,068,542	8,218	11,076,760	1,144,858	-1,144,908	8,786,994	2,834,449	576,309	41,580	293,358	237,310
2001	12,645,707	11,318,053	10,105	11,328,158	1,165,776	-992,797	9,169,585	2,821,427	654,695	42,133	300,137	243,644
2002	11,535,289	9,853,922	9,460	9,863,382	1,020,608	-556,997	8,285,777	2,572,999	676,513	41,276	279,468	215,538
2003	11,718,366	9,891,866	6,018	9,897,884	1,027,830	-476,215	8,393,839	2,592,487	732,040	42,036	278,768	210,519
2004	12,023,818	10,279,616	10,420	10,290,036	1,096,365	-693,131	8,500,540	2,775,619	747,659	42,984	279,728	214,515
2005	12,904,847	10,654,708	8,647	10,663,355	1,134,702	-756,806	8,771,847	3,289,536	843,464	46,049	280,241	218,044
2006	13,881,261	11,187,758	7,032	11,194,790	1,187,091	-757,229	9,250,470	3,786,551	844,240	48,836	284,243	221,750
2007	14,547,608	11,695,477	7,085	11,702,562	1,250,510	-931,009	9,521,043	4,098,317	928,248	50,613	287,428	228,962
2008	15,060,376	11,926,862	6,891	11,933,753	1,285,109	-908,099	9,740,545	4,159,680	1,160,151	51,779	290,859	235,192
2009	13,696,406	11,344,781	10,378	11,355,159	1,218,922	-1,325,961	8,810,276	3,634,274	1,251,856	46,715	293,190	228,871
2010	14,815,455	11,719,225	9,071	11,728,296	1,243,235	-787,287	9,697,774	3,687,045	1,430,636	50,064	295,930	227,803
2011	15,632,452	12,225,111	16,642	12,241,753	1,177,083	-940,549	10,124,121	4,043,906	1,464,425	52,018	300,518	234,434
2012	16,700,010	12,961,278	9,907	12,971,185	1,233,999	-986,009	10,751,177	4,482,196	1,466,637	54,749	305,028	239,480
2013	17,505,391	13,612,955	12,758	13,625,713	1,438,949	-953,065	11,233,699	4,730,914	1,540,778	56,515	309,749	245,009
2014	18,896,217	14,485,732	10,512	14,496,244	1,530,978	-1,003,300	11,961,966	5,286,721	1,647,530	60,467	312,505	252,668
2015	20,412,704	15,192,915	12,721	15,205,636	1,621,673	-826,204	12,757,759	5,870,139	1,784,806	64,197	317,968	258,539
2016	20,924,309	15,534,199	14,216	15,548,415	1,668,718	-936,045	12,943,652	6,114,001	1,866,656	65,150	321,173	264,032
2017	21,939,604	16,449,872	15,293	16,465,165	1,757,590	-1,083,880	13,623,695	6,397,537	1,918,372	68,027	322,514	268,671
2018	23,866,572	23,856,283	10,289	17,444,309	1,868,223	-1,188,125	14,387,961	7,367,866	2,110,745	73,518	324,636	273,867
2019	24,962,717	24,953,968	8,749	19,241,035	2,027,876	-1,942,506	15,270,653	7,445,488	2,246,576	76,527	326,196	281,568

Personal Income and Employment by Area: Bowling Green, KY

(Thousands of dollars, except as noted.)

Year	Personal income, total	Earnings by place of work			Less: Contributions for government social insurance	Plus: Adjustment for residence	Equals: Net earnings by place of residence	Plus: Dividends, interest, and rent	Plus: Personal current transfer receipts	Per capita personal income (dollars)	Population (persons)	Total employment
		Nonfarm	Farm	Total								
1970	238,044	175,431	15,726	191,157	11,945	710	179,922	29,864	28,258	2,655	89,652	37,297
1971	265,227	195,047	17,127	212,174	13,712	744	199,206	33,690	32,331	2,836	93,520	38,393
1972	303,342	224,576	21,037	245,613	16,575	766	229,804	38,107	35,431	3,183	95,307	40,228
1973	350,258	259,340	25,936	285,276	21,794	2,357	265,839	42,966	41,453	3,669	95,464	42,648
1974	387,810	286,550	22,853	309,403	25,070	3,170	287,503	50,095	50,212	4,002	96,904	43,625
1975	427,934	311,056	15,600	326,656	26,799	3,162	303,019	58,089	66,826	4,351	98,351	43,179
1976	485,803	358,953	14,572	373,525	31,446	5,009	347,088	64,516	74,199	4,832	100,546	45,371
1977	541,776	397,195	22,342	419,537	34,784	7,967	392,720	73,739	75,317	5,294	102,335	46,883
1978	620,309	465,232	21,200	486,432	41,834	8,768	453,366	85,380	81,563	5,953	104,207	50,148
1979	707,127	522,879	26,878	549,757	48,699	12,358	513,416	98,483	95,228	6,694	105,640	50,732
1980	776,348	551,391	16,764	568,155	51,615	13,489	530,029	125,350	120,969	7,218	107,557	49,865
1981	902,933	629,693	27,548	657,241	63,699	15,670	609,212	156,278	137,443	8,239	109,593	50,960
1982	963,143	649,035	23,333	672,368	66,817	23,721	629,272	180,851	153,020	8,384	114,875	50,359
1983	999,561	696,520	-5,907	690,613	71,491	21,752	640,874	194,702	163,985	8,554	116,854	51,861
1984	1,135,188	780,102	26,201	806,303	81,520	19,740	744,523	219,855	170,810	9,975	113,805	53,904
1985	1,195,288	847,991	13,813	861,804	90,459	20,072	791,417	225,528	178,343	10,562	113,170	54,825
1986	1,207,908	846,391	13,792	860,183	93,862	22,487	788,808	230,222	188,878	10,735	112,523	55,198
1987	1,275,438	894,216	21,528	915,744	98,646	25,649	842,747	235,002	197,689	11,365	112,227	55,910
1988	1,404,839	995,269	24,017	1,019,286	110,514	23,971	932,743	260,010	212,086	12,507	112,325	57,594
1989	1,536,005	1,069,756	36,531	1,106,287	121,280	19,333	1,004,340	296,062	235,603	13,632	112,679	59,974
1990	1,608,506	1,114,048	36,270	1,150,318	129,977	20,252	1,040,593	304,727	263,186	14,076	114,270	61,201
1991	1,723,952	1,197,080	37,618	1,234,698	141,901	18,917	1,111,714	314,046	298,192	14,915	115,583	62,846
1992	1,881,486	1,338,490	43,313	1,381,803	158,802	16,766	1,239,767	318,876	322,843	16,012	117,502	65,051
1993	1,992,916	1,430,073	37,730	1,467,803	172,045	20,304	1,316,062	336,443	340,411	16,563	120,327	66,995
1994	2,138,330	1,573,545	34,123	1,607,668	192,986	16,269	1,430,951	350,451	356,928	17,429	122,686	69,464
1995	2,249,560	1,669,832	14,256	1,684,088	205,612	13,615	1,492,091	373,529	383,940	17,947	125,345	72,461
1996	2,414,904	1,767,588	31,371	1,798,959	215,456	9,334	1,592,837	405,232	416,835	18,904	127,749	73,893
1997	2,591,321	1,903,766	32,931	1,936,697	229,465	10,223	1,717,455	430,857	443,009	19,919	130,090	75,666
1998	2,717,012	2,010,486	12,190	2,022,676	240,271	13,702	1,796,107	463,686	457,219	20,546	132,238	75,648
1999	2,855,100	2,165,497	3,828	2,169,325	257,540	12,565	1,924,350	457,160	473,590	21,347	133,747	77,333
2000	3,093,191	2,293,106	34,044	2,327,150	263,296	14,898	2,078,752	506,524	507,915	22,850	135,367	78,805
2001	3,218,289	2,364,156	31,734	2,395,890	267,659	18,233	2,146,464	509,957	561,868	23,508	136,901	79,048
2002	3,323,645	2,480,671	22,281	2,502,952	279,955	23,278	2,246,275	469,550	607,820	23,996	138,510	78,927
2003	3,452,571	2,598,906	24,638	2,623,544	290,813	30,275	2,363,006	463,276	626,289	24,500	140,921	80,185
2004	3,692,323	2,744,151	46,712	2,790,863	303,789	24,894	2,511,968	503,078	677,277	25,812	143,044	82,086
2005	3,917,433	2,925,981	60,945	2,986,926	327,754	24,464	2,683,636	513,428	720,369	26,847	145,918	84,829
2006	4,104,360	3,040,998	55,777	3,096,775	344,983	19,985	2,771,777	550,735	781,848	27,486	149,324	86,880
2007	4,324,832	3,176,551	26,156	3,202,707	361,929	13,310	2,854,088	619,014	851,730	28,507	151,710	89,670
2008	4,565,557	3,275,586	16,390	3,291,976	379,143	15,328	2,928,161	660,575	976,821	29,548	154,513	89,166
2009	4,476,562	3,080,716	23,938	3,104,654	367,218	-4,361	2,733,075	640,685	1,102,802	28,517	156,978	85,556
2010	4,730,041	3,266,380	27,799	3,294,179	378,583	-1,076	2,914,520	638,772	1,176,749	29,691	159,309	86,256
2011	4,991,877	3,408,552	52,425	3,460,977	351,015	-19,283	3,090,679	701,648	1,199,550	31,022	160,913	89,444
2012	5,171,416	3,585,357	56,517	3,641,874	366,459	-20,007	3,255,408	719,834	1,196,174	31,864	162,296	90,993
2013	5,244,652	3,686,970	96,904	3,783,874	426,784	-43,617	3,313,473	708,063	1,223,116	31,932	164,246	92,301
2014	5,526,824	3,858,004	68,714	3,926,718	451,904	-56,194	3,418,620	767,659	1,340,545	33,250	166,221	94,216
2015	5,835,113	4,062,970	61,068	4,124,038	476,547	-59,480	3,588,011	824,811	1,422,291	34,505	169,108	96,162
2016	5,985,001	4,218,462	31,988	4,250,450	502,244	-66,061	3,682,145	860,127	1,442,729	34,829	171,839	99,565
2017	6,230,922	4,369,481	41,367	4,410,848	519,406	-46,651	3,844,791	894,912	1,491,219	35,639	174,835	101,028
2018	6,400,089	6,372,514	27,575	4,513,483	534,866	-56,394	3,922,223	935,266	1,542,600	36,186	176,864	102,878
2019	6,652,350	6,624,307	28,043	4,692,457	548,044	-67,644	4,076,769	949,605	1,625,976	37,114	179,240	104,102

Personal Income and Employment by Area: Bremerton-Silverdale-Port Orchard, WA

(Thousands of dollars, except as noted.)

Year	Personal income, total	Derivation of personal income									Per capita personal income (dollars)	Population (persons)	Total employment
		Earnings by place of work			Less: Contributions for government social insurance	Plus: Adjustment for residence	Equals: Net earnings by place of residence	Plus: Dividends, interest, and rent	Plus: Personal current transfer receipts				
		Nonfarm	Farm	Total									
1970	486,434	391,738	1,502	393,240	17,268	-42,165	333,807	117,933	34,694		4,787	101,617	45,195
1971	507,925	401,290	1,060	402,350	18,254	-46,638	337,458	128,587	41,880		4,999	101,606	41,911
1972	550,509	432,237	1,156	433,393	20,733	-47,840	364,820	138,859	46,830		5,385	102,225	41,798
1973	629,457	489,297	2,012	491,309	26,640	-49,714	414,955	160,827	53,675		5,607	112,257	45,114
1974	742,964	582,283	1,568	583,851	32,475	-59,689	491,687	189,692	61,585		6,636	111,965	49,047
1975	858,418	673,210	1,237	674,447	40,020	-65,973	568,454	213,532	76,432		7,207	119,117	51,652
1976	955,374	751,785	1,182	752,967	47,753	-66,976	638,238	231,812	85,324		7,897	120,976	54,063
1977	1,101,571	868,973	1,259	870,232	56,003	-73,202	741,027	267,355	93,189		8,749	125,902	58,694
1978	1,260,302	970,341	1,744	972,085	63,907	-65,994	842,184	316,688	101,430		9,502	132,640	61,793
1979	1,449,681	1,098,866	1,980	1,100,846	74,979	-53,386	972,481	364,338	112,862		10,301	140,733	65,222
1980	1,625,238	1,180,646	1,577	1,182,223	82,672	-31,881	1,067,670	415,982	141,586		10,925	148,762	67,650
1981	1,785,897	1,275,129	1,644	1,276,773	97,426	-40,319	1,139,028	478,356	168,513		11,529	154,907	68,860
1982	1,981,503	1,411,352	1,663	1,413,015	105,653	-59,487	1,247,875	548,595	185,033		12,779	155,059	70,104
1983	2,208,199	1,600,922	1,159	1,602,081	131,219	-65,729	1,405,133	606,663	196,403		13,757	160,515	73,806
1984	2,323,081	1,658,720	406	1,659,126	141,762	-54,598	1,462,766	648,266	212,049		14,363	161,742	75,920
1985	2,450,140	1,708,620	133	1,708,753	155,676	-30,562	1,522,515	698,109	229,516		14,981	163,546	77,990
1986	2,521,180	1,708,605	-354	1,708,251	162,310	3,016	1,548,957	726,235	245,988		15,346	164,293	77,909
1987	2,709,242	1,844,068	1,287	1,845,355	179,383	27,602	1,693,574	753,507	262,161		15,959	169,760	83,191
1988	2,998,253	2,085,596	577	2,086,173	211,614	24,680	1,899,239	819,661	279,353		16,757	178,929	90,373
1989	3,260,819	2,206,752	3,607	2,210,359	231,970	55,871	2,034,260	916,407	310,152		17,871	182,461	92,716
1990	3,784,198	2,518,561	2,237	2,520,798	274,093	217,275	2,463,980	975,648	344,570		19,722	191,879	99,487
1991	4,157,382	2,789,438	3,826	2,793,264	308,907	220,130	2,704,487	1,051,366	401,529		20,825	199,636	103,816
1992	4,501,517	3,008,567	3,536	3,012,103	340,130	266,715	2,938,688	1,111,377	451,452		21,481	209,562	105,396
1993	4,743,043	3,010,174	3,068	3,013,242	347,167	391,393	3,057,468	1,185,134	500,441		22,451	211,262	103,073
1994	4,957,911	3,104,821	3,211	3,108,032	362,329	418,926	3,164,629	1,262,156	531,126		23,122	214,422	106,538
1995	5,229,188	3,220,839	1,691	3,222,530	377,135	430,611	3,276,006	1,377,463	575,719		23,408	223,391	108,268
1996	5,495,060	3,332,704	1,399	3,334,103	385,052	420,946	3,369,997	1,517,192	607,871		24,252	226,584	112,627
1997	5,942,242	3,493,289	2,134	3,495,423	396,145	598,614	3,697,892	1,600,463	643,887		25,903	229,403	111,977
1998	6,176,159	3,537,432	720	3,538,152	401,458	746,110	3,882,804	1,622,387	670,968		26,985	228,878	110,034
1999	6,474,160	3,699,802	918	3,700,720	414,137	834,946	4,121,529	1,644,625	708,006		28,223	229,393	110,431
2000	7,091,562	3,943,478	1,281	3,944,759	444,603	1,068,776	4,568,932	1,742,968	779,662		30,473	232,720	112,566
2001	7,341,601	4,138,066	890	4,138,956	467,175	1,047,814	4,719,595	1,747,088	874,918		31,306	234,513	113,167
2002	7,673,681	4,617,413	1,071	4,618,484	526,058	961,616	5,054,042	1,682,021	937,618		32,225	238,129	117,072
2003	8,081,121	4,926,815	2,718	4,929,533	562,593	917,830	5,284,770	1,805,616	990,735		33,705	239,758	119,293
2004	8,609,407	5,292,128	1,941	5,294,069	609,263	925,073	5,609,879	1,975,074	1,024,454		35,582	241,960	121,918
2005	9,050,749	5,598,099	831	5,598,930	647,190	919,949	5,871,689	2,075,977	1,103,083		37,742	239,806	124,980
2006	9,555,848	5,847,290	2,152	5,849,442	682,502	874,922	6,041,862	2,316,552	1,197,434		38,995	245,054	127,063
2007	10,010,328	5,964,686	1,632	5,966,318	700,185	926,488	6,192,621	2,526,539	1,291,168		41,008	244,105	127,595
2008	10,541,931	6,164,839	-749	6,164,090	723,862	873,451	6,313,679	2,734,978	1,493,274		42,695	246,912	127,474
2009	10,323,531	6,176,304	401	6,176,705	746,258	805,379	6,235,826	2,424,944	1,662,761		41,493	248,800	123,188
2010	10,607,283	6,394,586	-1,272	6,393,314	764,443	766,892	6,395,763	2,366,322	1,845,198		42,150	251,658	120,811
2011	10,920,638	6,451,873	291	6,452,164	707,421	713,183	6,457,926	2,608,286	1,854,426		42,952	254,250	120,718
2012	11,365,363	6,608,066	-479	6,607,587	712,656	738,189	6,633,120	2,859,708	1,872,535		44,692	254,306	121,380
2013	11,360,931	6,587,546	724	6,588,270	795,463	862,389	6,655,196	2,800,935	1,904,800		45,006	252,434	121,561
2014	12,085,515	6,848,792	746	6,849,538	830,461	961,884	6,980,961	3,038,482	2,066,072		47,697	253,381	124,403
2015	12,624,551	7,198,501	4,277	7,202,778	876,727	961,433	7,287,484	3,218,993	2,118,074		48,711	259,175	127,312
2016	13,215,905	7,550,658	1,895	7,552,553	911,301	1,052,041	7,693,293	3,283,362	2,239,250		50,230	263,109	129,915
2017	13,988,937	7,928,562	2,601	7,931,163	962,890	1,263,215	8,231,488	3,439,192	2,318,257		52,508	266,414	131,380
2018	15,159,557	15,160,061	-504	8,459,704	1,013,786	1,271,444	8,717,362	3,986,192	2,456,003		56,297	269,276	135,908
2019	15,982,626	15,982,270	356	8,950,877	1,066,150	1,438,700	9,323,427	4,060,927	2,598,272		58,874	271,473	139,206

Personal Income and Employment by Area: Bridgeport-Stamford-Norwalk, CT

(Thousands of dollars, except as noted.)

Year	Personal income, total	Earnings by place of work			Less: Contributions for government social insurance	Plus: Adjustment for residence	Equals: Net earnings by place of residence	Plus: Dividends, interest, and rent	Plus: Personal current transfer receipts	Per capita personal income (dollars)	Population (persons)	Total employment
		Nonfarm	Farm	Total								
1970	4,860,504	3,147,197	3,681	3,150,878	208,962	665,217	3,607,133	969,894	283,477	6,130	792,934	366,252
1971	5,101,426	3,251,071	3,673	3,254,744	223,363	679,467	3,710,848	1,039,763	350,815	6,435	792,758	358,267
1972	5,483,660	3,537,389	3,649	3,541,038	258,000	702,508	3,985,546	1,124,024	374,090	6,959	788,034	364,054
1973	5,883,424	3,911,903	4,252	3,916,155	330,354	698,151	4,283,952	1,192,810	406,662	7,480	786,524	379,191
1974	6,352,715	4,229,786	4,041	4,233,827	374,258	717,665	4,577,234	1,300,388	475,093	8,059	788,324	383,909
1975	6,814,123	4,464,601	3,695	4,468,296	386,283	775,075	4,857,088	1,334,125	622,910	8,576	794,554	374,936
1976	7,449,088	4,970,834	3,072	4,973,906	437,127	811,283	5,348,062	1,430,568	670,458	9,341	797,444	385,892
1977	8,289,329	5,643,127	3,313	5,646,440	498,579	872,536	6,020,397	1,566,193	702,739	10,228	810,423	403,360
1978	9,308,626	6,427,273	3,316	6,430,589	585,428	966,337	6,811,498	1,758,611	738,517	11,597	802,642	425,460
1979	10,522,084	7,296,754	2,917	7,299,671	692,806	1,082,157	7,689,022	2,012,196	820,866	13,109	802,656	442,700
1980	12,114,690	8,285,890	2,688	8,288,578	789,350	1,234,151	8,733,379	2,431,320	949,991	14,980	808,703	455,859
1981	13,778,176	9,249,786	2,181	9,251,967	949,492	1,354,594	9,657,069	3,047,512	1,073,595	16,943	813,186	470,540
1982	14,892,004	9,924,754	3,067	9,927,821	1,048,044	1,444,001	10,323,778	3,374,846	1,193,380	18,207	817,943	474,803
1983	15,790,894	10,612,277	2,425	10,614,702	1,128,848	1,557,939	11,043,793	3,460,588	1,286,513	19,214	821,854	476,184
1984	17,748,238	12,032,503	2,881	12,035,384	1,308,932	1,661,584	12,388,036	4,015,430	1,344,772	21,510	825,107	495,194
1985	19,125,106	13,146,476	2,624	13,149,100	1,448,341	1,845,563	13,546,322	4,148,942	1,429,842	23,031	830,396	509,468
1986	20,490,336	14,290,306	2,965	14,293,271	1,579,604	1,884,766	14,598,433	4,376,546	1,515,357	24,634	831,797	519,808
1987	22,322,461	15,825,783	3,085	15,828,868	1,717,306	2,004,167	16,115,729	4,640,769	1,565,963	26,950	828,277	525,397
1988	24,980,133	17,752,236	2,656	17,754,892	1,932,958	2,175,903	17,997,837	5,291,854	1,690,442	30,220	826,605	537,634
1989	27,114,309	18,556,240	2,065	18,558,305	2,015,062	2,193,847	18,737,090	6,491,874	1,885,345	32,766	827,517	532,086
1990	27,933,582	19,191,242	3,099	19,194,341	2,057,938	1,815,410	18,951,813	6,873,370	2,108,399	33,701	828,860	521,951
1991	28,246,727	19,492,459	3,962	19,496,421	2,126,970	1,795,318	19,164,769	6,726,335	2,355,623	33,906	833,094	503,321
1992	31,689,819	21,065,940	5,910	21,071,850	2,232,533	2,923,827	21,763,144	7,151,225	2,775,450	37,980	834,372	501,927
1993	32,629,970	22,181,213	8,461	22,189,674	2,333,814	2,285,973	22,141,833	7,581,865	2,906,272	38,894	838,945	512,679
1994	33,471,898	22,923,375	9,607	22,932,982	2,452,079	2,033,100	22,514,003	7,954,305	3,003,590	39,730	842,482	508,287
1995	36,425,112	24,736,400	10,395	24,746,795	2,636,559	2,592,670	24,702,906	8,497,768	3,224,438	42,951	848,057	518,746
1996	39,005,828	26,343,803	5,162	26,348,965	2,785,707	3,161,417	26,724,675	8,971,062	3,310,091	45,652	854,421	528,175
1997	41,990,761	29,305,153	4,646	29,309,799	3,007,275	2,478,555	28,781,079	9,806,739	3,402,943	48,769	861,020	537,529
1998	46,409,607	32,008,342	6,901	32,015,243	3,184,139	3,677,052	32,508,156	10,488,886	3,412,565	53,427	868,651	551,305
1999	49,497,064	34,919,382	10,098	34,929,480	3,371,946	3,364,443	34,921,977	11,075,606	3,499,481	56,436	877,043	563,031
2000	55,077,663	39,248,422	11,380	39,259,802	3,622,577	3,214,954	38,852,179	12,525,916	3,699,568	62,279	884,364	577,741
2001	59,024,534	42,880,869	11,820	42,892,689	3,734,864	3,100,931	42,258,756	12,844,074	3,921,704	66,390	889,063	576,192
2002	57,844,797	41,948,341	11,785	41,960,126	3,798,008	3,486,105	41,648,223	12,006,929	4,189,645	64,783	892,900	574,103
2003	57,962,922	42,139,530	11,390	42,150,920	3,886,095	3,517,429	41,782,254	11,929,123	4,251,545	64,666	896,342	575,380
2004	61,738,273	42,614,889	12,640	42,627,529	4,027,408	4,418,506	43,018,627	14,156,614	4,563,032	68,791	897,472	583,542
2005	66,978,056	44,840,627	14,829	44,855,456	4,175,830	4,857,027	45,536,653	16,822,131	4,619,272	74,615	897,653	591,253
2006	74,442,192	47,270,420	16,251	47,286,671	4,359,447	5,573,534	48,500,758	21,045,980	4,895,454	83,059	896,254	600,698
2007	82,439,394	51,799,497	19,324	51,818,821	4,656,868	6,848,105	54,010,058	23,276,630	5,152,706	91,855	897,498	617,956
2008	90,605,692	58,529,955	17,861	58,547,816	4,892,936	8,207,554	61,862,434	22,859,114	5,884,144	100,247	903,824	621,959
2009	89,552,649	62,472,700	18,618	62,491,318	4,713,627	6,574,007	64,351,698	18,697,716	6,503,235	98,364	910,421	608,209
2010	95,621,625	64,789,280	17,612	64,806,892	4,772,230	8,447,019	68,481,681	20,224,743	6,915,201	103,965	919,749	605,628
2011	96,668,717	63,667,897	14,260	63,682,157	4,356,656	8,686,351	68,011,852	21,740,540	6,916,325	104,012	929,398	621,735
2012	97,162,840	60,000,645	19,771	60,020,416	4,414,138	10,502,419	66,108,697	24,053,275	7,000,868	103,768	936,345	628,379
2013	91,893,783	56,951,229	25,460	56,976,689	5,099,406	9,852,297	61,729,580	23,082,967	7,081,236	97,462	942,865	639,196
2014	97,580,063	58,767,387	17,195	58,784,582	5,270,865	10,037,154	63,550,871	26,745,411	7,283,781	103,091	946,547	646,628
2015	99,450,654	58,695,321	20,613	58,715,934	5,424,974	10,610,104	63,901,064	28,010,340	7,539,250	104,893	948,116	657,223
2016	101,227,241	59,804,546	17,821	59,822,367	5,511,682	10,047,134	64,357,819	29,052,389	7,817,033	106,646	949,191	664,137
2017	104,589,841	58,890,629	18,163	58,908,792	5,505,824	12,562,583	65,965,551	30,676,670	7,947,620	110,104	949,921	665,436
2018	110,852,692	110,833,118	19,574	60,665,570	5,658,400	13,722,081	68,729,251	33,676,547	8,446,894	117,432	943,971	663,549
2019	114,517,862	114,491,594	26,268	62,084,830	5,754,637	15,330,231	71,660,424	34,275,157	8,582,281	121,397	943,332	666,826

Personal Income and Employment by Area: Brownsville-Harlingen, TX

(Thousands of dollars, except as noted.)

Year	Personal income, total	Earnings by place of work			Less: Contributions for government social insurance	Plus: Adjustment for residence	Equals: Net earnings by place of residence	Plus: Dividends, interest, and rent	Plus: Personal current transfer receipts	Per capita personal income (dollars)	Population (persons)	Total employment
		Nonfarm	Farm	Total								
1970	313,753	235,891	12,535	248,426	15,000	-8,878	224,548	50,419	38,786	2,222	141,196	48,384
1971	365,169	265,273	24,210	289,483	17,408	-9,731	262,344	57,081	45,744	2,471	147,753	50,443
1972	413,943	311,343	20,676	332,019	21,566	-12,223	298,230	64,453	51,260	2,628	157,489	54,936
1973	485,003	367,116	15,921	383,037	29,725	-15,229	338,083	75,667	71,253	2,905	166,939	59,244
1974	571,166	422,375	25,565	447,940	35,323	-17,547	395,070	90,871	85,225	3,317	172,211	62,830
1975	653,609	486,103	17,041	503,144	40,246	-21,223	441,675	106,211	105,723	3,575	182,806	64,977
1976	729,412	547,870	16,964	564,834	45,664	-23,177	495,993	115,036	118,383	3,851	189,415	67,457
1977	800,019	593,551	25,495	619,046	49,589	-24,873	544,584	129,059	126,376	4,109	194,722	69,508
1978	943,986	707,392	33,308	740,700	60,254	-27,499	652,947	150,912	140,127	4,745	198,941	74,442
1979	1,075,955	816,103	13,414	829,517	72,680	-27,998	728,839	179,309	167,807	5,235	205,544	77,871
1980	1,235,507	921,222	3,944	925,166	82,787	-27,631	814,748	218,291	202,468	5,829	211,944	81,655
1981	1,455,488	1,048,635	39,017	1,087,652	101,802	-22,495	963,355	266,447	225,686	6,610	220,184	84,935
1982	1,561,377	1,108,240	15,480	1,123,720	108,940	-23,753	991,027	318,927	251,423	6,767	230,718	85,599
1983	1,672,892	1,122,637	30,554	1,153,191	107,925	-22,308	1,022,958	355,239	294,695	7,003	238,878	83,585
1984	1,774,807	1,170,093	28,770	1,198,863	114,124	-22,305	1,062,434	391,208	321,165	7,323	242,355	83,931
1985	1,926,454	1,251,313	43,113	1,294,426	122,365	-22,590	1,149,471	431,440	345,543	7,834	245,894	85,022
1986	1,983,233	1,295,455	15,734	1,311,189	124,438	-22,434	1,164,317	443,972	374,944	7,901	250,996	83,543
1987	2,043,684	1,318,754	41,152	1,359,906	125,588	-22,625	1,211,693	441,640	390,351	8,055	253,714	85,358
1988	2,205,592	1,436,577	50,888	1,487,465	143,188	-21,344	1,322,933	467,138	415,521	8,669	254,410	88,741
1989	2,380,309	1,558,053	28,628	1,586,681	160,254	-22,753	1,403,674	511,734	464,901	9,280	256,512	93,483
1990	2,650,173	1,756,567	39,592	1,796,159	177,535	-26,635	1,591,989	516,989	541,195	10,126	261,728	98,639
1991	2,857,614	1,881,741	30,741	1,912,482	194,117	-26,856	1,691,509	535,712	630,393	10,613	269,261	101,267
1992	3,203,167	2,065,785	38,156	2,103,941	211,567	-30,382	1,861,992	565,295	775,880	11,550	277,322	104,646
1993	3,476,116	2,254,178	57,997	2,312,175	232,090	-32,174	2,047,911	575,123	853,082	12,057	288,297	109,851
1994	3,700,012	2,405,663	51,942	2,457,605	251,640	-33,139	2,172,826	597,991	929,195	12,445	297,316	115,588
1995	3,869,868	2,480,523	25,422	2,505,945	260,821	-31,483	2,213,641	653,237	1,002,990	12,691	304,928	117,889
1996	4,086,295	2,583,709	48,255	2,631,964	269,176	-27,407	2,335,381	662,672	1,088,242	13,093	312,086	121,253
1997	4,365,735	2,811,319	44,581	2,855,900	289,749	-26,725	2,539,426	686,635	1,139,674	13,717	318,281	124,620
1998	4,652,402	3,039,491	69,786	3,109,277	308,587	-27,514	2,773,176	731,710	1,147,516	14,335	324,556	127,625
1999	4,812,673	3,183,321	73,284	3,256,605	320,998	-22,899	2,912,708	724,326	1,175,639	14,572	330,277	132,109
2000	5,181,592	3,417,713	67,296	3,485,009	342,345	-21,320	3,121,344	793,529	1,266,719	15,416	336,123	139,353
2001	5,701,043	3,871,867	62,748	3,934,615	370,866	-69,123	3,494,626	815,514	1,390,903	16,652	342,368	142,995
2002	6,089,719	4,143,338	55,241	4,198,579	397,227	-76,743	3,724,609	806,315	1,558,795	17,390	350,194	148,213
2003	6,408,601	4,272,540	93,308	4,365,848	418,315	-70,064	3,877,469	868,239	1,662,893	17,877	358,492	150,342
2004	6,609,610	4,440,793	81,556	4,522,349	437,404	-62,384	4,022,561	841,633	1,745,416	18,044	366,299	154,155
2005	6,990,927	4,566,777	81,096	4,647,873	459,399	-42,931	4,145,543	896,840	1,948,544	18,721	373,429	156,329
2006	7,483,539	4,921,344	65,196	4,986,540	490,192	-34,922	4,461,426	950,035	2,072,078	19,685	380,169	162,680
2007	7,981,577	5,109,869	63,202	5,173,071	522,876	-19,399	4,630,796	1,033,963	2,316,818	20,661	386,306	167,167
2008	8,554,557	5,311,560	40,911	5,352,471	544,268	-3,384	4,804,819	1,165,488	2,584,250	21,767	393,000	169,857
2009	8,886,806	5,471,975	32,722	5,504,697	562,517	-13,130	4,929,050	1,093,378	2,864,378	22,200	400,303	170,020
2010	9,522,683	5,848,917	47,486	5,896,403	597,145	-23,918	5,275,340	1,095,711	3,151,632	23,363	407,590	171,929
2011	9,964,151	6,093,006	42,209	6,135,215	550,462	-31,058	5,553,695	1,185,108	3,225,348	24,131	412,917	178,631
2012	10,235,440	6,330,028	36,451	6,366,479	571,957	-30,975	5,763,547	1,295,793	3,176,100	24,642	415,370	181,256
2013	10,438,841	6,464,960	64,117	6,529,077	655,974	-24,638	5,848,465	1,324,219	3,266,157	25,027	417,095	185,550
2014	10,870,391	6,724,699	31,360	6,756,059	681,528	-18,958	6,055,573	1,417,912	3,396,906	25,954	418,838	189,017
2015	11,247,720	6,917,613	33,337	6,950,950	709,090	-26,701	6,215,159	1,438,182	3,594,379	26,807	419,579	190,118
2016	11,559,021	7,035,510	38,833	7,074,343	736,740	-46,191	6,291,412	1,493,544	3,774,065	27,406	421,766	192,466
2017	11,754,457	7,088,222	64,470	7,152,692	755,969	-34,374	6,362,349	1,560,804	3,831,304	27,741	423,725	193,572
2018	12,216,651	12,172,510	44,141	7,392,308	785,159	-29,105	6,578,044	1,640,409	3,998,198	28,940	422,139	196,292
2019	12,664,258	12,623,974	40,284	7,705,348	816,159	-21,537	6,867,652	1,679,674	4,116,932	29,928	423,163	199,947

Personal Income and Employment by Area: Brunswick, GA

(Thousands of dollars, except as noted.)

Year	Personal income, total	Earnings by place of work			Less: Contributions for government social insurance	Plus: Adjustment for residence	Equals: Net earnings by place of residence	Plus: Dividends, interest, and rent	Plus: Personal current transfer receipts	Per capita personal income (dollars)	Population (persons)	Total employment
		Nonfarm	Farm	Total								
1970	217,294	170,827	2,545	173,372	10,952	2,535	164,955	34,841	17,498	3,390	64,102	27,191
1971	248,873	196,850	2,304	199,154	13,264	2,749	188,639	39,534	20,700	3,782	65,809	28,897
1972	275,680	217,472	2,732	220,204	15,250	3,828	208,782	43,607	23,291	4,082	67,537	29,346
1973	297,353	229,832	4,341	234,173	18,125	4,829	220,877	48,693	27,783	4,344	68,446	29,715
1974	314,290	235,988	4,817	240,805	19,641	6,201	227,365	52,381	34,544	4,638	67,760	29,309
1975	320,878	227,190	5,782	232,972	18,695	7,249	221,526	52,935	46,417	4,840	66,301	27,827
1976	367,868	266,859	5,543	272,402	22,053	7,772	258,121	59,975	49,772	5,504	66,832	29,663
1977	412,371	302,830	4,017	306,847	24,900	8,840	290,787	68,329	53,255	6,041	68,260	31,063
1978	469,980	342,739	5,484	348,223	28,580	10,391	330,034	81,261	58,685	6,865	68,464	32,995
1979	531,687	385,094	3,838	388,932	33,403	12,738	368,267	96,225	67,195	7,564	70,289	33,871
1980	600,992	425,002	2,186	427,188	37,008	16,925	407,105	113,949	79,938	8,353	71,952	34,773
1981	667,188	454,115	3,723	457,838	42,747	19,961	435,052	140,276	91,860	9,175	72,718	34,166
1982	706,194	464,925	4,853	469,778	44,653	21,601	446,726	158,128	101,340	9,592	73,627	33,888
1983	756,277	497,565	3,778	501,343	48,038	22,239	475,544	170,970	109,763	10,162	74,420	34,276
1984	839,210	552,992	5,345	558,337	54,688	25,732	529,381	190,643	119,186	11,113	75,513	35,831
1985	920,227	618,061	4,013	622,074	62,484	24,486	584,076	208,724	127,427	12,026	76,517	37,907
1986	993,481	666,243	4,978	671,221	68,210	27,883	630,894	226,041	136,546	12,757	77,877	38,823
1987	1,054,558	707,612	3,121	710,733	72,101	29,283	667,915	241,538	145,105	13,341	79,049	39,594
1988	1,150,821	772,898	5,119	778,017	81,220	28,963	725,760	265,763	159,298	14,337	80,269	41,522
1989	1,271,085	823,750	8,088	831,838	87,379	30,895	775,354	324,164	171,567	15,613	81,414	42,364
1990	1,356,242	871,336	6,950	878,286	91,814	33,871	820,343	345,886	190,013	16,452	82,437	42,569
1991	1,426,502	900,538	7,553	908,091	96,001	43,029	855,119	350,195	221,188	17,124	83,303	42,130
1992	1,538,624	973,310	8,274	981,584	102,507	43,025	922,102	371,247	245,275	18,261	84,259	42,703
1993	1,625,010	1,026,748	7,183	1,033,931	109,033	42,316	967,214	392,853	264,943	18,978	85,624	44,165
1994	1,731,405	1,079,618	6,499	1,086,117	116,267	47,788	1,017,638	425,255	288,512	20,019	86,487	45,056
1995	1,871,148	1,160,986	5,703	1,166,689	124,503	50,984	1,093,170	466,961	311,017	21,379	87,522	47,089
1996	2,025,088	1,241,338	5,420	1,246,758	131,581	53,320	1,168,497	521,602	334,989	22,872	88,541	48,188
1997	2,138,358	1,304,075	4,864	1,308,939	135,852	58,135	1,231,222	560,559	346,577	23,752	90,027	48,883
1998	2,274,777	1,408,496	5,060	1,413,556	143,870	68,851	1,338,537	583,447	352,793	24,954	91,160	50,359
1999	2,349,605	1,468,638	5,340	1,473,978	148,574	73,638	1,399,042	584,256	366,307	25,423	92,420	50,905
2000	2,488,967	1,544,424	4,867	1,549,291	155,640	65,682	1,459,333	639,959	389,675	26,664	93,344	52,025
2001	2,573,087	1,596,451	5,619	1,602,070	164,136	59,104	1,497,038	660,220	415,829	27,070	95,052	52,363
2002	2,667,879	1,681,416	3,545	1,684,961	172,591	54,306	1,566,676	636,221	464,982	27,614	96,612	52,596
2003	2,823,955	1,821,422	3,686	1,825,108	185,578	45,728	1,685,258	664,060	474,637	28,763	98,180	52,535
2004	3,071,615	1,983,838	3,921	1,987,759	207,193	33,457	1,814,023	738,916	518,676	30,753	99,879	54,370
2005	3,272,830	2,123,203	3,725	2,126,928	216,392	30,503	1,941,039	789,608	542,183	32,234	101,532	56,363
2006	3,546,437	2,312,205	1,146	2,313,351	239,006	18,453	2,092,798	874,753	578,886	33,868	104,715	58,121
2007	3,648,183	2,327,124	1,690	2,328,814	239,320	9,656	2,099,150	929,758	619,275	33,989	107,334	59,407
2008	3,610,665	2,254,007	1,273	2,255,280	252,584	-5,620	1,997,076	913,457	700,132	32,950	109,579	59,054
2009	3,461,295	2,149,672	1,217	2,150,889	240,785	862	1,910,966	790,944	759,385	31,087	111,343	55,728
2010	3,598,086	2,249,219	1,239	2,250,458	243,940	7,122	2,013,640	762,237	822,209	31,974	112,530	53,860
2011	3,771,286	2,226,378	1,292	2,227,670	217,481	8,125	2,018,314	892,149	860,823	33,390	112,945	53,751
2012	3,769,403	2,224,266	2,930	2,227,196	222,403	4,104	2,008,897	898,733	861,773	33,251	113,361	54,206
2013	3,808,035	2,268,331	3,519	2,271,850	255,852	4,295	2,020,293	897,502	890,240	33,445	113,860	54,752
2014	3,996,423	2,310,857	2,273	2,313,130	258,476	11,939	2,066,593	991,342	938,488	34,832	114,735	55,910
2015	4,262,695	2,469,422	3,249	2,472,671	275,062	9,330	2,206,939	1,069,656	986,100	36,741	116,020	57,061
2016	4,399,116	2,578,779	3,389	2,582,168	293,904	18,733	2,306,997	1,067,887	1,024,232	37,614	116,955	58,337
2017	4,544,845	2,662,558	2,627	2,665,185	305,482	15,251	2,374,954	1,106,290	1,063,601	38,477	118,119	58,874
2018	4,963,920	4,964,443	-523	2,852,570	327,068	5,694	2,531,196	1,309,444	1,123,280	41,967	118,282	61,187
2019	5,093,781	5,095,005	-1,224	2,929,907	337,704	11,443	2,603,646	1,313,246	1,176,889	42,885	118,779	61,788

Personal Income and Employment by Area: Buffalo-Cheektowaga, NY

(Thousands of dollars, except as noted.)

Year	Personal income, total	Earnings by place of work			Less: Contributions for government social insurance	Plus: Adjustment for residence	Equals: Net earnings by place of residence	Plus: Dividends, interest, and rent	Plus: Personal current transfer receipts	Per capita personal income (dollars)	Population (persons)	Total employment
		Nonfarm	Farm	Total								
1970	5,668,577	4,726,169	22,870	4,749,039	357,861	-65,438	4,325,740	793,271	549,566	4,194	1,351,513	568,934
1971	6,108,318	5,045,253	22,715	5,067,968	392,449	-72,100	4,603,419	831,633	673,266	4,509	1,354,743	567,469
1972	6,463,718	5,358,152	18,241	5,376,393	439,976	-75,416	4,861,001	869,349	733,368	4,796	1,347,603	566,533
1973	7,018,358	5,874,983	26,612	5,901,595	559,600	-79,245	5,262,750	956,667	798,941	5,262	1,333,861	585,656
1974	7,575,057	6,237,591	25,992	6,263,583	613,643	-78,942	5,570,998	1,082,439	921,620	5,744	1,318,687	586,402
1975	8,181,205	6,467,022	23,307	6,490,329	623,846	-79,680	5,786,803	1,181,521	1,212,881	6,231	1,312,980	568,364
1976	8,816,270	7,026,697	23,390	7,050,087	691,508	-87,641	6,270,938	1,242,949	1,302,383	6,766	1,303,095	569,298
1977	9,606,553	7,699,188	22,196	7,721,384	753,883	-97,786	6,869,715	1,365,810	1,371,028	7,448	1,289,794	577,315
1978	10,367,645	8,389,444	27,648	8,417,092	840,374	-104,683	7,472,035	1,469,604	1,426,006	8,125	1,276,092	585,744
1979	11,384,785	9,203,500	31,775	9,235,275	949,644	-111,376	8,174,255	1,656,334	1,554,196	9,010	1,263,570	597,758
1980	12,362,259	9,593,044	31,575	9,624,619	985,941	-110,055	8,528,623	1,985,543	1,848,093	9,959	1,241,275	583,672
1981	13,489,641	10,277,495	34,392	10,311,887	1,125,826	-112,834	9,073,227	2,373,960	2,042,454	10,943	1,232,720	575,313
1982	14,206,810	10,360,665	32,821	10,393,486	1,144,119	-104,891	9,144,476	2,716,537	2,345,797	11,611	1,223,579	552,973
1983	14,899,860	10,730,086	24,781	10,754,867	1,191,178	-101,940	9,461,749	2,900,392	2,537,719	12,309	1,210,449	542,712
1984	16,286,109	11,788,276	31,688	11,819,964	1,329,736	-103,711	10,386,517	3,258,826	2,640,766	13,600	1,197,531	560,459
1985	17,216,569	12,622,536	34,497	12,657,033	1,447,002	-108,043	11,101,988	3,382,270	2,732,311	14,445	1,191,856	572,233
1986	18,118,687	13,354,940	39,283	13,394,223	1,548,370	-106,435	11,739,418	3,490,408	2,888,861	15,296	1,184,555	585,218
1987	18,859,407	14,049,820	45,235	14,095,055	1,606,660	-101,381	12,387,014	3,514,490	2,957,903	15,986	1,179,756	593,226
1988	20,208,866	15,274,567	39,417	15,313,984	1,777,758	-105,557	13,430,669	3,631,944	3,146,253	17,109	1,181,174	611,066
1989	21,653,398	16,189,409	43,670	16,233,079	1,869,984	-104,205	14,258,890	4,033,217	3,361,291	18,258	1,185,954	623,408
1990	23,061,417	17,086,455	42,119	17,128,574	1,890,005	-107,287	15,131,282	4,277,274	3,652,861	19,364	1,190,943	630,513
1991	23,541,813	17,404,398	35,470	17,439,868	1,994,519	-109,638	15,335,711	4,222,687	3,983,415	19,700	1,194,992	622,358
1992	24,696,198	18,336,720	36,249	18,372,969	2,068,492	-114,500	16,189,977	4,132,941	4,373,280	20,606	1,198,490	619,834
1993	25,198,310	18,683,220	37,038	18,720,258	2,125,441	-117,044	16,477,773	4,142,234	4,578,303	20,986	1,200,744	620,260
1994	26,119,373	19,353,292	31,806	19,385,098	2,223,142	-120,362	17,041,594	4,251,776	4,826,003	21,757	1,200,479	633,711
1995	27,236,237	19,965,145	26,445	19,991,590	2,294,800	-129,294	17,567,496	4,612,390	5,056,351	22,737	1,197,885	626,083
1996	28,053,194	20,504,777	31,638	20,536,415	2,313,895	-144,685	18,077,835	4,728,256	5,247,103	23,492	1,194,167	626,699
1997	29,053,334	21,277,274	26,443	21,303,717	2,362,260	-150,298	18,791,159	4,970,851	5,291,324	24,493	1,186,175	631,833
1998	29,990,367	21,995,986	33,540	22,029,526	2,421,097	-171,229	19,437,200	5,088,426	5,464,741	25,449	1,178,462	627,096
1999	31,195,074	23,311,324	43,617	23,354,941	2,509,677	-186,096	20,659,168	4,956,285	5,579,621	26,592	1,173,102	638,318
2000	32,839,116	24,628,699	47,912	24,676,611	2,628,277	-204,560	21,843,774	5,250,214	5,745,128	28,090	1,169,060	646,437
2001	32,980,975	24,366,486	52,046	24,418,532	2,695,014	-184,030	21,539,488	5,322,223	6,119,264	28,308	1,165,067	634,355
2002	33,514,184	24,952,207	46,400	24,998,607	2,795,662	-180,011	22,022,934	5,029,070	6,462,180	28,850	1,161,678	630,515
2003	34,655,394	25,753,527	52,710	25,806,237	2,893,911	-174,710	22,737,616	5,279,003	6,638,775	29,877	1,159,918	631,286
2004	36,075,474	27,112,512	57,701	27,170,213	3,043,193	-184,928	23,942,092	5,119,960	7,013,422	31,205	1,156,070	635,979
2005	36,651,960	27,329,722	52,958	27,382,680	3,119,545	-164,255	24,098,880	5,264,078	7,289,002	31,911	1,148,563	636,763
2006	38,440,127	28,599,384	49,472	28,648,856	3,243,924	-162,920	25,242,012	5,496,412	7,701,703	33,669	1,141,712	636,520
2007	40,348,725	29,614,169	71,682	29,685,851	3,328,662	-139,052	26,218,137	6,082,669	8,047,919	35,466	1,137,678	643,412
2008	42,072,025	30,314,871	91,485	30,406,356	3,449,906	-108,762	26,847,688	6,316,476	8,907,861	37,023	1,136,364	648,214
2009	42,563,653	30,270,211	61,929	30,332,140	3,419,092	-106,444	26,806,604	6,062,336	9,694,713	37,489	1,135,377	635,320
2010	44,088,783	31,350,082	88,812	31,438,894	3,487,809	-139,987	27,811,098	6,047,897	10,229,788	38,820	1,135,710	634,444
2011	45,943,255	32,382,808	96,626	32,479,434	3,254,462	-213,535	29,011,437	6,573,561	10,358,257	40,441	1,136,059	642,219
2012	47,651,263	33,526,206	101,910	33,628,116	3,317,178	-297,012	30,013,926	7,298,628	10,338,709	41,957	1,135,717	646,715
2013	48,171,541	34,356,457	123,556	34,480,013	3,826,998	-361,639	30,291,376	7,379,007	10,501,158	42,367	1,136,993	651,220
2014	49,522,448	35,036,395	109,254	35,145,649	3,984,489	-398,606	30,762,554	8,003,454	10,756,440	43,520	1,137,924	656,972
2015	51,560,888	36,348,312	91,388	36,439,700	4,141,480	-438,605	31,859,615	8,446,655	11,254,618	45,362	1,136,662	663,440
2016	52,424,465	37,069,874	65,869	37,135,743	4,259,261	-451,672	32,424,810	8,542,636	11,457,019	46,192	1,134,914	667,485
2017	54,926,413	38,387,066	69,758	38,456,824	4,409,864	-471,118	33,575,842	8,979,580	12,370,991	48,314	1,136,856	670,495
2018	56,783,377	56,752,074	31,303	40,312,777	4,513,430	-521,443	35,277,904	9,440,753	12,064,720	50,261	1,129,777	677,973
2019	59,028,041	58,978,777	49,264	41,688,379	4,629,018	-554,789	36,504,572	9,631,663	12,891,806	52,331	1,127,983	682,705

Personal Income and Employment by Area: Burlington, NC

(Thousands of dollars, except as noted.)

Year	Personal income, total	Earnings by place of work			Less: Contributions for government social insurance	Plus: Adjustment for residence	Equals: Net earnings by place of residence	Plus: Dividends, interest, and rent	Plus: Personal current transfer receipts	Per capita personal income (dollars)	Population (persons)	Total employment
		Nonfarm	Farm	Total								
1970	350,273	292,866	6,208	299,074	21,451	8,984	286,607	40,056	23,610	3,617	96,843	51,242
1971	381,007	314,564	5,430	319,994	24,016	12,575	308,553	43,718	28,736	3,868	98,499	51,105
1972	424,017	348,621	6,033	354,654	27,936	17,226	343,944	47,873	32,200	4,251	99,740	52,100
1973	469,926	383,222	9,782	393,004	35,009	21,217	379,212	53,137	37,577	4,702	99,940	53,563
1974	504,551	397,986	9,484	407,470	37,926	27,630	397,174	60,448	46,929	5,083	99,272	52,836
1975	536,960	402,929	6,373	409,302	37,596	32,948	404,654	66,561	65,745	5,466	98,243	49,823
1976	590,057	433,619	11,436	445,055	41,198	40,692	444,549	72,477	73,031	5,977	98,721	49,923
1977	628,721	453,265	9,621	462,886	42,848	52,776	472,814	80,789	75,118	6,383	98,505	49,601
1978	697,983	496,298	8,532	504,830	48,507	72,615	528,938	90,053	78,992	7,083	98,540	50,016
1979	781,945	552,483	6,792	559,275	55,701	88,374	591,948	100,174	89,823	7,895	99,048	53,068
1980	871,795	592,943	4,996	597,939	60,008	101,791	639,722	124,940	107,133	8,759	99,532	52,664
1981	979,962	662,094	9,242	671,336	71,609	100,131	699,858	156,363	123,741	9,791	100,083	53,335
1982	1,050,004	686,110	9,436	695,546	74,489	99,631	720,688	186,295	143,021	10,396	101,000	52,891
1983	1,133,432	760,024	4,830	764,854	82,845	100,760	782,769	200,420	150,243	11,160	101,559	53,988
1984	1,254,093	848,649	10,577	859,226	94,675	103,009	867,560	232,009	154,524	12,331	101,706	56,603
1985	1,334,700	908,102	6,762	914,864	102,634	104,358	916,588	250,858	167,254	13,018	102,524	57,844
1986	1,448,617	1,004,694	7,089	1,011,783	116,026	98,867	994,624	275,628	178,365	13,994	103,515	59,960
1987	1,548,484	1,104,383	5,294	1,109,677	125,289	95,262	1,079,650	280,705	188,129	14,737	105,072	62,866
1988	1,682,733	1,215,900	8,774	1,224,674	140,611	89,085	1,173,148	304,999	204,586	15,826	106,327	66,241
1989	1,829,543	1,295,831	14,869	1,310,700	150,086	82,898	1,243,512	359,610	226,421	17,031	107,425	67,397
1990	1,901,481	1,351,755	19,328	1,371,083	160,375	74,882	1,285,590	370,697	245,194	17,494	108,695	68,152
1991	1,981,909	1,408,424	18,350	1,426,774	170,158	70,134	1,326,750	375,255	279,904	17,893	110,762	66,347
1992	2,111,525	1,499,798	18,130	1,517,928	178,542	80,636	1,420,022	384,995	306,508	18,715	112,825	67,347
1993	2,245,397	1,600,013	16,625	1,616,638	192,222	80,759	1,505,175	411,205	329,017	19,580	114,678	68,752
1994	2,379,702	1,696,634	15,536	1,712,170	206,111	87,961	1,594,020	438,081	347,601	20,376	116,788	69,706
1995	2,545,725	1,780,465	10,378	1,790,843	216,596	100,358	1,674,605	485,286	385,834	21,429	118,796	71,463
1996	2,695,792	1,871,189	10,954	1,882,143	226,641	103,465	1,758,967	522,115	414,710	22,231	121,263	73,122
1997	2,900,497	2,031,817	10,023	2,041,840	242,913	107,055	1,905,982	561,083	433,432	23,414	123,877	74,821
1998	3,108,824	2,178,210	9,317	2,187,527	260,532	134,533	2,061,528	600,878	446,418	24,628	126,232	78,580
1999	3,278,069	2,361,889	12,115	2,374,004	282,326	126,220	2,217,898	591,327	468,844	25,462	128,743	80,175
2000	3,444,901	2,447,515	16,135	2,463,650	292,749	140,918	2,311,819	630,731	502,351	26,212	131,423	81,244
2001	3,588,562	2,482,777	16,481	2,499,258	296,194	182,235	2,385,299	636,528	566,735	26,912	133,346	77,847
2002	3,650,103	2,502,125	5,171	2,507,296	293,838	216,186	2,429,644	613,617	606,842	26,990	135,239	76,384
2003	3,766,080	2,498,106	10,726	2,508,832	299,426	288,394	2,497,800	627,656	640,624	27,690	136,009	75,173
2004	3,848,228	2,623,545	11,196	2,634,741	311,194	212,403	2,535,950	623,171	689,107	27,963	137,619	75,967
2005	4,004,478	2,695,913	14,720	2,710,633	325,522	238,814	2,623,925	639,750	740,803	28,745	139,311	76,703
2006	4,346,676	2,847,193	12,589	2,859,782	342,219	279,891	2,797,454	720,780	828,442	30,727	141,462	77,138
2007	4,653,404	2,938,128	11,611	2,949,739	354,728	345,637	2,940,648	835,209	877,547	32,156	144,712	80,082
2008	4,849,735	2,987,076	5,659	2,992,735	361,101	380,557	3,012,191	834,236	1,003,308	32,834	147,704	78,758
2009	4,720,490	2,749,568	2,932	2,752,500	336,694	441,618	2,857,424	762,489	1,100,577	31,480	149,954	74,921
2010	4,834,308	2,846,114	2,605	2,848,719	342,402	441,402	2,947,719	730,628	1,155,961	31,912	151,490	74,330
2011	5,042,233	2,943,838	-534	2,943,304	324,302	439,783	3,058,785	819,402	1,164,046	32,987	152,857	76,422
2012	5,246,696	3,130,221	5,692	3,135,913	336,892	404,739	3,203,760	847,951	1,194,985	34,187	153,471	77,711
2013	5,259,359	3,144,992	4,504	3,149,496	390,015	451,899	3,211,380	834,512	1,213,467	34,059	154,417	77,885
2014	5,524,438	3,203,777	7,833	3,211,610	397,771	533,945	3,347,784	929,447	1,247,207	35,482	155,698	78,855
2015	5,784,891	3,285,111	4,323	3,289,434	408,741	596,191	3,476,884	989,109	1,318,898	36,755	157,389	79,324
2016	5,994,562	3,454,927	874	3,455,801	429,935	598,735	3,624,601	1,013,610	1,356,351	37,625	159,325	81,209
2017	6,307,062	3,599,310	1,235	3,600,545	443,947	671,629	3,828,227	1,060,814	1,418,021	38,839	162,391	82,156
2018	6,650,506	6,655,916	-5,410	3,733,060	455,274	750,538	4,028,324	1,130,642	1,491,540	39,940	166,514	84,139
2019	6,982,583	6,986,853	-4,270	3,946,448	480,919	780,595	4,246,124	1,152,913	1,583,546	41,193	169,509	86,304

Personal Income and Employment by Area: Burlington-South Burlington, VT

(Thousands of dollars, except as noted.)

		Derivation of personal income										
		Earnings by place of work			Less: Contributions for government social insurance	Plus: Adjustment for residence	Equals: Net earnings by place of residence	Plus: Dividends, interest, and rent	Plus: Personal current transfer receipts	Per capita personal income (dollars)	Population (persons)	Total employment
Year	Personal income, total	Nonfarm	Farm	Total								
1970............	516,335	422,616	17,722	440,338	29,444	-13,527	397,367	72,287	46,681	3,834	134,673	62,022
1971............	556,777	447,386	17,720	465,106	31,994	-12,818	420,294	80,023	56,460	4,048	137,553	62,103
1972............	606,443	484,457	19,304	503,761	36,122	-13,220	454,419	87,894	64,130	4,314	140,585	62,800
1973............	654,967	521,330	20,573	541,903	44,911	-12,976	484,016	97,541	73,410	4,650	140,865	64,201
1974............	706,184	553,004	16,913	569,917	49,146	-12,374	508,397	109,757	88,030	4,985	141,657	64,786
1975............	791,194	604,097	17,982	622,079	52,565	-13,623	555,891	125,097	110,206	5,509	143,608	64,467
1976............	880,961	681,928	22,301	704,229	60,602	-15,170	628,457	134,176	118,328	6,067	145,209	67,585
1977............	960,758	755,626	18,942	774,568	67,583	-16,735	690,250	150,250	120,258	6,513	147,509	70,446
1978............	1,114,324	893,339	27,525	920,864	82,639	-21,653	816,572	171,296	126,456	7,478	149,023	76,185
1979............	1,265,516	1,023,961	29,838	1,053,799	98,499	-26,303	928,997	192,999	143,520	8,350	151,554	80,057
1980............	1,428,519	1,134,802	30,079	1,164,881	109,727	-29,188	1,025,966	233,625	168,928	9,191	155,430	82,463
1981............	1,622,347	1,283,722	32,918	1,316,640	133,162	-36,152	1,147,326	283,346	191,675	10,332	157,017	85,578
1982............	1,768,338	1,389,929	31,780	1,421,709	147,354	-42,601	1,231,754	328,992	207,592	11,145	158,663	87,158
1983............	1,913,244	1,523,752	21,355	1,545,107	163,393	-49,561	1,332,153	360,259	220,832	11,936	160,287	89,680
1984............	2,106,272	1,687,829	22,047	1,709,876	186,031	-56,226	1,467,619	411,747	226,906	13,024	161,724	94,035
1985............	2,313,562	1,866,984	27,639	1,894,623	209,699	-64,958	1,619,966	455,093	238,503	14,129	163,751	98,992
1986............	2,495,723	2,029,452	27,935	2,057,387	228,907	-71,776	1,756,704	493,329	245,690	15,050	165,834	103,108
1987............	2,708,768	2,233,000	36,515	2,269,515	247,883	-80,470	1,941,162	516,264	251,342	16,147	167,755	107,321
1988............	2,991,002	2,490,757	34,060	2,524,817	284,100	-97,568	2,143,149	580,640	267,213	17,443	171,477	113,250
1989............	3,346,857	2,739,025	35,548	2,774,573	309,471	-108,811	2,356,291	694,040	296,526	19,127	174,979	117,499
1990............	3,521,968	2,895,469	33,930	2,929,399	346,095	-117,385	2,465,919	726,502	329,547	19,813	177,757	117,930
1991............	3,614,329	2,964,492	28,614	2,993,106	357,372	-118,632	2,517,102	734,489	362,738	20,141	179,447	115,960
1992............	3,852,004	3,133,575	49,875	3,183,450	373,108	-123,622	2,686,720	755,307	409,977	21,261	181,178	117,796
1993............	4,023,183	3,296,137	39,987	3,336,124	394,254	-129,512	2,812,358	777,683	433,142	21,876	183,909	120,276
1994............	4,184,528	3,388,569	40,336	3,428,905	409,134	-129,998	2,889,773	840,583	454,172	22,355	187,186	123,280
1995............	4,461,385	3,560,273	31,957	3,592,230	434,510	-142,111	3,015,609	950,454	495,322	23,568	189,300	125,287
1996............	4,741,595	3,810,527	46,011	3,856,538	460,096	-159,377	3,237,065	991,872	512,658	24,820	191,043	128,300
1997............	5,001,261	4,007,208	34,235	4,041,443	480,696	-169,545	3,391,202	1,067,106	542,953	25,908	193,040	130,011
1998............	5,367,554	4,352,659	44,123	4,396,782	513,716	-185,351	3,697,715	1,106,472	563,367	27,570	194,691	133,049
1999............	5,783,085	4,757,783	47,902	4,805,685	552,638	-201,416	4,051,631	1,125,123	606,331	29,352	197,026	136,879
2000............	6,295,298	5,207,839	51,158	5,258,997	595,562	-223,176	4,440,259	1,193,307	661,732	31,540	199,600	142,039
2001............	6,594,958	5,460,384	52,174	5,512,558	630,201	-231,906	4,650,451	1,218,346	726,161	32,752	201,361	144,163
2002............	6,743,870	5,606,012	39,763	5,645,775	634,572	-230,736	4,780,467	1,185,494	777,909	33,213	203,052	143,707
2003............	7,066,430	5,817,168	48,415	5,865,583	660,647	-235,735	4,969,201	1,281,963	815,266	34,605	204,201	144,044
2004............	7,445,785	6,132,343	65,426	6,197,769	695,390	-241,367	5,261,012	1,337,234	847,539	36,206	205,652	147,053
2005............	7,647,435	6,311,090	66,625	6,377,715	724,231	-247,779	5,405,705	1,316,789	924,941	37,009	206,637	147,964
2006............	8,172,739	6,536,953	41,277	6,578,230	758,595	-240,416	5,579,219	1,576,112	1,017,408	39,401	207,426	149,069
2007............	8,615,383	6,758,765	72,496	6,831,261	800,297	-251,526	5,779,438	1,695,848	1,140,097	41,374	208,232	151,286
2008............	9,111,415	7,057,271	71,419	7,128,690	833,866	-254,021	6,040,803	1,780,496	1,290,116	43,526	209,332	151,588
2009............	8,972,211	7,059,412	39,949	7,099,361	833,051	-245,536	6,020,774	1,554,913	1,396,524	42,636	210,435	149,147
2010............	9,238,298	7,298,604	62,007	7,360,611	852,794	-256,331	6,251,486	1,497,245	1,489,567	43,677	211,514	150,311
2011............	9,932,380	7,614,009	84,215	7,698,224	796,124	-241,024	6,661,076	1,751,456	1,519,848	46,680	212,774	153,443
2012............	10,317,112	7,892,529	79,512	7,972,041	834,949	-266,780	6,870,312	1,892,974	1,553,826	48,269	213,744	156,025
2013............	10,537,013	8,149,744	97,334	8,247,078	975,939	-264,887	7,006,252	1,906,064	1,624,697	49,023	214,940	157,590
2014............	10,988,514	8,298,332	114,730	8,413,062	1,017,843	-244,196	7,151,023	2,130,899	1,706,592	50,830	216,182	159,995
2015............	11,448,627	8,606,671	70,172	8,676,843	1,061,951	-250,567	7,364,325	2,284,617	1,799,685	52,804	216,812	162,273
2016............	11,785,629	8,878,271	59,811	8,938,082	1,091,661	-251,851	7,594,570	2,352,748	1,838,311	54,204	217,429	163,814
2017............	12,183,237	9,184,149	57,361	9,241,510	1,133,328	-225,043	7,883,139	2,436,891	1,863,207	55,785	218,395	164,709
2018............	12,545,471	12,489,156	56,315	9,512,991	1,159,574	-231,295	8,122,122	2,516,942	1,906,407	57,041	219,939	165,754
2019............	12,929,749	12,849,018	80,731	9,863,675	1,173,222	-221,274	8,469,179	2,526,512	1,934,058	58,662	220,411	167,476

Personal Income and Employment by Area: California-Lexington Park, MD

(Thousands of dollars, except as noted.)

Year	Personal income, total	Earnings by place of work			Less: Contributions for government social insurance	Plus: Adjustment for residence	Equals: Net earnings by place of residence	Plus: Dividends, interest, and rent	Plus: Personal current transfer receipts	Per capita personal income (dollars)	Population (persons)	Total employment
		Nonfarm	Farm	Total								
1970	205,033	147,579	5,694	153,273	7,478	9,180	154,975	40,708	9,350	4,286	47,840	19,164
1971	230,307	162,424	4,453	166,877	8,459	16,464	174,882	44,176	11,249	4,594	50,127	19,026
1972	259,542	180,400	5,240	185,640	9,625	21,320	197,335	49,277	12,930	5,109	50,805	19,653
1973	278,652	184,440	8,012	192,452	10,637	28,303	210,118	53,378	15,156	5,581	49,928	19,221
1974	314,963	206,087	7,933	214,020	12,701	34,066	235,385	61,333	18,245	6,096	51,667	20,064
1975	313,494	194,757	6,410	201,167	12,572	40,585	229,180	61,405	22,909	5,944	52,738	18,610
1976	347,827	213,201	7,717	220,918	14,073	48,689	255,534	67,077	25,216	6,474	53,724	18,852
1977	383,723	229,288	7,698	236,986	15,214	58,547	280,319	75,729	27,675	7,038	54,522	19,582
1978	429,820	247,819	10,702	258,521	16,768	70,747	312,500	86,780	30,540	7,575	56,744	20,556
1979	464,968	265,540	7,430	272,970	19,870	83,876	336,976	92,906	35,086	7,943	58,541	20,935
1980	527,810	299,399	3,785	303,184	22,922	97,923	378,185	107,048	42,577	8,771	60,176	21,211
1981	637,140	360,097	11,537	371,634	26,509	114,503	459,628	127,687	49,825	10,414	61,182	22,032
1982	695,208	388,632	18,623	407,255	29,106	116,780	494,929	144,883	55,396	11,268	61,697	22,268
1983	736,046	422,493	9,533	432,026	34,543	123,654	521,137	154,754	60,155	11,786	62,450	23,501
1984	807,286	465,867	8,430	474,297	39,891	133,613	568,019	173,738	65,529	12,764	63,245	24,650
1985	880,016	508,956	12,874	521,830	45,530	146,604	622,904	186,830	70,282	13,619	64,618	25,721
1986	950,696	563,958	4,446	568,404	52,568	159,571	675,407	201,441	73,848	14,281	66,570	27,230
1987	1,042,225	628,687	5,201	633,888	59,506	169,875	744,257	215,780	82,188	15,087	69,083	29,457
1988	1,178,101	736,180	6,935	743,115	73,916	182,863	852,062	236,792	89,247	16,412	71,785	32,351
1989	1,293,795	809,524	3,530	813,054	83,119	195,682	925,617	266,060	102,118	17,453	74,130	34,042
1990	1,395,218	882,991	5,634	888,625	93,090	206,199	1,001,734	279,085	114,399	18,271	76,361	35,990
1991	1,475,771	946,457	6,380	952,837	101,081	194,623	1,046,379	297,347	132,045	18,932	77,952	36,785
1992	1,554,785	994,877	4,799	999,676	106,975	195,047	1,087,748	312,585	154,452	19,727	78,815	36,686
1993	1,585,392	1,004,048	4,259	1,008,307	108,684	201,152	1,100,775	322,931	161,686	20,327	77,994	35,928
1994	1,638,346	1,039,231	5,236	1,044,467	114,623	200,746	1,130,590	341,066	166,690	20,808	78,737	36,940
1995	1,713,367	1,091,329	-5,492	1,085,837	119,644	196,155	1,162,348	372,544	178,475	21,627	79,222	38,098
1996	1,842,676	1,192,243	14,510	1,206,753	130,378	184,227	1,260,602	393,490	188,584	22,853	80,633	40,147
1997	2,113,630	1,460,019	7,330	1,467,349	159,123	149,108	1,457,334	459,194	197,102	25,415	83,165	44,464
1998	2,353,645	1,709,910	1,114	1,711,024	183,865	116,209	1,643,368	507,522	202,755	27,701	84,967	47,377
1999	2,443,185	1,772,182	2,619	1,774,801	190,597	120,945	1,705,149	521,508	216,528	28,533	85,627	48,147
2000	2,636,231	1,941,485	10,795	1,952,280	206,222	105,661	1,851,719	550,814	233,698	30,477	86,498	49,501
2001	2,682,482	1,957,713	10,929	1,968,642	210,328	135,972	1,894,286	527,112	261,084	30,673	87,455	47,090
2002	2,916,007	2,175,502	-4,701	2,170,801	232,318	142,907	2,081,390	543,435	291,182	32,465	89,819	49,310
2003	3,172,593	2,402,817	6,149	2,408,966	256,921	139,447	2,291,492	571,492	309,609	34,360	92,333	51,659
2004	3,422,428	2,582,730	8,189	2,590,919	280,805	190,741	2,500,855	586,871	334,702	36,064	94,900	52,800
2005	3,654,570	2,685,268	5,095	2,690,363	290,721	274,106	2,673,748	612,087	368,735	37,726	96,871	53,234
2006	3,922,358	2,898,916	3,329	2,902,245	318,660	272,546	2,856,131	674,001	392,226	39,680	98,849	54,953
2007	4,200,817	3,052,797	2,505	3,055,302	339,933	295,570	3,010,939	757,180	432,698	41,758	100,599	56,573
2008	4,477,356	3,116,763	3,043	3,119,806	352,595	367,348	3,134,559	835,777	507,020	43,930	101,921	56,063
2009	4,675,706	3,372,049	3,028	3,375,077	379,999	310,046	3,305,124	829,623	540,959	45,275	103,273	56,276
2010	4,953,711	3,721,687	-331	3,721,356	422,440	217,945	3,516,861	839,095	597,755	46,837	105,764	57,614
2011	5,257,249	3,996,247	2,751	3,998,998	402,889	118,793	3,714,902	912,281	630,066	48,866	107,585	58,334
2012	5,354,226	4,035,182	58	4,035,240	408,618	127,299	3,753,921	949,409	650,896	49,198	108,831	58,503
2013	5,358,790	4,049,610	-3,577	4,046,033	463,363	120,824	3,703,494	979,706	675,590	49,039	109,275	59,094
2014	5,548,373	4,157,395	-6,443	4,150,952	474,083	128,790	3,805,659	1,022,117	720,597	50,432	110,016	59,501
2015	5,798,688	4,298,216	-7,580	4,290,636	490,638	180,032	3,980,030	1,057,200	761,458	52,193	111,100	60,300
2016	5,962,892	4,388,167	-7,028	4,381,139	498,324	211,076	4,093,891	1,068,902	800,099	53,319	111,835	60,435
2017	6,187,732	4,533,615	-7,844	4,525,771	516,874	246,450	4,255,347	1,113,072	819,313	54,921	112,667	60,982
2018	6,404,219	6,407,644	-3,425	4,672,480	531,436	238,261	4,379,305	1,156,519	868,395	56,815	112,720	62,333
2019	6,649,699	6,646,759	2,940	4,959,645	562,841	165,665	4,562,469	1,172,395	914,835	58,582	113,510	64,287

Personal Income and Employment by Area: Canton-Massillon, OH

(Thousands of dollars, except as noted.)

Year	Personal income, total	Earnings by place of work			Less: Contributions for government social insurance	Plus: Adjustment for residence	Equals: Net earnings by place of residence	Plus: Dividends, interest, and rent	Plus: Personal current transfer receipts	Per capita personal income (dollars)	Population (persons)	Total employment
		Nonfarm	Farm	Total								
1970	1,539,014	1,257,308	6,263	1,263,571	86,403	32,588	1,209,756	204,466	124,792	3,902	394,389	166,024
1971	1,594,880	1,266,119	7,849	1,273,968	89,495	43,474	1,227,947	218,615	148,318	4,019	396,830	160,591
1972	1,767,736	1,416,355	7,807	1,424,162	105,412	52,319	1,371,069	232,722	163,945	4,480	394,589	163,820
1973	1,991,029	1,613,297	9,499	1,622,796	139,857	59,081	1,542,020	258,597	190,412	4,919	404,798	173,392
1974	2,228,143	1,791,284	10,639	1,801,923	161,136	65,845	1,706,632	296,003	225,508	5,483	406,348	179,109
1975	2,393,365	1,852,965	14,869	1,867,834	162,465	73,265	1,778,634	320,367	294,364	5,947	402,470	173,184
1976	2,607,650	2,026,060	15,741	2,041,801	180,923	82,159	1,943,037	342,940	321,673	6,510	400,573	173,726
1977	2,889,951	2,249,265	13,768	2,263,033	200,669	112,452	2,174,816	380,708	334,427	7,201	401,304	177,260
1978	3,219,758	2,529,202	8,722	2,537,924	233,670	133,927	2,438,181	425,251	356,326	7,967	404,117	184,559
1979	3,618,783	2,836,297	7,293	2,843,590	272,784	154,282	2,725,088	484,643	409,052	8,982	402,887	189,646
1980	3,960,435	2,948,295	297	2,948,592	282,431	174,671	2,840,832	597,744	521,859	9,794	404,365	186,051
1981	4,377,425	3,211,721	2,760	3,214,481	329,515	176,999	3,061,965	736,985	578,475	10,856	403,233	184,686
1982	4,520,150	3,144,256	4,582	3,148,838	326,647	188,297	3,010,488	818,427	691,235	11,255	401,616	177,193
1983	4,673,058	3,194,008	-311	3,193,697	334,666	204,919	3,063,950	868,682	740,426	11,691	399,727	172,450
1984	5,082,542	3,513,085	10,183	3,523,268	378,965	220,889	3,365,192	962,772	754,578	12,734	399,131	179,713
1985	5,308,867	3,659,949	12,457	3,672,406	400,955	235,901	3,507,352	1,001,813	799,702	13,388	396,527	183,119
1986	5,454,943	3,703,347	12,327	3,715,674	417,024	263,292	3,561,942	1,033,654	859,347	13,860	393,569	185,112
1987	5,716,044	3,940,389	14,925	3,955,314	443,742	265,131	3,776,703	1,041,977	897,364	14,577	392,135	191,292
1988	6,115,930	4,259,918	14,230	4,274,148	494,459	278,247	4,057,936	1,118,347	939,647	15,532	393,752	194,561
1989	6,556,918	4,483,325	19,738	4,503,063	522,312	303,825	4,284,576	1,270,035	1,002,307	16,622	394,481	198,003
1990	6,931,864	4,723,907	17,440	4,741,347	560,477	311,808	4,492,678	1,313,115	1,126,071	17,567	394,606	201,081
1991	7,042,221	4,813,851	9,328	4,823,179	582,378	322,021	4,562,822	1,287,546	1,191,853	17,737	397,025	200,722
1992	7,530,403	5,160,203	20,514	5,180,717	617,528	340,888	4,904,077	1,317,828	1,308,498	18,854	399,399	199,451
1993	7,861,478	5,424,606	16,229	5,440,835	661,054	364,750	5,144,531	1,365,318	1,351,629	19,551	402,098	202,448
1994	8,293,385	5,766,366	25,708	5,792,074	711,120	391,221	5,472,175	1,456,998	1,364,212	20,548	403,612	207,012
1995	8,681,847	5,995,431	27,036	6,022,467	749,400	416,943	5,690,010	1,558,783	1,433,054	21,441	404,924	212,418
1996	9,048,955	6,186,992	26,678	6,213,670	762,440	452,524	5,903,754	1,643,588	1,501,613	22,293	405,915	215,591
1997	9,423,245	6,412,641	27,659	6,440,300	772,726	476,334	6,143,908	1,739,802	1,539,535	23,197	406,235	218,984
1998	10,111,443	6,956,008	54,885	7,010,893	807,271	500,235	6,703,857	1,809,580	1,598,006	24,893	406,189	224,798
1999	10,418,068	7,180,885	46,529	7,227,414	824,802	532,880	6,935,492	1,828,027	1,654,549	25,598	406,983	226,886
2000	10,998,364	7,560,069	35,204	7,595,273	837,972	560,094	7,317,395	1,913,633	1,767,336	27,031	406,887	232,230
2001	11,108,027	7,564,434	33,110	7,597,544	853,492	606,301	7,350,353	1,847,098	1,910,576	27,342	406,256	225,330
2002	11,273,504	7,629,000	26,139	7,655,139	843,586	676,437	7,487,990	1,743,952	2,041,562	27,765	406,039	221,364
2003	11,603,888	7,763,278	25,417	7,788,695	868,856	768,246	7,688,085	1,772,999	2,142,804	28,578	406,046	217,698
2004	11,969,590	8,094,418	29,860	8,124,278	916,589	818,160	8,025,849	1,751,561	2,192,180	29,485	405,960	218,617
2005	12,347,308	8,253,621	31,681	8,285,302	948,774	912,148	8,248,676	1,764,696	2,333,936	30,475	405,168	220,170
2006	12,872,494	8,319,521	25,266	8,344,787	962,325	1,081,278	8,463,740	1,941,747	2,467,007	31,757	405,343	216,097
2007	13,525,028	8,516,401	32,064	8,548,465	983,455	1,164,629	8,729,639	2,161,008	2,634,381	33,318	405,939	217,378
2008	13,996,849	8,686,058	33,281	8,719,339	1,016,361	1,132,431	8,835,409	2,211,169	2,950,271	34,463	406,140	215,543
2009	13,443,130	8,160,398	39,792	8,200,190	973,870	1,021,740	8,248,060	1,965,747	3,229,323	33,183	405,127	205,924
2010	13,761,187	8,265,656	44,436	8,310,092	969,438	1,100,755	8,441,409	1,913,648	3,406,130	34,044	404,214	203,967
2011	14,705,332	8,801,349	58,654	8,860,003	935,786	1,127,463	9,051,680	2,171,907	3,481,745	36,463	403,291	209,428
2012	15,300,503	9,193,126	47,415	9,240,541	964,807	1,207,115	9,482,849	2,393,373	3,424,281	37,929	403,403	213,719
2013	15,483,113	9,622,396	62,556	9,684,952	1,088,758	1,074,700	9,670,894	2,268,846	3,543,373	38,393	403,281	217,118
2014	16,127,210	9,991,075	58,868	10,049,943	1,120,318	1,070,142	9,999,767	2,494,881	3,632,562	39,950	403,680	220,079
2015	16,631,998	10,026,005	33,826	10,059,831	1,128,648	1,276,941	10,208,124	2,656,689	3,767,185	41,328	402,435	219,177
2016	16,590,847	9,928,267	29,823	9,958,090	1,146,554	1,274,304	10,085,840	2,648,065	3,856,942	41,357	401,165	219,985
2017	17,140,770	10,378,890	28,430	10,407,320	1,224,076	1,225,468	10,408,712	2,774,018	3,958,040	42,860	399,927	221,971
2018	17,793,419	17,779,419	14,000	10,681,646	1,247,083	1,327,789	10,762,352	3,005,987	4,025,080	44,670	398,330	222,134
2019	18,310,362	18,302,465	7,897	10,936,942	1,275,657	1,434,228	11,095,513	3,036,705	4,178,144	46,061	397,520	222,779

Personal Income and Employment by Area: Cape Coral-Fort Myers, FL

(Thousands of dollars, except as noted.)

Year	Personal income, total	Earnings by place of work			Less: Contributions for government social insurance	Plus: Adjustment for residence	Equals: Net earnings by place of residence	Plus: Dividends, interest, and rent	Plus: Personal current transfer receipts	Per capita personal income (dollars)	Population (persons)	Total employment
		Nonfarm	Farm	Total								
1970	424,777	255,307	7,788	263,095	16,301	5,688	252,482	122,719	49,576	3,954	107,430	42,485
1971	481,303	281,710	8,448	290,158	18,792	5,892	277,258	141,942	62,103	4,116	116,946	44,589
1972	566,888	337,228	9,099	346,327	23,700	6,875	329,502	161,431	75,955	4,440	127,672	49,836
1973	700,122	418,684	10,076	428,760	33,844	9,862	404,778	199,141	96,203	5,100	137,276	58,032
1974	822,773	483,494	9,569	493,063	41,155	10,583	462,491	243,677	116,605	5,604	146,825	61,830
1975	916,640	503,421	15,192	518,613	42,100	8,456	484,969	277,494	154,177	5,917	154,905	61,397
1976	1,045,610	577,994	17,346	595,340	48,458	8,386	555,268	316,668	173,674	6,550	159,632	65,373
1977	1,224,202	680,308	18,233	698,541	57,763	10,705	651,483	376,352	196,367	7,036	173,998	73,310
1978	1,483,214	833,626	23,175	856,801	72,566	14,151	798,386	456,106	228,722	8,109	182,920	83,121
1979	1,761,290	986,198	24,644	1,010,842	90,397	14,876	935,321	553,556	272,413	9,145	192,597	90,770
1980	2,149,997	1,146,092	25,998	1,172,090	106,373	17,288	1,083,005	733,490	333,502	10,334	208,050	96,755
1981	2,569,819	1,313,646	22,103	1,335,749	131,787	18,978	1,222,940	943,339	403,540	11,745	218,795	103,581
1982	2,744,856	1,363,942	27,149	1,391,091	142,832	16,969	1,265,228	1,006,855	472,773	11,886	230,932	106,186
1983	3,093,013	1,542,321	39,899	1,582,220	160,655	14,593	1,436,158	1,133,657	523,198	12,805	241,554	113,430
1984	3,531,951	1,774,399	39,545	1,813,944	189,367	16,479	1,641,056	1,321,244	569,651	13,835	255,299	121,575
1985	3,987,867	2,003,597	43,315	2,046,912	218,359	18,900	1,847,453	1,502,095	638,319	14,930	267,107	129,854
1986	4,441,540	2,253,269	50,847	2,304,116	252,185	18,722	2,070,653	1,664,855	706,032	15,835	280,483	136,443
1987	4,920,677	2,556,640	58,630	2,615,270	282,950	19,805	2,352,125	1,803,634	764,918	16,665	295,262	138,260
1988	5,486,734	2,881,768	58,449	2,940,217	329,695	23,554	2,634,076	2,011,611	841,047	17,881	306,842	149,455
1989	6,386,328	3,197,310	61,650	3,258,960	372,326	24,713	2,911,347	2,518,329	956,652	19,818	322,253	159,512
1990	6,807,498	3,426,826	41,827	3,468,653	394,898	30,003	3,103,758	2,651,395	1,052,345	20,080	339,012	164,024
1991	6,933,177	3,616,892	48,490	3,665,382	417,708	-93,352	3,154,322	2,606,869	1,171,986	19,749	351,069	163,361
1992	7,308,276	3,871,763	46,252	3,918,015	445,103	-147,040	3,325,872	2,645,164	1,337,240	20,319	359,679	162,757
1993	7,782,306	4,134,713	49,101	4,183,814	472,610	-79,233	3,631,971	2,720,752	1,429,583	21,094	368,938	170,194
1994	8,330,303	4,468,729	39,826	4,508,555	518,294	-69,540	3,920,721	2,878,991	1,530,591	21,868	380,928	178,317
1995	9,093,151	4,768,774	41,282	4,810,056	549,600	-75,801	4,184,655	3,253,328	1,655,168	23,207	391,823	186,043
1996	9,535,549	5,136,363	30,688	5,167,051	582,228	-150,179	4,434,644	3,338,998	1,761,907	23,796	400,723	191,718
1997	10,162,884	5,292,558	33,445	5,326,003	604,113	-57,310	4,664,580	3,657,513	1,840,791	24,737	410,841	196,507
1998	10,962,952	5,885,618	43,275	5,928,893	656,736	-145,508	5,126,649	3,975,468	1,860,835	25,985	421,889	205,733
1999	11,538,383	6,446,621	45,651	6,492,272	710,017	-147,080	5,635,175	3,952,373	1,950,835	26,710	431,981	211,109
2000	12,710,375	6,961,704	43,776	7,005,480	764,422	-7,656	6,233,402	4,378,323	2,098,650	28,607	444,311	219,932
2001	14,302,245	8,167,560	42,924	8,210,484	886,105	-9,902	7,314,477	4,705,290	2,282,478	31,022	461,037	232,767
2002	14,799,383	8,748,005	45,561	8,793,566	943,875	-21,899	7,827,792	4,508,578	2,463,013	30,904	478,889	240,323
2003	15,984,759	9,739,725	43,820	9,783,545	1,049,738	-22,867	8,710,940	4,628,795	2,645,024	32,120	497,662	258,600
2004	18,593,586	11,282,868	42,389	11,325,257	1,210,610	-74,365	10,040,282	5,681,098	2,872,206	35,591	522,431	276,146
2005	20,767,776	12,523,544	45,654	12,569,198	1,361,579	-52,907	11,154,712	6,516,696	3,096,368	37,417	555,029	300,554
2006	24,113,537	14,475,819	35,446	14,511,265	1,548,833	-91,054	12,871,378	7,868,003	3,374,156	41,384	582,678	316,326
2007	24,754,053	14,264,308	25,811	14,290,119	1,563,192	37,587	12,764,514	8,314,993	3,674,546	40,935	604,716	315,773
2008	25,177,524	13,424,417	25,755	13,450,172	1,514,409	-16,034	11,919,729	9,006,796	4,250,999	41,208	610,984	298,689
2009	24,275,885	12,542,672	30,727	12,573,399	1,449,151	9,058	11,133,306	8,432,451	4,710,128	39,647	612,297	284,886
2010	24,286,546	12,753,521	41,223	12,794,744	1,432,490	-148,347	11,213,907	7,888,837	5,183,802	39,142	620,467	284,625
2011	26,197,166	13,053,824	41,131	13,094,955	1,331,097	-21,680	11,742,178	8,995,585	5,459,403	41,512	631,077	292,596
2012	26,802,947	13,517,932	56,596	13,574,528	1,395,604	-209,241	11,969,683	9,261,413	5,571,851	41,582	644,580	301,974
2013	27,238,646	13,865,747	61,481	13,927,228	1,630,182	-113,873	12,183,173	9,234,034	5,821,439	41,244	660,431	314,673
2014	30,255,203	15,095,215	53,503	15,148,718	1,762,741	-291,979	13,093,998	10,891,172	6,270,033	44,608	678,241	334,645
2015	32,629,000	16,466,384	69,350	16,535,734	1,905,137	-504,616	14,125,981	11,802,529	6,700,490	46,585	700,421	353,153
2016	34,835,737	17,579,670	65,086	17,644,756	2,046,749	-603,466	14,994,541	12,831,910	7,009,286	48,215	722,506	364,211
2017	36,786,500	18,787,629	52,097	18,839,726	2,166,961	-699,990	15,972,775	13,466,696	7,347,029	49,764	739,224	372,280
2018	38,547,795	38,489,321	58,474	19,479,883	2,267,794	-753,169	16,458,920	14,263,573	7,825,302	51,093	754,470	391,979
2019	40,119,053	40,052,400	66,653	20,579,971	2,426,123	-774,087	17,379,761	14,398,293	8,340,999	52,064	770,577	403,070

Personal Income and Employment by Area: Cape Girardeau, MO-IL

(Thousands of dollars, except as noted.)

Year	Personal income, total	Earnings by place of work			Less: Contributions for government social insurance	Plus: Adjustment for residence	Equals: Net earnings by place of residence	Plus: Dividends, interest, and rent	Plus: Personal current transfer receipts	Per capita personal income (dollars)	Population (persons)	Total employment
		Nonfarm	Farm	Total								
1970	222,083	169,627	9,171	178,798	11,405	-6,509	160,884	33,039	28,160	3,153	70,436	30,842
1971	242,481	185,875	8,250	194,125	12,963	-7,055	174,107	36,531	31,843	3,373	71,899	31,125
1972	262,465	198,524	10,466	208,990	14,450	-6,576	187,964	40,310	34,191	3,564	73,647	31,770
1973	296,723	217,718	18,539	236,257	18,254	-6,082	211,921	45,786	39,016	4,048	73,297	33,247
1974	330,521	250,830	10,119	260,949	21,944	-7,705	231,300	52,907	46,314	4,431	74,588	34,420
1975	379,546	274,221	17,405	291,626	23,478	-8,765	259,383	60,443	59,720	5,087	74,605	34,141
1976	422,961	317,320	15,432	332,752	27,451	-10,990	294,311	66,143	62,507	5,506	76,817	36,445
1977	463,456	349,977	14,501	364,478	30,208	-11,215	323,055	75,134	65,267	5,973	77,598	37,517
1978	526,451	401,003	19,953	420,956	35,866	-12,988	372,102	83,560	70,789	6,678	78,829	39,115
1979	589,997	444,672	24,964	469,636	41,160	-14,618	413,858	95,695	80,444	7,380	79,941	39,912
1980	632,790	466,106	2,883	468,989	43,073	-11,193	414,723	120,146	97,921	7,758	81,562	39,014
1981	720,486	496,981	16,547	513,528	49,323	-11,267	452,938	147,219	120,329	8,782	82,038	39,055
1982	755,887	513,919	10,882	524,801	51,882	-12,557	460,362	176,084	119,441	9,266	81,576	39,480
1983	802,466	561,348	-1,820	559,528	56,354	-16,825	486,349	187,345	128,772	9,841	81,546	40,586
1984	892,923	616,270	13,170	629,440	63,602	-17,580	548,258	210,896	133,769	10,925	81,732	41,905
1985	948,768	656,136	16,431	672,567	68,883	-18,391	585,293	221,826	141,649	11,541	82,211	43,356
1986	996,935	714,065	2,341	716,406	75,566	-22,000	618,840	230,111	147,984	12,103	82,368	44,845
1987	1,063,917	775,813	9,625	785,438	81,133	-23,305	681,000	231,063	151,854	12,892	82,524	46,098
1988	1,115,402	826,657	4,319	830,976	89,028	-23,958	717,990	237,809	159,603	13,475	82,775	46,557
1989	1,204,185	877,513	12,982	890,495	95,487	-25,682	769,326	258,739	176,120	14,555	82,734	47,610
1990	1,238,100	911,743	9,411	921,154	102,290	-30,307	788,557	259,892	189,651	14,910	83,037	49,146
1991	1,301,814	947,215	6,612	953,827	108,025	-33,450	812,352	274,223	215,239	15,518	83,892	48,247
1992	1,403,424	1,030,767	14,305	1,045,072	116,490	-44,219	884,363	285,820	233,241	16,488	85,118	49,450
1993	1,474,699	1,084,704	10,172	1,094,876	123,263	-49,132	922,481	304,338	247,880	17,187	85,803	50,713
1994	1,560,150	1,165,094	8,418	1,173,512	133,147	-53,235	987,130	314,072	258,948	18,085	86,267	52,387
1995	1,662,831	1,248,750	3,121	1,251,871	142,368	-62,958	1,046,545	338,814	277,472	19,095	87,084	54,098
1996	1,736,429	1,286,209	9,210	1,295,419	144,810	-67,070	1,083,539	360,114	292,776	19,738	87,975	54,280
1997	1,828,121	1,351,047	8,961	1,360,008	150,825	-71,907	1,137,276	383,562	307,283	20,711	88,270	54,484
1998	1,933,178	1,449,492	3,270	1,452,762	161,180	-81,892	1,209,690	400,708	322,780	21,799	88,682	56,838
1999	2,041,622	1,586,002	2,332	1,588,334	175,468	-100,140	1,312,726	399,268	329,628	22,681	90,016	58,769
2000	2,180,881	1,670,686	10,129	1,680,815	181,444	-107,855	1,391,516	433,619	355,746	24,091	90,527	59,512
2001	2,265,046	1,715,256	13,124	1,728,380	186,856	-110,703	1,430,821	438,397	395,828	24,829	91,226	57,816
2002	2,351,673	1,803,446	7,327	1,810,773	195,024	-118,160	1,497,589	422,443	431,641	25,647	91,694	57,787
2003	2,456,915	1,871,087	22,035	1,893,122	201,823	-120,353	1,570,946	433,240	452,729	26,752	91,840	58,156
2004	2,621,811	1,984,976	37,878	2,022,854	210,578	-115,199	1,697,077	442,324	482,410	28,272	92,734	58,289
2005	2,701,868	2,094,001	19,298	2,113,299	223,291	-119,045	1,770,963	410,224	520,681	28,998	93,173	59,727
2006	2,856,544	2,211,379	12,078	2,223,457	238,399	-131,728	1,853,330	452,975	550,239	30,335	94,167	61,015
2007	3,047,410	2,326,385	6,426	2,332,811	255,213	-144,093	1,933,505	521,837	592,068	32,208	94,616	62,379
2008	3,114,754	2,273,926	29,685	2,303,611	255,109	-137,335	1,911,167	548,034	655,553	32,776	95,031	61,857
2009	3,105,759	2,277,226	13,267	2,290,493	255,777	-144,297	1,890,419	508,181	707,159	32,475	95,634	60,395
2010	3,191,464	2,327,552	19,880	2,347,432	256,053	-140,841	1,950,538	487,330	753,596	33,090	96,448	59,229
2011	3,331,026	2,367,987	23,347	2,391,334	234,207	-121,762	2,035,365	531,863	763,798	34,363	96,937	59,171
2012	3,543,765	2,494,947	17,665	2,512,612	242,173	-108,906	2,161,533	610,534	771,698	36,461	97,193	59,680
2013	3,568,600	2,572,261	36,801	2,609,062	279,783	-108,301	2,220,978	558,727	788,895	36,719	97,187	60,558
2014	3,629,417	2,573,246	37,202	2,610,448	283,069	-92,958	2,234,421	593,479	801,517	37,265	97,396	60,046
2015	3,820,899	2,701,456	9,986	2,711,442	295,779	-79,356	2,336,307	635,953	848,639	39,297	97,231	60,266
2016	3,858,269	2,705,916	19,590	2,725,506	301,492	-84,767	2,339,247	650,693	868,329	39,741	97,085	60,535
2017	4,000,271	2,791,103	20,484	2,811,587	308,095	-75,910	2,427,582	683,861	888,828	41,333	96,782	60,677
2018	4,155,068	4,152,299	2,769	2,883,322	320,662	-88,398	2,474,262	749,716	931,090	42,894	96,868	61,477
2019	4,312,900	4,299,787	13,113	3,009,299	332,811	-88,880	2,587,608	758,715	966,577	44,571	96,765	62,193

Personal Income and Employment by Area: Carbondale-Marion, IL

(Thousands of dollars, except as noted.)

Year	Personal income, total	Earnings by place of work			Less: Contributions for government social insurance	Plus: Adjustment for residence	Equals: Net earnings by place of residence	Plus: Dividends, interest, and rent	Plus: Personal current transfer receipts	Per capita personal income (dollars)	Population (persons)	Total employment
		Nonfarm	Farm	Total								
1970	324,924	258,599	2,145	260,744	15,052	-2,209	243,483	42,515	38,926	3,112	104,404	40,154
1971	364,863	286,980	2,871	289,851	17,188	-2,617	270,046	46,932	47,885	3,415	106,828	41,453
1972	401,416	312,025	3,009	315,034	19,471	-1,349	294,214	52,115	55,087	3,705	108,334	42,454
1973	456,578	342,541	9,466	352,007	24,400	-1,292	326,315	60,142	70,121	4,271	106,903	43,396
1974	495,243	364,480	9,510	373,990	27,065	1,189	348,114	69,309	77,820	4,615	107,320	44,408
1975	587,924	417,458	12,813	430,271	29,669	2,761	403,363	81,695	102,866	5,329	110,316	44,949
1976	660,254	484,980	8,797	493,777	36,115	1,508	459,170	89,371	111,713	5,790	114,039	47,991
1977	720,975	530,488	11,370	541,858	40,062	4,761	506,557	100,353	114,065	6,229	115,743	49,432
1978	786,172	585,648	8,304	593,952	45,110	4,783	553,625	111,423	121,124	6,748	116,505	50,217
1979	884,913	641,961	11,013	652,974	51,396	15,846	617,424	128,234	139,255	7,505	117,908	51,476
1980	972,624	683,292	2,196	685,488	54,271	19,040	650,257	157,300	165,067	8,195	118,692	51,285
1981	1,075,070	727,487	7,504	734,991	61,069	17,946	691,868	193,438	189,764	8,921	120,509	51,216
1982	1,181,923	778,860	3,490	782,350	66,357	24,409	740,402	241,355	200,166	9,823	120,316	51,051
1983	1,254,280	836,669	-520	836,149	71,714	15,516	779,951	257,279	217,050	10,396	120,650	52,036
1984	1,359,665	912,161	2,643	914,804	80,827	14,991	848,968	287,902	222,795	11,343	119,864	53,250
1985	1,414,180	928,017	11,698	939,715	83,347	25,275	881,643	302,305	230,232	11,785	119,997	53,361
1986	1,448,925	962,489	-4,184	958,305	86,303	25,458	897,460	317,460	234,005	12,113	119,619	54,938
1987	1,514,826	1,011,748	6,915	1,018,663	89,066	20,023	949,620	320,595	244,611	12,632	119,923	55,376
1988	1,569,041	1,049,891	8,316	1,058,207	96,661	23,924	985,470	325,656	257,915	13,157	119,255	55,452
1989	1,690,108	1,102,139	21,601	1,123,740	103,011	27,381	1,048,110	366,563	275,435	14,211	118,928	56,439
1990	1,756,374	1,187,537	9,269	1,196,806	109,136	23,847	1,111,517	353,680	291,177	14,788	118,770	58,256
1991	1,818,343	1,246,499	6,273	1,252,772	119,032	9,367	1,143,107	364,592	310,644	15,335	118,578	58,784
1992	1,963,415	1,340,694	12,146	1,352,840	126,134	5,121	1,231,827	373,646	357,942	16,396	119,749	59,722
1993	2,007,125	1,370,579	13,889	1,384,468	130,850	-1,659	1,251,959	382,558	372,608	16,600	120,909	60,133
1994	2,121,111	1,469,618	16,030	1,485,648	143,723	919	1,342,844	400,297	377,970	17,467	121,436	62,968
1995	2,235,413	1,533,939	8,874	1,542,813	150,424	-4,602	1,387,787	444,498	403,128	18,394	121,529	63,549
1996	2,324,611	1,573,953	14,467	1,588,420	152,865	-6,679	1,428,876	471,986	423,749	19,132	121,503	63,587
1997	2,419,295	1,633,675	14,443	1,648,118	156,971	-9,627	1,481,520	499,138	438,637	19,863	121,801	64,237
1998	2,532,983	1,712,070	14,522	1,726,592	164,507	-15,049	1,547,036	532,332	453,615	20,817	121,676	65,029
1999	2,639,209	1,850,094	7,913	1,858,007	173,486	-26,423	1,658,098	524,328	456,783	21,722	121,502	67,486
2000	2,768,092	1,946,526	10,992	1,957,518	179,181	-30,863	1,747,474	540,106	480,512	22,893	120,912	69,016
2001	3,009,692	2,142,388	6,777	2,149,165	191,497	-41,622	1,916,046	581,166	512,480	24,819	121,267	69,573
2002	3,130,398	2,297,071	-1,400	2,295,671	205,894	-55,184	2,034,593	548,243	547,562	25,853	121,086	69,564
2003	3,206,009	2,328,126	3,155	2,331,281	211,945	-58,502	2,060,834	575,803	569,372	26,324	121,792	69,391
2004	3,316,708	2,398,556	17,449	2,416,005	220,729	-65,723	2,129,553	583,588	603,567	27,000	122,841	69,792
2005	3,445,739	2,538,882	7,977	2,546,859	242,540	-84,742	2,219,577	560,283	665,879	27,815	123,881	71,440
2006	3,599,420	2,680,038	9,466	2,689,504	254,821	-100,384	2,334,299	588,313	676,808	28,889	124,594	72,504
2007	3,743,427	2,751,629	6,390	2,758,019	263,812	-105,007	2,389,200	609,828	744,399	30,015	124,719	72,760
2008	3,937,228	2,832,566	20,309	2,852,875	272,914	-125,844	2,454,117	670,144	812,967	31,428	125,279	72,413
2009	4,080,404	2,904,327	3,716	2,908,043	278,134	-144,030	2,485,879	694,222	900,303	32,412	125,893	72,044
2010	4,331,547	3,114,423	10,511	3,124,934	293,574	-159,029	2,672,331	682,761	976,455	34,157	126,813	72,125
2011	4,464,670	3,199,390	20,058	3,219,448	274,600	-177,890	2,766,958	745,313	952,399	35,144	127,041	72,703
2012	4,531,243	3,252,500	9,310	3,261,810	282,104	-188,373	2,791,333	794,139	945,771	36,033	125,752	72,457
2013	4,588,457	3,277,592	45,130	3,322,722	315,164	-207,611	2,799,947	796,606	991,904	36,111	127,067	71,428
2014	4,671,658	3,330,498	26,974	3,357,472	322,947	-216,730	2,817,795	847,210	1,006,653	36,868	126,712	71,906
2015	4,814,628	3,420,234	12,856	3,433,090	330,852	-237,353	2,864,885	887,916	1,061,827	37,942	126,896	72,857
2016	4,838,622	3,452,427	8,527	3,460,954	338,445	-261,166	2,861,343	905,148	1,072,131	38,198	126,672	73,182
2017	4,957,681	3,519,506	16,986	3,536,492	347,104	-270,696	2,918,692	941,419	1,097,570	39,468	125,612	73,252
2018	5,532,805	5,521,340	11,465	3,798,777	378,851	-141,226	3,278,700	963,715	1,290,390	40,476	136,694	76,649
2019	5,665,870	5,661,953	3,917	3,870,079	390,533	-127,433	3,352,113	984,406	1,329,351	41,733	135,764	77,735

Personal Income and Employment by Area: Carson City, NV

(Thousands of dollars, except as noted.)

Year	Personal income, total	Earnings by place of work			Less: Contributions for government social insurance	Plus: Adjustment for residence	Equals: Net earnings by place of residence	Plus: Dividends, interest, and rent	Plus: Personal current transfer receipts	Per capita personal income (dollars)	Population (persons)	Total employment
		Nonfarm	Farm	Total								
1970	86,094	65,872	47	65,919	2,301	842	64,460	16,519	5,115	5,367	16,041	8,194
1971	104,264	78,136	305	78,441	2,907	2,438	77,972	19,716	6,576	5,655	18,439	9,095
1972	122,082	90,520	155	90,675	3,824	4,421	91,272	22,899	7,911	6,107	19,991	9,860
1973	142,199	105,907	460	106,367	5,579	6,513	107,301	25,575	9,323	6,418	22,158	11,152
1974	163,239	121,672	96	121,768	6,755	7,175	122,188	29,322	11,729	6,856	23,808	12,036
1975	189,435	138,032	137	138,169	7,117	7,685	138,737	33,800	16,898	7,433	25,484	12,528
1976	220,730	162,807	143	162,950	8,899	7,350	161,401	40,294	19,035	8,459	26,094	13,820
1977	256,190	190,877	134	191,011	11,001	6,348	186,358	47,840	21,992	9,374	27,331	15,384
1978	311,643	237,818	116	237,934	14,851	2,251	225,334	60,625	25,684	10,398	29,972	17,838
1979	352,566	271,089	122	271,211	18,744	-2,476	249,991	72,998	29,577	11,093	31,782	19,081
1980	397,895	295,960	234	296,194	20,592	4	275,606	85,528	36,761	12,310	32,323	19,360
1981	452,262	338,030	153	338,183	24,862	-7,787	305,534	102,505	44,223	13,510	33,475	19,536
1982	475,708	341,380	164	341,544	25,085	-6,997	309,462	119,063	47,183	13,859	34,324	18,960
1983	503,576	362,389	163	362,552	29,896	-12,149	320,507	129,624	53,445	14,532	34,654	19,392
1984	552,520	397,542	274	397,816	35,190	-13,078	349,548	146,102	56,870	15,670	35,260	20,535
1985	601,045	438,202	115	438,317	41,267	-21,131	375,919	162,230	62,896	16,517	36,389	21,622
1986	646,402	470,487	104	470,591	45,552	-26,442	398,597	178,467	69,338	17,430	37,086	22,495
1987	672,934	509,136	221	509,357	49,982	-35,743	423,632	175,029	74,273	17,991	37,403	24,244
1988	736,821	564,654	116	564,770	57,172	-41,237	466,361	190,478	79,982	19,199	38,379	25,165
1989	808,735	606,056	153	606,209	62,183	-49,839	494,187	221,764	92,784	20,393	39,657	25,785
1990	872,217	658,267	190	658,457	69,064	-41,374	548,019	221,937	102,261	21,423	40,714	26,766
1991	941,474	705,768	152	705,920	73,328	-50,234	582,358	236,183	122,933	22,456	41,926	27,173
1992	1,025,626	777,146	140	777,286	79,210	-58,763	639,313	251,337	134,976	23,724	43,231	27,073
1993	1,080,695	834,535	176	834,711	86,047	-80,502	668,162	271,130	141,403	24,246	44,572	28,566
1994	1,163,386	916,896	79	916,975	96,962	-99,375	720,638	299,546	143,202	25,232	46,108	30,498
1995	1,260,239	1,002,315	-8	1,002,307	106,936	-119,214	776,157	327,565	156,517	26,382	47,768	32,941
1996	1,338,679	1,076,306	-105	1,076,201	110,691	-146,982	818,528	357,054	163,097	27,159	49,290	34,369
1997	1,431,386	1,171,737	-179	1,171,558	116,711	-172,289	882,558	377,557	171,271	28,365	50,463	35,519
1998	1,526,658	1,274,413	-6	1,274,407	122,451	-183,328	968,628	378,714	179,316	30,015	50,864	36,263
1999	1,590,269	1,369,872	117	1,369,989	128,616	-211,838	1,029,535	379,654	181,080	30,610	51,953	37,564
2000	1,750,671	1,484,649	139	1,484,788	122,044	-220,960	1,141,784	413,634	195,253	33,303	52,568	39,240
2001	1,252,164	997,010	315	997,325	127,172	-231,773	638,380	397,682	216,102	23,417	53,472	41,635
2002	1,095,751	882,445	565	883,010	131,364	-257,767	493,879	362,425	239,447	20,104	54,503	41,771
2003	1,167,997	920,810	302	921,112	134,489	-282,172	504,451	410,644	252,902	21,146	55,234	41,908
2004	1,185,455	938,014	301	938,315	138,796	-322,089	477,430	444,369	263,656	21,171	55,995	43,058
2005	1,386,285	1,158,762	298	1,159,060	146,934	-365,798	646,328	460,005	279,952	24,763	55,982	43,878
2006	1,691,451	1,493,084	322	1,493,406	156,129	-392,100	945,177	455,810	290,464	30,526	55,410	43,921
2007	1,621,198	1,452,036	195	1,452,231	177,871	-450,252	824,108	488,088	309,002	29,323	55,288	42,266
2008	1,658,971	1,509,886	1,168	1,511,054	181,826	-488,368	840,860	470,614	347,497	29,863	55,552	41,157
2009	2,286,837	2,117,882	1,441	2,119,323	167,012	-510,821	1,441,490	454,116	391,231	41,278	55,401	39,407
2010	2,442,605	2,299,171	2,441	2,301,612	165,668	-533,699	1,602,245	413,360	427,000	44,421	54,988	38,440
2011	2,363,973	2,149,681	3,393	2,153,074	151,544	-532,168	1,469,362	462,068	432,543	43,215	54,703	38,076
2012	2,153,762	1,945,635	3,582	1,949,217	159,178	-524,803	1,265,236	447,608	440,918	39,619	54,362	37,406
2013	2,206,574	2,004,365	3,764	2,008,129	171,349	-539,468	1,297,312	461,659	447,603	41,021	53,791	37,531
2014	2,274,840	2,006,519	5,103	2,011,622	179,509	-557,419	1,274,694	504,284	495,862	42,006	54,155	37,575
2015	2,461,958	2,171,110	4,489	2,175,599	183,629	-600,795	1,391,175	534,754	536,029	45,488	54,123	37,675
2016	2,454,615	2,102,280	3,466	2,105,746	183,816	-584,595	1,337,335	557,567	559,713	45,219	54,283	38,257
2017	2,682,333	2,358,458	3,750	2,362,208	204,304	-649,504	1,508,400	589,390	584,543	48,997	54,745	39,869
2018	2,804,115	2,802,919	1,196	2,387,287	210,564	-592,634	1,584,089	613,071	606,955	50,797	55,202	39,484
2019	2,933,904	2,933,008	896	2,501,568	226,586	-612,006	1,662,976	623,299	647,629	52,470	55,916	40,470

Personal Income and Employment by Area: Casper, WY

(Thousands of dollars, except as noted.)

Year	Personal income, total	Earnings by place of work			Less: Contributions for government social insurance	Plus: Adjustment for residence	Equals: Net earnings by place of residence	Plus: Dividends, interest, and rent	Plus: Personal current transfer receipts	Per capita personal income (dollars)	Population (persons)	Total employment
		Nonfarm	Farm	Total								
1970	241,410	188,187	4,641	192,828	12,904	6,633	186,557	39,276	15,577	4,698	51,381	25,733
1971	259,416	201,896	2,614	204,510	14,304	7,402	197,608	44,035	17,773	4,977	52,121	26,453
1972	276,780	215,571	4,135	219,706	16,194	7,371	210,883	46,949	18,948	5,212	53,106	27,009
1973	317,814	247,875	7,885	255,760	21,425	6,133	240,468	55,207	22,139	6,018	52,814	28,431
1974	389,544	312,607	5,375	317,982	26,848	6,833	297,967	66,489	25,088	7,281	53,504	30,410
1975	468,746	389,022	2,302	391,324	32,946	7,283	365,661	72,880	30,205	8,357	56,088	33,334
1976	517,903	434,447	1,994	436,441	39,067	5,594	402,968	82,115	32,820	8,843	58,567	35,183
1977	632,083	544,927	1,847	546,774	47,380	3,957	503,351	93,416	35,316	10,273	61,526	39,229
1978	769,151	678,521	1,662	680,183	61,393	-603	618,187	111,199	39,765	11,740	65,515	44,060
1979	883,607	786,350	2,593	788,943	75,562	-5,854	707,527	129,485	46,595	12,927	68,354	46,821
1980	1,016,095	896,573	1,898	898,471	86,058	-13,176	799,237	161,742	55,116	14,011	72,523	48,294
1981	1,180,992	1,026,343	1,174	1,027,517	106,676	-10,562	910,279	205,009	65,704	15,738	75,042	51,043
1982	1,206,850	1,003,390	3,855	1,007,245	107,639	-7,792	891,814	238,202	76,834	15,654	77,094	49,117
1983	1,122,025	878,412	7,597	886,009	92,206	-3,794	790,009	240,988	91,028	14,707	76,292	44,001
1984	1,149,274	899,112	3,260	902,372	97,199	-1,058	804,115	255,788	89,371	15,708	73,166	44,094
1985	1,135,127	864,391	2,436	866,827	95,245	2,316	773,898	262,493	98,736	15,861	71,569	42,169
1986	1,032,877	748,539	839	749,378	83,057	5,496	671,817	253,385	107,675	14,931	69,177	37,710
1987	1,037,545	752,602	1,434	754,036	80,841	6,040	679,235	248,885	109,425	16,073	64,552	36,574
1988	1,049,271	750,229	988	751,217	87,737	8,298	671,778	262,786	114,707	16,786	62,507	37,519
1989	1,177,887	844,153	-123	844,030	91,643	11,744	764,131	287,172	126,584	19,084	61,722	37,111
1990	1,300,666	934,077	-415	933,662	105,507	13,547	841,702	319,015	139,949	21,219	61,296	38,058
1991	1,307,580	883,181	3,403	886,584	107,684	12,180	791,080	363,490	153,010	20,984	62,312	38,809
1992	1,385,029	924,194	2,646	926,840	110,741	12,014	828,113	384,754	172,162	21,954	63,087	38,045
1993	1,459,222	972,736	2,716	975,452	115,007	11,615	872,060	396,854	190,308	22,807	63,981	38,759
1994	1,500,533	1,000,710	1,633	1,002,343	119,060	11,880	895,163	413,021	192,349	22,973	65,316	39,738
1995	1,525,891	1,024,082	1,098	1,025,180	121,354	10,863	914,689	404,629	206,573	23,230	65,687	40,383
1996	1,589,804	1,070,284	782	1,071,066	123,361	10,381	958,086	414,874	216,844	24,140	65,859	40,551
1997	1,730,814	1,194,660	2,625	1,197,285	131,861	10,045	1,075,469	433,477	221,868	26,101	66,311	41,280
1998	1,803,374	1,230,220	1,420	1,231,640	137,166	8,824	1,103,298	470,474	229,602	27,264	66,146	41,582
1999	1,906,250	1,323,556	2,592	1,326,148	144,108	7,132	1,189,172	481,091	235,987	28,760	66,282	42,325
2000	2,155,219	1,535,293	2,137	1,537,430	164,005	2,549	1,375,974	524,299	254,946	32,359	66,603	43,624
2001	2,113,140	1,489,692	3,642	1,493,334	169,590	3,509	1,327,253	515,951	269,936	31,550	66,978	44,539
2002	2,160,180	1,548,525	3,272	1,551,797	171,609	2,946	1,383,134	485,303	291,743	31,977	67,554	44,730
2003	2,287,726	1,652,444	5,521	1,657,965	183,913	293	1,474,345	495,705	317,676	33,522	68,246	45,554
2004	2,417,422	1,770,214	4,576	1,774,790	204,198	-3,291	1,567,301	517,702	332,419	35,017	69,035	47,196
2005	2,736,102	1,982,354	7,511	1,989,865	225,303	-6,200	1,758,362	632,797	344,943	39,131	69,922	48,826
2006	3,203,912	2,397,724	1,260	2,398,984	287,633	-9,988	2,101,363	749,906	352,643	45,249	70,806	50,902
2007	3,308,237	2,526,219	-437	2,525,782	312,679	-6,076	2,207,027	727,762	373,448	45,716	72,365	52,732
2008	3,850,489	2,994,274	-1,071	2,993,203	340,285	54	2,652,972	757,242	440,275	52,258	73,682	53,987
2009	3,365,489	2,601,280	325	2,601,605	314,443	-2,058	2,285,104	605,306	475,079	44,731	75,238	51,712
2010	3,745,140	2,866,167	1,256	2,867,423	327,771	-13,480	2,526,172	709,646	509,322	49,633	75,456	51,833
2011	4,094,062	3,100,951	8,921	3,109,872	320,922	-32,173	2,756,777	830,521	506,764	53,572	76,421	53,356
2012	4,751,192	3,641,539	1,436	3,642,975	356,996	-42,913	3,243,066	1,009,106	499,020	60,461	78,583	55,493
2013	5,078,184	3,882,898	5,524	3,888,422	408,056	-45,315	3,435,051	1,121,247	521,886	62,616	81,101	56,646
2014	5,732,223	4,309,710	10,460	4,320,170	445,882	-50,306	3,823,982	1,366,229	542,012	70,387	81,439	57,780
2015	6,021,575	4,277,130	7,190	4,284,320	428,635	-28,208	3,827,477	1,617,977	576,121	73,314	82,134	57,150
2016	5,246,528	3,766,463	3,514	3,769,977	382,199	-3,140	3,384,638	1,256,843	605,047	64,858	80,892	53,911
2017	5,331,515	3,808,422	3,254	3,811,676	396,746	-6,698	3,408,232	1,299,845	623,438	67,023	79,547	53,739
2018	5,647,104	5,645,500	1,604	4,358,980	425,951	-8,587	3,924,442	1,064,287	658,375	71,324	79,175	54,082
2019	5,764,702	5,763,244	1,458	4,424,158	437,705	15,233	4,001,686	1,065,908	697,108	72,187	79,858	55,034

Personal Income and Employment by Area: Cedar Rapids, IA

(Thousands of dollars, except as noted.)

Year	Personal income, total	Earnings by place of work			Less: Contributions for government social insurance	Plus: Adjustment for residence	Equals: Net earnings by place of residence	Plus: Dividends, interest, and rent	Plus: Personal current transfer receipts	Per capita personal income (dollars)	Population (persons)	Total employment
		Nonfarm	Farm	Total								
1970	867,743	679,218	45,908	725,126	51,334	-2,882	670,910	134,314	62,519	4,209	206,165	96,649
1971	907,248	707,397	41,325	748,722	55,651	-4,373	688,698	145,349	73,201	4,372	207,532	94,803
1972	981,866	759,844	52,935	812,779	63,501	-5,226	744,052	157,433	80,381	4,721	207,990	96,324
1973	1,117,635	853,889	84,216	938,105	82,738	-7,020	848,347	177,093	92,195	5,400	206,982	100,990
1974	1,220,471	954,387	61,195	1,015,582	95,619	-8,229	911,734	201,519	107,218	5,871	207,881	104,894
1975	1,361,320	1,043,807	68,297	1,112,104	102,083	-8,965	1,001,056	226,327	133,937	6,481	210,055	105,550
1976	1,485,204	1,178,599	42,148	1,220,747	116,619	-11,145	1,092,983	244,575	147,646	7,023	211,491	108,639
1977	1,624,848	1,297,383	39,153	1,336,536	127,413	-13,161	1,195,962	274,570	154,316	7,706	210,846	110,943
1978	1,842,812	1,460,396	77,545	1,537,941	148,920	-18,597	1,370,424	305,064	167,324	8,732	211,033	114,026
1979	2,051,499	1,679,912	40,486	1,720,398	178,273	-26,118	1,516,007	346,999	188,493	9,680	211,937	121,050
1980	2,207,069	1,766,082	4,504	1,770,586	185,620	-26,026	1,558,940	418,960	229,169	10,330	213,666	119,634
1981	2,434,346	1,850,059	45,517	1,895,576	206,607	-29,124	1,659,845	516,285	258,216	11,454	212,534	116,231
1982	2,520,131	1,832,522	14,324	1,846,846	206,424	-30,294	1,610,128	608,216	301,787	11,979	210,374	111,314
1983	2,570,471	1,895,554	-19,506	1,876,048	213,291	-26,154	1,636,603	613,294	320,574	12,344	208,238	110,835
1984	2,827,567	2,036,395	51,007	2,087,402	234,825	-24,354	1,828,223	677,907	321,437	13,596	207,969	113,084
1985	2,966,502	2,185,531	35,174	2,220,705	255,289	-32,133	1,933,283	694,984	338,235	14,331	206,995	115,476
1986	3,118,213	2,311,408	59,524	2,370,932	274,778	-35,343	2,060,811	702,978	354,424	15,147	205,865	117,488
1987	3,313,101	2,507,122	71,887	2,579,009	296,097	-38,284	2,244,628	706,440	362,033	16,116	205,577	119,721
1988	3,484,804	2,712,436	22,352	2,734,788	329,956	-40,599	2,364,233	739,203	381,368	16,801	207,415	125,116
1989	3,856,667	2,934,587	81,773	3,016,360	354,020	-42,079	2,620,261	828,473	407,933	18,406	209,528	129,901
1990	4,039,220	3,113,667	83,721	3,197,388	386,919	-47,345	2,763,124	826,293	449,803	19,125	211,200	131,540
1991	4,162,304	3,237,493	48,500	3,285,993	405,898	-46,218	2,833,877	846,707	481,720	19,500	213,453	132,831
1992	4,412,071	3,433,228	87,268	3,520,496	427,000	-50,178	3,043,318	844,925	523,828	20,349	216,818	133,978
1993	4,585,152	3,646,243	35,798	3,682,041	457,550	-56,146	3,168,345	871,470	545,337	20,847	219,948	136,563
1994	4,933,129	3,927,887	85,138	4,013,025	498,316	-63,500	3,451,209	908,317	573,603	22,150	222,711	140,427
1995	5,223,835	4,165,021	44,740	4,209,761	528,393	-77,691	3,603,677	1,009,905	610,253	23,078	226,357	146,630
1996	5,586,117	4,352,447	115,314	4,467,761	532,629	-87,329	3,847,803	1,092,874	645,440	24,507	227,938	149,382
1997	5,912,525	4,620,115	100,181	4,720,296	580,125	-99,070	4,041,101	1,201,894	669,530	25,652	230,490	152,680
1998	6,479,473	5,216,993	67,573	5,284,566	645,874	-133,066	4,505,626	1,284,839	689,008	27,880	232,402	157,170
1999	6,816,453	5,607,686	60,402	5,668,088	684,543	-150,861	4,832,684	1,258,845	724,924	28,961	235,365	161,738
2000	7,285,359	5,972,706	78,402	6,051,108	721,437	-181,137	5,148,534	1,359,749	777,076	30,617	237,950	164,865
2001	7,425,115	5,981,819	93,973	6,075,792	720,710	-156,157	5,198,925	1,364,579	861,611	30,919	240,145	163,779
2002	7,556,361	5,947,686	87,852	6,035,538	713,594	-127,157	5,194,787	1,392,800	968,774	31,212	242,099	160,448
2003	7,694,142	6,103,847	85,318	6,189,165	738,934	-115,796	5,334,435	1,380,606	979,101	31,628	243,272	159,065
2004	8,082,885	6,447,451	140,029	6,587,480	771,074	-96,036	5,720,370	1,347,640	1,014,875	32,977	245,108	161,774
2005	8,396,379	6,732,390	93,787	6,826,177	809,927	-90,573	5,925,677	1,371,102	1,099,600	33,957	247,265	164,717
2006	8,917,953	7,047,904	71,796	7,119,700	847,858	-93,786	6,178,056	1,535,377	1,204,520	35,740	249,524	168,369
2007	9,638,330	7,542,681	106,996	7,649,677	907,831	-104,875	6,636,971	1,712,363	1,288,996	38,140	252,709	172,462
2008	10,258,012	7,926,142	109,537	8,035,679	962,583	-128,252	6,944,844	1,831,611	1,481,557	40,148	255,503	174,581
2009	10,182,917	7,822,135	75,774	7,897,909	953,304	-91,746	6,852,859	1,727,538	1,602,520	39,638	256,896	172,876
2010	10,587,905	8,120,697	83,548	8,204,245	991,674	-57,518	7,155,053	1,721,231	1,711,621	40,976	258,395	173,011
2011	11,127,303	8,387,198	188,653	8,575,851	926,521	-127,562	7,521,768	1,861,043	1,744,492	42,667	260,796	175,478
2012	11,742,280	8,762,733	138,597	8,901,330	944,189	-113,346	7,843,795	2,149,079	1,749,406	44,862	261,740	176,557
2013	11,871,341	8,923,242	229,828	9,153,070	1,077,564	-30,534	8,044,972	2,046,306	1,780,063	45,233	262,449	177,261
2014	12,332,349	9,362,175	86,133	9,448,308	1,111,507	-83,594	8,253,207	2,190,804	1,888,338	46,720	263,963	178,989
2015	12,807,477	9,584,409	62,773	9,647,182	1,136,738	-44,521	8,465,923	2,325,101	2,016,453	48,151	265,984	181,100
2016	13,064,503	9,795,216	21,792	9,817,008	1,175,111	-50,958	8,590,939	2,402,262	2,071,302	48,762	267,925	181,335
2017	13,445,883	10,109,686	20,896	10,130,582	1,212,994	-51,689	8,865,899	2,506,189	2,073,795	49,746	270,293	181,875
2018	14,218,156	14,136,700	81,456	10,621,264	1,274,617	-230,545	9,116,102	2,805,892	2,296,162	52,261	272,061	182,251
2019	14,509,845	14,360,230	149,615	10,709,437	1,288,463	-151,829	9,269,145	2,800,940	2,439,760	53,143	273,032	184,455

Personal Income and Employment by Area: Chambersburg-Waynesboro, PA

(Thousands of dollars, except as noted.)

Year	Personal income, total	Earnings by place of work			Less: Contributions for government social insurance	Plus: Adjustment for residence	Equals: Net earnings by place of residence	Plus: Dividends, interest, and rent	Plus: Personal current transfer receipts	Per capita personal income (dollars)	Population (persons)	Total employment
		Nonfarm	Farm	Total								
1970	402,056	309,060	16,046	325,106	18,784	5,766	312,088	56,053	33,915	3,976	101,127	45,763
1971	425,498	324,248	13,591	337,839	20,346	5,906	323,399	62,672	39,427	4,128	103,082	44,890
1972	477,416	365,265	15,581	380,846	24,028	6,773	363,591	69,487	44,338	4,630	103,103	46,239
1973	536,494	412,697	17,730	430,427	31,392	7,042	406,077	81,097	49,320	5,144	104,285	48,655
1974	598,323	454,468	20,778	475,246	36,378	8,300	447,168	92,240	58,915	5,611	106,640	50,542
1975	657,255	498,091	13,610	511,701	38,922	5,461	478,240	102,310	76,705	6,083	108,052	50,373
1976	715,956	534,221	17,185	551,406	42,775	8,489	517,120	111,164	87,672	6,498	110,183	50,555
1977	779,494	572,139	15,349	587,488	45,380	18,131	560,239	125,589	93,666	7,072	110,218	50,537
1978	878,988	646,979	19,434	666,413	52,338	21,139	635,214	144,298	99,476	7,907	111,166	51,634
1979	963,986	698,445	23,399	721,844	59,353	30,962	693,453	160,694	109,839	8,594	112,172	52,438
1980	1,059,936	768,492	15,522	784,014	66,285	20,079	737,808	196,440	125,688	9,313	113,810	53,620
1981	1,180,283	829,800	24,183	853,983	76,659	21,831	799,155	235,591	145,537	10,326	114,302	53,452
1982	1,245,982	812,820	25,195	838,015	75,731	28,294	790,578	276,179	179,225	10,864	114,688	52,664
1983	1,300,079	826,574	21,758	848,332	79,810	37,685	806,207	293,795	200,077	11,276	115,293	51,891
1984	1,415,951	899,524	40,751	940,275	91,648	54,666	903,293	323,083	189,575	12,156	116,482	52,342
1985	1,524,474	969,709	43,945	1,013,654	100,315	59,405	972,744	352,817	198,913	13,043	116,882	53,479
1986	1,607,610	1,003,965	52,853	1,056,818	106,556	71,896	1,022,158	373,769	211,683	13,686	117,464	54,682
1987	1,701,619	1,085,071	40,582	1,125,653	114,902	83,772	1,094,523	390,407	216,689	14,443	117,819	56,100
1988	1,820,976	1,170,801	40,010	1,210,811	128,795	99,761	1,181,777	410,274	228,925	15,308	118,953	58,222
1989	1,963,437	1,267,849	46,972	1,314,821	139,385	113,546	1,288,982	430,003	244,452	16,392	119,780	60,503
1990	2,106,171	1,337,049	39,001	1,376,050	148,842	130,521	1,357,729	476,726	271,716	17,334	121,503	62,343
1991	2,195,668	1,381,189	29,346	1,410,535	156,037	134,849	1,389,347	487,051	319,270	17,845	123,039	61,587
1992	2,314,959	1,445,747	53,088	1,498,835	165,136	151,350	1,485,049	494,420	335,490	18,655	124,095	61,679
1993	2,414,863	1,508,199	44,271	1,552,470	176,823	163,469	1,539,116	523,157	352,590	19,310	125,056	62,013
1994	2,507,603	1,584,387	39,805	1,624,192	188,917	181,351	1,616,626	529,021	361,956	19,901	126,002	62,399
1995	2,595,338	1,633,690	27,916	1,661,606	194,707	202,646	1,669,545	548,017	377,776	20,520	126,479	63,732
1996	2,775,625	1,723,243	47,791	1,771,034	200,937	217,740	1,787,837	583,275	404,513	21,873	126,897	65,054
1997	2,881,522	1,775,823	42,297	1,818,120	207,474	241,628	1,852,274	608,506	420,742	22,565	127,696	66,252
1998	3,073,067	1,874,924	54,958	1,929,882	215,656	267,058	1,981,284	652,254	439,529	23,916	128,492	65,520
1999	3,172,023	1,905,835	57,776	1,963,611	217,466	305,872	2,052,017	649,121	470,885	24,613	128,875	64,503
2000	3,353,248	1,982,095	61,459	2,043,554	224,819	335,075	2,153,810	696,842	502,596	25,845	129,745	65,163
2001	3,538,175	2,060,147	71,433	2,131,580	232,527	390,571	2,289,624	694,222	554,329	27,091	130,604	64,999
2002	3,641,096	2,152,137	32,174	2,184,311	243,423	424,741	2,365,629	687,843	587,624	27,584	131,998	65,382
2003	3,859,964	2,271,187	64,998	2,336,185	255,349	468,447	2,549,283	695,638	615,043	28,896	133,583	66,732
2004	4,211,903	2,512,914	95,674	2,608,588	280,557	534,891	2,862,922	693,357	655,624	31,029	135,742	69,437
2005	4,562,247	2,740,864	93,402	2,834,266	310,316	631,558	3,155,508	694,437	712,302	32,839	138,927	72,375
2006	4,876,973	2,909,751	72,303	2,982,054	334,002	689,558	3,337,610	765,012	774,351	34,243	142,421	74,675
2007	5,201,761	3,032,124	107,302	3,139,426	349,669	702,207	3,491,964	878,561	831,236	35,914	144,840	76,580
2008	5,351,866	3,073,170	113,044	3,186,214	356,339	679,569	3,509,444	922,735	919,687	36,399	147,032	77,395
2009	5,223,782	2,939,870	70,221	3,010,091	351,199	641,259	3,300,151	857,008	1,066,623	35,139	148,662	73,881
2010	5,394,365	3,040,427	91,399	3,131,826	362,491	680,490	3,449,825	817,729	1,126,811	35,979	149,930	73,831
2011	5,716,539	3,142,058	123,130	3,265,188	340,136	762,720	3,687,772	885,997	1,142,770	37,870	150,952	74,708
2012	5,849,904	3,232,541	124,421	3,356,962	347,155	764,370	3,774,177	920,147	1,155,580	38,619	151,477	75,353
2013	5,946,523	3,341,763	141,305	3,483,068	400,032	748,355	3,831,391	914,664	1,200,468	39,159	151,855	76,279
2014	6,241,966	3,450,448	168,171	3,618,619	414,147	772,414	3,976,886	1,002,243	1,262,837	40,942	152,459	77,202
2015	6,420,837	3,628,225	103,956	3,732,181	433,121	755,926	4,054,986	1,032,136	1,333,715	41,993	152,903	78,894
2016	6,526,284	3,674,882	52,154	3,727,036	443,519	804,299	4,087,816	1,036,740	1,401,728	42,499	153,564	79,459
2017	6,765,678	3,827,140	79,979	3,907,119	464,566	823,176	4,265,729	1,086,977	1,412,972	43,866	154,234	80,000
2018	7,156,703	7,101,134	55,569	4,096,591	485,760	863,291	4,474,122	1,141,612	1,540,969	46,298	154,579	81,022
2019	7,431,056	7,354,802	76,254	4,245,458	503,495	911,299	4,653,262	1,164,086	1,613,708	47,934	155,027	81,956

Personal Income and Employment by Area: Champaign-Urbana, IL

(Thousands of dollars, except as noted.)

Year	Personal income, total	Earnings by place of work			Less: Contributions for government social insurance	Plus: Adjustment for residence	Equals: Net earnings by place of residence	Plus: Dividends, interest, and rent	Plus: Personal current transfer receipts	Per capita personal income (dollars)	Population (persons)	Total employment
		Nonfarm	Farm	Total								
1970	798,136	604,676	38,946	643,622	32,629	-6,309	604,684	148,450	45,002	4,093	195,003	92,168
1971	892,758	663,881	59,975	723,856	37,394	-6,483	679,979	159,560	53,219	4,564	195,599	94,618
1972	948,496	711,012	47,080	758,092	41,835	-5,245	711,012	176,661	60,823	4,868	194,839	95,753
1973	1,095,132	769,489	103,088	872,577	51,561	-4,257	816,759	206,273	72,100	5,508	198,829	99,841
1974	1,177,786	832,723	98,889	931,612	59,138	-4,248	868,226	226,601	82,959	5,906	199,411	101,332
1975	1,386,487	951,798	146,278	1,098,076	66,143	-6,546	1,025,387	255,680	105,420	7,008	197,848	103,387
1976	1,459,308	1,036,596	116,436	1,153,032	74,742	-3,591	1,074,699	270,833	113,776	7,266	200,853	104,608
1977	1,559,213	1,107,687	116,575	1,224,262	80,335	1,079	1,145,006	296,176	118,031	7,710	202,220	106,004
1978	1,664,757	1,212,826	85,953	1,298,779	90,163	2,422	1,211,038	326,724	126,995	8,192	203,216	107,412
1979	1,835,510	1,312,709	112,465	1,425,174	102,411	5,704	1,328,467	367,572	139,471	9,190	199,739	109,443
1980	1,922,947	1,382,678	39,793	1,422,471	106,373	12,124	1,328,222	426,202	168,523	9,576	200,808	108,626
1981	2,170,414	1,494,721	82,765	1,577,486	123,365	14,156	1,468,277	502,651	199,486	10,706	202,737	108,357
1982	2,322,548	1,581,468	54,692	1,636,160	131,302	9,112	1,513,970	592,133	216,445	11,419	203,390	108,510
1983	2,393,816	1,681,030	-10,191	1,670,839	141,172	6,904	1,536,571	617,561	239,684	11,854	201,935	107,989
1984	2,696,969	1,823,441	85,634	1,909,075	158,361	16,041	1,766,755	680,880	249,334	13,341	202,158	110,746
1985	2,834,224	1,933,532	108,823	2,042,355	171,638	8,716	1,879,433	697,967	256,824	13,998	202,468	113,254
1986	2,969,832	2,093,305	90,222	2,183,527	186,822	-20,147	1,976,558	730,069	263,205	14,555	204,047	118,091
1987	3,111,488	2,248,864	70,748	2,319,612	198,396	-32,873	2,088,343	749,828	273,317	15,228	204,329	120,675
1988	3,278,349	2,430,877	47,518	2,478,395	225,642	-37,256	2,215,497	780,276	282,576	16,009	204,777	123,729
1989	3,535,412	2,523,637	99,706	2,623,343	237,274	-42,407	2,343,662	886,790	304,960	17,406	203,114	123,578
1990	3,716,621	2,749,546	97,719	2,847,265	257,135	-56,283	2,533,847	855,167	327,607	18,298	203,117	125,903
1991	3,751,030	2,812,559	44,233	2,856,792	270,875	-55,607	2,530,310	865,282	355,438	18,286	205,133	124,402
1992	4,026,525	2,998,252	90,344	3,088,596	285,716	-64,284	2,738,596	888,398	399,531	19,370	207,870	124,588
1993	4,046,830	2,964,511	103,642	3,068,153	285,674	-57,003	2,725,476	897,634	423,720	19,788	204,513	120,796
1994	4,187,478	3,070,580	134,730	3,205,310	301,781	-58,358	2,845,171	911,457	430,850	20,664	202,646	123,137
1995	4,339,292	3,213,985	32,677	3,246,662	317,013	-63,094	2,866,555	1,012,806	459,931	21,362	203,128	125,336
1996	4,633,206	3,335,484	127,332	3,462,816	327,309	-63,227	3,072,280	1,074,596	486,330	22,557	205,401	126,882
1997	4,874,557	3,485,619	107,009	3,592,628	339,176	-69,717	3,183,735	1,186,207	504,615	23,525	207,211	128,334
1998	5,106,439	3,682,572	59,266	3,741,838	355,053	-67,505	3,319,280	1,266,421	520,738	24,614	207,458	130,766
1999	5,351,639	3,969,078	44,175	4,013,253	375,045	-76,241	3,561,967	1,246,147	543,525	25,569	209,300	133,627
2000	5,788,711	4,267,494	85,604	4,353,098	394,999	-92,101	3,865,998	1,352,569	570,144	27,484	210,623	136,731
2001	6,167,542	4,649,290	87,722	4,737,012	417,796	-131,471	4,187,745	1,360,815	618,982	29,029	212,461	136,688
2002	6,316,331	4,942,449	67,448	5,009,897	442,875	-182,064	4,384,958	1,263,430	667,943	29,442	214,532	135,927
2003	6,522,601	5,053,149	90,291	5,143,440	457,498	-202,289	4,483,653	1,338,216	700,732	29,991	217,483	135,768
2004	6,831,346	5,232,971	175,593	5,408,564	473,999	-244,623	4,689,942	1,405,559	735,845	31,163	219,215	137,054
2005	6,881,792	5,359,915	82,025	5,441,940	495,298	-251,598	4,695,044	1,374,508	812,240	31,083	221,400	136,950
2006	7,260,964	5,607,887	115,978	5,723,865	511,961	-289,834	4,922,070	1,497,148	841,746	32,325	224,622	138,012
2007	7,702,196	5,874,603	191,564	6,066,167	540,180	-319,473	5,206,514	1,575,788	919,894	33,856	227,498	140,253
2008	8,193,240	6,133,893	282,708	6,416,601	567,368	-375,181	5,474,052	1,676,359	1,042,829	35,875	228,381	141,155
2009	8,619,432	6,279,978	164,707	6,444,685	569,445	-298,558	5,576,682	1,883,587	1,159,163	37,342	230,826	138,581
2010	9,029,615	6,735,845	178,066	6,913,911	590,935	-297,005	6,025,971	1,725,251	1,278,393	38,865	232,333	136,800
2011	9,380,193	6,814,573	296,747	7,111,320	541,624	-247,112	6,322,584	1,822,712	1,234,897	40,191	233,391	136,316
2012	9,608,115	7,079,120	180,038	7,259,158	563,296	-226,265	6,469,597	1,915,097	1,223,421	40,977	234,478	136,493
2013	10,056,242	7,441,152	376,271	7,817,423	643,090	-233,384	6,940,949	1,837,975	1,277,318	42,660	235,731	137,204
2014	10,360,842	7,779,399	161,768	7,941,167	666,274	-212,099	7,062,794	1,962,180	1,335,868	43,711	237,028	138,417
2015	10,611,525	8,024,262	-4,122	8,020,140	685,991	-204,041	7,130,108	2,073,730	1,407,687	44,544	238,228	140,374
2016	10,561,783	7,780,562	105,628	7,886,190	681,774	-194,639	7,009,777	2,118,678	1,433,328	44,167	239,135	140,126
2017	10,608,630	7,783,865	30,806	7,814,671	691,681	-201,952	6,921,038	2,210,453	1,477,139	44,365	239,124	141,242
2018	10,257,582	10,112,605	144,977	7,688,749	685,790	-295,887	6,707,072	2,124,528	1,425,982	45,331	226,284	135,289
2019	10,536,670	10,460,767	75,903	7,906,017	713,529	-315,115	6,877,373	2,166,669	1,492,628	46,616	226,033	137,330

Personal Income and Employment by Area: Charleston, WV

(Thousands of dollars, except as noted.)

Year	Personal income, total	Earnings by place of work: Nonfarm	Earnings by place of work: Farm	Earnings by place of work: Total	Less: Contributions for government social insurance	Plus: Adjustment for residence	Equals: Net earnings by place of residence	Plus: Dividends, interest, and rent	Plus: Personal current transfer receipts	Per capita personal income (dollars)	Population (persons)	Total employment
1970	993,837	873,810	234	874,044	65,362	-36,987	771,695	120,420	101,722	3,765	263,984	112,925
1971	1,071,943	933,887	192	934,079	72,695	-42,079	819,305	131,103	121,535	4,042	265,194	113,601
1972	1,171,846	1,032,731	240	1,032,971	84,627	-58,908	889,436	142,658	139,752	4,423	264,953	116,423
1973	1,279,952	1,138,833	262	1,139,095	108,477	-76,255	954,363	160,684	164,905	4,868	262,931	119,946
1974	1,413,891	1,265,509	139	1,265,648	124,719	-101,014	1,039,915	188,040	185,936	5,406	261,523	123,324
1975	1,587,047	1,419,875	164	1,420,039	138,115	-124,406	1,157,518	210,944	218,585	5,983	265,278	125,757
1976	1,759,365	1,592,240	195	1,592,435	158,063	-147,225	1,287,147	230,787	241,431	6,597	266,697	129,397
1977	1,952,255	1,786,995	292	1,787,287	175,948	-172,848	1,438,491	257,857	255,907	7,250	269,295	132,961
1978	2,167,029	2,018,647	335	2,018,982	204,935	-213,731	1,600,316	284,610	282,103	7,971	271,875	138,957
1979	2,418,669	2,270,984	448	2,271,432	240,654	-262,931	1,767,847	319,768	331,054	8,870	272,681	142,342
1980	2,605,697	2,396,460	356	2,396,816	259,227	-292,278	1,845,311	381,288	379,098	9,538	273,195	138,180
1981	2,840,831	2,509,715	133	2,509,848	290,164	-295,652	1,924,032	469,478	447,321	10,403	273,065	131,513
1982	3,046,381	2,664,954	284	2,665,238	317,090	-326,453	2,021,695	534,338	490,348	11,207	271,826	128,902
1983	3,111,775	2,629,830	447	2,630,277	315,041	-317,382	1,997,854	564,301	549,620	11,540	269,657	124,483
1984	3,318,347	2,786,090	1,038	2,787,128	339,576	-326,912	2,120,640	624,699	573,008	12,427	267,030	125,051
1985	3,463,300	2,910,274	701	2,910,975	357,693	-341,596	2,211,686	656,502	595,112	13,181	262,742	125,298
1986	3,512,860	2,943,246	819	2,944,065	377,669	-359,756	2,206,640	671,978	634,242	13,574	258,796	125,037
1987	3,534,260	2,945,756	12	2,945,768	381,504	-358,393	2,205,871	674,313	654,076	13,801	256,091	124,011
1988	3,825,349	3,161,494	134	3,161,628	412,899	-339,137	2,409,592	721,446	694,311	15,275	250,433	125,278
1989	4,034,982	3,287,816	221	3,288,037	435,334	-353,568	2,499,135	807,073	728,774	16,379	246,351	125,964
1990	4,296,318	3,540,261	677	3,540,938	477,024	-401,959	2,661,955	856,780	777,583	17,671	243,124	129,747
1991	4,477,881	3,714,592	622	3,715,214	514,962	-432,609	2,767,643	829,532	880,706	18,418	243,125	130,517
1992	4,768,059	3,929,614	928	3,930,542	548,653	-482,870	2,899,019	856,355	1,012,685	19,535	244,084	132,244
1993	4,957,134	4,083,410	450	4,083,860	588,138	-493,996	3,001,726	873,475	1,081,933	20,316	244,001	134,391
1994	5,191,393	4,315,915	338	4,316,253	618,857	-534,192	3,163,204	932,303	1,095,886	21,356	243,093	138,091
1995	5,347,220	4,489,501	70	4,489,571	653,956	-582,872	3,252,743	976,176	1,118,301	22,021	242,822	140,818
1996	5,532,883	4,651,499	-819	4,650,680	678,621	-639,379	3,332,680	1,028,389	1,171,814	22,837	242,282	142,338
1997	5,691,420	4,824,347	-1,130	4,823,217	697,090	-685,132	3,440,995	1,055,285	1,195,140	23,610	241,059	144,325
1998	6,032,522	5,089,131	-1,142	5,087,989	737,635	-699,521	3,650,833	1,157,018	1,224,671	25,217	239,229	145,734
1999	6,180,113	5,327,480	-1,166	5,326,314	764,431	-734,496	3,827,387	1,112,834	1,239,892	26,042	237,312	147,614
2000	6,519,389	5,613,762	-725	5,613,037	823,224	-784,824	4,004,989	1,207,489	1,306,911	27,681	235,518	148,787
2001	6,678,752	5,694,743	-822	5,693,921	802,582	-832,134	4,059,205	1,179,344	1,440,203	28,612	233,423	147,209
2002	6,841,608	5,765,118	-1,188	5,763,930	779,072	-868,187	4,116,671	1,155,282	1,569,655	29,478	232,093	145,606
2003	6,873,446	5,819,928	-569	5,819,359	806,578	-891,080	4,121,701	1,154,187	1,597,558	29,682	231,566	144,477
2004	6,898,333	6,027,680	-106	6,027,574	820,355	-953,131	4,254,088	1,072,809	1,571,436	29,879	230,874	144,232
2005	7,249,141	6,382,459	-410	6,382,049	850,024	-1,060,975	4,471,050	1,151,701	1,626,390	31,650	229,041	144,540
2006	7,673,054	6,710,009	-803	6,709,206	854,633	-1,197,342	4,657,231	1,291,896	1,723,927	33,691	227,750	145,601
2007	7,927,942	6,816,640	-1,261	6,815,379	831,352	-1,231,581	4,752,446	1,351,028	1,824,468	34,899	227,165	146,588
2008	8,385,002	7,104,849	-200	7,104,649	831,576	-1,284,288	4,988,785	1,381,349	2,014,868	36,969	226,811	146,575
2009	8,395,907	7,164,827	-140	7,164,687	846,929	-1,346,988	4,970,770	1,261,710	2,163,427	36,918	227,421	144,581
2010	8,635,941	7,294,475	-472	7,294,003	855,686	-1,350,620	5,087,697	1,281,823	2,266,421	38,060	226,901	143,898
2011	8,968,729	7,589,454	-225	7,589,229	785,086	-1,432,507	5,371,636	1,343,444	2,253,649	39,716	225,823	144,234
2012	9,166,858	7,677,830	310	7,678,140	791,274	-1,458,362	5,428,504	1,426,974	2,311,380	40,616	225,696	144,231
2013	9,008,092	7,524,374	376	7,524,750	870,971	-1,385,770	5,268,009	1,371,477	2,368,606	40,099	224,644	142,098
2014	9,220,014	7,582,626	-90	7,582,536	892,969	-1,384,517	5,305,050	1,435,082	2,479,882	41,382	222,802	140,932
2015	9,256,904	7,531,764	-20	7,531,744	899,430	-1,418,221	5,214,093	1,469,198	2,573,613	42,032	220,236	138,707
2016	9,152,396	7,350,509	-280	7,350,229	897,036	-1,430,795	5,022,398	1,499,876	2,630,122	42,035	217,735	135,749
2017	9,317,388	7,435,691	-630	7,435,061	922,966	-1,452,442	5,059,653	1,554,649	2,703,086	43,457	214,406	134,397
2018	11,503,784	11,512,701	-8,917	9,012,112	1,095,860	-1,553,531	6,362,721	1,828,820	3,312,243	44,198	260,280	152,384
2019	11,639,393	11,645,823	-6,430	8,585,871	1,043,468	-1,150,131	6,392,272	1,839,202	3,407,919	45,276	257,074	147,626

Personal Income and Employment by Area: Charleston-North Charleston, SC

(Thousands of dollars, except as noted.)

Year	Personal income, total	Earnings by place of work			Less: Contributions for government social insurance	Plus: Adjustment for residence	Equals: Net earnings by place of residence	Plus: Dividends, interest, and rent	Plus: Personal current transfer receipts	Per capita personal income (dollars)	Population (persons)	Total employment
		Nonfarm	Farm	Total								
1970	1,279,669	1,056,968	7,639	1,064,607	59,898	-11,367	993,342	216,524	69,803	3,801	336,669	152,101
1971	1,383,879	1,130,473	7,446	1,137,919	66,798	-11,343	1,059,778	238,548	85,553	4,011	345,034	151,142
1972	1,517,813	1,232,701	9,813	1,242,514	75,438	-10,819	1,156,257	263,516	98,040	4,286	354,123	153,558
1973	1,680,008	1,364,230	10,318	1,374,548	94,055	-12,543	1,267,950	294,968	117,090	4,634	362,524	162,266
1974	1,959,389	1,576,872	15,077	1,591,949	113,060	-14,022	1,464,867	346,905	147,617	5,189	377,614	172,300
1975	2,213,586	1,756,358	19,661	1,776,019	128,328	-16,947	1,630,744	388,448	194,394	5,691	388,945	176,227
1976	2,459,268	1,977,834	12,311	1,990,145	148,863	-21,212	1,820,070	424,015	215,183	6,111	402,464	183,691
1977	2,651,205	2,136,753	8,786	2,145,539	159,554	-24,348	1,961,637	463,506	226,062	6,511	407,216	188,099
1978	3,009,689	2,408,891	15,418	2,424,309	181,834	-28,414	2,214,061	545,654	249,974	7,209	417,483	197,797
1979	3,372,609	2,698,623	20,159	2,718,782	212,054	-34,732	2,471,996	612,965	287,648	7,933	425,158	204,605
1980	3,809,937	3,020,853	6,976	3,027,829	237,871	-41,007	2,748,951	707,666	353,320	8,786	433,615	209,543
1981	4,325,681	3,408,083	10,642	3,418,725	287,607	-45,365	3,085,753	832,985	406,943	9,715	445,278	217,214
1982	4,676,711	3,626,698	23,524	3,650,222	308,623	-46,431	3,295,168	937,168	444,375	10,317	453,298	217,116
1983	5,039,496	3,909,629	10,127	3,919,756	349,967	-40,132	3,529,657	1,033,966	475,873	10,934	460,906	222,685
1984	5,573,828	4,339,955	19,015	4,358,970	403,264	-50,105	3,905,601	1,158,709	509,518	11,927	467,325	236,807
1985	5,934,775	4,635,729	8,199	4,643,928	444,899	-56,914	4,142,115	1,246,149	546,511	12,645	469,353	246,759
1986	6,361,315	4,964,353	7,302	4,971,655	493,245	-59,917	4,418,493	1,359,572	583,250	13,227	480,947	255,473
1987	6,797,770	5,323,389	11,954	5,335,343	528,764	-62,639	4,743,940	1,451,630	602,200	13,862	490,378	263,378
1988	7,329,506	5,787,906	17,965	5,805,871	601,080	-69,612	5,135,179	1,551,970	642,357	14,874	492,783	270,818
1989	7,956,613	6,149,175	13,890	6,163,065	653,838	-75,414	5,433,813	1,723,378	799,422	15,824	502,823	275,672
1990	8,658,930	6,731,605	12,967	6,744,572	739,637	-85,291	5,919,644	1,864,973	874,313	17,017	508,851	289,036
1991	9,034,156	6,961,780	19,060	6,980,840	777,915	-77,665	6,125,260	1,954,240	954,656	17,246	523,852	287,878
1992	9,495,342	7,237,437	16,418	7,253,855	813,485	-64,278	6,376,092	2,019,035	1,100,215	17,903	530,382	283,152
1993	9,860,162	7,402,313	23,960	7,426,273	843,836	-58,346	6,524,091	2,137,955	1,198,116	18,537	531,913	282,830
1994	10,089,234	7,417,182	34,106	7,451,288	861,532	-42,789	6,546,967	2,240,729	1,301,538	19,059	529,376	280,828
1995	10,310,767	7,435,391	31,774	7,467,165	869,583	-27,616	6,569,966	2,330,876	1,409,925	19,745	522,192	281,375
1996	10,813,743	7,691,660	27,846	7,719,506	889,684	-19,559	6,810,263	2,484,964	1,518,516	20,877	517,970	282,824
1997	11,576,341	8,250,086	28,077	8,278,163	958,508	-16,237	7,303,418	2,676,616	1,596,307	21,910	528,354	293,859
1998	12,564,973	9,068,067	20,573	9,088,640	1,053,237	-12,938	8,022,465	2,873,752	1,668,756	23,456	535,674	304,992
1999	13,443,604	9,889,082	24,118	9,913,200	1,142,910	-10,635	8,759,655	2,918,993	1,764,956	24,614	546,169	316,969
2000	14,569,805	10,713,020	25,266	10,738,286	1,227,919	-1,877	9,508,490	3,168,555	1,892,760	26,447	550,916	323,851
2001	14,924,586	10,896,374	26,859	10,923,233	1,271,569	-8,593	9,643,071	3,181,907	2,099,608	26,799	556,901	327,147
2002	15,625,032	11,566,180	16,081	11,582,261	1,353,488	-18,219	10,210,554	3,135,416	2,279,062	27,646	565,179	333,500
2003	16,378,648	12,252,126	25,908	12,278,034	1,440,587	-26,183	10,811,264	3,161,924	2,405,460	28,565	573,376	341,030
2004	17,742,036	13,231,252	21,931	13,253,183	1,548,462	-33,531	11,671,190	3,474,573	2,596,273	30,213	587,231	353,803
2005	19,384,317	14,313,955	23,840	14,337,795	1,659,581	-45,995	12,632,219	3,945,704	2,806,394	32,398	598,313	364,423
2006	21,155,362	15,397,210	15,758	15,412,968	1,819,614	-48,102	13,545,252	4,604,640	3,005,470	34,429	614,463	374,776
2007	22,875,052	16,690,687	15,394	16,706,081	1,957,941	-61,154	14,686,986	5,005,965	3,182,101	36,403	628,384	391,799
2008	23,320,656	16,703,046	10,143	16,713,189	2,017,422	-62,455	14,633,312	4,966,905	3,720,439	36,234	643,613	394,806
2009	22,657,806	16,082,697	16,301	16,098,998	1,973,274	-41,180	14,084,544	4,449,531	4,123,731	34,568	655,447	381,979
2010	24,296,348	17,202,262	17,751	17,220,013	2,050,295	-28,344	15,141,374	4,641,916	4,513,058	36,401	667,466	384,824
2011	26,397,237	18,667,465	14,919	18,682,384	1,952,530	-19,534	16,710,320	5,062,554	4,624,363	38,748	681,261	399,885
2012	28,942,468	20,747,454	18,538	20,765,992	2,053,143	-8,038	18,704,811	5,564,824	4,672,833	41,525	696,993	408,522
2013	28,767,808	20,713,789	28,378	20,742,167	2,365,833	-7,854	18,368,480	5,545,452	4,853,876	40,438	711,407	418,728
2014	31,283,960	22,207,748	14,937	22,222,685	2,517,779	2,622	19,707,528	6,393,126	5,183,306	43,045	726,770	432,506
2015	33,614,523	23,854,666	9,824	23,864,490	2,683,787	-14,046	21,166,657	6,887,198	5,560,668	45,116	745,061	448,862
2016	35,242,387	24,961,523	12,293	24,973,816	2,805,592	-39,872	22,128,352	7,320,687	5,793,348	46,256	761,904	467,956
2017	37,084,960	26,407,643	7,325	26,414,968	2,986,386	-49,040	23,379,542	7,732,902	5,972,516	47,800	775,831	478,810
2018	40,353,521	40,348,551	4,970	27,960,792	3,179,471	-70,653	24,710,668	9,258,639	6,384,214	51,202	788,122	501,446
2019	42,607,758	42,601,363	6,395	29,738,649	3,383,383	-85,406	26,269,860	9,546,964	6,790,934	53,119	802,122	514,430

Personal Income and Employment by Area: Charlotte-Concord-Gastonia, NC-SC

(Thousands of dollars, except as noted.)

Year	Personal income, total	Earnings by place of work			Less: Contributions for government social insurance	Plus: Adjustment for residence	Equals: Net earnings by place of residence	Plus: Dividends, interest, and rent	Plus: Personal current transfer receipts	Per capita personal income (dollars)	Population (persons)	Total employment
		Nonfarm	Farm	Total								
1970	3,570,757	3,182,109	23,102	3,205,211	225,700	-51,022	2,928,489	397,045	245,223	3,613	988,444	503,563
1971	3,904,425	3,458,387	27,218	3,485,605	254,522	-55,099	3,175,984	439,309	289,132	3,875	1,007,583	511,003
1972	4,403,475	3,924,723	32,679	3,957,402	303,176	-64,005	3,590,221	487,622	325,632	4,284	1,027,951	534,518
1973	4,912,458	4,369,985	64,193	4,434,178	387,915	-69,663	3,976,600	550,750	385,108	4,710	1,042,990	557,073
1974	5,344,543	4,677,751	51,734	4,729,485	429,910	-72,566	4,227,009	634,981	482,553	5,071	1,054,007	556,610
1975	5,752,816	4,834,237	43,467	4,877,704	434,093	-78,175	4,365,436	696,736	690,644	5,435	1,058,573	531,234
1976	6,427,283	5,484,004	48,150	5,532,154	504,519	-87,701	4,939,934	762,400	724,949	6,031	1,065,660	552,899
1977	7,124,675	6,140,199	44,271	6,184,470	562,819	-101,503	5,520,148	852,106	752,421	6,619	1,076,317	576,425
1978	8,074,560	7,015,507	58,283	7,073,790	662,281	-120,818	6,290,691	973,865	810,004	7,374	1,095,051	604,651
1979	9,125,808	7,957,450	66,030	8,023,480	778,268	-147,938	7,097,274	1,112,460	916,074	8,182	1,115,330	631,747
1980	10,266,424	8,787,537	33,877	8,821,414	859,393	-175,236	7,786,785	1,388,427	1,091,212	8,984	1,142,703	636,966
1981	11,555,367	9,741,341	40,927	9,782,268	1,021,767	-208,766	8,551,735	1,745,865	1,257,767	9,963	1,159,800	644,468
1982	12,379,107	10,197,544	58,007	10,255,551	1,081,665	-223,361	8,950,525	2,012,197	1,416,385	10,520	1,176,768	634,435
1983	13,563,373	11,250,363	47,855	11,298,218	1,203,729	-244,188	9,850,301	2,188,033	1,525,039	11,430	1,186,619	648,334
1984	15,390,998	12,767,309	134,902	12,902,211	1,399,933	-274,575	11,227,703	2,561,987	1,601,308	12,755	1,206,699	687,850
1985	16,698,309	13,855,878	155,607	14,011,485	1,538,805	-300,085	12,172,595	2,794,495	1,731,219	13,577	1,229,877	711,901
1986	18,098,776	15,137,698	144,780	15,282,478	1,717,076	-331,024	13,234,378	3,029,630	1,834,768	14,506	1,247,714	738,057
1987	19,784,206	16,822,651	85,527	16,908,178	1,881,794	-379,226	14,647,158	3,232,579	1,904,469	15,551	1,272,213	768,719
1988	21,875,684	18,554,858	124,151	18,679,009	2,116,214	-420,953	16,141,842	3,669,664	2,064,178	16,865	1,297,129	803,761
1989	23,890,954	20,072,039	161,528	20,233,567	2,287,189	-461,682	17,484,696	4,094,975	2,311,283	18,091	1,320,598	826,270
1990	25,648,599	21,567,003	206,836	21,773,839	2,521,599	-507,093	18,745,147	4,346,334	2,557,118	19,001	1,349,847	844,984
1991	26,613,112	22,040,075	237,338	22,277,413	2,611,399	-496,537	19,169,477	4,485,207	2,958,428	19,272	1,380,932	830,828
1992	28,830,767	23,923,406	233,381	24,156,787	2,794,437	-520,667	20,841,683	4,707,698	3,281,386	20,516	1,405,306	844,448
1993	30,863,992	25,528,199	246,803	25,775,002	2,995,693	-541,191	22,238,118	5,049,808	3,576,066	21,497	1,435,716	873,760
1994	33,368,371	27,661,930	245,601	27,907,531	3,279,929	-584,722	24,042,880	5,577,332	3,748,159	22,694	1,470,366	909,458
1995	36,286,667	29,931,378	275,626	30,207,004	3,542,791	-636,842	26,027,371	6,126,134	4,133,162	24,046	1,509,023	948,911
1996	39,213,260	32,078,331	258,514	32,336,845	3,751,922	-664,292	27,920,631	6,803,150	4,489,479	25,288	1,550,697	975,193
1997	42,249,833	34,750,688	237,600	34,988,288	4,042,307	-721,183	30,224,798	7,333,232	4,691,803	26,492	1,594,838	1,014,492
1998	46,213,279	38,261,913	268,750	38,530,663	4,425,876	-783,422	33,321,365	7,974,969	4,916,945	28,180	1,639,936	1,045,077
1999	49,342,174	41,245,902	305,794	41,551,696	4,777,793	-867,722	35,906,181	8,223,752	5,212,241	29,255	1,686,617	1,083,959
2000	52,929,457	44,200,097	291,811	44,491,908	5,098,582	-936,576	38,456,750	8,836,565	5,636,142	30,620	1,728,616	1,115,568
2001	52,021,808	42,838,844	329,867	43,168,711	5,315,683	-1,004,669	36,848,359	8,828,687	6,344,762	29,400	1,769,476	1,121,045
2002	53,596,920	44,388,744	205,620	44,594,364	5,463,967	-1,042,828	38,087,569	8,570,192	6,939,159	29,667	1,806,638	1,123,996
2003	56,852,951	47,187,112	243,952	47,431,064	5,715,277	-1,042,047	40,673,740	8,832,606	7,346,605	30,873	1,841,489	1,127,253
2004	63,364,708	52,521,887	279,897	52,801,784	6,024,274	-1,129,493	45,648,017	9,800,003	7,916,688	33,704	1,880,010	1,155,661
2005	70,154,895	58,058,495	315,550	58,374,045	6,558,915	-1,214,328	50,600,802	10,982,307	8,571,786	36,271	1,934,168	1,198,944
2006	79,349,790	66,009,605	279,234	66,288,839	7,204,020	-1,238,812	57,846,007	12,093,023	9,410,760	39,492	2,009,239	1,252,774
2007	89,000,460	74,270,489	233,424	74,503,913	7,849,293	-1,237,834	65,416,786	13,378,422	10,205,252	42,662	2,086,153	1,309,517
2008	99,325,263	82,220,845	162,106	82,382,951	8,147,463	-1,191,781	73,043,707	14,414,573	11,866,983	46,160	2,151,756	1,311,813
2009	91,373,637	73,649,522	166,098	73,815,620	7,729,979	-921,458	65,164,183	12,609,844	13,599,610	41,612	2,195,856	1,259,733
2010	86,142,948	67,380,109	161,668	67,541,777	7,562,640	-768,717	59,210,420	12,247,503	14,685,025	38,747	2,223,196	1,253,117
2011	91,110,779	70,261,537	175,258	70,436,795	7,169,935	-647,663	62,619,197	13,603,835	14,887,747	40,383	2,256,180	1,307,403
2012	103,157,607	80,917,877	280,518	81,198,395	7,680,192	-537,213	72,980,990	15,058,706	15,117,911	44,972	2,293,822	1,336,776
2013	98,684,419	77,583,920	347,781	77,931,701	8,943,754	-365,113	68,622,834	14,624,673	15,436,912	42,281	2,334,036	1,372,726
2014	105,336,372	82,268,831	370,086	82,638,917	9,520,191	-515,531	72,603,195	16,524,735	16,208,442	44,331	2,376,148	1,426,460
2015	113,238,106	88,182,366	413,603	88,595,969	10,183,181	-583,775	77,829,013	18,226,555	17,182,538	46,713	2,424,115	1,480,794
2016	118,709,834	92,871,749	305,865	93,177,614	10,627,194	-608,474	81,941,946	18,930,557	17,837,331	47,954	2,475,519	1,531,472
2017	125,653,500	98,737,721	343,177	99,080,898	11,151,750	-674,518	87,254,630	19,871,134	18,527,736	49,758	2,525,305	1,572,986
2018	135,599,272	135,311,968	287,304	105,849,551	11,657,544	-702,247	93,489,760	22,276,504	19,833,008	52,295	2,592,950	1,636,445
2019	142,170,385	141,886,268	284,117	111,611,042	12,303,886	-768,274	98,538,882	22,702,408	20,929,095	53,916	2,636,883	1,683,494

Personal Income and Employment by Area: Charlottesville, VA

(Thousands of dollars, except as noted.)

Year	Personal income, total	Earnings by place of work			Less: Contributions for government social insurance	Plus: Adjustment for residence	Equals: Net earnings by place of residence	Plus: Dividends, interest, and rent	Plus: Personal current transfer receipts	Per capita personal income (dollars)	Population (persons)	Total employment
		Nonfarm	Farm	Total								
1970	382,009	306,035	7,606	313,641	19,212	-19,465	274,964	77,462	29,583	3,415	111,846	51,870
1971	418,835	332,208	7,062	339,270	21,688	-18,976	298,606	85,070	35,159	3,684	113,689	52,468
1972	479,147	366,133	7,473	373,606	25,221	-3,395	344,990	94,025	40,132	4,031	118,870	54,890
1973	552,697	420,065	11,906	431,971	32,841	-3,687	395,443	109,148	48,106	4,519	122,296	58,728
1974	617,706	463,653	11,765	475,418	37,815	-3,840	433,763	125,306	58,637	4,923	125,476	60,912
1975	682,296	499,850	7,047	506,897	39,984	2,629	469,542	134,944	77,810	5,219	130,734	60,189
1976	762,356	555,719	5,038	560,757	44,944	10,489	526,302	150,331	85,723	5,755	132,458	62,508
1977	837,372	611,855	4,325	616,180	50,026	10,983	577,137	168,612	91,623	6,273	133,491	64,427
1978	957,134	707,233	10,296	717,529	58,754	5,344	664,119	193,906	99,109	7,090	135,000	68,132
1979	1,062,765	809,740	9,895	819,635	70,191	-9,646	739,798	209,791	113,176	7,764	136,881	71,979
1980	1,208,283	908,115	5,051	913,166	79,955	-17,691	815,520	258,036	134,727	8,753	138,046	74,348
1981	1,372,332	989,058	3,310	992,368	93,685	-11,935	886,748	329,759	155,825	9,810	139,886	74,591
1982	1,505,033	1,064,286	1,726	1,066,012	102,224	-14,597	949,191	384,760	171,082	10,686	140,835	75,162
1983	1,639,061	1,184,304	308	1,184,612	116,121	-21,679	1,046,812	405,538	186,711	11,516	142,328	77,404
1984	1,824,054	1,310,255	4,960	1,315,215	132,138	-21,569	1,161,508	464,016	198,530	12,697	143,655	80,110
1985	1,974,578	1,425,294	3,726	1,429,020	146,738	-23,996	1,258,286	505,588	210,704	13,519	146,056	82,356
1986	2,132,538	1,551,877	4,783	1,556,660	165,238	-23,794	1,367,628	544,802	220,108	14,601	146,055	86,235
1987	2,305,118	1,685,215	9,041	1,694,256	178,297	-21,543	1,494,416	582,920	227,782	15,508	148,641	90,858
1988	2,610,003	1,919,924	9,720	1,929,644	206,942	-23,492	1,699,210	668,532	242,261	17,250	151,301	91,623
1989	2,861,492	2,061,740	14,215	2,075,955	223,857	-21,609	1,830,489	760,593	270,410	18,532	154,409	94,636
1990	3,075,262	2,191,381	16,958	2,208,339	240,899	-20,628	1,946,812	837,636	290,814	19,476	157,899	95,934
1991	3,251,634	2,297,763	16,746	2,314,509	253,534	-19,591	2,041,384	887,839	322,411	20,252	160,559	95,320
1992	3,497,935	2,435,807	15,763	2,451,570	267,841	-20,334	2,163,395	962,261	372,279	21,439	163,154	96,170
1993	3,752,715	2,612,224	13,869	2,626,093	284,848	-26,502	2,314,743	1,038,022	399,950	22,512	166,695	99,792
1994	3,956,587	2,750,452	14,130	2,764,582	299,974	-30,125	2,434,483	1,106,125	415,979	23,242	170,234	101,956
1995	4,234,263	2,870,389	15,150	2,885,539	311,424	-34,392	2,539,723	1,237,075	457,465	24,439	173,261	104,722
1996	4,482,129	3,050,323	15,355	3,065,678	329,990	-44,071	2,691,617	1,303,849	486,663	25,397	176,481	107,633
1997	4,819,459	3,293,134	9,436	3,302,570	352,469	-47,354	2,902,747	1,406,135	510,577	26,803	179,813	110,980
1998	5,188,439	3,602,582	8,988	3,611,570	382,339	-62,902	3,166,329	1,502,665	519,445	28,317	183,230	115,714
1999	5,465,635	3,830,139	7,825	3,837,964	406,243	-67,803	3,363,918	1,552,994	548,723	29,206	187,141	118,612
2000	5,955,862	4,186,663	13,871	4,200,534	436,588	-84,121	3,679,825	1,678,081	597,956	31,246	190,613	122,142
2001	6,262,818	4,405,533	7,704	4,413,237	466,258	-94,844	3,852,135	1,751,716	658,967	32,347	193,611	121,814
2002	6,412,594	4,610,787	4,520	4,615,307	488,553	-110,552	4,016,202	1,707,136	689,256	32,659	196,350	122,780
2003	6,834,310	4,820,659	-398	4,820,261	509,150	-121,297	4,189,814	1,907,292	737,204	34,412	198,602	123,298
2004	7,322,831	5,180,137	5,674	5,185,811	548,582	-136,926	4,500,303	2,047,622	774,906	36,435	200,985	126,942
2005	7,888,267	5,542,091	2,867	5,544,958	592,721	-164,438	4,787,799	2,253,721	846,747	38,484	204,975	130,861
2006	8,648,416	5,901,126	-8,750	5,892,376	635,868	-196,369	5,060,139	2,663,468	924,809	41,475	208,519	135,499
2007	9,204,793	6,224,916	-11,508	6,213,408	676,895	-221,271	5,315,242	2,905,422	984,129	43,546	211,383	139,136
2008	9,598,148	6,468,986	4,085	6,473,071	707,819	-244,089	5,521,163	2,961,289	1,115,696	44,711	214,672	140,581
2009	9,228,984	6,451,553	6,997	6,458,550	710,177	-233,676	5,514,697	2,515,804	1,198,483	42,495	217,176	137,893
2010	9,681,058	6,755,829	9,019	6,764,848	727,333	-211,523	5,825,992	2,557,044	1,298,022	44,201	219,025	137,159
2011	10,219,798	6,849,498	11,811	6,861,309	660,395	-202,576	5,998,338	2,887,160	1,334,300	46,255	220,947	138,801
2012	11,095,485	7,278,302	21,998	7,300,300	685,406	-195,339	6,419,555	3,316,301	1,359,629	49,834	222,649	140,856
2013	10,991,450	7,337,006	13,970	7,350,976	798,759	-177,297	6,374,920	3,198,292	1,418,238	49,056	224,057	142,429
2014	11,696,722	7,685,178	8,491	7,693,669	837,128	-193,944	6,662,597	3,538,736	1,495,389	51,687	226,297	145,985
2015	12,479,110	8,249,242	7,193	8,256,435	897,530	-231,758	7,127,147	3,766,289	1,585,674	54,537	228,818	150,735
2016	13,037,269	8,506,286	3,975	8,510,261	924,221	-243,218	7,342,822	4,044,391	1,650,056	56,399	231,160	154,607
2017	13,739,226	9,013,290	5,063	9,018,353	980,982	-276,871	7,760,500	4,259,645	1,719,081	58,767	233,793	157,714
2018	14,721,107	14,731,872	-10,765	9,180,839	1,005,018	-398,468	7,777,353	5,280,803	1,662,951	67,735	217,335	155,749
2019	15,084,997	15,087,463	-2,466	9,453,698	1,032,099	-406,342	8,015,257	5,292,901	1,776,839	69,003	218,615	160,315

Personal Income and Employment by Area: Chattanooga, TN-GA

(Thousands of dollars, except as noted.)

Year	Personal income, total	Earnings by place of work			Less: Contributions for government social insurance	Plus: Adjustment for residence	Equals: Net earnings by place of residence	Plus: Dividends, interest, and rent	Plus: Personal current transfer receipts	Per capita personal income (dollars)	Population (persons)	Total employment
		Nonfarm	Farm	Total								
1970	1,330,318	1,169,675	4,311	1,173,986	76,760	-43,113	1,054,113	163,961	112,244	3,575	372,113	172,095
1971	1,474,581	1,286,539	3,807	1,290,346	86,418	-46,757	1,157,171	185,424	131,986	3,876	380,419	174,934
1972	1,674,323	1,471,219	5,289	1,476,508	103,374	-52,526	1,320,608	206,648	147,067	4,326	387,034	186,173
1973	1,872,144	1,645,219	9,097	1,654,316	133,722	-55,932	1,464,662	232,672	174,810	4,739	395,063	196,966
1974	2,054,698	1,779,157	4,370	1,783,527	149,824	-59,310	1,574,393	269,803	210,502	5,154	398,683	197,405
1975	2,230,144	1,866,010	7,212	1,873,222	152,748	-54,890	1,665,584	291,987	272,573	5,554	401,552	190,016
1976	2,492,020	2,092,790	9,431	2,102,221	174,051	-51,873	1,876,297	317,315	298,408	6,140	405,890	196,745
1977	2,755,079	2,327,332	6,532	2,333,864	191,994	-62,047	2,079,823	356,215	319,041	6,703	411,025	201,417
1978	3,145,986	2,683,708	5,564	2,689,272	222,836	-75,066	2,391,370	408,219	346,397	7,563	415,992	211,442
1979	3,430,114	2,893,475	7,112	2,900,587	250,372	-80,228	2,569,987	458,947	401,180	8,096	423,664	214,637
1980	3,723,675	3,037,880	5,674	3,043,554	263,229	-80,633	2,699,692	539,426	484,557	8,712	427,429	208,292
1981	4,085,895	3,251,775	8,296	3,260,071	304,253	-83,778	2,872,040	661,753	552,102	9,491	430,519	206,190
1982	4,329,526	3,351,053	9,992	3,361,045	319,349	-79,210	2,962,486	768,457	598,583	10,135	427,203	199,884
1983	4,557,833	3,516,322	4,627	3,520,949	343,115	-71,071	3,106,763	810,737	640,333	10,769	423,243	199,125
1984	4,953,151	3,815,634	10,868	3,826,502	385,049	-72,288	3,369,165	911,372	672,614	11,678	424,137	206,887
1985	5,276,069	4,064,629	9,024	4,073,653	420,743	-69,584	3,583,326	976,474	716,269	12,428	424,535	211,855
1986	5,638,776	4,383,968	9,036	4,393,004	464,410	-85,131	3,843,463	1,033,810	761,503	13,273	424,816	218,811
1987	6,115,956	4,829,699	6,719	4,836,418	507,109	-89,610	4,239,699	1,079,405	796,852	14,245	429,335	229,011
1988	6,668,836	5,256,800	9,993	5,266,793	566,692	-94,921	4,605,180	1,211,172	852,484	15,394	433,218	235,200
1989	7,076,123	5,448,067	15,959	5,464,026	598,981	-98,410	4,766,635	1,367,059	942,429	16,304	434,018	240,365
1990	7,498,710	5,750,245	15,581	5,765,826	637,022	-89,725	5,039,079	1,434,336	1,025,295	17,289	433,718	243,572
1991	7,747,533	5,893,734	18,198	5,911,932	664,466	-91,520	5,155,946	1,423,444	1,168,143	17,692	437,902	243,018
1992	8,336,210	6,284,235	19,817	6,304,052	701,306	-64,594	5,538,152	1,476,252	1,321,806	18,878	441,576	245,510
1993	8,920,828	6,763,107	20,399	6,783,506	757,314	-68,373	5,957,819	1,548,877	1,414,132	19,939	447,416	254,759
1994	9,341,819	7,123,340	22,557	7,145,897	810,876	-92,961	6,242,060	1,612,442	1,487,317	20,629	452,845	261,969
1995	9,921,900	7,519,582	14,640	7,534,222	857,439	-105,977	6,570,806	1,745,503	1,605,591	21,659	458,090	266,963
1996	10,504,425	7,945,480	16,684	7,962,164	893,109	-93,577	6,975,478	1,849,956	1,678,991	22,732	462,090	273,762
1997	11,056,648	8,511,578	17,224	8,528,802	943,645	-113,277	7,471,880	1,840,884	1,743,884	23,688	466,756	276,491
1998	11,916,080	9,153,506	21,914	9,175,420	983,559	-101,354	8,090,507	2,069,136	1,756,437	25,346	470,131	282,947
1999	12,646,532	9,860,405	19,584	9,879,989	1,058,967	-118,792	8,702,230	2,103,347	1,840,955	26,691	473,820	291,583
2000	13,375,131	10,430,505	16,622	10,447,127	1,113,624	-134,478	9,199,025	2,197,120	1,978,986	28,003	477,630	298,758
2001	13,422,502	10,321,957	30,395	10,352,352	1,129,226	-135,925	9,087,201	2,182,079	2,153,222	27,859	481,798	295,485
2002	13,715,205	10,560,237	12,842	10,573,079	1,160,547	-120,526	9,292,006	2,098,206	2,324,993	28,223	485,957	293,159
2003	14,302,544	11,067,607	12,589	11,080,196	1,211,925	-125,631	9,742,640	2,137,767	2,422,137	29,184	490,089	295,067
2004	15,009,136	11,585,114	24,968	11,610,082	1,258,412	-89,697	10,261,973	2,166,767	2,580,396	30,339	494,709	297,575
2005	15,655,754	12,049,676	29,785	12,079,461	1,313,554	-105,337	10,660,570	2,243,162	2,752,022	31,339	499,564	302,725
2006	16,694,722	12,677,865	8,493	12,686,358	1,381,430	-134,447	11,170,481	2,581,243	2,942,998	32,963	506,473	308,555
2007	17,497,360	13,039,024	11,613	13,050,637	1,437,626	-122,934	11,490,077	2,792,492	3,214,791	34,101	513,100	313,955
2008	18,187,862	13,430,273	29,445	13,459,718	1,499,277	-201,798	11,758,643	2,834,717	3,594,502	35,059	518,778	309,896
2009	17,918,771	13,073,106	26,593	13,099,699	1,457,864	-142,288	11,499,547	2,603,604	3,815,620	34,191	524,082	291,690
2010	18,938,892	13,781,876	16,285	13,798,161	1,515,959	-198,457	12,083,745	2,698,261	4,156,886	35,788	529,196	290,655
2011	20,019,637	14,500,414	7,345	14,507,759	1,402,888	-216,560	12,888,311	2,871,607	4,259,719	37,522	533,540	297,413
2012	21,198,232	15,387,589	44,607	15,432,196	1,447,672	-258,930	13,725,594	3,186,084	4,286,554	39,394	538,108	300,036
2013	21,160,225	15,486,507	58,108	15,544,615	1,654,814	-267,061	13,622,740	3,101,579	4,435,906	39,038	542,036	303,348
2014	21,908,778	15,786,261	57,649	15,843,910	1,689,595	-122,563	14,031,752	3,324,448	4,552,578	40,272	544,017	303,855
2015	23,070,212	16,566,680	61,694	16,628,374	1,772,732	-189,326	14,666,316	3,637,185	4,766,711	42,158	547,232	310,991
2016	23,735,641	17,149,425	31,845	17,181,270	1,830,828	-152,166	15,198,276	3,656,342	4,881,023	43,003	551,957	318,368
2017	24,782,011	18,120,237	45,683	18,165,920	1,941,922	-337,800	15,886,198	3,850,649	5,045,164	44,528	556,548	324,573
2018	25,828,981	25,786,382	42,599	18,736,119	2,016,607	-417,962	16,301,550	4,283,580	5,243,851	46,055	560,832	335,261
2019	26,776,612	26,760,903	15,709	19,548,932	2,114,595	-530,918	16,903,419	4,335,597	5,537,596	47,376	565,194	341,472

Personal Income and Employment by Area: Cheyenne, WY

(Thousands of dollars, except as noted.)

Year	Personal income, total	Earnings by place of work			Less: Contributions for government social insurance	Plus: Adjustment for residence	Equals: Net earnings by place of residence	Plus: Dividends, interest, and rent	Plus: Personal current transfer receipts	Per capita personal income (dollars)	Population (persons)	Total employment
		Nonfarm	Farm	Total								
1970	252,643	194,127	4,016	198,143	14,212	-933	182,998	50,776	18,869	4,462	56,619	28,563
1971	278,822	214,779	3,692	218,471	16,164	-1,574	200,733	56,613	21,476	4,812	57,944	29,358
1972	316,308	248,403	5,405	253,808	19,435	-2,894	231,479	61,832	22,997	5,272	59,997	31,164
1973	368,918	299,024	2,699	301,723	26,358	-4,924	270,441	71,862	26,615	5,907	62,458	33,858
1974	421,372	339,216	5,972	345,188	30,392	-6,058	308,738	82,317	30,317	6,504	64,789	34,558
1975	460,198	369,276	3,179	372,455	32,738	-7,183	332,534	91,017	36,647	7,118	64,656	34,715
1976	499,110	401,915	2,462	404,377	37,177	-8,805	358,395	99,945	40,770	7,608	65,603	35,707
1977	545,964	439,633	1,956	441,589	40,521	-10,254	390,814	110,483	44,667	8,233	66,313	36,652
1978	633,865	513,924	3,702	517,626	48,371	-13,259	455,996	128,116	49,753	9,461	67,001	39,071
1979	714,130	582,650	3,925	586,575	57,616	-16,372	512,587	143,894	57,649	10,325	69,168	41,258
1980	815,794	654,505	5,503	660,008	63,994	-19,446	576,568	172,098	67,128	11,824	68,994	42,593
1981	913,139	720,837	4,130	724,967	75,197	-19,777	629,993	203,850	79,296	13,012	70,176	42,834
1982	986,599	763,875	2,479	766,354	80,704	-20,797	664,853	233,079	88,667	13,871	71,129	43,159
1983	1,017,431	770,854	3,502	774,356	80,500	-20,521	673,335	242,078	102,018	13,955	72,907	41,915
1984	1,079,459	819,217	1,091	820,308	87,568	-21,390	711,350	263,043	105,066	14,718	73,345	42,415
1985	1,127,157	852,893	828	853,721	92,828	-22,115	738,778	277,475	110,904	15,419	73,102	42,570
1986	1,172,405	878,550	4,623	883,173	96,753	-21,676	764,744	287,554	120,107	15,756	74,411	42,461
1987	1,189,497	881,608	8,265	889,873	98,059	-20,752	771,062	293,943	124,492	15,839	75,101	43,181
1988	1,223,589	907,476	7,579	915,055	107,833	-21,294	785,928	307,074	130,587	16,419	74,523	43,939
1989	1,308,019	954,078	8,791	962,869	112,896	-21,744	828,229	336,722	143,068	17,756	73,667	44,287
1990	1,400,438	997,700	14,182	1,011,882	122,599	-22,116	867,167	379,246	154,025	19,138	73,175	44,257
1991	1,463,370	1,053,903	14,714	1,068,617	130,928	-21,637	916,052	376,522	170,796	19,781	73,978	45,286
1992	1,549,319	1,129,599	16,041	1,145,640	139,826	-22,010	983,804	375,946	189,569	20,433	75,826	46,097
1993	1,631,027	1,199,571	19,740	1,219,311	147,894	-20,663	1,050,754	375,384	204,889	21,047	77,495	47,556
1994	1,721,747	1,259,646	9,595	1,269,241	155,020	-17,720	1,096,501	405,913	219,333	21,826	78,885	48,911
1995	1,806,934	1,286,473	15,818	1,302,291	157,386	-14,328	1,130,577	447,087	229,270	22,725	79,513	49,370
1996	1,868,181	1,305,018	12,029	1,317,047	159,500	-11,386	1,146,161	482,603	239,417	23,298	80,186	49,791
1997	1,962,802	1,337,613	24,662	1,362,275	165,561	-9,471	1,187,243	528,670	246,889	24,435	80,328	50,275
1998	2,112,908	1,442,052	16,567	1,458,619	176,008	-8,275	1,274,336	587,208	251,364	26,240	80,522	50,884
1999	2,230,005	1,536,445	13,621	1,550,066	186,812	-6,981	1,356,273	610,832	262,900	27,528	81,009	51,821
2000	2,380,982	1,635,750	15,282	1,651,032	195,864	-2,791	1,452,377	642,454	286,151	29,098	81,825	53,509
2001	2,486,526	1,737,212	19,801	1,757,013	207,338	-7,773	1,541,902	630,149	314,475	30,120	82,554	52,757
2002	2,637,450	1,889,208	5,651	1,894,859	218,963	-17,577	1,658,319	638,172	340,959	31,690	83,226	54,629
2003	2,813,991	2,012,166	13,053	2,025,219	236,407	-24,978	1,763,834	679,525	370,632	33,466	84,084	55,774
2004	2,977,947	2,132,226	13,531	2,145,757	252,873	-31,234	1,861,650	715,810	400,487	34,860	85,427	56,596
2005	3,127,863	2,239,784	18,302	2,258,086	263,575	-37,310	1,957,201	744,904	425,758	36,484	85,732	57,722
2006	3,419,006	2,500,343	13,054	2,513,397	323,956	-47,317	2,142,124	817,718	459,164	39,381	86,819	58,704
2007	3,584,357	2,603,796	19,318	2,623,114	341,251	-51,025	2,230,838	862,540	490,979	40,892	87,654	61,107
2008	3,945,640	2,786,630	30,296	2,816,926	353,669	-58,583	2,404,674	967,963	573,003	44,295	89,077	62,254
2009	3,761,963	2,750,685	25,250	2,775,935	357,519	-77,264	2,341,152	797,068	623,743	41,601	90,430	61,625
2010	3,955,192	2,838,972	32,740	2,871,712	362,183	-89,780	2,419,749	856,293	679,150	42,889	92,219	61,441
2011	4,416,002	3,024,727	70,491	3,095,218	344,661	-109,548	2,641,009	1,084,770	690,223	47,696	92,587	62,826
2012	4,600,922	3,226,485	38,292	3,264,777	369,815	-133,614	2,761,348	1,148,843	690,731	48,582	94,704	63,565
2013	4,637,670	3,397,663	39,540	3,437,203	424,333	-153,791	2,859,079	1,073,610	704,981	48,445	95,731	65,587
2014	4,742,714	3,460,363	49,547	3,509,910	443,135	-155,454	2,911,321	1,094,456	736,937	49,340	96,123	66,307
2015	4,827,334	3,510,538	28,212	3,538,750	446,153	-157,060	2,935,537	1,115,429	776,368	49,764	97,005	67,062
2016	4,772,775	3,485,814	20,494	3,506,308	446,465	-158,117	2,901,726	1,063,054	807,995	48,718	97,968	67,533
2017	4,971,731	3,617,844	27,728	3,645,572	464,901	-162,960	3,017,711	1,105,551	848,469	50,563	98,327	67,939
2018	5,205,696	5,194,469	11,227	3,810,743	471,448	-172,721	3,166,574	1,142,661	896,461	52,655	98,865	70,779
2019	5,384,262	5,372,411	11,851	3,968,963	489,757	-183,986	3,295,220	1,155,302	933,740	54,113	99,500	72,107

Personal Income and Employment by Area: Chicago-Naperville-Elgin, IL-IN-WI

(Thousands of dollars, except as noted.)

Year	Personal income, total	Derivation of personal income					Equals: Net earnings by place of residence	Plus: Dividends, interest, and rent	Plus: Personal current transfer receipts	Per capita personal income (dollars)	Population (persons)	Total employment
		Earnings by place of work			Less: Contributions for government social insurance	Plus: Adjustment for residence						
		Nonfarm	Farm	Total								
1970	39,042,067	33,236,351	86,734	33,323,085	2,242,085	-220,877	30,860,123	5,547,563	2,634,381	4,945	7,895,845	3,748,330
1971	41,693,277	35,164,992	126,592	35,291,584	2,443,040	-244,656	32,603,888	5,907,509	3,181,880	5,241	7,955,398	3,702,932
1972	45,123,683	38,201,968	88,392	38,290,360	2,799,518	-282,518	35,208,324	6,315,266	3,600,093	5,660	7,972,491	3,731,149
1973	49,732,970	42,130,409	182,890	42,313,299	3,579,992	-323,899	38,409,408	7,039,001	4,284,561	6,243	7,966,188	3,874,673
1974	54,553,129	45,828,588	148,968	45,977,556	4,034,979	-355,799	41,586,778	8,058,457	4,907,894	6,842	7,973,418	3,934,993
1975	58,433,668	47,799,792	229,126	48,028,918	4,091,563	-373,026	43,564,329	8,592,841	6,276,498	7,315	7,988,641	3,831,128
1976	64,192,731	52,906,047	158,417	53,064,464	4,622,553	-385,479	48,056,432	9,175,117	6,961,182	8,009	8,014,978	3,918,359
1977	71,017,879	59,068,433	161,840	59,230,273	5,147,532	-420,169	53,662,572	10,062,019	7,293,288	8,825	8,047,518	4,032,483
1978	78,718,037	65,965,004	168,100	66,133,104	5,908,887	-471,484	59,752,733	11,183,394	7,781,910	9,757	8,067,880	4,165,078
1979	86,307,014	72,420,326	198,815	72,619,141	6,739,277	-549,764	65,330,100	12,548,879	8,428,035	10,714	8,055,256	4,212,288
1980	94,171,212	76,333,919	73,393	76,407,312	7,075,545	-549,110	68,782,657	15,125,229	10,263,326	11,694	8,052,943	4,122,105
1981	103,627,947	81,715,572	171,801	81,887,373	8,119,333	-532,929	73,235,111	18,680,720	11,712,116	12,892	8,038,127	4,108,351
1982	109,546,668	83,822,464	126,959	83,949,423	8,481,571	-536,551	74,931,301	21,833,292	12,782,075	13,613	8,047,477	4,025,482
1983	115,032,419	87,965,256	-55,778	87,909,478	8,964,223	-522,985	78,422,270	22,966,534	13,643,615	14,299	8,044,580	3,992,825
1984	126,082,430	96,611,498	128,843	96,740,341	10,162,988	-549,846	86,027,507	26,055,572	13,999,351	15,628	8,067,923	4,150,208
1985	132,939,813	102,665,752	184,891	102,850,643	10,958,616	-559,835	91,332,192	27,022,489	14,585,132	16,469	8,072,070	4,206,304
1986	140,682,691	109,791,496	169,806	109,961,302	11,741,284	-592,810	97,627,208	27,920,476	15,135,007	17,415	8,078,098	4,297,096
1987	150,034,541	118,922,940	208,759	119,131,699	12,511,093	-687,125	105,933,481	28,736,589	15,364,471	18,525	8,099,059	4,429,471
1988	163,636,534	130,986,934	127,766	131,114,700	14,014,942	-769,460	116,330,298	31,423,977	15,882,259	20,160	8,116,756	4,560,934
1989	173,570,066	138,222,041	323,630	138,545,671	14,916,130	-824,615	122,804,926	33,859,973	16,905,167	21,289	8,153,134	4,646,403
1990	185,617,214	146,689,250	253,715	146,942,965	15,585,480	-888,115	130,469,370	36,622,105	18,525,739	22,627	8,203,210	4,719,223
1991	190,171,343	150,385,797	96,837	150,482,634	16,335,975	-929,968	133,216,691	36,970,400	19,984,252	22,900	8,304,560	4,690,670
1992	205,137,770	162,159,225	181,171	162,340,396	17,251,406	-1,051,239	144,037,751	38,151,586	22,948,433	24,384	8,412,788	4,668,331
1993	213,324,335	168,909,187	167,898	169,077,085	18,167,401	-1,147,986	149,761,698	39,370,681	24,191,956	25,059	8,512,911	4,745,984
1994	224,768,787	177,411,966	258,907	177,670,873	19,346,697	-1,259,920	157,064,256	42,397,641	25,306,890	26,118	8,605,735	4,860,416
1995	240,472,614	188,258,913	115,890	188,374,803	20,441,215	-1,377,373	166,556,215	47,059,038	26,857,361	27,662	8,693,383	4,989,418
1996	255,530,533	199,112,850	251,170	199,364,020	21,398,761	-1,524,040	176,441,219	50,779,417	28,309,897	29,096	8,782,253	5,072,565
1997	271,320,981	212,456,555	226,612	212,683,167	22,676,284	-1,679,736	188,327,147	54,227,302	28,766,532	30,614	8,862,719	5,159,787
1998	290,219,984	227,396,945	164,548	227,561,493	24,078,958	-1,891,667	201,590,868	59,380,449	29,248,667	32,430	8,949,190	5,291,308
1999	304,242,459	242,852,778	137,640	242,990,418	25,310,222	-2,081,340	215,598,856	58,878,550	29,765,053	33,671	9,035,654	5,357,397
2000	329,131,722	260,611,635	171,115	260,782,750	26,717,579	-2,294,321	231,770,850	65,497,532	31,863,340	36,116	9,113,234	5,462,648
2001	339,345,030	269,996,256	186,933	270,183,189	27,152,182	-2,482,647	240,548,360	64,304,692	34,491,978	37,008	9,169,580	5,450,274
2002	343,260,435	273,760,755	140,544	273,901,299	27,430,645	-2,610,018	243,860,636	62,233,262	37,166,537	37,286	9,206,032	5,386,960
2003	348,230,607	278,568,893	189,269	278,758,162	28,186,417	-2,713,809	247,857,936	61,716,091	38,656,580	37,715	9,233,303	5,387,028
2004	361,115,061	289,207,298	386,026	289,593,324	29,883,372	-2,899,830	256,810,122	64,347,102	39,957,837	38,994	9,260,676	5,446,229
2005	378,098,652	298,975,560	238,731	299,214,291	31,491,180	-3,150,194	264,572,917	69,604,144	43,921,591	40,760	9,276,302	5,528,261
2006	404,953,720	315,442,397	234,603	315,677,000	32,960,486	-3,408,058	279,308,456	81,122,967	44,522,297	43,554	9,297,749	5,627,599
2007	429,148,694	329,019,542	445,907	329,465,449	34,449,849	-3,547,516	291,468,084	88,527,797	49,152,813	45,961	9,337,140	5,733,881
2008	435,995,123	329,697,565	439,264	330,136,829	34,986,401	-3,551,570	291,598,858	89,992,721	54,403,544	46,459	9,384,555	5,715,056
2009	408,720,581	308,745,517	203,044	308,948,561	33,126,963	-2,998,139	272,823,459	74,521,777	61,375,345	43,345	9,429,498	5,515,227
2010	418,598,811	315,159,842	231,820	315,391,662	33,512,140	-3,000,880	278,878,642	72,746,336	66,973,833	44,196	9,471,312	5,470,609
2011	439,463,437	327,925,371	521,964	328,447,335	31,420,766	-3,130,112	293,896,457	81,430,868	64,136,112	46,273	9,497,177	5,581,826
2012	464,532,051	345,987,639	345,915	346,333,554	32,998,829	-3,273,757	310,060,968	90,073,414	64,397,669	48,766	9,525,765	5,643,024
2013	474,359,278	360,248,682	719,667	360,968,349	38,155,633	-3,291,241	319,521,475	87,896,996	66,940,807	49,679	9,548,402	5,730,418
2014	504,032,757	377,548,833	299,766	377,848,599	39,455,254	-3,272,829	335,120,516	100,626,062	68,286,179	52,718	9,560,874	5,832,155
2015	529,332,727	394,039,330	22,793	394,062,123	40,851,354	-3,580,790	349,629,979	107,538,150	72,164,598	55,384	9,557,503	5,964,397
2016	537,423,216	400,110,847	240,011	400,350,858	41,662,001	-3,670,817	355,018,040	109,678,179	72,726,997	56,296	9,546,326	6,039,246
2017	555,922,382	413,336,663	33,875	413,370,538	43,017,199	-3,891,010	366,462,329	114,504,448	74,955,605	58,315	9,533,040	6,104,559
2018	584,625,041	584,435,755	189,286	433,026,090	45,399,058	-4,113,135	383,513,897	123,390,598	77,720,546	61,642	9,484,158	6,135,579
2019	600,616,821	600,442,310	174,511	446,553,091	46,732,383	-4,233,329	395,587,379	124,244,800	80,784,642	63,500	9,458,539	6,216,332

Personal Income and Employment by Area: Chico, CA

(Thousands of dollars, except as noted.)

Year	Personal income, total	Earnings by place of work			Less: Contributions for government social insurance	Plus: Adjustment for residence	Equals: Net earnings by place of residence	Plus: Dividends, interest, and rent	Plus: Personal current transfer receipts	Per capita personal income (dollars)	Population (persons)	Total employment
		Nonfarm	Farm	Total								
1970	381,579	226,169	24,434	250,603	14,475	6,603	242,731	75,745	63,103	3,716	102,682	36,830
1971	415,603	245,668	24,962	270,630	16,360	7,415	261,685	83,366	70,552	3,924	105,916	38,010
1972	461,533	273,571	28,920	302,491	19,113	8,632	292,010	92,503	77,020	4,093	112,775	40,361
1973	536,861	308,483	46,152	354,635	24,717	10,218	340,136	107,837	88,888	4,742	113,223	42,508
1974	630,119	341,944	70,657	412,601	28,409	12,178	396,370	125,323	108,426	5,372	117,295	44,300
1975	699,800	385,750	52,089	437,839	31,333	15,044	421,550	144,403	133,847	5,754	121,626	45,985
1976	766,349	448,738	29,862	478,600	36,886	17,894	459,608	157,418	149,323	6,112	125,377	48,998
1977	861,046	504,728	38,057	542,785	42,231	21,127	521,681	179,095	160,270	6,651	129,470	51,665
1978	974,489	579,081	31,548	610,629	49,225	25,708	587,112	210,537	176,840	7,394	131,797	54,807
1979	1,130,636	653,895	56,369	710,264	58,625	29,538	681,177	247,487	201,972	8,162	138,531	58,299
1980	1,320,695	741,991	61,407	803,398	65,175	32,436	770,659	309,880	240,156	9,119	144,828	60,482
1981	1,467,413	789,069	56,521	845,590	75,524	33,286	803,352	376,235	287,826	9,885	148,451	61,097
1982	1,532,666	803,809	42,256	846,065	78,860	34,777	801,982	408,439	322,245	10,089	151,913	59,921
1983	1,647,030	875,651	16,628	892,279	87,126	34,913	840,066	456,215	350,749	10,677	154,263	62,688
1984	1,803,653	965,397	31,211	996,608	99,960	37,453	934,101	496,849	372,703	11,504	156,791	64,197
1985	1,946,271	1,056,120	33,846	1,089,966	111,319	39,682	1,018,329	526,799	401,143	12,113	160,680	66,863
1986	2,079,377	1,150,414	27,616	1,178,030	122,664	44,484	1,099,850	546,773	432,754	12,739	163,233	68,099
1987	2,257,359	1,271,158	64,147	1,335,305	137,044	47,262	1,245,523	555,159	456,677	13,520	166,970	71,391
1988	2,468,501	1,411,174	80,281	1,491,455	157,578	51,066	1,384,943	591,651	491,907	14,359	171,909	76,545
1989	2,663,869	1,525,321	43,753	1,569,074	174,453	54,397	1,449,018	671,924	542,927	15,086	176,583	79,880
1990	2,872,915	1,672,337	63,550	1,735,887	187,601	59,937	1,608,223	683,454	581,238	15,643	183,652	84,276
1991	3,052,820	1,774,585	64,187	1,838,772	200,253	63,722	1,702,241	700,923	649,656	16,266	187,678	85,153
1992	3,239,403	1,859,396	80,716	1,940,112	209,022	67,796	1,798,886	706,903	733,614	17,013	190,409	84,849
1993	3,340,767	1,905,387	83,170	1,988,557	214,257	71,090	1,845,390	727,466	767,911	17,325	192,831	84,708
1994	3,480,305	2,041,969	64,102	2,106,071	228,399	73,431	1,951,103	740,294	788,908	17,880	194,648	88,262
1995	3,589,571	2,075,376	46,513	2,121,889	230,371	81,829	1,973,347	790,745	825,479	18,306	196,083	89,235
1996	3,798,320	2,194,163	58,420	2,252,583	234,610	86,177	2,104,150	833,892	860,278	19,347	196,327	91,583
1997	4,034,871	2,353,526	75,495	2,429,021	245,932	93,018	2,276,107	894,242	864,522	20,379	197,994	93,148
1998	4,238,403	2,499,915	14,212	2,514,127	256,909	101,508	2,358,726	969,370	910,307	21,193	199,993	94,625
1999	4,412,897	2,658,288	44,542	2,702,830	272,895	110,869	2,540,804	933,424	938,669	21,924	201,282	97,199
2000	4,742,588	2,890,524	59,537	2,950,061	292,111	123,407	2,781,357	985,222	976,009	23,270	203,807	98,639
2001	5,167,986	3,214,580	59,442	3,274,022	333,459	132,905	3,073,468	1,025,169	1,069,349	25,064	206,193	99,172
2002	5,315,013	3,426,545	66,023	3,492,568	360,959	134,194	3,265,803	925,568	1,123,642	25,416	209,120	101,094
2003	5,576,133	3,552,921	91,464	3,644,385	376,812	143,785	3,411,358	977,730	1,187,045	26,367	211,481	100,790
2004	5,950,239	3,752,384	102,305	3,854,689	414,246	151,353	3,591,796	1,098,967	1,259,476	27,927	213,065	101,812
2005	6,170,006	3,900,127	115,707	4,015,834	437,978	158,527	3,736,383	1,111,723	1,321,900	28,731	214,752	103,948
2006	6,553,340	4,105,830	78,178	4,184,008	447,064	167,978	3,904,922	1,216,427	1,431,991	30,224	216,824	105,268
2007	6,859,094	4,203,643	104,981	4,308,624	452,326	178,600	4,034,898	1,305,467	1,518,729	31,541	217,469	106,781
2008	7,034,312	4,105,166	151,281	4,256,447	455,815	186,852	3,987,484	1,352,067	1,694,761	32,115	219,034	103,874
2009	7,047,335	4,042,429	212,164	4,254,593	454,280	157,224	3,957,537	1,243,055	1,846,743	32,066	219,777	99,078
2010	7,307,770	4,176,259	201,616	4,377,875	451,222	146,891	4,073,544	1,229,115	2,005,111	33,224	219,957	97,799
2011	7,574,070	4,272,003	216,770	4,488,773	422,856	130,661	4,196,578	1,366,907	2,010,585	34,427	220,003	97,756
2012	7,784,914	4,366,644	236,206	4,602,850	434,148	118,931	4,287,633	1,450,102	2,047,179	35,231	220,969	100,633
2013	8,133,014	4,545,099	348,036	4,893,135	502,890	110,254	4,500,499	1,505,710	2,126,805	36,674	221,768	104,338
2014	8,492,494	4,724,175	183,671	4,907,846	524,046	113,221	4,497,021	1,732,617	2,262,856	37,976	223,629	107,497
2015	9,152,079	5,035,200	204,305	5,239,505	552,895	117,237	4,803,847	1,913,413	2,434,819	40,709	224,818	110,139
2016	9,498,336	5,239,392	185,480	5,424,872	581,215	114,650	4,958,307	2,023,518	2,516,511	41,931	226,525	112,625
2017	9,925,515	5,536,968	249,647	5,786,615	614,078	119,314	5,291,851	2,125,247	2,508,417	43,287	229,294	114,627
2018	10,267,576	10,065,471	202,105	6,046,214	656,086	114,034	5,504,162	2,131,114	2,632,300	44,576	230,339	114,472
2019	10,490,209	10,261,186	229,023	6,231,741	672,042	136,717	5,696,416	2,165,766	2,628,027	47,860	219,186	113,221

Personal Income and Employment by Area: Cincinnati, OH-KY-IN

(Thousands of dollars, except as noted.)

Year	Personal income, total	Earnings by place of work Nonfarm	Farm	Total	Less: Contributions for government social insurance	Plus: Adjustment for residence	Equals: Net earnings by place of residence	Plus: Dividends, interest, and rent	Plus: Personal current transfer receipts	Per capita personal income (dollars)	Population (persons)	Total employment
1970	6,912,576	5,628,139	40,395	5,668,534	375,829	49,721	5,342,426	1,041,278	528,872	4,106	1,683,357	717,838
1971	7,226,566	5,806,640	34,064	5,840,704	398,814	44,196	5,486,086	1,114,606	625,874	4,274	1,690,881	706,103
1972	7,855,798	6,338,865	41,085	6,379,950	459,114	55,070	5,975,906	1,186,085	693,807	4,650	1,689,419	719,327
1973	8,699,916	7,058,616	51,828	7,110,444	590,318	59,107	6,579,233	1,312,659	808,024	5,119	1,699,443	749,255
1974	9,555,877	7,636,619	68,025	7,704,644	662,115	55,402	7,097,931	1,489,821	968,125	5,629	1,697,582	757,725
1975	10,288,933	8,034,595	68,008	8,102,603	679,411	52,718	7,475,910	1,607,125	1,205,898	6,070	1,695,118	742,023
1976	11,375,486	8,976,233	67,242	9,043,475	776,392	63,428	8,330,511	1,727,135	1,317,840	6,673	1,704,762	759,472
1977	12,649,315	10,075,974	63,076	10,139,050	873,120	72,973	9,338,903	1,914,756	1,395,656	7,377	1,714,809	787,208
1978	14,123,449	11,412,646	46,675	11,459,321	1,020,929	74,983	10,513,375	2,122,602	1,487,472	8,172	1,728,350	824,603
1979	15,721,207	12,696,209	42,197	12,738,406	1,186,960	75,274	11,626,720	2,394,649	1,699,838	9,057	1,735,736	843,934
1980	17,422,886	13,549,956	39,232	13,589,188	1,260,328	68,775	12,397,635	2,924,217	2,101,034	9,996	1,743,032	840,256
1981	19,152,012	14,468,567	40,325	14,508,892	1,436,896	79,607	13,151,603	3,655,538	2,344,871	10,963	1,747,031	829,486
1982	20,264,386	14,886,162	70,631	14,956,793	1,504,010	89,687	13,542,470	4,036,971	2,684,945	11,573	1,751,052	812,056
1983	21,541,896	15,839,233	654	15,839,887	1,628,333	100,805	14,312,359	4,342,005	2,887,532	12,297	1,751,730	815,951
1984	23,731,687	17,497,225	58,149	17,555,374	1,833,247	126,428	15,848,555	4,852,781	3,030,351	13,486	1,759,676	850,061
1985	25,388,148	18,879,228	56,936	18,936,164	2,009,271	148,210	17,075,103	5,078,283	3,234,762	14,347	1,769,618	880,814
1986	26,950,995	20,254,515	18,728	20,273,243	2,225,351	155,931	18,203,823	5,348,965	3,398,207	15,117	1,782,790	909,075
1987	28,668,980	21,833,787	21,856	21,855,643	2,400,246	155,884	19,611,281	5,533,608	3,524,091	15,923	1,800,487	939,655
1988	30,872,030	23,459,811	28,797	23,488,608	2,651,022	190,136	21,027,722	6,106,358	3,737,950	17,042	1,811,516	970,621
1989	33,434,666	25,098,557	55,762	25,154,319	2,852,722	202,168	22,503,765	6,951,882	3,979,019	18,362	1,820,832	995,454
1990	36,029,560	27,006,672	52,890	27,059,562	3,132,668	202,046	24,128,940	7,492,678	4,407,942	19,611	1,837,214	1,015,267
1991	37,089,143	28,025,896	47,051	28,072,947	3,329,567	222,057	24,965,437	7,314,940	4,808,766	19,952	1,858,915	1,016,454
1992	39,852,332	30,262,851	69,950	30,332,801	3,576,150	221,079	26,977,730	7,595,174	5,279,428	21,214	1,878,558	1,026,671
1993	41,614,861	31,580,115	49,054	31,629,169	3,756,467	249,331	28,122,033	7,968,268	5,524,560	21,901	1,900,124	1,043,171
1994	43,800,294	33,285,961	60,742	33,346,703	4,029,069	279,279	29,596,913	8,467,047	5,736,334	22,891	1,913,442	1,071,538
1995	46,188,097	34,954,790	15,287	34,970,077	4,268,072	299,525	31,001,530	9,097,871	6,088,696	23,971	1,926,822	1,101,936
1996	49,149,374	37,076,603	40,972	37,117,575	4,476,519	293,047	32,934,103	9,882,239	6,333,032	25,338	1,939,779	1,131,097
1997	52,501,626	39,792,873	65,864	39,858,737	4,708,798	303,418	35,453,357	10,516,355	6,531,914	26,838	1,956,236	1,158,927
1998	56,491,171	43,146,172	45,625	43,191,797	4,967,857	282,153	38,506,093	11,369,487	6,615,591	28,659	1,971,116	1,194,392
1999	58,883,162	45,889,168	18,180	45,907,348	5,284,226	278,872	40,901,994	11,149,950	6,831,218	29,672	1,984,493	1,214,973
2000	62,247,284	48,200,458	79,068	48,279,526	5,406,178	294,341	43,167,689	11,767,683	7,311,912	31,131	1,999,554	1,235,864
2001	64,880,379	50,326,450	59,916	50,386,366	5,557,958	292,789	45,121,197	11,736,884	8,022,298	32,243	2,012,228	1,227,320
2002	66,418,453	51,698,913	14,480	51,713,393	5,649,069	295,028	46,359,352	11,464,574	8,594,527	32,874	2,020,396	1,219,242
2003	68,419,005	53,347,843	25,498	53,373,341	5,866,472	295,717	47,802,586	11,683,753	8,932,666	33,679	2,031,529	1,226,328
2004	72,033,803	55,940,299	78,677	56,018,976	6,195,716	239,959	50,063,219	12,567,657	9,402,927	35,263	2,042,753	1,241,509
2005	75,022,909	58,010,603	56,395	58,066,998	6,422,561	200,022	51,844,459	13,169,754	10,008,696	36,510	2,054,879	1,258,897
2006	79,346,061	60,006,663	47,516	60,054,179	6,665,655	283,248	53,671,772	15,043,355	10,630,934	38,332	2,069,960	1,268,954
2007	82,017,288	61,925,301	33,809	61,959,110	6,896,815	212,717	55,275,012	15,404,102	11,338,174	39,355	2,084,042	1,284,177
2008	84,540,722	62,734,922	19,638	62,754,560	7,127,237	198,867	55,826,190	15,769,805	12,944,727	40,353	2,095,040	1,279,660
2009	82,051,822	61,572,115	46,725	61,618,840	7,025,553	128,108	54,721,395	13,273,525	14,056,902	38,930	2,107,649	1,239,043
2010	85,715,774	64,618,642	28,184	64,646,826	7,146,450	60,698	57,561,074	13,178,610	14,976,090	40,475	2,117,729	1,229,401
2011	92,138,508	68,382,458	70,486	68,452,944	6,675,606	69,394	61,846,732	14,953,835	15,337,941	43,409	2,122,544	1,244,021
2012	95,601,934	70,896,581	45,403	70,941,984	6,873,536	68,594	64,137,042	16,381,896	15,082,996	44,923	2,128,106	1,255,411
2013	96,586,764	72,294,303	126,905	72,421,208	7,797,733	115,200	64,738,675	16,353,530	15,494,559	45,213	2,136,269	1,269,521
2014	100,236,140	73,877,678	34,970	73,912,648	8,058,354	111,054	65,965,348	17,891,782	16,379,010	46,696	2,146,562	1,290,566
2015	104,813,951	76,482,975	3,091	76,486,066	8,378,967	100,004	68,207,103	19,471,522	17,135,326	48,622	2,155,674	1,314,909
2016	107,967,380	79,112,672	8,170	79,120,842	8,774,949	51,954	70,397,847	19,990,379	17,579,154	49,846	2,166,029	1,337,044
2017	112,301,873	82,533,754	-24,636	82,509,118	9,254,524	102,370	73,356,964	20,927,709	18,017,200	51,536	2,179,082	1,356,969
2018	119,565,639	119,556,739	8,900	86,302,330	9,559,619	486,736	77,229,447	23,520,686	18,815,506	54,055	2,211,936	1,392,046
2019	124,461,934	124,467,780	-5,846	90,563,837	9,997,214	447,057	81,013,680	23,717,105	19,731,149	56,033	2,221,208	1,414,594

Personal Income and Employment by Area: Clarksville, TN-KY

(Thousands of dollars, except as noted.)

Year	Personal income, total	Earnings by place of work			Less: Contributions for government social insurance	Plus: Adjustment for residence	Equals: Net earnings by place of residence	Plus: Dividends, interest, and rent	Plus: Personal current transfer receipts	Per capita personal income (dollars)	Population (persons)	Total employment
		Nonfarm	Farm	Total								
1970	463,454	354,164	15,890	370,054	21,775	1,699	349,978	79,015	34,461	3,612	128,304	62,242
1971	521,409	397,658	20,030	417,688	25,845	1,828	393,671	87,377	40,361	3,946	132,120	63,181
1972	558,891	428,780	23,281	452,061	28,838	-1,493	421,730	92,497	44,664	4,282	130,523	62,873
1973	734,687	570,281	31,550	601,831	41,057	-7,140	553,634	128,267	52,786	5,059	145,221	74,314
1974	820,430	637,109	26,176	663,285	48,129	-7,921	607,235	149,850	63,345	5,451	150,507	75,527
1975	857,553	658,768	17,110	675,878	52,597	-6,413	616,868	161,113	79,572	5,789	148,128	73,152
1976	995,464	772,477	21,803	794,280	63,869	-7,878	722,533	187,008	85,923	6,562	151,709	79,719
1977	1,067,383	811,457	36,406	847,863	65,767	-4,161	777,935	197,880	91,568	6,817	156,582	78,755
1978	1,172,444	893,432	27,245	920,677	71,696	-6,391	842,590	229,976	99,878	7,455	157,269	80,086
1979	1,303,823	979,508	41,820	1,021,328	81,232	-4,999	935,097	253,116	115,610	8,158	159,822	80,031
1980	1,371,628	1,013,595	17,832	1,031,427	85,368	1,375	947,434	283,816	140,378	8,573	159,999	78,851
1981	1,546,004	1,141,440	34,486	1,175,926	101,188	-15,706	1,059,032	327,068	159,904	9,589	161,222	79,659
1982	1,658,087	1,203,100	28,822	1,231,922	104,253	-13,723	1,113,946	366,238	177,903	9,984	166,069	78,823
1983	1,719,478	1,288,028	-14,518	1,273,510	115,463	-13,274	1,144,773	386,258	188,447	10,327	166,510	79,185
1984	1,882,074	1,369,288	31,278	1,400,566	127,470	-6,408	1,266,688	416,898	198,488	11,257	167,189	81,128
1985	2,010,419	1,460,435	28,672	1,489,107	137,774	1,373	1,352,706	446,654	211,059	11,725	171,467	82,547
1986	2,119,127	1,546,539	21,627	1,568,166	149,810	6,081	1,424,437	471,853	222,837	12,397	170,942	83,901
1987	2,272,627	1,660,836	25,809	1,686,645	161,872	14,575	1,539,348	500,585	232,694	13,213	171,998	86,982
1988	2,432,753	1,782,209	24,288	1,806,497	181,357	21,803	1,646,943	533,621	252,189	13,979	174,027	88,495
1989	2,588,368	1,839,899	37,711	1,877,610	192,354	29,761	1,715,017	591,417	281,934	14,662	176,531	90,093
1990	2,588,750	1,822,845	32,107	1,854,952	196,307	40,777	1,699,422	573,002	316,326	14,314	180,857	87,447
1991	2,777,276	1,960,370	28,318	1,988,688	214,457	41,896	1,816,127	597,132	364,017	15,421	180,093	87,685
1992	3,306,544	2,394,728	43,760	2,438,488	265,243	35,295	2,208,540	692,561	405,443	17,406	189,963	97,180
1993	3,437,595	2,484,904	33,852	2,518,756	280,040	36,279	2,274,995	738,208	424,392	17,940	191,616	99,926
1994	3,617,678	2,587,409	43,322	2,630,731	290,403	42,022	2,382,350	787,486	447,842	18,391	196,709	102,624
1995	3,895,693	2,770,909	30,410	2,801,319	306,003	40,951	2,536,267	861,197	498,229	19,378	201,040	107,625
1996	4,136,965	2,922,443	49,821	2,972,264	320,710	42,979	2,694,533	915,815	526,617	19,860	208,307	109,895
1997	4,290,274	3,057,319	43,952	3,101,271	335,237	52,683	2,818,717	910,986	560,571	20,187	212,526	112,425
1998	4,588,521	3,223,995	23,058	3,247,053	348,409	62,480	2,961,124	1,042,090	585,307	21,343	214,986	113,432
1999	4,868,510	3,480,365	5,351	3,485,716	376,521	60,806	3,170,001	1,075,565	622,944	22,407	217,276	118,256
2000	5,352,564	3,825,362	47,728	3,873,090	405,253	65,516	3,533,353	1,137,722	681,489	24,228	220,923	121,022
2001	5,378,909	3,841,245	47,337	3,888,582	420,803	45,291	3,513,070	1,107,723	758,116	24,121	223,001	120,958
2002	5,710,485	4,146,762	30,329	4,177,091	453,712	28,648	3,752,027	1,133,540	824,918	25,482	224,096	122,111
2003	6,088,115	4,482,702	41,463	4,524,165	481,703	4,249	4,046,711	1,154,342	887,062	27,192	223,891	123,153
2004	6,565,148	4,925,147	71,544	4,996,691	522,900	-8,007	4,465,784	1,141,869	957,495	28,681	228,899	126,813
2005	7,357,400	5,710,604	93,271	5,803,875	597,894	-91,322	5,114,659	1,208,608	1,034,133	30,961	237,633	133,697
2006	7,921,384	6,174,645	71,437	6,246,082	649,845	-129,612	5,466,625	1,329,977	1,124,782	33,364	237,426	136,582
2007	8,210,785	6,337,532	34,192	6,371,724	671,542	-130,821	5,569,361	1,415,772	1,225,652	33,128	247,849	138,849
2008	8,766,484	6,712,068	46,383	6,758,451	719,834	-201,897	5,836,720	1,508,983	1,420,781	35,302	248,331	139,223
2009	8,959,532	6,779,377	52,514	6,831,891	741,556	-170,098	5,920,237	1,493,373	1,545,922	34,924	256,545	137,188
2010	9,446,851	7,150,462	22,457	7,172,919	780,391	-183,694	6,208,834	1,528,694	1,709,323	36,109	261,619	138,915
2011	10,306,044	7,683,883	66,467	7,750,350	757,089	-203,291	6,789,970	1,707,464	1,808,610	39,014	264,163	142,490
2012	10,501,934	7,773,593	70,627	7,844,220	763,743	-167,861	6,912,616	1,760,460	1,828,858	38,328	274,004	142,647
2013	10,375,766	7,536,350	134,560	7,670,910	825,418	-132,313	6,713,179	1,757,708	1,904,879	38,142	272,031	142,662
2014	10,511,134	7,558,377	50,076	7,608,453	837,504	-101,957	6,668,992	1,826,203	2,015,939	38,023	276,442	144,083
2015	10,862,594	7,712,512	57,466	7,769,978	856,271	-84,719	6,828,988	1,862,806	2,170,800	38,814	279,865	146,544
2016	10,835,910	7,585,936	21,291	7,607,227	837,745	-60,661	6,708,821	1,873,148	2,253,941	38,584	280,843	146,217
2017	11,305,053	7,897,061	33,033	7,930,094	878,427	-47,853	7,003,814	1,941,239	2,360,000	39,661	285,042	147,614
2018	12,320,446	12,298,212	22,234	8,433,381	926,356	63,678	7,570,703	1,996,694	2,753,049	40,488	304,301	157,413
2019	12,891,821	12,859,813	32,008	8,851,801	967,212	58,976	7,943,565	2,027,261	2,920,995	41,881	307,820	160,846

Personal Income and Employment by Area: Cleveland, TN

(Thousands of dollars, except as noted.)

Year	Personal income, total	Earnings by place of work			Less: Contributions for government social insurance	Plus: Adjustment for residence	Equals: Net earnings by place of residence	Plus: Dividends, interest, and rent	Plus: Personal current transfer receipts	Per capita personal income (dollars)	Population (persons)	Total employment
		Nonfarm	Farm	Total								
1970	194,832	162,070	1,834	163,904	10,907	2,891	155,888	21,776	17,168	3,100	62,840	28,344
1971	219,046	182,333	1,642	183,975	12,691	3,605	174,889	24,270	19,887	3,352	65,350	29,244
1972	250,052	209,708	2,478	212,186	15,388	4,579	201,377	26,910	21,765	3,719	67,241	31,705
1973	289,286	241,832	4,671	246,503	20,176	5,569	231,896	31,443	25,947	4,154	69,648	34,135
1974	306,477	248,205	1,718	249,923	21,519	7,385	235,789	36,749	33,939	4,275	71,692	32,962
1975	328,845	256,727	1,754	258,481	21,615	5,185	242,051	42,087	44,707	4,542	72,406	30,714
1976	373,202	293,661	2,363	296,024	25,427	10,653	281,250	44,653	47,299	5,048	73,937	32,387
1977	405,364	307,285	3,381	310,666	26,937	20,899	304,628	49,130	51,606	5,342	75,881	33,401
1978	463,234	361,237	1,083	362,320	32,219	21,888	351,989	55,502	55,743	5,966	77,652	35,414
1979	524,542	404,388	2,423	406,811	37,619	26,497	395,689	62,875	65,978	6,587	79,631	36,135
1980	600,426	451,872	4,438	456,310	41,941	26,364	440,733	77,040	82,653	7,380	81,363	36,047
1981	679,756	507,718	7,806	515,524	50,809	27,805	492,520	95,686	91,550	8,284	82,061	36,618
1982	724,715	528,431	7,029	535,460	53,899	29,804	511,365	112,099	101,251	8,823	82,139	36,932
1983	798,079	594,647	3,427	598,074	60,906	29,205	566,373	123,442	108,264	9,680	82,449	37,384
1984	885,383	654,245	11,349	665,594	69,126	33,524	629,992	140,243	115,148	10,584	83,652	39,385
1985	947,214	704,741	7,979	712,720	75,125	35,663	673,258	151,555	122,401	11,211	84,486	39,808
1986	1,011,521	736,719	12,234	748,953	80,203	47,574	716,324	163,397	131,800	11,919	84,865	40,542
1987	1,098,514	809,196	6,728	815,924	86,928	54,090	783,086	177,599	137,829	12,872	85,340	42,402
1988	1,183,209	859,208	7,790	866,998	94,423	71,293	843,868	189,668	149,673	13,678	86,505	43,780
1989	1,296,710	916,032	18,674	934,706	100,873	80,223	914,056	217,094	165,560	14,922	86,902	44,308
1990	1,361,760	962,812	16,411	979,223	106,456	81,257	954,024	222,660	185,076	15,530	87,684	43,815
1991	1,435,420	1,013,578	20,118	1,033,696	114,229	77,395	996,862	222,775	215,783	16,137	88,954	43,128
1992	1,585,623	1,123,040	19,717	1,142,757	124,999	82,863	1,100,621	231,327	253,675	17,556	90,317	44,380
1993	1,646,763	1,150,811	20,987	1,171,798	129,003	97,991	1,140,786	234,923	271,054	17,904	91,979	45,808
1994	1,756,417	1,238,505	17,079	1,255,584	140,271	98,985	1,214,298	261,179	280,940	18,854	93,161	46,481
1995	1,852,505	1,300,093	10,124	1,310,217	146,305	101,286	1,265,198	280,141	307,166	19,473	95,133	48,418
1996	1,993,616	1,406,596	13,214	1,419,810	154,757	100,678	1,365,731	300,297	327,588	20,585	96,848	50,123
1997	2,155,431	1,557,220	5,690	1,562,910	166,490	97,664	1,494,084	316,826	344,521	21,550	100,019	51,829
1998	2,348,971	1,688,769	10,176	1,698,945	173,033	107,919	1,633,831	360,737	354,403	23,085	101,755	51,846
1999	2,416,500	1,740,269	8,715	1,748,984	182,631	111,191	1,677,544	369,017	369,939	23,465	102,982	52,450
2000	2,460,197	1,722,547	6,423	1,728,970	182,997	128,758	1,674,731	386,635	398,831	23,579	104,338	52,528
2001	2,481,132	1,655,376	25,895	1,681,271	185,478	140,352	1,636,145	399,342	445,645	23,564	105,295	53,704
2002	2,538,680	1,720,649	4,519	1,725,168	193,616	155,759	1,687,311	374,992	476,377	23,955	105,979	53,647
2003	2,680,341	1,790,500	6,216	1,796,716	201,000	186,850	1,782,566	388,565	509,210	25,108	106,754	54,086
2004	2,857,415	1,937,543	19,925	1,957,468	216,022	177,443	1,918,889	389,756	548,770	26,433	108,099	55,465
2005	2,956,030	1,962,492	22,071	1,984,563	219,303	205,704	1,970,964	394,380	590,686	27,018	109,410	55,733
2006	3,157,823	2,043,266	6,446	2,049,712	226,658	273,500	2,096,554	419,790	641,479	28,404	111,177	56,345
2007	3,355,350	2,106,790	3,988	2,110,778	234,833	297,162	2,173,107	474,605	707,638	29,710	112,935	56,070
2008	3,540,240	2,113,583	12,461	2,126,044	239,447	331,413	2,218,010	522,173	800,057	30,972	114,306	55,208
2009	3,455,829	2,014,254	19,089	2,033,343	236,865	298,917	2,095,395	499,192	861,242	30,027	115,090	53,667
2010	3,579,734	2,097,077	26,733	2,123,810	241,480	300,603	2,182,933	442,090	954,711	30,883	115,913	53,265
2011	3,808,093	2,228,325	25,655	2,253,980	230,357	302,238	2,325,861	516,007	966,225	32,664	116,583	54,831
2012	4,045,808	2,474,230	27,303	2,501,533	245,511	256,575	2,512,597	559,000	974,211	34,381	117,674	56,876
2013	4,073,814	2,543,444	54,868	2,598,312	287,633	201,790	2,512,469	567,784	993,561	34,412	118,383	60,381
2014	4,223,364	2,660,647	57,947	2,718,594	298,363	172,811	2,593,042	600,050	1,030,272	35,342	119,501	62,262
2015	4,413,855	2,692,168	40,997	2,733,165	304,178	232,166	2,661,153	674,696	1,078,006	36,610	120,565	61,936
2016	4,469,107	2,745,557	24,900	2,770,457	311,296	247,881	2,707,042	656,097	1,105,968	36,881	121,177	62,632
2017	4,649,999	2,790,796	32,252	2,823,048	317,740	313,236	2,818,544	690,815	1,140,640	38,016	122,317	61,946
2018	4,784,442	4,768,557	15,885	2,907,179	331,053	323,116	2,899,242	670,971	1,214,229	38,594	123,968	62,640
2019	4,977,562	4,977,811	-249	3,047,915	351,247	314,763	3,011,431	681,789	1,284,342	39,839	124,942	64,896

Personal Income and Employment by Area: Cleveland-Elyria, OH

(Thousands of dollars, except as noted.)

Year	Personal income, total	Derivation of personal income			Less: Contributions for government social insurance	Plus: Adjustment for residence	Equals: Net earnings by place of residence	Plus: Dividends, interest, and rent	Plus: Personal current transfer receipts	Per capita personal income (dollars)	Population (persons)	Total employment
		Earnings by place of work										
		Nonfarm	Farm	Total								
1970	10,739,310	9,265,524	19,843	9,285,367	615,025	-286,840	8,383,502	1,563,124	792,684	4,631	2,318,811	1,076,814
1971	11,259,149	9,579,995	26,837	9,606,832	653,378	-305,674	8,647,780	1,662,229	949,140	4,869	2,312,528	1,044,149
1972	12,122,234	10,377,214	28,586	10,405,800	747,243	-333,289	9,325,268	1,751,339	1,045,627	5,322	2,277,630	1,053,824
1973	13,319,112	11,511,398	20,630	11,532,028	964,373	-386,076	10,181,579	1,933,610	1,203,923	5,878	2,266,062	1,095,299
1974	14,613,538	12,493,333	27,215	12,520,548	1,082,844	-437,928	10,999,776	2,199,298	1,414,464	6,502	2,247,641	1,114,246
1975	15,457,357	12,922,717	37,515	12,960,232	1,088,512	-478,207	11,393,513	2,321,621	1,742,223	6,908	2,237,565	1,077,447
1976	16,767,087	14,216,214	39,604	14,255,818	1,227,678	-556,120	12,472,020	2,447,461	1,847,606	7,553	2,219,936	1,088,064
1977	18,581,102	15,973,198	35,760	16,008,958	1,377,706	-655,152	13,976,100	2,664,318	1,940,684	8,394	2,213,651	1,114,106
1978	20,527,552	17,785,247	35,968	17,821,215	1,585,566	-765,894	15,469,755	2,964,130	2,093,667	9,302	2,206,866	1,148,501
1979	22,408,647	19,369,101	28,215	19,397,316	1,799,238	-879,608	16,718,470	3,322,545	2,367,632	10,257	2,184,615	1,159,618
1980	24,310,668	20,080,895	27,342	20,108,237	1,851,713	-945,404	17,311,120	3,974,859	3,024,689	11,191	2,172,438	1,133,733
1981	26,500,199	21,402,715	31,574	21,434,289	2,110,018	-1,026,226	18,298,045	4,881,341	3,320,813	12,257	2,162,129	1,112,891
1982	27,714,318	21,587,658	29,419	21,617,077	2,157,804	-1,021,570	18,437,703	5,418,939	3,857,676	12,886	2,150,690	1,072,341
1983	29,110,176	22,541,029	29,722	22,570,751	2,293,980	-1,053,273	19,223,498	5,736,053	4,150,625	13,561	2,146,550	1,058,826
1984	31,917,925	24,857,262	34,010	24,891,272	2,586,673	-1,156,170	21,148,429	6,449,386	4,320,110	14,906	2,141,290	1,090,297
1985	33,862,734	26,504,152	30,694	26,534,846	2,793,441	-1,228,522	22,512,883	6,768,987	4,580,864	15,889	2,131,240	1,106,952
1986	35,188,992	27,642,351	28,348	27,670,699	2,998,393	-1,261,039	23,411,267	6,905,934	4,871,791	16,594	2,120,606	1,123,074
1987	36,909,884	29,256,843	43,283	29,300,126	3,175,125	-1,319,711	24,805,290	7,056,260	5,048,334	17,461	2,113,892	1,145,205
1988	39,873,290	31,881,886	72,163	31,954,049	3,540,963	-1,427,920	26,985,166	7,609,770	5,278,354	18,969	2,102,075	1,171,445
1989	42,411,894	33,661,202	92,851	33,754,053	3,777,616	-1,526,393	28,450,044	8,334,778	5,627,072	20,161	2,103,702	1,194,435
1990	45,294,907	35,534,500	91,401	35,625,901	4,077,758	-1,658,953	29,889,190	9,210,505	6,195,212	21,525	2,104,288	1,206,598
1991	45,865,297	35,967,900	64,799	36,032,699	4,222,480	-1,660,691	30,149,528	9,056,318	6,659,451	21,660	2,117,512	1,192,489
1992	48,108,841	37,974,810	120,349	38,095,159	4,431,334	-1,781,332	31,882,493	8,995,635	7,230,713	22,575	2,131,036	1,181,133
1993	49,991,115	39,298,637	115,739	39,414,376	4,636,173	-1,807,043	32,971,160	9,464,338	7,555,617	23,356	2,140,398	1,195,585
1994	52,498,143	41,807,523	110,591	41,918,114	4,994,766	-1,965,583	34,957,765	9,738,409	7,801,969	24,460	2,146,303	1,223,705
1995	55,073,147	43,425,785	111,046	43,536,831	5,246,490	-2,075,032	36,215,309	10,612,654	8,245,184	25,613	2,150,203	1,251,048
1996	57,314,432	44,919,621	110,572	45,030,193	5,370,277	-2,208,654	37,451,262	11,365,209	8,497,961	26,613	2,153,598	1,268,542
1997	60,274,826	47,458,441	111,744	47,570,185	5,550,527	-2,497,579	39,522,079	11,996,623	8,756,124	28,000	2,152,676	1,290,060
1998	63,489,338	49,987,166	118,657	50,105,823	5,695,634	-2,704,627	41,705,562	13,002,107	8,781,669	29,508	2,151,568	1,305,773
1999	65,344,967	52,420,534	123,577	52,544,111	5,938,787	-3,063,285	43,542,039	12,785,796	9,017,132	30,394	2,149,943	1,324,094
2000	68,673,859	54,993,962	97,698	55,091,660	6,021,111	-3,318,379	45,752,170	13,385,744	9,535,945	31,978	2,147,532	1,341,671
2001	68,536,467	54,501,337	103,652	54,604,989	6,010,848	-3,400,755	45,193,386	13,116,469	10,226,612	32,000	2,141,787	1,322,201
2002	68,728,603	54,453,608	94,326	54,547,934	5,906,187	-3,327,372	45,314,375	12,607,834	10,806,394	32,173	2,136,201	1,294,109
2003	70,126,990	56,290,876	71,601	56,362,477	6,154,488	-3,414,902	46,793,087	11,989,910	11,343,993	32,906	2,131,150	1,291,744
2004	72,892,419	58,593,854	116,240	58,710,094	6,508,595	-3,629,648	48,571,851	12,526,351	11,794,217	34,336	2,122,934	1,296,299
2005	75,255,689	59,553,495	125,555	59,679,050	6,651,173	-3,620,776	49,407,101	13,501,189	12,347,399	35,638	2,111,699	1,299,430
2006	79,574,471	62,410,685	86,128	62,496,813	6,960,253	-3,845,196	51,691,364	15,034,508	12,848,599	37,903	2,099,415	1,309,383
2007	83,181,468	64,290,494	102,337	64,392,831	7,126,159	-3,865,797	53,400,875	16,177,378	13,603,215	39,769	2,091,596	1,316,266
2008	85,609,597	65,019,022	91,461	65,110,483	7,288,676	-3,620,444	54,201,363	16,292,221	15,116,013	41,058	2,085,110	1,302,283
2009	81,301,774	61,284,667	102,227	61,386,894	6,977,213	-3,327,934	51,081,747	14,074,690	16,145,337	39,067	2,081,063	1,251,077
2010	82,445,042	62,087,605	103,139	62,190,744	6,994,678	-3,380,035	51,816,031	13,683,902	16,945,109	39,722	2,075,557	1,243,015
2011	87,682,840	65,271,102	114,752	65,385,854	6,604,575	-3,615,335	55,165,944	15,189,343	17,327,553	42,380	2,068,991	1,260,014
2012	91,784,605	68,475,584	129,206	68,604,790	6,856,993	-3,915,499	57,832,298	16,910,731	17,041,576	44,454	2,064,711	1,277,714
2013	92,568,404	70,783,580	139,279	70,922,859	7,732,642	-3,988,880	59,201,337	15,941,554	17,425,513	44,809	2,065,844	1,290,660
2014	97,137,374	72,764,300	130,622	72,894,922	7,900,948	-3,898,434	61,095,540	17,805,881	18,235,953	47,012	2,066,227	1,299,937
2015	100,422,993	74,787,272	127,552	74,914,824	8,116,739	-3,851,432	62,946,653	18,539,332	18,937,008	48,682	2,062,842	1,313,243
2016	102,508,660	75,964,676	149,487	76,114,163	8,388,197	-3,808,848	63,917,118	19,176,775	19,414,767	49,760	2,060,065	1,323,727
2017	106,554,764	79,202,972	116,973	79,319,945	8,847,585	-3,947,901	66,524,459	20,122,564	19,907,741	51,755	2,058,844	1,331,464
2018	110,433,483	110,357,616	75,867	81,348,413	9,020,946	-4,285,063	68,042,404	22,165,465	20,225,614	53,770	2,053,795	1,348,640
2019	113,588,996	113,515,246	73,750	84,308,760	9,359,978	-4,743,398	70,205,384	22,362,106	21,021,506	55,451	2,048,449	1,366,976

Personal Income and Employment by Area: Coeur d'Alene, ID

(Thousands of dollars, except as noted.)

Year	Personal income, total	Earnings by place of work			Less: Contributions for government social insurance	Plus: Adjustment for residence	Equals: Net earnings by place of residence	Plus: Dividends, interest, and rent	Plus: Personal current transfer receipts	Per capita personal income (dollars)	Population (persons)	Total employment
		Nonfarm	Farm	Total								
1970	128,305	73,697	2,621	76,318	5,381	19,416	90,353	23,733	14,219	3,606	35,579	12,625
1971	144,854	83,293	2,309	85,602	6,311	21,534	100,825	27,061	16,968	3,953	36,644	13,312
1972	167,854	99,844	3,474	103,318	7,992	23,533	118,859	29,712	19,283	4,283	39,195	14,772
1973	189,600	119,658	-2,546	117,112	11,145	26,406	132,373	34,293	22,934	4,459	42,519	16,223
1974	226,270	132,897	5,892	138,789	12,506	31,147	157,430	40,687	28,153	5,073	44,600	17,126
1975	258,825	146,483	4,059	150,542	13,391	36,093	173,244	49,070	36,511	5,464	47,365	17,382
1976	299,824	175,897	4,336	180,233	16,255	41,164	205,142	54,520	40,162	6,140	48,828	19,043
1977	345,686	209,355	2,752	212,107	19,534	45,764	238,337	64,401	42,948	6,704	51,565	20,572
1978	414,419	253,716	4,235	257,951	23,770	55,165	289,346	77,393	47,680	7,482	55,386	22,466
1979	475,380	289,101	3,523	292,624	28,596	64,247	328,275	90,284	56,821	8,095	58,728	24,047
1980	527,870	302,354	3,992	306,346	29,744	73,117	349,719	108,860	69,291	8,798	59,996	23,469
1981	575,842	315,204	2,922	318,126	33,338	79,541	364,329	131,478	80,035	9,467	60,827	23,099
1982	600,503	310,392	2,918	313,310	33,498	71,656	351,468	152,863	96,172	9,618	62,436	22,576
1983	679,298	362,177	5,631	367,808	39,518	76,449	404,739	173,466	101,093	10,785	62,987	24,041
1984	748,375	407,933	4,995	412,928	46,351	83,776	450,353	194,261	103,761	11,427	65,494	26,144
1985	793,754	426,584	3,827	430,411	49,274	85,468	466,605	214,916	112,233	11,886	66,783	26,831
1986	827,347	446,205	3,458	449,663	52,293	87,858	485,228	222,841	119,278	12,393	66,761	27,960
1987	856,137	475,753	147	475,900	54,613	94,272	515,559	216,961	123,617	12,940	66,160	29,674
1988	941,881	527,218	3,150	530,368	63,210	106,935	574,093	233,216	134,572	14,088	66,859	31,474
1989	1,049,203	591,079	3,829	594,908	72,137	117,228	639,999	260,978	148,226	15,489	67,738	33,071
1990	1,150,054	667,785	5,524	673,309	85,508	127,284	715,085	272,166	162,803	16,326	70,443	35,431
1991	1,247,483	737,398	2,405	739,803	96,752	127,420	770,471	291,255	185,757	16,870	73,946	38,117
1992	1,421,786	860,885	4,753	865,638	110,936	138,587	893,289	320,329	208,168	18,327	77,577	41,164
1993	1,577,666	968,572	5,297	973,869	125,377	143,321	991,813	356,770	229,083	19,088	82,654	44,016
1994	1,737,402	1,088,379	570	1,088,949	141,171	157,630	1,105,408	388,517	243,477	19,733	88,046	48,249
1995	1,867,673	1,132,332	339	1,132,671	148,654	170,330	1,154,347	442,958	270,368	20,152	92,677	50,172
1996	2,010,419	1,206,336	1,380	1,207,716	154,829	192,665	1,245,552	471,112	293,755	20,814	96,590	51,999
1997	2,132,629	1,275,589	-898	1,274,691	163,795	214,740	1,325,636	496,981	310,012	21,303	100,108	54,341
1998	2,295,920	1,401,944	1,090	1,403,034	175,767	244,964	1,472,231	496,942	326,747	22,352	102,717	55,676
1999	2,432,945	1,507,297	1,902	1,509,199	183,862	267,873	1,593,210	488,205	351,530	22,878	106,346	57,772
2000	2,620,919	1,659,765	2,872	1,662,637	198,607	240,520	1,704,550	530,141	386,228	23,938	109,487	59,995
2001	2,804,277	1,796,108	3,530	1,799,638	210,469	227,309	1,816,478	542,476	445,323	25,141	111,542	61,217
2002	2,891,465	1,891,994	4,059	1,896,053	222,605	222,242	1,895,690	512,468	483,307	25,438	113,667	62,919
2003	3,054,857	1,975,205	3,202	1,978,407	237,222	230,974	1,972,159	568,144	514,554	26,219	116,512	64,164
2004	3,333,907	2,158,926	4,187	2,163,113	262,863	239,348	2,139,598	635,844	558,465	27,552	121,002	68,866
2005	3,675,588	2,373,789	3,290	2,377,079	294,548	228,299	2,310,830	755,225	609,533	29,178	125,972	73,502
2006	4,021,006	2,653,411	1,744	2,655,155	332,799	208,325	2,530,681	836,336	653,989	31,048	129,510	77,152
2007	4,290,590	2,774,358	2,062	2,776,420	352,942	227,027	2,650,505	929,020	711,065	32,306	132,811	80,534
2008	4,418,647	2,725,601	-1,531	2,724,070	353,834	264,239	2,634,475	954,913	829,259	32,579	135,627	80,340
2009	4,328,071	2,558,152	273	2,558,425	341,867	313,622	2,530,180	883,349	914,542	31,498	137,407	76,284
2010	4,456,968	2,602,289	-2,206	2,600,083	359,998	336,164	2,576,249	871,726	1,008,993	32,098	138,856	75,121
2011	4,749,635	2,638,930	3,373	2,642,303	329,602	414,788	2,727,489	999,404	1,022,742	33,714	140,881	75,818
2012	5,043,804	2,687,913	4,132	2,692,045	333,041	547,081	2,906,085	1,091,415	1,046,304	35,502	142,071	75,139
2013	5,239,339	2,893,628	6,478	2,900,106	386,891	532,655	3,045,870	1,113,422	1,080,047	36,413	143,887	77,720
2014	5,606,276	3,024,145	4,177	3,028,322	401,597	564,534	3,191,259	1,263,978	1,151,039	38,253	146,556	80,311
2015	6,023,193	3,254,203	2,272	3,256,475	425,290	556,999	3,388,184	1,414,272	1,220,737	40,312	149,414	82,640
2016	6,298,078	3,452,793	2,281	3,455,074	450,256	585,529	3,590,347	1,424,925	1,282,806	41,125	153,144	84,999
2017	6,656,049	3,690,412	1,870	3,692,282	480,813	600,758	3,812,227	1,501,517	1,342,305	42,224	157,637	87,636
2018	7,320,336	7,318,838	1,498	3,990,929	518,496	669,046	4,141,479	1,709,626	1,469,231	45,409	161,209	91,417
2019	7,728,980	7,728,162	818	4,233,369	549,888	728,248	4,411,729	1,729,281	1,587,970	46,645	165,697	94,185

Personal Income and Employment by Area: College Station-Bryan, TX

(Thousands of dollars, except as noted.)

Year	Personal income, total	Earnings by place of work			Less: Contributions for government social insurance	Plus: Adjustment for residence	Equals: Net earnings by place of residence	Plus: Dividends, interest, and rent	Plus: Personal current transfer receipts	Per capita personal income (dollars)	Population (persons)	Total employment
		Nonfarm	Farm	Total								
1970............	239,328	175,727	9,198	184,925	11,227	67	173,765	40,225	25,338	2,901	82,495	33,470
1971............	273,855	204,457	8,439	212,896	13,554	-418	198,924	45,721	29,210	3,229	84,820	35,764
1972............	313,756	228,045	17,136	245,181	15,656	-159	229,366	52,246	32,144	3,483	90,094	37,801
1973............	349,995	253,478	14,939	268,417	19,832	889	249,474	62,083	38,438	3,687	94,934	39,127
1974............	384,608	276,825	7,244	284,069	22,472	2,363	263,960	74,108	46,540	3,861	99,612	39,846
1975............	439,121	317,036	-2,657	314,379	25,202	3,532	292,709	87,888	58,524	4,449	98,699	41,325
1976............	508,891	370,375	3,632	374,007	29,612	4,330	348,725	96,480	63,686	4,983	102,118	44,451
1977............	579,396	424,639	6,122	430,761	34,291	5,755	402,225	109,327	67,844	5,486	105,615	48,208
1978............	671,254	496,345	7,202	503,547	40,972	6,793	469,368	126,102	75,784	5,992	112,021	51,286
1979............	763,510	565,527	7,896	573,423	48,901	9,181	533,703	144,082	85,725	6,521	117,089	53,353
1980............	902,991	667,756	194	667,950	57,432	11,575	622,093	181,082	99,816	7,360	122,685	57,181
1981............	1,143,205	871,905	14,397	886,302	81,533	-5,411	799,358	230,816	113,031	8,737	130,852	63,834
1982............	1,296,359	957,990	9,929	967,919	90,480	-3,472	873,967	294,018	128,374	9,099	142,471	66,877
1983............	1,410,044	1,031,014	5,877	1,036,891	94,658	-5,074	937,159	332,196	140,689	9,591	147,011	68,500
1984............	1,551,996	1,123,356	4,258	1,127,614	103,557	-795	1,023,262	378,565	150,169	10,364	149,749	70,778
1985............	1,621,915	1,149,608	2,369	1,151,977	105,487	2,815	1,049,305	412,410	160,200	10,620	152,724	71,201
1986............	1,625,456	1,154,713	-8,884	1,145,829	104,172	4,815	1,046,472	405,573	173,411	10,560	153,931	69,985
1987............	1,666,036	1,171,910	5,750	1,177,660	103,761	6,139	1,080,038	403,496	182,502	10,942	152,259	71,753
1988............	1,768,139	1,272,115	3,305	1,275,420	119,754	2,524	1,158,190	417,952	191,997	11,719	150,882	74,831
1989............	1,927,466	1,374,458	11,017	1,385,475	131,463	-3,105	1,250,907	462,613	213,946	12,818	150,375	77,282
1990............	2,043,366	1,480,269	13,272	1,493,541	139,619	-1,242	1,352,680	454,739	235,947	13,488	151,495	79,083
1991............	2,163,816	1,570,220	14,666	1,584,886	152,142	1,780	1,434,524	471,125	258,167	14,045	154,062	81,933
1992............	2,317,612	1,691,121	20,737	1,711,858	163,031	147	1,548,974	471,794	296,844	14,640	158,308	83,359
1993............	2,486,992	1,819,336	18,552	1,837,888	175,008	-4,050	1,658,830	516,959	311,203	15,096	164,742	87,560
1994............	2,601,084	1,925,310	18,169	1,943,479	188,508	-6,590	1,748,381	526,806	325,897	15,491	167,911	90,558
1995............	2,741,565	1,990,436	11,857	2,002,293	195,985	-7,923	1,798,385	580,984	362,196	16,069	170,608	92,132
1996............	2,888,041	2,093,838	-883	2,092,955	204,183	-9,269	1,879,503	620,335	388,203	16,758	172,341	93,646
1997............	3,161,697	2,321,249	8,985	2,330,234	224,079	-10,138	2,096,017	656,621	409,059	17,954	176,098	97,342
1998............	3,350,286	2,503,138	-1,658	2,501,480	240,604	-14,063	2,246,813	679,393	424,080	18,665	179,498	100,944
1999............	3,515,520	2,652,241	27,165	2,679,406	252,813	-16,569	2,410,024	669,994	435,502	19,281	182,327	100,840
2000............	3,769,818	2,847,417	11,517	2,858,934	269,367	-19,758	2,569,809	735,141	464,868	20,294	185,760	104,085
2001............	4,038,511	3,086,973	26,826	3,113,799	284,046	-24,635	2,805,118	726,758	506,635	21,446	188,315	107,288
2002............	4,182,181	3,184,108	45,688	3,229,796	291,673	-31,934	2,906,189	721,076	554,916	21,780	192,016	108,148
2003............	4,517,033	3,401,210	63,150	3,464,360	317,190	-49,382	3,097,788	812,481	606,764	23,019	196,234	109,810
2004............	4,711,026	3,572,589	60,605	3,633,194	333,919	-41,012	3,258,263	815,883	636,880	23,629	199,374	111,780
2005............	5,022,791	3,793,927	49,417	3,843,344	354,367	-33,275	3,455,702	869,410	697,679	24,682	203,500	115,746
2006............	5,440,591	4,119,815	29,651	4,149,466	376,630	-41,280	3,731,556	966,374	742,661	26,030	209,014	119,940
2007............	5,778,146	4,289,701	27,179	4,316,880	399,549	-40,195	3,877,136	1,081,752	819,258	27,127	213,000	120,087
2008............	6,414,808	4,564,243	-12,959	4,551,284	421,316	-25,489	4,104,479	1,365,162	945,167	29,337	218,658	123,029
2009............	6,539,865	4,771,046	-9,794	4,761,252	443,978	-44,862	4,272,412	1,236,635	1,030,818	29,051	225,114	127,108
2010............	6,972,643	5,027,625	14,027	5,041,652	461,514	-28,942	4,551,196	1,271,709	1,149,738	30,389	229,449	128,073
2011............	7,296,920	5,144,394	-4,215	5,140,179	422,387	11,367	4,729,159	1,383,885	1,183,876	31,527	231,451	128,362
2012............	7,764,213	5,426,142	759	5,426,901	441,606	36,055	5,021,350	1,557,307	1,185,556	33,163	234,126	131,867
2013............	8,093,680	5,739,793	52,524	5,792,317	519,470	35,624	5,308,471	1,557,719	1,227,490	34,033	237,820	137,260
2014............	8,726,393	6,171,940	32,747	6,204,687	556,634	53,836	5,701,889	1,719,852	1,304,652	35,980	242,533	141,934
2015............	9,116,788	6,434,581	56,585	6,491,166	586,411	34,237	5,938,992	1,766,933	1,410,863	36,447	250,138	146,143
2016............	9,292,800	6,506,119	9,134	6,515,253	600,175	3,711	5,918,789	1,896,657	1,477,354	36,553	254,230	149,026
2017............	9,729,227	6,880,346	11,849	6,892,195	640,333	-25,744	6,226,118	1,989,215	1,513,894	37,704	258,044	151,720
2018............	10,583,596	10,564,274	19,322	7,328,239	680,886	-16,746	6,630,607	2,358,302	1,594,687	40,498	261,335	158,548
2019............	11,050,339	11,042,444	7,895	7,657,470	709,562	-18,091	6,929,817	2,416,523	1,703,999	41,742	264,728	162,558

Personal Income and Employment by Area: Colorado Springs, CO

(Thousands of dollars, except as noted.)

Year	Personal income, total	Earnings by place of work			Less: Contributions for government social insurance	Plus: Adjustment for residence	Equals: Net earnings by place of residence	Plus: Dividends, interest, and rent	Plus: Personal current transfer receipts	Per capita personal income (dollars)	Population (persons)	Total employment
		Nonfarm	Farm	Total								
1970	1,072,245	797,479	2,787	800,266	44,176	-1,431	754,659	256,190	61,396	4,439	241,543	116,502
1971	1,171,605	873,849	2,542	876,391	50,659	720	826,452	270,050	75,103	4,614	253,897	117,553
1972	1,372,920	1,036,652	2,983	1,039,635	63,176	3,817	980,276	304,806	87,838	5,020	273,474	128,822
1973	1,580,510	1,192,341	5,401	1,197,742	80,698	10,160	1,127,204	348,639	104,667	5,358	294,996	140,951
1974	1,736,052	1,294,218	3,687	1,297,905	91,168	15,798	1,222,535	393,970	119,547	5,793	299,705	142,577
1975	1,868,907	1,357,894	4,571	1,362,465	97,001	21,608	1,287,072	430,007	151,828	6,234	299,777	139,515
1976	2,016,953	1,464,140	5,370	1,469,510	106,204	29,776	1,393,082	460,611	163,260	6,777	297,633	143,093
1977	2,188,790	1,573,271	5,306	1,578,577	114,467	39,738	1,503,848	512,179	172,763	7,119	307,449	147,428
1978	2,528,015	1,809,887	4,390	1,814,277	132,674	50,253	1,731,856	606,473	189,686	8,101	312,072	154,227
1979	2,888,059	2,083,521	1,307	2,084,828	161,856	63,743	1,986,715	687,031	214,313	9,107	317,132	164,283
1980	3,281,712	2,336,633	2,454	2,339,087	185,717	81,271	2,234,641	793,160	253,911	10,250	320,180	170,287
1981	3,848,756	2,738,309	471	2,738,780	233,888	85,164	2,590,056	955,362	303,338	11,653	330,278	178,535
1982	4,259,676	3,016,989	2,944	3,019,933	259,813	88,409	2,848,529	1,069,367	341,780	12,476	341,418	185,178
1983	4,674,710	3,317,823	2,039	3,319,862	295,714	87,858	3,112,006	1,181,120	381,584	13,222	353,551	192,322
1984	5,294,525	3,804,454	1,309	3,805,763	353,241	86,829	3,539,351	1,336,311	418,863	14,516	364,735	209,639
1985	5,822,397	4,205,563	70	4,205,633	402,736	86,991	3,889,888	1,482,220	450,289	15,277	381,127	220,895
1986	6,273,129	4,557,466	-280	4,557,186	442,102	85,509	4,200,593	1,584,557	487,979	15,913	394,224	226,673
1987	6,658,876	4,838,504	1,600	4,840,104	467,635	85,321	4,457,790	1,667,196	533,890	16,369	406,810	229,718
1988	7,052,499	5,185,712	289	5,186,001	520,170	87,236	4,753,067	1,729,632	569,800	17,273	408,302	236,180
1989	7,409,205	5,327,103	467	5,327,570	551,517	90,538	4,866,591	1,904,595	638,019	18,082	409,747	238,697
1990	7,608,768	5,437,106	-297	5,436,809	578,739	104,702	4,962,772	1,949,153	696,843	18,557	410,017	235,412
1991	8,091,293	5,851,287	380	5,851,667	637,897	106,627	5,320,397	1,982,929	787,967	19,393	417,227	241,791
1992	8,833,091	6,426,039	2,367	6,428,406	703,765	108,413	5,833,054	2,111,089	888,948	20,274	435,686	250,936
1993	9,392,302	6,838,459	1,656	6,840,115	760,643	111,913	6,191,385	2,249,493	951,424	20,786	451,855	262,001
1994	10,176,944	7,428,476	-983	7,427,493	830,835	109,639	6,706,297	2,452,867	1,017,780	21,517	472,965	279,017
1995	11,140,692	8,038,681	-1,140	8,037,541	890,427	109,933	7,257,047	2,738,880	1,144,765	22,882	486,869	291,270
1996	12,002,210	8,705,752	-1,053	8,704,699	958,233	112,962	7,859,428	2,951,757	1,191,025	24,172	496,543	303,895
1997	12,719,484	9,328,054	-285	9,327,769	1,023,592	123,854	8,428,031	3,059,898	1,231,555	25,132	506,107	315,465
1998	14,081,471	10,509,130	301	10,509,431	1,084,615	136,164	9,560,980	3,243,132	1,277,359	27,195	517,799	326,466
1999	15,200,670	11,521,836	1,521	11,523,357	1,170,527	156,118	10,508,948	3,318,068	1,373,654	28,716	529,338	334,576
2000	16,645,272	12,695,641	3,994	12,699,635	1,280,838	177,419	11,596,216	3,591,769	1,457,287	30,791	540,593	345,217
2001	17,347,775	13,233,676	5,866	13,239,542	1,350,375	184,267	12,073,434	3,645,557	1,628,784	31,142	557,057	349,511
2002	17,715,135	13,553,324	3,883	13,557,207	1,415,819	175,949	12,317,337	3,567,345	1,830,453	31,316	565,688	347,088
2003	18,163,926	13,850,516	1,085	13,851,601	1,455,412	183,430	12,579,619	3,636,064	1,948,243	31,910	569,231	347,795
2004	18,911,630	14,465,867	8,437	14,474,304	1,562,530	194,033	13,105,807	3,758,298	2,047,525	32,700	578,345	353,744
2005	20,122,018	15,430,176	4,848	15,435,024	1,674,176	204,677	13,965,525	3,919,503	2,236,990	34,234	587,778	365,026
2006	21,291,364	16,066,939	1,067	16,068,006	1,752,455	229,881	14,545,432	4,312,798	2,433,134	35,336	602,532	371,136
2007	22,456,259	16,555,032	-2,046	16,552,986	1,805,208	260,042	15,007,820	4,803,026	2,645,413	36,844	609,490	378,789
2008	23,331,276	16,775,664	-3,661	16,772,003	1,855,722	280,320	15,196,601	4,956,036	3,178,639	37,592	620,644	378,125
2009	23,674,394	17,022,066	-1,213	17,020,853	1,886,211	309,946	15,444,588	4,625,859	3,603,947	37,519	630,998	371,574
2010	24,842,210	17,673,790	-816	17,672,974	1,958,299	358,191	16,072,866	4,605,245	4,164,099	38,201	650,299	372,146
2011	26,486,793	18,408,382	3,784	18,412,166	1,861,762	424,969	16,975,373	5,158,024	4,353,396	40,134	659,959	378,167
2012	27,559,861	18,922,418	1,765	18,924,183	1,912,978	673,067	17,684,272	5,470,810	4,404,779	41,241	668,271	379,506
2013	27,977,519	19,369,755	5,030	19,374,785	2,145,874	559,810	17,788,721	5,637,164	4,551,634	41,308	677,296	386,398
2014	29,675,047	20,284,093	3,810	20,287,903	2,253,806	667,815	18,701,912	6,093,220	4,879,915	43,307	685,223	394,845
2015	31,174,710	21,044,363	5,488	21,049,851	2,356,341	700,240	19,393,750	6,463,396	5,317,564	44,802	695,830	404,608
2016	32,030,733	21,593,934	8,105	21,602,039	2,419,179	624,699	19,807,559	6,674,681	5,548,493	45,066	710,746	413,072
2017	33,681,358	22,843,731	8,798	22,852,529	2,555,709	718,127	21,014,947	6,954,480	5,711,931	46,529	723,878	422,552
2018	36,128,371	36,127,458	913	24,142,556	2,675,048	693,936	22,161,444	7,503,154	6,463,773	49,007	737,202	436,707
2019	38,125,082	38,126,267	-1,185	25,527,993	2,819,427	858,362	23,566,928	7,750,198	6,807,956	51,120	745,791	447,972

Personal Income and Employment by Area: Columbia, MO

(Thousands of dollars, except as noted.)

Year	Personal income, total	Earnings by place of work			Less: Contributions for government social insurance	Plus: Adjustment for residence	Equals: Net earnings by place of residence	Plus: Dividends, interest, and rent	Plus: Personal current transfer receipts	Per capita personal income (dollars)	Population (persons)	Total employment
		Nonfarm	Farm	Total								
1970	285,184	240,607	3,792	244,399	14,721	-7,685	221,993	45,819	17,372	3,518	81,073	39,470
1971	316,338	264,748	4,649	269,397	16,668	-7,452	245,277	51,041	20,020	3,831	82,578	40,284
1972	351,410	293,659	4,267	297,926	18,832	-7,579	271,515	57,606	22,289	4,181	84,046	41,917
1973	400,911	327,026	11,501	338,527	24,222	-7,418	306,887	66,862	27,162	4,525	88,593	44,491
1974	452,747	367,822	8,518	376,340	28,234	-7,460	340,646	79,342	32,759	4,978	90,958	45,535
1975	513,216	414,633	2,514	417,147	31,481	-7,702	377,964	92,329	42,923	5,781	88,769	46,649
1976	586,161	474,602	3,918	478,520	36,313	-6,847	435,360	102,606	48,195	6,335	92,528	49,134
1977	654,451	527,709	6,431	534,140	40,445	-4,546	489,149	114,481	50,821	6,952	94,134	51,203
1978	739,584	598,491	5,950	604,441	47,635	-1,584	555,222	128,587	55,775	7,634	96,886	53,672
1979	838,394	673,322	10,408	683,730	55,730	-594	627,406	146,693	64,295	8,586	97,649	56,890
1980	942,492	743,655	758	744,413	60,654	989	684,748	179,313	78,431	9,352	100,776	57,601
1981	1,033,646	785,110	6,557	791,667	68,617	2,285	725,335	217,099	91,212	10,118	102,163	56,917
1982	1,121,500	828,243	3,079	831,322	73,046	1,063	759,339	262,496	99,665	10,886	103,024	56,723
1983	1,238,841	928,372	-574	927,798	82,481	-4,973	840,344	286,862	111,635	11,962	103,564	59,821
1984	1,335,217	1,000,234	1,682	1,001,916	91,460	-10,936	899,520	317,904	117,793	12,773	104,531	62,097
1985	1,428,310	1,081,368	9,767	1,091,135	101,030	-20,248	969,857	333,943	124,510	13,629	104,800	64,693
1986	1,522,601	1,168,848	608	1,169,456	110,932	-24,193	1,034,331	355,938	132,332	14,358	106,045	67,855
1987	1,628,955	1,265,547	1,953	1,267,500	119,102	-29,962	1,118,436	370,345	140,174	15,170	107,382	69,530
1988	1,732,743	1,368,761	1,682	1,370,443	136,520	-38,361	1,195,562	387,917	149,264	15,849	109,331	72,316
1989	1,862,641	1,472,229	6,610	1,478,839	148,002	-42,897	1,287,940	406,639	168,062	16,755	111,171	73,951
1990	2,009,729	1,600,279	4,558	1,604,837	165,780	-53,702	1,385,355	439,595	184,779	17,812	112,827	76,763
1991	2,169,259	1,728,180	4,930	1,733,110	181,303	-62,908	1,488,899	464,463	215,897	18,835	115,171	78,338
1992	2,354,002	1,902,649	2,660	1,905,309	197,728	-72,560	1,635,021	487,627	231,354	20,008	117,651	80,387
1993	2,513,059	1,997,235	5,222	2,002,457	208,164	-78,994	1,715,299	537,595	260,165	20,885	120,329	83,169
1994	2,687,395	2,160,567	1,758	2,162,325	226,726	-97,936	1,837,663	576,773	272,959	21,881	122,817	86,022
1995	2,855,792	2,271,998	-1,921	2,270,077	237,823	-105,748	1,926,506	631,423	297,863	22,752	125,520	89,182
1996	3,057,214	2,437,075	5,949	2,443,024	251,607	-119,976	2,071,441	673,041	312,732	23,816	128,366	92,799
1997	3,272,038	2,557,729	3,168	2,560,897	262,942	-127,487	2,170,468	775,864	325,706	24,981	130,981	94,940
1998	3,424,511	2,743,426	2,182	2,745,608	280,545	-142,192	2,322,871	758,926	342,714	25,826	132,601	96,122
1999	3,585,711	2,921,668	-2,740	2,918,928	294,537	-152,213	2,472,178	750,576	362,957	26,743	134,081	96,953
2000	3,826,867	3,107,304	4,004	3,111,308	310,736	-169,998	2,630,574	794,783	401,510	28,151	135,940	100,521
2001	4,020,997	3,292,879	4,296	3,297,175	329,669	-176,476	2,791,030	778,172	451,795	29,099	138,181	101,796
2002	4,145,233	3,466,722	2,523	3,469,245	343,917	-190,284	2,935,044	727,956	482,233	29,463	140,695	102,670
2003	4,332,428	3,562,844	8,107	3,570,951	352,821	-186,353	3,031,777	794,314	506,337	30,293	143,019	103,060
2004	4,644,451	3,761,093	19,274	3,780,367	372,170	-199,765	3,208,432	899,060	536,959	31,954	145,348	105,536
2005	4,831,584	3,938,351	3,833	3,942,184	394,994	-224,079	3,323,111	923,939	584,534	32,473	148,786	108,633
2006	5,146,867	4,135,484	4,909	4,140,393	420,031	-235,335	3,485,027	1,035,512	626,328	33,687	152,784	111,093
2007	5,412,829	4,245,694	4,818	4,250,512	437,676	-240,249	3,572,587	1,165,461	674,781	34,772	155,666	112,770
2008	5,818,184	4,377,938	7,878	4,385,816	453,930	-183,699	3,748,187	1,269,423	800,574	36,803	158,089	112,735
2009	6,105,665	4,490,880	9,985	4,500,865	456,835	-183,301	3,860,729	1,374,995	869,941	38,026	160,565	110,552
2010	6,108,868	4,700,816	11,201	4,712,017	469,019	-219,426	4,023,572	1,120,031	965,265	37,439	163,168	111,844
2011	6,432,132	4,920,932	16,638	4,937,570	440,297	-232,988	4,264,285	1,163,148	1,004,699	38,743	166,019	115,066
2012	6,819,337	5,232,294	7,319	5,239,613	464,635	-273,261	4,501,717	1,295,151	1,022,469	40,429	168,674	118,612
2013	7,028,464	5,545,988	23,524	5,569,512	552,113	-303,084	4,714,315	1,273,852	1,040,297	41,117	170,937	121,775
2014	7,262,070	5,679,835	23,445	5,703,280	570,608	-305,396	4,827,276	1,362,344	1,072,450	42,029	172,787	122,892
2015	7,600,058	5,909,394	56	5,909,450	602,676	-314,761	4,992,013	1,475,219	1,132,826	43,580	174,395	125,202
2016	7,735,966	6,015,739	2,093	6,017,832	622,562	-329,767	5,065,503	1,489,783	1,180,680	43,816	176,555	126,761
2017	7,985,993	6,191,617	12,505	6,204,122	641,193	-349,507	5,213,422	1,569,675	1,202,896	44,797	178,271	128,221
2018	9,409,471	9,392,615	16,856	6,815,272	710,527	-141,086	5,963,659	1,884,879	1,560,933	45,512	206,746	143,658
2019	9,884,411	9,845,593	38,818	7,249,260	756,444	-175,883	6,316,933	1,923,399	1,644,079	47,482	208,173	144,993

Personal Income and Employment by Area: Columbia, SC

(Thousands of dollars, except as noted.)

Year	Personal income, total	Earnings by place of work			Less: Contributions for government social insurance	Plus: Adjustment for residence	Equals: Net earnings by place of residence	Plus: Dividends, interest, and rent	Plus: Personal current transfer receipts	Per capita personal income (dollars)	Population (persons)	Total employment
		Nonfarm	Farm	Total								
1970	1,458,229	1,201,538	16,335	1,217,873	75,700	3,781	1,145,954	214,869	97,406	3,598	405,343	198,370
1971	1,616,213	1,329,307	18,059	1,347,366	87,312	59	1,260,113	241,138	114,962	3,842	420,632	204,042
1972	1,823,762	1,504,783	19,471	1,524,254	102,692	-2,007	1,419,555	271,112	133,095	4,265	427,654	213,386
1973	2,066,739	1,709,134	30,056	1,739,190	133,028	-7,773	1,598,389	307,624	160,726	4,713	438,518	225,415
1974	2,366,539	1,953,031	27,300	1,980,331	157,478	-17,789	1,805,064	360,780	200,695	5,198	455,302	237,022
1975	2,609,730	2,107,240	20,220	2,127,460	168,366	-23,138	1,935,956	401,503	272,271	5,651	461,809	235,356
1976	2,864,484	2,340,665	22,657	2,363,322	192,250	-31,126	2,139,946	431,774	292,764	6,131	467,203	240,094
1977	3,126,547	2,575,393	17,681	2,593,074	210,735	-37,931	2,344,408	477,280	304,859	6,547	477,566	247,405
1978	3,486,845	2,881,165	22,598	2,903,763	240,838	-46,195	2,616,730	535,739	334,376	7,215	483,307	255,079
1979	3,918,442	3,234,514	38,056	3,272,570	280,476	-59,818	2,932,276	601,479	384,687	7,968	491,796	263,946
1980	4,364,480	3,550,356	11,064	3,561,420	308,873	-68,581	3,183,966	714,638	465,876	8,733	499,796	267,308
1981	4,884,473	3,892,115	20,223	3,912,338	362,580	-67,307	3,482,451	864,101	537,921	9,667	505,283	268,434
1982	5,230,157	4,104,020	23,009	4,127,029	389,853	-66,546	3,670,630	980,864	578,663	10,303	507,615	268,213
1983	5,719,181	4,536,553	5,736	4,542,289	445,301	-72,302	4,024,686	1,072,990	621,505	11,141	513,337	276,269
1984	6,348,484	5,050,832	39,351	5,090,183	513,530	-75,959	4,500,694	1,192,313	655,477	12,239	518,709	289,340
1985	6,844,835	5,465,683	24,303	5,489,986	567,218	-75,135	4,847,633	1,291,023	706,179	13,130	521,313	298,320
1986	7,369,987	5,921,990	22,745	5,944,735	633,376	-77,944	5,233,415	1,392,933	743,639	13,949	528,371	308,968
1987	7,889,174	6,391,718	22,246	6,413,964	679,178	-76,109	5,658,677	1,464,565	765,932	14,806	532,846	314,930
1988	8,530,135	6,944,769	30,612	6,975,381	773,397	-82,102	6,119,882	1,590,593	819,660	15,870	537,516	327,808
1989	9,243,178	7,403,954	36,732	7,440,686	833,624	-75,081	6,531,981	1,771,070	940,127	16,994	543,917	335,359
1990	9,824,889	7,847,709	30,645	7,878,354	906,993	-101,390	6,869,971	1,905,495	1,049,423	17,811	551,633	341,316
1991	10,307,314	8,091,255	49,811	8,141,066	945,457	-75,699	7,119,910	1,969,747	1,217,657	18,300	563,238	336,460
1992	10,910,866	8,577,220	44,069	8,621,289	995,843	-92,263	7,533,183	2,021,627	1,356,056	19,064	572,323	340,420
1993	11,428,631	8,933,708	34,259	8,967,967	1,046,068	-55,597	7,866,302	2,111,091	1,451,238	19,638	581,956	344,577
1994	12,159,886	9,459,480	53,843	9,513,323	1,124,681	-77,629	8,311,013	2,280,325	1,568,548	20,614	589,879	356,921
1995	12,971,726	10,040,859	48,331	10,089,190	1,195,160	-73,669	8,820,361	2,478,015	1,673,350	21,650	599,158	369,402
1996	13,929,763	10,742,757	60,899	10,803,656	1,257,023	-85,793	9,460,840	2,671,134	1,797,789	22,875	608,946	382,266
1997	14,776,849	11,442,836	64,606	11,507,442	1,338,110	-84,631	10,084,701	2,815,955	1,876,193	23,843	619,752	393,077
1998	16,054,707	12,490,556	78,087	12,568,643	1,454,543	-87,387	11,026,713	3,053,628	1,974,366	25,445	630,966	405,382
1999	16,823,863	13,268,852	73,988	13,342,840	1,534,020	-115,584	11,693,236	3,035,683	2,094,944	26,282	640,126	413,431
2000	18,048,745	14,149,775	69,282	14,219,057	1,623,335	-99,471	12,496,251	3,293,876	2,258,618	27,786	649,567	422,563
2001	18,467,120	14,375,388	86,135	14,461,523	1,663,788	-125,806	12,671,929	3,259,037	2,536,154	28,018	659,125	416,234
2002	19,058,295	14,875,691	48,461	14,924,152	1,716,542	-153,666	13,053,944	3,241,853	2,762,498	28,612	666,087	415,110
2003	19,773,855	15,517,714	84,096	15,601,810	1,799,123	-189,905	13,612,782	3,249,847	2,911,226	29,248	676,083	418,233
2004	20,901,569	16,383,540	115,779	16,499,319	1,904,529	-236,574	14,358,216	3,396,842	3,146,511	30,274	690,421	424,587
2005	22,007,265	17,212,058	100,608	17,312,666	1,990,070	-292,613	15,029,983	3,586,954	3,390,328	31,477	699,160	433,120
2006	23,861,594	18,541,208	86,348	18,627,556	2,177,546	-359,446	16,090,564	4,099,889	3,671,141	33,369	715,091	446,637
2007	25,214,752	19,439,853	57,118	19,496,971	2,270,778	-389,221	16,836,972	4,455,911	3,921,869	34,515	730,546	459,367
2008	26,451,691	20,106,862	59,398	20,166,260	2,364,142	-397,121	17,404,997	4,487,628	4,559,066	35,470	745,740	459,041
2009	25,982,477	19,512,768	72,451	19,585,219	2,321,070	-356,113	16,908,036	4,138,291	4,936,150	34,214	759,400	443,153
2010	26,528,184	19,612,487	85,115	19,697,602	2,320,156	-339,557	17,037,889	4,052,944	5,437,351	34,466	769,685	438,955
2011	27,731,598	20,278,150	42,571	20,320,721	2,142,986	-364,595	17,813,140	4,412,307	5,506,151	35,716	776,454	446,229
2012	28,901,414	21,208,495	77,390	21,285,885	2,196,535	-363,413	18,725,937	4,682,925	5,492,552	36,889	783,462	453,369
2013	29,669,782	22,092,194	149,325	22,241,519	2,567,004	-402,678	19,271,837	4,725,637	5,672,308	37,501	791,164	463,131
2014	31,373,596	23,409,496	50,152	23,459,648	2,704,507	-494,448	20,260,693	5,036,974	6,075,929	39,261	799,106	473,871
2015	33,429,653	24,875,589	61,316	24,936,905	2,858,469	-561,809	21,516,627	5,421,194	6,491,832	41,315	809,147	489,386
2016	34,300,262	25,616,638	37,821	25,654,459	2,939,130	-612,302	22,103,027	5,502,046	6,695,189	41,960	817,443	498,550
2017	35,615,262	26,443,634	41,574	26,485,208	3,046,416	-536,142	22,902,650	5,794,034	6,918,578	43,168	825,033	502,586
2018	37,355,418	37,281,685	73,733	27,366,732	3,131,880	-452,152	23,782,700	6,254,557	7,318,161	44,915	831,690	511,034
2019	39,006,819	38,970,306	36,513	28,520,171	3,276,350	-450,929	24,792,892	6,419,914	7,794,013	46,523	838,433	517,807

Personal Income and Employment by Area: Columbus, GA-AL

(Thousands of dollars, except as noted.)

Year	Personal income, total	Earnings by place of work			Less: Contributions for government social insurance	Plus: Adjustment for residence	Equals: Net earnings by place of residence	Plus: Dividends, interest, and rent	Plus: Personal current transfer receipts	Per capita personal income (dollars)	Population (persons)	Total employment
		Nonfarm	Farm	Total								
1970.............	967,543	776,328	3,997	780,325	48,135	-9,177	723,013	175,263	69,267	3,799	254,664	122,623
1971.............	1,021,290	820,138	4,129	824,267	53,641	-10,832	759,794	179,939	81,557	4,026	253,660	120,026
1972.............	1,060,253	848,124	4,756	852,880	57,423	-11,271	784,186	182,951	93,116	4,294	246,940	115,160
1973.............	1,147,277	911,466	6,869	918,335	68,631	-12,801	836,903	201,389	108,985	4,829	237,599	116,481
1974.............	1,257,757	983,462	5,792	989,254	77,488	-16,961	894,805	227,772	135,180	5,148	244,309	117,043
1975.............	1,343,420	1,037,990	4,544	1,042,534	82,792	-23,824	935,918	240,156	167,346	5,384	249,515	114,971
1976.............	1,485,062	1,161,899	7,064	1,168,963	95,139	-33,629	1,040,195	262,229	182,638	5,823	255,031	119,819
1977.............	1,625,200	1,292,253	3,966	1,296,219	105,274	-44,260	1,146,685	288,881	189,634	6,410	253,528	124,514
1978.............	1,808,318	1,431,563	6,433	1,437,996	117,541	-55,195	1,265,260	336,183	206,875	6,964	259,685	127,399
1979.............	1,931,077	1,513,396	8,641	1,522,037	130,139	-57,951	1,333,947	361,754	235,376	7,424	260,109	126,043
1980.............	2,118,690	1,625,606	5,831	1,631,437	140,572	-59,755	1,431,110	412,719	274,861	8,151	259,921	125,648
1981.............	2,362,778	1,760,596	11,671	1,772,267	161,373	-34,081	1,576,813	472,872	313,093	9,112	259,295	123,547
1982.............	2,581,586	1,900,790	10,761	1,911,551	172,386	-39,894	1,699,271	543,502	338,813	9,804	263,318	126,188
1983.............	2,732,469	2,025,101	6,895	2,031,996	190,739	-44,393	1,796,864	572,860	362,745	10,436	261,838	126,279
1984.............	3,040,241	2,277,241	8,984	2,286,225	220,617	-54,542	2,011,066	646,139	383,036	11,561	262,983	133,890
1985.............	3,265,662	2,459,460	5,799	2,465,259	242,463	-65,966	2,156,830	700,715	408,117	12,344	264,556	136,899
1986.............	3,491,651	2,646,520	4,482	2,651,002	264,403	-72,866	2,313,733	751,839	426,079	13,106	266,407	139,494
1987.............	3,699,763	2,834,227	7,097	2,841,324	283,897	-81,802	2,475,625	786,296	437,842	13,827	267,567	141,956
1988.............	3,937,472	3,000,047	9,422	3,009,469	312,128	-85,665	2,611,676	864,431	461,365	14,770	266,586	144,303
1989.............	4,075,458	3,072,703	9,688	3,082,391	325,525	-92,864	2,664,002	898,156	513,300	15,342	265,634	142,868
1990.............	4,304,282	3,238,224	7,902	3,246,126	345,930	-94,610	2,805,586	933,423	565,273	16,125	266,931	142,037
1991.............	4,502,606	3,361,678	11,981	3,373,659	363,117	-108,763	2,901,779	969,035	631,792	16,907	266,314	138,678
1992.............	4,895,487	3,653,209	11,533	3,664,742	395,434	-134,678	3,134,630	1,059,157	701,700	17,756	275,715	142,086
1993.............	5,044,598	3,754,066	12,340	3,766,406	409,945	-153,830	3,202,631	1,104,818	737,149	18,169	277,655	144,549
1994.............	5,270,251	3,898,302	15,542	3,913,844	426,661	-172,482	3,314,701	1,163,995	791,555	18,763	280,889	145,839
1995.............	5,491,266	4,043,618	10,178	4,053,796	439,992	-185,058	3,428,746	1,212,453	850,067	19,635	279,663	147,697
1996.............	5,698,929	4,236,806	14,706	4,251,512	458,775	-215,707	3,577,030	1,227,986	893,913	20,373	279,725	152,880
1997.............	6,060,075	4,561,830	13,875	4,575,705	490,039	-257,252	3,828,414	1,309,965	921,696	21,574	280,896	157,278
1998.............	6,505,502	4,924,439	16,589	4,941,028	521,601	-293,027	4,126,400	1,435,772	943,330	23,177	280,686	162,370
1999.............	6,765,672	5,194,762	22,509	5,217,271	549,085	-326,843	4,341,343	1,433,362	990,967	24,086	280,899	163,745
2000.............	7,120,364	5,432,698	15,264	5,447,962	569,901	-357,225	4,520,836	1,545,807	1,053,721	25,211	282,431	166,348
2001.............	7,468,436	5,674,901	20,006	5,694,907	594,399	-399,695	4,700,813	1,610,314	1,157,309	26,330	283,646	163,525
2002.............	7,761,527	5,864,018	15,859	5,879,877	610,197	-442,030	4,827,650	1,664,574	1,269,303	27,195	285,398	161,670
2003.............	7,994,688	6,084,965	19,951	6,104,916	629,388	-516,973	4,958,555	1,730,111	1,306,022	28,658	278,969	160,677
2004.............	8,311,642	6,294,069	19,035	6,313,104	668,236	-591,922	5,052,946	1,860,571	1,398,125	29,175	284,887	162,954
2005.............	8,716,892	6,632,332	19,051	6,651,383	703,743	-776,241	5,171,399	2,036,204	1,509,289	30,441	286,358	165,736
2006.............	9,121,897	6,931,368	13,978	6,945,346	742,770	-922,044	5,280,532	2,244,539	1,596,826	31,550	289,129	168,304
2007.............	9,274,682	7,106,262	9,481	7,115,743	762,496	-1,065,242	5,288,005	2,269,295	1,717,382	32,398	286,274	168,355
2008.............	9,497,429	7,434,180	15,300	7,449,480	823,786	-1,331,300	5,294,394	2,262,799	1,940,236	33,094	286,985	172,005
2009.............	9,360,007	7,542,180	15,161	7,557,341	840,937	-1,499,210	5,217,194	2,060,121	2,082,692	31,949	292,968	172,149
2010.............	9,839,360	7,879,866	11,374	7,891,240	878,740	-1,503,683	5,508,817	2,052,722	2,277,821	33,184	296,507	174,188
2011.............	10,656,151	8,210,215	10,527	8,220,742	820,963	-1,497,541	5,902,238	2,347,195	2,406,718	35,232	302,453	179,575
2012.............	10,885,761	8,545,732	19,952	8,565,684	855,793	-1,626,971	6,082,920	2,393,508	2,409,333	35,107	310,072	180,348
2013.............	10,867,723	8,531,123	35,492	8,566,615	961,838	-1,707,427	5,897,350	2,468,403	2,501,970	34,415	315,784	180,876
2014.............	11,172,726	8,558,001	21,655	8,579,656	964,637	-1,664,750	5,950,269	2,611,504	2,610,953	35,691	313,038	179,697
2015.............	11,685,576	8,740,187	23,883	8,764,070	985,525	-1,655,302	6,123,243	2,836,191	2,726,142	37,629	310,545	179,086
2016.............	11,834,863	8,536,450	19,952	8,556,402	959,644	-1,410,171	6,186,587	2,848,906	2,799,370	38,586	306,712	175,019
2017.............	12,227,338	8,865,209	21,522	8,886,731	998,901	-1,510,053	6,377,777	2,948,135	2,901,426	40,247	303,811	176,662
2018.............	13,040,174	13,033,438	6,736	9,285,848	1,049,691	-1,546,691	6,689,466	3,196,789	3,153,919	40,980	318,211	182,286
2019.............	13,542,897	13,537,359	5,538	9,655,724	1,092,954	-1,573,094	6,989,676	3,243,692	3,309,529	42,183	321,048	186,138

Personal Income and Employment by Area: Columbus, IN

(Thousands of dollars, except as noted.)

Year	Personal income, total	Earnings by place of work			Less: Contributions for government social insurance	Plus: Adjustment for residence	Equals: Net earnings by place of residence	Plus: Dividends, interest, and rent	Plus: Personal current transfer receipts	Per capita personal income (dollars)	Population (persons)	Total employment
		Nonfarm	Farm	Total								
1970	238,843	265,039	3,416	268,455	17,850	-58,896	191,709	33,176	13,958	4,184	57,080	32,082
1971	261,594	282,359	5,698	288,057	19,784	-60,499	207,774	37,204	16,616	4,537	57,662	32,179
1972	285,134	307,801	4,624	312,425	22,947	-63,887	225,591	40,728	18,815	4,845	58,851	32,600
1973	332,282	356,150	12,215	368,365	30,828	-73,882	263,655	46,444	22,183	5,564	59,716	35,298
1974	373,571	403,896	10,806	414,702	36,163	-84,379	294,160	53,609	25,802	6,200	60,249	36,323
1975	380,739	390,507	7,833	398,340	34,116	-76,970	287,254	58,974	34,511	6,258	60,844	33,996
1976	437,420	462,798	12,561	475,359	41,400	-96,326	337,633	64,082	35,705	7,134	61,316	35,623
1977	495,850	539,452	7,900	547,352	47,605	-113,660	386,087	71,939	37,824	7,950	62,371	37,582
1978	550,984	609,589	7,443	617,032	55,638	-130,820	430,574	78,504	41,906	8,711	63,254	39,086
1979	608,115	687,200	4,795	691,995	65,182	-152,334	474,479	86,162	47,474	9,485	64,113	40,753
1980	623,160	658,768	1,774	660,542	62,493	-143,579	454,470	108,231	60,459	9,593	64,960	37,946
1981	703,651	728,834	4,143	732,977	74,793	-159,201	498,983	136,912	67,756	10,943	64,301	38,067
1982	712,995	695,270	3,942	699,212	72,517	-141,961	484,734	148,009	80,252	11,142	63,992	35,323
1983	759,805	743,070	-1,617	741,453	78,199	-145,820	517,434	157,624	84,747	11,916	63,765	35,344
1984	917,429	911,817	13,083	924,900	98,989	-182,858	643,053	187,036	87,340	14,432	63,567	37,712
1985	932,749	898,158	9,932	908,090	98,711	-163,978	645,401	194,419	92,929	14,713	63,398	37,442
1986	923,800	879,346	6,887	886,233	97,528	-150,726	637,979	188,125	97,696	14,677	62,940	37,657
1987	1,019,865	1,002,494	5,872	1,008,366	108,090	-171,116	729,160	191,035	99,670	16,079	63,427	38,972
1988	1,078,724	1,051,930	1,467	1,053,397	115,962	-166,340	771,095	201,664	105,965	17,016	63,395	40,195
1989	1,150,473	1,060,263	8,580	1,068,843	116,697	-148,862	803,284	232,067	115,122	18,153	63,375	40,871
1990	1,204,019	1,095,690	7,761	1,103,451	124,521	-140,685	838,245	241,295	124,479	18,856	63,855	42,137
1991	1,223,379	1,128,809	400	1,129,209	131,024	-151,044	847,141	240,892	135,346	18,867	64,843	42,105
1992	1,359,185	1,276,994	8,547	1,285,541	147,202	-184,484	953,855	248,611	156,719	20,761	65,467	44,050
1993	1,472,526	1,420,880	7,836	1,428,716	165,337	-223,872	1,039,507	267,589	165,430	22,191	66,357	46,277
1994	1,570,771	1,524,128	4,260	1,528,388	178,444	-238,573	1,111,371	287,691	171,709	23,349	67,273	48,419
1995	1,696,662	1,614,573	2,103	1,616,676	189,198	-252,260	1,175,218	341,717	179,727	24,801	68,410	49,868
1996	1,771,766	1,656,196	15,960	1,672,156	191,464	-267,226	1,213,466	363,246	195,054	25,666	69,031	50,171
1997	1,861,557	1,753,770	9,042	1,762,812	201,100	-285,052	1,276,660	385,782	199,115	26,759	69,568	51,045
1998	2,020,667	1,909,550	4,959	1,914,509	213,218	-312,028	1,389,263	420,575	210,829	28,754	70,275	52,869
1999	2,093,466	2,009,145	720	2,009,865	223,325	-318,862	1,467,678	407,186	218,602	29,636	70,639	52,944
2000	2,236,130	2,126,433	10,554	2,136,987	231,664	-342,622	1,562,701	438,013	235,416	31,160	71,763	52,846
2001	2,155,059	1,952,872	11,863	1,964,735	218,591	-283,116	1,463,028	426,776	265,255	29,886	72,110	50,295
2002	2,194,719	1,975,423	1,436	1,976,859	221,526	-257,611	1,497,722	412,707	284,290	30,529	71,890	49,158
2003	2,273,194	2,032,215	13,076	2,045,291	231,597	-257,668	1,556,026	418,776	298,392	31,442	72,299	48,777
2004	2,387,975	2,177,306	22,385	2,199,691	250,193	-289,936	1,659,562	409,790	318,623	32,765	72,882	50,421
2005	2,441,382	2,273,213	12,950	2,286,163	261,213	-323,289	1,701,661	391,648	348,073	33,144	73,660	51,636
2006	2,648,774	2,423,695	10,232	2,433,927	281,630	-346,170	1,806,127	466,467	376,180	35,550	74,508	52,453
2007	2,737,262	2,527,229	11,072	2,538,301	294,244	-383,939	1,860,118	479,375	397,769	36,368	75,265	53,859
2008	2,891,651	2,654,424	21,570	2,675,994	308,877	-436,097	1,931,020	500,181	460,450	38,008	76,080	54,442
2009	2,739,434	2,410,766	28,229	2,438,995	285,740	-367,706	1,785,549	443,060	510,825	35,779	76,566	50,963
2010	2,884,487	2,551,553	7,249	2,558,802	297,775	-354,828	1,906,199	435,667	542,621	37,554	76,809	50,843
2011	3,125,554	2,825,410	22,078	2,847,488	294,199	-456,148	2,097,141	486,023	542,390	40,289	77,579	54,100
2012	3,398,893	3,179,278	24,784	3,204,062	326,437	-591,251	2,286,374	549,010	563,509	43,071	78,914	57,396
2013	3,379,837	3,154,148	60,492	3,214,640	368,950	-564,351	2,281,339	528,783	569,715	42,475	79,572	57,351
2014	3,584,373	3,359,936	33,067	3,393,003	389,236	-591,554	2,412,213	573,813	598,347	44,609	80,350	59,056
2015	3,707,101	3,540,847	10,441	3,551,288	413,778	-665,284	2,472,226	606,490	628,385	45,606	81,286	60,067
2016	3,780,976	3,615,736	18,485	3,634,221	410,066	-695,333	2,528,822	607,507	644,647	46,181	81,873	60,675
2017	3,921,838	3,752,018	12,027	3,764,045	419,720	-725,759	2,618,566	637,837	665,435	47,804	82,040	61,149
2018	4,238,170	4,217,718	20,452	4,040,650	454,171	-790,146	2,796,333	751,044	690,793	51,234	82,722	61,956
2019	4,402,236	4,381,910	20,326	4,136,798	473,356	-748,140	2,915,302	758,639	728,295	52,546	83,779	62,220

Personal Income and Employment by Area: Columbus, OH

(Thousands of dollars, except as noted.)

Year	Personal income, total	Earnings by place of work			Less: Contributions for government social insurance	Plus: Adjustment for residence	Equals: Net earnings by place of residence	Plus: Dividends, interest, and rent	Plus: Personal current transfer receipts	Per capita personal income (dollars)	Population (persons)	Total employment
		Nonfarm	Farm	Total								
1970	4,968,990	4,158,986	53,117	4,212,103	255,499	-13,377	3,943,227	676,637	349,126	4,061	1,223,517	547,892
1971	5,458,636	4,557,086	45,568	4,602,654	286,905	-18,713	4,297,036	750,203	411,397	4,378	1,246,879	559,807
1972	5,989,818	5,012,476	58,579	5,071,055	332,507	-23,089	4,715,459	814,676	459,683	4,759	1,258,508	585,094
1973	6,652,006	5,574,927	69,628	5,644,555	427,157	-25,458	5,191,940	914,853	545,213	5,232	1,271,417	610,863
1974	7,312,298	6,007,561	100,605	6,108,166	477,150	-26,863	5,604,153	1,042,202	665,943	5,682	1,286,905	619,395
1975	7,847,629	6,277,019	95,947	6,372,966	487,253	-30,747	5,854,966	1,128,666	863,997	6,038	1,299,613	608,330
1976	8,620,957	6,961,090	91,912	7,053,002	554,547	-33,276	6,465,179	1,215,221	940,557	6,619	1,302,532	620,404
1977	9,594,795	7,827,893	90,878	7,918,771	625,734	-39,334	7,253,703	1,350,317	990,775	7,292	1,315,830	642,252
1978	10,614,320	8,728,771	85,091	8,813,862	721,267	-45,812	8,046,783	1,507,739	1,059,798	8,018	1,323,883	669,335
1979	11,803,035	9,686,036	123,960	9,809,996	837,183	-52,602	8,920,211	1,686,556	1,196,268	8,872	1,330,412	687,708
1980	12,975,478	10,378,815	66,247	10,445,062	900,504	-63,572	9,480,986	2,034,954	1,459,538	9,762	1,329,236	695,825
1981	14,232,984	11,194,518	6,487	11,201,005	1,037,963	-67,261	10,095,781	2,464,091	1,673,112	10,617	1,340,612	689,230
1982	15,251,563	11,726,956	25,071	11,752,027	1,093,306	-88,359	10,570,362	2,767,405	1,913,796	11,348	1,343,981	680,904
1983	16,477,889	12,727,787	-10,765	12,717,022	1,220,698	-109,713	11,386,611	3,022,501	2,068,777	12,188	1,351,988	690,537
1984	18,347,133	14,248,862	107,378	14,356,240	1,398,990	-140,536	12,816,714	3,379,878	2,150,541	13,470	1,362,111	726,332
1985	19,845,598	15,606,512	114,542	15,721,054	1,565,680	-184,658	13,970,716	3,568,676	2,306,206	14,439	1,374,432	760,496
1986	21,096,622	16,780,235	93,278	16,873,513	1,734,416	-224,227	14,914,870	3,748,760	2,432,992	15,199	1,388,054	787,782
1987	22,393,952	18,059,786	71,251	18,131,037	1,872,917	-262,106	15,996,014	3,866,577	2,531,361	15,932	1,405,633	823,595
1988	24,329,289	19,774,678	86,205	19,860,883	2,098,442	-331,281	17,431,160	4,203,521	2,694,608	17,012	1,430,091	848,911
1989	26,596,663	21,362,530	99,899	21,462,429	2,280,710	-399,247	18,782,472	4,921,333	2,892,858	18,369	1,447,914	876,674
1990	28,251,968	22,788,408	104,717	22,893,125	2,493,677	-450,009	19,949,439	5,105,579	3,196,950	19,242	1,468,263	894,479
1991	29,386,946	23,755,872	42,654	23,798,526	2,670,032	-462,922	20,665,572	5,174,862	3,546,512	19,689	1,492,559	898,033
1992	31,746,301	25,693,055	118,915	25,811,970	2,899,512	-507,699	22,404,759	5,406,788	3,934,754	20,919	1,517,612	909,049
1993	33,518,973	27,102,667	111,147	27,213,814	3,083,895	-536,334	23,593,585	5,802,609	4,122,779	21,757	1,540,611	930,524
1994	35,813,171	28,958,344	141,493	29,099,837	3,359,274	-576,201	25,164,362	6,344,121	4,304,688	22,954	1,560,222	964,490
1995	37,589,154	30,531,351	104,343	30,635,694	3,583,732	-629,522	26,422,440	6,585,178	4,581,536	23,799	1,579,412	1,001,985
1996	39,460,101	32,171,506	147,669	32,319,175	3,743,954	-677,696	27,897,525	6,873,435	4,689,141	24,769	1,593,111	1,023,195
1997	42,456,133	34,509,309	204,551	34,713,860	3,916,245	-763,713	30,033,902	7,588,234	4,833,997	26,319	1,613,135	1,044,212
1998	45,643,343	37,692,726	142,351	37,835,077	4,130,792	-861,347	32,842,938	7,818,706	4,981,699	27,888	1,636,690	1,074,387
1999	48,190,798	40,285,312	106,766	40,392,078	4,419,902	-940,715	35,031,461	7,897,893	5,261,444	29,062	1,658,194	1,096,790
2000	52,202,457	43,775,730	156,430	43,932,160	4,623,523	-1,045,656	38,262,981	8,285,427	5,654,049	31,035	1,682,068	1,132,103
2001	53,173,364	44,279,579	150,075	44,429,654	4,741,456	-1,121,142	38,567,056	8,353,297	6,253,011	31,154	1,706,779	1,142,117
2002	54,746,972	45,642,469	80,335	45,722,804	4,808,282	-1,163,370	39,751,152	8,180,249	6,815,571	31,713	1,726,352	1,136,086
2003	56,699,102	47,114,805	101,315	47,216,120	4,983,428	-1,214,113	41,018,579	8,466,024	7,214,499	32,413	1,749,262	1,137,227
2004	59,432,916	49,665,498	179,810	49,845,308	5,315,215	-1,332,615	43,197,478	8,577,711	7,657,727	33,586	1,769,572	1,151,480
2005	62,048,567	51,369,868	96,487	51,466,355	5,481,189	-1,397,536	44,587,630	9,188,331	8,272,606	34,642	1,791,126	1,166,767
2006	65,670,059	53,800,779	93,387	53,894,166	5,762,738	-1,457,117	46,674,311	10,151,340	8,844,408	36,142	1,816,992	1,181,275
2007	69,297,117	56,317,498	132,431	56,449,929	5,992,663	-1,476,843	48,980,423	10,819,951	9,496,743	37,630	1,841,539	1,205,643
2008	71,944,859	57,421,007	128,613	57,549,620	6,209,516	-1,446,888	49,893,216	11,117,722	10,933,921	38,563	1,865,647	1,204,031
2009	70,978,224	56,166,335	191,215	56,357,550	6,138,319	-1,367,045	48,852,186	10,206,312	11,919,726	37,603	1,887,548	1,174,285
2010	73,622,930	58,101,193	190,278	58,291,471	6,180,839	-1,393,636	50,716,996	10,092,883	12,813,051	38,620	1,906,365	1,173,163
2011	79,499,092	61,687,384	345,000	62,032,384	5,866,488	-1,472,125	54,693,771	11,444,810	13,360,511	41,274	1,926,142	1,200,586
2012	85,104,819	66,166,937	220,829	66,387,766	6,142,786	-1,669,381	58,575,599	13,465,517	13,063,703	43,719	1,946,644	1,228,248
2013	86,824,467	69,093,962	408,808	69,502,770	6,996,415	-1,753,619	60,752,736	12,694,655	13,377,076	44,048	1,971,120	1,256,856
2014	91,057,072	71,682,327	228,066	71,910,393	7,261,686	-1,824,212	62,824,495	14,095,422	14,137,155	45,564	1,998,460	1,285,553
2015	95,925,297	74,928,339	102,271	75,030,610	7,616,311	-1,884,308	65,529,991	15,595,306	14,800,000	47,413	2,023,198	1,315,385
2016	98,657,437	77,010,320	126,101	77,136,421	7,956,272	-2,002,857	67,177,292	16,271,198	15,208,947	48,197	2,046,977	1,344,770
2017	103,195,243	81,011,060	86,134	81,097,194	8,487,194	-2,098,361	70,511,639	17,089,593	15,594,011	49,644	2,078,725	1,370,011
2018	107,553,917	107,404,129	149,788	83,901,306	8,684,932	-2,333,370	72,883,004	18,573,941	16,096,972	51,114	2,104,194	1,395,186
2019	111,370,103	111,317,808	52,295	87,106,257	9,023,062	-2,450,449	75,632,746	18,843,331	16,894,026	52,477	2,122,271	1,418,008

Personal Income and Employment by Area: Corpus Christi, TX

(Thousands of dollars, except as noted.)

Year	Personal income, total	Earnings by place of work			Less: Contributions for government social insurance	Plus: Adjustment for residence	Equals: Net earnings by place of residence	Plus: Dividends, interest, and rent	Plus: Personal current transfer receipts	Per capita personal income (dollars)	Population (persons)	Total employment
		Nonfarm	Farm	Total								
1970	1,072,943	885,238	14,784	900,022	51,642	-14,011	834,369	165,509	73,065	3,636	295,082	126,000
1971	1,174,065	965,963	14,510	980,473	58,101	-14,803	907,569	179,767	86,729	3,865	303,749	128,721
1972	1,276,672	1,042,115	20,263	1,062,378	65,233	-16,171	980,974	195,117	100,581	4,086	312,437	129,292
1973	1,422,778	1,144,257	40,995	1,185,252	82,891	-18,263	1,084,098	215,842	122,838	4,563	311,819	134,114
1974	1,619,615	1,296,369	40,590	1,336,959	96,621	-21,415	1,218,923	250,973	149,719	5,210	310,879	137,156
1975	1,834,018	1,473,831	29,555	1,503,386	107,771	-25,320	1,370,295	279,495	184,228	5,787	316,939	138,280
1976	2,095,395	1,713,890	33,517	1,747,407	125,053	-30,660	1,591,694	300,713	202,988	6,487	323,036	142,172
1977	2,217,943	1,813,094	21,713	1,834,807	134,752	-29,861	1,670,194	331,068	216,681	6,825	324,964	145,244
1978	2,560,177	2,122,210	18,406	2,140,616	161,523	-39,385	1,939,708	383,081	237,388	7,814	327,620	154,230
1979	2,945,208	2,461,309	21,507	2,482,816	198,186	-49,272	2,235,358	438,865	270,985	8,797	334,805	162,460
1980	3,294,818	2,749,986	-14,783	2,735,203	225,898	-52,945	2,456,360	522,863	315,595	9,628	342,213	166,236
1981	3,828,183	3,111,272	44,999	3,156,271	280,185	-49,788	2,826,298	652,005	349,880	10,997	348,104	175,453
1982	4,123,312	3,313,585	12,212	3,325,797	309,970	-64,722	2,951,105	778,841	393,366	11,454	359,988	180,014
1983	4,285,205	3,310,589	18,277	3,328,866	308,004	-57,774	2,963,088	860,662	461,455	11,654	367,695	176,099
1984	4,532,470	3,461,613	24,334	3,485,947	331,130	-54,536	3,100,281	943,878	488,311	12,254	369,879	178,794
1985	4,784,425	3,600,449	32,145	3,632,594	349,986	-49,544	3,233,064	1,040,620	510,741	12,911	370,569	180,370
1986	4,746,523	3,482,442	13,963	3,496,405	333,115	-43,439	3,119,851	1,054,516	572,156	12,676	374,442	170,111
1987	4,710,517	3,392,641	40,530	3,433,171	320,232	-32,258	3,080,681	1,021,279	608,557	12,742	369,672	171,076
1988	4,929,074	3,573,510	36,296	3,609,806	352,965	-34,841	3,222,000	1,070,103	636,971	13,432	366,973	172,794
1989	5,187,667	3,697,931	-1,111	3,696,820	372,376	-33,143	3,291,301	1,199,326	697,040	14,161	366,328	173,076
1990	5,603,771	4,093,068	2,719	4,095,787	407,484	-31,174	3,657,129	1,179,264	767,378	15,217	368,255	178,082
1991	5,969,118	4,335,047	43,331	4,378,378	443,257	-38,427	3,896,694	1,200,524	871,900	15,992	373,245	181,527
1992	6,457,746	4,629,666	30,655	4,660,321	470,390	-43,873	4,146,058	1,281,556	1,030,132	17,081	378,071	182,760
1993	6,753,977	4,931,511	39,245	4,970,756	502,521	-45,653	4,422,582	1,256,798	1,074,597	17,508	385,768	188,525
1994	7,143,164	5,194,116	53,812	5,247,928	534,800	-51,760	4,661,368	1,320,695	1,161,101	18,220	392,050	193,248
1995	7,469,196	5,329,797	72,122	5,401,919	552,531	-58,843	4,790,545	1,416,095	1,262,556	18,924	394,701	197,179
1996	7,964,093	5,768,821	5,115	5,773,936	591,130	-67,386	5,115,420	1,496,350	1,352,323	19,984	398,529	203,672
1997	8,454,758	6,129,857	41,118	6,170,975	622,733	-69,876	5,478,366	1,568,119	1,408,273	21,005	402,504	209,271
1998	8,918,663	6,506,325	33,993	6,540,318	656,280	-74,055	5,809,983	1,655,125	1,453,555	22,086	403,818	213,226
1999	9,150,387	6,733,541	102,846	6,836,387	670,100	-79,491	6,086,796	1,600,739	1,462,852	22,641	404,155	212,816
2000	9,519,201	6,965,989	71,904	7,037,893	694,128	-83,991	6,259,774	1,731,128	1,528,299	23,594	403,458	216,468
2001	10,229,604	7,676,488	14,794	7,691,282	741,812	-116,448	6,833,022	1,747,095	1,649,487	25,406	402,647	218,448
2002	10,522,351	7,938,951	15,769	7,954,720	772,528	-148,460	7,033,732	1,695,770	1,792,849	25,937	405,692	219,204
2003	11,076,396	8,362,044	96,608	8,458,652	824,411	-200,261	7,433,980	1,729,642	1,912,774	27,220	406,915	222,177
2004	11,614,114	8,860,938	121,426	8,982,364	865,059	-264,858	7,852,447	1,739,287	2,022,380	28,194	411,936	223,193
2005	12,510,822	9,452,536	51,319	9,503,855	922,629	-267,883	8,313,343	1,978,882	2,218,597	30,052	416,308	227,248
2006	13,360,579	10,339,596	1,251	10,340,847	989,135	-435,506	8,916,206	2,080,207	2,364,166	31,847	419,530	231,771
2007	13,865,116	10,472,052	64,269	10,536,321	1,042,718	-529,157	8,964,446	2,307,097	2,593,573	32,980	420,407	238,828
2008	15,305,672	11,640,788	26,118	11,666,906	1,120,456	-691,277	9,855,173	2,571,432	2,879,067	36,169	423,168	244,005
2009	14,550,880	10,744,439	26,494	10,770,933	1,089,579	-542,847	9,138,507	2,300,810	3,111,563	34,056	427,262	239,855
2010	15,580,425	11,148,240	172,655	11,320,895	1,130,699	-422,279	9,767,917	2,381,346	3,431,162	36,414	427,872	238,829
2011	16,884,580	11,826,509	215,538	12,042,047	1,054,656	-274,510	10,712,881	2,642,472	3,529,227	39,184	430,908	241,996
2012	17,766,178	12,588,206	40,916	12,629,122	1,126,338	-179,963	11,322,821	2,950,646	3,492,711	40,694	436,575	249,137
2013	18,418,388	13,196,791	131,186	13,327,977	1,314,910	-86,489	11,926,578	2,902,285	3,589,525	41,594	442,812	254,662
2014	19,412,769	13,870,023	39,378	13,909,401	1,384,082	-77,527	12,447,792	3,194,089	3,770,888	43,364	447,671	259,360
2015	19,340,838	13,631,402	-7,749	13,623,653	1,395,775	-104,684	12,123,194	3,213,101	4,004,543	42,756	452,355	260,059
2016	18,605,412	13,004,776	27,989	13,032,765	1,389,053	-252,387	11,391,325	2,991,469	4,222,618	40,975	454,066	257,327
2017	19,151,847	13,236,480	94,739	13,331,219	1,439,611	-205,807	11,685,801	3,121,145	4,344,901	42,184	454,008	257,817
2018	18,724,313	18,669,793	54,520	13,386,454	1,428,910	-449,835	11,507,709	3,127,667	4,088,937	43,677	428,697	253,651
2019	19,366,168	19,325,222	40,946	13,773,164	1,455,101	-385,807	11,932,256	3,184,748	4,249,164	45,140	429,024	255,282

Personal Income and Employment by Area: Corvallis, OR

(Thousands of dollars, except as noted.)

Year	Personal income, total	Nonfarm	Farm	Total	Less: Contributions for government social insurance	Plus: Adjustment for residence	Equals: Net earnings by place of residence	Plus: Dividends, interest, and rent	Plus: Personal current transfer receipts	Per capita personal income (dollars)	Population (persons)	Total employment
1970	183,578	134,535	3,433	137,968	9,350	3,667	132,285	38,670	12,623	3,403	53,943	19,498
1971	205,429	149,891	3,253	153,144	10,653	4,572	147,063	43,658	14,708	3,740	54,929	20,207
1972	232,456	169,342	4,151	173,493	12,614	6,328	167,207	48,778	16,471	3,866	60,135	21,016
1973	263,806	188,695	7,172	195,867	16,164	8,837	188,540	55,152	20,114	4,448	59,313	22,257
1974	299,249	208,349	8,217	216,566	18,409	11,940	210,097	64,254	24,898	4,887	61,230	23,381
1975	338,181	234,630	4,033	238,663	20,124	14,727	233,266	73,162	31,753	5,488	61,618	24,344
1976	389,271	272,697	5,906	278,603	23,621	18,516	273,498	80,894	34,879	6,248	62,299	25,929
1977	446,823	319,660	5,389	325,049	28,481	20,496	317,064	91,855	37,904	6,815	65,569	28,314
1978	514,888	372,914	5,090	378,004	34,732	23,441	366,713	106,666	41,509	7,690	66,955	30,807
1979	569,961	407,035	6,139	413,174	39,681	28,321	401,814	120,739	47,408	8,361	68,171	30,922
1980	629,806	436,130	6,890	443,020	43,078	32,430	432,372	141,987	55,447	9,198	68,471	30,495
1981	706,844	480,849	9,536	490,385	51,101	33,438	472,722	172,195	61,927	10,190	69,369	30,876
1982	745,397	510,570	8,591	519,161	55,909	26,470	489,722	185,338	70,337	10,731	69,461	31,071
1983	798,385	542,406	10,905	553,311	60,004	26,286	519,593	202,819	75,973	11,699	68,245	31,395
1984	858,862	580,422	14,585	595,007	65,980	27,920	556,947	221,983	79,932	12,729	67,474	32,566
1985	888,296	590,442	15,656	606,098	66,999	30,460	569,559	233,502	85,235	13,204	67,275	33,707
1986	937,245	635,723	19,477	655,200	72,524	26,593	609,269	244,719	83,257	14,001	66,940	35,204
1987	990,373	684,582	16,704	701,286	76,909	26,063	650,440	251,543	88,390	14,653	67,590	36,280
1988	1,063,347	752,431	23,404	775,835	89,034	25,898	712,699	258,209	92,439	15,666	67,876	37,645
1989	1,170,796	820,494	18,932	839,426	96,679	23,954	766,701	304,831	99,264	16,755	69,879	38,457
1990	1,226,515	868,393	17,570	885,963	104,845	25,074	806,192	311,674	108,649	17,261	71,059	39,188
1991	1,279,973	909,801	15,276	925,077	110,006	25,743	840,814	323,167	115,992	17,900	71,507	39,115
1992	1,368,381	987,886	12,485	1,000,371	118,561	22,193	904,003	337,386	126,992	18,844	72,618	39,372
1993	1,479,727	1,093,560	17,297	1,110,857	131,750	8,954	988,061	358,683	132,983	19,997	73,997	41,016
1994	1,591,629	1,200,624	21,742	1,222,366	146,441	1,459	1,077,384	370,614	143,631	21,086	75,481	42,864
1995	1,744,720	1,299,198	18,212	1,317,410	159,999	-7,508	1,149,903	433,576	161,241	22,802	76,517	44,979
1996	1,929,118	1,442,262	25,420	1,467,682	180,491	-21,546	1,265,645	491,568	171,905	24,804	77,776	48,096
1997	2,074,710	1,577,311	25,086	1,602,397	194,761	-34,854	1,372,782	525,100	176,828	26,409	78,560	49,568
1998	2,158,319	1,644,178	24,245	1,668,423	201,579	-33,501	1,433,343	537,895	187,081	27,340	78,943	50,743
1999	2,181,868	1,652,069	30,850	1,682,919	199,773	-29,732	1,453,414	523,527	204,927	27,882	78,254	50,485
2000	2,296,481	1,745,987	28,512	1,774,499	212,636	-45,008	1,516,855	566,648	212,978	29,353	78,236	51,408
2001	2,387,093	1,822,814	38,241	1,861,055	210,891	-45,090	1,605,074	548,234	233,785	30,412	78,491	48,298
2002	2,427,899	1,849,796	38,299	1,888,095	213,697	-35,190	1,639,208	539,403	249,288	30,272	80,203	45,836
2003	2,567,795	1,909,748	42,912	1,952,660	220,301	-40,056	1,692,303	612,105	263,387	31,969	80,322	45,891
2004	2,620,431	1,973,614	45,125	2,018,739	228,537	-83,706	1,706,496	645,220	268,715	32,694	80,149	47,624
2005	2,674,303	2,058,759	35,462	2,094,221	240,166	-84,847	1,769,208	612,746	292,349	33,039	80,943	48,107
2006	2,812,806	2,143,796	37,836	2,181,632	252,430	-81,606	1,847,596	648,621	316,589	34,321	81,957	48,815
2007	2,929,666	2,188,415	29,197	2,217,612	260,660	-66,124	1,890,828	700,235	338,603	34,994	83,718	48,386
2008	3,091,611	2,212,583	25,497	2,238,080	265,582	-48,864	1,923,634	770,943	397,034	36,739	84,150	48,213
2009	2,965,230	2,207,420	24,293	2,231,713	263,245	-137,821	1,830,647	694,796	439,787	34,726	85,390	47,494
2010	3,077,657	2,279,643	21,114	2,300,757	271,759	-140,326	1,888,672	709,219	479,766	35,970	85,561	47,457
2011	3,261,808	2,316,366	27,569	2,343,935	244,850	-151,098	1,947,987	833,245	480,576	37,939	85,976	48,590
2012	3,310,592	2,410,269	32,358	2,442,627	253,838	-171,590	2,017,199	824,029	469,364	38,331	86,368	48,486
2013	3,313,536	2,425,676	35,808	2,461,484	290,380	-158,386	2,012,718	811,740	489,078	38,559	85,934	48,184
2014	3,512,756	2,494,758	32,356	2,527,114	302,004	-134,466	2,090,644	908,069	514,043	40,397	86,956	49,242
2015	3,707,774	2,611,951	35,488	2,647,439	313,324	-159,804	2,174,311	984,170	549,293	42,083	88,106	50,368
2016	3,898,501	2,706,225	35,984	2,742,209	327,158	-105,077	2,309,974	1,023,993	564,534	43,658	89,296	49,984
2017	4,117,613	2,853,581	33,284	2,886,865	347,105	-75,294	2,464,466	1,072,603	580,544	45,273	90,951	51,185
2018	4,351,272	4,329,799	21,473	3,053,723	360,784	-160,262	2,532,677	1,203,250	615,345	47,070	92,442	52,756
2019	4,534,024	4,518,235	15,789	3,126,370	371,823	-94,375	2,660,172	1,220,379	653,473	48,725	93,053	53,199

Personal Income and Employment by Area: Crestview-Fort Walton Beach-Destin, FL

(Thousands of dollars, except as noted.)

Year	Personal income, total	Earnings by place of work			Less: Contributions for government social insurance	Plus: Adjustment for residence	Equals: Net earnings by place of residence	Plus: Dividends, interest, and rent	Plus: Personal current transfer receipts	Per capita personal income (dollars)	Population (persons)	Total employment
		Nonfarm	Farm	Total								
1970	397,526	320,410	1,010	321,420	17,638	-22,403	281,379	92,961	23,186	3,797	104,708	43,341
1971	451,674	365,524	2,955	368,479	21,210	-25,032	322,237	102,043	27,394	4,194	107,706	45,369
1972	512,479	413,090	3,357	416,447	24,411	-27,783	364,253	115,408	32,818	4,547	112,702	46,894
1973	559,571	440,551	7,473	448,024	28,184	-27,264	392,576	127,077	39,918	4,872	114,864	49,238
1974	617,777	478,596	9,103	487,699	32,799	-26,278	428,622	141,985	47,170	5,302	116,509	51,718
1975	691,636	520,856	9,441	530,297	36,987	-27,385	465,925	161,890	63,821	5,583	123,878	51,954
1976	757,512	573,751	5,722	579,473	41,822	-31,306	506,345	180,898	70,269	6,100	124,190	53,408
1977	830,796	626,811	2,592	629,403	45,680	-32,180	551,543	203,270	75,983	6,522	127,380	55,208
1978	949,826	702,757	6,354	709,111	51,189	-33,630	624,292	242,590	82,944	7,374	128,807	58,497
1979	1,042,862	762,910	8,298	771,208	58,529	-35,615	677,064	268,535	97,263	7,920	131,677	60,253
1980	1,158,307	827,984	3,131	831,115	62,925	-36,598	731,592	310,371	116,344	8,768	132,104	60,453
1981	1,355,782	974,409	1,404	975,813	79,429	-43,819	852,565	365,094	138,123	10,014	135,394	63,432
1982	1,483,117	1,060,369	2,488	1,062,857	87,829	-46,562	928,466	395,833	158,818	10,649	139,276	65,789
1983	1,632,927	1,164,725	1,356	1,166,081	102,149	-46,609	1,017,323	439,044	176,560	11,298	144,536	69,831
1984	1,834,874	1,305,357	3,932	1,309,289	118,650	-50,444	1,140,195	501,841	192,838	12,279	149,428	75,701
1985	1,987,754	1,400,002	2,645	1,402,647	131,934	-47,872	1,222,841	551,186	213,727	12,848	154,718	79,525
1986	2,163,609	1,531,459	3,898	1,535,357	149,316	-51,256	1,334,785	598,054	230,770	13,569	159,450	84,261
1987	2,353,072	1,673,457	3,871	1,677,328	163,337	-53,044	1,460,947	646,622	245,503	14,345	164,034	86,072
1988	2,557,660	1,802,928	7,717	1,810,645	183,804	-65,426	1,561,415	726,626	269,619	15,310	167,059	88,777
1989	2,800,987	1,931,770	8,849	1,940,619	200,434	-62,308	1,677,877	818,689	304,421	16,493	169,832	91,122
1990	3,048,476	2,047,442	7,352	2,054,794	216,146	-14,630	1,824,018	887,741	336,717	17,694	172,290	91,622
1991	3,258,442	2,191,957	7,569	2,199,526	234,359	-33,655	1,931,512	942,659	384,271	18,325	177,811	94,263
1992	3,553,894	2,359,319	8,806	2,368,125	254,874	-3,601	2,109,650	1,007,803	436,441	19,389	183,299	96,788
1993	3,791,859	2,505,998	7,412	2,513,410	272,059	-31,395	2,209,956	1,110,731	471,172	20,090	188,744	100,240
1994	3,981,554	2,605,404	7,325	2,612,729	285,679	-31,456	2,295,594	1,182,242	503,718	20,561	193,649	105,827
1995	4,309,037	2,817,684	7,071	2,824,755	304,730	-99,185	2,420,840	1,313,402	574,795	21,820	197,484	109,725
1996	4,587,952	3,040,468	10,114	3,050,582	327,754	-133,987	2,588,841	1,409,360	589,751	22,806	201,172	114,103
1997	4,877,442	3,197,909	9,292	3,207,201	347,886	-120,858	2,738,457	1,511,785	627,200	23,814	204,814	118,905
1998	5,167,514	3,395,559	4,895	3,400,454	368,075	-163,154	2,869,225	1,650,855	647,434	24,999	206,708	122,256
1999	5,495,672	3,590,191	7,235	3,597,426	386,769	-158,668	3,051,989	1,747,125	696,558	26,305	208,918	124,906
2000	5,801,225	3,855,011	3,353	3,858,364	413,892	-215,937	3,228,535	1,808,054	764,636	27,370	211,955	129,035
2001	6,145,246	4,150,979	3,174	4,154,153	439,687	-229,929	3,484,537	1,802,882	857,827	28,589	214,955	123,262
2002	6,607,923	4,622,763	-4,630	4,618,133	486,859	-285,554	3,845,720	1,825,051	937,152	30,010	220,192	128,008
2003	7,247,346	5,205,623	507	5,206,130	542,287	-343,061	4,320,782	1,915,154	1,011,410	32,466	223,227	134,491
2004	7,918,591	5,850,618	2,257	5,852,875	610,719	-396,745	4,845,411	1,984,771	1,088,409	34,425	230,024	145,298
2005	8,539,536	6,356,687	2,284	6,358,971	665,704	-447,163	5,246,104	2,148,896	1,144,536	36,582	233,437	150,544
2006	9,084,145	6,619,892	4,385	6,624,277	718,273	-481,458	5,424,546	2,444,612	1,214,987	38,620	235,216	155,241
2007	9,336,566	6,593,403	3,608	6,597,011	727,009	-516,367	5,353,635	2,700,374	1,282,557	39,725	235,032	155,616
2008	9,368,969	6,396,600	2,427	6,399,027	720,548	-532,892	5,145,587	2,753,762	1,469,620	39,815	235,315	150,985
2009	9,040,336	6,241,552	1,184	6,242,736	728,251	-548,546	4,965,939	2,467,570	1,606,827	38,357	235,687	146,856
2010	9,566,896	6,458,983	2,563	6,461,546	742,749	-571,295	5,147,502	2,594,921	1,824,473	40,550	235,927	144,422
2011	9,935,560	6,672,860	4,036	6,676,896	699,477	-618,628	5,358,791	2,679,979	1,896,790	41,629	238,668	148,422
2012	10,701,063	7,284,628	6,641	7,291,269	761,321	-704,352	5,825,596	3,017,889	1,857,578	43,329	246,972	151,356
2013	10,844,841	7,489,604	4,356	7,493,960	868,799	-731,759	5,893,402	3,008,481	1,942,958	43,050	251,914	155,639
2014	11,544,768	7,712,937	11,454	7,724,391	895,906	-732,411	6,096,074	3,360,468	2,088,226	45,127	255,831	158,397
2015	12,246,003	8,076,980	16,066	8,093,046	931,307	-744,680	6,417,059	3,607,192	2,221,752	46,956	260,796	163,165
2016	12,820,853	8,444,978	3,820	8,448,798	970,518	-768,408	6,709,872	3,784,375	2,326,606	48,316	265,355	168,004
2017	13,461,786	8,897,621	5,243	8,902,864	1,020,664	-806,440	7,075,760	3,945,699	2,440,327	49,611	271,346	171,258
2018	14,719,045	14,706,525	12,520	9,508,114	1,074,115	-849,307	7,584,692	4,480,721	2,653,632	53,010	277,666	178,972
2019	15,456,503	15,440,898	15,605	10,165,644	1,158,408	-925,442	8,081,794	4,541,941	2,832,768	54,270	284,809	184,130

Personal Income and Employment by Area: Cumberland, MD-WV

(Thousands of dollars, except as noted.)

Year	Personal income, total	Earnings by place of work			Less: Contributions for government social insurance	Plus: Adjustment for residence	Equals: Net earnings by place of residence	Plus: Dividends, interest, and rent	Plus: Personal current transfer receipts	Per capita personal income (dollars)	Population (persons)	Total employment
		Nonfarm	Farm	Total								
1970	356,715	312,900	927	313,827	24,342	-16,997	272,488	37,925	46,302	3,329	107,140	42,280
1971	385,369	330,253	911	331,164	26,475	-15,047	289,642	40,826	54,901	3,577	107,735	41,720
1972	416,815	352,062	1,034	353,096	29,385	-13,265	310,446	43,942	62,427	3,807	109,483	41,890
1973	454,127	382,041	1,507	383,548	36,229	-13,120	334,199	49,681	70,247	4,186	108,476	42,897
1974	492,609	408,275	1,269	409,544	40,100	-16,764	352,680	57,331	82,598	4,516	109,091	42,044
1975	530,985	412,802	1,056	413,858	39,740	-14,308	359,810	63,995	107,180	4,903	108,304	40,012
1976	572,138	448,160	568	448,728	43,766	-15,627	389,335	70,221	112,582	5,290	108,148	39,976
1977	635,602	506,203	561	506,764	49,281	-18,480	439,003	78,999	117,600	5,892	107,873	40,722
1978	698,318	560,358	1,506	561,864	56,213	-19,548	486,103	86,768	125,447	6,518	107,138	42,694
1979	773,257	612,568	1,558	614,126	63,670	-17,884	532,572	96,270	144,415	7,163	107,955	42,382
1980	861,065	654,571	1,299	655,870	68,487	-16,712	570,671	120,694	169,700	7,983	107,868	42,213
1981	939,893	687,247	590	687,837	77,975	-11,664	598,198	147,334	194,361	8,701	108,027	41,782
1982	998,653	693,114	703	693,817	80,802	-7,662	605,353	176,683	216,617	9,307	107,298	40,498
1983	1,053,386	718,611	2,040	720,651	84,752	-4,970	630,929	186,810	235,647	9,924	106,147	40,484
1984	1,116,190	759,600	2,909	762,509	93,196	-5,439	663,874	207,213	245,103	10,682	104,497	40,688
1985	1,173,066	794,867	2,419	797,286	99,367	-4,048	693,871	220,027	259,168	11,345	103,396	41,264
1986	1,198,124	802,512	2,684	805,196	103,360	-143	701,693	231,871	264,560	11,670	102,668	40,906
1987	1,266,928	854,754	1,439	856,193	108,253	-78	747,862	233,333	285,733	12,388	102,270	42,300
1988	1,343,924	928,205	1,185	929,390	123,070	-1,823	804,497	238,536	300,891	13,152	102,187	43,808
1989	1,435,674	967,968	1,388	969,356	128,927	-1,033	839,396	275,001	321,277	14,063	102,086	44,253
1990	1,509,208	1,007,002	1,622	1,008,624	132,333	8,436	884,727	279,638	344,843	14,849	101,634	44,793
1991	1,560,142	1,016,568	967	1,017,535	133,761	10,177	893,951	286,586	379,605	15,280	102,101	44,400
1992	1,609,264	1,024,395	1,954	1,026,349	134,115	13,211	905,445	280,577	423,242	15,729	102,312	43,742
1993	1,661,886	1,066,450	2,083	1,068,533	139,819	11,659	940,373	284,516	436,997	16,236	102,359	43,705
1994	1,726,488	1,107,793	2,166	1,109,959	144,814	9,941	975,086	303,506	447,896	16,842	102,508	44,034
1995	1,781,012	1,132,264	823	1,133,087	148,127	9,550	994,510	316,216	470,286	17,341	102,704	44,466
1996	1,846,848	1,172,719	992	1,173,711	153,051	7,442	1,028,102	331,525	487,221	18,031	102,424	45,200
1997	1,930,600	1,228,414	-525	1,227,889	158,815	3,270	1,072,344	361,152	497,104	18,843	102,457	45,957
1998	1,982,945	1,266,304	108	1,266,412	160,072	3,955	1,110,295	369,186	503,464	19,305	102,718	46,271
1999	2,051,741	1,320,591	126	1,320,717	165,147	5,968	1,161,538	362,424	527,779	20,025	102,458	46,460
2000	2,153,849	1,386,992	1,054	1,388,046	172,771	7,132	1,222,407	384,411	547,031	21,146	101,858	47,376
2001	2,523,433	1,717,190	273	1,717,463	195,246	14,263	1,536,480	395,100	591,853	24,838	101,596	47,090
2002	2,638,558	1,836,441	328	1,836,769	203,551	9,258	1,642,476	369,474	626,608	26,005	101,462	46,958
2003	2,734,413	1,901,216	2,004	1,903,220	210,813	10,307	1,702,714	366,531	665,168	26,951	101,457	46,793
2004	2,829,385	1,969,359	3,950	1,973,309	218,087	8,139	1,763,361	388,293	677,731	27,832	101,658	47,694
2005	2,784,086	1,887,675	3,231	1,890,906	222,972	13,369	1,681,303	378,639	724,144	27,518	101,172	48,486
2006	2,770,619	1,842,098	1,072	1,843,170	228,490	16,027	1,630,707	389,165	750,747	27,350	101,304	48,721
2007	2,836,669	1,809,793	-786	1,809,007	228,499	26,027	1,606,535	431,519	798,615	27,816	101,981	48,389
2008	3,034,629	1,875,905	5	1,875,910	235,024	24,961	1,665,847	483,833	884,949	29,617	102,462	48,378
2009	3,142,187	1,931,752	-160	1,931,592	241,388	6,096	1,696,300	487,915	957,972	30,453	103,181	48,072
2010	3,274,219	2,027,046	-203	2,026,843	252,207	-12,245	1,762,391	491,160	1,020,668	31,739	103,161	48,285
2011	3,386,375	2,075,308	65	2,075,373	230,949	-24,964	1,819,460	534,706	1,032,209	33,001	102,615	48,584
2012	3,426,121	2,086,365	-2,155	2,084,210	231,033	-31,163	1,822,014	555,860	1,048,247	33,648	101,821	48,372
2013	3,463,693	2,119,001	-180	2,118,821	262,121	-37,394	1,819,306	563,413	1,080,974	34,203	101,268	48,051
2014	3,556,886	2,133,198	-666	2,132,532	266,325	-33,348	1,832,859	585,941	1,138,086	35,365	100,576	47,949
2015	3,658,167	2,206,197	-1,858	2,204,339	278,777	-37,752	1,887,810	608,434	1,161,923	36,631	99,864	48,301
2016	3,738,672	2,227,282	-1,939	2,225,343	282,723	-39,468	1,903,152	622,585	1,212,935	37,569	99,516	47,861
2017	3,835,161	2,272,607	-5,053	2,267,554	290,215	-38,749	1,938,590	653,199	1,243,372	38,803	98,837	47,685
2018	3,891,961	3,893,910	-1,949	2,306,642	294,610	-39,106	1,972,926	653,636	1,265,399	39,757	97,894	47,450
2019	4,007,649	4,009,683	-2,034	2,374,591	302,146	-39,083	2,033,362	668,609	1,305,678	41,195	97,284	47,591

Personal Income and Employment by Area: Dallas-Fort Worth-Arlington, TX

(Thousands of dollars, except as noted.)

Year	Personal income, total	Earnings by place of work			Less: Contributions for government social insurance	Plus: Adjustment for residence	Equals: Net earnings by place of residence	Plus: Dividends, interest, and rent	Plus: Personal current transfer receipts	Per capita personal income (dollars)	Population (persons)	Total employment
		Nonfarm	Farm	Total								
1970	10,545,542	8,981,425	39,410	9,020,835	588,164	-19,523	8,413,148	1,514,566	617,828	4,332	2,434,181	1,192,710
1971	11,277,664	9,452,237	34,789	9,487,026	634,413	11,163	8,863,776	1,674,374	739,514	4,550	2,478,739	1,193,666
1972	12,497,876	10,484,822	47,357	10,532,179	739,267	30,378	9,823,290	1,844,371	830,215	5,010	2,494,430	1,251,641
1973	14,020,526	11,780,249	81,724	11,861,973	960,442	40,291	10,941,822	2,093,376	985,328	5,500	2,549,156	1,329,267
1974	15,872,127	13,242,064	30,445	13,272,509	1,104,244	57,862	12,226,127	2,473,606	1,172,394	6,055	2,621,429	1,373,955
1975	17,701,993	14,554,019	33,749	14,587,768	1,183,094	75,648	13,480,322	2,709,412	1,512,259	6,634	2,668,519	1,372,695
1976	19,776,572	16,538,704	57,461	16,596,165	1,377,182	56,301	15,275,284	2,878,646	1,622,642	7,221	2,738,645	1,432,668
1977	22,134,245	18,929,201	16,900	18,946,101	1,595,697	-66,381	17,284,023	3,149,322	1,700,900	7,927	2,792,291	1,514,786
1978	25,721,166	22,152,524	38,316	22,190,840	1,912,937	-141,898	20,136,005	3,688,265	1,896,896	8,993	2,860,247	1,621,566
1979	29,835,185	25,888,747	41,806	25,930,553	2,339,737	-179,998	23,410,818	4,288,730	2,135,637	10,132	2,944,580	1,722,152
1980	34,682,915	29,899,406	-1,690	29,897,716	2,720,561	-223,281	26,953,874	5,239,358	2,489,683	11,344	3,057,465	1,795,112
1981	40,009,203	34,198,647	49,945	34,248,592	3,347,388	-231,232	30,669,972	6,492,834	2,846,397	12,737	3,141,226	1,877,705
1982	44,545,589	37,397,808	51,598	37,449,406	3,739,342	-287,777	33,422,287	7,874,844	3,248,458	13,685	3,255,044	1,927,039
1983	49,396,186	41,481,125	51,241	41,532,366	4,156,712	-354,822	37,020,832	8,822,543	3,552,811	14,672	3,366,597	1,997,325
1984	56,277,143	47,617,966	46,326	47,664,292	4,904,822	-419,496	42,339,974	10,168,711	3,768,458	16,154	3,483,781	2,168,499
1985	62,493,040	52,831,984	25,465	52,857,449	5,523,559	-497,485	46,836,405	11,579,502	4,077,133	17,240	3,624,952	2,297,002
1986	66,122,416	55,970,190	-844	55,969,346	5,798,886	-554,993	49,615,467	12,057,619	4,449,330	17,576	3,762,028	2,325,559
1987	68,490,940	58,166,909	10,756	58,177,665	5,929,767	-599,226	51,648,672	12,133,200	4,709,068	17,806	3,846,478	2,400,673
1988	72,428,887	61,561,518	13,230	61,574,748	6,426,900	-633,100	54,514,748	12,918,884	4,995,255	18,604	3,893,126	2,433,185
1989	77,232,775	65,389,882	43,067	65,432,949	6,835,300	-703,446	57,894,203	13,824,177	5,514,395	19,537	3,953,105	2,465,294
1990	83,386,617	70,343,790	53,108	70,396,898	7,245,131	-758,136	62,393,631	14,833,249	6,159,737	20,621	4,043,744	2,522,308
1991	86,498,849	73,112,738	48,648	73,161,386	7,719,174	-822,793	64,619,419	14,977,848	6,901,582	20,869	4,144,813	2,546,010
1992	92,983,781	78,418,699	72,152	78,490,851	8,201,798	-897,199	69,391,854	15,428,066	8,163,861	21,976	4,231,065	2,558,964
1993	98,716,611	83,765,367	65,492	83,830,859	8,733,904	-949,600	74,147,355	15,786,457	8,782,799	22,842	4,321,701	2,631,521
1994	105,315,356	89,317,557	76,248	89,393,805	9,447,713	-1,031,161	78,914,931	16,932,416	9,468,009	23,794	4,426,050	2,723,712
1995	113,303,501	95,941,456	33,318	95,974,774	10,164,002	-1,138,505	84,672,267	18,357,783	10,273,451	24,978	4,536,179	2,830,895
1996	123,505,879	104,839,585	25,250	104,864,835	10,969,460	-1,275,518	92,619,857	19,893,805	10,992,217	26,479	4,664,290	2,940,089
1997	135,440,045	116,084,529	67,224	116,151,753	12,087,897	-1,497,919	102,565,937	21,351,954	11,522,154	28,167	4,808,429	3,074,940
1998	150,053,427	129,825,776	42,346	129,868,122	13,347,004	-1,708,680	114,812,438	23,294,645	11,946,344	30,267	4,957,705	3,194,239
1999	159,117,536	139,504,335	97,576	139,601,911	14,396,709	-1,894,117	123,311,085	23,560,529	12,245,922	31,191	5,101,405	3,302,302
2000	176,206,039	154,546,878	41,566	154,588,444	15,684,076	-2,150,623	136,753,745	26,320,156	13,132,138	33,657	5,235,385	3,436,524
2001	183,847,633	161,546,718	69,054	161,615,772	16,203,227	-2,172,250	143,240,295	26,066,952	14,540,386	34,195	5,376,413	3,485,148
2002	185,269,254	162,396,712	64,996	162,461,708	16,222,173	-2,092,536	144,146,999	24,951,583	16,170,672	33,790	5,482,944	3,447,658
2003	188,870,395	163,823,558	130,358	163,953,916	16,729,066	-1,992,833	145,232,017	26,453,007	17,185,371	33,873	5,575,785	3,455,935
2004	196,481,993	170,245,165	140,543	170,385,708	17,536,886	-2,058,811	150,790,011	27,549,503	18,142,479	34,675	5,666,333	3,523,116
2005	214,833,928	181,987,856	118,700	182,106,556	18,561,837	-2,053,083	161,491,636	33,147,366	20,194,926	37,191	5,776,543	3,646,950
2006	236,575,955	199,281,707	113,421	199,395,128	19,650,553	-2,129,794	177,614,781	37,105,798	21,855,376	39,809	5,942,755	3,793,235
2007	250,584,533	207,093,359	100,836	207,194,195	20,764,779	-2,144,513	184,284,903	42,211,947	24,087,683	41,202	6,081,907	3,942,822
2008	270,162,614	215,504,102	22,253	215,526,355	21,425,039	-2,054,484	192,046,832	50,012,531	28,103,251	43,497	6,211,115	4,024,677
2009	251,525,163	201,487,963	902	201,488,865	20,993,739	-1,806,434	178,688,692	41,782,702	31,053,769	39,662	6,341,740	3,944,140
2010	264,556,519	211,164,794	20,606	211,185,400	21,721,630	-1,639,253	187,824,517	42,007,968	34,724,034	41,005	6,451,833	3,958,888
2011	294,823,363	229,549,342	5,145	229,554,487	20,291,212	-1,653,558	207,609,717	51,183,513	36,030,133	44,864	6,571,537	4,099,721
2012	313,040,929	245,444,382	68,168	245,512,550	21,421,722	-1,740,524	222,350,304	54,528,010	36,162,615	46,681	6,706,020	4,222,790
2013	321,034,152	258,458,732	165,905	258,624,637	25,454,258	-1,715,926	231,454,453	52,043,960	37,535,739	47,091	6,817,243	4,352,128
2014	347,197,652	276,684,095	116,510	276,800,605	26,953,544	-1,903,171	247,943,890	59,431,507	39,822,255	49,951	6,950,715	4,498,865
2015	361,077,787	286,599,763	171,480	286,771,243	28,802,535	-2,221,478	255,747,230	62,821,040	42,509,517	50,849	7,101,031	4,668,473
2016	375,997,723	294,565,324	37,150	294,602,474	30,226,667	-2,584,751	261,791,056	69,525,742	44,680,925	51,837	7,253,424	4,828,196
2017	392,145,456	308,008,679	39,216	308,047,895	31,959,416	-2,715,374	273,373,105	72,943,380	45,828,971	52,995	7,399,662	4,947,059
2018	423,961,883	424,114,265	-152,382	335,762,408	33,502,154	-3,544,016	298,716,238	78,156,604	47,089,041	56,864	7,455,756	5,085,031
2019	444,730,277	444,867,098	-136,821	354,620,865	35,065,983	-3,907,207	315,647,675	79,477,336	49,605,266	58,725	7,573,136	5,226,844

Personal Income and Employment by Area: Dalton, GA

(Thousands of dollars, except as noted.)

Year	Personal income, total	Derivation of personal income								Per capita personal income (dollars)	Population (persons)	Total employment
		Earnings by place of work			Less: Contributions for government social insurance	Plus: Adjustment for residence	Equals: Net earnings by place of residence	Plus: Dividends, interest, and rent	Plus: Personal current transfer receipts			
		Nonfarm	Farm	Total								
1970	226,414	216,086	1,961	218,047	14,777	-17,244	186,026	23,412	16,976	3,302	68,569	35,168
1971	261,434	250,526	1,661	252,187	17,866	-19,826	214,495	27,731	19,208	3,668	71,282	37,695
1972	308,176	298,195	2,312	300,507	22,166	-23,763	254,578	32,270	21,328	4,181	73,703	41,452
1973	352,394	338,969	6,935	345,904	28,752	-26,394	290,758	36,323	25,313	4,572	77,080	43,738
1974	368,916	350,741	2,108	352,849	30,881	-27,036	294,932	41,509	32,475	4,641	79,491	42,486
1975	390,877	345,986	7,050	353,036	29,680	-25,210	298,146	45,394	47,337	4,936	79,193	39,069
1976	449,453	413,024	6,373	419,397	36,331	-30,444	352,622	49,729	47,102	5,630	79,835	42,562
1977	507,878	477,596	5,544	483,140	41,985	-36,857	404,298	55,433	48,147	6,203	81,872	45,560
1978	569,576	535,049	7,840	542,889	48,285	-40,370	454,234	63,446	51,896	6,826	83,444	47,923
1979	637,591	597,910	6,303	604,213	55,821	-44,599	503,793	73,639	60,159	7,512	84,874	49,185
1980	687,094	633,071	1,856	634,927	59,510	-49,270	526,147	87,986	72,961	8,012	85,754	48,891
1981	753,069	683,023	3,224	686,247	68,680	-56,357	561,210	107,843	84,016	8,679	86,771	48,672
1982	787,997	698,261	4,025	702,286	70,769	-61,810	569,707	125,232	93,058	9,039	87,177	46,909
1983	893,820	817,804	3,407	821,211	84,276	-78,978	657,957	136,877	98,986	10,198	87,649	50,744
1984	999,164	928,458	6,665	935,123	98,633	-94,550	741,940	151,416	105,808	11,188	89,307	54,398
1985	1,076,073	1,005,792	5,828	1,011,620	108,630	-108,117	794,873	167,440	113,760	11,869	90,663	56,119
1986	1,182,219	1,125,642	7,744	1,133,386	123,034	-128,881	881,471	179,902	120,846	12,826	92,171	58,945
1987	1,298,855	1,263,199	4,010	1,267,209	136,072	-153,868	977,269	196,135	125,451	13,766	94,353	62,232
1988	1,406,602	1,369,835	8,831	1,378,666	150,179	-172,975	1,055,512	217,200	133,890	14,606	96,302	65,112
1989	1,523,230	1,447,870	13,693	1,461,563	159,680	-189,612	1,112,271	260,337	150,622	15,570	97,831	66,708
1990	1,594,884	1,517,577	12,135	1,529,712	167,188	-205,558	1,156,966	269,356	168,562	16,117	98,957	67,995
1991	1,652,362	1,551,461	13,775	1,565,236	173,148	-216,677	1,175,411	281,057	195,894	16,460	100,385	66,329
1992	1,809,155	1,739,010	13,431	1,752,441	190,828	-254,775	1,306,838	281,818	220,499	17,769	101,814	69,845
1993	1,941,850	1,898,056	15,688	1,913,744	209,087	-289,727	1,414,930	292,431	234,489	18,755	103,540	73,741
1994	2,082,676	2,027,206	18,282	2,045,488	224,844	-318,611	1,502,033	323,708	256,935	19,615	106,177	76,724
1995	2,188,957	2,099,390	16,696	2,116,086	231,754	-334,129	1,550,203	356,828	281,926	20,124	108,771	78,552
1996	2,344,575	2,229,592	21,771	2,251,363	243,654	-363,782	1,643,927	394,117	306,531	21,109	111,071	80,144
1997	2,455,130	2,355,967	21,618	2,377,585	254,299	-389,889	1,733,397	409,313	312,420	21,600	113,661	81,060
1998	2,626,498	2,544,839	28,777	2,573,616	272,825	-426,690	1,874,101	434,056	318,341	22,757	115,417	82,126
1999	2,711,134	2,652,304	28,180	2,680,484	283,031	-447,055	1,950,398	420,067	340,669	22,976	118,000	83,196
2000	2,893,158	2,859,875	23,481	2,883,356	305,756	-506,969	2,070,631	452,933	369,594	23,919	120,959	87,006
2001	3,212,863	3,134,462	32,936	3,167,398	324,501	-533,712	2,309,185	488,429	415,249	25,907	124,015	85,876
2002	3,306,438	3,220,564	22,627	3,243,191	332,181	-566,386	2,344,624	485,995	475,819	26,198	126,208	86,500
2003	3,437,335	3,369,082	19,092	3,388,174	347,956	-612,609	2,427,609	523,453	486,273	26,755	128,476	86,673
2004	3,552,234	3,517,515	24,667	3,542,182	386,133	-647,205	2,508,844	522,320	521,070	27,053	131,307	88,308
2005	3,549,876	3,535,019	22,567	3,557,586	389,894	-676,733	2,490,959	498,428	560,489	26,514	133,885	89,189
2006	3,632,265	3,595,683	-483	3,595,200	394,120	-711,155	2,489,925	529,762	612,578	26,594	136,581	90,340
2007	3,741,255	3,612,654	8,326	3,620,980	394,960	-741,219	2,484,801	589,619	666,835	26,956	138,792	89,950
2008	3,736,009	3,407,563	19,472	3,427,035	388,889	-695,803	2,342,343	625,372	768,294	26,607	140,415	84,979
2009	3,557,300	3,175,897	15,604	3,191,501	364,657	-674,540	2,152,304	551,754	853,242	25,248	140,897	77,658
2010	3,652,153	3,206,025	9,844	3,215,869	365,007	-657,936	2,192,926	529,700	929,527	25,662	142,315	76,810
2011	3,798,516	3,246,346	3,125	3,249,471	339,828	-698,968	2,210,675	628,200	959,641	26,663	142,466	77,683
2012	3,922,810	3,378,819	34,637	3,413,456	350,837	-678,669	2,383,950	592,457	946,403	27,523	142,528	76,671
2013	4,111,355	3,560,907	46,279	3,607,186	409,424	-697,226	2,500,536	637,421	973,398	28,906	142,233	76,814
2014	4,424,547	3,885,876	49,128	3,935,004	440,316	-803,990	2,690,698	720,592	1,013,257	30,991	142,767	80,171
2015	4,742,840	4,079,183	48,319	4,127,502	459,032	-810,077	2,858,393	839,075	1,045,372	33,046	143,523	81,974
2016	4,890,315	4,251,635	26,350	4,277,985	477,574	-865,322	2,935,089	874,071	1,081,155	33,943	144,074	81,919
2017	5,072,458	4,268,140	38,944	4,307,084	476,094	-780,490	3,050,500	905,198	1,116,760	35,118	144,440	79,914
2018	5,291,383	5,244,914	46,469	4,339,137	477,448	-751,961	3,109,728	1,041,040	1,140,615	36,697	144,192	81,600
2019	5,418,976	5,401,514	17,462	4,325,361	478,978	-657,259	3,189,124	1,046,805	1,183,047	37,444	144,724	80,515

Personal Income and Employment by Area: Danville, IL

(Thousands of dollars, except as noted.)

Year	Personal income, total	Earnings by place of work			Less: Contributions for government social insurance	Plus: Adjustment for residence	Equals: Net earnings by place of residence	Plus: Dividends, interest, and rent	Plus: Personal current transfer receipts	Per capita personal income (dollars)	Population (persons)	Total employment
		Nonfarm	Farm	Total								
1970	373,467	304,412	13,951	318,363	20,397	-10,243	287,723	48,330	37,414	3,846	97,100	43,790
1971	414,577	333,407	21,318	354,725	22,802	-14,798	317,125	52,163	45,289	4,255	97,441	43,260
1972	449,098	370,566	17,581	388,147	26,546	-19,719	341,882	57,540	49,676	4,591	97,815	44,707
1973	529,893	426,433	39,440	465,873	35,525	-26,151	404,197	67,439	58,257	5,404	98,058	46,897
1974	558,284	445,175	38,951	484,126	38,523	-29,029	416,574	75,557	66,153	5,713	97,719	46,993
1975	623,023	472,955	54,161	527,116	39,974	-32,495	454,647	82,867	85,509	6,382	97,623	45,416
1976	674,821	537,858	44,156	582,014	46,452	-40,496	495,066	88,503	91,252	6,874	98,166	46,632
1977	720,640	584,000	41,993	625,993	50,321	-47,384	528,288	98,484	93,868	7,365	97,842	46,973
1978	779,928	650,821	31,194	682,015	57,774	-56,369	567,872	112,597	99,459	7,977	97,772	47,926
1979	841,483	681,808	48,559	730,367	62,548	-62,406	605,413	126,392	109,678	8,682	96,928	47,142
1980	865,521	687,293	14,957	702,250	62,509	-65,522	574,219	155,531	135,771	9,098	95,130	44,925
1981	964,702	726,477	30,391	756,868	71,108	-69,179	616,581	189,404	158,717	10,198	94,596	44,283
1982	1,001,723	724,682	18,848	743,530	72,098	-62,866	608,566	220,820	172,337	10,771	92,998	42,605
1983	1,008,751	753,304	-1,949	751,355	75,918	-61,656	613,781	214,760	180,210	10,875	92,758	42,368
1984	1,131,583	828,630	34,545	863,175	87,063	-66,032	710,080	240,827	180,676	12,281	92,141	42,881
1985	1,161,226	841,809	39,563	881,372	89,976	-63,658	727,738	244,219	189,269	12,679	91,584	42,021
1986	1,186,410	858,317	33,487	891,804	92,516	-59,737	739,551	249,579	197,280	12,959	91,551	42,054
1987	1,223,209	903,088	21,977	925,065	95,654	-58,103	771,308	248,491	203,410	13,455	90,909	42,017
1988	1,269,663	941,167	16,305	957,472	102,026	-53,168	802,278	255,469	211,916	14,134	89,831	42,051
1989	1,359,427	960,779	44,448	1,005,227	105,252	-48,630	851,345	287,066	221,016	15,319	88,740	41,546
1990	1,380,611	968,231	39,532	1,007,763	103,486	-36,920	867,357	270,864	242,390	15,661	88,155	41,527
1991	1,404,343	1,000,442	18,429	1,018,871	109,806	-37,298	871,767	271,671	260,905	15,961	87,986	41,296
1992	1,523,911	1,062,372	42,431	1,104,803	114,270	-39,303	951,230	276,814	295,867	17,328	87,944	41,311
1993	1,554,597	1,077,925	48,604	1,126,529	118,952	-37,074	970,503	278,195	305,899	17,719	87,738	40,834
1994	1,647,161	1,151,333	60,617	1,211,950	128,418	-39,610	1,043,922	290,906	312,333	18,734	87,922	42,042
1995	1,621,843	1,128,310	18,415	1,146,725	126,039	-30,257	990,429	303,657	327,757	18,734	86,570	41,796
1996	1,706,235	1,147,025	47,654	1,194,679	127,040	-27,277	1,040,362	324,652	341,221	20,003	85,298	42,425
1997	1,726,506	1,170,655	32,364	1,203,019	129,080	-23,568	1,050,371	330,870	345,265	20,247	85,274	42,515
1998	1,784,745	1,219,685	15,118	1,234,803	133,571	-25,432	1,075,800	355,050	353,895	20,998	84,996	42,324
1999	1,815,915	1,260,848	10,270	1,271,118	134,904	-19,156	1,117,058	341,637	357,220	21,547	84,276	42,214
2000	1,886,717	1,275,179	29,716	1,304,895	133,817	-9,630	1,161,448	352,443	372,826	22,509	83,821	42,344
2001	1,985,607	1,320,447	30,901	1,351,348	137,411	-2,108	1,211,829	376,418	397,360	23,738	83,646	40,683
2002	2,023,442	1,354,969	19,109	1,374,078	139,447	4,056	1,238,687	360,394	424,361	24,291	83,299	40,062
2003	2,150,492	1,443,235	36,063	1,479,298	149,072	-146	1,330,080	371,976	448,436	25,911	82,996	40,636
2004	2,209,243	1,487,897	61,077	1,548,974	156,192	2,572	1,395,354	346,321	467,568	26,632	82,955	40,029
2005	2,201,894	1,519,771	21,943	1,541,714	166,762	5,600	1,380,552	317,644	503,698	26,616	82,728	40,190
2006	2,287,011	1,572,013	40,942	1,612,955	171,034	9,670	1,451,591	312,086	523,334	27,649	82,715	39,863
2007	2,368,560	1,565,097	61,517	1,626,614	171,456	23,689	1,478,847	323,318	566,395	28,794	82,258	39,718
2008	2,517,880	1,587,287	100,285	1,687,572	175,866	31,123	1,542,829	370,278	604,773	30,732	81,930	39,183
2009	2,521,683	1,561,953	60,696	1,622,649	172,795	23,051	1,472,905	369,036	679,742	30,861	81,710	37,825
2010	2,647,682	1,638,120	76,674	1,714,794	178,474	22,610	1,558,930	365,930	722,822	32,432	81,639	37,284
2011	2,788,087	1,720,222	125,312	1,845,534	169,333	12,707	1,688,908	395,957	703,222	34,252	81,399	38,010
2012	2,784,932	1,751,191	83,347	1,834,538	173,878	12,590	1,673,250	417,882	693,800	34,457	80,823	38,165
2013	2,861,008	1,743,652	160,204	1,903,856	192,010	7,978	1,719,824	414,774	726,410	35,506	80,578	37,344
2014	2,862,240	1,779,103	84,560	1,863,663	196,603	10,326	1,677,386	441,264	743,590	35,868	79,800	37,663
2015	2,868,678	1,812,869	12,916	1,825,785	198,888	11,366	1,638,263	450,408	780,007	36,227	79,187	37,736
2016	2,873,484	1,780,621	47,435	1,828,056	197,667	12,516	1,642,905	448,304	782,275	36,577	78,560	36,587
2017	2,912,814	1,789,878	27,069	1,816,947	199,494	20,712	1,638,165	468,048	806,601	37,387	77,909	36,210
2018	3,004,944	2,937,881	67,063	1,878,516	204,672	25,163	1,699,007	469,096	836,841	39,177	76,702	35,462
2019	3,038,613	2,999,313	39,300	1,895,635	209,949	27,328	1,713,014	476,026	849,573	40,109	75,758	35,539

Personal Income and Employment by Area: Daphne-Fairhope-Foley, AL

(Thousands of dollars, except as noted.)

Year	Personal income, total	Earnings by place of work			Less: Contributions for government social insurance	Plus: Adjustment for residence	Equals: Net earnings by place of residence	Plus: Dividends, interest, and rent	Plus: Personal current transfer receipts	Per capita personal income (dollars)	Population (persons)	Total employment
		Nonfarm	Farm	Total								
1970............	172,745	79,248	5,789	85,037	6,071	47,185	126,151	28,828	17,766	2,905	59,474	19,749
1971............	196,684	89,196	8,786	97,982	6,919	51,482	142,545	33,364	20,775	3,270	60,142	20,505
1972............	223,797	104,139	9,606	113,745	8,432	57,438	162,751	37,514	23,532	3,584	62,435	21,727
1973............	268,069	121,106	20,473	141,579	11,236	63,826	194,169	45,617	28,283	4,176	64,196	23,015
1974............	305,794	137,576	17,877	155,453	13,293	73,014	215,174	55,843	34,777	4,628	66,072	23,738
1975............	345,248	151,882	16,280	168,162	14,678	83,503	236,987	63,422	44,839	5,088	67,861	24,458
1976............	406,080	180,248	27,854	208,102	17,557	94,603	285,148	71,220	49,712	5,781	70,244	25,750
1977............	435,048	202,296	9,603	211,899	19,860	107,108	299,147	82,483	53,418	6,009	72,399	26,965
1978............	496,475	218,663	20,914	239,577	21,592	124,081	342,066	95,253	59,156	6,660	74,550	27,291
1979............	542,296	244,352	4,309	248,661	24,913	138,082	361,830	109,267	71,199	7,080	76,594	27,875
1980............	615,733	263,431	1,749	265,180	26,777	159,044	397,447	134,553	83,733	7,801	78,931	27,777
1981............	717,874	291,361	10,495	301,856	32,333	184,421	453,944	168,087	95,843	8,941	80,287	28,722
1982............	759,626	306,308	438	306,746	34,707	192,619	464,658	188,246	106,722	9,226	82,331	29,388
1983............	844,438	349,814	6,907	356,721	39,188	203,122	520,655	205,632	118,151	10,055	83,978	31,306
1984............	940,987	395,399	4,842	400,241	45,369	224,335	579,207	233,008	128,772	10,847	86,752	33,057
1985............	1,048,339	437,883	14,040	451,923	49,964	250,708	652,667	255,836	139,836	11,726	89,401	33,969
1986............	1,115,365	469,386	9,187	478,573	53,058	270,666	696,181	271,500	147,684	12,215	91,311	34,674
1987............	1,182,205	499,048	14,112	513,160	56,032	289,608	746,736	283,649	151,820	12,683	93,214	36,081
1988............	1,281,576	528,899	14,640	543,539	61,784	315,329	797,084	316,101	168,391	13,540	94,649	37,654
1989............	1,436,895	568,898	18,028	586,926	67,236	347,393	867,083	377,268	192,544	14,937	96,198	38,889
1990............	1,566,530	631,608	11,511	643,119	74,864	390,110	958,365	397,921	210,244	15,831	98,955	40,545
1991............	1,736,418	697,625	17,516	715,141	82,626	448,657	1,081,172	414,972	240,274	16,954	102,420	42,388
1992............	1,930,098	773,910	20,742	794,652	90,355	506,108	1,210,405	441,852	277,841	18,107	106,595	44,246
1993............	2,128,721	860,852	26,233	887,085	101,563	564,261	1,349,783	478,258	300,680	19,106	111,416	47,280
1994............	2,346,375	965,130	21,661	986,791	116,178	601,469	1,472,082	538,851	335,442	20,129	116,565	50,770
1995............	2,557,326	1,073,129	22,922	1,096,051	129,352	621,992	1,588,691	600,128	368,507	21,153	120,896	54,511
1996............	2,801,985	1,194,516	23,839	1,218,355	140,649	669,688	1,747,394	652,671	401,920	22,342	125,412	56,932
1997............	3,050,203	1,299,527	23,367	1,322,894	154,451	740,059	1,908,502	714,133	427,568	23,434	130,164	60,806
1998............	3,313,100	1,498,614	4,949	1,503,563	171,529	745,606	2,077,640	786,084	449,376	24,643	134,444	64,758
1999............	3,490,161	1,625,770	20,689	1,646,459	187,352	760,813	2,219,920	798,724	471,517	25,373	137,555	67,472
2000............	3,781,887	1,746,938	15,186	1,762,124	199,875	816,514	2,378,763	882,140	520,984	26,757	141,342	69,423
2001............	3,928,935	1,808,269	10,662	1,818,931	211,491	828,822	2,436,262	902,088	590,585	27,119	144,875	70,661
2002............	4,054,363	1,922,298	3,460	1,925,758	224,876	823,431	2,524,313	879,480	650,570	27,402	147,957	71,892
2003............	4,249,802	2,047,201	16,717	2,063,918	240,077	846,720	2,670,561	869,172	710,069	28,050	151,509	73,844
2004............	4,740,854	2,264,675	19,201	2,283,876	263,116	884,707	2,905,467	1,052,904	782,483	30,338	156,266	77,691
2005............	5,237,162	2,575,798	9,596	2,585,394	298,743	927,632	3,214,283	1,174,494	848,385	32,292	162,183	82,612
2006............	5,847,880	2,887,750	17,407	2,905,157	333,566	976,514	3,548,105	1,371,159	928,616	34,784	168,121	87,768
2007............	6,215,336	2,994,484	15,883	3,010,367	355,021	1,049,847	3,705,193	1,502,362	1,007,781	36,051	172,404	92,728
2008............	6,286,039	2,861,480	10,184	2,871,664	360,128	1,151,309	3,662,845	1,481,240	1,141,954	35,751	175,827	92,684
2009............	6,224,967	2,705,574	15,500	2,721,074	344,003	1,248,139	3,625,210	1,343,769	1,255,988	34,698	179,406	89,324
2010............	6,643,563	2,794,361	5,327	2,799,688	353,166	1,367,980	3,814,502	1,387,883	1,441,178	36,282	183,110	89,246
2011............	7,051,666	2,899,092	8,060	2,907,152	328,267	1,530,395	4,109,280	1,457,559	1,484,827	37,804	186,534	92,000
2012............	7,253,460	3,002,939	14,369	3,017,308	337,507	1,568,206	4,248,007	1,502,006	1,503,447	38,166	190,048	93,226
2013............	7,441,318	3,197,592	36,821	3,234,413	401,285	1,552,687	4,385,815	1,483,086	1,572,417	38,212	194,736	96,471
2014............	7,875,234	3,417,850	12,617	3,430,467	425,029	1,596,969	4,602,407	1,602,542	1,670,285	39,561	199,064	99,837
2015............	8,400,864	3,655,192	10,418	3,665,610	451,987	1,697,525	4,911,148	1,721,651	1,768,065	41,412	202,863	103,943
2016............	8,923,673	3,875,851	15,316	3,891,167	475,684	1,856,832	5,272,315	1,783,054	1,868,304	43,004	207,509	107,855
2017............	9,372,465	4,121,131	18,477	4,139,608	506,289	1,944,944	5,578,263	1,855,948	1,938,254	44,079	212,628	110,457
2018............	10,065,966	10,050,356	15,610	4,357,139	549,170	2,041,739	5,849,708	2,090,788	2,125,470	46,205	217,855	115,748
2019............	10,600,260	10,584,338	15,922	4,661,559	582,063	2,099,348	6,178,844	2,112,917	2,308,499	47,485	223,234	119,535

Personal Income and Employment by Area: Davenport-Moline-Rock Island, IA-IL

(Thousands of dollars, except as noted.)

Year	Personal income, total	Derivation of personal income								Per capita personal income (dollars)	Population (persons)	Total employment
		Earnings by place of work			Less: Contributions for government social insurance	Plus: Adjustment for residence	Equals: Net earnings by place of residence	Plus: Dividends, interest, and rent	Plus: Personal current transfer receipts			
		Nonfarm	Farm	Total								
1970	1,622,020	1,314,949	48,364	1,363,313	86,a09	-23,965	1,253,339	247,937	120,744	4,271	379,817	169,173
1971	1,717,581	1,386,972	39,893	1,426,865	93,458	-24,620	1,308,787	267,879	140,915	4,505	381,302	167,145
1972	1,887,827	1,523,131	59,947	1,583,078	108,874	-27,326	1,446,878	288,283	152,666	4,942	382,010	171,157
1973	2,171,907	1,743,142	100,802	1,843,944	145,158	-34,572	1,664,214	329,699	177,994	5,648	384,562	183,158
1974	2,433,004	1,994,591	80,378	2,074,969	173,786	-45,473	1,855,710	376,985	200,309	6,229	390,568	193,442
1975	2,697,281	2,135,977	126,030	2,262,007	182,626	-50,025	2,029,356	417,038	250,887	6,809	396,120	192,380
1976	2,898,322	2,358,686	83,964	2,442,650	206,986	-61,919	2,173,745	443,408	281,169	7,267	398,850	194,882
1977	3,188,957	2,644,316	69,582	2,713,898	233,113	-79,809	2,400,976	489,416	298,565	7,967	400,292	199,126
1978	3,503,443	2,903,381	91,583	2,994,964	265,345	-93,679	2,635,940	544,638	322,865	8,709	402,294	202,184
1979	3,914,573	3,293,948	77,154	3,371,102	315,315	-111,632	2,944,155	610,723	359,695	9,699	403,603	207,010
1980	4,256,874	3,540,230	-3,913	3,536,317	335,077	-124,393	3,076,847	746,302	433,725	10,526	404,420	202,488
1981	4,741,795	3,758,083	68,794	3,826,877	380,316	-124,569	3,321,992	911,027	508,776	11,703	405,162	201,299
1982	4,903,774	3,642,553	38,353	3,680,906	362,166	-108,850	3,209,890	1,088,275	605,609	12,198	402,024	190,760
1983	4,879,252	3,610,918	-51,993	3,558,925	361,772	-102,481	3,094,672	1,118,034	666,546	12,291	396,986	186,120
1984	5,377,191	3,914,382	80,114	3,994,496	403,808	-110,539	3,480,149	1,239,019	658,023	13,686	392,904	190,977
1985	5,568,600	4,057,419	106,178	4,163,597	426,120	-111,729	3,625,748	1,257,944	684,908	14,396	386,807	191,204
1986	5,575,402	4,037,613	73,382	4,110,995	428,583	-101,697	3,580,715	1,285,377	709,310	14,671	380,036	188,955
1987	5,849,134	4,329,220	95,775	4,424,995	455,506	-108,218	3,861,271	1,270,606	717,257	15,625	374,353	191,033
1988	6,030,020	4,507,399	53,648	4,561,047	489,638	-103,667	3,967,742	1,311,630	750,648	16,277	370,464	194,882
1989	6,473,546	4,767,320	78,925	4,846,245	524,236	-105,354	4,216,655	1,463,879	793,012	17,550	368,854	199,096
1990	6,794,051	5,089,042	80,068	5,169,110	563,270	-110,837	4,495,003	1,442,286	856,762	18,446	368,316	203,953
1991	6,970,971	5,230,028	66,233	5,296,261	591,533	-114,757	4,589,971	1,461,014	919,986	18,791	370,975	207,790
1992	7,418,850	5,539,152	105,292	5,644,444	618,884	-119,908	4,905,652	1,486,175	1,027,023	19,860	373,565	207,908
1993	7,521,401	5,620,413	65,738	5,686,151	641,015	-114,245	4,930,891	1,520,586	1,069,924	20,100	374,198	206,295
1994	7,848,215	5,932,866	92,223	6,025,089	686,342	-124,994	5,213,753	1,550,447	1,084,015	20,961	374,425	209,569
1995	8,271,770	6,231,860	16,812	6,248,672	720,540	-130,454	5,397,678	1,712,562	1,161,530	22,059	374,979	214,131
1996	8,843,950	6,549,229	117,691	6,666,920	739,237	-128,012	5,799,671	1,844,775	1,199,504	23,602	374,708	218,500
1997	9,321,653	6,968,091	96,402	7,064,493	794,612	-147,431	6,122,450	1,990,561	1,208,642	24,857	375,006	223,429
1998	9,867,773	7,364,741	70,613	7,435,354	836,377	-148,741	6,450,236	2,155,999	1,261,538	26,276	375,549	229,670
1999	9,961,879	7,513,258	36,182	7,549,440	844,388	-140,449	6,564,603	2,082,127	1,315,149	26,447	376,678	229,932
2000	10,480,887	7,836,990	69,660	7,906,650	871,865	-141,403	6,893,382	2,190,401	1,397,104	27,892	375,763	231,704
2001	10,845,168	8,135,379	59,323	8,194,702	894,376	-153,147	7,147,179	2,183,092	1,514,897	28,954	374,561	228,307
2002	11,036,878	8,343,105	45,897	8,389,002	912,969	-168,561	7,307,472	2,087,381	1,642,025	29,531	373,740	224,701
2003	11,416,725	8,628,909	125,444	8,754,353	945,226	-176,239	7,632,888	2,106,349	1,677,488	30,610	372,975	223,492
2004	12,340,920	9,443,973	168,731	9,612,704	1,021,118	-189,513	8,402,073	2,188,778	1,750,069	33,109	372,740	226,886
2005	12,698,126	9,870,961	74,205	9,945,166	1,085,932	-204,505	8,654,729	2,148,949	1,894,448	34,055	372,876	231,269
2006	13,424,766	10,336,218	71,095	10,407,313	1,127,018	-212,555	9,067,740	2,330,344	2,026,682	35,918	373,762	231,766
2007	14,216,889	10,739,782	141,240	10,881,022	1,181,192	-162,027	9,537,803	2,488,734	2,190,352	37,899	375,121	233,972
2008	15,107,410	11,149,108	191,802	11,340,910	1,237,781	-155,311	9,947,818	2,686,793	2,472,799	40,129	376,467	234,372
2009	14,736,693	10,856,711	85,179	10,941,890	1,212,592	-179,334	9,549,964	2,420,871	2,765,858	38,975	378,108	225,854
2010	15,199,333	11,170,602	65,360	11,235,962	1,253,207	-226,874	9,755,881	2,397,182	3,046,270	40,026	379,741	223,989
2011	16,216,316	11,701,135	243,832	11,944,967	1,185,374	-261,252	10,498,341	2,745,742	2,972,233	42,617	380,509	227,447
2012	16,602,565	12,089,570	154,312	12,243,882	1,213,528	-279,868	10,750,486	2,931,920	2,920,159	43,432	382,269	228,828
2013	16,732,686	12,097,863	317,398	12,415,261	1,367,776	-282,504	10,764,981	2,951,475	3,016,230	43,620	383,597	228,835
2014	16,916,429	12,110,144	102,382	12,212,526	1,364,097	-253,398	10,595,031	3,191,455	3,129,943	44,075	383,814	230,114
2015	17,272,231	12,247,159	16,678	12,263,837	1,378,639	-243,943	10,641,255	3,350,528	3,280,448	45,054	383,365	229,856
2016	17,530,205	12,378,124	65,734	12,443,858	1,403,886	-203,716	10,836,256	3,390,880	3,303,069	45,810	382,671	228,265
2017	18,181,975	12,994,110	44,601	13,038,711	1,468,377	-269,556	11,300,778	3,539,950	3,341,247	47,564	382,263	229,417
2018	18,667,082	18,558,595	108,487	13,261,192	1,513,699	-269,792	11,477,701	3,673,031	3,516,350	49,118	380,044	230,160
2019	19,149,116	19,058,060	91,056	13,637,746	1,556,273	-301,252	11,780,221	3,691,331	3,677,564	50,502	379,172	231,801

Personal Income and Employment by Area: Dayton-Kettering, OH

(Thousands of dollars, except as noted.)

Year	Personal income, total	Earnings by place of work			Less: Contributions for government social insurance	Plus: Adjustment for residence	Equals: Net earnings by place of residence	Plus: Dividends, interest, and rent	Plus: Personal current transfer receipts	Per capita personal income (dollars)	Population (persons)	Total employment
		Nonfarm	Farm	Total								
1970	3,724,442	3,390,457	19,936	3,410,393	206,990	-242,805	2,960,598	543,195	220,649	4,556	817,533	388,647
1971	3,850,553	3,424,747	18,705	3,443,452	213,624	-233,979	2,995,849	585,702	269,002	4,717	816,329	370,912
1972	4,198,442	3,763,377	22,439	3,785,816	249,182	-252,601	3,284,033	616,987	297,422	5,158	813,964	380,981
1973	4,556,792	4,086,845	38,039	4,124,884	313,612	-271,616	3,539,656	671,252	345,884	5,652	806,273	389,418
1974	4,879,893	4,261,889	41,241	4,303,130	335,862	-267,085	3,700,183	748,201	431,509	6,109	798,827	389,620
1975	5,259,095	4,445,463	35,020	4,480,483	342,172	-252,970	3,885,341	818,851	554,903	6,593	797,720	377,791
1976	5,777,472	4,971,522	30,386	5,001,908	397,541	-287,581	4,316,786	876,501	584,185	7,276	794,070	386,876
1977	6,352,071	5,511,820	24,938	5,536,758	443,501	-321,804	4,771,453	971,897	608,721	8,056	788,517	399,513
1978	6,966,972	6,061,433	24,825	6,086,258	502,416	-354,280	5,229,562	1,082,236	655,174	8,835	788,528	414,200
1979	7,679,484	6,636,020	42,521	6,678,541	573,379	-397,072	5,708,090	1,207,651	763,743	9,705	791,260	421,805
1980	8,298,078	6,896,544	27,641	6,924,185	592,645	-405,543	5,925,997	1,424,698	947,383	10,477	792,002	412,506
1981	8,924,098	7,464,360	2,936	7,467,296	684,596	-624,734	6,157,966	1,712,568	1,053,564	11,284	790,829	408,425
1982	9,320,916	7,536,479	14,243	7,550,722	698,140	-622,600	6,229,982	1,868,202	1,222,732	11,856	786,167	394,889
1983	9,944,010	8,060,817	-10,541	8,050,276	778,279	-648,339	6,623,658	2,023,471	1,296,881	12,694	783,366	397,786
1984	11,015,219	9,009,710	36,095	9,045,805	897,233	-720,736	7,427,836	2,248,614	1,338,769	14,018	785,813	418,017
1985	11,794,419	9,735,177	49,998	9,785,175	998,701	-773,045	8,013,429	2,353,247	1,427,743	14,951	788,847	431,975
1986	12,433,030	10,281,818	35,647	10,317,465	1,092,539	-796,345	8,428,581	2,483,916	1,520,533	15,717	791,049	443,823
1987	12,913,874	10,672,036	29,137	10,701,173	1,134,955	-798,189	8,768,029	2,561,987	1,583,858	16,220	796,181	455,751
1988	13,950,371	11,648,723	35,824	11,684,547	1,283,792	-867,320	9,533,435	2,743,295	1,673,641	17,381	802,640	464,150
1989	14,961,083	12,273,783	47,404	12,321,187	1,363,771	-887,701	10,069,715	3,127,133	1,764,235	18,646	802,358	471,695
1990	15,592,863	12,712,259	45,026	12,757,285	1,450,064	-914,708	10,392,513	3,213,970	1,986,380	19,386	804,335	473,295
1991	16,195,814	13,084,446	27,917	13,112,363	1,529,416	-940,617	10,642,330	3,431,142	2,122,342	20,000	809,809	470,098
1992	16,894,463	13,721,775	53,109	13,774,884	1,603,407	-951,356	11,220,121	3,339,092	2,335,250	20,743	814,480	464,432
1993	17,556,271	14,359,306	41,646	14,400,952	1,695,609	-1,043,833	11,661,510	3,491,063	2,403,698	21,491	816,922	469,215
1994	18,396,461	15,117,514	45,918	15,163,432	1,812,080	-1,139,751	12,211,601	3,676,109	2,508,751	22,576	814,885	481,730
1995	19,494,409	15,864,914	30,974	15,895,888	1,915,624	-1,230,619	12,749,645	4,095,089	2,649,675	23,902	815,608	491,268
1996	20,222,281	16,405,037	44,535	16,449,572	1,962,614	-1,282,642	13,204,316	4,276,224	2,741,741	24,837	814,188	492,909
1997	21,220,106	17,230,660	66,260	17,296,920	2,022,001	-1,395,764	13,879,155	4,507,135	2,833,816	26,157	811,250	499,170
1998	22,062,689	17,840,225	46,723	17,886,948	2,030,387	-1,355,259	14,501,302	4,678,587	2,882,800	27,199	811,168	502,538
1999	22,574,101	18,413,785	26,549	18,440,334	2,092,884	-1,391,137	14,956,313	4,650,478	2,967,310	27,938	808,010	497,259
2000	23,728,063	19,185,952	42,182	19,228,134	2,113,710	-1,480,499	15,633,925	4,915,433	3,178,705	29,442	805,938	503,030
2001	24,307,765	19,566,553	48,764	19,615,317	2,150,185	-1,478,645	15,986,487	4,816,047	3,505,231	30,216	804,479	497,721
2002	24,616,187	19,841,703	25,580	19,867,283	2,149,017	-1,479,150	16,239,116	4,630,529	3,746,542	30,606	804,286	488,980
2003	25,108,567	20,321,200	38,601	20,359,801	2,222,736	-1,493,598	16,643,467	4,545,115	3,919,985	31,194	804,926	484,370
2004	25,747,510	21,126,077	53,913	21,179,990	2,333,908	-1,544,812	17,301,270	4,346,548	4,099,692	31,948	805,930	484,036
2005	26,248,663	21,334,814	41,269	21,376,083	2,372,460	-1,579,348	17,424,275	4,484,150	4,340,238	32,617	804,766	482,766
2006	27,674,327	22,097,126	39,614	22,136,740	2,472,685	-1,589,078	18,074,977	4,973,411	4,625,939	34,442	803,498	481,807
2007	28,449,698	22,087,806	46,398	22,134,204	2,471,427	-1,515,255	18,147,522	5,352,935	4,949,241	35,480	801,852	481,030
2008	29,041,747	21,906,106	30,297	21,936,403	2,497,925	-1,426,051	18,012,427	5,414,426	5,614,894	36,293	800,209	471,122
2009	28,396,522	21,007,014	53,315	21,060,329	2,413,732	-1,334,085	17,312,512	4,960,644	6,123,366	35,545	798,895	450,129
2010	29,087,348	21,482,383	43,729	21,526,112	2,433,199	-1,455,977	17,636,936	4,918,145	6,532,267	36,376	799,639	447,825
2011	30,847,757	22,507,133	66,956	22,574,089	2,292,497	-1,540,561	18,741,031	5,421,666	6,685,060	38,526	800,690	454,622
2012	31,732,388	23,291,906	46,307	23,338,213	2,352,969	-1,538,192	19,447,052	5,737,971	6,547,365	39,597	801,382	457,498
2013	32,097,469	23,801,912	116,962	23,918,874	2,607,835	-1,454,639	19,856,400	5,590,907	6,650,162	40,091	800,609	457,953
2014	33,343,639	24,477,058	42,393	24,519,451	2,680,491	-1,450,987	20,387,973	6,002,382	6,953,284	41,666	800,264	463,450
2015	34,525,470	25,173,562	13,957	25,187,519	2,773,844	-1,403,403	21,010,272	6,289,631	7,225,567	43,195	799,293	469,801
2016	35,244,187	25,672,589	13,627	25,686,216	2,882,831	-1,394,173	21,409,212	6,433,313	7,401,662	44,006	800,886	474,063
2017	36,722,858	26,814,680	8,757	26,823,437	3,049,461	-1,386,512	22,387,464	6,740,965	7,594,429	45,708	803,416	480,301
2018	38,483,906	38,453,039	30,867	28,047,791	3,133,421	-1,465,398	23,448,972	7,252,833	7,782,101	47,801	805,088	487,291
2019	39,703,066	39,698,275	4,791	29,160,596	3,262,072	-1,596,626	24,301,898	7,324,418	8,076,750	49,161	807,611	492,689

Personal Income and Employment by Area: Decatur, AL

(Thousands of dollars, except as noted.)

Year	Personal income, total	Derivation of personal income									Per capita personal income (dollars)	Population (persons)	Total employment
		Earnings by place of work			Less: Contributions for government social insurance	Plus: Adjustment for residence	Equals: Net earnings by place of residence	Plus: Dividends, interest, and rent	Plus: Personal current transfer receipts				
		Nonfarm	Farm	Total									
1970	350,823	250,850	13,280	264,130	18,331	38,890	284,689	34,748	31,386		3,341	105,018	41,444
1971	375,836	259,423	13,605	273,028	19,308	44,382	298,102	39,856	37,878		3,491	107,661	41,034
1972	407,614	285,521	15,993	301,514	22,367	43,641	322,788	43,186	41,640		3,716	109,678	42,354
1973	453,561	322,270	25,527	347,797	29,339	39,651	358,109	48,194	47,258		4,106	110,455	44,291
1974	492,008	371,689	10,504	382,193	35,236	34,359	381,316	55,450	55,242		4,359	112,864	46,325
1975	564,046	417,398	22,106	439,504	39,305	28,271	428,470	61,781	73,795		4,943	114,103	46,956
1976	623,154	457,488	28,380	485,868	43,614	31,851	474,105	67,845	81,204		5,387	115,667	47,493
1977	691,124	514,088	27,274	541,362	48,987	38,188	530,563	76,445	84,116		5,901	117,115	49,637
1978	781,117	600,536	21,239	621,775	58,622	39,714	602,867	88,721	89,529		6,548	119,287	52,721
1979	892,073	681,679	26,101	707,780	68,697	48,524	687,607	101,203	103,263		7,383	120,822	53,931
1980	957,906	694,627	10,421	705,048	69,838	69,996	705,206	125,596	127,104		7,954	120,435	51,505
1981	1,074,370	752,569	20,057	772,626	81,113	85,280	776,793	154,511	143,066		8,927	120,351	51,147
1982	1,132,143	771,157	14,944	786,101	85,213	92,499	793,387	177,439	161,317		9,350	121,091	49,815
1983	1,222,667	831,192	5,425	836,617	92,272	114,380	858,725	189,193	174,749		10,028	121,928	50,679
1984	1,397,534	927,618	26,803	954,421	104,560	144,518	994,379	215,966	187,189		11,314	123,522	53,337
1985	1,529,018	999,951	19,773	1,019,724	112,814	185,141	1,092,051	237,135	199,832		12,225	125,076	54,919
1986	1,630,068	1,054,073	25,274	1,079,347	118,461	207,277	1,168,163	251,635	210,270		12,883	126,532	56,295
1987	1,721,944	1,131,996	27,374	1,159,370	125,489	211,141	1,245,022	262,010	214,912		13,437	128,146	58,491
1988	1,876,472	1,209,923	41,230	1,251,153	138,353	249,350	1,362,150	289,046	225,276		14,544	129,017	60,490
1989	2,037,815	1,300,380	45,530	1,345,910	149,201	254,361	1,451,070	325,644	261,101		15,656	130,162	62,258
1990	2,174,460	1,404,547	33,469	1,438,016	163,235	260,888	1,535,669	348,035	290,756		16,458	132,118	65,211
1991	2,304,469	1,504,415	46,433	1,550,848	176,515	245,307	1,619,640	361,778	323,051		17,170	134,218	65,427
1992	2,473,319	1,597,818	43,713	1,641,531	184,643	293,168	1,750,056	358,389	364,874		18,192	135,959	65,640
1993	2,564,676	1,682,309	36,775	1,719,084	197,412	288,543	1,810,215	369,975	384,486		18,583	138,014	67,205
1994	2,729,151	1,741,331	51,368	1,792,699	205,850	323,328	1,910,177	409,215	409,759		19,642	138,947	67,605
1995	2,856,699	1,823,949	25,330	1,849,279	217,009	334,812	1,967,082	446,785	442,832		20,346	140,404	69,872
1996	2,969,447	1,911,547	40,469	1,952,016	224,534	300,111	2,027,593	473,629	468,225		20,973	141,587	71,005
1997	3,091,715	2,018,406	42,605	2,061,011	235,839	274,345	2,099,517	498,067	494,131		21,627	142,959	72,474
1998	3,308,280	2,178,344	57,964	2,236,308	251,529	275,818	2,260,597	538,820	508,863		22,944	144,192	74,066
1999	3,416,575	2,286,978	61,927	2,348,905	265,258	259,700	2,343,347	535,100	538,128		23,529	145,207	75,040
2000	3,512,752	2,318,222	43,601	2,361,823	269,729	265,431	2,357,525	574,704	580,523		24,044	146,095	75,786
2001	3,610,062	2,383,860	64,564	2,448,424	281,825	267,944	2,434,543	576,781	598,738		24,633	146,552	75,846
2002	3,610,706	2,328,583	33,752	2,362,335	274,587	316,905	2,404,653	569,177	636,876		24,653	146,464	73,525
2003	3,799,064	2,388,843	53,822	2,442,665	281,069	353,086	2,514,682	604,558	679,824		25,776	147,386	72,553
2004	4,022,154	2,566,223	87,523	2,653,746	298,093	337,421	2,693,074	622,432	706,648		27,301	147,324	74,234
2005	4,180,343	2,645,592	71,424	2,717,016	310,273	371,980	2,778,723	636,916	764,704		28,170	148,399	74,947
2006	4,389,390	2,749,465	17,725	2,767,190	323,724	421,658	2,865,124	686,912	837,354		29,357	149,519	75,300
2007	4,591,063	2,858,385	33,905	2,892,290	340,627	405,916	2,957,579	727,349	906,135		30,467	150,690	77,096
2008	4,749,203	2,873,383	45,546	2,918,929	347,875	370,196	2,941,250	796,722	1,011,231		31,267	151,890	76,549
2009	4,675,974	2,744,270	41,387	2,785,657	332,728	392,252	2,845,181	717,664	1,113,129		30,508	153,269	72,444
2010	4,830,519	2,838,224	29,023	2,867,247	348,004	365,041	2,884,284	744,083	1,202,152		31,377	153,949	71,651
2011	4,928,269	2,928,802	-3,351	2,925,451	321,786	359,850	2,963,515	756,102	1,208,652		31,991	154,054	73,429
2012	5,060,139	3,010,926	14,680	3,025,606	328,454	362,337	3,059,489	777,078	1,223,572		32,884	153,880	73,498
2013	5,147,432	3,047,560	81,396	3,128,956	375,728	366,583	3,119,811	770,313	1,257,308		33,618	153,114	73,777
2014	5,326,958	3,136,108	48,257	3,184,365	380,403	403,323	3,207,285	820,676	1,298,997		34,850	152,856	73,398
2015	5,399,425	3,118,340	39,140	3,157,480	382,573	424,196	3,199,103	848,856	1,351,466		35,444	152,336	73,080
2016	5,454,449	3,189,551	-2,606	3,186,945	390,758	403,159	3,199,346	865,204	1,389,899		35,872	152,051	73,381
2017	5,679,148	3,278,601	35,032	3,313,633	402,084	430,694	3,342,243	899,700	1,437,205		37,396	151,867	74,133
2018	5,917,497	5,915,627	1,870	3,465,822	432,577	414,005	3,447,250	959,842	1,510,405		38,894	152,144	75,691
2019	6,149,159	6,171,788	-22,629	3,723,142	461,485	352,658	3,614,315	974,791	1,560,053		40,295	152,603	78,044

Personal Income and Employment by Area: Decatur, IL

(Thousands of dollars, except as noted.)

Year	Personal income, total	Earnings by place of work			Less: Contributions for government social insurance	Plus: Adjustment for residence	Equals: Net earnings by place of residence	Plus: Dividends, interest, and rent	Plus: Personal current transfer receipts	Per capita personal income (dollars)	Population (persons)	Total employment
		Nonfarm	Farm	Total								
1970	534,200	488,789	10,288	499,077	34,906	-46,430	417,741	72,420	44,039	4,277	124,905	61,590
1971	572,760	516,740	12,685	529,425	37,852	-49,155	442,418	77,520	52,822	4,572	125,278	60,980
1972	620,388	568,459	10,017	578,476	43,869	-56,878	477,729	84,808	57,851	4,954	125,241	62,469
1973	694,282	625,380	23,435	648,815	55,686	-63,795	529,334	95,765	69,183	5,471	126,910	65,047
1974	769,313	698,627	25,338	723,965	64,811	-74,750	584,404	107,382	77,527	6,022	127,752	66,355
1975	841,296	730,642	37,107	767,749	66,126	-78,732	622,891	118,966	99,439	6,511	129,218	65,268
1976	919,355	820,774	28,793	849,567	75,820	-90,491	683,256	126,297	109,802	7,088	129,701	66,311
1977	1,002,082	904,795	28,199	932,994	83,754	-101,449	747,791	139,167	115,124	7,628	131,366	68,395
1978	1,101,786	1,018,082	21,022	1,039,104	96,485	-117,748	824,871	155,806	121,109	8,321	132,404	69,932
1979	1,176,523	1,073,949	26,143	1,100,092	105,044	-122,398	872,650	171,192	132,681	8,889	132,364	69,000
1980	1,292,317	1,153,101	7,733	1,160,834	112,300	-137,072	911,462	217,420	163,435	9,850	131,205	67,250
1981	1,445,131	1,231,812	25,701	1,257,513	128,901	-143,184	985,428	271,043	188,660	11,091	130,295	67,071
1982	1,488,283	1,199,761	17,011	1,216,772	126,890	-127,184	962,698	310,319	215,266	11,583	128,485	63,475
1983	1,479,684	1,195,349	-9,713	1,185,636	127,257	-116,645	941,734	310,069	227,881	11,657	126,932	60,376
1984	1,647,591	1,339,794	19,603	1,359,397	148,894	-127,377	1,083,126	343,648	220,817	13,073	126,033	62,722
1985	1,723,662	1,400,256	24,463	1,424,719	158,147	-130,489	1,136,083	355,470	232,109	13,793	124,970	62,271
1986	1,765,939	1,440,701	21,468	1,462,169	163,100	-147,547	1,151,522	367,872	246,545	14,384	122,775	62,625
1987	1,839,902	1,523,430	18,364	1,541,794	169,262	-158,174	1,214,358	373,331	252,213	15,265	120,527	62,642
1988	1,918,551	1,601,787	11,177	1,612,964	183,047	-152,525	1,277,392	379,486	261,673	16,119	119,024	63,093
1989	2,079,085	1,680,742	25,595	1,706,337	192,223	-159,311	1,354,803	443,696	280,586	17,661	117,723	64,147
1990	2,151,903	1,773,585	18,461	1,792,046	197,032	-159,738	1,435,276	412,249	304,378	18,350	117,271	64,900
1991	2,189,750	1,806,697	10,554	1,817,251	206,416	-158,589	1,452,246	408,214	329,290	18,560	117,984	65,857
1992	2,351,131	1,879,588	30,313	1,909,901	209,510	-161,039	1,539,352	441,003	370,776	19,875	118,297	65,119
1993	2,396,054	1,943,611	21,164	1,964,775	220,566	-169,068	1,575,141	430,571	390,342	20,317	117,933	65,228
1994	2,467,381	2,005,041	35,406	2,040,447	229,876	-175,665	1,634,906	437,672	394,803	21,001	117,490	65,479
1995	2,543,005	2,032,617	4,948	2,037,565	232,692	-173,821	1,631,052	494,258	417,695	21,682	117,289	65,836
1996	2,719,215	2,195,898	35,233	2,231,131	248,948	-199,862	1,782,321	498,177	438,717	23,326	116,573	68,553
1997	2,784,270	2,245,218	30,525	2,275,743	253,983	-206,579	1,815,181	519,520	449,569	24,063	115,706	68,850
1998	2,940,775	2,386,526	12,501	2,399,027	267,200	-221,328	1,910,499	567,692	462,584	25,472	115,453	68,933
1999	3,113,843	2,614,091	13,372	2,627,463	285,856	-247,578	2,094,029	548,154	471,660	27,044	115,142	71,554
2000	3,198,727	2,631,495	22,768	2,654,263	285,957	-251,727	2,116,579	589,316	492,832	27,937	114,499	71,803
2001	3,449,933	2,814,876	24,597	2,839,473	294,524	-223,745	2,321,204	597,387	531,342	30,368	113,604	68,070
2002	3,455,935	2,819,463	17,709	2,837,172	287,827	-192,312	2,357,033	518,806	580,096	30,702	112,564	65,473
2003	3,414,210	2,766,736	20,779	2,787,515	293,082	-195,778	2,298,655	516,448	599,107	30,601	111,572	64,829
2004	3,562,118	2,836,818	50,420	2,887,238	312,426	-192,341	2,382,471	563,529	616,118	32,039	111,181	65,063
2005	3,640,957	2,962,110	24,139	2,986,249	332,328	-216,240	2,437,681	541,662	661,614	32,777	111,083	65,139
2006	3,845,787	3,098,243	31,231	3,129,474	342,451	-200,649	2,586,374	579,443	679,970	34,707	110,808	65,741
2007	4,084,859	3,264,086	52,194	3,316,280	363,188	-213,932	2,739,160	601,323	744,376	36,883	110,751	66,941
2008	4,311,208	3,328,281	68,403	3,396,684	372,411	-190,324	2,833,949	674,114	803,145	38,984	110,588	66,551
2009	4,303,088	3,222,605	49,071	3,271,676	359,957	-170,022	2,741,697	663,834	897,557	38,860	110,732	64,187
2010	4,367,632	3,268,988	45,870	3,314,858	361,653	-190,080	2,763,125	639,851	964,656	39,427	110,777	63,818
2011	4,603,157	3,422,130	82,517	3,504,647	341,987	-196,861	2,965,799	710,079	927,279	41,601	110,649	65,204
2012	4,589,075	3,463,655	35,387	3,499,042	347,002	-257,607	2,894,433	754,213	940,429	41,679	110,105	64,625
2013	4,728,647	3,447,799	146,835	3,594,634	385,338	-224,456	2,984,840	759,751	984,056	43,171	109,533	63,052
2014	4,869,248	3,697,412	64,351	3,761,763	405,245	-283,024	3,073,494	798,130	997,624	44,866	108,529	63,091
2015	4,795,672	3,770,339	17,812	3,788,151	414,748	-437,412	2,935,991	813,675	1,046,006	44,645	107,419	63,030
2016	4,823,822	3,690,839	72,298	3,763,137	410,964	-429,912	2,922,261	848,550	1,053,011	45,230	106,651	62,608
2017	4,835,163	3,712,293	12,402	3,724,695	414,772	-444,387	2,865,536	885,480	1,084,147	45,701	105,801	62,526
2018	5,037,722	4,992,846	44,876	3,942,474	439,738	-462,874	3,039,862	875,674	1,122,186	48,206	104,504	62,249
2019	5,071,870	5,048,586	23,284	3,899,547	436,368	-432,870	3,030,309	883,477	1,158,084	48,764	104,009	61,206

Personal Income and Employment by Area: Deltona-Daytona Beach-Ormond Beach, FL

(Thousands of dollars, except as noted.)

| Year | Personal income, total | Derivation of personal income | | | | | Equals: Net earnings by place of residence | Plus: Dividends, interest, and rent | Plus: Personal current transfer receipts | Per capita personal income (dollars) | Population (persons) | Total employment |
| | | Earnings by place of work | | | Less: Contributions for government social insurance | Plus: Adjustment for residence | | | | | | |
		Nonfarm	Farm	Total								
1970	639,900	359,669	9,803	369,472	23,287	19,725	365,910	176,934	97,056	3,659	174,894	64,013
1971	714,677	399,988	11,223	411,211	27,196	20,456	404,471	196,772	113,434	3,928	181,923	67,875
1972	817,755	468,530	13,503	482,033	33,731	21,860	470,162	217,774	129,819	4,311	189,672	74,167
1973	968,502	563,638	17,467	581,105	46,286	24,516	559,335	252,842	156,325	4,748	203,993	82,359
1974	1,098,055	630,594	16,556	647,150	54,411	24,871	617,610	296,592	183,853	5,058	217,106	86,169
1975	1,220,491	667,839	21,824	689,663	56,789	26,874	659,748	328,800	231,943	5,424	225,008	85,659
1976	1,339,947	731,492	21,117	752,609	62,502	29,616	719,723	364,031	256,193	5,820	230,241	86,843
1977	1,500,427	811,580	19,171	830,751	69,862	33,186	794,075	420,703	285,649	6,309	237,833	91,275
1978	1,738,599	949,251	21,542	970,793	83,901	41,409	928,301	494,354	315,944	7,044	246,836	98,192
1979	2,025,975	1,099,207	20,979	1,120,186	102,201	48,652	1,066,637	590,349	368,989	7,767	260,852	104,567
1980	2,428,260	1,247,869	27,051	1,274,920	117,822	57,387	1,214,485	768,251	445,524	8,906	272,648	110,011
1981	2,857,102	1,397,086	27,496	1,424,582	142,423	77,320	1,359,479	972,134	525,489	10,059	284,026	114,209
1982	3,113,811	1,482,872	40,034	1,522,906	156,730	98,522	1,464,698	1,052,862	596,251	10,557	294,958	117,353
1983	3,493,310	1,657,339	44,242	1,701,581	174,334	122,416	1,649,663	1,181,022	662,625	11,440	305,348	123,065
1984	3,914,893	1,897,103	42,595	1,939,698	204,642	151,886	1,886,942	1,328,747	699,204	12,390	315,969	131,569
1985	4,327,149	2,124,848	40,643	2,165,491	233,859	180,917	2,112,549	1,455,460	759,140	13,198	327,855	140,900
1986	4,727,208	2,333,911	44,216	2,378,127	263,237	216,896	2,331,786	1,572,591	822,831	13,892	340,285	148,201
1987	5,121,555	2,596,306	41,088	2,637,394	288,771	257,582	2,606,205	1,637,436	877,914	14,445	354,554	149,553
1988	5,660,854	2,839,151	48,483	2,887,634	327,682	305,066	2,865,018	1,810,956	984,880	15,312	369,706	156,611
1989	6,229,772	2,983,452	47,893	3,031,345	355,332	356,069	3,032,082	2,109,174	1,088,516	16,207	384,379	156,972
1990	6,652,633	3,154,811	47,618	3,202,429	369,846	415,168	3,247,751	2,209,852	1,195,030	16,480	403,674	155,591
1991	6,874,294	3,272,734	56,995	3,329,729	387,560	429,510	3,371,679	2,166,372	1,336,243	16,541	415,595	155,691
1992	7,283,319	3,494,452	64,726	3,559,178	412,271	472,100	3,619,007	2,149,206	1,515,106	17,108	425,733	156,162
1993	7,705,254	3,738,673	61,361	3,800,034	440,756	509,667	3,868,945	2,202,018	1,634,291	17,693	435,486	162,045
1994	8,171,784	3,947,259	62,090	4,009,349	474,971	547,248	4,081,626	2,337,286	1,752,872	18,350	445,335	166,426
1995	8,781,837	4,221,394	59,703	4,281,097	508,047	583,368	4,356,418	2,531,935	1,893,484	19,367	453,432	173,778
1996	9,356,269	4,469,265	59,170	4,528,435	529,476	643,166	4,642,125	2,710,889	2,003,255	20,315	460,565	177,992
1997	9,917,969	4,680,035	67,347	4,747,382	554,799	724,253	4,916,836	2,904,405	2,096,728	21,062	470,889	180,114
1998	10,481,118	4,883,458	64,760	4,948,218	575,459	819,196	5,191,955	3,124,149	2,165,014	21,881	478,995	183,443
1999	10,971,953	5,256,778	67,523	5,324,301	610,568	906,693	5,620,426	3,104,289	2,247,238	22,544	486,692	187,376
2000	11,788,062	5,592,601	65,783	5,658,384	646,447	1,018,547	6,030,484	3,379,310	2,378,268	23,790	495,514	192,200
2001	12,940,321	6,385,296	66,948	6,452,244	718,318	1,152,404	6,886,330	3,438,517	2,615,474	25,622	505,047	214,468
2002	13,604,954	6,868,317	61,774	6,930,091	767,907	1,267,241	7,429,425	3,375,457	2,800,072	26,358	516,153	220,863
2003	14,517,696	7,427,610	56,432	7,484,042	830,139	1,402,101	8,056,004	3,482,583	2,979,109	27,443	529,021	229,419
2004	15,926,792	8,046,828	62,359	8,109,187	911,750	1,589,305	8,786,742	3,884,713	3,255,337	29,158	546,232	239,566
2005	17,254,262	8,583,049	75,133	8,658,182	991,792	1,948,377	9,614,767	4,082,723	3,556,772	30,630	563,305	253,529
2006	18,726,642	9,191,135	66,221	9,257,356	1,086,550	2,186,277	10,357,083	4,510,780	3,858,779	32,338	579,087	263,121
2007	19,721,302	9,231,634	69,155	9,300,789	1,114,930	2,390,241	10,576,100	5,049,847	4,095,355	33,457	589,451	265,560
2008	19,990,705	8,903,733	62,652	8,966,385	1,109,375	2,467,273	10,324,283	5,087,083	4,579,339	33,830	590,912	256,904
2009	18,789,991	8,300,641	67,105	8,367,746	1,062,645	2,251,835	9,556,936	4,244,362	4,988,693	31,881	589,388	244,590
2010	19,714,254	8,613,124	66,614	8,679,738	1,084,782	2,231,923	9,826,879	4,482,987	5,404,388	33,385	590,515	241,576
2011	20,377,586	8,759,670	58,180	8,817,850	997,861	2,196,722	10,016,711	4,774,264	5,586,611	34,424	591,964	245,674
2012	21,040,386	9,239,490	71,314	9,310,804	1,051,010	2,333,144	10,592,938	4,831,906	5,615,542	35,347	595,246	249,416
2013	21,280,552	9,377,363	67,750	9,445,113	1,199,113	2,377,379	10,623,379	4,828,893	5,828,280	35,427	600,681	254,041
2014	22,615,330	9,821,016	64,864	9,885,880	1,257,227	2,464,722	11,093,375	5,325,936	6,196,019	37,111	609,394	261,499
2015	23,966,014	10,332,906	84,595	10,417,501	1,315,499	2,646,093	11,748,095	5,646,011	6,571,908	38,515	622,251	269,013
2016	25,398,457	10,894,466	75,861	10,970,327	1,400,638	2,959,900	12,529,589	5,994,625	6,874,243	39,882	636,843	278,052
2017	26,703,045	11,316,376	74,383	11,390,759	1,464,028	3,283,299	13,210,030	6,279,642	7,213,373	41,132	649,202	282,576
2018	28,609,503	28,509,737	99,766	12,242,384	1,568,240	3,431,933	14,106,077	6,849,253	7,654,173	43,467	658,186	296,288
2019	29,917,225	29,802,464	114,761	12,752,417	1,659,641	3,792,241	14,885,017	6,928,000	8,104,208	44,762	668,365	300,524

Personal Income and Employment by Area: Denver-Aurora-Lakewood, CO

(Thousands of dollars, except as noted.)

Year	Personal income, total	Earnings by place of work			Less: Contributions for government social insurance	Plus: Adjustment for residence	Equals: Net earnings by place of residence	Plus: Dividends, interest, and rent	Plus: Personal current transfer receipts	Per capita personal income (dollars)	Population (persons)	Total employment
		Nonfarm	Farm	Total								
1970	5,351,690	4,403,071	26,626	4,429,697	270,949	-109,466	4,049,282	932,879	369,529	4,756	1,125,162	567,136
1971	6,094,357	5,053,265	23,366	5,076,631	320,688	-131,908	4,624,035	1,042,520	427,802	5,241	1,162,772	597,433
1972	6,853,290	5,762,156	25,378	5,787,534	387,316	-157,136	5,243,082	1,139,174	471,034	5,684	1,205,736	638,174
1973	7,737,318	6,568,662	24,903	6,593,565	508,353	-191,006	5,894,206	1,294,503	548,609	6,200	1,247,871	688,969
1974	8,578,515	7,183,300	32,259	7,215,559	566,765	-208,214	6,440,580	1,498,373	639,562	6,793	1,262,795	697,029
1975	9,496,789	7,791,838	37,955	7,829,793	597,161	-223,994	7,008,638	1,672,380	815,771	7,387	1,285,565	696,348
1976	10,499,533	8,708,263	20,824	8,729,087	680,395	-253,921	7,794,771	1,810,821	893,941	7,975	1,316,528	721,876
1977	11,794,472	9,896,069	23,133	9,919,202	779,024	-298,472	8,841,706	2,012,975	939,791	8,778	1,343,631	763,237
1978	13,650,331	11,591,379	23,197	11,614,576	936,019	-357,878	10,320,679	2,313,138	1,016,514	9,819	1,390,221	821,600
1979	15,561,186	13,377,621	13,171	13,390,792	1,137,696	-454,110	11,798,986	2,628,492	1,133,708	10,866	1,432,057	870,090
1980	17,850,113	15,219,049	25,601	15,244,650	1,310,693	-561,062	13,372,895	3,178,064	1,299,154	12,218	1,460,960	901,316
1981	20,573,043	17,376,595	11,188	17,387,783	1,620,340	-624,457	15,142,986	3,907,120	1,522,937	13,734	1,497,985	939,574
1982	22,833,423	19,151,580	6,212	19,157,792	1,831,815	-650,748	16,675,229	4,438,741	1,719,453	14,815	1,541,261	968,403
1983	24,592,766	20,348,236	26,176	20,374,412	1,974,064	-642,135	17,758,213	4,945,791	1,888,762	15,578	1,578,689	980,047
1984	26,831,886	22,248,352	14,552	22,262,904	2,229,228	-642,135	19,391,541	5,453,548	1,986,797	16,768	1,600,224	1,034,156
1985	28,530,685	23,602,827	19,681	23,622,508	2,418,292	-672,310	20,531,906	5,920,363	2,078,416	17,578	1,623,121	1,054,857
1986	29,500,834	24,316,255	19,923	24,336,178	2,515,287	-662,969	21,157,922	6,110,522	2,232,390	18,018	1,637,259	1,047,201
1987	30,299,202	24,797,776	29,466	24,827,242	2,545,953	-614,437	21,666,852	6,212,106	2,420,244	18,424	1,644,586	1,033,523
1988	31,823,983	26,000,447	28,334	26,028,781	2,755,193	-606,011	22,667,577	6,597,220	2,559,186	19,425	1,638,280	1,053,281
1989	34,369,476	27,507,728	22,435	27,530,163	2,951,815	-592,139	23,986,209	7,529,017	2,854,250	20,965	1,639,407	1,065,789
1990	36,448,193	29,346,793	14,816	29,361,609	3,221,649	-583,435	25,556,525	7,824,039	3,067,629	21,983	1,658,024	1,084,091
1991	38,680,251	31,355,518	10,303	31,365,821	3,524,055	-567,243	27,274,523	8,020,708	3,385,020	22,722	1,702,298	1,108,061
1992	41,775,503	34,248,653	29,343	34,277,996	3,808,347	-593,442	29,876,207	8,103,078	3,796,218	23,723	1,760,945	1,129,013
1993	45,261,221	37,206,046	43,203	37,249,249	4,179,058	-586,670	32,483,521	8,696,584	4,081,116	24,878	1,819,298	1,174,291
1994	48,525,423	39,521,899	16,130	39,538,029	4,464,304	-495,940	34,577,785	9,619,306	4,328,332	26,048	1,862,948	1,223,582
1995	52,734,135	42,410,544	30,701	42,441,245	4,763,892	-484,530	37,192,823	10,696,646	4,844,666	27,600	1,910,680	1,259,599
1996	56,935,003	45,859,517	20,003	45,879,520	5,092,702	-533,473	40,253,345	11,656,008	5,025,650	29,055	1,959,552	1,304,522
1997	61,360,455	49,757,078	27,672	49,784,750	5,494,671	-566,941	43,723,138	12,573,481	5,063,836	30,494	2,012,227	1,362,615
1998	67,789,295	55,481,178	24,582	55,505,760	5,730,471	-321,911	49,453,378	13,234,639	5,101,278	32,890	2,061,091	1,421,735
1999	73,469,135	61,510,032	28,850	61,538,882	6,276,909	-523,419	54,738,554	13,341,457	5,389,124	34,679	2,118,555	1,465,962
2000	82,569,558	68,859,102	24,780	68,883,882	6,951,624	-58,794	61,873,464	15,003,291	5,692,803	38,033	2,170,977	1,523,011
2001	85,941,086	71,556,760	36,317	71,593,077	7,264,826	-212,803	64,115,448	15,510,784	6,314,854	38,734	2,218,759	1,518,724
2002	86,590,843	72,209,192	32,868	72,242,060	7,553,325	-468,830	64,219,905	15,270,590	7,100,348	38,200	2,266,781	1,521,825
2003	87,654,128	72,917,388	19,915	72,937,303	7,660,597	-577,409	64,699,297	15,509,104	7,445,727	38,363	2,284,876	1,510,967
2004	90,552,968	75,630,328	49,980	75,680,308	8,141,576	-543,554	66,995,178	15,837,388	7,720,402	39,289	2,304,818	1,533,283
2005	96,744,351	80,100,444	51,354	80,151,798	8,620,198	-599,239	70,932,361	17,549,865	8,262,125	41,472	2,332,749	1,571,107
2006	105,082,291	85,712,069	39,153	85,751,222	9,141,048	-744,474	75,865,700	20,312,933	8,903,658	44,260	2,374,194	1,607,028
2007	111,102,591	89,279,766	56,366	89,336,132	9,577,780	-728,483	79,029,869	22,536,551	9,536,171	45,935	2,418,686	1,664,565
2008	114,199,833	90,970,030	42,293	91,012,323	10,039,912	-856,210	80,116,201	22,740,251	11,343,381	46,348	2,463,971	1,683,596
2009	107,642,059	84,735,263	52,361	84,787,624	9,653,356	-545,651	74,588,617	20,401,179	12,652,263	42,895	2,509,417	1,643,661
2010	111,188,479	87,355,388	45,839	87,401,227	9,763,596	-1,000,570	76,637,061	20,169,193	14,382,225	43,528	2,554,399	1,637,488
2011	123,111,670	93,772,072	82,933	93,855,005	9,232,256	-858,639	83,764,110	24,527,296	14,820,264	47,357	2,599,629	1,672,982
2012	131,791,137	100,065,475	55,652	100,121,127	9,746,788	-999,438	89,374,901	27,557,118	14,859,118	49,805	2,646,151	1,715,507
2013	139,679,709	110,111,704	53,439	110,165,143	11,438,220	-934,965	97,791,958	26,452,556	15,435,195	51,804	2,696,308	1,776,525
2014	153,090,246	120,260,041	47,373	120,307,414	12,367,454	-936,666	107,003,294	29,531,100	16,555,852	55,673	2,749,827	1,843,957
2015	159,190,300	123,408,162	60,981	123,469,143	13,105,891	-1,323,513	109,039,739	32,279,199	17,871,362	56,708	2,807,211	1,916,987
2016	161,732,732	124,302,899	49,109	124,352,008	13,533,477	-1,527,918	109,290,613	33,881,527	18,560,592	56,712	2,851,848	1,981,426
2017	172,311,370	133,636,776	64,520	133,701,296	14,337,896	-1,541,445	117,821,955	35,478,732	19,010,683	59,660	2,888,227	2,021,098
2018	189,649,107	189,628,665	20,442	146,373,025	15,393,511	-1,676,918	129,302,596	39,784,509	20,562,002	64,690	2,931,665	2,087,752
2019	199,503,851	199,483,683	20,168	155,403,543	16,243,364	-1,471,431	137,688,748	40,350,852	21,464,251	67,236	2,967,239	2,142,948

Personal Income and Employment by Area: Des Moines-West Des Moines, IA

(Thousands of dollars, except as noted.)

Year	Personal income, total	Earnings by place of work			Less: Contributions for government social insurance	Plus: Adjustment for residence	Equals: Net earnings by place of residence	Plus: Dividends, interest, and rent	Plus: Personal current transfer receipts	Per capita personal income (dollars)	Population (persons)	Total employment
		Nonfarm	Farm	Total								
1970	1,603,428	1,319,167	51,333	1,370,500	96,859	-41,294	1,232,347	244,005	127,076	4,399	364,467	187,011
1971	1,728,848	1,425,631	40,576	1,466,207	108,259	-44,687	1,313,261	269,095	146,492	4,675	369,809	189,174
1972	1,914,734	1,578,983	58,300	1,637,283	126,616	-50,454	1,460,213	294,837	159,684	5,130	373,239	195,315
1973	2,163,689	1,751,335	112,447	1,863,782	162,979	-55,698	1,645,105	331,931	186,653	5,706	379,164	203,486
1974	2,366,096	1,954,339	64,587	2,018,926	189,351	-62,567	1,767,008	380,750	218,338	6,173	383,309	207,989
1975	2,651,254	2,154,655	73,588	2,228,243	203,688	-68,675	1,955,880	419,829	275,545	6,864	386,229	211,349
1976	2,913,692	2,387,712	65,152	2,452,864	226,760	-73,641	2,152,463	455,013	306,216	7,493	388,848	218,073
1977	3,212,935	2,686,172	31,862	2,718,034	252,881	-83,121	2,382,032	510,565	320,338	8,276	388,226	226,273
1978	3,615,525	2,991,778	80,810	3,072,588	291,525	-91,193	2,689,870	572,962	352,693	9,267	390,158	234,444
1979	4,038,288	3,388,301	49,838	3,438,139	344,884	-101,732	2,991,523	653,053	393,712	10,344	390,395	241,384
1980	4,371,573	3,576,978	15,720	3,592,698	361,661	-108,243	3,122,794	782,119	466,660	11,133	392,658	241,141
1981	4,841,822	3,822,173	53,719	3,875,892	411,680	-115,397	3,348,815	957,537	535,470	12,303	393,561	236,774
1982	5,152,143	3,949,405	32,174	3,981,579	427,680	-117,920	3,435,979	1,108,870	607,294	13,122	392,625	233,881
1983	5,397,524	4,196,729	-8,792	4,187,937	454,509	-126,404	3,607,024	1,140,814	649,686	13,712	393,623	236,788
1984	5,880,834	4,583,650	28,443	4,612,093	510,009	-137,872	3,964,212	1,256,609	660,013	14,893	394,875	244,988
1985	6,164,620	4,820,407	41,488	4,861,895	544,317	-146,572	4,171,006	1,292,471	701,143	15,567	395,994	249,172
1986	6,445,693	5,073,675	59,709	5,133,384	586,402	-156,769	4,390,213	1,328,168	727,312	16,236	397,004	252,303
1987	6,840,440	5,467,207	79,243	5,546,450	629,331	-171,959	4,745,160	1,357,226	738,054	17,101	399,998	259,847
1988	7,390,708	6,023,074	39,021	6,062,095	711,416	-193,561	5,157,118	1,454,443	779,147	18,256	404,844	270,261
1989	8,040,434	6,483,734	93,387	6,577,121	762,743	-208,431	5,605,947	1,611,329	823,158	19,575	410,759	279,484
1990	8,678,919	6,982,320	72,630	7,054,950	847,489	-230,319	5,977,142	1,797,621	904,156	20,760	418,062	290,422
1991	8,965,868	7,350,899	55,449	7,406,348	899,799	-240,933	6,265,616	1,718,744	981,508	21,128	424,368	295,382
1992	9,599,392	7,923,998	87,279	8,011,277	964,092	-262,604	6,784,581	1,750,979	1,063,832	22,220	432,014	300,284
1993	9,975,691	8,327,881	17,551	8,345,432	1,014,808	-274,985	7,055,639	1,802,789	1,117,263	22,718	439,105	305,489
1994	10,677,069	8,864,871	97,543	8,962,414	1,094,395	-289,750	7,578,269	1,938,233	1,160,567	24,011	444,671	313,372
1995	11,391,115	9,424,764	56,275	9,481,039	1,161,305	-309,984	8,009,750	2,154,902	1,226,463	25,237	451,372	326,428
1996	12,178,313	9,978,493	132,079	10,110,572	1,190,682	-327,656	8,592,234	2,286,510	1,299,569	26,631	457,294	333,775
1997	12,887,104	10,611,962	107,054	10,719,016	1,290,994	-349,871	9,078,151	2,478,993	1,329,960	27,878	462,263	338,246
1998	13,958,681	11,522,600	69,447	11,592,047	1,379,639	-379,623	9,832,785	2,743,783	1,382,113	29,815	468,172	346,460
1999	14,648,422	12,393,315	41,269	12,434,584	1,477,429	-408,257	10,548,898	2,674,466	1,425,058	30,779	475,924	353,113
2000	15,576,448	13,047,772	59,691	13,107,463	1,533,626	-423,865	11,149,972	2,886,569	1,539,907	32,233	483,243	358,088
2001	16,319,381	13,768,386	45,554	13,813,940	1,612,765	-446,051	11,755,124	2,878,721	1,685,536	33,321	489,761	360,712
2002	16,853,132	14,275,003	57,664	14,332,667	1,675,760	-464,667	12,192,240	2,805,280	1,855,612	33,959	496,276	359,878
2003	17,439,634	14,950,715	67,999	15,018,714	1,768,012	-480,280	12,770,422	2,814,644	1,854,568	34,643	503,406	362,214
2004	18,911,879	16,087,248	175,286	16,262,534	1,877,656	-492,121	13,892,757	3,105,318	1,913,804	36,991	511,257	372,924
2005	19,900,914	16,953,998	135,674	17,089,672	1,974,927	-524,948	14,589,797	3,242,896	2,068,221	38,155	521,578	381,843
2006	21,452,461	17,986,284	106,939	18,093,223	2,080,897	-523,653	15,488,673	3,674,293	2,289,495	40,268	532,738	393,169
2007	22,659,633	18,804,882	171,924	18,976,806	2,201,295	-616,647	16,158,864	4,035,420	2,465,349	41,685	543,590	404,565
2008	23,741,761	19,487,622	201,135	19,688,757	2,303,813	-659,600	16,725,344	4,101,723	2,914,694	42,883	553,644	407,824
2009	23,308,551	19,223,131	146,707	19,369,838	2,303,812	-559,223	16,506,803	3,668,237	3,133,511	41,430	562,601	403,038
2010	24,316,896	19,899,923	94,542	19,994,465	2,373,851	-499,561	17,121,053	3,766,574	3,429,269	42,515	571,967	401,493
2011	25,457,717	20,222,082	239,210	20,461,292	2,195,413	-589,878	17,676,001	4,270,460	3,511,256	43,820	580,961	407,644
2012	27,273,335	21,574,896	192,794	21,767,690	2,281,448	-639,783	18,846,459	4,886,979	3,539,897	46,245	589,758	415,412
2013	27,679,084	22,338,082	220,680	22,558,762	2,665,840	-529,412	19,363,510	4,655,998	3,659,576	46,104	600,366	424,795
2014	29,647,889	23,872,152	112,726	23,984,878	2,776,411	-537,106	20,671,361	5,105,559	3,870,969	48,446	611,977	434,989
2015	31,316,959	24,929,402	78,403	25,007,805	2,873,015	-503,548	21,631,242	5,574,084	4,111,633	50,303	622,566	442,694
2016	32,514,557	26,033,115	24,805	26,057,920	3,044,843	-576,408	22,436,669	5,833,922	4,243,966	51,225	634,740	453,321
2017	33,781,235	27,253,405	3,870	27,257,275	3,184,541	-598,165	23,474,569	6,087,337	4,219,329	52,300	645,911	460,258
2018	37,229,450	37,083,602	145,848	28,847,852	3,404,365	-248,191	25,195,296	6,950,657	5,083,497	53,884	690,915	484,420
2019	38,488,124	38,287,371	200,753	29,855,844	3,522,832	-244,946	26,088,066	6,952,348	5,447,710	55,039	699,292	491,471

Personal Income and Employment by Area: Detroit-Warren-Dearborn, MI

(Thousands of dollars, except as noted.)

Year	Personal income, total	Earnings by place of work			Less: Contributions for government social insurance	Plus: Adjustment for residence	Equals: Net earnings by place of residence	Plus: Dividends, interest, and rent	Plus: Personal current transfer receipts	Per capita personal income (dollars)	Population (persons)	Total employment
		Nonfarm	Farm	Total								
1970	20,473,778	17,605,595	34,095	17,639,690	1,256,732	-159,525	16,223,433	2,652,970	1,597,375	4,612	4,439,498	1,819,813
1971	22,059,058	18,836,787	31,718	18,868,505	1,384,176	-163,954	17,320,375	2,817,309	1,921,374	4,946	4,459,793	1,803,088
1972	24,440,594	21,041,099	41,104	21,082,203	1,647,001	-194,485	19,240,717	3,002,171	2,197,706	5,488	4,453,517	1,854,501
1973	27,254,747	23,795,186	46,739	23,841,925	2,162,977	-205,465	21,473,483	3,271,605	2,509,659	6,144	4,435,796	1,939,903
1974	28,883,744	24,572,344	46,143	24,618,487	2,307,355	-272,983	22,038,149	3,724,458	3,121,137	6,532	4,422,090	1,926,974
1975	30,323,450	24,691,187	48,695	24,739,882	2,257,459	-276,919	22,205,504	4,022,648	4,095,298	6,900	4,394,458	1,808,270
1976	33,800,030	28,193,834	46,030	28,239,864	2,634,598	-247,928	25,357,338	4,297,514	4,145,178	7,750	4,361,574	1,876,295
1977	38,051,495	32,337,048	54,020	32,391,068	3,025,529	-259,649	29,105,890	4,714,191	4,231,414	8,744	4,351,973	1,960,763
1978	42,389,221	36,367,129	37,866	36,404,995	3,511,594	-272,371	32,621,030	5,251,067	4,517,124	9,730	4,356,619	2,043,005
1979	46,120,599	39,215,984	42,807	39,258,791	3,917,301	-295,693	35,045,797	5,840,040	5,234,762	10,586	4,356,811	2,045,908
1980	48,824,209	39,109,989	42,303	39,152,292	3,863,007	-295,440	34,993,845	6,825,800	7,004,564	11,250	4,339,778	1,921,891
1981	51,395,115	40,433,542	42,368	40,475,910	4,317,843	-219,346	35,938,721	8,154,598	7,301,796	12,020	4,275,732	1,876,138
1982	52,922,315	40,006,836	38,997	40,045,833	4,330,097	-214,096	35,501,640	9,336,076	8,084,599	12,532	4,223,098	1,789,482
1983	56,201,073	42,406,862	28,272	42,435,134	4,666,625	-160,427	37,608,082	10,009,789	8,583,202	13,429	4,185,050	1,798,974
1984	62,456,215	47,915,976	43,472	47,959,448	5,454,814	-172,234	42,332,400	11,467,499	8,656,316	14,932	4,182,763	1,897,635
1985	68,591,338	53,790,970	47,716	53,838,686	6,254,816	-203,195	47,380,675	12,354,345	8,856,318	16,347	4,195,986	2,012,186
1986	73,127,376	57,955,880	32,547	57,988,427	6,757,969	-269,732	50,960,726	12,906,970	9,259,680	17,330	4,219,771	2,067,378
1987	75,541,248	60,063,155	43,870	60,107,025	6,922,493	-322,849	52,861,683	13,235,783	9,443,782	17,810	4,241,494	2,118,647
1988	80,991,059	64,885,558	43,872	64,929,430	7,645,413	-370,301	56,913,716	14,245,785	9,831,558	19,128	4,234,083	2,168,474
1989	86,947,955	68,592,022	58,979	68,651,001	8,080,678	-361,934	60,208,389	16,187,839	10,551,727	20,517	4,237,904	2,227,089
1990	90,544,457	71,050,389	53,028	71,103,417	8,530,456	-373,478	62,199,483	16,984,466	11,360,508	21,300	4,250,986	2,244,909
1991	91,197,557	71,286,205	52,748	71,338,953	8,683,405	-387,980	62,267,568	16,403,285	12,526,704	21,280	4,285,663	2,181,991
1992	96,314,198	76,355,416	50,528	76,405,944	9,228,885	-555,608	66,621,451	16,432,536	13,260,211	22,296	4,319,806	2,182,305
1993	101,454,753	80,702,199	49,252	80,751,451	9,788,207	-775,673	70,187,571	17,097,700	14,169,482	23,351	4,344,712	2,209,546
1994	109,115,048	86,839,370	47,119	86,886,489	10,725,780	-938,142	75,222,567	19,607,988	14,284,493	24,995	4,365,423	2,279,342
1995	115,768,562	92,219,112	50,486	92,269,598	11,339,603	-1,317,006	79,612,989	21,095,523	15,060,050	26,313	4,399,746	2,339,032
1996	121,857,583	96,737,305	44,670	96,781,975	11,578,418	-1,524,152	83,679,405	22,392,749	15,785,429	27,488	4,433,102	2,391,801
1997	128,129,940	101,384,059	46,255	101,430,314	12,118,956	-1,579,550	87,731,808	23,518,061	16,880,071	28,855	4,440,400	2,425,583
1998	136,276,446	109,829,810	45,202	109,875,012	12,817,546	-1,894,327	95,163,139	24,498,924	16,614,383	30,681	4,441,717	2,463,358
1999	142,927,741	116,860,796	55,365	116,916,161	13,571,475	-1,982,089	101,362,597	23,981,631	17,583,513	32,136	4,447,649	2,511,959
2000	154,098,864	126,766,959	36,107	126,803,066	14,321,259	-2,449,788	110,032,019	26,090,098	17,976,747	34,586	4,455,503	2,580,828
2001	155,389,421	127,540,579	32,098	127,572,677	14,283,779	-2,502,466	110,786,432	24,733,929	19,869,060	34,826	4,461,855	2,536,678
2002	153,572,877	125,716,370	33,032	125,749,402	14,271,465	-2,402,026	109,075,911	24,020,580	20,476,386	34,461	4,456,433	2,500,131
2003	156,570,013	127,849,091	40,462	127,889,553	14,474,485	-2,674,803	110,740,265	24,462,135	21,367,613	35,158	4,453,371	2,486,062
2004	159,485,373	130,460,339	64,302	130,524,641	14,917,357	-2,716,213	112,891,071	24,401,099	22,193,203	35,873	4,445,887	2,487,090
2005	162,731,592	132,083,879	64,578	132,148,457	15,358,581	-3,039,316	113,750,560	25,372,156	23,608,876	36,725	4,431,048	2,503,800
2006	164,700,292	131,045,041	78,843	131,123,884	15,478,851	-2,804,443	112,840,590	26,849,048	25,010,654	37,350	4,409,697	2,474,998
2007	169,060,614	131,778,100	66,791	131,844,891	15,637,977	-2,791,512	113,415,402	28,354,011	27,291,201	38,624	4,377,116	2,470,996
2008	169,218,238	128,760,349	71,015	128,831,364	15,513,105	-3,013,310	110,304,949	27,887,960	31,025,329	38,995	4,339,504	2,413,765
2009	158,591,604	115,922,844	49,700	115,972,544	14,141,218	-1,878,189	99,953,137	23,872,460	34,766,007	36,781	4,311,728	2,255,835
2010	162,617,739	119,038,448	60,733	119,099,181	14,283,013	-2,418,748	102,397,420	23,231,433	36,988,886	37,895	4,291,287	2,258,061
2011	174,353,352	126,667,778	108,849	126,776,627	13,404,715	-2,111,404	111,260,508	26,230,713	36,862,131	40,655	4,288,618	2,329,607
2012	182,336,969	133,549,883	95,974	133,645,857	14,022,911	-2,433,483	117,189,463	28,486,393	36,661,113	42,447	4,295,646	2,372,902
2013	183,655,689	136,827,229	85,152	136,912,381	16,308,667	-2,210,565	118,393,149	28,497,330	36,765,210	42,725	4,298,541	2,415,202
2014	193,504,001	142,702,290	59,658	142,761,948	16,834,688	-2,551,921	123,375,339	31,985,383	38,143,279	44,966	4,303,366	2,458,072
2015	205,643,798	150,613,834	61,292	150,675,126	17,613,230	-2,558,218	130,503,678	34,788,703	40,351,417	47,799	4,302,282	2,508,178
2016	211,758,002	155,714,080	54,626	155,768,706	18,108,766	-2,919,715	134,740,225	35,722,109	41,295,668	49,179	4,305,869	2,547,231
2017	219,371,807	162,826,062	21,267	162,847,329	18,874,343	-3,232,755	140,740,231	37,143,978	41,487,598	50,863	4,313,002	2,585,962
2018	227,218,784	227,158,680	60,104	167,548,960	19,704,644	-3,443,349	144,400,967	40,154,064	42,663,753	52,572	4,322,084	2,627,875
2019	234,001,030	233,929,960	71,070	171,912,593	20,035,346	-3,259,078	148,618,169	40,417,678	44,965,183	54,172	4,319,629	2,659,945

Personal Income and Employment by Area: Dothan, AL

(Thousands of dollars, except as noted.)

Year	Personal income, total	Earnings by place of work			Less: Contributions for government social insurance	Plus: Adjustment for residence	Equals: Net earnings by place of residence	Plus: Dividends, interest, and rent	Plus: Personal current transfer receipts	Per capita personal income (dollars)	Population (persons)	Total employment
		Nonfarm	Farm	Total								
1970	278,801	176,422	18,077	194,499	13,404	33,743	214,838	34,597	29,366	3,026	92,122	41,593
1971	309,458	202,576	18,535	221,111	15,620	30,304	235,795	39,747	33,916	3,287	94,147	43,039
1972	349,141	236,764	26,184	262,948	19,290	24,201	267,859	43,535	37,747	3,567	97,881	45,497
1973	427,476	299,282	42,225	341,507	28,113	18,936	332,330	51,235	43,911	4,257	100,409	49,519
1974	477,002	343,152	34,200	377,352	33,309	18,523	362,566	61,501	52,935	4,526	105,391	51,163
1975	519,787	350,060	40,273	390,333	33,496	21,286	378,123	71,999	69,665	4,811	108,046	49,593
1976	598,322	425,514	38,312	463,826	41,836	21,820	443,810	78,332	76,180	5,450	109,777	51,727
1977	642,890	473,313	24,878	498,191	46,582	22,871	474,480	87,443	80,967	5,794	110,966	53,046
1978	728,189	537,027	33,225	570,252	53,830	22,535	538,957	100,998	88,234	6,457	112,772	54,447
1979	792,719	572,646	31,322	603,968	59,219	30,298	575,047	114,813	102,859	6,976	113,631	54,259
1980	870,374	655,750	-14,240	641,510	68,002	32,645	606,153	143,581	120,640	7,601	114,505	55,050
1981	1,038,673	691,486	44,870	736,356	77,054	64,388	723,690	176,978	138,005	8,987	115,576	54,328
1982	1,064,555	700,654	24,051	724,705	79,005	73,451	719,151	192,579	152,825	9,172	116,060	52,319
1983	1,121,096	749,082	9,441	758,523	84,617	76,092	749,998	204,776	166,322	9,667	115,974	52,832
1984	1,267,023	820,164	55,594	875,758	94,794	78,841	859,805	231,273	175,945	10,876	116,501	54,538
1985	1,329,945	883,993	28,328	912,321	102,348	81,062	891,035	249,691	189,219	11,336	117,318	55,398
1986	1,416,153	956,258	22,117	978,375	109,452	82,499	951,422	265,170	199,561	12,039	117,628	56,956
1987	1,517,449	1,037,794	35,133	1,072,927	117,653	82,672	1,037,946	271,967	207,536	12,754	118,980	59,215
1988	1,656,851	1,127,224	59,962	1,187,186	131,995	80,068	1,135,259	298,867	222,725	13,888	119,302	61,390
1989	1,839,932	1,234,438	75,457	1,309,895	144,223	71,898	1,237,570	351,214	251,148	15,403	119,455	64,645
1990	1,887,410	1,319,482	53,615	1,373,097	155,000	29,317	1,247,414	372,117	267,879	15,621	120,826	66,534
1991	1,983,201	1,376,551	82,868	1,459,419	163,317	19,532	1,315,634	378,193	289,374	16,188	122,507	67,078
1992	2,155,078	1,506,764	76,357	1,583,121	176,485	35,014	1,441,650	384,526	328,902	17,431	123,636	68,384
1993	2,195,197	1,555,054	62,167	1,617,221	184,224	23,562	1,456,559	393,337	345,301	17,565	124,976	69,447
1994	2,328,710	1,623,796	79,605	1,703,401	194,602	20,669	1,529,468	428,959	370,283	18,624	125,036	69,704
1995	2,477,812	1,718,817	76,707	1,795,524	207,125	19,157	1,607,556	466,407	403,849	19,685	125,872	71,949
1996	2,547,319	1,777,315	63,168	1,840,483	211,223	11,889	1,641,149	476,995	429,175	20,048	127,060	72,959
1997	2,664,477	1,855,721	46,335	1,902,056	220,356	26,823	1,708,523	505,529	450,425	20,806	128,062	74,932
1998	2,850,876	1,983,475	55,439	2,038,914	231,918	41,493	1,848,489	549,271	453,116	22,112	128,927	75,252
1999	2,977,198	2,045,876	78,733	2,124,609	239,342	64,556	1,949,823	549,218	478,157	22,907	129,970	75,357
2000	3,065,877	2,103,806	38,648	2,142,454	247,014	70,657	1,966,097	588,748	511,032	23,399	131,024	75,270
2001	3,329,585	2,212,312	94,751	2,307,063	256,021	79,644	2,130,686	619,152	579,747	25,337	131,413	74,332
2002	3,433,007	2,283,023	94,598	2,377,621	264,630	102,809	2,215,800	594,121	623,086	26,014	131,967	73,972
2003	3,551,492	2,369,435	85,777	2,455,212	275,618	118,749	2,298,343	586,319	666,830	26,586	133,586	74,707
2004	3,814,308	2,523,057	85,951	2,609,008	292,749	132,455	2,448,714	638,117	727,477	28,242	135,057	77,191
2005	4,061,850	2,660,101	89,363	2,749,464	308,847	148,281	2,588,898	690,009	782,943	29,726	136,643	78,855
2006	4,311,827	2,812,336	57,703	2,870,039	329,989	195,293	2,735,343	724,339	852,145	31,005	139,070	80,328
2007	4,578,334	2,879,297	55,975	2,935,272	342,318	226,038	2,818,992	834,586	924,756	32,434	141,157	82,333
2008	4,691,707	2,830,732	57,850	2,888,582	344,538	247,750	2,791,794	873,576	1,026,337	32,819	142,958	80,560
2009	4,677,487	2,770,934	38,924	2,809,858	338,722	304,914	2,776,050	785,850	1,115,587	32,393	144,396	77,260
2010	4,940,194	2,840,735	35,615	2,876,350	349,017	343,739	2,871,072	842,963	1,226,159	33,867	145,870	76,393
2011	5,102,929	2,887,104	30,987	2,918,091	316,458	349,892	2,951,525	892,237	1,259,167	34,808	146,604	76,925
2012	5,169,750	2,949,305	25,346	2,974,651	320,460	364,774	3,018,965	878,384	1,272,401	35,062	147,447	76,750
2013	5,196,761	3,027,157	68,844	3,096,001	370,058	309,668	3,035,611	859,258	1,301,892	35,247	147,439	76,940
2014	5,329,483	3,091,718	27,440	3,119,158	376,018	292,475	3,035,615	914,200	1,379,668	36,052	147,826	77,307
2015	5,501,775	3,193,427	26,244	3,219,671	388,653	283,995	3,115,013	950,361	1,436,401	37,177	147,990	78,018
2016	5,624,307	3,257,329	23,368	3,280,697	395,218	295,953	3,181,432	978,581	1,464,294	38,058	147,781	77,808
2017	5,839,310	3,378,078	43,769	3,421,847	410,853	292,942	3,303,936	1,018,328	1,517,046	39,478	147,914	78,838
2018	6,191,069	6,108,245	82,824	3,601,446	436,947	304,079	3,468,578	1,114,168	1,608,323	41,761	148,249	79,741
2019	6,443,785	6,359,320	84,465	3,755,617	452,059	310,049	3,613,607	1,129,221	1,700,957	43,143	149,358	81,396

Personal Income and Employment by Area: Dover, DE

(Thousands of dollars, except as noted.)

Year	Personal income, total	Earnings by place of work			Less: Contributions for government social insurance	Plus: Adjustment for residence	Equals: Net earnings by place of residence	Plus: Dividends, interest, and rent	Plus: Personal current transfer receipts	Per capita personal income (dollars)	Population (persons)	Total employment
		Nonfarm	Farm	Total								
1970	329,298	278,854	9,441	288,295	18,575	-15,601	254,119	53,737	21,442	3,985	82,633	42,223
1971	366,988	310,011	9,377	319,388	21,322	-15,923	282,143	59,234	25,611	4,236	86,628	43,110
1972	408,579	343,571	11,098	354,669	24,323	-15,582	314,764	65,369	28,446	4,565	89,512	45,268
1973	456,659	370,705	24,117	394,822	29,554	-14,087	351,181	72,425	33,053	5,058	90,286	46,076
1974	510,034	406,440	29,191	435,631	33,776	-14,561	387,294	82,590	40,150	5,603	91,026	45,692
1975	562,531	442,630	21,485	464,115	37,052	-14,248	412,815	92,126	57,590	6,080	92,521	44,751
1976	607,527	477,290	20,993	498,283	41,024	-12,981	444,278	100,515	62,734	6,431	94,465	44,883
1977	649,026	515,906	11,058	526,964	43,991	-13,072	469,901	111,225	67,900	6,742	96,264	45,851
1978	716,082	553,939	18,542	572,481	48,484	-7,114	516,883	125,887	73,312	7,288	98,251	45,902
1979	771,030	587,704	14,983	602,687	53,413	-2,193	547,081	139,724	84,225	7,775	99,166	46,424
1980	842,712	631,423	-63	631,360	58,556	4,109	576,913	165,643	100,156	8,575	98,280	46,321
1981	949,603	696,007	10,271	706,278	69,248	7,624	644,654	191,535	113,414	9,659	98,317	46,451
1982	1,026,420	747,928	9,497	757,425	74,883	11,834	694,376	210,139	121,905	10,344	99,225	47,096
1983	1,090,616	785,065	10,206	795,271	79,384	20,652	736,539	222,848	131,229	10,803	100,953	47,036
1984	1,193,297	859,394	15,794	875,188	87,901	24,726	812,013	245,469	135,815	11,784	101,261	48,525
1985	1,286,780	931,003	12,394	943,397	95,516	31,182	879,063	263,717	144,000	12,515	102,818	51,069
1986	1,388,580	1,010,584	12,461	1,023,045	105,128	32,184	950,101	283,927	154,552	13,261	104,713	52,893
1987	1,495,350	1,093,487	9,590	1,103,077	112,217	38,754	1,029,614	304,024	161,712	14,072	106,263	54,198
1988	1,638,237	1,185,429	26,827	1,212,256	128,408	45,280	1,129,128	330,319	178,790	15,316	106,965	55,677
1989	1,799,718	1,291,494	25,551	1,317,045	140,250	48,822	1,225,617	379,140	194,961	16,503	109,052	57,099
1990	1,913,129	1,403,891	21,541	1,425,432	150,359	50,540	1,325,613	374,591	212,925	17,137	111,638	58,224
1991	2,032,361	1,467,999	24,819	1,492,818	159,055	42,593	1,376,356	407,548	248,457	17,783	114,288	59,918
1992	2,143,911	1,559,597	28,902	1,588,499	168,611	33,120	1,453,008	414,969	275,934	18,533	115,682	61,604
1993	2,209,117	1,625,135	20,250	1,645,385	177,808	22,458	1,490,035	419,506	299,576	18,723	117,987	62,713
1994	2,313,151	1,709,259	24,506	1,733,765	188,586	14,551	1,559,730	452,778	300,643	19,432	119,039	63,944
1995	2,466,683	1,821,555	13,066	1,834,621	202,186	256	1,632,691	492,776	341,216	20,434	120,715	65,999
1996	2,644,216	1,914,314	25,237	1,939,551	209,957	-5,152	1,724,442	530,416	389,358	21,773	121,447	67,066
1997	2,705,802	1,941,933	15,958	1,957,891	211,276	6,399	1,753,014	554,981	397,807	22,103	122,419	66,499
1998	2,944,272	2,136,507	25,618	2,162,125	224,793	3,728	1,941,060	570,084	433,128	23,733	124,056	67,593
1999	3,159,582	2,357,061	25,467	2,382,528	236,636	-1,564	2,144,328	575,150	440,104	25,154	125,611	70,155
2000	3,462,370	2,602,664	30,733	2,633,397	245,923	-3,311	2,384,163	600,913	477,294	27,214	127,229	71,832
2001	3,485,763	2,577,598	33,580	2,611,178	247,663	-7,454	2,356,061	609,568	520,134	26,974	129,228	72,004
2002	3,696,742	2,814,479	12,730	2,827,209	284,854	-30,570	2,511,785	618,366	566,591	28,043	131,824	73,663
2003	3,944,688	2,971,093	24,193	2,995,286	299,736	-25,412	2,670,138	654,998	619,552	29,306	134,605	75,124
2004	4,285,749	3,249,185	45,623	3,294,808	328,424	-33,726	2,932,658	675,974	677,117	30,757	139,342	78,240
2005	4,492,907	3,383,451	52,936	3,436,387	350,949	-29,524	3,055,914	688,110	748,883	31,075	144,585	81,729
2006	4,855,663	3,585,733	46,039	3,631,772	374,340	27,006	3,284,438	750,107	821,118	32,435	149,704	83,361
2007	5,107,946	3,664,695	52,305	3,717,000	394,204	34,468	3,357,264	846,412	904,270	33,175	153,969	84,923
2008	5,234,526	3,558,297	48,967	3,607,264	405,184	64,867	3,266,947	909,180	1,058,399	33,146	157,925	84,602
2009	5,458,585	3,630,143	72,586	3,702,729	405,581	120,123	3,417,271	876,940	1,164,374	34,099	160,081	81,628
2010	5,513,788	3,672,197	67,701	3,739,898	407,573	32,469	3,364,794	881,410	1,267,584	33,833	162,973	81,669
2011	5,835,406	3,802,343	79,698	3,882,041	370,879	28,946	3,540,108	959,357	1,335,941	35,334	165,149	83,855
2012	5,967,753	3,869,478	97,258	3,966,736	391,044	15,796	3,591,488	1,001,417	1,374,848	35,641	167,442	84,764
2013	6,126,335	3,953,878	125,376	4,079,254	454,133	47,032	3,672,153	1,006,696	1,447,486	36,218	169,150	86,586
2014	6,369,739	4,096,134	132,843	4,228,977	479,099	9,631	3,759,509	1,064,920	1,545,310	37,106	171,664	87,649
2015	6,546,305	4,168,356	99,255	4,267,611	490,154	30,933	3,808,390	1,115,198	1,622,717	37,767	173,332	88,491
2016	6,805,126	4,350,252	100,652	4,450,904	503,746	22,350	3,969,508	1,126,324	1,709,294	38,941	174,754	90,458
2017	7,126,715	4,458,285	110,329	4,568,614	518,860	90,631	4,140,385	1,175,978	1,810,352	40,304	176,824	91,545
2018	7,434,085	7,305,048	129,037	4,840,017	546,093	25,780	4,319,704	1,199,539	1,914,842	41,638	178,540	94,151
2019	7,791,288	7,665,614	125,674	5,099,363	576,276	30,626	4,553,713	1,223,161	2,014,414	43,097	180,786	95,847

Personal Income and Employment by Area: Dubuque, IA

(Thousands of dollars, except as noted.)

Year	Personal income, total	Earnings by place of work			Less: Contributions for government social insurance	Plus: Adjustment for residence	Equals: Net earnings by place of residence	Plus: Dividends, interest, and rent	Plus: Personal current transfer receipts	Per capita personal income (dollars)	Population (persons)	Total employment
		Nonfarm	Farm	Total								
1970	337,786	307,536	17,404	324,940	23,291	-44,302	257,347	53,394	27,045	3,721	90,790	43,244
1971	359,129	331,103	14,793	345,896	26,066	-49,402	270,428	57,715	30,986	3,915	91,739	42,981
1972	395,076	371,627	15,811	387,438	30,892	-57,756	298,790	62,315	33,971	4,260	92,731	44,134
1973	447,182	422,366	22,897	445,263	40,709	-67,567	336,987	70,607	39,588	4,772	93,700	47,239
1974	496,919	486,881	13,798	500,679	48,829	-83,056	368,794	81,629	46,496	5,299	93,779	48,892
1975	546,504	516,800	20,357	537,157	50,614	-88,482	398,061	88,916	59,527	5,774	94,655	48,652
1976	595,507	573,928	13,839	587,767	57,048	-99,337	431,382	97,669	66,456	6,223	95,687	49,568
1977	672,610	665,079	12,712	677,791	65,783	-121,728	490,280	111,401	70,929	7,135	94,270	51,642
1978	748,022	731,010	27,794	758,804	74,826	-137,240	546,738	123,429	77,855	7,982	93,716	52,499
1979	807,693	808,131	15,871	824,002	85,847	-156,094	582,061	138,694	86,938	8,645	93,425	53,560
1980	856,714	846,784	-3,233	843,551	89,565	-169,579	584,407	167,324	104,983	9,143	93,701	52,948
1981	944,822	862,351	16,276	878,627	96,839	-161,420	620,368	205,592	118,862	10,126	93,307	50,728
1982	955,294	794,332	5,392	799,724	90,003	-131,970	577,751	234,822	142,721	10,385	91,992	47,472
1983	981,524	817,102	-12,104	804,998	92,792	-127,843	584,363	245,724	151,437	10,870	90,296	47,693
1984	1,104,426	898,295	30,820	929,115	105,242	-138,338	685,535	269,773	149,118	12,324	89,616	49,513
1985	1,144,351	932,711	27,501	960,212	110,615	-139,541	710,056	280,084	154,211	12,844	89,096	49,643
1986	1,170,040	924,084	38,284	962,368	111,192	-127,164	724,012	288,907	157,121	13,331	87,771	49,358
1987	1,265,517	1,040,545	46,379	1,086,924	123,784	-144,570	818,570	288,527	158,420	14,525	87,125	51,309
1988	1,304,156	1,082,791	29,898	1,112,689	132,632	-144,506	835,551	302,703	165,902	14,930	87,351	52,579
1989	1,405,943	1,130,826	50,926	1,181,752	137,134	-144,691	899,927	326,610	179,406	16,227	86,644	53,836
1990	1,467,082	1,189,145	49,245	1,238,390	148,355	-151,890	938,145	334,986	193,951	16,968	86,462	55,086
1991	1,514,201	1,245,508	35,645	1,281,153	156,991	-156,853	967,309	339,980	206,912	17,407	86,988	56,048
1992	1,642,851	1,353,425	55,414	1,408,839	169,294	-169,792	1,069,753	349,670	223,428	18,739	87,672	56,773
1993	1,695,548	1,418,303	36,742	1,455,045	178,349	-171,571	1,105,125	354,321	236,102	19,211	88,261	57,566
1994	1,818,686	1,543,263	48,326	1,591,589	196,176	-182,267	1,213,146	360,996	244,544	20,514	88,654	58,805
1995	1,923,481	1,634,454	29,762	1,664,216	207,539	-195,227	1,261,450	404,483	257,548	21,627	88,938	60,614
1996	2,007,121	1,622,889	58,676	1,681,565	198,749	-197,429	1,285,387	444,763	276,971	22,527	89,097	60,234
1997	2,081,386	1,703,508	48,299	1,751,807	214,751	-209,668	1,327,388	469,013	284,985	23,387	88,996	61,363
1998	2,219,058	1,779,884	41,126	1,821,010	223,409	-217,955	1,379,646	534,500	304,912	24,996	88,775	61,304
1999	2,233,420	1,829,015	29,371	1,858,386	227,345	-218,595	1,412,446	505,506	315,468	25,113	88,934	61,845
2000	2,366,650	1,896,204	48,391	1,944,595	232,991	-225,429	1,486,175	546,172	334,303	26,532	89,201	62,242
2001	2,408,823	1,900,513	43,056	1,943,569	231,545	-216,138	1,495,886	549,051	363,886	27,086	88,932	61,990
2002	2,468,754	1,969,498	31,739	2,001,237	239,481	-212,718	1,549,038	524,813	394,903	27,698	89,132	61,804
2003	2,540,645	2,064,672	35,637	2,100,309	254,800	-217,498	1,628,011	515,555	397,079	28,226	90,012	62,344
2004	2,623,489	2,142,236	57,173	2,199,409	268,985	-242,459	1,687,965	522,715	412,809	29,001	90,462	63,647
2005	2,716,339	2,233,959	45,539	2,279,498	283,573	-252,747	1,743,178	535,472	437,689	29,926	90,769	65,285
2006	2,972,328	2,389,117	30,253	2,419,370	296,355	-258,143	1,864,872	619,203	488,253	32,571	91,258	67,149
2007	3,238,318	2,523,323	42,455	2,565,778	305,928	-257,905	2,001,945	704,851	531,522	35,149	92,130	67,770
2008	3,381,529	2,608,543	30,877	2,639,420	320,286	-251,745	2,067,389	715,443	598,697	36,550	92,519	67,401
2009	3,305,377	2,589,579	6,461	2,596,040	321,010	-247,823	2,027,207	663,086	615,084	35,562	92,948	66,382
2010	3,467,167	2,770,242	24,724	2,794,966	349,020	-282,320	2,163,626	644,933	658,608	36,912	93,930	67,896
2011	3,700,440	2,907,201	60,532	2,967,733	331,794	-317,660	2,318,279	719,835	662,326	39,117	94,599	69,906
2012	3,906,499	3,126,009	69,108	3,195,117	346,497	-375,643	2,472,977	771,383	662,139	41,066	95,128	71,133
2013	3,945,678	3,158,797	85,252	3,244,049	392,217	-364,984	2,486,848	765,464	693,366	41,149	95,888	71,687
2014	4,128,797	3,289,991	62,594	3,352,585	397,880	-387,596	2,567,109	836,711	724,977	42,826	96,408	72,537
2015	4,315,713	3,358,795	90,315	3,449,110	402,837	-410,172	2,636,101	911,480	768,132	44,578	96,813	73,546
2016	4,347,455	3,406,938	41,367	3,448,305	413,342	-414,277	2,620,686	934,565	792,204	44,956	96,704	72,830
2017	4,462,884	3,535,983	26,112	3,562,095	431,874	-434,468	2,695,753	975,747	791,384	45,990	97,041	73,281
2018	4,857,757	4,796,160	61,597	3,754,342	455,342	-456,768	2,842,232	1,145,780	869,745	50,120	96,922	73,451
2019	5,013,959	4,927,584	86,375	3,914,465	473,164	-482,533	2,958,768	1,143,832	911,359	51,525	97,311	74,041

Personal Income and Employment by Area: Duluth, MN-WI

(Thousands of dollars, except as noted.)

Year	Personal income, total	Earnings by place of work			Less: Contributions for government social insurance	Plus: Adjustment for residence	Equals: Net earnings by place of residence	Plus: Dividends, interest, and rent	Plus: Personal current transfer receipts	Per capita personal income (dollars)	Population (persons)	Total employment
		Nonfarm	Farm	Total								
1970	1,049,497	828,978	3,931	832,909	60,088	-6,895	765,926	156,091	127,480	3,570	293,960	115,741
1971	1,132,812	890,539	3,502	894,041	66,901	-7,548	819,592	167,388	145,832	3,824	296,224	116,412
1972	1,224,210	963,080	3,989	967,069	76,060	-8,217	882,792	177,287	164,131	4,142	295,529	118,378
1973	1,339,703	1,052,051	6,388	1,058,439	94,972	-8,284	955,183	198,412	186,108	4,584	292,286	121,637
1974	1,471,299	1,136,578	4,775	1,141,353	107,630	-7,288	1,026,435	228,212	216,652	5,095	288,748	123,186
1975	1,713,412	1,326,197	3,549	1,329,746	124,602	-2,570	1,202,574	255,139	255,699	5,896	290,582	126,320
1976	1,928,015	1,506,276	4,370	1,510,646	142,497	2,238	1,370,387	273,230	284,398	6,536	294,985	130,460
1977	1,996,351	1,527,893	6,518	1,534,411	144,800	-5,759	1,383,852	301,289	311,210	6,765	295,109	128,310
1978	2,290,895	1,798,715	7,071	1,805,786	173,075	-1,661	1,631,050	328,989	330,856	7,777	294,586	133,882
1979	2,530,495	1,984,698	7,888	1,992,586	197,885	3,946	1,798,647	364,790	367,058	8,543	296,193	137,174
1980	2,769,373	2,085,219	7,481	2,092,700	206,539	-10,992	1,875,169	444,462	449,742	9,343	296,407	135,992
1981	3,056,061	2,259,939	8,649	2,268,588	242,547	-17,106	2,008,935	545,982	501,144	10,359	295,015	133,167
1982	3,037,474	2,065,951	6,837	2,072,788	227,149	-18,607	1,827,032	609,784	600,658	10,395	292,192	122,580
1983	3,061,711	2,002,974	4,722	2,007,696	221,818	-14,251	1,771,627	644,937	645,147	10,684	286,582	117,782
1984	3,267,436	2,162,574	4,884	2,167,458	247,187	-13,731	1,906,540	708,869	652,027	11,627	281,016	120,193
1985	3,362,193	2,205,443	6,222	2,211,665	256,484	-14,727	1,940,454	737,897	683,842	12,182	275,987	120,332
1986	3,472,524	2,277,552	11,792	2,289,344	270,970	-19,262	1,999,112	770,889	702,523	12,793	271,434	121,403
1987	3,588,068	2,407,989	3,552	2,411,541	283,103	-23,760	2,104,678	768,562	714,828	13,335	269,076	123,967
1988	3,769,511	2,598,808	2,386	2,601,194	320,562	-23,526	2,257,106	789,365	723,040	14,093	267,468	127,214
1989	4,134,686	2,841,717	5,961	2,847,678	352,729	-22,922	2,472,027	889,902	772,757	15,413	268,268	131,705
1990	4,403,781	3,043,512	3,747	3,047,259	376,401	25,628	2,696,486	891,749	815,546	16,326	269,746	134,052
1991	4,576,088	3,234,527	1,700	3,236,227	403,328	-27,641	2,805,258	904,302	866,528	16,870	271,256	137,205
1992	4,850,559	3,456,422	4,799	3,461,221	423,798	-33,287	3,004,136	906,591	939,832	17,772	272,939	139,402
1993	4,959,750	3,541,162	4,697	3,545,859	438,076	-37,872	3,069,911	919,273	970,566	18,139	273,424	139,020
1994	5,189,680	3,715,358	5,411	3,720,769	464,395	-43,893	3,212,481	966,285	1,010,914	18,952	273,834	141,956
1995	5,511,765	3,912,526	2,895	3,915,421	487,298	-43,870	3,384,253	1,070,203	1,057,309	20,280	271,777	145,458
1996	5,805,483	4,110,844	2,958	4,113,802	506,276	-47,815	3,559,711	1,146,934	1,098,838	21,310	272,433	148,086
1997	6,019,195	4,293,547	2,008	4,295,555	530,306	-53,517	3,711,732	1,191,279	1,116,184	21,999	273,609	150,364
1998	6,435,609	4,646,681	3,499	4,650,180	564,603	-63,798	4,021,779	1,258,476	1,155,354	23,526	273,552	153,154
1999	6,691,669	4,921,226	3,279	4,924,505	596,285	-71,764	4,256,456	1,245,783	1,189,430	24,362	274,682	156,046
2000	7,120,262	5,230,257	2,348	5,232,605	625,155	-77,794	4,529,656	1,336,332	1,254,274	25,819	275,775	159,051
2001	7,262,893	5,199,090	2,729	5,201,819	626,523	-77,313	4,497,983	1,349,061	1,415,849	26,225	276,946	157,065
2002	7,566,141	5,425,124	1,824	5,426,948	649,341	-85,698	4,691,909	1,349,389	1,524,843	27,329	276,852	157,080
2003	7,791,929	5,525,706	4,270	5,529,976	664,176	-84,887	4,780,913	1,429,389	1,581,627	28,108	277,209	156,621
2004	8,084,310	5,800,675	4,573	5,805,248	692,645	-78,444	5,034,159	1,389,666	1,660,485	29,176	277,087	157,218
2005	8,127,386	5,867,802	3,175	5,870,977	719,139	-76,268	5,075,570	1,324,652	1,727,164	29,374	276,682	158,903
2006	8,561,867	6,100,342	4,212	6,104,554	755,181	-78,447	5,270,926	1,424,892	1,866,049	30,942	276,710	160,902
2007	9,077,056	6,389,976	5,420	6,395,396	788,564	-84,438	5,522,394	1,539,468	2,015,194	32,744	277,209	163,123
2008	9,664,103	6,794,592	291	6,794,883	834,626	-88,061	5,872,196	1,592,714	2,199,193	34,693	278,561	162,868
2009	9,565,143	6,559,373	-1,770	6,557,603	810,267	-99,902	5,647,434	1,478,624	2,439,085	34,227	279,465	157,544
2010	10,162,467	7,073,242	3,510	7,076,752	845,952	-101,068	6,129,732	1,466,023	2,566,712	36,336	279,677	157,284
2011	10,758,195	7,472,458	3,756	7,476,214	799,959	-117,104	6,559,151	1,633,637	2,565,407	38,456	279,753	158,359
2012	10,969,979	7,571,890	1,842	7,573,732	805,202	-121,368	6,647,162	1,753,727	2,569,090	39,271	279,339	158,929
2013	10,987,240	7,604,853	6,033	7,610,886	931,565	-138,264	6,541,057	1,787,527	2,658,656	39,319	279,439	160,981
2014	11,378,574	7,788,190	6,776	7,794,966	949,667	-142,590	6,702,709	1,911,796	2,764,069	40,688	279,651	162,477
2015	11,676,324	7,883,264	7,206	7,890,470	965,137	-143,520	6,781,813	2,043,794	2,850,717	41,821	279,197	163,240
2016	11,724,555	7,863,228	3,715	7,866,943	962,236	-158,081	6,746,626	2,045,721	2,932,208	42,030	278,954	162,825
2017	12,124,781	8,125,662	-3,554	8,122,108	1,003,625	-160,857	6,957,626	2,138,746	3,028,409	43,492	278,782	163,876
2018	13,307,077	13,307,422	-345	8,860,474	1,109,863	-145,655	7,604,956	2,357,841	3,344,280	46,004	289,260	170,715
2019	13,759,223	13,757,190	2,033	9,146,015	1,147,958	-148,954	7,849,103	2,378,192	3,531,928	47,654	288,732	171,192

Personal Income and Employment by Area: Durham-Chapel Hill, NC

(Thousands of dollars, except as noted.)

Year	Personal income, total	Earnings by place of work			Less: Contributions for government social insurance	Plus: Adjustment for residence	Equals: Net earnings by place of residence	Plus: Dividends, interest, and rent	Plus: Personal current transfer receipts	Per capita personal income (dollars)	Population (persons)	Total employment
		Nonfarm	Farm	Total								
1970	896,581	757,721	22,672	780,393	50,259	-21,428	708,706	118,834	69,041	3,637	246,517	120,512
1971	1,010,661	862,391	24,128	886,519	59,151	-31,986	795,382	133,342	81,937	4,000	252,666	125,379
1972	1,118,503	958,548	26,764	985,312	68,592	-39,393	877,327	149,408	91,768	4,282	261,180	130,456
1973	1,233,761	1,046,288	45,351	1,091,639	86,838	-46,040	958,761	169,736	105,264	4,625	266,750	133,616
1974	1,363,250	1,157,774	36,434	1,194,208	99,818	-57,753	1,036,637	197,200	129,413	5,020	271,564	136,334
1975	1,527,220	1,278,443	42,026	1,320,469	109,791	-75,803	1,134,875	222,253	170,092	5,640	270,769	134,827
1976	1,690,429	1,422,098	47,767	1,469,865	124,369	-87,822	1,257,674	244,678	188,077	6,143	275,162	139,310
1977	1,875,322	1,600,483	46,880	1,647,363	138,761	-110,435	1,398,167	275,896	201,259	6,670	281,149	145,598
1978	2,108,943	1,836,976	45,608	1,882,584	165,451	-136,434	1,580,699	313,146	215,098	7,420	284,208	152,779
1979	2,340,659	2,060,026	33,060	2,093,086	193,578	-159,879	1,739,629	356,628	244,402	8,089	289,360	159,411
1980	2,642,356	2,283,907	29,054	2,312,961	215,340	-185,895	1,911,726	441,354	289,276	9,023	292,831	161,496
1981	2,996,125	2,548,198	49,217	2,597,415	259,568	-220,612	2,117,235	550,180	328,710	10,129	295,796	164,424
1982	3,271,417	2,789,460	46,400	2,835,860	285,480	-265,038	2,285,342	632,778	353,297	10,951	298,730	165,394
1983	3,549,486	3,082,842	29,439	3,112,281	319,465	-308,992	2,483,824	683,769	381,893	11,742	302,298	169,000
1984	4,055,512	3,555,700	57,383	3,613,083	375,208	-389,444	2,848,431	803,508	403,573	13,212	306,946	181,343
1985	4,483,187	4,037,273	39,559	4,076,832	433,856	-478,133	3,164,843	889,894	428,450	14,331	312,842	194,306
1986	4,850,330	4,401,453	45,407	4,446,860	484,101	-538,987	3,423,772	976,809	449,749	15,113	320,939	202,479
1987	5,241,180	4,834,783	41,562	4,876,345	523,175	-626,201	3,726,969	1,041,383	472,828	16,011	327,345	210,424
1988	5,745,334	5,306,392	50,485	5,356,877	593,447	-700,672	4,062,758	1,167,837	514,739	17,239	333,279	219,599
1989	6,407,741	5,836,526	73,992	5,910,518	652,385	-826,920	4,431,213	1,406,073	570,455	18,860	339,747	227,827
1990	6,889,138	6,379,292	76,802	6,456,094	732,505	-940,086	4,783,503	1,471,143	634,492	19,859	346,907	234,238
1991	7,303,956	6,937,599	81,031	7,018,630	806,872	-1,153,298	5,058,460	1,515,289	730,207	20,596	354,625	240,084
1992	7,966,650	7,666,502	70,716	7,737,218	877,736	-1,329,660	5,529,822	1,630,580	806,248	21,962	362,754	246,553
1993	8,482,748	8,134,028	82,794	8,216,822	932,898	-1,430,448	5,853,476	1,736,975	892,297	22,793	372,169	253,905
1994	8,941,962	8,585,093	75,492	8,660,585	1,002,171	-1,534,853	6,123,561	1,884,946	933,455	23,527	380,071	259,586
1995	9,509,941	9,219,347	77,519	9,296,866	1,078,060	-1,746,463	6,472,343	2,000,286	1,037,312	24,498	388,187	269,469
1996	10,159,357	9,870,034	78,209	9,948,243	1,149,885	-1,926,881	6,871,477	2,171,756	1,116,124	25,657	395,974	279,035
1997	10,825,403	10,713,078	74,928	10,788,006	1,241,276	-2,267,901	7,278,829	2,376,644	1,169,930	26,724	405,085	288,450
1998	11,549,555	11,640,739	83,861	11,724,600	1,346,231	-2,539,341	7,839,028	2,518,196	1,192,331	27,968	412,954	300,040
1999	12,269,088	12,797,568	80,230	12,877,798	1,474,643	-2,936,696	8,466,459	2,561,326	1,241,303	29,196	420,226	308,913
2000	13,146,794	14,285,195	80,179	14,365,374	1,626,544	-3,626,162	9,112,668	2,696,885	1,337,241	30,853	426,116	316,136
2001	13,615,141	14,640,503	96,644	14,737,147	1,669,258	-3,629,708	9,438,181	2,682,528	1,494,432	31,283	435,229	311,848
2002	13,692,533	14,668,481	38,584	14,707,065	1,658,150	-3,613,246	9,435,669	2,630,256	1,626,608	30,994	441,780	310,867
2003	14,137,925	15,087,206	46,816	15,134,022	1,725,565	-3,668,178	9,740,279	2,693,892	1,703,754	31,671	446,402	311,704
2004	15,864,507	16,332,386	68,131	16,400,517	1,822,798	-3,664,702	10,913,017	3,127,834	1,823,656	35,151	451,323	320,642
2005	16,994,730	17,008,912	74,830	17,083,742	1,898,992	-3,635,686	11,549,064	3,451,950	1,993,716	37,083	458,287	325,596
2006	18,410,582	18,482,912	73,869	18,556,781	2,051,287	-4,008,096	12,497,398	3,772,238	2,140,946	39,319	468,238	336,467
2007	19,954,327	19,943,948	66,928	20,010,876	2,226,193	-4,362,902	13,421,781	4,201,447	2,331,099	41,684	478,699	349,474
2008	20,903,083	20,576,827	50,154	20,626,981	2,309,446	-4,428,404	13,889,131	4,330,322	2,683,630	42,666	489,919	351,975
2009	20,531,927	20,446,456	49,684	20,496,140	2,312,411	-4,494,894	13,688,835	3,873,049	2,970,043	41,084	499,753	347,001
2010	21,446,116	21,476,132	53,782	21,529,914	2,367,251	-4,723,691	14,438,972	3,808,385	3,198,759	42,173	508,532	345,440
2011	22,444,209	21,042,971	27,413	21,070,384	2,093,900	-4,190,725	14,785,759	4,344,636	3,313,814	43,538	515,514	346,747
2012	23,690,511	22,241,760	56,362	22,298,122	2,177,343	-4,555,234	15,565,545	4,727,902	3,397,064	45,150	524,708	354,394
2013	23,760,300	22,802,078	62,524	22,864,602	2,585,593	-4,796,163	15,482,846	4,795,224	3,482,230	44,583	532,944	360,034
2014	25,493,388	23,899,898	99,956	23,999,854	2,723,101	-4,965,561	16,311,192	5,499,512	3,682,684	47,056	541,769	370,097
2015	27,045,047	24,692,295	96,421	24,788,716	2,807,496	-4,890,117	17,091,103	6,035,154	3,918,790	49,142	550,346	381,746
2016	28,292,743	25,377,826	70,988	25,448,814	2,884,115	-4,824,906	17,739,793	6,484,962	4,067,988	50,620	558,920	397,207
2017	29,663,279	26,519,035	77,724	26,596,759	3,000,274	-4,960,203	18,636,282	6,799,480	4,227,517	52,277	567,428	403,327
2018	33,613,793	33,577,956	35,837	29,561,186	3,303,488	-5,256,798	21,000,900	7,678,372	4,934,521	52,727	637,501	446,038
2019	35,068,510	35,027,802	40,708	31,338,494	3,499,469	-5,804,402	22,034,623	7,820,193	5,213,694	54,423	644,367	457,392

Personal Income and Employment by Area: East Stroudsburg, PA

(Thousands of dollars, except as noted.)

Year	Personal income, total	Earnings by place of work			Less: Contributions for government social insurance	Plus: Adjustment for residence	Equals: Net earnings by place of residence	Plus: Dividends, interest, and rent	Plus: Personal current transfer receipts	Per capita personal income (dollars)	Population (persons)	Total employment
		Nonfarm	Farm	Total								
1970	194,209	182,295	827	183,122	10,715	-31,752	140,655	35,461	18,093	4,274	45,441	25,965
1971	213,335	196,699	428	197,127	12,257	-32,102	152,768	39,287	21,280	4,607	46,302	26,505
1972	248,897	225,488	371	225,859	14,780	-30,103	180,976	43,302	24,619	5,088	48,917	27,900
1973	288,633	255,839	1,253	257,092	19,290	-27,452	210,350	49,387	28,896	5,582	51,711	30,353
1974	332,565	284,289	444	284,733	22,923	-21,738	240,072	57,013	35,480	6,060	54,877	31,305
1975	376,892	310,120	1,209	311,329	24,286	-21,927	265,116	63,225	48,551	6,539	57,637	31,147
1976	419,438	340,807	1,441	342,248	27,013	-20,304	294,931	69,090	55,417	6,948	60,370	31,868
1977	466,232	374,938	1,261	376,199	29,933	-18,455	327,811	78,578	59,843	7,418	62,848	33,116
1978	527,126	428,874	605	429,479	34,743	-20,408	374,328	87,436	65,362	8,043	65,535	34,888
1979	594,040	464,086	1,693	465,779	39,493	-7,479	418,807	100,718	74,515	8,747	67,911	35,265
1980	671,280	502,881	847	503,728	43,763	-1,091	458,874	123,937	88,469	9,638	69,649	35,960
1981	748,267	543,688	1,354	545,042	50,517	-2,152	492,373	153,781	102,113	10,618	70,470	36,945
1982	820,383	575,935	628	576,563	53,316	-3,409	519,838	183,750	116,795	11,444	71,688	37,363
1983	886,219	621,275	-703	620,572	60,457	3,873	563,988	192,646	129,585	12,231	72,455	38,614
1984	996,821	705,394	127	705,521	71,441	12,221	646,301	215,952	134,568	13,552	73,556	41,607
1985	1,101,908	772,694	490	773,184	80,655	20,504	713,033	243,869	145,006	14,643	75,250	43,899
1986	1,225,161	858,957	-310	858,647	91,421	34,923	802,149	266,866	156,146	15,682	78,127	46,679
1987	1,358,778	975,575	-184	975,391	104,863	38,173	908,701	287,301	162,776	16,642	81,647	49,932
1988	1,520,404	1,077,847	258	1,078,105	119,941	64,965	1,023,129	319,368	177,907	17,442	87,169	52,588
1989	1,661,775	1,172,745	307	1,173,052	129,279	80,753	1,124,526	344,087	193,162	17,974	92,452	54,322
1990	1,753,086	1,198,259	1,230	1,199,489	134,266	91,776	1,156,999	374,386	221,701	18,094	96,889	54,242
1991	1,824,976	1,191,145	805	1,191,950	134,807	142,673	1,199,816	362,986	262,174	17,986	101,469	51,670
1992	1,954,018	1,223,833	652	1,224,485	139,601	219,505	1,304,389	359,511	290,118	18,495	105,649	51,456
1993	2,099,128	1,272,615	376	1,272,991	148,043	274,122	1,399,070	390,352	309,706	19,072	110,062	52,129
1994	2,241,252	1,342,685	813	1,343,498	159,585	308,249	1,492,162	410,471	338,619	19,531	114,752	54,504
1995	2,387,172	1,412,106	221	1,412,327	167,964	333,079	1,577,442	448,581	361,149	20,048	119,070	55,406
1996	2,553,234	1,485,514	874	1,486,388	172,585	377,439	1,691,242	470,421	391,571	20,706	123,307	56,753
1997	2,745,753	1,556,759	300	1,557,059	179,586	449,521	1,826,994	504,257	414,502	21,540	127,470	58,180
1998	2,978,781	1,664,753	67	1,664,820	189,520	514,905	1,990,205	547,980	440,596	22,738	131,007	59,561
1999	3,185,248	1,795,717	-421	1,795,296	202,208	590,379	2,183,467	534,784	466,997	23,606	134,936	61,565
2000	3,554,963	2,006,772	945	2,007,717	222,797	677,943	2,462,863	585,206	506,894	25,445	139,710	65,634
2001	3,796,541	2,176,915	-112	2,176,803	239,633	695,600	2,632,770	608,094	555,677	26,406	143,775	67,036
2002	3,996,348	2,343,141	-558	2,342,583	259,696	704,460	2,787,347	595,714	613,287	26,851	148,833	68,786
2003	4,210,885	2,492,342	828	2,493,170	274,943	732,387	2,950,614	605,012	655,259	27,339	154,027	70,438
2004	4,510,155	2,745,961	2,171	2,748,132	300,564	763,525	3,211,093	591,147	707,915	28,513	158,181	72,677
2005	4,779,477	2,913,729	1,266	2,914,995	324,017	818,830	3,409,808	620,956	748,713	29,495	162,045	74,896
2006	5,059,159	3,109,251	1,116	3,110,367	347,584	852,622	3,615,405	646,283	797,471	30,627	165,185	77,436
2007	5,391,367	3,246,699	-601	3,246,098	366,335	908,481	3,788,244	740,972	862,151	32,216	167,352	79,621
2008	5,586,425	3,337,135	1,360	3,338,495	380,165	827,629	3,785,959	787,816	1,012,650	33,139	168,576	80,002
2009	5,443,630	3,244,682	2,329	3,247,011	375,063	709,276	3,581,224	754,503	1,107,903	32,137	169,390	77,120
2010	5,415,490	3,364,629	2,727	3,367,356	386,051	525,387	3,506,692	709,987	1,198,811	31,879	169,876	76,353
2011	5,675,283	3,390,590	2,421	3,393,011	353,271	619,104	3,658,844	793,183	1,223,256	33,392	169,961	75,724
2012	5,625,122	3,396,615	4,008	3,400,623	351,987	561,528	3,610,164	801,041	1,213,917	33,329	168,775	75,092
2013	5,874,147	3,381,459	4,053	3,385,512	391,240	827,103	3,821,375	799,131	1,253,641	35,051	167,588	74,392
2014	6,126,126	3,398,996	4,108	3,403,104	392,861	929,417	3,939,660	876,099	1,310,367	36,564	167,547	73,913
2015	6,369,391	3,591,469	3,069	3,594,538	411,589	906,861	4,089,810	898,965	1,380,616	38,178	166,835	75,437
2016	6,558,179	3,681,053	2,161	3,683,214	425,656	937,027	4,194,585	896,115	1,467,479	39,385	166,516	76,886
2017	6,840,517	3,816,734	2,139	3,818,873	445,496	1,044,276	4,417,653	936,234	1,486,630	40,706	168,046	78,000
2018	7,155,522	7,154,981	541	3,897,137	453,150	1,060,338	4,504,325	1,002,077	1,649,120	42,267	169,294	78,544
2019	7,461,802	7,460,056	1,746	4,083,390	476,673	1,113,689	4,720,406	1,025,445	1,715,951	43,823	170,271	80,089

Personal Income and Employment by Area: Eau Claire, WI

(Thousands of dollars, except as noted.)

| Year | Personal income, total | Derivation of personal income | | | | | | | | Per capita personal income (dollars) | Population (persons) | Total employment |
| | | Earnings by place of work | | | Less: Contributions for government social insurance | Plus: Adjustment for residence | Equals: Net earnings by place of residence | Plus: Dividends, interest, and rent | Plus: Personal current transfer receipts | | | |
		Nonfarm	Farm	Total								
1970	419,956	338,337	18,916	357,253	24,606	-15,205	317,442	60,574	41,940	3,634	115,555	51,672
1971	458,788	366,348	19,437	385,785	27,578	-15,059	343,148	66,738	48,902	3,868	118,617	52,507
1972	498,973	396,468	21,232	417,700	31,497	-14,966	371,237	72,549	55,187	4,117	121,204	53,066
1973	544,971	421,461	27,307	448,768	38,435	-13,749	396,584	82,783	65,604	4,532	120,238	53,548
1974	593,854	448,670	23,743	472,413	42,635	-12,378	417,400	95,445	81,009	4,900	121,193	53,903
1975	654,586	478,280	23,005	501,285	44,802	-10,849	445,634	105,868	103,084	5,278	124,012	54,581
1976	718,124	522,433	22,471	544,904	49,332	-8,453	487,119	114,646	116,359	5,768	124,496	55,598
1977	809,882	591,713	33,334	625,047	55,755	-8,927	560,365	128,716	120,801	6,376	127,012	58,235
1978	903,140	663,937	32,358	696,295	64,252	-8,085	623,958	145,308	133,874	7,006	128,912	60,913
1979	1,001,516	721,254	39,869	761,123	73,061	-5,310	682,752	163,382	155,382	7,746	129,293	62,962
1980	1,134,990	788,012	38,953	826,965	80,069	-3,752	743,144	203,928	187,918	8,637	131,405	63,315
1981	1,258,094	867,406	28,946	896,352	94,693	-6,369	795,290	253,342	209,462	9,460	132,986	63,776
1982	1,335,786	897,855	31,085	928,940	98,771	-5,587	824,582	284,237	226,967	9,988	133,738	63,651
1983	1,418,059	962,471	17,044	979,515	104,736	-6,070	868,709	303,807	245,543	10,620	133,527	63,838
1984	1,540,874	1,036,771	36,546	1,073,317	114,793	-6,756	951,768	333,284	255,822	11,483	134,188	65,777
1985	1,624,946	1,091,947	38,545	1,130,492	121,819	-6,865	1,001,808	348,985	274,153	12,116	134,120	66,855
1986	1,738,763	1,188,545	46,202	1,234,747	132,621	-9,456	1,092,670	365,859	280,234	12,951	134,252	69,351
1987	1,836,251	1,280,738	46,161	1,326,899	140,459	-8,519	1,177,921	367,429	290,901	13,578	135,233	71,536
1988	1,932,390	1,382,778	35,469	1,418,247	158,022	-8,101	1,252,124	379,880	300,386	14,196	136,125	73,958
1989	2,103,205	1,458,885	58,235	1,517,120	168,017	-6,236	1,342,867	438,623	321,715	15,331	137,187	74,933
1990	2,210,384	1,549,512	45,879	1,595,391	184,659	-3,909	1,406,823	457,352	346,209	16,044	137,771	75,588
1991	2,291,073	1,634,203	29,109	1,663,312	196,411	-5,928	1,460,973	457,717	372,383	16,444	139,325	77,150
1992	2,473,941	1,770,557	39,166	1,809,723	210,432	-6,098	1,593,193	478,354	402,394	17,594	140,614	78,688
1993	2,556,898	1,849,389	28,959	1,878,348	219,142	-4,464	1,654,742	496,495	405,661	18,008	141,985	79,787
1994	2,731,707	1,993,723	39,188	2,032,911	238,979	-8,667	1,785,265	531,646	414,796	19,103	142,998	83,136
1995	2,890,743	2,122,856	23,168	2,146,024	256,322	-13,876	1,875,826	578,603	436,314	20,082	143,950	87,319
1996	3,073,447	2,260,603	48,049	2,308,652	271,154	-19,616	2,017,882	604,820	450,745	21,219	144,842	90,392
1997	3,291,681	2,463,325	27,624	2,490,949	293,360	-29,143	2,168,446	659,539	463,696	22,571	145,834	92,863
1998	3,555,786	2,683,325	41,695	2,725,020	316,442	-34,822	2,373,756	703,263	478,767	24,277	146,470	95,170
1999	3,725,935	2,878,236	40,283	2,918,519	339,429	-36,658	2,542,432	691,809	491,694	25,281	147,378	98,899
2000	3,988,503	3,086,019	23,291	3,109,310	358,894	-42,184	2,708,232	749,710	530,561	26,830	148,656	99,914
2001	4,130,438	3,097,389	30,283	3,127,672	349,893	-40,232	2,737,547	798,596	594,295	27,600	149,655	95,828
2002	4,259,017	3,247,083	26,993	3,274,076	363,063	-46,614	2,864,399	756,365	638,253	28,234	150,846	95,806
2003	4,380,990	3,349,585	39,377	3,388,962	375,660	-45,407	2,967,895	755,100	657,995	28,857	151,816	96,732
2004	4,556,432	3,516,014	57,308	3,573,322	396,051	-28,359	3,148,912	728,231	679,289	29,699	153,419	98,739
2005	4,738,847	3,643,923	44,223	3,688,146	419,561	-31,023	3,237,562	768,288	732,997	30,611	154,809	100,615
2006	5,080,038	3,903,679	31,940	3,935,619	450,264	-43,341	3,442,014	869,820	768,204	32,530	156,167	103,409
2007	5,418,293	4,123,968	51,452	4,175,420	473,842	-54,827	3,646,751	933,282	838,260	34,368	157,654	105,103
2008	5,653,069	4,218,685	53,682	4,272,367	489,409	-61,422	3,721,536	993,887	937,646	35,621	158,700	104,841
2009	5,774,343	4,257,365	17,249	4,274,614	490,112	-50,536	3,733,966	966,082	1,074,295	36,029	160,271	101,939
2010	5,997,854	4,429,002	54,236	4,483,238	507,210	-57,029	3,918,999	922,225	1,156,630	37,102	161,658	102,785
2011	6,324,030	4,576,027	96,049	4,672,076	468,984	-58,524	4,144,568	1,045,160	1,134,302	38,826	162,881	104,747
2012	6,600,036	4,762,943	80,816	4,843,759	485,896	-71,067	4,286,796	1,151,485	1,161,755	40,271	163,889	106,085
2013	6,633,955	4,797,992	78,514	4,876,506	552,230	-72,296	4,251,980	1,179,205	1,202,770	40,256	164,795	106,199
2014	6,955,929	5,000,377	78,826	5,079,203	577,504	-60,399	4,441,300	1,270,148	1,244,481	42,162	164,981	107,798
2015	7,103,364	5,096,133	74,000	5,170,133	593,693	-82,191	4,494,249	1,312,256	1,296,859	42,932	165,455	108,604
2016	7,161,637	5,139,281	41,601	5,180,882	598,435	-89,641	4,492,806	1,350,198	1,318,633	43,025	166,452	109,272
2017	7,494,218	5,416,881	33,376	5,450,257	634,405	-109,324	4,706,528	1,407,806	1,379,884	44,746	167,484	110,510
2018	8,018,914	7,977,551	41,363	5,800,828	663,261	-122,962	5,014,605	1,558,150	1,446,159	47,600	168,464	111,750
2019	8,288,411	8,233,893	54,518	6,019,412	690,288	-150,070	5,179,054	1,574,584	1,534,773	48,956	169,304	112,887

Personal Income and Employment by Area: El Centro, CA

(Thousands of dollars, except as noted.)

Year	Personal income, total	Earnings by place of work			Less: Contributions for government social insurance	Plus: Adjustment for residence	Equals: Net earnings by place of residence	Plus: Dividends, interest, and rent	Plus: Personal current transfer receipts	Per capita personal income (dollars)	Population (persons)	Total employment
		Nonfarm	Farm	Total								
1970	299,115	175,395	102,809	278,204	12,340	-39,358	226,506	35,112	37,497	3,999	74,795	34,273
1971	301,362	187,379	88,107	275,486	13,656	-38,450	223,380	37,989	39,993	4,022	74,931	34,377
1972	384,220	203,216	148,542	351,758	15,533	-37,939	298,286	42,324	43,610	5,064	75,869	35,499
1973	425,947	232,410	155,052	387,462	20,286	-39,142	328,034	50,959	46,954	5,348	79,648	37,260
1974	488,692	268,810	177,654	446,464	24,223	-47,271	374,970	57,885	55,837	5,994	81,526	39,718
1975	523,162	305,287	168,146	473,433	26,376	-57,783	389,274	65,016	68,872	6,304	82,989	42,553
1976	581,199	343,522	181,160	524,682	30,301	-65,269	429,112	67,212	84,875	6,816	85,264	44,782
1977	603,258	373,672	166,362	540,034	32,857	-71,274	435,903	73,034	94,321	6,936	86,981	44,503
1978	656,466	414,805	168,076	582,881	36,740	-77,911	468,230	84,373	103,863	7,420	88,474	44,679
1979	929,275	466,456	371,339	837,795	43,714	-76,661	717,420	97,418	114,437	10,315	90,086	46,745
1980	892,604	501,697	271,261	772,958	46,460	-87,007	639,491	119,747	133,366	9,641	92,584	45,523
1981	937,766	534,114	203,896	738,010	52,687	-53,920	631,403	147,688	158,675	9,944	94,301	43,663
1982	1,039,053	549,167	267,565	816,732	54,739	-61,416	700,577	164,268	174,208	10,859	95,688	43,260
1983	1,100,336	550,956	290,123	841,079	56,053	-60,135	724,891	184,073	191,372	11,357	96,890	42,970
1984	1,127,019	600,390	255,088	855,478	63,262	-65,130	727,086	188,991	210,942	11,562	97,475	42,308
1985	1,123,270	635,816	200,804	836,620	66,587	-64,735	705,298	190,390	227,582	11,323	99,199	41,051
1986	1,161,225	700,264	174,015	874,279	74,683	-63,037	736,559	194,658	230,008	11,743	98,885	42,325
1987	1,363,167	768,105	303,976	1,072,081	81,927	-62,779	927,375	197,166	238,626	13,621	100,077	43,579
1988	1,568,327	881,931	393,506	1,275,437	98,187	-65,519	1,111,731	204,377	252,219	15,394	101,881	47,530
1989	1,688,937	966,360	385,739	1,352,099	110,979	-67,273	1,173,847	234,710	280,380	16,060	105,166	52,145
1990	1,789,097	1,045,624	369,225	1,414,849	118,763	-64,759	1,231,327	241,450	316,320	16,141	110,839	52,121
1991	1,874,590	1,094,401	359,154	1,453,555	123,658	-57,914	1,271,983	244,914	357,693	16,003	117,143	51,265
1992	2,015,111	1,232,205	297,403	1,529,608	135,611	-63,856	1,330,141	249,669	435,301	16,274	123,823	52,634
1993	2,262,259	1,315,565	431,050	1,746,615	144,367	-62,945	1,539,303	262,817	460,139	17,040	132,758	55,335
1994	2,284,882	1,371,806	382,693	1,754,499	150,955	-65,039	1,538,505	282,712	463,665	17,011	134,315	56,933
1995	2,360,428	1,372,800	396,911	1,769,711	149,162	-60,419	1,560,130	307,361	492,937	17,231	136,986	58,101
1996	2,345,878	1,406,497	306,694	1,713,191	146,736	-56,152	1,510,303	316,234	519,341	17,001	137,987	58,050
1997	2,440,859	1,492,990	312,060	1,805,050	151,731	-53,773	1,599,546	331,269	510,044	17,608	138,624	59,914
1998	2,629,171	1,601,412	352,679	1,954,091	159,715	-49,135	1,745,241	344,827	539,103	18,832	139,615	61,395
1999	2,718,591	1,679,382	336,057	2,015,439	169,696	-42,253	1,803,490	348,189	566,912	19,273	141,056	63,093
2000	2,729,511	1,760,164	256,305	2,016,469	176,722	-33,083	1,806,664	349,976	572,871	19,167	142,410	60,311
2001	3,015,226	1,940,927	263,770	2,204,697	201,616	-1,292	2,001,789	391,132	622,305	20,982	143,707	59,479
2002	3,397,289	2,116,860	420,783	2,537,643	224,188	-13,561	2,299,894	404,768	692,627	23,327	145,640	63,149
2003	3,545,428	2,291,170	331,018	2,622,188	246,737	-24,601	2,350,850	459,707	734,871	23,797	148,984	65,353
2004	3,660,540	2,399,849	337,987	2,737,836	264,132	-30,088	2,443,616	462,099	754,825	24,042	152,259	65,534
2005	3,845,072	2,550,118	359,518	2,909,636	281,823	-48,341	2,579,472	467,932	797,668	24,630	156,113	67,019
2006	4,129,836	2,763,435	358,924	3,122,359	297,424	-66,805	2,758,130	483,351	888,355	25,730	160,505	71,933
2007	4,379,331	2,920,499	367,418	3,287,917	306,836	-100,968	2,880,113	520,767	978,451	26,607	164,596	74,210
2008	4,772,695	3,018,166	571,810	3,589,976	323,826	-139,253	3,126,897	560,775	1,085,023	28,423	167,917	74,053
2009	4,855,601	3,031,927	488,567	3,520,494	328,891	-144,503	3,047,100	578,399	1,230,102	28,229	172,008	72,584
2010	5,146,224	3,176,001	468,957	3,644,958	327,185	-147,385	3,170,388	597,862	1,377,974	29,444	174,778	72,573
2011	5,584,740	3,312,875	693,469	4,006,344	310,398	-151,912	3,544,034	664,066	1,376,640	31,703	176,157	73,804
2012	5,672,248	3,398,162	636,749	4,034,911	319,759	-157,064	3,558,088	729,156	1,385,004	32,003	177,241	75,293
2013	5,808,922	3,453,971	714,727	4,168,698	359,239	-163,797	3,645,662	731,574	1,431,686	32,769	177,267	77,668
2014	5,843,786	3,531,426	568,729	4,100,155	374,147	-167,872	3,558,136	783,939	1,501,711	32,671	178,868	80,242
2015	6,346,537	3,684,483	778,150	4,462,633	384,540	-179,917	3,898,176	832,611	1,615,750	35,290	179,839	81,468
2016	6,355,736	3,710,298	664,744	4,375,042	395,171	-171,304	3,808,567	868,406	1,678,763	35,118	180,980	79,735
2017	6,619,469	3,840,775	781,925	4,622,700	413,686	-180,449	4,028,565	912,284	1,678,620	36,206	182,830	79,738
2018	6,822,928	6,103,545	719,383	4,703,959	428,732	-179,438	4,095,789	967,664	1,759,475	37,587	181,523	80,859
2019	7,329,602	6,406,247	923,355	5,096,482	459,301	-185,978	4,451,203	994,022	1,884,377	40,447	181,215	82,159

Personal Income and Employment by Area: Elizabethtown-Fort Knox, KY

(Thousands of dollars, except as noted.)

Year	Personal income, total	Earnings by place of work			Less: Contributions for government social insurance	Plus: Adjustment for residence	Equals: Net earnings by place of residence	Plus: Dividends, interest, and rent	Plus: Personal current transfer receipts	Per capita personal income (dollars)	Population (persons)	Total employment
		Nonfarm	Farm	Total								
1970	491,984	398,423	12,529	410,952	23,039	-14,461	373,452	98,882	19,650	4,570	107,652	63,118
1971	506,089	410,110	12,972	423,082	25,386	-13,153	384,543	98,997	22,549	4,693	107,830	58,437
1972	542,596	436,669	15,160	451,829	27,167	-11,239	413,423	104,010	25,163	5,120	105,967	55,176
1973	560,221	437,445	20,332	457,777	28,728	-7,041	422,008	107,957	30,256	5,651	99,133	53,229
1974	652,568	507,481	21,922	529,403	35,205	-8,168	486,030	128,841	37,697	6,222	104,885	56,273
1975	671,920	527,785	8,542	536,327	39,119	-9,799	487,409	135,350	49,161	6,085	110,417	55,211
1976	706,293	550,417	11,074	561,491	41,609	-7,908	511,974	139,162	55,157	5,984	118,037	54,863
1977	813,909	630,775	15,044	645,819	47,522	-5,233	593,064	164,089	56,756	6,840	118,999	58,950
1978	870,028	663,260	13,202	676,462	49,187	-891	626,384	183,007	60,637	7,440	116,940	58,530
1979	963,407	726,754	18,573	745,327	55,912	1,808	691,223	200,731	71,453	8,099	118,949	58,857
1980	1,043,585	774,609	12,994	787,603	60,353	6,490	733,740	222,770	87,075	8,467	123,258	59,302
1981	1,120,007	824,555	23,285	847,840	67,596	-1,735	778,509	238,939	102,559	9,239	121,230	55,951
1982	1,224,859	902,266	19,247	921,513	73,092	-6,467	841,954	270,514	112,391	10,139	120,805	57,731
1983	1,301,661	970,267	-4,977	965,290	82,238	-4,472	878,580	301,075	122,006	10,686	121,809	59,250
1984	1,419,848	1,040,392	20,621	1,061,013	89,965	-6,182	964,866	323,023	131,959	11,617	122,225	59,602
1985	1,507,158	1,115,054	13,121	1,128,175	98,762	-7,492	1,021,921	343,728	141,509	12,271	122,818	61,588
1986	1,570,448	1,159,048	10,639	1,169,687	107,212	-4,045	1,058,430	360,946	151,072	12,745	123,219	62,886
1987	1,646,379	1,216,479	15,614	1,232,093	114,431	-1,060	1,116,602	372,470	157,307	13,379	123,053	63,165
1988	1,740,487	1,287,933	13,949	1,301,882	127,116	3,614	1,178,380	389,243	172,864	13,939	124,869	64,064
1989	1,867,718	1,356,676	27,634	1,384,310	137,220	1,961	1,249,051	421,558	197,109	15,005	124,472	65,539
1990	1,952,934	1,417,728	27,448	1,445,176	149,829	-1,596	1,293,751	441,466	217,717	15,565	125,466	66,277
1991	2,026,159	1,465,668	26,767	1,492,435	157,434	3,573	1,338,574	437,630	249,955	16,677	121,495	63,642
1992	2,221,243	1,601,058	31,941	1,632,999	174,927	12,968	1,471,040	469,946	280,257	18,501	120,059	64,628
1993	2,261,877	1,616,181	28,089	1,644,270	179,628	26,923	1,491,565	480,250	290,062	17,880	126,505	64,846
1994	2,353,163	1,650,695	29,606	1,680,301	185,251	42,886	1,537,936	512,089	303,138	18,338	128,321	65,357
1995	2,427,074	1,676,822	12,002	1,688,824	187,469	58,150	1,559,505	537,840	329,729	18,753	129,423	66,847
1996	2,551,053	1,737,716	25,435	1,763,151	193,965	70,444	1,639,630	558,547	352,876	19,792	128,895	67,246
1997	2,657,710	1,821,853	13,987	1,835,840	203,643	87,851	1,720,048	558,277	379,385	20,415	130,182	67,884
1998	2,853,723	1,918,497	2,078	1,920,575	213,770	112,510	1,819,315	636,028	398,380	21,713	131,428	69,443
1999	2,979,911	2,028,470	-17,686	2,010,784	226,410	138,522	1,922,896	643,148	413,867	22,480	132,558	70,620
2000	3,295,707	2,218,645	10,401	2,229,046	241,336	158,738	2,146,448	697,415	451,844	24,502	134,506	72,649
2001	3,422,083	2,316,789	12,327	2,329,116	253,373	150,293	2,226,036	695,069	500,978	25,226	135,657	73,306
2002	3,485,469	2,403,553	-8,206	2,395,347	263,545	134,731	2,266,533	669,041	549,895	25,518	136,591	72,023
2003	3,633,788	2,583,778	-117	2,583,661	281,482	95,338	2,397,517	663,719	572,552	26,654	136,333	73,739
2004	3,817,351	2,742,619	12,367	2,754,986	296,701	79,623	2,537,908	653,816	625,627	27,616	138,230	74,797
2005	3,967,100	2,840,721	28,777	2,869,498	306,621	68,515	2,631,392	666,343	669,365	28,301	140,177	73,784
2006	4,173,502	3,056,116	19,705	3,075,821	333,357	-5,567	2,736,897	703,281	733,324	29,627	140,870	76,298
2007	4,359,182	3,126,494	7,646	3,134,140	342,919	-13,447	2,777,774	784,623	796,785	30,732	141,844	76,947
2008	4,594,617	3,324,964	-2,568	3,322,396	367,072	-114,141	2,841,183	838,283	915,151	32,133	142,988	76,798
2009	4,790,052	3,451,678	3,633	3,455,311	387,612	-121,719	2,945,980	820,282	1,023,790	33,304	143,829	75,095
2010	5,069,272	3,905,188	-5,338	3,899,850	430,212	-368,992	3,100,646	859,373	1,109,253	33,828	149,853	78,858
2011	5,325,372	4,215,031	13,216	4,228,247	420,164	-581,445	3,226,638	969,174	1,129,560	35,193	151,319	80,821
2012	5,425,698	4,047,365	15,737	4,063,102	408,705	-346,262	3,308,135	975,858	1,141,705	35,813	151,500	78,596
2013	5,380,919	3,962,025	71,963	4,033,988	449,434	-346,336	3,238,218	967,030	1,175,671	35,365	152,155	78,171
2014	5,607,995	3,948,330	31,728	3,980,058	446,815	-160,940	3,372,303	973,240	1,262,452	36,981	151,646	76,902
2015	5,730,738	3,859,854	24,593	3,884,447	446,848	-17,379	3,420,220	974,589	1,335,929	38,696	148,095	76,536
2016	5,896,287	3,898,448	9,366	3,907,814	451,805	101,173	3,557,182	978,326	1,360,779	39,588	148,940	77,269
2017	6,138,270	4,000,247	7,385	4,007,632	461,070	171,946	3,718,508	1,012,393	1,407,369	40,805	150,430	76,754
2018	6,351,661	6,375,735	-24,074	4,080,861	474,149	199,000	3,805,712	1,054,503	1,491,446	41,460	153,201	78,005
2019	6,630,660	6,640,086	-9,426	4,207,642	482,006	264,885	3,990,521	1,067,035	1,573,104	43,076	153,928	78,529

Personal Income and Employment by Area: Elkhart-Goshen, IN

(Thousands of dollars, except as noted.)

Year	Personal income, total	Derivation of personal income			Less: Contributions for government social insurance	Plus: Adjustment for residence	Equals: Net earnings by place of residence	Plus: Dividends, interest, and rent	Plus: Personal current transfer receipts	Per capita personal income (dollars)	Population (persons)	Total employment
		Earnings by place of work										
		Nonfarm	Farm	Total								
1970	552,330	558,921	6,678	565,599	39,107	-84,845	441,647	75,883	34,800	4,362	126,624	71,287
1971	601,971	610,634	8,364	618,998	44,415	-97,279	477,304	83,731	40,936	4,739	127,025	73,110
1972	683,157	714,024	8,090	722,114	55,043	-119,974	547,097	90,643	45,417	5,271	129,596	80,429
1973	759,373	796,745	15,797	812,542	70,119	-137,515	604,908	101,066	53,399	5,740	132,290	84,783
1974	749,526	758,336	8,299	766,635	69,608	-128,774	568,253	114,582	66,691	5,656	132,510	77,343
1975	785,862	762,915	14,151	777,066	68,709	-132,132	576,225	122,928	86,709	5,977	131,484	73,077
1976	908,745	942,599	15,240	957,839	86,525	-176,615	694,699	132,572	81,474	6,916	131,402	82,175
1977	1,021,030	1,088,803	10,433	1,099,236	101,518	-211,138	786,580	147,905	86,545	7,644	133,567	87,444
1978	1,141,941	1,247,694	4,913	1,252,607	119,592	-251,937	881,078	166,552	94,311	8,428	135,493	93,129
1979	1,203,224	1,286,651	3,826	1,290,477	126,331	-260,684	903,462	186,875	112,887	8,803	136,687	89,398
1980	1,226,176	1,224,092	8,290	1,232,382	118,426	-245,510	868,446	216,102	141,628	8,931	137,292	80,021
1981	1,353,592	1,332,543	6,274	1,338,817	137,810	-264,066	936,941	261,466	155,185	9,892	136,836	81,375
1982	1,443,216	1,403,536	2,142	1,405,678	148,234	-281,887	975,557	295,620	172,039	10,445	138,179	82,288
1983	1,645,532	1,695,142	-736	1,694,406	179,196	-355,256	1,159,954	311,213	174,365	11,730	140,286	91,798
1984	1,885,250	1,950,161	14,866	1,965,027	212,635	-409,292	1,343,100	357,397	184,753	13,029	144,701	100,401
1985	1,993,676	2,050,682	14,229	2,064,911	228,276	-427,103	1,409,532	381,274	202,870	13,536	147,287	101,827
1986	2,160,033	2,242,074	14,300	2,256,374	250,771	-465,717	1,539,886	402,986	217,161	14,498	148,990	106,079
1987	2,354,303	2,476,699	17,339	2,494,038	273,523	-514,418	1,706,097	425,584	222,622	15,574	151,167	112,993
1988	2,542,726	2,706,767	9,082	2,715,849	306,591	-562,980	1,846,278	457,778	238,670	16,520	153,917	118,921
1989	2,732,709	2,807,367	24,021	2,831,388	319,493	-572,219	1,939,676	539,416	253,617	17,538	155,813	119,871
1990	2,803,794	2,822,729	20,457	2,843,186	330,838	-558,262	1,954,086	569,489	280,219	17,914	156,517	117,792
1991	2,854,501	2,854,635	11,015	2,865,650	336,297	-557,371	1,971,982	567,403	315,116	18,050	158,141	113,810
1992	3,141,154	3,178,927	18,894	3,197,821	369,889	-627,461	2,200,471	577,726	362,957	19,577	160,454	117,964
1993	3,350,572	3,431,207	18,421	3,449,628	399,069	-673,830	2,376,729	593,909	379,934	20,492	163,510	123,339
1994	3,619,981	3,765,878	16,011	3,781,889	444,647	-743,793	2,593,449	629,615	396,917	21,742	166,498	129,440
1995	3,812,383	3,942,977	10,087	3,953,064	468,165	-765,387	2,719,512	681,485	411,386	22,443	169,869	134,046
1996	3,977,379	4,047,205	21,687	4,068,892	480,126	-779,650	2,809,116	724,322	443,941	23,046	172,582	133,328
1997	4,141,940	4,180,777	26,012	4,206,789	495,175	-799,408	2,912,206	773,276	456,458	23,631	175,274	134,160
1998	4,491,824	4,584,103	25,812	4,609,915	534,681	-880,246	3,194,988	808,837	487,999	25,251	177,885	140,573
1999	4,789,195	5,000,052	12,762	5,012,814	576,084	-968,374	3,468,356	807,547	513,292	26,512	180,645	146,242
2000	5,038,221	5,215,659	16,832	5,232,491	593,743	-1,011,425	3,627,323	858,129	552,769	27,469	183,412	147,774
2001	4,938,397	4,933,784	27,500	4,961,284	558,095	-953,677	3,449,512	863,568	625,317	26,736	184,708	137,494
2002	5,112,529	5,237,871	21,759	5,259,630	592,996	-1,033,099	3,633,535	819,910	659,084	27,704	184,543	137,557
2003	5,297,126	5,483,030	37,691	5,520,721	625,035	-1,117,229	3,778,457	834,126	684,543	28,304	187,149	140,017
2004	5,600,902	6,079,768	51,344	6,131,112	691,342	-1,353,370	4,086,400	787,180	727,322	29,585	189,316	148,000
2005	5,864,112	6,396,016	36,485	6,432,501	732,632	-1,459,080	4,240,789	822,705	800,618	30,504	192,242	150,926
2006	6,124,176	6,633,219	26,728	6,659,947	761,053	-1,589,518	4,309,376	942,851	871,949	31,398	195,047	153,411
2007	6,299,930	6,624,585	37,292	6,661,877	760,667	-1,572,003	4,329,207	1,051,408	919,315	32,093	196,304	152,211
2008	6,135,705	6,005,156	36,443	6,041,599	702,700	-1,359,553	3,979,346	1,057,871	1,098,488	31,026	197,762	140,901
2009	5,596,773	4,914,416	11,470	4,925,886	594,486	-917,944	3,413,456	894,397	1,288,920	28,336	197,514	120,605
2010	5,982,244	5,451,546	35,541	5,487,087	652,006	-1,083,490	3,751,591	914,092	1,316,561	30,297	197,452	126,843
2011	6,395,099	5,711,253	65,826	5,777,079	614,706	-1,120,021	4,042,352	1,042,488	1,310,259	32,236	198,383	130,784
2012	6,895,794	6,444,020	63,180	6,507,200	673,007	-1,311,378	4,522,815	1,029,886	1,343,093	34,638	199,084	136,452
2013	7,127,959	6,870,601	103,987	6,974,588	815,693	-1,454,655	4,704,240	1,081,664	1,342,055	35,575	200,366	142,382
2014	7,707,065	7,543,981	107,902	7,651,883	878,360	-1,648,858	5,124,665	1,156,717	1,425,683	38,216	201,673	148,074
2015	8,108,594	7,998,163	75,027	8,073,190	935,036	-1,747,916	5,390,238	1,230,030	1,488,326	39,865	203,401	151,709
2016	8,536,950	8,712,896	38,256	8,751,152	991,155	-1,973,989	5,786,008	1,230,441	1,520,501	41,818	204,146	154,728
2017	9,050,652	9,949,145	32,438	9,981,583	1,114,643	-2,684,008	6,182,932	1,302,736	1,564,984	44,143	205,032	164,226
2018	9,531,126	9,451,559	79,567	10,101,819	1,116,530	-2,560,847	6,424,442	1,529,115	1,577,569	46,354	205,617	166,134
2019	9,692,815	9,629,274	63,541	9,734,735	1,079,534	-2,175,555	6,479,646	1,538,525	1,674,644	46,975	206,341	162,215

Personal Income and Employment by Area: Elmira, NY

(Thousands of dollars, except as noted.)

Year	Personal income, total	Earnings by place of work			Less: Contributions for government social insurance	Plus: Adjustment for residence	Equals: Net earnings by place of residence	Plus: Dividends, interest, and rent	Plus: Personal current transfer receipts	Per capita personal income (dollars)	Population (persons)	Total employment
		Nonfarm	Farm	Total								
1970	396,780	335,313	2,368	337,681	25,373	-12,399	299,909	53,299	43,572	3,911	101,457	45,446
1971	417,926	347,540	2,230	349,770	27,192	-12,258	310,320	55,746	51,860	4,135	101,080	44,720
1972	450,654	375,041	2,196	377,237	30,787	-12,053	334,397	60,356	55,901	4,433	101,665	44,763
1973	493,677	413,405	2,892	416,297	39,391	-11,728	365,178	66,953	61,546	4,915	100,452	47,207
1974	534,102	431,076	2,210	433,286	42,454	-7,486	383,346	76,704	74,052	5,344	99,936	46,263
1975	573,579	441,164	1,974	443,138	42,399	-4,851	395,888	82,717	94,974	5,707	100,497	44,186
1976	619,058	479,784	2,702	482,486	47,320	-5,821	429,345	87,803	101,910	6,190	100,008	44,018
1977	663,650	500,579	2,167	502,746	49,351	695	454,090	96,318	113,242	6,681	99,335	43,206
1978	714,037	546,455	2,186	548,641	55,145	3,982	497,478	101,245	115,314	7,235	98,689	43,898
1979	774,162	585,742	2,967	588,709	60,779	8,535	536,465	110,354	127,343	7,793	99,339	44,018
1980	866,444	638,179	3,316	641,495	65,977	11,908	587,426	132,748	146,270	8,892	97,443	43,155
1981	949,566	687,973	3,108	691,081	75,556	7,810	623,335	160,268	165,963	9,850	96,406	43,073
1982	998,061	684,350	3,010	687,360	75,753	10,379	621,986	187,261	188,814	10,393	96,032	40,676
1983	1,045,639	706,479	2,736	709,215	78,723	11,496	641,988	195,761	207,890	11,046	94,659	39,693
1984	1,129,476	766,289	3,740	770,029	86,977	11,202	694,254	214,628	220,594	12,120	93,190	40,900
1985	1,159,337	778,630	4,238	782,868	89,739	18,782	711,911	221,603	225,823	12,574	92,200	41,191
1986	1,220,687	820,878	5,105	825,983	96,525	21,794	751,252	234,062	235,373	13,388	91,179	42,328
1987	1,299,640	913,947	5,771	919,718	105,457	10,338	824,599	237,949	237,092	14,154	91,819	44,422
1988	1,395,009	1,001,625	4,398	1,006,023	118,303	11,924	899,644	246,879	248,486	14,977	93,142	46,262
1989	1,535,913	1,094,119	4,544	1,098,663	127,681	9,090	980,072	294,302	261,539	16,219	94,701	47,884
1990	1,612,204	1,147,490	4,132	1,151,622	127,221	10,605	1,035,006	296,903	280,295	16,919	95,292	48,188
1991	1,665,578	1,178,931	3,035	1,181,966	133,598	8,796	1,057,164	301,178	307,236	17,532	95,001	47,118
1992	1,728,476	1,225,409	3,014	1,228,423	136,941	-230	1,091,252	297,012	340,212	18,203	94,954	46,818
1993	1,757,154	1,252,064	3,197	1,255,261	142,315	-8,945	1,104,001	300,272	352,881	18,553	94,711	46,964
1994	1,820,741	1,307,149	2,784	1,309,933	150,604	-19,537	1,139,792	310,120	370,829	19,342	94,132	47,823
1995	1,890,135	1,356,925	2,175	1,359,100	156,193	-23,720	1,179,187	324,623	386,325	20,178	93,675	47,762
1996	1,957,988	1,405,460	3,161	1,408,621	160,241	-27,928	1,220,452	334,964	402,572	21,060	92,972	48,771
1997	2,022,561	1,474,302	1,506	1,475,808	165,208	-41,805	1,268,795	343,788	409,978	21,946	92,162	49,516
1998	2,092,163	1,547,533	2,626	1,550,159	172,207	-50,812	1,327,140	345,709	419,314	22,793	91,791	50,968
1999	2,177,526	1,618,285	2,624	1,620,909	175,117	-45,224	1,400,568	337,959	438,999	23,854	91,284	51,569
2000	2,305,865	1,672,978	2,705	1,675,683	180,729	8,745	1,503,699	358,810	443,356	25,313	91,094	51,377
2001	2,320,694	1,668,533	3,073	1,671,606	185,828	-3,329	1,482,449	362,184	476,061	25,564	90,780	49,776
2002	2,305,052	1,668,132	1,249	1,669,381	187,974	-16,560	1,464,847	318,951	521,254	25,438	90,613	48,141
2003	2,349,528	1,701,103	2,136	1,703,239	192,036	-21,127	1,490,076	320,369	539,083	26,061	90,154	47,038
2004	2,431,245	1,750,990	2,768	1,753,758	198,673	-29,364	1,525,721	331,808	573,716	27,081	89,777	46,333
2005	2,534,935	1,839,560	2,316	1,841,876	214,037	-31,036	1,596,803	341,327	596,805	28,527	88,860	46,498
2006	2,663,154	1,914,719	1,422	1,916,141	223,712	5,605	1,698,034	339,626	625,494	30,013	88,732	47,090
2007	2,778,926	1,989,116	1,989	1,991,105	229,744	-14,274	1,747,087	376,406	655,433	31,353	88,634	47,911
2008	2,974,123	2,096,938	1,884	2,098,822	243,955	-21,377	1,833,490	418,957	721,676	33,605	88,503	47,835
2009	2,989,004	2,054,454	87	2,054,541	235,740	-15,137	1,803,664	394,443	790,897	33,641	88,849	45,895
2010	3,135,386	2,211,111	1,705	2,212,816	249,700	-42,309	1,920,807	381,987	832,592	35,235	88,985	45,941
2011	3,281,569	2,289,437	2,710	2,292,147	234,526	-27,361	2,030,260	421,793	829,516	36,879	88,983	46,425
2012	3,358,955	2,347,191	2,849	2,350,040	235,926	-32,618	2,081,496	448,850	828,609	37,658	89,197	45,982
2013	3,375,627	2,360,273	3,621	2,363,894	267,866	-21,074	2,074,954	452,375	848,298	38,197	88,374	45,277
2014	3,453,757	2,388,275	2,953	2,391,228	276,387	-13,010	2,101,831	486,164	865,762	39,510	87,414	45,297
2015	3,494,790	2,386,128	851	2,386,979	276,548	-25,413	2,085,018	502,510	907,262	40,156	87,030	45,094
2016	3,486,380	2,339,041	1,062	2,340,103	275,494	-9,865	2,054,744	507,863	923,773	40,520	86,040	44,038
2017	3,642,730	2,372,997	1,136	2,374,133	281,057	18,518	2,111,594	530,482	1,000,654	42,577	85,557	43,788
2018	3,735,959	3,733,733	2,226	2,457,849	286,328	41,607	2,213,128	559,158	963,673	44,510	83,935	43,684
2019	3,874,102	3,870,785	3,317	2,506,830	290,309	58,814	2,275,335	570,888	1,027,879	46,421	83,456	43,630

Personal Income and Employment by Area: El Paso, TX

(Thousands of dollars, except as noted.)

Year	Personal income, total	Earnings by place of work			Less: Contributions for government social insurance	Plus: Adjustment for residence	Equals: Net earnings by place of residence	Plus: Dividends, interest, and rent	Plus: Personal current transfer receipts	Per capita personal income (dollars)	Population (persons)	Total employment
		Nonfarm	Farm	Total								
1970	1,203,259	973,527	9,345	982,872	62,026	-22,756	898,090	218,760	86,409	3,316	362,854	150,442
1971	1,316,139	1,072,835	7,844	1,080,679	71,639	-32,199	976,841	236,278	103,020	3,542	371,562	155,024
1972	1,427,111	1,168,213	13,411	1,181,624	81,214	-48,817	1,051,593	255,821	119,697	3,748	380,771	158,645
1973	1,630,778	1,347,813	10,984	1,358,797	105,969	-63,759	1,189,069	298,364	143,345	4,069	400,736	172,265
1974	1,831,322	1,504,699	11,675	1,516,374	122,106	-76,391	1,317,877	344,888	168,557	4,422	414,149	178,186
1975	1,939,079	1,650,839	11,999	1,662,838	135,057	-180,306	1,347,475	376,772	214,832	4,509	430,008	183,213
1976	2,161,399	1,845,061	16,226	1,861,287	153,446	-198,826	1,509,015	408,068	244,316	4,879	443,031	189,986
1977	2,380,879	2,036,842	20,615	2,057,457	168,057	-224,304	1,665,096	452,808	262,975	5,260	452,639	194,248
1978	2,668,601	2,290,265	12,779	2,303,044	192,179	-249,540	1,861,325	514,473	292,803	5,762	463,126	200,883
1979	3,036,740	2,583,433	10,812	2,594,245	227,863	-248,753	2,117,629	576,343	342,768	6,394	474,925	208,458
1980	3,371,958	2,851,352	6,588	2,857,940	253,028	-311,008	2,293,904	671,261	406,793	6,931	486,485	214,832
1981	4,064,006	3,239,015	20,461	3,259,476	308,726	-128,327	2,822,423	790,063	451,520	8,120	500,476	223,237
1982	4,390,171	3,442,956	6,794	3,449,750	326,341	-157,921	2,965,488	919,803	504,880	8,525	514,949	222,683
1983	4,728,022	3,635,297	17,879	3,653,176	343,899	-152,590	3,156,687	1,003,255	568,080	9,023	523,973	219,571
1984	5,096,456	3,935,097	15,534	3,950,631	383,119	-181,848	3,385,664	1,095,811	614,981	9,573	532,385	227,764
1985	5,502,556	4,238,111	17,161	4,255,272	416,452	-198,636	3,640,184	1,205,685	656,687	10,161	541,534	232,617
1986	5,806,357	4,470,682	8,031	4,478,713	438,314	-195,351	3,845,048	1,248,068	713,241	10,513	552,279	235,285
1987	6,029,678	4,645,236	19,333	4,664,569	453,731	-214,745	3,996,093	1,276,536	757,049	10,725	562,186	245,513
1988	6,454,997	5,017,373	18,127	5,035,500	508,260	-231,511	4,295,729	1,348,297	810,971	11,292	571,624	254,501
1989	7,067,940	5,375,779	16,492	5,392,271	554,062	-242,817	4,595,392	1,537,271	935,277	12,106	583,850	264,114
1990	7,634,080	5,714,230	12,285	5,726,515	581,941	-267,853	4,876,721	1,694,930	1,062,429	12,761	598,255	269,064
1991	7,942,059	6,040,646	7,748	6,048,394	624,970	-296,909	5,126,515	1,598,686	1,216,858	12,997	611,092	271,145
1992	8,771,712	6,659,925	26,917	6,686,842	688,724	-318,195	5,679,923	1,621,602	1,470,187	14,102	622,040	281,367
1993	9,242,850	7,005,752	23,325	7,029,077	731,023	-330,787	5,967,267	1,682,845	1,592,738	14,511	636,952	288,491
1994	9,749,666	7,426,708	31,411	7,458,119	774,093	-367,066	6,316,960	1,729,969	1,702,737	15,021	649,075	295,015
1995	10,234,554	7,715,170	27,551	7,742,721	802,130	-381,764	6,558,827	1,823,720	1,852,007	15,569	657,359	299,334
1996	10,632,063	7,885,941	25,758	7,911,699	813,916	-393,012	6,704,771	1,894,071	2,033,221	16,118	659,655	298,829
1997	11,373,629	8,455,018	31,215	8,486,233	865,889	-433,301	7,187,043	2,049,941	2,136,645	17,019	668,300	307,305
1998	12,002,268	8,983,520	37,465	9,020,985	913,758	-461,794	7,645,433	2,230,893	2,125,942	17,795	674,484	313,506
1999	12,264,865	9,318,037	32,288	9,350,325	942,936	-476,669	7,930,720	2,168,329	2,165,816	18,071	678,720	317,940
2000	13,066,818	9,963,918	28,706	9,992,624	984,600	-497,230	8,510,794	2,273,012	2,283,012	19,073	685,086	325,078
2001	13,632,407	10,347,298	29,458	10,376,756	1,019,086	-367,751	8,989,919	2,161,551	2,480,937	19,684	692,568	324,108
2002	14,345,732	10,837,513	31,476	10,868,989	1,064,814	-376,248	9,427,927	2,172,951	2,744,854	20,498	699,844	331,527
2003	14,911,123	11,314,505	42,132	11,356,637	1,124,126	-370,521	9,861,990	2,114,868	2,934,265	21,045	708,545	336,122
2004	15,731,941	11,966,213	36,655	12,002,868	1,187,470	-337,792	10,477,606	2,224,752	3,029,583	21,820	720,997	342,434
2005	16,770,640	12,521,173	36,554	12,557,727	1,250,725	-286,786	11,020,216	2,418,762	3,331,662	22,926	731,511	351,148
2006	17,771,192	13,191,529	20,388	13,211,917	1,313,759	-311,214	11,586,944	2,646,968	3,537,280	23,750	748,254	363,333
2007	18,874,732	13,716,866	23,232	13,740,098	1,396,064	-335,955	12,008,079	2,967,091	3,899,562	24,867	759,040	375,521
2008	19,932,716	14,068,657	12,025	14,080,682	1,450,836	-344,337	12,285,509	3,241,350	4,405,857	25,776	773,304	381,999
2009	20,905,265	14,701,719	9,903	14,711,622	1,526,138	-381,621	12,803,863	3,233,863	4,867,539	26,456	790,182	382,242
2010	22,904,539	16,161,701	18,224	16,179,925	1,657,124	-347,639	14,175,162	3,290,729	5,438,648	28,383	806,983	389,852
2011	24,459,937	17,026,028	12,760	17,038,788	1,563,687	-306,918	15,168,183	3,659,101	5,632,653	29,730	822,747	402,636
2012	25,676,790	17,739,970	7,611	17,747,581	1,639,491	-270,008	15,838,082	4,259,451	5,579,257	30,770	834,478	406,476
2013	25,281,231	17,588,135	17,119	17,605,254	1,838,180	-167,730	15,599,344	3,941,466	5,740,421	30,331	833,522	411,096
2014	26,631,124	18,203,084	15,045	18,218,129	1,898,773	-136,775	16,182,581	4,415,554	6,032,989	31,827	836,753	415,341
2015	27,575,767	18,920,962	17,531	18,938,493	1,985,508	-191,999	16,760,986	4,427,887	6,386,894	32,973	836,326	423,791
2016	28,359,126	19,355,179	8,747	19,363,926	2,045,839	-246,928	17,071,159	4,605,905	6,682,062	33,712	841,220	432,049
2017	29,209,182	20,016,073	12,096	20,028,169	2,135,301	-283,318	17,609,550	4,812,171	6,787,461	34,575	844,818	437,144
2018	30,533,172	30,519,553	13,619	21,045,401	2,211,159	-169,915	18,664,327	4,853,712	7,015,133	36,279	841,613	450,307
2019	31,766,708	31,753,280	13,428	21,998,134	2,292,250	-203,667	19,502,217	4,955,303	7,309,188	37,633	844,124	460,601

Personal Income and Employment by Area: Enid, OK

(Thousands of dollars, except as noted.)

Year	Personal income, total	Earnings by place of work			Less: Contributions for government social insurance	Plus: Adjustment for residence	Equals: Net earnings by place of residence	Plus: Dividends, interest, and rent	Plus: Personal current transfer receipts	Per capita personal income (dollars)	Population (persons)	Total employment
		Nonfarm	Farm	Total								
1970	220,525	166,678	8,631	175,309	11,088	-2,899	161,322	39,804	19,399	3,901	56,532	27,435
1971	240,055	178,534	10,934	189,468	12,299	-3,212	173,957	43,734	22,364	4,166	57,616	27,233
1972	259,831	196,276	11,158	207,434	13,972	-3,625	189,837	45,394	24,600	4,511	57,604	27,881
1973	289,212	214,464	16,047	230,511	17,570	-3,914	209,027	51,890	28,295	5,115	56,540	28,388
1974	320,536	240,903	12,184	253,087	20,314	-4,312	228,461	58,966	33,109	5,568	57,571	29,130
1975	359,151	270,396	9,176	279,572	22,654	-4,663	252,255	66,454	40,442	6,115	58,729	29,368
1976	398,849	300,179	11,996	312,175	25,466	-5,485	281,224	72,464	45,161	6,633	60,129	29,733
1977	451,706	346,053	10,672	356,725	29,242	-5,644	321,839	81,213	48,654	7,393	61,098	31,156
1978	505,892	397,053	2,592	399,645	34,472	-6,976	358,197	94,515	53,180	8,169	61,926	32,482
1979	594,705	454,123	19,567	473,690	40,859	-7,145	425,686	108,030	60,989	9,551	62,264	33,792
1980	694,855	529,905	12,190	542,095	47,952	-7,285	486,858	137,626	70,371	10,998	63,179	35,874
1981	825,882	634,097	-2,412	631,685	61,671	-5,745	564,269	180,440	81,173	12,804	64,500	38,599
1982	908,798	658,696	20,290	678,986	65,953	-5,431	607,602	206,109	95,087	13,444	67,597	38,596
1983	889,002	641,599	-1,483	640,116	63,240	-9,440	567,436	216,796	104,770	13,224	67,225	36,727
1984	951,281	660,272	25,158	685,430	66,602	-10,526	608,302	232,914	110,065	14,466	65,759	36,862
1985	937,021	643,775	12,083	655,858	66,345	-8,527	580,986	236,027	120,008	14,606	64,151	35,121
1986	912,366	613,712	21,029	634,741	64,342	-6,325	564,074	217,857	130,435	14,586	62,550	32,271
1987	881,225	587,530	18,944	606,474	62,250	-3,540	540,684	209,302	131,239	14,722	59,858	31,523
1988	918,649	599,302	33,457	632,759	67,383	-3,391	561,985	217,828	138,836	15,924	57,691	31,608
1989	954,368	613,127	35,200	648,327	69,388	-686	578,253	228,402	147,713	16,691	57,178	31,302
1990	982,357	639,771	30,832	670,603	74,187	-783	595,633	226,728	159,996	17,330	56,686	31,722
1991	988,747	658,766	7,459	666,225	78,644	-4,160	583,421	226,918	178,408	17,504	56,486	32,187
1992	1,050,094	682,126	18,974	701,100	81,154	-6,919	613,027	242,506	194,561	18,494	56,780	31,861
1993	1,081,363	717,264	19,081	736,345	86,160	-7,870	642,315	230,425	208,623	19,012	56,879	32,707
1994	1,133,191	748,281	20,343	768,624	90,287	-8,893	669,444	247,220	216,527	19,778	57,296	33,416
1995	1,151,110	760,362	3,273	763,635	91,903	-8,459	663,273	255,901	231,936	19,868	57,939	33,519
1996	1,194,696	775,439	7,042	782,481	92,905	-9,612	679,964	274,242	240,490	20,672	57,794	33,499
1997	1,293,667	844,995	23,345	868,340	98,343	-11,154	758,843	283,655	251,169	22,370	57,831	34,343
1998	1,340,005	860,952	21,705	882,657	99,713	-11,914	771,030	308,656	260,319	23,055	58,122	34,609
1999	1,330,778	862,383	18,653	881,036	100,653	-13,548	766,835	309,100	254,843	22,867	58,197	34,232
2000	1,398,716	891,784	24,460	916,244	102,943	-13,372	799,929	334,815	263,972	24,232	57,721	34,319
2001	1,456,797	948,756	15,557	964,313	109,627	-14,280	840,406	330,272	286,119	25,433	57,279	33,369
2002	1,508,632	995,385	20,111	1,015,496	115,844	-18,453	881,199	321,937	305,496	26,352	57,249	33,265
2003	1,599,530	1,051,517	43,994	1,095,511	121,019	-20,358	954,134	326,236	319,160	27,949	57,230	33,999
2004	1,713,156	1,124,567	52,688	1,177,255	129,510	-21,797	1,025,948	340,319	346,889	29,815	57,459	34,452
2005	1,796,408	1,216,666	39,612	1,256,278	136,455	-21,715	1,098,108	344,288	354,012	31,319	57,358	34,825
2006	2,005,594	1,314,996	44,053	1,359,049	145,352	-20,179	1,193,518	423,327	388,749	34,745	57,723	35,569
2007	2,092,038	1,350,898	17,851	1,368,749	154,300	-25,084	1,189,365	488,370	414,303	35,975	58,153	36,830
2008	2,234,248	1,465,186	21,998	1,487,184	161,364	-31,649	1,294,171	486,877	453,200	37,968	58,845	38,102
2009	2,166,441	1,457,551	2,738	1,460,289	164,783	-39,589	1,255,917	434,302	476,222	36,114	59,989	37,704
2010	2,372,274	1,598,600	9,912	1,608,512	173,085	-46,291	1,389,136	484,053	499,085	39,059	60,736	38,004
2011	2,509,582	1,658,838	30,362	1,689,200	165,616	-46,362	1,477,222	530,759	501,601	41,369	60,664	38,074
2012	2,712,599	1,796,085	48,778	1,844,863	180,102	-60,540	1,604,221	599,791	508,587	44,273	61,270	39,161
2013	2,671,709	1,890,788	40,094	1,930,882	209,941	-63,604	1,657,337	508,794	505,578	42,904	62,272	39,623
2014	2,851,506	2,022,554	53,362	2,075,916	221,220	-69,133	1,785,563	559,720	506,223	45,476	62,704	40,235
2015	2,783,831	1,987,404	15,682	2,003,086	220,314	-73,134	1,709,638	555,583	518,610	44,074	63,163	39,845
2016	2,733,218	1,957,882	3,483	1,961,365	225,646	-85,790	1,649,929	553,409	529,880	43,813	62,384	39,696
2017	2,624,702	1,743,849	5,096	1,748,945	203,113	-33,876	1,511,956	569,109	543,637	42,622	61,581	37,930
2018	2,667,845	2,665,745	2,100	1,747,232	203,120	-25,227	1,518,885	594,685	554,275	43,667	61,095	37,222
2019	2,741,380	2,725,559	15,821	1,788,028	205,854	-21,840	1,560,334	604,182	576,864	44,899	61,056	37,423

Personal Income and Employment by Area: Erie, PA

(Thousands of dollars, except as noted.)

Year	Personal income, total	Earnings by place of work			Less: Contributions for government social insurance	Plus: Adjustment for residence	Equals: Net earnings by place of residence	Plus: Dividends, interest, and rent	Plus: Personal current transfer receipts	Per capita personal income (dollars)	Population (persons)	Total employment
		Nonfarm	Farm	Total								
1970	1,032,554	874,070	9,693	883,763	65,451	-14,813	803,499	129,382	99,673	3,907	264,315	117,410
1971	1,114,365	945,500	7,669	953,169	73,696	-17,222	862,251	137,096	115,018	4,148	268,634	118,885
1972	1,215,863	1,040,511	6,961	1,047,472	85,357	-19,558	942,557	144,961	128,345	4,464	272,384	121,771
1973	1,356,689	1,172,171	13,611	1,185,782	110,177	-22,308	1,053,297	161,374	142,018	4,942	274,509	128,972
1974	1,518,598	1,310,640	13,040	1,323,680	128,119	-26,417	1,169,144	182,506	166,948	5,516	275,306	133,424
1975	1,650,464	1,377,633	12,089	1,389,722	130,633	-28,723	1,230,366	199,742	220,356	5,910	279,275	131,019
1976	1,762,065	1,452,937	13,712	1,466,649	140,390	-28,375	1,297,884	212,574	251,607	6,262	281,390	128,968
1977	1,926,260	1,603,342	15,839	1,619,181	157,429	-31,394	1,430,358	234,711	261,191	6,879	280,019	131,617
1978	2,133,750	1,794,375	19,266	1,813,641	181,303	-35,723	1,596,615	257,994	279,141	7,664	278,420	136,329
1979	2,351,026	1,976,366	15,477	1,991,843	205,530	-39,030	1,747,283	290,632	313,111	8,433	278,792	137,775
1980	2,572,414	2,091,398	10,104	2,101,502	214,290	-41,132	1,846,080	357,630	368,704	9,186	280,043	134,200
1981	2,827,865	2,239,417	16,432	2,255,849	244,875	-45,621	1,965,353	442,663	419,849	10,080	280,529	131,270
1982	2,984,718	2,289,517	10,085	2,299,602	254,517	-49,390	1,995,695	506,723	482,300	10,610	281,320	128,148
1983	3,080,333	2,318,991	7,358	2,326,349	260,836	-49,879	2,015,634	532,148	532,551	10,935	281,683	124,998
1984	3,310,930	2,537,766	10,711	2,548,477	298,687	-56,030	2,193,760	595,051	522,119	11,786	280,928	128,793
1985	3,479,883	2,668,220	13,588	2,681,808	317,654	-61,846	2,302,308	632,345	545,230	12,536	277,584	130,880
1986	3,607,065	2,741,417	15,076	2,756,493	325,801	-66,196	2,364,496	661,235	581,334	13,016	277,123	131,407
1987	3,757,515	2,878,186	21,354	2,899,540	336,665	-70,451	2,492,424	671,633	593,458	13,626	275,759	133,889
1988	4,019,275	3,129,085	14,988	3,144,073	373,075	-78,674	2,692,324	704,058	622,893	14,630	274,732	138,424
1989	4,404,653	3,379,005	21,128	3,400,133	393,719	-87,655	2,918,759	822,705	663,189	15,989	275,474	141,704
1990	4,658,382	3,605,066	23,708	3,628,774	423,356	-97,078	3,108,340	821,766	728,276	16,884	275,911	145,501
1991	4,911,352	3,779,019	23,928	3,802,947	449,018	-104,717	3,249,212	829,896	832,244	17,668	277,973	145,836
1992	5,231,718	4,031,863	36,226	4,068,089	477,472	-115,153	3,475,464	865,161	891,093	18,715	279,548	146,388
1993	5,483,858	4,230,493	25,935	4,256,428	508,745	-122,734	3,624,949	918,448	940,461	19,530	280,796	148,918
1994	5,711,514	4,369,077	21,488	4,390,565	537,160	-125,821	3,727,584	1,021,164	962,766	20,279	281,649	149,803
1995	5,876,065	4,527,431	15,063	4,542,494	557,374	-133,657	3,851,463	1,015,469	1,009,133	20,828	282,127	153,226
1996	6,178,960	4,639,289	28,540	4,667,829	562,161	-138,863	3,966,805	1,135,309	1,076,846	21,866	282,582	154,003
1997	6,465,592	4,845,324	19,469	4,864,793	582,948	-146,456	4,135,389	1,228,703	1,101,500	22,878	282,609	155,708
1998	6,647,425	4,991,938	23,396	5,015,334	594,444	-152,531	4,268,359	1,266,252	1,112,814	23,592	281,764	156,304
1999	6,841,796	5,268,700	31,915	5,300,615	617,585	-165,525	4,517,505	1,167,372	1,156,919	24,323	281,294	160,400
2000	7,145,629	5,426,173	29,401	5,455,574	629,898	-174,993	4,650,683	1,270,693	1,224,253	25,447	280,803	163,440
2001	7,306,576	5,548,634	25,505	5,574,139	635,251	-186,510	4,752,378	1,227,168	1,327,030	26,035	280,647	161,055
2002	7,464,258	5,607,113	17,123	5,624,236	639,111	-190,808	4,794,317	1,241,260	1,428,681	26,622	280,379	158,749
2003	7,568,004	5,645,700	26,197	5,671,897	638,942	-196,820	4,836,135	1,223,601	1,508,268	27,014	280,153	157,208
2004	7,894,869	5,961,389	19,693	5,981,082	671,673	-201,811	5,107,598	1,230,279	1,556,992	28,413	277,864	159,170
2005	8,138,081	6,197,481	19,055	6,216,536	715,798	-210,621	5,290,117	1,182,714	1,665,250	29,357	277,211	161,240
2006	8,601,430	6,426,262	16,776	6,443,038	744,207	-216,551	5,482,280	1,365,419	1,753,731	30,897	278,389	161,898
2007	9,095,516	6,641,399	16,066	6,657,465	767,540	-225,800	5,664,125	1,553,396	1,877,995	32,650	278,573	163,256
2008	9,470,231	6,760,807	13,353	6,774,160	781,656	-218,375	5,774,129	1,568,866	2,127,236	33,982	278,686	162,487
2009	9,355,776	6,464,082	7,710	6,471,792	760,584	-189,409	5,521,799	1,404,198	2,429,779	33,433	279,838	156,498
2010	9,708,470	6,673,579	11,196	6,684,775	779,809	-188,816	5,716,150	1,399,480	2,592,840	34,577	280,775	156,247
2011	10,386,678	7,178,301	18,521	7,196,822	751,002	-213,599	6,232,221	1,557,059	2,597,398	36,925	281,288	159,178
2012	10,705,224	7,307,149	27,054	7,334,203	758,146	-212,942	6,363,115	1,839,417	2,502,692	38,029	281,503	160,356
2013	10,643,469	7,444,015	19,658	7,463,673	861,107	-199,783	6,402,783	1,607,703	2,632,983	37,925	280,647	160,541
2014	10,945,994	7,540,310	18,324	7,558,634	872,930	-198,429	6,487,275	1,790,473	2,668,246	39,184	279,351	161,111
2015	11,299,548	7,792,410	13,535	7,805,945	904,509	-191,485	6,709,951	1,811,746	2,777,851	40,630	278,111	161,317
2016	11,370,780	7,626,451	8,791	7,635,242	899,812	-186,097	6,549,333	1,883,214	2,938,233	41,151	276,321	158,823
2017	11,499,800	7,668,471	7,446	7,675,917	915,371	-152,741	6,607,805	1,967,805	2,924,190	41,887	274,541	158,554
2018	12,229,735	12,218,894	10,841	7,959,535	943,025	-172,332	6,844,178	2,260,787	3,124,770	45,038	271,544	158,433
2019	12,509,662	12,490,325	19,337	8,180,847	966,660	-211,383	7,002,804	2,296,728	3,210,130	46,379	269,728	159,017

Personal Income and Employment by Area: Eugene-Springfield, OR

(Thousands of dollars, except as noted.)

Year	Personal income, total	Earnings by place of work			Less: Contributions for government social insurance	Plus: Adjustment for residence	Equals: Net earnings by place of residence	Plus: Dividends, interest, and rent	Plus: Personal current transfer receipts	Per capita personal income (dollars)	Population (persons)	Total employment
		Nonfarm	Farm	Total								
1970	790,124	621,254	6,452	627,706	49,259	8,542	586,989	131,403	71,732	3,651	216,409	85,936
1971	879,451	692,758	5,215	697,973	56,290	9,497	651,180	145,222	83,049	3,983	220,797	90,186
1972	997,847	798,153	6,534	804,687	68,255	10,105	746,537	158,553	92,757	4,395	227,016	96,964
1973	1,130,280	906,120	11,626	917,746	88,722	10,947	839,971	179,716	110,593	4,898	230,743	103,424
1974	1,260,360	978,382	15,718	994,100	98,024	12,657	908,733	210,351	141,276	5,328	236,565	105,876
1975	1,401,281	1,053,462	9,081	1,062,543	101,333	14,525	975,735	241,064	184,482	5,831	240,324	106,648
1976	1,623,286	1,251,885	12,309	1,264,194	122,087	16,756	1,158,863	267,512	196,911	6,601	245,932	114,312
1977	1,861,298	1,455,925	9,812	1,465,737	144,512	18,971	1,340,196	305,464	215,638	7,388	251,925	122,378
1978	2,139,948	1,684,533	7,703	1,692,236	170,596	21,750	1,543,390	360,246	236,312	8,223	260,240	130,003
1979	2,403,456	1,874,776	10,665	1,885,441	195,854	27,639	1,717,226	419,670	266,560	8,974	267,827	133,161
1980	2,602,364	1,946,630	5,590	1,952,220	203,446	33,881	1,782,655	498,487	321,222	9,439	275,708	131,154
1981	2,775,658	1,983,381	13,181	1,996,562	222,567	24,719	1,798,714	603,863	373,081	10,018	277,068	126,204
1982	2,775,517	1,900,988	9,777	1,910,765	217,298	24,260	1,717,727	641,577	416,213	10,191	272,346	118,130
1983	2,958,424	2,028,661	4,847	2,033,508	233,172	26,017	1,826,353	688,188	443,883	11,020	268,453	121,237
1984	3,199,434	2,220,843	14,399	2,235,242	263,752	25,668	1,997,158	745,244	457,032	11,944	267,878	127,016
1985	3,346,049	2,325,967	15,078	2,341,045	278,457	25,767	2,088,355	775,026	482,668	12,530	267,051	129,177
1986	3,494,361	2,442,536	20,513	2,463,049	292,120	25,690	2,196,619	805,608	492,134	13,125	266,239	132,737
1987	3,728,839	2,662,080	18,942	2,681,022	315,104	25,038	2,390,956	826,734	511,149	13,881	268,636	139,567
1988	4,091,201	2,933,454	31,426	2,964,880	361,121	26,120	2,629,879	916,291	545,031	14,985	273,014	146,319
1989	4,497,330	3,159,084	30,636	3,189,720	390,738	24,929	2,823,911	1,076,608	596,811	16,139	278,665	151,322
1990	4,749,152	3,362,480	33,135	3,395,615	422,888	27,283	3,000,010	1,099,093	650,049	16,707	284,261	154,526
1991	4,942,665	3,475,986	25,783	3,501,769	440,054	29,390	3,091,105	1,131,324	720,236	17,133	288,490	152,184
1992	5,252,388	3,704,663	26,624	3,731,287	466,027	29,869	3,295,129	1,150,375	806,884	17,958	292,482	153,541
1993	5,624,250	3,950,642	39,806	3,990,448	494,180	28,868	3,525,136	1,233,175	865,939	18,919	297,281	156,357
1994	6,036,094	4,293,508	35,161	4,328,669	538,188	29,209	3,819,690	1,309,361	907,043	19,999	301,819	164,297
1995	6,452,420	4,466,458	27,241	4,493,699	562,765	34,489	3,965,423	1,475,944	1,011,053	21,038	306,704	167,644
1996	6,870,127	4,733,782	25,572	4,759,354	605,433	37,165	4,191,086	1,609,536	1,069,505	22,090	311,004	173,379
1997	7,276,385	5,078,260	25,440	5,103,700	640,341	37,429	4,500,788	1,672,374	1,103,223	22,984	316,579	177,912
1998	7,670,710	5,397,826	15,137	5,412,963	677,272	32,764	4,768,455	1,701,914	1,200,341	23,998	319,646	181,115
1999	7,899,634	5,606,560	15,656	5,622,216	697,280	30,168	4,955,104	1,645,913	1,298,617	24,550	321,778	184,549
2000	8,394,799	5,934,551	15,178	5,949,729	732,125	29,534	5,247,138	1,783,510	1,364,151	25,951	323,492	186,789
2001	8,795,874	6,166,390	18,503	6,184,893	748,825	14,083	5,450,151	1,825,422	1,520,301	27,076	324,855	185,129
2002	8,872,974	6,315,116	18,110	6,333,226	773,283	652	5,560,595	1,739,720	1,572,659	27,093	327,506	184,589
2003	9,083,162	6,546,399	29,370	6,575,769	800,740	-14,491	5,760,538	1,688,306	1,634,318	27,454	330,845	185,159
2004	9,661,179	6,965,168	31,951	6,997,119	860,691	-32,895	6,103,533	1,852,751	1,704,895	29,071	332,327	191,076
2005	10,301,209	7,442,951	29,251	7,472,202	924,078	-54,346	6,493,778	2,004,930	1,802,501	30,674	335,831	196,415
2006	11,286,304	7,975,035	39,448	8,014,483	983,895	-72,022	6,958,566	2,390,486	1,937,252	33,202	339,926	201,138
2007	11,542,265	8,102,580	38,602	8,141,182	1,012,384	-89,076	7,039,722	2,437,557	2,064,986	33,471	344,844	205,433
2008	11,852,668	8,067,221	40,369	8,107,590	1,018,065	-99,797	6,989,728	2,533,374	2,329,566	34,042	348,176	201,514
2009	11,535,236	7,535,530	38,344	7,573,874	959,310	-75,269	6,539,295	2,289,896	2,706,045	32,878	350,850	189,685
2010	11,889,739	7,715,151	33,350	7,748,501	983,761	-70,908	6,693,832	2,312,721	2,883,186	33,789	351,880	187,126
2011	12,321,230	7,878,802	38,897	7,917,699	897,421	-70,076	6,950,202	2,455,873	2,915,155	34,863	353,419	189,044
2012	12,880,388	8,289,561	46,014	8,335,575	932,867	-68,791	7,333,917	2,633,094	2,913,377	36,335	354,486	189,457
2013	12,934,935	8,431,273	52,973	8,484,246	1,079,550	-65,485	7,339,211	2,583,333	3,012,391	36,432	355,041	191,204
2014	13,827,725	8,817,889	49,585	8,867,474	1,139,131	-67,639	7,660,704	2,868,734	3,298,287	38,672	357,564	195,773
2015	14,879,842	9,451,038	52,586	9,503,624	1,203,278	-75,557	8,224,789	3,144,157	3,510,896	41,136	361,721	200,897
2016	15,553,827	9,918,433	51,909	9,970,342	1,255,418	-67,099	8,647,825	3,267,250	3,638,752	42,233	368,283	203,746
2017	16,275,162	10,479,272	49,032	10,528,304	1,339,281	-69,562	9,119,461	3,419,953	3,735,748	43,430	374,748	207,602
2018	17,460,343	17,409,909	50,434	11,049,759	1,381,561	-66,022	9,602,176	3,848,422	4,009,745	46,124	378,549	213,465
2019	18,087,217	18,044,212	43,005	11,462,861	1,442,485	-65,060	9,955,316	3,907,954	4,223,947	47,340	382,067	216,272

Personal Income and Employment by Area: Evansville, IN-KY

(Thousands of dollars, except as noted.)

Year	Personal income, total	Earnings by place of work			Less: Contributions for government social insurance	Plus: Adjustment for residence	Equals: Net earnings by place of residence	Plus: Dividends, interest, and rent	Plus: Personal current transfer receipts	Per capita personal income (dollars)	Population (persons)	Total employment
		Nonfarm	Farm	Total								
1970	949,474	831,356	6,874	838,230	57,264	-57,900	723,066	140,278	86,130	3,725	254,890	118,647
1971	1,042,382	897,264	16,810	914,074	64,130	-61,476	788,468	154,108	99,806	4,044	257,776	121,245
1972	1,131,669	983,940	15,568	999,508	74,477	-69,189	855,842	165,904	109,923	4,384	258,125	124,254
1973	1,292,367	1,108,139	33,292	1,141,431	96,499	-73,780	971,152	188,286	132,929	4,969	260,065	130,416
1974	1,415,870	1,200,170	25,662	1,225,832	108,186	-77,528	1,040,118	218,779	156,973	5,434	260,547	129,898
1975	1,557,836	1,281,996	24,500	1,306,496	113,155	-72,907	1,120,434	241,653	195,749	5,970	260,965	127,384
1976	1,744,746	1,460,432	29,192	1,489,624	131,133	-86,889	1,271,602	265,907	207,237	6,647	262,498	133,259
1977	2,012,432	1,713,916	26,138	1,740,054	151,081	-100,161	1,488,812	302,808	220,812	7,564	266,046	139,775
1978	2,252,233	1,949,581	16,816	1,966,397	177,541	-118,834	1,670,022	342,175	240,036	8,331	270,348	146,579
1979	2,500,776	2,152,238	26,957	2,179,195	203,196	-132,555	1,843,444	382,697	274,635	9,165	272,865	148,866
1980	2,733,336	2,266,959	18,288	2,285,247	215,759	-140,803	1,928,685	478,485	326,166	9,887	276,466	146,600
1981	3,016,477	2,417,357	14,470	2,431,827	248,251	-140,233	2,043,343	597,766	375,368	10,902	276,701	145,853
1982	3,199,760	2,500,387	11,966	2,512,353	263,673	-136,868	2,111,812	674,025	413,923	11,519	277,792	144,080
1983	3,337,875	2,622,082	-24,714	2,597,368	275,498	-139,789	2,182,081	709,488	446,306	11,993	278,314	143,145
1984	3,733,480	2,924,062	22,230	2,946,292	315,667	-155,717	2,474,908	787,188	471,384	13,360	279,451	148,687
1985	3,922,567	3,058,474	15,490	3,073,964	337,196	-156,070	2,580,698	842,919	498,950	13,998	280,221	149,820
1986	4,064,600	3,153,899	16,298	3,170,197	352,470	-153,517	2,664,210	870,089	530,301	14,528	279,786	150,742
1987	4,196,686	3,281,954	11,856	3,293,810	360,659	-147,745	2,785,406	868,065	543,215	15,023	279,347	152,301
1988	4,500,810	3,535,865	10,569	3,546,434	398,862	-160,263	2,987,309	938,361	575,140	16,136	278,923	155,991
1989	4,827,390	3,687,445	33,366	3,720,811	419,194	-160,296	3,141,321	1,056,979	629,090	17,307	278,930	158,985
1990	5,114,966	3,922,661	10,152	3,932,813	457,802	-168,193	3,306,818	1,119,470	688,678	18,308	279,384	161,461
1991	5,268,274	4,105,751	-6,760	4,098,991	484,657	-174,894	3,439,440	1,073,855	754,979	18,730	281,270	161,774
1992	5,694,486	4,427,157	28,439	4,455,596	515,557	-198,143	3,741,896	1,104,806	847,784	20,038	284,179	164,642
1993	5,979,454	4,674,717	16,998	4,691,715	550,692	-217,135	3,923,888	1,157,092	898,474	20,854	286,723	169,312
1994	6,242,059	4,878,218	18,122	4,896,340	584,389	-238,672	4,073,279	1,237,132	931,648	21,623	288,681	174,356
1995	6,449,760	5,010,893	6,702	5,017,595	602,783	-245,369	4,169,443	1,318,836	961,481	22,244	289,950	177,218
1996	6,867,883	5,313,183	52,924	5,366,107	633,377	-278,699	4,454,031	1,398,060	1,015,792	23,509	292,136	179,775
1997	7,194,717	5,657,704	23,574	5,681,278	670,544	-310,124	4,700,610	1,460,445	1,033,662	24,481	293,894	182,816
1998	7,739,805	6,091,662	12,250	6,103,912	710,749	-299,669	5,093,494	1,576,294	1,070,017	26,280	294,517	183,227
1999	7,930,616	6,346,737	4,679	6,351,416	741,752	-315,197	5,294,467	1,523,991	1,112,158	26,828	295,610	185,640
2000	8,412,075	6,635,421	41,242	6,676,663	763,431	-314,978	5,598,254	1,625,808	1,188,013	28,373	296,480	188,367
2001	8,774,812	6,947,248	45,299	6,992,547	781,347	-346,605	5,864,595	1,615,581	1,294,636	29,542	297,027	189,688
2002	8,975,644	7,196,859	15,013	7,211,872	808,749	-360,653	6,042,470	1,559,076	1,374,098	30,081	298,383	188,934
2003	9,196,681	7,346,603	48,974	7,395,577	831,116	-356,782	6,207,679	1,569,481	1,419,521	30,592	300,628	188,816
2004	9,520,816	7,548,546	78,710	7,627,256	855,288	-339,747	6,432,221	1,583,998	1,504,597	31,494	302,310	187,460
2005	9,908,047	7,862,355	77,258	7,939,613	899,799	-360,133	6,679,681	1,608,680	1,619,686	32,609	303,844	188,590
2006	10,553,432	8,311,760	63,343	8,375,103	950,741	-380,093	7,044,269	1,752,323	1,756,840	34,539	305,549	189,353
2007	10,685,861	8,256,188	54,183	8,310,371	954,062	-390,085	6,966,224	1,872,667	1,846,970	34,754	307,468	189,398
2008	11,263,013	8,552,450	93,097	8,645,547	998,876	-426,264	7,220,407	1,938,405	2,104,201	36,495	308,614	189,148
2009	11,078,696	8,342,401	87,576	8,429,977	974,487	-349,282	7,106,208	1,719,351	2,253,137	35,718	310,170	183,626
2010	11,785,203	8,912,119	34,768	8,946,887	1,006,035	-312,022	7,628,830	1,761,574	2,394,799	37,799	311,787	184,471
2011	12,605,967	9,371,692	113,497	9,485,189	921,319	-278,618	8,285,252	1,928,997	2,391,718	40,322	312,631	188,291
2012	13,080,952	9,454,217	53,563	9,507,780	926,991	-190,238	8,390,551	2,223,896	2,466,505	41,732	313,452	188,271
2013	12,690,756	9,115,372	233,003	9,348,375	1,047,265	-116,794	8,184,316	2,009,815	2,496,625	40,358	314,454	186,857
2014	13,186,056	9,446,094	100,276	9,546,370	1,094,221	-117,238	8,334,911	2,175,648	2,675,497	41,853	315,055	189,282
2015	13,563,492	9,627,981	58,045	9,686,026	1,135,708	-129,876	8,420,442	2,335,460	2,807,590	42,999	315,439	191,185
2016	13,743,278	9,730,565	43,059	9,773,624	1,133,364	-115,587	8,524,673	2,332,695	2,885,910	43,533	315,700	191,949
2017	14,286,049	10,113,468	62,930	10,176,398	1,176,708	-139,868	8,859,822	2,445,597	2,980,630	45,256	315,669	193,934
2018	14,810,042	14,771,298	38,744	10,418,754	1,225,180	-158,858	9,034,716	2,656,998	3,118,328	47,067	314,660	195,465
2019	15,406,351	15,359,920	46,431	10,857,383	1,277,587	-150,151	9,429,645	2,685,085	3,291,621	48,896	315,086	196,211

Personal Income and Employment by Area: Fairbanks, AK

(Thousands of dollars, except as noted.)

Year	Personal income, total	Earnings by place of work			Less: Contributions for government social insurance	Plus: Adjustment for residence	Equals: Net earnings by place of residence	Plus: Dividends, interest, and rent	Plus: Personal current transfer receipts	Per capita personal income (dollars)	Population (persons)	Total employment
		Nonfarm	Farm	Total								
1970	278,000	251,770	204	251,974	16,197	-10,816	224,961	45,117	7,922	6,051	45,940	23,571
1971	290,765	270,347	203	270,550	17,661	-20,842	232,047	48,301	10,417	6,152	47,260	23,042
1972	310,392	296,147	334	296,481	19,878	-30,049	246,554	51,911	11,927	6,509	47,690	23,612
1973	328,225	312,778	325	313,103	23,188	-35,913	254,002	56,336	17,887	6,888	47,654	23,221
1974	453,568	509,522	560	510,082	45,652	-94,118	370,312	66,370	16,886	9,356	48,480	28,366
1975	808,224	934,522	905	935,427	92,818	-136,400	706,209	81,971	20,044	15,613	51,765	38,163
1976	853,100	945,688	943	946,631	95,099	-114,199	737,333	91,765	24,002	15,239	55,983	36,768
1977	765,561	819,917	704	820,621	77,007	-117,926	625,688	102,826	37,047	13,811	55,433	34,246
1978	737,979	707,912	884	708,796	62,669	-65,693	580,434	116,434	41,111	13,339	55,325	31,953
1979	756,770	729,717	438	730,155	66,245	-65,855	598,055	122,151	36,564	13,782	54,910	32,015
1980	826,592	788,250	272	788,522	67,972	-72,008	648,542	138,686	39,364	15,161	54,520	31,780
1981	941,399	895,633	30	895,663	82,597	-81,623	731,443	160,729	49,227	16,640	56,576	33,124
1982	1,194,321	1,070,101	5	1,070,106	99,139	-91,359	879,608	200,102	114,611	19,937	59,905	36,850
1983	1,271,568	1,170,511	-237	1,170,274	108,703	-102,343	959,228	227,223	85,117	19,356	65,695	38,748
1984	1,328,195	1,247,388	-879	1,246,509	122,340	-135,328	988,841	248,402	90,952	19,446	68,300	41,113
1985	1,425,756	1,323,381	-1,903	1,321,478	129,256	-152,881	1,039,341	273,658	112,757	19,959	71,433	42,878
1986	1,398,719	1,245,323	-943	1,244,380	115,724	-139,393	989,263	279,585	129,871	19,025	73,520	41,269
1987	1,368,064	1,185,755	527	1,186,282	109,801	-129,908	946,573	285,869	135,622	18,606	73,528	42,080
1988	1,406,800	1,200,925	848	1,201,773	117,071	-128,112	956,590	303,531	146,679	18,667	75,364	42,911
1989	1,535,059	1,253,789	-338	1,253,451	122,923	-88,941	1,041,587	330,440	163,032	19,905	77,121	43,488
1990	1,586,890	1,318,497	777	1,319,274	134,191	-123,168	1,061,915	339,442	185,533	20,327	78,067	43,739
1991	1,653,668	1,379,678	1,557	1,381,235	142,481	-132,571	1,106,183	349,799	197,686	20,548	80,479	44,917
1992	1,784,644	1,493,547	2,452	1,495,999	156,612	-149,132	1,190,255	373,847	220,542	21,630	82,506	45,630
1993	1,863,705	1,524,482	1,486	1,525,968	161,877	-151,533	1,212,558	408,003	243,144	22,460	82,979	46,493
1994	1,879,554	1,527,702	312	1,528,014	164,413	-145,660	1,217,941	414,489	247,124	22,506	83,512	46,423
1995	1,959,578	1,585,299	1,216	1,586,515	170,479	-156,030	1,260,006	443,451	256,121	23,914	81,941	46,681
1996	2,011,923	1,620,618	111	1,620,729	173,795	-164,431	1,282,503	455,741	273,679	24,275	82,880	47,330
1997	2,105,279	1,696,642	271	1,696,913	182,291	-177,090	1,337,532	472,507	295,240	25,524	82,483	48,611
1998	2,211,035	1,780,539	641	1,781,180	189,355	-181,737	1,410,088	479,341	321,606	26,543	83,299	49,469
1999	2,284,083	1,828,744	567	1,829,311	191,633	-190,440	1,447,238	489,643	347,202	27,390	83,390	49,335
2000	2,455,218	1,951,993	399	1,952,392	201,949	-207,277	1,543,166	521,145	390,907	29,579	83,005	50,450
2001	2,535,219	2,021,037	2,036	2,023,073	208,023	-183,774	1,631,276	491,566	412,377	29,892	84,814	51,232
2002	2,702,139	2,188,990	2,278	2,191,268	224,781	-167,072	1,799,415	483,674	419,050	31,386	86,095	52,613
2003	2,871,225	2,346,977	3,946	2,350,923	238,105	-147,783	1,965,035	499,264	406,926	33,046	86,885	52,971
2004	3,024,919	2,479,650	3,973	2,483,623	255,847	-119,413	2,108,363	518,847	397,709	33,971	89,043	54,102
2005	3,317,349	2,691,677	5,616	2,697,293	278,753	-84,752	2,333,788	560,219	423,342	36,684	90,431	55,121
2006	3,633,124	2,919,276	4,796	2,924,072	312,163	-36,583	2,575,326	607,435	450,363	40,125	90,545	56,731
2007	3,917,343	2,998,798	4,931	3,003,729	317,033	23,629	2,710,325	696,772	510,246	41,877	93,545	57,967
2008	4,322,142	3,100,915	1,270	3,102,185	328,694	88,490	2,861,981	764,442	695,719	45,712	94,552	58,040
2009	4,292,947	3,192,774	3,414	3,196,188	336,199	86,588	2,946,577	747,076	599,294	45,076	95,238	57,509
2010	4,526,325	3,335,241	3,623	3,338,864	343,881	79,192	3,074,175	775,583	676,567	46,057	98,276	57,318
2011	4,970,113	3,635,293	3,341	3,638,634	335,975	77,550	3,380,209	887,042	702,862	50,645	98,136	58,909
2012	5,071,247	3,733,503	5,792	3,739,295	349,590	67,096	3,456,801	936,938	677,508	50,534	100,354	59,373
2013	4,918,998	3,652,722	1,911	3,654,633	382,233	64,718	3,337,118	911,389	670,491	48,752	100,898	58,144
2014	5,160,031	3,697,804	4,219	3,702,023	378,070	74,136	3,398,089	950,265	811,677	51,960	99,308	57,188
2015	5,339,118	3,826,382	3,636	3,830,018	388,496	78,393	3,519,915	986,830	832,373	53,582	99,643	58,065
2016	5,316,097	3,785,827	5,176	3,791,003	386,124	70,042	3,474,921	1,011,503	829,673	52,843	100,602	58,427
2017	5,433,509	3,838,494	4,406	3,842,900	397,620	69,360	3,514,640	1,053,566	865,303	54,497	99,703	58,629
2018	5,689,172	5,685,423	3,749	3,958,242	405,440	69,965	3,622,767	1,111,160	955,245	57,720	98,565	58,844
2019	5,806,852	5,801,413	5,439	4,016,990	408,906	72,444	3,680,528	1,123,788	1,002,536	59,958	96,849	58,474

Personal Income and Employment by Area: Fargo, ND-MN

(Thousands of dollars, except as noted.)

Year	Personal income, total	Derivation of personal income								Per capita personal income (dollars)	Population (persons)	Total employment
		Earnings by place of work			Less: Contributions for government social insurance	Plus: Adjustment for residence	Equals: Net earnings by place of residence	Plus: Dividends, interest, and rent	Plus: Personal current transfer receipts			
		Nonfarm	Farm	Total								
1970	462,348	361,915	26,901	388,816	28,348	-5,513	354,955	71,315	36,078	3,831	120,690	57,963
1971	509,069	392,060	32,997	425,057	31,523	-6,368	387,166	78,783	43,120	4,123	123,471	58,638
1972	565,942	432,614	43,016	475,630	36,305	-7,404	431,921	85,331	48,690	4,511	125,464	60,388
1973	740,158	493,239	148,456	641,695	47,657	-8,724	585,314	98,645	56,199	5,863	126,247	64,939
1974	775,821	552,470	107,712	660,182	55,300	-10,016	594,866	115,532	65,423	6,084	127,527	66,730
1975	804,871	613,867	53,703	667,570	60,545	-11,089	595,936	131,978	76,957	6,242	128,935	68,868
1976	954,422	711,829	100,034	811,863	71,960	-13,660	726,243	143,295	84,884	7,244	131,761	72,986
1977	966,351	792,758	13,485	806,243	78,082	-16,702	711,459	162,641	92,251	7,239	133,484	75,490
1978	1,164,667	899,988	90,175	990,163	91,267	-20,479	878,417	183,566	102,684	8,549	136,239	78,760
1979	1,241,704	996,539	47,748	1,044,287	105,121	-23,809	915,357	209,604	116,743	9,063	137,013	80,905
1980	1,282,880	1,031,439	-10,742	1,020,697	108,371	-25,814	886,512	257,728	138,640	9,298	137,979	78,475
1981	1,480,087	1,110,942	34,643	1,145,585	123,868	-27,913	993,804	327,889	158,394	10,637	139,144	77,415
1982	1,590,659	1,159,755	29,562	1,189,317	131,226	-27,365	1,030,726	383,351	176,582	11,344	140,221	76,983
1983	1,688,887	1,240,660	37,578	1,278,238	142,297	-27,895	1,108,046	385,339	195,502	11,861	142,387	79,004
1984	1,845,072	1,354,008	55,770	1,409,778	160,412	-29,543	1,219,823	415,563	209,686	12,797	144,178	82,450
1985	1,926,305	1,433,338	39,665	1,473,003	174,605	-30,232	1,268,166	434,406	223,733	13,182	146,132	84,299
1986	2,052,916	1,525,323	65,203	1,590,526	190,012	-29,970	1,370,544	442,794	239,578	13,941	147,258	85,952
1987	2,174,116	1,624,747	87,881	1,712,628	202,064	-30,064	1,480,500	436,799	256,817	14,633	148,578	89,329
1988	2,237,854	1,727,719	43,833	1,771,552	222,884	-30,925	1,517,743	452,765	267,346	14,872	150,478	92,213
1989	2,417,863	1,843,034	40,085	1,883,119	240,368	-31,437	1,611,314	509,405	297,144	15,925	151,829	94,155
1990	2,609,655	1,981,888	80,174	2,062,062	271,881	-32,461	1,757,720	525,149	326,786	16,973	153,752	96,333
1991	2,710,777	2,100,563	64,604	2,165,167	294,377	-36,981	1,833,809	543,756	333,212	17,429	155,533	100,109
1992	2,944,037	2,252,448	97,922	2,350,370	313,892	-40,252	1,996,226	579,564	368,247	18,612	158,182	102,535
1993	3,046,222	2,393,887	30,961	2,424,848	336,103	-43,728	2,045,017	607,823	393,382	18,983	160,472	104,841
1994	3,298,751	2,572,735	91,129	2,663,864	362,866	-48,204	2,252,794	645,449	400,508	20,248	162,919	109,730
1995	3,473,885	2,706,890	51,556	2,758,446	378,920	-53,013	2,326,513	724,958	422,414	21,044	165,081	113,090
1996	3,770,530	2,890,201	136,773	3,026,974	400,545	-57,562	2,568,867	760,764	440,899	22,620	166,691	115,991
1997	3,951,158	3,087,997	65,393	3,153,390	421,829	-64,461	2,667,100	827,250	456,808	23,415	168,747	118,867
1998	4,299,178	3,376,136	71,915	3,448,051	453,932	-74,523	2,919,596	897,683	481,899	25,157	170,893	121,710
1999	4,558,123	3,606,690	96,598	3,703,288	476,985	-81,307	3,144,996	899,880	513,247	26,364	172,892	123,691
2000	5,000,759	3,946,395	98,584	4,044,979	512,075	-89,308	3,443,596	1,003,626	553,537	28,581	174,970	126,440
2001	5,039,176	3,982,345	90,341	4,072,686	516,223	-94,605	3,461,858	997,900	579,418	28,465	177,033	128,846
2002	5,300,693	4,186,896	90,053	4,276,949	540,080	-96,855	3,640,014	1,038,669	622,010	29,631	178,891	129,742
2003	5,579,328	4,417,522	139,651	4,557,173	571,971	-103,024	3,882,178	1,042,767	654,383	30,733	181,539	131,637
2004	5,932,440	4,780,845	119,502	4,900,347	610,954	-111,504	4,177,889	1,058,327	696,224	31,818	186,448	135,324
2005	6,263,971	5,045,765	113,463	5,159,228	639,237	-120,046	4,399,945	1,128,878	735,148	33,090	189,303	139,308
2006	6,804,180	5,428,348	123,474	5,551,822	674,123	-134,329	4,743,370	1,263,158	797,652	35,180	193,412	144,064
2007	7,312,114	5,740,605	145,469	5,886,074	708,965	-140,480	5,036,629	1,405,207	870,278	37,095	197,121	148,966
2008	8,043,197	6,089,259	178,794	6,268,053	747,598	-146,117	5,374,338	1,652,875	1,015,984	39,947	201,346	151,713
2009	7,950,261	6,225,223	52,474	6,277,697	783,789	-162,930	5,330,978	1,527,168	1,092,115	38,552	206,223	151,422
2010	8,445,101	6,384,631	134,892	6,519,523	771,123	-169,230	5,579,170	1,670,561	1,195,370	40,340	209,350	152,299
2011	9,154,680	6,871,979	132,353	7,004,332	758,644	-195,099	6,050,589	1,871,631	1,232,460	43,039	212,706	156,425
2012	10,228,149	7,544,095	266,069	7,810,164	775,446	-209,092	6,825,626	2,153,362	1,249,161	47,140	216,972	161,529
2013	10,562,492	8,045,955	169,185	8,215,140	928,779	-231,707	7,054,654	2,200,350	1,307,488	47,264	223,477	166,066
2014	11,305,015	8,812,191	35,456	8,847,647	1,009,272	-251,944	7,586,431	2,346,464	1,372,120	49,584	227,998	171,419
2015	11,686,661	9,124,836	-840	9,123,996	1,069,950	-277,406	7,776,640	2,464,967	1,445,054	50,160	232,987	174,403
2016	12,038,661	9,297,554	64,284	9,361,838	1,102,953	-282,631	7,976,254	2,550,539	1,511,868	50,693	237,483	176,359
2017	12,242,895	9,471,036	-12,001	9,459,035	1,143,504	-295,826	8,019,705	2,661,428	1,561,762	50,725	241,356	177,714
2018	13,025,395	12,970,768	54,627	9,901,239	1,181,053	-306,959	8,413,227	2,933,682	1,678,486	53,315	244,311	180,087
2019	13,521,155	13,451,127	70,028	10,345,110	1,216,759	-323,484	8,804,867	2,953,201	1,763,087	54,932	246,145	183,648

Personal Income and Employment by Area: Farmington, NM

(Thousands of dollars, except as noted.)

| Year | Personal income, total | Derivation of personal income | | | | | Equals: Net earnings by place of residence | Plus: Dividends, interest, and rent | Plus: Personal current transfer receipts | Per capita personal income (dollars) | Population (persons) | Total employment |
| | | Earnings by place of work | | | Less: Contributions for government social insurance | Plus: Adjustment for residence | | | | | | |
		Nonfarm	Farm	Total								
1970	142,881	114,267	1,940	116,207	7,015	1,483	110,675	16,931	15,275	2,707	52,779	16,564
1971	169,166	138,014	1,434	139,448	8,874	1,095	131,669	19,602	17,895	3,138	53,916	17,929
1972	196,092	159,271	1,861	161,132	10,557	1,102	151,677	22,671	21,744	3,517	55,756	18,919
1973	231,880	190,934	2,493	193,427	14,961	625	179,091	26,211	26,578	3,949	58,722	21,634
1974	281,735	231,832	2,617	234,449	18,932	-95	215,422	31,952	34,361	4,609	61,123	24,337
1975	330,766	269,538	2,067	271,605	21,833	-476	249,296	39,869	41,601	5,117	64,638	26,037
1976	388,734	322,765	1,509	324,274	26,842	-1,819	295,613	45,593	47,528	5,703	68,161	27,389
1977	464,962	398,173	2,605	400,778	33,905	-6,503	360,370	53,296	51,296	6,514	71,376	30,699
1978	547,021	484,735	-835	483,900	42,910	-11,789	429,201	61,858	55,962	7,281	75,134	33,028
1979	603,458	534,884	-1,030	533,854	48,919	-17,273	467,662	70,772	65,024	7,647	78,915	34,065
1980	705,424	633,084	-2,554	630,530	57,992	-27,037	545,501	86,254	73,669	8,569	82,318	36,207
1981	827,140	744,103	-277	743,826	73,413	-33,574	636,839	109,148	81,153	9,641	85,794	38,634
1982	864,389	756,826	-2,089	754,737	75,962	-33,125	645,650	133,644	85,095	9,730	88,833	37,760
1983	852,747	706,122	2,322	708,444	70,334	-27,335	610,775	143,820	98,152	9,401	90,708	35,488
1984	888,571	727,078	2,359	729,437	74,216	-24,925	630,296	155,670	102,605	9,728	91,339	35,364
1985	944,181	767,645	4,056	771,701	79,346	-26,175	666,180	170,749	107,252	10,303	91,644	36,677
1986	949,129	753,247	5,969	759,216	78,176	-24,865	656,175	175,019	117,935	10,143	93,577	35,730
1987	927,185	716,349	13,662	730,011	72,747	-21,284	635,980	170,662	120,543	10,047	92,289	34,608
1988	977,868	759,373	23,430	782,803	81,894	-22,870	678,039	173,633	126,196	10,625	92,031	36,149
1989	1,078,673	834,745	29,476	864,221	91,184	-25,552	747,485	189,075	142,113	11,672	92,413	37,919
1990	1,194,625	961,062	29,246	990,308	111,589	-29,917	848,802	194,758	151,065	13,046	91,567	40,164
1991	1,294,574	1,036,456	25,319	1,061,775	121,371	-31,740	908,664	211,915	173,995	13,808	93,755	42,648
1992	1,382,774	1,101,192	31,061	1,132,253	127,329	-32,119	972,805	217,081	192,888	14,520	95,233	43,061
1993	1,497,682	1,188,491	38,632	1,227,123	137,673	-34,399	1,055,051	231,407	211,224	15,310	97,821	44,491
1994	1,609,242	1,269,470	38,871	1,308,341	148,593	-36,437	1,123,311	249,276	236,655	16,075	100,106	46,604
1995	1,726,308	1,354,505	42,618	1,397,123	157,750	-38,218	1,201,155	270,082	255,071	17,026	101,390	49,846
1996	1,803,323	1,380,975	37,394	1,418,369	159,973	-35,828	1,222,568	290,117	290,638	17,354	103,911	50,807
1997	1,914,781	1,438,097	70,613	1,508,710	165,344	-36,747	1,306,619	314,238	293,924	18,149	105,501	52,569
1998	1,992,677	1,507,873	54,905	1,562,778	173,867	-37,617	1,351,294	320,139	321,244	18,355	108,565	53,560
1999	2,050,004	1,568,884	44,525	1,613,409	181,862	-35,726	1,395,821	310,392	343,791	18,210	112,574	54,235
2000	2,186,881	1,696,172	31,985	1,728,157	188,995	-33,991	1,505,171	317,804	363,906	19,161	114,131	54,446
2001	2,384,894	1,856,583	18,884	1,875,467	214,303	-34,674	1,626,490	353,832	404,572	20,605	115,745	56,802
2002	2,463,988	1,910,674	9,208	1,919,882	219,937	-27,039	1,672,906	347,313	443,769	20,631	119,430	57,347
2003	2,594,762	2,001,762	7,788	2,009,550	228,879	-20,209	1,760,462	359,668	474,632	21,347	121,553	58,042
2004	2,813,318	2,193,855	7,276	2,201,131	248,775	-15,601	1,936,755	379,956	496,607	22,839	123,179	60,223
2005	3,102,026	2,390,818	6,783	2,397,601	267,181	-7,315	2,123,105	440,259	538,662	24,854	124,809	62,057
2006	3,409,120	2,663,972	264	2,664,236	299,538	3,768	2,368,466	465,280	575,374	27,267	125,028	64,092
2007	3,689,138	2,845,190	10,599	2,855,789	324,538	23,464	2,554,715	511,907	622,516	29,244	126,149	65,736
2008	4,084,330	3,133,898	13,097	3,146,995	358,156	31,660	2,820,499	548,012	715,819	32,184	126,905	67,365
2009	3,900,112	2,888,646	16,521	2,905,167	335,826	11,377	2,580,718	526,406	792,988	30,150	129,359	64,351
2010	3,962,264	2,909,561	14,131	2,923,692	334,004	-8,977	2,580,711	516,720	864,833	30,431	130,205	62,510
2011	4,211,719	3,101,532	31,538	3,133,070	317,885	-34,802	2,780,383	557,976	873,360	32,486	129,649	63,442
2012	4,272,541	3,164,437	25,093	3,189,530	325,120	-58,462	2,805,948	602,863	863,730	32,948	129,677	64,476
2013	4,155,362	3,143,200	14,406	3,157,606	372,185	-76,213	2,709,208	585,281	860,873	32,131	129,324	64,533
2014	4,344,513	3,215,463	20,360	3,235,823	385,195	-76,116	2,774,512	630,234	939,767	33,689	128,958	65,401
2015	4,369,417	3,200,217	-15,043	3,185,174	395,715	-81,410	2,708,049	650,797	1,010,571	34,103	128,125	65,100
2016	4,223,209	3,001,711	-12,186	2,989,525	369,776	-68,481	2,551,268	630,474	1,041,467	33,053	127,772	62,525
2017	4,283,860	3,061,241	-16,921	3,044,320	379,404	-74,085	2,590,831	651,164	1,041,865	33,751	126,926	62,716
2018	4,427,385	4,410,650	16,735	3,114,790	387,069	-73,148	2,654,573	655,856	1,116,956	35,278	125,499	61,264
2019	4,462,308	4,439,672	22,636	3,091,130	380,746	-73,406	2,636,978	665,318	1,160,012	35,999	123,958	60,719

Personal Income and Employment by Area: Fayetteville, NC

(Thousands of dollars, except as noted.)

Year	Personal income, total	Earnings by place of work			Less: Contributions for government social insurance	Plus: Adjustment for residence	Equals: Net earnings by place of residence	Plus: Dividends, interest, and rent	Plus: Personal current transfer receipts	Per capita personal income (dollars)	Population (persons)	Total employment
		Nonfarm	Farm	Total								
1970	895,508	756,061	12,471	768,532	46,776	-44,509	677,247	176,742	41,519	3,920	228,446	112,945
1971	943,591	802,118	12,250	814,368	53,127	-46,677	714,564	178,763	50,264	4,081	231,237	109,455
1972	1,079,144	923,693	14,413	938,106	62,149	-55,238	820,719	199,575	58,850	4,635	232,815	113,149
1973	1,217,676	1,041,004	16,664	1,057,668	75,642	-61,609	920,417	229,333	67,926	5,100	238,764	119,544
1974	1,405,028	1,189,674	17,555	1,207,229	90,462	-67,085	1,049,682	271,240	84,106	5,601	250,874	124,799
1975	1,514,949	1,258,022	13,314	1,271,336	100,659	-66,055	1,104,622	295,511	114,816	5,988	252,984	123,017
1976	1,618,849	1,336,989	17,565	1,354,554	110,252	-69,067	1,175,235	311,763	131,851	6,282	257,713	123,376
1977	1,725,916	1,410,413	14,753	1,425,166	114,407	-67,226	1,243,533	342,258	140,125	6,577	262,434	123,810
1978	1,891,547	1,518,122	13,994	1,532,116	122,616	-65,395	1,344,105	396,691	150,751	7,134	265,132	123,934
1979	2,033,223	1,640,744	9,296	1,650,040	138,588	-70,511	1,440,941	423,243	169,039	7,708	263,783	126,562
1980	2,347,916	1,874,637	6,546	1,881,183	156,816	-73,040	1,651,327	493,607	202,982	8,749	268,372	132,509
1981	2,600,610	2,073,528	11,003	2,084,531	182,868	-75,443	1,826,220	543,232	231,158	9,601	270,877	131,023
1982	2,806,231	2,222,490	16,299	2,238,789	192,186	-81,353	1,965,250	588,911	252,070	10,299	272,471	130,296
1983	3,073,279	2,443,763	7,674	2,451,437	220,950	-87,676	2,142,811	653,920	276,548	11,126	276,236	134,692
1984	3,375,291	2,680,611	15,688	2,696,299	248,824	-96,353	2,351,122	727,528	296,641	12,035	280,454	140,886
1985	3,582,929	2,842,152	12,212	2,854,364	268,890	-100,270	2,485,204	778,919	318,806	12,648	283,286	143,770
1986	3,808,289	3,008,205	18,349	3,026,554	291,300	-103,773	2,631,481	843,074	333,734	13,406	284,080	145,243
1987	4,013,967	3,188,939	17,097	3,206,036	311,027	-111,062	2,783,947	886,199	343,821	13,937	288,001	149,275
1988	4,262,191	3,416,052	22,814	3,438,866	350,797	-120,553	2,967,516	917,637	377,038	14,854	286,942	151,677
1989	4,539,251	3,574,701	26,197	3,600,898	372,502	-119,180	3,109,216	1,002,280	427,755	15,393	294,889	155,228
1990	4,681,857	3,680,857	38,352	3,719,209	397,072	-136,705	3,185,432	1,019,251	477,174	15,670	298,784	153,724
1991	4,915,528	3,869,784	30,448	3,900,232	423,656	-155,835	3,320,741	1,053,244	541,543	16,225	302,956	152,205
1992	5,884,299	4,735,632	28,091	4,763,723	523,865	-218,392	4,021,466	1,262,397	600,436	19,282	305,176	169,016
1993	6,131,748	4,862,968	28,512	4,891,480	549,440	-226,130	4,115,910	1,347,924	667,914	19,471	314,917	172,380
1994	6,273,478	4,937,656	29,614	4,967,270	550,402	-233,412	4,183,456	1,392,714	697,308	19,685	318,691	174,463
1995	6,599,849	5,107,865	18,412	5,126,277	560,183	-249,327	4,316,767	1,498,273	784,809	20,462	322,543	178,702
1996	6,871,863	5,243,121	35,109	5,278,230	573,485	-259,793	4,444,952	1,568,917	857,994	21,153	324,870	179,262
1997	7,114,105	5,492,371	41,694	5,534,065	598,707	-278,229	4,657,129	1,543,836	913,140	21,580	329,662	181,817
1998	7,473,835	5,740,495	15,793	5,756,288	625,961	-295,961	4,834,366	1,690,815	948,654	22,574	331,086	185,997
1999	7,806,704	5,997,083	14,775	6,011,858	656,098	-319,793	5,035,967	1,741,293	1,029,444	23,343	334,441	189,034
2000	8,214,675	6,307,419	40,231	6,347,650	689,397	-355,782	5,302,471	1,805,805	1,106,399	24,327	337,678	191,268
2001	8,353,621	6,460,101	44,661	6,504,762	710,254	-418,502	5,376,006	1,745,225	1,232,390	24,639	339,038	183,880
2002	8,826,180	7,051,012	8,839	7,059,851	772,538	-615,217	5,672,096	1,801,850	1,352,234	25,847	341,482	187,778
2003	9,212,829	7,660,743	7,495	7,668,238	840,441	-908,077	5,919,720	1,841,831	1,451,278	27,111	339,823	191,621
2004	9,671,537	8,158,394	39,854	8,198,248	894,120	-1,098,375	6,205,753	1,893,416	1,572,368	27,973	345,748	195,171
2005	10,196,311	8,992,624	38,620	9,031,244	980,545	-1,608,227	6,442,472	2,001,262	1,752,577	29,684	343,493	201,031
2006	10,558,532	9,565,386	55,396	9,620,782	1,042,029	-1,986,729	6,592,024	2,064,558	1,901,950	30,278	348,725	204,148
2007	10,902,321	10,284,245	26,278	10,310,523	1,122,517	-2,639,246	6,548,760	2,279,641	2,073,920	31,080	350,780	209,743
2008	11,500,839	11,048,647	39,752	11,088,399	1,207,579	-3,097,012	6,783,808	2,362,544	2,354,487	32,332	355,712	213,688
2009	11,611,350	11,472,750	31,396	11,504,146	1,275,930	-3,558,161	6,670,055	2,382,434	2,558,861	32,017	362,658	214,117
2010	12,146,553	12,088,225	37,597	12,125,822	1,346,537	-3,844,558	6,934,727	2,429,914	2,781,912	32,416	374,710	214,883
2011	12,666,499	12,398,089	42,951	12,441,040	1,272,943	-4,107,446	7,060,651	2,660,677	2,945,171	33,301	380,366	216,810
2012	12,960,116	12,475,612	58,047	12,533,659	1,279,187	-4,029,228	7,225,244	2,690,141	3,044,731	34,039	380,740	214,982
2013	12,909,208	12,211,733	66,852	12,278,585	1,405,052	-3,800,621	7,072,912	2,724,542	3,111,754	33,577	384,464	213,529
2014	13,178,812	12,066,450	62,564	12,129,014	1,400,717	-3,624,136	7,104,161	2,824,870	3,249,781	34,288	384,360	211,975
2015	13,513,863	12,280,278	39,965	12,320,243	1,432,215	-3,739,594	7,148,434	2,899,230	3,466,199	35,142	384,554	212,157
2016	13,560,851	12,204,270	40,173	12,244,443	1,418,519	-3,779,061	7,046,863	2,920,396	3,593,592	35,073	386,646	214,111
2017	14,062,512	12,610,609	53,472	12,664,081	1,470,093	-3,900,605	7,293,383	3,031,761	3,737,368	36,369	386,662	214,727
2018	19,265,143	19,189,892	75,251	14,605,808	1,673,242	-2,630,602	10,301,964	3,756,732	5,206,447	36,874	522,461	259,355
2019	20,122,626	20,046,700	75,926	15,116,028	1,729,939	-2,610,676	10,775,413	3,825,450	5,521,763	38,204	526,719	263,547

Personal Income and Employment by Area: Fayetteville-Springdale-Rogers, AR

(Thousands of dollars, except as noted.)

Year	Personal income, total	Earnings by place of work			Less: Contributions for government social insurance	Plus: Adjustment for residence	Equals: Net earnings by place of residence	Plus: Dividends, interest, and rent	Plus: Personal current transfer receipts	Per capita personal income (dollars)	Population (persons)	Total employment
		Nonfarm	Farm	Total								
1970	412,591	315,125	11,894	327,019	22,812	-10,792	293,415	68,372	50,804	2,742	150,488	70,807
1971	468,205	348,047	18,310	366,357	25,755	-10,367	330,235	78,002	59,968	3,008	155,659	71,683
1972	553,810	400,938	39,992	440,930	31,077	-10,377	399,476	87,464	66,870	3,365	164,587	75,556
1973	663,756	456,983	72,183	529,166	40,696	-10,478	477,992	105,917	79,847	3,914	169,595	78,403
1974	704,052	510,139	23,347	533,486	47,146	-10,577	475,763	129,865	98,424	4,012	175,478	80,412
1975	834,946	540,622	75,475	616,097	48,945	-10,832	556,320	150,501	128,125	4,683	178,301	78,703
1976	942,247	642,039	61,328	703,367	58,721	-12,264	632,382	168,312	141,553	5,135	183,484	83,760
1977	1,056,713	739,566	51,710	791,276	68,496	-13,649	709,131	195,819	151,763	5,543	190,629	88,950
1978	1,224,928	852,691	73,510	926,201	81,127	-16,091	828,983	228,264	167,681	6,265	195,519	93,869
1979	1,368,526	962,084	59,363	1,021,447	94,495	-19,580	907,372	268,628	192,526	6,813	200,858	97,375
1980	1,542,368	1,056,612	42,790	1,099,402	103,799	-22,786	972,817	338,947	230,604	7,510	205,371	99,074
1981	1,766,790	1,170,397	60,434	1,230,831	125,196	-30,143	1,075,492	424,026	267,272	8,543	206,809	101,476
1982	1,884,290	1,214,692	61,102	1,275,794	131,870	-32,426	1,111,498	480,480	292,312	9,053	208,135	101,411
1983	2,068,897	1,353,619	67,759	1,421,378	148,333	-38,382	1,234,663	514,095	320,139	9,805	211,010	104,781
1984	2,375,253	1,549,935	137,228	1,687,163	174,083	-46,545	1,466,535	570,414	338,304	11,052	214,918	110,511
1985	2,591,283	1,683,659	163,140	1,846,799	190,645	-52,753	1,603,401	627,320	360,562	11,864	218,411	114,621
1986	2,864,747	1,860,110	230,081	2,090,191	211,461	-60,740	1,817,990	666,028	380,729	12,914	221,825	119,025
1987	3,011,835	2,066,897	169,772	2,236,669	233,366	-68,045	1,935,258	677,422	399,155	13,265	227,055	125,866
1988	3,278,023	2,297,924	163,036	2,460,960	269,759	-82,574	2,108,627	747,739	421,657	14,196	230,907	132,435
1989	3,612,924	2,507,900	205,230	2,713,130	294,318	-94,504	2,324,308	824,431	464,185	15,404	234,537	136,787
1990	3,852,885	2,714,888	161,597	2,876,485	332,716	-115,946	2,427,823	919,567	505,495	15,955	241,478	139,593
1991	4,159,396	2,934,727	154,255	3,088,982	360,900	-116,161	2,611,921	987,661	559,814	16,593	250,665	146,715
1992	4,654,255	3,300,099	178,397	3,478,496	403,544	-115,004	2,959,948	1,074,025	620,282	17,891	260,143	153,194
1993	5,045,330	3,592,067	163,215	3,755,282	440,864	-124,150	3,190,268	1,192,157	662,905	18,476	273,070	163,449
1994	5,548,566	3,974,636	180,065	4,154,701	493,471	-146,682	3,514,548	1,324,361	709,657	19,430	285,563	172,371
1995	6,096,510	4,323,668	180,164	4,503,832	533,319	-156,741	3,813,772	1,509,413	773,325	20,345	299,657	183,452
1996	6,592,046	4,566,174	223,540	4,789,714	559,345	-171,345	4,059,024	1,704,612	828,410	21,127	312,015	189,353
1997	7,105,019	4,882,456	234,173	5,116,629	598,209	-196,551	4,321,869	1,900,744	882,406	22,089	321,648	193,813
1998	7,819,599	5,375,227	240,645	5,615,872	653,051	-197,149	4,765,672	2,119,757	934,170	23,736	329,438	197,050
1999	8,396,280	5,894,211	271,437	6,165,648	715,643	-209,640	5,240,365	2,180,240	975,675	24,780	338,827	202,983
2000	9,081,002	6,394,158	225,071	6,619,229	773,626	-224,788	5,620,815	2,410,717	1,049,470	25,980	349,532	209,503
2001	9,778,662	6,885,200	278,416	7,163,616	814,944	-239,381	6,109,291	2,494,003	1,175,368	27,288	358,350	218,192
2002	10,332,713	7,498,475	188,982	7,687,457	882,797	-246,483	6,558,177	2,509,525	1,265,011	28,106	367,634	225,733
2003	11,070,835	8,032,463	198,321	8,230,784	938,881	-250,412	7,041,491	2,696,831	1,332,513	29,175	379,457	231,646
2004	12,458,590	8,837,724	337,346	9,175,070	1,014,836	-248,864	7,911,370	3,112,055	1,435,165	31,726	392,694	240,227
2005	13,797,667	9,567,982	248,390	9,816,372	1,103,058	-241,960	8,471,354	3,763,827	1,562,486	33,819	407,987	253,989
2006	15,289,564	10,200,115	123,545	10,323,660	1,200,243	-227,644	8,895,773	4,652,918	1,740,873	36,059	424,016	263,632
2007	16,638,527	10,468,269	176,504	10,644,773	1,245,648	-205,536	9,193,589	5,529,258	1,915,680	38,115	436,539	267,837
2008	17,690,004	10,620,104	159,986	10,780,090	1,307,532	-176,410	9,296,148	6,180,716	2,213,140	39,611	446,592	266,222
2009	16,732,318	10,483,103	28,489	10,511,592	1,301,258	-159,648	9,050,686	5,227,331	2,454,301	36,763	455,143	258,329
2010	17,545,153	11,034,977	30,069	11,065,046	1,355,253	-162,985	9,546,808	5,292,279	2,706,066	37,708	465,290	259,740
2011	19,979,114	11,619,102	-27,580	11,591,522	1,288,390	-161,587	10,141,545	7,042,293	2,795,276	42,053	475,098	266,924
2012	23,315,791	12,555,553	90,502	12,646,055	1,341,180	-191,158	11,113,717	9,345,496	2,856,578	48,164	484,093	273,161
2013	23,250,978	13,546,377	228,843	13,775,220	1,610,951	-219,120	11,945,149	8,337,896	2,967,933	47,187	492,739	279,918
2014	26,654,376	14,430,180	351,876	14,782,056	1,721,015	-245,417	12,815,624	10,661,706	3,177,046	53,077	502,187	291,344
2015	28,853,065	15,348,388	229,632	15,578,020	1,834,335	-266,334	13,477,351	12,008,705	3,367,009	56,215	513,262	302,627
2016	30,315,265	16,128,136	136,231	16,264,367	1,909,469	-288,349	14,066,549	12,752,465	3,496,251	57,724	525,176	315,014
2017	31,938,654	17,054,058	231,143	17,285,201	2,027,991	-327,437	14,929,773	13,414,780	3,594,101	59,425	537,463	322,018
2018	35,143,183	34,930,588	212,595	17,600,713	2,050,475	-387,245	15,162,993	16,356,220	3,623,970	66,909	525,239	321,447
2019	36,251,158	36,194,844	56,314	18,447,252	2,190,735	-421,338	15,835,179	16,534,041	3,881,938	67,771	534,904	328,133

Personal Income and Employment by Area: Flagstaff, AZ

(Thousands of dollars, except as noted.)

Year	Personal income, total	Earnings by place of work			Less: Contributions for government social insurance	Plus: Adjustment for residence	Equals: Net earnings by place of residence	Plus: Dividends, interest, and rent	Plus: Personal current transfer receipts	Per capita personal income (dollars)	Population (persons)	Total employment
		Nonfarm	Farm	Total								
1970	161,686	132,931	2,083	135,014	7,929	-8,930	118,155	27,929	15,602	3,288	49,180	20,148
1971	191,445	162,410	2,268	164,678	10,419	-13,511	140,748	31,211	19,486	3,590	53,330	21,705
1972	232,114	207,239	3,051	210,290	14,192	-21,420	174,678	35,213	22,223	3,988	58,203	24,041
1973	274,482	248,659	4,013	252,672	19,668	-25,647	207,357	41,102	26,023	4,452	61,654	26,189
1974	296,520	262,069	150	262,219	21,044	-21,542	219,633	46,865	30,022	4,574	64,831	26,719
1975	335,707	276,024	5,866	281,890	21,637	-16,201	244,052	51,260	40,395	4,808	69,825	26,902
1976	361,820	292,722	1,493	294,215	22,768	-10,177	261,270	55,485	45,065	5,449	66,403	27,565
1977	397,913	321,980	1,148	323,128	25,138	-5,960	292,030	63,450	42,433	5,772	68,939	29,570
1978	470,375	379,802	6,516	386,318	30,620	-6,757	348,941	74,313	47,121	6,642	70,815	32,397
1979	520,701	420,865	646	421,511	35,957	-6,140	379,414	86,365	54,922	7,098	73,357	33,879
1980	600,418	474,627	2,285	476,912	41,461	-5,742	429,709	104,306	66,403	7,944	75,579	35,165
1981	665,849	513,603	666	514,269	48,110	-2,137	464,022	127,641	74,186	8,559	77,794	35,739
1982	713,246	530,367	3,444	533,811	50,961	169	483,019	149,521	80,706	9,011	79,156	35,849
1983	783,166	573,780	3,431	577,211	57,080	-871	519,260	173,080	90,826	9,655	81,118	37,242
1984	872,848	642,102	5,768	647,870	64,982	-4,049	578,839	196,345	97,664	10,436	83,640	39,790
1985	956,449	707,414	935	708,349	73,183	-5,919	629,247	219,122	108,080	11,328	84,431	41,603
1986	1,054,836	788,879	3,307	792,186	82,627	-8,346	701,213	239,127	114,496	12,045	87,575	43,483
1987	1,124,707	844,065	1,538	845,603	88,022	-9,829	747,752	251,087	125,868	12,444	90,380	45,220
1988	1,207,907	911,094	678	911,772	99,815	-14,652	797,305	273,192	137,410	12,939	93,355	46,586
1989	1,281,478	928,295	-305	927,990	104,398	-15,740	807,852	309,757	163,869	13,462	95,194	47,115
1990	1,388,541	1,006,709	775	1,007,484	116,587	-20,241	870,656	335,403	182,482	14,299	97,106	48,543
1991	1,485,117	1,078,998	1,751	1,080,749	126,058	-22,486	932,205	349,910	203,002	14,904	99,647	49,766
1992	1,629,994	1,184,719	2,163	1,186,882	138,436	-25,497	1,022,949	375,294	231,751	15,903	102,498	51,643
1993	1,723,819	1,252,786	107	1,252,893	147,040	-24,798	1,081,055	396,156	246,608	16,329	105,570	53,787
1994	1,872,310	1,347,781	-1,110	1,346,671	157,844	-23,859	1,164,968	446,444	260,898	17,228	108,680	56,507
1995	2,001,700	1,416,351	-1,248	1,415,103	158,661	-23,422	1,233,020	504,281	264,399	18,041	110,954	58,867
1996	2,149,711	1,522,068	899	1,522,967	174,577	-23,145	1,325,245	539,953	284,513	19,077	112,686	61,574
1997	2,303,810	1,618,796	734	1,619,530	181,721	-18,896	1,418,913	590,411	294,486	20,130	114,444	62,567
1998	2,457,638	1,718,819	4,577	1,723,396	190,811	-15,932	1,516,653	630,644	310,341	21,394	114,874	65,405
1999	2,583,559	1,813,712	9,544	1,823,256	200,315	-13,820	1,609,121	643,299	331,139	22,406	115,307	66,761
2000	2,774,397	1,944,066	4,261	1,948,327	213,779	-11,272	1,723,276	702,146	348,975	23,759	116,773	69,832
2001	2,932,557	2,038,508	9,119	2,047,627	226,594	-4,873	1,816,160	705,887	410,510	24,793	118,283	66,819
2002	3,066,787	2,153,906	428	2,154,334	239,810	2,277	1,916,801	693,751	456,235	25,281	121,308	67,698
2003	3,222,536	2,288,713	-115	2,288,598	250,755	9,125	2,046,968	672,559	503,009	26,225	122,882	69,161
2004	3,476,352	2,465,444	1,743	2,467,187	268,694	17,403	2,215,896	738,056	522,400	27,785	125,117	72,523
2005	3,744,862	2,613,239	32	2,613,271	288,079	32,195	2,357,387	813,418	574,057	29,481	127,025	74,562
2006	4,119,871	2,836,261	-22	2,836,239	307,268	43,340	2,572,311	935,078	612,482	32,013	128,695	76,556
2007	4,416,384	3,076,489	17,917	3,094,406	336,655	43,759	2,801,510	951,165	663,709	33,857	130,442	79,194
2008	4,716,122	3,187,844	9,925	3,197,769	350,892	42,819	2,889,696	1,053,339	773,087	35,768	131,853	78,696
2009	4,517,343	3,028,485	5,388	3,033,873	341,473	51,875	2,744,275	910,346	862,722	33,844	133,477	76,109
2010	4,622,891	3,132,093	5,746	3,137,839	350,340	63,229	2,850,728	823,852	948,311	34,342	134,612	76,341
2011	4,971,530	3,317,502	6,682	3,324,184	324,541	86,414	3,086,057	943,589	941,884	37,051	134,181	76,961
2012	5,005,591	3,256,347	1,002	3,257,349	322,951	108,991	3,043,389	1,041,667	920,535	36,805	136,002	78,072
2013	5,235,880	3,456,554	2,961	3,459,515	382,960	128,956	3,205,511	1,086,240	944,129	38,373	136,448	80,103
2014	5,605,538	3,612,219	3,031	3,615,250	399,895	135,128	3,350,483	1,217,721	1,037,334	40,854	137,209	81,656
2015	5,935,647	3,815,840	5,773	3,821,613	424,255	144,728	3,542,086	1,322,255	1,071,306	42,800	138,682	83,523
2016	6,203,928	3,956,692	4,487	3,961,179	436,278	152,067	3,676,968	1,416,538	1,110,422	44,289	140,079	85,092
2017	6,513,074	4,161,966	7,676	4,169,642	458,950	162,054	3,872,746	1,480,558	1,159,770	46,266	140,776	86,303
2018	6,965,148	6,940,566	24,582	4,442,445	479,921	155,772	4,118,296	1,633,063	1,213,789	48,870	142,523	87,132
2019	7,057,376	7,050,336	7,040	4,446,792	486,098	171,918	4,132,612	1,648,855	1,275,909	49,189	143,476	87,159

Personal Income and Employment by Area: Flint, MI

(Thousands of dollars, except as noted.)

		Earnings by place of work			Less: Contributions for government social insurance	Plus: Adjustment for residence	Equals: Net earnings by place of residence	Plus: Dividends, interest, and rent	Plus: Personal current transfer receipts	Per capita personal income (dollars)	Population (persons)	Total employment
Year	Personal income, total	Nonfarm	Farm	Total								
1970	1,771,022	1,618,255	3,749	1,622,004	113,439	-119,282	1,389,283	218,119	163,620	3,970	446,058	169,418
1971	2,050,637	1,926,510	3,188	1,929,698	138,409	-154,672	1,636,617	232,021	181,999	4,574	448,310	180,597
1972	2,232,036	2,115,753	5,044	2,120,797	164,610	-174,935	1,781,252	246,822	203,962	4,975	448,656	181,540
1973	2,452,316	2,368,810	6,331	2,375,141	213,069	-199,956	1,962,116	263,227	226,973	5,428	451,762	190,536
1974	2,474,702	2,265,756	6,992	2,272,748	211,254	-185,181	1,876,313	291,930	306,459	5,497	450,155	181,085
1975	2,695,600	2,418,511	7,264	2,425,775	222,103	-204,701	1,998,971	311,066	385,563	6,032	446,850	172,646
1976	3,205,305	3,025,601	6,365	3,031,966	283,603	-283,283	2,465,080	346,210	394,015	7,205	444,880	184,610
1977	3,692,290	3,590,047	5,861	3,595,908	336,765	-356,096	2,903,047	391,656	397,587	8,269	446,546	197,459
1978	4,042,108	3,975,603	1,933	3,977,536	387,416	-396,187	3,193,933	431,999	416,176	8,990	449,607	205,560
1979	4,414,030	4,291,343	4,071	4,295,414	427,340	-427,461	3,440,613	485,648	487,769	9,785	451,082	209,373
1980	4,644,626	4,176,568	3,704	4,180,272	408,258	-413,108	3,358,906	563,140	722,580	10,341	449,131	193,291
1981	5,064,084	4,628,517	4,682	4,633,199	493,230	-463,852	3,676,117	674,951	713,016	11,434	442,878	196,257
1982	5,039,827	4,339,488	-159	4,339,329	468,809	-408,904	3,461,616	776,863	801,348	11,530	437,115	180,848
1983	5,492,110	4,828,984	2,642	4,831,626	531,404	-466,921	3,833,301	830,625	828,184	12,696	432,600	184,486
1984	6,109,702	5,469,115	5,904	5,475,019	624,808	-524,443	4,325,768	947,380	836,554	14,200	430,254	194,055
1985	6,637,303	6,008,042	4,895	6,012,937	705,066	-561,600	4,746,271	1,020,657	870,375	15,390	431,268	202,416
1986	6,962,585	6,236,728	3,838	6,240,566	732,763	-554,803	4,953,000	1,090,954	918,631	16,078	433,037	205,863
1987	6,661,000	5,698,352	4,050	5,702,402	661,344	-421,645	4,619,413	1,075,417	966,170	15,371	433,335	202,507
1988	6,894,660	5,769,787	3,977	5,773,764	685,436	-378,341	4,709,987	1,146,076	1,038,597	16,031	430,096	194,226
1989	7,224,829	5,982,754	6,405	5,989,159	714,198	-370,688	4,904,273	1,184,987	1,135,569	16,843	428,946	198,317
1990	7,558,747	6,128,473	5,372	6,133,845	741,866	-353,885	5,038,094	1,299,104	1,221,549	17,540	430,938	201,117
1991	7,929,183	6,395,000	1,817	6,396,817	786,256	-356,856	5,253,705	1,285,177	1,390,301	18,389	431,184	196,856
1992	8,182,401	6,499,758	1,331	6,501,089	789,813	-291,065	5,420,211	1,296,746	1,465,444	18,987	430,944	195,695
1993	8,539,785	6,717,044	1,467	6,718,511	823,066	-248,481	5,646,964	1,337,384	1,555,437	19,828	430,702	195,165
1994	9,421,322	7,556,622	-1,445	7,555,177	930,484	-287,550	6,337,143	1,521,565	1,562,614	21,872	430,742	205,760
1995	9,932,124	7,821,296	1,510	7,822,806	957,530	-235,380	6,629,896	1,618,088	1,684,140	22,977	432,261	214,744
1996	10,362,715	7,855,211	-1,952	7,853,259	933,462	-128,532	6,791,265	1,690,559	1,880,891	23,916	433,302	218,418
1997	10,527,497	7,909,096	-2,213	7,906,883	937,396	-17,786	6,951,701	1,789,657	1,786,139	24,314	432,978	218,542
1998	10,819,281	8,131,759	-2,760	8,128,999	942,670	120,122	7,306,451	1,770,934	1,741,896	24,978	433,160	217,360
1999	11,151,806	8,222,323	2,631	8,224,954	956,751	248,024	7,516,227	1,766,442	1,869,137	25,671	434,409	214,621
2000	11,714,357	8,496,090	-2,081	8,494,009	970,839	391,559	7,914,729	1,842,654	1,956,974	26,808	436,965	215,500
2001	11,669,306	8,213,631	-5,569	8,208,062	953,701	505,479	7,759,840	1,753,343	2,156,123	26,607	438,584	208,522
2002	11,766,625	8,255,490	-890	8,254,600	963,434	511,326	7,802,492	1,723,010	2,241,123	26,739	440,062	206,216
2003	12,135,618	8,312,599	2,313	8,314,912	965,243	612,741	7,962,410	1,794,726	2,378,482	27,475	441,689	204,035
2004	12,357,008	8,490,076	6,623	8,496,699	1,003,440	721,729	8,214,988	1,673,447	2,468,573	27,923	442,534	205,076
2005	12,527,585	8,208,000	7,747	8,215,747	980,365	978,901	8,214,283	1,695,844	2,617,458	28,310	442,508	199,141
2006	12,904,691	8,413,025	8,577	8,421,602	1,027,454	970,398	8,364,546	1,769,349	2,770,796	29,251	441,164	199,333
2007	13,024,999	8,167,142	8,378	8,175,520	1,005,866	971,150	8,140,804	1,836,288	3,047,907	29,730	438,109	197,347
2008	13,094,262	7,734,411	11,875	7,746,286	969,629	1,011,757	7,788,414	1,816,413	3,489,435	30,235	433,082	189,381
2009	12,616,803	7,296,062	5,098	7,301,160	924,427	688,279	7,065,012	1,663,475	3,888,316	29,479	427,989	181,507
2010	12,902,553	7,425,432	9,887	7,435,319	918,996	541,625	7,057,948	1,636,481	4,208,124	30,363	424,938	179,309
2011	13,526,409	7,730,570	22,046	7,752,616	852,305	632,653	7,532,964	1,820,815	4,172,630	32,061	421,901	182,703
2012	13,841,129	7,925,397	22,126	7,947,523	871,551	790,020	7,865,992	1,858,731	4,116,406	33,108	418,054	182,470
2013	14,075,225	8,048,586	25,775	8,074,361	1,004,991	809,160	7,878,530	1,936,510	4,260,185	33,876	415,489	185,571
2014	14,542,513	8,227,423	12,935	8,240,358	1,024,387	818,020	8,033,991	2,118,088	4,390,434	35,240	412,673	187,635
2015	15,252,089	8,624,827	25,711	8,650,538	1,062,329	852,495	8,440,704	2,188,273	4,623,112	37,178	410,249	187,290
2016	15,716,548	8,725,971	19,725	8,745,696	1,075,587	972,492	8,642,601	2,356,260	4,717,687	38,464	408,607	186,040
2017	16,147,159	8,975,501	6,536	8,982,037	1,111,433	1,072,486	8,943,090	2,451,394	4,752,675	39,636	407,385	187,721
2018	16,518,658	16,509,368	9,290	9,218,067	1,166,077	1,195,071	9,247,061	2,485,696	4,785,901	40,618	406,688	188,307
2019	17,015,416	17,004,058	11,358	9,519,142	1,194,213	1,164,804	9,489,733	2,513,910	5,011,773	41,929	405,813	190,303

Personal Income and Employment by Area: Florence, SC

(Thousands of dollars, except as noted.)

Year	Personal income, total	Earnings by place of work			Less: Contributions for government social insurance	Plus: Adjustment for residence	Equals: Net earnings by place of residence	Plus: Dividends, interest, and rent	Plus: Personal current transfer receipts	Per capita personal income (dollars)	Population (persons)	Total employment
		Nonfarm	Farm	Total								
1970	406,157	335,541	23,087	358,628	23,637	-14,584	320,407	44,564	41,186	2,838	143,122	68,218
1971	445,235	367,395	23,811	391,206	26,699	-15,648	348,859	49,311	47,065	3,058	145,616	69,457
1972	501,497	419,930	24,895	444,825	31,941	-18,444	394,440	54,827	52,230	3,411	147,002	72,381
1973	576,880	485,934	30,377	516,311	42,491	-22,080	451,740	63,233	61,907	3,797	151,937	76,728
1974	674,759	556,988	43,467	600,455	50,584	-27,202	522,669	71,430	80,660	4,281	157,632	78,964
1975	713,992	562,197	31,022	593,219	49,699	-24,181	519,339	81,545	113,108	4,438	160,899	74,439
1976	792,398	647,423	23,012	670,435	58,461	-27,504	584,470	88,827	119,101	4,881	162,337	76,550
1977	870,486	719,410	20,706	740,116	65,020	-29,942	645,154	99,658	125,674	5,230	166,445	77,460
1978	994,242	816,651	32,603	849,254	75,495	-32,210	741,549	111,762	140,931	5,879	169,123	79,149
1979	1,099,503	915,714	21,030	936,744	87,479	-37,987	811,278	125,807	162,418	6,400	171,805	80,572
1980	1,223,173	1,014,044	1,734	1,015,778	96,820	-44,287	874,671	155,996	192,506	7,061	173,231	81,883
1981	1,400,222	1,127,787	25,746	1,153,533	115,644	-52,448	985,441	195,872	218,909	8,044	174,072	82,700
1982	1,462,646	1,133,795	33,593	1,167,388	119,110	-48,188	1,000,090	225,773	236,783	8,387	174,401	79,678
1983	1,557,357	1,220,378	11,315	1,231,693	130,065	-45,508	1,056,120	248,956	252,281	8,959	173,824	80,119
1984	1,737,405	1,371,216	23,390	1,394,606	151,219	-53,936	1,189,451	282,357	265,597	9,934	174,898	83,677
1985	1,832,209	1,422,115	22,453	1,444,568	158,687	-51,826	1,234,055	306,751	291,403	10,444	175,430	82,212
1986	1,928,084	1,527,243	-3,836	1,523,407	174,548	-49,323	1,299,536	323,624	304,924	11,004	175,210	83,463
1987	2,067,273	1,621,557	28,369	1,649,926	182,753	-46,687	1,420,486	334,820	311,967	11,826	174,806	84,803
1988	2,254,760	1,773,409	39,132	1,812,541	207,128	-50,803	1,554,610	367,572	332,578	12,904	174,734	88,568
1989	2,481,749	1,897,413	37,198	1,934,611	225,135	-51,146	1,658,330	438,539	384,880	14,128	175,658	91,566
1990	2,655,971	2,058,136	23,238	2,081,374	247,476	-52,701	1,781,197	446,632	428,142	15,030	176,706	93,814
1991	2,829,845	2,166,822	33,573	2,200,395	262,966	-60,015	1,877,414	458,678	493,753	15,763	179,519	94,063
1992	3,024,174	2,304,152	36,008	2,340,160	277,060	-61,101	2,001,999	463,520	558,655	16,612	182,044	95,003
1993	3,186,980	2,439,147	29,036	2,468,183	296,509	-64,948	2,106,726	483,562	596,692	17,303	184,186	96,466
1994	3,365,240	2,541,304	43,427	2,584,731	312,172	-64,294	2,208,265	521,236	635,739	18,118	185,744	98,121
1995	3,530,073	2,689,484	23,097	2,712,581	329,940	-72,024	2,310,617	546,847	672,609	18,799	187,778	100,459
1996	3,778,617	2,857,197	44,991	2,902,188	344,323	-82,434	2,475,431	584,273	718,913	20,000	188,929	102,855
1997	3,956,507	3,005,831	40,799	3,046,630	360,923	-88,509	2,597,198	614,862	744,447	20,750	190,674	106,126
1998	4,185,589	3,210,444	17,350	3,227,794	384,709	-94,785	2,748,300	659,443	777,846	21,836	191,680	107,187
1999	4,334,464	3,333,481	20,786	3,354,267	395,262	-94,334	2,864,671	645,911	823,882	22,500	192,641	107,966
2000	4,624,383	3,521,866	50,162	3,572,028	416,543	-101,366	3,054,119	705,110	865,154	23,925	193,290	108,664
2001	4,810,558	3,591,338	67,434	3,658,772	427,543	-106,652	3,124,577	735,608	950,373	24,766	194,240	106,048
2002	4,940,458	3,727,652	-7,323	3,720,329	441,809	-110,648	3,167,872	732,729	1,039,857	25,259	195,590	106,518
2003	5,104,408	3,802,498	47,272	3,849,770	451,545	-106,893	3,291,332	730,233	1,082,843	25,904	197,053	105,208
2004	5,360,660	3,950,385	37,918	3,988,303	470,779	-107,883	3,409,641	777,538	1,173,481	27,073	198,010	105,332
2005	5,533,787	4,041,258	24,405	4,065,663	482,259	-105,234	3,478,170	803,498	1,252,119	27,785	199,167	105,676
2006	5,929,913	4,282,967	22,623	4,305,590	521,617	-116,161	3,667,812	929,186	1,332,915	29,515	200,913	107,464
2007	6,201,434	4,455,872	8,375	4,464,247	540,977	-121,821	3,801,449	997,073	1,402,912	30,663	202,246	109,510
2008	6,438,176	4,502,363	14,416	4,516,779	550,831	-128,412	3,837,536	1,007,169	1,593,471	31,590	203,805	109,121
2009	6,297,908	4,333,832	11,220	4,345,052	538,097	-149,826	3,657,129	915,355	1,725,424	30,748	204,825	104,986
2010	6,445,824	4,408,284	8,513	4,416,797	543,286	-167,749	3,705,762	891,390	1,848,672	31,341	205,667	104,404
2011	6,726,232	4,558,156	17,753	4,575,909	503,161	-189,317	3,883,431	993,169	1,849,632	32,680	205,822	106,929
2012	6,858,670	4,730,567	24,713	4,755,280	513,945	-218,780	4,022,555	990,752	1,845,363	33,271	206,146	107,460
2013	6,979,014	4,925,104	31,994	4,957,098	599,189	-254,271	4,103,638	1,010,976	1,864,400	33,868	206,066	108,522
2014	7,193,114	5,055,479	-6,410	5,049,069	610,975	-263,369	4,174,725	1,055,792	1,962,597	34,829	206,525	109,048
2015	7,524,696	5,267,537	-30,388	5,237,149	636,914	-278,494	4,321,741	1,137,496	2,065,459	36,473	206,307	110,745
2016	7,703,891	5,296,965	-1,786	5,295,179	643,296	-269,712	4,382,171	1,208,332	2,113,388	37,431	205,818	111,513
2017	8,005,211	5,512,362	-4,592	5,507,770	671,790	-268,307	4,567,673	1,271,083	2,166,455	38,892	205,831	112,812
2018	8,324,125	8,320,563	3,562	5,754,464	702,463	-283,242	4,768,759	1,329,493	2,225,873	40,598	205,036	116,274
2019	8,696,180	8,673,040	23,140	6,040,906	734,402	-290,438	5,016,066	1,382,531	2,297,583	42,439	204,911	117,902

Personal Income and Employment by Area: Florence-Muscle Shoals, AL

(Thousands of dollars, except as noted.)

| Year | Personal income, total | Derivation of personal income | | | | | | | | | Per capita personal income (dollars) | Population (persons) | Total employment |
| | | Earnings by place of work | | | Less: Contributions for government social insurance | Plus: Adjustment for residence | Equals: Net earnings by place of residence | Plus: Dividends, interest, and rent | Plus: Personal current transfer receipts | | | |
		Nonfarm	Farm	Total								
1970	364,774	287,164	11,269	298,433	19,076	2,687	282,044	46,066	36,664	3,089	118,093	45,574
1971	407,840	318,621	13,503	332,124	21,253	1,580	312,451	52,655	42,734	3,383	120,545	46,466
1972	445,489	358,547	14,600	373,147	25,604	-4,397	343,146	55,976	46,367	3,664	121,579	48,921
1973	491,305	395,681	19,485	415,166	33,191	-7,031	374,944	62,878	53,483	3,976	123,562	50,449
1974	546,775	444,839	13,243	458,082	38,994	-9,088	410,000	72,785	63,990	4,405	124,134	51,771
1975	599,466	470,334	11,781	482,115	40,917	-9,315	431,883	82,063	85,520	4,741	126,431	50,742
1976	692,149	554,355	23,631	577,986	48,689	-22,388	506,909	91,098	94,142	5,413	127,873	53,503
1977	763,431	630,581	17,434	648,015	55,060	-32,363	560,592	104,147	98,692	5,863	130,206	55,877
1978	875,787	733,682	18,412	752,094	64,530	-39,858	647,706	121,832	106,249	6,641	131,868	59,286
1979	975,515	791,588	28,891	820,479	72,305	-34,423	713,751	139,753	122,011	7,250	134,560	59,603
1980	1,078,322	855,949	12,059	868,008	77,974	-37,922	752,112	175,164	151,046	7,969	135,322	58,791
1981	1,195,164	902,580	22,282	924,862	89,305	-20,524	815,033	212,734	167,397	8,781	136,104	57,118
1982	1,241,658	911,897	22,328	934,225	92,173	-18,223	823,829	231,877	185,952	9,188	135,139	55,778
1983	1,289,950	943,668	1,285	944,953	98,913	-6,182	839,858	243,868	206,224	9,623	134,050	56,395
1984	1,395,554	993,222	13,187	1,006,409	106,894	4,489	904,004	271,514	220,036	10,455	133,488	57,561
1985	1,475,173	1,029,173	12,687	1,041,860	112,866	24,358	953,352	289,951	231,870	11,062	133,350	57,338
1986	1,554,521	1,077,852	7,737	1,085,589	118,286	40,267	1,007,570	304,641	242,310	11,719	132,653	57,115
1987	1,635,178	1,124,151	13,778	1,137,929	122,477	57,339	1,072,791	313,560	248,827	12,403	131,839	58,321
1988	1,777,323	1,216,672	18,618	1,235,290	137,899	80,045	1,177,436	343,336	256,551	13,554	131,132	60,565
1989	1,893,865	1,276,150	14,515	1,290,665	147,401	82,228	1,225,492	380,964	287,409	14,483	130,762	62,347
1990	2,078,612	1,396,662	9,946	1,406,608	161,988	111,392	1,356,012	408,367	314,233	15,766	131,838	64,761
1991	2,173,766	1,460,542	19,772	1,480,314	170,877	107,923	1,417,360	407,649	348,757	16,255	133,733	66,343
1992	2,321,763	1,565,121	23,991	1,589,112	180,401	112,866	1,521,577	410,469	389,717	17,176	135,174	67,141
1993	2,414,084	1,633,439	16,628	1,650,067	192,102	120,224	1,578,189	425,201	410,694	17,625	136,971	68,977
1994	2,555,253	1,724,956	32,016	1,756,972	204,809	117,419	1,669,582	448,898	436,773	18,545	137,786	69,508
1995	2,702,119	1,806,876	3,344	1,810,220	217,006	129,057	1,722,271	506,908	472,940	19,445	138,962	72,519
1996	2,819,101	1,865,923	25,920	1,891,843	221,563	124,747	1,795,027	523,975	500,099	20,091	140,318	73,172
1997	2,909,428	1,912,989	15,974	1,928,963	226,908	129,863	1,831,918	550,852	526,658	20,585	141,339	73,294
1998	2,975,149	1,894,596	15,560	1,910,156	222,525	147,908	1,835,539	590,323	549,287	20,946	142,041	71,742
1999	3,042,427	1,950,726	11,379	1,962,105	229,243	157,117	1,889,979	582,776	569,672	21,380	142,305	71,492
2000	3,160,871	1,979,834	18,250	1,998,084	231,976	163,177	1,929,285	628,803	602,783	22,098	143,036	71,922
2001	3,259,440	1,998,908	20,577	2,019,485	237,371	171,354	1,953,468	636,418	669,554	22,860	142,584	70,339
2002	3,287,368	2,006,045	6,649	2,012,694	236,329	173,100	1,949,465	621,233	716,670	23,124	142,163	67,794
2003	3,443,415	2,086,850	32,653	2,119,503	245,314	191,443	2,065,632	622,324	755,459	24,184	142,382	67,531
2004	3,664,208	2,233,813	49,874	2,283,687	260,371	201,117	2,224,433	627,586	812,189	25,604	143,112	68,949
2005	3,880,307	2,363,160	48,551	2,411,711	279,324	217,446	2,349,833	665,366	865,108	27,000	143,717	71,142
2006	4,099,148	2,515,973	38,746	2,554,719	298,490	232,950	2,489,179	677,039	932,930	28,327	144,707	73,600
2007	4,325,090	2,563,441	30,077	2,593,518	310,370	243,345	2,526,493	804,016	994,581	29,707	145,593	74,996
2008	4,419,627	2,536,000	32,488	2,568,488	318,338	252,182	2,502,332	825,374	1,091,921	30,132	146,675	74,033
2009	4,406,196	2,533,895	26,349	2,560,244	316,607	221,315	2,464,952	766,676	1,174,568	29,984	146,952	72,415
2010	4,615,833	2,683,486	1,227	2,684,713	335,193	220,421	2,569,941	773,975	1,271,917	31,345	147,260	72,486
2011	4,749,033	2,736,640	1,377	2,738,017	307,986	219,599	2,649,630	832,423	1,266,980	32,276	147,137	73,883
2012	4,810,077	2,766,116	4,087	2,770,203	309,254	225,850	2,686,799	851,861	1,271,417	32,672	147,221	73,577
2013	4,850,236	2,827,024	54,636	2,881,660	354,023	204,406	2,732,043	827,364	1,290,829	32,946	147,216	73,905
2014	5,066,025	2,948,249	21,765	2,970,014	366,087	203,412	2,807,339	919,520	1,339,166	34,359	147,444	74,934
2015	5,168,856	3,032,631	8,204	3,040,835	375,144	187,648	2,853,339	929,463	1,386,054	35,215	146,780	75,210
2016	5,249,488	3,047,186	-10,467	3,036,719	379,528	198,857	2,856,048	972,264	1,421,176	35,797	146,646	75,521
2017	5,422,139	3,115,966	5,769	3,121,735	390,088	208,227	2,939,874	1,011,800	1,470,465	36,876	147,038	75,883
2018	5,579,182	5,586,541	-7,359	3,158,040	407,183	235,208	2,986,065	1,072,615	1,520,502	37,797	147,608	76,475
2019	5,785,895	5,792,792	-6,897	3,258,289	414,972	256,564	3,099,881	1,088,084	1,597,930	39,102	147,970	77,351

Personal Income and Employment by Area: Fond du Lac, WI

(Thousands of dollars, except as noted.)

Year	Personal income, total	Derivation of personal income									Per capita personal income (dollars)	Population (persons)	Total employment
		Earnings by place of work			Less: Contributions for government social insurance	Plus: Adjustment for residence	Equals: Net earnings by place of residence	Plus: Dividends, interest, and rent	Plus: Personal current transfer receipts				
		Nonfarm	Farm	Total									
1970.........	322,337	245,447	18,456	263,903	18,807	-2,948	242,148	51,698	28,491	3,820	84,380	39,020
1971.........	344,029	256,193	21,497	277,690	20,238	-439	257,013	54,692	32,324	4,117	83,569	38,765
1972.........	375,685	283,304	20,008	303,312	23,510	2,230	282,032	57,881	35,772	4,406	85,264	40,118
1973.........	423,011	320,486	21,909	342,395	30,581	4,070	315,884	65,629	41,498	4,889	86,518	41,920
1974.........	463,052	342,328	21,018	363,346	33,885	9,154	338,615	74,774	49,663	5,349	86,561	42,694
1975.........	510,326	358,433	25,368	383,801	34,687	14,014	363,128	82,665	64,533	5,857	87,138	41,961
1976.........	565,686	406,292	22,955	429,247	39,852	17,934	407,329	88,011	70,346	6,515	86,830	42,917
1977.........	637,421	447,527	39,691	487,218	44,127	23,397	466,488	97,760	73,173	7,271	87,670	44,071
1978.........	702,220	499,994	32,151	532,145	50,575	32,239	513,809	107,829	80,582	8,005	87,720	44,857
1979.........	794,391	561,380	40,505	601,885	59,087	40,462	583,260	119,385	91,746	9,010	88,172	46,299
1980.........	864,166	584,669	35,167	619,836	61,496	45,419	603,759	147,047	113,360	9,718	88,924	45,661
1981.........	949,353	648,281	24,762	673,043	73,081	43,431	643,393	181,025	124,935	10,720	88,556	46,334
1982.........	1,000,826	663,058	21,333	684,391	75,710	43,957	652,638	205,956	142,232	11,327	88,361	45,665
1983.........	1,041,471	698,402	6,129	704,531	79,161	49,116	674,486	217,047	149,938	11,796	88,289	45,170
1984.........	1,161,467	779,539	23,085	802,624	90,274	52,567	764,917	245,159	151,391	13,116	88,552	46,517
1985.........	1,215,461	812,202	25,336	837,538	94,159	55,589	798,968	254,242	162,251	13,666	88,942	46,739
1986.........	1,277,850	847,996	33,960	881,956	98,070	65,577	849,463	261,565	166,822	14,373	88,909	45,908
1987.........	1,365,050	929,495	41,385	970,880	105,180	70,435	936,135	260,461	168,454	15,331	89,038	46,598
1988.........	1,428,705	1,005,506	20,739	1,026,245	117,347	76,933	985,831	268,031	174,843	15,912	89,787	47,180
1989.........	1,607,235	1,142,789	45,809	1,188,598	132,902	66,671	1,122,367	293,847	191,021	17,908	89,748	50,119
1990.........	1,688,612	1,205,476	39,054	1,244,530	145,119	81,364	1,180,775	301,987	205,850	18,701	90,296	51,402
1991.........	1,725,333	1,235,946	34,829	1,270,775	151,298	80,649	1,200,126	305,500	219,707	18,905	91,265	51,910
1992.........	1,855,836	1,348,197	37,534	1,385,731	163,385	84,970	1,307,316	309,439	239,081	20,161	92,049	52,863
1993.........	1,959,430	1,441,595	27,400	1,468,995	175,227	86,871	1,380,639	329,843	248,948	21,097	92,876	54,466
1994.........	2,103,886	1,549,146	42,564	1,591,710	189,851	93,629	1,495,488	351,107	257,291	22,449	93,717	55,863
1995.........	2,197,751	1,599,473	26,664	1,626,137	196,601	100,715	1,530,251	396,440	271,060	23,254	94,509	56,839
1996.........	2,317,192	1,659,296	43,435	1,702,731	202,376	106,941	1,607,296	425,486	284,410	24,256	95,529	57,633
1997.........	2,426,645	1,733,499	27,387	1,760,886	211,527	111,298	1,660,657	472,352	293,636	25,278	95,998	57,950
1998.........	2,568,251	1,847,042	41,761	1,888,803	224,813	115,714	1,779,704	483,516	305,031	26,611	96,512	59,514
1999.........	2,634,975	1,903,914	36,959	1,940,873	232,476	126,455	1,834,852	486,709	313,414	27,169	96,985	59,881
2000.........	2,789,530	2,020,475	22,116	2,042,591	241,625	133,365	1,934,331	513,137	342,062	28,643	97,390	60,814
2001.........	2,831,522	1,994,474	29,469	2,023,943	235,571	160,123	1,948,495	501,834	381,193	28,936	97,856	58,683
2002.........	2,932,157	2,082,438	24,001	2,106,439	242,588	161,076	2,024,927	495,449	411,781	29,890	98,097	58,998
2003.........	2,996,770	2,102,689	42,628	2,145,317	247,994	176,898	2,074,221	497,053	425,496	30,433	98,470	58,352
2004.........	3,096,011	2,193,977	49,293	2,243,270	260,099	196,056	2,179,227	484,174	432,610	31,295	98,929	58,529
2005.........	3,191,798	2,257,130	45,873	2,303,003	270,870	207,974	2,240,107	488,368	463,323	32,144	99,297	58,968
2006.........	3,333,207	2,327,685	35,224	2,362,909	281,068	222,048	2,303,889	537,481	491,837	33,359	99,920	59,304
2007.........	3,538,262	2,402,597	66,688	2,469,285	291,601	242,390	2,420,074	585,040	533,148	35,200	100,520	59,937
2008.........	3,722,576	2,491,794	64,051	2,555,845	305,265	249,489	2,500,069	628,078	594,429	36,813	101,122	59,767
2009.........	3,605,289	2,371,627	19,281	2,390,908	292,019	231,050	2,329,939	575,653	699,697	35,566	101,370	56,808
2010.........	3,743,592	2,435,894	63,103	2,498,997	298,106	229,456	2,430,347	560,048	753,197	36,852	101,585	56,460
2011.........	3,892,626	2,505,054	108,690	2,613,744	279,847	231,005	2,564,902	609,636	718,088	38,223	101,841	57,214
2012.........	4,070,219	2,646,654	104,391	2,751,045	292,631	210,122	2,668,536	673,895	727,788	39,973	101,823	57,437
2013.........	4,067,256	2,701,397	108,899	2,810,296	334,806	188,469	2,663,959	652,725	750,572	39,960	101,783	58,964
2014.........	4,291,992	2,818,599	133,976	2,952,575	346,395	196,062	2,802,242	704,149	785,601	42,098	101,952	59,867
2015.........	4,454,931	2,935,146	109,545	3,044,691	358,684	198,305	2,884,312	755,164	815,455	43,712	101,916	60,075
2016.........	4,515,520	3,017,803	82,198	3,100,001	363,920	195,184	2,931,265	756,239	828,016	44,179	102,210	60,173
2017.........	4,691,921	3,130,688	78,939	3,209,627	378,808	212,564	3,043,383	782,710	865,828	45,753	102,548	60,349
2018.........	4,976,108	4,914,496	61,612	3,380,622	399,036	199,200	3,180,786	864,647	930,675	48,311	103,001	61,270
2019.........	5,164,866	5,068,429	96,437	3,530,092	415,341	206,140	3,320,891	872,522	971,453	49,949	103,403	62,207

Personal Income and Employment by Area: Fort Collins, CO

(Thousands of dollars, except as noted.)

Year	Personal income, total	Earnings by place of work			Less: Contributions for government social insurance	Plus: Adjustment for residence	Equals: Net earnings by place of residence	Plus: Dividends, interest, and rent	Plus: Personal current transfer receipts	Per capita personal income (dollars)	Population (persons)	Total employment
		Nonfarm	Farm	Total								
1970	313,677	208,982	6,352	215,334	10,780	10,531	215,085	71,132	27,460	3,443	91,095	35,982
1971	368,477	241,027	11,168	252,195	12,652	15,147	254,690	81,986	31,801	3,794	97,125	37,219
1972	428,182	287,685	8,067	295,752	16,568	20,953	300,137	92,060	35,985	4,002	106,999	41,926
1973	500,034	333,401	9,374	342,775	22,325	28,122	348,572	108,156	43,306	4,447	112,441	45,809
1974	577,813	378,997	8,603	387,600	26,294	37,079	398,385	128,229	51,199	4,817	119,945	48,576
1975	676,045	432,904	12,393	445,297	29,156	45,535	461,676	149,076	65,293	5,606	120,593	51,021
1976	782,016	513,053	9,461	522,514	35,067	57,830	545,277	165,255	71,484	6,348	123,187	55,630
1977	898,522	601,869	5,331	607,200	42,418	68,661	633,443	188,208	76,871	6,808	131,973	60,594
1978	1,065,075	723,405	6,673	730,078	52,744	84,224	761,558	218,268	85,249	7,730	137,780	66,489
1979	1,255,180	864,441	399	864,840	66,507	101,647	899,980	258,248	96,952	8,628	145,474	71,512
1980	1,436,880	958,536	127	958,663	75,088	119,479	1,003,054	317,500	116,326	9,573	150,091	73,957
1981	1,631,363	1,054,111	7,402	1,061,513	88,905	131,876	1,104,484	386,013	140,866	10,638	153,347	74,913
1982	1,786,871	1,136,352	5,147	1,141,499	97,245	151,874	1,196,128	429,889	160,854	11,352	157,410	76,547
1983	1,976,418	1,249,884	10,291	1,260,175	109,134	166,883	1,317,924	481,841	176,653	12,214	161,816	80,642
1984	2,171,404	1,394,294	8,358	1,402,652	126,427	181,030	1,457,255	527,366	186,783	13,154	165,073	86,194
1985	2,336,369	1,495,821	6,159	1,501,980	139,172	194,165	1,556,973	578,781	200,615	13,769	169,687	88,750
1986	2,500,223	1,618,044	5,133	1,623,177	153,186	201,889	1,671,880	609,959	218,384	14,347	174,271	91,424
1987	2,672,269	1,739,402	4,839	1,744,241	162,522	213,223	1,794,942	637,240	240,087	15,046	177,612	92,603
1988	2,856,494	1,875,881	8,116	1,883,997	184,099	232,046	1,931,944	671,281	253,269	15,816	180,610	98,006
1989	3,133,629	2,036,601	13,274	2,049,875	205,906	249,525	2,093,494	755,653	284,482	17,076	183,507	101,762
1990	3,367,283	2,227,547	13,687	2,241,234	232,183	267,881	2,276,932	784,245	306,106	17,978	187,299	105,353
1991	3,589,411	2,397,691	13,097	2,410,788	256,406	291,957	2,446,339	804,572	338,500	18,583	193,154	110,094
1992	3,920,444	2,653,828	17,321	2,671,149	280,347	307,507	2,698,309	840,109	382,026	19,581	200,212	113,837
1993	4,289,008	2,924,534	21,225	2,945,759	314,947	321,978	2,952,790	927,215	409,003	20,606	208,143	121,231
1994	4,650,188	3,224,557	16,963	3,241,520	352,302	333,719	3,222,937	993,311	433,940	21,442	216,868	128,209
1995	5,068,498	3,464,978	13,973	3,478,951	378,997	352,543	3,452,497	1,129,324	486,677	22,754	222,750	134,280
1996	5,554,984	3,858,405	22,078	3,880,483	417,305	363,199	3,826,377	1,220,444	508,163	24,327	228,350	143,321
1997	6,019,839	4,170,154	22,625	4,192,779	445,415	395,887	4,143,251	1,358,690	517,898	25,754	233,746	148,781
1998	6,484,138	4,538,775	21,216	4,559,991	454,298	452,499	4,558,192	1,392,396	533,550	26,931	240,765	154,951
1999	6,937,741	4,888,876	17,691	4,906,567	485,220	503,442	4,924,789	1,442,446	570,506	28,101	246,884	159,167
2000	7,819,835	5,546,268	13,743	5,560,011	547,163	592,449	5,605,297	1,606,018	608,520	30,900	253,072	166,868
2001	8,367,212	6,052,944	17,855	6,070,799	592,762	592,491	6,070,528	1,613,612	683,072	32,115	260,541	170,194
2002	8,461,451	6,274,352	7,481	6,281,833	634,158	514,182	6,161,857	1,538,821	760,773	31,885	265,372	171,113
2003	8,527,371	6,333,366	2,498	6,335,864	645,201	517,085	6,207,748	1,524,721	794,902	31,765	268,448	171,677
2004	8,860,686	6,522,130	18,578	6,540,708	686,674	531,583	6,385,617	1,643,300	831,769	32,635	271,510	176,191
2005	9,358,231	6,815,658	19,842	6,835,500	726,883	537,424	6,646,041	1,797,448	914,742	34,016	275,116	180,859
2006	10,050,169	7,175,125	14,444	7,189,569	764,783	563,136	6,987,922	2,057,578	1,004,669	35,802	280,713	184,627
2007	10,800,468	7,505,817	25,138	7,530,955	802,051	588,808	7,317,712	2,390,348	1,092,408	37,749	286,112	190,983
2008	11,086,749	7,508,917	21,346	7,530,263	817,909	613,206	7,325,560	2,438,131	1,323,058	38,014	291,650	192,586
2009	10,904,899	7,400,649	19,329	7,419,978	803,660	551,696	7,168,014	2,247,134	1,489,751	36,754	296,696	188,924
2010	11,216,727	7,576,807	27,625	7,604,432	822,054	540,145	7,322,523	2,220,780	1,673,424	37,336	300,427	189,251
2011	11,907,560	7,842,605	30,332	7,872,937	783,034	569,242	7,659,145	2,518,620	1,729,795	39,038	305,027	193,349
2012	12,697,717	8,377,921	33,090	8,411,011	827,258	600,391	8,184,144	2,770,404	1,743,169	40,892	310,521	196,967
2013	13,443,111	8,889,599	38,251	8,927,850	933,156	637,288	8,631,982	2,983,940	1,827,189	42,560	315,859	203,384
2014	14,626,567	9,543,476	43,623	9,587,099	1,011,097	702,995	9,278,997	3,375,566	1,972,004	45,189	323,673	210,392
2015	15,645,207	10,151,286	47,919	10,199,205	1,084,170	709,556	9,824,591	3,692,294	2,128,322	47,005	332,840	217,135
2016	16,347,449	10,679,302	42,243	10,721,545	1,148,164	657,772	10,231,153	3,891,687	2,224,609	48,289	338,531	226,300
2017	17,384,075	11,482,712	55,042	11,537,754	1,224,635	707,327	11,020,446	4,084,105	2,279,524	50,539	343,976	232,282
2018	19,008,370	18,981,094	27,276	12,292,674	1,308,782	779,616	11,763,508	4,661,815	2,583,047	54,207	350,660	240,021
2019	19,944,871	19,908,454	36,417	12,992,023	1,381,243	866,913	12,477,693	4,736,423	2,730,755	55,884	356,899	245,338

Personal Income and Employment by Area: Fort Smith, AR-OK

(Thousands of dollars, except as noted.)

Year	Personal income, total	Derivation of personal income								Per capita personal income (dollars)	Population (persons)	Total employment
		Earnings by place of work			Less: Contributions for government social insurance	Plus: Adjustment for residence	Equals: Net earnings by place of residence	Plus: Dividends, interest, and rent	Plus: Personal current transfer receipts			
		Nonfarm	Farm	Total								
1970	466,259	358,754	10,804	369,558	26,257	-5,275	338,026	64,117	64,116	2,891	161,302	63,978
1971	523,088	396,392	12,403	408,795	29,933	-3,034	375,828	71,696	75,564	3,139	166,652	66,079
1972	585,188	446,382	16,324	462,706	35,379	-4,926	422,401	78,211	84,576	3,429	170,641	69,301
1973	668,147	504,024	25,669	529,693	46,121	-6,001	477,571	91,186	99,390	3,861	173,030	72,952
1974	765,079	581,384	19,627	601,011	54,915	-7,339	538,757	108,817	117,505	4,277	178,875	76,608
1975	854,776	632,230	19,367	651,597	58,104	-7,886	585,607	121,081	148,088	4,115	207,746	76,082
1976	962,779	725,125	18,936	744,061	68,361	-7,735	667,965	132,522	162,292	5,115	188,214	79,870
1977	1,087,611	838,612	16,361	854,973	79,970	-9,847	765,156	150,787	171,668	5,596	194,364	84,651
1978	1,229,277	960,522	11,478	972,000	94,147	-12,559	865,294	176,471	187,512	6,199	198,313	89,078
1979	1,377,579	1,054,483	21,150	1,075,633	106,792	-13,335	955,506	203,775	218,298	6,826	201,812	89,789
1980	1,546,557	1,148,928	9,011	1,157,939	114,137	-12,606	1,031,196	254,551	260,810	7,594	203,668	89,678
1981	1,755,949	1,276,023	22,295	1,298,318	136,486	-18,783	1,143,049	317,951	294,949	8,613	203,878	92,299
1982	1,836,866	1,296,325	12,381	1,308,706	141,865	-19,330	1,147,511	364,595	324,760	9,001	204,078	89,608
1983	1,973,228	1,418,773	11,829	1,430,602	157,205	-24,369	1,249,028	377,587	346,613	9,520	207,278	93,043
1984	2,191,936	1,605,453	13,707	1,619,160	182,941	-29,670	1,406,549	426,369	359,018	10,416	210,446	98,057
1985	2,344,884	1,717,087	16,340	1,733,427	197,098	-32,890	1,503,439	460,335	381,110	11,049	212,229	100,810
1986	2,494,394	1,849,920	24,613	1,874,533	212,533	-37,116	1,624,884	471,856	397,654	11,635	214,383	103,742
1987	2,648,495	2,014,925	20,187	2,035,112	228,643	-43,491	1,762,978	473,604	411,913	12,201	217,078	108,679
1988	2,821,071	2,150,044	24,423	2,174,467	253,138	-48,234	1,873,095	509,356	438,620	12,938	218,039	112,329
1989	2,989,752	2,245,833	37,611	2,283,444	263,533	-58,504	1,961,407	546,251	482,094	13,653	218,975	113,097
1990	3,131,696	2,371,934	24,139	2,396,073	289,452	-66,738	2,039,883	564,595	527,218	14,248	219,804	114,149
1991	3,285,532	2,478,247	26,621	2,504,868	303,297	-55,264	2,146,307	554,151	585,074	14,744	222,842	116,211
1992	3,607,601	2,731,862	35,627	2,767,489	331,416	-60,066	2,376,007	569,943	661,651	15,941	226,308	118,602
1993	3,752,811	2,852,884	45,470	2,898,354	350,115	-63,079	2,485,160	572,904	694,747	16,238	231,118	124,499
1994	4,051,154	3,093,319	60,742	3,154,061	384,468	-71,001	2,698,592	617,918	734,644	17,310	234,032	128,786
1995	4,281,397	3,251,524	39,525	3,291,049	401,122	-74,709	2,815,218	671,241	794,938	17,879	239,471	133,767
1996	4,496,824	3,377,518	53,384	3,430,902	411,636	-71,317	2,947,949	709,055	839,820	18,466	243,520	136,556
1997	4,732,813	3,561,080	60,439	3,621,519	430,819	-71,885	3,118,815	751,068	862,930	19,173	246,842	138,117
1998	5,027,532	3,805,982	59,761	3,865,743	455,380	-77,050	3,333,313	814,008	880,211	20,154	249,460	140,029
1999	5,223,860	3,986,959	78,430	4,065,389	478,725	-76,879	3,509,785	797,065	917,010	20,686	252,529	142,424
2000	5,574,386	4,270,115	69,390	4,339,505	505,845	-75,437	3,758,223	849,722	966,441	21,764	256,126	144,518
2001	5,699,504	4,238,586	83,666	4,322,252	509,073	-74,585	3,738,594	878,808	1,082,102	22,084	258,087	144,267
2002	5,816,374	4,295,711	77,538	4,373,249	512,826	-72,645	3,787,778	839,000	1,189,596	22,361	260,117	143,080
2003	6,069,797	4,520,583	57,653	4,578,236	532,559	-75,079	3,970,598	838,607	1,260,592	23,176	261,903	143,170
2004	6,528,454	4,867,652	93,885	4,961,537	563,774	-78,660	4,319,103	850,249	1,359,102	24,726	264,035	145,176
2005	6,872,902	5,135,739	83,134	5,218,873	600,154	-88,490	4,530,229	902,074	1,440,599	25,769	266,708	149,247
2006	7,383,988	5,500,306	39,354	5,539,660	652,096	-95,206	4,792,358	1,006,492	1,585,138	27,240	271,075	152,732
2007	7,704,164	5,582,671	33,670	5,616,341	669,361	-96,348	4,850,632	1,153,134	1,700,398	28,086	274,305	155,860
2008	8,119,550	5,651,814	41,763	5,693,577	693,427	-86,444	4,913,706	1,283,949	1,921,895	29,384	276,322	155,012
2009	8,000,577	5,384,131	12,003	5,396,134	671,693	-63,921	4,660,520	1,227,024	2,113,033	28,685	278,908	149,499
2010	8,303,703	5,582,898	82,028	5,664,926	697,095	-55,010	4,912,821	1,134,118	2,256,764	29,584	280,686	147,415
2011	8,856,661	5,846,691	95,606	5,942,297	650,538	-45,155	5,246,604	1,297,627	2,312,430	31,494	281,216	145,446
2012	9,183,403	6,009,758	124,738	6,134,496	655,669	-28,123	5,450,704	1,387,596	2,345,103	32,678	281,027	145,348
2013	9,187,473	6,021,581	160,659	6,182,240	733,240	-6,861	5,442,139	1,341,133	2,404,201	32,794	280,156	144,446
2014	9,533,302	6,182,504	165,039	6,347,543	757,345	-10,455	5,579,743	1,428,951	2,524,608	34,065	279,858	145,414
2015	9,751,440	6,199,923	164,583	6,364,506	766,335	10,620	5,608,791	1,535,514	2,607,135	34,778	280,393	146,292
2016	9,810,642	6,283,478	107,316	6,390,794	770,126	782	5,621,450	1,490,440	2,698,752	34,909	281,032	147,262
2017	10,146,080	6,448,694	134,711	6,583,405	783,912	12,665	5,812,158	1,574,419	2,759,503	35,968	282,086	146,629
2018	9,291,140	9,258,603	32,537	6,080,366	745,449	-62,879	5,272,038	1,538,073	2,481,029	37,120	250,298	134,796
2019	9,609,548	9,603,980	5,568	6,250,735	780,073	-63,558	5,407,104	1,582,080	2,620,364	38,382	250,368	135,452

Personal Income and Employment by Area: Fort Wayne, IN

(Thousands of dollars, except as noted.)

Year	Personal income, total	Earnings by place of work			Less: Contributions for government social insurance	Plus: Adjustment for residence	Equals: Net earnings by place of residence	Plus: Dividends, interest, and rent	Plus: Personal current transfer receipts	Per capita personal income (dollars)	Population (persons)	Total employment
		Nonfarm	Farm	Total								
1970	1,344,891	1,230,094	16,694	1,246,788	84,534	-105,879	1,056,375	201,647	86,869	4,092	328,656	161,511
1971	1,457,060	1,312,822	25,182	1,338,004	93,298	-111,303	1,133,403	219,528	104,129	4,373	333,164	161,889
1972	1,609,556	1,473,598	20,761	1,494,359	111,541	-124,201	1,258,617	235,121	115,818	4,787	336,249	169,353
1973	1,815,005	1,640,355	48,325	1,688,680	143,480	-134,565	1,410,635	266,483	137,887	5,364	338,398	177,766
1974	1,971,311	1,785,961	29,248	1,815,209	162,478	-146,510	1,506,221	307,298	157,792	5,801	339,819	181,183
1975	2,068,003	1,789,601	37,895	1,827,496	160,154	-140,224	1,527,118	336,444	204,441	6,090	339,555	171,717
1976	2,314,529	2,043,139	37,029	2,080,168	185,573	-156,908	1,737,687	364,284	212,558	6,833	338,719	178,522
1977	2,598,589	2,327,244	33,271	2,360,515	211,259	-178,429	1,970,827	407,929	219,833	7,653	339,540	186,924
1978	2,904,203	2,637,023	21,395	2,658,418	246,446	-199,154	2,212,818	449,791	241,594	8,451	343,658	194,996
1979	3,226,819	2,921,962	27,928	2,949,890	282,399	-218,504	2,448,987	501,573	276,259	9,337	345,596	198,262
1980	3,432,417	2,964,538	24,654	2,989,192	284,910	-210,035	2,494,247	596,460	341,710	9,935	345,480	188,701
1981	3,742,757	3,156,732	3,073	3,159,805	326,300	-219,470	2,614,035	733,546	395,176	10,917	342,832	187,540
1982	3,828,809	3,090,414	9,876	3,100,290	324,805	-204,648	2,570,837	815,205	442,767	11,240	340,642	179,724
1983	3,962,692	3,210,181	-10,192	3,199,989	339,241	-199,324	2,661,424	827,246	474,022	11,718	338,181	179,245
1984	4,413,032	3,581,712	22,941	3,604,653	388,068	-210,979	3,005,606	916,343	491,083	13,069	337,671	188,092
1985	4,763,564	3,918,659	11,685	3,930,344	432,651	-232,020	3,265,673	982,924	514,967	13,968	341,030	196,048
1986	5,206,052	4,339,874	18,399	4,358,273	481,318	-259,967	3,616,988	1,045,539	543,525	15,066	345,561	205,357
1987	5,600,519	4,745,331	23,661	4,768,992	519,846	-283,544	3,965,602	1,084,472	550,445	15,953	351,063	214,510
1988	6,135,115	5,181,971	13,141	5,195,112	582,586	-309,862	4,302,664	1,227,837	604,614	17,381	352,986	222,312
1989	6,677,700	5,571,054	20,838	5,591,892	626,465	-325,756	4,639,671	1,389,248	648,781	18,856	354,134	229,759
1990	6,971,492	5,801,951	34,492	5,836,443	672,046	-342,486	4,821,911	1,452,573	697,008	19,618	355,358	230,671
1991	7,029,692	5,876,709	15,755	5,892,464	693,978	-360,359	4,838,127	1,415,321	776,244	19,606	358,547	229,542
1992	7,646,379	6,356,537	25,215	6,381,752	740,403	-377,351	5,263,998	1,471,311	911,070	21,139	361,726	233,513
1993	7,947,234	6,684,705	30,087	6,714,792	782,068	-397,047	5,535,677	1,471,638	939,919	21,770	365,059	237,212
1994	8,425,690	7,074,314	27,727	7,102,041	838,448	-402,559	5,861,034	1,569,872	994,784	22,913	367,729	242,100
1995	8,894,037	7,412,385	15,027	7,427,412	877,663	-391,327	6,158,422	1,717,022	1,018,593	23,977	370,934	247,340
1996	9,334,281	7,702,715	40,260	7,742,975	900,962	-411,392	6,430,621	1,838,640	1,065,020	24,902	374,837	249,925
1997	9,802,772	8,111,499	59,087	8,170,586	945,142	-456,325	6,769,119	1,950,236	1,083,417	25,888	378,663	255,042
1998	10,533,381	8,736,543	30,911	8,767,454	997,040	-458,139	7,312,275	2,081,076	1,140,030	27,488	383,203	259,620
1999	10,930,794	9,250,391	1,204	9,251,595	1,044,037	-487,057	7,720,501	2,025,102	1,185,191	28,258	386,827	260,196
2000	11,531,409	9,630,688	19,436	9,650,124	1,075,044	-528,090	8,046,990	2,178,976	1,305,443	29,489	391,039	262,844
2001	11,505,687	9,476,547	30,052	9,506,599	1,078,110	-501,138	7,927,351	2,132,951	1,445,385	29,233	393,580	258,569
2002	11,726,539	9,621,006	5,160	9,626,166	1,098,309	-459,781	8,068,076	2,123,147	1,535,316	29,601	396,147	255,715
2003	11,727,472	9,609,540	42,535	9,652,075	1,112,549	-396,166	8,143,360	1,989,824	1,594,288	29,393	398,993	252,021
2004	12,224,638	9,862,363	72,445	9,934,808	1,151,453	-363,475	8,419,880	2,109,563	1,695,195	30,517	400,583	254,367
2005	12,608,912	10,226,262	39,474	10,265,736	1,202,689	-367,307	8,695,740	2,055,473	1,857,699	31,269	403,240	256,935
2006	13,578,463	10,837,794	41,231	10,879,025	1,267,689	-395,823	9,215,513	2,353,843	2,009,107	33,380	406,783	261,893
2007	14,136,838	11,127,765	49,122	11,176,887	1,304,940	-384,173	9,487,774	2,546,044	2,103,020	34,461	410,223	265,241
2008	14,420,084	11,079,218	78,642	11,157,860	1,310,811	-391,448	9,455,601	2,508,731	2,455,752	34,995	412,062	262,561
2009	13,818,824	10,449,035	74,038	10,523,073	1,259,884	-373,669	8,889,520	2,212,094	2,717,210	33,344	414,438	250,600
2010	14,296,912	10,818,054	42,063	10,860,117	1,283,250	-371,605	9,205,262	2,180,436	2,911,214	34,291	416,927	249,765
2011	15,246,487	11,376,993	87,486	11,464,479	1,191,135	-382,441	9,890,903	2,431,967	2,923,617	36,313	419,867	255,085
2012	16,078,266	11,860,235	124,367	11,984,602	1,221,348	-380,279	10,382,975	2,661,516	3,033,775	38,130	421,669	257,727
2013	16,173,823	11,965,212	221,571	12,186,783	1,397,820	-290,163	10,498,800	2,616,278	3,058,745	38,132	424,155	257,907
2014	17,028,761	12,580,268	120,117	12,700,385	1,456,286	-263,674	10,980,425	2,797,761	3,250,575	39,944	426,321	261,740
2015	17,817,540	13,118,488	7,652	13,126,140	1,528,872	-204,354	11,392,914	3,005,430	3,419,196	41,542	428,909	266,812
2016	18,391,007	13,553,273	68,609	13,621,882	1,549,723	-286,083	11,786,076	3,097,756	3,507,175	42,641	431,296	269,305
2017	19,176,861	14,118,052	24,930	14,142,982	1,603,394	-252,062	12,287,526	3,258,436	3,630,899	44,124	434,617	272,396
2018	19,015,375	18,962,604	52,771	14,223,571	1,623,880	-457,517	12,142,174	3,343,646	3,529,555	46,478	409,126	263,869
2019	19,636,577	19,596,132	40,445	14,787,475	1,703,426	-551,354	12,532,695	3,379,738	3,724,144	47,516	413,263	268,332

Personal Income and Employment by Area: Fresno, CA

(Thousands of dollars, except as noted.)

Year	Personal income, total	Earnings by place of work			Less: Contributions for government social insurance	Plus: Adjustment for residence	Equals: Net earnings by place of residence	Plus: Dividends, interest, and rent	Plus: Personal current transfer receipts	Per capita personal income (dollars)	Population (persons)	Total employment
		Nonfarm	Farm	Total								
1970	1,653,102	1,109,998	163,187	1,273,185	75,618	-4,476	1,193,091	232,777	227,234	3,984	414,886	180,330
1971	1,799,992	1,225,503	164,215	1,389,718	85,514	-7,487	1,296,717	255,099	248,176	4,238	424,697	185,808
1972	2,036,193	1,390,133	213,278	1,603,411	100,608	-11,442	1,491,361	285,236	259,596	4,714	431,918	198,065
1973	2,339,957	1,570,947	293,372	1,864,319	129,483	-16,508	1,718,328	336,201	285,428	5,320	439,865	206,954
1974	2,740,807	1,763,526	430,003	2,193,529	149,994	-23,959	2,019,576	389,487	331,744	6,092	449,886	216,106
1975	2,963,789	1,964,177	335,593	2,299,770	162,430	-33,144	2,104,196	445,799	413,794	6,385	464,183	222,296
1976	3,397,744	2,227,009	456,376	2,683,385	187,712	-43,594	2,452,079	485,010	460,655	7,121	477,162	231,059
1977	3,628,639	2,495,762	367,290	2,863,052	214,584	-54,572	2,593,896	546,221	488,522	7,420	489,016	239,078
1978	4,040,140	2,864,223	324,389	3,188,612	250,027	-68,567	2,870,018	632,586	537,536	8,120	497,564	249,946
1979	4,792,511	3,311,998	539,229	3,851,227	303,647	-88,968	3,458,612	740,893	593,006	9,465	506,332	267,295
1980	5,540,745	3,628,152	717,272	4,345,424	326,936	-107,200	3,911,288	926,504	702,953	10,703	517,679	275,120
1981	5,809,316	3,879,272	444,440	4,323,712	379,992	-93,593	3,850,127	1,120,000	839,189	10,984	528,891	275,530
1982	6,125,148	4,010,237	471,836	4,482,073	401,117	-100,053	3,980,903	1,207,863	936,382	11,311	541,500	277,400
1983	6,443,188	4,302,610	347,771	4,650,381	437,230	-102,263	4,110,888	1,306,445	1,025,855	11,591	555,873	284,985
1984	7,119,275	4,687,867	487,089	5,174,956	495,426	-109,563	4,569,967	1,444,314	1,104,994	12,444	572,091	289,156
1985	7,644,924	4,986,147	583,227	5,569,374	532,729	-114,982	4,921,663	1,513,971	1,209,290	13,089	584,070	292,647
1986	8,160,310	5,335,201	634,627	5,969,828	579,005	-117,592	5,273,231	1,576,115	1,310,964	13,747	593,621	296,092
1987	8,910,556	5,873,438	806,603	6,680,041	641,395	-126,559	5,912,087	1,628,426	1,370,043	14,636	608,831	308,325
1988	9,572,858	6,374,272	855,872	7,230,144	718,300	-138,381	6,373,463	1,713,876	1,485,519	15,252	627,658	320,730
1989	10,378,753	6,867,247	832,276	7,699,523	785,036	-157,434	6,757,053	1,983,393	1,638,307	15,949	650,755	328,682
1990	11,305,019	7,597,429	880,645	8,478,074	861,373	-181,107	7,435,594	2,012,808	1,856,617	16,815	672,302	342,583
1991	11,853,761	8,138,502	690,165	8,828,667	924,760	-184,097	7,719,810	2,044,894	2,089,057	17,140	691,569	351,296
1992	12,614,523	8,519,837	743,824	9,263,661	961,799	-178,295	8,123,567	2,044,048	2,446,908	17,760	710,263	347,643
1993	13,359,184	8,957,593	890,254	9,847,847	1,007,233	-189,181	8,651,433	2,116,418	2,591,333	18,379	726,859	356,938
1994	13,672,905	9,296,839	828,600	10,125,439	1,043,404	-190,868	8,891,167	2,203,064	2,578,674	18,481	739,835	364,559
1995	14,222,713	9,619,847	725,940	10,345,787	1,062,270	-189,176	9,094,341	2,437,970	2,690,402	18,975	749,534	377,757
1996	14,865,185	9,940,951	834,813	10,775,764	1,063,581	-186,490	9,525,693	2,517,410	2,822,082	19,523	761,409	384,048
1997	15,268,932	10,297,980	829,925	11,127,905	1,082,842	-168,788	9,876,275	2,590,427	2,802,230	19,794	771,391	379,588
1998	16,233,690	11,076,614	705,103	11,781,717	1,136,945	-164,956	10,479,816	2,730,056	3,023,818	20,849	778,615	392,386
1999	17,133,655	11,660,991	897,326	12,558,317	1,195,780	-159,393	11,203,144	2,747,044	3,183,467	21,705	789,405	395,669
2000	18,513,075	13,044,566	807,023	13,851,589	1,302,738	-151,134	12,397,717	2,842,178	3,273,180	23,104	801,288	400,136
2001	19,279,959	13,553,352	610,836	14,164,188	1,459,012	-170,559	12,534,617	3,052,947	3,692,395	23,714	813,021	399,740
2002	20,667,227	14,607,061	823,694	15,430,755	1,595,778	-204,057	13,630,920	3,092,015	3,944,292	24,907	829,762	410,513
2003	22,247,954	15,463,196	1,180,051	16,643,247	1,706,215	-205,959	14,731,073	3,296,281	4,220,600	26,261	847,193	411,423
2004	23,637,889	16,604,990	1,364,846	17,969,836	1,886,991	-232,098	15,850,747	3,344,062	4,443,080	27,453	861,035	416,389
2005	24,608,466	17,364,903	1,283,544	18,648,447	1,983,101	-237,363	16,427,983	3,517,410	4,663,073	28,206	872,470	424,613
2006	26,231,982	18,641,556	1,196,994	19,838,550	2,046,598	-213,424	17,578,528	3,660,976	4,992,478	29,679	883,862	435,397
2007	27,520,808	19,244,174	1,227,101	20,471,275	2,079,998	-231,384	18,159,893	3,992,311	5,368,604	30,717	895,933	445,265
2008	28,143,040	19,159,318	842,503	20,001,821	2,125,391	-212,406	17,664,024	4,465,008	6,014,008	30,939	909,630	441,468
2009	28,208,477	18,450,463	1,293,827	19,744,290	2,075,859	-227,758	17,440,673	4,112,439	6,655,365	30,612	921,478	424,077
2010	29,561,648	18,941,164	1,403,238	20,344,402	2,056,735	-246,042	18,041,625	4,119,155	7,400,868	31,711	932,218	420,791
2011	31,409,742	19,736,471	1,757,821	21,494,292	1,935,985	-254,809	19,303,498	4,661,724	7,444,520	33,402	940,360	426,268
2012	32,440,966	20,249,572	1,685,731	21,935,303	1,984,469	-206,536	19,744,298	5,106,933	7,589,735	34,262	946,851	439,605
2013	33,311,673	20,991,319	1,620,910	22,612,229	2,306,366	-207,667	20,098,196	5,263,238	7,950,239	34,926	953,787	455,462
2014	35,738,055	22,029,115	1,705,613	23,734,728	2,409,360	-208,505	21,116,863	6,135,903	8,485,289	37,105	963,170	465,176
2015	38,466,667	23,338,546	1,830,295	25,168,841	2,532,826	-281,907	22,354,108	6,852,447	9,260,112	39,561	972,333	476,054
2016	39,391,217	24,354,549	1,399,011	25,753,560	2,669,850	-283,797	22,799,913	6,985,273	9,606,031	40,214	979,534	487,228
2017	41,024,026	25,507,729	1,841,892	27,349,621	2,789,128	-284,628	24,275,865	7,367,964	9,380,197	41,470	989,255	495,917
2018	43,088,095	41,197,302	1,890,793	28,818,842	2,944,238	-324,146	25,550,458	7,680,392	9,857,245	43,438	991,950	508,813
2019	45,445,944	43,283,932	2,162,012	30,618,900	3,143,688	-362,100	27,113,112	7,841,228	10,491,604	45,487	999,101	523,122

Personal Income and Employment by Area: Gadsden, AL

(Thousands of dollars, except as noted.)

| Year | Personal income, total | Derivation of personal income | | | | | | | | | Per capita personal income (dollars) | Population (persons) | Total employment |
| | | Earnings by place of work | | | Less: Contributions for government social insurance | Plus: Adjustment for residence | Equals: Net earnings by place of residence | Plus: Dividends, interest, and rent | Plus: Personal current transfer receipts | | | |
		Nonfarm	Farm	Total								
1970	283,339	229,243	2,232	231,475	16,770	6,374	221,079	29,382	32,878	3,010	94,134	35,044
1971	311,494	242,333	2,771	245,104	18,185	11,363	238,282	32,903	40,309	3,283	94,887	35,388
1972	349,727	274,756	3,487	278,243	21,681	13,044	269,606	36,166	43,955	3,652	95,758	36,119
1973	387,651	304,307	5,490	309,797	27,982	14,122	295,937	41,468	50,246	4,035	96,072	37,400
1974	425,798	329,803	2,314	332,117	31,337	16,052	316,832	49,118	59,848	4,409	96,579	37,366
1975	471,815	346,616	5,355	351,971	32,685	19,206	338,492	56,235	77,088	4,818	97,936	36,837
1976	515,075	378,681	5,050	383,731	36,323	23,586	370,994	61,110	82,971	5,204	98,984	36,805
1977	589,445	448,970	5,004	453,974	43,210	23,590	434,354	68,414	86,677	5,884	100,171	39,116
1978	670,912	519,574	6,142	525,716	51,079	25,699	500,336	78,024	92,552	6,595	101,731	41,070
1979	752,567	584,238	5,449	589,687	59,354	27,393	557,726	88,366	106,475	7,311	102,937	42,239
1980	821,916	614,799	-41	614,758	62,117	35,288	587,929	107,562	126,425	7,971	103,112	41,418
1981	915,406	664,594	8,550	673,144	72,394	40,580	641,330	130,223	143,853	8,875	103,143	40,735
1982	928,164	638,288	4,786	643,074	71,414	46,895	618,555	146,207	163,402	9,053	102,524	38,726
1983	986,146	677,930	5,322	683,252	77,162	46,113	652,203	157,702	176,241	9,602	102,707	38,722
1984	1,078,216	744,516	4,324	748,840	86,808	50,694	712,726	179,019	186,471	10,539	102,307	40,376
1985	1,130,889	771,669	6,044	777,713	90,103	57,510	745,120	191,196	194,573	11,056	102,291	40,925
1986	1,177,473	789,320	8,419	797,739	91,110	62,145	768,774	204,701	203,998	11,582	101,664	40,944
1987	1,249,587	866,238	3,147	869,385	98,401	64,708	835,692	206,093	207,802	12,334	101,314	41,863
1988	1,329,676	920,953	8,917	929,870	107,870	73,322	895,322	219,977	214,377	13,201	100,728	42,754
1989	1,412,547	934,795	13,807	948,602	109,714	82,360	921,248	247,157	244,142	14,079	100,327	43,434
1990	1,458,035	947,542	12,087	959,629	111,742	86,859	934,746	257,877	265,412	14,608	99,809	43,565
1991	1,499,998	962,533	12,656	975,189	114,402	91,643	952,430	251,349	296,219	14,945	100,365	43,913
1992	1,614,531	1,050,939	13,248	1,064,187	123,013	92,086	1,033,260	251,444	329,827	15,993	100,950	44,463
1993	1,692,700	1,101,830	13,949	1,115,779	131,091	99,478	1,084,166	263,503	345,031	16,708	101,310	46,081
1994	1,793,727	1,182,869	17,652	1,200,521	141,431	87,771	1,146,861	274,616	372,250	17,549	102,213	46,709
1995	1,856,191	1,232,100	9,837	1,241,937	149,036	81,420	1,174,321	290,878	390,992	18,137	102,342	47,735
1996	1,944,422	1,229,260	16,302	1,245,562	147,524	128,938	1,226,976	300,631	416,815	18,866	103,063	48,513
1997	2,041,488	1,280,513	20,697	1,301,210	153,033	138,860	1,287,037	321,507	432,944	19,605	104,129	49,701
1998	2,124,446	1,334,617	20,001	1,354,618	157,471	141,853	1,339,000	336,433	449,013	20,356	104,367	49,727
1999	2,169,667	1,344,520	21,306	1,365,826	157,854	161,326	1,369,298	332,400	467,969	20,862	104,002	49,023
2000	2,250,683	1,377,546	17,878	1,395,424	160,962	167,009	1,401,471	353,381	495,831	21,791	103,286	49,443
2001	2,304,386	1,356,832	23,460	1,380,292	162,238	172,714	1,390,768	370,004	543,614	22,378	102,976	48,338
2002	2,377,330	1,412,155	16,875	1,429,030	169,540	175,431	1,434,921	363,498	578,911	23,084	102,988	49,064
2003	2,459,105	1,436,301	20,162	1,456,463	173,156	189,074	1,472,381	381,754	604,970	23,869	103,025	48,002
2004	2,592,371	1,526,427	31,060	1,557,487	183,166	204,238	1,578,559	386,611	627,201	25,149	103,080	49,327
2005	2,680,162	1,589,152	12,419	1,601,571	192,031	217,959	1,627,499	381,424	671,239	25,977	103,174	50,115
2006	2,774,856	1,638,182	-4,299	1,633,883	198,733	231,052	1,666,202	389,225	719,429	26,803	103,528	49,828
2007	2,951,225	1,674,162	2,985	1,677,147	205,144	249,022	1,721,025	454,585	775,615	28,406	103,893	49,838
2008	3,046,789	1,676,379	4,734	1,681,113	211,569	251,964	1,721,508	477,120	848,161	29,238	104,206	49,618
2009	3,039,768	1,650,623	4,666	1,655,289	207,513	225,109	1,672,885	448,295	918,588	29,162	104,239	46,996
2010	3,177,599	1,715,204	4,145	1,719,349	216,826	216,942	1,719,465	467,931	990,203	30,420	104,457	46,792
2011	3,223,417	1,752,751	-8,038	1,744,713	198,801	209,508	1,755,420	481,789	986,208	30,889	104,354	48,421
2012	3,286,139	1,777,916	-3,037	1,774,879	200,879	211,572	1,785,572	506,558	994,009	31,520	104,257	48,495
2013	3,279,165	1,785,220	16,093	1,801,313	227,218	208,203	1,782,298	476,809	1,020,058	31,571	103,865	48,600
2014	3,396,465	1,844,493	11,973	1,856,466	232,793	215,972	1,839,645	502,320	1,054,500	32,856	103,374	49,586
2015	3,513,350	1,897,542	15,202	1,912,744	239,812	222,092	1,895,024	533,539	1,084,787	34,129	102,942	49,755
2016	3,573,119	1,940,048	3,299	1,943,347	244,244	231,770	1,930,873	537,081	1,105,165	34,783	102,726	50,633
2017	3,706,264	1,988,175	11,300	1,999,475	251,274	242,421	1,990,622	559,781	1,155,861	36,069	102,755	50,804
2018	3,821,755	3,809,823	11,932	2,042,662	262,891	253,997	2,033,768	566,056	1,221,931	37,245	102,611	50,728
2019	3,919,481	3,918,820	661	2,060,734	262,926	277,667	2,075,475	574,983	1,269,023	38,326	102,268	50,285

Personal Income and Employment by Area: Gainesville, FL

(Thousands of dollars, except as noted.)

Year	Personal income, total	Earnings by place of work			Less: Contributions for government social insurance	Plus: Adjustment for residence	Equals: Net earnings by place of residence	Plus: Dividends, interest, and rent	Plus: Personal current transfer receipts	Per capita personal income (dollars)	Population (persons)	Total employment
		Nonfarm	Farm	Total								
1970	357,683	293,873	7,286	301,159	16,834	-12,638	271,687	59,490	26,506	3,289	108,745	50,213
1971	411,352	335,053	9,489	344,542	20,266	-15,492	308,784	69,083	33,485	3,651	112,666	52,801
1972	489,251	405,125	10,011	415,136	25,691	-20,574	368,871	81,372	39,008	3,949	123,894	58,353
1973	577,199	480,081	14,785	494,866	35,519	-25,260	434,087	96,986	46,126	4,429	130,322	63,584
1974	649,392	536,739	12,339	549,078	41,868	-27,995	479,215	114,305	55,872	4,776	135,976	66,040
1975	724,464	583,393	12,518	595,911	45,622	-28,950	521,339	129,336	73,789	5,268	137,514	66,766
1976	786,807	631,390	12,808	644,198	51,462	-31,533	561,203	140,834	84,770	5,711	137,769	66,895
1977	864,086	700,045	7,984	708,029	57,914	-35,166	614,949	156,497	92,640	6,058	142,625	70,025
1978	988,750	799,121	12,297	811,418	69,143	-39,829	702,446	181,862	104,442	6,676	148,102	74,708
1979	1,117,094	892,236	19,483	911,719	81,590	-43,192	786,937	206,493	123,664	7,363	151,718	78,191
1980	1,289,205	1,007,536	17,545	1,025,081	90,425	-49,663	884,993	256,428	147,784	8,154	158,113	81,820
1981	1,472,713	1,124,259	16,891	1,141,150	109,255	-48,359	983,536	317,128	172,049	9,106	161,727	83,589
1982	1,626,496	1,230,772	24,066	1,254,838	122,497	-55,691	1,076,650	360,178	189,668	9,801	165,951	86,074
1983	1,805,152	1,371,360	22,341	1,393,701	136,448	-65,504	1,191,749	401,443	211,960	10,688	168,900	88,731
1984	2,033,459	1,563,482	19,767	1,583,249	158,498	-79,480	1,345,271	459,630	228,558	11,764	172,859	94,216
1985	2,246,516	1,746,180	17,559	1,763,739	179,980	-91,384	1,492,375	504,400	249,741	12,675	177,239	99,763
1986	2,404,582	1,866,024	16,930	1,882,954	195,812	-99,118	1,588,024	547,422	269,136	13,385	179,646	104,449
1987	2,585,939	2,009,862	15,531	2,025,393	206,174	-107,818	1,711,401	586,235	288,303	14,158	182,650	105,549
1988	2,823,524	2,205,604	20,755	2,226,359	236,123	-122,169	1,868,067	640,845	314,612	15,210	185,638	109,865
1989	3,117,916	2,389,807	24,108	2,413,915	256,282	-137,157	2,020,476	734,220	363,220	16,521	188,728	112,555
1990	3,338,016	2,568,285	23,443	2,591,728	272,992	-152,794	2,165,942	771,756	400,318	17,343	192,474	116,385
1991	3,517,630	2,707,499	26,863	2,734,362	289,668	-163,338	2,281,356	785,491	450,783	17,713	198,591	117,284
1992	3,726,564	2,880,388	39,066	2,919,454	308,246	-179,308	2,431,900	783,278	511,386	18,269	203,980	117,689
1993	3,948,578	3,065,625	38,006	3,103,631	325,364	-193,303	2,584,964	815,059	548,555	18,929	208,594	122,951
1994	4,150,834	3,242,901	34,269	3,277,170	347,643	-219,934	2,709,593	862,948	578,293	19,679	210,925	126,720
1995	4,427,468	3,394,994	28,505	3,423,499	363,962	-231,923	2,827,614	973,367	626,487	20,489	216,093	130,710
1996	4,637,667	3,566,515	29,770	3,596,285	380,520	-261,211	2,954,554	1,021,996	661,117	21,114	219,654	134,282
1997	4,904,857	3,760,862	36,206	3,797,068	402,714	-288,217	3,106,137	1,116,668	682,052	21,952	223,439	135,691
1998	5,216,599	4,069,121	37,507	4,106,628	434,074	-327,762	3,344,792	1,184,325	687,482	23,014	226,674	140,985
1999	5,435,611	4,279,773	39,633	4,319,406	454,626	-308,327	3,556,453	1,169,936	709,222	23,642	229,909	144,422
2000	5,774,649	4,541,266	33,864	4,575,130	480,155	-340,965	3,754,010	1,239,972	780,667	24,778	233,054	148,576
2001	6,127,153	4,812,664	38,615	4,851,279	509,807	-364,224	3,977,248	1,277,832	872,073	25,962	236,001	153,003
2002	6,316,303	5,061,384	21,955	5,083,339	533,484	-387,525	4,162,330	1,209,135	944,838	26,415	239,116	154,387
2003	6,552,273	5,198,667	20,334	5,219,001	549,159	-379,751	4,290,091	1,248,725	1,013,457	27,072	242,033	155,446
2004	7,284,674	5,871,490	26,501	5,897,991	620,095	-470,028	4,807,868	1,479,980	996,826	29,717	245,138	159,696
2005	7,842,917	6,247,887	27,072	6,274,959	663,870	-487,276	5,123,813	1,602,035	1,117,069	31,427	249,557	161,888
2006	8,419,564	6,652,269	21,551	6,673,820	714,586	-526,307	5,432,927	1,829,196	1,157,441	32,924	255,729	165,760
2007	8,834,745	6,903,017	16,159	6,919,176	748,409	-549,663	5,621,104	1,979,859	1,233,782	34,072	259,295	167,416
2008	9,138,993	6,965,513	16,499	6,982,012	765,807	-570,361	5,645,844	2,065,300	1,427,849	34,924	261,685	166,028
2009	8,836,347	6,838,830	15,909	6,854,739	761,591	-570,925	5,522,223	1,784,705	1,529,419	33,536	263,486	159,649
2010	9,257,866	7,010,802	30,969	7,041,771	768,588	-585,976	5,687,207	1,867,829	1,702,830	34,987	264,607	157,626
2011	9,653,803	7,032,900	38,027	7,070,927	689,653	-612,276	5,768,998	2,094,790	1,790,015	36,180	266,825	158,531
2012	9,708,887	7,210,915	64,302	7,275,217	715,823	-660,922	5,898,472	2,055,460	1,754,955	36,154	268,543	159,797
2013	9,783,840	7,393,372	63,072	7,456,444	832,098	-691,021	5,933,325	2,030,121	1,820,394	36,289	269,608	161,685
2014	10,436,196	7,690,760	87,027	7,777,787	867,393	-686,726	6,223,668	2,228,621	1,983,907	38,264	272,745	166,036
2015	10,909,130	8,003,344	91,827	8,095,171	896,805	-703,201	6,495,165	2,342,311	2,071,654	39,427	276,689	170,311
2016	11,354,672	8,304,648	67,857	8,372,505	934,579	-744,698	6,693,228	2,491,554	2,169,890	40,329	281,551	173,602
2017	11,876,633	8,725,083	69,180	8,794,263	980,516	-820,725	6,993,022	2,617,077	2,266,534	41,718	284,687	177,016
2018	14,196,596	14,064,654	131,942	10,005,912	1,122,600	-611,080	8,272,232	3,057,626	2,866,738	43,291	327,933	198,868
2019	14,771,206	14,602,567	168,639	10,438,067	1,183,427	-639,312	8,615,328	3,105,824	3,050,054	44,880	329,128	202,377

Personal Income and Employment by Area: Gainesville, GA

(Thousands of dollars, except as noted.)

Year	Personal income, total	Earnings by place of work			Less: Contributions for government social insurance	Plus: Adjustment for residence	Equals: Net earnings by place of residence	Plus: Dividends, interest, and rent	Plus: Personal current transfer receipts	Per capita personal income (dollars)	Population (persons)	Total employment
		Nonfarm	Farm	Total								
1970	196,115	166,060	3,899	169,959	10,560	-984	158,415	22,573	15,127	3,279	59,814	29,685
1971	211,988	176,451	3,140	179,591	11,564	239	168,266	25,655	18,067	3,419	62,007	30,211
1972	241,760	199,657	4,894	204,551	13,765	1,616	192,402	28,815	20,543	3,813	63,406	30,977
1973	275,604	217,549	12,623	230,172	17,172	3,451	216,451	34,675	24,478	4,187	65,831	31,482
1974	300,115	237,747	5,711	243,458	19,557	3,811	227,712	41,882	30,521	4,494	66,786	32,098
1975	337,306	245,702	15,535	261,237	19,800	5,242	246,679	47,460	43,167	4,884	69,063	31,241
1976	381,368	286,568	16,659	303,227	23,544	6,513	286,196	50,643	44,529	5,477	69,626	33,292
1977	431,665	331,720	15,914	347,634	27,087	8,017	328,564	55,649	47,452	6,064	71,185	35,486
1978	497,468	386,312	17,534	403,846	32,505	9,659	381,000	64,226	52,242	6,858	72,534	37,509
1979	559,831	444,692	9,311	454,003	39,116	11,140	426,027	74,510	59,294	7,537	74,275	39,816
1980	637,061	487,502	2,974	490,476	42,989	19,235	466,722	96,914	73,425	8,374	76,074	39,846
1981	716,441	533,787	5,942	539,729	50,546	20,331	509,514	123,313	83,614	9,229	77,629	40,631
1982	769,971	557,933	10,285	568,218	53,837	24,027	538,408	137,704	93,859	9,767	78,832	40,711
1983	844,841	614,201	9,698	623,899	59,650	26,538	590,787	152,728	101,326	10,524	80,278	42,095
1984	986,980	711,590	29,324	740,914	71,046	28,735	698,603	181,249	107,128	12,033	82,024	45,932
1985	1,085,046	799,866	24,107	823,973	81,984	29,615	771,604	199,983	113,459	12,891	84,174	48,216
1986	1,204,312	880,117	40,447	920,564	91,438	30,729	859,855	223,891	120,566	13,834	87,054	49,668
1987	1,279,647	974,783	25,526	1,000,309	101,462	25,453	924,300	229,255	126,092	14,363	89,092	51,538
1988	1,397,799	1,058,771	35,774	1,094,545	113,502	23,561	1,004,604	254,040	139,155	15,263	91,583	53,765
1989	1,522,304	1,123,222	49,850	1,173,072	121,110	17,584	1,069,546	299,121	153,637	16,218	93,865	55,176
1990	1,613,754	1,199,398	41,786	1,241,184	129,249	9,654	1,121,589	319,047	173,118	16,772	96,215	55,485
1991	1,692,195	1,239,543	41,418	1,280,961	135,421	16,961	1,162,501	327,637	202,057	17,003	99,525	55,068
1992	1,838,303	1,357,096	38,613	1,395,709	145,832	21,789	1,271,666	333,972	232,665	17,990	102,186	56,420
1993	1,992,980	1,497,728	40,924	1,538,652	161,353	10,821	1,388,120	354,753	250,107	18,819	105,903	60,311
1994	2,185,594	1,650,342	37,617	1,687,959	178,913	6,591	1,515,637	396,313	273,644	19,864	110,029	64,802
1995	2,337,505	1,761,205	33,533	1,794,738	190,092	13,408	1,618,054	417,690	301,761	20,421	114,464	67,737
1996	2,542,486	1,882,168	39,090	1,921,258	200,645	29,986	1,750,599	466,498	325,389	21,339	119,147	69,621
1997	2,699,384	2,016,335	34,976	2,051,311	212,011	30,223	1,869,523	495,240	334,621	21,731	124,219	71,817
1998	3,000,257	2,245,116	48,776	2,293,892	230,680	42,724	2,105,936	549,828	344,493	23,225	129,182	74,904
1999	3,292,398	2,510,516	46,581	2,557,097	254,113	50,162	2,353,146	575,064	364,188	24,428	134,781	77,324
2000	3,576,484	2,711,986	37,046	2,749,032	274,545	47,380	2,521,867	646,844	407,773	25,366	140,993	81,590
2001	3,766,106	2,812,035	53,698	2,865,733	290,758	72,104	2,647,079	667,298	451,729	25,769	146,148	81,018
2002	3,945,712	2,950,927	32,724	2,983,651	303,385	75,605	2,755,871	671,718	518,123	26,265	150,229	81,381
2003	4,229,402	3,190,145	32,623	3,222,768	320,759	84,179	2,986,188	712,772	530,442	27,542	153,561	83,278
2004	4,563,083	3,375,356	49,663	3,425,019	350,878	190,507	3,264,648	707,070	591,365	29,179	156,385	85,877
2005	4,929,725	3,610,590	46,771	3,657,361	372,970	150,995	3,435,386	835,419	658,920	30,623	160,979	89,023
2006	5,272,938	3,795,261	16,484	3,811,745	399,417	200,742	3,613,070	937,328	722,540	31,665	166,524	92,744
2007	5,553,728	3,914,410	15,606	3,930,016	413,818	265,155	3,781,353	989,954	782,421	32,206	172,446	97,240
2008	5,530,130	3,927,608	19,995	3,947,603	439,757	62,677	3,570,523	1,049,617	909,990	31,195	177,277	97,443
2009	5,411,867	3,726,029	12,345	3,738,374	413,604	63,916	3,388,686	1,004,134	1,019,047	30,318	178,503	91,963
2010	5,503,160	3,824,005	4,351	3,828,356	423,458	58,923	3,463,821	912,698	1,126,641	30,563	180,059	92,717
2011	5,941,660	4,184,770	-7,176	4,177,594	403,048	-45,486	3,729,060	1,028,779	1,183,821	32,563	182,467	95,786
2012	6,137,356	4,256,896	18,039	4,274,935	411,050	64,142	3,928,027	1,023,952	1,185,377	33,283	184,401	96,011
2013	6,369,991	4,527,825	21,797	4,549,622	493,630	46,781	4,102,773	1,025,143	1,242,075	34,107	186,765	99,657
2014	6,822,873	4,869,993	27,825	4,897,818	524,073	48,590	4,422,335	1,119,227	1,281,311	36,008	189,480	102,061
2015	7,452,247	5,310,774	26,245	5,337,019	568,320	6,150	4,774,849	1,301,477	1,375,921	38,712	192,506	107,186
2016	7,832,366	5,575,932	12,075	5,588,007	596,871	71,583	5,062,719	1,349,232	1,420,415	39,913	196,237	111,233
2017	8,216,290	6,029,574	21,301	6,050,875	641,945	-59,526	5,349,404	1,398,682	1,468,204	41,219	199,335	114,986
2018	8,956,711	8,947,686	9,025	6,422,770	683,696	-46,365	5,692,709	1,713,232	1,550,770	44,442	201,538	119,266
2019	9,317,545	9,321,702	-4,157	6,661,687	724,513	14,231	5,951,405	1,721,926	1,644,214	45,576	204,441	121,156

Personal Income and Employment by Area: Gettysburg, PA

(Thousands of dollars, except as noted.)

Year	Personal income, total	Earnings by place of work			Less: Contributions for government social insurance	Plus: Adjustment for residence	Equals: Net earnings by place of residence	Plus: Dividends, interest, and rent	Plus: Personal current transfer receipts	Per capita personal income (dollars)	Population (persons)	Total employment
		Nonfarm	Farm	Total								
1970	220,477	127,784	8,495	136,279	9,340	45,619	172,558	30,080	17,839	3,857	57,165	24,009
1971	237,257	135,820	6,958	142,778	10,344	51,401	183,835	32,904	20,518	4,047	58,628	23,992
1972	267,285	148,867	7,988	156,855	11,787	61,140	206,208	36,362	24,715	4,395	60,815	24,380
1973	301,015	164,296	11,039	175,335	14,854	70,682	231,163	42,540	27,312	4,806	62,627	25,256
1974	335,085	175,629	15,221	190,850	16,536	80,121	254,435	48,094	32,556	5,275	63,523	24,999
1975	363,640	184,376	9,788	194,164	16,850	87,465	264,779	55,566	43,295	5,697	63,834	24,443
1976	414,886	211,826	16,688	228,514	19,568	98,477	307,423	59,358	48,105	6,439	64,435	25,654
1977	458,548	230,076	18,720	248,796	21,206	114,087	341,677	66,439	50,432	7,012	65,398	26,298
1978	511,846	264,210	10,236	274,446	24,871	133,925	383,500	74,873	53,473	7,728	66,235	27,477
1979	574,470	289,874	10,133	300,007	28,216	155,522	427,313	87,782	59,375	8,522	67,409	28,152
1980	643,770	316,371	5,865	322,236	31,259	173,845	464,822	109,956	68,992	9,396	68,513	28,790
1981	710,744	345,427	6,185	351,612	36,658	182,038	496,992	133,857	79,895	10,226	69,506	28,581
1982	767,808	361,305	15,662	376,967	38,529	181,085	519,523	154,994	93,291	10,903	70,422	28,659
1983	804,716	394,083	8,998	403,081	42,342	185,341	546,080	157,149	101,487	11,386	70,679	29,204
1984	886,368	436,075	18,378	454,453	48,502	203,780	609,731	176,805	99,832	12,610	70,290	30,229
1985	950,348	472,516	17,063	489,579	53,468	217,442	653,553	190,050	106,745	13,377	71,043	31,718
1986	1,026,278	511,426	27,130	538,556	58,291	228,438	708,703	203,880	113,695	14,157	72,492	32,650
1987	1,097,423	567,064	21,028	588,092	64,203	246,419	770,308	209,055	118,060	14,835	73,976	34,638
1988	1,201,940	630,820	22,895	653,715	72,596	266,978	848,097	224,757	129,086	15,957	75,326	35,985
1989	1,307,944	691,461	19,197	710,658	78,200	279,016	911,474	256,011	140,459	17,073	76,609	36,964
1990	1,397,840	737,450	29,588	767,038	83,836	295,928	979,130	261,659	157,051	17,740	78,797	37,551
1991	1,449,162	753,256	31,501	784,757	87,711	297,569	994,615	271,356	183,191	17,995	80,531	37,987
1992	1,541,070	816,671	40,966	857,637	94,768	298,829	1,061,698	278,002	201,370	18,846	81,771	38,543
1993	1,590,800	860,235	33,922	894,157	101,617	302,232	1,094,772	284,243	211,785	19,163	83,013	38,395
1994	1,630,088	896,407	19,829	916,236	108,842	302,310	1,109,704	295,550	224,834	19,363	84,186	39,636
1995	1,728,939	918,521	29,863	948,384	112,176	311,242	1,147,450	343,791	237,698	20,325	85,063	40,120
1996	1,837,041	941,005	41,584	982,589	112,157	334,327	1,204,759	374,568	257,714	21,299	86,252	40,211
1997	1,967,209	977,396	33,758	1,011,154	114,458	394,644	1,291,340	409,281	266,588	22,418	87,751	40,491
1998	2,085,014	1,057,905	25,231	1,083,136	120,725	397,152	1,359,563	448,138	277,313	23,408	89,074	43,308
1999	2,226,847	1,173,198	32,651	1,205,849	129,700	411,820	1,487,969	443,109	295,769	24,643	90,363	44,773
2000	2,409,446	1,249,309	19,880	1,269,189	137,388	469,514	1,601,315	485,670	322,461	26,345	91,457	46,362
2001	2,607,522	1,331,603	32,258	1,363,861	146,441	523,107	1,740,527	507,830	359,165	28,162	92,591	42,614
2002	2,714,406	1,406,502	19,211	1,425,713	153,904	564,013	1,835,822	496,930	381,654	28,897	93,934	43,293
2003	2,891,035	1,495,200	32,810	1,528,010	161,750	623,818	1,990,078	501,116	399,841	30,272	95,503	43,866
2004	3,024,538	1,588,908	22,234	1,611,142	172,377	675,208	2,113,973	481,297	429,268	31,085	97,300	44,833
2005	3,184,428	1,686,829	18,661	1,705,490	185,542	736,568	2,256,516	461,431	466,481	32,294	98,606	46,439
2006	3,338,642	1,747,351	8,684	1,756,035	199,633	773,744	2,330,146	505,928	502,568	33,420	99,899	47,899
2007	3,539,589	1,776,563	30,447	1,807,010	205,116	820,587	2,422,481	572,158	544,950	35,219	100,502	48,286
2008	3,714,611	1,732,356	66,327	1,798,683	206,023	894,293	2,486,953	605,597	622,061	36,758	101,056	47,539
2009	3,692,569	1,656,842	59,337	1,716,179	201,833	873,585	2,387,931	536,653	767,985	36,469	101,252	45,689
2010	3,784,592	1,721,556	56,711	1,778,267	205,143	900,878	2,474,002	549,419	761,171	37,300	101,464	45,039
2011	3,935,064	1,776,467	56,848	1,833,315	191,147	941,158	2,583,326	604,492	747,246	38,784	101,460	44,677
2012	4,048,791	1,822,563	78,871	1,901,434	195,499	945,379	2,651,314	646,965	750,512	39,997	101,228	45,139
2013	4,131,957	1,923,056	74,905	1,997,961	230,446	932,292	2,699,807	662,981	769,169	40,887	101,059	47,114
2014	4,368,460	1,991,849	81,706	2,073,555	238,979	1,008,599	2,843,175	717,408	807,877	43,153	101,231	47,549
2015	4,556,497	2,056,702	65,222	2,121,924	244,839	1,033,494	2,910,579	783,924	861,994	44,831	101,637	47,644
2016	4,601,294	2,103,923	42,554	2,146,477	253,209	988,885	2,882,153	818,772	900,369	45,251	101,684	48,581
2017	4,816,605	2,214,182	62,655	2,276,837	270,068	1,033,267	3,040,036	861,396	915,173	47,067	102,336	49,193
2018	4,986,055	4,963,522	22,533	2,324,680	277,779	1,059,607	3,106,508	887,413	992,134	48,379	103,062	49,106
2019	5,169,186	5,139,193	29,993	2,419,816	288,861	1,085,626	3,216,581	906,300	1,046,305	50,182	103,009	49,506

Personal Income and Employment by Area: Glens Falls, NY

(Thousands of dollars, except as noted.)

Year	Personal income, total	Earnings by place of work Nonfarm	Earnings by place of work Farm	Earnings by place of work Total	Less: Contributions for government social insurance	Plus: Adjustment for residence	Equals: Net earnings by place of residence	Plus: Dividends, interest, and rent	Plus: Personal current transfer receipts	Per capita personal income (dollars)	Population (persons)	Total employment
1970	370,853	296,401	9,468	305,869	22,577	-2,946	280,346	49,620	40,887	3,614	102,612	43,236
1971	398,502	313,681	9,831	323,512	24,786	-5,209	293,517	55,570	49,415	3,807	104,666	43,913
1972	426,819	335,677	10,127	345,804	27,754	-7,268	310,782	62,395	53,642	4,030	105,917	44,230
1973	465,658	365,632	11,125	376,757	34,816	-8,843	333,098	71,137	61,423	4,378	106,354	45,768
1974	507,356	392,985	9,488	402,473	38,663	-10,694	353,116	80,230	74,010	4,753	106,739	46,106
1975	550,664	405,548	7,154	412,702	39,089	-10,840	362,773	88,338	99,553	5,081	108,378	44,892
1976	600,360	451,064	9,186	460,250	44,431	-12,579	403,240	93,763	103,357	5,513	108,894	46,339
1977	647,233	492,063	6,145	498,208	48,256	-17,165	432,787	104,268	110,178	5,893	109,831	47,327
1978	711,564	551,820	10,298	562,118	55,170	-24,050	482,898	110,443	118,223	6,449	110,335	48,379
1979	779,711	605,743	14,680	620,423	62,393	-31,440	526,590	125,346	127,775	7,059	110,464	49,743
1980	869,768	652,921	15,690	668,611	67,336	-36,254	565,021	154,125	150,622	7,927	109,725	49,896
1981	965,096	705,103	15,255	720,358	77,390	-37,415	605,553	187,679	171,864	8,787	109,830	50,090
1982	1,048,683	746,098	16,038	762,136	82,735	-35,763	643,638	212,418	192,627	9,554	109,768	50,097
1983	1,128,992	797,043	14,578	811,621	88,645	-33,967	689,009	236,482	203,501	10,259	110,046	50,967
1984	1,263,830	906,295	14,725	921,020	102,388	-35,462	783,170	268,855	211,805	11,434	110,536	52,557
1985	1,353,577	965,146	15,939	981,085	110,118	-28,379	842,588	287,305	223,684	12,147	111,433	53,905
1986	1,472,546	1,070,654	17,836	1,088,490	123,438	-30,789	934,263	306,118	232,165	13,118	112,257	56,468
1987	1,601,833	1,183,461	18,413	1,201,874	134,970	-30,310	1,036,594	328,281	236,958	14,045	114,046	57,673
1988	1,756,523	1,317,205	14,952	1,332,157	153,030	-29,409	1,149,718	352,710	254,095	15,188	115,651	60,396
1989	1,906,821	1,370,907	19,982	1,390,889	158,086	-16,979	1,215,824	420,276	270,721	16,295	117,016	60,320
1990	1,998,011	1,418,909	22,262	1,441,171	157,428	-8,934	1,274,809	426,033	297,169	16,786	119,027	60,604
1991	2,054,214	1,447,568	16,786	1,464,354	164,915	-41	1,299,398	423,335	331,481	17,078	120,286	59,605
1992	2,214,533	1,551,649	22,557	1,574,206	172,985	6,686	1,407,907	427,850	378,776	18,258	121,290	59,655
1993	2,268,337	1,589,942	22,127	1,612,069	178,490	15,201	1,448,780	426,575	392,982	18,506	122,572	60,889
1994	2,353,423	1,654,966	17,571	1,672,537	188,805	17,416	1,501,148	434,087	418,188	19,167	122,783	63,236
1995	2,472,394	1,714,967	13,731	1,728,698	193,808	25,277	1,560,167	469,228	442,999	20,020	123,496	64,371
1996	2,570,081	1,754,698	23,186	1,777,884	194,754	37,117	1,620,247	484,409	465,425	20,791	123,615	63,799
1997	2,679,720	1,838,420	9,380	1,847,800	199,577	53,437	1,701,660	507,249	470,811	21,714	123,410	63,862
1998	2,807,300	1,890,558	24,182	1,914,740	204,778	70,462	1,780,424	530,880	495,996	22,743	123,436	62,144
1999	2,913,438	1,966,985	23,760	1,990,745	206,746	93,592	1,877,591	520,028	515,819	23,481	124,074	63,464
2000	3,142,024	2,150,218	20,324	2,170,542	222,553	114,458	2,062,447	544,091	535,486	25,288	124,250	64,595
2001	3,167,962	2,089,308	25,354	2,114,662	228,593	147,006	2,033,075	557,718	577,169	25,436	124,548	65,139
2002	3,224,852	2,158,186	16,214	2,174,400	240,909	150,412	2,083,903	517,145	623,804	25,814	124,926	65,403
2003	3,386,784	2,287,046	20,521	2,307,567	254,547	159,151	2,212,171	519,990	654,623	26,891	125,944	66,490
2004	3,652,824	2,468,469	29,267	2,497,736	273,301	191,757	2,416,192	536,900	699,732	28,795	126,854	68,542
2005	3,766,793	2,561,320	28,489	2,589,809	290,462	181,258	2,480,605	549,912	736,276	29,503	127,674	69,447
2006	3,922,289	2,656,976	17,789	2,674,765	303,119	218,750	2,590,396	540,028	791,865	30,565	128,325	70,191
2007	4,057,649	2,711,498	21,074	2,732,572	307,285	229,400	2,654,687	564,707	838,255	31,505	128,794	71,096
2008	4,342,835	2,829,919	21,546	2,851,465	325,242	188,029	2,714,252	692,319	936,264	33,639	129,100	72,890
2009	4,468,284	2,865,154	12,851	2,878,005	325,611	208,706	2,761,100	665,388	1,041,796	34,699	128,771	71,224
2010	4,662,891	2,991,598	31,435	3,023,033	333,816	187,249	2,876,466	674,261	1,112,164	36,144	129,008	70,234
2011	4,847,568	3,030,326	47,047	3,077,373	310,064	214,260	2,981,569	736,109	1,129,890	37,636	128,803	70,770
2012	4,975,129	3,152,898	47,119	3,200,017	318,724	175,536	3,056,829	785,166	1,133,134	38,746	128,405	70,839
2013	5,055,767	3,166,376	59,085	3,225,461	361,540	256,578	3,120,499	795,105	1,140,163	39,541	127,862	70,564
2014	5,154,706	3,241,790	69,811	3,311,601	378,915	183,220	3,115,906	844,484	1,194,316	40,467	127,379	71,320
2015	5,269,934	3,338,194	39,969	3,378,163	391,934	151,522	3,137,751	890,004	1,242,179	41,593	126,701	71,768
2016	5,385,832	3,394,196	34,903	3,429,099	401,394	184,281	3,211,986	905,644	1,268,202	42,635	126,325	71,329
2017	5,660,949	3,563,652	38,493	3,602,145	420,919	164,364	3,345,590	949,786	1,365,573	44,874	126,152	71,976
2018	5,851,973	5,831,775	20,198	3,663,474	421,148	245,357	3,487,683	1,027,391	1,336,899	46,633	125,489	71,725
2019	6,110,108	6,075,726	34,382	3,783,756	430,627	269,859	3,622,988	1,048,027	1,439,093	48,823	125,148	71,784

Personal Income and Employment by Area: Goldsboro, NC

(Thousands of dollars, except as noted.)

Year	Personal income, total	Earnings by place of work			Less: Contributions for government social insurance	Plus: Adjustment for residence	Equals: Net earnings by place of residence	Plus: Dividends, interest, and rent	Plus: Personal current transfer receipts	Per capita personal income (dollars)	Population (persons)	Total employment
		Nonfarm	Farm	Total								
1970	287,524	231,276	16,522	247,798	15,680	-13,255	218,863	45,911	22,750	3,353	85,747	42,648
1971	314,929	253,442	17,910	271,352	17,999	-14,972	238,381	49,683	26,865	3,581	87,943	43,039
1972	355,430	282,502	23,683	306,185	20,513	-15,628	270,044	54,623	30,763	3,943	90,151	43,682
1973	393,421	303,687	35,177	338,864	24,689	-14,463	299,712	59,977	33,732	4,355	90,338	44,400
1974	446,433	340,317	40,079	380,396	28,817	-16,734	334,845	70,375	41,213	4,863	91,807	45,687
1975	479,207	357,004	36,633	393,637	31,216	-14,561	347,860	77,419	53,928	5,181	92,498	44,628
1976	521,085	390,154	35,703	425,857	35,037	-13,861	376,959	84,659	59,467	5,582	93,352	45,876
1977	551,523	421,116	21,812	442,928	37,333	-12,618	392,977	95,911	62,635	5,825	94,674	46,344
1978	618,738	464,609	33,578	498,187	41,876	-12,063	444,248	107,345	67,145	6,393	96,788	46,994
1979	671,208	519,193	18,240	537,433	48,700	-11,014	477,719	117,333	76,156	6,910	97,135	48,534
1980	739,544	561,213	13,743	574,956	52,559	-10,891	511,506	136,787	91,251	7,600	97,314	48,041
1981	815,058	600,252	26,141	626,393	60,103	-14,058	552,232	157,208	105,618	8,311	98,066	47,291
1982	875,938	635,369	28,662	664,031	63,595	-17,091	583,345	177,153	115,440	8,883	98,603	46,959
1983	935,715	690,958	16,564	707,522	70,066	-17,294	620,162	190,574	124,979	9,414	99,391	47,490
1984	1,062,173	751,523	61,483	813,006	78,344	-16,233	718,429	211,997	131,747	10,580	100,393	48,551
1985	1,107,760	786,648	55,857	842,505	83,299	-13,452	745,754	220,788	141,218	10,947	101,193	48,845
1986	1,154,436	821,094	53,196	874,290	88,997	-11,929	773,364	230,970	150,102	11,521	100,205	48,493
1987	1,201,745	882,543	28,753	911,296	95,038	-10,412	805,846	240,608	155,291	11,864	101,296	49,782
1988	1,301,456	960,115	30,270	990,385	107,845	-15,596	866,944	265,736	168,776	12,726	102,269	52,540
1989	1,428,127	1,018,678	46,259	1,064,937	114,807	-12,413	937,717	304,473	185,937	13,740	103,938	52,694
1990	1,542,500	1,074,164	56,241	1,130,405	123,204	17,181	1,024,382	309,966	208,152	14,705	104,896	53,244
1991	1,628,725	1,105,557	73,633	1,179,190	128,107	20,249	1,071,332	317,899	239,494	15,287	106,545	51,973
1992	1,768,834	1,186,551	69,324	1,255,875	136,880	50,575	1,169,570	334,572	264,692	16,437	107,614	52,502
1993	1,866,996	1,256,753	73,468	1,330,221	146,115	45,901	1,230,007	342,855	294,134	17,227	108,374	53,661
1994	1,982,989	1,309,248	79,421	1,388,669	152,634	71,720	1,307,755	367,738	307,496	18,116	109,459	55,617
1995	2,102,483	1,385,452	73,618	1,459,070	161,288	60,401	1,358,183	400,455	343,845	18,843	111,578	57,476
1996	2,212,889	1,437,978	82,389	1,520,367	165,815	62,704	1,417,256	423,731	371,902	19,601	112,898	57,498
1997	2,322,481	1,511,699	82,324	1,594,023	173,536	49,655	1,470,142	457,017	395,322	20,487	113,366	59,127
1998	2,390,885	1,584,247	59,431	1,643,678	182,322	35,955	1,497,311	488,316	405,258	21,078	113,429	58,373
1999	2,481,021	1,642,987	43,209	1,686,196	190,142	63,705	1,559,759	489,886	431,376	21,922	113,176	58,682
2000	2,612,468	1,717,943	50,595	1,768,538	198,294	72,444	1,642,688	514,133	455,647	22,987	113,648	59,844
2001	2,764,352	1,828,022	56,717	1,884,739	209,699	75,818	1,750,858	519,238	494,256	24,263	113,934	59,739
2002	2,840,131	1,905,838	36,721	1,942,559	218,422	72,107	1,796,244	510,961	532,926	24,847	114,305	59,786
2003	2,888,159	1,923,770	16,096	1,939,866	223,402	83,671	1,800,135	520,543	567,481	25,203	114,595	58,552
2004	3,082,955	2,050,306	34,250	2,084,556	236,175	88,848	1,937,229	537,608	608,118	26,467	116,484	58,827
2005	3,223,446	2,113,889	56,820	2,170,709	245,602	96,217	2,021,324	543,263	658,859	27,549	117,009	58,868
2006	3,380,057	2,221,475	37,307	2,258,782	259,380	97,942	2,097,344	560,944	721,769	28,758	117,534	59,751
2007	3,627,551	2,303,274	69,496	2,372,770	272,745	117,046	2,217,071	642,516	767,964	30,498	118,942	61,543
2008	3,756,727	2,326,995	106,538	2,433,533	276,384	115,560	2,272,709	634,809	849,209	31,330	119,910	60,722
2009	3,776,180	2,323,882	92,346	2,416,228	279,591	86,704	2,223,341	620,736	932,103	31,152	121,217	59,757
2010	3,877,472	2,391,115	110,379	2,501,494	283,111	77,272	2,295,655	603,350	978,467	31,559	122,864	58,747
2011	4,030,065	2,472,332	101,431	2,573,763	269,417	59,565	2,363,911	658,079	1,008,075	32,480	124,080	60,034
2012	4,224,252	2,582,681	141,260	2,723,941	276,031	39,949	2,487,859	703,810	1,032,583	33,917	124,547	59,949
2013	4,179,702	2,551,097	163,800	2,714,897	309,384	34,849	2,440,362	684,093	1,055,247	33,514	124,715	59,386
2014	4,349,534	2,565,326	202,029	2,767,355	311,125	67,358	2,523,588	732,437	1,093,509	34,890	124,664	59,086
2015	4,439,760	2,589,403	160,984	2,750,387	316,806	76,734	2,510,315	786,489	1,142,956	35,674	124,454	58,954
2016	4,434,246	2,595,401	103,429	2,698,830	316,578	87,762	2,470,014	788,623	1,175,609	35,623	124,476	58,860
2017	4,610,060	2,664,047	134,440	2,798,487	324,046	95,127	2,569,568	823,682	1,216,810	37,126	124,172	59,195
2018	4,735,428	4,662,661	72,767	2,846,194	330,310	117,308	2,633,192	853,190	1,249,046	38,425	123,237	59,708
2019	4,912,230	4,835,020	77,210	2,963,411	345,951	129,827	2,747,287	872,231	1,292,712	39,894	123,131	60,002

Personal Income and Employment by Area: Grand Forks, ND-MN

(Thousands of dollars, except as noted.)

Year	Personal income, total	Earnings by place of work			Less: Contributions for government social insurance	Plus: Adjustment for residence	Equals: Net earnings by place of residence	Plus: Dividends, interest, and rent	Plus: Personal current transfer receipts	Per capita personal income (dollars)	Population (persons)	Total employment
		Nonfarm	Farm	Total								
1970	358,608	247,966	33,965	281,931	18,853	4,879	267,957	61,147	29,504	3,738	95,935	43,052
1971	392,498	269,553	34,767	304,320	21,288	7,785	290,817	67,120	34,561	4,010	97,885	43,405
1972	442,727	300,299	47,267	347,566	24,388	7,675	330,853	73,963	37,911	4,490	98,607	44,636
1973	580,655	339,134	142,350	481,484	30,746	1,052	451,790	86,188	42,677	5,818	99,795	46,958
1974	604,087	376,816	119,775	496,591	36,013	-4,430	456,148	97,751	50,188	6,035	100,100	48,256
1975	644,297	414,932	102,682	517,614	40,614	-4,337	472,663	111,422	60,212	6,561	98,203	48,980
1976	683,917	485,209	67,380	552,589	48,357	-7,470	496,762	121,311	65,844	6,797	100,617	51,544
1977	679,040	500,791	29,499	530,290	48,635	-7,202	474,453	133,621	70,966	6,661	101,935	51,571
1978	819,219	549,210	105,612	654,822	54,218	-8,021	592,583	147,963	78,673	8,093	101,225	52,678
1979	851,678	599,987	72,976	672,963	61,546	-9,252	602,165	162,500	87,013	8,401	101,383	52,989
1980	885,826	643,622	19,371	662,993	66,540	-10,034	586,419	195,762	103,645	8,764	101,074	53,483
1981	1,002,265	698,397	30,374	728,771	75,838	-9,498	643,435	239,878	118,952	9,887	101,367	52,972
1982	1,095,948	741,001	37,012	778,013	80,770	-9,023	688,220	275,959	131,769	10,760	101,851	53,099
1983	1,168,682	783,530	47,597	831,127	86,799	-7,839	736,489	283,591	148,602	11,335	103,104	54,018
1984	1,303,531	830,392	111,083	941,475	94,693	-8,065	838,717	304,682	160,132	12,565	103,741	54,465
1985	1,317,111	875,412	62,395	937,807	102,024	-8,259	827,524	318,005	171,582	12,700	103,712	55,684
1986	1,419,084	920,225	110,567	1,030,792	110,241	-8,929	911,622	327,769	179,693	13,731	103,349	55,969
1987	1,471,031	975,157	110,250	1,085,407	117,601	-9,350	958,456	322,733	189,842	14,224	103,422	57,658
1988	1,474,407	1,018,897	63,615	1,082,512	128,680	-8,138	945,694	332,242	196,471	14,131	104,341	58,645
1989	1,561,546	1,074,278	56,876	1,131,154	137,303	-7,758	986,093	362,592	212,861	15,001	104,094	59,627
1990	1,654,164	1,119,893	89,844	1,209,737	148,093	-7,858	1,053,786	371,963	228,415	16,032	103,177	59,698
1991	1,686,811	1,184,404	64,659	1,249,063	159,621	-10,696	1,078,746	375,201	232,864	16,371	103,034	61,249
1992	1,824,367	1,252,808	121,728	1,374,536	169,609	-14,019	1,190,908	374,235	259,224	17,512	104,181	61,836
1993	1,823,335	1,326,213	29,754	1,355,967	181,395	-17,530	1,157,042	395,427	270,866	17,458	104,443	63,139
1994	1,950,802	1,399,164	63,520	1,462,684	191,770	-20,806	1,250,108	427,994	272,700	18,473	105,601	65,108
1995	2,025,516	1,467,099	42,450	1,509,549	199,214	-25,651	1,284,684	453,021	287,811	19,172	105,650	66,896
1996	2,177,493	1,526,145	129,960	1,656,105	206,135	-28,969	1,421,001	459,374	297,118	20,651	105,443	67,548
1997	2,147,195	1,586,608	31,905	1,618,513	212,440	-33,015	1,373,058	475,814	298,323	20,717	103,643	65,519
1998	2,273,834	1,643,083	96,213	1,739,296	219,425	-36,686	1,483,185	495,622	295,027	22,752	99,938	65,303
1999	2,270,850	1,678,306	61,419	1,739,725	222,496	-38,384	1,478,845	480,850	311,155	23,191	97,919	64,607
2000	2,399,869	1,724,420	107,074	1,831,494	228,382	-41,347	1,561,765	502,523	335,581	24,638	97,405	64,457
2001	2,432,614	1,794,739	60,123	1,854,862	230,233	-44,746	1,579,883	495,852	356,879	25,166	96,663	65,352
2002	2,547,943	1,897,052	56,899	1,953,951	240,278	-49,791	1,663,882	501,862	382,199	26,440	96,367	65,622
2003	2,745,204	2,012,883	145,604	2,158,487	253,892	-57,343	1,847,252	498,252	399,700	28,517	96,267	66,495
2004	2,796,342	2,137,147	63,304	2,200,451	267,546	-63,269	1,869,636	504,325	422,381	28,486	98,164	67,733
2005	2,910,196	2,226,870	78,592	2,305,462	278,755	-68,010	1,958,697	502,010	449,489	29,764	97,777	69,046
2006	3,096,706	2,329,903	109,283	2,439,186	288,254	-73,252	2,077,680	540,069	478,957	31,514	98,266	69,872
2007	3,320,296	2,424,853	148,497	2,573,350	299,272	-78,429	2,195,649	609,833	514,814	34,017	97,606	70,645
2008	3,610,991	2,499,977	237,730	2,737,707	307,913	-82,198	2,347,596	683,510	579,885	36,812	98,092	69,995
2009	3,524,378	2,566,130	101,707	2,667,837	323,477	-83,537	2,260,823	645,511	618,044	35,985	97,941	69,557
2010	3,723,522	2,662,216	149,684	2,811,900	318,656	-82,637	2,410,607	649,652	663,263	37,767	98,592	69,234
2011	3,990,545	2,762,425	142,929	2,905,354	306,320	-69,067	2,529,967	779,470	681,108	40,695	98,061	69,292
2012	4,422,933	2,944,168	281,826	3,225,994	310,444	-46,733	2,868,817	869,430	684,686	44,655	99,047	71,410
2013	4,514,001	3,049,128	283,175	3,332,303	362,873	-39,344	2,930,086	878,678	705,237	44,821	100,712	71,774
2014	4,577,492	3,217,212	93,011	3,310,223	386,306	-42,926	2,880,991	957,482	739,019	45,190	101,295	72,276
2015	4,684,668	3,355,166	24,820	3,379,986	407,786	-45,722	2,926,478	991,240	766,950	46,010	101,819	72,859
2016	4,810,279	3,467,046	49,526	3,516,572	418,605	-52,721	3,045,246	968,677	796,356	47,053	102,231	72,651
2017	4,933,945	3,545,438	36,756	3,582,194	430,450	-44,975	3,106,769	1,006,652	820,524	48,176	102,414	72,485
2018	5,114,605	5,048,202	66,403	3,686,739	437,452	-53,191	3,196,096	1,050,426	868,083	50,258	101,766	72,189
2019		5,159,239	78,111	3,789,561	445,971	-75,409	3,268,181	1,064,900	904,269	51,950	100,815	72,249

Personal Income and Employment by Area: Grand Island, NE

(Thousands of dollars, except as noted.)

Year	Personal income, total	Earnings by place of work			Less: Contributions for government social insurance	Plus: Adjustment for residence	Equals: Net earnings by place of residence	Plus: Dividends, interest, and rent	Plus: Personal current transfer receipts	Per capita personal income (dollars)	Population (persons)	Total employment
		Nonfarm	Farm	Total								
1970............	257,019	170,309	36,916	207,225	11,911	-5,111	190,203	44,110	22,706	3,824	67,211	31,910
1971............	271,900	179,178	37,327	216,505	12,841	-4,888	198,776	47,803	25,321	4,034	67,395	31,655
1972............	300,622	199,281	39,107	238,388	14,654	-5,343	218,391	54,303	27,928	4,428	67,890	33,218
1973............	351,679	226,718	54,970	281,688	19,273	-6,081	256,334	62,144	33,201	5,121	68,678	35,148
1974............	376,782	246,664	49,501	296,165	21,797	-6,204	268,164	70,233	38,385	5,483	68,715	35,595
1975............	437,270	269,390	72,115	341,505	23,314	-6,868	311,323	80,412	45,535	6,253	69,925	35,293
1976............	447,374	307,060	40,153	347,213	26,855	-7,306	313,052	86,103	48,219	6,388	70,033	36,625
1977............	459,313	338,885	8,055	346,940	29,475	-8,263	309,202	97,742	52,369	6,449	71,220	37,764
1978............	563,425	376,710	63,368	440,078	33,695	-9,079	397,304	108,389	57,732	7,884	71,462	39,141
1979............	588,735	423,392	27,977	451,369	39,400	-10,638	401,331	122,475	64,929	8,132	72,400	39,560
1980............	602,738	465,096	-33,537	431,559	43,359	-13,003	375,197	151,159	76,382	8,262	72,954	40,087
1981............	758,159	505,234	39,462	544,696	50,049	-12,520	482,127	186,795	89,237	10,277	73,771	40,254
1982............	776,854	507,440	10,899	518,339	51,424	-11,602	455,313	221,409	100,132	10,453	74,317	38,976
1983............	803,797	522,489	11,381	533,870	53,185	-10,919	469,766	225,160	108,871	10,853	74,064	39,138
1984............	927,062	558,584	81,854	640,438	58,537	-10,171	571,730	240,568	114,764	12,500	74,167	39,328
1985............	932,677	567,298	71,892	639,190	61,318	-9,468	568,404	243,596	120,677	12,659	73,677	38,879
1986............	975,902	592,097	91,630	683,727	65,846	-9,997	607,884	241,256	126,762	13,477	72,410	38,811
1987............	1,012,470	619,051	106,083	725,134	68,955	-8,988	647,191	235,446	129,833	14,071	71,955	39,539
1988............	1,081,672	653,541	133,897	787,438	75,952	-7,152	704,334	240,742	136,596	15,060	71,826	40,534
1989............	1,154,190	692,075	127,812	819,887	80,722	-6,345	732,820	275,795	145,575	16,089	71,740	41,448
1990............	1,209,581	748,261	134,690	882,951	89,958	-6,380	786,613	266,465	156,503	16,783	72,071	42,489
1991............	1,280,768	793,710	142,669	936,379	96,197	-8,050	832,132	280,173	168,463	17,605	72,752	43,359
1992............	1,334,544	849,171	127,794	976,965	101,326	-8,272	867,367	282,857	184,320	18,162	73,479	44,308
1993............	1,363,086	908,934	85,512	994,446	108,969	-9,303	876,174	293,396	193,516	18,302	74,477	45,175
1994............	1,481,224	987,461	111,096	1,098,557	118,562	-9,890	970,105	305,931	205,188	19,727	75,088	47,719
1995............	1,545,879	1,034,258	94,093	1,128,351	122,434	-9,572	996,345	333,576	215,958	20,349	75,970	47,414
1996............	1,688,168	1,081,746	155,638	1,237,384	127,485	-10,110	1,099,789	357,367	231,012	22,058	76,534	48,688
1997............	1,710,751	1,139,982	102,854	1,242,836	135,455	-10,668	1,096,713	373,008	241,030	22,206	77,040	49,347
1998............	1,808,650	1,197,816	92,068	1,289,884	140,939	-9,834	1,139,111	412,719	256,820	23,324	77,545	50,196
1999............	1,861,941	1,249,832	78,710	1,328,542	145,617	-9,345	1,173,580	414,300	274,061	23,906	77,886	50,770
2000............	1,951,125	1,302,535	80,460	1,382,995	150,607	-10,709	1,221,679	444,212	285,234	25,137	77,621	50,928
2001............	2,062,827	1,388,936	85,434	1,474,370	159,556	-15,238	1,299,576	447,674	315,577	26,683	77,308	50,403
2002............	2,098,114	1,453,117	59,577	1,512,694	165,813	-19,107	1,327,774	431,728	338,612	27,063	77,526	49,739
2003............	2,243,078	1,495,290	132,514	1,627,804	171,562	-23,682	1,432,560	453,251	357,267	28,779	77,941	49,965
2004............	2,265,243	1,545,525	133,792	1,679,317	176,975	-26,851	1,475,491	414,551	375,201	28,962	78,215	50,269
2005............	2,350,016	1,619,788	159,668	1,779,456	190,000	-32,732	1,556,724	398,535	394,757	30,074	78,140	51,315
2006............	2,435,777	1,727,764	92,541	1,820,305	206,910	-35,666	1,577,729	436,689	421,359	31,007	78,556	52,459
2007............	2,680,711	1,844,382	157,292	2,001,674	220,890	-44,022	1,736,762	500,132	443,817	33,938	78,988	53,461
2008............	2,865,354	1,897,580	150,988	2,048,568	228,540	-53,998	1,766,030	601,776	497,548	35,841	79,947	54,433
2009............	2,809,347	1,892,215	147,847	2,040,062	228,181	-57,188	1,754,693	535,472	519,182	34,611	81,169	54,166
2010............	2,874,585	1,966,377	136,455	2,102,832	239,598	-62,312	1,800,922	519,518	554,145	35,030	82,061	53,946
2011............	3,188,735	2,039,906	289,559	2,329,465	217,569	-70,483	2,041,413	590,533	556,789	38,570	82,675	55,054
2012............	3,330,637	2,169,900	259,542	2,429,442	223,990	-80,300	2,125,152	644,562	560,923	39,952	83,365	56,099
2013............	3,343,362	2,210,038	317,112	2,527,150	257,851	-87,401	2,181,898	594,732	566,732	39,850	83,899	56,793
2014............	3,433,064	2,359,504	215,240	2,574,744	271,772	-94,797	2,208,175	635,138	589,751	40,656	84,442	57,172
2015............	3,558,339	2,428,195	192,404	2,620,599	275,948	-94,786	2,249,865	692,636	615,838	42,048	84,626	56,949
2016............	3,541,748	2,462,923	112,408	2,575,331	282,060	-94,795	2,198,476	705,211	638,061	41,683	84,968	57,149
2017............	3,672,840	2,539,810	133,312	2,673,122	297,467	-99,613	2,276,042	736,205	660,593	43,187	85,045	57,709
2018............	3,310,290	3,232,736	77,554	2,474,329	275,961	-154,287	2,044,081	651,336	614,873	43,859	75,476	51,673
2019............	3,436,663	3,317,307	119,356	2,585,357	286,336	-165,342	2,133,679	658,889	644,095	45,487	75,553	51,822

Personal Income and Employment by Area: Grand Junction, CO

(Thousands of dollars, except as noted.)

Year	Personal income, total	Derivation of personal income									Per capita personal income (dollars)	Population (persons)	Total employment
		Earnings by place of work			Less: Contributions for government social insurance	Plus: Adjustment for residence	Equals: Net earnings by place of residence	Plus: Dividends, interest, and rent	Plus: Personal current transfer receipts				
		Nonfarm	Farm	Total									
1970	193,533	138,826	3,993	142,819	8,195	121	134,745	35,603	23,185		3,552	54,479	23,121
1971	214,485	149,183	7,157	156,340	8,932	453	147,861	39,596	27,028		3,878	55,311	23,077
1972	236,705	168,812	4,600	173,412	10,758	1,085	163,739	43,570	29,396		4,159	56,912	24,258
1973	275,667	193,357	8,130	201,487	14,205	2,062	189,344	51,947	34,376		4,756	57,962	26,242
1974	326,263	232,044	6,702	238,746	17,459	3,077	224,364	62,191	39,708		5,532	58,973	28,069
1975	383,882	275,267	7,304	282,571	20,538	3,683	265,716	70,980	47,186		6,068	63,261	30,541
1976	429,725	311,045	5,577	316,622	23,291	5,450	298,781	79,703	51,241		6,450	66,628	32,111
1977	516,171	386,961	3,986	390,947	28,908	6,548	368,587	92,818	54,766		7,526	68,585	35,299
1978	600,883	456,683	827	457,510	35,274	8,449	430,685	110,150	60,048		8,320	72,223	37,820
1979	693,452	524,270	4,395	528,665	43,288	10,824	496,201	128,941	68,310		9,012	76,946	40,671
1980	815,643	609,596	2,580	612,176	51,893	13,732	574,015	160,526	81,102		9,851	82,796	43,710
1981	987,643	743,970	2,350	746,320	69,526	15,786	692,580	199,535	95,528		11,267	87,659	48,937
1982	1,093,557	798,516	-1,789	796,727	76,842	21,073	740,958	238,686	113,913		11,615	94,152	50,531
1983	1,108,483	768,535	1,206	769,741	73,346	23,077	719,472	255,218	133,793		11,545	96,012	48,319
1984	1,105,881	749,044	1,610	750,654	72,847	21,440	699,247	265,029	141,605		11,703	94,496	46,669
1985	1,102,098	730,827	-854	729,973	73,140	21,662	678,495	275,756	147,847		12,332	89,368	44,600
1986	1,082,075	688,008	-4,408	683,600	71,250	22,458	634,808	284,196	163,071		12,383	87,386	42,603
1987	1,168,654	752,858	-1,131	751,727	75,766	22,254	698,215	291,344	179,095		13,365	87,443	42,211
1988	1,277,022	839,702	433	840,135	87,270	22,207	775,072	312,100	189,850		14,369	88,872	45,112
1989	1,370,073	881,899	2,537	884,436	96,136	23,659	811,959	346,945	211,169		15,018	91,231	47,556
1990	1,470,377	958,419	2,293	960,712	107,105	28,304	881,911	361,624	226,842		15,683	93,757	49,479
1991	1,568,876	1,034,550	4,680	1,039,230	119,169	26,522	946,583	369,072	253,221		16,283	96,348	50,610
1992	1,709,903	1,131,597	8,463	1,140,060	128,847	23,770	1,034,983	391,717	283,203		17,452	97,977	51,414
1993	1,825,477	1,211,686	10,155	1,221,841	139,318	25,404	1,107,927	409,862	307,688		18,150	100,579	53,284
1994	1,940,144	1,286,510	7,041	1,293,551	149,380	30,782	1,174,953	439,289	325,902		18,768	103,373	55,648
1995	2,114,524	1,365,684	6,204	1,371,888	158,716	32,017	1,245,189	503,788	365,547		19,954	105,968	58,004
1996	2,245,219	1,462,006	8,137	1,470,143	167,445	33,633	1,336,331	529,494	379,394		20,764	108,131	61,078
1997	2,442,397	1,613,502	8,572	1,622,074	181,526	36,097	1,476,645	576,333	389,419		22,090	110,566	63,850
1998	2,656,272	1,764,478	12,211	1,776,689	183,059	39,817	1,633,447	592,689	430,136		23,572	112,686	66,443
1999	2,793,849	1,884,287	8,016	1,892,303	193,575	42,442	1,741,170	595,507	457,172		24,331	114,827	68,110
2000	3,022,612	2,033,166	8,630	2,041,796	204,229	47,355	1,884,922	659,079	478,611		25,696	117,631	69,890
2001	3,273,192	2,239,100	12,979	2,252,079	225,828	51,528	2,077,779	671,566	523,847		27,392	119,496	71,083
2002	3,390,632	2,379,679	13,516	2,393,195	250,205	53,855	2,196,845	616,624	577,163		27,692	122,440	72,725
2003	3,485,729	2,444,409	9,150	2,453,559	260,211	60,165	2,253,513	636,959	595,257		27,887	124,994	73,953
2004	3,655,656	2,541,330	14,632	2,555,962	282,780	71,125	2,344,307	678,302	633,047		28,632	127,678	76,252
2005	3,964,891	2,749,334	17,916	2,767,250	310,413	98,234	2,555,071	722,499	687,321		30,454	130,194	79,069
2006	4,390,798	3,051,552	11,901	3,063,453	342,096	144,929	2,866,286	785,263	739,249		32,605	134,665	82,251
2007	4,941,947	3,406,313	10,889	3,417,202	382,902	186,706	3,221,006	940,813	780,128		35,443	139,434	87,490
2008	5,463,061	3,716,675	7,816	3,724,491	424,450	222,995	3,523,036	1,064,477	875,548		38,162	143,155	90,899
2009	5,105,027	3,470,543	6,505	3,477,048	396,099	177,414	3,258,363	935,973	910,691		34,528	147,851	86,309
2010	4,992,788	3,277,432	7,347	3,284,779	374,119	186,511	3,097,171	893,200	1,002,417		34,098	146,424	83,210
2011	5,209,240	3,341,833	14,071	3,355,904	352,844	218,517	3,221,577	969,350	1,018,313		35,371	147,276	83,893
2012	5,458,050	3,474,464	14,094	3,488,558	363,340	254,447	3,379,665	1,059,818	1,018,567		37,027	147,406	84,751
2013	5,550,898	3,573,731	11,095	3,584,826	403,793	281,986	3,463,019	1,038,309	1,049,570		37,697	147,250	84,923
2014	5,887,231	3,703,413	23,290	3,726,703	420,509	308,914	3,615,108	1,147,759	1,124,364		39,991	147,215	86,644
2015	5,974,294	3,725,093	22,111	3,747,204	429,245	270,097	3,588,056	1,171,358	1,214,880		40,335	148,116	86,352
2016	5,979,808	3,671,804	13,475	3,685,279	427,488	227,935	3,485,726	1,216,016	1,278,066		39,920	149,794	86,586
2017	6,292,523	3,921,919	17,113	3,939,032	457,838	232,659	3,713,853	1,270,564	1,308,106		41,503	151,616	88,682
2018	6,944,767	6,936,298	8,469	4,269,132	493,948	249,090	4,024,274	1,391,149	1,529,344		45,405	152,951	90,710
2019	7,204,611	7,197,273	7,338	4,438,357	513,433	256,535	4,181,459	1,414,691	1,608,461		46,719	154,210	92,118

Personal Income and Employment by Area: Grand Rapids-Kentwood, MI

(Thousands of dollars, except as noted.)

Year	Personal income, total	Earnings by place of work			Less: Contributions for government social insurance	Plus: Adjustment for residence	Equals: Net earnings by place of residence	Plus: Dividends, interest, and rent	Plus: Personal current transfer receipts	Per capita personal income (dollars)	Population (persons)	Total employment
		Nonfarm	Farm	Total								
1970	2,418,757	1,995,172	34,693	2,029,865	144,453	-19,801	1,865,611	340,079	213,067	3,916	617,650	260,078
1971	2,614,403	2,144,596	31,639	2,176,235	160,305	-19,674	1,996,256	365,097	253,050	4,211	620,779	264,236
1972	2,911,575	2,406,416	39,810	2,446,226	189,300	-19,529	2,237,397	395,001	279,177	4,644	626,892	276,468
1973	3,253,585	2,725,480	50,705	2,776,185	248,822	-22,981	2,504,382	432,221	316,982	5,099	638,073	292,681
1974	3,562,594	2,933,280	55,816	2,989,096	277,431	-25,952	2,685,713	490,557	386,324	5,539	643,154	298,385
1975	3,854,169	3,036,890	50,408	3,087,298	277,745	-20,311	2,789,242	553,894	511,033	5,945	648,334	289,665
1976	4,302,756	3,483,005	48,437	3,531,442	327,765	-23,930	3,179,747	591,122	531,887	6,577	654,247	305,252
1977	4,853,772	4,004,902	64,106	4,069,008	378,367	-34,851	3,655,790	656,805	541,177	7,323	662,779	323,181
1978	5,537,622	4,657,898	74,469	4,732,367	453,517	-48,157	4,230,693	736,118	570,811	8,238	672,225	345,133
1979	6,195,436	5,251,728	76,263	5,327,991	535,810	-69,424	4,722,757	831,020	641,659	9,043	685,105	356,907
1980	6,758,881	5,504,029	80,761	5,584,790	559,568	-69,024	4,956,198	1,001,936	800,747	9,695	697,163	349,556
1981	7,399,160	5,927,038	77,555	6,004,593	648,341	-80,415	5,275,837	1,227,350	895,973	10,507	704,228	350,029
1982	7,844,634	6,053,208	92,839	6,146,047	670,446	-92,153	5,383,448	1,440,882	1,020,304	11,106	706,354	344,069
1983	8,454,528	6,624,570	60,933	6,685,503	747,007	-121,327	5,817,169	1,561,002	1,076,357	11,918	709,384	356,659
1984	9,482,044	7,558,586	97,112	7,655,698	882,329	-165,514	6,607,855	1,791,389	1,082,800	13,176	719,650	378,005
1985	10,274,630	8,248,273	125,919	8,374,192	973,045	-190,916	7,210,231	1,916,781	1,147,618	14,060	730,764	396,691
1986	10,956,729	8,838,909	94,631	8,933,540	1,040,299	-178,311	7,714,930	2,027,931	1,213,868	14,788	740,945	405,607
1987	11,763,944	9,578,448	110,195	9,688,643	1,105,433	-214,571	8,368,639	2,133,636	1,261,669	15,604	753,914	423,569
1988	12,752,234	10,534,633	98,368	10,633,001	1,256,808	-265,862	9,110,331	2,320,225	1,321,678	16,569	769,644	441,855
1989	13,863,932	11,378,744	149,788	11,528,532	1,341,168	-303,157	9,884,207	2,513,548	1,466,177	17,729	782,004	458,586
1990	14,854,523	12,081,321	133,568	12,214,889	1,451,923	-335,861	10,427,105	2,813,241	1,614,177	18,675	795,411	473,830
1991	15,479,383	12,410,455	141,032	12,551,487	1,510,578	-329,917	10,710,992	2,937,928	1,830,463	19,096	810,613	472,642
1992	16,758,325	13,410,128	138,874	13,549,002	1,619,270	-382,758	11,546,974	3,252,790	1,958,561	20,355	823,316	479,549
1993	17,645,753	14,373,687	127,202	14,500,889	1,748,982	-447,585	12,304,322	3,250,454	2,090,977	21,115	835,716	492,605
1994	19,234,448	15,785,277	112,139	15,897,416	1,964,860	-557,955	13,374,601	3,750,336	2,109,511	22,642	849,497	519,290
1995	20,532,133	17,002,467	117,484	17,119,951	2,121,869	-676,006	14,322,076	4,024,245	2,185,812	23,744	864,714	546,139
1996	21,845,200	18,044,525	123,971	18,168,496	2,213,624	-756,397	15,198,475	4,351,317	2,295,408	24,823	880,047	559,946
1997	23,294,662	19,194,666	127,828	19,322,494	2,363,732	-866,338	16,092,424	4,719,533	2,482,705	26,057	893,999	575,693
1998	24,911,416	20,781,025	134,484	20,915,509	2,511,963	-955,227	17,448,319	4,943,120	2,519,977	27,481	906,489	583,976
1999	26,169,496	22,106,748	152,531	22,259,279	2,650,208	-1,095,463	18,513,608	4,950,099	2,705,789	28,425	920,648	596,451
2000	28,082,957	23,841,192	124,889	23,966,081	2,791,098	-1,250,757	19,924,226	5,284,862	2,873,869	30,063	934,152	616,446
2001	28,677,359	24,011,153	127,413	24,138,566	2,697,767	-1,247,006	20,193,793	5,243,890	3,239,676	30,361	944,552	608,301
2002	28,722,425	24,308,726	129,714	24,438,440	2,735,971	-1,199,956	20,502,513	4,792,691	3,427,221	30,165	952,185	600,829
2003	29,594,605	24,598,367	137,638	24,736,005	2,774,126	-1,198,829	20,763,050	5,217,784	3,613,771	30,852	959,259	599,899
2004	31,334,775	25,260,267	187,199	25,447,466	2,904,716	-1,287,870	21,254,880	6,291,880	3,788,015	32,468	965,089	611,040
2005	32,288,482	26,036,668	172,420	26,209,088	3,036,192	-1,379,906	21,792,990	6,463,461	4,032,031	33,263	970,713	619,764
2006	34,123,280	26,743,859	199,409	26,943,268	3,153,943	-1,287,838	22,501,487	7,238,538	4,383,255	34,941	976,610	618,219
2007	35,244,471	26,847,512	214,197	27,061,709	3,187,164	-1,197,572	22,676,973	7,759,591	4,807,907	35,904	981,643	618,822
2008	37,000,121	26,947,237	233,547	27,180,784	3,221,981	-985,230	22,973,573	8,451,467	5,575,081	37,580	984,563	607,354
2009	34,049,931	25,298,645	194,014	25,492,659	3,043,259	-748,413	21,700,987	6,188,745	6,160,199	34,489	987,281	572,336
2010	36,095,497	26,173,460	257,965	26,431,425	3,093,773	-586,377	22,751,275	6,677,988	6,666,234	36,482	989,416	573,948
2011	39,390,035	27,449,077	383,753	27,832,830	2,891,756	-601,528	24,339,546	8,375,649	6,674,840	39,505	997,100	596,964
2012	42,410,757	29,400,594	273,597	29,674,191	3,073,038	-618,566	25,982,587	9,787,441	6,640,729	42,090	1,007,613	615,802
2013	42,776,507	30,651,631	378,079	31,029,710	3,612,562	-701,838	26,715,310	9,303,126	6,758,071	41,973	1,019,146	634,782
2014	45,192,710	32,557,035	281,901	32,838,936	3,804,256	-851,501	28,183,179	9,953,874	7,055,657	43,887	1,029,762	653,526
2015	48,146,357	34,714,913	244,504	34,959,417	4,016,681	-939,218	30,003,518	10,678,594	7,464,245	46,336	1,039,064	673,834
2016	49,640,339	36,170,629	222,955	36,393,584	4,164,677	-1,189,698	31,039,209	10,940,350	7,660,780	47,329	1,048,826	696,475
2017	51,537,967	37,947,470	167,274	38,114,744	4,342,776	-1,316,948	32,455,020	11,365,871	7,717,076	48,661	1,059,113	709,224
2018	52,555,045	52,337,573	217,472	40,057,326	4,634,045	-1,765,010	33,658,271	10,850,483	8,046,291	49,054	1,071,370	732,702
2019	54,223,857	54,032,439	191,418	41,438,774	4,772,992	-1,953,398	34,712,384	10,925,519	8,585,954	50,330	1,077,370	741,654

Personal Income and Employment by Area: Grants Pass, OR

(Thousands of dollars, except as noted.)

Year	Personal income, total	Earnings by place of work			Less: Contributions for government social insurance	Plus: Adjustment for residence	Equals: Net earnings by place of residence	Plus: Dividends, interest, and rent	Plus: Personal current transfer receipts	Per capita personal income (dollars)	Population (persons)	Total employment
		Nonfarm	Farm	Total								
1970	127,591	84,708	1,526	86,234	6,304	439	80,369	27,610	19,612	3,515	36,304	12,674
1971	145,879	97,541	756	98,297	7,507	763	91,553	31,251	23,075	3,755	38,848	13,786
1972	164,653	112,117	246	112,363	9,217	1,163	104,309	34,611	25,733	4,085	40,305	14,944
1973	189,515	128,229	688	128,917	11,930	1,500	118,487	39,534	31,494	4,392	43,151	16,085
1974	210,775	131,836	2,143	133,979	12,576	2,481	123,884	46,312	40,579	4,603	45,787	15,850
1975	244,329	148,887	2,164	151,051	13,613	2,464	139,902	53,550	50,877	5,087	48,032	16,628
1976	288,436	184,198	2,857	187,055	17,001	2,488	172,542	60,980	54,914	5,688	50,710	18,506
1977	328,896	211,863	2,509	214,372	20,079	2,836	197,129	71,580	60,187	6,259	52,549	19,980
1978	378,846	247,264	1,869	249,133	23,949	3,295	228,479	84,367	66,000	6,794	55,762	21,235
1979	422,703	269,795	2,398	272,193	27,102	4,392	249,483	98,518	74,702	7,301	57,893	22,222
1980	470,230	277,918	3,929	281,847	28,014	5,255	259,088	120,942	90,200	7,977	58,948	22,300
1981	509,163	281,703	2,732	284,435	30,389	4,082	258,128	146,508	104,527	8,600	59,202	21,755
1982	526,423	273,541	2,478	276,019	30,290	3,901	249,630	161,151	115,642	9,052	58,154	21,089
1983	585,847	302,726	2,473	305,199	33,996	5,462	276,665	185,485	123,697	10,180	57,548	21,796
1984	637,966	332,766	2,819	335,585	38,447	7,612	304,750	203,389	129,827	10,798	59,083	22,691
1985	682,639	354,174	2,161	356,335	41,573	7,614	322,376	222,737	137,526	11,252	60,666	23,251
1986	717,762	373,838	1,591	375,429	43,644	9,298	341,083	234,385	142,294	11,824	60,702	23,778
1987	747,132	404,470	1,206	405,676	47,005	10,745	369,416	229,258	148,458	12,200	61,238	24,388
1988	804,406	448,091	1,426	449,517	54,412	11,923	407,028	236,760	160,618	13,033	61,721	25,684
1989	890,844	482,737	2,335	485,072	59,498	11,803	437,377	273,318	180,149	14,400	61,865	26,508
1990	936,461	511,815	2,100	513,915	63,479	14,406	464,842	272,989	198,630	14,868	62,985	26,838
1991	980,341	516,620	2,494	519,114	65,289	16,434	470,259	286,686	223,396	15,181	64,575	26,716
1992	1,037,962	544,658	1,564	546,222	68,861	20,249	497,610	293,900	246,452	15,845	65,507	27,206
1993	1,117,044	586,946	4,314	591,260	73,697	22,483	540,046	311,642	265,356	16,549	67,500	27,970
1994	1,195,664	626,934	5,559	632,493	79,320	27,199	580,372	326,398	288,894	17,227	69,406	29,344
1995	1,286,063	645,406	5,102	650,508	83,051	30,847	598,304	358,998	328,761	18,034	71,313	29,760
1996	1,369,702	692,375	3,890	696,265	88,809	35,021	642,477	378,112	349,113	18,942	72,310	30,589
1997	1,448,015	741,202	3,505	744,707	93,532	39,940	691,115	392,400	364,500	19,716	73,442	31,808
1998	1,525,449	797,896	4,311	802,207	99,068	45,096	748,235	388,838	388,376	20,488	74,455	32,339
1999	1,591,660	845,805	1,351	847,156	104,471	50,794	793,479	373,650	424,531	21,163	75,209	33,340
2000	1,683,442	878,821	684	879,505	108,782	60,684	831,407	407,989	444,046	22,194	75,851	33,734
2001	1,776,100	920,955	1,903	922,858	111,719	68,112	879,251	400,584	496,265	23,232	76,452	33,417
2002	1,818,172	976,260	964	977,224	120,061	73,697	930,860	368,338	518,974	23,396	77,712	33,916
2003	1,909,059	1,061,180	2,654	1,063,834	130,071	77,918	1,011,681	370,108	527,270	24,233	78,779	35,230
2004	2,066,435	1,174,394	4,691	1,179,085	144,774	84,734	1,119,045	407,718	539,672	25,918	79,729	36,699
2005	2,187,991	1,254,032	4,346	1,258,378	158,279	90,566	1,190,665	434,978	562,348	27,126	80,660	37,991
2006	2,337,549	1,319,637	2,346	1,321,983	167,348	90,290	1,244,925	493,837	598,787	28,646	81,601	38,788
2007	2,420,345	1,293,615	-106	1,293,509	169,037	110,455	1,234,927	547,173	638,245	29,608	81,746	38,856
2008	2,412,997	1,232,736	-2,409	1,230,327	165,925	96,250	1,160,652	539,924	712,421	29,288	82,389	37,739
2009	2,412,699	1,187,042	-1,182	1,185,860	163,172	89,751	1,112,439	487,322	812,938	29,311	82,315	35,858
2010	2,487,189	1,215,925	-745	1,215,180	166,894	86,831	1,135,117	471,344	880,728	30,015	82,866	34,891
2011	2,560,693	1,228,546	1,771	1,230,317	152,957	79,111	1,156,471	502,012	902,210	30,976	82,666	35,008
2012	2,666,060	1,278,244	4,038	1,282,282	156,457	103,120	1,228,945	529,005	908,110	32,225	82,732	34,959
2013	2,708,669	1,273,705	5,164	1,278,869	176,371	134,177	1,236,675	527,849	944,145	32,592	83,108	35,028
2014	2,889,878	1,360,203	5,129	1,365,332	189,277	110,167	1,286,222	576,655	1,027,001	34,672	83,350	36,084
2015	3,081,483	1,472,888	4,677	1,477,565	200,749	100,840	1,377,656	615,936	1,087,891	36,501	84,422	37,059
2016	3,216,169	1,562,216	5,014	1,567,230	210,645	103,642	1,460,227	640,492	1,115,450	37,687	85,338	37,649
2017	3,358,766	1,670,221	4,834	1,675,055	227,005	98,897	1,546,947	668,945	1,142,874	38,896	86,352	38,671
2018	3,652,347	3,650,045	2,302	1,843,603	242,361	110,658	1,711,900	717,895	1,222,552	41,909	87,150	39,779
2019	3,810,451	3,810,364	87	1,950,884	258,059	98,533	1,791,358	728,900	1,290,193	43,554	87,487	40,997

Personal Income and Employment by Area: Great Falls, MT

(Thousands of dollars, except as noted.)

		Derivation of personal income										
		Earnings by place of work			Less: Contributions for government social insurance	Plus: Adjustment for residence	Equals: Net earnings by place of residence	Plus: Dividends, interest, and rent	Plus: Personal current transfer receipts	Per capita personal income (dollars)	Population (persons)	Total employment
Year	Personal income, total	Nonfarm	Farm	Total								
1970............	357,739	274,671	13,037	287,708	20,138	-2,111	265,459	65,329	26,951	4,349	82,258	37,297
1971............	384,731	293,892	13,295	307,187	21,982	-2,088	283,117	69,545	32,069	4,556	84,453	37,626
1972............	429,950	328,497	17,116	345,613	25,407	-2,093	318,113	75,876	35,961	5,068	84,842	38,689
1973............	468,382	355,573	17,888	373,461	30,802	-1,945	340,714	86,205	41,463	5,528	84,728	39,742
1974............	516,168	389,822	17,376	407,198	34,694	-1,442	371,062	97,763	47,343	6,064	85,126	40,285
1975............	558,424	417,570	16,120	433,690	37,319	420	396,791	105,311	56,322	6,594	84,693	39,860
1976............	619,187	476,800	10,105	486,905	43,737	1,464	444,632	113,283	61,272	7,296	84,869	42,084
1977............	670,908	523,517	3,862	527,379	48,578	3,160	481,961	124,099	64,848	7,779	86,247	43,274
1978............	740,513	571,385	7,251	578,636	54,438	6,830	531,028	137,934	71,551	8,550	86,611	44,429
1979............	798,576	609,316	5,506	614,822	60,509	10,180	564,493	152,585	81,498	9,453	84,475	44,026
1980............	847,771	620,563	6,544	627,107	62,439	16,247	580,915	173,132	93,724	10,515	80,627	42,836
1981............	911,044	654,362	4,250	658,612	70,056	9,533	598,089	205,865	107,090	11,362	80,183	42,087
1982............	956,506	670,222	4,248	674,470	72,419	8,405	610,456	228,024	118,026	11,988	79,791	41,059
1983............	1,019,329	710,399	10,537	720,936	77,767	7,234	650,403	238,315	130,611	12,643	80,621	41,553
1984............	1,075,396	741,781	8,905	750,686	84,046	6,851	673,491	262,350	139,555	13,389	80,318	41,719
1985............	1,084,569	742,958	1,261	744,219	85,621	6,025	664,623	273,396	146,550	13,627	79,591	40,524
1986............	1,118,501	757,102	9,147	766,249	89,223	4,320	681,346	279,348	157,807	14,307	78,179	40,276
1987............	1,150,773	777,522	9,394	786,916	91,849	3,831	698,898	284,027	167,848	14,804	77,733	40,260
1988............	1,215,641	830,277	5,527	835,804	103,647	2,181	734,338	303,252	178,051	15,649	77,681	42,046
1989............	1,303,500	875,469	20,390	895,859	109,806	2,000	788,053	326,201	189,246	16,691	78,098	42,690
1990............	1,352,856	920,421	12,318	932,739	122,123	2,415	813,031	334,319	205,506	17,392	77,788	43,160
1991............	1,421,630	978,542	18,455	996,997	132,082	948	865,863	337,959	217,808	18,075	78,651	44,293
1992............	1,479,441	1,029,610	16,016	1,045,626	141,655	291	904,262	343,061	232,118	18,556	79,727	44,595
1993............	1,572,673	1,079,972	35,116	1,115,088	151,703	-738	962,647	360,736	249,290	19,409	81,028	44,940
1994............	1,594,870	1,107,873	12,336	1,120,209	155,313	-1,055	963,841	374,031	256,998	19,418	82,134	46,791
1995............	1,676,640	1,142,382	15,472	1,157,854	156,308	-2,638	998,908	404,670	273,062	20,397	82,201	47,358
1996............	1,730,378	1,183,971	7,935	1,191,906	156,317	-3,493	1,032,096	416,224	282,058	20,992	82,429	47,981
1997............	1,780,473	1,199,096	9,215	1,208,311	154,218	-4,108	1,049,985	440,509	289,979	22,019	80,861	47,438
1998............	1,880,474	1,265,147	8,516	1,273,663	159,070	-6,373	1,108,220	472,406	299,848	23,299	80,709	48,102
1999............	1,899,560	1,291,078	9,690	1,300,768	161,459	-7,906	1,131,403	472,136	296,021	23,569	80,596	47,682
2000............	1,985,176	1,331,049	2,228	1,333,277	166,538	-9,304	1,157,435	496,972	330,769	24,716	80,318	47,944
2001............	2,069,433	1,395,999	4,962	1,400,961	175,485	-10,347	1,215,129	501,330	352,974	25,850	80,055	47,844
2002............	2,152,842	1,484,453	1,813	1,486,266	185,822	-11,928	1,288,516	502,024	362,302	26,962	79,848	47,693
2003............	2,236,762	1,560,008	5,085	1,565,093	194,437	-12,113	1,358,543	502,105	376,114	28,088	79,633	47,643
2004............	2,364,363	1,651,711	16,647	1,668,358	206,069	-14,084	1,448,205	517,536	398,622	29,482	80,198	48,326
2005............	2,460,353	1,725,949	18,291	1,744,240	216,694	-16,083	1,511,463	519,510	429,380	30,739	80,041	48,759
2006............	2,666,746	1,840,334	10,134	1,850,468	232,648	-19,363	1,598,457	608,484	459,805	33,341	79,984	49,919
2007............	2,793,119	1,904,173	15,033	1,919,206	243,637	-21,269	1,654,300	656,083	482,736	34,871	80,099	50,132
2008............	2,917,524	1,974,944	16,230	1,991,174	253,308	-20,894	1,716,972	653,829	546,723	36,229	80,529	50,810
2009............	2,949,357	2,032,147	10,118	2,042,265	259,110	-22,514	1,760,641	597,211	591,505	36,556	80,680	50,231
2010............	3,125,087	2,131,006	15,552	2,146,558	267,307	-20,799	1,858,452	628,605	638,030	38,349	81,491	49,971
2011............	3,229,267	2,162,386	21,205	2,183,591	247,202	-11,934	1,924,455	674,457	630,355	39,538	81,674	49,736
2012............	3,296,474	2,178,466	19,210	2,197,676	247,452	5,033	1,955,257	704,899	636,318	40,400	81,596	49,761
2013............	3,272,559	2,162,526	20,860	2,183,386	277,157	11,011	1,917,240	706,087	649,232	39,851	82,119	50,033
2014............	3,431,157	2,257,871	14,644	2,272,515	290,695	14,305	1,996,125	758,318	676,714	41,848	81,991	50,084
2015............	3,538,787	2,319,858	14,817	2,334,675	296,444	6,989	2,045,220	788,101	705,466	43,246	81,829	50,297
2016............	3,604,156	2,326,319	8,151	2,334,470	291,021	-1,984	2,041,465	805,861	756,830	44,229	81,488	50,148
2017............	3,752,776	2,399,564	9,261	2,408,825	302,637	1,041	2,107,229	839,620	805,927	45,959	81,654	50,443
2018............	3,911,977	3,890,975	21,002	2,502,684	323,728	6,177	2,185,133	902,602	824,242	47,889	81,688	50,590
2019............	4,052,262	4,025,694	26,568	2,597,557	333,620	7,472	2,271,409	919,183	861,670	49,803	81,366	51,202

Personal Income and Employment by Area: Greeley, CO

(Thousands of dollars, except as noted.)

Year	Personal income, total	Earnings by place of work			Less: Contributions for government social insurance	Plus: Adjustment for residence	Equals: Net earnings by place of residence	Plus: Dividends, interest, and rent	Plus: Personal current transfer receipts	Per capita personal income (dollars)	Population (persons)	Total employment
		Nonfarm	Farm	Total								
1970	331,691	170,975	74,032	245,007	10,272	17,255	251,990	50,900	28,801	3,685	90,012	34,611
1971	368,062	197,135	70,784	267,919	12,225	21,518	277,212	57,097	33,753	3,925	93,779	35,647
1972	431,460	244,014	77,292	321,306	16,200	24,968	330,074	64,144	37,242	4,332	99,597	39,546
1973	513,873	293,321	93,932	387,253	22,619	28,633	393,267	76,129	44,477	4,922	104,411	44,129
1974	613,721	344,588	127,349	471,937	27,829	30,523	474,631	87,798	51,292	5,679	108,059	47,670
1975	670,486	376,142	120,928	497,070	29,231	38,025	505,864	102,237	62,385	6,181	108,479	47,671
1976	726,285	439,870	100,074	539,944	34,841	43,656	548,759	109,805	67,721	6,599	110,052	49,788
1977	745,537	478,520	49,520	528,040	38,072	58,979	548,947	123,442	73,148	6,624	112,555	51,346
1978	871,664	536,035	72,424	608,459	42,909	80,550	646,100	142,967	82,597	7,585	114,919	52,739
1979	978,249	604,891	59,800	664,691	50,846	102,936	716,781	168,738	92,730	8,139	120,194	53,520
1980	1,065,290	655,293	16,013	671,306	55,380	129,636	745,562	206,871	112,857	8,607	123,767	54,564
1981	1,232,706	709,558	68,999	778,557	63,899	140,449	855,107	247,066	130,533	9,879	124,780	55,002
1982	1,295,207	769,127	33,936	803,063	70,895	140,138	872,306	276,728	146,173	10,301	125,733	55,718
1983	1,405,402	845,887	40,986	886,873	78,878	131,316	939,311	305,177	160,914	10,849	129,542	58,126
1984	1,549,866	916,915	85,385	1,002,300	88,737	134,174	1,047,737	331,457	170,672	11,852	130,764	59,839
1985	1,605,619	996,896	56,504	1,053,400	99,499	117,776	1,071,677	355,279	178,663	12,219	131,402	60,864
1986	1,643,095	1,036,242	69,237	1,105,479	106,056	107,015	1,106,438	346,348	190,309	12,475	131,715	60,862
1987	1,715,610	1,075,134	93,869	1,169,003	108,873	96,737	1,156,867	356,958	201,785	13,025	131,713	61,351
1988	1,817,102	1,162,629	119,612	1,282,241	123,424	73,192	1,232,009	369,991	215,102	13,782	131,842	65,219
1989	1,980,673	1,260,501	150,496	1,410,997	136,556	61,342	1,335,783	411,360	233,530	14,982	132,202	66,292
1990	2,052,824	1,332,867	158,672	1,491,539	146,974	58,020	1,402,585	401,996	248,243	15,533	132,161	66,690
1991	2,158,526	1,427,706	140,126	1,567,832	163,701	70,484	1,474,615	411,318	272,593	16,077	134,262	68,491
1992	2,336,869	1,540,781	133,374	1,674,155	173,718	108,144	1,608,581	421,424	306,864	16,988	137,560	69,676
1993	2,590,543	1,688,187	180,102	1,868,289	193,207	133,523	1,808,605	453,427	328,511	18,168	142,586	73,905
1994	2,767,862	1,836,512	142,257	1,978,769	211,562	157,873	1,925,080	492,375	350,407	18,787	147,328	77,289
1995	2,939,796	1,942,759	114,611	2,057,370	221,986	184,968	2,020,352	521,489	397,955	19,323	152,140	79,705
1996	3,208,174	2,076,067	152,216	2,228,283	231,869	228,382	2,224,796	573,652	409,726	20,547	156,140	82,605
1997	3,467,474	2,218,265	188,080	2,406,345	243,969	280,704	2,443,080	605,679	418,715	21,467	161,525	86,239
1998	3,836,544	2,479,772	185,670	2,665,442	247,932	348,822	2,766,332	642,954	427,258	23,036	166,547	89,357
1999	4,221,834	2,749,869	208,377	2,958,246	271,280	415,698	3,102,664	657,646	461,524	24,216	174,342	92,082
2000	4,655,125	3,025,098	176,691	3,201,789	294,496	526,439	3,433,732	729,006	492,387	25,457	182,861	95,735
2001	5,009,329	3,201,258	270,794	3,472,052	325,591	555,525	3,701,986	757,583	549,760	26,041	192,360	103,132
2002	5,016,032	3,388,536	146,963	3,535,499	357,227	524,563	3,702,835	706,880	606,317	24,803	202,234	104,924
2003	5,249,292	3,505,388	145,553	3,650,941	371,937	586,260	3,865,264	741,220	642,808	25,133	208,858	108,331
2004	5,778,374	3,726,321	190,647	3,916,968	405,901	799,692	4,310,759	785,127	682,488	26,836	215,322	112,357
2005	6,355,911	3,957,480	235,929	4,193,409	432,469	963,199	4,724,139	882,785	748,987	28,517	222,879	116,668
2006	6,883,808	4,281,676	179,502	4,461,178	466,128	1,146,785	5,141,835	932,072	809,901	29,838	230,703	121,484
2007	7,594,475	4,572,964	243,088	4,816,052	502,028	1,335,699	5,649,723	1,075,001	869,751	31,951	237,692	126,301
2008	8,192,532	4,749,475	238,103	4,987,578	526,843	1,465,975	5,926,710	1,237,014	1,028,808	33,653	243,442	125,730
2009	8,067,808	4,469,462	184,776	4,654,238	496,841	1,587,297	5,744,694	1,153,399	1,169,715	32,506	248,193	122,003
2010	8,395,847	4,629,190	271,800	4,900,990	512,342	1,510,426	5,899,074	1,144,820	1,351,953	33,031	254,182	121,409
2011	9,060,387	5,060,056	290,053	5,350,109	504,479	1,529,199	6,374,829	1,278,189	1,407,369	35,046	258,528	126,413
2012	9,785,716	5,613,721	340,796	5,954,517	549,915	1,535,893	6,940,495	1,422,722	1,422,499	37,102	263,754	129,876
2013	10,473,700	6,235,534	371,742	6,607,276	660,631	1,607,264	7,553,909	1,442,472	1,477,319	38,820	269,804	136,790
2014	11,677,642	7,221,184	421,107	7,642,291	757,431	1,519,514	8,404,374	1,675,229	1,598,039	42,374	275,584	145,955
2015	12,474,877	7,540,375	523,603	8,063,978	796,925	1,708,116	8,975,169	1,762,781	1,736,927	43,867	284,382	149,826
2016	12,875,331	7,392,789	433,319	7,826,108	785,509	2,159,957	9,200,556	1,846,264	1,828,511	43,757	294,243	148,289
2017	13,428,252	7,809,349	428,578	8,237,927	856,644	2,237,587	9,618,870	1,932,941	1,876,441	44,080	304,633	154,659
2018	15,122,272	14,656,970	465,302	9,212,826	943,834	2,486,327	10,755,319	2,287,788	2,079,165	48,035	314,815	162,281
2019	16,288,858	15,722,388	566,470	9,942,356	1,015,758	2,816,214	11,742,812	2,343,731	2,202,315	50,198	324,492	167,913

Personal Income and Employment by Area: Green Bay, WI

(Thousands of dollars, except as noted.)

Year	Personal income, total	Earnings by place of work			Less: Contributions for government social insurance	Plus: Adjustment for residence	Equals: Net earnings by place of residence	Plus: Dividends, interest, and rent	Plus: Personal current transfer receipts	Per capita personal income (dollars)	Population (persons)	Total employment
		Nonfarm	Farm	Total								
1970	723,595	568,772	26,951	595,723	42,146	-2,902	550,675	113,239	59,681	3,554	203,616	84,132
1971	787,959	616,445	28,725	645,170	47,141	-3,678	594,351	124,304	69,304	3,814	206,593	84,910
1972	872,204	690,828	29,312	720,140	55,645	-4,683	659,812	135,357	77,035	4,184	208,479	89,459
1973	972,298	770,852	33,593	804,445	71,346	-3,882	729,217	153,938	89,143	4,609	210,941	94,338
1974	1,097,809	868,232	31,139	899,371	83,458	-4,612	811,301	177,764	108,744	5,172	212,277	98,309
1975	1,222,330	950,818	32,090	982,908	89,570	-4,320	889,018	196,751	136,561	5,675	215,386	100,255
1976	1,361,715	1,063,775	36,830	1,100,605	101,874	-2,297	996,434	211,575	153,706	6,257	217,622	103,497
1977	1,542,093	1,207,214	52,286	1,259,500	114,792	-859	1,143,849	236,141	162,103	7,053	218,655	107,283
1978	1,736,528	1,372,594	48,825	1,421,419	133,934	1,719	1,289,204	266,289	181,035	7,884	220,260	112,205
1979	1,942,531	1,508,557	67,284	1,575,841	153,374	8,535	1,431,002	299,291	212,238	8,798	220,801	114,982
1980	2,165,761	1,624,828	70,215	1,695,043	165,303	9,919	1,539,659	370,327	255,775	9,654	224,345	115,673
1981	2,369,968	1,751,084	53,614	1,804,698	190,829	7,175	1,621,044	456,285	292,639	10,481	226,129	114,829
1982	2,532,151	1,851,639	49,943	1,901,582	204,176	-1,303	1,696,103	512,388	323,660	11,142	227,271	115,900
1983	2,706,237	2,013,353	28,352	2,041,705	221,114	-11,241	1,809,350	546,656	350,231	11,857	228,249	117,407
1984	3,006,969	2,253,006	46,873	2,299,879	254,312	-18,931	2,026,636	619,045	361,288	13,020	230,950	122,659
1985	3,229,540	2,435,652	56,057	2,491,709	277,836	-26,487	2,187,386	661,959	380,195	13,903	232,292	126,109
1986	3,431,905	2,633,306	55,903	2,689,209	299,488	-33,444	2,356,277	683,684	391,944	14,622	234,712	131,147
1987	3,591,445	2,796,453	62,502	2,858,955	312,667	-40,046	2,506,242	679,599	405,604	15,156	236,959	132,768
1988	3,792,400	2,988,209	38,158	3,026,367	344,451	-50,500	2,631,416	739,637	421,347	15,837	239,462	136,000
1989	4,176,682	3,187,002	96,220	3,283,222	364,293	-58,638	2,860,291	861,849	454,542	17,314	241,229	138,858
1990	4,473,948	3,530,005	76,628	3,606,633	420,243	-79,617	3,106,773	879,423	487,752	18,282	244,716	145,741
1991	4,692,872	3,718,119	56,536	3,774,655	447,195	-62,196	3,265,264	891,510	536,098	18,845	249,019	147,990
1992	5,080,648	4,062,741	73,858	4,136,599	482,357	-65,812	3,588,430	913,343	578,875	20,076	253,077	152,470
1993	5,401,186	4,373,207	57,581	4,430,788	517,199	-91,534	3,822,055	971,521	607,610	20,943	257,897	157,686
1994	5,770,787	4,716,105	72,490	4,788,595	565,259	-128,942	4,094,394	1,047,494	628,899	22,021	262,056	164,348
1995	6,120,445	4,979,922	46,735	5,026,657	601,021	-160,361	4,265,275	1,186,000	669,170	22,943	266,765	170,096
1996	6,546,122	5,271,944	72,413	5,344,357	631,804	-179,216	4,533,337	1,312,818	699,967	24,166	270,879	174,894
1997	7,059,587	5,758,015	54,416	5,812,431	685,183	-220,022	4,907,226	1,428,288	724,073	25,748	274,177	179,143
1998	7,530,993	6,143,632	90,304	6,233,936	725,345	-238,480	5,270,111	1,516,048	744,834	27,194	276,931	183,607
1999	7,886,307	6,634,854	94,194	6,729,048	784,256	-323,117	5,621,675	1,492,692	771,940	28,155	280,100	190,780
2000	8,441,311	7,138,862	68,234	7,207,096	833,331	-400,819	5,972,946	1,640,609	827,756	29,798	283,282	196,203
2001	8,635,499	7,176,226	87,080	7,263,306	822,957	-392,524	6,047,825	1,664,147	923,527	30,217	285,783	195,881
2002	8,955,407	7,481,396	80,186	7,561,582	855,591	-394,352	6,311,639	1,634,198	1,009,570	31,018	288,713	195,984
2003	9,312,755	7,834,797	119,501	7,954,298	892,015	-393,271	6,669,012	1,595,025	1,048,718	31,984	291,169	199,248
2004	9,800,728	8,282,921	139,290	8,422,211	942,950	-429,356	7,049,905	1,662,562	1,088,261	33,271	294,570	204,045
2005	10,134,225	8,514,521	122,277	8,636,798	979,182	-411,017	7,246,599	1,703,910	1,183,716	34,145	296,800	205,762
2006	10,720,139	8,849,909	100,421	8,950,330	1,025,801	-429,885	7,494,644	1,943,884	1,281,611	35,889	298,702	206,832
2007	11,269,932	9,125,987	162,892	9,288,879	1,059,617	-429,426	7,799,836	2,073,737	1,396,359	37,418	301,190	209,193
2008	11,778,221	9,379,838	161,186	9,541,024	1,099,837	-424,746	8,016,441	2,170,479	1,591,301	38,940	302,468	207,798
2009	11,582,049	9,238,113	66,590	9,304,703	1,084,496	-416,336	7,803,871	1,946,520	1,831,658	38,013	304,686	202,060
2010	12,077,647	9,452,526	141,294	9,593,820	1,111,826	-437,306	8,044,688	2,046,290	1,986,669	39,373	306,750	201,974
2011	12,776,901	9,933,265	223,992	10,157,257	1,036,846	-465,489	8,654,922	2,176,001	1,945,978	41,396	308,651	204,703
2012	13,510,923	10,411,654	242,604	10,654,258	1,073,272	-458,087	9,122,899	2,421,680	1,966,344	43,488	310,682	206,579
2013	13,656,626	10,760,901	259,238	11,020,139	1,244,283	-501,321	9,274,535	2,362,726	2,019,365	43,771	312,000	208,635
2014	14,243,691	11,033,095	332,619	11,365,714	1,275,366	-465,927	9,624,421	2,524,799	2,094,471	45,354	314,054	211,036
2015	14,812,980	11,465,984	317,318	11,783,302	1,326,685	-517,803	9,938,814	2,679,948	2,194,218	46,923	315,687	213,929
2016	15,032,898	11,672,046	249,390	11,921,436	1,343,601	-522,628	10,055,207	2,736,697	2,240,994	47,357	317,441	215,935
2017	15,583,737	12,106,105	226,202	12,332,307	1,403,228	-527,205	10,401,874	2,846,421	2,335,442	48,692	320,050	218,886
2018	16,575,483	16,415,343	160,140	12,928,400	1,460,284	-605,067	10,863,049	3,222,838	2,489,596	51,575	321,384	221,628
2019	17,107,901	16,868,448	239,453	13,355,526	1,509,813	-607,778	11,237,935	3,246,855	2,623,111	52,981	322,906	222,360

Personal Income and Employment by Area: Greensboro-High Point, NC

(Thousands of dollars, except as noted.)

Year	Personal income, total	Earnings by place of work			Less: Contributions for government social insurance	Plus: Adjustment for residence	Equals: Net earnings by place of residence	Plus: Dividends, interest, and rent	Plus: Personal current transfer receipts	Per capita personal income (dollars)	Population (persons)	Total employment
		Nonfarm	Farm	Total								
1970	1,732,134	1,582,881	25,267	1,608,148	112,594	-84,167	1,411,387	208,940	111,807	3,948	438,730	247,290
1971	1,898,502	1,735,432	29,467	1,764,899	128,225	-98,959	1,537,715	228,812	131,975	4,237	448,079	251,788
1972	2,112,332	1,951,088	29,637	1,980,725	151,619	-114,907	1,714,199	251,481	146,652	4,637	455,577	262,903
1973	2,343,880	2,161,142	48,538	2,209,680	192,675	-128,401	1,888,604	283,978	171,298	5,087	460,732	272,867
1974	2,552,770	2,331,214	42,217	2,373,431	215,681	-143,080	2,014,670	327,723	210,377	5,501	464,097	272,067
1975	2,729,702	2,391,914	46,541	2,438,455	216,506	-149,287	2,072,662	356,806	300,234	5,851	466,520	258,218
1976	2,998,783	2,651,047	47,890	2,698,937	245,749	-166,917	2,286,271	390,453	322,059	6,362	471,352	268,292
1977	3,321,180	2,960,163	46,006	3,006,169	273,013	-188,910	2,544,246	438,513	338,421	6,959	477,233	278,421
1978	3,780,639	3,433,254	49,194	3,482,448	326,691	-237,130	2,918,627	494,830	367,182	7,836	482,440	291,685
1979	4,169,668	3,803,078	32,284	3,835,362	375,104	-268,693	3,191,565	560,256	417,847	8,558	487,216	298,117
1980	4,619,368	4,112,067	23,149	4,135,216	406,218	-298,967	3,430,031	688,846	500,491	9,366	493,196	296,162
1981	5,168,724	4,491,894	43,888	4,535,782	475,054	-334,560	3,726,168	865,537	577,019	10,400	496,975	298,011
1982	5,488,160	4,688,531	47,363	4,735,894	500,111	-354,412	3,881,371	964,100	642,689	10,962	500,656	295,265
1983	5,969,097	5,146,874	33,403	5,180,277	552,305	-395,415	4,232,557	1,050,816	685,724	11,838	504,241	302,975
1984	6,705,371	5,798,995	32,881	5,831,876	639,045	-448,454	4,744,377	1,241,849	719,145	13,189	508,397	320,355
1985	7,178,836	6,206,659	32,460	6,239,119	692,214	-476,702	5,070,203	1,340,831	767,802	14,014	512,256	327,294
1986	7,697,781	6,666,345	37,953	6,704,298	757,438	-511,721	5,435,139	1,447,623	815,019	14,896	516,765	338,297
1987	8,375,056	7,387,134	34,186	7,421,320	825,923	-575,556	6,019,841	1,504,676	850,539	16,007	523,217	351,897
1988	9,145,853	7,991,259	51,903	8,043,162	914,104	-624,503	6,504,555	1,719,580	921,718	17,256	530,011	364,650
1989	9,812,259	8,471,197	81,424	8,552,621	967,586	-658,708	6,926,327	1,862,159	1,023,773	18,329	535,336	368,711
1990	10,460,806	8,869,060	94,276	8,963,336	1,040,295	-689,531	7,233,510	2,111,550	1,115,746	19,279	542,612	373,827
1991	10,758,443	8,986,075	100,492	9,086,567	1,067,433	-654,972	7,364,162	2,130,009	1,264,272	19,462	552,787	365,866
1992	11,581,973	9,750,456	100,651	9,851,107	1,141,837	-696,522	8,012,748	2,183,002	1,386,223	20,624	561,591	368,982
1993	12,276,239	10,302,681	113,315	10,415,996	1,216,308	-775,697	8,423,991	2,341,727	1,510,521	21,489	571,281	381,473
1994	13,049,753	11,015,725	120,599	11,136,324	1,313,291	-825,774	8,997,259	2,476,745	1,575,749	22,426	581,897	391,593
1995	13,841,711	11,705,459	118,868	11,824,327	1,397,498	-940,721	9,486,108	2,597,711	1,757,892	23,287	594,390	405,535
1996	14,759,901	12,350,650	137,178	12,487,828	1,458,882	-1,023,858	10,005,088	2,842,477	1,912,336	24,389	605,175	414,861
1997	15,812,360	13,136,041	139,871	13,275,912	1,537,512	-1,056,843	10,681,557	3,127,490	2,003,313	25,689	615,526	423,430
1998	16,859,432	14,084,198	140,740	14,224,938	1,645,589	-1,099,608	11,479,741	3,291,487	2,088,204	26,894	626,891	427,270
1999	17,458,032	14,897,603	146,895	15,044,498	1,741,108	-1,192,187	12,111,203	3,158,406	2,188,423	27,406	637,026	434,398
2000	18,257,556	15,419,731	129,924	15,549,655	1,798,470	-1,183,164	12,568,021	3,346,647	2,342,888	28,288	645,409	437,861
2001	18,759,901	15,792,348	136,387	15,928,735	1,838,663	-1,224,241	12,865,831	3,286,177	2,607,893	28,740	652,741	436,712
2002	18,884,193	15,911,488	63,984	15,975,472	1,833,412	-1,259,081	12,882,979	3,191,898	2,809,316	28,706	657,855	431,446
2003	19,270,571	16,307,230	72,511	16,379,741	1,920,276	-1,338,785	13,120,680	3,225,890	2,924,001	29,060	663,140	430,127
2004	20,521,983	17,043,809	99,757	17,143,566	1,984,880	-1,295,527	13,863,159	3,496,910	3,161,914	30,735	667,711	437,752
2005	21,649,354	17,787,730	114,040	17,901,770	2,090,740	-1,369,302	14,441,728	3,805,894	3,401,732	31,975	677,080	445,612
2006	23,247,788	18,883,597	109,880	18,993,477	2,199,028	-1,425,998	15,368,451	4,185,751	3,693,586	33,710	689,637	455,391
2007	24,272,910	19,493,276	79,130	19,572,406	2,287,384	-1,529,783	15,755,239	4,565,820	3,951,851	34,652	700,485	464,629
2008	25,079,186	19,749,475	59,824	19,809,299	2,318,767	-1,535,470	15,955,062	4,601,569	4,522,555	35,253	711,405	460,767
2009	24,166,177	18,540,323	69,781	18,610,104	2,207,020	-1,376,184	15,026,900	4,036,730	5,102,547	33,615	718,902	437,294
2010	24,879,631	19,025,521	75,475	19,100,996	2,235,859	-1,375,932	15,489,205	3,966,452	5,423,974	34,308	725,174	434,446
2011	25,772,067	19,306,641	35,948	19,342,589	2,079,809	-1,356,298	15,906,482	4,327,097	5,538,488	35,283	730,431	443,003
2012	27,237,303	20,343,631	77,083	20,420,714	2,146,666	-1,399,568	16,874,480	4,746,712	5,616,111	37,013	735,879	445,779
2013	27,173,304	20,774,610	104,642	20,879,252	2,513,294	-1,465,717	16,900,241	4,574,326	5,698,737	36,667	741,089	450,703
2014	28,812,961	21,657,724	149,059	21,806,783	2,609,387	-1,448,602	17,748,794	5,141,531	5,922,636	38,573	746,975	457,076
2015	30,376,983	22,701,837	141,092	22,842,929	2,726,195	-1,423,304	18,693,430	5,458,387	6,225,166	40,387	752,140	466,135
2016	30,837,328	22,813,907	118,287	22,932,194	2,730,500	-1,466,768	18,734,926	5,676,406	6,425,996	40,760	756,564	470,895
2017	32,240,932	23,786,718	128,855	23,915,573	2,810,281	-1,471,666	19,633,626	5,944,542	6,662,764	42,356	761,184	473,746
2018	33,293,181	33,241,317	51,864	24,521,393	2,844,843	-1,550,875	20,125,675	6,277,330	6,890,176	43,437	766,473	478,379
2019	34,624,284	34,576,665	47,619	25,495,431	2,963,790	-1,536,720	20,994,921	6,377,589	7,251,774	44,859	771,851	486,387

Personal Income and Employment by Area: Greenville, NC

(Thousands of dollars, except as noted.)

Year	Personal income, total	Earnings by place of work			Less: Contributions for government social insurance	Plus: Adjustment for residence	Equals: Net earnings by place of residence	Plus: Dividends, interest, and rent	Plus: Personal current transfer receipts	Per capita personal income (dollars)	Population (persons)	Total employment
		Nonfarm	Farm	Total								
1970	217,915	137,288	31,833	169,121	9,442	7,107	166,786	30,911	20,218	2,941	74,101	32,746
1971	236,862	158,056	25,375	183,431	11,293	7,848	179,986	33,751	23,125	3,145	75,306	33,622
1972	265,316	177,025	28,590	205,615	13,155	10,292	202,752	37,703	24,861	3,539	74,977	34,854
1973	310,619	199,898	42,623	242,521	17,074	12,152	237,599	44,363	28,657	4,099	75,787	36,126
1974	352,192	224,206	44,966	269,172	19,969	15,769	264,972	51,862	35,358	4,636	75,977	37,100
1975	405,664	258,569	47,129	305,698	23,147	17,238	299,789	59,383	46,492	5,142	78,887	37,475
1976	462,176	296,537	51,297	347,834	27,161	21,331	342,004	66,428	53,744	5,767	80,147	39,729
1977	486,896	334,443	24,155	358,598	30,283	24,331	352,646	75,954	58,296	6,015	80,948	40,727
1978	566,804	379,836	47,162	426,998	35,460	27,257	418,795	84,327	63,682	6,915	81,969	41,601
1979	604,576	426,208	20,821	447,029	41,457	30,469	436,041	94,692	73,843	7,300	82,819	43,563
1980	700,605	475,032	28,325	503,357	46,473	35,653	492,537	118,435	89,633	7,735	90,580	43,433
1981	794,865	525,309	35,185	560,494	55,352	38,079	543,221	148,753	102,891	8,635	92,047	44,149
1982	867,221	566,857	41,688	608,545	60,823	37,344	585,066	169,323	112,832	9,285	93,400	44,824
1983	927,663	629,339	21,149	650,488	67,871	40,284	622,901	182,216	122,546	9,791	94,750	46,159
1984	1,059,713	730,122	35,167	765,289	80,509	40,104	724,884	206,255	128,574	11,020	96,164	48,581
1985	1,128,984	781,517	34,765	816,282	86,971	43,464	772,775	219,160	137,049	11,552	97,730	49,206
1986	1,219,372	861,438	31,169	892,607	97,342	43,334	838,599	235,758	145,015	12,239	99,626	51,663
1987	1,324,700	952,467	32,498	984,965	105,837	46,019	925,147	249,518	150,035	12,987	102,001	53,714
1988	1,474,065	1,063,172	43,205	1,106,377	122,968	48,572	1,031,981	281,088	160,996	14,132	104,306	57,254
1989	1,664,409	1,195,880	47,865	1,243,745	137,500	43,883	1,150,128	331,931	182,350	15,632	106,474	59,652
1990	1,816,345	1,322,371	54,999	1,377,370	153,437	34,813	1,258,746	345,113	212,486	16,655	109,054	62,264
1991	1,926,099	1,371,088	56,497	1,427,585	160,932	53,890	1,320,543	358,433	247,123	17,203	111,965	61,864
1992	2,066,552	1,500,945	42,116	1,543,061	173,496	48,821	1,418,386	371,921	276,245	18,077	114,318	62,509
1993	2,218,000	1,618,738	41,781	1,660,519	186,632	42,996	1,516,883	393,826	307,291	19,001	116,728	64,747
1994	2,349,434	1,739,749	43,301	1,783,050	202,221	13,487	1,594,316	433,862	321,256	19,629	119,694	67,248
1995	2,535,983	1,847,686	28,171	1,875,857	214,195	31,276	1,692,938	475,285	367,760	20,698	122,525	71,899
1996	2,683,537	1,951,259	51,852	2,003,111	223,116	-18,914	1,761,081	520,682	401,774	21,492	124,861	72,840
1997	2,921,499	2,099,700	61,051	2,160,751	238,592	-1,329	1,920,830	579,581	421,088	22,858	127,812	73,994
1998	3,006,396	2,207,378	25,190	2,232,568	252,510	6,117	1,986,175	609,559	410,662	23,034	130,519	74,574
1999	3,138,323	2,373,472	16,643	2,390,115	272,347	-43,849	2,073,919	606,919	457,485	23,676	132,554	77,601
2000	3,368,007	2,577,602	36,589	2,614,191	293,428	-62,513	2,258,250	632,633	477,124	25,079	134,298	79,638
2001	3,472,813	2,669,431	29,737	2,699,168	298,481	-73,790	2,326,897	626,951	518,965	25,422	136,605	80,176
2002	3,580,605	2,752,134	16,563	2,768,697	306,392	-93,400	2,368,905	640,874	570,826	25,736	139,128	80,735
2003	3,717,269	2,839,435	20,802	2,860,237	322,909	-110,582	2,426,746	682,925	607,598	26,250	141,610	81,225
2004	3,959,596	2,979,827	27,778	3,007,605	336,570	-108,263	2,562,772	738,670	658,154	27,405	144,486	83,747
2005	4,276,417	3,194,471	25,669	3,220,140	364,464	-101,364	2,754,312	793,316	728,789	28,909	147,929	86,281
2006	4,645,894	3,452,674	26,185	3,478,859	389,295	-115,212	2,974,352	854,183	817,359	30,378	152,934	89,256
2007	4,997,125	3,687,424	33,327	3,720,751	420,416	-114,369	3,185,966	917,382	893,777	31,732	157,479	93,882
2008	5,341,878	3,800,688	41,823	3,842,511	431,506	-108,133	3,302,872	1,016,781	1,022,225	32,951	162,116	94,593
2009	5,286,162	3,733,572	44,732	3,778,304	427,942	-104,795	3,245,567	934,846	1,105,749	31,925	165,581	91,737
2010	5,487,542	3,917,900	40,630	3,958,530	441,882	-123,268	3,393,380	915,414	1,178,748	32,501	168,843	91,866
2011	5,694,029	3,953,412	42,821	3,996,233	404,923	-109,858	3,481,452	992,656	1,219,921	33,336	170,806	93,859
2012	6,155,391	4,274,293	64,263	4,338,556	429,421	-136,325	3,772,810	1,118,304	1,264,277	35,576	173,023	95,599
2013	6,182,742	4,358,197	83,459	4,441,656	500,389	-134,247	3,807,020	1,080,021	1,295,701	35,445	174,434	96,308
2014	6,437,372	4,536,311	58,569	4,594,880	522,766	-157,223	3,914,891	1,173,420	1,349,061	36,768	175,079	97,846
2015	6,683,570	4,706,330	33,320	4,739,650	539,344	-182,087	4,018,219	1,258,650	1,406,701	37,924	176,237	98,450
2016	6,844,894	4,826,262	37,602	4,863,864	554,084	-184,209	4,125,571	1,268,040	1,451,283	38,535	177,627	99,313
2017	7,143,838	5,025,421	51,025	5,076,446	571,187	-189,590	4,315,669	1,330,829	1,497,340	39,900	179,042	100,492
2018	7,513,687	7,492,923	20,764	5,355,708	593,233	-222,045	4,540,430	1,414,884	1,558,373	41,841	179,575	102,543
2019	7,830,577	7,800,361	30,216	5,607,087	619,703	-253,124	4,734,260	1,453,633	1,642,684	43,325	180,742	103,958

Personal Income and Employment by Area: Greenville-Anderson, SC

(Thousands of dollars, except as noted.)

Year	Personal income, total	Earnings by place of work			Less: Contributions for government social insurance	Plus: Adjustment for residence	Equals: Net earnings by place of residence	Plus: Dividends, interest, and rent	Plus: Personal current transfer receipts	Per capita personal income (dollars)	Population (persons)	Total employment
		Nonfarm	Farm	Total								
1970	1,517,638	1,293,717	8,982	1,302,699	91,249	15,671	1,227,121	173,462	117,055	3,326	456,342	218,306
1971	1,662,943	1,412,959	11,057	1,424,016	103,491	14,053	1,334,578	192,023	136,342	3,556	467,592	222,013
1972	1,881,594	1,623,546	9,444	1,632,990	124,784	8,914	1,517,120	212,529	151,945	3,918	480,222	236,053
1973	2,156,975	1,876,081	15,114	1,891,195	165,193	3,580	1,729,582	245,943	181,450	4,389	491,446	252,272
1974	2,430,522	2,103,600	12,242	2,115,842	191,998	-5,886	1,917,958	285,791	226,773	4,811	505,159	260,780
1975	2,583,672	2,127,910	10,248	2,138,158	188,404	-2,358	1,947,396	315,266	321,010	5,048	511,828	245,959
1976	2,908,608	2,441,789	11,286	2,453,075	222,212	-1,082	2,229,781	343,912	334,915	5,683	511,833	258,160
1977	3,222,013	2,729,079	11,405	2,740,484	248,827	-8,633	2,483,024	386,767	352,222	6,135	525,157	267,903
1978	3,629,476	3,102,405	14,667	3,117,072	290,594	-15,926	2,810,552	434,931	383,993	6,795	534,157	279,956
1979	4,091,614	3,497,367	18,593	3,515,960	338,065	-24,405	3,153,490	494,864	443,260	7,533	543,173	288,304
1980	4,630,336	3,866,445	4,404	3,870,849	372,658	-26,156	3,472,035	619,322	538,979	8,338	555,331	291,377
1981	5,165,797	4,219,502	5,059	4,224,561	436,152	-29,495	3,758,914	775,871	631,012	9,156	564,171	292,183
1982	5,457,774	4,304,405	10,036	4,314,441	451,197	-26,750	3,836,494	916,959	704,321	9,596	568,779	286,688
1983	5,915,924	4,670,057	4,206	4,674,263	497,912	-27,013	4,149,338	1,014,889	751,697	10,349	571,626	291,548
1984	6,549,474	5,179,946	11,794	5,191,740	569,765	-26,911	4,595,064	1,164,789	789,621	11,373	575,900	304,398
1985	7,031,242	5,553,548	8,695	5,562,243	618,437	-28,007	4,915,799	1,254,248	861,195	12,092	581,502	310,248
1986	7,550,259	6,009,604	6,087	6,015,691	686,336	-35,717	5,293,638	1,343,779	912,842	12,873	586,510	318,643
1987	8,151,912	6,568,268	13,879	6,582,147	739,784	-36,905	5,805,458	1,404,849	941,605	13,755	592,638	328,469
1988	8,993,265	7,308,389	18,862	7,327,251	844,693	-50,015	6,432,543	1,555,172	1,005,550	14,944	601,817	345,744
1989	9,724,120	7,810,300	21,905	7,832,205	913,491	-63,625	6,855,089	1,739,230	1,129,801	15,928	610,505	356,698
1990	10,501,838	8,415,151	22,059	8,437,210	1,001,801	-87,539	7,347,870	1,896,301	1,257,667	16,931	620,288	364,023
1991	10,853,974	8,599,197	21,967	8,621,164	1,038,668	-79,447	7,503,049	1,908,866	1,442,059	17,268	628,575	358,319
1992	11,553,662	9,021,057	28,135	9,049,192	1,079,692	10,735	7,980,235	1,965,660	1,607,767	18,127	637,366	358,466
1993	12,294,952	9,686,658	31,473	9,718,131	1,169,456	-29,883	8,518,792	2,061,308	1,714,852	18,997	647,208	372,522
1994	13,164,535	10,332,964	33,321	10,366,285	1,262,494	-5,713	9,098,078	2,205,878	1,860,579	20,030	657,228	383,788
1995	14,225,499	11,116,545	22,907	11,139,452	1,364,194	13,361	9,788,619	2,466,719	1,970,161	21,278	668,549	398,851
1996	15,145,702	11,779,574	10,759	11,790,333	1,420,055	-7,333	10,362,945	2,673,983	2,108,774	22,232	681,257	409,377
1997	16,052,932	12,433,582	18,703	12,452,285	1,498,581	20,076	10,973,780	2,880,415	2,198,737	23,146	693,566	418,744
1998	17,294,547	13,357,101	19,993	13,377,094	1,608,087	72,280	11,841,287	3,137,081	2,316,179	24,486	706,300	427,192
1999	18,022,908	14,157,217	27,821	14,185,038	1,692,276	15,120	12,507,882	3,063,602	2,451,424	25,119	717,514	437,552
2000	19,352,244	15,124,937	31,760	15,156,697	1,796,844	-46,857	13,312,996	3,385,010	2,654,238	26,592	727,743	448,598
2001	20,200,522	15,713,625	29,280	15,742,905	1,859,079	-43,509	13,840,317	3,379,436	2,980,769	27,459	735,668	440,664
2002	20,448,164	15,722,938	21,007	15,743,945	1,854,726	-21,328	13,867,891	3,341,828	3,238,445	27,590	741,131	428,775
2003	20,758,418	16,040,080	14,498	16,054,578	1,909,853	-43,112	14,101,613	3,276,129	3,380,676	27,779	747,276	430,601
2004	21,345,320	16,172,728	26,354	16,199,082	1,950,341	43,127	14,291,868	3,376,805	3,676,647	28,302	754,196	435,716
2005	22,369,919	16,862,170	33,046	16,895,216	2,038,974	20,692	14,876,934	3,530,572	3,962,413	29,317	763,048	446,423
2006	24,145,356	17,830,724	11,076	17,841,800	2,208,205	71,551	15,705,146	4,125,766	4,314,444	31,055	777,494	457,273
2007	25,931,259	18,836,805	5,128	18,841,933	2,317,166	146,834	16,671,601	4,669,846	4,589,812	32,680	793,500	470,173
2008	26,968,915	19,232,450	-1,890	19,230,560	2,391,973	135,656	16,974,243	4,699,031	5,295,641	33,346	808,765	470,312
2009	25,971,422	18,136,234	16,233	18,152,467	2,288,166	147,472	16,011,773	4,057,152	5,902,497	31,700	819,279	445,295
2010	27,097,071	18,898,879	22,891	18,921,770	2,348,512	187,106	16,760,364	3,967,464	6,369,243	32,815	825,762	444,311
2011	28,631,927	20,049,308	6,128	20,055,436	2,240,299	103,277	17,918,414	4,322,384	6,391,129	34,346	833,632	462,592
2012	30,259,440	21,380,900	15,037	21,395,937	2,302,258	184,702	19,278,381	4,558,063	6,422,996	35,967	841,312	466,221
2013	30,866,977	22,067,891	34,435	22,102,326	2,677,304	270,034	19,695,056	4,621,697	6,550,224	36,363	848,866	476,286
2014	33,017,144	23,454,738	16,901	23,471,639	2,809,174	311,973	20,974,438	5,114,806	6,927,900	38,369	860,506	491,144
2015	35,159,088	24,949,285	25,828	24,975,113	2,960,025	287,161	22,302,249	5,544,980	7,311,859	40,297	872,507	507,269
2016	36,151,738	25,574,533	7,872	25,582,405	3,047,705	271,356	22,806,056	5,789,130	7,556,552	40,872	884,512	516,610
2017	37,747,410	26,696,771	5,731	26,702,502	3,198,070	324,010	23,828,442	6,118,037	7,800,931	42,132	895,923	524,838
2018	40,152,888	40,154,479	-1,591	28,107,726	3,373,093	241,931	24,976,564	7,050,830	8,125,494	44,269	907,028	545,399
2019	41,822,381	41,832,812	-10,431	29,212,410	3,503,851	297,354	26,005,913	7,264,773	8,551,695	45,436	920,477	554,401

Personal Income and Employment by Area: Gulfport-Biloxi, MS

(Thousands of dollars, except as noted.)

Year	Personal income, total	Earnings by place of work			Less: Contributions for government social insurance	Plus: Adjustment for residence	Equals: Net earnings by place of residence	Plus: Dividends, interest, and rent	Plus: Personal current transfer receipts	Per capita personal income (dollars)	Population (persons)	Total employment
		Nonfarm	Farm	Total								
1970.............	843,647	747,906	1,991	749,897	48,020	-56,548	645,329	143,140	55,178	3,493	241,495	109,735
1971.............	906,576	789,913	2,199	792,112	52,602	-51,346	688,164	152,543	65,869	3,607	251,347	111,651
1972.............	1,068,122	950,858	1,906	952,764	66,088	-63,543	823,133	169,776	75,213	4,128	258,728	120,441
1973.............	1,214,035	1,074,743	2,790	1,077,533	82,592	-67,901	927,040	196,689	90,306	4,473	271,384	128,013
1974.............	1,328,702	1,154,594	2,334	1,156,928	92,019	-69,835	995,074	221,529	112,099	4,823	275,483	128,526
1975.............	1,500,557	1,306,351	1,712	1,308,063	106,258	-82,745	1,119,060	242,722	138,775	5,418	276,941	131,617
1976.............	1,673,786	1,466,834	2,093	1,468,927	121,873	-91,365	1,255,689	262,183	155,914	5,869	285,195	137,857
1977.............	1,831,149	1,613,407	2,950	1,616,357	138,001	-104,224	1,374,132	286,658	170,359	6,283	291,439	142,534
1978.............	2,016,600	1,753,428	2,607	1,756,035	151,565	-108,322	1,496,148	329,372	191,080	6,797	296,689	142,259
1979.............	2,174,351	1,833,025	3,426	1,836,451	163,127	-94,951	1,578,373	366,086	229,892	7,280	298,661	138,800
1980.............	2,469,858	2,030,046	595	2,030,641	176,151	-94,953	1,759,537	438,319	272,002	8,202	301,117	142,303
1981.............	2,844,488	2,326,090	525	2,326,615	215,889	-114,387	1,996,339	531,624	316,525	9,347	304,337	144,575
1982.............	3,127,220	2,595,914	2,706	2,598,620	246,833	-156,171	2,195,616	580,277	351,327	10,056	310,986	148,783
1983.............	3,174,155	2,525,746	491	2,526,237	243,657	-125,318	2,157,262	613,263	403,630	10,064	315,399	141,240
1984.............	3,334,443	2,622,416	671	2,623,087	258,966	-123,555	2,240,566	672,823	421,054	10,610	314,280	143,148
1985.............	3,544,459	2,798,942	764	2,799,706	283,269	-144,841	2,371,596	726,841	446,022	11,147	317,972	147,352
1986.............	3,786,236	3,008,817	-564	3,008,253	308,351	-169,097	2,530,805	781,021	474,410	11,721	323,031	153,422
1987.............	3,893,055	3,091,395	837	3,092,232	316,701	-182,238	2,593,293	800,516	499,246	12,105	321,614	152,171
1988.............	4,112,745	3,256,542	1,467	3,258,009	349,138	-195,049	2,713,822	864,006	534,917	12,936	317,926	153,728
1989.............	4,361,896	3,365,596	1,603	3,367,199	362,300	-194,709	2,810,190	955,281	596,425	13,874	314,383	153,676
1990.............	4,567,144	3,542,930	1,563	3,544,493	399,762	-207,213	2,937,518	973,469	656,157	14,616	312,471	154,152
1991.............	4,840,436	3,780,762	1,477	3,782,239	434,237	-224,169	3,123,833	977,550	739,053	15,366	315,015	157,723
1992.............	5,251,445	4,113,710	2,913	4,116,623	471,416	-245,312	3,399,895	1,013,420	838,130	16,240	323,357	162,663
1993.............	5,829,635	4,646,759	1,236	4,647,995	536,147	-287,771	3,824,077	1,107,549	898,009	17,561	331,962	177,618
1994.............	6,298,442	5,039,080	26	5,039,106	596,904	-296,148	4,146,054	1,205,427	946,961	18,477	340,882	187,042
1995.............	6,589,498	5,146,581	-531	5,146,050	607,070	-294,883	4,244,097	1,294,127	1,051,274	19,046	345,981	185,900
1996.............	6,858,054	5,227,467	-2,101	5,225,366	617,575	-279,820	4,327,971	1,384,323	1,145,760	19,767	346,950	188,184
1997.............	7,240,813	5,521,496	-1,918	5,519,578	655,547	-299,495	4,564,536	1,469,708	1,206,569	20,625	351,065	194,086
1998.............	8,028,996	6,307,188	-1,416	6,305,772	753,688	-389,946	5,162,138	1,658,043	1,208,815	22,582	355,546	204,312
1999.............	8,405,673	6,687,132	188	6,687,320	798,581	-402,237	5,486,502	1,664,964	1,254,207	23,283	361,019	211,650
2000.............	8,920,944	7,004,428	1,233	7,005,661	823,822	-417,347	5,764,492	1,794,242	1,362,210	24,414	365,397	210,596
2001.............	9,035,222	6,911,080	3,469	6,914,549	786,706	-444,393	5,683,450	1,831,432	1,520,340	24,541	368,163	208,057
2002.............	9,211,207	7,055,884	1,832	7,057,716	806,911	-481,035	5,769,770	1,820,263	1,621,174	24,835	370,891	207,517
2003.............	9,579,222	7,457,464	1,902	7,459,366	849,359	-561,561	6,048,446	1,811,319	1,719,457	25,799	371,296	209,489
2004.............	9,899,395	7,791,780	2,257	7,794,037	889,969	-622,323	6,281,745	1,744,785	1,872,865	26,102	379,253	209,170
2005.............	10,904,863	8,061,143	1,423	8,062,566	923,377	-729,421	6,409,768	1,653,071	2,842,024	28,442	383,412	199,148
2006.............	10,482,649	8,210,468	1,417	8,211,885	961,844	-760,641	6,489,400	1,872,822	2,120,427	30,187	347,253	195,003
2007.............	12,701,694	8,862,962	-4,031	8,858,931	1,049,085	-879,810	6,930,036	3,758,034	2,013,624	35,600	356,789	207,835
2008.............	12,277,072	9,400,140	-6,649	9,393,491	1,099,463	-1,026,839	7,267,189	2,707,270	2,302,613	33,794	363,290	210,970
2009.............	12,335,307	9,378,323	-5,875	9,372,448	1,111,319	-1,032,323	7,228,806	2,651,235	2,455,266	33,558	367,577	206,518
2010.............	12,783,559	9,672,068	-8,624	9,663,444	1,123,391	-1,028,918	7,511,135	2,531,789	2,740,635	34,423	371,367	207,450
2011.............	12,866,269	9,521,059	-5,714	9,515,345	1,006,266	-974,400	7,534,679	2,454,274	2,877,316	34,258	375,571	205,784
2012.............	13,033,041	9,629,050	-6,752	9,622,298	1,024,728	-927,357	7,670,213	2,492,991	2,869,837	34,427	378,568	206,190
2013.............	13,054,594	9,735,612	542	9,736,154	1,174,929	-940,297	7,620,928	2,471,121	2,962,545	34,192	381,800	208,478
2014.............	13,461,500	9,913,244	-7,306	9,905,938	1,188,811	-910,045	7,807,082	2,559,145	3,095,273	34,917	385,531	208,634
2015.............	13,643,205	9,883,522	-6,048	9,877,474	1,209,613	-918,782	7,749,079	2,645,981	3,248,145	35,162	388,012	208,160
2016.............	13,931,854	10,035,817	-7,854	10,027,963	1,230,009	-931,853	7,866,101	2,695,830	3,369,923	35,646	390,836	209,582
2017.............	14,261,290	10,217,975	-7,899	10,210,076	1,254,447	-924,225	8,031,404	2,805,438	3,424,448	36,175	394,232	210,109
2018.............	15,271,584	15,272,851	-1,267	10,712,789	1,322,904	-853,911	8,535,974	2,901,609	3,834,001	36,827	414,686	220,092
2019.............	15,784,326	15,785,117	-791	11,004,942	1,362,189	-870,317	8,772,436	2,944,210	4,067,680	37,792	417,665	223,055

Personal Income and Employment by Area: Hagerstown-Martinsburg, MD-WV

(Thousands of dollars, except as noted.)

Year	Personal income, total	Earnings by place of work			Less: Contributions for government social insurance	Plus: Adjustment for residence	Equals: Net earnings by place of residence	Plus: Dividends, interest, and rent	Plus: Personal current transfer receipts	Per capita personal income (dollars)	Population (persons)	Total employment
		Nonfarm	Farm	Total								
1970	529,615	416,554	11,573	428,127	30,006	21,607	419,728	63,383	46,504	3,773	140,356	61,187
1971	579,295	441,017	10,561	451,578	32,550	31,297	450,325	69,962	59,008	4,072	142,270	60,568
1972	642,962	495,442	12,910	508,352	38,553	34,977	504,776	77,166	61,020	4,443	144,718	62,605
1973	712,792	550,756	15,830	566,586	48,918	39,066	556,734	87,914	68,144	4,847	147,060	65,091
1974	799,667	614,376	17,050	631,426	56,559	42,362	617,229	102,360	80,078	5,347	149,552	66,441
1975	881,803	661,091	13,828	674,919	59,782	47,549	662,686	114,294	104,823	5,815	151,655	65,786
1976	960,251	717,182	10,573	727,755	65,495	58,299	720,559	124,046	115,646	6,244	153,782	66,479
1977	1,066,638	814,076	9,073	823,149	75,148	59,319	807,320	138,761	120,557	6,883	154,974	68,660
1978	1,202,992	918,234	18,477	936,711	85,635	67,200	918,276	156,987	127,729	7,674	156,758	71,340
1979	1,345,129	1,034,800	17,323	1,052,123	100,560	68,021	1,019,584	179,383	146,162	8,467	158,863	73,750
1980	1,449,053	1,062,953	10,237	1,073,190	103,211	86,518	1,056,497	215,204	177,352	9,057	159,999	71,741
1981	1,589,205	1,141,098	9,391	1,150,489	118,001	93,328	1,125,816	260,101	203,288	9,915	160,281	71,196
1982	1,691,793	1,149,118	9,169	1,158,287	120,861	102,656	1,140,082	313,139	238,572	10,523	160,772	69,372
1983	1,777,698	1,214,042	9,288	1,223,330	131,440	97,126	1,189,016	328,998	259,684	10,918	162,823	70,800
1984	1,990,476	1,380,275	17,047	1,397,322	154,420	102,113	1,345,015	377,033	268,428	12,075	164,837	73,953
1985	2,119,446	1,467,960	18,508	1,486,468	166,993	112,032	1,431,507	400,475	287,464	12,709	166,763	75,989
1986	2,255,665	1,548,910	24,866	1,573,776	178,749	135,407	1,530,434	426,287	298,944	13,360	168,834	78,736
1987	2,425,713	1,682,980	22,279	1,705,259	192,889	151,257	1,663,627	441,029	321,057	14,153	171,398	82,899
1988	2,620,163	1,819,763	22,460	1,842,223	214,711	177,666	1,805,178	470,073	344,912	15,077	173,783	86,869
1989	2,853,045	1,954,309	19,599	1,973,908	231,566	196,916	1,939,258	539,763	374,024	16,113	177,068	89,711
1990	2,981,526	2,078,559	23,169	2,101,728	250,305	173,217	2,024,640	552,925	403,961	16,401	181,790	91,971
1991	3,071,235	2,184,028	21,715	2,205,743	268,834	108,808	2,045,717	565,686	459,832	16,541	185,679	92,208
1992	3,232,194	2,298,187	31,988	2,330,175	283,423	92,847	2,139,599	569,048	523,547	17,095	189,071	91,949
1993	3,360,762	2,380,033	20,418	2,400,451	296,787	105,011	2,208,675	597,855	554,232	17,575	191,225	93,693
1994	3,582,059	2,532,846	17,635	2,550,481	317,112	124,771	2,358,140	646,548	577,371	18,517	193,451	95,211
1995	3,741,579	2,677,223	8,978	2,686,201	335,630	110,924	2,461,495	686,736	593,348	19,105	195,846	99,247
1996	3,974,297	2,798,848	14,789	2,813,637	348,519	141,603	2,606,721	730,783	636,793	20,067	198,049	101,073
1997	4,319,515	3,003,168	10,476	3,013,644	368,868	229,964	2,874,740	795,957	648,818	21,603	199,951	103,427
1998	4,498,452	3,192,937	15,299	3,208,236	385,913	157,068	2,979,391	837,746	681,315	22,186	202,761	105,167
1999	4,701,546	3,429,196	15,729	3,444,925	409,403	111,864	3,147,386	832,815	721,345	22,874	205,544	107,031
2000	5,136,262	3,632,896	16,202	3,649,098	433,503	265,844	3,481,439	891,368	763,455	24,645	208,408	109,258
2001	5,626,691	3,930,938	19,417	3,950,355	467,805	347,352	3,829,902	941,420	855,369	26,601	211,521	114,045
2002	5,891,381	4,039,913	8,826	4,048,739	477,374	436,710	4,008,075	938,185	945,121	27,312	215,706	114,201
2003	6,250,980	4,251,256	21,855	4,273,111	505,310	560,655	4,328,456	912,509	1,010,015	28,234	221,396	115,877
2004	6,775,267	4,558,450	32,267	4,590,717	539,504	706,398	4,757,611	987,428	1,030,228	29,758	227,681	118,519
2005	7,296,886	4,847,541	31,004	4,878,545	575,755	901,438	5,204,228	987,506	1,105,152	31,157	234,198	122,850
2006	7,876,530	5,133,484	27,157	5,160,641	607,242	1,038,600	5,591,999	1,100,645	1,183,886	32,736	240,604	125,819
2007	8,320,072	5,192,310	28,623	5,220,933	610,954	1,188,911	5,798,890	1,230,019	1,291,163	33,917	245,305	127,278
2008	8,663,133	5,179,398	30,263	5,209,661	614,477	1,242,733	5,837,917	1,327,995	1,497,221	34,889	248,303	125,911
2009	8,618,243	5,056,504	25,894	5,082,398	601,157	1,222,858	5,704,099	1,279,814	1,634,330	34,503	249,783	122,122
2010	8,954,941	5,213,639	28,012	5,241,651	623,694	1,291,153	5,909,110	1,260,519	1,785,312	35,487	252,341	121,714
2011	9,400,130	5,492,555	45,565	5,538,120	585,146	1,247,034	6,200,008	1,362,064	1,838,058	36,956	254,363	124,361
2012	9,721,885	5,756,835	60,082	5,816,917	612,860	1,215,043	6,419,100	1,434,463	1,868,322	37,994	255,881	127,966
2013	9,818,739	5,877,772	57,937	5,935,709	693,144	1,185,768	6,428,333	1,432,457	1,957,949	38,149	257,380	129,300
2014	10,195,157	6,049,387	58,631	6,108,018	709,679	1,211,245	6,609,584	1,531,983	2,053,590	39,345	259,123	130,403
2015	10,604,700	6,225,904	29,671	6,255,575	735,091	1,337,921	6,858,405	1,598,478	2,147,817	40,679	260,695	131,299
2016	10,980,006	6,347,395	24,227	6,371,622	751,336	1,485,582	7,105,868	1,626,784	2,247,354	41,736	263,080	132,058
2017	11,408,218	6,602,951	20,025	6,622,976	785,486	1,560,552	7,398,042	1,703,305	2,306,871	42,969	265,498	132,934
2018	12,521,492	12,497,262	24,230	7,041,011	842,373	1,806,261	8,004,899	1,873,489	2,643,104	43,824	285,722	140,340
2019	13,045,602	12,988,132	57,470	7,210,066	862,269	2,023,152	8,370,949	1,903,452	2,771,201	45,281	288,104	140,857

Personal Income and Employment by Area: Hammond, LA

(Thousands of dollars, except as noted.)

| Year | Personal income, total | Derivation of personal income | | | | | | | | Per capita personal income (dollars) | Population (persons) | Total employment |
| | | Earnings by place of work | | | Less: Contributions for government social insurance | Plus: Adjustment for residence | Equals: Net earnings by place of residence | Plus: Dividends, interest, and rent | Plus: Personal current transfer receipts | | | |
		Nonfarm	Farm	Total								
1970	155,386	92,684	9,962	102,646	5,808	12,770	109,608	19,447	26,331	2,346	66,244	20,955
1971	172,304	99,361	12,708	112,069	6,320	14,793	120,542	21,298	30,464	2,518	68,421	21,042
1972	191,624	111,771	13,297	125,068	7,388	17,725	135,405	23,458	32,761	2,803	68,368	22,132
1973	221,073	127,091	17,087	144,178	9,546	20,763	155,395	27,758	37,920	3,207	68,944	23,356
1974	246,895	139,869	12,603	152,472	10,737	26,110	167,845	34,186	44,864	3,527	70,000	23,840
1975	287,159	151,486	16,710	168,196	11,233	34,234	191,197	39,119	56,843	3,987	72,031	23,535
1976	326,518	171,822	15,038	186,860	12,930	45,232	219,162	43,822	63,534	4,400	74,202	24,397
1977	368,182	193,437	15,626	209,063	14,430	53,638	248,271	50,386	69,525	4,826	76,299	24,835
1978	417,571	225,679	11,984	237,663	17,242	64,465	284,886	57,144	75,541	5,349	78,065	26,739
1979	476,084	251,175	9,122	260,297	19,426	83,092	323,963	64,789	87,332	5,968	79,771	26,121
1980	550,410	275,442	7,470	282,912	21,049	100,702	362,565	80,636	107,209	6,793	81,026	27,010
1981	623,041	306,832	7,413	314,245	24,519	114,797	404,523	98,855	119,663	7,580	82,194	27,882
1982	688,997	325,855	6,516	332,371	25,612	119,746	426,505	118,070	144,422	8,138	84,663	28,300
1983	746,838	349,457	7,721	357,178	26,796	116,784	447,166	138,009	161,663	8,628	86,562	28,974
1984	797,869	384,254	8,146	392,400	30,162	117,027	479,265	149,218	169,386	9,063	88,037	29,761
1985	844,941	407,758	13,146	420,904	32,175	111,116	499,845	162,228	182,868	9,507	88,876	30,136
1986	866,835	423,075	16,492	439,567	33,353	103,401	509,615	165,513	191,707	9,714	89,239	30,240
1987	870,683	424,920	20,654	445,574	33,584	100,001	511,991	159,468	199,224	9,897	87,971	29,887
1988	903,581	435,394	20,048	455,442	37,054	111,084	529,472	165,154	208,955	10,384	87,019	30,165
1989	965,358	462,187	22,992	485,179	41,367	115,890	559,702	174,180	231,476	11,169	86,429	30,880
1990	1,038,985	504,404	18,542	522,946	45,965	128,229	605,210	174,921	258,854	12,116	85,754	31,266
1991	1,134,263	565,490	15,416	580,906	52,909	133,241	661,238	180,896	292,129	13,115	86,485	32,005
1992	1,257,041	635,286	21,559	656,845	58,929	141,865	739,781	182,972	334,288	14,264	88,124	33,722
1993	1,369,982	696,338	21,192	717,530	64,390	143,434	796,574	193,917	379,491	15,241	89,885	35,685
1994	1,490,974	752,348	23,940	776,288	71,411	155,376	860,253	212,248	418,473	16,255	91,726	37,632
1995	1,564,101	800,723	25,547	826,270	76,855	165,856	915,271	225,687	423,143	16,679	93,775	39,337
1996	1,630,230	842,588	28,427	871,015	81,835	175,604	964,784	238,102	427,344	17,187	94,851	40,716
1997	1,724,504	896,674	20,373	917,047	86,394	194,278	1,024,931	253,893	445,680	17,868	96,515	41,476
1998	1,811,954	946,882	24,539	971,421	90,979	218,644	1,099,086	270,002	442,866	18,443	98,246	41,204
1999	1,875,834	1,014,851	25,309	1,040,160	96,629	222,633	1,166,164	269,298	440,372	18,826	99,643	42,758
2000	1,996,088	1,101,390	21,034	1,122,424	102,926	231,556	1,251,054	283,441	461,593	19,819	100,716	44,352
2001	2,163,338	1,166,515	21,916	1,188,431	110,355	244,223	1,322,299	282,751	558,288	21,281	101,657	46,530
2002	2,242,370	1,226,381	13,665	1,240,046	116,284	260,478	1,384,240	286,117	572,013	21,874	102,511	46,879
2003	2,341,833	1,324,890	11,775	1,336,665	124,029	263,123	1,475,759	300,301	565,773	22,565	103,782	48,697
2004	2,543,779	1,465,534	19,201	1,484,735	134,381	253,860	1,604,214	296,390	643,175	24,149	105,335	50,294
2005	2,807,808	1,620,955	12,429	1,633,384	146,162	267,489	1,754,711	311,257	741,840	26,244	106,987	52,420
2006	3,256,757	1,907,766	16,427	1,924,193	174,219	350,717	2,100,691	379,361	776,705	28,543	114,102	57,421
2007	3,533,237	1,991,608	16,014	2,007,622	183,589	383,861	2,207,894	506,166	819,177	30,252	116,792	59,683
2008	3,797,407	2,112,130	11,970	2,124,100	195,852	425,265	2,353,513	521,747	922,147	32,013	118,621	60,137
2009	3,752,529	2,079,951	6,511	2,086,462	192,291	384,253	2,278,424	491,428	982,677	31,269	120,009	59,761
2010	3,986,966	2,386,208	11,008	2,397,216	214,601	302,084	2,484,699	453,411	1,048,856	32,819	121,485	60,129
2011	4,176,404	2,509,209	13,243	2,522,452	206,187	288,331	2,604,596	497,490	1,074,318	34,057	122,629	60,288
2012	4,306,991	2,458,021	13,945	2,471,966	199,908	396,326	2,668,384	526,910	1,111,697	34,836	123,637	60,275
2013	4,314,259	2,372,300	16,977	2,389,277	222,294	467,853	2,634,836	525,609	1,153,814	34,392	125,443	60,200
2014	4,457,259	2,456,509	14,638	2,471,147	229,394	500,588	2,742,341	553,548	1,161,370	35,109	126,954	60,818
2015	4,643,079	2,354,028	10,558	2,364,586	225,617	666,260	2,805,229	544,771	1,293,079	36,067	128,735	60,732
2016	4,808,463	2,423,723	6,235	2,429,958	234,525	649,175	2,844,608	590,424	1,373,431	36,812	130,623	62,695
2017	5,010,211	2,547,662	5,098	2,552,760	244,757	629,300	2,937,303	618,762	1,454,146	37,814	132,497	64,354
2018	5,047,372	5,044,002	3,370	2,586,242	253,627	668,292	3,000,907	662,830	1,383,635	37,713	133,837	65,300
2019	5,228,657	5,226,020	2,637	2,714,244	263,440	650,578	3,101,382	671,969	1,455,306	38,800	134,758	65,972

Personal Income and Employment by Area: Hanford-Corcoran, CA

(Thousands of dollars, except as noted.)

Year	Personal income, total	Earnings by place of work			Less: Contributions for government social insurance	Plus: Adjustment for residence	Equals: Net earnings by place of residence	Plus: Dividends, interest, and rent	Plus: Personal current transfer receipts	Per capita personal income (dollars)	Population (persons)	Total employment
		Nonfarm	Farm	Total								
1970	265,191	175,825	37,589	213,414	11,865	-8,679	192,870	43,833	28,488	3,984	66,570	28,533
1971	278,879	191,990	32,327	224,317	13,714	-8,561	202,042	46,309	30,528	4,197	66,450	29,151
1972	314,305	208,843	45,745	254,588	15,460	-8,092	231,036	50,634	32,635	4,611	68,161	29,839
1973	345,342	229,881	49,406	279,287	18,610	-7,992	252,685	58,022	34,635	5,056	68,308	30,582
1974	437,143	254,002	108,358	362,360	21,533	-7,783	333,044	63,756	40,343	6,329	69,067	31,905
1975	445,741	273,562	83,520	357,082	23,364	-8,100	325,618	69,573	50,550	6,315	70,590	32,738
1976	532,959	285,581	150,747	436,328	25,188	-6,386	404,754	71,307	56,898	7,432	71,708	32,207
1977	531,403	315,464	110,503	425,967	28,226	-6,872	390,869	79,788	60,746	7,333	72,467	33,077
1978	525,109	351,796	48,869	400,665	31,315	-6,554	362,796	93,740	68,573	7,139	73,556	33,605
1979	684,421	394,720	147,861	542,581	36,572	-5,747	500,262	107,816	76,343	9,304	73,562	35,517
1980	846,922	419,904	246,478	666,382	37,787	-4,077	624,518	129,044	93,360	11,404	74,265	35,016
1981	828,510	486,981	126,860	613,841	46,727	-3,357	563,757	156,148	108,605	10,869	76,229	35,983
1982	892,113	519,191	139,665	658,856	49,548	-2,700	606,608	170,100	115,405	11,406	78,213	34,679
1983	858,897	550,976	51,580	602,556	53,930	-3,003	545,623	191,537	121,737	10,586	81,138	35,641
1984	999,413	608,023	125,454	733,477	62,251	-6,245	664,981	206,783	127,649	12,041	83,004	36,754
1985	1,006,438	622,559	107,477	730,036	64,022	-5,716	660,298	208,851	137,289	11,812	85,205	36,258
1986	1,007,552	632,734	82,972	715,706	66,238	-4,883	644,585	212,718	150,249	11,665	86,372	36,047
1987	1,157,771	691,427	170,505	861,932	72,961	-12,208	776,763	224,355	156,653	13,152	88,032	36,612
1988	1,243,853	800,009	149,802	949,811	87,444	-24,926	837,441	237,436	168,976	13,161	94,510	39,367
1989	1,382,176	917,990	150,800	1,068,790	99,417	-40,996	928,377	268,562	185,237	13,843	99,850	41,267
1990	1,393,565	938,368	117,547	1,055,915	102,318	-37,194	916,403	271,235	205,927	13,678	101,885	40,087
1991	1,495,923	995,724	157,140	1,152,864	111,478	-44,469	996,917	266,312	232,694	14,338	104,334	41,203
1992	1,630,271	1,035,715	207,796	1,243,511	116,239	-42,021	1,085,251	269,205	275,815	15,177	107,414	41,535
1993	1,719,615	1,098,392	208,763	1,307,155	124,648	-42,907	1,139,600	285,508	294,507	15,753	109,161	43,577
1994	1,782,529	1,149,491	201,742	1,351,233	128,725	-44,300	1,178,208	310,646	293,675	15,977	111,565	44,229
1995	1,802,543	1,187,253	165,464	1,352,717	130,220	-44,008	1,178,489	317,052	307,002	15,834	113,840	45,163
1996	1,929,607	1,228,973	219,171	1,448,144	131,371	-40,775	1,275,998	331,163	322,446	16,719	115,411	47,583
1997	1,972,942	1,303,109	173,915	1,477,024	136,100	-40,667	1,300,257	351,562	321,123	16,896	116,769	48,573
1998	2,013,425	1,333,866	119,950	1,453,816	135,158	-24,769	1,293,889	369,134	350,402	16,577	121,457	47,999
1999	2,145,619	1,412,665	157,289	1,569,954	143,528	-23,215	1,403,211	372,749	369,659	16,975	126,402	48,316
2000	2,266,557	1,516,274	153,947	1,670,221	153,816	-24,455	1,491,950	393,287	381,320	17,457	129,835	49,518
2001	2,489,041	1,610,764	207,143	1,817,907	171,804	-8,638	1,637,465	423,905	427,671	18,731	132,881	48,875
2002	2,751,946	1,903,255	183,530	2,086,785	200,190	-51,166	1,835,429	454,541	461,976	20,329	135,369	53,293
2003	3,109,361	2,118,089	299,129	2,417,218	224,736	-90,746	2,101,736	502,621	505,004	22,306	139,393	55,626
2004	3,374,497	2,280,691	418,034	2,698,725	249,996	-119,388	2,329,341	507,973	537,183	23,499	143,601	56,222
2005	3,482,098	2,376,094	391,110	2,767,204	259,066	-117,082	2,391,056	521,644	569,398	23,990	145,147	57,079
2006	3,506,827	2,550,289	192,700	2,742,989	271,456	-108,764	2,362,769	534,552	609,506	23,741	147,712	57,125
2007	4,008,807	2,678,836	508,134	3,186,970	276,396	-131,465	2,779,109	571,427	658,271	26,651	150,420	58,761
2008	3,915,777	2,781,593	236,723	3,018,316	292,229	-175,078	2,551,009	617,302	747,466	25,757	152,027	58,713
2009	3,777,859	2,714,114	95,213	2,809,327	291,777	-176,322	2,341,228	623,859	812,772	24,809	152,278	56,878
2010	4,070,314	2,799,327	223,525	3,022,852	291,865	-214,507	2,516,480	647,471	906,363	26,707	152,404	56,175
2011	4,516,225	2,867,364	573,951	3,441,315	275,058	-243,946	2,922,311	682,939	910,975	29,706	152,030	56,158
2012	4,424,671	2,864,136	444,889	3,309,025	275,956	-250,097	2,782,972	720,703	920,996	29,251	151,265	56,739
2013	4,477,749	2,914,012	406,620	3,320,632	306,388	-235,550	2,778,694	735,161	963,894	29,718	150,675	57,516
2014	4,846,014	3,081,797	503,675	3,585,472	320,573	-262,098	3,002,801	825,670	1,017,543	32,337	149,862	59,748
2015	4,888,581	3,172,355	269,696	3,442,051	332,648	-213,785	2,895,618	887,665	1,105,298	32,486	150,482	60,587
2016	5,012,486	3,188,696	212,527	3,401,223	337,648	-139,450	2,924,125	942,449	1,145,912	33,462	149,797	60,752
2017	5,302,517	3,297,583	383,418	3,681,001	353,894	-136,912	3,190,195	985,150	1,127,172	35,326	150,101	61,723
2018	5,595,305	5,116,612	478,693	3,953,950	372,016	-183,504	3,398,430	1,024,634	1,172,241	36,961	151,382	63,654
2019	6,030,809	5,370,941	659,868	4,336,231	401,790	-207,093	3,727,348	1,047,531	1,255,930	39,433	152,940	65,092

Personal Income and Employment by Area: Harrisburg-Carlisle, PA

(Thousands of dollars, except as noted.)

Year	Personal income, total	Earnings by place of work			Less: Contributions for government social insurance	Plus: Adjustment for residence	Equals: Net earnings by place of residence	Plus: Dividends, interest, and rent	Plus: Personal current transfer receipts	Per capita personal income (dollars)	Population (persons)	Total employment
		Nonfarm	Farm	Total								
1970	1,758,789	1,560,954	20,955	1,581,909	110,101	-106,855	1,364,953	245,001	148,835	4,275	411,421	212,257
1971	1,917,418	1,706,275	14,838	1,721,113	124,668	-126,574	1,469,871	272,500	175,047	4,599	416,883	214,199
1972	2,121,103	1,910,446	14,822	1,925,268	145,631	-157,035	1,622,602	301,387	197,114	5,030	421,671	223,174
1973	2,356,228	2,156,395	22,403	2,178,798	187,977	-190,961	1,799,860	339,716	216,652	5,519	426,925	233,699
1974	2,599,131	2,383,862	22,150	2,406,012	215,859	-234,788	1,955,365	388,242	255,524	6,067	428,390	239,598
1975	2,821,295	2,521,931	17,999	2,539,930	222,482	-256,242	2,061,206	432,620	327,469	6,575	429,067	235,721
1976	3,088,512	2,789,215	22,334	2,811,549	253,182	-301,773	2,256,594	472,452	359,466	7,174	430,488	239,343
1977	3,368,794	3,083,367	15,433	3,098,800	281,710	-358,783	2,458,307	530,428	380,059	7,746	434,923	244,658
1978	3,691,961	3,419,471	16,109	3,435,580	320,415	-420,237	2,694,928	589,596	407,437	8,454	436,716	251,930
1979	4,054,250	3,787,793	21,438	3,809,231	368,646	-502,307	2,938,278	657,051	458,921	9,178	441,734	257,914
1980	4,473,051	4,119,103	3,739	4,122,842	400,551	-589,267	3,133,024	809,261	530,766	9,969	448,717	260,074
1981	4,961,310	4,448,631	13,774	4,462,405	462,945	-625,109	3,374,351	982,956	604,003	10,975	452,040	259,996
1982	5,432,382	4,709,298	18,666	4,727,964	493,249	-649,964	3,584,751	1,160,145	687,486	12,047	450,941	259,191
1983	5,795,021	5,028,179	10,726	5,038,905	535,159	-678,339	3,825,407	1,231,002	738,612	12,790	453,087	260,817
1984	6,339,855	5,541,161	39,001	5,580,162	615,633	-737,641	4,226,888	1,366,611	746,356	13,926	455,244	271,598
1985	6,807,984	5,932,606	38,270	5,970,876	670,934	-761,516	4,538,426	1,469,261	800,297	14,915	456,461	279,915
1986	7,316,877	6,410,164	39,315	6,449,479	733,678	-821,765	4,894,036	1,566,770	856,071	15,914	459,787	288,050
1987	7,794,042	6,906,025	35,700	6,941,725	783,928	-859,359	5,298,438	1,616,214	879,390	16,850	462,555	299,738
1988	8,438,709	7,552,283	22,946	7,575,229	887,071	-912,004	5,776,154	1,724,195	938,360	18,099	466,243	310,881
1989	9,279,115	8,155,649	40,703	8,196,352	941,695	-962,377	6,292,280	1,980,825	1,006,010	19,716	470,638	320,922
1990	9,905,094	8,739,119	38,935	8,778,054	1,015,958	-994,629	6,767,467	2,012,124	1,125,503	20,815	475,860	327,398
1991	10,438,253	9,218,616	23,514	9,242,130	1,082,773	-1,092,637	7,066,720	2,078,327	1,293,206	21,657	481,975	329,899
1992	11,022,202	9,848,115	49,123	9,897,238	1,150,845	-1,201,056	7,545,337	2,105,579	1,371,286	22,657	486,480	332,619
1993	11,464,584	10,313,123	42,620	10,355,743	1,220,846	-1,293,108	7,841,789	2,183,443	1,439,352	23,309	491,859	336,584
1994	11,938,573	10,821,713	44,246	10,865,959	1,306,071	-1,383,393	8,176,495	2,281,460	1,480,618	24,062	496,159	345,672
1995	12,490,168	11,282,037	26,713	11,308,750	1,359,786	-1,502,117	8,446,847	2,487,118	1,556,203	25,040	498,803	353,789
1996	13,192,157	11,873,357	53,202	11,926,559	1,401,137	-1,638,746	8,886,676	2,647,207	1,658,274	26,280	501,990	360,378
1997	13,845,272	12,531,392	27,454	12,558,846	1,467,197	-1,732,115	9,359,534	2,777,010	1,708,728	27,491	503,624	364,360
1998	14,609,431	13,347,757	37,548	13,385,305	1,541,738	-1,899,027	9,944,540	2,908,073	1,756,818	28,844	506,506	370,887
1999	15,155,445	13,979,510	34,938	14,014,448	1,600,680	-1,986,138	10,427,630	2,870,740	1,857,075	29,823	508,176	373,847
2000	15,865,097	14,514,089	51,106	14,565,195	1,639,948	-2,042,311	10,882,936	3,016,541	1,965,620	31,142	509,451	377,751
2001	16,668,100	15,323,664	49,032	15,372,696	1,720,160	-2,113,951	11,538,585	2,980,018	2,149,497	32,594	511,391	374,212
2002	17,251,421	15,990,748	23,146	16,013,894	1,801,381	-2,222,639	11,989,874	2,956,651	2,304,896	33,462	515,553	376,379
2003	17,878,616	16,544,346	57,242	16,601,588	1,853,338	-2,288,727	12,459,523	3,013,982	2,405,111	34,438	519,152	377,860
2004	18,580,498	17,523,366	87,473	17,610,839	1,951,285	-2,530,803	13,128,751	2,957,347	2,494,400	35,603	521,882	382,824
2005	19,237,130	18,068,097	76,621	18,144,718	2,022,863	-2,586,780	13,535,075	2,976,532	2,725,523	36,588	525,775	386,116
2006	20,030,772	18,714,964	61,009	18,775,973	2,104,067	-2,772,613	13,899,293	3,231,960	2,899,519	37,633	532,268	393,455
2007	21,126,780	19,410,618	100,630	19,511,248	2,169,880	-2,857,076	14,484,292	3,585,096	3,057,392	39,323	537,268	397,219
2008	21,851,766	19,681,763	111,474	19,793,237	2,216,871	-2,941,554	14,634,812	3,729,168	3,487,786	40,295	542,301	397,581
2009	21,644,049	19,395,947	68,869	19,464,816	2,214,584	-2,999,982	14,250,250	3,499,767	3,894,032	39,578	546,874	389,711
2010	22,310,735	19,858,178	82,431	19,940,609	2,260,581	-3,048,866	14,631,162	3,442,700	4,236,873	40,557	550,108	387,050
2011	23,434,153	20,565,251	127,441	20,692,692	2,090,176	-3,227,808	15,374,708	3,750,139	4,309,306	42,444	552,121	391,078
2012	24,329,791	21,146,222	134,955	21,281,177	2,133,960	-3,262,604	15,884,613	4,083,991	4,361,187	43,831	555,085	393,306
2013	24,668,507	22,106,883	160,627	22,267,510	2,498,589	-3,542,350	16,226,571	3,962,609	4,479,327	44,183	558,323	398,124
2014	25,760,515	22,865,650	184,072	23,049,722	2,586,386	-3,673,544	16,789,792	4,337,756	4,632,967	45,877	561,510	403,008
2015	26,995,324	23,990,007	117,291	24,107,298	2,712,485	-3,843,201	17,551,612	4,550,077	4,893,635	47,754	565,301	409,542
2016	27,261,695	24,131,921	51,393	24,183,314	2,745,677	-3,862,899	17,574,738	4,527,372	5,159,585	47,995	568,008	412,835
2017	28,323,471	25,175,984	86,258	25,262,242	2,894,284	-3,999,326	18,368,632	4,748,935	5,205,904	49,525	571,903	417,872
2018	29,975,666	29,921,122	54,544	26,379,877	2,995,316	-4,145,042	19,239,519	5,086,593	5,649,554	52,209	574,149	423,488
2019	31,134,512	31,052,559	81,953	27,538,467	3,126,957	-4,392,122	20,019,388	5,192,677	5,922,447	53,871	577,941	430,851

Personal Income and Employment by Area: Harrisonburg, VA

(Thousands of dollars, except as noted.)

Year	Personal income, total	Earnings by place of work			Less: Contributions for government social insurance	Plus: Adjustment for residence	Equals: Net earnings by place of residence	Plus: Dividends, interest, and rent	Plus: Personal current transfer receipts	Per capita personal income (dollars)	Population (persons)	Total employment
		Nonfarm	Farm	Total								
1970	210,184	159,308	12,492	171,800	10,339	8,817	170,278	25,491	14,415	3,347	62,807	31,524
1971	229,751	176,658	12,350	189,008	11,932	7,283	184,359	28,595	16,797	3,529	65,099	32,660
1972	253,679	193,377	15,843	209,220	13,760	7,118	202,578	31,893	19,208	3,721	68,174	33,531
1973	294,399	222,196	23,025	245,221	18,182	6,335	233,374	38,404	22,621	4,248	69,311	35,796
1974	303,767	236,044	7,781	243,825	20,082	6,971	230,714	45,086	27,967	4,237	71,687	35,967
1975	333,756	249,944	11,408	261,352	20,724	2,530	243,158	49,898	40,700	4,543	73,459	35,112
1976	372,627	287,316	10,015	297,331	24,226	2,083	275,188	55,956	41,483	5,023	74,179	36,872
1977	413,003	319,000	11,996	330,996	26,990	544	304,550	64,616	43,837	5,498	75,123	37,960
1978	462,426	359,285	14,429	373,714	30,889	-1,674	341,151	72,758	48,517	6,038	76,581	38,530
1979	520,307	409,958	12,404	422,362	36,745	-7,855	377,762	87,727	54,818	6,769	76,866	40,432
1980	589,540	456,943	6,669	463,612	41,118	-9,633	412,861	111,088	65,591	7,647	77,093	41,367
1981	652,992	488,353	9,645	497,998	47,159	-12,103	438,736	135,909	78,347	8,320	78,483	40,603
1982	707,705	534,390	6,509	540,899	52,748	-16,796	471,355	152,807	83,543	8,949	79,086	41,535
1983	767,527	582,123	7,545	589,668	57,810	-18,349	513,509	162,394	91,624	9,645	79,575	43,301
1984	878,856	644,472	39,436	683,908	65,629	-18,823	599,456	182,142	97,258	11,024	79,725	44,841
1985	950,585	698,847	45,043	743,890	72,863	-22,617	648,410	195,349	106,826	11,821	80,416	46,105
1986	1,070,477	804,368	62,602	866,970	86,474	-32,815	747,681	211,386	111,410	13,146	81,428	48,414
1987	1,122,254	880,142	33,168	913,310	94,127	-33,757	785,426	221,245	115,583	13,543	82,868	49,974
1988	1,252,258	967,379	47,932	1,015,311	106,028	-38,916	870,367	251,798	130,093	14,745	84,927	51,531
1989	1,380,963	1,040,573	73,416	1,113,989	115,263	-43,427	955,299	287,395	138,269	15,957	86,545	52,875
1990	1,445,744	1,102,078	71,671	1,173,749	122,934	-50,622	1,000,193	290,135	155,416	16,270	88,857	54,138
1991	1,515,686	1,157,523	72,910	1,230,433	130,379	-60,434	1,039,620	304,149	171,917	16,670	90,921	54,601
1992	1,642,250	1,266,277	91,635	1,357,912	141,737	-73,959	1,142,216	308,897	191,137	17,642	93,087	56,747
1993	1,744,362	1,359,286	93,859	1,453,145	151,741	-85,787	1,215,617	326,995	201,750	18,298	95,333	58,861
1994	1,836,663	1,454,191	91,837	1,546,028	161,951	-96,375	1,287,702	340,232	208,729	18,812	97,631	60,901
1995	1,908,047	1,512,773	85,100	1,597,873	168,027	-106,463	1,323,383	357,725	226,939	19,078	100,011	62,815
1996	1,985,399	1,563,057	82,479	1,645,536	171,045	-109,937	1,364,554	380,638	240,207	19,341	102,652	63,643
1997	2,094,973	1,687,792	67,985	1,755,777	182,829	-123,374	1,449,574	398,832	246,567	20,102	104,218	65,073
1998	2,235,520	1,798,793	85,944	1,884,737	191,849	-136,888	1,556,000	422,756	256,764	21,187	105,512	65,511
1999	2,340,249	1,928,816	81,427	2,010,243	205,633	-157,027	1,647,583	421,605	271,061	21,808	107,311	68,004
2000	2,512,138	2,053,095	95,406	2,148,501	215,833	-173,068	1,759,600	461,209	291,329	23,172	108,414	69,394
2001	2,747,179	2,229,623	153,535	2,383,158	240,341	-198,151	1,944,666	478,952	323,561	24,903	110,317	71,676
2002	2,695,858	2,301,909	51,779	2,353,688	249,133	-220,057	1,884,498	463,105	348,255	24,038	112,152	72,157
2003	2,879,276	2,438,935	65,085	2,504,020	261,725	-254,856	1,987,439	522,268	369,569	25,446	113,151	72,919
2004	3,050,773	2,542,505	113,908	2,656,413	275,389	-247,978	2,133,046	513,583	404,144	26,635	114,542	74,115
2005	3,221,007	2,657,973	145,184	2,803,157	290,146	-265,027	2,247,984	526,166	446,857	27,624	116,602	74,983
2006	3,364,584	2,832,426	76,732	2,909,158	316,211	-311,429	2,281,518	592,490	490,576	28,308	118,858	77,390
2007	3,544,186	2,932,318	106,992	3,039,310	328,432	-342,676	2,368,202	654,122	521,862	29,333	120,825	79,009
2008	3,715,373	3,014,238	104,301	3,118,539	341,769	-355,431	2,421,339	701,515	592,519	30,364	122,361	79,039
2009	3,646,840	2,989,926	66,743	3,056,669	340,462	-365,037	2,351,170	662,433	633,237	29,376	124,144	77,220
2010	3,835,087	3,075,477	115,018	3,190,495	346,798	-353,819	2,489,878	662,158	683,051	30,579	125,416	77,309
2011	4,049,755	3,138,247	132,067	3,270,314	317,574	-367,987	2,584,753	747,606	717,396	31,926	126,847	78,824
2012	4,250,447	3,293,688	111,797	3,405,485	329,161	-372,843	2,703,481	815,448	731,518	33,082	128,481	79,301
2013	4,319,120	3,360,052	165,845	3,525,897	380,953	-358,070	2,786,874	793,835	738,411	33,468	129,052	79,909
2014	4,580,582	3,460,052	198,074	3,658,126	390,370	-346,492	2,921,264	867,944	791,374	35,092	130,532	80,925
2015	4,813,506	3,678,708	147,883	3,826,591	411,251	-344,375	3,070,965	912,862	829,679	36,655	131,319	82,093
2016	4,869,316	3,737,433	112,900	3,850,333	422,559	-364,450	3,063,324	944,392	861,600	36,545	133,241	84,313
2017	5,114,886	3,893,243	150,410	4,043,653	442,476	-378,609	3,222,568	993,605	898,713	38,045	134,442	85,366
2018	5,434,131	5,277,349	156,782	4,251,374	461,919	-380,881	3,408,574	1,083,406	942,151	40,328	134,749	86,463
2019	5,575,624	5,474,412	101,212	4,395,486	486,030	-429,517	3,479,939	1,097,840	997,845	41,312	134,964	88,530

Personal Income and Employment by Area: Hartford-East Hartford-Middletown, CT

(Thousands of dollars, except as noted.)

Year	Personal income, total	Earnings by place of work			Less: Contributions for government social insurance	Plus: Adjustment for residence	Equals: Net earnings by place of residence	Plus: Dividends, interest, and rent	Plus: Personal current transfer receipts	Per capita personal income (dollars)	Population (persons)	Total employment
		Nonfarm	Farm	Total								
1970	5,171,164	4,382,190	37,659	4,419,849	293,222	-178,390	3,948,237	837,241	385,686	4,983	1,037,762	515,814
1971	5,395,535	4,476,209	34,903	4,511,112	309,310	-172,558	4,029,244	879,270	487,021	5,155	1,046,710	504,925
1972	5,783,030	4,851,833	32,162	4,883,995	356,062	-185,231	4,342,702	930,871	509,457	5,503	1,050,940	514,795
1973	6,343,191	5,387,507	38,187	5,425,694	455,426	-210,705	4,759,563	1,037,071	546,557	6,031	1,051,711	538,925
1974	6,962,111	5,840,648	53,090	5,893,738	515,034	-238,519	5,140,185	1,178,313	643,613	6,602	1,054,609	551,581
1975	7,500,799	6,140,389	40,568	6,180,957	528,872	-267,332	5,384,753	1,267,437	848,609	7,139	1,050,706	539,442
1976	8,014,376	6,582,807	43,958	6,626,765	579,288	-286,404	5,761,073	1,344,305	908,998	7,649	1,047,780	544,412
1977	8,754,771	7,252,770	43,950	7,296,720	650,126	-315,200	6,331,394	1,477,326	946,051	8,409	1,041,160	560,291
1978	9,761,716	8,269,703	39,082	8,308,785	764,832	-378,481	7,165,472	1,636,876	959,368	9,325	1,046,844	589,554
1979	11,040,256	9,452,555	39,097	9,491,652	909,025	-476,857	8,105,770	1,853,752	1,080,734	10,531	1,048,331	614,832
1980	12,564,493	10,559,925	46,358	10,606,283	1,004,620	-574,712	9,026,951	2,289,381	1,248,161	11,927	1,053,458	629,793
1981	13,960,708	11,475,731	41,916	11,517,647	1,172,453	-633,163	9,712,031	2,808,227	1,440,450	13,188	1,058,562	632,664
1982	15,089,526	12,238,619	47,685	12,286,304	1,267,473	-688,284	10,330,547	3,158,677	1,600,302	14,234	1,060,120	629,064
1983	16,156,298	13,197,026	50,346	13,247,372	1,378,411	-757,302	11,111,659	3,311,366	1,733,273	15,126	1,068,101	636,326
1984	17,990,270	14,777,920	53,766	14,831,686	1,579,981	-880,412	12,371,293	3,799,160	1,819,817	16,747	1,074,268	666,698
1985	19,348,449	16,206,894	58,141	16,265,035	1,750,056	-1,026,210	13,488,769	3,922,535	1,937,145	17,889	1,081,595	692,320
1986	21,041,995	17,892,877	64,897	17,957,774	1,939,613	-1,198,652	14,819,509	4,171,009	2,051,477	19,263	1,092,348	723,469
1987	23,023,590	19,938,607	66,046	20,004,653	2,126,561	-1,376,167	16,501,925	4,395,130	2,126,535	20,809	1,106,430	745,697
1988	25,234,539	21,868,359	84,760	21,953,119	2,387,606	-1,530,090	18,035,423	4,899,576	2,299,540	22,507	1,121,183	767,174
1989	27,418,784	23,219,803	77,794	23,297,597	2,517,746	-1,692,058	19,087,793	5,739,061	2,591,930	24,409	1,123,307	766,227
1990	28,313,207	24,047,525	102,455	24,149,980	2,579,643	-1,913,925	19,656,412	5,760,408	2,896,387	25,166	1,125,047	758,360
1991	28,578,741	24,265,381	88,972	24,354,353	2,641,821	-1,872,015	19,840,517	5,486,089	3,252,135	25,347	1,127,479	724,845
1992	29,840,621	25,028,753	93,327	25,122,080	2,694,450	-1,886,543	20,541,087	5,485,098	3,814,436	26,523	1,125,083	709,988
1993	30,699,193	25,702,048	97,715	25,799,763	2,765,965	-1,903,408	21,130,390	5,597,582	3,971,221	27,273	1,125,634	710,405
1994	31,403,791	26,294,783	79,656	26,374,439	2,867,030	-1,891,772	21,615,637	5,679,678	4,108,476	27,891	1,125,949	698,042
1995	32,409,889	26,836,961	81,929	26,918,890	2,952,749	-1,781,485	22,184,656	5,827,236	4,397,997	28,821	1,124,531	708,359
1996	33,649,580	27,697,988	68,047	27,766,035	3,044,154	-1,619,123	23,102,758	6,035,793	4,511,029	29,874	1,126,396	715,650
1997	35,686,266	29,605,234	62,968	29,668,202	3,199,897	-1,608,984	24,859,321	6,195,985	4,630,960	31,609	1,128,992	722,220
1998	37,999,259	31,962,098	71,910	32,034,008	3,362,301	-1,723,468	26,948,239	6,342,555	4,708,465	33,499	1,134,353	733,474
1999	40,003,279	34,401,456	72,652	34,474,108	3,536,467	-1,950,035	28,987,606	6,208,905	4,806,768	35,050	1,141,318	745,821
2000	43,727,593	37,524,738	88,871	37,613,609	3,753,931	-1,947,231	31,912,447	6,763,080	5,052,066	37,995	1,150,872	762,284
2001	45,253,523	38,692,120	81,841	38,773,961	3,855,347	-1,993,367	32,925,247	6,974,320	5,353,956	39,062	1,158,513	765,606
2002	45,573,415	39,188,330	73,421	39,261,751	4,025,568	-1,866,608	33,369,575	6,462,910	5,740,930	38,985	1,169,000	757,708
2003	46,636,437	39,652,134	73,144	39,725,278	4,089,061	-1,752,993	33,883,224	6,889,033	5,864,180	39,543	1,179,394	752,250
2004	49,440,735	42,473,824	74,177	42,548,001	4,355,010	-1,934,681	36,258,310	7,014,136	6,168,289	41,807	1,182,605	763,538
2005	51,561,794	44,368,030	66,187	44,434,217	4,530,285	-1,973,328	37,930,604	7,235,585	6,395,605	43,405	1,187,929	775,261
2006	55,319,219	46,775,490	63,727	46,839,217	4,693,398	-1,920,368	40,225,451	8,240,503	6,853,265	46,342	1,193,725	786,925
2007	58,570,078	48,744,446	79,884	48,824,330	4,878,964	-2,112,346	41,833,020	9,439,673	7,297,385	48,874	1,198,395	801,933
2008	60,708,419	49,213,021	76,610	49,289,631	4,988,521	-1,903,031	42,398,079	9,951,898	8,358,442	50,404	1,204,436	807,415
2009	60,007,555	48,223,561	74,816	48,298,377	4,882,075	-1,755,606	41,660,696	9,068,810	9,278,049	49,609	1,209,604	785,190
2010	61,539,251	49,460,554	80,739	49,541,293	4,915,727	-1,739,375	42,886,191	8,747,104	9,905,956	50,677	1,214,343	774,625
2011	64,216,022	51,231,781	75,807	51,307,588	4,593,817	-1,943,610	44,770,161	9,516,728	9,929,133	52,761	1,217,106	786,151
2012	66,241,812	52,344,755	95,102	52,439,857	4,751,954	-2,009,194	45,678,709	10,520,969	10,042,134	54,472	1,216,064	791,456
2013	66,745,133	53,555,620	91,802	53,647,422	5,552,855	-2,139,710	45,954,857	10,610,823	10,179,453	54,846	1,216,966	798,580
2014	69,523,631	55,607,806	78,360	55,686,166	5,749,423	-2,361,623	47,575,120	11,498,716	10,449,795	57,208	1,215,275	807,029
2015	71,625,836	57,472,916	80,626	57,553,542	5,950,375	-2,502,363	49,100,804	11,702,941	10,822,091	59,047	1,213,041	813,794
2016	72,437,757	57,893,683	63,607	57,957,290	6,042,108	-2,393,770	49,521,412	11,779,611	11,136,734	59,862	1,210,075	816,290
2017	74,252,861	59,232,105	59,830	59,291,935	6,228,612	-2,438,419	50,624,904	12,307,058	11,320,899	61,353	1,210,259	822,170
2018	76,525,205	76,475,968	49,237	61,211,466	6,453,203	-2,419,591	52,338,672	12,127,416	12,059,117	63,446	1,206,139	824,366
2019	78,476,365	78,413,398	62,967	62,963,998	6,633,999	-2,515,994	53,814,005	12,337,938	12,324,422	65,132	1,204,877	831,128

Personal Income and Employment by Area: Hattiesburg, MS

(Thousands of dollars, except as noted.)

Year	Personal income, total	Earnings by place of work			Less: Contributions for government social insurance	Plus: Adjustment for residence	Equals: Net earnings by place of residence	Plus: Dividends, interest, and rent	Plus: Personal current transfer receipts	Per capita personal income (dollars)	Population (persons)	Total employment
		Nonfarm	Farm	Total								
1970	225,607	177,307	4,196	181,503	12,383	-74	169,046	29,620	26,941	2,742	82,290	33,601
1971	250,584	195,461	4,164	199,625	13,978	73	185,720	33,697	31,167	2,984	83,983	35,050
1972	283,106	221,480	4,590	226,070	16,506	193	209,757	37,896	35,453	3,243	87,298	37,235
1973	320,040	245,733	8,399	254,132	20,913	850	234,069	44,309	41,662	3,588	89,186	38,607
1974	362,770	275,395	6,110	281,505	24,295	944	258,154	53,038	51,578	3,988	90,966	39,612
1975	402,726	300,874	5,691	306,565	26,179	1,789	282,175	57,176	63,375	4,375	92,048	39,716
1976	458,073	346,316	6,391	352,707	30,522	2,364	324,549	62,824	70,700	4,902	93,441	41,341
1977	518,117	395,522	7,741	403,263	34,591	3,255	371,927	70,182	76,008	5,432	95,376	43,243
1978	578,619	440,281	8,334	448,615	39,365	4,936	414,186	79,743	84,690	5,977	96,810	44,696
1979	644,162	482,697	11,511	494,208	44,782	7,272	456,698	89,612	97,852	6,551	98,328	45,088
1980	724,251	530,030	5,523	535,553	49,257	8,043	494,339	113,988	115,924	7,222	100,284	45,403
1981	812,820	582,062	5,230	587,292	58,512	6,118	534,898	145,405	132,517	7,935	102,434	45,484
1982	858,873	603,365	9,239	612,604	62,413	4,047	554,238	160,002	144,633	8,247	104,145	45,036
1983	929,035	682,770	4,944	687,714	71,411	-17,468	598,835	170,160	160,040	8,694	106,863	47,090
1984	999,766	720,180	6,410	726,590	76,966	-10,844	638,780	192,340	168,646	9,285	107,674	47,377
1985	1,045,549	728,112	7,722	735,834	79,176	4,718	661,376	209,260	174,913	9,702	107,761	47,057
1986	1,096,216	775,583	7,520	783,103	85,344	-1,062	696,697	219,177	180,342	10,124	108,276	47,970
1987	1,164,035	834,398	8,302	842,700	91,608	-5,214	745,878	226,030	192,127	10,738	108,400	49,468
1988	1,237,918	893,336	10,026	903,362	102,495	-6,468	794,399	237,121	206,398	11,461	108,015	50,464
1989	1,362,173	974,158	11,126	985,284	111,165	-10,074	864,045	270,786	227,342	12,469	109,245	51,867
1990	1,446,152	1,058,033	5,456	1,063,489	124,938	-13,389	925,162	271,904	249,086	13,195	109,601	52,390
1991	1,502,120	1,081,069	6,003	1,087,072	130,549	-10,966	945,557	277,988	278,575	13,593	110,509	52,773
1992	1,622,547	1,162,732	9,012	1,171,744	138,705	-15,706	1,017,333	293,584	311,630	14,587	111,229	53,563
1993	1,733,867	1,241,861	9,715	1,251,576	147,626	-15,152	1,088,798	314,674	330,395	15,421	112,437	55,796
1994	1,875,606	1,358,433	14,191	1,372,624	162,289	-19,228	1,191,107	336,744	347,755	16,461	113,942	58,389
1995	2,018,606	1,449,442	12,874	1,462,316	172,288	-24,438	1,265,590	371,582	381,434	17,367	116,231	61,030
1996	2,135,047	1,528,976	14,408	1,543,384	179,153	-23,981	1,340,250	388,933	405,864	18,070	118,152	62,103
1997	2,296,720	1,642,024	16,490	1,658,514	191,108	-23,486	1,443,920	429,742	423,058	19,200	119,618	64,061
1998	2,426,619	1,724,170	19,187	1,743,357	200,487	-20,247	1,522,623	479,990	424,006	19,999	121,340	66,653
1999	2,522,730	1,813,344	18,320	1,831,664	210,509	-24,058	1,597,097	485,351	440,282	20,577	122,598	68,862
2000	2,648,141	1,863,615	17,360	1,880,975	214,504	-24,103	1,642,368	532,493	473,280	21,297	124,342	69,431
2001	2,833,099	1,998,577	22,356	2,020,933	226,813	-31,184	1,762,936	535,223	534,940	22,646	125,102	69,121
2002	2,964,234	2,106,011	16,303	2,122,314	238,941	-39,751	1,843,622	532,791	587,821	23,490	126,193	69,773
2003	3,019,871	2,185,622	15,868	2,201,490	247,169	-42,549	1,911,772	496,093	612,006	23,709	127,371	70,371
2004	3,213,013	2,323,833	30,909	2,354,742	264,644	-51,560	2,038,538	515,358	659,117	24,914	128,966	70,778
2005	3,448,118	2,468,200	30,416	2,498,616	278,051	-55,148	2,165,417	535,462	747,239	26,359	130,815	72,565
2006	3,765,658	2,760,681	23,964	2,784,645	317,223	-74,647	2,392,775	627,132	745,751	28,067	134,167	77,786
2007	3,943,803	2,865,118	21,223	2,886,341	332,902	-82,637	2,470,802	685,568	787,433	28,725	137,293	80,259
2008	4,160,863	2,919,390	9,488	2,928,878	337,868	-83,007	2,508,003	760,840	892,020	29,869	139,305	79,761
2009	4,231,705	2,929,440	11,821	2,941,261	343,126	-54,864	2,543,271	726,342	962,092	29,956	141,266	78,381
2010	4,435,356	3,030,106	8,245	3,038,351	346,465	-24,512	2,667,374	709,128	1,058,854	30,954	143,289	78,562
2011	4,663,796	3,082,181	-3,090	3,079,091	317,369	9,645	2,771,367	782,506	1,109,923	32,107	145,256	79,317
2012	4,944,329	3,255,237	1,156	3,256,393	332,988	34,319	2,957,724	882,660	1,103,945	33,745	146,520	80,455
2013	4,991,603	3,308,342	30,009	3,338,351	380,387	63,770	3,021,734	846,415	1,123,454	33,791	147,718	81,363
2014	5,225,572	3,468,828	16,620	3,485,448	397,171	70,476	3,158,753	897,135	1,169,684	35,327	147,919	83,463
2015	5,403,183	3,591,462	11,965	3,603,427	419,191	52,376	3,236,612	947,199	1,219,372	36,376	148,538	85,091
2016	5,510,821	3,649,105	8,939	3,658,044	426,773	30,721	3,261,992	983,486	1,265,343	37,000	148,943	85,359
2017	5,648,035	3,742,216	10,031	3,752,247	441,572	26,358	3,337,033	1,024,930	1,286,072	37,938	148,877	87,023
2018	6,446,610	6,355,549	91,061	4,182,503	493,038	110,011	3,799,476	1,125,255	1,521,879	38,306	168,292	96,149
2019	6,588,139	6,531,655	56,484	4,242,019	508,001	115,178	3,849,196	1,138,419	1,600,524	39,018	168,849	97,120

Personal Income and Employment by Area: Hickory-Lenoir-Morganton, NC

(Thousands of dollars, except as noted.)

		Derivation of personal income										
		Earnings by place of work			Less: Contributions for government social insurance	Plus: Adjustment for residence	Equals: Net earnings by place of residence	Plus: Dividends, interest, and rent	Plus: Personal current transfer receipts	Per capita personal income (dollars)	Population (persons)	Total employment
Year	Personal income, total	Nonfarm	Farm	Total								
1970............	784,523	713,459	5,822	719,281	51,357	-23,029	644,895	86,257	53,371	3,436	228,324	123,300
1971............	866,297	785,457	7,418	792,875	58,880	-25,108	708,887	95,199	62,211	3,695	234,432	126,489
1972............	980,621	901,560	4,440	906,000	70,924	-28,007	807,069	105,342	68,210	4,078	240,460	133,573
1973............	1,106,372	1,008,941	17,369	1,026,310	90,692	-30,299	905,319	119,939	81,114	4,476	247,184	139,492
1974............	1,187,079	1,063,524	12,392	1,075,916	99,690	-30,382	945,844	139,272	101,963	4,722	251,418	138,142
1975............	1,257,076	1,056,724	12,323	1,069,047	97,494	-26,341	945,212	151,529	160,335	4,962	253,359	129,718
1976............	1,414,855	1,225,822	15,129	1,240,951	116,385	-32,821	1,091,745	165,410	157,700	5,553	254,783	137,473
1977............	1,593,399	1,395,622	18,542	1,414,164	132,099	-37,335	1,244,730	185,145	163,524	6,187	257,538	143,921
1978............	1,760,066	1,551,002	15,989	1,566,991	151,127	-39,311	1,376,553	208,652	174,861	6,710	262,291	148,852
1979............	1,936,487	1,693,762	15,718	1,709,480	170,929	-40,681	1,497,870	237,047	201,570	7,288	265,722	150,985
1980............	2,158,080	1,830,125	11,711	1,841,836	183,352	-41,466	1,617,018	294,605	246,457	7,961	271,068	151,175
1981............	2,430,415	2,028,459	20,220	2,048,679	217,563	-48,764	1,782,352	367,170	280,893	8,912	272,705	153,144
1982............	2,574,701	2,089,696	17,859	2,107,555	224,665	-50,410	1,832,480	416,490	325,731	9,364	274,966	150,999
1983............	2,852,208	2,354,136	16,805	2,370,941	255,634	-59,225	2,056,082	452,170	343,956	10,347	275,660	156,262
1984............	3,196,501	2,641,839	30,453	2,672,292	295,026	-68,055	2,309,211	526,525	360,765	11,459	278,940	164,550
1985............	3,388,460	2,794,099	29,010	2,823,109	315,256	-68,794	2,439,059	561,908	387,493	11,981	282,830	167,043
1986............	3,686,292	3,051,532	33,545	3,085,077	350,071	-75,541	2,659,465	612,262	414,565	12,977	284,074	172,324
1987............	3,980,000	3,348,547	22,195	3,370,742	377,613	-82,637	2,910,492	640,851	428,657	13,905	286,235	178,889
1988............	4,359,547	3,653,979	23,866	3,677,845	420,871	-90,229	3,166,745	726,791	466,011	15,060	289,487	185,685
1989............	4,742,121	3,861,043	44,579	3,905,622	443,266	-92,308	3,370,048	852,415	519,658	16,289	291,125	189,029
1990............	4,965,260	4,031,894	54,256	4,086,150	474,202	-93,216	3,518,732	875,337	571,191	16,918	293,489	191,322
1991............	5,122,563	4,081,079	64,011	4,145,090	485,908	-90,920	3,568,262	889,428	664,873	17,246	297,026	187,870
1992............	5,557,612	4,492,475	71,782	4,564,257	526,798	-104,012	3,933,447	904,690	719,475	18,465	300,989	193,366
1993............	5,911,871	4,780,030	77,439	4,857,469	566,701	-109,425	4,181,343	941,459	789,069	19,332	305,812	198,101
1994............	6,295,271	5,096,740	78,139	5,174,879	610,972	-113,116	4,450,791	1,025,383	819,097	20,242	310,993	201,756
1995............	6,615,773	5,225,176	75,032	5,300,208	628,501	-100,268	4,571,439	1,119,264	925,070	20,899	316,556	206,522
1996............	6,986,474	5,437,075	80,034	5,517,109	648,959	-101,226	4,766,924	1,211,226	1,008,324	21,704	321,905	208,510
1997............	7,436,275	5,766,804	83,910	5,850,714	681,434	-97,363	5,071,917	1,298,986	1,065,372	22,705	327,516	211,062
1998............	7,910,552	6,149,800	92,049	6,241,849	730,047	-99,149	5,412,653	1,384,637	1,113,262	23,765	332,861	213,060
1999............	8,311,800	6,504,145	96,133	6,600,278	768,441	-96,545	5,735,292	1,404,265	1,172,243	24,594	337,955	216,340
2000............	8,710,256	6,803,751	89,654	6,893,405	802,122	-99,426	5,991,857	1,462,136	1,256,263	25,376	343,247	221,379
2001............	8,973,809	6,829,102	92,276	6,921,378	808,511	-74,891	6,037,976	1,509,374	1,426,459	25,865	346,952	215,026
2002............	8,942,174	6,746,980	54,244	6,801,224	785,700	-58,428	5,957,096	1,436,994	1,548,084	25,674	348,299	206,898
2003............	9,042,293	6,692,166	56,346	6,748,512	797,555	-35,409	5,915,548	1,500,050	1,626,695	25,874	349,472	201,090
2004............	9,491,121	7,039,404	65,505	7,104,909	828,509	-19,954	6,256,446	1,498,096	1,736,579	27,023	351,224	203,385
2005............	9,968,165	7,170,171	100,233	7,270,404	860,725	19,824	6,429,503	1,646,498	1,892,164	28,146	354,159	203,025
2006............	10,478,168	7,552,721	88,960	7,641,681	901,190	-9,944	6,730,547	1,676,493	2,071,128	29,310	357,492	205,211
2007............	10,887,807	7,665,897	58,075	7,723,972	920,673	11,128	6,814,427	1,851,975	2,221,405	30,178	360,791	205,462
2008............	11,123,394	7,604,883	24,235	7,629,118	915,375	39,770	6,753,513	1,864,591	2,505,290	30,559	364,003	200,169
2009............	10,824,454	6,954,106	48,540	7,002,646	847,907	73,589	6,228,328	1,703,806	2,892,320	29,604	365,639	185,648
2010............	11,054,020	7,158,782	51,768	7,210,550	864,134	72,385	6,418,801	1,631,489	3,003,730	30,235	365,602	182,847
2011............	11,312,004	7,246,417	20,099	7,266,516	815,299	70,062	6,521,279	1,782,805	3,007,920	31,031	364,536	185,630
2012............	11,791,498	7,501,254	41,059	7,542,313	822,972	91,197	6,810,538	1,923,070	3,057,890	32,429	363,606	185,886
2013............	11,728,171	7,559,557	95,669	7,655,226	950,102	87,840	6,792,964	1,861,514	3,073,693	32,272	363,413	187,055
2014............	12,310,178	7,865,209	139,357	8,004,566	986,277	127,326	7,145,615	2,018,314	3,146,249	33,938	362,725	188,500
2015............	12,983,622	8,238,997	150,939	8,389,936	1,033,382	138,712	7,495,266	2,169,659	3,318,697	35,763	363,044	191,529
2016............	13,340,193	8,441,893	111,091	8,552,984	1,056,574	150,019	7,646,429	2,285,923	3,407,841	36,598	364,506	194,800
2017............	14,067,291	8,965,429	120,960	9,086,389	1,105,943	147,186	8,127,632	2,397,862	3,541,797	38,379	366,534	198,700
2018............	14,563,744	14,500,702	63,042	9,400,811	1,130,645	158,322	8,428,488	2,468,986	3,666,270	39,527	368,449	199,452
2019............	15,093,644	15,042,332	51,312	9,705,834	1,174,334	176,659	8,708,159	2,516,648	3,868,837	40,826	369,711	201,902

Personal Income and Employment by Area: Hilton Head Island-Bluffton, SC

(Thousands of dollars, except as noted.)

| Year | Personal income, total | Derivation of personal income | | | | | | | | | Per capita personal income (dollars) | Population (persons) | Total employment |
| | | Earnings by place of work | | | Less: Contributions for government social insurance | Plus: Adjustment for residence | Equals: Net earnings by place of residence | Plus: Dividends, interest, and rent | Plus: Personal current transfer receipts | | | |
		Nonfarm	Farm	Total								
1970	266,573	199,240	4,221	203,461	12,006	4,872	196,327	56,914	13,332	4,224	63,110	34,783
1971	270,191	202,275	4,282	206,557	13,002	4,711	198,266	56,195	15,730	4,179	64,658	32,961
1972	326,122	248,954	4,614	253,568	16,252	3,954	241,270	66,636	18,216	4,743	68,755	35,347
1973	365,162	280,043	3,754	283,797	20,026	2,965	266,736	76,815	21,611	5,321	68,623	37,134
1974	393,386	293,067	5,248	298,315	22,034	3,859	280,140	85,961	27,285	5,933	66,303	36,514
1975	434,814	312,863	6,507	319,370	24,645	5,268	299,993	96,610	38,211	5,791	75,090	36,956
1976	512,916	369,939	4,328	374,267	29,810	6,623	351,080	117,781	44,055	6,570	78,071	40,575
1977	557,655	401,628	3,417	405,045	32,099	6,390	379,336	132,675	45,644	7,274	76,668	41,908
1978	620,329	440,125	2,761	442,886	35,133	5,554	413,307	155,924	51,098	7,899	78,535	43,150
1979	698,738	495,328	3,202	498,530	41,307	3,591	460,814	176,334	61,590	8,764	79,724	44,712
1980	795,986	557,774	396	558,170	46,426	2,366	514,110	206,145	75,731	9,884	80,532	46,210
1981	957,453	663,141	579	663,720	58,587	6,585	611,718	257,181	88,554	11,546	82,926	46,448
1982	1,013,318	690,976	3,044	694,020	61,621	7,778	640,177	277,863	95,278	11,848	85,527	46,606
1983	1,068,526	729,606	6	729,612	67,731	8,013	669,894	294,895	103,737	12,229	87,375	47,483
1984	1,233,893	851,902	-714	851,188	82,141	4,762	773,809	345,918	114,166	13,670	90,263	51,207
1985	1,353,277	937,203	-1,446	935,757	93,582	2,551	844,726	384,712	123,839	14,697	92,077	54,742
1986	1,475,579	1,018,037	508	1,018,545	104,259	4,790	919,076	423,452	133,051	15,666	94,192	56,562
1987	1,560,551	1,055,800	2,219	1,058,019	108,382	9,401	959,038	461,507	140,006	16,219	96,218	57,567
1988	1,676,998	1,119,053	3,149	1,122,202	119,791	15,898	1,018,309	509,133	149,556	17,039	98,423	58,897
1989	1,838,580	1,181,398	3,522	1,184,920	128,926	18,814	1,074,808	590,521	173,251	18,359	100,147	60,252
1990	2,031,884	1,279,139	3,677	1,282,816	143,710	16,965	1,156,071	682,051	193,762	19,774	102,754	61,850
1991	2,119,190	1,309,073	5,364	1,314,437	149,813	18,060	1,182,684	711,537	224,969	19,999	105,964	60,325
1992	2,336,051	1,425,795	3,751	1,429,546	163,687	17,969	1,283,828	794,313	257,910	21,340	109,469	61,579
1993	2,494,089	1,498,321	13,358	1,511,679	174,901	19,813	1,356,591	854,040	283,458	21,958	113,587	63,720
1994	2,743,540	1,642,656	9,740	1,652,396	194,233	18,933	1,477,096	949,902	316,542	23,253	117,989	66,792
1995	2,944,891	1,804,789	8,815	1,813,604	213,245	8,319	1,608,678	990,104	346,109	24,096	122,214	71,135
1996	3,238,165	1,948,874	5,183	1,954,057	227,817	17,956	1,744,196	1,111,831	382,138	25,481	127,083	74,453
1997	3,576,440	2,116,373	5,582	2,121,955	247,887	8,334	1,882,402	1,281,613	412,425	27,095	131,994	78,311
1998	3,924,097	2,316,514	6,592	2,323,106	271,066	3,717	2,055,757	1,422,162	446,178	28,846	136,035	81,074
1999	4,195,892	2,545,248	9,812	2,555,060	294,660	-12,247	2,248,153	1,466,869	480,870	30,312	138,422	84,993
2000	4,502,385	2,706,826	8,601	2,715,427	314,195	-18,944	2,382,288	1,592,632	527,465	31,479	143,027	88,583
2001	4,772,115	2,926,818	9,910	2,936,728	335,758	-19,084	2,581,886	1,589,056	601,173	32,558	146,574	92,982
2002	4,889,305	3,024,449	10,843	3,035,292	349,161	-15,691	2,670,440	1,559,240	659,625	32,510	150,392	94,863
2003	5,161,166	3,241,118	21,259	3,262,377	377,504	-15,542	2,869,331	1,575,070	716,765	33,903	152,234	97,376
2004	5,713,652	3,500,374	28,165	3,528,539	410,841	-12,053	3,105,645	1,833,526	774,481	36,211	157,787	101,288
2005	6,241,338	3,773,408	24,829	3,798,237	440,990	-8,224	3,349,023	2,042,794	849,521	38,210	163,343	105,260
2006	7,023,167	4,096,116	28,547	4,124,663	492,784	2,980	3,634,859	2,444,447	943,861	41,406	169,619	109,635
2007	7,482,346	4,329,805	12,912	4,342,717	519,885	21,242	3,844,074	2,609,983	1,028,289	42,908	174,382	112,983
2008	7,625,081	4,276,908	23,372	4,300,280	520,680	38,468	3,818,068	2,615,263	1,191,750	42,357	180,019	110,918
2009	7,366,712	3,993,588	22,110	4,015,698	497,123	43,922	3,562,497	2,460,681	1,343,534	40,043	183,971	105,838
2010	7,182,985	3,951,855	26,000	3,977,855	488,729	49,751	3,538,877	2,180,142	1,463,966	38,253	187,776	103,807
2011	7,652,849	4,049,783	22,150	4,071,933	451,948	62,585	3,682,570	2,439,451	1,530,828	40,446	189,211	104,363
2012	8,107,530	4,298,950	16,116	4,315,066	470,593	64,276	3,908,749	2,625,882	1,572,899	41,943	193,299	106,089
2013	8,343,430	4,493,210	18,606	4,511,816	542,076	65,753	4,035,493	2,643,517	1,664,420	42,238	197,536	108,036
2014	9,140,091	4,784,469	11,760	4,796,229	572,401	72,362	4,296,190	3,061,903	1,781,998	45,249	201,995	111,529
2015	9,866,906	5,104,281	16,302	5,120,583	609,473	65,572	4,576,682	3,364,538	1,925,686	47,551	207,501	115,575
2016	10,233,851	5,286,516	13,730	5,300,246	633,084	62,276	4,729,438	3,487,137	2,017,276	48,371	211,568	118,873
2017	10,648,551	5,463,561	11,165	5,474,726	662,168	71,433	4,883,991	3,676,989	2,087,571	49,459	215,302	122,328
2018	11,688,294	11,681,898	6,396	5,647,403	698,760	82,347	5,030,990	4,395,151	2,262,153	53,610	218,023	127,879
2019	12,343,180	12,337,012	6,168	6,047,845	746,446	68,057	5,369,456	4,529,675	2,444,049	55,551	222,195	130,831

Personal Income and Employment by Area: Hinesville, GA

(Thousands of dollars, except as noted.)

Year	Personal income, total	Earnings by place of work			Less: Contributions for government social insurance	Plus: Adjustment for residence	Equals: Net earnings by place of residence	Plus: Dividends, interest, and rent	Plus: Personal current transfer receipts	Per capita personal income (dollars)	Population (persons)	Total employment
		Nonfarm	Farm	Total								
1970	76,182	69,871	971	70,842	3,612	-15,192	52,038	18,977	5,167	3,576	21,303	9,248
1971	81,026	73,877	1,172	75,049	4,095	-15,067	55,887	18,749	6,390	3,753	21,587	9,029
1972	88,560	79,395	1,184	80,579	4,411	-14,059	62,109	19,458	6,993	4,045	21,894	8,729
1973	95,721	83,692	1,648	85,340	4,854	-14,302	66,184	21,462	8,075	4,516	21,198	8,747
1974	106,241	92,488	1,473	93,961	5,503	-15,517	72,941	23,150	10,150	5,014	21,188	9,148
1975	124,820	103,795	1,017	104,812	6,553	-12,661	85,598	26,095	13,127	5,005	24,937	9,529
1976	172,775	188,499	734	189,233	13,903	-64,524	110,806	47,879	14,090	5,980	28,894	15,280
1977	228,210	266,272	-512	265,760	19,864	-102,625	143,271	70,274	14,665	6,787	33,625	20,349
1978	267,881	304,939	1,463	306,402	21,728	-120,805	163,869	87,554	16,458	7,042	38,038	21,446
1979	309,234	352,061	1,416	353,477	25,705	-138,622	189,150	101,054	19,030	7,856	39,364	22,895
1980	356,727	398,492	986	399,478	29,189	-148,494	221,795	111,886	23,046	8,298	42,989	24,553
1981	398,316	443,478	940	444,418	33,385	-155,526	255,507	116,158	26,651	8,576	46,444	26,045
1982	449,527	490,269	1,455	491,724	36,015	-161,725	293,984	125,961	29,582	9,257	48,561	26,948
1983	454,769	487,866	1,604	489,470	38,682	-156,903	293,885	128,505	32,379	9,545	47,647	25,701
1984	488,877	517,505	1,431	518,936	41,864	-160,001	317,071	135,712	36,094	9,771	50,034	25,809
1985	528,780	557,970	599	558,569	46,189	-168,505	343,875	145,931	38,974	10,314	51,268	26,658
1986	558,583	584,465	770	585,235	49,627	-176,841	358,767	158,273	41,543	10,765	51,890	27,196
1987	593,298	612,650	366	613,016	53,134	-178,405	381,477	168,156	43,665	10,941	54,228	28,028
1988	616,917	642,680	800	643,480	59,925	-188,242	395,313	174,163	47,441	11,060	55,780	27,945
1989	658,073	666,133	1,200	667,333	63,613	-186,668	417,052	187,714	53,307	11,429	57,578	28,135
1990	661,699	596,900	743	597,643	58,718	-109,372	429,553	169,575	62,571	11,168	59,247	24,410
1991	722,835	688,479	1,200	689,679	69,660	-161,302	458,717	191,740	72,378	12,016	60,158	25,608
1992	864,430	871,334	1,504	872,838	92,266	-243,358	537,214	241,742	85,474	13,284	65,072	29,828
1993	907,488	849,496	1,405	850,901	91,634	-193,799	565,468	248,538	93,482	14,006	64,792	29,680
1994	954,332	876,294	1,744	878,038	91,285	-198,157	588,596	264,264	101,472	14,074	67,809	30,543
1995	1,026,812	930,826	1,482	932,308	93,857	-211,560	626,891	288,071	111,850	14,997	68,468	32,025
1996	1,080,060	953,228	1,722	954,950	95,815	-201,751	657,384	300,189	122,487	15,481	69,766	32,488
1997	1,122,243	1,009,225	1,817	1,011,042	100,400	-203,774	706,868	286,903	128,472	15,701	71,477	32,627
1998	1,165,074	1,036,761	2,480	1,039,241	102,701	-223,067	713,473	319,029	132,572	16,401	71,035	32,828
1999	1,237,592	1,068,254	3,138	1,071,392	105,026	-192,882	773,484	321,494	142,614	17,166	72,095	32,807
2000	1,300,297	1,159,678	3,118	1,162,796	114,134	-239,751	808,911	334,285	157,101	18,014	72,181	34,607
2001	1,370,347	1,233,903	4,471	1,238,374	123,958	-256,574	857,842	334,258	178,247	19,049	71,939	34,716
2002	1,451,400	1,321,527	3,433	1,324,960	132,020	-287,216	905,724	340,939	204,737	19,774	73,399	34,713
2003	1,598,395	1,528,123	3,831	1,531,954	150,519	-358,032	1,023,403	364,867	210,125	22,433	71,252	35,794
2004	1,691,755	1,641,711	4,243	1,645,954	166,570	-396,429	1,082,955	372,538	236,262	22,675	74,609	37,376
2005	1,757,525	1,848,759	3,900	1,852,659	183,338	-572,588	1,096,733	395,830	264,962	23,006	76,395	37,293
2006	1,879,090	1,949,051	2,428	1,951,479	195,037	-566,928	1,189,514	406,918	282,658	24,988	75,199	37,608
2007	1,916,296	2,075,984	3,000	2,078,984	205,465	-705,323	1,168,196	441,219	306,881	25,185	76,089	38,874
2008	2,044,377	2,345,922	3,622	2,349,544	239,914	-894,016	1,215,614	478,016	350,747	27,121	75,379	41,570
2009	2,116,001	2,363,803	2,887	2,366,690	246,337	-841,975	1,278,378	458,356	379,267	26,173	80,848	41,165
2010	2,184,301	2,564,604	2,748	2,567,352	271,739	-1,015,178	1,280,435	477,529	426,337	28,245	77,334	42,508
2011	2,375,367	2,704,016	3,004	2,707,020	263,363	-1,055,023	1,388,634	524,751	461,982	29,582	80,297	44,250
2012	2,367,029	2,657,993	4,256	2,662,249	262,510	-995,996	1,403,743	515,064	448,222	29,419	80,459	43,430
2013	2,383,600	2,618,488	6,911	2,625,399	284,880	-941,943	1,398,576	511,614	473,410	30,210	78,900	43,176
2014	2,459,450	2,549,545	5,835	2,555,380	278,684	-834,192	1,442,504	510,577	506,369	30,284	81,212	42,012
2015	2,518,412	2,545,909	5,500	2,551,409	278,851	-809,133	1,463,425	510,918	544,069	31,724	79,385	41,513
2016	2,533,873	2,480,060	4,857	2,484,917	269,698	-760,947	1,454,272	502,161	577,440	31,680	79,984	40,774
2017	2,606,949	2,532,575	4,161	2,536,736	278,973	-769,805	1,487,958	514,055	604,936	32,425	80,400	41,423
2018	2,739,287	2,736,492	2,795	2,621,239	283,467	-758,503	1,579,269	516,510	643,508	34,371	79,697	42,816
2019	2,831,749	2,829,665	2,084	2,665,377	288,144	-756,857	1,620,376	524,252	687,121	34,962	80,994	43,145

Personal Income and Employment by Area: Homosassa Springs, FL

(Thousands of dollars, except as noted.)

Year	Personal income, total	Earnings by place of work			Less: Contributions for government social insurance	Plus: Adjustment for residence	Equals: Net earnings by place of residence	Plus: Dividends, interest, and rent	Plus: Personal current transfer receipts	Per capita personal income (dollars)	Population (persons)	Total employment
		Nonfarm	Farm	Total								
1970	63,421	35,041	678	35,719	2,186	-1,249	32,284	19,180	11,957	3,203	19,799	6,020
1971	76,322	40,929	795	41,724	2,741	-1,234	37,749	23,066	15,507	3,365	22,680	6,864
1972	95,300	53,382	1,015	54,397	3,804	-2,118	48,475	26,951	19,874	3,542	26,906	8,318
1973	128,831	77,449	1,403	78,852	6,375	-4,742	67,735	35,003	26,093	3,829	33,646	10,406
1974	143,423	73,420	1,064	74,484	6,439	-1,982	66,063	43,948	33,412	3,851	37,239	10,038
1975	166,390	75,222	1,144	76,366	6,531	-1,571	68,264	49,888	48,238	4,175	39,855	9,797
1976	184,511	85,307	1,259	86,566	7,386	-1,648	77,532	56,670	50,309	4,472	41,261	10,225
1977	214,481	96,935	1,277	98,212	8,587	-737	88,888	67,976	57,617	4,721	45,432	11,298
1978	259,922	116,001	1,533	117,534	10,487	324	107,371	85,459	67,092	5,375	48,361	12,617
1979	317,379	140,283	1,520	141,803	13,412	-16	128,375	107,129	81,875	6,152	51,586	14,045
1980	395,705	171,115	1,412	172,527	16,575	-1,208	154,744	140,461	100,500	7,102	55,719	15,605
1981	485,018	208,787	669	209,456	21,753	-1,676	186,027	177,098	121,893	8,127	59,678	17,682
1982	546,771	239,393	1,306	240,699	26,216	-4,893	209,590	192,545	144,636	8,687	62,938	18,878
1983	618,839	255,254	743	255,997	27,762	1,709	229,944	220,110	168,785	9,257	66,850	19,846
1984	759,551	304,519	901	305,420	33,645	3,346	275,121	292,126	192,304	10,690	71,051	21,909
1985	891,898	381,495	223	381,718	43,101	-1,079	337,538	342,218	212,142	11,936	74,724	24,290
1986	964,889	377,798	266	378,064	44,255	10,193	344,002	387,113	233,774	12,198	79,104	25,542
1987	1,062,137	443,599	-472	443,127	50,824	13,832	406,135	403,483	252,519	12,780	83,112	26,811
1988	1,175,099	467,778	39	467,817	56,724	23,189	434,282	452,999	287,818	13,661	86,021	27,981
1989	1,332,866	519,534	242	519,776	65,527	27,136	481,385	535,673	315,808	14,875	89,607	29,039
1990	1,429,401	547,819	129	547,948	68,280	30,514	510,182	569,145	350,074	15,103	94,645	29,942
1991	1,513,828	606,784	692	607,476	75,406	32,426	564,496	551,122	398,210	15,515	97,569	30,207
1992	1,609,740	663,014	1,314	664,328	81,939	36,770	619,159	536,089	454,492	16,064	100,210	30,105
1993	1,698,253	711,859	999	712,858	87,648	43,854	669,064	545,347	483,842	16,653	101,978	31,764
1994	1,818,061	755,961	977	756,938	95,342	51,934	713,530	584,757	519,774	17,410	104,429	33,496
1995	1,899,323	778,770	617	779,387	99,307	62,224	742,304	590,925	566,094	17,655	107,581	34,117
1996	2,019,182	818,976	626	819,602	102,910	72,172	788,864	625,849	604,469	18,364	109,954	35,859
1997	2,177,620	889,315	1,288	890,603	111,376	77,935	857,162	688,249	632,209	19,448	111,972	36,610
1998	2,320,638	935,509	1,638	937,147	116,114	90,667	911,700	756,046	652,892	20,295	114,344	38,580
1999	2,477,313	1,024,157	2,957	1,027,114	123,987	99,394	1,002,521	797,844	676,948	21,240	116,634	40,133
2000	2,674,598	1,079,942	2,660	1,082,602	130,395	110,746	1,062,953	886,558	725,087	22,542	118,649	41,747
2001	2,827,031	1,189,915	2,970	1,192,885	141,404	118,580	1,170,061	871,121	785,849	23,326	121,197	41,251
2002	2,917,004	1,233,417	2,377	1,235,794	146,150	132,335	1,221,979	856,854	838,171	23,621	123,491	41,905
2003	3,078,162	1,324,854	1,748	1,326,602	157,304	151,121	1,320,419	865,983	891,760	24,388	126,215	42,829
2004	3,277,428	1,409,693	1,729	1,411,422	170,865	170,447	1,411,004	889,156	977,268	25,242	129,840	44,819
2005	3,613,455	1,588,999	1,680	1,590,679	195,407	193,727	1,588,999	947,084	1,077,372	27,008	133,791	47,674
2006	3,934,256	1,751,467	2,166	1,753,633	222,376	212,931	1,744,188	1,008,872	1,181,196	28,545	137,826	50,648
2007	4,171,631	1,758,328	1,751	1,760,079	230,168	224,562	1,754,473	1,146,259	1,270,899	29,591	140,974	51,287
2008	4,280,083	1,682,618	1,652	1,684,270	228,552	232,933	1,688,651	1,175,966	1,415,466	30,116	142,122	49,583
2009	4,163,606	1,664,128	1,775	1,665,903	231,258	207,061	1,641,706	998,754	1,523,146	29,450	141,381	47,289
2010	4,326,171	1,738,168	1,584	1,739,752	239,108	196,563	1,697,207	1,007,046	1,621,918	30,643	141,178	46,761
2011	4,414,575	1,729,685	1,102	1,730,787	219,658	203,719	1,714,848	1,024,304	1,675,423	31,586	139,765	46,578
2012	4,498,839	1,788,193	2,603	1,790,796	228,286	214,962	1,777,472	1,035,052	1,686,315	32,320	139,198	46,871
2013	4,596,130	1,777,534	2,399	1,779,933	253,311	220,640	1,747,262	1,126,459	1,722,409	33,098	138,865	46,808
2014	4,789,352	1,783,107	5,218	1,788,325	255,037	244,768	1,778,056	1,177,497	1,833,799	34,476	138,920	47,079
2015	5,038,411	1,858,713	3,657	1,862,370	263,209	271,306	1,870,467	1,238,378	1,929,566	35,875	140,443	47,825
2016	5,216,693	1,886,308	2,245	1,888,553	273,185	292,882	1,908,250	1,290,173	2,018,270	36,483	142,990	48,760
2017	5,444,144	1,944,198	2,694	1,946,892	284,840	312,969	1,975,021	1,349,025	2,120,098	37,379	145,647	48,999
2018	5,615,058	5,613,876	1,182	2,003,578	300,315	339,794	2,043,057	1,395,468	2,176,533	38,021	147,682	50,932
2019	5,844,856	5,843,108	1,748	2,054,705	316,086	363,451	2,102,070	1,411,522	2,331,264	39,055	149,657	51,397

Personal Income and Employment by Area: Hot Springs, AR

(Thousands of dollars, except as noted.)

Year	Personal income, total	Earnings by place of work			Less: Contributions for government social insurance	Plus: Adjustment for residence	Equals: Net earnings by place of residence	Plus: Dividends, interest, and rent	Plus: Personal current transfer receipts	Per capita personal income (dollars)	Population (persons)	Total employment
		Nonfarm	Farm	Total								
1970	173,467	119,289	641	119,930	8,762	-1,571	109,597	37,543	26,327	3,176	54,620	23,344
1971	200,806	139,363	719	140,082	10,589	-1,719	127,774	42,337	30,695	3,510	57,207	25,542
1972	227,659	159,222	1,156	160,378	12,631	-1,443	146,304	46,817	34,538	3,845	59,206	26,849
1973	260,759	180,998	2,534	183,532	16,531	-1,700	165,301	53,861	41,597	4,251	61,347	28,786
1974	298,775	204,407	1,321	205,728	19,377	-938	185,413	63,626	49,736	4,691	63,691	29,920
1975	325,437	209,333	2,726	212,059	19,256	-2,398	190,405	71,302	63,730	5,080	64,058	27,808
1976	370,291	242,384	2,507	244,891	22,333	-949	221,609	80,088	68,594	5,634	65,728	29,099
1977	417,981	275,434	1,754	277,188	25,723	-280	251,185	92,960	73,836	6,190	67,520	30,813
1978	470,699	307,926	2,692	310,618	29,330	545	281,833	107,601	81,265	6,872	68,495	31,529
1979	525,701	337,778	2,588	340,366	33,365	714	307,715	124,754	93,232	7,507	70,026	31,939
1980	603,823	369,045	2,229	371,274	36,186	2,563	337,651	157,200	108,972	8,559	70,545	31,739
1981	681,007	391,403	2,699	394,102	41,789	1,359	353,672	199,633	127,702	9,667	70,445	31,654
1982	732,189	413,381	2,682	416,063	45,082	-3,473	367,508	224,427	140,254	10,381	70,534	31,979
1983	765,712	438,565	1,524	440,089	48,177	-277	391,635	222,344	151,733	10,716	71,455	32,719
1984	837,059	473,557	1,806	475,363	53,759	2,854	424,458	252,442	160,159	11,598	72,172	33,519
1985	891,564	497,825	1,429	499,254	57,652	2,247	443,849	277,151	170,564	12,347	72,209	34,063
1986	937,601	519,566	2,412	521,978	60,434	1,635	463,179	291,075	183,347	12,935	72,487	34,160
1987	974,954	546,713	863	547,576	63,590	1,967	485,953	295,014	193,987	13,311	73,244	34,459
1988	1,028,191	571,580	1,125	572,705	69,363	4,117	507,459	312,355	208,377	14,119	72,821	34,781
1989	1,137,699	604,959	2,193	607,152	74,204	6,208	539,156	369,341	229,202	15,543	73,195	35,525
1990	1,202,719	638,633	1,272	639,905	81,091	9,261	568,075	384,870	249,774	16,350	73,563	35,662
1991	1,271,051	682,663	1,532	684,195	86,841	6,726	604,080	384,381	282,590	16,983	74,844	36,928
1992	1,383,018	745,386	1,842	747,228	94,627	6,072	658,673	407,581	316,764	18,066	76,553	38,245
1993	1,488,981	809,422	4,640	814,062	103,034	3,742	714,770	437,976	336,235	18,951	78,568	40,364
1994	1,577,635	871,695	5,867	877,562	113,501	2,184	766,245	461,584	349,806	19,556	80,673	41,171
1995	1,680,736	937,569	7,341	944,910	121,724	420	823,606	480,916	376,214	20,493	82,015	43,164
1996	1,765,555	972,955	7,369	980,324	125,848	786	855,262	514,027	396,266	21,115	83,615	43,870
1997	1,863,919	1,019,293	8,089	1,027,382	132,076	-500	894,806	549,223	419,890	21,923	85,021	45,357
1998	1,983,525	1,099,347	7,695	1,107,042	140,574	-1,689	964,779	581,835	436,911	23,018	86,172	45,848
1999	2,015,093	1,152,918	6,924	1,159,842	147,049	-3,476	1,009,317	559,992	445,784	23,115	87,177	46,295
2000	2,105,090	1,208,787	3,928	1,212,715	153,070	-3,617	1,056,028	578,448	470,614	23,837	88,311	47,186
2001	2,180,453	1,259,323	3,438	1,262,761	156,158	7,077	1,113,680	547,698	519,075	24,491	89,032	48,005
2002	2,218,413	1,305,901	1,619	1,307,520	161,008	19,251	1,165,763	506,371	546,279	24,751	89,630	47,862
2003	2,314,274	1,379,705	2,429	1,382,134	169,390	30,622	1,243,366	503,299	567,609	25,577	90,483	48,612
2004	2,439,849	1,446,524	3,607	1,450,131	177,333	32,730	1,305,528	534,987	599,334	26,787	91,084	49,727
2005	2,615,673	1,519,912	3,761	1,523,673	188,749	42,784	1,377,708	594,445	643,520	28,402	92,096	51,052
2006	2,834,868	1,599,181	4,456	1,603,637	202,247	67,415	1,468,805	657,592	708,471	30,133	94,077	52,168
2007	2,966,364	1,626,971	7,501	1,634,472	209,643	87,704	1,512,533	698,756	755,075	31,306	94,753	52,990
2008	2,989,077	1,620,097	6,067	1,626,164	214,860	95,614	1,506,918	648,925	833,234	31,255	95,636	52,336
2009	2,983,040	1,608,168	3,182	1,611,350	216,082	85,353	1,480,621	593,307	909,112	31,125	95,840	51,467
2010	3,039,203	1,665,153	2,280	1,667,433	220,796	69,331	1,515,968	565,778	957,457	31,633	96,077	50,918
2011	3,193,104	1,745,502	1,303	1,746,805	208,967	67,460	1,605,298	611,871	975,935	32,975	96,834	51,177
2012	3,338,656	1,841,173	2,266	1,843,439	213,512	51,523	1,681,450	668,403	988,803	34,430	96,969	51,561
2013	3,272,745	1,851,718	5,278	1,856,996	239,897	21,625	1,638,724	624,851	1,009,170	33,523	97,627	51,640
2014	3,448,144	1,887,874	5,627	1,893,501	247,520	25,774	1,671,755	706,575	1,069,814	35,286	97,720	52,146
2015	3,544,220	1,932,414	3,985	1,936,399	255,195	34,122	1,715,326	710,526	1,118,368	36,264	97,734	52,068
2016	3,618,239	1,984,700	3,992	1,988,692	258,391	37,934	1,768,235	688,044	1,161,960	36,834	98,231	52,114
2017	3,774,529	2,080,924	5,917	2,086,841	269,692	36,978	1,854,127	731,480	1,188,922	38,259	98,658	52,517
2018	3,916,903	3,915,384	1,519	2,149,788	282,923	22,887	1,889,752	791,629	1,235,522	39,578	98,966	53,315
2019	4,081,660	4,079,585	2,075	2,221,910	292,489	21,061	1,950,482	816,228	1,314,950	41,069	99,386	54,293

Personal Income and Employment by Area: Houma-Thibodaux, LA

(Thousands of dollars, except as noted.)

Year	Personal income, total	Earnings by place of work			Less: Contributions for -government social insurance	Plus: Adjustment for residence	Equals: Net earnings by place of residence	Plus: Dividends, interest, and rent	Plus: Personal current transfer receipts	Per capita personal income (dollars)	Population (persons)	Total employment
		Nonfarm	Farm	Total								
1970	423,303	328,870	9,719	338,589	21,274	29,133	346,448	47,657	29,198	2,910	145,445	50,412
1971	468,085	363,406	10,296	373,702	24,071	30,669	380,300	53,522	34,263	3,163	147,993	51,619
1972	516,657	402,699	11,561	414,260	28,022	32,663	418,901	59,174	38,582	3,413	151,395	53,708
1973	583,587	456,134	20,999	477,133	36,898	31,238	471,473	66,501	45,613	3,816	152,931	56,711
1974	685,979	525,971	34,047	560,018	43,757	35,480	551,741	80,827	53,411	4,432	154,770	59,281
1975	791,965	624,045	15,974	640,019	51,256	41,742	630,505	96,568	64,892	4,984	158,910	62,632
1976	922,987	735,221	24,000	759,221	61,058	44,598	742,761	106,845	73,381	5,671	162,751	66,030
1977	1,044,855	840,102	26,866	866,968	70,733	47,446	843,681	120,779	80,395	6,283	166,289	69,860
1978	1,229,617	1,022,063	11,096	1,033,159	88,373	57,282	1,002,068	137,090	90,459	7,248	169,656	75,915
1979	1,417,748	1,194,781	10,196	1,204,977	107,246	60,569	1,158,300	155,954	103,494	8,148	173,998	79,997
1980	1,686,588	1,402,591	7,637	1,410,228	124,425	69,867	1,355,670	205,089	125,829	9,458	178,317	84,311
1981	1,982,295	1,621,737	12,222	1,633,959	154,750	91,968	1,571,177	264,898	146,220	10,787	183,763	88,068
1982	2,100,905	1,648,024	12,443	1,660,467	160,941	101,437	1,600,963	325,181	174,761	11,153	188,371	87,004
1983	2,026,473	1,477,704	7,082	1,484,786	140,742	104,600	1,448,644	355,846	221,983	10,674	189,850	78,980
1984	2,112,315	1,528,496	1,389	1,529,885	150,224	114,505	1,494,166	391,839	226,310	11,145	189,525	79,729
1985	2,161,592	1,541,748	1,402	1,543,150	151,877	120,042	1,511,315	407,687	242,590	11,397	189,669	79,101
1986	2,043,388	1,372,901	2,912	1,375,813	131,002	112,971	1,357,782	396,592	289,014	10,831	188,665	71,653
1987	1,982,983	1,319,396	5,552	1,324,948	124,085	108,649	1,309,512	381,935	291,536	10,723	184,936	70,421
1988	2,106,898	1,405,752	8,702	1,414,454	140,681	126,961	1,400,734	406,929	299,235	11,456	183,916	71,686
1989	2,245,153	1,459,834	9,953	1,469,787	147,345	140,830	1,463,272	452,594	329,287	12,253	183,230	71,631
1990	2,449,660	1,638,318	5,470	1,643,788	170,148	161,035	1,634,675	452,468	362,517	13,397	182,852	75,007
1991	2,591,535	1,719,511	6,979	1,726,490	182,082	166,839	1,711,247	456,314	423,974	14,049	184,458	75,913
1992	2,708,122	1,742,531	9,646	1,752,177	180,380	164,456	1,736,253	470,802	501,067	14,594	185,561	73,772
1993	2,859,910	1,861,746	11,240	1,872,986	196,269	154,328	1,831,045	476,975	551,890	15,369	186,083	77,661
1994	3,063,879	1,995,190	9,383	2,004,573	215,175	158,227	1,947,625	501,883	614,371	16,378	187,077	79,935
1995	3,209,393	2,074,168	10,704	2,084,872	223,948	166,285	2,027,209	557,169	625,015	17,074	187,973	82,540
1996	3,436,755	2,261,051	8,758	2,269,809	243,694	166,024	2,192,139	603,804	640,812	18,157	189,283	86,114
1997	3,819,586	2,606,894	9,871	2,616,765	278,714	165,980	2,504,031	665,850	649,705	19,962	191,339	92,368
1998	4,046,332	2,819,076	8,663	2,827,739	301,210	169,977	2,696,506	711,108	638,718	20,894	193,664	97,205
1999	3,989,669	2,766,418	10,281	2,776,699	291,840	153,362	2,638,221	694,183	657,265	20,505	194,569	95,887
2000	4,328,919	3,039,474	9,093	3,048,567	311,883	138,158	2,874,842	771,370	682,707	22,253	194,531	98,985
2001	4,745,744	3,407,810	9,210	3,417,020	358,268	141,195	3,199,947	759,134	786,663	24,292	195,360	99,867
2002	4,901,691	3,556,404	8,248	3,564,652	374,120	141,422	3,331,954	745,689	824,048	24,921	196,692	102,116
2003	5,036,720	3,677,295	8,117	3,685,412	386,143	147,099	3,446,368	743,185	847,167	25,418	198,156	103,898
2004	5,182,389	3,754,583	8,791	3,763,374	391,040	151,577	3,523,911	719,386	939,092	25,995	199,363	104,125
2005	5,807,109	4,194,455	11,032	4,205,487	422,028	118,387	3,901,846	859,714	1,045,549	28,968	200,467	108,049
2006	6,944,030	5,199,614	28,262	5,227,876	515,947	61,646	4,773,575	1,085,280	1,085,175	33,976	204,379	115,415
2007	7,733,545	5,921,219	12,791	5,934,010	586,578	3,740	5,351,172	1,238,401	1,143,972	37,651	205,401	120,804
2008	8,388,010	6,264,134	30,222	6,294,356	622,315	-21,726	5,650,315	1,442,974	1,294,721	40,511	207,056	123,100
2009	8,049,525	5,995,116	30,113	6,025,229	605,212	-88,445	5,331,572	1,364,744	1,353,209	38,743	207,769	119,739
2010	8,167,340	6,344,661	40,158	6,384,819	626,591	-165,252	5,592,976	1,103,610	1,470,754	39,219	208,251	119,412
2011	8,188,769	6,329,070	40,552	6,369,622	565,649	-229,068	5,574,905	1,140,341	1,473,523	39,255	208,604	118,227
2012	8,688,027	6,768,924	37,304	6,806,228	602,401	-390,484	5,813,343	1,390,559	1,484,125	41,590	208,897	121,800
2013	8,922,294	7,299,930	33,469	7,333,399	748,656	-624,574	5,960,169	1,410,897	1,551,228	42,500	209,938	126,518
2014	9,542,124	7,754,809	28,372	7,783,181	782,249	-681,669	6,319,263	1,670,564	1,552,297	45,135	211,413	129,133
2015	9,244,147	7,141,637	30,062	7,171,699	737,617	-589,710	5,844,372	1,686,642	1,713,133	43,545	212,291	124,421
2016	8,624,373	6,178,685	22,309	6,200,994	644,923	-406,085	5,149,986	1,635,649	1,838,738	40,731	211,740	116,658
2017	8,716,294	6,077,938	20,692	6,098,630	633,329	-365,188	5,100,113	1,688,769	1,927,412	41,405	210,512	114,094
2018	8,906,282	8,884,719	21,563	6,393,263	675,229	-425,959	5,292,075	1,620,484	1,993,723	42,584	209,144	115,448
2019	9,140,203	9,115,067	25,136	6,563,512	688,644	-448,708	5,426,160	1,628,382	2,085,661	43,927	208,075	116,349

Personal Income and Employment by Area: Houston-The Woodlands-Sugar Land, TX

(Thousands of dollars, except as noted.)

| Year | Personal income, total | Derivation of personal income | | | | | | | | Per capita personal income (dollars) | Population (persons) | Total employment |
| | | Earnings by place of work | | | Less: Contributions for government social insurance | Plus: Adjustment for residence | Equals: Net earnings by place of residence | Plus: Dividends, interest, and rent | Plus: Personal current transfer receipts | | | |
		Nonfarm	Farm	Total								
1970	9,359,224	8,128,677	28,654	8,157,331	527,413	-74,349	7,555,569	1,305,406	498,249	4,240	2,207,116	1,022,725
1971	10,267,131	8,894,756	28,463	8,923,219	594,467	-117,671	8,211,081	1,458,027	598,023	4,513	2,275,020	1,053,329
1972	11,387,434	9,901,050	32,560	9,933,610	697,119	-153,914	9,082,577	1,620,638	684,219	4,881	2,333,148	1,105,219
1973	12,901,143	11,326,510	64,053	11,390,563	931,233	-205,257	10,254,073	1,831,342	815,728	5,371	2,401,849	1,187,670
1974	15,333,368	13,502,750	60,173	13,562,923	1,140,478	-216,332	12,206,113	2,164,938	962,317	6,183	2,479,921	1,264,423
1975	18,149,058	15,962,486	60,526	16,023,012	1,320,396	-165,827	14,536,789	2,416,939	1,195,330	7,014	2,587,627	1,336,396
1976	20,806,358	18,545,698	27,670	18,573,368	1,570,081	-118,601	16,884,686	2,594,763	1,326,909	7,717	2,696,239	1,417,454
1977	23,738,842	21,411,387	67,965	21,479,352	1,816,811	-185,043	19,477,498	2,848,120	1,413,224	8,477	2,800,536	1,511,549
1978	28,053,834	25,502,679	32,374	25,535,053	2,223,125	-231,447	23,080,481	3,386,542	1,586,811	9,622	2,915,493	1,631,614
1979	32,753,401	29,880,688	67,348	29,948,036	2,726,076	-285,482	26,936,478	4,007,910	1,809,013	10,800	3,032,641	1,734,505
1980	38,342,568	34,806,575	44,589	34,851,164	3,205,119	-344,911	31,301,134	4,901,945	2,139,489	12,085	3,172,859	1,823,264
1981	45,604,291	41,379,084	37,608	41,416,692	4,104,376	-364,642	36,947,674	6,196,987	2,459,630	13,780	3,309,381	1,961,475
1982	50,603,018	45,112,034	17,728	45,129,762	4,584,155	-387,445	40,158,162	7,537,275	2,907,581	14,438	3,504,930	2,009,330
1983	51,615,508	44,694,129	43,932	44,738,061	4,497,421	-366,729	39,873,911	8,279,561	3,462,036	14,316	3,605,388	1,927,450
1984	54,984,610	47,258,042	21,480	47,279,522	4,858,734	-382,208	42,038,580	9,309,380	3,636,650	15,178	3,622,633	1,979,788
1985	57,793,830	48,932,715	91,236	49,023,951	5,058,357	-308,419	43,657,175	10,270,837	3,865,818	15,927	3,628,588	1,979,670
1986	57,624,679	48,113,481	49,160	48,162,641	4,916,134	-272,658	42,973,849	10,283,816	4,367,014	15,710	3,668,133	1,894,904
1987	58,410,772	48,745,125	42,192	48,787,317	4,881,212	-224,470	43,681,635	10,177,848	4,551,289	16,109	3,626,052	1,925,079
1988	63,013,300	52,787,551	112,518	52,900,069	5,486,529	-289,877	47,123,663	11,162,352	4,727,285	17,430	3,615,294	2,000,883
1989	68,672,225	57,955,088	87,195	58,042,283	6,026,368	-345,623	51,670,292	11,855,555	5,146,378	18,711	3,670,089	2,075,840
1990	75,811,049	64,229,024	70,910	64,299,934	6,578,646	-431,247	57,290,041	12,763,722	5,757,286	20,079	3,775,620	2,171,989
1991	80,189,049	68,217,795	95,407	68,313,202	7,166,962	-488,862	60,657,378	13,058,815	6,472,856	20,641	3,884,885	2,231,824
1992	86,984,024	73,858,873	86,891	73,945,764	7,594,953	-517,876	65,832,935	13,343,092	7,807,997	21,802	3,989,770	2,228,085
1993	91,238,366	77,380,665	80,701	77,461,366	7,899,739	-540,777	69,020,850	13,666,607	8,550,909	22,387	4,075,564	2,271,445
1994	95,209,292	80,350,595	100,474	80,451,069	8,337,138	-572,265	71,541,666	14,431,027	9,236,599	22,923	4,153,355	2,333,616
1995	102,555,928	85,862,865	109,662	85,972,527	8,851,912	-622,251	76,498,364	15,981,616	10,075,948	24,259	4,227,574	2,402,453
1996	111,691,346	94,023,956	86,489	94,110,445	9,450,817	-699,915	83,959,713	17,042,104	10,689,529	25,887	4,314,589	2,471,047
1997	123,473,024	105,106,474	103,190	105,209,664	10,346,003	-813,227	94,050,434	18,264,916	11,157,674	28,016	4,407,210	2,579,858
1998	135,682,671	116,187,125	96,728	116,283,853	11,307,087	-915,769	104,060,997	20,222,056	11,399,618	30,059	4,513,913	2,704,046
1999	142,313,795	122,882,811	119,355	123,002,166	11,887,878	-966,359	110,147,929	20,305,784	11,860,082	30,785	4,622,857	2,735,747
2000	156,340,177	134,785,426	86,633	134,872,059	12,816,910	-1,116,483	120,938,666	22,799,331	12,602,180	33,140	4,717,507	2,817,971
2001	164,765,751	143,046,975	91,011	143,137,986	13,603,411	-1,277,626	128,256,949	22,647,956	13,860,846	34,199	4,817,815	2,877,532
2002	163,805,402	141,227,640	98,590	141,326,230	13,726,085	-1,304,586	126,295,559	22,145,671	15,364,172	33,179	4,937,081	2,901,048
2003	170,545,050	145,782,848	143,051	145,925,899	14,246,884	-1,312,866	130,366,149	23,776,076	16,402,825	33,863	5,036,393	2,921,541
2004	183,516,155	157,582,145	159,325	157,741,470	15,097,326	-1,491,241	141,152,903	25,053,857	17,309,395	35,755	5,132,602	2,974,098
2005	201,474,018	169,551,763	150,889	169,702,652	16,153,198	-1,736,719	151,812,735	30,231,958	19,429,325	38,495	5,233,729	3,078,388
2006	225,855,731	189,306,211	155,725	189,461,936	17,472,182	-2,084,706	169,905,048	35,209,515	20,741,168	41,643	5,423,615	3,209,343
2007	241,389,766	201,894,405	115,840	202,010,245	19,068,874	-2,517,084	180,424,287	38,198,837	22,766,642	43,565	5,540,882	3,331,799
2008	269,180,303	219,569,956	94,266	219,664,222	20,213,918	-2,735,468	196,714,836	46,172,203	26,293,264	47,421	5,676,381	3,456,148
2009	253,135,078	206,067,421	69,279	206,136,700	19,990,690	-2,496,857	183,649,153	40,564,912	28,921,013	43,448	5,826,108	3,431,276
2010	267,817,259	217,718,918	60,139	217,779,057	20,546,425	-2,417,936	194,814,696	40,251,626	32,750,937	45,031	5,947,419	3,435,171
2011	291,011,520	235,971,237	43,018	236,014,255	19,425,557	-2,806,666	213,782,032	43,073,728	34,155,760	48,038	6,057,947	3,546,818
2012	321,849,013	258,966,085	78,594	259,044,679	20,883,791	-3,262,915	234,897,973	52,963,006	33,988,034	52,048	6,183,726	3,675,499
2013	326,298,579	267,753,821	139,295	267,893,116	25,025,010	-3,500,260	239,367,846	51,684,230	35,246,503	51,552	6,329,553	3,809,211
2014	354,491,321	290,190,214	105,604	290,295,818	26,752,898	-3,872,809	259,670,111	57,428,975	37,392,235	54,563	6,496,862	3,949,297
2015	362,014,112	290,155,191	139,872	290,295,063	27,696,023	-3,851,610	258,747,430	63,073,612	40,193,070	54,322	6,664,187	4,047,837
2016	348,362,610	280,928,635	66,728	280,995,363	27,532,364	-3,673,110	249,789,889	55,914,443	42,658,278	51,245	6,798,010	4,040,483
2017	363,677,100	293,008,886	87,345	293,096,231	28,606,367	-3,344,982	261,144,882	58,419,441	44,112,777	52,765	6,892,427	4,084,715
2018	398,715,792	398,688,141	27,651	316,339,334	30,099,500	-3,586,971	282,652,863	70,424,233	45,638,696	57,154	6,976,147	4,296,886
2019	416,121,512	416,083,078	38,434	331,466,308	31,180,912	-3,763,153	296,522,243	71,486,389	48,112,880	58,890	7,066,141	4,401,003

Personal Income and Employment by Area: Huntington-Ashland, WV-KY-OH

(Thousands of dollars, except as noted.)

Year	Personal income, total	Earnings by place of work			Less: Contributions for government social insurance	Plus: Adjustment for residence	Equals: Net earnings by place of residence	Plus: Dividends, interest, and rent	Plus: Personal current transfer receipts	Per capita personal income (dollars)	Population (persons)	Total employment
		Nonfarm	Farm	Total								
1970	1,061,462	857,286	4,535	861,821	66,999	9,325	804,147	126,820	130,495	3,175	334,330	119,730
1971	1,160,546	923,446	3,869	927,315	73,953	14,265	867,627	139,138	153,781	3,412	340,145	121,125
1972	1,246,078	978,721	5,675	984,396	81,687	22,351	925,060	150,575	170,443	3,628	343,475	120,225
1973	1,377,893	1,080,280	7,086	1,087,366	102,949	27,085	1,011,502	169,962	196,429	4,017	342,989	123,834
1974	1,552,031	1,193,458	6,952	1,200,410	117,003	41,787	1,125,194	198,127	228,710	4,507	344,384	126,438
1975	1,733,898	1,297,338	7,304	1,304,642	125,815	53,081	1,231,908	222,855	279,135	4,995	347,122	126,903
1976	1,959,834	1,492,663	6,858	1,499,521	147,512	57,738	1,409,747	246,611	303,476	5,516	355,311	131,120
1977	2,196,243	1,685,871	5,480	1,691,351	165,477	69,580	1,595,454	280,731	320,058	6,085	360,951	136,556
1978	2,467,240	1,919,632	4,395	1,924,027	194,916	81,807	1,810,918	307,691	348,631	6,766	364,651	141,485
1979	2,773,857	2,157,547	2,983	2,160,530	226,166	96,091	2,030,455	344,191	399,211	7,497	370,018	143,365
1980	3,049,638	2,268,394	1,439	2,269,833	238,617	110,021	2,141,237	419,254	489,147	8,171	373,228	141,228
1981	3,299,515	2,400,698	2,632	2,403,330	271,413	103,947	2,235,864	512,416	551,235	8,852	372,735	138,629
1982	3,444,302	2,402,798	4,214	2,407,012	280,021	122,566	2,249,557	585,926	608,819	9,287	370,867	132,782
1983	3,548,829	2,409,359	-247	2,409,112	283,358	129,416	2,255,170	620,604	673,055	9,541	371,942	129,173
1984	3,822,421	2,586,737	6,685	2,593,422	311,280	150,405	2,432,547	693,126	696,748	10,361	368,941	131,431
1985	4,024,213	2,719,706	3,597	2,723,303	331,973	166,246	2,557,576	723,641	742,996	11,008	365,559	132,535
1986	4,143,169	2,787,128	1,026	2,788,154	353,825	176,771	2,611,100	750,755	781,314	11,473	361,118	133,493
1987	4,313,934	2,948,968	-1,505	2,947,463	371,417	177,330	2,753,376	746,120	814,438	12,049	358,041	135,685
1988	4,573,525	3,169,933	-1,587	3,168,346	414,365	179,757	2,933,738	783,506	856,281	12,885	354,959	139,421
1989	4,879,764	3,345,023	447	3,345,470	441,148	186,775	3,091,097	874,051	914,616	13,805	353,470	142,984
1990	5,197,872	3,589,578	3,579	3,593,157	481,096	204,166	3,316,227	888,590	993,055	14,744	352,539	148,238
1991	5,426,046	3,698,340	5,010	3,703,350	503,022	217,675	3,418,003	900,025	1,108,018	15,291	354,853	148,269
1992	5,883,409	4,018,230	6,060	4,024,290	538,780	238,521	3,724,031	916,932	1,242,446	16,481	356,976	151,101
1993	6,088,680	4,129,321	3,146	4,132,467	571,443	262,601	3,823,625	947,059	1,317,996	16,901	360,258	152,539
1994	6,338,896	4,321,992	5,192	4,327,184	599,514	265,036	3,992,706	983,590	1,362,600	17,527	361,659	156,273
1995	6,551,783	4,362,824	1,321	4,364,145	614,520	312,979	4,062,604	1,048,263	1,440,916	18,064	362,701	159,781
1996	6,808,380	4,457,383	-24	4,457,359	631,305	350,363	4,176,417	1,117,236	1,514,727	18,755	363,025	161,222
1997	7,169,614	4,687,313	2,050	4,689,363	655,381	375,208	4,409,190	1,187,730	1,572,694	19,738	363,240	163,757
1998	7,440,873	4,836,468	681	4,837,149	681,362	380,971	4,536,758	1,280,222	1,623,893	20,512	362,749	165,849
1999	7,601,262	4,980,673	-2,955	4,977,718	701,224	400,416	4,676,910	1,242,635	1,681,717	20,980	362,305	166,898
2000	7,965,159	5,190,487	1,265	5,191,752	739,539	414,508	4,866,721	1,317,991	1,780,447	21,992	362,183	167,419
2001	8,389,131	5,412,846	-2,099	5,410,747	744,474	429,224	5,095,497	1,329,065	1,964,569	23,247	360,868	165,386
2002	8,683,434	5,594,871	-5,935	5,588,936	751,659	437,645	5,274,922	1,293,093	2,115,419	24,080	360,609	164,855
2003	8,872,656	5,795,973	-1,476	5,794,497	788,398	422,956	5,429,055	1,260,750	2,182,851	24,515	361,922	166,029
2004	9,068,846	6,045,124	-2	6,045,122	813,956	406,157	5,637,323	1,198,126	2,233,397	25,068	361,774	167,969
2005	9,402,923	6,266,232	-957	6,265,275	844,192	427,379	5,848,462	1,205,874	2,348,587	25,985	361,864	168,972
2006	10,015,084	6,627,434	-3,951	6,623,483	864,949	453,930	6,212,464	1,301,755	2,500,865	27,600	362,868	170,979
2007	10,585,550	6,931,945	-7,187	6,924,758	877,728	421,633	6,468,663	1,462,478	2,654,409	29,141	363,249	174,932
2008	11,294,665	7,294,364	-6,447	7,287,917	902,522	386,400	6,771,795	1,577,407	2,945,463	31,038	363,898	175,291
2009	11,474,467	7,256,839	-3,043	7,253,796	907,676	435,744	6,781,864	1,512,665	3,179,938	31,460	364,731	169,689
2010	11,803,297	7,464,473	-4,463	7,460,010	924,320	482,174	7,017,864	1,455,573	3,329,860	32,334	365,040	168,930
2011	12,288,958	7,718,357	-2,368	7,715,989	846,846	436,318	7,305,461	1,610,401	3,373,096	33,675	364,927	169,348
2012	12,539,358	7,884,801	-210	7,884,591	870,133	437,495	7,451,953	1,684,081	3,403,324	34,374	364,794	170,514
2013	12,422,861	7,918,847	2,614	7,921,461	975,180	406,639	7,352,920	1,604,476	3,465,465	34,139	363,889	169,741
2014	12,836,257	8,101,831	-1,105	8,100,726	1,010,637	399,691	7,489,780	1,705,757	3,640,720	35,377	362,837	169,719
2015	13,141,779	8,161,319	1,781	8,163,100	1,023,303	468,434	7,608,231	1,761,522	3,772,026	36,408	360,957	168,438
2016	13,135,325	7,982,401	-838	7,981,563	1,025,555	556,283	7,512,291	1,778,962	3,844,072	36,603	358,857	166,717
2017	13,419,673	8,117,011	-5,661	8,111,350	1,059,971	582,798	7,634,177	1,847,250	3,938,246	37,646	356,474	167,351
2018	14,494,768	14,503,369	-8,601	8,805,199	1,109,300	630,231	8,326,130	1,986,431	4,182,207	40,368	359,069	172,660
2019	14,721,817	14,727,800	-5,983	9,079,812	1,133,475	438,022	8,384,359	2,012,146	4,325,312	41,368	355,873	173,996

Personal Income and Employment by Area: Huntsville, AL

(Thousands of dollars, except as noted.)

Year	Personal income, total	Derivation of personal income								Per capita personal income (dollars)	Population (persons)	Total employment
		Earnings by place of work			Less: Contributions for government social insurance	Plus: Adjustment for residence	Equals: Net earnings by place of residence	Plus: Dividends, interest, and rent	Plus: Personal current transfer receipts			
		Nonfarm	Farm	Total								
1970	904,666	873,867	19,625	893,492	43,750	-126,294	723,448	133,007	48,211	3,962	228,314	107,133
1971	999,215	955,338	26,234	981,572	48,042	-144,472	789,058	154,603	55,554	4,335	230,509	106,235
1972	1,083,376	1,029,043	26,466	1,055,509	55,275	-147,449	852,785	168,389	62,202	4,663	232,339	109,439
1973	1,167,328	1,086,939	35,145	1,122,084	68,262	-147,250	906,572	186,355	74,401	5,005	233,247	111,439
1974	1,257,789	1,154,541	29,060	1,183,601	76,269	-150,845	956,487	209,969	91,333	5,424	231,872	112,513
1975	1,339,700	1,205,924	21,649	1,227,573	81,776	-154,615	991,182	226,889	121,629	5,770	232,194	110,559
1976	1,487,058	1,332,981	31,163	1,364,144	95,385	-159,128	1,109,631	245,271	132,156	6,337	234,646	113,836
1977	1,626,884	1,482,801	18,543	1,501,344	109,274	-172,591	1,219,479	271,369	136,036	6,866	236,952	119,368
1978	1,830,708	1,662,427	24,866	1,687,293	126,390	-187,817	1,373,086	311,502	146,120	7,689	238,094	125,751
1979	2,019,757	1,831,386	33,993	1,865,379	145,226	-216,300	1,503,853	345,885	170,019	8,417	239,958	126,654
1980	2,232,060	2,012,098	6,819	2,018,917	157,763	-251,689	1,609,465	412,593	210,002	9,162	243,620	126,604
1981	2,507,130	2,237,668	29,027	2,266,695	190,810	-291,987	1,783,898	490,528	232,704	10,201	245,771	128,803
1982	2,743,765	2,442,661	28,965	2,471,626	213,585	-323,357	1,934,684	551,924	257,157	11,012	249,166	131,353
1983	3,024,815	2,809,057	-7,338	2,801,719	263,464	-384,785	2,153,470	591,960	279,385	11,915	253,867	139,295
1984	3,462,975	3,244,000	23,922	3,267,922	312,351	-460,090	2,495,481	672,356	295,138	13,401	258,407	149,177
1985	3,844,542	3,677,065	18,660	3,695,725	365,035	-545,450	2,785,240	740,936	318,366	14,530	264,588	158,683
1986	4,172,807	4,038,312	10,465	4,048,777	407,722	-603,322	3,037,733	797,364	337,710	15,441	270,237	166,030
1987	4,552,696	4,420,443	13,831	4,434,274	445,998	-646,247	3,342,029	865,399	345,268	16,454	276,697	174,660
1988	4,987,694	4,878,755	28,462	4,907,217	508,593	-740,551	3,658,073	963,425	366,196	17,577	283,769	182,016
1989	5,414,253	5,178,900	20,431	5,199,331	546,312	-765,364	3,887,655	1,105,746	420,852	18,696	289,588	186,585
1990	5,788,609	5,560,434	14,241	5,574,675	604,328	-829,780	4,140,567	1,181,084	466,958	19,666	294,353	191,461
1991	6,154,316	5,840,931	30,927	5,871,858	640,791	-832,534	4,398,533	1,221,703	534,080	20,375	302,052	192,008
1992	6,694,265	6,378,932	32,797	6,411,729	699,801	-918,549	4,793,379	1,293,851	607,035	21,513	311,170	195,615
1993	6,873,823	6,538,408	18,591	6,556,999	726,486	-941,644	4,888,869	1,334,485	650,469	21,414	320,998	200,042
1994	7,106,675	6,691,189	42,729	6,733,918	762,922	-985,929	4,985,067	1,441,410	680,198	21,825	325,620	196,887
1995	7,446,835	6,941,009	6,460	6,947,469	796,018	-1,037,016	5,114,435	1,589,373	743,027	22,873	325,571	200,903
1996	7,759,869	7,047,168	37,511	7,084,679	811,714	-989,520	5,283,445	1,679,751	796,673	23,692	327,532	204,454
1997	8,269,832	7,431,943	8,422	7,440,365	861,785	-949,176	5,629,404	1,801,077	839,351	25,039	330,281	209,852
1998	8,861,866	7,954,029	24,699	7,978,728	917,217	-988,959	6,072,552	1,923,556	865,758	26,333	336,527	216,761
1999	9,075,793	8,172,540	27,566	8,200,106	952,310	-999,169	6,248,627	1,906,523	920,643	26,727	339,572	218,936
2000	9,775,629	8,740,684	31,325	8,772,009	1,015,421	-1,059,724	6,696,864	2,073,297	1,005,468	28,420	343,972	224,393
2001	10,045,512	8,995,422	26,206	9,021,628	1,034,389	-1,099,829	6,887,410	2,025,861	1,132,241	28,829	348,453	226,046
2002	10,384,307	9,419,376	-4,547	9,414,829	1,082,576	-1,164,233	7,168,020	1,978,583	1,237,704	29,325	354,116	225,574
2003	11,018,280	10,008,306	55,213	10,063,519	1,151,578	-1,250,196	7,661,745	2,017,083	1,339,452	30,613	359,920	230,523
2004	11,777,501	10,541,192	78,233	10,619,425	1,203,659	-1,268,339	8,147,427	2,192,105	1,437,969	32,245	365,248	237,472
2005	12,666,929	11,252,033	61,251	11,313,284	1,288,577	-1,349,335	8,675,372	2,418,036	1,573,521	33,980	372,777	244,689
2006	13,700,908	12,121,847	54,294	12,176,141	1,388,149	-1,475,261	9,312,731	2,656,164	1,732,013	35,789	382,821	252,344
2007	14,763,343	12,825,620	35,555	12,861,175	1,478,082	-1,491,648	9,891,445	2,965,806	1,906,092	37,669	391,922	263,130
2008	15,863,844	13,400,036	55,978	13,456,014	1,566,758	-1,475,356	10,413,900	3,255,566	2,194,378	39,427	402,361	267,107
2009	16,025,728	13,748,559	35,195	13,783,754	1,601,339	-1,511,384	10,671,031	2,962,329	2,392,368	38,880	412,182	262,881
2010	16,864,018	14,210,953	838	14,211,791	1,670,117	-1,471,486	11,070,188	3,105,312	2,688,518	40,221	419,279	262,764
2011	17,763,358	14,662,082	34,007	14,696,089	1,525,538	-1,485,955	11,684,596	3,267,160	2,811,602	41,791	425,049	266,691
2012	18,287,609	14,923,818	38,916	14,962,734	1,558,473	-1,456,825	11,947,436	3,490,445	2,849,728	42,542	429,876	267,871
2013	18,444,945	15,220,288	90,486	15,310,774	1,814,591	-1,437,912	12,058,271	3,428,180	2,958,494	42,375	435,275	271,678
2014	19,152,151	15,737,690	34,482	15,772,172	1,872,669	-1,500,865	12,398,638	3,632,024	3,121,489	43,507	440,212	274,632
2015	20,028,140	16,354,869	36,022	16,390,891	1,946,220	-1,537,404	12,907,267	3,817,557	3,303,316	45,071	444,373	280,652
2016	20,761,244	16,890,912	8,516	16,899,428	1,994,177	-1,509,599	13,395,652	3,948,056	3,417,536	46,215	449,232	287,058
2017	21,738,101	17,716,028	32,479	17,748,507	2,088,325	-1,567,707	14,092,475	4,113,847	3,531,779	47,729	455,448	292,917
2018	23,251,202	23,242,725	8,477	18,701,564	2,220,337	-1,587,392	14,893,835	4,506,977	3,850,390	50,199	463,181	301,888
2019	24,586,808	24,573,166	13,642	19,932,993	2,356,523	-1,645,814	15,930,656	4,559,303	4,096,849	52,110	471,824	310,152

Personal Income and Employment by Area: Idaho Falls, ID

(Thousands of dollars, except as noted.)

Year	Personal income, total	Earnings by place of work			Less: Contributions for government social insurance	Plus: Adjustment for residence	Equals: Net earnings by place of residence	Plus: Dividends, interest, and rent	Plus: Personal current transfer receipts	Per capita personal income (dollars)	Population (persons)	Total employment
		Nonfarm	Farm	Total								
1970	249,121	198,596	24,705	223,301	14,927	-10,811	197,563	34,689	16,869	3,705	67,248	31,286
1971	269,269	212,764	23,431	236,195	16,559	-10,097	209,539	39,780	19,950	4,001	67,297	31,832
1972	304,063	241,079	26,886	267,965	19,582	-10,943	237,440	43,715	22,908	4,370	69,575	33,559
1973	351,493	266,228	44,126	310,354	24,925	-11,685	273,744	51,777	25,972	5,006	70,208	34,784
1974	410,130	302,807	57,679	360,486	29,228	-11,978	319,280	60,750	30,100	5,605	73,174	36,116
1975	444,191	347,607	34,227	381,834	33,247	-13,891	334,696	71,791	37,704	5,906	75,210	37,509
1976	500,212	408,781	27,596	436,377	39,932	-18,324	378,121	77,337	44,754	6,487	77,106	40,884
1977	553,282	469,082	20,883	489,965	46,295	-23,854	419,816	87,235	46,231	6,943	79,685	43,056
1978	616,679	536,043	21,740	557,783	53,797	-32,363	471,623	97,935	47,121	7,444	82,839	45,361
1979	664,981	583,963	15,097	599,060	61,177	-37,303	500,580	108,652	55,749	7,902	84,150	44,826
1980	748,365	627,866	31,508	659,374	65,989	-37,807	555,578	126,756	66,031	8,808	84,969	44,180
1981	819,037	667,660	40,290	707,950	74,874	-41,904	591,172	151,485	76,380	9,496	86,247	42,968
1982	861,468	687,115	38,654	725,769	78,757	-45,064	601,948	176,989	82,531	10,023	85,951	42,575
1983	934,549	741,751	50,722	792,473	85,383	-53,762	653,328	191,574	89,647	10,764	86,820	43,606
1984	1,013,489	817,070	41,824	858,894	96,249	-53,399	709,246	210,053	94,190	11,556	87,700	44,662
1985	1,104,973	897,409	41,031	938,440	107,543	-58,347	772,550	230,968	101,455	12,538	88,130	46,059
1986	1,148,805	949,246	40,198	989,444	114,285	-67,189	807,970	232,031	108,804	12,948	88,724	46,656
1987	1,206,166	1,003,024	46,630	1,049,654	118,797	-71,136	859,721	232,376	114,069	13,419	89,885	47,643
1988	1,284,775	1,066,947	41,180	1,108,127	125,814	-66,438	915,875	244,333	124,567	14,226	90,313	49,146
1989	1,411,362	1,139,087	62,426	1,201,513	136,728	-67,336	997,449	278,162	135,751	15,569	90,651	50,522
1990	1,526,182	1,256,424	76,906	1,333,330	162,007	-79,336	1,091,987	284,342	149,853	16,569	92,109	53,055
1991	1,594,702	1,345,490	56,415	1,401,905	176,974	-94,526	1,130,405	296,781	167,516	16,827	94,772	55,402
1992	1,730,733	1,444,051	65,525	1,509,576	187,529	-98,697	1,223,350	316,630	190,753	17,770	97,397	56,340
1993	1,832,141	1,520,859	76,074	1,596,933	197,824	-106,344	1,292,765	331,296	208,080	18,514	98,961	58,099
1994	1,897,700	1,576,824	49,431	1,626,255	209,700	-100,477	1,316,078	359,809	221,813	18,914	100,332	59,318
1995	1,977,785	1,601,801	59,956	1,661,757	217,304	-99,172	1,345,281	388,224	244,280	19,623	100,789	58,985
1996	2,036,575	1,661,754	64,420	1,726,174	224,566	-139,057	1,362,551	413,029	260,995	20,202	100,809	60,883
1997	2,124,714	1,743,803	48,598	1,792,401	234,734	-143,215	1,414,452	437,547	272,715	20,932	101,505	62,038
1998	2,234,201	1,859,080	62,680	1,921,760	248,314	-151,122	1,522,324	434,547	277,330	21,813	102,425	63,214
1999	2,365,128	1,954,862	72,803	2,027,665	258,050	-146,309	1,623,306	443,213	298,609	22,863	103,450	64,963
2000	2,526,370	2,080,952	80,240	2,161,192	274,220	-158,336	1,728,636	468,641	329,093	24,048	105,055	66,613
2001	2,720,949	2,239,280	76,805	2,316,085	267,143	-193,621	1,855,321	501,393	364,235	25,649	106,082	67,441
2002	2,848,892	2,341,230	110,245	2,451,475	279,253	-194,554	1,977,668	480,959	390,265	26,435	107,768	68,159
2003	2,983,031	2,446,016	62,414	2,508,430	294,923	-195,111	2,018,396	548,824	415,811	27,134	109,937	70,441
2004	3,252,470	2,581,460	102,969	2,684,429	311,420	-179,185	2,193,824	603,675	454,971	28,740	113,168	72,823
2005	3,527,326	2,752,800	72,234	2,825,034	333,388	-184,490	2,307,156	723,296	496,874	30,354	116,208	76,232
2006	3,930,731	3,066,014	90,871	3,156,885	368,773	-195,770	2,592,342	788,211	550,178	32,761	119,981	79,150
2007	4,213,646	3,207,009	135,694	3,342,703	390,283	-199,333	2,753,087	876,037	584,522	33,925	124,203	82,923
2008	4,348,926	3,180,720	136,616	3,317,336	401,827	-172,303	2,743,206	930,137	675,583	33,883	128,353	82,656
2009	4,229,421	3,269,615	97,431	3,367,046	410,042	-163,250	2,793,754	712,062	723,605	32,133	131,621	80,095
2010	4,386,201	3,395,392	88,385	3,483,777	435,459	-193,223	2,855,095	739,022	792,084	32,779	133,813	80,052
2011	4,591,232	3,340,142	123,713	3,463,855	388,488	-198,645	2,876,722	914,793	799,717	34,028	134,926	80,140
2012	4,876,179	3,443,475	101,683	3,545,158	391,065	-160,012	2,994,081	1,058,363	823,735	35,814	136,153	79,832
2013	4,911,577	3,591,116	111,651	3,702,767	441,543	-153,302	3,107,922	950,529	853,126	35,902	136,807	81,086
2014	5,095,465	3,735,299	94,485	3,829,784	452,743	-142,415	3,234,626	991,847	868,992	36,973	137,815	82,789
2015	5,586,540	4,048,699	101,055	4,149,754	481,023	-175,808	3,492,923	1,165,586	928,031	40,057	139,464	85,508
2016	5,932,855	4,222,088	88,311	4,310,399	504,322	-196,185	3,609,892	1,356,398	966,565	41,662	142,405	88,647
2017	6,263,528	4,506,284	84,014	4,590,298	536,665	-227,868	3,825,765	1,429,155	1,008,608	43,006	145,643	90,866
2018	6,844,788	6,758,968	85,820	4,999,076	577,357	-266,314	4,155,405	1,598,151	1,091,232	46,113	148,436	94,318
2019	7,189,022	7,084,739	104,283	5,314,936	611,245	-291,510	4,412,181	1,608,308	1,168,533	47,443	151,530	97,417

Personal Income and Employment by Area: Indianapolis-Carmel-Anderson, IN

(Thousands of dollars, except as noted.)

Year	Personal income, total	Earnings by place of work			Less: Contributions for government social insurance	Plus: Adjustment for residence	Equals: Net earnings by place of residence	Plus: Dividends, interest, and rent	Plus: Personal current transfer receipts	Per capita personal income (dollars)	Population (persons)	Total employment
		Nonfarm	Farm	Total								
1970	5,360,907	4,622,519	39,661	4,662,180	310,573	-84,768	4,266,839	739,463	354,605	4,164	1,287,512	599,216
1971	5,839,732	4,978,349	70,109	5,048,458	346,518	-95,670	4,606,270	812,287	421,175	4,506	1,295,884	600,061
1972	6,365,329	5,482,566	56,661	5,539,227	404,591	-106,019	5,028,617	870,883	465,829	4,872	1,306,519	616,990
1973	7,184,781	6,138,364	152,176	6,290,540	522,040	-121,213	5,647,287	979,685	557,809	5,478	1,311,545	646,904
1974	7,780,405	6,615,844	91,430	6,707,274	584,815	-131,081	5,991,378	1,125,819	663,208	5,892	1,320,524	656,064
1975	8,387,294	6,899,935	137,348	7,037,283	599,376	-139,061	6,298,846	1,243,125	845,323	6,362	1,318,435	637,432
1976	9,268,165	7,728,948	139,556	7,868,504	683,115	-153,850	7,031,539	1,336,461	900,165	7,010	1,322,178	654,608
1977	10,288,075	8,706,575	91,621	8,798,196	771,125	-171,716	7,855,355	1,484,625	948,095	7,749	1,327,653	676,374
1978	11,464,111	9,736,240	100,568	9,836,808	887,910	-191,630	8,757,268	1,664,203	1,042,640	8,574	1,337,003	701,877
1979	12,664,452	10,755,794	91,570	10,847,364	1,017,331	-212,498	9,617,535	1,852,067	1,194,850	9,435	1,342,252	718,694
1980	13,863,701	11,281,584	71,980	11,353,564	1,059,244	-217,028	10,077,292	2,260,333	1,526,076	10,279	1,348,738	706,615
1981	15,190,610	12,131,363	55,427	12,186,790	1,227,322	-225,997	10,733,471	2,783,736	1,673,403	11,247	1,350,644	699,352
1982	15,720,656	12,254,495	47,358	12,301,853	1,262,594	-208,770	10,830,489	3,047,390	1,842,777	11,633	1,351,396	681,888
1983	16,745,780	13,091,688	-12,281	13,079,407	1,354,195	-201,043	11,524,169	3,230,212	1,991,399	12,381	1,352,538	690,577
1984	18,595,927	14,633,969	91,586	14,725,555	1,547,881	-260,579	12,917,095	3,588,011	2,090,821	13,664	1,360,966	724,435
1985	19,978,591	15,837,763	91,139	15,928,902	1,707,527	-284,544	13,936,831	3,833,871	2,207,889	14,612	1,367,229	748,013
1986	21,288,267	17,030,091	52,965	17,083,056	1,846,264	-312,443	14,924,349	4,023,180	2,340,738	15,479	1,375,291	774,534
1987	22,729,803	18,361,542	78,028	18,439,570	1,969,893	-321,382	16,148,295	4,191,441	2,390,067	16,370	1,388,481	801,322
1988	24,601,442	19,975,913	34,077	20,009,990	2,210,822	-334,944	17,464,224	4,588,349	2,548,869	17,595	1,398,243	826,484
1989	26,893,524	21,482,143	107,608	21,589,751	2,383,415	-369,621	18,836,715	5,279,662	2,777,147	19,048	1,411,888	856,717
1990	28,818,108	22,980,471	102,593	23,083,064	2,636,267	-397,893	20,048,904	5,747,817	3,021,387	20,134	1,431,307	881,268
1991	30,124,193	24,337,484	23,006	24,360,490	2,823,491	-409,169	21,127,830	5,637,070	3,359,293	20,669	1,457,442	887,840
1992	32,604,860	26,165,767	93,135	26,258,902	3,012,842	-360,895	22,885,165	5,855,270	3,864,425	22,015	1,481,005	898,464
1993	34,567,038	27,711,309	120,286	27,831,595	3,201,070	-359,879	24,270,646	6,195,997	4,100,395	22,961	1,505,485	922,306
1994	36,964,595	29,621,276	94,716	29,715,992	3,476,896	-356,744	25,882,352	6,785,940	4,296,303	24,169	1,529,405	948,056
1995	38,684,993	30,873,402	43,899	30,917,301	3,642,370	-346,062	26,928,869	7,394,706	4,361,418	24,934	1,551,504	975,060
1996	40,957,147	32,614,207	137,691	32,751,898	3,801,785	-371,019	28,579,094	7,841,308	4,536,745	26,027	1,573,626	992,151
1997	43,291,995	34,702,931	135,600	34,838,531	4,032,517	-395,362	30,410,652	8,183,773	4,697,570	27,145	1,594,815	1,015,309
1998	47,558,389	38,270,405	82,284	38,352,689	4,339,653	-478,054	33,534,982	9,186,422	4,836,985	29,440	1,615,438	1,044,041
1999	49,985,270	40,931,923	52,781	40,984,704	4,606,376	-510,985	35,867,343	9,018,044	5,099,883	30,488	1,639,509	1,070,835
2000	54,520,213	44,493,137	99,289	44,592,426	4,924,340	-560,648	39,107,438	9,862,820	5,549,955	32,765	1,663,995	1,099,383
2001	56,382,995	45,999,363	116,763	46,116,126	5,039,789	-644,793	40,431,544	9,806,233	6,145,218	33,418	1,687,209	1,095,475
2002	57,208,581	46,824,827	55,940	46,880,767	5,147,929	-667,603	41,065,235	9,564,114	6,579,232	33,494	1,708,018	1,089,132
2003	58,240,591	47,640,695	140,850	47,781,545	5,310,240	-686,371	41,784,934	9,559,545	6,896,112	33,679	1,729,297	1,096,058
2004	61,099,478	50,084,514	235,555	50,320,069	5,612,409	-766,909	43,940,751	9,863,514	7,295,213	34,901	1,750,639	1,114,589
2005	63,485,929	51,987,105	148,890	52,135,995	5,887,014	-805,520	45,443,461	10,093,108	7,949,360	35,808	1,772,959	1,133,886
2006	68,052,649	55,021,414	128,023	55,149,437	6,242,263	-835,701	48,071,473	11,412,149	8,569,027	37,792	1,800,724	1,153,305
2007	70,137,979	56,357,800	169,460	56,527,260	6,437,311	-811,353	49,278,596	11,799,083	9,060,300	38,400	1,826,515	1,176,677
2008	74,001,523	58,461,554	264,826	58,726,380	6,674,876	-767,475	51,284,029	12,067,158	10,650,336	39,994	1,850,321	1,180,108
2009	73,964,754	58,378,065	292,435	58,670,500	6,540,780	-813,877	51,315,843	10,799,062	11,849,849	39,480	1,873,460	1,141,299
2010	78,042,433	61,761,057	212,516	61,973,573	6,650,553	-856,638	54,466,382	10,646,261	12,929,790	41,238	1,892,470	1,141,412
2011	83,786,350	65,525,318	317,994	65,843,312	6,138,130	-756,793	58,948,389	11,782,656	13,055,305	43,857	1,910,429	1,165,477
2012	87,958,715	68,666,381	180,323	68,846,704	6,426,397	-626,210	61,794,097	12,824,932	13,339,686	45,598	1,928,986	1,190,492
2013	89,258,553	70,389,473	730,288	71,119,761	7,554,321	-603,953	62,961,487	12,727,438	13,569,628	45,698	1,953,213	1,214,279
2014	92,977,389	72,840,302	369,880	73,210,182	7,817,133	-587,937	64,805,112	13,739,049	14,433,228	47,176	1,970,850	1,239,192
2015	97,253,487	76,156,651	63,847	76,220,498	8,201,978	-531,170	67,487,350	14,688,660	15,077,477	48,948	1,986,872	1,269,165
2016	101,836,116	80,055,491	181,348	80,236,839	8,486,801	-591,641	71,158,397	15,316,025	15,361,694	50,776	2,005,612	1,298,988
2017	106,415,302	84,016,669	82,917	84,099,586	8,848,629	-627,028	74,623,929	16,101,253	15,690,120	52,457	2,028,614	1,318,788
2018	112,423,871	112,311,239	112,632	87,438,813	9,286,837	-566,144	77,585,832	18,418,167	16,419,872	54,778	2,052,368	1,354,093
2019	116,920,707	116,838,445	82,262	91,299,505	9,758,595	-633,344	80,907,566	18,628,876	17,384,265	56,360	2,074,537	1,382,816

Personal Income and Employment by Area: Iowa City, IA

(Thousands of dollars, except as noted.)

Year	Personal income, total	Earnings by place of work			Less: Contributions for government social insurance	Plus: Adjustment for residence	Equals: Net earnings by place of residence	Plus: Dividends, interest, and rent	Plus: Personal current transfer receipts	Per capita personal income (dollars)	Population (persons)	Total employment
		Nonfarm	Farm	Total								
1970	344,368	252,377	28,880	281,257	18,405	-4,060	258,792	63,584	21,992	3,774	91,237	44,389
1971	373,977	278,994	25,278	304,272	21,175	-4,434	278,663	69,347	25,967	4,039	92,581	45,252
1972	408,804	295,816	35,247	331,063	23,487	-1,627	305,949	75,610	27,245	4,417	92,551	45,759
1973	475,914	331,842	55,593	387,435	30,370	-63	357,002	87,063	31,849	5,049	94,258	48,094
1974	510,072	374,099	33,921	408,020	36,076	699	372,643	100,138	37,291	5,339	95,544	50,462
1975	603,951	420,639	61,549	482,188	40,020	2,621	444,789	113,544	45,618	6,293	95,973	52,099
1976	658,636	482,778	39,319	522,097	45,784	4,516	480,829	127,411	50,396	6,667	98,784	54,408
1977	742,509	555,447	33,628	589,075	51,730	3,831	541,176	147,932	53,401	7,485	99,194	56,853
1978	857,185	628,384	60,378	688,762	61,179	4,806	632,389	165,812	58,984	8,604	99,624	59,367
1979	939,303	696,009	47,130	743,139	70,908	9,314	681,545	190,988	66,770	9,233	101,738	60,040
1980	1,025,778	762,195	19,130	781,325	77,533	12,160	715,952	231,024	78,802	10,026	102,308	61,267
1981	1,171,524	819,717	52,002	871,719	88,949	17,524	800,294	280,061	91,169	11,278	103,873	60,386
1982	1,252,508	871,463	39,792	911,255	95,657	13,743	829,341	321,514	101,653	11,963	104,697	61,469
1983	1,329,515	955,722	15,720	971,442	104,077	8,346	875,711	343,776	110,028	12,558	105,874	62,017
1984	1,483,287	1,034,760	63,644	1,098,404	115,033	5,829	989,200	380,251	113,836	13,845	107,132	64,839
1985	1,546,071	1,089,623	53,494	1,143,117	123,179	7,948	1,027,886	393,844	124,341	14,275	108,304	65,524
1986	1,625,031	1,159,225	51,982	1,211,207	134,748	6,884	1,083,343	411,646	130,042	14,905	109,024	66,717
1987	1,712,764	1,240,814	58,387	1,299,201	143,026	8,453	1,164,628	411,722	136,414	15,569	110,013	67,957
1988	1,812,251	1,366,548	28,662	1,395,210	163,850	6,309	1,237,669	428,799	145,783	16,152	112,201	70,554
1989	2,039,035	1,513,547	54,196	1,567,743	179,342	-75	1,388,326	491,220	159,489	17,892	113,962	73,114
1990	2,156,494	1,618,888	58,582	1,677,470	194,937	-1,045	1,481,488	501,287	173,719	18,557	116,212	75,272
1991	2,262,137	1,722,505	43,157	1,765,662	206,707	-5,743	1,553,212	522,342	186,583	19,283	117,311	77,243
1992	2,422,145	1,841,677	58,207	1,899,884	217,347	-5,799	1,676,738	545,129	200,278	20,280	119,436	78,669
1993	2,544,162	1,944,021	32,319	1,976,340	227,463	-10,078	1,738,799	591,467	213,896	21,020	121,037	81,316
1994	2,760,047	2,106,782	63,227	2,170,009	249,094	-19,265	1,901,650	632,641	225,756	22,424	123,084	84,043
1995	2,884,690	2,212,381	27,996	2,240,377	260,281	-23,981	1,956,115	687,306	241,269	23,127	124,733	87,281
1996	3,089,305	2,321,242	72,285	2,393,527	263,873	-27,391	2,102,263	729,215	257,827	24,576	125,704	88,742
1997	3,261,362	2,448,788	77,451	2,526,239	285,923	-28,400	2,211,916	779,280	270,166	25,670	127,050	90,147
1998	3,473,938	2,660,824	38,181	2,699,005	308,010	-26,951	2,364,044	832,539	277,355	27,071	128,325	93,857
1999	3,677,729	2,896,256	24,210	2,920,466	331,844	-35,371	2,553,251	829,939	294,539	28,205	130,392	95,422
2000	4,032,153	3,211,957	43,068	3,255,025	361,484	-51,433	2,842,108	865,535	324,510	30,507	132,173	97,843
2001	4,180,499	3,365,797	46,197	3,411,994	376,231	-98,373	2,937,390	889,929	353,180	31,056	134,610	101,247
2002	4,334,532	3,543,834	35,069	3,578,903	393,484	-137,253	3,048,166	894,584	391,782	31,858	136,056	103,321
2003	4,467,906	3,710,064	37,229	3,747,293	414,172	-168,232	3,164,889	912,576	390,441	32,408	137,863	105,134
2004	4,732,037	3,909,479	92,051	4,001,530	433,211	-215,143	3,353,176	965,075	413,786	33,764	140,149	107,207
2005	4,858,556	4,066,088	67,557	4,133,645	450,949	-252,358	3,430,338	976,291	451,927	34,300	141,650	109,151
2006	5,187,197	4,285,480	72,423	4,357,903	474,417	-285,462	3,598,024	1,091,521	497,652	36,098	143,698	111,747
2007	5,580,448	4,562,302	83,631	4,645,933	508,041	-323,209	3,814,683	1,214,449	551,316	38,189	146,129	114,856
2008	5,961,081	4,794,306	93,873	4,888,179	538,039	-323,218	4,026,922	1,274,328	659,831	40,061	148,799	116,152
2009	5,982,909	4,886,018	59,064	4,945,082	545,022	-361,993	4,038,067	1,257,091	687,751	39,477	151,556	116,043
2010	6,133,072	5,041,477	62,286	5,103,763	561,769	-388,363	4,153,631	1,230,513	748,928	40,090	152,983	115,917
2011	6,695,537	5,211,325	165,980	5,377,305	520,783	-338,494	4,518,028	1,398,427	779,082	43,060	155,493	119,002
2012	7,068,895	5,505,368	153,070	5,658,438	542,425	-348,676	4,767,337	1,510,997	790,561	44,546	158,686	121,282
2013	7,323,885	5,833,154	204,156	6,037,310	636,841	-422,110	4,978,359	1,525,108	820,418	45,323	161,594	123,992
2014	7,754,001	6,171,912	151,808	6,323,720	659,912	-396,639	5,267,169	1,621,581	865,251	47,247	164,117	124,912
2015	8,026,310	6,363,658	108,201	6,471,859	677,758	-442,627	5,351,474	1,747,939	926,897	48,161	166,655	126,640
2016	8,275,164	6,568,243	36,717	6,604,960	704,823	-447,695	5,452,442	1,852,659	970,063	49,040	168,742	129,620
2017	8,602,601	6,801,913	61,887	6,863,800	732,081	-448,488	5,683,231	1,942,988	976,382	50,164	171,491	130,900
2018	9,459,396	9,273,231	186,165	7,277,288	758,618	-340,639	6,178,031	2,190,908	1,090,457	54,803	172,607	131,025
2019	9,665,204	9,436,993	228,211	7,458,555	772,928	-408,220	6,277,407	2,206,938	1,180,859	55,834	173,105	131,752

Personal Income and Employment by Area: Ithaca, NY

(Thousands of dollars, except as noted.)

Year	Personal income, total	Nonfarm	Farm	Total	Less: Contributions for government social insurance	Plus: Adjustment for residence	Equals: Net earnings by place of residence	Plus: Dividends, interest, and rent	Plus: Personal current transfer receipts	Per capita personal income (dollars)	Population (persons)	Total employment
1970	271,269	236,134	4,196	240,330	16,309	-20,643	203,378	45,649	22,242	3,523	77,008	31,858
1971	294,050	251,453	4,118	255,571	17,878	-20,846	216,847	49,515	27,688	3,805	77,277	32,074
1972	322,700	277,365	4,935	282,300	20,756	-23,888	237,656	54,134	30,910	4,029	80,102	33,322
1973	362,411	313,742	9,405	323,147	27,404	-28,274	267,469	60,705	34,237	4,349	83,324	35,318
1974	403,237	352,450	6,680	359,130	32,015	-33,404	293,711	68,707	40,819	4,712	85,580	37,573
1975	431,758	362,864	7,334	370,198	33,070	-34,553	302,575	74,270	54,913	5,052	85,471	36,913
1976	455,987	383,542	7,249	390,791	35,377	-35,343	320,071	78,517	57,399	5,298	86,067	37,712
1977	473,732	390,126	6,288	396,414	36,238	-34,468	325,708	86,784	61,240	5,490	86,287	38,255
1978	518,008	433,202	7,527	440,729	42,019	-38,273	360,437	92,078	65,493	5,992	86,457	39,942
1979	567,246	475,124	9,980	485,104	47,948	-43,727	393,429	102,542	71,275	6,508	87,161	41,218
1980	652,170	540,195	8,416	548,611	54,902	-51,772	441,937	126,423	83,810	7,468	87,331	41,835
1981	754,540	616,279	9,996	626,275	66,918	-57,250	502,107	157,550	94,883	8,560	88,150	43,881
1982	840,569	695,191	9,818	705,009	73,620	-66,837	564,552	171,732	104,285	9,502	88,458	45,648
1983	950,308	795,641	8,255	803,896	83,920	-78,166	641,810	194,399	114,099	10,698	88,828	48,064
1984	1,062,926	900,504	10,705	911,209	95,917	-86,543	728,749	214,348	119,829	11,932	89,080	50,756
1985	1,137,413	973,550	13,415	986,965	105,424	-96,482	785,059	225,062	127,292	12,667	89,791	52,407
1986	1,217,340	1,048,076	12,947	1,061,023	115,514	-102,515	842,994	240,826	133,520	13,573	89,687	54,502
1987	1,296,586	1,136,011	10,312	1,146,323	123,762	-111,024	911,537	249,146	135,903	14,364	90,264	55,893
1988	1,389,244	1,226,604	11,747	1,238,351	138,425	-121,893	978,033	266,659	144,552	15,119	91,888	58,258
1989	1,556,344	1,346,359	15,043	1,361,402	150,636	-133,080	1,077,686	323,696	154,962	16,688	93,262	60,237
1990	1,618,413	1,395,401	16,417	1,411,818	149,888	-141,085	1,120,845	328,713	168,855	17,173	94,241	60,340
1991	1,662,267	1,435,577	16,652	1,452,229	158,268	-150,020	1,143,941	330,577	187,749	17,446	95,283	60,526
1992	1,744,481	1,488,179	25,689	1,513,868	160,008	-156,245	1,197,615	335,859	211,007	18,231	95,685	59,647
1993	1,775,998	1,502,659	33,802	1,536,461	162,169	-164,510	1,209,782	346,869	219,347	18,476	96,122	59,660
1994	1,844,869	1,586,272	24,187	1,610,459	175,117	-181,222	1,254,120	363,436	227,313	19,136	96,409	60,253
1995	1,928,260	1,635,949	23,837	1,659,786	181,551	-193,555	1,284,680	393,760	249,820	19,906	96,870	60,082
1996	1,954,698	1,634,953	25,893	1,660,846	181,412	-196,039	1,283,395	414,988	256,315	20,298	96,298	58,651
1997	2,022,092	1,737,912	10,029	1,747,941	192,824	-215,993	1,339,124	422,092	260,876	21,016	96,216	58,558
1998	2,105,416	1,797,884	13,350	1,811,234	200,197	-235,942	1,375,095	453,604	276,717	21,923	96,036	57,896
1999	2,243,093	1,984,828	13,566	1,998,394	216,490	-275,376	1,506,528	451,247	285,318	23,207	96,656	61,479
2000	2,365,892	2,077,015	17,245	2,094,260	226,797	-290,858	1,576,605	489,730	299,557	24,490	96,608	62,504
2001	2,503,383	2,203,643	18,594	2,222,237	244,051	-304,997	1,673,189	504,129	326,065	25,687	97,458	64,225
2002	2,563,183	2,331,511	10,095	2,341,606	263,058	-332,238	1,746,310	461,921	354,952	26,094	98,227	64,594
2003	2,692,822	2,481,982	12,539	2,494,521	283,560	-363,920	1,847,041	477,340	368,441	27,187	99,049	66,031
2004	2,851,707	2,605,296	16,134	2,621,430	293,714	-373,781	1,953,935	505,886	391,886	28,651	99,531	67,459
2005	2,875,015	2,644,289	14,557	2,658,846	302,597	-388,852	1,967,397	501,026	406,592	28,914	99,433	68,246
2006	3,011,152	2,775,914	10,322	2,786,236	315,944	-406,968	2,063,324	518,529	429,299	30,217	99,651	68,278
2007	3,191,345	2,888,470	18,781	2,907,251	324,405	-413,071	2,169,775	568,710	452,860	31,942	99,910	69,485
2008	3,441,248	3,057,871	20,006	3,077,877	351,023	-434,682	2,292,172	638,892	510,184	34,281	100,383	70,253
2009	3,478,744	3,131,083	10,659	3,141,742	355,236	-466,427	2,320,079	598,511	560,154	34,274	101,497	68,613
2010	3,569,514	3,195,235	18,415	3,213,650	356,135	-476,489	2,381,026	584,011	604,477	35,076	101,764	67,611
2011	3,738,377	3,261,890	22,779	3,284,669	327,659	-489,171	2,467,839	656,514	614,024	36,655	101,987	67,421
2012	3,907,523	3,437,821	20,882	3,458,703	339,277	-530,999	2,588,427	718,121	600,975	37,912	103,067	68,184
2013	3,958,430	3,479,093	24,948	3,504,041	386,096	-524,003	2,593,942	750,351	614,137	38,010	104,143	68,895
2014	4,067,596	3,513,207	26,979	3,540,186	396,248	-530,602	2,613,336	823,821	630,439	39,004	104,286	67,847
2015	4,246,999	3,656,709	13,630	3,670,339	414,739	-532,701	2,722,899	862,931	661,169	40,726	104,283	69,660
2016	4,233,704	3,705,940	12,033	3,717,973	421,608	-601,700	2,694,665	862,351	676,688	40,490	104,561	69,857
2017	4,440,812	3,862,646	12,384	3,875,030	440,272	-621,906	2,812,852	902,596	725,364	42,373	104,802	69,737
2018	4,621,168	4,610,057	11,111	4,015,903	455,532	-623,414	2,936,957	953,657	730,554	45,120	102,419	70,078
2019	4,750,972	4,731,228	19,744	4,045,451	452,868	-602,489	2,990,094	966,374	794,504	46,496	102,180	69,392

Personal Income and Employment by Area: Jackson, MI

(Thousands of dollars, except as noted.)

Year	Personal income, total	Earnings by place of work			Less: Contributions for government social insurance	Plus: Adjustment for residence	Equals: Net earnings by place of residence	Plus: Dividends, interest, and rent	Plus: Personal current transfer receipts	Per capita personal income (dollars)	Population (persons)	Total employment
		Nonfarm	Farm	Total								
1970	584,669	480,910	6,320	487,230	34,559	7,225	459,896	74,513	50,260	4,082	143,227	58,293
1971	610,313	488,957	5,032	493,989	36,270	12,886	470,605	78,483	61,225	4,250	143,589	56,632
1972	686,460	560,197	6,598	566,795	44,160	15,317	537,952	84,046	64,462	4,755	144,372	59,352
1973	772,999	634,747	9,711	644,458	58,182	20,765	607,041	93,496	72,462	5,313	145,481	62,549
1974	828,625	672,318	3,531	675,849	63,956	21,257	633,150	106,901	88,574	5,641	146,903	62,188
1975	907,391	703,745	8,532	712,277	65,210	22,433	669,500	119,346	118,545	6,135	147,902	60,080
1976	981,361	750,851	6,588	757,439	70,800	38,279	724,918	127,665	128,778	6,609	148,498	60,290
1977	1,091,243	841,405	6,622	848,027	79,826	51,413	819,614	142,471	129,158	7,260	150,313	62,569
1978	1,229,816	962,270	4,487	966,757	93,660	64,487	937,584	155,861	136,371	8,117	151,502	65,436
1979	1,348,062	1,042,928	3,241	1,046,169	105,633	77,711	1,018,247	174,074	155,741	8,881	151,789	65,967
1980	1,436,360	1,058,381	1,934	1,060,315	105,607	81,281	1,035,989	206,111	194,260	9,478	151,554	62,760
1981	1,549,914	1,119,591	5,662	1,125,253	120,698	80,832	1,085,387	247,413	217,114	10,233	151,459	62,048
1982	1,589,960	1,099,663	3,562	1,103,225	120,194	76,595	1,059,626	282,552	247,782	10,586	150,195	58,972
1983	1,650,938	1,119,695	-6,602	1,113,093	123,429	85,070	1,074,734	310,668	265,536	11,160	147,930	57,854
1984	1,764,489	1,182,823	5,205	1,188,028	135,043	99,092	1,152,077	347,669	264,743	12,138	145,374	58,403
1985	1,843,509	1,223,763	7,805	1,231,568	142,157	113,853	1,203,264	364,371	275,874	12,749	144,602	59,140
1986	1,944,221	1,296,592	5,415	1,302,007	150,672	113,037	1,264,372	386,001	293,848	13,376	145,355	60,642
1987	2,087,854	1,437,206	11,410	1,448,616	164,651	102,930	1,386,895	397,110	303,849	14,130	147,758	62,691
1988	2,196,361	1,513,779	7,773	1,521,552	180,075	116,534	1,458,011	416,832	321,518	14,805	148,357	63,018
1989	2,380,392	1,625,741	15,571	1,641,312	191,220	112,710	1,562,802	472,062	345,528	15,996	148,816	65,309
1990	2,456,766	1,686,143	9,843	1,695,986	200,410	113,644	1,609,220	473,175	374,371	16,364	150,128	65,679
1991	2,508,078	1,699,562	5,075	1,704,637	204,988	118,715	1,618,364	469,119	420,595	16,605	151,039	64,640
1992	2,652,804	1,795,129	4,868	1,799,997	214,691	136,774	1,722,080	479,883	450,841	17,514	151,465	65,537
1993	2,801,739	1,895,789	2,106	1,897,895	228,257	142,608	1,812,246	506,327	483,166	18,379	152,445	66,378
1994	2,976,825	2,019,463	1,032	2,020,495	248,591	161,288	1,933,192	557,626	486,007	19,547	152,288	68,008
1995	3,155,630	2,136,255	1,839	2,138,094	264,250	166,847	2,040,691	606,829	508,110	20,583	153,313	70,813
1996	3,296,485	2,231,711	1,558	2,233,269	269,764	181,293	2,144,798	622,740	528,947	21,366	154,289	72,489
1997	3,468,826	2,330,312	471	2,330,783	282,425	205,748	2,254,106	658,162	556,558	22,332	155,331	73,186
1998	3,588,395	2,424,176	1,044	2,425,220	290,915	238,333	2,372,638	655,529	560,228	23,004	155,991	72,741
1999	3,833,793	2,643,432	4,576	2,648,008	314,985	260,178	2,593,201	634,999	605,593	24,406	157,085	75,602
2000	4,040,175	2,765,447	4,304	2,769,751	326,581	289,834	2,733,004	682,883	624,288	25,461	158,679	77,800
2001	4,123,010	2,793,374	880	2,794,254	320,100	282,016	2,756,170	669,905	696,935	25,806	159,772	76,959
2002	4,162,045	2,821,238	153	2,821,391	325,126	295,178	2,791,443	643,349	727,253	25,868	160,893	76,539
2003	4,233,328	2,817,119	-948	2,816,171	323,332	309,466	2,802,305	663,514	767,509	26,112	162,119	75,903
2004	4,367,040	2,989,153	7,306	2,996,459	343,809	288,830	2,941,480	633,702	791,858	26,934	162,140	77,085
2005	4,463,967	3,062,990	5,874	3,068,864	359,845	277,155	2,986,174	635,641	842,152	27,378	163,047	77,179
2006	4,550,013	3,089,314	8,274	3,097,588	366,161	272,065	3,003,492	639,466	907,055	27,848	163,387	75,802
2007	4,677,260	3,103,132	7,437	3,110,569	371,721	264,630	3,003,478	683,741	990,041	28,639	163,316	75,170
2008	4,785,759	3,105,599	-1,008	3,104,591	376,203	241,667	2,970,055	697,908	1,117,796	29,758	160,825	74,162
2009	4,695,243	2,937,190	1,269	2,938,459	358,440	186,206	2,766,225	680,016	1,249,002	29,324	160,114	70,410
2010	4,849,365	3,048,735	12,673	3,061,408	363,255	160,568	2,858,721	653,442	1,337,202	30,286	160,119	69,182
2011	5,024,270	3,165,410	25,511	3,190,921	344,025	126,376	2,973,272	716,230	1,334,768	31,475	159,625	72,195
2012	5,148,292	3,300,655	4,557	3,305,212	356,683	95,884	3,044,413	762,461	1,341,418	32,195	159,908	72,243
2013	5,240,092	3,457,268	28,737	3,486,005	420,803	28,133	3,093,335	775,670	1,371,087	32,841	159,558	73,852
2014	5,423,370	3,530,054	12,423	3,542,477	428,377	45,086	3,159,186	829,807	1,434,377	34,036	159,343	74,227
2015	5,703,865	3,662,880	6,307	3,669,187	440,971	55,004	3,283,220	902,117	1,518,528	35,830	159,191	74,854
2016	5,896,412	3,832,392	-2,924	3,829,468	457,628	47,248	3,419,088	919,315	1,558,009	37,268	158,215	75,638
2017	6,039,314	3,940,712	-11,429	3,929,283	470,427	55,695	3,514,551	954,093	1,570,670	38,069	158,640	75,514
2018	6,211,490	6,213,630	-2,140	4,061,509	495,465	57,927	3,623,971	978,570	1,608,949	39,173	158,566	76,029
2019	6,401,733	6,403,167	-1,434	4,151,430	502,540	59,282	3,708,172	990,726	1,702,835	40,387	158,510	75,844

Personal Income and Employment by Area: Jackson, MS

(Thousands of dollars, except as noted.)

Year	Personal income, total	Earnings by place of work			Less: Contributions for government social insurance	Plus: Adjustment for residence	Equals: Net earnings by place of residence	Plus: Dividends, interest, and rent	Plus: Personal current transfer receipts	Per capita personal income (dollars)	Population (persons)	Total employment
		Nonfarm	Farm	Total								
1970	1,169,060	940,224	50,369	990,593	63,915	-12,406	914,272	149,918	104,870	3,234	361,473	170,261
1971	1,301,693	1,039,078	57,412	1,096,490	73,056	-13,500	1,009,934	167,182	124,577	3,521	369,687	175,421
1972	1,466,101	1,176,282	64,881	1,241,163	86,602	-15,638	1,138,923	184,746	142,432	3,876	378,229	182,347
1973	1,686,270	1,349,531	90,830	1,440,361	114,495	-20,045	1,305,821	213,825	166,624	4,378	385,151	194,536
1974	1,912,388	1,526,913	76,358	1,603,271	133,895	-16,478	1,452,898	253,652	205,838	4,818	396,911	200,851
1975	2,056,099	1,612,632	44,671	1,657,303	139,323	-5,091	1,512,889	284,363	258,847	5,082	404,561	194,047
1976	2,319,273	1,803,225	74,095	1,877,320	159,022	2,298	1,720,596	308,141	290,536	5,641	411,149	198,388
1977	2,605,251	2,062,144	61,160	2,123,304	180,875	6,074	1,948,503	344,230	312,518	6,238	417,649	207,091
1978	2,985,707	2,379,007	62,119	2,441,126	214,810	17,222	2,243,538	398,397	343,772	6,990	427,123	219,759
1979	3,417,328	2,694,498	87,364	2,781,862	253,438	38,374	2,566,798	463,429	387,101	7,871	434,186	226,855
1980	3,735,115	2,929,599	26,842	2,956,441	274,623	15,216	2,697,034	576,277	461,804	8,478	440,574	225,694
1981	4,153,650	3,158,574	34,497	3,193,071	318,814	28,295	2,902,552	721,236	529,862	9,344	444,541	224,409
1982	4,374,546	3,253,427	62,076	3,315,503	335,421	20,213	3,000,295	802,452	571,799	9,760	448,195	219,440
1983	4,646,101	3,490,000	20,107	3,510,107	362,829	27,183	3,174,461	842,933	628,707	10,274	452,220	222,590
1984	5,098,415	3,831,054	86,329	3,917,383	409,134	11,198	3,519,447	930,162	648,806	11,161	456,787	230,375
1985	5,371,781	4,087,570	46,240	4,133,810	446,933	-3,023	3,683,854	1,004,283	683,644	11,553	464,955	234,972
1986	5,625,605	4,311,667	39,452	4,351,119	476,306	-17,947	3,856,866	1,040,800	727,939	12,027	467,741	238,293
1987	5,973,414	4,570,773	70,985	4,641,758	501,189	-25,690	4,114,879	1,085,588	772,947	12,731	469,189	241,648
1988	6,405,601	4,900,131	85,723	4,985,854	557,801	-25,250	4,402,803	1,173,291	829,507	13,667	468,678	248,098
1989	7,028,472	5,263,982	77,521	5,341,503	595,516	-31,878	4,714,109	1,408,467	905,896	14,956	469,951	253,316
1990	7,386,961	5,593,677	67,312	5,660,989	657,579	-32,766	4,970,644	1,423,278	993,039	15,597	473,615	255,177
1991	7,777,023	5,872,557	74,803	5,947,360	704,996	-39,717	5,202,647	1,457,532	1,116,844	16,287	477,502	257,780
1992	8,354,284	6,317,067	74,220	6,391,287	749,201	-42,015	5,600,071	1,500,485	1,253,728	17,317	482,440	262,586
1993	8,877,636	6,734,864	73,656	6,808,520	797,752	-49,914	5,960,854	1,564,390	1,352,392	18,230	486,974	272,370
1994	9,589,368	7,253,366	102,556	7,355,922	865,582	-57,237	6,433,103	1,701,355	1,454,910	19,455	492,911	281,002
1995	10,302,550	7,789,564	73,314	7,862,878	923,054	-69,124	6,870,700	1,849,372	1,582,478	20,682	498,145	289,786
1996	10,912,754	8,168,427	120,867	8,289,294	955,556	-79,752	7,253,986	1,976,927	1,681,841	21,598	505,267	295,891
1997	11,622,486	8,691,909	104,279	8,796,188	1,011,505	-96,715	7,687,968	2,191,986	1,742,532	22,744	511,024	302,489
1998	12,410,692	9,356,616	115,026	9,471,642	1,079,164	-107,961	8,284,517	2,377,480	1,748,695	23,972	517,713	309,660
1999	12,777,169	9,784,986	109,091	9,894,077	1,130,631	-120,863	8,642,583	2,337,652	1,796,934	24,500	521,516	313,373
2000	13,560,980	10,310,403	83,830	10,394,233	1,176,532	-138,783	9,078,918	2,541,172	1,940,890	25,765	526,339	316,370
2001	14,281,902	10,763,590	137,842	10,901,432	1,217,507	-147,146	9,536,779	2,554,281	2,190,842	27,034	528,292	318,245
2002	14,618,141	11,098,102	48,337	11,146,439	1,260,388	-141,206	9,744,845	2,508,986	2,364,310	27,533	530,930	318,603
2003	15,242,102	11,622,798	116,457	11,739,255	1,312,954	-160,718	10,265,583	2,507,190	2,469,329	28,458	535,600	323,301
2004	16,171,757	12,353,760	194,862	12,548,622	1,404,748	-198,637	10,945,237	2,586,567	2,639,953	29,829	542,144	328,806
2005	17,363,974	12,970,482	193,771	13,164,253	1,448,298	-210,937	11,505,018	3,035,658	2,823,298	31,718	547,444	333,786
2006	18,762,041	13,818,051	86,933	13,904,984	1,580,637	-238,921	12,085,426	3,674,098	3,002,517	33,692	556,877	344,273
2007	19,231,347	14,078,558	110,839	14,189,397	1,633,497	-252,430	12,303,470	3,745,353	3,182,524	34,394	559,153	350,842
2008	20,708,088	15,074,870	79,429	15,154,299	1,719,963	-230,180	13,204,156	3,867,523	3,636,409	36,859	561,812	353,078
2009	19,833,959	14,273,948	104,820	14,378,768	1,683,128	-255,838	12,439,802	3,486,511	3,907,646	35,143	564,376	347,789
2010	20,621,474	14,822,718	103,703	14,926,421	1,701,450	-259,329	12,965,642	3,396,132	4,259,700	36,251	568,849	347,079
2011	21,931,784	15,499,293	57,953	15,557,246	1,579,175	-309,979	13,668,092	3,831,332	4,432,360	38,208	574,014	353,069
2012	22,765,413	16,116,207	65,832	16,182,039	1,626,815	-315,329	14,239,895	4,113,120	4,412,398	39,493	576,440	354,673
2013	23,073,577	16,792,428	196,313	16,988,741	1,898,877	-425,260	14,664,604	3,883,689	4,525,284	39,973	577,229	359,847
2014	24,021,757	17,433,182	125,723	17,558,905	1,971,415	-440,085	15,147,405	4,185,239	4,689,113	41,520	578,559	366,589
2015	24,260,795	17,345,502	70,617	17,416,119	2,028,005	-461,233	14,926,881	4,438,949	4,894,965	41,918	578,766	372,039
2016	24,557,829	17,411,071	39,336	17,450,407	2,044,027	-451,196	14,955,184	4,532,174	5,070,471	42,373	579,558	374,889
2017	24,968,718	17,604,704	65,849	17,670,553	2,084,612	-437,889	15,148,052	4,699,560	5,121,106	43,145	578,715	377,451
2018	25,983,190	25,874,550	108,640	18,105,598	2,154,569	-373,347	15,577,682	4,910,274	5,495,234	43,496	597,376	383,285
2019	26,608,102	26,524,865	83,237	18,512,903	2,221,512	-361,654	15,929,737	4,940,614	5,737,751	44,734	594,806	386,772

Personal Income and Employment by Area: Jackson, TN

(Thousands of dollars, except as noted.)

Year	Personal income, total	Earnings by place of work Nonfarm	Farm	Total	Less: Contributions for government social insurance	Plus: Adjustment for residence	Equals: Net earnings by place of residence	Plus: Dividends, interest, and rent	Plus: Personal current transfer receipts	Per capita personal income (dollars)	Population (persons)	Total employment
1970	269,815	209,180	13,008	222,188	14,425	1,472	209,235	30,516	30,064	2,983	90,439	41,609
1971	301,085	231,735	17,810	249,545	16,233	-863	232,449	34,537	34,099	3,261	92,319	42,190
1972	334,930	267,310	14,517	281,827	19,475	-3,617	258,735	38,699	37,496	3,531	94,860	45,340
1973	380,494	300,088	22,036	322,124	24,814	-6,314	290,996	44,476	45,022	3,980	95,609	47,469
1974	418,028	345,677	8,372	354,049	30,102	-12,328	311,619	51,799	54,610	4,330	96,538	48,962
1975	462,505	371,145	8,638	379,783	31,703	-15,578	332,502	59,284	70,719	4,737	97,641	47,350
1976	512,759	418,531	9,335	427,866	36,392	-20,509	370,965	64,264	77,530	5,202	98,570	48,158
1977	569,044	477,073	8,000	485,073	41,703	-28,027	415,343	72,430	81,271	5,715	99,563	49,487
1978	628,988	527,432	10,746	538,178	46,912	-32,004	459,262	81,774	87,952	6,317	99,563	49,960
1979	684,079	578,689	5,172	583,861	53,566	-39,386	490,909	92,378	100,792	6,762	101,162	50,542
1980	738,104	605,500	-3,475	602,025	56,056	-45,962	500,007	114,993	123,104	7,210	102,369	49,086
1981	811,291	636,123	4,408	640,531	62,639	-44,656	533,236	140,665	137,390	7,893	102,788	47,615
1982	859,434	644,333	4,601	648,934	64,169	-44,699	540,066	168,732	150,636	8,366	102,728	46,149
1983	923,100	710,964	-7,837	703,127	71,432	-47,468	584,227	177,885	160,988	9,026	102,276	47,546
1984	1,046,698	802,617	12,393	815,010	84,022	-52,537	678,451	202,410	165,837	10,180	102,820	51,276
1985	1,099,909	850,048	1,621	851,669	90,239	-53,854	707,576	215,275	177,058	10,594	103,826	51,084
1986	1,176,843	919,726	4,848	924,574	99,596	-59,625	765,353	220,978	190,512	11,355	103,639	52,206
1987	1,277,256	985,644	30,992	1,016,636	105,690	-60,767	850,179	226,068	201,009	12,345	103,462	53,337
1988	1,375,379	1,071,694	24,912	1,096,606	118,914	-60,364	917,328	243,284	214,767	13,264	103,695	55,784
1989	1,474,301	1,171,024	19,309	1,190,333	131,705	-71,021	987,607	253,934	232,760	14,186	103,923	58,447
1990	1,600,587	1,271,312	16,924	1,288,236	143,303	-81,279	1,063,654	284,128	252,805	15,305	104,582	59,632
1991	1,680,920	1,332,275	27,594	1,359,869	152,484	-86,219	1,121,166	278,640	281,114	15,839	106,123	60,230
1992	1,866,010	1,498,727	40,605	1,539,332	168,540	-101,609	1,269,183	282,101	314,726	17,301	107,853	63,184
1993	1,964,131	1,596,524	27,732	1,624,256	180,258	-112,908	1,331,090	291,245	341,796	17,891	109,784	65,375
1994	2,134,214	1,752,362	45,076	1,797,438	200,519	-130,766	1,466,153	309,409	358,652	19,139	111,509	69,405
1995	2,260,006	1,863,506	29,647	1,893,153	213,596	-144,740	1,534,817	327,715	397,474	19,898	113,582	71,076
1996	2,389,569	1,967,373	37,090	2,004,463	221,727	-159,876	1,622,860	352,015	414,694	20,725	115,301	71,865
1997	2,559,871	2,163,147	25,704	2,188,851	242,154	-189,250	1,757,447	371,620	430,804	21,887	116,961	75,450
1998	2,789,247	2,379,326	9,550	2,388,876	258,017	-212,979	1,917,880	423,529	447,838	23,436	119,013	77,269
1999	2,904,793	2,514,168	2,557	2,516,725	273,692	-235,903	2,007,130	432,066	465,597	24,038	120,842	79,257
2000	3,119,808	2,693,563	19,311	2,712,874	288,166	-259,602	2,165,106	450,746	503,956	25,542	122,142	80,714
2001	2,983,235	2,507,106	14,380	2,521,486	282,837	-263,181	1,975,468	457,622	550,145	24,178	123,387	77,909
2002	3,058,745	2,577,453	-210	2,577,243	294,044	-263,112	2,020,087	440,465	598,193	24,689	123,890	76,964
2003	3,227,498	2,696,121	21,067	2,717,188	304,175	-278,433	2,134,580	451,898	641,020	26,052	123,886	77,452
2004	3,430,422	2,899,657	18,274	2,917,931	321,700	-300,176	2,296,055	457,722	676,645	27,367	125,351	78,654
2005	3,544,837	2,996,643	33,508	3,030,151	332,467	-332,240	2,365,444	454,829	724,564	28,091	126,192	79,507
2006	3,667,756	3,090,048	35,014	3,125,062	343,510	-344,558	2,436,994	467,740	763,022	28,744	127,602	80,146
2007	3,874,852	3,230,337	8,634	3,238,971	358,285	-377,822	2,502,864	527,355	844,633	30,241	128,134	81,346
2008	4,009,143	3,232,151	36,716	3,268,867	366,448	-391,204	2,511,215	565,037	932,891	31,213	128,445	81,050
2009	4,052,701	3,150,304	33,874	3,184,178	360,333	-339,401	2,484,444	562,297	1,005,960	31,376	129,164	77,290
2010	4,259,672	3,309,937	8,106	3,318,043	368,025	-354,508	2,595,510	556,393	1,107,769	32,759	130,031	77,501
2011	4,632,455	3,566,259	50,786	3,617,045	343,039	-392,814	2,881,192	623,430	1,127,833	35,713	129,714	79,545
2012	4,686,810	3,726,205	-20,177	3,706,028	351,506	-438,192	2,916,330	639,065	1,131,415	36,009	130,155	80,983
2013	4,658,888	3,737,332	20,992	3,758,324	399,863	-481,206	2,877,255	627,983	1,153,650	35,734	130,376	81,562
2014	4,639,167	3,798,132	-49,617	3,748,515	406,424	-517,752	2,824,339	656,707	1,158,121	35,738	129,810	82,369
2015	4,828,516	3,900,135	-46,193	3,853,942	418,775	-519,950	2,915,217	697,786	1,215,513	37,377	129,184	83,023
2016	4,964,870	4,044,359	-49,240	3,995,119	436,542	-562,338	2,996,239	724,448	1,244,183	38,463	129,083	85,128
2017	5,128,153	4,193,147	-70,794	4,122,353	456,850	-586,020	3,079,483	764,191	1,284,479	39,681	129,235	85,487
2018	7,164,271	7,204,604	-40,333	5,153,484	575,765	-321,845	4,255,874	1,009,943	1,898,454	40,178	178,315	107,628
2019	7,466,160	7,466,442	-282	5,374,616	595,529	-342,950	4,436,137	1,025,079	2,004,944	41,794	178,644	109,211

Personal Income and Employment by Area: Jacksonville, FL

(Thousands of dollars, except as noted.)

Year	Personal income, total	Earnings by place of work			Less: Contributions for government social insurance	Plus: Adjustment for residence	Equals: Net earnings by place of residence	Plus: Dividends, interest, and rent	Plus: Personal current transfer receipts	Per capita personal income (dollars)	Population (persons)	Total employment
		Nonfarm	Farm	Total								
1970	2,567,000	2,114,878	13,021	2,127,899	135,388	-12,090	1,980,421	409,149	177,430	4,118	623,388	295,684
1971	2,840,266	2,332,698	15,481	2,348,179	155,780	-13,747	2,178,652	452,843	208,771	4,475	634,713	301,891
1972	3,189,179	2,625,387	17,939	2,643,326	183,196	-15,387	2,444,743	498,579	245,857	4,935	646,275	313,941
1973	3,576,714	2,951,238	22,872	2,974,110	235,105	-17,600	2,721,405	560,453	294,856	5,421	659,829	332,075
1974	4,037,450	3,303,980	26,398	3,330,378	272,986	-20,804	3,036,588	657,261	343,601	5,871	687,746	345,616
1975	4,422,511	3,540,411	33,133	3,573,544	290,668	-22,670	3,260,206	721,995	440,310	6,403	690,714	341,634
1976	4,737,665	3,786,512	32,329	3,818,841	319,292	-25,046	3,474,503	767,905	495,257	6,782	698,553	340,298
1977	5,172,586	4,145,695	25,448	4,171,143	350,583	-29,579	3,790,981	846,601	535,004	7,338	704,888	349,448
1978	5,780,316	4,638,128	17,301	4,655,429	401,184	-31,398	4,222,847	972,313	585,156	8,076	715,770	368,161
1979	6,356,757	5,078,857	14,875	5,093,732	460,712	-32,343	4,600,677	1,088,595	667,485	8,807	721,782	371,167
1980	7,255,473	5,688,556	20,702	5,709,258	517,785	-33,196	5,158,277	1,312,363	784,833	9,786	741,394	381,950
1981	8,275,617	6,405,018	34,314	6,439,332	624,302	-36,377	5,778,653	1,591,677	905,287	10,955	755,420	390,199
1982	9,061,807	6,947,284	53,584	7,000,868	690,891	-24,581	6,285,396	1,764,248	1,012,163	11,793	768,427	397,586
1983	9,888,233	7,612,807	48,983	7,661,790	769,182	-31,186	6,861,422	1,920,117	1,106,694	12,623	783,354	411,897
1984	11,143,991	8,642,815	45,034	8,687,849	897,080	-35,688	7,755,081	2,219,827	1,169,083	13,858	804,178	442,276
1985	12,241,386	9,543,628	41,498	9,585,126	1,005,112	-37,216	8,542,798	2,449,373	1,249,215	14,789	827,746	470,849
1986	13,305,113	10,427,117	46,883	10,474,000	1,129,350	-32,231	9,312,419	2,665,830	1,326,864	15,594	853,211	493,439
1987	14,366,224	11,296,748	48,872	11,345,620	1,211,438	-10,755	10,123,427	2,848,491	1,394,306	16,423	874,757	503,658
1988	15,543,633	12,191,677	55,776	12,247,453	1,355,028	-4,925	10,887,500	3,128,457	1,527,676	17,340	896,417	519,933
1989	17,005,492	12,973,452	51,174	13,024,626	1,448,341	10,052	11,586,337	3,687,497	1,731,658	18,805	904,284	536,809
1990	18,327,614	13,916,376	59,205	13,975,581	1,553,282	32,226	12,454,525	3,971,597	1,901,492	19,661	932,169	555,661
1991	19,025,780	14,449,029	60,202	14,509,231	1,627,259	36,270	12,918,242	3,964,947	2,142,591	19,910	955,572	555,630
1992	20,155,442	15,363,270	56,741	15,420,011	1,733,723	44,234	13,730,522	3,960,395	2,464,525	20,615	977,699	555,070
1993	21,337,411	16,253,606	55,119	16,308,725	1,823,866	43,100	14,527,959	4,159,628	2,649,824	21,542	990,520	568,743
1994	22,511,450	17,124,875	51,594	17,176,469	1,928,864	41,921	15,289,526	4,446,291	2,775,633	22,411	1,004,478	582,196
1995	24,212,435	18,259,675	48,373	18,308,048	2,042,844	34,463	16,299,667	4,910,671	3,002,097	23,723	1,020,631	603,371
1996	26,014,364	19,617,974	54,202	19,672,176	2,176,148	20,583	17,516,611	5,323,778	3,173,975	24,720	1,052,363	630,841
1997	27,676,463	20,976,000	61,165	21,037,165	2,327,388	5,447	18,715,224	5,662,142	3,299,097	25,696	1,077,069	648,513
1998	30,037,316	22,790,872	69,420	22,860,292	2,491,426	-5,807	20,363,059	6,333,239	3,341,018	27,434	1,094,889	671,238
1999	31,310,296	23,841,114	71,207	23,912,321	2,602,713	-655	21,308,953	6,515,611	3,485,732	28,209	1,109,951	687,819
2000	34,139,422	26,097,668	71,479	26,169,147	2,809,077	-19,811	23,340,259	7,037,712	3,761,451	30,312	1,126,282	715,920
2001	35,251,499	26,796,632	85,413	26,882,045	2,938,300	-38,467	23,905,278	7,204,994	4,141,227	30,704	1,148,091	682,257
2002	36,584,456	28,001,791	72,611	28,074,402	3,062,951	-68,456	24,942,995	7,085,112	4,556,349	31,232	1,171,363	685,898
2003	38,928,279	30,014,986	62,850	30,077,836	3,269,761	-82,790	26,725,285	7,310,278	4,892,716	32,629	1,193,042	706,052
2004	41,886,489	31,993,812	71,411	32,065,223	3,495,589	-145,695	28,423,939	8,173,445	5,289,105	34,253	1,222,866	728,218
2005	45,472,796	34,246,197	71,653	34,317,850	3,747,900	-171,880	30,398,070	9,330,705	5,744,021	36,405	1,249,072	752,286
2006	49,683,433	36,796,169	61,299	36,857,468	4,128,642	-217,784	32,511,042	10,914,870	6,257,521	38,745	1,282,311	781,243
2007	51,869,602	37,917,238	63,878	37,981,116	4,264,951	-231,680	33,484,485	11,640,835	6,744,282	39,692	1,306,788	794,744
2008	52,423,886	37,052,349	52,262	37,104,611	4,249,651	-187,749	32,667,211	11,928,031	7,828,644	39,633	1,322,728	783,542
2009	49,594,700	35,137,191	43,111	35,180,302	4,104,344	-76,866	30,999,092	9,902,793	8,692,815	37,150	1,334,972	750,560
2010	52,262,151	36,477,233	48,679	36,525,912	4,197,699	7,447	32,335,660	10,210,509	9,715,982	38,744	1,348,910	746,907
2011	54,867,880	37,030,940	30,724	37,061,664	3,856,076	64,674	33,270,262	11,455,701	10,141,917	40,286	1,361,962	762,037
2012	57,247,865	38,740,061	32,590	38,772,651	4,062,478	72,413	34,782,586	12,417,638	10,047,641	41,542	1,378,059	771,167
2013	57,946,468	39,895,290	40,147	39,935,437	4,689,475	106,420	35,352,382	12,163,511	10,430,575	41,562	1,394,206	787,575
2014	61,302,311	41,917,597	38,326	41,955,923	4,919,206	59,527	37,096,244	12,985,159	11,220,908	43,239	1,417,740	810,766
2015	65,217,127	44,179,264	53,334	44,232,598	5,136,358	45,832	39,142,072	14,181,512	11,893,543	45,102	1,445,986	839,150
2016	67,820,553	45,977,020	33,510	46,010,530	5,355,650	23,849	40,678,729	14,691,494	12,450,330	45,933	1,476,503	863,794
2017	71,707,293	48,925,574	33,462	48,959,036	5,669,344	-8,046	43,281,646	15,336,070	13,089,577	47,647	1,504,980	889,431
2018	77,124,644	77,085,626	39,018	52,759,053	6,051,827	-7,136	46,700,090	16,624,157	13,800,397	50,321	1,532,663	938,974
2019	80,191,700	80,146,669	45,031	55,114,572	6,402,701	-6,239	48,705,632	16,801,603	14,684,465	51,421	1,559,514	962,081

Personal Income and Employment by Area: Jacksonville, NC

(Thousands of dollars, except as noted.)

Year	Personal income, total	Earnings by place of work			Less: Contributions for government social insurance	Plus: Adjustment for residence	Equals: Net earnings by place of residence	Plus: Dividends, interest, and rent	Plus: Personal current transfer receipts	Per capita personal income (dollars)	Population (persons)	Total employment
		Nonfarm	Farm	Total								
1970	469,455	387,871	6,832	394,703	23,178	-10,622	360,903	96,734	11,818	4,576	102,582	63,781
1971	454,696	381,011	5,501	386,512	24,401	-11,196	350,915	89,706	14,075	4,509	100,831	56,615
1972	504,609	422,174	6,898	429,072	27,138	-11,986	389,948	98,491	16,170	5,330	94,669	55,778
1973	548,029	451,825	12,176	464,001	30,157	-12,840	421,004	108,671	18,354	5,881	93,193	55,913
1974	638,970	525,931	11,996	537,927	37,150	-14,725	486,052	130,787	22,131	6,631	96,362	59,332
1975	717,056	586,542	14,622	601,164	45,481	-15,531	540,152	146,977	29,927	6,361	112,734	62,166
1976	758,046	619,248	11,994	631,242	49,730	-15,706	565,806	157,783	34,457	6,576	115,272	62,032
1977	800,311	651,778	6,364	658,142	51,230	-16,926	589,986	173,609	36,716	6,877	116,382	62,822
1978	882,656	703,220	8,889	712,109	54,031	-18,155	639,923	203,192	39,541	7,451	118,455	63,952
1979	906,526	724,563	4,673	729,236	57,850	-18,387	652,999	207,492	46,035	8,011	113,156	61,681
1980	956,728	757,109	7,614	764,723	60,076	-18,985	685,662	214,721	56,345	8,428	113,515	60,235
1981	1,231,227	987,034	7,606	994,640	81,794	-17,691	895,155	270,536	65,536	10,605	116,100	62,778
1982	1,333,970	1,059,261	11,799	1,071,060	85,350	-16,697	969,013	290,497	74,460	11,221	118,881	62,899
1983	1,434,585	1,145,114	4,867	1,149,981	97,164	-17,228	1,035,589	317,304	81,692	11,549	124,216	66,943
1984	1,606,763	1,283,199	3,660	1,286,859	112,447	-16,632	1,157,780	359,610	89,373	12,524	128,297	69,653
1985	1,771,396	1,418,385	1,713	1,420,098	125,829	-17,746	1,276,523	397,627	97,246	13,295	133,240	72,992
1986	1,858,766	1,474,006	2,639	1,476,645	134,088	-15,520	1,327,037	426,376	105,353	13,455	138,143	73,307
1987	1,988,812	1,570,567	7,133	1,577,700	144,848	-15,119	1,417,733	460,863	110,216	14,088	141,166	77,154
1988	2,075,055	1,643,768	4,219	1,647,987	161,757	-12,476	1,473,754	479,324	121,977	14,542	142,695	77,449
1989	2,237,858	1,751,909	4,745	1,756,654	175,342	-11,933	1,569,379	529,997	138,482	15,002	149,174	80,413
1990	2,108,899	1,624,641	18,608	1,643,249	169,454	-16,633	1,457,162	498,626	153,111	14,050	150,098	73,735
1991	2,159,313	1,642,416	27,745	1,670,161	174,542	-11,292	1,484,327	499,214	175,772	14,268	151,342	71,053
1992	2,543,504	1,963,168	24,415	1,987,583	214,925	-21,223	1,751,435	597,639	194,430	17,377	146,370	78,921
1993	2,544,441	1,912,752	32,473	1,945,225	214,636	-15,069	1,715,520	611,732	217,189	17,217	147,789	79,122
1994	2,736,073	2,041,898	32,768	2,074,666	222,585	-14,988	1,837,093	666,213	232,767	18,643	146,760	80,724
1995	2,866,410	2,101,260	31,653	2,132,913	222,558	-11,550	1,898,805	700,909	266,696	19,465	147,258	83,029
1996	2,994,879	2,164,203	35,414	2,199,617	229,257	-5,315	1,965,045	733,849	295,985	20,146	148,658	84,330
1997	3,201,094	2,298,137	35,197	2,333,334	243,953	-4,131	2,085,250	803,519	312,325	21,636	147,955	86,093
1998	3,332,435	2,411,819	13,744	2,425,563	255,504	1,376	2,171,435	828,005	332,995	22,102	150,773	86,108
1999	3,502,914	2,527,615	16,338	2,543,953	268,261	4,483	2,280,175	863,800	358,939	23,411	149,628	87,777
2000	3,619,602	2,581,409	33,097	2,614,506	275,415	9,829	2,348,920	887,057	383,625	24,022	150,678	87,507
2001	3,772,095	2,736,528	35,247	2,771,775	291,416	2,089	2,482,448	860,150	429,497	24,970	151,068	88,590
2002	3,802,600	2,776,774	12,987	2,789,761	294,301	-3,047	2,492,413	842,476	467,711	24,789	153,397	90,613
2003	4,152,277	3,117,344	6,990	3,124,334	329,509	-25,163	2,769,662	881,088	501,527	27,593	150,481	92,408
2004	4,636,550	3,561,554	11,467	3,573,021	378,179	-48,619	3,146,223	932,347	557,980	29,191	158,837	95,728
2005	5,067,922	3,915,158	27,398	3,942,556	414,080	-68,037	3,460,439	988,898	618,585	32,238	157,205	99,289
2006	5,376,469	4,181,771	8,549	4,190,320	452,126	-83,672	3,654,522	1,039,252	682,695	33,356	161,185	102,152
2007	5,974,723	4,670,767	22,740	4,693,507	502,503	-116,376	4,074,628	1,160,776	739,319	36,597	163,256	104,594
2008	6,678,575	5,253,674	38,670	5,292,344	561,674	-164,745	4,565,925	1,259,935	852,715	39,504	169,059	109,708
2009	7,258,857	5,781,798	34,652	5,816,450	632,060	-215,196	4,969,194	1,353,599	936,064	41,943	173,064	113,560
2010	7,821,017	6,226,878	56,648	6,283,526	675,364	-247,420	5,360,742	1,422,417	1,037,858	41,848	186,889	114,629
2011	8,073,259	6,303,439	49,746	6,353,185	634,304	-257,564	5,461,317	1,520,658	1,091,284	43,636	185,013	114,456
2012	8,176,417	6,299,064	67,420	6,366,484	643,493	-254,165	5,468,826	1,575,711	1,131,880	42,872	190,719	113,433
2013	8,114,979	6,157,883	134,517	6,292,400	691,145	-244,181	5,357,074	1,580,206	1,177,699	42,183	192,377	113,476
2014	8,226,458	6,136,826	139,324	6,276,150	692,280	-234,484	5,349,386	1,626,191	1,250,881	42,876	191,866	112,765
2015	8,308,684	6,093,418	119,246	6,212,664	692,454	-219,070	5,301,140	1,635,083	1,372,461	43,031	193,088	110,282
2016	8,834,884	6,530,566	95,106	6,625,672	735,937	-238,613	5,651,122	1,735,884	1,447,878	45,967	192,199	111,827
2017	8,719,755	6,331,828	110,986	6,442,814	720,239	-226,300	5,496,275	1,707,952	1,515,528	44,972	193,893	114,936
2018	9,132,278	9,084,028	48,250	6,710,849	739,707	-231,007	5,740,135	1,705,371	1,686,772	46,377	196,915	115,183
2019	9,407,046	9,359,081	47,965	6,882,828	756,454	-228,009	5,898,365	1,717,349	1,791,332	47,525	197,938	114,581

Personal Income and Employment by Area: Janesville-Beloit, WI

(Thousands of dollars, except as noted.)

Year	Personal income, total	Earnings by place of work			Less: Contributions for government social insurance	Plus: Adjustment for residence	Equals: Net earnings by place of residence	Plus: Dividends, interest, and rent	Plus: Personal current transfer receipts	Per capita personal income (dollars)	Population (persons)	Total employment
		Nonfarm	Farm	Total								
1970	508,949	375,550	15,862	391,412	27,547	26,750	390,615	73,909	44,425	3,859	131,872	53,249
1971	554,306	405,743	18,858	424,601	30,633	26,140	420,108	80,143	54,055	4,191	132,257	53,167
1972	597,945	438,445	18,644	457,089	35,424	29,198	450,863	86,080	61,002	4,487	133,253	53,902
1973	675,634	502,648	27,163	529,811	46,955	30,845	513,701	95,047	66,886	5,019	134,603	57,505
1974	732,589	543,377	20,932	564,309	52,883	31,782	543,208	106,539	82,842	5,387	135,984	59,092
1975	789,143	564,013	24,949	588,962	53,851	29,997	565,108	116,622	107,413	5,732	137,680	58,336
1976	886,974	673,086	11,494	684,580	64,971	26,211	645,820	125,638	115,516	6,455	137,402	60,119
1977	1,002,959	776,744	22,736	799,480	74,572	24,746	749,654	139,568	113,737	7,275	137,859	62,999
1978	1,113,290	868,548	21,388	889,936	86,392	32,246	835,790	153,315	124,185	8,064	138,065	64,619
1979	1,234,630	955,810	28,106	983,916	98,137	33,792	919,571	168,707	146,352	8,831	139,809	66,458
1980	1,320,334	932,825	28,814	961,639	94,885	41,361	908,115	202,935	209,284	9,480	139,269	63,602
1981	1,469,057	1,042,565	26,676	1,069,241	113,731	40,377	995,887	248,224	224,946	10,619	138,336	64,284
1982	1,485,534	1,014,534	13,209	1,027,743	112,561	41,601	956,783	284,140	244,611	10,773	137,893	61,023
1983	1,605,844	1,144,744	-1,542	1,143,202	126,634	39,358	1,055,926	305,664	244,254	11,675	137,549	62,519
1984	1,789,236	1,280,520	12,983	1,293,503	145,659	52,690	1,200,534	338,855	249,847	13,010	137,523	65,192
1985	1,888,355	1,350,155	18,198	1,368,353	156,866	62,931	1,274,418	349,038	264,899	13,712	137,713	65,868
1986	1,958,185	1,359,842	23,452	1,383,294	156,925	85,072	1,311,441	369,088	277,656	14,236	137,555	66,699
1987	2,033,381	1,400,451	36,795	1,437,246	158,400	99,535	1,378,381	366,737	288,263	14,991	135,641	68,104
1988	2,206,337	1,582,383	16,307	1,598,690	184,087	115,125	1,529,728	383,285	293,324	16,153	136,588	70,857
1989	2,355,648	1,649,706	35,354	1,685,060	193,402	130,629	1,622,287	420,559	312,802	17,050	138,161	71,522
1990	2,494,373	1,764,660	30,483	1,795,143	214,277	140,084	1,720,950	436,876	336,547	17,835	139,859	73,269
1991	2,550,011	1,760,612	22,044	1,782,656	215,679	145,160	1,712,137	454,662	383,212	18,057	141,219	71,991
1992	2,818,423	2,027,663	31,349	2,059,012	245,807	128,273	1,941,478	471,619	405,326	19,722	142,904	75,226
1993	2,943,921	2,132,308	19,344	2,151,652	258,685	135,774	2,028,741	498,985	416,195	20,391	144,372	76,394
1994	3,124,299	2,286,242	29,048	2,315,290	277,868	151,810	2,189,232	515,144	419,923	21,402	145,982	78,980
1995	3,315,600	2,435,468	23,590	2,459,058	295,923	152,581	2,315,716	556,072	443,812	22,376	148,179	82,349
1996	3,444,607	2,501,199	34,925	2,536,124	299,102	159,787	2,396,809	588,570	459,228	22,974	149,937	82,642
1997	3,624,936	2,656,207	22,985	2,679,192	313,931	166,044	2,531,305	625,320	468,311	24,143	150,145	84,076
1998	3,802,017	2,763,896	27,031	2,790,927	323,369	184,816	2,652,374	672,914	476,729	25,208	150,827	83,619
1999	3,903,910	2,857,959	28,459	2,886,418	334,925	202,514	2,754,007	652,622	497,281	25,761	151,541	84,649
2000	4,077,645	2,937,423	21,376	2,958,799	340,681	225,805	2,843,923	688,730	544,992	26,745	152,464	84,977
2001	4,206,381	2,979,790	27,152	3,006,942	350,877	231,875	2,887,940	708,880	609,561	27,461	153,174	83,958
2002	4,335,941	3,104,837	19,733	3,124,570	361,346	231,054	2,994,278	686,674	654,989	28,224	153,628	83,122
2003	4,485,378	3,240,077	33,860	3,273,937	376,851	229,391	3,126,477	683,309	675,592	29,075	154,268	83,550
2004	4,644,186	3,313,045	49,241	3,362,286	386,508	287,926	3,263,704	682,722	697,760	29,831	155,685	84,840
2005	4,794,903	3,389,575	37,738	3,427,313	401,677	320,082	3,345,718	698,504	750,681	30,587	156,761	85,936
2006	5,145,319	3,673,931	32,578	3,706,509	439,899	311,739	3,578,349	776,035	790,935	32,455	158,538	87,118
2007	5,295,140	3,644,309	44,838	3,689,147	438,700	333,670	3,584,117	858,009	853,014	33,113	159,912	87,009
2008	5,403,846	3,559,317	30,643	3,589,960	433,989	354,366	3,510,337	909,818	983,691	33,638	160,647	84,580
2009	5,285,996	3,272,405	26,111	3,298,516	398,873	398,580	3,298,223	842,467	1,145,306	32,953	160,411	78,107
2010	5,419,568	3,264,949	38,882	3,303,831	399,323	374,604	3,279,112	928,480	1,211,976	33,817	160,263	77,420
2011	5,711,510	3,430,403	71,869	3,502,272	375,072	453,625	3,580,825	968,617	1,162,068	35,723	159,882	77,870
2012	5,987,361	3,662,872	37,120	3,699,992	396,364	392,366	3,695,994	1,101,898	1,189,469	37,400	160,092	79,446
2013	6,168,321	3,965,537	84,570	4,050,107	474,815	285,774	3,861,066	1,087,220	1,220,035	38,462	160,373	80,894
2014	6,220,493	3,885,856	39,780	3,925,636	473,394	362,205	3,814,447	1,132,681	1,273,365	38,644	160,970	82,079
2015	6,438,886	4,048,777	30,289	4,079,066	491,898	355,576	3,942,744	1,173,094	1,323,048	39,978	161,059	83,354
2016	6,589,945	4,175,297	23,176	4,198,473	505,185	369,737	4,063,025	1,190,734	1,336,186	40,825	161,421	84,084
2017	6,821,151	4,350,038	17,953	4,367,991	529,750	349,887	4,188,128	1,237,246	1,395,777	42,026	162,309	85,359
2018	7,214,503	7,189,258	25,245	4,628,738	556,819	320,152	4,392,071	1,354,709	1,467,723	44,295	162,874	86,332
2019	7,552,841	7,520,145	32,696	4,863,337	587,752	370,433	4,646,018	1,368,530	1,538,293	46,236	163,354	87,689

Personal Income and Employment by Area: Jefferson City, MO

(Thousands of dollars, except as noted.)

Year	Personal income, total	Earnings by place of work			Less: Contributions for government social insurance	Plus: Adjustment for residence	Equals: Net earnings by place of residence	Plus: Dividends, interest, and rent	Plus: Personal current transfer receipts	Per capita personal income (dollars)	Population (persons)	Total employment
		Nonfarm	Farm	Total								
1970	342,121	265,871	17,635	283,506	16,832	-8,684	257,990	52,799	31,332	3,639	94,027	47,791
1971	371,341	291,732	14,825	306,557	19,137	-10,723	276,697	58,903	35,741	3,926	94,588	48,879
1972	406,798	316,119	19,926	336,045	21,652	-11,969	302,424	65,672	38,702	4,166	97,637	50,046
1973	465,525	350,251	35,029	385,280	27,702	-13,646	343,932	76,362	45,231	4,726	98,495	52,912
1974	514,010	393,519	25,828	419,347	32,363	-15,738	371,246	89,718	53,046	5,143	99,942	54,087
1975	560,744	421,875	19,171	441,046	33,845	-17,562	389,639	102,264	68,841	5,495	102,037	53,159
1976	628,573	491,201	14,904	506,105	39,834	-24,515	441,756	112,340	74,477	6,060	103,718	55,939
1977	702,792	560,481	19,949	580,430	45,955	-35,386	499,089	126,394	77,309	6,689	105,067	59,122
1978	809,163	664,645	27,687	692,332	57,196	-50,724	584,412	140,490	84,261	7,477	108,217	63,595
1979	896,624	738,510	30,741	769,251	66,049	-60,044	643,158	158,025	95,441	8,172	109,714	64,788
1980	992,623	815,622	3,830	819,452	71,753	-71,472	676,227	200,054	116,342	8,759	113,330	65,774
1981	1,130,066	897,104	16,658	913,762	85,063	-77,297	751,402	245,406	133,258	9,876	114,422	66,216
1982	1,235,960	966,390	12,608	978,998	93,981	-86,028	798,989	288,751	148,220	10,728	115,211	65,896
1983	1,326,342	1,032,427	3,568	1,035,995	100,137	-84,266	851,592	313,954	160,796	11,389	116,456	67,159
1984	1,441,180	1,085,083	19,960	1,105,043	106,525	-74,361	924,157	348,874	168,149	12,282	117,342	68,046
1985	1,495,213	1,094,732	22,559	1,117,291	107,857	-61,483	947,951	369,649	177,613	12,780	117,000	67,660
1986	1,608,769	1,196,428	21,281	1,217,709	119,473	-67,254	1,030,982	390,649	187,138	13,592	118,360	69,180
1987	1,678,323	1,260,239	23,077	1,283,316	124,791	-69,140	1,089,385	399,225	189,713	14,076	119,231	69,132
1988	1,753,421	1,341,431	15,683	1,357,114	140,418	-67,557	1,149,139	406,545	197,737	14,655	119,646	70,870
1989	1,920,764	1,446,941	23,913	1,470,854	152,246	-72,008	1,246,600	457,000	217,164	15,973	120,250	73,463
1990	2,018,562	1,559,467	21,113	1,580,580	167,205	-83,079	1,330,296	449,889	238,377	16,668	121,107	75,568
1991	2,144,345	1,644,181	18,083	1,662,264	178,156	-88,557	1,395,551	472,036	276,758	17,420	123,100	76,650
1992	2,289,461	1,773,417	17,008	1,790,425	190,254	-95,943	1,504,228	481,859	303,374	18,345	124,802	77,896
1993	2,405,852	1,856,797	16,679	1,873,476	199,701	-100,530	1,573,245	509,405	323,202	18,994	126,662	79,861
1994	2,548,476	1,983,027	4,921	1,987,948	214,580	-106,865	1,666,503	537,300	344,673	19,834	128,490	82,641
1995	2,708,402	2,118,785	-4,155	2,114,630	229,148	-118,395	1,767,087	573,486	367,829	20,651	131,148	85,679
1996	2,899,119	2,259,849	19,850	2,279,699	240,978	-130,198	1,908,523	610,075	380,521	21,700	133,601	88,188
1997	3,101,355	2,425,120	21,067	2,446,187	256,540	-144,513	2,045,134	658,905	397,316	22,853	135,707	90,574
1998	3,238,990	2,548,816	8,891	2,557,707	268,657	-152,478	2,136,572	688,164	414,254	23,596	137,268	92,096
1999	3,413,983	2,763,728	-4,584	2,759,144	287,921	-173,270	2,297,953	682,516	433,514	24,608	138,736	93,723
2000	3,612,010	2,903,311	10,394	2,913,705	301,096	-184,985	2,427,624	725,231	459,155	25,748	140,285	95,500
2001	3,744,920	3,015,686	13,394	3,029,080	313,499	-201,145	2,514,436	719,453	511,031	26,561	140,991	96,794
2002	3,796,362	3,093,238	4,601	3,097,839	319,957	-203,963	2,573,919	677,159	545,284	26,699	142,190	95,941
2003	3,986,782	3,257,233	17,211	3,274,444	335,366	-230,067	2,709,011	707,010	570,761	27,846	143,171	97,932
2004	4,247,353	3,443,767	80,953	3,524,720	350,871	-235,883	2,937,966	697,154	612,233	29,777	142,637	98,610
2005	4,376,648	3,565,422	57,552	3,622,974	367,770	-242,833	3,012,371	705,241	659,036	30,299	144,450	99,222
2006	4,637,728	3,757,045	49,400	3,806,445	386,093	-241,183	3,179,169	757,164	701,395	31,841	145,654	99,545
2007	4,865,818	3,854,611	53,244	3,907,855	401,578	-252,042	3,254,235	853,753	757,830	33,224	146,455	100,715
2008	5,186,861	4,018,085	78,909	4,096,994	421,323	-273,927	3,401,744	925,278	859,839	35,096	147,792	101,618
2009	5,119,639	3,976,565	47,974	4,024,539	414,925	-295,229	3,314,385	873,107	932,147	34,388	148,880	100,049
2010	5,227,586	4,069,481	64,657	4,134,138	421,323	-312,570	3,400,245	823,411	1,003,930	34,857	149,974	99,159
2011	5,363,530	4,095,764	78,985	4,174,749	381,216	-323,241	3,470,292	875,372	1,017,866	35,676	150,340	98,429
2012	5,554,587	4,161,391	51,594	4,212,985	382,567	-316,915	3,513,503	1,006,106	1,034,978	36,944	150,351	97,656
2013	5,666,248	4,395,629	86,427	4,482,056	446,898	-346,233	3,688,925	912,661	1,064,662	37,612	150,650	98,057
2014	5,862,736	4,470,487	140,815	4,611,302	458,492	-350,725	3,802,085	968,893	1,091,758	38,890	150,751	98,209
2015	5,999,380	4,581,075	68,323	4,649,398	476,884	-363,007	3,809,507	1,029,822	1,160,051	39,742	150,958	98,931
2016	6,016,298	4,599,579	36,920	4,636,499	491,715	-366,603	3,778,181	1,038,863	1,199,254	39,723	151,455	100,719
2017	6,228,372	4,728,219	55,832	4,784,051	504,754	-370,212	3,909,085	1,089,651	1,229,636	41,121	151,465	101,588
2018	6,393,650	6,390,380	3,270	4,839,628	514,251	-389,940	3,935,437	1,168,531	1,289,682	42,199	151,512	101,580
2019	6,675,625	6,664,125	11,500	5,067,513	539,994	-411,719	4,115,800	1,188,712	1,371,113	44,141	151,235	103,215

Personal Income and Employment by Area: Johnson City, TN

(Thousands of dollars, except as noted.)

Year	Personal income, total	Earnings by place of work			Less: Contributions for government social insurance	Plus: Adjustment for residence	Equals: Net earnings by place of residence	Plus: Dividends, interest, and rent	Plus: Personal current transfer receipts	Per capita personal income (dollars)	Population (persons)	Total employment
		Nonfarm	Farm	Total								
1970	399,260	283,219	7,417	290,636	18,568	36,480	308,548	46,788	43,924	3,002	132,997	51,412
1971	442,056	317,167	6,578	323,745	21,424	36,652	338,973	52,757	50,326	3,241	136,401	53,402
1972	494,553	355,301	10,656	365,957	25,215	39,926	380,668	58,854	55,031	3,529	140,121	56,559
1973	561,016	409,661	13,635	423,296	33,261	40,407	430,442	66,783	63,791	3,980	140,947	60,518
1974	618,936	445,610	10,492	456,102	37,493	44,492	463,101	77,246	78,589	4,320	143,257	60,850
1975	656,423	437,761	7,022	444,783	35,459	51,423	460,747	87,020	108,656	4,511	145,524	55,431
1976	728,393	491,869	11,555	503,424	40,948	59,464	521,940	92,739	113,714	4,867	149,645	57,109
1977	802,321	546,191	9,283	555,474	45,671	71,439	581,242	103,325	117,754	5,371	149,374	59,709
1978	918,853	629,814	9,013	638,827	53,515	88,273	673,585	118,985	126,283	6,094	150,780	62,719
1979	1,033,038	707,064	4,474	711,538	63,248	101,892	750,182	137,525	145,331	6,727	153,562	64,552
1980	1,172,305	783,979	7,798	791,777	70,751	109,669	830,695	169,912	171,698	7,518	155,925	66,128
1981	1,316,291	858,016	14,605	872,621	83,424	121,557	910,754	206,690	198,847	8,330	158,024	65,685
1982	1,377,633	878,357	13,403	891,760	86,848	118,993	923,905	232,024	221,704	8,696	158,424	64,173
1983	1,471,834	945,994	4,682	950,676	94,516	124,980	981,140	251,350	239,344	9,257	158,995	64,560
1984	1,603,935	1,036,645	10,254	1,046,899	107,358	127,354	1,066,895	285,595	251,445	10,041	159,742	67,109
1985	1,689,743	1,089,982	10,028	1,100,010	114,429	142,887	1,128,468	296,850	264,425	10,599	159,422	67,936
1986	1,808,207	1,176,558	5,215	1,181,773	126,535	152,564	1,207,802	318,647	281,758	11,349	159,326	69,445
1987	1,918,038	1,271,104	7,170	1,278,274	136,009	155,758	1,298,023	323,608	296,407	12,038	159,337	72,376
1988	2,059,479	1,361,853	10,211	1,372,064	152,084	169,513	1,389,493	352,003	317,983	12,938	159,181	75,181
1989	2,227,164	1,436,197	11,320	1,447,517	162,954	193,774	1,478,337	396,477	352,350	13,970	159,430	77,238
1990	2,402,074	1,567,238	17,634	1,584,872	178,343	207,179	1,613,708	400,346	388,020	14,925	160,942	80,870
1991	2,531,865	1,646,317	19,679	1,665,996	190,435	208,654	1,684,215	410,076	437,574	15,525	163,079	80,820
1992	2,744,462	1,819,474	22,254	1,841,728	208,268	207,427	1,840,887	414,114	489,461	16,650	164,834	83,910
1993	2,869,754	1,883,846	22,440	1,906,286	215,761	230,210	1,920,735	422,685	526,334	17,174	167,100	85,376
1994	2,977,181	1,995,543	21,143	2,016,686	233,661	194,648	1,977,673	448,397	551,111	17,583	169,319	88,631
1995	3,170,334	2,104,697	14,908	2,119,605	248,129	206,493	2,077,969	489,331	603,034	18,469	171,654	91,968
1996	3,354,781	2,208,066	7,894	2,215,960	257,747	230,464	2,188,677	526,984	639,120	19,248	174,296	93,587
1997	3,555,236	2,376,632	12,082	2,388,714	273,736	219,192	2,334,170	549,909	671,157	20,103	176,853	95,673
1998	3,809,623	2,547,861	10,984	2,558,845	287,385	213,403	2,484,863	613,080	711,680	21,333	178,581	96,099
1999	3,874,014	2,651,017	7,567	2,658,584	298,780	155,243	2,515,047	619,165	739,802	21,505	180,145	97,479
2000	4,120,690	2,856,665	13,316	2,869,981	318,515	106,503	2,657,969	647,381	815,340	22,648	181,944	99,329
2001	4,276,691	2,916,257	7,002	2,923,259	327,879	127,902	2,723,282	671,912	881,497	23,474	182,187	98,166
2002	4,391,905	2,987,733	3,121	2,990,854	338,198	135,335	2,787,991	635,789	968,125	23,873	183,973	96,239
2003	4,567,077	3,105,074	3,946	3,109,020	348,931	144,509	2,904,598	649,669	1,012,810	24,549	186,040	97,295
2004	4,945,851	3,391,794	5,326	3,397,120	376,733	147,731	3,168,118	688,580	1,089,153	26,404	187,317	100,015
2005	5,093,851	3,519,750	6,878	3,526,628	394,839	131,605	3,263,394	667,368	1,163,089	26,926	189,182	102,263
2006	5,406,226	3,677,951	2,644	3,680,595	414,490	177,785	3,443,890	726,907	1,235,429	28,166	191,943	103,414
2007	5,764,858	3,846,536	-2,895	3,843,641	437,566	173,133	3,579,208	827,063	1,358,587	29,744	193,819	106,084
2008	6,041,097	3,929,452	-2,466	3,926,986	455,147	179,211	3,651,050	876,152	1,513,895	30,784	196,242	105,554
2009	6,079,361	3,900,494	5,909	3,906,403	456,342	143,864	3,593,925	867,276	1,618,160	30,751	197,698	101,327
2010	6,357,342	3,962,948	816	3,963,764	459,179	205,104	3,709,689	877,746	1,769,907	31,945	199,010	100,747
2011	6,752,843	4,178,552	-979	4,177,573	429,051	257,584	4,006,106	934,208	1,812,529	33,849	199,499	103,422
2012	6,965,256	4,373,787	2,798	4,376,585	435,044	234,750	4,176,291	967,416	1,821,549	34,782	200,256	103,604
2013	6,950,380	4,342,817	4,765	4,347,582	488,256	267,407	4,126,733	972,597	1,851,050	34,698	200,313	101,654
2014	7,124,784	4,394,083	8,516	4,402,599	493,723	280,599	4,189,475	1,034,277	1,901,032	35,640	199,911	102,024
2015	7,456,831	4,604,147	9,503	4,613,650	515,772	279,766	4,377,644	1,088,560	1,990,627	37,244	200,217	103,321
2016	7,624,492	4,698,814	-4,256	4,694,558	526,702	261,187	4,429,043	1,159,188	2,036,261	37,868	201,343	104,139
2017	7,913,921	4,920,472	2,022	4,922,494	556,681	226,648	4,592,461	1,222,022	2,099,438	39,168	202,053	105,111
2018	8,167,988	8,170,350	-2,362	5,084,677	577,861	256,395	4,763,211	1,244,331	2,160,446	40,256	202,900	106,793
2019	8,392,139	8,395,034	-2,895	5,222,287	591,961	205,503	4,835,829	1,262,548	2,293,762	41,209	203,649	107,558

Personal Income and Employment by Area: Johnstown, PA

(Thousands of dollars, except as noted.)

Year	Personal income, total	Earnings by place of work			Less: Contributions for government social insurance	Plus: Adjustment for residence	Equals: Net earnings by place of residence	Plus: Dividends, interest, and rent	Plus: Personal current transfer receipts	Per capita personal income (dollars)	Population (persons)	Total employment
		Nonfarm	Farm	Total								
1970	607,109	520,299	2,913	523,212	39,131	-33,390	450,691	64,614	91,804	3,246	187,061	70,524
1971	652,058	546,212	2,272	548,484	42,709	-35,117	470,658	68,879	112,521	3,453	188,837	70,619
1972	729,191	618,943	1,235	620,178	50,029	-41,017	529,132	73,513	126,546	3,848	189,521	71,565
1973	810,449	686,485	4,001	690,486	63,793	-45,292	581,401	83,154	145,894	4,282	189,286	73,454
1974	915,701	781,170	3,920	785,090	75,704	-54,371	655,015	96,054	164,632	4,858	188,475	74,173
1975	1,052,072	887,051	3,081	890,132	83,580	-63,706	742,846	111,633	197,593	5,572	188,819	76,041
1976	1,149,286	958,304	3,689	961,993	91,481	-65,987	804,525	120,748	224,013	6,046	190,087	76,121
1977	1,262,593	1,041,240	3,134	1,044,374	98,398	-69,171	876,805	135,930	249,858	6,635	190,302	76,013
1978	1,361,707	1,099,172	6,242	1,105,414	105,791	-68,354	931,269	153,374	277,064	7,237	188,155	74,653
1979	1,521,037	1,239,482	7,715	1,247,197	122,559	-85,132	1,039,506	176,438	305,093	8,161	186,373	76,327
1980	1,594,958	1,210,659	9,740	1,220,399	120,236	-78,987	1,021,176	222,144	351,638	8,716	182,986	71,866
1981	1,716,391	1,246,443	13,143	1,259,586	133,237	-73,017	1,053,332	273,077	389,982	9,456	181,509	69,018
1982	1,764,176	1,189,815	4,771	1,194,586	129,013	-53,757	1,011,816	310,815	441,545	9,878	178,601	65,149
1983	1,796,066	1,146,506	2,825	1,149,331	124,334	-42,414	982,583	338,630	474,853	10,147	176,996	62,516
1984	1,901,340	1,229,874	6,383	1,236,257	140,633	-40,069	1,055,555	376,530	469,255	10,820	175,730	63,475
1985	1,937,778	1,244,431	4,915	1,249,346	144,362	-35,815	1,069,169	390,713	477,896	11,214	172,797	64,019
1986	1,957,248	1,226,039	4,333	1,230,372	145,986	-31,281	1,053,105	404,341	499,802	11,486	170,400	64,855
1987	2,019,148	1,288,327	3,779	1,292,106	151,505	-24,581	1,116,020	395,776	507,352	11,981	168,535	66,371
1988	2,209,157	1,482,240	574	1,482,814	173,230	-27,356	1,282,228	404,130	522,799	13,308	166,006	68,288
1989	2,360,720	1,570,265	3,398	1,573,663	183,133	-31,027	1,359,503	457,059	544,158	14,397	163,970	69,263
1990	2,485,662	1,655,592	5,587	1,661,179	193,552	-26,802	1,440,825	453,256	591,581	15,255	162,938	71,269
1991	2,630,127	1,717,959	5,359	1,723,318	202,554	-22,261	1,498,503	449,496	682,128	16,188	162,473	70,635
1992	2,729,538	1,778,494	8,837	1,787,331	209,030	-6,225	1,572,076	447,468	709,994	16,823	162,247	70,141
1993	2,799,978	1,814,365	8,520	1,822,885	218,475	5,337	1,609,747	449,740	740,491	17,308	161,770	70,383
1994	2,887,963	1,883,497	7,006	1,890,503	232,805	12,598	1,670,296	467,425	750,242	17,964	160,766	71,846
1995	2,995,364	1,939,322	5,389	1,944,711	240,731	10,014	1,713,994	510,982	770,388	18,734	159,892	73,380
1996	3,073,460	1,940,042	8,967	1,949,009	237,144	20,471	1,732,336	528,742	812,382	19,380	158,588	73,457
1997	3,166,958	1,992,758	2,679	1,995,437	243,537	26,392	1,778,292	561,272	827,394	20,121	157,396	73,397
1998	3,309,236	2,118,843	2,245	2,121,088	251,288	27,903	1,897,703	581,589	829,944	21,257	155,677	74,169
1999	3,435,513	2,235,900	625	2,236,525	262,887	29,888	2,003,526	567,565	864,422	22,321	153,911	75,076
2000	3,529,501	2,232,539	3,120	2,235,659	260,881	46,805	2,021,583	602,483	905,435	23,204	152,107	75,088
2001	3,723,119	2,327,849	-1,257	2,326,592	267,609	60,928	2,119,911	631,656	971,552	24,672	150,902	72,951
2002	3,785,767	2,362,918	-2,518	2,360,400	271,738	74,643	2,163,305	596,397	1,026,065	25,267	149,831	71,797
2003	3,905,606	2,445,189	4,070	2,449,259	278,920	83,911	2,254,250	600,535	1,050,821	26,241	148,836	71,477
2004	4,021,382	2,556,723	2,497	2,559,220	291,415	88,986	2,356,791	568,173	1,096,418	27,192	147,886	72,180
2005	4,139,691	2,635,215	5,303	2,640,518	311,725	95,680	2,424,473	554,177	1,161,041	28,166	146,975	72,655
2006	4,292,358	2,724,360	7,113	2,731,473	324,573	77,782	2,484,682	595,895	1,211,781	29,381	146,093	74,221
2007	4,520,099	2,795,398	8,220	2,803,618	336,402	81,176	2,548,392	681,056	1,290,651	31,112	145,283	74,950
2008	4,735,969	2,868,385	12,647	2,881,032	347,884	87,045	2,620,193	710,911	1,404,865	32,742	144,646	75,025
2009	4,720,043	2,817,606	6,727	2,824,333	347,349	101,100	2,578,084	697,719	1,444,240	32,736	144,186	72,738
2010	4,708,067	2,917,948	5,816	2,923,764	356,545	-20,831	2,546,388	655,100	1,506,579	32,820	143,452	72,287
2011	5,043,540	2,979,699	15,920	2,995,619	328,453	147,921	2,815,087	715,681	1,512,772	35,378	142,561	72,198
2012	5,092,909	2,974,401	17,078	2,991,479	325,523	179,166	2,845,122	749,648	1,498,139	35,988	141,518	71,679
2013	5,097,678	2,977,152	15,405	2,992,557	362,494	206,490	2,836,553	735,785	1,525,340	36,740	138,749	70,681
2014	5,199,802	2,986,984	14,252	3,001,236	375,299	225,584	2,851,521	780,847	1,567,434	37,848	137,386	69,917
2015	5,335,383	3,021,200	9,950	3,031,150	373,940	232,932	2,890,142	804,981	1,640,260	39,273	135,854	69,189
2016	5,348,141	2,967,019	8,411	2,975,430	373,872	223,536	2,825,094	803,528	1,719,519	39,818	134,313	68,066
2017	5,453,233	2,990,097	9,961	3,000,058	383,367	267,895	2,884,586	843,991	1,724,656	40,985	133,054	67,239
2018	5,710,818	5,709,787	1,031	3,120,551	395,379	276,082	3,001,254	896,981	1,812,583	43,445	131,449	66,032
2019	5,872,588	5,866,744	5,844	3,210,819	404,488	275,133	3,081,464	917,822	1,873,302	45,107	130,192	66,018

Personal Income and Employment by Area: Jonesboro, AR

(Thousands of dollars, except as noted.)

Year	Personal income, total	Earnings by place of work			Less: Contributions for government social insurance	Plus: Adjustment for residence	Equals: Net earnings by place of residence	Plus: Dividends, interest, and rent	Plus: Personal current transfer receipts	Per capita personal income (dollars)	Population (persons)	Total employment
		Nonfarm	Farm	Total								
1970	232,177	146,372	43,150	189,522	11,136	3,789	182,175	25,548	24,454	2,919	79,540	34,569
1971	251,604	164,558	38,960	203,518	12,866	3,752	194,404	28,764	28,436	3,050	82,495	35,576
1972	278,732	188,955	37,116	226,071	15,373	3,709	214,407	31,858	32,467	3,330	83,698	36,928
1973	340,701	207,580	72,099	279,679	19,394	3,969	264,254	37,607	38,840	4,010	84,953	37,486
1974	382,837	227,529	78,869	306,398	21,956	4,146	288,588	46,024	48,225	4,465	85,734	37,982
1975	408,780	257,744	54,099	311,843	24,362	3,836	291,317	55,182	62,281	4,735	86,332	38,045
1976	438,467	300,452	36,526	336,978	28,746	3,042	311,274	59,555	67,638	4,971	88,200	39,374
1977	491,063	337,792	44,679	382,471	32,614	1,791	351,648	66,348	73,067	5,478	89,644	41,014
1978	630,210	386,681	126,999	513,680	38,343	1,378	476,715	74,094	79,401	6,981	90,272	42,812
1979	629,548	431,483	67,534	499,017	44,209	280	455,088	84,795	89,665	6,931	90,835	42,949
1980	650,383	455,975	28,711	484,686	46,459	148	438,375	103,206	108,802	7,205	90,274	42,267
1981	738,967	474,473	67,706	542,179	52,321	-315	489,543	128,440	120,984	8,202	90,094	40,797
1982	768,278	490,565	51,517	542,082	54,932	183	487,333	149,963	130,982	8,603	89,303	40,231
1983	787,400	527,441	25,220	552,661	59,214	93	493,540	150,691	143,169	8,841	89,065	40,737
1984	907,637	594,052	64,617	658,669	68,381	223	590,511	166,019	151,107	10,151	89,417	42,557
1985	948,682	630,009	51,211	681,220	73,061	512	608,671	180,280	159,731	10,571	89,745	43,490
1986	967,408	677,597	17,228	694,825	78,652	135	616,308	186,098	165,002	10,769	89,832	44,766
1987	1,060,016	745,089	50,416	795,505	85,954	-737	708,814	181,335	169,867	11,642	91,051	46,963
1988	1,159,019	805,294	78,456	883,750	96,410	580	787,920	192,991	178,108	12,606	91,939	48,776
1989	1,221,318	863,127	46,661	909,788	103,622	1,084	807,250	214,972	199,096	13,173	92,714	49,447
1990	1,288,921	906,721	43,599	950,320	112,976	4,871	842,215	228,126	218,580	13,712	93,999	49,752
1991	1,378,040	951,822	67,661	1,019,483	118,918	7,372	907,937	225,712	244,391	14,627	94,210	49,788
1992	1,514,843	1,048,408	89,017	1,137,425	130,022	6,749	1,014,152	231,475	269,216	15,781	95,994	51,479
1993	1,577,750	1,115,099	74,143	1,189,242	138,930	5,848	1,056,160	240,164	281,426	16,110	97,939	52,981
1994	1,656,838	1,182,789	81,584	1,264,373	148,863	6,386	1,121,896	247,693	287,249	16,757	98,872	53,314
1995	1,795,999	1,263,900	98,035	1,361,935	158,288	4,583	1,208,230	276,768	311,001	17,812	100,831	56,015
1996	1,902,309	1,321,408	113,473	1,434,881	164,198	5,299	1,275,982	298,024	328,303	18,532	102,652	56,986
1997	1,992,389	1,398,162	108,787	1,506,949	172,907	5,343	1,339,385	310,812	342,192	19,134	104,130	57,997
1998	2,110,451	1,508,926	90,009	1,598,935	182,681	5,668	1,421,922	331,263	357,266	19,984	105,607	59,098
1999	2,217,860	1,625,636	79,814	1,705,450	194,296	2,149	1,513,303	330,683	373,874	20,813	106,563	60,455
2000	2,337,178	1,701,763	90,537	1,792,300	202,406	2,084	1,591,978	349,294	395,906	21,613	108,136	61,241
2001	2,403,345	1,695,634	93,165	1,788,799	201,817	-2,814	1,584,168	367,263	451,914	22,095	108,774	61,014
2002	2,467,829	1,775,898	43,900	1,819,798	209,111	-13,894	1,596,793	366,109	504,927	22,601	109,191	61,139
2003	2,706,348	1,863,458	184,526	2,047,984	218,204	-24,578	1,805,202	372,658	528,488	24,564	110,177	61,586
2004	2,795,296	1,994,517	166,359	2,160,876	231,097	-35,313	1,894,466	325,722	575,108	25,099	111,370	62,829
2005	2,885,903	2,089,201	102,429	2,191,630	244,733	-38,572	1,908,325	355,869	621,709	25,637	112,570	63,514
2006	3,024,608	2,153,942	114,187	2,268,129	259,162	-44,734	1,964,233	385,623	674,752	26,386	114,629	64,964
2007	3,186,881	2,208,325	109,534	2,317,859	268,241	-41,248	2,008,370	444,439	734,072	27,435	116,163	64,741
2008	3,348,650	2,292,084	109,163	2,401,247	286,437	-64,406	2,050,404	465,609	832,637	28,399	117,915	64,977
2009	3,413,900	2,295,941	99,885	2,395,826	290,642	-60,180	2,045,004	452,789	916,107	28,422	120,114	64,443
2010	3,606,628	2,462,350	94,156	2,556,506	305,297	-60,891	2,190,318	432,301	984,009	29,744	121,255	65,208
2011	3,865,422	2,584,049	122,442	2,706,491	289,073	-48,206	2,369,212	480,819	1,015,391	31,490	122,750	67,910
2012	4,056,821	2,743,593	79,196	2,822,789	297,068	-30,808	2,494,913	529,996	1,031,912	32,680	124,136	68,060
2013	4,174,415	2,818,110	190,627	3,008,737	339,301	-32,991	2,636,445	488,390	1,049,580	33,213	125,685	69,162
2014	4,240,836	2,924,116	41,613	2,965,729	355,710	-31,108	2,578,911	535,343	1,126,582	33,479	126,670	70,420
2015	4,344,912	3,020,445	1,767	3,022,212	370,664	-39,233	2,612,315	565,042	1,167,555	33,863	128,307	72,438
2016	4,437,517	3,103,790	-7,669	3,096,121	377,175	-62,139	2,656,807	567,319	1,213,391	34,190	129,789	74,428
2017	4,595,101	3,225,112	15,577	3,240,689	392,170	-84,103	2,764,416	600,082	1,230,603	35,005	131,269	76,313
2018	4,846,214	4,792,478	53,736	3,429,815	411,626	-105,925	2,912,264	652,283	1,281,667	36,515	132,719	78,214
2019	5,103,025	5,009,029	93,996	3,634,369	435,089	-119,621	3,079,659	671,900	1,351,466	38,122	133,860	79,784

Personal Income and Employment by Area: Joplin, MO

(Thousands of dollars, except as noted.)

Year	Personal income, total	Earnings by place of work			Less: Contributions for government social insurance	Plus: Adjustment for residence	Equals: Net earnings by place of residence	Plus: Dividends, interest, and rent	Plus: Personal current transfer receipts	Per capita personal income (dollars)	Population (persons)	Total employment
		Nonfarm	Farm	Total								
1970	354,813	273,450	10,341	283,791	18,399	-6,324	259,068	50,657	45,088	3,139	113,028	48,807
1971	379,110	291,191	9,671	300,862	20,308	-8,264	272,290	55,148	51,672	3,314	114,407	49,252
1972	428,365	331,460	15,571	347,031	24,322	-9,849	312,860	60,360	55,145	3,650	117,364	52,210
1973	485,292	368,637	26,756	395,393	31,341	-10,957	353,095	68,326	63,871	4,064	119,399	55,584
1974	523,487	407,601	9,893	417,494	35,911	-12,970	368,613	79,832	75,042	4,328	120,962	55,905
1975	568,447	423,422	10,444	433,866	36,445	-12,682	384,739	88,212	95,496	4,693	121,126	53,422
1976	632,272	474,540	14,454	488,994	41,337	-14,227	433,430	97,416	101,426	5,192	121,777	55,436
1977	702,099	534,084	13,728	547,812	46,634	-15,924	485,254	111,778	105,067	5,675	123,716	57,532
1978	786,186	607,725	14,860	622,585	54,953	-19,920	547,712	124,480	113,994	6,294	124,905	59,753
1979	879,690	678,401	16,617	695,018	63,378	-21,304	610,336	141,139	128,215	6,940	126,753	61,872
1980	979,951	724,351	17,943	742,294	67,466	-23,754	651,074	174,134	154,743	7,665	127,845	61,478
1981	1,100,055	801,562	15,893	817,455	79,874	-27,315	710,266	212,948	176,841	8,535	128,894	62,909
1982	1,178,246	838,831	6,326	845,157	84,985	-32,243	727,929	251,660	198,657	9,118	129,226	62,312
1983	1,269,131	905,250	6,240	911,490	91,712	-35,713	784,065	273,355	211,711	9,790	129,634	64,321
1984	1,403,816	1,013,969	5,248	1,019,217	105,788	-41,985	871,444	312,544	219,828	10,743	130,678	67,177
1985	1,493,928	1,092,186	7,212	1,099,398	116,190	-47,730	935,478	325,524	232,926	11,360	131,504	69,624
1986	1,590,326	1,169,757	14,388	1,184,145	124,873	-55,234	1,004,038	339,450	246,838	12,033	132,165	71,862
1987	1,671,774	1,263,879	7,274	1,271,153	132,982	-61,637	1,076,534	338,141	257,099	12,543	133,284	73,545
1988	1,783,976	1,340,886	12,251	1,353,137	145,718	-64,608	1,142,811	362,215	278,950	13,346	133,670	74,700
1989	1,898,391	1,415,771	20,801	1,436,572	155,491	-66,999	1,214,082	389,996	294,313	14,125	134,404	75,726
1990	2,000,160	1,499,680	14,731	1,514,411	169,119	-74,123	1,271,169	410,139	318,852	14,792	135,219	77,595
1991	2,115,915	1,589,294	12,284	1,601,578	181,051	-79,848	1,340,679	405,465	369,771	15,478	136,705	78,870
1992	2,312,996	1,731,192	14,248	1,745,440	195,106	-87,409	1,462,925	449,168	400,903	16,656	138,865	81,177
1993	2,456,286	1,845,759	13,136	1,858,895	209,232	-95,612	1,554,051	468,117	434,118	17,352	141,558	84,247
1994	2,645,707	2,014,517	11,926	2,026,443	230,112	-109,248	1,687,083	503,273	455,351	18,346	144,212	88,024
1995	2,801,857	2,142,519	7,933	2,150,452	245,997	-116,625	1,787,830	523,310	490,717	19,092	146,755	90,789
1996	2,965,766	2,258,581	21,944	2,280,525	256,494	-123,538	1,900,493	539,381	525,892	19,844	149,456	93,362
1997	3,157,183	2,414,215	22,213	2,436,428	274,230	-136,764	2,025,434	574,147	557,602	20,791	151,852	95,844
1998	3,316,092	2,548,530	22,394	2,570,924	289,694	-144,713	2,136,517	603,258	576,317	21,524	154,066	98,516
1999	3,469,462	2,691,431	15,778	2,707,209	303,575	-148,092	2,255,542	605,238	608,682	22,266	155,822	99,452
2000	3,663,051	2,814,860	8,374	2,823,234	313,644	-151,922	2,357,668	654,380	651,003	23,233	157,665	100,269
2001	3,883,005	2,990,232	21,161	3,011,393	329,644	-159,064	2,522,685	628,195	732,125	24,488	158,567	99,129
2002	3,962,631	3,091,631	15,338	3,106,969	335,678	-171,294	2,599,997	575,550	787,084	24,752	160,092	97,883
2003	4,086,655	3,182,840	29,452	3,212,292	347,507	-185,691	2,679,094	580,495	827,066	25,221	162,037	97,823
2004	4,361,967	3,332,363	68,002	3,400,365	363,436	-192,359	2,844,570	652,589	864,808	26,598	163,997	98,482
2005	4,451,225	3,388,473	64,999	3,453,472	376,618	-194,260	2,882,594	636,479	932,152	26,789	166,160	99,546
2006	4,694,716	3,582,006	41,883	3,623,889	404,196	-211,602	3,008,091	709,703	976,922	27,829	168,701	102,126
2007	4,936,466	3,698,859	41,759	3,740,618	425,543	-209,940	3,105,135	778,946	1,052,385	28,830	171,224	105,104
2008	5,273,285	3,822,556	84,094	3,906,650	448,293	-203,112	3,255,245	843,025	1,175,015	30,527	172,744	105,170
2009	5,289,113	3,799,232	49,588	3,848,820	441,888	-186,564	3,220,368	792,951	1,275,794	30,329	174,394	101,990
2010	5,393,523	3,856,626	61,737	3,918,363	442,524	-181,811	3,294,028	749,666	1,349,829	30,674	175,835	100,016
2011	5,696,067	4,010,695	56,266	4,066,961	414,457	-181,418	3,471,086	839,734	1,385,247	32,247	176,638	101,070
2012	6,017,856	4,216,297	58,701	4,274,998	422,457	-173,067	3,679,474	995,005	1,343,377	34,512	174,368	102,073
2013	5,931,072	4,290,230	82,835	4,373,065	482,860	-171,222	3,718,983	850,864	1,361,225	33,865	175,140	101,929
2014	6,189,604	4,345,813	134,941	4,480,754	490,123	-134,740	3,855,891	930,145	1,403,568	35,189	175,894	101,444
2015	6,468,309	4,569,073	99,926	4,668,999	516,639	-122,599	4,029,761	961,924	1,476,624	36,599	176,733	101,605
2016	6,571,480	4,599,573	65,679	4,665,252	524,786	-92,335	4,048,131	993,233	1,530,116	37,019	177,517	101,785
2017	6,756,499	4,714,017	71,486	4,785,503	538,858	-95,018	4,151,627	1,039,025	1,565,847	37,850	178,507	102,183
2018	7,201,720	7,165,131	36,589	5,032,869	559,475	-117,253	4,356,141	1,213,597	1,631,982	40,320	178,613	103,600
2019	7,438,057	7,414,046	24,011	5,201,257	586,068	-100,473	4,514,716	1,226,475	1,696,866	41,423	179,564	104,944

Personal Income and Employment by Area: Kahului-Wailuku-Lahaina, HI

(Thousands of dollars, except as noted.)

Year	Personal income, total	Earnings by place of work			Less: Contributions for government social insurance	Plus: Adjustment for residence	Equals: Net earnings by place of residence	Plus: Dividends, interest, and rent	Plus: Personal current transfer receipts	Per capita personal income (dollars)	Population (persons)	Total employment
		Nonfarm	Farm	Total								
1970	199,508	124,379	37,343	161,722	9,259	33	152,496	31,550	15,462	4,338	45,995	22,016
1971	220,100	135,780	37,904	173,684	10,635	-55	162,994	36,754	20,352	4,250	51,784	22,664
1972	242,138	148,307	39,733	188,040	12,183	-104	175,753	41,218	25,167	4,703	51,488	23,264
1973	268,541	165,033	38,686	203,719	15,878	-219	187,622	50,240	30,679	5,096	52,693	24,568
1974	357,443	191,969	89,294	281,263	19,580	-722	260,961	58,908	37,574	6,661	53,661	26,464
1975	379,559	233,660	54,923	288,583	21,968	-2,371	264,244	66,618	48,697	6,698	56,669	29,157
1976	423,121	269,325	54,157	323,482	25,324	-3,083	295,075	72,317	55,729	7,032	60,173	31,192
1977	475,251	315,645	55,733	371,378	29,810	-4,017	337,551	81,038	56,662	7,572	62,763	33,058
1978	529,548	365,868	47,483	413,351	36,293	-4,767	372,291	95,966	61,291	8,030	65,950	35,880
1979	612,079	424,955	53,938	478,893	43,393	-5,641	429,859	114,786	67,434	8,802	69,537	37,847
1980	733,508	469,621	97,238	566,859	47,270	-6,073	513,516	138,903	81,089	10,241	71,624	39,255
1981	769,699	515,529	51,457	566,986	55,584	-4,128	507,274	166,686	95,739	10,395	74,043	38,790
1982	838,061	569,940	58,659	628,599	62,351	-4,242	562,006	169,266	106,789	10,869	77,103	40,711
1983	979,608	634,055	103,443	737,498	68,462	-3,693	665,343	196,377	117,888	12,236	80,060	43,194
1984	1,038,831	705,774	69,577	775,351	77,922	-3,750	693,679	222,365	122,787	12,521	82,969	44,749
1985	1,127,368	788,252	63,316	851,568	88,160	-4,534	758,874	239,058	129,436	13,240	85,147	48,048
1986	1,228,301	865,151	73,511	938,662	97,650	-4,753	836,259	257,201	134,841	14,056	87,389	50,149
1987	1,329,873	961,975	73,277	1,035,252	108,359	-4,900	921,993	268,924	138,956	14,690	90,532	53,953
1988	1,500,439	1,124,023	66,870	1,190,893	128,164	-5,472	1,057,257	295,268	147,914	16,002	93,767	58,381
1989	1,748,023	1,324,148	60,850	1,384,998	149,806	-8,235	1,226,957	357,131	163,935	18,055	96,819	62,829
1990	1,953,686	1,503,118	67,682	1,570,800	177,004	-9,771	1,384,025	389,246	180,415	19,209	101,709	66,255
1991	2,080,622	1,618,460	67,274	1,685,734	192,438	-10,153	1,483,143	394,395	203,084	19,703	105,599	69,643
1992	2,302,938	1,760,085	97,223	1,857,308	208,876	-9,965	1,638,467	418,835	245,636	21,209	108,585	72,764
1993	2,441,170	1,861,638	57,066	1,918,704	215,201	-9,403	1,694,100	484,897	262,173	21,807	111,944	72,912
1994	2,539,146	1,942,678	58,477	2,001,155	228,246	-10,547	1,762,362	495,926	280,858	22,127	114,754	73,468
1995	2,620,030	1,972,859	59,511	2,032,370	229,713	-9,454	1,793,203	505,445	321,382	22,223	117,895	73,984
1996	2,652,637	1,988,076	56,091	2,044,167	233,397	-10,586	1,800,184	510,737	341,716	21,979	120,689	74,645
1997	2,744,581	2,043,023	57,536	2,100,559	238,101	-10,989	1,851,469	555,363	337,749	22,355	122,772	75,979
1998	2,887,074	2,124,904	65,049	2,189,953	245,746	-12,084	1,932,123	601,695	353,256	23,162	124,648	78,154
1999	3,114,478	2,318,242	70,622	2,388,864	264,067	-14,833	2,109,964	626,347	378,167	24,687	126,160	80,371
2000	3,331,040	2,481,256	62,275	2,543,531	281,362	-16,679	2,245,490	686,980	398,570	25,806	129,078	82,260
2001	3,546,343	2,675,614	66,466	2,742,080	298,538	-14,901	2,428,641	696,643	421,059	26,779	132,428	85,069
2002	3,742,787	2,850,122	72,141	2,922,263	318,036	-12,850	2,591,377	692,425	458,985	27,810	134,583	85,815
2003	3,981,918	3,092,773	73,624	3,166,397	345,829	-10,435	2,810,133	692,579	479,206	28,939	137,596	87,997
2004	4,350,123	3,332,273	78,718	3,410,991	362,204	-8,327	3,040,460	789,125	520,538	30,934	140,625	91,839
2005	4,709,925	3,617,779	84,978	3,702,757	395,208	-7,140	3,300,409	844,824	564,692	32,834	143,448	96,095
2006	5,071,817	3,818,015	94,979	3,912,994	430,575	-4,681	3,477,738	1,000,832	593,247	34,792	145,776	98,710
2007	5,383,571	3,985,578	94,137	4,079,715	455,502	-2,703	3,621,510	1,104,348	657,713	36,347	148,117	102,898
2008	5,637,459	3,981,217	77,588	4,058,805	454,037	2,030	3,606,798	1,249,227	781,434	37,230	151,424	101,182
2009	5,350,898	3,722,263	76,675	3,798,938	423,252	8,213	3,383,899	1,100,617	866,382	34,884	153,393	94,943
2010	5,527,863	3,745,763	78,694	3,824,457	441,206	13,074	3,396,325	1,149,411	982,127	35,646	155,078	93,935
2011	5,863,040	3,914,963	84,128	3,999,091	423,108	17,772	3,593,755	1,247,639	1,021,646	37,361	156,928	95,096
2012	6,305,988	4,243,652	103,146	4,346,798	444,975	20,958	3,922,781	1,383,676	999,531	39,715	158,782	97,164
2013	6,317,802	4,352,033	93,320	4,445,353	525,287	25,608	3,945,674	1,341,314	1,030,814	39,218	161,095	100,042
2014	6,733,445	4,579,694	85,120	4,664,814	528,944	27,164	4,163,034	1,462,691	1,107,720	41,181	163,509	102,724
2015	7,164,176	4,888,770	76,564	4,965,334	557,636	28,278	4,435,976	1,583,079	1,145,121	43,557	164,477	104,658
2016	7,456,421	5,050,957	62,944	5,113,901	575,581	29,743	4,568,063	1,688,018	1,200,340	45,062	165,472	106,840
2017	7,856,029	5,349,687	78,696	5,428,383	614,498	29,764	4,843,649	1,763,721	1,248,659	47,226	166,348	109,054
2018	8,212,150	8,181,518	30,632	5,715,303	652,591	30,510	5,093,222	1,832,615	1,286,313	49,157	167,058	110,356
2019	8,600,887	8,568,443	32,444	6,013,209	689,524	29,647	5,353,332	1,866,142	1,381,413	51,348	167,503	113,729

Personal Income and Employment by Area: Kalamazoo-Portage, MI

(Thousands of dollars, except as noted.)

Year	Personal income, total	Earnings by place of work			Less: Contributions for government social insurance	Plus: Adjustment for residence	Equals: Net earnings by place of residence	Plus: Dividends, interest, and rent	Plus: Personal current transfer receipts	Per capita personal income (dollars)	Population (persons)	Total employment
		Nonfarm	Farm	Total								
1970	1,024,094	834,532	18,026	852,558	59,929	-3,231	789,398	149,462	85,234	3,971	257,900	108,004
1971	1,083,816	873,031	17,465	890,496	64,642	-1,949	823,905	157,410	102,501	4,173	259,747	106,654
1972	1,187,917	961,313	20,557	981,870	74,874	-652	906,344	168,247	113,326	4,515	263,099	110,715
1973	1,330,915	1,079,201	29,593	1,108,794	97,611	-2,783	1,008,400	190,740	131,775	5,076	262,173	115,785
1974	1,471,063	1,178,093	27,751	1,205,844	110,553	-9,137	1,086,154	221,445	163,464	5,564	264,388	118,408
1975	1,618,247	1,258,389	28,432	1,286,821	114,779	-12,593	1,159,449	240,637	218,161	6,062	266,969	117,797
1976	1,775,166	1,413,221	20,303	1,433,524	131,604	-17,193	1,284,727	259,005	231,434	6,584	269,631	121,403
1977	1,985,399	1,598,931	29,010	1,627,941	147,877	-21,208	1,458,856	289,184	237,359	7,298	272,051	126,334
1978	2,213,477	1,798,316	30,743	1,829,059	170,622	-25,045	1,633,392	321,308	258,777	8,073	274,191	131,628
1979	2,447,355	2,017,573	21,330	2,038,903	200,012	-42,898	1,795,993	358,432	292,930	8,858	276,290	134,464
1980	2,672,972	2,138,880	12,626	2,151,506	211,258	-57,678	1,882,570	427,968	362,434	9,559	279,626	132,685
1981	2,955,316	2,316,453	21,181	2,337,634	246,051	-56,063	2,035,520	524,096	395,700	10,526	280,754	132,264
1982	3,092,685	2,348,534	20,089	2,368,623	253,826	-50,003	2,064,794	590,864	437,027	11,019	280,662	129,119
1983	3,300,427	2,500,724	15,861	2,516,585	274,339	-48,809	2,193,437	638,325	468,665	11,818	279,280	129,086
1984	3,591,333	2,716,635	28,677	2,745,312	308,601	-46,801	2,389,910	719,873	481,550	12,849	279,510	132,514
1985	3,847,126	2,934,373	43,510	2,977,883	338,590	-54,157	2,585,136	752,427	509,563	13,707	280,675	136,989
1986	4,129,760	3,160,197	35,216	3,195,413	365,172	-39,247	2,790,994	802,182	536,584	14,587	283,122	141,796
1987	4,420,491	3,402,637	51,943	3,454,580	386,888	-35,723	3,031,969	838,276	550,246	15,439	286,324	148,346
1988	4,759,164	3,740,676	44,055	3,784,731	436,953	-37,860	3,309,918	877,089	572,157	16,418	289,882	153,749
1989	5,204,218	3,980,662	60,902	4,041,564	461,156	-35,942	3,544,466	1,034,786	624,966	17,816	292,105	159,164
1990	5,381,969	4,121,475	51,771	4,173,246	487,081	-27,914	3,658,251	1,043,560	680,158	18,290	294,251	161,538
1991	5,655,166	4,331,163	57,279	4,388,442	517,848	-23,630	3,846,964	1,051,342	756,860	19,095	296,165	163,402
1992	5,969,442	4,582,609	57,236	4,639,845	544,711	-8,790	4,086,344	1,076,295	806,803	19,937	299,414	164,582
1993	6,308,395	4,823,755	50,729	4,874,484	576,255	2,937	4,301,166	1,135,754	871,475	20,843	302,658	167,830
1994	6,684,124	5,041,778	47,794	5,089,572	614,936	31,658	4,506,294	1,304,394	873,436	21,962	304,355	170,650
1995	7,021,344	5,300,857	54,012	5,354,869	648,377	38,271	4,744,763	1,329,059	947,522	22,908	306,504	175,650
1996	7,380,403	5,588,009	49,406	5,637,415	669,041	38,474	5,006,848	1,408,014	965,541	23,880	309,056	177,475
1997	7,659,961	5,739,872	55,568	5,795,440	688,364	77,067	5,184,143	1,451,857	1,023,961	24,676	310,425	178,617
1998	8,009,072	6,053,057	58,477	6,111,534	716,503	89,568	5,484,599	1,511,352	1,013,121	25,674	311,947	177,380
1999	8,261,984	6,280,014	61,850	6,341,864	736,450	105,288	5,710,702	1,444,257	1,107,025	26,343	313,627	178,146
2000	8,605,467	6,471,138	67,496	6,538,634	752,904	124,254	5,909,984	1,546,371	1,149,112	27,297	315,250	180,572
2001	9,092,938	6,907,029	68,032	6,975,061	756,711	88,362	6,306,712	1,496,216	1,290,010	28,729	316,512	179,844
2002	9,326,202	7,126,619	65,070	7,191,689	786,523	84,738	6,489,904	1,497,798	1,338,500	29,262	318,714	179,202
2003	9,595,061	7,364,922	66,381	7,431,303	812,712	45,003	6,663,594	1,524,666	1,406,801	29,905	320,856	177,994
2004	9,817,961	7,344,368	93,892	7,438,260	830,334	76,569	6,684,495	1,648,082	1,485,384	30,706	319,746	179,683
2005	10,015,830	7,372,022	80,720	7,452,742	852,915	106,588	6,706,415	1,727,520	1,581,895	31,273	320,268	181,523
2006	10,497,849	7,619,818	96,172	7,715,990	892,131	112,733	6,936,592	1,863,623	1,697,634	32,684	321,197	182,576
2007	10,891,092	7,830,839	100,570	7,931,409	925,193	122,032	7,128,248	1,899,295	1,863,549	33,816	322,070	184,879
2008	11,482,410	8,065,132	97,391	8,162,523	963,446	160,057	7,359,134	1,995,558	2,127,718	35,509	323,363	182,099
2009	11,254,292	7,757,222	94,676	7,851,898	930,363	141,665	7,063,200	1,857,818	2,333,274	34,564	325,604	175,629
2010	11,577,809	7,919,653	120,023	8,039,676	930,351	191,863	7,301,188	1,779,582	2,497,039	35,421	326,865	172,314
2011	12,282,123	8,084,844	186,016	8,270,860	846,383	194,824	7,619,301	2,144,856	2,517,966	37,405	328,352	172,996
2012	12,644,009	8,416,544	110,747	8,527,291	879,110	204,155	7,852,336	2,309,801	2,481,872	38,279	330,308	173,841
2013	12,961,034	8,653,610	167,910	8,821,520	1,025,007	225,414	8,021,927	2,395,582	2,543,525	39,018	332,184	176,085
2014	13,400,999	8,820,049	107,936	8,927,985	1,047,395	264,069	8,144,659	2,602,055	2,654,285	40,149	333,779	179,054
2015	14,250,108	9,363,493	100,248	9,463,741	1,098,385	276,778	8,642,134	2,791,421	2,816,553	42,596	334,538	181,588
2016	14,683,214	9,783,440	125,526	9,908,966	1,140,639	291,844	9,060,171	2,729,592	2,893,451	43,667	336,257	184,685
2017	15,134,770	10,283,356	80,118	10,363,474	1,190,018	225,853	9,399,309	2,829,920	2,905,541	44,733	338,338	186,770
2018	12,778,555	12,719,568	58,987	9,272,447	1,073,679	-282,224	7,916,544	2,596,367	2,265,644	48,279	264,680	158,117
2019	13,118,941	13,050,609	68,332	9,660,937	1,110,542	-440,221	8,110,174	2,610,694	2,398,073	49,493	265,066	159,623

Personal Income and Employment by Area: Kankakee, IL

(Thousands of dollars, except as noted.)

Year	Personal income, total	Earnings by place of work			Less: Contributions for government social insurance	Plus: Adjustment for residence	Equals: Net earnings by place of residence	Plus: Dividends, interest, and rent	Plus: Personal current transfer receipts	Per capita personal income (dollars)	Population (persons)	Total employment
		Nonfarm	Farm	Total								
1970	374,165	287,108	11,263	298,371	19,044	13,017	292,344	50,444	31,377	3,844	97,342	39,706
1971	414,326	310,688	18,119	328,807	21,318	14,675	322,164	54,359	37,803	4,200	98,659	40,376
1972	449,044	341,706	12,309	354,015	24,795	16,894	346,114	60,005	42,925	4,504	99,695	40,906
1973	513,219	373,462	30,151	403,613	31,456	19,694	391,851	68,386	52,982	5,166	99,351	42,692
1974	553,924	405,097	23,455	428,552	35,238	22,246	415,560	77,069	61,295	5,551	99,787	43,581
1975	607,935	412,224	36,404	448,628	34,949	26,458	440,137	87,154	80,644	6,080	99,990	42,589
1976	653,633	445,681	30,555	476,236	38,528	32,936	470,644	92,157	90,832	6,507	100,458	42,763
1977	719,099	491,423	30,958	522,381	42,611	39,799	519,569	101,895	97,635	7,076	101,619	44,000
1978	791,542	545,425	27,246	572,671	48,497	49,309	573,483	112,909	105,150	7,683	103,025	45,063
1979	865,021	584,871	33,924	618,795	54,028	58,966	623,733	125,840	115,448	8,299	104,238	44,868
1980	924,442	607,234	10,574	617,808	55,847	64,991	626,952	157,531	139,959	8,985	102,886	43,027
1981	1,038,412	651,774	27,418	679,192	64,401	66,403	681,194	194,539	162,679	10,127	102,544	43,280
1982	1,082,227	654,843	18,876	673,719	65,026	67,399	676,092	225,023	181,112	10,692	101,218	41,632
1983	1,092,859	667,295	-1,245	666,050	66,316	68,982	668,716	225,791	198,352	10,977	99,560	40,857
1984	1,182,279	698,087	24,129	722,216	71,530	79,457	730,143	251,827	200,309	12,001	98,513	41,023
1985	1,219,117	723,948	29,777	753,725	75,637	83,448	761,536	252,085	205,496	12,563	97,039	41,045
1986	1,266,413	758,244	28,807	787,051	79,429	87,192	794,814	259,591	212,008	13,202	95,926	41,221
1987	1,327,206	815,370	25,452	840,822	84,303	91,790	848,309	262,516	216,381	13,870	95,692	42,154
1988	1,406,788	867,158	33,595	900,753	92,654	99,526	907,625	271,061	228,102	14,734	95,481	42,337
1989	1,508,945	911,043	43,751	954,794	98,324	105,489	961,959	304,229	242,757	15,782	95,611	42,756
1990	1,641,340	1,012,318	60,016	1,072,334	106,983	103,992	1,069,343	306,962	265,035	16,998	96,560	45,566
1991	1,664,898	1,055,434	38,170	1,093,604	114,440	107,255	1,086,419	293,510	284,969	17,059	97,598	47,700
1992	1,789,950	1,122,429	42,895	1,165,324	119,928	115,052	1,160,448	304,449	325,053	18,041	99,215	45,999
1993	1,896,814	1,215,709	50,451	1,266,160	131,719	114,605	1,249,046	309,956	337,812	18,824	100,766	47,610
1994	1,996,534	1,294,961	53,546	1,348,507	142,625	120,356	1,326,238	324,035	346,261	19,625	101,736	50,134
1995	2,128,529	1,387,561	35,545	1,423,106	153,522	120,890	1,390,474	364,426	373,629	20,884	101,923	52,190
1996	2,228,451	1,418,261	52,412	1,470,673	154,895	133,964	1,449,742	387,111	391,598	21,784	102,296	51,612
1997	2,294,289	1,465,262	30,408	1,495,670	159,395	148,634	1,484,909	407,927	401,453	22,285	102,951	52,245
1998	2,381,607	1,512,696	21,850	1,534,546	163,146	169,291	1,540,691	431,785	409,131	23,073	103,222	53,006
1999	2,463,312	1,592,738	18,531	1,611,269	168,868	189,759	1,632,160	415,514	415,638	23,760	103,675	53,241
2000	2,632,231	1,687,502	28,639	1,716,141	175,943	208,469	1,748,667	447,751	435,813	25,348	103,842	54,118
2001	2,756,598	1,751,718	23,880	1,775,598	182,946	237,350	1,830,002	458,134	468,462	26,381	104,490	53,784
2002	2,833,919	1,820,547	15,617	1,836,164	189,306	247,941	1,894,799	432,411	506,709	27,007	104,932	52,857
2003	2,907,722	1,826,008	16,194	1,842,202	191,356	268,490	1,919,336	454,007	534,379	27,485	105,794	52,113
2004	2,996,568	1,876,667	49,630	1,926,297	200,805	295,659	2,021,151	418,722	556,695	28,072	106,744	52,379
2005	3,122,240	1,945,204	35,185	1,980,389	214,232	337,573	2,103,730	399,988	618,522	28,932	107,917	53,554
2006	3,306,580	2,045,268	38,600	2,083,868	225,240	366,876	2,225,504	437,934	643,142	30,132	109,735	54,878
2007	3,503,371	2,106,024	76,545	2,182,569	234,685	384,713	2,332,597	465,434	705,340	31,421	111,499	55,452
2008	3,677,318	2,150,696	101,666	2,252,362	240,596	373,908	2,385,674	518,509	773,135	32,641	112,658	55,182
2009	3,628,577	2,136,240	68,710	2,204,950	236,176	293,165	2,261,939	494,854	871,784	32,081	113,107	54,090
2010	3,720,500	2,168,962	54,432	2,223,394	238,501	319,991	2,304,884	477,933	937,683	32,803	113,418	53,693
2011	3,837,359	2,238,044	86,981	2,325,025	223,521	322,875	2,424,379	509,813	903,167	33,816	113,477	53,599
2012	3,878,902	2,358,967	52,503	2,411,470	236,832	268,857	2,443,495	533,295	902,112	34,341	112,952	54,818
2013	4,007,456	2,435,043	108,841	2,543,884	269,508	275,395	2,549,771	530,250	927,435	35,715	112,207	55,124
2014	4,047,459	2,507,886	54,932	2,562,818	277,854	252,606	2,537,570	568,561	941,328	36,338	111,384	55,371
2015	4,145,016	2,584,724	-7,004	2,577,720	284,439	267,923	2,561,204	592,840	990,972	37,425	110,756	55,565
2016	4,270,269	2,615,764	71,674	2,687,438	289,164	261,544	2,659,818	616,312	994,139	38,802	110,053	55,138
2017	4,369,097	2,740,635	27,628	2,768,263	303,766	237,401	2,701,898	641,386	1,025,813	39,862	109,605	57,054
2018	4,550,632	4,511,121	39,511	2,863,022	316,562	279,278	2,825,738	648,382	1,076,512	41,387	109,953	56,346
2019	4,689,720	4,652,959	36,761	3,001,934	331,704	242,690	2,912,920	659,889	1,116,911	42,687	109,862	57,058

Personal Income and Employment by Area: Kansas City, MO-KS

(Thousands of dollars, except as noted.)

Year	Personal income, total	Earnings by place of work			Less: Contributions for government social insurance	Plus: Adjustment for residence	Equals: Net earnings by place of residence	Plus: Dividends, interest, and rent	Plus: Personal current transfer receipts	Per capita personal income (dollars)	Population (persons)	Total employment
		Nonfarm	Farm	Total								
1970.............	6,169,809	5,158,197	69,514	5,227,711	347,962	-33,526	4,846,223	879,775	443,811	4,346	1,419,593	674,424
1971.............	6,725,331	5,595,335	73,673	5,669,008	390,806	-34,424	5,243,778	965,919	515,634	4,695	1,432,356	679,124
1972.............	7,371,520	6,140,083	96,596	6,236,679	452,442	-35,334	5,748,903	1,054,654	567,963	5,120	1,439,848	697,223
1973.............	8,099,191	6,738,317	139,328	6,877,645	574,782	-36,305	6,266,558	1,168,589	664,044	5,568	1,454,634	727,985
1974.............	8,769,756	7,240,121	70,030	7,310,151	637,906	-33,670	6,638,575	1,352,257	778,924	6,044	1,450,974	734,327
1975.............	9,649,950	7,825,073	73,351	7,898,424	677,428	-37,882	7,183,114	1,474,431	992,405	6,684	1,443,816	727,345
1976.............	10,609,345	8,742,798	50,836	8,793,634	772,971	-44,874	7,975,789	1,575,007	1,058,549	7,306	1,452,126	751,366
1977.............	11,816,254	9,797,017	83,989	9,881,006	861,914	-55,016	8,964,076	1,738,988	1,113,190	8,120	1,455,117	776,160
1978.............	13,124,062	10,954,612	94,470	11,049,082	996,230	-61,952	9,990,900	1,941,426	1,191,736	8,935	1,468,792	807,453
1979.............	14,672,460	12,193,464	153,550	12,347,014	1,149,435	-70,298	11,127,281	2,198,680	1,346,499	9,943	1,475,676	828,859
1980.............	16,045,353	13,021,290	7,307	13,028,597	1,224,137	-76,412	11,728,048	2,680,720	1,636,585	10,811	1,484,234	821,393
1981.............	17,650,245	13,876,092	99,884	13,975,976	1,399,849	-83,329	12,492,798	3,279,326	1,878,121	11,848	1,489,775	814,405
1982.............	18,927,613	14,519,770	34,995	14,554,765	1,495,497	-87,283	12,971,985	3,892,099	2,063,529	12,664	1,494,551	808,137
1983.............	20,011,290	15,482,528	-19,609	15,462,919	1,612,417	-92,196	13,758,306	4,090,884	2,162,100	13,317	1,502,652	812,620
1984.............	22,231,657	17,270,105	12,963	17,283,068	1,846,369	-93,130	15,343,569	4,630,012	2,258,076	14,638	1,518,797	856,338
1985.............	24,066,925	18,816,530	107,515	18,924,045	2,056,544	-137,357	16,730,144	4,939,970	2,396,811	15,665	1,536,347	889,683
1986.............	25,602,564	20,192,538	68,334	20,260,872	2,220,942	-159,229	17,880,701	5,169,878	2,551,985	16,470	1,554,473	916,814
1987.............	27,190,369	21,620,669	75,366	21,696,035	2,345,522	-174,089	19,176,424	5,350,169	2,663,776	17,246	1,576,591	941,024
1988.............	28,922,680	22,922,233	69,250	22,991,483	2,566,560	-181,644	20,243,279	5,813,532	2,865,869	18,145	1,593,958	960,486
1989.............	30,773,818	24,223,330	103,879	24,327,209	2,711,475	-182,651	21,433,083	6,254,247	3,086,488	19,201	1,602,744	975,387
1990.............	32,210,378	25,380,669	55,057	25,435,726	2,964,632	-225,927	22,245,167	6,614,119	3,351,092	19,896	1,618,905	985,056
1991.............	33,743,201	26,428,389	23,415	26,451,804	3,126,474	-242,345	23,082,985	6,855,956	3,804,260	20,619	1,636,516	981,595
1992.............	36,232,652	28,549,610	103,864	28,653,474	3,342,084	-286,900	25,024,490	7,052,005	4,156,157	21,915	1,653,327	988,989
1993.............	38,073,218	30,125,270	34,715	30,159,985	3,523,700	-308,698	26,327,587	7,295,096	4,450,535	22,744	1,673,964	1,013,149
1994.............	40,341,404	31,940,776	89,670	32,030,446	3,772,849	-361,296	27,896,301	7,765,910	4,679,193	23,815	1,693,952	1,037,813
1995.............	42,675,082	33,740,224	7,622	33,747,846	3,955,817	-392,203	29,399,826	8,264,963	5,010,293	24,948	1,710,587	1,069,637
1996.............	45,301,736	35,806,521	121,449	35,927,970	4,151,627	-442,821	31,333,522	8,701,114	5,267,100	26,135	1,733,398	1,093,386
1997.............	48,052,227	38,174,909	111,615	38,286,524	4,413,127	-498,104	33,375,293	9,295,661	5,381,273	27,356	1,756,537	1,131,838
1998.............	51,618,674	41,143,594	64,375	41,207,969	4,716,704	-557,056	35,934,209	10,145,192	5,539,273	29,049	1,776,976	1,162,276
1999.............	54,453,363	44,255,862	36,660	44,292,522	5,060,339	-635,431	38,596,752	10,060,332	5,796,279	30,307	1,796,711	1,182,542
2000.............	58,475,222	47,485,220	61,218	47,546,438	5,395,456	-719,949	41,431,033	10,830,704	6,213,485	32,166	1,817,929	1,202,207
2001.............	58,612,296	47,439,060	91,953	47,531,013	5,572,852	-733,621	41,224,540	10,549,255	6,838,501	31,897	1,837,551	1,208,113
2002.............	60,033,871	48,909,845	20,646	48,930,491	5,691,860	-742,014	42,496,617	10,254,298	7,282,956	32,297	1,858,778	1,200,000
2003.............	61,270,279	49,804,556	76,578	49,881,134	5,842,597	-755,625	43,282,912	10,369,993	7,617,374	32,675	1,875,142	1,198,497
2004.............	63,077,655	51,316,717	241,702	51,558,419	6,098,930	-743,409	44,716,080	10,385,403	7,976,172	33,337	1,892,097	1,214,807
2005.............	66,154,499	53,855,622	135,726	53,991,348	6,359,755	-768,809	46,862,784	10,795,259	8,496,456	34,646	1,909,428	1,233,735
2006.............	73,025,453	58,763,633	82,105	58,845,738	6,759,037	-788,246	51,298,455	12,593,491	9,133,507	37,802	1,931,764	1,255,225
2007.............	78,373,243	62,346,144	120,530	62,466,674	7,110,877	-829,499	54,526,298	13,984,325	9,862,620	40,095	1,954,688	1,286,659
2008.............	83,746,293	65,177,023	164,372	65,341,395	7,411,498	-839,786	57,090,111	15,311,446	11,344,736	42,427	1,973,888	1,288,893
2009.............	82,029,573	64,479,852	171,051	64,650,903	7,277,844	-644,660	56,728,399	13,012,403	12,288,771	41,121	1,994,834	1,254,465
2010.............	82,558,151	64,177,849	119,032	64,296,881	7,304,873	-568,358	56,423,650	12,883,101	13,251,400	41,004	2,013,412	1,237,277
2011.............	87,180,560	66,295,338	201,874	66,497,212	6,705,668	-488,066	59,303,478	14,398,194	13,478,888	43,055	2,024,880	1,254,941
2012.............	92,957,823	71,447,898	117,296	71,565,194	6,979,678	-393,226	64,192,290	15,224,222	13,541,311	45,601	2,038,501	1,269,552
2013.............	94,490,496	74,151,380	260,757	74,412,137	8,133,854	-285,614	65,992,669	14,620,870	13,876,957	46,002	2,054,039	1,288,951
2014.............	98,025,498	76,123,315	206,168	76,329,483	8,452,137	-306,273	67,571,073	16,050,362	14,404,063	47,364	2,069,602	1,313,822
2015.............	103,011,484	79,966,982	-27,494	79,939,488	8,987,125	-371,544	70,580,819	17,208,877	15,221,788	49,401	2,085,221	1,342,547
2016.............	104,692,209	80,321,745	51,420	80,373,165	9,062,593	-301,204	71,009,368	17,944,782	15,738,059	49,702	2,106,382	1,367,989
2017.............	108,373,694	82,998,303	107,921	83,106,224	9,357,071	-294,482	73,454,671	18,777,341	16,141,682	50,906	2,128,912	1,385,161
2018.............	114,691,816	114,629,600	62,216	87,543,303	9,774,533	-421,875	77,346,895	20,312,186	17,032,735	53,484	2,144,427	1,406,538
2019.............	118,708,230	118,523,960	184,270	91,002,414	10,161,933	-482,803	80,357,678	20,480,989	17,869,563	55,009	2,157,990	1,425,225

Personal Income and Employment by Area: Kennewick-Richland, WA

(Thousands of dollars, except as noted.)

Year	Personal income, total	Earnings by place of work			Less: Contributions for government social insurance	Plus: Adjustment for residence	Equals: Net earnings by place of residence	Plus: Dividends, interest, and rent	Plus: Personal current transfer receipts	Per capita personal income (dollars)	Population (persons)	Total employment
		Nonfarm	Farm	Total								
1970	382,393	297,502	25,178	322,680	24,115	553	299,118	49,341	33,934	4,090	93,499	40,817
1971	403,538	308,377	26,738	335,115	26,085	119	309,149	54,984	39,405	4,289	94,080	40,315
1972	451,875	341,910	38,957	380,867	30,826	-1,475	348,566	61,045	42,264	4,753	95,067	41,832
1973	523,780	392,533	57,633	450,166	41,352	-4,858	403,956	73,021	46,803	5,501	95,211	44,867
1974	634,502	471,785	84,601	556,386	51,670	-8,891	495,825	84,289	54,388	6,431	98,666	49,005
1975	764,899	594,964	84,272	679,236	65,038	-16,353	597,845	100,652	66,402	7,282	105,045	54,232
1976	857,709	684,978	79,488	764,466	75,583	-18,344	670,539	112,492	74,678	7,601	112,838	58,982
1977	1,001,877	868,960	50,060	919,020	96,883	-33,539	788,598	134,023	79,256	8,375	119,629	64,042
1978	1,228,865	1,084,451	72,695	1,157,146	124,589	-49,876	982,681	160,140	86,044	9,510	129,214	71,236
1979	1,418,757	1,281,988	58,472	1,340,460	152,526	-59,727	1,128,207	191,426	99,124	10,286	137,929	77,504
1980	1,594,474	1,349,092	107,312	1,456,404	159,895	-62,359	1,234,150	232,040	128,284	10,957	145,515	78,001
1981	1,881,536	1,675,968	95,127	1,771,095	217,248	-104,700	1,449,147	283,518	148,871	12,592	149,418	82,905
1982	1,950,930	1,663,589	87,982	1,751,571	216,889	-89,311	1,445,371	322,781	182,778	12,745	153,079	77,676
1983	1,989,897	1,632,158	93,703	1,725,861	210,908	-68,500	1,446,453	342,487	200,957	13,322	149,371	74,772
1984	1,978,250	1,513,389	126,040	1,639,429	199,586	-45,382	1,394,461	370,960	212,829	13,418	147,429	71,264
1985	2,006,634	1,578,698	71,484	1,650,182	210,827	-47,764	1,391,591	391,053	223,990	13,707	146,400	72,013
1986	2,102,949	1,629,793	98,519	1,728,312	218,866	-45,946	1,463,500	401,749	237,700	14,350	146,551	72,890
1987	2,176,813	1,681,752	105,728	1,787,480	225,286	-45,205	1,516,989	409,301	250,523	14,753	147,547	76,282
1988	2,242,461	1,711,011	123,261	1,834,272	236,351	-44,705	1,553,216	412,757	276,488	15,281	146,750	76,763
1989	2,396,892	1,785,798	123,374	1,909,172	246,957	-40,653	1,621,562	476,529	298,801	16,404	146,117	78,677
1990	2,633,067	2,030,622	127,930	2,158,552	286,225	-48,263	1,824,064	480,404	328,599	17,399	151,331	84,264
1991	2,879,090	2,210,477	116,961	2,327,438	315,115	-22,007	1,990,316	507,401	381,373	18,457	155,993	86,871
1992	3,205,242	2,469,799	144,861	2,614,660	349,838	-23,399	2,241,423	543,360	420,459	19,825	161,680	89,400
1993	3,558,964	2,714,808	217,013	2,931,821	377,536	-24,295	2,529,990	578,588	450,386	21,175	168,075	93,769
1994	3,827,224	3,008,774	186,200	3,194,974	429,446	-30,291	2,735,237	616,785	475,202	21,875	174,957	100,015
1995	3,909,404	2,971,296	215,708	3,187,004	428,019	-22,365	2,736,620	656,606	516,178	21,659	180,501	97,934
1996	4,052,626	2,948,025	281,136	3,229,161	416,240	-14,156	2,798,765	698,422	555,439	22,316	181,605	97,910
1997	4,150,810	3,025,474	226,829	3,252,303	411,766	-10,146	2,830,391	741,158	579,261	22,570	183,909	98,810
1998	4,351,507	3,185,984	244,470	3,430,454	433,364	870	2,997,960	747,077	606,470	23,359	186,290	98,097
1999	4,570,079	3,392,668	221,052	3,613,720	446,774	8,716	3,175,662	739,677	654,740	24,177	189,025	101,094
2000	4,917,548	3,585,883	263,398	3,849,281	481,824	15,860	3,383,317	797,550	736,681	25,520	192,696	102,447
2001	5,332,576	3,919,513	252,573	4,172,086	509,989	16,490	3,678,587	828,757	825,232	27,149	196,420	106,138
2002	5,631,999	4,261,726	279,688	4,541,414	563,442	17,012	3,994,984	784,827	852,188	27,787	202,688	109,060
2003	6,030,730	4,514,714	358,560	4,873,274	595,000	24,481	4,302,755	809,240	918,735	28,849	209,043	111,933
2004	6,360,307	4,864,248	314,398	5,178,646	642,401	26,228	4,562,473	853,282	944,552	29,741	213,854	113,664
2005	6,608,314	5,048,348	319,900	5,368,248	670,151	29,383	4,727,480	859,277	1,021,557	30,163	219,086	116,263
2006	6,864,546	5,096,609	352,794	5,449,403	671,382	46,621	4,824,642	938,445	1,101,459	30,625	224,149	117,441
2007	7,583,527	5,529,584	404,353	5,933,937	728,330	46,575	5,252,182	1,125,917	1,205,428	33,079	229,255	123,032
2008	8,298,847	5,947,072	328,849	6,275,921	778,985	51,473	5,548,409	1,337,424	1,413,014	34,965	237,348	127,067
2009	8,809,440	6,378,850	358,415	6,737,265	847,427	43,622	5,933,460	1,309,468	1,566,512	35,869	245,600	129,446
2010	9,641,778	7,115,608	383,008	7,498,616	912,509	34,357	6,620,464	1,288,028	1,733,286	37,729	255,553	134,755
2011	10,284,480	7,359,411	492,375	7,851,786	855,345	29,589	7,026,030	1,491,097	1,767,353	39,027	263,522	137,296
2012	10,263,353	7,070,797	509,470	7,580,267	809,514	72,392	6,843,145	1,596,039	1,824,169	38,263	268,235	138637
2013	10,203,725	7,104,337	530,457	7,634,794	923,698	83,086	6,794,182	1,556,572	1,852,971	37,655	270,980	139,040
2014	10,653,495	7,330,173	449,654	7,779,827	963,714	91,247	6,907,360	1,692,626	2,053,509	38,852	274,207	141,373
2015	11,566,384	7,855,173	754,653	8,609,826	1,020,403	76,228	7,665,651	1,815,893	2,084,840	41,460	278,980	145,230
2016	11,874,984	8,160,666	599,408	8,760,074	1,058,089	85,232	7,787,217	1,870,181	2,217,586	41,843	283,799	148,526
2017	12,312,528	8,534,081	556,983	9,091,064	1,109,788	72,569	8,053,845	1,965,653	2,293,030	42,414	290,296	151,445
2018	13,154,449	12,619,161	535,288	9,573,516	1,168,555	78,887	8,483,848	2,239,084	2,431,517	44,548	295,289	156,333
2019	13,851,313	13,234,784	616,529	10,159,581	1,228,642	70,574	9,001,513	2,277,997	2,571,803	46,231	299,612	160,235

Personal Income and Employment by Area: Killeen-Temple, TX

(Thousands of dollars, except as noted.)

Year	Personal income, total	Earnings by place of work			Less: Contributions for government social insurance	Plus: Adjustment for residence	Equals: Net earnings by place of residence	Plus: Dividends, interest, and rent	Plus: Personal current transfer receipts	Per capita personal income (dollars)	Population (persons)	Total employment
		Nonfarm	Farm	Total								
1970	748,345	597,282	6,948	604,230	36,662	-13,348	554,220	153,901	40,224	4,410	169,695	89,828
1971	809,895	650,281	5,616	655,897	42,553	-12,151	601,193	161,896	46,806	4,644	174,387	90,083
1972	983,904	790,808	10,687	801,495	51,897	-13,039	736,559	193,728	53,617	5,081	193,630	97,294
1973	1,137,414	888,878	26,109	914,987	62,086	-3,559	849,342	224,455	63,617	5,248	216,716	102,623
1974	1,257,555	989,954	5,656	995,610	72,599	819	923,830	259,042	74,683	5,669	221,833	106,605
1975	1,410,652	1,101,052	6,746	1,107,798	85,600	-2,353	1,019,845	297,248	93,559	6,380	221,119	110,740
1976	1,567,438	1,225,124	4,861	1,229,985	97,634	4,614	1,136,965	326,238	104,235	6,819	229,880	115,223
1977	1,669,358	1,299,360	-4,065	1,295,295	102,590	5,241	1,197,946	358,650	112,762	7,180	232,517	117,302
1978	1,862,386	1,427,039	2,093	1,429,132	111,551	-204	1,317,377	419,298	125,711	7,859	236,961	120,403
1979	1,899,568	1,442,481	2,644	1,445,125	118,080	3,477	1,330,522	422,093	146,953	8,163	232,714	114,795
1980	2,156,912	1,621,366	-3,352	1,618,014	132,995	8,282	1,493,301	488,849	174,762	9,462	227,951	117,723
1981	2,450,680	1,858,642	8,900	1,867,542	159,975	-13,481	1,694,086	558,168	198,426	10,531	232,715	121,283
1982	2,677,896	2,018,611	6,046	2,024,657	170,762	-14,745	1,839,150	620,066	218,680	11,202	239,048	121,716
1983	2,887,904	2,163,268	-2,144	2,161,124	188,938	-13,979	1,958,207	688,741	240,956	11,921	242,252	122,761
1984	3,123,342	2,335,619	439	2,336,058	209,963	-11,974	2,114,121	750,892	258,329	12,764	244,697	126,897
1985	3,359,414	2,498,086	-5,052	2,493,034	228,543	-12,639	2,251,852	824,242	283,320	13,297	252,645	131,716
1986	3,539,987	2,633,785	-6,190	2,627,595	243,038	-18,992	2,365,565	866,900	307,522	13,971	253,385	133,296
1987	3,661,865	2,713,229	2,846	2,716,075	250,254	-23,820	2,442,001	890,434	329,430	14,100	259,706	137,444
1988	3,890,447	2,903,587	442	2,904,029	283,667	-28,334	2,592,028	940,935	357,484	14,828	262,373	139,949
1989	4,051,729	2,965,417	7,253	2,972,670	296,528	-28,094	2,648,048	1,007,107	396,574	15,206	266,463	140,155
1990	4,170,021	3,070,759	4,510	3,075,269	310,506	-32,843	2,731,920	990,857	447,244	15,472	269,515	139,118
1991	4,065,537	2,944,663	9,484	2,954,147	303,482	-21,645	2,629,020	947,984	488,533	15,304	265,657	128,838
1992	4,718,136	3,450,897	9,043	3,459,940	361,663	-27,040	3,071,237	1,062,426	584,473	17,428	270,722	139,350
1993	5,248,592	3,874,091	9,453	3,883,544	411,515	-31,496	3,440,533	1,185,690	622,369	18,314	286,593	151,294
1994	5,705,706	4,238,387	7,485	4,245,872	444,099	-32,735	3,769,038	1,291,633	645,035	18,532	307,884	162,733
1995	6,039,084	4,453,068	-73	4,452,995	458,481	-26,274	3,968,240	1,369,480	701,364	19,281	313,222	169,153
1996	6,316,799	4,600,007	2,812	4,602,819	473,084	-10,976	4,118,759	1,445,765	752,275	19,826	318,613	170,885
1997	6,480,237	4,776,377	2,363	4,778,740	487,424	13,395	4,304,711	1,378,402	797,124	20,136	321,821	172,991
1998	6,945,975	5,016,445	-5,193	5,011,252	506,799	47,122	4,551,575	1,555,851	838,549	21,350	325,335	176,092
1999	7,422,232	5,343,100	10,188	5,353,288	535,396	90,303	4,908,195	1,630,159	883,878	22,804	325,473	179,581
2000	7,839,432	5,625,492	5,480	5,630,972	561,098	117,911	5,187,785	1,674,898	976,749	23,543	332,989	182,507
2001	8,329,744	6,092,130	4,920	6,097,050	602,166	95,123	5,590,007	1,652,110	1,087,627	24,761	336,409	181,905
2002	8,800,903	6,533,244	8,914	6,542,158	644,568	49,990	5,947,580	1,661,550	1,191,773	25,792	341,231	184,092
2003	9,420,284	7,082,753	24,662	7,107,415	701,512	28,816	6,434,719	1,656,427	1,329,138	27,475	342,865	185,268
2004	9,918,315	7,465,559	27,681	7,493,240	746,261	20,081	6,767,060	1,739,564	1,411,691	28,359	349,745	187,498
2005	10,885,203	8,247,402	23,661	8,271,063	818,661	4,066	7,456,468	1,878,902	1,549,833	30,445	357,533	194,934
2006	12,005,233	9,232,496	20,445	9,252,941	906,031	-22,240	8,324,670	2,011,671	1,668,892	32,850	365,460	203,763
2007	13,203,373	10,067,447	3,064	10,070,511	991,951	-38,500	9,040,060	2,304,907	1,858,406	34,672	380,804	214,008
2008	14,453,322	10,919,265	-34,230	10,885,035	1,085,261	-82,450	9,717,324	2,591,317	2,144,681	36,848	392,237	222,216
2009	14,812,157	11,289,291	-41,104	11,248,187	1,153,538	-127,983	9,966,666	2,579,316	2,266,175	37,464	395,375	220,670
2010	15,172,661	11,355,474	-26,759	11,328,715	1,173,156	-140,882	10,014,677	2,543,139	2,614,845	37,163	408,277	216,539
2011	15,971,118	11,685,336	-29,763	11,655,573	1,099,683	-174,280	10,381,610	2,803,991	2,785,517	38,730	412,376	219,858
2012	16,162,340	11,700,040	-6,049	11,693,991	1,104,926	-176,664	10,412,401	2,913,564	2,836,375	38,161	423,529	219,547
2013	15,922,798	11,494,731	5,371	11,500,102	1,207,467	-202,940	10,089,695	2,836,467	2,996,636	37,548	424,069	218,809
2014	16,406,213	11,661,432	-8,281	11,653,151	1,224,367	-211,494	10,217,290	2,985,235	3,203,688	38,458	426,600	219,108
2015	17,180,922	12,158,862	18,772	12,177,634	1,289,161	-221,609	10,666,864	3,023,792	3,490,266	39,703	432,741	224,592
2016	17,367,638	12,067,148	-4,749	12,062,399	1,293,396	-200,137	10,568,866	3,108,293	3,690,479	39,761	436,803	224,477
2017	18,093,765	12,587,204	1,019	12,588,223	1,359,526	-195,928	11,032,769	3,210,238	3,850,758	40,773	443,773	226,994
2018	18,800,567	18,833,208	-32,641	12,962,539	1,383,330	-179,471	11,399,738	3,210,196	4,190,633	41,661	451,272	232,121
2019	19,726,228	19,760,818	-34,590	13,603,970	1,443,893	-171,146	11,988,931	3,277,782	4,459,515	42,855	460,303	237,122

Personal Income and Employment by Area: Kingsport-Bristol, TN-VA

(Thousands of dollars, except as noted.)

Year	Personal income, total	Earnings by place of work			Less: Contributions for government social insurance	Plus: Adjustment for residence	Equals: Net earnings by place of residence	Plus: Dividends, interest, and rent	Plus: Personal current transfer receipts	Per capita personal income (dollars)	Population (persons)	Total employment
		Nonfarm	Farm	Total								
1970	756,289	657,355	19,281	676,636	43,978	-29,013	603,645	83,145	69,499	3,128	241,800	103,480
1971	815,430	699,806	16,521	716,327	48,661	-25,377	642,289	92,330	80,811	3,301	247,013	103,817
1972	905,205	769,693	23,320	793,013	56,042	-24,552	712,419	102,083	90,703	3,625	249,683	106,749
1973	1,020,110	863,873	27,630	891,503	72,613	-23,459	795,431	116,176	108,503	4,028	253,233	112,348
1974	1,142,412	967,469	21,652	989,121	84,923	-27,950	876,248	134,502	131,662	4,439	257,350	115,905
1975	1,245,816	1,037,484	12,733	1,050,217	88,947	-41,942	919,328	154,390	172,098	4,779	260,702	114,222
1976	1,397,018	1,171,544	19,217	1,190,761	101,998	-48,104	1,040,659	169,393	186,966	5,282	264,479	119,484
1977	1,556,484	1,329,485	13,402	1,342,887	115,508	-60,005	1,167,374	192,127	196,983	5,819	267,499	124,891
1978	1,765,212	1,532,092	16,489	1,548,581	133,630	-86,041	1,328,910	219,250	217,052	6,497	271,688	131,666
1979	1,942,752	1,692,646	6,596	1,699,242	151,086	-110,267	1,437,889	251,023	253,840	7,064	275,007	133,425
1980	2,124,978	1,779,746	9,212	1,788,958	159,005	-117,623	1,512,330	311,848	300,800	7,623	278,763	130,586
1981	2,418,900	1,986,809	23,148	2,009,957	191,421	-133,767	1,684,769	385,645	348,486	8,639	279,993	131,108
1982	2,564,038	2,035,633	19,381	2,055,014	206,451	-100,961	1,747,602	434,168	382,268	9,144	280,418	128,310
1983	2,707,146	2,131,874	7,064	2,138,938	218,001	-98,156	1,822,781	471,004	413,361	9,699	279,113	127,756
1984	2,913,286	2,246,681	13,856	2,260,537	235,450	-87,676	1,937,411	537,104	438,771	10,461	278,485	129,086
1985	3,139,534	2,456,970	14,105	2,471,075	261,926	-97,035	2,112,114	561,798	465,622	11,298	277,884	132,126
1986	3,316,776	2,604,902	4,864	2,609,766	285,255	-97,743	2,226,768	593,278	496,730	11,979	276,878	133,598
1987	3,488,475	2,745,119	14,931	2,760,050	298,286	-93,670	2,368,094	598,835	521,546	12,584	277,217	136,288
1988	3,763,391	2,961,603	18,197	2,979,800	330,066	-104,253	2,545,481	658,955	558,955	13,644	275,824	139,584
1989	4,039,813	3,176,435	21,918	3,198,353	358,458	-117,313	2,722,582	701,860	615,371	14,655	275,656	143,467
1990	4,356,278	3,379,242	28,262	3,407,504	383,983	-117,090	2,906,431	775,503	674,344	15,772	276,205	147,539
1991	4,605,142	3,565,438	29,767	3,595,205	410,767	-125,344	3,059,094	791,712	754,336	16,515	278,847	148,554
1992	4,907,001	3,789,679	39,437	3,829,116	431,847	-120,006	3,277,263	783,452	846,286	17,383	282,292	151,184
1993	5,062,326	3,910,474	31,123	3,941,597	448,578	-132,514	3,360,505	799,940	901,881	17,754	285,142	153,439
1994	5,221,189	3,959,881	27,311	3,987,192	458,289	-95,866	3,433,037	839,507	948,645	18,216	286,625	153,499
1995	5,554,474	4,183,207	15,043	4,198,250	483,661	-110,917	3,603,672	917,637	1,033,165	19,169	289,762	158,102
1996	5,857,460	4,414,634	2,027	4,416,661	500,828	-139,533	3,776,300	996,313	1,084,847	20,049	292,153	158,808
1997	6,085,311	4,505,090	6,655	4,511,745	505,902	-111,564	3,894,279	1,048,570	1,142,462	20,681	294,250	160,258
1998	6,420,693	4,650,940	8,213	4,659,153	512,556	-92,894	4,053,703	1,178,670	1,188,320	21,667	296,333	158,389
1999	6,716,466	4,825,182	9,366	4,834,548	527,387	-21,954	4,285,207	1,198,513	1,232,746	22,549	297,863	159,345
2000	7,078,274	4,927,108	24,280	4,951,388	537,426	28,269	4,442,231	1,305,985	1,330,058	23,710	298,534	158,601
2001	7,277,087	5,074,232	17,871	5,092,103	575,413	-8,782	4,507,908	1,315,318	1,453,861	24,367	298,648	158,986
2002	7,445,794	5,193,069	11,074	5,204,143	594,505	-11,039	4,598,599	1,283,757	1,563,438	24,880	299,267	158,930
2003	7,731,722	5,437,319	-1,873	5,435,446	619,789	-31,075	4,784,582	1,311,924	1,635,216	25,741	300,370	158,839
2004	8,111,469	5,725,664	8,586	5,734,250	646,429	-27,037	5,060,784	1,302,739	1,747,946	26,978	300,668	157,418
2005	8,402,971	5,900,428	8,568	5,908,996	670,806	-16,772	5,221,418	1,291,074	1,890,479	27,777	302,519	159,083
2006	9,002,263	6,288,996	-9,235	6,279,761	722,081	-80,437	5,477,243	1,475,040	2,049,980	29,561	304,535	161,822
2007	9,541,719	6,524,342	-18,023	6,506,319	750,932	-86,091	5,669,296	1,648,484	2,223,939	31,100	306,805	162,848
2008	10,114,729	6,791,719	-14,245	6,777,474	786,456	-108,386	5,882,632	1,749,379	2,482,718	32,833	308,069	163,301
2009	9,903,974	6,533,639	-11,552	6,522,087	766,996	-73,269	5,681,822	1,542,630	2,679,522	32,021	309,293	157,034
2010	10,107,867	6,680,859	-10,837	6,670,022	782,445	-115,689	5,771,888	1,468,550	2,867,429	32,659	309,494	154,844
2011	10,752,722	7,113,443	-6,970	7,106,473	739,785	-174,862	6,191,826	1,638,918	2,921,978	34,799	308,993	158,091
2012	11,213,785	7,400,001	-8,652	7,391,349	747,437	-156,646	6,487,266	1,789,140	2,937,379	36,343	308,555	157,063
2013	10,998,392	7,289,113	-1,281	7,287,832	833,853	-170,110	6,283,869	1,709,144	3,005,379	35,733	307,793	156,863
2014	11,051,640	7,162,741	8,600	7,171,341	833,513	-175,869	6,161,959	1,830,100	3,059,581	35,975	307,203	157,347
2015	11,297,258	7,236,416	1,385	7,237,801	853,443	-165,774	6,218,584	1,880,809	3,197,865	36,897	306,182	156,738
2016	11,387,835	7,214,126	-26,488	7,187,638	862,278	-139,801	6,185,559	1,929,379	3,272,897	37,228	305,893	157,805
2017	11,905,359	7,523,456	-24,421	7,499,035	894,954	-107,706	6,496,375	2,027,052	3,381,932	38,823	306,659	157,736
2018	12,329,340	12,349,923	-20,583	7,815,767	930,649	-146,816	6,738,302	2,116,651	3,474,387	40,195	306,736	158,606
2019	12,570,113	12,591,990	-21,877	7,845,704	940,338	-96,188	6,809,178	2,137,500	3,623,435	40,918	307,202	158,812

Personal Income and Employment by Area: Kingston, NY

(Thousands of dollars, except as noted.)

Year	Personal income, total	Derivation of personal income									Per capita personal income (dollars)	Population (persons)	Total employment
		Earnings by place of work			Less: Contributions for government social insurance	Plus: Adjustment for residence	Equals: Net earnings by place of residence	Plus: Dividends, interest, and rent	Plus: Personal current transfer receipts				
		Nonfarm	Farm	Total									
1970	574,715	408,659	6,869	415,528	31,226	42,656	426,958	92,490	55,267	4,040	142,242	52,414
1971	623,694	434,425	6,704	441,129	34,452	51,529	458,206	99,732	65,756	4,251	146,705	53,640
1972	675,172	463,921	4,043	467,964	38,536	62,140	491,568	107,667	75,937	4,498	150,111	54,890
1973	754,760	514,178	7,123	521,301	49,347	70,847	542,801	123,627	88,332	4,934	152,980	57,237
1974	828,152	543,464	8,995	552,459	53,684	81,243	580,018	142,095	106,039	5,376	154,057	57,453
1975	913,241	564,474	9,644	574,118	54,755	92,992	612,355	156,217	144,669	5,853	156,022	55,738
1976	967,361	593,541	8,456	601,997	58,960	103,865	646,902	162,711	157,748	6,131	157,793	55,635
1977	1,038,576	634,078	9,387	643,465	62,659	120,240	701,046	176,929	160,601	6,592	157,559	56,665
1978	1,143,405	708,103	10,910	719,013	71,437	139,471	787,047	188,084	168,274	7,209	158,617	58,794
1979	1,271,278	792,499	13,556	806,055	82,280	160,972	884,747	204,431	182,100	7,965	159,606	61,376
1980	1,420,810	855,033	12,069	867,102	89,455	185,478	963,125	244,954	212,731	8,986	158,111	61,668
1981	1,575,049	924,422	10,227	934,649	102,508	203,748	1,035,889	296,028	243,132	9,992	157,625	61,536
1982	1,769,422	1,045,447	12,650	1,058,097	116,493	219,266	1,160,870	342,018	266,534	11,215	157,770	63,222
1983	1,943,945	1,193,234	6,514	1,199,748	134,108	222,073	1,287,713	373,463	282,769	12,271	158,414	66,330
1984	2,185,698	1,365,290	8,563	1,373,853	156,527	242,039	1,459,365	431,737	294,596	13,699	159,557	69,296
1985	2,348,100	1,468,029	11,961	1,479,990	170,522	266,506	1,575,974	462,489	309,637	14,687	159,880	71,174
1986	2,526,813	1,627,393	12,194	1,639,587	191,321	275,582	1,723,848	482,628	320,337	15,816	159,760	74,612
1987	2,650,981	1,704,139	15,992	1,720,131	196,061	300,025	1,824,095	500,151	326,735	16,378	161,865	73,866
1988	2,825,364	1,795,549	18,746	1,814,295	211,745	333,553	1,936,103	538,794	350,467	17,345	162,889	76,380
1989	3,082,747	1,904,405	19,024	1,923,429	220,621	354,067	2,056,875	641,057	384,815	18,756	164,359	76,774
1990	3,207,655	1,978,148	18,161	1,996,309	219,512	376,801	2,153,598	630,270	423,787	19,318	166,049	77,348
1991	3,378,129	2,098,553	23,424	2,121,977	238,891	376,771	2,259,857	645,881	472,391	20,004	168,869	77,826
1992	3,584,672	2,192,767	18,949	2,211,716	244,835	403,842	2,370,723	673,237	540,712	20,979	170,872	78,504
1993	3,519,350	2,073,378	18,762	2,092,140	232,371	443,940	2,303,709	644,944	570,697	20,391	172,594	76,404
1994	3,528,255	2,006,115	16,512	2,022,627	226,596	466,460	2,262,491	652,226	613,538	20,483	172,252	76,405
1995	3,605,143	1,944,036	16,993	1,961,029	219,587	518,840	2,260,282	698,706	646,155	20,916	172,362	74,331
1996	3,707,142	1,942,217	14,804	1,957,021	215,026	573,216	2,315,211	713,199	678,732	21,403	173,205	74,388
1997	3,881,535	2,051,499	13,923	2,065,422	222,365	606,784	2,449,841	739,463	692,231	22,289	174,148	75,635
1998	4,180,072	2,212,794	12,085	2,224,879	238,236	673,725	2,660,368	780,342	739,362	23,875	175,085	77,766
1999	4,418,059	2,388,061	19,247	2,407,308	250,908	745,784	2,902,184	761,850	754,025	25,028	176,526	80,901
2000	4,732,846	2,551,539	18,365	2,569,904	268,289	827,780	3,129,395	809,531	793,920	26,617	177,810	83,102
2001	4,884,075	2,576,336	19,102	2,595,438	275,273	886,434	3,206,599	821,668	855,808	27,371	178,440	84,862
2002	4,919,835	2,682,874	7,983	2,690,857	290,988	887,495	3,287,364	719,702	912,769	27,313	180,128	85,462
2003	5,089,882	2,809,730	15,162	2,824,892	304,573	899,628	3,419,947	718,585	951,350	28,130	180,942	86,617
2004	5,563,052	2,981,808	12,644	2,994,452	320,172	1,095,122	3,769,402	791,768	1,001,882	30,592	181,847	86,991
2005	5,849,959	3,076,880	8,187	3,085,067	337,282	1,168,314	3,916,099	886,247	1,047,613	32,065	182,438	87,641
2006	6,217,491	3,360,208	13,327	3,373,535	372,788	1,151,941	4,152,688	951,399	1,113,404	34,004	182,845	88,732
2007	6,519,005	3,463,090	26,287	3,489,377	384,211	1,221,246	4,326,412	1,011,960	1,180,633	35,658	182,818	89,799
2008	6,794,504	3,512,311	28,577	3,540,888	395,887	1,172,870	4,317,871	1,161,024	1,315,609	37,093	183,174	89,273
2009	6,788,764	3,512,775	23,491	3,536,266	390,153	1,039,557	4,185,670	1,147,778	1,455,316	37,171	182,638	87,247
2010	6,997,629	3,666,760	27,327	3,694,087	395,474	1,040,170	4,338,783	1,097,132	1,561,714	38,358	182,428	86,535
2011	7,253,169	3,681,235	22,606	3,703,841	360,738	1,098,911	4,442,014	1,206,185	1,604,970	39,740	182,516	86,146
2012	7,476,002	3,800,008	24,431	3,824,439	364,992	1,062,439	4,521,886	1,316,528	1,637,588	41,147	181,689	85,986
2013	7,514,628	3,866,930	28,508	3,895,438	417,952	1,058,709	4,536,195	1,319,237	1,659,196	41,525	180,965	86,816
2014	7,788,353	3,923,548	21,542	3,945,090	434,803	1,091,603	4,601,890	1,448,656	1,737,807	43,086	180,763	88,659
2015	8,057,368	4,039,623	23,329	4,062,952	453,269	1,124,603	4,734,286	1,489,664	1,833,418	44,775	179,952	89,279
2016	8,299,497	4,143,370	22,678	4,166,048	469,925	1,180,227	4,876,350	1,559,466	1,863,681	46,225	179,546	90,282
2017	8,757,593	4,299,975	23,820	4,323,795	489,856	1,263,188	5,097,127	1,635,556	2,024,910	48,811	179,417	91,160
2018	9,026,113	9,014,804	11,309	4,519,340	503,063	1,288,395	5,304,672	1,757,899	1,963,542	50,590	178,418	92,069
2019	9,412,460	9,397,226	15,234	4,657,487	514,047	1,384,789	5,528,229	1,793,335	2,090,896	53,006	177,573	92,527

Personal Income and Employment by Area: Knoxville, TN

(Thousands of dollars, except as noted.)

Year	Personal income, total	Earnings by place of work			Less: Contributions for government social insurance	Plus: Adjustment for residence	Equals: Net earnings by place of residence	Plus: Dividends, interest, and rent	Plus: Personal current transfer receipts	Per capita personal income (dollars)	Population (persons)	Total employment
		Nonfarm	Farm	Total								
1970	1,680,029	1,386,721	10,161	1,396,882	89,115	-11,835	1,295,932	212,269	171,828	3,179	528,426	214,863
1971	1,852,013	1,516,930	9,787	1,526,717	100,676	-11,161	1,414,880	235,236	201,897	3,422	541,129	218,824
1972	2,050,991	1,681,597	14,737	1,696,334	117,150	-8,761	1,570,423	258,268	222,300	3,737	548,773	227,791
1973	2,308,986	1,884,751	21,507	1,906,258	150,269	-11,029	1,744,960	297,651	266,375	4,170	553,697	239,669
1974	2,592,488	2,093,078	17,094	2,110,172	172,065	-13,735	1,924,372	350,601	317,515	4,626	560,437	243,085
1975	2,914,956	2,284,083	11,946	2,296,029	184,289	-12,055	2,099,685	409,641	405,630	5,106	570,915	242,890
1976	3,299,657	2,603,859	24,786	2,628,645	213,154	-13,196	2,402,295	450,660	446,702	5,655	583,484	255,754
1977	3,697,468	2,962,892	17,342	2,980,234	241,560	-18,588	2,720,086	509,185	468,197	6,221	594,330	266,898
1978	4,226,526	3,409,806	16,052	3,425,858	280,965	-15,947	3,128,946	581,128	516,452	7,023	601,788	279,856
1979	4,746,730	3,813,980	13,358	3,827,338	327,653	-21,823	3,477,862	663,148	605,720	7,751	612,421	290,671
1980	5,280,415	4,113,604	20,384	4,133,988	353,824	-29,585	3,750,579	812,551	717,285	8,466	623,731	291,449
1981	5,902,130	4,504,518	28,817	4,533,335	420,463	-21,549	4,091,323	993,926	816,881	9,364	630,304	295,737
1982	6,341,916	4,784,834	25,314	4,810,148	461,203	-30,721	4,318,224	1,138,247	885,445	9,964	636,499	299,009
1983	6,694,130	5,032,922	12,007	5,044,929	493,333	-23,414	4,528,182	1,200,232	965,716	10,487	638,326	291,743
1984	7,312,091	5,485,558	23,314	5,508,872	560,310	-27,183	4,921,379	1,379,158	1,011,554	11,486	636,588	301,274
1985	7,730,785	5,823,193	16,093	5,839,286	607,134	-26,043	5,206,109	1,453,396	1,071,280	12,139	636,844	306,615
1986	8,164,676	6,175,165	13,926	6,189,091	661,427	-36,821	5,490,843	1,519,250	1,154,583	12,884	633,710	314,957
1987	8,822,278	6,759,068	14,322	6,773,390	714,866	-39,597	6,018,927	1,582,590	1,220,761	13,857	636,657	327,828
1988	9,686,119	7,502,996	13,375	7,516,371	815,405	-54,274	6,646,692	1,735,486	1,303,941	15,079	642,344	344,316
1989	10,243,893	7,894,761	20,362	7,915,123	874,218	-51,370	6,989,535	1,808,441	1,445,917	15,815	647,744	351,772
1990	11,022,808	8,363,701	22,419	8,386,120	933,748	-35,455	7,416,917	2,011,612	1,594,279	16,866	653,537	358,570
1991	11,609,330	8,800,752	24,568	8,825,320	1,002,648	-72,966	7,749,706	2,055,216	1,804,408	17,454	665,146	360,963
1992	12,578,914	9,652,786	30,375	9,683,161	1,086,651	-104,972	8,491,538	2,061,560	2,025,816	18,555	677,924	371,887
1993	13,413,355	10,335,383	30,355	10,365,738	1,167,112	-119,225	9,079,401	2,166,017	2,167,937	19,468	688,984	385,921
1994	14,075,225	10,837,851	24,992	10,862,843	1,256,249	-127,853	9,478,741	2,324,540	2,271,944	20,064	701,511	398,164
1995	14,971,059	11,412,913	21,094	11,434,007	1,327,501	-148,408	9,958,098	2,545,011	2,467,950	20,958	714,347	407,652
1996	15,659,428	11,900,196	10,497	11,910,693	1,364,047	-168,746	10,377,900	2,696,483	2,585,045	21,607	724,741	411,103
1997	16,518,900	12,559,459	15,120	12,574,579	1,431,113	-205,679	10,937,787	2,895,457	2,685,656	22,562	732,158	415,188
1998	18,162,256	13,825,942	18,687	13,844,629	1,522,624	-204,338	12,117,667	3,264,684	2,779,905	24,632	737,355	425,392
1999	18,618,371	14,204,786	23,997	14,228,783	1,582,636	-178,714	12,467,433	3,250,107	2,900,831	25,042	743,499	430,837
2000	20,028,463	15,227,807	30,981	15,258,788	1,674,283	-192,249	13,392,256	3,449,086	3,187,121	26,710	749,847	440,925
2001	20,248,336	15,203,821	40,254	15,244,075	1,691,939	-212,132	13,340,004	3,472,246	3,436,086	26,767	756,459	436,861
2002	21,046,744	16,029,170	40,422	16,069,592	1,797,385	-241,837	14,030,370	3,320,960	3,695,414	27,571	763,352	440,108
2003	21,883,807	16,722,548	25,386	16,747,934	1,874,543	-240,272	14,633,119	3,408,217	3,842,471	28,343	772,111	445,509
2004	23,173,165	17,893,601	20,504	17,914,105	1,987,247	-264,378	15,662,480	3,436,170	4,074,515	29,704	780,124	459,111
2005	24,284,094	18,777,468	16,101	18,793,569	2,075,562	-311,243	16,406,764	3,531,442	4,345,888	30,713	790,669	467,944
2006	25,825,628	19,866,807	3,901	19,870,708	2,191,562	-363,262	17,315,884	3,867,567	4,642,177	32,087	804,860	479,051
2007	27,177,235	20,582,707	-11,067	20,571,640	2,298,239	-408,449	17,864,952	4,251,549	5,060,734	33,286	816,480	487,735
2008	28,344,674	20,871,557	-11,115	20,860,442	2,377,820	-466,769	18,015,853	4,648,900	5,679,921	34,270	827,099	490,369
2009	27,832,568	20,312,239	-3,410	20,308,829	2,345,420	-507,216	17,456,193	4,265,944	6,110,431	33,378	833,862	470,298
2010	29,073,095	21,104,853	1,420	21,106,273	2,412,266	-473,743	18,220,264	4,237,160	6,615,671	34,662	838,748	469,153
2011	30,910,415	22,145,398	-2,204	22,143,194	2,244,097	-598,708	19,300,389	4,877,570	6,732,456	36,667	843,001	477,626
2012	32,558,852	23,165,449	12,087	23,177,536	2,271,088	-464,007	20,442,441	5,266,800	6,849,611	38,428	847,269	477,017
2013	32,579,701	23,687,708	17,942	23,705,650	2,618,907	-481,903	20,604,840	4,929,053	7,045,808	38,267	851,377	480,213
2014	34,070,487	24,639,571	18,176	24,657,747	2,702,179	-480,640	21,474,928	5,415,486	7,180,073	39,816	855,695	488,720
2015	35,802,191	25,790,559	18,610	25,809,169	2,825,605	-487,559	22,496,005	5,748,613	7,557,573	41,611	860,398	497,823
2016	36,925,695	26,790,260	2,915	26,793,175	2,929,347	-491,057	23,372,771	5,800,013	7,752,911	42,547	867,870	507,654
2017	38,507,106	27,963,968	8,123	27,972,091	3,076,958	-467,370	24,427,763	6,103,369	7,975,974	43,903	877,104	511,639
2018	39,926,820	39,927,053	-233	28,909,249	3,171,045	-681,608	25,056,596	6,644,774	8,225,450	46,360	861,234	516,068
2019	41,323,565	41,322,435	1,130	29,756,942	3,271,842	-590,949	25,894,151	6,714,961	8,714,453	47,550	869,046	525,301

Personal Income and Employment by Area: Kokomo, IN

(Thousands of dollars, except as noted.)

Year	Personal income, total	Earnings by place of work			Less: Contributions for government social insurance	Plus: Adjustment for residence	Equals: Net earnings by place of residence	Plus: Dividends, interest, and rent	Plus: Personal current transfer receipts	Per capita personal income (dollars)	Population (persons)	Total employment
		Nonfarm	Farm	Total								
1970	331,938	339,172	5,101	344,273	22,733	-52,896	268,644	41,170	22,124	3,982	83,353	42,282
1971	384,616	400,068	7,664	407,732	27,903	-65,921	313,908	45,197	25,511	4,584	83,904	44,735
1972	429,095	460,468	5,807	466,275	34,537	-78,852	352,886	48,118	28,091	5,058	84,832	46,840
1973	498,639	535,902	17,916	553,818	46,926	-94,878	412,014	54,917	31,708	5,815	85,745	50,105
1974	506,802	533,449	9,731	543,180	48,464	-94,141	400,575	62,950	43,277	5,811	87,215	47,441
1975	529,985	520,790	17,570	538,360	46,757	-92,491	399,112	70,449	60,424	6,098	86,906	43,959
1976	603,238	646,150	10,822	656,972	58,907	-124,706	473,359	77,332	52,547	6,958	86,700	47,377
1977	672,470	746,027	5,793	751,820	67,991	-152,531	531,298	87,137	54,035	7,719	87,123	49,509
1978	739,370	827,340	9,483	836,823	77,815	-174,283	584,725	94,161	60,484	8,474	87,248	50,886
1979	782,962	868,097	7,452	875,549	84,319	-185,636	605,594	102,436	74,932	8,968	87,305	49,709
1980	839,617	862,252	1,444	863,696	83,180	-187,632	592,884	123,519	123,214	9,676	86,774	45,809
1981	887,944	921,843	85	921,928	95,940	-197,215	628,773	149,943	109,228	10,313	86,098	46,275
1982	883,200	865,791	2,790	868,581	91,592	-176,894	600,095	161,716	121,389	10,390	85,004	42,641
1983	974,632	993,201	-1,920	991,281	106,423	-208,022	676,836	172,420	125,376	11,530	84,532	43,455
1984	1,114,265	1,164,886	7,157	1,172,043	128,577	-250,029	793,437	192,841	127,987	13,160	84,671	47,020
1985	1,209,975	1,285,017	8,624	1,293,641	143,969	-278,525	871,147	205,765	133,063	14,326	84,459	47,707
1986	1,233,883	1,289,057	6,711	1,295,768	143,515	-271,605	880,648	212,780	140,455	14,730	83,768	47,674
1987	1,256,526	1,302,142	9,828	1,311,970	143,223	-267,045	901,702	209,759	145,065	15,266	82,308	48,068
1988	1,367,182	1,450,340	5,576	1,455,916	163,395	-302,451	990,070	221,496	155,616	16,880	80,994	48,902
1989	1,472,569	1,534,112	10,431	1,544,543	173,296	-317,319	1,053,928	247,436	171,205	18,236	80,751	49,968
1990	1,515,935	1,541,538	13,107	1,554,645	180,308	-304,114	1,070,223	255,881	189,831	18,721	80,976	50,562
1991	1,551,343	1,587,854	8,786	1,596,640	187,804	-319,740	1,089,096	252,272	209,975	18,936	81,924	50,375
1992	1,662,725	1,715,362	12,379	1,727,741	199,092	-359,591	1,169,058	252,889	240,778	20,145	82,537	52,015
1993	1,770,673	1,857,559	15,884	1,873,443	218,365	-404,640	1,250,438	268,474	251,761	21,264	83,271	53,683
1994	1,884,528	2,043,334	16,630	2,059,964	240,029	-467,548	1,352,387	274,408	257,733	22,547	83,584	53,788
1995	1,979,095	2,129,197	8,025	2,137,222	236,695	-505,926	1,394,601	320,316	264,178	23,587	83,905	56,546
1996	2,042,827	2,162,744	21,936	2,184,680	229,036	-525,716	1,429,928	331,109	281,790	24,131	84,656	56,874
1997	2,080,986	2,175,566	20,605	2,196,171	227,438	-528,344	1,440,389	351,374	289,223	24,578	84,669	56,082
1998	2,204,766	2,327,553	11,951	2,339,504	232,284	-568,732	1,538,488	369,047	297,231	26,135	84,361	56,595
1999	2,312,948	2,500,430	7,155	2,507,585	245,559	-627,794	1,634,232	362,811	315,905	27,284	84,772	57,213
2000	2,406,448	2,558,018	13,580	2,571,598	248,837	-648,040	1,674,721	391,292	340,435	28,331	84,940	57,398
2001	2,354,937	2,448,629	15,228	2,463,857	281,622	-594,994	1,587,241	383,042	384,654	27,735	84,909	54,466
2002	2,395,617	2,506,249	9,722	2,515,971	287,595	-600,244	1,628,132	364,242	403,243	28,329	84,563	53,920
2003	2,446,666	2,531,807	14,876	2,546,683	291,765	-597,455	1,657,463	367,157	422,046	28,942	84,538	52,448
2004	2,519,188	2,629,356	24,887	2,654,243	300,112	-620,624	1,733,507	334,194	451,487	29,887	84,291	52,038
2005	2,559,067	2,617,770	15,628	2,633,398	300,181	-605,810	1,727,407	339,020	492,640	30,327	84,382	51,636
2006	2,650,856	2,665,025	10,558	2,675,583	310,452	-615,261	1,749,870	362,928	538,058	31,579	83,943	51,247
2007	2,759,075	2,687,272	12,261	2,699,533	314,196	-595,188	1,790,149	403,437	565,489	32,947	83,743	50,656
2008	2,712,827	2,393,985	24,741	2,418,726	285,908	-469,668	1,663,150	406,508	643,169	32,500	83,472	48,220
2009	2,526,355	2,000,794	10,623	2,011,417	246,460	-325,463	1,439,494	379,667	707,194	30,548	82,701	43,224
2010	2,571,457	2,029,463	3,401	2,032,864	246,312	-323,821	1,462,731	368,294	740,432	31,075	82,750	44,555
2011	2,733,268	2,162,099	20,410	2,182,509	233,900	-364,208	1,584,401	404,398	744,469	33,020	82,775	45,557
2012	2,855,306	2,263,219	25,977	2,289,196	241,939	-382,668	1,664,589	421,802	768,915	34,481	82,807	46,485
2013	2,894,950	2,354,032	55,367	2,409,399	291,083	-423,447	1,694,869	414,490	785,591	35,002	82,707	47,657
2014	3,024,826	2,474,197	25,886	2,500,083	303,282	-433,713	1,763,088	439,230	822,508	36,637	82,563	48,400
2015	3,104,623	2,537,308	-5,724	2,531,584	314,250	-434,101	1,783,233	461,965	859,425	37,717	82,314	48,601
2016	3,205,581	2,602,038	14,364	2,616,402	318,043	-447,893	1,850,466	476,150	878,965	38,932	82,339	49,830
2017	3,305,648	2,673,001	-291	2,672,710	318,794	-454,422	1,899,494	498,223	907,931	40,135	82,363	49,959
2018	3,466,287	3,450,659	15,628	2,687,889	321,955	-359,932	2,006,002	526,874	933,411	42,140	82,257	48,870
2019	3,542,015	3,534,829	7,186	2,741,273	332,689	-373,963	2,034,621	534,563	972,831	42,911	82,544	48,258

Personal Income and Employment by Area: La Crosse-Onalaska, WI-MN

(Thousands of dollars, except as noted.)

Year	Personal income, total	Earnings by place of work			Less: Contributions for government social insurance	Plus: Adjustment for residence	Equals: Net earnings by place of residence	Plus: Dividends, interest, and rent	Plus: Personal current transfer receipts	Per capita personal income (dollars)	Population (persons)	Total employment
		Nonfarm	Farm	Total								
1970	351,917	265,134	18,975	284,109	19,719	-6,989	257,401	58,922	35,594	3,581	98,260	42,995
1971	379,780	284,348	19,289	303,637	21,845	-7,215	274,577	63,301	41,902	3,825	99,301	43,907
1972	413,433	312,253	21,855	334,108	25,281	-8,400	300,427	67,254	45,752	4,187	98,738	45,533
1973	468,010	352,671	31,478	384,149	32,705	-9,942	341,502	73,946	52,562	4,672	100,165	48,430
1974	514,132	391,540	24,873	416,413	37,822	-11,753	366,838	83,326	63,968	5,050	101,810	49,921
1975	566,448	428,642	19,890	448,532	40,610	-13,097	394,825	93,088	78,535	5,414	104,618	50,747
1976	637,150	492,901	19,442	512,343	47,636	-16,096	448,611	103,081	85,458	6,143	103,720	53,331
1977	718,376	552,252	30,107	582,359	53,355	-19,477	509,527	117,690	91,159	6,757	106,314	55,192
1978	803,419	632,290	28,734	661,024	62,648	-24,020	574,356	128,712	100,351	7,337	109,509	57,889
1979	898,823	712,223	27,666	739,889	73,651	-26,480	639,758	141,662	117,403	8,072	111,346	60,200
1980	1,021,439	791,881	25,165	817,046	81,539	-31,203	704,304	177,119	140,016	9,312	109,696	61,582
1981	1,139,565	868,894	25,271	894,165	95,804	-38,062	760,299	219,989	159,277	10,315	110,473	62,428
1982	1,218,145	903,873	24,697	928,570	100,726	-38,787	789,057	253,596	175,492	10,974	111,000	61,655
1983	1,293,441	972,405	9,211	981,616	107,946	-42,044	831,626	270,392	191,423	11,640	111,122	62,200
1984	1,416,499	1,059,573	25,696	1,085,269	120,446	-45,464	919,359	299,460	197,680	12,622	112,222	64,086
1985	1,492,240	1,110,621	30,350	1,140,971	127,277	-47,789	965,905	313,127	213,208	13,213	112,937	64,642
1986	1,569,389	1,161,748	41,491	1,203,239	133,262	-49,390	1,020,587	330,597	218,205	13,875	113,108	65,626
1987	1,674,088	1,254,420	46,390	1,300,810	141,399	-53,645	1,105,766	343,930	224,392	14,662	114,178	67,341
1988	1,771,034	1,375,472	26,650	1,402,122	161,277	-60,672	1,180,173	357,121	233,740	15,403	114,981	70,751
1989	1,943,296	1,479,517	45,117	1,524,634	174,225	-64,302	1,286,107	403,642	253,547	16,797	115,693	70,706
1990	2,092,451	1,562,487	47,337	1,609,824	190,348	-65,650	1,353,826	467,936	270,689	17,920	116,769	72,019
1991	2,141,819	1,634,282	34,342	1,668,624	201,250	-69,287	1,398,087	456,374	287,358	18,197	117,700	73,440
1992	2,281,479	1,761,316	33,911	1,795,227	213,581	-74,424	1,507,222	461,929	312,328	19,139	119,207	75,248
1993	2,420,515	1,878,634	23,131	1,901,765	226,964	-79,069	1,595,732	502,357	322,426	20,071	120,597	77,177
1994	2,563,583	2,004,817	25,708	2,030,525	244,263	-83,919	1,702,343	532,033	329,207	21,038	121,856	79,874
1995	2,640,060	2,052,175	12,051	2,064,226	251,076	-83,820	1,729,330	558,719	352,011	21,480	122,910	81,628
1996	2,792,695	2,193,133	26,283	2,219,416	266,816	-90,450	1,862,150	571,145	359,400	22,536	123,920	83,209
1997	2,947,156	2,350,771	19,722	2,370,493	283,334	-98,561	1,988,598	587,783	370,775	23,668	124,521	85,030
1998	3,162,618	2,514,344	29,424	2,543,768	300,088	-103,770	2,139,910	644,677	378,031	25,226	125,371	86,896
1999	3,274,537	2,617,847	24,211	2,642,058	311,887	-97,344	2,232,827	644,041	397,669	25,980	126,041	87,257
2000	3,451,767	2,732,021	14,949	2,746,970	322,952	-99,162	2,324,856	693,281	433,630	27,175	127,021	88,620
2001	3,602,170	2,834,617	17,959	2,852,576	331,754	-113,360	2,407,462	708,578	486,130	28,225	127,624	88,333
2002	3,692,910	2,922,021	14,492	2,936,513	339,715	-105,986	2,490,812	667,829	534,269	28,792	128,261	87,533
2003	3,845,196	3,050,196	26,758	3,076,954	353,386	-110,875	2,612,693	683,160	549,343	29,859	128,780	88,472
2004	3,997,506	3,174,819	38,406	3,213,225	365,231	-125,167	2,722,827	709,024	565,655	30,990	128,992	88,138
2005	4,158,349	3,293,899	36,912	3,330,811	382,385	-131,369	2,817,057	740,240	601,052	32,099	129,549	89,432
2006	4,394,588	3,457,759	27,703	3,485,462	404,670	-144,487	2,936,305	822,711	635,572	33,766	130,147	91,459
2007	4,629,220	3,573,578	27,743	3,601,321	421,718	-154,799	3,024,804	914,954	689,462	35,286	131,190	92,487
2008	4,906,229	3,718,281	31,633	3,749,914	440,932	-171,457	3,137,525	997,915	770,789	37,191	131,920	92,633
2009	4,974,574	3,777,476	13,266	3,790,742	444,713	-189,439	3,156,590	935,060	882,924	37,383	133,072	90,829
2010	5,077,993	3,900,569	28,412	3,928,981	462,045	-207,216	3,259,720	859,191	959,082	37,923	133,903	91,117
2011	5,377,474	4,028,212	52,982	4,081,194	428,269	-228,052	3,424,873	1,025,230	927,371	40,102	134,094	92,209
2012	5,682,599	4,223,468	57,557	4,281,025	442,636	-255,502	3,582,887	1,148,703	951,009	42,001	135,298	93,979
2013	5,625,416	4,341,667	44,485	4,386,152	513,989	-276,431	3,595,732	1,050,093	979,591	41,480	135,618	95,065
2014	5,966,346	4,562,799	46,557	4,609,356	535,180	-288,030	3,786,146	1,143,312	1,036,888	43,835	136,108	95,427
2015	6,165,735	4,681,695	31,581	4,713,276	548,966	-287,967	3,876,343	1,210,573	1,078,819	45,219	136,354	95,886
2016	6,306,828	4,818,330	15,860	4,834,190	559,879	-324,212	3,950,099	1,257,474	1,099,255	46,224	136,442	96,719
2017	6,494,495	4,937,002	11,569	4,948,571	581,806	-326,922	4,039,843	1,306,615	1,148,037	47,428	136,934	97,306
2018	6,891,419	6,865,374	26,045	5,203,911	604,905	-345,934	4,253,072	1,424,502	1,213,845	50,445	136,613	97,901
2019	7,108,822	7,069,769	39,053	5,403,454	629,366	-368,417	4,405,671	1,435,019	1,268,132	52,035	136,616	98,153

Personal Income and Employment by Area: Lafayette, LA

(Thousands of dollars, except as noted.)

Year	Personal income, total	Earnings by place of work			Less: Contributions for government social insurance	Plus: Adjustment for residence	Equals: Net earnings by place of residence	Plus: Dividends, interest, and rent	Plus: Personal current transfer receipts	Per capita personal income (dollars)	Population (persons)	Total employment
		Nonfarm	Farm	Total								
1970	805,165	584,621	39,652	624,273	36,957	24,925	612,241	109,467	83,457	2,707	297,437	106,400
1971	884,670	645,894	38,897	684,791	41,721	23,475	666,545	122,172	95,953	2,932	301,678	108,662
1972	985,311	729,548	45,181	774,729	49,714	21,077	746,092	134,920	104,299	3,201	307,819	113,843
1973	1,152,474	825,043	101,536	926,579	65,085	17,213	878,707	152,911	120,856	3,689	312,430	119,859
1974	1,347,267	952,477	122,915	1,075,392	77,644	17,866	1,015,614	187,384	144,269	4,248	317,134	124,542
1975	1,562,706	1,128,221	105,665	1,233,886	91,074	18,513	1,161,325	224,040	177,341	4,844	322,597	130,569
1976	1,724,255	1,333,387	42,940	1,376,327	109,380	13,869	1,280,816	246,297	197,142	5,211	330,873	137,893
1977	1,992,514	1,574,370	50,850	1,625,220	128,516	6,313	1,503,017	279,570	209,927	5,899	337,770	147,120
1978	2,381,562	1,960,774	35,423	1,996,197	164,968	-2,722	1,828,507	324,157	228,898	6,917	344,306	161,185
1979	2,787,799	2,320,543	53,177	2,373,720	204,852	-15,882	2,152,986	374,480	260,333	7,925	351,776	170,540
1980	3,334,622	2,773,721	27,202	2,800,923	244,515	-32,872	2,523,536	501,041	310,045	9,226	361,450	181,105
1981	4,095,563	3,456,825	16,031	3,472,856	329,428	-61,617	3,081,811	670,453	343,299	11,035	371,133	199,253
1982	4,572,504	3,752,185	42,429	3,794,614	370,924	-77,237	3,346,453	823,010	403,041	11,855	385,710	205,964
1983	4,550,157	3,528,606	27,416	3,556,022	341,351	-63,472	3,151,199	895,901	503,057	11,556	393,737	193,845
1984	4,700,343	3,651,637	12,044	3,663,681	364,278	-57,348	3,242,055	953,725	504,563	11,961	392,956	193,564
1985	4,913,527	3,748,245	28,171	3,776,416	379,562	-57,444	3,339,410	1,040,782	533,335	12,423	395,505	192,643
1986	4,645,752	3,370,084	16,568	3,386,652	334,428	-35,476	3,016,748	994,395	634,609	11,700	397,056	174,850
1987	4,402,044	3,143,569	22,222	3,165,791	306,254	-15,162	2,844,375	925,071	632,598	11,313	389,109	164,848
1988	4,756,912	3,434,996	79,750	3,514,746	352,178	-16,763	3,145,805	964,861	646,246	12,393	383,841	171,932
1989	5,111,895	3,646,308	65,716	3,712,024	376,285	-11,263	3,324,476	1,075,130	712,289	13,319	383,800	177,407
1990	5,550,876	4,079,953	36,132	4,116,085	432,146	-18,684	3,665,255	1,105,216	780,405	14,478	383,397	186,879
1991	5,837,167	4,272,778	43,202	4,315,980	464,821	-21,801	3,829,358	1,111,155	896,654	15,033	388,299	191,220
1992	6,136,561	4,406,144	61,344	4,467,488	470,247	-2,034	3,995,207	1,112,651	1,028,703	15,633	392,531	188,119
1993	6,524,512	4,676,688	72,349	4,749,037	503,980	-5,552	4,239,505	1,163,828	1,121,179	16,396	397,922	195,210
1994	7,013,882	5,037,096	54,811	5,091,907	554,587	-24,162	4,513,158	1,241,963	1,258,761	17,431	402,385	201,325
1995	7,421,515	5,295,005	89,238	5,384,243	582,134	-47,360	4,754,749	1,367,119	1,299,647	18,250	406,658	208,746
1996	8,010,673	5,806,145	99,344	5,905,489	636,479	-76,643	5,192,367	1,492,500	1,325,806	19,480	411,228	217,292
1997	8,806,045	6,521,408	85,973	6,607,381	707,931	-100,298	5,799,152	1,644,060	1,362,833	21,140	416,562	228,667
1998	9,349,456	6,991,300	78,049	7,069,349	751,691	-126,093	6,191,565	1,755,718	1,402,173	22,203	421,081	237,170
1999	9,319,881	6,831,560	72,812	6,904,372	723,676	-93,214	6,087,482	1,760,558	1,471,841	21,975	424,114	232,472
2000	9,935,457	7,309,973	71,407	7,381,380	761,358	-116,591	6,503,431	1,915,780	1,516,246	23,369	425,158	236,014
2001	10,792,612	8,058,627	76,068	8,134,695	861,628	-154,234	7,118,833	1,920,471	1,753,308	25,290	426,750	241,219
2002	10,991,658	8,263,055	45,386	8,308,441	879,517	-148,809	7,280,115	1,853,518	1,858,025	25,541	430,358	241,717
2003	11,374,959	8,594,489	89,885	8,684,374	898,686	-129,827	7,655,861	1,859,836	1,859,262	26,276	432,900	243,521
2004	11,760,813	8,903,213	76,039	8,979,252	927,099	-171,060	7,881,093	1,836,481	2,043,239	26,973	436,018	244,291
2005	13,164,920	9,904,598	55,129	9,959,727	999,165	-238,892	8,721,670	2,169,045	2,274,205	29,925	439,936	252,865
2006	15,129,980	11,407,239	66,167	11,473,406	1,141,128	-301,433	10,030,845	2,715,666	2,383,469	33,567	450,740	266,576
2007	16,037,803	12,112,623	69,011	12,181,634	1,229,186	-361,561	10,590,887	2,951,395	2,495,521	35,301	454,315	274,647
2008	18,056,366	13,133,252	133,622	13,266,874	1,313,846	-407,875	11,545,153	3,639,007	2,872,206	39,329	459,111	281,721
2009	16,972,147	12,476,093	126,111	12,602,204	1,273,471	-322,983	11,005,750	2,955,161	3,011,236	36,578	463,998	277,490
2010	17,942,262	13,076,439	138,501	13,214,940	1,308,472	-256,005	11,650,463	3,079,552	3,212,247	38,366	467,661	278,005
2011	18,630,531	13,614,753	114,328	13,729,081	1,226,981	-196,938	12,305,162	3,053,522	3,271,847	39,581	470,693	284,493
2012	20,607,829	14,719,390	145,351	14,864,741	1,305,208	-154,378	13,405,155	3,880,970	3,321,704	43,450	474,293	292,872
2013	21,018,517	15,773,472	172,308	15,945,780	1,552,322	-22,348	14,371,110	3,199,218	3,448,189	43,806	479,811	299,502
2014	22,260,492	16,643,980	125,542	16,769,522	1,607,167	24,502	15,186,857	3,578,992	3,494,643	45,888	485,104	303,453
2015	21,122,053	15,108,772	63,230	15,172,002	1,521,048	130,168	13,781,122	3,460,663	3,880,268	43,103	490,041	295,324
2016	19,811,130	13,173,077	47,694	13,220,771	1,356,942	287,904	12,151,733	3,466,482	4,192,915	40,296	491,646	286,607
2017	20,225,360	13,261,893	81,149	13,343,042	1,374,309	277,318	12,246,051	3,588,518	4,390,791	41,145	491,558	286,782
2018	21,309,936	21,216,372	93,564	13,903,670	1,462,276	322,970	12,764,364	4,002,389	4,543,183	43,518	489,680	289,651
2019	21,775,660	21,691,268	84,392	14,147,074	1,479,884	325,225	12,992,415	4,023,822	4,759,423	44,512	489,207	292,176

Personal Income and Employment by Area: Lafayette-West Lafayette, IN

(Thousands of dollars, except as noted.)

Year	Personal income, total	Earnings by place of work			Less: Contributions for government social insurance	Plus: Adjustment for residence	Equals: Net earnings by place of residence	Plus: Dividends, interest, and rent	Plus: Personal current transfer receipts	Per capita personal income (dollars)	Population (persons)	Total employment
		Nonfarm	Farm	Total								
1970.............	507,331	412,779	20,631	433,410	28,045	-14,774	390,591	83,303	33,437	3,660	138,617	62,709
1971.............	562,517	439,001	35,303	474,304	30,892	-13,844	429,568	92,990	39,959	3,995	140,794	63,225
1972.............	604,019	479,613	27,485	507,098	35,671	-14,346	457,081	101,326	45,612	4,184	144,368	64,982
1973.............	716,411	531,175	75,074	606,249	45,500	-15,013	545,736	116,880	53,795	5,009	143,014	67,510
1974.............	755,819	581,705	49,767	631,472	52,537	-18,171	560,764	133,882	61,173	5,205	145,206	68,865
1975.............	853,224	611,047	87,733	698,780	54,672	-18,540	625,568	149,874	77,782	5,883	145,041	68,001
1976.............	907,714	679,066	62,857	741,923	61,149	-17,271	663,503	162,371	81,840	6,179	146,905	70,142
1977.............	987,994	770,336	37,801	808,137	68,649	-21,066	718,422	183,537	86,035	6,650	148,579	72,763
1978.............	1,120,873	879,573	47,200	926,773	80,449	-25,245	821,079	203,944	95,850	7,456	150,334	75,536
1979.............	1,245,382	974,236	53,338	1,027,574	92,420	-28,212	906,942	229,571	108,869	8,209	151,718	75,825
1980.............	1,335,883	1,035,609	19,870	1,055,479	97,674	-30,111	927,694	278,477	129,712	8,794	151,907	76,075
1981.............	1,499,152	1,108,911	41,251	1,150,162	113,096	-28,849	1,008,217	341,048	149,887	9,822	152,637	75,590
1982.............	1,576,984	1,139,611	38,427	1,178,038	118,701	-31,409	1,027,928	380,814	168,242	10,258	153,738	74,541
1983.............	1,620,823	1,188,320	-2,527	1,185,793	123,193	-29,644	1,032,956	404,239	183,628	10,529	153,944	74,681
1984.............	1,800,695	1,299,011	48,005	1,347,016	137,269	-31,101	1,178,646	429,164	192,885	11,727	153,552	77,450
1985.............	1,903,656	1,372,142	52,368	1,424,510	147,204	-34,398	1,242,908	456,939	203,809	12,343	154,225	78,778
1986.............	1,996,757	1,470,444	36,502	1,506,946	158,406	-41,227	1,307,313	474,395	215,049	12,944	154,265	80,336
1987.............	2,110,956	1,583,438	45,674	1,629,112	167,220	-50,073	1,411,819	480,781	218,356	13,634	154,829	82,628
1988.............	2,214,919	1,718,330	11,447	1,729,777	189,751	-51,313	1,488,713	495,832	230,374	14,157	156,458	85,370
1989.............	2,472,054	1,875,447	55,990	1,931,437	207,583	-61,024	1,662,830	559,334	249,890	15,555	158,926	87,860
1990.............	2,625,434	2,034,920	50,175	2,085,095	231,032	-76,281	1,777,782	578,459	269,193	16,504	159,075	90,758
1991.............	2,707,383	2,178,241	-3,015	2,175,226	250,304	-89,610	1,835,312	581,789	290,282	16,751	161,622	92,258
1992.............	2,927,312	2,328,803	38,090	2,366,893	264,547	-101,193	2,001,153	599,127	327,032	17,856	163,942	93,614
1993.............	3,073,903	2,440,601	41,225	2,481,826	278,886	-105,298	2,097,642	632,196	344,065	18,424	166,846	95,426
1994.............	3,264,594	2,596,669	52,280	2,648,949	299,855	-117,383	2,231,711	674,355	358,528	19,342	168,780	97,690
1995.............	3,446,261	2,778,689	3,352	2,782,041	320,351	-139,157	2,322,533	756,343	367,385	20,132	171,187	101,510
1996.............	3,644,275	2,894,448	77,639	2,972,087	328,711	-156,796	2,486,580	770,623	387,072	21,024	173,337	103,302
1997.............	3,871,340	3,094,530	69,596	3,164,126	350,340	-183,586	2,630,200	839,283	401,857	22,188	174,481	105,842
1998.............	4,132,719	3,359,792	27,745	3,387,537	369,592	-203,246	2,814,699	882,174	435,846	23,507	175,806	109,947
1999.............	4,256,589	3,522,860	21,320	3,544,180	384,560	-220,901	2,938,719	859,969	457,901	24,002	177,346	112,335
2000.............	4,580,624	3,782,629	25,857	3,808,486	404,831	-244,256	3,159,399	923,760	497,465	25,601	178,921	113,695
2001.............	4,611,965	3,781,011	39,892	3,820,903	416,636	-260,302	3,143,965	927,003	540,997	25,522	180,706	109,292
2002.............	4,663,089	3,843,698	30,035	3,873,733	421,569	-274,112	3,178,052	907,303	577,734	25,652	181,781	108,659
2003.............	4,690,708	3,885,903	46,986	3,932,889	429,752	-284,505	3,218,632	866,981	605,095	25,546	183,621	106,008
2004.............	4,938,104	4,064,944	89,747	4,154,691	452,136	-280,645	3,421,910	872,607	643,587	26,693	184,996	106,887
2005.............	5,154,204	4,278,923	62,830	4,341,753	479,863	-302,396	3,559,494	890,513	704,197	27,413	188,023	108,909
2006.............	5,431,835	4,401,107	55,227	4,456,334	497,833	-273,521	3,684,980	983,727	763,128	28,282	192,060	111,329
2007.............	5,712,288	4,574,082	88,103	4,662,185	517,703	-291,103	3,853,379	1,049,420	809,489	29,271	195,149	113,268
2008.............	6,157,041	4,766,027	140,851	4,906,878	541,592	-288,697	4,076,589	1,127,502	952,950	31,103	197,954	113,469
2009.............	6,009,868	4,631,108	76,959	4,708,067	529,006	-284,843	3,894,218	1,074,238	1,041,412	29,933	200,775	109,675
2010.............	6,242,300	4,768,467	94,683	4,863,150	536,381	-279,388	4,047,381	1,049,660	1,145,259	30,886	202,105	109,442
2011.............	6,709,056	5,055,813	176,473	5,232,286	501,788	-303,522	4,426,976	1,154,296	1,127,784	32,814	204,455	113,096
2012.............	6,995,876	5,352,894	108,763	5,461,657	525,399	-329,864	4,606,394	1,237,080	1,152,402	33,737	207,365	116,268
2013.............	7,138,422	5,366,489	316,050	5,682,539	602,858	-315,354	4,764,327	1,212,533	1,161,562	33,956	210,227	116,817
2014.............	7,413,817	5,678,759	156,447	5,835,206	633,743	-322,630	4,878,833	1,293,592	1,241,392	34,908	212,381	119,121
2015.............	7,595,722	5,879,498	37,921	5,917,419	663,548	-336,915	4,916,956	1,381,911	1,296,855	35,385	214,657	120,203
2016.............	7,897,225	6,081,335	85,306	6,166,641	676,204	-359,125	5,131,312	1,430,754	1,335,159	36,343	217,296	122,090
2017.............	8,179,575	6,356,874	35,797	6,392,671	703,723	-389,817	5,299,131	1,506,910	1,373,534	37,309	219,239	123,355
2018.............	9,155,463	9,063,067	92,396	7,046,239	772,680	-333,819	5,939,740	1,711,191	1,504,532	39,645	230,938	129,958
2019.............	9,358,207	9,286,763	71,444	7,143,479	794,031	-321,210	6,028,238	1,735,681	1,594,288	40,164	233,002	132,073

Personal Income and Employment by Area: Lake Charles, LA

(Thousands of dollars, except as noted.)

Year	Personal income, total	Earnings by place of work			Less: Contributions for government social insurance	Plus: Adjustment for residence	Equals: Net earnings by place of residence	Plus: Dividends, interest, and rent	Plus: Personal current transfer receipts	Per capita personal income (dollars)	Population (persons)	Total employment
		Nonfarm	Farm	Total								
1970	491,476	408,068	8,433	416,501	26,515	-3,039	386,947	59,370	45,159	3,200	153,590	57,589
1971	529,251	439,671	8,758	448,429	29,222	-5,714	413,493	65,351	50,407	3,422	154,666	57,881
1972	556,300	457,816	8,903	466,719	31,780	-5,935	429,004	70,912	56,384	3,540	157,151	57,794
1973	626,807	515,599	18,047	533,646	41,616	-10,313	481,717	78,029	67,061	3,945	158,870	60,991
1974	712,607	590,165	16,504	606,669	49,209	-15,434	542,026	93,025	77,556	4,472	159,343	62,986
1975	811,538	669,467	15,228	684,695	54,433	-21,300	608,962	106,385	96,191	5,060	160,391	65,067
1976	919,711	790,080	2,070	792,150	65,168	-28,884	698,098	115,252	106,361	5,652	162,731	68,125
1977	1,036,821	894,285	8,560	902,845	73,112	-36,865	792,868	127,998	115,955	6,263	165,539	71,271
1978	1,224,395	1,090,022	10,762	1,100,784	91,950	-59,417	949,417	151,283	123,695	7,304	167,630	78,314
1979	1,407,862	1,283,800	11,753	1,295,553	112,962	-85,509	1,097,082	174,199	136,581	8,189	171,913	82,909
1980	1,641,103	1,492,938	8,637	1,501,575	130,913	-112,164	1,258,498	215,691	166,914	9,248	177,456	86,336
1981	1,898,005	1,722,383	3,871	1,726,254	162,348	-127,778	1,436,128	276,345	185,532	10,502	180,724	89,401
1982	1,942,542	1,644,337	5,670	1,650,007	157,870	-105,339	1,386,798	326,660	229,084	10,565	183,865	82,812
1983	2,038,162	1,661,668	4,750	1,666,418	157,302	-108,239	1,400,877	364,576	272,709	11,036	184,681	80,277
1984	2,058,711	1,630,558	2,356	1,632,914	156,757	-94,455	1,381,702	402,166	274,843	11,171	184,287	78,899
1985	2,122,274	1,659,056	4,615	1,663,671	160,808	-95,607	1,407,256	433,837	281,181	11,595	183,031	78,558
1986	2,129,263	1,643,559	61	1,643,620	158,069	-95,019	1,390,532	429,743	308,988	11,745	181,297	76,259
1987	2,193,774	1,712,486	1,930	1,714,416	162,760	-95,225	1,456,431	423,178	314,165	12,173	180,214	77,853
1988	2,327,620	1,796,623	13,651	1,810,274	179,495	-95,490	1,535,289	465,706	326,625	13,007	178,955	79,865
1989	2,467,738	1,920,278	2,519	1,922,797	195,459	-106,515	1,620,823	479,152	367,763	13,881	177,773	82,655
1990	2,749,054	2,170,146	4,960	2,175,106	227,865	-125,659	1,821,582	519,860	407,612	15,486	177,524	87,736
1991	2,908,113	2,306,447	2,286	2,308,733	247,094	-131,832	1,929,807	523,967	454,339	16,207	179,439	89,353
1992	3,055,947	2,404,060	4,581	2,408,641	254,461	-133,887	2,020,293	529,334	506,320	16,908	180,736	88,809
1993	3,204,424	2,483,285	5,344	2,488,629	264,065	-143,262	2,081,302	566,643	556,479	17,598	182,093	89,641
1994	3,455,815	2,665,015	1,629	2,666,644	287,657	-157,124	2,221,863	611,965	621,987	18,763	184,181	93,804
1995	3,674,810	2,832,378	6,465	2,838,843	305,109	-169,093	2,364,641	667,761	642,408	19,693	186,607	97,914
1996	3,897,417	3,061,153	2,306	3,063,459	330,253	-187,238	2,545,968	698,284	653,165	20,585	189,335	102,120
1997	4,109,314	3,286,609	3,640	3,290,249	353,288	-199,666	2,737,295	699,461	672,558	21,506	191,076	105,423
1998	4,241,445	3,377,266	6,882	3,384,148	369,902	-214,006	2,800,240	765,323	675,882	22,037	192,470	107,839
1999	4,314,501	3,432,825	6,198	3,439,023	370,431	-216,882	2,851,710	751,226	711,565	22,308	193,408	107,766
2000	4,479,503	3,547,016	5,291	3,552,307	374,473	-217,516	2,960,318	786,871	732,314	23,151	193,491	108,617
2001	4,688,908	3,671,268	11,315	3,682,583	382,945	-238,312	3,061,326	796,681	830,901	24,273	193,171	108,198
2002	4,778,433	3,751,561	5,455	3,757,016	394,247	-236,560	3,126,209	784,360	867,864	24,718	193,321	108,036
2003	4,805,805	3,792,365	10,657	3,803,022	395,209	-228,971	3,178,842	739,737	887,226	24,702	194,552	107,586
2004	5,043,469	4,005,443	11,237	4,016,680	410,074	-253,921	3,352,685	722,297	968,487	25,805	195,444	106,568
2005	5,505,312	4,310,694	4,350	4,315,044	431,046	-292,334	3,591,664	763,486	1,150,162	28,051	196,263	108,680
2006	5,959,204	4,635,513	13,588	4,649,101	460,006	-305,236	3,883,859	991,795	1,083,550	30,866	193,069	110,930
2007	6,583,448	4,892,002	3,489	4,895,491	489,501	-327,641	4,078,349	1,383,374	1,121,725	33,831	194,598	113,094
2008	7,016,589	5,261,541	2,266	5,263,807	522,330	-377,730	4,363,747	1,367,135	1,285,707	35,733	196,362	115,652
2009	6,711,682	5,069,188	6,096	5,075,284	507,067	-315,749	4,252,468	1,107,574	1,351,640	33,896	198,010	112,613
2010	6,881,161	5,138,247	8,532	5,146,779	505,242	-288,013	4,353,524	1,073,607	1,454,030	34,416	199,943	110,785
2011	7,189,538	5,313,807	8,120	5,321,927	475,308	-305,922	4,540,697	1,167,264	1,481,577	35,863	200,475	112,346
2012	7,630,345	5,604,168	15,931	5,620,099	495,004	-315,707	4,809,388	1,290,387	1,530,570	37,938	201,126	114,545
2013	7,769,202	5,907,800	25,214	5,933,014	586,735	-368,871	4,977,408	1,210,491	1,581,303	38,422	202,209	117,149
2014	8,391,097	6,800,429	21,413	6,821,842	667,450	-634,814	5,519,578	1,286,140	1,585,379	41,263	203,356	123,642
2015	8,965,984	7,326,804	11,589	7,338,393	728,823	-760,727	5,848,843	1,366,400	1,750,741	43,660	205,357	128,993
2016	9,241,323	7,903,311	8,330	7,911,641	799,670	-1,057,850	6,054,121	1,336,376	1,850,826	44,533	207,518	135,600
2017	9,724,922	8,587,784	10,406	8,598,190	875,052	-1,323,961	6,399,177	1,390,274	1,935,471	46,451	209,357	142,545
2018	10,204,086	10,208,511	-4,425	9,030,209	941,112	-1,396,998	6,692,099	1,522,970	1,989,017	48,547	210,190	145,917
2019	10,445,141	10,451,090	-5,949	8,940,298	921,408	-1,196,970	6,821,920	1,532,747	2,090,474	49,642	210,409	143,349

Personal Income and Employment by Area: Lake Havasu City-Kingman, AZ

(Thousands of dollars, except as noted.)

Year	Personal income, total	Earnings by place of work			Less: Contributions for government social insurance	Plus: Adjustment for residence	Equals: Net earnings by place of residence	Plus: Dividends, interest, and rent	Plus: Personal current transfer receipts	Per capita personal income (dollars)	Population (persons)	Total employment
		Nonfarm	Farm	Total								
1970	102,490	66,091	1,274	67,365	4,225	11,209	74,349	18,445	9,696	3,891	26,338	9,297
1971	118,683	73,925	2,040	75,965	4,937	13,553	84,581	21,589	12,513	4,130	28,736	9,969
1972	135,971	83,329	3,489	86,818	5,873	14,746	95,691	24,804	15,476	4,374	31,084	10,832
1973	163,490	97,737	5,483	103,220	7,882	18,447	113,785	30,171	19,534	4,804	34,030	11,853
1974	182,255	115,194	686	115,880	9,800	16,123	122,203	36,302	23,750	4,983	36,572	13,269
1975	211,573	125,660	9,382	135,042	10,576	15,944	140,410	42,053	29,110	5,372	39,388	13,882
1976	230,847	141,398	54	141,452	11,874	18,049	147,627	47,091	36,129	5,437	42,458	14,593
1977	269,381	160,553	2,912	163,465	13,812	21,870	171,523	55,967	41,891	6,220	43,312	15,773
1978	328,934	196,295	3,876	200,171	17,289	26,737	209,619	69,182	50,133	7,148	46,017	17,606
1979	397,496	247,144	1,930	249,074	23,306	27,618	253,386	83,844	60,266	7,676	51,783	20,022
1980	460,917	268,553	4,924	273,477	25,668	31,928	279,737	105,262	75,918	8,169	56,423	21,285
1981	515,652	282,505	3,578	286,083	29,311	36,741	293,513	128,316	93,823	8,798	58,607	21,566
1982	548,776	270,741	4,562	275,303	28,949	42,111	288,465	149,880	110,431	8,775	62,539	20,609
1983	614,716	289,999	7,597	297,596	31,045	49,929	316,480	174,940	123,296	9,604	64,005	21,081
1984	716,005	341,804	5,857	347,661	37,252	56,842	367,251	211,921	136,833	10,629	67,364	23,340
1985	815,304	389,168	2,387	391,555	43,430	66,435	414,560	244,637	156,107	11,521	70,769	25,423
1986	910,427	432,044	1,266	433,310	48,416	77,985	462,879	273,129	174,419	12,080	75,366	26,881
1987	1,001,345	485,900	1,456	487,356	54,319	92,319	525,356	280,404	195,585	12,952	77,314	29,243
1988	1,120,161	536,321	3,910	540,231	62,328	112,478	590,381	308,988	220,792	13,597	82,381	31,315
1989	1,258,408	595,501	6,951	602,452	72,849	136,044	665,647	343,048	249,713	14,458	87,040	33,410
1990	1,445,167	702,053	8,192	710,245	86,995	164,857	788,107	374,259	282,801	15,134	95,491	36,930
1991	1,546,282	759,732	7,829	767,561	94,310	170,535	843,786	379,424	323,072	15,121	102,263	38,893
1992	1,653,450	811,377	7,696	819,073	100,658	182,942	901,357	385,755	366,338	15,219	108,644	39,206
1993	1,797,994	875,755	6,157	881,912	109,043	198,515	971,384	425,138	401,472	15,539	115,706	40,507
1994	1,988,757	957,454	5,223	962,677	120,219	216,911	1,059,369	486,091	443,297	16,181	122,906	43,326
1995	2,041,225	982,316	1,863	984,179	120,797	234,062	1,097,444	459,983	483,798	15,669	130,274	43,977
1996	2,196,237	1,046,698	3,450	1,050,148	131,001	255,698	1,174,845	494,357	527,035	16,097	136,436	46,030
1997	2,382,431	1,158,289	2,951	1,161,240	139,899	277,141	1,298,482	524,153	559,796	16,906	140,922	47,793
1998	2,576,973	1,250,558	4,018	1,254,576	149,045	302,842	1,408,373	557,087	611,513	17,753	145,155	49,316
1999	2,745,344	1,351,280	6,174	1,357,454	160,454	332,622	1,529,622	563,716	652,006	18,260	150,351	51,247
2000	2,972,148	1,472,338	7,868	1,480,206	174,489	355,097	1,660,814	608,859	702,475	19,026	156,215	54,312
2001	3,252,557	1,630,318	7,331	1,637,649	193,606	389,455	1,833,498	635,654	783,405	20,289	160,312	57,796
2002	3,452,334	1,777,994	5,179	1,783,173	211,404	418,687	1,990,456	598,897	862,981	20,778	166,155	59,875
2003	3,716,916	1,905,194	8,573	1,913,767	226,657	472,110	2,159,220	618,129	939,567	21,531	172,633	63,760
2004	4,107,483	2,093,064	11,869	2,104,933	249,049	563,921	2,419,805	664,210	1,023,468	22,753	180,521	67,457
2005	4,508,922	2,281,505	11,255	2,292,760	278,894	621,982	2,635,848	749,035	1,124,039	23,885	188,773	72,539
2006	4,797,570	2,490,628	9,590	2,500,218	305,773	601,381	2,795,826	761,920	1,239,824	24,456	196,168	75,359
2007	4,980,373	2,472,704	6,380	2,479,084	313,332	593,428	2,759,180	877,836	1,343,357	24,932	199,760	74,677
2008	5,085,767	2,439,089	5,676	2,444,765	316,552	547,036	2,675,249	902,327	1,508,191	25,419	200,078	70,529
2009	5,057,614	2,279,732	3,912	2,283,644	302,516	571,976	2,553,104	822,252	1,682,258	25,327	199,696	65,562
2010	5,114,627	2,284,675	3,449	2,288,124	308,727	562,784	2,542,181	791,526	1,780,920	25,533	200,315	64,092
2011	5,162,489	2,271,687	17,720	2,289,407	283,958	496,448	2,501,897	849,362	1,811,230	25,464	202,733	64,077
2012	5,282,867	2,309,146	2,767	2,311,913	286,607	520,994	2,546,300	885,339	1,851,228	25,990	203,262	63,231
2013	5,433,435	2,438,730	12,722	2,451,452	330,224	492,817	2,614,045	895,377	1,924,013	26,762	203,026	63,999
2014	5,765,508	2,550,566	12,177	2,562,743	341,482	535,770	2,757,031	987,174	2,021,303	28,357	203,320	65,391
2015	5,991,713	2,636,644	15,867	2,652,511	356,335	536,084	2,832,260	1,052,708	2,106,745	29,296	204,524	66,887
2016	6,167,703	2,692,124	9,028	2,701,152	371,187	577,552	2,907,517	1,080,726	2,179,460	30,030	205,385	67,897
2017	6,395,143	2,824,095	7,075	2,831,170	396,504	551,341	2,986,007	1,131,686	2,277,450	30,865	207,200	69,608
2018	6,980,623	6,952,161	28,462	3,039,851	426,158	646,385	3,260,078	1,278,921	2,441,624	33,354	209,292	71,815
2019	7,297,603	7,273,860	23,743	3,156,497	448,090	683,731	3,392,138	1,312,354	2,593,111	34,393	212,181	73,421

Personal Income and Employment by Area: Lakeland-Winter Haven, FL

(Thousands of dollars, except as noted.)

| | | | | | Derivation of personal income | | | | | | | |
| | | Earnings by place of work | | | Less: Contributions for government social insurance | Plus: Adjustment for residence | Equals: Net earnings by place of residence | Plus: Dividends, interest, and rent | Plus: Personal current transfer receipts | Per capita personal income (dollars) | Population (persons) | Total employment |
Year	Personal income, total	Nonfarm	Farm	Total								
1970	804,411	584,104	54,769	638,873	38,981	-22,544	577,348	145,461	81,602	3,492	230,334	97,281
1971	895,766	644,399	62,637	707,036	44,615	-23,517	638,904	159,356	97,506	3,709	241,479	100,888
1972	1,029,634	746,353	76,593	822,946	54,268	-27,489	741,189	175,690	112,755	4,079	252,394	107,814
1973	1,199,202	891,703	73,763	965,466	74,503	-34,508	856,455	208,355	134,392	4,576	262,049	118,069
1974	1,383,145	1,044,138	75,436	1,119,574	91,301	-44,243	984,030	244,445	154,670	5,047	274,042	125,364
1975	1,564,674	1,170,262	79,911	1,250,173	100,928	-56,828	1,092,417	273,124	199,133	5,501	284,417	128,059
1976	1,690,740	1,244,502	91,047	1,335,549	108,871	-57,797	1,168,881	297,710	224,149	5,839	289,562	128,195
1977	1,904,825	1,395,553	116,831	1,512,384	122,456	-68,148	1,321,780	337,426	245,619	6,434	296,048	134,567
1978	2,198,857	1,599,310	156,694	1,756,004	143,986	-80,311	1,531,707	396,279	270,871	7,301	301,183	142,680
1979	2,511,872	1,842,204	154,007	1,996,211	173,781	-98,243	1,724,187	469,946	317,739	8,032	312,723	149,427
1980	2,985,678	2,132,894	203,370	2,336,264	202,950	-117,504	2,015,810	592,688	377,180	9,214	324,038	156,846
1981	3,308,242	2,358,635	135,209	2,493,844	241,458	-125,421	2,126,965	738,586	442,691	9,935	332,973	160,268
1982	3,452,120	2,358,083	132,440	2,490,523	247,168	-111,860	2,131,495	808,479	512,146	10,155	339,930	155,026
1983	3,752,174	2,508,403	171,774	2,680,177	263,157	-99,305	2,317,715	878,123	556,336	10,842	346,080	157,947
1984	4,110,432	2,805,097	122,032	2,927,129	301,586	-90,952	2,534,591	996,704	579,137	11,598	354,414	165,687
1985	4,441,065	3,010,169	127,755	3,137,924	329,542	-83,599	2,724,783	1,084,720	631,562	12,207	363,802	173,302
1986	4,743,098	3,178,503	117,296	3,295,799	356,930	-68,405	2,870,464	1,182,613	690,021	12,748	372,057	176,446
1987	5,144,012	3,483,511	136,969	3,620,480	383,942	-65,200	3,171,338	1,245,250	727,424	13,533	380,106	178,789
1988	5,688,370	3,820,099	190,740	4,010,839	434,129	-59,470	3,517,240	1,349,844	821,286	14,617	389,160	188,505
1989	6,252,503	4,131,686	148,850	4,280,536	475,193	-61,495	3,743,848	1,601,237	907,418	15,701	398,231	195,457
1990	6,556,679	4,303,229	120,957	4,424,186	489,615	-25,670	3,908,901	1,642,391	1,005,387	16,080	407,756	194,693
1991	6,815,714	4,398,968	134,981	4,533,949	504,114	61,879	4,091,714	1,599,215	1,124,785	16,418	415,136	191,941
1992	7,203,889	4,648,776	78,279	4,727,055	530,097	99,681	4,296,639	1,612,433	1,294,817	17,024	423,171	188,240
1993	7,598,387	4,888,768	84,171	4,972,939	553,994	183,094	4,602,039	1,591,359	1,404,989	17,703	429,224	192,484
1994	8,221,179	5,279,642	87,382	5,367,024	604,922	234,620	4,996,722	1,716,141	1,508,316	18,749	438,480	199,641
1995	8,853,107	5,584,518	96,626	5,681,144	636,279	339,012	5,383,877	1,849,748	1,619,482	19,798	447,182	205,287
1996	9,396,345	5,976,920	80,402	6,057,322	670,561	338,439	5,725,200	1,949,323	1,721,822	20,673	454,512	210,699
1997	9,746,932	6,128,069	89,533	6,217,602	692,674	440,210	5,965,138	1,987,083	1,794,711	21,028	463,519	214,741
1998	10,678,516	6,693,894	132,364	6,826,258	746,304	506,341	6,586,295	2,219,997	1,872,224	22,650	471,450	223,190
1999	11,218,075	7,116,170	115,792	7,231,962	781,582	674,472	7,124,852	2,159,283	1,933,940	23,466	478,047	227,091
2000	11,730,807	7,269,959	120,892	7,390,851	808,731	760,536	7,342,656	2,334,507	2,053,644	24,162	485,515	234,576
2001	12,681,673	8,098,941	102,568	8,201,509	886,154	710,179	8,025,534	2,425,203	2,230,936	25,728	492,917	232,840
2002	12,925,873	8,346,928	118,487	8,465,415	908,615	725,143	8,281,943	2,228,921	2,415,009	25,776	501,469	235,387
2003	13,611,705	8,791,254	94,501	8,885,755	956,143	713,200	8,642,812	2,359,950	2,608,943	26,531	513,058	238,688
2004	14,723,982	9,349,574	92,706	9,442,280	1,028,382	726,585	9,140,483	2,716,919	2,866,580	27,903	527,685	249,751
2005	16,064,215	10,205,860	134,671	10,340,531	1,138,913	716,856	9,918,474	3,062,087	3,083,654	29,348	547,373	266,193
2006	16,799,499	10,539,449	150,439	10,689,888	1,227,149	695,547	10,158,286	3,299,301	3,341,912	29,560	568,324	275,020
2007	17,471,820	10,688,255	91,006	10,779,261	1,253,064	686,555	10,212,752	3,586,799	3,672,269	29,816	585,982	276,628
2008	17,966,738	10,594,989	80,873	10,675,862	1,265,064	617,218	10,028,016	3,744,011	4,194,711	30,206	594,801	268,495
2009	17,228,147	10,210,169	106,907	10,317,076	1,250,578	485,581	9,552,079	3,157,948	4,518,120	28,777	598,683	258,199
2010	18,387,470	10,461,764	125,968	10,587,732	1,250,476	437,820	9,775,076	3,705,806	4,906,588	30,486	603,135	255,704
2011	19,457,677	10,620,827	133,028	10,753,855	1,144,245	416,173	10,025,783	4,302,003	5,129,891	31,902	609,924	258,249
2012	19,546,204	11,122,917	146,897	11,269,814	1,197,353	398,293	10,470,754	3,931,537	5,143,913	31,749	615,639	261,791
2013	19,615,810	11,524,415	123,104	11,647,519	1,392,944	325,796	10,580,371	3,704,570	5,330,869	31,487	622,981	266,989
2014	20,733,698	11,896,097	108,829	12,004,926	1,441,167	400,472	10,964,231	4,096,468	5,672,999	32,644	635,152	273,852
2015	21,785,997	12,392,577	126,800	12,519,377	1,491,295	445,613	11,473,695	4,331,178	5,981,124	33,535	649,644	281,016
2016	22,387,332	12,762,237	96,303	12,858,540	1,557,351	480,018	11,781,207	4,356,769	6,249,356	33,563	667,018	287,212
2017	23,486,598	13,411,542	74,467	13,486,009	1,638,049	481,425	12,329,385	4,554,084	6,603,129	34,213	686,483	294,603
2018	25,288,404	25,195,872	92,532	14,505,064	1,753,545	494,427	13,245,946	5,118,937	6,923,521	35,789	706,597	312,797
2019	26,562,710	26,422,643	140,067	15,395,158	1,891,268	542,095	14,045,985	5,184,788	7,331,937	36,649	724,777	322,930

Personal Income and Employment by Area: Lancaster, PA

(Thousands of dollars, except as noted.)

Year	Personal income, total	Earnings by place of work			Less: Contributions for government social insurance	Plus: Adjustment for residence	Equals: Net earnings by place of residence	Plus: Dividends, interest, and rent	Plus: Personal current transfer receipts	Per capita personal income (dollars)	Population (persons)	Total employment
		Nonfarm	Farm	Total								
1970	1,391,393	1,059,372	84,767	1,144,139	78,563	42,606	1,108,182	182,577	100,634	4,331	321,290	156,017
1971	1,454,953	1,116,689	66,208	1,182,897	86,287	48,751	1,145,361	193,890	115,702	4,447	327,155	156,834
1972	1,616,518	1,258,627	65,432	1,324,059	102,540	56,771	1,278,290	208,956	129,272	4,867	332,160	163,540
1973	1,831,295	1,428,735	87,805	1,516,540	134,168	65,280	1,447,652	240,102	143,541	5,437	336,819	172,896
1974	1,976,296	1,532,955	68,078	1,601,033	149,336	78,236	1,529,933	271,772	174,591	5,810	340,170	173,356
1975	2,128,090	1,595,007	62,793	1,657,800	150,550	88,929	1,596,179	300,811	231,100	6,172	344,814	168,983
1976	2,345,672	1,790,272	51,857	1,842,129	172,580	101,587	1,771,136	326,352	248,184	6,752	347,407	173,386
1977	2,594,683	2,012,731	28,510	2,041,241	193,513	116,154	1,963,882	368,503	262,298	7,390	351,084	179,617
1978	2,972,383	2,299,560	70,842	2,370,402	226,062	133,832	2,278,172	410,765	283,446	8,381	354,667	187,604
1979	3,337,881	2,563,110	90,470	2,653,580	261,659	155,987	2,547,908	464,992	324,981	9,289	359,329	192,732
1980	3,610,692	2,707,502	46,456	2,753,958	279,918	181,615	2,655,655	576,941	378,096	9,935	363,420	194,330
1981	4,000,474	2,902,309	83,261	2,985,570	320,438	195,278	2,860,410	706,863	433,201	10,901	366,979	193,300
1982	4,303,177	3,025,906	69,015	3,094,921	338,229	198,595	2,955,287	842,032	505,858	11,599	370,992	191,675
1983	4,603,334	3,282,674	52,440	3,335,114	370,797	199,558	3,163,875	895,905	543,554	12,235	376,234	194,960
1984	5,154,347	3,662,780	147,665	3,810,445	431,253	211,263	3,590,455	1,011,721	552,171	13,532	380,892	203,704
1985	5,546,988	3,975,471	116,493	4,091,964	472,106	216,995	3,836,853	1,111,415	598,720	14,399	385,245	210,863
1986	6,046,419	4,345,460	167,565	4,513,025	516,025	219,696	4,216,696	1,188,332	641,391	15,411	392,339	218,827
1987	6,531,002	4,774,976	168,649	4,943,625	560,536	231,498	4,614,587	1,244,960	671,455	16,255	401,773	228,379
1988	7,052,177	5,282,181	81,846	5,364,027	627,239	244,879	4,981,667	1,341,012	729,498	17,194	410,152	237,036
1989	7,887,990	5,727,587	178,115	5,905,702	666,534	259,862	5,499,030	1,593,151	795,809	18,890	417,585	244,037
1990	8,253,673	6,099,780	110,193	6,209,973	717,200	264,732	5,757,505	1,632,441	863,727	19,423	424,947	250,269
1991	8,493,752	6,235,028	83,396	6,318,424	740,612	275,491	5,853,303	1,644,646	995,803	19,697	431,229	247,396
1992	9,083,365	6,670,842	146,879	6,817,721	787,280	288,418	6,318,859	1,699,463	1,065,043	20,839	435,886	249,064
1993	9,652,801	7,049,622	148,174	7,197,796	845,373	288,318	6,640,741	1,891,525	1,120,535	21,886	441,056	251,472
1994	9,876,689	7,343,425	123,479	7,466,904	895,352	298,940	6,870,492	1,837,180	1,169,017	22,132	446,254	255,573
1995	10,275,090	7,668,162	77,836	7,745,998	929,798	306,171	7,122,371	1,913,774	1,238,945	22,742	451,817	263,269
1996	10,916,661	7,994,597	183,834	8,178,431	946,195	320,010	7,552,246	2,031,523	1,332,892	23,951	455,783	266,835
1997	11,584,904	8,547,278	149,084	8,696,362	996,179	337,155	8,037,338	2,167,264	1,380,302	25,180	460,085	273,421
1998	12,170,246	8,929,601	140,947	9,070,548	1,035,042	359,356	8,394,862	2,326,129	1,449,255	26,214	464,272	272,593
1999	12,686,151	9,426,029	114,586	9,540,615	1,078,043	376,553	8,839,125	2,308,626	1,538,400	27,114	467,879	276,989
2000	13,760,359	10,188,376	167,337	10,355,713	1,146,931	393,303	9,602,085	2,506,907	1,651,367	29,156	471,955	282,826
2001	14,525,000	10,846,497	179,171	11,025,668	1,201,685	422,900	10,246,883	2,455,973	1,822,144	30,548	475,483	287,532
2002	14,693,234	11,222,436	97,535	11,319,971	1,240,880	425,803	10,504,894	2,224,070	1,964,270	30,603	480,118	287,524
2003	15,337,459	11,594,430	178,030	11,772,460	1,276,445	434,314	10,930,329	2,314,020	2,093,110	31,616	485,119	287,563
2004	16,377,672	12,358,303	265,426	12,623,729	1,342,907	464,120	11,744,942	2,443,745	2,188,985	33,425	489,977	294,482
2005	17,164,504	12,965,009	261,808	13,226,817	1,412,188	478,030	12,292,659	2,452,770	2,419,075	34,695	494,722	300,350
2006	17,820,135	13,297,550	205,329	13,502,879	1,469,461	533,394	12,566,812	2,663,654	2,589,669	35,575	500,922	303,188
2007	18,629,768	13,415,607	307,657	13,723,264	1,481,733	573,452	12,814,983	3,035,039	2,779,746	36,771	506,639	307,737
2008	19,296,524	13,516,689	228,915	13,745,604	1,513,079	572,415	12,804,940	3,308,151	3,183,433	37,692	511,957	308,123
2009	18,882,798	12,980,030	125,049	13,105,079	1,478,431	646,318	12,272,966	3,061,644	3,548,188	36,554	516,577	299,341
2010	19,750,248	13,512,785	263,959	13,776,744	1,514,004	751,975	13,014,715	2,927,142	3,808,391	37,959	520,307	298,774
2011	20,812,985	13,834,991	322,160	14,157,151	1,395,397	893,140	13,654,894	3,307,408	3,850,683	39,736	523,786	300,897
2012	21,627,909	14,276,402	330,328	14,606,730	1,424,267	961,920	14,144,383	3,587,997	3,895,529	41,050	526,870	305,697
2013	22,191,961	14,887,009	401,957	15,288,966	1,644,672	1,044,652	14,688,946	3,512,967	3,990,048	41,860	530,149	309,698
2014	23,524,783	15,690,392	494,765	16,185,157	1,722,457	1,050,193	15,512,893	3,876,185	4,135,705	44,075	533,746	316,924
2015	24,866,409	16,913,187	297,835	17,211,022	1,830,617	1,048,274	16,428,679	4,102,787	4,334,943	46,346	536,534	324,102
2016	25,514,554	17,484,628	105,742	17,590,370	1,902,106	1,055,710	16,743,974	4,247,641	4,522,939	47,325	539,137	330,755
2017	26,714,515	18,403,811	182,247	18,586,058	2,007,033	1,109,822	17,688,847	4,467,811	4,557,857	49,207	542,903	335,713
2018	28,608,117	28,392,792	215,325	19,854,369	2,097,371	1,090,807	18,847,805	4,830,652	4,929,660	52,591	543,969	341,734
2019	29,640,682	29,441,859	198,823	20,598,394	2,180,728	1,119,738	19,537,404	4,943,436	5,159,842	54,314	545,724	347,010

Personal Income and Employment by Area: Lansing-East Lansing, MI

(Thousands of dollars, except as noted.)

Year	Personal income, total	Earnings by place of work			Less: Contributions for government social insurance	Plus: Adjustment for residence	Equals: Net earnings by place of residence	Plus: Dividends, interest, and rent	Plus: Personal current transfer receipts	Per capita personal income (dollars)	Population (persons)	Total employment
		Nonfarm	Farm	Total								
1970	1,495,784	1,269,779	22,940	1,292,719	86,343	-34,127	1,172,249	208,840	114,695	3,946	379,047	158,585
1971	1,693,566	1,466,952	20,531	1,487,483	102,438	-55,360	1,329,685	228,673	135,208	4,428	382,476	163,734
1972	1,873,250	1,630,931	27,688	1,658,619	121,231	-66,858	1,470,530	252,296	150,424	4,848	386,369	169,358
1973	2,077,275	1,835,573	31,672	1,867,245	157,845	-79,880	1,629,520	279,352	168,403	5,286	392,980	176,554
1974	2,188,334	1,834,643	35,555	1,870,198	162,471	-57,794	1,649,933	317,646	220,755	5,509	397,253	176,321
1975	2,437,112	2,005,650	33,314	2,038,964	174,693	-71,622	1,792,649	361,131	283,332	6,114	398,619	177,812
1976	2,731,051	2,331,656	24,793	2,356,449	207,138	-104,706	2,044,605	392,211	294,235	6,818	400,590	184,014
1977	3,072,820	2,644,562	29,327	2,673,889	234,369	-130,469	2,309,051	439,136	324,633	7,599	404,394	190,769
1978	3,392,620	2,996,173	20,992	3,017,165	274,162	-157,516	2,585,487	489,279	317,854	8,276	409,950	200,143
1979	3,786,474	3,343,526	28,336	3,371,862	315,533	-181,459	2,874,870	552,577	359,027	9,154	413,652	206,975
1980	4,145,242	3,505,631	25,126	3,530,757	322,550	-189,799	3,018,408	655,281	471,553	9,867	420,109	204,514
1981	4,547,576	3,855,771	33,643	3,889,414	387,823	-227,371	3,274,220	770,494	502,862	10,811	420,637	203,789
1982	4,722,294	3,885,629	14,054	3,899,683	393,485	-224,824	3,281,374	885,996	554,924	11,382	414,906	196,333
1983	5,143,867	4,309,729	6,816	4,316,545	446,673	-274,619	3,595,253	966,893	581,721	12,466	412,647	200,932
1984	5,566,408	4,627,712	24,922	4,652,634	492,443	-280,964	3,879,227	1,079,975	607,206	13,482	412,862	204,494
1985	5,997,322	5,072,485	28,171	5,100,656	559,288	-311,486	4,229,882	1,142,980	624,460	14,430	415,612	215,819
1986	6,389,365	5,399,117	22,605	5,421,722	598,253	-314,381	4,509,088	1,216,686	663,591	15,131	422,282	222,907
1987	6,594,284	5,494,743	31,248	5,525,991	602,002	-284,229	4,639,760	1,254,436	700,088	15,456	426,652	232,298
1988	6,996,185	5,897,770	23,640	5,921,410	672,780	-301,297	4,947,333	1,322,333	726,519	16,283	429,673	237,230
1989	7,555,816	6,295,076	51,818	6,346,894	714,993	-311,669	5,320,232	1,442,452	793,132	17,550	430,527	243,788
1990	7,902,111	6,563,813	40,127	6,603,940	754,900	-316,225	5,532,815	1,506,976	862,320	18,232	433,414	248,011
1991	8,266,911	6,883,101	25,930	6,909,031	803,645	-334,601	5,770,785	1,531,918	964,208	18,918	436,979	248,866
1992	8,711,034	7,279,076	29,953	7,309,029	842,607	-348,433	6,117,989	1,588,039	1,005,006	19,837	439,128	249,680
1993	8,975,449	7,394,457	28,731	7,423,188	857,338	-323,545	6,242,305	1,642,703	1,090,441	20,342	441,234	249,094
1994	9,590,301	7,910,601	25,464	7,936,065	934,929	-346,912	6,654,224	1,828,361	1,107,716	21,665	442,671	256,015
1995	10,011,131	8,278,822	27,552	8,306,374	980,290	-357,121	6,968,963	1,888,925	1,153,243	22,578	443,395	268,156
1996	10,508,406	8,642,327	33,210	8,675,537	997,635	-367,182	7,310,720	1,990,963	1,206,723	23,506	447,043	272,297
1997	11,001,409	8,951,631	31,741	8,983,372	1,033,672	-366,324	7,583,376	2,123,013	1,295,020	24,562	447,895	271,236
1998	11,307,980	9,280,855	35,056	9,315,911	1,056,604	-355,864	7,903,443	2,095,833	1,308,704	25,276	447,384	272,104
1999	11,953,744	9,972,232	48,301	10,020,533	1,133,245	-385,813	8,501,475	2,053,855	1,398,414	26,736	447,095	276,294
2000	12,550,675	10,489,413	27,287	10,516,700	1,177,740	-402,463	8,936,497	2,151,154	1,463,024	27,969	448,735	279,789
2001	12,951,796	10,815,679	27,441	10,843,120	1,195,475	-447,875	9,199,770	2,119,364	1,632,662	28,651	452,051	278,614
2002	12,953,591	11,043,063	24,622	11,067,685	1,231,211	-537,228	9,299,246	1,962,433	1,691,912	28,443	455,420	277,265
2003	13,178,719	11,135,527	34,795	11,170,322	1,239,897	-599,333	9,331,092	2,066,301	1,781,326	28,751	458,376	277,463
2004	13,520,156	11,243,099	70,946	11,314,045	1,256,145	-493,848	9,564,052	2,093,902	1,862,202	29,282	461,724	275,123
2005	13,718,649	11,332,859	51,017	11,383,876	1,285,463	-518,189	9,580,224	2,143,891	1,994,534	29,646	462,743	271,952
2006	14,181,861	11,680,311	58,885	11,739,196	1,346,740	-585,945	9,806,511	2,226,091	2,149,259	30,607	463,349	272,826
2007	14,591,852	11,792,787	67,618	11,860,405	1,371,584	-618,466	9,870,355	2,352,888	2,368,609	31,461	463,804	274,225
2008	15,144,911	11,916,600	68,923	11,985,523	1,402,265	-664,705	9,918,553	2,488,229	2,738,129	32,665	463,638	270,061
2009	14,780,656	11,390,757	36,061	11,426,818	1,338,974	-621,117	9,466,727	2,271,480	3,042,449	31,914	463,147	257,497
2010	15,509,006	11,975,353	83,563	12,058,916	1,380,025	-687,986	9,990,905	2,245,429	3,272,672	33,411	464,189	257,686
2011	16,005,349	12,030,507	179,335	12,209,842	1,230,827	-697,900	10,281,115	2,450,482	3,273,752	34,347	465,984	260,495
2012	16,272,287	12,124,992	105,024	12,230,016	1,248,391	-680,163	10,301,462	2,709,069	3,261,756	34,870	466,660	259,225
2013	16,403,690	12,469,124	135,884	12,605,008	1,457,472	-736,119	10,411,417	2,648,380	3,343,893	35,064	467,828	261,365
2014	17,120,593	12,787,101	85,882	12,872,983	1,495,765	-727,307	10,649,911	2,953,255	3,517,427	36,459	469,585	264,690
2015	17,964,599	13,403,669	43,798	13,447,467	1,547,780	-737,749	11,161,938	3,064,712	3,737,949	38,135	471,076	267,594
2016	18,647,022	13,991,068	41,966	14,033,034	1,608,033	-782,771	11,642,230	3,151,471	3,853,321	39,314	474,310	271,439
2017	19,176,950	14,475,797	-15,634	14,460,163	1,661,999	-784,005	12,014,159	3,280,648	3,882,143	40,148	477,656	275,517
2018	22,606,483	22,575,184	31,299	15,960,028	1,883,152	-129,123	13,947,753	3,881,759	4,776,971	41,202	548,674	300,855
2019	23,389,059	23,319,959	69,100	16,482,528	1,930,578	-138,100	14,413,850	3,937,340	5,037,869	42,495	550,391	303,038

Personal Income and Employment by Area: Laredo, TX

(Thousands of dollars, except as noted.)

Year	Personal income, total	Earnings by place of work			Less: Contributions for government social insurance	Plus: Adjustment for residence	Equals: Net earnings by place of residence	Plus: Dividends, interest, and rent	Plus: Personal current transfer receipts	Per capita personal income (dollars)	Population (persons)	Total employment
		Nonfarm	Farm	Total								
1970	182,339	148,940	3,057	151,997	9,355	-6,614	136,028	26,908	19,403	2,480	73,536	27,042
1971	197,620	160,158	4,055	164,213	10,408	-7,881	145,924	29,265	22,431	2,548	77,556	26,710
1972	220,806	180,117	3,804	183,921	12,054	-9,644	162,223	33,058	25,525	2,725	81,025	27,421
1973	236,894	193,246	4,793	198,039	14,681	-11,745	171,613	34,890	30,391	2,851	83,080	28,534
1974	242,858	195,468	3,075	198,543	16,009	-13,392	169,142	31,894	41,822	3,141	77,327	28,206
1975	280,802	225,483	2,604	228,087	18,440	-16,652	192,995	34,875	52,932	3,383	83,006	29,172
1976	315,306	257,838	1,274	259,112	21,264	-18,238	219,610	37,659	58,037	3,564	88,481	30,810
1977	353,652	293,594	895	294,489	24,151	-20,362	249,976	41,780	61,896	3,864	91,535	32,558
1978	404,598	335,136	753	335,889	27,980	-21,926	285,983	50,368	68,247	4,315	93,776	34,251
1979	471,397	385,312	4,058	389,370	33,811	-23,487	332,072	60,384	78,941	4,868	96,844	36,084
1980	558,776	461,411	-189	461,222	41,358	-29,385	390,479	74,428	93,869	5,561	100,481	38,920
1981	673,332	549,253	82	549,335	53,540	-21,138	474,657	94,852	103,823	6,408	105,077	42,261
1982	727,949	571,934	3,387	575,321	56,014	-23,214	496,093	112,443	119,413	6,552	111,106	42,033
1983	722,900	527,107	-2,178	524,929	49,979	-21,025	453,925	121,967	147,008	6,263	115,419	37,681
1984	780,395	578,509	-2,660	575,849	56,077	-24,618	495,154	136,318	148,923	6,695	116,566	39,429
1985	846,527	644,650	-6,055	638,595	63,528	-28,700	546,367	146,960	153,200	7,164	118,164	42,213
1986	883,094	662,819	-5,409	657,410	64,312	-27,396	565,702	149,927	167,465	7,238	122,011	41,857
1987	928,656	700,009	-1,422	698,587	66,954	-28,954	602,679	150,937	175,040	7,457	124,528	43,947
1988	1,031,112	792,458	-1,595	790,863	78,923	-30,282	681,658	164,029	185,425	8,146	126,575	46,882
1989	1,165,152	886,758	-482	886,276	89,321	-32,409	764,546	183,427	217,179	8,967	129,943	50,230
1990	1,314,914	1,011,975	1,399	1,013,374	99,842	-35,655	877,877	187,912	249,125	9,781	134,430	53,910
1991	1,481,511	1,147,790	1,924	1,149,714	116,074	-40,331	993,309	200,509	287,693	10,576	140,082	57,729
1992	1,712,818	1,304,340	1,666	1,306,006	130,193	-44,505	1,131,308	229,520	351,990	11,650	147,026	60,857
1993	1,885,877	1,455,104	-406	1,454,698	144,729	-49,309	1,260,660	251,245	373,972	12,203	154,536	65,418
1994	2,070,719	1,614,502	-1,622	1,612,880	162,665	-54,234	1,395,981	257,766	416,972	12,853	161,107	69,329
1995	2,162,955	1,616,084	-803	1,615,281	162,391	-51,570	1,401,320	293,578	468,057	12,916	167,466	68,700
1996	2,332,538	1,730,822	-2,648	1,728,174	172,940	-54,560	1,500,674	314,325	517,539	13,594	171,583	70,431
1997	2,556,556	1,924,038	-390	1,923,648	193,219	-60,237	1,670,192	341,739	544,625	14,432	177,140	75,384
1998	2,705,256	2,049,169	2,566	2,051,735	206,035	-60,021	1,785,679	372,108	547,469	14,783	182,994	78,704
1999	2,817,586	2,151,340	8,200	2,159,540	218,126	-62,139	1,879,275	380,090	558,221	14,907	189,014	81,214
2000	3,069,067	2,347,214	9,208	2,356,422	235,889	-67,012	2,053,521	422,504	593,042	15,773	194,576	85,583
2001	3,747,447	2,965,545	14,027	2,979,572	265,924	-83,565	2,630,083	466,266	651,098	18,705	200,347	90,442
2002	3,982,598	3,159,452	14,812	3,174,264	285,143	-92,312	2,796,809	448,932	736,857	19,333	206,001	95,631
2003	4,187,376	3,267,602	23,207	3,290,809	305,192	-96,490	2,889,127	504,109	794,140	19,772	211,786	98,782
2004	4,295,023	3,369,094	20,734	3,389,828	321,688	-101,475	2,966,665	500,091	828,267	19,715	217,858	103,893
2005	4,784,054	3,714,846	10,087	3,724,933	351,724	-108,319	3,264,890	580,407	938,757	21,386	223,703	108,658
2006	5,191,225	3,990,964	12,641	4,003,605	368,244	-108,902	3,526,459	661,049	1,003,717	22,639	229,307	113,275
2007	5,433,108	4,084,367	2,482	4,086,849	388,575	-111,162	3,587,112	720,562	1,125,434	23,160	234,594	117,861
2008	6,215,392	4,568,467	-2,029	4,566,438	410,677	-108,212	4,047,549	873,589	1,294,254	25,867	240,287	119,894
2009	6,028,274	4,270,727	-4,224	4,266,503	404,822	-105,374	3,756,307	813,918	1,458,049	24,514	245,908	118,445
2010	6,516,524	4,660,857	-5,467	4,655,390	435,005	-106,069	4,114,316	783,533	1,618,675	25,928	251,327	119,888
2011	7,110,002	5,080,036	1,553	5,081,589	416,876	-104,187	4,560,526	891,787	1,657,689	27,817	255,598	126,846
2012	7,412,271	5,287,755	1,737	5,289,492	437,279	-97,012	4,755,201	1,008,997	1,648,073	28,513	259,964	128,758
2013	7,539,619	5,351,493	17,075	5,368,568	501,131	-76,856	4,790,581	1,057,003	1,692,035	28,563	263,962	132,186
2014	7,823,025	5,559,755	14,729	5,574,484	519,905	-67,928	4,986,651	1,063,683	1,772,691	29,281	267,168	135,720
2015	7,979,831	5,614,278	21,295	5,635,573	541,170	-94,844	4,999,559	1,103,018	1,877,254	29,577	269,795	139,026
2016	8,102,983	5,607,825	748	5,608,573	552,554	-122,134	4,933,885	1,192,588	1,976,510	29,747	272,401	139,772
2017	8,246,035	5,687,059	-2,361	5,684,698	570,795	-104,128	5,009,775	1,241,834	1,994,426	30,008	274,794	141,616
2018	8,663,833	8,660,067	3,766	6,067,944	599,365	-92,527	5,376,052	1,251,670	2,036,111	31,491	275,120	144,274
2019	8,981,800	8,980,298	1,502	6,340,985	619,976	-105,256	5,615,753	1,278,055	2,087,992	32,466	276,652	148,363

Personal Income and Employment by Area: Las Cruces, NM

(Thousands of dollars, except as noted.)

Year	Personal income, total	Earnings by place of work			Less: Contributions for government social insurance	Plus: Adjustment for residence	Equals: Net earnings by place of residence	Plus: Dividends, interest, and rent	Plus: Personal current transfer receipts	Per capita personal income (dollars)	Population (persons)	Total employment
		Nonfarm	Farm	Total								
1970	228,654	179,992	12,396	192,388	8,393	-7,128	176,867	33,883	17,904	3,255	70,254	27,080
1971	258,499	201,793	14,117	215,910	9,841	-9,006	197,063	39,537	21,899	3,554	72,726	28,316
1972	282,005	216,482	15,179	231,661	11,044	-7,422	213,195	44,161	24,649	3,684	76,553	29,477
1973	311,428	236,988	16,334	253,322	14,266	-6,964	232,092	50,351	28,985	4,049	76,909	30,621
1974	358,809	258,971	28,036	287,007	16,312	-6,599	264,096	59,152	35,561	4,548	78,888	31,045
1975	392,408	277,990	16,500	294,490	17,752	1,175	277,913	70,047	44,448	4,787	81,979	31,211
1976	444,278	315,981	22,899	338,880	20,374	-1,548	316,958	77,039	50,281	5,211	85,259	32,448
1977	494,883	362,914	20,042	382,956	24,369	-3,966	354,621	86,662	53,600	5,604	88,302	35,175
1978	568,285	414,060	24,856	438,916	28,803	-4,403	405,710	102,735	59,840	6,164	92,193	37,771
1979	621,528	455,273	14,132	469,405	33,333	-3,067	433,005	117,998	70,525	6,630	93,741	39,643
1980	702,558	486,953	21,677	508,630	35,824	1,380	474,186	142,026	86,346	7,242	97,012	39,628
1981	811,807	544,423	35,568	579,991	43,145	4,760	541,606	171,615	98,586	8,149	99,623	40,165
1982	904,449	596,421	32,691	629,112	48,468	8,417	589,061	204,893	110,495	8,743	103,448	41,829
1983	1,026,637	673,980	46,103	720,083	57,163	9,322	672,242	230,893	123,502	9,539	107,627	44,305
1984	1,126,676	740,969	41,180	782,149	64,306	12,808	730,651	258,915	137,110	10,017	112,474	46,879
1985	1,233,770	798,558	49,585	848,143	71,816	18,442	794,769	291,491	147,510	10,607	116,321	48,564
1986	1,332,333	846,845	67,614	914,459	78,524	26,879	862,814	311,866	157,653	11,059	120,474	49,986
1987	1,423,598	903,131	65,169	968,300	84,078	35,159	919,381	332,044	172,173	11,386	125,032	52,506
1988	1,499,691	946,044	66,638	1,012,682	94,931	44,420	962,171	349,847	187,673	11,535	130,016	55,774
1989	1,663,014	1,021,714	93,269	1,114,983	104,886	45,867	1,055,964	394,996	212,054	12,508	132,957	57,095
1990	1,784,665	1,098,787	103,630	1,202,417	118,717	54,573	1,138,273	404,520	241,872	13,066	136,593	57,771
1991	1,911,004	1,189,970	87,239	1,277,209	130,352	66,502	1,213,359	422,096	275,549	13,531	141,228	59,961
1992	2,099,588	1,301,388	102,692	1,404,080	141,765	81,056	1,343,371	443,799	312,418	14,283	146,995	60,744
1993	2,239,522	1,384,856	86,376	1,471,232	151,673	95,860	1,415,419	476,111	347,992	14,633	153,049	61,738
1994	2,330,012	1,415,925	75,878	1,491,803	159,767	110,897	1,442,933	505,306	381,773	14,791	157,530	62,238
1995	2,539,316	1,511,295	100,397	1,611,692	170,318	120,042	1,561,416	546,851	431,049	15,771	161,014	65,557
1996	2,654,863	1,568,447	76,986	1,645,433	177,394	129,003	1,597,042	588,315	469,506	16,030	165,618	67,010
1997	2,794,236	1,632,149	104,121	1,736,270	185,515	144,038	1,694,793	616,330	483,113	16,526	169,081	68,290
1998	2,980,035	1,760,777	112,492	1,873,269	201,388	156,247	1,828,128	635,009	516,898	17,320	172,057	69,944
1999	3,067,299	1,829,059	112,265	1,941,324	213,429	174,051	1,901,946	615,268	550,085	17,639	173,889	72,267
2000	3,243,254	1,975,603	80,172	2,055,775	223,570	188,888	2,021,093	629,658	592,503	18,523	175,098	74,836
2001	3,642,499	2,221,309	112,816	2,334,125	243,433	169,986	2,260,678	701,734	680,087	20,638	176,496	78,825
2002	3,851,503	2,436,766	94,776	2,531,542	264,739	154,891	2,421,694	668,720	761,089	21,581	178,464	80,989
2003	4,095,813	2,645,829	116,042	2,761,871	286,991	141,966	2,616,846	662,373	816,594	22,499	182,045	83,352
2004	4,349,239	2,829,251	152,523	2,981,774	306,367	100,674	2,776,081	699,594	873,564	23,517	184,939	86,099
2005	4,707,074	3,097,431	172,194	3,269,625	336,910	38,868	2,971,583	785,656	949,835	24,879	189,199	89,628
2006	4,991,655	3,313,584	123,364	3,436,948	366,469	45,532	3,116,011	835,765	1,039,879	25,770	193,701	91,995
2007	5,350,103	3,442,702	177,466	3,620,168	389,990	37,157	3,267,335	933,619	1,149,149	27,041	197,853	94,725
2008	5,597,617	3,572,065	108,721	3,680,786	413,616	26,239	3,293,409	976,891	1,327,317	27,869	200,855	95,890
2009	5,948,539	3,728,021	127,406	3,855,427	429,207	81,625	3,507,845	941,606	1,499,088	28,961	205,401	94,906
2010	6,344,861	3,912,498	222,393	4,134,891	443,131	87,010	3,778,770	938,675	1,627,416	30,197	210,114	95,627
2011	6,553,180	3,953,595	196,818	4,150,413	403,185	111,841	3,859,069	1,041,328	1,652,783	30,786	212,860	97,248
2012	6,713,668	3,959,092	129,593	4,088,685	407,245	171,835	3,853,275	1,219,903	1,640,490	31,365	214,050	97,093
2013	6,495,350	3,956,438	134,822	4,091,260	468,585	143,467	3,766,142	1,084,399	1,644,809	30,434	213,425	98,951
2014	6,787,201	4,042,013	114,824	4,156,837	483,161	134,706	3,808,382	1,165,894	1,812,925	31,835	213,200	99,307
2015	7,168,283	4,181,051	149,359	4,330,410	516,602	157,121	3,970,929	1,227,714	1,969,640	33,628	213,165	99,872
2016	7,389,930	4,309,687	181,406	4,491,093	528,559	158,579	4,121,113	1,261,890	2,006,927	34,553	213,874	100,598
2017	7,623,197	4,434,690	185,289	4,619,979	534,588	225,678	4,311,069	1,306,388	2,005,740	35,362	215,579	99,901
2018	7,863,764	7,743,044	120,720	4,765,469	560,323	188,187	4,393,333	1,304,004	2,166,427	36,192	217,278	102,367
2019	8,238,087	8,099,111	138,976	4,950,897	583,810	265,916	4,633,003	1,319,681	2,285,403	37,756	218,195	103,693

Personal Income and Employment by Area: Las Vegas-Henderson-Paradise, NV

(Thousands of dollars, except as noted.)

Year	Personal income, total	Earnings by place of work			Less: Contributions for government social insurance	Plus: Adjustment for residence	Equals: Net earnings by place of residence	Plus: Dividends, interest, and rent	Plus: Personal current transfer receipts	Per capita personal income (dollars)	Population (persons)	Total employment
		Nonfarm	Farm	Total								
1970	1,429,017	1,180,655	1,732	1,182,387	82,314	41,419	1,141,492	211,557	75,968	5,176	276,079	134,095
1971	1,582,762	1,301,670	1,334	1,303,004	93,505	37,347	1,246,846	238,405	97,511	5,402	293,008	138,801
1972	1,747,451	1,447,250	1,318	1,448,568	109,842	26,181	1,364,907	265,291	117,253	5,684	307,426	145,742
1973	1,984,224	1,677,474	1,418	1,678,892	146,925	12,703	1,544,670	302,171	137,383	6,212	319,399	160,282
1974	2,221,573	1,845,898	2,006	1,847,904	164,868	13,850	1,696,886	350,892	173,795	6,594	336,930	168,726
1975	2,515,704	2,038,508	2,074	2,040,582	180,969	15,006	1,874,619	398,951	242,134	7,160	351,339	174,218
1976	2,863,774	2,335,534	2,783	2,338,317	213,203	9,012	2,134,126	454,439	275,209	7,750	369,529	186,546
1977	3,296,192	2,723,422	2,580	2,726,002	251,966	931	2,474,967	517,855	303,370	8,453	389,965	204,806
1978	3,959,777	3,293,521	2,496	3,296,017	314,392	-2,960	2,978,665	642,527	338,585	9,590	412,913	228,609
1979	4,631,857	3,856,001	1,518	3,857,519	388,226	-10,567	3,458,726	765,266	407,865	10,495	441,358	251,535
1980	5,359,706	4,367,073	3,213	4,370,286	443,251	-3,508	3,923,527	933,019	503,160	11,423	469,185	265,076
1981	6,162,457	4,920,769	1,887	4,922,656	530,878	19,508	4,411,286	1,128,864	622,307	12,506	492,747	272,538
1982	6,629,060	5,103,473	2,477	5,105,950	541,265	40,724	4,605,409	1,326,890	696,761	12,904	513,708	269,949
1983	7,092,525	5,443,056	926	5,443,982	597,931	43,564	4,889,615	1,446,134	756,776	13,377	530,195	274,043
1984	7,685,375	5,869,268	2,951	5,872,219	670,344	52,388	5,254,263	1,613,093	818,019	14,104	544,893	286,101
1985	8,375,859	6,356,946	2,478	6,359,424	739,665	69,681	5,689,440	1,779,991	906,428	14,928	561,081	300,096
1986	9,142,842	6,937,323	1,535	6,938,858	825,195	64,130	6,177,793	1,941,284	1,023,765	15,742	580,775	316,982
1987	10,067,109	7,766,744	2,128	7,768,872	930,044	46,213	6,885,041	2,078,122	1,103,946	16,456	611,763	345,999
1988	11,504,022	8,971,169	2,161	8,973,330	1,086,946	42,522	7,928,906	2,343,693	1,231,423	17,769	647,410	375,496
1989	13,196,124	10,218,492	2,945	10,221,437	1,263,165	13,806	8,972,078	2,796,324	1,427,722	19,084	691,467	412,843
1990	15,093,525	11,841,257	3,280	11,844,537	1,541,960	-15,835	10,286,742	3,147,173	1,659,610	19,960	756,170	452,016
1991	16,727,113	12,877,528	3,501	12,881,029	1,653,818	-2,894	11,224,317	3,433,258	2,069,538	20,497	816,085	465,549
1992	18,671,191	14,327,433	4,769	14,332,202	1,812,173	-11,810	12,508,219	3,797,102	2,365,870	21,778	857,357	472,519
1993	20,550,154	15,885,082	5,733	15,890,815	2,021,746	-83,001	13,786,068	4,235,704	2,528,382	22,774	902,338	504,060
1994	23,043,214	17,922,081	5,450	17,927,531	2,295,749	-143,308	15,488,474	4,857,758	2,696,982	23,692	972,624	567,840
1995	25,587,458	19,882,711	5,574	19,888,285	2,551,332	-189,245	17,147,708	5,518,262	2,921,488	24,702	1,035,847	606,312
1996	28,648,985	22,357,483	6,320	22,363,803	2,809,592	-279,104	19,275,107	6,204,871	3,169,007	26,047	1,099,894	662,190
1997	31,677,828	24,752,452	6,527	24,758,979	3,033,850	-302,979	21,422,150	6,853,726	3,401,952	26,909	1,177,230	713,369
1998	36,077,820	28,188,695	6,871	28,195,566	3,280,705	-317,567	24,597,294	7,833,040	3,647,486	28,833	1,251,258	749,408
1999	39,344,966	31,281,166	6,434	31,287,600	3,531,451	-350,779	27,405,370	8,112,794	3,826,802	29,779	1,321,254	803,146
2000	43,337,526	34,131,998	5,112	34,137,110	3,489,358	-371,878	30,275,874	8,940,620	4,121,032	31,091	1,393,909	853,137
2001	46,367,048	36,905,547	5,103	36,910,650	3,741,988	-414,649	32,754,013	8,925,637	4,687,398	31,747	1,460,500	882,073
2002	48,283,011	38,223,367	3,954	38,227,321	3,908,978	-423,369	33,894,974	9,080,787	5,307,250	31,703	1,522,962	896,528
2003	51,578,290	40,220,622	3,437	40,224,059	3,964,985	-461,398	35,797,676	10,065,933	5,714,681	32,559	1,584,166	941,654
2004	57,787,769	45,189,560	3,464	45,193,024	4,393,181	-555,331	40,244,512	11,392,694	6,150,563	34,754	1,662,773	1,011,906
2005	65,883,025	50,641,606	3,126	50,644,732	4,878,488	-616,635	45,149,609	14,086,596	6,646,820	38,093	1,729,522	1,087,078
2006	71,247,941	54,943,632	3,887	54,947,519	5,710,201	-578,268	48,659,050	15,408,726	7,180,165	39,499	1,803,774	1,145,464
2007	74,577,710	56,921,694	2,624	56,924,318	6,034,265	-547,282	50,342,771	16,367,140	7,867,799	39,928	1,867,817	1,174,103
2008	73,285,040	54,067,867	4,286	54,072,153	5,658,995	-484,852	47,928,306	15,990,619	9,366,115	38,322	1,912,349	1,160,263
2009	68,076,424	49,279,252	4,331	49,283,583	5,419,677	-449,997	43,413,909	13,941,996	10,720,519	35,102	1,939,407	1,081,892
2010	70,001,222	50,038,582	3,734	50,042,316	5,289,625	-377,701	44,374,990	13,760,269	11,865,963	35,845	1,952,906	1,056,986
2011	72,858,166	51,746,037	4,284	51,750,321	5,001,060	-278,599	46,470,662	14,395,752	11,991,752	37,049	1,966,521	1,076,766
2012	77,839,744	53,527,489	1,876	53,529,365	5,288,759	-316,612	47,923,994	17,827,283	12,088,467	38,992	1,996,290	1,092,996
2013	77,846,855	55,285,799	2,212	55,288,011	5,810,936	-327,318	49,149,757	16,362,492	12,334,606	38,423	2,026,056	1,125,631
2014	83,548,431	57,983,722	2,497	57,986,219	6,448,919	-359,424	51,177,876	19,010,628	13,359,927	40,459	2,064,991	1,169,854
2015	90,036,449	61,343,442	2,796	61,346,238	6,904,165	-356,322	54,085,751	21,270,377	14,680,321	42,665	2,110,330	1,216,212
2016	92,750,753	62,899,304	1,650	62,900,954	7,169,726	-415,036	55,316,192	21,944,994	15,489,567	43,005	2,156,724	1,263,416
2017	97,457,342	65,994,078	1,437	65,995,515	7,340,383	-378,359	58,276,773	22,989,431	16,191,138	44,217	2,204,079	1,297,670
2018	106,317,025	106,317,210	-185	71,542,830	7,904,147	-515,120	63,123,563	25,635,803	17,557,659	47,759	2,226,115	1,354,799
2019	110,628,465	110,627,157	1,308	75,317,611	8,691,256	-530,071	66,096,284	25,859,765	18,672,416	48,806	2,266,715	1,397,879

Personal Income and Employment by Area: Lawrence, KS

(Thousands of dollars, except as noted.)

Year	Personal income, total	Earnings by place of work			Less: Contributions for government social insurance	Plus: Adjustment for residence	Equals: Net earnings by place of residence	Plus: Dividends, interest, and rent	Plus: Personal current transfer receipts	Per capita personal income (dollars)	Population (persons)	Total employment
		Nonfarm	Farm	Total								
1970	189,361	142,025	2,913	144,938	10,193	8,576	143,321	32,485	13,555	3,252	58,233	23,010
1971	213,246	161,457	4,306	165,763	12,103	7,864	161,524	36,144	15,578	3,577	59,621	24,197
1972	229,915	168,765	5,104	173,869	13,315	11,364	171,918	39,849	18,148	3,784	60,767	24,524
1973	254,888	186,789	6,280	193,069	17,182	12,738	188,625	44,338	21,925	4,121	61,848	25,994
1974	284,949	214,048	2,360	216,408	20,658	11,429	207,179	51,485	26,285	4,534	62,844	27,633
1975	323,561	237,196	4,435	241,631	22,712	12,337	231,256	60,123	32,182	5,341	60,580	27,762
1976	364,929	274,812	3,491	278,303	26,556	12,679	264,426	64,704	35,799	5,934	61,498	29,598
1977	418,143	316,234	7,089	323,323	30,394	13,500	306,429	71,205	40,509	6,644	62,932	31,544
1978	465,468	355,024	4,192	359,216	35,431	16,802	340,587	80,154	44,727	7,086	65,685	33,135
1979	518,678	396,388	4,206	400,594	41,165	19,444	378,873	92,052	47,753	7,775	66,710	34,211
1980	571,918	419,356	-20	419,336	43,725	23,859	399,470	114,536	57,912	8,405	68,045	34,501
1981	643,120	451,328	2,407	453,735	50,291	30,125	433,569	142,623	66,928	9,244	69,569	33,622
1982	674,394	460,947	353	461,300	51,836	35,502	444,966	160,011	69,417	9,641	69,948	33,433
1983	724,190	492,959	-3,135	489,824	54,363	40,770	476,231	172,916	75,043	10,353	69,947	33,914
1984	799,122	537,198	1,966	539,164	59,561	48,678	528,281	194,114	76,727	11,316	70,618	35,192
1985	864,981	569,561	7,741	577,302	63,298	56,939	570,943	211,225	82,813	11,988	72,151	36,131
1986	934,057	626,540	5,794	632,334	69,329	62,871	625,876	225,279	82,902	12,531	74,538	37,149
1987	983,375	657,993	8,028	666,021	72,255	69,053	662,819	231,915	88,641	12,914	76,148	39,566
1988	1,068,926	721,227	10,187	731,414	83,155	76,146	724,405	247,165	97,356	13,569	78,779	42,190
1989	1,181,331	794,481	8,100	802,581	90,618	82,085	794,048	278,529	108,754	14,750	80,092	43,552
1990	1,242,686	849,239	5,626	854,865	102,000	88,542	841,407	278,856	122,423	15,113	82,229	44,906
1991	1,319,533	900,019	4,465	904,484	109,468	98,469	893,485	288,268	137,780	15,768	83,683	46,550
1992	1,437,674	974,359	11,483	985,842	117,094	110,528	979,276	303,259	155,139	16,839	85,379	47,328
1993	1,528,457	1,038,426	2,834	1,041,260	124,409	124,739	1,041,590	319,477	167,390	17,383	87,926	48,723
1994	1,648,908	1,109,372	5,717	1,115,089	135,054	137,113	1,117,148	359,051	172,709	18,386	89,683	49,946
1995	1,750,526	1,173,731	1,989	1,175,720	141,405	151,082	1,185,397	381,558	183,571	19,151	91,408	53,006
1996	1,860,095	1,232,841	9,201	1,242,042	146,670	168,413	1,263,785	405,773	190,537	19,919	93,381	54,732
1997	2,036,292	1,355,899	8,054	1,363,953	161,080	182,491	1,385,364	448,292	202,636	21,277	95,706	57,637
1998	2,214,229	1,478,444	504	1,478,948	173,287	206,192	1,511,853	487,522	214,854	22,695	97,566	59,943
1999	2,309,930	1,556,298	-2,401	1,553,897	182,295	234,450	1,606,052	478,133	225,745	23,218	99,490	62,118
2000	2,497,551	1,671,754	-5,718	1,666,036	196,728	260,619	1,729,927	519,019	248,605	24,914	100,247	63,729
2001	2,691,165	1,861,995	-3,140	1,858,855	214,525	257,261	1,901,591	515,487	274,087	26,574	101,269	67,353
2002	2,765,826	1,911,803	-7,079	1,904,724	219,043	263,175	1,948,856	524,375	292,595	26,970	102,552	65,803
2003	2,838,131	1,941,453	-1,843	1,939,610	224,232	263,653	1,979,031	551,802	307,298	27,403	103,570	66,165
2004	2,898,111	2,021,920	7,936	2,029,856	234,594	249,150	2,044,412	533,805	319,894	27,647	104,826	67,337
2005	3,039,109	2,088,059	1,900	2,089,959	243,740	274,094	2,120,313	581,227	337,569	28,757	105,681	67,579
2006	3,274,573	2,176,057	-2,956	2,173,101	253,544	296,941	2,216,498	699,458	358,617	30,550	107,187	68,153
2007	3,426,751	2,223,437	1,914	2,225,351	256,662	336,988	2,305,677	726,117	394,957	31,761	107,892	69,124
2008	3,644,069	2,363,317	4,128	2,367,445	266,391	348,189	2,449,243	722,555	472,271	33,429	109,010	67,975
2009	3,698,644	2,369,330	13,295	2,382,625	270,322	345,737	2,458,040	728,302	512,302	33,612	110,039	67,419
2010	3,748,735	2,386,088	6,115	2,392,203	273,069	391,712	2,510,846	674,997	562,892	33,704	111,224	66,702
2011	3,930,344	2,428,594	14,678	2,443,272	242,698	396,412	2,596,986	749,938	583,420	34,973	112,381	66,327
2012	4,086,588	2,467,583	9,710	2,477,293	246,711	474,050	2,704,632	804,335	577,621	36,096	113,215	66,197
2013	4,199,002	2,581,031	29,070	2,610,101	289,447	469,336	2,789,990	812,430	596,582	36,655	114,554	67,805
2014	4,403,290	2,707,699	17,866	2,725,565	303,577	480,863	2,902,851	877,144	623,295	37,854	116,323	69,517
2015	4,675,838	2,859,702	10,787	2,870,489	319,443	523,743	3,074,789	944,258	656,791	39,671	117,866	70,420
2016	4,810,329	2,966,003	15,118	2,981,121	325,938	468,247	3,123,430	1,003,254	683,645	40,256	119,492	71,511
2017	4,996,007	3,083,190	17,655	3,100,845	338,482	491,359	3,253,722	1,042,053	700,232	41,360	120,793	72,384
2018	5,321,380	5,308,691	12,689	3,202,779	351,719	588,269	3,439,329	1,145,888	736,163	43,939	121,109	74,410
2019	5,521,639	5,499,352	22,287	3,327,268	367,371	622,032	3,581,929	1,157,339	782,371	45,163	122,259	75,267

Personal Income and Employment by Area: Lawton, OK

(Thousands of dollars, except as noted.)

Year	Personal income, total	Earnings by place of work			Less: Contributions for government social insurance	Plus: Adjustment for residence	Equals: Net earnings by place of residence	Plus: Dividends, interest, and rent	Plus: Personal current transfer receipts	Per capita personal income (dollars)	Population (persons)	Total employment
		Nonfarm	Farm	Total								
1970	474,227	374,178	6,559	380,737	21,692	-8,085	350,960	98,035	25,232	4,130	114,835	57,235
1971	477,877	376,915	5,259	382,174	23,342	-8,435	350,397	98,092	29,388	4,166	114,717	53,368
1972	488,467	382,516	7,874	390,390	23,936	-8,844	357,610	98,147	32,710	4,561	107,106	50,475
1973	547,261	417,401	18,630	436,031	28,238	-9,675	398,118	111,374	37,769	5,005	109,334	51,921
1974	601,813	461,535	11,260	472,795	32,850	-10,389	429,556	126,662	45,595	5,431	110,808	53,070
1975	644,183	489,898	9,177	499,075	37,042	-10,527	451,506	136,542	56,135	5,721	112,591	53,108
1976	746,867	571,485	10,070	581,555	44,720	-10,773	526,062	158,260	62,545	6,164	121,157	56,963
1977	793,076	611,743	1,099	612,842	47,460	-11,188	554,194	172,660	66,222	6,476	122,462	57,631
1978	877,968	678,582	1,598	680,180	53,308	-15,422	611,450	196,142	70,376	7,057	124,413	58,416
1979	974,090	729,988	18,862	748,850	59,447	-11,862	677,541	214,574	81,975	7,971	122,200	58,783
1980	1,063,769	793,776	5,723	799,499	64,973	-8,850	725,676	242,471	95,622	8,847	120,234	59,943
1981	1,226,622	905,657	13,931	919,588	77,698	-6,092	835,798	282,984	107,840	10,073	121,777	60,159
1982	1,388,372	1,035,816	9,655	1,045,471	87,837	-10,703	946,931	321,085	120,356	10,982	126,418	63,838
1983	1,461,836	1,075,200	8,504	1,083,704	93,866	-10,191	979,647	351,286	130,903	11,325	129,084	63,134
1984	1,554,491	1,149,242	4,486	1,153,728	102,427	-11,491	1,039,810	376,771	137,910	12,140	128,046	64,339
1985	1,658,380	1,224,058	12,685	1,236,743	111,421	-13,857	1,111,465	399,995	146,920	13,031	127,261	65,425
1986	1,722,616	1,272,786	24,740	1,297,526	118,538	-16,188	1,162,800	406,251	153,565	13,683	125,897	64,430
1987	1,777,007	1,331,655	12,310	1,343,965	125,431	-19,141	1,199,393	414,582	163,032	14,182	125,301	65,717
1988	1,794,611	1,334,787	22,196	1,356,983	134,684	-16,025	1,206,274	411,833	176,504	14,556	123,289	64,438
1989	1,829,424	1,343,760	17,241	1,361,001	138,495	-14,968	1,207,538	430,977	190,909	15,368	119,044	63,133
1990	1,900,927	1,386,326	27,272	1,413,598	147,994	-14,148	1,251,456	438,808	210,663	16,094	118,112	62,529
1991	1,952,710	1,436,876	13,199	1,450,075	157,106	-15,065	1,277,904	442,271	232,535	16,563	117,896	60,909
1992	2,205,964	1,641,892	20,012	1,661,904	181,848	-22,261	1,457,795	486,173	261,996	17,313	127,413	65,370
1993	2,197,770	1,611,894	19,351	1,631,245	182,537	-18,488	1,430,220	495,129	272,421	17,514	125,485	64,545
1994	2,225,033	1,623,666	11,813	1,635,479	183,414	-16,913	1,435,152	499,667	290,214	17,754	125,323	63,353
1995	2,300,015	1,646,448	2,162	1,648,610	185,112	-16,592	1,446,906	536,210	316,899	18,637	123,412	64,135
1996	2,360,609	1,664,511	9,673	1,674,184	185,858	-13,949	1,474,377	553,557	332,675	19,136	123,357	64,864
1997	2,392,990	1,702,736	12,275	1,715,011	189,191	-10,752	1,515,068	537,519	340,403	19,535	122,497	64,740
1998	2,502,805	1,766,176	11,404	1,777,580	195,291	-11,733	1,570,556	585,262	346,987	20,502	122,076	64,171
1999	2,568,937	1,794,498	17,240	1,811,738	199,703	-11,159	1,600,876	595,315	372,746	20,964	122,542	64,417
2000	2,689,059	1,865,730	19,278	1,885,008	206,075	-8,451	1,670,482	624,118	394,459	22,097	121,695	64,749
2001	2,889,179	2,039,629	10,597	2,050,226	221,370	-17,673	1,811,183	636,476	441,520	24,086	119,955	64,488
2002	3,014,098	2,156,654	18,638	2,175,292	234,076	-28,518	1,912,698	629,181	472,219	25,141	119,889	64,635
2003	3,191,062	2,327,355	19,839	2,347,194	250,550	-43,943	2,052,701	621,820	516,541	27,162	117,484	64,923
2004	3,293,476	2,438,817	31,791	2,470,608	267,170	-57,120	2,146,318	608,369	538,789	26,920	122,341	66,046
2005	3,444,918	2,548,270	35,864	2,584,134	274,270	-67,939	2,241,925	615,875	587,118	28,359	121,475	64,462
2006	3,769,223	2,835,082	14,084	2,849,166	302,852	-87,941	2,458,373	675,797	635,053	30,649	122,980	67,139
2007	3,943,278	2,927,956	3,719	2,931,675	315,554	-99,072	2,517,049	737,911	688,318	31,342	125,814	68,756
2008	4,231,985	3,103,150	21,192	3,124,342	333,294	-114,718	2,676,330	782,650	773,005	34,083	124,166	69,391
2009	4,339,306	3,228,907	-12,194	3,216,713	355,353	-120,833	2,740,527	767,551	831,228	34,403	126,131	69,558
2010	4,685,181	3,520,607	-5,497	3,515,110	384,202	-130,445	3,000,463	786,662	898,056	35,607	131,579	71,532
2011	4,836,047	3,509,519	10,574	3,520,093	352,280	-113,376	3,054,437	853,743	927,867	36,596	132,146	69,613
2012	4,835,607	3,435,341	26,015	3,461,356	346,864	-92,973	3,021,519	859,849	954,239	36,511	132,442	68,302
2013	4,864,452	3,454,933	25,883	3,480,816	389,770	-84,669	3,006,377	879,937	978,138	37,241	130,620	68,862
2014	4,963,651	3,459,888	59,802	3,519,690	389,063	-80,048	3,050,579	896,695	1,016,377	38,015	130,572	68,606
2015	5,082,288	3,555,533	33,696	3,589,229	397,291	-87,488	3,104,450	917,558	1,060,280	39,252	129,480	68,968
2016	4,972,848	3,455,966	827	3,456,793	389,564	-97,824	2,969,405	906,607	1,096,836	39,061	127,311	68,490
2017	5,089,702	3,521,201	-947	3,520,254	402,739	-94,574	3,022,941	937,263	1,129,498	39,967	127,349	68,511
2018	5,160,729	5,154,827	5,902	3,553,031	405,419	-95,307	3,052,305	925,591	1,182,833	40,845	126,348	68,473
2019	5,396,858	5,383,346	13,512	3,700,835	420,092	-97,035	3,183,708	949,947	1,263,203	42,692	126,415	69,339

Personal Income and Employment by Area: Lebanon, PA

(Thousands of dollars, except as noted.)

Year	Personal income, total	Earnings by place of work			Less: Contributions for government social insurance	Plus: Adjustment for residence	Equals: Net earnings by place of residence	Plus: Dividends, interest, and rent	Plus: Personal current transfer receipts	Per capita personal income (dollars)	Population (persons)	Total employment
		Nonfarm	Farm	Total								
1970	391,453	298,815	11,617	310,432	20,759	19,833	309,506	47,907	34,040	3,907	100,193	44,662
1971	404,211	306,448	9,638	316,086	21,967	18,236	312,355	52,181	39,675	3,928	102,907	43,469
1972	447,121	342,576	9,890	352,466	25,787	19,329	346,008	56,886	44,227	4,324	103,414	44,721
1973	496,917	379,209	12,642	391,851	33,035	23,374	382,190	65,090	49,637	4,729	105,069	45,978
1974	552,795	420,008	10,251	430,259	38,229	26,580	418,610	74,675	59,510	5,249	105,311	46,696
1975	608,263	453,233	8,655	461,888	39,642	20,145	442,391	83,740	82,132	4,894	124,289	46,734
1976	663,856	494,491	9,602	504,093	43,853	26,255	486,495	90,724	86,637	6,135	108,206	46,955
1977	736,809	549,915	8,027	557,942	48,559	33,321	542,704	102,161	91,944	6,819	108,055	47,783
1978	815,150	603,635	10,665	614,300	54,533	42,959	602,726	115,077	97,347	7,457	109,308	48,272
1979	917,852	671,491	14,272	685,763	62,616	56,864	680,011	129,274	108,567	8,337	110,096	49,036
1980	1,003,263	704,701	8,178	712,879	66,213	70,289	716,955	161,714	124,594	9,218	108,839	48,871
1981	1,108,773	739,817	12,109	751,926	74,753	90,543	767,716	197,012	144,045	10,112	109,645	48,150
1982	1,173,241	727,547	10,790	738,337	74,059	110,562	774,840	229,964	168,437	10,610	110,574	46,129
1983	1,240,662	757,908	10,838	768,746	79,392	123,749	813,103	245,855	181,704	11,258	110,199	45,813
1984	1,345,183	802,345	24,989	827,334	88,124	152,585	891,795	272,683	180,705	12,201	110,250	46,912
1985	1,425,678	840,161	25,334	865,495	93,751	167,294	939,038	293,958	192,682	12,916	110,382	47,415
1986	1,515,240	874,113	32,066	906,179	97,923	191,796	1,000,052	308,833	206,355	13,680	110,764	47,688
1987	1,612,240	950,214	28,399	978,613	106,467	215,662	1,087,808	315,363	209,069	14,441	111,646	50,000
1988	1,749,890	1,055,604	14,420	1,070,024	120,929	241,298	1,190,393	333,402	226,095	15,535	112,643	52,423
1989	1,925,481	1,129,960	23,680	1,153,640	127,606	275,678	1,301,712	380,312	243,457	17,038	113,009	52,792
1990	2,027,721	1,170,877	31,606	1,202,483	133,393	289,932	1,359,022	397,729	270,970	17,770	114,109	52,552
1991	2,129,806	1,195,964	26,362	1,222,326	138,596	323,655	1,407,385	406,958	315,463	18,480	115,248	52,326
1992	2,247,926	1,277,068	28,901	1,305,969	147,783	351,273	1,509,459	407,349	331,118	19,368	116,066	52,293
1993	2,342,535	1,314,541	24,837	1,339,378	155,620	387,085	1,570,843	418,798	352,894	20,062	116,764	51,088
1994	2,453,208	1,400,028	23,340	1,423,368	166,279	409,686	1,666,775	427,021	359,412	20,893	117,415	51,472
1995	2,530,553	1,381,406	16,045	1,397,451	166,169	469,945	1,701,227	448,651	380,675	21,480	117,809	52,277
1996	2,664,623	1,398,455	28,451	1,426,906	164,900	525,979	1,787,985	468,698	407,940	22,507	118,391	52,193
1997	2,801,704	1,473,706	26,696	1,500,402	172,786	556,098	1,883,714	497,463	420,527	23,593	118,753	53,347
1998	2,982,799	1,544,604	29,248	1,573,852	179,237	609,017	2,003,632	542,484	436,683	24,942	119,590	51,923
1999	3,091,745	1,641,066	20,649	1,661,715	187,998	613,924	2,087,641	536,920	467,184	25,777	119,944	52,886
2000	3,247,184	1,737,945	38,391	1,776,336	198,705	605,962	2,183,593	568,788	494,803	26,990	120,309	54,561
2001	3,468,720	1,928,060	40,987	1,969,047	215,421	623,154	2,376,780	557,204	534,736	28,678	120,954	58,544
2002	3,550,175	1,992,970	21,047	2,014,017	221,528	659,939	2,452,418	523,037	574,720	29,172	121,698	58,829
2003	3,675,964	2,083,577	47,465	2,131,042	230,400	665,950	2,566,592	509,971	599,401	29,849	123,154	59,506
2004	3,984,663	2,224,449	73,651	2,298,100	245,325	724,106	2,776,881	568,737	639,045	31,968	124,644	60,913
2005	4,172,366	2,322,361	67,542	2,389,903	259,682	776,053	2,906,274	563,802	702,290	33,062	126,197	62,302
2006	4,377,775	2,470,225	44,405	2,514,630	280,114	784,010	3,018,526	618,222	741,027	34,121	128,302	64,150
2007	4,597,950	2,535,641	64,522	2,600,163	287,742	793,001	3,105,422	706,202	786,326	35,319	130,182	65,328
2008	4,792,814	2,557,543	66,455	2,623,998	294,976	806,237	3,135,259	756,079	901,476	36,427	131,574	64,936
2009	4,738,709	2,520,242	51,965	2,572,207	295,988	735,100	3,011,319	714,296	1,013,094	35,640	132,959	64,003
2010	4,931,472	2,674,360	59,934	2,734,294	311,430	742,869	3,165,733	693,011	1,072,728	36,904	133,628	64,608
2011	5,169,183	2,802,588	87,228	2,889,816	294,583	728,149	3,323,382	757,798	1,088,003	38,450	134,438	66,020
2012	5,285,870	2,902,837	93,330	2,996,167	302,554	680,831	3,374,444	814,435	1,096,991	39,019	135,468	67,515
2013	5,391,831	2,954,056	127,279	3,081,335	341,424	717,407	3,457,318	802,524	1,131,989	39,728	135,720	67,425
2014	5,615,637	2,989,236	148,358	3,137,594	346,858	773,949	3,564,685	874,944	1,176,008	41,137	136,510	67,212
2015	5,907,184	3,109,859	99,047	3,208,906	357,552	855,353	3,706,707	950,655	1,249,822	42,949	137,540	66,996
2016	6,097,478	3,200,384	42,234	3,242,618	371,622	901,406	3,772,402	1,018,820	1,306,256	44,007	138,557	67,379
2017	6,379,068	3,360,136	68,318	3,428,454	392,362	951,992	3,988,084	1,071,395	1,319,589	45,645	139,754	67,873
2018	6,721,612	6,679,518	42,094	3,573,981	408,090	989,429	4,155,320	1,124,523	1,441,769	47,557	141,339	68,469
2019	6,937,119	6,905,341	31,778	3,758,811	432,235	963,757	4,290,333	1,149,972	1,496,814	48,924	141,793	69,994

Personal Income and Employment by Area: Lewiston, ID-WA

(Thousands of dollars, except as noted.)

Year	Personal income, total	Earnings by place of work			Less: Contributions for government social insurance	Plus: Adjustment for residence	Equals: Net earnings by place of residence	Plus: Dividends, interest, and rent	Plus: Personal current transfer receipts	Per capita personal income (dollars)	Population (persons)	Total employment
		Nonfarm	Farm	Total								
1970	166,225	115,690	8,313	124,003	9,095	4,896	119,804	28,181	18,240	3,760	44,211	17,980
1971	181,691	127,026	8,214	135,240	10,329	4,341	129,252	31,868	20,571	4,056	44,792	18,651
1972	203,450	142,757	11,849	154,606	12,020	3,283	145,869	34,459	23,122	4,384	46,404	18,905
1973	228,028	161,996	15,283	177,279	15,830	877	162,326	39,323	26,379	4,909	46,454	20,121
1974	264,950	182,986	25,104	208,090	18,365	-1,615	188,110	45,392	31,448	5,679	46,658	20,911
1975	290,248	206,659	13,662	220,321	20,154	-1,031	199,136	52,835	38,277	6,209	46,744	21,367
1976	317,152	232,783	12,210	244,993	23,000	-1,725	220,268	55,180	41,704	6,660	47,617	22,040
1977	345,508	259,594	10,087	269,681	25,749	-4,144	239,788	61,530	44,190	7,213	47,898	22,824
1978	387,945	295,864	10,330	306,194	29,545	-5,900	270,749	68,503	48,693	7,992	48,543	23,861
1979	428,688	333,801	8,658	342,459	35,020	-11,042	296,397	76,522	55,769	8,744	49,026	24,620
1980	480,292	358,439	15,518	373,957	37,639	-13,004	323,314	91,021	65,957	9,590	50,082	24,405
1981	520,159	372,463	18,414	390,877	42,011	-12,380	336,486	109,169	74,504	10,368	50,169	23,670
1982	546,709	368,653	19,741	388,394	42,465	-10,409	335,520	127,544	83,645	10,966	49,856	22,989
1983	601,076	399,246	27,815	427,061	46,124	-9,347	371,590	141,109	88,377	12,101	49,673	23,660
1984	626,335	419,818	16,212	436,030	50,195	-8,228	377,607	155,853	92,875	12,461	50,264	23,775
1985	639,323	423,522	4,636	428,158	51,026	-6,531	370,601	167,807	100,915	12,721	50,257	23,403
1986	662,296	434,370	11,266	445,636	52,988	-4,807	387,841	168,726	105,729	13,275	49,891	23,465
1987	681,648	457,146	8,254	465,400	55,791	-4,977	404,632	165,890	111,126	13,616	50,063	24,138
1988	729,895	494,108	12,478	506,586	62,664	-2,210	441,712	169,262	118,921	14,599	49,995	25,462
1989	795,736	529,533	18,246	547,779	67,867	-393	479,519	189,659	126,558	15,614	50,964	26,044
1990	853,804	578,610	21,540	600,150	77,582	1,310	523,878	192,184	137,742	16,570	51,526	26,983
1991	901,816	616,733	10,877	627,610	83,610	364	544,364	199,620	157,832	17,182	52,487	27,518
1992	985,763	689,699	9,824	699,523	92,283	-1,673	605,567	208,553	171,643	18,381	53,629	28,639
1993	1,067,086	742,210	23,147	765,357	99,583	-2,502	663,272	220,782	183,032	19,490	54,750	29,620
1994	1,117,613	796,689	7,128	803,817	107,177	-3,639	693,001	229,392	195,220	19,962	55,987	31,132
1995	1,162,691	796,278	10,704	806,982	107,804	-2,827	696,351	254,768	211,572	20,500	56,718	31,384
1996	1,232,323	838,195	13,468	851,663	111,092	-5,414	735,157	273,500	223,666	21,495	57,332	32,113
1997	1,290,985	894,615	426	895,041	116,075	-7,940	771,026	288,742	231,217	22,307	57,874	33,058
1998	1,358,769	954,521	6,457	960,978	121,624	-9,839	829,515	284,630	244,624	23,380	58,116	33,458
1999	1,418,007	1,012,036	8,571	1,020,607	124,741	-11,683	884,183	279,793	254,031	24,431	58,042	33,588
2000	1,481,615	1,041,145	19,696	1,060,841	129,407	-12,685	918,749	289,548	273,318	25,570	57,944	34,320
2001	1,534,229	1,062,263	19,933	1,082,196	132,703	-13,731	935,762	298,674	299,793	26,707	57,446	33,539
2002	1,548,444	1,090,821	16,610	1,107,431	136,005	-12,675	958,751	275,597	314,096	26,882	57,601	33,446
2003	1,609,843	1,125,622	18,641	1,144,263	141,174	-13,277	989,812	289,713	330,318	27,669	58,183	33,600
2004	1,681,643	1,161,869	23,535	1,185,404	145,310	-12,410	1,027,684	303,607	350,352	28,706	58,581	33,585
2005	1,712,873	1,181,917	21,925	1,203,842	150,957	-13,545	1,039,340	305,952	367,581	29,042	58,979	33,984
2006	1,830,700	1,262,437	16,447	1,278,884	161,548	-12,486	1,104,850	328,528	397,322	30,693	59,646	34,467
2007	1,963,198	1,322,009	21,389	1,343,398	169,787	-10,974	1,162,637	369,999	430,562	32,770	59,908	35,176
2008	2,067,678	1,349,073	24,171	1,373,244	174,135	-12,335	1,186,774	408,532	472,372	34,345	60,203	34,975
2009	2,051,549	1,322,441	17,763	1,340,204	173,102	-11,575	1,155,527	388,704	507,318	33,930	60,464	33,927
2010	2,138,401	1,384,231	22,378	1,406,609	182,320	-12,420	1,211,869	380,497	546,035	35,030	61,044	33,982
2011	2,210,600	1,386,738	24,928	1,411,666	164,252	-13,571	1,233,843	429,691	547,066	36,010	61,388	33,980
2012	2,274,070	1,417,211	22,186	1,439,397	165,131	-12,418	1,261,848	468,465	543,757	37,037	61,400	33,494
2013	2,328,061	1,498,662	21,922	1,520,584	190,921	-18,753	1,310,910	454,607	562,544	37,601	61,915	34,430
2014	2,416,314	1,529,940	-821	1,529,119	197,328	-18,517	1,313,274	503,483	599,557	38,962	62,017	34,864
2015	2,520,445	1,604,820	7,233	1,612,053	205,585	-19,261	1,387,207	525,937	607,301	40,581	62,109	35,266
2016	2,607,746	1,675,251	-16	1,675,235	214,687	-20,248	1,440,300	531,661	635,785	41,787	62,406	35,870
2017	2,726,464	1,751,517	253	1,751,770	224,923	-22,211	1,504,636	559,942	661,886	43,332	62,920	36,370
2018	2,906,903	2,901,267	5,636	1,796,500	229,155	-19,246	1,548,099	657,781	701,023	46,235	62,872	36,124
2019	3,001,480	2,995,673	5,807	1,851,135	238,405	-17,549	1,595,181	666,896	739,403	47,650	62,990	36,318

Personal Income and Employment by Area: Lewiston-Auburn, ME

(Thousands of dollars, except as noted.)

Year	Personal income, total	Earnings by place of work			Less: Contributions for government social insurance	Plus: Adjustment for residence	Equals: Net earnings by place of residence	Plus: Dividends, interest, and rent	Plus: Personal current transfer receipts	Per capita personal income (dollars)	Population (persons)	Total employment
		Nonfarm	Farm	Total								
1970	339,559	245,390	6,907	252,297	19,291	21,803	254,809	46,393	38,357	3,713	91,463	42,844
1971	350,474	240,860	7,099	247,959	19,477	25,854	254,336	49,865	46,273	3,773	92,881	40,634
1972	373,641	255,844	9,495	265,339	21,738	27,410	271,011	53,438	49,192	3,985	93,756	40,343
1973	423,220	288,072	18,096	306,168	27,820	29,065	307,413	58,582	57,225	4,451	95,076	42,562
1974	459,977	308,823	13,975	322,798	30,844	32,348	324,302	67,275	68,400	4,798	95,870	43,143
1975	506,117	329,092	14,041	343,133	32,268	35,036	345,901	74,436	85,780	5,298	95,535	42,320
1976	579,076	381,103	23,386	404,489	38,489	43,097	409,097	78,590	91,389	5,962	97,130	44,591
1977	622,266	416,443	18,291	434,734	42,096	46,293	438,931	87,384	95,951	6,338	98,181	46,014
1978	683,401	465,446	15,016	480,462	48,555	54,180	486,087	95,442	101,872	6,914	98,837	47,120
1979	750,882	509,826	12,901	522,727	54,493	63,221	531,455	103,342	116,085	7,535	99,656	47,810
1980	843,510	553,477	11,128	564,605	59,010	77,759	583,354	123,770	136,386	8,475	99,531	47,774
1981	920,680	583,782	13,423	597,205	66,270	85,622	616,557	147,758	156,365	9,251	99,522	47,298
1982	994,172	600,158	15,140	615,298	68,408	100,216	647,106	176,253	170,813	10,056	98,860	45,953
1983	1,075,398	655,243	13,366	668,609	74,858	107,146	700,897	189,208	185,293	10,834	99,262	46,577
1984	1,180,324	729,743	20,067	749,810	85,417	111,488	775,881	210,700	193,743	11,801	100,018	48,103
1985	1,242,315	773,236	17,568	790,804	90,215	112,663	813,252	224,272	204,791	12,409	100,114	48,570
1986	1,336,704	837,104	14,671	851,775	97,136	127,450	882,089	242,490	212,125	13,340	100,204	50,078
1987	1,455,273	939,048	14,137	953,185	107,058	138,865	984,992	254,351	215,930	14,355	101,378	51,603
1988	1,595,764	1,028,427	12,437	1,040,864	119,791	163,975	1,085,048	280,150	230,566	15,409	103,559	53,611
1989	1,733,855	1,097,709	10,731	1,108,440	126,141	184,319	1,166,618	321,098	246,139	16,470	105,276	54,122
1990	1,785,505	1,113,528	17,088	1,130,616	134,139	195,162	1,191,639	315,952	277,914	16,938	105,412	53,181
1991	1,788,322	1,115,132	16,841	1,131,973	136,424	167,018	1,162,567	306,877	318,878	17,036	104,973	50,918
1992	1,861,172	1,155,416	16,732	1,172,148	142,774	180,542	1,209,916	298,742	352,514	17,838	104,335	50,835
1993	1,925,212	1,217,047	22,212	1,239,259	154,004	172,019	1,257,274	298,868	369,070	18,429	104,464	52,166
1994	2,015,499	1,287,349	27,361	1,314,710	164,818	168,189	1,318,081	310,208	387,210	19,359	104,112	53,466
1995	2,070,025	1,327,018	10,621	1,337,639	171,013	162,335	1,328,961	336,455	404,609	19,948	103,769	53,265
1996	2,165,578	1,378,531	21,502	1,400,033	174,536	153,081	1,378,578	354,899	432,101	21,032	102,966	53,134
1997	2,270,628	1,448,483	14,203	1,462,686	182,904	174,217	1,453,999	367,510	449,119	22,149	102,518	53,271
1998	2,360,011	1,557,054	13,637	1,570,691	194,455	161,145	1,537,381	362,882	459,748	22,886	103,120	55,697
1999	2,483,646	1,702,606	23,816	1,726,422	208,786	145,825	1,663,461	354,363	465,822	24,019	103,403	58,684
2000	2,640,465	1,828,505	23,546	1,852,051	220,048	130,307	1,762,310	388,021	490,134	25,425	103,852	60,420
2001	2,734,944	1,874,917	24,369	1,899,286	226,267	138,779	1,811,798	395,589	527,557	26,232	104,260	59,480
2002	2,895,797	2,012,772	23,317	2,036,089	235,756	113,608	1,913,941	418,573	563,283	27,562	105,063	60,214
2003	3,032,318	2,087,279	30,885	2,118,164	242,031	123,088	1,999,221	414,977	618,120	28,569	106,140	60,114
2004	3,114,809	2,162,790	23,164	2,185,954	248,568	145,535	2,082,921	380,170	651,718	29,147	106,867	60,631
2005	3,178,102	2,202,154	8,921	2,211,075	255,619	137,193	2,092,649	367,971	717,482	29,604	107,352	60,554
2006	3,330,745	2,344,001	10,641	2,354,642	274,258	123,283	2,203,667	404,930	722,148	30,860	107,932	61,323
2007	3,476,906	2,427,109	17,463	2,444,572	288,397	103,570	2,259,745	447,971	769,190	32,272	107,739	62,993
2008	3,621,974	2,472,240	29,494	2,501,734	296,394	78,538	2,283,878	450,191	887,905	33,449	108,284	62,500
2009	3,624,099	2,419,408	21,623	2,441,031	289,614	61,988	2,213,405	437,177	973,517	33,609	107,830	60,515
2010	3,658,554	2,472,053	22,074	2,494,127	298,760	28,178	2,223,545	466,257	968,752	33,973	107,690	60,259
2011	3,756,958	2,496,413	24,447	2,520,860	272,561	6,080	2,254,379	488,909	1,013,670	34,983	107,395	60,362
2012	3,822,381	2,562,892	38,830	2,601,722	280,756	-3,136	2,317,830	504,514	1,000,037	35,559	107,495	60,347
2013	3,793,494	2,584,105	39,369	2,623,474	323,972	-6,109	2,293,393	490,795	1,009,306	35,364	107,271	60,398
2014	3,900,699	2,701,662	22,521	2,724,183	333,627	-46,440	2,344,116	528,572	1,028,011	36,357	107,290	61,285
2015	4,056,671	2,788,581	37,379	2,825,960	348,646	-31,051	2,446,263	541,718	1,068,690	37,876	107,104	61,733
2016	4,116,134	2,858,424	12,077	2,870,501	352,641	-59,836	2,458,024	564,305	1,093,805	38,372	107,269	62,446
2017	4,292,403	2,953,342	10,635	2,963,977	363,465	-28,883	2,571,629	588,683	1,132,091	39,873	107,651	62,493
2018	4,464,983	4,435,134	29,849	3,103,285	380,906	-42,651	2,679,728	608,623	1,176,632	41,375	107,914	63,255
2019	4,652,478	4,625,950	26,528	3,262,915	399,204	-54,331	2,809,380	617,954	1,225,144	42,968	108,277	63,892

Personal Income and Employment by Area: Lexington-Fayette, KY

(Thousands of dollars, except as noted.)

Year	Personal income, total	Earnings by place of work			Less: Contributions for government social insurance	Plus: Adjustment for residence	Equals: Net earnings by place of residence	Plus: Dividends, interest, and rent	Plus: Personal current transfer receipts	Per capita personal income (dollars)	Population (persons)	Total employment
		Nonfarm	Farm	Total								
1970	1,017,530	857,895	42,124	900,019	54,163	-49,882	795,974	147,327	74,229	3,804	267,481	140,584
1971	1,127,053	949,712	39,006	988,718	61,436	-52,159	875,123	165,006	86,924	4,118	273,697	143,669
1972	1,251,564	1,055,175	51,243	1,106,418	72,088	-61,923	972,407	182,977	96,180	4,440	281,894	148,727
1973	1,400,290	1,196,803	54,506	1,251,309	94,851	-71,630	1,084,828	204,737	110,725	4,868	287,662	158,535
1974	1,560,999	1,325,589	56,972	1,382,561	108,738	-83,358	1,190,465	236,865	133,669	5,270	296,218	162,910
1975	1,710,621	1,417,655	60,952	1,478,607	115,190	-84,944	1,278,473	257,114	175,034	5,747	297,670	157,519
1976	1,934,689	1,627,457	71,845	1,699,302	135,761	-104,743	1,458,798	285,649	190,242	6,377	303,393	166,412
1977	2,150,870	1,802,950	94,260	1,897,210	150,367	-118,230	1,628,613	318,572	203,685	6,973	308,473	170,538
1978	2,444,284	2,029,243	148,323	2,177,566	175,832	-139,295	1,862,439	362,713	219,132	7,841	311,728	180,152
1979	2,731,660	2,297,636	141,902	2,439,538	206,600	-166,088	2,066,850	417,484	247,326	8,622	316,817	184,649
1980	3,034,438	2,437,328	193,405	2,630,733	221,253	-173,540	2,235,940	501,868	296,630	9,537	318,175	183,059
1981	3,438,971	2,664,961	258,179	2,923,140	260,843	-186,483	2,475,814	626,296	336,861	10,751	319,884	183,889
1982	3,696,393	2,822,928	231,382	3,054,310	281,232	-195,340	2,577,738	755,718	362,937	11,469	322,286	185,181
1983	4,024,789	3,083,752	280,225	3,363,977	310,274	-218,600	2,835,103	795,589	394,097	12,413	324,231	191,185
1984	4,557,690	3,502,078	364,345	3,866,423	359,216	-258,001	3,249,206	893,314	415,170	14,018	325,133	200,185
1985	4,852,230	3,792,516	341,328	4,133,844	396,859	-285,048	3,451,937	955,883	444,410	14,682	330,485	205,232
1986	4,992,158	3,988,198	253,497	4,241,695	433,192	-295,642	3,512,861	1,012,278	467,019	14,894	335,169	212,210
1987	5,285,964	4,279,590	238,901	4,518,491	463,752	-322,510	3,732,229	1,062,367	491,368	15,592	339,008	216,098
1988	5,881,666	4,827,944	245,711	5,073,655	520,277	-352,113	4,201,265	1,147,142	533,259	17,138	343,186	223,962
1989	6,321,218	5,208,599	233,857	5,442,456	570,760	-400,890	4,470,806	1,253,762	596,650	18,328	344,891	230,602
1990	6,893,882	5,737,963	242,676	5,980,639	652,399	-465,640	4,862,600	1,374,410	656,872	19,688	350,161	235,619
1991	7,320,865	6,058,058	248,903	6,306,961	692,106	-469,386	5,145,469	1,429,296	746,100	20,572	355,861	237,345
1992	7,837,414	6,483,642	314,329	6,797,971	739,905	-507,662	5,550,404	1,463,270	823,740	21,579	363,195	242,428
1993	8,150,083	6,757,974	281,970	7,039,944	778,884	-510,742	5,750,318	1,523,419	876,346	22,037	369,839	248,440
1994	8,471,303	6,998,601	278,514	7,277,115	825,454	-546,720	5,904,941	1,653,252	913,110	22,561	375,478	251,588
1995	9,028,358	7,412,527	279,784	7,692,311	878,581	-602,243	6,211,487	1,832,808	984,063	23,753	380,096	264,124
1996	9,661,628	7,992,998	321,845	8,314,843	937,877	-698,997	6,677,969	1,935,190	1,048,469	25,023	386,117	272,024
1997	10,316,250	8,544,408	387,127	8,931,535	999,011	-776,624	7,155,900	2,051,339	1,109,011	26,380	391,065	279,832
1998	11,100,423	9,158,863	448,361	9,607,224	1,069,447	-811,958	7,725,819	2,233,573	1,141,031	27,906	397,775	286,606
1999	11,756,212	9,783,837	547,130	10,330,967	1,148,367	-846,332	8,336,268	2,245,409	1,174,535	29,071	404,393	293,947
2000	12,683,617	10,402,017	643,031	11,045,048	1,192,481	-920,499	8,932,068	2,457,737	1,293,812	30,941	409,924	300,557
2001	12,745,430	10,585,664	402,456	10,988,120	1,215,144	-956,318	8,816,658	2,478,987	1,449,785	30,747	414,520	297,666
2002	12,991,399	10,941,938	390,681	11,332,619	1,256,338	-993,258	9,083,023	2,332,647	1,575,729	31,047	418,448	293,692
2003	13,349,646	11,396,697	287,994	11,684,691	1,292,944	-1,039,267	9,352,480	2,366,732	1,630,434	31,414	424,953	296,949
2004	14,170,955	12,050,187	342,351	12,392,538	1,340,919	-1,079,548	9,972,071	2,450,383	1,748,501	32,938	430,229	301,335
2005	14,905,445	12,610,352	293,756	12,904,108	1,393,135	-1,154,514	10,356,459	2,686,086	1,862,900	34,117	436,898	307,901
2006	16,073,430	13,301,421	303,575	13,604,996	1,476,249	-1,219,607	10,909,140	3,151,204	2,013,086	36,065	445,685	316,801
2007	16,913,219	13,979,046	246,710	14,225,756	1,556,041	-1,288,165	11,381,550	3,347,118	2,184,551	37,407	452,138	324,498
2008	17,407,850	14,389,110	-45,080	14,344,030	1,618,946	-1,252,460	11,472,624	3,382,462	2,552,764	37,834	460,112	322,909
2009	16,958,860	13,687,273	4,717	13,691,990	1,573,437	-1,130,416	10,988,137	3,136,925	2,833,798	36,289	467,328	312,564
2010	17,568,795	14,039,628	39,806	14,079,434	1,589,355	-1,056,986	11,433,093	3,002,189	3,133,513	37,119	473,306	312,898
2011	18,551,165	14,518,441	55,957	14,574,398	1,456,059	-1,083,991	12,034,348	3,330,832	3,185,985	38,764	478,570	317,157
2012	19,435,624	15,169,412	145,867	15,315,279	1,514,020	-1,117,592	12,683,667	3,564,336	3,187,621	40,116	484,490	321,742
2013	20,117,058	15,589,618	624,497	16,214,115	1,770,036	-1,126,488	13,317,591	3,504,538	3,294,929	41,104	489,413	327,531
2014	21,164,751	16,282,488	537,644	16,820,132	1,855,412	-1,207,380	13,757,340	3,844,310	3,563,101	42,836	494,089	335,617
2015	22,212,054	17,151,392	514,909	17,666,301	1,976,570	-1,288,278	14,401,453	4,051,362	3,759,239	44,377	500,528	345,796
2016	22,636,223	17,489,299	479,902	17,969,201	2,035,764	-1,432,493	14,500,944	4,457,027	3,678,252	44,669	506,760	351,572
2017	23,223,253	17,932,803	509,748	18,442,551	2,090,461	-1,517,405	14,834,685	4,658,993	3,729,575	45,300	512,650	356,987
2018	24,729,052	24,104,552	624,500	18,962,514	2,112,203	-1,502,619	15,347,692	5,483,551	3,897,809	48,023	514,938	357,809
2019	25,648,827	24,981,735	667,092	19,784,491	2,183,328	-1,609,636	15,991,527	5,548,664	4,108,636	49,606	517,056	361,874

Personal Income and Employment by Area: Lima, OH

(Thousands of dollars, except as noted.)

Year	Personal income, total	Earnings by place of work			Less: Contributions for government social insurance	Plus: Adjustment for residence	Equals: Net earnings by place of residence	Plus: Dividends, interest, and rent	Plus: Personal current transfer receipts	Per capita personal income (dollars)	Population (persons)	Total employment
		Nonfarm	Farm	Total								
1970	439,385	419,832	4,748	424,580	28,588	-51,050	344,942	59,351	35,092	3,955	111,084	56,153
1971	465,872	433,323	4,889	438,212	30,076	-47,402	360,734	62,791	42,347	4,181	111,437	54,945
1972	489,289	452,316	6,580	458,896	33,227	-47,821	377,848	66,074	45,367	4,422	110,643	54,610
1973	554,243	523,367	9,359	532,726	44,576	-59,143	429,007	73,044	52,192	5,027	110,245	57,847
1974	607,835	571,175	10,743	581,918	50,375	-67,191	464,352	81,822	61,661	5,494	110,637	58,786
1975	647,153	592,884	8,751	601,635	50,985	-71,164	479,486	88,010	79,657	5,840	110,806	56,340
1976	699,455	642,001	10,327	652,328	56,239	-76,457	519,632	94,956	84,867	6,367	109,853	56,613
1977	775,298	733,388	6,671	740,059	64,248	-95,838	579,973	106,674	88,651	7,018	110,465	58,352
1978	861,705	837,741	6,315	844,056	76,299	-116,955	650,802	117,121	93,782	7,846	109,828	60,165
1979	953,492	931,402	7,214	938,616	88,075	-137,447	713,094	131,439	108,959	8,571	111,247	61,611
1980	1,034,998	954,363	7,039	961,402	88,646	-145,698	727,058	163,769	144,171	9,226	112,188	58,688
1981	1,098,158	980,401	-194	980,207	97,348	-146,869	735,990	200,889	161,279	9,829	111,726	57,444
1982	1,147,388	1,007,272	-1,951	1,005,321	101,638	-155,678	748,005	219,439	179,944	10,447	109,826	55,345
1983	1,223,736	1,080,158	-5,489	1,074,669	110,331	-169,124	795,214	235,444	193,078	11,234	108,936	55,927
1984	1,385,983	1,237,251	14,176	1,251,427	129,461	-199,519	922,447	265,217	198,319	12,641	109,642	58,993
1985	1,466,696	1,341,397	12,473	1,353,870	142,609	-222,020	989,241	273,412	204,043	13,382	109,601	61,057
1986	1,548,122	1,449,376	10,201	1,459,577	158,698	-246,519	1,054,360	281,631	212,131	14,105	109,755	62,105
1987	1,585,393	1,494,184	10,926	1,505,110	164,129	-250,705	1,090,276	281,175	213,942	14,397	110,123	62,506
1988	1,667,335	1,563,857	12,609	1,576,466	176,828	-258,948	1,140,690	294,753	231,892	15,087	110,518	64,316
1989	1,750,403	1,597,140	22,643	1,619,783	182,532	-261,467	1,175,784	326,731	247,888	15,874	110,270	65,527
1990	1,815,379	1,635,960	26,710	1,662,670	190,919	-265,352	1,206,399	332,341	276,639	16,527	109,841	65,107
1991	1,852,229	1,676,769	16,968	1,693,737	199,575	-269,672	1,224,490	331,839	295,900	16,851	109,916	64,909
1992	1,979,850	1,750,331	18,530	1,768,861	207,498	-263,603	1,297,760	340,737	341,353	17,959	110,242	63,879
1993	1,994,037	1,790,955	12,010	1,802,965	213,805	-273,608	1,315,552	344,317	334,168	18,085	110,262	64,648
1994	2,113,276	1,883,849	14,207	1,898,056	227,168	-285,339	1,385,549	372,297	355,430	19,188	110,138	65,381
1995	2,167,849	1,877,951	4,325	1,882,276	227,671	-263,976	1,390,629	402,144	375,076	19,736	109,841	66,147
1996	2,224,976	1,895,983	6,756	1,902,739	226,168	-259,872	1,416,699	422,463	385,814	20,306	109,573	66,212
1997	2,296,398	1,933,167	20,069	1,953,236	224,798	-269,304	1,459,134	442,080	395,184	21,039	109,150	66,563
1998	2,439,688	2,057,428	7,448	2,064,876	230,519	-287,615	1,546,742	482,710	410,236	22,465	108,599	67,726
1999	2,564,162	2,250,359	875	2,251,234	249,302	-350,157	1,651,775	488,081	424,306	23,700	108,192	71,158
2000	2,693,867	2,375,739	13,401	2,389,140	252,349	-379,848	1,756,943	490,207	446,717	24,808	108,589	72,973
2001	2,737,251	2,382,326	12,328	2,394,654	259,990	-369,227	1,765,437	486,889	484,925	25,223	108,523	69,825
2002	2,795,584	2,434,841	-2,053	2,432,788	261,682	-359,597	1,811,509	476,217	507,858	25,761	108,518	69,133
2003	2,876,216	2,508,788	3,752	2,512,540	272,397	-352,164	1,887,979	455,975	532,262	26,776	107,418	68,371
2004	2,942,437	2,605,735	19,340	2,625,075	289,405	-374,212	1,961,458	424,287	556,692	27,544	106,826	68,615
2005	3,013,752	2,655,186	12,959	2,668,145	299,329	-366,918	2,001,898	417,439	594,415	28,203	106,861	68,553
2006	3,164,347	2,736,630	14,680	2,751,310	307,081	-354,541	2,089,688	440,279	634,380	29,652	106,716	67,907
2007	3,318,085	2,772,376	14,701	2,787,077	310,142	-323,940	2,152,995	487,620	677,470	31,092	106,717	66,745
2008	3,400,437	2,744,274	14,407	2,758,681	311,433	-296,703	2,150,545	502,849	747,043	31,847	106,773	65,417
2009	3,402,639	2,744,411	19,943	2,764,354	312,192	-339,020	2,113,142	463,512	825,985	31,944	106,518	62,898
2010	3,491,317	2,812,047	32,378	2,844,425	312,278	-367,742	2,164,405	454,769	872,143	32,824	106,366	62,432
2011	3,635,704	2,881,227	46,990	2,928,217	290,059	-399,785	2,238,373	498,135	899,196	34,307	105,975	62,950
2012	3,748,688	2,949,246	27,639	2,976,885	298,528	-393,136	2,285,221	576,587	886,880	35,623	105,233	63,339
2013	3,733,234	3,008,671	41,991	3,050,662	330,996	-406,447	2,313,219	515,116	904,899	35,546	105,025	63,602
2014	3,857,927	3,070,444	18,443	3,088,887	335,550	-388,812	2,364,525	560,591	932,811	36,797	104,843	63,377
2015	3,990,098	3,115,349	-10,779	3,104,570	339,811	-350,916	2,413,843	598,900	977,355	38,332	104,093	63,532
2016	4,057,889	3,203,879	-2,663	3,201,216	358,733	-386,376	2,456,107	603,143	998,639	39,159	103,626	63,358
2017	4,223,346	3,361,305	-7,534	3,353,771	380,681	-404,464	2,568,626	631,921	1,022,799	40,925	103,198	64,007
2018	4,373,564	4,356,958	16,606	3,459,651	386,933	-412,924	2,659,794	664,217	1,049,553	42,575	102,725	63,626
2019	4,481,729	4,473,130	8,599	3,564,787	398,787	-448,145	2,717,855	673,043	1,090,831	43,788	102,351	63,768

Personal Income and Employment by Area: Lincoln, NE

(Thousands of dollars, except as noted.)

Year	Personal income, total	Earnings by place of work			Less: Contributions for government social insurance	Plus: Adjustment for residence	Equals: Net earnings by place of residence	Plus: Dividends, interest, and rent	Plus: Personal current transfer receipts	Per capita personal income (dollars)	Population (persons)	Total employment
		Nonfarm	Farm	Total								
1970	761,119	608,314	15,182	623,496	40,790	-6,171	576,535	129,698	54,886	4,153	183,265	94,866
1971	834,654	664,518	18,341	682,859	45,895	-7,420	629,544	142,287	62,823	4,446	187,741	98,445
1972	918,081	733,434	19,078	752,512	52,849	-8,983	690,680	157,073	70,328	4,705	195,133	102,842
1973	1,035,680	824,266	30,980	855,246	69,063	-11,138	775,045	176,253	84,382	5,280	196,134	107,748
1974	1,148,954	925,745	21,704	947,449	81,359	-14,011	852,079	200,984	95,891	5,756	199,608	111,765
1975	1,303,224	1,018,528	45,582	1,064,110	87,628	-16,032	960,450	223,085	119,689	6,552	198,905	112,328
1976	1,421,987	1,151,154	19,752	1,170,906	100,169	-18,503	1,052,234	241,615	128,138	7,145	199,025	116,047
1977	1,554,224	1,264,079	14,912	1,278,991	110,723	-19,926	1,148,342	270,128	135,754	7,743	200,719	119,912
1978	1,768,411	1,415,813	55,099	1,470,912	128,277	-23,080	1,319,555	297,763	151,093	8,711	203,010	123,341
1979	1,931,967	1,570,522	26,032	1,596,554	147,910	-26,869	1,421,775	341,196	168,996	9,453	204,382	127,203
1980	2,095,217	1,689,474	-10,358	1,679,116	158,154	-29,388	1,491,574	404,293	199,350	10,007	209,378	127,424
1981	2,368,019	1,830,003	23,553	1,853,556	184,336	-33,852	1,635,368	500,104	232,547	11,185	211,713	125,565
1982	2,573,068	1,908,397	44,769	1,953,166	196,722	-35,309	1,721,135	596,349	255,584	12,089	212,839	123,845
1983	2,687,403	2,025,454	18,131	2,043,585	209,412	-38,474	1,795,699	614,565	277,139	12,546	214,209	124,320
1984	2,924,125	2,223,999	22,541	2,246,540	236,591	-43,916	1,966,033	671,779	286,313	13,523	216,231	128,322
1985	3,123,414	2,375,135	36,630	2,411,765	259,391	-46,389	2,105,985	705,601	311,828	14,351	217,648	132,780
1986	3,261,137	2,504,488	45,520	2,550,008	283,776	-51,466	2,214,766	722,603	323,768	14,896	218,934	134,997
1987	3,451,673	2,703,200	41,939	2,745,139	306,228	-57,545	2,381,366	736,620	333,687	15,660	220,410	140,194
1988	3,724,621	2,900,111	61,759	2,961,870	343,753	-62,871	2,555,246	814,992	354,383	16,693	223,119	146,113
1989	3,991,872	3,121,506	59,010	3,180,516	368,854	-69,400	2,742,262	863,997	385,613	17,630	226,420	149,477
1990	4,302,681	3,379,562	63,057	3,442,619	412,491	-77,428	2,952,700	929,241	420,740	18,696	230,144	155,589
1991	4,513,709	3,547,152	45,534	3,592,686	434,956	-83,056	3,074,674	982,679	456,356	19,337	233,419	156,858
1992	4,836,798	3,802,221	59,416	3,861,637	456,948	-92,375	3,312,314	1,025,903	498,581	20,337	237,827	158,269
1993	5,081,565	4,029,718	31,059	4,060,777	484,027	-102,357	3,474,393	1,067,686	539,486	20,931	242,779	162,253
1994	5,480,020	4,314,357	58,159	4,372,516	520,710	-112,431	3,739,375	1,180,727	559,918	22,283	245,933	169,247
1995	5,879,906	4,613,025	17,899	4,630,924	546,447	-119,231	3,965,246	1,312,771	601,889	23,473	250,498	172,577
1996	6,286,324	4,851,905	94,383	4,946,288	577,489	-128,618	4,240,181	1,400,887	645,256	24,759	253,904	177,454
1997	6,575,773	5,122,993	53,369	5,176,362	615,519	-139,184	4,421,659	1,484,973	669,141	25,547	257,404	180,195
1998	7,161,527	5,579,685	54,298	5,633,983	663,623	-157,927	4,812,433	1,614,657	734,437	27,437	261,021	184,836
1999	7,544,065	5,927,873	47,648	5,975,521	698,063	-170,234	5,107,224	1,664,353	772,488	28,589	263,880	189,577
2000	8,198,331	6,436,624	43,775	6,480,399	741,392	-186,868	5,552,139	1,827,026	819,166	30,586	268,042	193,410
2001	8,369,259	6,681,116	45,303	6,726,419	767,732	-202,813	5,755,874	1,694,877	918,508	30,856	271,237	196,992
2002	8,753,071	7,055,273	14,517	7,069,790	805,752	-213,177	6,050,861	1,709,393	992,817	31,833	274,972	198,177
2003	9,120,901	7,249,100	61,695	7,310,795	831,581	-221,382	6,257,832	1,816,394	1,046,675	32,669	279,194	200,972
2004	9,455,247	7,574,216	88,364	7,662,580	865,452	-220,550	6,576,578	1,770,842	1,107,827	33,557	281,768	203,838
2005	9,817,908	7,887,230	58,445	7,945,675	911,890	-229,699	6,804,086	1,830,781	1,183,041	34,392	285,469	206,855
2006	10,389,660	8,247,573	29,531	8,277,104	970,086	-227,710	7,079,308	2,047,273	1,263,079	35,958	288,940	209,583
2007	10,989,135	8,569,546	69,524	8,639,070	1,002,094	-210,286	7,426,690	2,212,814	1,349,631	37,569	292,502	213,477
2008	11,515,752	8,767,611	98,187	8,865,798	1,023,671	-220,792	7,621,335	2,358,122	1,536,295	38,871	296,258	212,954
2009	11,304,605	8,761,289	87,406	8,848,695	1,019,574	-233,048	7,596,073	2,095,409	1,613,123	37,728	299,633	209,775
2010	11,680,093	9,018,280	91,314	9,109,594	1,056,439	-258,511	7,794,644	2,132,359	1,753,090	38,551	302,980	208,789
2011	12,383,034	9,228,795	181,892	9,410,687	958,711	-307,597	8,144,379	2,449,583	1,789,072	40,369	306,746	210,610
2012	13,127,060	9,837,686	93,114	9,930,800	989,942	-341,735	8,599,123	2,711,210	1,816,727	42,268	310,564	215,151
2013	13,217,034	10,059,502	202,943	10,262,445	1,152,330	-369,773	8,740,342	2,622,445	1,854,247	42,023	314,522	218,785
2014	13,880,839	10,587,524	136,981	10,724,505	1,206,372	-386,690	9,131,443	2,811,287	1,938,109	43,397	319,858	222,020
2015	14,566,101	11,049,264	106,719	11,155,983	1,259,045	-399,412	9,497,526	3,018,071	2,050,504	45,029	323,481	226,769
2016	14,998,490	11,359,744	75,370	11,435,114	1,295,797	-400,579	9,738,738	3,119,317	2,140,435	45,778	327,633	229,407
2017	15,556,190	11,746,236	98,952	11,845,188	1,356,114	-420,863	10,068,211	3,261,811	2,226,168	46,924	331,519	230,099
2018	16,539,079	16,481,159	57,920	12,478,907	1,427,301	-472,677	10,578,929	3,517,243	2,442,907	49,548	333,800	235,618
2019	17,098,776	17,034,036	64,740	12,932,600	1,483,065	-488,377	10,961,158	3,554,427	2,583,191	50,833	336,374	238,292

Personal Income and Employment by Area: Little Rock-North Little Rock-Conway, AR

(Thousands of dollars, except as noted.)

Year	Personal income, total	Earnings by place of work			Less: Contributions for government social insurance	Plus: Adjustment for residence	Equals: Net earnings by place of residence	Plus: Dividends, interest, and rent	Plus: Personal current transfer receipts	Per capita personal income (dollars)	Population (persons)	Total employment
		Nonfarm	Farm	Total								
1970	1,450,105	1,195,466	28,284	1,223,750	85,462	-22,602	1,115,686	212,105	122,314	3,635	398,923	189,395
1971	1,637,474	1,351,485	29,033	1,380,518	99,363	-27,327	1,253,828	238,788	144,858	3,989	410,511	196,544
1972	1,855,105	1,542,392	36,863	1,579,255	119,038	-29,083	1,431,134	261,792	162,179	4,397	421,948	209,206
1973	2,127,721	1,751,201	68,368	1,819,569	155,333	-35,216	1,629,020	295,990	202,711	4,901	434,101	221,631
1974	2,415,090	1,963,866	72,021	2,035,887	180,073	-35,516	1,820,298	346,681	248,111	5,364	450,208	229,229
1975	2,686,035	2,144,029	53,257	2,197,286	192,768	-35,115	1,969,403	396,535	320,097	5,906	454,800	226,577
1976	2,986,826	2,424,519	40,363	2,464,882	221,591	-36,549	2,206,742	429,553	350,531	6,451	463,036	234,682
1977	3,296,427	2,702,565	41,072	2,743,637	249,469	-37,769	2,456,399	473,904	366,124	7,000	470,916	243,509
1978	3,760,823	3,065,938	70,406	3,136,344	290,242	-36,380	2,809,722	544,482	406,619	7,845	479,418	254,644
1979	4,186,018	3,405,122	49,201	3,454,323	334,368	-14,005	3,105,950	614,411	465,657	8,623	485,427	260,249
1980	4,659,808	3,718,187	28,470	3,746,657	364,058	-20,345	3,362,254	742,492	555,062	9,400	495,743	259,470
1981	5,129,744	4,005,442	38,154	4,043,596	423,958	-34,267	3,585,371	914,702	629,671	10,291	498,489	257,023
1982	5,490,849	4,248,231	21,921	4,270,152	457,671	-47,239	3,765,242	1,040,629	684,978	10,953	501,306	256,891
1983	5,923,152	4,626,428	18,750	4,645,178	504,405	-54,245	4,086,528	1,089,248	747,376	11,724	505,195	264,519
1984	6,479,257	5,064,971	35,275	5,100,246	567,820	-60,883	4,471,543	1,222,768	784,946	12,688	510,658	275,936
1985	7,004,721	5,492,804	35,424	5,528,228	623,358	-72,796	4,832,074	1,332,626	840,021	13,567	516,324	284,898
1986	7,454,320	5,854,297	26,615	5,880,912	669,379	-72,437	5,139,096	1,420,197	895,027	14,277	522,119	289,743
1987	7,761,114	6,149,972	45,518	6,195,490	700,160	-87,015	5,408,315	1,426,652	926,147	14,710	527,622	295,390
1988	8,218,799	6,494,406	75,779	6,570,185	770,332	-94,651	5,705,202	1,538,431	975,166	15,544	528,733	304,689
1989	8,878,036	6,900,422	63,311	6,963,733	818,996	-105,848	6,038,889	1,746,313	1,092,834	16,674	532,436	312,014
1990	9,435,305	7,417,202	50,965	7,468,167	917,204	-122,068	6,428,895	1,819,351	1,187,059	17,589	536,444	317,357
1991	10,012,498	7,934,088	49,661	7,983,749	980,039	-148,948	6,854,762	1,832,357	1,325,379	18,442	542,913	324,532
1992	10,859,711	8,656,144	64,548	8,720,692	1,060,472	-173,689	7,486,531	1,908,491	1,464,689	19,662	552,311	331,121
1993	11,386,531	9,096,830	57,578	9,154,408	1,111,552	-194,986	7,847,870	1,988,771	1,549,890	20,265	561,887	341,004
1994	12,005,290	9,606,281	63,673	9,669,954	1,191,713	-221,502	8,256,739	2,124,406	1,624,145	21,103	568,889	347,270
1995	12,797,950	10,202,122	59,899	10,262,021	1,260,003	-252,130	8,749,888	2,288,683	1,759,379	22,205	576,345	361,633
1996	13,625,516	10,773,247	83,088	10,856,335	1,319,934	-281,281	9,255,120	2,453,610	1,916,786	23,297	584,861	370,043
1997	14,280,904	11,358,757	73,912	11,432,669	1,388,622	-310,118	9,733,929	2,572,610	1,974,365	24,135	591,707	376,359
1998	15,295,577	12,223,870	60,985	12,284,855	1,476,276	-347,229	10,461,350	2,822,935	2,011,292	25,585	597,826	382,432
1999	15,906,996	12,838,448	66,956	12,905,404	1,542,730	-383,706	10,978,968	2,824,366	2,103,662	26,280	605,291	387,438
2000	16,809,492	13,541,813	71,602	13,613,415	1,612,187	-418,570	11,582,658	2,940,781	2,286,053	27,452	612,313	392,022
2001	17,833,435	14,445,131	76,119	14,521,250	1,680,385	-465,424	12,375,441	2,911,910	2,546,084	28,851	618,126	395,201
2002	18,418,538	14,881,788	50,918	14,932,706	1,718,383	-487,639	12,726,684	2,940,270	2,751,584	29,509	624,166	393,400
2003	19,453,955	15,707,138	104,906	15,812,044	1,799,892	-519,191	13,492,961	3,057,474	2,903,520	30,829	631,032	397,411
2004	20,469,067	16,547,239	109,232	16,656,471	1,878,183	-555,657	14,222,631	3,119,549	3,126,887	32,005	639,558	403,985
2005	21,962,453	17,564,439	57,202	17,621,641	1,976,408	-580,833	15,064,400	3,517,217	3,380,836	33,852	648,784	412,763
2006	23,199,053	18,306,852	67,081	18,373,933	2,117,583	-631,790	15,624,560	3,887,788	3,686,705	35,059	661,719	423,919
2007	24,853,038	19,493,198	78,560	19,571,758	2,249,437	-769,468	16,552,853	4,277,279	4,022,906	37,014	671,441	432,635
2008	25,378,153	19,187,355	61,172	19,248,527	2,306,297	-698,290	16,243,940	4,607,002	4,527,211	37,217	681,888	433,707
2009	25,344,440	19,303,231	38,809	19,342,040	2,330,859	-649,035	16,362,146	4,080,803	4,901,491	36,630	691,903	426,980
2010	25,835,617	19,415,687	24,994	19,440,681	2,346,504	-612,094	16,482,083	4,019,858	5,333,676	36,790	702,245	427,388
2011	27,093,687	19,955,858	14,386	19,970,244	2,183,635	-644,412	17,142,197	4,474,084	5,477,406	38,151	710,178	435,010
2012	28,911,563	20,943,259	33,740	20,976,999	2,236,908	-592,594	18,147,497	5,177,450	5,586,616	40,330	716,876	435,672
2013	28,460,073	21,242,099	109,586	21,351,685	2,549,866	-672,772	18,129,047	4,608,880	5,722,146	39,394	722,455	438,749
2014	29,733,511	21,929,437	66,706	21,996,143	2,641,337	-691,753	18,663,053	4,959,786	6,110,672	40,879	727,363	441,874
2015	30,712,945	22,425,897	27,702	22,453,599	2,726,570	-735,480	18,991,549	5,281,646	6,439,750	42,066	730,107	448,503
2016	31,297,404	22,816,894	21,323	22,838,217	2,733,099	-736,510	19,368,608	5,216,701	6,712,095	42,671	733,461	453,112
2017	32,250,196	23,358,586	41,823	23,400,409	2,783,847	-740,676	19,875,886	5,517,018	6,857,292	43,679	738,344	456,941
2018	33,355,595	33,337,457	18,138	23,910,334	2,887,343	-832,471	20,190,520	6,090,287	7,074,788	45,070	740,081	463,348
2019	34,565,252	34,536,024	29,228	24,637,371	2,991,070	-849,357	20,796,944	6,272,399	7,495,909	46,560	742,384	467,388

Personal Income and Employment by Area: Logan, UT-ID

(Thousands of dollars, except as noted.)

Year	Personal income, total	Earnings by place of work			Less: Contributions for government social insurance	Plus: Adjustment for residence	Equals: Net earnings by place of residence	Plus: Dividends, interest, and rent	Plus: Personal current transfer receipts	Per capita personal income (dollars)	Population (persons)	Total employment
		Nonfarm	Farm	Total								
1970	142,719	86,078	14,685	100,763	5,819	10,307	105,251	24,791	12,677	2,865	49,811	19,220
1971	159,132	94,999	15,313	110,312	6,628	11,930	115,614	28,571	14,947	3,133	50,796	19,811
1972	180,672	108,052	18,233	126,285	7,903	13,271	131,653	32,203	16,816	3,416	52,893	20,828
1973	202,208	122,470	21,084	143,554	10,481	13,859	146,932	35,522	19,754	3,716	54,413	22,111
1974	227,739	137,895	23,551	161,446	12,370	15,826	164,902	40,522	22,315	4,082	55,792	23,183
1975	252,002	156,895	17,379	174,274	13,729	18,489	179,034	45,642	27,326	4,384	57,480	23,664
1976	289,615	186,124	17,899	204,023	16,419	20,959	208,563	50,696	30,356	4,911	58,974	25,332
1977	318,071	207,964	13,463	221,427	18,121	24,211	227,517	57,793	32,761	5,228	60,841	26,351
1978	363,517	239,975	14,333	254,308	21,308	28,234	261,234	66,372	35,911	5,823	62,424	27,771
1979	412,925	275,882	11,630	287,512	25,753	33,639	295,398	76,626	40,901	6,439	64,124	29,228
1980	467,845	304,979	12,162	317,141	29,480	39,020	326,681	92,695	48,469	7,011	66,734	30,090
1981	517,200	331,033	7,358	338,391	34,407	44,931	348,915	110,204	58,081	7,469	69,244	29,973
1982	556,313	340,354	11,617	351,971	35,436	49,524	366,059	126,075	64,179	7,783	71,482	29,880
1983	608,451	376,033	9,287	385,320	38,861	54,243	400,702	138,642	69,107	8,265	73,620	30,808
1984	667,326	413,702	12,819	426,521	43,782	59,899	442,638	151,118	73,570	8,925	74,772	31,754
1985	716,586	440,197	15,646	455,843	47,165	67,155	475,833	160,483	80,270	9,521	75,261	32,227
1986	777,944	485,805	21,073	506,878	52,725	71,217	525,370	169,448	83,126	10,283	75,651	33,320
1987	846,227	522,209	33,077	555,286	56,726	78,944	577,504	177,152	91,571	11,068	76,454	34,995
1988	897,416	567,102	34,688	601,790	65,303	83,469	619,956	183,173	94,287	11,558	77,643	36,896
1989	985,686	625,543	40,451	665,994	73,152	87,105	679,947	200,319	105,420	12,496	78,881	39,229
1990	1,049,954	684,099	45,831	729,930	81,411	89,104	737,623	197,489	114,842	13,171	79,719	40,769
1991	1,118,403	743,145	42,607	785,752	89,444	91,446	787,754	205,630	125,019	13,579	82,362	41,907
1992	1,212,930	813,171	50,395	863,566	96,617	96,825	863,774	208,967	140,189	14,220	85,299	42,939
1993	1,312,112	884,289	51,483	935,772	105,471	98,462	928,763	230,158	153,191	14,881	88,175	44,894
1994	1,396,025	970,935	44,482	1,015,417	116,911	99,594	998,100	241,895	156,030	15,307	91,202	48,049
1995	1,490,544	1,022,994	39,471	1,062,465	123,620	104,255	1,043,100	275,362	172,082	15,824	94,198	50,269
1996	1,604,257	1,092,675	47,950	1,140,625	128,601	108,655	1,120,679	303,879	179,699	16,572	96,807	52,531
1997	1,730,781	1,185,898	46,597	1,232,495	137,296	116,770	1,211,969	332,724	186,088	17,523	98,774	54,389
1998	1,864,244	1,250,095	65,862	1,315,957	145,350	125,130	1,295,737	373,234	195,273	18,473	100,916	55,955
1999	1,931,681	1,313,066	64,843	1,377,909	152,513	122,288	1,347,684	376,278	207,719	19,025	101,532	57,125
2000	2,008,020	1,355,812	43,170	1,398,982	157,431	131,273	1,372,824	408,650	226,546	19,455	103,211	58,582
2001	2,159,237	1,453,528	68,348	1,521,876	167,909	128,528	1,482,495	425,547	251,195	20,703	104,294	59,183
2002	2,209,108	1,541,845	35,101	1,576,946	177,743	123,920	1,523,123	415,113	270,872	20,611	107,180	60,144
2003	2,348,584	1,676,378	34,934	1,711,312	193,853	121,265	1,638,724	424,760	285,100	21,582	108,819	62,064
2004	2,546,513	1,802,585	60,136	1,862,721	211,458	122,539	1,773,802	464,952	307,759	22,980	110,813	64,377
2005	2,620,921	1,864,540	38,436	1,902,976	220,531	130,576	1,813,021	474,265	333,635	23,281	112,580	65,734
2006	2,775,384	1,988,335	23,734	2,012,069	232,571	141,642	1,921,140	492,899	361,345	24,491	113,321	68,179
2007	3,026,468	2,118,745	46,746	2,165,491	249,013	146,207	2,062,685	564,130	399,653	26,113	115,901	71,644
2008	3,344,419	2,290,621	51,370	2,341,991	266,422	148,930	2,224,499	648,062	471,858	28,012	119,394	72,983
2009	3,361,712	2,311,351	28,373	2,339,724	265,798	140,800	2,214,726	630,392	516,594	27,320	123,048	71,800
2010	3,568,695	2,464,090	48,672	2,512,762	279,986	134,641	2,367,417	625,463	575,815	28,288	126,156	71,850
2011	3,824,871	2,605,352	65,541	2,670,893	260,617	135,864	2,546,140	687,556	591,175	29,971	127,619	73,553
2012	3,995,055	2,653,354	65,757	2,719,111	260,010	149,923	2,609,024	804,807	581,224	31,052	128,656	74,294
2013	4,022,448	2,747,810	84,630	2,832,440	306,775	171,813	2,697,478	731,208	593,762	30,979	129,843	75,295
2014	4,254,276	2,846,015	98,079	2,944,094	322,771	182,776	2,804,099	821,867	628,310	32,529	130,784	77,426
2015	4,564,787	3,021,916	94,863	3,116,779	332,961	193,478	2,977,296	922,997	664,494	34,395	132,718	79,622
2016	4,788,420	3,245,895	62,144	3,308,039	353,276	203,829	3,158,592	920,622	709,206	35,290	135,689	81,228
2017	5,056,942	3,453,513	70,912	3,524,425	378,738	215,182	3,360,869	968,752	727,321	36,644	138,002	83,200
2018	5,584,640	5,515,555	69,085	3,811,527	401,032	236,010	3,646,505	1,157,167	780,968	39,861	140,104	85,544
2019	5,881,417	5,804,268	77,149	4,019,477	424,222	253,692	3,848,947	1,198,433	834,037	41,370	142,165	87,960

Personal Income and Employment by Area: Longview, TX

(Thousands of dollars, except as noted.)

Year	Personal income, total	Earnings by place of work			Less: Contributions for government social insurance	Plus: Adjustment for residence	Equals: Net earnings by place of residence	Plus: Dividends, interest, and rent	Plus: Personal current transfer receipts	Per capita personal income (dollars)	Population (persons)	Total employment
		Nonfarm	Farm	Total								
1970.............	432,135	308,328	3,621	311,949	19,889	24,579	316,639	66,311	49,185	3,297	131,055	53,026
1971.............	473,200	340,009	2,366	342,375	22,565	25,076	344,886	72,336	55,978	3,541	133,616	54,346
1972.............	526,660	376,422	7,382	383,804	26,067	27,418	385,155	79,211	62,294	3,825	137,697	56,603
1973.............	596,152	426,223	12,755	438,978	34,476	28,926	433,428	89,010	73,714	4,254	140,153	59,291
1974.............	694,824	501,511	12,161	513,672	41,875	30,466	502,263	105,193	87,368	4,857	143,059	62,300
1975.............	795,160	568,982	3,785	572,767	46,219	35,547	562,095	125,425	107,640	5,407	147,050	64,378
1976.............	922,874	685,315	4,128	689,443	56,627	34,208	667,024	137,912	117,938	6,143	150,221	68,830
1977.............	1,025,983	762,977	2,988	765,965	63,446	40,004	742,523	156,505	126,955	6,603	155,386	71,742
1978.............	1,187,253	890,733	5,108	895,841	75,591	45,900	866,150	180,046	141,057	7,429	159,818	76,038
1979.............	1,358,644	1,035,803	4,321	1,040,124	92,299	43,777	991,602	207,229	159,813	8,199	165,709	79,930
1980.............	1,570,275	1,171,201	-372	1,170,829	105,502	51,300	1,116,627	267,433	186,215	9,199	170,696	82,526
1981.............	1,867,981	1,388,593	797	1,389,390	135,515	53,727	1,307,602	346,788	213,591	10,668	175,096	89,406
1982.............	2,081,883	1,480,783	12,637	1,493,420	148,512	52,525	1,397,433	434,644	249,806	11,308	184,111	91,268
1983.............	2,161,571	1,490,039	4,438	1,494,477	147,543	40,314	1,387,248	491,439	282,884	11,556	187,045	88,609
1984.............	2,311,503	1,584,937	5,936	1,590,873	160,976	53,320	1,483,217	534,573	293,713	12,401	186,400	90,541
1985.............	2,463,271	1,651,178	4,222	1,655,400	169,884	67,090	1,552,606	600,221	310,444	13,284	185,436	91,871
1986.............	2,481,459	1,643,533	4,911	1,648,444	167,096	58,607	1,539,955	599,374	342,130	13,493	183,911	88,573
1987.............	2,476,045	1,650,892	-138	1,650,754	165,730	61,546	1,546,570	572,551	356,924	13,624	181,744	91,065
1988.............	2,614,944	1,759,714	200	1,759,914	183,535	66,355	1,642,734	601,851	370,359	14,475	180,657	92,809
1989.............	2,771,835	1,804,317	13,548	1,817,865	190,398	68,022	1,695,489	677,017	399,329	15,459	179,308	91,708
1990.............	2,917,207	1,932,355	16,475	1,948,830	199,402	79,128	1,828,556	648,581	440,070	16,188	180,206	94,053
1991.............	3,037,707	2,022,799	18,908	2,041,707	214,382	77,478	1,904,803	650,826	482,078	16,640	182,550	95,739
1992.............	3,242,022	2,181,380	28,511	2,209,891	228,364	63,371	2,044,898	642,157	554,967	17,643	183,757	96,484
1993.............	3,318,827	2,216,722	25,190	2,241,912	232,014	83,765	2,093,663	633,500	591,664	17,942	184,979	98,115
1994.............	3,479,568	2,348,524	23,536	2,372,060	248,598	58,504	2,181,966	669,447	628,155	18,683	186,238	100,672
1995.............	3,678,091	2,449,490	11,758	2,461,248	261,970	68,253	2,267,531	728,398	682,162	19,497	188,646	102,590
1996.............	3,913,247	2,632,141	10,242	2,642,383	277,748	68,560	2,433,195	757,394	722,658	20,536	190,556	105,595
1997.............	4,168,805	2,866,432	20,789	2,887,221	298,681	42,766	2,631,306	781,153	756,346	21,697	192,139	109,323
1998.............	4,362,775	3,042,894	22,168	3,065,062	315,698	17,113	2,766,477	824,561	771,737	22,592	193,114	110,870
1999.............	4,455,582	3,119,858	34,084	3,153,942	321,745	13,743	2,845,940	823,347	786,295	22,945	194,184	111,103
2000.............	4,822,802	3,364,585	27,091	3,391,676	338,757	18,821	3,071,740	927,027	824,035	24,845	194,113	113,712
2001.............	5,120,962	3,673,644	40,258	3,713,902	373,334	-53,143	3,287,425	935,273	898,264	26,211	195,374	116,694
2002.............	5,134,660	3,568,413	44,826	3,613,239	362,028	15,340	3,266,541	886,964	981,155	25,965	197,750	113,474
2003.............	5,364,176	3,704,403	45,874	3,750,277	382,331	22,349	3,390,295	946,882	1,026,999	26,882	199,547	113,280
2004.............	5,472,447	3,841,139	42,736	3,883,875	400,702	34,297	3,517,470	878,812	1,076,165	27,195	201,231	113,660
2005.............	5,976,997	4,277,445	32,777	4,310,222	442,535	-14,045	3,853,642	959,076	1,164,279	29,434	203,062	117,359
2006.............	6,663,279	4,883,399	16,536	4,899,935	482,333	-36,622	4,380,980	1,052,814	1,229,485	32,419	205,537	121,298
2007.............	7,129,667	5,161,622	17,165	5,178,787	523,088	-83,011	4,572,688	1,221,477	1,335,502	34,308	207,813	126,813
2008.............	8,237,197	5,938,076	-2,307	5,935,769	570,989	-167,391	5,197,389	1,555,819	1,483,989	39,214	210,058	131,128
2009.............	7,740,369	5,431,009	-4,519	5,426,490	556,183	-196,715	4,673,592	1,448,547	1,618,230	36,319	213,121	128,334
2010.............	7,929,595	5,839,390	10,607	5,849,997	599,600	-244,024	5,006,373	1,172,141	1,751,081	36,928	214,731	130,743
2011.............	8,740,874	6,257,056	1,208	6,258,264	568,307	-286,347	5,403,610	1,549,871	1,787,393	40,464	216,016	132,662
2012.............	8,821,865	6,569,335	19,031	6,588,366	602,085	-304,536	5,681,745	1,363,579	1,776,541	40,711	216,693	137,021
2013.............	8,778,684	6,742,011	40,274	6,782,285	699,178	-381,681	5,701,426	1,244,626	1,832,632	40,592	216,265	139,078
2014.............	9,192,281	6,979,538	43,298	7,022,836	720,086	-423,596	5,879,154	1,396,081	1,917,046	42,469	216,445	140,387
2015.............	8,868,248	6,469,652	57,898	6,527,550	694,694	-388,401	5,444,455	1,398,485	2,025,308	40,837	217,162	138,713
2016.............	8,623,258	6,040,214	25,448	6,065,662	673,027	-368,973	5,023,662	1,444,977	2,154,619	39,681	217,314	136,424
2017.............	8,749,076	6,119,161	31,418	6,150,579	697,911	-400,429	5,052,239	1,510,290	2,186,547	40,229	217,481	136,280
2018.............	11,927,686	11,910,585	17,101	8,248,366	923,171	-293,366	7,031,829	2,016,886	2,878,971	41,805	285,315	172,769
2019.............	12,312,747	12,316,158	-3,411	8,518,687	940,062	-316,536	7,262,089	2,055,161	2,995,497	42,953	286,657	174,874

Personal Income and Employment by Area: Longview, WA

(Thousands of dollars, except as noted.)

Year	Personal income, total	Earnings by place of work			Less: Contributions for government social insurance	Plus: Adjustment for residence	Equals: Net earnings by place of residence	Plus: Dividends, interest, and rent	Plus: Personal current transfer receipts	Per capita personal income (dollars)	Population (persons)	Total employment
		Nonfarm	Farm	Total								
1970	274,017	243,870	2,108	245,978	22,330	-12,156	211,492	35,172	27,353	3,983	68,799	29,467
1971	285,111	247,004	2,301	249,305	23,414	-11,683	214,208	38,153	32,750	4,083	69,830	28,695
1972	322,011	286,469	3,030	289,499	28,573	-14,451	246,475	41,290	34,246	4,660	69,102	30,465
1973	364,830	325,522	6,572	332,094	37,278	-17,067	277,749	47,421	39,660	5,126	71,174	32,414
1974	415,761	370,547	6,439	376,986	43,530	-21,077	312,379	56,157	47,225	5,774	72,006	33,292
1975	476,003	422,291	5,023	427,314	48,366	-24,976	353,972	63,974	58,057	6,394	74,445	34,143
1976	538,891	498,857	5,355	504,212	58,514	-39,452	406,246	69,345	63,300	7,249	74,340	35,416
1977	579,382	529,984	3,537	533,521	61,768	-39,331	432,422	77,622	69,338	7,760	74,659	35,411
1978	641,679	581,592	6,920	588,512	69,021	-42,967	476,524	88,945	76,210	8,495	75,532	35,985
1979	715,480	639,634	8,125	647,759	77,342	-47,517	522,900	103,283	89,297	9,159	78,118	36,487
1980	801,254	706,760	4,568	711,328	85,927	-58,814	566,587	123,681	110,986	10,066	79,601	37,129
1981	855,922	731,944	6,468	738,412	95,066	-56,299	587,047	147,122	121,753	10,745	79,657	36,029
1982	877,213	706,263	7,424	713,687	93,703	-49,030	570,954	165,096	141,163	11,103	79,006	34,093
1983	947,460	758,964	7,525	766,489	102,389	-53,278	610,822	184,686	151,952	12,007	78,908	34,630
1984	999,166	795,732	7,438	803,170	111,335	-49,979	641,856	197,453	159,857	12,626	79,138	35,602
1985	1,020,930	788,948	8,431	797,379	110,318	-43,725	643,336	208,127	169,467	12,984	78,627	35,058
1986	1,063,558	817,574	8,571	826,145	114,439	-40,562	671,144	215,333	177,081	13,700	77,632	35,534
1987	1,110,951	872,300	5,495	877,795	121,803	-43,108	712,884	213,377	184,690	14,165	78,428	37,670
1988	1,197,856	955,100	6,574	961,674	136,437	-43,348	781,889	226,639	189,328	15,061	79,531	39,451
1989	1,312,840	1,026,077	9,732	1,035,809	145,867	-43,866	846,076	261,453	205,311	16,212	80,982	40,985
1990	1,410,879	1,118,843	10,582	1,129,425	161,250	-44,735	923,440	261,613	225,826	17,106	82,478	42,731
1991	1,530,092	1,210,750	12,040	1,222,790	176,574	-56,409	989,807	282,082	258,203	18,171	84,207	43,637
1992	1,574,445	1,204,947	13,060	1,218,007	172,426	-41,090	1,004,491	285,103	284,851	18,454	85,316	42,176
1993	1,640,894	1,251,714	13,214	1,264,928	181,554	-43,207	1,040,167	289,725	311,002	18,969	86,506	42,678
1994	1,724,984	1,328,882	11,345	1,340,227	192,804	-54,152	1,093,271	303,729	327,984	19,649	87,791	44,279
1995	1,795,948	1,372,206	10,264	1,382,470	198,976	-52,115	1,131,379	319,435	345,134	20,115	89,284	45,260
1996	1,869,179	1,411,803	8,959	1,420,762	197,846	-47,190	1,175,726	341,377	352,076	20,694	90,325	46,179
1997	1,941,944	1,438,446	7,117	1,445,563	192,889	-40,751	1,211,923	365,224	364,797	21,254	91,367	46,315
1998	2,037,000	1,507,223	7,488	1,514,711	200,348	-38,655	1,275,708	374,449	386,843	22,069	92,301	46,458
1999	2,132,570	1,589,674	7,662	1,597,336	205,288	-42,231	1,349,817	372,402	410,351	22,975	92,820	47,768
2000	2,223,877	1,645,205	4,851	1,650,056	218,063	-38,015	1,393,978	395,934	433,965	23,917	92,984	48,330
2001	2,349,155	1,691,118	4,953	1,696,071	226,888	-21,765	1,447,418	408,224	493,513	25,096	93,608	47,910
2002	2,358,662	1,676,647	3,646	1,680,293	222,756	4,955	1,462,492	372,721	523,449	25,006	94,325	46,430
2003	2,437,436	1,704,175	7,775	1,711,950	227,401	37,318	1,521,867	371,708	543,861	25,789	94,516	46,147
2004	2,562,359	1,771,010	7,318	1,778,328	239,378	86,596	1,625,546	377,559	559,254	26,819	95,541	46,412
2005	2,746,263	1,884,685	2,069	1,886,754	256,892	142,509	1,772,371	379,385	594,507	28,448	96,536	47,467
2006	2,946,347	1,961,359	-24	1,961,335	264,259	207,787	1,904,863	392,172	649,312	29,712	99,162	48,319
2007	3,242,834	2,119,911	-561	2,119,350	278,573	213,841	2,054,618	482,348	705,868	32,189	100,744	49,380
2008	3,419,215	2,135,266	1,175	2,136,441	278,159	206,246	2,064,528	545,189	809,498	33,625	101,688	48,587
2009	3,392,671	2,037,018	2,801	2,039,819	275,260	173,877	1,938,436	529,663	924,572	33,220	102,126	46,239
2010	3,602,219	2,299,669	4,283	2,303,952	298,240	89,271	2,094,983	510,032	997,204	35,194	102,353	45,873
2011	3,648,912	2,254,114	7,430	2,261,544	272,455	113,883	2,102,972	565,369	980,571	35,672	102,291	45,880
2012	3,836,823	2,436,240	6,886	2,443,126	279,672	90,206	2,253,660	587,405	995,758	37,746	101,649	45,861
2013	3,887,625	2,541,525	7,892	2,549,417	324,477	51,037	2,275,977	595,748	1,015,900	38,309	101,481	46,456
2014	4,058,007	2,635,232	6,928	2,642,160	340,938	10,311	2,311,533	654,791	1,091,683	39,869	101,784	48,218
2015	4,233,436	2,708,645	17,114	2,725,759	350,114	48,715	2,424,360	687,943	1,121,133	41,093	103,020	48,559
2016	4,367,097	2,693,033	17,678	2,710,711	353,345	133,774	2,491,140	694,934	1,181,023	41,688	104,756	48,801
2017	4,585,187	2,803,018	18,598	2,821,616	372,197	176,851	2,626,270	733,058	1,225,859	42,888	106,910	49,665
2018	4,885,518	4,863,228	22,290	2,953,378	387,601	212,283	2,778,060	847,286	1,260,172	44,923	108,752	50,667
2019	5,142,891	5,125,279	17,612	3,128,787	405,406	221,175	2,944,556	870,101	1,328,234	46,503	110,593	51,607

Personal Income and Employment by Area: Los Angeles-Long Beach-Anaheim, CA

(Thousands of dollars, except as noted.)

Year	Personal income, total	Derivation of personal income								Per capita personal income (dollars)	Population (persons)	Total employment
		Earnings by place of work			Less: Contributions for government social insurance	Plus: Adjustment for residence	Equals: Net earnings by place of residence	Plus: Dividends, interest, and rent	Plus: Personal current transfer receipts			
		Nonfarm	Farm	Total								
1970	42,898,309	35,477,189	66,565	35,543,754	2,395,587	-780,077	32,368,090	6,588,317	3,941,902	5,062	8,475,377	3,938,904
1971	44,962,023	36,759,101	64,606	36,823,707	2,548,382	-971,593	33,303,732	7,066,371	4,591,920	5,236	8,587,868	3,890,306
1972	48,982,924	40,567,852	78,966	40,646,818	2,973,135	-1,207,361	36,466,322	7,597,646	4,918,956	5,700	8,593,421	4,034,431
1973	53,179,424	44,483,547	94,016	44,577,563	3,757,828	-1,409,001	39,410,734	8,379,692	5,388,998	6,150	8,647,592	4,258,523
1974	58,755,856	48,584,652	111,613	48,696,265	4,214,122	-1,628,292	42,853,851	9,556,937	6,345,068	6,711	8,754,864	4,372,383
1975	64,589,683	52,389,382	102,827	52,492,209	4,418,812	-1,799,274	46,274,123	10,404,577	7,910,983	7,304	8,842,499	4,367,984
1976	71,531,619	58,791,328	124,366	58,915,694	5,066,226	-2,010,333	51,839,135	11,024,916	8,667,568	7,962	8,984,368	4,520,496
1977	79,408,612	66,386,922	139,889	66,526,811	5,818,748	-2,417,011	58,291,052	11,993,009	9,124,551	8,761	9,063,784	4,733,736
1978	90,398,475	76,611,969	133,347	76,745,316	6,892,751	-2,864,364	66,988,201	13,620,952	9,789,322	9,821	9,204,893	5,044,872
1979	102,138,575	87,340,061	187,217	87,527,278	8,234,187	-3,332,339	75,960,752	15,658,137	10,519,686	10,991	9,292,983	5,314,599
1980	115,300,613	96,965,793	267,554	97,233,347	8,975,819	-4,027,096	84,230,432	19,049,691	12,020,490	12,195	9,454,611	5,404,030
1981	129,996,980	107,551,171	228,530	107,779,701	10,795,659	-4,596,711	92,387,331	23,579,797	14,029,852	13,522	9,613,602	5,490,043
1982	138,320,599	112,998,736	253,341	113,252,077	11,580,792	-5,010,937	96,660,348	26,247,365	15,412,886	14,095	9,813,347	5,398,676
1983	148,472,241	121,526,229	310,139	121,836,368	12,641,973	-5,613,165	103,581,230	28,493,676	16,397,335	14,833	10,009,841	5,496,333
1984	164,224,282	135,345,465	318,906	135,664,371	14,595,207	-6,471,654	114,597,510	32,723,808	16,902,964	16,156	10,165,047	5,772,337
1985	177,250,747	147,249,103	316,614	147,565,717	16,037,576	-7,382,219	124,145,922	34,894,148	18,210,677	17,118	10,354,836	5,967,933
1986	189,742,328	159,613,704	301,198	159,914,902	17,526,767	-8,322,840	134,065,295	36,240,181	19,436,852	17,862	10,622,535	6,154,066
1987	204,800,735	176,172,958	299,373	176,472,331	19,283,345	-9,568,987	147,619,999	37,072,534	20,108,202	18,901	10,835,330	6,389,935
1988	220,419,002	191,114,270	325,423	191,439,693	21,470,922	-10,671,083	159,297,688	39,962,807	21,158,507	20,037	11,000,781	6,660,585
1989	233,985,898	200,934,238	345,310	201,279,548	22,709,207	-11,806,804	166,763,537	44,314,768	22,907,593	20,933	11,177,630	6,773,734
1990	251,230,793	214,141,690	377,725	214,519,415	23,982,890	-13,665,422	176,871,103	49,194,448	25,165,242	22,238	11,297,143	6,881,721
1991	255,593,617	216,050,544	310,597	216,361,141	24,281,688	-13,199,420	178,880,033	48,882,605	27,830,979	22,419	11,400,816	6,700,497
1992	267,793,738	223,782,190	277,269	224,059,459	24,789,754	-12,911,995	186,357,710	49,089,593	32,346,435	23,181	11,552,438	6,471,123
1993	270,571,376	224,582,107	282,541	224,864,648	24,834,589	-13,017,954	187,012,105	49,409,586	34,149,685	23,259	11,632,798	6,397,429
1994	277,469,993	228,868,687	274,942	229,143,629	25,480,488	-12,819,200	190,843,941	51,274,895	35,351,157	23,790	11,663,207	6,402,534
1995	289,416,398	235,778,197	319,223	236,097,420	25,913,590	-12,865,864	197,317,966	55,263,926	36,834,506	24,752	11,692,693	6,550,063
1996	306,055,522	247,567,022	323,988	247,891,010	26,499,315	-12,764,236	208,627,459	58,771,742	38,656,321	26,001	11,771,038	6,656,417
1997	323,174,030	262,890,272	364,919	263,255,191	27,831,330	-13,905,135	221,518,726	62,887,055	38,768,249	27,121	11,915,815	6,736,278
1998	352,331,421	285,689,526	411,870	286,101,396	29,795,724	-14,126,996	242,178,676	69,144,332	41,008,413	29,150	12,086,776	7,020,536
1999	369,840,604	303,490,236	441,804	303,932,040	31,532,370	-14,210,576	258,189,094	68,448,512	43,202,998	30,183	12,253,223	7,121,223
2000	395,435,615	324,205,955	463,293	324,669,248	33,580,848	-14,915,022	276,173,378	74,322,806	44,939,431	31,909	12,392,704	7,216,670
2001	411,089,020	335,106,592	393,286	335,499,878	35,406,470	-15,732,824	284,360,584	76,522,331	50,206,105	32,857	12,511,491	7,247,391
2002	422,127,291	345,691,801	410,526	346,102,327	36,949,442	-16,231,687	292,921,198	75,327,326	53,878,767	33,465	12,614,158	7,236,765
2003	444,643,741	363,596,204	459,087	364,055,291	39,073,582	-16,786,986	308,194,723	79,628,594	56,820,424	35,021	12,696,521	7,270,628
2004	472,850,183	391,538,637	418,917	391,957,554	42,807,245	-17,817,967	331,332,342	82,093,556	59,424,285	37,130	12,734,974	7,374,051
2005	504,577,166	409,449,610	420,858	409,870,468	44,577,221	-18,363,897	346,929,350	95,736,322	61,911,494	39,648	12,726,428	7,475,717
2006	544,864,016	433,798,266	461,093	434,259,359	45,773,250	-19,663,003	368,823,106	110,203,762	65,837,148	43,004	12,670,216	7,603,489
2007	562,606,706	442,605,230	389,672	442,994,902	46,280,539	-20,201,192	376,513,171	116,964,976	69,128,559	44,538	12,631,988	7,727,181
2008	570,770,452	437,980,026	382,779	438,362,805	46,930,801	-19,722,303	371,709,701	121,434,690	77,626,061	44,968	12,692,740	7,623,443
2009	549,632,542	417,950,448	355,998	418,306,446	45,012,876	-18,360,708	354,932,862	109,242,933	85,456,747	43,025	12,774,577	7,303,651
2010	578,117,602	437,376,022	304,215	437,680,237	45,346,180	-17,791,763	374,542,294	109,030,498	94,544,810	45,019	12,841,606	7,244,649
2011	616,258,336	460,760,318	259,221	461,019,539	42,582,559	-18,623,846	399,813,134	121,299,687	95,145,515	47,626	12,939,463	7,398,718
2012	663,033,578	490,250,757	312,332	490,563,089	44,145,559	-19,146,220	427,271,310	139,688,992	96,073,276	50,840	13,041,538	7,684,611
2013	661,003,474	500,355,905	309,113	500,665,018	51,140,613	-19,096,866	430,427,539	130,751,574	99,824,361	50,334	13,132,253	7,926,256
2014	704,229,720	521,767,622	294,123	522,061,745	53,651,996	-19,260,137	449,149,612	148,958,332	106,121,776	53,313	13,209,445	8,163,661
2015	753,843,484	548,560,601	309,493	548,870,094	56,317,041	-19,167,539	473,385,514	165,520,116	114,937,854	56,749	13,283,824	8,402,247
2016	776,513,342	565,461,860	271,931	565,733,791	58,189,070	-20,957,139	486,587,582	171,027,001	118,898,759	58,261	13,328,261	8,563,547
2017	802,394,129	589,617,982	323,401	589,941,383	60,421,289	-23,240,756	506,279,338	179,372,675	116,742,116	60,087	13,353,907	8,691,132
2018	846,486,801	846,295,746	191,055	610,729,194	63,533,420	-22,752,206	524,443,568	197,840,606	124,202,627	63,886	13,249,879	8,850,436
2019	881,215,471	880,958,915	256,556	638,104,274	66,416,741	-23,383,284	548,304,249	200,961,106	131,950,116	66,684	13,214,799	9,027,619

Personal Income and Employment by Area: Louisville/Jefferson County, KY-IN

(Thousands of dollars, except as noted.)

Year	Personal income, total	Earnings by place of work			Less: Contributions for government social insurance	Plus: Adjustment for residence	Equals: Net earnings by place of residence	Plus: Dividends, interest, and rent	Plus: Personal current transfer receipts	Per capita personal income (dollars)	Population (persons)	Total employment
		Nonfarm	Farm	Total								
1970	3,820,968	3,210,852	41,471	3,252,323	223,314	-15,020	3,013,989	514,798	292,181	3,952	966,908	446,276
1971	4,099,843	3,407,887	43,840	3,451,727	244,722	-19,594	3,187,411	561,297	351,135	4,179	981,174	447,479
1972	4,508,151	3,780,800	48,027	3,828,827	287,478	-28,832	3,512,517	604,240	391,394	4,581	983,998	459,721
1973	5,033,586	4,243,437	60,149	4,303,586	371,632	-39,444	3,892,510	676,659	464,417	5,051	996,523	481,524
1974	5,517,618	4,565,353	68,263	4,633,616	413,747	-42,322	4,177,547	781,863	558,208	5,488	1,005,432	489,621
1975	5,890,816	4,716,300	54,950	4,771,250	417,596	-40,599	4,313,055	851,949	725,812	5,839	1,008,789	470,167
1976	6,474,476	5,228,719	60,122	5,288,841	471,191	-42,715	4,774,935	918,284	781,257	6,387	1,013,771	477,680
1977	7,202,842	5,887,979	63,950	5,951,929	529,935	-46,334	5,375,660	1,023,914	803,268	7,092	1,015,639	494,112
1978	8,026,281	6,636,639	50,516	6,687,155	611,688	-47,391	6,028,076	1,139,236	858,969	7,848	1,022,668	516,166
1979	8,847,180	7,265,633	50,623	7,316,256	693,242	-53,509	6,569,505	1,289,908	987,767	8,615	1,026,904	521,237
1980	9,692,544	7,656,435	48,608	7,705,043	729,738	-56,205	6,919,100	1,564,468	1,208,976	9,463	1,024,218	512,145
1981	10,739,846	8,252,131	76,117	8,328,248	846,518	-56,407	7,425,323	1,948,854	1,365,669	10,494	1,023,428	508,363
1982	11,361,296	8,384,560	89,059	8,473,619	875,073	-39,711	7,558,835	2,288,755	1,513,706	11,081	1,025,301	492,030
1983	12,019,904	8,933,007	33,528	8,966,535	938,500	-43,763	7,984,272	2,421,827	1,613,805	11,732	1,024,512	493,381
1984	13,210,185	9,817,215	118,551	9,935,766	1,055,205	-66,247	8,814,314	2,714,697	1,681,174	12,917	1,022,721	509,674
1985	13,909,034	10,346,913	112,848	10,459,761	1,128,342	-74,391	9,257,028	2,874,790	1,777,216	13,623	1,020,967	518,551
1986	14,572,810	10,854,795	103,562	10,958,357	1,220,063	-78,143	9,660,151	3,036,733	1,875,926	14,288	1,019,913	531,916
1987	15,387,719	11,580,569	117,671	11,698,240	1,295,341	-85,145	10,317,754	3,134,253	1,935,712	15,080	1,020,403	543,749
1988	16,822,610	12,740,405	119,520	12,859,925	1,441,135	-95,761	11,323,029	3,442,498	2,057,083	16,498	1,019,654	564,610
1989	18,142,144	13,542,935	196,800	13,739,735	1,537,577	-94,984	12,107,174	3,774,370	2,260,600	17,770	1,020,953	577,251
1990	19,238,493	14,310,534	172,686	14,483,220	1,677,135	-77,982	12,728,103	4,052,750	2,457,640	18,761	1,025,448	592,058
1991	20,031,421	14,856,420	156,551	15,012,971	1,766,056	-91,107	13,155,808	4,140,587	2,735,026	19,343	1,035,577	589,956
1992	21,577,444	16,145,247	113,191	16,258,438	1,907,344	-115,525	14,235,569	4,339,547	3,002,328	20,630	1,045,950	600,441
1993	22,572,958	17,042,715	98,241	17,140,956	2,032,341	-149,039	14,959,576	4,482,863	3,130,519	21,357	1,056,941	616,676
1994	23,772,055	18,049,131	87,372	18,136,503	2,192,088	-183,399	15,761,016	4,733,291	3,277,748	22,287	1,066,643	634,530
1995	25,110,941	18,961,179	45,519	19,006,698	2,305,462	-198,180	16,503,056	5,124,932	3,482,953	23,323	1,076,646	655,893
1996	26,485,862	19,820,478	74,027	19,894,505	2,389,301	-222,010	17,283,194	5,516,437	3,686,231	24,406	1,085,228	665,467
1997	27,924,269	20,962,239	58,311	21,020,550	2,516,575	-244,469	18,259,506	5,788,166	3,876,597	25,525	1,094,013	681,426
1998	30,200,622	22,842,487	60,053	22,902,540	2,716,538	-298,344	19,887,658	6,345,156	3,967,808	27,384	1,102,866	695,896
1999	31,527,372	24,447,025	28,393	24,475,418	2,909,034	-362,979	21,203,405	6,258,923	4,065,044	28,306	1,113,813	709,867
2000	33,826,855	26,048,880	89,719	26,138,599	3,014,456	-420,662	22,703,481	6,762,394	4,360,980	30,093	1,124,086	724,376
2001	34,768,474	26,878,613	72,425	26,951,038	3,110,115	-448,966	23,391,957	6,623,412	4,753,105	30,709	1,132,204	717,887
2002	35,421,803	27,345,829	30,827	27,376,656	3,176,340	-453,176	23,747,140	6,575,706	5,098,957	31,064	1,140,281	708,895
2003	36,295,360	28,190,063	57,267	28,247,330	3,247,029	-440,600	24,559,701	6,459,861	5,275,798	31,514	1,151,726	707,763
2004	38,347,565	29,939,661	85,638	30,025,299	3,397,780	-461,166	26,166,353	6,555,625	5,625,587	33,004	1,161,921	715,855
2005	39,815,047	30,814,169	49,689	30,863,858	3,505,103	-474,615	26,884,140	6,921,281	6,009,626	33,954	1,172,611	728,041
2006	42,597,029	32,165,983	47,511	32,213,494	3,690,237	-433,057	28,090,200	8,060,572	6,446,257	35,881	1,187,190	742,303
2007	44,418,350	33,386,736	43,947	33,430,683	3,868,527	-466,287	29,095,869	8,401,915	6,920,566	36,932	1,202,720	756,832
2008	45,572,211	33,404,954	40,619	33,445,573	3,952,351	-386,394	29,106,828	8,601,941	7,863,442	37,451	1,216,853	753,045
2009	44,546,332	32,576,903	29,306	32,606,209	3,899,426	-408,529	28,298,254	7,541,847	8,706,231	36,277	1,227,965	729,252
2010	46,459,792	33,711,648	23,625	33,735,273	3,965,144	-189,921	29,580,208	7,576,349	9,303,235	37,541	1,237,565	725,159
2011	49,006,807	35,239,961	59,947	35,299,908	3,648,132	6,568	31,658,344	7,916,446	9,432,017	39,379	1,244,490	735,122
2012	52,274,407	37,344,272	61,978	37,406,250	3,844,165	-233,150	33,328,935	9,438,832	9,506,640	41,741	1,252,357	749,870
2013	51,901,058	38,191,830	206,611	38,398,441	4,477,062	-272,350	33,649,029	8,579,889	9,672,140	41,085	1,263,269	764,439
2014	54,519,294	39,835,249	114,309	39,949,558	4,701,187	-406,142	34,842,229	9,234,333	10,442,732	42,896	1,270,951	781,884
2015	57,520,720	42,146,476	85,376	42,231,852	5,004,786	-609,091	36,617,975	9,915,502	10,987,243	45,009	1,277,992	800,429
2016	59,059,169	43,799,141	39,723	43,838,864	5,183,168	-839,427	37,816,269	10,091,985	11,150,915	45,966	1,284,848	817,970
2017	61,196,779	45,507,282	22,222	45,529,504	5,351,554	-954,557	39,223,393	10,476,323	11,497,063	47,294	1,293,953	827,588
2018	63,652,743	63,599,537	53,206	46,941,165	5,512,416	-1,174,366	40,254,383	11,878,263	11,520,097	50,437	1,262,023	828,689
2019	65,954,660	65,910,766	43,894	49,002,013	5,725,010	-1,308,728	41,968,275	11,965,540	12,020,845	52,134	1,265,108	837,815

Personal Income and Employment by Area: Lubbock, TX

(Thousands of dollars, except as noted.)

Year	Personal income, total	Earnings by place of work Nonfarm	Farm	Total	Less: Contributions for government social insurance	Plus: Adjustment for residence	Equals: Net earnings by place of residence	Plus: Dividends, interest, and rent	Plus: Personal current transfer receipts	Per capita personal income (dollars)	Population (persons)	Total employment
1970	727,087	533,818	72,755	606,573	32,937	-1,711	571,925	109,849	45,313	3,665	198,372	89,704
1971	744,276	572,888	36,994	609,882	36,625	-1,626	571,631	119,421	53,224	3,657	203,502	90,946
1972	836,301	646,093	42,473	688,566	43,026	-2,402	643,138	132,929	60,234	3,980	210,117	96,524
1973	1,017,162	726,950	128,140	855,090	56,164	-3,917	795,009	149,038	73,115	4,840	210,167	102,204
1974	1,062,522	835,745	39,322	875,067	66,753	-5,234	803,080	174,571	84,871	4,970	213,786	106,461
1975	1,163,883	919,912	16,898	936,810	72,294	-5,652	858,864	200,995	104,024	5,385	216,123	107,353
1976	1,353,581	1,049,798	64,733	1,114,531	84,120	-6,996	1,023,415	217,755	112,411	6,204	218,179	112,458
1977	1,533,010	1,183,170	91,656	1,274,826	95,619	-9,115	1,170,092	243,382	119,536	6,923	221,434	118,015
1978	1,686,400	1,336,251	61,042	1,397,293	110,060	-10,588	1,276,645	275,371	134,384	7,496	224,976	121,963
1979	1,900,130	1,497,212	76,650	1,573,862	129,659	-13,776	1,430,427	313,220	156,483	8,366	227,137	122,321
1980	2,085,251	1,661,255	23,238	1,684,493	145,428	-13,303	1,525,762	377,589	181,900	9,084	229,562	124,241
1981	2,415,914	1,793,157	128,361	1,921,518	168,020	-12,483	1,741,015	467,131	207,768	10,473	230,672	124,379
1982	2,574,425	1,919,228	53,595	1,972,823	181,998	-9,493	1,781,332	559,917	233,176	11,073	232,493	125,658
1983	2,844,144	2,101,300	79,715	2,181,015	197,026	-13,552	1,970,437	611,971	261,736	12,059	235,862	126,896
1984	2,965,254	2,170,234	66,769	2,237,003	205,249	-7,688	2,024,066	655,748	285,440	12,496	237,294	126,165
1985	3,141,737	2,295,354	59,799	2,355,153	219,087	-7,907	2,128,159	703,964	309,614	13,341	235,499	127,720
1986	3,189,005	2,348,151	34,368	2,382,519	222,947	-12,273	2,147,299	703,746	337,960	13,517	235,917	125,110
1987	3,321,960	2,343,976	142,163	2,486,139	222,187	-1,761	2,262,191	694,152	365,617	14,110	235,440	129,492
1988	3,511,268	2,519,661	145,844	2,665,505	247,887	-3,960	2,413,658	707,229	390,381	14,854	236,385	131,935
1989	3,645,095	2,625,134	79,322	2,704,456	262,524	-9,791	2,432,141	780,941	432,013	15,368	237,184	131,633
1990	3,912,018	2,825,466	131,118	2,956,584	277,252	-2,107	2,677,225	751,537	483,256	16,493	237,193	134,323
1991	3,987,165	2,957,733	47,069	3,004,802	296,464	-2,744	2,705,594	747,148	534,423	16,642	239,584	135,650
1992	4,275,318	3,105,408	115,664	3,221,072	308,706	-13,049	2,899,317	741,036	634,965	17,727	241,180	134,968
1993	4,545,047	3,288,856	169,934	3,458,790	326,178	-15,083	3,117,529	757,158	670,360	18,543	245,109	139,393
1994	4,781,209	3,489,819	134,153	3,623,972	349,420	-19,007	3,255,545	796,812	728,852	19,162	249,516	141,802
1995	4,980,851	3,614,435	91,851	3,706,286	364,715	-24,753	3,316,818	876,686	787,347	19,750	252,199	146,373
1996	5,289,323	3,790,123	139,585	3,929,708	378,064	-29,956	3,521,688	920,233	847,402	20,861	253,555	147,374
1997	5,495,428	3,981,279	128,863	4,110,142	393,844	-32,856	3,683,442	926,176	885,810	21,620	254,178	150,419
1998	5,733,007	4,295,901	74,900	4,370,801	416,963	-41,369	3,912,469	985,657	834,881	22,615	253,502	151,104
1999	5,863,078	4,421,911	90,276	4,512,187	423,366	-45,919	4,042,902	951,836	868,340	23,037	254,507	151,946
2000	6,212,215	4,727,713	41,836	4,769,549	448,345	-55,290	4,265,914	1,026,936	919,365	24,205	256,651	155,675
2001	6,360,822	4,786,222	56,871	4,843,093	462,169	-55,594	4,325,330	1,039,187	996,305	24,463	260,015	157,772
2002	6,578,907	5,005,602	54,939	5,060,541	483,543	-70,120	4,506,878	998,135	1,073,894	25,045	262,680	157,232
2003	6,910,957	5,102,812	122,685	5,225,497	503,852	-70,375	4,651,270	1,109,310	1,150,377	25,948	266,338	156,117
2004	7,118,928	5,299,307	188,937	5,488,244	524,237	-68,313	4,895,694	1,026,498	1,196,736	26,517	268,466	158,613
2005	7,565,753	5,530,920	208,504	5,739,424	549,042	-81,516	5,108,866	1,147,360	1,309,527	27,972	270,478	161,147
2006	7,969,996	5,951,019	75,091	6,026,110	579,446	-81,696	5,364,968	1,193,190	1,411,838	29,043	274,419	164,127
2007	8,462,188	6,037,602	175,498	6,213,100	597,360	-73,564	5,542,176	1,389,128	1,530,884	30,498	277,466	166,211
2008	8,997,953	6,334,375	19,897	6,354,272	626,444	-34,914	5,692,914	1,607,795	1,697,244	32,099	280,321	170,038
2009	9,184,854	6,463,646	62,578	6,526,224	646,478	-24,654	5,855,092	1,496,959	1,832,803	32,088	286,236	170,816
2010	9,842,853	6,811,601	168,216	6,979,817	671,532	17,525	6,325,810	1,514,166	2,002,877	33,682	292,226	170,484
2011	10,233,804	7,005,551	-12,165	6,993,386	611,302	96,098	6,478,182	1,675,608	2,080,014	34,654	295,315	174,057
2012	10,850,165	7,362,736	-32,413	7,330,323	639,497	191,690	6,882,516	1,915,155	2,052,494	36,422	297,902	176,461
2013	11,266,727	7,722,698	204,378	7,927,076	752,799	235,416	7,409,693	1,745,163	2,111,871	37,399	301,258	181,110
2014	11,779,958	8,152,293	-28,712	8,123,581	792,218	280,536	7,611,899	1,959,250	2,208,809	38,467	306,233	184,432
2015	12,220,091	8,460,692	3,797	8,464,489	833,748	232,289	7,863,030	2,018,429	2,338,632	39,404	310,125	188,201
2016	12,535,691	8,607,764	-51,849	8,555,915	865,261	153,733	7,844,387	2,245,850	2,445,454	39,921	314,013	193,632
2017	13,053,322	8,897,205	8,067	8,905,272	906,549	206,498	8,205,221	2,356,570	2,491,531	41,180	316,983	196,607
2018	13,680,735	13,651,312	29,423	9,356,584	944,652	241,847	8,653,779	2,421,983	2,604,973	42,854	319,239	200,917
2019	14,233,889	14,197,667	36,222	9,743,235	977,007	266,116	9,032,344	2,477,882	2,723,663	44,169	322,257	204,363

Personal Income and Employment by Area: Lynchburg, VA

(Thousands of dollars, except as noted.)

Year	Personal income, total	Earnings by place of work			Less: Contributions for government social insurance	Plus: Adjustment for residence	Equals: Net earnings by place of residence	Plus: Dividends, interest, and rent	Plus: Personal current transfer receipts	Per capita personal income (dollars)	Population (persons)	Total employment
		Nonfarm	Farm	Total								
1970............	547,509	472,206	9,319	481,525	31,116	-26,330	424,079	75,244	48,186	3,289	166,469	79,441
1971............	587,464	504,460	8,535	512,995	34,589	-30,739	447,667	82,670	57,127	3,428	171,359	79,326
1972............	657,724	575,398	9,656	585,054	41,585	-40,432	503,037	90,628	64,059	3,764	174,732	82,093
1973............	737,153	644,213	13,386	657,599	53,726	-45,041	558,832	103,314	75,007	4,177	176,483	86,237
1974............	823,007	714,378	13,987	728,365	61,975	-51,373	615,017	119,232	88,758	4,617	178,257	88,455
1975............	894,903	745,675	7,790	753,465	62,991	-42,580	647,894	128,750	118,259	4,856	184,275	85,436
1976............	1,004,788	846,797	6,035	852,832	72,634	-45,667	734,531	141,546	128,711	5,418	185,470	89,082
1977............	1,121,386	945,660	3,417	949,077	81,181	-47,207	820,689	159,905	140,792	6,006	186,723	91,298
1978............	1,275,770	1,083,347	4,841	1,088,188	95,045	-55,066	938,077	180,566	157,127	6,672	191,211	95,509
1979............	1,443,773	1,223,282	5,991	1,229,273	111,791	-61,112	1,056,370	207,533	179,870	7,448	193,855	99,044
1980............	1,607,090	1,308,883	1,023	1,309,906	119,808	-63,517	1,126,581	260,030	220,479	8,257	194,636	97,473
1981............	1,782,308	1,400,922	3,913	1,404,835	138,455	-64,800	1,201,580	323,711	257,017	9,089	196,102	96,671
1982............	1,900,788	1,440,062	-3,295	1,436,767	144,672	-54,140	1,237,955	375,113	287,720	9,641	197,158	95,302
1983............	2,070,894	1,552,528	953	1,553,481	158,174	-45,584	1,349,723	407,473	313,698	10,506	197,122	95,745
1984............	2,297,990	1,720,334	3,257	1,723,591	180,864	-38,718	1,504,009	464,211	329,770	11,591	198,260	99,984
1985............	2,455,570	1,816,934	803	1,817,737	194,439	-22,129	1,601,169	492,838	361,563	12,335	199,074	102,302
1986............	2,622,256	1,938,447	916	1,939,363	213,488	-9,377	1,716,498	514,591	391,167	13,086	200,383	103,804
1987............	2,843,193	2,088,859	7,842	2,096,701	227,523	5,716	1,874,894	551,001	417,298	14,111	201,487	108,094
1988............	3,061,488	2,221,508	8,971	2,230,479	248,829	20,049	2,001,699	612,306	447,483	15,069	203,166	109,641
1989............	3,347,570	2,371,309	13,715	2,385,024	268,223	37,284	2,154,085	715,677	477,808	16,345	204,803	112,967
1990............	3,502,166	2,499,655	14,603	2,514,258	284,313	57,530	2,287,475	703,874	510,817	16,926	206,913	115,259
1991............	3,607,438	2,569,006	11,071	2,580,077	295,244	62,796	2,347,629	715,862	543,947	17,263	208,971	114,238
1992............	3,827,638	2,704,000	12,641	2,716,641	306,734	77,106	2,487,013	732,444	608,181	17,980	212,888	114,404
1993............	4,051,149	2,899,911	5,357	2,905,268	329,660	87,355	2,662,963	764,715	623,471	18,852	214,890	117,353
1994............	4,257,699	3,049,551	9,034	3,058,585	346,479	98,953	2,811,059	791,578	655,062	19,555	217,728	120,192
1995............	4,443,256	3,134,649	4,530	3,139,179	355,677	115,837	2,899,339	839,154	704,763	20,232	219,612	122,217
1996............	4,638,387	3,237,784	3,755	3,241,539	365,273	128,260	3,004,526	893,201	740,660	20,906	221,872	123,775
1997............	4,863,143	3,419,938	685	3,420,623	382,495	141,842	3,179,970	917,232	765,941	21,695	224,156	125,140
1998............	5,176,217	3,632,268	3,828	3,636,096	400,557	164,647	3,400,186	973,197	802,834	22,937	225,675	125,567
1999............	5,454,843	3,888,300	-1,754	3,886,546	426,803	178,118	3,637,861	962,673	854,309	23,995	227,337	128,961
2000............	5,812,484	4,082,567	10,769	4,093,336	440,851	201,019	3,853,504	1,044,307	914,673	25,398	228,855	131,133
2001............	5,954,674	4,076,674	2,414	4,079,088	459,821	205,875	3,825,142	1,103,844	1,025,688	25,946	229,499	127,137
2002............	6,028,551	4,093,841	-735	4,093,106	464,589	213,318	3,841,835	1,098,583	1,088,133	26,171	230,356	124,534
2003............	6,261,364	4,247,204	-9,139	4,238,065	479,313	210,407	3,969,159	1,126,959	1,165,246	26,915	232,634	124,264
2004............	6,566,045	4,461,839	-3,069	4,458,770	511,258	216,780	4,164,292	1,178,666	1,223,087	27,991	234,574	126,419
2005............	6,897,237	4,722,203	-3,847	4,718,356	549,814	220,808	4,389,350	1,197,688	1,310,199	28,917	238,515	129,811
2006............	7,386,182	4,982,359	-22,382	4,959,977	586,604	221,873	4,595,246	1,332,786	1,458,150	30,369	243,213	132,755
2007............	7,765,971	5,196,334	-24,411	5,171,923	612,007	226,100	4,786,016	1,428,356	1,551,599	31,463	246,827	135,949
2008............	8,186,108	5,324,766	-18,623	5,306,143	633,480	228,366	4,901,029	1,507,688	1,777,391	32,837	249,299	137,054
2009............	8,095,004	5,231,608	-14,073	5,217,535	626,489	225,774	4,816,820	1,355,211	1,922,973	32,194	251,441	133,014
2010............	8,322,933	5,341,561	-12,865	5,328,696	639,615	223,559	4,912,640	1,319,542	2,090,751	32,897	253,000	131,504
2011............	8,687,118	5,385,589	-5,481	5,380,108	581,406	242,927	5,041,629	1,442,454	2,203,035	34,177	254,183	131,578
2012............	9,018,392	5,551,968	18	5,551,986	592,346	257,466	5,217,106	1,619,430	2,181,856	35,289	255,555	132,229
2013............	9,015,579	5,641,137	-4,205	5,636,932	685,063	258,756	5,210,625	1,546,616	2,258,338	35,114	256,752	132,785
2014............	9,401,809	5,818,916	-4,517	5,814,399	704,432	260,476	5,370,443	1,709,272	2,322,094	36,469	257,802	134,280
2015............	9,747,090	5,968,281	-4,050	5,964,231	721,248	288,046	5,531,029	1,789,783	2,426,278	37,623	259,072	135,079
2016............	9,763,714	5,919,645	-18,431	5,901,214	726,487	283,577	5,458,304	1,781,845	2,523,565	37,539	260,092	135,161
2017............	10,073,918	6,119,105	-27,865	6,091,240	758,582	278,462	5,611,120	1,863,591	2,599,207	38,560	261,254	136,125
2018............	10,619,217	10,638,351	-19,134	6,352,445	790,395	288,822	5,850,872	2,079,923	2,688,422	40,394	262,893	138,984
2019............	10,875,932	10,889,101	-13,169	6,490,596	809,809	298,878	5,979,665	2,094,700	2,801,567	41,265	263,566	140,395

Personal Income and Employment by Area: Macon-Bibb County, GA

(Thousands of dollars, except as noted.)

Year	Personal income, total	Earnings by place of work			Less: Contributions for government social insurance	Plus: Adjustment for residence	Equals: Net earnings by place of residence	Plus: Dividends, interest, and rent	Plus: Personal current transfer receipts	Per capita personal income (dollars)	Population (persons)	Total employment
		Nonfarm	Farm	Total								
1970	664,522	453,972	5,480	459,452	29,751	92,391	522,092	84,817	57,613	3,667	181,228	78,317
1971	732,150	495,189	6,314	501,503	33,500	98,912	566,915	96,346	68,889	3,940	185,839	79,907
1972	795,018	545,837	6,403	552,240	38,739	98,209	611,710	104,987	78,321	4,219	188,436	81,664
1973	856,424	596,161	9,270	605,431	48,637	95,145	651,939	116,182	88,303	4,539	188,667	83,070
1974	945,818	663,483	6,565	670,048	56,266	92,922	706,704	131,618	107,496	4,996	189,318	85,187
1975	1,047,179	726,728	6,406	733,134	60,628	92,610	765,116	146,321	135,742	5,458	191,852	85,941
1976	1,138,426	803,285	7,557	810,842	68,332	90,120	832,630	157,814	147,982	5,921	192,268	87,195
1977	1,231,221	870,916	5,885	876,801	73,582	98,538	901,757	175,529	153,935	6,292	195,693	87,585
1978	1,341,220	959,621	7,626	967,247	83,090	95,486	979,643	195,696	165,881	6,790	197,518	88,125
1979	1,488,345	1,082,640	8,213	1,090,853	97,897	89,177	1,082,133	218,651	187,561	7,497	198,531	89,341
1980	1,660,351	1,211,020	3,215	1,214,235	109,783	73,345	1,177,797	261,796	220,758	8,351	198,810	91,031
1981	1,876,514	1,335,345	4,189	1,339,534	130,634	97,210	1,306,110	319,994	250,410	9,395	199,746	91,575
1982	2,012,774	1,414,743	6,712	1,421,455	140,826	100,751	1,381,380	360,862	270,532	10,020	200,885	91,762
1983	2,165,903	1,528,127	4,380	1,532,507	152,985	94,033	1,473,555	396,771	295,577	10,699	202,440	92,018
1984	2,377,497	1,699,389	7,142	1,706,531	175,195	89,478	1,620,814	443,478	313,205	11,684	203,490	95,941
1985	2,528,505	1,826,714	7,939	1,834,653	192,199	82,643	1,725,097	466,087	337,321	12,376	204,300	97,593
1986	2,694,161	1,981,740	8,443	1,990,183	210,655	58,584	1,838,112	497,780	358,269	13,182	204,377	99,644
1987	2,875,064	2,151,765	11,064	2,162,829	226,332	24,200	1,960,697	536,591	377,776	14,022	205,043	101,989
1988	3,106,124	2,330,908	15,057	2,345,965	253,819	10,072	2,102,218	588,240	415,666	15,071	206,097	105,223
1989	3,343,748	2,457,819	17,966	2,475,785	268,615	7,373	2,214,543	680,778	448,427	16,169	206,803	106,740
1990	3,482,850	2,596,757	19,002	2,615,759	282,424	-43,720	2,289,615	702,885	490,350	16,810	207,190	108,636
1991	3,654,861	2,687,702	20,952	2,708,654	296,447	-50,100	2,362,107	725,171	567,583	17,457	209,358	106,541
1992	3,890,153	2,877,444	20,696	2,898,140	313,038	-39,517	2,545,585	718,749	625,819	18,462	210,716	107,456
1993	4,057,527	2,987,869	23,445	3,011,314	326,647	-48,346	2,636,321	752,831	668,375	19,005	213,497	111,132
1994	4,297,360	3,162,059	24,655	3,186,714	347,432	-63,202	2,776,080	803,057	718,223	19,949	215,416	113,744
1995	4,600,725	3,375,736	19,344	3,395,080	370,203	-54,567	2,970,310	877,075	753,340	21,204	216,979	118,082
1996	4,920,854	3,544,448	16,840	3,561,288	389,881	21,561	3,192,968	928,317	799,569	22,500	218,702	121,131
1997	5,077,295	3,728,143	17,764	3,745,907	408,023	-41,540	3,296,344	958,307	822,644	22,989	220,860	122,871
1998	5,370,462	3,943,828	20,479	3,964,307	424,429	-15,330	3,524,548	1,019,037	826,877	24,220	221,736	123,933
1999	5,549,852	4,124,315	26,541	4,150,856	439,740	-5,875	3,705,241	982,563	862,048	24,995	222,038	125,300
2000	5,814,628	4,202,019	23,909	4,225,928	446,287	39,601	3,819,242	1,078,915	916,471	26,144	222,407	126,496
2001	5,942,982	4,254,559	30,298	4,284,857	453,101	31,819	3,863,575	1,099,987	979,420	26,666	222,869	123,568
2002	6,215,050	4,383,081	21,429	4,404,510	467,972	44,320	3,980,858	1,107,263	1,126,929	27,664	224,661	123,274
2003	6,309,802	4,499,838	23,474	4,523,312	476,836	50,319	4,096,795	1,079,418	1,133,589	27,921	225,987	124,397
2004	6,530,719	4,731,513	26,653	4,758,166	512,874	691	4,245,983	1,090,907	1,193,829	28,720	227,394	126,769
2005	6,753,429	4,819,841	29,114	4,848,955	521,900	16,815	4,343,870	1,110,244	1,299,315	29,604	228,125	127,960
2006	7,041,408	4,989,215	14,252	5,003,467	541,999	-12,653	4,448,815	1,209,257	1,383,336	30,661	229,655	128,869
2007	7,256,296	4,922,460	18,251	4,940,711	535,592	43,722	4,448,841	1,321,842	1,485,613	31,487	230,452	129,865
2008	7,488,157	5,063,461	23,856	5,087,317	577,014	-27,403	4,482,900	1,344,295	1,660,962	32,372	231,314	131,938
2009	7,404,462	5,010,777	22,412	5,033,189	569,045	-89,449	4,374,695	1,247,356	1,782,411	31,907	232,065	126,729
2010	7,591,169	5,106,356	22,642	5,128,998	576,797	-108,725	4,443,476	1,210,497	1,937,196	32,689	232,223	126,182
2011	8,010,419	5,242,544	30,142	5,272,686	523,424	-152,787	4,596,475	1,415,284	1,998,660	34,420	232,728	128,211
2012	7,927,873	5,363,273	40,534	5,403,807	535,248	-242,067	4,626,492	1,330,164	1,971,217	34,051	232,823	129,506
2013	7,986,539	5,561,492	45,220	5,606,712	628,231	-325,246	4,653,235	1,330,885	2,002,419	34,530	231,290	130,171
2014	8,348,121	5,816,744	45,570	5,862,314	650,315	-384,287	4,827,712	1,436,762	2,083,647	36,210	230,547	133,172
2015	8,654,169	6,048,060	51,633	6,099,693	675,255	-466,391	4,958,047	1,538,709	2,157,413	37,640	229,919	135,132
2016	8,765,972	6,082,197	42,288	6,124,485	679,589	-442,435	5,002,461	1,539,403	2,224,108	38,252	229,163	133,820
2017	9,033,001	6,278,257	43,010	6,321,267	703,533	-495,516	5,122,218	1,600,122	2,310,661	39,460	228,914	135,342
2018	9,405,674	9,382,196	23,478	6,478,469	730,412	-505,993	5,242,064	1,800,729	2,362,881	40,967	229,594	138,325
2019	9,703,865	9,689,365	14,500	6,653,731	751,502	-487,150	5,415,079	1,816,924	2,471,862	42,191	229,996	139,879

Personal Income and Employment by Area: Madera, CA

(Thousands of dollars, except as noted.)

Year	Personal income, total	Derivation of personal income									Per capita personal income (dollars)	Population (persons)	Total employment
		Earnings by place of work			Less: Contributions for government social insurance	Plus: Adjustment for residence	Equals: Net earnings by place of residence	Plus: Dividends, interest, and rent	Plus: Personal current transfer receipts				
		Nonfarm	Farm	Total									
1970	157,504	77,600	31,793	109,393	5,536	4,117	107,974	24,016	25,514		3,776	41,707	16,486
1971	172,911	87,734	31,328	119,062	6,478	5,925	118,509	26,382	28,020		4,044	42,754	17,136
1972	203,344	101,333	42,466	143,799	7,799	8,456	144,456	30,122	28,766		4,705	43,223	18,531
1973	252,612	114,738	67,670	182,408	10,095	11,556	183,869	36,730	32,013		5,682	44,458	19,251
1974	288,523	129,786	76,193	205,979	11,862	14,683	208,800	41,798	37,925		6,263	46,071	20,413
1975	303,984	147,138	57,037	204,175	13,043	16,991	208,123	48,018	47,843		6,344	47,917	21,108
1976	351,479	169,492	69,799	239,291	15,238	21,020	245,073	52,088	54,318		7,072	49,699	22,320
1977	404,651	192,466	84,098	276,564	17,549	26,612	285,627	59,394	59,630		7,667	52,777	23,161
1978	443,859	224,422	68,117	292,539	20,658	34,823	306,704	71,974	65,181		7,963	55,741	24,123
1979	599,802	271,185	149,895	421,080	25,567	43,401	438,914	88,157	72,731		9,969	60,169	26,794
1980	679,239	296,759	158,035	454,794	27,387	51,617	479,024	112,352	87,863		10,620	63,961	27,854
1981	665,972	318,383	81,551	399,934	31,941	56,724	424,717	135,973	105,282		9,908	67,214	28,249
1982	687,423	324,111	77,066	401,177	33,232	59,124	427,069	147,097	113,257		9,928	69,240	28,791
1983	699,323	351,466	40,329	391,795	36,685	63,411	418,521	156,285	124,517		9,780	71,504	30,018
1984	780,203	394,232	59,288	453,520	42,339	69,856	481,037	169,759	129,407		10,688	72,996	29,837
1985	830,324	423,961	53,885	477,846	46,061	74,742	506,527	175,251	148,546		11,054	75,118	30,233
1986	922,147	471,010	78,828	549,838	51,630	78,322	576,530	183,283	162,334		11,982	76,960	30,149
1987	1,049,058	540,669	125,140	665,809	59,764	81,084	687,129	193,015	168,914		13,279	79,003	32,257
1988	1,133,911	585,973	120,682	706,655	67,278	89,250	728,627	212,196	193,088		13,868	81,762	33,655
1989	1,222,046	615,483	111,293	726,776	71,317	109,158	764,617	247,460	209,969		14,411	84,797	34,542
1990	1,330,613	679,841	111,716	791,557	77,542	121,671	835,686	263,111	231,816		14,930	89,125	35,423
1991	1,418,479	762,409	90,776	853,185	87,066	120,407	886,526	265,164	266,789		14,936	94,973	38,461
1992	1,602,982	826,780	164,280	991,060	94,001	121,154	1,018,213	270,847	313,922		16,105	99,536	38,949
1993	1,665,036	886,417	129,811	1,016,228	99,760	124,899	1,041,367	284,026	339,643		16,004	104,039	39,682
1994	1,700,029	940,685	94,313	1,034,998	105,318	125,166	1,054,846	300,134	345,049		15,830	107,396	41,256
1995	1,729,154	955,518	66,891	1,022,409	108,669	124,663	1,038,403	323,595	367,156		15,820	109,300	44,780
1996	1,886,968	998,930	136,248	1,135,178	109,957	122,880	1,148,101	344,145	394,722		16,678	113,143	46,793
1997	2,030,119	1,091,316	176,901	1,268,217	116,813	116,193	1,267,597	362,920	399,602		17,435	116,442	48,055
1998	2,130,181	1,240,423	91,598	1,332,021	128,752	109,005	1,312,274	391,777	426,130		17,879	119,143	52,112
1999	2,250,425	1,303,914	131,265	1,435,179	137,399	113,086	1,410,866	387,522	452,037		18,464	121,883	52,404
2000	2,356,465	1,344,791	151,869	1,496,660	142,081	129,054	1,483,633	407,977	464,855		19,067	123,587	51,446
2001	2,560,931	1,550,605	105,360	1,655,965	165,852	138,005	1,628,118	419,160	513,653		20,393	125,581	50,566
2002	2,770,787	1,672,768	149,884	1,822,652	182,266	157,491	1,797,877	421,581	551,329		21,585	128,369	51,998
2003	2,980,474	1,822,057	151,096	1,973,153	201,227	147,578	1,919,504	474,078	586,892		22,454	132,738	54,041
2004	3,312,361	1,945,894	354,595	2,300,489	222,441	156,689	2,234,737	469,434	608,190		24,159	137,106	56,155
2005	3,459,649	2,080,092	345,690	2,425,782	238,778	149,124	2,336,128	482,946	640,575		24,657	140,313	57,801
2006	3,645,416	2,315,048	249,677	2,564,725	253,507	110,787	2,422,005	528,160	695,251		25,382	143,622	60,055
2007	3,974,257	2,408,923	361,264	2,770,187	258,740	116,823	2,628,270	599,811	746,176		27,208	146,067	60,959
2008	3,983,184	2,395,321	297,273	2,692,594	262,155	90,010	2,520,449	620,795	841,940		26,848	148,359	59,936
2009	3,863,788	2,373,468	137,375	2,510,843	265,121	96,438	2,342,160	593,134	928,494		25,891	149,234	58,448
2010	4,294,627	2,434,268	381,488	2,815,756	258,826	114,710	2,671,640	600,998	1,021,989		28,434	151,037	57,484
2011	4,550,509	2,505,485	490,410	2,995,895	244,299	108,021	2,859,617	660,800	1,030,092		29,962	151,876	57,253
2012	4,806,494	2,616,924	676,415	3,293,339	256,460	40,129	3,077,008	683,559	1,045,927		31,642	151,900	59,606
2013	5,021,922	2,702,160	801,189	3,503,349	295,921	22,077	3,229,505	718,770	1,073,647		33,078	151,819	61,067
2014	5,495,393	2,806,203	1,017,533	3,823,736	306,730	16,258	3,533,264	831,740	1,130,389		35,661	154,103	62,848
2015	5,601,678	2,873,941	786,881	3,660,822	312,836	92,173	3,440,159	941,714	1,219,805		36,275	154,423	61,528
2016	5,752,450	3,066,900	671,933	3,738,833	335,435	76,679	3,480,077	1,014,777	1,257,596		37,121	154,966	63,843
2017	6,087,194	3,226,957	827,237	4,054,194	356,411	66,799	3,764,582	1,071,000	1,251,612		38,799	156,890	64,828
2018	6,133,070	5,522,160	610,910	4,014,353	370,746	98,759	3,742,366	1,088,559	1,302,145		39,094	156,882	66,075
2019	6,492,474	5,791,277	701,197	4,275,469	396,366	116,993	3,996,096	1,107,125	1,389,253		41,267	157,327	67,715

Personal Income and Employment by Area: Madison, WI

(Thousands of dollars, except as noted.)

					Derivation of personal income							
		Earnings by place of work			Less: Contributions for government social insurance	Plus: Adjustment for residence	Equals: Net earnings by place of residence	Plus: Dividends, interest, and rent	Plus: Personal current transfer receipts	Per capita personal income (dollars)	Population (persons)	Total employment
Year	Personal income, total	Nonfarm	Farm	Total								
1970	1,708,448	1,316,440	87,386	1,403,826	90,597	-18,928	1,294,301	293,796	120,351	4,524	377,631	191,581
1971	1,854,242	1,421,354	91,918	1,513,272	101,500	-19,685	1,392,087	323,086	139,069	4,846	382,627	194,234
1972	1,997,037	1,529,585	94,778	1,624,363	115,366	-18,198	1,490,799	351,273	154,965	5,219	382,656	200,459
1973	2,225,349	1,693,667	119,509	1,813,176	147,243	-16,418	1,649,515	394,456	181,378	5,766	385,942	208,252
1974	2,423,637	1,852,574	97,909	1,950,483	169,979	-16,747	1,763,757	446,644	213,236	6,172	392,653	212,493
1975	2,710,063	2,030,435	115,196	2,145,631	184,359	-17,051	1,944,221	497,860	267,982	6,920	391,644	216,816
1976	2,970,088	2,279,797	90,258	2,370,055	209,710	-13,796	2,146,549	541,772	281,767	7,488	396,665	227,364
1977	3,305,419	2,525,419	116,541	2,641,960	232,485	-8,929	2,400,546	604,477	300,396	8,234	401,437	235,127
1978	3,713,483	2,855,398	123,377	2,978,775	270,539	-5,121	2,703,115	681,225	329,143	9,141	406,224	243,149
1979	4,110,390	3,132,711	146,018	3,278,729	311,040	1,637	2,969,326	760,594	380,470	10,037	409,524	250,720
1980	4,584,488	3,413,658	147,235	3,560,893	341,201	-2,230	3,217,462	912,629	454,397	10,977	417,638	255,057
1981	4,992,447	3,646,271	135,612	3,781,883	391,202	-6	3,390,675	1,096,387	505,385	11,862	420,874	253,625
1982	5,385,057	3,897,883	109,991	4,007,874	417,110	-11,063	3,579,701	1,254,049	551,307	12,739	422,726	253,833
1983	5,716,609	4,168,577	31,920	4,200,497	438,106	-12,197	3,750,194	1,360,663	605,752	13,438	425,420	257,282
1984	6,261,877	4,558,053	92,057	4,650,110	482,639	-13,984	4,153,487	1,485,193	623,197	14,568	429,829	267,580
1985	6,721,761	4,938,119	104,018	5,042,137	525,882	-26,352	4,489,903	1,564,283	667,575	15,472	434,452	276,651
1986	7,189,445	5,312,413	144,315	5,456,728	565,268	-39,449	4,852,011	1,640,936	696,498	16,365	439,308	283,663
1987	7,715,532	5,801,217	168,547	5,969,764	607,559	-53,341	5,308,864	1,688,572	718,096	17,347	444,766	295,146
1988	8,084,248	6,250,324	76,938	6,327,262	688,813	-61,951	5,576,498	1,756,712	751,038	17,889	451,906	305,036
1989	8,980,302	6,802,542	178,065	6,980,607	753,182	-76,401	6,151,024	2,008,138	821,140	19,676	456,408	315,061
1990	9,637,953	7,421,863	140,059	7,561,922	855,604	-93,280	6,613,038	2,135,393	889,522	20,763	464,185	326,175
1991	10,158,404	7,921,260	105,479	8,026,739	923,289	-119,696	6,983,754	2,200,953	973,697	21,426	474,124	332,549
1992	11,084,296	8,657,116	140,284	8,797,400	996,869	-141,416	7,659,115	2,351,514	1,073,667	22,916	483,693	340,984
1993	11,743,501	9,279,813	94,381	9,374,194	1,061,193	-162,896	8,150,105	2,465,140	1,128,256	23,753	494,411	349,725
1994	12,505,071	9,895,627	121,567	10,017,194	1,149,866	-183,307	8,684,021	2,657,535	1,163,515	24,892	502,367	359,601
1995	13,272,015	10,407,456	76,177	10,483,633	1,211,728	-200,827	9,071,078	2,952,607	1,248,330	26,039	509,694	367,663
1996	13,998,192	10,859,504	133,845	10,993,349	1,263,846	-224,362	9,505,141	3,176,373	1,316,678	27,116	516,235	374,687
1997	14,914,973	11,677,144	87,598	11,764,742	1,351,134	-259,272	10,154,336	3,381,758	1,378,879	28,475	523,795	381,856
1998	16,004,958	12,554,806	127,719	12,682,525	1,441,825	-299,083	10,941,617	3,690,950	1,372,391	30,366	527,073	390,131
1999	16,778,458	13,430,633	141,874	13,572,507	1,549,306	-350,075	11,673,126	3,666,224	1,439,108	31,575	531,380	399,716
2000	18,193,867	14,628,035	99,766	14,727,801	1,664,914	-412,186	12,650,701	3,980,225	1,562,941	33,850	537,485	409,450
2001	19,350,676	15,837,257	138,054	15,975,311	1,745,886	-483,566	13,745,859	3,876,350	1,728,467	35,521	544,773	414,371
2002	20,125,658	16,778,587	118,694	16,897,281	1,840,633	-563,987	14,492,661	3,771,350	1,861,647	36,439	552,305	417,989
2003	20,823,989	17,365,295	160,527	17,525,822	1,914,370	-611,071	15,000,381	3,885,296	1,938,312	37,243	559,138	422,526
2004	21,767,475	18,290,810	222,206	18,513,016	2,021,862	-720,164	15,770,990	3,987,730	2,008,755	38,434	566,363	432,853
2005	22,705,353	19,028,305	192,750	19,221,055	2,109,803	-798,422	16,312,830	4,218,453	2,174,070	39,623	573,036	442,110
2006	24,295,908	19,918,208	171,312	20,089,520	2,223,323	-840,448	17,025,749	4,944,877	2,325,282	41,868	580,296	447,330
2007	25,436,935	20,571,322	239,995	20,811,317	2,307,957	-907,126	17,596,234	5,235,151	2,605,550	43,281	587,711	454,846
2008	26,092,041	20,927,531	187,946	21,115,477	2,374,933	-922,554	17,817,990	5,331,315	2,942,736	43,893	594,452	454,618
2009	25,636,642	20,573,694	122,966	20,696,660	2,328,257	-963,861	17,404,542	4,967,882	3,264,218	42,606	601,715	444,144
2010	26,339,379	20,939,396	203,258	21,142,654	2,377,965	-972,607	17,792,082	4,963,375	3,583,922	43,423	606,578	444,555
2011	28,321,082	22,289,544	323,991	22,613,535	2,242,907	-1,114,215	19,256,413	5,556,230	3,508,439	46,183	613,240	454,166
2012	29,703,340	23,298,067	244,241	23,542,308	2,322,223	-1,095,237	20,124,848	5,989,162	3,589,330	47,916	619,909	462,205
2013	30,700,141	24,593,495	342,603	24,936,098	2,779,728	-1,164,058	20,992,312	6,003,270	3,704,559	48,998	626,560	468,463
2014	32,090,514	25,564,026	282,902	25,846,928	2,869,129	-1,257,998	21,719,801	6,503,841	3,866,872	50,702	632,924	478,101
2015	34,027,214	27,005,124	226,508	27,231,632	3,027,474	-1,324,683	22,879,475	7,077,181	4,070,558	53,233	639,214	488,879
2016	35,333,247	28,227,696	165,403	28,393,099	3,142,156	-1,478,207	23,772,736	7,399,550	4,160,961	54,574	647,432	502,251
2017	36,825,809	29,427,153	161,952	29,589,105	3,288,953	-1,517,370	24,782,782	7,699,604	4,343,423	56,289	654,230	506,853
2018	39,325,386	39,189,632	135,754	31,051,598	3,414,908	-1,613,415	26,023,275	8,646,243	4,655,868	59,591	659,927	512,106
2019	41,279,684	41,083,363	196,321	33,013,449	3,632,009	-1,759,324	27,622,116	8,746,123	4,911,445	62,087	664,865	522,164

Personal Income and Employment by Area: Manchester-Nashua, NH

(Thousands of dollars, except as noted.)

					Derivation of personal income							
		Earnings by place of work			Less: Contributions for government social insurance	Plus: Adjustment for residence	Equals: Net earnings by place of residence	Plus: Dividends, interest, and rent	Plus: Personal current transfer receipts	Per capita personal income (dollars)	Population (persons)	Total employment
Year	Personal income, total	Nonfarm	Farm	Total								
1970	961,049	790,738	3,474	794,212	51,606	679	743,285	144,957	72,807	4,245	226,390	115,787
1971	1,027,801	829,329	3,064	832,393	56,139	5,277	781,531	158,168	88,102	4,328	237,461	114,427
1972	1,119,971	899,311	3,113	902,424	64,221	13,875	852,078	172,363	95,530	4,748	235,887	115,341
1973	1,257,989	1,015,714	4,381	1,020,095	83,627	20,612	957,080	188,675	112,234	5,251	239,589	122,872
1974	1,385,255	1,097,185	2,685	1,099,870	93,381	31,323	1,037,812	212,725	134,718	5,686	243,605	125,196
1975	1,509,213	1,158,130	3,301	1,161,431	96,173	38,495	1,103,753	231,058	174,402	6,080	248,215	121,735
1976	1,718,541	1,330,041	3,868	1,333,909	111,678	55,789	1,278,020	254,812	185,709	6,718	255,826	129,826
1977	1,965,431	1,514,419	4,452	1,518,871	127,409	89,041	1,480,503	290,200	194,728	7,475	262,922	137,799
1978	2,299,436	1,760,599	5,581	1,766,180	151,020	141,574	1,756,734	329,780	212,922	8,559	268,671	147,386
1979	2,640,750	2,027,604	4,870	2,032,474	181,677	172,350	2,023,147	375,983	241,620	9,595	275,208	155,080
1980	3,041,125	2,277,113	2,559	2,279,672	204,182	217,796	2,293,286	465,114	282,725	10,932	278,189	159,785
1981	3,437,093	2,529,616	3,425	2,533,041	243,930	241,265	2,530,376	577,071	329,646	12,110	283,833	162,816
1982	3,802,574	2,774,331	4,012	2,778,343	274,341	252,767	2,756,769	688,393	357,412	13,234	287,334	166,065
1983	4,212,238	3,161,244	3,488	3,164,732	317,734	261,831	3,108,829	722,370	381,039	14,484	290,819	174,012
1984	4,819,673	3,665,172	3,817	3,668,989	380,778	286,526	3,574,737	845,704	399,232	16,169	298,089	189,171
1985	5,314,856	4,092,400	5,022	4,097,422	435,028	309,996	3,972,390	923,778	418,688	17,285	307,490	199,943
1986	5,860,757	4,567,324	5,080	4,572,404	489,177	310,582	4,393,809	1,025,236	441,712	18,531	316,260	208,594
1987	6,431,102	5,123,463	9,013	5,132,476	541,236	296,319	4,887,559	1,093,359	450,184	19,836	324,218	214,561
1988	6,980,236	5,554,163	10,442	5,564,605	600,714	323,415	5,287,306	1,202,776	490,154	21,196	329,319	220,131
1989	7,366,468	5,697,606	6,849	5,704,455	617,690	353,846	5,440,611	1,370,572	555,285	21,986	335,057	215,952
1990	7,348,699	5,663,611	7,989	5,671,600	631,768	303,373	5,343,205	1,381,334	624,160	21,821	336,768	208,783
1991	7,627,991	5,685,850	8,088	5,693,938	642,201	341,752	5,393,489	1,395,773	838,729	22,631	337,066	199,944
1992	7,969,910	6,104,347	7,564	6,111,911	684,290	295,866	5,723,487	1,355,420	891,003	23,367	341,078	202,042
1993	8,210,679	6,220,447	6,256	6,226,703	696,541	410,964	5,941,126	1,405,352	864,201	23,803	344,944	204,282
1994	8,759,634	6,532,366	5,723	6,538,089	740,156	500,159	6,298,092	1,502,657	958,885	25,086	349,190	209,544
1995	9,340,234	6,898,603	5,160	6,903,763	785,395	557,951	6,676,319	1,629,126	1,034,789	26,411	353,651	212,713
1996	10,041,720	7,486,169	5,126	7,491,295	841,908	585,806	7,235,193	1,775,995	1,030,532	28,001	358,624	218,719
1997	10,916,779	8,125,875	4,700	8,130,575	903,787	679,363	7,906,151	1,939,932	1,070,696	29,970	364,261	225,406
1998	12,062,034	9,069,530	3,949	9,073,479	978,970	699,800	8,794,309	2,151,880	1,115,845	32,548	370,595	233,399
1999	13,044,109	9,891,345	6,394	9,897,739	1,049,913	873,650	9,721,476	2,180,928	1,141,705	34,654	376,407	238,338
2000	14,817,603	11,130,903	6,002	11,136,905	1,162,891	1,135,191	11,109,205	2,489,674	1,218,724	38,773	382,162	246,068
2001	14,846,851	10,965,049	5,176	10,970,225	1,162,758	1,190,780	10,998,247	2,519,912	1,328,692	38,323	387,414	245,028
2002	14,919,866	11,095,646	5,738	11,101,384	1,163,039	1,113,805	11,052,150	2,422,594	1,445,122	38,289	389,665	242,388
2003	15,347,687	11,650,098	5,884	11,655,982	1,235,530	999,703	11,420,155	2,450,841	1,476,691	39,206	391,461	246,090
2004	16,370,678	12,344,680	5,893	12,350,573	1,324,295	1,064,676	12,090,954	2,681,441	1,598,283	41,505	394,428	250,596
2005	16,767,811	12,917,452	3,271	12,920,723	1,378,334	955,282	12,497,671	2,606,246	1,663,894	42,302	396,381	255,100
2006	17,928,326	13,526,473	2,850	13,529,323	1,424,652	1,104,642	13,209,313	2,946,161	1,772,852	45,027	398,169	256,756
2007	18,836,632	14,090,457	778	14,091,235	1,501,604	1,013,247	13,602,878	3,307,359	1,926,395	47,228	398,843	260,416
2008	19,381,634	14,289,445	1,203	14,290,648	1,549,496	986,503	13,727,655	3,411,505	2,242,474	48,508	399,556	258,229
2009	18,878,448	13,869,344	-1,001	13,868,343	1,514,567	774,076	13,127,852	3,314,258	2,436,338	47,179	400,148	250,764
2010	19,345,988	14,198,391	-1,094	14,197,297	1,543,834	1,106,501	13,759,964	2,972,019	2,614,005	48,240	401,038	247,058
2011	20,494,600	14,845,106	-2,801	14,842,305	1,441,909	941,328	14,341,724	3,582,946	2,569,930	51,003	401,829	249,484
2012	21,521,516	15,168,391	1,123	15,169,514	1,473,945	1,034,456	14,730,025	4,183,817	2,607,674	53,441	402,715	250,653
2013	21,244,073	15,417,219	3,151	15,420,370	1,692,853	980,875	14,708,392	3,882,552	2,653,129	52,666	403,371	254,367
2014	21,793,706	16,348,872	-1,644	16,347,228	1,772,361	748,628	15,323,495	3,640,639	2,829,572	53,803	405,062	258,616
2015	22,550,386	16,867,487	-444	16,867,043	1,831,253	863,919	15,899,709	3,617,397	3,033,280	55,542	406,009	264,891
2016	23,398,126	17,413,763	-1,952	17,411,811	1,896,854	991,292	16,506,249	3,677,089	3,214,788	57,388	407,718	269,178
2017	24,608,221	18,239,517	-2,514	18,237,003	2,003,598	1,196,883	17,430,288	3,843,607	3,334,326	60,064	409,697	272,228
2018	25,338,570	25,337,290	1,280	19,019,817	2,076,244	1,045,999	17,989,572	3,844,912	3,504,086	61,111	414,630	276,114
2019	26,363,623	26,359,361	4,262	19,849,207	2,160,086	1,187,683	18,876,804	3,890,787	3,596,032	63,218	417,025	280,504

Personal Income and Employment by Area: Manhattan, KS

(Thousands of dollars, except as noted.)

Year	Personal income, total	Earnings by place of work			Less: Contributions for government social insurance	Plus: Adjustment for residence	Equals: Net earnings by place of residence	Plus: Dividends, interest, and rent	Plus: Personal current transfer receipts	Per capita personal income (dollars)	Population (persons)	Total employment
		Nonfarm	Farm	Total								
1970	289,990	119,461	6,205	125,666	7,980	111,367	229,053	47,236	13,701	4,214	68,809	21,881
1971	318,404	138,350	5,617	143,967	9,592	116,135	250,510	52,300	15,594	4,540	70,127	23,477
1972	339,912	149,388	8,926	158,314	10,975	119,274	266,613	55,676	17,623	4,879	69,674	23,827
1973	368,583	159,355	12,980	172,335	13,580	125,947	284,702	63,102	20,779	5,065	72,765	24,363
1974	407,550	178,938	11,472	190,410	16,209	135,125	309,326	73,615	24,609	5,495	74,161	25,624
1975	446,565	203,994	10,758	214,752	18,551	140,027	336,228	80,249	30,088	5,962	74,899	26,460
1976	482,402	230,629	7,675	238,304	21,194	145,417	362,527	85,854	34,021	6,233	77,389	27,641
1977	526,936	261,338	3,182	264,520	23,924	151,968	392,564	96,910	37,462	6,983	75,461	29,291
1978	582,620	295,073	7,468	302,541	28,062	156,424	430,903	110,272	41,445	7,568	76,980	30,448
1979	632,536	315,107	5,094	320,201	31,057	173,885	463,029	123,736	45,771	8,182	77,305	30,601
1980	709,697	340,426	-3,482	336,944	33,768	206,668	509,844	144,802	55,051	9,024	78,646	30,601
1981	807,205	374,612	10,916	385,528	39,956	227,881	573,453	171,430	62,322	10,093	79,976	30,908
1982	870,898	397,055	9,603	406,658	42,754	242,079	605,983	197,832	67,083	10,788	80,726	31,468
1983	914,083	416,171	7,266	423,437	43,923	250,332	629,846	209,388	74,849	11,056	82,675	31,585
1984	972,971	453,944	8,182	462,126	48,262	251,803	665,667	229,203	78,101	11,894	81,804	32,746
1985	1,048,034	480,988	17,971	498,959	51,750	270,391	717,600	244,328	86,106	13,018	80,504	33,518
1986	1,086,125	505,915	13,479	519,394	54,185	277,770	742,979	257,964	85,182	13,543	80,200	33,800
1987	1,124,768	536,920	15,618	552,538	57,329	277,500	772,709	262,476	89,583	13,925	80,773	35,862
1988	1,171,817	571,988	14,442	586,430	64,382	283,219	805,267	272,667	93,883	14,349	81,667	37,095
1989	1,253,745	619,302	9,033	628,335	68,951	287,419	846,803	302,688	104,254	15,146	82,780	37,881
1990	1,261,579	647,831	13,690	661,521	75,231	271,510	857,800	292,288	111,491	15,137	83,343	38,985
1991	1,290,981	692,056	8,561	700,617	81,733	247,194	866,078	302,129	122,774	15,877	81,311	40,004
1992	1,466,960	763,646	17,072	780,718	89,294	305,628	997,052	333,696	136,212	17,304	84,774	40,430
1993	1,465,052	774,305	12,293	786,598	89,952	290,594	987,240	335,520	142,292	17,381	84,291	41,564
1994	1,556,099	832,644	15,603	848,247	98,486	304,562	1,054,323	357,859	143,917	18,204	85,482	42,235
1995	1,578,362	873,973	3,304	877,277	102,753	287,836	1,062,360	362,557	153,445	18,407	85,748	43,743
1996	1,583,264	920,749	17,937	938,686	107,215	224,339	1,055,810	368,985	158,469	19,107	82,862	44,143
1997	1,625,675	956,368	10,659	967,027	112,128	222,814	1,077,713	381,343	166,619	19,912	81,644	44,564
1998	1,691,917	993,533	6,640	1,000,173	115,741	227,277	1,111,709	412,128	168,080	20,866	81,084	45,021
1999	1,773,855	1,057,079	9,971	1,067,050	122,566	233,578	1,178,062	418,922	176,871	21,910	80,961	45,615
2000	1,890,022	1,161,062	8,240	1,169,302	134,363	233,385	1,268,324	427,620	194,078	23,179	81,539	46,873
2001	2,035,313	1,294,706	13,834	1,308,540	146,809	243,224	1,404,955	418,809	211,549	25,012	81,374	47,834
2002	2,098,792	1,341,279	3,664	1,344,943	151,836	258,890	1,451,997	422,435	224,360	25,846	81,205	47,798
2003	2,214,136	1,398,847	14,526	1,413,373	159,344	279,807	1,533,836	442,773	237,527	27,052	81,847	48,281
2004	2,317,966	1,469,215	22,211	1,491,426	167,557	308,235	1,632,104	440,360	245,502	27,790	83,411	47,988
2005	2,425,544	1,532,418	17,189	1,549,607	176,338	343,004	1,716,273	450,309	258,962	28,809	84,195	48,841
2006	2,645,846	1,651,355	5,977	1,657,332	188,720	387,017	1,855,629	513,818	276,399	30,536	86,648	50,057
2007	2,883,158	1,745,164	9,662	1,754,826	198,937	440,401	1,996,290	587,452	299,416	32,866	87,724	52,054
2008	3,220,457	1,917,957	13,625	1,931,582	213,444	503,085	2,221,223	645,570	353,664	35,653	90,328	53,747
2009	3,285,457	1,887,332	25,353	1,912,685	212,229	558,341	2,258,797	651,577	375,083	36,024	91,201	53,038
2010	3,538,379	1,940,644	19,409	1,960,053	219,284	724,097	2,464,866	660,946	412,567	37,917	93,320	52,509
2011	3,746,711	2,011,770	44,140	2,055,910	197,570	743,876	2,602,216	711,165	433,330	39,286	95,370	52,133
2012	3,817,148	2,102,176	37,198	2,139,374	205,918	690,022	2,623,478	763,330	430,340	38,710	98,608	53,167
2013	3,744,723	2,106,454	69,711	2,176,165	232,817	610,142	2,553,490	745,073	446,160	38,167	98,113	53,858
2014	3,874,217	2,204,093	47,323	2,251,416	243,947	597,508	2,604,977	802,610	466,630	39,737	97,497	54,613
2015	4,032,301	2,291,089	39,318	2,330,407	256,535	611,867	2,685,739	853,378	493,184	40,935	98,506	54,979
2016	4,032,301	2,291,089	39,318	2,330,407	256,535	611,867	2,685,739	853,378	493,184	40,935	98,506	54,979
2017	4,059,844	2,355,475	41,032	2,396,507	258,757	556,631	2,694,381	857,424	508,039	41,852	97,004	54,992
2018	5,950,233	5,924,508	25,725	4,697,781	511,465	-267,916	3,918,400	1,241,503	790,330	45,181	131,698	90,547
2019	6,132,748	6,083,763	48,985	4,842,542	527,004	-277,609	4,037,929	1,253,217	841,602	47,072	130,285	91,283

Personal Income and Employment by Area: Mankato, MN

(Thousands of dollars, except as noted.)

Year	Personal income, total	Earnings by place of work			Less: Contributions for government social insurance	Plus: Adjustment for residence	Equals: Net earnings by place of residence	Plus: Dividends, interest, and rent	Plus: Personal current transfer receipts	Per capita personal income (dollars)	Population (persons)	Total employment
		Nonfarm	Farm	Total								
1970	264,523	181,093	29,959	211,052	12,252	-954	197,846	45,102	21,575	3,434	77,037	32,324
1971	280,227	199,226	23,124	222,350	14,015	-2,141	206,194	49,222	24,811	3,592	78,012	32,665
1972	305,079	213,266	29,059	242,325	15,686	-2,016	224,623	52,926	27,530	3,937	77,494	34,258
1973	379,991	240,844	69,116	309,960	20,598	-3,140	286,222	61,588	32,181	4,944	76,854	36,352
1974	406,071	271,570	53,774	325,344	24,431	-4,673	296,240	71,574	38,257	5,240	77,488	37,064
1975	438,278	298,401	44,128	342,529	26,495	-6,458	309,576	81,837	46,865	5,668	77,328	37,194
1976	452,057	330,594	19,745	350,339	29,938	-8,012	312,389	87,667	52,001	5,809	77,818	37,739
1977	538,793	364,602	62,841	427,443	33,056	-9,703	384,684	98,636	55,473	6,901	78,073	39,224
1978	598,122	414,191	65,510	479,701	38,944	-12,069	428,688	109,183	60,251	7,677	77,906	40,917
1979	639,361	461,106	47,155	508,261	45,017	-14,614	448,630	122,661	68,070	8,148	78,471	42,687
1980	689,137	489,996	32,905	522,901	47,553	-16,386	458,962	148,308	81,867	8,681	79,381	42,871
1981	764,949	529,639	34,659	564,298	55,025	-16,468	492,805	179,740	92,404	9,591	79,753	43,218
1982	810,490	552,547	19,326	571,873	58,109	-16,479	497,285	210,242	102,963	10,136	79,958	43,012
1983	839,592	589,845	-6,280	583,565	62,631	-16,743	504,191	224,045	111,356	10,522	79,795	43,112
1984	960,800	636,944	42,219	679,163	69,110	-13,609	596,444	248,193	116,163	12,043	79,784	43,684
1985	1,000,129	657,324	47,123	704,447	72,838	-10,972	620,637	254,889	124,603	12,471	80,198	44,449
1986	1,041,753	690,146	45,184	735,330	78,541	-9,726	647,063	263,869	130,821	12,975	80,288	44,537
1987	1,144,918	748,250	80,606	828,856	84,844	-10,632	733,380	273,365	138,173	14,244	80,379	45,846
1988	1,159,810	809,357	42,856	852,213	95,148	-9,481	747,584	267,913	144,313	14,254	81,366	47,128
1989	1,288,175	864,863	73,909	938,772	101,569	-6,927	830,276	304,351	153,548	15,795	81,555	47,596
1990	1,355,221	931,697	59,515	991,212	109,677	-4,752	876,783	314,401	164,037	16,470	82,283	48,587
1991	1,389,310	989,991	29,459	1,019,450	118,050	-11,133	890,267	325,278	173,765	16,788	82,758	49,463
1992	1,504,342	1,095,190	44,590	1,139,780	128,820	-16,600	994,360	323,887	186,095	18,135	82,954	51,307
1993	1,541,598	1,158,705	-331	1,158,374	136,851	-22,569	998,954	347,445	195,199	18,510	83,283	52,620
1994	1,679,712	1,239,692	51,008	1,290,700	148,154	-26,556	1,115,990	359,065	204,657	20,064	83,717	54,719
1995	1,746,853	1,295,081	22,553	1,317,634	154,359	-29,089	1,134,186	395,310	217,357	20,662	84,545	55,982
1996	1,883,239	1,360,297	81,129	1,441,426	160,183	-31,249	1,249,994	408,995	224,250	22,179	84,912	56,419
1997	1,924,793	1,414,337	51,682	1,466,019	166,294	-34,530	1,265,195	431,587	228,011	22,672	84,897	56,660
1998	2,098,592	1,582,272	53,040	1,635,312	182,558	-47,075	1,405,679	461,302	231,611	24,756	84,771	60,139
1999	2,167,940	1,652,269	43,173	1,695,442	192,115	-52,584	1,450,743	473,257	243,940	25,474	85,105	61,312
2000	2,269,434	1,739,647	59,137	1,798,784	200,945	-58,597	1,539,242	467,799	262,393	26,422	85,892	61,984
2001	2,480,657	1,915,843	48,419	1,964,262	214,998	-65,880	1,683,384	497,461	299,812	28,479	87,105	61,726
2002	2,575,596	2,042,286	41,787	2,084,073	226,585	-76,087	1,781,401	470,201	323,994	29,233	88,107	62,351
2003	2,711,182	2,108,077	60,975	2,169,052	237,200	-86,977	1,844,875	521,092	345,215	30,348	89,336	62,587
2004	2,845,153	2,212,074	125,812	2,337,886	248,187	-93,668	1,996,031	488,231	360,891	31,560	90,152	63,325
2005	2,936,670	2,320,041	146,326	2,466,367	265,780	-114,752	2,085,835	472,970	377,865	32,232	91,111	65,189
2006	3,162,843	2,514,438	131,872	2,646,310	289,662	-133,449	2,223,199	518,498	421,146	34,053	92,879	67,013
2007	3,232,835	2,532,140	98,367	2,630,507	293,160	-139,048	2,198,299	574,556	459,980	34,405	93,963	67,773
2008	3,349,876	2,484,904	163,775	2,648,679	295,701	-147,859	2,205,119	618,098	526,659	35,217	95,121	67,301
2009	3,214,063	2,403,424	102,877	2,506,301	288,583	-144,662	2,073,056	555,977	585,030	33,441	96,111	65,739
2010	3,355,872	2,456,161	145,838	2,601,999	290,729	-157,467	2,153,803	558,770	643,299	34,653	96,841	65,596
2011	3,668,135	2,596,646	221,430	2,818,076	275,133	-177,472	2,365,471	664,635	638,029	37,697	97,306	66,932
2012	3,920,996	2,760,100	262,136	3,022,236	287,787	-191,127	2,543,322	738,896	638,778	40,017	97,984	67,085
2013	3,987,569	2,848,560	266,533	3,115,093	338,106	-177,599	2,599,388	729,589	658,592	40,803	97,727	68,260
2014	4,194,664	3,028,577	218,336	3,246,913	352,031	-190,906	2,703,976	793,196	697,492	42,545	98,594	68,772
2015	4,326,639	3,154,387	160,190	3,314,577	363,406	-188,236	2,762,935	842,904	720,800	43,677	99,059	70,114
2016	4,325,197	3,232,456	65,307	3,297,763	373,820	-201,178	2,722,765	850,048	752,384	43,295	99,900	70,681
2017	4,518,740	3,392,183	72,976	3,465,159	395,739	-214,978	2,854,442	888,313	775,985	44,767	100,939	71,923
2018	4,734,877	4,638,670	96,207	3,609,531	415,730	-232,289	2,961,512	949,997	823,368	46,614	101,577	72,209
2019	4,914,860	4,782,275	132,585	3,775,830	432,078	-239,756	3,103,996	954,281	856,583	48,219	101,927	73,016

Personal Income and Employment by Area: Mansfield, OH

(Thousands of dollars, except as noted.)

Year	Personal income, total	Earnings by place of work			Less: Contributions for government social insurance	Plus: Adjustment for residence	Equals: Net earnings by place of residence	Plus: Dividends, interest, and rent	Plus: Personal current transfer receipts	Per capita personal income (dollars)	Population (persons)	Total employment
		Nonfarm	Farm	Total								
1970	516,298	469,915	2,941	472,856	31,347	-27,267	414,242	65,513	36,543	3,976	129,838	60,931
1971	567,752	518,416	1,989	520,405	36,010	-30,507	453,888	70,589	43,275	4,387	129,411	63,089
1972	606,042	554,492	3,572	558,064	40,680	-33,389	483,995	74,974	47,073	4,632	130,847	63,607
1973	670,311	618,207	4,793	623,000	53,147	-37,425	532,428	83,357	54,526	5,120	130,923	66,236
1974	707,235	629,762	5,918	635,680	56,036	-34,472	545,172	94,271	67,792	5,425	130,356	64,297
1975	746,455	636,939	7,033	643,972	55,070	-33,286	555,616	100,804	90,035	5,703	130,887	60,904
1976	822,879	716,878	8,277	725,155	63,706	-39,105	622,344	107,710	92,825	6,274	131,160	61,493
1977	924,472	823,791	6,640	830,431	74,107	-48,160	708,164	119,352	96,956	7,083	130,524	64,527
1978	1,002,098	893,232	4,947	898,179	82,483	-49,941	765,755	131,348	104,995	7,657	130,866	65,594
1979	1,097,045	969,585	4,548	974,133	92,464	-52,503	829,166	148,581	119,298	8,427	130,178	65,972
1980	1,190,148	1,009,230	153	1,009,383	95,333	-55,893	858,157	183,705	148,286	9,077	131,116	65,230
1981	1,326,930	1,113,393	327	1,113,720	112,650	-69,082	931,988	226,779	168,163	10,171	130,465	65,158
1982	1,348,026	1,066,001	3,203	1,069,204	107,859	-64,687	896,658	248,107	203,261	10,438	129,141	61,624
1983	1,481,979	1,208,763	-2,432	1,206,331	126,327	-83,038	996,966	270,494	214,519	11,572	128,066	63,435
1984	1,615,110	1,320,629	6,262	1,326,891	141,117	-89,481	1,096,293	300,940	217,877	12,570	128,485	66,715
1985	1,715,525	1,421,297	7,323	1,428,620	154,326	-101,702	1,172,592	309,786	233,147	13,384	128,181	67,043
1986	1,788,723	1,476,521	5,310	1,481,831	164,713	-104,322	1,212,796	322,524	253,403	14,038	127,418	68,043
1987	1,841,310	1,531,199	6,927	1,538,126	170,131	-105,948	1,262,047	321,937	257,326	14,459	127,345	69,183
1988	1,938,842	1,636,096	6,640	1,642,736	187,832	-113,146	1,341,758	330,262	266,822	15,246	127,167	70,397
1989	2,050,664	1,702,809	10,767	1,713,576	196,549	-118,077	1,398,950	364,327	287,387	16,199	126,590	71,654
1990	2,110,444	1,720,229	9,376	1,729,605	201,886	-114,084	1,413,635	374,360	322,449	16,728	126,160	70,803
1991	2,112,274	1,704,297	1,482	1,705,779	202,509	-103,217	1,400,053	363,928	348,293	16,627	127,040	68,169
1992	2,212,074	1,751,265	14,244	1,765,509	204,693	-95,621	1,465,195	368,405	378,474	17,353	127,475	68,884
1993	2,338,330	1,886,585	5,787	1,892,372	225,177	-101,956	1,565,239	378,323	394,768	18,298	127,792	71,627
1994	2,451,765	1,960,444	11,829	1,972,273	236,861	-88,755	1,646,657	392,408	412,700	19,112	128,281	72,358
1995	2,530,497	2,024,062	14,140	2,038,202	246,504	-93,381	1,698,317	398,479	433,701	19,736	128,217	74,128
1996	2,651,396	2,110,894	16,478	2,127,372	253,674	-99,849	1,773,849	422,556	454,991	20,570	128,894	74,963
1997	2,790,263	2,214,945	17,427	2,232,372	258,857	-102,710	1,870,805	451,309	468,149	21,652	128,868	75,038
1998	2,871,401	2,254,415	14,627	2,269,042	256,895	-93,857	1,918,290	472,850	480,261	22,339	128,540	72,778
1999	2,960,700	2,347,402	9,902	2,357,304	264,069	-96,541	1,996,694	462,136	501,870	22,910	129,233	73,336
2000	3,091,340	2,430,549	10,520	2,441,069	264,559	-95,106	2,081,404	485,665	524,271	23,991	128,853	73,985
2001	3,245,700	2,532,755	11,061	2,543,816	277,173	-91,688	2,174,955	486,316	584,429	25,320	128,187	74,473
2002	3,360,241	2,627,282	3,807	2,631,089	280,966	-85,796	2,264,327	472,876	623,038	26,178	128,363	73,890
2003	3,467,133	2,684,865	4,263	2,689,128	290,301	-80,077	2,318,750	486,203	662,180	27,021	128,312	72,842
2004	3,511,678	2,749,543	9,782	2,759,325	304,770	-104,117	2,350,438	469,084	692,156	27,415	128,094	72,726
2005	3,539,964	2,741,300	6,739	2,748,039	306,017	-100,719	2,341,303	473,922	724,739	27,716	127,724	72,383
2006	3,641,891	2,809,844	6,865	2,816,709	317,216	-117,986	2,381,507	490,764	769,620	28,611	127,292	72,402
2007	3,736,049	2,750,732	7,881	2,758,613	308,912	-88,223	2,361,478	554,305	820,266	29,419	126,995	71,443
2008	3,878,436	2,749,561	8,323	2,757,884	317,476	-74,681	2,365,727	600,689	912,020	30,750	126,128	70,018
2009	3,740,646	2,537,465	9,642	2,547,107	297,904	-63,969	2,185,234	552,532	1,002,880	29,852	125,308	65,881
2010	3,775,544	2,535,692	21,234	2,556,926	293,057	-61,257	2,202,612	532,932	1,040,000	30,408	124,161	64,781
2011	3,986,603	2,614,726	34,567	2,649,293	274,293	-59,820	2,315,180	603,625	1,067,798	32,377	123,130	66,089
2012	4,038,830	2,656,747	21,964	2,678,711	276,441	-30,794	2,371,476	607,898	1,059,456	32,936	122,625	64,818
2013	4,112,909	2,684,501	42,894	2,727,395	301,289	17,388	2,443,494	599,799	1,069,616	33,629	122,303	64,764
2014	4,288,828	2,773,052	37,510	2,810,562	311,217	19,480	2,518,825	645,599	1,124,404	35,164	121,965	65,552
2015	4,408,372	2,805,667	7,272	2,812,939	313,146	56,222	2,556,015	687,269	1,165,088	36,241	121,641	65,057
2016	4,418,827	2,812,290	2,426	2,814,716	322,098	47,981	2,540,599	683,982	1,194,246	36,469	121,167	64,960
2017	4,579,612	2,931,443	-2,552	2,928,891	341,419	51,538	2,639,010	716,823	1,223,779	37,977	120,589	64,606
2018	4,766,061	4,746,769	19,292	3,085,613	353,224	24,478	2,756,867	769,596	1,239,598	39,393	120,987	65,391
2019	4,907,564	4,895,334	12,230	3,108,036	356,922	76,295	2,827,409	779,374	1,300,781	40,507	121,154	65,105

Personal Income and Employment by Area: McAllen-Edinburg-Mission, TX

(Thousands of dollars, except as noted.)

Year	Personal income, total	Earnings by place of work			Less: Contributions for government social insurance	Plus: Adjustment for residence	Equals: Net earnings by place of residence	Plus: Dividends, interest, and rent	Plus: Personal current transfer receipts	Per capita personal income (dollars)	Population (persons)	Total employment
		Nonfarm	Farm	Total								
1970	364,139	260,864	22,601	283,465	15,860	-9,141	258,464	59,886	45,789	1,989	183,040	55,167
1971	428,483	296,938	37,595	334,533	18,581	-8,638	307,314	67,788	53,381	2,216	193,397	58,147
1972	479,788	346,602	25,965	372,567	22,664	-8,990	340,913	77,030	61,845	2,342	204,904	64,427
1973	571,221	405,838	26,895	432,733	31,119	-9,421	392,193	91,716	87,312	2,632	217,004	69,841
1974	671,642	475,413	30,438	505,851	37,482	-11,518	456,851	110,674	104,117	3,001	223,800	74,338
1975	791,763	555,034	34,284	589,318	42,731	-12,780	533,807	130,410	127,546	3,316	238,746	77,588
1976	903,307	658,565	22,947	681,512	51,002	-14,133	616,377	145,074	141,856	3,628	249,003	82,908
1977	1,051,173	734,940	70,547	805,487	57,494	-15,582	732,411	166,181	152,581	4,063	258,732	87,780
1978	1,185,172	831,701	64,062	895,763	66,294	-14,859	814,610	194,956	175,606	4,454	266,103	90,869
1979	1,326,959	934,978	39,547	974,525	78,510	-13,656	882,359	227,993	216,607	4,817	275,488	93,698
1980	1,550,674	1,078,146	28,323	1,106,469	92,606	-14,859	999,004	283,521	268,149	5,412	286,540	99,240
1981	1,848,512	1,234,897	86,461	1,321,358	116,678	-8,014	1,196,666	351,133	300,713	6,191	298,559	106,048
1982	2,023,439	1,336,876	67,723	1,404,599	128,049	-9,088	1,267,462	421,021	334,956	6,459	313,256	110,680
1983	2,160,148	1,387,666	48,611	1,436,277	129,299	-9,757	1,297,221	462,487	400,440	6,617	326,453	108,973
1984	2,354,671	1,502,659	52,377	1,555,036	142,003	-9,061	1,403,972	511,545	439,154	7,038	334,571	110,090
1985	2,587,303	1,648,875	44,532	1,693,407	156,625	-8,546	1,528,236	570,943	488,124	7,584	341,145	113,109
1986	2,685,917	1,714,213	30,958	1,745,171	160,769	-8,836	1,575,566	586,222	524,129	7,663	350,514	112,319
1987	2,795,855	1,781,761	53,465	1,835,226	166,031	-9,065	1,660,130	589,005	546,720	7,803	358,307	117,858
1988	3,074,496	2,001,417	65,415	2,066,832	193,315	-8,300	1,865,217	613,521	595,758	8,412	365,499	124,638
1989	3,369,972	2,152,316	46,903	2,199,219	214,557	-5,100	1,979,562	704,448	685,962	8,936	377,106	131,460
1990	3,685,707	2,343,101	60,723	2,403,824	229,546	-3,836	2,170,442	713,232	802,033	9,519	387,200	134,822
1991	4,066,060	2,564,273	81,093	2,645,366	256,872	-4,084	2,384,410	760,187	921,463	10,075	403,571	138,175
1992	4,512,124	2,788,544	83,404	2,871,948	276,611	-1,656	2,593,681	766,739	1,151,704	10,634	424,312	142,423
1993	4,890,266	3,055,318	113,222	3,168,540	304,283	-2,325	2,861,932	786,619	1,241,715	10,928	447,508	148,166
1994	5,313,250	3,335,923	100,392	3,436,315	337,829	-6,002	3,092,484	836,523	1,384,243	11,331	468,906	155,816
1995	5,645,401	3,494,633	83,306	3,577,939	355,901	-6,263	3,215,775	898,866	1,530,760	11,578	487,593	163,571
1996	6,085,455	3,771,188	60,367	3,831,555	378,066	-8,099	3,445,390	951,870	1,688,195	12,088	503,411	171,626
1997	6,588,265	4,186,474	60,429	4,246,903	413,115	-11,486	3,822,302	992,814	1,773,149	12,672	519,903	182,919
1998	7,091,156	4,558,472	111,074	4,669,546	443,519	-11,719	4,214,308	1,042,307	1,834,541	13,182	537,929	188,244
1999	7,423,072	4,857,744	122,054	4,979,798	472,252	-16,449	4,491,097	1,048,311	1,883,664	13,354	555,875	199,684
2000	8,109,236	5,393,201	111,147	5,504,348	512,439	-18,981	4,972,928	1,131,607	2,004,701	14,147	573,216	212,033
2001	8,742,718	5,883,660	126,783	6,010,443	552,375	-96,632	5,361,436	1,176,921	2,204,361	14,816	590,067	220,968
2002	9,453,353	6,350,748	110,857	6,461,605	596,009	-90,806	5,774,790	1,164,043	2,514,520	15,484	610,520	230,567
2003	10,212,426	6,874,129	154,949	7,029,078	654,808	-82,502	6,291,768	1,181,287	2,739,371	16,147	632,475	242,793
2004	11,086,510	7,592,041	140,485	7,732,526	717,097	-69,603	6,945,826	1,252,280	2,888,404	16,958	653,779	256,668
2005	12,083,397	8,095,657	158,990	8,254,647	782,345	-59,886	7,412,416	1,392,021	3,278,960	17,902	674,982	270,969
2006	13,016,953	8,807,383	106,362	8,913,745	841,074	-21,467	8,051,204	1,431,058	3,534,691	18,720	695,352	282,999
2007	13,888,971	9,178,517	94,000	9,272,517	905,229	-4,975	8,362,313	1,566,529	3,960,129	19,418	715,264	302,755
2008	15,077,915	9,563,376	44,060	9,607,436	946,296	29,028	8,690,168	1,888,217	4,499,530	20,467	736,694	308,229
2009	15,991,827	10,046,419	38,709	10,085,128	997,710	67,161	9,154,579	1,835,711	5,001,537	21,112	757,468	310,579
2010	17,090,699	10,711,782	66,503	10,778,285	1,049,164	93,841	9,822,962	1,807,671	5,460,066	21,939	779,015	316,440
2011	18,063,642	11,300,163	45,310	11,345,473	980,105	157,562	10,522,930	1,953,354	5,587,358	22,732	794,639	329,907
2012	18,709,340	11,781,758	57,329	11,839,087	1,013,455	248,708	11,074,340	2,165,539	5,469,461	23,192	806,725	335,365
2013	19,263,889	12,290,492	83,084	12,373,576	1,175,876	324,566	11,522,266	2,152,836	5,588,787	23,564	817,526	342,957
2014	20,203,308	12,936,004	54,954	12,990,958	1,233,659	376,803	12,134,102	2,235,523	5,833,683	24,365	829,210	353,695
2015	21,019,698	13,365,570	68,160	13,433,730	1,294,058	346,420	12,486,092	2,373,524	6,160,082	25,020	840,113	361,691
2016	21,541,969	13,586,637	49,705	13,636,342	1,342,752	268,276	12,561,866	2,486,359	6,493,744	25,338	850,187	368,164
2017	22,047,447	13,991,623	50,115	14,041,738	1,402,985	292,598	12,931,351	2,607,145	6,508,951	25,617	860,661	374,436
2018	22,949,668	22,808,209	141,459	14,806,916	1,463,589	271,966	13,615,293	2,685,261	6,649,114	26,615	862,298	387,937
2019	23,815,443	23,681,018	134,425	15,394,490	1,513,368	296,786	14,177,908	2,754,058	6,883,477	27,415	868,707	396,490

Personal Income and Employment by Area: Medford, OR

(Thousands of dollars, except as noted.)

Year	Personal income, total	Earnings by place of work			Less: Contributions for government social insurance	Plus: Adjustment for residence	Equals: Net earnings by place of residence	Plus: Dividends, interest, and rent	Plus: Personal current transfer receipts	Per capita personal income (dollars)	Population (persons)	Total employment
		Nonfarm	Farm	Total								
1970	332,495	235,360	5,186	240,546	18,016	4,488	227,018	66,784	38,693	3,486	95,374	36,133
1971	380,955	270,822	8,211	279,033	21,443	4,906	262,496	74,284	44,175	3,829	99,487	39,058
1972	431,925	315,140	6,464	321,604	26,338	5,515	300,781	81,932	49,212	4,260	101,396	41,785
1973	493,284	357,936	9,492	367,428	34,228	5,701	338,901	94,253	60,130	4,600	107,245	44,421
1974	558,936	392,826	10,847	403,673	38,393	5,140	370,420	110,978	77,538	5,039	110,926	45,606
1975	631,982	431,477	9,193	440,670	40,680	5,661	405,651	126,796	99,535	5,499	114,924	46,756
1976	720,268	503,909	10,334	514,243	47,733	7,192	473,702	137,426	109,140	6,120	117,683	49,250
1977	821,643	585,794	8,841	594,635	56,268	8,152	546,519	155,328	119,796	6,717	122,329	52,964
1978	954,398	685,593	11,085	696,678	67,432	8,997	638,243	185,293	130,862	7,549	126,435	57,334
1979	1,073,460	761,390	16,388	777,778	77,611	9,066	709,233	216,461	147,766	8,263	129,918	58,937
1980	1,196,911	810,659	20,498	831,157	83,028	9,296	757,425	263,115	176,371	9,004	132,929	58,583
1981	1,282,978	824,827	12,612	837,439	90,124	11,231	758,546	320,775	203,657	9,536	134,546	57,391
1982	1,317,243	808,493	10,891	819,384	90,009	11,801	741,176	348,092	227,975	9,841	133,847	54,859
1983	1,432,497	890,677	5,080	895,757	100,092	12,197	807,862	384,272	240,363	10,760	133,130	57,463
1984	1,596,051	1,018,091	11,081	1,029,172	117,621	11,714	923,265	424,232	248,554	11,838	134,830	60,553
1985	1,687,489	1,075,541	12,473	1,088,014	125,208	12,434	975,240	446,002	266,247	12,368	136,444	61,517
1986	1,781,914	1,149,334	13,786	1,163,120	133,867	11,846	1,041,099	470,866	269,949	12,969	137,397	63,925
1987	1,899,744	1,263,653	6,955	1,270,608	146,275	11,682	1,136,015	480,402	283,327	13,606	139,626	67,656
1988	2,075,750	1,380,746	9,246	1,389,992	165,594	12,519	1,236,917	533,806	305,027	14,736	140,860	71,400
1989	2,280,964	1,473,649	13,546	1,487,195	176,766	14,277	1,324,706	616,745	339,513	15,890	143,549	72,786
1990	2,431,840	1,597,449	10,885	1,608,334	195,763	13,899	1,426,470	634,381	370,989	16,499	147,392	75,872
1991	2,570,550	1,654,405	16,701	1,671,106	205,922	13,418	1,478,602	672,587	419,361	17,028	150,956	76,214
1992	2,761,971	1,808,225	16,851	1,825,076	224,257	11,803	1,612,622	691,816	457,533	17,822	154,975	78,291
1993	2,976,728	1,957,182	19,986	1,977,168	240,025	11,393	1,748,536	738,357	489,835	18,715	159,054	80,714
1994	3,236,236	2,155,409	15,642	2,171,051	264,507	9,377	1,915,921	798,127	522,188	19,790	163,527	85,896
1995	3,443,551	2,225,294	14,502	2,239,796	276,436	9,649	1,973,009	889,500	581,042	20,573	167,378	88,260
1996	3,667,830	2,348,369	20,101	2,368,470	295,222	9,815	2,083,063	961,991	622,776	21,485	170,715	91,601
1997	3,832,637	2,470,427	19,388	2,489,815	309,399	9,581	2,189,997	1,002,639	640,001	22,087	173,523	95,490
1998	4,062,078	2,657,190	14,939	2,672,129	329,882	9,032	2,351,279	1,022,215	688,584	22,996	176,645	97,290
1999	4,330,856	2,896,065	14,277	2,910,342	352,882	8,565	2,566,025	1,011,748	753,083	24,159	179,264	100,050
2000	4,620,655	3,068,911	10,209	3,079,120	376,502	7,217	2,709,835	1,110,379	800,441	25,420	181,775	103,307
2001	4,957,164	3,314,083	12,986	3,327,069	393,415	1,141	2,934,795	1,123,476	898,893	26,965	183,835	103,859
2002	5,064,691	3,481,959	11,118	3,493,077	416,721	-4,308	3,072,048	1,038,744	953,899	27,127	186,704	103,968
2003	5,403,152	3,684,355	16,269	3,700,624	442,468	-7,553	3,250,603	1,144,153	1,008,396	28,462	189,838	107,562
2004	5,694,773	3,936,469	18,391	3,954,860	479,127	-11,098	3,464,635	1,187,507	1,042,631	29,632	192,185	111,967
2005	5,955,425	4,068,291	17,707	4,085,998	506,726	-14,044	3,565,228	1,279,204	1,110,993	30,588	194,701	115,395
2006	6,507,805	4,309,632	17,126	4,326,758	534,109	-9,501	3,783,148	1,528,365	1,196,292	33,058	196,858	117,401
2007	6,718,036	4,389,655	18,273	4,407,928	553,438	-26,326	3,828,164	1,611,936	1,277,936	33,733	199,152	119,400
2008	6,867,053	4,316,063	16,489	4,332,552	548,924	-13,126	3,770,502	1,649,501	1,447,050	34,137	201,162	116,112
2009	6,619,763	4,073,813	20,119	4,093,932	528,825	-25,284	3,539,823	1,433,126	1,646,814	32,722	202,301	110,154
2010	6,742,263	4,121,719	17,665	4,139,384	539,501	-32,057	3,567,826	1,398,072	1,776,365	33,159	203,334	109,131
2011	7,108,360	4,224,602	21,013	4,245,615	491,550	-32,154	3,721,911	1,567,691	1,818,758	34,742	204,607	109,021
2012	7,417,346	4,469,476	22,923	4,492,399	513,256	-65,709	3,913,434	1,654,010	1,849,902	36,047	205,768	109,916
2013	7,544,596	4,665,314	29,079	4,694,393	605,565	-107,970	3,980,858	1,635,513	1,928,225	36,420	207,155	112,515
2014	8,188,001	4,907,659	29,435	4,937,094	642,352	-82,831	4,211,911	1,855,646	2,120,444	39,151	209,140	114,770
2015	8,765,804	5,257,126	29,153	5,286,279	675,872	-70,336	4,540,071	1,965,741	2,259,992	41,374	211,868	117,751
2016	9,216,498	5,556,577	29,009	5,585,586	709,935	-72,641	4,803,010	2,083,819	2,329,669	42,926	214,706	120,129
2017	9,647,267	5,882,500	28,362	5,910,862	761,091	-66,912	5,082,859	2,173,103	2,391,305	44,360	217,479	122,840
2018	10,237,971	10,224,469	13,502	6,183,258	787,486	-78,861	5,316,911	2,347,512	2,573,548	46,661	219,411	126,178
2019	10,669,698	10,663,784	5,914	6,482,437	829,429	-70,501	5,582,507	2,375,604	2,711,587	48,291	220,944	127,649

Personal Income and Employment by Area: Memphis, TN-MS-AR

(Thousands of dollars, except as noted.)

Year	Personal income, total	Earnings by place of work			Less: Contributions for government social insurance	Plus: Adjustment for residence	Equals: Net earnings by place of residence	Plus: Dividends, interest, and rent	Plus: Personal current transfer receipts	Per capita personal income (dollars)	Population (persons)	Total employment
		Nonfarm	Farm	Total								
1970	3,229,613	2,679,114	62,006	2,741,120	175,962	-18,809	2,546,349	425,768	257,496	3,510	920,140	414,524
1971	3,624,452	3,015,320	62,028	3,077,348	205,060	-26,376	2,845,912	471,932	306,608	3,898	929,937	429,167
1972	4,111,964	3,455,097	65,820	3,520,917	244,395	-34,025	3,242,497	526,139	343,328	4,354	944,488	455,373
1973	4,578,628	3,846,863	95,319	3,942,182	312,264	-40,872	3,589,046	586,740	402,842	4,829	948,225	472,452
1974	5,070,704	4,222,041	62,031	4,284,072	354,055	-44,368	3,885,649	684,763	500,292	5,279	960,477	479,924
1975	5,499,540	4,441,414	57,072	4,498,486	367,248	-46,943	4,084,295	748,835	666,410	5,707	963,646	463,926
1976	5,986,228	4,830,102	74,410	4,904,512	409,053	-45,638	4,449,821	789,075	747,332	6,175	969,411	466,956
1977	6,574,703	5,357,506	87,727	5,445,233	455,179	-47,728	4,942,326	856,322	776,055	6,742	975,249	481,178
1978	7,425,542	6,093,997	87,774	6,181,771	526,033	-47,431	5,608,307	970,350	846,885	7,550	983,532	500,999
1979	8,302,175	6,801,353	95,662	6,897,015	612,009	-57,224	6,227,782	1,098,387	976,006	8,332	996,459	513,957
1980	9,186,803	7,431,885	13,508	7,445,393	667,951	-67,021	6,710,421	1,312,527	1,163,855	9,135	1,005,686	514,719
1981	10,051,415	7,945,322	53,659	7,998,981	768,297	-75,513	7,155,171	1,587,546	1,308,698	10,030	1,002,176	503,394
1982	10,607,099	8,244,044	43,806	8,287,850	812,081	-99,911	7,375,858	1,829,973	1,401,268	10,551	1,005,293	491,268
1983	11,380,242	8,927,920	-600	8,927,320	889,537	-116,241	7,921,542	1,940,558	1,518,142	11,270	1,009,767	501,064
1984	12,619,130	9,921,053	55,925	9,976,978	1,019,561	-129,361	8,828,056	2,209,482	1,581,592	12,453	1,013,317	522,360
1985	13,491,104	10,691,672	56,140	10,747,812	1,115,344	-140,658	9,491,810	2,334,629	1,664,665	13,172	1,024,191	533,858
1986	14,343,210	11,474,106	18,234	11,492,340	1,222,958	-151,471	10,117,911	2,449,485	1,775,814	13,870	1,034,093	551,772
1987	15,508,814	12,491,033	79,696	12,570,729	1,324,233	-148,350	11,098,146	2,556,316	1,854,352	14,811	1,047,141	573,250
1988	16,788,787	13,495,440	103,910	13,599,350	1,475,289	-137,576	11,986,485	2,828,789	1,973,513	15,815	1,061,590	595,468
1989	18,248,432	14,508,060	65,713	14,573,773	1,597,346	-171,666	12,804,761	3,308,474	2,135,197	17,037	1,071,132	616,435
1990	19,329,117	15,476,334	68,692	15,545,026	1,725,528	-203,334	13,616,164	3,394,277	2,318,676	17,921	1,078,598	623,835
1991	20,169,832	16,175,300	73,987	16,249,287	1,829,252	-219,218	14,200,817	3,382,847	2,586,168	18,475	1,091,735	618,879
1992	21,774,865	17,538,461	102,131	17,640,592	1,954,502	-243,593	15,442,497	3,457,263	2,875,105	19,716	1,104,416	620,945
1993	23,154,570	18,720,852	73,792	18,794,644	2,081,818	-275,221	16,437,605	3,604,062	3,112,903	20,724	1,117,303	638,087
1994	24,935,746	20,287,342	116,421	20,403,763	2,283,519	-325,473	17,794,771	3,861,754	3,279,221	22,009	1,132,959	671,106
1995	26,801,668	21,719,247	75,325	21,794,572	2,433,562	-369,735	18,991,275	4,194,999	3,615,394	23,342	1,148,208	688,368
1996	28,445,916	22,998,929	140,308	23,139,237	2,537,179	-416,237	20,185,821	4,444,003	3,816,092	24,488	1,161,613	702,296
1997	30,008,135	24,447,377	94,099	24,541,476	2,691,289	-468,111	21,382,076	4,718,983	3,907,076	25,593	1,172,495	721,454
1998	33,726,822	27,765,110	48,011	27,813,121	2,929,320	-541,752	24,342,049	5,279,189	4,105,584	28,413	1,187,032	740,753
1999	34,744,048	28,884,979	52,658	28,937,637	3,080,996	-595,866	25,260,775	5,247,062	4,236,211	28,885	1,202,822	751,200
2000	36,018,707	29,798,456	46,488	29,844,944	3,174,013	-648,310	26,022,621	5,488,692	4,507,394	29,614	1,216,257	763,639
2001	38,104,073	31,639,709	147,416	31,787,125	3,380,171	-677,924	27,729,030	5,457,759	4,917,284	31,115	1,224,627	760,358
2002	39,032,722	32,653,902	32,878	32,686,780	3,528,958	-696,011	28,461,811	5,299,478	5,271,433	31,602	1,235,125	756,819
2003	40,338,785	33,504,201	158,695	33,662,896	3,620,376	-718,387	29,324,133	5,416,029	5,598,623	32,338	1,247,414	759,011
2004	42,134,253	35,114,722	181,926	35,296,648	3,775,652	-762,164	30,758,832	5,528,989	5,846,432	33,468	1,258,948	767,768
2005	43,661,218	36,031,024	153,656	36,184,680	3,865,382	-775,879	31,543,419	5,866,588	6,251,211	34,326	1,271,965	779,343
2006	46,523,229	38,119,270	124,004	38,243,274	4,084,777	-806,179	33,352,318	6,634,254	6,536,657	36,012	1,291,868	798,441
2007	48,457,231	39,290,132	115,087	39,405,219	4,267,677	-848,544	34,288,998	7,030,897	7,137,336	37,210	1,302,273	813,800
2008	48,841,706	38,644,547	104,957	38,749,504	4,285,995	-837,048	33,626,461	7,156,306	8,058,939	37,260	1,310,829	810,392
2009	47,303,938	36,917,242	109,755	37,026,997	4,157,802	-761,715	32,107,480	6,562,732	8,633,726	35,898	1,317,719	782,051
2010	49,047,076	37,696,870	36,623	37,733,493	4,181,223	-746,950	32,805,320	6,687,558	9,554,198	36,981	1,326,280	780,211
2011	51,556,541	39,062,731	115,592	39,178,323	3,828,418	-773,160	34,576,745	7,209,215	9,770,581	38,696	1,332,338	794,484
2012	54,059,140	41,027,936	47,366	41,075,302	3,904,981	-807,986	36,362,335	7,809,301	9,887,504	40,337	1,340,171	799,259
2013	53,949,310	41,284,811	298,299	41,583,110	4,473,213	-779,865	36,330,032	7,471,611	10,147,667	40,231	1,340,975	803,257
2014	55,307,160	42,340,629	28,064	42,368,693	4,580,187	-786,275	37,002,231	8,022,500	10,282,429	41,200	1,342,422	816,181
2015	57,214,996	43,670,466	-32,687	43,637,779	4,717,280	-807,662	38,112,837	8,316,737	10,785,422	42,588	1,343,439	828,695
2016	58,776,978	44,872,162	-32,729	44,839,433	4,842,272	-856,452	39,140,709	8,589,019	11,047,250	43,694	1,345,193	842,754
2017	60,614,441	46,220,010	-21,261	46,198,749	5,039,314	-876,809	40,282,626	9,030,516	11,301,299	44,958	1,348,260	848,929
2018	62,663,644	62,631,912	31,732	47,650,691	5,222,743	-971,333	41,456,615	9,653,734	11,553,295	46,677	1,342,497	862,397
2019	64,590,483	64,506,487	83,996	49,093,605	5,477,874	-993,043	42,622,688	9,755,500	12,212,295	47,985	1,346,045	875,032

Personal Income and Employment by Area: Merced, CA

(Thousands of dollars, except as noted.)

Year	Personal income, total	Earnings by place of work			Less: Contributions for government social insurance	Plus: Adjustment for residence	Equals: Net earnings by place of residence	Plus: Dividends, interest, and rent	Plus: Personal current transfer receipts	Per capita personal income (dollars)	Population (persons)	Total employment
		Nonfarm	Farm	Total								
1970	434,859	250,899	78,531	329,430	17,297	3,889	316,022	69,432	49,405	4,131	105,275	45,456
1971	460,187	276,214	69,534	345,748	20,013	4,009	329,744	75,213	55,230	4,260	108,032	47,188
1972	517,524	305,479	88,135	393,614	22,997	4,804	375,421	83,926	58,177	4,681	110,548	49,741
1973	612,840	341,807	130,956	472,763	28,522	4,907	449,148	99,070	64,622	5,355	114,436	51,449
1974	685,840	385,206	137,450	522,656	33,496	5,443	494,603	113,996	77,241	5,815	117,949	54,411
1975	783,346	426,877	167,674	594,551	37,128	4,103	561,526	126,213	95,607	6,450	121,456	56,336
1976	878,577	486,963	186,623	673,586	43,470	3,221	633,337	135,638	109,602	6,953	126,358	58,502
1977	964,456	545,897	191,997	737,894	49,215	3,848	692,527	151,964	119,965	7,619	126,591	60,515
1978	1,017,192	620,943	134,596	755,539	55,799	5,790	705,530	177,983	133,679	7,920	128,435	61,473
1979	1,170,290	693,339	179,664	873,003	63,665	9,295	818,633	202,344	149,313	8,881	131,775	64,328
1980	1,331,927	747,337	223,498	970,835	67,547	10,589	913,877	239,657	178,393	9,821	135,625	64,044
1981	1,362,937	802,049	127,573	929,622	77,661	16,004	867,965	282,867	212,105	9,761	139,632	62,729
1982	1,461,800	861,647	118,986	980,633	84,178	18,868	915,323	310,042	236,435	10,239	142,766	62,096
1983	1,528,943	916,685	83,605	1,000,290	91,329	22,110	931,071	335,859	262,013	10,355	147,657	62,975
1984	1,773,556	1,030,951	167,318	1,198,269	106,646	26,559	1,118,182	370,819	284,555	11,718	151,357	64,798
1985	1,911,489	1,118,344	171,155	1,289,499	116,771	32,444	1,205,172	387,791	318,526	12,258	155,939	66,196
1986	2,060,070	1,194,808	202,346	1,397,154	126,063	40,180	1,311,271	404,857	343,942	12,957	158,988	67,501
1987	2,285,290	1,318,563	271,136	1,589,699	137,528	53,453	1,505,624	421,915	357,751	14,024	162,956	70,309
1988	2,395,633	1,409,767	258,992	1,668,759	154,488	66,018	1,580,289	430,496	384,848	14,281	167,749	73,220
1989	2,610,501	1,497,751	283,848	1,781,599	166,916	76,733	1,691,416	494,799	424,286	15,091	172,988	74,815
1990	2,786,599	1,607,353	285,166	1,892,519	178,913	90,856	1,804,462	510,953	471,184	15,485	179,953	76,728
1991	2,911,291	1,679,683	275,569	1,955,252	190,027	96,776	1,862,001	517,874	531,416	15,644	186,091	78,038
1992	3,108,931	1,751,785	298,703	2,050,488	197,766	106,911	1,959,633	517,970	631,328	16,407	189,489	76,943
1993	3,207,165	1,796,353	308,550	2,104,903	204,979	117,898	2,017,822	523,982	665,361	16,606	193,137	78,232
1994	3,284,026	1,819,611	326,879	2,146,490	206,089	132,272	2,072,673	532,480	678,873	16,603	197,798	77,678
1995	3,171,229	1,752,652	218,588	1,971,240	197,363	157,534	1,931,411	527,945	711,873	16,238	195,291	77,043
1996	3,484,054	1,799,133	399,358	2,198,491	194,827	184,826	2,188,490	547,927	747,637	17,884	194,819	77,229
1997	3,595,354	1,922,956	358,554	2,281,510	203,569	219,706	2,297,647	561,183	736,524	18,130	198,312	77,931
1998	3,824,171	2,098,350	299,252	2,397,602	215,286	255,929	2,438,245	609,531	776,395	18,907	202,264	82,507
1999	4,016,274	2,211,430	291,519	2,502,949	229,183	304,963	2,578,729	617,880	819,665	19,427	206,734	83,851
2000	4,242,176	2,352,118	246,546	2,598,664	243,538	385,739	2,740,865	655,407	845,904	19,986	212,258	83,061
2001	4,615,574	2,523,778	298,821	2,822,599	269,346	394,953	2,948,206	709,702	957,666	21,093	218,816	82,590
2002	4,918,182	2,789,249	315,588	3,104,837	303,314	375,403	3,176,926	706,165	1,035,091	21,825	225,351	87,067
2003	5,394,821	3,036,090	433,510	3,469,600	332,958	395,344	3,531,986	760,261	1,102,574	23,280	231,735	87,520
2004	5,910,302	3,222,920	683,673	3,906,593	363,568	435,934	3,978,959	763,774	1,167,569	24,919	237,180	87,874
2005	6,140,026	3,419,519	612,984	4,032,503	381,609	497,065	4,147,959	765,279	1,226,788	25,314	242,554	87,573
2006	6,300,539	3,656,372	401,879	4,058,251	393,059	497,928	4,163,120	809,764	1,327,655	25,681	245,338	90,187
2007	7,017,024	3,665,731	874,155	4,539,886	395,284	535,143	4,679,745	910,379	1,426,900	28,233	248,540	92,968
2008	6,823,858	3,581,620	561,349	4,142,969	401,957	530,070	4,271,082	943,341	1,609,435	27,237	250,538	90,756
2009	6,898,078	3,673,337	462,908	4,136,245	410,772	470,290	4,195,763	914,245	1,788,070	27,341	252,302	88,875
2010	7,300,407	3,741,625	586,866	4,328,491	399,376	455,391	4,384,506	925,055	1,990,846	28,431	256,772	88,611
2011	7,924,519	3,787,343	959,579	4,746,922	371,663	521,266	4,896,525	1,033,373	1,994,621	30,525	259,607	88,469
2012	8,112,642	3,954,101	913,790	4,867,891	390,387	470,065	4,947,569	1,132,197	2,032,876	31,035	261,407	92,113
2013	8,690,667	4,078,919	1,252,077	5,330,996	446,489	477,938	5,362,445	1,198,992	2,129,230	33,081	262,712	94,673
2014	9,488,457	4,270,481	1,503,636	5,774,117	462,867	509,518	5,820,768	1,395,252	2,272,437	35,768	265,281	97,956
2015	9,686,983	4,532,197	1,039,255	5,571,452	484,366	552,576	5,639,662	1,573,286	2,474,035	36,226	267,406	100,098
2016	9,913,086	4,700,270	887,549	5,587,819	517,122	634,016	5,704,713	1,644,200	2,564,173	36,868	268,878	101,040
2017	10,556,722	4,988,430	1,264,727	6,253,157	551,301	626,368	6,328,224	1,734,895	2,493,603	38,716	272,673	103,945
2018	10,696,798	9,820,721	876,077	6,017,391	573,803	864,581	6,308,169	1,771,637	2,616,992	39,018	274,151	106,173
2019	11,406,396	10,321,479	1,084,917	6,533,381	622,417	900,456	6,811,420	1,810,059	2,784,917	41,077	277,680	107,288

Personal Income and Employment by Area: Miami-Fort Lauderdale-Pompano Beach, FL

(Thousands of dollars, except as noted.)

Year	Personal income, total	Derivation of personal income									Per capita personal income (dollars)	Population (persons)	Total employment
		Earnings by place of work			Less: Contributions for government social insurance	Plus: Adjustment for residence	Equals: Net earnings by place of residence	Plus: Dividends, interest, and rent	Plus: Personal current transfer receipts				
		Nonfarm	Farm	Total									
1970	10,723,332	7,570,402	105,059	7,675,461	490,761	-12,205	7,172,495	2,659,151	891,686	4,755	2,255,202	1,054,067
1971	11,973,429	8,308,995	122,138	8,431,133	560,807	-16,498	7,853,828	3,031,972	1,087,629	5,063	2,364,750	1,087,984
1972	13,740,830	9,599,126	131,527	9,730,653	685,284	-20,550	9,024,819	3,421,480	1,294,531	5,543	2,478,824	1,178,470
1973	16,065,434	11,326,691	139,634	11,466,325	933,948	-29,219	10,503,158	3,990,093	1,572,183	6,168	2,604,637	1,304,027
1974	18,109,416	12,365,697	201,117	12,566,814	1,064,125	-29,226	11,473,463	4,697,119	1,938,834	6,595	2,745,960	1,330,500
1975	19,421,822	12,579,507	226,346	12,805,853	1,059,036	-29,180	11,717,637	5,107,965	2,596,220	6,845	2,837,578	1,275,484
1976	21,171,455	13,680,499	233,926	13,914,425	1,168,205	-26,213	12,720,007	5,586,433	2,865,015	7,341	2,884,080	1,292,596
1977	23,699,865	15,373,859	208,539	15,582,398	1,322,007	-32,310	14,228,081	6,362,645	3,109,139	8,068	2,937,632	1,367,587
1978	27,264,542	17,882,167	195,555	18,077,722	1,585,493	-48,109	16,444,120	7,376,673	3,443,749	9,079	3,002,966	1,485,993
1979	31,531,438	20,620,971	210,600	20,831,571	1,919,378	-69,043	18,843,150	8,734,555	3,953,733	10,100	3,121,950	1,567,870
1980	37,275,817	23,914,041	291,109	24,205,150	2,247,862	-92,270	21,865,018	10,748,744	4,662,055	11,452	3,254,936	1,663,461
1981	43,322,662	26,903,058	323,739	27,226,797	2,720,704	-39,422	24,466,671	13,463,775	5,392,216	12,793	3,386,317	1,715,798
1982	46,093,564	28,320,823	422,817	28,743,640	2,943,142	-48,518	25,751,980	14,309,555	6,032,029	13,361	3,449,745	1,720,145
1983	50,351,579	31,038,118	715,874	31,753,992	3,233,549	-70,133	28,450,310	15,348,907	6,552,362	14,359	3,506,541	1,771,008
1984	55,603,387	34,386,680	450,907	34,837,587	3,677,992	-90,906	31,068,689	17,516,809	7,017,889	15,618	3,560,292	1,862,036
1985	60,295,902	37,502,274	454,282	37,956,556	4,075,773	-111,884	33,768,899	19,063,328	7,463,675	16,597	3,632,834	1,921,376
1986	64,607,910	40,538,030	537,808	41,075,838	4,520,079	-120,123	36,435,636	20,203,433	7,968,841	17,418	3,709,283	1,976,279
1987	70,039,163	44,844,978	590,313	45,435,291	4,932,983	-140,525	40,361,783	21,299,216	8,378,164	18,445	3,797,118	1,983,981
1988	76,339,041	49,129,398	621,712	49,751,110	5,554,394	-157,717	44,038,999	23,211,834	9,088,208	19,616	3,891,758	2,077,107
1989	84,613,056	51,724,493	555,191	52,279,684	5,905,326	-157,569	46,216,789	28,163,578	10,232,689	21,238	3,984,047	2,124,442
1990	90,431,751	54,865,738	431,771	55,297,509	6,200,007	-183,751	48,913,751	30,376,230	11,141,770	22,172	4,078,578	2,151,815
1991	94,407,722	56,931,782	512,637	57,444,419	6,462,509	-177,290	50,804,620	31,004,997	12,598,105	22,603	4,176,731	2,129,237
1992	99,527,890	60,974,711	600,067	61,574,778	6,856,548	-166,722	54,551,508	30,384,500	14,591,882	23,347	4,262,995	2,133,944
1993	105,628,246	65,856,904	661,304	66,518,208	7,360,272	-169,949	58,987,987	31,179,397	15,460,862	24,337	4,340,175	2,221,343
1994	110,638,688	69,319,487	484,294	69,803,781	7,836,300	-175,188	61,792,293	32,481,126	16,365,269	24,890	4,445,162	2,289,282
1995	118,870,020	73,641,770	516,285	74,158,055	8,275,297	-174,552	65,708,206	35,410,789	17,751,025	26,141	4,547,191	2,367,458
1996	126,518,278	78,465,201	417,206	78,882,407	8,695,324	-179,933	70,007,150	37,705,770	18,805,358	27,194	4,652,414	2,423,829
1997	132,453,908	82,220,890	450,641	82,671,531	9,113,267	-167,907	73,390,357	39,760,131	19,303,420	27,884	4,750,249	2,495,838
1998	142,832,382	89,430,354	548,389	89,978,743	9,749,850	-173,540	80,055,353	43,126,658	19,650,371	29,530	4,836,853	2,580,377
1999	149,317,626	95,628,247	630,980	96,259,227	10,377,349	-177,720	85,704,158	43,251,273	20,362,195	30,275	4,932,004	2,668,615
2000	162,347,856	104,880,353	574,363	105,454,716	11,201,074	-196,716	94,056,926	46,623,901	21,667,029	32,302	5,025,895	2,759,068
2001	170,915,803	112,291,613	629,770	112,921,383	12,206,605	-427,793	100,286,985	47,153,972	23,474,846	33,442	5,110,780	2,854,679
2002	176,395,219	117,288,340	616,882	117,905,222	12,636,163	-641,576	104,627,483	46,676,812	25,090,924	33,940	5,197,205	2,884,746
2003	182,169,695	122,046,832	549,030	122,595,862	13,120,081	-857,475	108,618,306	46,817,857	26,733,532	34,622	5,261,713	2,947,087
2004	198,303,832	131,242,940	521,431	131,764,371	14,090,209	-1,038,087	116,636,075	53,127,191	28,540,566	37,161	5,336,368	3,033,206
2005	216,853,367	141,896,971	592,893	142,489,864	15,338,875	-1,491,277	125,659,712	60,627,089	30,566,566	40,075	5,411,148	3,153,331
2006	235,721,342	150,301,515	591,611	150,893,126	16,485,417	-1,720,866	132,686,843	71,201,732	31,832,767	43,413	5,429,748	3,234,598
2007	245,235,052	152,605,444	559,218	153,164,662	17,001,437	-1,758,335	134,404,890	77,597,547	33,232,615	45,221	5,422,987	3,292,421
2008	241,218,860	146,317,418	505,364	146,822,782	16,900,674	-1,863,514	128,058,594	75,651,061	37,509,205	44,223	5,454,633	3,238,672
2009	220,806,180	135,501,338	551,849	136,053,187	16,192,828	-1,692,151	118,168,208	61,974,302	40,663,670	40,113	5,504,624	3,113,043
2010	239,771,459	145,411,180	553,734	145,964,914	16,566,177	-1,214,351	128,184,386	67,307,894	44,279,179	42,940	5,583,888	3,125,007
2011	252,185,201	150,484,885	456,672	150,941,557	15,284,203	-1,409,564	134,247,790	72,276,315	45,661,096	44,272	5,696,288	3,232,075
2012	263,804,080	154,693,534	528,062	155,221,596	15,843,184	-2,011,976	137,366,436	81,945,948	44,491,696	45,634	5,780,894	3,317,113
2013	262,233,595	160,559,625	592,729	161,152,354	18,581,183	-2,232,147	140,339,024	76,389,596	45,504,975	44,727	5,862,992	3,435,012
2014	285,921,011	172,642,522	535,046	173,177,568	19,708,476	-2,285,580	151,183,512	86,968,867	47,768,632	48,105	5,943,656	3,586,619
2015	308,132,986	183,398,129	706,968	184,105,097	20,774,626	-2,442,002	160,888,469	97,315,307	49,929,210	51,134	6,026,044	3,752,715
2016	315,177,363	190,760,161	633,271	191,393,432	21,618,066	-3,116,510	166,658,856	96,423,512	52,094,995	51,606	6,107,433	3,837,553
2017	330,928,703	200,354,058	549,113	200,903,171	22,594,724	-3,410,175	174,898,272	101,407,812	54,622,619	53,732	6,158,824	3,904,280
2018	363,413,990	362,632,975	781,015	216,963,606	24,024,929	-3,473,277	189,465,400	119,670,328	54,278,262	59,151	6,143,837	4,108,797
2019	375,944,348	375,059,596	884,752	227,165,944	25,417,098	-3,762,863	197,985,983	121,137,426	56,820,939	60,966	6,166,488	4,201,387

Personal Income and Employment by Area: Michigan City-La Porte, IN

(Thousands of dollars, except as noted.)

Year	Personal income, total	Earnings by place of work			Less: Contributions for government social insurance	Plus: Adjustment for residence	Equals: Net earnings by place of residence	Plus: Dividends, interest, and rent	Plus: Personal current transfer receipts	Per capita personal income (dollars)	Population (persons)	Total employment
		Nonfarm	Farm	Total								
1970	405,753	319,798	5,729	325,527	22,456	20,794	323,865	52,362	29,526	3,847	105,461	45,672
1971	430,233	326,695	10,528	337,223	23,782	24,105	337,546	57,107	35,580	4,047	106,310	44,103
1972	472,811	362,812	7,144	369,956	27,838	31,250	373,368	61,092	38,351	4,429	106,744	45,366
1973	539,615	403,999	16,325	420,324	35,558	40,068	424,834	70,270	44,511	5,037	107,134	47,958
1974	588,706	436,701	8,392	445,093	40,261	50,675	455,507	81,867	51,332	5,493	107,180	48,730
1975	640,124	444,936	17,067	462,003	40,208	59,369	481,164	91,172	67,788	5,963	107,353	46,388
1976	706,083	493,075	16,159	509,234	45,038	71,727	535,923	98,545	71,615	6,562	107,604	47,203
1977	783,754	551,728	8,926	560,654	50,054	88,834	599,434	110,281	74,039	7,224	108,496	48,332
1978	889,401	624,138	13,976	638,114	58,176	106,904	686,842	121,496	81,063	8,174	108,807	50,502
1979	980,714	678,623	9,852	688,475	65,577	128,351	751,249	135,872	93,593	8,986	109,142	50,703
1980	1,062,542	718,909	4,803	723,712	69,332	126,985	781,365	166,472	114,705	9,779	108,657	49,332
1981	1,153,658	751,346	5,889	757,235	77,837	135,856	815,254	204,356	134,048	10,631	108,515	48,011
1982	1,165,620	748,457	886	749,343	79,295	125,490	795,538	216,731	153,351	10,779	108,140	46,152
1983	1,181,177	766,599	-8,369	758,230	81,529	108,903	785,604	226,069	169,504	11,015	107,230	45,219
1984	1,277,160	820,235	10,149	830,384	89,348	111,613	852,649	252,554	171,957	11,939	106,976	46,096
1985	1,335,047	870,773	8,641	879,414	96,368	111,823	894,869	261,048	179,130	12,515	106,680	47,280
1986	1,388,792	917,291	7,760	925,051	102,005	103,385	926,431	270,192	192,169	13,139	105,696	48,106
1987	1,467,077	981,898	14,118	996,016	107,304	108,724	997,436	272,452	197,189	13,866	105,806	49,835
1988	1,565,711	1,074,771	4,993	1,079,764	123,643	113,211	1,069,332	291,099	205,280	14,779	105,941	51,945
1989	1,707,099	1,139,715	22,362	1,162,077	131,127	119,488	1,150,438	335,279	221,382	16,029	106,502	53,294
1990	1,778,907	1,193,902	20,991	1,214,893	139,609	119,409	1,194,693	345,706	238,508	16,585	107,257	53,683
1991	1,816,875	1,236,959	2,954	1,239,913	146,180	118,611	1,212,344	345,889	258,642	16,799	108,151	53,728
1992	1,957,682	1,319,951	19,383	1,339,334	154,983	126,091	1,310,442	350,506	296,734	17,972	108,928	53,920
1993	2,030,568	1,374,752	14,238	1,388,990	162,404	128,006	1,354,592	360,172	315,804	18,551	109,461	54,837
1994	2,135,740	1,446,160	19,164	1,465,324	172,869	142,006	1,434,461	376,263	325,016	19,483	109,620	55,637
1995	2,228,727	1,493,922	13,892	1,507,814	179,301	144,695	1,473,208	424,648	330,871	20,340	109,571	57,043
1996	2,332,475	1,532,927	22,259	1,555,186	182,094	154,641	1,527,733	453,571	351,171	21,246	109,783	56,722
1997	2,470,404	1,632,939	23,965	1,656,904	192,651	154,283	1,618,536	490,359	361,509	22,504	109,774	57,371
1998	2,593,048	1,740,085	18,884	1,758,969	200,631	164,043	1,722,381	500,004	370,663	23,583	109,954	58,248
1999	2,624,977	1,789,742	9,345	1,799,087	206,167	163,766	1,756,686	483,918	384,373	23,857	110,028	58,957
2000	2,782,139	1,896,580	13,320	1,909,900	216,581	156,338	1,849,657	526,595	405,887	25,264	110,121	59,904
2001	2,849,079	1,921,488	19,422	1,940,910	220,586	171,118	1,891,442	513,031	444,606	25,883	110,077	58,597
2002	2,888,464	1,947,200	10,812	1,958,012	224,665	191,509	1,924,856	491,638	471,970	26,365	109,555	57,869
2003	2,960,981	1,945,097	23,301	1,968,398	226,092	225,750	1,968,056	502,569	490,356	27,158	109,027	56,932
2004	3,026,107	2,009,860	41,547	2,051,407	235,273	225,381	2,041,515	466,540	518,052	27,784	108,914	56,935
2005	3,134,370	2,083,178	22,694	2,105,872	247,471	260,453	2,118,854	452,715	562,801	28,614	109,541	57,591
2006	3,311,102	2,149,383	26,352	2,175,735	256,234	296,071	2,215,572	493,797	601,733	30,199	109,641	57,497
2007	3,466,037	2,217,598	26,968	2,244,566	266,546	316,480	2,294,500	540,348	631,189	31,269	110,846	57,996
2008	3,635,758	2,246,625	29,983	2,276,608	271,945	340,169	2,344,832	569,199	721,727	32,676	111,267	57,091
2009	3,434,595	2,133,135	14,638	2,147,773	260,167	241,945	2,129,551	501,816	803,228	30,813	111,465	54,442
2010	3,559,091	2,160,112	32,075	2,192,187	259,881	294,297	2,226,603	476,434	856,054	31,932	111,458	53,238
2011	3,778,761	2,239,615	50,099	2,289,714	238,793	347,500	2,398,421	532,883	847,457	33,948	111,309	53,913
2012	3,990,801	2,315,329	54,183	2,369,512	243,121	383,772	2,510,163	608,619	872,019	35,859	111,290	53,668
2013	3,990,161	2,336,067	86,742	2,422,809	279,622	388,775	2,531,962	574,215	883,984	35,814	111,414	53,428
2014	4,084,729	2,402,426	38,443	2,440,869	286,310	378,900	2,533,459	618,176	933,094	36,563	111,717	53,500
2015	4,164,086	2,396,577	4,093	2,400,670	288,878	450,460	2,562,252	630,962	970,872	37,574	110,825	53,280
2016	4,284,157	2,438,411	13,746	2,452,157	290,698	475,538	2,636,997	654,369	992,791	38,873	110,208	53,113
2017	4,429,050	2,504,593	1,175	2,505,768	297,780	513,856	2,721,844	686,186	1,021,020	40,253	110,029	53,127
2018	4,659,156	4,632,273	26,883	2,596,568	311,716	527,028	2,811,880	776,061	1,071,215	42,363	109,981	53,278
2019	4,825,145	4,802,162	22,983	2,645,619	320,410	574,805	2,900,014	785,750	1,139,381	43,910	109,888	53,548

Personal Income and Employment by Area: Midland, MI

(Thousands of dollars, except as noted.)

		Derivation of personal income										
		Earnings by place of work			Less: Contributions for government social insurance	Plus: Adjustment for residence	Equals: Net earnings by place of residence	Plus: Dividends, interest, and rent	Plus: Personal current transfer receipts	Per capita personal income (dollars)	Population (persons)	Total employment
Year	Personal income, total	Nonfarm	Farm	Total								
1970	277,325	285,670	1,613	287,283	20,219	-51,018	216,046	46,103	15,176	4,336	63,956	28,920
1971	299,208	301,232	1,394	302,626	22,121	-49,458	231,047	48,866	19,295	4,600	65,050	27,915
1972	321,559	317,665	2,621	320,286	24,578	-48,235	247,473	52,486	21,600	4,925	65,286	27,970
1973	352,547	350,732	3,187	353,919	31,828	-50,754	271,337	56,352	24,858	5,310	66,390	29,341
1974	410,969	406,363	7,733	414,096	38,416	-61,308	314,372	62,574	34,023	6,119	67,168	28,737
1975	449,291	438,157	4,214	442,371	40,362	-64,940	337,069	70,659	41,563	6,547	68,626	30,639
1976	511,778	508,866	2,797	511,663	47,602	-73,031	391,030	77,753	42,995	7,382	69,324	32,404
1977	594,681	603,469	4,500	607,969	56,695	-89,582	461,692	87,179	45,810	8,389	70,888	35,226
1978	663,859	672,619	3,989	676,608	64,444	-92,878	519,286	95,591	48,982	9,233	71,900	35,972
1979	730,776	738,168	3,508	741,676	74,550	-99,421	567,705	108,066	55,005	9,989	73,158	36,279
1980	773,486	735,259	2,014	737,273	73,494	-89,820	573,959	126,860	72,667	10,469	73,882	34,846
1981	854,851	791,988	2,026	794,014	85,842	-91,281	616,891	160,902	77,058	11,408	74,936	34,356
1982	904,532	823,353	1,165	824,518	92,225	-99,958	632,335	185,238	86,959	12,095	74,784	33,960
1983	953,477	841,331	-235	841,096	94,247	-89,066	657,783	200,940	94,754	12,680	75,198	33,798
1984	1,022,239	851,133	2,194	853,327	96,306	-62,394	694,627	225,008	102,604	13,480	75,835	33,330
1985	1,093,068	881,598	2,030	883,628	100,225	-41,815	741,588	243,691	107,789	15,078	72,492	33,734
1986	1,174,550	959,534	1,050	960,584	108,944	-43,366	808,274	250,469	115,807	16,179	72,598	34,691
1987	1,271,864	1,036,999	2,758	1,039,757	115,912	-47,231	876,614	273,798	121,452	17,410	73,054	36,329
1988	1,400,428	1,154,807	4,046	1,158,853	132,013	-48,428	978,412	295,422	126,594	18,908	74,065	37,224
1989	1,551,684	1,231,158	7,238	1,238,396	141,271	-52,154	1,044,971	366,182	140,531	20,754	74,767	39,737
1990	1,644,668	1,306,722	2,919	1,309,641	153,520	-48,783	1,107,338	383,173	154,157	21,640	76,002	41,424
1991	1,698,467	1,330,532	2,997	1,333,529	157,915	-28,573	1,147,041	379,751	171,675	22,135	76,733	41,784
1992	1,826,089	1,469,540	3,582	1,473,122	173,186	-49,563	1,250,373	391,414	184,302	23,456	77,853	43,653
1993	1,912,487	1,505,679	4,413	1,510,092	178,711	-25,394	1,305,987	404,280	202,220	24,328	78,614	43,354
1994	1,993,816	1,525,778	1,693	1,527,471	185,902	-4,758	1,336,811	450,098	206,907	25,126	79,352	43,013
1995	2,111,747	1,629,057	2,723	1,631,780	197,828	-12,731	1,421,221	474,534	215,992	26,449	79,841	43,166
1996	2,251,232	1,736,784	1,452	1,738,236	206,769	10,999	1,542,466	485,918	222,848	27,828	80,897	44,035
1997	2,316,023	1,798,138	1,115	1,799,253	212,924	-6,371	1,579,958	489,726	246,339	28,366	81,648	44,500
1998	2,477,685	1,879,423	859	1,880,282	219,695	31,880	1,692,467	533,707	251,511	30,186	82,081	44,439
1999	2,517,881	1,904,508	2,739	1,907,247	222,736	43,789	1,728,300	514,512	275,069	30,483	82,599	45,798
2000	2,636,745	2,088,256	2,099	2,090,355	244,437	-31,238	1,814,680	527,486	294,579	31,801	82,913	47,165
2001	2,798,301	2,236,470	1,332	2,237,802	233,432	-46,886	1,957,484	512,396	328,421	33,482	83,576	45,811
2002	2,787,587	2,190,300	1,648	2,191,948	231,501	-17,522	1,942,925	499,739	344,923	33,319	83,664	45,388
2003	2,894,328	2,269,834	1,426	2,271,260	236,073	-6,349	2,028,838	503,692	361,798	34,451	84,012	44,687
2004	3,123,295	2,433,534	4,494	2,438,028	258,827	-48,218	2,130,983	610,936	381,376	37,156	84,058	44,371
2005	3,110,003	2,376,273	5,596	2,381,869	258,627	6,768	2,130,010	569,950	410,043	37,055	83,930	44,863
2006	3,240,864	2,425,465	2,997	2,428,462	269,858	21,187	2,179,791	627,027	434,046	38,723	83,693	45,446
2007	3,343,083	2,491,025	5,476	2,496,501	282,154	21,866	2,236,213	629,459	477,411	39,989	83,600	46,416
2008	3,608,710	2,669,677	9,159	2,678,836	302,324	-16,887	2,359,625	703,800	545,285	43,164	83,605	46,547
2009	3,476,823	2,571,054	2,559	2,573,613	294,528	55,340	2,334,425	552,155	590,243	41,569	83,639	45,169
2010	3,563,912	2,693,922	6,561	2,700,483	298,866	14,120	2,415,737	516,711	631,464	42,604	83,653	45,043
2011	3,792,745	2,804,658	18,456	2,823,114	278,813	42,574	2,586,875	574,531	631,339	45,282	83,759	45,974
2012	3,778,443	2,685,462	13,673	2,699,135	280,205	68,485	2,487,415	656,603	634,425	45,170	83,650	45,863
2013	3,690,179	2,644,190	9,943	2,654,133	324,141	65,375	2,395,367	646,030	648,782	44,168	83,549	46,560
2014	3,409,096	2,233,181	1,148	2,234,329	365,840	98,080	1,966,569	758,885	683,642	40,866	83,421	47,554
2015	3,395,980	2,148,172	355	2,148,527	382,855	79,260	1,844,932	820,877	730,171	40,607	83,630	47,798
2016	3,929,482	2,639,407	-2,410	2,636,997	356,586	65,514	2,345,925	833,603	749,954	47,097	83,433	47,578
2017	4,581,092	3,550,112	-9,164	3,540,948	379,458	-199,349	2,962,141	863,040	755,911	54,922	83,411	47,337
2018	4,524,934	4,525,412	-478	3,373,522	387,182	-148,857	2,837,483	891,103	796,348	54,371	83,223	47,743
2019	4,654,376	4,654,797	-421	3,404,813	390,304	-102,972	2,911,537	894,119	848,720	55,972	83,156	48,064

Personal Income and Employment by Area: Midland, TX

(Thousands of dollars, except as noted.)

Year	Personal income, total	Earnings by place of work			Less: Contributions for government social insurance	Plus: Adjustment for residence	Equals: Net earnings by place of residence	Plus: Dividends, interest, and rent	Plus: Personal current transfer receipts	Per capita personal income (dollars)	Population (persons)	Total employment
		Nonfarm	Farm	Total								
1970	328,929	277,558	8,502	286,060	16,115	-7,782	262,163	53,050	13,716	4,679	70,297	34,454
1971	355,615	301,824	7,968	309,792	17,843	-8,549	283,400	56,237	15,978	4,987	71,302	35,324
1972	384,016	326,266	7,542	333,808	19,843	-8,860	305,105	60,738	18,173	5,373	71,477	35,958
1973	437,833	360,467	20,683	381,150	25,760	-10,138	345,252	70,440	22,141	6,144	71,259	37,635
1974	491,237	417,190	2,960	420,150	30,516	-11,597	378,037	86,365	26,835	6,701	73,313	39,497
1975	595,384	522,571	-1,933	520,638	37,720	-17,134	465,784	97,785	31,815	7,872	75,637	43,247
1976	688,235	593,053	13,799	606,852	42,464	-18,467	545,921	106,781	35,533	8,830	77,943	43,997
1977	776,522	677,281	17,684	694,965	50,590	-25,750	618,625	120,021	37,876	9,803	79,216	48,808
1978	928,623	828,981	7,603	836,584	62,781	-34,602	739,201	146,086	43,336	11,474	80,934	52,831
1979	1,084,219	941,549	32,756	974,305	74,353	-39,898	860,054	174,651	49,514	12,978	83,546	54,875
1980	1,286,647	1,177,604	-11,224	1,166,380	96,272	-59,704	1,010,404	218,600	57,643	14,506	88,700	61,483
1981	1,656,134	1,453,620	33,403	1,487,023	131,837	-69,448	1,285,738	305,806	64,590	17,625	93,964	71,676
1982	1,868,698	1,634,787	21,385	1,656,172	157,802	-75,718	1,422,652	372,033	74,013	17,975	103,959	77,759
1983	1,813,014	1,526,316	3,763	1,530,079	148,806	-64,716	1,316,557	403,577	92,880	16,159	112,195	73,906
1984	1,891,028	1,562,175	-6,629	1,555,546	157,124	-57,698	1,340,724	449,202	101,102	16,896	111,919	74,561
1985	2,054,538	1,660,032	1,141	1,661,173	171,287	-54,549	1,435,337	508,277	110,924	18,023	113,997	76,826
1986	1,965,416	1,537,951	6,383	1,544,334	154,851	-49,153	1,340,330	492,584	132,502	16,760	117,265	68,942
1987	1,906,573	1,456,826	30,395	1,487,221	145,530	-37,450	1,304,241	463,420	138,912	16,979	112,287	69,786
1988	2,099,675	1,600,115	26,466	1,626,581	164,594	-37,719	1,424,268	530,163	145,244	18,841	111,439	71,380
1989	2,215,008	1,667,737	4,013	1,671,750	167,598	-27,531	1,476,621	574,966	163,421	19,867	111,494	68,991
1990	2,417,622	1,732,693	20,527	1,753,220	170,704	-18,709	1,563,807	673,960	179,855	21,659	111,624	68,901
1991	2,405,765	1,704,105	2,682	1,706,787	178,546	-15,811	1,512,430	688,934	204,401	21,210	113,427	70,299
1992	2,584,971	1,824,349	20,668	1,845,017	185,283	-14,069	1,645,665	692,332	246,974	22,415	115,325	68,743
1993	2,755,869	1,951,608	28,854	1,980,462	195,575	-9,093	1,775,794	714,251	265,824	23,664	116,456	71,541
1994	2,817,180	1,942,231	11,153	1,953,384	195,530	4	1,757,858	767,421	291,901	23,930	117,728	72,932
1995	2,887,389	2,043,332	8,911	2,052,243	202,016	3,397	1,853,624	719,229	314,536	24,368	118,493	73,505
1996	3,142,235	2,253,914	170	2,254,084	212,205	5,456	2,047,335	757,104	337,796	26,363	119,192	74,051
1997	3,571,682	2,641,052	21,220	2,662,272	237,930	1,291	2,425,633	792,718	353,331	29,350	121,691	78,960
1998	3,641,971	2,679,311	-6,554	2,672,757	238,763	15,913	2,449,907	835,352	356,712	29,562	123,197	79,647
1999	3,514,835	2,493,359	19,973	2,513,332	223,788	17,602	2,307,146	836,123	371,566	28,707	122,440	76,928
2000	3,874,127	2,719,902	-1,135	2,718,767	237,610	30,912	2,512,069	970,750	391,308	32,209	120,280	77,716
2001	5,801,734	4,749,730	5,752	4,755,482	326,231	23,940	4,453,191	929,127	419,416	47,997	120,877	78,340
2002	5,832,450	4,824,942	633	4,825,575	329,212	30,738	4,527,101	846,967	458,382	47,662	122,371	78,309
2003	6,383,623	5,293,014	35,009	5,328,023	358,015	25,928	4,995,936	902,276	485,411	51,599	123,717	81,345
2004	6,595,146	5,437,986	23,878	5,461,864	381,819	20,970	5,101,015	983,287	510,844	52,700	125,144	82,457
2005	7,534,661	6,205,245	34,306	6,239,551	435,994	-16,617	5,786,940	1,200,283	547,438	59,345	126,963	86,823
2006	8,179,244	6,668,786	13,462	6,682,248	473,655	-22,745	6,185,848	1,407,962	585,434	62,779	130,287	92,598
2007	8,039,679	6,314,746	45,533	6,360,279	504,770	12,953	5,868,462	1,512,218	658,999	60,246	133,448	97,097
2008	11,714,315	9,792,700	-24,910	9,767,790	650,648	-44,751	9,072,391	1,919,003	722,921	85,469	137,060	105,642
2009	8,675,957	6,975,945	7,789	6,983,734	559,596	-11,171	6,412,967	1,493,354	769,636	61,554	140,948	102,364
2010	10,251,948	8,533,062	40,472	8,573,534	637,193	-118,492	7,817,849	1,595,244	838,855	72,305	141,788	107,924
2011	14,191,645	12,430,779	3,955	12,434,734	708,769	-173,991	11,551,974	1,789,029	850,642	97,832	145,061	113,311
2012	16,267,566	14,187,906	394	14,188,300	800,471	-338,755	13,049,074	2,383,105	835,387	106,847	152,251	126,039
2013	17,366,875	15,792,816	24,131	15,816,947	994,477	-438,602	14,383,868	2,131,785	851,222	110,201	157,593	133,204
2014	18,984,561	17,320,433	586	17,321,019	1,117,335	-646,223	15,557,461	2,533,933	893,167	117,163	162,036	141,092
2015	14,840,580	12,951,545	20,295	12,971,840	997,262	-537,897	11,436,681	2,463,897	940,002	88,501	167,688	141,903
2016	12,775,577	10,477,706	5,670	10,483,376	887,767	-466,906	9,128,703	2,643,484	1,003,390	75,523	169,161	140,625
2017	12,642,258	10,446,298	3,693	10,449,991	969,636	-616,824	8,863,531	2,760,586	1,018,141	74,072	170,675	148,836
2018	22,679,972	22,644,236	35,736	20,543,800	1,422,396	-979,216	18,142,188	3,504,928	1,032,856	127,283	178,186	158,443
2019	23,513,106	23,514,435	-1,329	21,460,387	1,489,035	-1,095,525	18,875,827	3,567,461	1,069,818	128,766	182,603	162,703

Personal Income and Employment by Area: Milwaukee-Waukesha, WI

(Thousands of dollars, except as noted.)

Year	Personal income, total	Earnings by place of work			Less: Contributions for government social insurance	Plus: Adjustment for residence	Equals: Net earnings by place of residence	Plus: Dividends, interest, and rent	Plus: Personal current transfer receipts	Per capita personal income (dollars)	Population (persons)	Total employment
		Nonfarm	Farm	Total								
1970	6,418,920	5,365,616	22,593	5,388,209	393,284	-108,182	4,886,743	995,361	536,816	4,570	1,404,488	659,946
1971	6,824,581	5,640,215	26,072	5,666,287	428,350	-119,326	5,118,611	1,071,160	634,810	4,857	1,405,231	655,077
1972	7,440,734	6,206,286	23,554	6,229,840	499,766	-138,434	5,591,640	1,143,239	705,855	5,255	1,416,024	671,565
1973	8,211,703	6,947,193	28,048	6,975,241	648,379	-162,233	6,164,629	1,256,193	790,881	5,827	1,409,344	707,070
1974	9,017,395	7,565,349	23,235	7,588,584	731,201	-187,190	6,670,193	1,432,008	915,194	6,398	1,409,473	721,019
1975	9,729,832	7,980,681	29,193	8,009,874	752,534	-201,553	7,055,787	1,540,515	1,133,530	6,974	1,395,236	705,141
1976	10,579,079	8,789,971	27,862	8,817,833	844,519	-233,015	7,740,299	1,628,018	1,210,762	7,558	1,399,726	718,806
1977	11,669,454	9,793,781	40,202	9,833,983	940,487	-273,294	8,620,202	1,770,268	1,278,984	8,371	1,394,089	744,641
1978	12,981,107	10,993,424	39,093	11,032,517	1,087,913	-319,901	9,624,703	1,933,345	1,423,059	9,344	1,389,196	773,376
1979	14,416,450	12,205,380	47,736	12,253,116	1,256,825	-375,138	10,621,153	2,179,056	1,616,241	10,333	1,395,212	794,684
1980	15,861,064	12,943,741	52,592	12,996,333	1,324,228	-414,992	11,257,113	2,650,173	1,953,778	11,356	1,396,659	783,371
1981	17,381,143	13,753,251	46,335	13,799,586	1,504,611	-441,360	11,853,615	3,277,777	2,249,751	12,489	1,391,672	769,054
1982	18,377,569	14,150,386	39,592	14,189,978	1,561,049	-441,702	12,187,227	3,656,421	2,533,921	13,206	1,391,628	746,855
1983	19,055,332	14,536,177	21,344	14,557,521	1,603,592	-437,376	12,516,553	3,804,391	2,734,388	13,735	1,387,307	735,233
1984	20,876,909	16,058,439	30,560	16,088,999	1,816,823	-480,804	13,791,372	4,311,077	2,774,460	15,075	1,384,897	771,524
1985	21,969,014	16,913,597	34,538	16,948,135	1,928,278	-502,368	14,517,489	4,518,740	2,932,785	15,812	1,389,361	782,599
1986	23,061,724	17,833,942	38,849	17,872,791	2,031,939	-524,424	15,316,428	4,681,961	3,063,335	16,575	1,391,362	794,602
1987	24,372,842	19,082,113	40,547	19,122,660	2,134,088	-545,886	16,442,686	4,797,324	3,132,832	17,433	1,398,088	815,518
1988	26,338,127	20,805,707	28,981	20,834,688	2,401,141	-585,526	17,848,021	5,228,810	3,261,296	18,685	1,409,602	847,896
1989	28,499,063	22,180,765	54,825	22,235,590	2,557,497	-617,951	19,060,142	5,946,265	3,492,656	20,047	1,421,621	867,258
1990	30,025,107	23,538,894	38,823	23,577,717	2,830,199	-638,247	20,109,271	6,174,167	3,741,669	20,919	1,435,303	881,288
1991	31,020,343	24,344,100	35,545	24,379,645	2,955,609	-672,422	20,751,614	6,215,462	4,053,267	21,397	1,449,760	874,176
1992	33,195,783	26,240,001	47,706	26,287,707	3,155,661	-765,859	22,366,187	6,430,529	4,399,067	22,694	1,462,728	882,783
1993	34,793,728	27,630,930	37,627	27,668,557	3,318,792	-851,404	23,498,361	6,689,006	4,606,361	23,657	1,470,728	893,226
1994	36,651,180	29,114,093	38,932	29,153,025	3,551,456	-951,836	24,649,733	7,216,733	4,784,714	24,827	1,476,272	915,146
1995	38,531,916	30,465,172	30,041	30,495,213	3,723,666	-1,047,814	25,723,733	7,773,329	5,034,854	26,011	1,481,347	932,863
1996	40,506,865	31,983,353	36,415	32,019,768	3,875,309	-1,127,016	27,017,443	8,347,530	5,141,892	27,258	1,486,045	942,951
1997	42,916,031	34,110,390	26,294	34,136,684	4,114,381	-1,253,473	28,768,830	8,837,796	5,309,405	28,852	1,487,435	959,068
1998	45,821,365	36,523,291	34,555	36,557,846	4,363,496	-1,362,762	30,831,588	9,555,759	5,434,018	30,733	1,490,926	978,150
1999	47,688,519	38,551,066	35,752	38,586,818	4,618,169	-1,376,654	32,591,995	9,425,341	5,671,183	31,872	1,496,255	989,784
2000	50,596,969	40,621,551	30,404	40,651,955	4,803,281	-1,558,219	34,290,455	10,239,338	6,067,176	33,677	1,502,420	1,004,465
2001	53,265,135	43,113,840	42,544	43,156,384	4,923,487	-1,737,109	36,495,788	9,977,038	6,792,309	35,339	1,507,257	1,007,270
2002	54,002,969	43,957,240	43,841	44,001,081	4,994,475	-1,847,969	37,158,637	9,585,634	7,258,698	35,663	1,514,251	993,676
2003	54,660,528	44,741,398	61,608	44,803,006	5,107,747	-1,970,784	37,724,475	9,511,495	7,424,558	35,967	1,519,746	991,375
2004	56,911,013	46,637,605	66,922	46,704,527	5,335,988	-1,994,725	39,373,814	9,987,258	7,549,941	37,385	1,522,302	1,000,338
2005	59,139,788	48,103,070	51,636	48,154,706	5,526,656	-2,159,125	40,468,925	10,669,686	8,001,177	38,847	1,522,391	1,008,163
2006	63,690,555	51,053,618	47,649	51,101,267	5,866,764	-2,371,248	42,863,255	12,450,878	8,376,422	41,794	1,523,907	1,019,482
2007	66,035,817	52,639,033	58,203	52,697,236	6,052,072	-2,508,163	44,137,001	12,919,592	8,979,224	43,147	1,530,492	1,032,273
2008	67,919,557	53,805,908	52,653	53,858,561	6,238,800	-2,628,678	44,991,083	12,997,381	9,931,093	44,154	1,538,232	1,031,665
2009	66,515,545	51,762,274	43,342	51,805,616	6,009,265	-2,421,660	43,374,691	11,453,924	11,686,930	42,924	1,549,613	990,276
2010	67,891,039	52,384,645	59,139	52,443,784	6,107,049	-2,299,527	44,037,208	11,282,443	12,571,388	43,613	1,556,675	981,214
2011	71,718,944	54,916,103	78,082	54,994,185	5,713,115	-2,446,568	46,834,502	12,861,557	12,022,885	45,924	1,561,671	994,345
2012	75,216,782	56,824,775	77,268	56,902,043	5,845,449	-2,291,362	48,765,232	14,196,430	12,255,120	47,977	1,567,759	1,000,506
2013	74,911,503	58,018,805	82,795	58,101,600	6,738,265	-2,366,449	48,996,886	13,439,958	12,474,659	47,662	1,571,740	1,014,555
2014	77,664,448	59,380,966	76,092	59,457,058	6,907,339	-2,303,028	50,246,691	14,455,060	12,962,697	49,311	1,575,007	1,025,408
2015	80,746,010	61,070,998	79,128	61,150,126	7,122,076	-2,393,386	51,634,664	15,700,236	13,411,110	51,223	1,576,376	1,037,411
2016	82,373,077	62,271,245	61,535	62,332,780	7,216,826	-2,492,364	52,623,590	16,293,897	13,455,590	52,262	1,576,143	1,044,646
2017	85,031,675	63,906,299	55,115	63,961,414	7,461,729	-2,475,905	54,023,780	16,931,705	14,076,190	53,946	1,576,236	1,052,678
2018	89,771,409	89,735,717	35,692	66,779,617	7,666,009	-2,643,082	56,470,526	18,515,121	14,785,762	57,034	1,573,995	1,064,144
2019	92,079,893	92,025,519	54,374	68,771,825	7,902,838	-2,724,961	58,144,026	18,606,992	15,328,875	58,457	1,575,179	1,071,038

Personal Income and Employment by Area: Minneapolis-St. Paul-Bloomington, MN-WI

(Thousands of dollars, except as noted.)

Year	Personal income, total	Earnings by place of work			Less: Contributions for government social insurance	Plus: Adjustment for residence	Equals: Net earnings by place of residence	Plus: Dividends, interest, and rent	Plus: Personal current transfer receipts	Per capita personal income (dollars)	Population (persons)	Total employment
		Nonfarm	Farm	Total								
1970	9,799,885	8,116,302	119,802	8,236,104	562,908	-54,519	7,618,677	1,439,880	741,328	4,701	2,084,574	1,001,143
1971	10,461,635	8,584,788	110,803	8,695,591	615,651	-52,664	8,027,276	1,565,973	868,386	4,972	2,104,296	997,890
1972	11,265,064	9,257,248	126,846	9,384,094	698,206	-55,524	8,630,364	1,676,116	958,584	5,344	2,107,895	1,038,036
1973	12,562,725	10,313,609	220,351	10,533,960	901,524	-62,315	9,570,121	1,857,463	1,135,141	5,909	2,125,921	1,097,783
1974	13,833,383	11,301,724	176,524	11,478,248	1,021,370	-65,745	10,391,133	2,127,763	1,314,487	6,449	2,145,063	1,123,468
1975	15,036,015	12,079,658	156,192	12,235,850	1,062,096	-70,917	11,102,837	2,333,013	1,600,165	6,980	2,154,275	1,115,829
1976	16,465,168	13,427,432	93,501	13,520,933	1,213,136	-81,602	12,226,195	2,488,950	1,750,023	7,595	2,167,976	1,147,906
1977	18,421,847	15,115,585	220,262	15,335,847	1,364,717	-100,752	13,870,378	2,752,591	1,798,878	8,453	2,179,319	1,198,787
1978	20,682,175	17,189,476	203,531	17,393,007	1,605,920	-117,304	15,669,783	3,086,065	1,926,327	9,400	2,200,167	1,259,054
1979	23,463,609	19,755,166	179,973	19,935,139	1,922,843	-146,912	17,865,384	3,461,122	2,137,103	10,547	2,224,748	1,330,627
1980	26,383,863	21,825,635	134,141	21,959,776	2,123,744	-162,636	19,673,396	4,175,078	2,535,389	11,654	2,263,881	1,360,454
1981	29,275,599	23,712,312	143,873	23,856,185	2,470,430	-181,003	21,204,752	5,158,076	2,912,771	12,773	2,291,962	1,357,542
1982	31,686,609	25,071,403	128,051	25,199,454	2,663,778	-187,176	22,348,500	6,093,051	3,245,058	13,674	2,317,206	1,336,848
1983	33,952,221	27,097,156	22,122	27,119,278	2,917,886	-203,902	23,997,490	6,466,146	3,488,585	14,560	2,331,850	1,356,281
1984	38,258,350	30,721,539	164,108	30,885,647	3,395,249	-242,524	27,247,874	7,364,992	3,645,484	16,246	2,354,976	1,445,106
1985	41,345,856	33,361,839	166,120	33,527,959	3,745,159	-272,482	29,510,318	7,914,734	3,920,804	17,293	2,390,959	1,497,630
1986	44,051,911	35,701,423	183,657	35,885,080	4,109,624	-289,928	31,485,528	8,436,890	4,129,493	18,142	2,428,147	1,533,116
1987	47,336,517	38,733,501	235,882	38,969,383	4,420,030	-314,109	34,235,244	8,810,626	4,290,647	19,173	2,468,889	1,602,851
1988	50,999,930	41,953,711	130,610	42,084,321	4,930,661	-344,757	36,808,903	9,592,717	4,598,310	20,210	2,523,553	1,654,072
1989	55,220,512	44,779,239	271,369	45,050,608	5,246,246	-343,566	39,460,796	10,749,278	5,010,438	21,550	2,562,410	1,689,977
1990	58,785,816	47,429,087	229,560	47,658,647	5,611,922	-333,678	41,713,047	11,636,272	5,436,497	22,557	2,606,156	1,721,797
1991	61,009,424	49,453,164	159,429	49,612,593	5,917,282	-356,073	43,339,238	11,767,787	5,902,399	23,054	2,646,336	1,728,757
1992	65,669,362	53,722,932	174,768	53,897,700	6,352,891	-411,862	47,132,947	12,102,044	6,434,371	24,424	2,688,729	1,756,753
1993	68,499,181	56,133,953	86,016	56,219,969	6,662,201	-445,363	49,112,405	12,555,145	6,831,631	25,052	2,734,239	1,794,801
1994	72,979,163	59,528,904	168,202	59,697,106	7,156,731	-507,471	52,032,904	13,755,460	7,190,799	26,283	2,776,675	1,853,150
1995	77,995,652	63,200,827	90,313	63,291,140	7,570,558	-566,829	55,153,753	15,194,444	7,647,455	27,666	2,819,211	1,911,772
1996	83,339,377	67,541,915	187,685	67,729,600	8,021,382	-645,523	59,062,695	16,251,189	8,025,493	29,124	2,861,505	1,951,582
1997	89,333,015	72,555,017	119,595	72,674,612	8,562,965	-726,606	63,385,041	17,794,927	8,153,047	30,772	2,903,107	1,989,738
1998	97,049,118	79,404,616	190,399	79,595,015	9,227,186	-827,544	69,540,285	19,051,969	8,456,864	32,937	2,946,520	2,047,473
1999	102,516,865	84,935,211	180,438	85,115,649	9,897,495	-985,859	74,232,295	19,390,075	8,894,495	34,232	2,994,735	2,096,145
2000	111,937,718	92,832,456	171,423	93,003,879	10,687,181	-1,163,913	81,152,785	21,188,921	9,596,012	36,768	3,044,425	2,151,783
2001	116,048,381	96,464,153	152,195	96,616,348	11,038,007	-1,281,026	84,297,315	20,997,633	10,753,433	37,597	3,086,645	2,167,201
2002	118,322,844	98,089,745	170,151	98,259,896	11,222,918	-1,308,404	85,728,574	20,865,959	11,728,311	37,970	3,116,197	2,156,254
2003	123,285,679	101,813,765	231,601	102,045,366	11,723,437	-1,376,579	88,945,350	22,087,331	12,252,998	39,220	3,143,413	2,165,919
2004	131,076,538	108,721,290	316,221	109,037,511	12,399,142	-1,528,021	95,110,348	23,100,868	12,865,322	41,324	3,171,902	2,199,628
2005	135,678,594	111,690,486	324,694	112,015,180	12,959,318	-1,615,081	97,440,781	24,685,458	13,552,355	42,412	3,199,046	2,242,751
2006	143,559,033	115,467,033	291,603	115,758,636	13,524,716	-1,623,501	100,610,419	28,015,795	14,932,819	44,386	3,234,367	2,278,366
2007	152,338,505	121,653,302	295,497	121,948,799	14,096,466	-1,684,985	106,167,348	29,681,383	16,489,774	46,592	3,269,613	2,310,499
2008	156,560,886	123,559,243	375,550	123,934,793	14,465,497	-1,644,035	107,825,261	29,803,470	18,932,155	47,425	3,301,252	2,302,230
2009	148,518,461	116,783,539	258,827	117,042,366	13,836,434	-1,268,534	101,937,398	25,891,057	20,690,006	44,593	3,330,508	2,227,304
2010	154,445,129	120,648,327	323,908	120,972,235	14,049,086	-1,249,822	105,673,327	26,276,242	22,495,560	46,032	3,355,196	2,220,306
2011	165,407,010	127,726,426	421,261	128,147,687	13,177,503	-1,342,293	113,627,891	29,117,268	22,661,851	48,812	3,388,629	2,271,607
2012	175,768,780	134,623,958	556,154	135,180,112	13,764,428	-1,324,088	120,091,596	32,928,185	22,748,999	51,362	3,422,188	2,300,866
2013	177,392,089	139,129,284	448,743	139,578,027	16,264,664	-1,310,711	122,002,652	31,768,506	23,620,931	51,295	3,458,299	2,341,833
2014	189,179,472	146,471,386	351,873	146,823,259	16,839,213	-1,350,640	128,633,406	35,657,201	24,888,865	54,156	3,493,226	2,383,234
2015	198,936,810	153,210,026	402,125	153,612,151	17,475,989	-1,361,292	134,774,870	38,311,001	25,850,939	56,495	3,521,325	2,431,868
2016	205,435,268	158,135,626	240,005	158,375,631	17,947,634	-1,394,539	139,033,458	39,638,428	26,763,382	57,751	3,557,276	2,468,929
2017	215,086,450	166,178,707	132,013	166,310,720	18,737,646	-1,495,753	146,077,321	41,400,806	27,608,323	59,736	3,600,618	2,509,028
2018	227,122,134	226,948,581	173,553	172,273,568	19,650,854	-1,741,740	150,880,974	46,852,771	29,388,389	62,914	3,610,061	2,533,230
2019	233,890,054	233,666,392	223,662	178,485,038	20,294,047	-1,833,476	156,357,515	46,798,987	30,733,552	64,255	3,640,043	2,565,549

Personal Income and Employment by Area: Missoula, MT

(Thousands of dollars, except as noted.)

Year	Personal income, total	Derivation of personal income			Less: Contributions for government social insurance	Plus: Adjustment for residence	Equals: Net earnings by place of residence	Plus: Dividends, interest, and rent	Plus: Personal current transfer receipts	Per capita personal income (dollars)	Population (persons)	Total employment
		Earnings by place of work										
		Nonfarm	Farm	Total								
1970	208,980	173,995	696	174,691	13,535	-5,092	156,064	34,810	18,106	3,574	58,472	25,139
1971	233,708	194,017	977	194,994	15,269	-5,764	173,961	38,324	21,423	3,896	59,990	26,508
1972	263,307	221,506	1,412	222,918	18,329	-8,015	196,574	42,382	24,351	4,253	61,918	28,195
1973	290,502	243,366	2,012	245,378	23,012	-9,280	213,086	48,531	28,885	4,509	64,424	29,798
1974	329,287	272,000	1,830	273,830	26,113	-10,928	236,789	57,230	35,268	4,914	67,007	30,952
1975	367,339	295,014	1,130	296,144	26,809	-11,672	257,663	66,425	43,251	5,478	67,056	31,090
1976	421,544	346,931	1,104	348,035	32,426	-14,908	300,701	73,432	47,411	6,062	69,539	33,780
1977	491,819	415,461	176	415,637	39,930	-20,077	355,630	84,894	51,295	6,930	70,970	36,648
1978	572,589	490,751	1,716	492,467	48,972	-25,212	418,283	98,461	55,845	7,928	72,226	40,008
1979	639,139	544,983	1,559	546,542	56,986	-30,859	458,697	114,584	65,858	8,627	74,088	40,389
1980	694,462	572,923	1,393	574,316	61,324	-33,542	479,450	135,570	79,442	9,124	76,115	39,442
1981	736,988	576,096	435	576,531	65,004	-22,824	488,703	156,594	91,691	9,653	76,352	37,592
1982	771,101	586,216	309	586,525	67,402	-25,984	493,139	179,891	98,071	10,248	75,242	36,696
1983	827,333	645,419	1,154	646,573	75,130	-29,372	542,071	179,948	105,314	10,948	75,571	38,399
1984	908,109	710,418	155	710,573	84,485	-31,930	594,158	202,346	111,605	11,813	76,875	40,726
1985	952,215	743,286	-522	742,764	89,956	-32,139	620,669	211,090	120,456	12,243	77,774	41,567
1986	985,599	766,659	955	767,614	94,262	-31,563	641,789	213,464	130,346	12,644	77,949	41,942
1987	1,025,302	797,419	-243	797,176	97,936	-31,731	667,509	218,322	139,471	13,199	77,680	43,048
1988	1,085,840	844,354	-516	843,838	109,213	-33,722	700,903	235,109	149,828	13,999	77,564	44,555
1989	1,162,487	902,230	369	902,599	118,659	-36,861	747,079	248,296	167,112	14,905	77,995	45,814
1990	1,254,609	980,021	197	980,218	137,269	-40,329	802,620	266,717	185,272	15,865	79,080	47,616
1991	1,333,097	1,045,332	284	1,045,616	148,125	-43,356	854,135	284,037	194,925	16,438	81,098	49,299
1992	1,463,872	1,168,467	293	1,168,760	165,648	-51,008	952,104	300,187	211,581	17,521	83,549	51,852
1993	1,571,964	1,268,176	700	1,268,876	184,306	-56,127	1,028,443	319,590	223,931	18,227	86,243	54,021
1994	1,665,826	1,332,212	-1,778	1,330,434	191,727	-58,399	1,080,308	355,025	230,493	18,922	88,037	56,003
1995	1,779,791	1,400,291	-2,871	1,397,420	196,342	-64,169	1,136,909	393,170	249,712	19,685	90,413	58,094
1996	1,886,245	1,480,167	-4,343	1,475,824	198,806	-71,175	1,205,843	421,187	259,215	20,514	91,947	60,152
1997	1,993,492	1,551,695	-4,406	1,547,289	202,649	-75,323	1,269,317	460,870	263,305	21,401	93,151	61,250
1998	2,139,890	1,655,481	-2,582	1,652,899	210,240	-83,013	1,359,646	507,713	272,531	22,802	93,847	62,905
1999	2,210,428	1,745,093	-1,462	1,743,631	220,943	-92,443	1,430,245	513,307	266,876	23,319	94,791	64,766
2000	2,409,616	1,880,192	-1,758	1,878,434	238,255	-103,029	1,537,150	569,741	302,725	25,054	96,178	66,193
2001	2,455,522	1,923,211	632	1,923,843	251,331	-114,615	1,557,897	558,581	339,044	25,202	97,435	68,296
2002	2,590,007	2,056,624	3,102	2,059,726	270,125	-128,147	1,661,454	576,664	351,889	26,170	98,968	69,240
2003	2,749,520	2,189,698	193	2,189,891	284,812	-141,374	1,763,705	619,122	366,693	27,502	99,976	70,828
2004	2,916,813	2,326,354	805	2,327,159	297,659	-162,085	1,867,415	665,042	384,356	28,898	100,934	72,124
2005	3,062,793	2,429,596	457	2,430,053	314,779	-183,077	1,932,197	715,820	414,776	29,940	102,298	73,462
2006	3,336,960	2,574,273	-1,569	2,572,704	333,570	-195,989	2,043,145	844,737	449,078	31,972	104,372	75,245
2007	3,575,216	2,714,004	-660	2,713,344	356,513	-216,358	2,140,473	953,717	481,026	33,693	106,110	77,712
2008	3,792,908	2,798,281	-4,275	2,794,006	365,800	-233,539	2,194,667	1,032,081	566,160	35,202	107,747	76,966
2009	3,862,925	2,795,478	-1,591	2,793,887	363,686	-235,697	2,194,504	1,048,240	620,181	35,532	108,717	75,735
2010	3,745,913	2,817,404	-1,780	2,815,624	363,416	-218,700	2,233,508	822,718	689,687	34,231	109,432	75,059
2011	4,027,927	2,931,222	5,360	2,936,582	339,388	-233,008	2,364,186	979,037	684,704	36,560	110,172	76,137
2012	4,302,675	3,022,127	-3,342	3,018,785	344,103	-216,674	2,458,008	1,140,923	703,744	38,757	111,016	76,750
2013	4,294,473	3,114,758	473	3,115,231	400,399	-201,973	2,512,859	1,059,995	721,619	38,490	111,575	77,715
2014	4,598,583	3,259,326	-2,518	3,256,808	419,234	-196,867	2,640,707	1,198,297	759,579	40,890	112,462	78,859
2015	5,124,439	3,452,816	-1,017	3,451,799	437,954	-206,773	2,807,072	1,512,446	804,921	45,038	113,780	80,129
2016	5,224,836	3,571,760	542	3,572,302	441,907	-246,972	2,883,423	1,469,666	871,747	45,082	115,896	82,156
2017	5,499,692	3,764,964	4,129	3,769,093	466,506	-265,366	3,037,221	1,533,596	928,875	46,829	117,441	83,506
2018	5,908,024	5,906,489	1,535	4,015,677	514,504	-276,120	3,225,053	1,696,124	986,847	49,798	118,640	85,980
2019	6,110,361	6,109,069	1,292	4,189,807	533,516	-289,957	3,366,334	1,709,906	1,034,121	51,090	119,600	87,572

Personal Income and Employment by Area: Mobile, AL

(Thousands of dollars, except as noted.)

Year	Personal income, total	Earnings by place of work			Less: Contributions for government social insurance	Plus: Adjustment for residence	Equals: Net earnings by place of residence	Plus: Dividends, interest, and rent	Plus: Personal current transfer receipts	Per capita personal income (dollars)	Population (persons)	Total employment
		Nonfarm	Farm	Total								
1970	950,622	776,889	6,544	783,433	58,025	-2,326	723,082	131,975	95,565	2,986	318,311	121,223
1971	1,027,930	825,238	7,528	832,766	62,798	-2,940	767,028	148,212	112,690	3,180	323,278	121,416
1972	1,136,937	914,253	8,338	922,591	72,892	13	849,712	162,187	125,038	3,506	324,325	126,180
1973	1,275,686	1,035,877	11,743	1,047,620	94,645	-2,850	950,125	181,105	144,456	3,931	324,541	133,484
1974	1,457,868	1,178,172	13,415	1,191,587	110,620	-7,644	1,073,323	210,522	174,023	4,426	329,414	137,961
1975	1,668,401	1,327,852	12,485	1,340,337	123,512	-5,359	1,211,466	235,975	220,960	4,977	335,235	141,132
1976	1,892,953	1,529,252	12,637	1,541,889	145,266	-8,544	1,388,079	257,268	247,606	5,489	344,892	147,159
1977	2,107,884	1,714,100	12,734	1,726,834	163,618	-3,680	1,559,536	285,762	262,586	5,969	353,134	153,854
1978	2,377,508	1,963,194	17,104	1,980,298	189,999	-26,781	1,763,518	327,592	286,398	6,603	360,079	162,577
1979	2,621,543	2,145,330	9,494	2,154,824	214,504	-40,682	1,899,638	375,142	346,763	7,247	361,747	163,160
1980	2,985,727	2,422,449	17,588	2,440,037	240,700	-58,168	2,141,169	459,181	385,377	8,153	366,205	167,983
1981	3,309,347	2,642,091	22,705	2,664,796	283,445	-65,288	2,316,063	554,080	439,204	8,934	370,432	168,136
1982	3,464,998	2,669,532	29,045	2,698,577	292,805	-48,945	2,356,827	615,456	492,715	9,245	374,782	161,111
1983	3,598,230	2,764,785	31,713	2,796,498	305,718	-71,221	2,419,559	631,990	546,681	9,548	376,842	159,696
1984	3,867,076	2,975,399	20,464	2,995,863	334,876	-87,751	2,573,236	709,040	584,800	10,279	376,211	164,970
1985	4,167,354	3,238,122	23,788	3,261,910	365,657	-110,365	2,785,888	761,056	620,410	11,000	378,847	169,061
1986	4,356,691	3,378,798	23,981	3,402,779	379,534	-117,993	2,905,252	802,493	648,946	11,413	381,729	169,068
1987	4,519,065	3,523,388	25,781	3,549,169	390,640	-132,906	3,025,623	826,089	667,353	11,778	383,696	171,067
1988	4,787,229	3,743,181	33,858	3,777,039	429,411	-143,719	3,203,909	889,364	693,956	12,548	381,501	175,349
1989	5,192,778	3,989,561	36,765	4,026,326	457,726	-172,421	3,396,179	1,008,188	788,411	13,706	378,869	177,801
1990	5,526,649	4,259,829	36,842	4,296,671	496,091	-191,639	3,608,941	1,053,403	864,305	14,576	379,167	181,716
1991	5,916,282	4,639,982	43,056	4,683,038	543,551	-254,753	3,884,734	1,068,649	962,899	15,448	382,978	188,154
1992	6,354,170	4,981,720	33,632	5,015,352	577,618	-304,668	4,133,066	1,119,027	1,102,077	16,373	388,097	191,637
1993	6,636,961	5,252,583	26,390	5,278,973	612,971	-355,009	4,310,993	1,159,320	1,166,648	16,856	393,740	199,587
1994	6,941,100	5,517,191	18,733	5,535,924	652,873	-395,694	4,487,357	1,217,367	1,236,376	17,542	395,685	201,086
1995	7,256,961	5,651,910	19,287	5,671,197	674,469	-420,269	4,576,459	1,337,737	1,342,765	18,341	395,664	204,219
1996	7,559,744	5,947,096	19,882	5,966,978	706,195	-474,123	4,786,660	1,362,392	1,410,692	19,082	396,163	208,206
1997	7,894,324	6,276,111	25,674	6,301,785	745,207	-550,518	5,006,060	1,423,783	1,464,481	19,839	397,917	213,334
1998	8,491,708	6,734,821	20,630	6,755,451	782,811	-511,770	5,460,870	1,537,667	1,493,171	21,310	398,479	216,432
1999	8,542,329	6,808,617	24,319	6,832,936	796,211	-539,025	5,497,700	1,507,704	1,536,925	21,392	399,323	216,083
2000	8,834,334	6,949,410	24,458	6,973,868	810,335	-589,671	5,573,862	1,624,294	1,636,178	22,082	400,073	217,097
2001	9,272,089	7,353,249	20,773	7,374,022	845,499	-585,561	5,942,962	1,533,587	1,795,540	23,173	400,129	215,385
2002	9,410,878	7,470,816	20,281	7,491,097	861,616	-577,066	6,052,415	1,497,796	1,860,667	23,613	398,549	213,117
2003	9,638,393	7,505,729	28,451	7,534,180	869,041	-549,272	6,115,867	1,574,566	1,947,960	24,212	398,082	211,180
2004	10,062,488	7,736,000	35,283	7,771,283	894,440	-546,473	6,330,370	1,664,404	2,067,714	25,285	397,959	212,787
2005	10,863,211	8,387,187	25,123	8,412,310	975,132	-572,321	6,864,857	1,667,657	2,330,697	27,230	398,942	218,945
2006	11,995,713	9,363,532	38,170	9,401,702	1,063,431	-601,275	7,736,996	1,874,921	2,383,796	29,772	402,916	226,409
2007	12,412,795	9,607,827	28,617	9,636,444	1,115,047	-612,456	7,908,941	2,015,945	2,487,909	30,595	405,715	233,054
2008	12,886,607	9,723,228	25,614	9,748,842	1,156,765	-642,288	7,949,789	2,110,418	2,826,400	31,493	409,196	234,073
2009	12,592,489	9,521,417	36,312	9,557,729	1,132,896	-740,269	7,684,564	1,943,970	2,963,955	30,565	411,994	225,897
2010	13,217,713	9,887,628	25,311	9,912,939	1,177,659	-863,463	7,871,817	2,049,909	3,295,987	31,979	413,320	226,900
2011	13,915,628	10,531,831	27,693	10,559,524	1,106,314	-1,045,833	8,407,377	2,142,891	3,365,360	33,675	413,232	233,197
2012	13,857,580	10,424,654	42,908	10,467,562	1,098,431	-1,046,211	8,322,920	2,178,780	3,355,880	33,494	413,737	229,435
2013	14,036,932	10,520,212	47,516	10,567,728	1,258,436	-986,758	8,322,534	2,303,962	3,410,436	33,911	413,929	228,792
2014	14,354,642	10,800,276	28,226	10,828,502	1,286,751	-1,022,540	8,519,211	2,258,352	3,577,079	34,647	414,314	231,064
2015	14,893,696	11,228,274	34,930	11,263,204	1,334,136	-1,132,918	8,796,150	2,391,526	3,706,020	35,924	414,588	233,931
2016	14,990,948	11,429,607	40,054	11,469,661	1,355,053	-1,299,851	8,814,757	2,412,989	3,763,202	36,136	414,852	235,988
2017	15,353,110	11,718,838	37,862	11,756,700	1,395,059	-1,399,923	8,961,718	2,512,282	3,879,110	37,089	413,955	237,745
2018	16,657,010	16,610,818	46,192	12,486,358	1,502,984	-1,417,046	9,566,328	2,801,048	4,289,634	38,709	430,310	243,683
2019	17,192,338	17,151,741	40,597	12,871,436	1,535,691	-1,466,670	9,869,075	2,830,943	4,492,320	40,025	429,536	246,248

Personal Income and Employment by Area: Modesto, CA

(Thousands of dollars, except as noted.)

Year	Personal income, total	Earnings by place of work			Less: Contributions for government social insurance	Plus: Adjustment for residence	Equals: Net earnings by place of residence	Plus: Dividends, interest, and rent	Plus: Personal current transfer receipts	Per capita personal income (dollars)	Population (persons)	Total employment
		Nonfarm	Farm	Total								
1970	790,180	502,478	62,878	565,356	35,779	30,049	559,626	116,867	113,687	4,040	195,578	83,872
1971	854,198	549,964	59,022	608,986	40,386	32,435	601,035	128,315	124,848	4,277	199,698	85,423
1972	963,489	622,412	78,807	701,219	48,113	34,458	687,564	142,323	133,602	4,778	201,644	90,511
1973	1,102,270	693,587	121,303	814,890	61,200	38,011	791,701	165,623	144,946	5,123	215,178	93,856
1974	1,255,143	782,516	136,115	918,631	70,941	43,049	890,739	191,301	173,103	5,641	222,484	98,381
1975	1,389,427	876,020	98,255	974,275	76,874	48,513	945,914	221,512	222,001	6,054	229,518	100,774
1976	1,557,694	999,983	91,410	1,091,393	88,930	54,876	1,057,339	245,322	255,033	6,592	236,293	104,388
1977	1,806,559	1,149,766	146,629	1,296,395	104,000	61,534	1,253,929	280,185	272,445	7,314	246,995	110,136
1978	2,021,879	1,317,105	136,991	1,454,096	121,266	69,710	1,402,540	324,101	295,238	8,176	247,280	116,129
1979	2,301,197	1,504,583	154,380	1,658,963	145,834	79,472	1,592,601	378,986	329,610	8,819	260,933	122,698
1980	2,594,554	1,634,898	157,655	1,792,553	155,561	88,897	1,725,889	474,097	394,568	9,687	267,852	123,136
1981	2,876,552	1,783,228	117,691	1,900,919	183,803	104,759	1,821,875	587,111	467,566	10,455	275,137	124,323
1982	3,101,512	1,886,216	120,912	2,007,128	196,831	123,528	1,933,825	649,713	517,974	11,048	280,737	124,463
1983	3,292,851	2,002,223	95,376	2,097,599	211,373	145,592	2,031,818	705,151	555,882	11,414	288,504	125,566
1984	3,676,102	2,229,810	136,281	2,366,091	242,741	182,877	2,306,227	779,153	590,722	12,509	293,879	128,705
1985	4,024,487	2,428,184	189,065	2,617,249	267,479	216,522	2,566,292	815,334	642,861	13,358	301,285	134,089
1986	4,345,529	2,649,850	188,103	2,837,953	293,716	248,773	2,793,010	855,573	696,946	13,966	311,154	137,844
1987	4,773,624	2,958,354	259,365	3,217,719	328,670	277,828	3,166,877	875,250	731,497	14,762	323,380	146,944
1988	5,207,829	3,258,154	256,249	3,514,403	372,344	320,571	3,462,630	950,133	795,066	15,497	336,063	156,458
1989	5,750,412	3,575,663	246,647	3,822,310	412,036	362,129	3,772,403	1,114,348	863,661	16,289	353,017	165,120
1990	6,278,916	3,912,080	288,259	4,200,339	448,542	405,019	4,156,816	1,157,251	964,849	16,730	375,312	171,839
1991	6,621,270	4,079,862	301,706	4,381,568	469,969	435,102	4,346,701	1,187,042	1,087,527	17,146	386,163	174,223
1992	6,985,482	4,299,538	292,584	4,592,122	492,696	455,548	4,554,974	1,167,096	1,263,412	17,697	394,725	173,045
1993	7,278,578	4,493,899	279,017	4,772,916	515,383	471,133	4,728,666	1,199,212	1,350,700	18,115	401,805	174,101
1994	7,461,839	4,628,972	252,861	4,881,833	528,258	504,910	4,858,485	1,240,801	1,362,553	18,367	406,274	174,328
1995	7,689,849	4,717,530	192,942	4,910,472	529,377	548,792	4,929,887	1,328,925	1,431,037	18,740	410,337	177,970
1996	8,220,856	4,947,496	332,517	5,280,013	538,160	584,730	5,326,583	1,395,068	1,499,205	19,802	415,159	183,775
1997	8,792,202	5,411,414	362,751	5,774,165	577,438	642,604	5,839,331	1,460,578	1,492,293	20,871	421,264	187,933
1998	9,571,251	5,969,107	384,758	6,353,865	622,773	689,947	6,421,039	1,575,819	1,574,393	22,323	428,754	198,000
1999	10,035,727	6,415,743	256,341	6,672,084	668,282	785,114	6,788,916	1,577,375	1,669,436	22,881	438,609	202,754
2000	10,943,607	7,077,587	216,298	7,293,885	720,998	948,763	7,521,650	1,651,519	1,770,438	24,348	449,471	205,267
2001	11,621,311	7,446,690	316,254	7,762,944	811,672	935,258	7,886,530	1,737,532	1,997,249	25,059	463,761	211,128
2002	12,232,334	7,931,068	322,270	8,253,338	880,235	930,869	8,303,972	1,744,465	2,183,897	25,619	477,469	215,168
2003	12,893,953	8,427,177	364,707	8,791,884	945,549	960,448	8,806,783	1,793,359	2,293,811	26,457	487,357	217,369
2004	13,847,124	8,964,597	645,606	9,610,203	1,037,635	1,016,330	9,588,898	1,880,347	2,377,879	28,110	492,613	219,983
2005	14,404,639	9,389,360	598,217	9,987,577	1,099,156	1,034,728	9,923,149	2,019,236	2,462,254	28,808	500,020	224,867
2006	15,027,448	9,649,721	560,343	10,210,064	1,089,142	1,159,125	10,280,047	2,122,501	2,624,900	29,778	504,651	225,192
2007	15,772,825	9,830,508	633,287	10,463,795	1,087,183	1,249,772	10,626,384	2,330,232	2,816,209	31,059	507,834	228,447
2008	15,959,269	9,737,804	482,774	10,220,578	1,101,500	1,272,671	10,391,749	2,356,339	3,211,181	31,352	509,032	223,665
2009	15,779,648	9,496,330	500,747	9,997,077	1,088,156	1,149,192	10,058,113	2,177,110	3,544,425	30,848	511,536	212,934
2010	16,541,939	9,815,997	553,152	10,369,149	1,081,650	1,140,368	10,427,867	2,211,599	3,902,473	32,105	515,242	210,904
2011	17,297,182	10,112,823	689,924	10,802,747	1,011,028	1,163,803	10,955,522	2,456,293	3,885,367	33,390	518,034	212,134
2012	18,023,970	10,358,808	789,549	11,148,357	1,039,227	1,276,296	11,385,426	2,685,461	3,953,083	34,572	521,349	218,345
2013	18,616,665	10,646,186	955,440	11,601,626	1,196,713	1,342,294	11,747,207	2,746,356	4,123,102	35,486	524,625	224,463
2014	20,374,984	11,181,601	1,432,239	12,613,840	1,252,970	1,438,095	12,798,965	3,184,915	4,391,104	38,476	529,544	230,637
2015	21,900,270	12,054,515	1,250,526	13,305,041	1,339,110	1,590,764	13,556,695	3,594,068	4,749,507	40,935	535,000	237,761
2016	22,360,836	12,557,381	837,802	13,395,183	1,407,505	1,655,222	13,642,900	3,805,301	4,912,635	41,305	541,353	242,765
2017	23,446,103	13,134,022	1,098,357	14,232,379	1,471,970	1,844,717	14,605,126	4,000,978	4,839,999	42,793	547,899	246,865
2018	23,915,119	23,080,806	834,313	14,634,352	1,558,180	1,739,164	14,815,336	4,088,056	5,011,727	43,631	548,126	252,909
2019	25,188,224	24,150,542	1,037,682	15,494,665	1,655,929	1,852,374	15,691,110	4,180,563	5,316,551	45,742	550,660	257,494

Personal Income and Employment by Area: Monroe, LA

(Thousands of dollars, except as noted.)

					Derivation of personal income							
		Earnings by place of work			Less: Contributions for government social insurance	Plus: Adjustment for residence	Equals: Net earnings by place of residence	Plus: Dividends, interest, and rent	Plus: Personal current transfer receipts	Per capita personal income (dollars)	Population (persons)	Total employment
Year	Personal income, total	Nonfarm	Farm	Total								
1970	369,753	287,206	5,537	292,743	18,552	-4,210	269,981	53,828	45,944	2,758	134,052	49,954
1971	417,790	324,448	7,137	331,585	21,650	-4,055	305,880	59,898	52,012	3,059	136,572	52,109
1972	465,499	364,509	6,923	371,432	25,623	-3,419	342,390	65,754	57,355	3,316	140,389	54,220
1973	521,184	409,294	9,969	419,263	33,180	-3,230	382,853	72,666	65,665	3,660	142,397	58,132
1974	581,313	450,820	4,903	455,723	37,586	-1,335	416,802	86,536	77,975	4,020	144,601	58,242
1975	657,201	493,959	6,719	500,678	40,178	-160	460,340	98,496	98,365	4,424	148,558	57,979
1976	766,408	592,253	10,866	603,119	49,545	-1,045	552,529	106,562	107,317	5,021	152,634	61,479
1977	854,758	662,495	13,048	675,543	54,637	3,128	624,034	118,430	112,294	5,534	154,446	63,178
1978	994,605	781,335	11,131	792,466	66,187	6,941	733,220	137,988	123,397	6,392	155,598	66,282
1979	1,107,073	855,644	14,055	869,699	74,866	13,789	808,622	157,856	140,595	7,023	157,646	66,963
1980	1,231,775	917,390	5,210	922,600	79,986	23,292	865,906	194,743	171,126	7,658	160,840	67,917
1981	1,380,792	1,014,942	7,587	1,022,529	93,632	19,856	948,753	241,539	190,500	8,509	162,278	68,401
1982	1,478,864	1,051,668	7,714	1,059,382	98,181	17,131	978,332	282,062	218,470	9,082	162,833	68,211
1983	1,599,046	1,135,902	7,129	1,143,031	105,205	14,469	1,052,295	306,448	240,303	9,712	164,650	69,765
1984	1,728,582	1,230,593	16,330	1,246,923	116,967	9,814	1,139,770	338,326	250,486	10,415	165,968	71,694
1985	1,842,497	1,311,773	10,285	1,322,058	126,095	3,632	1,199,595	372,365	270,537	11,040	166,887	73,963
1986	1,929,440	1,366,511	17,834	1,384,345	130,745	-1,941	1,251,659	384,753	293,028	11,416	169,012	73,356
1987	1,950,862	1,393,407	20,690	1,414,097	131,335	-3,924	1,278,838	372,631	299,393	11,646	167,513	73,825
1988	2,051,909	1,473,267	23,833	1,497,100	144,227	-6,814	1,346,059	387,439	318,411	12,373	165,842	73,947
1989	2,203,002	1,559,135	27,526	1,586,661	154,608	-8,685	1,423,368	432,645	346,989	13,424	164,107	74,432
1990	2,339,961	1,678,577	21,941	1,700,518	169,683	-10,137	1,520,698	436,570	382,693	14,361	162,944	75,648
1991	2,467,514	1,758,354	24,938	1,783,292	182,439	-11,004	1,589,849	443,444	434,221	15,035	164,119	76,682
1992	2,666,479	1,900,621	34,992	1,935,613	194,168	-13,954	1,727,491	446,372	492,616	16,036	166,280	78,203
1993	2,812,901	1,984,673	45,266	2,029,939	204,446	-17,178	1,808,315	463,005	541,581	16,812	167,314	81,017
1994	2,994,076	2,097,381	52,565	2,149,946	220,475	-23,087	1,906,384	489,088	598,604	17,841	167,822	81,542
1995	3,180,418	2,245,192	47,290	2,292,482	236,940	-32,022	2,023,520	554,796	602,102	18,841	168,806	84,945
1996	3,350,197	2,338,849	60,329	2,399,178	247,955	-38,165	2,113,058	572,111	665,028	19,792	169,266	86,982
1997	3,367,914	2,397,377	42,549	2,439,926	253,919	-40,647	2,145,360	590,439	632,115	19,819	169,934	87,893
1998	3,531,817	2,503,673	32,123	2,535,796	266,700	-43,391	2,225,705	658,804	647,308	20,757	170,152	90,035
1999	3,686,028	2,682,806	30,323	2,713,129	281,970	-56,858	2,374,301	658,471	653,256	21,692	169,927	92,393
2000	3,966,684	2,917,050	28,331	2,945,381	295,389	-62,637	2,587,355	697,302	682,027	23,329	170,033	95,093
2001	4,061,455	2,929,988	40,596	2,970,584	302,260	-75,092	2,593,232	677,923	790,300	23,951	169,572	98,472
2002	4,237,886	3,118,354	27,658	3,146,012	320,152	-87,719	2,738,141	661,162	838,583	24,877	170,352	100,218
2003	4,269,869	3,127,912	36,596	3,164,508	318,491	-86,791	2,759,226	669,145	841,498	24,925	171,306	99,865
2004	4,476,206	3,248,256	62,892	3,311,148	326,439	-92,991	2,891,718	647,030	937,458	26,029	171,969	100,220
2005	4,700,034	3,350,265	54,646	3,404,911	332,614	-95,391	2,976,906	714,662	1,008,466	27,288	172,241	99,880
2006	5,054,487	3,520,495	36,780	3,557,275	351,675	-97,815	3,107,785	860,033	1,086,669	29,032	174,102	101,130
2007	5,213,765	3,650,809	28,155	3,678,964	363,169	-121,398	3,194,397	873,480	1,145,888	29,977	173,927	102,068
2008	5,529,744	3,695,416	26,834	3,722,250	369,505	-101,729	3,251,016	987,505	1,291,223	31,703	174,425	101,856
2009	5,655,695	3,791,086	31,671	3,822,757	378,753	-96,586	3,347,418	943,686	1,364,591	32,196	175,667	100,439
2010	5,765,491	3,943,011	36,543	3,979,554	389,081	-92,967	3,497,506	829,412	1,438,573	32,609	176,806	100,262
2011	6,019,999	3,981,213	26,669	4,007,882	355,060	-77,198	3,575,624	974,190	1,470,185	33,945	177,348	102,480
2012	6,172,524	4,081,564	35,517	4,117,081	365,712	-82,066	3,669,303	999,015	1,504,206	34,722	177,769	103,394
2013	6,256,790	4,150,791	55,756	4,206,547	424,105	-67,798	3,714,644	994,051	1,548,095	35,050	178,510	104,666
2014	6,354,909	4,267,583	47,894	4,315,477	431,824	-91,011	3,792,642	1,020,387	1,541,880	35,515	178,938	105,781
2015	6,668,293	4,409,734	49,678	4,459,412	450,294	-115,302	3,893,816	1,065,315	1,709,162	37,168	179,410	106,274
2016	6,861,885	4,489,234	29,421	4,518,655	461,271	-145,779	3,911,605	1,081,109	1,869,171	38,218	179,546	106,879
2017	7,021,311	4,582,894	46,526	4,629,420	471,436	-138,446	4,019,538	1,116,855	1,884,918	39,347	178,445	106,797
2018	8,249,670	8,159,188	90,482	5,171,147	539,709	-9,790	4,621,648	1,356,337	2,271,685	40,812	202,138	116,394
2019	8,375,896	8,293,900	81,996	5,160,820	536,657	5,340	4,629,503	1,363,550	2,382,843	41,825	200,261	116,093

Personal Income and Employment by Area: Monroe, MI

(Thousands of dollars, except as noted.)

Year	Personal income, total	Earnings by place of work			Less: Contributions for government social insurance	Plus: Adjustment for residence	Equals: Net earnings by place of residence	Plus: Dividends, interest, and rent	Plus: Personal current transfer receipts	Per capita personal income (dollars)	Population (persons)	Total employment
		Nonfarm	Farm	Total								
1970	447,425	210,184	9,339	219,523	14,721	156,788	361,590	54,347	31,488	3,740	119,640	28,386
1971	490,338	233,671	7,299	240,970	16,779	168,702	392,893	59,701	37,744	4,033	121,589	29,043
1972	560,418	273,988	12,706	286,694	20,988	186,524	452,230	66,454	41,734	4,541	123,422	30,768
1973	637,123	316,224	13,417	329,641	28,072	212,547	514,116	75,001	48,006	5,126	124,301	32,201
1974	680,892	330,847	8,861	339,708	30,754	224,401	533,355	85,267	62,270	5,451	124,906	32,581
1975	732,876	339,486	16,178	355,664	30,582	224,995	550,077	94,322	88,477	5,803	126,297	31,334
1976	829,067	388,015	9,801	397,816	35,212	274,987	637,591	100,511	90,965	6,520	127,148	32,540
1977	944,403	449,249	12,484	461,733	40,796	318,843	739,780	112,584	92,039	7,265	129,995	33,950
1978	1,057,320	501,580	10,288	511,868	46,921	369,199	834,146	123,282	99,892	7,983	132,450	34,920
1979	1,172,775	533,031	16,792	549,823	51,719	415,932	914,036	139,946	118,793	8,733	134,285	34,884
1980	1,273,733	544,803	20,439	565,242	52,494	425,214	937,962	166,768	169,003	9,454	134,732	33,246
1981	1,377,975	639,071	13,626	652,697	68,849	413,014	996,862	202,710	178,403	10,228	134,729	34,698
1982	1,442,527	685,282	6,945	692,227	75,038	388,160	1,005,349	231,776	205,402	10,901	132,334	34,361
1983	1,548,486	755,372	3,366	758,738	82,542	405,904	1,082,100	252,695	213,691	11,831	130,888	35,020
1984	1,659,148	707,857	18,996	726,853	78,043	510,498	1,159,308	286,509	213,331	12,680	130,851	33,976
1985	1,757,755	728,921	15,385	744,306	81,723	576,156	1,238,739	302,273	216,743	13,481	130,386	35,020
1986	1,920,452	883,092	13,375	896,467	99,617	574,345	1,371,195	321,000	228,257	14,643	131,150	37,893
1987	1,991,738	941,070	13,857	954,927	105,040	579,138	1,429,025	327,313	235,400	15,106	131,852	39,715
1988	2,155,014	1,054,616	14,276	1,068,892	121,542	618,135	1,565,485	344,976	244,553	16,321	132,040	40,868
1989	2,281,017	1,148,509	16,162	1,164,671	134,626	622,803	1,652,848	361,940	266,229	17,189	132,700	43,343
1990	2,351,795	1,209,003	17,769	1,226,772	143,891	592,864	1,675,745	382,498	293,552	17,565	133,892	45,406
1991	2,399,561	1,245,617	8,131	1,253,748	150,623	581,136	1,684,261	381,203	334,097	17,819	134,664	46,113
1992	2,595,382	1,359,545	12,379	1,371,924	162,837	644,336	1,853,423	389,604	352,355	19,186	135,277	46,355
1993	2,762,164	1,417,824	11,056	1,428,880	171,030	721,994	1,979,844	406,328	375,992	20,366	135,623	46,938
1994	3,079,088	1,540,762	12,100	1,552,862	187,904	837,851	2,202,809	489,666	386,613	22,511	136,783	48,731
1995	3,240,237	1,618,691	17,231	1,635,922	196,616	880,604	2,319,910	519,448	400,879	23,373	138,631	50,033
1996	3,391,007	1,679,288	14,046	1,693,334	199,212	931,258	2,425,380	548,666	416,961	24,200	140,123	50,605
1997	3,587,984	1,784,394	19,730	1,804,124	210,010	975,871	2,569,985	570,622	447,377	25,317	141,725	52,094
1998	3,818,100	1,919,961	20,743	1,940,704	221,259	1,067,969	2,787,414	583,197	447,489	26,698	143,009	53,783
1999	4,112,085	2,120,045	21,704	2,141,749	243,204	1,162,904	3,061,449	570,989	479,647	28,452	144,525	56,396
2000	4,343,397	2,238,418	20,262	2,258,680	253,597	1,205,851	3,210,934	621,770	510,693	29,675	146,364	58,727
2001	4,471,432	2,323,708	14,945	2,338,653	260,999	1,229,040	3,306,694	595,693	569,045	30,293	147,605	59,030
2002	4,490,951	2,417,519	18,808	2,436,327	276,938	1,168,740	3,328,129	576,212	586,610	30,230	148,561	58,898
2003	4,642,339	2,488,186	18,684	2,506,870	282,536	1,198,861	3,423,195	600,897	618,247	31,001	149,747	58,696
2004	4,841,092	2,543,853	23,587	2,567,440	291,324	1,335,757	3,611,873	583,832	645,387	32,035	151,117	58,876
2005	4,979,758	2,513,361	20,959	2,534,320	295,452	1,436,291	3,675,159	608,607	695,992	32,681	152,374	59,054
2006	5,134,191	2,626,584	27,061	2,653,645	313,614	1,427,096	3,767,127	609,575	757,489	33,456	153,460	59,603
2007	5,288,827	2,578,552	27,199	2,605,751	311,455	1,496,141	3,790,437	671,468	826,922	34,472	153,424	59,132
2008	5,343,286	2,507,635	16,785	2,524,420	307,500	1,434,150	3,651,070	722,294	969,922	34,968	152,806	57,260
2009	5,042,561	2,287,783	22,578	2,310,361	284,745	1,291,925	3,317,541	642,129	1,082,891	33,110	152,296	53,469
2010	5,186,485	2,337,182	26,849	2,364,031	285,087	1,321,312	3,400,256	634,864	1,151,365	34,139	151,924	52,532
2011	5,469,008	2,381,311	51,552	2,432,863	258,950	1,467,462	3,641,375	678,590	1,149,043	36,110	151,453	53,377
2012	5,645,000	2,536,242	26,475	2,562,717	276,087	1,500,791	3,787,421	715,932	1,141,647	37,449	150,737	54,458
2013	5,729,624	2,629,046	53,621	2,682,667	324,878	1,469,042	3,826,831	725,528	1,177,265	38,183	150,057	56,250
2014	5,987,718	2,717,283	25,011	2,742,294	335,161	1,548,737	3,955,870	788,096	1,243,752	39,972	149,796	57,543
2015	6,305,530	2,842,304	18,232	2,860,536	345,314	1,649,311	4,164,533	832,559	1,308,438	42,214	149,369	57,966
2016	6,524,480	2,903,417	18,924	2,922,341	349,833	1,719,164	4,291,672	882,202	1,350,606	43,723	149,223	58,033
2017	6,788,553	3,002,713	4,177	3,006,890	360,457	1,858,019	4,504,452	913,200	1,370,901	45,363	149,649	57,823
2018	7,040,382	7,023,227	17,155	3,109,429	376,698	1,925,402	4,658,133	966,535	1,415,714	46,881	150,174	57,956
2019	7,311,437	7,288,220	23,217	3,192,363	382,674	2,008,802	4,818,491	976,574	1,516,372	48,581	150,500	57,697

Personal Income and Employment by Area: Montgomery, AL

(Thousands of dollars, except as noted.)

Year	Personal income, total	Earnings by place of work			Less: Contributions for government social insurance	Plus: Adjustment for residence	Equals: Net earnings by place of residence	Plus: Dividends, interest, and rent	Plus: Personal current transfer receipts	Per capita personal income (dollars)	Population (persons)	Total employment
		Nonfarm	Farm	Total								
1970	821,743	648,601	20,376	668,977	45,411	-2,883	620,683	129,782	71,278	3,435	239,239	109,720
1971	932,728	734,677	23,155	757,832	52,137	-3,781	701,914	147,823	82,991	3,846	242,500	112,842
1972	1,082,001	854,494	32,191	886,685	63,004	-4,927	818,754	170,200	93,047	4,288	252,309	119,422
1973	1,224,140	962,843	42,950	1,005,793	80,874	-6,957	917,962	195,847	110,331	4,744	258,064	124,450
1974	1,359,239	1,072,465	25,326	1,097,791	93,246	-10,014	994,531	228,732	135,976	5,151	263,893	126,242
1975	1,469,402	1,137,036	21,515	1,158,551	100,379	-11,539	1,046,633	248,750	174,019	5,524	265,984	124,938
1976	1,646,376	1,271,461	42,584	1,314,045	115,289	-15,561	1,183,195	269,571	193,610	6,094	270,156	127,870
1977	1,792,684	1,413,534	19,548	1,433,082	128,629	-21,154	1,283,299	300,436	208,949	6,570	272,860	132,672
1978	2,041,480	1,606,309	33,859	1,640,168	148,010	-29,809	1,462,349	347,640	231,491	7,376	276,789	139,055
1979	2,270,352	1,785,676	40,331	1,826,007	171,725	-41,172	1,613,110	387,081	270,161	8,056	281,831	142,495
1980	2,507,508	1,946,081	18,150	1,964,231	188,418	-43,970	1,731,843	458,664	317,001	8,751	286,531	142,176
1981	2,761,064	2,074,007	17,490	2,091,497	215,256	-29,463	1,846,778	556,811	357,475	9,574	288,378	139,589
1982	2,945,695	2,165,214	27,443	2,192,657	227,512	-31,417	1,933,728	613,204	398,763	10,183	289,284	137,511
1983	3,217,601	2,402,691	19,706	2,422,397	256,127	-42,377	2,123,893	665,759	427,949	11,105	289,744	141,881
1984	3,537,963	2,661,352	21,969	2,683,321	287,780	-51,895	2,343,646	740,936	453,381	12,100	292,394	147,345
1985	3,823,104	2,899,209	29,648	2,928,857	315,600	-62,721	2,550,536	795,894	476,674	12,985	294,421	150,916
1986	4,084,174	3,135,792	23,556	3,159,348	339,756	-71,924	2,747,668	839,756	496,750	13,709	297,919	156,125
1987	4,372,989	3,366,284	43,316	3,409,600	359,967	-83,824	2,965,809	898,158	509,022	14,510	301,371	160,694
1988	4,701,889	3,611,645	53,144	3,664,789	403,537	-95,245	3,166,007	996,910	538,972	15,532	302,729	166,464
1989	5,103,772	3,807,685	49,481	3,857,166	426,323	-104,099	3,326,744	1,164,083	612,945	16,734	305,003	169,489
1990	5,364,632	4,003,332	50,701	4,054,033	455,455	-111,635	3,486,943	1,191,565	686,124	17,529	306,042	170,900
1991	5,655,230	4,207,688	63,503	4,271,191	481,977	-116,986	3,672,228	1,226,560	756,442	18,176	311,129	171,043
1992	6,083,594	4,523,547	43,101	4,566,648	513,121	-126,539	3,926,988	1,297,482	859,124	19,192	316,981	175,249
1993	6,370,097	4,760,072	29,227	4,789,299	541,797	-134,807	4,112,695	1,334,993	922,409	19,740	322,707	179,984
1994	6,792,001	5,091,592	29,287	5,120,879	583,257	-144,367	4,393,255	1,427,138	971,608	20,729	327,654	183,466
1995	7,188,896	5,302,616	13,297	5,315,913	609,465	-153,064	4,553,384	1,579,601	1,055,911	21,676	331,647	189,986
1996	7,524,350	5,554,393	23,807	5,578,200	634,896	-165,318	4,777,986	1,632,649	1,113,715	22,460	335,014	194,046
1997	7,937,695	5,816,476	38,983	5,855,459	667,339	-179,617	5,008,503	1,761,694	1,167,498	23,422	338,906	197,762
1998	8,415,175	6,239,652	34,635	6,274,287	703,270	-197,355	5,373,662	1,847,523	1,193,990	24,597	342,120	201,452
1999	8,769,604	6,596,901	50,102	6,647,003	741,330	-217,042	5,688,631	1,835,569	1,245,404	25,453	344,540	205,388
2000	9,224,316	6,875,011	42,499	6,917,510	770,641	-230,656	5,916,213	1,986,075	1,322,028	26,577	347,080	206,869
2001	9,316,037	6,941,495	53,726	6,995,221	798,430	-258,064	5,938,727	1,979,863	1,397,447	26,715	348,725	209,312
2002	9,716,854	7,308,363	34,777	7,343,140	841,093	-284,212	6,217,835	1,969,890	1,529,129	27,685	350,984	210,012
2003	10,200,906	7,648,606	61,456	7,710,062	878,499	-309,575	6,521,988	2,040,712	1,638,206	28,946	352,411	212,969
2004	10,894,293	8,076,540	103,275	8,179,815	917,383	-322,500	6,939,932	2,232,691	1,721,670	30,687	355,009	216,880
2005	11,414,631	8,490,466	106,724	8,597,190	965,286	-350,143	7,281,761	2,280,364	1,852,506	31,826	358,659	222,859
2006	12,105,134	8,992,695	95,843	9,088,538	1,025,720	-388,006	7,674,812	2,425,259	2,005,063	33,075	365,989	227,676
2007	12,542,575	9,255,158	60,916	9,316,074	1,065,298	-422,537	7,828,239	2,542,382	2,171,954	33,955	369,390	234,199
2008	12,804,287	9,300,404	53,973	9,354,377	1,110,327	-453,299	7,790,751	2,588,605	2,424,931	34,583	370,249	231,517
2009	12,714,021	9,251,823	64,150	9,315,973	1,098,806	-466,928	7,750,239	2,362,538	2,601,244	34,190	371,860	223,844
2010	13,102,262	9,405,184	60,859	9,466,043	1,116,396	-482,005	7,867,642	2,354,175	2,880,445	34,927	375,128	220,603
2011	13,641,275	9,585,782	54,862	9,640,644	1,010,916	-515,218	8,114,510	2,556,641	2,970,124	36,329	375,497	221,792
2012	13,706,425	9,577,108	80,955	9,658,063	1,012,549	-528,406	8,117,108	2,640,995	2,948,322	36,580	374,695	218,631
2013	13,835,033	9,775,119	136,500	9,911,619	1,161,847	-539,399	8,210,373	2,604,681	3,019,979	37,008	373,835	219,378
2014	14,230,494	9,972,361	113,452	10,085,813	1,179,524	-546,589	8,359,700	2,740,860	3,129,934	38,129	373,222	221,243
2015	14,833,924	10,337,598	123,130	10,460,728	1,216,568	-571,761	8,672,399	2,866,835	3,294,690	39,759	373,097	222,799
2016	15,185,010	10,749,060	73,054	10,822,114	1,253,571	-598,985	8,969,558	2,880,031	3,335,421	40,659	373,475	225,583
2017	15,723,625	11,075,379	92,826	11,168,205	1,286,818	-598,343	9,283,044	2,986,797	3,453,784	42,053	373,903	227,461
2018	16,175,960	16,111,882	64,078	11,241,751	1,325,946	-597,220	9,318,585	3,153,741	3,703,634	43,365	373,022	227,910
2019	16,749,561	16,701,578	47,983	11,681,382	1,370,967	-627,325	9,683,090	3,199,498	3,866,973	44,870	373,290	229,408

Personal Income and Employment by Area: Morgantown, WV

(Thousands of dollars, except as noted.)

Year	Personal income, total	Earnings by place of work			Less: Contributions for government social insurance	Plus: Adjustment for residence	Equals: Net earnings by place of residence	Plus: Dividends, interest, and rent	Plus: Personal current transfer receipts	Per capita personal income (dollars)	Population (persons)	Total employment
		Nonfarm	Farm	Total								
1970	266,124	213,095	847	213,942	14,864	4,512	203,590	34,199	28,335	2,983	89,219	34,394
1971	296,621	236,461	952	237,413	17,315	3,306	223,404	38,242	34,975	3,271	90,684	35,273
1972	340,664	276,990	870	277,860	21,296	-358	256,206	43,192	41,266	3,622	94,067	37,872
1973	364,176	293,102	1,016	294,118	25,961	-3,432	264,725	49,168	50,283	3,791	96,069	38,107
1974	403,584	326,114	47	326,161	29,918	-7,206	289,037	57,364	57,183	4,106	98,296	38,804
1975	458,241	370,883	-100	370,783	33,555	-11,189	326,039	64,298	67,904	4,685	97,808	40,252
1976	511,329	419,851	-102	419,749	38,650	-18,190	362,909	72,906	75,514	5,135	99,573	42,073
1977	574,724	472,629	-184	472,445	42,227	-19,927	410,291	83,603	80,830	5,659	101,553	43,083
1978	645,097	532,986	905	533,891	48,968	-27,495	457,428	95,938	91,731	6,255	103,131	44,710
1979	695,822	570,263	312	570,575	55,473	-32,905	482,197	106,847	106,778	6,669	104,338	43,728
1980	775,551	623,361	32	623,393	63,757	-41,419	518,217	134,231	123,103	7,328	105,829	43,877
1981	872,076	679,195	-2,339	676,856	73,808	-38,063	564,985	165,406	141,685	8,141	107,115	43,092
1982	953,020	754,738	-2,007	752,731	85,550	-49,347	617,834	185,814	149,372	8,878	107,348	43,856
1983	1,018,515	786,567	-461	786,106	90,595	-51,575	643,936	207,955	166,624	9,436	107,934	44,249
1984	1,097,543	854,460	1,748	856,208	100,426	-54,576	701,206	223,035	173,302	10,141	108,233	45,127
1985	1,154,420	899,735	1,867	901,602	107,846	-58,776	734,980	236,524	182,916	10,811	106,785	46,436
1986	1,194,627	927,208	2,476	929,684	117,075	-66,016	746,593	250,818	197,216	11,254	106,152	47,850
1987	1,249,857	985,257	-576	984,681	125,455	-71,385	787,841	257,750	204,266	11,812	105,816	49,184
1988	1,391,272	1,097,171	-372	1,096,799	140,715	-64,059	892,025	278,488	220,759	13,195	105,441	50,388
1989	1,461,720	1,129,622	1,329	1,130,951	148,822	-56,605	925,524	298,985	237,211	13,922	104,993	51,305
1990	1,573,196	1,221,234	178	1,221,412	162,961	-58,103	1,000,348	317,898	254,950	15,026	104,696	53,460
1991	1,668,693	1,287,530	-1,523	1,286,007	175,060	-59,758	1,051,189	326,704	290,800	15,708	106,229	54,423
1992	1,825,250	1,384,288	638	1,384,926	191,376	-69,566	1,123,984	354,641	346,625	16,984	107,468	56,208
1993	1,880,315	1,421,435	814	1,422,249	202,955	-71,936	1,147,358	363,494	369,463	17,317	108,582	56,446
1994	1,978,030	1,522,433	1,007	1,523,440	217,818	-80,263	1,225,359	379,950	372,721	18,065	109,494	58,961
1995	2,038,247	1,532,728	-1,598	1,531,130	223,573	-76,227	1,231,330	421,262	385,655	18,488	110,247	59,587
1996	2,111,787	1,553,855	48	1,553,903	224,494	-73,527	1,255,882	444,792	411,113	19,102	110,553	59,610
1997	2,166,258	1,566,618	-2,136	1,564,482	223,570	-63,502	1,277,410	464,642	424,206	19,554	110,781	59,184
1998	2,266,635	1,651,870	-2,359	1,649,511	238,968	-78,661	1,331,882	500,125	434,628	20,435	110,918	59,873
1999	2,361,175	1,761,749	-3,454	1,758,295	252,997	-88,580	1,416,718	501,262	443,195	21,293	110,888	60,730
2000	2,554,433	1,952,745	-603	1,952,142	285,711	-106,902	1,559,529	525,608	469,296	22,943	111,338	62,298
2001	2,716,085	2,071,511	-1,146	2,070,365	287,987	-120,849	1,661,529	527,660	526,896	24,086	112,764	63,393
2002	2,868,192	2,196,233	-4,367	2,191,866	285,618	-133,694	1,772,554	519,950	575,688	25,084	114,343	64,332
2003	2,918,690	2,279,211	-6,906	2,272,305	308,883	-145,885	1,817,537	513,079	588,074	25,060	116,466	64,987
2004	3,140,423	2,508,951	-4,073	2,504,878	325,070	-142,106	2,037,702	521,225	581,496	26,600	118,062	67,260
2005	3,392,787	2,713,676	-4,798	2,708,878	344,938	-145,149	2,218,791	568,455	605,541	28,288	119,937	69,278
2006	3,588,869	2,822,442	-5,413	2,817,029	352,998	-158,943	2,305,088	640,458	643,323	29,443	121,894	70,374
2007	3,726,079	2,894,750	-6,766	2,887,984	348,316	-177,858	2,361,810	678,453	685,816	30,169	123,507	73,433
2008	3,974,567	3,090,124	-4,962	3,085,162	358,801	-211,544	2,514,817	697,792	761,958	31,729	125,267	75,367
2009	4,150,104	3,316,977	-6,442	3,310,535	385,374	-259,782	2,665,379	668,537	816,188	32,550	127,498	76,187
2010	4,479,833	3,587,356	-7,493	3,579,863	414,131	-285,986	2,879,746	702,546	897,541	34,370	130,340	77,855
2011	4,722,429	3,654,621	-4,630	3,649,991	373,535	-240,869	3,035,587	776,003	910,839	35,687	132,329	78,369
2012	4,910,266	3,831,431	-5,702	3,825,729	388,851	-277,836	3,159,042	830,391	920,833	36,541	134,378	80,642
2013	4,921,636	3,949,764	-4,262	3,945,502	453,935	-315,861	3,175,706	801,894	944,036	36,304	135,566	81,740
2014	5,195,283	4,135,725	-5,917	4,129,808	476,774	-314,920	3,338,114	854,317	1,002,852	37,958	136,871	82,811
2015	5,412,337	4,356,758	-5,896	4,350,862	503,827	-379,359	3,467,676	897,768	1,046,893	39,292	137,745	84,100
2016	5,413,794	4,345,824	-7,257	4,338,567	512,558	-419,630	3,406,379	947,203	1,060,212	39,094	138,482	83,943
2017	5,651,673	4,609,583	-10,844	4,598,739	557,507	-471,646	3,569,586	986,121	1,095,966	40,745	138,709	85,451
2018	6,017,885	6,022,601	-4,716	4,766,415	556,651	-455,483	3,754,281	1,082,673	1,180,931	43,231	139,204	86,921
2019	6,181,584	6,182,641	-1,057	4,926,763	574,101	-482,727	3,869,935	1,094,169	1,217,480	44,458	139,044	87,598

Personal Income and Employment by Area: Morristown, TN

(Thousands of dollars, except as noted.)

Year	Personal income, total	Earnings by place of work			Less: Contributions for government social insurance	Plus: Adjustment for residence	Equals: Net earnings by place of residence	Plus: Dividends, interest, and rent	Plus: Personal current transfer receipts	Per capita personal income (dollars)	Population (persons)	Total employment
		Nonfarm	Farm	Total								
1970	179,394	173,340	5,207	178,547	11,370	-25,057	142,120	19,569	17,705	2,800	64,065	33,308
1971	204,490	200,430	4,924	205,354	13,742	-29,404	162,208	22,375	19,907	3,074	66,514	34,956
1972	238,260	234,131	7,545	241,676	16,982	-34,378	190,316	25,517	22,427	3,468	68,704	38,430
1973	271,360	261,617	10,577	272,194	21,721	-36,315	214,158	29,398	27,804	3,849	70,499	39,656
1974	294,122	280,304	7,171	287,475	24,229	-37,751	225,495	34,201	34,426	4,055	72,527	38,744
1975	310,344	276,401	3,538	279,939	23,614	-33,885	222,440	37,700	50,204	4,256	72,914	34,813
1976	351,199	317,460	8,141	325,601	27,710	-38,339	259,552	41,127	50,520	4,708	74,589	37,232
1977	392,143	364,842	4,401	369,243	32,177	-45,333	291,733	46,623	53,787	5,109	76,762	39,929
1978	449,752	420,011	5,354	425,365	37,669	-50,493	337,203	54,155	58,394	5,706	78,827	42,110
1979	502,123	461,486	4,013	465,499	42,794	-51,864	370,841	62,358	68,924	6,309	79,591	42,332
1980	547,966	472,209	2,456	474,665	43,459	-47,996	383,210	78,554	86,202	6,774	80,893	40,018
1981	604,583	500,382	5,204	505,586	49,754	-45,185	410,647	97,104	96,832	7,376	81,970	38,986
1982	645,973	523,790	3,537	527,327	52,848	-49,789	424,690	113,394	107,889	7,737	83,487	38,391
1983	700,057	576,930	-2,351	574,579	58,734	-55,455	460,390	122,642	117,025	8,090	86,535	39,955
1984	781,134	650,446	2,817	653,263	68,632	-62,947	521,684	136,730	122,720	9,049	86,327	41,739
1985	817,891	669,169	4,029	673,198	71,304	-58,449	543,445	144,072	130,374	9,790	83,544	41,597
1986	868,226	708,951	2,150	711,101	77,163	-57,073	576,865	149,531	141,830	10,440	83,162	42,533
1987	936,639	770,994	2,867	773,861	83,417	-59,066	631,378	155,473	149,788	11,350	82,524	43,935
1988	1,028,950	846,857	2,661	849,518	94,372	-59,232	695,914	170,426	162,610	12,367	83,204	45,919
1989	1,140,557	939,395	4,338	943,733	105,373	-72,215	766,145	196,708	177,704	13,729	83,074	48,607
1990	1,235,957	1,016,828	5,154	1,021,982	114,538	-67,968	839,476	197,760	198,721	14,750	83,791	50,379
1991	1,295,635	1,049,126	5,660	1,054,786	119,909	-75,624	859,253	200,584	235,798	15,284	84,770	49,816
1992	1,427,387	1,156,195	7,254	1,163,449	130,645	-76,896	955,908	199,488	271,991	16,533	86,338	51,670
1993	1,522,301	1,235,762	6,078	1,241,840	141,173	-80,510	1,020,157	209,017	293,127	17,203	88,492	53,277
1994	1,591,202	1,278,431	5,285	1,283,716	149,203	-72,662	1,061,851	224,145	305,206	17,640	90,206	53,805
1995	1,707,904	1,347,071	1,844	1,348,915	157,114	-62,742	1,129,059	249,665	329,180	18,428	92,682	54,986
1996	1,803,777	1,413,407	-2,300	1,411,107	163,214	-62,827	1,185,066	268,698	350,013	18,951	95,181	55,998
1997	1,955,568	1,517,534	2,026	1,519,560	172,478	-50,659	1,296,423	286,942	372,203	20,036	97,602	56,824
1998	2,150,908	1,657,129	4,145	1,661,274	182,957	-36,696	1,441,621	321,042	388,245	21,617	99,503	57,994
1999	2,237,182	1,762,223	3,891	1,766,114	195,082	-68,904	1,502,128	327,817	407,237	22,064	101,395	59,986
2000	2,332,730	1,825,941	8,022	1,833,963	203,977	-92,141	1,537,845	345,430	449,455	22,693	102,796	61,433
2001	2,395,902	1,821,394	9,093	1,830,487	206,467	-81,699	1,542,321	358,012	495,569	23,077	103,821	57,997
2002	2,466,341	1,863,269	6,220	1,869,489	211,918	-73,613	1,583,958	340,585	541,798	23,733	103,919	57,111
2003	2,566,386	1,959,015	7,294	1,966,309	222,962	-89,042	1,654,305	346,222	565,859	24,374	105,291	57,762
2004	2,694,588	2,114,225	8,013	2,122,238	237,868	-102,929	1,781,441	321,620	591,527	25,346	106,314	59,166
2005	2,757,508	2,091,962	10,040	2,102,002	236,680	-60,090	1,805,232	312,300	639,976	25,603	107,703	58,718
2006	2,878,569	2,123,894	6,671	2,130,565	240,770	-27,934	1,861,861	334,950	681,758	26,238	109,708	59,216
2007	3,014,006	2,158,605	1,857	2,160,462	248,780	-30,518	1,881,164	379,348	753,494	26,965	111,776	59,564
2008	3,166,250	2,162,523	-230	2,162,293	253,466	-23,668	1,885,159	424,182	856,909	27,991	113,115	58,838
2009	3,167,686	2,019,104	2,729	2,021,833	241,599	28,101	1,808,335	424,557	934,794	27,880	113,618	54,545
2010	3,288,422	2,119,784	6,221	2,126,005	251,186	-6,278	1,868,541	414,724	1,005,157	28,790	114,219	54,257
2011	3,505,549	2,181,897	2,729	2,184,626	231,030	79,314	2,032,910	446,827	1,025,812	30,565	114,692	54,687
2012	3,573,093	2,323,338	3,261	2,326,599	237,069	-565	2,088,965	459,401	1,024,727	31,094	114,914	55,154
2013	3,622,712	2,347,629	6,056	2,353,685	268,612	21,975	2,107,048	462,100	1,053,564	31,474	115,102	55,404
2014	3,762,628	2,443,158	9,383	2,452,541	275,658	15,280	2,192,163	492,379	1,078,086	32,623	115,336	56,265
2015	3,951,447	2,557,246	8,230	2,565,476	286,063	15,647	2,295,060	528,554	1,127,833	33,956	116,371	57,074
2016	4,029,223	2,606,363	920	2,607,283	294,363	18,842	2,331,762	542,292	1,155,169	34,475	116,874	58,071
2017	4,163,886	2,723,699	8,183	2,731,882	311,307	-15,120	2,405,455	569,490	1,188,941	35,263	118,081	58,941
2018	5,164,293	5,169,051	-4,758	3,080,808	358,759	239,552	2,961,601	691,760	1,510,932	36,425	141,778	67,502
2019	5,346,273	5,353,044	-6,771	3,207,594	374,832	224,023	3,056,785	702,835	1,586,653	37,452	142,749	68,900

Personal Income and Employment by Area: Mount Vernon-Anacortes, WA

(Thousands of dollars, except as noted.)

Year	Personal income, total	Earnings by place of work			Less: Contributions for government social insurance	Plus: Adjustment for residence	Equals: Net earnings by place of residence	Plus: Dividends, interest, and rent	Plus: Personal current transfer receipts	Per capita personal income (dollars)	Population (persons)	Total employment
		Nonfarm	Farm	Total								
1970	210,795	141,229	11,282	152,511	11,412	7,281	148,380	37,494	24,921	4,021	52,419	21,242
1971	230,211	153,460	13,347	166,807	12,966	6,666	160,507	41,403	28,301	4,369	52,694	21,537
1972	252,938	172,325	14,626	186,951	15,490	5,487	176,948	45,513	30,477	4,759	53,145	22,736
1973	295,178	204,667	21,565	226,232	21,484	3,742	208,490	51,704	34,984	5,544	53,244	24,711
1974	326,194	215,809	26,573	242,382	22,871	4,979	224,490	58,799	42,905	6,024	54,151	24,990
1975	364,169	238,472	25,179	263,651	24,749	4,920	243,822	68,001	52,346	6,816	53,431	25,161
1976	415,084	288,481	23,491	311,972	30,573	1,063	282,462	75,232	57,390	7,351	56,468	26,771
1977	445,393	303,666	20,725	324,391	32,150	4,190	296,431	87,078	61,884	7,716	57,722	26,893
1978	506,036	352,263	18,807	371,070	37,624	5,526	338,972	100,852	66,212	8,503	59,516	28,633
1979	584,006	399,018	26,152	425,170	43,649	8,588	390,109	118,432	75,465	9,505	61,443	29,681
1980	659,107	429,456	24,671	454,127	47,239	8,273	415,161	148,103	95,843	10,220	64,491	29,998
1981	729,974	465,388	21,994	487,382	56,258	7,366	438,490	180,668	110,816	11,097	65,779	30,968
1982	784,219	482,315	22,382	504,697	59,947	7,341	452,091	206,539	125,589	11,738	66,812	30,991
1983	861,793	528,545	31,270	559,815	66,188	4,978	498,605	225,055	138,133	12,656	68,094	32,337
1984	905,850	538,015	28,703	566,718	69,957	8,803	505,564	252,966	147,320	13,167	68,795	32,176
1985	959,680	564,778	28,368	593,146	72,868	12,611	532,889	271,950	154,841	13,880	69,139	32,600
1986	1,019,315	601,228	35,546	636,774	78,055	18,410	577,129	279,166	163,020	14,489	70,353	33,374
1987	1,049,750	606,607	47,568	654,175	78,676	26,374	601,873	277,060	170,817	14,742	71,206	34,918
1988	1,167,720	688,936	53,987	742,923	91,067	30,689	682,545	301,348	183,827	15,892	73,477	37,811
1989	1,338,342	791,395	55,908	847,303	106,387	33,532	774,448	364,984	198,910	17,597	76,054	40,078
1990	1,462,704	895,756	55,632	951,388	122,256	39,460	868,592	378,142	215,970	18,180	80,457	42,865
1991	1,583,606	984,040	55,087	1,039,127	135,814	38,954	942,267	398,168	243,171	18,906	83,761	44,137
1992	1,712,498	1,056,331	66,374	1,122,705	145,824	45,697	1,022,578	410,718	279,202	19,810	86,445	44,728
1993	1,815,703	1,111,181	76,876	1,188,057	152,711	51,776	1,087,122	426,824	301,757	20,280	89,530	45,889
1994	1,941,787	1,196,398	74,805	1,271,203	166,432	45,221	1,149,992	466,941	324,854	21,146	91,829	48,619
1995	2,080,172	1,260,151	81,677	1,341,828	176,352	45,561	1,211,037	517,318	351,817	22,117	94,053	49,832
1996	2,227,233	1,301,820	84,985	1,386,805	175,792	57,486	1,268,499	582,036	376,698	23,263	95,743	51,671
1997	2,361,174	1,400,126	82,817	1,482,943	180,821	72,963	1,375,085	600,283	385,806	24,207	97,539	52,910
1998	2,561,316	1,540,170	87,614	1,627,784	193,760	89,126	1,523,150	633,453	404,713	25,636	99,909	53,846
1999	2,734,138	1,715,720	92,672	1,808,392	210,679	78,617	1,676,330	627,150	430,658	26,884	101,701	56,204
2000	2,920,145	1,853,748	83,347	1,937,095	231,506	69,827	1,775,416	682,799	461,930	28,236	103,420	58,486
2001	2,985,783	1,847,470	93,837	1,941,307	235,388	81,016	1,786,935	685,159	513,689	28,563	104,534	58,680
2002	3,069,581	1,936,308	80,287	2,016,595	247,162	108,207	1,877,640	648,436	543,505	29,078	105,563	58,710
2003	3,238,088	2,030,660	101,138	2,131,798	260,227	135,967	2,007,538	665,116	565,434	30,159	107,369	59,854
2004	3,392,498	2,162,028	84,133	2,246,161	275,001	118,681	2,089,841	715,976	586,681	31,115	109,030	60,779
2005	3,601,915	2,347,227	87,318	2,434,545	303,119	122,288	2,253,714	723,059	625,142	32,543	110,683	63,202
2006	3,964,523	2,484,993	90,145	2,575,138	317,718	152,267	2,409,687	886,227	668,609	35,202	112,621	64,921
2007	4,282,336	2,584,479	94,470	2,678,949	334,215	205,681	2,550,415	1,013,282	718,639	37,543	114,066	66,686
2008	4,529,058	2,668,249	107,367	2,775,616	343,325	175,980	2,608,271	1,096,840	823,947	39,108	115,808	66,360
2009	4,433,145	2,524,300	125,241	2,649,541	335,780	183,629	2,497,390	1,007,400	928,355	38,034	116,557	63,177
2010	4,448,061	2,589,829	113,906	2,703,735	341,268	154,212	2,516,679	911,577	1,019,805	38,034	116,951	62,291
2011	4,662,445	2,623,368	112,857	2,736,225	316,638	200,693	2,620,280	1,017,396	1,024,769	39,654	117,578	62,388
2012	4,950,021	2,795,539	115,792	2,911,331	325,476	194,154	2,780,009	1,139,943	1,030,069	42,044	117,733	62,620
2013	5,045,590	2,963,529	142,815	3,106,344	383,258	164,626	2,887,712	1,105,135	1,052,743	42,653	118,295	64,896
2014	5,319,176	3,110,352	135,396	3,245,748	402,638	128,042	2,971,152	1,206,449	1,141,575	44,361	119,907	66,277
2015	5,609,450	3,237,940	190,096	3,428,036	420,749	119,611	3,126,898	1,311,208	1,171,344	46,201	121,414	66,725
2016	5,865,229	3,358,962	180,236	3,539,198	431,443	166,429	3,274,184	1,350,231	1,240,814	47,534	123,390	67,695
2017	6,218,753	3,621,480	180,793	3,802,273	468,329	179,386	3,513,330	1,421,658	1,283,765	49,505	125,619	69,146
2018	6,656,585	6,535,281	121,304	4,062,904	499,863	70,964	3,634,005	1,661,493	1,361,087	52,072	127,835	70,912
2019	7,042,338	6,902,994	139,344	4,331,850	529,556	97,669	3,899,963	1,695,837	1,446,538	54,505	129,205	72,221

Personal Income and Employment by Area: Muncie, IN

(Thousands of dollars, except as noted.)

Year	Personal income, total	Earnings by place of work			Less: Contributions for government social insurance	Plus: Adjustment for residence	Equals: Net earnings by place of residence	Plus: Dividends, interest, and rent	Plus: Personal current transfer receipts	Per capita personal income (dollars)	Population (persons)	Total employment
		Nonfarm	Farm	Total								
1970	453,679	398,132	4,642	402,774	26,965	-19,063	356,746	64,129	32,804	3,506	129,415	54,161
1971	495,858	422,022	8,306	430,328	29,576	-15,021	385,731	70,305	39,822	3,799	130,524	53,900
1972	525,032	444,527	5,567	450,094	33,280	-11,531	405,283	75,122	44,627	3,937	133,342	54,086
1973	596,151	496,955	14,805	511,760	42,844	-8,954	459,962	83,914	52,275	4,482	133,005	55,918
1974	647,781	541,518	7,282	548,800	48,890	-9,909	490,001	95,856	61,924	4,935	131,273	56,276
1975	686,269	538,737	12,836	551,573	48,237	-6,185	497,151	106,361	82,757	5,266	130,324	53,413
1976	752,516	598,265	9,773	608,038	53,908	-1,661	552,469	115,032	85,015	5,766	130,508	54,644
1977	841,773	678,215	6,761	684,976	60,869	-1,438	622,669	128,705	90,399	6,467	130,160	57,114
1978	930,089	745,110	8,060	753,170	68,838	2,496	686,828	143,156	100,105	7,170	129,712	57,799
1979	1,026,345	822,227	6,886	829,113	78,526	-370	750,217	161,478	114,650	7,980	128,611	59,035
1980	1,125,163	858,189	2,578	860,767	81,171	-3,111	776,485	197,858	150,820	8,763	128,394	57,729
1981	1,218,563	900,763	1,571	902,334	92,243	540	810,631	244,599	163,333	9,570	127,338	56,902
1982	1,233,758	874,294	4,049	878,343	91,568	5,878	792,653	260,455	180,650	9,801	125,887	54,123
1983	1,310,010	938,943	-4,074	934,869	98,405	9,087	845,551	271,654	192,805	10,559	124,068	54,000
1984	1,430,165	1,025,955	8,332	1,034,287	109,770	15,135	939,652	289,966	200,547	11,574	123,569	55,565
1985	1,493,179	1,072,384	5,784	1,078,168	116,765	18,346	979,749	305,723	207,707	12,235	122,044	56,476
1986	1,572,043	1,145,382	5,656	1,151,038	125,155	13,460	1,039,343	315,527	217,173	13,017	120,770	57,543
1987	1,636,580	1,208,244	9,926	1,218,170	130,697	11,162	1,098,635	316,063	221,882	13,516	121,082	58,948
1988	1,749,526	1,306,406	4,447	1,310,853	145,694	16,740	1,181,899	333,956	233,671	14,499	120,662	60,820
1989	1,884,434	1,373,438	9,547	1,382,985	154,616	23,517	1,251,886	377,393	255,155	15,709	119,962	61,574
1990	2,003,361	1,461,454	9,279	1,470,733	168,665	21,441	1,323,509	397,497	282,355	16,726	119,774	62,976
1991	2,074,910	1,537,656	4,990	1,542,646	179,242	10,114	1,373,518	395,267	306,125	17,295	119,973	62,840
1992	2,169,482	1,664,256	8,886	1,673,142	191,084	-47,599	1,434,459	392,655	342,368	18,026	120,352	65,363
1993	2,241,264	1,721,570	11,760	1,733,330	199,661	-52,524	1,481,145	397,827	362,292	18,533	120,935	65,781
1994	2,365,872	1,837,554	15,737	1,853,291	215,603	-72,259	1,565,429	422,564	377,879	19,632	120,514	67,867
1995	2,462,428	1,914,997	8,157	1,923,154	224,657	-83,797	1,614,700	467,799	379,929	20,400	120,707	69,973
1996	2,536,454	1,918,513	11,212	1,929,725	222,557	-58,073	1,649,095	486,653	400,706	21,035	120,582	68,253
1997	2,613,740	2,008,351	16,568	2,024,919	232,241	-71,144	1,721,534	484,507	407,699	21,684	120,539	68,126
1998	2,752,185	2,051,152	13,413	2,064,565	232,569	-31,882	1,800,114	526,456	425,615	23,032	119,495	68,306
1999	2,829,369	2,097,870	10,358	2,108,228	236,184	-9,952	1,862,092	513,735	453,542	23,822	118,772	68,754
2000	2,994,658	2,201,452	12,916	2,214,368	245,065	-5,754	1,963,549	547,728	483,381	25,213	118,776	69,098
2001	3,065,010	2,208,034	14,706	2,222,740	250,885	-14,889	1,956,966	570,321	537,723	25,482	120,281	68,548
2002	3,059,612	2,209,891	4,730	2,214,621	250,859	-6,250	1,957,512	542,214	559,886	25,508	119,949	65,882
2003	3,119,020	2,249,641	12,937	2,262,578	256,666	-17,353	1,988,559	553,618	576,843	26,006	119,935	64,632
2004	3,146,155	2,282,392	23,185	2,305,577	260,189	6,480	2,051,868	488,873	605,414	26,452	118,938	63,457
2005	3,178,503	2,285,023	14,831	2,299,854	266,334	22,166	2,055,686	464,182	658,635	26,898	118,170	62,542
2006	3,188,740	2,295,400	10,729	2,306,129	271,068	-28,098	2,006,963	474,923	706,854	27,178	117,326	63,302
2007	3,222,455	2,310,820	9,488	2,320,308	275,480	-68,980	1,975,848	518,757	727,850	27,489	117,229	63,379
2008	3,312,800	2,307,920	17,673	2,325,593	277,978	-111,888	1,935,727	546,958	830,115	28,313	117,007	62,103
2009	3,249,375	2,200,346	11,975	2,212,321	269,990	-121,284	1,821,047	509,258	919,070	27,657	117,490	59,146
2010	3,312,450	2,187,357	9,868	2,197,225	264,906	-107,974	1,824,345	503,983	984,122	28,156	117,647	57,777
2011	3,459,191	2,272,279	23,915	2,296,194	243,454	-119,181	1,933,559	545,927	979,705	29,354	117,844	58,559
2012	3,627,469	2,398,828	20,367	2,419,195	254,452	-143,723	2,021,020	587,727	1,018,722	31,017	116,950	58,940
2013	3,645,882	2,439,399	46,521	2,485,920	294,856	-155,200	2,035,864	583,783	1,026,235	31,224	116,764	58,993
2014	3,780,014	2,513,788	14,351	2,528,139	302,421	-147,498	2,078,220	614,561	1,087,233	32,461	116,448	58,556
2015	3,880,216	2,600,175	-9,699	2,590,476	315,004	-170,489	2,104,983	641,111	1,134,122	33,505	115,811	59,583
2016	3,983,776	2,636,313	6,611	2,642,924	314,193	-150,982	2,177,749	641,935	1,164,092	34,497	115,483	60,282
2017	4,119,161	2,730,591	-5,793	2,724,798	324,095	-158,570	2,242,133	673,951	1,203,077	35,762	115,184	60,167
2018	4,222,330	4,211,924	10,406	2,762,883	333,174	-167,420	2,262,289	712,195	1,247,846	36,942	114,297	60,091
2019	4,351,803	4,343,869	7,934	2,887,498	350,344	-213,284	2,323,870	721,673	1,306,260	38,129	114,135	60,082

Personal Income and Employment by Area: Muskegon, MI

(Thousands of dollars, except as noted.)

Year	Personal income, total	Earnings by place of work			Less: Contributions for government social insurance	Plus: Adjustment for residence	Equals: Net earnings by place of residence	Plus: Dividends, interest, and rent	Plus: Personal current transfer receipts	Per capita personal income (dollars)	Population (persons)	Total employment
		Nonfarm	Farm	Total								
1970	580,833	502,485	3,319	505,804	36,139	-23,834	445,831	67,863	67,139	3,686	157,595	61,851
1971	601,588	499,296	3,304	502,600	37,037	-19,104	446,459	72,066	83,063	3,799	158,338	59,280
1972	668,217	562,195	3,743	565,938	44,138	-22,281	499,519	77,269	91,429	4,226	158,137	61,124
1973	727,752	621,504	3,694	625,198	56,776	-26,740	541,682	84,338	101,732	4,631	157,135	63,037
1974	805,200	679,210	5,755	684,965	63,978	-31,455	589,532	96,443	119,225	5,151	156,315	64,536
1975	880,409	712,195	4,593	716,788	65,004	-33,296	618,488	107,755	154,166	5,634	156,266	63,935
1976	959,264	787,449	4,627	792,076	73,762	-34,110	684,204	113,032	162,028	6,095	157,395	65,187
1977	1,051,818	872,209	5,573	877,782	81,465	-33,802	762,515	123,098	166,205	6,678	157,496	66,515
1978	1,179,804	982,422	7,285	989,707	95,122	-35,263	859,322	138,824	181,658	7,502	157,258	68,481
1979	1,295,276	1,072,957	5,242	1,078,199	108,592	-35,326	934,281	157,027	203,968	8,194	158,067	68,649
1980	1,395,210	1,108,549	5,379	1,113,928	110,521	-38,716	964,691	187,799	242,720	8,839	157,850	66,135
1981	1,505,262	1,162,622	7,758	1,170,380	125,075	-41,412	1,003,893	225,800	275,569	9,494	158,550	64,362
1982	1,575,139	1,154,252	9,653	1,163,905	125,615	-34,949	1,003,341	260,890	310,908	10,090	156,114	61,143
1983	1,639,741	1,192,327	7,477	1,199,804	131,908	-27,090	1,040,806	269,668	329,267	10,613	154,496	60,591
1984	1,809,110	1,335,798	8,729	1,344,527	154,387	-25,795	1,164,345	312,480	332,285	11,683	154,844	64,284
1985	1,916,564	1,420,334	12,683	1,433,017	166,241	-23,985	1,242,791	324,979	348,794	12,313	155,654	66,520
1986	1,984,921	1,474,821	8,086	1,482,907	172,581	-30,062	1,280,264	338,761	365,896	12,739	155,812	67,445
1987	2,075,511	1,511,736	8,319	1,520,055	173,494	-14,652	1,331,909	368,113	375,489	13,275	156,345	67,252
1988	2,165,811	1,587,473	7,751	1,595,224	188,961	-586	1,405,677	369,914	390,220	13,739	157,643	68,222
1989	2,313,446	1,669,433	10,877	1,680,310	197,412	6,304	1,489,202	403,140	421,104	14,608	158,365	69,448
1990	2,431,375	1,738,463	7,588	1,746,051	208,189	8,270	1,546,132	425,737	459,506	15,255	159,384	70,361
1991	2,499,662	1,746,604	9,589	1,756,193	211,795	17,735	1,562,133	427,202	510,327	15,537	160,885	68,332
1992	2,640,606	1,856,422	10,002	1,866,424	223,688	36,027	1,678,763	432,168	529,675	16,286	162,135	68,157
1993	2,751,922	1,917,508	8,785	1,926,293	233,846	54,267	1,746,714	450,380	554,828	16,874	163,082	67,576
1994	2,938,274	2,033,507	8,135	2,041,642	254,701	86,535	1,873,476	509,412	555,386	17,952	163,678	69,480
1995	3,082,029	2,131,597	9,654	2,141,251	270,894	98,905	1,969,262	532,146	580,621	18,741	164,457	71,863
1996	3,246,918	2,230,168	8,884	2,239,052	279,187	121,891	2,081,756	553,967	611,195	19,588	165,763	73,599
1997	3,463,258	2,378,999	9,540	2,388,539	297,185	144,462	2,235,816	585,282	642,160	20,729	167,077	75,236
1998	3,654,793	2,570,631	11,277	2,581,908	317,126	159,168	2,423,950	584,250	646,593	21,736	168,147	77,667
1999	3,879,278	2,744,430	11,905	2,756,335	335,486	171,223	2,592,072	580,521	706,685	22,909	169,331	81,008
2000	4,081,733	2,872,463	7,757	2,880,220	350,599	198,559	2,728,180	618,924	734,629	23,954	170,396	83,059
2001	4,147,379	2,824,957	8,372	2,833,329	329,755	206,920	2,710,494	608,899	827,986	24,246	171,055	79,334
2002	4,177,683	2,838,399	6,182	2,844,581	332,029	208,243	2,720,795	589,497	867,391	24,351	171,563	78,856
2003	4,278,848	2,877,411	9,508	2,886,919	338,038	198,414	2,747,295	618,509	913,044	24,838	172,269	79,851
2004	4,369,235	2,975,734	13,972	2,989,706	356,069	196,620	2,830,257	599,708	939,270	25,289	172,771	81,907
2005	4,505,600	3,038,062	13,722	3,051,784	373,747	234,846	2,912,883	594,859	997,858	25,953	173,608	82,256
2006	4,691,004	3,133,500	14,862	3,148,362	390,076	238,015	2,996,301	625,190	1,069,513	27,005	173,710	82,617
2007	4,839,045	3,143,484	19,754	3,163,238	393,949	247,799	3,017,088	653,552	1,168,405	27,853	173,738	81,964
2008	4,918,262	3,152,085	20,213	3,172,298	398,910	153,832	2,927,220	676,565	1,314,477	28,291	173,846	80,353
2009	4,768,347	2,934,018	14,607	2,948,625	372,728	109,638	2,685,535	622,071	1,460,741	27,602	172,755	75,602
2010	4,955,354	3,040,949	23,854	3,064,803	380,354	90,075	2,774,524	624,021	1,556,809	28,827	171,898	74,814
2011	5,188,257	3,155,642	40,058	3,195,700	354,811	99,127	2,940,016	713,780	1,534,461	30,524	169,975	76,745
2012	5,387,609	3,320,569	20,637	3,341,206	371,161	113,007	3,083,052	774,658	1,529,899	31,676	170,087	77,708
2013	5,457,599	3,369,522	37,346	3,406,868	424,411	132,896	3,115,353	772,685	1,569,561	31,694	172,196	78,230
2014	5,753,599	3,506,993	28,861	3,535,854	439,648	190,210	3,286,416	834,795	1,632,388	33,418	172,171	79,815
2015	6,061,868	3,665,716	23,697	3,689,413	453,057	203,183	3,439,539	887,070	1,735,259	35,167	172,373	80,440
2016	6,262,673	3,706,954	28,164	3,735,118	456,506	299,060	3,577,672	907,793	1,777,208	36,179	173,102	79,879
2017	6,452,555	3,867,607	17,590	3,885,197	474,800	318,503	3,728,900	942,543	1,781,112	37,149	173,693	81,174
2018	6,646,850	6,631,298	15,552	3,955,755	496,115	338,239	3,797,879	994,263	1,854,708	38,289	173,599	81,388
2019	6,879,677	6,863,926	15,751	3,980,563	497,548	427,761	3,910,776	1,005,327	1,963,574	39,637	173,566	80,904

Personal Income and Employment by Area: Myrtle Beach-Conway-North Myrtle Beach, SC-NC

(Thousands of dollars, except as noted.)

Year	Personal income, total	Earnings by place of work			Less: Contributions for government social insurance	Plus: Adjustment for residence	Equals: Net earnings by place of residence	Plus: Dividends, interest, and rent	Plus: Personal current transfer receipts	Per capita personal income (dollars)	Population (persons)	Total employment
		Nonfarm	Farm	Total								
1970	285,259	204,494	19,298	223,792	13,478	6,039	216,353	42,169	26,737	2,993	95,303	42,155
1971	335,024	240,583	18,453	259,036	16,402	9,073	251,707	52,169	31,148	3,312	101,165	45,218
1972	391,975	288,747	22,502	311,249	20,303	6,150	297,096	59,818	35,061	3,652	107,339	48,709
1973	450,877	333,232	27,197	360,429	26,458	5,982	339,953	69,526	41,398	3,977	113,376	52,009
1974	513,110	372,614	36,788	409,402	31,109	2,325	380,618	79,473	53,019	4,337	118,307	53,860
1975	578,653	422,534	28,498	451,032	35,517	-2,511	413,004	91,816	73,833	4,743	121,997	55,574
1976	641,890	479,653	22,519	502,172	40,806	-4,428	456,938	101,264	83,688	5,035	127,490	58,366
1977	708,269	540,277	17,141	557,418	45,663	-8,564	503,191	117,371	87,707	5,532	128,032	62,138
1978	829,350	619,934	36,238	656,172	53,200	-11,309	591,663	140,742	96,945	6,277	132,125	66,349
1979	914,703	697,988	15,134	713,122	62,065	-15,805	635,252	164,883	114,568	6,798	134,546	68,739
1980	1,042,425	771,768	12,589	784,357	68,908	-20,136	695,313	204,648	142,464	7,524	138,543	70,280
1981	1,207,439	864,210	27,210	891,420	83,236	-22,806	785,378	252,684	169,377	8,415	143,488	72,021
1982	1,335,999	945,094	17,925	963,019	93,370	-24,540	845,109	296,735	194,155	9,028	147,977	75,532
1983	1,541,279	1,102,138	14,018	1,116,156	109,956	-18,355	987,845	340,251	213,183	9,926	155,270	80,547
1984	1,759,761	1,266,857	10,611	1,277,468	131,306	-20,986	1,125,176	404,284	230,301	10,757	163,585	88,239
1985	1,956,690	1,391,938	18,514	1,410,452	147,079	-21,673	1,241,700	458,698	256,292	11,420	171,336	91,199
1986	2,114,823	1,487,991	-2,657	1,485,334	161,192	1,164	1,325,306	508,918	280,599	11,911	177,546	93,765
1987	2,317,270	1,621,672	21,732	1,643,404	173,473	11,217	1,481,148	539,388	296,734	12,638	183,363	95,855
1988	2,540,020	1,762,174	24,547	1,786,721	195,414	24,720	1,616,027	600,109	323,884	13,576	187,091	100,892
1989	2,812,270	1,887,664	27,082	1,914,746	213,944	39,742	1,740,544	685,199	386,527	14,744	190,746	103,297
1990	3,025,598	2,031,032	28,366	2,059,398	235,653	56,799	1,880,544	708,634	436,420	15,402	196,448	107,397
1991	3,210,173	2,168,175	37,160	2,205,335	256,757	31,685	1,980,263	734,531	495,379	15,846	202,583	108,714
1992	3,425,074	2,282,384	39,524	2,321,908	268,812	46,847	2,099,943	754,392	570,739	16,443	208,302	109,888
1993	3,584,083	2,359,916	36,261	2,396,177	281,331	45,682	2,160,528	798,071	625,484	17,197	208,415	111,547
1994	3,914,430	2,577,562	35,349	2,612,911	313,926	41,679	2,340,664	872,083	701,683	18,150	215,675	118,839
1995	4,349,220	2,872,774	23,808	2,896,582	349,625	37,615	2,584,572	987,844	776,804	19,350	224,765	128,781
1996	4,806,958	3,147,288	33,975	3,181,263	373,954	52,001	2,859,310	1,096,336	851,312	20,452	235,041	135,319
1997	5,287,584	3,469,655	39,667	3,509,322	411,646	63,604	3,161,280	1,215,559	910,745	21,574	245,090	144,171
1998	5,718,037	3,803,526	1,544	3,805,070	451,428	84,939	3,438,581	1,295,962	983,494	22,457	254,627	149,824
1999	6,125,468	4,155,680	13,674	4,169,354	490,065	94,428	3,773,717	1,300,586	1,051,165	23,273	263,200	155,162
2000	6,572,759	4,364,716	42,355	4,407,071	518,334	100,589	3,989,326	1,439,731	1,143,702	24,188	271,736	158,299
2001	6,842,989	4,480,149	60,989	4,541,138	537,167	69,926	4,073,897	1,484,806	1,284,286	24,616	277,987	161,326
2002	7,000,020	4,630,612	-10,711	4,619,901	556,979	75,498	4,138,420	1,447,859	1,413,741	24,573	284,862	163,517
2003	7,430,618	4,988,183	22,389	5,010,572	606,460	25,778	4,429,890	1,467,015	1,533,713	25,420	292,309	168,876
2004	8,207,500	5,522,004	24,193	5,546,197	666,223	21,874	4,901,848	1,593,749	1,711,903	27,139	302,421	178,122
2005	9,055,067	6,058,704	23,011	6,081,715	728,854	46,964	5,399,825	1,762,684	1,892,558	28,498	317,745	189,671
2006	10,018,548	6,635,200	12,074	6,647,274	822,288	87,903	5,912,889	1,998,639	2,107,020	29,805	336,132	202,101
2007	10,735,319	6,785,274	7,369	6,792,643	847,290	187,110	6,132,463	2,312,701	2,290,155	30,544	351,472	208,184
2008	11,143,356	6,584,502	30,169	6,614,671	836,634	212,783	5,990,820	2,479,193	2,673,343	30,625	363,866	204,744
2009	11,031,762	6,140,380	35,706	6,176,086	802,381	345,904	5,719,609	2,255,516	3,056,637	29,702	371,417	194,533
2010	11,303,645	6,205,609	36,715	6,242,324	813,277	382,603	5,811,650	2,146,880	3,345,115	29,864	378,506	192,085
2011	11,855,806	6,365,617	29,918	6,395,535	762,394	382,092	6,015,233	2,373,808	3,466,765	30,720	385,932	197,161
2012	12,409,616	6,669,963	39,119	6,709,082	784,706	376,319	6,300,695	2,509,828	3,599,093	31,525	393,648	200,115
2013	13,028,581	7,104,306	54,229	7,158,535	923,330	425,912	6,661,117	2,547,118	3,820,346	32,245	404,054	205,937
2014	14,076,682	7,556,886	49,996	7,606,882	975,996	421,973	7,052,859	2,872,563	4,151,260	33,810	416,347	211,158
2015	15,300,069	8,068,687	26,359	8,095,046	1,033,278	473,264	7,535,032	3,242,810	4,522,227	35,458	431,502	216,841
2016	16,256,068	8,474,900	34,988	8,509,888	1,090,386	633,965	8,053,467	3,441,987	4,760,614	36,303	447,793	224,541
2017	17,216,612	9,084,407	41,405	9,125,812	1,179,467	684,639	8,630,984	3,634,595	4,951,033	37,092	464,165	231,898
2018	18,928,980	18,933,277	-4,297	9,707,714	1,262,195	696,498	9,142,017	4,133,535	5,653,428	39,355	480,985	240,796
2019	20,121,637	20,123,416	-1,779	10,227,696	1,334,649	862,031	9,755,078	4,248,246	6,118,313	40,494	496,901	246,096

Personal Income and Employment by Area: Napa, CA

(Thousands of dollars, except as noted.)

Year	Personal income, total	Earnings by place of work			Less: Contributions for government social insurance	Plus: Adjustment for residence	Equals: Net earnings by place of residence	Plus: Dividends, interest, and rent	Plus: Personal current transfer receipts	Per capita personal income (dollars)	Population (persons)	Total employment
		Nonfarm	Farm	Total								
1970............	381,497	200,291	6,511	206,802	11,903	65,775	260,674	82,224	38,599	4,795	79,562	27,680
1971............	416,801	217,607	6,258	223,865	13,468	70,994	281,391	92,646	42,764	5,097	81,771	28,531
1972............	448,277	232,249	7,762	240,011	15,010	75,874	300,875	101,594	45,808	5,387	83,208	29,297
1973............	508,478	267,159	13,400	280,559	19,876	80,542	341,225	114,786	52,467	5,797	87,718	31,552
1974............	578,763	302,113	9,589	311,702	23,560	95,826	383,968	132,347	62,448	6,377	90,759	33,495
1975............	674,732	346,569	15,444	362,013	26,750	111,299	446,562	149,514	78,656	7,207	93,627	35,667
1976............	745,064	379,543	16,148	395,691	29,226	126,868	493,333	162,843	88,888	7,846	94,964	36,033
1977............	827,296	412,087	21,533	433,620	32,188	144,783	546,215	183,287	97,794	8,571	96,521	36,858
1978............	943,170	471,624	26,011	497,635	37,931	166,309	626,013	212,576	104,581	9,780	96,437	38,852
1979............	1,055,709	542,121	20,588	562,709	46,332	175,840	692,217	242,296	121,196	10,687	98,789	41,207
1980............	1,166,017	582,073	20,909	602,982	49,794	187,810	740,998	286,374	138,645	11,739	99,331	43,047
1981............	1,326,710	662,298	22,664	684,962	62,311	197,520	820,171	346,476	160,063	13,312	99,662	44,376
1982............	1,427,348	690,523	37,653	728,176	66,593	215,123	876,706	376,406	174,236	14,107	101,178	44,528
1983............	1,519,183	733,184	19,871	753,055	72,031	235,458	916,482	413,993	188,708	14,960	101,549	45,542
1984............	1,658,126	829,270	19,956	849,226	84,904	245,371	1,009,693	453,931	194,502	16,272	101,902	47,379
1985............	1,788,105	900,721	21,142	921,863	93,809	261,734	1,089,788	487,774	210,543	17,358	103,014	49,000
1986............	1,920,241	995,525	30,221	1,025,746	105,436	270,878	1,191,188	505,749	223,304	18,422	104,237	51,024
1987............	2,007,907	1,069,171	23,722	1,092,893	113,218	281,208	1,260,883	516,964	230,060	19,121	105,010	52,434
1988............	2,184,268	1,195,782	28,504	1,224,286	132,032	293,245	1,385,499	553,574	245,195	20,581	106,130	54,863
1989............	2,416,052	1,265,289	59,217	1,324,506	141,886	308,321	1,490,941	654,841	270,270	22,235	108,662	56,480
1990............	2,568,559	1,390,694	45,325	1,436,019	155,675	339,481	1,619,825	659,425	289,309	23,081	111,284	59,343
1991............	2,715,890	1,488,245	54,906	1,543,151	167,013	345,002	1,721,140	675,745	319,005	24,199	112,233	60,173
1992............	2,842,249	1,594,834	44,668	1,639,502	177,659	326,086	1,787,929	691,221	363,099	24,862	114,322	60,221
1993............	2,959,035	1,665,021	33,636	1,698,657	185,461	320,854	1,834,050	741,264	383,721	25,737	114,972	60,849
1994............	3,089,928	1,755,620	35,649	1,791,269	194,629	333,985	1,930,625	769,558	389,745	26,620	116,077	62,499
1995............	3,225,147	1,863,604	40,338	1,903,942	205,052	301,113	2,000,003	818,442	406,702	27,637	116,697	64,022
1996............	3,460,698	2,010,971	53,432	2,064,403	214,396	289,237	2,139,244	893,629	427,825	29,329	117,996	67,250
1997............	3,717,064	2,194,095	98,409	2,292,504	233,144	253,070	2,312,430	966,959	437,675	31,025	119,808	70,898
1998............	4,022,735	2,440,831	63,703	2,504,534	254,403	249,485	2,499,616	1,057,998	465,121	33,086	121,583	77,036
1999............	4,368,254	2,803,319	76,809	2,880,128	289,604	229,023	2,819,547	1,084,113	464,594	35,507	123,026	81,319
2000............	4,813,769	3,084,190	139,774	3,223,964	318,179	232,753	3,138,538	1,187,982	487,249	38,645	124,565	82,348
2001............	5,218,803	3,660,354	136,466	3,796,820	378,150	132,526	3,551,196	1,144,416	523,191	41,152	126,818	83,462
2002............	5,301,667	3,865,271	149,315	4,014,586	404,704	53,834	3,663,716	1,082,508	555,443	41,180	128,744	85,105
2003............	5,368,028	3,964,656	117,209	4,081,865	427,803	-30,482	3,623,580	1,158,516	585,932	41,249	130,138	85,767
2004............	5,443,667	4,049,495	95,622	4,145,117	463,163	-95,571	3,586,383	1,240,901	616,383	41,750	130,387	87,004
2005............	5,768,900	4,174,010	151,967	4,325,977	475,505	-74,076	3,776,396	1,341,042	651,462	44,246	130,381	87,728
2006............	6,146,388	4,391,241	88,961	4,480,202	480,276	-80,967	3,918,959	1,523,273	704,156	46,762	131,440	88,027
2007............	6,366,947	4,606,215	67,281	4,673,496	499,580	-159,611	4,014,305	1,606,563	746,079	48,022	132,583	91,173
2008............	6,406,833	4,652,354	44,876	4,697,230	514,604	-269,148	3,913,478	1,654,266	839,089	47,779	134,093	91,679
2009............	6,237,934	4,504,042	107,205	4,611,247	499,292	-230,628	3,881,327	1,450,850	905,757	46,111	135,280	88,602
2010............	6,385,064	4,626,054	85,443	4,711,497	490,105	-259,215	3,962,177	1,433,399	989,488	46,676	136,794	87,944
2011............	6,732,921	4,698,049	59,827	4,757,876	452,371	-244,356	4,061,149	1,665,614	1,006,158	48,823	137,905	89,319
2012............	7,450,101	5,094,743	206,272	5,301,015	477,361	-279,752	4,543,902	1,891,429	1,014,770	53,646	138,876	92,257
2013............	7,711,457	5,538,092	197,251	5,735,343	572,909	-295,240	4,867,194	1,799,857	1,044,406	55,090	139,978	96,114
2014............	8,394,533	6,079,360	190,304	6,269,664	616,804	-403,976	5,248,884	2,056,293	1,089,356	59,570	140,918	99,898
2015............	9,068,054	6,626,255	91,369	6,717,624	663,653	-374,489	5,679,482	2,226,732	1,161,840	64,082	141,507	103,165
2016............	9,558,456	6,933,805	130,167	7,063,972	694,032	-270,512	6,099,428	2,258,167	1,200,861	67,480	141,649	103,176
2017............	10,033,630	7,127,457	242,098	7,369,555	718,220	-189,029	6,462,306	2,365,767	1,205,557	71,174	140,973	104,826
2018............	9,998,840	9,825,402	173,438	7,225,768	744,455	-484,155	5,997,158	2,748,068	1,253,614	72,043	138,789	107,598
2019............	10,429,596	10,218,137	211,459	7,549,276	782,868	-451,071	6,315,337	2,774,353	1,339,906	75,717	137,744	109,197

Personal Income and Employment by Area: Naples-Marco Island, FL

(Thousands of dollars, except as noted.)

Year	Personal income, total	Earnings by place of work			Less: Contributions for government social insurance	Plus: Adjustment for residence	Equals: Net earnings by place of residence	Plus: Dividends, interest, and rent	Plus: Personal current transfer receipts	Per capita personal income (dollars)	Population (persons)	Total employment
		Nonfarm	Farm	Total								
1970	208,518	126,251	9,560	135,811	7,829	-11,869	116,113	77,669	14,736	5,364	38,874	19,784
1971	248,158	142,417	12,446	154,863	9,157	-11,225	134,481	93,439	20,238	5,814	42,683	21,385
1972	290,752	162,864	15,182	178,046	11,053	-11,510	155,483	110,868	24,401	5,916	49,144	22,959
1973	368,203	214,688	16,135	230,823	16,968	-14,942	198,913	138,061	31,229	6,724	54,757	28,113
1974	426,924	236,006	18,908	254,914	19,697	-15,257	219,960	168,112	38,852	7,311	58,396	30,121
1975	456,499	232,806	21,777	254,583	18,884	-10,919	224,780	178,930	52,789	7,177	63,602	28,974
1976	523,920	264,984	22,891	287,875	20,883	-9,240	257,752	206,728	59,440	7,923	66,125	29,334
1977	620,590	324,165	21,698	345,863	26,089	-10,612	309,162	243,861	67,567	8,942	69,404	34,304
1978	756,148	404,583	25,432	430,015	33,747	-13,342	382,926	294,875	78,347	10,103	74,844	40,053
1979	892,743	476,453	35,609	512,062	41,994	-13,099	456,969	342,120	93,654	10,902	81,890	44,215
1980	1,082,132	555,386	37,864	593,250	49,835	-13,171	530,244	437,362	114,526	12,367	87,504	46,868
1981	1,341,559	645,952	37,397	683,349	63,122	-13,292	606,935	595,549	139,075	14,352	93,473	50,278
1982	1,446,414	657,479	49,704	707,183	67,559	-8,947	630,677	648,171	167,566	14,478	99,902	51,225
1983	1,647,968	722,358	84,208	806,566	73,794	-6,628	726,144	733,883	187,941	15,806	104,265	55,623
1984	1,904,028	832,272	78,778	911,050	87,495	-9,320	814,235	882,167	207,626	17,293	110,105	61,169
1985	2,119,244	948,845	88,742	1,037,587	102,725	-11,856	923,006	966,155	230,083	18,335	115,584	65,543
1986	2,397,468	1,069,544	104,993	1,174,537	119,764	-11,800	1,042,973	1,097,283	257,212	19,763	121,311	71,756
1987	2,773,825	1,285,247	122,892	1,408,139	141,862	-15,835	1,250,442	1,242,720	280,663	21,684	127,921	74,893
1988	3,383,296	1,491,305	142,264	1,633,569	169,085	-21,502	1,442,982	1,617,650	322,664	24,985	135,413	83,812
1989	3,859,997	1,697,170	177,436	1,874,606	196,272	-25,905	1,652,429	1,844,790	362,778	26,659	144,790	89,342
1990	4,151,199	1,835,917	114,906	1,950,823	211,501	-29,203	1,710,119	2,026,528	414,552	26,857	154,568	92,101
1991	4,642,765	1,966,306	163,669	2,129,975	226,354	100,981	2,004,602	2,161,104	477,059	28,312	163,988	94,434
1992	5,238,715	2,135,932	207,357	2,343,289	243,320	161,865	2,261,834	2,413,706	563,175	30,444	172,077	96,093
1993	5,674,400	2,337,418	204,490	2,541,908	264,512	97,714	2,375,110	2,685,233	614,057	31,300	181,288	101,102
1994	6,243,328	2,583,059	154,108	2,737,167	295,029	92,194	2,534,332	3,035,261	673,735	32,665	191,132	104,131
1995	6,792,820	2,821,678	147,719	2,969,397	316,757	106,301	2,758,941	3,301,497	732,382	34,026	199,639	107,407
1996	7,500,818	3,092,576	134,526	3,227,102	342,643	184,819	3,069,278	3,642,239	789,301	35,854	209,205	113,188
1997	8,363,682	3,500,077	142,932	3,643,009	386,804	100,338	3,356,543	4,167,984	839,155	37,858	220,923	119,660
1998	9,313,989	3,821,332	164,529	3,985,861	417,181	195,648	3,764,328	4,672,545	877,116	39,911	233,371	128,002
1999	10,026,272	4,252,919	154,215	4,407,134	457,397	202,008	4,151,745	4,930,343	944,184	40,908	245,094	133,485
2000	10,804,584	4,724,567	156,123	4,880,690	507,357	67,461	4,440,794	5,326,482	1,037,308	42,535	254,015	143,309
2001	12,166,356	5,621,460	147,768	5,769,228	592,234	80,670	5,257,664	5,759,307	1,149,385	46,043	264,240	151,622
2002	12,726,576	5,999,728	164,283	6,164,011	631,310	108,032	5,640,733	5,846,688	1,239,155	46,196	275,490	157,775
2003	13,507,187	6,526,796	142,672	6,669,468	692,883	110,527	6,087,112	6,085,202	1,334,873	47,340	285,321	168,142
2004	15,705,208	6,913,798	144,696	7,058,494	756,929	176,567	6,478,132	7,778,545	1,448,531	53,054	296,021	177,642
2005	18,020,573	7,760,561	177,813	7,938,374	843,319	166,181	7,261,236	9,152,661	1,606,676	58,613	307,452	182,757
2006	20,829,534	8,392,260	166,503	8,558,763	927,494	231,092	7,862,361	11,233,606	1,733,567	66,629	312,621	190,179
2007	21,773,560	8,285,943	155,811	8,441,754	933,083	163,909	7,672,580	12,241,306	1,859,674	69,246	314,437	186,380
2008	21,574,166	7,409,466	143,663	7,553,129	881,691	299,380	6,970,818	12,473,279	2,130,069	68,134	316,641	178,682
2009	18,245,590	6,763,865	150,456	6,914,321	833,442	311,284	6,392,163	9,481,942	2,371,485	57,289	318,485	169,935
2010	20,229,837	7,378,019	137,659	7,515,678	854,699	515,545	7,176,524	10,455,874	2,597,439	62,709	322,601	170,283
2011	21,341,492	7,634,405	116,674	7,751,079	790,943	445,361	7,405,497	11,227,419	2,708,576	65,132	327,667	176,891
2012	23,781,957	7,786,197	132,568	7,918,765	824,244	689,663	7,784,184	13,272,781	2,724,992	71,513	332,556	183,066
2013	23,486,915	7,986,856	154,200	8,141,056	956,974	640,997	7,825,079	12,847,124	2,814,712	69,184	339,483	190,509
2014	27,008,941	8,977,862	122,254	9,100,116	1,051,485	825,481	8,874,112	15,137,515	2,997,314	77,564	348,216	200,956
2015	29,847,567	9,720,236	137,367	9,857,603	1,124,078	1,058,842	9,792,367	16,848,034	3,207,166	83,561	357,194	210,259
2016	31,384,045	10,310,592	114,093	10,424,685	1,197,409	1,161,537	10,388,813	17,635,498	3,359,734	85,727	366,095	217,129
2017	32,749,753	10,575,030	101,766	10,676,796	1,231,288	1,275,502	10,721,010	18,512,552	3,516,191	87,829	372,880	220,839
2018	37,178,408	37,082,514	95,894	11,610,068	1,336,137	1,351,230	11,625,161	21,818,086	3,735,161	98,303	378,201	231,736
2019	38,252,405	38,146,991	105,414	12,269,267	1,431,749	1,390,668	12,228,186	21,972,789	4,051,430	99,382	384,902	238,593

Personal Income and Employment by Area: Nashville-Davidson—Murfreesboro—Franklin, TN

(Thousands of dollars, except as noted.)

Year	Personal income, total	Derivation of personal income									Per capita personal income (dollars)	Population (persons)	Total employment
		Earnings by place of work			Less: Contributions for government social insurance	Plus: Adjustment for residence	Equals: Net earnings by place of residence	Plus: Dividends, interest, and rent	Plus: Personal current transfer receipts				
		Nonfarm	Farm	Total									
1970.............	2,872,703	2,378,911	54,080	2,432,991	155,235	-4,047	2,273,709	377,994	221,000	3,614	794,960	388,326
1971.............	3,127,554	2,578,373	49,397	2,627,770	173,003	-2,692	2,452,075	415,766	259,713	3,877	806,661	390,781
1972.............	3,518,921	2,928,581	59,226	2,987,807	207,389	-7,469	2,772,949	459,890	286,082	4,235	831,002	414,671
1973.............	4,015,481	3,348,960	84,658	3,433,618	272,313	-10,030	3,151,275	526,552	337,654	4,768	842,119	441,535
1974.............	4,475,688	3,717,199	62,857	3,780,056	315,214	-13,497	3,451,345	615,312	409,031	5,205	859,921	454,143
1975.............	4,839,952	3,917,438	37,484	3,954,922	325,367	-13,857	3,615,698	681,491	542,763	5,504	879,430	437,309
1976.............	5,466,439	4,468,518	62,377	4,530,895	377,132	-21,419	4,132,344	740,503	593,592	6,134	891,221	457,484
1977.............	6,150,674	5,084,056	65,171	5,149,227	427,494	-30,362	4,691,371	836,500	622,803	6,759	909,992	481,268
1978.............	7,046,834	5,884,783	67,651	5,952,434	502,365	-45,738	5,404,331	959,994	682,509	7,574	930,403	503,047
1979.............	7,912,979	6,593,672	63,285	6,656,957	587,718	-50,306	6,018,933	1,099,383	794,663	8,339	948,910	520,756
1980.............	8,740,913	7,073,328	45,449	7,118,777	632,400	-54,846	6,431,531	1,331,103	978,279	9,045	966,369	516,142
1981.............	9,856,746	7,874,030	72,860	7,946,890	761,086	-86,645	7,099,159	1,644,062	1,113,525	10,111	974,846	523,293
1982.............	10,546,452	8,244,805	71,894	8,316,699	818,066	-65,467	7,433,166	1,876,293	1,236,993	10,752	980,868	519,035
1983.............	11,368,590	9,052,629	-3,235	9,049,394	911,747	-66,384	8,071,263	1,978,561	1,318,766	11,480	990,291	530,629
1984.............	12,865,634	10,262,939	72,091	10,335,030	1,064,235	-88,792	9,182,003	2,295,194	1,388,437	12,799	1,005,226	566,641
1985.............	14,113,608	11,428,448	53,779	11,482,227	1,201,456	-123,065	10,157,706	2,470,487	1,485,415	13,828	1,020,620	597,123
1986.............	15,434,061	12,671,885	15,911	12,687,796	1,359,711	-155,373	11,172,712	2,663,261	1,598,088	14,823	1,041,249	628,746
1987.............	16,734,170	13,876,218	14,390	13,890,608	1,475,492	-197,297	12,217,819	2,822,395	1,693,956	15,701	1,065,808	657,288
1988.............	18,117,640	14,957,303	18,111	14,975,414	1,621,148	-215,445	13,138,821	3,137,078	1,841,741	16,764	1,080,719	672,526
1989.............	19,312,897	15,864,193	31,653	15,895,846	1,740,006	-260,339	13,895,501	3,386,182	2,031,214	17,653	1,094,048	684,522
1990.............	20,498,382	16,621,308	37,556	16,658,864	1,841,007	-303,771	14,514,086	3,709,124	2,275,172	18,492	1,108,523	692,179
1991.............	21,745,132	17,714,414	51,092	17,765,506	1,990,439	-364,496	15,410,571	3,733,051	2,601,510	19,230	1,130,775	699,011
1992.............	24,080,861	19,823,983	67,458	19,891,441	2,191,637	-429,337	17,270,467	3,892,151	2,918,243	20,834	1,155,871	715,870
1993.............	25,949,147	21,516,392	64,248	21,580,640	2,376,204	-482,392	18,722,044	4,115,926	3,111,177	21,878	1,186,057	752,674
1994.............	28,050,027	23,455,860	60,778	23,516,638	2,629,669	-538,212	20,348,757	4,438,414	3,262,856	23,008	1,219,138	796,197
1995.............	30,648,767	25,530,111	43,113	25,573,224	2,847,785	-608,130	22,117,309	4,942,804	3,588,654	24,501	1,250,936	825,158
1996.............	32,586,978	27,193,917	-13,087	27,180,830	2,977,182	-647,541	23,556,107	5,255,880	3,774,991	25,415	1,282,177	849,563
1997.............	34,792,349	29,239,931	26,655	29,266,586	3,201,904	-710,360	25,354,322	5,511,880	3,926,147	26,498	1,313,031	879,964
1998.............	39,078,405	32,708,010	-6,726	32,701,284	3,418,912	-750,429	28,531,943	6,410,477	4,135,985	29,185	1,338,997	910,453
1999.............	41,159,423	34,772,957	-39,381	34,733,576	3,643,682	-823,750	30,266,144	6,570,033	4,323,246	30,208	1,362,545	930,969
2000.............	44,458,273	37,548,149	22,293	37,570,442	3,886,847	-904,860	32,778,735	6,964,946	4,714,592	32,044	1,387,417	953,958
2001.............	45,400,247	38,257,732	3,007	38,260,739	4,007,964	-879,137	33,373,638	6,826,258	5,200,351	32,217	1,409,191	950,262
2002.............	46,874,573	39,914,881	-40,946	39,873,935	4,186,792	-875,057	34,812,086	6,473,701	5,588,786	32,828	1,427,867	949,117
2003.............	48,919,440	41,548,747	-47,647	41,501,100	4,349,000	-891,814	36,260,286	6,691,003	5,968,151	33,737	1,450,015	960,064
2004.............	52,097,251	44,219,712	-8,303	44,211,409	4,617,354	-913,116	38,680,939	7,021,663	6,394,649	35,238	1,478,449	992,080
2005.............	54,901,135	46,326,393	-5,319	46,321,074	4,861,320	-922,083	40,537,671	7,479,221	6,884,243	36,327	1,511,310	1,024,302
2006.............	59,732,571	50,256,025	-30,738	50,225,287	5,197,542	-998,540	44,029,205	8,420,229	7,283,137	38,453	1,553,397	1,054,627
2007.............	62,776,028	51,901,941	-77,775	51,824,166	5,476,174	-981,300	45,366,692	9,368,196	8,041,140	39,423	1,592,365	1,079,668
2008.............	65,631,907	52,975,253	-15,822	52,959,431	5,674,310	-968,953	46,316,168	10,098,231	9,217,508	40,341	1,626,925	1,073,450
2009.............	66,076,076	53,771,178	-34,944	53,736,234	5,601,073	-826,871	47,308,290	8,843,228	9,924,558	39,943	1,654,243	1,034,690
2010.............	69,921,618	55,969,083	-38,753	55,930,330	5,713,092	-783,267	49,433,971	9,455,059	11,032,588	41,725	1,675,757	1,035,716
2011.............	74,609,090	59,418,691	-11,790	59,406,901	5,311,368	-793,442	53,302,091	10,052,723	11,254,276	43,944	1,697,833	1,063,725
2012.............	80,032,440	63,929,080	66,329	63,995,409	5,612,375	-913,451	57,469,583	11,236,158	11,326,699	46,350	1,726,698	1,097,326
2013.............	81,778,431	66,819,717	95,225	66,914,942	6,610,198	-968,348	59,336,396	10,703,338	11,738,697	46,521	1,757,891	1,133,289
2014.............	88,091,942	72,237,082	56,435	72,293,517	7,030,716	-1,034,302	64,228,499	11,808,025	12,055,418	49,138	1,792,756	1,180,581
2015.............	94,768,760	77,758,831	47,398	77,806,229	7,593,427	-1,132,993	69,079,809	12,900,240	12,788,711	51,800	1,829,513	1,228,733
2016.............	100,136,564	82,360,644	1,487	82,362,131	7,957,857	-1,296,343	73,107,931	13,881,885	13,146,748	53,582	1,868,855	1,278,929
2017.............	106,463,757	88,290,181	1,926	88,292,107	8,535,053	-1,422,294	78,334,760	14,632,555	13,496,442	55,944	1,903,045	1,315,055
2018.............	111,957,997	112,025,207	-67,210	92,142,752	8,942,619	-1,811,410	81,388,723	16,466,883	14,102,391	58,779	1,904,726	1,369,274
2019.............	117,373,879	117,442,373	-68,494	97,244,743	9,496,373	-1,960,842	85,787,528	16,642,277	14,944,074	60,680	1,934,317	1,414,855

Personal Income and Employment by Area: New Bern, NC

(Thousands of dollars, except as noted.)

Year	Personal income, total	Earnings by place of work			Less: Contributions for government social insurance	Plus: Adjustment for residence	Equals: Net earnings by place of residence	Plus: Dividends, interest, and rent	Plus: Personal current transfer receipts	Per capita personal income (dollars)	Population (persons)	Total employment
		Nonfarm	Farm	Total								
1970	286,284	229,469	15,138	244,607	12,390	-13,232	218,985	47,616	19,683	3,488	82,081	40,058
1971	300,887	247,778	11,597	259,375	13,749	-16,696	228,930	49,119	22,838	3,587	83,889	38,574
1972	334,128	269,626	18,626	288,252	15,358	-18,796	254,098	53,366	26,664	3,925	85,129	38,318
1973	394,009	312,781	26,311	339,092	19,658	-21,141	298,293	65,748	29,968	4,502	87,526	40,884
1974	434,747	344,290	26,683	370,973	23,207	-22,831	324,935	73,667	36,145	5,020	86,605	41,460
1975	474,739	370,115	25,448	395,563	26,471	-23,745	345,347	82,400	46,992	5,344	88,837	41,185
1976	463,825	357,054	24,001	381,055	25,898	-21,912	333,245	77,350	53,230	5,094	91,051	37,864
1977	517,429	404,858	14,147	419,005	29,647	-22,907	366,451	93,006	57,972	5,685	91,010	40,592
1978	617,906	479,328	24,300	503,628	35,161	-29,375	439,092	115,841	62,973	6,751	91,529	43,032
1979	674,689	533,663	10,629	544,292	41,013	-30,258	473,021	130,400	71,268	7,443	90,650	44,787
1980	786,728	604,323	16,815	621,138	46,284	-32,283	542,571	158,627	85,530	8,603	91,445	46,872
1981	838,031	644,322	16,948	661,270	51,043	-49,501	560,726	179,291	98,014	9,073	92,365	43,576
1982	942,033	717,127	26,122	743,249	56,875	-56,953	629,421	202,965	109,647	10,009	94,122	45,190
1983	989,594	770,861	6,322	777,183	65,449	-58,565	653,169	218,452	117,973	10,381	95,328	46,894
1984	1,136,252	878,967	20,643	899,610	76,938	-63,452	759,220	250,529	126,503	11,683	97,256	49,839
1985	1,226,427	958,230	13,553	971,783	86,660	-70,552	814,571	274,052	137,804	12,281	99,860	51,285
1986	1,314,841	1,021,827	15,701	1,037,528	95,177	-74,935	867,416	299,284	148,141	13,108	100,306	52,168
1987	1,374,376	1,052,231	23,782	1,076,013	100,713	-70,135	905,165	311,661	157,550	13,744	99,999	52,819
1988	1,470,965	1,127,392	25,509	1,152,901	113,405	-77,603	961,893	335,801	173,271	14,522	101,292	53,217
1989	1,599,622	1,190,726	25,672	1,216,398	122,442	-81,110	1,012,846	391,507	195,269	15,720	101,757	54,451
1990	1,650,899	1,212,698	26,557	1,239,255	129,664	-73,156	1,036,435	398,392	216,072	16,041	102,918	54,413
1991	1,744,002	1,260,166	35,313	1,295,479	136,845	-80,120	1,078,514	413,505	251,983	16,728	104,258	53,677
1992	1,928,283	1,414,134	29,937	1,444,071	154,766	-91,728	1,197,577	452,590	278,116	18,251	105,655	55,701
1993	1,984,678	1,415,588	31,525	1,447,113	157,550	-86,760	1,202,803	473,388	308,487	18,746	105,871	55,763
1994	2,087,530	1,484,901	31,139	1,516,040	165,790	-92,204	1,258,046	506,784	322,700	19,612	106,443	56,340
1995	2,224,058	1,557,251	29,094	1,586,345	173,313	-96,514	1,316,518	544,561	362,979	20,565	108,147	58,223
1996	2,398,467	1,658,302	44,778	1,703,080	184,524	-102,302	1,416,254	590,662	391,551	21,834	109,848	60,554
1997	2,561,587	1,744,128	52,150	1,796,278	193,807	-97,973	1,504,498	647,480	409,609	22,977	111,484	62,242
1998	2,673,510	1,872,841	21,825	1,894,666	208,638	-106,051	1,579,977	668,056	425,477	23,745	112,591	64,020
1999	2,796,816	1,963,534	20,620	1,984,154	219,899	-108,319	1,655,936	680,189	460,691	24,514	114,091	64,804
2000	2,989,056	2,078,516	66,499	2,145,015	232,725	-113,909	1,798,381	702,839	487,836	25,957	115,156	65,818
2001	3,063,179	2,104,473	80,082	2,184,555	235,425	-121,240	1,827,890	697,071	538,218	26,319	116,388	64,919
2002	3,050,818	2,132,717	28,743	2,161,460	239,096	-117,553	1,804,811	673,291	572,716	26,377	115,664	64,573
2003	3,232,527	2,303,741	28,732	2,332,473	260,728	-138,826	1,932,919	695,044	604,564	27,921	115,776	65,373
2004	3,491,620	2,491,071	55,662	2,546,733	280,508	-154,739	2,111,486	730,084	650,050	29,966	116,520	67,058
2005	3,750,431	2,653,337	92,335	2,745,672	300,060	-171,183	2,274,429	773,908	702,094	31,841	117,787	68,387
2006	3,933,143	2,789,532	63,901	2,853,433	317,728	-173,072	2,362,633	812,480	758,030	32,799	119,915	69,504
2007	4,222,491	2,967,207	41,346	3,008,553	339,712	-197,846	2,470,995	934,732	816,764	34,933	120,873	70,196
2008	4,411,457	3,019,489	43,232	3,062,721	346,540	-186,868	2,529,313	968,250	913,894	36,015	122,491	69,705
2009	4,417,477	3,041,343	41,956	3,083,299	354,304	-232,701	2,496,294	920,386	1,000,797	35,283	125,202	67,944
2010	4,562,858	3,151,331	52,999	3,204,330	363,932	-251,803	2,588,595	908,924	1,065,339	35,809	127,421	67,088
2011	4,711,068	3,173,171	56,944	3,230,115	337,791	-281,588	2,610,736	1,002,310	1,098,022	36,752	128,185	66,549
2012	4,862,182	3,270,826	78,520	3,349,346	348,280	-304,788	2,696,278	1,035,374	1,130,530	37,859	128,430	66,858
2013	4,787,254	3,196,494	71,895	3,268,389	384,783	-288,548	2,595,058	1,034,924	1,157,272	37,634	127,206	66,968
2014	4,928,578	3,268,014	49,064	3,317,078	395,172	-301,328	2,620,578	1,111,535	1,196,465	38,853	126,852	67,108
2015	5,072,452	3,353,929	18,023	3,371,952	405,466	-308,078	2,658,408	1,153,053	1,260,991	40,397	125,564	67,450
2016	5,147,387	3,386,977	22,941	3,409,918	408,343	-311,804	2,689,771	1,157,455	1,300,161	41,087	125,281	68,263
2017	5,235,088	3,329,945	28,896	3,358,841	402,282	-253,176	2,703,383	1,177,739	1,353,966	41,926	124,864	68,057
2018	5,421,548	5,402,649	18,899	3,498,148	414,563	-258,555	2,825,030	1,210,115	1,386,403	43,517	124,584	67,552
2019	5,690,657	5,645,766	44,891	3,708,569	435,876	-281,455	2,991,238	1,232,545	1,466,874	45,788	124,284	68,395

Personal Income and Employment by Area: New Haven-Milford, CT

(Thousands of dollars, except as noted.)

Year	Personal income, total	Earnings by place of work			Less: Contributions for government social insurance	Plus: Adjustment for residence	Equals: Net earnings by place of residence	Plus: Dividends, interest, and rent	Plus: Personal current transfer receipts	Per capita personal income (dollars)	Population (persons)	Total employment
		Nonfarm	Farm	Total								
1970	3,590,216	2,760,353	7,183	2,767,536	188,141	96,473	2,675,868	594,547	319,801	4,803	747,435	341,697
1971	3,810,156	2,882,319	7,292	2,889,611	203,266	99,169	2,785,514	629,329	395,313	5,033	757,031	335,504
1972	4,112,415	3,138,423	7,069	3,145,492	234,151	114,248	3,025,589	670,534	416,292	5,424	758,131	342,677
1973	4,482,966	3,443,164	8,267	3,451,431	296,384	134,906	3,289,953	742,518	450,495	5,924	756,777	357,175
1974	4,889,082	3,684,913	7,802	3,692,715	330,304	158,023	3,520,434	839,886	528,762	6,439	759,277	364,298
1975	5,244,296	3,764,841	8,099	3,772,940	329,632	190,058	3,633,366	900,869	710,061	6,904	759,648	349,425
1976	5,615,847	4,039,411	7,787	4,047,198	359,127	222,825	3,910,896	954,001	750,950	7,406	758,263	351,258
1977	6,151,807	4,438,053	9,735	4,447,788	396,063	264,928	4,316,653	1,049,528	785,626	8,117	757,917	361,753
1978	6,799,915	4,939,406	11,701	4,951,107	452,783	327,551	4,825,875	1,168,388	805,652	8,981	757,121	374,218
1979	7,571,868	5,478,014	10,419	5,488,433	524,191	404,746	5,368,988	1,313,599	889,281	9,960	760,219	385,300
1980	8,484,836	5,890,414	11,139	5,901,553	563,729	519,787	5,857,611	1,623,467	1,003,758	11,134	762,066	386,193
1981	9,468,123	6,318,965	8,176	6,327,141	648,154	622,376	6,301,363	1,984,139	1,182,621	12,403	763,373	385,348
1982	10,143,334	6,640,676	12,366	6,653,042	692,012	696,675	6,657,705	2,171,674	1,313,955	13,261	764,877	381,104
1983	10,920,825	7,217,360	12,025	7,229,385	757,949	742,720	7,214,156	2,289,546	1,417,123	14,165	770,970	385,388
1984	12,214,612	8,147,769	12,890	8,160,659	877,892	835,865	8,118,632	2,624,324	1,471,656	15,735	776,264	406,456
1985	13,068,809	8,816,021	12,253	8,828,274	961,245	935,065	8,802,094	2,716,377	1,550,338	16,689	783,092	416,819
1986	14,067,275	9,534,083	13,458	9,547,541	1,042,786	1,038,690	9,543,445	2,890,314	1,633,516	17,817	789,528	428,205
1987	15,334,181	10,654,077	12,641	10,666,718	1,151,944	1,120,314	10,635,088	3,015,372	1,683,721	19,252	796,486	441,230
1988	16,920,792	11,854,486	13,924	11,868,410	1,306,442	1,229,962	11,791,930	3,316,171	1,812,691	21,116	801,339	455,617
1989	18,240,437	12,455,333	11,670	12,467,003	1,368,849	1,329,074	12,427,228	3,780,281	2,032,928	22,687	804,000	453,175
1990	18,766,936	12,731,771	13,039	12,744,810	1,381,440	1,382,171	12,745,541	3,750,794	2,270,601	23,302	805,366	445,131
1991	18,977,915	12,984,378	11,418	12,995,796	1,436,140	1,335,227	12,894,883	3,546,826	2,536,206	23,502	807,490	426,841
1992	19,968,736	13,639,580	13,825	13,653,405	1,486,998	1,314,011	13,480,418	3,490,682	2,997,636	24,694	808,659	424,565
1993	20,740,836	14,144,222	17,019	14,161,241	1,540,077	1,374,035	13,995,199	3,619,489	3,126,148	25,638	808,977	429,976
1994	21,360,761	14,527,521	15,310	14,542,831	1,597,601	1,453,729	14,398,959	3,701,968	3,259,834	26,398	809,178	425,475
1995	22,321,221	14,995,960	16,502	15,012,462	1,665,622	1,549,737	14,896,577	3,941,078	3,483,566	27,586	809,157	432,879
1996	23,026,714	15,670,023	13,890	15,683,913	1,738,809	1,467,156	15,412,260	4,050,468	3,563,986	28,393	811,000	442,172
1997	24,263,555	16,725,898	13,178	16,739,076	1,831,397	1,524,483	16,432,162	4,171,838	3,659,555	29,826	813,505	446,766
1998	25,549,502	17,945,626	15,391	17,961,017	1,916,099	1,593,836	17,638,754	4,209,995	3,700,753	31,260	817,313	455,111
1999	26,903,547	18,998,882	17,509	19,016,391	1,982,874	1,873,298	18,906,815	4,208,827	3,787,905	32,793	820,396	460,583
2000	29,170,429	20,724,489	20,168	20,744,657	2,098,394	1,876,552	20,522,815	4,650,736	3,996,878	35,362	824,911	470,567
2001	30,675,817	21,989,599	20,368	22,009,967	2,192,188	1,982,639	21,800,418	4,639,993	4,235,406	36,964	829,875	474,576
2002	31,066,990	22,731,892	23,693	22,755,585	2,334,919	1,706,135	22,126,801	4,396,376	4,543,813	37,202	835,099	474,530
2003	31,455,167	22,920,017	23,353	22,943,370	2,388,535	1,668,745	22,223,580	4,609,224	4,622,363	37,360	841,939	472,083
2004	32,654,837	23,894,575	25,727	23,920,302	2,507,983	1,694,307	23,106,626	4,630,668	4,917,543	38,667	844,505	482,152
2005	33,850,958	24,504,213	27,748	24,531,961	2,561,576	1,983,582	23,953,967	4,801,019	5,095,972	39,958	847,162	485,556
2006	36,103,735	25,641,142	27,513	25,668,655	2,637,124	2,198,945	25,230,476	5,458,293	5,414,966	42,465	850,207	491,429
2007	38,004,892	26,347,244	31,159	26,378,403	2,716,429	2,313,280	25,975,254	6,306,788	5,722,850	44,523	853,598	498,327
2008	38,974,544	26,647,618	32,984	26,680,602	2,784,242	2,064,191	25,960,551	6,480,003	6,533,990	45,498	856,622	496,820
2009	37,954,686	25,998,913	34,775	26,033,688	2,725,994	1,366,066	24,673,760	6,045,824	7,235,102	44,132	860,025	483,308
2010	38,831,237	26,542,041	34,620	26,576,661	2,743,089	1,437,846	25,271,418	5,859,287	7,700,532	44,963	863,618	477,548
2011	40,426,436	27,014,561	26,475	27,041,036	2,547,834	1,709,674	26,202,876	6,483,330	7,740,230	46,751	864,725	482,732
2012	41,616,667	27,695,617	33,989	27,729,606	2,639,652	1,635,559	26,725,513	7,040,094	7,851,060	48,093	865,335	487,938
2013	42,013,479	28,238,838	30,616	28,269,454	3,056,332	1,611,569	26,824,691	7,296,384	7,892,404	48,595	864,558	492,768
2014	43,436,747	28,958,533	24,186	28,982,719	3,132,438	1,888,243	27,738,524	7,616,980	8,081,243	50,270	864,073	496,915
2015	44,633,486	29,861,893	26,193	29,888,086	3,227,517	1,614,695	28,275,264	7,992,380	8,365,842	51,803	861,594	501,059
2016	45,106,708	30,405,377	28,579	30,433,956	3,302,737	1,516,132	28,647,351	7,848,231	8,611,126	52,451	859,973	504,410
2017	46,930,537	31,322,541	26,343	31,348,884	3,423,400	2,041,506	29,966,990	8,215,572	8,747,975	54,543	860,435	508,506
2018	47,801,068	47,772,186	28,882	32,004,969	3,528,694	1,896,345	30,372,620	8,108,171	9,320,277	55,779	856,971	511,150
2019	49,360,086	49,326,551	33,535	32,977,312	3,629,724	2,291,440	31,639,028	8,257,184	9,463,874	57,748	854,757	515,387

Personal Income and Employment by Area: New Orleans-Metairie, LA

(Thousands of dollars, except as noted.)

Year	Personal income, total	Earnings by place of work			Less: Contributions for government social insurance	Plus: Adjustment for residence	Equals: Net earnings by place of residence	Plus: Dividends, interest, and rent	Plus: Personal current transfer receipts	Per capita personal income (dollars)	Population (persons)	Total employment
		Nonfarm	Farm	Total								
1970	4,300,405	3,687,179	10,681	3,697,860	241,315	-111,456	3,345,089	600,296	355,020	3,750	1,146,894	504,994
1971	4,646,375	3,963,952	11,797	3,975,749	266,323	-132,441	3,576,985	658,144	411,246	3,983	1,166,467	508,631
1972	5,077,018	4,355,333	14,514	4,369,847	307,439	-154,871	3,907,537	711,210	458,271	4,276	1,187,285	526,614
1973	5,591,596	4,802,185	22,938	4,825,123	390,737	-172,319	4,262,067	789,363	540,166	4,670	1,197,218	548,458
1974	6,302,891	5,347,613	31,416	5,379,029	446,765	-203,708	4,728,556	943,799	630,536	5,240	1,202,899	563,281
1975	7,101,589	6,018,452	13,862	6,032,314	493,477	-243,251	5,295,586	1,033,246	772,757	5,835	1,217,164	581,071
1976	7,969,835	6,848,418	15,927	6,864,345	572,554	-289,431	6,002,360	1,108,962	858,513	6,427	1,239,970	600,729
1977	8,844,129	7,649,764	14,610	7,664,374	636,449	-329,431	6,698,494	1,217,885	927,750	7,045	1,255,289	617,879
1978	10,030,800	8,731,336	11,747	8,743,083	740,630	-387,270	7,615,183	1,404,702	1,010,915	7,897	1,270,252	640,835
1979	11,305,254	9,895,502	11,342	9,906,844	872,300	-472,185	8,562,359	1,597,616	1,145,279	8,794	1,285,635	657,374
1980	12,972,514	11,253,188	9,160	11,262,348	985,674	-587,254	9,689,420	1,927,135	1,355,959	9,915	1,308,411	679,099
1981	14,871,507	12,772,706	12,294	12,785,000	1,201,115	-622,317	10,961,568	2,389,249	1,520,690	11,244	1,322,669	695,393
1982	16,023,828	13,467,443	13,603	13,481,046	1,291,861	-645,369	11,543,816	2,757,061	1,722,951	11,950	1,340,939	692,756
1983	16,765,831	13,745,419	14,467	13,759,886	1,312,453	-659,576	11,787,857	3,037,307	1,940,667	12,407	1,351,273	679,426
1984	17,875,664	14,545,801	8,367	14,554,168	1,420,914	-676,923	12,456,331	3,386,572	2,032,761	13,237	1,350,467	693,125
1985	18,574,004	14,744,956	11,223	14,756,179	1,445,102	-638,592	12,672,485	3,703,040	2,198,479	13,760	1,349,897	681,199
1986	18,892,004	14,771,492	12,490	14,783,982	1,430,585	-577,817	12,775,580	3,734,619	2,381,805	14,022	1,347,337	660,295
1987	19,076,986	14,919,564	11,818	14,931,382	1,421,105	-560,103	12,950,174	3,706,418	2,420,394	14,372	1,327,369	650,890
1988	19,960,654	15,641,137	17,881	15,659,018	1,557,720	-571,016	13,530,282	3,862,733	2,567,639	15,233	1,310,318	664,408
1989	21,099,327	16,364,374	17,963	16,382,337	1,638,471	-581,261	14,162,605	4,141,853	2,794,869	16,269	1,296,918	668,800
1990	22,547,350	17,560,423	8,413	17,568,836	1,807,204	-640,125	15,121,507	4,351,908	3,073,935	17,546	1,285,014	681,627
1991	23,666,685	18,369,775	9,733	18,379,508	1,937,658	-646,168	15,795,682	4,333,496	3,537,507	18,276	1,294,966	685,564
1992	25,301,998	19,390,972	14,708	19,405,680	2,014,170	-647,112	16,744,398	4,483,503	4,074,097	19,358	1,307,069	683,945
1993	26,422,766	20,052,448	19,104	20,071,552	2,088,595	-639,201	17,343,756	4,624,312	4,454,698	20,089	1,315,265	695,199
1994	27,922,811	21,172,538	14,246	21,186,784	2,243,430	-664,756	18,278,598	4,773,581	4,870,632	21,099	1,323,418	705,084
1995	29,487,214	22,293,618	15,692	22,309,310	2,357,522	-705,890	19,245,898	5,294,513	4,946,803	22,168	1,330,188	724,157
1996	30,461,203	22,974,303	13,828	22,988,131	2,427,218	-725,063	19,835,850	5,592,430	5,032,923	22,884	1,331,131	732,972
1997	32,129,269	24,329,973	15,079	24,345,052	2,564,260	-766,006	21,014,786	6,000,616	5,113,867	24,093	1,333,525	747,596
1998	33,610,579	25,711,172	16,509	25,727,681	2,723,496	-802,998	22,201,187	6,284,291	5,125,101	25,167	1,335,520	756,651
1999	34,393,762	26,588,208	17,049	26,605,257	2,776,012	-780,058	23,049,187	6,107,648	5,236,927	25,698	1,338,370	760,569
2000	36,372,188	27,958,350	15,318	27,973,668	2,840,824	-785,920	24,346,924	6,656,540	5,368,724	27,158	1,339,280	770,060
2001	38,814,556	30,083,144	15,637	30,098,781	2,979,655	-843,767	26,275,359	6,447,128	6,092,069	28,869	1,344,528	775,759
2002	39,990,034	31,238,515	14,922	31,253,437	3,078,836	-898,749	27,275,852	6,352,724	6,361,458	29,521	1,354,638	774,909
2003	41,004,944	32,358,859	16,146	32,375,005	3,169,408	-948,118	28,257,479	6,440,641	6,306,824	30,037	1,365,146	779,325
2004	41,734,610	32,626,848	16,655	32,643,503	3,241,327	-1,051,758	28,350,418	6,504,866	6,879,326	30,293	1,377,699	783,035
2005	43,586,638	32,349,981	17,187	32,367,168	3,140,974	-1,012,713	28,213,481	6,754,745	8,618,412	31,438	1,386,429	699,855
2006	42,274,224	32,418,464	36,802	32,455,266	3,130,020	-1,664,615	27,660,631	8,525,738	6,087,855	40,641	1,040,195	648,243
2007	48,873,805	34,213,305	21,773	34,235,078	3,344,570	-1,839,599	29,050,909	13,606,416	6,216,480	44,578	1,096,365	691,840
2008	50,241,731	37,204,815	27,249	37,232,064	3,556,440	-2,015,445	31,660,179	11,335,580	7,245,972	44,233	1,135,831	715,249
2009	48,106,382	36,229,532	28,504	36,258,036	3,558,117	-1,495,895	31,204,024	9,119,170	7,783,188	41,193	1,167,842	715,352
2010	50,718,765	38,433,218	36,663	38,469,881	3,694,010	-1,615,520	33,160,351	8,858,293	8,700,121	42,426	1,195,455	725,378
2011	51,522,137	38,733,342	36,937	38,770,279	3,385,702	-1,808,049	33,576,528	9,094,143	8,851,466	42,448	1,213,780	730,928
2012	55,168,697	39,999,775	30,956	40,030,731	3,449,396	-1,516,462	35,064,873	11,087,891	9,015,933	44,929	1,227,902	745,943
2013	55,440,576	40,586,559	37,492	40,624,051	3,982,190	-1,244,700	35,397,161	10,667,365	9,376,050	44,667	1,241,194	762,251
2014	59,028,600	43,690,172	26,129	43,716,301	4,162,899	-1,251,219	38,302,183	11,230,558	9,495,859	47,162	1,251,626	776,394
2015	60,688,394	43,959,843	25,804	43,985,647	4,328,725	-1,125,234	38,531,688	11,641,662	10,515,044	48,031	1,263,526	791,161
2016	60,983,377	43,276,987	19,445	43,296,432	4,329,113	-1,055,624	37,911,695	11,929,897	11,141,785	47,973	1,271,195	797,046
2017	62,682,846	44,083,790	16,591	44,100,381	4,432,479	-985,454	38,682,448	12,379,289	11,621,109	49,134	1,275,762	798,242
2018	67,270,399	67,262,421	7,978	47,230,603	4,710,110	-845,357	41,675,136	13,550,860	12,044,403	52,963	1,270,133	810,813
2019	69,069,320	69,061,033	8,287	48,679,658	4,826,587	-1,045,605	42,807,466	13,625,083	12,636,771	54,363	1,270,530	822,910

Personal Income and Employment by Area: New York-Newark-Jersey City, NY-NJ-PA

(Thousands of dollars, except as noted.)

Year	Personal income, total	Earnings by place of work			Less: Contributions for government social insurance	Plus: Adjustment for residence	Equals: Net earnings by place of residence	Plus: Dividends, interest, and rent	Plus: Personal current transfer receipts	Per capita personal income (dollars)	Population (persons)	Total employment
		Nonfarm	Farm	Total								
1970	90,396,327	90,340,705	55,622	73,488,033	5,439,016	-1,021,953	67,027,064	15,042,767	8,326,496	5,290	17,089,280	8,073,922
1971	96,410,189	96,358,821	51,368	77,548,455	5,921,565	-1,137,523	70,489,367	15,854,269	10,066,553	5,617	17,162,560	7,922,322
1972	103,427,115	103,382,954	44,161	83,459,004	6,692,402	-1,346,955	75,419,647	16,706,039	11,301,429	6,039	17,125,818	7,943,751
1973	110,001,431	109,933,449	67,982	89,161,002	8,282,485	-1,555,808	79,322,709	18,149,572	12,529,150	6,480	16,974,851	8,045,221
1974	118,338,536	118,266,144	72,392	94,284,596	9,026,239	-1,764,662	83,493,695	20,294,458	14,550,383	7,020	16,857,193	7,950,778
1975	127,505,633	127,445,152	60,481	99,151,203	9,286,653	-2,019,246	87,845,304	21,405,185	18,255,144	7,599	16,778,386	7,718,680
1976	135,572,917	135,514,037	58,880	105,814,046	10,084,830	-2,291,086	93,438,130	22,595,218	19,539,569	8,112	16,712,756	7,696,630
1977	146,764,176	146,692,379	71,797	115,092,008	10,869,973	-2,664,934	101,557,101	24,774,428	20,432,647	8,850	16,584,115	7,778,853
1978	160,679,003	160,592,836	86,167	127,330,660	12,303,380	-3,054,267	111,973,013	27,284,928	21,421,062	9,757	16,468,444	7,991,342
1979	175,867,875	175,773,380	94,495	140,047,685	14,032,271	-3,513,876	122,501,538	30,387,610	22,978,727	10,724	16,400,125	8,177,740
1980	196,782,794	196,668,273	114,521	154,018,033	15,480,830	-4,025,024	134,512,179	36,085,460	26,185,155	12,015	16,377,893	8,250,921
1981	220,230,388	220,102,393	127,995	169,273,836	18,179,113	-4,312,846	146,781,877	43,930,884	29,517,627	13,426	16,403,191	8,336,160
1982	239,087,400	238,958,562	128,838	182,138,826	19,905,658	-4,729,503	157,503,665	49,587,444	31,996,291	14,544	16,439,430	8,370,456
1983	258,892,128	258,756,651	135,477	198,279,909	21,808,259	-5,088,414	171,383,236	52,870,737	34,638,155	15,629	16,564,621	8,492,281
1984	286,792,373	286,639,841	152,532	218,857,702	24,806,010	-5,574,227	188,477,465	61,654,128	36,660,780	17,216	16,658,685	8,785,468
1985	307,455,061	307,300,289	154,772	237,240,394	27,207,944	-6,105,132	203,927,318	64,810,866	38,716,877	18,376	16,730,929	8,994,880
1986	329,302,718	329,145,209	157,509	257,707,513	29,941,921	-6,338,617	221,426,975	66,977,068	40,898,675	19,590	16,810,158	9,183,635
1987	354,272,209	354,087,459	184,750	282,391,802	32,261,772	-6,817,359	243,312,671	68,855,640	42,103,898	21,015	16,858,269	9,264,870
1988	391,092,698	390,908,105	184,593	312,683,187	35,900,009	-7,473,120	269,310,058	77,017,624	44,765,016	23,146	16,896,865	9,423,421
1989	420,552,012	420,376,837	175,175	328,755,966	37,268,626	-7,664,727	283,822,613	87,659,722	49,069,677	24,914	16,880,387	9,446,416
1990	449,446,258	449,281,467	164,791	348,924,459	37,600,715	-7,607,723	303,716,021	91,663,464	54,066,773	26,612	16,888,902	9,344,755
1991	448,688,350	448,546,521	141,829	342,787,208	38,386,930	-7,747,481	296,652,797	91,206,963	60,828,590	26,426	16,979,004	9,029,995
1992	477,406,170	477,260,006	146,164	367,737,037	40,355,169	-9,414,298	317,967,570	90,867,626	68,570,974	27,894	17,114,713	8,955,065
1993	492,838,676	492,690,346	148,330	378,821,666	41,431,938	-9,285,921	328,103,807	91,929,579	72,805,290	28,532	17,273,224	8,981,162
1994	509,563,177	509,419,840	143,337	390,430,947	43,437,061	-9,389,853	337,604,033	96,391,419	75,567,725	29,273	17,407,324	8,987,008
1995	541,587,941	541,443,782	144,159	411,458,090	45,240,843	-10,585,115	355,632,132	105,210,376	80,745,433	30,869	17,544,499	9,117,756
1996	574,778,359	574,634,949	143,410	437,597,532	47,073,060	-12,098,296	378,426,176	112,332,828	84,019,355	32,507	17,681,708	9,249,305
1997	611,686,455	611,559,919	126,536	469,440,839	49,278,444	-12,652,655	407,509,740	119,983,271	84,193,444	34,296	17,835,528	9,400,699
1998	651,587,260	651,445,437	141,823	503,649,278	52,101,921	-14,956,723	436,590,634	127,669,272	87,327,354	36,183	18,007,924	9,607,048
1999	689,743,290	689,598,553	144,737	540,674,592	54,860,805	-14,900,907	470,912,880	128,377,711	90,452,699	37,914	18,192,429	9,842,948
2000	752,632,081	752,451,707	180,374	592,925,397	59,450,226	-16,700,995	516,774,176	140,481,174	95,376,731	41,002	18,356,204	10,175,147
2001	781,490,771	781,336,757	154,014	619,947,407	61,773,537	-17,299,870	540,874,000	137,964,258	102,652,513	42,296	18,476,764	10,250,875
2002	779,638,097	779,460,210	177,887	618,564,713	62,592,980	-17,544,438	538,427,295	129,593,196	111,617,606	42,019	18,554,586	10,187,653
2003	788,802,401	788,619,145	183,256	623,727,377	64,018,552	-18,198,133	541,510,692	131,631,517	115,660,192	42,411	18,598,803	10,217,610
2004	825,617,646	825,434,270	183,376	650,971,454	67,179,410	-20,435,820	563,356,224	138,891,860	123,369,562	44,393	18,597,871	10,371,671
2005	862,421,257	862,235,603	185,654	673,640,569	70,323,124	-22,422,383	580,895,062	158,821,349	122,704,846	46,445	18,568,830	10,533,708
2006	935,138,611	934,934,780	203,831	719,692,750	74,166,717	-25,146,205	620,379,828	184,543,082	130,215,701	50,442	18,538,752	10,720,893
2007	1,008,722,284	1,008,526,992	195,292	770,187,829	79,135,159	-29,078,877	661,973,793	210,779,078	135,969,413	54,313	18,572,325	11,017,676
2008	1,024,525,568	1,024,253,946	271,622	775,057,204	81,671,048	-29,714,571	663,671,585	211,955,221	148,898,762	54,869	18,672,355	11,117,086
2009	994,467,589	994,181,950	285,639	749,679,837	78,915,782	-24,002,702	646,761,353	184,151,423	163,554,813	52,897	18,800,157	10,893,447
2010	1,033,820,797	1,033,557,859	262,938	784,299,598	80,697,953	-25,883,751	677,717,894	181,853,391	174,249,512	54,632	18,923,407	10,924,348
2011	1,094,617,223	1,094,384,299	232,924	815,447,411	74,269,556	-26,940,069	714,237,786	203,586,517	176,792,920	57,452	19,052,774	11,240,143
2012	1,152,045,984	1,151,765,932	280,052	854,434,481	76,223,064	-28,610,839	749,600,578	227,969,445	174,475,961	60,160	19,149,689	11,396,724
2013	1,166,746,613	1,166,487,731	258,882	879,342,623	89,884,962	-27,451,751	762,005,910	229,224,218	175,516,485	60,684	19,226,449	11,634,909
2014	1,223,930,339	1,223,741,779	188,560	916,275,580	94,547,821	-28,916,411	792,811,348	251,315,274	179,803,717	63,479	19,280,929	11,919,980
2015	1,279,279,091	1,279,083,908	195,183	950,606,564	98,651,932	-29,701,532	822,253,100	268,633,680	188,392,311	66,212	19,320,968	12,210,602
2016	1,328,347,854	1,328,174,796	173,058	982,280,266	100,986,455	-29,231,760	852,062,051	281,913,479	194,372,324	68,703	19,334,778	12,418,037
2017	1,412,351,029	1,412,178,675	172,354	1,038,814,447	106,594,092	-32,368,291	899,852,064	305,443,965	207,055,000	73,093	19,322,607	12,576,761
2018	1,475,920,082	1,475,754,192	165,890	1,091,167,963	110,711,187	-35,144,832	945,311,944	327,669,588	202,938,550	76,565	19,276,644	12,884,057
2019	1,534,294,144	1,534,062,686	231,458	1,138,701,907	114,885,016	-37,766,460	986,050,431	332,474,124	215,769,589	79,844	19,216,182	13,142,753

Personal Income and Employment by Area: Niles, MI

(Thousands of dollars, except as noted.)

Year	Personal income, total	Earnings by place of work			Less: Contributions for government social insurance	Plus: Adjustment for residence	Equals: Net earnings by place of residence	Plus: Dividends, interest, and rent	Plus: Personal current transfer receipts	Per capita personal income (dollars)	Population (persons)	Total employment
		Nonfarm	Farm	Total								
1970	666,696	546,019	13,052	559,071	39,687	-10,848	508,536	93,336	64,824	4,066	163,981	74,168
1971	717,542	586,702	12,290	598,992	43,922	-12,948	542,122	98,540	76,880	4,343	165,230	73,938
1972	808,588	679,053	11,695	690,748	53,707	-17,187	619,854	105,678	83,056	4,810	168,102	78,406
1973	895,502	754,205	15,564	769,769	69,060	-17,940	682,769	116,362	96,371	5,248	170,653	81,115
1974	974,624	796,330	22,494	818,824	75,629	-18,182	725,013	132,310	117,301	5,666	172,002	80,618
1975	1,031,937	804,883	15,667	820,550	74,539	-15,095	730,916	143,838	157,183	5,951	173,395	76,020
1976	1,102,463	859,801	13,170	872,971	80,940	-9,851	782,180	153,215	167,068	6,304	174,881	77,131
1977	1,228,915	973,031	20,099	993,130	91,954	-12,492	888,684	170,555	169,676	7,028	174,870	80,061
1978	1,344,483	1,062,997	22,766	1,085,763	103,327	-8,030	974,406	186,530	183,547	7,752	173,427	81,369
1979	1,434,755	1,121,221	10,930	1,132,151	113,332	-3,241	1,015,578	207,295	211,882	8,263	173,635	80,344
1980	1,525,164	1,127,396	10,910	1,138,306	113,486	-540	1,024,280	246,919	253,965	8,904	171,288	75,636
1981	1,659,127	1,191,069	14,545	1,205,614	129,067	574	1,077,121	299,537	282,469	9,705	170,961	73,651
1982	1,725,497	1,189,713	16,173	1,205,886	130,946	2,382	1,077,322	340,255	307,920	10,342	166,840	70,908
1983	1,789,859	1,232,584	10,889	1,243,473	137,640	5,089	1,110,922	352,433	326,504	10,892	164,326	70,184
1984	1,934,226	1,342,440	15,670	1,358,110	155,332	8,530	1,211,308	393,883	329,035	11,844	163,308	71,984
1985	2,036,097	1,415,625	24,911	1,440,536	165,932	8,940	1,283,544	408,086	344,467	12,496	162,945	73,946
1986	2,158,762	1,536,716	16,730	1,553,446	180,070	4,415	1,377,791	419,981	360,990	13,292	162,415	75,938
1987	2,309,300	1,666,538	28,463	1,695,001	191,830	5,731	1,508,902	428,538	371,860	14,170	162,973	78,673
1988	2,429,013	1,754,125	20,933	1,775,058	208,736	13,657	1,579,979	462,170	386,864	14,902	163,001	80,352
1989	2,592,513	1,845,320	30,772	1,876,092	218,200	14,224	1,672,116	511,803	408,594	15,989	162,143	81,954
1990	2,678,822	1,923,656	18,952	1,942,608	231,038	13,325	1,724,895	511,466	442,461	16,596	161,415	82,670
1991	2,756,531	1,962,365	22,914	1,985,279	238,957	16,890	1,763,212	505,325	487,994	17,055	161,622	81,364
1992	2,961,887	2,120,627	24,690	2,145,317	255,654	18,768	1,908,431	532,796	520,660	18,285	161,982	81,260
1993	3,139,298	2,284,249	19,862	2,304,111	278,217	19,983	2,045,877	537,014	556,407	19,347	162,266	81,681
1994	3,317,067	2,402,562	20,202	2,422,764	300,932	25,096	2,146,928	610,879	559,260	20,431	162,353	85,310
1995	3,490,921	2,516,923	22,834	2,539,757	314,856	34,909	2,259,810	655,828	575,283	21,414	163,022	88,048
1996	3,606,947	2,578,165	19,748	2,597,913	316,430	42,537	2,324,020	688,492	594,435	22,146	162,873	88,373
1997	3,840,424	2,734,934	24,180	2,759,114	334,147	42,472	2,467,439	727,772	645,213	23,647	162,407	88,512
1998	3,961,563	2,845,060	24,055	2,869,115	340,598	61,709	2,590,226	737,144	634,193	24,447	162,046	90,479
1999	4,193,250	3,063,067	29,509	3,092,576	360,311	63,699	2,795,964	709,575	687,711	25,880	162,028	89,527
2000	4,389,140	3,195,502	25,938	3,221,440	370,470	73,171	2,924,141	752,218	712,781	27,015	162,471	90,418
2001	4,542,720	3,218,339	33,411	3,251,750	355,894	91,834	2,987,690	746,560	808,470	28,189	161,153	87,082
2002	4,584,969	3,304,278	26,138	3,330,416	364,947	78,828	3,044,297	716,689	823,983	28,548	160,604	85,403
2003	4,682,449	3,297,676	34,699	3,332,375	365,744	97,937	3,064,568	750,734	867,147	29,208	160,314	84,103
2004	4,873,485	3,444,498	47,101	3,491,599	383,639	104,581	3,212,541	765,339	895,605	30,508	159,742	84,376
2005	4,877,817	3,428,495	39,333	3,467,828	394,397	111,771	3,185,202	750,853	941,762	30,773	158,510	84,908
2006	5,118,938	3,539,616	48,386	3,588,002	409,497	159,486	3,337,991	773,264	1,007,683	32,494	157,537	84,495
2007	5,380,329	3,665,644	59,223	3,724,867	428,288	137,878	3,434,457	851,752	1,094,120	34,187	157,378	86,793
2008	5,638,651	3,656,805	46,090	3,702,895	437,410	178,727	3,444,212	956,524	1,237,915	35,828	157,380	85,422
2009	5,367,013	3,483,369	36,101	3,519,470	418,191	98,683	3,199,962	824,971	1,342,080	34,172	157,059	80,366
2010	5,646,484	3,651,816	45,294	3,697,110	427,925	101,984	3,371,169	840,562	1,434,753	36,026	156,735	80,301
2011	5,869,143	3,603,676	69,185	3,672,861	382,846	135,204	3,425,219	1,014,741	1,429,183	37,433	156,792	80,616
2012	5,899,219	3,624,587	56,182	3,680,769	387,452	200,169	3,493,486	985,045	1,420,688	37,714	156,421	80,626
2013	5,954,635	3,809,063	55,504	3,864,567	457,248	147,031	3,554,350	966,222	1,434,063	38,208	155,847	80,940
2014	6,233,911	3,925,903	43,652	3,969,555	474,834	175,275	3,669,996	1,075,230	1,488,685	40,044	155,677	82,489
2015	6,559,558	4,122,401	44,759	4,167,160	493,185	109,712	3,783,687	1,204,991	1,570,880	42,374	154,802	83,451
2016	6,782,561	4,206,700	47,560	4,254,260	502,839	217,787	3,969,208	1,204,377	1,608,976	43,998	154,157	82,748
2017	7,116,498	4,342,744	36,734	4,379,478	517,912	394,010	4,255,576	1,251,211	1,609,711	46,133	154,259	83,594
2018	7,299,007	7,252,535	46,472	4,477,215	539,285	320,746	4,258,676	1,388,974	1,651,357	47,461	153,790	83,419
2019	7,399,551	7,348,980	50,571	4,555,829	546,708	245,756	4,254,877	1,399,323	1,745,351	48,237	153,401	83,526

Personal Income and Employment by Area: North Port-Sarasota-Bradenton, FL

(Thousands of dollars, except as noted.)

		Derivation of personal income										
		Earnings by place of work			Less: Contributions for government social insurance	Plus: Adjustment for residence	Equals: Net earnings by place of residence	Plus: Dividends, interest, and rent	Plus: Personal current transfer receipts	Per capita personal income (dollars)	Population (persons)	Total employment
Year	Personal income, total	Nonfarm	Farm	Total								
1970	980,330	504,474	18,012	522,486	33,169	-5,753	483,564	363,853	132,913	4,457	219,936	86,898
1971	1,112,894	566,278	21,641	587,919	38,956	-5,054	543,909	407,924	161,061	4,786	232,523	91,869
1972	1,283,455	666,653	25,314	691,967	48,314	-4,779	638,874	454,839	189,742	5,245	244,710	99,827
1973	1,532,026	813,255	27,042	840,297	67,612	-7,418	765,267	533,683	233,076	5,787	264,738	113,242
1974	1,747,243	902,560	28,319	930,879	79,394	-8,017	843,468	628,415	275,360	6,192	282,181	117,686
1975	1,907,301	924,571	30,883	955,454	79,931	-6,189	869,334	690,820	347,147	6,602	288,894	114,242
1976	2,152,544	1,047,108	33,441	1,080,549	89,893	-5,415	985,241	784,879	382,424	7,256	296,666	119,612
1977	2,489,070	1,214,865	32,209	1,247,074	105,433	-6,511	1,135,130	926,606	427,334	8,116	306,701	130,788
1978	2,950,698	1,466,006	37,440	1,503,446	130,343	-8,201	1,364,902	1,103,473	482,323	9,161	322,092	144,674
1979	3,450,344	1,690,972	51,405	1,742,377	157,614	-11,360	1,573,403	1,311,766	565,175	10,190	338,608	153,849
1980	4,137,609	1,916,918	71,451	1,988,369	180,928	-12,157	1,795,284	1,666,869	675,456	11,664	354,724	160,146
1981	4,935,749	2,152,201	62,577	2,214,778	218,919	8,750	2,004,609	2,134,104	797,036	13,334	370,172	166,835
1982	5,291,219	2,263,193	91,159	2,354,352	241,096	28,554	2,141,810	2,241,201	908,208	13,753	384,723	172,913
1983	5,970,132	2,567,549	140,496	2,708,045	272,030	53,104	2,489,119	2,482,003	999,010	14,942	399,556	183,463
1984	6,696,326	2,927,954	94,846	3,022,800	319,317	85,995	2,789,478	2,848,549	1,058,299	16,191	413,582	196,895
1985	7,368,070	3,167,307	94,367	3,261,674	353,652	126,462	3,034,484	3,178,932	1,154,654	17,270	426,636	204,184
1986	8,018,025	3,455,183	102,700	3,557,883	396,180	171,110	3,332,813	3,430,705	1,254,507	18,283	438,539	213,336
1987	8,724,069	3,904,690	111,600	4,016,290	441,934	221,358	3,795,714	3,587,610	1,340,745	19,376	450,241	215,825
1988	9,579,370	4,250,039	129,257	4,379,296	499,472	285,029	4,164,853	3,944,639	1,469,878	20,697	462,830	227,771
1989	11,182,418	4,620,544	127,372	4,747,916	554,788	348,031	4,541,159	5,036,045	1,605,214	23,481	476,235	237,209
1990	11,916,349	5,020,773	100,338	5,121,111	589,888	408,588	4,939,811	5,237,795	1,738,743	24,156	493,311	246,876
1991	12,152,170	5,334,006	120,688	5,454,694	630,499	337,313	5,161,508	5,097,744	1,892,918	24,059	505,103	251,512
1992	12,898,651	5,820,568	136,436	5,957,004	680,413	381,087	5,657,678	5,141,488	2,099,485	25,232	511,201	257,502
1993	13,435,528	6,273,631	139,204	6,412,835	728,539	295,151	5,979,447	5,226,947	2,229,134	25,793	520,892	269,675
1994	14,401,508	6,790,615	117,265	6,907,880	802,290	285,672	6,391,262	5,632,936	2,377,310	27,058	532,241	286,866
1995	15,347,839	7,581,935	117,902	7,699,837	892,232	122,623	6,930,228	5,890,843	2,526,768	28,330	541,758	309,665
1996	16,304,836	7,767,724	107,746	7,875,470	898,128	410,581	7,387,923	6,253,832	2,663,081	29,591	551,004	304,542
1997	17,386,400	8,308,507	132,073	8,440,580	962,960	450,745	7,928,365	6,698,474	2,759,561	30,975	561,309	317,015
1998	18,991,489	8,954,953	158,915	9,113,868	1,025,285	652,933	8,741,516	7,384,956	2,865,017	33,144	573,004	321,983
1999	19,831,802	9,631,197	159,969	9,791,166	1,085,400	880,898	9,586,664	7,282,838	2,962,300	34,082	581,892	329,161
2000	21,417,957	10,627,431	163,214	10,790,645	1,180,689	700,840	10,310,796	7,986,705	3,120,456	36,130	592,809	353,692
2001	21,433,548	10,391,700	169,717	10,561,417	1,184,832	709,952	10,086,537	7,989,557	3,357,454	35,370	605,988	324,277
2002	22,084,574	11,426,412	178,698	11,605,110	1,292,899	589,354	10,901,565	7,618,615	3,564,394	35,589	620,540	343,092
2003	23,134,916	12,194,551	162,400	12,356,951	1,359,226	516,247	11,513,972	7,871,788	3,749,156	36,441	634,862	348,500
2004	25,860,267	13,755,348	166,939	13,922,287	1,527,604	499,843	12,894,526	8,982,515	3,983,226	39,546	653,934	367,129
2005	28,541,125	15,342,949	216,076	15,559,025	1,711,537	378,323	14,225,811	10,059,962	4,255,352	42,298	674,757	387,813
2006	31,010,570	16,370,758	203,779	16,574,537	1,857,585	313,859	15,030,811	11,380,118	4,599,641	45,262	685,132	399,382
2007	31,536,980	15,736,378	187,782	15,924,160	1,843,734	295,068	14,375,494	12,260,336	4,901,150	45,591	691,735	397,906
2008	30,655,428	14,258,217	162,723	14,420,940	1,738,466	343,830	13,026,304	12,112,300	5,516,824	44,049	695,944	372,080
2009	27,978,312	13,142,110	169,953	13,312,063	1,659,161	376,040	12,028,942	9,915,071	6,034,299	40,085	697,973	355,547
2010	29,378,973	13,396,399	174,858	13,571,257	1,651,603	472,362	12,392,016	10,515,480	6,471,477	41,768	703,383	346,051
2011	31,285,433	13,861,001	139,448	14,000,449	1,533,793	547,095	13,013,751	11,558,348	6,713,334	44,076	709,806	352,488
2012	31,838,897	14,156,361	153,781	14,310,142	1,590,327	565,985	13,285,800	11,791,854	6,761,243	44,180	720,659	361,757
2013	32,831,627	14,849,782	169,539	15,019,321	1,866,695	576,497	13,729,123	12,080,965	7,021,539	44,828	732,386	375,452
2014	36,495,218	16,213,001	151,639	16,364,640	2,004,815	576,450	14,936,275	14,041,434	7,517,509	48,779	748,180	394,106
2015	39,726,292	17,797,591	170,265	17,967,856	2,154,269	591,444	16,405,031	15,284,087	8,037,174	51,713	768,207	411,427
2016	41,439,291	18,658,834	136,828	18,795,662	2,269,421	585,408	17,111,649	15,960,844	8,366,798	52,558	788,442	419,591
2017	43,475,538	19,643,211	121,552	19,764,763	2,389,574	582,922	17,958,111	16,748,133	8,769,294	54,028	804,690	428,310
2018	46,866,563	46,705,307	161,256	21,399,030	2,576,562	610,911	19,433,379	18,036,134	9,397,050	57,104	820,716	449,945
2019	48,613,206	48,417,433	195,773	22,289,717	2,735,334	706,321	20,260,704	18,201,617	10,150,885	58,081	836,995	461,954

Personal Income and Employment by Area: Norwich-New London, CT

(Thousands of dollars, except as noted.)

Year	Personal income, total	Earnings by place of work Nonfarm	Farm	Total	Less: Contributions for government social insurance	Plus: Adjustment for residence	Equals: Net earnings by place of residence	Plus: Dividends, interest, and rent	Plus: Personal current transfer receipts	Per capita personal income (dollars)	Population (persons)	Total employment
1970	1,008,957	824,578	8,094	832,672	52,910	-39,085	740,677	196,971	71,309	4,360	231,405	102,499
1971	1,089,406	889,425	8,046	897,471	60,164	-44,709	792,598	211,530	85,278	4,656	233,975	103,331
1972	1,198,510	975,833	8,926	984,759	69,019	-48,262	867,478	235,528	95,504	5,018	238,857	104,979
1973	1,323,721	1,094,458	11,330	1,105,788	86,485	-57,752	961,551	257,823	104,347	5,559	238,138	109,925
1974	1,476,722	1,237,671	6,002	1,243,673	102,790	-73,596	1,067,287	286,834	122,601	6,195	238,362	115,819
1975	1,577,780	1,272,595	10,476	1,283,071	105,536	-71,607	1,105,928	312,521	159,331	6,530	241,627	112,930
1976	1,709,395	1,394,392	11,625	1,406,017	118,516	-77,840	1,209,661	326,218	173,516	7,065	241,968	116,012
1977	1,896,632	1,569,033	13,141	1,582,174	138,790	-91,808	1,351,576	362,075	182,981	7,861	241,265	122,050
1978	2,049,957	1,656,323	8,360	1,664,683	147,775	-81,593	1,435,315	415,903	198,739	8,445	242,732	121,499
1979	2,260,639	1,826,902	9,990	1,836,892	168,617	-83,669	1,584,606	460,340	215,693	9,388	240,812	123,476
1980	2,566,067	2,032,729	11,647	2,044,376	183,291	-90,734	1,770,351	547,964	247,752	10,726	239,228	126,114
1981	2,926,267	2,309,541	18,060	2,327,601	223,217	-115,386	1,988,998	651,469	285,800	12,093	241,985	129,103
1982	3,212,936	2,549,499	22,255	2,571,754	251,097	-141,363	2,179,294	719,228	314,414	13,219	243,051	131,160
1983	3,530,809	2,856,192	24,081	2,880,273	288,556	-163,766	2,427,951	764,395	338,463	14,306	246,802	135,782
1984	3,922,341	3,145,076	38,287	3,183,363	326,082	-166,590	2,690,691	870,807	360,843	15,753	248,990	140,610
1985	4,157,101	3,332,122	37,036	3,369,158	348,267	-155,280	2,865,611	906,252	385,238	16,749	248,201	143,521
1986	4,304,251	3,353,329	38,619	3,391,948	346,231	-110,581	2,935,136	958,571	410,544	17,302	248,765	144,825
1987	4,655,438	3,636,935	43,265	3,680,200	372,044	-92,885	3,215,271	1,014,594	425,573	18,581	250,549	149,270
1988	4,944,654	3,860,267	38,843	3,899,110	407,836	-77,896	3,413,378	1,072,245	459,031	19,552	252,893	151,325
1989	5,375,950	4,107,397	36,125	4,143,522	433,533	-86,475	3,623,514	1,235,481	516,955	21,181	253,805	152,415
1990	5,597,212	4,123,638	44,215	4,167,853	433,970	52,655	3,786,538	1,229,126	581,548	21,909	255,474	149,439
1991	5,689,125	4,242,618	40,538	4,283,156	454,987	10,904	3,839,073	1,196,133	653,919	22,244	255,761	143,950
1992	6,036,794	4,411,978	42,499	4,454,477	470,077	83,420	4,067,820	1,200,577	768,397	23,926	252,306	141,923
1993	6,266,538	4,614,692	54,397	4,669,089	491,002	28,971	4,207,058	1,253,977	805,503	24,682	253,886	143,783
1994	6,585,322	5,002,731	48,516	5,051,247	542,941	-77,498	4,430,808	1,326,630	827,884	25,762	255,618	145,989
1995	6,881,678	5,321,951	34,773	5,356,724	581,631	-195,648	4,579,445	1,415,788	886,445	26,691	257,828	151,338
1996	7,127,062	5,534,907	37,243	5,572,150	604,401	-236,645	4,731,104	1,478,557	917,401	27,545	258,741	153,594
1997	7,571,275	5,964,492	35,484	5,999,976	636,423	-277,513	5,086,040	1,538,945	946,290	29,271	258,662	157,056
1998	7,987,842	6,219,907	37,409	6,257,316	649,285	-199,519	5,408,512	1,603,025	976,305	31,126	256,626	157,246
1999	8,348,447	6,587,785	38,018	6,625,803	664,632	-203,273	5,757,898	1,589,158	1,001,391	32,413	257,568	158,947
2000	8,836,277	6,884,984	41,753	6,926,737	682,769	-131,672	6,112,296	1,676,410	1,047,571	34,006	259,848	162,098
2001	9,238,583	7,194,670	45,596	7,240,266	704,213	-125,311	6,410,742	1,707,391	1,120,450	35,343	261,396	163,919
2002	9,553,666	7,528,663	51,633	7,580,296	760,615	-175,962	6,643,719	1,703,063	1,206,884	36,093	264,698	167,600
2003	9,987,238	7,885,662	48,372	7,934,034	786,535	-236,670	6,910,829	1,832,755	1,243,654	37,464	266,584	168,575
2004	10,701,435	8,479,603	46,249	8,525,852	831,955	-175,761	7,518,136	1,871,467	1,311,832	39,842	268,595	169,467
2005	11,024,366	8,802,997	41,437	8,844,434	858,496	-206,216	7,779,722	1,876,332	1,368,312	40,882	269,664	172,255
2006	11,561,394	9,080,418	38,106	9,118,524	882,400	-195,358	8,040,766	2,046,006	1,474,622	42,691	270,814	172,895
2007	12,200,333	9,309,821	42,830	9,352,651	908,889	-75,001	8,368,761	2,244,546	1,587,026	45,075	270,669	174,716
2008	12,653,532	9,508,526	54,190	9,562,716	942,977	-199,238	8,420,501	2,410,111	1,822,920	46,412	272,634	176,181
2009	12,574,656	9,453,576	53,645	9,507,221	941,026	-295,401	8,270,794	2,269,738	2,034,124	45,955	273,630	171,178
2010	12,730,513	9,522,294	47,011	9,569,305	936,267	-307,092	8,325,946	2,206,384	2,198,183	46,456	274,036	168,288
2011	13,229,656	9,593,739	45,305	9,639,044	858,369	-197,653	8,583,022	2,433,039	2,213,595	48,420	273,226	168,024
2012	13,559,865	9,591,433	62,639	9,654,072	871,161	-144,129	8,638,782	2,691,773	2,229,310	49,438	274,280	166,652
2013	13,532,743	9,561,018	65,430	9,626,448	987,752	21,604	8,660,300	2,605,667	2,266,776	49,500	273,388	165,947
2014	13,915,482	9,662,946	42,444	9,705,390	1,004,400	143,745	8,844,735	2,738,735	2,332,012	51,185	271,864	164,546
2015	14,499,291	9,884,581	53,887	9,938,468	1,030,478	260,838	9,168,828	2,907,753	2,422,710	53,648	270,266	164,688
2016	14,724,604	10,269,376	47,529	10,316,905	1,068,075	162,981	9,411,811	2,812,787	2,500,006	54,676	269,307	165,629
2017	15,260,910	10,768,290	39,670	10,807,960	1,118,835	88,912	9,778,037	2,937,555	2,545,318	56,725	269,033	167,739
2018	15,421,095	15,351,594	69,501	10,929,688	1,141,626	70,405	9,858,467	2,857,712	2,704,916	57,912	266,285	167,628
2019	15,837,267	15,765,677	71,590	11,137,971	1,170,010	146,744	10,114,705	2,912,951	2,809,611	59,717	265,206	167,200

Personal Income and Employment by Area: Ocala, FL

(Thousands of dollars, except as noted.)

Year	Personal income, total	Earnings by place of work			Less: Contributions for government social insurance	Plus: Adjustment for residence	Equals: Net earnings by place of residence	Plus: Dividends, interest, and rent	Plus: Personal current transfer receipts	Per capita personal income (dollars)	Population (persons)	Total employment
		Nonfarm	Farm	Total								
1970	228,020	151,527	10,838	162,365	9,942	5,163	157,586	43,619	26,815	3,243	70,320	28,119
1971	264,761	174,869	11,581	186,450	12,020	6,115	180,545	51,201	33,015	3,452	76,690	30,308
1972	314,537	208,462	13,638	222,100	15,029	8,338	215,409	59,517	39,611	3,880	81,072	32,968
1973	382,637	252,427	15,795	268,222	20,854	10,472	257,840	74,699	50,098	4,265	89,718	36,754
1974	424,854	271,214	9,833	281,047	23,546	11,828	269,329	90,753	64,772	4,361	97,426	37,392
1975	463,166	280,611	8,011	288,622	24,147	14,187	278,662	101,142	83,362	4,644	99,728	36,675
1976	514,585	308,808	6,790	315,598	27,176	16,915	305,337	110,296	98,952	4,889	105,252	37,671
1977	576,504	344,768	6,406	351,174	30,542	19,304	339,936	125,714	110,854	5,252	109,765	39,712
1978	668,831	401,363	6,772	408,135	36,357	21,981	393,759	150,969	124,103	5,938	112,629	43,276
1979	785,914	472,472	5,470	477,942	44,930	23,639	456,651	182,100	147,163	6,672	117,793	46,365
1980	958,921	547,299	9,789	557,088	52,422	27,503	532,169	244,884	181,868	7,720	124,218	50,295
1981	1,133,868	623,975	1,985	625,960	64,198	39,039	600,801	315,396	217,671	8,662	130,907	52,796
1982	1,277,019	676,871	14,606	691,477	71,612	50,664	670,529	352,289	254,201	9,295	137,381	54,974
1983	1,444,615	767,700	17,815	785,515	80,556	58,896	763,855	398,212	282,548	9,958	145,069	58,774
1984	1,640,913	886,544	20,324	906,868	95,426	72,250	883,692	457,569	299,652	10,830	151,521	63,433
1985	1,865,116	998,809	25,105	1,023,914	109,924	89,753	1,003,743	521,537	339,836	11,696	159,464	68,511
1986	2,080,906	1,122,175	30,358	1,152,533	126,021	102,930	1,129,442	573,041	378,423	12,448	167,170	73,388
1987	2,286,904	1,247,957	27,728	1,275,685	138,434	121,210	1,258,461	613,405	415,038	13,115	174,370	74,876
1988	2,536,349	1,373,285	33,223	1,406,508	157,498	144,799	1,393,809	677,810	464,730	14,069	180,277	77,900
1989	2,842,484	1,487,741	32,666	1,520,407	174,992	169,026	1,514,441	791,519	536,524	15,155	187,560	79,822
1990	3,089,135	1,584,235	33,303	1,617,538	184,262	199,936	1,633,212	851,576	604,347	15,673	197,095	81,784
1991	3,178,850	1,651,947	32,379	1,684,326	193,640	133,289	1,623,975	859,278	695,597	15,600	203,775	81,874
1992	3,408,460	1,771,490	45,330	1,816,820	207,277	139,488	1,749,031	864,420	795,009	16,278	209,388	82,420
1993	3,665,782	1,926,896	53,045	1,979,941	225,314	154,397	1,909,024	900,159	856,599	17,065	214,818	86,980
1994	3,959,387	2,068,885	54,190	2,123,075	245,865	182,789	2,059,999	966,263	933,125	17,714	223,523	89,626
1995	4,277,453	2,218,703	55,084	2,273,787	261,688	173,431	2,185,530	1,082,102	1,009,821	18,548	230,611	92,766
1996	4,617,111	2,429,561	55,140	2,484,701	280,098	156,461	2,361,064	1,180,440	1,075,607	19,511	236,637	98,351
1997	4,917,850	2,554,042	66,722	2,620,764	295,990	198,880	2,523,654	1,256,733	1,137,463	20,216	243,264	102,369
1998	5,363,782	2,771,134	63,007	2,834,141	317,260	245,523	2,762,404	1,384,858	1,216,520	21,448	250,086	107,202
1999	5,665,490	2,974,559	56,858	3,031,417	336,418	284,985	2,979,984	1,407,708	1,277,798	22,221	254,964	110,338
2000	6,076,719	3,110,302	32,989	3,143,291	350,230	387,444	3,180,505	1,533,713	1,362,501	23,352	260,221	113,425
2001	6,414,941	3,337,243	36,351	3,373,594	381,846	370,412	3,362,160	1,561,202	1,491,579	24,248	264,553	111,456
2002	6,567,287	3,552,051	37,356	3,589,407	403,859	345,995	3,531,543	1,430,687	1,605,057	24,170	271,716	114,392
2003	6,978,474	3,851,926	21,204	3,873,130	439,516	326,838	3,760,452	1,498,418	1,719,604	24,915	280,091	119,807
2004	7,615,332	4,139,888	23,674	4,163,562	483,475	324,793	4,004,880	1,715,135	1,895,317	26,155	291,164	126,037
2005	8,488,351	4,576,528	13,110	4,589,638	540,148	318,363	4,367,853	2,003,045	2,117,453	27,963	303,558	134,595
2006	9,409,827	5,044,239	17,693	5,061,932	614,820	287,005	4,734,117	2,345,365	2,330,345	29,749	316,310	143,125
2007	9,833,755	5,077,022	-17,364	5,059,658	627,976	266,575	4,698,257	2,618,316	2,517,182	30,199	325,634	145,863
2008	9,942,073	4,919,679	-40,906	4,878,773	624,601	219,969	4,474,141	2,619,429	2,848,503	30,123	330,052	140,813
2009	9,621,606	4,520,718	-39,619	4,481,099	594,417	236,945	4,123,627	2,363,447	3,134,532	29,079	330,880	131,466
2010	9,972,773	4,568,133	-22,201	4,545,932	594,042	250,310	4,202,200	2,393,974	3,376,599	30,098	331,344	128,566
2011	10,392,454	4,610,450	-59,925	4,550,525	548,945	265,191	4,266,771	2,623,481	3,502,202	31,274	332,307	129,797
2012	10,601,097	4,792,198	26,675	4,818,873	572,253	252,404	4,499,024	2,567,123	3,534,950	31,739	334,004	132,017
2013	10,468,087	4,892,614	-1,792	4,890,822	653,461	250,035	4,487,396	2,358,045	3,622,646	31,222	335,274	134,618
2014	11,055,432	5,078,839	17,792	5,096,631	678,733	261,657	4,679,555	2,571,014	3,804,863	32,673	338,368	138,701
2015	11,557,764	5,310,159	21,733	5,331,892	702,733	286,671	4,915,830	2,649,482	3,992,452	33,720	342,757	141,954
2016	12,162,027	5,655,141	16,872	5,672,013	748,551	294,763	5,218,225	2,776,547	4,167,255	34,934	348,139	146,341
2017	12,708,667	5,801,096	60,881	5,861,977	774,506	338,355	5,425,826	2,904,120	4,378,721	35,864	354,353	148,193
2018	13,363,961	13,351,763	12,198	6,126,739	825,249	372,840	5,674,330	3,126,140	4,563,491	37,219	359,062	155,440
2019	13,999,019	13,972,848	26,171	6,459,774	883,433	405,350	5,981,691	3,166,242	4,851,086	38,293	365,579	159,229

Personal Income and Employment by Area: Ocean City, NJ

(Thousands of dollars, except as noted.)

Year	Personal income, total	Earnings by place of work			Less: Contributions for government social insurance	Plus: Adjustment for residence	Equals: Net earnings by place of residence	Plus: Dividends, interest, and rent	Plus: Personal current transfer receipts	Per capita personal income (dollars)	Population (persons)	Total employment
		Nonfarm	Farm	Total								
1970	261,323	151,397	1,101	152,498	11,075	25,634	167,057	60,153	34,113	4,337	60,259	25,672
1971	292,415	168,190	962	169,152	12,787	26,784	183,149	67,702	41,564	4,606	63,485	26,985
1972	333,999	190,401	1,019	191,420	15,084	33,244	209,580	75,505	48,914	5,036	66,321	28,236
1973	393,430	227,699	1,460	229,159	20,299	39,212	248,072	87,912	57,446	5,769	68,194	30,935
1974	441,926	246,154	1,582	247,736	22,708	46,879	271,907	101,901	68,118	6,144	71,929	30,751
1975	503,624	270,699	1,387	272,086	24,926	55,495	302,655	113,843	87,126	6,804	74,014	31,385
1976	568,484	305,685	1,313	306,998	27,963	65,176	344,211	124,376	99,897	7,398	76,838	32,553
1977	631,487	338,815	883	339,698	31,255	75,048	383,491	140,519	107,477	8,070	78,248	34,569
1978	710,744	383,200	1,093	384,293	35,993	89,114	437,414	156,072	117,258	8,900	79,862	36,393
1979	790,161	413,999	981	414,980	40,783	111,040	485,237	173,819	131,105	9,669	81,725	37,189
1980	915,302	453,260	557	453,817	44,694	137,946	547,069	217,899	150,334	11,061	82,754	38,264
1981	1,037,390	485,257	1,037	486,294	51,461	167,294	602,127	264,065	171,198	12,270	84,550	39,013
1982	1,122,061	509,761	1,647	511,408	54,472	178,275	635,211	296,327	190,523	13,185	85,104	39,669
1983	1,215,357	565,725	2,287	568,012	62,140	191,757	697,629	311,838	205,890	14,187	85,665	42,138
1984	1,335,103	626,495	2,308	628,803	71,701	208,607	765,709	354,959	214,435	15,330	87,092	43,146
1985	1,438,733	689,826	2,381	692,207	79,433	222,972	835,746	382,978	220,009	16,230	88,647	43,532
1986	1,549,740	755,144	2,461	757,605	88,217	234,715	904,103	415,132	230,505	17,194	90,130	44,391
1987	1,655,731	826,555	1,996	828,551	97,329	250,322	981,544	434,631	239,556	17,990	92,038	44,431
1988	1,805,903	928,587	2,216	930,803	112,132	267,562	1,086,233	464,162	255,508	19,426	92,961	46,515
1989	1,943,603	980,201	2,274	982,475	118,262	279,156	1,143,369	525,925	274,309	20,496	94,830	47,087
1990	2,040,511	1,015,630	2,425	1,018,055	118,685	309,461	1,208,831	531,847	299,833	21,396	95,368	47,010
1991	2,090,885	1,031,464	2,088	1,033,552	123,706	313,807	1,223,653	519,378	347,854	21,554	97,006	46,586
1992	2,240,070	1,106,230	2,240	1,108,470	131,728	328,195	1,304,937	524,227	410,906	22,830	98,121	47,721
1993	2,346,534	1,147,829	2,833	1,150,662	135,222	358,326	1,373,766	536,709	436,059	23,822	98,504	47,462
1994	2,417,588	1,195,960	3,379	1,199,339	143,375	360,307	1,416,271	553,331	447,986	24,282	99,561	47,835
1995	2,553,398	1,243,912	2,923	1,246,835	148,403	376,241	1,474,673	599,263	479,462	25,431	100,405	48,319
1996	2,674,570	1,293,094	2,485	1,295,579	154,359	390,421	1,531,641	640,105	502,824	26,517	100,861	49,078
1997	2,888,597	1,397,775	2,297	1,400,072	160,756	441,200	1,680,516	685,952	522,129	28,493	101,380	50,322
1998	3,042,894	1,449,669	3,604	1,453,273	165,875	497,999	1,785,397	721,028	536,469	29,867	101,883	51,329
1999	3,166,218	1,548,811	4,309	1,553,120	173,335	510,252	1,890,037	723,099	553,082	31,000	102,135	52,030
2000	3,386,818	1,641,421	5,603	1,647,024	181,897	542,592	2,007,719	797,873	581,226	33,102	102,314	54,163
2001	3,619,501	1,825,266	5,651	1,830,917	198,948	539,637	2,171,606	818,195	629,700	35,477	102,023	55,135
2002	3,735,529	1,945,189	6,235	1,951,424	212,463	518,215	2,257,176	769,251	709,102	36,733	101,694	55,661
2003	3,795,543	2,062,560	6,029	2,068,589	222,014	484,429	2,331,004	779,472	685,067	37,317	101,710	56,471
2004	3,992,699	2,223,110	6,107	2,229,217	240,873	459,034	2,447,378	861,689	683,632	39,735	100,482	58,373
2005	4,077,735	2,354,232	6,369	2,360,601	264,609	417,028	2,513,020	835,025	729,690	41,078	99,269	60,454
2006	4,174,361	2,382,678	7,117	2,389,795	270,288	398,432	2,517,939	857,618	798,804	42,296	98,695	60,128
2007	4,197,024	2,285,626	7,404	2,293,030	272,714	412,114	2,432,430	919,980	844,614	42,964	97,686	59,741
2008	4,194,600	2,242,894	7,068	2,249,962	275,609	307,067	2,281,420	988,995	924,185	42,999	97,550	59,281
2009	4,207,605	2,202,163	6,362	2,208,525	273,228	249,286	2,184,583	995,784	1,027,238	43,271	97,238	58,521
2010	4,342,943	2,259,469	5,778	2,265,247	278,254	249,142	2,236,135	1,015,392	1,091,416	44,670	97,222	58,088
2011	4,527,809	2,251,075	4,882	2,255,957	255,771	292,563	2,292,749	1,127,723	1,107,337	46,891	96,561	58,106
2012	4,693,197	2,340,686	5,486	2,346,172	259,893	322,178	2,408,457	1,183,419	1,101,321	48,691	96,387	58,053
2013	4,731,939	2,437,473	6,374	2,443,847	297,411	289,879	2,436,315	1,186,471	1,109,153	49,443	95,704	58,720
2014	4,883,092	2,562,930	5,688	2,568,618	309,427	237,492	2,496,683	1,245,371	1,141,038	51,322	95,146	59,768
2015	5,096,939	2,659,446	6,038	2,665,484	320,592	233,049	2,577,941	1,328,846	1,190,152	53,981	94,421	60,288
2016	5,247,741	2,734,073	6,104	2,740,177	327,008	282,599	2,695,768	1,324,453	1,227,520	55,875	93,920	60,668
2017	5,456,352	2,836,103	5,745	2,841,848	338,999	305,614	2,808,463	1,389,378	1,258,511	58,324	93,553	61,937
2018	5,571,180	5,566,189	4,991	2,975,983	350,741	312,409	2,937,651	1,348,742	1,284,787	60,264	92,446	62,116
2019	5,773,945	5,768,405	5,540	3,105,555	366,700	313,069	3,051,924	1,369,311	1,352,710	62,734	92,039	63,074

Personal Income and Employment by Area: Odessa, TX

(Thousands of dollars, except as noted.)

					Derivation of personal income							
		Earnings by place of work			Less: Contributions for government social insurance	Plus: Adjustment for residence	Equals: Net earnings by place of residence	Plus: Dividends, interest, and rent	Plus: Personal current transfer receipts	Per capita personal income (dollars)	Population (persons)	Total employment
Year	Personal income, total	Nonfarm	Farm	Total								
1970	342,782	301,150	460	301,610	18,409	7,072	290,273	35,455	17,054	3,698	92,704	38,555
1971	367,519	321,697	99	321,796	20,093	7,271	308,974	38,512	20,033	3,926	93,609	39,295
1972	405,464	356,961	-680	356,281	23,239	7,691	340,733	42,015	22,716	4,291	94,500	40,684
1973	451,399	397,916	225	398,141	30,713	8,140	375,568	48,411	27,420	4,840	93,264	43,432
1974	542,855	479,145	610	479,755	37,996	9,519	451,278	58,976	32,601	5,616	96,667	46,851
1975	653,641	571,871	55	571,926	44,309	15,237	542,854	71,025	39,762	6,562	99,614	49,230
1976	795,881	709,582	298	709,880	52,843	16,327	673,364	78,591	43,926	7,773	102,392	51,191
1977	897,303	801,150	74	801,224	61,468	21,501	761,257	88,971	47,075	8,570	104,702	54,572
1978	1,031,873	920,635	743	921,378	73,925	29,019	876,472	102,072	53,329	9,538	108,189	58,659
1979	1,126,926	998,173	221	998,394	85,385	34,562	947,571	117,137	62,218	10,114	111,422	59,768
1980	1,349,255	1,174,121	72	1,174,193	102,391	54,480	1,126,282	150,639	72,334	11,527	117,052	64,450
1981	1,751,450	1,546,000	1,095	1,547,095	144,618	59,842	1,462,319	206,623	82,508	14,191	123,418	73,670
1982	1,890,841	1,620,139	1,234	1,621,373	158,107	64,563	1,527,829	266,375	96,637	13,954	135,501	74,922
1983	1,754,371	1,431,154	383	1,431,537	139,207	52,217	1,344,547	286,986	122,838	12,709	138,041	67,260
1984	1,759,958	1,407,125	475	1,407,600	142,278	51,889	1,317,211	314,051	128,696	13,133	134,006	66,031
1985	1,812,286	1,444,681	696	1,445,377	150,025	46,565	1,341,917	334,562	135,807	13,603	133,225	67,259
1986	1,616,613	1,215,730	509	1,216,239	123,137	44,198	1,137,300	314,542	164,771	12,101	133,588	57,894
1987	1,545,593	1,154,249	598	1,154,847	116,067	33,551	1,072,331	306,355	166,907	12,347	125,180	55,809
1988	1,601,855	1,200,397	232	1,200,629	126,055	33,441	1,108,015	323,821	170,019	13,123	122,067	57,518
1989	1,664,648	1,221,551	127	1,221,678	127,452	27,279	1,121,505	346,788	196,355	13,904	119,722	55,919
1990	1,708,198	1,268,409	-158	1,268,251	131,684	23,840	1,160,407	329,234	218,557	14,397	118,652	57,211
1991	1,810,723	1,357,487	-590	1,356,897	143,785	17,958	1,231,070	326,327	253,326	15,095	119,955	58,006
1992	1,861,672	1,364,858	-233	1,364,625	142,361	15,820	1,238,084	321,258	302,330	15,382	121,027	56,475
1993	1,930,173	1,424,822	-532	1,424,290	149,040	9,580	1,284,830	318,666	326,677	15,949	121,018	56,906
1994	1,993,286	1,473,181	-185	1,472,996	155,738	667	1,317,925	324,020	351,341	16,438	121,258	58,224
1995	2,055,845	1,499,812	-1,185	1,498,627	158,991	-1,990	1,337,646	343,962	374,237	16,988	121,017	58,734
1996	2,142,612	1,565,046	-2,232	1,562,814	163,408	-6,811	1,392,595	355,801	394,216	17,632	121,519	59,531
1997	2,341,644	1,753,101	-1,810	1,751,291	179,062	-9,729	1,562,500	372,236	406,908	19,233	121,749	61,867
1998	2,514,713	1,945,227	-1,614	1,943,613	196,917	-30,423	1,716,273	393,045	405,395	20,355	123,544	64,989
1999	2,382,551	1,795,910	-1,469	1,794,441	177,728	-24,985	1,591,728	365,638	425,185	19,457	122,450	60,926
2000	2,569,355	1,965,182	-852	1,964,330	190,295	-38,711	1,735,324	395,271	438,760	21,288	120,694	62,662
2001	2,785,510	2,164,186	-575	2,163,611	215,174	-38,117	1,910,320	402,841	472,349	23,058	120,802	64,327
2002	2,843,754	2,195,815	446	2,196,261	218,109	-47,003	1,931,149	389,600	523,005	23,271	122,199	64,267
2003	2,900,618	2,201,603	1,009	2,202,612	226,611	-42,566	1,933,435	409,382	557,801	23,632	122,739	64,158
2004	2,979,900	2,292,716	997	2,293,713	238,204	-36,078	2,019,431	385,575	574,894	24,000	124,163	65,340
2005	3,325,727	2,534,399	852	2,535,251	266,432	-5,935	2,262,884	438,853	623,990	26,526	125,378	67,933
2006	3,866,820	3,052,978	566	3,053,544	308,696	-7,333	2,737,515	481,609	647,696	30,334	127,476	72,744
2007	4,291,650	3,469,661	849	3,470,510	351,128	-53,035	3,066,347	530,330	694,973	32,897	130,459	76,549
2008	4,960,889	3,981,037	-1,820	3,979,217	394,560	-7,471	3,577,186	627,038	756,665	37,282	133,064	81,181
2009	4,486,526	3,563,001	-2,005	3,560,996	361,089	-110,681	3,089,226	577,927	819,373	32,765	136,930	77,006
2010	4,794,782	3,832,553	-2,409	3,830,144	387,840	-118,030	3,324,274	559,950	910,558	34,978	137,079	78,317
2011	5,527,046	4,640,990	-2,357	4,638,633	420,322	-272,935	3,945,376	683,165	898,505	39,589	139,611	85,207
2012	6,460,741	5,655,202	-2,267	5,652,935	489,178	-379,786	4,783,971	803,950	872,820	44,725	144,455	91,845
2013	6,566,858	6,093,039	-1,495	6,091,544	589,948	-491,949	5,009,647	679,157	878,054	43,881	149,651	94,474
2014	7,374,465	6,722,536	-1,978	6,720,558	649,465	-430,506	5,640,587	817,520	916,358	47,711	154,566	100,266
2015	6,700,435	5,910,305	-1,011	5,909,294	590,024	-400,158	4,919,112	800,595	980,728	41,921	159,835	96,837
2016	5,976,672	5,002,947	-2,545	5,000,402	520,738	-361,386	4,118,278	811,603	1,046,791	37,928	157,580	90,048
2017	6,417,181	5,518,312	-2,803	5,515,509	591,762	-415,943	4,507,804	855,476	1,053,901	40,851	157,087	94,517
2018	7,846,736	7,845,851	885	6,988,652	720,771	-364,398	5,903,483	866,728	1,076,525	48,449	161,960	104,366
2019	8,337,928	8,338,381	-453	7,426,975	752,436	-336,158	6,338,381	893,150	1,106,397	50,161	166,223	107,412

Personal Income and Employment by Area: Ogden-Clearfield, UT

(Thousands of dollars, except as noted.)

Year	Personal income, total	Earnings by place of work			Less: Contributions for government social insurance	Plus: Adjustment for residence	Equals: Net earnings by place of residence	Plus: Dividends, interest, and rent	Plus: Personal current transfer receipts	Per capita personal income (dollars)	Population (persons)	Total employment
		Nonfarm	Farm	Total								
1970	969,165	736,060	19,328	755,388	36,595	24,125	742,918	161,646	64,601	3,747	258,652	101,375
1971	1,105,674	848,798	18,875	867,673	42,032	9,697	835,338	194,041	76,295	4,165	265,466	102,505
1972	1,187,967	897,136	21,518	918,654	49,285	22,305	891,674	210,639	85,654	4,379	271,286	106,947
1973	1,288,341	956,805	29,967	986,772	61,191	32,578	958,159	228,315	101,867	4,675	275,564	109,681
1974	1,428,952	1,058,738	25,577	1,084,315	71,464	41,988	1,054,839	258,192	115,921	5,109	279,691	112,270
1975	1,572,838	1,167,556	15,280	1,182,836	79,865	45,407	1,148,378	282,220	142,240	5,487	286,672	114,043
1976	1,763,256	1,318,691	15,401	1,334,092	92,699	54,155	1,295,548	313,031	154,677	6,012	293,292	118,620
1977	1,955,618	1,458,309	10,038	1,468,347	104,226	72,824	1,436,945	351,641	167,032	6,489	301,368	123,292
1978	2,244,010	1,656,985	13,471	1,670,456	121,620	93,536	1,642,372	415,834	185,804	7,217	310,926	130,121
1979	2,523,051	1,853,976	15,558	1,869,534	145,163	115,748	1,840,119	470,656	212,276	7,866	320,746	136,040
1980	2,833,369	2,032,680	12,117	2,044,797	159,248	149,395	2,034,944	548,746	249,679	8,543	331,666	137,885
1981	3,179,999	2,273,345	6,066	2,279,411	190,343	157,393	2,246,461	640,494	293,044	9,342	340,400	140,230
1982	3,466,831	2,433,209	7,952	2,441,161	206,927	178,716	2,412,950	720,311	333,570	9,940	348,770	141,296
1983	3,740,197	2,596,199	5,019	2,601,218	232,532	221,385	2,590,071	788,429	361,697	10,511	355,842	143,806
1984	4,131,769	2,895,050	7,831	2,902,881	269,072	240,057	2,873,866	883,293	374,610	11,429	361,527	152,784
1985	4,505,025	3,193,429	5,909	3,199,338	310,562	253,156	3,141,932	951,540	411,553	12,272	367,103	161,151
1986	4,766,979	3,374,296	12,637	3,386,933	334,104	267,333	3,320,162	1,007,262	439,555	12,792	372,647	166,082
1987	4,965,969	3,452,378	35,064	3,487,442	343,673	317,093	3,460,862	1,045,851	459,256	13,093	379,274	171,824
1988	5,262,010	3,664,639	52,004	3,716,643	384,819	346,550	3,678,374	1,097,135	486,501	13,803	381,216	178,142
1989	5,636,414	3,922,772	47,140	3,969,912	421,983	374,148	3,922,077	1,179,405	534,932	14,635	385,120	184,178
1990	6,111,853	4,215,190	60,135	4,275,325	471,422	497,683	4,301,586	1,220,435	589,832	15,679	389,815	190,389
1991	6,477,232	4,497,255	54,339	4,551,594	511,109	521,926	4,562,411	1,272,190	642,631	16,257	398,436	192,203
1992	6,957,437	4,779,187	73,622	4,852,809	544,894	629,575	4,937,490	1,307,141	712,806	17,021	408,757	193,998
1993	7,421,599	5,055,433	75,662	5,131,095	583,898	719,306	5,266,503	1,374,831	780,265	17,675	419,888	199,000
1994	7,913,976	5,360,880	55,777	5,416,657	630,691	810,357	5,596,323	1,511,590	806,063	18,362	430,988	213,802
1995	8,562,691	5,749,554	44,342	5,793,896	679,335	886,761	6,001,322	1,690,396	870,973	19,428	440,732	220,335
1996	9,253,574	6,161,854	49,938	6,211,792	723,711	993,911	6,481,992	1,845,281	926,301	20,530	450,737	233,975
1997	9,971,026	6,597,480	53,417	6,650,897	766,366	1,157,574	7,042,105	1,960,702	968,219	21,643	460,703	244,207
1998	10,746,094	6,951,991	54,154	7,006,145	806,334	1,316,458	7,516,269	2,213,864	1,015,961	22,854	470,206	248,177
1999	11,226,487	7,234,177	48,133	7,282,310	836,286	1,494,242	7,940,266	2,211,978	1,074,243	23,438	478,978	251,600
2000	11,976,345	7,645,893	34,947	7,680,840	884,895	1,614,349	8,410,294	2,417,968	1,148,083	24,546	487,906	257,400
2001	12,747,397	8,219,151	46,865	8,266,016	946,366	1,697,407	9,017,057	2,461,088	1,269,252	25,728	495,459	259,182
2002	13,183,468	8,645,331	23,763	8,669,094	995,204	1,702,840	9,376,730	2,419,869	1,386,869	26,145	504,247	263,457
2003	13,762,780	9,084,871	28,892	9,113,763	1,056,444	1,701,102	9,758,421	2,519,646	1,484,713	26,827	513,021	266,987
2004	14,438,647	9,585,977	42,100	9,628,077	1,133,092	1,846,177	10,341,162	2,544,095	1,553,390	27,640	522,374	276,026
2005	15,463,287	10,082,373	38,854	10,121,227	1,194,259	2,032,680	10,959,648	2,823,848	1,679,791	29,043	532,425	283,624
2006	17,021,471	11,133,567	31,230	11,164,797	1,298,207	2,306,463	12,173,053	3,027,918	1,820,500	31,189	545,746	294,833
2007	18,633,475	11,725,488	40,122	11,765,610	1,369,526	2,653,831	13,049,915	3,588,900	1,994,660	33,169	561,767	308,361
2008	19,394,983	11,895,045	37,791	11,932,836	1,402,039	2,760,106	13,290,903	3,743,504	2,360,576	33,611	577,040	309,968
2009	18,909,643	11,524,244	27,443	11,551,687	1,369,317	2,705,123	12,887,493	3,435,545	2,586,605	32,117	588,773	301,210
2010	19,335,715	11,725,620	38,274	11,763,894	1,385,082	2,765,444	13,144,256	3,303,629	2,887,830	32,241	599,724	297,159
2011	20,617,524	12,244,041	78,414	12,322,455	1,304,301	2,996,285	14,014,439	3,626,364	2,976,721	34,040	605,681	304,022
2012	21,748,275	12,926,662	66,473	12,993,135	1,350,863	3,229,462	14,871,734	3,913,769	2,962,772	35,521	612,257	308,441
2013	22,218,283	13,286,542	94,861	13,381,403	1,575,328	3,396,113	15,202,188	3,974,217	3,041,878	35,751	621,468	315,442
2014	23,375,717	13,995,849	107,674	14,103,523	1,659,561	3,486,982	15,930,944	4,285,593	3,159,180	37,052	630,889	324,272
2015	24,888,778	14,871,609	86,744	14,958,353	1,732,343	3,653,991	16,880,001	4,659,579	3,349,198	38,848	640,663	335,561
2016	26,331,173	15,733,381	56,901	15,790,282	1,829,282	3,937,224	17,898,224	4,915,267	3,517,682	40,324	652,995	346,571
2017	27,728,432	16,623,145	56,982	16,680,127	1,963,707	4,198,827	18,915,247	5,170,871	3,642,314	41,674	665,358	356,319
2018	29,705,915	29,673,470	32,445	17,656,816	2,059,833	4,275,663	19,872,646	5,939,983	3,893,286	44,096	673,660	369,335
2019	31,541,823	31,468,677	73,146	18,552,448	2,159,085	4,828,015	21,221,378	6,141,746	4,178,699	46,123	683,864	378,978

Personal Income and Employment by Area: Oklahoma City, OK

(Thousands of dollars, except as noted.)

Year	Personal income, total	Earnings by place of work Nonfarm	Farm	Total	Less: Contributions for government social insurance	Plus: Adjustment for residence	Equals: Net earnings by place of residence	Plus: Dividends, interest, and rent	Plus: Personal current transfer receipts	Per capita personal income (dollars)	Population (persons)	Total employment
1970	3,017,627	2,484,654	27,488	2,512,142	143,758	-51,610	2,316,774	464,939	235,914	4,144	728,165	354,356
1971	3,364,882	2,741,764	26,904	2,768,668	164,431	-50,514	2,553,723	534,130	277,029	4,479	751,178	364,970
1972	3,694,011	3,051,263	24,884	3,076,147	194,150	-70,361	2,811,636	572,407	309,968	4,796	770,165	385,385
1973	4,089,347	3,349,156	61,343	3,410,499	249,832	-77,259	3,083,408	649,403	356,536	5,210	784,927	398,352
1974	4,571,230	3,727,100	40,620	3,767,720	288,038	-76,960	3,402,722	746,500	422,008	5,766	792,748	407,075
1975	5,025,160	4,021,527	34,624	4,056,151	309,340	-64,598	3,682,213	811,597	531,350	6,296	798,210	406,103
1976	5,510,871	4,415,814	30,336	4,446,150	347,102	-60,130	4,038,918	890,986	580,967	6,818	808,238	411,197
1977	6,194,095	5,057,117	17,862	5,074,979	398,459	-95,441	4,581,079	1,004,204	608,812	7,547	820,775	432,760
1978	7,111,495	5,879,414	13,197	5,892,611	480,958	-126,266	5,285,387	1,173,766	652,342	8,495	837,101	465,144
1979	8,191,439	6,780,232	37,811	6,818,043	580,145	-146,557	6,091,341	1,350,876	749,222	9,615	851,930	488,083
1980	9,603,583	7,950,111	23,121	7,973,232	688,884	-183,866	7,100,482	1,639,324	863,777	10,946	877,354	513,837
1981	11,191,572	9,218,441	5,797	9,224,238	861,510	-181,364	8,181,364	2,032,778	977,430	12,467	897,677	543,150
1982	12,613,485	10,246,235	16,888	10,263,123	981,046	-173,809	9,108,268	2,413,691	1,091,526	13,457	937,318	568,698
1983	13,051,527	10,446,756	4,078	10,450,834	1,000,019	-203,821	9,246,994	2,616,315	1,188,218	13,428	971,970	562,358
1984	14,018,964	11,171,586	10,990	11,182,576	1,089,785	-213,296	9,879,495	2,901,319	1,238,150	14,252	983,657	574,026
1985	14,536,744	11,400,213	26,215	11,426,428	1,130,774	-200,088	10,095,566	3,094,470	1,346,708	14,715	987,888	562,905
1986	14,538,004	11,313,973	49,383	11,363,356	1,144,357	-185,922	10,033,077	3,056,356	1,448,571	14,774	983,997	542,698
1987	14,551,571	11,325,693	42,464	11,368,157	1,153,140	-171,629	10,043,388	2,987,537	1,520,646	15,002	970,003	543,299
1988	15,220,534	11,850,729	57,831	11,908,560	1,271,501	-181,277	10,455,782	3,127,521	1,637,231	15,749	966,423	549,865
1989	16,348,811	12,568,148	64,905	12,633,053	1,357,679	-166,664	11,108,710	3,496,439	1,743,662	16,855	969,976	557,627
1990	17,025,368	13,126,286	51,645	13,177,931	1,467,296	-181,919	11,528,716	3,604,672	1,891,980	17,507	972,512	567,554
1991	17,567,437	13,569,205	41,302	13,610,507	1,554,084	-183,099	11,873,324	3,604,553	2,089,560	17,854	983,942	568,264
1992	18,687,635	14,426,436	61,647	14,488,083	1,644,894	-197,307	12,645,882	3,680,751	2,361,002	18,717	998,407	574,498
1993	19,594,349	15,197,954	54,227	15,252,181	1,749,775	-212,283	13,290,123	3,839,193	2,465,033	19,305	1,014,998	586,259
1994	20,579,604	15,830,712	63,012	15,893,724	1,853,382	-225,995	13,814,347	4,103,365	2,661,892	19,993	1,029,338	599,649
1995	21,552,827	16,526,980	7,759	16,534,739	1,943,716	-242,302	14,348,721	4,329,708	2,874,398	20,737	1,039,343	621,260
1996	22,910,729	17,561,956	19,233	17,581,189	2,028,027	-240,728	15,312,434	4,583,465	3,014,830	21,781	1,051,886	640,572
1997	23,928,988	18,386,764	27,930	18,414,694	2,099,330	-250,415	16,064,949	4,745,099	3,118,940	22,462	1,065,333	652,676
1998	25,483,579	19,522,769	13,887	19,536,656	2,209,087	-258,424	17,069,145	5,175,663	3,238,771	23,701	1,075,233	667,154
1999	26,495,227	20,350,961	36,648	20,387,609	2,314,528	-300,054	17,773,027	5,308,558	3,413,642	24,344	1,088,347	679,360
2000	29,193,097	22,374,597	34,232	22,408,829	2,498,503	-343,523	19,566,803	5,909,165	3,717,129	26,584	1,098,132	698,058
2001	31,427,445	24,231,233	42,071	24,273,304	2,660,654	-344,329	21,268,321	6,006,408	4,152,716	28,342	1,108,860	707,782
2002	32,269,267	25,068,072	61,176	25,129,248	2,769,050	-356,670	22,003,528	6,015,520	4,250,219	28,754	1,122,241	703,510
2003	34,323,429	26,967,698	48,668	27,016,366	2,912,457	-359,100	23,744,809	6,039,298	4,539,322	30,256	1,134,419	703,638
2004	36,241,044	28,437,526	86,662	28,524,188	3,090,463	-395,445	25,038,280	6,433,453	4,769,311	31,637	1,145,524	718,972
2005	39,447,749	30,630,618	98,240	30,728,858	3,217,045	-397,590	27,114,223	7,075,083	5,258,443	33,968	1,161,308	733,082
2006	43,414,374	33,159,799	44,774	33,204,573	3,428,080	-412,303	29,364,190	8,268,676	5,781,508	36,709	1,182,668	749,113
2007	44,679,795	33,347,154	58,530	33,405,684	3,580,531	-353,910	29,471,243	8,977,969	6,230,583	37,244	1,199,665	764,900
2008	49,045,360	36,812,820	66,913	36,879,733	3,760,016	-375,380	32,744,337	9,188,476	7,112,547	40,312	1,216,645	780,121
2009	47,030,579	35,071,389	-10,074	35,061,315	3,746,802	-386,149	30,928,364	8,400,988	7,701,227	37,996	1,237,780	766,965
2010	48,668,843	36,108,497	31,038	36,139,535	3,845,149	-413,153	31,881,233	8,483,764	8,303,846	38,695	1,257,743	771,479
2011	52,056,589	38,215,970	68,708	38,284,678	3,708,646	-466,318	34,109,714	9,483,744	8,463,131	40,793	1,276,130	790,633
2012	55,011,578	40,360,747	110,988	40,471,735	3,928,284	-482,158	36,061,293	10,271,124	8,679,161	42,413	1,297,041	814,008
2013	56,618,873	42,432,516	112,919	42,545,435	4,552,915	-513,668	37,478,852	10,171,211	8,968,810	42,910	1,319,469	832,874
2014	59,988,733	44,731,010	158,455	44,889,465	4,693,859	-497,546	39,698,060	10,948,399	9,342,274	44,911	1,335,736	846,309
2015	61,525,255	45,720,592	88,140	45,808,732	4,789,300	-521,737	40,497,695	11,279,805	9,747,755	45,369	1,356,118	857,526
2016	61,347,558	44,777,099	35,399	44,812,498	4,823,867	-513,343	39,475,288	11,733,913	10,138,357	44,699	1,372,463	861,565
2017	65,170,028	48,168,954	24,363	48,193,317	5,073,714	-592,973	42,526,630	12,217,535	10,425,863	47,097	1,383,737	870,743
2018	66,345,545	66,376,442	-30,897	48,663,689	5,262,377	-677,644	42,723,668	12,774,567	10,847,310	47,607	1,393,605	883,183
2019	68,841,224	68,855,391	-14,167	50,445,621	5,446,240	-649,802	44,349,579	12,958,450	11,533,195	48,860	1,408,950	897,278

Personal Income and Employment by Area: Olympia-Lacey-Tumwater, WA

(Thousands of dollars, except as noted.)

Year	Personal income, total	Earnings by place of work			Less: Contributions for government social insurance	Plus: Adjustment for residence	Equals: Net earnings by place of residence	Plus: Dividends, interest, and rent	Plus: Personal current transfer receipts	Per capita personal income (dollars)	Population (persons)	Total employment
		Nonfarm	Farm	Total								
1970............	357,422	257,443	5,347	262,790	19,590	9,066	252,266	74,654	30,502	4,612	77,498	34,767
1971............	395,612	282,099	4,690	286,789	22,570	12,001	276,220	82,623	36,769	4,950	79,920	35,873
1972............	427,521	302,358	6,506	308,864	25,336	12,561	296,089	89,073	42,359	5,216	81,970	36,700
1973............	487,701	336,283	15,247	351,530	32,489	19,457	338,498	100,428	48,775	5,742	84,930	37,999
1974............	554,735	378,724	14,107	392,831	38,280	24,275	378,826	116,368	59,541	6,201	89,466	39,450
1975............	633,132	428,183	11,846	440,029	42,959	27,113	424,183	135,535	73,414	6,753	93,760	41,096
1976............	726,738	494,329	12,270	506,599	50,440	35,592	491,751	152,802	82,185	7,431	97,798	43,594
1977............	823,320	558,826	11,627	570,453	57,128	46,068	559,393	175,852	88,075	7,729	106,529	45,440
1978............	981,445	671,900	17,035	688,935	71,083	57,249	675,101	208,296	98,048	8,702	112,782	49,562
1979............	1,128,038	756,875	18,956	775,831	81,440	76,925	771,316	244,725	111,997	9,465	119,176	53,380
1980............	1,300,439	833,419	19,121	852,540	92,880	103,080	862,740	294,814	142,885	10,377	125,325	55,242
1981............	1,467,770	904,824	19,848	924,672	108,596	134,400	950,476	351,806	165,488	11,349	129,326	55,939
1982............	1,553,849	916,616	21,445	938,061	112,255	151,499	977,305	392,764	183,780	11,762	132,109	55,768
1983............	1,681,245	1,000,683	19,571	1,020,254	124,859	140,246	1,035,641	443,697	201,907	12,556	133,899	58,575
1984............	1,845,594	1,123,256	17,246	1,140,502	142,948	139,820	1,137,374	493,966	214,254	13,598	135,721	61,228
1985............	2,024,542	1,231,413	17,362	1,248,775	158,993	155,616	1,245,398	540,737	238,407	14,604	138,632	63,934
1986............	2,190,308	1,339,786	16,932	1,356,718	176,564	173,805	1,353,959	575,460	260,889	15,425	141,998	67,550
1987............	2,335,758	1,445,632	12,531	1,458,163	189,590	195,022	1,463,595	592,468	279,695	16,019	145,813	71,492
1988............	2,543,013	1,575,925	12,051	1,587,976	215,743	225,336	1,597,569	637,126	308,318	16,904	150,439	75,337
1989............	2,851,672	1,742,739	19,838	1,762,577	236,833	241,308	1,767,052	737,489	347,131	18,355	155,365	79,332
1990............	3,160,408	1,961,185	19,785	1,980,970	265,618	309,793	2,025,145	758,094	377,169	19,387	163,014	83,933
1991............	3,511,663	2,215,612	21,606	2,237,218	299,051	325,281	2,263,448	818,916	429,299	20,731	169,388	87,571
1992............	3,866,667	2,449,048	25,923	2,474,971	326,309	380,674	2,529,336	851,708	485,623	21,919	176,407	90,233
1993............	4,143,497	2,635,703	26,964	2,662,667	348,416	395,367	2,709,618	907,201	526,678	22,635	183,054	92,374
1994............	4,347,026	2,745,385	28,357	2,773,742	368,276	415,392	2,820,858	967,420	558,748	23,247	186,997	96,701
1995............	4,593,766	2,864,437	26,118	2,890,555	384,235	448,991	2,955,311	1,030,561	607,894	23,924	192,013	97,945
1996............	4,856,469	2,986,163	28,790	3,014,953	386,722	490,570	3,118,801	1,098,341	639,327	24,747	196,247	101,394
1997............	5,193,718	3,172,363	29,377	3,201,740	394,405	591,031	3,398,366	1,136,127	659,225	26,032	199,512	103,918
1998............	5,540,546	3,437,166	34,681	3,471,847	428,253	620,857	3,664,451	1,186,298	689,797	27,422	202,050	106,533
1999............	5,793,262	3,694,592	33,051	3,727,643	447,239	588,434	3,868,838	1,186,152	738,272	28,277	204,873	108,667
2000............	6,416,042	4,017,070	22,702	4,039,772	489,668	784,277	4,334,381	1,278,855	802,806	30,804	208,287	110,972
2001............	6,821,865	4,335,305	24,902	4,360,207	510,946	769,992	4,619,253	1,306,244	896,368	32,115	212,421	111,844
2002............	7,021,506	4,576,859	19,033	4,595,892	544,573	756,964	4,808,283	1,260,106	953,117	32,460	216,313	114,979
2003............	7,333,685	4,775,666	33,357	4,809,023	573,100	729,508	4,965,431	1,361,596	1,006,658	33,411	219,499	118,075
2004............	7,705,778	4,974,487	29,711	5,004,198	601,519	785,674	5,188,353	1,465,020	1,052,405	34,557	222,985	120,654
2005............	8,100,952	5,266,694	22,325	5,289,019	642,786	803,618	5,449,851	1,522,289	1,128,812	35,683	227,023	124,210
2006............	8,696,020	5,602,447	22,728	5,625,175	684,382	820,973	5,761,766	1,701,409	1,232,845	37,372	232,688	128,590
2007............	9,445,118	6,012,698	23,705	6,036,403	729,321	844,135	6,151,217	1,947,019	1,346,882	39,723	237,772	133,305
2008............	10,097,763	6,290,955	37,403	6,328,358	751,939	840,703	6,417,122	2,129,394	1,551,247	41,328	244,332	134,597
2009............	10,001,050	6,173,095	40,529	6,213,624	763,813	813,915	6,263,726	1,997,159	1,740,165	40,014	249,936	130,603
2010............	10,228,260	6,277,337	41,073	6,318,410	770,699	759,175	6,306,886	1,988,521	1,932,853	40,435	252,954	128,661
2011............	10,503,230	6,264,223	45,055	6,309,278	702,658	767,333	6,373,953	2,171,086	1,958,191	40,990	256,241	128,331
2012............	10,955,297	6,543,531	55,802	6,599,333	709,557	806,559	6,696,335	2,289,173	1,969,789	42,393	258,421	130,341
2013............	11,147,378	6,869,626	76,494	6,946,120	834,435	691,131	6,802,816	2,308,539	2,036,023	42,580	261,798	133,678
2014............	11,701,992	7,135,916	80,052	7,215,968	877,315	640,065	6,978,718	2,506,836	2,216,438	44,164	264,969	137,151
2015............	12,238,957	7,373,061	126,237	7,499,298	918,561	674,364	7,255,101	2,677,939	2,305,917	45,643	268,148	140,195
2016............	12,868,692	7,795,388	106,272	7,901,660	966,127	747,773	7,683,306	2,746,103	2,439,283	46,979	273,923	144,630
2017............	13,705,325	8,356,269	104,557	8,460,826	1,042,694	866,997	8,285,129	2,883,206	2,536,990	48,845	280,588	148,735
2018............	14,437,014	14,357,561	79,453	9,160,702	1,123,301	441,154	8,478,555	3,244,500	2,713,959	50,469	286,056	154,781
2019............	15,348,436	15,268,553	79,883	9,686,472	1,179,571	612,093	9,118,994	3,336,711	2,892,731	52,828	290,536	157,297

Personal Income and Employment by Area: Omaha-Council Bluffs, NE-IA

(Thousands of dollars, except as noted.)

Year	Personal income, total	Derivation of personal income									Per capita personal income (dollars)	Population (persons)	Total employment
		Earnings by place of work			Less: Contributions for government social insurance	Plus: Adjustment for residence	Equals: Net earnings by place of residence	Plus: Dividends, interest, and rent	Plus: Personal current transfer receipts			
		Nonfarm	Farm	Total									
1970	2,658,127	2,116,323	83,142	2,199,465	148,476	-19,851	2,031,138	421,134	205,855	4,275	621,778	297,197
1971	2,865,198	2,278,984	85,385	2,364,369	165,260	-20,673	2,178,436	452,896	233,866	4,521	633,774	301,792
1972	3,145,062	2,492,519	111,595	2,604,114	188,058	-20,522	2,395,534	491,936	257,592	4,886	643,739	308,000
1973	3,540,683	2,757,779	180,756	2,938,535	237,937	-19,679	2,680,919	551,880	307,884	5,461	648,329	318,343
1974	3,807,732	3,019,017	96,778	3,115,795	270,557	-15,226	2,830,012	622,810	354,910	5,832	652,850	324,237
1975	4,208,664	3,248,219	128,980	3,377,199	285,951	-9,372	3,081,876	680,934	445,854	6,484	649,131	321,665
1976	4,587,524	3,627,621	80,493	3,708,114	324,424	-5,899	3,377,791	735,142	474,591	6,989	656,376	330,324
1977	5,033,558	3,976,861	103,766	4,080,627	355,442	-3,453	3,721,732	816,588	495,238	7,683	655,126	339,330
1978	5,651,599	4,422,594	172,349	4,594,943	405,439	1,217	4,190,721	910,036	550,842	8,584	658,391	350,508
1979	6,191,919	4,917,955	97,417	5,015,372	469,203	3,890	4,550,059	1,023,908	617,952	9,414	657,736	359,581
1980	6,836,142	5,344,448	41,975	5,386,423	507,665	12,439	4,891,197	1,221,998	722,947	10,437	654,969	356,972
1981	7,651,517	5,791,831	125,271	5,917,102	586,703	-5,105	5,325,294	1,502,898	823,325	11,636	657,562	357,821
1982	8,299,628	6,153,201	105,617	6,258,818	635,310	-10,353	5,613,155	1,785,367	901,106	12,561	660,724	356,924
1983	8,698,224	6,553,252	44,620	6,597,872	685,649	-13,209	5,899,014	1,830,985	968,225	13,108	663,573	363,321
1984	9,612,823	7,210,488	122,261	7,332,749	774,541	-16,021	6,542,187	2,045,923	1,024,713	14,377	668,605	375,618
1985	10,246,847	7,681,521	209,689	7,891,210	844,222	-17,304	7,029,684	2,123,578	1,093,585	15,264	671,289	386,904
1986	10,667,961	8,085,405	163,430	8,248,835	913,550	-19,646	7,315,639	2,208,245	1,144,077	15,865	672,408	392,455
1987	11,206,099	8,573,341	156,780	8,730,121	961,734	-18,557	7,749,830	2,279,801	1,176,468	16,663	672,505	405,568
1988	11,895,105	9,150,158	145,083	9,295,241	1,067,328	-20,736	8,207,177	2,450,364	1,237,564	17,570	677,009	416,931
1989	12,670,227	9,747,638	149,828	9,897,466	1,136,374	-23,078	8,738,014	2,613,737	1,318,476	18,608	680,885	428,864
1990	13,701,977	10,481,838	161,014	10,642,852	1,272,819	-24,871	9,345,162	2,912,137	1,444,678	19,918	687,913	439,366
1991	14,311,637	10,972,034	159,207	11,131,241	1,344,446	-31,476	9,755,319	2,985,473	1,570,845	20,550	696,443	440,334
1992	15,219,607	11,682,087	200,167	11,882,254	1,412,508	-38,352	10,431,394	3,077,640	1,710,573	21,608	704,360	442,339
1993	15,732,403	12,162,962	87,622	12,250,584	1,473,216	-39,351	10,738,017	3,173,526	1,820,860	22,218	708,077	450,793
1994	16,888,275	13,022,545	185,663	13,208,208	1,581,812	-45,886	11,580,510	3,395,545	1,912,220	23,616	715,120	466,628
1995	18,195,224	14,101,757	62,935	14,164,692	1,687,153	-60,089	12,417,450	3,750,268	2,027,506	25,101	724,894	477,507
1996	19,651,089	15,125,447	249,890	15,375,337	1,798,568	-77,564	13,499,205	4,010,272	2,141,612	26,666	736,937	491,378
1997	20,730,341	16,040,743	188,442	16,229,185	1,935,009	-96,453	14,197,723	4,304,942	2,227,676	27,775	746,356	499,983
1998	22,317,953	17,165,317	127,937	17,293,254	2,053,627	-107,923	15,131,704	4,854,770	2,331,479	29,606	753,844	516,047
1999	23,726,698	18,473,195	120,821	18,594,016	2,193,107	-131,089	16,269,820	4,986,705	2,470,173	31,154	761,603	527,810
2000	25,328,726	19,566,422	151,266	19,717,688	2,296,117	-148,151	17,273,420	5,448,930	2,606,376	32,925	769,291	538,603
2001	26,240,528	20,350,850	154,642	20,505,492	2,366,596	-154,841	17,984,055	5,396,970	2,859,503	33,808	776,165	538,485
2002	27,145,954	21,112,244	111,612	21,223,856	2,448,152	-170,235	18,605,469	5,458,899	3,081,586	34,644	783,567	534,297
2003	28,062,873	21,876,681	174,387	22,051,068	2,554,928	-186,294	19,309,846	5,544,463	3,208,564	35,429	792,086	536,725
2004	30,041,243	23,444,927	327,929	23,772,856	2,689,023	-198,348	20,885,485	5,794,300	3,361,458	37,401	803,214	544,747
2005	31,099,257	23,975,309	251,121	24,226,430	2,834,357	-222,915	21,169,158	6,329,718	3,600,381	38,191	814,309	552,642
2006	33,554,482	25,803,315	156,705	25,960,020	3,071,262	-259,635	22,629,123	7,015,057	3,910,302	40,674	824,961	564,063
2007	35,538,195	26,674,043	230,270	26,904,313	3,151,848	-270,182	23,482,283	7,906,724	4,149,188	42,583	834,554	574,920
2008	37,399,658	27,894,336	315,976	28,210,312	3,278,580	-271,504	24,660,228	7,976,869	4,762,561	44,254	845,119	580,743
2009	36,836,001	28,122,045	372,711	28,494,756	3,284,992	-222,943	24,986,821	6,860,341	4,988,839	43,021	856,233	572,076
2010	38,934,563	29,558,213	287,637	29,845,850	3,386,299	-163,131	26,296,420	7,216,867	5,421,276	44,853	868,050	568,925
2011	42,514,737	32,199,498	518,964	32,718,462	3,115,419	-131,817	29,471,226	7,462,125	5,581,386	48,496	876,667	574,938
2012	44,504,461	33,383,704	376,024	33,759,728	3,209,086	-81,681	30,468,961	8,420,961	5,614,539	50,259	885,500	583,893
2013	43,649,618	32,914,446	685,413	33,599,859	3,667,182	-41,231	29,891,446	8,031,677	5,726,495	48,766	895,082	592,997
2014	47,050,932	35,736,425	391,652	36,128,077	3,838,137	-22,940	32,267,000	8,825,725	5,958,207	52,034	904,241	603,968
2015	49,051,027	37,094,110	397,265	37,491,375	4,028,226	-32,753	33,430,396	9,321,603	6,299,028	53,648	914,305	616,031
2016	49,182,895	36,883,631	298,020	37,181,651	4,097,280	-27,115	33,057,256	9,605,802	6,519,837	53,228	924,003	623,500
2017	50,973,238	38,326,039	233,858	38,559,897	4,288,003	-19,958	34,251,936	10,010,056	6,711,246	54,615	933,316	629,430
2018	53,987,434	53,833,730	153,704	40,372,789	4,466,177	21,647	35,928,259	10,819,595	7,239,580	57,374	940,970	639,207
2019	55,966,372	55,692,176	274,196	42,086,343	4,661,687	14,082	37,438,738	10,879,346	7,648,288	58,947	949,442	648,397

Personal Income and Employment by Area: Orlando-Kissimmee-Sanford, FL

(Thousands of dollars, except as noted.)

Year	Personal income, total	Earnings by place of work			Less: Contributions for government social insurance	Plus: Adjustment for residence	Equals: Net earnings by place of residence	Plus: Dividends, interest, and rent	Plus: Personal current transfer receipts	Per capita personal income (dollars)	Population (persons)	Total employment
		Nonfarm	Farm	Total								
1970	2,090,897	1,475,800	96,216	1,572,016	95,062	21,012	1,497,966	409,705	183,226	3,959	528,201	232,835
1971	2,437,079	1,741,054	108,392	1,849,446	117,558	18,945	1,750,833	464,677	221,569	4,362	558,715	252,062
1972	2,891,041	2,104,942	129,052	2,233,994	149,361	18,016	2,102,649	534,268	254,124	4,820	599,794	289,075
1973	3,413,913	2,562,815	130,585	2,693,400	208,780	12,732	2,497,352	613,688	302,873	5,300	644,122	323,363
1974	3,739,141	2,759,499	128,252	2,887,751	233,515	11,735	2,665,971	705,075	368,095	5,495	680,514	326,248
1975	4,010,805	2,825,531	150,953	2,976,484	235,913	6,317	2,746,888	771,442	492,475	5,816	689,597	315,687
1976	4,430,995	3,137,586	168,736	3,306,322	268,006	-2,942	3,035,374	849,409	546,212	6,286	704,932	327,025
1977	4,932,360	3,498,088	193,055	3,691,143	301,156	-6,855	3,383,132	958,454	590,774	6,797	725,644	344,104
1978	5,766,388	4,115,821	248,997	4,364,818	363,424	-17,613	3,983,781	1,132,571	650,036	7,698	749,095	375,240
1979	6,652,604	4,784,260	244,634	5,028,894	441,872	-25,285	4,561,737	1,328,287	762,580	8,519	780,907	396,668
1980	7,919,092	5,556,322	327,856	5,884,178	516,163	-37,826	5,330,189	1,669,404	919,499	9,738	813,225	418,551
1981	9,161,188	6,441,513	237,729	6,679,242	640,439	-53,329	5,985,474	2,096,766	1,078,948	10,835	845,498	441,015
1982	10,207,566	7,244,703	280,905	7,525,608	736,135	-95,159	6,694,314	2,288,017	1,225,235	11,635	877,348	463,274
1983	11,470,503	8,263,247	351,236	8,614,483	845,668	-136,517	7,632,298	2,500,647	1,337,558	12,520	916,199	494,692
1984	12,908,737	9,562,360	229,751	9,792,111	1,004,967	-189,229	8,597,915	2,891,393	1,419,429	13,480	957,644	537,857
1985	14,299,095	10,763,771	210,047	10,973,818	1,151,298	-247,651	9,574,869	3,183,673	1,540,553	14,352	996,347	573,928
1986	15,736,018	12,065,859	202,627	12,268,486	1,323,854	-324,095	10,620,537	3,454,366	1,661,115	15,153	1,038,445	615,381
1987	17,148,572	13,361,815	188,910	13,550,725	1,451,403	-416,091	11,683,231	3,695,828	1,769,513	15,847	1,082,164	636,135
1988	19,132,731	15,031,321	217,068	15,248,389	1,671,735	-502,114	13,074,540	4,096,041	1,962,150	17,083	1,119,977	672,874
1989	21,334,241	16,525,533	193,250	16,718,783	1,850,633	-604,232	14,263,918	4,815,612	2,254,711	18,212	1,171,413	713,886
1990	23,034,557	17,978,789	163,502	18,142,291	2,002,469	-715,400	15,424,422	5,092,778	2,517,357	18,565	1,240,724	739,630
1991	24,088,713	18,653,927	199,941	18,853,868	2,093,957	-655,956	16,103,955	5,128,714	2,856,044	18,771	1,283,301	737,044
1992	25,678,596	20,103,559	184,609	20,288,168	2,247,476	-718,926	17,321,766	5,012,544	3,344,286	19,470	1,318,902	755,421
1993	27,385,805	21,526,255	184,234	21,710,489	2,389,448	-795,098	18,525,943	5,196,230	3,663,632	20,180	1,357,101	788,146
1994	28,895,407	22,778,146	164,982	22,943,128	2,568,550	-881,051	19,493,527	5,465,882	3,935,998	20,724	1,394,315	813,296
1995	31,064,780	24,346,099	177,566	24,523,665	2,723,278	-924,260	20,876,127	5,917,631	4,271,022	21,748	1,428,415	840,455
1996	33,510,459	26,340,074	159,583	26,499,657	2,922,086	-1,002,497	22,575,074	6,370,388	4,564,997	22,802	1,469,619	885,718
1997	36,086,442	28,601,905	186,603	28,788,508	3,176,978	-1,156,342	24,455,188	6,834,139	4,797,115	23,739	1,520,145	935,200
1998	39,371,422	31,675,530	197,641	31,873,171	3,493,768	-1,353,022	27,026,381	7,412,408	4,932,633	25,111	1,567,910	987,408
1999	42,147,877	34,580,251	197,969	34,778,220	3,771,177	-1,523,649	29,483,394	7,527,134	5,137,349	26,211	1,607,993	1,032,530
2000	45,719,726	37,588,649	197,064	37,785,713	4,065,800	-1,766,325	31,953,588	8,212,423	5,553,715	27,594	1,656,890	1,071,873
2001	47,025,603	38,554,189	195,950	38,750,139	4,293,386	-1,885,195	32,571,558	8,297,416	6,156,629	27,495	1,710,359	1,083,195
2002	48,858,181	40,201,120	180,943	40,382,063	4,453,669	-1,991,426	33,936,968	8,091,216	6,829,997	27,755	1,760,345	1,082,826
2003	51,882,103	42,778,661	151,485	42,930,146	4,725,893	-2,128,007	36,076,246	8,402,195	7,403,662	28,640	1,811,544	1,121,204
2004	56,533,444	47,016,314	173,837	47,190,151	5,204,583	-2,405,502	39,580,066	8,944,985	8,008,393	30,102	1,878,077	1,179,837
2005	62,036,220	51,836,608	191,092	52,027,700	5,774,167	-2,824,754	43,428,779	9,949,951	8,657,490	31,719	1,955,794	1,250,750
2006	67,685,828	55,671,850	186,847	55,858,697	6,273,737	-3,067,033	46,517,927	11,834,570	9,333,331	33,507	2,020,057	1,303,562
2007	70,781,126	57,477,171	172,367	57,649,538	6,518,866	-3,228,492	47,902,180	12,854,047	10,024,899	34,395	2,057,865	1,340,657
2008	71,317,749	56,531,706	169,941	56,701,647	6,575,649	-3,254,856	46,871,142	12,818,973	11,627,634	34,164	2,087,489	1,316,027
2009	67,727,403	52,734,142	191,418	52,925,560	6,239,517	-2,975,078	43,710,965	11,151,608	12,864,830	32,069	2,111,917	1,253,746
2010	71,182,976	54,077,079	208,045	54,285,124	6,308,005	-2,970,898	45,006,221	11,650,356	14,526,399	33,274	2,139,317	1,254,307
2011	75,389,242	55,722,084	191,677	55,913,761	5,793,966	-3,008,672	47,111,123	12,992,157	15,285,962	34,639	2,176,424	1,295,438
2012	78,521,664	59,334,127	241,145	59,575,272	6,176,484	-3,339,394	50,059,394	13,278,663	15,183,607	35,252	2,227,414	1,335,426
2013	80,783,780	62,286,964	258,147	62,545,111	7,274,954	-3,478,600	51,791,557	13,264,061	15,728,162	35,554	2,272,175	1,374,927
2014	86,943,807	66,633,310	258,647	66,891,957	7,740,331	-3,616,739	55,534,887	14,498,597	16,910,323	37,348	2,327,929	1,438,261
2015	93,990,187	71,890,156	355,851	72,246,007	8,247,668	-3,887,361	60,110,978	15,963,229	17,915,980	39,310	2,391,028	1,504,918
2016	98,347,658	76,170,613	279,709	76,450,322	8,734,988	-4,388,703	63,326,631	16,376,417	18,644,610	40,087	2,453,333	1,567,954
2017	104,106,800	81,196,552	230,769	81,427,321	9,257,951	-4,815,351	67,354,019	17,147,047	19,605,734	41,480	2,509,831	1,616,966
2018	112,563,950	112,329,566	234,384	87,562,546	9,943,952	-5,140,740	72,477,854	19,266,910	20,819,186	43,717	2,574,838	1,727,406
2019	117,774,061	117,491,477	282,584	92,449,792	10,640,642	-5,548,158	76,260,992	19,528,329	21,984,740	45,156	2,608,147	1,776,688

Personal Income and Employment by Area: Oshkosh-Neenah, WI

(Thousands of dollars, except as noted.)

		Derivation of personal income										
		Earnings by place of work			Less: Contributions for government social insurance	Plus: Adjustment for residence	Equals: Net earnings by place of residence	Plus: Dividends, interest, and rent	Plus: Personal current transfer receipts	Per capita personal income (dollars)	Population (persons)	Total employment
Year	Personal income, total	Nonfarm	Farm	Total								
1970	507,667	426,630	8,094	434,724	31,107	-23,835	379,782	86,312	41,573	3,899	130,213	58,052
1971	532,948	441,404	8,734	450,138	33,318	-24,933	391,887	91,773	49,288	4,061	131,228	57,187
1972	575,795	483,646	9,278	492,924	38,654	-29,932	424,338	97,177	54,280	4,375	131,616	58,727
1973	639,027	543,038	10,572	553,610	50,124	-34,170	469,316	106,937	62,774	4,896	130,530	61,323
1974	705,292	592,502	11,118	603,620	56,715	-38,572	508,333	120,816	76,143	5,462	129,132	62,563
1975	778,467	645,338	11,649	656,987	60,727	-44,291	551,969	131,687	94,811	5,969	130,425	62,538
1976	856,350	723,404	8,554	731,958	69,024	-50,845	612,089	141,797	102,464	6,559	130,569	64,799
1977	959,040	814,165	15,525	829,690	76,947	-59,724	693,019	157,453	108,568	7,342	130,632	66,556
1978	1,064,165	917,622	12,376	929,998	89,300	-69,056	771,642	173,338	119,185	8,190	129,936	68,792
1979	1,189,621	1,022,195	16,827	1,039,022	103,272	-74,109	861,641	193,782	134,198	9,092	130,845	71,146
1980	1,310,233	1,082,976	17,305	1,100,281	109,167	-77,430	913,684	233,378	163,171	9,945	131,746	69,583
1981	1,429,996	1,157,088	12,466	1,169,554	124,390	-83,999	961,165	286,401	182,430	10,888	131,335	68,777
1982	1,521,673	1,206,581	10,160	1,216,741	131,822	-88,737	996,182	319,574	205,917	11,587	131,330	68,279
1983	1,632,491	1,303,772	1,762	1,305,534	142,548	-99,589	1,063,397	346,379	222,715	12,411	131,539	68,795
1984	1,790,336	1,441,315	8,571	1,449,886	161,739	-112,060	1,176,087	386,301	227,948	13,450	133,106	72,636
1985	1,903,171	1,541,980	7,785	1,549,765	174,897	-120,610	1,254,258	408,876	240,037	14,180	134,219	74,641
1986	2,006,905	1,642,673	9,520	1,652,193	186,159	-131,553	1,334,481	425,127	247,297	14,825	135,372	76,626
1987	2,120,623	1,763,203	11,760	1,774,963	197,085	-142,325	1,435,553	431,070	254,000	15,556	136,319	78,525
1988	2,251,572	1,896,669	5,323	1,901,992	218,356	-153,409	1,530,227	456,815	264,530	16,297	138,161	80,578
1989	2,451,696	1,990,637	14,624	2,005,261	228,125	-145,417	1,631,719	534,137	285,840	17,638	139,004	81,836
1990	2,634,503	2,184,047	12,963	2,197,010	261,182	-166,885	1,768,943	558,232	307,328	18,702	140,871	86,195
1991	2,754,628	2,332,957	9,998	2,342,955	280,841	-194,163	1,867,951	556,143	330,534	19,228	143,263	88,504
1992	3,001,652	2,579,159	13,232	2,592,391	306,477	-233,981	2,051,933	591,435	358,284	20,637	145,449	90,993
1993	3,105,381	2,706,721	5,775	2,712,496	323,819	-260,812	2,127,865	603,017	374,499	20,978	148,031	92,431
1994	3,316,816	2,856,093	15,263	2,871,356	343,770	-266,661	2,260,925	666,747	389,144	22,280	148,867	94,352
1995	3,517,557	3,058,483	6,186	3,064,669	367,889	-301,646	2,395,134	710,844	411,579	23,338	150,725	97,363
1996	3,688,179	3,156,890	12,232	3,169,122	377,150	-290,469	2,501,503	761,112	425,564	24,231	152,206	98,410
1997	3,865,559	3,337,565	7,138	3,344,703	396,056	-317,706	2,630,941	795,319	439,299	25,179	153,525	99,045
1998	4,140,167	3,639,227	12,837	3,652,064	429,602	-409,274	2,813,188	877,920	449,059	26,807	154,444	101,732
1999	4,295,570	3,890,440	12,225	3,902,665	455,407	-478,738	2,968,520	862,872	464,178	27,571	155,801	103,893
2000	4,556,160	4,120,342	7,322	4,127,664	478,865	-475,679	3,173,120	885,374	497,666	29,001	157,103	106,300
2001	4,720,497	4,253,394	6,496	4,259,890	493,270	-493,772	3,272,848	897,374	550,275	29,846	158,163	106,369
2002	4,827,847	4,403,250	8,801	4,412,051	506,592	-551,264	3,354,195	878,165	595,487	30,338	159,134	107,051
2003	4,979,985	4,497,772	15,900	4,513,672	517,225	-572,458	3,423,989	946,716	609,280	31,234	159,440	106,191
2004	5,277,295	4,765,542	16,303	4,781,845	546,676	-526,104	3,709,065	939,831	628,399	32,956	160,130	107,034
2005	5,432,589	4,907,219	17,335	4,924,554	566,068	-562,694	3,795,792	964,484	672,313	33,649	161,451	108,304
2006	5,788,640	5,057,303	12,241	5,069,544	587,797	-583,094	3,898,653	1,171,054	718,933	35,573	162,727	109,149
2007	6,010,236	5,274,139	21,853	5,295,992	608,388	-612,950	4,074,654	1,164,645	770,937	36,640	164,037	110,165
2008	6,166,334	5,431,020	27,613	5,458,633	634,769	-686,083	4,137,781	1,145,177	883,376	37,392	164,910	111,420
2009	5,990,500	5,240,799	8,684	5,249,483	615,821	-690,048	3,943,614	1,027,892	1,018,994	35,994	166,429	107,969
2010	6,210,543	5,461,114	14,164	5,475,278	648,600	-737,987	4,088,691	1,035,816	1,086,036	37,175	167,064	108,916
2011	6,573,804	5,674,155	28,631	5,702,786	598,929	-814,861	4,288,996	1,229,354	1,055,454	39,247	167,497	111,014
2012	6,777,266	5,827,332	26,526	5,853,858	609,455	-798,697	4,445,706	1,263,593	1,067,967	40,210	168,545	110,642
2013	6,731,435	5,995,907	27,112	6,023,019	709,621	-885,012	4,428,386	1,203,907	1,099,142	39,765	169,279	111,756
2014	7,020,323	6,152,441	27,704	6,180,145	724,118	-872,138	4,583,889	1,292,962	1,143,472	41,468	169,295	112,469
2015	7,342,592	6,334,659	27,683	6,362,342	746,488	-878,048	4,737,806	1,400,373	1,204,413	43,407	169,157	113,091
2016	7,559,233	6,569,525	15,758	6,585,283	767,977	-936,803	4,880,503	1,463,679	1,215,051	44,583	169,555	115,484
2017	7,813,771	6,794,273	17,800	6,812,073	802,647	-986,186	5,023,240	1,520,884	1,269,647	45,852	170,414	116,711
2018	8,197,668	8,183,664	14,004	6,984,866	807,478	-973,405	5,203,983	1,649,227	1,344,458	47,974	170,878	116,253
2019	8,470,908	8,445,548	25,360	7,245,864	840,304	-1,001,005	5,404,555	1,660,570	1,405,783	49,276	171,907	116,006

Personal Income and Employment by Area: Owensboro, KY

(Thousands of dollars, except as noted.)

Year	Personal income, total	Earnings by place of work			Less: Contributions for government social insurance	Plus: Adjustment for residence	Equals: Net earnings by place of residence	Plus: Dividends, interest, and rent	Plus: Personal current transfer receipts	Per capita personal income (dollars)	Population (persons)	Total employment
		Nonfarm	Farm	Total								
1970	320,584	255,753	11,629	267,382	17,575	-1,232	248,575	41,388	30,621	3,348	95,768	42,800
1971	346,680	270,549	12,931	283,480	19,049	751	265,182	45,118	36,380	3,575	96,960	42,627
1972	385,742	296,311	15,826	312,137	22,120	6,029	296,046	49,231	40,465	3,968	97,215	43,642
1973	428,085	325,627	25,247	350,874	28,023	3,235	326,086	54,150	47,849	4,364	98,090	45,008
1974	476,524	359,775	24,164	383,939	32,271	3,164	354,832	62,435	59,257	4,814	98,996	46,164
1975	518,329	385,142	16,717	401,859	34,050	5,519	373,328	70,276	74,725	5,193	99,816	44,188
1976	577,142	433,257	18,542	451,799	38,732	8,008	421,075	77,790	78,277	5,749	100,389	45,399
1977	648,219	481,530	26,841	508,371	42,776	13,433	479,028	88,556	80,635	6,433	100,759	46,935
1978	726,593	560,633	15,482	576,115	51,356	14,556	539,315	101,407	85,871	7,125	101,985	49,522
1979	822,467	625,831	19,612	645,443	59,521	21,366	607,288	116,545	98,634	7,969	103,209	49,610
1980	913,637	691,076	3,400	694,476	66,050	19,807	648,233	148,122	117,282	8,791	103,927	49,868
1981	1,026,691	748,621	22,733	771,354	76,964	15,095	709,485	183,996	133,210	9,849	104,247	49,877
1982	1,081,238	764,057	15,520	779,577	79,631	19,445	719,391	215,285	146,562	10,324	104,731	49,194
1983	1,122,302	830,883	-22,117	808,766	86,159	17,917	740,524	224,725	157,053	10,646	105,422	50,297
1984	1,254,372	876,692	34,038	910,730	93,698	20,473	837,505	248,390	168,477	11,775	106,527	51,708
1985	1,284,177	897,363	21,806	919,169	97,176	20,509	842,502	262,378	179,297	12,092	106,197	51,751
1986	1,310,777	923,335	17,374	940,709	103,153	16,489	854,045	266,964	189,768	12,396	105,746	52,395
1987	1,352,898	963,108	15,413	978,521	106,507	15,735	887,749	268,309	196,840	12,878	105,054	52,141
1988	1,448,635	1,047,980	17,796	1,065,776	116,803	14,206	963,179	276,846	208,610	13,859	104,527	52,711
1989	1,567,523	1,095,825	47,480	1,143,305	124,637	14,288	1,032,956	303,753	230,814	14,992	104,559	54,131
1990	1,650,826	1,158,564	42,261	1,200,825	136,171	14,063	1,078,717	321,599	250,510	15,765	104,716	54,954
1991	1,713,422	1,198,480	33,325	1,231,805	142,422	11,556	1,100,939	329,770	282,713	16,288	105,194	54,878
1992	1,837,714	1,278,481	56,361	1,334,842	149,956	7,763	1,192,649	337,646	307,419	17,334	106,017	55,861
1993	1,901,877	1,355,874	45,428	1,401,302	162,107	4,918	1,244,113	343,251	314,513	17,834	106,646	57,276
1994	2,025,354	1,444,381	53,978	1,498,359	176,059	1,540	1,323,840	368,425	333,089	18,834	107,539	59,266
1995	2,093,512	1,502,993	31,868	1,534,861	184,350	-1,103	1,349,408	385,892	358,212	19,342	108,234	60,800
1996	2,197,463	1,534,198	64,763	1,598,961	187,131	-1,830	1,410,000	410,924	376,539	20,239	108,573	60,962
1997	2,338,396	1,673,182	43,614	1,716,796	202,595	-10,643	1,503,558	436,786	398,052	21,483	108,851	62,246
1998	2,422,470	1,740,643	29,201	1,769,844	211,952	-7,994	1,549,898	465,614	406,958	22,209	109,075	62,960
1999	2,502,976	1,836,875	26,715	1,863,590	222,740	-6,958	1,633,892	442,589	426,495	22,851	109,533	63,701
2000	2,691,093	1,923,184	62,272	1,985,456	226,118	-9,334	1,750,004	485,685	455,404	24,450	110,064	64,172
2001	2,756,526	1,962,014	63,219	2,025,233	229,522	-7,224	1,788,487	472,960	495,079	25,061	109,991	62,827
2002	2,836,736	2,037,694	19,692	2,057,386	236,200	3,721	1,824,907	478,611	533,218	25,744	110,190	62,105
2003	2,927,792	2,090,266	36,440	2,126,706	240,168	11,658	1,898,196	481,737	547,859	26,440	110,735	62,423
2004	3,099,842	2,194,609	82,131	2,276,740	247,387	19,432	2,048,785	462,932	588,125	27,927	110,999	62,784
2005	3,259,546	2,276,443	111,464	2,387,907	257,871	24,801	2,154,837	474,859	629,850	29,242	111,469	62,984
2006	3,474,230	2,426,690	88,854	2,515,544	274,462	28,796	2,269,878	520,514	683,838	30,978	112,152	64,127
2007	3,712,221	2,585,815	67,895	2,653,710	291,722	37,128	2,399,116	573,771	739,334	32,881	112,900	65,389
2008	4,120,808	2,849,689	80,703	2,930,392	316,142	37,696	2,651,946	632,962	835,900	36,258	113,651	65,107
2009	3,963,880	2,626,638	109,955	2,736,593	304,199	18,574	2,450,968	586,705	926,207	34,654	114,385	63,026
2010	4,033,451	2,711,610	62,215	2,773,825	308,368	10,889	2,476,346	573,218	983,887	35,143	114,772	63,217
2011	4,192,636	2,710,574	120,680	2,831,254	279,257	-4,234	2,547,763	649,090	995,783	36,370	115,276	64,634
2012	4,219,654	2,772,574	94,933	2,867,507	293,757	-42,535	2,531,215	698,169	990,270	36,373	116,012	66,237
2013	4,321,707	2,840,277	205,737	3,046,014	340,569	-62,668	2,642,777	665,963	1,012,967	37,136	116,374	66,029
2014	4,498,930	2,935,882	136,093	3,071,975	354,101	-60,134	2,657,740	742,317	1,098,873	38,612	116,516	66,080
2015	4,614,698	3,067,784	74,806	3,142,590	371,985	-81,837	2,688,768	767,815	1,158,115	39,305	117,408	67,052
2016	4,542,969	3,034,923	50,907	3,085,830	375,396	-78,978	2,631,456	741,405	1,170,108	38,525	117,923	67,691
2017	4,663,386	3,056,417	81,231	3,137,648	383,546	-66,296	2,687,806	773,730	1,201,850	39,395	118,376	68,167
2018	4,882,979	4,803,895	79,084	3,258,399	395,526	-73,199	2,789,674	846,783	1,246,522	41,075	118,879	67,858
2019	4,999,502	4,932,489	67,013	3,330,922	401,835	-84,182	2,844,905	857,182	1,297,415	41,858	119,440	68,091

Personal Income and Employment by Area: Oxnard-Thousand Oaks-Ventura, CA

(Thousands of dollars, except as noted.)

| Year | Personal income, total | Derivation of personal income | | | | | | | | | Per capita personal income (dollars) | Population (persons) | Total employment |
| | | Earnings by place of work | | | Less: Contributions for government social insurance | Plus: Adjustment for residence | Equals: Net earnings by place of residence | Plus: Dividends, interest, and rent | Plus: Personal current transfer receipts | | | |
		Nonfarm	Farm	Total								
1970	1,675,029	993,450	70,144	1,063,594	59,659	266,591	1,270,526	276,675	127,828	4,394	381,174	135,394
1971	1,846,661	1,087,352	77,954	1,165,306	66,834	287,697	1,386,169	309,432	151,060	4,667	395,691	140,085
1972	2,086,155	1,221,184	91,278	1,312,462	79,079	340,746	1,574,129	342,236	169,790	5,107	408,523	147,656
1973	2,368,468	1,352,274	129,273	1,481,547	99,113	401,405	1,783,839	391,554	193,075	5,646	419,461	155,861
1974	2,697,313	1,508,134	139,016	1,647,150	114,703	473,033	2,005,480	454,295	237,538	6,217	433,885	164,301
1975	3,067,325	1,696,502	143,245	1,839,747	128,038	534,204	2,245,913	512,953	308,459	6,833	448,918	171,738
1976	3,415,649	1,894,313	110,060	2,004,373	145,545	635,485	2,494,313	565,057	356,279	7,418	460,485	176,285
1977	3,925,078	2,169,151	148,233	2,317,384	171,933	764,228	2,909,679	637,153	378,246	8,200	478,695	188,053
1978	4,631,103	2,530,991	191,946	2,722,937	206,263	940,953	3,457,627	755,761	417,715	9,373	494,086	202,771
1979	5,233,301	2,859,840	153,355	3,013,195	245,491	1,153,980	3,921,684	847,914	463,703	10,218	512,189	213,342
1980	6,075,966	3,212,435	161,842	3,374,277	270,790	1,379,112	4,482,599	1,045,953	547,414	11,403	532,827	221,151
1981	6,889,811	3,585,011	155,419	3,740,430	327,718	1,547,680	4,960,392	1,278,549	650,870	12,610	546,389	225,479
1982	7,502,143	3,908,134	206,124	4,114,258	366,910	1,616,401	5,363,749	1,420,477	717,917	13,346	562,142	229,893
1983	8,134,982	4,256,520	213,837	4,470,357	413,523	1,741,025	5,797,859	1,578,228	758,895	14,133	575,586	237,557
1984	9,076,701	4,810,054	238,127	5,048,181	488,379	1,915,735	6,475,537	1,793,120	808,044	15,416	588,790	248,225
1985	9,880,063	5,326,172	217,602	5,543,774	551,106	2,083,634	7,076,302	1,922,421	881,340	16,390	602,819	260,105
1986	10,817,704	5,881,893	317,243	6,199,136	616,305	2,255,143	7,837,974	2,027,747	951,983	17,578	615,422	270,559
1987	11,796,155	6,527,630	387,110	6,914,740	694,225	2,491,653	8,712,168	2,097,563	986,424	18,663	632,062	287,425
1988	12,944,377	7,317,836	445,607	7,763,443	804,748	2,646,744	9,605,439	2,282,859	1,056,079	19,888	650,851	305,846
1989	13,967,127	7,805,015	427,647	8,232,662	870,346	2,809,535	10,171,851	2,646,108	1,149,168	21,013	664,692	317,976
1990	14,970,554	8,453,809	465,101	8,918,910	938,783	3,079,208	11,059,335	2,664,566	1,246,653	22,340	670,117	327,267
1991	15,621,492	8,925,682	438,537	9,364,219	993,420	3,157,377	11,528,176	2,696,861	1,396,455	23,119	675,706	332,915
1992	16,207,128	9,482,041	285,341	9,767,382	1,048,851	3,190,239	11,908,770	2,707,122	1,591,236	23,690	684,143	332,193
1993	16,983,115	9,803,744	414,090	10,217,834	1,084,064	3,310,079	12,443,849	2,855,184	1,684,082	24,615	689,943	335,316
1994	17,665,815	10,297,146	358,400	10,655,546	1,145,221	3,373,256	12,883,581	3,070,044	1,712,190	25,291	698,509	344,984
1995	18,835,782	10,587,326	441,879	11,029,205	1,164,919	3,642,324	13,506,610	3,526,477	1,802,695	26,775	703,486	352,089
1996	19,600,729	11,124,804	332,740	11,457,544	1,195,213	3,721,707	13,984,038	3,712,716	1,903,975	27,598	710,215	358,399
1997	21,018,291	11,784,445	413,120	12,197,565	1,254,224	4,153,317	15,096,658	3,977,527	1,944,106	29,147	721,107	357,142
1998	22,051,972	12,631,099	406,776	13,037,875	1,339,466	4,085,732	15,784,141	4,223,387	2,044,444	30,176	730,779	371,587
1999	23,607,596	13,854,545	461,734	14,316,279	1,451,002	4,191,007	17,056,284	4,390,702	2,160,610	31,758	743,357	385,759
2000	25,822,440	15,580,589	424,619	16,005,208	1,609,561	4,375,904	18,771,551	4,765,204	2,285,685	34,134	756,506	395,387
2001	27,357,448	17,130,336	305,730	17,436,066	1,802,749	4,511,675	20,144,992	4,676,319	2,536,137	35,683	766,689	407,454
2002	28,144,639	17,881,679	370,195	18,251,874	1,906,699	4,557,627	20,902,802	4,520,484	2,721,353	36,107	779,489	415,664
2003	29,797,711	19,211,972	366,809	19,578,781	2,070,441	4,495,294	22,003,634	4,899,766	2,894,311	37,811	788,070	422,993
2004	31,884,532	20,618,575	523,616	21,142,191	2,296,975	4,832,256	23,677,472	5,194,819	3,012,241	40,157	793,994	428,584
2005	33,177,599	21,517,750	509,445	22,027,195	2,412,869	4,686,667	24,300,993	5,692,643	3,183,963	41,775	794,197	435,416
2006	35,582,708	22,294,218	648,308	22,942,526	2,451,966	4,999,418	25,489,978	6,664,577	3,428,153	44,580	798,183	441,017
2007	36,938,844	22,953,655	622,807	23,576,462	2,477,639	4,986,481	26,085,304	7,203,644	3,649,896	46,172	800,027	447,553
2008	37,152,444	22,245,760	667,213	22,912,973	2,459,404	5,216,431	25,670,000	7,263,945	4,218,499	46,075	806,353	441,320
2009	36,256,168	22,053,638	848,878	22,902,516	2,449,366	4,578,077	25,031,227	6,537,790	4,687,151	44,479	815,130	427,303
2010	37,868,923	23,195,123	931,952	24,127,075	2,463,452	4,584,226	26,247,849	6,414,006	5,207,068	45,885	825,298	424,867
2011	39,908,241	23,979,345	824,729	24,804,074	2,298,787	4,728,110	27,233,397	7,405,012	5,269,832	48,025	830,990	430,069
2012	41,704,333	24,457,367	1,054,420	25,511,787	2,329,430	5,283,274	28,465,631	7,956,647	5,282,055	49,937	835,143	438,470
2013	42,313,336	24,859,934	1,248,104	26,108,038	2,669,771	5,267,946	28,706,213	8,118,977	5,488,146	50,363	840,175	446,562
2014	44,708,130	25,779,490	1,207,222	26,986,712	2,768,935	5,575,070	29,792,847	9,119,398	5,795,885	52,925	844,749	456,390
2015	47,194,829	26,707,051	1,464,754	28,171,805	2,846,311	6,183,950	31,509,444	9,468,408	6,216,977	55,594	848,925	460,851
2016	48,381,341	26,921,408	1,230,371	28,151,779	2,899,712	6,524,333	31,776,400	10,166,379	6,438,562	56,846	851,096	463,261
2017	50,550,958	27,829,752	1,347,770	29,177,522	2,996,371	7,263,325	33,444,476	10,627,314	6,479,168	59,178	854,223	468,725
2018	52,500,391	51,486,202	1,014,189	29,441,601	3,101,166	7,202,832	33,543,267	12,080,848	6,876,276	61,900	848,142	473,480
2019	54,749,053	53,503,883	1,245,170	31,147,731	3,292,872	7,263,657	35,118,516	12,243,854	7,386,683	64,715	846,006	482,248

Personal Income and Employment by Area: Palm Bay-Melbourne-Titusville, FL

(Thousands of dollars, except as noted.)

Year	Personal income, total	Earnings by place of work			Less: Contributions for government social insurance	Plus: Adjustment for residence	Equals: Net earnings by place of residence	Plus: Dividends, interest, and rent	Plus: Personal current transfer receipts	Per capita personal income (dollars)	Population (persons)	Total employment
		Nonfarm	Farm	Total								
1970	960,656	824,515	3,649	828,164	48,418	-25,113	754,633	150,345	55,678	4,183	229,660	96,024
1971	997,539	816,909	5,158	822,067	49,360	-19,279	753,428	173,574	70,537	4,305	231,701	92,542
1972	1,098,130	882,554	7,339	889,893	56,797	-17,371	815,725	196,562	85,843	4,764	230,503	95,402
1973	1,214,884	957,791	9,272	967,063	71,295	-13,390	882,378	228,012	104,494	5,100	238,222	101,054
1974	1,288,875	973,540	8,879	982,419	75,325	-11,004	896,090	263,759	129,026	5,405	238,464	99,316
1975	1,425,801	1,047,870	6,844	1,054,714	80,238	-13,507	960,969	297,553	167,279	5,910	241,241	97,287
1976	1,545,551	1,120,597	6,191	1,126,788	87,661	-10,513	1,028,614	331,243	185,694	6,419	240,791	98,836
1977	1,722,462	1,250,238	6,385	1,256,623	100,298	-9,675	1,146,650	375,662	200,150	7,134	241,451	103,907
1978	2,011,797	1,458,540	7,983	1,466,523	120,935	-9,244	1,336,344	450,487	224,966	8,014	251,031	113,104
1979	2,362,778	1,724,273	10,283	1,734,556	150,984	-10,221	1,573,351	528,441	260,986	8,983	263,038	121,837
1980	2,823,655	2,014,927	13,200	2,028,127	178,073	-8,382	1,841,672	669,611	312,372	10,243	275,664	129,188
1981	3,259,509	2,273,293	9,240	2,282,533	216,346	-8,218	2,057,969	830,821	370,719	11,398	285,963	133,908
1982	3,581,183	2,479,572	12,079	2,491,651	243,013	-9,954	2,238,684	918,016	424,483	11,973	299,098	138,412
1983	3,982,208	2,772,922	13,416	2,786,338	277,932	-13,214	2,495,192	1,018,054	468,962	12,846	310,006	147,424
1984	4,530,774	3,187,974	10,245	3,198,219	330,120	-16,119	2,851,980	1,168,255	510,539	14,037	322,780	159,722
1985	5,015,727	3,545,117	10,256	3,555,373	375,182	-15,706	3,164,485	1,289,170	562,072	14,886	336,935	170,814
1986	5,347,897	3,734,718	9,107	3,743,825	407,335	-9,341	3,327,149	1,398,322	622,426	15,315	349,183	175,694
1987	5,767,566	4,048,894	9,653	4,058,547	437,498	-5,669	3,615,380	1,483,410	668,776	16,038	359,628	176,540
1988	6,370,868	4,501,813	15,615	4,517,428	500,038	-4,057	4,013,333	1,616,634	740,901	17,147	371,547	187,777
1989	7,150,560	4,916,005	14,347	4,930,352	551,202	-599	4,378,551	1,914,197	857,812	18,601	384,423	196,440
1990	7,626,357	5,236,681	14,051	5,250,732	585,860	749	4,665,621	1,995,220	965,516	18,914	403,209	202,232
1991	8,022,074	5,533,472	16,213	5,549,685	624,172	-2,683	4,922,830	1,996,133	1,103,111	19,306	415,512	203,022
1992	8,561,401	5,919,345	14,610	5,933,955	666,016	5,229	5,273,168	2,006,707	1,281,526	20,117	425,584	203,939
1993	8,923,620	6,109,457	13,347	6,122,804	685,358	23,368	5,460,814	2,077,915	1,384,891	20,454	436,282	206,630
1994	9,295,180	6,252,356	12,453	6,264,809	725,784	44,783	5,583,808	2,208,483	1,502,889	20,926	444,198	209,999
1995	9,788,712	6,407,829	11,076	6,418,905	745,828	68,157	5,741,234	2,417,623	1,629,855	21,690	451,310	211,373
1996	10,219,494	6,551,493	8,958	6,560,451	766,054	98,717	5,893,114	2,578,897	1,747,483	22,417	455,889	215,068
1997	10,930,629	6,982,652	10,210	6,992,862	816,791	123,097	6,299,168	2,788,663	1,842,798	23,675	461,686	223,138
1998	11,546,814	7,393,662	14,001	7,407,663	859,734	163,082	6,711,011	2,926,447	1,909,356	24,693	467,624	230,763
1999	12,004,015	7,753,218	15,783	7,769,001	894,939	205,353	7,079,415	2,905,440	2,019,160	25,425	472,138	234,135
2000	13,216,815	8,632,969	16,542	8,649,511	983,084	232,838	7,899,265	3,165,267	2,152,283	27,661	477,819	242,259
2001	13,811,392	8,990,141	16,267	9,006,408	1,008,906	244,642	8,242,144	3,205,939	2,363,309	28,393	486,429	244,989
2002	14,268,508	9,349,789	17,678	9,367,467	1,046,382	260,098	8,581,183	3,126,128	2,561,197	28,801	495,425	244,592
2003	15,194,100	9,983,007	14,822	9,997,829	1,121,554	280,756	9,157,031	3,285,328	2,751,741	30,096	504,847	252,217
2004	16,382,833	10,963,742	14,128	10,977,870	1,236,580	302,271	10,043,561	3,340,307	2,998,965	31,583	518,722	261,987
2005	17,623,694	11,895,394	18,420	11,913,814	1,342,369	332,231	10,903,676	3,538,265	3,181,753	33,258	529,907	272,273
2006	18,875,425	12,542,757	16,268	12,559,025	1,437,776	374,129	11,495,378	3,949,280	3,430,767	35,272	535,138	278,457
2007	19,589,968	12,590,196	11,595	12,601,791	1,460,937	430,799	11,571,653	4,366,303	3,652,012	36,297	539,719	277,306
2008	20,098,093	12,571,473	9,083	12,580,556	1,483,129	446,931	11,544,358	4,430,405	4,123,330	37,056	542,378	269,411
2009	19,276,155	12,116,437	9,964	12,126,401	1,454,584	388,127	11,059,944	3,797,641	4,418,570	35,558	542,109	258,623
2010	19,983,099	12,470,738	16,995	12,487,733	1,477,339	374,803	11,385,197	3,850,868	4,747,034	36,735	543,976	256,563
2011	20,799,080	12,526,890	15,492	12,542,382	1,337,808	379,112	11,583,686	4,242,327	4,973,067	38,203	544,439	257,435
2012	20,812,141	12,499,163	23,123	12,522,286	1,355,247	416,931	11,583,970	4,239,008	4,989,163	38,027	547,293	258,429
2013	20,861,592	12,484,141	21,762	12,505,903	1,527,213	430,724	11,409,414	4,319,446	5,132,732	37,878	550,754	260,570
2014	21,853,051	12,664,234	25,401	12,689,635	1,553,150	479,394	11,615,879	4,778,678	5,458,494	39,284	556,277	265,389
2015	23,259,278	13,416,966	35,930	13,452,896	1,627,559	498,644	12,323,981	5,142,201	5,793,096	41,035	566,822	272,836
2016	24,297,936	13,970,526	28,404	13,998,930	1,706,541	524,430	12,816,819	5,447,145	6,033,972	42,045	577,899	279,817
2017	25,682,911	14,879,793	34,173	14,913,966	1,812,870	556,795	13,657,891	5,688,296	6,336,724	43,592	589,162	287,251
2018	27,354,878	27,337,763	17,115	15,987,546	1,937,460	609,970	14,660,056	6,108,114	6,586,708	45,959	595,203	303,723
2019	28,839,354	28,819,067	20,287	17,121,769	2,094,453	607,565	15,634,881	6,191,313	7,013,160	47,911	601,942	313,828

Personal Income and Employment by Area: Panama City, FL

(Thousands of dollars, except as noted.)

| Year | Personal income, total | Derivation of personal income | | | | | | | | Per capita personal income (dollars) | Population (persons) | Total employment |
| | | Earnings by place of work | | | Less: Contributions for government social insurance | Plus: Adjustment for residence | Equals: Net earnings by place of residence | Plus: Dividends, interest, and rent | Plus: Personal current transfer receipts | | | |
		Nonfarm	Farm	Total								
1970	295,964	238,906	174	239,080	14,055	-1,960	223,065	50,356	22,543	3,450	85,792	35,240
1971	323,060	256,606	210	256,816	15,682	-1,926	239,208	57,039	26,813	3,659	88,300	35,430
1972	358,760	283,390	210	283,600	18,042	-2,102	263,456	63,199	32,105	4,003	89,621	36,514
1973	411,431	324,755	439	325,194	23,516	-2,673	299,005	73,167	39,259	4,485	91,744	39,716
1974	470,682	368,908	796	369,704	28,237	-3,757	337,710	85,311	47,661	4,868	96,694	42,168
1975	527,353	402,200	793	402,993	30,812	-4,703	367,478	97,201	62,674	5,299	99,527	42,716
1976	596,019	459,916	656	460,572	36,025	-7,145	417,402	108,418	70,199	5,825	102,320	45,048
1977	644,969	491,314	448	491,762	38,689	-7,051	446,022	121,499	77,448	6,205	103,944	46,176
1978	740,384	560,790	341	561,131	44,703	-8,585	507,843	147,486	85,055	7,035	105,250	48,370
1979	818,099	611,933	277	612,210	51,796	-10,624	549,790	170,495	97,814	7,572	108,048	49,098
1980	930,336	674,518	301	674,819	57,183	-9,282	608,354	205,110	116,872	8,538	108,965	50,033
1981	1,064,830	767,481	170	767,651	70,068	-10,389	687,194	242,336	135,300	9,591	111,027	51,966
1982	1,168,232	826,531	304	826,835	76,994	-12,482	737,359	275,842	155,031	10,187	114,679	53,880
1983	1,281,370	909,719	275	909,994	86,226	-13,872	809,896	300,923	170,551	10,964	116,871	56,082
1984	1,444,872	1,039,607	321	1,039,928	101,135	-17,861	920,932	341,323	182,617	12,020	120,204	60,969
1985	1,574,306	1,136,205	375	1,136,580	113,154	-19,154	1,004,272	372,831	197,203	12,605	124,892	65,284
1986	1,702,034	1,225,373	537	1,225,910	125,384	-19,352	1,081,174	407,338	213,522	13,153	129,400	67,908
1987	1,780,431	1,279,057	621	1,279,678	129,866	-18,300	1,131,512	421,750	227,169	13,412	132,748	67,445
1988	1,929,509	1,387,241	565	1,387,806	145,912	-17,557	1,224,337	456,052	249,120	14,257	135,342	69,027
1989	2,086,314	1,446,472	279	1,446,751	154,759	-16,512	1,275,480	522,751	288,083	15,202	137,241	70,569
1990	2,262,923	1,569,300	138	1,569,438	168,708	-18,841	1,381,889	559,897	321,137	16,302	138,809	73,233
1991	2,432,462	1,696,540	-25	1,696,515	183,471	-22,112	1,490,932	576,921	364,609	17,200	141,422	74,997
1992	2,600,719	1,805,051	-263	1,804,788	196,082	-25,506	1,583,200	602,194	415,325	17,957	144,829	76,244
1993	2,786,071	1,917,383	-32	1,917,351	208,335	-28,973	1,680,043	659,091	446,937	18,669	149,232	78,539
1994	2,901,686	1,999,541	372	1,999,913	219,331	-31,371	1,749,211	668,922	483,553	19,053	152,295	79,835
1995	3,142,205	2,115,487	653	2,116,140	229,649	-33,393	1,853,098	747,651	541,456	20,285	154,905	81,750
1996	3,308,369	2,239,376	1,170	2,240,546	241,829	-37,568	1,961,149	796,173	551,047	20,981	157,681	84,598
1997	3,470,376	2,350,753	1,766	2,352,519	254,651	-40,080	2,057,788	834,409	578,179	21,769	159,420	85,586
1998	3,627,425	2,460,643	1,461	2,462,104	267,703	-42,472	2,151,929	890,091	585,405	22,715	159,691	86,984
1999	3,745,459	2,549,212	1,359	2,550,571	275,159	-42,552	2,232,860	889,792	622,807	23,285	160,855	87,306
2000	3,899,534	2,598,972	1,070	2,600,042	280,213	-42,857	2,276,972	954,142	668,420	23,930	162,959	87,746
2001	4,291,485	2,915,888	1,064	2,916,952	311,555	-47,475	2,557,922	994,268	739,295	25,997	165,075	88,813
2002	4,529,019	3,155,650	861	3,156,511	334,456	-53,632	2,768,423	947,032	813,564	27,017	167,638	90,750
2003	4,848,954	3,410,212	585	3,410,797	360,916	-57,467	2,992,414	984,221	872,319	28,471	170,310	93,235
2004	5,238,961	3,685,881	724	3,686,605	394,778	-67,786	3,224,041	1,079,033	935,887	30,064	174,259	98,640
2005	5,676,880	4,037,157	823	4,037,980	435,728	-83,479	3,518,773	1,161,412	996,695	31,768	178,698	102,904
2006	6,088,855	4,327,939	755	4,328,694	476,017	-85,426	3,767,251	1,269,110	1,052,494	33,547	181,500	106,196
2007	6,283,930	4,286,266	689	4,286,955	479,640	-72,044	3,735,271	1,439,078	1,109,581	34,669	181,253	106,775
2008	6,490,130	4,295,955	593	4,296,548	488,693	-68,665	3,739,190	1,485,315	1,265,625	35,637	182,118	104,896
2009	6,315,633	4,156,760	525	4,157,285	485,666	-48,786	3,622,833	1,318,634	1,374,166	34,437	183,397	101,535
2010	6,642,079	4,286,541	616	4,287,157	496,072	-49,858	3,741,227	1,353,080	1,547,772	35,897	185,031	100,997
2011	6,826,573	4,262,275	706	4,262,981	447,669	-37,325	3,777,987	1,451,304	1,597,282	36,844	185,281	101,869
2012	6,864,496	4,321,379	662	4,322,041	459,228	-17,783	3,845,030	1,452,465	1,567,001	36,606	187,524	102,158
2013	6,950,441	4,424,174	831	4,425,005	526,256	-4,173	3,894,576	1,446,920	1,608,945	36,484	190,509	104,207
2014	7,393,935	4,684,756	949	4,685,705	557,130	-7,446	4,121,129	1,561,189	1,711,617	38,069	194,227	108,180
2015	7,828,223	4,932,943	829	4,933,772	579,702	-19,185	4,334,885	1,701,666	1,791,672	39,712	197,124	110,850
2016	8,082,160	5,073,324	1,084	5,074,408	598,938	-32,921	4,442,549	1,776,630	1,862,981	40,595	199,092	112,727
2017	8,340,995	5,180,523	996	5,181,519	611,954	-32,001	4,537,564	1,854,053	1,949,378	41,763	199,723	113,302
2018	8,043,321	8,042,351	970	5,184,995	609,016	-140,023	4,435,956	1,688,740	1,918,625	43,188	186,240	109,765
2019	7,982,208	7,980,660	1,548	5,189,542	616,756	-149,688	4,423,098	1,678,767	1,880,343	45,690	174,705	105,766

Personal Income and Employment by Area: Parkersburg-Vienna, WV

(Thousands of dollars, except as noted.)

Year	Personal income, total	Earnings by place of work			Less: Contributions for government social insurance	Plus: Adjustment for residence	Equals: Net earnings by place of residence	Plus: Dividends, interest, and rent	Plus: Personal current transfer receipts	Per capita personal income (dollars)	Population (persons)	Total employment
		Nonfarm	Farm	Total								
1970	318,216	265,753	716	266,469	20,162	1,957	248,264	39,781	30,171	3,509	90,698	37,759
1971	337,191	281,115	831	281,946	22,081	-935	258,930	42,875	35,386	3,742	90,111	38,352
1972	369,651	314,547	1,037	315,584	26,269	-5,806	283,509	46,904	39,238	4,062	91,003	39,746
1973	406,901	349,601	1,456	351,057	33,776	-7,880	309,401	52,316	45,184	4,429	91,866	42,037
1974	463,093	397,299	819	398,118	40,232	-10,347	347,539	60,887	54,667	5,024	92,182	43,648
1975	495,791	401,490	280	401,770	39,454	-7,941	354,375	68,177	73,239	5,322	93,160	41,134
1976	547,765	449,447	-144	449,303	44,953	-8,070	396,280	73,983	77,502	5,820	94,121	42,127
1977	622,084	514,767	-243	514,524	51,319	-8,240	454,965	82,680	84,439	6,551	94,964	44,102
1978	701,671	585,813	151	585,964	60,451	-5,687	519,826	91,768	90,077	7,255	96,719	46,028
1979	772,357	648,676	219	648,895	69,301	-14,120	565,474	103,962	102,921	7,928	97,422	46,895
1980	849,513	696,324	344	696,668	75,171	-22,970	598,527	125,863	125,123	8,620	98,551	46,059
1981	931,764	757,522	-821	756,701	87,222	-31,702	637,777	153,807	140,180	9,461	98,486	45,220
1982	966,490	776,733	-1,633	775,100	91,943	-41,391	641,766	169,896	154,828	9,913	97,500	44,032
1983	1,023,366	814,630	-1,352	813,278	97,825	-47,167	668,286	186,640	168,440	10,510	97,368	44,220
1984	1,105,997	880,315	-197	880,118	108,095	-48,810	723,213	207,160	175,624	11,407	96,959	45,190
1985	1,171,487	930,261	103	930,364	115,381	-53,259	761,724	220,432	189,331	12,149	96,427	45,545
1986	1,200,824	953,390	-393	952,997	122,683	-55,034	775,280	224,256	201,288	12,515	95,949	45,461
1987	1,238,924	998,037	-848	997,189	130,717	-66,039	800,433	228,566	209,925	13,113	94,480	47,158
1988	1,342,717	1,101,076	-690	1,100,386	147,160	-76,351	876,875	241,124	224,718	14,301	93,892	47,850
1989	1,409,867	1,123,379	-473	1,122,906	152,118	-70,857	899,931	270,823	239,113	15,216	92,654	48,408
1990	1,495,189	1,183,029	109	1,183,138	162,087	-77,527	943,524	292,215	259,450	16,225	92,156	48,937
1991	1,538,877	1,208,214	-631	1,207,583	170,145	-81,763	955,675	291,791	291,411	16,628	92,547	48,290
1992	1,646,844	1,299,458	-114	1,299,344	183,199	-86,378	1,029,767	281,206	335,871	17,680	93,148	49,325
1993	1,722,038	1,359,514	-88	1,359,426	195,216	-89,645	1,074,565	287,566	359,907	18,365	93,766	50,279
1994	1,780,961	1,412,973	48	1,413,021	201,174	-91,617	1,120,230	299,876	360,855	18,908	94,190	51,179
1995	1,847,871	1,457,850	-335	1,457,515	208,383	-95,613	1,153,519	322,559	371,793	19,569	94,428	51,896
1996	1,922,582	1,525,764	-135	1,525,629	218,300	-116,681	1,190,648	335,978	395,956	20,386	94,308	52,966
1997	1,989,927	1,583,280	-543	1,582,737	224,583	-118,738	1,239,416	342,477	408,034	21,118	94,229	53,811
1998	2,053,753	1,601,616	-1,698	1,599,918	228,663	-104,996	1,266,259	365,656	421,838	21,840	94,035	53,323
1999	2,140,217	1,665,102	-2,112	1,662,990	235,228	-112,907	1,314,855	394,211	431,151	22,778	93,958	53,370
2000	2,227,995	1,761,423	-1,867	1,759,556	255,487	-133,765	1,370,304	403,021	454,670	23,775	93,711	54,205
2001	2,299,364	1,774,623	-2,470	1,772,153	249,284	-108,907	1,413,962	381,837	503,565	24,583	93,536	53,714
2002	2,398,512	1,798,856	-3,623	1,795,233	248,655	-78,922	1,467,656	379,971	550,885	25,673	93,424	52,634
2003	2,420,175	1,814,758	-2,586	1,812,172	255,810	-76,294	1,480,068	377,656	562,451	26,031	92,974	52,167
2004	2,490,105	1,901,234	-2,098	1,899,136	264,543	-99,186	1,535,407	393,130	561,568	26,861	92,705	52,520
2005	2,508,856	1,904,309	-2,938	1,901,371	262,512	-90,906	1,547,953	370,184	590,719	27,077	92,655	52,249
2006	2,685,008	2,016,089	-4,151	2,011,938	265,674	-97,569	1,648,695	399,551	636,762	29,076	92,343	52,837
2007	2,805,475	2,009,265	-5,203	2,004,062	253,597	-65,659	1,684,806	442,368	678,301	30,397	92,295	52,695
2008	2,934,926	2,023,897	-3,781	2,020,116	247,241	-50,636	1,722,239	459,832	752,855	31,719	92,528	51,861
2009	2,937,360	1,994,318	-4,171	1,990,147	247,270	-72,474	1,670,403	434,918	832,039	31,740	92,544	50,384
2010	3,008,121	2,037,973	-4,212	2,033,761	250,143	-86,561	1,697,057	432,607	878,457	32,449	92,703	50,082
2011	3,165,602	2,122,035	-3,094	2,118,941	231,803	-90,326	1,796,812	474,796	893,994	34,178	92,620	50,711
2012	3,293,114	2,207,702	-3,572	2,204,130	238,844	-91,914	1,873,372	518,246	901,496	35,652	92,367	51,018
2013	3,288,922	2,214,031	-2,085	2,211,946	268,328	-52,523	1,891,095	481,622	916,205	35,617	92,341	50,539
2014	3,462,480	2,279,299	-3,055	2,276,244	278,706	-3,361	1,994,177	513,285	955,018	37,537	92,242	50,367
2015	3,483,525	2,259,847	-2,881	2,256,966	281,495	-4,662	1,970,809	524,813	987,903	37,820	92,109	49,694
2016	3,448,897	2,166,934	-4,079	2,162,855	277,744	19,119	1,904,230	537,102	1,007,565	37,698	91,488	48,416
2017	3,513,581	2,186,200	-5,978	2,180,222	287,542	27,455	1,920,135	558,161	1,035,285	38,654	90,898	47,575
2018	3,893,418	3,900,782	-7,364	2,407,654	298,596	115,577	2,224,635	600,346	1,068,437	43,265	89,991	46,795
2019	3,927,966	3,933,734	-5,768	2,484,092	306,406	44,882	2,222,568	602,991	1,102,407	43,967	89,339	47,220

Personal Income and Employment by Area: Pensacola-Ferry Pass-Brent, FL

(Thousands of dollars, except as noted.)

Year	Personal income, total	Earnings by place of work			Less: Contributions for government social insurance	Plus: Adjustment for residence	Equals: Net earnings by place of residence	Plus: Dividends, interest, and rent	Plus: Personal current transfer receipts	Per capita personal income (dollars)	Population (persons)	Total employment
		Nonfarm	Farm	Total								
1970	972,357	794,688	3,947	798,635	44,344	-2,881	751,410	162,500	58,447	3,983	244,134	104,526
1971	1,100,934	895,132	5,392	900,524	52,591	-2,529	845,404	187,255	68,275	4,384	251,153	107,815
1972	1,233,579	1,002,625	5,444	1,008,069	61,568	-186	946,315	207,360	79,904	4,725	261,051	111,779
1973	1,323,451	1,059,444	12,847	1,072,291	73,602	1,476	1,000,165	225,422	97,864	5,005	264,441	114,005
1974	1,479,983	1,172,003	15,565	1,187,568	85,207	857	1,103,218	259,423	117,342	5,532	267,551	117,846
1975	1,639,777	1,275,812	16,176	1,291,988	93,858	702	1,198,832	288,913	152,032	5,948	275,666	119,341
1976	1,738,312	1,347,341	9,495	1,356,836	101,929	7,883	1,262,790	303,945	171,577	6,158	282,287	118,547
1977	1,897,906	1,467,712	5,051	1,472,763	111,237	10,067	1,371,593	341,027	185,286	6,650	285,381	121,814
1978	2,131,332	1,618,448	11,976	1,630,424	124,900	13,710	1,519,234	405,824	206,274	7,441	286,428	126,124
1979	2,378,340	1,802,495	9,538	1,812,033	146,096	14,948	1,680,885	459,220	238,235	8,225	289,161	128,844
1980	2,628,307	1,944,806	2,698	1,947,504	160,743	22,367	1,809,128	538,028	281,151	9,006	291,830	131,667
1981	3,010,209	2,213,251	4,358	2,217,609	195,341	26,237	2,048,505	633,233	328,471	10,052	299,477	135,907
1982	3,275,608	2,386,495	3,212	2,389,707	215,098	32,554	2,207,163	702,945	365,500	10,778	303,905	136,941
1983	3,552,331	2,586,381	3,495	2,589,876	241,151	32,475	2,381,200	769,782	401,349	11,375	312,280	140,353
1984	3,898,962	2,813,639	9,967	2,823,606	269,943	38,773	2,592,436	876,086	430,440	12,368	315,257	148,279
1985	4,151,703	2,978,060	8,145	2,986,205	292,900	41,407	2,734,712	953,014	463,977	12,944	320,743	154,423
1986	4,441,997	3,180,697	7,457	3,188,154	322,615	48,517	2,914,056	1,032,161	495,780	13,562	327,528	161,370
1987	4,701,642	3,356,802	12,090	3,368,892	338,530	56,194	3,086,556	1,088,069	527,017	14,040	334,873	161,606
1988	5,017,997	3,554,814	15,904	3,570,718	373,388	76,587	3,273,917	1,169,458	574,622	15,028	333,905	162,727
1989	5,431,454	3,740,755	13,018	3,753,773	399,157	81,778	3,436,394	1,329,245	665,815	15,898	341,654	165,545
1990	5,771,141	3,979,135	16,662	3,995,797	426,961	50,140	3,618,976	1,418,903	733,262	16,694	345,706	167,249
1991	6,083,425	4,156,584	17,949	4,174,533	451,021	82,930	3,806,442	1,447,026	829,957	17,234	352,981	168,899
1992	6,484,828	4,476,474	22,207	4,498,681	489,554	55,126	4,064,253	1,468,710	951,865	17,915	361,975	172,885
1993	6,770,377	4,613,137	23,817	4,636,954	505,620	94,647	4,225,981	1,526,153	1,018,243	18,413	367,689	174,170
1994	7,079,281	4,786,058	21,746	4,807,804	529,859	108,091	4,386,036	1,603,811	1,089,434	18,939	373,790	178,056
1995	7,523,876	4,946,295	12,332	4,958,627	546,166	189,476	4,601,937	1,738,239	1,183,700	19,789	380,205	183,511
1996	8,116,714	5,302,499	21,581	5,324,080	579,626	234,978	4,979,432	1,897,777	1,239,505	20,894	388,477	190,014
1997	8,598,097	5,629,591	15,609	5,645,200	616,172	238,705	5,267,733	2,034,927	1,295,437	21,499	399,925	198,535
1998	9,132,026	5,959,463	10,244	5,969,707	647,224	298,998	5,621,481	2,208,220	1,302,325	22,332	408,930	204,939
1999	9,470,171	6,192,478	16,158	6,208,636	670,496	311,066	5,849,206	2,232,142	1,388,823	23,097	410,026	207,920
2000	10,106,156	6,519,689	21,790	6,541,479	704,176	387,591	6,224,894	2,377,103	1,504,159	24,465	413,085	212,573
2001	10,874,231	7,031,146	16,454	7,047,600	756,938	399,008	6,689,670	2,500,054	1,684,507	25,951	419,037	209,983
2002	11,228,474	7,227,765	13,097	7,240,862	778,728	448,499	6,910,633	2,470,336	1,847,505	26,420	425,006	209,430
2003	11,816,073	7,635,700	23,867	7,659,567	820,420	498,373	7,337,520	2,472,832	2,005,721	27,603	428,066	213,127
2004	12,587,320	8,159,147	15,827	8,174,974	888,254	548,044	7,834,764	2,549,834	2,202,722	28,905	435,466	219,672
2005	13,349,933	8,696,029	18,121	8,714,150	951,780	596,544	8,358,914	2,708,968	2,282,051	30,377	439,471	223,707
2006	14,359,371	9,291,236	24,188	9,315,424	1,043,899	632,524	8,904,049	3,025,434	2,429,888	32,386	443,378	229,442
2007	14,959,375	9,446,042	10,045	9,456,087	1,068,131	691,800	9,079,756	3,267,167	2,612,452	33,726	443,551	232,026
2008	15,298,063	9,385,936	10,677	9,396,613	1,078,753	726,277	9,044,137	3,279,119	2,974,807	34,347	445,392	225,906
2009	15,121,125	9,226,486	1,199	9,227,685	1,079,489	722,179	8,870,375	3,023,453	3,227,297	33,861	446,559	217,869
2010	15,806,512	9,503,240	8,482	9,511,722	1,098,278	746,687	9,160,131	3,092,014	3,554,367	35,052	450,947	217,732
2011	16,589,195	9,799,304	19,974	9,819,278	1,027,465	792,749	9,584,562	3,303,655	3,700,978	36,452	455,093	220,462
2012	17,101,919	10,121,864	800	10,122,664	1,068,082	873,168	9,927,750	3,515,790	3,658,379	37,043	461,672	221,297
2013	17,122,600	10,173,377	10,628	10,184,005	1,206,127	903,798	9,881,676	3,462,288	3,778,636	36,650	467,188	225,227
2014	17,955,802	10,511,747	-10,889	10,500,858	1,245,617	949,357	10,204,598	3,732,574	4,018,630	38,133	470,871	229,477
2015	18,880,364	11,028,855	-4,388	11,024,467	1,298,593	964,669	10,690,543	3,950,671	4,239,150	39,673	475,894	233,458
2016	19,510,648	11,396,056	-8,237	11,387,819	1,346,883	966,984	11,007,920	4,081,853	4,420,875	40,498	481,774	239,669
2017	20,286,214	11,846,716	-4,122	11,842,594	1,403,533	992,168	11,431,229	4,223,888	4,631,097	41,589	487,784	244,310
2018	21,492,072	21,475,161	16,911	12,608,257	1,483,423	1,046,481	12,171,315	4,386,277	4,934,480	43,471	494,399	255,027
2019	22,591,862	22,559,543	32,319	13,403,741	1,591,705	1,115,153	12,927,189	4,461,891	5,202,782	44,947	502,629	262,091

Personal Income and Employment by Area: Peoria, IL

(Thousands of dollars, except as noted.)

Year	Personal income, total	Earnings by place of work			Less: Contributions for government social insurance	Plus: Adjustment for residence	Equals: Net earnings by place of residence	Plus: Dividends, interest, and rent	Plus: Personal current transfer receipts	Per capita personal income (dollars)	Population (persons)	Total employment
		Nonfarm	Farm	Total								
1970	1,566,479	1,311,884	39,905	1,351,789	88,889	-35,925	1,226,975	224,479	115,025	4,304	363,968	164,383
1971	1,708,997	1,425,476	45,525	1,471,001	99,872	-38,738	1,332,391	240,697	135,909	4,627	369,391	164,742
1972	1,838,676	1,537,555	39,836	1,577,391	113,722	-41,394	1,422,275	262,222	154,179	4,922	373,551	165,245
1973	2,121,271	1,753,150	88,311	1,841,461	151,297	-50,287	1,639,877	301,331	180,063	5,666	374,401	175,153
1974	2,383,613	1,991,148	89,396	2,080,544	178,108	-62,688	1,839,748	343,264	200,601	6,336	376,199	181,638
1975	2,721,430	2,213,786	132,393	2,346,179	193,838	-74,379	2,077,962	389,931	253,537	7,195	378,257	186,144
1976	2,932,753	2,429,021	103,506	2,532,527	217,688	-82,740	2,232,099	416,448	284,206	7,691	381,346	190,624
1977	3,189,400	2,658,038	97,330	2,755,368	237,167	-95,924	2,422,277	464,767	302,356	8,347	382,124	191,841
1978	3,555,865	3,043,587	78,840	3,122,427	281,109	-122,735	2,718,583	513,432	323,850	9,271	383,538	197,934
1979	3,811,586	3,206,616	92,214	3,298,830	306,869	-127,977	2,863,984	581,760	365,842	9,926	384,001	194,459
1980	4,152,487	3,495,257	12,668	3,507,925	335,921	-159,488	3,012,516	692,834	447,137	10,708	387,782	192,228
1981	4,590,050	3,663,265	105,728	3,768,993	378,117	-160,475	3,230,401	841,253	518,396	11,851	387,307	188,890
1982	4,648,202	3,458,035	75,482	3,533,517	360,299	-127,828	3,045,390	993,201	609,611	12,118	383,564	175,891
1983	4,475,914	3,218,657	-30,363	3,188,294	334,538	-89,466	2,764,290	1,036,069	675,555	11,830	378,344	166,495
1984	4,904,749	3,513,964	74,008	3,587,972	379,187	-97,346	3,111,439	1,146,516	646,794	13,190	371,853	172,623
1985	5,048,977	3,593,985	117,205	3,711,190	391,886	-91,840	3,227,464	1,149,571	671,942	13,853	364,457	171,203
1986	5,183,687	3,708,276	85,667	3,793,943	404,254	-97,582	3,292,107	1,187,035	704,545	14,486	357,835	172,056
1987	5,379,524	3,933,749	71,899	4,005,648	421,471	-104,884	3,479,293	1,171,204	729,027	15,156	354,936	174,514
1988	5,828,808	4,435,594	30,787	4,466,381	488,524	-123,582	3,854,275	1,216,444	758,089	16,433	354,697	181,969
1989	6,319,323	4,743,202	73,465	4,816,667	524,846	-121,533	4,170,288	1,338,123	810,912	17,689	357,249	187,671
1990	6,678,156	5,027,591	78,385	5,105,976	541,467	-109,815	4,454,694	1,348,129	875,333	18,588	359,269	191,515
1991	6,703,395	5,012,644	51,657	5,064,301	554,846	-99,052	4,410,403	1,356,859	936,133	18,543	361,500	191,716
1992	7,135,289	5,254,481	101,801	5,356,282	569,526	-98,213	4,688,543	1,385,121	1,061,625	19,699	362,223	190,752
1993	7,443,162	5,580,805	77,400	5,658,205	616,566	-122,822	4,918,817	1,429,844	1,094,501	20,533	362,492	194,442
1994	7,902,183	5,934,012	128,785	6,062,797	660,417	-115,865	5,286,515	1,495,052	1,120,616	21,779	362,843	199,927
1995	8,143,940	6,057,979	33,904	6,091,883	672,712	-96,944	5,322,227	1,626,668	1,195,045	22,228	366,385	202,647
1996	8,693,351	6,391,537	149,453	6,540,990	708,637	-125,173	5,707,180	1,722,951	1,263,220	23,719	366,521	210,524
1997	9,166,699	6,775,842	125,888	6,901,730	748,438	-141,771	6,011,521	1,873,010	1,282,168	25,003	366,624	214,200
1998	9,703,645	7,255,943	91,861	7,347,804	792,963	-146,310	6,408,531	1,999,861	1,295,253	26,441	366,997	218,478
1999	9,952,015	7,583,273	65,055	7,648,328	813,153	-136,638	6,698,537	1,931,719	1,321,759	27,074	367,581	218,280
2000	10,401,944	7,760,626	106,859	7,867,485	822,356	-132,697	6,912,432	2,095,162	1,394,350	28,370	366,659	220,599
2001	10,681,924	8,063,941	90,727	8,154,668	862,218	-126,500	7,165,950	2,032,578	1,483,396	29,218	365,600	216,712
2002	10,794,256	8,290,409	56,843	8,347,252	881,057	-117,329	7,348,866	1,854,845	1,590,545	29,467	366,312	212,245
2003	11,094,565	8,454,203	100,724	8,554,927	902,757	-118,270	7,533,900	1,900,701	1,659,964	30,292	366,256	209,745
2004	11,793,099	9,052,105	186,467	9,238,572	987,873	-145,352	8,105,347	1,957,827	1,729,925	32,050	367,962	213,341
2005	12,372,082	9,792,819	78,090	9,870,909	1,078,833	-198,861	8,593,215	1,905,840	1,873,027	33,459	369,772	216,653
2006	13,448,387	10,683,434	88,031	10,771,465	1,155,232	-237,592	9,378,641	2,136,922	1,932,824	36,182	371,687	222,145
2007	14,207,860	11,140,970	192,949	11,333,919	1,206,365	-270,275	9,857,279	2,233,774	2,116,807	37,971	374,179	226,638
2008	14,954,838	11,472,408	272,962	11,745,370	1,253,091	-265,140	10,227,139	2,405,824	2,321,875	39,775	375,982	227,619
2009	14,739,575	11,023,037	172,288	11,195,325	1,203,489	-222,274	9,769,562	2,356,481	2,613,532	38,852	379,373	216,612
2010	15,104,767	11,322,914	118,138	11,441,052	1,239,902	-244,586	9,956,564	2,330,956	2,817,247	39,856	378,982	216,991
2011	16,523,404	12,465,281	303,395	12,768,676	1,213,334	-350,777	11,204,565	2,608,348	2,710,491	43,521	379,665	221,377
2012	17,134,757	13,222,575	169,617	13,392,192	1,293,634	-432,545	11,666,013	2,768,598	2,700,146	45,075	380,137	224,706
2013	16,692,887	12,491,174	397,388	12,888,562	1,399,517	-374,681	11,114,364	2,741,367	2,837,156	43,749	381,557	219,484
2014	16,936,710	12,600,622	142,455	12,743,077	1,405,318	-368,870	10,968,889	3,086,918	2,880,903	44,639	379,412	218,834
2015	17,439,282	12,872,893	-1,425	12,871,468	1,423,863	-311,813	11,135,792	3,263,876	3,039,614	46,221	377,300	218,339
2016	17,527,085	12,742,365	148,578	12,890,943	1,405,863	-329,524	11,155,556	3,288,587	3,082,942	46,664	375,600	214,608
2017	17,495,442	12,519,445	40,589	12,560,034	1,384,001	-270,773	10,905,260	3,417,329	3,172,853	46,977	372,427	211,972
2018	19,524,347	19,329,022	195,325	13,854,767	1,516,122	-21,042	12,317,603	3,537,535	3,669,209	48,408	403,328	224,449
2019	19,666,390	19,559,596	106,794	13,800,950	1,520,441	3,002	12,283,511	3,566,052	3,816,827	49,097	400,561	224,181

Personal Income and Employment by Area: Philadelphia-Camden-Wilmington, PA-NJ-DE-MD

(Thousands of dollars, except as noted.)

Year	Personal income, total	Earnings by place of work			Less: Contributions for government social insurance	Plus: Adjustment for residence	Equals: Net earnings by place of residence	Plus: Dividends, interest, and rent	Plus: Personal current transfer receipts	Per capita personal income (dollars)	Population (persons)	Total employment
		Nonfarm	Farm	Total								
1970	24,520,198	20,039,390	94,448	20,133,838	1,436,557	52,200	18,749,481	3,683,033	2,087,684	4,599	5,331,133	2,424,294
1971	26,125,091	21,114,400	99,205	21,213,605	1,571,650	73,436	19,715,391	3,944,720	2,464,980	4,872	5,362,194	2,392,220
1972	28,339,983	22,923,197	91,533	23,014,730	1,793,297	124,808	21,346,241	4,212,154	2,781,588	5,293	5,353,850	2,424,493
1973	30,621,832	24,856,753	135,537	24,992,290	2,243,235	189,927	22,938,982	4,588,136	3,094,714	5,758	5,317,951	2,467,445
1974	33,305,265	26,643,145	135,103	26,778,248	2,492,914	247,132	24,532,466	5,113,733	3,659,066	6,289	5,295,959	2,453,221
1975	35,981,127	28,016,022	110,152	28,126,174	2,557,693	280,537	25,849,018	5,441,504	4,690,605	6,804	5,288,609	2,376,788
1976	39,176,435	30,459,484	139,511	30,598,995	2,831,890	360,665	28,127,770	5,850,128	5,198,537	7,418	5,280,969	2,398,310
1977	42,605,446	33,095,270	132,403	33,227,673	3,069,436	435,113	30,593,350	6,433,671	5,578,425	8,093	5,264,778	2,415,937
1978	46,787,916	36,643,060	134,332	36,777,392	3,490,984	514,103	33,800,511	7,055,916	5,931,489	8,916	5,247,420	2,480,533
1979	51,530,923	40,225,755	136,126	40,361,881	3,982,608	594,235	36,973,508	7,892,111	6,665,304	9,819	5,248,348	2,531,977
1980	57,084,565	43,529,772	89,436	43,619,208	4,330,334	732,389	40,021,263	9,498,434	7,564,868	10,886	5,244,018	2,533,311
1981	63,222,516	47,034,778	127,745	47,162,523	5,003,327	845,587	43,004,783	11,695,986	8,521,747	12,042	5,250,278	2,530,893
1982	68,344,102	49,701,183	151,116	49,852,299	5,378,387	904,056	45,377,968	13,480,270	9,485,864	13,001	5,257,004	2,524,306
1983	72,951,858	53,427,724	143,538	53,571,262	5,875,092	979,185	48,675,355	14,095,860	10,180,643	13,865	5,261,664	2,558,593
1984	79,503,431	58,523,873	202,459	58,726,332	6,681,102	1,101,664	53,146,894	15,860,311	10,496,226	15,060	5,279,124	2,645,844
1985	85,574,904	63,363,634	225,204	63,588,838	7,331,153	1,180,665	57,438,350	17,070,567	11,065,987	16,163	5,294,461	2,722,101
1986	90,999,442	67,783,561	214,907	67,998,468	7,908,084	1,311,575	61,401,959	17,920,683	11,676,800	17,056	5,335,416	2,785,227
1987	97,572,391	73,863,745	199,920	74,063,665	8,538,491	1,444,385	66,969,559	18,606,829	11,996,003	18,125	5,383,434	2,876,967
1988	105,911,474	80,579,558	182,308	80,761,866	9,540,574	1,573,396	72,794,688	20,379,331	12,737,455	19,536	5,421,382	2,951,624
1989	114,591,373	85,840,356	185,138	86,025,494	10,048,583	1,639,604	77,616,515	23,228,385	13,746,473	21,086	5,434,490	2,987,983
1990	121,241,003	90,232,511	213,732	90,446,243	10,567,223	1,710,198	81,589,218	24,843,271	14,808,514	22,266	5,445,186	2,986,306
1991	125,340,682	92,022,458	204,036	92,226,494	10,899,355	1,907,443	83,234,582	24,893,484	17,212,616	22,873	5,479,918	2,912,895
1992	132,190,614	97,329,071	225,644	97,554,715	11,453,320	1,999,852	88,101,247	25,309,965	18,779,402	24,019	5,503,640	2,891,738
1993	136,875,461	100,649,048	239,650	100,888,698	11,911,185	2,122,342	91,099,855	26,034,028	19,741,578	24,738	5,533,081	2,910,168
1994	141,508,926	104,213,364	244,090	104,457,454	12,570,444	2,228,945	94,115,955	27,147,808	20,245,163	25,441	5,562,336	2,922,050
1995	148,930,267	108,636,644	233,869	108,870,513	13,031,443	2,405,513	98,244,583	29,377,217	21,308,467	26,660	5,586,177	2,963,541
1996	156,972,264	114,018,430	281,357	114,299,787	13,469,802	2,372,665	103,202,650	31,188,508	22,581,106	28,020	5,602,154	2,998,593
1997	165,382,500	120,802,405	273,455	121,075,860	14,146,652	2,637,368	109,566,576	32,861,578	22,954,346	29,451	5,615,600	3,061,561
1998	177,481,851	130,407,357	277,968	130,685,325	15,018,450	2,650,191	118,317,066	35,826,426	23,338,359	31,468	5,640,015	3,127,485
1999	185,557,412	138,410,317	259,226	138,669,543	15,724,565	2,663,679	125,608,657	35,671,034	24,277,721	32,754	5,665,210	3,179,438
2000	200,907,011	149,121,941	306,785	149,428,726	16,672,815	2,996,110	135,752,021	39,004,449	26,150,541	35,297	5,691,968	3,250,559
2001	209,871,254	157,464,714	269,347	157,734,061	17,235,301	3,121,758	143,620,518	38,390,530	27,860,206	36,730	5,713,954	3,267,912
2002	214,635,735	162,058,357	266,085	162,324,442	17,825,404	3,214,533	147,713,571	37,056,579	29,865,585	37,371	5,743,383	3,266,732
2003	222,521,028	168,575,831	273,023	168,848,854	18,446,925	3,306,371	153,708,300	37,892,118	30,920,610	38,539	5,773,864	3,280,167
2004	235,678,253	179,781,765	318,494	180,100,259	19,507,061	3,571,846	164,165,044	39,944,353	31,568,856	40,602	5,804,535	3,324,106
2005	244,539,533	185,144,008	298,309	185,442,317	20,359,515	3,757,312	168,840,114	41,758,731	33,940,688	41,951	5,829,139	3,384,631
2006	260,519,835	193,459,221	285,186	193,744,407	21,467,374	4,054,352	176,331,385	48,590,234	35,598,216	44,487	5,856,125	3,436,677
2007	275,953,313	203,007,495	149,238	203,156,733	22,486,817	4,456,079	185,125,995	52,683,425	38,143,893	46,914	5,882,126	3,488,513
2008	281,583,364	203,664,107	173,388	203,837,495	23,235,707	4,840,798	185,442,586	53,519,667	42,621,111	47,670	5,906,917	3,501,145
2009	275,596,452	200,242,229	231,880	200,474,109	22,880,607	4,663,730	182,257,232	46,828,115	46,511,105	46,385	5,941,539	3,415,648
2010	287,193,133	207,664,270	225,995	207,890,265	23,217,669	5,040,567	189,713,163	46,455,178	51,024,792	48,096	5,971,189	3,410,339
2011	303,810,556	216,889,628	253,048	217,142,676	21,306,009	5,309,989	201,146,656	51,071,892	51,592,008	50,665	5,996,406	3,451,664
2012	319,545,636	226,399,854	358,806	226,758,660	21,941,710	5,840,881	210,657,831	57,229,399	51,658,406	53,073	6,020,821	3,476,792
2013	322,258,219	234,391,311	352,042	234,743,353	25,493,597	5,997,108	215,246,864	54,405,863	52,605,492	53,395	6,035,329	3,525,841
2014	337,001,050	242,236,730	366,614	242,603,344	26,410,654	6,499,615	222,692,305	59,607,530	54,701,215	55,675	6,053,028	3,586,414
2015	351,293,623	250,944,764	327,719	251,272,483	27,451,565	6,550,673	230,371,591	63,281,018	57,641,014	57,906	6,066,589	3,646,653
2016	362,699,062	258,565,066	243,880	258,808,946	28,143,063	6,839,528	237,505,411	64,468,436	60,725,215	59,682	6,077,152	3,729,105
2017	377,223,079	270,558,535	243,240	270,801,775	29,538,080	6,709,815	247,973,510	67,848,516	61,401,053	61,879	6,096,120	3,786,405
2018	391,224,070	390,867,383	356,687	274,790,415	30,293,896	7,450,123	251,946,642	74,037,164	65,240,264	64,228	6,091,208	3,849,638
2019	406,399,941	405,911,661	488,280	286,808,091	31,381,973	7,915,342	263,341,460	75,375,656	67,682,825	66,596	6,102,434	3,918,093

Personal Income and Employment by Area: Phoenix-Mesa-Chandler, AZ

(Thousands of dollars, except as noted.)

Year	Personal income, total	Earnings by place of work			Less: Contributions for government social insurance	Plus: Adjustment for residence	Equals: Net earnings by place of residence	Plus: Dividends, interest, and rent	Plus: Personal current transfer receipts	Per capita personal income (dollars)	Population (persons)	Total employment
		Nonfarm	Farm	Total								
1970	4,435,397	3,376,315	105,153	3,481,468	230,632	-21,339	3,229,497	869,987	335,913	4,225	1,049,680	456,574
1971	5,038,059	3,818,694	120,929	3,939,623	272,161	-21,368	3,646,094	991,866	400,099	4,579	1,100,219	478,419
1972	5,785,408	4,458,900	98,528	4,557,428	335,218	-14,476	4,207,734	1,117,667	460,007	4,970	1,163,970	522,280
1973	6,707,040	5,203,336	106,777	5,310,113	448,512	-11,443	4,850,158	1,298,017	558,865	5,419	1,237,668	574,470
1974	7,613,878	5,681,015	247,112	5,928,127	506,663	-19,760	5,401,704	1,525,580	686,594	5,848	1,301,957	592,448
1975	8,141,145	5,864,612	94,831	5,959,443	515,861	-28,218	5,415,364	1,737,879	987,902	6,086	1,337,680	573,360
1976	9,126,107	6,605,949	206,113	6,812,062	585,353	-38,357	6,188,352	1,876,238	1,061,517	6,679	1,366,423	603,064
1977	10,352,142	7,674,347	159,414	7,833,761	686,978	-39,000	7,107,783	2,119,572	1,124,787	7,306	1,416,931	654,968
1978	12,273,363	9,255,747	162,453	9,418,200	851,039	-36,532	8,530,629	2,482,221	1,260,513	8,313	1,476,485	728,998
1979	14,595,699	11,111,150	246,899	11,358,049	1,067,111	-42,081	10,248,857	2,910,022	1,436,820	9,439	1,546,348	792,672
1980	16,893,996	12,533,395	296,437	12,829,832	1,214,376	-54,931	11,560,525	3,599,788	1,733,683	10,479	1,612,182	820,853
1981	19,335,537	14,067,071	256,213	14,323,284	1,466,097	-51,903	12,805,284	4,484,477	2,045,776	11,655	1,658,988	843,575
1982	20,654,673	14,737,498	222,721	14,960,219	1,559,860	-42,589	13,357,770	5,025,307	2,271,596	12,088	1,708,649	847,957
1983	22,914,802	16,351,347	175,169	16,526,516	1,751,677	-30,908	14,743,931	5,687,902	2,482,969	13,006	1,761,819	895,053
1984	26,163,791	18,829,845	320,170	19,150,015	2,069,986	-33,099	17,046,930	6,438,186	2,678,675	14,239	1,837,457	988,892
1985	29,431,887	21,334,931	288,071	21,623,002	2,383,883	-41,013	19,198,106	7,307,865	2,925,916	15,234	1,931,978	1,074,363
1986	32,324,473	23,604,280	286,319	23,890,599	2,650,089	-44,240	21,196,270	7,889,458	3,238,745	16,055	2,013,320	1,130,847
1987	34,961,445	25,591,638	356,798	25,948,436	2,847,742	-36,320	23,064,374	8,363,994	3,533,077	16,628	2,102,571	1,175,415
1988	37,813,719	27,914,751	389,911	28,304,662	3,196,896	-50,403	25,057,363	8,877,549	3,878,807	17,485	2,162,647	1,224,682
1989	40,573,599	29,020,120	423,994	29,444,114	3,409,779	-15,279	26,019,056	10,083,185	4,471,358	18,297	2,217,530	1,247,064
1990	42,474,931	30,593,481	384,406	30,977,887	3,695,289	-12,219	27,270,379	10,282,503	4,922,049	18,885	2,249,116	1,266,338
1991	44,433,254	32,272,730	443,627	32,716,357	3,916,461	-4,641	28,795,255	10,153,980	5,484,019	19,159	2,319,206	1,263,249
1992	47,360,604	34,772,605	386,057	35,158,662	4,180,070	2,848	30,981,440	10,150,719	6,228,445	19,744	2,398,760	1,271,798
1993	50,723,694	37,487,249	422,391	37,909,640	4,508,566	13,764	33,414,838	10,611,833	6,697,023	20,356	2,491,818	1,328,795
1994	55,941,697	41,527,630	367,401	41,895,031	4,998,511	11,949	36,908,469	11,896,110	7,137,118	21,405	2,613,502	1,416,403
1995	61,693,123	45,740,134	406,849	46,146,983	5,289,086	-22,678	40,835,219	13,222,803	7,635,101	22,483	2,744,046	1,508,585
1996	67,546,444	50,860,346	443,806	51,304,152	5,996,757	-56,114	45,251,281	14,178,482	8,116,681	23,653	2,855,711	1,614,248
1997	73,890,376	55,763,048	422,315	56,185,363	6,482,785	-38,212	49,664,366	15,758,527	8,467,483	24,932	2,963,714	1,702,231
1998	80,746,460	62,364,632	455,635	62,820,267	7,128,742	-33,934	55,657,591	16,367,427	8,721,442	26,263	3,074,532	1,791,395
1999	85,737,771	67,092,192	443,376	67,535,568	7,661,580	-15,848	59,858,140	16,592,191	9,287,440	26,976	3,178,349	1,857,012
2000	94,079,123	74,076,763	361,990	74,438,753	8,419,870	-2,490	66,016,393	18,205,426	9,857,304	28,740	3,273,477	1,929,164
2001	96,749,035	76,025,167	348,160	76,373,327	8,754,785	75,431	67,693,973	17,885,688	11,169,374	28,762	3,363,736	1,952,759
2002	100,261,692	78,149,230	332,579	78,481,809	8,988,529	120,150	69,613,430	18,174,786	12,473,476	29,041	3,452,470	1,963,854
2003	106,057,360	81,805,251	374,555	82,179,806	9,285,771	173,784	73,067,819	19,369,475	13,620,066	29,990	3,536,388	2,015,185
2004	117,061,376	90,591,327	535,077	91,126,404	10,128,473	225,973	81,223,904	20,802,433	15,035,039	32,183	3,637,332	2,104,069
2005	131,188,776	100,891,507	474,809	101,366,316	11,172,214	260,135	90,454,237	24,060,121	16,674,418	34,755	3,774,696	2,245,171
2006	147,093,905	112,864,316	382,819	113,247,135	12,293,605	303,548	101,257,078	27,600,362	18,236,465	37,579	3,914,212	2,363,627
2007	154,783,876	117,290,930	424,187	117,715,117	12,966,264	398,191	105,147,044	29,813,203	19,823,629	38,521	4,018,128	2,425,683
2008	153,843,772	114,030,300	360,618	114,390,918	12,968,481	526,137	101,948,574	28,585,853	23,309,345	37,465	4,106,372	2,378,751
2009	143,988,766	104,559,444	214,567	104,774,011	12,243,537	507,303	93,037,777	24,791,327	26,159,662	34,666	4,153,609	2,246,716
2010	146,615,714	104,753,834	259,159	105,012,993	12,358,976	535,458	93,189,475	24,596,215	28,830,024	34,874	4,204,148	2,209,907
2011	154,622,571	109,546,401	487,174	110,033,575	11,481,464	562,182	99,114,293	26,685,978	28,822,300	36,400	4,247,852	2,264,667
2012	163,674,620	115,915,133	444,364	116,359,497	11,956,991	592,572	104,995,078	29,803,669	28,875,873	37,873	4,321,686	2,311,182
2013	168,082,126	121,625,266	554,052	122,179,318	14,077,657	631,442	108,733,103	29,421,624	29,927,399	38,283	4,390,565	2,375,865
2014	179,115,906	127,981,993	585,637	128,567,630	14,652,345	656,298	114,571,583	32,839,190	31,705,133	40,064	4,470,712	2,441,128
2015	189,729,276	134,933,915	548,572	135,482,487	15,541,242	659,914	120,601,159	36,109,471	33,018,646	41,624	4,558,145	2,529,228
2016	197,440,915	141,384,402	556,672	141,941,074	16,271,459	645,100	126,314,715	37,305,766	33,820,434	42,474	4,648,498	2,612,783
2017	208,895,905	150,481,078	733,825	151,214,903	17,288,314	667,947	134,594,536	39,082,968	35,218,401	44,096	4,737,270	2,681,110
2018	225,676,984	225,073,141	603,843	161,718,965	18,478,366	692,491	143,933,090	44,432,351	37,311,543	46,539	4,849,209	2,790,209
2019	237,836,502	237,192,508	643,994	171,659,944	19,663,349	723,649	152,720,244	45,329,467	39,786,791	48,065	4,948,203	2,886,513

Personal Income and Employment by Area: Pine Bluff, AR

(Thousands of dollars, except as noted.)

Year	Personal income, total	Earnings by place of work			Less: Contributions for government social insurance	Plus: Adjustment for residence	Equals: Net earnings by place of residence	Plus: Dividends, interest, and rent	Plus: Personal current transfer receipts	Per capita personal income (dollars)	Population (persons)	Total employment
		Nonfarm	Farm	Total								
1970	290,916	216,093	19,611	235,704	16,562	1,788	220,930	35,845	34,141	2,784	104,477	38,872
1971	320,454	233,791	24,064	257,855	18,270	1,696	241,281	39,906	39,267	3,090	103,719	39,197
1972	347,493	255,891	24,640	280,531	21,138	1,531	260,924	43,541	43,028	3,313	104,888	39,993
1973	405,124	285,991	44,097	330,088	27,314	1,070	303,844	49,656	51,624	3,887	104,231	41,117
1974	434,033	316,994	27,289	344,283	31,299	113	313,097	58,518	62,418	4,124	105,251	42,161
1975	476,783	332,287	34,207	366,494	31,913	-1,420	333,161	64,977	78,645	4,526	105,335	40,227
1976	535,406	374,787	39,947	414,734	36,522	-1,184	377,028	71,360	87,018	5,047	106,074	40,529
1977	592,237	423,222	39,313	462,535	41,774	-1,271	419,490	80,641	92,106	5,555	106,613	42,336
1978	679,727	504,132	48,248	552,380	50,778	-11,840	489,762	89,213	100,752	6,264	108,520	45,097
1979	758,571	587,653	44,581	632,234	61,539	-24,914	545,781	99,879	112,911	6,861	110,555	46,194
1980	825,794	657,337	14,601	671,938	68,113	-33,603	570,222	123,430	132,142	7,374	111,988	46,894
1981	908,859	661,580	39,133	700,713	73,591	-22,534	604,588	151,669	152,602	8,123	111,883	44,628
1982	919,753	646,749	23,206	669,955	74,269	-14,987	580,699	175,109	163,945	8,321	110,538	42,054
1983	964,914	691,675	11,379	703,054	80,028	-15,621	607,405	180,666	176,843	8,776	109,954	42,484
1984	1,051,281	745,001	28,861	773,862	89,511	-16,917	667,434	201,445	182,402	9,595	109,561	42,993
1985	1,100,703	783,931	26,203	810,134	95,465	-19,881	694,788	214,862	191,053	10,108	108,892	43,590
1986	1,183,695	882,991	23,889	906,880	108,926	-37,279	760,675	223,358	199,662	10,916	108,437	45,357
1987	1,209,269	872,370	39,024	911,394	105,889	-24,161	781,344	221,166	206,759	11,130	108,653	44,835
1988	1,309,406	933,750	66,385	1,000,135	119,358	-26,497	854,280	240,320	214,806	12,061	108,561	46,386
1989	1,365,021	968,517	42,115	1,010,632	125,893	-28,507	856,232	269,303	239,486	12,641	107,985	47,039
1990	1,426,971	1,038,584	34,870	1,073,454	137,678	-35,547	900,229	268,526	258,216	13,341	106,958	47,603
1991	1,463,798	1,027,682	46,134	1,073,816	132,871	-22,336	918,609	263,139	282,050	13,646	107,267	47,185
1992	1,575,596	1,099,015	66,146	1,165,161	139,970	-21,556	1,003,635	258,144	313,817	14,644	107,590	47,356
1993	1,638,622	1,146,494	52,152	1,198,646	146,765	-20,790	1,031,091	280,574	326,957	15,274	107,282	48,353
1994	1,711,484	1,174,682	83,601	1,258,283	150,940	-15,787	1,091,556	275,762	344,166	15,878	107,791	47,473
1995	1,772,981	1,227,698	54,941	1,282,639	157,250	-14,774	1,110,615	293,907	368,459	16,460	107,714	48,926
1996	1,859,345	1,254,948	94,248	1,349,196	159,871	-11,388	1,177,937	304,141	377,267	17,263	107,707	49,406
1997	1,903,658	1,300,372	83,386	1,383,758	165,901	-9,281	1,208,576	303,791	391,291	17,672	107,720	49,381
1998	1,993,502	1,366,548	76,277	1,442,825	172,916	-8,088	1,261,821	325,495	406,186	18,555	107,440	49,260
1999	2,027,777	1,410,344	84,910	1,495,254	177,056	-7,323	1,310,875	311,340	405,562	18,909	107,241	49,241
2000	2,112,930	1,487,956	73,583	1,561,539	184,671	-8,032	1,368,836	317,864	426,230	19,713	107,184	49,436
2001	2,201,738	1,520,876	86,656	1,607,532	188,925	-3,058	1,415,549	319,477	466,712	20,681	106,464	49,489
2002	2,256,268	1,566,447	52,241	1,618,688	192,930	-1,520	1,424,238	323,256	508,774	21,293	105,965	48,574
2003	2,385,208	1,635,962	115,265	1,751,227	199,549	-7,801	1,543,877	312,105	529,226	22,616	105,465	48,948
2004	2,497,018	1,736,018	132,215	1,868,233	210,283	-37,539	1,620,411	309,798	566,809	23,857	104,665	49,671
2005	2,513,556	1,776,328	95,012	1,871,340	214,380	-55,904	1,601,056	319,073	593,427	24,188	103,917	49,426
2006	2,562,954	1,834,126	68,110	1,902,236	225,650	-83,207	1,593,379	327,877	641,698	24,854	103,121	49,191
2007	2,680,268	1,826,126	94,697	1,920,823	226,999	-51,499	1,642,325	353,930	684,013	26,298	101,921	48,352
2008	2,726,113	1,836,522	87,386	1,923,908	232,793	-75,810	1,615,305	359,444	751,364	26,910	101,305	47,892
2009	2,740,856	1,848,708	58,101	1,906,809	236,993	-98,273	1,571,543	355,510	813,803	27,247	100,593	47,573
2010	2,784,747	1,914,182	46,678	1,960,860	244,581	-128,584	1,587,695	336,043	861,009	27,822	100,093	47,239
2011	2,856,669	1,924,163	53,936	1,978,099	221,774	-120,900	1,635,425	359,915	861,329	28,851	99,016	47,240
2012	2,914,398	1,964,684	94,451	2,059,135	223,074	-167,863	1,668,198	386,486	859,714	29,926	97,388	46,585
2013	2,942,899	1,889,242	176,283	2,065,525	241,202	-110,661	1,713,662	361,400	867,837	30,739	95,737	45,147
2014	2,951,595	1,880,255	117,140	1,997,395	243,749	-89,044	1,664,602	377,789	909,204	31,119	94,850	43,939
2015	2,953,846	1,841,853	93,942	1,935,795	240,981	-77,009	1,617,805	387,627	948,414	31,430	93,983	43,821
2016	2,975,533	1,856,757	114,804	1,971,561	241,291	-114,694	1,615,576	386,754	973,203	32,199	92,412	43,522
2017	2,996,481	1,895,843	88,567	1,984,410	245,904	-139,313	1,599,193	406,959	990,329	32,942	90,963	43,096
2018	3,066,965	2,984,525	82,440	2,000,351	250,733	-123,510	1,626,108	425,359	1,015,498	34,365	89,246	42,830
2019	3,126,791	3,047,835	78,956	2,022,736	255,864	-131,653	1,635,219	433,856	1,057,716	35,611	87,804	42,396

Personal Income and Employment by Area: Pittsburgh, PA

(Thousands of dollars, except as noted.)

Year	Personal income, total	Earnings by place of work			Less: Contributions for government social insurance	Plus: Adjustment for residence	Equals: Net earnings by place of residence	Plus: Dividends, interest, and rent	Plus: Personal current transfer receipts	Per capita personal income (dollars)	Population (persons)	Total employment
		Nonfarm	Farm	Total								
1970	11,286,375	9,279,300	33,266	9,312,566	683,635	-29,634	8,599,297	1,521,282	1,165,796	4,091	2,758,743	1,132,359
1971	11,887,371	9,662,772	35,548	9,698,320	738,906	-37,685	8,921,729	1,598,328	1,367,314	4,306	2,760,937	1,113,813
1972	12,858,851	10,479,485	41,854	10,521,339	840,895	-45,876	9,634,568	1,688,684	1,535,599	4,673	2,751,873	1,124,028
1973	14,023,848	11,530,303	40,406	11,570,709	1,065,963	-57,855	10,446,891	1,859,448	1,717,509	5,137	2,730,057	1,154,111
1974	15,575,362	12,762,748	43,833	12,806,581	1,226,950	-85,046	11,494,585	2,108,740	1,972,037	5,762	2,703,028	1,167,040
1975	17,206,793	13,822,385	46,381	13,868,766	1,299,014	-100,947	12,468,805	2,289,266	2,448,722	6,371	2,700,715	1,159,949
1976	18,750,712	15,035,208	57,588	15,092,796	1,434,009	-105,426	13,553,361	2,459,345	2,738,006	6,960	2,693,955	1,169,981
1977	20,644,417	16,679,938	59,236	16,739,174	1,585,810	-128,573	15,024,791	2,723,794	2,895,832	7,693	2,683,597	1,185,498
1978	22,691,978	18,459,573	53,682	18,513,255	1,802,874	-153,678	16,556,703	3,008,296	3,126,979	8,484	2,674,747	1,210,116
1979	25,139,310	20,459,137	59,775	20,518,912	2,070,691	-183,553	18,264,668	3,384,715	3,489,927	9,452	2,659,625	1,231,366
1980	27,592,002	21,660,418	42,172	21,702,590	2,199,143	-191,313	19,312,134	4,215,001	4,064,867	10,426	2,646,406	1,214,171
1981	30,417,265	23,249,238	62,251	23,311,489	2,531,332	-204,533	20,575,624	5,278,652	4,562,989	11,562	2,630,712	1,200,978
1982	32,030,452	23,083,568	55,200	23,138,768	2,558,140	-97,502	20,483,126	6,153,783	5,393,543	12,224	2,620,312	1,156,673
1983	32,710,924	23,151,437	34,791	23,186,228	2,589,793	-43,873	20,552,562	6,320,839	5,837,523	12,548	2,606,777	1,121,342
1984	34,750,629	24,628,553	66,774	24,695,327	2,854,867	-26,397	21,814,063	7,066,504	5,870,062	13,459	2,581,947	1,133,457
1985	36,109,709	25,570,865	63,081	25,633,946	3,002,045	-8,046	22,623,855	7,455,062	6,030,792	14,201	2,542,677	1,144,718
1986	37,211,076	26,206,318	54,693	26,261,011	3,099,254	2,867	23,164,624	7,669,258	6,377,194	14,786	2,516,600	1,149,933
1987	38,725,790	27,752,365	50,953	27,803,318	3,232,771	10,858	24,581,405	7,618,145	6,526,240	15,522	2,494,837	1,176,201
1988	41,950,618	30,422,119	44,317	30,466,436	3,578,101	14,111	26,902,446	8,234,881	6,813,291	16,917	2,479,863	1,207,101
1989	44,984,999	32,247,720	56,804	32,304,524	3,754,299	16,778	28,567,003	9,293,963	7,124,033	18,213	2,469,921	1,228,910
1990	48,111,189	34,315,014	85,280	34,400,294	4,036,295	-5,653	30,358,346	9,876,141	7,876,702	19,481	2,469,681	1,257,869
1991	50,328,425	35,744,233	64,794	35,809,027	4,255,383	-36,916	31,516,728	9,819,260	8,992,437	20,318	2,476,980	1,250,192
1992	52,948,437	38,344,335	79,522	38,423,857	4,546,032	-84,786	33,793,039	9,705,879	9,449,519	21,298	2,486,034	1,259,326
1993	54,739,112	39,813,557	61,947	39,875,504	4,796,859	-121,255	34,957,390	9,778,151	10,003,571	21,975	2,490,949	1,267,305
1994	56,480,779	41,306,138	39,116	41,345,254	5,068,509	-138,297	36,138,448	10,094,525	10,247,806	22,711	2,486,989	1,282,644
1995	58,677,747	42,510,302	23,790	42,534,092	5,224,775	-159,045	37,150,272	10,849,943	10,677,532	23,659	2,480,098	1,296,271
1996	61,306,402	43,998,179	42,879	44,041,058	5,299,995	-184,908	38,556,155	11,512,353	11,237,894	24,808	2,471,209	1,303,923
1997	64,561,216	46,611,419	11,972	46,623,391	5,543,863	-214,747	40,864,781	12,255,503	11,440,932	26,242	2,460,208	1,320,252
1998	67,230,988	48,872,672	20,934	48,893,606	5,728,629	-243,632	42,921,345	12,843,829	11,465,814	27,444	2,449,747	1,332,351
1999	70,455,876	52,483,838	18,895	52,502,733	6,057,608	-311,466	46,133,659	12,429,402	11,892,815	28,893	2,438,518	1,354,381
2000	74,767,739	55,449,575	44,158	55,493,733	6,299,083	-353,546	48,841,104	13,509,276	12,417,359	30,790	2,428,303	1,380,946
2001	76,711,418	57,173,836	21,415	57,195,251	6,521,994	-432,315	50,240,942	13,285,849	13,184,627	31,732	2,417,480	1,386,079
2002	77,659,188	58,181,701	23,044	58,204,745	6,653,141	-476,062	51,075,542	12,753,138	13,830,508	32,246	2,408,348	1,377,923
2003	79,190,638	59,105,899	55,227	59,161,126	6,721,072	-480,320	51,959,734	12,849,488	14,381,416	32,980	2,401,168	1,364,807
2004	82,343,867	61,968,166	53,427	62,021,593	6,990,966	-527,129	54,503,498	12,987,291	14,853,078	34,466	2,389,107	1,372,751
2005	85,236,967	64,106,761	36,885	64,143,646	7,311,757	-541,763	56,290,126	13,006,384	15,940,457	35,897	2,374,483	1,378,023
2006	90,654,096	66,863,213	49,917	66,913,130	7,674,059	-628,346	58,610,725	15,220,263	16,823,108	38,347	2,364,039	1,389,178
2007	95,387,998	69,387,049	35,331	69,422,380	7,940,319	-611,918	60,870,143	16,630,092	17,887,763	40,437	2,358,914	1,409,989
2008	99,484,504	72,028,146	33,923	72,062,069	8,236,487	-614,098	63,211,484	16,755,401	19,517,619	42,212	2,356,802	1,414,771
2009	96,929,896	69,917,097	29,755	69,946,852	8,146,996	-470,461	61,329,395	14,991,637	20,608,864	41,152	2,355,432	1,385,475
2010	100,906,381	73,253,124	46,150	73,299,274	8,444,413	-501,570	64,353,291	14,674,438	21,878,652	42,812	2,356,983	1,390,551
2011	106,429,090	76,817,410	58,934	76,876,344	7,929,716	-582,395	68,364,233	16,330,895	21,733,962	45,104	2,359,626	1,413,965
2012	110,377,142	78,980,848	85,473	79,066,321	8,134,731	-532,803	70,398,787	18,257,324	21,721,031	46,765	2,360,263	1,432,340
2013	111,162,109	82,177,007	100,327	82,277,334	9,436,858	-534,631	72,305,845	17,053,882	21,802,382	47,103	2,359,977	1,440,804
2014	115,574,375	84,646,521	102,830	84,749,351	9,691,264	-550,346	74,507,741	18,671,889	22,394,745	49,041	2,356,699	1,449,877
2015	120,111,869	88,185,104	55,919	88,241,023	10,072,894	-712,676	77,455,453	19,389,259	23,267,157	51,130	2,349,139	1,459,369
2016	120,908,136	87,467,249	40,992	87,508,241	10,116,053	-731,283	76,660,905	19,812,162	24,435,069	51,636	2,341,536	1,464,176
2017	125,648,489	91,776,651	46,076	91,822,727	10,694,288	-814,536	80,313,903	20,777,755	24,556,831	53,849	2,333,367	1,479,848
2018	135,191,378	135,182,450	8,928	98,710,525	11,186,608	-910,663	86,613,254	22,788,822	25,789,302	58,206	2,322,653	1,496,627
2019	139,582,271	139,527,789	54,482	102,362,801	11,543,276	-1,022,039	89,797,486	23,229,912	26,554,873	60,227	2,317,600	1,514,579

Personal Income and Employment by Area: Pittsfield, MA

(Thousands of dollars, except as noted.)

Year	Personal income, total	Earnings by place of work			Less: Contributions for government social insurance	Plus: Adjustment for residence	Equals: Net earnings by place of residence	Plus: Dividends, interest, and rent	Plus: Personal current transfer receipts	Per capita personal income (dollars)	Population (persons)	Total employment
		Nonfarm	Farm	Total								
1970	617,044	483,166	3,850	487,016	32,373	-3,355	451,288	97,099	68,657	4,117	149,893	66,119
1971	657,388	510,589	3,674	514,263	35,381	-2,942	475,940	102,987	78,461	4,354	150,987	65,091
1972	706,423	550,362	3,487	553,849	40,377	-2,114	511,358	110,296	84,769	4,745	148,869	65,585
1973	779,029	615,450	3,547	618,997	52,376	-1,649	564,972	118,250	95,807	5,208	149,573	69,449
1974	845,894	665,072	3,067	668,139	58,309	-613	609,217	128,383	108,294	5,653	149,649	70,334
1975	906,579	678,703	3,696	682,399	57,405	2,048	627,042	133,712	145,825	6,093	148,788	67,804
1976	958,249	716,704	3,568	720,272	61,743	5,004	663,533	141,123	153,593	6,547	146,360	66,846
1977	1,018,502	758,234	3,476	761,710	65,540	8,290	704,460	154,669	159,373	7,033	144,826	67,029
1978	1,119,412	840,858	4,563	845,421	75,018	11,558	781,961	168,554	168,897	7,649	146,354	68,925
1979	1,235,616	919,454	4,285	923,739	85,047	16,074	854,766	188,675	192,175	8,496	145,437	71,249
1980	1,378,108	993,177	4,098	997,275	91,459	20,510	926,326	232,303	219,479	9,499	145,081	71,264
1981	1,521,777	1,071,558	3,527	1,075,085	106,361	17,275	985,999	286,264	249,514	10,522	144,629	70,426
1982	1,651,218	1,132,450	4,247	1,136,697	114,762	12,738	1,034,673	342,402	274,143	11,615	142,162	69,487
1983	1,757,622	1,214,423	5,004	1,219,427	124,006	8,175	1,103,596	358,900	295,126	12,380	141,969	69,795
1984	1,949,744	1,360,789	6,718	1,367,507	142,937	2,695	1,227,265	411,455	311,024	13,753	141,767	72,759
1985	2,067,119	1,468,209	6,393	1,474,602	154,863	-4,547	1,315,192	427,554	324,373	14,667	140,938	74,546
1986	2,208,129	1,583,822	7,153	1,590,975	169,895	-11,783	1,409,297	459,513	339,319	15,728	140,396	77,067
1987	2,328,491	1,691,754	5,607	1,697,361	178,957	-19,259	1,499,145	479,190	350,156	16,600	140,268	76,319
1988	2,510,104	1,823,597	4,308	1,827,905	196,152	-28,564	1,603,189	528,072	378,843	17,957	139,787	78,504
1989	2,697,840	1,921,883	4,253	1,926,136	207,654	-41,245	1,677,237	601,804	418,799	19,299	139,790	79,087
1990	2,773,638	1,952,357	4,723	1,957,080	206,803	-50,866	1,699,411	613,381	460,846	19,894	139,423	77,748
1991	2,796,745	1,884,720	4,606	1,889,326	203,878	-44,005	1,641,443	627,253	528,049	20,170	138,661	73,552
1992	2,827,965	1,947,641	6,006	1,953,647	208,414	-38,662	1,706,571	574,541	546,853	20,521	137,809	73,706
1993	2,940,269	1,999,234	3,839	2,003,073	216,245	-35,854	1,750,974	625,470	563,825	21,440	137,139	75,102
1994	3,042,065	2,051,924	3,836	2,055,760	222,327	-31,104	1,802,329	643,287	596,449	22,176	137,176	75,643
1995	3,168,181	2,126,956	2,251	2,129,207	231,994	-29,002	1,868,211	673,304	626,666	23,145	136,885	75,632
1996	3,351,222	2,241,361	3,080	2,244,441	239,526	-25,780	1,979,135	728,478	643,609	24,523	136,657	76,886
1997	3,522,742	2,372,122	3,455	2,375,577	251,705	-24,135	2,099,737	756,965	666,040	25,788	136,602	77,231
1998	3,694,657	2,485,609	3,980	2,489,589	262,025	-18,764	2,208,800	829,873	655,984	27,214	135,763	78,323
1999	3,858,297	2,648,390	4,693	2,653,083	272,067	-13,474	2,367,542	811,472	679,283	28,532	135,227	79,056
2000	4,112,645	2,804,649	4,787	2,809,436	284,489	-3,008	2,521,939	883,441	707,265	30,516	134,769	79,393
2001	4,220,947	2,842,878	3,854	2,846,732	296,753	-8,362	2,541,617	910,853	768,477	31,517	133,928	79,964
2002	4,284,195	2,986,149	3,480	2,989,629	314,155	-24,203	2,651,271	806,568	826,356	32,084	133,529	80,215
2003	4,301,305	2,971,324	3,406	2,974,730	312,289	-25,989	2,636,452	784,059	880,794	32,238	133,423	79,900
2004	4,597,368	3,163,035	5,375	3,168,410	342,234	-32,553	2,793,623	883,031	920,714	34,547	133,076	80,034
2005	4,748,387	3,300,047	3,737	3,303,784	365,101	-40,943	2,897,740	859,835	990,812	35,820	132,563	81,565
2006	4,980,818	3,427,231	1,437	3,428,668	374,614	-48,329	3,005,725	931,052	1,044,041	37,740	131,977	82,231
2007	5,172,156	3,499,055	864	3,499,919	384,327	-53,995	3,061,597	1,028,456	1,082,103	39,218	131,883	83,314
2008	5,367,279	3,530,569	1,896	3,532,465	391,823	-62,948	3,077,694	1,073,892	1,215,693	40,856	131,372	83,438
2009	5,287,236	3,433,695	2,751	3,436,446	381,616	-67,432	2,987,398	983,678	1,316,160	40,279	131,264	81,386
2010	5,418,950	3,523,765	3,633	3,527,398	379,031	-65,822	3,082,545	952,101	1,384,304	41,273	131,294	80,930
2011	5,694,621	3,635,313	3,473	3,638,786	355,174	-70,417	3,213,195	1,079,593	1,401,833	43,641	130,488	81,165
2012	5,889,216	3,727,286	7,878	3,735,164	361,226	-72,986	3,300,952	1,154,368	1,433,896	45,248	130,154	82,425
2013	5,914,538	3,770,318	9,936	3,780,254	408,622	-73,555	3,298,077	1,172,112	1,444,349	45,738	129,313	83,431
2014	6,223,806	3,889,470	3,270	3,892,740	423,423	-69,458	3,399,859	1,334,334	1,489,613	48,380	128,645	84,024
2015	6,536,174	4,065,619	121	4,065,740	434,599	-70,539	3,560,602	1,388,123	1,587,449	51,213	127,628	86,281
2016	6,659,161	4,176,620	-1,591	4,175,029	448,924	-74,510	3,651,595	1,356,850	1,650,716	52,493	126,858	85,684
2017	6,832,930	4,277,031	-401	4,276,630	462,507	-68,111	3,746,012	1,413,773	1,673,145	54,095	126,313	86,114
2018	7,132,374	7,135,374	-3,000	4,382,163	476,239	-70,164	3,835,760	1,548,522	1,748,092	56,651	125,901	85,848
2019	7,284,151	7,285,766	-1,615	4,484,135	487,123	-58,452	3,938,560	1,561,007	1,784,584	58,299	124,944	86,326

Personal Income and Employment by Area: Pocatello, ID

(Thousands of dollars, except as noted.)

Year	Personal income, total	Earnings by place of work			Less: Contributions for government social insurance	Plus: Adjustment for residence	Equals: Net earnings by place of residence	Plus: Dividends, interest, and rent	Plus: Personal current transfer receipts	Per capita personal income (dollars)	Population (persons)	Total employment
		Nonfarm	Farm	Total								
1970	180,403	133,357	3,631	136,988	11,199	12,441	138,230	25,631	16,542	3,449	52,301	21,284
1971	197,548	145,649	3,624	149,273	12,336	11,737	148,674	29,185	19,689	3,711	53,234	21,673
1972	221,291	163,697	4,820	168,517	14,415	13,033	167,135	31,959	22,197	4,079	54,256	22,338
1973	245,415	188,273	1,123	189,396	19,082	14,360	184,674	35,639	25,102	4,493	54,619	23,949
1974	288,684	218,585	7,129	225,714	22,900	15,586	218,400	41,295	28,989	5,136	56,204	25,253
1975	332,065	251,085	3,668	254,753	25,495	17,814	247,072	48,818	36,175	5,818	57,076	26,556
1976	389,601	305,171	4,574	309,745	31,431	18,696	297,010	52,799	39,792	6,488	60,045	28,815
1977	428,435	335,614	2,607	338,221	34,826	22,721	326,116	59,545	42,774	6,868	62,378	30,488
1978	484,031	379,983	3,615	383,598	39,846	24,299	368,051	68,215	47,765	7,584	63,821	31,826
1979	533,850	421,919	2,156	424,075	46,323	23,402	401,154	77,567	55,129	8,229	64,871	32,145
1980	578,044	444,269	4,848	449,117	49,240	26,114	425,991	86,005	66,048	8,805	65,650	30,930
1981	625,003	468,157	5,630	473,787	55,897	33,272	451,162	100,041	73,800	9,401	66,486	30,178
1982	665,608	481,563	5,353	486,916	59,787	37,468	464,597	118,138	82,873	9,922	67,081	29,433
1983	709,757	501,745	6,435	508,180	62,289	46,608	492,499	128,757	88,501	10,545	67,307	29,207
1984	744,846	525,044	3,059	528,103	68,115	53,527	513,515	139,326	92,005	11,098	67,114	29,669
1985	804,872	565,893	4,749	570,642	74,743	57,555	553,454	152,717	98,701	12,004	67,051	30,216
1986	800,033	546,567	5,512	552,079	73,232	62,558	541,405	155,761	102,867	11,933	67,043	28,847
1987	816,251	552,322	3,786	556,108	71,438	74,937	559,607	151,050	105,594	12,341	66,140	28,462
1988	850,233	580,138	2,416	582,554	80,078	81,132	583,608	154,657	111,968	12,963	65,588	29,680
1989	911,170	616,344	5,353	621,697	86,943	84,433	619,187	169,817	122,166	13,833	65,869	30,423
1990	959,674	652,753	7,369	660,122	95,648	90,773	655,247	172,360	132,067	14,484	66,258	30,888
1991	1,025,897	685,579	6,828	692,407	100,821	109,375	700,961	177,746	147,190	15,235	67,338	31,624
1992	1,114,719	750,325	10,965	761,290	106,527	107,164	761,927	185,081	167,711	16,115	69,173	32,944
1993	1,199,290	813,472	10,158	823,630	115,189	109,709	818,150	202,267	178,873	16,946	70,770	34,329
1994	1,261,196	857,730	6,749	864,479	120,591	111,904	855,792	216,800	188,604	17,403	72,468	35,875
1995	1,326,803	886,314	9,322	895,636	125,308	111,926	882,254	240,448	204,101	18,026	73,603	36,418
1996	1,394,924	947,208	8,287	955,495	131,525	105,758	929,728	250,699	214,497	18,844	74,026	38,085
1997	1,454,686	987,733	4,435	992,168	135,579	111,733	968,322	264,540	221,824	19,491	74,635	38,859
1998	1,523,758	1,062,487	6,676	1,069,163	141,422	112,154	1,039,895	259,494	224,369	20,354	74,864	39,955
1999	1,572,556	1,121,101	9,052	1,130,153	145,787	96,315	1,080,681	258,630	233,245	20,821	75,527	41,174
2000	1,641,240	1,170,040	8,943	1,178,983	151,319	99,970	1,127,634	266,298	247,308	21,673	75,728	42,453
2001	1,730,295	1,192,934	8,532	1,201,466	153,563	122,085	1,169,988	280,497	279,810	22,679	76,296	43,013
2002	1,782,337	1,223,876	12,127	1,236,003	156,530	106,212	1,185,685	289,602	307,050	23,302	76,487	42,855
2003	1,854,152	1,282,697	8,396	1,291,093	162,762	97,979	1,226,310	306,722	321,120	24,297	76,312	43,780
2004	1,966,512	1,385,712	11,226	1,396,938	175,830	88,251	1,309,359	310,487	346,666	25,594	76,834	45,355
2005	2,046,658	1,456,676	8,656	1,465,332	187,525	85,482	1,363,289	316,214	367,155	26,436	77,419	46,608
2006	2,170,243	1,524,768	8,763	1,533,531	197,808	96,631	1,432,354	340,355	397,534	27,650	78,491	47,498
2007	2,284,849	1,580,412	10,645	1,591,057	204,685	103,076	1,489,448	369,116	426,285	28,799	79,338	48,138
2008	2,368,344	1,602,804	11,363	1,614,167	207,738	109,271	1,515,700	364,125	488,519	29,381	80,609	46,718
2009	2,353,713	1,526,448	8,138	1,534,586	202,870	134,873	1,466,589	359,038	528,086	28,706	81,994	44,853
2010	2,422,488	1,542,800	8,697	1,551,497	212,021	144,094	1,483,570	354,002	584,916	29,178	83,024	43,978
2011	2,525,711	1,554,775	15,683	1,570,458	193,377	167,214	1,544,295	385,692	595,724	30,212	83,599	44,145
2012	2,593,837	1,581,943	12,196	1,594,139	194,828	184,625	1,583,936	407,619	602,282	30,981	83,724	44,074
2013	2,658,595	1,633,520	12,985	1,646,505	216,467	191,385	1,621,423	424,832	612,340	31,874	83,410	44,646
2014	2,757,768	1,687,783	11,142	1,698,925	224,756	196,247	1,670,416	459,852	627,500	33,022	83,514	45,309
2015	2,911,085	1,785,780	12,539	1,798,319	232,758	194,668	1,760,229	497,182	653,674	34,659	83,992	46,202
2016	3,008,320	1,839,648	9,536	1,849,184	239,732	214,898	1,824,350	504,352	679,618	35,652	84,379	46,558
2017	3,153,879	1,917,888	13,356	1,931,244	250,214	234,725	1,915,755	528,983	709,141	36,987	85,269	47,160
2018	3,615,429	3,569,384	46,045	2,223,456	284,874	216,701	2,155,283	646,291	813,855	38,310	94,374	52,621
2019	3,778,833	3,720,485	58,348	2,327,590	295,799	231,764	2,263,555	658,504	856,774	39,573	95,489	53,809

Personal Income and Employment by Area: Portland-South Portland, ME

(Thousands of dollars, except as noted.)

Year	Personal income, total	Earnings by place of work			Less: Contributions for government social insurance	Plus: Adjustment for residence	Equals: Net earnings by place of residence	Plus: Dividends, interest, and rent	Plus: Personal current transfer receipts	Per capita personal income (dollars)	Population (persons)	Total employment
		Nonfarm	Farm	Total								
1970	1,309,394	1,052,479	7,804	1,060,283	71,698	-38,473	950,112	239,994	119,288	3,985	328,590	156,769
1971	1,412,610	1,119,076	7,885	1,126,961	78,837	-36,951	1,011,173	260,636	140,801	4,202	336,169	155,953
1972	1,564,546	1,247,512	8,971	1,256,483	92,402	-42,343	1,121,738	284,116	158,692	4,562	342,955	160,994
1973	1,715,429	1,352,873	14,673	1,367,546	114,173	-39,605	1,213,768	312,092	189,569	4,908	349,490	165,759
1974	1,876,732	1,458,545	12,171	1,470,716	127,325	-50,650	1,292,741	353,833	230,158	5,270	356,106	169,317
1975	2,075,896	1,583,433	10,744	1,594,177	135,312	-66,038	1,392,827	387,620	295,449	5,752	360,891	170,259
1976	2,336,245	1,809,000	17,917	1,826,917	157,854	-75,808	1,593,255	419,222	323,768	6,397	365,186	177,404
1977	2,572,894	2,004,274	8,929	2,013,203	175,222	-84,894	1,753,087	474,479	345,328	6,906	372,562	184,124
1978	2,882,269	2,264,861	10,650	2,275,511	204,215	-95,892	1,975,404	536,078	370,787	7,628	377,860	193,643
1979	3,193,454	2,515,682	6,276	2,521,958	234,416	-104,731	2,182,811	592,287	418,356	8,335	383,159	200,253
1980	3,620,239	2,807,558	4,152	2,811,710	260,393	-117,323	2,433,994	701,123	485,122	9,385	385,753	204,838
1981	4,021,609	3,087,550	6,089	3,093,639	305,905	-169,384	2,618,350	847,736	555,523	10,284	391,072	207,150
1982	4,443,130	3,355,873	8,144	3,364,017	338,426	-192,715	2,832,876	1,004,799	605,455	11,266	394,395	210,235
1983	4,812,060	3,656,001	2,920	3,658,921	377,092	-191,734	3,090,095	1,069,537	652,428	12,052	399,275	217,658
1984	5,390,352	4,093,914	9,110	4,103,024	438,249	-191,245	3,473,530	1,227,545	689,277	13,294	405,463	228,798
1985	5,920,385	4,507,243	6,880	4,514,123	484,748	-170,169	3,859,206	1,325,572	735,607	14,377	411,789	239,590
1986	6,533,722	5,016,674	9,923	5,026,597	547,026	-164,003	4,315,568	1,450,286	767,868	15,631	417,991	254,199
1987	7,150,723	5,565,047	8,278	5,573,325	606,622	-161,697	4,805,006	1,555,960	789,757	16,832	424,840	265,537
1988	7,965,763	6,252,052	7,575	6,259,627	694,910	-183,844	5,380,873	1,745,449	839,441	18,370	433,634	281,206
1989	8,627,292	6,711,790	5,378	6,717,168	738,713	-212,618	5,765,837	1,958,625	902,830	19,663	438,759	287,046
1990	9,007,684	6,951,046	13,093	6,964,139	807,287	-223,226	5,933,626	2,067,306	1,006,752	20,343	442,790	285,041
1991	9,111,913	6,885,007	10,943	6,895,950	807,394	-180,000	5,908,556	2,046,643	1,156,714	20,457	445,414	273,772
1992	9,561,977	7,195,091	15,223	7,210,314	854,237	-153,002	6,203,075	2,085,985	1,272,917	21,396	446,901	274,413
1993	9,907,560	7,382,640	12,704	7,395,344	895,274	-95,209	6,404,861	2,160,766	1,341,933	22,034	449,643	276,688
1994	10,397,073	7,727,257	10,031	7,737,288	956,241	-48,463	6,732,584	2,262,296	1,402,193	22,916	453,695	283,211
1995	10,991,776	8,008,107	11,513	8,019,620	997,819	6,300	7,028,101	2,479,954	1,483,721	24,025	457,522	285,360
1996	11,705,993	8,405,806	10,943	8,416,749	1,035,159	59,434	7,441,024	2,674,795	1,590,174	25,235	463,883	290,659
1997	12,502,054	9,010,082	9,895	9,019,977	1,106,313	89,294	8,002,958	2,832,264	1,666,832	26,591	470,167	299,375
1998	13,337,411	9,724,590	11,029	9,735,619	1,179,976	145,922	8,701,565	2,926,522	1,709,324	28,053	475,444	307,580
1999	14,155,823	10,519,756	11,685	10,531,441	1,256,114	192,173	9,467,500	2,919,588	1,768,735	29,371	481,966	313,419
2000	15,323,335	11,227,090	15,799	11,242,889	1,315,947	302,248	10,229,190	3,195,799	1,898,346	31,325	489,179	323,073
2001	16,232,737	11,969,046	14,888	11,983,934	1,376,874	286,447	10,893,507	3,288,324	2,050,906	32,795	494,975	329,579
2002	16,761,631	12,444,606	14,496	12,459,102	1,384,245	258,697	11,333,554	3,240,179	2,187,898	33,511	500,178	330,414
2003	17,571,042	13,070,823	14,431	13,085,254	1,437,165	197,454	11,845,543	3,354,996	2,370,503	34,804	504,858	335,323
2004	18,704,204	13,955,232	14,552	13,969,784	1,530,513	169,725	12,608,996	3,573,752	2,521,456	36,788	508,428	343,215
2005	19,093,917	14,124,194	11,045	14,135,239	1,562,846	186,006	12,758,399	3,602,043	2,733,475	37,418	510,287	343,183
2006	20,392,890	14,931,892	10,731	14,942,623	1,673,043	204,307	13,473,887	4,121,256	2,797,747	39,938	510,614	348,308
2007	21,175,467	15,365,666	9,323	15,374,989	1,753,098	190,927	13,812,818	4,361,005	3,001,644	41,337	512,265	353,971
2008	21,894,483	15,671,941	19,722	15,691,663	1,806,137	180,772	14,066,298	4,330,741	3,497,444	42,580	514,191	353,530
2009	21,533,567	15,429,899	24,037	15,453,936	1,767,911	214,475	13,900,500	3,849,061	3,784,006	41,835	514,728	343,960
2010	22,207,022	15,933,761	33,977	15,967,738	1,818,282	300,728	14,450,184	3,877,372	3,879,466	43,214	513,879	342,237
2011	23,267,162	16,260,514	31,179	16,291,693	1,667,495	391,131	15,015,329	4,228,308	4,023,525	45,098	515,929	345,578
2012	23,984,970	16,694,539	33,171	16,727,710	1,723,810	445,410	15,449,310	4,514,641	4,021,019	46,314	517,872	347,932
2013	24,080,859	16,953,350	35,045	16,988,395	2,010,591	516,387	15,494,191	4,441,423	4,145,245	46,309	519,999	351,283
2014	25,381,046	17,567,946	31,149	17,599,095	2,059,784	600,205	16,139,516	4,945,286	4,296,244	48,525	523,049	356,001
2015	26,634,034	18,405,645	26,224	18,431,869	2,188,551	613,901	16,857,219	5,265,110	4,511,705	50,684	525,492	362,352
2016	27,697,564	19,178,447	23,804	19,202,251	2,259,989	629,327	17,571,589	5,482,031	4,643,944	52,432	528,261	369,483
2017	29,053,073	20,237,642	23,641	20,261,283	2,375,142	608,017	18,494,158	5,749,025	4,809,890	54,603	532,083	376,290
2018	30,997,140	30,983,403	13,737	21,322,754	2,513,605	641,554	19,450,703	6,435,786	5,110,651	57,913	535,232	384,132
2019	32,310,227	32,293,835	16,392	22,422,434	2,633,682	669,694	20,458,446	6,459,056	5,392,725	60,000	538,500	391,110

Personal Income and Employment by Area: Portland-Vancouver-Hillsboro, OR-WA

(Thousands of dollars, except as noted.)

Year	Personal income, total	Earnings by place of work			Less: Contributions for government social insurance	Plus: Adjustment for residence	Equals: Net earnings by place of residence	Plus: Dividends, interest, and rent	Plus: Personal current transfer receipts	Per capita personal income (dollars)	Population (persons)	Total employment
		Nonfarm	Farm	Total								
1970	4,839,750	3,841,363	48,010	3,889,373	294,374	9,352	3,604,351	807,901	427,498	4,460	1,085,025	497,091
1971	5,289,170	4,160,169	44,528	4,204,697	328,026	23,091	3,899,762	892,268	497,140	4,785	1,105,374	506,310
1972	5,892,337	4,690,577	48,379	4,738,956	392,279	37,872	4,384,549	968,100	539,688	5,195	1,134,259	535,293
1973	6,599,173	5,270,140	83,122	5,353,262	510,759	47,463	4,889,966	1,075,874	633,333	5,700	1,157,768	564,082
1974	7,470,277	5,904,154	79,239	5,983,393	586,768	58,077	5,454,702	1,248,745	766,830	6,359	1,174,809	583,002
1975	8,291,936	6,364,377	72,248	6,436,625	616,976	99,017	5,918,666	1,397,285	975,985	6,953	1,192,510	587,075
1976	9,287,115	7,220,112	70,781	7,290,893	712,908	125,697	6,703,682	1,518,155	1,065,278	7,656	1,213,090	609,841
1977	10,335,263	8,167,539	71,689	8,239,228	813,974	78,467	7,503,721	1,698,889	1,132,653	8,319	1,242,430	640,432
1978	11,888,345	9,536,300	69,748	9,606,048	977,647	48,857	8,677,258	1,979,454	1,231,633	9,322	1,275,246	683,210
1979	13,497,187	10,906,532	82,997	10,989,529	1,162,884	14,792	9,841,437	2,285,654	1,370,096	10,285	1,312,315	719,013
1980	15,113,387	11,935,285	81,851	12,017,136	1,272,567	3,955	10,748,524	2,756,416	1,608,447	11,222	1,346,705	728,447
1981	16,542,871	12,643,346	83,103	12,726,449	1,436,597	14,146	11,303,998	3,377,901	1,860,972	12,124	1,364,523	717,025
1982	17,183,283	12,717,462	69,321	12,786,783	1,470,701	40,716	11,356,798	3,709,743	2,116,742	12,512	1,373,347	694,891
1983	18,134,873	13,260,740	74,090	13,334,830	1,550,685	61,243	11,845,388	3,990,696	2,298,789	13,227	1,371,007	703,207
1984	19,798,807	14,616,848	109,744	14,726,592	1,768,828	58,169	13,015,933	4,419,867	2,363,007	14,343	1,380,339	734,223
1985	20,856,719	15,482,959	109,246	15,592,205	1,885,163	50,850	13,757,892	4,646,372	2,452,455	14,989	1,391,424	754,432
1986	22,119,353	16,557,928	158,946	16,716,874	2,010,221	51,015	14,757,668	4,848,796	2,512,889	15,690	1,409,733	775,492
1987	23,367,978	17,724,844	150,209	17,875,053	2,121,464	49,291	15,802,880	4,962,510	2,602,588	16,419	1,423,238	803,521
1988	25,621,787	19,732,690	182,506	19,915,196	2,435,516	49,649	17,529,329	5,342,723	2,749,735	17,620	1,454,141	845,832
1989	28,352,210	21,597,097	187,842	21,784,939	2,663,638	57,593	19,178,894	6,154,949	3,018,367	19,064	1,487,217	883,562
1990	31,092,474	23,954,711	240,900	24,195,611	3,033,477	55,643	21,217,777	6,605,003	3,269,694	20,243	1,535,965	918,239
1991	32,816,993	25,387,312	267,345	25,654,657	3,253,596	64,719	22,465,780	6,718,655	3,632,558	20,708	1,584,767	929,685
1992	35,246,718	27,456,074	246,867	27,702,941	3,492,382	59,318	24,269,877	6,941,302	4,035,539	21,680	1,625,751	941,423
1993	37,848,194	29,485,790	249,269	29,735,059	3,752,649	49,986	26,032,396	7,508,121	4,307,677	22,668	1,669,701	969,806
1994	40,815,645	31,747,442	230,689	31,978,131	4,077,627	42,763	27,943,267	8,424,925	4,447,453	23,894	1,708,216	1,022,108
1995	44,305,203	34,294,787	238,680	34,533,467	4,428,385	5,812	30,110,894	9,311,202	4,883,107	25,328	1,749,224	1,065,398
1996	48,349,768	37,666,234	268,174	37,934,408	4,895,457	-31,434	33,007,517	10,126,701	5,215,550	26,905	1,797,066	1,112,001
1997	52,050,493	40,966,216	318,191	41,284,407	5,236,441	-68,052	35,979,914	10,711,969	5,358,610	28,290	1,839,867	1,160,405
1998	54,878,933	43,727,458	319,646	44,047,104	5,546,839	-74,085	38,426,180	11,022,898	5,429,855	29,263	1,875,365	1,188,161
1999	57,281,732	46,061,977	327,765	46,389,742	5,773,690	-75,570	40,540,482	10,871,166	5,870,084	30,049	1,906,262	1,203,732
2000	62,929,380	50,806,441	298,757	51,105,198	6,332,901	-126,097	44,646,200	11,942,633	6,340,547	32,525	1,934,792	1,230,760
2001	63,929,584	51,119,521	327,285	51,446,806	6,315,077	-93,420	45,038,309	11,737,557	7,153,718	32,433	1,971,152	1,230,201
2002	64,296,980	51,055,621	321,028	51,376,649	6,309,234	-56,242	45,011,173	11,412,848	7,872,959	32,102	2,002,918	1,213,408
2003	66,501,216	52,474,216	406,426	52,880,642	6,481,393	-8,121	46,391,128	12,053,325	8,056,763	32,854	2,024,115	1,216,494
2004	70,630,609	56,050,146	423,755	56,473,901	6,968,444	6,278	49,511,735	12,897,710	8,221,164	34,635	2,039,297	1,248,863
2005	74,641,931	59,226,008	432,970	59,658,978	7,316,915	-8,986	52,333,077	13,651,435	8,657,419	36,106	2,067,325	1,289,785
2006	81,701,865	64,043,533	488,643	64,532,176	7,863,814	-35,885	56,632,477	15,766,784	9,302,604	38,847	2,103,164	1,330,456
2007	86,404,669	67,088,308	475,399	67,563,707	8,223,900	684	59,340,491	16,991,991	10,072,187	40,417	2,137,828	1,368,280
2008	90,841,147	68,154,997	514,100	68,669,097	8,352,696	133,765	60,450,166	18,546,626	11,844,355	41,807	2,172,853	1,367,770
2009	86,755,892	64,269,554	465,073	64,734,627	8,031,351	294,058	56,997,334	16,167,402	13,591,156	39,314	2,206,737	1,310,373
2010	88,948,950	65,633,990	405,877	66,039,867	8,285,248	465,165	58,219,784	15,884,796	14,844,370	39,854	2,231,876	1,306,785
2011	94,877,986	69,028,828	466,178	69,495,006	7,734,541	377,714	62,138,179	17,810,279	14,929,528	42,003	2,258,821	1,333,678
2012	101,391,134	73,929,644	532,006	74,461,650	8,140,359	331,388	66,652,679	19,854,462	14,883,993	44,369	2,285,177	1,358,131
2013	102,907,013	76,819,728	603,047	77,422,775	9,584,922	326,351	68,164,204	19,358,113	15,384,696	44,562	2,309,289	1,389,557
2014	110,739,675	81,130,318	565,884	81,696,202	10,154,503	435,026	71,976,725	22,052,849	16,710,101	47,275	2,342,444	1,433,568
2015	119,339,086	86,990,314	702,758	87,693,072	10,765,217	437,051	77,364,906	24,351,994	17,622,186	50,097	2,382,181	1,481,131
2016	124,974,141	91,590,721	625,550	92,216,271	11,247,917	278,597	81,246,951	25,503,719	18,223,471	51,576	2,423,102	1,521,173
2017	131,861,371	97,793,864	579,213	98,373,077	12,113,670	217,992	86,477,399	26,679,647	18,704,325	53,751	2,453,168	1,557,228
2018	143,214,639	142,832,559	382,080	104,220,078	12,601,768	294,713	91,913,023	31,558,372	19,743,244	57,903	2,473,350	1,606,393
2019	149,346,827	149,003,931	342,896	109,742,844	13,281,356	98,484	96,559,972	31,943,742	20,843,113	59,921	2,492,412	1,642,485

Personal Income and Employment by Area: Port St. Lucie, FL

(Thousands of dollars, except as noted.)

Year	Personal income, total	Earnings by place of work			Less: Contributions for government social insurance	Plus: Adjustment for residence	Equals: Net earnings by place of residence	Plus: Dividends, interest, and rent	Plus: Personal current transfer receipts	Per capita personal income (dollars)	Population (persons)	Total employment
		Nonfarm	Farm	Total								
1970............	314,908	185,400	23,641	209,041	12,412	309	196,938	82,937	35,033	3,949	79,741	33,285
1971............	365,479	209,249	28,337	237,586	14,601	2,417	225,402	96,936	43,141	4,321	84,589	35,253
1972............	441,651	257,116	34,881	291,997	18,903	2,425	275,519	113,292	52,840	4,901	90,118	39,752
1973............	539,533	318,856	34,460	353,316	26,816	3,947	330,447	141,545	67,541	5,239	102,977	44,659
1974............	618,281	355,871	35,234	391,105	31,474	4,798	364,429	171,150	82,702	5,482	112,792	46,293
1975............	692,720	380,117	38,997	419,114	33,146	5,579	391,547	194,063	107,110	5,883	117,754	46,049
1976............	790,994	434,172	46,111	480,283	37,833	7,740	450,190	219,681	121,123	6,482	122,024	48,072
1977............	910,728	489,023	58,524	547,547	43,123	11,867	516,291	257,575	136,862	7,175	126,939	51,647
1978............	1,086,736	579,065	77,889	656,954	51,937	16,306	621,323	310,262	155,151	8,113	133,944	56,962
1979............	1,304,264	704,186	80,958	785,144	66,063	17,067	736,148	381,803	186,313	9,108	143,206	62,851
1980............	1,663,682	882,979	122,384	1,005,363	83,903	2,941	924,401	511,443	227,838	10,819	153,770	68,854
1981............	1,933,556	979,152	85,659	1,064,811	99,992	20,592	985,411	678,023	270,122	11,806	163,782	71,320
1982............	2,143,899	1,051,361	98,310	1,149,671	111,108	31,735	1,070,298	756,970	316,631	12,350	173,600	74,297
1983............	2,409,474	1,140,439	154,046	1,294,485	119,742	56,745	1,231,488	823,248	354,738	13,282	181,413	77,623
1984............	2,638,384	1,236,869	101,719	1,338,588	132,984	90,490	1,296,094	955,144	387,146	13,895	189,879	81,858
1985............	2,950,357	1,345,705	110,120	1,455,825	148,160	118,861	1,426,526	1,090,650	433,181	14,917	197,784	86,119
1986............	3,274,971	1,508,008	110,034	1,618,042	170,297	139,868	1,587,613	1,206,032	481,326	15,824	206,964	90,815
1987............	3,647,109	1,724,234	135,300	1,859,534	192,185	159,502	1,826,851	1,296,794	523,464	16,742	217,839	93,920
1988............	4,258,597	1,941,389	220,566	2,161,955	223,813	187,039	2,125,181	1,541,257	592,159	18,708	227,640	101,218
1989............	4,874,855	2,141,027	167,524	2,308,551	252,123	208,584	2,265,012	1,921,420	688,423	20,377	239,233	107,262
1990............	5,337,847	2,277,859	124,563	2,402,422	264,565	237,932	2,375,789	2,189,201	772,857	20,957	254,702	109,748
1991............	5,540,206	2,342,531	149,173	2,491,704	273,643	248,702	2,466,763	2,185,934	887,509	21,054	263,143	108,584
1992............	5,829,248	2,530,054	106,874	2,636,928	292,540	267,351	2,611,739	2,183,318	1,034,191	21,613	269,716	108,447
1993............	6,178,666	2,685,556	103,939	2,789,495	308,989	280,618	2,761,124	2,297,835	1,119,707	22,287	277,235	111,244
1994............	6,509,197	2,805,913	88,625	2,894,538	330,635	304,064	2,867,967	2,433,697	1,207,533	22,839	285,006	113,621
1995............	7,144,672	2,959,179	97,094	3,056,273	349,116	324,949	3,032,106	2,803,206	1,309,360	24,592	290,527	117,523
1996............	7,648,009	3,141,218	59,515	3,200,733	365,916	363,205	3,198,022	3,047,073	1,402,914	25,669	297,947	122,505
1997............	8,149,594	3,307,848	61,224	3,369,072	386,018	394,662	3,377,716	3,286,499	1,485,379	26,728	304,912	126,227
1998............	8,809,664	3,523,315	105,598	3,628,913	407,982	446,781	3,667,712	3,593,880	1,548,072	28,310	311,185	133,060
1999............	9,242,946	3,777,610	89,817	3,867,427	430,797	496,449	3,933,079	3,699,933	1,609,934	29,220	316,323	136,633
2000............	9,899,941	4,024,672	83,733	4,108,405	458,233	567,652	4,217,824	3,961,311	1,720,806	30,858	320,819	141,761
2001............	10,698,222	4,525,801	67,306	4,593,107	507,141	725,168	4,811,134	4,036,935	1,850,153	32,585	328,315	143,578
2002............	11,018,687	4,915,101	66,462	4,981,563	545,876	883,507	5,319,194	3,717,799	1,981,694	32,528	338,741	148,128
2003............	11,783,308	5,265,221	51,727	5,316,948	588,229	1,080,239	5,808,958	3,866,432	2,107,918	33,521	351,522	155,145
2004............	13,407,416	5,909,236	64,059	5,973,295	663,328	1,196,364	6,506,331	4,598,050	2,303,035	36,406	368,277	166,986
2005............	14,895,420	6,553,542	101,807	6,655,349	746,806	1,515,109	7,423,652	5,086,223	2,385,545	38,803	383,877	179,580
2006............	16,371,867	6,955,788	95,564	7,051,352	819,006	1,665,396	7,897,742	5,906,549	2,567,576	41,233	397,053	187,529
2007............	17,227,178	7,121,674	68,055	7,189,729	858,233	1,794,828	8,126,324	6,351,203	2,749,651	41,976	410,402	189,637
2008............	17,389,591	6,699,225	62,842	6,762,067	846,043	1,899,021	7,815,045	6,449,866	3,124,680	41,650	417,520	183,487
2009............	15,939,306	6,443,445	62,864	6,506,309	816,720	1,775,016	7,464,605	5,057,678	3,417,023	37,964	419,850	175,818
2010............	16,414,379	6,710,438	70,068	6,780,506	820,553	1,498,057	7,458,010	5,249,059	3,707,310	38,605	425,193	176,756
2011............	17,507,010	6,840,565	81,546	6,922,111	754,986	1,622,430	7,789,555	5,851,812	3,865,643	40,870	428,363	179,263
2012............	19,202,462	7,122,779	106,036	7,228,815	787,212	2,186,419	8,628,022	6,729,510	3,844,930	44,428	432,217	181,956
2013............	18,869,985	7,239,318	95,488	7,334,806	900,839	2,293,899	8,727,866	6,138,629	4,003,490	43,188	436,927	185,840
2014............	20,715,012	7,665,552	92,817	7,758,369	950,011	2,372,479	9,180,837	7,267,637	4,266,538	46,672	443,840	194,098
2015............	22,104,975	8,204,763	127,743	8,332,506	1,005,677	2,468,219	9,795,048	7,776,469	4,533,458	48,727	453,650	202,464
2016............	23,613,991	8,509,915	79,693	8,589,608	1,058,780	2,960,785	10,491,613	8,365,959	4,756,419	50,831	464,563	210,088
2017............	24,825,580	8,886,299	61,642	8,947,941	1,108,004	3,218,784	11,058,721	8,776,083	4,990,776	52,438	473,429	214,527
2018............	26,162,619	26,072,226	90,393	9,578,161	1,184,953	3,219,758	11,612,966	9,262,414	5,287,239	54,373	481,167	226,382
2019............	27,249,575	27,131,483	118,092	10,130,175	1,270,429	3,414,911	12,274,657	9,347,636	5,627,282	55,691	489,297	233,225

Personal Income and Employment by Area: Poughkeepsie-Newburgh-Middletown, NY

(Thousands of dollars, except as noted.)

Year	Personal income, total	Earnings by place of work			Less: Contributions for government social insurance	Plus: Adjustment for residence	Equals: Net earnings by place of residence	Plus: Dividends, interest, and rent	Plus: Personal current transfer receipts	Per capita personal income (dollars)	Population (persons)	Total employment
		Nonfarm	Farm	Total								
1970	1,928,321	1,905,425	22,896	1,509,513	111,073	64,522	1,462,962	309,887	155,472	4,319	446,438	186,898
1971	2,134,783	2,113,367	21,416	1,639,510	124,703	91,649	1,606,456	340,092	188,235	4,672	456,961	189,327
1972	2,357,479	2,339,576	17,903	1,793,401	143,246	122,935	1,773,090	374,687	209,702	5,130	459,527	192,493
1973	2,610,794	2,587,484	23,310	1,965,250	180,420	164,138	1,948,968	415,400	246,426	5,570	468,716	201,165
1974	2,872,515	2,851,400	21,115	2,111,175	199,764	204,484	2,115,895	463,282	293,338	6,043	475,356	203,257
1975	3,165,617	3,140,932	24,685	2,227,161	207,727	251,725	2,271,159	505,336	389,122	6,550	483,292	199,854
1976	3,397,625	3,373,601	24,024	2,350,271	224,775	304,987	2,430,483	528,605	438,537	7,026	483,589	199,394
1977	3,705,209	3,678,748	26,461	2,549,206	243,325	360,164	2,666,045	573,952	465,212	7,564	489,832	203,486
1978	4,119,419	4,092,673	26,746	2,840,325	277,283	435,227	2,998,269	622,850	498,300	8,306	495,984	212,224
1979	4,623,555	4,589,988	33,567	3,176,483	320,495	511,560	3,367,548	716,209	539,798	9,209	502,051	221,762
1980	5,208,461	5,170,852	37,609	3,448,452	345,202	623,051	3,726,301	853,256	628,904	10,296	505,849	222,410
1981	5,914,329	5,880,993	33,336	3,831,059	407,158	727,497	4,151,398	1,036,763	726,168	11,604	509,660	225,577
1982	6,574,113	6,544,067	30,046	4,238,267	453,901	789,831	4,574,197	1,198,967	800,949	12,796	513,751	230,042
1983	7,118,887	7,099,422	19,465	4,609,171	499,453	863,291	4,973,009	1,293,204	852,674	13,710	519,246	233,972
1984	7,969,083	7,940,672	28,411	5,218,644	576,101	962,456	5,604,999	1,480,817	883,267	15,147	526,116	244,050
1985	8,612,665	8,584,859	27,806	5,688,903	637,186	1,058,279	6,109,996	1,574,588	928,081	16,193	531,875	254,676
1986	9,256,140	9,224,690	31,450	6,122,576	694,576	1,176,496	6,604,496	1,662,352	989,292	17,195	538,304	261,524
1987	9,852,451	9,813,365	39,086	6,560,340	735,400	1,272,072	7,097,012	1,746,773	1,008,666	17,984	547,857	264,793
1988	10,647,116	10,609,163	37,953	7,117,616	820,862	1,399,174	7,695,928	1,867,905	1,083,283	19,092	557,662	275,305
1989	11,593,991	11,550,197	43,794	7,609,508	864,832	1,432,133	8,176,809	2,212,576	1,204,606	20,618	562,322	278,982
1990	12,231,579	12,194,781	36,798	8,004,625	876,976	1,570,627	8,698,276	2,216,581	1,316,722	21,495	569,041	279,509
1991	12,591,290	12,549,622	41,668	8,124,661	908,731	1,658,055	8,873,985	2,258,960	1,458,345	21,936	573,990	273,759
1992	13,109,160	13,076,512	32,648	8,388,603	925,403	1,735,858	9,199,058	2,238,017	1,672,085	22,586	580,407	273,282
1993	13,298,761	13,246,478	52,283	8,333,717	921,386	1,899,743	9,312,074	2,222,387	1,764,300	22,749	584,584	269,630
1994	13,513,941	13,477,320	36,621	8,235,150	922,593	2,051,293	9,363,850	2,297,945	1,852,146	23,077	585,604	272,756
1995	14,178,331	14,147,320	31,011	8,484,600	949,931	2,185,870	9,720,539	2,486,943	1,970,849	24,032	589,989	270,432
1996	14,849,290	14,823,541	25,749	8,795,353	971,608	2,375,895	10,199,640	2,582,688	2,066,962	24,957	594,986	274,599
1997	15,670,427	15,653,061	17,366	9,063,722	986,979	2,798,718	10,875,461	2,685,239	2,109,727	26,126	599,795	277,738
1998	16,575,447	16,543,570	31,877	9,642,542	1,044,416	2,867,628	11,465,754	2,795,598	2,314,095	27,353	605,983	282,874
1999	17,652,548	17,608,952	43,596	10,608,481	1,105,679	2,981,416	12,484,218	2,783,131	2,385,199	28,740	614,216	293,769
2000	18,981,243	18,927,533	53,710	11,273,342	1,177,748	3,406,863	13,502,457	2,973,540	2,505,246	30,428	623,806	301,872
2001	19,915,261	19,864,592	50,669	11,917,251	1,275,439	3,599,254	14,241,066	2,979,800	2,694,395	31,492	632,386	303,862
2002	20,203,655	20,173,471	30,184	12,310,252	1,336,694	3,675,651	14,649,209	2,636,207	2,918,239	31,535	640,675	308,074
2003	21,128,926	21,096,633	32,293	12,920,449	1,413,899	3,779,699	15,286,249	2,807,638	3,035,039	32,531	649,508	313,034
2004	22,228,806	22,196,715	32,091	13,554,598	1,490,200	3,989,446	16,053,844	2,851,107	3,323,855	33,896	655,793	320,334
2005	23,286,043	23,254,263	31,780	14,079,643	1,560,870	4,171,966	16,690,739	3,197,356	3,397,948	35,342	658,884	325,155
2006	24,768,015	24,735,841	32,174	14,665,121	1,627,978	4,591,863	17,629,006	3,538,981	3,600,028	37,435	661,620	327,925
2007	26,288,823	26,263,929	24,894	15,174,477	1,664,645	5,013,751	18,523,583	3,943,424	3,821,816	39,605	663,783	331,551
2008	27,348,409	27,302,169	46,240	15,592,925	1,736,445	4,978,377	18,834,857	4,207,539	4,306,013	41,035	666,468	332,459
2009	26,927,502	26,885,508	41,994	15,724,885	1,741,503	4,272,542	18,255,924	3,904,087	4,767,491	40,252	668,966	325,667
2010	27,458,091	27,404,388	53,703	16,200,166	1,770,234	4,138,680	18,568,612	3,750,463	5,139,016	40,911	671,173	323,882
2011	28,641,808	28,593,384	48,424	16,538,357	1,628,442	4,393,527	19,303,442	4,072,579	5,265,787	42,607	672,230	328,527
2012	29,784,003	29,720,637	63,366	17,068,692	1,649,486	4,633,561	20,052,767	4,398,211	5,333,025	44,406	670,722	328,574
2013	30,162,483	30,103,576	58,907	17,360,201	1,891,091	4,829,554	20,298,664	4,452,112	5,411,707	44,979	670,588	332,270
2014	31,020,386	30,974,472	45,914	17,565,202	1,957,925	4,896,315	20,503,592	4,837,602	5,679,192	46,301	669,972	336,416
2015	32,408,766	32,372,146	36,620	18,108,071	2,036,450	5,148,532	21,220,153	5,175,852	6,012,761	48,383	669,842	342,370
2016	33,245,350	33,210,037	35,313	18,466,641	2,079,043	5,280,326	21,667,924	5,422,770	6,154,656	49,559	670,828	343,525
2017	34,859,033	34,815,133	43,900	19,338,738	2,180,220	5,290,274	22,448,792	5,830,874	6,579,367	51,773	673,303	347,985
2018	36,054,013	36,015,238	38,775	20,195,654	2,248,098	5,653,023	23,600,579	5,967,551	6,485,883	53,329	676,065	354,476
2019	37,859,352	37,803,033	56,319	21,090,600	2,332,806	6,029,683	24,787,477	6,084,781	6,987,094	55,745	679,158	360,090

Personal Income and Employment by Area: Prescott Valley-Prescott, AZ

(Thousands of dollars, except as noted.)

| Year | Personal income, total | Derivation of personal income | | | | | | | | Per capita personal income (dollars) | Population (persons) | Total employment |
| | | Earnings by place of work | | | Less: Contributions for government social insurance | Plus: Adjustment for residence | Equals: Net earnings by place of residence | Plus: Dividends, interest, and rent | Plus: Personal current transfer receipts | | | |
		Nonfarm	Farm	Total								
1970	144,363	80,740	2,618	83,358	5,139	2,433	80,652	44,292	19,419	3,843	37,570	12,550
1971	171,295	95,709	3,448	99,157	6,313	4,200	97,044	50,845	23,406	4,240	40,403	13,909
1972	203,467	114,316	5,913	120,229	7,929	6,226	118,526	57,461	27,480	4,535	44,864	15,086
1973	241,208	134,784	8,017	142,801	10,487	8,490	140,804	68,156	32,248	5,030	47,951	16,708
1974	263,506	148,131	552	148,683	12,164	8,397	144,916	80,726	37,864	5,246	50,233	17,382
1975	299,669	159,161	7,979	167,140	12,876	8,034	162,298	89,212	48,159	5,970	50,194	17,370
1976	332,974	184,318	2,119	186,437	14,689	7,212	178,960	98,264	55,750	5,973	55,746	18,441
1977	384,717	212,962	4,211	217,173	17,527	8,112	207,758	114,748	62,211	6,440	59,742	20,271
1978	449,804	238,570	7,945	246,515	19,845	14,422	241,092	137,416	71,296	7,211	62,377	21,755
1979	517,155	276,862	1,932	278,794	24,174	17,305	271,925	163,633	81,597	7,854	65,842	23,433
1980	617,566	313,072	5,298	318,370	28,012	19,000	309,358	207,521	100,687	8,989	68,705	24,767
1981	713,095	344,130	1,853	345,983	33,682	21,001	333,302	259,296	120,497	10,060	70,883	25,230
1982	760,465	347,549	3,847	351,396	35,049	22,031	338,378	284,117	137,970	10,275	74,009	25,227
1983	840,906	384,232	4,085	388,317	39,454	26,930	375,793	314,582	150,531	10,954	76,769	26,696
1984	948,174	420,851	6,213	427,064	44,122	35,143	418,085	365,638	164,451	11,907	79,633	28,552
1985	1,067,781	476,148	1,593	477,741	51,314	41,622	468,049	419,193	180,539	12,921	82,642	31,802
1986	1,187,527	533,455	3,059	536,514	57,507	49,878	528,885	459,869	198,773	13,339	89,025	34,400
1987	1,275,393	583,022	2,537	585,559	62,972	55,901	578,488	475,623	221,282	13,595	93,811	36,621
1988	1,410,400	640,432	327	640,759	72,277	63,402	631,884	530,068	248,448	14,176	99,493	38,956
1989	1,546,082	671,762	3,236	674,998	81,399	69,192	662,791	603,571	279,720	14,916	103,651	40,422
1990	1,658,590	728,783	5,446	734,229	89,827	77,789	722,191	622,271	314,128	15,242	108,818	42,267
1991	1,772,412	806,902	5,430	812,332	98,982	82,414	795,764	624,351	352,297	15,669	113,119	44,202
1992	1,918,275	902,200	6,620	908,820	110,219	91,511	890,112	630,173	397,990	16,198	118,427	46,644
1993	2,084,370	1,003,163	2,783	1,005,946	123,138	99,291	982,099	673,103	429,168	16,653	125,164	49,463
1994	2,374,726	1,158,743	-296	1,158,447	141,596	109,155	1,126,006	782,188	466,532	17,992	131,986	55,718
1995	2,533,393	1,227,366	-765	1,226,601	145,686	122,775	1,203,690	821,025	508,678	18,108	139,901	57,666
1996	2,752,664	1,318,743	4,724	1,323,467	158,302	136,751	1,301,916	901,199	549,549	18,801	146,414	60,672
1997	2,995,160	1,470,415	6,124	1,476,539	171,423	150,082	1,455,198	962,967	576,995	19,715	151,924	64,787
1998	3,243,973	1,570,217	12,707	1,582,924	182,163	168,148	1,568,909	1,047,870	627,194	20,572	157,686	67,473
1999	3,399,517	1,671,013	24,213	1,695,226	193,466	184,979	1,686,739	1,050,335	662,443	20,863	162,943	66,576
2000	3,649,716	1,769,977	17,673	1,787,650	206,659	206,654	1,787,645	1,141,368	720,703	21,646	168,608	69,991
2001	3,844,812	1,905,268	23,894	1,929,162	223,293	210,728	1,916,597	1,130,647	797,568	22,271	172,636	76,403
2002	3,984,975	2,054,057	10,578	2,064,635	241,534	209,287	2,032,388	1,069,578	883,009	22,468	177,362	78,539
2003	4,250,723	2,209,410	14,383	2,223,793	257,168	213,578	2,180,203	1,120,311	950,209	23,344	182,090	80,739
2004	4,722,581	2,417,503	16,065	2,433,568	281,922	225,180	2,376,826	1,279,680	1,066,075	25,144	187,822	84,763
2005	5,323,133	2,696,065	16,550	2,712,615	318,061	239,453	2,634,007	1,516,889	1,172,237	27,239	195,424	90,797
2006	5,857,709	3,017,430	11,801	3,029,231	359,867	255,819	2,925,183	1,614,542	1,317,984	28,703	204,082	95,889
2007	6,322,466	3,148,514	10,353	3,158,867	382,800	268,160	3,044,227	1,840,678	1,437,561	30,284	208,773	98,495
2008	6,432,599	3,147,369	8,109	3,155,478	391,420	263,872	3,027,930	1,780,367	1,624,302	30,456	211,211	95,085
2009	6,118,330	2,915,656	2,043	2,917,699	374,256	233,650	2,777,093	1,527,690	1,813,547	28,973	211,172	89,442
2010	6,077,090	2,803,537	2,540	2,806,077	369,687	224,810	2,661,200	1,472,861	1,943,029	28,806	210,969	87,118
2011	6,312,934	2,775,698	7,520	2,783,218	337,779	229,630	2,675,069	1,629,998	2,007,867	29,936	210,883	87,057
2012	6,544,765	2,871,337	7,095	2,878,432	347,191	228,396	2,759,637	1,713,639	2,071,489	30,899	211,809	88,290
2013	6,845,763	3,057,309	7,787	3,065,096	404,635	220,063	2,880,524	1,773,379	2,191,860	31,960	214,198	90,104
2014	7,432,353	3,300,844	8,976	3,309,820	426,237	227,460	3,111,043	2,008,771	2,312,539	34,170	217,509	92,499
2015	7,824,286	3,481,667	8,197	3,489,864	450,822	239,607	3,278,649	2,110,911	2,434,726	35,465	220,621	94,931
2016	8,137,520	3,700,079	10,192	3,710,271	484,114	241,835	3,467,992	2,154,961	2,514,567	36,269	224,363	97,420
2017	8,532,977	3,895,603	12,363	3,907,966	515,784	259,557	3,651,739	2,255,312	2,625,926	37,398	228,168	99,344
2018	9,371,726	9,361,660	10,066	4,178,417	558,518	273,185	3,893,084	2,618,785	2,859,857	40,435	231,772	102,155
2019	9,731,391	9,726,144	5,247	4,282,435	582,998	287,584	3,987,021	2,663,777	3,080,593	41,393	235,099	103,773

Personal Income and Employment by Area: Providence-Warwick, RI-MA

(Thousands of dollars, except as noted.)

Year	Personal income, total	Earnings by place of work — Nonfarm	Earnings by place of work — Farm	Earnings by place of work — Total	Less: Contributions for government social insurance	Plus: Adjustment for residence	Equals: Net earnings by place of residence	Plus: Dividends, interest, and rent	Plus: Personal current transfer receipts	Per capita personal income (dollars)	Population (persons)	Total employment
1970	5,814,992	4,387,300	16,934	4,404,234	328,715	188,818	4,264,337	921,850	628,805	4,165	1,396,129	629,664
1971	6,202,171	4,612,057	15,023	4,627,080	358,216	211,732	4,480,596	979,264	742,311	4,389	1,413,149	623,177
1972	6,770,032	5,073,636	14,154	5,087,790	411,755	235,873	4,911,908	1,046,956	811,168	4,734	1,430,040	639,853
1973	7,284,619	5,452,140	12,997	5,465,137	514,209	271,749	5,222,677	1,142,054	919,888	5,068	1,437,274	652,677
1974	7,710,883	5,598,805	13,930	5,612,735	553,187	319,367	5,378,915	1,247,976	1,083,992	5,459	1,412,609	640,670
1975	8,369,663	5,793,686	14,558	5,808,244	556,877	350,698	5,602,065	1,334,317	1,433,281	5,952	1,406,082	615,617
1976	9,182,532	6,499,990	15,516	6,515,506	636,881	392,095	6,270,720	1,427,191	1,484,621	6,486	1,415,810	641,578
1977	10,070,327	7,158,790	14,737	7,173,527	701,293	456,438	6,928,672	1,587,021	1,554,634	7,082	1,422,032	665,492
1978	11,091,486	7,962,515	19,317	7,981,832	803,514	526,850	7,705,168	1,734,397	1,651,921	7,780	1,425,662	687,471
1979	12,330,433	8,834,566	17,291	8,851,857	921,195	611,522	8,542,184	1,939,167	1,849,082	8,622	1,430,055	699,681
1980	13,796,860	9,541,656	18,875	9,560,531	996,188	720,575	9,284,918	2,373,232	2,138,710	9,688	1,424,092	699,678
1981	15,287,047	10,257,155	23,193	10,280,348	1,140,405	803,131	9,943,074	2,907,291	2,436,682	10,691	1,429,942	696,826
1982	16,522,724	10,809,823	42,156	10,851,979	1,215,934	881,739	10,517,784	3,339,083	2,665,857	11,544	1,431,288	687,087
1983	17,877,820	11,763,581	54,607	11,818,188	1,337,787	988,956	11,469,357	3,576,713	2,831,750	12,465	1,434,222	697,303
1984	19,714,204	13,050,642	54,689	13,105,331	1,540,711	1,143,170	12,707,790	4,077,253	2,929,161	13,673	1,441,812	730,198
1985	21,238,561	14,203,849	60,588	14,264,437	1,660,354	1,250,734	13,854,817	4,277,502	3,106,242	14,630	1,451,669	752,699
1986	22,775,483	15,389,867	65,343	15,455,210	1,810,674	1,337,555	14,982,091	4,539,208	3,254,184	15,573	1,462,482	774,732
1987	24,381,511	16,656,773	60,720	16,717,493	1,943,190	1,514,026	16,288,329	4,735,649	3,357,533	16,485	1,478,976	783,574
1988	26,808,521	18,364,247	60,575	18,424,822	2,170,331	1,679,706	17,934,197	5,263,120	3,611,204	17,949	1,493,594	804,366
1989	28,931,015	19,391,205	50,346	19,441,551	2,266,866	1,764,485	18,939,170	5,999,583	3,992,262	19,239	1,503,781	805,887
1990	29,813,538	19,749,929	47,613	19,797,542	2,389,123	1,874,500	19,282,919	6,077,820	4,452,799	19,702	1,513,216	786,517
1991	30,160,084	19,451,557	50,386	19,501,943	2,411,286	1,865,165	18,955,822	5,877,131	5,327,131	19,852	1,519,234	749,079
1992	31,581,582	20,678,158	45,545	20,723,703	2,560,911	1,936,178	20,098,970	5,915,004	5,567,608	20,745	1,522,392	760,306
1993	32,903,703	21,616,178	46,008	21,662,186	2,707,000	1,976,073	20,931,259	6,062,672	5,909,772	21,532	1,528,117	772,176
1994	34,122,785	22,536,267	40,456	22,576,723	2,849,013	2,135,055	21,862,765	6,248,699	6,011,321	22,272	1,532,065	778,499
1995	35,896,275	23,541,977	40,440	23,582,417	2,957,763	2,220,465	22,845,119	6,709,312	6,341,844	23,373	1,535,833	784,811
1996	37,277,821	24,425,830	44,400	24,470,230	3,032,165	2,315,182	23,753,247	7,039,344	6,485,230	24,180	1,541,702	791,039
1997	39,465,746	25,725,074	35,823	25,760,897	3,177,135	2,607,517	25,191,279	7,451,928	6,822,539	25,480	1,548,897	802,598
1998	41,720,383	27,522,364	30,321	27,552,685	3,349,029	2,886,316	27,089,972	7,730,386	6,900,025	26,772	1,558,350	815,590
1999	43,898,696	29,390,292	31,357	29,421,649	3,514,350	3,148,297	29,055,596	7,678,368	7,164,732	27,932	1,571,610	832,845
2000	47,394,354	31,618,439	35,429	31,653,868	3,732,495	3,665,617	31,586,990	8,337,940	7,469,424	29,881	1,586,085	855,161
2001	50,147,686	33,350,990	35,881	33,386,871	3,911,308	3,849,012	33,324,575	8,527,654	8,295,457	31,432	1,595,424	855,796
2002	52,041,805	34,940,473	43,709	34,984,182	4,040,819	3,815,990	34,759,353	8,478,445	8,804,007	32,350	1,608,716	859,087
2003	54,412,516	36,658,678	43,343	36,702,021	4,229,572	3,868,244	36,340,693	8,938,514	9,133,309	33,637	1,617,623	865,534
2004	56,978,329	38,552,441	46,722	38,599,163	4,495,357	4,225,194	38,329,000	8,999,905	9,649,424	35,160	1,620,567	877,834
2005	58,513,890	39,700,952	41,931	39,742,883	4,684,909	4,194,178	39,252,152	9,095,198	10,166,540	36,268	1,613,353	883,474
2006	61,860,624	41,752,397	43,446	41,795,843	4,919,800	4,366,591	41,242,634	10,032,943	10,585,047	38,481	1,607,583	889,734
2007	64,383,851	42,484,854	40,982	42,525,836	5,060,242	4,595,815	42,061,409	10,950,631	11,371,811	40,175	1,602,603	898,480
2008	66,213,379	42,818,738	49,903	42,868,641	5,151,085	4,414,987	42,132,543	11,296,029	12,784,807	41,346	1,601,459	886,236
2009	64,471,077	41,085,810	47,557	41,133,367	5,043,299	4,078,232	40,168,300	10,313,750	13,989,027	40,270	1,600,970	855,319
2010	67,518,867	43,600,660	44,878	43,645,538	5,160,892	3,910,275	42,394,921	10,295,329	14,828,617	42,137	1,602,351	852,089
2011	70,183,709	44,678,092	34,186	44,712,278	4,808,107	4,176,492	44,080,663	11,175,767	14,927,279	43,823	1,601,522	860,585
2012	72,885,547	46,529,399	41,110	46,570,509	4,926,023	4,441,388	46,085,874	11,928,790	14,870,883	45,440	1,604,011	865,547
2013	73,292,493	47,579,413	40,046	47,619,459	5,642,596	4,474,711	46,451,574	11,775,637	15,065,282	45,653	1,605,438	881,151
2014	76,432,735	49,364,471	40,173	49,404,644	5,891,543	4,345,229	47,858,330	12,710,665	15,863,740	47,469	1,610,173	898,770
2015	79,923,923	51,270,180	42,041	51,312,221	6,127,155	4,642,908	49,827,974	13,451,175	16,644,774	49,545	1,613,155	919,792
2016	81,364,156	51,762,308	30,584	51,792,892	6,248,754	5,133,224	50,677,362	13,734,742	16,952,052	50,353	1,615,878	929,470
2017	84,737,026	53,673,331	28,118	53,701,449	6,481,087	5,657,775	52,878,137	14,359,647	17,499,242	52,271	1,621,122	940,118
2018	87,981,541	87,954,223	27,318	56,100,051	6,789,343	5,988,750	55,299,458	14,833,076	17,849,007	54,230	1,622,379	954,815
2019	91,200,004	91,175,542	24,462	57,995,808	7,007,684	6,835,512	57,823,636	14,902,395	18,473,973	56,138	1,624,578	965,516

Personal Income and Employment by Area: Provo-Orem, UT

(Thousands of dollars, except as noted.)

Year	Personal income, total	Earnings by place of work			Less: Contributions for government social insurance	Plus: Adjustment for residence	Equals: Net earnings by place of residence	Plus: Dividends, interest, and rent	Plus: Personal current transfer receipts	Per capita personal income (dollars)	Population (persons)	Total employment
		Nonfarm	Farm	Total								
1970	398,439	296,737	9,575	306,312	20,247	24,775	310,840	52,323	35,276	2,774	143,630	52,365
1971	442,217	324,740	9,460	334,200	22,891	28,744	340,053	59,468	42,696	2,936	150,643	54,182
1972	512,139	381,335	7,560	388,895	28,013	34,594	395,476	67,824	48,839	3,204	159,828	58,707
1973	589,542	435,843	17,429	453,272	37,403	39,989	455,858	75,966	57,718	3,523	167,341	63,657
1974	663,155	490,487	12,655	503,142	43,894	46,645	505,893	89,473	67,789	3,802	174,411	66,614
1975	737,418	536,507	8,587	545,094	47,786	54,792	552,100	99,527	85,791	4,112	179,319	66,238
1976	859,244	630,401	10,408	640,809	55,472	68,045	653,382	112,959	92,903	4,639	185,213	70,264
1977	992,780	735,778	8,495	744,273	64,506	81,958	761,725	130,406	100,649	5,060	196,202	75,348
1978	1,147,489	854,554	6,739	861,293	77,072	92,833	877,054	155,641	114,794	5,610	204,554	80,873
1979	1,317,997	986,055	10,277	996,332	94,196	101,583	1,003,719	182,810	131,468	6,110	215,721	84,123
1980	1,467,753	1,071,011	7,749	1,078,760	102,125	113,441	1,090,076	219,479	158,198	6,511	225,440	83,779
1981	1,645,443	1,190,030	6,033	1,196,063	122,784	128,500	1,201,779	260,207	183,457	7,088	232,150	84,370
1982	1,732,578	1,188,833	7,346	1,196,179	122,681	144,660	1,218,158	296,981	217,439	7,268	238,395	85,064
1983	1,848,030	1,251,552	8,125	1,259,677	128,847	153,627	1,284,457	329,349	234,224	7,592	243,424	87,034
1984	2,050,889	1,404,257	9,736	1,413,993	147,731	171,106	1,437,368	370,909	242,612	8,301	247,068	92,533
1985	2,192,544	1,500,322	10,980	1,511,302	160,485	185,636	1,536,453	397,736	258,355	8,743	250,774	95,049
1986	2,317,461	1,591,324	9,930	1,601,254	170,807	182,401	1,612,848	420,107	284,506	9,151	253,249	97,302
1987	2,452,731	1,656,233	14,360	1,670,593	177,161	180,691	1,674,123	436,928	341,680	9,574	256,199	101,692
1988	2,699,332	1,892,175	22,414	1,914,589	214,749	178,669	1,878,509	467,392	353,431	10,381	260,016	110,799
1989	2,962,413	2,084,605	21,389	2,105,994	241,905	186,129	2,050,218	522,410	389,785	11,130	266,166	117,040
1990	3,276,112	2,390,593	23,080	2,413,673	285,763	191,350	2,319,260	531,844	425,008	12,102	270,713	125,706
1991	3,604,614	2,664,385	28,856	2,693,241	324,901	199,076	2,567,416	567,115	470,083	12,922	278,950	131,672
1992	3,920,647	2,915,232	31,985	2,947,217	351,576	220,403	2,816,044	582,916	521,687	13,522	289,947	133,739
1993	4,265,447	3,161,303	27,338	3,188,641	381,571	240,549	3,047,619	648,668	569,160	14,124	302,004	138,561
1994	4,680,990	3,505,538	23,570	3,529,108	427,534	263,012	3,364,586	732,890	583,514	14,864	314,918	151,987
1995	5,164,548	3,889,150	19,596	3,908,746	480,668	279,192	3,707,270	830,576	626,702	15,881	325,204	161,158
1996	5,671,772	4,250,640	23,519	4,274,159	512,061	312,503	4,074,601	931,912	665,259	16,797	337,667	172,108
1997	6,033,550	4,517,010	25,750	4,542,760	537,910	354,429	4,359,279	992,580	681,691	17,344	347,876	180,366
1998	6,698,785	4,990,322	33,302	5,023,624	587,400	383,775	4,819,999	1,161,224	717,562	18,546	361,197	188,543
1999	7,116,989	5,354,072	26,234	5,380,306	627,607	411,993	5,164,692	1,193,760	758,537	19,250	369,707	195,570
2000	7,707,963	5,732,323	29,655	5,761,978	674,154	447,895	5,535,719	1,351,917	820,327	20,280	380,079	203,516
2001	8,069,547	5,957,027	27,541	5,984,568	700,341	505,179	5,789,406	1,364,962	915,179	20,478	394,059	207,244
2002	8,331,145	6,044,110	19,985	6,064,095	709,273	544,578	5,899,400	1,414,777	1,016,968	20,537	405,672	208,369
2003	8,710,995	6,281,510	29,631	6,311,141	744,754	585,564	6,151,951	1,472,090	1,086,954	21,001	414,780	211,327
2004	9,444,123	6,963,870	43,568	7,007,438	822,951	692,587	6,877,074	1,412,052	1,154,997	22,220	425,023	222,605
2005	10,608,867	7,577,751	44,599	7,622,350	897,055	827,516	7,552,811	1,789,676	1,266,380	24,132	439,623	236,232
2006	11,957,495	8,514,085	24,828	8,538,913	995,544	1,065,487	8,608,856	1,985,380	1,363,259	26,138	457,471	250,781
2007	13,406,647	9,248,152	47,276	9,295,428	1,084,134	1,284,606	9,495,900	2,409,178	1,501,569	27,978	479,181	268,048
2008	14,336,109	9,390,668	30,043	9,420,711	1,105,773	1,499,766	9,814,704	2,718,316	1,803,089	28,808	497,639	268,390
2009	13,619,305	8,851,828	28,077	8,879,905	1,059,396	1,513,305	9,333,814	2,294,875	1,990,616	26,445	515,010	262,149
2010	13,946,179	8,875,420	45,988	8,921,408	1,067,189	1,634,743	9,488,962	2,224,163	2,233,054	26,302	530,238	259,785
2011	15,101,155	9,462,975	70,968	9,533,943	1,019,828	1,734,079	10,248,194	2,547,667	2,305,294	27,905	541,171	269,378
2012	16,507,003	10,431,190	79,401	10,510,591	1,096,362	1,870,827	11,285,056	2,944,274	2,277,673	30,009	550,071	278,458
2013	17,405,689	11,443,532	94,464	11,537,996	1,335,980	1,831,900	12,033,916	3,023,430	2,348,343	30,977	561,895	289,895
2014	18,982,231	12,408,854	108,167	12,517,021	1,426,932	2,003,762	13,093,851	3,489,550	2,398,830	33,225	571,320	301,436
2015	20,798,716	13,738,886	96,020	13,834,906	1,538,051	2,042,266	14,339,121	3,905,836	2,553,759	35,640	583,583	317,189
2016	22,387,758	14,817,071	67,011	14,884,082	1,650,739	2,286,417	15,519,760	4,157,952	2,710,046	37,221	601,478	334,975
2017	23,517,994	15,705,631	62,335	15,767,966	1,797,016	2,393,699	16,364,649	4,365,188	2,788,157	38,075	617,675	348,323
2018	26,093,360	26,051,911	41,449	17,596,255	1,972,771	2,426,523	18,050,007	5,096,433	2,946,920	41,212	633,149	371,186
2019	27,824,776	27,793,170	31,606	19,160,287	2,115,827	2,334,176	19,378,636	5,284,280	3,161,860	42,923	648,252	382,745

Personal Income and Employment by Area: Pueblo, CO

(Thousands of dollars, except as noted.)

Year	Personal income, total	Earnings by place of work Nonfarm	Farm	Total	Less: Contributions for government social insurance	Plus: Adjustment for residence	Equals: Net earnings by place of residence	Plus: Dividends, interest, and rent	Plus: Personal current transfer receipts	Per capita personal income (dollars)	Population (persons)	Total employment
1970	417,116	326,012	2,799	328,811	18,433	-8,376	302,002	66,804	48,310	3,518	118,574	46,458
1971	460,152	355,264	2,040	357,304	20,388	-8,401	328,515	74,775	56,862	3,811	120,746	46,902
1972	510,393	397,917	3,621	401,538	24,406	-8,818	368,314	80,827	61,252	4,182	122,032	49,018
1973	579,201	456,895	3,679	460,574	33,443	-11,671	415,460	92,241	71,500	4,646	124,680	51,840
1974	647,868	507,264	3,556	510,820	38,730	-13,356	458,734	107,065	82,069	5,199	124,611	52,526
1975	715,356	542,635	5,049	547,684	41,357	-12,245	494,082	121,682	99,592	5,649	126,644	51,414
1976	775,126	588,483	5,562	594,045	46,026	-12,147	535,872	128,438	110,816	6,168	125,675	52,192
1977	830,738	630,970	3,157	634,127	50,559	-11,326	572,242	138,996	119,500	6,665	124,638	51,961
1978	920,575	702,864	2,408	705,272	58,442	-12,419	634,411	155,054	131,110	7,426	123,963	53,178
1979	1,027,687	788,450	2,784	791,234	68,723	-14,219	708,292	173,498	145,897	8,164	125,884	54,608
1980	1,125,975	828,401	3,717	832,118	72,490	-13,702	745,926	207,750	172,299	8,935	126,012	53,070
1981	1,250,489	892,401	6,589	898,990	83,788	-13,956	801,246	245,776	203,467	9,935	125,863	51,665
1982	1,281,596	853,858	4,088	857,946	81,074	-10,318	766,554	276,883	238,159	10,228	125,299	49,099
1983	1,302,162	806,536	6,344	812,880	76,284	-4,752	731,844	302,290	268,028	10,356	125,737	47,022
1984	1,381,429	847,337	6,076	853,413	83,176	-2,331	767,906	336,873	276,650	11,124	124,183	47,903
1985	1,455,503	894,266	4,593	898,859	89,995	-305	808,559	365,513	281,431	11,752	123,851	48,921
1986	1,516,899	922,944	6,196	929,140	93,809	1,317	836,648	381,858	298,393	12,222	124,111	49,175
1987	1,539,556	922,410	7,908	930,318	92,412	2,829	840,735	381,747	317,074	12,385	124,312	48,884
1988	1,625,495	990,693	8,405	999,098	105,236	3,311	897,173	389,205	339,117	13,136	123,745	51,235
1989	1,741,207	1,066,164	7,117	1,073,281	117,186	1,438	957,533	414,197	369,477	14,083	123,639	52,619
1990	1,822,794	1,135,879	5,452	1,141,331	126,029	887	1,016,189	413,401	393,204	14,803	123,134	55,119
1991	1,909,055	1,180,490	4,628	1,185,118	135,039	3,787	1,053,866	406,597	448,592	15,465	123,447	54,874
1992	2,031,755	1,254,031	5,394	1,259,425	141,534	9,535	1,127,426	398,616	505,713	16,334	124,387	55,461
1993	2,151,753	1,329,059	7,188	1,336,247	153,975	13,802	1,196,074	412,052	543,627	16,991	126,644	56,530
1994	2,308,666	1,451,207	2,425	1,453,632	168,608	17,458	1,302,482	434,053	572,131	17,926	128,787	59,435
1995	2,522,345	1,541,813	-547	1,541,266	178,535	21,745	1,384,476	479,356	658,513	19,274	130,865	61,533
1996	2,638,546	1,618,536	186	1,618,722	187,794	28,498	1,459,426	517,434	661,686	19,886	132,686	64,066
1997	2,828,144	1,770,986	-37	1,770,949	201,946	32,531	1,601,534	545,881	680,729	20,982	134,792	66,762
1998	2,989,705	1,892,900	-404	1,892,496	200,751	41,659	1,733,404	560,024	696,277	21,713	137,690	69,410
1999	3,165,760	2,012,041	-716	2,011,325	207,082	52,081	1,856,324	558,664	750,772	22,583	140,184	70,034
2000	3,370,511	2,136,113	1,152	2,137,265	215,151	68,075	1,990,189	592,927	787,395	23,769	141,800	70,788
2001	3,512,272	2,192,809	5,526	2,198,335	232,050	68,325	2,034,610	624,580	853,082	24,388	144,014	71,286
2002	3,637,009	2,264,757	-2,697	2,262,060	249,019	62,929	2,075,970	620,646	940,393	24,820	146,537	70,850
2003	3,771,588	2,329,929	543	2,330,472	255,164	61,587	2,136,895	656,018	978,675	25,500	147,907	70,865
2004	3,893,988	2,487,244	10,144	2,497,388	276,430	57,530	2,278,488	592,666	1,022,834	26,195	148,654	70,866
2005	4,002,198	2,525,092	7,717	2,532,809	285,099	67,940	2,315,650	587,344	1,099,204	26,712	149,825	71,955
2006	4,176,067	2,649,713	4,172	2,653,885	300,326	73,383	2,426,942	594,678	1,154,447	27,469	152,026	73,457
2007	4,486,199	2,806,233	9,850	2,816,083	322,429	60,471	2,554,125	712,217	1,219,857	28,921	155,121	75,882
2008	4,478,185	2,864,272	2,527	2,866,799	334,562	54,494	2,586,731	765,061	1,126,393	28,569	156,748	76,134
2009	4,530,418	2,848,106	2,620	2,850,726	332,283	29,707	2,548,150	748,437	1,233,831	28,702	157,846	74,761
2010	4,712,429	2,909,926	6,299	2,916,225	338,241	24,332	2,602,316	743,773	1,366,340	29,552	159,463	74,419
2011	4,924,867	3,019,557	13,489	3,033,046	323,829	7,192	2,716,409	798,190	1,410,268	30,748	160,171	75,213
2012	5,085,250	3,114,592	6,292	3,120,884	333,424	-1,303	2,786,157	870,792	1,428,301	31,637	160,735	75,114
2013	5,161,280	3,164,510	6,306	3,170,816	368,986	13,262	2,815,092	868,318	1,477,870	32,044	161,070	75,148
2014	5,478,029	3,336,724	4,732	3,341,456	393,364	218	2,948,310	938,230	1,591,489	33,937	161,419	76,177
2015	5,789,351	3,459,451	7,573	3,467,024	413,314	381	3,054,091	1,009,755	1,725,505	35,508	163,043	77,338
2016	5,975,250	3,554,222	4,889	3,559,111	426,006	-1,557	3,131,548	1,044,716	1,798,986	36,250	164,834	78,647
2017	6,198,065	3,708,376	8,798	3,717,174	446,322	-5,162	3,265,690	1,096,410	1,835,965	37,231	166,475	79,650
2018	6,578,511	6,571,929	6,582	3,908,225	469,712	-8,102	3,430,411	1,203,154	1,944,946	39,293	167,422	81,072
2019	6,851,552	6,844,658	6,894	4,108,321	495,396	-14,622	3,598,303	1,229,800	2,023,449	40,680	168,424	82,308

Personal Income and Employment by Area: Punta Gorda, FL

(Thousands of dollars, except as noted.)

Year	Personal income, total	Earnings by place of work			Less: Contributions for government social insurance	Plus: Adjustment for residence	Equals: Net earnings by place of residence	Plus: Dividends, interest, and rent	Plus: Personal current transfer receipts	Per capita personal income (dollars)	Population (persons)	Total employment
		Nonfarm	Farm	Total								
1970	104,816	49,972	1,445	51,417	3,282	620	48,755	36,936	19,125	3,747	27,977	8,072
1971	123,756	58,030	1,667	59,697	4,050	515	56,162	44,343	23,251	4,119	30,046	8,996
1972	154,008	77,599	1,915	79,514	5,624	111	74,001	51,720	28,287	4,759	32,364	10,711
1973	187,787	92,696	1,975	94,671	7,591	1,067	88,147	64,473	35,167	5,107	36,771	12,355
1974	215,874	99,322	2,118	101,440	8,688	1,889	94,641	79,150	42,083	5,206	41,468	12,512
1975	241,617	101,005	2,556	103,561	8,787	2,458	97,232	92,273	52,112	5,517	43,796	12,707
1976	278,804	118,785	3,428	122,213	10,214	2,477	114,476	105,099	59,229	6,294	44,299	13,487
1977	330,545	142,985	3,963	146,948	12,511	2,404	136,841	124,680	69,024	7,024	47,062	15,343
1978	400,771	176,874	5,226	182,100	15,797	2,346	168,649	152,129	79,993	7,867	50,945	17,656
1979	470,130	196,875	6,258	203,133	18,416	4,865	189,582	184,396	96,152	8,502	55,299	18,195
1980	579,716	232,381	8,615	240,996	22,005	6,091	225,082	233,650	120,984	9,748	59,472	19,577
1981	695,885	269,592	4,781	274,373	27,682	8,673	255,364	292,266	148,255	10,974	63,412	21,295
1982	749,629	271,497	6,998	278,495	29,458	13,486	262,523	312,823	174,283	11,030	67,961	21,403
1983	845,399	307,113	9,099	316,212	33,087	17,190	300,315	354,923	190,161	11,820	71,524	22,702
1984	986,678	343,816	6,478	350,294	37,893	23,147	335,548	444,565	206,565	12,951	76,183	24,000
1985	1,117,862	384,272	6,489	390,761	43,555	28,703	375,909	511,744	230,209	13,820	80,886	26,318
1986	1,244,686	435,209	6,475	441,684	50,794	32,368	423,258	567,189	254,239	14,460	86,079	28,995
1987	1,379,140	502,491	6,934	509,425	57,694	39,263	490,994	612,737	275,409	15,032	91,745	30,055
1988	1,576,533	588,677	12,578	601,255	69,739	44,164	575,680	691,921	308,932	16,212	97,247	32,981
1989	1,874,843	666,924	10,764	677,688	81,958	49,725	645,455	866,821	362,567	18,019	104,050	36,229
1990	2,022,784	725,921	10,902	736,823	87,588	57,216	706,451	909,954	406,379	17,929	112,821	38,654
1991	2,092,792	756,163	16,356	772,519	92,120	63,282	743,681	888,604	460,507	17,764	117,813	39,216
1992	2,224,363	825,403	13,367	838,770	100,349	67,226	805,647	890,049	528,667	18,404	120,861	39,827
1993	2,347,470	879,405	13,998	893,403	106,622	74,031	860,812	912,655	574,003	18,911	124,134	41,205
1994	2,528,248	938,938	11,591	950,529	116,547	80,676	914,658	981,472	632,118	19,840	127,434	43,349
1995	2,707,341	990,033	11,731	1,001,764	123,536	92,570	970,798	1,054,324	682,219	20,709	130,731	44,270
1996	2,882,374	1,067,133	8,462	1,075,595	130,437	95,327	1,040,485	1,120,161	721,728	21,739	132,587	46,679
1997	3,083,185	1,110,758	10,933	1,121,691	135,545	110,127	1,096,273	1,234,146	752,766	22,845	134,959	48,085
1998	3,304,271	1,217,075	15,711	1,232,786	145,467	122,938	1,210,257	1,303,417	790,597	24,014	137,598	51,813
1999	3,446,363	1,340,430	13,276	1,353,706	156,780	135,489	1,332,415	1,293,597	820,351	24,575	140,240	54,226
2000	3,709,485	1,464,363	13,559	1,477,922	168,378	152,818	1,462,362	1,376,433	870,690	26,074	142,266	56,385
2001	3,876,103	1,616,115	8,565	1,624,680	186,097	177,542	1,616,125	1,316,736	943,242	26,492	146,311	55,287
2002	3,920,279	1,693,746	10,723	1,704,469	195,026	228,898	1,738,341	1,187,166	994,772	26,114	150,123	54,855
2003	4,099,525	1,767,572	11,916	1,779,488	203,715	282,725	1,858,498	1,195,057	1,045,970	26,753	153,235	55,225
2004	4,490,839	1,898,390	13,736	1,912,126	224,996	278,950	1,966,080	1,356,452	1,168,307	28,467	157,755	57,451
2005	4,787,584	2,052,046	23,361	2,075,407	247,338	356,169	2,184,238	1,446,410	1,156,936	30,836	155,262	59,929
2006	5,177,994	2,219,346	30,693	2,250,039	281,411	388,396	2,357,024	1,567,865	1,253,105	32,960	157,099	64,678
2007	5,391,127	2,173,910	21,509	2,195,419	281,190	394,386	2,308,615	1,747,074	1,335,438	33,749	159,742	64,346
2008	5,337,154	2,062,729	24,564	2,087,293	277,660	302,428	2,112,061	1,727,706	1,497,387	33,260	160,467	61,774
2009	5,020,082	1,945,124	32,666	1,977,790	269,733	263,690	1,971,747	1,415,222	1,633,113	31,448	159,629	59,476
2010	5,129,562	2,024,418	43,041	2,067,459	277,021	192,136	1,982,574	1,395,974	1,751,014	32,086	159,869	59,627
2011	5,358,323	2,084,695	44,159	2,128,854	260,828	152,524	2,020,550	1,532,701	1,805,072	33,514	159,881	60,926
2012	5,551,813	2,184,303	63,292	2,247,595	273,916	156,698	2,130,377	1,567,478	1,853,958	34,095	162,833	61,871
2013	5,731,387	2,258,188	60,904	2,319,092	316,131	180,857	2,183,818	1,627,950	1,919,619	34,772	164,830	63,458
2014	6,189,429	2,349,280	56,775	2,406,055	328,525	211,188	2,288,718	1,844,177	2,056,534	36,768	168,336	65,561
2015	6,654,943	2,522,500	67,031	2,589,531	346,358	241,683	2,484,856	1,972,869	2,197,218	38,507	172,824	68,115
2016	7,046,749	2,651,274	52,417	2,703,691	368,725	285,099	2,620,065	2,124,313	2,302,371	39,554	178,157	69,745
2017	7,382,653	2,762,273	54,800	2,817,073	388,482	311,978	2,740,569	2,227,048	2,415,036	40,557	182,033	70,542
2018	7,725,742	7,695,216	30,526	2,966,378	418,032	311,013	2,859,359	2,273,604	2,592,779	41,795	184,849	73,802
2019	8,083,940	8,049,511	34,429	3,136,445	449,476	301,271	2,988,240	2,301,411	2,794,289	42,793	188,910	75,702

Personal Income and Employment by Area: Racine, WI

(Thousands of dollars, except as noted.)

Year	Personal income, total	Earnings by place of work			Less: Contributions for government social insurance	Plus: Adjustment for residence	Equals: Net earnings by place of residence	Plus: Dividends, interest, and rent	Plus: Personal current transfer receipts	Per capita personal income (dollars)	Population (persons)	Total employment
		Nonfarm	Farm	Total								
1970	704,171	506,929	8,788	515,717	36,912	60,994	539,799	105,212	59,160	4,121	170,861	65,523
1971	745,366	529,734	10,607	540,341	40,077	62,059	562,323	111,939	71,104	4,375	170,371	64,391
1972	825,049	594,902	9,099	604,001	47,589	68,011	624,423	118,702	81,924	4,845	170,296	67,536
1973	922,302	676,807	12,091	688,898	62,908	74,842	700,832	129,699	91,771	5,405	170,642	72,370
1974	1,030,446	757,626	9,860	767,486	73,325	81,340	775,501	146,323	108,622	6,001	171,715	74,830
1975	1,137,080	821,882	17,565	839,447	77,691	77,814	839,570	163,119	134,391	6,539	173,903	74,659
1976	1,243,957	919,871	14,053	933,924	88,352	80,262	925,834	172,374	145,749	7,221	172,264	76,731
1977	1,373,950	1,021,698	24,379	1,046,077	97,927	86,166	1,034,316	186,725	152,909	8,009	171,543	78,866
1978	1,546,280	1,163,971	18,325	1,182,296	115,034	102,986	1,170,248	208,053	167,979	9,002	171,762	81,566
1979	1,733,512	1,302,854	17,773	1,320,627	133,883	126,128	1,312,872	231,239	189,401	10,063	172,266	84,225
1980	1,887,080	1,353,485	16,142	1,369,627	138,305	142,501	1,373,823	280,845	232,412	10,909	172,979	81,694
1981	2,049,865	1,424,138	16,407	1,440,545	156,343	148,378	1,432,580	349,590	267,695	11,921	171,952	79,864
1982	2,099,884	1,379,544	9,325	1,388,869	152,944	167,329	1,403,254	388,329	308,301	12,274	171,080	76,027
1983	2,191,594	1,428,010	-897	1,427,113	157,879	175,635	1,444,869	417,178	329,547	12,911	169,741	75,330
1984	2,414,377	1,590,188	11,588	1,601,776	180,511	191,179	1,612,444	472,818	329,115	14,234	169,619	79,329
1985	2,500,324	1,634,236	11,683	1,645,919	186,383	202,396	1,661,932	488,624	349,768	14,684	170,270	78,935
1986	2,631,436	1,754,803	13,822	1,768,625	199,841	199,294	1,768,078	499,775	363,583	15,511	169,655	80,809
1987	2,788,794	1,867,970	17,342	1,885,312	208,179	230,885	1,908,018	511,945	368,831	16,387	170,181	82,839
1988	3,014,421	2,021,541	15,401	2,036,942	233,497	265,388	2,068,833	565,639	379,949	17,532	171,934	85,849
1989	3,241,385	2,193,274	14,220	2,207,494	253,176	265,602	2,219,920	610,677	410,788	18,665	173,657	87,306
1990	3,452,812	2,342,401	11,249	2,353,650	281,741	296,198	2,368,107	643,817	440,888	19,672	175,518	89,786
1991	3,620,822	2,443,140	12,447	2,455,587	296,607	304,695	2,463,675	676,324	480,823	20,355	177,885	89,881
1992	3,806,979	2,558,130	26,826	2,584,956	306,654	356,286	2,634,588	655,692	516,699	21,120	180,251	89,115
1993	4,004,447	2,680,610	22,638	2,703,248	322,586	409,737	2,790,399	684,863	529,185	22,030	181,776	90,045
1994	4,240,801	2,807,911	23,509	2,831,420	342,972	462,697	2,951,145	752,110	537,546	23,131	183,338	91,293
1995	4,435,200	2,856,324	21,941	2,878,265	351,129	514,228	3,041,364	828,225	565,611	23,999	184,808	93,148
1996	4,660,527	2,989,572	19,427	3,008,999	363,022	537,673	3,183,650	892,355	584,522	25,103	185,658	94,284
1997	4,973,349	3,246,982	16,886	3,263,868	389,886	572,974	3,446,956	926,844	599,549	26,649	186,621	94,788
1998	5,199,848	3,376,647	15,408	3,392,055	404,201	620,311	3,608,165	985,240	606,443	27,705	187,689	95,393
1999	5,267,107	3,510,978	15,001	3,525,979	422,203	574,742	3,678,518	957,754	630,835	27,963	188,361	94,131
2000	5,548,132	3,543,314	15,088	3,558,402	420,600	704,630	3,842,432	1,016,751	688,949	29,370	188,904	94,602
2001	5,862,422	3,716,244	18,496	3,734,740	427,265	756,319	4,063,794	1,031,769	766,859	31,010	189,047	95,781
2002	6,017,639	3,829,632	17,464	3,847,096	436,099	778,715	4,189,712	1,008,558	819,369	31,700	189,833	94,908
2003	6,204,797	3,935,890	24,728	3,960,618	450,844	799,492	4,309,266	1,049,576	845,955	32,512	190,845	94,955
2004	6,493,774	4,106,028	25,425	4,131,453	471,771	842,777	4,502,459	1,134,460	856,855	33,856	191,808	96,430
2005	6,601,459	4,186,205	19,185	4,205,390	484,666	886,199	4,606,923	1,070,935	923,601	34,160	193,251	97,069
2006	7,002,165	4,312,681	26,360	4,339,041	505,067	964,809	4,798,783	1,227,754	975,628	36,109	193,915	97,225
2007	7,276,866	4,436,524	28,369	4,464,893	518,112	989,655	4,936,436	1,282,502	1,057,928	37,433	194,395	97,383
2008	7,691,316	4,475,277	24,468	4,499,745	527,760	1,057,648	5,029,633	1,466,089	1,195,594	39,497	194,730	96,571
2009	7,343,247	4,261,155	23,255	4,284,410	505,263	967,891	4,747,038	1,185,976	1,410,233	37,633	195,130	92,186
2010	7,429,651	4,354,457	19,085	4,373,542	516,805	883,969	4,740,706	1,183,686	1,505,259	38,022	195,406	91,779
2011	7,778,867	4,575,848	24,375	4,600,223	486,426	919,083	5,032,880	1,290,507	1,455,480	39,906	194,931	93,336
2012	8,122,819	4,754,782	19,579	4,774,361	502,940	860,948	5,132,369	1,505,936	1,484,514	41,731	194,645	94,216
2013	7,937,101	4,750,081	21,146	4,771,227	567,904	907,092	5,110,415	1,303,665	1,523,021	40,755	194,753	93,408
2014	8,272,075	4,901,366	12,961	4,914,327	583,741	885,986	5,216,572	1,478,180	1,577,323	42,441	194,908	94,837
2015	8,697,754	4,968,006	13,194	4,981,200	595,338	990,728	5,376,590	1,674,169	1,646,995	44,658	194,763	95,303
2016	8,782,735	4,992,699	10,768	5,003,467	599,767	1,043,899	5,447,599	1,664,220	1,670,916	45,037	195,010	94,657
2017	9,100,130	5,152,565	8,374	5,160,939	625,689	1,090,071	5,625,321	1,726,813	1,747,996	46,412	196,071	95,358
2018	9,760,878	9,750,492	10,386	5,421,330	649,264	1,095,418	5,867,484	2,055,411	1,837,983	49,710	196,357	96,783
2019	9,981,409	9,966,359	15,050	5,518,213	664,534	1,171,452	6,025,131	2,062,023	1,894,255	50,845	196,311	96,966

Personal Income and Employment by Area: Raleigh-Cary, NC

(Thousands of dollars, except as noted.)

Year	Personal income, total	Earnings by place of work			Less: Contributions for government social insurance	Plus: Adjustment for residence	Equals: Net earnings by place of residence	Plus: Dividends, interest, and rent	Plus: Personal current transfer receipts	Per capita personal income (dollars)	Population (persons)	Total employment
		Nonfarm	Farm	Total								
1970	1,196,842	956,524	50,778	1,007,302	63,442	18,228	962,088	156,372	78,382	3,750	319,135	165,563
1971	1,319,245	1,047,907	48,736	1,096,643	71,831	26,250	1,051,062	175,796	92,387	4,014	328,641	168,259
1972	1,494,638	1,190,116	59,681	1,249,797	86,153	30,301	1,193,945	197,306	103,387	4,425	337,793	177,550
1973	1,701,509	1,363,857	71,393	1,435,250	114,504	33,354	1,354,100	227,690	119,719	4,904	346,989	188,533
1974	1,932,923	1,524,338	86,463	1,610,801	133,023	40,186	1,517,964	266,592	148,367	5,419	356,680	195,217
1975	2,156,884	1,647,284	95,251	1,742,535	142,702	54,489	1,654,322	299,696	202,866	5,945	362,809	190,837
1976	2,383,131	1,834,193	89,164	1,923,357	162,059	64,763	1,826,061	331,124	225,946	6,461	368,858	197,595
1977	2,638,378	2,062,310	64,738	2,127,048	180,758	79,323	2,025,613	374,585	238,180	6,994	377,230	205,674
1978	3,014,777	2,361,147	92,034	2,453,181	214,033	90,108	2,329,256	426,671	258,850	7,830	385,013	214,810
1979	3,417,079	2,755,899	40,794	2,796,693	260,627	94,582	2,630,648	489,039	297,392	8,686	393,407	229,255
1980	3,892,536	3,074,966	45,642	3,120,608	293,787	104,576	2,931,397	604,729	356,410	9,628	404,305	233,851
1981	4,391,883	3,345,694	75,283	3,420,977	344,406	146,172	3,222,743	752,037	417,103	10,660	411,982	236,605
1982	4,815,126	3,628,274	74,247	3,702,521	380,184	178,684	3,501,021	856,717	457,388	11,470	419,800	239,666
1983	5,413,843	4,145,100	47,984	4,193,084	438,319	201,859	3,956,624	957,815	499,404	12,550	431,398	252,652
1984	6,360,203	4,872,431	81,770	4,954,201	523,564	248,566	4,679,203	1,146,131	534,869	14,193	448,113	273,343
1985	7,278,175	5,655,921	82,595	5,738,516	616,390	295,483	5,417,609	1,284,090	576,476	15,561	467,729	294,465
1986	7,977,405	6,235,133	49,645	6,284,778	691,844	346,665	5,939,599	1,419,449	618,357	16,510	483,172	307,223
1987	8,704,245	6,770,978	69,832	6,840,810	736,800	433,633	6,537,643	1,517,654	648,948	17,602	494,491	320,160
1988	9,662,714	7,441,720	96,170	7,537,890	834,329	490,429	7,193,990	1,758,616	710,108	18,902	511,200	336,952
1989	10,704,458	8,061,082	107,346	8,168,428	901,823	591,684	7,858,289	2,039,866	806,303	20,299	527,344	350,715
1990	11,576,807	8,706,809	137,296	8,844,105	998,559	672,128	8,517,674	2,159,395	899,738	21,092	548,874	361,542
1991	12,297,883	9,065,403	151,425	9,216,828	1,054,473	863,943	9,026,298	2,243,955	1,027,630	21,647	568,119	361,975
1992	13,607,161	10,090,907	154,988	10,245,895	1,153,124	1,002,967	10,095,738	2,356,255	1,155,168	23,112	588,751	373,756
1993	14,820,083	10,998,081	162,058	11,160,139	1,253,742	1,067,189	10,973,586	2,560,952	1,285,545	24,193	612,576	394,846
1994	16,037,524	11,932,341	160,415	12,092,756	1,380,843	1,131,981	11,843,894	2,847,672	1,345,958	25,132	638,140	413,368
1995	17,535,413	12,882,755	140,888	13,023,643	1,491,560	1,294,903	12,826,986	3,183,977	1,524,450	26,317	666,317	433,235
1996	19,205,602	14,087,067	148,754	14,235,821	1,623,545	1,405,852	14,018,128	3,551,047	1,636,427	27,654	694,496	456,366
1997	21,345,498	15,545,165	197,289	15,742,454	1,794,732	1,653,957	15,601,679	4,010,736	1,733,083	29,584	721,528	484,256
1998	23,317,070	17,204,704	166,502	17,371,206	1,986,008	1,827,947	17,213,145	4,286,325	1,817,600	31,086	750,079	512,369
1999	24,996,522	18,540,217	160,949	18,701,166	2,154,115	2,114,083	18,661,134	4,414,540	1,920,848	32,179	776,786	520,966
2000	27,560,682	20,275,147	209,874	20,485,021	2,356,853	2,645,880	20,774,048	4,718,978	2,067,656	34,273	804,157	539,376
2001	29,536,285	22,063,839	191,043	22,254,882	2,512,142	2,667,455	22,410,195	4,751,195	2,374,895	35,453	833,100	548,246
2002	30,184,789	22,561,609	77,121	22,638,730	2,552,641	2,814,423	22,900,512	4,636,592	2,647,685	35,135	859,117	551,503
2003	31,413,780	23,222,989	68,026	23,291,015	2,685,284	3,103,941	23,709,672	4,877,813	2,826,295	35,563	883,333	559,703
2004	33,658,077	24,671,322	113,785	24,785,107	2,826,632	3,234,542	25,193,017	5,430,637	3,034,423	37,007	909,510	578,156
2005	36,643,468	26,070,699	112,737	26,183,436	3,027,212	3,602,430	26,758,654	6,496,184	3,388,630	38,787	944,725	605,919
2006	41,045,134	28,838,626	96,630	28,935,256	3,308,405	4,239,047	29,865,898	7,435,710	3,743,526	41,492	989,219	640,331
2007	44,715,857	30,767,080	87,857	30,854,937	3,571,527	5,076,891	32,360,301	8,257,886	4,097,670	43,226	1,034,476	677,941
2008	47,855,083	32,317,239	121,900	32,439,139	3,694,208	5,432,269	34,177,200	8,814,304	4,863,579	44,427	1,077,163	684,070
2009	46,276,810	30,773,816	130,241	30,904,057	3,590,316	5,813,492	33,127,233	7,610,009	5,539,568	41,689	1,110,061	665,891
2010	48,591,482	32,304,902	101,041	32,405,943	3,714,879	6,208,676	34,899,740	7,611,645	6,080,097	42,722	1,137,393	666,828
2011	50,761,818	33,605,538	105,033	33,710,571	3,513,233	5,641,080	35,838,418	8,615,639	6,307,761	43,634	1,163,343	688,337
2012	54,209,563	36,065,865	135,015	36,200,880	3,679,854	5,914,313	38,435,339	9,352,278	6,421,946	45,596	1,188,920	708,499
2013	54,832,457	37,572,231	107,600	37,679,831	4,399,571	5,705,871	38,986,131	9,279,462	6,566,864	45,150	1,214,464	728,477
2014	59,027,566	40,335,423	150,068	40,485,491	4,702,691	5,658,230	41,441,030	10,666,868	6,919,668	47,503	1,242,613	757,085
2015	63,673,248	43,742,963	112,559	43,855,522	5,077,468	5,570,180	44,348,234	11,893,249	7,431,765	50,023	1,272,875	792,689
2016	66,502,795	46,278,280	112,535	46,390,815	5,332,874	5,456,412	46,514,353	12,181,538	7,806,904	50,964	1,304,896	819,902
2017	70,016,292	49,034,215	131,941	49,166,156	5,594,034	5,589,940	49,162,062	12,738,000	8,116,230	52,444	1,335,079	839,913
2018	76,531,044	76,441,379	89,665	53,467,937	5,969,165	5,850,104	53,348,876	14,347,389	8,834,779	56,207	1,361,590	876,277
2019	80,458,462	80,349,591	108,871	56,627,935	6,337,673	6,197,155	56,487,417	14,581,429	9,389,616	57,851	1,390,785	903,481

Personal Income and Employment by Area: Rapid City, SD

(Thousands of dollars, except as noted.)

Year	Personal income, total	Earnings by place of work			Less: Contributions for government social insurance	Plus: Adjustment for residence	Equals: Net earnings by place of residence	Plus: Dividends, interest, and rent	Plus: Personal current transfer receipts	Per capita personal income (dollars)	Population (persons)	Total employment
		Nonfarm	Farm	Total								
1970	321,371	237,753	12,570	250,323	15,427	4,031	238,927	58,276	24,168	3,935	81,667	37,761
1971	362,172	272,160	13,455	285,615	18,244	2,298	269,669	64,790	27,713	4,279	84,645	39,342
1972	416,104	313,888	18,840	332,728	21,475	2,425	313,678	71,802	30,624	4,720	88,158	41,056
1973	474,757	349,942	32,633	382,575	27,099	2,269	357,745	82,979	34,033	5,396	87,982	43,482
1974	505,322	380,719	14,705	395,424	30,697	3,244	367,971	96,993	40,358	5,658	89,308	43,651
1975	563,501	414,847	19,374	434,221	34,279	4,760	404,702	108,992	49,807	6,279	89,744	44,004
1976	619,358	465,223	11,385	476,608	38,464	6,232	444,376	119,766	55,216	6,607	93,739	45,978
1977	685,169	513,094	10,741	523,835	40,910	8,081	491,006	136,310	57,853	7,092	96,608	48,360
1978	793,371	589,590	18,138	607,728	47,425	10,535	570,838	160,088	62,445	8,041	98,670	51,590
1979	885,017	650,920	22,537	673,457	55,530	13,347	631,274	180,989	72,754	8,848	100,024	52,967
1980	939,925	669,346	14,881	684,227	57,159	15,699	642,767	211,238	85,920	9,667	97,234	51,844
1981	1,031,689	709,810	16,466	726,276	64,237	15,827	677,866	251,502	102,321	10,566	97,645	50,991
1982	1,111,070	756,721	13,588	770,309	69,082	12,661	713,888	281,481	115,701	11,237	98,875	51,796
1983	1,186,853	827,982	12,515	840,497	77,075	10,720	774,142	285,852	126,859	11,827	100,353	54,204
1984	1,313,093	922,447	19,837	942,284	87,847	8,792	863,229	315,120	134,744	12,709	103,323	58,045
1985	1,360,335	964,840	6,798	971,638	94,902	7,386	884,122	331,281	144,932	12,935	105,166	58,311
1986	1,437,281	1,016,545	15,237	1,031,782	103,590	5,803	933,995	348,395	154,891	13,503	106,441	59,737
1987	1,525,536	1,094,269	11,223	1,105,492	113,141	4,145	996,496	367,598	161,442	14,024	108,783	63,586
1988	1,606,114	1,164,917	6,051	1,170,968	124,709	2,161	1,048,420	387,090	170,604	14,687	109,358	62,921
1989	1,724,166	1,236,415	10,028	1,246,443	134,164	1,168	1,113,447	420,455	190,264	15,861	108,707	64,630
1990	1,861,069	1,346,699	15,712	1,362,411	153,789	-8,895	1,199,727	455,065	206,277	16,946	109,825	67,637
1991	1,969,908	1,430,796	7,924	1,438,720	165,032	-8,025	1,265,663	480,431	223,814	17,510	112,499	69,532
1992	2,120,623	1,527,924	14,180	1,542,104	175,285	-5,160	1,361,659	512,410	246,554	18,483	114,732	70,921
1993	2,232,143	1,606,477	20,354	1,626,831	183,490	-3,775	1,439,566	526,501	266,076	19,215	116,165	72,557
1994	2,319,720	1,662,486	5,715	1,668,201	191,339	333	1,477,195	553,639	288,886	19,823	117,020	75,111
1995	2,453,052	1,715,315	14,584	1,729,899	196,496	910	1,534,313	603,846	314,893	20,789	117,995	75,455
1996	2,525,880	1,741,434	2,759	1,744,193	200,527	2,618	1,546,284	643,418	336,178	21,429	117,871	75,634
1997	2,635,140	1,808,684	7,235	1,815,919	208,796	1,385	1,608,508	683,438	343,194	22,372	117,790	76,299
1998	2,859,294	1,949,310	13,491	1,962,801	223,159	-944	1,738,698	763,140	357,456	24,181	118,245	78,869
1999	3,024,243	2,063,710	30,613	2,094,323	239,761	-4,596	1,849,966	797,366	376,911	25,375	119,182	81,704
2000	3,193,698	2,155,303	32,305	2,187,608	252,493	-5,048	1,930,067	855,857	407,774	26,511	120,469	84,037
2001	3,437,777	2,356,522	36,123	2,392,645	269,164	-7,523	2,115,958	870,066	451,753	28,250	121,692	82,165
2002	3,583,425	2,512,231	15,959	2,528,190	284,991	-10,388	2,232,811	866,391	484,223	29,176	122,822	82,848
2003	3,798,572	2,649,292	47,294	2,696,586	300,205	-11,016	2,385,365	907,643	505,564	30,813	123,278	83,438
2004	4,098,550	2,834,921	39,295	2,874,216	316,231	-12,741	2,545,244	1,010,281	543,025	32,679	125,419	85,201
2005	4,305,661	2,952,024	55,444	3,007,468	325,534	-7,608	2,674,326	1,048,934	582,401	34,172	125,998	86,298
2006	4,520,253	3,049,727	12,369	3,062,096	342,572	-6,582	2,712,942	1,175,653	631,658	35,461	127,471	87,312
2007	4,806,326	3,150,936	20,770	3,171,706	358,093	-419	2,813,194	1,303,917	689,215	37,282	128,918	88,943
2008	5,051,455	3,272,442	33,275	3,305,717	375,769	-126	2,929,822	1,320,216	801,417	38,526	131,119	90,452
2009	5,054,210	3,322,337	3,786	3,326,123	381,291	-7,007	2,937,825	1,262,002	854,383	37,929	133,254	89,742
2010	5,326,465	3,492,308	12,027	3,504,335	398,308	-6,422	3,099,605	1,271,969	954,891	39,454	135,004	89,607
2011	5,608,849	3,613,591	50,570	3,664,161	368,290	-9,563	3,286,308	1,338,971	983,570	41,172	136,229	91,147
2012	5,883,324	3,781,572	40,843	3,822,415	382,141	-6,642	3,433,632	1,452,469	997,223	42,530	138,334	91,928
2013	5,869,994	3,878,276	33,118	3,911,394	440,900	5,708	3,476,202	1,358,111	1,035,681	41,704	140,755	92,963
2014	6,364,716	4,095,747	56,291	4,152,038	462,417	17,888	3,707,509	1,575,560	1,081,647	44,598	142,713	94,000
2015	6,569,707	4,237,441	43,392	4,280,833	475,251	7,069	3,812,651	1,618,034	1,139,022	45,828	143,357	94,108
2016	6,704,039	4,301,031	24,209	4,325,240	489,222	-12,211	3,823,807	1,692,347	1,187,885	46,273	144,879	95,155
2017	6,913,945	4,412,034	27,294	4,439,328	509,637	-12,329	3,917,362	1,774,547	1,222,036	47,082	146,850	96,598
2018	7,026,924	7,002,796	24,128	4,478,846	513,028	-74,412	3,891,406	1,861,149	1,274,369	50,137	140,154	93,553
2019	7,295,050	7,297,476	-2,426	4,651,159	541,674	-67,251	4,042,234	1,885,260	1,367,556	51,335	142,107	94,606

Personal Income and Employment by Area: Reading, PA

(Thousands of dollars, except as noted.)

Year	Personal income, total	Earnings by place of work			Less: Contributions for government social insurance	Plus: Adjustment for residence	Equals: Net earnings by place of residence	Plus: Dividends, interest, and rent	Plus: Personal current transfer receipts	Per capita personal income (dollars)	Population (persons)	Total employment
		Nonfarm	Farm	Total								
1970	1,252,791	1,027,771	18,618	1,046,389	79,002	4,950	972,337	165,861	114,593	4,221	296,772	146,430
1971	1,332,288	1,086,941	13,346	1,100,287	86,780	9,547	1,023,054	176,031	133,203	4,449	299,474	145,699
1972	1,478,467	1,201,563	20,067	1,221,630	100,840	18,095	1,138,885	189,007	150,575	4,914	300,891	148,292
1973	1,645,877	1,340,100	23,025	1,363,125	129,077	29,047	1,263,095	213,654	169,128	5,396	305,011	154,355
1974	1,811,050	1,442,564	21,103	1,463,667	143,747	42,512	1,362,432	243,787	204,831	5,924	305,720	155,151
1975	1,956,345	1,485,548	19,342	1,504,890	144,415	56,246	1,416,721	268,965	270,659	6,375	306,891	149,308
1976	2,169,731	1,654,554	25,018	1,679,572	163,067	66,675	1,583,180	293,008	293,543	7,034	308,452	153,056
1977	2,415,498	1,852,844	23,147	1,875,991	181,730	81,997	1,776,258	331,538	307,702	7,877	306,642	156,627
1978	2,698,350	2,080,827	22,645	2,103,472	209,603	104,298	1,998,167	367,848	332,335	8,729	309,110	161,553
1979	3,024,076	2,320,728	25,717	2,346,445	241,628	129,276	2,234,093	420,005	369,978	9,691	312,055	164,360
1980	3,366,073	2,493,025	23,303	2,516,328	260,503	156,543	2,412,368	520,983	432,722	10,754	313,016	165,898
1981	3,729,154	2,713,378	34,842	2,748,220	303,546	153,436	2,598,110	643,184	487,860	11,861	314,414	165,448
1982	3,980,903	2,809,421	34,229	2,843,650	319,571	154,913	2,678,992	740,376	561,535	12,654	314,597	163,637
1983	4,282,832	3,041,658	40,381	3,082,039	349,732	147,328	2,879,635	797,115	606,082	13,588	315,184	164,855
1984	4,670,276	3,374,686	62,824	3,437,510	405,486	142,924	3,174,948	890,388	604,940	14,700	317,711	171,552
1985	4,903,232	3,520,221	53,764	3,573,985	427,431	151,455	3,298,009	957,669	647,554	15,414	318,105	172,691
1986	5,151,473	3,706,100	51,486	3,757,586	449,792	153,178	3,460,972	1,004,629	685,872	16,079	320,394	173,929
1987	5,468,098	4,002,755	60,684	4,063,439	479,089	153,774	3,738,124	1,027,773	702,201	16,884	323,871	179,717
1988	5,915,967	4,387,905	48,387	4,436,292	534,326	152,741	4,054,707	1,116,921	744,339	18,038	327,977	184,644
1989	6,538,477	4,830,076	63,531	4,893,607	575,104	130,818	4,449,321	1,294,207	794,949	19,580	333,938	189,338
1990	6,746,828	4,984,826	68,319	5,053,145	597,324	127,069	4,582,890	1,288,258	875,680	19,972	337,812	190,057
1991	6,993,289	5,060,132	63,660	5,123,792	610,832	153,938	4,666,898	1,305,758	1,020,633	20,410	342,637	185,735
1992	7,504,851	5,488,015	84,278	5,572,293	654,974	170,897	5,088,216	1,321,296	1,095,339	21,687	346,050	186,648
1993	7,861,371	5,786,372	72,384	5,858,756	704,888	194,990	5,348,858	1,372,445	1,140,068	22,449	350,186	188,584
1994	8,243,934	6,126,077	81,336	6,207,413	753,245	209,160	5,663,328	1,414,862	1,165,744	23,282	354,092	190,821
1995	8,607,203	6,304,713	60,382	6,365,095	772,717	246,626	5,839,004	1,546,362	1,221,837	24,097	357,193	194,899
1996	9,043,801	6,505,984	69,451	6,575,435	777,716	301,052	6,098,771	1,642,545	1,302,485	25,095	360,380	197,093
1997	9,458,239	6,777,448	61,859	6,839,307	808,392	358,448	6,389,363	1,732,423	1,336,453	26,003	363,739	202,003
1998	9,934,374	6,994,905	67,093	7,061,998	828,932	438,373	6,671,439	1,890,398	1,372,537	27,063	367,082	206,229
1999	10,360,158	7,300,423	65,566	7,365,989	848,998	519,846	7,036,837	1,869,954	1,453,367	27,929	370,942	211,470
2000	11,103,780	7,700,150	87,715	7,787,865	884,909	611,914	7,514,870	2,033,673	1,555,237	29,646	374,546	215,764
2001	11,552,756	7,982,919	90,747	8,073,666	917,155	687,551	7,844,062	1,998,960	1,709,734	30,604	377,487	207,227
2002	11,887,279	8,191,034	65,363	8,256,397	934,076	736,965	8,059,286	1,972,784	1,855,209	31,173	381,338	204,712
2003	12,251,029	8,316,600	88,143	8,404,743	940,383	871,974	8,336,334	1,993,603	1,921,092	31,751	385,846	202,718
2004	12,689,794	8,629,336	104,769	8,734,105	974,133	952,068	8,712,040	1,959,252	2,018,502	32,467	390,848	206,368
2005	13,342,564	9,015,691	91,982	9,107,673	1,025,204	1,086,392	9,168,861	1,963,542	2,210,161	33,699	395,933	210,061
2006	14,287,615	9,610,398	68,196	9,678,594	1,104,508	1,049,134	9,623,220	2,297,076	2,367,319	35,556	401,834	216,496
2007	14,948,640	9,957,695	42,303	9,999,998	1,138,799	1,064,344	9,925,543	2,542,454	2,480,643	36,890	405,223	219,162
2008	15,383,176	9,964,232	54,972	10,019,204	1,153,976	1,090,015	9,955,243	2,611,412	2,816,521	37,728	407,737	217,938
2009	14,967,753	9,596,817	42,753	9,639,570	1,126,608	997,777	9,510,739	2,287,495	3,169,519	36,515	409,904	210,367
2010	15,678,834	10,031,751	62,992	10,094,743	1,164,143	1,101,947	10,032,547	2,228,945	3,417,342	38,056	411,989	211,636
2011	16,476,385	10,480,336	81,654	10,561,990	1,088,004	1,124,460	10,598,446	2,439,271	3,438,668	39,908	412,857	214,240
2012	17,199,309	10,716,749	103,002	10,819,751	1,109,921	1,122,123	10,831,953	2,898,861	3,468,495	41,592	413,522	215,262
2013	16,940,856	10,896,172	122,007	11,018,179	1,269,835	1,135,053	10,883,397	2,537,987	3,519,472	40,919	414,011	216,796
2014	17,730,082	11,278,190	141,441	11,419,631	1,326,507	1,145,104	11,238,228	2,882,347	3,609,507	42,760	414,642	219,940
2015	18,580,911	11,927,636	98,586	12,026,222	1,394,341	1,151,653	11,783,534	3,016,626	3,780,751	44,745	415,261	222,809
2016	18,972,501	12,196,901	47,357	12,244,258	1,426,849	1,150,128	11,967,537	3,030,834	3,974,130	45,636	415,732	224,803
2017	19,765,386	12,718,214	66,612	12,784,826	1,489,323	1,277,726	12,573,229	3,184,760	4,007,397	47,302	417,854	226,259
2018	20,790,624	20,682,519	108,105	13,400,589	1,546,091	1,265,246	13,119,744	3,356,667	4,314,213	49,439	420,529	228,850
2019	21,605,098	21,473,727	131,371	13,832,473	1,592,963	1,475,178	13,714,688	3,429,428	4,460,982	51,299	421,164	232,853

Personal Income and Employment by Area: Redding, CA

(Thousands of dollars, except as noted.)

Year	Personal income, total	Earnings by place of work			Less: Contributions for government social insurance	Plus: Adjustment for residence	Equals: Net earnings by place of residence	Plus: Dividends, interest, and rent	Plus: Personal current transfer receipts	Per capita personal income (dollars)	Population (persons)	Total employment
		Nonfarm	Farm	Total								
1970	315,205	230,080	2,632	232,712	14,211	4,024	222,525	47,107	45,573	4,042	77,980	29,369
1971	348,129	254,054	2,018	256,072	16,311	3,852	243,613	52,903	51,613	4,383	79,434	30,699
1972	382,075	282,111	664	282,775	19,267	4,031	267,539	58,831	55,705	4,737	80,656	32,031
1973	434,362	320,437	4,603	325,040	25,065	3,584	303,559	69,563	61,240	5,156	84,249	34,817
1974	497,975	353,208	7,558	360,766	28,046	2,681	335,401	83,022	79,552	5,747	86,651	35,762
1975	562,845	393,190	6,204	399,394	30,253	2,038	371,179	95,312	96,354	6,112	92,082	37,593
1976	646,233	464,503	5,855	470,358	36,409	1,569	435,518	106,639	104,076	6,809	94,909	40,685
1977	728,667	524,941	6,150	531,091	42,076	823	489,838	123,464	115,365	7,275	100,157	43,503
1978	851,500	619,697	7,998	627,695	50,726	-681	576,288	147,668	127,544	8,221	103,572	47,369
1979	974,419	700,816	9,184	710,000	60,515	-2,305	647,180	174,743	152,496	8,685	112,199	49,477
1980	1,083,423	738,493	12,312	750,805	63,131	-3,551	684,123	212,327	186,973	9,293	116,590	50,551
1981	1,179,141	760,374	11,264	771,638	70,663	-2,386	698,589	253,461	227,091	9,804	120,270	50,078
1982	1,260,842	795,568	12,814	808,382	75,412	-2,303	730,667	280,679	249,496	10,376	121,513	49,830
1983	1,371,034	863,849	10,392	874,241	83,221	-417	790,603	317,541	262,890	11,164	122,807	51,243
1984	1,513,727	964,903	10,951	975,854	97,058	-521	878,275	352,570	282,882	12,079	125,322	53,517
1985	1,615,823	1,016,394	10,711	1,027,105	104,331	1,614	924,388	381,998	309,437	12,578	128,461	54,432
1986	1,744,320	1,109,173	8,259	1,117,432	115,821	1,880	1,003,491	404,732	336,097	13,406	130,119	56,501
1987	1,897,407	1,253,978	8,784	1,262,762	132,282	152	1,130,632	410,304	356,471	14,271	132,958	60,612
1988	2,093,170	1,409,168	9,280	1,418,448	153,691	-2,794	1,261,963	443,310	387,897	15,320	136,627	64,192
1989	2,323,011	1,545,319	10,319	1,555,638	170,893	-4,557	1,380,188	513,663	429,160	16,476	140,997	66,910
1990	2,541,648	1,695,634	10,535	1,706,169	185,725	-6,500	1,513,944	552,545	475,159	17,103	148,606	71,727
1991	2,713,034	1,813,165	9,100	1,822,265	198,716	-6,704	1,616,845	565,958	530,231	17,646	153,746	73,820
1992	2,896,498	1,914,669	9,719	1,924,388	208,119	-2,451	1,713,818	570,315	612,365	18,473	156,800	73,116
1993	3,010,702	1,978,490	10,573	1,989,063	215,942	-28	1,773,093	588,392	649,217	19,087	157,735	73,197
1994	3,135,342	2,090,798	12,873	2,103,671	226,616	3,511	1,880,566	600,728	654,048	19,766	158,621	75,586
1995	3,249,393	2,142,199	8,563	2,150,762	229,121	10,097	1,931,738	627,324	690,331	20,411	159,198	75,741
1996	3,378,817	2,205,640	9,557	2,215,197	228,109	15,230	2,002,318	646,450	730,049	21,152	159,737	77,057
1997	3,562,687	2,334,825	13,056	2,347,881	238,471	19,667	2,129,077	692,978	740,632	22,161	160,761	78,613
1998	3,773,976	2,427,596	11,137	2,438,733	243,353	26,986	2,222,366	736,245	815,365	23,291	162,034	79,004
1999	3,945,294	2,566,345	12,442	2,578,787	256,958	34,949	2,356,778	727,998	860,518	24,356	161,987	81,009
2000	4,199,895	2,725,458	12,445	2,737,903	273,177	43,121	2,507,847	779,405	912,643	25,669	163,615	83,530
2001	4,616,134	3,023,982	14,316	3,038,298	313,532	39,583	2,764,349	827,168	1,024,617	27,740	166,408	85,889
2002	4,797,550	3,258,778	15,007	3,273,785	345,404	32,869	2,961,250	743,101	1,093,199	28,188	170,198	88,589
2003	4,973,083	3,406,718	17,706	3,424,424	367,155	25,023	3,082,292	778,647	1,112,144	28,713	173,202	89,688
2004	5,138,923	3,490,757	18,015	3,508,772	395,733	-12,790	3,100,249	873,366	1,165,308	29,388	174,867	90,490
2005	5,260,540	3,570,588	17,904	3,588,492	415,443	-31,710	3,141,339	894,513	1,224,688	29,955	175,615	91,346
2006	5,609,091	3,753,356	11,705	3,765,061	423,978	-57,063	3,284,020	987,720	1,337,351	31,840	176,166	93,130
2007	5,827,967	3,851,701	7,836	3,859,537	429,052	-97,864	3,332,621	1,070,004	1,425,342	33,011	176,548	94,482
2008	5,870,392	3,683,594	18,697	3,702,291	420,971	-93,457	3,187,863	1,095,752	1,586,777	33,120	177,247	90,773
2009	5,865,530	3,548,384	26,421	3,574,805	410,202	-77,408	3,087,195	1,027,113	1,751,222	33,086	177,279	86,195
2010	6,135,906	3,643,651	36,778	3,680,429	406,157	-57,836	3,216,436	1,022,012	1,897,458	34,611	177,284	84,019
2011	6,317,057	3,680,197	36,374	3,716,571	378,740	-61,569	3,276,262	1,132,000	1,908,795	35,570	177,595	84,116
2012	6,473,558	3,695,595	50,294	3,745,889	379,742	-45,591	3,320,556	1,196,139	1,956,863	36,385	177,917	84,888
2013	6,626,497	3,758,937	35,707	3,794,644	426,667	5,075	3,373,052	1,220,434	2,033,011	37,135	178,445	85,742
2014	7,089,824	3,958,609	44,045	4,002,654	448,690	7,110	3,561,074	1,380,627	2,148,123	39,612	178,983	88,047
2015	7,539,383	4,184,740	48,688	4,233,428	470,418	7,438	3,770,448	1,468,424	2,300,511	42,244	178,472	89,938
2016	7,745,218	4,323,628	33,415	4,357,043	492,044	25,490	3,890,489	1,485,302	2,369,427	43,324	178,774	90,507
2017	8,040,889	4,550,870	58,049	4,608,919	516,770	40,742	4,132,891	1,560,251	2,347,747	44,691	179,921	91,443
2018	8,372,513	8,332,976	39,537	4,786,221	548,810	22,656	4,260,067	1,679,434	2,433,012	46,589	179,709	92,242
2019	8,722,632	8,669,188	53,444	5,017,447	578,594	9,212	4,448,065	1,709,770	2,564,797	48,438	180,080	93,816

Personal Income and Employment by Area: Reno, NV

(Thousands of dollars, except as noted.)

Year	Personal income, total	Earnings by place of work			Less: Contributions for government social insurance	Plus: Adjustment for residence	Equals: Net earnings by place of residence	Plus: Dividends, interest, and rent	Plus: Personal current transfer receipts	Per capita personal income (dollars)	Population (persons)	Total employment
		Nonfarm	Farm	Total								
1970	672,283	537,954	1,110	539,064	36,240	-5,370	497,454	132,957	41,872	5,473	122,838	68,813
1971	759,099	610,678	1,099	611,777	42,479	-9,815	559,483	148,904	50,712	5,874	129,234	73,393
1972	851,823	689,353	1,411	690,764	51,278	-13,413	626,073	166,438	59,312	6,257	136,146	77,256
1973	960,495	785,071	1,992	787,063	67,580	-18,402	701,081	192,086	67,328	6,772	141,828	83,477
1974	1,059,905	847,665	896	848,561	74,021	-20,648	753,892	224,170	81,843	7,147	148,306	85,698
1975	1,205,657	951,412	1,284	952,696	80,698	-24,514	847,484	245,010	113,163	7,875	153,109	89,100
1976	1,393,220	1,124,512	1,588	1,126,100	98,386	-31,633	996,081	274,585	122,554	8,726	159,670	96,622
1977	1,644,823	1,364,377	1,022	1,365,399	122,155	-42,058	1,201,186	309,839	133,798	9,745	168,795	108,044
1978	2,037,436	1,712,238	773	1,713,011	159,462	-48,413	1,505,136	380,896	151,404	11,402	178,694	124,884
1979	2,366,064	1,994,605	-679	1,993,926	196,099	-57,946	1,739,881	451,717	174,466	12,551	188,511	134,856
1980	2,658,764	2,194,200	3,015	2,197,215	215,531	-64,293	1,917,391	535,755	205,618	13,503	196,906	135,996
1981	2,961,553	2,370,660	2,127	2,372,787	247,641	-60,469	2,064,677	651,233	245,643	14,539	203,693	136,031
1982	3,140,573	2,426,863	2,459	2,429,322	253,427	-58,788	2,117,107	750,552	272,914	14,929	210,363	133,990
1983	3,338,389	2,556,233	1,746	2,557,979	276,750	-51,492	2,229,737	804,199	304,453	15,676	212,962	133,936
1984	3,654,583	2,809,526	1,057	2,810,583	317,274	-54,312	2,438,997	893,749	321,837	16,748	218,215	141,249
1985	3,939,588	3,008,364	333	3,008,697	346,641	-53,726	2,608,330	983,941	347,317	17,611	223,695	145,142
1986	4,216,417	3,248,279	86	3,248,365	385,249	-55,724	2,807,392	1,029,507	379,518	18,318	230,182	151,010
1987	4,549,692	3,538,196	1,571	3,539,767	420,097	-60,711	3,058,959	1,093,052	397,681	19,177	237,251	160,239
1988	4,992,050	3,925,748	1,742	3,927,490	467,724	-68,414	3,391,352	1,178,505	422,193	20,426	244,395	167,081
1989	5,402,955	4,165,551	1,999	4,167,550	501,844	-65,580	3,600,126	1,320,350	482,479	21,550	250,718	170,932
1990	5,965,065	4,556,301	1,341	4,557,642	570,290	-101,097	3,886,255	1,540,999	537,811	23,015	259,178	175,220
1991	6,454,376	4,833,979	1,789	4,835,768	598,456	-96,722	4,140,590	1,660,907	652,879	24,205	266,660	174,711
1992	7,085,632	5,293,466	591	5,294,057	647,724	-108,673	4,537,660	1,824,424	723,548	25,902	273,556	175,503
1993	7,373,493	5,545,640	9,233	5,554,873	687,324	-102,243	4,765,306	1,870,304	737,883	26,213	281,288	182,728
1994	7,993,228	5,963,949	3,433	5,967,382	743,289	-110,487	5,113,606	2,146,221	733,401	27,445	291,248	192,012
1995	8,680,469	6,414,679	3,957	6,418,636	799,510	-118,493	5,500,633	2,379,749	800,087	28,911	300,246	200,861
1996	9,372,446	6,916,145	5,137	6,921,282	838,500	-125,501	5,957,281	2,575,799	839,366	30,217	310,169	209,606
1997	9,976,725	7,421,169	3,325	7,424,494	872,068	-123,824	6,428,602	2,674,738	873,385	31,233	319,425	218,118
1998	10,986,506	8,176,640	4,103	8,180,743	915,475	-148,577	7,116,691	2,965,763	904,052	33,497	327,980	225,042
1999	11,810,647	8,899,423	4,195	8,903,618	954,952	-140,517	7,808,149	3,081,024	921,474	35,127	336,225	227,450
2000	13,006,735	9,621,386	5,650	9,627,036	938,083	-143,067	8,545,886	3,478,701	982,148	37,725	344,782	237,815
2001	14,068,357	10,519,129	4,324	10,523,453	1,013,371	-171,872	9,338,210	3,631,480	1,098,667	39,591	355,341	242,495
2002	14,171,699	10,552,808	3,836	10,556,644	1,023,671	-159,109	9,373,864	3,579,971	1,217,864	38,752	365,706	243,158
2003	14,946,920	11,080,875	3,498	11,084,373	1,046,458	-170,740	9,867,175	3,788,082	1,291,663	39,783	375,713	248,625
2004	16,307,712	11,858,467	4,892	11,863,359	1,105,125	-170,722	10,587,512	4,324,202	1,395,998	42,214	386,308	259,523
2005	17,586,989	12,636,900	4,564	12,641,464	1,168,449	-193,541	11,279,474	4,814,887	1,492,628	44,350	396,546	269,843
2006	18,408,961	13,371,288	6,283	13,377,571	1,307,355	-213,056	11,857,160	4,939,542	1,612,259	45,525	404,366	278,718
2007	18,694,926	13,258,238	2,921	13,261,159	1,350,587	-166,875	11,743,697	5,193,746	1,757,483	45,296	412,724	286,859
2008	18,129,092	12,254,884	5,589	12,260,473	1,250,837	-91,598	10,918,038	5,141,037	2,070,017	43,279	418,892	278,417
2009	17,532,270	11,781,736	8,273	11,790,009	1,218,365	-30,707	10,540,937	4,609,630	2,381,703	41,567	421,787	259,859
2010	18,681,140	12,819,352	8,438	12,827,790	1,219,626	56,082	11,664,246	4,393,981	2,622,913	43,853	425,991	253,315
2011	19,569,773	12,687,517	10,904	12,698,421	1,140,429	120,640	11,678,632	5,206,903	2,684,238	45,667	428,536	255,352
2012	18,943,995	12,115,939	10,785	12,126,724	1,180,338	135,893	11,082,279	5,158,736	2,702,980	43,830	432,212	255,675
2013	19,185,899	12,064,176	11,726	12,075,902	1,309,926	197,718	10,963,694	5,428,587	2,793,618	43,988	436,163	263,928
2014	20,503,881	12,577,875	18,104	12,595,979	1,445,033	222,058	11,373,004	6,106,151	3,024,726	46,409	441,807	269,281
2015	22,703,269	14,009,477	21,509	14,030,986	1,553,270	192,938	12,670,654	6,731,445	3,301,170	50,651	448,230	278,642
2016	23,741,770	14,635,642	12,747	14,648,389	1,637,566	144,850	13,155,673	7,116,975	3,469,122	52,018	456,418	290,044
2017	25,766,205	16,336,404	11,366	16,347,770	1,780,780	125,922	14,692,912	7,464,919	3,608,374	55,460	464,593	302,609
2018	28,989,976	28,982,563	7,413	18,037,660	1,949,111	68,232	16,156,781	9,019,632	3,813,563	61,900	468,335	316,138
2019	30,121,290	30,113,424	7,866	19,054,793	2,123,035	64,222	16,995,980	9,079,582	4,045,728	63,328	475,642	323,849

Personal Income and Employment by Area: Richmond, VA

(Thousands of dollars, except as noted.)

Year	Personal income, total	Earnings by place of work			Less: Contributions for government social insurance	Plus: Adjustment for residence	Equals: Net earnings by place of residence	Plus: Dividends, interest, and rent	Plus: Personal current transfer receipts	Per capita personal income (dollars)	Population (persons)	Total employment
		Nonfarm	Farm	Total								
1970	2,889,290	2,489,464	16,378	2,505,842	157,625	-85,357	2,262,860	430,650	195,780	4,028	717,320	363,604
1971	3,189,968	2,713,033	15,031	2,728,064	178,873	-70,217	2,478,974	474,541	236,453	4,376	729,032	368,947
1972	3,503,510	2,988,003	19,800	3,007,803	206,223	-90,730	2,710,850	517,069	275,591	4,787	731,939	378,331
1973	3,924,521	3,361,068	30,585	3,391,653	267,295	-113,722	3,010,636	589,474	324,411	5,294	741,343	401,104
1974	4,406,894	3,755,135	30,463	3,785,598	308,978	-131,389	3,345,231	683,197	378,466	5,892	747,915	417,651
1975	4,914,915	4,073,624	24,993	4,098,617	329,345	-84,551	3,684,721	747,404	482,790	6,477	758,781	413,944
1976	5,412,019	4,505,538	21,381	4,526,919	372,334	-91,831	4,062,754	815,697	533,568	7,006	772,532	424,700
1977	6,008,192	5,019,395	9,842	5,029,237	413,127	-89,895	4,526,215	910,414	571,563	7,636	786,806	438,435
1978	6,809,525	5,691,929	27,261	5,719,190	476,683	-106,208	5,136,299	1,045,524	627,702	8,568	794,750	457,990
1979	7,691,213	6,390,017	574	6,390,591	559,694	-76,486	5,754,411	1,218,808	717,994	9,568	803,835	471,434
1980	8,646,386	7,043,315	-9,013	7,034,302	620,379	-105,486	6,308,437	1,480,082	857,867	10,673	810,116	472,830
1981	9,714,915	7,717,858	25,268	7,743,126	728,564	-117,420	6,897,142	1,825,426	992,347	11,880	817,739	470,744
1982	10,489,952	8,231,154	9,663	8,240,817	787,999	-118,119	7,334,699	2,068,008	1,087,245	12,735	823,713	469,070
1983	11,273,448	8,857,329	-5,256	8,852,073	865,206	-110,959	7,875,908	2,225,562	1,171,978	13,581	830,095	475,270
1984	12,414,800	9,678,885	38,965	9,717,850	971,997	-106,587	8,639,266	2,532,240	1,243,294	14,840	836,596	489,234
1985	13,388,204	10,524,074	21,982	10,546,056	1,084,788	-111,042	9,350,226	2,706,614	1,331,364	15,832	845,645	509,452
1986	14,396,285	11,358,169	23,463	11,381,632	1,210,734	-112,456	10,058,442	2,919,897	1,417,946	16,790	857,407	529,695
1987	15,745,663	12,587,692	27,226	12,614,918	1,330,296	-130,021	11,154,601	3,112,096	1,478,966	18,032	873,222	556,131
1988	17,319,415	13,855,985	45,223	13,901,208	1,506,070	-147,108	12,248,030	3,482,317	1,589,068	19,485	888,857	568,478
1989	18,938,800	14,912,495	54,279	14,966,774	1,629,292	-157,335	13,180,147	4,020,958	1,737,695	20,968	903,206	583,119
1990	19,903,032	15,560,480	59,009	15,619,489	1,716,924	-166,416	13,736,149	4,296,202	1,870,681	21,640	919,735	589,433
1991	20,366,986	15,963,431	46,424	16,009,855	1,780,784	-187,892	14,041,179	4,264,430	2,061,377	21,810	933,839	578,586
1992	21,591,753	16,895,312	51,478	16,946,790	1,872,196	-214,790	14,859,804	4,412,597	2,319,352	22,706	950,908	579,119
1993	22,636,372	17,649,270	37,840	17,687,110	1,961,632	-246,377	15,479,101	4,675,804	2,481,467	23,443	965,604	587,075
1994	23,945,230	18,693,416	57,663	18,751,079	2,067,567	-287,981	16,395,531	4,972,752	2,576,947	24,458	979,035	605,263
1995	25,149,932	19,601,189	54,871	19,656,060	2,164,345	-326,899	17,164,816	5,191,148	2,793,968	25,354	991,943	621,056
1996	26,400,160	20,575,645	73,411	20,649,056	2,256,604	-362,426	18,030,026	5,421,897	2,948,237	26,292	1,004,116	632,125
1997	28,149,889	22,189,575	44,214	22,233,789	2,414,993	-433,157	19,385,639	5,722,594	3,041,656	27,652	1,017,990	650,624
1998	30,000,199	23,801,516	26,574	23,828,090	2,552,483	-462,935	20,812,672	6,070,888	3,116,639	29,089	1,031,320	661,987
1999	31,527,717	25,403,263	25,452	25,428,715	2,730,221	-509,774	22,188,720	6,075,707	3,263,290	30,148	1,045,761	677,738
2000	34,052,485	27,313,288	44,676	27,357,964	2,888,096	-563,771	23,906,097	6,658,558	3,487,830	32,156	1,058,966	694,731
2001	36,459,546	29,337,539	24,438	29,361,977	3,111,822	-548,614	25,701,541	6,890,002	3,868,003	34,048	1,070,817	698,884
2002	37,344,193	29,957,030	23,002	29,980,032	3,206,937	-500,335	26,272,760	7,020,401	4,051,032	34,438	1,084,389	700,097
2003	39,225,538	31,060,463	26,770	31,087,233	3,313,118	-449,906	27,324,209	7,575,969	4,325,360	35,704	1,098,631	702,035
2004	41,706,625	33,206,329	36,861	33,243,190	3,584,126	-429,064	29,230,000	7,949,530	4,527,095	37,375	1,115,900	717,512
2005	44,694,577	35,401,918	31,378	35,433,296	3,839,282	-402,234	31,191,780	8,567,793	4,935,004	39,376	1,135,074	736,833
2006	48,039,453	37,112,616	16,232	37,128,848	4,070,646	-336,965	32,721,237	9,913,152	5,405,064	41,510	1,157,286	752,506
2007	50,558,299	39,029,809	14,641	39,044,450	4,279,108	-289,508	34,475,834	10,280,328	5,802,137	43,052	1,174,344	771,046
2008	52,338,366	39,523,769	33,421	39,557,190	4,387,585	-234,270	34,935,335	10,709,268	6,693,763	44,015	1,189,113	770,886
2009	49,940,398	37,825,039	36,573	37,861,612	4,255,344	-182,469	33,423,799	9,207,951	7,308,648	41,592	1,200,712	747,991
2010	51,651,122	39,108,380	22,081	39,130,461	4,351,693	-147,518	34,631,250	9,080,419	7,939,453	42,686	1,210,039	744,104
2011	54,974,632	40,711,350	71,145	40,782,495	4,031,240	-150,496	36,600,759	10,146,481	8,227,392	45,089	1,219,241	757,400
2012	58,534,547	42,859,279	80,439	42,939,718	4,190,340	-157,054	38,592,324	11,625,917	8,316,306	47,461	1,233,321	770,586
2013	58,922,032	44,402,413	86,564	44,488,977	4,943,892	-149,986	39,395,099	10,855,892	8,671,041	47,298	1,245,755	783,093
2014	62,003,545	46,440,987	41,379	46,482,366	5,123,345	-163,486	41,195,535	11,817,347	8,990,663	49,264	1,258,597	796,770
2015	65,919,882	49,287,869	12,626	49,300,495	5,416,199	-200,058	43,684,238	12,670,469	9,565,175	51,904	1,270,027	821,707
2016	67,388,282	50,212,697	10,377	50,223,074	5,532,352	-225,450	44,465,272	12,995,246	9,927,764	52,557	1,282,205	840,293
2017	70,660,099	52,712,671	7,011	52,719,682	5,809,869	-243,210	46,666,603	13,603,365	10,390,131	54,597	1,294,204	852,393
2018	73,178,594	73,168,315	10,279	53,647,231	5,958,808	-593,588	47,094,835	15,349,449	10,734,310	57,124	1,281,053	862,933
2019	75,741,839	75,715,431	26,408	55,793,236	6,193,708	-625,545	48,973,983	15,426,077	11,341,779	58,628	1,291,900	877,697

Personal Income and Employment by Area: Riverside-San Bernardino-Ontario, CA

(Thousands of dollars, except as noted.)

Year	Personal income, total	Earnings by place of work			Less: Contributions for government social insurance	Plus: Adjustment for residence	Equals: Net earnings by place of residence	Plus: Dividends, interest, and rent	Plus: Personal current transfer receipts	Per capita personal income (dollars)	Population (persons)	Total employment
		Nonfarm	Farm	Total								
1970	4,910,718	3,135,466	112,771	3,248,237	204,697	439,194	3,482,734	856,272	571,712	4,294	1,143,539	418,790
1971	5,326,325	3,341,866	94,990	3,436,856	225,316	540,962	3,752,502	927,001	646,822	4,548	1,171,161	422,980
1972	5,948,005	3,683,519	144,267	3,827,786	260,583	672,950	4,240,153	1,006,723	701,129	5,001	1,189,476	436,775
1973	6,614,417	4,046,761	168,227	4,214,988	323,838	809,591	4,700,741	1,123,933	789,743	5,502	1,202,185	458,353
1974	7,425,733	4,414,477	167,136	4,581,613	364,732	958,866	5,175,747	1,286,663	963,323	6,038	1,229,743	468,665
1975	8,414,136	4,779,190	224,490	5,003,680	389,832	1,129,521	5,743,369	1,445,689	1,225,078	6,739	1,248,571	473,347
1976	9,506,530	5,383,473	257,788	5,641,261	442,192	1,334,345	6,533,414	1,589,439	1,383,677	7,412	1,282,517	491,513
1977	10,697,117	6,088,613	259,954	6,348,567	510,694	1,568,986	7,406,859	1,783,419	1,506,839	7,938	1,347,627	524,096
1978	12,367,023	7,121,761	255,381	7,377,142	610,948	1,870,814	8,637,008	2,077,828	1,652,187	8,614	1,435,733	566,072
1979	14,020,247	8,080,842	197,276	8,278,118	725,753	2,197,277	9,749,642	2,412,501	1,858,104	9,367	1,496,847	596,581
1980	16,168,124	8,889,079	263,796	9,152,875	780,376	2,592,939	10,965,438	2,967,331	2,235,355	10,282	1,572,429	609,845
1981	18,559,946	9,768,364	284,213	10,052,577	929,185	3,121,272	12,244,664	3,606,111	2,709,171	11,413	1,626,183	618,273
1982	20,053,701	10,207,063	335,822	10,542,885	992,886	3,488,818	13,038,817	4,022,272	2,992,612	11,890	1,686,602	618,248
1983	22,048,306	11,154,689	389,914	11,544,603	1,111,544	3,966,401	14,399,460	4,454,987	3,193,859	12,646	1,743,463	645,466
1984	24,849,226	12,688,834	434,226	13,123,060	1,310,782	4,639,709	16,451,987	5,005,730	3,391,509	13,721	1,811,019	685,286
1985	27,754,307	14,311,988	459,539	14,771,527	1,503,117	5,346,532	18,614,942	5,414,795	3,724,570	14,623	1,897,927	736,046
1986	30,855,008	16,059,254	519,696	16,578,950	1,708,433	6,067,605	20,938,122	5,838,247	4,078,639	15,463	1,995,378	781,634
1987	34,194,067	18,165,339	513,690	18,679,029	1,935,780	6,976,851	23,720,100	6,123,890	4,350,077	16,112	2,122,256	829,482
1988	38,084,692	20,304,888	586,423	20,891,311	2,242,076	7,903,555	26,552,790	6,717,965	4,813,937	16,798	2,267,166	889,223
1989	42,656,093	22,371,229	558,642	22,929,871	2,509,048	8,860,607	29,281,430	8,013,026	5,361,637	17,500	2,437,479	947,954
1990	47,168,306	24,489,966	610,184	25,100,150	2,724,088	10,424,343	32,800,405	8,356,588	6,011,313	17,932	2,630,471	1,003,046
1991	48,901,773	25,989,035	527,988	26,517,023	2,894,892	9,989,314	33,611,445	8,464,754	6,825,574	17,853	2,739,150	1,037,939
1992	51,266,697	27,686,170	530,221	28,216,391	3,054,213	9,716,436	34,878,614	8,476,718	7,911,365	18,171	2,821,341	1,035,249
1993	52,632,062	28,276,224	516,656	28,792,880	3,138,414	9,773,034	35,427,500	8,697,854	8,506,708	18,374	2,864,517	1,039,281
1994	54,106,404	29,562,571	562,443	30,125,014	3,293,135	9,565,778	36,397,657	8,976,703	8,732,044	18,622	2,905,505	1,065,322
1995	56,101,159	30,907,941	550,028	31,457,969	3,397,410	9,400,045	37,460,604	9,428,308	9,212,247	19,019	2,949,807	1,099,819
1996	58,776,228	32,522,674	668,841	33,191,515	3,466,710	9,275,386	39,000,191	10,038,252	9,737,785	19,656	2,990,316	1,132,225
1997	62,292,447	34,886,249	558,232	35,444,481	3,667,079	10,054,415	41,831,817	10,614,506	9,846,124	20,475	3,042,372	1,168,111
1998	67,816,125	38,830,759	741,612	39,572,371	4,005,391	10,395,776	45,962,756	11,424,532	10,428,837	21,818	3,108,220	1,244,588
1999	71,798,973	42,456,017	697,651	43,153,668	4,384,883	10,516,676	49,285,461	11,549,408	10,964,104	22,511	3,189,513	1,311,728
2000	77,283,676	46,390,367	449,493	46,839,860	4,760,005	11,266,356	53,346,211	12,425,596	11,511,869	23,584	3,277,022	1,355,540
2001	83,353,711	49,756,930	584,207	50,341,137	5,368,291	11,956,884	56,929,730	13,647,671	12,776,310	24,680	3,377,365	1,402,821
2002	88,013,751	53,811,820	503,115	54,314,935	5,904,099	12,453,465	60,864,301	13,403,824	13,745,626	25,241	3,486,938	1,458,784
2003	95,104,356	58,481,718	617,364	59,099,082	6,503,460	13,188,151	65,783,773	14,550,724	14,769,859	26,288	3,617,771	1,517,838
2004	103,328,315	65,629,651	744,341	66,373,992	7,554,519	14,016,711	72,836,184	14,814,933	15,677,198	27,513	3,755,607	1,611,428
2005	111,247,926	71,433,127	656,527	72,089,654	8,200,388	14,865,199	78,754,465	15,844,645	16,648,816	28,704	3,875,709	1,698,878
2006	120,093,982	76,883,156	466,219	77,349,375	8,506,433	15,998,708	84,841,650	17,169,267	18,083,065	30,125	3,986,510	1,766,253
2007	125,592,646	78,249,349	713,184	78,962,533	8,456,163	16,838,485	87,344,855	18,773,302	19,474,489	30,878	4,067,344	1,799,604
2008	127,136,028	75,977,213	611,389	76,588,602	8,355,041	16,442,876	84,676,437	19,977,582	22,482,009	30,907	4,113,447	1,747,886
2009	124,019,399	71,769,075	390,814	72,159,889	8,006,199	16,024,519	80,178,209	18,860,181	24,981,009	29,807	4,160,685	1,665,991
2010	127,900,880	73,371,907	479,630	73,851,537	7,949,392	15,706,641	81,608,786	18,483,055	27,809,039	30,142	4,243,235	1,638,713
2011	135,988,208	77,617,868	681,618	78,299,486	7,573,961	16,779,648	87,505,173	20,400,758	28,082,277	31,638	4,298,271	1,678,261
2012	139,909,018	80,091,067	599,859	80,690,926	7,745,084	17,199,623	90,145,465	21,351,016	28,412,537	32,227	4,341,405	1,727,702
2013	144,112,444	83,444,029	510,772	83,954,801	8,978,803	17,480,722	92,456,720	22,228,166	29,427,558	32,916	4,378,138	1,788,303
2014	152,634,806	88,246,094	722,121	88,968,215	9,570,442	17,470,404	96,868,177	24,679,405	31,087,224	34,488	4,425,776	1,868,345
2015	162,960,457	95,415,371	735,318	96,150,689	10,314,300	16,938,594	102,774,983	26,680,906	33,504,568	36,433	4,472,874	1,944,515
2016	170,445,698	99,687,181	634,047	100,321,228	10,792,302	18,530,264	108,059,190	27,650,273	34,736,235	37,679	4,523,653	1,995,590
2017	178,882,553	105,387,883	795,336	106,183,219	11,371,674	20,296,914	115,108,459	29,021,277	34,752,817	39,052	4,580,670	2,052,926
2018	186,261,819	185,681,782	580,037	111,480,145	12,188,884	20,178,691	119,469,952	30,332,603	36,459,264	40,382	4,612,542	2,124,375
2019	196,452,976	195,701,271	751,705	118,271,664	13,017,314	21,018,032	126,272,382	31,129,204	39,051,390	42,242	4,650,631	2,186,300

Personal Income and Employment by Area: Roanoke, VA

(Thousands of dollars, except as noted.)

Year	Personal income, total	Earnings by place of work			Less: Contributions for government social insurance	Plus: Adjustment for residence	Equals: Net earnings by place of residence	Plus: Dividends, interest, and rent	Plus: Personal current transfer receipts	Per capita personal income (dollars)	Population (persons)	Total employment
		Nonfarm	Farm	Total								
1970	858,818	730,643	5,166	735,809	51,639	-17,093	667,077	114,101	77,640	3,708	231,596	113,547
1971	938,685	794,236	5,124	799,360	57,676	-19,726	721,958	126,245	90,482	3,938	238,357	115,420
1972	1,036,415	884,884	6,865	891,749	67,325	-28,058	796,366	138,359	101,690	4,257	243,439	120,323
1973	1,166,816	1,001,613	8,755	1,010,368	86,635	-34,251	889,482	158,871	118,463	4,702	248,131	128,106
1974	1,295,167	1,094,586	10,001	1,104,587	97,675	-37,637	969,275	185,867	140,025	5,153	251,318	131,119
1975	1,423,222	1,160,547	7,237	1,167,784	100,252	-27,964	1,039,568	202,276	181,378	5,616	253,423	128,335
1976	1,582,041	1,297,444	6,213	1,303,657	114,726	-25,349	1,163,582	219,675	198,784	6,190	255,587	131,459
1977	1,735,818	1,426,642	5,681	1,432,323	127,564	-22,541	1,282,218	239,864	213,736	6,711	258,644	135,493
1978	1,970,463	1,610,288	7,666	1,617,954	145,076	-9,154	1,463,724	268,415	238,324	7,578	260,021	140,517
1979	2,152,211	1,764,198	6,158	1,770,356	165,451	-27,549	1,577,356	308,356	266,499	8,219	261,869	141,562
1980	2,370,883	1,901,839	148	1,901,987	178,693	-46,885	1,676,409	381,926	312,548	9,101	260,501	140,251
1981	2,618,711	2,047,711	3,461	2,051,172	207,136	-51,690	1,792,346	470,983	355,382	10,007	261,693	138,411
1982	2,780,681	2,126,898	1,017	2,127,915	220,821	-57,125	1,849,969	544,808	385,904	10,623	261,751	138,094
1983	3,019,996	2,330,508	4,006	2,334,514	245,691	-62,051	2,026,772	578,670	414,554	11,541	261,672	140,118
1984	3,389,261	2,621,925	7,535	2,629,460	286,004	-73,820	2,269,636	686,962	432,663	12,904	262,643	146,364
1985	3,653,313	2,858,005	8,502	2,866,507	317,600	-85,205	2,463,702	726,862	462,749	13,880	263,208	152,702
1986	3,876,557	3,038,603	10,437	3,049,040	348,615	-90,241	2,610,184	773,877	492,496	14,704	263,645	155,869
1987	4,135,333	3,278,186	12,646	3,290,832	371,674	-98,532	2,820,626	801,213	513,494	15,603	265,026	160,150
1988	4,374,680	3,434,023	15,906	3,449,929	399,155	-106,690	2,944,084	894,919	535,677	16,458	265,805	159,825
1989	4,755,538	3,664,584	21,315	3,685,899	425,194	-121,032	3,139,673	1,032,903	582,962	17,828	266,749	164,203
1990	5,025,194	3,904,116	25,411	3,929,527	457,682	-140,300	3,331,545	1,066,956	626,693	18,651	269,440	166,966
1991	5,161,248	4,008,534	22,642	4,031,176	474,463	-151,806	3,404,907	1,073,299	683,042	18,912	272,906	164,617
1992	5,450,633	4,287,022	22,515	4,309,537	499,944	-174,329	3,635,264	1,061,382	753,987	19,896	273,951	166,401
1993	5,736,462	4,549,155	17,606	4,566,761	530,207	-198,509	3,838,045	1,106,195	792,222	20,736	276,643	169,750
1994	6,018,218	4,758,678	18,740	4,777,418	551,815	-221,263	4,004,340	1,164,712	849,166	21,557	279,176	175,063
1995	6,330,237	4,994,027	14,725	5,008,752	582,236	-247,484	4,179,032	1,248,448	902,757	22,533	280,938	179,737
1996	6,638,372	5,196,877	12,302	5,209,179	601,512	-268,955	4,338,712	1,357,391	942,269	23,464	282,915	183,486
1997	6,909,629	5,426,825	6,988	5,433,813	625,354	-288,335	4,520,124	1,418,453	971,052	24,279	284,593	183,985
1998	7,349,518	5,873,925	9,714	5,883,639	664,502	-329,381	4,889,756	1,451,130	1,008,632	25,719	285,762	191,061
1999	7,617,797	6,136,355	4,443	6,140,798	693,661	-357,139	5,089,998	1,475,312	1,052,487	26,525	287,193	190,906
2000	8,011,322	6,391,352	9,930	6,401,282	713,014	-395,257	5,293,011	1,600,491	1,117,820	27,750	288,699	194,558
2001	8,500,124	6,754,335	7,297	6,761,632	756,393	-410,301	5,594,938	1,676,917	1,228,269	29,357	289,547	191,045
2002	8,780,213	6,975,774	2,460	6,978,234	783,767	-423,350	5,771,117	1,701,343	1,307,753	30,228	290,466	188,705
2003	9,023,350	7,137,330	-3,478	7,133,852	799,103	-433,924	5,900,825	1,728,014	1,394,511	30,893	292,082	187,372
2004	9,506,136	7,518,435	9,567	7,528,002	849,728	-464,950	6,213,324	1,813,010	1,479,802	32,362	293,745	190,307
2005	9,878,433	7,802,613	9,952	7,812,565	893,853	-491,503	6,427,209	1,848,477	1,602,747	33,327	296,405	194,972
2006	10,379,613	8,143,446	143	8,143,589	951,045	-519,783	6,672,761	1,956,303	1,750,549	34,607	299,930	200,015
2007	11,046,954	8,532,735	3,520	8,536,255	993,885	-548,218	6,994,152	2,177,613	1,875,189	36,476	302,858	202,744
2008	11,575,155	8,781,705	7,359	8,789,064	1,028,990	-577,482	7,182,592	2,289,530	2,103,033	37,877	305,596	201,279
2009	11,376,981	8,637,433	4,284	8,641,717	1,018,593	-567,705	7,055,419	2,037,913	2,283,649	36,960	307,816	193,947
2010	11,617,436	8,679,843	7,929	8,687,772	1,018,177	-551,994	7,117,601	2,049,356	2,450,479	37,643	308,625	190,548
2011	12,113,465	8,888,892	18,398	8,907,290	941,373	-580,019	7,385,898	2,235,061	2,492,506	39,175	309,212	192,046
2012	12,812,843	9,246,345	19,665	9,266,010	970,726	-598,024	7,697,260	2,562,579	2,553,004	41,258	310,556	193,632
2013	12,630,609	9,335,938	15,167	9,351,105	1,112,343	-595,190	7,643,572	2,357,962	2,629,075	40,484	311,993	194,153
2014	13,068,629	9,505,931	18,313	9,524,244	1,131,465	-608,190	7,784,589	2,564,958	2,719,082	41,773	312,847	195,968
2015	13,827,076	10,054,223	9,819	10,064,042	1,181,665	-658,252	8,224,125	2,752,522	2,850,429	44,137	313,278	196,560
2016	13,760,661	9,876,157	514	9,876,671	1,175,114	-626,627	8,074,930	2,750,722	2,935,009	43,949	313,102	197,189
2017	14,113,140	9,998,297	-8,614	9,989,683	1,194,410	-620,161	8,175,112	2,882,386	3,055,642	44,928	314,128	196,648
2018	14,741,327	14,753,412	-12,085	10,230,868	1,232,856	-638,750	8,359,262	3,209,188	3,172,877	47,092	313,033	198,428
2019	15,151,947	15,159,370	-7,423	10,528,887	1,269,617	-657,622	8,601,648	3,229,109	3,321,190	48,374	313,222	200,538

Personal Income and Employment by Area: Rochester, MN

(Thousands of dollars, except as noted.)

Year	Personal income, total	Earnings by place of work			Less: Contributions for government social insurance	Plus: Adjustment for residence	Equals: Net earnings by place of residence	Plus: Dividends, interest, and rent	Plus: Personal current transfer receipts	Per capita personal income (dollars)	Population (persons)	Total employment
		Nonfarm	Farm	Total								
1970	531,247	386,908	54,160	441,068	26,598	-3,571	410,899	79,110	41,238	3,888	136,645	61,810
1971	566,507	415,324	51,141	466,465	29,647	-4,464	432,354	86,631	47,522	4,105	138,020	62,584
1972	625,050	457,361	61,672	519,033	34,157	-5,673	479,203	93,502	52,345	4,478	139,574	66,413
1973	741,615	516,543	108,372	624,915	44,716	-7,622	572,577	107,062	61,976	5,288	140,244	70,682
1974	782,079	562,304	81,076	643,380	50,508	-8,512	584,360	123,485	74,234	5,529	141,439	72,619
1975	865,503	633,726	68,272	701,998	55,511	-11,901	634,586	142,159	88,758	6,088	142,168	73,701
1976	944,395	719,060	52,250	771,310	64,229	-14,830	692,251	154,826	97,318	6,563	143,886	76,699
1977	1,098,729	802,415	106,467	908,882	71,851	-18,514	818,517	176,384	103,828	7,551	145,499	78,691
1978	1,238,530	929,187	112,323	1,041,510	86,719	-25,225	929,566	195,132	113,832	8,484	145,983	81,851
1979	1,331,857	1,037,311	72,670	1,109,981	100,475	-28,452	981,054	221,003	129,800	9,017	147,713	84,728
1980	1,487,851	1,142,203	64,120	1,206,323	110,485	-32,394	1,063,444	268,928	155,479	10,022	148,456	86,430
1981	1,654,915	1,237,975	70,431	1,308,406	128,063	-33,592	1,146,751	327,141	181,023	11,049	149,775	86,334
1982	1,834,583	1,343,421	74,810	1,418,231	143,134	-38,412	1,236,685	396,519	201,379	12,196	150,427	86,370
1983	1,889,385	1,449,568	-5,787	1,443,781	156,269	-42,342	1,245,170	422,567	221,648	12,437	151,922	88,143
1984	2,200,996	1,637,710	89,078	1,726,788	181,227	-50,056	1,495,505	466,819	238,672	14,374	153,128	91,755
1985	2,307,593	1,735,272	77,798	1,813,070	195,256	-54,814	1,563,000	490,741	253,852	14,918	154,688	92,865
1986	2,426,063	1,816,262	107,005	1,923,267	209,000	-57,444	1,656,823	503,224	266,016	15,673	154,797	92,206
1987	2,575,865	1,934,281	146,085	2,080,366	220,219	-64,215	1,795,932	504,411	275,522	16,568	155,475	94,618
1988	2,677,274	2,102,498	87,019	2,189,517	247,634	-72,277	1,869,606	515,320	292,348	16,854	158,849	98,326
1989	2,992,209	2,292,336	135,285	2,427,621	269,737	-81,994	2,075,890	594,514	321,805	18,586	160,993	101,567
1990	3,192,837	2,506,340	126,270	2,632,610	296,815	-93,328	2,242,467	608,476	341,894	19,537	163,427	104,645
1991	3,316,577	2,650,254	96,584	2,746,838	318,121	-96,462	2,332,255	619,461	364,861	19,959	166,169	106,918
1992	3,530,002	2,838,454	76,200	2,914,654	337,124	-99,931	2,477,599	657,451	394,952	20,992	168,159	108,570
1993	3,585,134	2,959,484	41,748	3,001,232	352,450	-102,613	2,546,169	627,419	411,546	20,925	171,334	110,560
1994	3,758,141	3,023,006	101,797	3,124,803	364,228	-100,983	2,659,592	658,938	439,611	21,791	172,466	110,937
1995	3,900,797	3,114,067	49,006	3,163,073	375,712	-100,557	2,686,804	741,500	472,493	22,582	172,741	113,113
1996	4,237,574	3,346,391	107,306	3,453,697	400,010	-107,489	2,946,198	791,197	500,179	24,331	174,161	114,704
1997	4,436,559	3,569,824	68,056	3,637,880	426,904	-118,813	3,092,163	834,307	510,089	25,172	176,251	118,626
1998	4,900,681	3,982,545	100,032	4,082,577	470,099	-137,135	3,475,343	905,296	520,042	27,304	179,488	123,856
1999	5,223,095	4,325,049	77,950	4,402,999	510,888	-154,195	3,737,916	926,572	558,607	28,620	182,498	127,906
2000	5,554,880	4,585,413	57,502	4,642,915	539,296	-163,877	3,939,742	1,010,203	604,935	29,934	185,573	131,560
2001	6,007,974	5,004,801	40,062	5,044,863	573,397	-178,629	4,292,837	1,035,846	679,291	31,991	187,803	132,985
2002	6,279,349	5,284,584	21,104	5,305,688	604,079	-187,517	4,514,092	1,020,377	744,880	32,937	190,646	134,146
2003	6,717,540	5,653,561	53,626	5,707,187	650,274	-210,094	4,846,819	1,072,054	798,667	34,794	193,067	136,828
2004	6,980,218	5,933,557	118,743	6,052,300	679,451	-211,892	5,160,957	974,545	844,716	35,741	195,300	138,421
2005	7,047,412	5,976,409	146,595	6,123,004	697,207	-212,263	5,213,534	956,157	877,721	35,740	197,188	139,865
2006	7,436,191	6,214,741	104,251	6,318,992	733,906	-201,234	5,383,852	1,096,008	956,331	37,225	199,763	141,771
2007	7,930,965	6,496,341	124,928	6,621,269	766,853	-197,129	5,657,287	1,237,760	1,035,918	39,305	201,782	143,695
2008	8,311,766	6,664,079	154,942	6,819,021	792,032	-186,646	5,840,343	1,310,518	1,160,905	40,708	204,181	142,489
2009	8,226,681	6,676,547	67,478	6,744,025	799,929	-215,876	5,728,220	1,222,607	1,275,854	39,917	206,097	139,773
2010	8,825,736	7,111,674	133,605	7,245,279	830,188	-186,486	6,228,605	1,210,573	1,386,558	42,596	207,194	138,061
2011	9,148,383	7,053,967	245,279	7,299,246	734,741	-180,362	6,384,143	1,368,303	1,395,937	43,888	208,450	139,594
2012	9,653,980	7,414,603	303,984	7,718,587	764,247	-186,206	6,768,134	1,488,323	1,397,523	46,067	209,562	142,449
2013	9,660,640	7,617,243	190,382	7,807,625	900,848	-201,457	6,705,320	1,512,688	1,442,632	45,664	211,560	144,443
2014	10,032,623	7,834,001	138,857	7,972,858	918,350	-202,869	6,851,639	1,660,986	1,519,998	47,178	212,654	145,360
2015	10,396,377	8,170,793	63,005	8,233,798	953,518	-227,384	7,052,896	1,768,463	1,575,018	48,620	213,829	147,961
2016	10,702,224	8,519,808	-53,924	8,465,884	990,356	-241,684	7,233,844	1,829,775	1,638,605	49,525	216,096	149,509
2017	11,100,859	8,906,976	-67,166	8,839,810	1,036,616	-302,969	7,500,225	1,908,775	1,691,859	50,856	218,280	151,110
2018	12,071,724	12,010,821	60,903	9,615,475	1,129,881	-349,137	8,136,457	2,097,245	1,838,022	54,918	219,814	152,998
2019	12,438,700	12,327,290	111,410	9,944,586	1,159,396	-377,439	8,407,751	2,101,181	1,929,768	56,050	221,921	155,074

Personal Income and Employment by Area: Rochester, NY

(Thousands of dollars, except as noted.)

Year	Personal income, total	Earnings by place of work			Less: Contributions for government social insurance	Plus: Adjustment for residence	Equals: Net earnings by place of residence	Plus: Dividends, interest, and rent	Plus: Personal current transfer receipts	Per capita personal income (dollars)	Population (persons)	Total employment
		Nonfarm	Farm	Total								
1970	4,543,716	3,774,719	64,553	3,839,272	276,964	-46,065	3,516,243	656,574	370,899	4,623	982,845	439,999
1971	4,870,129	4,012,962	61,581	4,074,543	304,319	-49,932	3,720,292	695,348	454,489	4,927	988,371	440,497
1972	5,244,349	4,371,248	41,128	4,412,376	352,229	-51,695	4,008,452	741,030	494,867	5,292	991,017	447,820
1973	5,757,009	4,798,117	72,803	4,870,920	448,781	-54,291	4,367,848	832,100	557,061	5,808	991,293	464,379
1974	6,304,031	5,220,989	84,056	5,305,045	507,725	-58,456	4,738,864	941,762	623,405	6,373	989,197	475,220
1975	6,814,001	5,484,338	65,112	5,549,450	521,206	-61,152	4,967,092	1,008,879	838,030	6,839	996,288	464,343
1976	7,260,204	5,896,373	57,078	5,953,451	572,254	-61,683	5,319,514	1,061,870	878,820	7,280	997,313	468,201
1977	7,870,948	6,424,789	60,062	6,484,851	622,054	-71,141	5,791,656	1,162,967	916,325	7,874	999,583	477,239
1978	8,531,744	7,045,322	66,337	7,111,659	698,906	-75,168	6,337,585	1,224,560	969,599	8,569	995,677	489,129
1979	9,465,090	7,842,783	80,471	7,923,254	805,638	-81,155	7,036,461	1,385,622	1,043,007	9,501	996,204	501,248
1980	10,647,796	8,648,149	68,504	8,716,653	886,640	-88,518	7,741,495	1,673,854	1,232,447	10,710	994,186	499,705
1981	11,953,264	9,561,796	83,508	9,645,304	1,041,775	-96,816	8,506,713	2,061,846	1,384,705	11,974	998,299	504,102
1982	13,021,657	10,302,710	71,042	10,373,752	1,137,881	-124,035	9,111,836	2,375,837	1,533,984	12,970	1,003,975	508,477
1983	13,611,691	10,651,487	35,353	10,686,840	1,181,442	-130,530	9,374,868	2,553,694	1,683,129	13,518	1,006,962	504,266
1984	14,916,845	11,624,049	57,621	11,681,670	1,312,840	-149,789	10,219,041	2,908,837	1,788,967	14,875	1,002,789	522,629
1985	15,997,616	12,620,376	69,579	12,689,955	1,444,272	-183,241	11,062,442	3,040,201	1,894,973	15,956	1,002,633	541,363
1986	16,847,852	13,303,278	83,299	13,386,577	1,549,087	-201,120	11,636,370	3,166,703	2,044,779	16,793	1,003,295	549,723
1987	17,474,726	13,877,368	100,828	13,978,196	1,589,925	-224,320	12,163,951	3,214,982	2,095,793	17,421	1,003,095	552,418
1988	18,953,572	15,185,577	102,315	15,287,892	1,774,322	-256,855	13,256,715	3,421,915	2,274,942	18,770	1,009,766	575,050
1989	20,782,822	16,269,777	107,259	16,377,036	1,881,934	-288,626	14,206,476	4,107,984	2,468,362	20,382	1,019,683	585,517
1990	21,598,616	16,873,844	103,722	16,977,566	1,870,985	-344,381	14,762,200	4,127,258	2,709,158	21,013	1,027,880	589,401
1991	22,464,069	17,603,528	92,143	17,695,671	1,998,597	-364,028	15,333,046	4,114,549	3,016,474	21,678	1,036,248	591,189
1992	23,555,008	18,490,932	101,400	18,592,332	2,061,092	-376,912	16,154,328	4,017,109	3,383,571	22,477	1,047,976	592,760
1993	24,178,184	19,004,638	110,352	19,114,990	2,131,981	-401,766	16,581,243	4,004,825	3,592,116	22,913	1,055,228	601,469
1994	24,867,803	19,484,024	91,886	19,575,910	2,216,694	-416,834	16,942,382	4,091,797	3,833,624	23,518	1,057,376	607,597
1995	26,005,032	20,253,521	73,772	20,327,293	2,297,160	-449,681	17,580,452	4,384,955	4,039,625	24,581	1,057,933	606,742
1996	26,944,000	20,802,572	92,886	20,895,458	2,341,806	-416,963	18,136,689	4,591,152	4,216,159	25,426	1,059,684	607,448
1997	28,029,188	21,652,744	89,680	21,742,424	2,402,551	-429,860	18,910,013	4,880,852	4,238,323	26,443	1,060,003	611,491
1998	29,281,688	22,507,752	98,589	22,606,341	2,452,560	-467,404	19,686,377	5,097,590	4,497,721	27,630	1,059,773	617,789
1999	30,365,026	23,653,099	128,573	23,781,672	2,509,413	-466,870	20,805,389	4,879,457	4,680,180	28,638	1,060,310	627,638
2000	31,958,827	24,824,504	131,775	24,956,279	2,603,917	-460,815	21,891,547	5,148,053	4,919,227	29,967	1,066,482	637,905
2001	32,654,842	25,305,511	150,023	25,455,534	2,730,345	-482,769	22,242,420	5,184,383	5,228,039	30,570	1,068,215	629,922
2002	32,849,382	25,516,306	114,848	25,631,154	2,782,890	-481,883	22,366,381	4,834,122	5,648,879	30,690	1,070,355	618,390
2003	33,459,762	26,193,807	144,350	26,338,157	2,865,708	-480,832	22,991,617	4,660,194	5,807,951	31,215	1,071,918	618,045
2004	34,725,085	27,035,670	151,908	27,187,578	2,977,687	-456,889	23,753,002	4,760,712	6,211,371	32,378	1,072,494	622,352
2005	35,524,589	27,522,025	121,405	27,643,430	3,094,180	-454,110	24,095,140	5,045,475	6,383,974	33,188	1,070,418	628,582
2006	36,977,295	28,442,351	132,552	28,574,903	3,200,414	-403,258	24,971,231	5,253,969	6,752,095	34,546	1,070,370	627,477
2007	38,877,608	29,518,349	249,120	29,767,469	3,291,034	-372,989	26,103,446	5,677,013	7,097,149	36,265	1,072,040	634,312
2008	40,974,726	30,224,495	291,684	30,516,179	3,402,391	-369,457	26,744,331	6,250,194	7,980,201	38,105	1,075,302	636,153
2009	41,191,834	30,273,897	163,586	30,437,483	3,362,951	-390,978	26,683,554	5,808,138	8,700,142	38,213	1,077,941	622,597
2010	42,861,936	31,579,932	270,427	31,850,359	3,430,814	-361,813	28,057,732	5,546,755	9,257,449	39,677	1,080,280	620,717
2011	44,927,946	32,551,865	300,233	32,852,098	3,191,440	-376,337	29,284,321	6,258,176	9,385,449	41,513	1,082,275	629,224
2012	47,198,784	33,832,132	305,679	34,137,811	3,254,592	-341,334	30,541,885	7,213,675	9,443,224	43,590	1,082,782	632,101
2013	46,907,901	34,200,677	361,262	34,561,939	3,738,271	-313,585	30,510,083	6,829,471	9,568,347	43,281	1,083,791	634,861
2014	47,842,141	34,168,932	316,288	34,485,220	3,846,139	-233,369	30,405,712	7,507,777	9,928,652	44,184	1,082,785	638,728
2015	50,076,306	35,673,451	200,949	35,874,400	4,023,881	-246,479	31,604,040	8,040,206	10,432,060	46,350	1,080,385	644,273
2016	50,650,138	35,897,030	175,401	36,072,431	4,092,976	-271,819	31,707,636	8,307,900	10,634,602	46,970	1,078,352	648,597
2017	52,967,833	37,047,961	187,130	37,235,091	4,236,325	-240,136	32,758,630	8,702,250	11,506,953	49,138	1,077,948	651,112
2018	54,775,889	54,643,268	132,621	38,479,118	4,294,669	-239,601	33,944,848	9,650,986	11,180,055	51,115	1,071,621	658,642
2019	56,936,973	56,745,573	191,400	39,679,121	4,398,814	-187,193	35,093,114	9,794,177	12,049,682	53,230	1,069,644	663,545

Personal Income and Employment by Area: Rockford, IL

(Thousands of dollars, except as noted.)

Year	Personal income, total	Earnings by place of work			Less: Contributions for government social insurance	Plus: Adjustment for residence	Equals: Net earnings by place of residence	Plus: Dividends, interest, and rent	Plus: Personal current transfer receipts	Per capita personal income (dollars)	Population (persons)	Total employment
		Nonfarm	Farm	Total								
1970.............	1,156,998	1,035,712	7,477	1,043,189	70,694	-47,053	925,442	150,923	80,633	4,259	271,661	127,617
1971.............	1,222,779	1,076,529	10,151	1,086,680	75,477	-49,191	962,012	160,534	100,233	4,510	271,149	123,947
1972.............	1,345,050	1,195,710	10,445	1,206,155	89,405	-54,089	1,062,661	172,444	109,945	4,961	271,136	129,119
1973.............	1,512,261	1,355,735	17,225	1,372,960	117,718	-61,946	1,193,296	193,662	125,303	5,535	273,201	137,581
1974.............	1,646,252	1,469,984	7,638	1,477,622	132,750	-64,978	1,279,894	220,675	145,683	5,992	274,734	139,257
1975.............	1,767,024	1,503,986	20,025	1,524,011	130,653	-64,179	1,329,179	244,670	193,175	6,443	274,255	133,933
1976.............	1,951,534	1,678,631	14,558	1,693,189	148,983	-67,732	1,476,474	262,294	212,766	7,132	273,627	136,512
1977.............	2,143,587	1,865,124	12,755	1,877,879	167,649	-73,687	1,636,543	288,163	218,881	7,831	273,731	140,705
1978.............	2,407,127	2,148,911	12,304	2,161,215	200,479	-97,243	1,863,493	321,729	221,905	8,719	276,063	147,308
1979.............	2,666,729	2,377,406	18,108	2,395,514	228,962	-107,646	2,058,906	361,673	246,150	9,629	276,951	150,437
1980.............	2,874,426	2,457,490	-577	2,456,913	233,655	-111,107	2,112,151	448,106	314,169	10,272	279,829	144,840
1981.............	3,194,602	2,645,891	16,659	2,662,550	268,965	-115,980	2,277,605	557,030	359,967	11,385	280,591	144,654
1982.............	3,295,387	2,565,655	12,458	2,578,113	262,571	-91,201	2,224,341	646,725	424,321	11,815	278,911	137,928
1983.............	3,408,355	2,657,579	-11,555	2,646,024	274,372	-90,827	2,280,825	682,678	444,852	12,289	277,354	136,046
1984.............	3,814,562	3,013,873	24,062	3,037,935	324,914	-112,051	2,600,970	782,837	430,755	13,770	277,028	143,578
1985.............	4,033,822	3,215,941	40,072	3,256,013	353,131	-125,638	2,777,244	801,484	455,094	14,478	278,623	147,717
1986.............	4,259,643	3,440,924	30,056	3,470,980	377,817	-144,736	2,948,427	830,303	480,913	15,287	278,638	151,509
1987.............	4,480,571	3,651,401	27,066	3,678,467	393,105	-148,015	3,137,347	838,118	505,106	16,056	279,051	154,960
1988.............	4,888,050	4,080,969	15,656	4,096,625	449,313	-169,655	3,477,657	883,657	526,736	17,472	279,763	161,185
1989.............	5,228,103	4,249,693	28,887	4,278,580	468,941	-162,768	3,646,871	1,014,445	566,787	18,568	281,563	163,402
1990.............	5,406,988	4,428,040	30,072	4,458,112	476,477	-165,565	3,816,070	973,457	617,461	18,992	284,702	167,347
1991.............	5,497,536	4,449,379	12,533	4,461,912	489,174	-128,105	3,844,633	973,997	678,906	18,964	289,895	165,457
1992.............	5,934,172	4,692,422	21,945	4,714,367	506,653	-108,370	4,099,344	1,045,977	788,851	20,164	294,298	165,482
1993.............	6,169,996	4,892,878	12,180	4,905,058	536,299	-100,567	4,268,192	1,072,386	829,418	20,664	298,582	168,660
1994.............	6,641,656	5,368,671	27,611	5,396,282	594,036	-123,354	4,678,892	1,128,461	834,303	21,980	302,172	175,923
1995.............	7,105,540	5,736,995	18,000	5,754,995	632,099	-119,336	5,003,560	1,206,442	895,538	23,246	305,671	184,417
1996.............	7,456,330	5,931,013	42,600	5,973,613	646,241	-115,225	5,212,147	1,301,033	943,150	24,080	309,644	186,765
1997.............	7,786,871	6,155,794	28,260	6,184,054	666,793	-99,952	5,417,309	1,398,331	971,231	24,931	312,342	188,652
1998.............	8,200,250	6,476,377	27,894	6,504,271	694,598	-107,003	5,702,670	1,479,171	1,018,409	26,030	315,025	191,098
1999.............	8,496,940	6,770,719	20,107	6,790,826	714,536	-76,077	6,000,213	1,454,763	1,041,964	26,754	317,596	192,185
2000.............	8,891,827	6,994,786	23,148	7,017,934	726,990	-66,529	6,224,415	1,561,420	1,105,992	27,698	321,033	194,248
2001.............	9,028,135	7,022,150	18,446	7,040,596	744,069	-12,509	6,284,018	1,505,489	1,238,628	27,931	323,229	190,203
2002.............	9,271,460	7,223,105	10,540	7,233,645	761,026	14,363	6,486,982	1,432,576	1,351,902	28,462	325,747	188,465
2003.............	9,533,368	7,308,989	10,590	7,319,579	775,629	58,552	6,602,502	1,502,587	1,428,279	28,935	329,472	187,307
2004.............	9,784,681	7,502,155	27,742	7,529,897	811,121	122,611	6,841,387	1,443,010	1,500,284	29,452	332,230	189,270
2005.............	10,193,712	7,803,106	11,298	7,814,404	872,262	190,862	7,133,004	1,417,657	1,643,051	30,347	335,903	189,252
2006.............	11,037,081	8,310,280	10,125	8,320,405	921,579	282,744	7,681,570	1,622,534	1,732,977	32,348	341,202	192,536
2007.............	11,669,599	8,633,913	35,599	8,669,512	954,330	357,241	8,072,423	1,676,049	1,921,127	33,581	347,503	196,276
2008.............	11,939,230	8,585,976	30,447	8,616,423	950,494	395,579	8,061,508	1,714,837	2,162,885	34,118	349,937	193,038
2009.............	11,567,100	7,929,107	1,647	7,930,754	875,266	353,079	7,408,567	1,665,731	2,492,802	33,071	349,766	180,372
2010.............	11,831,377	8,056,170	3,641	8,059,811	894,266	301,571	7,467,116	1,659,019	2,705,242	33,882	349,194	178,730
2011.............	12,282,306	8,439,284	56,276	8,495,560	854,915	277,430	7,918,075	1,795,436	2,568,795	35,324	347,701	182,051
2012.............	12,583,344	8,730,857	13,731	8,744,588	895,130	259,589	8,109,047	1,915,776	2,558,521	36,389	345,803	183,925
2013.............	12,850,290	8,866,561	88,583	8,955,144	1,012,450	310,894	8,253,588	1,911,867	2,684,835	37,283	344,671	183,164
2014.............	13,241,090	9,193,663	33,714	9,227,377	1,034,384	262,922	8,455,915	2,081,616	2,703,559	38,670	342,412	186,124
2015.............	13,698,108	9,521,950	10,287	9,532,237	1,052,516	270,883	8,750,604	2,110,374	2,837,130	40,203	340,725	187,466
2016.............	13,833,213	9,540,656	60,726	9,601,382	1,061,294	275,297	8,815,385	2,148,242	2,869,586	40,728	339,650	186,253
2017.............	14,273,265	9,883,206	-4,653	9,878,553	1,098,034	303,609	9,084,128	2,234,518	2,954,619	42,192	338,291	185,866
2018.............	14,842,571	14,833,823	8,748	10,428,594	1,171,127	257,311	9,514,778	2,251,325	3,076,468	44,029	337,110	187,478
2019.............	15,052,234	15,052,562	-328	10,492,096	1,179,096	286,503	9,599,503	2,275,559	3,177,172	44,783	336,116	187,023

Personal Income and Employment by Area: Rocky Mount, NC

(Thousands of dollars, except as noted.)

Year	Personal income, total	Earnings by place of work			Less: Contributions for government social insurance	Plus: Adjustment for residence	Equals: Net earnings by place of residence	Plus: Dividends, interest, and rent	Plus: Personal current transfer receipts	Per capita personal income (dollars)	Population (persons)	Total employment
		Nonfarm	Farm	Total								
1970	333,106	242,455	32,529	274,984	17,855	4,101	261,230	39,404	32,472	2,986	111,571	53,924
1971	364,218	272,178	28,080	300,258	20,676	4,257	283,839	43,190	37,189	3,243	112,296	54,910
1972	421,041	317,025	36,223	353,248	25,068	3,000	331,180	48,555	41,306	3,707	113,571	58,004
1973	492,168	369,709	52,346	422,055	33,369	582	389,268	55,678	47,222	4,278	115,045	61,874
1974	553,096	414,334	56,786	471,120	39,137	359	432,342	63,533	57,221	4,752	116,381	63,125
1975	595,696	434,918	53,180	488,098	40,477	125	447,746	70,136	77,814	5,040	118,189	60,327
1976	673,334	500,034	61,036	561,070	47,479	-2,738	510,853	77,751	84,730	5,629	119,609	62,983
1977	715,562	554,134	37,517	591,651	52,255	-4,172	535,224	88,615	91,723	5,894	121,414	64,333
1978	808,523	623,600	53,060	676,660	60,064	-7,143	609,453	99,633	99,437	6,605	122,406	65,387
1979	855,459	689,839	13,722	703,561	68,664	-7,809	627,088	113,155	115,216	6,941	123,247	66,769
1980	948,514	740,481	15,654	756,135	73,744	-8,992	673,399	138,051	137,064	7,683	123,463	65,511
1981	1,106,869	829,235	51,760	880,995	88,646	-13,378	778,971	170,280	157,618	8,899	124,388	66,742
1982	1,183,916	864,496	57,823	922,319	93,013	-14,710	814,596	194,130	175,190	9,432	125,524	64,937
1983	1,260,798	955,638	34,109	989,747	103,210	-18,240	868,297	203,957	188,544	9,969	126,478	66,048
1984	1,422,878	1,064,211	66,167	1,130,378	118,052	-24,708	987,618	235,952	199,308	11,194	127,115	68,538
1985	1,516,599	1,145,223	62,735	1,207,958	129,135	-28,253	1,050,570	253,437	212,592	11,775	128,799	69,053
1986	1,607,566	1,256,602	47,421	1,304,023	144,462	-39,821	1,119,740	266,015	221,811	12,382	129,830	71,452
1987	1,717,662	1,357,616	60,304	1,417,920	153,734	-51,489	1,212,697	275,404	229,561	13,100	131,116	71,862
1988	1,894,660	1,501,142	81,572	1,582,714	174,782	-63,524	1,344,408	303,914	246,338	14,372	131,826	75,005
1989	2,041,531	1,582,409	82,267	1,664,676	184,173	-71,766	1,408,737	360,785	272,009	15,424	132,358	76,775
1990	2,125,903	1,645,906	96,111	1,742,017	196,221	-90,294	1,455,502	366,181	304,220	15,904	133,668	76,391
1991	2,210,385	1,719,375	96,229	1,815,604	207,524	-111,281	1,496,799	367,380	346,206	16,396	134,810	76,478
1992	2,351,824	1,829,863	90,608	1,920,471	218,040	-110,446	1,591,985	375,431	384,408	17,306	135,899	77,279
1993	2,485,837	1,909,455	94,901	2,004,356	228,571	-103,069	1,672,716	395,752	417,369	18,111	137,253	77,560
1994	2,605,480	1,997,106	109,109	2,106,215	241,277	-102,528	1,762,410	411,687	431,383	18,746	138,990	77,617
1995	2,766,386	2,106,980	112,631	2,219,611	254,933	-127,072	1,837,606	444,905	483,875	19,688	140,508	80,590
1996	2,985,395	2,185,720	117,978	2,303,698	261,394	-77,236	1,965,068	490,661	529,666	21,088	141,570	81,061
1997	3,195,701	2,282,622	148,423	2,431,045	270,265	-36,202	2,124,578	520,654	550,469	22,378	142,807	79,237
1998	3,289,978	2,357,162	127,184	2,484,346	279,931	-35,943	2,168,472	554,060	567,446	23,022	142,903	78,718
1999	3,356,548	2,439,149	70,097	2,509,246	290,405	-28,264	2,190,577	547,251	618,720	23,418	143,333	78,734
2000	3,516,877	2,529,017	122,546	2,651,563	301,371	-37,893	2,312,299	575,741	628,837	24,570	143,139	79,541
2001	3,696,423	2,636,071	112,087	2,748,158	310,330	-26,009	2,411,819	592,368	692,236	25,664	144,034	78,749
2002	3,674,933	2,631,103	48,588	2,679,691	308,748	-8,698	2,362,245	560,715	751,973	25,397	144,698	77,715
2003	3,773,645	2,690,441	50,241	2,740,682	321,482	7,745	2,426,945	566,374	780,326	25,938	145,487	76,799
2004	3,978,467	2,803,954	77,648	2,881,602	331,359	150	2,550,393	599,462	828,612	27,189	146,326	77,368
2005	4,127,041	2,847,525	107,551	2,955,076	341,731	13,771	2,627,116	600,901	899,024	28,070	147,027	77,492
2006	4,328,296	2,975,226	82,500	3,057,726	357,337	22,253	2,722,642	636,315	969,339	29,195	148,256	79,869
2007	4,550,512	3,063,648	63,364	3,127,012	372,658	56,213	2,810,567	714,164	1,025,781	30,409	149,644	81,585
2008	4,800,024	3,082,915	79,731	3,162,646	376,997	66,832	2,852,481	774,554	1,172,989	31,759	151,138	80,079
2009	4,793,670	2,976,789	89,071	3,065,860	366,331	52,424	2,751,953	748,579	1,293,138	31,594	151,729	76,106
2010	4,863,937	3,032,674	70,180	3,102,854	367,378	83,450	2,818,926	689,127	1,355,884	31,914	152,407	74,961
2011	4,974,630	3,007,748	68,821	3,076,569	335,585	80,220	2,821,204	770,536	1,382,890	32,769	151,808	76,701
2012	5,133,909	3,108,733	75,451	3,184,184	340,317	67,848	2,911,715	795,344	1,426,850	34,022	150,901	74,498
2013	4,997,071	3,026,105	40,618	3,066,723	378,871	52,132	2,739,984	823,944	1,433,143	33,336	149,899	73,881
2014	5,218,903	3,098,686	39,330	3,138,016	387,132	69,764	2,820,648	906,575	1,491,680	34,992	149,147	73,827
2015	5,361,873	3,207,219	18,534	3,225,753	401,414	52,153	2,876,492	942,239	1,543,142	36,303	147,699	74,071
2016	5,403,156	3,163,165	21,622	3,184,787	397,115	84,227	2,871,899	956,735	1,574,522	36,681	147,301	74,141
2017	5,568,520	3,190,467	40,127	3,230,594	399,760	105,823	2,936,657	1,001,848	1,630,015	37,949	146,738	73,657
2018	5,831,032	5,777,975	53,057	3,400,432	411,244	125,038	3,114,226	1,082,222	1,634,584	39,917	146,078	74,354
2019	6,041,241	5,962,545	78,696	3,535,966	424,163	134,804	3,246,607	1,105,639	1,688,995	41,444	145,770	74,955

Personal Income and Employment by Area: Rome, GA

(Thousands of dollars, except as noted.)

Year	Personal income, total	Earnings by place of work Nonfarm	Farm	Total	Less: Contributions for government social insurance	Plus: Adjustment for residence	Equals: Net earnings by place of residence	Plus: Dividends, interest, and rent	Plus: Personal current transfer receipts	Per capita personal income (dollars)	Population (persons)	Total employment
1970	249,840	213,913	1,300	215,213	14,268	-1,910	199,035	28,791	22,014	3,374	74,051	34,937
1971	272,366	231,703	1,480	233,183	16,110	-2,657	214,416	32,193	25,757	3,596	75,747	35,869
1972	304,137	261,379	1,752	263,131	19,108	-4,167	239,856	35,731	28,550	3,988	76,267	37,626
1973	343,221	296,170	2,816	298,986	24,839	-4,241	269,906	40,048	33,267	4,448	77,161	39,299
1974	378,749	322,845	1,544	324,389	28,021	-5,082	291,286	45,896	41,567	4,857	77,988	39,874
1975	403,089	325,740	1,467	327,207	27,711	-5,296	294,200	51,935	56,954	5,108	78,917	37,308
1976	447,558	367,645	1,443	369,088	31,912	-6,161	331,015	56,565	59,978	5,630	79,499	38,135
1977	489,905	404,988	1,192	406,180	35,013	-6,494	364,673	62,561	62,671	6,084	80,526	38,921
1978	533,718	441,624	1,222	442,846	39,348	-5,707	397,791	68,932	66,995	6,655	80,194	39,774
1979	592,760	488,966	3,957	492,923	45,262	-7,307	440,354	77,597	74,809	7,450	79,565	40,267
1980	654,346	521,924	925	522,849	48,203	-6,347	468,299	96,455	89,592	8,194	79,860	39,476
1981	718,459	555,272	2,734	558,006	54,995	-6,744	496,267	118,916	103,276	8,987	79,948	39,772
1982	747,798	563,932	4,178	568,110	56,719	-10,482	500,909	132,261	114,628	9,360	79,897	38,189
1983	800,844	604,816	1,948	606,764	61,168	-12,451	533,145	144,665	123,034	10,116	79,163	37,795
1984	869,932	655,564	2,528	658,092	68,094	-11,108	578,890	160,885	130,157	10,981	79,223	39,730
1985	925,102	700,726	1,250	701,976	74,220	-10,795	616,961	169,026	139,115	11,634	79,520	40,092
1986	1,000,069	761,145	583	761,728	81,288	-12,066	668,374	184,185	147,510	12,532	79,804	41,120
1987	1,076,317	828,892	-317	828,575	87,534	-13,544	727,497	194,587	154,233	13,407	80,281	42,515
1988	1,158,233	888,941	2,433	891,374	96,776	-14,024	780,574	207,733	169,926	14,291	81,046	43,653
1989	1,241,132	937,347	3,481	940,828	102,938	-15,783	822,107	238,611	180,414	15,268	81,290	44,055
1990	1,329,271	1,009,357	3,517	1,012,874	110,076	-23,092	879,706	250,317	199,248	16,313	81,483	44,628
1991	1,405,143	1,070,441	4,878	1,075,319	118,413	-33,187	923,719	255,408	226,016	17,079	82,274	44,515
1992	1,511,817	1,165,599	6,001	1,171,600	126,865	-42,110	1,002,625	259,181	250,011	18,193	83,100	45,569
1993	1,569,706	1,206,685	5,358	1,212,043	131,717	-43,000	1,037,326	265,297	267,083	18,666	84,094	47,211
1994	1,671,089	1,293,448	6,647	1,300,095	142,393	-51,271	1,106,431	282,337	282,321	19,680	84,911	49,360
1995	1,728,012	1,301,422	5,181	1,306,603	143,174	-43,610	1,119,819	305,360	302,833	20,078	86,063	49,299
1996	1,840,615	1,378,724	7,193	1,385,917	149,583	-49,917	1,186,417	333,993	320,205	21,142	87,061	49,613
1997	1,909,106	1,420,160	6,980	1,427,140	151,216	-47,639	1,228,285	352,578	328,243	21,697	87,991	50,251
1998	1,978,998	1,467,168	7,916	1,475,084	156,805	-40,163	1,278,116	361,235	339,647	22,278	88,833	49,963
1999	2,079,406	1,569,848	7,629	1,577,477	164,849	-41,232	1,371,396	345,121	362,889	23,192	89,659	49,836
2000	2,170,925	1,598,953	6,026	1,604,979	168,078	-34,627	1,402,274	383,754	384,897	23,899	90,837	50,348
2001	2,298,435	1,705,546	9,422	1,714,968	179,471	-62,607	1,472,890	400,476	425,069	25,207	91,181	50,251
2002	2,386,660	1,786,759	4,637	1,791,396	187,416	-82,816	1,521,164	389,419	476,077	25,775	92,597	50,114
2003	2,470,309	1,866,190	6,356	1,872,546	193,893	-99,458	1,579,195	415,388	475,726	26,409	93,539	50,560
2004	2,610,975	2,012,541	10,648	2,023,189	215,246	-125,780	1,682,163	399,388	529,424	27,772	94,014	51,690
2005	2,627,080	1,929,912	12,026	1,941,938	208,442	-103,210	1,630,286	425,907	570,887	27,849	94,332	51,414
2006	2,717,069	2,038,418	5,541	2,043,959	221,141	-138,420	1,684,398	438,132	594,539	28,551	95,165	52,717
2007	2,808,408	2,033,082	10,283	2,043,365	219,276	-135,280	1,688,809	497,473	622,126	29,467	95,308	52,357
2008	2,864,912	2,055,635	11,408	2,067,043	234,015	-148,396	1,684,632	507,228	673,052	29,867	95,922	51,533
2009	2,833,878	2,047,078	9,910	2,056,988	230,775	-190,307	1,635,906	454,669	743,303	29,402	96,383	49,708
2010	2,918,037	2,087,623	6,919	2,094,542	236,264	-206,658	1,651,620	454,367	812,050	30,261	96,428	49,387
2011	3,019,176	2,106,859	4,121	2,110,980	211,589	-222,246	1,677,145	488,342	853,689	31,378	96,221	49,159
2012	3,055,976	2,170,371	16,400	2,186,771	218,350	-235,565	1,732,856	484,669	838,451	31,833	96,000	49,239
2013	3,096,718	2,220,967	21,959	2,242,926	250,638	-233,913	1,758,375	485,043	853,300	32,284	95,921	49,429
2014	3,254,929	2,321,078	24,719	2,345,797	258,934	-231,655	1,855,208	514,962	884,759	33,920	95,959	50,605
2015	3,411,439	2,405,785	26,139	2,431,924	267,905	-231,823	1,932,196	565,504	913,739	35,446	96,243	51,176
2016	3,493,406	2,457,020	12,632	2,469,652	275,361	-231,691	1,962,600	591,081	939,725	36,156	96,620	51,882
2017	3,631,557	2,526,083	17,947	2,544,030	283,642	-208,471	2,051,917	613,612	966,028	37,204	97,613	52,461
2018	3,760,045	3,749,493	10,552	2,603,493	292,075	-198,715	2,112,703	655,612	991,730	38,382	97,964	53,214
2019	3,872,375	3,864,753	7,622	2,655,075	300,706	-184,842	2,169,527	660,960	1,041,888	39,314	98,498	53,789

Personal Income and Employment by Area: Sacramento-Roseville-Folsom, CA

(Thousands of dollars, except as noted.)

Year	Personal income, total	Earnings by place of work			Less: Contributions for government social insurance	Plus: Adjustment for residence	Equals: Net earnings by place of residence	Plus: Dividends, interest, and rent	Plus: Personal current transfer receipts	Per capita personal income (dollars)	Population (persons)	Total employment
		Nonfarm	Farm	Total								
1970	4,056,127	3,019,145	78,526	3,097,671	167,543	46,767	2,976,895	667,330	411,902	4,761	852,036	360,459
1971	4,462,068	3,312,958	79,496	3,392,454	189,765	46,656	3,249,345	745,796	466,927	5,093	876,053	368,520
1972	4,928,736	3,674,421	99,494	3,773,915	223,152	48,815	3,599,578	824,161	504,997	5,460	902,647	385,583
1973	5,445,749	4,031,560	137,550	4,169,110	277,364	53,004	3,944,750	942,008	558,991	6,012	905,830	400,639
1974	6,137,885	4,441,915	192,552	4,634,467	315,137	59,040	4,378,370	1,092,913	666,602	6,619	927,304	417,125
1975	6,886,120	4,928,191	162,706	5,090,897	347,042	73,596	4,817,451	1,233,363	835,306	7,257	948,850	431,998
1976	7,619,961	5,541,048	109,773	5,650,821	401,160	77,921	5,327,582	1,358,501	933,878	7,847	971,060	450,281
1977	8,521,066	6,224,320	134,273	6,358,593	461,389	86,478	5,983,682	1,527,523	1,009,861	8,521	1,000,056	471,705
1978	9,760,416	7,156,718	141,698	7,298,416	547,397	103,593	6,854,612	1,785,780	1,120,024	9,378	1,040,724	504,114
1979	11,064,177	8,108,914	160,588	8,269,502	656,579	107,234	7,720,157	2,060,878	1,283,142	10,326	1,071,481	532,619
1980	12,427,490	8,744,342	214,973	8,959,315	690,972	132,075	8,400,418	2,486,906	1,540,166	11,227	1,106,955	544,041
1981	13,762,492	9,487,978	150,893	9,638,871	817,934	117,513	8,938,450	2,970,629	1,853,413	12,143	1,133,346	557,728
1982	14,772,197	10,104,581	117,568	10,222,149	889,275	124,855	9,457,729	3,287,053	2,027,415	12,642	1,168,540	565,530
1983	15,968,174	10,974,796	70,342	11,045,138	1,005,026	131,656	10,171,768	3,646,950	2,149,456	13,374	1,193,993	586,240
1984	17,914,310	12,445,247	159,386	12,604,633	1,184,438	135,814	11,556,009	4,085,170	2,273,131	14,703	1,218,388	613,520
1985	19,823,351	13,983,584	158,081	14,141,665	1,353,674	131,066	12,919,057	4,426,572	2,477,722	15,849	1,250,764	649,028
1986	21,645,699	15,511,373	154,651	15,666,024	1,529,413	132,797	14,269,408	4,691,999	2,684,292	16,844	1,285,092	678,664
1987	23,462,946	17,127,656	194,126	17,321,782	1,701,695	130,664	15,750,751	4,871,151	2,841,044	17,625	1,331,264	718,562
1988	25,581,391	18,839,745	194,123	19,033,868	1,947,474	140,321	17,226,715	5,257,135	3,097,541	18,552	1,378,887	756,390
1989	28,335,790	20,683,946	199,257	20,883,203	2,153,381	123,653	18,853,475	6,054,295	3,428,020	19,836	1,428,491	791,265
1990	31,027,352	22,952,847	219,420	23,172,267	2,372,660	117,914	20,917,521	6,279,222	3,830,609	20,393	1,521,462	837,598
1991	32,889,865	24,411,529	189,703	24,601,232	2,541,216	75,526	22,135,542	6,477,264	4,277,059	20,989	1,566,994	846,203
1992	34,867,420	25,780,556	192,455	25,973,011	2,668,907	20,321	23,324,425	6,572,785	4,970,210	21,910	1,591,373	838,258
1993	35,759,371	26,310,906	236,163	26,547,069	2,739,299	38,692	23,846,462	6,694,507	5,218,402	22,237	1,608,074	837,172
1994	37,791,252	28,056,083	232,174	28,288,257	2,921,374	-8,253	25,358,630	7,120,544	5,312,078	23,307	1,621,444	870,499
1995	40,329,219	29,820,984	215,440	30,036,424	3,057,859	-79,255	26,899,310	7,822,312	5,607,597	24,515	1,645,098	886,610
1996	42,252,093	31,183,514	236,265	31,419,779	3,130,865	-98,637	28,190,277	8,150,930	5,910,886	25,262	1,672,583	914,825
1997	45,030,721	33,521,185	224,093	33,745,278	3,325,745	-160,274	30,259,259	8,813,320	5,958,142	26,481	1,700,488	938,908
1998	48,605,943	36,574,979	198,079	36,773,058	3,593,508	-187,080	32,992,470	9,292,754	6,320,719	28,066	1,731,847	973,971
1999	52,212,596	39,828,950	273,415	40,102,365	3,921,445	-166,246	36,014,674	9,516,935	6,680,987	29,545	1,767,237	1,017,726
2000	57,018,505	44,126,618	233,133	44,359,751	4,286,203	-145,306	39,928,242	10,102,115	6,988,148	31,538	1,807,949	1,041,891
2001	62,331,887	48,812,679	203,317	49,015,996	4,839,635	-176,967	43,999,394	10,527,238	7,805,255	33,398	1,866,310	1,084,938
2002	64,934,763	51,459,767	203,160	51,662,927	5,162,239	-193,945	46,306,743	10,322,496	8,305,524	33,759	1,923,508	1,099,722
2003	68,983,458	54,378,964	218,631	54,597,595	5,525,135	-187,992	48,884,468	11,313,708	8,785,282	35,007	1,970,542	1,124,044
2004	73,334,232	57,972,715	253,909	58,226,624	6,059,543	-292,307	51,874,774	12,125,879	9,333,579	36,509	2,008,663	1,157,385
2005	76,761,190	61,023,372	234,424	61,257,796	6,413,768	-382,290	54,461,738	12,414,740	9,884,712	37,723	2,034,850	1,191,410
2006	81,690,229	64,201,333	214,970	64,416,303	6,547,339	-368,764	57,500,200	13,377,714	10,812,315	39,696	2,057,885	1,214,206
2007	85,056,346	65,680,356	318,910	65,999,266	6,549,561	-333,427	59,116,278	14,365,988	11,574,080	40,849	2,082,217	1,232,558
2008	87,909,372	65,743,061	338,935	66,081,996	6,639,581	-288,976	59,153,439	15,599,672	13,156,261	41,697	2,108,310	1,209,043
2009	86,213,023	63,114,944	402,341	63,517,285	6,434,870	-159,773	56,922,642	14,652,177	14,638,204	40,425	2,132,657	1,162,375
2010	88,560,317	63,767,081	299,079	64,066,160	6,350,936	-36,426	57,678,798	14,503,192	16,378,327	41,116	2,153,935	1,136,573
2011	93,540,278	66,428,184	339,795	66,767,979	5,959,493	16,413	60,824,899	16,183,569	16,531,810	43,027	2,174,008	1,139,388
2012	97,785,691	69,138,651	443,320	69,581,971	6,161,265	179,451	63,600,157	17,383,972	16,801,562	44,596	2,192,724	1,176,096
2013	101,408,457	72,259,016	479,609	72,738,625	7,143,476	205,493	65,800,642	17,962,381	17,645,434	45,812	2,213,564	1,211,645
2014	108,063,287	75,936,373	504,757	76,441,130	7,510,918	194,374	69,124,586	20,002,224	18,936,477	48,254	2,239,455	1,241,830
2015	115,685,773	80,860,423	465,426	81,325,849	7,952,344	380,991	73,754,496	21,391,203	20,540,074	51,033	2,266,892	1,279,035
2016	119,989,645	83,761,544	460,312	84,221,856	8,306,128	461,960	76,377,688	22,307,035	21,304,922	52,278	2,295,233	1,309,574
2017	125,039,082	88,125,216	564,062	88,689,278	8,691,413	575,775	80,573,640	23,411,028	21,054,414	53,783	2,324,884	1,332,525
2018	132,323,857	131,947,556	376,301	92,931,321	9,286,477	637,045	84,281,889	25,421,337	22,620,631	56,502	2,341,940	1,378,465
2019	139,088,819	138,614,835	473,984	98,115,756	9,843,895	718,519	88,990,380	26,049,117	24,049,322	58,843	2,363,730	1,412,094

Personal Income and Employment by Area: Saginaw, MI

(Thousands of dollars, except as noted.)

Year	Personal income, total	Earnings by place of work — Nonfarm	Earnings by place of work — Farm	Earnings by place of work — Total	Less: Contributions for government social insurance	Plus: Adjustment for residence	Equals: Net earnings by place of residence	Plus: Dividends, interest, and rent	Plus: Personal current transfer receipts	Per capita personal income (dollars)	Population (persons)	Total employment
1970	833,147	725,462	9,119	734,581	51,926	-38,394	644,261	112,392	76,494	3,781	220,370	84,309
1971	967,531	865,612	7,978	873,590	63,632	-52,762	757,196	120,325	90,010	4,335	223,170	89,057
1972	1,073,395	964,157	11,033	975,190	75,246	-58,727	841,217	129,388	102,790	4,790	224,074	92,541
1973	1,201,599	1,086,788	19,860	1,106,648	98,608	-66,015	942,025	141,516	118,058	5,336	225,199	96,459
1974	1,268,242	1,084,061	39,378	1,123,439	101,700	-56,915	964,824	159,063	144,355	5,614	225,920	95,113
1975	1,373,369	1,157,164	19,777	1,176,941	106,544	-58,140	1,012,257	177,262	183,850	6,084	225,723	92,153
1976	1,569,810	1,393,476	13,623	1,407,099	130,291	-84,150	1,192,658	190,532	186,620	6,942	226,118	96,864
1977	1,756,811	1,595,456	14,954	1,610,410	148,983	-110,293	1,351,134	213,583	192,094	7,744	226,861	100,874
1978	1,949,817	1,794,530	14,664	1,809,194	172,866	-129,099	1,507,229	232,162	210,426	8,585	227,115	104,515
1979	2,106,754	1,915,839	16,481	1,932,320	190,933	-140,635	1,600,752	259,852	246,150	9,292	226,732	105,175
1980	2,229,860	1,868,510	19,111	1,887,621	183,724	-133,175	1,570,722	308,356	350,782	9,807	227,373	98,304
1981	2,375,494	2,017,804	14,596	2,032,400	214,908	-156,920	1,660,572	368,161	346,761	10,599	224,132	98,329
1982	2,375,661	1,902,316	3,440	1,905,756	205,352	-137,680	1,562,724	418,210	394,727	10,753	220,925	91,223
1983	2,529,764	2,058,947	-1,869	2,057,078	227,716	-162,989	1,666,373	450,756	412,635	11,616	217,784	91,228
1984	2,758,499	2,273,797	10,295	2,284,092	260,828	-199,036	1,824,228	508,736	425,535	12,729	216,710	94,924
1985	2,939,403	2,492,114	8,707	2,500,821	291,692	-243,514	1,965,615	536,252	437,536	13,669	215,040	98,880
1986	3,019,514	2,556,163	2,888	2,559,051	300,357	-256,911	2,001,783	556,742	460,989	14,046	214,972	99,967
1987	3,082,536	2,634,909	16,687	2,651,596	304,617	-292,725	2,054,254	556,365	471,917	14,398	214,098	103,044
1988	3,227,836	2,801,764	13,870	2,815,634	332,057	-329,793	2,153,784	581,928	492,124	15,117	213,522	105,620
1989	3,422,445	2,910,020	23,482	2,933,502	345,747	-357,693	2,230,062	655,736	536,647	16,121	212,303	107,071
1990	3,522,299	2,976,864	15,114	2,991,978	358,915	-352,085	2,280,978	655,820	585,501	16,609	212,071	106,622
1991	3,621,768	3,057,343	14,911	3,072,254	373,654	-368,169	2,330,431	644,447	646,890	17,053	212,384	105,668
1992	3,799,081	3,233,318	13,108	3,246,426	388,938	-394,114	2,463,374	654,486	681,221	17,885	212,421	107,274
1993	3,991,889	3,377,601	16,127	3,393,728	412,583	-407,990	2,573,155	688,362	730,372	18,815	212,165	107,006
1994	4,230,696	3,624,150	1,699	3,625,849	446,685	-445,374	2,733,790	753,479	743,427	19,931	212,262	109,557
1995	4,412,972	3,737,765	11,843	3,749,608	460,296	-432,932	2,856,380	790,809	765,783	20,808	212,076	112,965
1996	4,612,938	3,901,180	7,989	3,909,169	466,412	-439,928	3,002,829	822,060	788,049	21,767	211,927	115,285
1997	4,844,658	4,059,224	6,680	4,065,904	481,095	-441,197	3,143,612	851,159	849,887	22,916	211,406	116,361
1998	4,936,617	4,223,787	2,212	4,225,999	491,016	-492,135	3,242,848	843,102	850,667	23,414	210,839	114,873
1999	5,178,231	4,510,783	19,876	4,530,659	518,341	-572,911	3,439,407	809,376	929,448	24,611	210,400	116,817
2000	5,421,571	4,680,876	8,449	4,689,325	530,035	-550,231	3,609,059	846,867	965,645	25,829	209,899	118,358
2001	5,388,898	4,595,219	-1,232	4,593,987	540,393	-559,351	3,494,243	833,912	1,060,743	25,728	209,460	117,341
2002	5,305,995	4,537,002	14,380	4,551,382	533,237	-549,067	3,469,078	738,708	1,098,209	25,348	209,323	114,780
2003	5,405,793	4,637,530	12,397	4,649,927	541,051	-580,000	3,528,876	725,893	1,151,024	25,895	208,755	114,389
2004	5,585,388	4,654,030	18,550	4,672,580	549,110	-525,058	3,598,412	791,476	1,195,500	26,790	208,489	113,429
2005	5,594,903	4,623,695	17,799	4,641,494	551,201	-549,674	3,540,619	790,930	1,263,354	26,981	207,368	112,826
2006	5,705,175	4,725,583	23,739	4,749,322	577,488	-570,402	3,601,432	782,448	1,321,295	27,719	205,822	111,712
2007	5,829,464	4,617,266	28,171	4,645,437	567,053	-546,865	3,531,519	855,656	1,442,289	28,696	203,144	110,931
2008	5,933,010	4,442,442	34,554	4,476,996	551,425	-497,012	3,428,559	888,416	1,616,035	29,376	201,966	106,908
2009	5,857,627	4,351,939	11,687	4,363,626	544,337	-543,823	3,275,466	811,405	1,770,756	29,166	200,835	103,080
2010	6,086,307	4,484,996	13,545	4,498,541	548,664	-546,451	3,403,426	788,475	1,894,406	30,454	199,851	102,853
2011	6,321,942	4,683,316	43,573	4,726,889	509,909	-632,376	3,584,604	862,740	1,874,598	31,795	198,833	106,093
2012	6,403,252	4,756,187	45,896	4,802,083	518,920	-647,619	3,635,544	897,065	1,870,643	32,299	198,250	106,832
2013	6,454,145	4,815,337	27,497	4,842,834	593,390	-644,312	3,605,132	917,275	1,931,738	32,821	196,645	107,255
2014	6,645,226	4,919,859	-3,624	4,916,235	606,574	-685,327	3,624,334	1,013,441	2,007,451	34,068	195,055	107,394
2015	6,907,941	5,043,590	-5,063	5,038,527	617,700	-685,377	3,735,450	1,044,707	2,127,784	35,774	193,097	107,872
2016	7,056,032	5,211,729	-15,889	5,195,840	634,493	-739,129	3,822,218	1,056,432	2,177,382	36,696	192,285	108,052
2017	7,310,793	5,331,512	-32,603	5,298,909	649,971	-622,415	4,026,523	1,097,745	2,186,525	38,090	191,934	107,748
2018	7,540,269	7,536,504	3,765	5,523,602	684,732	-701,756	4,137,114	1,149,827	2,253,328	39,521	190,791	108,136
2019	7,723,177	7,719,237	3,940	5,620,273	692,203	-729,984	4,198,086	1,162,980	2,362,111	40,533	190,539	108,305

Personal Income and Employment by Area: St. Cloud, MN

(Thousands of dollars, except as noted.)

Year	Personal income, total	Earnings by place of work			Less: Contributions for government social insurance	Plus: Adjustment for residence	Equals: Net earnings by place of residence	Plus: Dividends, interest, and rent	Plus: Personal current transfer receipts	Per capita personal income (dollars)	Population (persons)	Total employment
		Nonfarm	Farm	Total								
1970	357,436	258,985	33,599	292,584	17,712	-2,265	272,607	50,671	34,158	3,061	116,762	45,611
1971	386,589	281,632	29,727	311,359	19,811	-900	290,648	55,791	40,150	3,249	118,978	46,936
1972	426,393	309,563	34,216	343,779	22,669	883	321,993	60,241	44,159	3,563	119,660	49,580
1973	503,680	351,670	60,194	411,864	29,713	1,753	383,904	68,432	51,344	4,130	121,957	53,110
1974	556,113	402,792	48,200	450,992	35,883	894	416,003	79,044	61,066	4,497	123,661	55,774
1975	609,861	447,005	35,997	483,002	38,868	-169	443,965	90,991	74,905	4,829	126,283	56,483
1976	671,498	498,887	29,564	528,451	44,340	553	484,664	100,148	86,686	5,268	127,477	57,890
1977	763,536	549,214	54,897	604,111	48,945	1,835	557,001	115,303	91,232	5,874	129,994	59,900
1978	852,919	632,903	48,700	681,603	58,620	1,617	624,600	130,054	98,265	6,504	131,145	62,454
1979	961,603	730,534	42,507	773,041	70,525	-575	701,941	148,882	110,780	7,262	132,420	66,254
1980	1,065,857	797,952	29,890	827,842	76,943	-2,327	748,572	183,939	133,346	7,967	133,782	67,330
1981	1,201,287	882,347	42,718	925,065	91,716	-10,459	822,890	224,004	154,393	8,885	135,211	67,644
1982	1,300,980	926,627	45,042	971,669	98,108	-14,993	858,568	268,456	173,956	9,558	136,115	67,216
1983	1,354,161	987,690	6,554	994,244	105,252	-17,157	871,835	292,813	189,513	9,881	137,048	68,777
1984	1,534,274	1,093,977	49,024	1,143,001	118,888	-16,492	1,007,621	325,392	201,261	11,115	138,037	71,557
1985	1,628,625	1,156,771	58,156	1,214,927	127,546	-16,302	1,071,079	344,888	212,658	11,684	139,387	73,891
1986	1,753,669	1,263,620	69,841	1,333,461	142,823	-22,147	1,168,491	365,177	220,001	12,447	140,892	77,336
1987	1,863,932	1,373,562	70,479	1,444,041	155,225	-28,693	1,260,123	375,928	227,881	13,097	142,314	81,199
1988	1,981,998	1,520,001	46,186	1,566,187	178,235	-39,393	1,348,559	394,048	239,391	13,681	144,873	85,778
1989	2,198,078	1,656,907	89,932	1,746,839	194,523	-48,594	1,503,722	429,925	264,431	14,944	147,087	89,177
1990	2,329,886	1,764,780	86,059	1,850,839	208,383	-57,778	1,584,678	464,090	281,118	15,525	150,078	90,903
1991	2,414,386	1,866,203	54,334	1,920,537	223,180	-62,850	1,634,507	474,475	305,404	15,904	151,812	93,550
1992	2,608,717	2,039,064	64,252	2,103,316	240,982	-65,160	1,797,174	481,860	329,683	17,003	153,430	95,350
1993	2,716,359	2,168,034	43,475	2,211,509	258,124	-72,862	1,880,523	490,547	345,289	17,469	155,495	97,771
1994	2,873,286	2,296,169	59,763	2,355,932	276,656	-72,780	2,006,496	505,859	360,931	18,270	157,264	100,598
1995	3,014,647	2,416,425	24,637	2,441,062	290,978	-80,986	2,069,098	559,687	385,862	18,933	159,224	105,687
1996	3,273,661	2,579,640	80,604	2,660,244	306,917	-84,797	2,268,530	594,334	410,797	20,389	160,563	108,022
1997	3,386,964	2,704,388	40,355	2,744,743	321,415	-88,058	2,335,270	631,329	420,365	20,877	162,234	107,758
1998	3,782,234	3,054,756	88,684	3,143,440	361,069	-121,432	2,660,939	680,986	440,309	23,154	163,352	110,718
1999	3,959,803	3,181,294	86,353	3,267,647	375,872	-82,309	2,809,466	687,180	463,157	23,932	165,463	112,488
2000	4,243,872	3,400,899	69,031	3,469,930	398,395	-75,326	2,996,209	747,248	500,415	25,240	168,139	115,436
2001	4,571,443	3,648,912	67,566	3,716,478	422,741	-58,756	3,234,981	772,947	563,515	26,798	170,587	119,810
2002	4,808,353	3,864,304	64,639	3,928,943	446,856	-61,192	3,420,895	768,570	618,888	27,774	173,123	121,271
2003	5,048,037	3,986,479	104,658	4,091,137	465,032	-58,501	3,567,604	824,682	655,751	28,819	175,161	120,862
2004	5,302,879	4,228,422	152,110	4,380,532	493,983	-32,306	3,854,243	752,398	696,238	29,983	176,860	123,417
2005	5,452,867	4,352,964	153,051	4,506,015	514,182	-41,254	3,950,579	761,372	740,916	30,425	179,222	125,143
2006	5,742,515	4,533,327	140,372	4,673,699	546,799	-71,822	4,055,078	860,641	826,796	31,574	181,873	127,619
2007	6,104,168	4,756,275	138,903	4,895,178	573,390	-122,931	4,198,857	983,968	921,343	33,067	184,598	130,268
2008	6,443,968	4,862,534	224,255	5,086,789	590,080	-158,481	4,338,228	1,025,413	1,080,327	34,551	186,507	129,574
2009	6,240,493	4,793,954	110,951	4,904,905	585,162	-265,051	4,054,692	990,510	1,195,291	33,174	188,114	126,361
2010	6,502,293	4,887,575	169,178	5,056,753	589,580	-245,449	4,221,724	949,750	1,330,819	34,365	189,210	126,070
2011	7,001,098	5,170,656	209,534	5,380,190	556,404	-268,453	4,555,333	1,081,824	1,363,941	36,835	190,064	128,919
2012	7,354,231	5,419,029	289,761	5,708,790	582,463	-272,305	4,854,022	1,159,119	1,341,090	38,594	190,553	130,849
2013	7,499,648	5,664,581	210,696	5,875,277	688,081	-262,327	4,924,869	1,184,619	1,390,160	39,144	191,592	132,712
2014	7,968,349	6,040,340	244,972	6,285,312	711,816	-319,440	5,254,056	1,255,483	1,458,810	41,296	192,958	134,408
2015	8,264,132	6,266,439	216,829	6,483,268	738,130	-386,830	5,358,308	1,390,926	1,514,898	42,391	194,951	136,435
2016	8,366,947	6,454,957	130,740	6,585,697	761,633	-434,672	5,389,392	1,395,205	1,582,350	42,680	196,039	137,279
2017	8,680,497	6,774,326	79,470	6,853,796	796,086	-463,596	5,594,114	1,462,261	1,624,122	43,894	197,759	139,083
2018	9,255,764	9,120,933	134,831	7,146,023	835,213	-462,503	5,848,307	1,638,855	1,768,602	46,240	200,166	138,452
2019	9,580,328	9,397,366	182,962	7,405,098	859,969	-446,032	6,099,097	1,643,063	1,838,168	47,436	201,964	140,170

Personal Income and Employment by Area: St. George, UT

(Thousands of dollars, except as noted.)

Year	Personal income, total	Earnings by place of work			Less: Contributions for government social insurance	Plus: Adjustment for residence	Equals: Net earnings by place of residence	Plus: Dividends, interest, and rent	Plus: Personal current transfer receipts	Per capita personal income (dollars)	Population (persons)	Total employment
		Nonfarm	Farm	Total								
1970	40,890	27,300	2,048	29,348	1,684	869	28,533	7,736	4,621	2,940	13,907	4,819
1971	45,422	29,763	1,736	31,499	1,903	1,201	30,797	9,085	5,540	3,021	15,037	5,015
1972	52,409	34,658	1,700	36,358	2,345	1,355	35,368	10,605	6,436	3,376	15,526	5,512
1973	60,744	39,214	2,851	42,065	3,041	1,644	40,668	12,223	7,853	3,709	16,379	5,916
1974	66,587	42,128	1,988	44,116	3,364	2,033	42,785	14,497	9,305	3,680	18,092	5,985
1975	77,215	47,779	1,533	49,312	3,693	2,425	48,044	17,358	11,813	4,173	18,504	6,192
1976	92,191	58,536	1,635	60,171	4,506	2,859	58,524	20,139	13,528	4,645	19,846	6,898
1977	107,325	67,768	1,709	69,477	5,261	3,545	67,761	24,032	15,532	5,141	20,877	7,443
1978	129,654	80,468	1,976	82,444	6,373	4,487	80,558	30,826	18,270	5,805	22,335	8,170
1979	155,888	98,170	2,130	100,300	8,500	5,158	96,958	37,310	21,620	6,490	24,019	9,054
1980	178,589	106,873	1,285	108,158	9,509	6,030	104,679	47,391	26,519	6,745	26,478	9,442
1981	198,424	113,099	611	113,710	11,006	6,553	109,257	56,312	32,855	7,069	28,070	9,582
1982	215,582	119,667	250	119,917	11,822	6,654	114,749	63,156	37,677	7,315	29,472	9,772
1983	242,970	136,435	-19	136,416	13,208	6,853	130,061	70,020	42,889	7,847	30,963	10,358
1984	296,237	173,570	228	173,798	16,853	6,874	163,819	84,734	47,684	9,027	32,816	11,851
1985	341,552	206,233	321	206,554	20,649	6,329	192,234	94,686	54,632	9,551	35,761	13,471
1986	392,178	239,819	578	240,397	24,226	5,958	222,129	107,621	62,428	9,928	39,503	14,907
1987	433,803	260,181	51	260,232	26,301	6,592	240,523	120,607	72,673	10,140	42,781	16,230
1988	474,564	281,832	811	282,643	30,569	7,710	259,784	134,246	80,534	10,634	44,627	17,503
1989	535,760	311,485	1,128	312,613	35,775	8,658	285,496	158,870	91,394	11,462	46,744	18,975
1990	614,437	377,613	1,938	379,551	43,608	8,727	344,670	164,331	105,436	12,493	49,183	21,258
1991	699,822	441,530	638	442,168	51,360	7,258	398,066	177,236	124,520	13,251	52,811	22,774
1992	778,219	488,031	1,521	489,552	56,973	8,970	441,549	193,219	143,451	13,811	56,349	24,084
1993	909,186	574,127	1,774	575,901	67,564	9,462	517,799	223,796	167,591	14,989	60,656	27,249
1994	1,053,848	697,198	203	697,401	83,211	7,888	622,078	250,440	181,330	15,849	66,493	33,162
1995	1,170,382	773,408	-872	772,536	93,859	9,211	687,888	275,806	206,688	16,197	72,261	35,711
1996	1,304,781	853,687	-1,000	852,687	101,009	12,264	763,942	310,138	230,701	16,804	77,647	38,801
1997	1,415,135	914,889	-480	914,409	106,487	15,588	823,510	339,029	252,596	17,359	81,520	40,701
1998	1,568,406	990,887	-318	990,569	115,943	17,986	892,612	407,257	268,537	18,487	84,837	42,689
1999	1,664,476	1,055,570	-688	1,054,882	123,208	21,451	953,125	423,951	287,400	18,904	88,049	44,820
2000	1,781,960	1,100,294	-631	1,099,663	131,496	24,824	992,991	468,295	320,674	19,538	91,206	47,299
2001	1,942,338	1,225,603	713	1,226,316	145,862	24,976	1,105,430	480,915	355,993	20,551	94,512	50,066
2002	2,032,511	1,327,386	-2,008	1,325,378	159,947	24,722	1,190,153	449,858	392,500	20,474	99,274	52,665
2003	2,201,984	1,457,597	80	1,457,677	177,298	25,605	1,305,984	467,546	428,454	21,135	104,188	55,712
2004	2,492,759	1,674,105	1,148	1,675,253	206,538	26,260	1,494,975	511,636	486,148	22,619	110,207	61,676
2005	2,876,650	1,933,330	911	1,934,241	240,398	26,431	1,720,274	615,558	540,818	24,174	119,000	67,944
2006	3,237,391	2,239,229	-1,560	2,237,669	274,617	25,802	1,988,854	657,905	590,632	25,532	126,796	73,427
2007	3,512,666	2,317,283	-4,389	2,312,894	288,266	26,418	2,051,046	804,284	657,336	26,555	132,277	77,265
2008	3,617,681	2,207,692	-4,313	2,203,379	281,333	30,316	1,952,362	904,174	761,145	26,689	135,552	75,466
2009	3,502,501	2,008,015	-3,257	2,004,758	263,436	33,931	1,775,253	862,125	865,123	25,549	137,088	71,644
2010	3,609,346	2,006,110	-2,780	2,003,330	261,467	37,210	1,779,073	883,410	946,863	26,080	138,393	70,275
2011	3,792,906	2,099,310	-238	2,099,072	249,739	41,264	1,890,597	926,700	975,609	26,847	141,276	72,101
2012	4,041,365	2,254,945	-527	2,254,418	262,306	48,854	2,040,966	1,005,448	994,951	28,023	144,216	74,752
2013	4,317,567	2,482,282	2,797	2,485,079	314,672	53,491	2,223,898	1,053,468	1,040,201	29,356	147,077	77,948
2014	4,711,149	2,707,747	2,161	2,709,908	340,015	51,367	2,421,260	1,202,276	1,087,613	31,163	151,179	82,089
2015	5,111,613	2,923,464	2,589	2,926,053	357,264	50,755	2,619,544	1,324,116	1,167,953	33,035	154,731	85,582
2016	5,505,008	3,240,263	227	3,240,490	395,314	44,607	2,889,783	1,372,627	1,242,598	34,571	159,237	90,752
2017	5,824,877	3,480,663	-572	3,480,091	433,695	41,665	3,088,061	1,443,918	1,292,898	35,161	165,662	94,227
2018	6,871,840	6,873,374	-1,534	4,012,027	484,644	32,934	3,560,317	1,890,568	1,420,955	40,053	171,567	100,814
2019	7,259,617	7,260,446	-829	4,220,486	511,611	35,874	3,744,749	1,955,414	1,559,454	40,886	177,556	104,156

Personal Income and Employment by Area: St. Joseph, MO-KS

(Thousands of dollars, except as noted.)

Year	Personal income, total	Earnings by place of work			Less: Contributions for government social insurance	Plus: Adjustment for residence	Equals: Net earnings by place of residence	Plus: Dividends, interest, and rent	Plus: Personal current transfer receipts	Per capita personal income (dollars)	Population (persons)	Total employment
		Nonfarm	Farm	Total								
1970	413,434	288,499	28,192	316,691	19,881	3,501	300,311	65,563	47,560	3,581	115,462	49,904
1971	446,250	310,367	27,784	338,151	22,133	4,880	320,898	70,775	54,577	3,812	117,065	50,202
1972	488,578	333,766	37,538	371,304	24,893	6,155	352,566	76,404	59,608	4,122	118,538	50,712
1973	543,724	359,429	53,986	413,415	31,136	7,793	390,072	84,689	68,963	4,597	118,278	51,864
1974	569,972	390,077	31,642	421,719	35,070	8,081	394,730	96,190	79,052	4,827	118,091	52,490
1975	625,486	419,929	30,026	449,955	36,835	11,366	424,486	105,131	95,869	5,259	118,925	52,020
1976	676,430	475,341	15,865	491,206	42,255	12,388	461,339	111,996	103,095	5,645	119,830	53,138
1977	747,067	518,123	25,614	543,737	46,062	15,909	513,584	124,890	108,593	6,221	120,097	53,528
1978	825,459	568,154	35,404	603,558	52,061	20,676	572,173	137,472	115,814	6,880	119,976	54,529
1979	923,074	624,010	45,851	669,861	59,164	25,409	636,106	155,967	131,001	7,718	119,604	55,845
1980	1,000,651	683,798	7,578	691,376	64,792	25,566	652,150	192,119	156,382	8,391	119,251	56,082
1981	1,135,885	729,394	37,359	766,753	74,086	27,895	720,562	236,329	178,994	9,579	118,583	55,596
1982	1,216,697	772,982	20,054	793,036	80,240	25,565	738,361	283,589	194,747	10,325	117,842	55,548
1983	1,255,123	804,379	-5,093	799,286	83,608	26,891	742,569	303,831	208,723	10,674	117,584	56,265
1984	1,370,360	871,392	9,717	881,109	92,793	26,492	814,808	335,702	219,850	11,677	117,358	57,192
1985	1,459,619	908,627	47,897	956,524	98,336	27,991	886,179	343,486	229,954	12,502	116,748	57,089
1986	1,497,233	939,828	34,300	974,128	101,853	28,907	901,182	352,346	243,705	12,852	116,500	56,485
1987	1,535,306	987,650	30,352	1,018,002	106,092	28,768	940,678	347,790	246,838	13,221	116,125	56,308
1988	1,603,664	1,071,267	16,741	1,088,008	119,703	26,188	994,493	357,909	251,262	13,910	115,289	57,352
1989	1,739,065	1,156,207	19,612	1,175,819	130,067	22,633	1,068,385	394,219	276,461	15,003	115,917	59,405
1990	1,778,507	1,203,202	25,060	1,228,262	137,542	16,373	1,107,093	381,892	289,522	15,331	116,008	60,198
1991	1,870,030	1,249,225	22,232	1,271,457	145,062	16,440	1,142,835	392,344	334,851	16,047	116,534	59,704
1992	1,977,413	1,306,180	38,199	1,344,379	149,136	22,601	1,217,844	403,589	355,980	16,847	117,377	59,547
1993	2,031,490	1,358,948	15,992	1,374,940	156,546	22,107	1,240,501	408,289	382,700	17,194	118,153	60,305
1994	2,150,095	1,433,949	41,352	1,475,301	166,286	27,220	1,336,235	416,388	397,472	18,203	118,119	60,738
1995	2,209,207	1,507,543	9,551	1,517,094	174,647	28,859	1,371,306	420,265	417,636	18,578	118,915	62,607
1996	2,351,240	1,541,726	62,340	1,604,066	176,031	35,364	1,463,399	450,696	437,145	19,727	119,187	62,179
1997	2,488,193	1,662,989	55,857	1,718,846	187,013	35,586	1,567,419	483,235	437,539	20,733	120,013	63,975
1998	2,584,055	1,774,970	35,275	1,810,245	198,625	36,940	1,648,560	486,527	448,968	21,357	120,992	65,446
1999	2,721,793	1,914,542	15,250	1,929,792	211,669	39,721	1,757,844	486,212	477,737	22,381	121,611	67,135
2000	2,923,415	2,048,987	26,881	2,075,868	224,002	43,873	1,895,739	514,105	513,571	23,559	124,091	68,339
2001	2,974,066	2,056,804	19,830	2,076,634	229,766	51,586	1,898,454	515,120	560,492	23,997	123,936	68,251
2002	3,032,654	2,141,143	-1,530	2,139,613	237,457	50,023	1,952,179	483,925	596,550	24,478	123,894	67,734
2003	3,113,900	2,189,041	11,748	2,200,789	243,650	45,643	2,002,782	495,634	615,484	25,128	123,923	68,092
2004	3,311,388	2,346,109	71,039	2,417,148	257,647	39,877	2,199,378	463,892	648,118	26,842	123,366	69,045
2005	3,392,760	2,434,178	45,292	2,479,470	271,801	30,902	2,238,571	460,554	693,635	27,475	123,484	69,535
2006	3,579,029	2,623,875	31,436	2,655,311	296,877	-3,971	2,354,463	492,251	732,315	28,812	124,222	71,478
2007	3,759,828	2,722,821	61,309	2,784,130	315,532	-32,560	2,436,038	548,671	775,119	29,963	125,483	74,526
2008	4,000,967	2,845,157	65,213	2,910,370	329,247	-58,502	2,522,621	612,339	866,007	31,734	126,077	75,019
2009	3,977,953	2,808,713	77,133	2,885,846	325,199	-124,208	2,436,439	597,154	944,360	31,322	127,001	73,068
2010	3,968,769	2,841,319	35,484	2,876,803	323,966	-125,157	2,427,680	545,307	995,782	31,182	127,277	70,878
2011	4,227,560	2,917,338	83,364	3,000,702	299,499	-104,457	2,596,746	618,284	1,012,530	33,121	127,639	70,968
2012	4,367,071	3,135,365	44,139	3,179,504	311,803	-175,994	2,691,707	651,957	1,023,407	34,148	127,886	71,403
2013	4,449,745	3,213,676	124,067	3,337,743	359,455	-186,033	2,792,255	637,512	1,019,978	34,859	127,651	72,283
2014	4,505,594	3,259,287	81,761	3,341,048	368,698	-198,388	2,773,962	687,037	1,044,595	35,392	127,306	72,020
2015	4,563,195	3,342,353	9,215	3,351,568	386,205	-220,808	2,744,555	723,756	1,094,884	35,969	126,864	73,042
2016	4,601,597	3,371,047	28,760	3,399,807	393,975	-239,452	2,766,380	726,359	1,108,858	36,254	126,927	73,674
2017	4,741,039	3,495,662	33,415	3,529,077	407,658	-278,886	2,842,533	761,822	1,136,684	37,350	126,935	73,517
2018	4,840,654	4,813,982	26,672	3,591,768	412,222	-258,607	2,920,939	736,950	1,182,765	38,418	125,998	72,709
2019	5,025,839	4,949,101	76,738	3,759,930	431,807	-281,753	3,046,370	745,575	1,233,894	40,135	125,223	72,815

Personal Income and Employment by Area: St. Louis, MO-IL

(Thousands of dollars, except as noted.)

Year	Personal income, total	Earnings by place of work			Less: Contributions for government social insurance	Plus: Adjustment for residence	Equals: Net earnings by place of residence	Plus: Dividends, interest, and rent	Plus: Personal current transfer receipts	Per capita personal income (dollars)	Population (persons)	Total employment
		Nonfarm	Farm	Total								
1970	11,000,702	9,006,214	63,227	9,069,441	597,235	-15,927	8,456,279	1,662,650	881,773	4,365	2,520,475	1,119,503
1971	11,736,076	9,519,993	68,615	9,588,608	652,043	-17,253	8,919,312	1,772,811	1,043,953	4,668	2,514,268	1,108,632
1972	12,587,409	10,229,514	82,504	10,312,018	737,233	-19,706	9,555,079	1,899,282	1,133,048	5,023	2,506,053	1,120,309
1973	13,688,693	11,063,790	167,605	11,231,395	922,267	-42,015	10,267,113	2,095,321	1,326,259	5,489	2,493,703	1,155,750
1974	14,864,310	11,889,861	139,496	12,029,357	1,025,821	-65,160	10,938,376	2,385,057	1,540,877	5,986	2,483,293	1,165,071
1975	16,147,882	12,567,195	174,401	12,741,596	1,065,530	-78,602	11,597,464	2,586,215	1,964,203	6,503	2,483,274	1,144,591
1976	17,633,355	13,984,487	114,400	14,098,887	1,205,364	-129,380	12,764,143	2,777,740	2,091,472	7,101	2,483,161	1,174,761
1977	19,445,715	15,599,210	117,394	15,716,604	1,348,283	-177,931	14,190,390	3,089,157	2,166,168	7,852	2,476,457	1,208,780
1978	21,572,058	17,457,800	120,904	17,578,704	1,558,154	-230,083	15,790,467	3,432,529	2,349,062	8,699	2,479,899	1,251,667
1979	23,848,861	19,248,226	155,522	19,403,748	1,777,353	-285,212	17,341,183	3,872,768	2,634,910	9,599	2,484,555	1,285,355
1980	26,137,634	20,404,036	27,574	20,431,610	1,870,047	-315,297	18,246,266	4,661,425	3,229,943	10,510	2,486,989	1,260,871
1981	29,034,514	22,140,569	109,614	22,250,183	2,175,703	-385,480	19,689,000	5,791,552	3,553,962	11,673	2,487,360	1,257,134
1982	31,261,136	23,225,143	44,461	23,269,604	2,326,902	-374,710	20,567,992	6,834,650	3,858,494	12,598	2,481,504	1,247,588
1983	33,506,155	24,998,758	-17,801	24,980,957	2,531,847	-367,839	22,081,271	7,265,416	4,159,468	13,485	2,484,786	1,260,590
1984	36,970,323	27,687,282	77,105	27,764,387	2,894,145	-391,324	24,478,918	8,161,579	4,329,826	14,806	2,496,966	1,314,730
1985	39,370,361	29,680,497	26,835	29,707,332	3,167,919	-393,375	26,146,038	8,666,055	4,558,268	15,661	2,513,864	1,347,519
1986	41,603,025	31,499,199	67,476	31,566,675	3,395,482	-398,472	27,772,721	9,098,792	4,731,512	16,450	2,529,039	1,385,583
1987	43,924,851	33,522,476	101,578	33,624,054	3,567,501	-390,140	29,666,413	9,389,500	4,868,938	17,268	2,543,754	1,403,758
1988	46,887,898	35,977,104	77,380	36,054,484	3,937,046	-386,681	31,730,757	10,051,400	5,105,741	18,367	2,552,771	1,427,738
1989	50,139,906	38,095,922	207,195	38,303,117	4,186,353	-389,975	33,726,789	10,882,008	5,531,109	19,625	2,554,879	1,452,169
1990	52,807,581	39,840,607	125,746	39,966,353	4,493,631	-371,476	35,101,246	11,700,813	6,005,522	20,588	2,565,020	1,464,298
1991	54,053,990	40,335,399	77,097	40,412,496	4,633,512	-368,334	35,410,650	11,815,333	6,828,007	20,956	2,579,363	1,442,695
1992	57,183,643	42,531,335	181,608	42,712,943	4,825,152	-374,638	37,513,153	12,283,165	7,387,325	22,075	2,590,410	1,439,015
1993	59,539,972	44,105,797	130,440	44,236,237	5,027,815	-386,503	38,821,919	12,889,873	7,828,180	22,848	2,605,968	1,468,529
1994	62,724,268	46,599,541	147,419	46,746,960	5,400,715	-422,911	40,923,334	13,656,805	8,144,129	23,970	2,616,756	1,496,005
1995	66,484,767	49,464,297	47,068	49,511,365	5,725,922	-455,454	43,329,989	14,535,648	8,619,130	25,285	2,629,433	1,529,685
1996	69,654,390	51,836,192	178,404	52,014,596	5,942,880	-492,103	45,579,613	15,230,695	8,844,082	26,383	2,640,161	1,555,249
1997	73,913,556	55,200,184	166,447	55,366,631	6,303,331	-532,696	48,530,604	16,210,545	9,172,407	27,880	2,651,165	1,579,818
1998	77,707,545	58,030,430	135,961	58,166,391	6,597,976	-555,125	51,013,290	17,228,889	9,465,366	29,246	2,657,031	1,603,406
1999	80,527,933	61,207,796	103,792	61,311,588	6,892,404	-603,846	53,815,338	16,895,307	9,817,288	30,201	2,666,413	1,620,760
2000	85,825,787	64,946,486	150,002	65,096,488	7,250,091	-652,147	57,194,250	18,216,558	10,414,979	32,039	2,678,822	1,642,704
2001	88,244,104	67,091,732	155,461	67,247,193	7,427,797	-667,647	59,151,749	17,738,569	11,353,786	32,803	2,690,131	1,641,921
2002	90,725,488	69,379,548	72,587	69,452,135	7,621,908	-684,702	61,145,525	17,582,801	11,997,162	33,601	2,700,121	1,638,359
2003	93,708,057	71,173,934	190,477	71,364,411	7,853,140	-702,579	62,808,692	18,459,221	12,440,144	34,565	2,711,031	1,641,157
2004	97,417,895	73,992,093	358,676	74,350,769	8,098,003	-700,014	65,552,752	18,872,096	12,993,047	35,791	2,721,868	1,648,824
2005	101,538,243	76,837,669	182,683	77,020,352	8,475,005	-707,874	67,837,473	19,735,487	13,965,283	37,189	2,730,316	1,669,564
2006	108,453,209	80,699,238	180,010	80,879,248	8,962,956	-706,814	71,209,478	22,496,580	14,747,151	39,520	2,744,265	1,690,675
2007	112,784,148	83,119,481	191,276	83,310,757	9,349,247	-664,688	73,296,822	23,621,926	15,865,400	40,929	2,755,581	1,714,159
2008	118,433,498	86,909,181	301,318	87,210,499	9,789,557	-694,553	76,726,389	24,004,081	17,703,028	42,790	2,767,776	1,714,077
2009	114,104,324	84,126,634	214,212	84,340,846	9,378,055	-482,007	74,480,784	20,423,240	19,200,300	41,054	2,779,404	1,660,457
2010	118,254,730	85,736,860	256,827	85,993,687	9,394,663	-263,988	76,335,036	21,358,421	20,561,273	42,387	2,789,860	1,644,561
2011	122,390,434	88,003,107	380,249	88,383,356	8,676,396	-240,060	79,466,900	22,291,020	20,632,514	43,808	2,793,774	1,664,110
2012	130,132,363	91,500,542	205,401	91,705,943	8,905,081	-342,203	82,458,659	26,869,680	20,804,024	46,540	2,796,137	1,667,792
2013	129,117,041	93,684,334	554,118	94,238,452	10,326,379	-345,199	83,566,874	24,136,962	21,413,205	46,119	2,799,644	1,686,296
2014	134,090,479	95,363,547	317,410	95,680,957	10,605,594	-371,271	84,704,092	27,329,127	22,057,260	47,823	2,803,901	1,702,952
2015	138,690,458	98,559,752	5,827	98,565,579	11,106,692	-393,583	87,065,304	28,373,586	23,251,568	49,403	2,807,321	1,733,548
2016	142,141,637	100,357,900	185,419	100,543,319	11,335,399	-410,473	88,797,447	29,472,415	23,871,775	50,642	2,806,782	1,755,690
2017	147,099,975	103,694,657	112,101	103,806,758	11,674,722	-428,141	91,703,895	30,924,242	24,471,838	52,398	2,807,338	1,774,691
2018	154,995,620	154,852,703	142,917	108,557,879	12,167,069	-491,722	95,899,088	33,615,828	25,480,704	55,277	2,803,958	1,792,387
2019	159,567,017	159,471,008	96,009	112,322,741	12,638,405	-549,650	99,134,686	33,901,956	26,530,375	56,923	2,803,228	1,813,241

Personal Income and Employment by Area: Salem, OR

(Thousands of dollars, except as noted.)

| Year | Personal income, total | Earnings by place of work | | | Less: Contributions for government social insurance | Plus: Adjustment for residence | Equals: Net earnings by place of residence | Plus: Dividends, interest, and rent | Plus: Personal current transfer receipts | Per capita personal income (dollars) | Population (persons) | Total employment |
		Nonfarm	Farm	Total								
1970	707,190	497,430	23,467	520,897	36,554	8,890	493,233	138,172	75,785	3,769	187,645	76,935
1971	783,788	551,053	23,671	574,724	42,020	11,900	544,604	152,032	87,152	4,058	193,158	78,983
1972	875,726	623,246	21,463	644,709	50,028	16,462	611,143	167,036	97,547	4,445	197,027	82,993
1973	1,010,102	700,872	48,661	749,533	64,980	22,016	706,569	189,186	114,347	5,061	199,576	88,074
1974	1,156,016	786,042	55,197	841,239	75,685	28,500	794,054	220,482	141,480	5,590	206,796	91,136
1975	1,293,023	869,591	43,561	913,152	81,630	33,280	864,802	254,670	173,551	6,115	211,453	93,710
1976	1,486,085	1,014,105	49,548	1,063,653	95,898	42,857	1,010,612	282,866	192,607	6,796	218,659	99,232
1977	1,674,490	1,154,268	43,377	1,197,645	110,810	53,904	1,140,739	325,096	208,655	7,330	228,455	106,818
1978	1,914,276	1,329,344	38,807	1,368,151	131,790	71,191	1,307,552	376,137	230,587	8,075	237,065	113,216
1979	2,193,942	1,498,602	43,798	1,542,400	154,503	113,832	1,501,729	431,433	260,780	9,006	243,606	118,107
1980	2,452,241	1,579,499	60,347	1,639,846	164,441	143,393	1,618,798	519,896	313,547	9,776	250,849	117,287
1981	2,631,835	1,663,400	54,163	1,717,563	185,419	110,829	1,642,973	626,323	362,539	10,355	254,150	115,262
1982	2,710,730	1,646,286	49,451	1,695,737	185,816	105,304	1,615,225	690,736	404,769	10,637	254,850	111,166
1983	2,868,017	1,727,168	43,087	1,770,255	194,488	104,292	1,680,059	751,649	436,309	11,230	255,400	113,893
1984	3,078,392	1,872,442	53,676	1,926,118	216,849	104,844	1,814,113	813,410	450,869	12,000	256,540	117,372
1985	3,263,800	2,011,294	58,153	2,069,447	235,002	97,362	1,931,807	853,345	478,648	12,638	258,250	121,772
1986	3,446,279	2,134,365	88,334	2,222,699	249,493	93,138	2,066,344	883,071	496,864	13,233	260,438	125,261
1987	3,637,644	2,320,091	88,904	2,408,995	267,136	86,404	2,228,263	890,274	519,107	13,829	263,037	132,049
1988	3,980,311	2,561,451	142,866	2,704,317	310,080	88,211	2,482,448	940,907	556,956	14,839	268,239	137,126
1989	4,380,607	2,830,347	126,180	2,956,527	343,335	85,297	2,698,489	1,065,533	616,585	16,011	273,600	141,107
1990	4,737,469	3,135,137	141,187	3,276,324	386,738	75,760	2,965,346	1,098,870	673,253	16,928	279,862	146,094
1991	5,049,509	3,357,825	156,888	3,514,713	418,866	75,571	3,171,418	1,140,066	738,025	17,582	287,202	147,147
1992	5,404,705	3,631,579	167,302	3,798,881	448,813	81,060	3,431,128	1,158,711	814,866	18,319	295,039	149,319
1993	5,772,272	3,884,549	165,973	4,050,522	478,794	91,775	3,663,503	1,228,881	879,888	19,038	303,205	154,522
1994	6,202,984	4,240,353	167,168	4,407,521	525,098	105,599	3,988,022	1,304,003	910,959	19,969	310,626	161,451
1995	6,624,550	4,446,719	145,375	4,592,094	555,452	133,999	4,170,641	1,438,859	1,015,050	20,856	317,638	165,842
1996	7,134,004	4,769,686	195,494	4,965,180	600,873	166,841	4,531,148	1,520,990	1,081,866	21,988	324,457	172,393
1997	7,438,303	4,934,337	208,048	5,142,385	622,115	199,517	4,719,787	1,600,740	1,117,776	22,426	331,688	176,546
1998	7,854,677	5,285,780	203,888	5,489,668	661,176	215,218	5,043,710	1,610,642	1,200,325	23,220	338,269	178,362
1999	8,280,040	5,641,810	226,326	5,868,136	697,332	221,906	5,392,710	1,563,898	1,323,432	24,071	343,985	181,037
2000	8,684,542	5,955,241	179,144	6,134,385	733,103	269,546	5,670,828	1,673,104	1,340,610	24,955	348,007	183,466
2001	8,804,937	5,918,597	202,573	6,121,170	722,960	242,202	5,640,412	1,666,409	1,498,116	25,044	351,581	182,319
2002	8,916,333	6,187,320	179,447	6,366,767	760,527	179,488	5,785,728	1,558,050	1,572,555	24,999	356,668	184,073
2003	9,302,876	6,425,471	236,882	6,662,353	792,642	113,687	5,983,398	1,685,461	1,634,017	25,814	360,377	187,787
2004	9,659,668	6,678,260	248,811	6,927,071	837,289	104,151	6,193,933	1,752,956	1,712,779	26,559	363,708	192,318
2005	10,169,207	7,119,875	257,584	7,377,459	895,410	84,509	6,566,558	1,766,133	1,836,516	27,630	368,046	197,802
2006	11,213,739	7,765,817	316,315	8,082,132	973,152	68,595	7,177,575	2,052,874	1,983,290	29,958	374,317	202,453
2007	11,613,114	7,964,555	300,092	8,264,647	1,014,511	31,906	7,282,042	2,175,588	2,155,484	30,581	379,755	207,319
2008	12,257,097	8,208,399	302,618	8,511,017	1,044,239	-73,684	7,393,094	2,306,840	2,557,163	31,913	384,075	205,685
2009	12,054,414	7,957,532	267,573	8,225,105	1,016,369	-182,714	7,026,022	2,149,031	2,879,361	31,042	388,323	198,184
2010	12,296,948	8,142,866	256,779	8,399,645	1,032,969	-301,570	7,065,106	2,085,559	3,146,283	31,414	391,453	195,920
2011	12,750,696	8,204,543	265,718	8,470,261	920,320	-252,852	7,297,089	2,228,587	3,225,020	32,402	393,520	194,633
2012	13,166,423	8,472,082	295,610	8,767,692	947,860	-190,764	7,629,068	2,344,722	3,192,633	33,267	395,782	194,151
2013	13,505,532	8,814,149	338,902	9,153,051	1,115,089	-214,443	7,823,519	2,373,017	3,308,996	33,937	397,963	197,390
2014	14,507,321	9,409,148	315,741	9,724,889	1,200,116	-292,949	8,231,824	2,597,867	3,677,630	36,077	402,117	204,138
2015	15,614,140	10,086,318	366,601	10,452,919	1,266,972	-290,433	8,895,514	2,789,526	3,929,100	38,239	408,326	209,466
2016	16,461,364	10,793,703	342,082	11,135,785	1,344,560	-307,956	9,483,269	2,929,581	4,048,514	39,456	417,208	214,614
2017	17,368,676	11,670,178	318,923	11,989,101	1,460,307	-388,477	10,140,317	3,088,536	4,139,823	40,869	424,982	224,936
2018	18,520,089	18,257,833	262,256	12,707,092	1,527,856	-423,489	10,755,747	3,368,956	4,395,386	43,030	430,404	227,895
2019	19,399,478	19,156,869	242,609	13,319,881	1,613,676	-392,785	11,313,420	3,457,093	4,628,965	44,709	433,903	232,196

Personal Income and Employment by Area: Salinas, CA

(Thousands of dollars, except as noted.)

Year	Personal income, total	Earnings by place of work			Less: Contributions for government social insurance	Plus: Adjustment for residence	Equals: Net earnings by place of residence	Plus: Dividends, interest, and rent	Plus: Personal current transfer receipts	Per capita personal income (dollars)	Population (persons)	Total employment
		Nonfarm	Farm	Total								
1970	1,364,273	908,393	109,573	1,017,966	59,309	-5,039	953,618	318,375	92,280	5,496	248,235	134,519
1971	1,537,357	1,026,264	131,596	1,157,860	70,447	-6,561	1,080,852	350,977	105,528	6,083	252,730	140,268
1972	1,643,539	1,078,857	166,158	1,245,015	76,423	-7,441	1,161,151	366,542	115,846	6,467	254,140	136,674
1973	1,839,849	1,205,691	195,923	1,401,614	94,561	-9,913	1,297,140	412,540	130,169	7,208	255,261	144,582
1974	2,050,129	1,301,198	253,541	1,554,739	106,099	-12,791	1,435,849	460,329	153,951	7,779	263,534	147,280
1975	2,188,715	1,419,258	209,655	1,628,913	117,505	-15,952	1,495,456	495,044	198,215	8,077	270,976	150,780
1976	2,290,452	1,493,285	201,272	1,694,557	125,970	-15,459	1,553,128	519,021	218,303	8,300	275,942	148,250
1977	2,521,308	1,652,411	220,800	1,873,211	140,822	-16,524	1,715,865	576,585	228,858	8,955	281,545	154,161
1978	2,899,743	1,857,164	299,584	2,156,748	158,856	-15,010	1,982,882	666,541	250,320	10,206	284,129	158,622
1979	3,121,866	2,016,145	273,706	2,289,851	179,633	-17,501	2,092,717	752,302	276,847	10,882	286,882	162,099
1980	3,501,254	2,145,504	343,054	2,488,558	186,003	-12,708	2,289,847	877,336	334,071	11,974	292,406	160,320
1981	4,033,236	2,365,806	427,400	2,793,206	221,643	-2,554	2,569,009	1,076,644	387,583	13,459	299,677	161,159
1982	4,272,966	2,537,836	432,145	2,969,981	239,698	-4,451	2,725,832	1,146,642	400,492	13,953	306,241	161,196
1983	4,758,124	2,720,079	634,627	3,354,706	264,688	1,956	3,091,974	1,231,943	434,207	15,168	313,698	164,668
1984	5,114,759	3,006,222	558,396	3,564,618	304,397	5,627	3,265,848	1,394,145	454,766	15,911	321,458	170,038
1985	5,407,320	3,306,951	482,151	3,789,102	338,804	102	3,450,400	1,466,090	490,830	16,481	328,102	175,384
1986	5,844,931	3,586,025	572,946	4,158,971	371,761	1,492	3,788,702	1,526,682	529,547	17,403	335,849	176,778
1987	6,250,071	3,910,850	614,300	4,525,150	409,511	4,394	4,120,033	1,585,503	544,535	18,314	341,268	183,254
1988	6,594,700	4,202,186	558,487	4,760,673	460,039	13,453	4,314,087	1,692,935	587,678	19,063	345,947	190,927
1989	6,966,343	4,411,361	490,591	4,901,952	489,844	21,186	4,433,294	1,886,993	646,056	19,911	349,872	194,992
1990	7,392,202	4,715,713	541,806	5,257,519	529,597	24,555	4,752,477	1,920,821	718,904	20,675	357,535	200,058
1991	7,561,106	4,952,300	414,620	5,366,920	561,913	29,166	4,834,173	1,926,851	800,082	20,726	364,805	200,838
1992	8,218,602	5,274,926	607,943	5,882,869	598,204	31,581	5,316,246	1,978,495	923,861	22,101	371,860	195,598
1993	8,362,212	5,137,732	779,971	5,917,703	582,567	51,624	5,386,760	2,000,616	974,836	22,540	371,002	191,239
1994	8,382,230	5,092,900	765,365	5,858,265	572,436	73,055	5,358,884	2,037,825	985,521	23,789	352,363	183,917
1995	8,927,730	5,298,408	888,082	6,186,490	585,085	99,359	5,700,764	2,192,815	1,034,151	25,114	355,486	187,617
1996	9,262,660	5,615,374	717,944	6,333,318	598,841	120,498	5,854,975	2,320,897	1,086,788	25,572	362,215	195,179
1997	10,006,265	5,939,085	980,677	6,919,762	622,192	149,070	6,446,640	2,452,090	1,107,535	26,556	376,794	197,557
1998	10,941,630	6,463,260	1,063,161	7,526,421	659,478	178,068	7,045,011	2,721,682	1,174,937	28,208	387,889	208,782
1999	11,644,938	7,069,718	1,111,316	8,181,034	722,519	221,690	7,680,205	2,725,250	1,239,483	29,387	396,267	218,234
2000	12,838,491	7,660,250	1,377,199	9,037,449	776,463	360,279	8,621,265	2,932,343	1,284,883	31,858	402,990	218,487
2001	12,943,849	8,100,201	1,101,554	9,201,755	876,017	262,067	8,587,805	2,950,713	1,405,331	31,797	407,082	217,510
2002	13,087,436	8,491,992	1,206,069	9,698,061	931,657	192,870	8,959,274	2,615,266	1,512,896	32,000	408,977	221,129
2003	13,739,960	8,924,459	1,334,863	10,259,322	998,374	160,161	9,421,109	2,735,240	1,583,611	33,535	409,725	223,693
2004	14,165,417	9,151,144	1,103,064	10,254,208	1,076,381	156,293	9,334,120	3,180,476	1,650,821	34,657	408,731	222,456
2005	14,737,704	9,491,733	1,182,208	10,673,941	1,106,011	130,296	9,698,226	3,316,715	1,722,763	36,377	405,139	221,519
2006	15,998,343	10,059,586	1,212,734	11,272,320	1,127,782	162,089	10,306,627	3,844,979	1,846,737	39,814	401,831	219,477
2007	16,620,656	10,465,288	1,113,966	11,579,254	1,147,486	173,220	10,604,988	4,077,261	1,938,407	41,306	402,376	224,438
2008	16,658,202	10,570,986	963,492	11,534,478	1,180,782	91,771	10,445,467	4,019,784	2,192,951	41,028	406,022	223,750
2009	16,647,065	10,358,460	1,486,379	11,844,839	1,172,207	14,871	10,687,503	3,552,132	2,407,430	40,577	410,263	217,029
2010	17,256,773	10,901,009	1,339,454	12,240,463	1,180,070	-23,064	11,037,329	3,556,406	2,663,038	41,435	416,475	220,156
2011	17,837,598	11,165,586	1,139,764	12,305,350	1,099,407	-34,647	11,171,296	3,965,075	2,701,227	42,353	421,162	221,085
2012	18,671,400	11,515,948	1,374,325	12,890,273	1,135,055	-97,301	11,657,917	4,295,522	2,717,961	43,820	426,094	225,859
2013	19,149,968	11,747,399	1,737,766	13,485,165	1,297,723	-131,544	12,055,898	4,262,155	2,831,915	44,703	428,382	230,857
2014	20,400,730	12,358,554	1,766,116	14,124,670	1,350,971	-119,669	12,654,030	4,781,863	2,964,837	47,398	430,416	238,959
2015	22,310,851	13,215,820	2,372,133	15,587,953	1,416,683	-128,079	14,043,191	5,087,483	3,180,177	51,553	432,774	244,341
2016	22,828,552	13,782,501	1,966,474	15,748,975	1,495,117	-101,375	14,152,483	5,385,064	3,291,005	52,316	436,363	248,168
2017	23,819,797	14,490,415	2,083,774	16,574,189	1,575,219	-86,417	14,912,553	5,636,738	3,270,506	54,395	437,907	250,413
2018	24,576,499	22,679,160	1,897,339	17,071,196	1,635,960	-103,119	15,332,117	5,784,191	3,460,191	56,634	433,950	256,579
2019	25,973,189	23,600,558	2,372,631	18,184,377	1,738,022	-19,595	16,426,760	5,875,145	3,671,284	59,838	434,061	261,783

Personal Income and Employment by Area: Salisbury, MD-DE

(Thousands of dollars, except as noted.)

Year	Personal income, total	Earnings by place of work			Less: Contributions for government social insurance	Plus: Adjustment for residence	Equals: Net earnings by place of residence	Plus: Dividends, interest, and rent	Plus: Personal current transfer receipts	Per capita personal income (dollars)	Population (persons)	Total employment
		Nonfarm	Farm	Total								
1970	658,152	486,145	39,134	525,279	33,261	7,876	499,894	95,352	62,906	3,681	178,804	92,457
1971	711,893	526,723	34,025	560,748	37,313	9,158	532,593	105,311	73,989	3,858	184,503	94,642
1972	806,771	594,576	50,343	644,919	44,245	8,497	609,171	116,941	80,659	4,316	186,939	99,270
1973	954,731	665,628	108,938	774,566	57,552	7,754	724,768	136,066	93,897	4,998	191,029	102,800
1974	986,538	718,379	51,919	770,298	64,473	8,269	714,094	158,241	114,203	5,034	195,957	101,927
1975	1,127,097	762,703	102,351	865,054	67,220	8,557	806,391	172,061	148,645	5,637	199,933	99,153
1976	1,214,565	846,600	83,284	929,884	75,284	9,219	863,819	188,973	161,773	5,961	203,759	100,183
1977	1,284,161	910,541	55,376	965,917	81,243	10,762	895,436	212,180	176,545	6,210	206,805	101,923
1978	1,431,621	1,036,920	55,028	1,091,948	94,793	5,284	1,002,439	236,443	192,739	6,846	209,113	107,617
1979	1,549,797	1,119,731	42,052	1,161,783	107,333	1,835	1,056,285	270,081	223,431	7,310	212,004	108,124
1980	1,685,752	1,189,237	2,748	1,191,985	114,582	-2,116	1,075,287	339,495	270,970	7,923	212,780	106,381
1981	1,900,453	1,265,302	39,464	1,304,766	131,338	-3,226	1,170,202	415,923	314,328	8,923	212,984	107,068
1982	2,101,050	1,351,180	71,747	1,422,927	142,762	-4,274	1,275,891	483,343	341,816	9,842	213,485	108,398
1983	2,297,712	1,524,082	62,937	1,587,019	162,602	-9,357	1,415,060	513,204	369,448	10,637	216,011	116,348
1984	2,615,628	1,710,511	128,482	1,838,993	187,167	-7,875	1,643,951	578,964	392,713	11,869	220,383	121,778
1985	2,866,288	1,898,715	135,396	2,034,111	210,083	-8,010	1,816,018	625,504	424,766	12,735	225,063	127,936
1986	3,195,261	2,083,972	213,375	2,297,347	232,978	-1,797	2,062,572	683,353	449,336	13,918	229,583	132,093
1987	3,439,578	2,303,173	168,265	2,471,438	253,922	5,930	2,223,446	729,510	486,622	14,758	233,065	137,270
1988	3,783,146	2,493,068	239,183	2,732,251	284,727	17,149	2,464,673	788,307	530,166	15,862	238,509	141,970
1989	4,114,163	2,640,770	261,186	2,901,956	304,720	29,539	2,626,775	911,154	576,234	16,959	242,598	143,143
1990	4,290,855	2,848,500	168,364	3,016,864	326,820	42,834	2,732,878	913,988	643,989	17,327	247,645	146,525
1991	4,549,706	2,965,262	157,351	3,122,613	343,089	58,931	2,838,455	984,261	726,990	17,895	254,246	145,358
1992	4,778,332	3,115,036	134,066	3,249,102	356,748	75,917	2,968,271	1,002,392	807,669	18,327	260,733	145,227
1993	4,973,953	3,243,376	135,303	3,378,679	375,201	92,658	3,096,136	1,014,358	863,459	18,570	267,853	147,101
1994	5,326,648	3,437,550	144,446	3,581,996	402,858	112,107	3,291,245	1,105,982	929,421	19,397	274,618	150,301
1995	5,676,887	3,614,769	113,580	3,728,349	423,941	133,694	3,438,102	1,215,308	1,023,477	20,171	281,441	157,221
1996	6,135,543	3,780,624	166,396	3,947,020	437,628	156,437	3,665,829	1,328,534	1,141,180	21,262	288,563	160,039
1997	6,499,903	4,025,886	135,267	4,161,153	460,761	174,254	3,874,646	1,446,075	1,179,182	22,051	294,772	164,110
1998	7,065,294	4,384,856	176,501	4,561,357	487,942	204,393	4,277,808	1,513,290	1,274,196	23,447	301,328	166,774
1999	7,618,103	4,795,480	179,994	4,975,474	514,594	237,388	4,698,268	1,559,272	1,360,563	24,775	307,487	171,319
2000	8,233,415	5,181,591	170,416	5,352,007	540,312	273,448	5,085,143	1,692,347	1,455,925	26,242	313,744	176,762
2001	8,931,902	5,565,061	261,579	5,826,640	577,153	307,465	5,556,952	1,756,266	1,618,684	27,988	319,128	179,323
2002	9,171,908	5,845,312	90,914	5,936,226	610,928	344,187	5,669,485	1,757,071	1,745,352	28,216	325,063	182,888
2003	9,845,563	6,267,003	205,138	6,472,141	650,030	378,553	6,200,664	1,762,353	1,882,546	29,641	332,157	184,905
2004	10,942,209	6,951,648	306,011	7,257,659	717,144	423,285	6,963,800	1,952,573	2,025,836	32,323	338,528	191,815
2005	11,515,078	7,256,435	321,491	7,577,926	776,317	469,174	7,270,783	2,033,879	2,210,416	33,309	345,704	197,589
2006	12,154,419	7,649,210	227,415	7,876,625	834,141	508,821	7,551,305	2,240,568	2,362,546	34,351	353,828	203,079
2007	12,800,591	7,722,737	231,207	7,953,944	869,763	558,034	7,642,215	2,580,640	2,577,736	35,467	360,918	205,892
2008	13,487,641	7,733,308	274,934	8,008,242	888,804	589,706	7,709,144	2,824,392	2,954,105	36,774	366,772	203,789
2009	13,258,432	7,411,032	292,737	7,703,769	877,825	589,346	7,415,290	2,613,972	3,229,170	35,780	370,558	198,311
2010	13,608,606	7,575,350	260,991	7,836,341	905,564	592,160	7,522,937	2,597,226	3,488,443	36,307	374,823	197,126
2011	14,317,898	7,764,306	229,372	7,993,678	815,731	623,732	7,801,679	2,904,654	3,611,565	37,845	378,331	196,549
2012	14,977,602	8,119,102	284,719	8,403,821	849,043	645,758	8,200,536	3,061,559	3,715,507	39,257	381,524	199,150
2013	15,663,722	8,623,983	490,851	9,114,834	982,694	643,079	8,775,219	3,006,769	3,881,734	40,689	384,965	201,905
2014	16,546,005	9,024,419	528,836	9,553,255	1,034,525	660,103	9,178,833	3,260,261	4,106,911	42,492	389,391	206,058
2015	17,873,899	9,989,886	411,794	10,401,680	1,108,652	678,190	9,971,218	3,534,261	4,368,420	45,320	394,393	210,641
2016	18,091,202	10,022,077	331,624	10,353,701	1,140,276	678,070	9,891,495	3,612,075	4,587,632	45,225	400,025	215,345
2017	18,692,090	10,126,542	445,722	10,572,264	1,181,802	689,850	10,080,312	3,805,579	4,806,199	46,056	405,853	218,884
2018	19,923,630	19,428,857	494,773	11,189,165	1,253,450	717,956	10,653,671	4,145,217	5,124,742	48,594	409,999	224,246
2019	20,567,257	20,187,893	379,364	11,507,610	1,309,549	739,583	10,937,644	4,187,766	5,441,847	49,473	415,726	227,831

Personal Income and Employment by Area: Salt Lake City, UT

(Thousands of dollars, except as noted.)

Year	Personal income, total	Earnings by place of work			Less: Contributions for government social insurance	Plus: Adjustment for residence	Equals: Net earnings by place of residence	Plus: Dividends, interest, and rent	Plus: Personal current transfer receipts	Per capita personal income (dollars)	Population (persons)	Total employment
		Nonfarm	Farm	Total								
1970	1,887,139	1,625,670	6,530	1,632,200	109,178	-61,575	1,461,447	282,894	142,798	3,908	482,939	228,004
1971	2,096,973	1,785,767	6,465	1,792,232	124,888	-54,279	1,613,065	317,060	166,848	4,203	498,890	235,582
1972	2,340,137	2,008,657	8,087	2,016,744	147,664	-73,160	1,795,920	353,522	190,695	4,585	510,409	248,748
1973	2,596,645	2,259,655	11,838	2,271,493	192,936	-88,875	1,989,682	386,153	220,810	4,955	524,033	265,327
1974	2,930,323	2,561,674	7,010	2,568,684	225,365	-108,929	2,234,390	446,637	249,296	5,463	536,395	278,466
1975	3,277,475	2,825,191	5,609	2,830,800	244,183	-119,688	2,466,929	492,684	317,862	5,942	551,569	282,198
1976	3,687,002	3,212,485	6,480	3,218,965	282,242	-137,783	2,798,940	544,888	343,174	6,471	569,758	295,659
1977	4,174,375	3,682,801	4,582	3,687,383	323,489	-167,761	3,196,133	610,506	367,736	7,115	586,735	312,954
1978	4,790,945	4,255,876	4,779	4,260,655	381,656	-207,657	3,671,342	713,905	405,698	7,906	605,964	333,838
1979	5,366,122	4,790,583	5,104	4,795,687	452,551	-245,076	4,098,060	809,542	458,520	8,574	625,894	346,245
1980	6,010,564	5,311,974	3,846	5,315,820	505,939	-295,099	4,514,782	956,891	538,891	9,244	650,232	350,072
1981	6,786,354	5,926,180	3,152	5,929,332	608,290	-323,929	4,997,113	1,156,489	632,752	10,141	669,210	353,355
1982	7,377,345	6,341,284	-435	6,340,849	662,047	-354,269	5,324,533	1,326,210	726,602	10,773	684,802	359,618
1983	7,938,532	6,850,557	3,928	6,854,485	720,356	-436,077	5,698,052	1,457,690	782,790	11,334	700,444	367,055
1984	8,749,272	7,590,719	4,728	7,595,447	819,857	-485,244	6,290,346	1,651,742	807,184	12,272	712,930	388,686
1985	9,326,090	8,078,911	4,001	8,082,912	883,267	-521,418	6,678,227	1,768,486	879,377	12,937	720,877	403,373
1986	9,778,716	8,452,917	4,672	8,457,589	928,001	-557,301	6,972,287	1,858,594	947,835	13,396	729,985	409,417
1987	10,253,312	8,920,379	3,937	8,924,316	972,698	-633,092	7,318,526	1,946,270	988,516	13,932	735,973	423,933
1988	10,856,706	9,483,961	9,538	9,493,499	1,079,208	-678,064	7,736,227	2,086,810	1,033,669	14,642	741,463	438,149
1989	11,553,943	10,081,428	9,004	10,090,432	1,166,002	-728,361	8,196,069	2,212,979	1,144,895	15,494	745,687	451,777
1990	12,463,161	10,985,013	12,261	10,997,274	1,314,893	-881,417	8,800,964	2,406,452	1,255,745	16,472	756,611	470,479
1991	13,277,724	11,829,034	8,911	11,837,945	1,434,865	-999,305	9,403,775	2,484,278	1,389,671	17,060	778,307	481,251
1992	14,300,298	12,948,213	11,970	12,960,183	1,557,242	-1,188,871	10,214,070	2,564,901	1,521,327	17,825	802,260	489,997
1993	15,339,419	14,057,428	14,575	14,072,003	1,697,018	-1,348,789	11,026,196	2,690,359	1,622,864	18,557	826,621	518,184
1994	16,634,537	15,340,434	9,681	15,350,115	1,863,865	-1,494,530	11,991,720	2,992,243	1,650,574	19,602	848,617	547,370
1995	18,166,502	16,617,738	8,896	16,626,634	2,023,177	-1,641,756	12,961,701	3,425,198	1,779,603	20,969	866,353	571,123
1996	19,820,021	18,097,994	6,920	18,104,914	2,154,586	-1,848,172	14,102,156	3,846,942	1,870,923	22,410	884,440	602,150
1997	21,523,760	19,840,938	6,029	19,846,967	2,331,286	-2,093,772	15,421,909	4,166,408	1,935,443	23,793	904,628	624,849
1998	23,148,945	21,294,628	5,275	21,299,903	2,485,051	-2,325,586	16,489,266	4,654,712	2,004,967	25,239	917,191	645,322
1999	24,474,982	22,929,698	8,830	22,938,528	2,633,050	-2,563,981	17,741,497	4,624,154	2,109,331	26,340	929,195	656,570
2000	26,305,209	24,534,035	7,820	24,541,855	2,823,963	-2,756,536	18,961,356	5,079,958	2,263,895	27,909	942,537	677,903
2001	26,724,866	24,901,793	10,222	24,912,015	2,922,942	-2,901,974	19,087,099	5,164,717	2,473,050	28,011	954,081	680,542
2002	27,411,496	25,186,236	4,018	25,190,254	2,959,451	-2,933,696	19,297,107	5,410,100	2,704,289	28,460	963,150	674,074
2003	28,015,374	25,631,619	4,598	25,636,217	3,035,689	-2,965,694	19,634,834	5,523,764	2,856,776	28,839	971,454	671,950
2004	29,674,202	27,422,989	5,562	27,428,551	3,267,302	-3,258,686	20,902,563	5,765,738	3,005,901	30,217	982,034	685,605
2005	32,595,526	29,809,732	5,241	29,814,973	3,542,607	-3,603,624	22,668,742	6,652,965	3,273,819	32,686	997,221	712,951
2006	36,498,191	33,444,689	7,903	33,452,592	3,867,470	-4,114,909	25,470,213	7,437,238	3,590,740	35,843	1,018,281	745,183
2007	38,952,027	36,067,143	6,124	36,073,267	4,170,145	-4,751,856	27,151,266	7,929,078	3,871,683	37,543	1,037,540	781,703
2008	40,352,873	36,662,264	6,959	36,669,223	4,253,775	-5,022,842	27,392,606	8,465,431	4,494,836	38,232	1,055,462	787,814
2009	38,350,203	35,203,945	8,462	35,212,407	4,138,456	-5,104,555	25,969,396	7,391,194	4,989,613	35,707	1,074,013	761,073
2010	39,391,250	35,909,933	9,984	35,919,917	4,187,366	-5,324,758	26,407,793	7,464,166	5,519,291	36,090	1,091,460	756,966
2011	42,521,738	38,188,928	13,774	38,202,702	3,971,256	-5,729,995	28,501,451	8,280,373	5,739,914	38,394	1,107,497	776,331
2012	45,679,053	41,534,191	13,548	41,547,739	4,208,808	-6,310,624	31,028,307	8,991,193	5,659,553	40,630	1,124,277	797,545
2013	46,958,055	43,393,580	17,508	43,411,088	4,984,807	-6,527,049	31,899,232	9,191,292	5,867,531	41,138	1,141,470	820,433
2014	49,576,275	45,409,615	16,544	45,426,159	5,219,000	-6,711,237	33,495,922	10,071,762	6,008,591	43,008	1,152,719	839,681
2015	53,358,610	48,320,607	32,343	48,352,950	5,457,880	-7,114,342	35,780,728	11,266,284	6,311,598	45,722	1,167,013	866,965
2016	55,960,332	51,148,443	15,947	51,164,390	5,742,511	-7,796,676	37,625,203	11,661,746	6,673,383	47,185	1,185,978	897,518
2017	58,524,742	53,753,883	17,101	53,770,984	6,136,718	-8,253,531	39,380,735	12,248,738	6,895,269	48,645	1,203,105	918,695
2018	63,554,301	63,546,796	7,505	56,933,388	6,431,062	-8,715,183	41,787,143	14,510,318	7,256,840	52,150	1,218,681	948,248
2019	67,119,992	67,114,722	5,270	60,443,696	6,809,905	-9,276,074	44,357,717	14,980,362	7,781,913	54,450	1,232,696	974,919

Personal Income and Employment by Area: San Angelo, TX

(Thousands of dollars, except as noted.)

Year	Personal income, total	Earnings by place of work			Less: Contributions for government social insurance	Plus: Adjustment for residence	Equals: Net earnings by place of residence	Plus: Dividends, interest, and rent	Plus: Personal current transfer receipts	Per capita personal income (dollars)	Population (persons)	Total employment
		Nonfarm	Farm	Total								
1970	274,804	200,845	11,960	212,805	12,175	-94	200,536	50,442	23,826	3,797	72,383	33,632
1971	295,431	221,069	7,648	228,717	13,922	-597	214,198	53,903	27,330	3,979	74,244	34,481
1972	325,078	242,286	9,757	252,043	15,884	-1,022	235,137	59,636	30,305	4,415	73,632	35,458
1973	364,407	272,260	10,577	282,837	20,456	-1,595	260,786	67,532	36,089	4,799	75,927	37,376
1974	400,364	300,193	6,631	306,824	23,377	-2,089	281,358	76,814	42,192	5,204	76,932	38,027
1975	458,843	339,823	7,359	347,182	26,122	-874	320,186	88,024	50,633	5,831	78,694	39,156
1976	520,931	386,881	14,493	401,374	30,055	-3,325	367,994	96,928	56,009	6,521	79,880	40,777
1977	574,895	435,151	7,780	442,931	34,248	-4,698	403,985	111,059	59,851	7,137	80,554	43,162
1978	659,714	506,560	5,521	512,081	40,621	-5,442	466,018	127,224	66,472	8,046	81,991	45,910
1979	728,495	564,323	2,204	566,527	47,902	-6,486	512,139	140,857	75,499	8,647	84,252	46,828
1980	835,588	639,423	-4,482	634,941	54,785	-8,351	571,805	176,953	86,830	9,635	86,724	48,508
1981	1,008,691	733,106	20,265	753,371	67,730	-7,551	678,090	232,060	98,541	11,373	88,690	50,976
1982	1,131,947	812,924	16,104	829,028	77,391	-7,104	744,533	276,856	110,558	12,246	92,432	53,252
1983	1,218,655	858,708	21,544	880,252	81,255	-7,444	791,553	304,214	122,888	12,671	96,176	53,418
1984	1,305,164	902,172	22,545	924,717	87,329	-4,926	832,462	340,087	132,615	13,326	97,944	54,135
1985	1,330,473	927,533	-13,455	914,078	91,362	-3,077	819,639	366,551	144,283	13,543	98,243	54,124
1986	1,367,478	942,635	2,047	944,682	92,510	-4,088	848,084	362,410	156,984	13,808	99,036	52,823
1987	1,392,153	954,221	12,341	966,562	93,117	-3,104	870,341	356,408	165,404	14,026	99,256	54,435
1988	1,467,300	1,003,300	9,633	1,012,933	100,836	-681	911,416	375,191	180,693	14,642	100,211	55,049
1989	1,558,304	1,022,367	8,076	1,030,443	104,775	1,493	927,161	430,120	201,023	15,378	101,335	54,853
1990	1,616,148	1,073,970	17,952	1,091,922	108,624	5,729	989,027	410,439	216,682	16,174	99,924	54,813
1991	1,671,451	1,139,415	9,223	1,148,638	118,242	5,826	1,036,222	404,375	230,854	16,762	99,719	55,746
1992	1,771,929	1,204,794	13,004	1,217,798	124,399	5,743	1,099,142	406,353	266,434	17,525	101,111	55,914
1993	1,870,317	1,285,193	14,606	1,299,799	132,702	5,071	1,172,168	417,373	280,776	18,364	101,848	57,157
1994	1,939,695	1,317,899	17,100	1,334,999	137,890	5,368	1,202,477	442,908	294,310	18,802	103,167	58,121
1995	2,068,811	1,398,587	11,466	1,410,053	146,192	4,253	1,268,114	476,806	323,891	19,962	103,639	60,203
1996	2,146,922	1,439,705	7,661	1,447,366	149,427	4,443	1,302,382	497,528	347,012	20,530	104,574	61,413
1997	2,262,222	1,523,799	11,208	1,535,007	155,652	8,014	1,387,369	510,590	364,263	21,492	105,261	61,580
1998	2,396,391	1,658,495	5,120	1,663,615	166,782	6,604	1,503,437	523,529	369,425	22,653	105,787	62,568
1999	2,445,851	1,690,721	18,080	1,708,801	170,502	5,816	1,544,115	517,377	384,359	23,149	105,657	62,422
2000	2,560,400	1,747,516	12,313	1,759,829	175,518	7,594	1,591,905	568,565	399,930	24,191	105,841	63,558
2001	2,810,958	1,967,328	30,221	1,997,549	190,727	5,832	1,812,654	567,274	431,030	26,620	105,596	63,898
2002	2,854,318	2,023,239	20,067	2,043,306	195,769	1,352	1,848,889	535,489	469,940	26,996	105,732	63,887
2003	2,978,926	2,086,897	33,804	2,120,701	206,475	2,245	1,916,471	560,497	501,958	28,103	106,002	63,558
2004	3,023,017	2,137,088	31,204	2,168,292	215,759	120	1,952,653	544,739	525,625	28,419	106,373	62,843
2005	3,244,113	2,249,403	36,315	2,285,718	223,666	4,041	2,066,093	606,602	571,418	30,436	106,587	63,244
2006	3,425,245	2,405,615	16,240	2,421,855	230,323	10,449	2,201,981	620,244	603,020	31,782	107,774	64,468
2007	3,604,711	2,435,321	31,437	2,466,758	238,673	24,241	2,252,326	689,393	662,992	33,288	108,289	65,127
2008	4,133,064	2,741,304	-371	2,740,933	257,838	44,061	2,527,156	880,099	725,809	37,845	109,210	66,020
2009	3,902,433	2,612,821	14,294	2,627,115	260,339	19,623	2,386,399	735,326	780,708	35,327	110,466	66,060
2010	4,135,308	2,746,802	36,612	2,783,414	272,363	11,537	2,522,588	757,900	854,820	36,829	112,284	66,639
2011	4,368,770	2,805,908	34,126	2,840,034	253,265	29,038	2,615,807	875,060	877,903	38,544	113,345	67,391
2012	4,642,765	2,992,369	17,130	3,009,499	266,943	14,312	2,756,868	1,018,123	867,774	40,410	114,891	69,369
2013	4,773,730	3,099,389	64,179	3,163,568	311,219	10,657	2,863,006	1,016,575	894,149	41,035	116,333	71,234
2014	5,249,507	3,399,753	48,271	3,448,024	333,207	12,381	3,127,198	1,185,246	937,063	44,497	117,975	72,445
2015	5,122,050	3,293,041	48,156	3,341,197	335,210	8,309	3,014,296	1,114,425	993,329	42,991	119,141	73,145
2016	5,032,190	3,163,190	25,984	3,189,174	332,309	-15,203	2,841,662	1,141,914	1,048,614	42,159	119,362	72,659
2017	5,121,743	3,187,016	32,719	3,219,735	344,246	-10,391	2,865,098	1,190,231	1,066,414	42,847	119,535	73,075
2018	5,784,930	5,767,604	17,326	3,659,470	375,403	-869	3,283,198	1,359,540	1,142,192	47,875	120,834	74,243
2019	6,016,858	5,993,352	23,506	3,824,802	388,905	10,273	3,446,170	1,391,815	1,178,873	49,308	122,027	74,749

Personal Income and Employment by Area: San Antonio-New Braunfels, TX

(Thousands of dollars, except as noted.)

Year	Personal income, total	Earnings by place of work			Less: Contributions for government social insurance	Plus: Adjustment for residence	Equals: Net earnings by place of residence	Plus: Dividends, interest, and rent	Plus: Personal current transfer receipts	Per capita personal income (dollars)	Population (persons)	Total employment
		Nonfarm	Farm	Total								
1970	3,684,643	2,808,085	33,294	2,841,379	159,637	-2,265	2,679,477	731,642	273,524	3,847	957,715	421,654
1971	4,105,585	3,137,631	20,888	3,158,519	186,884	-3,174	2,968,461	817,555	319,569	4,157	987,523	433,674
1972	4,520,504	3,451,810	35,480	3,487,290	213,133	-5,444	3,268,713	891,805	359,986	4,481	1,008,844	443,581
1973	5,041,111	3,811,954	64,331	3,876,285	266,226	-7,895	3,602,164	1,001,863	437,084	4,852	1,038,887	462,283
1974	5,562,333	4,159,699	47,989	4,207,688	302,457	-2,549	3,902,682	1,133,577	526,074	5,271	1,055,225	467,397
1975	6,080,004	4,450,355	47,328	4,497,683	326,809	11,658	4,182,532	1,229,972	667,500	5,712	1,064,486	461,538
1976	6,675,840	4,925,366	40,937	4,966,303	369,354	22,298	4,619,247	1,328,332	728,261	6,161	1,083,489	475,281
1977	7,294,609	5,433,993	20,951	5,454,944	409,680	3,287	5,048,551	1,476,700	769,358	6,598	1,105,551	493,057
1978	8,225,297	6,147,597	12,971	6,160,568	475,334	-3,858	5,681,376	1,695,356	848,565	7,319	1,123,898	515,788
1979	9,307,841	6,954,727	18,472	6,973,199	566,623	2,683	6,409,259	1,920,480	978,102	8,174	1,138,722	535,097
1980	10,651,527	7,921,124	-20,539	7,900,585	654,032	7,779	7,254,332	2,265,769	1,131,426	9,167	1,161,968	557,276
1981	12,197,582	9,017,941	12,971	9,030,912	797,533	22,431	8,255,810	2,669,754	1,272,018	10,275	1,187,117	575,836
1982	13,487,947	9,808,557	11,466	9,820,023	881,171	17,696	8,956,548	3,120,992	1,410,407	11,036	1,222,136	594,500
1983	14,773,312	10,655,606	39,080	10,694,686	976,871	13,015	9,730,830	3,499,009	1,543,473	11,781	1,254,044	611,333
1984	16,570,645	11,970,928	45,086	12,016,014	1,122,939	9,729	10,902,804	3,989,121	1,678,720	12,906	1,283,925	646,427
1985	18,205,892	13,143,116	6,805	13,149,921	1,253,018	11,498	11,908,401	4,506,136	1,791,355	13,819	1,317,439	676,534
1986	19,211,657	13,868,942	12,769	13,881,711	1,318,806	6,446	12,569,351	4,706,010	1,936,296	14,161	1,356,676	685,123
1987	19,644,068	14,195,585	12,077	14,207,662	1,340,468	4,256	12,871,450	4,703,536	2,069,082	14,153	1,387,997	702,912
1988	20,828,129	15,147,620	4,503	15,152,123	1,479,625	3,852	13,676,350	4,941,439	2,210,340	14,936	1,394,458	706,182
1989	22,074,120	15,717,375	31,683	15,749,058	1,567,485	6,649	14,188,222	5,366,478	2,519,420	15,753	1,401,286	713,903
1990	23,224,842	16,526,592	49,940	16,576,532	1,641,022	11,226	14,946,736	5,433,198	2,844,908	16,461	1,410,902	723,234
1991	24,416,180	17,484,395	47,919	17,532,314	1,782,766	15,707	15,765,255	5,526,800	3,124,125	17,026	1,434,060	736,292
1992	26,616,269	19,065,737	71,050	19,136,787	1,937,420	24,978	17,224,345	5,740,114	3,651,810	18,164	1,465,365	752,583
1993	28,290,688	20,432,597	84,225	20,516,822	2,082,417	34,023	18,468,428	5,987,500	3,834,760	18,882	1,498,269	780,913
1994	30,307,687	21,965,642	70,316	22,035,958	2,252,551	38,147	19,821,554	6,353,107	4,133,026	19,742	1,535,185	813,191
1995	32,571,622	23,445,175	61,379	23,506,554	2,412,350	47,951	21,142,155	6,925,206	4,504,261	20,745	1,570,083	847,156
1996	34,380,363	24,775,742	31,257	24,806,999	2,528,201	70,634	22,349,432	7,186,809	4,844,122	21,495	1,599,427	872,230
1997	36,929,120	26,490,210	69,316	26,559,526	2,710,987	91,674	23,940,213	7,895,387	5,093,520	22,674	1,628,676	908,164
1998	39,778,215	28,941,233	60,288	29,001,521	2,918,263	133,187	26,216,445	8,320,922	5,240,848	23,965	1,659,847	931,942
1999	42,103,098	31,240,513	76,901	31,317,414	3,125,547	164,899	28,356,766	8,354,588	5,391,744	24,928	1,689,009	954,739
2000	46,114,509	34,520,529	62,957	34,583,486	3,353,732	212,225	31,441,979	8,964,409	5,708,121	26,811	1,720,003	980,454
2001	48,316,212	36,502,963	71,646	36,574,609	3,536,335	264,991	33,303,265	8,767,601	6,245,346	27,639	1,748,123	993,949
2002	49,770,874	37,763,276	101,424	37,864,700	3,672,280	282,954	34,475,374	8,514,525	6,780,975	27,896	1,784,153	1,004,351
2003	52,655,957	39,856,262	115,505	39,971,767	3,923,100	364,449	36,413,116	8,881,028	7,361,813	28,998	1,815,846	1,010,902
2004	55,164,166	41,781,281	111,933	41,893,214	4,156,254	498,474	38,235,434	9,089,078	7,839,654	29,696	1,857,602	1,028,529
2005	59,416,921	44,057,714	94,676	44,152,390	4,392,382	568,083	40,328,091	10,351,580	8,737,250	31,333	1,896,328	1,064,972
2006	64,969,586	48,043,599	59,558	48,103,157	4,702,399	775,063	44,175,821	11,323,359	9,470,406	33,209	1,956,361	1,110,198
2007	69,296,706	50,137,096	55,350	50,192,446	4,992,629	972,458	46,172,275	12,637,298	10,487,133	34,450	2,011,543	1,153,153
2008	74,682,114	52,743,996	-16,685	52,727,311	5,199,967	1,222,057	48,749,401	13,999,778	11,932,935	36,231	2,061,275	1,178,789
2009	72,859,018	51,583,381	-18,310	51,565,071	5,306,376	1,039,011	47,297,706	12,462,982	13,098,330	34,601	2,105,672	1,171,263
2010	77,285,401	54,219,435	-2,749	54,216,686	5,573,113	921,228	49,564,801	13,113,036	14,607,564	35,897	2,152,961	1,179,723
2011	84,274,754	57,578,291	-1,659	57,576,632	5,210,341	901,494	53,267,785	15,768,113	15,238,856	38,418	2,193,620	1,205,858
2012	87,649,529	60,575,864	16,535	60,592,399	5,467,347	960,106	56,085,158	16,291,427	15,272,944	39,192	2,236,395	1,236,539
2013	91,145,110	64,460,693	95,732	64,556,425	6,445,941	864,279	58,974,763	16,360,566	15,809,781	39,978	2,279,878	1,270,468
2014	99,274,676	70,204,510	57,843	70,262,353	6,876,079	1,006,917	64,393,191	18,118,091	16,763,394	42,636	2,328,419	1,312,470
2015	103,457,659	71,937,177	112,621	72,049,798	7,297,228	968,196	65,720,766	19,802,168	17,934,725	43,487	2,379,054	1,355,451
2016	106,197,224	74,532,405	26,955	74,559,360	7,681,334	895,172	67,773,198	19,550,784	18,873,242	43,771	2,426,211	1,407,272
2017	110,855,039	78,189,018	25,599	78,214,617	8,113,492	960,314	71,061,439	20,411,056	19,382,544	44,808	2,473,974	1,436,173
2018	118,958,647	118,978,435	-19,788	84,098,070	8,503,738	1,062,177	76,656,509	22,012,091	20,290,047	47,349	2,512,379	1,489,074
2019	124,191,616	124,221,893	-30,277	88,153,210	8,853,219	1,105,849	80,405,840	22,384,952	21,400,824	48,684	2,550,960	1,519,276

Personal Income and Employment by Area: San Diego-Chula Vista-Carlsbad, CA

(Thousands of dollars, except as noted.)

| | | | | | Derivation of personal income | | | | | | | |
| | | Earnings by place of work | | | Less: Contributions for government social insurance | Plus: Adjustment for residence | Equals: Net earnings by place of residence | Plus: Dividends, interest, and rent | Plus: Personal current transfer receipts | Per capita personal income (dollars) | Population (persons) | Total employment |
Year	Personal income, total	Nonfarm	Farm	Total								
1970	7,021,079	5,197,882	55,543	5,253,425	330,158	-31,761	4,891,506	1,593,087	536,486	5,140	1,365,976	647,900
1971	7,542,007	5,552,875	53,571	5,606,446	366,432	-34,848	5,205,166	1,712,595	624,246	5,418	1,391,925	649,466
1972	8,389,601	6,185,140	66,676	6,251,816	421,658	-39,672	5,790,486	1,901,618	697,497	5,854	1,433,126	672,285
1973	9,259,626	6,782,180	93,067	6,875,247	513,822	-42,635	6,318,790	2,140,191	800,645	6,175	1,499,594	707,773
1974	10,346,671	7,432,299	90,285	7,522,584	582,505	-36,744	6,903,335	2,458,996	984,340	6,716	1,540,667	738,023
1975	11,572,053	8,121,710	127,474	8,249,184	641,270	-28,094	7,579,820	2,721,783	1,270,450	7,157	1,616,907	755,698
1976	12,917,968	9,111,012	140,674	9,251,686	733,932	-11,769	8,505,985	2,970,690	1,441,293	7,863	1,642,781	786,899
1977	14,430,966	10,243,704	145,540	10,389,244	841,360	-24,610	9,523,274	3,350,314	1,557,378	8,412	1,715,527	837,772
1978	16,558,724	11,843,665	121,391	11,965,056	989,270	-15,953	10,959,833	3,898,085	1,700,806	9,327	1,775,410	901,275
1979	18,772,293	13,466,406	115,005	13,581,411	1,184,792	6,180	12,402,799	4,456,856	1,912,638	10,272	1,827,602	951,199
1980	21,673,970	15,231,915	130,630	15,362,545	1,306,937	12,741	14,068,349	5,345,045	2,260,576	11,556	1,875,620	988,237
1981	24,710,161	16,898,694	136,921	17,035,615	1,565,281	138,157	15,608,491	6,394,583	2,707,087	12,823	1,927,018	994,581
1982	26,771,408	18,157,216	146,039	18,303,255	1,707,103	146,070	16,742,222	7,037,567	2,991,619	13,573	1,972,354	1,001,945
1983	28,899,057	19,592,410	152,031	19,744,441	1,907,010	174,796	18,012,227	7,674,025	3,212,805	14,320	2,018,133	1,036,404
1984	32,418,187	22,291,784	166,620	22,458,404	2,257,329	179,666	20,380,741	8,652,472	3,384,974	15,688	2,066,419	1,099,543
1985	35,569,628	24,746,996	197,066	24,944,062	2,543,992	198,416	22,598,486	9,304,937	3,666,205	16,730	2,126,090	1,160,801
1986	38,773,644	27,301,007	230,526	27,531,533	2,850,882	225,645	24,906,296	9,879,126	3,988,222	17,650	2,196,834	1,215,030
1987	41,871,173	30,029,243	212,305	30,241,548	3,155,298	262,122	27,348,372	10,287,290	4,235,511	18,402	2,275,309	1,277,030
1988	46,018,825	33,402,677	182,362	33,585,039	3,636,499	291,390	30,239,930	11,176,389	4,602,506	19,464	2,364,284	1,349,526
1989	50,000,601	35,620,581	230,526	35,851,107	3,928,187	333,883	32,256,803	12,702,625	5,041,173	20,455	2,444,380	1,396,314
1990	52,763,858	37,736,038	298,772	38,034,810	4,155,899	377,878	34,256,789	12,955,258	5,551,811	21,002	2,512,365	1,426,402
1991	55,032,226	39,699,075	241,204	39,940,279	4,392,161	334,774	35,882,892	12,991,145	6,158,189	21,555	2,553,122	1,436,665
1992	57,832,374	41,538,542	197,911	41,736,453	4,583,742	328,248	37,480,959	13,361,265	6,990,150	22,302	2,593,126	1,406,200
1993	59,175,096	42,104,423	211,031	42,315,454	4,665,573	312,453	37,962,334	13,825,830	7,386,932	22,762	2,599,776	1,402,948
1994	60,899,000	43,361,620	224,569	43,586,189	4,840,970	288,938	39,034,157	14,305,363	7,559,480	23,291	2,614,685	1,408,463
1995	63,689,849	44,858,354	246,325	45,104,679	4,934,866	281,857	40,451,670	15,277,759	7,960,420	24,275	2,623,697	1,440,496
1996	67,919,229	48,108,712	281,483	48,390,195	5,143,278	269,236	43,516,153	16,062,608	8,340,468	25,615	2,651,549	1,479,423
1997	72,640,103	52,055,833	320,278	52,376,111	5,532,467	249,861	47,093,505	17,082,524	8,464,074	26,978	2,692,600	1,521,768
1998	80,653,171	58,525,799	352,838	58,878,637	6,097,149	241,128	53,022,616	18,831,837	8,798,718	29,471	2,736,720	1,608,669
1999	87,247,277	65,104,996	360,400	65,465,396	6,743,671	182,201	58,903,926	19,077,792	9,265,559	31,276	2,789,593	1,656,003
2000	95,741,844	72,297,291	359,299	72,656,590	7,495,956	138,277	65,298,911	20,760,076	9,682,857	33,863	2,827,366	1,696,594
2001	98,574,007	74,783,608	347,415	75,131,023	7,944,179	-75,720	67,111,124	20,814,696	10,648,187	34,350	2,869,672	1,713,767
2002	102,632,994	79,031,111	362,136	79,393,247	8,474,995	-320,939	70,597,313	20,793,022	11,242,659	35,386	2,900,355	1,749,463
2003	108,487,447	84,394,532	401,227	84,795,759	9,096,337	-535,389	75,164,033	21,478,174	11,845,240	37,221	2,914,702	1,782,103
2004	117,398,423	92,149,911	446,795	92,596,706	10,097,202	-765,967	81,733,537	23,240,745	12,424,141	40,068	2,930,007	1,812,986
2005	123,075,207	96,631,938	465,757	97,097,695	10,555,955	-948,877	85,592,863	24,408,031	13,074,313	41,885	2,938,375	1,837,287
2006	129,688,924	101,188,657	419,036	101,607,693	10,803,629	-1,176,916	89,627,148	26,005,602	14,056,174	44,003	2,947,289	1,861,439
2007	133,384,851	102,231,468	401,541	102,633,009	10,867,329	-1,492,316	90,273,364	28,207,974	14,903,513	44,824	2,975,742	1,890,307
2008	136,405,729	101,931,305	460,373	102,391,678	11,158,296	-1,908,296	89,325,086	30,055,456	17,025,187	45,136	3,022,116	1,882,625
2009	131,894,754	98,337,506	533,177	98,870,683	10,939,103	-1,974,541	85,957,039	27,187,216	18,750,499	43,086	3,061,203	1,821,926
2010	136,918,739	101,230,863	588,005	101,818,868	11,086,243	-2,053,304	88,679,321	27,286,469	20,952,949	44,113	3,103,793	1,804,107
2011	146,013,646	105,786,678	510,954	106,297,632	10,441,514	-2,167,842	93,688,276	31,024,453	21,300,917	46,505	3,139,767	1,828,222
2012	153,444,873	111,586,952	627,409	112,214,361	10,833,798	-2,226,207	99,154,356	32,828,892	21,461,625	48,256	3,179,798	1,877,293
2013	159,087,705	116,817,984	684,226	117,502,210	12,571,917	-2,210,375	102,719,918	33,934,054	22,433,733	49,460	3,216,522	1,920,961
2014	169,896,807	122,754,938	643,494	123,398,432	13,188,315	-2,243,994	107,966,123	38,008,679	23,922,005	52,166	3,256,875	1,973,127
2015	180,101,999	129,197,592	721,819	129,919,411	13,794,864	-2,294,187	113,830,360	40,560,960	25,710,679	54,742	3,290,044	2,030,156
2016	186,149,364	133,371,718	678,226	134,049,944	14,238,749	-2,371,780	117,439,415	42,109,396	26,600,553	56,116	3,317,200	2,073,606
2017	193,296,405	139,415,475	703,407	140,118,882	14,824,948	-2,426,539	122,867,395	43,916,018	26,512,992	57,913	3,337,685	2,112,512
2018	203,855,654	203,366,803	488,851	146,876,841	15,713,596	-2,606,776	128,556,469	47,378,016	27,921,169	61,147	3,333,861	2,160,038
2019	212,748,650	212,133,690	614,960	154,054,906	16,497,035	-2,682,974	134,874,897	48,052,877	29,820,876	63,729	3,338,330	2,204,327

Personal Income and Employment by Area: San Francisco-Oakland-Berkeley, CA

(Thousands of dollars, except as noted.)

Year	Personal income, total	Earnings by place of work			Less: Contributions for government social insurance	Plus: Adjustment for residence	Equals: Net earnings by place of residence	Plus: Dividends, interest, and rent	Plus: Personal current transfer receipts	Per capita personal income (dollars)	Population (persons)	Total employment
		Nonfarm	Farm	Total								
1970	17,758,252	14,344,577	54,040	14,398,617	916,727	-490,495	12,991,395	3,279,499	1,487,358	5,713	3,108,460	1,559,634
1971	18,922,324	15,107,827	50,566	15,158,393	993,263	-478,952	13,686,178	3,531,384	1,704,762	6,066	3,119,247	1,528,383
1972	20,547,981	16,463,802	63,355	16,527,157	1,140,417	-500,443	14,886,297	3,835,355	1,826,329	6,555	3,134,632	1,561,571
1973	22,058,296	17,686,918	67,268	17,754,186	1,417,530	-524,958	15,811,698	4,234,443	2,012,155	7,011	3,146,217	1,614,085
1974	24,304,358	19,257,861	72,533	19,330,394	1,598,743	-570,040	17,161,611	4,810,231	2,332,516	7,710	3,152,349	1,648,391
1975	26,876,119	21,067,667	78,432	21,146,099	1,712,018	-633,633	18,800,448	5,188,400	2,887,271	8,510	3,158,346	1,670,337
1976	29,450,851	23,293,131	72,610	23,365,741	1,922,349	-729,849	20,713,543	5,577,687	3,159,621	9,241	3,187,017	1,693,226
1977	32,224,427	25,722,822	63,551	25,786,373	2,145,087	-877,371	22,763,915	6,141,226	3,319,286	10,072	3,199,300	1,733,826
1978	36,044,414	29,064,238	78,859	29,143,097	2,482,258	-1,037,572	25,623,267	6,906,482	3,514,665	11,216	3,213,638	1,817,444
1979	40,234,936	32,491,677	103,502	32,595,179	2,914,715	-1,162,758	28,517,706	7,859,777	3,857,453	12,470	3,226,421	1,895,178
1980	45,536,329	36,128,140	116,289	36,244,429	3,211,117	-1,360,286	31,673,026	9,490,730	4,372,573	13,964	3,260,930	1,955,758
1981	51,417,855	39,683,581	110,412	39,793,993	3,831,802	-1,415,484	34,546,707	11,850,527	5,020,621	15,601	3,295,803	1,971,802
1982	55,089,850	42,154,077	116,698	42,270,775	4,167,479	-1,377,655	36,725,641	12,916,948	5,447,261	16,524	3,333,995	1,960,504
1983	59,916,850	45,840,294	118,991	45,959,285	4,611,921	-1,304,199	40,043,165	14,070,916	5,802,769	17,695	3,386,080	1,996,122
1984	66,381,238	50,547,490	117,042	50,664,532	5,280,746	-1,296,720	44,087,066	16,292,810	6,001,362	19,364	3,428,080	2,066,961
1985	71,115,447	54,432,869	123,645	54,556,514	5,767,651	-1,292,156	47,496,707	17,227,865	6,390,875	20,439	3,479,465	2,120,828
1986	75,679,506	58,894,918	129,897	59,024,815	6,313,809	-1,542,347	51,168,659	17,710,919	6,799,928	21,476	3,523,866	2,168,002
1987	79,968,993	62,997,206	135,832	63,133,038	6,741,661	-1,517,760	54,873,617	18,034,249	7,061,127	22,470	3,558,999	2,224,223
1988	87,495,963	69,140,538	133,159	69,273,697	7,561,469	-1,496,250	60,215,978	19,749,693	7,530,292	24,281	3,603,440	2,310,192
1989	93,615,657	72,588,296	136,327	72,724,623	8,042,499	-1,647,205	63,034,919	22,298,220	8,282,518	25,599	3,656,981	2,351,774
1990	99,034,323	76,827,714	145,811	76,973,525	8,475,271	-1,647,022	66,851,232	23,168,925	9,014,166	26,624	3,719,675	2,399,266
1991	103,542,135	81,079,411	114,587	81,193,998	8,973,128	-1,772,324	70,448,546	23,306,974	9,786,615	27,535	3,760,370	2,388,786
1992	109,633,758	85,745,583	130,332	85,875,915	9,415,352	-1,628,458	74,832,105	23,671,595	11,130,058	28,809	3,805,588	2,347,136
1993	113,895,634	88,617,212	133,073	88,750,285	9,715,926	-1,592,355	77,442,004	24,809,821	11,643,809	29,663	3,839,619	2,358,677
1994	118,135,753	91,758,127	141,876	91,900,003	10,124,732	-1,545,241	80,230,030	26,094,009	11,811,714	30,606	3,859,905	2,385,264
1995	126,463,480	97,177,962	120,170	97,298,132	10,561,012	-1,293,394	85,443,726	28,658,956	12,360,798	32,561	3,883,894	2,436,826
1996	136,900,716	104,260,168	128,917	104,389,085	11,038,955	-186,488	93,163,642	30,914,496	12,822,578	34,895	3,923,208	2,492,590
1997	146,246,324	112,099,461	192,729	112,292,190	11,815,241	284,037	100,760,986	32,613,479	12,871,859	36,693	3,985,694	2,550,128
1998	162,545,383	124,195,303	181,331	124,376,634	12,843,879	874,651	112,407,406	36,591,238	13,546,739	40,182	4,045,185	2,639,817
1999	177,755,158	137,455,287	193,137	137,648,424	14,147,782	2,761,491	126,262,133	37,451,510	14,041,515	43,465	4,089,620	2,697,881
2000	204,672,428	160,621,125	207,119	160,828,244	16,333,959	3,790,105	148,284,390	41,839,384	14,548,654	49,487	4,135,875	2,770,316
2001	207,254,080	165,694,576	218,358	165,912,934	16,944,742	892,730	149,860,922	41,429,224	15,963,934	49,644	4,174,788	2,747,283
2002	201,372,766	161,500,778	208,305	161,709,083	16,718,368	-530,321	144,460,394	39,488,631	17,423,741	48,424	4,158,544	2,679,890
2003	204,474,783	163,459,706	230,921	163,690,627	17,030,698	-1,068,468	145,591,461	40,723,601	18,159,721	49,319	4,145,965	2,653,534
2004	216,294,694	171,161,545	190,116	171,351,661	18,185,450	-1,085,899	152,080,312	45,343,846	18,870,536	52,329	4,133,400	2,659,356
2005	230,832,589	179,562,232	179,093	179,741,325	18,862,141	-1,884,774	158,994,410	52,093,969	19,744,210	55,786	4,137,858	2,682,602
2006	252,262,890	190,428,689	177,070	190,605,759	19,407,582	-1,781,739	169,416,438	61,668,937	21,177,515	60,805	4,148,724	2,728,960
2007	263,823,978	197,767,931	166,120	197,934,051	19,945,631	-991,895	176,996,525	64,510,893	22,316,560	63,061	4,183,637	2,785,090
2008	268,451,669	198,276,430	162,475	198,438,905	20,584,543	-506,141	177,348,221	65,969,677	25,133,771	63,255	4,243,932	2,785,616
2009	255,768,839	192,400,365	162,894	192,563,259	19,970,857	-759,376	171,833,026	56,103,017	27,832,796	59,442	4,302,830	2,687,707
2010	265,878,289	198,611,192	163,012	198,774,204	19,940,246	1,368,042	180,202,000	55,050,523	30,625,766	61,194	4,344,810	2,663,490
2011	288,152,330	209,392,915	180,336	209,573,251	18,695,662	2,958,213	193,835,802	63,782,720	30,533,808	65,501	4,399,218	2,715,302
2012	313,987,946	232,838,802	194,314	233,033,116	20,167,025	-2,242,789	210,623,302	72,733,094	30,631,550	70,351	4,463,172	2,836,176
2013	321,909,866	242,920,075	204,151	243,124,226	24,147,571	-294,915	218,681,740	71,346,535	31,881,591	71,082	4,528,717	2,943,008
2014	350,349,154	258,318,001	252,697	258,570,698	25,829,284	2,891,817	235,633,231	80,968,276	33,747,647	76,230	4,595,964	3,059,283
2015	384,389,575	278,757,565	289,630	279,047,195	27,746,060	4,406,002	255,707,137	92,366,833	36,315,605	82,523	4,657,985	3,183,834
2016	406,159,774	298,391,842	250,054	298,641,896	29,409,155	1,172,945	270,405,686	98,225,574	37,528,514	86,434	4,699,077	3,278,341
2017	432,359,944	321,539,376	288,445	321,827,821	31,332,430	1,872,193	292,367,584	102,750,195	37,242,165	91,459	4,727,357	3,346,854
2018	473,747,078	473,579,034	168,044	343,057,792	33,587,441	1,868,183	311,338,534	122,780,608	39,627,936	100,236	4,726,314	3,407,818
2019	496,466,826	496,224,062	242,764	367,550,166	35,854,113	-1,173,565	330,522,488	124,062,316	41,882,022	104,921	4,731,803	3,480,410

Personal Income and Employment by Area: San Jose-Sunnyvale-Santa Clara, CA

(Thousands of dollars, except as noted.)

Year	Personal income, total	Earnings by place of work			Less: Contributions for government social insurance	Plus: Adjustment for residence	Equals: Net earnings by place of residence	Plus: Dividends, interest, and rent	Plus: Personal current transfer receipts	Per capita personal income (dollars)	Population (persons)	Total employment
		Nonfarm	Farm	Total								
1970	5,534,127	4,215,123	48,867	4,263,990	284,661	369,993	4,349,322	778,460	406,345	5,079	1,089,674	465,696
1971	5,956,579	4,512,419	51,593	4,564,012	314,276	359,172	4,608,908	865,550	482,121	5,322	1,119,155	468,263
1972	6,610,349	5,105,259	57,898	5,163,157	377,334	345,027	5,130,850	958,148	521,351	5,709	1,157,841	500,625
1973	7,382,556	5,842,144	78,728	5,920,872	500,555	312,063	5,732,380	1,077,020	573,156	6,238	1,183,576	544,854
1974	8,276,698	6,583,684	81,853	6,665,537	579,590	275,225	6,361,172	1,242,730	672,796	6,986	1,184,823	576,125
1975	9,188,573	7,128,079	82,909	7,210,988	611,469	307,357	6,906,876	1,385,904	895,793	7,571	1,213,688	578,145
1976	10,249,199	8,144,218	68,233	8,212,451	715,209	283,406	7,780,648	1,501,242	967,309	8,342	1,228,572	616,284
1977	11,480,890	9,395,211	82,006	9,477,217	844,061	198,177	8,831,333	1,654,395	995,162	9,153	1,254,396	654,919
1978	13,179,444	11,023,393	83,357	11,106,750	1,020,884	120,313	10,206,179	1,909,494	1,063,771	10,264	1,284,003	708,398
1979	15,251,451	13,075,768	94,626	13,170,394	1,267,871	-7,988	11,894,535	2,216,740	1,140,176	11,771	1,295,698	770,291
1980	17,602,148	14,989,183	104,694	15,093,877	1,427,082	-122,071	13,544,724	2,734,551	1,322,873	13,268	1,326,709	814,696
1981	19,988,425	16,953,841	84,949	17,038,790	1,745,222	-297,037	14,996,531	3,439,545	1,552,349	14,799	1,350,627	832,437
1982	21,901,335	18,880,173	95,526	18,975,699	1,986,212	-553,198	16,436,289	3,798,939	1,666,107	15,964	1,371,955	848,645
1983	24,162,929	21,260,706	99,450	21,360,156	2,288,892	-899,858	18,171,406	4,206,123	1,785,400	17,237	1,401,776	879,267
1984	27,008,475	24,142,733	118,983	24,261,716	2,709,798	-1,290,765	20,261,153	4,928,494	1,818,828	18,951	1,425,185	936,276
1985	28,687,588	25,858,401	125,325	25,983,726	2,923,564	-1,628,498	21,431,664	5,283,407	1,972,517	19,786	1,449,912	949,532
1986	29,803,632	26,940,110	141,408	27,081,518	3,055,230	-1,756,278	22,270,010	5,406,699	2,126,923	20,391	1,461,582	947,268
1987	31,654,585	29,223,076	148,800	29,371,876	3,286,046	-2,187,548	23,898,282	5,543,602	2,212,701	21,380	1,480,543	978,952
1988	34,665,513	32,562,121	141,139	32,703,260	3,759,631	-2,680,069	26,263,560	6,031,959	2,369,994	23,009	1,506,608	1,023,025
1989	37,225,649	34,670,071	138,039	34,808,110	3,986,593	-3,006,249	27,815,268	6,785,190	2,625,191	24,263	1,534,258	1,036,067
1990	39,066,135	36,884,217	126,958	37,011,175	4,221,001	-3,843,936	28,946,238	7,234,820	2,885,077	25,448	1,535,142	1,052,577
1991	40,673,301	38,446,217	112,918	38,559,135	4,432,029	-3,919,521	30,207,585	7,290,649	3,175,067	26,233	1,550,447	1,040,251
1992	43,751,012	41,359,128	120,834	41,479,962	4,679,201	-4,238,479	32,562,282	7,483,879	3,704,851	27,863	1,570,207	1,017,714
1993	44,617,672	42,028,294	155,773	42,184,067	4,811,069	-4,526,487	32,846,511	7,882,502	3,888,659	28,085	1,588,680	1,023,035
1994	46,467,773	43,900,717	169,310	44,070,027	5,087,957	-4,941,200	34,040,870	8,511,997	3,914,906	29,003	1,602,152	1,036,627
1995	51,206,472	48,574,157	197,267	48,771,424	5,549,180	-5,606,237	37,616,007	9,493,318	4,097,147	31,559	1,622,579	1,075,809
1996	55,716,545	54,086,068	178,138	54,264,206	6,102,632	-7,212,730	40,948,844	10,463,513	4,304,188	33,709	1,652,864	1,131,518
1997	61,817,008	61,240,640	193,098	61,433,738	6,802,807	-8,603,956	46,026,975	11,480,361	4,309,672	36,706	1,684,121	1,175,557
1998	67,149,081	66,855,801	197,634	67,053,435	7,335,512	-9,951,158	49,766,765	12,862,517	4,519,799	39,314	1,708,031	1,221,008
1999	75,273,260	78,376,188	222,136	78,598,324	8,430,548	-12,965,383	57,202,393	13,344,869	4,725,998	43,688	1,722,965	1,226,104
2000	93,814,304	100,391,771	323,462	100,715,233	10,304,020	-16,684,824	73,726,389	15,152,494	4,935,421	53,956	1,738,728	1,283,119
2001	88,366,401	90,192,228	249,237	90,441,465	9,439,742	-13,060,106	67,941,617	14,969,875	5,454,909	50,706	1,742,726	1,245,499
2002	82,823,906	81,390,844	221,729	81,612,573	8,583,901	-10,860,634	62,168,038	14,391,752	6,264,116	48,030	1,724,404	1,151,605
2003	83,526,111	80,492,685	229,641	80,722,326	8,520,856	-10,313,102	61,888,368	15,110,342	6,527,401	48,596	1,718,790	1,111,274
2004	86,223,893	83,344,479	242,673	83,587,152	9,016,307	-10,728,414	63,842,431	15,830,451	6,551,011	50,188	1,718,016	1,110,182
2005	91,392,488	85,947,093	230,703	86,177,796	9,230,775	-10,456,823	66,490,198	18,047,835	6,854,455	52,829	1,729,959	1,120,373
2006	100,767,124	93,074,697	224,681	93,299,378	9,686,061	-11,365,850	72,247,467	21,093,648	7,426,009	57,737	1,745,283	1,146,729
2007	109,229,362	100,438,524	203,296	100,641,820	10,203,086	-12,762,078	77,676,656	23,651,191	7,901,515	61,848	1,766,098	1,183,453
2008	109,096,441	99,703,319	175,459	99,878,778	10,498,778	-12,418,334	76,961,666	23,052,236	9,082,539	60,770	1,795,231	1,186,385
2009	102,772,999	94,416,797	241,568	94,658,365	10,086,317	-11,075,614	73,496,434	19,010,842	10,265,723	56,482	1,819,573	1,130,469
2010	111,487,846	103,246,559	230,168	103,476,727	10,533,755	-12,578,492	80,364,480	19,792,525	11,330,841	60,523	1,842,074	1,126,570
2011	122,475,560	112,512,237	196,412	112,708,649	10,001,877	-14,898,051	87,808,721	23,422,402	11,244,437	65,500	1,869,846	1,159,903
2012	136,098,647	118,466,828	246,406	118,713,234	10,451,716	-10,482,534	97,778,984	27,117,798	11,201,865	71,685	1,898,569	1,206,137
2013	138,431,157	125,761,793	293,640	126,055,433	12,881,765	-13,396,010	99,777,658	27,102,607	11,550,892	71,789	1,928,305	1,254,614
2014	152,141,978	137,905,999	305,408	138,211,407	14,045,205	-16,619,854	107,546,348	32,357,271	12,238,359	77,853	1,954,220	1,300,041
2015	168,014,581	153,534,820	428,888	153,963,708	15,373,819	-19,902,503	118,687,386	36,156,198	13,170,997	84,960	1,977,584	1,358,709
2016	180,899,908	163,173,320	388,105	163,561,425	16,101,886	-18,433,126	129,026,413	38,297,400	13,576,095	90,863	1,990,910	1,395,306
2017	193,098,172	178,563,149	394,907	178,958,056	17,417,174	-22,005,769	139,535,113	40,096,674	13,466,385	96,623	1,998,463	1,427,593
2018	216,457,424	216,211,358	246,066	195,345,310	18,818,972	-21,453,464	155,072,874	47,271,278	14,113,272	108,565	1,993,804	1,459,165
2019	227,095,402	226,806,497	288,905	204,217,254	19,640,247	-20,103,215	164,473,792	47,711,943	14,909,667	114,080	1,990,660	1,490,982

Personal Income and Employment by Area: San Luis Obispo-Paso Robles, CA

(Thousands of dollars, except as noted.)

Year	Personal income, total	Earnings by place of work			Less: Contributions for government social insurance	Plus: Adjustment for residence	Equals: Net earnings by place of residence	Plus: Dividends, interest, and rent	Plus: Personal current transfer receipts	Per capita personal income (dollars)	Population (persons)	Total employment
		Nonfarm	Farm	Total								
1970	410,874	250,223	17,638	267,861	14,935	13,385	266,311	88,796	55,767	3,866	106,280	38,922
1971	455,874	282,363	17,908	300,271	17,428	13,938	296,781	98,500	60,593	4,171	109,301	40,811
1972	513,809	321,221	23,147	344,368	21,113	14,896	338,151	110,387	65,271	4,449	115,484	43,478
1973	581,196	358,830	27,270	386,100	26,863	17,791	377,028	130,047	74,121	4,850	119,843	45,667
1974	673,901	399,905	40,083	439,988	31,041	21,526	430,473	152,011	91,417	5,368	125,535	48,387
1975	767,457	451,386	33,698	485,084	34,418	27,141	477,807	176,413	113,237	6,069	126,456	50,574
1976	874,841	522,678	33,850	556,528	40,031	32,959	549,456	195,569	129,816	6,516	134,260	53,644
1977	975,928	585,484	27,105	612,589	45,708	41,666	608,547	225,112	142,269	7,040	138,635	56,552
1978	1,152,991	695,073	44,864	739,937	55,958	47,902	731,881	264,676	156,434	7,902	145,914	60,728
1979	1,312,402	792,040	41,414	833,454	67,457	59,134	825,131	311,928	175,343	8,700	150,850	65,290
1980	1,486,564	843,427	45,673	889,100	70,113	72,362	891,349	388,567	206,648	9,481	156,786	66,956
1981	1,672,093	925,234	49,536	974,770	85,267	66,813	956,316	472,008	243,769	10,329	161,886	68,339
1982	1,796,170	958,879	62,286	1,021,165	90,931	74,490	1,004,724	526,235	265,211	10,784	166,563	68,574
1983	2,166,411	1,280,798	68,083	1,348,881	127,760	49,927	1,271,048	613,373	281,990	12,642	171,365	75,005
1984	2,382,952	1,412,144	53,564	1,465,708	144,599	68,057	1,389,166	688,539	305,247	13,420	177,566	79,834
1985	2,551,924	1,480,246	53,258	1,533,504	149,855	88,468	1,472,117	746,023	333,784	13,776	185,248	84,089
1986	2,778,742	1,626,663	72,418	1,699,081	165,384	94,957	1,628,654	790,888	359,200	14,435	192,497	87,984
1987	3,019,418	1,829,764	84,857	1,914,621	186,139	93,763	1,822,245	819,199	377,974	15,147	199,345	92,685
1988	3,313,775	2,022,158	88,696	2,110,854	212,600	102,754	2,001,008	906,757	406,010	16,223	204,261	98,930
1989	3,667,188	2,181,670	91,975	2,273,645	234,621	107,789	2,146,813	1,074,119	446,256	17,192	213,314	103,273
1990	3,833,545	2,346,773	72,761	2,419,534	250,092	111,320	2,280,762	1,069,765	483,018	17,563	218,276	106,051
1991	4,009,496	2,489,432	47,156	2,536,588	264,916	123,747	2,395,419	1,086,865	527,212	18,234	219,895	110,470
1992	4,249,317	2,637,813	63,697	2,701,510	279,130	129,695	2,552,075	1,100,167	597,075	19,154	221,848	110,178
1993	4,403,078	2,697,296	77,927	2,775,223	284,869	134,940	2,625,294	1,141,854	635,930	19,712	223,370	109,848
1994	4,571,999	2,795,346	70,575	2,865,921	297,402	142,581	2,711,100	1,202,877	658,022	20,210	226,228	112,959
1995	4,835,554	2,974,326	74,240	3,048,566	311,092	150,667	2,888,141	1,257,428	689,985	21,082	229,370	116,952
1996	5,211,367	3,215,172	76,942	3,292,114	324,625	159,140	3,126,629	1,353,854	730,884	22,369	232,976	120,730
1997	5,670,563	3,501,976	125,149	3,627,125	348,348	173,190	3,451,967	1,469,847	748,749	23,967	236,601	125,634
1998	6,147,338	3,822,562	101,266	3,923,828	374,399	189,506	3,738,935	1,623,061	785,342	25,612	240,020	131,952
1999	6,504,221	4,105,521	108,469	4,213,990	403,465	209,896	4,020,421	1,667,380	816,420	26,714	243,480	137,881
2000	7,058,288	4,388,050	165,767	4,553,817	432,236	249,840	4,371,421	1,821,680	865,187	28,479	247,839	138,477
2001	7,688,672	4,903,034	130,152	5,033,186	490,281	266,238	4,809,143	1,928,889	950,640	30,576	251,462	140,627
2002	7,962,860	5,251,897	131,585	5,383,482	531,550	278,630	5,130,562	1,830,103	1,002,195	31,463	253,083	144,119
2003	8,296,586	5,484,445	133,202	5,617,647	561,091	316,541	5,373,097	1,884,356	1,039,133	32,577	254,674	144,119
2004	8,839,528	5,880,755	122,643	6,003,398	621,243	351,923	5,734,078	2,028,231	1,077,219	34,416	256,842	146,485
2005	9,243,300	6,085,618	125,267	6,210,885	652,301	395,798	5,954,382	2,140,869	1,148,049	35,742	258,615	149,346
2006	10,008,874	6,422,519	123,926	6,546,445	666,938	434,208	6,313,715	2,459,087	1,236,072	38,422	260,498	152,479
2007	10,592,263	6,587,739	123,309	6,711,048	675,502	489,421	6,524,967	2,760,769	1,306,527	40,310	262,770	156,737
2008	10,603,088	6,589,361	81,440	6,670,801	692,649	525,299	6,503,451	2,604,127	1,495,510	39,808	266,358	154,624
2009	10,474,303	6,426,909	135,950	6,562,859	681,664	499,524	6,380,719	2,459,744	1,633,840	39,062	268,145	149,202
2010	10,849,987	6,631,090	167,580	6,798,670	680,795	499,020	6,616,895	2,440,911	1,792,181	40,212	269,819	147,777
2011	11,577,475	6,969,948	160,836	7,130,784	648,330	511,807	6,994,261	2,773,238	1,809,976	42,698	271,150	151,009
2012	12,255,640	7,283,761	275,310	7,559,071	666,511	533,437	7,425,997	2,998,748	1,830,895	44,667	274,378	155,745
2013	12,679,893	7,639,943	316,159	7,956,102	775,482	532,882	7,713,502	3,064,680	1,901,711	45,946	275,973	159,397
2014	13,516,440	8,001,706	249,409	8,251,115	818,208	562,938	7,995,845	3,493,006	2,027,589	48,527	278,534	164,718
2015	14,505,638	8,535,161	291,520	8,826,681	868,055	596,059	8,554,685	3,779,751	2,171,202	51,732	280,402	169,464
2016	14,905,254	8,738,462	322,923	9,061,385	892,042	598,037	8,767,380	3,897,111	2,240,763	52,803	282,282	169,962
2017	15,680,360	9,233,507	393,327	9,626,834	938,935	635,023	9,322,922	4,081,707	2,275,731	55,328	283,405	173,773
2018	16,465,164	16,252,325	212,839	9,970,172	1,006,140	655,360	9,619,392	4,408,756	2,437,016	58,108	283,354	175,375
2019	17,270,828	17,013,753	257,075	10,585,957	1,073,263	678,338	10,191,032	4,477,866	2,601,930	61,004	283,111	178,476

Personal Income and Employment by Area: Santa Cruz-Watsonville, CA

(Thousands of dollars, except as noted.)

Year	Personal income, total	Earnings by place of work			Less: Contributions for government social insurance	Plus: Adjustment for residence	Equals: Net earnings by place of residence	Plus: Dividends, interest, and rent	Plus: Personal current transfer receipts	Per capita personal income (dollars)	Population (persons)	Total employment
		Nonfarm	Farm	Total								
1970	558,375	311,740	19,379	331,119	20,780	47,906	358,245	129,153	70,977	4,475	124,788	49,358
1971	623,329	338,430	21,178	359,608	23,013	59,872	396,467	143,587	83,275	4,799	129,886	50,838
1972	707,795	384,651	24,048	408,699	27,479	74,952	456,172	159,149	92,474	4,989	141,878	55,131
1973	820,147	435,469	35,687	471,156	35,479	94,099	529,776	180,893	109,478	5,643	145,347	58,086
1974	937,464	484,551	35,625	520,176	40,742	117,270	596,704	210,309	130,451	6,257	149,828	61,601
1975	1,063,053	531,506	31,297	562,803	43,402	146,286	665,687	236,587	160,779	6,702	158,622	64,137
1976	1,217,157	622,603	36,258	658,861	50,905	174,909	782,865	259,135	175,157	7,244	168,026	68,940
1977	1,397,624	724,164	43,947	768,111	61,098	211,965	918,978	293,199	185,447	7,980	175,132	73,750
1978	1,611,473	839,356	50,910	890,266	72,490	256,893	1,074,669	336,234	200,570	9,216	174,865	77,918
1979	1,837,404	929,807	62,176	991,983	84,499	323,095	1,230,579	388,844	217,981	9,984	184,041	81,923
1980	2,135,900	1,036,844	65,159	1,102,003	92,240	392,587	1,402,350	480,840	252,710	11,283	189,305	84,798
1981	2,424,888	1,146,481	77,394	1,223,875	111,055	427,150	1,539,970	596,637	288,281	12,526	193,590	87,088
1982	2,594,812	1,215,440	80,138	1,295,578	120,503	465,163	1,640,238	648,461	306,113	13,148	197,353	87,797
1983	2,917,647	1,383,343	127,879	1,511,222	138,701	503,257	1,875,778	714,829	327,040	14,449	201,921	93,297
1984	3,238,443	1,570,778	129,453	1,700,231	164,062	556,295	2,092,464	806,842	339,137	15,723	205,964	97,417
1985	3,433,684	1,696,925	98,634	1,795,559	180,272	590,728	2,206,015	861,651	366,018	16,186	212,143	102,627
1986	3,683,657	1,850,595	135,321	1,985,916	198,743	605,165	2,392,338	901,146	390,173	17,002	216,661	103,042
1987	3,951,216	2,063,958	152,067	2,216,025	222,579	640,708	2,634,154	915,085	401,977	17,862	221,202	108,605
1988	4,325,897	2,334,269	160,563	2,494,832	261,690	685,327	2,918,469	984,514	422,914	19,167	225,700	117,109
1989	4,591,240	2,431,467	154,686	2,586,153	278,669	722,516	3,030,000	1,080,275	480,965	19,836	231,463	119,693
1990	4,982,518	2,736,409	187,277	2,923,686	309,712	748,190	3,362,164	1,109,924	510,430	21,699	229,616	125,068
1991	5,180,197	2,935,028	174,555	3,109,583	337,218	772,217	3,544,582	1,106,664	528,951	22,529	229,935	129,334
1992	5,538,322	3,121,225	214,771	3,335,996	357,756	822,740	3,800,980	1,128,475	608,867	23,779	232,912	126,162
1993	5,753,255	3,185,084	225,216	3,410,300	363,592	852,348	3,899,056	1,206,085	648,114	24,442	235,386	128,059
1994	5,977,393	3,308,486	211,314	3,519,800	377,774	889,950	4,031,976	1,298,688	646,729	25,145	237,714	129,313
1995	6,380,484	3,519,154	214,646	3,733,800	395,564	988,306	4,326,542	1,379,597	674,345	26,660	239,324	133,854
1996	6,871,429	3,761,809	227,894	3,989,703	406,366	1,110,516	4,693,853	1,483,544	694,032	28,492	241,168	136,690
1997	7,418,152	4,000,069	239,582	4,239,651	423,064	1,285,058	5,101,645	1,612,971	703,536	30,236	245,344	136,897
1998	8,058,306	4,395,922	215,350	4,611,272	453,680	1,423,765	5,581,357	1,760,437	716,512	32,119	250,889	145,249
1999	8,868,463	4,687,851	372,744	5,060,595	486,462	1,732,596	6,306,729	1,816,150	745,584	34,961	253,667	146,085
2000	10,269,082	5,491,706	294,745	5,786,451	554,320	2,267,192	7,499,323	2,004,203	765,556	40,139	255,835	145,981
2001	10,186,256	5,878,369	263,618	6,141,987	597,266	1,903,049	7,447,770	1,894,656	843,830	39,783	256,045	145,357
2002	9,967,470	5,921,052	241,757	6,162,809	596,148	1,620,000	7,186,661	1,866,568	914,241	39,160	254,531	143,460
2003	10,074,916	5,919,255	290,432	6,209,687	602,844	1,573,253	7,180,096	1,931,842	962,978	39,818	253,021	141,691
2004	10,447,215	5,963,331	309,456	6,272,787	635,418	1,652,710	7,290,079	2,168,001	989,135	41,399	252,356	141,559
2005	10,543,553	6,031,797	289,556	6,321,353	651,418	1,629,677	7,299,612	2,201,854	1,042,087	41,943	251,377	140,941
2006	11,181,590	6,320,069	248,387	6,568,456	665,307	1,610,090	7,513,239	2,551,978	1,116,373	44,439	251,616	142,051
2007	11,757,090	6,400,816	275,002	6,675,818	666,715	1,663,386	7,672,489	2,886,105	1,198,496	46,415	253,304	145,223
2008	12,120,091	6,405,635	281,688	6,687,323	677,216	1,661,784	7,671,891	3,074,038	1,374,162	47,248	256,520	142,699
2009	11,826,543	6,597,242	377,777	6,975,019	686,795	1,545,634	7,833,858	2,450,394	1,542,291	45,485	260,009	139,005
2010	12,789,341	7,439,480	398,869	7,838,349	697,465	1,615,215	8,756,099	2,325,358	1,707,884	48,589	263,216	138,372
2011	13,302,889	7,395,286	359,442	7,754,728	642,276	1,773,106	8,885,558	2,712,279	1,705,052	50,180	265,103	138,208
2012	14,173,085	7,445,582	413,734	7,859,316	639,597	2,055,692	9,275,411	3,170,996	1,726,678	53,124	266,794	140,225
2013	14,551,892	7,849,602	465,933	8,315,535	752,216	2,135,983	9,699,302	3,049,875	1,802,715	54,017	269,395	144,623
2014	15,328,295	8,212,556	457,533	8,670,089	792,357	2,085,285	9,963,017	3,458,365	1,906,913	56,452	271,529	149,214
2015	16,347,740	8,356,194	543,655	8,899,849	824,214	2,473,332	10,548,967	3,745,028	2,053,745	59,598	274,299	153,530
2016	16,766,106	8,466,541	527,169	8,993,710	861,910	2,556,203	10,688,003	3,935,176	2,142,927	60,924	275,196	154,836
2017	17,665,129	8,826,816	564,359	9,391,175	899,626	2,908,300	11,399,849	4,114,959	2,150,321	64,028	275,897	156,392
2018	18,697,119	18,326,275	370,844	9,595,021	941,346	3,188,789	11,842,464	4,560,325	2,294,330	68,277	273,841	156,783
2019	19,559,977	19,129,184	430,793	10,339,629	1,011,706	3,166,184	12,494,107	4,633,028	2,432,842	71,592	273,213	159,825

Personal Income and Employment by Area: Santa Fe, NM

(Thousands of dollars, except as noted.)

Year	Personal income, total	Earnings by place of work			Less: Contributions for government social insurance	Plus: Adjustment for residence	Equals: Net earnings by place of residence	Plus: Dividends, interest, and rent	Plus: Personal current transfer receipts	Per capita personal income (dollars)	Population (persons)	Total employment
		Nonfarm	Farm	Total								
1970	206,513	138,862	1,931	140,793	7,853	11,240	144,180	43,510	18,823	3,753	55,026	22,514
1971	230,769	157,567	1,472	159,039	9,362	10,996	160,673	48,906	21,190	4,058	56,874	24,070
1972	263,733	181,577	1,202	182,779	11,241	13,834	185,372	55,306	23,055	4,452	59,243	26,263
1973	298,254	206,172	2,590	208,762	14,970	15,722	209,514	62,235	26,505	4,870	61,246	28,068
1974	342,090	233,644	3,170	236,814	17,567	17,806	237,053	72,880	32,157	5,406	63,278	29,166
1975	384,068	259,740	2,160	261,900	19,143	21,688	264,445	79,169	40,454	5,825	65,930	29,184
1976	435,599	294,860	1,583	296,443	21,533	26,792	301,702	89,860	44,037	6,305	69,090	30,690
1977	493,716	338,586	1,087	339,673	25,169	31,800	346,304	101,742	45,670	6,895	71,604	33,009
1978	575,018	393,001	2,639	395,640	30,115	36,578	402,103	121,592	51,323	7,913	72,669	35,227
1979	642,811	432,145	2,461	434,606	34,969	41,637	441,274	142,400	59,137	8,531	75,353	36,981
1980	725,023	478,778	533	479,311	39,903	45,468	484,876	169,115	71,032	9,556	75,872	37,378
1981	836,968	532,646	557	533,203	47,544	54,661	540,320	216,360	80,288	10,838	77,222	38,104
1982	945,909	584,071	1,011	585,082	53,555	62,007	593,534	266,449	85,926	11,806	80,118	40,035
1983	1,041,065	657,184	-385	656,799	60,722	68,843	664,920	285,662	90,483	12,657	82,250	42,732
1984	1,162,144	731,894	1,292	733,186	68,491	81,771	746,466	318,674	97,004	13,818	84,106	44,481
1985	1,289,046	797,634	3,175	800,809	76,060	96,780	821,529	362,336	105,181	15,046	85,676	46,724
1986	1,405,171	887,304	1,874	889,178	85,081	100,773	904,870	386,682	113,619	15,765	89,134	48,864
1987	1,484,602	928,245	1,061	929,306	88,325	118,810	959,791	402,236	122,575	16,081	92,323	50,998
1988	1,597,071	995,549	2,567	998,116	101,408	118,115	1,014,823	449,391	132,857	16,899	94,507	54,052
1989	1,754,997	1,096,266	1,094	1,097,360	113,377	128,567	1,112,550	491,998	150,449	18,100	96,962	56,683
1990	1,901,683	1,207,432	2,134	1,209,566	132,417	131,170	1,208,319	529,732	163,632	19,096	99,587	58,372
1991	2,059,287	1,349,144	4,009	1,353,153	149,872	115,583	1,318,864	560,738	179,685	20,084	102,536	63,309
1992	2,264,977	1,482,232	3,207	1,485,439	162,909	138,794	1,461,324	602,190	201,463	21,362	106,030	65,129
1993	2,488,321	1,653,323	2,611	1,655,934	180,393	121,509	1,597,050	667,816	223,455	22,636	109,927	68,364
1994	2,696,822	1,763,895	3,931	1,767,826	197,198	131,254	1,701,882	756,046	238,894	23,668	113,944	70,827
1995	2,996,553	1,910,188	2,885	1,913,073	214,154	133,337	1,832,256	896,305	267,992	25,295	118,462	75,227
1996	3,150,699	1,949,078	3,345	1,952,423	219,167	131,795	1,865,051	990,572	295,076	26,032	121,031	75,777
1997	3,345,694	2,085,409	2,042	2,087,451	231,305	128,474	1,984,620	1,052,396	308,678	26,944	124,172	77,163
1998	3,593,793	2,221,322	3,024	2,224,346	247,340	160,937	2,137,943	1,132,307	323,543	28,532	125,956	78,737
1999	3,710,326	2,273,784	6,992	2,280,776	257,759	181,995	2,205,012	1,153,005	352,309	28,995	127,966	79,221
2000	4,140,801	2,530,467	5,937	2,536,404	274,923	210,149	2,471,630	1,289,893	379,278	31,923	129,713	81,236
2001	4,397,932	2,740,275	7,524	2,747,799	297,072	214,435	2,665,162	1,314,825	417,945	33,557	131,057	84,055
2002	4,546,345	2,952,840	6,386	2,959,226	317,647	227,048	2,868,627	1,215,401	462,317	34,041	133,555	85,360
2003	4,672,577	3,008,976	4,919	3,013,895	327,268	260,452	2,947,079	1,231,847	493,651	34,557	135,213	87,912
2004	4,933,197	3,138,913	4,476	3,143,389	342,702	240,138	3,040,825	1,359,994	532,378	36,170	136,391	90,099
2005	5,332,752	3,321,402	5,173	3,326,575	362,227	224,682	3,189,030	1,566,604	577,118	38,753	137,610	93,143
2006	5,793,630	3,595,250	9,284	3,604,534	397,226	194,030	3,401,338	1,757,829	634,463	41,745	138,786	94,699
2007	6,175,931	3,851,284	3,247	3,854,531	430,067	111,255	3,535,719	1,942,266	697,946	44,048	140,210	98,058
2008	6,400,806	3,965,833	6,577	3,972,410	450,882	69,872	3,591,400	1,990,533	818,873	45,170	141,704	98,098
2009	6,192,918	3,786,745	4,183	3,790,928	431,988	128,458	3,487,398	1,794,172	911,348	43,245	143,205	93,942
2010	6,253,365	3,805,422	2,021	3,807,443	430,968	167,419	3,543,894	1,700,585	1,008,886	43,269	144,523	92,489
2011	6,610,037	3,855,017	1,800	3,856,817	388,564	179,610	3,647,863	1,927,912	1,034,262	45,448	145,442	92,417
2012	6,929,344	3,919,788	767	3,920,555	394,044	248,185	3,774,696	2,103,093	1,051,555	47,406	146,169	91,816
2013	6,939,290	4,018,870	-3,231	4,015,639	460,875	222,890	3,777,654	2,061,422	1,100,214	47,330	146,616	92,784
2014	7,481,855	4,066,371	-734	4,065,637	470,038	250,745	3,846,344	2,428,968	1,206,543	50,903	146,983	93,260
2015	7,696,147	4,149,947	-2,654	4,147,293	498,462	249,002	3,897,833	2,502,446	1,295,868	52,257	147,276	94,396
2016	8,036,896	4,139,553	-3,102	4,136,451	499,333	383,317	4,020,435	2,672,556	1,343,905	54,324	147,943	94,508
2017	8,263,561	4,193,319	-4,127	4,189,192	501,965	451,716	4,138,943	2,763,616	1,361,002	55,553	148,750	94,550
2018	8,790,396	8,790,874	-478	4,290,734	520,081	459,428	4,230,081	3,077,044	1,483,271	58,696	149,761	94,229
2019	9,063,004	9,062,632	372	4,469,730	546,247	504,053	4,427,536	3,065,510	1,569,958	60,276	150,358	96,346

Personal Income and Employment by Area: Santa Maria-Santa Barbara, CA

(Thousands of dollars, except as noted.)

Year	Personal income, total	Earnings by place of work Nonfarm	Earnings by place of work Farm	Earnings by place of work Total	Less: Contributions for government social insurance	Plus: Adjustment for residence	Equals: Net earnings by place of residence	Plus: Dividends, interest, and rent	Plus: Personal current transfer receipts	Per capita personal income (dollars)	Population (persons)	Total employment
1970	1,338,257	919,747	35,407	955,154	57,246	-5,141	892,767	338,219	107,271	5,044	265,291	116,626
1971	1,429,790	971,262	38,675	1,009,937	62,188	-4,287	943,462	364,294	122,034	5,297	269,930	117,818
1972	1,570,222	1,058,954	53,455	1,112,409	70,796	-3,337	1,038,276	396,865	135,081	5,670	276,957	121,263
1973	1,743,627	1,173,238	66,679	1,239,917	89,602	-4,758	1,145,557	445,275	152,795	6,285	277,414	129,723
1974	1,920,803	1,274,843	69,400	1,344,243	100,943	-6,187	1,237,113	503,815	179,875	6,899	278,431	134,399
1975	2,119,517	1,404,119	68,732	1,472,851	109,221	-8,321	1,355,309	542,625	221,583	7,499	282,626	138,012
1976	2,347,422	1,584,603	68,134	1,652,737	124,281	-11,050	1,517,406	585,336	244,680	8,206	286,075	141,699
1977	2,583,164	1,757,286	74,682	1,831,968	142,677	-16,131	1,673,160	651,148	258,856	8,896	290,381	149,056
1978	2,951,811	2,036,819	80,906	2,117,725	169,472	-20,552	1,927,701	748,797	275,313	9,993	295,397	160,992
1979	3,314,174	2,277,681	94,856	2,372,537	201,658	-26,716	2,144,163	866,477	303,534	11,218	295,423	168,561
1980	3,773,852	2,499,834	132,061	2,631,895	218,153	-35,381	2,378,361	1,044,032	351,459	12,572	300,191	168,218
1981	4,302,836	2,748,752	123,347	2,872,099	261,865	-40,516	2,569,718	1,315,651	417,467	14,081	305,588	171,396
1982	4,651,106	2,946,588	149,116	3,095,704	288,350	-51,437	2,755,917	1,443,696	451,493	14,856	313,073	172,644
1983	5,036,726	3,205,696	170,756	3,376,452	318,987	-48,541	3,008,924	1,546,947	480,855	15,628	322,294	176,829
1984	5,669,668	3,725,344	133,162	3,858,506	386,737	-76,545	3,395,224	1,771,327	503,117	17,226	329,133	185,802
1985	6,103,760	4,089,207	134,969	4,224,176	429,226	-95,055	3,699,895	1,864,780	539,085	18,028	338,569	192,555
1986	6,499,147	4,405,664	154,335	4,559,999	465,482	-103,463	3,991,054	1,930,766	577,327	18,803	345,651	197,339
1987	6,868,749	4,688,973	180,566	4,869,539	492,097	-99,101	4,278,341	1,987,910	602,498	19,512	352,021	200,745
1988	7,424,092	5,060,178	204,678	5,264,856	545,355	-108,219	4,611,282	2,168,512	644,298	20,865	355,810	207,750
1989	8,026,689	5,397,950	217,498	5,615,448	589,949	-124,673	4,900,826	2,420,244	705,619	21,949	365,695	212,536
1990	8,303,443	5,604,470	239,916	5,844,386	616,109	-136,186	5,092,091	2,435,076	776,276	22,408	370,565	214,939
1991	8,770,037	6,032,922	205,414	6,238,336	661,552	-152,820	5,423,964	2,489,356	856,717	23,392	374,910	220,855
1992	9,134,464	6,224,176	170,978	6,395,154	675,919	-158,000	5,561,235	2,609,488	963,741	24,165	378,003	214,252
1993	9,333,973	6,252,664	239,029	6,491,693	679,767	-160,829	5,651,097	2,660,184	1,022,692	24,559	380,064	215,117
1994	9,654,421	6,250,292	219,509	6,469,801	690,897	-169,619	5,609,285	3,004,409	1,040,727	25,127	384,226	216,284
1995	9,863,506	6,376,221	276,876	6,653,097	699,213	-182,304	5,771,580	2,998,942	1,092,984	25,647	384,582	221,933
1996	10,319,542	6,622,239	281,121	6,903,360	707,206	-194,728	6,001,426	3,174,001	1,144,115	26,727	386,108	225,153
1997	10,720,989	6,948,609	330,822	7,279,431	737,196	-219,875	6,322,360	3,233,741	1,164,888	27,399	391,290	226,970
1998	11,737,445	7,535,112	317,224	7,852,336	782,421	-241,034	6,828,881	3,700,736	1,207,828	29,735	394,738	235,910
1999	12,354,139	7,934,433	350,133	8,284,566	828,788	-267,400	7,188,378	3,902,537	1,263,224	31,126	396,906	239,821
2000	13,467,748	8,820,933	388,110	9,209,043	925,442	-324,259	7,959,342	4,178,632	1,329,774	33,670	399,990	244,170
2001	13,722,573	9,276,103	303,980	9,580,083	984,906	-353,493	8,241,684	4,037,738	1,443,151	34,037	403,164	243,235
2002	13,683,755	9,638,099	346,249	9,984,348	1,035,512	-376,053	8,572,783	3,593,499	1,517,473	33,772	405,178	244,532
2003	14,425,764	10,243,927	381,583	10,625,510	1,116,233	-431,734	9,077,543	3,765,194	1,583,027	35,461	406,810	248,298
2004	16,106,028	11,167,310	376,511	11,543,821	1,238,443	-485,955	9,819,423	4,638,957	1,647,648	39,545	407,284	250,723
2005	17,091,378	11,727,565	411,861	12,139,426	1,294,775	-547,026	10,297,625	5,065,428	1,728,325	41,883	408,079	253,193
2006	18,486,804	12,033,899	405,405	12,439,304	1,290,371	-582,193	10,566,740	6,057,835	1,862,229	45,301	408,085	253,267
2007	18,975,209	12,396,493	394,956	12,791,449	1,312,651	-646,127	10,832,671	6,182,344	1,960,194	46,141	411,243	258,250
2008	19,022,250	12,590,920	399,458	12,990,378	1,359,075	-693,353	10,937,950	5,864,992	2,219,308	45,742	415,859	258,059
2009	18,592,918	12,511,866	664,289	13,176,155	1,356,505	-667,281	11,152,369	5,030,973	2,409,576	44,231	420,356	249,731
2010	19,341,353	12,984,126	577,880	13,562,006	1,344,424	-662,774	11,554,808	5,153,519	2,633,026	45,580	424,338	245,732
2011	20,811,129	13,571,564	501,621	14,073,185	1,274,280	-697,296	12,101,609	6,042,998	2,666,522	48,846	426,058	250,715
2012	22,029,683	14,189,115	639,077	14,828,192	1,323,156	-740,048	12,764,988	6,589,397	2,675,298	51,133	430,827	256,831
2013	22,058,509	14,384,242	813,775	15,198,017	1,499,306	-723,053	12,975,658	6,301,201	2,781,650	50,595	435,980	260,888
2014	23,628,757	15,005,202	842,758	15,847,960	1,571,267	-755,120	13,521,573	7,158,466	2,948,718	53,625	440,628	269,484
2015	25,378,342	15,918,520	1,080,379	16,998,899	1,651,002	-825,991	14,521,906	7,708,872	3,147,564	57,168	443,927	273,832
2016	25,454,080	16,064,043	884,247	16,948,290	1,682,315	-800,283	14,465,692	7,725,397	3,262,991	57,034	446,296	274,783
2017	26,646,853	16,908,721	968,225	17,876,946	1,758,633	-842,168	15,276,145	8,080,969	3,289,739	59,460	448,150	277,989
2018	28,224,056	27,458,714	765,342	18,686,608	1,851,364	-880,697	15,954,547	8,839,700	3,429,809	63,314	445,780	281,463
2019	29,502,767	28,555,420	947,347	19,784,344	1,972,459	-919,618	16,892,267	8,939,563	3,670,937	66,076	446,499	291,191

Personal Income and Employment by Area: Santa Rosa-Petaluma, CA

(Thousands of dollars, except as noted.)

Year	Personal income, total	Earnings by place of work			Less: Contributions for government social insurance	Plus: Adjustment for residence	Equals: Net earnings by place of residence	Plus: Dividends, interest, and rent	Plus: Personal current transfer receipts	Per capita personal income (dollars)	Population (persons)	Total employment
		Nonfarm	Farm	Total								
1970	957,026	508,418	24,485	532,903	32,136	136,914	637,681	203,063	116,282	4,646	206,003	74,003
1971	1,063,234	564,137	18,145	582,282	37,082	160,204	705,404	226,888	130,942	5,006	212,402	76,798
1972	1,205,719	643,504	25,319	668,823	44,342	186,463	810,944	254,154	140,621	5,380	224,091	82,982
1973	1,370,646	730,719	33,869	764,588	57,607	212,227	919,208	292,662	158,776	5,760	237,957	88,869
1974	1,552,265	813,707	27,524	841,231	66,380	246,577	1,021,428	339,694	191,143	6,387	243,028	93,352
1975	1,773,564	899,385	29,681	929,066	71,589	286,827	1,144,304	384,132	245,128	7,003	253,255	96,964
1976	2,023,175	1,053,365	33,457	1,086,822	84,482	323,872	1,326,212	423,641	273,322	7,703	262,654	103,354
1977	2,289,555	1,196,930	41,600	1,238,530	97,929	371,928	1,512,529	482,121	294,905	8,381	273,175	109,903
1978	2,664,526	1,421,880	46,255	1,468,135	119,024	436,620	1,785,731	559,454	319,341	9,467	281,442	118,796
1979	3,043,203	1,639,325	45,489	1,684,814	145,084	493,544	2,033,274	649,894	360,035	10,427	291,859	127,676
1980	3,477,261	1,798,627	39,817	1,838,444	156,982	579,299	2,260,761	797,080	419,420	11,530	301,586	133,637
1981	3,965,958	1,980,612	67,446	2,048,058	188,696	640,176	2,499,538	972,384	494,036	12,851	308,609	137,159
1982	4,236,873	2,100,006	57,548	2,157,554	204,122	690,400	2,643,832	1,063,534	529,507	13,466	314,636	138,573
1983	4,650,295	2,343,445	42,214	2,385,659	231,616	741,749	2,895,792	1,196,838	557,665	14,461	321,580	145,902
1984	5,220,940	2,725,524	54,957	2,780,481	280,949	804,132	3,303,664	1,337,185	580,091	15,973	326,863	155,144
1985	5,668,660	2,997,409	58,263	3,055,672	313,966	853,688	3,595,394	1,449,710	623,556	16,903	335,355	161,324
1986	6,130,011	3,292,610	60,464	3,353,074	347,162	918,852	3,924,764	1,532,792	672,455	17,754	345,270	166,384
1987	6,575,465	3,629,302	72,134	3,701,436	384,317	966,815	4,283,934	1,588,220	703,311	18,465	356,111	174,046
1988	7,211,764	4,032,568	81,747	4,114,315	439,938	1,039,378	4,713,755	1,740,998	757,011	19,603	367,893	186,395
1989	8,058,225	4,410,114	110,172	4,520,286	489,567	1,115,310	5,146,029	2,074,167	838,029	21,171	380,633	193,548
1990	8,677,571	4,841,062	101,673	4,942,735	535,389	1,261,228	5,668,574	2,103,478	905,519	22,222	390,495	204,435
1991	9,067,260	5,140,837	117,482	5,258,319	575,025	1,239,784	5,923,078	2,144,425	999,757	22,786	397,937	207,198
1992	9,587,374	5,475,542	112,314	5,587,856	604,671	1,250,062	6,233,247	2,217,461	1,136,666	23,664	405,151	207,086
1993	10,061,979	5,751,934	93,382	5,845,316	633,729	1,312,207	6,523,794	2,344,986	1,193,199	24,500	410,687	210,765
1994	10,550,598	6,079,918	93,567	6,173,485	668,508	1,356,787	6,861,764	2,457,091	1,231,743	25,353	416,152	218,474
1995	11,021,041	6,280,805	82,049	6,362,854	687,577	1,384,980	7,060,257	2,667,312	1,293,472	26,099	422,286	221,033
1996	11,878,837	6,840,345	108,322	6,948,667	722,347	1,392,784	7,619,104	2,901,663	1,358,070	27,728	428,399	232,015
1997	12,984,551	7,621,946	168,525	7,790,471	796,448	1,508,679	8,502,702	3,104,575	1,377,274	29,703	437,141	242,030
1998	14,133,890	8,588,576	132,986	8,721,562	877,951	1,525,461	9,369,072	3,332,298	1,432,520	31,697	445,901	254,209
1999	14,958,731	9,331,035	123,983	9,455,018	956,400	1,543,551	10,042,169	3,430,305	1,486,257	32,991	453,421	263,310
2000	17,042,031	10,601,529	191,064	10,792,593	1,089,290	2,008,982	11,712,285	3,774,277	1,555,469	37,014	460,421	267,725
2001	17,821,758	11,566,905	176,014	11,742,919	1,194,289	1,855,405	12,404,035	3,705,632	1,712,091	38,302	465,293	272,782
2002	17,824,431	11,889,753	166,868	12,056,621	1,231,870	1,702,837	12,527,588	3,476,834	1,820,009	38,308	465,298	272,287
2003	18,090,265	11,915,181	114,068	12,029,249	1,254,207	1,699,028	12,474,070	3,689,287	1,926,908	38,780	466,489	268,461
2004	18,313,674	12,216,862	137,089	12,353,951	1,346,584	1,549,909	12,557,276	3,759,889	1,996,509	39,232	466,809	271,429
2005	18,911,246	12,475,593	200,257	12,675,850	1,390,771	1,514,195	12,799,274	4,006,038	2,105,934	40,587	465,938	271,468
2006	20,238,216	13,020,091	118,873	13,138,964	1,407,076	1,490,771	13,222,659	4,717,029	2,298,528	43,505	465,188	274,369
2007	20,894,788	13,227,076	137,543	13,364,619	1,415,605	1,492,477	13,441,491	5,015,815	2,437,482	44,709	467,356	279,979
2008	20,656,813	13,050,659	103,237	13,153,896	1,434,715	1,244,346	12,963,527	4,921,723	2,771,563	43,664	473,091	276,221
2009	20,058,536	12,468,829	188,275	12,657,104	1,366,304	1,397,031	12,687,831	4,297,617	3,073,088	41,834	479,479	262,782
2010	20,821,336	13,162,783	131,631	13,294,414	1,379,832	1,167,173	13,081,755	4,337,136	3,402,445	42,946	484,827	260,148
2011	21,972,758	13,645,327	119,466	13,764,793	1,294,000	1,171,205	13,641,998	4,905,817	3,424,943	45,043	487,822	263,452
2012	23,005,070	13,734,992	317,763	14,052,755	1,286,393	1,552,054	14,318,416	5,221,845	3,464,809	46,878	490,740	267,006
2013	24,027,228	14,411,607	342,349	14,753,956	1,514,049	1,762,870	15,002,777	5,450,191	3,574,260	48,539	495,007	277,115
2014	25,733,587	15,396,796	379,605	15,776,401	1,615,613	1,446,686	15,607,474	6,281,921	3,844,192	51,512	499,563	288,743
2015	27,838,517	16,666,116	355,111	17,021,227	1,741,321	1,598,455	16,878,361	6,822,898	4,137,258	55,445	502,096	296,943
2016	28,851,729	17,267,246	449,429	17,716,675	1,813,523	1,704,187	17,607,339	6,959,767	4,284,623	57,264	503,833	299,549
2017	30,397,470	18,033,861	533,967	18,567,828	1,895,126	2,129,373	18,802,075	7,287,941	4,307,454	60,286	504,217	304,489
2018	31,612,355	31,407,951	204,404	19,187,520	2,034,081	1,482,985	18,636,424	8,390,156	4,585,775	63,397	498,643	309,070
2019	32,972,432	32,714,097	258,335	20,194,866	2,149,136	1,557,141	19,602,871	8,504,016	4,865,545	66,700	494,336	313,181

Personal Income and Employment by Area: Savannah, GA

(Thousands of dollars, except as noted.)

Year	Personal income, total	Earnings by place of work			Less: Contributions for government social insurance	Plus: Adjustment for residence	Equals: Net earnings by place of residence	Plus: Dividends, interest, and rent	Plus: Personal current transfer receipts	Per capita personal income (dollars)	Population (persons)	Total employment
		Nonfarm	Farm	Total								
1970	745,764	614,061	3,000	617,061	39,518	-8,341	569,202	107,281	69,281	3,608	206,709	96,506
1971	790,868	638,493	3,745	642,238	42,696	-6,742	592,800	113,677	84,391	3,891	203,279	94,486
1972	844,303	684,288	3,687	687,975	48,026	-5,898	634,051	115,795	94,457	4,133	204,260	93,250
1973	923,475	748,569	5,257	753,826	60,968	-3,909	688,949	124,682	109,844	4,509	204,809	96,053
1974	1,020,920	812,730	5,277	818,007	68,884	-2,323	746,800	141,300	132,820	4,982	204,936	96,696
1975	1,192,441	931,552	4,551	936,103	76,871	-6,142	853,090	173,038	166,313	5,612	212,479	100,738
1976	1,356,515	1,039,889	3,848	1,043,737	87,331	32,875	989,281	186,220	181,014	6,204	218,664	103,097
1977	1,512,469	1,149,844	2,004	1,151,848	96,166	61,432	1,117,114	206,717	188,638	6,730	224,727	104,468
1978	1,713,715	1,300,239	6,907	1,307,146	111,123	77,737	1,273,760	235,764	204,191	7,580	226,093	108,230
1979	1,871,658	1,407,150	8,823	1,415,973	125,085	90,134	1,381,022	261,677	228,959	8,158	229,430	108,522
1980	2,108,663	1,553,612	2,042	1,555,654	138,005	95,705	1,513,354	324,155	271,154	9,101	231,691	109,966
1981	2,418,147	1,723,166	8,243	1,731,409	164,800	138,435	1,705,044	403,949	309,154	10,286	235,102	112,942
1982	2,618,390	1,853,501	10,972	1,864,473	182,852	142,180	1,823,801	459,064	335,525	10,950	239,114	114,351
1983	2,791,993	1,976,952	9,157	1,986,109	197,362	133,255	1,922,002	499,944	370,047	11,616	240,354	114,335
1984	3,050,478	2,169,922	7,643	2,177,565	223,190	132,201	2,086,576	571,272	392,630	12,581	242,463	118,390
1985	3,283,995	2,358,033	5,621	2,363,654	247,098	133,296	2,249,852	616,664	417,479	13,426	244,606	122,010
1986	3,545,327	2,614,577	4,027	2,618,604	277,737	100,385	2,441,252	661,033	443,042	14,332	247,365	126,772
1987	3,773,609	2,785,345	4,794	2,790,139	292,431	107,918	2,605,626	701,354	466,629	15,021	251,216	130,214
1988	4,039,638	2,982,046	5,151	2,987,197	323,056	100,449	2,764,590	780,940	494,108	15,900	254,061	134,151
1989	4,385,120	3,181,316	6,282	3,187,598	347,578	76,530	2,916,550	920,705	547,865	17,165	255,475	137,367
1990	4,650,792	3,488,236	4,147	3,492,383	380,909	-32,187	3,079,287	969,543	601,962	17,946	259,160	142,254
1991	4,858,666	3,532,700	5,417	3,538,117	388,471	25,720	3,175,366	1,007,337	675,963	18,496	262,690	138,590
1992	5,288,764	3,831,893	6,243	3,838,136	414,262	93,096	3,516,970	1,027,361	744,433	19,745	267,853	143,404
1993	5,501,003	4,014,389	3,211	4,017,600	433,637	34,611	3,618,574	1,080,783	801,646	20,159	272,886	145,860
1994	5,849,796	4,219,185	5,350	4,224,535	463,607	22,443	3,783,371	1,206,304	860,121	21,074	277,581	150,429
1995	6,193,056	4,448,800	2,922	4,451,722	487,444	29,381	3,993,659	1,280,609	918,788	22,029	281,126	155,080
1996	6,572,324	4,747,715	3,820	4,751,535	518,847	-10,484	4,222,204	1,384,018	966,102	23,184	283,480	158,374
1997	6,802,210	4,867,313	3,409	4,870,722	531,790	-17,129	4,321,803	1,500,321	980,086	23,726	286,697	162,397
1998	7,340,212	5,308,230	1,265	5,309,495	576,323	-15,775	4,717,397	1,637,683	985,132	25,448	288,441	164,741
1999	7,637,153	5,634,636	4,163	5,638,799	606,506	-50,602	4,981,691	1,616,825	1,038,637	26,189	291,618	167,970
2000	8,068,425	5,886,203	4,140	5,890,343	630,315	-22,750	5,237,278	1,728,793	1,102,354	27,470	293,721	172,243
2001	8,271,965	6,035,552	6,424	6,041,976	642,025	-8,315	5,391,636	1,691,633	1,188,696	27,839	297,133	172,488
2002	8,606,246	6,233,004	4,954	6,237,958	663,427	20,436	5,594,967	1,667,061	1,344,218	28,531	301,644	173,541
2003	9,121,842	6,614,535	6,948	6,621,483	696,077	72,026	5,997,432	1,773,857	1,350,553	29,948	304,585	177,613
2004	9,731,680	7,127,020	7,323	7,134,343	768,944	73,841	6,439,240	1,863,879	1,428,561	31,337	310,553	183,261
2005	10,411,291	7,576,606	8,619	7,585,225	813,638	192,223	6,963,810	1,922,241	1,525,240	33,101	314,528	190,505
2006	11,299,860	8,211,978	9,415	8,221,393	885,612	183,137	7,518,918	2,163,238	1,617,704	35,086	322,065	198,121
2007	12,094,641	8,624,522	8,680	8,633,202	924,969	258,186	7,966,419	2,397,536	1,730,686	36,657	329,943	207,508
2008	12,608,636	8,766,346	7,905	8,774,251	979,887	401,130	8,195,494	2,426,396	1,986,746	37,617	335,185	205,696
2009	12,550,552	8,703,483	7,066	8,710,549	968,504	361,027	8,103,072	2,269,811	2,177,669	36,482	344,017	198,549
2010	13,092,022	8,848,332	7,695	8,856,027	984,032	512,491	8,384,486	2,279,283	2,428,253	37,547	348,687	196,887
2011	14,101,833	9,188,179	6,504	9,194,683	909,711	541,324	8,826,296	2,706,629	2,568,908	39,630	355,839	200,445
2012	14,277,255	9,571,726	10,306	9,582,032	947,486	493,418	9,127,964	2,643,354	2,505,937	39,428	362,109	203,237
2013	14,554,618	9,955,796	10,535	9,966,331	1,109,055	448,700	9,305,976	2,660,516	2,588,126	39,828	365,438	208,594
2014	15,348,173	10,494,842	5,903	10,500,745	1,159,172	347,443	9,689,016	2,921,436	2,737,721	41,264	371,950	214,858
2015	16,233,361	11,143,906	10,530	11,154,436	1,232,800	290,253	10,211,889	3,149,531	2,871,941	42,870	378,664	223,203
2016	16,546,855	11,403,857	9,026	11,412,883	1,257,079	221,846	10,377,650	3,184,679	2,984,526	43,115	383,785	228,040
2017	17,130,789	11,880,873	7,725	11,888,598	1,316,362	188,523	10,760,759	3,287,958	3,082,072	44,204	387,543	231,755
2018	18,319,186	18,307,673	11,513	12,769,647	1,407,660	84,296	11,446,283	3,654,446	3,218,457	47,038	389,453	241,848
2019	18,829,571	18,816,976	12,595	13,140,635	1,453,902	75,028	11,761,761	3,683,732	3,384,078	47,869	393,353	246,639

Personal Income and Employment by Area: Scranton—Wilkes-Barre, PA

(Thousands of dollars, except as noted.)

Year	Personal income, total	Earnings by place of work			Less: Contributions for government social insurance	Plus: Adjustment for residence	Equals: Net earnings by place of residence	Plus: Dividends, interest, and rent	Plus: Personal current transfer receipts	Per capita personal income (dollars)	Population (persons)	Total employment
		Nonfarm	Farm	Total								
1970	2,147,763	1,639,360	5,903	1,645,263	123,705	45,680	1,567,238	275,347	305,178	3,602	596,204	255,288
1971	2,344,677	1,753,755	6,397	1,760,152	137,169	44,112	1,667,095	299,011	378,571	3,901	601,087	253,153
1972	2,590,425	1,930,929	5,327	1,936,256	156,322	42,974	1,822,908	324,211	443,306	4,272	606,331	258,007
1973	2,870,429	2,132,743	6,904	2,139,647	197,262	42,932	1,985,317	370,410	514,702	4,737	605,941	266,382
1974	3,082,235	2,229,467	6,496	2,235,963	213,816	44,955	2,067,102	424,184	590,949	5,083	606,407	260,623
1975	3,361,969	2,349,313	10,455	2,359,768	218,479	40,726	2,182,015	458,819	721,135	5,529	608,007	251,998
1976	3,649,913	2,567,537	10,704	2,578,241	243,952	37,345	2,371,634	489,134	789,145	6,045	603,751	251,764
1977	3,986,753	2,831,788	14,436	2,846,224	267,387	34,840	2,613,677	544,290	828,786	6,598	604,269	254,824
1978	4,399,963	3,175,778	11,739	3,187,517	306,458	36,478	2,917,537	597,577	884,849	7,290	603,524	261,329
1979	4,857,926	3,441,042	15,603	3,456,645	342,349	32,312	3,146,608	663,218	1,048,100	8,074	601,656	265,502
1980	5,242,373	3,561,643	14,502	3,576,145	360,355	32,482	3,248,272	818,118	1,175,983	8,781	597,021	259,934
1981	5,737,807	3,790,638	16,908	3,807,546	411,740	34,446	3,430,252	1,007,268	1,300,287	9,656	594,227	257,840
1982	6,207,667	3,957,695	13,128	3,970,823	435,352	32,154	3,567,625	1,204,378	1,435,664	10,502	591,104	252,572
1983	6,593,764	4,191,476	12,266	4,203,742	464,791	34,712	3,773,663	1,269,782	1,550,319	11,218	587,760	252,296
1984	6,970,919	4,439,219	19,731	4,458,950	509,762	51,157	4,000,345	1,403,446	1,567,128	11,933	584,185	254,756
1985	7,395,405	4,733,455	20,804	4,754,259	550,505	49,125	4,252,879	1,535,823	1,606,703	12,756	579,742	259,357
1986	7,756,387	5,005,375	18,539	5,023,914	585,002	40,548	4,479,460	1,606,822	1,670,105	13,409	578,457	263,798
1987	8,121,953	5,380,313	17,082	5,397,395	622,977	46,287	4,820,705	1,610,273	1,690,975	14,099	576,085	269,274
1988	8,716,038	5,874,494	12,117	5,886,611	695,418	34,776	5,225,969	1,727,240	1,762,829	15,134	575,917	278,326
1989	9,466,942	6,351,552	17,620	6,369,172	742,280	25,387	5,652,279	1,982,492	1,832,171	16,439	575,871	283,746
1990	9,948,061	6,709,686	19,382	6,729,068	785,703	27,539	5,970,904	2,012,671	1,964,486	17,268	576,090	288,238
1991	10,350,677	6,884,143	14,794	6,898,937	818,685	6,901	6,087,153	2,010,100	2,253,424	17,901	578,212	284,245
1992	10,848,943	7,361,071	24,814	7,385,885	874,744	-44,622	6,466,519	2,000,867	2,381,557	18,718	579,606	285,358
1993	11,168,065	7,672,302	19,231	7,691,533	930,333	-80,230	6,680,970	1,990,269	2,496,826	19,244	580,330	286,290
1994	11,571,051	8,015,042	15,462	8,030,504	986,339	-72,646	6,971,519	2,074,780	2,524,752	19,992	578,788	289,245
1995	12,076,971	8,343,793	8,860	8,352,653	1,025,320	-92,245	7,235,088	2,242,002	2,599,881	20,931	576,980	293,803
1996	12,585,597	8,551,079	14,813	8,565,892	1,026,042	-68,427	7,471,423	2,387,019	2,727,155	21,930	573,886	294,639
1997	13,127,841	8,982,449	10,638	8,993,087	1,064,932	-76,031	7,852,124	2,498,761	2,776,956	23,056	569,384	297,412
1998	13,627,667	9,296,379	13,069	9,309,448	1,088,726	-60,332	8,160,390	2,670,355	2,796,922	24,068	566,216	296,660
1999	14,122,546	9,804,808	11,454	9,816,262	1,128,448	-62,592	8,625,222	2,597,445	2,899,879	25,077	563,157	300,626
2000	15,073,076	10,501,260	19,556	10,520,816	1,187,472	-52,929	9,280,415	2,797,429	2,995,232	26,922	559,879	308,211
2001	15,612,622	10,948,909	12,887	10,961,796	1,243,868	-49,040	9,668,888	2,754,613	3,189,121	28,006	557,476	306,843
2002	15,837,702	11,121,351	11,892	11,133,243	1,263,368	-3,173	9,866,702	2,627,575	3,343,425	28,500	555,702	301,409
2003	16,199,080	11,367,410	19,609	11,387,019	1,288,912	22,567	10,120,674	2,640,171	3,438,235	29,162	555,483	301,889
2004	16,950,437	11,902,505	16,154	11,918,659	1,351,274	66,908	10,634,293	2,692,465	3,623,679	30,514	555,495	304,761
2005	17,448,015	12,247,535	13,268	12,260,803	1,427,984	119,783	10,952,602	2,644,571	3,850,842	31,345	556,652	308,372
2006	18,204,768	12,592,480	15,499	12,607,979	1,481,284	174,037	11,300,732	2,842,013	4,062,023	32,647	557,626	311,527
2007	19,185,457	12,987,520	11,413	12,998,933	1,528,983	234,398	11,704,348	3,183,745	4,297,364	34,258	560,032	316,218
2008	20,014,947	13,153,078	14,583	13,167,661	1,561,283	280,527	11,886,905	3,360,564	4,767,478	35,642	561,548	316,876
2009	19,947,728	12,948,693	16,607	12,965,300	1,556,278	269,030	11,678,052	3,098,698	5,170,978	35,435	562,933	309,015
2010	20,554,643	13,379,820	18,820	13,398,640	1,594,706	270,962	12,074,896	3,028,511	5,451,236	36,459	563,771	308,777
2011	21,308,374	13,772,969	19,185	13,792,154	1,484,197	247,691	12,555,648	3,250,705	5,502,021	37,807	563,604	311,684
2012	21,790,286	13,983,254	32,391	14,015,645	1,499,745	215,432	12,731,332	3,600,691	5,458,263	38,656	563,694	312,973
2013	21,631,259	14,322,364	33,912	14,356,276	1,718,252	153,358	12,791,382	3,398,180	5,441,697	38,523	561,521	315,608
2014	22,382,016	14,799,102	37,592	14,836,694	1,779,666	139,823	13,196,851	3,643,096	5,542,069	39,965	560,034	319,488
2015	23,223,060	15,316,152	20,900	15,337,052	1,839,948	131,365	13,628,469	3,818,311	5,776,280	41,652	557,555	321,177
2016	23,682,673	15,489,256	13,017	15,502,273	1,881,344	124,454	13,745,383	3,938,203	5,999,087	42,658	555,171	323,618
2017	24,415,781	16,043,247	16,704	16,059,951	1,967,749	129,221	14,221,423	4,128,726	6,065,632	43,959	555,426	325,807
2018	25,535,827	25,540,515	-4,688	16,630,748	2,024,852	136,149	14,742,045	4,324,074	6,469,708	45,993	555,215	325,946
2019	26,245,576	26,243,815	1,761	17,008,837	2,065,049	184,543	15,128,331	4,408,111	6,709,134	47,385	553,885	327,904

Personal Income and Employment by Area: Seattle-Tacoma-Bellevue, WA

(Thousands of dollars, except as noted.)

Year	Personal income, total	Earnings by place of work			Less: Contributions for government social insurance	Plus: Adjustment for residence	Equals: Net earnings by place of residence	Plus: Dividends, interest, and rent	Plus: Personal current transfer receipts	Per capita personal income (dollars)	Population (persons)	Total employment
		Nonfarm	Farm	Total								
1970	8,731,054	7,010,889	26,946	7,037,835	559,723	18,717	6,496,829	1,472,418	761,807	4,758	1,834,990	824,119
1971	8,942,817	7,011,821	28,446	7,040,267	580,348	14,736	6,474,655	1,569,989	898,173	4,873	1,835,190	786,245
1972	9,425,134	7,460,267	33,366	7,493,633	653,159	9,385	6,849,859	1,637,838	937,437	5,219	1,806,099	789,860
1973	10,474,443	8,405,539	49,155	8,454,694	840,240	386	7,614,840	1,814,212	1,045,391	5,816	1,800,981	834,401
1974	11,829,739	9,434,527	47,977	9,482,504	969,872	19,750	8,532,382	2,095,568	1,201,789	6,450	1,833,981	869,673
1975	13,418,533	10,562,573	50,176	10,612,749	1,076,303	64,080	9,600,526	2,324,517	1,493,490	7,190	1,866,276	887,648
1976	14,884,770	11,826,526	51,174	11,877,700	1,233,342	99,984	10,744,342	2,517,491	1,622,937	7,891	1,886,242	919,384
1977	16,563,011	13,425,500	54,295	13,479,795	1,428,946	51,537	12,102,386	2,796,774	1,663,851	8,641	1,916,683	968,408
1978	19,374,731	16,003,912	49,467	16,053,379	1,756,897	29,335	14,325,817	3,250,009	1,798,905	9,829	1,971,129	1,046,539
1979	22,582,576	18,823,493	56,541	18,880,034	2,138,583	110,838	16,852,289	3,760,509	1,969,778	11,113	2,032,131	1,123,231
1980	25,831,708	21,064,163	44,721	21,108,884	2,359,828	106,492	18,855,548	4,580,204	2,395,956	12,267	2,105,824	1,159,283
1981	28,854,599	23,169,342	55,977	23,225,319	2,781,762	-30,272	20,413,285	5,622,808	2,818,506	13,410	2,151,691	1,167,540
1982	30,910,389	24,269,417	47,955	24,317,372	2,960,991	-15,123	21,341,258	6,408,799	3,160,332	14,193	2,177,909	1,160,929
1983	32,566,753	25,224,672	54,058	25,278,730	3,113,281	-18,794	22,146,655	6,928,901	3,491,197	14,884	2,188,099	1,179,085
1984	35,133,760	27,286,909	55,652	27,342,561	3,469,223	-65,902	23,807,436	7,706,293	3,620,031	15,854	2,216,022	1,236,653
1985	38,025,357	29,686,537	62,125	29,748,662	3,803,822	-116,746	25,828,094	8,320,911	3,876,352	16,840	2,258,026	1,290,615
1986	40,973,901	32,448,010	70,168	32,518,178	4,169,389	-193,404	28,155,385	8,690,212	4,128,304	17,807	2,301,024	1,346,586
1987	43,772,479	35,065,262	75,522	35,140,784	4,481,173	-265,029	30,394,582	9,016,249	4,361,648	18,577	2,356,263	1,422,816
1988	48,226,800	38,848,802	77,155	38,925,957	5,073,601	-299,246	33,553,110	9,841,474	4,832,216	19,876	2,426,393	1,505,432
1989	53,437,443	42,791,792	91,413	42,883,205	5,572,026	-361,987	36,949,192	11,164,024	5,324,227	21,433	2,493,214	1,587,002
1990	58,868,037	47,565,802	94,275	47,660,077	6,338,120	-580,054	40,741,903	12,275,373	5,850,761	22,828	2,578,807	1,653,020
1991	62,573,349	50,799,730	89,714	50,889,444	6,838,633	-638,777	43,412,034	12,600,877	6,560,438	23,786	2,630,705	1,661,101
1992	67,420,070	55,510,917	117,051	55,627,968	7,472,266	-799,040	47,356,662	12,896,430	7,166,978	25,055	2,690,858	1,669,827
1993	70,062,830	57,287,857	110,486	57,398,343	7,697,910	-969,695	48,730,738	13,677,645	7,654,447	25,567	2,740,325	1,687,223
1994	73,519,995	59,550,610	105,935	59,656,545	8,113,599	-1,029,263	50,513,683	14,972,153	8,034,159	26,502	2,774,159	1,728,057
1995	78,008,350	62,510,103	95,132	62,605,235	8,532,251	-1,110,019	52,962,965	16,499,296	8,546,089	27,715	2,814,630	1,750,246
1996	84,207,951	67,638,554	100,263	67,738,817	9,072,702	-1,231,685	57,434,430	17,868,613	8,904,908	29,476	2,856,795	1,807,825
1997	91,931,211	74,960,322	91,990	75,052,312	9,785,287	-1,661,519	63,605,506	19,100,603	9,225,102	31,504	2,918,071	1,887,996
1998	102,413,093	85,258,298	116,424	85,374,722	10,957,785	-2,005,132	72,411,805	20,447,537	9,553,751	34,381	2,978,761	1,957,069
1999	111,580,954	94,339,843	121,948	94,461,791	11,578,130	-2,152,778	80,730,883	20,766,019	10,084,052	36,952	3,019,651	1,997,050
2000	119,075,381	100,503,322	91,384	100,594,706	12,561,324	-2,602,948	85,430,434	23,046,025	10,598,922	39,013	3,052,187	2,050,200
2001	120,829,181	101,280,065	107,779	101,387,844	12,097,161	-2,664,862	86,625,821	22,262,040	11,941,320	39,066	3,092,927	2,040,022
2002	122,531,715	101,766,329	91,941	101,858,270	12,190,110	-2,663,787	87,004,373	22,640,712	12,886,630	39,294	3,118,302	1,999,926
2003	126,123,268	103,915,450	132,709	104,048,159	12,636,559	-2,708,706	88,702,894	24,051,994	13,368,380	40,256	3,133,021	2,002,177
2004	136,401,504	108,827,979	113,725	108,941,704	13,372,332	-2,817,407	92,751,965	30,383,893	13,265,646	43,179	3,158,967	2,040,998
2005	141,328,945	115,210,552	105,080	115,315,632	14,180,061	-2,990,999	98,144,572	29,295,411	13,888,962	44,189	3,198,265	2,099,077
2006	156,113,084	125,068,026	92,252	125,160,278	15,123,126	-3,142,280	106,894,872	34,427,769	14,790,443	47,930	3,257,081	2,169,876
2007	169,728,942	134,266,754	91,140	134,357,894	15,992,032	-3,520,692	114,845,170	38,921,672	15,962,100	51,363	3,304,467	2,252,591
2008	175,720,787	137,118,369	107,397	137,225,766	16,322,453	-3,577,579	117,325,734	39,905,234	18,489,819	52,375	3,355,042	2,272,430
2009	163,997,325	128,897,511	113,742	129,011,253	15,956,705	-3,434,337	109,620,211	33,261,236	21,115,878	48,025	3,414,797	2,182,713
2010	167,667,652	131,330,913	108,479	131,439,392	16,362,537	-3,212,668	111,864,187	32,353,519	23,449,946	48,627	3,448,049	2,154,810
2011	179,195,871	139,046,427	119,911	139,166,338	15,450,355	-3,175,668	120,540,315	35,540,090	23,115,466	51,245	3,496,870	2,190,360
2012	198,177,002	151,786,088	125,670	151,911,758	16,079,948	-3,210,931	132,620,879	42,579,112	22,977,011	55,790	3,552,220	2,258,786
2013	204,033,607	160,560,624	170,653	160,731,277	19,015,885	-3,172,396	138,542,996	42,079,448	23,411,163	56,510	3,610,580	2,313,266
2014	223,340,147	170,635,867	184,462	170,820,329	20,047,747	-3,236,047	147,536,535	50,443,722	25,359,890	60,902	3,667,189	2,380,537
2015	237,223,771	179,409,560	289,325	179,698,885	21,241,757	-3,355,226	155,101,902	56,296,151	25,825,718	63,623	3,728,606	2,454,268
2016	250,948,009	190,654,625	218,951	190,873,576	22,262,196	-3,806,495	164,804,885	58,930,560	27,212,564	65,993	3,802,660	2,527,356
2017	267,653,492	205,833,183	223,248	206,056,431	23,973,967	-4,388,296	177,694,168	61,811,758	28,147,566	69,214	3,867,046	2,583,679
2018	294,409,674	294,278,691	130,983	224,639,038	25,622,998	-3,959,728	195,056,312	70,222,871	29,130,491	74,815	3,935,179	2,668,890
2019	310,717,787	310,565,294	152,493	240,647,763	27,086,988	-4,625,592	208,935,183	71,198,721	30,583,883	78,073	3,979,845	2,739,330

Personal Income and Employment by Area: Sebastian-Vero Beach, FL

(Thousands of dollars, except as noted.)

Year	Personal income, total	Earnings by place of work			Less: Contributions for government social insurance	Plus: Adjustment for residence	Equals: Net earnings by place of residence	Plus: Dividends, interest, and rent	Plus: Personal current transfer receipts	Per capita personal income (dollars)	Population (persons)	Total employment
		Nonfarm	Farm	Total								
1970	147,387	85,590	5,816	91,406	5,485	-396	85,525	44,173	17,689	4,072	36,192	15,206
1971	173,674	100,446	8,454	108,900	6,783	-1,543	100,574	51,617	21,483	4,617	37,617	16,339
1972	209,071	123,376	12,145	135,521	8,814	-2,677	124,030	59,839	25,202	5,153	40,570	18,541
1973	250,946	151,902	12,463	164,365	12,477	-4,264	147,624	73,026	30,296	5,747	43,668	21,051
1974	281,597	162,102	14,098	176,200	14,028	-4,152	158,020	87,514	36,063	6,146	45,818	21,271
1975	304,978	169,386	12,033	181,419	14,352	-4,354	162,713	96,337	45,928	6,453	47,259	21,020
1976	350,589	196,505	12,234	208,739	16,601	-5,952	186,186	112,204	52,199	7,277	48,176	22,091
1977	404,668	221,991	15,598	237,589	19,349	-6,589	211,651	134,092	58,925	8,016	50,485	23,515
1978	486,509	264,691	20,580	285,271	23,668	-8,358	253,245	166,600	66,664	9,126	53,309	25,884
1979	576,112	304,667	21,828	326,495	28,335	-7,975	290,185	204,766	81,161	9,948	57,912	27,380
1980	698,671	335,779	34,903	370,682	30,950	-4,152	335,580	262,803	100,288	11,505	60,728	28,130
1981	848,789	396,955	24,184	421,139	39,720	-8,402	373,017	354,669	121,103	13,274	63,946	29,823
1982	890,445	388,328	26,785	415,113	40,811	-2,699	371,603	369,442	149,400	13,192	67,499	30,005
1983	994,919	416,631	47,608	464,239	43,849	-1,117	419,273	408,709	166,937	14,129	70,419	31,067
1984	1,142,565	480,384	43,885	524,269	51,911	-5,586	466,772	494,497	181,296	15,484	73,792	33,139
1985	1,296,847	534,884	55,544	590,428	59,593	-7,141	523,694	573,522	199,631	17,091	75,879	35,176
1986	1,433,307	610,458	56,815	667,273	69,320	-7,272	590,681	621,808	220,818	18,195	78,776	37,595
1987	1,606,315	683,276	74,750	758,026	76,745	-5,526	675,755	691,989	238,571	19,789	81,171	37,686
1988	1,859,059	769,114	113,426	882,540	89,616	-8,204	784,720	816,564	257,775	22,162	83,885	41,082
1989	2,081,819	885,334	88,911	974,245	105,386	-14,947	853,912	932,252	295,655	23,781	87,542	43,275
1990	2,296,583	943,785	63,267	1,007,052	109,888	-14,212	882,952	1,091,809	321,822	25,205	91,115	44,005
1991	2,425,511	921,811	75,091	996,902	109,894	-3,166	883,842	1,188,854	352,815	25,916	93,593	43,445
1992	2,563,399	987,513	61,340	1,048,853	116,950	1,397	933,300	1,224,762	405,337	26,696	96,023	42,812
1993	2,665,024	1,041,154	54,148	1,095,302	122,579	4,788	977,511	1,258,392	429,121	27,315	97,566	43,672
1994	2,852,067	1,118,441	49,310	1,167,751	133,668	2,018	1,036,101	1,350,106	465,860	28,561	99,858	45,180
1995	3,146,915	1,193,591	46,581	1,240,172	142,418	2,726	1,100,480	1,552,159	494,276	30,874	101,929	47,392
1996	3,380,726	1,304,404	32,527	1,336,931	152,074	-2,054	1,182,803	1,671,033	526,890	32,638	103,583	49,354
1997	3,628,890	1,373,159	30,739	1,403,898	160,700	-836	1,242,362	1,832,826	553,702	34,141	106,291	51,903
1998	3,922,336	1,476,135	48,551	1,524,686	170,949	-1,541	1,352,196	1,992,036	578,104	35,998	108,961	53,805
1999	4,117,031	1,633,856	39,142	1,672,998	185,502	-5,614	1,481,882	2,039,512	595,637	36,992	111,294	54,638
2000	4,397,450	1,729,519	42,819	1,772,338	194,832	3,310	1,580,816	2,181,316	635,318	38,805	113,323	55,510
2001	4,862,704	1,910,348	35,762	1,946,110	210,965	69,343	1,804,488	2,372,169	686,047	42,117	115,456	58,381
2002	4,985,470	1,993,985	41,048	2,035,033	219,549	123,367	1,938,851	2,309,516	737,103	42,198	118,144	59,597
2003	5,255,580	2,173,523	35,762	2,209,285	241,693	154,578	2,122,170	2,355,398	778,012	43,633	120,450	63,547
2004	6,142,306	2,308,609	41,949	2,350,558	261,718	236,063	2,324,903	2,968,631	848,772	49,138	125,001	65,719
2005	6,860,492	2,498,051	59,504	2,557,555	285,443	372,385	2,644,497	3,354,075	861,920	53,616	127,955	68,831
2006	7,956,294	2,742,009	60,777	2,802,786	318,605	480,266	2,964,447	4,067,328	924,519	60,521	131,463	72,591
2007	8,284,140	2,851,469	42,196	2,893,665	335,634	487,267	3,045,298	4,249,525	989,317	61,563	134,564	73,481
2008	8,399,479	2,783,178	36,267	2,819,445	338,870	521,389	3,001,964	4,278,833	1,118,682	61,635	136,277	71,663
2009	7,092,202	2,539,838	43,745	2,583,583	319,541	475,209	2,739,251	3,117,331	1,235,620	51,762	137,016	68,431
2010	7,305,892	2,527,230	48,826	2,576,056	312,140	372,375	2,636,291	3,337,091	1,332,510	52,836	138,275	67,970
2011	8,033,703	2,567,747	52,501	2,620,248	287,946	489,605	2,821,907	3,824,920	1,386,876	57,761	139,086	69,292
2012	8,518,012	2,750,313	61,868	2,812,181	306,815	563,472	3,068,838	4,046,327	1,402,847	60,627	140,499	70,303
2013	8,566,625	2,770,865	54,872	2,825,737	348,242	713,281	3,190,776	3,931,909	1,443,940	60,353	141,942	71,335
2014	9,613,971	3,028,190	49,545	3,077,735	375,114	705,347	3,407,968	4,656,475	1,549,528	66,500	144,571	73,889
2015	10,135,233	3,225,147	56,774	3,281,921	394,140	781,982	3,669,763	4,791,899	1,673,571	68,653	147,629	76,234
2016	10,775,473	3,337,503	41,097	3,378,600	413,221	953,629	3,919,008	5,097,037	1,759,428	71,181	151,382	77,587
2017	11,312,198	3,455,702	25,644	3,481,346	429,333	1,072,588	4,124,601	5,343,255	1,844,342	73,274	154,383	79,136
2018	12,473,322	12,411,011	62,311	3,740,973	460,724	1,111,289	4,391,538	6,087,050	1,994,734	79,353	157,187	83,116
2019	12,924,659	12,845,596	79,063	3,907,808	488,680	1,233,785	4,652,913	6,121,215	2,150,531	80,818	159,923	85,014

Personal Income and Employment by Area: Sebring-Avon Park, FL

(Thousands of dollars, except as noted.)

Year	Personal income, total	Earnings by place of work			Less: Contributions for government social insurance	Plus: Adjustment for residence	Equals: Net earnings by place of residence	Plus: Dividends, interest, and rent	Plus: Personal current transfer receipts	Per capita personal income (dollars)	Population (persons)	Total employment
		Nonfarm	Farm	Total								
1970	103,745	51,193	14,987	66,180	3,500	859	63,539	25,359	14,847	3,470	29,898	10,437
1971	117,865	57,785	16,873	74,658	4,108	828	71,378	28,555	17,932	3,691	31,931	10,970
1972	132,818	63,355	19,949	83,304	4,775	747	79,276	32,241	21,301	3,917	33,912	11,766
1973	155,727	75,313	20,943	96,256	6,415	408	90,249	39,105	26,373	4,333	35,937	12,899
1974	174,908	86,401	19,001	105,402	7,790	40	97,652	45,967	31,289	4,370	40,025	13,681
1975	198,890	93,321	21,470	114,791	8,307	156	106,640	52,585	39,665	4,843	41,070	13,811
1976	221,719	102,630	25,706	128,336	9,181	-203	118,952	57,953	44,814	5,332	41,584	13,930
1977	253,442	114,837	32,067	146,904	10,338	-742	135,824	67,448	50,170	6,040	41,962	14,676
1978	304,020	135,417	43,977	179,394	12,224	-1,582	165,588	81,705	56,727	6,975	43,588	16,021
1979	348,484	153,261	45,732	198,993	14,574	-2,589	181,830	98,686	67,968	7,604	45,828	16,722
1980	421,175	172,302	61,071	233,373	16,722	-3,072	213,579	124,883	82,713	8,756	48,102	17,930
1981	458,704	191,640	41,125	232,765	20,064	-6,964	205,737	153,653	99,314	9,117	50,315	18,584
1982	513,806	198,387	45,893	244,280	21,532	-6,801	215,947	181,334	116,525	9,827	52,286	19,097
1983	581,960	223,785	66,188	289,973	24,163	-7,743	258,067	197,299	126,594	10,843	53,670	20,205
1984	638,800	255,553	48,537	304,090	28,196	-8,196	267,698	234,487	136,615	11,482	55,636	21,386
1985	717,314	288,219	54,179	342,398	32,660	-9,160	300,578	264,035	152,701	12,473	57,508	22,542
1986	792,242	320,022	55,851	375,873	37,136	-9,564	329,173	294,117	168,952	13,343	59,375	23,609
1987	853,488	348,498	62,912	411,410	39,969	-7,259	364,182	306,238	183,068	13,740	62,119	23,712
1988	966,416	383,325	100,182	483,507	46,334	-6,786	430,387	334,813	201,216	15,024	64,325	24,811
1989	1,068,549	419,852	75,559	495,411	52,743	-5,239	437,429	397,428	233,692	16,109	66,334	25,945
1990	1,127,130	452,357	65,763	518,120	55,550	-3,616	458,954	408,671	259,505	16,279	69,238	27,382
1991	1,179,693	479,665	78,212	557,877	59,257	-4,010	494,610	396,876	288,207	16,473	71,614	28,117
1992	1,238,380	512,127	67,731	579,858	63,165	-3,217	513,476	394,034	330,870	16,782	73,790	28,451
1993	1,302,405	543,816	70,537	614,353	67,327	-3,109	543,917	400,841	357,647	17,069	76,301	28,985
1994	1,384,708	583,705	65,487	649,192	73,382	-2,252	573,558	415,772	395,378	17,589	78,724	30,386
1995	1,468,514	606,837	70,553	677,390	76,868	-177	600,345	447,433	420,736	18,176	80,792	30,952
1996	1,529,380	625,373	54,005	679,378	77,797	2,639	604,220	479,864	445,296	18,490	82,713	31,677
1997	1,598,139	659,145	55,855	715,000	81,298	5,128	638,830	496,671	462,638	18,950	84,334	32,801
1998	1,700,121	669,075	97,468	766,543	82,955	8,590	692,178	527,303	480,640	19,873	85,551	34,156
1999	1,736,579	702,483	98,878	801,361	85,495	10,967	726,833	510,735	499,011	20,052	86,604	35,518
2000	1,805,474	730,839	75,426	806,265	87,531	16,817	735,551	542,272	527,651	20,654	87,417	32,853
2001	1,913,724	809,782	56,153	865,935	99,525	20,202	786,612	554,388	572,724	21,622	88,510	32,571
2002	2,005,447	885,152	61,324	946,476	108,644	20,910	858,742	536,764	609,941	22,298	89,939	34,134
2003	2,084,512	950,288	50,738	1,001,026	116,209	23,543	908,360	536,973	639,179	22,921	90,943	35,970
2004	2,206,271	1,030,319	55,640	1,085,959	127,157	33,100	991,902	528,313	686,056	23,703	93,079	36,151
2005	2,366,429	1,099,998	79,699	1,179,697	139,574	41,735	1,081,858	551,894	732,677	24,750	95,614	37,340
2006	2,549,454	1,174,660	102,977	1,277,637	153,696	51,395	1,175,336	591,662	782,456	26,071	97,788	38,629
2007	2,678,415	1,198,152	76,985	1,275,137	160,996	56,171	1,170,312	679,444	828,659	27,048	99,023	40,082
2008	2,737,730	1,151,275	79,990	1,231,265	159,967	63,310	1,134,608	693,477	909,645	27,496	99,568	38,869
2009	2,713,767	1,146,708	94,863	1,241,571	161,749	55,667	1,135,489	590,750	987,528	27,424	98,956	37,758
2010	2,841,572	1,170,604	100,404	1,271,008	163,196	58,933	1,166,745	626,248	1,048,579	28,809	98,635	37,513
2011	2,918,216	1,192,099	96,325	1,288,424	152,478	59,091	1,195,037	651,081	1,072,098	29,641	98,451	37,769
2012	2,934,597	1,206,297	127,689	1,333,986	154,973	64,601	1,243,614	615,395	1,075,588	29,882	98,205	38,022
2013	2,934,293	1,211,095	123,942	1,335,037	172,450	66,662	1,229,249	607,318	1,097,726	29,920	98,071	37,525
2014	3,063,361	1,220,189	131,334	1,351,523	174,560	70,983	1,247,946	660,625	1,154,790	31,106	98,482	38,222
2015	3,237,173	1,277,584	163,931	1,441,515	180,862	73,488	1,334,141	686,928	1,216,104	32,407	99,891	38,831
2016	3,324,368	1,331,562	115,443	1,447,005	191,299	77,827	1,333,533	729,712	1,261,123	32,734	101,558	39,591
2017	3,441,046	1,386,621	79,264	1,465,885	200,752	83,304	1,348,437	767,333	1,325,276	33,446	102,883	40,056
2018	3,520,298	3,443,728	76,570	1,527,024	210,362	92,231	1,408,893	753,903	1,357,502	33,548	104,933	40,788
2019	3,662,511	3,561,016	101,495	1,601,282	222,286	100,689	1,479,685	764,525	1,418,301	34,480	106,221	41,266

Personal Income and Employment by Area: Sheboygan, WI

(Thousands of dollars, except as noted.)

Year	Personal income, total	Earnings by place of work			Less: Contributions for government social insurance	Plus: Adjustment for residence	Equals: Net earnings by place of residence	Plus: Dividends, interest, and rent	Plus: Personal current transfer receipts	Per capita personal income (dollars)	Population (persons)	Total employment
		Nonfarm	Farm	Total								
1970	381,796	297,865	11,237	309,102	22,448	-363	286,291	63,572	31,933	3,947	96,726	44,180
1971	406,232	312,983	11,680	324,663	24,438	908	301,133	68,592	36,507	4,184	97,081	44,145
1972	450,864	350,540	12,363	362,903	28,890	2,693	336,706	73,776	40,382	4,622	97,541	45,544
1973	498,159	387,255	14,081	401,336	36,779	5,105	369,662	82,037	46,460	5,042	98,803	47,761
1974	550,696	423,289	13,011	436,300	42,015	7,650	401,935	93,348	55,413	5,509	99,963	48,662
1975	596,734	437,391	17,304	454,695	42,067	9,005	421,633	102,789	72,312	5,945	100,372	47,393
1976	670,106	503,690	17,416	521,106	49,220	11,811	483,697	109,892	76,517	6,711	99,858	49,028
1977	755,393	572,442	22,151	594,593	55,830	14,434	553,197	122,138	80,058	7,517	100,495	51,286
1978	848,398	654,404	18,225	672,629	65,778	18,432	625,283	134,477	88,638	8,460	100,282	53,344
1979	960,559	739,436	22,579	762,015	77,325	23,533	708,223	150,465	101,871	9,536	100,727	55,367
1980	1,053,121	774,657	22,940	797,597	80,593	24,894	741,898	184,302	126,921	10,437	100,907	54,206
1981	1,153,895	837,311	16,912	854,223	93,101	20,687	781,809	228,497	143,589	11,475	100,554	54,019
1982	1,188,391	837,283	14,448	851,731	93,595	18,039	776,175	247,213	165,003	11,793	100,770	52,305
1983	1,239,568	883,067	2,021	885,088	98,920	14,921	801,089	263,032	175,447	12,323	100,592	51,763
1984	1,373,210	994,065	9,803	1,003,868	114,462	10,049	899,455	295,978	177,777	13,588	101,060	54,410
1985	1,423,695	1,025,862	12,451	1,038,313	118,610	7,287	926,990	309,043	187,662	14,092	101,028	54,488
1986	1,497,511	1,089,659	17,831	1,107,490	125,483	2,563	984,570	320,018	192,923	14,828	100,995	54,967
1987	1,576,558	1,165,242	21,558	1,186,800	131,329	-284	1,055,187	325,434	195,937	15,556	101,347	56,142
1988	1,692,951	1,281,860	10,271	1,292,131	148,829	-8,487	1,134,815	352,838	205,298	16,595	102,018	58,606
1989	1,852,265	1,386,232	28,321	1,414,553	160,340	-17,981	1,236,232	392,284	223,749	17,978	103,032	60,778
1990	1,920,385	1,442,748	22,717	1,465,465	172,766	-22,067	1,270,632	407,612	242,141	18,441	104,137	62,116
1991	1,974,006	1,490,765	17,541	1,508,306	180,485	-21,099	1,306,722	403,996	263,288	18,851	104,714	62,581
1992	2,145,138	1,626,472	22,572	1,649,044	194,812	-23,077	1,431,155	433,174	280,809	20,309	105,627	63,543
1993	2,282,740	1,766,222	16,296	1,782,518	213,150	-27,446	1,541,922	452,596	288,222	21,388	106,729	65,899
1994	2,444,121	1,909,135	20,155	1,929,290	232,315	-27,939	1,669,036	484,529	290,556	22,611	108,093	68,711
1995	2,579,717	1,983,885	15,082	1,998,967	242,258	-27,598	1,729,111	542,316	308,290	23,522	109,672	70,153
1996	2,690,924	2,051,025	25,566	2,076,591	249,267	-24,007	1,803,317	564,053	323,554	24,300	110,737	69,931
1997	2,791,720	2,149,203	18,727	2,167,930	259,090	-19,296	1,889,544	572,534	329,642	25,030	111,536	70,790
1998	2,999,112	2,302,110	29,778	2,331,888	276,405	-19,762	2,035,721	623,461	339,930	26,784	111,973	72,156
1999	3,140,632	2,491,032	29,928	2,520,960	299,463	-27,958	2,193,539	597,403	349,690	28,019	112,088	74,285
2000	3,344,186	2,653,717	21,716	2,675,433	314,356	-30,651	2,330,426	643,956	369,804	29,663	112,739	76,014
2001	3,446,918	2,713,160	29,747	2,742,907	315,950	-29,111	2,397,846	641,021	408,051	30,497	113,023	72,890
2002	3,580,235	2,856,885	28,993	2,885,878	324,776	-32,910	2,528,192	611,914	440,129	31,613	113,251	71,835
2003	3,640,515	2,911,613	33,909	2,945,522	334,449	-36,333	2,574,740	613,138	452,637	32,094	113,433	71,910
2004	3,849,406	3,121,461	33,944	3,155,405	359,193	-34,788	2,761,424	623,754	464,228	33,817	113,832	72,930
2005	3,910,649	3,147,572	28,453	3,176,025	367,761	-40,450	2,767,814	646,869	495,966	34,168	114,454	75,062
2006	4,097,341	3,234,902	24,867	3,259,769	381,209	-32,770	2,845,790	722,696	528,855	35,699	114,775	75,474
2007	4,305,133	3,341,763	43,701	3,385,464	392,887	-36,987	2,955,590	776,431	573,112	37,378	115,178	75,974
2008	4,588,390	3,446,080	48,617	3,494,697	404,880	-28,455	3,061,362	880,619	646,409	39,674	115,652	75,544
2009	4,472,549	3,364,839	31,087	3,395,926	393,795	-40,983	2,961,148	747,970	763,431	38,703	115,562	71,260
2010	4,491,367	3,343,147	45,422	3,388,569	395,970	-44,508	2,948,091	734,400	808,876	38,881	115,517	69,978
2011	4,697,244	3,399,856	68,405	3,468,261	363,765	-43,664	3,060,832	862,939	773,473	40,768	115,218	69,971
2012	5,048,106	3,595,995	73,419	3,669,414	377,923	-64,328	3,227,163	1,046,887	774,056	43,975	114,794	70,308
2013	4,949,290	3,685,036	65,363	3,750,399	436,119	-87,954	3,226,326	935,117	787,847	43,142	114,720	71,763
2014	5,207,504	3,833,366	77,848	3,911,214	453,089	-98,097	3,360,028	1,029,222	818,254	45,276	115,017	73,207
2015	5,408,197	3,980,410	68,407	4,048,817	464,645	-95,716	3,488,456	1,063,824	855,917	46,921	115,261	73,440
2016	5,510,729	4,168,613	55,520	4,224,133	480,956	-114,908	3,628,269	1,010,216	872,244	47,867	115,127	73,767
2017	5,776,492	4,390,028	51,043	4,441,071	503,027	-122,770	3,815,274	1,050,811	910,407	50,081	115,344	74,926
2018	6,137,617	6,103,422	34,195	4,631,979	524,220	-136,325	3,971,434	1,197,859	968,324	53,263	115,233	75,337
2019	6,309,435	6,259,350	50,085	4,775,684	542,029	-138,155	4,095,500	1,203,519	1,010,416	54,703	115,340	75,714

Personal Income and Employment by Area: Sherman-Denison, TX

(Thousands of dollars, except as noted.)

Year	Personal income, total	Earnings by place of work			Less: Contributions for government social insurance	Plus: Adjustment for residence	Equals: Net earnings by place of residence	Plus: Dividends, interest, and rent	Plus: Personal current transfer receipts	Per capita personal income (dollars)	Population (persons)	Total employment
		Nonfarm	Farm	Total								
1970	287,412	230,159	1,806	231,965	15,720	-4,417	211,828	45,942	29,642	3,478	82,644	38,706
1971	281,123	218,099	2,094	220,193	15,732	-2,774	201,687	44,657	34,779	3,482	80,725	35,761
1972	309,089	240,745	4,397	245,142	18,457	-3,840	222,845	48,338	37,906	4,015	76,977	36,851
1973	350,654	266,832	9,335	276,167	23,650	-3,723	248,794	56,489	45,371	4,544	77,168	37,720
1974	388,371	299,154	-1,537	297,617	27,275	-3,273	267,069	67,981	53,321	4,905	79,176	38,648
1975	423,246	307,599	-1,624	305,975	27,180	-667	278,128	75,740	69,378	5,146	82,243	36,797
1976	475,796	345,489	7,204	352,693	30,962	-343	321,388	80,472	73,936	5,658	84,093	37,567
1977	529,118	397,084	-981	396,103	35,971	-643	359,489	89,133	80,496	6,292	84,089	39,578
1978	622,806	479,226	2,139	481,365	44,532	-2,783	434,050	99,349	89,407	7,346	84,776	42,554
1979	730,686	574,360	6,745	581,105	55,802	-4,159	521,144	111,066	98,476	8,351	87,500	45,113
1980	822,433	627,836	1,175	629,011	61,252	-1,051	566,708	140,597	115,128	9,126	90,118	44,931
1981	917,831	683,663	798	684,461	71,476	-80	612,905	171,575	133,351	10,071	91,140	45,027
1982	996,473	698,393	2,306	700,699	74,483	4,055	630,271	214,350	151,852	10,848	91,857	44,236
1983	1,086,038	752,624	5,191	757,815	79,010	4,385	683,190	237,172	165,676	11,733	92,562	44,445
1984	1,194,496	828,377	6,602	834,979	89,718	6,753	752,014	268,765	173,717	12,745	93,722	45,965
1985	1,293,339	885,112	9,291	894,403	96,420	8,897	806,880	302,164	184,295	13,639	94,827	47,323
1986	1,344,696	931,768	561	932,329	101,066	6,687	837,950	309,403	197,343	13,893	96,787	47,263
1987	1,359,328	948,109	-1,165	946,944	102,795	6,101	850,250	302,644	206,434	14,202	95,717	48,538
1988	1,416,400	1,008,909	-1,424	1,007,485	112,486	4,602	899,601	302,810	213,989	14,871	95,246	48,810
1989	1,468,209	1,022,459	-1,238	1,021,221	114,886	6,441	912,776	329,432	226,001	15,374	95,499	48,602
1990	1,532,353	1,083,358	919	1,084,277	118,312	6,552	972,517	310,714	249,122	16,110	95,120	49,556
1991	1,577,346	1,118,317	2,127	1,120,444	124,164	5,175	1,001,455	307,089	268,802	16,400	96,178	49,176
1992	1,636,028	1,141,896	6,504	1,148,400	125,335	9,429	1,032,494	298,040	305,494	16,977	96,370	48,581
1993	1,686,429	1,184,670	1,366	1,186,036	131,527	11,957	1,066,466	296,846	323,117	17,301	97,474	48,917
1994	1,768,372	1,237,192	5,219	1,242,411	138,242	13,164	1,117,333	310,599	340,440	17,888	98,857	50,201
1995	1,877,209	1,305,599	-1,279	1,304,320	146,903	14,440	1,171,857	333,587	371,765	18,708	100,342	52,249
1996	2,009,744	1,390,397	1,164	1,391,561	155,227	19,235	1,255,569	357,825	396,350	19,513	102,993	53,694
1997	2,160,449	1,507,357	2,126	1,509,483	164,401	26,088	1,371,170	374,794	414,485	20,552	105,122	56,132
1998	2,284,641	1,602,126	784	1,602,910	173,428	36,867	1,466,349	390,761	427,531	21,348	107,020	55,290
1999	2,400,362	1,702,202	6,374	1,708,576	183,024	39,696	1,565,248	391,634	443,480	21,987	109,173	56,291
2000	2,599,036	1,842,324	1,090	1,843,414	194,649	47,105	1,695,870	432,528	470,638	23,428	110,939	57,537
2001	2,698,986	1,856,417	-563	1,855,854	197,317	90,182	1,748,719	438,148	512,119	24,027	112,330	59,963
2002	2,750,154	1,846,339	5,004	1,851,343	195,224	120,379	1,776,498	417,470	556,186	24,286	113,239	59,732
2003	2,857,262	1,892,488	10,560	1,903,048	204,892	133,309	1,831,465	434,263	591,534	24,971	114,421	60,176
2004	2,998,013	1,937,979	13,421	1,951,400	212,166	203,533	1,942,767	438,899	616,347	26,070	114,998	60,290
2005	3,164,013	2,001,152	6,472	2,007,624	220,425	244,549	2,031,748	458,978	673,287	27,355	115,666	61,002
2006	3,422,950	2,141,270	4,445	2,145,715	227,862	303,982	2,221,835	480,488	720,627	29,213	117,174	62,162
2007	3,681,652	2,186,149	8,542	2,194,691	234,135	364,264	2,324,820	570,776	786,056	31,113	118,331	63,164
2008	3,949,903	2,219,858	-1,028	2,218,830	239,152	415,996	2,395,674	684,661	869,568	33,239	118,834	63,208
2009	3,809,816	2,181,417	-7,106	2,174,311	241,599	320,992	2,253,704	606,889	949,223	31,730	120,069	62,365
2010	3,907,857	2,269,210	-4,049	2,265,161	252,000	285,630	2,298,791	575,395	1,033,671	32,287	121,034	61,568
2011	4,128,428	2,365,936	2,662	2,368,598	232,167	300,552	2,436,983	627,356	1,064,089	34,015	121,372	62,940
2012	4,345,998	2,463,104	6,080	2,469,184	238,293	358,442	2,589,333	692,395	1,064,270	35,696	121,750	63,217
2013	4,437,818	2,570,130	26,496	2,596,626	280,489	334,742	2,650,879	668,515	1,118,424	36,288	122,295	64,726
2014	4,719,494	2,619,423	15,291	2,634,714	287,249	440,060	2,787,525	749,059	1,182,910	38,202	123,540	66,129
2015	4,900,237	2,679,805	22,277	2,702,082	297,190	489,584	2,894,476	763,825	1,241,936	39,030	125,549	67,191
2016	5,177,290	2,713,702	11,834	2,725,536	307,437	594,724	3,012,823	861,565	1,302,902	40,383	128,206	67,910
2017	5,409,499	2,847,903	11,688	2,859,591	326,301	638,180	3,171,470	903,736	1,334,293	41,250	131,140	68,806
2018	5,683,293	5,711,515	-28,222	3,011,460	342,507	714,358	3,383,311	903,756	1,396,226	42,480	133,787	71,615
2019	5,991,490	6,009,786	-18,296	3,150,619	353,415	803,025	3,600,229	925,313	1,465,948	43,987	136,212	73,149

Personal Income and Employment by Area: Shreveport-Bossier City, LA

(Thousands of dollars, except as noted.)

Year	Personal income, total	Earnings by place of work			Less: Contributions for government social insurance	Plus: Adjustment for residence	Equals: Net earnings by place of residence	Plus: Dividends, interest, and rent	Plus: Personal current transfer receipts	Per capita personal income (dollars)	Population (persons)	Total employment
		Nonfarm	Farm	Total								
1970	1,254,974	998,298	20,875	1,019,173	64,683	-24,388	930,102	204,148	120,724	3,500	358,599	156,510
1971	1,355,283	1,067,545	24,297	1,091,842	70,745	-25,045	996,052	218,523	140,708	3,732	363,150	156,487
1972	1,470,474	1,160,349	28,537	1,188,886	80,267	-27,428	1,081,191	234,425	154,858	4,002	367,392	158,719
1973	1,626,009	1,286,557	33,249	1,319,806	101,687	-32,155	1,185,964	264,720	175,325	4,397	369,828	166,046
1974	1,838,298	1,452,681	17,995	1,470,676	118,454	-36,213	1,316,009	319,578	202,711	4,930	372,886	171,606
1975	2,060,643	1,610,754	16,932	1,627,686	129,900	-39,572	1,458,214	353,695	248,734	5,408	381,019	174,633
1976	2,273,754	1,789,322	26,541	1,815,863	147,346	-44,284	1,624,233	375,745	273,776	5,877	386,919	178,905
1977	2,526,869	2,011,351	27,547	2,038,898	163,843	-48,961	1,826,094	411,151	289,624	6,481	389,881	184,422
1978	2,851,164	2,281,377	24,296	2,305,673	189,172	-58,899	2,057,602	476,208	317,354	7,242	393,685	189,618
1979	3,196,279	2,550,354	36,753	2,587,107	220,088	-67,453	2,299,566	536,407	360,306	8,032	397,929	192,590
1980	3,641,883	2,852,213	14,678	2,866,891	245,946	-77,955	2,542,990	667,154	431,739	9,019	403,812	197,589
1981	4,187,148	3,289,408	16,314	3,305,722	303,614	-130,166	2,871,942	831,578	483,628	10,256	408,275	205,422
1982	4,524,825	3,422,564	9,175	3,431,739	321,100	-90,400	3,020,239	950,422	554,164	10,915	414,540	206,376
1983	4,811,341	3,559,962	13,518	3,573,480	333,114	-92,610	3,147,756	1,053,096	610,489	11,508	418,102	204,949
1984	5,214,317	3,875,564	16,055	3,891,619	375,108	-100,975	3,415,536	1,160,890	637,891	12,411	420,125	211,853
1985	5,500,871	4,015,985	17,067	4,033,052	392,953	-98,228	3,541,871	1,260,432	698,568	12,995	423,310	212,767
1986	5,547,118	3,943,917	22,942	3,966,859	380,780	-85,995	3,500,084	1,277,520	769,514	13,035	425,565	201,775
1987	5,629,095	4,027,837	30,791	4,058,628	381,700	-78,828	3,598,100	1,251,114	779,881	13,388	420,448	198,273
1988	5,836,284	4,173,960	31,384	4,205,344	412,351	-76,472	3,716,521	1,297,706	822,057	14,110	413,628	197,372
1989	6,090,108	4,298,815	26,206	4,325,021	427,416	-63,215	3,834,390	1,359,085	896,633	14,903	408,649	195,216
1990	6,467,303	4,520,746	21,652	4,542,398	460,476	-52,627	4,029,295	1,460,591	977,417	16,118	401,238	196,252
1991	6,694,776	4,645,364	15,054	4,660,418	487,952	-55,654	4,116,812	1,463,349	1,114,615	16,731	400,139	196,602
1992	7,202,886	5,002,578	16,400	5,018,978	520,688	-70,617	4,427,673	1,504,815	1,270,398	17,884	402,750	198,843
1993	7,652,877	5,275,071	15,535	5,290,606	553,633	-85,802	4,651,171	1,574,784	1,426,922	18,853	405,929	204,276
1994	8,053,205	5,577,889	18,448	5,596,337	595,227	-97,577	4,903,533	1,637,705	1,511,967	19,727	408,225	207,412
1995	8,353,506	5,805,944	13,126	5,819,070	620,327	-124,853	5,073,890	1,755,378	1,524,238	20,303	411,451	214,651
1996	8,637,192	6,009,804	17,880	6,027,684	638,629	-122,334	5,266,721	1,828,457	1,542,014	20,897	413,330	217,592
1997	9,022,761	6,308,082	12,491	6,320,573	666,706	-138,400	5,515,467	1,931,269	1,576,025	21,687	416,050	221,717
1998	9,413,374	6,586,018	7,279	6,593,297	699,952	-150,068	5,743,277	2,034,633	1,635,464	22,683	414,997	224,278
1999	9,687,819	6,880,296	18,821	6,899,117	721,635	-163,435	6,014,047	1,980,026	1,693,746	23,249	416,699	226,764
2000	10,227,807	7,296,508	16,561	7,313,069	749,877	-170,479	6,392,713	2,105,059	1,730,035	24,477	417,850	228,426
2001	11,224,590	8,172,892	19,816	8,192,708	805,616	-185,033	7,202,059	2,064,099	1,958,432	26,877	417,622	228,119
2002	11,504,330	8,453,447	15,699	8,469,146	827,203	-193,159	7,448,784	1,971,067	2,084,479	27,525	417,953	225,624
2003	11,791,425	8,689,502	23,277	8,712,779	853,492	-214,498	7,644,789	2,009,500	2,137,136	28,193	418,234	228,894
2004	12,179,694	8,904,752	28,573	8,933,325	892,901	-242,118	7,798,306	2,026,607	2,354,781	28,883	421,695	233,337
2005	13,225,866	9,584,833	18,652	9,603,485	937,543	-266,573	8,399,369	2,319,768	2,506,729	31,171	424,302	241,070
2006	14,274,237	10,247,108	22,582	10,269,690	1,005,686	-287,769	8,976,235	2,637,810	2,660,192	33,130	430,852	246,426
2007	14,569,319	10,435,204	19,680	10,454,884	1,040,890	-306,504	9,107,490	2,654,807	2,807,022	33,765	431,496	251,910
2008	16,694,069	11,775,754	-16,452	11,759,302	1,121,611	-328,156	10,309,535	3,216,925	3,167,609	38,500	433,607	256,165
2009	15,960,838	11,117,949	-895	11,117,054	1,096,768	-286,631	9,733,655	2,874,324	3,352,859	36,609	435,976	252,251
2010	16,991,588	12,010,381	3,124	12,013,505	1,159,541	-295,453	10,558,511	2,894,878	3,538,199	38,517	441,148	255,354
2011	17,488,940	11,781,932	2,049	11,783,981	1,064,553	-290,673	10,428,755	3,494,355	3,565,830	39,299	445,027	260,804
2012	18,029,766	11,890,010	11,269	11,901,279	1,063,058	-209,912	10,628,309	3,733,685	3,667,772	40,207	448,421	260,971
2013	18,384,236	12,517,082	23,506	12,540,588	1,207,140	-147,612	11,185,836	3,398,818	3,799,582	41,130	446,977	258,225
2014	19,723,039	13,745,664	6,062	13,751,726	1,269,411	-146,090	12,336,225	3,562,336	3,824,478	44,314	445,070	259,181
2015	19,418,887	12,950,503	61	12,950,564	1,265,856	-153,445	11,531,263	3,681,183	4,206,441	43,688	444,486	260,265
2016	18,826,689	12,188,225	-3,886	12,184,339	1,235,022	-161,416	10,787,901	3,521,227	4,517,561	42,556	442,403	259,067
2017	18,811,186	11,943,894	-3,477	11,940,417	1,247,439	-162,913	10,530,065	3,644,188	4,636,933	42,662	440,933	258,382
2018	18,672,868	18,685,776	-12,908	12,001,560	1,251,252	-344,135	10,406,173	4,002,388	4,264,307	47,002	397,281	239,195
2019	19,068,236	19,084,785	-16,549	12,232,241	1,265,876	-342,502	10,623,863	4,026,413	4,417,960	48,310	394,706	239,375

Personal Income and Employment by Area: Sierra Vista-Douglas, AZ

(Thousands of dollars, except as noted.)

Year	Personal income, total	Earnings by place of work			Less: Contributions for government social insurance	Plus: Adjustment for residence	Equals: Net earnings by place of residence	Plus: Dividends, interest, and rent	Plus: Personal current transfer receipts	Per capita personal income (dollars)	Population (persons)	Total employment
		Nonfarm	Farm	Total								
1970	258,346	203,119	6,493	209,612	11,329	-5,870	192,413	49,208	16,725	4,116	62,770	26,150
1971	310,805	244,189	9,400	253,589	14,297	-7,278	232,014	59,060	19,731	4,629	67,149	28,259
1972	350,963	271,112	11,193	282,305	16,344	-6,178	259,783	68,456	22,724	4,947	70,938	29,255
1973	393,750	297,934	14,483	312,417	19,246	-5,914	287,257	78,582	27,911	5,281	74,558	30,088
1974	422,424	317,600	13,649	331,249	21,768	-6,334	303,147	85,896	33,381	5,546	76,165	30,429
1975	444,691	322,041	13,448	335,489	22,551	-6,672	306,266	91,726	46,699	5,781	76,922	29,245
1976	486,415	344,990	21,298	366,288	24,075	-6,629	335,584	98,275	52,556	6,161	78,946	29,568
1977	527,949	381,694	11,603	393,297	26,597	-7,110	359,590	112,587	55,772	6,543	80,688	30,807
1978	598,871	426,557	16,333	442,890	30,254	-7,242	405,394	131,060	62,417	7,201	83,160	32,605
1979	644,379	453,440	10,252	463,692	33,640	-3,221	426,831	146,184	71,364	7,470	86,268	32,952
1980	729,673	506,074	8,623	514,697	38,656	-997	475,044	171,504	83,125	8,468	86,172	34,124
1981	811,048	551,094	11,386	562,480	45,082	-1,438	515,960	196,227	98,861	9,213	88,036	33,576
1982	859,250	566,938	13,785	580,723	46,391	-1,852	532,480	216,803	109,967	9,723	88,373	33,110
1983	937,995	612,771	18,706	631,477	52,544	-2,729	576,204	240,927	120,864	10,554	88,872	33,925
1984	1,033,492	683,141	14,677	697,818	59,650	-4,676	633,492	268,507	131,493	11,365	90,937	35,381
1985	1,085,132	712,871	10,723	723,594	65,788	-4,600	653,206	292,271	139,655	11,899	91,192	36,956
1986	1,152,180	748,877	16,665	765,542	70,853	-4,564	690,125	312,951	149,104	12,245	94,093	38,102
1987	1,227,098	799,353	18,986	818,339	75,676	-7,681	734,982	329,131	162,985	12,691	96,690	38,917
1988	1,294,453	830,427	30,623	861,050	83,964	-7,841	769,245	347,465	177,743	13,440	96,316	39,320
1989	1,358,577	858,318	19,773	878,091	91,079	-8,955	778,057	375,639	204,881	13,927	97,551	39,979
1990	1,439,562	921,108	18,913	940,021	100,320	-13,217	826,484	386,800	226,278	14,702	97,918	40,361
1991	1,527,274	977,710	19,896	997,606	107,427	-13,326	876,853	394,491	255,930	15,418	99,058	39,034
1992	1,654,714	1,057,205	28,782	1,085,987	118,798	-13,602	953,587	408,982	292,145	16,310	101,453	40,872
1993	1,719,311	1,079,140	26,738	1,105,878	123,757	-10,149	971,972	431,244	316,095	16,468	104,403	42,304
1994	1,814,646	1,138,452	9,385	1,147,837	130,616	-7,220	1,010,001	467,343	337,302	16,599	109,323	44,449
1995	1,886,593	1,156,136	6,900	1,163,036	129,596	-4,111	1,029,329	498,374	358,890	16,773	112,480	44,987
1996	1,986,665	1,192,173	23,873	1,216,046	136,244	-1,090	1,078,712	527,644	380,309	17,600	112,880	46,281
1997	2,068,792	1,245,208	30,516	1,275,724	141,091	644	1,135,277	532,443	401,072	18,004	114,907	47,434
1998	2,202,974	1,318,984	27,370	1,346,354	148,438	3,413	1,201,329	581,733	419,912	18,976	116,091	47,790
1999	2,281,510	1,352,495	34,101	1,386,596	152,316	8,593	1,242,873	591,513	447,124	19,579	116,530	48,312
2000	2,444,761	1,467,725	38,279	1,506,004	164,773	9,765	1,350,996	630,978	462,787	20,695	118,132	50,495
2001	2,637,453	1,586,948	46,986	1,633,934	176,006	-242	1,457,686	652,017	527,750	22,201	118,798	50,753
2002	2,771,101	1,707,269	33,468	1,740,737	190,031	-4,794	1,545,912	635,168	590,021	23,122	119,847	50,600
2003	3,024,788	1,904,894	34,976	1,939,870	207,520	-8,629	1,723,721	647,863	653,204	25,073	120,638	52,389
2004	3,247,831	1,994,347	42,983	2,037,330	223,076	-11,086	1,803,168	720,507	724,156	26,355	123,234	53,549
2005	3,530,600	2,173,709	68,570	2,242,279	245,388	-17,372	1,979,519	752,038	799,043	28,068	125,786	55,625
2006	3,739,833	2,329,209	34,963	2,364,172	262,463	-14,701	2,087,008	777,241	875,584	29,392	127,241	56,566
2007	4,025,825	2,473,657	46,228	2,519,885	282,288	-15,798	2,221,799	852,118	951,908	31,401	128,206	58,186
2008	4,259,200	2,615,371	23,478	2,638,849	303,764	-20,432	2,314,653	861,065	1,083,482	33,011	129,023	57,354
2009	4,440,968	2,714,177	27,540	2,741,717	318,508	-41,651	2,381,558	816,804	1,242,606	34,140	130,081	56,700
2010	4,550,397	2,823,679	31,495	2,855,174	333,490	-59,536	2,462,148	790,890	1,297,359	34,530	131,782	56,554
2011	4,681,207	2,849,267	54,184	2,903,451	305,686	-71,474	2,526,291	870,998	1,283,918	35,210	132,952	56,143
2012	4,531,332	2,732,283	40,306	2,772,589	296,824	-75,799	2,399,966	869,782	1,261,584	34,374	131,826	54,888
2013	4,463,184	2,607,504	64,584	2,672,088	318,979	-74,783	2,278,326	883,635	1,301,223	34,510	129,332	53,141
2014	4,556,979	2,573,093	47,514	2,620,607	313,295	-68,759	2,238,553	926,200	1,392,226	35,866	127,054	52,294
2015	4,662,523	2,593,296	49,311	2,642,607	317,361	-66,627	2,258,619	953,767	1,450,137	36,979	126,084	51,819
2016	4,728,614	2,594,722	84,496	2,679,218	318,863	-69,017	2,291,338	948,230	1,489,046	37,722	125,355	51,259
2017	4,902,154	2,660,018	96,576	2,756,594	331,445	-68,968	2,356,181	981,895	1,564,078	39,294	124,756	51,028
2018	5,045,137	5,030,551	14,586	2,782,305	342,359	-67,133	2,372,813	1,034,535	1,637,789	39,911	126,411	51,236
2019	5,259,219	5,236,817	22,402	2,883,243	357,360	-66,455	2,459,428	1,050,575	1,749,216	41,766	125,922	52,115

Personal Income and Employment by Area: Sioux City, IA-NE-SD

(Thousands of dollars, except as noted.)

Year	Personal income, total	Earnings by place of work			Less: Contributions for government social insurance	Plus: Adjustment for residence	Equals: Net earnings by place of residence	Plus: Dividends, interest, and rent	Plus: Personal current transfer receipts	Per capita personal income (dollars)	Population (persons)	Total employment
		Nonfarm	Farm	Total								
1970	595,480	423,596	48,259	471,855	31,052	1,783	442,586	93,075	59,819	3,772	157,876	72,833
1971	641,193	455,503	50,410	505,913	34,480	1,858	473,291	101,857	66,045	4,017	159,627	73,517
1972	728,675	497,777	85,119	582,896	39,538	1,465	544,823	112,097	71,755	4,561	159,765	75,422
1973	870,085	557,264	151,976	709,240	51,321	1,403	659,322	128,205	82,558	5,434	160,131	79,574
1974	879,866	628,764	69,123	697,887	60,531	-757	636,599	146,810	96,457	5,488	160,327	82,025
1975	999,517	701,743	83,071	784,814	66,143	-2,682	715,989	165,735	117,793	6,174	161,899	82,537
1976	1,054,368	794,915	29,894	824,809	74,913	-4,226	745,670	179,231	129,467	6,438	163,760	84,198
1977	1,170,067	844,291	66,679	910,970	78,691	-3,956	828,323	202,354	139,390	7,099	164,822	83,528
1978	1,329,850	932,203	117,995	1,050,198	89,994	-7,482	952,722	219,098	158,030	8,166	162,857	84,631
1979	1,386,120	994,978	79,542	1,074,520	100,511	-6,339	967,670	241,373	177,077	8,574	161,674	84,150
1980	1,442,107	1,060,544	364	1,060,908	106,764	-6,856	947,288	292,240	202,579	8,985	160,495	82,883
1981	1,704,006	1,160,244	88,028	1,248,272	124,067	-11,400	1,112,805	364,014	227,187	10,583	161,009	82,444
1982	1,725,922	1,154,268	36,541	1,190,809	125,121	-9,889	1,055,799	417,256	252,867	10,806	159,718	79,728
1983	1,752,372	1,218,700	-22,461	1,196,239	131,102	-9,631	1,055,506	426,465	270,401	11,042	158,696	80,852
1984	1,929,198	1,280,698	56,366	1,337,064	140,345	-8,323	1,188,396	458,078	282,724	12,190	158,265	83,017
1985	2,030,281	1,328,920	86,220	1,415,140	149,234	-8,712	1,257,194	470,214	302,873	12,964	156,606	82,318
1986	2,078,239	1,375,170	84,161	1,459,331	158,678	-9,310	1,291,343	471,825	315,071	13,420	154,861	82,879
1987	2,229,851	1,493,058	132,283	1,625,341	173,110	-11,021	1,441,210	466,247	322,394	14,523	153,535	84,732
1988	2,304,788	1,589,597	95,614	1,685,211	189,691	-10,028	1,485,492	482,754	336,542	14,912	154,564	86,760
1989	2,487,085	1,711,916	129,645	1,841,561	204,508	-10,700	1,626,353	509,975	350,757	16,124	154,246	90,853
1990	2,652,770	1,812,322	141,578	1,953,900	222,806	-12,885	1,718,209	557,595	376,966	17,109	155,053	93,372
1991	2,739,976	1,889,282	126,810	2,016,092	235,119	-16,506	1,764,467	569,520	405,989	17,499	156,583	92,809
1992	2,996,327	2,084,099	169,772	2,253,871	256,338	-21,400	1,976,133	585,480	434,714	18,938	158,214	94,798
1993	3,071,296	2,217,802	113,321	2,331,123	273,320	-23,602	2,034,201	588,883	448,212	19,151	160,369	98,232
1994	3,299,239	2,398,790	161,436	2,560,226	298,459	-28,000	2,233,767	599,586	465,886	20,331	162,280	101,761
1995	3,515,048	2,599,306	108,218	2,707,524	323,906	-35,977	2,347,641	678,966	488,441	21,426	164,052	105,716
1996	3,888,198	2,776,245	234,945	3,011,190	331,923	-41,166	2,638,101	739,891	510,206	23,443	165,859	107,604
1997	3,957,039	2,881,866	176,123	3,057,989	352,899	-41,382	2,663,708	774,211	519,120	23,818	166,138	108,743
1998	4,204,534	3,104,846	139,519	3,244,365	375,056	-47,916	2,821,393	858,586	524,555	25,244	166,559	108,475
1999	4,292,876	3,227,400	114,599	3,341,999	386,514	-46,991	2,908,494	834,168	550,214	25,606	167,651	109,275
2000	4,511,598	3,367,629	115,179	3,482,808	399,793	-47,265	3,035,750	884,240	591,608	26,893	167,762	109,035
2001	4,638,676	3,400,596	129,271	3,529,867	403,945	-42,654	3,083,268	926,147	629,261	27,770	167,040	108,991
2002	4,701,287	3,435,572	107,736	3,543,308	406,242	-34,919	3,102,147	905,796	693,344	28,228	166,544	106,273
2003	4,827,414	3,527,709	153,312	3,681,021	417,629	-27,808	3,235,584	907,676	684,154	29,040	166,232	105,154
2004	5,266,249	3,848,113	257,689	4,105,802	439,463	-17,765	3,648,574	911,423	706,252	31,690	166,178	104,144
2005	5,608,074	4,150,448	228,841	4,379,289	468,515	-8,119	3,902,655	946,812	758,607	34,021	164,840	105,096
2006	5,897,891	4,382,007	135,024	4,517,031	486,481	9,728	4,040,278	1,025,720	831,893	35,670	165,345	106,343
2007	6,534,743	4,774,481	193,052	4,967,533	524,313	19,544	4,462,764	1,194,136	877,843	39,459	165,607	109,349
2008	7,125,950	5,148,231	304,116	5,452,347	563,235	36,771	4,925,883	1,208,943	991,124	42,877	166,196	110,418
2009	6,634,613	4,755,845	220,298	4,976,143	543,701	50,373	4,482,815	1,110,012	1,041,786	39,598	167,549	108,706
2010	6,921,218	4,911,884	257,910	5,169,794	548,710	51,146	4,672,230	1,126,773	1,122,215	40,994	168,834	107,749
2011	6,930,672	4,645,180	416,146	5,061,326	486,566	74,022	4,648,782	1,152,196	1,129,694	41,036	168,892	107,925
2012	7,149,844	4,748,452	328,608	5,077,060	488,965	79,220	4,667,315	1,349,785	1,132,744	42,421	168,544	108,683
2013	7,349,724	4,870,472	605,070	5,475,542	571,638	67,162	4,971,066	1,223,241	1,155,417	43,623	168,481	110,720
2014	7,585,213	5,139,240	395,135	5,534,375	596,488	60,082	4,997,969	1,383,150	1,204,094	45,029	168,452	112,088
2015	8,026,774	5,492,002	366,042	5,858,044	632,421	49,024	5,274,647	1,482,707	1,269,420	47,599	168,634	113,291
2016	8,169,950	5,735,675	267,607	6,003,282	674,761	32,154	5,360,675	1,494,146	1,315,129	48,329	169,049	112,898
2017	8,087,235	5,569,061	219,823	5,788,884	648,689	81,710	5,221,905	1,552,450	1,312,880	47,962	168,618	111,517
2018	7,363,690	7,263,814	99,876	5,192,874	584,018	-33,219	4,575,637	1,568,796	1,219,257	51,212	143,787	96,161
2019	7,644,480	7,524,536	119,944	5,403,934	608,998	-16,652	4,778,284	1,577,084	1,289,112	52,829	144,701	96,535

Personal Income and Employment by Area: Sioux Falls, SD

(Thousands of dollars, except as noted.)

Year	Personal income, total	Earnings by place of work			Less: Contributions for government social insurance	Plus: Adjustment for residence	Equals: Net earnings by place of residence	Plus: Dividends, interest, and rent	Plus: Personal current transfer receipts	Per capita personal income (dollars)	Population (persons)	Total employment
		Nonfarm	Farm	Total								
1970	464,373	345,033	37,216	382,249	23,339	-3,952	354,958	68,819	40,596	3,740	124,171	60,271
1971	508,717	372,189	44,678	416,867	25,680	-3,979	387,208	74,776	46,733	4,067	125,075	60,995
1972	576,394	406,967	68,995	475,962	29,026	-4,130	442,806	81,583	52,005	4,571	126,094	61,395
1973	690,876	470,628	110,766	581,394	39,254	-4,514	537,626	92,948	60,302	5,443	126,920	65,595
1974	748,516	533,493	84,047	617,540	45,948	-4,921	566,671	110,909	70,936	5,847	128,011	67,350
1975	834,582	587,571	91,591	679,162	49,977	-4,611	624,574	124,846	85,162	6,468	129,032	68,274
1976	879,337	677,670	34,355	712,025	57,694	-4,679	649,652	136,837	92,848	6,710	131,050	71,764
1977	1,003,511	762,078	55,482	817,560	63,196	-5,282	749,082	156,347	98,082	7,550	132,916	75,138
1978	1,175,124	886,224	86,077	972,301	75,500	-5,994	890,807	177,855	106,462	8,804	133,481	79,276
1979	1,294,634	979,601	89,002	1,068,603	89,215	-5,635	973,753	200,590	120,291	9,568	135,312	80,201
1980	1,359,268	1,045,472	22,147	1,067,619	95,428	-5,236	966,955	251,262	141,051	9,766	139,185	79,520
1981	1,573,555	1,123,309	81,250	1,204,559	109,346	-7,776	1,087,437	320,173	165,945	11,309	139,142	78,983
1982	1,640,084	1,177,308	36,974	1,214,282	116,631	-9,103	1,088,548	366,536	185,000	11,653	140,747	79,169
1983	1,739,611	1,287,535	19,856	1,307,391	128,284	-11,861	1,167,246	373,474	198,891	12,162	143,042	82,261
1984	1,935,290	1,408,896	55,064	1,463,960	143,639	-14,298	1,306,023	418,660	210,607	13,248	146,081	86,170
1985	2,051,370	1,480,644	82,031	1,562,675	155,526	-16,146	1,391,003	433,759	226,608	13,867	147,929	88,138
1986	2,145,550	1,568,979	73,364	1,642,343	169,658	-18,092	1,454,593	451,362	239,595	14,517	147,796	89,382
1987	2,277,497	1,660,434	111,179	1,771,613	181,315	-20,091	1,570,207	458,792	248,498	15,319	148,672	93,682
1988	2,470,026	1,816,639	121,128	1,937,767	203,012	-23,973	1,710,782	494,384	264,860	16,308	151,460	97,090
1989	2,660,528	1,986,552	86,492	2,073,044	223,377	-26,575	1,823,092	552,526	284,910	17,476	152,240	100,812
1990	2,934,681	2,220,258	102,230	2,322,488	263,350	-30,347	2,028,791	601,426	304,464	19,038	154,148	105,115
1991	3,109,908	2,393,099	100,859	2,493,958	286,243	-32,946	2,174,769	608,275	326,864	19,817	156,928	109,696
1992	3,370,262	2,593,646	139,119	2,732,765	305,621	-37,754	2,389,390	626,714	354,158	20,965	160,753	113,135
1993	3,507,369	2,752,666	71,005	2,823,671	322,597	-42,413	2,458,661	676,625	372,083	21,375	164,088	116,256
1994	3,890,048	2,995,324	189,709	3,185,033	353,167	-48,651	2,783,215	715,467	391,366	23,157	167,987	122,281
1995	4,044,494	3,169,342	66,490	3,235,832	372,509	-53,059	2,810,264	811,142	423,088	23,694	170,698	125,850
1996	4,444,635	3,347,992	222,166	3,570,158	392,470	-59,131	3,118,557	875,952	450,126	25,550	173,960	129,330
1997	4,612,824	3,560,297	147,579	3,707,876	417,714	-69,368	3,220,794	922,838	469,192	26,246	175,756	132,805
1998	5,053,527	3,917,372	150,347	4,067,719	454,263	-82,034	3,531,422	1,035,417	486,688	28,238	178,964	136,890
1999	5,384,437	4,287,949	98,540	4,386,489	499,913	-96,576	3,790,000	1,084,574	509,863	29,401	183,138	142,582
2000	5,801,760	4,577,829	121,896	4,699,725	535,022	-111,921	4,052,782	1,193,578	555,400	30,810	188,310	147,233
2001	5,972,147	4,727,662	87,506	4,815,168	552,358	-118,847	4,143,963	1,225,846	602,338	31,155	191,693	148,941
2002	6,209,059	5,006,591	59,415	5,066,006	581,992	-129,244	4,354,770	1,201,736	652,553	31,933	194,442	150,765
2003	6,581,408	5,262,827	119,925	5,382,752	613,631	-133,877	4,635,244	1,267,621	678,543	33,271	197,813	152,571
2004	7,122,368	5,633,606	184,156	5,817,762	646,333	-141,006	5,030,423	1,360,782	731,163	35,202	202,328	155,870
2005	7,788,507	6,130,035	119,129	6,249,164	684,361	-150,473	5,414,330	1,566,752	807,425	37,698	206,605	160,492
2006	8,729,099	6,841,319	106,616	6,947,935	750,703	-155,641	6,041,591	1,792,328	895,180	41,258	211,576	165,729
2007	9,579,629	7,388,283	168,791	7,557,074	809,424	-156,665	6,590,985	2,032,269	956,375	44,157	216,943	171,417
2008	10,229,134	7,726,043	211,638	7,937,681	850,913	-164,531	6,922,237	2,188,323	1,118,574	46,101	221,887	175,343
2009	10,049,877	7,731,775	257,535	7,989,310	849,098	-159,396	6,980,816	1,887,714	1,181,347	44,486	225,913	173,762
2010	10,594,513	8,061,124	225,572	8,286,696	871,305	-151,366	7,264,025	2,042,406	1,288,082	46,239	229,123	174,143
2011	10,990,522	8,048,347	425,932	8,474,279	790,612	-160,947	7,522,720	2,149,238	1,318,564	47,311	232,305	177,722
2012	11,711,231	8,892,779	199,533	9,092,312	849,800	-165,548	8,076,964	2,305,944	1,328,323	49,425	236,948	181,848
2013	11,731,704	8,917,254	354,984	9,272,238	985,381	-157,303	8,129,554	2,214,774	1,387,376	48,433	242,227	185,909
2014	12,778,979	9,869,501	196,092	10,065,593	1,061,629	-159,351	8,844,613	2,470,228	1,464,138	51,809	246,657	191,037
2015	13,867,060	10,666,330	165,700	10,832,030	1,118,701	-180,133	9,533,196	2,794,231	1,539,633	55,364	250,469	194,314
2016	14,233,087	10,962,385	126,628	11,089,013	1,161,242	-182,815	9,744,956	2,874,777	1,613,354	55,954	254,372	197,544
2017	14,495,462	11,067,595	125,836	11,193,431	1,195,443	-192,526	9,805,462	3,021,377	1,668,623	55,947	259,094	200,621
2018	15,891,144	15,734,835	156,309	12,144,619	1,271,180	-212,137	10,661,302	3,384,126	1,845,716	60,237	263,810	205,197
2019	16,631,099	16,447,549	183,550	12,832,980	1,359,531	-234,036	11,239,413	3,417,683	1,974,003	62,003	268,232	210,100

Personal Income and Employment by Area: South Bend-Mishawaka, IN-MI

(Thousands of dollars, except as noted.)

Year	Personal income, total	Earnings by place of work			Less: Contributions for government social insurance	Plus: Adjustment for residence	Equals: Net earnings by place of residence	Plus: Dividends, interest, and rent	Plus: Personal current transfer receipts	Per capita personal income (dollars)	Population (persons)	Total employment
		Nonfarm	Farm	Total								
1970	1,110,466	852,197	7,575	859,772	57,910	62,403	864,265	156,667	89,534	3,855	288,051	115,959
1971	1,185,112	883,810	9,614	893,424	62,256	73,020	904,188	169,200	111,724	4,122	287,489	113,550
1972	1,320,268	993,533	13,150	1,006,683	74,400	90,577	1,022,860	180,535	116,873	4,558	289,656	118,965
1973	1,473,106	1,104,983	23,862	1,128,845	95,536	102,991	1,136,300	200,717	136,089	5,089	289,459	125,314
1974	1,585,458	1,189,067	15,973	1,205,040	106,729	96,462	1,194,773	229,099	161,586	5,496	288,497	126,842
1975	1,714,007	1,236,664	32,921	1,269,585	109,135	95,523	1,255,973	255,539	202,495	5,945	288,309	123,186
1976	1,879,499	1,370,286	25,181	1,395,467	122,910	124,590	1,397,147	270,170	212,182	6,546	287,124	125,452
1977	2,070,331	1,522,377	14,792	1,537,169	137,336	150,918	1,550,751	297,846	221,734	7,188	288,007	129,758
1978	2,311,819	1,699,477	23,147	1,722,624	158,574	176,095	1,740,145	331,025	240,649	7,967	290,181	134,190
1979	2,527,132	1,861,451	19,796	1,881,247	179,831	181,961	1,883,377	368,595	275,160	8,665	291,639	135,847
1980	2,732,474	1,931,582	5,766	1,937,348	184,702	174,208	1,926,854	460,088	345,532	9,390	290,984	130,558
1981	3,001,856	2,069,665	8,387	2,078,052	213,252	176,335	2,041,135	571,334	389,387	10,358	289,810	129,347
1982	3,134,345	2,122,056	8,766	2,130,822	222,222	177,371	2,085,971	617,413	430,961	10,893	287,735	126,263
1983	3,337,791	2,236,100	2,936	2,239,036	235,260	215,140	2,218,916	657,767	461,108	11,645	286,626	127,770
1984	3,695,626	2,501,646	20,435	2,522,081	269,474	233,466	2,486,073	733,306	476,247	12,822	288,222	135,669
1985	3,873,265	2,630,419	14,099	2,644,518	288,088	238,778	2,595,208	774,118	503,939	13,385	289,373	137,736
1986	4,111,016	2,800,494	24,678	2,825,172	307,980	259,326	2,776,518	801,391	533,107	14,205	289,411	141,018
1987	4,376,395	3,036,124	36,483	3,072,607	329,889	274,517	3,017,235	813,875	545,285	15,042	290,952	146,392
1988	4,643,820	3,254,332	19,540	3,273,872	365,772	282,831	3,190,931	872,266	580,623	15,862	292,757	149,826
1989	4,946,490	3,407,194	41,183	3,448,377	384,834	276,024	3,339,567	980,345	626,578	16,740	295,488	151,731
1990	5,136,215	3,556,091	42,019	3,598,110	413,197	250,927	3,435,840	1,015,200	685,175	17,283	297,187	153,679
1991	5,267,245	3,665,861	25,953	3,691,814	432,885	244,338	3,503,267	1,007,968	756,010	17,633	298,719	153,036
1992	5,674,845	3,938,136	35,995	3,974,131	461,097	281,559	3,794,593	1,027,850	852,402	18,859	300,909	155,304
1993	6,029,051	4,202,048	30,101	4,232,149	494,335	294,547	4,032,361	1,102,700	893,990	19,787	304,704	158,330
1994	6,409,497	4,475,499	29,192	4,504,691	537,634	335,861	4,302,918	1,174,187	932,392	20,863	307,216	163,946
1995	6,721,909	4,722,084	18,038	4,740,122	571,582	334,369	4,502,909	1,268,423	950,577	21,679	310,072	168,659
1996	7,021,997	4,893,172	29,566	4,922,738	584,743	332,780	4,670,775	1,351,203	1,000,019	22,498	312,119	169,345
1997	7,373,806	5,130,739	31,633	5,162,372	613,749	328,736	4,877,359	1,462,661	1,033,786	23,515	313,574	172,747
1998	7,933,206	5,581,979	18,760	5,600,739	649,269	331,248	5,282,718	1,605,678	1,044,810	25,220	314,556	175,639
1999	8,264,789	5,928,923	10,354	5,939,277	680,285	369,586	5,628,578	1,536,559	1,099,652	26,171	315,804	175,066
2000	8,624,442	6,141,967	22,101	6,164,068	698,806	362,941	5,828,203	1,635,164	1,161,075	27,207	316,991	177,109
2001	8,860,489	6,285,732	24,146	6,309,878	702,018	319,976	5,927,836	1,650,897	1,281,756	27,960	316,897	174,081
2002	9,098,062	6,465,796	10,712	6,476,508	721,112	365,908	6,121,304	1,631,740	1,345,018	28,730	316,678	172,073
2003	9,229,504	6,627,443	28,871	6,656,314	747,872	389,114	6,297,556	1,539,373	1,392,575	29,157	316,545	171,686
2004	9,732,008	6,964,915	58,339	7,023,254	787,935	527,256	6,762,575	1,508,634	1,460,799	30,717	316,831	173,844
2005	10,063,429	7,084,079	37,173	7,121,252	813,660	620,263	6,927,855	1,565,249	1,570,325	31,724	317,221	174,433
2006	10,696,411	7,373,751	32,677	7,406,428	849,529	687,084	7,243,983	1,761,735	1,690,693	33,660	317,778	175,052
2007	11,080,745	7,508,979	40,525	7,549,504	874,206	710,168	7,385,466	1,917,156	1,778,123	34,772	318,668	176,316
2008	11,246,309	7,595,316	29,478	7,624,794	898,799	566,967	7,292,962	1,907,906	2,045,441	35,148	319,966	173,666
2009	10,554,208	7,080,213	23,239	7,103,452	847,931	328,977	6,584,498	1,720,266	2,249,444	33,066	319,189	164,720
2010	10,874,921	7,166,455	42,088	7,208,543	842,191	403,898	6,770,250	1,710,232	2,394,439	34,088	319,022	163,945
2011	11,524,338	7,548,404	102,651	7,651,055	777,055	382,678	7,256,678	1,891,326	2,376,334	36,143	318,854	166,847
2012	12,062,435	7,852,092	55,381	7,907,473	797,400	449,071	7,559,144	2,075,903	2,427,388	37,913	318,160	165,809
2013	12,240,559	8,019,887	73,879	8,093,766	911,070	618,847	7,801,543	1,995,079	2,443,937	38,432	318,498	165,629
2014	12,887,381	8,404,281	15,413	8,419,694	947,389	701,799	8,174,104	2,148,381	2,564,896	40,366	319,267	168,314
2015	13,664,380	8,840,668	-3,363	8,837,305	995,675	805,466	8,647,096	2,326,196	2,691,088	42,748	319,651	171,852
2016	13,898,849	9,043,002	-2,201	9,040,801	1,017,608	777,820	8,801,013	2,342,251	2,755,585	43,323	320,822	175,495
2017	14,700,797	9,322,530	-11,263	9,311,267	1,044,355	1,147,331	9,414,243	2,458,539	2,828,015	45,681	321,815	176,231
2018	15,263,634	15,249,910	13,724	9,642,584	1,093,269	1,095,366	9,644,681	2,709,623	2,909,330	47,300	322,697	179,014
2019	15,544,754	15,537,773	6,981	10,025,284	1,140,878	829,135	9,713,541	2,734,771	3,096,442	48,035	323,613	181,357

Personal Income and Employment by Area: Spartanburg, SC

(Thousands of dollars, except as noted.)

Year	Personal income, total	Earnings by place of work			Less: Contributions for government social insurance	Plus: Adjustment for residence	Equals: Net earnings by place of residence	Plus: Dividends, interest, and rent	Plus: Personal current transfer receipts	Per capita personal income (dollars)	Population (persons)	Total employment
		Nonfarm	Farm	Total								
1970	647,309	580,899	7,033	587,932	42,161	-22,232	523,539	65,956	57,814	3,179	203,598	95,324
1971	709,991	635,744	8,587	644,331	47,844	-24,279	572,208	73,146	64,637	3,418	207,746	97,322
1972	793,946	717,621	4,674	722,295	56,420	-25,175	640,700	81,250	71,996	3,695	214,876	102,291
1973	906,158	817,382	9,843	827,225	73,332	-26,814	727,079	93,747	85,332	4,156	218,059	108,377
1974	1,002,081	887,826	8,428	896,254	82,767	-26,329	787,158	108,478	106,445	4,541	220,651	109,521
1975	1,088,851	923,592	13,616	937,208	83,413	-34,317	819,478	119,620	149,753	4,898	222,317	104,514
1976	1,227,461	1,076,300	6,180	1,082,480	99,800	-38,651	944,029	130,791	152,641	5,544	221,399	112,098
1977	1,327,798	1,161,159	4,676	1,165,835	107,962	-37,427	1,020,446	146,472	160,880	5,861	226,538	112,592
1978	1,498,157	1,317,978	6,481	1,324,459	126,129	-40,197	1,158,133	165,648	174,376	6,555	228,545	116,562
1979	1,672,526	1,459,039	7,135	1,466,174	143,708	-38,733	1,283,733	187,533	201,260	7,251	230,660	118,727
1980	1,886,083	1,607,515	3,485	1,611,000	157,816	-43,939	1,409,245	233,673	243,165	8,040	234,585	119,546
1981	2,099,054	1,741,510	5,909	1,747,419	182,659	-43,528	1,521,232	292,052	285,770	8,856	237,011	119,197
1982	2,191,017	1,753,894	166	1,754,060	186,510	-40,464	1,527,086	340,229	323,702	9,190	238,425	115,589
1983	2,372,532	1,899,113	850	1,899,963	205,296	-40,205	1,654,462	378,338	339,732	9,902	239,608	116,366
1984	2,646,242	2,133,726	11,636	2,145,362	238,004	-44,269	1,863,089	430,461	352,692	10,909	242,564	121,852
1985	2,814,057	2,267,837	-2,360	2,265,477	256,019	-37,154	1,972,304	462,666	379,087	11,463	245,495	123,771
1986	2,992,450	2,406,564	516	2,407,080	278,219	-25,467	2,103,394	491,609	397,447	12,141	246,475	125,105
1987	3,226,898	2,625,978	6,225	2,632,203	298,691	-24,192	2,309,320	511,633	405,945	12,986	248,494	128,824
1988	3,529,801	2,884,362	10,271	2,894,633	337,264	-17,964	2,539,405	559,601	430,795	14,044	251,333	134,930
1989	3,804,630	3,071,664	8,263	3,079,927	363,431	-12,462	2,704,034	617,925	482,671	14,908	255,211	140,069
1990	4,076,249	3,247,909	5,417	3,253,326	391,774	2,393	2,863,945	678,267	534,037	15,806	257,888	141,738
1991	4,245,422	3,343,650	9,759	3,353,409	408,489	-11,517	2,933,403	699,654	612,365	16,255	261,183	138,353
1992	4,494,572	3,643,511	9,165	3,652,676	440,454	-107,789	3,104,433	717,714	672,425	17,049	263,625	141,135
1993	4,797,199	3,879,885	10,793	3,890,678	474,297	-88,023	3,328,358	754,650	714,191	18,058	265,660	144,593
1994	5,068,300	4,113,805	9,902	4,123,707	509,446	-123,864	3,490,397	811,660	766,243	18,876	268,510	150,032
1995	5,380,897	4,386,208	7,790	4,393,998	544,512	-148,785	3,700,701	856,949	823,247	19,808	271,652	154,425
1996	5,675,220	4,555,652	3,877	4,559,529	555,383	-133,876	3,870,270	921,804	883,146	20,664	274,644	156,444
1997	5,983,091	4,800,357	5,730	4,806,087	582,935	-156,043	4,067,109	996,405	919,577	21,592	277,093	159,044
1998	6,235,432	5,039,806	6,290	5,046,096	614,589	-206,817	4,224,690	1,047,578	963,164	22,318	279,388	159,862
1999	6,584,069	5,297,644	8,679	5,306,323	637,484	-151,137	4,517,702	1,039,032	1,027,335	23,360	281,850	160,084
2000	7,025,820	5,532,993	9,537	5,542,530	662,862	-132,366	4,747,302	1,167,696	1,110,822	24,703	284,414	161,104
2001	7,217,078	5,614,447	6,480	5,620,927	684,983	-131,147	4,804,797	1,168,167	1,244,114	25,210	286,282	158,986
2002	7,441,901	5,768,278	5,375	5,773,653	699,778	-160,893	4,912,982	1,180,051	1,348,868	25,825	288,166	156,367
2003	7,575,460	5,910,301	11,030	5,921,331	716,140	-153,028	5,052,163	1,110,835	1,412,462	26,146	289,742	156,147
2004	7,994,908	6,229,494	1,407	6,230,901	746,108	-242,405	5,242,388	1,243,538	1,508,982	27,464	291,107	156,034
2005	8,438,264	6,421,808	11,747	6,433,555	770,713	-241,778	5,421,064	1,396,435	1,620,765	28,729	293,722	157,497
2006	9,071,284	6,862,300	13,109	6,875,409	839,427	-320,588	5,715,394	1,601,511	1,754,379	30,426	298,146	160,868
2007	9,627,605	7,162,690	16,969	7,179,659	869,933	-377,726	5,932,000	1,833,096	1,862,509	31,745	303,275	164,825
2008	10,142,182	7,304,664	21,191	7,325,855	901,840	-358,533	6,065,482	1,944,171	2,132,529	32,839	308,845	164,754
2009	9,572,539	6,737,541	26,096	6,763,637	853,376	-319,124	5,591,137	1,600,475	2,380,927	30,638	312,435	154,178
2010	9,874,875	6,983,370	29,208	7,012,578	864,185	-368,173	5,780,220	1,565,340	2,529,315	31,481	313,673	152,528
2011	10,441,035	7,222,807	18,431	7,241,238	807,398	-391,567	6,042,273	1,885,691	2,513,071	33,161	314,862	157,691
2012	11,167,674	7,653,646	17,634	7,671,280	830,692	-450,359	6,390,229	2,251,177	2,526,268	35,275	316,589	160,343
2013	10,983,910	7,968,205	23,141	7,991,346	970,867	-585,531	6,434,948	1,975,685	2,573,277	34,470	318,651	166,423
2014	11,971,985	8,460,948	15,841	8,476,789	1,019,685	-619,512	6,837,592	2,409,576	2,724,817	37,273	321,197	171,286
2015	12,627,268	8,985,092	19,443	9,004,535	1,070,928	-615,382	7,318,225	2,436,737	2,872,306	38,909	324,532	175,418
2016	13,107,544	9,362,694	11,932	9,374,626	1,122,141	-651,299	7,601,186	2,535,404	2,970,954	39,871	328,751	181,985
2017	13,675,870	9,879,332	7,644	9,886,976	1,191,557	-756,349	7,939,070	2,672,174	3,064,626	40,898	334,391	188,632
2018	13,525,267	13,525,342	-75	9,898,826	1,190,611	-753,834	7,954,381	2,723,584	2,847,302	43,055	314,137	186,820
2019	14,124,521	14,121,610	2,911	10,431,106	1,254,571	-852,019	8,324,516	2,805,864	2,994,141	44,169	319,785	192,272

Personal Income and Employment by Area: Spokane-Spokane Valley, WA

(Thousands of dollars, except as noted.)

Year	Personal income, total	Derivation of personal income									Per capita personal income (dollars)	Population (persons)	Total employment
		Earnings by place of work			Less: Contributions for government social insurance	Plus: Adjustment for residence	Equals: Net earnings by place of residence	Plus: Dividends, interest, and rent	Plus: Personal current transfer receipts				
		Nonfarm	Farm	Total									
1970	1,204,080	907,081	23,387	930,468	73,775	-16,053	840,640	219,368	144,072		3,851	312,662	129,507
1971	1,316,565	985,526	23,187	1,008,713	83,296	-13,715	911,702	240,949	163,914		4,105	320,760	130,877
1972	1,454,773	1,091,713	31,408	1,123,121	96,852	-12,838	1,013,431	261,651	179,691		4,482	324,588	135,558
1973	1,608,272	1,205,850	44,486	1,250,336	123,183	-16,438	1,110,715	292,514	205,043		4,864	330,672	140,777
1974	1,843,346	1,360,492	69,245	1,429,737	142,743	-19,832	1,267,162	337,007	239,177		5,456	337,833	147,280
1975	2,039,739	1,479,525	61,514	1,541,039	152,627	-19,213	1,369,199	381,059	289,481		5,986	340,737	145,992
1976	2,281,143	1,706,727	45,867	1,752,594	179,804	-20,113	1,552,677	411,250	317,216		6,574	346,996	154,184
1977	2,529,255	1,921,192	35,768	1,956,960	203,587	-20,152	1,733,221	463,002	333,032		7,170	352,737	160,857
1978	2,888,804	2,232,348	35,661	2,268,009	242,846	-23,099	2,002,064	528,315	358,425		7,978	362,077	171,110
1979	3,268,176	2,500,904	49,342	2,550,246	281,438	-6,327	2,262,481	599,512	406,183		8,826	370,294	176,121
1980	3,658,198	2,716,350	41,158	2,757,508	305,563	-8,927	2,443,018	720,199	494,981		9,609	380,713	177,638
1981	4,010,103	2,930,967	44,896	2,975,863	353,372	-40,019	2,582,472	864,856	562,775		10,409	385,240	176,434
1982	4,207,167	2,968,379	34,231	3,002,610	363,285	-46,466	2,592,859	983,928	630,380		10,896	386,115	173,325
1983	4,546,102	3,186,841	53,286	3,240,127	396,794	-52,345	2,790,988	1,083,489	671,625		11,732	387,506	178,995
1984	4,850,285	3,424,052	38,570	3,462,622	443,708	-62,362	2,956,552	1,189,213	704,520		12,350	392,732	185,944
1985	5,033,674	3,505,860	29,999	3,535,859	458,758	-63,400	3,013,701	1,258,833	761,140		12,741	395,083	187,899
1986	5,242,537	3,650,089	46,683	3,696,772	482,390	-69,667	3,144,715	1,296,214	801,608		13,311	393,851	191,101
1987	5,431,263	3,850,142	18,018	3,868,160	503,753	-75,868	3,288,539	1,300,367	842,357		13,820	393,013	196,927
1988	5,757,028	4,110,721	32,933	4,143,654	555,532	-86,889	3,501,233	1,341,024	914,771		14,652	392,929	201,707
1989	6,259,058	4,365,692	37,217	4,402,909	589,948	-94,505	3,718,456	1,546,040	994,562		15,824	395,554	205,459
1990	6,716,147	4,804,803	30,216	4,835,019	655,351	-101,701	4,077,967	1,541,024	1,097,156		16,663	403,054	213,149
1991	7,295,392	5,220,565	23,257	5,243,822	713,976	-106,234	4,423,612	1,613,563	1,258,217		17,635	413,678	219,425
1992	7,901,004	5,717,126	31,939	5,749,065	777,561	-120,740	4,850,764	1,666,274	1,383,966		18,553	425,854	224,934
1993	8,402,002	6,122,581	38,158	6,160,739	838,582	-130,654	5,191,503	1,747,069	1,463,430		19,207	437,440	229,463
1994	8,894,319	6,519,901	23,304	6,543,205	897,617	-147,248	5,498,340	1,879,622	1,516,357		19,981	445,129	242,655
1995	9,268,137	6,722,454	33,186	6,755,640	927,247	-160,592	5,667,801	1,992,973	1,607,363		20,468	452,821	245,905
1996	9,741,788	7,035,557	34,719	7,070,276	945,082	-178,410	5,946,784	2,124,432	1,670,572		21,287	457,647	250,642
1997	10,298,882	7,450,070	26,485	7,476,555	961,232	-196,844	6,318,479	2,247,038	1,733,365		22,369	460,412	254,871
1998	10,876,615	8,025,461	25,052	8,050,513	1,016,527	-223,399	6,810,587	2,278,310	1,787,718		23,430	464,219	258,203
1999	11,351,212	8,457,401	20,554	8,477,955	1,033,732	-243,903	7,200,320	2,235,732	1,915,160		24,327	466,608	260,710
2000	12,267,367	9,170,201	25,998	9,196,199	1,132,590	-218,534	7,845,075	2,407,300	2,014,992		26,063	470,685	267,891
2001	12,453,842	9,095,881	22,594	9,118,475	1,146,603	-207,531	7,764,341	2,446,347	2,243,154		26,222	474,933	268,588
2002	12,777,582	9,301,006	32,295	9,333,301	1,172,209	-200,582	7,960,510	2,456,115	2,360,957		26,655	479,375	266,648
2003	13,261,035	9,648,873	49,696	9,698,569	1,227,573	-207,277	8,263,719	2,531,548	2,465,768		27,437	483,328	270,596
2004	13,911,171	10,248,294	33,019	10,281,313	1,314,365	-212,480	8,754,468	2,622,470	2,534,233		28,475	488,534	275,957
2005	14,485,803	10,842,631	21,860	10,864,491	1,407,460	-195,287	9,261,744	2,504,170	2,719,889		29,299	494,408	283,759
2006	15,612,829	11,561,581	14,774	11,576,355	1,489,207	-166,127	9,921,021	2,756,157	2,935,651		31,066	502,564	293,798
2007	16,912,401	12,245,778	19,033	12,264,811	1,557,833	-168,631	10,538,347	3,185,808	3,188,246		33,030	512,037	303,178
2008	18,131,361	12,641,507	9,420	12,650,927	1,591,506	-191,798	10,867,623	3,624,472	3,639,266		34,959	518,646	303,214
2009	17,811,208	12,184,233	18,392	12,202,625	1,589,242	-231,018	10,382,365	3,360,424	4,068,419		33,937	524,826	291,777
2010	18,265,098	12,396,388	32,904	12,429,292	1,610,230	-245,278	10,573,784	3,233,933	4,457,381		34,566	528,416	285,665
2011	19,040,161	12,730,765	43,476	12,774,241	1,505,115	-299,529	10,969,597	3,627,871	4,442,693		35,947	529,674	286,724
2012	19,853,763	13,365,451	32,575	13,398,026	1,534,078	-400,648	11,463,300	3,926,791	4,463,672		37,331	531,837	291,816
2013	20,052,157	13,777,862	36,990	13,814,852	1,771,193	-366,414	11,677,245	3,849,316	4,525,596		37,513	534,546	296,578
2014	21,277,760	14,267,507	19,975	14,287,482	1,839,715	-385,805	12,061,962	4,223,758	4,992,040		39,453	539,319	301,856
2015	22,327,041	14,933,053	65,734	14,998,787	1,929,279	-373,716	12,695,792	4,556,233	5,075,016		40,925	545,559	306,358
2016	23,267,540	15,598,876	40,445	15,639,321	1,987,865	-409,008	13,242,448	4,642,645	5,382,447		41,940	554,777	313,055
2017	24,452,640	16,492,622	34,536	16,527,158	2,113,778	-422,366	13,991,014	4,888,091	5,573,535		43,338	564,236	317,902
2018	25,876,063	25,836,710	39,353	17,351,226	2,194,287	-518,732	14,638,207	5,539,570	5,698,286		46,304	558,827	323,149
2019	27,190,815	27,136,511	54,304	18,358,952	2,295,871	-577,786	15,485,295	5,672,124	6,033,396		47,827	568,521	330,522

Personal Income and Employment by Area: Springfield, IL

(Thousands of dollars, except as noted.)

Year	Personal income, total	Earnings by place of work			Less: Contributions for government social insurance	Plus: Adjustment for residence	Equals: Net earnings by place of residence	Plus: Dividends, interest, and rent	Plus: Personal current transfer receipts	Per capita personal income (dollars)	Population (persons)	Total employment
		Nonfarm	Farm	Total								
1970	793,627	656,376	24,255	680,631	38,683	-26,656	615,292	119,402	58,933	4,619	171,806	90,195
1971	888,773	736,448	30,181	766,629	44,476	-32,655	689,498	130,509	68,766	5,064	175,525	92,866
1972	966,057	793,177	34,982	828,159	49,801	-35,992	742,366	145,256	78,435	5,472	176,557	93,833
1973	1,076,590	856,215	58,475	914,690	61,209	-39,450	814,031	167,768	94,791	6,028	178,605	96,418
1974	1,199,367	953,354	61,155	1,014,509	70,797	-46,115	897,597	192,624	109,146	6,681	179,531	99,017
1975	1,350,941	1,045,381	80,270	1,125,651	77,368	-51,543	996,740	213,598	140,603	7,344	183,947	100,341
1976	1,444,065	1,140,058	59,592	1,199,650	86,496	-53,686	1,059,468	228,825	155,772	7,707	187,362	101,727
1977	1,550,499	1,219,356	65,617	1,284,973	93,099	-56,355	1,135,519	252,450	162,530	8,229	188,410	103,960
1978	1,706,750	1,367,710	50,614	1,418,324	107,116	-64,825	1,246,383	283,411	176,956	9,086	187,846	107,229
1979	1,826,772	1,435,609	54,873	1,490,482	116,210	-66,032	1,308,240	322,610	195,922	9,744	187,471	106,604
1980	1,965,909	1,517,872	23,097	1,540,969	119,965	-73,244	1,347,760	382,365	235,784	10,469	187,780	103,610
1981	2,194,208	1,626,163	60,846	1,687,009	138,179	-85,139	1,463,691	455,746	274,771	11,703	187,489	102,830
1982	2,372,886	1,725,218	39,850	1,765,068	147,959	-90,741	1,526,368	549,120	297,398	12,700	186,844	103,591
1983	2,457,447	1,817,016	-1,026	1,815,990	156,440	-96,226	1,563,324	576,238	317,885	13,099	187,611	104,656
1984	2,688,967	1,957,808	42,698	2,000,506	173,027	-103,870	1,723,609	633,819	331,539	14,322	187,747	106,763
1985	2,824,113	2,079,115	44,712	2,123,827	188,037	-114,270	1,821,520	653,795	348,798	15,014	188,104	110,181
1986	3,028,221	2,287,758	38,283	2,326,041	208,804	-134,868	1,982,369	684,499	361,353	16,166	187,316	115,910
1987	3,228,427	2,502,139	43,335	2,545,474	228,130	-154,131	2,163,213	691,606	373,608	17,210	187,591	117,958
1988	3,411,382	2,711,348	13,684	2,725,032	256,930	-171,380	2,296,722	724,334	390,326	18,096	188,519	120,710
1989	3,726,487	2,857,275	57,818	2,915,093	272,203	-174,211	2,468,679	842,493	415,315	19,722	188,954	122,213
1990	3,943,407	3,139,570	43,726	3,183,296	295,291	-196,675	2,691,330	800,699	451,378	20,775	189,818	125,747
1991	4,061,743	3,245,981	26,475	3,272,456	314,841	-210,657	2,746,958	830,542	484,243	21,095	192,544	125,206
1992	4,351,038	3,481,695	54,624	3,536,319	335,406	-239,654	2,961,259	846,661	543,118	22,245	195,599	126,634
1993	4,502,212	3,628,128	31,549	3,659,677	352,480	-253,649	3,053,548	884,116	564,548	22,679	198,516	125,314
1994	4,768,786	3,843,519	62,712	3,906,231	381,047	-268,845	3,256,339	934,046	578,401	23,710	201,132	128,409
1995	4,968,596	3,984,542	11,303	3,995,845	395,248	-278,543	3,322,054	1,022,890	623,652	24,646	201,598	130,309
1996	5,269,183	4,162,744	74,866	4,237,610	411,567	-296,002	3,530,041	1,087,205	651,937	26,069	202,123	131,736
1997	5,430,507	4,258,226	69,524	4,327,750	419,173	-309,533	3,599,044	1,161,719	669,744	26,899	201,884	131,819
1998	5,703,449	4,527,711	42,744	4,570,455	443,131	-333,563	3,793,761	1,237,456	672,232	28,274	201,722	133,299
1999	5,881,035	4,766,846	31,247	4,798,093	456,392	-355,477	3,986,224	1,214,082	680,729	29,208	201,347	134,275
2000	6,271,018	5,049,641	57,576	5,107,217	471,726	-380,836	4,254,655	1,288,859	727,504	31,102	201,628	137,874
2001	6,518,529	5,319,527	60,375	5,379,902	489,799	-430,041	4,460,062	1,281,004	777,463	32,202	202,427	137,075
2002	6,657,785	5,500,073	44,016	5,544,089	509,532	-450,336	4,584,221	1,248,280	825,284	32,752	203,281	134,989
2003	6,671,580	5,373,036	74,105	5,447,141	506,316	-426,307	4,514,518	1,290,366	866,696	32,720	203,901	131,001
2004	6,764,609	5,434,190	128,601	5,562,791	518,006	-424,103	4,620,682	1,234,835	909,092	33,075	204,526	130,500
2005	6,844,404	5,577,072	62,937	5,640,009	549,264	-426,588	4,664,157	1,194,258	985,989	33,389	204,988	130,874
2006	7,064,738	5,667,995	79,841	5,747,836	557,800	-410,884	4,779,152	1,267,463	1,018,123	34,314	205,887	130,286
2007	7,367,475	5,766,672	141,133	5,907,805	577,494	-381,649	4,948,662	1,301,648	1,117,165	35,631	206,771	130,144
2008	7,690,633	5,873,651	171,529	6,045,180	596,670	-361,174	5,087,336	1,366,200	1,237,097	36,997	207,874	128,936
2009	7,882,957	5,977,082	108,906	6,085,988	604,147	-368,354	5,113,487	1,405,406	1,364,064	37,736	208,900	127,554
2010	8,255,206	6,316,338	79,555	6,395,893	630,524	-390,254	5,375,115	1,379,323	1,500,768	39,225	210,460	127,802
2011	8,635,454	6,437,463	162,797	6,600,260	581,916	-377,801	5,640,543	1,524,695	1,470,216	40,798	211,666	129,076
2012	8,644,532	6,426,613	71,989	6,498,602	587,130	-381,600	5,529,872	1,628,801	1,485,859	40,774	212,010	127,805
2013	8,894,347	6,509,254	226,581	6,735,835	657,629	-364,279	5,713,927	1,637,858	1,542,562	42,037	211,585	126,346
2014	9,166,063	6,751,289	79,968	6,831,257	683,479	-392,924	5,754,854	1,807,633	1,603,576	43,341	211,487	128,087
2015	9,317,436	6,987,228	-34,660	6,952,568	710,439	-478,939	5,763,190	1,854,059	1,700,187	44,161	210,990	129,778
2016	9,450,266	6,943,037	34,437	6,977,474	713,928	-474,733	5,788,813	1,937,453	1,724,000	45,003	209,990	129,766
2017	9,634,500	7,035,945	21,025	7,056,970	726,044	-494,425	5,836,501	2,023,164	1,774,835	46,165	208,697	129,405
2018	9,971,208	9,873,394	97,814	7,429,291	767,218	-506,514	6,155,559	1,938,833	1,876,816	47,955	207,928	128,848
2019	10,198,822	10,155,350	43,472	7,550,187	782,689	-504,028	6,263,470	1,973,529	1,961,823	49,301	206,868	128,706

Personal Income and Employment by Area: Springfield, MA

(Thousands of dollars, except as noted.)

Year	Personal income, total	Earnings by place of work			Less: Contributions for government social insurance	Plus: Adjustment for residence	Equals: Net earnings by place of residence	Plus: Dividends, interest, and rent	Plus: Personal current transfer receipts	Per capita personal income (dollars)	Population (persons)	Total employment
		Nonfarm	Farm	Total								
1970	2,369,382	1,798,520	13,029	1,811,549	113,961	53,790	1,751,378	369,756	248,248	4,057	584,006	249,926
1971	2,511,903	1,886,518	11,044	1,897,562	123,208	52,009	1,826,363	389,227	296,313	4,292	585,290	247,098
1972	2,707,309	2,040,540	9,290	2,049,830	139,561	61,306	1,971,575	410,895	324,839	4,569	592,484	250,911
1973	2,960,932	2,236,239	12,735	2,248,974	175,238	74,355	2,148,091	445,940	366,901	4,978	594,809	259,342
1974	3,181,882	2,347,932	16,997	2,364,929	190,893	91,654	2,265,690	482,233	433,959	5,361	593,517	260,953
1975	3,468,645	2,418,427	12,688	2,431,115	189,414	102,632	2,344,333	510,249	614,063	5,856	592,358	250,085
1976	3,693,009	2,633,762	14,052	2,647,814	210,688	114,009	2,551,135	539,271	602,603	6,258	590,171	251,721
1977	4,036,798	2,909,334	14,935	2,924,269	233,761	131,280	2,821,788	590,613	624,397	6,879	586,804	259,644
1978	4,461,089	3,248,547	17,019	3,265,566	269,317	160,096	3,156,345	644,424	660,320	7,646	583,481	270,979
1979	4,977,340	3,607,782	13,837	3,621,619	311,234	199,567	3,509,952	723,560	743,828	8,544	582,523	278,090
1980	5,571,209	3,903,596	17,596	3,921,192	336,772	243,957	3,828,377	892,305	850,527	9,561	582,692	281,837
1981	6,123,437	4,177,851	17,961	4,195,812	386,304	267,378	4,076,886	1,081,797	964,754	10,471	584,790	278,651
1982	6,629,919	4,376,474	14,274	4,390,748	410,648	280,074	4,260,174	1,302,473	1,067,272	11,417	580,705	274,230
1983	7,074,439	4,734,913	17,120	4,752,033	450,363	288,137	4,589,807	1,337,336	1,147,296	12,160	581,778	278,420
1984	7,836,604	5,259,331	23,012	5,282,343	517,994	321,412	5,085,761	1,541,031	1,209,812	13,444	582,893	290,483
1985	8,374,821	5,679,189	22,469	5,701,658	561,195	347,191	5,487,654	1,614,461	1,272,706	14,366	582,962	298,323
1986	8,967,507	6,129,694	24,049	6,153,743	618,070	381,502	5,917,175	1,701,809	1,348,523	15,370	583,433	306,741
1987	9,735,390	6,778,098	27,143	6,805,241	674,299	409,591	6,540,533	1,793,229	1,401,628	16,498	590,082	311,695
1988	10,627,333	7,446,664	34,057	7,480,721	756,074	436,884	7,161,531	1,955,075	1,510,727	17,802	596,967	320,757
1989	11,515,045	7,799,744	28,154	7,827,898	791,005	456,490	7,493,383	2,285,744	1,735,918	19,121	602,229	319,997
1990	11,641,632	7,869,130	30,490	7,899,620	789,881	473,984	7,583,723	2,137,440	1,920,469	19,282	603,765	313,127
1991	11,863,531	7,787,551	27,645	7,815,196	796,793	476,905	7,495,308	2,096,641	2,271,582	19,678	602,886	298,962
1992	12,189,895	8,133,746	23,653	8,157,399	823,940	481,607	7,815,066	2,046,464	2,328,365	20,234	602,439	301,351
1993	12,499,739	8,378,061	21,645	8,399,706	853,670	467,785	8,013,821	2,099,525	2,386,393	20,730	602,990	302,284
1994	13,038,427	8,707,582	21,970	8,729,552	890,633	484,916	8,323,835	2,171,390	2,543,202	21,582	604,128	304,888
1995	13,599,043	8,920,143	21,449	8,941,592	923,241	477,129	8,495,480	2,426,677	2,676,886	22,518	603,922	305,322
1996	14,170,010	9,341,399	22,172	9,363,571	949,610	501,635	8,915,596	2,530,105	2,724,309	23,486	603,331	308,475
1997	14,836,951	9,798,384	21,429	9,819,813	996,891	522,926	9,345,848	2,657,972	2,833,131	24,537	604,675	312,467
1998	15,368,892	10,231,538	15,017	10,246,555	1,033,591	563,094	9,776,058	2,754,619	2,838,215	25,369	605,809	316,875
1999	15,989,823	10,787,328	17,122	10,804,450	1,071,045	615,658	10,349,063	2,690,929	2,949,831	26,336	607,147	321,946
2000	17,061,014	11,526,104	23,181	11,549,285	1,130,601	687,968	11,106,652	2,835,419	3,118,943	28,020	608,897	329,185
2001	18,044,470	12,305,173	20,194	12,325,367	1,220,392	680,912	11,785,887	2,838,819	3,419,764	29,626	609,075	332,345
2002	18,516,692	12,732,747	22,752	12,755,499	1,263,404	624,863	12,116,958	2,660,397	3,739,337	30,244	612,241	329,737
2003	19,148,250	13,109,032	20,024	13,129,056	1,294,662	607,808	12,442,202	2,707,201	3,998,847	31,120	615,294	327,408
2004	19,840,178	13,729,064	21,209	13,750,273	1,387,440	636,117	12,998,950	2,640,587	4,200,641	32,215	615,860	330,174
2005	20,600,538	14,147,429	20,900	14,168,329	1,469,418	632,438	13,331,349	2,664,744	4,604,445	33,414	616,530	330,955
2006	21,563,536	14,586,182	15,521	14,601,703	1,498,739	650,934	13,753,898	3,007,446	4,802,192	34,916	617,576	331,269
2007	22,575,861	15,034,257	13,378	15,047,635	1,544,216	726,039	14,229,458	3,380,761	4,965,642	36,514	618,276	336,485
2008	23,578,437	15,467,464	8,798	15,476,262	1,600,094	658,564	14,534,732	3,392,522	5,651,183	38,050	619,668	335,970
2009	23,756,437	15,274,734	9,030	15,283,764	1,587,947	632,603	14,328,420	3,249,484	6,178,533	38,274	620,687	327,112
2010	24,450,470	15,738,499	11,577	15,750,076	1,597,712	705,492	14,857,856	3,134,688	6,457,926	39,218	623,455	327,016
2011	25,671,120	16,290,351	5,971	16,296,322	1,502,401	812,940	15,606,861	3,522,369	6,541,890	40,998	626,157	329,942
2012	27,048,432	17,199,333	11,478	17,210,811	1,565,887	872,117	16,517,041	3,874,247	6,657,144	43,132	627,115	339,950
2013	27,281,492	17,532,686	8,185	17,540,871	1,778,664	921,762	16,683,969	3,884,269	6,713,254	43,412	628,437	344,851
2014	28,370,575	18,057,614	5,525	18,063,139	1,848,145	943,205	17,158,199	4,276,664	6,935,712	44,998	630,479	348,191
2015	29,899,478	18,798,499	4,853	18,803,352	1,885,899	982,448	17,899,901	4,531,331	7,468,246	47,407	630,696	359,285
2016	30,501,641	19,153,050	1,600	19,154,650	1,937,828	996,321	18,213,143	4,523,221	7,765,277	48,365	630,661	364,398
2017	31,356,885	19,791,898	-780	19,791,118	2,014,502	1,024,958	18,801,574	4,710,744	7,844,567	49,643	631,652	367,916
2018	36,629,063	36,623,600	5,463	22,339,521	2,296,963	1,585,537	21,628,095	5,888,754	9,112,214	52,317	700,138	410,881
2019	37,643,308	37,633,858	9,450	23,171,518	2,372,417	1,623,378	22,422,479	5,970,699	9,250,130	53,978	697,382	416,676

Personal Income and Employment by Area: Springfield, MO

(Thousands of dollars, except as noted.)

Year	Personal income, total	Earnings by place of work			Less: Contributions for government social insurance	Plus: Adjustment for residence	Equals: Net earnings by place of residence	Plus: Dividends, interest, and rent	Plus: Personal current transfer receipts	Per capita personal income (dollars)	Population (persons)	Total employment
		Nonfarm	Farm	Total								
1970	701,954	555,435	16,899	572,334	38,236	-15,082	519,016	105,513	77,425	3,332	210,653	97,284
1971	769,880	606,699	17,126	623,825	42,946	-15,894	564,985	117,001	87,894	3,531	218,024	100,075
1972	865,244	684,061	22,901	706,962	50,738	-17,390	638,834	129,024	97,386	3,832	225,777	105,645
1973	977,830	766,252	35,536	801,788	65,543	-19,137	717,108	146,627	114,095	4,227	231,356	110,471
1974	1,062,911	825,668	21,499	847,167	72,837	-19,867	754,463	171,956	136,492	4,513	235,542	109,821
1975	1,175,914	875,606	25,039	900,645	75,374	-20,151	805,120	193,452	177,342	4,971	236,572	107,489
1976	1,332,580	1,014,050	30,991	1,045,041	88,263	-23,170	933,608	212,752	186,220	5,527	241,105	113,331
1977	1,480,066	1,142,472	24,874	1,167,346	99,859	-25,850	1,041,637	243,208	195,221	5,988	247,152	119,130
1978	1,692,043	1,313,407	35,266	1,348,673	118,477	-29,785	1,200,411	276,568	215,064	6,689	252,970	125,953
1979	1,890,888	1,468,989	27,809	1,496,798	137,093	-33,317	1,326,388	319,680	244,820	7,385	256,053	130,864
1980	2,141,112	1,604,901	29,827	1,634,728	149,283	-39,351	1,446,094	398,397	296,621	8,249	259,555	131,378
1981	2,397,773	1,742,939	47,968	1,790,907	174,136	-44,574	1,572,197	485,429	340,147	9,184	261,087	132,649
1982	2,589,950	1,859,877	21,229	1,881,106	189,951	-46,624	1,644,531	578,187	367,232	9,874	262,312	134,650
1983	2,808,534	2,024,641	14,861	2,039,502	206,065	-50,694	1,782,743	627,433	398,358	10,522	266,915	139,611
1984	3,130,280	2,264,931	19,031	2,283,962	236,219	-58,790	1,988,953	726,469	414,858	11,524	271,631	147,471
1985	3,346,403	2,430,795	19,928	2,450,723	258,740	-64,467	2,127,516	771,993	446,894	12,086	276,883	153,042
1986	3,595,922	2,633,717	21,354	2,655,071	282,259	-70,456	2,302,356	814,736	478,830	12,783	281,312	158,763
1987	3,797,339	2,821,909	18,293	2,840,202	297,371	-73,435	2,469,396	826,297	501,646	13,229	287,040	161,311
1988	4,067,099	3,034,576	21,912	3,056,488	329,702	-78,990	2,647,796	886,556	532,747	13,948	291,591	168,214
1989	4,425,129	3,268,638	40,960	3,309,598	357,176	-84,973	2,867,449	973,290	584,390	15,009	294,823	172,646
1990	4,674,543	3,465,471	33,517	3,498,988	390,862	-92,317	3,015,809	1,012,521	646,213	15,563	300,354	177,682
1991	5,035,969	3,716,714	24,062	3,740,776	422,924	-104,684	3,213,168	1,067,984	754,817	16,400	307,066	179,784
1992	5,495,411	4,082,276	19,502	4,101,778	459,246	-118,839	3,523,693	1,154,147	817,571	17,469	314,578	184,602
1993	5,923,210	4,414,247	16,398	4,430,645	497,638	-120,786	3,812,221	1,214,889	896,100	18,312	323,461	194,731
1994	6,397,830	4,794,406	2,814	4,797,220	545,151	-124,912	4,127,157	1,338,861	931,812	19,218	332,908	204,646
1995	6,771,444	5,101,160	76	5,101,236	578,148	-135,449	4,387,639	1,374,379	1,009,426	19,860	340,951	211,443
1996	7,169,472	5,380,337	700	5,381,037	601,224	-147,850	4,631,963	1,456,476	1,081,033	20,702	346,324	215,750
1997	7,599,491	5,660,716	3,120	5,663,836	628,278	-161,621	4,873,937	1,572,649	1,152,905	21,546	352,705	221,150
1998	8,112,436	6,080,850	7,992	6,088,842	668,763	-161,160	5,258,919	1,669,468	1,184,049	22,631	358,461	224,809
1999	8,524,059	6,541,190	-3,519	6,537,671	711,621	-169,978	5,656,072	1,631,928	1,236,059	23,425	363,882	229,377
2000	8,977,946	6,790,875	-2,352	6,788,523	739,911	-180,791	5,867,821	1,768,377	1,341,748	24,270	369,920	234,283
2001	9,726,184	7,387,151	8,422	7,395,573	789,160	-173,953	6,432,460	1,780,116	1,513,608	25,922	375,215	235,317
2002	10,115,623	7,766,416	7,433	7,773,849	820,368	-165,954	6,787,527	1,679,233	1,648,863	26,583	380,529	237,008
2003	10,729,884	8,208,270	21,053	8,229,323	867,432	-161,372	7,200,519	1,776,280	1,753,085	27,723	387,040	241,499
2004	11,429,595	8,823,930	65,136	8,889,066	922,253	-181,429	7,785,384	1,746,029	1,898,182	28,961	394,660	246,956
2005	12,051,353	9,357,180	49,183	9,406,363	991,576	-188,358	8,226,429	1,775,848	2,049,076	29,913	402,883	256,341
2006	12,717,084	9,731,290	23,384	9,754,674	1,052,971	-191,039	8,510,664	2,018,044	2,188,376	30,735	413,765	263,627
2007	13,426,436	9,992,734	7,616	10,000,350	1,110,453	-183,522	8,706,375	2,360,246	2,359,815	31,731	423,127	270,226
2008	14,170,870	10,033,944	12,754	10,046,698	1,137,215	-156,934	8,752,549	2,726,158	2,692,163	33,010	429,289	267,387
2009	13,852,316	9,907,962	-15,906	9,892,056	1,106,472	-197,723	8,587,861	2,318,327	2,946,128	31,902	434,220	258,981
2010	13,960,032	9,908,708	-519	9,908,189	1,098,058	-165,028	8,645,103	2,170,541	3,144,388	31,924	437,283	254,756
2011	14,492,462	10,020,354	20,488	10,040,842	1,017,589	-166,257	8,856,996	2,367,915	3,267,551	32,922	440,209	258,567
2012	15,262,825	10,565,813	-4,861	10,560,952	1,055,006	-183,721	9,322,225	2,584,053	3,356,547	34,361	444,188	263,488
2013	15,403,608	10,905,002	22,629	10,927,631	1,224,857	-193,877	9,508,897	2,464,138	3,430,573	34,355	448,360	266,178
2014	16,168,958	11,381,758	64,920	11,446,678	1,284,048	-209,814	9,952,816	2,679,030	3,537,112	35,807	451,556	271,253
2015	17,105,407	12,077,092	24,991	12,102,083	1,369,104	-229,355	10,503,624	2,885,949	3,715,834	37,554	455,484	276,467
2016	17,330,272	12,242,286	-10,540	12,231,746	1,403,131	-253,433	10,575,182	2,915,073	3,840,017	37,848	457,897	278,845
2017	18,017,702	12,738,241	-11,098	12,727,143	1,452,507	-258,215	11,016,421	3,066,229	3,935,052	38,968	462,369	282,200
2018	19,230,402	19,227,035	3,367	13,548,843	1,530,628	-285,833	11,732,382	3,398,384	4,099,636	41,243	466,273	288,306
2019	20,037,243	20,033,697	3,546	14,238,123	1,611,676	-330,362	12,296,085	3,449,157	4,292,001	42,605	470,300	282,200

Personal Income and Employment by Area: Springfield, OH

(Thousands of dollars, except as noted.)

Year	Personal income, total	Earnings by place of work			Less: Contributions for government social insurance	Plus: Adjustment for residence	Equals: Net earnings by place of residence	Plus: Dividends, interest, and rent	Plus: Personal current transfer receipts	Per capita personal income (dollars)	Population (persons)	Total employment
		Nonfarm	Farm	Total								
1970	624,985	400,905	8,847	409,752	26,066	109,962	493,648	84,677	46,660	3,965	157,639	55,081
1971	701,759	462,524	8,279	470,803	31,270	111,595	551,128	94,620	56,011	4,386	160,007	57,561
1972	735,920	484,167	7,107	491,274	34,671	116,064	572,667	100,481	62,772	4,661	157,903	57,769
1973	802,916	530,319	13,268	543,587	43,832	120,777	620,532	109,245	73,139	5,102	157,377	59,907
1974	860,916	553,163	17,001	570,164	47,645	127,197	649,716	121,058	90,142	5,525	155,828	59,056
1975	916,174	554,517	23,663	578,180	46,403	134,405	666,182	134,128	115,864	5,924	154,645	55,640
1976	989,647	605,349	18,344	623,693	51,447	143,196	715,442	142,575	131,630	6,522	151,748	56,507
1977	1,079,820	680,408	13,125	693,533	58,395	154,529	789,667	158,063	132,090	7,163	150,753	58,103
1978	1,192,800	768,492	13,498	781,990	68,507	165,316	878,799	175,560	138,441	7,916	150,681	60,630
1979	1,306,649	836,865	17,051	853,916	77,425	178,009	954,500	195,135	157,014	8,665	150,789	61,472
1980	1,415,166	864,123	12,589	876,712	78,966	196,323	994,069	229,570	191,527	9,425	150,149	59,719
1981	1,480,026	888,972	946	889,918	86,067	182,324	986,175	269,707	224,144	9,902	149,463	58,312
1982	1,525,851	856,688	3,414	860,102	83,835	188,219	964,486	298,015	263,350	10,322	147,821	54,398
1983	1,612,044	927,370	-3,750	923,620	92,758	189,132	1,019,994	312,430	279,620	10,956	147,142	54,481
1984	1,800,730	1,077,698	12,321	1,090,019	110,922	195,511	1,174,608	344,457	281,665	12,242	147,100	57,693
1985	1,903,421	1,143,469	17,380	1,160,849	120,282	199,632	1,240,199	362,558	300,664	12,942	147,075	59,175
1986	2,002,549	1,227,097	12,845	1,239,942	132,919	198,814	1,305,837	377,513	319,199	13,586	147,403	60,508
1987	2,074,743	1,299,395	16,410	1,315,805	142,395	194,092	1,367,502	378,368	328,873	14,065	147,514	62,208
1988	2,260,471	1,455,756	23,751	1,479,507	165,889	195,611	1,509,229	401,702	349,540	15,274	147,992	63,505
1989	2,386,486	1,498,221	28,153	1,526,374	173,317	205,501	1,558,558	456,893	371,035	16,155	147,720	65,358
1990	2,520,855	1,534,793	26,221	1,561,014	180,739	249,723	1,629,998	474,340	416,517	17,079	147,596	65,336
1991	2,596,523	1,574,084	13,086	1,587,170	190,487	260,969	1,657,652	489,879	448,992	17,574	147,747	64,309
1992	2,749,563	1,708,571	32,470	1,741,041	206,264	240,157	1,774,934	484,224	490,405	18,630	147,584	64,709
1993	2,838,718	1,757,296	20,648	1,777,944	214,469	281,668	1,845,143	485,357	508,218	19,253	147,442	64,554
1994	2,976,943	1,840,584	21,952	1,862,536	225,275	309,166	1,946,427	507,183	523,333	20,203	147,355	65,631
1995	3,129,076	1,916,494	25,776	1,942,270	236,632	339,080	2,044,718	536,652	547,706	21,244	147,289	67,425
1996	3,231,731	1,942,099	23,535	1,965,634	234,640	363,133	2,094,127	563,077	574,527	21,967	147,116	67,183
1997	3,416,525	2,039,770	32,666	2,072,436	238,006	392,247	2,226,677	596,712	593,136	23,358	146,268	67,932
1998	3,588,961	2,242,249	17,576	2,259,825	249,202	338,266	2,348,889	629,049	611,023	24,625	145,742	70,742
1999	3,669,904	2,340,199	10,372	2,350,571	258,742	335,583	2,427,412	622,089	620,403	25,282	145,159	71,410
2000	3,804,873	2,360,232	15,167	2,375,399	252,890	390,869	2,513,378	626,268	665,227	26,312	144,605	72,418
2001	3,857,353	2,362,953	22,811	2,385,764	263,449	394,476	2,516,791	620,957	719,605	26,824	143,803	68,606
2002	3,841,037	2,285,094	16,563	2,301,657	248,056	429,698	2,483,299	596,193	761,545	26,817	143,229	66,993
2003	3,907,167	2,260,975	20,367	2,281,342	248,885	461,420	2,493,877	607,243	806,047	27,562	141,758	66,257
2004	3,977,704	2,289,763	38,590	2,328,353	259,281	500,208	2,569,280	568,345	840,079	28,135	141,380	65,548
2005	4,052,115	2,325,152	35,061	2,360,213	266,294	524,075	2,617,994	554,188	879,933	28,664	141,367	65,001
2006	4,212,231	2,439,313	37,175	2,476,488	281,999	515,400	2,709,889	589,063	913,279	29,944	140,668	65,338
2007	4,322,493	2,435,530	36,578	2,472,108	282,438	519,462	2,709,132	640,322	973,039	30,913	139,829	65,336
2008	4,428,930	2,500,236	27,563	2,527,799	295,994	463,537	2,695,342	656,084	1,077,504	31,770	139,404	64,851
2009	4,398,826	2,432,091	29,988	2,462,079	293,382	416,154	2,584,851	628,137	1,185,838	31,697	138,778	62,359
2010	4,458,378	2,429,812	24,065	2,453,877	286,650	422,391	2,589,618	618,267	1,250,493	32,245	138,265	61,102
2011	4,676,837	2,541,051	34,157	2,575,208	272,546	401,701	2,704,363	675,266	1,297,208	33,951	137,754	62,236
2012	4,740,964	2,610,868	17,047	2,627,915	276,302	422,194	2,773,807	698,199	1,268,958	34,577	137,115	62,301
2013	4,793,269	2,669,582	32,306	2,701,888	304,554	393,477	2,790,811	696,144	1,306,314	35,098	136,567	62,742
2014	4,917,178	2,710,624	7,918	2,718,542	308,939	416,888	2,826,491	735,105	1,355,582	36,094	136,233	63,202
2015	5,051,817	2,735,909	-4,660	2,731,249	312,027	458,192	2,877,414	760,652	1,413,751	37,249	135,624	62,501
2016	5,122,686	2,762,167	-3,170	2,758,997	322,590	465,764	2,902,171	780,684	1,439,831	38,053	134,621	61,636
2017	5,286,633	2,909,201	-4,683	2,904,518	346,296	437,765	2,995,987	816,402	1,474,244	39,289	134,557	62,039
2018	5,456,881	5,439,819	17,062	2,995,479	350,320	486,806	3,131,965	838,930	1,485,986	40,563	134,528	62,076
2019	5,606,209	5,601,598	4,611	3,049,471	358,650	528,584	3,219,405	848,775	1,538,029	41,811	134,083	62,218

Personal Income and Employment by Area: State College, PA

(Thousands of dollars, except as noted.)

Year	Personal income, total	Earnings by place of work			Less: Contributions for government social insurance	Plus: Adjustment for residence	Equals: Net earnings by place of residence	Plus: Dividends, interest, and rent	Plus: Personal current transfer receipts	Per capita personal income (dollars)	Population (persons)	Total employment
		Nonfarm	Farm	Total								
1970	311,381	273,733	3,052	276,785	18,156	-16,982	241,647	44,711	25,023	3,130	99,495	40,640
1971	338,460	298,151	2,130	300,281	20,603	-19,595	260,083	49,439	28,938	3,342	101,263	41,670
1972	377,376	328,554	2,779	331,333	23,205	-19,625	288,503	55,616	33,257	3,630	103,971	43,904
1973	428,240	368,886	4,835	373,721	29,201	-19,128	325,392	64,283	38,565	4,077	105,034	46,470
1974	475,413	406,481	5,993	412,474	33,778	-22,228	356,468	73,036	45,909	4,404	107,957	47,629
1975	530,466	437,745	4,983	442,728	35,719	-22,626	384,383	83,170	62,913	4,933	107,533	47,752
1976	591,914	490,628	6,455	497,083	41,155	-25,474	430,454	91,650	69,810	5,379	110,048	50,025
1977	658,606	551,484	5,645	557,129	46,198	-29,616	481,315	103,454	73,837	5,832	112,939	51,750
1978	725,643	610,308	3,635	613,943	52,860	-31,860	529,223	116,136	80,284	6,519	111,315	53,267
1979	819,564	683,709	8,034	691,743	61,587	-36,696	593,460	133,084	93,020	7,288	112,459	55,133
1980	909,436	736,592	8,177	744,769	67,291	-41,526	635,952	161,053	112,431	8,039	113,131	56,510
1981	993,763	784,453	9,782	794,235	77,473	-38,351	678,411	193,640	121,712	8,687	114,390	55,794
1982	1,077,007	839,029	7,119	846,148	83,543	-43,274	719,331	223,181	134,495	9,389	114,706	55,674
1983	1,170,705	908,436	3,508	911,944	91,290	-50,043	770,611	248,141	151,953	10,075	116,203	56,956
1984	1,276,452	1,006,173	10,481	1,016,654	105,992	-58,040	852,622	274,333	149,497	11,062	115,390	59,461
1985	1,350,471	1,063,136	9,944	1,073,080	114,232	-60,784	898,064	293,311	159,096	11,585	116,567	60,583
1986	1,434,656	1,140,065	7,686	1,147,751	124,853	-65,640	957,258	314,989	162,409	12,189	117,697	63,132
1987	1,556,360	1,258,169	9,246	1,267,415	136,804	-77,711	1,052,900	329,393	174,067	13,027	119,468	66,110
1988	1,724,182	1,406,658	13,392	1,420,050	159,195	-88,348	1,172,507	361,808	189,867	14,312	120,473	68,862
1989	1,933,517	1,577,695	16,006	1,593,701	174,932	-110,922	1,307,847	421,938	203,732	15,842	122,049	71,931
1990	2,049,768	1,688,862	12,166	1,701,028	188,123	-121,009	1,391,896	433,680	224,192	16,368	125,231	74,221
1991	2,186,645	1,807,604	5,159	1,812,763	203,344	-133,048	1,476,371	456,486	253,788	17,283	126,518	75,902
1992	2,325,635	1,918,670	16,831	1,935,501	213,881	-138,637	1,582,983	468,442	274,210	18,186	127,881	76,642
1993	2,397,361	1,988,224	9,622	1,997,846	223,710	-143,493	1,630,643	479,493	287,225	18,451	129,930	78,826
1994	2,528,888	2,106,336	11,365	2,117,701	238,159	-148,807	1,730,735	515,876	282,277	19,327	130,847	80,708
1995	2,653,619	2,202,699	4,197	2,206,896	249,105	-162,343	1,795,448	557,325	300,846	20,111	131,951	84,000
1996	2,812,860	2,307,483	15,646	2,323,129	254,588	-176,022	1,892,519	595,894	324,447	20,976	134,102	85,877
1997	2,980,772	2,467,545	8,575	2,476,120	271,755	-194,192	2,010,173	629,958	340,641	22,105	134,849	87,914
1998	3,142,739	2,592,692	16,798	2,609,490	278,451	-208,142	2,122,897	660,581	359,261	23,339	134,657	90,593
1999	3,307,832	2,751,243	12,424	2,763,667	291,205	-229,928	2,242,534	699,018	366,280	24,445	135,315	93,184
2000	3,471,091	2,919,438	18,923	2,938,361	306,020	-256,951	2,375,390	700,184	395,517	25,529	135,965	95,959
2001	3,654,124	3,121,884	13,825	3,135,709	318,608	-294,912	2,522,189	686,256	445,679	26,552	137,620	97,495
2002	3,826,896	3,362,720	8,284	3,371,004	339,953	-343,580	2,687,471	658,329	481,096	27,176	140,821	100,705
2003	3,987,389	3,476,205	16,082	3,492,287	344,282	-364,358	2,783,647	705,841	497,901	27,898	142,926	100,925
2004	4,260,991	3,737,121	20,935	3,758,056	365,491	-423,963	2,968,602	770,146	522,243	29,541	144,238	103,041
2005	4,513,040	4,047,109	15,544	4,062,653	394,061	-476,672	3,191,920	769,163	551,957	31,008	145,543	104,606
2006	4,720,270	4,205,817	12,969	4,218,786	411,042	-540,388	3,267,356	857,488	595,426	31,736	148,734	106,074
2007	4,910,296	4,334,637	17,608	4,352,245	426,270	-600,270	3,325,705	937,422	647,169	32,845	149,498	107,699
2008	5,194,643	4,533,865	10,557	4,544,422	444,398	-646,344	3,453,680	986,659	754,304	34,255	151,645	108,962
2009	5,217,415	4,502,449	3,696	4,506,145	449,197	-632,163	3,424,785	978,880	813,750	34,089	153,052	108,969
2010	5,500,656	4,753,478	15,916	4,769,394	467,331	-669,251	3,632,812	981,242	886,602	35,654	154,280	108,939
2011	5,807,279	4,934,557	24,584	4,959,141	434,028	-708,268	3,816,845	1,086,080	904,354	37,457	155,039	111,163
2012	6,016,617	5,088,068	29,594	5,117,662	441,725	-710,018	3,965,919	1,161,290	889,408	38,591	155,909	111,266
2013	6,272,537	5,419,705	34,992	5,454,697	518,117	-738,491	4,198,089	1,153,338	921,110	39,625	158,298	113,149
2014	6,619,644	5,682,454	39,395	5,721,849	546,110	-789,143	4,386,596	1,248,487	984,561	41,467	159,637	114,274
2015	6,666,239	5,719,926	19,413	5,739,339	563,169	-805,910	4,370,260	1,296,085	999,894	41,520	160,553	115,479
2016	6,843,106	5,844,981	4,186	5,849,167	577,927	-839,255	4,431,985	1,348,120	1,063,001	42,220	162,083	117,566
2017	7,181,690	6,133,138	15,838	6,148,976	607,855	-860,236	4,680,885	1,423,237	1,077,568	44,152	162,660	119,085
2018	7,457,920	7,445,214	12,706	6,349,269	625,945	-910,685	4,812,639	1,496,613	1,148,668	45,866	162,601	116,515
2019	7,723,642	7,696,068	27,574	6,541,174	642,984	-925,151	4,973,039	1,539,287	1,211,316	47,564	162,385	116,024

Personal Income and Employment by Area: Staunton, VA

(Thousands of dollars, except as noted.)

Year	Personal income, total	Earnings by place of work			Less: Contributions for government social insurance	Plus: Adjustment for residence	Equals: Net earnings by place of residence	Plus: Dividends, interest, and rent	Plus: Personal current transfer receipts	Per capita personal income (dollars)	Population (persons)	Total employment
		Nonfarm	Farm	Total								
1970	298,781	258,450	6,640	265,090	16,761	-8,534	239,795	38,419	20,567	3,488	85,665	41,054
1971	315,732	268,852	6,450	275,302	18,116	-8,684	248,502	42,696	24,534	3,600	87,707	40,415
1972	346,385	294,291	8,144	302,435	21,001	-10,247	271,187	47,384	27,814	3,916	88,454	41,457
1973	392,997	331,105	13,216	344,321	27,310	-11,942	305,069	54,404	33,524	4,461	88,087	43,253
1974	434,939	369,435	9,811	379,246	31,707	-14,974	332,565	62,467	39,907	4,890	88,941	45,156
1975	468,654	378,060	9,283	387,343	31,546	-12,881	342,916	69,658	56,080	5,200	90,122	42,447
1976	519,353	427,717	7,125	434,842	36,294	-14,820	383,728	76,531	59,094	5,750	90,316	44,035
1977	571,105	475,350	1,262	476,612	40,483	-16,042	420,087	85,705	65,313	6,308	90,541	45,245
1978	629,926	522,859	1,061	523,920	45,569	-15,611	462,740	96,678	70,508	6,949	90,646	46,008
1979	698,779	572,543	2,405	574,948	51,953	-11,666	511,329	105,967	81,483	7,689	90,886	46,584
1980	774,955	637,445	971	638,416	58,333	-26,470	553,613	124,748	96,594	8,513	91,031	47,059
1981	858,637	684,397	-160	684,237	67,467	-27,600	589,170	155,417	114,050	9,404	91,309	47,007
1982	911,676	689,957	161	690,118	69,050	-17,642	603,426	180,983	127,267	9,942	91,701	45,701
1983	983,143	731,014	1,047	732,061	73,617	-9,640	648,804	196,087	138,252	10,706	91,828	45,092
1984	1,106,492	807,518	12,191	819,709	83,645	-9,462	726,602	234,409	145,481	12,058	91,764	46,741
1985	1,169,839	842,040	14,542	856,582	88,637	-5,221	762,724	250,295	156,820	12,737	91,846	47,500
1986	1,255,038	894,406	19,478	913,884	96,820	2,176	819,240	268,838	166,960	13,602	92,272	48,454
1987	1,350,162	980,786	17,277	998,063	105,404	5,919	898,578	278,346	173,238	14,404	93,737	51,201
1988	1,471,085	1,073,224	23,989	1,097,213	118,561	12,056	990,708	299,892	180,485	15,483	95,015	52,603
1989	1,609,297	1,135,215	32,172	1,167,387	126,230	22,545	1,063,702	351,784	193,811	16,672	96,527	53,093
1990	1,707,685	1,196,910	35,524	1,232,434	135,108	31,047	1,128,373	370,694	208,618	17,408	98,096	54,582
1991	1,736,283	1,203,780	32,799	1,236,579	136,997	37,309	1,136,891	368,895	230,497	17,519	99,110	53,191
1992	1,828,832	1,261,113	35,482	1,296,595	142,180	44,043	1,198,458	369,954	260,420	18,276	100,067	52,582
1993	1,912,124	1,325,462	32,834	1,358,296	149,081	50,017	1,259,232	379,880	273,012	18,901	101,163	53,648
1994	2,005,090	1,387,261	36,185	1,423,446	155,086	54,859	1,323,219	395,002	286,869	19,607	102,263	54,075
1995	2,098,439	1,421,494	32,039	1,453,533	158,982	59,518	1,354,069	433,583	310,787	20,236	103,697	54,791
1996	2,205,714	1,490,984	32,012	1,522,996	165,164	61,534	1,419,366	460,166	326,182	21,008	104,994	56,133
1997	2,333,443	1,615,870	15,239	1,631,109	177,963	63,009	1,516,155	479,485	337,803	22,016	105,988	58,271
1998	2,502,062	1,742,386	20,070	1,762,456	186,774	73,082	1,648,764	501,884	351,414	23,410	106,879	59,935
1999	2,551,231	1,770,773	16,349	1,787,122	191,532	85,112	1,680,702	500,767	369,762	23,590	108,150	60,837
2000	2,720,461	1,860,722	26,909	1,887,631	198,440	95,503	1,784,694	539,937	395,830	24,929	109,129	61,784
2001	2,783,550	1,844,689	35,872	1,880,561	210,409	118,321	1,788,473	551,608	443,469	25,397	109,602	60,313
2002	2,848,543	1,905,562	20,936	1,926,498	216,341	143,644	1,853,801	520,926	473,816	25,794	110,436	59,698
2003	3,007,655	1,983,307	8,281	1,991,588	222,686	174,762	1,943,664	557,713	506,278	26,963	111,549	59,782
2004	3,322,913	2,227,530	30,398	2,257,928	242,202	175,687	2,191,413	595,844	535,656	29,471	112,751	61,591
2005	3,433,491	2,270,937	39,881	2,310,818	256,183	199,113	2,253,748	592,464	587,279	30,096	114,085	63,083
2006	3,605,605	2,295,444	16,447	2,311,891	264,541	249,854	2,297,204	659,327	649,074	31,013	116,262	63,738
2007	3,967,911	2,517,875	22,066	2,539,941	282,031	284,109	2,542,019	739,976	685,916	33,710	117,708	64,894
2008	4,179,290	2,634,503	16,009	2,650,512	296,172	293,924	2,648,264	762,113	768,913	35,292	118,420	64,776
2009	4,153,708	2,578,696	13,439	2,592,135	292,604	307,086	2,606,617	710,701	836,390	35,025	118,593	62,262
2010	4,249,786	2,618,630	26,488	2,645,118	292,741	309,388	2,661,765	697,364	890,657	35,918	118,318	61,243
2011	4,354,143	2,550,275	42,917	2,593,192	266,482	337,016	2,663,726	768,094	922,323	36,659	118,775	61,537
2012	4,433,116	2,555,633	34,206	2,589,839	268,674	353,127	2,674,292	841,285	917,539	37,425	118,452	61,959
2013	4,479,976	2,616,233	48,449	2,664,682	312,098	354,888	2,707,472	823,758	948,746	37,604	119,137	62,618
2014	4,700,031	2,722,764	58,629	2,781,393	322,051	348,453	2,807,795	898,120	994,116	39,346	119,454	63,243
2015	4,889,339	2,829,428	45,105	2,874,533	332,205	360,182	2,902,510	945,611	1,041,218	40,746	119,995	64,161
2016	4,957,348	2,860,969	26,347	2,887,316	340,364	373,958	2,920,910	961,033	1,075,405	41,026	120,833	65,273
2017	5,177,207	2,963,093	38,712	3,001,805	355,141	402,116	3,048,780	1,007,086	1,121,341	42,436	121,999	65,133
2018	5,436,837	5,407,994	28,843	3,130,219	372,773	405,866	3,163,312	1,105,358	1,168,167	44,336	122,628	65,925
2019	5,621,379	5,609,159	12,220	3,218,758	388,250	439,748	3,270,256	1,117,460	1,233,663	45,658	123,120	67,443

Personal Income and Employment by Area: Stockton, CA

(Thousands of dollars, except as noted.)

Year	Personal income, total	Earnings by place of work			Less: Contributions for government social insurance	Plus: Adjustment for residence	Equals: Net earnings by place of residence	Plus: Dividends, interest, and rent	Plus: Personal current transfer receipts	Per capita personal income (dollars)	Population (persons)	Total employment
		Nonfarm	Farm	Total								
1970	1,278,250	900,345	103,228	1,003,573	56,978	-12,632	933,963	192,386	151,901	4,385	291,488	125,639
1971	1,390,528	983,384	104,415	1,087,799	64,433	-12,392	1,010,974	211,696	167,858	4,695	296,167	127,686
1972	1,528,236	1,075,883	123,592	1,199,475	74,314	-10,252	1,114,909	231,936	181,391	5,090	300,221	132,230
1973	1,704,543	1,175,239	167,599	1,342,838	93,705	-9,771	1,239,362	263,967	201,214	5,609	303,896	135,549
1974	1,936,888	1,307,453	209,817	1,517,270	108,102	-10,577	1,398,591	301,505	236,792	6,316	306,658	139,715
1975	2,130,146	1,419,692	190,228	1,609,920	114,391	-12,728	1,482,801	341,834	305,511	6,877	309,750	141,773
1976	2,320,183	1,578,559	171,009	1,749,568	130,539	-10,572	1,608,457	365,596	346,130	7,304	317,671	144,612
1977	2,556,555	1,742,951	186,272	1,929,223	147,382	-8,841	1,773,000	406,789	376,766	7,968	320,840	147,548
1978	2,868,968	1,993,874	171,395	2,165,269	171,671	-5,743	1,987,855	465,357	415,756	8,624	332,685	153,412
1979	3,245,393	2,235,724	212,841	2,448,565	203,261	-6,497	2,238,807	536,233	470,353	9,591	338,384	162,770
1980	3,690,850	2,398,775	287,853	2,686,628	215,941	-840	2,469,847	659,293	561,710	10,536	350,304	165,174
1981	4,075,817	2,624,958	212,959	2,837,917	257,384	18,131	2,598,664	810,227	666,926	11,276	361,462	167,276
1982	4,347,135	2,755,500	187,057	2,942,557	275,474	35,927	2,703,010	893,149	750,976	11,640	373,479	167,744
1983	4,579,513	2,892,580	123,438	3,016,018	293,830	67,792	2,789,980	974,631	814,902	11,873	385,721	169,304
1984	5,152,677	3,239,905	201,377	3,441,282	341,175	97,843	3,197,950	1,093,271	861,456	12,923	398,731	176,594
1985	5,582,735	3,526,682	203,962	3,730,644	375,824	130,603	3,485,423	1,163,001	934,311	13,419	416,042	181,855
1986	6,027,045	3,857,793	197,371	4,055,164	415,127	161,831	3,801,868	1,225,135	1,000,042	13,991	430,786	186,320
1987	6,557,228	4,226,092	297,989	4,524,081	455,068	198,732	4,267,745	1,244,470	1,045,013	14,711	445,726	195,501
1988	7,080,526	4,552,682	347,160	4,899,842	510,396	246,418	4,635,864	1,313,957	1,130,705	15,489	457,138	205,322
1989	7,667,579	4,871,224	317,769	5,188,993	549,747	302,129	4,941,375	1,490,859	1,235,345	16,424	466,863	209,243
1990	8,146,661	5,199,586	297,728	5,497,314	583,569	356,913	5,270,658	1,506,922	1,369,081	16,827	484,131	214,261
1991	8,542,060	5,477,326	261,403	5,738,729	622,224	376,352	5,492,857	1,521,913	1,527,290	17,337	492,694	216,618
1992	9,149,223	5,723,020	327,706	6,050,726	642,485	424,885	5,833,126	1,526,125	1,789,972	18,288	500,278	212,460
1993	9,543,968	5,943,726	374,500	6,318,226	668,946	452,432	6,101,712	1,573,831	1,868,425	18,847	506,385	214,476
1994	9,904,668	6,198,071	377,300	6,575,371	697,511	474,603	6,352,463	1,659,827	1,892,378	19,337	512,212	220,269
1995	10,231,273	6,312,788	351,001	6,663,789	704,740	546,338	6,505,387	1,748,653	1,977,233	19,754	517,923	224,933
1996	10,809,337	6,546,643	421,581	6,968,224	708,979	624,645	6,883,890	1,848,538	2,076,909	20,603	524,657	228,643
1997	11,536,532	7,121,856	449,033	7,570,889	759,186	700,851	7,512,554	1,956,082	2,067,896	21,689	531,908	233,118
1998	12,304,414	7,604,021	375,012	7,979,033	791,859	833,945	8,021,119	2,065,912	2,217,383	22,775	540,257	238,983
1999	13,110,805	8,134,641	406,711	8,541,352	851,232	990,100	8,680,220	2,106,309	2,324,276	23,733	552,424	249,510
2000	14,288,856	8,887,001	382,967	9,269,968	919,591	1,284,022	9,634,399	2,257,715	2,396,742	25,162	567,885	254,521
2001	15,616,572	9,894,834	423,307	10,318,141	1,061,648	1,305,521	10,562,014	2,340,017	2,714,541	26,415	591,207	260,519
2002	16,333,659	10,526,474	418,163	10,944,637	1,145,359	1,333,945	11,133,223	2,289,772	2,910,664	26,819	609,041	266,758
2003	17,476,595	11,267,519	506,560	11,774,079	1,243,209	1,413,713	11,944,583	2,416,508	3,115,504	27,883	626,778	274,428
2004	18,671,110	12,058,522	573,154	12,631,676	1,371,078	1,593,796	12,854,394	2,526,080	3,290,636	29,042	642,898	279,725
2005	19,757,562	12,726,472	583,566	13,310,038	1,438,041	1,837,998	13,709,995	2,602,169	3,445,398	30,073	656,985	283,427
2006	20,907,859	13,242,706	441,858	13,684,564	1,450,929	2,038,144	14,271,779	2,921,007	3,715,073	31,544	662,812	287,112
2007	21,610,450	13,175,390	597,980	13,773,370	1,448,365	2,105,141	14,430,146	3,217,211	3,963,093	32,347	668,080	293,377
2008	21,700,946	12,922,478	533,138	13,455,616	1,461,477	1,953,257	13,947,396	3,305,052	4,448,498	32,308	671,692	287,022
2009	21,765,614	12,827,444	563,924	13,391,368	1,446,057	1,830,667	13,775,978	3,056,638	4,932,998	32,115	677,736	275,719
2010	22,503,652	13,270,968	452,655	13,723,623	1,424,413	1,656,031	13,955,241	3,006,033	5,542,378	32,743	687,291	268,668
2011	23,243,047	13,344,555	560,118	13,904,673	1,317,574	1,762,963	14,350,062	3,323,833	5,569,152	33,440	695,071	269,966
2012	24,074,531	13,531,332	928,681	14,460,013	1,337,265	1,692,063	14,814,811	3,584,911	5,674,809	34,345	700,958	276,843
2013	25,014,730	13,983,059	987,632	14,970,691	1,540,968	2,057,879	15,487,602	3,647,006	5,880,122	35,545	703,747	285,328
2014	26,773,886	14,518,996	1,152,262	15,671,258	1,604,350	2,138,509	16,205,417	4,235,141	6,333,328	37,527	713,452	294,311
2015	28,834,765	15,936,252	870,571	16,806,823	1,739,583	2,145,713	17,212,953	4,698,265	6,923,547	39,835	723,846	310,444
2016	30,102,917	16,621,541	555,516	17,177,057	1,832,299	2,740,734	18,085,492	4,847,118	7,170,307	40,996	734,294	319,751
2017	31,920,185	17,670,466	760,173	18,430,639	1,940,700	3,350,881	19,840,820	5,109,399	6,969,966	42,822	745,424	329,770
2018	33,634,157	32,816,770	817,387	19,566,240	2,067,879	3,420,861	20,919,222	5,364,651	7,350,284	44,697	752,491	339,762
2019	35,926,949	34,913,653	1,013,296	20,795,848	2,207,730	3,967,668	22,555,786	5,481,616	7,889,547	47,139	762,148	347,851

Personal Income and Employment by Area: Sumter, SC

(Thousands of dollars, except as noted.)

Year	Personal income, total	Earnings by place of work			Less: Contributions for government social insurance	Plus: Adjustment for residence	Equals: Net earnings by place of residence	Plus: Dividends, interest, and rent	Plus: Personal current transfer receipts	Per capita personal income (dollars)	Population (persons)	Total employment
		Nonfarm	Farm	Total								
1970	236,568	197,814	8,070	205,884	12,920	-16,679	176,285	41,765	18,518	2,967	79,727	36,298
1971	257,261	215,608	7,350	222,958	14,916	-16,603	191,439	43,965	21,857	3,142	81,867	36,617
1972	288,789	240,828	9,756	250,584	17,055	-17,870	215,659	48,408	24,722	3,427	84,259	37,059
1973	313,671	260,350	8,984	269,334	20,429	-18,361	230,544	53,417	29,710	3,772	83,151	37,868
1974	348,497	276,618	14,233	290,851	22,726	-16,841	251,284	59,237	37,976	4,183	83,313	37,426
1975	382,668	300,154	9,449	309,603	24,951	-18,576	266,076	66,588	50,004	4,482	85,380	37,204
1976	419,381	333,267	8,919	342,186	28,667	-19,299	294,220	71,008	54,153	4,920	85,241	37,621
1977	455,349	363,469	7,882	371,351	31,105	-20,287	319,959	79,569	55,821	5,259	86,589	38,477
1978	514,153	410,972	6,443	417,415	35,512	-22,485	359,418	93,003	61,732	5,922	86,824	39,864
1979	564,290	446,299	9,548	455,847	40,200	-23,490	392,157	101,433	70,700	6,445	87,556	40,248
1980	620,161	485,622	555	486,177	43,263	-24,468	418,446	115,532	86,183	6,989	88,736	40,098
1981	685,923	525,064	4,277	529,341	50,062	-23,649	455,630	131,772	98,521	7,586	90,420	40,072
1982	744,160	568,062	2,676	570,738	53,926	-27,702	489,110	148,998	106,052	8,102	91,845	39,657
1983	804,042	615,574	113	615,687	60,094	-27,684	527,909	161,714	114,419	8,677	92,663	40,634
1984	908,566	680,992	20,031	701,023	68,582	-28,687	603,754	183,526	121,286	9,599	94,657	42,253
1985	973,153	735,743	13,053	748,796	75,166	-31,498	642,132	199,030	131,991	10,099	96,362	43,248
1986	1,026,048	778,971	8,303	787,274	81,799	-29,645	675,830	211,670	138,548	10,461	98,084	43,739
1987	1,098,950	834,731	13,242	847,973	87,275	-29,463	731,235	226,238	141,477	11,054	99,420	44,627
1988	1,179,160	901,610	16,398	918,008	98,520	-31,821	787,667	241,424	150,069	11,818	99,777	45,935
1989	1,284,777	950,253	18,564	968,817	106,153	-29,830	832,834	275,457	176,486	12,604	101,933	46,844
1990	1,416,072	1,026,547	16,575	1,043,122	117,376	10,053	935,799	288,681	191,592	13,983	101,271	48,598
1991	1,461,353	1,055,017	20,191	1,075,208	122,604	-14,669	937,935	298,559	224,859	14,239	102,630	47,713
1992	1,555,887	1,108,309	18,333	1,126,642	129,044	-983	996,615	308,383	250,889	15,079	103,179	48,403
1993	1,621,011	1,185,646	12,573	1,198,219	139,899	-36,502	1,021,818	333,978	265,215	15,405	105,224	50,751
1994	1,719,270	1,231,928	16,496	1,248,424	145,939	-26,636	1,075,849	350,496	292,925	16,290	105,542	51,597
1995	1,794,871	1,299,557	7,866	1,307,423	153,397	-38,000	1,116,026	369,625	309,220	16,956	105,852	53,220
1996	1,883,985	1,345,977	22,158	1,368,135	157,072	-42,290	1,168,773	385,687	329,525	17,784	105,938	53,549
1997	1,975,098	1,424,360	13,541	1,437,901	165,684	-50,094	1,222,123	406,048	346,927	18,726	105,475	54,482
1998	2,058,661	1,493,830	9,514	1,503,344	174,604	-62,879	1,265,861	428,408	364,392	19,519	105,468	54,838
1999	2,144,754	1,547,037	11,628	1,558,665	179,539	-40,760	1,338,366	424,078	382,310	20,460	104,827	55,120
2000	2,248,134	1,634,647	11,876	1,646,523	189,411	-66,259	1,390,853	448,614	408,667	21,451	104,802	56,101
2001	2,314,204	1,641,920	20,433	1,662,353	193,522	-52,791	1,416,040	445,760	452,404	22,118	104,629	54,499
2002	2,432,651	1,718,212	9,149	1,727,361	201,217	-50,105	1,476,039	459,865	496,747	23,085	105,380	54,107
2003	2,538,940	1,805,542	15,700	1,821,242	209,941	-44,912	1,566,389	453,836	518,715	24,155	105,112	53,882
2004	2,693,703	1,899,862	25,039	1,924,901	221,715	-35,610	1,667,576	461,548	564,579	25,389	106,099	54,520
2005	2,797,412	1,953,070	29,848	1,982,918	227,347	-21,974	1,733,597	458,317	605,498	26,370	106,082	54,892
2006	2,944,756	2,036,949	14,415	2,051,364	243,720	-7,069	1,800,575	496,204	647,977	27,793	105,953	54,656
2007	3,083,186	2,092,127	15,538	2,107,665	249,546	9,047	1,867,166	526,931	689,089	29,083	106,014	54,814
2008	3,180,122	2,067,760	9,966	2,077,726	249,326	25,873	1,854,273	542,955	782,894	29,871	106,463	53,301
2009	3,129,821	2,005,296	9,197	2,014,493	244,644	2,582	1,772,431	508,752	848,638	29,250	107,004	50,995
2010	3,221,169	2,084,241	10,744	2,094,985	253,418	-40,507	1,801,060	504,179	915,930	29,940	107,586	51,069
2011	3,385,617	2,225,419	8,906	2,234,325	244,963	-91,892	1,897,470	563,822	924,325	31,555	107,291	52,845
2012	3,588,023	2,467,856	24,454	2,492,310	267,184	-170,162	2,054,964	609,091	923,968	33,251	107,908	53,812
2013	3,587,636	2,489,379	38,076	2,527,455	299,258	-195,377	2,032,820	605,077	949,739	33,285	107,784	53,937
2014	3,702,137	2,555,093	9,550	2,564,643	306,054	-188,388	2,070,201	631,048	1,000,888	34,374	107,702	54,636
2015	3,804,840	2,585,679	10,404	2,596,083	310,409	-182,070	2,103,604	647,630	1,053,606	35,468	107,276	54,936
2016	3,827,529	2,588,398	10,575	2,598,973	311,461	-190,887	2,096,625	649,397	1,081,507	35,676	107,287	54,521
2017	3,941,257	2,663,638	10,375	2,674,013	323,386	-193,940	2,156,687	671,255	1,113,315	36,887	106,847	54,830
2018	5,232,598	5,223,609	8,989	3,209,078	394,339	13,260	2,827,999	858,740	1,545,859	37,335	140,151	67,438
2019	5,434,249	5,431,490	2,759	3,332,386	408,601	11,885	2,935,670	884,742	1,613,837	38,687	140,466	67,761

Personal Income and Employment by Area: Syracuse, NY

(Thousands of dollars, except as noted.)

Year	Personal income, total	Earnings by place of work			Less: Contributions for government social insurance	Plus: Adjustment for residence	Equals: Net earnings by place of residence	Plus: Dividends, interest, and rent	Plus: Personal current transfer receipts	Per capita personal income (dollars)	Population (persons)	Total employment
		Nonfarm	Farm	Total								
1970	2,562,246	2,134,132	25,826	2,159,958	159,044	-33,036	1,967,878	340,052	254,316	4,019	637,540	270,461
1971	2,778,329	2,306,288	24,874	2,331,162	177,611	-38,056	2,115,495	363,062	299,772	4,341	640,019	274,853
1972	2,988,887	2,511,740	22,314	2,534,054	203,519	-42,388	2,288,147	387,583	313,157	4,657	641,826	278,450
1973	3,249,712	2,745,827	28,770	2,774,597	257,308	-45,379	2,471,910	429,851	347,951	5,059	642,407	289,236
1974	3,554,107	2,981,044	26,392	3,007,436	287,568	-51,434	2,668,434	483,366	402,307	5,527	642,995	294,880
1975	3,809,864	3,033,376	21,614	3,054,990	287,290	-49,100	2,718,600	530,198	561,066	5,897	646,105	283,301
1976	4,082,945	3,304,762	22,888	3,327,650	320,529	-54,277	2,952,844	555,628	574,473	6,305	647,543	286,493
1977	4,481,088	3,685,085	16,810	3,701,895	355,778	-64,346	3,281,771	609,125	590,192	6,924	647,200	295,258
1978	4,896,592	4,067,724	24,111	4,091,835	402,548	-69,348	3,619,939	645,953	630,700	7,570	646,806	304,167
1979	5,464,280	4,573,614	31,021	4,604,635	468,697	-82,013	4,053,925	727,557	682,798	8,476	644,646	311,104
1980	6,097,030	4,961,922	31,312	4,993,234	507,669	-88,758	4,396,807	894,498	805,725	9,486	642,764	307,311
1981	6,713,000	5,373,948	35,167	5,409,115	586,156	-106,136	4,716,823	1,089,539	906,638	10,477	640,720	308,076
1982	7,334,814	5,798,723	28,946	5,827,669	637,151	-127,880	5,062,638	1,253,475	1,018,701	11,453	640,442	308,937
1983	7,943,906	6,324,443	21,258	6,345,701	698,934	-151,038	5,495,729	1,372,833	1,075,344	12,355	642,984	314,098
1984	8,865,683	7,123,028	30,728	7,153,756	805,381	-177,606	6,170,769	1,553,423	1,141,491	13,714	646,469	327,908
1985	9,448,823	7,686,438	34,666	7,721,104	878,188	-200,342	6,642,574	1,601,715	1,204,534	14,528	650,383	340,140
1986	9,968,180	8,096,865	40,575	8,137,440	935,677	-208,608	6,993,155	1,688,512	1,286,513	15,368	648,635	346,353
1987	10,271,856	8,367,092	43,463	8,410,555	957,853	-210,060	7,242,642	1,716,933	1,312,281	15,883	646,725	348,298
1988	11,025,902	9,056,761	33,579	9,090,340	1,056,380	-228,915	7,805,045	1,822,040	1,398,817	16,980	649,352	359,990
1989	12,115,751	9,786,475	46,201	9,832,676	1,126,183	-257,955	8,448,538	2,147,651	1,519,562	18,502	654,842	367,410
1990	12,789,116	10,350,434	47,141	10,397,575	1,142,373	-297,707	8,957,495	2,173,676	1,657,945	19,333	661,505	374,714
1991	13,058,689	10,456,521	39,919	10,496,440	1,182,353	-302,545	9,011,542	2,201,779	1,845,368	19,619	665,618	368,948
1992	13,797,739	11,070,719	38,854	11,109,573	1,228,735	-324,647	9,556,191	2,178,239	2,063,309	20,640	668,488	367,160
1993	14,078,481	11,240,892	49,706	11,290,598	1,254,904	-333,319	9,702,375	2,217,476	2,158,630	21,003	670,309	367,707
1994	14,410,697	11,466,575	39,718	11,506,293	1,295,586	-342,938	9,867,769	2,265,703	2,277,225	21,589	667,499	369,006
1995	14,863,453	11,663,818	27,362	11,691,180	1,319,060	-359,649	10,012,471	2,425,544	2,425,438	22,372	664,389	365,912
1996	15,192,888	11,828,229	41,231	11,869,460	1,316,544	-391,843	10,161,073	2,502,805	2,529,010	23,006	660,384	367,025
1997	15,707,277	12,292,180	24,415	12,316,595	1,350,626	-389,595	10,576,374	2,599,743	2,531,160	23,972	655,229	366,983
1998	16,430,561	12,783,876	47,366	12,831,242	1,386,050	-366,844	11,078,348	2,660,792	2,691,421	25,220	651,499	366,462
1999	17,155,185	13,574,521	54,396	13,628,917	1,431,954	-385,205	11,811,758	2,620,688	2,722,739	26,381	650,297	374,195
2000	18,105,879	14,260,420	59,220	14,319,640	1,496,406	-362,613	12,460,621	2,772,528	2,872,730	27,857	649,961	378,485
2001	18,281,252	14,330,667	72,027	14,402,694	1,565,740	-371,287	12,465,667	2,738,452	3,077,133	28,095	650,697	376,302
2002	18,690,021	14,831,163	48,898	14,880,061	1,640,854	-394,255	12,844,952	2,553,639	3,291,430	28,655	652,241	371,452
2003	19,429,339	15,316,832	54,784	15,371,616	1,698,398	-399,304	13,273,914	2,704,179	3,451,246	29,659	655,091	372,360
2004	20,305,638	16,100,150	68,478	16,168,628	1,772,947	-367,136	14,028,545	2,626,947	3,650,146	30,947	656,149	375,373
2005	20,944,151	16,487,709	66,300	16,554,009	1,845,025	-389,479	14,319,505	2,839,220	3,785,426	31,975	655,021	379,598
2006	21,915,843	17,217,647	52,249	17,269,896	1,911,833	-416,774	14,941,289	2,979,774	3,994,780	33,443	655,321	380,463
2007	23,216,544	18,054,740	89,920	18,144,660	1,985,199	-428,372	15,731,089	3,318,014	4,167,441	35,380	656,209	386,623
2008	24,138,932	18,294,915	91,947	18,386,862	2,047,108	-404,339	15,935,415	3,563,308	4,640,209	36,634	658,913	386,944
2009	24,503,152	18,315,950	46,519	18,362,469	2,028,805	-374,859	15,958,805	3,422,518	5,121,829	37,078	660,857	377,832
2010	25,271,068	18,834,047	82,355	18,916,402	2,052,361	-324,844	16,539,197	3,242,562	5,489,309	38,107	663,154	373,991
2011	26,218,457	19,110,921	103,384	19,214,305	1,879,432	-332,628	17,002,245	3,596,415	5,619,797	39,559	662,770	377,100
2012	27,264,592	19,825,842	94,956	19,920,798	1,921,942	-322,542	17,676,314	3,956,363	5,631,915	41,213	661,548	379,080
2013	27,433,518	20,142,254	112,486	20,254,740	2,201,634	-295,711	17,757,395	3,955,878	5,720,245	41,380	662,958	380,095
2014	28,235,020	20,494,602	119,436	20,614,038	2,280,013	-279,800	18,054,225	4,278,027	5,902,768	42,669	661,725	381,268
2015	29,366,171	21,169,344	58,254	21,227,598	2,367,114	-287,922	18,572,562	4,588,557	6,205,052	44,504	659,850	382,371
2016	29,761,420	21,468,298	41,871	21,510,169	2,418,975	-298,669	18,792,525	4,648,099	6,320,796	45,304	656,931	383,404
2017	30,972,555	22,056,830	51,120	22,107,950	2,488,322	-346,272	19,273,356	4,866,627	6,832,572	47,298	654,841	384,114
2018	32,483,834	32,419,905	63,929	23,597,074	2,580,126	-360,858	20,656,090	5,206,717	6,621,027	49,954	650,281	387,251
2019	33,759,608	33,657,374	102,234	24,377,196	2,641,615	-368,528	21,367,053	5,301,761	7,090,794	52,051	648,593	391,208

Personal Income and Employment by Area: Tallahassee, FL

(Thousands of dollars, except as noted.)

Year	Personal income, total	Earnings by place of work			Less: Contributions for government social insurance	Plus: Adjustment for residence	Equals: Net earnings by place of residence	Plus: Dividends, interest, and rent	Plus: Personal current transfer receipts	Per capita personal income (dollars)	Population (persons)	Total employment
		Nonfarm	Farm	Total								
1970	491,814	399,417	18,424	417,841	23,566	-13,928	380,347	75,481	35,986	3,107	158,300	68,040
1971	567,235	463,338	17,662	481,000	28,966	-15,277	436,757	87,983	42,495	3,438	165,004	71,779
1972	669,418	551,421	16,968	568,389	35,850	-17,809	514,730	103,944	50,744	3,855	173,644	77,730
1973	785,602	645,787	20,466	666,253	48,662	-19,745	597,846	125,713	62,043	4,329	181,470	83,485
1974	884,309	717,696	18,682	736,378	56,903	-20,902	658,573	149,911	75,825	4,673	189,245	86,579
1975	977,884	779,457	17,403	796,860	62,054	-21,220	713,586	166,058	98,240	5,229	186,999	87,284
1976	1,063,676	845,362	18,407	863,769	70,559	-21,125	772,085	181,158	110,433	5,612	189,529	88,025
1977	1,160,438	924,104	12,405	936,509	78,583	-20,235	837,691	200,799	121,948	5,960	194,690	90,724
1978	1,304,352	1,037,771	16,526	1,054,297	92,922	-21,553	939,822	230,728	133,802	6,519	200,091	94,497
1979	1,485,497	1,178,811	20,378	1,199,189	111,764	-23,534	1,063,891	265,915	155,691	7,278	204,111	99,612
1980	1,704,539	1,322,513	19,914	1,342,427	122,191	-24,934	1,195,302	322,578	186,659	7,996	213,167	104,810
1981	1,932,538	1,482,934	15,531	1,498,465	148,207	-26,752	1,323,506	395,100	213,932	8,874	217,765	107,359
1982	2,107,823	1,593,554	23,265	1,616,819	162,314	-30,299	1,424,206	449,757	233,860	9,513	221,584	108,947
1983	2,328,388	1,755,153	24,597	1,779,750	177,507	-32,848	1,569,395	501,653	257,340	10,340	225,185	112,794
1984	2,553,190	1,928,535	26,125	1,954,660	198,603	-34,805	1,721,252	556,913	275,025	11,130	229,399	117,358
1985	2,771,177	2,104,870	26,093	2,130,963	219,344	-38,678	1,872,941	600,144	298,092	11,888	233,106	123,662
1986	3,077,005	2,365,868	29,076	2,394,944	250,568	-43,390	2,100,986	660,104	315,915	13,047	235,840	131,759
1987	3,362,973	2,614,843	29,532	2,644,375	270,086	-50,974	2,323,315	704,069	335,589	13,953	241,026	135,906
1988	3,736,245	2,933,807	34,484	2,968,291	316,602	-55,746	2,595,943	772,235	368,067	15,141	246,756	143,371
1989	4,168,470	3,211,390	39,370	3,250,760	345,898	-62,431	2,842,431	901,442	424,597	16,429	253,724	150,382
1990	4,540,385	3,523,250	37,538	3,560,788	374,654	-68,203	3,117,931	956,164	466,290	17,383	261,192	156,015
1991	4,830,859	3,762,671	47,278	3,809,949	401,890	-75,814	3,332,245	970,241	528,373	17,793	271,509	158,565
1992	5,132,150	4,020,962	47,474	4,068,436	429,303	-81,776	3,557,357	971,361	603,432	18,593	276,025	161,167
1993	5,472,834	4,295,830	47,845	4,343,675	453,609	-88,104	3,801,962	1,029,920	640,952	19,242	284,421	166,471
1994	5,833,475	4,590,133	45,320	4,635,453	489,181	-98,756	4,047,516	1,105,761	680,198	19,929	292,713	172,345
1995	6,336,012	4,924,978	46,894	4,971,872	523,726	-107,498	4,340,648	1,254,435	740,929	21,222	298,563	179,081
1996	6,676,310	5,211,643	44,556	5,256,199	551,491	-117,510	4,587,198	1,317,545	771,567	22,038	302,943	181,936
1997	7,021,126	5,495,050	53,182	5,548,232	583,043	-127,289	4,837,900	1,378,126	805,100	22,765	308,414	188,091
1998	7,552,934	5,948,879	54,853	6,003,732	629,147	-144,063	5,230,522	1,484,473	837,939	24,155	312,685	191,646
1999	7,994,277	6,376,036	58,579	6,434,615	673,917	-159,105	5,601,593	1,512,649	880,035	25,232	316,825	195,883
2000	8,413,816	6,705,268	55,660	6,760,928	707,286	-169,503	5,884,139	1,593,651	936,026	26,184	321,336	201,044
2001	9,022,253	7,226,567	59,649	7,286,216	755,723	-184,527	6,345,966	1,639,116	1,037,171	27,813	324,386	204,473
2002	9,271,879	7,459,730	53,547	7,513,277	778,121	-195,449	6,539,707	1,594,256	1,137,916	28,273	327,940	198,342
2003	9,685,847	7,705,643	44,749	7,750,392	802,743	-207,051	6,740,598	1,724,065	1,221,184	28,974	334,289	200,990
2004	10,313,282	8,137,193	48,912	8,186,105	851,600	-215,436	7,119,069	1,919,787	1,274,426	30,407	339,179	205,899
2005	10,965,588	8,542,478	48,899	8,591,377	899,608	-231,918	7,459,851	2,112,587	1,393,150	31,853	344,257	212,085
2006	11,546,072	8,922,143	49,531	8,971,674	953,571	-250,910	7,767,193	2,325,490	1,453,389	32,934	350,580	216,913
2007	12,086,857	9,294,872	38,429	9,333,301	999,718	-267,379	8,066,204	2,445,338	1,575,315	33,823	357,357	220,398
2008	12,326,071	9,327,997	44,925	9,372,922	1,014,242	-287,348	8,071,332	2,431,078	1,823,661	34,122	361,238	217,761
2009	12,157,668	9,104,793	39,139	9,143,932	999,014	-261,028	7,883,890	2,319,491	1,954,287	33,337	364,690	210,705
2010	12,811,474	9,281,682	45,160	9,326,842	1,001,496	-265,073	8,060,273	2,568,476	2,182,725	34,688	369,339	209,441
2011	13,519,895	9,315,534	39,293	9,354,827	893,020	-251,127	8,210,680	3,016,613	2,292,602	36,423	371,194	211,131
2012	13,416,715	9,649,035	55,246	9,704,281	918,130	-242,980	8,543,171	2,641,148	2,232,396	35,752	375,272	210,402
2013	13,185,715	9,541,867	60,456	9,602,323	1,041,482	-229,356	8,331,485	2,538,965	2,315,265	35,330	373,212	211,733
2014	13,970,121	9,938,450	66,888	10,005,338	1,091,290	-234,999	8,679,049	2,769,724	2,521,348	37,201	375,532	217,297
2015	14,480,737	10,172,580	80,240	10,252,820	1,117,955	-240,559	8,894,306	2,919,305	2,667,126	38,314	377,947	219,402
2016	14,999,467	10,499,720	67,736	10,567,456	1,161,936	-243,689	9,161,831	3,094,394	2,743,242	39,572	379,047	223,570
2017	15,685,315	10,984,045	66,347	11,050,392	1,215,444	-258,903	9,576,045	3,234,853	2,874,417	40,994	382,627	226,969
2018	16,529,184	16,461,864	67,320	11,621,326	1,279,221	-287,742	10,054,363	3,381,469	3,093,352	43,009	384,318	235,311
2019	17,127,856	17,027,014	100,842	12,100,686	1,347,766	-290,208	10,462,712	3,435,037	3,230,107	44,232	387,227	239,871

Personal Income and Employment by Area: Tampa-St. Petersburg-Clearwater, FL

(Thousands of dollars, except as noted.)

Year	Personal income, total	Earnings by place of work			Less: Contributions for government social insurance	Plus: Adjustment for residence	Equals: Net earnings by place of residence	Plus: Dividends, interest, and rent	Plus: Personal current transfer receipts	Per capita personal income (dollars)	Population (persons)	Total employment
		Nonfarm	Farm	Total								
1970	4,329,776	2,829,055	43,720	2,872,775	186,697	25,929	2,712,007	1,063,264	554,505	3,875	1,117,227	439,739
1971	4,872,882	3,171,668	50,731	3,222,399	217,856	28,540	3,033,083	1,184,145	655,654	4,127	1,180,716	460,528
1972	5,671,208	3,768,453	64,599	3,833,052	271,412	32,708	3,594,348	1,316,842	760,018	4,530	1,251,917	509,052
1973	6,638,176	4,446,246	72,983	4,519,229	369,372	42,299	4,192,156	1,525,278	920,742	4,978	1,333,538	565,986
1974	7,488,493	4,931,707	65,798	4,997,505	427,349	48,861	4,619,017	1,786,106	1,083,370	5,370	1,394,490	581,774
1975	8,233,437	5,176,323	78,963	5,255,286	438,549	52,743	4,869,480	1,986,268	1,377,689	5,774	1,425,848	564,107
1976	8,950,891	5,602,729	84,829	5,687,558	481,335	55,520	5,261,743	2,169,230	1,519,918	6,163	1,452,426	567,011
1977	10,169,956	6,410,543	91,282	6,501,825	544,288	65,375	6,022,912	2,478,619	1,668,425	6,880	1,478,254	597,815
1978	11,705,963	7,455,204	102,214	7,557,418	649,760	74,814	6,982,472	2,871,616	1,851,875	7,713	1,517,764	644,879
1979	13,479,977	8,565,514	103,451	8,668,965	783,780	86,492	7,971,677	3,374,301	2,133,999	8,568	1,573,352	679,429
1980	15,913,401	9,767,227	137,091	9,904,318	903,469	97,561	9,098,410	4,280,111	2,534,880	9,781	1,626,975	717,538
1981	18,423,485	11,000,672	113,744	11,114,416	1,099,800	92,195	10,106,811	5,361,318	2,955,356	10,983	1,677,405	753,441
1982	20,022,699	11,799,994	159,858	11,959,852	1,223,135	70,923	10,807,640	5,871,460	3,343,599	11,623	1,722,726	776,167
1983	22,282,228	13,342,460	199,741	13,542,201	1,389,413	44,329	12,197,117	6,450,776	3,634,335	12,558	1,774,374	821,026
1984	24,870,472	15,127,525	161,407	15,288,932	1,623,627	19,202	13,684,507	7,390,732	3,795,233	13,622	1,825,777	883,678
1985	27,136,994	16,665,179	152,397	16,817,576	1,820,009	-1,719	14,995,848	8,060,397	4,080,749	14,458	1,877,018	932,733
1986	29,234,365	18,123,147	159,092	18,282,239	2,026,789	-29,924	16,225,526	8,624,099	4,384,740	15,198	1,923,591	969,125
1987	31,157,648	19,790,203	152,513	19,942,716	2,189,286	-56,128	17,697,302	8,834,597	4,625,749	15,839	1,967,197	983,589
1988	33,848,439	21,736,261	191,645	21,927,906	2,476,426	-89,113	19,362,367	9,482,869	5,003,203	16,877	2,005,545	1,029,281
1989	37,628,205	23,331,506	194,477	23,525,983	2,694,959	-109,553	20,721,471	11,301,445	5,605,289	18,451	2,039,321	1,052,726
1990	39,444,797	24,859,946	174,027	25,033,973	2,834,593	-158,490	22,040,890	11,357,244	6,046,663	18,983	2,077,857	1,074,649
1991	40,554,113	25,780,658	196,034	25,976,692	2,967,958	-172,166	22,836,568	11,045,508	6,672,037	19,211	2,110,974	1,060,636
1992	42,692,004	27,741,661	198,060	27,939,721	3,181,097	-233,452	24,525,172	10,652,425	7,514,407	19,994	2,135,204	1,062,769
1993	45,371,607	29,507,125	193,303	29,700,428	3,365,923	-211,116	26,123,389	11,200,820	8,047,398	20,967	2,163,912	1,093,939
1994	47,604,258	31,624,671	175,092	31,799,763	3,642,029	-241,576	27,916,158	11,149,385	8,538,715	21,695	2,194,294	1,137,326
1995	51,264,737	33,788,107	184,475	33,972,582	3,880,883	-170,942	29,920,757	12,251,351	9,092,629	23,030	2,226,036	1,178,494
1996	54,399,379	36,349,360	169,905	36,519,265	4,126,779	-424,151	31,968,335	12,895,745	9,535,299	24,108	2,256,460	1,230,493
1997	57,872,609	38,881,308	192,798	39,074,106	4,419,311	-540,281	34,114,514	13,930,415	9,827,680	25,192	2,297,251	1,275,654
1998	61,968,524	42,638,751	242,665	42,881,416	4,787,704	-770,629	37,323,083	14,715,460	9,929,981	26,518	2,336,822	1,341,749
1999	64,825,338	46,213,437	235,916	46,449,353	5,155,467	-1,131,354	40,162,532	14,466,698	10,196,108	27,363	2,369,105	1,396,874
2000	70,133,388	50,083,888	238,821	50,322,709	5,519,213	-1,000,016	43,803,480	15,629,205	10,700,703	29,173	2,404,013	1,447,354
2001	72,565,771	51,638,492	258,564	51,897,056	5,747,132	-876,395	45,273,529	15,725,113	11,567,129	29,691	2,444,015	1,413,290
2002	75,132,593	54,203,076	261,417	54,464,493	6,006,482	-762,585	47,695,426	15,075,636	12,361,531	30,205	2,487,445	1,442,072
2003	79,163,784	56,952,278	227,902	57,180,180	6,280,112	-614,511	50,285,557	15,805,391	13,072,836	31,294	2,529,652	1,453,478
2004	85,287,872	61,418,769	235,858	61,654,627	6,788,877	-457,071	54,408,679	16,897,598	13,981,595	32,958	2,587,771	1,507,186
2005	92,026,869	65,819,016	272,511	66,091,527	7,305,033	-240,759	58,545,735	18,430,610	15,050,524	34,706	2,651,580	1,557,459
2006	98,473,133	69,204,910	277,575	69,482,485	7,832,700	-8,329	61,641,456	20,615,975	16,215,702	36,472	2,699,935	1,591,049
2007	102,383,223	70,674,861	244,123	70,918,984	8,070,516	199,461	63,047,929	22,006,109	17,329,185	37,547	2,726,780	1,608,915
2008	103,333,590	69,682,627	243,422	69,926,049	8,092,368	409,757	62,243,438	21,585,088	19,505,064	37,617	2,746,981	1,553,818
2009	100,445,702	67,201,466	248,116	67,449,582	7,931,532	407,341	59,925,391	19,363,107	21,157,204	36,342	2,763,937	1,484,482
2010	107,212,826	69,159,552	233,314	69,392,866	7,985,136	449,752	61,857,482	22,141,899	23,213,445	38,448	2,788,500	1,464,392
2011	114,763,764	71,239,892	199,575	71,439,467	7,366,566	497,592	64,570,493	26,001,649	24,191,622	40,565	2,829,142	1,485,034
2012	114,018,518	74,544,553	229,649	74,774,202	7,765,779	518,994	67,527,417	22,730,234	23,760,867	40,046	2,847,187	1,516,827
2013	114,120,702	76,389,386	236,344	76,625,730	9,000,650	569,302	68,194,382	21,462,829	24,463,491	39,728	2,872,530	1,558,597
2014	121,600,707	79,936,293	227,168	80,163,461	9,392,476	607,988	71,378,973	24,069,375	26,152,359	41,689	2,916,839	1,604,935
2015	129,117,120	84,758,917	269,127	85,028,044	9,875,210	630,534	75,783,368	25,820,775	27,512,977	43,419	2,973,756	1,664,419
2016	133,669,830	87,994,700	200,813	88,195,513	10,334,565	664,309	78,525,257	26,580,912	28,563,661	44,021	3,036,525	1,709,460
2017	139,318,600	91,321,057	190,503	91,511,560	10,724,697	751,050	81,537,913	27,785,848	29,994,839	45,067	3,091,399	1,739,910
2018	149,314,487	149,105,767	208,720	97,806,665	11,388,432	874,284	87,292,517	30,708,936	31,313,034	47,332	3,154,649	1,835,600
2019	156,253,370	155,979,533	273,837	103,472,730	12,176,366	819,987	92,116,351	31,133,432	33,003,587	48,908	3,194,831	1,886,364

Personal Income and Employment by Area: Terre Haute, IN

(Thousands of dollars, except as noted.)

Year	Personal income, total	Earnings by place of work			Less: Contributions for government social insurance	Plus: Adjustment for residence	Equals: Net earnings by place of residence	Plus: Dividends, interest, and rent	Plus: Personal current transfer receipts	Per capita personal income (dollars)	Population (persons)	Total employment
		Nonfarm	Farm	Total								
1970	603,941	483,409	10,413	493,822	33,374	-6,706	453,742	85,712	64,487	3,441	175,500	72,023
1971	647,877	496,848	19,716	516,564	35,422	-3,421	477,721	93,900	76,256	3,659	177,082	71,460
1972	689,170	525,299	16,170	541,469	39,329	580	502,720	100,672	85,778	3,902	176,637	71,698
1973	792,760	582,778	39,723	622,501	49,979	-43	572,479	114,952	105,329	4,516	175,537	73,710
1974	850,208	633,933	23,053	656,986	57,249	-1,227	598,510	132,142	119,556	4,920	172,796	74,911
1975	945,926	678,164	37,641	715,805	60,382	-2,026	653,397	150,212	142,317	5,470	172,939	73,605
1976	1,038,257	757,027	36,068	793,095	68,053	-1,494	723,548	162,155	152,554	5,978	173,680	74,743
1977	1,137,631	846,890	26,421	873,311	75,704	-3,207	794,400	183,000	160,231	6,518	174,548	76,933
1978	1,263,000	957,166	25,441	982,607	87,664	-7,761	887,182	203,169	172,649	7,234	174,590	79,642
1979	1,400,392	1,074,224	20,467	1,094,691	101,665	-16,832	976,194	227,102	197,096	8,029	174,406	82,452
1980	1,533,824	1,143,790	14,757	1,158,547	108,436	-25,407	1,024,704	277,003	232,117	8,695	176,395	81,575
1981	1,648,564	1,186,811	8,823	1,195,634	121,289	-24,507	1,049,838	336,035	262,691	9,407	175,255	78,331
1982	1,722,246	1,194,644	9,136	1,203,780	124,639	-25,896	1,053,245	379,032	289,969	9,854	174,781	75,509
1983	1,773,126	1,219,551	-11,604	1,207,947	126,947	-21,772	1,059,228	400,892	313,006	10,212	173,625	74,293
1984	1,923,321	1,308,374	19,567	1,327,941	139,476	-20,686	1,167,779	432,771	322,771	11,137	172,695	75,547
1985	2,005,549	1,363,066	18,956	1,382,022	148,066	-17,202	1,216,754	452,533	336,262	11,660	172,000	76,009
1986	2,092,656	1,429,253	17,126	1,446,379	155,779	-14,341	1,276,259	467,731	348,666	12,268	170,581	76,417
1987	2,154,513	1,493,607	15,205	1,508,812	160,498	-12,668	1,335,646	464,779	354,088	12,733	169,209	77,280
1988	2,240,616	1,560,768	8,188	1,568,956	174,291	-10,298	1,384,367	488,083	368,166	13,322	168,190	78,360
1989	2,450,012	1,665,379	25,585	1,690,964	187,756	-10,755	1,492,453	555,803	401,756	14,649	167,248	80,505
1990	2,564,412	1,781,005	17,295	1,798,300	205,465	-15,365	1,577,470	561,276	425,666	15,392	166,606	82,626
1991	2,677,949	1,902,001	-555	1,901,446	222,827	-26,533	1,652,086	567,634	458,229	16,041	166,943	83,969
1992	2,892,934	2,054,193	32,077	2,086,270	238,136	-30,494	1,817,640	559,126	516,168	17,207	168,127	86,041
1993	3,006,738	2,145,643	28,252	2,173,895	250,731	-37,063	1,886,101	574,697	545,940	17,731	169,575	87,972
1994	3,135,063	2,231,284	28,139	2,259,423	264,485	-34,645	1,960,293	601,909	572,861	18,444	169,975	89,740
1995	3,243,009	2,307,640	12,029	2,319,669	275,892	-39,453	2,004,324	658,955	579,730	18,974	170,921	91,712
1996	3,338,059	2,323,150	27,565	2,350,715	275,538	-38,877	2,036,300	690,747	611,012	19,443	171,682	90,589
1997	3,422,138	2,373,689	26,266	2,399,955	281,254	-42,091	2,076,610	716,710	628,818	19,935	171,665	89,365
1998	3,638,528	2,540,377	12,911	2,553,288	294,203	-37,812	2,221,273	762,653	654,602	21,248	171,237	89,175
1999	3,764,693	2,676,360	19,204	2,695,564	306,368	-41,180	2,348,016	724,449	692,228	21,986	171,235	89,837
2000	3,929,766	2,760,774	30,454	2,791,228	313,638	-44,432	2,433,158	775,141	721,467	23,001	170,855	90,967
2001	4,103,057	2,862,864	33,880	2,896,744	319,885	-42,884	2,533,975	775,185	793,897	24,065	170,497	88,755
2002	4,182,390	2,982,516	11,783	2,994,299	333,094	-49,700	2,611,505	736,556	834,329	24,594	170,055	87,917
2003	4,346,281	3,109,357	40,699	3,150,056	351,175	-59,661	2,739,220	746,460	860,601	25,501	170,438	88,672
2004	4,477,361	3,208,461	62,009	3,270,470	364,428	-60,340	2,845,702	723,981	907,678	26,337	170,001	89,092
2005	4,522,725	3,271,444	32,717	3,304,161	380,052	-60,481	2,863,628	676,846	982,251	26,505	170,634	88,835
2006	4,726,665	3,403,200	19,340	3,422,540	395,459	-63,917	2,963,164	712,701	1,050,800	27,524	171,730	89,219
2007	4,892,344	3,462,964	47,855	3,510,819	409,175	-68,211	3,033,433	772,393	1,086,518	28,446	171,987	89,912
2008	5,192,835	3,565,128	48,813	3,613,941	421,675	-76,738	3,115,528	838,727	1,238,580	30,197	171,967	88,702
2009	5,126,338	3,455,564	43,333	3,498,897	414,465	-74,953	3,009,479	777,397	1,339,462	29,771	172,190	86,554
2010	5,309,965	3,606,106	56,018	3,662,124	423,573	-97,056	3,141,495	749,785	1,418,685	30,830	172,231	86,127
2011	5,496,675	3,624,802	88,476	3,713,278	379,913	-93,438	3,239,927	831,085	1,425,663	31,884	172,396	86,211
2012	5,628,204	3,726,557	44,078	3,770,635	391,316	-102,470	3,276,849	873,960	1,477,395	32,656	172,348	86,821
2013	5,682,768	3,731,045	153,883	3,884,928	445,438	-96,917	3,342,573	865,066	1,475,129	33,084	171,767	86,550
2014	5,808,500	3,805,819	66,799	3,872,618	452,806	-91,590	3,328,222	916,142	1,564,136	33,983	170,922	86,553
2015	5,888,895	3,798,396	10,020	3,808,416	458,492	-70,361	3,279,563	967,232	1,642,100	34,573	170,334	85,996
2016	6,023,940	3,840,459	19,146	3,859,605	460,314	-52,853	3,346,438	986,710	1,690,792	35,389	170,220	86,095
2017	6,249,493	3,984,301	17,061	4,001,362	475,460	-58,928	3,466,974	1,035,180	1,747,339	36,769	169,965	86,034
2018	7,020,899	6,991,606	29,293	4,256,072	511,676	94,889	3,839,285	1,199,752	1,981,862	37,600	186,726	91,674
2019	7,240,598	7,224,846	15,752	4,390,795	530,654	82,168	3,942,309	1,217,968	2,080,321	38,851	186,367	91,506

Personal Income and Employment by Area: Texarkana, TX-AR

(Thousands of dollars, except as noted.)

Year	Personal income, total	Earnings by place of work			Less: Contributions for government social insurance	Plus: Adjustment for residence	Equals: Net earnings by place of residence	Plus: Dividends, interest, and rent	Plus: Personal current transfer receipts	Per capita personal income (dollars)	Population (persons)	Total employment
		Nonfarm	Farm	Total								
1970	376,236	324,456	11,436	335,892	18,697	-30,211	286,984	51,358	37,894	3,317	113,411	51,614
1971	401,204	335,787	9,817	345,604	19,670	-25,701	300,233	57,175	43,796	3,480	115,276	49,646
1972	451,345	374,221	13,100	387,321	22,977	-24,287	340,057	62,409	48,879	3,912	115,364	50,603
1973	500,642	405,085	17,198	422,283	28,914	-23,440	369,929	72,073	58,640	4,343	115,273	51,600
1974	557,896	441,474	16,765	458,239	32,689	-24,158	401,392	85,270	71,234	4,789	116,487	51,969
1975	612,547	469,308	10,204	479,512	33,445	-22,501	423,566	99,646	89,335	5,088	120,390	50,601
1976	688,992	528,222	11,390	539,612	38,716	-21,025	479,871	111,578	97,543	5,657	121,802	52,595
1977	758,960	583,833	9,404	593,237	43,510	-20,212	529,515	126,787	102,658	6,177	122,871	54,507
1978	853,414	659,800	10,235	670,035	51,017	-19,814	599,204	141,250	112,960	6,903	123,622	56,842
1979	975,042	770,277	21,406	791,683	63,966	-38,888	688,829	157,670	128,543	7,698	126,658	59,580
1980	1,060,243	799,347	6,746	806,093	64,733	-21,466	719,894	190,984	149,365	8,325	127,351	57,931
1981	1,189,283	876,037	11,872	887,909	75,730	-22,120	790,059	229,663	169,561	9,266	128,345	57,646
1982	1,280,745	937,625	10,523	948,148	82,646	-29,627	835,875	260,720	184,150	9,903	129,332	58,212
1983	1,374,736	1,003,663	7,881	1,011,544	92,070	-32,327	887,147	286,193	201,396	10,457	131,460	59,156
1984	1,524,552	1,110,664	21,099	1,131,763	105,168	-34,762	991,833	321,056	211,663	11,532	132,198	61,554
1985	1,617,159	1,172,824	16,009	1,188,833	114,106	-36,865	1,037,862	353,411	225,886	12,133	133,288	62,566
1986	1,666,693	1,203,071	21,265	1,224,336	118,805	-37,898	1,067,633	362,072	236,988	12,472	133,636	61,580
1987	1,705,511	1,242,492	19,495	1,261,987	122,375	-39,534	1,100,078	359,892	245,541	12,738	133,889	62,892
1988	1,780,082	1,290,326	31,411	1,321,737	133,327	-37,107	1,151,303	368,700	260,079	13,221	134,645	62,821
1989	1,906,304	1,373,138	34,858	1,407,996	144,821	-44,990	1,218,185	404,017	284,102	14,248	133,795	64,410
1990	2,016,915	1,487,624	29,284	1,516,908	161,228	-60,790	1,294,890	406,190	315,835	14,996	134,497	67,025
1991	2,104,913	1,533,055	32,544	1,565,599	168,451	-35,251	1,361,897	393,750	349,266	15,563	135,250	66,542
1992	2,218,602	1,577,584	32,928	1,610,512	173,066	-21,248	1,416,198	400,343	402,061	16,294	136,162	65,220
1993	2,296,434	1,634,262	32,845	1,667,107	179,675	-16,031	1,471,401	408,483	416,550	16,689	137,598	66,853
1994	2,408,242	1,689,673	36,552	1,726,225	188,344	-10,861	1,527,020	431,784	449,438	17,325	139,004	67,344
1995	2,542,984	1,767,390	32,753	1,800,143	196,884	-4,707	1,598,552	462,961	481,471	18,183	139,853	69,282
1996	2,678,317	1,844,765	40,961	1,885,726	202,969	-100	1,682,657	491,978	503,682	18,948	141,353	70,753
1997	2,831,747	1,960,556	49,125	2,009,681	213,779	5,639	1,801,541	505,038	525,168	19,957	141,893	71,877
1998	2,919,884	2,013,867	38,110	2,051,977	217,318	15,959	1,850,618	534,864	534,402	20,516	142,322	71,041
1999	3,044,068	2,128,799	51,551	2,180,350	228,119	9,228	1,961,459	543,995	538,614	21,280	143,051	72,551
2000	3,195,713	2,221,786	44,351	2,266,137	237,032	9,507	2,038,612	596,688	560,413	22,316	143,205	73,713
2001	3,379,625	2,330,750	51,415	2,382,165	245,137	6,839	2,143,867	621,085	614,673	23,653	142,882	73,705
2002	3,454,100	2,433,140	39,737	2,472,877	255,409	-4,740	2,212,728	581,849	659,523	24,129	143,149	73,435
2003	3,540,543	2,533,016	54,943	2,587,959	269,938	-12,809	2,305,212	536,237	699,094	24,659	143,582	73,161
2004	3,746,046	2,648,946	69,145	2,718,091	284,772	-23,883	2,409,436	592,158	744,452	26,015	143,996	73,880
2005	3,907,254	2,799,784	39,143	2,838,927	300,509	-35,284	2,503,134	599,700	804,420	27,033	144,534	75,734
2006	4,101,785	2,941,285	26,894	2,968,179	316,119	-43,774	2,608,286	627,470	866,029	28,085	146,051	76,838
2007	4,365,350	3,051,673	44,042	3,095,715	335,185	-60,203	2,700,327	722,919	942,104	29,844	146,273	78,664
2008	4,580,518	3,187,262	11,520	3,198,782	355,961	-96,008	2,746,813	783,191	1,050,514	31,055	147,495	80,187
2009	4,574,046	3,196,865	666	3,197,531	361,236	-114,038	2,722,257	727,971	1,123,818	30,751	148,743	78,630
2010	4,766,429	3,286,692	8,729	3,295,421	368,463	-81,156	2,845,802	702,975	1,217,652	31,920	149,324	77,899
2011	4,958,809	3,356,284	9,561	3,365,845	336,099	-81,516	2,948,230	776,617	1,233,962	33,147	149,602	79,003
2012	5,056,990	3,382,837	19,686	3,402,523	338,049	-92,854	2,971,620	852,960	1,232,410	33,784	149,684	78,650
2013	4,902,153	3,237,766	31,702	3,269,468	365,844	-76,938	2,826,686	801,335	1,274,132	32,757	149,653	77,544
2014	5,053,314	3,261,961	37,103	3,299,064	370,822	-73,444	2,854,798	859,472	1,339,044	33,797	149,519	77,424
2015	5,270,670	3,401,435	41,160	3,442,595	389,145	-90,888	2,962,562	907,916	1,400,192	35,199	149,739	78,409
2016	5,372,210	3,471,230	16,113	3,487,343	399,367	-96,206	2,991,770	920,165	1,460,275	35,771	150,185	79,178
2017	5,508,127	3,533,818	22,844	3,556,662	408,104	-91,867	3,056,691	963,323	1,488,113	36,634	150,355	78,619
2018	5,637,393	5,616,122	21,271	3,614,386	414,556	-91,911	3,107,919	986,458	1,543,016	37,747	149,347	79,172
2019	5,788,318	5,763,504	24,814	3,705,160	424,406	-99,076	3,181,678	1,003,726	1,602,914	38,910	148,761	80,158

Personal Income and Employment by Area: The Villages, FL

(Thousands of dollars, except as noted.)

Year	Personal income, total	Earnings by place of work			Less: Contributions for government social insurance	Plus: Adjustment for residence	Equals: Net earnings by place of residence	Plus: Dividends, interest, and rent	Plus: Personal current transfer receipts	Per capita personal income (dollars)	Population (persons)	Total employment
		Nonfarm	Farm	Total								
1970	39,947	25,114	3,231	28,345	2,089	1,295	27,551	6,161	6,235	2,669	14,967	4,545
1971	45,938	27,459	4,346	31,805	2,296	2,017	31,526	7,111	7,301	2,908	15,797	4,724
1972	54,241	30,437	5,783	36,220	2,573	3,120	36,767	8,313	9,161	3,051	17,780	5,092
1973	65,269	34,882	7,313	42,195	3,208	4,628	43,615	10,346	11,308	3,410	19,143	5,413
1974	72,053	37,386	6,521	43,907	3,671	5,946	46,182	12,183	13,688	3,523	20,453	5,460
1975	82,166	40,682	7,113	47,795	3,978	6,857	50,674	13,848	17,644	3,913	20,999	5,497
1976	90,468	43,529	7,752	51,281	4,320	8,259	55,220	14,984	20,264	4,102	22,056	5,668
1977	100,157	47,597	7,901	55,498	4,774	10,174	60,898	16,960	22,299	4,487	22,324	5,961
1978	118,028	55,776	9,951	65,727	5,571	12,393	72,549	21,504	23,975	5,169	22,835	6,565
1979	139,092	62,836	12,223	75,059	6,433	14,668	83,294	26,771	29,027	5,965	23,318	6,841
1980	160,289	68,177	10,541	78,718	7,014	18,367	90,071	35,085	35,133	6,559	24,439	6,802
1981	178,038	74,787	7,351	82,138	8,335	19,519	93,322	43,390	41,326	7,104	25,063	6,847
1982	197,747	82,967	9,983	92,950	9,516	19,660	103,094	47,707	46,946	7,658	25,822	6,869
1983	221,897	93,219	11,107	104,326	10,554	20,701	114,473	55,216	52,208	8,349	26,577	7,337
1984	244,871	103,933	9,452	113,385	12,037	23,965	125,313	63,653	55,905	8,949	27,362	7,732
1985	266,999	115,350	7,785	123,135	13,666	26,096	135,565	69,784	61,650	9,430	28,313	8,285
1986	288,735	121,570	8,230	129,800	14,984	29,877	144,693	76,318	67,724	9,882	29,217	8,497
1987	311,323	129,283	6,940	136,223	15,473	35,048	155,798	79,931	75,594	10,457	29,771	8,769
1988	340,492	140,682	9,304	149,986	17,524	39,445	171,907	83,386	85,199	11,289	30,161	9,022
1989	374,445	150,876	11,156	162,032	18,905	43,411	186,538	98,852	89,055	12,083	30,990	9,138
1990	391,807	152,270	10,551	162,821	18,910	46,841	190,752	102,657	98,398	12,289	31,882	9,144
1991	412,782	157,377	14,012	171,389	19,854	45,923	197,458	104,605	110,719	12,561	32,863	9,069
1992	447,580	169,549	16,043	185,592	21,429	48,245	212,408	104,485	130,687	13,240	33,804	9,142
1993	469,677	178,680	14,259	192,939	22,370	51,166	221,735	105,602	142,340	13,510	34,764	9,427
1994	502,119	190,402	11,644	202,046	24,207	53,339	231,178	112,996	157,945	13,890	36,149	9,665
1995	549,588	217,251	8,772	226,023	26,926	50,469	249,566	122,887	177,135	14,297	38,441	10,357
1996	611,563	256,038	7,118	263,156	30,351	45,150	277,955	137,397	196,211	14,265	42,871	11,189
1997	661,289	277,926	9,589	287,515	32,739	45,362	300,138	146,742	214,409	14,187	46,611	11,587
1998	716,554	293,558	9,831	303,389	34,565	49,007	317,831	165,865	232,858	14,693	48,767	12,004
1999	782,120	320,990	13,398	334,388	37,458	49,039	345,969	167,447	268,704	15,121	51,725	12,199
2000	835,710	339,359	13,361	352,720	39,668	49,136	362,188	173,262	300,260	15,552	53,738	12,646
2001	974,713	420,278	14,965	435,243	47,494	52,539	440,288	171,112	363,313	17,470	55,793	14,060
2002	1,076,926	464,906	9,671	474,577	51,828	52,205	474,954	191,734	410,238	18,088	59,539	15,461
2003	1,222,492	577,800	11,127	588,927	63,445	33,001	558,483	218,755	445,254	19,739	61,934	18,140
2004	1,427,543	620,485	11,481	631,966	69,595	88,742	651,113	276,927	499,503	22,148	64,456	20,022
2005	1,682,055	764,488	13,757	778,245	85,706	96,404	788,943	308,646	584,466	24,286	69,261	24,039
2006	1,975,708	896,780	13,220	910,000	121,823	98,047	886,224	373,821	715,663	25,927	76,202	26,589
2007	2,127,239	958,723	10,120	968,843	133,500	46,198	881,541	420,942	824,756	25,910	82,101	27,723
2008	2,374,163	973,083	8,635	981,718	144,535	45,880	883,063	490,602	1,000,498	27,468	86,433	28,378
2009	2,553,155	1,031,251	8,166	1,039,417	156,699	16,874	899,592	469,340	1,184,223	28,167	90,643	29,325
2010	2,807,088	1,114,648	9,235	1,123,883	168,160	-23,070	932,653	559,619	1,314,816	29,774	94,279	30,827
2011	3,285,313	1,243,050	7,543	1,250,593	171,660	-30,090	1,048,843	771,466	1,465,004	33,532	97,976	32,744
2012	3,712,859	1,316,449	16,254	1,332,703	183,956	43,656	1,192,403	955,283	1,565,173	36,509	101,698	34,451
2013	3,987,196	1,418,291	14,464	1,432,755	220,138	40,302	1,252,919	1,072,436	1,661,841	37,284	106,942	37,042
2014	4,355,208	1,464,566	21,545	1,486,111	231,957	-42,892	1,211,262	1,295,025	1,848,921	38,770	112,334	39,033
2015	4,725,493	1,519,581	29,505	1,549,086	245,218	-64,634	1,239,234	1,458,351	2,027,908	40,316	117,210	40,351
2016	5,177,088	1,616,930	21,204	1,638,134	266,702	11,436	1,382,868	1,648,723	2,145,497	42,393	122,121	41,503
2017	5,440,231	1,750,823	21,066	1,771,889	290,983	-6,372	1,474,534	1,716,284	2,249,413	43,464	125,165	42,983
2018	6,096,685	6,078,847	17,838	1,948,025	324,049	-45,012	1,578,964	2,082,937	2,434,784	47,364	128,719	45,176
2019	6,407,369	6,391,512	15,857	2,122,147	358,458	-84,042	1,679,647	2,091,593	2,636,129	48,387	132,420	47,422

Personal Income and Employment by Area: Toledo, OH

(Thousands of dollars, except as noted.)

Year	Personal income, total	Derivation of personal income									Per capita personal income (dollars)	Population (persons)	Total employment
		Earnings by place of work			Less: Contributions for government social insurance	Plus: Adjustment for residence	Equals: Net earnings by place of residence	Plus: Dividends, interest, and rent	Plus: Personal current transfer receipts				
		Nonfarm	Farm	Total									
1970	2,609,375	2,239,321	25,167	2,264,488	149,493	-85,418	2,029,577	368,524	211,274		4,295	607,493	277,346
1971	2,803,026	2,392,796	23,873	2,416,669	164,761	-84,540	2,167,368	393,992	241,666		4,567	613,790	277,628
1972	3,064,197	2,632,595	29,887	2,662,482	191,302	-92,016	2,379,164	420,258	264,775		4,956	618,239	283,180
1973	3,400,864	2,932,533	42,449	2,974,982	247,426	-102,961	2,624,595	468,538	307,731		5,474	621,256	295,425
1974	3,684,598	3,118,131	46,183	3,164,314	273,112	-110,320	2,780,882	531,446	372,270		5,915	622,934	294,935
1975	3,964,502	3,242,241	52,973	3,295,214	276,446	-112,416	2,906,352	565,961	492,189		6,387	620,746	285,579
1976	4,383,306	3,675,087	43,836	3,718,923	321,732	-138,952	3,258,239	604,680	520,387		7,126	615,085	292,558
1977	4,794,445	4,072,055	31,635	4,103,690	359,684	-169,198	3,574,808	666,973	552,664		7,811	613,830	299,282
1978	5,248,147	4,509,983	23,588	4,533,571	410,320	-198,514	3,924,737	737,816	585,594		8,588	611,100	307,404
1979	5,756,965	4,892,156	35,520	4,927,676	459,250	-223,401	4,245,025	836,143	675,797		9,357	615,273	312,170
1980	6,284,574	5,050,914	45,147	5,096,061	467,971	-228,093	4,399,997	1,000,701	883,876		10,183	617,164	301,227
1981	6,797,402	5,405,937	8,078	5,414,015	535,686	-240,371	4,637,958	1,207,116	952,328		11,017	616,977	298,217
1982	7,144,585	5,530,732	13,079	5,543,811	555,664	-240,536	4,747,611	1,335,511	1,061,463		11,617	614,991	289,638
1983	7,603,984	5,925,201	-8,666	5,916,535	605,550	-272,796	5,038,189	1,440,182	1,125,613		12,426	611,930	291,994
1984	8,427,894	6,638,133	52,912	6,691,045	695,246	-334,222	5,661,577	1,604,346	1,161,971		13,803	610,582	305,313
1985	8,975,065	7,174,063	40,848	7,214,911	764,196	-375,915	6,074,800	1,675,850	1,224,415		14,710	610,137	312,850
1986	9,363,799	7,481,854	33,956	7,515,810	818,123	-372,360	6,325,327	1,736,497	1,301,975		15,299	612,073	321,095
1987	9,794,601	7,864,800	40,103	7,904,903	856,486	-387,847	6,660,570	1,778,325	1,355,706		15,976	613,093	328,662
1988	10,415,640	8,432,431	51,846	8,484,277	948,668	-420,595	7,115,014	1,883,254	1,417,372		16,882	616,985	338,504
1989	11,132,878	8,882,634	65,124	8,947,758	1,003,998	-445,794	7,497,966	2,133,283	1,501,629		18,086	615,560	342,926
1990	11,563,741	9,110,989	84,577	9,195,566	1,042,495	-411,320	7,741,751	2,148,067	1,673,923		18,814	614,637	340,445
1991	11,654,052	9,118,531	72,457	9,190,988	1,072,860	-403,044	7,715,084	2,116,797	1,822,171		18,962	614,606	334,188
1992	12,445,740	9,835,035	77,652	9,912,687	1,151,810	-476,030	8,284,847	2,168,089	1,992,804		20,212	615,755	336,874
1993	12,921,719	10,323,544	68,729	10,392,273	1,219,926	-559,961	8,612,386	2,246,261	2,063,072		20,989	615,629	344,665
1994	13,571,163	11,023,593	76,590	11,100,183	1,318,078	-691,357	9,090,748	2,336,370	2,144,045		22,037	615,841	359,308
1995	14,201,141	11,430,907	62,893	11,493,800	1,377,179	-722,562	9,394,059	2,525,452	2,281,630		23,042	616,304	364,582
1996	14,708,355	11,793,924	85,339	11,879,263	1,410,732	-781,178	9,687,353	2,688,126	2,332,876		23,859	616,468	370,314
1997	15,451,299	12,373,944	106,693	12,480,637	1,438,837	-826,583	10,215,217	2,851,431	2,384,651		25,008	617,850	374,438
1998	16,071,232	12,958,650	73,877	13,032,527	1,453,582	-879,438	10,699,507	2,966,360	2,405,365		25,985	618,484	378,126
1999	16,605,823	13,727,793	56,003	13,783,796	1,535,545	-973,529	11,274,722	2,874,258	2,456,843		26,854	618,371	384,408
2000	17,270,361	14,134,898	74,430	14,209,328	1,526,367	-986,475	11,696,486	2,992,522	2,581,353		27,936	618,207	388,509
2001	17,850,061	14,631,595	54,884	14,686,479	1,588,960	-1,000,495	12,097,024	2,972,933	2,780,104		28,835	619,037	387,285
2002	18,184,128	14,923,952	26,957	14,950,909	1,590,257	-996,495	12,364,157	2,837,615	2,982,356		29,390	618,721	378,942
2003	18,691,998	15,290,352	49,681	15,340,033	1,649,229	-986,779	12,704,025	2,887,288	3,100,685		30,197	619,006	375,897
2004	19,082,592	15,659,066	87,966	15,747,032	1,723,302	-1,004,376	13,019,354	2,821,549	3,241,689		30,869	618,181	378,950
2005	19,492,032	15,916,280	82,716	15,998,996	1,762,198	-1,026,145	13,210,653	2,834,795	3,446,584		31,601	616,819	379,314
2006	20,521,621	16,590,498	83,198	16,673,696	1,835,230	-1,064,695	13,773,771	3,112,381	3,635,469		33,391	614,581	381,467
2007	21,285,294	16,943,212	76,100	17,019,312	1,866,437	-1,063,952	14,088,923	3,340,844	3,855,527		34,691	613,567	381,133
2008	21,639,581	16,802,113	63,328	16,865,441	1,872,538	-1,002,092	13,990,811	3,323,423	4,325,347		35,361	611,964	371,730
2009	21,028,815	15,892,964	81,050	15,974,014	1,789,524	-935,214	13,249,276	2,995,583	4,783,956		34,432	610,734	351,738
2010	21,687,225	16,335,784	60,974	16,396,758	1,799,944	-962,871	13,633,943	3,035,467	5,017,815		35,553	610,003	350,290
2011	22,843,714	17,024,055	130,005	17,154,060	1,706,844	-1,040,141	14,407,075	3,314,517	5,122,122		37,526	608,736	356,353
2012	23,356,607	17,620,093	102,101	17,722,194	1,756,225	-1,114,387	14,851,582	3,532,634	4,972,391		38,453	607,400	359,123
2013	23,675,815	18,150,019	118,696	18,268,715	1,945,738	-1,109,856	15,213,121	3,390,548	5,072,146		39,006	606,981	362,121
2014	24,827,207	18,964,777	63,726	19,028,503	2,032,391	-1,176,895	15,819,217	3,686,826	5,321,164		40,969	606,000	367,317
2015	25,863,875	19,777,053	19,017	19,796,070	2,104,153	-1,254,090	16,437,827	3,900,773	5,525,275		42,766	604,781	373,490
2016	26,417,277	20,264,220	34,949	20,299,169	2,203,800	-1,304,490	16,790,879	3,964,532	5,661,866		43,694	604,591	376,790
2017	27,065,046	20,697,230	3,319	20,700,549	2,278,015	-1,300,009	17,122,525	4,141,293	5,801,228		44,834	603,668	376,177
2018	30,173,121	30,116,602	56,519	22,602,721	2,459,223	-991,078	19,152,420	4,701,852	6,318,849		46,919	643,089	398,987
2019	31,019,188	30,960,075	59,113	23,234,049	2,528,690	-1,027,820	19,677,539	4,766,371	6,575,278		48,330	641,816	402,146

Personal Income and Employment by Area: Topeka, KS

(Thousands of dollars, except as noted.)

Year	Personal income, total	Earnings by place of work			Less: Contributions for government social insurance	Plus: Adjustment for residence	Equals: Net earnings by place of residence	Plus: Dividends, interest, and rent	Plus: Personal current transfer receipts	Per capita personal income (dollars)	Population (persons)	Total employment
		Nonfarm	Farm	Total								
1970	802,172	641,190	11,624	652,814	48,295	-8,105	596,414	133,384	72,374	4,058	197,701	95,350
1971	886,240	700,964	17,642	718,606	54,401	-7,652	656,553	145,447	84,240	4,459	198,772	96,314
1972	984,741	776,891	26,766	803,657	63,058	-8,167	732,432	159,529	92,780	4,855	202,849	98,653
1973	1,089,232	858,242	32,617	890,859	79,969	-5,194	805,696	175,202	108,334	5,378	202,528	102,182
1974	1,139,465	883,697	24,742	908,439	86,911	-1,049	820,479	193,419	125,567	5,869	194,147	100,477
1975	1,246,682	951,373	16,367	967,740	91,905	1,275	877,110	213,133	156,439	6,389	195,125	100,810
1976	1,368,024	1,054,648	7,967	1,062,615	103,140	5,138	964,613	229,716	173,695	6,921	197,659	102,988
1977	1,541,924	1,187,906	17,253	1,205,159	115,875	10,168	1,099,452	255,591	186,881	7,748	199,010	106,791
1978	1,718,465	1,334,487	8,779	1,343,266	133,652	16,830	1,226,444	285,700	206,321	8,577	200,351	110,694
1979	1,888,977	1,471,723	3,293	1,475,016	153,257	19,644	1,341,403	321,259	226,315	9,368	201,651	112,914
1980	2,097,532	1,588,924	-23,286	1,565,638	165,791	24,637	1,424,484	399,084	273,964	10,277	204,099	113,888
1981	2,383,769	1,719,443	14,567	1,734,010	192,745	22,485	1,563,750	506,255	313,764	11,662	204,404	113,415
1982	2,548,515	1,798,372	7,732	1,806,104	207,240	21,900	1,620,764	588,939	338,812	12,440	204,869	111,566
1983	2,664,391	1,914,482	-10,998	1,903,484	219,580	17,381	1,701,285	605,111	357,995	12,959	205,608	112,196
1984	2,901,972	2,096,098	4,394	2,100,492	245,738	15,547	1,870,301	667,178	364,493	14,087	206,005	116,313
1985	3,095,928	2,206,756	52,017	2,258,773	262,712	4,519	2,000,580	708,374	386,974	15,079	205,319	116,597
1986	3,220,458	2,330,572	24,206	2,354,778	277,956	-515	2,076,307	746,303	397,848	15,648	205,805	117,515
1987	3,348,520	2,451,489	19,201	2,470,690	287,955	-1,702	2,181,033	760,514	406,973	16,150	207,337	123,311
1988	3,559,539	2,630,043	10,724	2,640,767	321,777	-4,298	2,314,692	813,335	431,512	16,930	210,255	125,741
1989	3,728,296	2,760,234	11,434	2,771,668	338,488	-9,774	2,423,406	835,625	469,265	17,771	209,794	127,498
1990	3,892,288	2,885,320	27,169	2,912,489	366,941	-11,625	2,533,923	851,838	506,527	18,482	210,598	128,053
1991	4,000,153	2,972,900	8,296	2,981,196	380,200	-11,591	2,589,405	865,378	545,370	18,826	212,479	127,916
1992	4,259,396	3,140,681	50,149	3,190,830	397,766	-11,515	2,781,549	872,449	605,398	19,902	214,014	128,684
1993	4,448,500	3,332,287	9,926	3,342,213	422,498	-15,385	2,904,330	902,059	642,111	20,571	216,252	131,257
1994	4,693,229	3,519,283	25,671	3,544,954	450,037	-15,459	3,079,458	952,683	661,088	21,470	218,593	133,525
1995	4,881,315	3,645,931	321	3,646,252	458,509	-16,570	3,171,173	1,009,525	700,617	22,184	220,036	137,625
1996	5,154,841	3,788,233	54,404	3,842,637	471,844	-15,567	3,355,226	1,070,835	728,780	23,299	221,246	139,732
1997	5,326,760	3,905,728	24,545	3,930,273	486,893	-5,402	3,437,978	1,118,303	770,479	23,960	222,316	139,357
1998	5,655,684	4,172,144	8,265	4,180,409	514,282	-8,139	3,657,988	1,203,913	793,783	25,299	223,555	142,312
1999	5,809,234	4,349,440	-5,895	4,343,545	534,266	-3,881	3,805,398	1,168,255	835,581	25,961	223,772	142,676
2000	6,153,814	4,560,052	-11,832	4,548,220	558,151	1,377	3,991,446	1,264,050	898,318	27,367	224,859	145,358
2001	6,511,840	4,871,643	13,557	4,885,200	592,396	-52	4,292,752	1,231,975	987,113	28,930	225,090	147,052
2002	6,633,598	4,955,379	-9,174	4,946,205	600,631	8,554	4,354,128	1,210,422	1,069,048	29,436	225,355	144,100
2003	6,725,834	4,937,088	11,562	4,948,650	603,294	18,990	4,364,346	1,238,673	1,122,815	29,740	226,153	142,484
2004	6,920,874	5,119,503	47,291	5,166,794	623,003	27,490	4,571,281	1,171,903	1,177,690	30,468	227,155	141,376
2005	7,098,705	5,258,342	17,362	5,275,704	643,478	37,934	4,670,160	1,193,719	1,234,826	31,106	228,208	141,136
2006	7,465,097	5,384,854	-4,088	5,380,766	657,699	63,889	4,786,956	1,361,611	1,316,530	32,624	228,825	140,007
2007	7,999,198	5,693,542	15,345	5,708,887	687,576	68,785	5,090,096	1,487,273	1,421,829	34,775	230,025	143,461
2008	8,412,254	5,932,665	17,877	5,950,542	709,103	84,680	5,326,119	1,506,832	1,579,303	36,374	231,272	144,190
2009	8,438,981	5,949,831	36,115	5,985,946	715,237	20,238	5,290,947	1,431,688	1,716,346	36,289	232,548	141,300
2010	8,530,329	6,070,964	-1,040	6,069,924	730,154	-26,112	5,313,658	1,394,549	1,822,122	36,412	234,274	141,073
2011	8,964,109	6,266,709	48,064	6,314,773	663,174	-73,333	5,578,266	1,492,878	1,892,965	38,202	234,648	142,102
2012	9,133,370	6,451,455	39,009	6,490,464	680,171	-123,596	5,686,697	1,553,929	1,892,744	38,968	234,383	142,185
2013	9,186,515	6,593,625	95,746	6,689,371	784,065	-166,438	5,738,868	1,521,292	1,926,355	39,290	233,812	143,442
2014	9,500,489	6,840,154	34,201	6,874,355	810,477	-166,961	5,896,917	1,618,358	1,985,214	40,662	233,646	145,205
2015	9,713,928	6,982,879	1,246	6,984,125	832,492	-180,977	5,970,656	1,667,960	2,075,312	41,629	233,345	144,853
2016	10,024,138	7,167,013	19,824	7,186,837	842,055	-191,690	6,153,092	1,735,580	2,135,466	43,032	232,948	145,187
2017	10,271,159	7,320,603	12,950	7,333,553	860,134	-186,989	6,286,430	1,798,938	2,185,791	44,054	233,149	144,643
2018	10,737,323	10,692,284	45,039	7,672,188	905,214	-195,712	6,571,262	1,896,539	2,269,522	46,229	232,266	144,444
2019	10,999,549	10,897,779	101,770	7,780,130	919,608	-161,639	6,698,883	1,913,359	2,387,307	47,418	231,969	144,559

Personal Income and Employment by Area: Trenton-Princeton, NJ

(Thousands of dollars, except as noted.)

Year	Personal income, total	Earnings by place of work			Less: Contributions for government social insurance	Plus: Adjustment for residence	Equals: Net earnings by place of residence	Plus: Dividends, interest, and rent	Plus: Personal current transfer receipts	Per capita personal income (dollars)	Population (persons)	Total employment
		Nonfarm	Farm	Total								
1970	1,502,265	1,256,172	2,577	1,258,749	92,246	-13,057	1,153,446	237,973	110,846	4,924	305,091	153,757
1971	1,651,657	1,381,007	2,044	1,383,051	104,148	-22,573	1,256,330	261,181	134,146	5,351	308,680	153,733
1972	1,837,479	1,559,066	1,821	1,560,887	122,826	-37,860	1,400,201	287,152	150,126	5,842	314,505	161,814
1973	2,029,946	1,736,255	3,496	1,739,751	157,306	-39,270	1,543,175	314,842	171,929	6,440	315,209	166,704
1974	2,223,435	1,880,696	4,524	1,885,220	175,024	-39,310	1,670,886	350,596	201,953	7,011	317,113	169,496
1975	2,382,116	1,951,765	2,056	1,953,821	178,513	-26,107	1,749,201	368,233	264,682	7,550	315,506	163,246
1976	2,597,306	2,141,369	2,226	2,143,595	198,903	-34,758	1,909,934	398,059	289,313	8,298	313,004	166,848
1977	2,825,891	2,351,959	3,160	2,355,119	218,087	-60,324	2,076,708	440,765	308,418	9,074	311,427	169,701
1978	3,093,629	2,612,657	2,722	2,615,379	250,069	-92,598	2,272,712	486,366	334,551	9,923	311,764	175,837
1979	3,378,784	2,858,924	2,358	2,861,282	283,633	-121,920	2,455,729	546,419	376,636	10,899	309,998	180,281
1980	3,746,850	3,117,300	1,841	3,119,141	305,453	-165,310	2,648,378	660,015	438,457	12,173	307,796	182,263
1981	4,147,565	3,400,388	3,817	3,404,205	355,908	-206,494	2,841,803	824,520	481,242	13,512	306,944	182,845
1982	4,513,014	3,608,605	2,934	3,611,539	377,898	-229,663	3,003,978	974,129	534,907	14,658	307,882	181,854
1983	4,825,373	3,946,798	4,158	3,950,956	426,389	-279,165	3,245,402	1,007,204	572,767	15,513	311,052	185,431
1984	5,346,405	4,422,836	5,850	4,428,686	499,334	-337,844	3,591,508	1,157,736	597,161	17,187	311,067	194,000
1985	5,761,857	4,832,232	6,502	4,838,734	551,095	-388,126	3,899,513	1,232,156	630,188	18,342	314,133	199,290
1986	6,206,379	5,306,210	6,626	5,312,836	613,135	-449,881	4,249,820	1,296,824	659,735	19,483	318,557	207,145
1987	6,729,160	5,830,784	7,909	5,838,693	667,363	-506,716	4,664,614	1,380,045	684,501	20,880	322,280	212,933
1988	7,487,965	6,530,639	7,184	6,537,823	764,226	-580,149	5,193,448	1,567,650	726,867	22,958	326,162	218,832
1989	8,156,106	6,914,960	6,396	6,921,356	800,305	-663,732	5,457,319	1,914,511	784,276	25,000	326,246	219,559
1990	8,697,032	7,384,609	4,926	7,389,535	829,957	-711,777	5,847,801	1,988,896	860,335	26,639	326,477	219,736
1991	8,868,792	7,666,994	3,058	7,670,052	880,122	-912,431	5,877,499	2,005,533	985,760	26,982	328,694	216,604
1992	9,517,817	8,180,550	1,990	8,182,540	931,848	-866,984	6,383,708	2,005,288	1,128,821	28,783	330,674	217,454
1993	9,693,836	8,403,830	2,576	8,406,406	953,228	-945,918	6,507,260	1,987,130	1,199,446	29,085	333,292	219,615
1994	10,025,467	8,722,040	3,174	8,725,214	1,006,864	-1,012,916	6,705,434	2,109,274	1,210,759	29,906	335,229	220,293
1995	10,504,224	8,990,131	1,973	8,992,104	1,044,279	-1,052,076	6,895,749	2,315,835	1,292,640	31,126	337,476	222,501
1996	11,045,714	9,214,761	2,899	9,217,660	1,070,017	-866,524	7,281,119	2,437,355	1,327,240	32,569	339,146	220,840
1997	11,650,321	9,970,281	1,436	9,971,717	1,145,286	-1,110,449	7,715,982	2,576,622	1,357,717	34,190	340,755	224,588
1998	12,437,241	10,435,513	1,245	10,436,758	1,186,776	-965,290	8,284,692	2,788,787	1,363,762	36,153	344,013	225,414
1999	13,057,689	10,986,530	1,293	10,987,823	1,245,560	-912,577	8,829,686	2,810,593	1,417,410	37,475	348,435	228,946
2000	14,450,504	12,190,977	3,850	12,194,827	1,363,901	-1,016,691	9,814,235	3,118,713	1,517,556	41,115	351,465	242,173
2001	15,853,546	13,660,988	2,799	13,663,787	1,480,163	-1,126,802	11,056,822	3,098,281	1,698,443	44,807	353,816	247,570
2002	16,378,380	14,226,117	3,860	14,229,977	1,535,204	-1,295,738	11,399,035	3,098,753	1,880,592	46,015	355,935	249,453
2003	16,880,015	14,724,077	4,114	14,728,191	1,575,654	-1,307,075	11,845,462	3,205,550	1,829,003	47,056	358,724	252,631
2004	17,165,902	15,333,351	5,920	15,339,271	1,639,299	-1,524,663	12,175,309	3,180,539	1,810,054	47,518	361,248	257,984
2005	17,589,316	15,607,227	4,950	15,612,177	1,707,564	-1,522,180	12,382,433	3,291,060	1,915,823	48,587	362,015	259,714
2006	18,877,482	16,421,082	5,215	16,426,297	1,799,389	-1,613,423	13,013,485	3,769,955	2,094,042	52,027	362,840	265,427
2007	19,856,064	16,835,197	4,747	16,839,944	1,883,460	-1,283,313	13,673,171	3,980,284	2,202,609	54,687	363,088	264,782
2008	20,427,763	17,780,073	3,818	17,783,891	1,991,709	-1,889,990	13,902,192	4,036,080	2,489,491	56,102	364,119	265,799
2009	19,163,833	17,124,088	3,324	17,127,412	1,922,922	-2,312,246	12,892,244	3,530,163	2,741,426	52,448	365,388	259,117
2010	19,574,500	17,655,172	3,341	17,658,513	1,983,227	-2,536,981	13,138,305	3,468,241	2,967,954	53,202	367,930	260,107
2011	20,751,178	18,235,231	6,559	18,241,790	1,835,082	-2,559,461	13,847,247	3,898,857	3,005,074	56,358	368,201	262,910
2012	21,843,306	19,030,866	8,128	19,038,994	1,894,800	-2,581,017	14,563,177	4,311,895	2,968,234	58,969	370,419	263,963
2013	21,455,162	19,845,025	8,318	19,853,343	2,220,623	-3,249,034	14,383,686	4,046,346	3,025,130	57,623	372,337	267,420
2014	22,868,832	20,464,873	6,358	20,471,231	2,287,422	-3,013,687	15,170,122	4,552,572	3,146,138	61,315	372,974	272,630
2015	23,384,088	20,714,156	7,523	20,721,679	2,336,374	-3,143,892	15,241,413	4,881,003	3,261,672	62,674	373,104	276,171
2016	23,716,747	21,397,381	5,401	21,402,782	2,394,581	-3,691,687	15,316,514	5,017,303	3,382,930	63,471	373,660	282,861
2017	24,860,835	21,860,226	7,062	21,867,288	2,471,042	-3,225,357	16,170,889	5,226,682	3,463,264	66,343	374,733	284,811
2018	25,434,539	25,432,195	2,344	22,861,098	2,557,250	-3,769,850	16,533,998	5,441,733	3,458,808	69,080	368,188	290,138
2019	26,377,963	26,372,688	5,275	24,703,869	2,722,643	-4,708,370	17,272,856	5,478,684	3,626,423	71,790	367,430	298,894

Personal Income and Employment by Area: Tucson, AZ

(Thousands of dollars, except as noted.)

Year	Personal income, total	Earnings by place of work			Less: Contributions for government social insurance	Plus: Adjustment for residence	Equals: Net earnings by place of residence	Plus: Dividends, interest, and rent	Plus: Personal current transfer receipts	Per capita personal income (dollars)	Population (persons)	Total employment
		Nonfarm	Farm	Total								
1970	1,450,771	1,025,196	9,121	1,034,317	69,598	14,248	978,967	344,831	126,973	4,076	355,962	144,257
1971	1,674,034	1,188,318	8,350	1,196,668	83,587	16,944	1,130,025	391,000	153,009	4,402	380,255	153,910
1972	1,905,022	1,363,766	12,649	1,376,415	100,346	15,682	1,291,751	437,269	176,002	4,675	407,515	165,820
1973	2,167,818	1,551,236	21,896	1,573,132	129,373	23,267	1,467,026	490,888	209,904	5,058	428,558	177,412
1974	2,420,702	1,708,320	16,922	1,725,242	148,097	26,991	1,604,136	566,011	250,555	5,455	443,741	181,576
1975	2,651,180	1,800,181	14,095	1,814,276	156,145	26,964	1,685,095	630,129	335,956	5,767	459,738	180,791
1976	2,900,858	1,967,561	18,384	1,985,945	171,550	32,580	1,846,975	675,058	378,825	6,151	471,596	185,903
1977	3,209,600	2,195,387	11,834	2,207,221	191,389	35,536	2,051,368	756,391	401,841	6,638	483,484	193,919
1978	3,687,707	2,514,099	15,924	2,530,023	223,517	33,891	2,340,397	887,159	460,151	7,410	497,687	206,946
1979	4,323,806	3,005,810	16,282	3,022,092	280,713	43,094	2,784,473	1,029,904	509,429	8,262	523,341	224,813
1980	4,977,858	3,390,573	16,831	3,407,404	322,646	38,753	3,123,511	1,251,260	603,087	9,291	535,780	234,354
1981	5,783,187	3,836,259	14,326	3,850,585	392,153	78,362	3,536,794	1,540,944	705,449	10,465	552,627	240,604
1982	6,171,947	4,024,506	13,593	4,038,099	419,400	59,936	3,678,635	1,710,961	782,351	10,866	568,004	245,297
1983	6,720,540	4,366,338	14,128	4,380,466	462,151	45,170	3,963,485	1,907,118	849,937	11,544	582,172	253,316
1984	7,387,659	4,842,774	33,960	4,876,734	529,159	45,672	4,393,247	2,094,922	899,490	12,477	592,087	271,828
1985	8,089,874	5,325,158	25,642	5,350,800	589,883	48,139	4,809,056	2,315,886	964,932	13,424	602,647	291,177
1986	8,778,098	5,818,120	29,159	5,847,279	646,842	57,629	5,258,066	2,474,335	1,045,697	14,122	621,586	302,631
1987	9,288,965	6,169,748	27,872	6,197,620	679,503	63,858	5,581,975	2,562,568	1,144,422	14,505	640,419	308,273
1988	9,934,583	6,559,895	31,163	6,591,058	749,448	95,324	5,936,934	2,746,074	1,251,575	15,127	656,727	318,154
1989	10,668,032	6,717,781	24,366	6,742,147	789,961	90,360	6,042,546	3,184,808	1,440,678	16,061	664,200	318,020
1990	10,999,408	6,884,706	26,634	6,911,340	830,958	116,028	6,196,410	3,201,929	1,601,069	16,445	668,844	318,925
1991	11,640,270	7,437,719	23,808	7,461,527	906,588	110,716	6,665,655	3,204,771	1,769,844	17,123	679,813	323,434
1992	12,330,393	7,956,384	20,226	7,976,610	964,708	114,383	7,126,285	3,210,371	1,993,737	17,663	698,091	328,018
1993	13,445,904	8,653,599	28,241	8,681,840	1,044,439	105,292	7,742,693	3,544,127	2,159,084	18,685	719,598	343,969
1994	14,548,118	9,548,676	14,876	9,563,552	1,160,188	93,514	8,496,878	3,753,927	2,297,313	19,525	745,112	367,152
1995	15,521,408	10,082,827	12,521	10,095,348	1,180,975	108,447	9,022,820	4,058,346	2,440,242	20,205	768,212	381,587
1996	16,516,732	10,657,629	18,087	10,675,716	1,278,928	135,529	9,532,317	4,395,447	2,588,968	21,076	783,685	389,883
1997	17,418,989	11,332,721	18,217	11,350,938	1,338,365	116,161	10,128,734	4,590,829	2,699,426	21,814	798,521	399,857
1998	18,686,374	12,335,536	14,682	12,350,218	1,440,035	108,184	11,018,367	4,893,458	2,774,549	22,974	813,386	416,075
1999	19,633,938	13,201,066	21,400	13,222,466	1,551,573	96,845	11,767,738	4,922,849	2,943,351	23,687	828,905	425,172
2000	20,982,050	14,173,700	14,964	14,188,664	1,651,400	89,262	12,626,526	5,263,564	3,091,960	24,742	848,019	441,662
2001	22,709,028	15,572,638	10,975	15,583,613	1,737,877	82,066	13,927,802	5,280,610	3,500,616	26,428	859,280	436,864
2002	23,235,520	16,242,706	17,313	16,260,019	1,809,144	45,951	14,496,826	4,838,978	3,899,716	26,577	874,267	437,057
2003	24,531,177	17,119,782	22,230	17,142,012	1,880,224	19,680	15,281,468	5,002,562	4,247,147	27,691	885,893	441,824
2004	26,046,402	17,811,966	29,548	17,841,514	1,984,458	-12,219	15,844,837	5,589,878	4,611,687	28,897	901,342	458,654
2005	28,401,473	18,887,794	32,654	18,920,448	2,127,994	-24,715	16,767,739	6,571,920	5,061,814	30,861	920,298	473,271
2006	31,184,186	20,696,205	27,621	20,723,826	2,306,062	-72,275	18,345,489	7,322,193	5,516,504	33,142	940,930	491,400
2007	32,956,900	21,833,120	16,842	21,849,962	2,450,099	-91,073	19,308,790	7,686,606	5,961,504	34,478	955,869	504,656
2008	34,876,190	22,340,868	18,687	22,359,555	2,557,452	-92,109	19,709,994	8,270,906	6,895,290	36,037	967,778	500,711
2009	32,992,085	21,384,806	36,348	21,421,154	2,489,975	-53,881	18,877,298	6,567,528	7,547,259	33,818	975,580	481,987
2010	33,359,029	21,524,972	39,151	21,564,123	2,513,414	-31,208	19,019,501	6,238,017	8,101,511	33,986	981,540	476,945
2011	34,767,954	21,791,077	57,589	21,848,666	2,302,657	12,955	19,558,964	7,156,806	8,052,184	35,215	987,297	477,616
2012	36,064,014	22,721,650	51,437	22,773,087	2,349,909	42,611	20,465,789	7,560,333	8,037,892	36,372	991,528	484,507
2013	36,601,437	23,266,854	53,674	23,320,528	2,686,475	86,913	20,720,966	7,586,535	8,293,936	36,794	994,759	489,825
2014	38,154,664	23,506,532	64,440	23,570,972	2,722,855	104,762	20,952,879	8,334,396	8,867,389	38,120	1,000,916	495,805
2015	39,385,843	23,753,993	70,497	23,824,490	2,779,991	116,723	21,161,222	8,919,922	9,304,699	39,177	1,005,323	500,149
2016	40,387,893	24,444,994	66,702	24,511,696	2,874,095	99,226	21,736,827	9,066,475	9,584,591	39,889	1,012,519	507,500
2017	42,585,356	25,933,241	72,694	26,005,935	3,048,842	88,533	23,045,626	9,506,802	10,032,928	41,637	1,022,769	515,453
2018	45,623,879	45,588,272	35,607	27,471,836	3,222,833	123,620	24,372,623	10,630,018	10,621,238	44,015	1,036,554	524,652
2019	47,604,994	47,574,414	30,580	28,783,605	3,391,550	105,055	25,497,110	10,814,143	11,293,741	45,456	1,047,279	536,686

Personal Income and Employment by Area: Tulsa, OK

(Thousands of dollars, except as noted.)

| Year | Personal income, total | Derivation of personal income | | | | | Equals: Net earnings by place of residence | Plus: Dividends, interest, and rent | Plus: Personal current transfer receipts | Per capita personal income (dollars) | Population (persons) | Total employment |
| | | Earnings by place of work | | | Less: Contributions for government social insurance | Plus: Adjustment for residence | | | | | | |
		Nonfarm	Farm	Total								
1970	2,244,876	1,803,417	17,819	1,821,236	118,059	-13,643	1,689,534	344,994	210,348	3,916	573,235	253,693
1971	2,423,024	1,923,488	15,964	1,939,452	129,622	-11,000	1,798,830	380,481	243,713	4,162	582,203	255,389
1972	2,660,683	2,136,833	21,145	2,157,978	151,577	-12,550	1,993,851	400,704	266,128	4,494	592,055	270,578
1973	3,010,374	2,427,869	25,672	2,453,541	201,071	-12,440	2,240,030	465,639	304,705	5,000	602,108	286,825
1974	3,535,154	2,854,603	28,731	2,883,334	242,127	-8,842	2,632,365	545,238	357,551	5,777	611,968	301,297
1975	4,037,412	3,226,449	26,245	3,252,694	267,329	10,306	2,995,671	600,416	441,325	6,457	625,290	309,562
1976	4,496,483	3,619,842	27,581	3,647,423	307,343	19,613	3,359,693	651,137	485,653	7,043	638,395	324,739
1977	5,048,189	4,114,867	17,591	4,132,458	347,292	18,843	3,804,009	723,181	520,999	7,746	651,741	336,418
1978	5,741,100	4,735,201	5,321	4,740,522	412,300	16,667	4,344,889	837,483	558,728	8,645	664,120	356,285
1979	6,570,626	5,463,555	16,969	5,480,524	494,812	-27,859	4,957,853	969,043	643,730	9,522	690,017	372,697
1980	7,754,003	6,414,764	11,648	6,426,412	582,946	-43,751	5,799,715	1,207,172	747,116	10,834	715,729	396,414
1981	9,020,964	7,407,097	22,929	7,430,026	724,104	-57,943	6,647,979	1,521,306	851,679	12,345	730,726	416,102
1982	9,865,263	7,928,027	16,706	7,944,733	799,460	-57,708	7,087,565	1,796,927	980,771	13,070	754,809	420,399
1983	10,028,274	7,890,947	14,600	7,905,547	792,124	-47,832	7,065,591	1,877,904	1,084,779	12,977	772,780	406,405
1984	10,745,623	8,413,935	12,368	8,426,303	856,524	-36,843	7,532,936	2,096,210	1,116,477	13,874	774,500	416,659
1985	11,350,185	8,838,843	10,333	8,849,176	913,651	-45,139	7,890,386	2,270,928	1,188,871	14,679	773,203	421,361
1986	11,535,530	8,970,166	21,113	8,991,279	946,414	-49,220	7,995,645	2,265,666	1,274,219	14,869	775,798	409,752
1987	11,579,981	8,981,797	16,105	8,997,902	945,958	-44,968	8,006,976	2,241,869	1,331,136	15,025	770,713	411,356
1988	12,138,355	9,463,547	26,063	9,489,610	1,040,902	-51,303	8,397,405	2,334,196	1,406,754	16,000	758,652	413,701
1989	12,976,626	10,149,835	29,269	10,179,104	1,117,270	-79,229	8,982,605	2,483,922	1,510,099	17,134	757,345	418,975
1990	13,917,909	10,829,567	13,894	10,843,461	1,237,234	-48,716	9,557,511	2,736,295	1,624,103	18,238	763,119	430,763
1991	14,433,922	11,276,525	30,254	11,306,779	1,316,608	-50,808	9,939,363	2,721,628	1,772,931	18,630	774,765	437,718
1992	15,240,048	11,861,419	31,082	11,892,501	1,371,429	-67,034	10,454,038	2,802,560	1,983,450	19,395	785,755	438,214
1993	15,822,834	12,381,108	29,253	12,410,361	1,438,718	-88,452	10,883,191	2,822,969	2,116,674	19,899	795,139	444,889
1994	16,532,367	12,845,782	35,297	12,881,079	1,515,283	-101,367	11,264,429	3,042,329	2,225,609	20,653	800,473	453,942
1995	17,471,159	13,413,972	9,776	13,423,748	1,580,280	-111,073	11,732,395	3,321,052	2,417,712	21,684	805,725	466,011
1996	18,657,703	14,313,567	13,657	14,327,224	1,654,860	-125,433	12,546,931	3,561,314	2,549,458	22,857	816,284	481,882
1997	19,979,614	15,542,980	16,410	15,559,390	1,772,424	-167,194	13,619,772	3,662,496	2,697,346	24,089	829,391	499,806
1998	21,580,873	16,834,592	-13,913	16,820,679	1,913,669	-194,604	14,712,406	4,132,159	2,736,308	25,598	843,057	523,100
1999	21,875,928	16,922,920	7,294	16,930,214	1,948,747	-176,024	14,805,443	4,204,458	2,866,027	25,597	854,631	522,394
2000	23,724,842	18,137,745	119	18,137,864	2,060,399	-205,246	15,872,219	4,835,180	3,017,443	27,547	861,237	533,529
2001	23,939,838	18,244,880	5,015	18,249,895	2,166,703	-250,250	15,832,942	4,805,185	3,301,711	27,593	867,602	537,484
2002	24,184,341	18,376,323	29,293	18,405,616	2,194,956	-264,144	15,946,516	4,728,480	3,509,345	27,644	874,844	530,126
2003	24,667,407	18,589,816	397	18,590,213	2,174,120	-232,034	16,184,059	4,715,094	3,768,254	28,109	877,577	516,720
2004	28,033,347	21,643,863	38,561	21,682,424	2,368,691	-240,282	19,073,451	4,992,403	3,967,493	31,928	878,004	520,154
2005	31,613,488	24,355,045	54,334	24,409,379	2,545,651	-267,564	21,596,164	5,726,536	4,290,788	35,808	882,861	535,329
2006	36,424,852	27,994,685	26,875	28,021,560	2,741,575	-343,308	24,936,677	6,779,405	4,708,770	40,743	894,011	552,670
2007	37,483,075	27,910,069	33,505	27,943,574	2,872,346	-324,077	24,747,151	7,662,062	5,073,862	41,352	906,441	567,239
2008	42,667,826	32,103,601	8,175	32,111,776	2,999,508	-297,821	28,814,447	8,132,731	5,720,648	46,554	916,525	577,748
2009	37,167,872	27,173,394	-7,608	27,165,786	2,864,605	-244,174	24,057,007	6,975,653	6,135,212	39,973	929,824	559,559
2010	38,833,808	28,268,338	18,550	28,286,888	2,886,792	-86,926	25,313,170	6,904,577	6,616,061	41,322	939,776	550,837
2011	43,488,850	31,757,640	41,783	31,799,423	2,824,469	-57,708	28,917,246	7,886,869	6,684,735	46,007	945,261	556,518
2012	48,479,511	35,358,253	71,104	35,429,357	3,031,063	-3,033	32,395,261	9,240,592	6,843,658	50,913	952,199	570,545
2013	53,543,765	41,346,408	90,028	41,436,436	3,523,865	30,979	37,943,550	8,630,362	6,969,853	55,674	961,738	578,954
2014	57,525,574	44,483,415	184,163	44,667,578	3,624,030	48,517	41,092,065	9,168,769	7,264,740	59,352	969,234	587,968
2015	53,148,444	39,648,855	86,710	39,735,565	3,622,946	44,072	36,156,691	9,434,769	7,556,984	54,222	980,208	596,899
2016	47,650,906	33,841,048	53,771	33,894,819	3,510,973	34,506	30,418,352	9,391,424	7,841,130	48,256	987,465	599,116
2017	51,358,754	37,219,372	35,985	37,255,357	3,678,831	-30,770	33,545,756	9,778,923	8,034,075	51,841	990,706	604,091
2018	54,497,793	54,525,648	-27,855	39,158,700	3,870,510	-43,486	35,244,704	10,853,725	8,399,364	54,875	993,135	609,346
2019	56,462,371	56,484,808	-22,437	40,553,612	4,006,768	-4,000	36,542,844	10,967,613	8,951,914	56,540	998,626	618,254

Personal Income and Employment by Area: Tuscaloosa, AL

(Thousands of dollars, except as noted.)

Year	Personal income, total	Earnings by place of work			Less: Contributions for government social insurance	Plus: Adjustment for residence	Equals: Net earnings by place of residence	Plus: Dividends, interest, and rent	Plus: Personal current transfer receipts	Per capita personal income (dollars)	Population (persons)	Total employment
		Nonfarm	Farm	Total								
1970	421,024	327,971	8,305	336,276	24,205	5,543	317,614	52,181	51,229	2,760	152,542	57,595
1971	477,791	370,233	11,259	381,492	28,071	6,114	359,535	59,828	58,428	3,072	155,545	59,464
1972	532,848	414,748	12,425	427,173	33,056	6,949	401,066	66,929	64,853	3,356	158,760	62,219
1973	597,587	464,592	17,845	482,437	42,654	8,638	448,421	75,759	73,407	3,712	160,974	64,792
1974	670,897	521,898	11,386	533,284	49,216	10,546	494,614	88,919	87,364	4,109	163,262	65,272
1975	754,936	568,090	12,707	580,797	53,304	12,159	539,652	102,804	112,480	4,594	164,319	64,783
1976	828,130	629,200	12,343	641,543	60,305	13,250	594,488	112,340	121,302	4,973	166,525	66,406
1977	942,678	732,568	9,710	742,278	68,752	13,626	687,152	126,212	129,314	5,599	168,371	68,549
1978	1,056,880	809,188	16,161	825,349	76,359	18,058	767,048	147,319	142,513	6,148	171,898	68,430
1979	1,173,059	891,927	15,288	907,215	86,998	20,618	840,835	168,910	163,314	6,767	173,338	69,758
1980	1,254,670	928,704	2,427	931,131	93,515	20,427	858,043	202,684	193,943	7,170	174,982	69,209
1981	1,402,575	1,010,964	7,528	1,018,492	110,261	27,908	936,139	246,412	220,024	7,965	176,099	69,349
1982	1,500,180	1,067,772	3,663	1,071,435	119,399	24,976	977,012	278,967	244,201	8,590	174,646	68,387
1983	1,611,324	1,137,285	-850	1,136,435	126,028	34,618	1,045,025	299,974	266,325	9,200	175,147	68,723
1984	1,786,750	1,268,023	8,273	1,276,296	142,022	33,042	1,167,316	336,413	283,021	10,156	175,924	71,003
1985	1,937,109	1,370,063	11,303	1,381,366	153,294	33,882	1,261,954	366,788	308,367	10,882	178,012	72,404
1986	2,031,265	1,433,360	14,355	1,447,715	162,051	39,354	1,325,018	382,488	323,759	11,262	180,361	75,044
1987	2,188,710	1,576,096	14,976	1,591,072	173,297	47,278	1,465,053	393,390	330,267	11,994	182,481	78,163
1988	2,329,599	1,667,807	21,864	1,689,671	193,321	61,694	1,558,044	426,617	344,938	12,678	183,746	81,570
1989	2,581,097	1,798,129	22,661	1,820,790	207,102	69,786	1,683,474	502,265	395,358	13,932	185,270	83,909
1990	2,814,979	1,985,493	27,036	2,012,529	230,606	66,744	1,848,667	521,705	444,607	15,028	187,311	87,832
1991	2,957,443	2,069,579	33,430	2,103,009	240,550	67,775	1,930,234	539,215	487,994	15,566	189,990	87,718
1992	3,187,706	2,206,396	36,488	2,242,884	251,662	84,438	2,075,660	550,009	562,037	16,708	190,785	88,695
1993	3,371,503	2,355,708	38,419	2,394,127	271,523	79,834	2,202,438	571,042	598,023	17,508	192,574	92,593
1994	3,583,329	2,495,967	28,915	2,524,882	289,967	77,589	2,312,504	623,529	647,296	18,445	194,272	94,585
1995	3,792,597	2,626,327	21,336	2,647,663	306,908	70,259	2,411,014	684,474	697,109	19,196	197,577	96,915
1996	3,932,597	2,714,169	27,038	2,741,207	316,023	67,100	2,492,284	707,467	732,846	19,866	197,955	99,421
1997	4,146,730	2,883,207	32,316	2,915,523	336,479	52,148	2,631,192	742,850	772,688	20,762	199,727	102,688
1998	4,424,471	3,090,522	46,293	3,136,815	355,731	46,940	2,828,024	815,583	780,864	21,980	201,299	104,856
1999	4,659,653	3,297,909	66,087	3,363,996	377,850	33,596	3,019,742	815,835	824,076	23,019	202,429	105,743
2000	4,839,574	3,381,104	45,012	3,426,116	387,497	29,678	3,068,297	890,892	880,385	23,667	204,489	106,454
2001	4,988,630	3,523,366	54,419	3,577,785	406,581	17,131	3,188,335	891,037	909,258	24,253	205,692	107,783
2002	5,142,225	3,658,780	44,226	3,703,006	421,981	1,702	3,282,727	881,283	978,215	24,918	206,365	108,429
2003	5,361,294	3,795,045	60,540	3,855,585	436,157	-14,348	3,405,080	938,488	1,017,726	25,854	207,368	109,040
2004	5,654,235	4,024,851	75,283	4,100,134	458,099	-18,517	3,623,518	956,002	1,074,715	27,040	209,105	111,644
2005	6,091,370	4,410,659	74,875	4,485,534	502,242	-97,385	3,885,907	1,056,348	1,149,115	28,659	212,545	115,235
2006	6,477,769	4,741,520	51,046	4,792,566	539,852	-158,140	4,094,574	1,163,881	1,219,314	29,723	217,938	120,420
2007	6,846,911	4,911,978	45,155	4,957,133	565,567	-192,782	4,198,784	1,301,098	1,347,029	31,016	220,757	123,649
2008	7,091,201	4,988,462	41,945	5,030,407	586,926	-242,618	4,200,863	1,388,373	1,501,965	31,614	224,304	123,407
2009	7,103,788	4,847,042	44,725	4,891,767	569,115	-232,827	4,089,825	1,368,364	1,645,599	31,071	228,631	118,587
2010	7,335,590	5,085,937	40,074	5,126,011	599,370	-300,900	4,225,741	1,322,219	1,787,630	31,826	230,487	118,531
2011	7,577,481	5,329,572	19,642	5,349,214	555,954	-317,022	4,476,238	1,307,652	1,793,591	32,745	231,411	120,664
2012	7,852,251	5,506,605	30,712	5,537,317	572,827	-324,495	4,639,995	1,450,562	1,761,694	33,662	233,270	123,778
2013	7,991,410	5,672,341	91,638	5,763,979	666,890	-313,298	4,783,791	1,407,329	1,800,290	33,962	235,302	125,260
2014	8,276,046	5,910,261	56,480	5,966,741	692,399	-357,995	4,916,347	1,481,283	1,878,416	34,754	238,133	129,621
2015	8,483,415	6,059,202	60,941	6,120,143	709,243	-401,354	5,009,546	1,532,588	1,941,281	35,308	240,267	133,365
2016	8,604,631	6,072,977	39,774	6,112,751	709,024	-362,430	5,041,297	1,571,844	1,991,490	35,638	241,444	134,144
2017	8,949,117	6,349,782	46,547	6,396,329	741,265	-398,194	5,256,870	1,640,995	2,051,252	36,858	242,799	135,895
2018	9,655,490	9,611,711	43,779	6,725,173	798,356	-384,664	5,542,153	1,796,790	2,316,547	38,429	251,257	142,162
2019	10,015,806	9,986,418	29,388	7,060,183	833,348	-459,111	5,767,724	1,824,049	2,424,033	39,738	252,047	145,945

Personal Income and Employment by Area: Twin Falls, ID

(Thousands of dollars, except as noted.)

					Derivation of personal income							
		Earnings by place of work			Less: Contributions for government social insurance	Plus: Adjustment for residence	Equals: Net earnings by place of residence	Plus: Dividends, interest, and rent	Plus: Personal current transfer receipts	Per capita personal income (dollars)	Population (persons)	Total employment
Year	Personal income, total	Nonfarm	Farm	Total								
1970	193,857	115,179	34,956	150,135	8,618	749	142,266	32,921	18,670	3,692	52,509	25,303
1971	211,160	129,014	31,599	160,613	9,944	503	151,172	38,242	21,746	3,858	54,740	26,097
1972	244,241	143,728	44,508	188,236	11,512	819	177,543	41,913	24,785	4,305	56,740	26,921
1973	294,627	165,615	66,283	231,898	15,569	675	217,004	50,013	27,610	5,083	57,963	28,605
1974	360,419	195,209	92,805	288,014	18,974	195	269,235	58,740	32,444	6,030	59,768	30,370
1975	362,205	220,594	51,866	272,460	21,121	304	251,643	71,284	39,278	5,836	62,064	30,726
1976	383,853	249,634	41,282	290,916	24,143	255	267,028	73,680	43,145	6,122	62,700	32,480
1977	396,498	269,712	23,877	293,589	26,075	10	267,524	82,134	46,840	6,181	64,150	32,734
1978	450,350	308,982	28,809	337,791	30,090	-232	307,469	91,448	51,433	6,974	64,574	34,350
1979	498,926	349,981	23,720	373,701	36,079	-533	337,089	102,577	59,260	7,541	66,164	35,211
1980	584,032	371,461	52,978	424,439	38,634	251	386,056	127,299	70,677	8,591	67,983	34,801
1981	631,945	397,495	43,280	440,775	44,291	-2,075	394,409	155,972	81,564	9,189	68,769	34,410
1982	671,469	407,721	33,756	441,477	46,503	-2,588	392,386	187,158	91,925	9,640	69,657	33,845
1983	731,044	422,340	62,983	485,323	47,872	-2,292	435,159	196,534	99,351	10,315	70,873	34,040
1984	776,008	451,752	68,248	520,000	53,109	-2,610	464,281	208,112	103,615	10,978	70,686	34,048
1985	803,623	468,455	61,441	529,896	56,154	-3,281	470,461	222,236	110,926	11,484	69,977	33,630
1986	822,928	473,307	74,412	547,719	57,528	-2,942	487,249	219,319	116,360	11,869	69,333	33,517
1987	860,941	498,344	91,852	590,196	59,632	-2,383	528,181	212,946	119,814	12,571	68,487	34,073
1988	920,206	542,806	100,834	643,640	67,509	-1,125	575,006	215,885	129,315	13,455	68,393	35,116
1989	1,011,907	583,130	125,034	708,164	73,652	-497	634,015	239,658	138,234	14,815	68,305	35,955
1990	1,077,392	652,200	123,022	775,222	86,797	-1,520	686,905	242,550	147,937	15,607	69,033	38,157
1991	1,111,836	690,400	107,339	797,739	93,621	-789	703,329	246,680	161,827	15,752	70,584	38,905
1992	1,194,008	741,576	120,756	862,332	98,571	5	763,766	248,571	181,671	16,596	71,944	39,444
1993	1,307,901	799,106	163,535	962,641	106,760	959	856,840	260,286	190,775	17,818	73,402	40,806
1994	1,375,580	879,124	134,369	1,013,493	117,827	1,139	896,805	275,233	203,542	18,252	75,368	42,697
1995	1,479,017	925,342	148,083	1,073,425	124,249	1,672	950,848	305,790	222,379	19,311	76,590	44,397
1996	1,602,165	990,257	176,995	1,167,252	129,090	1,985	1,040,147	325,264	236,754	20,464	78,292	45,773
1997	1,650,079	1,027,697	161,088	1,188,785	133,314	2,615	1,058,086	345,450	246,543	20,705	79,696	47,072
1998	1,760,729	1,095,773	201,757	1,297,530	139,914	3,354	1,160,970	347,583	252,176	21,750	80,953	48,520
1999	1,810,072	1,153,765	192,924	1,346,689	144,148	5,521	1,208,062	337,028	264,982	22,095	81,923	48,686
2000	1,879,327	1,196,888	176,775	1,373,663	149,785	7,448	1,231,326	362,117	285,884	22,683	82,853	50,294
2001	2,010,418	1,233,672	223,721	1,457,393	154,733	6,684	1,309,344	382,600	318,474	24,183	83,135	50,131
2002	2,029,259	1,322,549	182,389	1,504,938	166,052	2,284	1,341,170	345,497	342,592	24,100	84,203	51,764
2003	2,085,605	1,370,263	163,089	1,533,352	175,088	-747	1,357,517	370,098	357,990	24,233	86,063	52,234
2004	2,282,849	1,432,111	268,128	1,700,239	182,858	643	1,518,024	382,619	382,206	26,048	87,640	52,721
2005	2,397,594	1,524,088	244,217	1,768,305	197,046	-386	1,570,873	415,141	411,580	26,793	89,487	54,863
2006	2,550,424	1,683,430	202,225	1,885,655	219,544	-4,526	1,661,585	436,092	452,747	27,696	92,085	56,593
2007	2,799,929	1,739,982	332,218	2,072,200	231,974	-5,792	1,834,434	480,108	485,387	29,689	94,310	57,877
2008	2,893,324	1,769,125	291,606	2,060,731	241,152	-10,835	1,808,744	519,172	565,408	30,026	96,360	58,300
2009	2,767,230	1,771,323	150,459	1,921,782	241,511	-13,873	1,666,398	487,870	612,962	28,148	98,310	56,659
2010	2,959,296	1,801,937	248,357	2,050,294	251,385	-13,265	1,785,644	483,723	689,929	29,588	100,016	55,501
2011	3,141,283	1,827,761	328,100	2,155,861	228,487	-11,423	1,915,951	530,175	695,157	31,232	100,579	56,044
2012	3,327,509	1,938,261	367,226	2,305,487	238,895	-13,018	2,053,574	583,497	690,438	32,963	100,947	56,340
2013	3,487,921	2,083,971	404,352	2,488,323	275,565	-12,878	2,199,880	589,350	698,691	34,092	102,309	58,148
2014	3,695,335	2,176,704	476,309	2,653,013	287,804	-19,326	2,345,883	618,400	731,052	35,651	103,653	60,162
2015	3,868,042	2,347,661	407,878	2,755,539	299,395	-28,478	2,427,666	680,020	760,356	36,863	104,929	61,241
2016	3,948,445	2,441,373	374,708	2,816,081	312,652	-27,132	2,476,297	695,138	777,010	36,973	106,793	62,274
2017	4,163,872	2,592,447	390,804	2,983,251	331,696	-30,222	2,621,333	733,712	808,827	38,288	108,751	63,997
2018	4,396,837	4,028,507	368,330	3,106,810	346,139	-35,957	2,724,714	821,911	850,212	39,937	110,095	65,207
2019	4,662,943	4,204,006	458,937	3,323,317	358,813	-45,208	2,919,296	832,778	910,869	41,899	111,290	66,637

Personal Income and Employment by Area: Tyler, TX

(Thousands of dollars, except as noted.)

Year	Personal income, total	Earnings by place of work			Less: Contributions for government social insurance	Plus: Adjustment for residence	Equals: Net earnings by place of residence	Plus: Dividends, interest, and rent	Plus: Personal current transfer receipts	Per capita personal income (dollars)	Population (persons)	Total employment
		Nonfarm	Farm	Total								
1970	351,219	290,251	2,119	292,370	19,129	-11,052	262,189	57,001	32,029	3,606	97,390	46,609
1971	386,169	316,918	3,785	320,703	21,431	-11,836	287,436	62,202	36,531	3,868	99,839	47,754
1972	438,298	367,053	3,343	370,396	26,074	-15,331	328,991	68,563	40,744	4,223	103,794	51,083
1973	500,311	415,053	8,045	423,098	34,373	-17,516	371,209	79,832	49,270	4,731	105,758	53,832
1974	570,348	464,251	8,027	472,278	39,172	-19,167	413,939	96,360	60,049	5,244	108,766	54,925
1975	637,891	506,514	3,205	509,719	41,468	-19,647	448,604	112,470	76,817	5,713	111,662	55,398
1976	733,407	589,520	7,480	597,000	48,693	-21,915	526,392	123,450	83,565	6,419	114,264	57,952
1977	841,790	694,847	5,332	700,179	57,449	-29,051	613,679	139,771	88,340	7,187	117,127	62,480
1978	973,776	810,559	3,889	814,448	68,508	-34,505	711,435	163,351	98,990	8,070	120,667	66,707
1979	1,127,369	936,018	10,433	946,451	83,063	-41,602	821,786	192,656	112,927	8,954	125,905	70,277
1980	1,283,749	1,027,624	10,260	1,037,884	91,630	-42,998	903,256	244,928	135,565	9,927	129,316	71,788
1981	1,495,480	1,178,122	11,480	1,189,602	113,283	-47,603	1,028,716	315,176	151,588	11,267	132,734	75,129
1982	1,704,299	1,303,250	17,550	1,320,800	128,982	-54,379	1,137,439	395,028	171,832	12,409	137,348	79,688
1983	1,856,465	1,411,313	23,739	1,435,052	139,100	-60,783	1,235,169	429,691	191,605	13,144	141,243	81,358
1984	2,035,226	1,567,583	21,554	1,589,137	160,465	-70,804	1,357,868	473,449	203,909	14,033	145,030	85,052
1985	2,151,033	1,629,148	8,798	1,637,946	169,055	-69,845	1,399,046	528,105	223,882	14,439	148,975	85,608
1986	2,221,483	1,657,042	18,574	1,675,616	170,825	-69,145	1,435,646	534,991	250,846	14,658	151,554	82,811
1987	2,239,646	1,657,258	18,204	1,675,462	168,973	-70,102	1,436,387	532,838	270,421	14,697	152,388	84,446
1988	2,335,766	1,707,916	12,720	1,720,636	179,711	-67,633	1,473,292	574,181	288,293	15,350	152,164	84,113
1989	2,470,890	1,764,444	16,008	1,780,452	187,529	-70,734	1,522,189	636,454	312,247	16,377	150,876	84,412
1990	2,606,041	1,876,359	14,867	1,891,226	195,386	-73,280	1,622,560	634,766	348,715	17,196	151,550	85,724
1991	2,708,520	1,970,747	12,758	1,983,505	211,493	-86,143	1,685,869	641,133	381,518	17,622	153,705	87,981
1992	2,882,811	2,131,086	13,160	2,144,246	225,167	-99,811	1,819,268	622,735	440,808	18,559	155,336	88,955
1993	3,045,388	2,274,492	14,024	2,288,516	240,888	-115,983	1,931,645	644,188	469,555	19,188	158,717	91,518
1994	3,192,026	2,379,674	13,799	2,393,473	254,151	-125,837	2,013,485	677,852	500,689	19,839	160,898	94,519
1995	3,408,371	2,507,993	14,219	2,522,212	267,755	-134,456	2,120,001	747,377	540,993	20,854	163,440	97,351
1996	3,631,056	2,693,197	12,463	2,705,660	283,333	-148,191	2,274,136	769,086	587,834	21,862	166,087	99,975
1997	3,899,334	2,959,420	22,403	2,981,823	305,022	-166,899	2,509,902	771,200	618,232	23,137	168,531	104,160
1998	4,207,754	3,200,704	27,999	3,228,703	328,140	-194,383	2,706,180	858,999	642,575	24,602	171,033	105,989
1999	4,357,033	3,368,536	34,136	3,402,672	342,995	-215,012	2,844,665	856,304	656,064	25,220	172,758	107,091
2000	4,762,552	3,693,998	28,594	3,722,592	365,009	-242,641	3,114,942	949,094	698,516	27,113	175,658	110,519
2001	5,009,411	3,931,127	35,625	3,966,752	387,295	-241,597	3,337,860	906,897	764,654	28,169	177,836	112,428
2002	5,164,689	4,070,184	38,130	4,108,314	400,139	-246,589	3,461,586	871,001	832,102	28,517	181,107	113,276
2003	5,425,113	4,250,597	34,158	4,284,755	426,463	-248,760	3,609,532	912,542	903,039	29,444	184,254	115,187
2004	5,768,612	4,646,169	30,764	4,676,933	465,835	-295,775	3,915,323	905,442	947,847	30,799	187,300	118,641
2005	6,494,115	5,177,114	32,830	5,209,944	502,092	-334,619	4,373,233	1,074,918	1,045,964	33,936	191,362	123,110
2006	7,121,807	5,712,486	26,020	5,738,506	532,215	-352,468	4,853,823	1,150,933	1,117,051	36,313	196,124	127,125
2007	7,324,890	5,686,609	19,636	5,706,245	551,409	-317,733	4,837,103	1,263,682	1,224,105	36,633	199,953	130,700
2008	8,679,258	6,718,435	15,360	6,733,795	601,304	-323,984	5,808,507	1,494,134	1,376,617	42,700	203,263	134,234
2009	8,043,696	6,116,204	19,087	6,135,291	590,870	-297,294	5,247,127	1,299,519	1,497,050	38,838	207,111	131,425
2010	8,863,787	6,787,163	21,224	6,808,387	619,764	-288,964	5,899,659	1,342,566	1,621,562	42,129	210,398	132,288
2011	10,022,147	7,732,725	17,150	7,749,875	577,574	-259,784	6,912,517	1,434,534	1,675,096	47,129	212,653	133,589
2012	10,244,634	7,833,363	27,116	7,860,479	587,854	-254,891	7,017,734	1,556,308	1,670,592	47,714	214,707	136,174
2013	10,593,764	8,209,902	35,912	8,245,814	683,602	-254,175	7,308,037	1,533,540	1,752,187	48,949	216,426	139,356
2014	11,273,857	8,666,815	28,221	8,695,036	712,575	-275,483	7,706,978	1,722,049	1,844,830	51,358	219,517	141,717
2015	10,568,786	7,831,455	36,639	7,868,094	721,540	-299,575	6,846,979	1,772,374	1,949,433	47,519	222,410	145,203
2016	10,536,401	7,629,169	28,318	7,657,487	735,587	-338,903	6,582,997	1,902,793	2,050,611	46,765	225,305	148,107
2017	10,748,612	7,741,675	25,688	7,767,363	758,417	-358,324	6,650,622	1,994,619	2,103,371	47,200	227,727	149,862
2018	12,700,793	12,692,037	8,756	9,711,453	837,093	-369,389	8,504,971	2,036,095	2,159,727	55,281	229,749	151,001
2019	13,102,118	13,095,529	6,589	9,982,916	857,605	-368,719	8,756,592	2,070,045	2,275,481	56,292	232,751	151,877

Personal Income and Employment by Area: Urban Honolulu, HI

(Thousands of dollars, except as noted.)

Year	Personal income, total	Earnings by place of work			Less: Contributions for government social insurance	Plus: Adjustment for residence	Equals: Net earnings by place of residence	Plus: Dividends, interest, and rent	Plus: Personal current transfer receipts	Per capita personal income (dollars)	Population (persons)	Total employment
		Nonfarm	Farm	Total								
1970	3,634,964	2,958,005	33,864	2,991,869	183,236	4,733	2,813,366	661,296	160,302	5,828	623,756	366,968
1971	3,926,337	3,153,668	32,321	3,185,989	203,001	5,034	2,988,022	728,002	210,313	6,202	633,043	367,494
1972	4,327,655	3,480,364	32,143	3,512,507	236,141	4,610	3,280,976	797,331	249,348	6,509	664,830	381,276
1973	4,791,314	3,870,404	31,032	3,901,436	300,444	4,394	3,605,386	905,061	280,867	7,007	683,772	398,757
1974	5,274,604	4,217,804	39,362	4,257,166	343,985	4,307	3,917,488	1,024,565	332,551	7,556	698,033	407,738
1975	5,821,193	4,616,636	40,096	4,656,732	380,298	6,294	4,282,728	1,105,665	432,800	8,224	707,866	415,990
1976	6,281,530	4,969,816	41,097	5,010,913	413,473	6,456	4,603,896	1,168,788	508,846	8,762	716,911	417,620
1977	6,771,327	5,354,178	47,097	5,401,275	442,424	6,313	4,965,164	1,270,914	535,249	9,213	734,962	418,536
1978	7,496,119	5,921,228	40,954	5,962,182	502,998	5,023	5,464,207	1,460,740	571,172	10,123	740,505	431,484
1979	8,372,875	6,641,373	43,531	6,684,904	589,044	4,651	6,100,511	1,643,308	629,056	11,113	753,428	454,142
1980	9,422,314	7,372,805	63,826	7,436,631	653,607	4,972	6,787,996	1,915,931	718,387	12,336	763,820	467,461
1981	10,313,480	7,950,314	45,816	7,996,130	750,841	4,969	7,250,258	2,222,532	840,690	13,436	767,573	461,302
1982	10,892,215	8,445,216	50,452	8,495,668	787,253	4,615	7,713,030	2,274,583	904,602	14,035	776,075	457,679
1983	11,852,319	9,068,558	72,563	9,141,121	865,649	4,652	8,280,124	2,582,378	989,817	15,020	789,097	463,241
1984	12,755,379	9,716,997	51,884	9,768,881	946,084	3,616	8,826,413	2,880,632	1,048,334	15,988	797,791	467,189
1985	13,549,475	10,353,793	55,720	10,409,513	1,027,509	4,982	9,386,986	3,054,689	1,107,800	16,846	804,294	477,011
1986	14,298,161	11,032,179	59,639	11,091,818	1,119,586	5,650	9,977,882	3,171,978	1,148,301	17,642	810,444	486,861
1987	15,228,178	11,922,435	58,526	11,980,961	1,220,266	6,027	10,766,722	3,272,209	1,189,247	18,606	818,447	509,161
1988	16,651,964	13,159,375	75,279	13,234,654	1,393,147	6,226	11,847,733	3,529,307	1,274,924	20,207	824,072	525,017
1989	18,429,324	14,449,342	68,648	14,517,990	1,530,993	10,499	12,997,496	4,018,982	1,412,846	22,168	831,337	540,855
1990	20,038,505	15,941,554	76,424	16,017,978	1,760,667	12,384	14,269,695	4,243,614	1,525,196	23,897	838,534	558,346
1991	21,105,032	16,853,115	67,200	16,920,315	1,883,622	10,653	15,047,346	4,394,601	1,663,085	24,815	850,510	569,711
1992	22,665,937	18,039,436	52,140	18,091,576	2,010,280	6,749	16,088,045	4,700,806	1,877,086	26,235	863,959	570,015
1993	23,390,411	18,380,701	76,253	18,456,954	2,044,634	5,563	16,417,883	4,904,373	2,068,155	26,875	870,348	566,606
1994	23,857,762	18,465,352	64,023	18,529,375	2,070,316	1,789	16,460,848	5,154,695	2,242,219	27,155	878,591	560,810
1995	24,342,583	18,404,319	71,016	18,475,335	2,060,576	-2,183	16,412,576	5,400,427	2,529,580	27,618	881,399	556,670
1996	24,282,200	18,332,011	66,664	18,398,675	2,055,206	-4,021	16,339,448	5,358,327	2,584,425	27,486	883,443	553,469
1997	25,101,536	18,850,953	66,597	18,917,550	2,085,664	-7,107	16,824,779	5,663,439	2,613,318	28,309	886,711	550,825
1998	25,542,879	19,029,970	71,789	19,101,759	2,108,546	-9,105	16,984,108	5,916,755	2,642,016	28,800	886,909	551,211
1999	26,270,596	19,589,857	90,061	19,679,918	2,144,039	-9,383	17,526,496	5,998,856	2,745,244	29,890	878,906	546,376
2000	27,698,372	20,687,415	83,373	20,770,788	2,249,280	-11,563	18,509,945	6,270,775	2,917,652	31,596	876,629	552,871
2001	28,738,100	21,777,581	78,931	21,856,512	2,372,021	-12,269	19,472,222	6,112,101	3,153,777	32,555	882,755	549,294
2002	29,937,496	23,083,897	86,994	23,170,891	2,516,001	-12,346	20,642,544	5,901,328	3,393,624	33,620	890,473	551,443
2003	31,215,818	24,445,346	89,094	24,534,440	2,697,166	-12,801	21,824,473	5,898,267	3,493,078	34,905	894,311	561,524
2004	33,424,009	26,090,365	74,935	26,165,300	2,829,704	-13,432	23,322,164	6,397,813	3,704,032	36,811	907,997	575,830
2005	35,767,141	27,819,048	68,103	27,887,151	3,010,547	-11,568	24,865,036	6,902,497	3,999,608	38,954	918,181	587,533
2006	38,301,624	29,390,591	66,117	29,456,708	3,240,728	-10,527	26,205,453	7,874,939	4,221,232	41,320	926,954	602,446
2007	40,245,095	30,387,458	66,030	30,453,488	3,382,606	-8,539	27,062,343	8,568,112	4,614,640	43,492	925,335	614,645
2008	42,190,859	31,183,638	91,736	31,275,374	3,467,235	-8,651	27,799,488	9,044,585	5,346,786	45,188	933,680	613,203
2009	42,616,645	31,146,190	112,727	31,258,917	3,473,792	-16,761	27,768,364	9,194,406	5,653,875	45,184	943,177	598,479
2010	43,342,396	31,895,061	108,012	32,003,073	3,659,540	-21,646	28,321,887	8,709,015	6,311,494	45,328	956,193	595,786
2011	45,446,147	33,113,013	111,154	33,224,167	3,485,142	-30,546	29,708,479	9,187,646	6,550,022	47,021	966,514	603,599
2012	47,163,235	34,584,969	111,358	34,696,327	3,603,904	-35,922	31,056,501	9,638,454	6,468,280	48,308	976,299	613,464
2013	47,883,947	35,639,933	103,138	35,743,071	4,195,207	-42,063	31,505,801	9,680,301	6,697,845	48,577	985,734	625,440
2014	50,398,758	36,991,207	89,191	37,080,398	4,230,150	-45,075	32,805,173	10,462,654	7,130,931	50,937	989,438	634,736
2015	52,693,399	38,709,838	90,225	38,800,063	4,412,351	-47,736	34,339,976	10,981,232	7,372,191	53,027	993,716	648,083
2016	54,329,238	39,681,418	82,843	39,764,261	4,497,523	-50,161	35,216,577	11,474,321	7,638,340	54,725	992,761	655,906
2017	56,083,760	40,844,195	84,020	40,928,215	4,639,953	-51,152	36,237,110	11,920,449	7,926,201	56,728	988,650	659,070
2018	58,129,300	58,063,916	65,384	42,628,005	4,829,085	-50,599	37,748,321	12,236,812	8,144,167	59,324	979,858	661,292
2019	59,617,709	59,550,718	66,991	43,770,194	4,986,561	-48,877	38,734,756	12,400,022	8,482,931	61,174	974,563	659,310

Personal Income and Employment by Area: Utica-Rome, NY

(Thousands of dollars, except as noted.)

Year	Personal income, total	Earnings by place of work			Less: Contributions for government social insurance	Plus: Adjustment for residence	Equals: Net earnings by place of residence	Plus: Dividends, interest, and rent	Plus: Personal current transfer receipts	Per capita personal income (dollars)	Population (persons)	Total employment
		Nonfarm	Farm	Total								
1970	1,324,477	1,060,561	20,517	1,081,078	77,266	-17,388	986,424	197,977	140,076	3,880	341,324	144,349
1971	1,413,713	1,110,302	20,540	1,130,842	83,159	-14,307	1,033,376	212,658	167,679	4,110	343,966	142,378
1972	1,494,219	1,165,518	19,851	1,185,369	91,493	-11,875	1,082,001	226,384	185,834	4,340	344,262	140,209
1973	1,617,724	1,262,975	22,213	1,285,188	113,937	-10,573	1,160,678	250,631	206,415	4,775	338,821	143,694
1974	1,736,217	1,333,690	18,273	1,351,963	124,340	-7,833	1,219,790	279,230	237,197	5,185	334,835	143,415
1975	1,880,517	1,387,031	14,400	1,401,431	127,841	-6,472	1,267,118	304,745	308,654	5,645	333,120	138,881
1976	1,992,681	1,471,966	16,023	1,487,989	138,815	-4,516	1,344,658	322,204	325,819	6,040	329,897	137,590
1977	2,119,146	1,562,799	10,130	1,572,929	147,764	-832	1,424,333	353,200	341,613	6,482	326,942	137,404
1978	2,301,630	1,719,066	14,066	1,733,132	166,510	797	1,567,419	377,472	356,739	7,070	325,540	141,015
1979	2,512,461	1,869,017	18,552	1,887,569	187,576	4,447	1,704,440	421,200	386,821	7,762	323,689	143,203
1980	2,801,291	2,016,424	18,482	2,034,906	201,409	7,642	1,841,139	510,294	449,858	8,748	320,223	142,202
1981	3,102,660	2,182,220	18,208	2,200,428	230,838	9,522	1,979,112	610,678	512,870	9,702	319,790	141,590
1982	3,377,079	2,310,389	18,059	2,328,448	243,903	9,457	2,094,002	703,139	579,938	10,560	319,788	140,336
1983	3,571,056	2,435,840	14,724	2,450,564	259,401	11,393	2,202,556	740,821	627,679	11,147	320,361	139,924
1984	3,927,276	2,705,873	19,088	2,724,961	294,788	8,611	2,438,784	835,714	652,778	12,269	320,097	144,968
1985	4,122,627	2,841,386	24,378	2,865,764	315,513	10,654	2,560,905	871,251	690,471	12,909	319,368	145,991
1986	4,318,788	2,983,477	29,378	3,012,855	336,839	9,648	2,685,664	905,821	727,303	13,626	316,950	148,023
1987	4,507,390	3,158,965	32,302	3,191,267	351,925	8,327	2,847,669	919,382	740,339	14,254	316,211	147,894
1988	4,789,374	3,419,559	25,449	3,445,008	389,858	5,051	3,060,201	942,428	786,745	15,188	315,341	152,786
1989	5,154,461	3,587,671	34,895	3,622,566	407,575	3,896	3,218,887	1,096,372	839,202	16,307	316,088	154,516
1990	5,437,480	3,799,410	35,831	3,835,241	414,060	1,375	3,422,556	1,110,793	904,131	17,149	317,074	156,491
1991	5,559,245	3,854,658	25,501	3,880,159	431,328	7,682	3,456,513	1,111,645	991,087	17,405	319,408	153,350
1992	5,888,314	4,080,340	32,105	4,112,445	449,332	6,365	3,669,478	1,107,459	1,111,377	18,377	320,421	154,175
1993	6,037,983	4,174,443	31,784	4,206,227	464,490	8,887	3,750,624	1,128,287	1,159,072	18,892	319,608	154,382
1994	6,177,547	4,263,976	31,234	4,295,210	481,799	9,837	3,823,248	1,132,104	1,222,195	19,426	318,002	156,706
1995	6,272,749	4,271,405	22,195	4,293,600	486,686	17,729	3,824,643	1,164,304	1,283,802	20,141	311,447	154,290
1996	6,332,442	4,270,347	37,531	4,307,878	480,426	22,893	3,850,345	1,172,302	1,309,795	20,715	305,700	151,768
1997	6,560,324	4,455,754	15,591	4,471,345	494,000	22,983	4,000,328	1,230,563	1,329,433	21,674	302,681	151,824
1998	6,836,628	4,609,564	35,382	4,644,946	504,636	24,773	4,165,083	1,236,379	1,435,166	22,742	300,619	153,524
1999	7,155,479	4,961,830	40,618	5,002,448	526,643	26,403	4,502,208	1,214,414	1,438,857	23,862	299,874	157,955
2000	7,486,127	5,229,804	36,211	5,266,015	553,834	22,753	4,734,934	1,260,526	1,490,667	24,987	299,597	160,777
2001	7,568,363	5,181,478	60,450	5,241,928	574,142	27,091	4,694,877	1,274,563	1,598,923	25,353	298,521	157,591
2002	7,599,553	5,301,858	44,187	5,346,045	594,568	34,837	4,786,314	1,114,047	1,699,192	25,498	298,049	156,713
2003	7,849,607	5,479,401	50,923	5,530,324	614,890	34,142	4,949,576	1,117,442	1,782,589	26,312	298,323	156,381
2004	8,271,175	5,732,006	61,603	5,793,609	644,365	37,720	5,186,964	1,192,674	1,891,537	27,664	298,986	157,189
2005	8,510,021	5,890,978	61,196	5,952,174	671,239	40,356	5,321,291	1,223,226	1,965,504	28,502	298,574	157,620
2006	8,934,777	6,287,598	47,669	6,335,267	713,591	39,707	5,661,383	1,210,348	2,063,046	29,957	298,258	158,777
2007	9,490,927	6,659,855	44,951	6,704,806	743,320	37,537	5,999,023	1,342,435	2,149,469	31,760	298,831	160,027
2008	9,964,012	6,756,696	47,540	6,804,236	765,360	39,089	6,077,965	1,489,486	2,396,561	33,337	298,886	160,584
2009	10,223,109	6,852,029	23,748	6,875,777	764,934	52,528	6,163,371	1,436,875	2,622,863	34,191	299,000	157,597
2010	10,611,359	7,059,473	45,434	7,104,907	777,724	75,644	6,402,827	1,410,526	2,798,006	35,459	299,257	156,996
2011	10,904,296	7,055,767	64,379	7,120,146	707,828	100,629	6,512,947	1,543,271	2,848,078	36,503	298,724	155,898
2012	11,187,909	7,157,658	58,249	7,215,907	711,773	128,465	6,632,599	1,707,136	2,848,174	37,517	298,207	154,968
2013	11,293,586	7,311,974	71,531	7,383,505	817,136	155,448	6,721,817	1,688,718	2,883,051	37,940	297,672	154,541
2014	11,363,924	7,222,450	76,037	7,298,487	825,727	171,143	6,643,903	1,783,508	2,936,513	38,309	296,636	154,516
2015	11,640,477	7,352,182	34,689	7,386,871	849,347	177,299	6,714,823	1,853,617	3,072,037	39,499	294,702	154,410
2016	11,856,191	7,506,469	31,752	7,538,221	872,790	172,603	6,838,034	1,891,176	3,126,981	40,361	293,752	155,453
2017	12,502,664	7,816,669	35,972	7,852,641	909,319	180,310	7,123,632	1,986,814	3,392,218	42,588	293,572	156,713
2018	12,807,674	12,775,519	32,155	8,200,669	928,465	193,746	7,465,950	2,091,522	3,250,202	43,984	291,187	156,415
2019	13,383,291	13,335,080	48,211	8,522,558	958,106	199,041	7,763,493	2,140,983	3,478,815	46,151	289,990	157,652

Personal Income and Employment by Area: Valdosta, GA

(Thousands of dollars, except as noted.)

Year	Personal income, total	Earnings by place of work			Less: Contributions for government social insurance	Plus: Adjustment for residence	Equals: Net earnings by place of residence	Plus: Dividends, interest, and rent	Plus: Personal current transfer receipts	Per capita personal income (dollars)	Population (persons)	Total employment
		Nonfarm	Farm	Total								
1970	245,043	179,555	19,547	199,102	11,387	-1,267	186,448	35,476	23,119	3,210	76,347	33,764
1971	271,673	197,873	21,745	219,618	13,112	-1,302	205,204	38,712	27,757	3,427	79,276	34,576
1972	304,782	223,945	23,089	247,034	15,309	-1,041	230,684	43,079	31,019	3,710	82,156	35,735
1973	336,050	244,220	27,018	271,238	18,758	-545	251,935	49,130	34,985	4,008	83,842	36,556
1974	374,522	263,142	32,732	295,874	21,127	-196	274,551	55,542	44,429	4,385	85,407	36,861
1975	389,535	267,730	25,892	293,622	21,582	711	272,751	61,894	54,890	4,555	85,511	35,575
1976	435,959	310,168	22,508	332,676	25,533	688	307,831	68,346	59,782	5,013	86,971	37,112
1977	464,895	345,112	6,920	352,032	28,215	1,545	325,362	76,658	62,875	5,242	88,679	38,149
1978	544,037	396,919	19,856	416,775	32,940	1,966	385,801	89,972	68,264	6,147	88,498	39,447
1979	600,913	440,089	16,711	456,800	38,008	2,005	420,797	101,181	78,935	6,641	90,486	40,040
1980	643,914	463,966	7,118	471,084	40,379	2,458	433,163	116,892	93,859	7,045	91,402	39,351
1981	731,592	510,249	16,829	527,078	47,574	1,699	481,203	139,466	110,923	7,941	92,131	40,149
1982	802,259	547,477	28,295	575,772	51,781	384	524,375	161,254	116,630	8,643	92,821	40,795
1983	853,320	594,023	15,095	609,118	56,949	1,019	553,188	173,641	126,491	9,051	94,274	42,007
1984	949,258	657,591	25,259	682,850	64,715	2,242	620,377	190,783	138,098	9,942	95,477	43,709
1985	1,019,389	711,373	25,615	736,988	71,622	1,608	666,974	203,746	148,669	10,604	96,133	44,826
1986	1,066,549	752,303	19,569	771,872	77,044	2,038	696,866	210,992	158,691	10,989	97,055	45,440
1987	1,150,168	799,885	32,496	832,381	81,333	4,833	755,881	224,802	169,485	11,753	97,863	46,586
1988	1,245,473	873,399	36,353	909,752	92,507	4,044	821,289	242,543	181,641	12,743	97,741	48,109
1989	1,358,741	945,522	37,295	982,817	100,863	-1,799	880,155	276,849	201,737	13,790	98,530	49,838
1990	1,428,007	989,328	37,252	1,026,580	106,271	-3,936	916,373	288,327	223,307	14,323	99,699	50,334
1991	1,517,159	1,039,801	45,082	1,084,883	113,106	-7,760	964,017	298,024	255,118	14,977	101,299	50,477
1992	1,627,552	1,118,863	48,259	1,167,122	120,951	-8,310	1,037,861	308,317	281,374	15,813	102,922	51,055
1993	1,722,639	1,187,933	40,102	1,228,035	129,100	-9,363	1,089,572	334,998	298,069	16,118	106,877	53,803
1994	1,847,255	1,260,115	52,868	1,312,983	137,631	-8,475	1,166,877	359,738	320,640	16,906	109,267	54,857
1995	2,011,392	1,368,451	59,701	1,428,152	147,906	-8,883	1,271,363	398,741	341,288	18,059	111,381	57,874
1996	2,121,489	1,454,549	49,757	1,504,306	155,630	-9,563	1,339,113	425,557	356,819	18,689	113,514	59,607
1997	2,249,466	1,553,060	49,694	1,602,754	164,051	-11,524	1,427,179	456,605	365,682	19,492	115,406	60,998
1998	2,384,880	1,678,265	37,090	1,715,355	174,843	-13,551	1,526,961	479,131	378,788	20,402	116,892	62,374
1999	2,492,252	1,749,804	55,911	1,805,715	180,918	-12,963	1,611,834	474,706	405,712	21,019	118,574	63,144
2000	2,611,699	1,797,444	57,645	1,855,089	185,144	-14,860	1,655,085	521,651	434,963	21,813	119,729	63,736
2001	2,727,826	1,875,355	56,674	1,932,029	193,453	-20,987	1,717,589	540,209	470,028	22,782	119,736	64,125
2002	2,876,107	2,022,883	46,236	2,069,119	208,548	-34,549	1,826,022	517,333	532,752	23,710	121,305	65,780
2003	3,007,188	2,145,532	68,824	2,214,356	218,162	-42,184	1,954,010	520,827	532,351	24,679	121,850	66,974
2004	3,142,214	2,245,924	55,199	2,301,123	236,633	-42,822	2,021,668	542,847	577,699	25,262	124,387	69,016
2005	3,331,717	2,384,000	65,752	2,449,752	249,001	-48,357	2,152,394	558,269	621,054	26,356	126,411	70,739
2006	3,448,743	2,465,930	51,475	2,517,405	264,660	-54,560	2,198,185	585,225	665,333	26,668	129,323	72,165
2007	3,629,090	2,546,257	50,508	2,596,765	270,835	-68,244	2,257,686	658,830	712,574	27,695	131,036	74,153
2008	3,820,636	2,639,300	59,686	2,698,986	297,767	-78,942	2,322,277	693,909	804,450	28,321	134,907	74,899
2009	3,898,117	2,617,913	55,100	2,673,013	295,647	-93,581	2,283,785	730,238	884,094	28,292	137,780	72,871
2010	4,058,515	2,684,231	35,797	2,720,028	300,785	-89,221	2,330,022	761,196	967,297	28,977	140,062	72,144
2011	4,284,774	2,692,936	63,904	2,756,840	271,005	-88,179	2,397,656	870,569	1,016,549	30,162	142,058	70,953
2012	4,288,115	2,800,056	49,517	2,849,573	282,378	-99,688	2,467,507	814,792	1,005,816	29,738	144,195	72,151
2013	4,358,610	2,921,489	52,474	2,973,963	321,608	-97,470	2,554,885	773,236	1,030,489	30,479	143,003	73,395
2014	4,544,161	3,048,012	28,519	3,076,531	333,956	-102,337	2,640,238	821,154	1,082,769	31,657	143,545	74,793
2015	4,719,390	3,126,431	39,176	3,165,607	342,259	-100,817	2,722,531	877,744	1,119,115	32,904	143,428	75,972
2016	4,862,501	3,191,001	35,055	3,226,056	349,677	-105,869	2,770,510	935,218	1,156,773	33,666	144,434	76,554
2017	5,052,383	3,339,765	20,642	3,360,407	367,870	-109,150	2,883,387	969,745	1,199,251	34,739	145,437	76,742
2018	5,325,097	5,297,690	27,407	3,554,174	385,771	-111,814	3,056,589	1,021,396	1,247,112	36,438	146,143	78,376
2019	5,541,534	5,494,777	46,757	3,710,129	401,564	-116,970	3,191,595	1,042,078	1,307,861	37,623	147,292	79,451

Personal Income and Employment by Area: Vallejo, CA

(Thousands of dollars, except as noted.)

Year	Personal income, total	Derivation of personal income								Per capita personal income (dollars)	Population (persons)	Total employment
		Earnings by place of work			Less: Contributions for government social insurance	Plus: Adjustment for residence	Equals: Net earnings by place of residence	Plus: Dividends, interest, and rent	Plus: Personal current transfer receipts			
		Nonfarm	Farm	Total								
1970	786,126	668,126	24,217	692,343	33,888	-113,252	545,203	173,084	67,839	4,538	173,238	77,595
1971	873,836	725,687	25,921	751,608	39,139	-108,009	604,460	191,340	78,036	4,896	178,481	77,695
1972	959,760	763,445	32,944	796,389	43,222	-84,029	669,138	206,576	84,046	5,295	181,259	76,710
1973	1,061,626	809,775	44,398	854,173	50,016	-64,012	740,145	227,516	93,965	5,794	183,223	77,022
1974	1,215,018	900,535	62,197	962,732	56,781	-57,824	848,127	254,051	112,840	6,482	187,439	80,026
1975	1,381,732	1,031,723	47,257	1,078,980	66,472	-60,827	951,681	290,793	139,258	7,214	191,535	83,585
1976	1,522,717	1,131,899	34,330	1,166,229	74,662	-40,221	1,051,346	314,590	156,781	7,692	197,971	85,184
1977	1,709,435	1,249,162	38,937	1,288,099	83,672	-13,849	1,190,578	346,660	172,197	8,350	204,713	87,746
1978	1,964,146	1,419,020	36,523	1,455,543	96,036	10,729	1,370,236	403,397	190,513	9,195	213,619	91,583
1979	2,210,169	1,530,739	41,130	1,571,869	111,544	82,226	1,542,551	449,014	218,604	9,847	224,455	94,584
1980	2,529,292	1,610,260	77,487	1,687,747	118,844	184,347	1,753,250	515,975	260,067	10,652	237,456	98,216
1981	2,844,830	1,796,582	41,290	1,837,872	142,319	234,035	1,929,588	605,745	309,497	11,564	246,003	100,008
1982	3,126,582	1,971,178	25,536	1,996,714	157,831	278,444	2,117,327	671,555	337,700	12,293	254,348	101,168
1983	3,450,873	2,176,364	21,415	2,197,779	184,630	331,938	2,345,087	747,452	358,334	13,253	260,386	103,847
1984	3,832,150	2,377,463	37,790	2,415,253	210,800	437,176	2,641,629	813,795	376,726	14,493	264,416	107,070
1985	4,257,748	2,630,390	42,855	2,673,245	241,095	524,413	2,956,563	884,982	416,203	15,675	271,634	111,397
1986	4,653,790	2,831,161	34,113	2,865,274	267,820	666,890	3,264,344	934,929	454,517	16,409	283,617	115,639
1987	5,037,305	3,009,140	50,884	3,060,024	288,555	817,772	3,589,241	966,941	481,123	16,970	296,835	119,521
1988	5,505,874	3,248,685	53,296	3,301,981	326,793	948,077	3,923,265	1,054,540	528,069	17,758	310,048	125,976
1989	6,104,537	3,518,273	67,131	3,585,404	361,330	1,098,706	4,322,780	1,196,235	585,522	18,721	326,074	131,381
1990	6,823,378	3,796,702	48,216	3,844,918	394,409	1,486,615	4,937,124	1,233,058	653,196	19,866	343,463	136,860
1991	7,095,025	3,888,819	49,734	3,938,553	412,107	1,591,718	5,118,164	1,243,500	733,361	20,037	354,104	137,031
1992	7,490,595	4,184,805	41,478	4,226,283	444,779	1,593,732	5,375,236	1,270,735	844,624	20,812	359,919	137,870
1993	7,767,482	4,338,413	44,964	4,383,377	463,885	1,638,898	5,558,390	1,329,583	879,509	21,325	364,251	139,183
1994	7,796,480	4,153,291	52,911	4,206,202	456,410	1,785,206	5,534,998	1,369,938	891,544	21,298	366,072	141,061
1995	8,006,341	4,156,411	29,342	4,185,753	450,192	1,872,123	5,607,684	1,456,622	942,035	21,911	365,395	139,996
1996	8,331,433	4,246,464	55,611	4,302,075	449,134	1,946,414	5,799,355	1,538,722	993,356	22,664	367,608	141,128
1997	8,865,485	4,483,694	36,132	4,519,826	468,093	2,207,501	6,259,234	1,603,740	1,002,511	23,840	371,881	143,144
1998	9,500,864	4,810,758	34,332	4,845,090	497,230	2,388,106	6,735,966	1,702,434	1,062,464	25,091	378,657	146,801
1999	10,169,242	5,231,496	46,471	5,277,967	539,582	2,546,205	7,284,590	1,737,121	1,147,531	26,233	387,657	152,966
2000	11,273,476	5,902,411	39,735	5,942,146	606,221	2,909,957	8,245,882	1,833,933	1,193,661	28,399	396,974	157,624
2001	12,246,147	6,711,916	47,541	6,759,457	703,326	2,946,240	9,002,371	1,927,942	1,315,834	30,297	404,209	167,983
2002	12,662,488	7,119,584	62,980	7,182,564	754,627	2,888,712	9,316,649	1,918,389	1,427,450	31,018	408,226	172,005
2003	13,164,373	7,530,859	63,175	7,594,034	815,167	2,814,281	9,593,148	2,041,162	1,530,063	32,233	408,409	175,902
2004	13,590,435	7,844,205	66,354	7,910,559	888,104	2,877,648	9,900,103	2,073,292	1,617,040	33,204	409,301	177,452
2005	14,012,653	8,119,323	80,958	8,200,281	928,905	2,876,256	10,147,632	2,128,729	1,736,292	34,330	408,181	179,244
2006	14,778,389	8,502,068	75,934	8,578,002	943,717	3,011,150	10,645,435	2,224,109	1,908,845	36,186	408,402	180,477
2007	15,385,245	8,772,392	95,848	8,868,240	944,328	3,031,131	10,955,043	2,399,737	2,030,465	37,686	408,243	181,321
2008	15,631,492	9,022,686	121,814	9,144,500	981,201	2,602,330	10,765,629	2,541,247	2,324,616	38,221	408,972	178,995
2009	15,395,664	9,194,619	101,658	9,296,277	1,000,538	2,096,316	10,392,055	2,405,184	2,598,425	37,524	410,290	174,328
2010	15,613,019	9,372,251	83,292	9,455,543	1,001,891	1,866,020	10,319,672	2,385,100	2,908,247	37,706	414,076	172,004
2011	16,252,685	9,491,520	99,182	9,590,702	925,721	2,027,027	10,692,008	2,620,019	2,940,658	39,008	416,652	169,810
2012	16,606,340	9,840,213	138,191	9,978,404	953,511	1,880,854	10,905,747	2,742,800	2,957,793	39,514	420,267	173,409
2013	17,346,253	10,309,744	135,067	10,444,811	1,109,833	1,985,941	11,320,919	2,905,962	3,119,372	40,874	424,384	178,391
2014	18,268,830	10,710,133	156,055	10,866,188	1,158,768	1,988,286	11,695,706	3,249,752	3,323,372	42,486	429,993	182,211
2015	19,554,495	11,183,718	164,768	11,348,486	1,217,978	2,390,804	12,521,312	3,429,155	3,604,028	44,979	434,751	188,007
2016	20,559,862	11,737,741	116,103	11,853,844	1,279,092	2,637,135	13,211,887	3,606,453	3,741,522	46,693	440,318	194,390
2017	21,879,096	12,308,913	143,672	12,452,585	1,339,829	3,252,319	14,365,075	3,775,746	3,738,275	49,116	445,458	197,480
2018	22,623,154	22,499,308	123,846	13,181,243	1,438,526	2,826,903	14,569,620	3,984,051	4,069,483	50,756	445,725	203,893
2019	23,951,255	23,814,323	136,932	13,935,887	1,525,781	3,117,222	15,527,328	4,065,708	4,358,219	53,505	447,643	207,214

Personal Income and Employment by Area: Victoria, TX

(Thousands of dollars, except as noted.)

		Earnings by place of work			Derivation of personal income							
Year	Personal income, total	Nonfarm	Farm	Total	Less: Contributions for government social insurance	Plus: Adjustment for residence	Equals: Net earnings by place of residence	Plus: Dividends, interest, and rent	Plus: Personal current transfer receipts	Per capita personal income (dollars)	Population (persons)	Total employment
1970	192,895	137,332	5,536	142,868	8,455	14,345	148,758	29,456	14,681	3,286	58,707	22,879
1971	212,966	154,479	2,694	157,173	9,867	15,898	163,204	32,801	16,961	3,570	59,656	24,144
1972	244,654	178,442	6,459	184,901	12,060	16,009	188,850	36,717	19,087	4,075	60,041	25,600
1973	272,284	193,907	10,068	203,975	15,270	18,287	206,992	41,829	23,463	4,422	61,570	26,406
1974	317,507	225,297	8,577	233,874	18,457	23,422	238,839	49,890	28,778	5,088	62,400	27,270
1975	370,669	264,375	6,762	271,137	21,345	27,103	276,895	57,988	35,786	5,789	64,032	28,572
1976	420,630	307,943	3,980	311,923	24,951	31,407	318,379	63,089	39,162	6,429	65,422	30,041
1977	469,067	347,441	-664	346,777	28,383	36,532	354,926	71,154	42,987	7,040	66,629	31,787
1978	549,409	414,129	-118	414,011	34,835	40,646	419,822	81,190	48,397	7,976	68,884	34,333
1979	643,009	471,868	10,476	482,344	41,645	53,094	493,793	93,851	55,365	8,966	71,718	35,474
1980	745,451	551,285	-5,627	545,658	49,406	61,193	557,445	121,439	66,567	9,993	74,599	37,678
1981	912,962	690,581	4,127	694,708	66,595	47,037	675,150	161,016	76,796	11,891	76,778	42,135
1982	1,002,672	731,251	-1,881	729,370	72,563	51,840	708,647	206,501	87,524	12,578	79,719	42,578
1983	1,007,915	702,531	-1,652	700,879	68,468	56,873	689,284	219,193	99,438	12,457	80,912	40,499
1984	1,082,268	749,603	-1,332	748,271	75,429	54,728	727,570	251,854	102,844	13,313	81,297	41,815
1985	1,135,975	772,260	-3,108	769,152	79,155	60,693	750,690	276,394	108,891	13,905	81,693	42,553
1986	1,115,631	725,579	-1,442	724,137	73,158	67,330	718,309	274,277	123,045	13,547	82,351	40,072
1987	1,111,571	711,764	1,204	712,968	70,983	67,750	709,735	270,834	131,002	13,704	81,112	40,743
1988	1,150,373	740,005	-1,215	738,790	76,486	70,353	732,657	280,567	137,149	14,349	80,171	40,664
1989	1,239,786	773,116	999	774,115	80,873	81,445	774,687	313,124	151,975	15,581	79,568	40,838
1990	1,355,036	838,447	3,144	841,591	85,927	93,017	848,681	341,307	165,048	16,820	80,560	41,598
1991	1,433,791	907,566	8,144	915,710	95,634	87,571	907,647	339,140	187,004	17,530	81,791	43,505
1992	1,539,494	954,385	5,790	960,175	99,325	105,461	966,311	353,943	219,240	18,480	83,304	43,216
1993	1,615,431	996,377	5,748	1,002,125	103,446	112,899	1,011,578	372,156	231,697	19,092	84,614	44,707
1994	1,667,090	1,062,588	11,512	1,074,100	111,089	116,730	1,079,741	335,675	251,674	19,408	85,899	45,882
1995	1,779,911	1,104,289	8,849	1,113,138	115,541	133,223	1,130,820	375,796	273,295	20,505	86,805	46,454
1996	1,890,636	1,176,643	-8,717	1,167,926	121,381	154,777	1,201,322	397,654	291,660	21,511	87,891	47,280
1997	1,974,213	1,252,358	1,174	1,253,532	128,314	131,455	1,256,673	413,549	303,991	22,276	88,626	48,767
1998	2,141,106	1,382,813	-8,938	1,373,875	138,921	146,342	1,381,296	453,023	306,787	23,789	90,004	49,732
1999	2,206,811	1,411,915	13,270	1,425,185	141,770	150,462	1,433,877	449,396	323,538	24,311	90,775	49,907
2000	2,395,198	1,574,579	5,872	1,580,451	154,011	161,108	1,587,548	468,361	339,289	26,337	90,944	51,226
2001	2,556,160	1,732,070	2,103	1,734,173	166,877	142,688	1,709,984	476,567	369,609	27,933	91,511	51,590
2002	2,564,830	1,771,258	2,608	1,773,866	170,843	122,319	1,725,342	440,707	398,781	27,993	91,624	51,457
2003	2,598,550	1,750,288	18,731	1,769,019	173,945	107,226	1,702,300	466,879	429,371	28,304	91,809	50,721
2004	2,683,564	1,829,171	19,751	1,848,922	182,530	97,744	1,764,136	468,684	450,744	29,236	91,789	50,878
2005	2,894,579	2,000,031	17,218	2,017,249	196,313	94,629	1,915,565	490,293	488,721	31,627	91,523	52,340
2006	3,147,646	2,254,366	13,683	2,268,049	212,540	66,821	2,122,330	505,082	520,234	34,345	91,649	54,220
2007	3,246,670	2,247,186	3,987	2,251,173	220,032	69,331	2,100,472	576,291	569,907	35,136	92,403	55,480
2008	3,521,361	2,485,517	-22,189	2,463,328	233,430	50,983	2,280,881	611,314	629,166	37,894	92,926	56,275
2009	3,211,054	2,191,291	-23,791	2,167,500	220,328	46,733	1,993,905	530,918	686,231	34,236	93,792	53,860
2010	3,422,674	2,359,256	-13,670	2,345,586	233,812	52,052	2,163,826	515,927	742,921	36,372	94,102	53,878
2011	3,688,731	2,530,737	-16,194	2,514,543	220,913	44,399	2,338,029	578,051	772,651	38,936	94,738	54,885
2012	4,042,566	2,799,571	-13,570	2,786,001	240,611	2,528	2,547,918	728,087	766,561	41,936	96,399	57,444
2013	4,215,360	3,002,734	-2,216	3,000,518	289,604	-23,891	2,687,023	742,439	785,898	43,230	97,509	59,164
2014	4,517,556	3,135,792	-5,744	3,130,048	301,241	-21,958	2,806,849	875,359	835,348	45,867	98,492	59,740
2015	4,448,896	2,949,027	-4,890	2,944,137	297,017	23,281	2,670,401	892,425	886,070	44,671	99,592	59,835
2016	4,194,194	2,637,195	-9,753	2,627,442	278,543	73,031	2,421,930	830,474	941,790	41,984	99,900	57,365
2017	4,221,351	2,609,438	-8,407	2,601,031	283,448	73,650	2,391,233	862,776	967,342	42,363	99,646	56,957
2018	4,649,847	4,658,133	-8,286	2,790,107	298,353	110,846	2,602,600	1,039,077	1,008,170	46,748	99,466	58,366
2019	4,855,536	4,860,090	-4,554	2,871,206	303,584	189,764	2,757,386	1,054,159	1,043,991	48,681	99,742	58,527

Personal Income and Employment by Area: Vineland-Bridgeton, NJ

(Thousands of dollars, except as noted.)

Year	Personal income, total	Earnings by place of work			Less: Contributions for government social insurance	Plus: Adjustment for residence	Equals: Net earnings by place of residence	Plus: Dividends, interest, and rent	Plus: Personal current transfer receipts	Per capita personal income (dollars)	Population (persons)	Total employment
		Nonfarm	Farm	Total								
1970	484,498	403,917	13,534	417,451	32,316	-7,091	378,044	54,022	52,432	3,961	122,309	58,153
1971	525,214	436,580	11,888	448,468	36,077	-9,770	402,621	59,956	62,637	4,143	126,773	58,260
1972	577,162	483,794	11,364	495,158	41,580	-15,010	438,568	66,635	71,959	4,473	129,031	60,730
1973	639,905	539,214	15,511	554,725	52,807	-19,435	482,483	76,995	80,427	4,894	130,746	62,667
1974	693,446	569,549	16,967	586,516	58,025	-22,032	506,459	87,503	99,484	5,202	133,306	61,865
1975	741,572	588,557	12,184	600,741	57,976	-27,571	515,194	93,345	133,033	5,520	134,350	58,858
1976	814,288	656,021	13,483	669,504	65,587	-34,083	569,834	100,486	143,968	6,016	135,359	60,950
1977	883,666	721,598	10,309	731,907	72,390	-37,815	621,702	111,782	150,182	6,537	135,184	61,741
1978	974,644	797,603	16,199	813,802	82,460	-37,034	694,308	120,413	159,923	7,240	134,615	62,802
1979	1,053,511	859,076	14,331	873,407	91,655	-39,914	741,838	132,006	179,667	7,864	133,966	63,029
1980	1,159,936	930,866	10,718	941,584	99,041	-48,923	793,620	161,323	204,993	8,716	133,088	64,876
1981	1,286,517	987,809	15,914	1,003,723	112,078	-40,414	851,231	197,953	237,333	9,621	133,726	63,534
1982	1,388,387	1,018,669	18,554	1,037,223	115,731	-21,940	899,552	226,777	262,058	10,400	133,494	61,162
1983	1,482,063	1,067,533	21,825	1,089,358	124,197	-13,436	951,725	247,902	282,436	11,186	132,497	61,559
1984	1,591,639	1,127,441	20,777	1,148,218	136,595	4,636	1,016,259	275,117	300,263	11,866	134,138	60,966
1985	1,692,975	1,196,725	22,782	1,219,507	144,627	17,146	1,092,026	291,934	309,015	12,533	135,083	61,704
1986	1,809,164	1,314,468	23,603	1,338,071	160,475	-4,859	1,172,737	312,042	324,385	13,332	135,700	63,622
1987	1,929,349	1,436,793	26,414	1,463,207	174,087	-19,104	1,270,016	324,086	335,247	14,187	135,995	65,766
1988	2,108,069	1,580,646	29,398	1,610,044	195,349	-14,684	1,400,011	348,696	359,362	15,436	136,569	67,638
1989	2,310,681	1,684,014	30,139	1,714,153	205,544	-15,063	1,493,546	425,260	391,875	16,759	137,881	68,023
1990	2,471,644	1,766,771	32,104	1,798,875	208,842	5,960	1,595,993	443,790	431,861	17,863	138,366	68,415
1991	2,554,847	1,799,297	33,009	1,832,306	217,177	-8,213	1,606,916	447,010	500,921	18,184	140,503	66,700
1992	2,740,973	1,902,369	38,743	1,941,112	227,537	2,177	1,715,752	438,789	586,432	19,313	141,921	67,268
1993	2,817,022	1,948,757	45,932	1,994,689	232,762	9,289	1,771,216	444,673	601,133	19,654	143,334	65,632
1994	2,879,171	2,035,465	50,870	2,086,335	245,727	-3,880	1,836,728	445,873	596,570	19,919	144,544	66,357
1995	2,961,425	2,121,108	49,193	2,170,301	255,416	-59,915	1,854,970	481,087	625,368	20,448	144,829	67,555
1996	3,036,571	2,194,100	49,380	2,243,480	263,686	-75,045	1,904,749	496,901	634,921	20,880	145,430	68,018
1997	3,193,119	2,321,683	44,188	2,365,871	272,780	-70,490	2,022,601	528,136	642,382	21,899	145,811	68,540
1998	3,267,940	2,397,366	50,612	2,447,978	278,371	-81,618	2,087,989	541,908	638,043	22,395	145,924	68,962
1999	3,359,214	2,459,441	34,542	2,493,983	281,849	-46,881	2,165,253	531,109	662,852	22,962	146,293	69,065
2000	3,490,376	2,565,271	52,183	2,617,454	296,482	-72,413	2,248,559	548,353	693,464	23,864	146,263	70,953
2001	3,707,414	2,709,981	43,670	2,753,651	312,103	-65,386	2,376,162	567,960	763,292	25,315	146,451	71,167
2002	3,914,410	2,821,686	47,260	2,868,946	321,545	-78,563	2,468,838	576,803	868,769	26,575	147,294	71,224
2003	4,051,368	2,978,433	48,499	3,026,932	334,284	-107,824	2,584,824	606,040	860,504	27,294	148,437	72,417
2004	4,170,697	3,174,412	51,559	3,225,971	360,163	-135,988	2,729,820	594,172	846,705	27,835	149,837	74,740
2005	4,319,296	3,313,415	52,581	3,365,996	384,995	-157,448	2,823,553	561,996	933,747	28,412	152,022	77,027
2006	4,542,673	3,401,093	70,129	3,471,222	395,545	-109,403	2,966,274	555,205	1,021,194	29,619	153,371	76,975
2007	4,696,379	3,473,912	78,696	3,552,608	417,027	-117,641	3,017,940	611,172	1,067,267	30,399	154,489	76,637
2008	4,922,764	3,548,420	74,017	3,622,437	431,345	-137,452	3,053,640	678,088	1,191,036	31,609	155,738	76,080
2009	5,085,778	3,558,578	71,267	3,629,845	431,173	-156,439	3,042,233	702,292	1,341,253	32,491	156,531	74,699
2010	5,247,882	3,589,921	67,492	3,657,413	434,002	-146,341	3,077,070	699,983	1,470,829	33,486	156,719	73,816
2011	5,389,575	3,606,085	61,759	3,667,844	398,126	-142,339	3,127,379	760,265	1,501,931	34,305	157,108	73,477
2012	5,364,278	3,672,664	75,648	3,748,312	400,911	-237,083	3,110,318	778,310	1,475,650	34,109	157,268	73,239
2013	5,378,084	3,700,111	66,246	3,766,357	449,890	-198,994	3,117,473	776,085	1,484,526	34,349	156,571	73,794
2014	5,533,866	3,871,440	62,905	3,934,345	466,531	-279,641	3,188,173	798,390	1,547,303	35,366	156,475	74,260
2015	5,715,734	3,948,428	80,647	4,029,075	479,111	-279,653	3,270,311	838,650	1,606,773	36,814	155,261	74,461
2016	5,757,613	4,037,329	77,899	4,115,228	488,334	-365,136	3,261,758	840,121	1,655,734	37,408	153,914	75,578
2017	5,932,723	4,141,039	64,549	4,205,588	501,702	-330,162	3,373,724	873,615	1,685,384	38,893	152,538	75,634
2018	5,963,194	5,899,118	64,076	4,288,886	510,230	-361,579	3,417,077	840,310	1,705,807	39,587	150,635	75,677
2019	6,166,042	6,080,178	85,864	4,465,861	525,454	-372,539	3,567,868	854,398	1,743,776	41,237	149,527	76,424

Personal Income and Employment by Area: Virginia Beach-Norfolk-Newport News, VA-NC

(Thousands of dollars, except as noted.)

Year	Personal income, total	Earnings by place of work			Less: Contributions for government social insurance	Plus: Adjustment for residence	Equals: Net earnings by place of residence	Plus: Dividends, interest, and rent	Plus: Personal current transfer receipts	Per capita personal income (dollars)	Population (persons)	Total employment
		Nonfarm	Farm	Total								
1970	4,631,568	3,765,653	21,017	3,786,670	217,484	-34,970	3,534,216	841,903	255,449	4,211	1,099,964	535,553
1971	5,070,040	4,122,410	13,745	4,136,155	250,128	-44,665	3,841,362	916,802	311,876	4,554	1,113,297	536,524
1972	5,602,009	4,582,873	28,147	4,611,020	289,659	-86,292	4,235,069	1,002,748	364,192	5,024	1,114,977	549,094
1973	6,221,222	5,076,358	42,099	5,118,457	355,467	-98,188	4,664,802	1,127,750	428,670	5,468	1,137,655	573,774
1974	6,916,687	5,608,583	31,439	5,640,022	410,330	-113,318	5,116,374	1,292,501	507,812	5,973	1,157,946	590,240
1975	7,430,141	5,919,741	35,620	5,955,361	443,770	-94,139	5,417,452	1,380,705	631,984	6,371	1,166,228	578,056
1976	8,067,566	6,450,780	31,692	6,482,472	495,932	-113,858	5,872,682	1,493,043	701,841	6,843	1,178,977	588,816
1977	8,898,113	7,129,921	14,563	7,144,484	551,779	-122,601	6,470,104	1,679,667	748,342	7,430	1,197,552	610,259
1978	10,045,421	7,989,913	22,154	8,012,067	618,009	-135,923	7,258,135	1,966,582	820,704	8,302	1,209,942	637,636
1979	11,022,930	8,696,173	-626	8,695,547	702,054	-93,955	7,899,538	2,184,368	939,024	9,115	1,209,282	645,753
1980	12,481,756	9,690,704	-131	9,690,573	773,379	-115,906	8,801,288	2,553,233	1,127,235	10,259	1,216,639	656,174
1981	14,208,440	10,933,720	31,032	10,964,752	928,769	-122,904	9,913,079	3,002,500	1,292,861	11,446	1,241,360	663,306
1982	15,539,134	11,935,088	15,869	11,950,957	1,015,746	-145,433	10,789,778	3,365,104	1,384,252	12,436	1,249,538	669,437
1983	16,758,217	12,958,037	-2,463	12,955,574	1,156,992	-146,867	11,651,715	3,615,308	1,491,194	13,084	1,280,795	689,339
1984	18,481,594	14,279,452	32,938	14,312,390	1,318,729	-149,142	12,844,519	4,056,608	1,580,467	14,130	1,307,970	721,529
1985	19,896,728	15,500,393	23,121	15,523,514	1,477,408	-148,996	13,897,110	4,319,070	1,680,548	15,068	1,320,458	753,916
1986	21,389,038	16,729,048	32,703	16,761,751	1,654,924	-146,468	14,960,359	4,649,763	1,778,916	15,803	1,353,468	782,672
1987	22,843,422	17,966,930	37,185	18,004,115	1,788,218	-146,358	16,069,539	4,920,394	1,853,489	16,400	1,392,921	817,041
1988	24,520,501	19,195,737	51,267	19,247,004	1,987,597	-129,439	17,129,968	5,404,773	1,985,760	17,271	1,419,734	833,888
1989	26,185,314	20,094,442	54,124	20,148,566	2,112,351	-110,005	17,926,210	6,009,519	2,249,585	18,227	1,436,650	848,379
1990	27,468,768	21,150,271	68,270	21,218,541	2,260,118	-110,888	18,847,535	6,184,250	2,436,983	18,811	1,460,246	860,162
1991	28,771,977	22,101,438	58,239	22,159,677	2,392,283	-113,677	19,653,717	6,375,784	2,742,476	19,535	1,472,822	849,974
1992	30,524,355	23,358,188	64,619	23,422,807	2,534,931	-113,236	20,774,640	6,682,514	3,067,201	20,273	1,505,656	854,326
1993	31,780,342	24,088,657	55,054	24,143,711	2,632,264	-107,017	21,404,430	7,088,441	3,287,471	20,813	1,526,947	862,226
1994	32,968,610	24,798,281	71,222	24,869,503	2,735,453	-100,591	22,033,459	7,426,358	3,508,793	21,453	1,536,791	865,351
1995	34,232,622	25,388,033	59,147	25,447,180	2,787,760	-93,195	22,566,225	7,873,491	3,792,906	22,169	1,544,193	880,792
1996	35,707,978	26,347,512	70,365	26,417,877	2,893,712	-80,463	23,443,702	8,229,948	4,034,328	23,016	1,551,433	896,189
1997	37,463,915	27,715,639	47,100	27,762,739	3,041,480	-64,216	24,657,043	8,657,295	4,149,577	24,067	1,556,639	910,489
1998	39,482,208	29,435,249	38,551	29,473,800	3,196,921	-53,513	26,223,366	9,023,115	4,235,727	25,353	1,557,271	923,212
1999	41,405,362	31,068,315	27,952	31,096,267	3,372,543	-27,029	27,696,695	9,218,585	4,490,082	26,401	1,568,344	932,627
2000	44,362,557	33,161,208	46,504	33,207,712	3,547,114	1,003	29,661,601	9,918,119	4,782,837	27,992	1,584,803	952,542
2001	46,633,105	35,194,632	34,532	35,229,164	3,773,178	-32,783	31,423,203	9,911,018	5,298,884	29,265	1,593,489	956,341
2002	48,939,858	37,393,685	35,007	37,428,692	4,013,198	-73,769	33,341,725	9,981,520	5,616,613	30,428	1,608,368	967,421
2003	52,430,106	40,231,118	57,509	40,288,627	4,283,320	-166,277	35,839,030	10,522,969	6,068,107	32,438	1,616,332	978,286
2004	56,140,751	43,450,677	61,311	43,511,988	4,632,673	-164,447	38,714,868	10,994,527	6,431,356	34,177	1,642,657	998,498
2005	58,929,825	45,425,480	77,672	45,503,152	4,883,981	-199,456	40,419,715	11,445,353	7,064,757	35,736	1,649,013	1,013,251
2006	62,931,448	47,831,723	65,109	47,896,832	5,224,308	-205,278	42,467,246	12,797,326	7,666,876	37,779	1,665,757	1,025,578
2007	65,687,007	49,678,931	51,647	49,730,578	5,428,045	-259,903	44,042,630	13,521,230	8,123,147	39,486	1,663,563	1,040,461
2008	67,239,346	49,841,920	54,883	49,896,803	5,536,546	-256,115	44,104,142	13,882,802	9,252,402	40,444	1,662,528	1,032,584
2009	66,273,429	48,980,848	50,661	49,031,509	5,521,732	-302,476	43,207,301	13,129,571	9,936,557	39,722	1,668,443	999,744
2010	68,178,476	49,881,626	33,804	49,915,430	5,620,508	-279,815	44,015,107	13,167,804	10,995,565	40,584	1,679,945	989,760
2011	71,150,772	50,605,970	58,487	50,664,457	5,156,638	-274,754	45,233,065	14,443,817	11,473,890	42,187	1,686,564	991,827
2012	73,819,680	52,189,723	61,654	52,251,377	5,317,559	-320,127	46,613,691	15,601,974	11,604,015	43,490	1,697,398	995,772
2013	73,824,173	52,668,220	63,781	52,732,001	6,053,584	-380,607	46,297,810	15,445,691	12,080,672	43,291	1,705,320	1,003,974
2014	76,690,152	54,403,974	18,874	54,422,848	6,237,523	-389,443	47,795,882	16,462,808	12,431,462	44,721	1,714,857	1,012,524
2015	80,255,309	56,709,377	-3,585	56,705,792	6,502,240	-368,753	49,834,799	17,158,379	13,262,131	46,650	1,720,356	1,029,133
2016	80,901,221	56,718,162	318	56,718,480	6,532,400	-446,682	49,739,398	17,435,897	13,725,926	46,960	1,722,766	1,039,585
2017	83,677,694	58,547,128	4,311	58,551,439	6,796,467	-483,130	51,271,842	18,145,277	14,260,575	48,502	1,725,246	1,049,393
2018	88,811,777	88,773,965	37,812	60,990,128	7,079,938	-72,608	53,837,582	19,729,642	15,244,553	50,355	1,763,713	1,088,564
2019	92,002,182	91,920,190	81,992	63,416,383	7,354,417	-96,032	55,965,934	19,892,543	16,143,705	52,011	1,768,901	1,102,751

Personal Income and Employment by Area: Visalia, CA

(Thousands of dollars, except as noted.)

Year	Personal income, total	Earnings by place of work			Less: Contributions for government social insurance	Plus: Adjustment for residence	Equals: Net earnings by place of residence	Plus: Dividends, interest, and rent	Plus: Personal current transfer receipts	Per capita personal income (dollars)	Population (persons)	Total employment
		Nonfarm	Farm	Total								
1970............	699,055	410,591	113,102	523,693	27,938	1,858	497,613	97,445	103,997	3,695	189,191	81,225
1971............	759,398	446,047	118,462	564,509	31,161	4,700	538,048	106,076	115,274	3,912	194,103	83,183
1972............	861,181	505,311	143,143	648,454	37,201	7,775	619,028	118,886	123,267	4,357	197,643	89,111
1973............	1,020,924	566,337	211,175	777,512	47,547	11,363	741,328	140,922	138,674	5,059	201,805	91,598
1974............	1,185,031	648,329	253,948	902,277	56,373	14,459	860,363	160,357	164,311	5,736	206,589	97,440
1975............	1,262,161	714,896	194,072	908,968	59,288	21,780	871,460	183,453	207,248	5,922	213,115	99,934
1976............	1,413,389	824,027	204,721	1,028,748	69,111	26,081	985,718	197,010	230,661	6,450	219,123	102,675
1977............	1,555,218	915,051	222,287	1,137,338	78,662	32,469	1,091,145	220,503	243,570	6,884	225,906	106,394
1978............	1,774,904	1,052,271	246,952	1,299,223	91,196	38,648	1,246,675	255,512	272,717	7,610	233,220	109,228
1979............	2,100,902	1,204,960	351,225	1,556,185	108,994	50,324	1,497,515	301,669	301,718	8,751	240,074	117,964
1980............	2,324,712	1,285,930	361,928	1,647,858	115,101	60,098	1,592,855	372,398	359,459	9,396	247,426	119,326
1981............	2,447,435	1,375,354	265,166	1,640,520	136,230	61,089	1,565,379	451,566	430,490	9,647	253,694	119,692
1982............	2,638,801	1,425,669	327,810	1,753,479	143,597	63,921	1,673,803	505,769	459,229	10,159	259,759	117,129
1983............	2,712,227	1,552,814	208,208	1,761,022	159,089	64,313	1,666,246	556,934	489,047	10,157	267,034	121,911
1984............	2,983,245	1,681,661	259,756	1,941,417	177,839	70,674	1,834,252	619,016	529,977	10,917	273,255	120,368
1985............	3,151,598	1,786,509	249,829	2,036,338	190,837	73,833	1,919,334	640,221	592,043	11,256	280,000	122,160
1986............	3,369,613	1,949,924	260,994	2,210,918	212,024	74,431	2,073,325	657,563	638,725	11,791	285,767	125,690
1987............	3,721,174	2,106,553	422,426	2,528,979	228,316	83,172	2,383,835	678,098	659,241	12,755	291,752	128,885
1988............	3,978,308	2,259,473	433,579	2,693,052	254,392	99,515	2,538,175	731,215	708,918	13,347	298,075	133,959
1989............	4,240,546	2,433,210	375,302	2,808,512	278,996	115,458	2,644,974	814,547	781,025	13,929	304,451	137,419
1990............	4,685,596	2,717,905	437,819	3,155,724	306,040	125,083	2,974,767	836,994	873,835	14,919	314,062	140,864
1991............	4,808,049	2,837,075	311,785	3,148,860	319,523	135,047	2,964,384	851,136	992,529	14,853	323,705	141,436
1992............	5,357,044	3,097,244	510,977	3,608,221	350,019	125,590	3,383,792	833,147	1,140,105	16,138	331,956	146,844
1993............	5,506,271	3,194,774	458,402	3,653,176	360,441	133,508	3,426,243	880,502	1,199,526	16,231	339,253	150,060
1994............	5,771,675	3,386,870	495,073	3,881,943	377,809	134,560	3,638,694	913,908	1,219,073	16,697	345,668	153,457
1995............	5,895,436	3,523,729	413,330	3,937,059	386,456	138,778	3,689,381	941,219	1,264,836	16,935	348,127	155,994
1996............	6,353,185	3,669,333	628,641	4,297,974	385,374	141,640	4,054,240	975,818	1,323,127	18,114	350,732	158,687
1997............	6,476,071	3,747,098	654,039	4,401,137	391,212	141,737	4,151,662	1,017,745	1,306,664	18,245	354,946	158,454
1998............	6,958,619	4,109,319	656,977	4,766,296	414,688	140,557	4,492,165	1,086,218	1,380,236	19,337	359,854	165,685
1999............	7,209,727	4,313,745	642,330	4,956,075	437,788	143,212	4,661,499	1,075,955	1,472,273	19,768	364,708	169,627
2000............	7,422,203	4,601,963	528,037	5,130,000	470,265	151,558	4,811,293	1,119,158	1,491,752	20,135	368,627	172,135
2001............	8,162,710	4,890,120	742,896	5,633,016	534,088	194,836	5,293,764	1,198,905	1,670,041	21,874	373,171	168,668
2002............	8,408,806	5,249,121	498,829	5,747,950	585,513	255,171	5,417,608	1,204,032	1,787,166	22,154	379,568	175,312
2003............	9,150,703	5,595,007	599,707	6,194,714	629,385	329,044	5,894,373	1,333,754	1,922,576	23,539	388,743	174,975
2004............	10,129,552	5,871,948	1,094,946	6,966,894	685,657	406,348	6,687,585	1,394,852	2,047,115	25,437	398,226	173,719
2005............	10,666,701	6,202,000	1,208,759	7,410,759	734,983	456,394	7,132,170	1,400,779	2,133,752	26,146	407,970	177,770
2006............	10,991,349	6,862,367	563,553	7,425,920	772,820	508,976	7,162,076	1,526,256	2,303,017	26,490	414,921	182,695
2007............	12,417,278	7,182,636	1,254,188	8,436,824	790,614	593,914	8,240,124	1,683,979	2,493,175	29,415	422,140	189,082
2008............	12,488,723	7,190,001	914,298	8,104,299	814,165	680,792	7,970,926	1,749,353	2,768,444	29,092	429,283	188,438
2009............	12,302,197	7,106,171	568,600	7,674,771	807,308	641,443	7,508,906	1,736,904	3,056,387	28,152	436,987	182,825
2010............	13,496,988	7,603,832	902,296	8,506,128	808,099	656,486	8,354,515	1,738,054	3,404,419	30,463	443,060	183,319
2011............	14,432,008	7,841,638	1,308,966	9,150,604	761,987	681,383	9,070,000	1,948,888	3,413,120	32,261	447,358	184,762
2012............	14,531,771	7,611,123	1,345,760	8,956,883	752,619	706,934	8,911,198	2,160,265	3,460,308	32,237	450,779	183,669
2013............	15,283,723	7,880,429	1,827,678	9,708,107	863,893	680,285	9,524,499	2,153,830	3,605,394	33,690	453,663	190,428
2014............	16,941,984	8,210,946	2,612,831	10,823,777	894,235	727,769	10,657,311	2,447,731	3,836,942	37,117	456,452	192,985
2015............	17,105,786	8,818,179	1,669,776	10,487,955	950,059	700,085	10,237,981	2,696,367	4,171,438	37,300	458,601	200,601
2016............	17,578,692	9,434,428	1,373,003	10,807,431	1,030,332	643,300	10,420,399	2,828,050	4,330,243	38,145	460,835	205,624
2017............	18,466,575	9,824,135	1,835,018	11,659,153	1,071,056	673,916	11,262,013	2,974,252	4,230,310	39,756	464,493	207,171
2018............	18,679,327	17,167,452	1,511,875	11,599,314	1,106,285	740,394	11,233,423	3,027,381	4,418,523	40,206	464,589	210,293
2019............	19,973,932	18,023,232	1,950,700	12,549,486	1,187,559	797,768	12,159,695	3,096,536	4,717,701	42,845	466,195	213,301

Personal Income and Employment by Area: Waco, TX

(Thousands of dollars, except as noted.)

Year	Personal income, total	Earnings by place of work			Less: Contributions for government social insurance	Plus: Adjustment for residence	Equals: Net earnings by place of residence	Plus: Dividends, interest, and rent	Plus: Personal current transfer receipts	Per capita personal income (dollars)	Population (persons)	Total employment
		Nonfarm	Farm	Total								
1970	556,788	421,624	11,223	432,847	26,930	1,428	407,345	86,733	62,710	3,374	165,008	72,540
1971	604,157	455,737	9,907	465,644	29,812	1,120	436,952	95,878	71,327	3,608	167,456	73,644
1972	668,055	507,739	9,600	517,339	34,736	907	483,510	105,689	78,856	3,907	170,979	77,099
1973	761,836	563,169	28,280	591,449	44,501	489	547,437	120,794	93,605	4,380	173,928	79,469
1974	828,262	617,405	6,428	623,833	50,124	185	573,894	141,911	112,457	4,678	177,057	80,372
1975	934,111	669,292	12,442	681,734	52,795	310	629,249	164,773	140,089	5,302	176,185	79,429
1976	1,049,382	773,660	12,136	785,796	61,837	-972	722,987	177,920	148,475	5,834	179,868	83,034
1977	1,133,212	847,726	194	847,920	68,812	-1,575	777,533	198,232	157,447	6,250	181,301	85,832
1978	1,284,680	970,655	2,092	972,747	80,694	-2,014	890,039	221,252	173,389	7,000	183,520	88,769
1979	1,431,169	1,085,036	2,361	1,087,397	95,001	-4,345	988,051	247,705	195,413	7,672	186,539	90,348
1980	1,617,123	1,195,746	-661	1,195,085	105,683	-5,599	1,083,803	307,123	226,197	8,537	189,416	92,112
1981	1,818,774	1,317,972	12,322	1,330,294	126,025	-9,249	1,195,020	370,701	253,053	9,487	191,717	93,873
1982	2,003,861	1,407,335	6,866	1,414,201	135,902	-7,916	1,270,383	456,893	276,585	10,331	193,961	94,587
1983	2,193,890	1,539,032	7,796	1,546,828	148,539	-6,674	1,391,615	502,779	299,496	11,099	197,671	96,325
1984	2,409,574	1,690,499	22,318	1,712,817	167,904	-9,820	1,535,093	561,664	312,817	12,059	199,820	100,053
1985	2,576,494	1,783,022	29,299	1,812,321	179,818	-12,354	1,620,149	621,703	334,642	12,805	201,204	101,927
1986	2,654,560	1,824,159	25,818	1,849,977	182,776	-17,300	1,649,901	642,681	361,978	12,976	204,568	100,542
1987	2,651,786	1,792,364	30,248	1,822,612	178,822	-18,166	1,625,624	644,389	381,773	12,966	204,519	101,805
1988	2,749,355	1,893,556	27,381	1,920,937	195,827	-19,777	1,705,333	641,034	402,988	13,454	204,348	103,130
1989	2,897,045	1,958,589	33,052	1,991,641	206,703	-21,540	1,763,398	701,713	431,934	14,096	205,516	103,364
1990	3,049,548	2,098,466	24,028	2,122,494	216,081	-19,173	1,887,240	685,999	476,309	14,698	207,477	104,832
1991	3,225,341	2,236,682	36,439	2,273,121	235,256	-23,614	2,014,251	689,207	521,883	15,393	209,531	107,920
1992	3,402,219	2,394,686	33,751	2,428,437	250,109	-29,044	2,149,284	662,451	590,484	16,103	211,278	109,069
1993	3,611,902	2,581,587	40,623	2,622,210	269,179	-31,655	2,321,376	668,242	622,284	16,847	214,400	112,112
1994	3,861,905	2,796,847	46,152	2,842,999	295,041	-33,603	2,514,355	687,755	659,795	17,644	218,877	115,322
1995	4,135,452	3,013,308	30,004	3,043,312	319,809	-38,197	2,685,306	749,402	700,744	18,702	221,128	119,892
1996	4,312,932	3,147,003	6,873	3,153,876	331,015	-36,693	2,786,168	789,059	737,705	19,212	224,497	121,857
1997	4,568,589	3,371,454	27,792	3,399,246	350,842	-38,400	3,010,004	794,315	764,270	20,165	226,561	124,685
1998	4,815,520	3,592,665	6,001	3,598,666	371,044	-41,010	3,186,612	851,219	777,689	21,079	228,450	126,949
1999	5,040,333	3,819,677	22,805	3,842,482	394,309	-43,412	3,404,761	835,805	799,767	21,903	230,120	129,275
2000	5,238,260	3,907,251	14,886	3,922,137	399,654	-37,797	3,484,686	902,461	851,113	22,531	232,489	130,926
2001	5,456,109	4,075,820	4,333	4,080,153	414,449	-58,924	3,606,780	920,339	928,990	23,379	233,379	130,991
2002	5,624,299	4,253,113	18,086	4,271,199	432,736	-82,698	3,755,765	855,750	1,012,784	23,968	234,661	131,509
2003	5,964,213	4,535,858	34,794	4,570,652	469,662	-115,422	3,985,568	894,466	1,084,179	25,184	236,830	133,443
2004	6,136,609	4,738,597	41,670	4,780,267	489,904	-130,409	4,159,954	848,546	1,128,109	25,631	239,419	135,175
2005	6,482,285	4,930,807	32,737	4,963,544	513,706	-154,656	4,295,182	958,278	1,228,825	26,922	240,784	137,127
2006	6,780,257	5,133,679	23,077	5,156,756	526,320	-173,285	4,457,151	1,021,972	1,301,134	27,972	242,397	138,958
2007	7,103,411	5,283,593	22,689	5,306,282	550,436	-190,457	4,565,389	1,115,208	1,422,814	29,058	244,453	141,938
2008	7,429,479	5,400,050	-1,337	5,398,713	566,342	-207,913	4,624,458	1,215,330	1,589,691	30,111	246,735	142,371
2009	7,500,535	5,466,666	-16,227	5,450,439	586,036	-215,316	4,649,087	1,140,912	1,710,536	30,069	249,441	141,710
2010	7,930,280	5,743,728	9,669	5,753,397	613,119	-220,631	4,919,647	1,138,966	1,871,667	31,246	253,804	141,538
2011	8,277,311	5,861,075	5,221	5,866,296	552,580	-217,992	5,095,724	1,254,275	1,927,312	32,374	255,676	142,734
2012	8,645,193	6,124,162	19,003	6,143,165	573,231	-225,155	5,344,779	1,384,696	1,915,718	33,658	256,853	144,437
2013	8,827,994	6,313,158	37,575	6,350,733	665,104	-221,264	5,464,365	1,404,669	1,958,960	34,132	258,646	147,091
2014	9,277,236	6,628,047	19,079	6,647,126	692,869	-210,594	5,743,663	1,477,433	2,056,140	35,641	260,298	149,906
2015	9,766,254	6,955,574	26,659	6,982,233	732,759	-221,153	6,028,321	1,564,891	2,173,042	37,191	262,598	152,148
2016	10,115,556	7,237,651	-25,077	7,212,574	777,676	-251,977	6,182,921	1,641,537	2,291,098	38,199	264,809	156,834
2017	10,549,888	7,586,954	-12,726	7,574,228	822,309	-260,176	6,491,743	1,721,663	2,336,482	39,263	268,696	159,531
2018	11,125,844	11,137,446	-11,602	7,998,736	857,309	-278,374	6,863,053	1,791,886	2,470,905	40,990	271,427	163,158
2019	11,428,760	11,440,319	-11,559	8,172,410	870,039	-258,448	7,043,923	1,825,625	2,559,212	41,723	273,920	164,711

Personal Income and Employment by Area: Walla Walla, WA

(Thousands of dollars, except as noted.)

Year	Personal income, total	Earnings by place of work			Less: Contributions for government social insurance	Plus: Adjustment for residence	Equals: Net earnings by place of residence	Plus: Dividends, interest, and rent	Plus: Personal current transfer receipts	Per capita personal income (dollars)	Population (persons)	Total employment
		Nonfarm	Farm	Total								
1970	190,553	122,938	24,354	147,292	9,432	-6,062	131,798	37,377	21,378	4,092	46,570	21,692
1971	201,097	131,729	21,337	153,066	10,491	-6,483	136,092	41,263	23,742	4,325	46,500	21,679
1972	231,438	143,852	34,890	178,742	12,046	-6,484	160,212	45,536	25,690	4,917	47,071	22,024
1973	283,216	155,778	66,895	222,673	15,114	-6,305	201,254	52,910	29,052	6,034	46,936	22,869
1974	300,911	174,294	58,480	232,774	17,652	-7,056	208,066	58,724	34,121	6,379	47,175	24,001
1975	334,380	195,750	58,327	254,077	19,834	-7,280	226,963	66,254	41,163	6,874	48,641	24,622
1976	360,085	229,818	49,542	279,360	23,958	-10,582	244,820	70,742	44,523	7,329	49,130	25,952
1977	378,174	250,902	34,556	285,458	26,377	-9,890	249,191	81,491	47,492	7,668	49,317	25,164
1978	431,213	290,543	42,100	332,643	31,794	-12,000	288,849	90,556	51,808	8,752	49,269	26,012
1979	486,594	354,177	37,504	391,681	40,942	-25,313	325,426	102,239	58,929	9,683	50,254	28,027
1980	554,630	377,239	54,672	431,911	43,582	-25,621	362,708	122,236	69,686	10,751	51,590	27,566
1981	603,113	391,147	52,133	443,280	48,085	-15,597	379,598	146,883	76,632	11,623	51,889	27,391
1982	615,887	398,711	38,482	437,193	49,100	-18,508	369,585	163,264	83,038	11,669	52,781	26,940
1983	685,863	421,205	73,447	494,652	52,897	-23,797	417,958	178,627	89,278	12,913	53,114	27,297
1984	703,053	451,013	57,500	508,513	58,895	-31,524	418,094	190,331	94,628	13,305	52,843	27,723
1985	699,352	451,512	37,594	489,106	59,562	-32,401	397,143	199,228	102,981	13,322	52,495	27,577
1986	720,538	450,531	56,754	507,285	60,087	-33,827	413,371	199,088	108,079	13,799	52,215	27,147
1987	712,423	455,621	49,384	505,005	60,730	-35,496	408,779	191,179	112,465	13,792	51,656	26,419
1988	732,799	485,852	46,905	532,757	67,137	-41,104	424,516	188,770	119,513	14,270	51,354	26,831
1989	782,321	517,682	38,851	556,533	71,142	-46,787	438,604	215,518	128,199	14,980	52,223	27,198
1990	827,292	547,234	58,122	605,356	77,088	-50,163	478,105	211,218	137,969	15,742	52,554	28,459
1991	870,339	584,204	46,526	630,730	82,212	-53,073	495,445	217,090	157,804	16,105	54,041	28,184
1992	943,078	643,429	48,250	691,679	90,070	-57,042	544,567	224,322	174,189	17,165	54,941	28,961
1993	1,018,390	682,540	77,839	760,379	96,268	-58,258	605,853	230,204	182,333	18,063	56,381	29,896
1994	1,042,115	728,767	51,427	780,194	102,548	-58,005	619,641	235,355	187,119	18,186	57,303	31,079
1995	1,089,502	747,274	55,885	803,159	106,284	-59,426	637,449	254,092	197,961	18,819	57,895	31,720
1996	1,194,761	774,112	106,840	880,952	107,087	-61,188	712,677	272,219	209,865	20,498	58,287	31,769
1997	1,198,235	799,912	69,057	868,969	106,719	-60,656	701,594	283,372	213,269	20,477	58,515	32,279
1998	1,277,200	848,783	86,280	935,063	111,409	-59,452	764,202	286,195	226,803	21,777	58,648	32,372
1999	1,316,518	879,669	85,979	965,648	112,940	-58,642	794,066	283,559	238,893	22,364	58,867	32,482
2000	1,456,410	931,673	150,294	1,081,967	121,919	-61,845	898,203	301,492	256,715	24,582	59,247	33,415
2001	1,518,170	973,155	143,233	1,116,388	127,429	-65,281	923,678	318,335	276,157	25,686	59,106	33,398
2002	1,505,348	1,016,459	111,737	1,128,196	132,351	-65,428	930,417	288,187	286,744	25,232	59,661	33,652
2003	1,592,620	1,062,421	145,767	1,208,188	139,161	-70,296	998,731	295,796	298,093	26,495	60,111	34,041
2004	1,654,112	1,119,363	124,318	1,243,681	146,337	-67,958	1,029,386	310,400	314,326	27,260	60,679	33,905
2005	1,695,392	1,166,722	106,689	1,273,411	150,032	-66,301	1,057,078	305,157	333,157	28,003	60,543	33,854
2006	1,770,267	1,206,100	107,427	1,313,527	156,348	-68,720	1,088,459	325,334	356,474	29,212	60,600	34,179
2007	1,942,507	1,275,747	123,918	1,399,665	165,863	-67,684	1,166,118	392,068	384,321	31,982	60,737	34,656
2008	2,141,030	1,336,662	149,977	1,486,639	176,300	-65,945	1,244,394	467,848	428,788	34,974	61,218	35,952
2009	2,129,858	1,355,966	144,703	1,500,669	182,945	-73,603	1,244,121	420,001	465,736	34,308	62,080	35,612
2010	2,205,976	1,415,963	156,115	1,572,078	190,186	-89,514	1,292,378	404,519	509,079	35,010	63,009	35,862
2011	2,328,440	1,434,722	188,472	1,623,194	174,909	-95,282	1,353,003	465,277	510,160	36,704	63,439	35,700
2012	2,396,488	1,481,482	207,542	1,689,024	176,228	-117,902	1,394,894	484,389	517,205	37,848	63,318	36,128
2013	2,430,964	1,513,972	205,126	1,719,098	197,836	-131,288	1,389,974	514,289	526,701	38,355	63,380	36,827
2014	2,517,771	1,569,531	158,557	1,728,088	208,807	-140,412	1,378,869	555,114	583,788	39,671	63,466	37,466
2015	2,677,931	1,599,248	265,513	1,864,761	213,148	-136,868	1,514,745	577,590	585,596	41,938	63,855	37,267
2016	2,708,485	1,668,911	208,217	1,877,128	221,316	-151,810	1,504,002	586,399	618,084	42,327	63,989	37,646
2017	2,788,566	1,723,848	189,442	1,913,290	233,414	-148,397	1,531,479	617,880	639,207	43,157	64,614	37,853
2018	2,814,320	2,670,208	144,112	1,892,152	229,300	-165,227	1,497,625	696,956	619,739	46,429	60,615	36,390
2019	2,943,477	2,787,932	155,545	1,978,667	241,244	-162,250	1,575,173	709,836	658,468	48,444	60,760	36,827

Personal Income and Employment by Area: Warner Robins, GA

(Thousands of dollars, except as noted.)

Year	Personal income, total	Earnings by place of work			Less: Contributions for government social insurance	Plus: Adjustment for residence	Equals: Net earnings by place of residence	Plus: Dividends, interest, and rent	Plus: Personal current transfer receipts	Per capita personal income (dollars)	Population (persons)	Total employment
		Nonfarm	Farm	Total								
1970	366,122	409,513	8,740	418,253	13,918	-123,053	281,282	65,626	19,214	4,174	87,709	50,074
1971	408,075	447,605	12,977	460,582	15,605	-133,940	311,037	73,889	23,149	4,492	90,839	49,359
1972	436,008	472,844	12,390	485,234	17,126	-135,975	332,133	77,782	26,093	4,688	93,008	48,562
1973	487,062	503,763	22,145	525,908	20,801	-134,696	370,411	86,724	29,927	5,180	94,022	49,211
1974	540,715	548,797	19,024	567,821	24,984	-137,744	405,093	98,137	37,485	5,611	96,373	50,280
1975	586,437	587,044	13,946	600,990	28,511	-143,165	429,314	108,059	49,064	5,969	98,251	49,765
1976	626,424	616,336	15,433	631,769	31,081	-143,918	456,770	113,595	56,059	6,290	99,591	49,403
1977	690,363	691,461	9,667	701,128	34,496	-161,994	504,638	127,969	57,756	6,849	100,792	50,158
1978	761,719	735,658	13,054	748,712	37,615	-160,494	550,603	148,260	62,856	7,434	102,471	51,101
1979	830,324	780,301	16,258	796,559	42,341	-158,126	596,092	162,078	72,154	7,953	104,400	50,783
1980	901,792	817,438	3,229	820,667	46,563	-144,870	629,234	186,377	86,181	8,499	106,108	51,799
1981	1,029,848	928,540	12,003	940,543	54,760	-175,152	710,631	219,784	99,433	9,578	107,518	51,524
1982	1,133,328	1,001,297	17,051	1,018,348	59,939	-182,945	775,464	250,936	106,928	10,486	108,084	52,289
1983	1,228,269	1,073,660	9,749	1,083,409	73,789	-175,622	833,998	275,708	118,563	11,266	109,024	53,163
1984	1,347,051	1,142,036	21,412	1,163,448	80,165	-169,354	913,929	304,661	128,461	12,321	109,327	54,057
1985	1,446,030	1,219,061	18,046	1,237,107	92,824	-163,325	980,958	324,480	140,592	13,052	110,786	56,151
1986	1,537,551	1,258,975	14,747	1,273,722	101,092	-130,378	1,042,252	345,939	149,360	13,695	112,267	58,757
1987	1,617,734	1,277,400	16,142	1,293,542	106,204	-92,016	1,095,322	365,072	157,340	14,207	113,865	59,213
1988	1,754,762	1,364,897	22,354	1,387,251	120,056	-80,847	1,186,348	396,666	171,748	15,104	116,176	60,188
1989	1,904,642	1,468,685	17,675	1,486,360	133,814	-81,057	1,271,489	444,358	188,795	16,208	117,510	62,194
1990	2,052,215	1,548,193	18,200	1,566,393	145,230	-34,293	1,386,870	454,541	210,804	17,236	119,068	62,862
1991	2,151,765	1,582,829	31,245	1,614,074	152,283	-11,055	1,450,736	459,141	241,888	17,806	120,842	61,259
1992	2,308,851	1,714,958	31,823	1,746,781	165,576	-19,025	1,562,180	472,845	273,826	18,706	123,430	63,510
1993	2,425,955	1,769,513	30,667	1,800,180	174,589	2,472	1,628,063	506,663	291,229	19,236	126,114	65,146
1994	2,534,774	1,817,581	36,603	1,854,184	182,434	32,092	1,703,842	521,466	309,466	19,582	129,441	67,590
1995	2,712,195	1,934,818	30,847	1,965,665	194,686	33,385	1,804,364	575,773	332,058	20,709	130,968	69,161
1996	2,852,993	2,100,951	32,238	2,133,189	211,457	-40,015	1,881,717	610,598	360,678	21,375	133,473	70,825
1997	3,036,095	2,169,042	36,736	2,205,778	219,440	28,464	2,014,802	649,560	371,733	22,203	136,742	70,836
1998	3,207,774	2,325,436	24,095	2,349,531	232,429	18,777	2,135,879	683,936	387,959	22,999	139,475	71,448
1999	3,424,554	2,492,868	40,020	2,532,888	248,348	26,327	2,310,867	696,826	416,861	24,113	142,022	74,014
2000	3,612,680	2,661,328	32,684	2,694,012	265,595	-8,584	2,419,833	745,211	447,636	24,946	144,820	76,035
2001	3,870,589	2,764,911	34,741	2,799,652	281,831	-24,032	2,493,789	874,811	501,989	26,263	147,377	76,656
2002	4,127,495	3,020,343	23,158	3,043,501	308,447	-61,466	2,673,588	886,909	566,998	27,348	150,927	78,645
2003	4,400,011	3,238,829	41,812	3,280,641	327,805	-85,740	2,867,096	941,827	591,088	28,508	154,342	80,709
2004	4,586,840	3,420,158	34,712	3,454,870	355,385	-60,124	3,039,361	896,562	650,917	28,814	159,187	83,129
2005	4,880,313	3,652,674	48,026	3,700,700	377,340	-106,102	3,217,258	931,371	731,684	30,154	161,847	85,551
2006	5,197,354	3,887,978	44,865	3,932,843	408,718	-102,271	3,421,854	977,923	797,577	31,372	165,671	89,197
2007	5,483,255	4,055,760	48,340	4,104,100	425,536	-173,185	3,505,379	1,099,696	878,180	32,200	170,285	92,375
2008	5,719,408	4,132,246	32,139	4,164,385	455,432	-152,881	3,556,072	1,138,433	1,024,903	32,911	173,782	92,271
2009	5,860,347	4,232,553	20,090	4,252,643	468,438	-145,182	3,639,023	1,112,331	1,108,993	33,148	176,793	92,253
2010	6,097,634	4,386,761	20,488	4,407,249	485,713	-173,337	3,748,199	1,119,638	1,229,797	33,787	180,472	92,444
2011	6,487,601	4,507,486	42,973	4,550,459	444,473	-181,677	3,924,309	1,272,610	1,290,682	35,354	183,502	94,350
2012	6,541,863	4,562,548	38,132	4,600,680	454,352	-128,168	4,018,160	1,224,487	1,299,216	35,277	185,443	94,683
2013	6,592,863	4,570,802	41,972	4,612,774	510,398	-72,405	4,029,971	1,222,954	1,339,938	35,371	186,394	95,260
2014	6,867,190	4,685,366	26,114	4,711,480	521,569	-28,475	4,161,436	1,288,849	1,416,905	36,619	187,533	95,536
2015	7,179,436	4,785,701	36,738	4,822,439	530,743	44,862	4,336,558	1,348,562	1,494,316	38,180	188,044	96,729
2016	7,351,485	4,912,441	32,436	4,944,877	544,769	16,279	4,416,387	1,380,774	1,554,324	38,678	190,068	97,908
2017	7,662,268	5,111,504	26,456	5,137,960	568,630	45,925	4,615,255	1,432,531	1,614,482	39,954	191,779	99,777
2018	7,662,276	7,649,192	13,084	5,164,352	569,516	19,650	4,614,486	1,449,505	1,598,285	41,896	182,886	98,857
2019	8,038,908	8,008,207	30,701	5,506,801	610,219	-36,554	4,860,028	1,477,882	1,700,998	43,358	185,409	102,035

Personal Income and Employment by Area: Washington-Arlington-Alexandria, DC-VA-MD-WV

(Thousands of dollars, except as noted.)

Year	Personal income, total	Earnings by place of work			Less: Contributions for government social insurance	Plus: Adjustment for residence	Equals: Net earnings by place of residence	Plus: Dividends, interest, and rent	Plus: Personal current transfer receipts	Per capita personal income (dollars)	Population (persons)	Total employment
		Nonfarm	Farm	Total								
1970	18,456,145	15,141,213	52,568	15,193,781	704,394	-28,237	14,461,150	3,246,936	748,059	5,813	3,174,781	1,635,996
1971	20,676,146	16,912,680	49,559	16,962,239	808,830	-163,226	15,990,183	3,772,386	913,577	6,404	3,228,473	1,676,874
1972	22,662,316	18,630,071	58,485	18,688,556	947,358	-271,953	17,469,245	4,126,351	1,066,720	6,872	3,297,994	1,728,072
1973	24,725,061	20,419,543	73,303	20,492,846	1,196,263	-380,342	18,916,241	4,554,701	1,254,119	7,453	3,317,553	1,785,895
1974	26,831,815	22,060,989	67,726	22,128,715	1,351,827	-511,475	20,265,413	5,077,117	1,489,285	8,060	3,329,115	1,820,202
1975	29,317,020	24,086,863	68,138	24,155,001	1,487,015	-688,584	21,979,402	5,476,024	1,861,594	8,738	3,354,959	1,837,675
1976	31,917,402	26,449,003	60,804	26,509,807	1,662,192	-851,275	23,996,340	5,927,432	1,993,630	9,459	3,374,253	1,868,791
1977	34,718,667	28,857,657	51,386	28,909,043	1,803,153	-1,027,224	26,078,666	6,540,710	2,099,291	10,265	3,382,257	1,919,713
1978	38,518,855	31,979,266	76,692	32,055,958	2,036,249	-1,283,659	28,736,050	7,515,406	2,267,399	11,291	3,411,506	2,000,343
1979	42,282,522	35,313,258	66,343	35,379,601	2,375,856	-1,649,706	31,354,039	8,364,883	2,563,600	12,368	3,418,637	2,061,280
1980	47,261,506	39,172,468	35,403	39,207,871	2,686,930	-1,989,981	34,530,960	9,754,485	2,976,061	13,727	3,442,968	2,096,829
1981	52,603,506	43,047,241	47,051	43,094,292	3,213,061	-2,175,626	37,705,605	11,459,972	3,437,929	15,024	3,501,294	2,118,775
1982	57,215,050	46,163,891	47,919	46,211,810	3,515,595	-2,242,044	40,454,171	12,922,283	3,838,596	16,146	3,543,649	2,120,432
1983	61,618,257	50,304,496	31,998	50,336,494	4,169,707	-2,316,507	43,850,280	13,631,361	4,136,616	17,136	3,595,901	2,185,742
1984	68,928,319	56,424,173	56,621	56,480,794	4,861,572	-2,558,620	49,060,602	15,408,629	4,459,088	18,769	3,672,371	2,319,314
1985	75,265,030	62,386,684	60,316	62,447,000	5,659,496	-2,787,613	53,999,891	16,597,282	4,667,857	20,056	3,752,795	2,449,391
1986	81,771,968	68,264,256	48,469	68,312,725	6,454,387	-2,812,904	59,045,434	17,805,898	4,920,636	21,259	3,846,429	2,578,468
1987	88,812,637	74,888,210	89,065	74,977,275	7,153,219	-3,037,137	64,786,919	18,869,833	5,155,885	22,497	3,947,690	2,713,726
1988	98,431,905	83,495,150	94,210	83,589,360	8,218,254	-3,330,391	72,040,715	20,842,337	5,548,853	24,330	4,045,716	2,823,319
1989	106,704,485	89,630,618	102,175	89,732,793	9,009,577	-3,543,839	77,179,377	23,592,716	5,932,392	25,889	4,121,547	2,898,376
1990	112,607,747	94,300,436	131,341	94,431,777	9,662,767	-3,611,204	81,157,806	24,950,082	6,499,859	26,983	4,173,328	2,930,896
1991	117,535,609	97,939,651	113,861	98,053,512	10,123,347	-3,579,333	84,350,832	25,920,639	7,264,138	27,753	4,235,129	2,864,621
1992	124,539,864	103,909,280	123,863	104,033,143	10,726,831	-3,756,515	89,549,797	26,766,598	8,223,469	28,962	4,300,061	2,851,903
1993	130,881,356	108,784,282	106,267	108,890,549	11,272,824	-3,996,860	93,620,865	28,488,669	8,771,822	30,005	4,362,043	2,898,087
1994	137,436,260	113,878,182	98,371	113,976,553	12,021,474	-4,250,159	97,704,920	30,509,855	9,221,485	31,080	4,422,005	2,933,968
1995	143,635,847	118,192,157	67,105	118,259,262	12,527,592	-4,305,816	101,425,854	32,507,071	9,702,922	32,089	4,476,203	2,984,951
1996	150,790,779	123,797,951	99,792	123,897,743	13,123,240	-4,598,986	106,175,517	34,190,675	10,424,587	33,236	4,536,908	3,030,891
1997	160,279,601	132,208,230	65,157	132,273,387	14,084,603	-5,055,591	113,133,193	36,471,637	10,674,771	34,828	4,602,056	3,098,310
1998	173,318,346	144,472,118	74,290	144,546,408	15,102,915	-5,375,491	124,068,002	37,875,730	11,374,614	37,095	4,672,330	3,171,026
1999	187,485,551	157,730,974	58,107	157,789,081	16,418,324	-5,084,287	136,286,470	39,230,316	11,968,765	39,358	4,763,645	3,256,656
2000	206,862,012	175,017,633	99,973	175,117,606	17,959,166	-5,914,158	151,244,282	42,799,014	12,818,716	42,535	4,863,388	3,402,899
2001	217,440,824	186,513,783	58,440	186,572,223	19,307,139	-6,456,266	160,808,818	42,571,312	14,060,694	43,748	4,970,350	3,466,368
2002	223,349,755	192,718,199	54,811	192,773,010	20,066,566	-6,873,266	165,833,178	42,256,069	15,260,508	44,177	5,055,829	3,503,099
2003	235,052,966	203,818,114	40,900	203,859,014	21,111,588	-7,674,884	175,072,542	43,731,284	16,249,140	45,867	5,124,633	3,556,598
2004	253,952,404	222,499,659	53,785	222,553,444	22,991,238	-8,635,425	190,926,781	45,994,696	17,030,927	48,838	5,199,870	3,653,953
2005	272,163,722	236,580,026	35,710	236,615,736	24,437,064	-9,969,090	202,209,582	51,516,335	18,437,805	51,609	5,273,577	3,739,388
2006	288,809,418	246,765,785	108	246,765,893	25,931,945	-10,274,031	210,559,917	58,775,014	19,474,487	54,299	5,318,889	3,805,018
2007	302,935,416	256,237,033	-7,264	256,229,769	27,115,667	-11,085,574	218,028,528	63,825,013	21,081,875	56,382	5,372,905	3,878,762
2008	316,119,644	264,948,051	37,584	264,985,635	28,496,613	-10,934,577	225,554,445	65,911,166	24,654,033	58,056	5,445,083	3,895,773
2009	313,083,844	267,849,160	47,541	267,896,701	29,018,926	-10,358,088	228,519,687	58,212,692	26,351,465	56,433	5,547,895	3,855,637
2010	330,571,177	283,272,967	38,963	283,311,930	30,322,698	-10,457,428	242,531,804	58,418,858	29,620,515	58,345	5,665,818	3,873,653
2011	354,275,509	296,349,496	72,094	296,421,590	27,896,434	-10,165,656	258,359,500	64,918,057	30,997,952	61,332	5,776,337	3,940,968
2012	368,484,874	304,276,899	127,695	304,404,594	28,693,159	-9,185,009	266,526,426	70,830,676	31,127,772	62,750	5,872,227	3,991,609
2013	364,228,989	304,250,932	130,919	304,381,851	33,033,252	-8,514,915	262,833,684	68,815,029	32,580,276	61,086	5,962,606	4,047,541
2014	380,127,084	313,263,856	78,713	313,342,569	33,934,920	-8,257,085	271,150,564	74,701,461	34,275,059	63,044	6,029,537	4,101,644
2015	401,008,701	329,773,753	28,642	329,802,395	35,502,681	-8,558,277	285,741,437	78,991,766	36,275,498	65,830	6,091,560	4,193,115
2016	414,918,704	341,188,926	22,761	341,211,687	36,611,989	-8,656,861	295,942,837	80,602,159	38,373,708	67,459	6,150,681	4,281,830
2017	432,558,000	355,941,167	-19,851	355,921,316	38,244,391	-9,053,239	308,623,686	84,347,125	39,587,189	69,581	6,216,589	4,339,883
2018	451,967,783	451,939,324	28,459	365,107,650	39,585,809	-8,974,251	316,547,590	93,674,993	41,745,200	72,340	6,247,841	4,434,939
2019	467,176,430	467,064,743	111,687	379,228,457	40,969,458	-9,178,139	329,080,860	94,002,109	44,093,461	74,385	6,280,487	4,518,171

Personal Income and Employment by Area: Waterloo-Cedar Falls, IA

(Thousands of dollars, except as noted.)

Year	Personal income, total	Earnings by place of work			Less: Contributions for government social insurance	Plus: Adjustment for residence	Equals: Net earnings by place of residence	Plus: Dividends, interest, and rent	Plus: Personal current transfer receipts	Per capita personal income (dollars)	Population (persons)	Total employment
		Nonfarm	Farm	Total								
1970	631,415	496,061	35,859	531,920	37,991	-21,117	472,812	100,737	57,866	3,717	169,857	76,398
1971	669,022	528,899	31,473	560,372	42,010	-23,504	494,858	109,180	64,984	3,929	170,283	75,817
1972	750,312	598,609	41,420	640,029	50,161	-27,391	562,477	118,889	68,946	4,424	169,595	77,925
1973	875,548	686,373	75,857	762,230	66,689	-33,698	661,843	134,288	79,417	5,146	170,158	83,267
1974	962,897	778,027	57,856	835,883	78,109	-39,889	717,885	152,724	92,288	5,658	170,178	85,777
1975	1,071,099	848,307	57,985	906,292	83,427	-43,798	779,067	172,278	119,754	6,264	170,987	85,435
1976	1,145,694	931,895	30,969	962,864	93,158	-47,159	822,547	188,543	134,604	6,660	172,038	86,484
1977	1,324,233	1,095,686	43,267	1,138,953	109,026	-60,399	969,528	214,651	140,054	7,664	172,797	91,066
1978	1,465,258	1,196,354	63,010	1,259,364	123,198	-67,283	1,068,883	240,315	156,060	8,401	174,425	92,582
1979	1,631,641	1,367,338	44,440	1,411,778	146,711	-82,044	1,183,023	273,851	174,767	9,329	174,893	95,443
1980	1,797,821	1,482,169	25,363	1,507,532	157,952	-91,002	1,258,578	331,689	207,554	10,147	177,172	95,288
1981	1,991,937	1,591,253	43,789	1,635,042	180,524	-98,235	1,356,283	404,391	231,263	11,262	176,866	93,456
1982	2,010,653	1,526,437	21,280	1,547,717	175,724	-89,730	1,282,263	452,358	276,032	11,460	175,444	88,697
1983	2,022,857	1,495,488	7,816	1,503,304	172,475	-82,639	1,248,190	474,244	300,423	11,633	173,893	86,524
1984	2,134,211	1,537,846	43,108	1,580,954	182,588	-83,309	1,315,057	519,539	299,615	12,438	171,586	85,792
1985	2,122,895	1,487,405	54,212	1,541,617	177,760	-75,214	1,288,643	518,556	315,696	12,709	167,036	82,930
1986	2,104,171	1,435,407	64,674	1,500,081	174,139	-65,159	1,260,783	514,864	328,524	12,970	162,232	80,235
1987	2,214,195	1,583,943	73,411	1,657,354	189,558	-80,814	1,386,982	499,498	327,715	13,930	158,953	82,491
1988	2,312,787	1,734,101	37,231	1,771,332	214,527	-94,259	1,462,546	511,388	338,853	14,709	157,238	85,872
1989	2,513,231	1,862,570	49,619	1,912,189	228,634	-104,546	1,579,009	569,322	364,900	15,899	158,077	88,775
1990	2,656,280	1,975,942	77,466	2,053,408	247,888	-113,194	1,692,326	569,837	394,117	16,703	159,026	91,900
1991	2,731,177	2,049,012	60,370	2,109,382	258,477	-114,774	1,736,131	573,253	421,793	17,018	160,489	93,283
1992	2,936,419	2,207,451	97,406	2,304,857	276,257	-125,233	1,903,367	577,140	455,912	18,209	161,261	94,400
1993	2,985,513	2,304,823	37,991	2,342,814	290,568	-129,605	1,922,641	578,883	483,989	18,406	162,204	95,937
1994	3,200,337	2,436,477	101,977	2,538,454	310,239	-134,712	2,093,503	602,316	504,518	19,707	162,400	96,870
1995	3,358,848	2,514,548	96,559	2,611,107	321,199	-136,956	2,152,952	673,743	532,153	20,687	162,363	99,104
1996	3,545,672	2,590,608	137,663	2,728,271	314,415	-142,065	2,271,791	717,462	556,419	21,751	163,010	100,755
1997	3,767,333	2,800,781	133,009	2,933,790	351,772	-156,766	2,425,252	774,639	567,442	23,126	162,902	103,664
1998	3,909,988	2,923,632	94,253	3,017,885	362,878	-159,969	2,495,038	820,217	594,733	23,937	163,342	105,588
1999	3,902,137	2,929,520	68,012	2,997,532	360,657	-155,316	2,481,559	805,300	615,278	23,864	163,516	104,942
2000	4,164,951	3,113,872	79,850	3,193,722	379,427	-172,992	2,641,303	874,222	649,426	25,443	163,699	106,241
2001	4,268,252	3,222,353	71,601	3,293,954	391,863	-187,299	2,714,792	842,086	711,374	26,091	163,590	104,894
2002	4,432,002	3,324,902	70,523	3,395,425	402,805	-200,665	2,791,955	861,984	778,063	27,251	162,634	104,571
2003	4,501,473	3,434,290	49,401	3,483,691	421,569	-212,256	2,849,866	870,646	780,961	27,720	162,388	104,473
2004	4,844,031	3,729,062	135,670	3,864,732	450,396	-232,538	3,181,798	854,509	807,724	29,756	162,793	106,240
2005	4,980,615	3,872,173	117,767	3,989,940	468,528	-249,057	3,272,355	856,694	851,566	30,507	163,260	107,311
2006	5,247,221	4,041,154	80,561	4,121,715	485,519	-265,211	3,370,985	948,035	928,201	32,000	163,976	108,753
2007	5,573,933	4,250,996	112,427	4,363,423	512,911	-290,868	3,559,644	1,039,903	974,386	33,923	164,310	110,709
2008	5,909,609	4,467,086	103,733	4,570,819	543,435	-305,329	3,722,055	1,106,129	1,081,425	35,659	165,724	111,092
2009	5,893,280	4,502,955	67,010	4,569,965	548,073	-318,822	3,703,070	1,044,521	1,145,689	35,242	167,225	110,044
2010	6,042,836	4,604,270	86,151	4,690,421	562,605	-331,530	3,796,286	1,025,893	1,220,657	35,988	167,913	109,771
2011	6,487,621	4,771,931	216,463	4,988,394	529,388	-361,314	4,097,692	1,129,213	1,260,716	38,542	168,325	111,902
2012	6,813,695	5,093,980	176,303	5,270,283	552,887	-394,889	4,322,507	1,246,610	1,244,578	40,383	168,725	113,816
2013	6,804,782	5,152,193	217,202	5,369,395	626,996	-402,899	4,339,500	1,194,616	1,270,666	40,100	169,697	114,443
2014	6,992,301	5,317,186	105,137	5,422,323	635,907	-397,124	4,389,292	1,276,161	1,326,848	41,086	170,189	114,650
2015	7,159,466	5,314,740	103,937	5,418,677	627,668	-398,812	4,392,197	1,365,937	1,401,332	41,966	170,602	113,758
2016	7,167,144	5,345,998	54,055	5,400,053	646,787	-392,372	4,360,894	1,370,079	1,436,171	42,186	169,894	112,978
2017	7,382,228	5,559,451	51,589	5,611,040	674,492	-410,878	4,525,670	1,427,566	1,428,992	43,452	169,892	112,983
2018	7,855,415	7,780,774	74,641	5,839,631	711,467	-430,492	4,697,672	1,603,384	1,554,359	46,499	168,936	114,087
2019	8,025,590	7,897,266	128,324	5,940,230	720,517	-425,082	4,794,631	1,603,234	1,627,725	47,623	168,522	113,858

Personal Income and Employment by Area: Watertown-Fort Drum, NY

(Thousands of dollars, except as noted.)

Year	Personal income, total	Earnings by place of work Nonfarm	Farm	Total	Less: Contributions for government social insurance	Plus: Adjustment for residence	Equals: Net earnings by place of residence	Plus: Dividends, interest, and rent	Plus: Personal current transfer receipts	Per capita personal income (dollars)	Population (persons)	Total employment
1970	313,911	233,051	13,226	246,277	17,886	1,332	229,723	45,347	38,841	3,535	88,789	36,388
1971	337,120	246,280	12,704	258,984	19,170	1,792	241,606	48,706	46,808	3,758	89,719	36,058
1972	354,161	258,045	12,596	270,641	21,020	1,164	250,785	52,350	51,026	3,902	90,773	36,058
1973	380,658	276,641	13,293	289,934	25,710	778	265,002	59,177	56,479	4,215	90,310	37,049
1974	412,204	297,281	10,516	307,797	28,471	-117	279,209	65,940	67,055	4,606	89,485	36,947
1975	450,975	315,477	7,626	323,103	29,592	-2,074	291,437	71,618	87,920	4,998	90,235	36,272
1976	480,436	336,374	10,448	346,822	32,046	-2,902	311,874	74,391	94,171	5,309	90,488	35,746
1977	507,630	360,887	5,744	366,631	34,443	-3,299	328,889	82,069	96,672	5,635	90,089	36,188
1978	560,769	406,740	10,688	417,428	39,685	-4,915	372,828	86,264	101,677	6,255	89,651	37,470
1979	617,790	453,821	11,220	465,041	45,747	-7,239	412,055	98,175	107,560	6,929	89,161	38,283
1980	686,675	493,802	8,382	502,184	49,402	-9,568	443,214	117,560	125,901	7,797	88,071	37,483
1981	749,470	527,057	7,048	534,105	55,388	-10,967	467,750	139,585	142,135	8,557	87,585	36,896
1982	824,343	555,255	9,497	564,752	58,787	-11,729	494,236	167,111	162,996	9,442	87,302	36,595
1983	880,079	597,922	7,740	605,662	63,922	-12,830	528,910	172,056	179,113	10,062	87,465	37,306
1984	976,056	674,029	9,639	683,668	73,089	-15,071	595,508	192,473	188,075	11,080	88,094	38,570
1985	1,058,050	741,730	12,640	754,370	81,387	-19,426	653,557	206,491	198,002	11,894	88,954	40,370
1986	1,168,512	841,825	15,534	857,359	92,370	-27,313	737,676	227,723	203,113	12,836	91,032	43,661
1987	1,374,848	1,059,911	17,406	1,077,317	114,820	-50,359	912,138	260,732	201,978	14,268	96,360	49,930
1988	1,581,005	1,280,260	12,875	1,293,135	143,014	-73,745	1,076,376	292,457	212,172	15,237	103,758	56,273
1989	1,787,872	1,422,493	19,483	1,441,976	156,679	-79,354	1,205,943	350,529	231,400	16,323	109,534	60,292
1990	1,852,405	1,457,107	20,830	1,477,937	156,051	-78,196	1,243,690	357,585	251,130	16,606	111,549	59,814
1991	1,946,410	1,515,191	13,645	1,528,836	165,526	-73,752	1,289,558	372,622	284,230	17,238	112,911	58,880
1992	2,055,931	1,573,569	18,860	1,592,429	172,555	-71,297	1,348,577	383,050	324,304	17,962	114,463	58,311
1993	2,059,712	1,555,290	17,626	1,572,916	173,235	-66,142	1,333,539	384,708	341,465	17,930	114,874	57,273
1994	2,119,244	1,599,431	15,834	1,615,265	177,783	-65,807	1,371,675	394,786	352,783	18,124	116,932	58,543
1995	2,201,951	1,643,327	9,650	1,652,977	180,459	-65,656	1,406,862	423,973	371,116	19,087	115,361	58,586
1996	2,261,624	1,672,858	20,720	1,693,578	182,095	-63,452	1,448,031	430,890	382,703	19,738	114,585	58,639
1997	2,318,594	1,733,861	8,033	1,741,894	186,017	-61,775	1,494,102	437,185	387,307	20,509	113,055	58,879
1998	2,436,714	1,813,967	8,916	1,822,883	193,052	-62,540	1,567,291	465,618	403,805	21,651	112,546	59,089
1999	2,548,053	1,904,832	8,920	1,913,752	197,763	-60,417	1,655,572	468,683	423,798	22,734	112,081	60,291
2000	2,692,809	2,010,563	7,663	2,018,226	207,851	-60,007	1,750,368	498,668	443,773	24,088	111,790	61,119
2001	2,714,889	2,014,208	11,694	2,025,902	217,321	-69,501	1,739,080	500,208	475,601	24,366	111,422	60,488
2002	2,842,346	2,122,015	15,503	2,137,518	230,596	-76,765	1,830,157	497,647	514,542	25,581	111,112	60,316
2003	3,020,134	2,279,687	24,887	2,304,574	245,508	-99,264	1,959,802	526,958	533,374	27,394	110,246	60,812
2004	3,215,898	2,451,609	37,924	2,489,533	267,055	-119,485	2,102,993	546,430	566,475	29,256	109,924	62,675
2005	3,514,490	2,779,078	38,427	2,817,505	302,268	-169,285	2,345,952	578,017	590,521	30,968	113,486	65,950
2006	3,813,590	3,151,982	26,188	3,178,170	343,212	-260,129	2,574,829	624,726	614,035	33,556	113,650	69,033
2007	4,058,799	3,312,916	39,912	3,352,828	357,326	-264,207	2,731,295	682,597	644,907	35,276	115,059	69,725
2008	4,341,008	3,518,761	42,604	3,561,365	382,812	-316,483	2,862,070	756,216	722,722	37,737	115,033	71,126
2009	4,531,018	3,679,478	20,635	3,700,113	401,460	-334,829	2,963,824	777,619	789,575	39,392	115,023	70,866
2010	4,830,213	3,923,471	43,213	3,966,684	428,610	-339,382	3,198,692	779,290	852,231	41,425	116,601	72,440
2011	5,049,427	4,025,162	66,609	4,091,771	404,189	-393,754	3,293,828	875,977	879,622	42,862	117,806	72,646
2012	5,098,854	3,966,860	57,123	4,023,983	399,622	-352,964	3,271,397	952,511	874,946	41,983	121,449	71,377
2013	5,012,091	3,888,942	72,148	3,961,090	432,652	-344,413	3,184,025	921,320	906,746	42,041	119,219	70,587
2014	5,058,669	3,853,741	83,054	3,936,795	436,065	-315,785	3,184,945	948,695	925,029	42,494	119,044	69,609
2015	5,037,142	3,833,305	40,294	3,873,599	435,675	-318,807	3,119,117	936,784	981,241	43,311	116,301	68,777
2016	4,937,010	3,741,368	34,606	3,775,974	425,653	-302,856	3,047,465	886,789	1,002,756	43,275	114,084	67,517
2017	5,146,329	3,845,057	40,346	3,885,403	441,383	-298,815	3,145,205	923,754	1,077,370	45,069	114,187	67,528
2018	5,235,284	5,188,555	46,729	3,977,049	440,485	-308,169	3,228,395	940,839	1,066,050	46,800	111,866	67,345
2019	5,421,948	5,361,374	60,574	4,089,094	449,617	-323,983	3,315,494	953,987	1,152,467	49,365	109,834	67,287

Personal Income and Employment by Area: Wausau-Weston, WI

(Thousands of dollars, except as noted.)

Year	Personal income, total	Earnings by place of work			Less: Contributions for government social insurance	Plus: Adjustment for residence	Equals: Net earnings by place of residence	Plus: Dividends, interest, and rent	Plus: Personal current transfer receipts	Per capita personal income (dollars)	Population (persons)	Total employment
		Nonfarm	Farm	Total								
1970	336,776	255,420	21,015	276,435	18,854	499	258,080	48,532	30,164	3,445	97,762	42,507
1971	364,714	275,088	21,010	296,098	21,036	1,009	276,071	53,374	35,269	3,678	99,164	42,664
1972	407,458	311,537	22,947	334,484	25,095	744	310,133	58,314	39,011	4,069	100,135	44,356
1973	461,198	356,405	27,446	383,851	32,904	512	351,459	65,565	44,174	4,534	101,722	46,586
1974	503,186	389,538	22,355	411,893	37,292	1,431	376,032	74,315	52,839	4,876	103,197	47,168
1975	565,233	428,179	25,566	453,745	40,005	1,149	414,889	83,428	66,916	5,395	104,779	48,012
1976	639,843	493,124	28,919	522,043	46,867	1,483	476,659	89,550	73,634	6,087	105,124	50,209
1977	736,095	573,300	39,645	612,945	54,446	665	559,164	99,555	77,376	6,876	107,054	53,684
1978	830,191	647,041	45,564	692,605	63,114	1,432	630,923	112,715	86,553	7,643	108,618	55,887
1979	925,333	707,553	56,237	763,790	71,903	2,247	694,134	128,913	102,286	8,368	110,574	56,769
1980	1,011,574	742,949	54,780	797,729	75,229	3,934	726,434	158,056	127,084	9,093	111,246	55,624
1981	1,092,193	795,894	46,290	842,184	86,030	3,874	760,028	193,551	138,614	9,850	110,887	55,453
1982	1,144,982	808,437	41,897	850,334	88,085	8,374	770,623	218,252	156,107	10,313	111,023	54,768
1983	1,199,293	869,107	21,343	890,450	94,425	10,774	806,799	224,839	167,655	10,809	110,953	55,723
1984	1,308,795	929,349	37,255	966,604	102,992	14,553	878,165	257,784	172,846	11,765	111,241	56,858
1985	1,392,973	997,293	36,975	1,034,268	111,513	13,963	936,718	273,212	183,043	12,520	111,260	57,757
1986	1,477,942	1,064,671	41,993	1,106,664	118,954	15,450	1,003,160	289,957	184,825	13,260	111,458	59,211
1987	1,569,556	1,153,438	51,154	1,204,592	127,228	15,968	1,093,332	289,214	187,010	14,007	112,058	61,043
1988	1,667,958	1,260,525	39,761	1,300,286	144,204	16,383	1,172,465	303,036	192,457	14,734	113,201	62,564
1989	1,855,697	1,360,382	76,151	1,436,533	156,596	15,391	1,295,328	346,812	213,557	16,233	114,318	64,559
1990	1,981,850	1,478,178	69,842	1,548,020	177,127	19,246	1,390,139	362,251	229,460	17,123	115,743	66,554
1991	2,068,665	1,571,719	47,284	1,619,003	189,912	16,506	1,445,597	368,767	254,301	17,685	116,972	68,392
1992	2,235,885	1,708,379	54,597	1,762,976	203,981	17,356	1,576,351	384,378	275,156	18,881	118,417	69,877
1993	2,348,607	1,810,486	42,451	1,852,937	216,374	16,017	1,652,580	405,417	290,610	19,565	120,044	70,906
1994	2,482,296	1,925,746	49,367	1,975,113	232,626	14,532	1,757,019	423,506	301,771	20,556	120,760	72,786
1995	2,605,618	2,028,304	31,637	2,059,941	245,485	8,973	1,823,429	460,354	321,835	21,419	121,649	74,772
1996	2,779,602	2,138,436	52,741	2,191,177	256,810	4,056	1,938,423	506,089	335,090	22,680	122,560	76,066
1997	2,953,168	2,317,566	27,508	2,345,074	276,444	-5,664	2,062,966	542,918	347,284	23,896	123,583	78,232
1998	3,154,973	2,440,292	49,838	2,490,130	287,043	-2,087	2,201,000	601,076	352,897	25,321	124,597	80,916
1999	3,304,132	2,623,976	44,441	2,668,417	308,512	-11,640	2,348,265	587,558	368,309	26,348	125,404	83,339
2000	3,525,868	2,812,887	26,255	2,839,142	325,374	-21,542	2,492,226	638,034	395,608	27,984	125,995	84,933
2001	3,699,414	2,976,210	44,514	3,020,724	340,937	-57,820	2,621,967	633,567	443,880	29,254	126,459	85,631
2002	3,825,570	3,139,302	35,277	3,174,579	355,955	-81,801	2,736,823	608,658	480,089	30,151	126,880	86,521
2003	3,961,344	3,249,093	52,610	3,301,703	368,713	-79,600	2,853,390	618,941	489,013	31,115	127,311	86,659
2004	4,119,779	3,438,672	61,301	3,499,973	391,171	-100,191	3,008,611	597,598	513,570	32,222	127,855	88,562
2005	4,318,763	3,626,212	52,567	3,678,779	414,777	-116,447	3,147,555	620,843	550,365	33,490	128,958	90,836
2006	4,518,355	3,778,378	37,712	3,816,090	437,497	-136,947	3,241,646	689,188	587,521	34,619	130,516	91,477
2007	4,745,097	3,893,361	65,236	3,958,597	452,787	-165,072	3,340,738	767,235	637,124	36,010	131,773	92,619
2008	4,956,253	3,970,945	58,339	4,029,284	465,197	-146,319	3,417,768	803,128	735,357	37,255	133,036	91,912
2009	4,974,150	3,830,142	19,606	3,849,748	449,744	-35,523	3,364,481	755,971	853,698	37,178	133,793	87,803
2010	5,005,781	3,825,671	57,418	3,883,089	449,642	-87,236	3,346,211	740,695	918,875	37,343	134,047	86,187
2011	5,298,706	3,975,835	101,595	4,077,430	418,504	-54,774	3,604,152	806,486	888,068	39,439	134,353	87,033
2012	5,581,116	4,169,824	101,816	4,271,640	434,515	-15,633	3,821,492	862,269	897,355	41,527	134,397	86,841
2013	5,609,399	4,251,084	94,215	4,345,299	499,520	-25,862	3,819,917	886,445	903,037	41,573	134,928	88,071
2014	5,901,506	4,429,677	131,039	4,560,716	518,228	-18,133	4,024,355	945,477	931,674	43,645	135,215	89,755
2015	6,074,581	4,555,007	97,799	4,652,806	534,178	-28,840	4,089,788	1,015,509	969,284	44,866	135,394	90,739
2016	6,246,164	4,620,931	71,760	4,692,691	535,046	54,179	4,211,824	1,050,759	983,581	46,201	135,195	91,208
2017	6,463,176	4,815,596	70,575	4,886,171	558,740	20,902	4,348,333	1,090,051	1,024,792	47,617	135,732	91,687
2018	8,103,082	8,018,277	84,805	5,896,214	670,390	138,503	5,364,327	1,341,999	1,396,756	49,684	163,094	107,455
2019	8,375,743	8,243,912	131,831	6,087,452	692,126	168,092	5,563,418	1,353,409	1,458,916	51,295	163,285	108,244

Personal Income and Employment by Area: Weirton-Steubenville, WV-OH

(Thousands of dollars, except as noted.)

Year	Personal income, total	Earnings by place of work			Less: Contributions for government social insurance	Plus: Adjustment for residence	Equals: Net earnings by place of residence	Plus: Dividends, interest, and rent	Plus: Personal current transfer receipts	Per capita personal income (dollars)	Population (persons)	Total employment
		Nonfarm	Farm	Total								
1970	603,659	559,411	947	560,358	41,075	-43,339	475,944	69,924	57,791	3,626	166,471	67,336
1971	655,277	607,649	1,121	608,770	46,459	-50,591	511,720	75,349	68,208	3,920	167,161	68,528
1972	714,183	665,855	1,194	667,049	53,066	-56,403	557,580	80,090	76,513	4,301	166,032	68,997
1973	767,566	710,436	1,697	712,133	66,289	-58,488	587,356	89,130	91,080	4,622	166,066	70,056
1974	879,832	820,599	1,973	822,572	79,983	-71,107	671,482	103,506	104,844	5,346	164,593	71,072
1975	961,462	872,396	1,547	873,943	85,142	-72,638	716,163	117,557	127,742	5,793	165,977	69,428
1976	1,080,647	1,004,027	1,375	1,005,402	98,476	-92,584	814,342	126,079	140,226	6,563	164,666	71,679
1977	1,179,504	1,088,456	1,262	1,089,718	106,240	-96,473	887,005	139,717	152,782	7,202	163,770	71,144
1978	1,271,763	1,161,052	1,474	1,162,526	116,877	-98,125	947,524	152,799	171,440	7,857	161,867	70,906
1979	1,419,618	1,302,284	1,753	1,304,037	135,487	-113,633	1,054,917	171,395	193,306	8,785	161,602	72,151
1980	1,527,137	1,334,690	1,901	1,336,591	139,169	-121,663	1,075,759	213,100	238,278	9,349	163,345	68,618
1981	1,644,418	1,380,663	1,807	1,382,470	154,031	-110,106	1,118,333	259,194	266,891	10,181	161,525	66,467
1982	1,639,708	1,292,762	2,234	1,294,996	148,079	-104,287	1,042,630	289,163	307,915	10,217	160,486	60,765
1983	1,617,420	1,222,736	717	1,223,453	141,218	-95,555	986,680	306,337	324,403	10,307	156,918	57,943
1984	1,713,492	1,278,264	438	1,278,702	151,493	-101,123	1,026,086	347,218	340,188	11,080	154,644	58,635
1985	1,733,479	1,267,767	1,224	1,268,991	151,475	-92,300	1,025,216	349,521	358,742	11,406	151,981	57,275
1986	1,821,619	1,357,102	375	1,357,477	167,499	-101,260	1,088,718	362,089	370,812	12,215	149,132	58,845
1987	1,863,147	1,399,105	324	1,399,429	170,958	-100,782	1,127,689	353,311	382,147	12,694	146,776	59,897
1988	1,956,394	1,500,832	-1,417	1,499,415	190,199	-112,010	1,197,206	362,168	397,020	13,473	145,205	60,005
1989	2,100,860	1,618,251	748	1,618,999	207,340	-124,689	1,286,970	402,900	410,990	14,602	143,873	61,112
1990	2,224,855	1,681,031	757	1,681,788	218,628	-112,185	1,350,975	427,101	446,779	15,638	142,270	62,123
1991	2,220,048	1,619,569	-1,147	1,618,422	214,424	-71,622	1,332,376	401,801	485,871	15,651	141,845	60,857
1992	2,342,245	1,729,900	2,438	1,732,338	223,164	-102,326	1,406,848	400,438	534,959	16,610	141,012	60,156
1993	2,402,267	1,752,906	1,689	1,754,595	238,794	-72,376	1,443,425	393,462	565,380	17,073	140,704	59,913
1994	2,501,287	1,814,775	2,781	1,817,556	245,634	-69,362	1,502,560	405,609	593,118	17,866	140,001	60,141
1995	2,550,358	1,796,315	1,328	1,797,643	249,019	-33,271	1,515,353	418,123	616,882	18,276	139,547	60,826
1996	2,635,974	1,829,905	449	1,830,354	252,899	-36,657	1,540,798	446,185	648,991	19,063	138,275	60,868
1997	2,649,444	1,746,627	1,456	1,748,083	236,953	-4,439	1,506,691	474,983	667,770	19,393	136,619	59,452
1998	2,796,175	1,875,068	1,891	1,876,959	254,449	-9,807	1,612,703	506,353	677,119	20,762	134,675	61,710
1999	2,837,353	1,879,832	2,141	1,881,973	251,557	17,306	1,647,722	490,368	699,263	21,289	133,276	60,934
2000	2,990,416	1,984,652	3,796	1,988,448	268,538	23,208	1,743,118	518,947	728,351	22,710	131,681	60,717
2001	3,168,308	2,049,360	4,316	2,053,676	268,160	62,751	1,848,267	523,959	796,082	24,241	130,701	60,250
2002	3,251,759	2,122,575	4,492	2,127,067	271,581	67,697	1,923,183	492,798	835,778	25,062	129,750	60,337
2003	3,262,097	2,119,135	3,585	2,122,720	276,505	83,391	1,929,606	473,323	859,168	25,260	129,141	59,545
2004	3,360,614	2,111,816	3,149	2,114,965	276,045	146,778	1,985,698	501,521	873,395	26,205	128,241	58,166
2005	3,374,504	2,117,694	2,023	2,119,717	279,266	182,018	2,022,469	459,205	892,830	26,474	127,464	58,048
2006	3,547,139	2,163,103	1,695	2,164,798	273,860	242,297	2,133,235	466,885	947,019	28,080	126,321	57,500
2007	3,695,819	2,227,208	1,213	2,228,421	275,221	237,833	2,191,033	524,976	979,810	29,511	125,236	57,963
2008	3,872,443	2,390,148	-1,125	2,389,023	294,695	160,864	2,255,192	538,851	1,078,400	30,990	124,959	58,237
2009	3,778,245	2,180,342	-198	2,180,144	274,513	202,490	2,108,121	499,765	1,170,359	30,290	124,734	54,820
2010	3,852,504	2,105,165	-443	2,104,722	261,635	304,861	2,147,948	483,886	1,220,670	30,987	124,326	52,804
2011	4,058,152	2,188,084	-249	2,187,835	244,968	362,781	2,305,648	526,598	1,225,906	32,873	123,449	52,893
2012	4,157,327	2,228,094	148	2,228,242	246,316	388,071	2,369,997	568,042	1,219,288	33,896	122,651	52,494
2013	4,181,407	2,210,690	1,328	2,212,018	268,642	443,538	2,386,914	546,178	1,248,315	34,243	122,110	52,091
2014	4,309,636	2,241,750	-126	2,241,624	275,749	462,390	2,428,265	580,771	1,300,600	35,481	121,463	51,778
2015	4,401,164	2,246,864	-389	2,246,475	277,181	491,185	2,460,479	594,930	1,345,755	36,488	120,621	51,269
2016	4,357,873	2,247,159	155	2,247,314	283,040	419,307	2,383,581	605,197	1,369,095	36,546	119,242	50,254
2017	4,507,201	2,321,343	-2,431	2,318,912	296,531	446,521	2,468,902	630,564	1,407,735	38,116	118,250	49,548
2018	4,753,425	4,759,012	-5,587	2,401,339	303,386	510,213	2,608,166	700,200	1,445,059	40,634	116,982	49,609
2019	4,893,403	4,898,512	-5,109	2,464,215	309,840	541,566	2,695,941	709,823	1,487,639	42,158	116,074	50,135

Personal Income and Employment by Area: Wenatchee, WA

(Thousands of dollars, except as noted.)

Year	Personal income, total	Earnings by place of work Nonfarm	Farm	Total	Less: Contributions for government social insurance	Plus: Adjustment for residence	Equals: Net earnings by place of residence	Plus: Dividends, interest, and rent	Plus: Personal current transfer receipts	Per capita personal income (dollars)	Population (persons)	Total employment
1970	233,154	158,823	19,635	178,458	12,977	-166	165,315	41,612	26,227	4,026	57,905	28,819
1971	266,510	170,446	36,117	206,563	14,632	-175	191,756	45,048	29,706	4,581	58,182	28,335
1972	284,714	182,550	37,258	219,808	16,352	298	203,754	48,961	31,999	4,906	58,036	28,518
1973	329,056	202,945	53,433	256,378	21,005	1,100	236,473	56,723	35,860	5,642	58,318	29,659
1974	369,509	228,690	57,772	286,462	24,447	1,148	263,163	64,136	42,210	6,207	59,531	31,056
1975	432,793	260,413	72,111	332,524	27,982	1,110	305,652	75,039	52,102	7,122	60,767	32,893
1976	464,732	308,579	52,827	361,406	33,902	-102	327,402	80,329	57,001	7,442	62,443	35,350
1977	522,482	353,189	54,629	407,818	39,188	-206	368,424	91,784	62,274	8,121	64,337	36,078
1978	580,874	387,544	59,826	447,370	43,600	3,773	407,543	105,791	67,540	8,857	65,586	36,913
1979	630,407	423,119	52,683	475,802	48,920	4,434	431,316	122,256	76,835	9,512	66,273	38,625
1980	707,702	442,319	67,814	510,133	51,477	5,284	463,940	148,941	94,821	10,470	67,591	38,992
1981	762,803	473,188	59,802	532,990	58,946	5,318	479,362	179,278	104,163	11,054	69,004	39,690
1982	814,883	488,827	62,204	551,031	62,109	5,850	494,772	202,136	117,975	11,704	69,622	39,743
1983	894,276	530,011	72,443	602,454	68,509	6,583	540,528	226,230	127,518	12,598	70,983	41,521
1984	963,699	578,274	72,225	650,499	77,530	5,218	578,187	249,804	135,708	13,306	72,428	42,260
1985	990,285	609,131	47,732	656,863	82,939	5,973	579,897	262,761	147,627	13,458	73,586	42,158
1986	1,059,312	629,815	84,637	714,452	85,979	8,430	636,903	266,508	155,901	14,342	73,859	41,969
1987	1,150,789	667,198	133,123	800,321	90,570	9,218	718,969	269,315	162,505	15,502	74,236	43,915
1988	1,135,140	716,588	59,442	776,030	99,539	10,850	687,341	275,309	172,490	14,935	76,006	44,589
1989	1,251,178	760,485	87,670	848,155	107,927	12,672	752,900	309,590	188,688	16,143	77,504	45,586
1990	1,332,739	824,485	84,403	908,888	119,201	16,328	806,015	318,061	208,663	16,899	78,865	48,257
1991	1,486,806	908,940	125,219	1,034,159	131,365	17,755	920,549	332,030	234,227	18,306	81,220	48,854
1992	1,629,985	990,816	154,948	1,145,764	142,013	20,502	1,024,253	344,939	260,793	19,504	83,570	48,476
1993	1,728,341	1,069,658	142,267	1,211,925	153,062	22,937	1,081,800	370,368	276,173	20,091	86,027	49,733
1994	1,807,351	1,144,770	114,513	1,259,283	164,070	24,287	1,119,500	393,048	294,803	20,363	88,755	52,796
1995	1,881,852	1,165,647	113,796	1,279,443	167,817	26,691	1,138,317	433,035	310,500	20,527	91,676	53,327
1996	2,042,695	1,225,759	166,444	1,392,203	170,726	29,290	1,250,767	461,277	330,651	21,850	93,486	53,993
1997	2,138,037	1,318,402	121,829	1,440,231	174,799	32,519	1,297,951	499,839	340,247	22,478	95,118	54,720
1998	2,249,348	1,405,478	128,181	1,533,659	182,381	37,588	1,388,866	499,120	361,362	23,233	96,819	55,168
1999	2,292,913	1,464,189	106,281	1,570,470	186,028	41,421	1,425,863	483,738	383,312	23,317	98,336	56,072
2000	2,444,726	1,525,601	131,549	1,657,150	198,835	43,132	1,501,447	522,912	420,367	24,614	99,322	56,928
2001	2,530,232	1,603,814	101,423	1,705,237	207,156	42,775	1,540,856	524,212	465,164	25,465	99,361	56,354
2002	2,586,874	1,682,906	120,997	1,803,903	218,174	39,977	1,625,706	479,114	482,054	25,924	99,786	56,612
2003	2,709,302	1,730,079	148,825	1,878,904	225,850	39,033	1,692,087	507,312	509,903	26,917	100,654	57,198
2004	2,849,995	1,827,218	170,870	1,998,088	242,472	38,562	1,794,178	532,882	522,935	27,950	101,968	58,759
2005	2,940,329	1,928,484	136,976	2,065,460	259,877	38,721	1,844,304	533,375	562,650	28,445	103,369	60,974
2006	3,128,930	2,045,386	135,729	2,181,115	274,750	37,895	1,944,260	577,758	606,912	29,773	105,094	62,332
2007	3,396,664	2,155,874	135,209	2,291,083	289,008	39,931	2,042,006	697,328	657,330	31,829	106,717	63,792
2008	3,718,672	2,233,640	157,527	2,391,167	301,628	43,165	2,132,704	841,836	744,132	34,423	108,029	64,605
2009	3,679,601	2,187,039	170,880	2,357,919	308,105	48,506	2,098,320	758,842	822,439	33,569	109,614	63,716
2010	3,785,058	2,212,570	184,330	2,396,900	311,351	54,448	2,139,997	745,935	899,126	34,012	111,286	62,778
2011	4,012,403	2,251,998	236,339	2,488,337	293,622	63,206	2,257,921	848,780	905,702	35,852	111,915	63,191
2012	4,348,769	2,418,175	269,528	2,687,703	300,379	78,041	2,465,365	965,319	918,085	38,562	112,774	64,483
2013	4,437,479	2,568,464	245,816	2,814,280	347,436	88,041	2,554,885	948,231	934,363	39,189	113,234	65,701
2014	4,741,962	2,715,698	219,316	2,935,014	372,826	95,354	2,657,542	1,053,849	1,030,571	41,597	113,997	67,547
2015	5,074,820	2,865,704	309,840	3,175,544	392,141	99,377	2,882,780	1,149,974	1,042,066	43,876	115,662	69,014
2016	5,326,857	2,946,473	305,508	3,251,981	400,205	106,052	2,957,828	1,254,377	1,114,652	45,435	117,240	69,857
2017	5,573,816	3,135,183	285,611	3,420,794	432,974	112,288	3,100,108	1,323,752	1,149,956	47,045	118,478	71,124
2018	5,924,225	5,729,126	195,099	3,559,383	446,064	123,794	3,237,113	1,501,784	1,185,328	49,575	119,501	73,081
2019	6,154,809	5,969,996	184,813	3,689,731	462,413	132,042	3,359,360	1,531,657	1,263,792	51,023	120,629	73,276

Personal Income and Employment by Area: Wheeling, WV-OH

(Thousands of dollars, except as noted.)

Year	Personal income, total	Earnings by place of work			Less: Contributions for government social insurance	Plus: Adjustment for residence	Equals: Net earnings by place of residence	Plus: Dividends, interest, and rent	Plus: Personal current transfer receipts	Per capita personal income (dollars)	Population (persons)	Total employment
		Nonfarm	Farm	Total								
1970	644,855	513,841	1,901	515,742	38,769	7,056	484,029	91,851	68,975	3,532	182,552	74,553
1971	688,713	541,975	2,345	544,320	42,239	7,153	509,234	98,826	80,653	3,699	186,174	74,644
1972	748,314	588,226	2,802	591,028	47,447	7,826	551,407	106,257	90,650	4,027	185,831	74,658
1973	817,931	641,793	3,185	644,978	60,044	7,197	592,131	118,050	107,750	4,416	185,230	76,692
1974	893,606	689,250	1,677	690,927	67,207	9,685	633,405	135,031	125,170	4,851	184,209	77,111
1975	992,231	756,596	2,702	759,298	71,683	4,363	691,978	147,633	152,620	5,360	185,114	76,968
1976	1,112,204	857,184	2,585	859,769	82,833	4,085	781,021	161,441	169,742	5,966	186,432	78,256
1977	1,232,362	957,365	1,932	959,297	92,719	2,979	869,557	180,780	182,025	6,637	185,683	79,725
1978	1,348,998	1,051,647	1,367	1,053,014	104,981	-842	947,191	197,318	204,489	7,282	185,256	81,408
1979	1,499,362	1,153,813	1,076	1,154,889	118,437	8,055	1,044,507	218,935	235,920	8,041	186,463	81,667
1980	1,620,122	1,175,054	732	1,175,786	121,537	16,009	1,070,258	274,588	275,276	8,741	185,340	78,635
1981	1,768,266	1,244,445	385	1,244,830	137,959	10,742	1,117,613	344,057	306,596	9,602	184,158	76,299
1982	1,850,522	1,255,148	-252	1,254,896	142,592	2,643	1,114,947	388,273	347,302	10,149	182,331	74,012
1983	1,882,262	1,218,777	-1,025	1,217,752	139,547	8,871	1,087,076	415,872	379,314	10,454	180,057	71,069
1984	1,985,983	1,275,937	501	1,276,438	148,814	14,913	1,142,537	455,364	388,082	11,234	176,777	70,504
1985	2,025,382	1,282,802	2,314	1,285,116	150,783	9,515	1,143,848	472,958	408,576	11,702	173,087	69,315
1986	2,066,117	1,296,187	1,747	1,297,934	156,896	7,945	1,148,983	491,249	425,885	12,246	168,724	68,607
1987	2,139,364	1,380,057	1,010	1,381,067	167,850	6,938	1,220,155	485,462	433,747	12,875	166,158	70,059
1988	2,223,793	1,456,222	-1,577	1,454,645	183,796	-7,541	1,263,308	505,751	454,734	13,581	163,741	71,434
1989	2,378,281	1,533,260	1,392	1,534,652	195,465	-7,099	1,332,088	567,464	478,729	14,711	161,663	71,939
1990	2,495,498	1,618,363	1,314	1,619,677	208,013	-2,194	1,409,470	578,010	508,018	15,699	158,961	72,385
1991	2,568,572	1,662,334	-2,791	1,659,543	219,889	-8,943	1,430,711	583,575	554,286	16,228	158,283	72,525
1992	2,730,575	1,731,967	2,101	1,734,068	230,546	20,565	1,524,087	587,680	618,808	17,225	158,525	71,690
1993	2,784,668	1,783,497	1,332	1,784,829	245,159	7,187	1,546,857	586,642	651,169	17,575	158,445	72,312
1994	2,905,485	1,887,290	1,625	1,888,915	258,848	3,300	1,633,367	605,120	666,998	18,396	157,944	74,195
1995	2,978,757	1,926,768	557	1,927,325	266,974	-9,016	1,651,335	639,718	687,704	19,033	156,502	75,761
1996	3,124,422	1,991,736	-1,726	1,990,010	274,725	8,480	1,723,765	675,457	725,200	19,856	157,354	76,900
1997	3,233,433	2,073,520	-1,875	2,071,645	279,854	1,465	1,793,256	698,360	741,817	20,714	156,100	77,888
1998	3,449,748	2,185,962	-531	2,185,431	293,377	12,240	1,904,294	754,180	791,274	22,176	155,562	79,973
1999	3,508,877	2,276,282	-490	2,275,792	303,703	9,921	1,982,010	725,924	800,943	22,751	154,230	79,789
2000	3,623,712	2,337,320	4,851	2,342,171	315,287	9,341	2,036,225	764,495	822,992	23,698	152,914	80,874
2001	4,007,583	2,657,847	4,463	2,662,310	325,937	5,833	2,342,206	762,571	902,806	26,413	151,728	79,685
2002	4,113,296	2,747,352	2,085	2,749,437	329,769	10,486	2,430,154	727,385	955,757	27,161	151,442	79,961
2003	4,183,958	2,837,003	242	2,837,245	347,751	7,468	2,496,962	711,095	975,901	27,770	150,666	79,043
2004	4,315,017	2,972,202	7,714	2,979,916	361,772	-38	2,618,106	699,408	997,503	28,731	150,186	80,122
2005	4,428,185	3,107,805	5,978	3,113,783	378,631	-9,563	2,725,589	683,489	1,019,107	29,632	149,438	81,069
2006	4,674,561	3,257,166	612	3,257,778	383,249	-11,446	2,863,083	736,376	1,075,102	31,329	149,208	81,521
2007	4,884,243	3,364,331	-3,416	3,360,915	381,011	3,014	2,982,918	780,612	1,120,713	32,840	148,727	81,881
2008	5,133,234	3,480,530	-6,959	3,473,571	390,501	11,522	3,094,592	829,949	1,208,693	34,667	148,073	81,915
2009	4,911,428	3,290,100	-7,782	3,282,318	386,043	-42,964	2,853,311	755,105	1,303,012	33,206	147,910	80,143
2010	4,877,428	3,235,238	-7,523	3,227,715	381,619	-73,859	2,772,237	748,178	1,357,013	32,978	147,901	80,099
2011	5,098,748	3,339,622	-5,257	3,334,365	351,774	-81,919	2,900,672	840,865	1,357,211	34,635	147,213	80,520
2012	5,297,760	3,528,683	-8,051	3,520,632	368,407	-123,155	3,029,070	899,220	1,369,470	36,168	146,477	81,080
2013	5,401,552	3,760,694	-3,957	3,756,737	433,190	-182,932	3,140,615	883,039	1,377,898	37,024	145,894	82,087
2014	5,686,672	3,938,482	-5,327	3,933,155	458,433	-205,081	3,269,641	970,217	1,446,814	39,244	144,906	82,648
2015	5,801,308	3,918,718	-6,824	3,911,894	457,219	-196,118	3,258,557	1,047,566	1,495,185	40,265	144,077	81,407
2016	5,907,235	3,943,594	-5,516	3,938,078	463,663	-199,293	3,275,122	1,103,668	1,528,445	41,347	142,871	80,248
2017	6,486,107	4,548,672	-14,162	4,534,510	532,156	-243,902	3,758,452	1,154,498	1,573,157	45,918	141,254	81,649
2018	6,886,865	6,900,520	-13,655	4,990,028	576,592	-355,034	4,058,402	1,220,824	1,607,639	49,171	140,059	83,099
2019	6,850,224	6,863,886	-13,662	4,793,849	550,167	-282,941	3,960,741	1,228,533	1,660,950	49,301	138,948	81,192

Personal Income and Employment by Area: Wichita, KS

(Thousands of dollars, except as noted.)

Year	Personal income, total	Earnings by place of work			Less: Contributions for government social insurance	Plus: Adjustment for residence	Equals: Net earnings by place of residence	Plus: Dividends, interest, and rent	Plus: Personal current transfer receipts	Per capita personal income (dollars)	Population (persons)	Total employment
		Nonfarm	Farm	Total								
1970	1,806,083	1,465,274	38,013	1,503,287	104,731	-14,008	1,384,548	255,444	166,091	4,038	447,283	210,746
1971	1,909,086	1,514,053	53,110	1,567,163	111,656	-14,399	1,441,108	276,796	191,182	4,320	441,929	205,860
1972	2,118,795	1,708,974	70,116	1,779,090	133,326	-18,883	1,626,881	298,740	193,174	4,847	437,170	216,199
1973	2,372,250	1,902,244	112,894	2,015,138	170,583	-22,036	1,822,519	329,582	220,149	5,408	438,655	227,741
1974	2,668,634	2,172,920	84,732	2,257,652	201,772	-27,764	2,028,116	391,666	248,852	5,990	445,506	238,535
1975	3,008,477	2,440,177	69,542	2,509,719	222,988	-29,545	2,257,186	444,905	306,386	6,682	450,230	241,789
1976	3,299,765	2,726,922	37,217	2,764,139	253,687	-35,991	2,474,461	479,899	345,405	7,216	457,265	250,873
1977	3,558,749	2,947,938	28,271	2,976,209	278,608	-38,860	2,658,741	529,766	370,242	7,735	460,059	254,590
1978	4,047,572	3,404,419	18,230	3,422,649	333,735	-47,554	3,041,360	606,582	399,630	8,728	463,740	267,224
1979	4,673,210	3,977,304	39,032	4,016,336	405,815	-61,039	3,549,482	687,620	436,108	9,918	471,185	282,468
1980	5,291,799	4,446,923	-3,519	4,443,404	441,881	-72,425	3,929,098	843,086	519,615	11,063	478,352	287,480
1981	5,995,338	4,914,776	6,350	4,921,126	520,677	-74,734	4,325,715	1,060,654	608,969	12,344	485,677	291,074
1982	6,408,344	4,971,980	53,353	5,025,333	539,381	-71,422	4,414,530	1,267,538	726,276	13,081	489,883	279,479
1983	6,568,763	5,093,624	20,837	5,114,461	552,892	-67,779	4,493,790	1,303,230	771,743	13,414	489,678	280,797
1984	7,191,364	5,616,795	41,780	5,658,575	626,164	-73,793	4,958,618	1,449,117	783,629	14,597	492,652	291,814
1985	7,484,936	5,836,181	11,388	5,847,569	660,583	-72,513	5,114,473	1,548,201	822,262	15,085	496,168	292,297
1986	7,980,322	6,235,768	64,481	6,300,249	704,738	-78,846	5,516,665	1,596,585	867,072	16,012	498,385	292,210
1987	8,337,822	6,598,624	61,968	6,660,592	735,034	-79,741	5,845,817	1,600,124	891,881	16,546	503,923	302,541
1988	8,870,295	6,990,836	72,104	7,062,940	805,481	-82,296	6,175,163	1,743,965	951,167	17,413	509,395	307,398
1989	9,437,042	7,424,776	50,847	7,475,623	850,684	-84,649	6,540,290	1,842,881	1,053,871	18,281	516,224	314,218
1990	10,055,953	7,897,061	65,913	7,962,974	957,321	-85,402	6,920,251	1,985,430	1,150,272	19,321	520,465	320,176
1991	10,588,514	8,261,416	47,959	8,309,375	1,017,595	-93,303	7,198,477	2,126,779	1,263,258	20,059	527,868	325,468
1992	11,355,526	8,938,946	83,115	9,022,061	1,090,884	-104,078	7,827,099	2,132,634	1,395,793	21,108	537,981	327,396
1993	11,797,706	9,188,157	71,012	9,259,169	1,116,201	-104,649	8,038,319	2,266,941	1,492,446	21,661	544,645	329,318
1994	12,069,154	9,403,740	81,079	9,484,819	1,179,481	-106,526	8,198,812	2,323,438	1,546,904	22,015	548,229	332,894
1995	12,812,617	9,956,995	31,207	9,988,202	1,245,267	-114,780	8,628,155	2,557,377	1,627,085	23,217	551,873	339,959
1996	13,789,567	10,705,838	74,450	10,780,288	1,346,719	-125,686	9,307,883	2,799,331	1,682,353	24,736	557,473	349,157
1997	14,990,176	11,680,601	120,596	11,801,197	1,473,465	-144,678	10,183,054	3,043,197	1,763,925	26,538	564,862	361,796
1998	15,918,901	12,532,287	48,100	12,580,387	1,585,732	-162,898	10,831,757	3,337,673	1,749,471	27,711	574,469	372,909
1999	16,050,413	12,654,950	58,218	12,713,168	1,599,275	-163,450	10,950,443	3,281,589	1,818,381	27,741	578,580	371,044
2000	16,770,555	12,994,921	42,218	13,037,139	1,634,381	-163,832	11,238,926	3,516,029	2,015,600	28,869	580,911	371,183
2001	17,839,238	13,869,693	8,054	13,877,747	1,613,528	-180,726	12,083,493	3,530,465	2,225,280	30,544	584,043	375,069
2002	17,895,491	13,916,676	20,062	13,936,738	1,619,974	-181,815	12,134,949	3,330,827	2,429,715	30,397	588,719	368,937
2003	17,952,182	13,777,463	114,543	13,892,006	1,623,208	-181,731	12,087,067	3,293,267	2,571,848	30,391	590,712	363,652
2004	18,789,653	14,299,862	161,285	14,461,147	1,714,110	-193,083	12,553,954	3,610,901	2,624,798	31,686	593,004	366,611
2005	19,584,561	14,600,599	140,543	14,741,142	1,818,607	-214,588	12,707,947	4,120,970	2,755,644	32,845	596,270	371,519
2006	22,130,074	16,030,425	179,366	16,209,791	1,955,654	-235,788	14,018,349	5,163,933	2,947,792	36,791	601,501	379,484
2007	23,353,602	16,653,546	118,988	16,772,534	2,023,020	-243,556	14,505,958	5,679,398	3,168,246	38,359	608,816	390,426
2008	25,815,952	18,203,140	189,054	18,392,194	2,116,229	-279,719	15,996,246	6,218,183	3,601,523	41,831	617,142	397,681
2009	24,472,167	17,157,295	143,589	17,300,884	2,018,476	-241,771	15,040,637	5,387,130	4,044,400	39,017	627,215	384,164
2010	24,384,209	17,909,025	140,290	18,049,315	2,043,747	-198,848	15,806,720	4,272,284	4,305,205	38,595	631,789	376,884
2011	27,335,190	19,454,537	111,346	19,565,883	1,894,949	-186,170	17,484,764	5,511,770	4,338,656	43,176	633,118	377,660
2012	28,959,960	20,055,176	188,100	20,243,276	1,931,037	-142,140	18,170,099	6,558,435	4,231,426	45,533	636,015	381,649
2013	29,447,331	20,869,014	283,507	21,152,521	2,249,591	-113,289	18,789,641	6,367,529	4,290,161	46,143	638,177	387,500
2014	30,988,236	21,300,767	142,351	21,443,118	2,312,670	-85,772	19,044,676	7,513,756	4,429,804	48,387	640,429	392,202
2015	30,295,580	21,394,785	114,478	21,509,263	2,396,347	-89,184	19,023,732	6,641,925	4,629,923	47,132	642,782	397,333
2016	30,103,395	21,202,484	185,642	21,388,126	2,357,087	-75,940	18,955,099	6,358,748	4,789,548	46,695	644,680	399,910
2017	30,801,323	21,571,717	160,295	21,732,012	2,399,611	-33,245	19,299,156	6,603,431	4,898,736	47,708	645,628	399,961
2018	32,125,008	32,075,217	49,791	21,985,920	2,472,700	-101,224	19,411,996	7,683,238	5,029,774	50,391	637,519	396,531
2019	33,374,235	33,194,287	179,948	23,083,973	2,602,246	-152,684	20,329,043	7,718,874	5,326,318	52,129	640,218	405,343

Personal Income and Employment by Area: Wichita Falls, TX

(Thousands of dollars, except as noted.)

Year	Personal income, total	Earnings by place of work			Less: Contributions for government social insurance	Plus: Adjustment for residence	Equals: Net earnings by place of residence	Plus: Dividends, interest, and rent	Plus: Personal current transfer receipts	Per capita personal income (dollars)	Population (persons)	Total employment
		Nonfarm	Farm	Total								
1970	574,667	443,324	4,504	447,828	25,967	-1,777	420,084	114,736	39,847	4,271	134,547	68,460
1971	645,432	500,386	5,309	505,695	30,869	-2,709	472,117	127,973	45,342	4,749	135,914	71,202
1972	674,171	521,053	5,494	526,547	32,823	-3,506	490,218	133,516	50,437	5,023	134,213	69,547
1973	750,253	570,747	12,043	582,790	40,178	-4,519	538,093	151,913	60,247	5,651	132,776	72,373
1974	842,465	639,305	17,915	657,220	47,369	-7,062	602,789	169,968	69,708	6,207	135,739	74,009
1975	906,418	683,863	13,239	697,102	51,542	-7,940	637,620	184,172	84,626	6,662	136,058	73,601
1976	1,004,485	773,977	11,610	785,587	59,718	-10,336	715,533	197,127	91,825	7,226	139,008	76,059
1977	1,068,280	829,237	6,475	835,712	64,364	-12,142	759,206	211,847	97,227	7,719	138,389	77,471
1978	1,196,734	936,713	2,831	939,544	73,381	-15,515	850,648	239,678	106,408	8,724	137,175	79,811
1979	1,343,033	1,047,148	9,006	1,056,154	86,157	-18,588	951,409	271,829	119,795	9,776	137,384	82,264
1980	1,481,526	1,150,728	-1,816	1,148,912	96,220	-23,307	1,029,385	316,740	135,401	10,698	138,486	84,353
1981	1,734,448	1,331,489	11,081	1,342,570	119,850	-26,159	1,196,561	386,493	151,394	12,362	140,309	88,921
1982	1,833,997	1,366,420	13,655	1,380,075	126,246	-24,315	1,229,514	433,966	170,517	12,840	142,833	88,337
1983	1,906,966	1,379,536	19,283	1,398,819	127,419	-22,135	1,249,265	469,620	188,081	13,232	144,114	85,451
1984	2,049,189	1,469,723	25,273	1,494,996	140,483	-22,099	1,332,414	518,607	198,168	14,210	144,209	86,935
1985	2,113,275	1,507,748	12,272	1,520,020	146,573	-21,035	1,352,412	550,939	209,924	14,628	144,471	87,027
1986	2,121,704	1,481,865	22,374	1,504,239	144,488	-19,074	1,340,677	549,287	231,740	14,648	144,842	82,505
1987	2,121,141	1,475,651	23,056	1,498,707	142,864	-17,068	1,338,775	539,723	242,643	14,892	142,433	81,957
1988	2,214,492	1,531,750	28,040	1,559,790	155,736	-16,545	1,387,509	568,215	258,768	15,663	141,380	81,928
1989	2,293,376	1,593,471	23,736	1,617,207	163,580	-14,779	1,438,848	578,552	275,976	16,271	140,953	81,822
1990	2,415,383	1,657,109	42,191	1,699,300	167,912	-22,164	1,509,224	606,776	299,383	17,215	140,303	81,730
1991	2,401,746	1,625,834	30,069	1,655,903	170,542	-20,373	1,464,988	608,661	328,097	17,270	139,070	79,063
1992	2,526,742	1,711,388	37,065	1,748,453	177,837	-20,887	1,549,729	599,438	377,575	18,206	138,786	78,932
1993	2,654,738	1,830,116	24,050	1,854,166	190,835	-23,536	1,639,795	616,685	398,258	18,774	141,403	82,583
1994	2,781,329	1,908,678	24,431	1,933,109	199,539	-25,947	1,707,623	651,893	421,813	19,317	143,986	84,658
1995	2,989,143	2,043,573	21,702	2,065,275	213,215	-29,808	1,822,252	714,053	452,838	20,232	147,740	87,085
1996	3,121,792	2,135,914	21,286	2,157,200	219,448	-30,997	1,906,755	735,203	479,834	20,651	151,170	88,384
1997	3,300,975	2,307,832	22,113	2,329,945	230,927	-31,631	2,067,387	732,135	501,453	21,791	151,480	89,491
1998	3,444,905	2,392,894	33,661	2,426,555	236,405	-30,952	2,159,198	783,144	502,563	22,783	151,206	89,655
1999	3,573,290	2,478,662	43,077	2,521,739	245,182	-30,721	2,245,836	808,083	519,371	23,606	151,374	88,964
2000	3,740,629	2,599,690	34,176	2,633,866	254,535	-32,188	2,347,143	845,120	548,366	24,634	151,847	90,930
2001	3,985,251	2,798,140	41,788	2,839,928	271,760	-30,946	2,537,222	854,111	593,918	26,433	150,770	90,627
2002	4,145,140	2,941,725	41,888	2,983,613	284,088	-28,177	2,671,348	834,083	639,709	27,452	150,995	89,770
2003	4,299,049	3,030,881	50,466	3,081,347	296,643	-22,197	2,762,507	854,137	682,405	28,528	150,694	89,026
2004	4,343,748	3,090,582	48,481	3,139,063	305,059	-15,656	2,818,348	802,761	722,639	28,571	152,033	87,369
2005	4,584,562	3,264,611	34,247	3,298,858	316,049	-6,014	2,976,795	835,912	771,855	30,331	151,152	85,765
2006	5,113,606	3,672,978	17,835	3,690,813	343,367	6,785	3,354,231	944,080	815,295	33,732	151,596	90,069
2007	5,211,237	3,651,018	13,150	3,664,168	353,989	18,372	3,328,551	991,822	890,864	34,594	150,641	90,385
2008	6,031,089	4,312,532	10,583	4,323,115	384,683	32,053	3,970,485	1,080,860	979,744	40,130	150,287	91,461
2009	5,484,091	3,779,174	-9,881	3,769,293	369,947	24,345	3,423,691	992,370	1,068,030	36,374	150,768	89,312
2010	5,702,034	3,954,581	-5,059	3,949,522	378,198	24,407	3,595,731	949,959	1,156,344	37,602	151,643	88,561
2011	6,331,162	4,404,504	1,793	4,406,297	350,351	21,726	4,077,672	1,068,041	1,185,449	42,130	150,276	87,265
2012	6,391,596	4,344,980	9,788	4,354,768	353,368	17,164	4,018,564	1,187,714	1,185,318	42,333	150,982	89,244
2013	6,457,672	4,494,289	18,303	4,512,592	399,938	14,189	4,126,843	1,098,727	1,232,102	42,659	151,380	89,008
2014	6,452,477	4,331,187	30,439	4,361,626	397,696	19,429	3,983,359	1,168,987	1,300,131	42,511	151,782	87,678
2015	6,147,595	3,940,688	37,087	3,977,775	392,994	15,827	3,600,608	1,180,424	1,366,563	40,990	149,979	88,140
2016	6,102,010	3,820,719	9,118	3,829,837	399,074	7,969	3,438,732	1,231,295	1,431,983	40,592	150,326	89,255
2017	6,142,570	3,790,021	-230	3,789,791	412,356	11,500	3,388,935	1,290,908	1,462,727	40,617	151,230	91,474
2018	6,529,713	6,524,404	5,309	4,005,277	425,770	18,352	3,597,859	1,413,804	1,518,050	43,256	150,955	89,715
2019	6,792,844	6,787,049	5,795	4,194,857	443,302	15,402	3,766,957	1,444,469	1,581,418	44,910	151,254	90,860

Personal Income and Employment by Area: Williamsport, PA

(Thousands of dollars, except as noted.)

Year	Personal income, total	Earnings by place of work			Less: Contributions for government social insurance	Plus: Adjustment for residence	Equals: Net earnings by place of residence	Plus: Dividends, interest, and rent	Plus: Personal current transfer receipts	Per capita personal income (dollars)	Population (persons)	Total employment
		Nonfarm	Farm	Total								
1970	411,949	351,224	3,655	354,879	26,745	-13,976	314,158	52,234	45,557	3,628	113,547	53,041
1971	436,332	367,561	2,763	370,324	28,974	-13,610	327,740	55,742	52,850	3,780	115,429	52,143
1972	480,933	406,612	2,080	408,692	33,627	-14,728	360,337	60,870	59,726	4,166	115,443	53,343
1973	538,407	459,906	5,231	465,137	43,423	-16,014	405,700	66,742	65,965	4,620	116,542	56,253
1974	592,531	497,016	6,364	503,380	48,661	-16,777	437,942	74,980	79,609	5,049	117,354	56,294
1975	644,690	521,412	5,317	526,729	49,365	-18,253	459,111	81,543	104,036	5,464	117,985	54,271
1976	709,786	577,654	6,010	583,664	55,905	-19,285	508,474	88,387	112,925	5,980	118,684	55,204
1977	776,113	634,961	5,930	640,891	61,927	-21,450	557,514	98,915	119,684	6,581	117,927	55,790
1978	865,105	719,522	4,877	724,399	71,902	-23,586	628,911	108,817	127,377	7,314	118,274	58,649
1979	947,090	779,232	8,306	787,538	80,034	-24,934	682,570	120,361	144,159	7,920	119,588	58,472
1980	1,026,380	808,711	6,340	815,051	82,731	-25,952	706,368	148,380	171,632	8,678	118,271	56,384
1981	1,126,684	862,723	10,760	873,483	94,270	-28,932	750,281	184,049	192,354	9,592	117,455	55,670
1982	1,187,939	882,320	9,655	891,975	98,007	-31,737	762,231	209,984	215,724	10,123	117,354	54,240
1983	1,226,835	889,632	1,486	891,118	99,398	-29,676	762,044	227,616	237,175	10,478	117,083	52,384
1984	1,325,397	974,344	9,562	983,906	113,145	-34,373	836,388	257,070	231,939	11,364	116,627	54,551
1985	1,394,043	1,029,434	9,553	1,038,987	120,571	-39,253	879,163	273,853	241,027	12,040	115,787	54,780
1986	1,482,767	1,109,139	7,883	1,117,022	130,133	-43,541	943,348	285,755	253,664	12,825	115,613	56,188
1987	1,593,793	1,222,379	7,793	1,230,172	141,692	-51,736	1,036,744	298,177	258,872	13,651	116,750	59,376
1988	1,723,399	1,343,730	8,936	1,352,666	158,859	-56,349	1,137,458	311,463	274,478	14,635	117,756	61,254
1989	1,864,425	1,415,164	11,994	1,427,158	164,131	-60,026	1,203,001	367,053	294,371	15,711	118,673	61,947
1990	1,918,569	1,444,061	12,709	1,456,770	169,624	-64,469	1,222,677	373,405	322,487	16,139	118,876	62,293
1991	1,999,795	1,482,365	6,141	1,488,506	175,516	-62,223	1,250,767	380,841	368,187	16,656	120,068	61,029
1992	2,107,315	1,562,554	17,758	1,580,312	184,990	-61,199	1,334,123	380,656	392,536	17,372	121,303	61,727
1993	2,188,316	1,610,893	17,926	1,628,819	194,211	-55,592	1,379,016	395,259	414,041	17,916	122,141	61,763
1994	2,228,055	1,649,704	15,949	1,665,653	203,888	-52,708	1,409,057	403,522	415,476	18,222	122,273	62,543
1995	2,318,213	1,714,145	7,926	1,722,071	209,749	-51,247	1,461,075	421,732	435,406	19,029	121,825	63,196
1996	2,422,144	1,771,052	15,708	1,786,760	212,016	-52,855	1,521,889	442,024	458,231	19,963	121,333	64,164
1997	2,526,395	1,848,837	6,787	1,855,624	218,869	-50,187	1,586,568	469,549	470,278	20,882	120,983	64,890
1998	2,634,754	1,930,779	8,671	1,939,450	225,633	-49,482	1,664,335	506,915	463,504	21,849	120,590	64,892
1999	2,685,498	2,000,829	6,927	2,007,756	232,440	-49,405	1,725,911	482,727	476,860	22,345	120,182	65,414
2000	2,833,508	2,103,358	11,429	2,114,787	242,868	-52,915	1,819,004	511,102	503,402	23,642	119,851	67,284
2001	2,995,376	2,240,528	9,165	2,249,693	254,040	-56,614	1,939,039	513,898	542,439	25,186	118,930	68,014
2002	3,071,529	2,246,152	6,739	2,252,891	252,835	-46,749	1,953,307	539,074	579,148	25,954	118,344	66,927
2003	3,169,710	2,303,449	15,164	2,318,613	258,133	-42,823	2,017,657	545,737	606,316	26,837	118,108	66,630
2004	3,280,736	2,419,883	22,624	2,442,507	270,746	-47,776	2,123,985	523,401	633,350	27,824	117,911	67,246
2005	3,337,856	2,491,320	19,145	2,510,465	283,129	-51,622	2,175,714	485,689	676,453	28,400	117,530	67,180
2006	3,434,869	2,524,998	16,406	2,541,404	290,503	-50,828	2,200,073	526,935	707,861	29,362	116,983	67,406
2007	3,594,920	2,600,322	14,886	2,615,208	298,593	-51,299	2,265,316	572,227	757,377	30,851	116,524	67,921
2008	3,751,090	2,622,705	10,176	2,632,881	304,550	-42,897	2,285,434	617,326	848,330	32,296	116,147	67,884
2009	3,773,857	2,568,715	6,521	2,575,236	303,381	-39,345	2,232,510	606,096	935,251	32,511	116,081	66,144
2010	3,967,805	2,755,527	11,380	2,766,907	322,320	-48,466	2,396,121	590,755	980,929	34,144	116,209	67,169
2011	4,316,113	3,062,614	16,545	3,079,159	320,134	-91,670	2,667,355	667,697	981,061	36,994	116,671	69,897
2012	4,440,852	3,200,981	20,174	3,221,155	332,299	-136,565	2,752,291	699,770	988,791	37,895	117,188	71,051
2013	4,455,078	3,240,812	15,855	3,256,667	375,347	-134,754	2,746,566	697,071	1,011,441	38,216	116,577	70,497
2014	4,615,421	3,340,907	15,677	3,356,584	391,899	-157,332	2,807,353	760,233	1,047,835	39,692	116,282	71,338
2015	4,668,778	3,364,549	6,758	3,371,307	397,811	-155,998	2,817,498	752,286	1,098,994	40,394	115,580	70,766
2016	4,587,911	3,131,822	785	3,132,607	376,510	-77,332	2,678,765	753,043	1,156,103	39,996	114,708	68,162
2017	4,706,848	3,244,129	5,908	3,250,037	396,344	-93,233	2,760,460	787,538	1,158,850	41,346	113,841	68,403
2018	4,961,200	4,950,375	10,825	3,404,814	410,820	-96,332	2,897,662	824,376	1,239,162	43,571	113,866	68,424
2019	5,091,802	5,071,029	20,773	3,473,632	416,209	-90,123	2,967,300	840,577	1,283,925	44,941	113,299	68,472

Personal Income and Employment by Area: Wilmington, NC

(Thousands of dollars, except as noted.)

Year	Personal income, total	Earnings by place of work			Less: Contributions for government social insurance	Plus: Adjustment for residence	Equals: Net earnings by place of residence	Plus: Dividends, interest, and rent	Plus: Personal current transfer receipts	Per capita personal income (dollars)	Population (persons)	Total employment
		Nonfarm	Farm	Total								
1970	327,087	262,927	10,504	273,431	18,307	-1,770	253,354	45,048	28,685	3,212	101,837	47,452
1971	358,922	289,002	9,525	298,527	20,660	-4,025	273,842	50,661	34,419	3,400	105,562	47,676
1972	417,525	339,820	9,578	349,398	25,410	-2,614	321,374	57,205	38,946	3,795	110,029	50,224
1973	479,995	394,734	11,934	406,668	34,045	-3,468	369,155	65,634	45,206	4,220	113,741	54,092
1974	530,365	424,060	10,382	434,442	38,188	1,414	397,668	76,758	55,939	4,552	116,500	54,463
1975	583,584	448,144	8,833	456,977	39,491	4,698	422,184	85,565	75,835	4,912	118,805	52,367
1976	652,765	501,693	8,679	510,372	44,899	7,349	472,822	94,667	85,276	5,414	120,568	54,105
1977	722,594	553,591	8,893	562,484	49,170	11,104	524,418	107,027	91,149	5,891	122,652	55,642
1978	811,457	624,292	10,567	634,859	56,948	12,665	590,576	123,819	97,062	6,645	122,115	57,773
1979	925,923	704,492	12,207	716,699	66,690	16,143	666,152	146,656	113,115	7,510	123,292	60,898
1980	1,051,344	778,317	13,609	791,926	73,770	18,189	736,345	179,868	135,131	8,328	126,245	61,704
1981	1,157,575	831,804	16,534	848,338	84,945	16,815	780,208	219,905	157,462	9,049	127,918	61,913
1982	1,231,636	868,767	12,260	881,027	90,921	20,893	810,999	243,571	177,066	9,446	130,392	61,420
1983	1,341,434	944,746	5,842	950,588	98,899	26,108	877,797	269,133	194,504	10,176	131,827	62,633
1984	1,494,919	1,050,486	10,013	1,060,499	111,780	25,947	974,666	315,750	204,503	11,164	133,911	66,887
1985	1,643,436	1,168,555	5,880	1,174,435	126,377	20,784	1,068,842	353,237	221,357	12,048	136,404	70,397
1986	1,826,460	1,328,929	5,593	1,334,522	146,475	5,907	1,193,954	389,464	243,042	13,096	139,471	74,836
1987	1,965,609	1,413,855	13,524	1,427,379	153,212	1,410	1,275,577	428,788	261,244	13,827	142,160	75,940
1988	2,164,239	1,558,529	12,586	1,571,115	174,670	-6,021	1,390,424	486,819	286,996	15,033	143,969	79,824
1989	2,355,383	1,703,585	13,925	1,717,510	191,848	-18,390	1,507,272	523,321	324,790	16,108	146,223	82,275
1990	2,577,345	1,828,866	18,259	1,847,125	211,041	-31,033	1,605,051	614,771	357,523	17,156	150,226	85,684
1991	2,784,739	1,937,471	27,367	1,964,838	226,428	-7,093	1,731,317	642,294	411,128	17,900	155,570	86,116
1992	3,022,479	2,122,050	30,177	2,152,227	244,476	-12,896	1,894,855	666,351	461,273	18,902	159,904	88,808
1993	3,273,164	2,274,752	32,573	2,307,325	262,179	-3,556	2,041,590	719,814	511,760	19,730	165,895	91,851
1994	3,586,727	2,477,209	32,810	2,510,019	290,621	2,373	2,221,771	833,960	530,996	20,825	172,233	96,120
1995	3,914,515	2,672,866	33,719	2,706,585	314,665	-1,584	2,390,336	922,530	601,649	21,851	179,144	101,327
1996	4,258,679	2,907,650	42,791	2,950,441	340,402	-23,304	2,586,735	1,018,291	653,653	22,958	185,496	106,945
1997	4,591,549	3,111,332	47,948	3,159,280	365,011	-39,774	2,754,495	1,151,565	685,489	24,021	191,148	113,067
1998	4,884,448	3,396,446	17,142	3,413,588	397,169	-66,585	2,949,834	1,213,579	721,035	24,853	196,533	116,103
1999	5,183,817	3,700,005	13,963	3,713,968	434,866	-90,038	3,189,064	1,230,566	764,187	26,009	199,312	119,821
2000	5,538,337	3,912,102	31,963	3,944,065	455,695	-93,222	3,395,148	1,328,314	814,875	27,404	202,099	121,732
2001	5,806,264	4,102,376	38,975	4,141,351	467,159	-83,662	3,590,530	1,301,059	914,675	28,186	205,996	125,064
2002	5,907,264	4,197,395	17,357	4,214,752	475,576	-90,652	3,648,524	1,259,314	999,426	28,055	210,563	127,090
2003	6,209,944	4,385,556	11,787	4,397,343	506,643	-57,589	3,833,111	1,330,322	1,046,511	28,900	214,877	130,232
2004	6,862,021	4,796,118	29,617	4,825,735	546,230	-50,696	4,228,809	1,505,750	1,127,462	30,841	222,498	136,557
2005	7,556,996	5,309,739	42,816	5,352,555	610,593	-78,762	4,663,200	1,678,318	1,215,478	32,729	230,897	144,084
2006	8,225,535	5,826,219	28,293	5,854,512	661,570	-148,571	5,044,371	1,869,830	1,311,334	34,522	238,272	150,847
2007	8,679,019	6,155,814	41,207	6,197,021	711,297	-235,290	5,250,434	2,023,555	1,405,030	35,640	243,520	158,078
2008	8,951,082	6,144,651	52,094	6,196,745	716,790	-190,391	5,289,564	2,074,388	1,587,130	36,055	248,260	156,516
2009	8,573,945	5,847,667	51,639	5,899,306	697,479	-257,354	4,944,473	1,855,213	1,774,259	34,049	251,814	149,467
2010	8,713,194	5,882,939	58,298	5,941,237	698,618	-219,279	5,023,340	1,792,114	1,897,740	34,076	255,700	147,606
2011	9,155,781	5,948,992	42,999	5,991,991	651,643	-185,604	5,154,744	2,027,361	1,973,676	35,318	259,242	151,006
2012	9,397,203	5,972,084	48,716	6,020,800	653,547	-133,528	5,233,725	2,137,732	2,025,746	35,745	262,899	152,682
2013	9,722,728	6,274,317	66,329	6,340,646	777,390	-132,283	5,430,973	2,193,401	2,098,354	36,296	267,870	156,292
2014	10,590,147	6,774,419	59,563	6,833,982	831,825	-106,264	5,895,893	2,504,976	2,189,278	38,916	272,125	161,741
2015	11,208,811	7,150,344	52,937	7,203,281	873,239	-162,677	6,167,365	2,708,813	2,332,633	40,436	277,197	166,292
2016	11,659,107	7,614,364	55,568	7,669,932	917,978	-333,122	6,418,832	2,815,124	2,425,151	41,325	282,131	172,751
2017	12,221,630	8,046,161	63,930	8,110,091	959,090	-397,855	6,753,146	2,947,373	2,521,111	42,413	288,156	175,951
2018	13,129,781	13,073,180	56,601	8,548,660	995,654	-424,158	7,128,848	3,307,686	2,693,247	44,618	294,273	182,202
2019	13,679,101	13,613,458	65,643	9,097,203	1,055,539	-562,501	7,479,163	3,366,654	2,833,284	45,975	297,533	188,464

Personal Income and Employment by Area: Winchester, VA-WV

(Thousands of dollars, except as noted.)

Year	Personal income, total	Earnings by place of work Nonfarm	Farm	Total	Less: Contributions for government social insurance	Plus: Adjustment for residence	Equals: Net earnings by place of residence	Plus: Dividends, interest, and rent	Plus: Personal current transfer receipts	Per capita personal income (dollars)	Population (persons)	Total employment
1970	180,907	142,653	2,873	145,526	9,607	4,385	140,304	24,386	16,217	3,255	55,578	27,231
1971	201,808	159,930	3,377	163,307	11,196	3,162	155,273	27,556	18,979	3,497	57,715	28,508
1972	223,153	177,058	4,151	181,209	13,030	3,024	171,203	30,811	21,139	3,835	58,191	29,150
1973	257,504	205,821	7,724	213,545	17,494	671	196,722	36,443	24,339	4,335	59,398	30,736
1974	291,957	234,272	9,152	243,424	20,715	-2,491	220,218	42,880	28,859	4,742	61,566	31,775
1975	308,011	245,694	6,299	251,993	21,065	-8,880	222,048	47,421	38,542	4,890	62,987	30,639
1976	346,187	284,745	4,398	289,143	24,797	-12,325	252,021	52,561	41,605	5,408	64,015	32,116
1977	386,363	321,706	4,078	325,784	28,167	-15,916	281,701	60,186	44,476	5,867	65,849	33,218
1978	445,347	370,638	12,744	383,382	33,036	-21,491	328,855	68,272	48,220	6,557	67,918	35,126
1979	487,659	406,503	13,121	419,624	37,630	-26,975	355,019	76,667	55,973	7,055	69,124	35,530
1980	530,210	438,929	3,881	442,810	40,757	-28,961	373,092	90,354	66,764	7,636	69,435	35,358
1981	599,318	478,298	5,750	484,048	47,696	-26,003	410,349	112,141	76,828	8,546	70,125	35,469
1982	644,532	499,261	5,584	504,845	50,636	-24,221	429,988	127,984	86,560	9,092	70,891	34,837
1983	700,421	541,218	3,724	544,942	55,310	-22,554	467,078	140,289	93,054	9,829	71,263	35,582
1984	794,716	608,208	7,330	615,538	63,192	-19,880	532,466	164,562	97,688	11,054	71,897	36,973
1985	874,059	672,410	4,858	677,268	71,095	-16,887	589,286	180,160	104,613	12,046	72,562	38,962
1986	978,945	761,663	11,008	772,671	82,865	-17,291	672,515	195,502	110,928	13,260	73,828	41,228
1987	1,085,096	856,376	12,518	868,894	92,881	-14,353	761,660	208,215	115,221	14,257	76,112	44,617
1988	1,206,529	945,609	10,723	956,332	104,281	-5,150	846,901	233,391	126,237	15,327	78,717	46,300
1989	1,338,592	1,019,989	8,936	1,028,925	114,052	7,307	922,180	277,925	138,487	16,433	81,456	48,563
1990	1,424,329	1,062,092	9,248	1,071,340	121,434	28,167	978,073	292,872	153,384	16,764	84,964	50,045
1991	1,456,973	1,073,662	12,241	1,085,903	124,789	25,577	986,691	297,331	172,951	16,750	86,981	49,180
1992	1,560,417	1,163,882	11,307	1,175,189	134,340	16,407	1,057,256	303,402	199,759	17,601	88,657	50,686
1993	1,662,582	1,250,540	9,805	1,260,345	144,157	15,888	1,132,076	322,371	208,135	18,340	90,652	52,047
1994	1,784,025	1,348,831	9,572	1,358,403	154,482	15,929	1,219,850	343,248	220,927	19,214	92,848	53,821
1995	1,912,081	1,421,658	12,342	1,434,000	162,475	17,048	1,288,573	383,153	240,355	20,191	94,698	55,672
1996	2,045,056	1,528,577	6,923	1,535,500	172,339	19,457	1,382,618	404,602	257,836	21,197	96,479	57,680
1997	2,144,365	1,607,588	5,293	1,612,881	180,788	29,352	1,461,445	413,766	269,154	21,836	98,202	58,997
1998	2,354,788	1,751,439	4,980	1,756,419	193,755	58,628	1,621,292	451,071	282,425	23,560	99,949	61,402
1999	2,498,143	1,870,105	5,780	1,875,885	206,152	80,868	1,750,601	449,976	297,566	24,629	101,429	62,096
2000	2,745,796	2,040,046	3,974	2,044,020	221,530	101,987	1,924,477	497,313	324,006	26,497	103,626	64,579
2001	2,957,335	2,136,668	6,181	2,142,849	238,480	160,566	2,064,935	526,499	365,901	27,833	106,252	65,186
2002	3,057,073	2,268,171	-2,297	2,265,874	253,841	152,626	2,164,659	497,023	395,391	28,061	108,945	66,069
2003	3,259,080	2,372,069	-3,039	2,369,030	264,067	212,162	2,317,125	519,090	422,865	29,239	111,464	66,412
2004	3,573,843	2,570,214	5,107	2,575,321	285,037	281,292	2,571,576	559,947	442,320	31,245	114,383	68,919
2005	3,906,949	2,822,515	-923	2,821,592	314,242	336,011	2,843,361	580,388	483,200	33,153	117,847	72,146
2006	4,250,284	2,977,121	-9,979	2,967,142	335,518	410,194	3,041,818	675,631	532,835	35,060	121,229	74,460
2007	4,412,509	3,011,422	-14,275	2,997,147	340,586	436,784	3,093,345	754,467	564,697	35,624	123,863	75,098
2008	4,614,352	2,971,484	-4,079	2,967,405	342,469	505,036	3,129,972	813,238	671,142	36,701	125,728	73,713
2009	4,511,273	2,908,104	-3,248	2,904,856	338,907	482,259	3,048,208	733,743	729,322	35,429	127,333	70,838
2010	4,702,353	3,030,441	-2,181	3,028,260	351,199	496,030	3,173,091	735,133	794,129	36,542	128,682	70,846
2011	4,981,354	3,176,664	1,782	3,178,446	328,482	519,807	3,369,771	806,269	805,314	38,325	129,977	73,097
2012	5,219,077	3,322,807	10,517	3,333,324	339,394	516,439	3,510,369	882,685	826,023	39,855	130,951	73,900
2013	5,228,903	3,434,008	2,484	3,436,492	399,958	463,091	3,499,625	864,878	864,400	39,514	132,330	75,339
2014	5,468,447	3,570,198	2,325	3,572,523	412,388	454,720	3,614,855	941,208	912,384	40,951	133,537	76,529
2015	5,796,015	3,808,439	-1,395	3,807,044	435,813	452,730	3,823,961	1,003,328	968,726	43,185	134,213	79,046
2016	6,058,674	3,903,472	-1,402	3,902,070	449,652	557,777	4,010,195	1,033,513	1,014,966	44,683	135,593	80,125
2017	6,347,759	4,111,888	2,147	4,114,035	475,600	572,081	4,210,516	1,083,707	1,053,536	46,036	137,887	81,675
2018	6,709,592	6,722,403	-12,811	4,289,235	496,899	577,365	4,369,701	1,210,883	1,129,008	48,100	139,492	83,297
2019	6,978,059	6,992,312	-14,253	4,513,711	524,552	565,675	4,554,834	1,224,019	1,199,206	49,643	140,566	84,832

Personal Income and Employment by Area: Winston-Salem, NC

(Thousands of dollars, except as noted.)

Year	Personal income, total	Earnings by place of work			Less: Contributions for government social insurance	Plus: Adjustment for residence	Equals: Net earnings by place of residence	Plus: Dividends, interest, and rent	Plus: Personal current transfer receipts	Per capita personal income (dollars)	Population (persons)	Total employment
		Nonfarm	Farm	Total								
1970	1,446,372	1,148,746	28,572	1,177,318	80,499	61,225	1,158,044	184,906	103,422	3,814	379,270	176,320
1971	1,574,441	1,243,206	30,541	1,273,747	90,286	67,666	1,251,127	200,669	122,645	4,055	388,244	178,777
1972	1,762,561	1,409,698	29,508	1,439,206	107,273	73,272	1,405,205	219,881	137,475	4,436	397,369	186,455
1973	1,992,434	1,604,394	45,796	1,650,190	140,746	75,694	1,585,138	248,772	158,524	4,947	402,778	197,084
1974	2,206,700	1,762,240	47,581	1,809,821	160,546	79,911	1,729,186	286,528	190,986	5,417	407,337	199,954
1975	2,410,149	1,880,544	43,895	1,924,439	168,190	78,456	1,834,705	310,567	264,877	5,855	411,650	193,474
1976	2,694,649	2,135,171	46,596	2,181,767	194,757	83,590	2,070,600	344,257	279,792	6,469	416,569	201,477
1977	2,991,631	2,398,943	40,238	2,439,181	217,575	87,865	2,309,471	388,543	293,617	7,085	422,231	210,239
1978	3,342,886	2,680,546	49,795	2,730,341	250,523	109,931	2,589,749	438,791	314,346	7,773	430,074	217,753
1979	3,701,489	2,983,833	33,880	3,017,713	290,181	120,419	2,847,951	494,103	359,435	8,453	437,876	224,330
1980	4,147,750	3,268,258	28,126	3,296,384	318,797	133,703	3,111,290	610,723	425,737	9,331	444,515	224,907
1981	4,698,878	3,605,381	54,839	3,660,220	377,432	154,884	3,437,672	773,049	488,157	10,459	449,284	228,321
1982	5,003,261	3,751,384	43,157	3,794,541	394,636	172,720	3,572,625	885,319	545,317	11,025	453,824	225,398
1983	5,414,802	4,073,725	24,697	4,098,422	430,034	208,519	3,876,907	949,708	588,187	11,839	457,356	229,151
1984	6,097,018	4,550,799	40,275	4,591,074	492,124	250,576	4,349,526	1,129,317	618,175	13,190	462,248	242,002
1985	6,615,240	4,961,656	40,881	5,002,537	543,113	268,365	4,727,789	1,223,298	664,153	14,131	468,149	251,201
1986	7,092,801	5,309,801	19,179	5,328,980	592,672	303,357	5,039,665	1,321,378	731,758	15,040	471,586	258,786
1987	7,706,261	5,820,736	22,124	5,842,860	637,994	352,325	5,557,191	1,411,355	737,715	16,083	479,157	268,061
1988	8,511,129	6,406,198	35,284	6,441,482	723,843	392,089	6,109,728	1,604,607	796,794	17,648	482,283	278,597
1989	9,200,503	6,772,581	42,576	6,815,157	763,721	440,164	6,491,600	1,821,116	887,787	18,955	485,397	281,675
1990	9,614,655	6,841,277	60,153	6,901,430	795,950	481,702	6,587,182	2,056,276	971,197	19,620	490,034	288,314
1991	9,836,797	6,995,841	70,763	7,066,604	823,929	464,187	6,706,862	2,029,327	1,100,608	19,814	496,463	283,093
1992	10,490,757	7,530,157	72,156	7,602,313	876,944	497,022	7,222,391	2,058,828	1,209,538	20,851	503,138	286,803
1993	11,077,410	7,896,906	63,196	7,960,102	931,081	570,766	7,599,787	2,151,707	1,325,916	21,633	512,062	294,537
1994	11,706,256	8,417,939	64,387	8,482,326	998,429	585,080	8,068,977	2,255,977	1,381,302	22,433	521,836	300,829
1995	12,584,951	8,883,846	48,271	8,932,117	1,057,656	679,315	8,553,776	2,486,379	1,544,796	23,714	530,693	308,135
1996	13,325,335	9,223,572	65,218	9,288,790	1,091,949	750,008	8,946,849	2,700,627	1,677,859	24,644	540,712	314,617
1997	14,155,489	9,876,386	56,926	9,933,312	1,158,296	771,186	9,546,202	2,857,503	1,751,784	25,757	549,576	320,761
1998	15,018,965	10,484,897	63,776	10,548,673	1,231,355	768,032	10,085,350	3,124,865	1,808,750	26,944	557,410	326,706
1999	15,516,825	10,892,914	69,651	10,962,565	1,278,363	827,643	10,511,845	3,095,296	1,909,684	27,516	563,928	330,837
2000	16,419,697	11,525,513	63,207	11,588,720	1,351,416	827,812	11,065,116	3,287,855	2,066,726	28,745	571,210	336,834
2001	16,846,683	11,790,250	61,806	11,852,056	1,371,367	853,007	11,333,696	3,223,426	2,289,561	29,137	578,186	328,671
2002	17,114,777	11,962,068	29,896	11,991,964	1,378,125	879,830	11,493,669	3,142,704	2,478,404	29,290	584,321	324,828
2003	17,708,736	12,330,437	36,651	12,367,088	1,444,619	923,096	11,845,565	3,243,658	2,619,513	30,068	588,964	323,784
2004	19,010,115	12,998,745	63,648	13,062,393	1,496,592	1,011,439	12,577,240	3,584,043	2,848,832	31,962	594,765	327,520
2005	19,824,769	13,430,615	70,734	13,501,349	1,572,676	1,097,799	13,026,472	3,721,057	3,077,240	32,888	602,805	334,166
2006	21,098,233	14,151,195	60,963	14,212,158	1,634,240	1,158,441	13,736,359	3,964,710	3,397,164	34,390	613,494	340,048
2007	22,104,931	14,512,145	58,777	14,570,922	1,694,133	1,238,978	14,115,767	4,323,768	3,665,396	35,478	623,068	345,798
2008	23,009,089	14,796,126	66,055	14,862,181	1,718,672	1,262,961	14,406,470	4,476,973	4,125,646	36,396	632,186	342,342
2009	22,090,594	14,176,029	57,641	14,233,670	1,675,872	1,112,725	13,670,523	3,804,596	4,615,475	34,642	637,688	329,508
2010	22,803,214	14,897,959	51,894	14,949,853	1,719,546	1,105,035	14,335,342	3,578,226	4,889,646	35,557	641,320	325,618
2011	23,204,641	14,585,537	37,265	14,622,802	1,578,811	1,118,235	14,162,226	4,049,456	4,992,959	35,995	644,663	328,719
2012	24,227,969	15,283,749	65,359	15,349,108	1,620,963	1,264,324	14,992,469	4,211,618	5,023,882	37,432	647,251	332,566
2013	24,036,984	15,278,191	62,729	15,340,920	1,870,223	1,386,759	14,857,456	4,044,234	5,135,294	36,954	650,449	335,637
2014	25,840,400	16,277,181	102,094	16,379,275	1,983,001	1,378,417	15,774,691	4,703,622	5,362,087	39,512	653,988	340,724
2015	27,042,110	17,072,868	87,448	17,160,316	2,072,502	1,356,691	16,444,505	4,949,353	5,648,252	41,154	657,101	346,949
2016	27,524,974	17,281,906	61,841	17,343,747	2,096,371	1,481,539	16,728,915	4,982,984	5,813,075	41,597	661,708	352,084
2017	28,850,825	18,284,923	69,939	18,354,862	2,186,265	1,416,433	17,585,030	5,217,075	6,048,720	43,207	667,733	354,792
2018	29,866,780	29,840,750	26,030	18,734,451	2,219,293	1,524,986	18,040,144	5,511,070	6,315,566	44,502	671,129	360,664
2019	31,031,767	31,000,019	31,748	19,643,151	2,327,271	1,500,834	18,816,714	5,592,724	6,622,329	45,904	676,008	369,073

Personal Income and Employment by Area: Worcester, MA-CT

(Thousands of dollars, except as noted.)

Year	Personal income, total	Earnings by place of work			Less: Contributions for government social insurance	Plus: Adjustment for residence	Equals: Net earnings by place of residence	Plus: Dividends, interest, and rent	Plus: Personal current transfer receipts	Per capita personal income (dollars)	Population (persons)	Total employment
		Nonfarm	Farm	Total								
1970	2,936,952	2,187,578	17,410	2,204,988	144,579	166,498	2,226,907	413,891	296,154	4,059	723,625	303,453
1971	3,122,407	2,276,258	17,035	2,293,293	155,062	192,965	2,331,196	435,877	355,334	4,280	729,613	299,766
1972	3,394,252	2,470,779	18,892	2,489,671	177,513	229,145	2,541,303	460,909	392,040	4,646	730,558	305,815
1973	3,761,499	2,759,923	23,340	2,783,263	228,772	266,797	2,821,288	503,462	436,749	5,113	735,701	320,736
1974	4,086,860	2,952,112	15,189	2,967,301	253,560	307,987	3,021,728	557,552	507,580	5,562	734,725	323,556
1975	4,428,904	3,016,742	15,877	3,032,619	249,893	341,857	3,124,583	588,729	715,592	6,040	733,288	309,349
1976	4,814,796	3,343,304	18,528	3,361,832	284,544	389,465	3,466,753	626,623	721,420	6,588	730,817	317,500
1977	5,248,947	3,632,445	16,555	3,649,000	311,374	478,967	3,816,593	688,081	744,273	7,184	730,608	324,246
1978	5,857,676	4,072,032	24,527	4,096,559	359,606	568,781	4,305,734	744,637	807,305	7,918	739,765	337,775
1979	6,536,437	4,515,531	20,310	4,535,841	417,250	681,121	4,799,712	825,565	911,160	8,816	741,446	348,159
1980	7,370,455	4,900,305	16,516	4,916,821	452,368	828,289	5,292,742	1,018,871	1,058,842	9,967	739,491	348,593
1981	8,215,810	5,360,624	20,046	5,380,670	523,478	906,595	5,763,787	1,247,419	1,204,604	11,086	741,103	347,686
1982	8,888,343	5,596,273	31,330	5,627,603	554,140	1,011,321	6,084,784	1,492,426	1,311,133	11,973	742,351	341,024
1983	9,507,163	5,944,602	27,918	5,972,520	596,891	1,147,366	6,522,995	1,610,405	1,373,763	12,822	741,465	343,763
1984	10,726,435	6,776,412	34,314	6,810,726	701,484	1,306,531	7,415,773	1,876,762	1,433,900	14,313	749,409	361,994
1985	11,569,696	7,403,902	29,516	7,433,418	772,509	1,433,828	8,094,737	1,965,862	1,509,097	15,270	757,692	374,819
1986	12,557,204	8,173,489	34,556	8,208,045	863,506	1,502,969	8,847,508	2,114,755	1,594,941	16,398	765,781	390,359
1987	13,678,868	9,132,808	29,315	9,162,123	950,689	1,593,017	9,804,451	2,228,574	1,645,843	17,580	778,071	397,657
1988	15,001,480	10,123,267	26,989	10,150,256	1,070,261	1,722,078	10,802,073	2,449,923	1,749,484	18,916	793,074	413,617
1989	15,957,729	10,582,805	25,262	10,608,067	1,110,465	1,769,635	11,267,237	2,714,797	1,975,695	19,744	808,224	410,592
1990	16,452,448	10,644,295	32,529	10,676,824	1,100,796	1,879,490	11,455,518	2,769,502	2,227,428	20,227	813,391	400,251
1991	16,563,540	10,577,781	32,476	10,610,257	1,110,664	1,805,909	11,305,502	2,725,437	2,532,601	20,386	812,492	382,147
1992	17,312,304	11,250,624	39,186	11,289,810	1,166,011	1,830,541	11,954,340	2,679,633	2,678,331	21,291	813,137	391,834
1993	17,924,129	11,880,588	36,463	11,917,051	1,240,207	1,730,714	12,407,558	2,762,183	2,754,388	21,923	817,597	401,887
1994	18,880,607	12,630,125	33,435	12,663,560	1,323,092	1,768,404	13,108,872	2,856,837	2,914,898	22,949	822,735	411,296
1995	19,755,621	12,978,514	23,408	13,001,922	1,367,829	1,980,201	13,614,294	3,053,282	3,088,045	23,927	825,647	415,200
1996	20,902,087	13,722,182	31,154	13,753,336	1,426,927	2,099,020	14,425,429	3,289,926	3,186,732	25,179	830,128	420,409
1997	22,445,708	14,575,797	31,150	14,606,947	1,506,638	2,548,721	15,649,030	3,506,377	3,290,301	26,824	836,766	429,799
1998	23,715,665	15,576,351	28,875	15,605,226	1,598,779	2,729,868	16,736,315	3,651,039	3,328,311	28,087	844,368	437,985
1999	25,055,501	16,376,252	37,620	16,413,872	1,661,956	3,259,443	18,011,359	3,616,924	3,427,218	29,362	853,319	442,402
2000	27,883,564	18,438,815	39,066	18,477,881	1,857,030	3,704,862	20,325,713	3,928,663	3,629,188	32,359	861,697	454,078
2001	28,940,870	18,979,911	30,865	19,010,776	1,926,871	3,869,118	20,953,023	4,042,234	3,945,613	33,224	871,081	457,330
2002	29,026,084	19,211,722	26,644	19,238,366	1,949,215	3,801,124	21,090,275	3,629,838	4,305,971	33,000	879,568	455,348
2003	30,143,621	19,926,839	28,916	19,955,755	2,008,939	3,877,346	21,824,162	3,776,278	4,543,181	33,979	887,129	457,339
2004	31,772,287	20,881,134	33,210	20,914,344	2,167,520	4,335,577	23,082,401	3,959,405	4,730,481	35,612	892,171	463,766
2005	33,007,460	21,359,256	26,679	21,385,935	2,265,370	4,809,996	23,930,561	4,032,459	5,044,440	36,802	896,901	467,587
2006	35,127,469	22,297,258	20,336	22,317,594	2,333,687	5,262,875	25,246,782	4,564,185	5,316,502	38,939	902,123	472,689
2007	36,994,049	22,965,199	21,209	22,986,408	2,396,603	5,748,021	26,337,826	5,057,180	5,599,043	40,854	905,524	478,942
2008	38,481,280	23,348,692	36,032	23,384,724	2,450,401	5,895,123	26,829,446	5,264,363	6,387,471	42,346	908,735	477,372
2009	37,918,430	22,734,028	29,311	22,763,339	2,396,435	5,605,946	25,972,850	4,891,199	7,054,381	41,515	913,363	464,206
2010	39,449,559	23,819,734	34,126	23,853,860	2,433,523	5,715,542	27,135,879	4,845,941	7,467,739	42,932	918,886	461,436
2011	41,411,544	25,043,922	34,246	25,078,168	2,312,544	5,779,215	28,544,839	5,401,546	7,465,159	44,896	922,380	469,335
2012	43,182,743	25,876,962	41,105	25,918,067	2,359,130	6,141,280	29,700,217	5,951,148	7,531,378	46,696	924,761	473,664
2013	43,146,206	26,495,143	43,471	26,538,614	2,727,776	5,754,629	29,565,467	5,998,794	7,581,945	46,470	928,480	485,083
2014	44,868,418	27,262,885	21,468	27,284,353	2,836,968	6,070,892	30,518,277	6,523,195	7,826,946	48,137	932,106	493,139
2015	47,111,225	28,394,061	19,532	28,413,593	2,907,638	6,359,257	31,865,212	6,894,380	8,351,633	50,395	934,835	509,651
2016	48,401,605	29,254,377	12,082	29,266,459	3,010,702	6,627,646	32,883,403	6,826,691	8,691,511	51,671	936,723	516,074
2017	50,646,528	30,818,489	14,907	30,833,396	3,171,241	7,031,981	34,694,136	7,123,774	8,828,618	53,738	942,475	524,444
2018	52,207,397	52,204,227	3,170	31,696,470	3,277,916	6,856,060	35,274,614	7,742,005	9,190,778	55,181	946,113	531,404
2019	54,204,431	54,192,249	12,182	32,859,125	3,386,449	7,416,120	36,888,796	7,861,298	9,454,337	57,214	947,404	538,423

Personal Income and Employment by Area: Yakima, WA

(Thousands of dollars, except as noted.)

Year	Personal income, total	Earnings by place of work			Less: Contributions for government social insurance	Plus: Adjustment for residence	Equals: Net earnings by place of residence	Plus: Dividends, interest, and rent	Plus: Personal current transfer receipts	Per capita personal income (dollars)	Population (persons)	Total employment
		Nonfarm	Farm	Total								
1970	514,992	329,853	45,375	375,228	27,791	8,438	355,875	83,553	75,564	3,537	145,600	63,707
1971	569,171	354,361	64,535	418,896	31,102	7,792	395,586	90,713	82,872	3,845	148,017	62,448
1972	629,237	389,841	76,739	466,580	35,780	8,699	439,499	98,973	90,765	4,180	150,541	64,284
1973	731,091	436,456	114,457	550,913	46,136	10,848	515,625	115,668	99,798	4,845	150,902	67,149
1974	839,680	494,599	137,963	632,562	53,685	13,765	592,642	131,246	115,792	5,409	155,229	69,450
1975	970,992	564,133	151,451	715,584	60,611	20,803	675,776	155,746	139,470	6,099	159,209	72,488
1976	1,016,332	647,718	101,320	749,038	72,029	23,159	700,168	165,139	151,025	6,271	162,074	77,178
1977	1,096,377	710,924	80,806	791,730	79,686	34,101	746,145	188,106	162,126	6,677	164,202	76,262
1978	1,291,969	814,489	134,548	949,037	92,894	44,234	900,377	215,769	175,823	7,763	166,436	78,991
1979	1,436,395	916,956	117,398	1,034,354	107,704	56,288	982,938	249,840	203,617	8,500	168,987	82,216
1980	1,572,482	973,163	116,390	1,089,553	114,788	58,548	1,033,313	295,439	243,730	9,083	173,118	82,688
1981	1,736,534	1,038,836	125,848	1,164,684	131,870	79,250	1,112,064	353,726	270,744	9,911	175,218	82,751
1982	1,828,637	1,057,033	133,228	1,190,261	135,778	69,674	1,124,157	399,479	305,001	10,342	176,825	81,334
1983	1,937,270	1,125,227	141,956	1,267,183	146,168	59,628	1,180,643	431,500	325,127	10,808	179,248	84,131
1984	2,082,747	1,194,894	177,018	1,371,912	161,293	48,837	1,259,456	474,247	349,044	11,557	180,209	84,048
1985	2,118,521	1,226,055	129,882	1,355,937	168,027	52,015	1,239,925	498,628	379,968	11,684	181,321	83,388
1986	2,254,408	1,271,311	195,348	1,466,659	175,992	53,260	1,343,927	513,104	397,377	12,458	180,961	84,095
1987	2,413,624	1,369,906	254,204	1,624,110	190,656	52,657	1,486,111	514,730	412,783	13,283	181,707	92,689
1988	2,485,110	1,469,506	211,266	1,680,772	210,961	55,506	1,525,317	518,897	440,896	13,400	185,454	96,178
1989	2,771,691	1,582,525	285,068	1,867,593	229,564	56,452	1,694,481	589,379	487,831	14,777	187,574	99,415
1990	3,031,486	1,747,375	266,181	2,013,556	257,487	63,279	1,819,348	667,692	544,446	16,001	189,454	101,956
1991	3,234,151	1,888,794	356,699	2,245,493	280,226	40,239	2,005,506	616,402	612,243	16,679	193,904	101,599
1992	3,523,192	2,072,349	382,568	2,454,917	307,326	40,115	2,187,706	644,709	690,777	17,706	198,983	102,197
1993	3,716,883	2,190,600	395,175	2,585,775	323,782	41,249	2,303,242	676,430	737,211	18,196	204,266	103,901
1994	3,873,016	2,333,425	358,599	2,692,024	341,767	42,844	2,393,101	724,559	755,356	18,534	208,963	108,409
1995	4,003,289	2,378,550	352,389	2,730,939	351,871	37,895	2,416,963	762,551	823,775	18,830	212,601	109,268
1996	4,271,553	2,472,624	427,577	2,900,201	352,463	33,638	2,581,376	826,859	863,318	19,872	214,951	111,266
1997	4,409,115	2,621,429	352,730	2,974,159	357,630	30,979	2,647,508	879,354	882,253	20,300	217,201	112,404
1998	4,652,543	2,819,617	407,412	3,227,029	376,463	25,926	2,876,492	881,100	894,951	21,172	219,748	112,073
1999	4,736,104	2,918,366	338,218	3,256,584	382,616	23,479	2,897,447	887,673	950,984	21,375	221,573	112,619
2000	5,011,656	3,037,836	409,241	3,447,077	405,275	19,221	3,061,023	936,470	1,014,163	22,513	222,615	112,920
2001	5,141,010	3,138,952	342,906	3,481,858	420,188	21,241	3,082,911	933,301	1,124,798	23,079	222,757	112,685
2002	5,216,420	3,253,223	367,089	3,620,312	435,840	23,881	3,208,353	857,929	1,150,138	23,350	223,402	112,734
2003	5,577,379	3,411,487	448,460	3,859,947	456,305	22,112	3,425,754	936,195	1,215,430	24,771	225,161	114,189
2004	5,823,093	3,560,481	521,941	4,082,422	480,912	22,187	3,623,697	948,029	1,251,367	25,621	227,280	113,223
2005	5,906,848	3,683,183	450,561	4,133,744	509,296	20,025	3,644,473	932,897	1,329,478	25,843	228,570	114,927
2006	6,153,717	3,860,306	413,852	4,274,158	531,502	13,599	3,756,255	984,532	1,412,930	26,684	230,617	117,779
2007	6,766,009	4,064,040	538,392	4,602,432	555,371	13,457	4,060,518	1,175,621	1,529,870	29,072	232,733	118,536
2008	7,384,511	4,281,593	547,374	4,828,967	593,618	8,990	4,244,339	1,401,222	1,738,950	31,387	235,272	121,722
2009	7,351,683	4,318,647	502,560	4,821,207	614,888	13,687	4,220,006	1,230,559	1,901,118	30,683	239,604	120,007
2010	7,807,410	4,475,432	611,204	5,086,636	631,559	20,411	4,475,488	1,224,513	2,107,409	31,961	244,283	119,123
2011	8,309,420	4,540,347	785,174	5,325,521	589,671	29,345	4,765,195	1,417,276	2,126,949	33,771	246,050	120,041
2012	8,817,896	4,817,007	850,266	5,667,273	610,036	14,082	5,071,319	1,613,887	2,132,690	35,783	246,428	124,847
2013	8,807,967	4,902,924	855,151	5,758,075	683,098	10,097	5,085,074	1,593,287	2,129,606	35,687	246,809	125,388
2014	9,342,879	5,046,853	922,584	5,969,437	721,588	9,940	5,257,789	1,677,345	2,407,745	37,816	247,064	127,312
2015	9,729,975	5,175,692	1,072,146	6,247,838	744,498	17,456	5,520,796	1,839,956	2,369,223	39,233	248,006	128,518
2016	9,964,842	5,393,515	1,027,756	6,421,271	765,623	18,556	5,674,204	1,757,390	2,533,248	39,968	249,323	130,545
2017	10,340,744	5,715,356	966,089	6,681,445	828,254	20,574	5,873,765	1,854,010	2,612,969	41,331	250,193	132,983
2018	11,001,031	10,144,592	856,439	7,036,148	847,141	22,529	6,211,536	2,150,849	2,638,646	43,905	250,562	134,982
2019	11,479,279	10,546,125	933,154	7,377,437	889,413	29,767	6,517,791	2,199,278	2,762,210	45,757	250,873	136,556

Personal Income and Employment by Area: York-Hanover, PA

(Thousands of dollars, except as noted.)

Year	Personal income, total	Earnings by place of work			Less: Contributions for government social insurance	Plus: Adjustment for residence	Equals: Net earnings by place of residence	Plus: Dividends, interest, and rent	Plus: Personal current transfer receipts	Per capita personal income (dollars)	Population (persons)	Total employment
		Nonfarm	Farm	Total								
1970	1,206,079	1,063,173	9,208	1,072,381	78,376	-31,911	962,094	153,738	90,247	4,411	273,427	139,933
1971	1,279,619	1,100,094	2,949	1,103,043	83,738	-12,199	1,007,106	168,431	104,082	4,587	278,991	137,875
1972	1,425,322	1,215,586	5,097	1,220,683	98,313	4,561	1,126,931	183,687	114,704	5,043	282,646	142,624
1973	1,589,893	1,330,118	14,619	1,344,737	123,335	29,057	1,250,459	209,367	130,067	5,557	286,122	147,199
1974	1,742,726	1,402,195	15,927	1,418,122	133,836	63,257	1,347,543	239,490	155,693	6,036	288,739	146,547
1975	1,899,048	1,455,589	13,416	1,469,005	133,920	88,997	1,424,082	267,599	207,367	6,486	292,808	140,987
1976	2,116,001	1,616,229	19,089	1,635,318	152,229	122,404	1,605,493	285,542	224,966	7,123	297,047	144,496
1977	2,360,782	1,804,018	15,226	1,819,244	170,638	160,373	1,808,979	317,269	234,534	7,852	300,642	148,395
1978	2,683,469	2,069,032	11,914	2,080,946	201,666	204,194	2,083,474	351,589	248,406	8,783	305,545	154,993
1979	3,034,776	2,313,487	22,491	2,335,978	233,864	253,654	2,355,768	400,633	278,375	9,780	310,297	160,882
1980	3,395,023	2,500,700	10,514	2,511,214	254,619	316,783	2,573,378	493,747	327,898	10,826	313,599	161,194
1981	3,726,704	2,693,415	19,911	2,713,326	293,384	323,098	2,743,040	604,794	378,870	11,821	315,266	159,431
1982	3,941,551	2,740,164	16,675	2,756,839	300,531	321,702	2,778,010	712,502	451,039	12,474	315,972	155,440
1983	4,121,294	2,843,039	2,225	2,845,264	317,874	349,470	2,876,860	757,994	486,440	13,037	316,125	154,109
1984	4,524,698	3,161,299	24,713	3,186,012	370,748	376,851	3,192,115	853,818	478,765	14,158	319,582	161,378
1985	4,828,656	3,384,335	20,956	3,405,291	400,799	388,545	3,393,037	924,947	510,672	15,082	320,150	165,404
1986	5,114,408	3,560,217	19,619	3,579,836	422,196	429,750	3,587,390	983,759	543,259	15,881	322,055	169,374
1987	5,461,816	3,888,224	19,581	3,907,805	455,349	439,617	3,892,073	1,010,477	559,266	16,758	325,922	176,386
1988	5,946,635	4,312,767	8,427	4,321,194	513,368	458,476	4,266,302	1,078,546	601,787	17,969	330,944	184,414
1989	6,456,078	4,585,005	20,529	4,605,534	535,964	473,422	4,542,992	1,258,989	654,097	19,211	336,068	188,133
1990	6,771,767	4,843,410	26,711	4,870,121	568,238	486,389	4,788,272	1,263,509	719,986	19,870	340,810	191,073
1991	7,078,679	5,018,191	13,380	5,031,571	594,222	520,292	4,957,641	1,296,188	824,850	20,446	346,209	188,389
1992	7,519,043	5,315,529	37,621	5,353,150	626,641	584,710	5,311,219	1,316,714	891,110	21,419	351,046	188,825
1993	7,911,940	5,519,147	24,733	5,543,880	665,167	639,199	5,517,912	1,461,353	932,675	22,215	356,156	190,523
1994	8,118,686	5,734,614	23,343	5,757,957	706,628	713,539	5,764,868	1,401,464	952,354	22,484	361,092	193,790
1995	8,560,821	6,020,193	11,880	6,032,073	739,982	770,955	6,063,046	1,488,587	1,009,188	23,390	365,997	198,685
1996	9,012,837	6,245,612	35,026	6,280,638	751,965	832,075	6,360,748	1,566,630	1,085,459	24,373	369,781	201,286
1997	9,477,674	6,592,550	12,813	6,605,363	783,392	866,812	6,688,783	1,663,830	1,125,061	25,429	372,706	204,054
1998	10,006,140	6,814,862	16,013	6,830,875	804,427	997,092	7,023,540	1,801,391	1,181,209	26,626	375,810	200,364
1999	10,390,210	7,116,768	9,134	7,125,902	833,167	1,093,718	7,386,453	1,756,175	1,247,582	27,422	378,905	204,405
2000	11,181,657	7,608,911	35,757	7,644,668	878,531	1,141,244	7,907,381	1,927,516	1,346,760	29,215	382,743	210,164
2001	11,525,083	7,800,016	26,391	7,826,407	894,576	1,222,233	8,154,064	1,871,174	1,499,845	29,875	385,773	211,514
2002	11,796,246	7,997,278	10,854	8,008,132	913,868	1,354,373	8,448,637	1,719,735	1,627,874	30,271	389,692	211,138
2003	12,471,136	8,381,488	65,392	8,446,880	946,759	1,446,316	8,946,437	1,787,994	1,736,705	31,565	395,093	211,658
2004	13,756,361	9,250,801	64,837	9,315,638	1,015,615	1,693,996	9,994,019	1,950,507	1,811,835	34,271	401,403	217,006
2005	14,764,296	10,064,916	44,137	10,109,053	1,111,218	1,822,760	10,820,595	1,943,234	2,000,467	36,093	409,066	223,488
2006	15,209,252	9,871,010	26,971	9,897,981	1,127,762	2,104,341	10,874,560	2,169,274	2,165,418	36,382	418,043	226,836
2007	16,640,602	10,675,869	39,726	10,715,595	1,179,812	2,282,372	11,818,155	2,508,058	2,314,389	39,162	424,919	231,790
2008	17,968,757	11,449,478	42,725	11,492,203	1,227,422	2,402,635	12,667,416	2,630,339	2,671,002	41,846	429,399	232,142
2009	17,348,082	10,584,795	29,859	10,614,654	1,184,654	2,429,951	11,859,951	2,488,983	2,999,148	40,063	433,022	223,008
2010	17,519,470	10,745,530	31,774	10,777,304	1,215,354	2,336,839	11,898,789	2,370,509	3,250,172	40,235	435,426	221,987
2011	18,053,496	10,851,737	35,717	10,887,454	1,130,539	2,391,291	12,148,206	2,631,622	3,273,668	41,341	436,702	224,717
2012	18,354,871	10,804,100	51,317	10,855,417	1,130,848	2,362,744	12,087,313	2,948,858	3,318,700	41,956	437,483	225,936
2013	18,331,878	10,983,660	51,089	11,034,749	1,298,367	2,402,772	12,139,154	2,774,470	3,418,254	41,765	438,926	227,260
2014	18,865,266	11,196,871	37,731	11,234,602	1,327,292	2,465,539	12,372,849	2,934,808	3,557,609	42,832	440,444	229,649
2015	19,743,521	11,702,148	17,747	11,719,895	1,384,175	2,594,314	12,930,034	3,074,424	3,739,063	44,687	441,822	231,838
2016	20,321,794	12,054,193	-6,954	12,047,239	1,439,311	2,675,092	13,283,020	3,093,691	3,945,083	45,790	443,809	235,774
2017	21,156,222	12,709,399	4,367	12,713,766	1,527,436	2,732,937	13,919,267	3,247,745	3,989,210	47,427	446,078	238,471
2018	22,342,240	22,342,044	196	13,264,749	1,575,114	2,853,172	14,542,807	3,472,314	4,327,119	49,888	447,847	240,494
2019	23,164,517	23,139,143	25,374	13,646,152	1,616,039	3,057,295	15,087,408	3,541,003	4,536,106	51,585	449,058	243,152

Personal Income and Employment by Area: Youngstown-Warren-Boardman, OH-PA

(Thousands of dollars, except as noted.)

Year	Personal income, total	Earnings by place of work			Less: Contributions for government social insurance	Plus: Adjustment for residence	Equals: Net earnings by place of residence	Plus: Dividends, interest, and rent	Plus: Personal current transfer receipts	Per capita personal income (dollars)	Population (persons)	Total employment
		Nonfarm	Farm	Total								
1970	2,586,501	2,238,856	8,172	2,247,028	154,468	-36,575	2,055,985	302,231	228,285	3,886	665,569	279,196
1971	2,757,559	2,363,330	7,656	2,370,986	167,755	-39,449	2,163,782	325,056	268,721	4,111	670,741	276,899
1972	3,046,740	2,635,873	8,730	2,644,603	197,250	-46,526	2,400,827	345,972	299,941	4,472	681,278	282,795
1973	3,438,961	3,016,279	14,941	3,031,220	263,301	-55,104	2,712,815	385,235	340,911	5,143	668,722	296,124
1974	3,758,820	3,251,298	15,570	3,266,868	294,955	-62,409	2,909,504	439,851	409,465	5,569	675,013	299,829
1975	3,976,949	3,292,945	17,575	3,310,520	292,039	-59,492	2,958,989	479,999	537,961	6,005	662,274	285,651
1976	4,373,755	3,629,637	20,754	3,650,391	325,744	-68,030	3,256,617	516,562	600,576	6,560	666,754	288,266
1977	4,840,148	4,063,895	17,270	4,081,165	366,240	-76,033	3,638,892	574,078	627,178	7,252	667,417	294,002
1978	5,315,357	4,472,435	12,833	4,485,268	416,924	-76,424	3,991,920	637,191	686,246	7,994	664,956	298,304
1979	5,857,395	4,905,322	13,963	4,919,285	474,007	-79,687	4,365,591	717,975	773,829	8,899	658,231	301,663
1980	6,365,198	5,035,540	8,081	5,043,621	481,906	-76,512	4,485,203	908,296	971,699	9,665	658,600	291,643
1981	6,947,526	5,379,300	12,046	5,391,346	552,630	-84,079	4,754,637	1,123,210	1,069,679	10,640	652,946	286,983
1982	6,934,357	4,925,211	9,375	4,934,586	509,401	-37,514	4,387,671	1,249,465	1,297,221	10,676	649,503	264,325
1983	7,237,696	5,124,635	1,050	5,125,685	538,677	-37,507	4,549,501	1,332,335	1,355,860	11,229	644,566	259,259
1984	7,866,481	5,649,422	17,182	5,666,604	611,158	-40,685	5,014,761	1,499,026	1,352,694	12,344	637,279	267,611
1985	8,216,618	5,885,405	19,729	5,905,134	645,437	-38,678	5,221,019	1,573,157	1,422,442	13,012	631,445	270,681
1986	8,452,983	5,982,789	16,567	5,999,356	667,063	-23,532	5,308,761	1,629,076	1,515,146	13,520	625,219	275,735
1987	8,642,591	6,135,992	22,379	6,158,371	684,228	-15,349	5,458,794	1,602,806	1,580,991	13,957	619,212	280,875
1988	9,360,441	6,773,995	29,579	6,803,574	774,133	-33,250	5,996,191	1,718,182	1,646,068	15,202	615,749	288,063
1989	10,059,013	7,234,872	35,429	7,270,301	835,787	-37,698	6,396,816	1,904,884	1,757,313	16,355	615,048	293,661
1990	10,431,129	7,383,589	33,616	7,417,205	870,440	-28,187	6,518,578	1,919,800	1,992,751	16,989	613,980	294,927
1991	10,700,232	7,555,122	19,772	7,574,894	915,359	-39,668	6,619,867	1,952,970	2,127,395	17,386	615,462	294,326
1992	11,275,211	7,973,450	38,592	8,012,042	955,716	-39,863	7,016,463	1,955,837	2,302,911	18,254	617,681	292,356
1993	11,611,003	8,251,065	25,312	8,276,377	1,010,518	-25,296	7,240,563	1,974,584	2,395,856	18,778	618,328	293,654
1994	12,191,023	8,745,285	26,268	8,771,553	1,081,259	-24,416	7,665,878	2,061,466	2,463,679	19,750	617,253	299,990
1995	12,704,098	8,991,516	21,431	9,012,947	1,121,229	4,143	7,895,861	2,221,992	2,586,245	20,637	615,595	309,477
1996	13,124,480	9,181,409	29,310	9,210,719	1,129,411	35,741	8,117,049	2,324,892	2,682,539	21,363	614,369	311,996
1997	13,706,351	9,564,928	22,530	9,587,458	1,139,754	42,072	8,489,776	2,469,263	2,747,312	22,400	611,902	315,429
1998	14,122,731	9,764,781	24,828	9,789,609	1,133,977	85,026	8,740,658	2,593,888	2,788,185	23,179	609,286	315,929
1999	14,481,948	10,137,844	21,532	10,159,376	1,166,572	91,035	9,083,839	2,539,099	2,859,010	23,898	605,978	317,483
2000	15,003,800	10,362,565	25,020	10,387,585	1,155,371	115,228	9,347,442	2,628,187	3,028,171	24,914	602,227	318,418
2001	15,560,429	10,683,630	18,625	10,702,255	1,190,590	158,201	9,669,866	2,616,836	3,273,727	25,972	599,116	311,150
2002	15,797,111	10,927,480	9,939	10,937,419	1,193,976	169,076	9,912,519	2,453,093	3,431,499	26,552	594,958	305,452
2003	16,338,308	11,309,812	17,884	11,327,696	1,244,562	191,066	10,274,200	2,498,510	3,565,598	27,598	592,016	302,591
2004	16,768,570	11,636,756	25,557	11,662,313	1,301,806	238,063	10,598,570	2,476,486	3,693,514	28,495	588,478	301,803
2005	17,217,462	11,904,728	18,376	11,923,104	1,348,413	261,790	10,836,481	2,475,620	3,905,361	29,471	584,222	303,520
2006	18,161,258	12,559,328	15,257	12,574,585	1,424,440	262,046	11,412,191	2,690,290	4,058,777	31,290	580,420	302,814
2007	18,605,349	12,382,431	30,547	12,412,978	1,414,585	310,985	11,309,378	3,032,011	4,263,960	32,327	575,543	301,433
2008	19,038,431	12,203,707	17,461	12,221,168	1,412,426	362,149	11,170,891	3,109,458	4,758,082	33,345	570,952	295,953
2009	18,100,449	11,079,743	11,292	11,091,035	1,317,140	376,897	10,150,792	2,733,737	5,215,920	31,858	568,156	280,869
2010	18,625,128	11,554,839	25,261	11,580,100	1,349,339	343,013	10,573,774	2,686,414	5,364,940	32,974	564,837	280,982
2011	19,830,050	12,319,379	52,453	12,371,832	1,290,793	347,938	11,428,977	2,956,270	5,444,803	35,268	562,271	285,225
2012	20,190,885	12,599,645	42,858	12,642,503	1,305,705	382,568	11,719,366	3,117,283	5,354,236	36,153	558,480	287,302
2013	20,209,474	12,642,090	48,038	12,690,128	1,426,425	437,788	11,701,491	3,023,046	5,484,937	36,364	555,758	287,506
2014	20,814,215	12,824,372	41,175	12,865,547	1,452,841	479,434	11,892,140	3,236,122	5,685,953	37,637	553,029	287,957
2015	21,391,849	13,114,845	4,638	13,119,483	1,486,887	485,966	12,118,562	3,392,350	5,880,937	38,976	548,846	287,933
2016	21,516,590	13,021,052	11,665	13,032,717	1,509,766	477,270	12,000,221	3,468,272	6,048,097	39,513	544,543	288,158
2017	22,028,738	13,200,727	5,580	13,206,307	1,553,976	554,145	12,206,476	3,639,763	6,182,499	40,649	541,926	285,175
2018	22,742,602	22,731,609	10,993	13,610,539	1,591,162	568,577	12,587,954	3,830,807	6,323,841	42,255	538,226	284,853
2019	23,140,742	23,130,518	10,224	13,649,654	1,595,974	673,772	12,727,452	3,878,714	6,534,576	43,167	536,081	283,700

Personal Income and Employment by Area: Yuba City, CA

(Thousands of dollars, except as noted.)

		Derivation of personal income										
		Earnings by place of work			Less: Contributions for government social insurance	Plus: Adjustment for residence	Equals: Net earnings by place of residence	Plus: Dividends, interest, and rent	Plus: Personal current transfer receipts	Per capita personal income (dollars)	Population (persons)	Total employment
Year	Personal income, total	Nonfarm	Farm	Total								
1970	381,992	247,601	45,848	293,449	17,043	-1,081	275,325	67,151	39,516	4,385	87,104	38,704
1971	416,455	269,274	52,357	321,631	19,232	-1,053	301,346	71,329	43,780	4,714	88,345	39,301
1972	453,626	290,533	63,161	353,694	21,250	-1,525	330,919	76,324	46,383	5,184	87,505	39,903
1973	511,582	304,200	96,542	400,742	24,323	-2,038	374,381	85,213	51,988	5,686	89,980	39,333
1974	589,712	336,569	125,115	461,684	27,903	-3,630	430,151	95,524	64,037	6,455	91,363	40,753
1975	639,526	374,793	111,918	486,711	31,194	-4,492	451,025	110,054	78,447	6,889	92,830	42,061
1976	647,325	410,241	71,770	482,011	35,046	-5,656	441,309	116,543	89,473	6,744	95,979	42,261
1977	729,495	447,835	99,000	546,835	38,607	-6,366	501,862	128,930	98,703	7,524	96,962	42,971
1978	800,278	504,366	85,799	590,165	43,672	-6,830	539,663	149,769	110,846	8,139	98,325	44,298
1979	894,183	559,315	95,175	654,490	49,749	-6,324	598,417	170,628	125,138	8,888	100,611	45,882
1980	1,012,341	601,249	121,553	722,802	52,199	-7,344	663,259	197,953	151,129	9,887	102,388	45,871
1981	1,101,199	641,567	119,557	761,124	60,425	-8,748	691,951	231,541	177,707	10,606	103,831	45,667
1982	1,118,935	665,971	75,625	741,596	62,819	-6,008	672,769	251,352	194,814	10,516	106,405	45,349
1983	1,151,034	691,779	41,179	732,958	66,645	692	667,005	270,596	213,433	10,610	108,483	45,038
1984	1,307,254	741,008	100,198	841,206	73,967	10,438	777,677	300,839	228,738	11,987	109,052	45,505
1985	1,412,011	779,330	127,016	906,346	79,025	22,850	850,171	314,183	247,657	12,729	110,929	46,019
1986	1,472,359	842,915	94,718	937,633	86,561	32,406	883,478	324,136	264,745	13,116	112,256	46,253
1987	1,582,880	899,183	123,432	1,022,615	93,710	44,673	973,578	334,836	274,466	13,818	114,554	48,049
1988	1,684,424	979,189	106,519	1,085,708	106,289	55,869	1,035,288	351,552	297,584	14,407	116,916	50,737
1989	1,844,201	1,056,469	105,023	1,161,492	116,786	69,504	1,114,210	400,703	329,288	15,405	119,714	53,653
1990	1,937,776	1,120,634	79,553	1,200,187	123,512	89,210	1,165,885	406,105	365,786	15,691	123,499	54,925
1991	2,111,973	1,191,846	121,389	1,313,235	133,488	89,124	1,268,871	429,192	413,910	16,672	126,677	56,571
1992	2,260,180	1,246,224	135,722	1,381,946	139,558	93,742	1,336,130	443,911	480,139	17,401	129,886	56,076
1993	2,329,892	1,271,636	151,036	1,422,672	142,812	96,344	1,376,204	449,940	503,748	17,657	131,950	56,416
1994	2,430,384	1,325,659	173,133	1,498,792	147,653	105,572	1,456,711	465,993	507,680	18,067	134,518	57,920
1995	2,524,598	1,380,505	160,978	1,541,483	151,059	115,902	1,506,326	486,488	531,784	18,656	135,323	59,036
1996	2,621,575	1,422,083	160,395	1,582,478	151,366	126,390	1,557,502	509,258	554,815	19,254	136,160	60,320
1997	2,732,275	1,527,763	139,784	1,667,547	157,720	142,043	1,651,870	524,956	555,449	20,028	136,425	60,517
1998	2,903,504	1,647,110	101,503	1,748,613	164,775	161,126	1,744,964	564,396	594,144	21,191	137,016	61,798
1999	3,149,018	1,759,555	199,079	1,958,634	177,675	182,379	1,963,338	552,388	633,292	22,803	138,097	63,347
2000	3,283,472	1,863,093	169,554	2,032,647	187,549	212,581	2,057,679	578,200	647,593	23,527	139,564	63,301
2001	3,408,197	1,984,893	125,132	2,110,025	212,204	222,767	2,120,588	571,133	716,476	24,105	141,387	61,499
2002	3,578,683	2,117,430	116,305	2,233,735	228,961	251,446	2,256,220	553,600	768,863	24,807	144,262	62,404
2003	3,857,126	2,262,049	153,349	2,415,398	245,998	282,847	2,452,247	582,935	821,944	26,167	147,404	62,573
2004	4,157,269	2,392,703	158,770	2,551,473	269,310	372,466	2,654,629	647,773	854,867	27,673	150,226	63,898
2005	4,409,164	2,496,039	121,454	2,617,493	281,570	508,040	2,843,963	684,867	880,334	28,437	155,049	64,648
2006	4,806,062	2,674,224	139,882	2,814,106	292,823	607,197	3,128,480	721,980	955,602	29,966	160,384	66,167
2007	5,149,468	2,809,052	160,506	2,969,558	300,487	672,571	3,341,642	782,575	1,025,251	31,453	163,720	67,736
2008	5,447,537	2,793,418	261,866	3,055,284	304,945	723,917	3,474,256	815,990	1,157,291	32,890	165,628	65,442
2009	5,499,867	2,802,294	353,425	3,155,719	310,255	582,729	3,428,193	805,090	1,266,584	33,137	165,973	63,426
2010	5,587,162	2,898,307	275,202	3,173,509	308,127	539,133	3,404,515	781,797	1,400,850	33,433	167,115	62,526
2011	5,783,221	2,958,370	288,149	3,246,519	290,405	548,621	3,504,735	849,082	1,429,404	34,615	167,071	62,563
2012	5,799,747	3,027,936	230,542	3,258,478	299,536	510,369	3,469,311	888,470	1,441,966	34,693	167,174	63,966
2013	6,059,132	3,116,124	320,274	3,436,398	341,214	534,761	3,629,945	933,753	1,495,434	36,096	167,861	65,459
2014	6,396,967	3,274,557	301,128	3,575,685	356,430	545,218	3,764,473	1,039,437	1,593,057	37,936	168,625	66,863
2015	6,741,301	3,458,433	179,121	3,637,554	372,912	614,546	3,879,188	1,136,335	1,725,778	39,719	169,725	68,743
2016	6,946,770	3,564,163	188,639	3,752,802	387,906	615,881	3,980,777	1,180,010	1,785,983	40,567	171,243	70,038
2017	7,237,745	3,745,970	272,645	4,018,615	408,311	636,253	4,246,557	1,238,091	1,753,097	41,673	173,679	71,557
2018	7,593,081	7,365,460	227,621	4,174,704	430,094	723,537	4,468,147	1,276,394	1,848,540	43,662	173,905	73,096
2019	8,041,182	7,772,190	268,992	4,476,062	464,016	722,201	4,734,247	1,307,074	1,999,861	45,782	175,639	75,581

Personal Income and Employment by Area: Yuma, AZ

(Thousands of dollars, except as noted.)

Year	Personal income, total	Earnings by place of work			Less: Contributions for government social insurance	Plus: Adjustment for residence	Equals: Net earnings by place of residence	Plus: Dividends, interest, and rent	Plus: Personal current transfer receipts	Per capita personal income (dollars)	Population (persons)	Total employment
		Nonfarm	Farm	Total								
1970	235,094	166,029	29,515	195,544	11,394	-7,832	176,318	42,539	16,237	3,828	61,415	29,730
1971	272,044	197,321	27,253	224,574	14,114	-8,281	202,179	50,514	19,351	4,195	64,853	31,172
1972	296,854	210,699	34,364	245,063	15,579	-9,060	220,424	54,072	22,358	4,421	67,150	31,018
1973	323,703	231,159	30,905	262,064	18,851	-9,420	233,793	62,827	27,083	4,713	68,685	31,328
1974	414,496	261,191	82,162	343,353	22,284	-11,295	309,774	72,681	32,041	5,806	71,396	32,675
1975	432,086	297,812	49,068	346,880	25,142	-14,734	307,004	82,298	42,784	6,223	69,434	33,614
1976	485,479	335,643	57,368	393,011	28,944	-16,513	347,554	88,321	49,604	6,348	76,476	35,033
1977	520,645	362,899	61,665	424,564	31,563	-20,921	372,080	96,629	51,936	6,553	79,454	36,573
1978	580,758	410,261	64,781	475,042	36,149	-28,224	410,669	112,713	57,376	7,198	80,680	38,692
1979	703,048	474,938	105,570	580,508	44,524	-33,164	502,820	131,658	68,570	8,419	83,512	39,541
1980	791,920	520,044	117,724	637,768	49,114	-37,484	551,170	155,490	85,260	8,665	91,393	40,634
1981	863,428	555,336	106,873	662,209	56,585	-22,536	583,088	178,186	102,154	9,402	91,834	40,844
1982	903,925	563,940	104,043	667,983	57,259	-20,977	589,747	202,453	111,725	9,629	93,878	40,449
1983	865,388	554,421	68,863	623,284	57,148	-17,587	548,549	207,200	109,639	10,299	84,027	38,578
1984	978,765	627,396	88,653	716,049	66,181	-18,540	631,328	235,898	111,539	11,465	85,373	40,324
1985	1,084,486	668,738	130,208	798,946	71,816	-17,213	709,917	260,738	113,831	12,384	87,572	41,031
1986	1,144,579	737,509	88,883	826,392	80,405	-14,977	731,010	284,635	128,934	12,647	90,505	42,571
1987	1,294,495	800,117	163,863	963,980	87,571	-12,610	863,799	289,346	141,350	13,967	92,684	45,954
1988	1,436,977	864,850	236,865	1,101,715	98,423	-8,111	995,181	288,803	152,993	14,804	97,064	48,117
1989	1,473,542	918,771	160,598	1,079,369	109,005	-988	969,376	312,368	191,798	14,254	103,380	50,231
1990	1,533,564	971,705	137,633	1,109,338	118,748	2,223	992,813	323,245	217,506	14,191	108,063	50,626
1991	1,688,767	1,070,171	171,190	1,241,361	130,802	-7,047	1,103,512	333,826	251,429	15,083	111,967	53,294
1992	1,818,271	1,151,568	162,719	1,314,287	141,263	-4,433	1,168,591	342,483	307,197	15,323	118,660	54,781
1993	1,979,645	1,201,331	245,996	1,447,327	148,331	-5,198	1,293,798	351,600	334,247	15,851	124,892	55,460
1994	2,014,037	1,284,795	153,413	1,438,208	157,771	-8,876	1,271,561	386,184	356,292	15,738	127,975	57,080
1995	2,355,018	1,355,256	376,898	1,732,154	158,176	-11,050	1,562,928	413,608	378,482	17,871	131,776	59,415
1996	2,273,318	1,421,267	196,477	1,617,744	169,677	-12,589	1,435,478	438,473	399,367	16,564	137,248	63,061
1997	2,454,744	1,546,450	216,401	1,762,851	179,788	-16,118	1,566,945	471,186	416,613	17,059	143,896	63,462
1998	2,687,018	1,633,708	324,637	1,958,345	187,860	-15,317	1,755,168	488,288	443,562	18,026	149,065	66,554
1999	2,713,222	1,692,126	258,433	1,950,559	194,492	-12,692	1,743,375	491,922	477,925	17,430	155,665	66,938
2000	2,878,896	1,772,768	307,903	2,080,671	202,805	-12,719	1,865,147	521,137	492,612	17,929	160,576	67,936
2001	3,057,053	1,935,107	237,813	2,172,920	226,046	-826	1,946,048	549,473	561,532	18,770	162,873	70,656
2002	3,313,674	2,071,415	324,186	2,395,601	246,650	832	2,149,783	536,653	627,238	20,035	165,398	72,784
2003	3,583,584	2,376,946	217,157	2,594,103	271,686	3,016	2,325,433	571,781	686,370	21,330	168,003	74,549
2004	4,011,268	2,644,438	324,175	2,968,613	301,169	2,594	2,670,038	604,245	736,985	23,210	172,824	78,518
2005	4,281,536	2,810,279	318,678	3,128,957	324,237	6,493	2,811,213	663,752	806,571	23,944	178,816	80,808
2006	4,528,146	3,083,977	225,376	3,309,353	351,815	11,363	2,968,901	686,237	873,008	24,630	183,848	83,776
2007	4,857,636	3,219,653	292,415	3,512,068	379,060	14,305	3,147,313	763,206	947,117	25,927	187,357	85,115
2008	5,041,311	3,297,855	187,854	3,485,709	396,181	19,539	3,109,067	813,276	1,118,968	26,366	191,202	83,665
2009	5,105,829	3,208,666	188,810	3,397,476	391,913	16,419	3,021,982	815,410	1,268,437	26,358	193,714	79,960
2010	5,361,748	3,273,668	311,122	3,584,790	400,555	21,984	3,206,219	761,794	1,393,735	27,200	197,124	79,901
2011	5,665,534	3,365,075	457,432	3,822,507	369,652	25,829	3,478,684	809,057	1,377,793	27,967	202,581	80,988
2012	5,606,527	3,454,632	270,635	3,725,267	378,927	33,448	3,379,788	866,656	1,360,083	27,741	202,105	82,389
2013	5,929,784	3,522,224	522,177	4,044,401	430,418	41,170	3,655,153	885,368	1,389,263	29,383	201,810	83,072
2014	5,942,092	3,644,358	300,058	3,944,416	439,996	43,875	3,548,295	932,973	1,460,824	29,266	203,039	83,682
2015	6,482,641	3,806,738	616,784	4,423,522	459,934	51,345	4,014,933	948,216	1,519,492	31,847	203,558	85,810
2016	6,833,428	3,981,885	725,692	4,707,577	487,594	48,056	4,268,039	1,013,943	1,551,446	33,259	205,463	88,692
2017	7,212,166	4,133,774	864,620	4,998,394	515,874	52,047	4,534,567	1,046,530	1,631,069	34,752	207,534	88,273
2018	7,408,956	6,797,910	611,046	5,046,671	546,361	51,770	4,552,080	1,143,251	1,713,625	35,012	211,612	89,875
2019	7,818,246	7,125,237	693,009	5,315,861	572,204	54,365	4,798,022	1,173,109	1,847,115	36,570	213,787	91,296

PART B

GROSS DOMESTIC PRODUCT (GDP) BY REGION, STATE, AND AREA

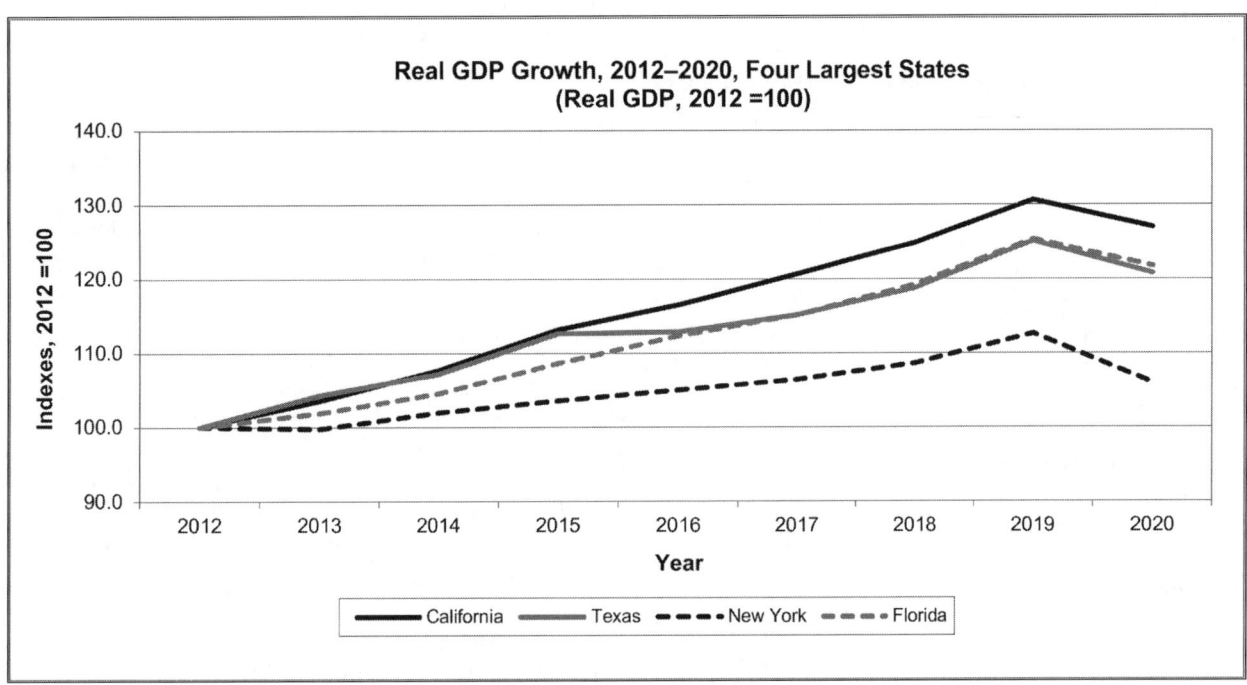

Real GDP Growth, 2012–2020, Four Largest States
(Real GDP, 2012 =100)

HIGHLIGHTS:

- GDP decreased in all states in 2020, and the nationwide GDP fell 3.5 percent. Utah had the smallest decrease of -0.1 percent, followed by Washington (-0.7 percent). The states with the greatest decline were Hawaii (-8.0 percent) and Wyoming (-7.0 percent).

- The three states with the largest GDP in 2020 were California ($2.7 trillion), Texas ($1.7 trillion), and New York ($1.4 trillion). Together, those three states produced 31.9 percent of the total U.S. GDP in 2020. The states with the lowest GDP were Vermont ($28.2 billion), Wyoming ($36.5 billion), and Montana ($46.5 billion).

- Midland, TX, experienced the largest growth in GDP among all metropolitan statistical areas (MSAs) from 2018 to 2019 at 18.7 percent. Rocky Mount, NC, experienced the largest decline in GDP from 2018 to 2019, at -18.9 percent. GDP declined by 0.1 percent or more in 39 MSAs.

- New York-Newark-Jersey City, NY-NJ-PA, which had the largest GDP among all MSAs, comprised 9.3 percent of the total U.S. metropolitan portion of GDP in 2019, followed by Los Angeles-Long Beach-Anaheim, CA, with 5.7 percent of the total GDP from all MSAs.

PART B NOTES AND DEFINITIONS: GROSS DOMESTIC PRODUCT BY REGION AND STATE

Source: U.S. Department of Commerce, Bureau of Economic Analysis (BEA), http://www.bea.gov

The following definitions are from the BEA. In a following section, further detail and explanation of the concepts is provided.

BEA definitions

Definitions. GDP by state is the state counterpart of the nation's gross domestic product (GDP), the BEA's featured and most comprehensive measure of U.S. economic activity. GDP by state is derived as the sum of the GDP originating in all the industries in a state.

The statistics of real GDP by state are prepared in chained (1997 or 2012) dollars. Real GDP by state is an inflation–adjusted measure of each state's gross product that is based on national prices for the goods and services produced within that state. The statistics of real GDP by state and of quantity indexes with a reference year of 2012 were derived by applying national chain–type price indexes to the current–dollar values of GDP by state for the 64 detailed NAICS–based industries for 1997 forward.

The chain–type index formula that is used in the national accounts is then used to calculate the values of total real GDP by state and of real GDP by state at more aggregated industry levels. Real GDP by state may reflect a substantial volume of output that is sold to other states and countries. To the extent that a state's output is produced and sold in national markets at relatively uniform prices (or sold locally at national prices), real GDP by state captures the differences across states that reflect the relative differences in the mix of goods and services that the states produce. However, real GDP by state does not capture geographic differences in the prices of goods and services that are produced and sold locally.

Relation of GDP by state to U.S. Gross Domestic Product (GDP). An industry's GDP by state, or its value added, in practice, is calculated as the sum of incomes earned by labor and capital and the costs incurred in the production of goods and services. That is, it includes the wages and salaries that workers earn, the income earned by individual or joint entrepreneurs as well as by corporations, and business taxes such as sales, property, and federal excise taxes—that count as a business expense.

GDP is calculated as the sum of what consumers, businesses, and government spend on final goods and services, plus investment and net foreign trade. In theory, incomes earned should equal what is spent, but due to different data sources, income earned, usually referred to as gross domestic income (GDI), does not always equal what is spent (GDP). The difference is referred to as the "statistical discrepancy."

Starting with the 2004 comprehensive revision, BEA's annual industry accounts and its GDP–by–state accounts allocate the statistical discrepancy across all private–sector industries. Therefore, the GDP–by–state statistics are now conceptually more similar to the GDP statistics in the national accounts than they had been in the past.

U.S. real GDP by state for the advance year, 2020, may differ from the Annual Industry Accounts' GDP by industry and, hence NIPA (national income and product accounts) GDP, because of different sources and vintages of data used to estimate GDP by state and NIPA GDP. For the revised years of 1997–2019, U.S. GDP by state is nearly identical to GDP by industry except for small differences resulting from GDP by state's exclusion of overseas Federal military and civilian activity (because it cannot be attributed to a particular state). The statistics of GDP by industry are from the 2020 annual update of the NIPAs, released in July 2020. However, because of revisions since July 2020, GDP in the NIPAs may differ from U.S. GDP by state.

BEA's national, international, regional, and industry statistics; the Survey of Current Business; and BEA news releases are available without charge on BEA's Web site at www.bea.gov. By visiting the site, you can also subscribe to receive free e–mail summaries of BEA releases and announcements.

Further notes

The value of an industry's GDP is equal to the market value of its gross output (which consists of sales or receipts and other operating income, taxes on production and imports, and inventory change) minus the value of its intermediate inputs (which consist of energy, raw materials, semifinished goods, and services that are purchased from domestic industries or foreign sources). In concept, this definition is equal to the sum of labor and property-type income earned in that industry in the production of GDP, plus commodity taxes. Property-type income is the sum of corporate profits, proprietors' income, rental income of persons, net interest, capital consumption allowances, business transfer payments, and the current surplus of government enterprises less subsidies.

In practice, GDP by state, like GDP by industry, is measured using the incomes data rather than data on gross output and intermediate inputs, which are not available on a sufficiently detailed and timely basis.

Therefore, the *value* of *GDP by state* is defined as the sum of labor and property-type incomes originating in each of 63 industries in that state, plus commodity taxes, and plus the allocated value of the statistical discrepancy between national GDP and national gross national income.

Chained-dollar estimates. The effect of the "chained-dollar" deflation procedure that BEA uses is to combine the real, inflation-adjusted, quantity changes in output between two adjacent time periods for individual products and industries using, as weights for the individual products, their average prices in those two periods. The estimates for successive time periods are then "chained" each to the previous one to provide a continuous index of real quantities that is not distorted by using prices from a single base year.

GDP by state is now calculated on a North American Industry Classification System (NAICS) basis back through 1997. Data for earlier years, beginning with 1977, were calculated on the Standard Industrial Classification (SIC) basis. According to BEA (in a "Cautionary note" on the Web site, dated June 7, 2007), "There is a discontinuity in the GDP by state time series at 1997, where the data change from SIC industry definitions to NAICS industry definitions. This discontinuity results from many sources, including differences in source data and different estimation methodologies. In addition, the NAICS-based GDP by state estimates are consistent with U.S. gross domestic product (GDP) while the SIC-based GDP by state estimates are consistent with U.S. gross domestic income (GDI). This data discontinuity may affect both the levels and the growth rates of the GDP by state estimates. Users of the GDP by state estimates are strongly cautioned against appending the two data series in an attempt to construct a single time series of GDP by state estimates for 1963 to 2006."

Patterns of Economic Change nevertheless provides SIC-based data for 1980 to 1997 for those who require information about economic growth before 1997 by state.

Gross Domestic Product by Region and State

(Millions of chained 1997 or 2012 dollars; index numbers)

Year	United States	New England	Mideast	Great Lakes	Plains	Southeast	Southwest	Rocky Mountain	Far West	Alabama	Alaska	Arizona	Arkansas
VALUE													
Chained 1997 Dollars													
1980	4,908,867	1,012,776	854,483	344,295	976,312	481,736	143,449	824,862	64,582	22,440	55,561	34,773	599,507
1981	5,042,118	1,028,056	861,593	355,679	1,008,512	508,762	148,620	851,427	65,771	25,866	57,106	36,018	619,243
1982	4,977,350	1,020,670	822,244	346,904	997,979	510,378	147,222	849,741	64,134	26,543	55,763	35,055	619,420
1983	5,120,074	1,055,252	849,428	349,664	1,037,194	509,902	148,939	874,727	67,305	25,822	58,950	36,179	641,585
1984	5,485,271	1,120,588	916,372	376,210	1,116,483	541,315	156,456	936,298	70,481	26,854	65,288	39,015	693,095
1985	5,704,145	1,158,560	946,668	386,662	1,166,972	564,578	160,383	979,706	73,801	29,834	69,447	39,403	728,599
1986	5,826,832	1,192,646	962,229	388,432	1,203,514	555,866	158,252	1,010,168	74,558	24,957	73,546	40,177	756,166
1987	6,076,695	1,253,511	988,285	401,771	1,265,154	556,371	160,106	1,071,727	78,659	29,525	76,600	41,566	802,816
1988	6,398,624	1,327,678	1,035,997	416,799	1,330,988	586,844	166,009	1,131,172	82,508	27,843	80,258	43,158	848,273
1989	6,540,047	1,340,174	1,057,952	427,444	1,361,603	598,852	169,205	1,177,017	82,408	28,986	80,971	44,012	880,307
1990	6,638,210	1,351,182	1,062,296	433,341	1,382,836	614,113	174,758	1,218,168	83,766	28,772	81,606	44,496	906,103
1991	6,627,809	1,330,568	1,057,697	438,079	1,397,392	625,303	179,276	1,207,739	86,116	25,821	81,946	46,498	893,112
1992	6,828,525	1,353,418	1,106,985	457,254	1,449,519	654,652	189,490	1,218,219	89,814	26,151	90,282	49,260	891,631
1993	6,967,716	1,366,936	1,133,832	459,352	1,498,996	681,390	201,103	1,225,572	91,168	26,048	94,916	50,756	888,070
1994	7,288,327	1,395,466	1,207,063	490,357	1,587,062	723,716	214,348	1,255,607	94,803	26,188	104,104	53,641	904,778
1995	7,539,096	1,426,803	1,235,447	505,631	1,651,779	759,372	226,604	1,300,697	98,024	27,609	112,020	55,836	940,599
1996	7,871,721	1,475,796	1,283,159	532,340	1,720,686	805,125	239,357	1,363,152	101,379	27,271	120,869	58,346	978,300
1997	8,284,432	1,535,947	1,345,334	558,791	1,802,254	866,050	253,743	1,443,206	104,805	27,581	129,279	60,333	1,037,091
Chained 2012 Dollars													
1997[1]	11,521,938	644,832	2,244,937	1,889,326	776,430	2,566,664	1,222,189	355,741	1,953,432	143,646	42,262	168,551	82,756
1998[1]	12,038,283	669,175	2,301,601	1,954,397	800,283	2,685,346	1,294,583	381,617	2,071,557	148,596	41,157	183,138	84,795
1999[1]	12,610,491	698,287	2,399,925	2,027,608	822,123	2,807,531	1,353,112	405,658	2,214,603	154,094	40,722	198,096	89,317
2000[1]	13,130,987	749,473	2,490,916	2,086,694	859,065	2,876,077	1,401,169	432,330	2,361,298	156,560	39,517	207,793	90,206
2001[1]	13,262,079	759,204	2,541,976	2,064,780	858,221	2,915,721	1,434,240	437,611	2,348,012	156,404	40,974	212,656	89,923
2002[1]	13,493,064	766,491	2,558,419	2,104,604	878,108	2,982,397	1,465,543	442,371	2,404,166	160,870	42,881	219,311	92,885
2003[1]	13,879,129	784,127	2,595,975	2,146,040	908,438	3,081,035	1,491,585	449,350	2,505,869	164,992	42,151	233,342	96,545
2004[1]	14,406,382	815,683	2,668,732	2,192,890	939,327	3,219,340	1,565,928	461,763	2,614,450	175,508	43,735	243,246	101,210
2005[1]	14,912,509	830,367	2,738,678	2,228,460	963,958	3,366,854	1,622,517	485,663	2,744,663	181,386	45,052	263,061	104,653
2006[1]	15,338,257	850,020	2,789,621	2,246,957	978,289	3,456,208	1,725,858	508,303	2,860,413	184,796	48,517	277,288	106,940
2007[1]	15,626,029	867,516	2,817,983	2,262,762	998,715	3,462,413	1,800,882	528,343	2,919,047	185,869	51,114	284,907	106,155
2008[1]	15,604,687	869,028	2,813,639	2,216,224	1,011,713	3,437,294	1,800,516	533,609	2,928,345	185,298	50,884	277,477	105,791
2009[1]	15,208,834	850,757	2,821,503	2,106,780	988,570	3,318,424	1,773,521	520,934	2,817,960	178,021	55,838	255,081	102,528
2010[1]	15,598,753	871,810	2,905,744	2,176,944	1,014,808	3,382,596	1,805,416	526,382	2,862,337	182,263	54,151	257,485	105,923
2011[1]	15,840,664	876,671	2,919,943	2,224,078	1,034,203	3,403,212	1,859,279	534,414	2,909,705	185,055	54,646	263,211	108,295
2012[1]	16,197,007	889,223	2,993,045	2,252,276	1,057,845	3,431,042	1,940,753	540,442	2,979,150	186,299	57,670	268,289	108,745
2013[1]	16,495,369	887,832	3,000,690	2,279,835	1,070,846	3,468,312	2,006,364	555,210	3,065,072	188,165	54,750	270,149	111,779
2014[1]	16,899,831	894,609	3,055,435	2,329,328	1,096,375	3,522,368	2,063,009	573,946	3,174,531	186,335	53,209	273,407	112,706
2015[1]	17,386,700	918,248	3,107,723	2,354,468	1,109,938	3,610,454	2,154,742	596,824	3,326,787	188,716	53,585	279,435	113,177
2016[1]	17,659,187	928,758	3,149,061	2,377,716	1,114,566	3,671,900	2,162,788	610,517	3,429,188	189,614	52,608	288,682	113,788
2017[1]	18,050,693	940,825	3,195,458	2,407,637	1,123,768	3,745,843	2,203,941	626,188	3,548,088	193,053	52,492	297,210	114,851
2018[1]	18,566,442	959,518	3,259,430	2,460,125	1,146,072	3,842,560	2,272,851	647,260	3,678,280	196,876	52,311	309,067	115,933
2019[1]	19,091,662	990,778	3,336,481	2,505,872	1,181,310	3,981,052	2,386,061	687,942	3,864,650	200,829	53,255	323,598	117,447
2020[1]	18,426,076	950,674	3,178,653	2,401,025	1,144,542	3,854,787	2,307,730	677,826	3,760,103	195,475	50,646	320,658	114,370

Gross Domestic Product by Region and State—*Continued*

(Millions of chained 1997 or 2012 dollars; index numbers)

Year	United States	New England	Mideast	Great Lakes	Plains	Southeast	Southwest	Rocky Mountain	Far West	Alabama	Alaska	Arizona	Arkansas
QUANTITY INDEX													
1997=100													
1980....................	59.3	56.6	65.9	63.5	61.6	54.2	55.6	56.5	57.2	61.6	81.4	43.0	57.6
1981....................	60.9	58.0	66.9	64.0	63.7	56.0	58.7	58.6	59.0	62.8	93.8	44.2	59.7
1982....................	60.1	58.6	66.5	61.1	62.1	55.4	58.9	58.0	58.9	61.2	96.2	43.1	58.1
1983....................	61.8	61.7	68.7	63.1	62.6	57.6	58.9	58.7	60.6	64.2	93.6	45.6	60.0
1984....................	66.2	67.3	73.0	68.1	67.3	61.9	62.5	61.7	64.9	67.3	97.4	50.5	64.7
1985....................	68.9	71.2	75.4	70.4	69.2	64.8	65.2	63.2	67.9	70.4	108.2	53.7	65.3
1986....................	70.3	74.7	77.6	71.5	69.5	66.8	64.2	62.4	70.0	71.1	90.5	56.9	66.6
1987....................	73.4	80.0	81.6	73.5	71.9	70.2	64.2	63.1	74.3	75.1	107.0	59.3	68.9
1988....................	77.2	85.0	86.4	77.0	74.6	73.9	67.8	65.4	78.4	78.7	101.0	62.1	71.5
1989....................	78.9	85.9	87.3	78.6	76.5	75.6	69.1	66.7	81.6	78.6	105.1	62.6	72.9
1990....................	80.1	84.5	88.0	79.0	77.6	76.7	70.9	68.9	84.4	79.9	104.3	63.1	73.8
1991....................	80.0	82.3	86.6	78.6	78.4	77.5	72.2	70.7	83.7	82.2	93.6	63.4	77.1
1992....................	82.4	83.7	88.1	82.3	81.8	80.4	75.6	74.7	84.4	85.7	94.8	69.8	81.6
1993....................	84.1	83.8	89.0	84.3	82.2	83.2	78.7	79.3	84.9	87.0	94.4	73.4	84.1
1994....................	88.0	86.8	90.9	89.7	87.8	88.1	83.6	84.5	87.0	90.5	94.9	80.5	88.9
1995....................	91.0	90.5	92.9	91.8	90.5	91.7	87.7	89.3	90.1	93.5	100.1	86.6	92.5
1996....................	95.0	94.4	96.1	95.4	95.3	95.5	93.0	94.3	94.5	96.7	98.9	93.5	96.7
1997....................	100.0	100.0	100.0	100.0	100.0	100.0	100.0	100.0	100.0	100.0	100.0	100.0	100.0
2012 = 100													
1997[1]....................	71.1	72.5	75.0	83.9	73.4	74.8	63.0	65.8	65.6	77.1	73.3	62.8	76.1
1998[1]....................	74.3	75.3	76.9	86.8	75.7	78.3	66.7	70.6	69.5	79.8	71.4	68.3	78.0
1999[1]....................	77.9	78.5	80.2	90.0	77.7	81.8	69.7	75.1	74.3	82.7	70.6	73.8	82.1
2000[1]....................	81.1	84.3	83.2	92.6	81.2	83.8	72.2	80.0	79.3	84.0	68.5	77.5	83.0
2001[1]....................	81.9	85.4	84.9	91.7	81.1	85.0	73.9	81.0	78.8	84.0	71.0	79.3	82.7
2002[1]....................	83.3	86.2	85.5	93.4	83.0	86.9	75.5	81.9	80.7	86.4	74.4	81.7	85.4
2003[1]....................	85.7	88.2	86.7	95.3	85.9	89.8	76.9	83.1	84.1	88.6	73.1	87.0	88.8
2004[1]....................	88.9	91.7	89.2	97.4	88.8	93.8	80.7	85.4	87.8	94.2	75.8	90.7	93.1
2005[1]....................	92.1	93.4	91.5	98.9	91.1	98.1	83.6	89.9	92.1	97.4	78.1	98.1	96.2
2006[1]....................	94.7	95.6	93.2	99.8	92.5	100.7	88.9	94.1	96.0	99.2	84.1	103.4	98.3
2007[1]....................	96.5	97.6	94.2	100.5	94.4	100.9	92.8	97.8	98.0	99.8	88.6	106.2	97.6
2008[1]....................	96.3	97.7	94.0	98.4	95.6	100.2	92.8	98.7	98.3	99.5	88.2	103.4	97.3
2009[1]....................	93.9	95.7	94.3	93.5	93.5	96.7	91.4	96.4	94.6	95.6	96.8	95.1	94.3
2010[1]....................	96.3	98.0	97.1	96.7	95.9	98.6	93.0	97.4	96.1	97.8	93.9	96.0	97.4
2011[1]....................	97.8	98.6	97.6	98.7	97.8	99.2	95.8	98.9	97.7	99.3	94.8	98.1	99.6
2012[1]....................	100.0	100.0	100.0	100.0	100.0	100.0	100.0	100.0	100.0	100.0	100.0	100.0	100.0
2013[1]....................	101.8	99.8	100.3	101.2	101.2	101.1	103.4	102.7	102.9	101.0	94.9	100.7	102.8
2014[1]....................	104.3	100.6	102.1	103.4	103.6	102.7	106.3	106.2	106.6	100.0	92.3	101.9	103.6
2015[1]....................	107.3	103.3	103.8	104.5	104.9	105.2	111.0	110.4	111.7	101.3	92.9	104.2	104.1
2016[1]....................	109.0	104.4	105.2	105.6	105.4	107.0	111.4	113.0	115.1	101.8	91.2	107.6	104.6
2017[1]....................	111.4	105.8	106.8	106.9	106.2	109.2	113.6	115.9	119.1	103.6	91.0	110.8	105.6
2018[1]....................	114.6	107.9	108.9	109.2	108.3	112.0	117.1	119.8	123.5	105.7	90.7	115.2	106.6
2019[1]....................	117.9	111.4	111.5	111.2	111.3	116.1	123.0	127.3	129.8	107.7	92.3	120.7	109.0
2020[1]....................	113.8	106.9	106.2	106.6	107.8	112.4	119.0	125.4	126.2	104.8	87.7	119.6	106.2

1 = NAICS basis, not continuous with previous years, which are based on the SIC.

Gross Domestic Product by Region and State—*Continued*

(Millions of chained 1997 or 2012 dollars; index numbers)

Year	California	Colorado	Connecticut	Delaware	District of Columbia	Florida	Georgia	Hawaii	Idaho	Illinois	Indiana	Iowa	Kansas	Kentucky
VALUE														
Chained 1997 Dollars														
1980............................	70,410	78,644	16,126	45,655	186,914	102,952	26,760	16,415	258,832	102,247	56,387	49,642	63,053	98,826
1981............................	73,467	80,480	16,456	44,856	195,993	107,314	26,654	16,493	262,248	103,494	58,097	51,081	64,756	101,477
1982............................	74,962	82,538	16,640	43,539	200,772	108,942	26,867	15,824	253,052	97,816	54,248	50,638	62,456	97,626
1983............................	75,947	86,663	17,959	43,965	212,495	116,030	27,932	16,597	255,786	100,129	52,043	50,956	62,542	96,515
1984............................	80,299	94,619	19,290	44,880	230,407	127,323	28,979	16,892	274,171	109,229	54,893	53,241	67,270	102,251
1985............................	82,357	99,671	20,492	45,563	242,870	136,869	29,973	17,274	282,224	111,327	56,009	55,267	69,294	104,078
1986............................	81,845	104,258	21,068	45,848	253,651	144,853	30,989	16,937	288,439	113,098	55,262	55,466	68,323	103,870
1987............................	83,322	112,210	22,563	47,149	270,018	152,163	32,376	17,350	297,698	117,397	56,536	57,350	70,822	104,284
1988............................	85,880	119,047	23,599	49,206	286,786	158,946	34,587	18,284	314,485	123,242	59,479	58,843	75,562	108,142
1989............................	86,898	120,607	25,312	50,146	297,215	162,167	36,643	19,453	320,572	127,701	61,636	59,286	77,233	108,117
1990............................	88,933	121,176	25,887	51,175	304,324	165,062	39,176	20,161	324,012	128,197	63,460	60,672	78,206	110,272
1991............................	90,780	118,216	26,930	50,241	305,979	167,209	39,756	20,593	323,641	128,215	63,818	61,275	78,908	110,055
1992............................	97,058	119,832	27,178	50,598	317,416	176,731	40,834	22,022	336,296	136,439	66,862	63,062	83,288	102,935
1993............................	103,457	118,315	26,946	51,310	329,410	184,789	40,152	23,940	343,470	140,645	66,913	63,516	85,810	105,296
1994............................	110,529	121,002	28,750	51,290	345,550	198,125	40,062	25,845	364,916	149,157	72,503	66,732	91,063	114,156
1995............................	116,821	128,538	29,941	49,889	358,419	209,292	39,552	27,996	374,858	153,785	74,568	67,531	94,259	120,333
1996............................	123,144	131,913	30,503	49,232	376,851	223,307	39,132	28,927	389,704	160,020	78,834	70,361	97,781	121,489
1997............................	133,204	140,280	31,450	49,702	393,075	235,200	39,064	30,312	408,048	167,366	83,113	74,147	103,621	126,003
Chained 2012 Dollars														
1997[1]............................	1,378,654	184,193	190,791	45,231	79,626	560,888	328,995	55,679	37,015	577,804	232,247	113,365	104,770	146,959
1998[1]............................	1,470,393	201,076	196,248	49,743	81,190	590,135	352,713	54,360	38,791	595,833	246,380	114,230	108,508	151,551
1999[1]............................	1,582,377	216,300	202,230	53,862	84,658	616,625	377,608	55,182	42,496	617,315	254,489	116,663	111,201	156,261
2000[1]............................	1,709,939	232,752	216,370	56,109	85,265	642,693	393,195	56,417	47,325	641,749	263,693	122,159	113,972	152,118
2001[1]............................	1,702,776	236,383	220,287	58,882	88,506	658,640	396,875	56,019	46,062	644,181	258,661	120,669	113,853	151,921
2002[1]............................	1,743,651	236,786	219,959	56,814	91,195	685,304	400,092	57,912	47,208	647,868	265,106	124,097	115,552	155,676
2003[1]............................	1,825,424	238,540	222,240	57,957	93,025	715,436	410,588	60,838	48,536	655,835	275,194	129,316	117,478	159,180
2004[1]............................	1,902,319	240,798	237,133	60,682	97,798	757,054	429,314	64,928	51,241	673,262	284,656	139,749	117,883	163,436
2005[1]............................	1,990,141	250,840	242,485	59,974	99,955	806,339	445,533	68,566	55,387	685,897	285,492	143,876	122,258	168,805
2006[1]............................	2,072,177	256,124	251,581	61,497	100,242	834,346	450,584	70,403	57,590	704,495	291,269	145,887	128,899	173,337
2007[1]............................	2,103,618	264,577	261,129	61,235	102,957	835,867	453,061	71,192	58,703	712,710	299,423	152,251	135,667	171,869
2008[1]............................	2,111,138	267,713	259,722	58,656	106,747	803,218	443,416	71,689	59,704	699,430	298,264	149,132	138,658	172,151
2009[1]............................	2,026,487	262,380	248,041	60,404	106,351	758,264	426,264	69,095	57,088	682,966	277,474	145,618	133,277	165,015
2010[1]............................	2,058,138	264,791	247,461	60,016	109,964	766,199	433,027	71,007	57,907	694,961	295,133	149,536	134,945	172,045
2011[1]............................	2,091,586	268,681	242,020	62,017	112,008	763,746	439,891	72,080	57,797	707,060	296,472	151,248	138,563	174,136
2012[1]............................	2,144,497	273,520	243,801	61,976	112,737	769,309	444,132	73,583	57,764	720,702	297,553	157,251	140,478	176,302
2013[1]............................	2,220,868	282,534	241,081	59,157	112,678	784,090	450,772	74,278	59,831	724,616	303,920	156,637	140,506	179,390
2014[1]............................	2,309,928	295,010	237,558	63,693	114,962	804,322	464,061	74,504	61,367	734,218	313,057	164,721	143,154	179,753
2015[1]............................	2,426,143	307,912	241,916	65,635	117,030	835,928	479,242	77,023	63,208	741,725	309,877	168,252	144,932	180,679
2016[1]............................	2,498,840	315,425	241,447	63,718	119,365	864,029	495,226	78,757	65,565	743,817	315,130	168,909	148,249	181,614
2017[1]............................	2,587,572	325,129	239,884	63,651	121,448	885,906	509,422	79,998	67,161	748,162	320,084	168,332	149,421	183,566
2018[1]............................	2,677,939	336,365	242,171	63,855	124,007	916,975	522,424	80,798	69,892	764,212	326,148	170,749	152,262	186,148
2019[1]............................	2,800,505	356,280	251,330	64,319	123,929	963,256	547,423	82,471	74,937	773,136	337,636	173,515	160,059	190,812
2020[1]............................	2,722,839	351,068	241,053	61,834	122,114	935,674	533,567	75,863	74,081	742,278	327,337	169,530	155,308	183,804

Gross Domestic Product by Region and State—*Continued*

(Millions of chained 1997 or 2012 dollars; index numbers)

Year	California	Colorado	Connecticut	Delaware	District of Columbia	Florida	Georgia	Hawaii	Idaho	Illinois	Indiana	Iowa	Kansas	Kentucky
QUANTITY INDEX														
1997=100														
1980..................	57.8	52.9	56.1	51.3	91.9	47.6	43.8	68.5	54.2	63.4	61.1	67.8	67.0	60.8
1981..................	59.7	55.2	57.4	52.3	90.3	49.9	45.6	68.2	54.4	64.3	61.8	69.9	68.9	62.5
1982..................	59.7	56.3	58.8	52.9	87.6	51.1	46.3	68.8	52.2	62.0	58.4	65.3	68.3	60.3
1983..................	61.9	57.0	61.8	57.1	88.5	54.1	49.3	71.5	54.8	62.7	59.8	62.6	68.7	60.4
1984..................	66.8	60.3	67.5	61.3	90.3	58.6	54.1	74.2	55.7	67.2	65.3	66.0	71.8	64.9
1985..................	70.3	61.8	71.1	65.2	91.7	61.8	58.2	76.7	57.0	69.2	66.5	67.4	74.5	66.9
1986..................	72.9	61.4	74.3	67.0	92.2	64.5	61.6	79.3	55.9	70.7	67.6	66.5	74.8	65.9
1987..................	77.4	62.6	80.0	71.7	94.9	68.7	64.7	82.9	57.2	73.0	70.1	68.0	77.3	68.3
1988..................	81.8	64.5	84.9	75.0	99.0	73.0	67.6	88.5	60.3	77.1	73.6	71.6	79.4	72.9
1989..................	84.9	65.2	86.0	80.5	100.9	75.6	68.9	93.8	64.2	78.6	76.3	74.2	80.0	74.5
1990..................	87.4	66.8	86.4	82.3	103.0	77.4	70.2	100.3	66.5	79.4	76.6	76.4	81.8	75.5
1991..................	86.1	68.2	84.3	85.6	101.1	77.8	71.1	101.8	67.9	79.3	76.6	76.8	82.6	76.2
1992..................	86.0	72.9	85.4	86.4	101.8	80.8	75.1	104.5	72.7	82.4	81.5	80.4	85.1	80.4
1993..................	85.6	77.7	84.3	85.7	103.2	83.8	78.6	102.8	79.0	84.2	84.0	80.5	85.7	82.8
1994..................	87.2	83.0	86.3	91.4	103.2	87.9	84.2	102.6	85.3	89.4	89.1	87.2	90.0	87.9
1995..................	90.7	87.7	91.6	95.2	100.4	91.2	89.0	101.2	92.4	91.9	91.9	89.7	91.1	91.0
1996..................	94.3	92.4	94.0	97.0	99.1	95.9	94.9	100.2	95.4	95.5	95.6	94.9	94.9	94.4
1997..................	100.0	100.0	100.0	100.0	100.0	100.0	100.0	100.0	100.0	100.0	100.0	100.0	100.0	100.0
2012 = 100														
1997[1]...............	64.3	67.3	78.3	73.0	70.6	72.9	74.1	75.7	64.1	80.2	78.1	72.1	74.6	83.4
1998[1]...............	68.6	73.5	80.5	80.3	72.0	76.7	79.4	73.9	67.2	82.7	82.8	72.6	77.2	86.0
1999[1]...............	73.8	79.1	82.9	86.9	75.1	80.2	85.0	75.0	73.6	85.7	85.5	74.2	79.2	88.6
2000[1]...............	79.7	85.1	88.7	90.5	75.6	83.5	88.5	76.7	81.9	89.0	88.6	77.7	81.1	86.3
2001[1]...............	79.4	86.4	90.4	95.0	78.5	85.6	89.4	76.1	79.7	89.4	86.9	76.7	81.0	86.2
2002[1]...............	81.3	86.6	90.2	91.7	80.9	89.1	90.1	78.7	81.7	89.9	89.1	78.9	82.3	88.3
2003[1]...............	85.1	87.2	91.2	93.5	82.5	93.0	92.4	82.7	84.0	91.0	92.5	82.2	83.6	90.3
2004[1]...............	88.7	88.0	97.3	97.9	86.7	98.4	96.7	88.2	88.7	93.4	95.7	88.9	83.9	92.7
2005[1]...............	92.8	91.7	99.5	96.8	88.7	104.8	100.3	93.2	95.9	95.2	95.9	91.5	87.0	95.7
2006[1]...............	96.6	93.6	103.2	99.2	88.9	108.5	101.5	95.7	99.7	97.8	97.9	92.8	91.8	98.3
2007[1]...............	98.1	96.7	107.1	98.8	91.3	108.7	102.0	96.8	101.6	98.9	100.6	96.8	96.6	97.5
2008[1]...............	98.4	97.9	106.5	94.6	94.7	104.4	99.8	97.4	103.4	97.0	100.2	94.8	98.7	97.6
2009[1]...............	94.5	95.9	101.7	97.5	94.3	98.6	96.0	93.9	98.8	94.8	93.3	92.6	94.9	93.6
2010[1]...............	96.0	96.8	101.5	96.8	97.5	99.6	97.5	96.5	100.2	96.4	99.2	95.1	96.1	97.6
2011[1]...............	97.5	98.2	99.3	100.1	99.4	99.3	99.0	98.0	100.1	98.1	99.6	96.2	98.6	98.8
2012[1]...............	100.0	100.0	100.0	100.0	100.0	100.0	100.0	100.0	100.0	100.0	100.0	100.0	100.0	100.0
2013[1]...............	103.6	103.3	98.9	95.5	99.9	101.9	101.5	100.9	103.6	100.5	102.1	99.6	100.0	101.8
2014[1]...............	107.7	107.9	97.4	102.8	102.0	104.6	104.5	101.3	106.2	101.9	105.2	104.8	101.9	102.0
2015[1]...............	113.1	112.6	99.2	105.9	103.8	108.7	107.9	104.7	109.4	102.9	104.1	107.0	103.2	102.5
2016[1]...............	116.5	115.3	99.0	102.8	105.9	112.3	111.5	107.0	113.5	103.2	105.9	107.4	105.5	103.0
2017[1]...............	120.7	118.9	98.4	102.7	107.7	115.2	114.7	108.7	116.3	103.8	107.6	107.0	106.4	104.1
2018[1]...............	124.9	123.0	99.3	103.0	110.0	119.2	117.6	109.8	121.0	106.0	109.6	108.6	108.4	105.6
2019[1]...............	130.6	130.2	103.0	104.0	110.1	125.3	123.4	111.9	129.7	107.2	113.4	109.9	113.7	108.2
2020[1]...............	127.0	128.3	98.7	99.9	108.4	121.7	120.3	103.0	128.2	103.0	109.9	107.4	110.3	104.2

1 = NAICS basis, not continuous with previous years, which are based on the SIC.

Gross Domestic Product by Region and State—*Continued*

(Millions of chained 1997 or 2012 dollars; index numbers)

Year	Louisiana	Maine	Maryland	Massachusetts	Michigan	Minnesota	Mississippi	Missouri	Montana	Nebraska	Nevada	New Hampshire	New Jersey
VALUE													
Chained 1997 Dollars													
1980	19,252	93,518	130,465	190,628	87,377	36,032	95,522	15,018	31,159	22,324	16,236	165,044	24,597
1981	19,384	95,346	133,647	190,543	89,820	37,270	96,740	15,606	32,929	23,256	16,905	169,389	24,949
1982	19,610	94,470	134,243	178,645	88,444	36,090	95,532	14,916	32,135	22,994	17,246	169,773	24,540
1983	20,471	99,052	142,103	190,879	91,405	36,857	98,611	14,932	31,360	23,738	18,344	181,669	24,951
1984	21,917	105,743	155,335	206,385	100,958	39,379	107,071	15,023	33,716	24,833	20,558	196,143	26,158
1985	22,858	111,803	164,593	215,019	104,958	40,474	108,667	14,635	34,881	25,888	22,435	206,429	27,135
1986	23,880	117,037	172,628	218,860	105,789	40,569	111,652	14,521	34,264	27,351	23,933	216,138	26,881
1987	25,426	123,260	183,712	221,362	110,916	43,229	116,060	14,624	34,351	29,144	26,669	230,997	26,932
1988	27,344	131,777	194,619	230,563	115,398	44,252	121,171	14,497	36,304	31,701	28,319	248,031	27,464
1989	27,882	134,612	195,609	234,224	118,868	44,669	123,688	15,089	37,389	34,125	28,278	251,515	28,056
1990	27,644	136,165	189,730	229,534	120,078	44,853	122,285	15,355	39,011	36,891	27,259	253,360	28,714
1991	26,836	133,662	183,996	225,576	120,067	45,841	124,167	15,739	40,250	37,713	27,411	252,718	31,980
1992	27,176	134,748	186,430	235,241	126,777	48,317	127,857	16,566	42,242	40,564	28,486	256,965	33,855
1993	27,337	137,003	187,751	242,175	127,068	50,440	128,278	17,285	42,385	43,994	28,832	259,805	37,463
1994	28,058	142,086	196,432	263,500	134,715	53,852	137,379	17,932	45,807	48,267	30,113	265,388	42,030
1995	28,769	144,424	203,189	264,125	138,724	56,528	144,371	18,036	46,556	51,081	32,379	271,764	42,733
1996	29,627	147,889	214,299	273,563	147,643	58,230	150,268	18,342	49,276	55,725	34,858	283,608	44,605
1997	30,775	154,783	226,880	286,408	156,650	59,875	158,308	18,932	50,308	59,467	36,935	292,671	48,683
Chained 2012 Dollars													
1997[1]	201,830	43,035	221,184	302,806	397,339	211,942	83,197	228,293	29,169	70,722	90,368	48,425	426,187
1998[1]	208,683	44,233	231,831	314,880	406,293	222,971	85,333	232,074	30,466	72,310	94,947	51,603	433,779
1999[1]	212,955	46,393	240,910	331,705	429,356	230,684	87,647	238,361	30,598	73,884	101,277	53,058	448,808
2000[1]	206,685	48,524	250,982	359,521	438,277	245,982	88,143	246,049	31,375	76,623	105,344	56,720	473,035
2001[1]	209,046	49,419	260,776	362,434	423,624	246,058	87,200	244,407	31,651	78,258	106,657	57,433	476,508
2002[1]	213,146	50,633	270,885	364,797	435,250	252,414	88,125	246,813	32,527	79,665	110,020	59,041	487,050
2003[1]	221,240	51,729	277,950	373,814	443,795	263,869	91,715	251,788	33,843	84,120	115,571	61,610	499,695
2004[1]	231,602	53,530	292,115	383,487	444,198	274,713	93,651	257,259	35,375	86,082	128,885	63,499	507,585
2005[1]	245,523	53,613	305,993	390,792	450,746	282,094	95,228	261,530	37,077	88,894	139,695	64,356	513,499
2006[1]	243,332	54,270	311,680	397,743	443,308	281,970	97,748	263,233	38,431	91,387	145,209	65,945	524,056
2007[1]	234,620	54,001	312,093	407,974	441,149	283,212	100,204	264,382	40,379	93,388	144,405	65,698	526,814
2008[1]	235,276	53,921	315,859	412,601	416,702	285,792	104,386	270,608	40,162	93,569	138,863	65,017	533,054
2009[1]	238,666	53,064	314,863	408,062	380,091	275,453	99,463	265,310	39,337	94,050	127,242	64,450	511,150
2010[1]	247,351	53,776	327,235	424,581	400,941	284,864	99,984	269,735	40,544	97,857	128,827	66,442	516,589
2011[1]	234,063	53,088	334,307	434,724	411,466	290,630	98,728	266,726	41,473	102,333	129,734	66,840	510,929
2012[1]	233,623	52,874	334,822	444,330	418,857	294,297	99,615	268,762	42,006	102,269	128,043	67,689	519,746
2013[1]	226,616	52,505	334,939	444,866	424,320	300,633	99,622	271,902	42,434	105,038	128,273	68,800	523,334
2014[1]	231,841	53,418	338,707	453,479	430,501	308,197	99,430	272,774	43,092	107,132	129,660	69,474	525,023
2015[1]	231,326	53,606	344,454	469,770	440,310	311,336	99,780	275,819	44,724	109,673	135,100	71,175	533,615
2016[1]	228,526	54,707	355,075	477,857	448,713	317,618	100,120	273,206	44,213	110,226	138,284	72,544	537,149
2017[1]	228,678	55,617	362,043	488,339	456,004	324,264	100,590	275,783	44,396	110,526	141,709	73,981	543,993
2018[1]	231,161	56,689	367,915	501,337	468,387	331,377	101,630	282,208	44,801	112,170	146,225	75,615	554,672
2019[1]	239,967	58,793	374,039	519,962	471,648	341,041	102,656	287,659	47,916	117,395	153,729	77,240	556,731
2020[1]	226,810	56,364	364,169	500,237	446,249	328,473	99,757	277,354	46,486	114,957	146,668	73,604	534,134

Gross Domestic Product by Region and State—*Continued*

(Millions of chained 1997 or 2012 dollars; index numbers)

Year	Louisiana	Maine	Maryland	Massachusetts	Michigan	Minnesota	Mississippi	Missouri	Montana	Nebraska	Nevada	New Hampshire	New Jersey
QUANTITY INDEX													
1997=100													
1980...........................	78.4	62.6	60.4	57.5	66.6	55.8	60.2	60.3	79.3	61.9	37.5	44.0	56.4
1981...........................	80.5	63.0	61.6	58.9	66.5	57.3	62.2	61.1	82.4	65.5	39.1	45.8	57.9
1982...........................	77.5	63.7	61.0	59.2	62.4	56.5	60.3	60.3	78.8	63.9	38.7	46.7	58.0
1983...........................	76.6	66.5	64.0	62.6	66.6	58.4	61.6	62.3	78.9	62.3	39.9	49.7	62.1
1984...........................	81.1	71.2	68.3	68.5	72.1	64.4	65.8	67.6	79.4	67.0	41.8	55.7	67.0
1985...........................	82.6	74.3	72.2	72.5	75.1	67.0	67.6	68.6	77.3	69.3	43.5	60.7	70.5
1986...........................	82.4	77.6	75.6	76.1	76.4	67.5	67.8	70.5	76.7	68.1	46.0	64.8	73.9
1987...........................	82.8	82.6	79.6	81.0	77.3	70.8	72.2	73.3	77.2	68.3	49.0	72.2	78.9
1988...........................	85.8	88.9	85.1	85.8	80.5	73.7	73.9	76.5	76.6	72.2	53.3	76.7	84.7
1989...........................	85.8	90.6	87.0	86.2	81.8	75.9	74.6	78.1	79.7	74.3	57.4	76.6	85.9
1990...........................	87.5	89.8	88.0	83.6	80.1	76.7	74.9	77.2	81.1	77.5	62.0	73.8	86.6
1991...........................	87.3	87.2	86.4	81.1	78.8	76.6	76.6	78.4	83.1	80.0	63.4	74.2	86.3
1992...........................	81.7	88.3	87.1	82.2	82.1	80.9	80.7	80.8	87.5	84.0	68.2	77.1	87.8
1993...........................	83.6	88.8	88.5	82.8	84.6	81.1	84.2	81.0	91.3	84.3	74.0	78.1	88.8
1994...........................	90.6	91.2	91.8	86.6	92.0	86.0	89.9	86.8	94.7	91.1	81.2	81.5	90.7
1995...........................	95.5	93.5	93.3	89.6	92.2	88.6	94.4	91.2	95.3	92.5	85.9	87.7	92.9
1996...........................	96.4	96.3	95.5	94.5	95.5	94.3	97.3	94.9	96.9	97.9	93.7	94.4	96.9
1997...........................	100.0	100.0	100.0	100.0	100.0	100.0	100.0	100.0	100.0	100.0	100.0	100.0	100.0
2012 = 100													
1997[1]...........................	86.4	81.4	66.1	68.1	94.9	72.0	83.5	84.9	69.4	69.2	70.6	71.5	82.0
1998[1]...........................	89.3	83.7	69.2	70.9	97.0	75.8	85.7	86.3	72.5	70.7	74.2	76.2	83.5
1999[1]...........................	91.2	87.7	72.0	74.7	102.5	78.4	88.0	88.7	72.8	72.2	79.1	78.4	86.4
2000[1]...........................	88.5	91.8	75.0	80.9	104.6	83.6	88.5	91.5	74.7	74.9	82.3	83.8	91.0
2001[1]...........................	89.5	93.5	77.9	81.6	101.1	83.6	87.5	90.9	75.3	76.5	83.3	84.8	91.7
2002[1]...........................	91.2	95.8	80.9	82.1	103.9	85.8	88.5	91.8	77.4	77.9	85.9	87.2	93.7
2003[1]...........................	94.7	97.8	83.0	84.1	106.0	89.7	92.1	93.7	80.6	82.3	90.3	91.0	96.1
2004[1]...........................	99.1	101.2	87.2	86.3	106.1	93.3	94.0	95.7	84.2	84.2	100.7	93.8	97.7
2005[1]...........................	105.1	101.4	91.4	88.0	107.6	95.9	95.6	97.3	88.3	86.9	109.1	95.1	98.8
2006[1]...........................	104.2	102.6	93.1	89.5	105.8	95.8	98.1	97.9	91.5	89.4	113.4	97.4	100.8
2007[1]...........................	100.4	102.1	93.2	91.8	105.3	96.2	100.6	98.4	96.1	91.3	112.8	97.1	101.4
2008[1]...........................	100.7	102.0	94.3	92.9	99.5	97.1	104.8	100.7	95.6	91.5	108.5	96.1	102.6
2009[1]...........................	102.2	100.4	94.0	91.8	90.7	93.6	99.8	98.7	93.6	92.0	99.4	95.2	98.3
2010[1]...........................	105.9	101.7	97.7	95.6	95.7	96.8	100.4	100.4	96.5	95.7	100.6	98.2	99.4
2011[1]...........................	100.2	100.4	99.8	97.8	98.2	98.8	99.1	99.2	98.7	100.1	101.3	98.7	98.3
2012[1]...........................	100.0	100.0	100.0	100.0	100.0	100.0	100.0	100.0	100.0	100.0	100.0	100.0	100.0
2013[1]...........................	97.0	99.3	100.0	100.1	101.3	102.2	100.0	101.2	101.0	102.7	100.2	101.6	100.7
2014[1]...........................	99.2	101.0	101.2	102.1	102.8	104.7	99.8	101.5	102.6	104.8	101.3	102.6	101.0
2015[1]...........................	99.0	101.4	102.9	105.7	105.1	105.8	100.2	102.6	106.5	107.2	105.5	105.2	102.7
2016[1]...........................	97.8	103.5	106.0	107.5	107.1	107.9	100.5	101.7	105.3	107.8	108.0	107.2	103.3
2017[1]...........................	97.9	105.2	108.1	109.9	108.9	110.2	101.0	102.6	105.7	108.1	110.7	109.3	104.7
2018[1]...........................	98.9	107.2	109.9	112.8	111.8	112.6	102.0	105.0	106.7	109.7	114.2	111.7	106.7
2019[1]...........................	102.8	111.2	111.8	117.0	112.6	115.1	103.1	107.0	114.0	114.4	120.3	114.2	107.2
2020[1]...........................	97.1	106.6	108.9	112.5	106.6	110.9	100.1	103.2	110.6	112.0	114.8	108.8	102.8

1 = NAICS basis, not continuous with previous years, which are based on the SIC.

Gross Domestic Product by Region and State—*Continued*

(Millions of chained 1997 or 2012 dollars; index numbers)

Year	New Mexico	New York	North Carolina	North Dakota	Ohio	Oklahoma	Oregon	Pennsylvania	Rhode Island	South Carolina	South Dakota	Tennessee
VALUE												
Chained 1997 Dollars												
1980	461,419	110,120	12,243	211,743	61,673	53,343	231,709	18,167	48,649	11,511	80,420	339,794
1981	469,897	113,991	14,085	213,962	65,276	51,928	232,708	18,609	50,326	12,201	82,680	361,250
1982	473,335	111,615	13,545	203,226	67,173	49,176	223,811	18,553	49,457	11,849	80,817	362,556
1983	483,340	117,269	13,282	211,442	63,976	49,722	229,968	19,086	52,632	11,778	85,226	362,005
1984	512,501	127,347	13,588	229,868	66,997	52,794	242,572	20,422	57,695	12,694	91,426	383,084
1985	526,285	135,374	13,668	238,150	68,101	54,080	248,495	21,754	59,771	13,174	94,918	400,230
1986	539,859	140,634	12,743	240,299	64,580	55,144	253,122	22,862	62,607	13,346	97,962	391,309
1987	562,846	147,274	13,074	247,287	63,487	56,988	266,991	23,871	67,198	13,623	104,884	389,772
1988	595,326	155,811	12,023	256,727	66,540	60,568	279,975	25,528	70,664	13,733	109,796	413,114
1989	594,267	160,953	12,733	262,187	66,722	62,292	284,585	26,214	72,984	13,961	110,896	423,660
1990	595,908	161,998	13,161	264,948	67,083	64,881	288,955	25,937	75,344	14,696	110,321	437,292
1991	577,446	162,239	13,118	263,064	67,424	65,969	289,708	25,005	76,010	15,411	114,266	444,358
1992	585,395	171,223	14,176	275,324	69,025	68,519	298,366	25,370	78,505	16,279	123,167	461,816
1993	588,213	176,678	13,987	277,702	70,761	72,548	303,021	25,653	81,301	17,208	128,543	478,420
1994	596,435	189,755	15,045	294,384	72,406	76,924	311,576	25,882	85,856	18,141	136,301	505,162
1995	608,937	199,056	15,325	304,834	73,889	81,919	321,832	26,552	89,046	18,520	140,814	530,666
1996	634,107	206,757	16,508	315,189	77,538	93,489	330,321	27,006	91,716	19,410	145,391	562,108
1997	664,679	221,259	16,501	332,476	81,106	100,363	342,662	28,717	96,465	19,765	152,687	606,982
Chained 2012 Dollars												
1997[1]	67,446	976,940	316,366	22,411	471,886	115,414	118,539	495,814	40,159	134,908	24,976	210,844
1998[1]	67,087	996,663	326,225	23,682	487,904	117,867	124,171	508,484	41,789	140,139	26,452	223,769
1999[1]	70,716	1,048,059	344,425	23,705	499,060	119,725	126,884	523,565	43,176	146,526	27,501	230,418
2000[1]	71,956	1,088,005	354,846	24,598	508,992	124,111	137,802	537,224	45,246	150,501	29,407	233,153
2001[1]	72,053	1,112,239	361,355	25,017	501,815	128,721	136,688	544,791	45,918	151,105	29,746	232,723
2002[1]	74,275	1,102,140	366,035	26,370	514,752	131,078	139,698	550,247	47,611	154,698	32,958	240,522
2003[1]	77,132	1,104,937	374,503	27,994	522,649	133,084	145,585	562,436	49,374	160,138	33,657	247,824
2004[1]	82,843	1,132,504	388,700	28,267	534,359	137,436	152,798	578,034	51,583	162,238	35,071	259,337
2005[1]	83,825	1,171,051	407,491	29,107	543,745	143,073	158,463	588,055	52,316	166,574	35,907	264,652
2006[1]	85,891	1,199,904	432,589	30,262	541,180	152,659	167,912	592,030	53,518	170,339	36,459	271,465
2007[1]	86,511	1,202,726	436,437	31,668	541,411	155,465	171,114	612,018	52,087	175,090	38,057	268,756
2008[1]	85,977	1,175,471	446,920	34,155	537,200	161,361	173,955	623,821	50,447	174,584	39,643	272,011
2009[1]	87,667	1,223,229	427,108	35,043	509,216	159,236	166,653	605,497	50,214	166,850	39,732	263,016
2010[1]	87,004	1,269,487	433,404	37,697	521,095	159,227	169,016	622,467	51,468	170,167	40,130	266,727
2011[1]	87,166	1,269,245	439,089	41,942	538,703	165,153	173,883	631,372	51,269	174,128	42,794	274,804
2012[1]	87,602	1,322,448	439,571	51,345	540,819	173,484	174,493	641,317	51,642	175,375	43,445	283,722
2013[1]	86,506	1,319,299	445,361	52,531	550,800	177,602	175,805	651,319	52,085	178,940	43,602	286,801
2014[1]	89,151	1,348,204	453,629	56,305	570,362	188,065	181,992	664,793	52,208	183,282	44,100	291,527
2015[1]	90,868	1,369,097	467,754	54,611	577,277	194,565	191,595	677,873	53,003	189,167	45,266	300,581
2016[1]	90,970	1,388,267	472,931	50,752	581,594	189,122	200,332	685,462	52,985	194,466	45,424	306,343
2017[1]	90,989	1,407,217	482,010	49,916	590,884	189,569	206,711	697,183	53,404	199,491	45,265	313,573
2018[1]	92,591	1,436,957	496,110	51,160	601,496	193,030	213,708	712,101	53,741	202,771	45,874	322,898
2019[1]	98,766	1,490,679	511,540	53,930	615,474	197,900	225,337	726,166	53,668	214,934	47,560	328,406
2020[1]	95,731	1,402,412	498,740	52,021	591,120	185,884	218,968	694,196	51,234	206,218	46,762	312,437

Gross Domestic Product by Region and State—*Continued*

(Millions of chained 1997 or 2012 dollars; index numbers)

Year	New Mexico	New York	North Carolina	North Dakota	Ohio	Oklahoma	Oregon	Pennsylvania	Rhode Island	South Carolina	South Dakota	Tennessee
QUANTITY INDEX												
1997=100												
1980..........................	50.5	69.4	49.8	74.2	63.7	76.0	53.2	67.6	63.3	50.4	58.2	52.7
1981..........................	51.2	70.7	51.5	85.4	64.4	80.5	51.7	67.9	64.8	52.2	61.7	54.2
1982..........................	50.4	71.2	50.4	82.1	61.1	82.8	49.0	65.3	64.6	51.3	60.0	52.9
1983..........................	51.3	72.7	53.0	80.5	63.6	78.9	49.5	67.1	66.5	54.6	59.6	55.8
1984..........................	53.7	77.1	57.6	82.3	69.1	82.6	52.6	70.8	71.1	59.8	64.2	59.9
1985..........................	55.7	79.2	61.2	82.8	71.6	84.0	53.9	72.5	75.8	62.0	66.7	62.2
1986..........................	55.2	81.2	63.6	77.2	72.3	79.6	54.9	73.9	79.6	64.9	67.5	64.2
1987..........................	55.3	84.7	66.6	79.2	74.4	78.3	56.8	77.9	83.1	69.7	68.9	68.7
1988..........................	56.4	89.6	70.4	72.9	77.2	82.0	60.3	81.7	88.9	73.3	69.5	71.9
1989..........................	57.6	89.4	72.7	77.2	78.9	82.3	62.1	83.1	91.3	75.7	70.6	72.6
1990..........................	59.0	89.7	73.2	79.8	79.7	82.7	64.6	84.3	90.3	78.1	74.4	72.3
1991..........................	65.7	86.9	73.3	79.5	79.1	83.1	65.7	84.5	87.1	78.8	78.0	74.8
1992..........................	69.5	88.1	77.4	85.9	82.8	85.1	68.3	87.1	88.3	81.4	82.4	80.7
1993..........................	77.0	88.5	79.9	84.8	83.5	87.2	72.3	88.4	89.3	84.3	87.1	84.2
1994..........................	86.3	89.7	85.8	91.2	88.5	89.3	76.6	90.9	90.1	89.0	91.8	89.3
1995..........................	87.8	91.6	90.0	92.9	91.7	91.1	81.6	93.9	92.5	92.3	93.7	92.2
1996..........................	91.6	95.4	93.4	100.0	94.8	95.6	93.2	96.4	94.0	95.1	98.2	95.2
1997..........................	100.0	100.0	100.0	100.0	100.0	100.0	100.0	100.0	100.0	100.0	100.0	100.0
2012 = 100												
1997[1]..........................	77.0	73.9	72.0	43.6	87.3	66.5	67.9	77.3	77.8	76.9	57.5	74.3
1998[1]..........................	76.6	75.4	74.2	46.1	90.2	67.9	71.2	79.3	80.9	79.9	60.9	78.9
1999[1]..........................	80.7	79.3	78.4	46.2	92.3	69.0	72.7	81.6	83.6	83.6	63.3	81.2
2000[1]..........................	82.1	82.3	80.7	47.9	94.1	71.5	79.0	83.8	87.6	85.8	67.7	82.2
2001[1]..........................	82.3	84.1	82.2	48.7	92.8	74.2	78.3	84.9	88.9	86.2	68.5	82.0
2002[1]..........................	84.8	83.3	83.3	51.4	95.2	75.6	80.1	85.8	92.2	88.2	75.9	84.8
2003[1]..........................	88.0	83.6	85.2	54.5	96.6	76.7	83.4	87.7	95.6	91.3	77.5	87.3
2004[1]..........................	94.6	85.6	88.4	55.1	98.8	79.2	87.6	90.1	99.9	92.5	80.7	91.4
2005[1]..........................	95.7	88.6	92.7	56.7	100.5	82.5	90.8	91.7	101.3	95.0	82.7	93.3
2006[1]..........................	98.0	90.7	98.4	58.9	100.1	88.0	96.2	92.3	103.6	97.1	83.9	95.7
2007[1]..........................	98.8	90.9	99.3	61.7	100.1	89.6	98.1	95.4	100.9	99.8	87.6	94.7
2008[1]..........................	98.1	88.9	101.7	66.5	99.3	93.0	99.7	97.3	97.7	99.5	91.3	95.9
2009[1]..........................	100.1	92.5	97.2	68.3	94.2	91.8	95.5	94.4	97.2	95.1	91.5	92.7
2010[1]..........................	99.3	96.0	98.6	73.4	96.4	91.8	96.9	97.1	99.7	97.0	92.4	94.0
2011[1]..........................	99.5	96.0	99.9	81.7	99.6	95.2	99.7	98.4	99.3	99.3	98.5	96.9
2012[1]..........................	100.0	100.0	100.0	100.0	100.0	100.0	100.0	100.0	100.0	100.0	100.0	100.0
2013[1]..........................	98.7	99.8	101.3	102.3	101.8	102.4	100.8	101.6	100.9	102.0	100.4	101.1
2014[1]..........................	101.8	101.9	103.2	109.7	105.5	108.4	104.3	103.7	101.1	104.5	101.5	102.8
2015[1]..........................	103.7	103.5	106.4	106.4	106.7	112.2	109.8	105.7	102.6	107.9	104.2	105.9
2016[1]..........................	103.8	105.0	107.6	98.8	107.5	109.0	114.8	106.9	102.6	110.9	104.6	108.0
2017[1]..........................	103.9	106.4	109.7	97.2	109.3	109.3	118.5	108.7	103.4	113.8	104.2	110.5
2018[1]..........................	105.7	108.7	112.9	99.6	111.2	111.3	122.5	111.0	104.1	115.6	105.6	113.8
2019[1]..........................	112.7	112.6	116.4	104.5	113.8	114.2	129.2	113.3	104.0	122.6	109.2	115.8
2020[1]..........................	109.2	106.0	113.5	100.8	109.3	107.3	125.5	108.4	99.3	117.6	107.4	110.2

1 = NAICS basis, not continuous with previous years, which are based on the SIC.

Gross Domestic Product by Region and State—*Continued*

(Millions of chained 1997 or 2012 dollars; index numbers)

Year	Texas	Utah	Vermont	Virginia	Washington	West Virginia	Wisconsin	Wyoming
VALUE								
Chained 1997 Dollars								
1980	27,127	8,540	115,633	100,522	29,233	91,254	13,547	271,111
1981	28,129	8,814	119,300	103,616	28,878	91,533	14,013	277,668
1982	27,956	8,777	119,714	103,652	28,069	89,641	13,124	280,768
1983	28,917	9,130	125,223	105,339	27,319	91,390	12,431	295,605
1984	31,159	9,590	133,820	109,176	28,766	96,922	13,028	322,249
1985	32,938	10,153	140,418	110,215	29,085	100,204	13,191	341,303
1986	32,467	10,597	147,618	115,190	28,673	101,810	12,581	358,010
1987	32,682	11,522	156,426	120,393	28,734	104,770	12,272	383,298
1988	34,413	12,521	164,558	127,672	30,865	111,180	13,050	407,276
1989	34,827	13,091	170,267	134,180	30,816	113,430	13,019	411,580
1990	36,697	13,313	173,022	141,946	31,349	115,638	13,673	404,914
1991	38,105	12,952	172,407	145,050	31,986	117,167	14,118	394,303
1992	39,564	13,562	175,795	150,245	32,880	123,617	14,327	400,774
1993	41,509	13,755	180,782	154,090	33,836	128,390	14,785	401,601
1994	44,958	14,178	188,082	159,470	35,963	135,190	15,105	415,642
1995	48,212	14,211	193,402	160,183	36,902	138,010	15,539	433,600
1996	52,980	14,839	201,703	169,162	37,750	144,558	15,968	452,476
1997	55,212	15,521	210,361	179,640	38,570	151,035	16,084	479,107
Chained 2012 Dollars								
1997[1]	872,763	80,683	20,026	301,623	271,601	59,237	209,257	25,240
1998[1]	928,374	85,720	20,697	317,197	289,102	60,165	217,254	25,841
1999[1]	965,677	89,270	21,843	332,146	310,332	62,170	226,298	26,822
2000[1]	998,297	92,508	23,023	346,161	312,230	62,052	233,085	27,708
2001[1]	1,021,889	93,887	23,714	358,519	305,055	62,017	236,113	29,241
2002[1]	1,041,811	95,693	24,455	362,262	310,338	62,805	240,996	29,876
2003[1]	1,048,299	97,649	25,301	376,114	316,224	62,839	247,867	30,612
2004[1]	1,102,696	102,725	26,564	393,446	322,003	63,721	256,003	31,530
2005[1]	1,132,796	109,146	26,909	415,087	343,362	65,549	262,161	33,121
2006[1]	1,210,287	118,721	27,132	423,738	356,691	66,435	266,471	37,527
2007[1]	1,274,303	124,498	26,802	427,001	378,205	66,522	267,936	40,335
2008[1]	1,275,774	123,483	27,437	425,804	382,381	67,888	264,632	42,633
2009[1]	1,271,436	120,792	26,997	425,583	372,728	67,565	257,143	41,385
2010[1]	1,301,727	123,330	28,111	437,268	381,253	68,444	264,841	39,801
2011[1]	1,343,791	127,060	28,733	441,609	387,832	69,658	270,373	39,396
2012[1]	1,411,379	128,721	28,887	444,950	400,863	69,399	274,344	38,432
2013[1]	1,472,104	131,902	28,499	446,560	411,141	70,159	276,190	38,504
2014[1]	1,512,351	135,890	28,491	445,527	425,334	69,846	281,232	38,561
2015[1]	1,589,956	141,348	28,805	454,098	443,357	69,498	285,271	39,567
2016[1]	1,593,149	146,875	29,257	455,393	460,081	68,663	288,416	38,077
2017[1]	1,624,949	150,791	29,644	463,426	479,158	69,647	292,477	38,258
2018[1]	1,676,679	157,233	30,013	476,388	506,706	71,321	299,835	38,369
2019[1]	1,764,357	168,793	29,806	489,168	548,687	72,340	308,045	39,214
2020[1]	1,703,074	168,622	28,196	476,950	544,632	68,353	294,185	36,475

Gross Domestic Product by Region and State—*Continued*

(Millions of chained 1997 or 2012 dollars; index numbers)

Year	Texas	Utah	Vermont	Virginia	Washington	West Virginia	Wisconsin	Wyoming
QUANTITY INDEX								
1997=100								
1980.....................	56.0	49.1	55.0	55.0	56.0	75.8	60.4	84.2
1981.....................	59.5	50.9	56.8	56.7	57.7	74.9	60.6	87.1
1982.....................	59.7	50.6	56.6	56.9	57.7	72.8	59.4	81.6
1983.....................	59.6	52.4	58.8	59.5	58.6	70.8	60.5	77.3
1984.....................	63.1	56.4	61.8	63.6	60.8	74.6	64.2	81.0
1985.....................	65.9	59.7	65.4	66.8	61.4	75.4	66.3	82.0
1986.....................	64.5	58.8	68.3	70.2	64.1	74.3	67.4	78.2
1987.....................	64.2	59.2	74.2	74.4	67.0	74.5	69.4	76.3
1988.....................	68.1	62.3	80.7	78.2	71.1	80.0	73.6	81.1
1989.....................	69.8	63.1	84.3	80.9	74.7	79.9	75.1	80.9
1990.....................	72.0	66.5	85.8	82.3	79.0	81.3	76.6	85.0
1991.....................	73.2	69.0	83.5	82.0	80.7	82.9	77.6	87.8
1992.....................	76.1	71.7	87.4	83.6	83.6	85.2	81.8	89.1
1993.....................	78.8	75.2	88.6	85.9	85.8	87.7	85.0	91.9
1994.....................	83.2	81.4	91.3	89.4	88.8	93.2	89.5	93.9
1995.....................	87.4	87.3	91.6	91.9	89.2	95.7	91.4	96.6
1996.....................	92.6	96.0	95.6	95.9	94.2	97.9	95.7	99.3
1997.....................	100.0	100.0	100.0	100.0	100.0	100.0	100.0	100.0
2012 = 100								
1997[1].................	61.8	62.7	69.3	67.8	67.8	85.4	76.3	65.7
1998[1].................	65.8	66.6	71.6	71.3	72.1	86.7	79.2	67.2
1999[1].................	68.4	69.4	75.6	74.6	77.4	89.6	82.5	69.8
2000[1].................	70.7	71.9	79.7	77.8	77.9	89.4	85.0	72.1
2001[1].................	72.4	72.9	82.1	80.6	76.1	89.4	86.1	76.1
2002[1].................	73.8	74.3	84.7	81.4	77.4	90.5	87.8	77.7
2003[1].................	74.3	75.9	87.6	84.5	78.9	90.5	90.3	79.7
2004[1].................	78.1	79.8	92.0	88.4	80.3	91.8	93.3	82.0
2005[1].................	80.3	84.8	93.2	93.3	85.7	94.5	95.6	86.2
2006[1].................	85.8	92.2	93.9	95.2	89.0	95.7	97.1	97.6
2007[1].................	90.3	96.7	92.8	96.0	94.3	95.9	97.7	105.0
2008[1].................	90.4	95.9	95.0	95.7	95.4	97.8	96.5	110.9
2009[1].................	90.1	93.8	93.5	95.6	93.0	97.4	93.7	107.7
2010[1].................	92.2	95.8	97.3	98.3	95.1	98.6	96.5	103.6
2011[1].................	95.2	98.7	99.5	99.2	96.7	100.4	98.6	102.5
2012[1].................	100.0	100.0	100.0	100.0	100.0	100.0	100.0	100.0
2013[1].................	104.3	102.5	98.7	100.4	102.6	101.1	100.7	100.2
2014[1].................	107.2	105.6	98.6	100.1	106.1	100.6	102.5	100.3
2015[1].................	112.7	109.8	99.7	102.1	110.6	100.1	104.0	103.0
2016[1].................	112.9	114.1	101.3	102.3	114.8	98.9	105.1	99.1
2017[1].................	115.1	117.1	102.6	104.2	119.5	100.4	106.6	99.5
2018[1].................	118.8	122.2	103.9	107.1	126.4	102.8	109.3	99.8
2019[1].................	125.1	131.1	103.2	109.9	137.0	104.3	112.2	102.0
2020[1].................	120.7	131.0	97.6	107.2	135.9	98.6	107.2	94.9

1 = NAICS basis, not continuous with previous years, which are based on the SIC.

Gross Domestic Product by Metropolitan Statistical Area

(Millions of chained 2012 dollars.)

Metropolitan Statistical Area	2001	2002	2003	2004	2005	2006	2007	2008	2009	2010	2011	2012	2013	2014	2015	2016	2017	2018	2019
Abilene, TX	4,855	4,904	4,976	5,109	5,204	5,674	5,911	6,027	5,884	6,081	6,106	6,286	6,306	6,398	6,306	6,224	6,302	6,621	6,812
Akron, OH	27,998	29,126	29,849	30,461	31,134	31,180	31,559	31,322	29,425	30,188	30,330	30,484	30,779	31,525	31,886	31,968	32,247	32,864	33,087
Albany, GA	5,478	5,559	5,601	5,664	5,808	5,791	5,671	5,552	5,456	5,330	5,416	5,436	5,402	5,334	5,305	5,392	5,383	5,462	5,699
Albany-Lebanon, OR	3,387	3,596	3,436	3,678	3,744	4,102	3,891	3,738	3,661	3,586	3,630	3,643	3,716	3,746	4,024	4,237	4,257	4,549	4,692
Albany-Schenectady-Troy, NY	42,278	42,844	44,113	44,981	45,543	46,912	47,045	47,686	48,647	48,811	48,853	49,077	49,690	50,316	51,589	53,030	54,313	55,124	56,461
Albuquerque, NM	29,908	30,208	33,167	37,651	37,558	38,076	37,473	37,154	38,444	37,640	37,228	37,058	35,983	36,868	37,412	38,017	37,829	38,477	39,251
Alexandria, LA	4,725	4,881	4,913	5,145	5,411	5,508	5,295	5,326	5,558	5,647	5,634	5,545	5,486	5,430	5,329	5,399	5,457	5,534	5,576
Allentown-Bethlehem-Easton, PA-NJ	42,205	42,128	38,204	35,120	35,187	35,264	36,863	37,198	36,101	37,141	37,291	37,188	37,685	38,334	39,226	40,063	40,191	40,544	41,913
Altoona, PA	4,602	4,584	4,704	4,864	5,031	5,217	5,180	5,191	5,109	5,194	5,142	5,155	5,204	5,248	5,303	5,337	5,468	5,489	5,647
Amarillo, TX	9,566	9,797	9,922	10,040	10,073	10,700	11,041	11,170	11,155	11,529	11,588	11,482	11,623	11,894	12,299	12,237	12,248	12,632	12,698
Ames, IA	4,004	4,174	4,329	4,495	4,586	4,724	4,807	4,978	4,801	4,812	5,030	5,289	5,546	5,691	5,665	5,594	5,691	5,837	5,837
Anchorage, AK	17,708	17,966	18,363	18,704	19,424	19,533	19,845	20,795	21,656	22,569	22,964	22,919	22,365	22,434	23,445	23,312	22,923	23,080	23,245
Ann Arbor, MI	18,972	20,060	20,431	20,226	20,602	20,044	20,436	19,300	17,890	18,452	18,652	19,041	19,254	19,538	20,388	20,953	21,512	22,225	22,431
Anniston-Oxford, AL	3,454	3,564	3,673	3,957	4,135	4,245	4,395	4,455	4,239	4,384	4,226	4,186	4,031	3,897	3,833	3,862	3,882	3,956	4,050
Appleton, WI	9,568	9,580	9,856	10,159	10,416	10,556	10,710	10,505	10,230	10,399	10,721	11,061	10,906	11,307	11,918	12,312	12,508	12,891	13,178
Asheville, NC	13,131	13,556	13,751	14,161	14,562	15,304	15,036	15,035	14,377	14,974	15,177	14,988	15,340	15,809	16,219	16,646	17,335	18,060	18,604
Athens-Clarke County, GA	6,580	6,682	7,013	7,155	7,285	7,387	7,488	7,514	7,457	7,491	7,464	7,733	7,881	8,073	8,347	8,481	8,944	9,306	9,151
Atlanta-Sandy Springs-Alpharetta, GA	255,588	258,265	265,862	279,097	291,832	292,849	293,958	285,603	272,399	277,408	283,394	287,374	293,252	306,798	321,771	336,828	351,449	366,280	371,827
Atlantic City-Hammonton, NJ	13,501	13,961	14,158	14,261	14,692	15,661	15,617	15,610	13,827	13,430	13,861	13,658	13,566	13,243	12,809	12,599	12,415	12,410	12,593
Auburn-Opelika, AL	3,019	3,173	3,325	3,676	3,800	3,931	4,086	4,064	4,014	4,105	4,465	4,617	4,700	4,731	4,926	5,087	5,174	5,220	5,266
Augusta-Richmond County, GA-SC	19,518	19,719	20,387	20,791	20,718	20,957	21,854	22,218	21,808	22,224	22,465	22,534	22,452	22,595	23,477	23,778	24,267	24,840	25,428
Austin-Round Rock-Georgetown, TX	61,180	62,775	64,513	67,523	73,018	81,417	85,475	89,190	87,079	92,603	96,446	98,832	103,345	109,028	118,091	124,294	132,449	138,796	143,076
Bakersfield, CA	27,619	31,297	31,272	34,099	36,486	42,296	46,050	44,754	47,450	45,064	43,919	47,559	46,625	47,383	47,842	47,776	48,400	49,292	51,417
Baltimore-Columbia-Towson, MD	131,483	135,707	138,078	143,849	151,059	155,589	155,960	156,519	155,874	160,999	164,058	165,595	166,886	169,887	174,179	179,128	182,180	185,477	188,615
Bangor, ME	5,632	5,783	5,756	5,935	5,966	6,029	5,939	5,876	5,850	5,828	5,681	5,607	5,540	5,569	5,560	5,680	5,714	5,890	6,034
Barnstable Town, MA	10,583	10,914	11,276	11,622	11,443	11,546	11,382	11,362	11,250	11,521	11,780	11,795	11,828	11,966	12,230	12,219	12,374	12,592	13,588
Baton Rouge, LA	37,628	40,176	41,694	45,875	50,474	49,339	45,585	44,276	44,537	46,497	51,638	51,574	51,606	56,680	56,639	54,141	50,721	53,053	53,348
Battle Creek, MI	5,609	5,670	5,770	5,888	5,996	6,123	6,179	5,959	5,471	5,565	5,454	5,405	5,523	5,539	5,713	5,837	5,868	5,893	5,848
Bay City, MI	3,522	3,541	3,579	3,561	3,565	3,625	3,609	3,507	3,411	3,524	3,517	3,506	3,515	3,335	3,362	3,329	3,276	3,320	3,323
Beaumont-Port Arthur, TX	23,329	22,550	22,947	26,927	24,308	24,557	26,768	25,748	25,966	28,315	28,201	28,430	28,341	23,741	23,778	24,846	25,456	27,094	26,978
Beckley, WV	3,796	3,832	3,774	3,854	4,048	4,046	4,081	4,257	4,208	4,352	4,425	4,276	4,166	3,875	3,771	3,560	3,656	3,769	3,844
Bellingham, WA	7,987	8,570	8,719	8,813	10,844	9,876	10,183	9,938	10,056	10,409	9,582	9,606	9,700	9,750	10,066	10,887	12,012	13,191	13,808
Bend, OR	4,534	4,759	5,018	5,181	5,684	6,029	6,167	5,920	5,392	5,218	5,213	5,408	5,742	6,265	6,839	7,414	8,103	8,482	8,670
Billings, MT	6,988	7,066	7,564	7,936	7,888	8,144	8,983	8,561	8,031	8,318	8,731	8,804	8,996	9,501	10,075	9,466	9,612	9,812	10,076
Binghamton, NY	8,065	8,004	7,986	8,050	8,256	8,891	9,340	9,839	9,985	10,411	10,328	10,463	10,457	10,310	10,332	10,103	10,077	10,249	10,652
Birmingham-Hoover, AL	46,269	47,850	48,553	51,012	52,425	51,829	52,238	52,447	49,731	50,129	51,303	52,031	51,828	51,777	52,600	52,860	53,733	54,962	55,428
Bismarck, ND	4,169	4,279	4,582	4,741	4,828	4,918	4,947	5,063	5,236	5,373	5,654	6,278	6,332	6,937	7,169	6,833	6,841	6,794	6,840
Blacksburg-Christiansburg, VA	5,443	5,517	5,856	5,914	6,260	6,664	6,834	6,409	6,058	6,093	6,267	6,229	6,272	6,504	6,706	6,766	6,524	6,747	6,864
Bloomington, IL	8,689	8,889	9,172	9,555	9,655	10,497	10,535	10,119	10,233	10,548	10,578	10,782	10,671	11,958	12,861	13,291	13,268	13,810	13,778
Bloomington, IN	4,970	5,108	5,250	5,383	5,604	5,755	5,632	5,642	5,583	5,648	5,678	5,710	5,788	6,072	6,041	6,182	6,434	6,619	6,644
Bloomsburg-Berwick, PA	3,116	3,283	3,274	3,446	3,542	3,779	3,701	3,749	3,744	3,899	4,026	4,025	4,096	4,017	4,090	4,080	4,075	4,080	4,123
Boise City, ID	18,461	18,999	20,141	21,593	23,874	24,006	24,204	24,837	23,732	23,935	23,924	24,142	25,219	26,392	26,989	28,303	30,084	32,266	33,376
Boston-Cambridge-Newton, MA-NH	286,818	286,304	294,087	303,060	310,665	315,164	324,976	327,217	325,616	340,447	348,154	356,855	358,488	365,033	380,881	388,346	398,751	414,346	423,726
Boulder, CO	17,926	16,675	16,798	17,344	17,702	18,284	19,307	20,087	19,811	20,304	20,293	20,434	20,985	21,706	22,690	23,506	25,036	25,929	27,510
Bowling Green, KY	4,500	4,662	4,859	5,066	5,388	5,643	5,588	5,657	5,230	5,689	5,692	5,863	5,918	6,040	6,102	6,241	6,357	6,432	6,550
Bremerton-Silverdale-Port Orchard, WA	8,393	8,845	9,002	9,339	9,728	9,951	10,055	10,389	10,141	10,087	9,994	9,895	9,818	10,000	10,266	10,669	11,016	11,591	12,065
Bridgeport-Stamford-Norwalk, CT	77,149	77,535	76,945	80,925	83,606	85,626	89,234	90,049	85,067	83,700	78,864	81,754	79,357	78,270	79,648	79,314	79,038	79,285	79,855
Brownsville-Harlingen, TX	7,275	7,626	7,761	7,877	8,091	8,511	8,555	8,672	8,677	9,069	9,280	9,386	9,514	9,471	9,533	9,713	9,804	10,092	10,373
Brunswick, GA	3,363	3,447	3,616	3,882	3,949	4,130	4,105	3,917	3,793	3,838	3,741	3,673	3,638	3,634	3,832	3,854	3,949	4,148	4,191
Buffalo-Cheektowaga, NY	47,742	48,990	49,684	51,129	51,703	54,219	54,610	54,888	54,822	56,625	56,142	57,449	57,283	58,193	59,284	59,756	59,930	61,089	63,027
Burlington, NC	4,602	4,832	4,810	5,059	5,065	5,305	5,223	5,203	4,837	5,070	5,178	5,131	5,122	5,111	5,154	5,338	5,382	5,478	5,624
Burlington-South Burlington, VT	8,861	9,105	9,703	10,329	10,452	10,667	10,424	10,966	10,887	11,472	11,745	11,830	11,582	11,639	11,938	12,161	12,306	12,560	12,534
California-Lexington Park, MD	3,937	4,233	4,494	4,692	4,843	5,108	5,222	5,253	5,466	5,890	6,145	6,144	6,082	6,166	6,265	6,391	6,416	6,585	6,806
Canton-Massillon, OH	14,707	14,999	15,025	15,244	15,455	15,111	14,831	14,752	13,782	14,431	15,592	15,197	16,259	17,864	18,338	18,162	18,218	18,545	18,618
Cape Coral-Fort Myers, FL	16,956	18,135	19,800	22,263	24,651	26,415	25,939	23,826	21,862	21,664	21,370	21,681	21,900	23,081	24,291	25,755	26,696	27,418	28,208

Gross Domestic Product by Metropolitan Statistical Area—*Continued*

(Millions of chained 2012 dollars.)

Metropolitan Statistical Area	2001	2002	2003	2004	2005	2006	2007	2008	2009	2010	2011	2012	2013	2014	2015	2016	2017	2018	2019
Cape Girardeau, MO-IL	3,310	3,403	3,459	3,614	3,782	3,920	3,936	3,955	3,877	3,864	3,842	3,820	3,803	3,800	3,925	3,976	4,002	4,086	4,149
Carbondale-Marion, IL	4,398	4,603	4,635	4,742	4,894	5,192	5,182	5,312	5,315	5,510	5,597	5,622	5,403	5,275	5,249	5,219	5,242	5,422	5,434
Carson City, NV	2,932	2,980	3,038	3,119	3,207	3,289	3,301	3,231	3,216	3,354	3,113	3,090	3,089	2,895	2,960	2,949	3,137	3,232	3,351
Casper, WY	3,156	3,251	3,324	3,549	3,842	4,354	4,459	4,582	4,269	4,462	4,733	5,302	5,402	5,825	5,786	5,225	5,112	5,627	5,603
Cedar Rapids, IA	10,605	10,499	11,253	12,289	12,917	12,854	13,970	13,867	14,278	15,092	15,449	15,285	15,255	15,866	16,675	16,737	16,544	16,964	16,916
Chambersburg-Waynesboro,	4,011	3,926	4,210	4,539	4,908	5,242	5,617	5,531	5,142	5,105	5,139	5,085	5,186	5,314	5,355	5,302	5,651	5,762	5,850
Champaign-Urbana, IL	8,625	8,979	9,010	9,157	9,214	9,516	9,720	10,041	9,950	10,347	10,396	10,440	10,794	10,994	10,852	10,737	10,654	10,745	10,733
Charleston, WV	13,729	13,747	13,673	13,570	13,981	14,130	14,043	13,997	13,997	13,715	13,661	13,040	12,782	12,421	12,171	11,941	11,649	12,326	11,795
Charleston-North Charleston,	21,574	22,376	23,591	24,929	26,463	27,212	28,196	28,143	27,333	28,403	29,835	31,499	31,356	32,418	33,930	35,690	36,965	38,404	39,548
Charlotte-Concord-Gastonia, NC-SC	92,815	95,126	99,350	104,842	112,368	119,267	120,867	128,017	117,766	114,327	120,388	127,585	125,827	129,446	134,805	138,625	143,827	148,298	150,589
Charlottesville, VA	7,941	8,074	8,446	8,915	9,419	9,810	10,177	10,244	10,338	10,774	10,809	11,067	10,874	11,023	11,199	11,506	12,008	12,197	12,316
Chattanooga, TN-GA	20,087	20,529	21,124	22,116	22,510	22,899	22,872	23,065	22,079	22,552	23,448	24,182	24,490	24,389	25,071	25,457	26,204	26,703	27,149
Cheyenne, WY	3,618	3,749	3,932	4,099	4,131	4,405	4,916	5,399	4,715	4,750	4,891	5,062	4,940	4,945	5,177	5,033	5,064	5,193	5,273
Chicago-Naperville-Elgin, IL-IN-WI	514,161	516,902	523,537	537,784	550,057	558,927	565,097	550,541	530,774	538,597	547,116	561,292	563,329	579,751	594,766	596,450	601,602	615,471	618,616
Chico, CA	6,598	7,127	7,498	7,678	7,895	8,384	8,272	7,971	7,971	7,957	7,957	7,712	7,922	7,937	8,269	8,781	9,195	9,367	9,897
Cincinnati, OH-KY-IN	101,547	103,909	105,750	107,378	109,781	109,222	109,741	109,250	105,185	108,781	112,272	113,190	114,012	117,043	120,187	124,272	126,548	129,839	133,731
Clarksville, TN-KY	7,575	8,227	8,469	9,151	9,981	10,595	10,333	10,600	10,631	10,926	11,516	11,602	11,313	11,203	11,275	10,885	10,997	11,140	11,290
Cleveland, TN	3,295	3,459	3,447	3,670	3,662	3,712	3,720	3,808	3,742	3,864	3,894	4,376	4,495	4,420	4,571	4,287	4,244	4,327	4,417
Cleveland-Elyria, OH	105,859	108,081	110,726	113,174	115,841	113,930	114,052	113,073	105,249	106,513	108,386	109,365	109,093	111,623	112,027	112,225	113,606	116,647	118,168
Coeur d'Alene, ID	3,488	3,564	3,701	3,937	4,297	4,550	4,779	4,707	4,395	4,564	4,399	4,430	4,648	4,762	4,892	5,127	5,351	5,674	5,789
College Station-Bryan, TX	7,069	7,364	7,604	7,727	8,338	9,138	10,002	10,473	11,301	10,687	10,494	10,574	11,319	12,063	12,818	12,889	13,416	13,857	14,098
Colorado Springs, CO	24,424	24,553	24,799	25,223	26,405	26,882	27,538	27,776	27,820	28,753	29,278	29,406	29,679	29,806	30,356	30,810	32,121	33,113	34,323
Columbia, MO	6,746	6,837	7,051	7,252	7,411	7,544	7,501	7,647	7,614	7,772	7,926	8,137	8,382	8,404	8,523	8,693	8,829	8,970	9,141
Columbia, SC	28,095	28,408	29,309	30,496	31,249	32,350	33,225	33,629	32,807	32,823	32,890	32,628	33,475	34,695	35,781	36,771	37,357	37,990	38,637
Columbus, GA-AL	11,095	11,461	11,445	11,700	11,957	12,321	12,713	12,746	12,899	13,095	13,324	13,440	13,174	13,132	13,268	12,907	13,119	13,458	13,596
Columbus, IN	3,565	3,456	3,630	3,805	4,025	4,469	4,983	5,315	4,395	5,329	5,450	5,882	6,183	5,921	5,776	5,637	5,757	6,078	6,045
Columbus, OH	85,619	87,126	89,319	92,279	95,310	93,693	94,631	93,489	90,530	93,356	96,864	100,757	103,774	107,394	109,356	111,322	113,818	116,225	117,001
Corpus Christi, TX	17,807	17,799	18,637	20,208	18,909	19,266	20,633	19,764	19,464	20,810	21,525	21,248	21,598	20,413	20,412	20,016	20,679	21,545	21,950
Corvallis, OR	2,650	2,695	2,745	2,865	3,013	3,340	3,647	3,827	3,776	3,872	4,023	3,961	3,855	3,828	3,905	4,005	4,217	4,391	4,457
Crestview-Fort Walton Beach-Destin, FL	8,720	9,489	10,337	11,411	12,283	11,965	11,816	11,359	10,886	10,715	10,769	11,308	11,511	11,615	11,962	12,253	12,821	13,235	13,935
Cumberland, MD-WV	3,154	3,208	3,170	3,185	3,217	3,384	3,373	3,413	3,398	3,616	3,632	3,549	3,549	3,501	3,576	3,615	3,609	3,576	3,675
Dallas-Fort Worth-Arlington, TX	277,828	284,973	287,650	303,272	317,728	335,638	349,044	354,118	342,724	349,012	361,325	374,743	385,096	400,172	419,841	432,613	448,957	464,390	472,334
Dalton, GA	5,743	6,009	6,086	6,746	6,982	6,992	7,071	6,689	6,077	5,736	5,780	5,953	5,876	6,038	6,258	6,483	6,437	6,394	6,350
Danville, IL	2,844	2,931	3,056	3,206	3,155	3,392	3,387	3,317	3,139	3,167	3,201	3,279	3,256	3,299	3,183	3,157	3,124	3,147	3,203
Daphne-Fairhope-Foley, AL	3,950	4,149	4,334	4,753	5,241	5,290	5,296	4,999	4,740	4,898	4,934	5,051	5,180	5,259	5,437	5,626	5,755	6,006	6,141
Davenport-Moline-Rock Island, IA-IL	16,825	16,721	17,142	18,172	18,541	18,926	19,308	19,623	18,768	19,225	19,888	20,542	19,940	20,219	19,817	19,365	19,419	19,654	20,023
Dayton-Kettering, OH	35,204	36,205	36,786	37,875	38,088	38,005	36,923	36,009	34,006	34,850	35,910	35,849	36,038	36,367	36,768	37,280	38,083	39,298	40,004
Decatur, AL	4,854	4,814	5,185	5,847	5,465	5,655	5,815	5,602	5,512	5,575	5,403	5,372	5,305	5,303	5,298	5,468	5,468	5,656	5,825
Decatur, IL	5,577	5,582	5,626	5,799	5,882	6,088	6,313	6,728	6,728	6,828	6,859	6,578	6,940	7,191	7,417	6,940	6,484	6,486	6,400
Deltona-Daytona Beach-Ormond Beach, FL	13,097	14,144	15,432	16,446	17,133	18,136	18,213	17,430	16,309	16,165	15,999	16,042	16,060	16,275	16,859	17,598	18,215	18,830	19,285
Denver-Aurora-Lakewood, CO	135,786	136,125	136,573	136,626	141,838	142,913	148,350	148,109	143,893	146,544	149,065	153,287	159,513	166,354	175,330	179,569	186,463	194,854	202,456
Des Moines-West Des Moines, IA	28,534	28,999	31,442	34,419	36,694	35,601	39,238	35,437	34,630	35,290	35,323	37,615	36,672	40,445	43,502	45,003	44,615	45,303	45,633
Detroit-Warren-Dearborn, MI	220,490	225,370	229,270	228,640	232,553	224,327	222,584	208,061	185,026	197,226	205,504	212,218	215,911	218,496	222,804	227,293	229,816	235,105	237,089
Dothan, AL	4,572	4,824	4,878	5,045	5,151	5,288	5,274	5,102	4,925	4,951	4,939	4,993	5,216	5,263	5,375	5,578	5,740	5,800	5,853
Dover, DE	5,728	5,901	5,971	6,521	6,560	6,853	6,894	6,802	6,957	6,804	6,704	6,495	6,388	6,543	6,769	6,712	6,745	7,018	7,275
Dubuque, IA	3,607	3,786	3,929	4,353	4,646	4,778	4,993	4,682	4,369	4,692	4,750	5,383	5,112	5,618	5,763	5,414	5,572	5,700	5,713
Duluth, MN-WI	11,473	11,978	12,107	12,832	12,997	13,034	12,768	13,165	12,472	13,674	14,143	13,511	14,181	14,259	12,819	13,444	13,653	14,300	14,962
Durham-Chapel Hill, NC	27,551	28,652	30,080	30,547	32,718	39,602	42,233	43,179	41,073	44,170	44,234	44,096	45,227	44,665	43,641	42,774	43,655	45,099	47,169
East Stroudsburg, PA	4,637	4,759	4,713	5,123	5,526	5,746	6,107	6,133	5,933	6,000	5,866	5,691	5,656	5,728	5,915	6,280	6,176	6,145	6,350
Eau Claire, WI	5,296	5,567	5,814	6,126	6,509	6,666	6,841	6,685	6,653	7,050	7,152	7,332	7,351	7,957	8,141	8,096	8,188	8,503	8,612
El Centro, CA	5,100	6,155	5,766	5,602	6,119	6,734	6,572	7,485	7,130	7,015	7,312	6,921	7,301	7,800	8,533	8,599	8,610	8,494	8,981
Elizabethtown-Fort Knox, KY	4,158	4,196	4,314	4,456	4,555	4,813	4,796	5,058	5,034	5,637	5,943	5,679	5,591	5,382	5,181	5,204	5,275	5,277	5,314
Elkhart-Goshen, IN	7,814	8,428	9,243	9,809	10,525	11,233	11,258	9,778	7,211	9,533	9,418	9,623	10,298	11,219	12,153	13,239	14,726	14,835	14,501
Elmira, NY	3,008	3,013	3,049	3,074	3,166	3,257	3,326	3,477	3,457	3,665	3,734	3,720	3,719	3,710	3,630	3,552	3,484	3,549	3,627
El Paso, TX	19,855	20,520	20,667	21,549	22,064	22,769	23,679	23,402	23,869	25,550	26,857	27,365	26,975	26,637	27,010	27,417	28,082	28,875	29,194
Enid, OK	1,967	2,017	2,112	2,174	2,268	2,379	2,541	2,789	2,867	2,992	3,062	3,509	3,627	4,109	4,083	4,365	3,184	3,187	3,201
Erie, PA	10,329	10,250	10,276	10,604	10,991	11,340	11,707	12,469	11,472	11,627	12,107	11,651	11,730	11,234	11,294	10,904	10,657	10,768	10,916
Eugene-Springfield, OR	11,084	11,332	11,556	12,104	12,664	13,403	13,573	13,409	12,556	12,597	12,699	12,757	12,792	12,980	13,745	14,249	14,805	15,228	15,482

Gross Domestic Product by Metropolitan Statistical Area—*Continued*

(Millions of chained 2012 dollars.)

Metropolitan Statistical Area	2001	2002	2003	2004	2005	2006	2007	2008	2009	2010	2011	2012	2013	2014	2015	2016	2017	2018	2019
Evansville, IN-KY	14,963	15,748	16,284	17,067	16,706	15,672	15,575	16,189	15,482	15,839	16,046	15,744	15,141	14,925	15,048	15,219	16,119	16,544	17,369
Fairbanks, AK	5,841	5,049	5,075	5,147	5,629	5,814	5,900	6,404	6,248	6,291	5,843	5,560	5,401	5,370	5,274	5,289	5,237	5,318	5,217
Fargo, ND-MN	7,816	8,305	8,735	9,093	9,421	9,758	10,060	10,376	10,149	10,549	11,102	12,013	11,980	12,898	13,135	12,988	13,201	13,443	13,574
Farmington, NM	6,569	6,589	6,485	6,618	6,647	6,877	7,056	6,902	6,980	6,529	6,495	6,408	6,320	6,583	6,864	6,384	6,316	5,846	5,907
Fayetteville, NC	14,606	15,133	15,607	16,282	17,296	17,896	17,873	18,530	19,185	19,634	19,801	19,228	19,026	18,868	19,026	18,885	18,863	19,078	19,298
Fayetteville-Springdale- Rogers, AR	13,347	14,370	15,308	16,801	17,925	17,934	17,347	17,119	16,318	17,227	17,613	18,257	19,474	20,441	21,316	21,900	23,045	23,727	23,863
Flagstaff, AZ	4,891	4,981	5,080	5,282	5,559	5,883	6,304	6,150	5,855	6,088	6,484	6,175	6,435	6,383	6,506	6,625	7,002	7,008	6,765
Flint, MI	14,014	14,788	15,180	15,098	15,222	15,125	14,834	13,465	12,302	12,973	13,159	13,111	13,688	14,000	14,601	14,687	14,662	14,835	14,995
Florence, SC	7,175	7,239	7,451	7,613	7,731	7,981	8,055	7,920	7,650	7,543	7,792	7,815	8,111	8,369	8,699	8,833	8,977	9,057	9,461
Florence-Muscle Shoals, AL	4,130	4,157	4,337	4,569	4,671	4,809	4,733	4,700	4,511	4,701	4,866	4,874	5,169	4,996	4,903	4,755	4,661	4,733	4,819
Fond du Lac, WI	3,668	3,620	3,754	3,954	4,029	4,123	4,157	4,178	3,942	4,148	4,317	4,513	4,570	4,754	4,731	4,661	4,693	4,773	4,904
Fort Collins, CO	10,322	10,965	11,057	11,231	11,457	11,895	12,230	12,557	12,388	12,668	12,813	13,108	13,737	14,395	15,160	15,784	16,970	17,852	18,268
Fort Smith, AR-OK	7,767	8,006	8,401	8,903	9,160	9,592	9,314	9,110	8,417	8,712	8,911	8,743	8,550	8,457	8,438	8,399	8,461	8,578	8,670
Fort Wayne, IN	15,399	15,772	16,437	16,769	17,125	17,766	18,175	17,251	15,900	16,357	16,572	17,299	17,299	18,560	19,387	19,680	20,301	21,027	21,554
Fresno, CA	28,319	30,838	32,988	34,024	35,515	38,282	37,213	35,973	36,015	36,160	36,474	35,316	36,702	38,239	40,050	41,503	43,125	44,264	46,009
Gadsden, AL	2,617	2,667	2,689	2,832	2,831	2,832	2,819	2,819	2,754	2,810	2,829	2,804	2,793	2,783	2,838	2,851	2,874	2,911	2,916
Gainesville, ...	10,247	10,509	10,576	11,468	11,825	12,373	12,958	12,654	12,247	12,160	11,950	11,970	12,031	12,397	12,729	13,075	13,372	13,840	14,204
Gainesville, ...	6,105	6,112	6,359	6,547	6,746	6,957	7,163	7,120	6,717	6,799	7,177	7,181	7,374	7,638	8,103	8,439	8,992	9,366	9,535
Gettysburg, ...	2,611	2,798	2,795	2,831	2,941	3,097	3,098	3,154	3,175	3,143	3,204	3,284	3,305	3,319	3,365	3,426	3,544	3,508	3,540
Glens Falls, ...	4,114	4,203	4,345	4,616	4,598	4,838	4,794	5,038	5,226	5,317	5,238	5,235	5,247	5,321	5,349	5,344	5,451	5,554	5,777
Goldsboro, ...	4,369	4,205	4,093	4,285	4,319	4,530	4,590	4,647	4,613	4,646	4,474	4,440	4,573	4,450	4,472	4,450	4,446	4,517	4,535
Grand Forks, ND-MN ..	3,484	3,664	3,951	3,827	3,925	4,197	4,224	4,462	4,315	4,433	4,499	4,790	4,804	4,787	4,829	4,949	5,030	5,036	5,013
Grand Island, NE	2,646	2,728	2,904	2,971	3,166	3,339	3,348	3,433	3,475	3,577	3,592	3,703	3,900	3,884	3,869	3,848	3,829	3,860	3,975
Grand Junction, CO	4,344	4,481	4,585	4,695	4,955	5,411	5,960	6,475	5,914	5,644	5,648	5,614	5,508	5,591	5,575	5,508	5,771	6,059	6,215
Grand Rapids- Kentwood, ...	42,905	44,189	45,210	46,282	47,388	47,239	47,101	45,593	42,500	44,161	45,051	46,126	47,090	48,530	50,738	51,945	53,312	54,901	55,051
Grants Pass, OR	1,740	1,832	1,911	2,005	2,110	2,218	2,243	2,130	2,088	2,080	2,068	2,051	2,037	2,114	2,256	2,353	2,490	2,602	2,723
Great Falls, MT	2,788	2,872	2,888	2,996	3,189	3,236	3,259	3,211	3,190	3,331	3,376	3,339	3,282	3,331	3,449	3,397	3,469	3,586	3,636
Greeley, CO	7,455	7,364	7,583	8,113	8,718	9,157	9,486	10,049	10,231	10,507	10,875	11,937	13,275	15,722	17,370	17,930	19,025	21,312	22,020
Green Bay, ...	13,877	14,186	14,649	15,096	15,403	15,673	15,767	15,724	15,215	15,976	16,187	16,667	16,450	17,667	18,177	18,441	18,303	18,947	19,113
Greensboro-High Point, ...	34,727	35,647	35,488	35,068	35,854	37,413	37,371	38,023	36,991	37,510	38,203	36,330	37,163	37,258	38,398	37,660	37,650	37,885	38,580
Greenville, NC	5,600	5,574	5,528	5,697	6,130	6,720	7,004	7,087	7,147	7,264	7,447	7,293	7,706	7,990	8,627	8,578	8,544	8,477	8,646
Greenville-Anderson,	31,949	33,382	34,456	31,474	31,606	31,744	32,831	33,015	31,138	31,992	33,469	33,729	34,917	36,100	37,609	38,648	39,796	41,392	42,440
Gulfport-Biloxi, MS	14,650	14,609	15,730	15,645	16,132	16,684	22,434	19,860	18,327	18,284	17,290	17,226	15,850	16,669	16,304	16,525	16,718	16,926	17,125
Hagerstown- Martinsburg, MD-WV	7,553	7,815	7,988	8,445	8,795	9,410	9,348	9,272	8,997	9,141	9,335	9,368	9,434	9,569	9,659	9,916	10,181	10,280	10,377
Hammond, ...	2,458	2,555	2,762	3,015	3,355	3,880	3,719	3,830	3,585	3,781	4,218	3,820	3,537	3,513	3,353	3,431	3,669	3,693	3,827
Hanford-Corcoran, CA ...	4,291	4,605	5,103	5,376	5,649	5,479	6,210	5,610	5,126	5,204	5,856	5,378	5,421	5,905	5,866	5,927	6,140	6,250	6,609
Harrisburg-Carlisle, PA	27,304	27,932	28,856	29,934	30,281	30,950	31,583	31,610	30,792	31,113	31,769	32,261	32,784	33,719	34,749	34,653	34,746	35,398	36,227
Harrisonburg, VA	7,122	6,237	6,181	6,314	6,720	6,850	6,867	6,775	7,075	7,446	7,498	7,661	7,783	7,534	7,324	7,091	7,114	7,216	7,194
Hartford-East Hartford- Middletown, CT	75,274	72,468	74,329	80,172	81,760	85,481	90,244	89,166	87,844	87,661	87,349	87,552	83,935	85,955	91,265	91,665	93,092	92,931	93,535
Hattiesburg, MS	4,413	4,553	4,758	4,951	5,143	5,421	5,212	5,537	5,484	5,559	5,496	5,596	5,609	5,563	5,610	5,542	5,630	5,646	5,602
Hickory-Lenoir- Morganton, NC	13,451	13,505	13,176	13,661	13,643	14,100	13,722	13,286	12,541	13,072	13,064	12,705	12,788	12,857	13,255	13,466	13,714	13,884	14,075
Hilton Head Island- Bluffton, SC	5,993	6,011	6,370	6,838	7,242	7,080	7,175	7,016	6,649	6,541	6,528	6,567	6,777	6,940	7,199	7,355	7,395	7,599	7,868
Hinesville, GA	2,401	2,473	2,681	2,820	2,996	3,058	3,198	3,463	3,486	3,660	3,811	3,712	3,624	3,463	3,402	3,327	3,311	3,333	3,305
Homosassa Springs, FL	3,408	3,506	3,599	3,812	3,977	4,472	4,510	4,312	3,911	3,646	3,529	3,532	3,512	3,437	3,356	3,368	3,367	3,456	3,879
Hot Springs, AR	2,526	2,616	2,691	2,759	2,843	2,849	2,792	2,747	2,661	2,773	2,979	2,894	2,872	2,871	2,910	2,904	2,958	2,993	3,031
Houma-Thibodaux, LA	10,349	9,955	9,483	9,346	9,631	11,250	11,384	11,221	11,284	10,944	10,485	10,691	10,990	11,216	10,202	8,960	8,714	8,964	9,159
Houston-The Woodlands-Sugar Land, TX	296,052	293,923	294,265	319,614	324,039	345,987	374,571	367,486	363,883	378,717	388,117	402,853	421,244	427,612	453,758	445,887	451,899	463,517	472,104
Huntington-Ashland, WV-KY-OH	12,399	12,641	12,833	13,228	13,339	13,558	13,477	14,091	14,113	13,906	13,742	14,447	15,574	14,889	14,854	14,375	14,466	15,043	15,385
Huntsville, AL	15,136	15,775	16,566	17,804	18,715	19,507	20,155	20,836	21,102	22,080	22,466	22,519	22,800	22,947	23,340	23,935	24,599	25,402	26,244
Idaho Falls, ...	4,159	4,426	4,431	4,632	4,797	5,273	5,343	5,404	5,422	5,383	5,332	5,328	5,437	5,483	5,822	6,048	6,460	6,874	7,102
Indianapolis-Carmel- Anderson, IN	95,061	96,209	99,280	104,567	105,260	106,889	110,436	113,659	110,465	114,028	114,000	113,206	115,863	118,495	115,487	117,580	119,098	123,442	126,096
Iowa City, IA	6,444	6,678	6,777	7,062	7,140	7,423	7,455	7,784	7,740	8,009	8,319	8,394	8,678	8,889	8,835	8,980	9,256	9,441	9,243
Ithaca, NY	4,415	4,580	4,792	4,895	4,896	5,003	4,976	5,210	5,279	5,472	5,401	5,396	5,390	5,322	5,370	5,408	5,448	5,530	5,495
Jackson, MI	4,909	5,071	5,047	5,176	5,263	5,272	5,251	4,997	4,611	4,850	5,032	5,076	5,154	5,062	5,173	5,342	5,456	5,611	5,684
Jackson, MS	21,108	21,583	22,305	22,902	23,316	23,669	22,893	24,069	24,069	23,149	23,514	23,618	23,688	24,257	24,588	24,715	24,563	24,552	24,578
Jackson, TN	6,401	6,364	6,500	6,652	6,764	7,001	6,860	7,014	7,057	7,516	8,071	7,167	7,189	7,057	7,191	7,325	7,525	7,711	7,798
Jacksonville, FL	53,264	54,814	57,615	60,162	62,892	65,759	66,162	63,661	60,309	60,508	59,822	60,551	61,782	63,210	65,944	68,037	70,851	73,616	75,768
Jacksonville, NC	5,269	5,128	5,342	5,812	6,196	6,413	6,859	7,531	8,072	8,457	8,407	8,264	8,060	7,903	7,749	8,128	7,956	8,073	8,030
Janesville-Beloit, WI	5,355	5,966	6,055	6,184	6,112	6,521	6,409	6,087	5,647	5,841	5,931	6,047	6,267	6,104	6,239	6,308	6,314	6,685	6,919

Gross Domestic Product by Metropolitan Statistical Area—*Continued*

(Millions of chained 2012 dollars.)

Metropolitan Statistical Area	2001	2002	2003	2004	2005	2006	2007	2008	2009	2010	2011	2012	2013	2014	2015	2016	2017	2018	2019
Jefferson City, MO	5,798	5,794	5,944	6,122	6,197	6,456	6,438	6,657	6,511	6,641	6,657	6,636	6,717	6,874	7,080	7,031	6,879	7,021	7,053
Johnson City, TN	5,197	5,347	5,591	5,997	6,091	6,326	6,410	6,535	6,356	6,210	6,396	6,509	6,460	6,317	6,602	6,475	6,621	6,789	6,903
Johnstown, PA	4,494	4,403	4,473	4,489	4,564	4,635	4,707	4,822	4,725	4,799	4,814	4,754	4,725	4,633	4,575	4,469	4,439	4,486	4,604
Jonesboro, AR	3,361	3,502	3,804	3,996	4,156	4,170	3,979	4,066	4,089	4,309	4,395	4,324	4,484	4,325	4,440	4,487	4,670	4,770	4,847
Joplin, MO	5,994	6,005	6,134	6,335	6,437	6,594	6,560	6,752	6,456	6,627	6,596	6,610	6,603	6,640	6,951	6,895	6,901	7,089	7,152
Kahului-Wailuku-Lahaina, HI	5,900	6,239	6,769	7,490	8,288	9,056	9,228	8,794	8,015	8,288	8,605	8,760	8,692	8,726	8,110	8,893	8,910	9,240	9,329
Kalamazoo-Portage, MI	10,752	11,508	11,496	11,502	11,365	11,221	11,383	11,037	10,790	10,903	10,864	10,899	11,046	11,020	11,422	11,689	12,181	12,623	12,819
Kankakee, IL	3,528	3,636	3,689	3,784	3,761	4,006	4,032	4,101	4,114	4,197	4,207	4,388	4,328	4,479	4,617	4,942	5,352	5,476	5,609
Kansas City, MO-KS	92,672	94,804	96,404	98,031	100,774	102,710	105,375	108,643	105,063	104,619	104,848	108,118	109,406	112,606	115,529	116,076	119,440	122,028	123,268
Kennewick-Richland, WA	8,985	9,658	9,722	9,921	10,447	11,046	11,167	11,232	11,845	12,996	12,677	12,168	12,177	12,428	13,057	13,685	13,920	14,590	15,155
Killeen-Temple, TX	11,050	11,452	11,997	12,480	13,394	14,568	15,327	16,269	16,442	16,353	16,653	16,488	16,052	15,956	16,563	16,182	16,493	16,795	17,047
Kingsport-Bristol, TN-VA	10,448	10,460	10,605	11,336	11,087	11,835	11,992	11,949	11,696	11,789	12,047	12,103	11,957	11,523	11,720	11,819	12,137	12,373	12,387
Kingston, NY	4,987	5,092	5,261	5,432	5,501	5,926	5,906	6,019	5,993	6,107	6,070	6,122	6,115	6,088	6,089	6,144	6,261	6,405	6,546
Knoxville, TN	28,092	29,585	30,728	32,416	33,347	34,149	34,069	34,584	33,000	33,299	34,484	34,801	34,953	35,399	36,409	37,296	38,246	39,345	39,784
Kokomo, IN	3,294	3,706	4,296	4,080	3,981	4,169	4,335	3,891	2,621	4,134	4,253	4,433	4,479	4,314	4,019	3,909	3,802	3,870	3,955
La Crosse-Onalaska, WI-MN	5,176	5,242	5,433	5,583	5,750	5,799	5,868	5,985	6,032	6,271	6,408	6,439	6,718	7,254	7,456	6,989	7,193	7,388	7,433
Lafayette, LA	19,987	18,902	18,583	18,919	19,421	22,207	21,893	22,477	22,251	22,424	22,643	23,437	23,034	23,098	21,489	19,540	19,498	20,065	20,368
Lafayette-West Lafayette, IN	7,036	7,216	7,472	7,720	7,904	8,329	8,584	8,519	7,739	8,237	8,428	8,367	8,718	8,983	9,057	9,478	9,909	10,339	10,411
Lake Charles, LA	14,799	15,756	18,669	20,247	24,211	20,685	17,430	15,343	13,015	11,839	14,124	13,591	11,754	12,189	12,304	13,207	15,547	16,436	16,984
Lake Havasu City-Kingman, AZ	3,777	4,138	4,270	4,597	4,878	5,187	5,310	5,048	4,649	4,613	4,564	4,515	4,626	4,723	4,785	4,908	4,815	4,944	5,201
Lakeland-Winter Haven, FL	17,190	17,761	18,288	19,079	20,219	21,592	21,833	21,179	19,795	19,851	19,783	19,955	20,364	20,146	21,235	21,986	23,186	23,983	24,838
Lancaster, PA	21,525	21,851	22,324	22,827	23,276	23,577	23,448	23,243	22,420	23,190	22,917	22,823	23,225	23,962	25,088	25,174	26,048	26,820	26,881
Lansing-East Lansing, MI	21,347	21,928	22,120	22,080	22,485	22,650	22,665	21,301	19,950	21,290	20,975	20,592	20,632	21,025	21,928	22,755	23,161	23,610	23,837
Laredo, TX	7,852	8,158	8,056	7,833	8,098	8,257	8,144	7,767	7,824	7,932	8,756	9,321	9,859	11,330	12,504	12,413	12,530	12,075	12,349
Las Cruces, NM	4,979	5,174	5,567	5,918	6,415	6,459	6,519	6,456	6,781	6,929	6,693	6,425	6,305	6,413	6,533	6,659	6,630	6,733	6,858
Las Vegas-Henderson-Paradise, NV	73,030	76,116	79,884	89,709	98,854	103,051	103,291	98,990	89,729	89,235	90,428	88,974	90,295	91,894	96,158	98,495	101,129	107,500	110,103
Lawrence, KS	3,714	3,804	3,746	3,796	3,779	3,754	3,788	3,973	3,931	3,894	3,951	3,962	4,026	4,115	4,184	4,307	4,403	4,503	4,456
Lawton, OK	3,734	3,886	4,178	4,351	4,275	4,483	4,539	4,714	4,883	5,088	4,969	4,744	4,753	4,742	4,897	4,785	4,633	4,627	4,685
Lebanon, PA	3,834	3,925	4,124	4,339	4,360	4,591	4,716	4,698	4,718	4,898	5,005	5,117	5,094	5,245	5,297	5,284	5,440	5,570	5,652
Lewiston, ID-WA	2,076	2,101	2,122	2,152	2,183	2,271	2,308	2,349	2,303	2,357	2,324	2,334	2,394	2,393	2,460	2,537	2,588	2,659	2,723
Lewiston-Auburn, ME .	3,478	3,755	3,868	3,938	3,887	3,993	4,095	4,186	4,045	3,972	3,955	4,045	4,012	4,045	4,119	4,169	4,132	4,257	4,318
Lexington-Fayette, KY .	19,389	20,338	20,627	21,431	22,384	23,155	23,273	22,867	21,173	22,083	22,245	22,660	23,604	24,309	25,363	25,959	26,031	26,402	26,819
Lima, OH	5,641	5,935	5,975	6,154	6,115	6,152	5,992	5,929	7,107	7,453	7,645	7,246	6,919	7,581	7,467	7,667	7,524	7,775	7,920
Lincoln, NE	13,255	13,348	13,861	14,014	14,583	14,907	15,172	14,716	14,440	14,842	14,952	15,078	15,116	15,715	16,159	16,427	17,371	17,587	17,926
Little Rock-North Little Rock-Conway, AR	26,596	27,325	28,530	29,490	31,039	31,693	32,528	32,162	31,321	31,142	31,667	31,669	31,919	32,042	32,506	32,601	32,728	33,229	33,523
Logan, UT-ID	2,923	2,931	3,112	3,255	3,273	3,518	3,724	3,937	4,045	4,332	4,467	4,235	4,299	4,454	4,624	4,833	5,091	5,368	5,507
Longview, TX	12,384	12,799	12,629	12,904	13,724	15,079	16,522	17,538	18,396	17,227	16,308	16,326	16,141	16,045	15,423	14,681	14,876	15,563	15,986
Longview, WA	3,308	3,224	3,365	3,422	3,595	3,842	4,077	3,926	3,821	4,141	4,011	4,127	4,244	4,240	4,319	4,341	4,482	4,710	4,925
Los Angeles-Long Beach-Anaheim, CA	642,548	660,139	694,565	722,872	749,846	773,376	777,111	781,358	742,588	760,005	771,891	786,046	804,143	830,698	869,758	889,801	922,011	937,167	960,250
Louisville/Jefferson County, KY-IN	51,048	51,291	52,601	54,241	55,794	57,293	57,222	56,449	53,438	55,977	56,834	58,763	58,919	59,581	61,240	62,631	62,509	63,551	64,569
Lubbock, TX	9,193	9,384	9,501	9,831	10,198	10,666	10,825	10,697	10,747	11,315	11,114	11,538	11,992	11,935	12,207	12,479	12,735	13,064	13,165
Lynchburg, VA	8,287	8,408	8,815	9,013	9,213	9,730	9,683	9,628	9,660	9,936	9,784	9,449	9,425	9,367	9,360	9,322	9,426	9,606	9,741
Macon-Bibb County, ..	10,103	10,078	9,846	10,132	10,018	10,060	9,847	9,945	9,672	9,741	9,909	9,942	9,947	9,970	10,083	10,043	10,135	10,531	10,486
Madera, CA	3,288	3,722	3,853	4,467	4,798	5,188	5,169	5,029	4,415	5,062	5,097	5,290	5,376	5,774	5,623	6,169	6,333	6,457	6,740
Madison, WI	29,927	30,964	31,995	33,431	34,861	34,888	35,604	35,001	34,529	35,576	36,696	37,514	38,052	39,390	41,052	42,429	43,239	45,140	46,327
Manchester-Nashua, NH	17,532	18,264	19,774	20,517	21,046	21,207	21,509	21,398	21,172	21,437	22,006	22,198	22,414	22,753	23,667	24,296	24,630	25,409	25,688
Manhattan, KS	4,737	4,752	4,941	5,154	5,295	5,723	6,171	6,522	6,495	6,835	7,086	6,987	6,723	6,512	6,624	6,414	6,327	6,277	6,121
Mankato, MN	3,705	3,891	3,879	4,146	4,314	4,682	4,570	4,627	4,438	4,621	4,765	4,916	5,036	5,235	5,248	5,174	5,231	5,347	5,445
Mansfield, OH	4,449	4,647	4,682	4,859	4,942	4,937	4,699	4,545	3,919	4,118	4,272	4,295	4,284	4,354	4,252	4,242	4,270	4,356	4,371
McAllen-Edinburg-Mission, TX	14,221	15,116	15,465	15,636	16,034	16,877	17,724	17,361	17,295	17,236	17,479	17,606	18,294	18,511	18,672	18,797	19,046	19,421	19,766
Medford, OR	6,017	6,298	6,495	6,781	6,889	7,244	7,415	7,316	7,031	6,822	6,816	6,688	6,916	7,087	7,440	7,767	8,138	8,381	8,613
Memphis, TN-MS-AR ..	62,290	63,283	64,037	65,391	66,287	66,315	64,870	64,412	61,822	61,925	62,447	64,189	64,536	63,953	65,292	66,147	66,966	68,306	68,353
Merced, CA	5,953	6,339	6,940	7,621	7,973	8,205	9,056	8,024	7,572	7,603	7,928	7,704	8,067	9,021	9,197	9,264	9,941	9,918	10,383
Miami-Fort Lauderdale-Pompano Beach, FL	227,330	235,551	243,706	256,711	273,400	277,878	275,982	264,869	249,460	256,952	257,241	257,308	264,714	274,142	286,750	297,035	309,117	321,547	327,129
Michigan City-La Porte, IN	3,845	3,840	3,837	3,981	3,902	3,996	4,057	4,087	3,735	3,890	3,834	3,843	3,869	3,988	3,840	3,830	3,833	3,865	3,894
Midland, MI	4,610	4,750	4,521	4,752	4,243	4,309	4,345	4,178	3,916	4,097	4,156	4,239	4,166	4,769	5,197	4,845	4,816	4,987	4,963
Midland, TX	6,632	6,811	6,526	6,868	7,294	8,559	9,514	10,518	11,312	12,309	14,363	18,104	18,702	20,288	22,500	23,191	27,111	34,028	40,382
Milwaukee-Waukesha, WI	78,828	79,095	81,367	82,969	85,524	86,786	87,246	86,178	83,440	85,467	87,323	87,643	87,470	87,852	89,138	89,788	90,440	93,082	93,888

Gross Domestic Product by Metropolitan Statistical Area—*Continued*

(Millions of chained 2012 dollars.)

Metropolitan Statistical Area	2001	2002	2003	2004	2005	2006	2007	2008	2009	2010	2011	2012	2013	2014	2015	2016	2017	2018	2019
Minneapolis-St. Paul-Bloomington, MN-WI	176,532	178,794	187,734	195,616	201,781	198,830	200,697	200,563	193,188	198,971	204,078	207,296	212,289	220,876	224,961	228,623	233,364	240,705	242,537
Missoula, MT	3,599	3,758	3,875	3,977	4,057	4,138	4,276	4,400	4,377	4,300	4,362	4,317	4,312	4,350	4,520	4,645	4,910	5,031	5,043
Mobile, AL	15,396	15,486	15,652	16,155	16,751	17,762	17,918	18,056	17,986	18,232	18,607	18,397	18,504	18,549	18,433	18,729	18,640	18,971	19,274
Modesto, CA	15,731	16,389	17,135	18,200	18,867	19,833	19,493	18,886	18,432	18,372	18,457	18,238	18,524	19,893	20,744	21,218	22,237	22,847	23,716
Monroe, LA	6,453	6,915	7,090	7,455	7,772	7,822	6,888	6,678	7,116	7,214	6,984	7,088	7,470	7,598	7,828	7,854	7,700	7,884	7,760
Monroe, MI	5,299	5,578	5,701	5,596	5,600	5,781	5,760	5,455	5,054	5,340	5,387	5,236	5,413	5,377	5,341	5,428	5,401	5,309	5,387
Montgomery, AL	13,531	13,813	14,170	14,811	15,294	15,718	15,621	15,443	14,948	15,359	15,560	15,590	15,607	15,405	15,718	16,014	15,933	16,031	16,178
Morgantown, WV	4,596	4,725	4,807	5,051	5,328	5,369	5,380	5,548	5,822	6,204	6,227	6,249	6,629	6,617	6,815	6,779	6,815	6,793	6,810
Morristown, TN	3,726	3,734	3,741	3,895	3,884	4,075	4,116	4,007	3,681	4,000	4,042	4,174	4,215	4,290	4,371	4,385	4,408	4,474	4,582
Mount Vernon-Anacortes, WA	5,168	6,208	5,936	5,562	6,788	6,427	6,595	6,698	6,885	6,898	5,702	5,564	5,907	6,189	7,201	7,115	7,196	7,544	7,765
Muncie, IN	4,201	4,177	4,289	4,177	4,109	4,181	3,990	3,908	3,746	4,037	4,306	3,590	3,636	3,642	3,636	3,610	3,674	3,683	3,760
Muskegon, MI	5,340	5,424	5,411	5,460	5,534	5,577	5,536	5,383	5,116	5,286	5,355	5,505	5,658	5,744	5,851	5,798	5,806	5,876	5,857
Myrtle Beach-Conway-North Myrtle Beach, SC-NC	11,007	11,214	11,732	12,509	13,466	13,243	13,382	12,851	12,138	12,247	12,450	12,380	12,774	13,332	13,691	14,219	14,946	15,326	15,831
Napa, CA	7,287	7,632	7,709	7,591	7,976	8,187	8,367	8,234	7,932	7,773	7,783	8,163	8,524	9,075	9,601	9,757	9,974	10,053	10,284
Naples-Marco Island, FL	11,922	12,489	13,062	13,631	15,070	15,264	14,918	13,489	12,319	12,585	12,462	12,446	12,704	13,460	14,306	14,907	15,160	15,761	16,352
Nashville-Davidson--Murfreesboro--Franklin, TN	67,202	69,817	73,207	77,772	80,385	83,511	83,219	86,655	84,776	86,094	89,181	94,198	96,317	100,919	107,697	110,936	114,606	118,460	121,217
New Bern, NC	4,292	4,225	4,406	4,588	4,909	5,000	5,171	5,085	4,951	5,077	4,984	4,929	5,130	5,290	5,276	4,916	4,883	4,936	5,120
New Haven-Milford, CT	41,623	42,857	42,888	45,842	46,385	47,987	48,182	48,524	46,559	47,045	46,525	45,431	45,589	45,167	45,696	46,342	46,679	47,660	48,368
New Orleans-Metairie, LA	73,324	74,972	78,750	81,032	83,716	78,703	82,598	86,421	85,837	92,807	70,812	71,495	68,882	69,962	70,443	70,553	73,960	74,913	77,291
New York-Newark-Jersey City, NY-NJ-PA	1,204,162	1,198,047	1,201,827	1,228,206	1,266,533	1,291,805	1,299,846	1,272,071	1,300,131	1,343,980	1,344,867	1,401,401	1,409,971	1,429,859	1,459,526	1,488,016	1,511,895	1,555,852	1,573,857
Niles, MI	6,225	6,373	6,462	6,646	6,479	6,743	7,032	6,566	5,739	6,346	6,392	6,362	6,449	6,491	6,622	6,906	7,232	7,140	7,043
North Port-Sarasota-Bradenton, FL	21,231	22,917	24,129	26,441	29,055	30,159	28,963	26,493	24,690	24,102	24,087	23,827	24,469	25,624	27,369	28,245	29,127	30,692	31,736
Norwich-New London, CT	14,406	15,129	15,994	17,728	18,385	19,547	20,886	19,319	17,174	17,023	16,842	16,725	17,138	16,116	16,561	16,545	17,283	17,218	17,345
Ocala, FL	6,470	6,736	7,170	7,585	8,255	9,259	9,372	9,114	8,220	8,086	7,892	7,795	7,841	7,916	8,133	8,617	8,680	8,962	9,331
Ocean City, NJ	4,391	4,604	4,831	5,031	5,187	5,252	5,170	4,992	4,815	4,881	4,854	4,832	4,839	4,883	4,867	4,855	4,801	4,736	5,071
Odessa, TX	5,651	6,060	5,780	5,997	6,151	7,207	7,958	8,631	8,864	9,363	10,918	12,860	13,034	13,146	11,653	10,231	11,096	12,985	13,450
Ogden-Clearfield, UT	16,509	16,951	17,319	17,718	18,649	20,481	21,148	20,954	20,976	21,200	21,292	21,007	21,856	22,093	22,724	23,771	25,230	26,103	27,150
Oklahoma City, OK	45,170	46,025	47,641	49,552	51,920	55,352	55,565	59,452	60,727	60,521	62,778	66,629	69,128	72,108	76,979	75,905	76,092	78,391	79,298
Olympia-Lacey-Tumwater, WA	8,542	8,657	8,786	8,871	9,237	9,723	10,278	10,587	10,261	10,295	10,128	10,220	10,396	10,657	10,642	11,203	11,686	12,486	12,795
Omaha-Council Bluffs, NE-IA	38,514	39,601	41,184	43,053	44,199	45,123	46,304	46,262	46,427	47,789	50,202	50,840	49,688	52,316	53,922	53,749	56,261	56,531	57,996
Orlando-Kissimmee-Sanford, FL	82,037	85,203	89,410	94,758	102,118	103,950	105,373	102,483	95,631	96,455	96,479	98,829	101,555	105,289	110,636	115,044	120,015	125,336	128,416
Oshkosh-Neenah, WI	7,795	8,534	8,593	8,705	8,787	8,917	8,911	8,732	8,537	8,745	8,861	8,973	8,876	8,982	8,995	9,266	9,258	9,484	9,725
Owensboro, KY	4,207	4,462	4,687	4,679	4,675	4,896	4,741	4,958	4,848	5,070	5,125	5,113	5,385	5,310	5,316	5,298	5,291	5,365	5,417
Oxnard-Thousand Oaks-Ventura, CA	36,573	37,574	40,042	44,211	46,427	52,306	55,781	50,806	50,054	49,497	46,542	45,712	46,497	46,549	47,061	46,985	46,652	47,163	48,497
Palm Bay-Melbourne-Titusville, FL	14,929	15,397	16,358	17,898	19,200	20,482	21,551	21,687	20,499	20,503	19,818	19,230	19,455	19,850	20,662	21,365	22,339	23,300	24,620
Panama City, FL	5,672	6,021	6,295	6,847	7,353	7,692	7,605	7,550	7,309	7,201	7,051	6,967	7,029	7,193	7,350	7,458	7,553	7,716	7,772
Parkersburg-Vienna, WV	3,445	3,572	3,567	3,564	3,528	3,710	3,540	3,595	3,698	3,624	3,608	3,543	3,396	3,372	3,328	3,238	3,194	3,216	3,253
Pensacola-Ferry Pass-Brent, FL	14,111	14,329	14,804	15,430	16,005	17,039	16,997	16,530	16,014	16,124	16,243	16,263	16,416	16,477	17,140	17,404	17,679	18,203	19,066
Peoria, IL	17,198	17,111	17,438	18,129	19,010	20,562	21,611	21,994	21,449	23,254	26,224	29,087	24,931	24,314	22,296	21,088	20,273	20,835	20,426
Philadelphia-Camden-Wilmington, PA-NJ-DE-MD	307,643	310,000	323,249	336,224	339,246	341,405	352,706	359,897	348,184	354,539	357,109	365,408	367,719	376,397	383,848	387,979	385,819	392,232	401,232
Phoenix-Mesa-Chandler, AZ	149,882	155,181	165,897	174,443	189,816	199,999	204,387	198,046	180,352	181,321	186,581	192,596	194,099	198,201	205,614	212,665	220,056	229,977	237,473
Pine Bluff, AR	3,593	3,566	3,698	3,857	3,844	3,892	3,702	3,732	3,648	3,750	3,680	3,712	3,809	3,593	3,441	3,404	3,335	3,312	3,259
Pittsburgh, PA	106,180	107,431	109,906	111,898	112,755	112,366	114,894	117,907	115,962	120,787	123,583	125,266	127,199	130,279	134,520	134,471	137,423	142,471	145,530
Pittsfield, MA	5,686	5,859	5,771	5,905	6,056	6,168	6,096	6,115	6,020	6,112	6,219	6,487	6,506	6,637	6,627	6,521	6,382	6,523	6,649
Pocatello, ID	2,721	2,582	2,601	2,780	2,943	3,019	3,048	3,132	3,008	2,979	2,964	2,955	2,931	2,878	2,932	2,945	3,033	3,141	3,230
Portland-South Portland, ME	22,658	22,924	23,843	24,880	24,944	24,918	24,816	25,004	24,749	25,091	25,002	25,075	24,822	25,550	25,941	26,696	27,448	28,328	28,785
Portland-Vancouver-Hillsboro, OR-WA	87,365	88,335	93,756	99,619	104,063	109,118	111,941	116,509	111,002	113,419	117,600	119,339	120,190	124,562	131,444	137,862	144,514	152,388	156,663
Port St. Lucie, FL	10,568	11,095	11,451	12,622	13,953	14,944	15,065	14,278	13,640	13,553	13,266	13,416	13,490	13,441	13,984	14,275	14,621	15,063	15,545
Poughkeepsie-Newburgh-Middletown,	21,267	21,588	22,783	23,565	24,071	24,420	24,688	25,630	25,776	26,382	26,244	26,570	26,531	26,447	27,063	27,278	27,838	28,794	29,747
Prescott Valley-Prescott, AZ	4,429	4,666	4,985	5,357	5,915	6,411	6,402	6,207	5,732	5,554	5,409	5,407	5,510	5,713	5,828	6,022	6,343	6,439	6,592

Gross Domestic Product by Metropolitan Statistical Area—*Continued*

(Millions of chained 2012 dollars.)

Metropolitan Statistical Area	2001	2002	2003	2004	2005	2006	2007	2008	2009	2010	2011	2012	2013	2014	2015	2016	2017	2018	2019
Providence-Warwick, -MA	65,571	67,599	69,807	71,905	72,594	74,843	73,152	72,095	70,962	72,677	72,885	73,190	73,501	74,497	76,585	76,638	77,138	78,023	79,008
Provo-Orem,	11,062	11,255	11,687	12,431	13,350	14,663	15,939	16,000	16,126	16,510	16,996	17,331	18,024	18,894	20,345	21,679	22,836	24,917	26,353
Pueblo, CO	4,471	4,549	4,671	4,911	4,614	4,890	4,926	5,232	5,188	5,318	5,480	5,631	5,526	5,462	5,649	5,782	5,928	6,061	6,268
Punta Gorda,	3,364	3,529	3,665	3,875	4,275	4,552	4,416	4,203	3,970	3,896	3,868	3,887	3,946	3,978	4,191	4,345	4,463	4,627	4,953
Racine, WI	7,920	7,938	8,100	8,364	8,276	8,544	8,269	7,998	7,703	8,158	8,091	8,060	7,805	7,868	7,741	7,651	7,531	7,743	7,799
Raleigh-Cary, NC	42,186	43,314	44,450	46,443	49,128	51,731	53,826	55,093	52,468	55,720	55,963	57,352	60,730	64,347	69,268	73,363	77,544	82,217	84,679
Rapid City, SD	4,305	4,852	4,888	4,724	4,881	4,713	4,813	4,935	4,834	4,985	5,095	5,173	5,133	5,296	5,392	5,404	5,510	5,585	5,657
Reading, PA	14,714	14,905	15,146	15,372	15,650	16,497	16,488	16,490	15,904	16,323	16,611	16,669	16,808	17,373	18,152	18,281	18,077	18,529	18,833
Redding, CA	6,120	6,853	7,098	7,028	6,924	7,520	7,351	6,931	6,590	6,779	6,943	6,692	6,799	6,913	7,134	7,446	7,852	7,827	8,413
Reno, NV	19,754	19,927	20,524	22,178	23,246	23,630	23,233	21,919	20,454	21,464	21,111	21,360	21,093	21,380	23,061	23,975	25,379	25,048	25,811
Richmond, VA	60,765	59,182	60,213	60,845	64,121	64,958	65,439	64,785	63,371	64,990	66,617	67,860	69,671	70,118	73,193	74,032	75,956	77,162	78,702
Riverside-San Bernardino-Ontario, CA	101,161	106,878	115,026	124,009	132,164	140,464	141,826	136,795	127,433	128,316	131,792	132,669	137,406	143,289	151,136	155,514	160,344	164,487	171,884
Roanoke, VA	13,287	13,228	13,415	13,428	14,038	14,676	15,049	14,953	14,447	14,562	14,619	14,533	14,726	14,810	15,262	14,991	14,905	15,106	15,407
Rochester, MN	7,839	8,377	9,016	9,478	9,644	9,959	9,991	10,247	10,062	10,651	10,677	10,875	11,214	11,188	11,549	11,762	12,193	12,740	12,894
Rochester, NY	50,034	50,812	51,349	51,342	51,766	53,075	53,176	53,565	53,737	55,031	53,982	54,310	53,663	52,986	54,107	54,274	54,661	55,374	56,728
Rockford, IL	12,859	13,091	13,370	13,706	13,985	14,803	14,992	14,762	13,527	13,745	14,193	14,198	13,911	14,122	14,222	14,213	14,457	14,922	14,843
Rocky Mount, NC	6,014	5,915	5,989	6,001	6,083	6,389	6,420	6,380	7,525	6,939	6,406	5,579	5,629	7,003	8,355	8,669	8,200	8,128	6,591
Rome, GA	4,105	3,651	3,683	3,841	3,736	3,842	3,885	3,866	3,738	3,750	3,756	3,681	3,601	3,726	3,865	3,972	3,880	3,882	3,961
Sacramento-Roseville-Folsom, CA	87,562	91,041	96,653	100,732	106,093	109,282	109,810	109,000	104,267	101,992	103,745	104,795	108,140	111,615	116,823	119,486	123,125	127,056	132,502
Saginaw, MI	7,678	7,861	8,203	8,059	8,143	8,063	7,858	7,331	6,859	7,330	7,437	7,397	7,476	7,351	7,402	7,573	7,461	7,642	7,666
St. Cloud, MN	7,281	7,501	7,565	7,904	7,998	8,208	8,206	8,371	8,124	8,194	8,435	8,425	8,662	9,068	9,254	9,528	9,711	9,818	9,822
St. George, UT	2,565	2,697	2,893	3,153	3,499	3,914	4,049	3,876	3,520	3,489	3,518	3,656	3,902	4,098	4,343	4,695	5,193	5,550	5,623
St. Joseph, MO-KS	4,352	4,463	4,540	4,790	4,774	4,943	5,014	5,181	5,083	5,108	5,118	5,486	5,604	5,395	5,233	5,257	5,428	5,511	5,626
St. Louis, -IL	131,942	133,753	137,841	140,064	142,189	141,644	142,227	146,239	142,691	144,857	144,509	145,746	144,482	144,258	146,348	146,024	147,958	150,858	152,402
Salem, OR	11,616	11,757	12,098	12,248	12,763	13,925	13,747	13,841	13,231	13,249	13,097	13,043	13,219	13,581	14,430	15,196	15,912	16,772	17,249
Salinas, CA	20,892	22,162	22,254	20,132	20,668	22,729	21,791	21,260	22,537	21,872	20,721	21,345	22,704	23,311	25,382	26,038	26,214	26,821	27,581
Salisbury, MD-DE	14,545	14,218	14,613	15,443	16,458	17,174	17,309	17,164	16,843	16,417	16,265	16,562	17,291	18,359	19,997	19,590	19,247	19,666	20,314
Salt Lake City, UT	50,988	52,014	52,551	55,615	58,792	63,095	66,161	65,112	63,199	64,807	67,667	69,286	70,426	72,477	75,299	78,243	80,548	85,199	88,155
San Angelo, TX	4,306	4,256	4,135	4,141	4,212	4,395	4,525	4,701	4,891	5,164	5,446	6,081	6,763	7,371	7,556	7,197	7,243	7,560	7,882
San Antonio-New Braunfels, TX	66,756	68,952	71,811	74,265	76,672	80,634	83,263	84,299	82,632	85,718	89,447	91,696	95,257	100,318	106,396	107,936	108,684	113,555	115,621
San Diego-Chula Vista-Carlsbad, CA	144,585	151,099	159,728	169,143	178,151	181,854	184,346	181,694	172,795	174,419	177,990	180,310	187,350	193,818	201,167	204,667	211,115	217,510	222,273
San Francisco-Oakland-Berkeley, CA	309,092	304,321	309,933	315,457	329,666	338,159	339,128	354,036	337,953	337,490	339,659	366,309	381,122	406,460	431,327	457,517	491,152	511,920	531,247
San Jose-Sunnyvale-Santa Clara, CA	117,253	112,251	118,848	123,949	131,701	141,665	154,536	162,559	159,286	173,300	186,677	193,278	211,305	227,332	249,529	265,882	284,621	306,243	320,444
San Luis Obispo-Paso Robles, CA	10,976	12,178	12,523	12,634	13,074	13,724	13,690	12,777	12,496	13,072	13,373	13,751	14,249	14,505	15,358	15,632	15,842	16,352	16,661
Santa Cruz-Watsonville, CA	10,972	10,976	11,167	11,031	11,044	11,504	11,461	11,332	11,456	12,274	12,122	11,944	12,323	12,744	13,012	13,209	13,388	13,838	14,407
Santa Fe, NM	5,517	6,191	5,640	5,711	5,917	6,094	6,372	6,605	6,090	6,080	5,969	5,904	5,882	5,806	5,838	5,809	5,769	5,865	5,977
Santa Maria-Santa Barbara, CA	18,036	18,832	19,680	20,440	21,366	22,147	22,454	22,437	22,724	22,491	22,728	23,166	23,615	24,339	25,818	25,972	26,806	27,672	28,412
Santa Rosa-Petaluma, CA	20,731	21,666	21,683	21,714	22,109	23,029	23,293	22,770	21,765	22,174	22,642	22,863	23,577	24,669	25,919	26,507	27,304	28,320	29,064
Savannah, GA	12,387	12,611	12,963	13,678	14,509	15,394	15,614	15,382	15,155	15,458	15,745	16,212	16,430	17,169	17,816	18,264	18,752	19,365	19,536
Scranton--Wilkes-Barre, PA	20,345	20,261	20,661	21,142	21,376	21,993	22,497	22,920	22,739	23,318	23,493	23,497	23,673	24,191	24,893	25,238	25,440	25,843	26,499
Seattle-Tacoma-Bellevue, WA	199,791	200,395	203,309	207,300	221,587	230,088	246,611	250,274	242,185	247,946	256,143	268,999	278,716	290,986	306,169	318,442	337,742	364,164	382,630
Sebastian-Vero Beach, FL	3,850	4,052	4,311	4,560	4,955	5,185	5,156	4,987	4,652	4,468	4,459	4,519	4,604	4,825	5,100	5,392	5,567	5,735	5,967
Sebring-Avon Park, FL	1,892	2,042	2,105	2,235	2,399	2,763	2,727	2,569	2,520	2,441	2,359	2,383	2,282	2,290	2,345	2,400	2,450	2,457	2,627
Sheboygan, WI	5,579	5,688	5,827	6,199	6,034	6,102	6,168	6,088	5,773	5,911	5,889	6,033	6,019	6,108	6,265	6,467	6,583	6,688	6,735
Sherman-Denison, TX .	3,072	3,137	3,208	3,414	3,419	3,699	3,722	3,787	3,794	3,854	4,071	4,185	4,214	4,279	4,412	4,454	4,587	4,798	4,866
Shreveport-Bossier City, LA	15,379	15,494	16,082	16,884	17,818	18,409	16,979	17,161	19,937	20,971	22,020	20,814	19,306	19,221	19,877	19,741	20,531	20,954	21,555
Sierra Vista-Douglas, AZ	3,367	3,420	3,672	3,799	4,048	4,277	4,541	4,559	4,569	4,715	4,691	4,472	4,352	4,249	4,325	4,437	4,372	4,416	4,589
Sioux City, IA-NE-SD ...	7,633	6,888	6,750	7,158	7,428	7,614	7,775	8,184	7,676	7,855	7,521	7,199	7,099	7,033	7,372	7,435	7,314	7,589	7,681
Sioux Falls, SD	8,997	10,500	10,446	12,225	13,078	14,225	14,521	14,818	15,209	14,856	15,820	17,052	16,463	17,109	17,371	17,520	17,568	18,056	18,367
South Bend-Mishawaka, IN-MI ...	11,581	11,931	12,485	12,808	12,814	13,125	13,196	12,750	11,522	12,125	12,203	12,310	12,401	12,911	13,107	13,102	13,227	13,686	14,032
Spartanburg,	9,850	10,169	10,634	11,260	11,617	12,286	12,161	11,947	10,890	11,389	11,554	11,286	11,474	11,640	12,110	12,835	13,702	14,141	14,675
Spokane-Spokane Valley, WA	17,425	17,400	17,833	18,446	19,331	20,368	21,274	21,578	20,870	20,875	20,957	21,098	21,530	22,015	22,410	23,101	24,175	25,754	26,873
Springfield, IL	9,843	10,041	9,817	9,852	9,809	10,084	10,117	10,080	10,108	10,337	10,380	10,162	10,146	10,326	10,330	10,319	10,458	10,860	10,944
Springfield, MA	26,176	26,529	27,142	27,398	27,378	27,568	27,478	27,680	27,109	27,805	28,382	28,740	28,701	29,024	29,779	29,968	30,361	30,723	31,177
Springfield, MO	13,903	14,273	14,910	15,581	16,283	16,436	16,508	16,764	16,311	16,209	16,085	16,221	16,118	16,603	17,151	17,195	17,430	17,946	18,068

Gross Domestic Product by Metropolitan Statistical Area—*Continued*

(Millions of chained 2012 dollars.)

Metropolitan Statistical Area	2001	2002	2003	2004	2005	2006	2007	2008	2009	2010	2011	2012	2013	2014	2015	2016	2017	2018	2019
Springfield, ...	4,307	4,360	4,306	4,466	4,450	4,618	4,354	4,233	4,023	4,077	4,178	4,135	4,164	4,207	4,211	4,191	4,216	4,293	4,328
State College, PA	5,436	5,590	5,724	5,989	6,330	6,311	6,412	6,604	6,628	6,876	7,085	7,224	7,339	7,417	7,529	7,726	7,912	7,900	7,983
Staunton, VA	4,494	4,260	4,184	4,458	4,648	4,752	4,837	4,847	4,950	5,033	4,884	4,675	4,710	4,719	4,707	4,669	4,700	4,767	4,848
Stockton, CA	20,788	21,805	22,880	24,007	25,239	25,685	25,403	24,549	23,842	23,299	23,152	23,490	24,337	25,317	26,893	27,434	28,468	29,554	30,486
Sumter, SC	3,608	3,654	3,785	3,879	3,918	4,113	4,168	4,058	3,941	4,048	4,088	4,250	4,288	4,133	4,152	4,147	4,342	4,437	4,575
Syracuse, NY	29,365	29,631	30,449	31,072	31,679	32,274	32,861	32,604	32,766	33,826	33,366	34,299	34,784	35,083	35,831	35,551	36,078	36,735	37,721
Tallahassee, ...	13,849	14,169	14,395	14,809	14,831	15,462	15,960	15,605	15,210	15,026	14,892	14,911	14,671	14,895	15,088	15,411	15,876	16,253	16,622
Tampa-St. Petersburg-Clearwater,	100,196	104,365	109,167	115,581	121,958	126,188	126,551	122,798	118,569	119,282	119,401	120,987	122,962	125,090	130,615	134,637	137,800	143,153	148,372
Terre Haute, IN	6,241	6,434	6,709	6,838	6,807	6,981	7,098	7,145	6,814	7,126	7,154	6,991	7,742	7,704	7,283	7,173	7,046	7,012	7,105
Texarkana, TX-AR	4,562	4,672	4,692	4,864	4,984	5,272	5,316	5,429	5,288	5,324	5,353	5,326	5,076	4,991	5,053	5,070	5,056	5,096	5,142
The Villages, ...	936	1,023	1,186	1,235	1,432	1,688	1,822	1,791	1,736	1,793	1,898	2,010	2,126	2,154	2,210	2,245	2,364	2,525	2,690
Toledo, OH	31,565	32,008	32,288	32,555	33,331	33,748	33,262	31,779	30,689	31,655	32,710	31,748	32,550	34,680	33,054	33,073	33,167	34,315	34,905
Topeka, KS	9,183	9,265	9,280	9,453	9,345	9,094	9,486	9,682	9,560	9,557	9,847	9,971	9,774	9,949	10,093	10,267	10,365	10,593	10,561
Trenton-Princeton, NJ .	24,556	25,301	25,830	26,126	26,464	26,761	26,408	27,512	26,481	26,693	26,782	28,353	28,495	28,141	28,694	29,707	29,667	30,121	31,468
Tucson, AZ	31,684	31,630	33,580	33,290	35,119	36,453	37,914	37,892	35,483	36,205	36,127	36,578	36,237	36,440	36,443	37,820	39,683	41,021	42,169
Tulsa, OK	38,068	38,032	37,444	38,473	40,674	44,706	44,729	46,091	43,563	42,767	45,172	47,440	48,198	51,537	52,817	49,664	50,635	52,593	54,232
Tuscaloosa, ...	8,237	8,700	9,170	9,808	10,265	10,351	10,821	10,325	9,503	9,827	10,652	10,189	10,474	10,168	9,922	10,068	10,392	10,663	11,046
Twin Falls, ID	2,989	3,035	3,054	3,219	3,387	3,609	3,802	3,757	3,405	3,611	3,578	3,737	3,915	4,135	4,259	4,489	4,567	4,740	4,901
Tyler, TX	7,381	7,394	7,544	8,423	8,814	9,367	9,377	9,304	9,170	9,406	9,452	9,655	9,741	9,717	9,907	9,982	9,895	10,273	10,390
Urban Honolulu, HI	42,666	43,808	45,639	48,381	50,439	51,285	51,936	52,917	51,888	53,260	54,035	54,967	55,591	55,742	58,503	59,331	60,743	61,309	61,094
Utica-Rome, ...	10,022	10,255	10,368	10,469	10,530	11,188	11,386	11,306	11,358	11,614	11,540	11,607	11,518	11,371	11,306	11,467	11,655	11,949	12,526
Valdosta, GA	3,980	4,148	4,305	4,340	4,511	4,670	4,696	4,771	4,703	4,725	4,669	4,691	4,673	4,676	4,745	4,810	4,923	5,071	5,172
Vallejo, CA	14,662	15,110	16,505	16,701	17,198	17,364	17,831	19,249	18,276	18,278	17,722	19,184	20,301	20,669	20,980	21,471	21,429	21,855	22,638
Victoria, TX	4,318	4,247	4,287	4,510	4,762	5,157	4,920	4,776	4,404	4,471	4,584	4,891	5,012	5,052	4,682	4,308	4,297	4,518	4,508
Vineland-Bridgeton, NJ	5,390	5,480	5,802	6,042	6,155	6,242	6,102	6,194	6,062	5,985	5,859	5,880	5,888	5,868	5,968	6,065	5,913	5,907	6,008
Virginia Beach-Norfolk-Newport News, VA-NC	72,930	74,170	77,558	81,272	84,762	85,470	86,244	85,850	85,065	85,135	84,961	84,115	84,503	83,830	86,340	86,059	86,529	87,872	89,523
Visalia, CA	11,388	10,717	11,414	12,645	14,000	13,870	15,259	14,407	13,104	14,181	14,733	13,982	14,423	16,238	16,393	17,362	18,223	18,271	19,351
Waco, TX	7,904	8,036	8,349	8,623	8,717	9,108	9,189	9,155	9,080	9,237	9,404	9,850	10,716	11,141	10,915	11,124	11,513	11,884	11,860
Walla Walla, WA	2,440	2,280	2,367	2,298	2,376	2,708	2,586	2,655	2,729	2,684	2,808	2,766	2,734	2,797	3,018	3,222	3,336	3,426	3,514
Warner Robins, GA	5,300	5,508	5,683	5,852	6,038	6,352	6,416	6,401	6,368	6,439	6,526	6,510	6,424	6,434	6,492	6,573	6,746	6,959	7,213
Washington-Arlington-Alexandria, DC-VA-MD-WV	332,430	344,821	358,157	381,067	400,320	401,226	405,860	414,855	415,637	432,841	441,528	444,840	442,709	447,671	456,753	468,369	476,310	484,615	492,130
Waterloo-Cedar Falls, IA	6,497	6,805	6,770	7,668	7,938	7,880	8,107	7,898	7,958	8,466	8,385	10,035	8,853	9,854	9,261	8,367	8,308	8,629	8,536
Watertown-Fort Drum, NY	4,479	4,503	4,684	4,932	5,434	5,985	6,053	6,325	6,465	6,765	6,894	6,665	6,508	6,348	6,116	5,910	5,827	5,851	5,873
Wausau-Weston, WI ...	6,681	6,850	7,140	7,443	7,704	7,877	7,896	7,754	7,439	7,580	7,877	7,997	8,060	8,419	8,618	8,873	8,949	9,300	9,467
Weirton-Steubenville, WV-OH	5,329	5,592	5,434	5,200	5,209	4,963	5,138	5,540	5,069	5,061	4,913	4,939	5,561	6,217	6,757	5,400	5,819	6,113	6,919
Wenatchee, ...	3,977	4,396	4,367	4,384	4,123	4,655	4,686	4,573	4,589	4,809	5,310	5,312	5,227	5,233	5,588	5,752	5,999	6,070	6,098
Wheeling, WV-OH	6,027	6,075	6,135	6,135	6,252	6,301	6,390	6,534	6,381	6,441	6,474	6,446	7,139	8,277	9,781	10,857	12,121	12,218	12,249
Wichita, KS	25,923	25,666	25,253	25,186	25,324	27,925	29,756	29,712	26,534	27,718	28,416	28,346	26,664	28,294	29,886	32,388	32,961	33,495	33,976
Wichita Falls, TX	5,397	5,482	5,408	5,353	5,313	5,704	5,708	5,768	5,735	5,723	5,681	5,914	5,872	5,817	5,727	5,800	5,844	5,954	6,154
Williamsport, PA	4,093	4,017	4,134	4,254	4,335	4,395	4,403	4,397	4,418	4,747	5,286	5,769	6,021	6,569	6,523	6,405	6,448	6,355	6,442
Wilmington, ...	8,706	8,919	9,181	9,474	10,196	10,771	11,291	11,429	10,915	11,136	11,193	10,515	11,112	11,599	11,778	12,229	12,289	12,829	13,276
Winchester, VA-WV	4,728	4,805	4,912	5,085	5,443	5,651	5,581	5,581	5,367	5,483	5,647	5,665	5,750	5,788	5,904	5,908	5,998	6,131	6,270
Winston-Salem, NC	26,880	26,785	27,532	28,648	29,102	30,233	29,723	30,612	29,530	29,488	28,200	28,299	28,676	29,254	29,403	29,555	30,010	30,228	30,879
Worcester, MA-CT	34,312	35,347	36,726	37,201	37,465	39,142	39,465	39,566	38,309	39,898	41,338	41,607	41,890	42,040	42,962	43,388	43,961	44,662	45,528
Yakima, WA	6,865	7,181	7,458	7,745	7,936	8,236	8,803	8,583	8,401	8,719	8,723	8,748	8,714	9,330	9,370	9,840	10,158	10,699	11,038
York-Hanover, PA	14,756	15,020	15,651	16,636	17,519	17,314	18,128	18,838	17,753	18,047	18,048	17,655	17,789	17,834	18,153	18,397	18,696	18,913	19,163
Youngstown-Warren-Boardman, OH-PA ...	20,337	20,998	21,157	21,638	21,988	22,141	21,648	21,022	18,953	19,604	20,336	19,931	19,926	19,831	19,751	19,567	19,148	19,455	19,795
Yuba City, ...	4,604	5,290	5,443	5,533	5,469	5,970	5,974	6,307	6,544	6,239	6,086	5,856	6,104	5,923	6,127	6,305	6,503	6,709	7,109
Yuma, AZ	4,839	5,572	5,431	5,963	6,394	6,830	7,207	6,662	6,366	6,633	6,480	6,016	6,323	6,232	6,714	7,134	7,405	7,566	7,927

Quantity Indexes for Real GDP by Metropolitan Area

(2012 = 100.0)

Metropolitan Statistical Area	2001	2002	2003	2004	2005	2006	2007	2008	2009	2010	2011	2012	2013	2014	2015	2016	2017	2018	2019
Abilene, TX	77.2	78.0	79.2	81.3	82.8	90.3	94.0	95.9	93.6	96.7	97.1	100.0	100.3	101.8	100.3	99.0	100.3	105.3	108.4
Akron, OH	91.8	95.5	97.9	99.9	102.1	102.3	103.5	102.8	96.5	99.0	99.5	100.0	101.0	103.4	104.6	104.9	105.8	107.8	108.5
Albany, GA	100.8	102.3	103.0	104.2	106.9	106.5	104.3	102.1	100.4	98.0	99.6	100.0	99.4	98.1	97.6	99.2	99.0	100.5	104.8
Albany-Lebanon, OR	93.0	98.7	94.3	101.0	102.8	112.6	106.8	102.6	100.5	98.5	99.7	100.0	102.0	102.8	110.5	116.3	116.9	124.9	128.8
Albany-Schenectady-Troy, NY	86.1	87.3	89.9	91.7	92.8	95.6	95.9	97.2	99.1	99.5	99.5	100.0	101.2	102.5	105.1	108.1	110.7	112.3	115.0
Albuquerque, NM	80.7	81.5	89.5	101.6	101.4	102.7	101.1	100.3	103.7	101.6	100.5	100.0	97.1	99.5	101.0	102.6	102.1	103.8	105.9
Alexandria, LA	85.2	88.0	88.6	92.8	97.6	99.3	95.5	96.0	100.2	101.8	101.6	100.0	98.9	97.9	96.1	97.4	98.4	99.8	100.5
Allentown-Bethlehem-Easton, PA-NJ	113.5	113.3	102.7	94.4	94.6	94.8	99.1	100.0	97.1	99.9	100.3	100.0	101.3	103.1	105.5	107.7	108.1	109.0	112.7
Altoona, PA	89.3	88.9	91.3	94.3	97.6	101.2	100.5	100.7	99.1	100.8	99.7	100.0	101.0	101.8	102.9	103.5	106.1	106.5	109.5
Amarillo, TX	83.3	85.3	86.4	87.4	87.7	93.2	96.2	97.3	97.2	100.4	100.9	100.0	101.2	103.6	107.1	106.6	106.7	110.0	110.6
Ames, IA	75.7	78.9	81.9	85.0	86.7	89.3	90.9	94.1	90.8	91.0	95.1	100.0	104.9	107.6	107.1	105.8	107.6	110.4	110.4
Anchorage, AK	77.3	78.4	80.1	81.6	84.8	85.2	86.6	90.7	94.5	98.5	100.2	100.0	97.6	97.9	102.3	101.7	100.0	100.7	101.4
Ann Arbor, MI	99.6	105.4	107.3	106.2	108.2	105.3	107.3	101.4	94.0	96.9	98.0	100.0	101.1	102.6	107.1	110.0	113.0	116.7	117.8
Anniston-Oxford, AL	82.5	85.1	87.7	94.5	98.8	101.4	105.0	106.4	101.3	104.7	101.0	100.0	96.3	93.1	91.6	92.3	92.7	94.5	96.8
Appleton, WI	86.5	86.6	89.1	91.8	94.2	95.4	96.8	95.0	92.5	94.0	96.9	100.0	98.6	102.2	107.8	111.3	113.1	116.5	119.1
Asheville, NC	87.6	90.4	91.8	94.5	97.2	102.1	100.3	100.3	95.9	99.9	101.3	100.0	102.4	105.5	108.2	111.1	115.7	120.5	124.1
Athens-Clarke County, GA	85.1	86.4	90.7	92.5	94.2	95.5	96.8	97.2	96.4	96.9	96.5	100.0	101.9	104.4	107.9	109.7	115.7	120.3	118.3
Atlanta-Sandy Springs-Alpharetta, GA	88.9	89.9	92.5	97.1	101.6	101.9	102.3	99.4	94.8	96.5	98.6	100.0	102.0	106.8	112.0	117.2	122.3	127.5	129.4
Atlantic City-Hammonton, NJ	98.9	102.2	103.7	104.4	107.6	114.7	114.3	114.3	101.2	98.3	101.5	100.0	99.3	97.0	93.8	92.2	90.9	90.9	92.2
Auburn-Opelika, AL	65.4	68.7	72.0	79.6	82.3	85.2	88.5	88.0	87.0	88.9	96.7	100.0	101.8	102.5	106.7	110.2	112.1	113.1	114.1
Augusta-Richmond County, GA-SC	86.6	87.5	90.5	92.3	91.9	93.0	97.0	98.6	96.8	98.6	99.7	100.0	99.6	100.3	104.2	105.5	107.7	110.2	112.8
Austin-Round Rock-Georgetown, TX	61.9	63.5	65.3	68.3	73.9	82.4	86.5	90.2	88.1	93.7	97.6	100.0	104.6	110.3	119.5	125.8	134.0	140.4	144.8
Bakersfield, CA	58.1	65.8	65.8	71.7	76.7	88.9	96.8	94.1	99.8	94.8	92.3	100.0	98.0	99.6	100.6	100.5	101.8	103.6	108.1
Baltimore-Columbia-Towson, MD	79.4	82.0	83.4	86.9	91.2	94.0	94.2	94.5	94.1	97.2	99.1	100.0	100.8	102.6	105.2	108.2	110.0	112.0	113.9
Bangor, ME	100.5	103.2	102.7	105.9	106.4	107.5	105.9	104.8	104.4	104.0	101.3	100.0	98.8	99.3	99.2	101.3	101.9	105.1	107.6
Barnstable Town, MA	89.7	92.5	95.6	98.5	97.0	97.9	96.5	96.3	95.4	97.7	99.9	100.0	100.3	101.5	103.7	103.6	104.9	106.8	115.2
Baton Rouge, LA	73.0	77.9	80.8	88.9	97.9	95.7	88.4	85.8	86.4	90.2	100.1	100.0	100.1	109.9	109.8	105.0	98.3	102.9	103.4
Battle Creek, MI	103.8	104.9	106.8	108.9	110.9	113.3	114.3	110.3	101.2	103.0	100.9	100.0	102.2	102.5	105.7	108.0	108.6	109.0	108.2
Bay City, MI	100.4	101.0	102.1	101.6	101.7	103.4	102.9	100.0	97.3	100.5	100.3	100.0	100.2	95.1	95.9	94.9	93.4	94.7	94.8
Beaumont-Port Arthur, TX	82.1	79.3	80.7	94.7	85.5	86.4	94.2	90.6	91.3	99.6	99.2	100.0	99.7	83.5	83.6	87.4	89.5	95.3	94.9
Beckley, WV	88.8	89.6	88.3	90.1	94.7	94.6	95.5	99.6	98.4	101.8	103.5	100.0	97.4	90.6	88.2	83.3	85.5	88.1	89.9
Bellingham, WA	83.1	89.2	90.8	91.7	112.9	102.8	106.0	103.5	104.7	108.4	99.8	100.0	101.0	101.5	104.8	113.3	125.0	137.3	143.7
Bend, OR	83.8	88.0	92.8	95.8	105.1	111.5	114.0	109.5	99.7	96.5	96.4	100.0	106.2	115.9	126.5	137.1	149.8	156.8	160.3
Billings, MT	79.4	80.3	85.9	90.1	89.6	92.5	102.0	97.2	91.2	94.5	99.2	100.0	102.2	107.9	114.4	107.5	109.2	111.5	114.4
Binghamton, NY	77.1	76.5	76.3	76.9	78.9	85.0	89.3	94.0	95.4	99.5	98.7	100.0	99.9	98.5	98.7	96.6	96.3	98.0	101.8
Birmingham-Hoover, AL	88.9	92.0	93.3	98.0	100.8	99.6	100.4	100.8	95.6	96.3	98.6	100.0	99.6	99.5	101.1	101.6	103.3	105.6	106.5
Bismarck, ND	66.4	68.2	73.0	75.5	76.9	78.3	78.8	80.7	83.4	85.6	90.1	100.0	100.9	110.5	114.2	108.8	109.0	108.2	109.0
Blacksburg-Christiansburg, VA	87.4	88.6	94.0	94.9	100.5	107.0	109.7	102.9	97.2	97.8	100.6	100.0	100.7	104.4	107.7	108.6	104.7	108.3	110.2
Bloomington, IL	80.6	82.4	85.1	88.6	89.6	97.4	97.7	93.9	94.9	97.8	98.1	100.0	99.0	110.9	119.3	123.3	123.1	128.1	127.8
Bloomington, IN	87.0	89.5	91.9	94.3	98.1	100.8	98.6	98.8	97.8	98.9	99.4	100.0	101.4	106.3	105.8	108.3	112.7	115.9	116.4
Bloomsburg-Berwick, PA	77.4	81.6	81.3	85.6	88.0	93.9	92.0	93.2	93.0	96.9	100.0	100.0	101.8	99.8	101.6	101.4	101.2	101.4	102.5
Boise City, ID	76.5	78.7	83.4	89.4	98.9	99.4	100.3	102.9	98.3	99.1	99.1	100.0	104.5	109.3	111.8	117.2	124.6	133.7	138.3
Boston-Cambridge-Newton, MA-NH	80.4	80.2	82.4	84.9	87.1	88.3	91.1	91.7	91.2	95.4	97.6	100.0	100.5	102.3	106.7	108.8	111.7	116.1	118.7
Boulder, CO	87.7	81.6	82.2	84.9	86.6	89.5	94.5	98.3	97.0	99.4	99.3	100.0	102.7	106.2	111.0	115.0	122.5	126.9	134.6
Bowling Green, KY	76.8	79.5	82.9	86.4	91.9	96.2	95.3	96.5	89.2	97.0	97.1	100.0	100.9	103.0	104.1	106.4	108.4	109.7	111.7
Bremerton-Silverdale-Port Orchard, WA	84.8	89.4	91.0	94.4	98.3	100.6	101.6	105.0	102.5	101.9	101.0	100.0	99.2	101.1	103.7	107.8	111.3	117.1	121.9
Bridgeport-Stamford-Norwalk, CT	94.4	94.8	94.1	99.0	102.3	104.7	109.2	110.1	104.1	102.4	96.5	100.0	97.1	95.7	97.4	97.0	96.7	97.0	97.7
Brownsville-Harlingen, TX	77.5	81.3	82.7	83.9	86.2	90.7	91.2	92.4	92.4	96.6	98.9	100.0	101.4	100.9	101.6	103.5	104.5	107.5	110.5
Brunswick, GA	91.6	93.8	98.5	105.7	107.5	112.5	111.8	106.6	103.3	104.5	101.9	100.0	99.1	98.9	104.3	104.9	107.5	112.9	114.1
Buffalo-Cheektowaga, NY	83.1	85.3	86.5	89.0	90.0	94.4	95.1	95.5	95.4	98.6	97.7	100.0	99.7	101.3	103.2	104.0	104.3	106.3	109.7
Burlington, NC	89.7	94.2	93.8	98.6	98.7	103.4	101.8	101.4	94.3	98.8	100.9	100.0	99.8	99.6	100.5	104.0	104.9	106.8	109.6
Burlington-South Burlington, VT	74.9	77.0	82.0	87.3	88.4	90.2	88.1	92.7	92.0	97.0	99.3	100.0	97.9	98.4	100.9	102.8	104.0	106.2	106.0
California-Lexington Park, MD	64.1	68.9	73.1	76.4	78.8	83.1	85.0	85.5	89.0	95.9	100.0	100.0	99.0	100.4	102.0	104.0	104.4	107.2	110.8
Canton-Massillon, OH	96.8	98.7	98.9	100.3	101.7	99.4	97.6	97.1	90.7	90.5	95.0	100.0	107.0	117.6	120.7	119.5	119.9	122.0	122.5
Cape Coral-Fort Myers, FL	78.2	83.6	91.3	102.7	113.7	121.8	119.6	109.9	100.8	99.9	98.6	100.0	101.0	106.5	112.0	118.8	123.1	126.5	130.1
Cape Girardeau, MO-IL	86.6	89.1	90.6	94.6	99.0	102.6	103.0	103.5	101.5	101.2	100.6	100.0	99.6	99.5	102.8	104.1	104.8	107.0	108.6
Carbondale-Marion, IL	78.2	81.9	82.4	84.3	87.1	92.3	92.2	94.5	94.5	98.0	99.6	100.0	96.1	93.8	93.4	92.8	93.2	96.4	96.7
Carson City, NV	94.9	96.4	98.3	100.9	103.8	106.4	106.8	104.5	104.1	108.5	100.7	100.0	99.9	93.7	95.8	95.4	101.5	104.6	108.4
Casper, WY	59.5	61.3	62.7	66.9	72.5	82.1	84.1	86.4	80.5	84.2	89.3	100.0	101.9	109.9	109.1	98.5	96.4	106.1	105.7
Cedar Rapids, IA	69.4	68.7	73.6	80.4	84.5	84.1	91.4	90.7	93.4	98.7	101.1	100.0	99.8	103.8	109.1	109.5	108.2	111.0	110.7
Chambersburg-Waynesboro, PA	78.9	77.2	82.8	89.3	96.5	103.1	110.5	108.8	101.1	100.4	101.1	100.0	102.0	104.5	105.3	104.3	111.1	113.3	115.0
Champaign-Urbana, IL	82.6	86.0	86.3	87.7	88.3	91.2	93.1	96.2	95.3	99.1	99.6	100.0	103.4	105.3	104.0	102.9	102.1	102.9	102.8
Charleston, WV	105.3	105.4	104.9	104.1	107.2	108.4	107.7	107.3	107.3	105.2	104.8	100.0	98.0	95.3	93.3	91.6	89.3	94.5	90.5
Charleston-North Charleston, SC	68.5	71.0	74.9	79.1	84.0	86.4	89.5	89.3	86.8	90.2	94.7	100.0	99.5	102.9	107.7	113.3	117.4	121.9	125.6
Charlotte-Concord-Gastonia, NC-SC	72.7	74.6	77.9	82.2	88.1	93.5	94.7	100.3	92.3	89.6	94.4	100.0	98.6	101.5	105.7	108.7	112.7	116.2	118.0
Charlottesville, VA	71.7	73.0	76.3	80.6	85.1	88.6	92.0	92.6	93.4	97.4	97.7	100.0	98.3	99.6	101.2	104.0	108.5	110.2	111.3
Chattanooga, TN-GA	83.1	84.9	87.4	91.5	93.1	94.7	94.6	95.4	91.3	93.3	97.0	100.0	101.3	100.9	103.7	105.3	108.4	110.4	112.3

Quantity Indexes for Real GDP by Metropolitan Area—*Continued*

(2012 = 100.0)

Metropolitan Statistical Area	2001	2002	2003	2004	2005	2006	2007	2008	2009	2010	2011	2012	2013	2014	2015	2016	2017	2018	2019
Cheyenne, WY	71.5	74.1	77.7	81.0	81.6	87.0	97.1	106.6	93.1	93.8	96.6	100.0	97.6	97.7	102.3	99.4	100.0	102.6	104.2
Chicago-Naperville-Elgin, IL-IN-WI	91.6	92.1	93.3	95.8	98.0	99.6	100.7	98.1	94.6	96.0	97.5	100.0	100.4	103.3	106.0	106.3	107.2	109.7	110.2
Chico, CA	85.6	92.4	97.2	99.6	102.4	108.7	107.3	103.4	103.4	103.2	103.2	100.0	102.7	102.9	107.2	113.9	119.2	121.5	128.3
Cincinnati, OH-KY-IN	89.7	91.8	93.4	94.9	97.0	96.5	97.0	96.5	92.9	96.1	99.2	100.0	100.7	103.4	106.2	109.8	111.8	114.7	118.1
Clarksville, TN-KY	65.3	70.9	73.0	78.9	86.0	91.3	89.1	91.4	91.6	94.2	99.3	100.0	97.5	96.6	97.2	93.8	94.8	96.0	97.3
Cleveland, TN	75.3	79.1	78.8	83.9	83.7	84.8	85.0	87.0	85.5	88.3	89.0	100.0	102.7	101.0	104.5	98.0	97.0	98.9	100.9
Cleveland-Elyria, OH	96.8	98.8	101.2	103.5	105.9	104.2	104.3	103.4	96.2	97.4	99.1	100.0	99.8	102.1	102.4	102.6	103.9	106.7	108.0
Coeur d'Alene, ID	78.7	80.5	83.6	88.9	97.0	102.7	107.9	106.3	99.2	103.0	99.3	100.0	104.9	107.5	110.4	115.7	120.8	128.1	130.7
College Station-Bryan, TX	66.9	69.6	71.9	73.1	78.9	86.4	94.6	99.0	106.9	101.1	99.2	100.0	107.0	114.1	121.2	121.9	126.9	131.1	133.3
Colorado Springs, CO	83.1	83.5	84.3	85.8	89.8	91.4	93.6	94.5	94.6	97.8	99.6	100.0	100.9	101.4	103.2	104.8	109.2	112.6	116.7
Columbia, MO	82.9	84.0	86.7	89.1	91.1	92.7	92.2	94.0	93.6	95.5	97.4	100.0	103.0	103.3	104.7	106.8	108.5	110.2	112.3
Columbia, SC	86.1	87.1	89.8	93.5	95.8	99.1	101.8	103.1	100.5	100.6	100.8	100.0	102.6	106.3	109.7	112.7	114.5	116.4	118.4
Columbus, GA-AL	82.5	85.3	85.5	87.0	89.0	91.7	94.6	94.8	96.0	97.4	99.1	100.0	98.0	97.7	98.7	96.0	97.6	100.1	101.2
Columbus, IN	60.6	58.8	61.7	64.7	68.4	76.0	84.7	90.4	74.7	90.6	92.7	100.0	105.1	100.7	98.2	95.8	97.9	103.3	102.8
Columbus, OH	85.0	86.5	88.6	91.6	94.6	93.0	93.9	92.8	89.9	92.7	96.1	100.0	103.0	106.6	108.5	110.5	113.0	115.4	116.1
Corpus Christi, TX	83.8	83.8	87.7	95.1	89.0	90.7	97.1	93.0	91.6	97.9	101.3	100.0	101.6	96.1	96.1	94.2	97.3	101.4	103.3
Corvallis, OR	66.9	68.1	69.3	72.3	76.1	84.3	92.1	96.6	95.3	97.8	101.6	100.0	97.3	96.7	98.6	101.1	106.5	110.9	112.5
Crestview-Fort Walton Beach-Destin, FL	77.1	83.9	91.4	100.9	108.6	105.8	104.5	100.5	96.3	94.8	95.2	100.0	101.8	102.7	105.8	108.4	113.4	117.0	123.2
Cumberland, MD-WV	88.9	90.4	89.3	89.8	90.7	95.4	95.1	96.2	95.7	101.9	102.3	100.0	100.0	98.7	100.8	101.9	101.7	100.8	103.5
Dallas-Fort Worth-Arlington, TX	74.1	76.0	76.8	80.9	84.8	89.6	93.1	94.5	91.5	93.1	96.4	100.0	102.8	106.8	112.0	115.4	119.8	123.9	126.0
Dalton, GA	96.5	100.9	102.2	113.3	117.3	117.5	118.8	112.4	102.1	96.4	97.1	100.0	98.7	101.4	105.1	108.9	108.1	107.4	106.7
Danville, IL	86.7	89.4	93.2	97.8	96.2	103.4	103.3	101.2	95.7	96.6	97.6	100.0	99.3	100.6	97.1	96.3	95.3	96.0	97.7
Daphne-Fairhope-Foley, AL	78.2	82.1	85.8	94.1	103.8	104.7	104.8	99.0	93.8	97.0	97.7	100.0	102.6	104.1	107.6	111.4	113.9	118.9	121.6
Davenport-Moline-Rock Island, IA-IL	81.9	81.4	83.4	88.5	90.3	92.1	94.0	95.5	91.4	93.6	96.8	100.0	97.1	98.4	96.5	94.3	94.5	95.7	97.5
Dayton-Kettering, OH	98.2	101.0	102.6	105.7	106.2	106.0	103.0	100.4	94.9	97.2	100.2	100.0	100.5	101.4	102.6	104.0	106.2	109.6	111.6
Decatur, AL	90.4	89.6	96.5	108.8	101.7	105.3	108.3	104.3	102.6	103.8	100.6	100.0	98.8	98.7	98.6	101.8	101.8	105.3	108.4
Decatur, IL	84.8	84.9	85.5	88.2	89.4	92.5	96.0	102.3	102.3	103.8	104.3	100.0	105.5	109.3	112.8	105.5	98.6	98.6	97.3
Deltona-Daytona Beach-Ormond Beach, FL	81.6	88.2	96.2	102.5	106.8	113.1	113.5	108.7	101.7	100.8	99.7	100.0	100.1	101.5	105.1	109.7	113.5	117.4	120.2
Denver-Aurora-Lakewood, CO	88.6	88.8	89.1	89.1	92.5	93.2	96.8	96.6	93.9	95.6	97.2	100.0	104.1	108.5	114.4	117.1	121.6	127.1	132.1
Des Moines-West Des Moines, IA	75.9	77.1	83.6	91.5	97.6	94.6	104.3	94.2	92.1	93.8	93.9	100.0	97.5	107.5	115.6	119.6	118.6	120.4	121.3
Detroit-Warren-Dearborn, MI	103.9	106.2	108.0	107.7	109.6	105.7	104.9	98.0	87.2	92.9	96.8	100.0	101.7	103.0	105.0	107.1	108.3	110.8	111.7
Dothan, AL	91.6	96.6	97.7	101.0	103.2	105.9	105.6	102.2	98.6	99.2	98.9	100.0	104.5	105.4	107.7	111.7	115.0	116.2	117.2
Dover, DE	88.2	90.9	91.9	100.4	101.0	105.5	106.2	104.7	107.1	104.8	103.2	100.0	98.4	100.7	104.2	103.4	103.9	108.1	112.0
Dubuque, IA	67.0	70.3	73.0	80.9	86.3	88.8	92.8	87.0	81.2	87.2	88.2	100.0	95.0	104.4	107.1	100.6	103.5	105.9	106.1
Duluth, MN-WI	84.9	88.7	89.6	95.0	96.2	96.5	94.5	97.4	92.3	101.2	104.7	100.0	105.0	105.5	94.9	99.5	101.1	105.8	110.7
Durham-Chapel Hill, NC	62.5	65.0	68.2	69.3	74.2	89.8	95.8	97.9	93.1	100.2	100.3	100.0	102.6	101.3	99.0	97.0	99.0	102.3	107.0
East Stroudsburg, PA	81.5	83.6	82.8	90.0	97.1	101.0	107.3	107.8	104.2	105.4	103.1	100.0	99.4	100.7	103.9	110.3	108.5	108.0	111.6
Eau Claire, WI	72.2	75.9	79.3	83.6	88.8	90.9	93.3	91.2	90.7	96.2	97.6	100.0	100.3	108.5	111.0	110.4	111.7	116.0	117.5
El Centro, CA	73.7	88.9	83.3	80.9	88.4	97.3	95.0	108.1	103.0	101.4	105.6	100.0	105.5	112.7	123.3	124.2	124.4	122.7	129.8
Elizabethtown-Fort Knox, KY	73.2	73.9	76.0	78.5	80.2	84.7	84.5	89.1	88.7	99.3	104.7	100.0	98.4	94.8	91.2	91.6	92.9	92.9	93.6
Elkhart-Goshen, IN	81.2	87.6	96.1	101.9	109.4	116.7	117.0	101.6	74.9	99.1	97.9	100.0	107.0	116.6	126.3	137.6	153.0	154.2	150.7
Elmira, NY	80.9	81.0	82.0	82.6	85.1	87.6	89.4	93.5	92.9	98.5	100.4	100.0	100.0	99.7	97.6	95.5	93.7	95.4	97.5
El Paso, TX	72.6	75.0	75.5	78.7	80.6	83.2	86.5	85.5	87.2	93.4	98.1	100.0	98.6	97.3	98.7	100.2	102.6	105.5	106.7
Enid, OK	56.1	57.5	60.2	61.9	64.6	67.8	72.4	79.5	81.7	85.2	87.2	100.0	103.4	117.1	116.3	124.4	90.7	90.8	91.2
Erie, PA	88.7	88.0	88.2	91.0	94.3	97.3	100.5	107.0	98.5	99.8	103.9	100.0	100.7	96.4	96.9	93.6	91.5	92.4	93.7
Eugene-Springfield, OR	86.9	88.8	90.6	94.9	99.3	105.1	106.4	105.1	98.4	98.7	99.5	100.0	100.3	101.7	107.7	111.7	116.0	119.4	121.4
Evansville, IN-KY	95.0	100.0	103.4	108.4	106.1	99.5	98.9	102.8	98.3	100.6	101.9	100.0	96.2	94.8	95.6	96.7	102.4	105.1	110.3
Fairbanks, AK	105.0	90.8	91.3	92.6	101.2	104.6	106.1	115.2	112.4	113.2	105.1	100.0	97.1	96.6	94.9	95.1	94.2	95.6	93.8
Fargo, ND-MN	65.1	69.1	72.7	75.7	78.4	81.2	83.7	86.4	84.5	87.8	92.4	100.0	99.7	107.4	109.3	108.1	109.9	111.9	113.0
Farmington, NM	102.5	102.8	101.2	103.3	103.7	107.3	110.1	107.7	108.9	101.9	101.4	100.0	98.6	102.7	107.1	99.6	98.6	91.2	92.2
Fayetteville, NC	76.0	78.7	81.2	84.7	90.0	93.1	93.0	96.4	99.8	102.1	103.0	100.0	98.9	98.1	98.9	98.2	98.1	99.2	100.4
Fayetteville-Springdale-Rogers, AR	73.1	78.7	83.8	92.0	98.2	98.2	95.0	93.8	89.4	94.4	96.5	100.0	106.7	112.0	116.8	120.0	126.2	130.0	130.7
Flagstaff, AZ	79.2	80.7	82.3	85.5	90.0	95.3	102.1	99.6	94.8	98.6	105.0	100.0	104.2	103.4	105.4	107.3	113.4	113.5	109.5
Flint, MI	106.9	112.8	115.8	115.2	116.1	115.4	113.1	102.7	93.8	99.0	100.4	100.0	104.4	106.8	111.4	112.0	111.8	113.2	114.4
Florence, SC	91.8	92.6	95.3	97.4	98.9	102.1	103.1	101.3	97.9	96.5	99.7	100.0	103.8	107.1	111.3	113.0	114.9	115.9	121.1
Florence-Muscle Shoals, AL	84.7	85.3	89.0	93.8	95.8	98.7	97.1	96.4	92.6	96.5	99.8	100.0	106.1	102.5	100.6	97.6	95.6	97.1	98.9
Fond du Lac, WI	81.3	80.2	83.2	87.6	89.3	91.3	92.1	92.6	87.4	91.9	95.6	100.0	101.3	105.3	104.8	103.3	104.0	105.8	108.7
Fort Collins, CO	78.7	83.7	84.4	85.7	87.4	90.7	93.3	95.8	94.5	96.6	97.7	100.0	104.8	109.8	115.7	120.4	129.5	136.2	139.4
Fort Smith, AR-OK	88.8	91.6	96.1	101.8	104.8	109.7	106.5	104.2	96.3	99.6	101.9	100.0	97.8	96.7	96.5	96.1	96.8	98.1	99.2
Fort Wayne, IN	89.0	91.2	95.0	96.9	99.0	102.7	105.1	99.7	91.9	94.6	95.8	100.0	100.0	107.3	112.1	113.8	117.4	121.5	124.6
Fresno, CA	80.2	87.3	93.4	96.3	100.6	108.4	105.4	101.9	102.0	102.4	103.3	100.0	103.9	108.3	113.4	117.5	122.1	125.3	130.3
Gadsden, AL	93.3	95.1	95.9	101.0	101.0	101.0	100.5	100.5	98.2	100.2	100.9	100.0	99.6	99.3	101.2	101.7	102.5	103.8	104.0
Gainesville, FL	85.6	87.8	88.4	95.8	98.8	103.4	108.3	105.7	102.3	101.6	99.8	100.0	100.5	103.6	106.3	109.2	111.7	115.6	118.7
Gainesville, GA	85.0	85.1	88.5	91.2	93.9	96.9	99.7	99.1	93.5	94.7	99.9	100.0	102.7	106.4	112.8	117.5	125.2	130.4	132.8
Gettysburg, PA	79.5	85.2	85.1	86.2	89.6	94.3	94.4	96.1	96.7	95.7	97.6	100.0	100.6	101.1	102.5	104.3	107.9	106.8	107.8
Glens Falls, NY	78.6	80.3	83.0	88.2	87.8	92.4	91.6	96.2	99.8	101.6	100.0	100.0	100.2	101.6	102.2	102.1	104.1	106.1	110.3
Goldsboro, NC	98.4	94.7	92.2	96.5	97.3	102.0	103.4	104.7	103.9	104.6	100.8	100.0	103.0	100.2	100.7	100.2	100.1	101.7	102.1
Grand Forks, ND-MN	72.7	76.5	82.5	79.9	81.9	87.6	88.2	93.2	90.1	92.6	93.9	100.0	100.3	99.9	100.8	103.3	105.0	105.1	104.7

Quantity Indexes for Real GDP by Metropolitan Area—*Continued*

(2012 = 100.0)

Metropolitan Statistical Area	2001	2002	2003	2004	2005	2006	2007	2008	2009	2010	2011	2012	2013	2014	2015	2016	2017	2018	2019
Grand Island, NE	71.4	73.7	78.4	80.2	85.5	90.2	90.4	92.7	93.8	96.6	97.0	100.0	105.3	104.9	104.5	103.9	103.4	104.2	107.4
Grand Junction, CO	77.4	79.8	81.7	83.6	88.3	96.4	106.2	115.4	105.4	100.6	100.6	100.0	98.1	99.6	99.3	98.1	102.8	107.9	110.7
Grand Rapids-Kentwood, MI	93.0	95.8	98.0	100.3	102.7	102.4	102.1	98.8	92.1	95.7	97.7	100.0	102.1	105.2	110.0	112.6	115.6	119.0	119.3
Grants Pass, OR	84.8	89.4	93.2	97.8	102.9	108.2	109.4	103.9	101.8	101.4	100.9	100.0	99.3	103.1	110.0	114.7	121.4	126.9	132.8
Great Falls, MT	83.5	86.0	86.5	89.7	95.5	96.9	97.6	96.2	95.5	99.8	101.1	100.0	98.3	99.8	103.3	101.7	103.9	107.4	108.9
Greeley, CO	62.5	61.7	63.5	68.0	73.0	76.7	79.5	84.2	85.7	88.0	91.1	100.0	111.2	131.7	145.5	150.2	159.4	178.5	184.5
Green Bay, WI	83.3	85.1	87.9	90.6	92.4	94.0	94.6	94.3	91.3	95.9	97.1	100.0	98.7	106.0	109.1	110.6	109.8	113.7	114.7
Greensboro-High Point, NC	95.6	98.1	97.7	96.5	98.7	103.0	102.9	104.7	101.8	103.2	105.2	100.0	102.3	102.6	105.7	103.7	103.6	104.3	106.2
Greenville, NC	76.8	76.4	75.8	78.1	84.1	92.1	96.0	97.2	98.0	99.6	102.1	100.0	105.7	109.6	118.3	117.6	117.2	116.2	118.5
Greenville-Anderson, SC	94.7	99.0	102.2	93.3	93.7	94.1	97.3	97.9	92.3	94.9	99.2	100.0	103.5	107.0	111.5	114.6	118.0	122.7	125.8
Gulfport-Biloxi, MS	85.0	84.8	91.3	90.8	93.6	96.9	130.2	115.3	106.4	106.1	100.4	100.0	92.0	96.8	94.6	95.9	97.0	98.3	99.4
Hagerstown-Martinsburg, MD-WV	80.6	83.4	85.3	90.1	93.9	100.4	99.8	90.0	96.0	97.6	99.6	100.0	100.7	102.1	103.1	105.8	108.7	109.7	110.8
Hammond, LA	64.3	66.9	72.3	78.9	87.8	101.6	97.4	100.3	93.8	99.0	110.4	100.0	92.6	92.0	87.8	89.8	96.0	96.7	100.2
Hanford-Corcoran, CA	79.8	85.6	94.9	100.0	105.0	101.9	115.5	104.3	95.3	96.8	108.9	100.0	100.8	109.8	109.1	110.2	114.2	116.2	122.9
Harrisburg-Carlisle, PA	84.6	86.6	89.4	92.8	93.9	95.9	97.9	98.0	95.4	96.4	98.5	100.0	101.6	104.5	107.7	107.4	107.7	109.7	112.3
Harrisonburg, VA	93.0	81.4	80.7	82.4	87.7	89.4	89.6	88.4	92.4	97.2	97.9	100.0	101.6	98.4	95.6	92.6	92.9	94.2	93.9
Hartford-East Hartford-Middletown, CT	86.0	82.8	84.9	91.6	93.4	97.6	103.1	101.8	100.3	100.1	99.8	100.0	95.9	98.2	104.2	104.7	106.3	106.1	106.8
Hattiesburg, MS	78.9	81.4	85.0	88.5	91.9	96.9	93.1	99.0	98.0	99.3	98.2	100.0	100.2	99.4	100.3	99.0	100.6	100.9	100.1
Hickory-Lenoir-Morganton, NC	105.9	106.3	103.7	107.5	107.4	111.0	108.0	104.6	98.7	102.9	102.8	100.0	100.6	101.2	104.3	106.0	107.9	109.3	110.8
Hilton Head Island-Bluffton, SC	91.3	91.5	97.0	104.1	110.3	107.8	109.3	106.8	101.2	99.6	99.4	100.0	103.2	105.7	109.6	112.0	112.6	115.7	119.8
Hinesville, GA	64.7	66.6	72.2	76.0	80.7	82.4	86.2	93.3	93.9	98.6	102.7	100.0	97.6	93.3	91.6	89.6	89.2	89.8	89.0
Homosassa Springs, FL	96.5	99.3	101.9	107.9	112.6	126.6	127.7	122.1	110.8	103.2	99.9	100.0	99.5	97.3	95.0	95.4	95.3	97.9	109.8
Hot Springs, AR	87.3	90.4	93.0	95.3	98.2	98.4	96.5	94.9	91.9	95.8	102.9	100.0	99.2	99.2	100.5	100.3	102.2	103.4	104.7
Houma-Thibodaux, LA	96.8	93.1	88.7	87.4	90.1	105.2	106.5	105.0	105.6	102.4	98.1	100.0	102.8	104.9	95.4	83.8	81.5	83.9	85.7
Houston-The Woodlands-Sugar Land, TX	73.5	73.0	73.0	79.3	80.4	85.9	93.0	91.2	90.3	94.0	96.3	100.0	104.6	106.1	112.6	110.7	112.2	115.1	117.2
Huntington-Ashland, WV-KY-OH	85.8	87.5	88.8	91.6	92.3	93.8	93.3	97.5	97.7	96.3	95.1	100.0	107.8	103.1	102.8	99.5	100.1	104.1	106.5
Huntsville, AL	67.2	70.1	73.6	79.1	83.1	86.6	89.5	92.5	93.7	98.0	99.8	100.0	101.2	101.9	103.6	106.3	109.2	112.8	116.5
Idaho Falls, ID	78.1	83.1	83.2	86.9	90.0	99.0	100.3	101.4	101.8	101.0	100.1	100.0	102.0	102.9	109.3	113.5	121.2	129.0	133.3
Indianapolis-Carmel-Anderson, IN	84.0	85.0	87.7	92.4	93.0	94.4	97.6	100.4	97.6	100.7	100.7	100.0	102.3	104.7	102.0	103.9	105.2	109.0	111.4
Iowa City, IA	76.8	79.6	80.7	84.1	85.1	88.4	88.8	92.7	92.2	95.4	99.1	100.0	103.4	105.9	105.3	107.0	110.3	112.5	110.1
Ithaca, NY	81.8	84.9	88.8	90.7	90.7	92.7	92.2	96.6	97.8	101.4	100.1	100.0	99.9	98.6	99.5	100.2	101.0	102.5	101.8
Jackson, MI	96.7	99.9	99.4	102.0	103.7	103.9	103.4	98.4	90.8	95.5	99.1	100.0	101.5	99.7	101.9	105.2	107.5	110.5	112.0
Jackson, MS	89.1	91.1	94.2	96.7	98.4	99.9	96.6	101.6	97.7	99.3	99.7	100.0	102.4	103.8	104.3	103.7	103.6	103.8	103.8
Jackson, TN	89.3	88.8	90.7	92.8	94.4	97.7	95.7	97.9	98.5	104.9	112.6	100.0	100.3	98.5	100.3	102.2	105.0	107.6	108.8
Jacksonville, FL	88.0	90.5	95.2	99.4	103.9	108.6	109.3	105.1	99.6	99.9	98.8	100.0	102.0	104.4	108.9	112.4	117.0	121.6	125.1
Jacksonville, NC	63.7	62.0	64.6	70.3	75.0	77.6	83.0	91.1	97.7	102.3	101.7	100.0	97.5	95.6	93.8	98.3	96.3	97.7	97.2
Janesville-Beloit, WI	88.6	98.7	100.1	102.3	101.1	107.8	106.0	100.7	93.4	96.6	98.1	100.0	103.6	100.9	103.2	104.3	104.4	110.5	114.4
Jefferson City, MO	87.4	87.3	89.6	92.3	93.4	97.3	97.0	100.3	98.1	100.1	100.3	100.0	101.2	103.6	106.7	106.0	103.7	105.8	106.3
Johnson City, TN	79.8	82.1	85.9	92.1	93.6	97.2	98.5	100.4	97.6	95.4	98.3	100.0	99.2	97.1	101.4	99.5	101.7	104.3	106.0
Johnstown, PA	94.5	92.6	94.1	94.4	96.0	97.5	99.0	101.4	99.4	101.0	101.3	100.0	99.4	97.5	96.2	94.0	93.4	94.4	96.9
Jonesboro, AR	77.7	81.0	88.0	92.4	96.1	96.4	92.0	94.0	94.6	99.6	101.6	100.0	103.7	100.0	102.7	103.8	108.0	110.3	112.1
Joplin, MO	90.7	90.9	92.8	95.8	97.4	99.8	99.2	102.1	97.7	100.3	99.8	100.0	99.9	100.5	105.2	104.3	104.4	107.3	108.2
Kahului-Wailuku-Lahaina, HI	67.3	71.2	77.3	85.5	94.6	103.4	105.3	100.4	91.5	94.6	98.2	100.0	99.2	99.6	92.6	101.5	101.7	105.5	106.5
Kalamazoo-Portage, MI	98.7	105.6	105.5	105.5	104.3	102.9	104.4	101.3	99.0	100.0	99.7	100.0	101.3	101.1	104.8	107.2	111.8	115.8	117.6
Kankakee, IL	80.4	82.9	84.1	86.2	85.7	91.3	91.9	93.5	93.8	95.7	95.9	100.0	98.6	102.1	105.2	112.6	122.0	124.8	127.8
Kansas City, MO-KS	85.7	87.7	89.2	90.7	93.2	95.0	97.5	100.5	97.2	96.8	97.0	100.0	101.2	104.2	106.9	107.4	110.5	112.9	114.0
Kennewick-Richland, WA	73.8	79.4	79.9	81.5	85.9	90.8	91.8	92.3	97.3	106.8	104.2	100.0	100.1	102.1	107.3	112.5	114.4	119.9	124.5
Killeen-Temple, TX	67.0	69.5	72.8	75.7	81.2	88.4	93.0	98.7	99.7	99.2	101.0	100.0	97.4	96.8	100.5	98.1	100.0	101.9	103.4
Kingsport-Bristol, TN-VA	86.3	86.4	87.6	93.7	91.6	97.8	99.1	98.7	96.6	97.4	99.5	100.0	98.8	95.2	96.8	97.6	100.3	102.2	102.3
Kingston, NY	81.5	83.2	85.9	88.7	89.9	96.8	96.5	98.3	97.9	99.8	99.2	100.0	99.9	99.4	99.5	100.4	102.3	104.6	106.9
Knoxville, TN	80.7	85.0	88.3	93.1	95.8	98.1	97.9	99.4	94.8	95.7	99.1	100.0	100.4	101.7	104.6	107.2	109.9	113.1	114.3
Kokomo, IN	74.3	83.6	96.9	92.0	89.8	94.0	97.8	87.8	59.1	93.3	96.0	100.0	101.1	97.3	90.7	88.2	85.8	87.3	89.2
La Crosse-Onalaska, WI-MN	80.4	81.4	84.4	86.7	89.3	90.1	91.1	92.9	93.7	97.4	99.5	100.0	104.3	112.6	115.8	108.5	111.7	114.7	115.4
Lafayette, LA	85.3	80.7	79.3	80.7	82.9	94.8	93.4	95.9	94.9	95.7	96.6	100.0	98.3	98.6	91.7	83.4	83.2	85.6	86.9
Lafayette-West Lafayette, IN	84.1	86.2	89.3	92.3	94.5	95.9	102.6	101.8	92.5	98.4	100.7	100.0	104.2	107.4	108.2	113.3	118.4	123.6	124.4
Lake Charles, LA	108.9	115.9	137.4	149.0	178.1	152.2	128.2	112.9	95.8	87.1	103.9	100.0	86.5	89.7	90.5	97.2	114.4	120.9	125.0
Lake Havasu City-Kingman, AZ	83.7	91.7	94.6	101.8	108.1	114.9	117.6	111.8	103.0	102.2	101.1	100.0	102.5	104.6	106.0	108.7	106.7	109.5	115.2
Lakeland-Winter Haven, FL	86.1	89.0	91.6	95.6	101.3	108.2	109.4	106.1	99.2	99.5	99.1	100.0	102.1	101.0	106.4	110.2	116.2	120.2	124.5
Lancaster, PA	94.3	95.7	97.8	100.0	102.0	103.3	102.7	101.8	98.2	101.6	100.4	100.0	101.8	105.0	109.9	110.3	114.1	117.5	117.8
Lansing-East Lansing, MI	103.7	106.5	107.4	107.2	109.2	110.0	110.1	103.4	96.9	103.4	101.9	100.0	100.2	102.1	106.5	110.5	112.5	114.7	115.8
Laredo, TX	84.2	87.5	86.4	84.0	86.9	88.6	87.4	83.3	83.9	85.1	93.9	100.0	105.8	121.5	134.1	133.2	134.4	129.5	132.5
Las Cruces, NM	77.5	80.5	86.6	92.1	99.8	100.5	101.5	100.5	105.5	107.8	104.2	100.0	98.1	99.8	101.7	103.6	103.2	104.8	106.7
Las Vegas-Henderson-Paradise, NV	82.1	85.5	89.8	100.8	111.1	115.8	116.1	111.3	100.8	100.3	101.6	100.0	101.5	103.3	108.1	110.7	113.7	120.8	123.7
Lawrence, KS	93.7	96.0	94.6	95.8	95.4	94.7	95.6	100.3	99.2	98.3	99.7	100.0	101.6	103.9	105.6	108.7	111.1	113.7	112.5
Lawton, OK	78.7	81.9	88.1	91.7	90.1	94.5	95.7	99.4	102.9	107.2	104.7	100.0	100.2	99.9	103.2	100.9	99.7	97.5	98.7
Lebanon, PA	74.9	76.7	80.6	84.8	85.2	89.7	92.2	91.8	92.2	95.7	97.8	100.0	99.5	102.5	103.5	103.3	106.3	108.8	110.4
Lewiston, ID-WA	88.9	90.0	90.9	92.2	93.5	97.3	98.9	100.6	98.7	101.0	99.5	100.0	102.5	102.5	105.4	108.7	110.9	113.9	116.7
Lewiston-Auburn, ME	86.0	92.8	95.6	97.4	96.1	98.7	101.2	103.5	100.0	98.2	97.8	100.0	99.2	100.0	101.8	103.0	102.1	105.2	106.7
Lexington-Fayette, KY	85.6	89.8	91.0	94.9	98.8	102.2	102.7	100.9	93.4	97.5	98.2	100.0	104.2	107.3	111.9	114.6	114.9	116.5	118.4
Lima, OH	77.8	81.9	82.5	84.9	84.4	84.9	82.7	81.8	98.1	102.9	105.5	100.0	95.5	104.6	103.0	105.8	103.8	107.3	109.3

Quantity Indexes for Real GDP by Metropolitan Area—*Continued*

(2012 = 100.0)

Metropolitan Statistical Area	2001	2002	2003	2004	2005	2006	2007	2008	2009	2010	2011	2012	2013	2014	2015	2016	2017	2018	2019
Lincoln, NE	87.9	88.5	91.9	92.9	96.7	98.9	100.6	97.6	95.8	98.4	99.2	100.0	100.3	104.2	107.2	108.9	115.2	116.6	118.9
Little Rock-North Little Rock-Conway, AR	84.0	86.3	90.1	93.1	98.0	100.1	102.7	101.6	98.9	98.3	100.0	100.0	100.8	101.2	102.6	102.9	103.3	104.9	105.9
Logan, UT-ID	69.0	69.2	73.5	76.9	77.3	83.1	87.9	93.0	95.5	102.3	105.5	100.0	101.5	105.2	109.2	114.1	120.2	126.8	130.1
Longview, TX	75.9	78.4	77.4	79.0	84.1	92.4	101.2	107.4	112.7	105.5	99.9	100.0	98.9	98.3	94.5	89.9	91.1	95.3	97.9
Longview, WA	80.1	78.1	81.5	82.9	87.1	93.1	98.8	95.1	92.6	100.3	97.2	100.0	102.8	102.7	104.6	105.2	108.6	114.1	119.3
Los Angeles-Long Beach-Anaheim, CA	81.7	84.0	88.4	92.0	95.4	98.4	98.9	99.4	94.5	96.7	98.2	100.0	102.3	105.7	110.7	113.2	117.3	119.2	122.2
Louisville/Jefferson County, KY-IN	86.9	87.3	89.5	92.3	94.9	97.5	97.4	96.1	90.9	95.3	96.7	100.0	100.3	101.4	104.2	106.6	106.4	108.1	109.9
Lubbock, TX	79.7	81.3	82.3	85.2	88.4	92.4	93.8	92.7	93.1	98.1	96.3	100.0	103.9	103.4	105.8	108.2	110.4	113.2	114.1
Lynchburg, VA	87.7	89.0	93.3	95.4	97.5	103.0	102.5	101.9	102.2	105.2	103.5	100.0	99.7	99.1	99.1	98.7	99.8	101.7	103.1
Macon-Bibb County, GA	101.6	101.4	99.0	101.9	100.8	101.2	99.0	100.0	97.3	98.0	99.7	100.0	100.0	100.3	101.4	101.0	101.9	105.9	105.5
Madera, CA	62.2	70.4	72.8	84.4	90.7	98.1	97.7	95.1	83.5	95.7	96.4	100.0	101.6	109.2	106.3	116.6	119.7	122.1	127.4
Madison, WI	79.8	82.5	85.3	89.1	92.9	93.0	94.9	93.3	92.0	94.8	97.8	100.0	101.4	105.0	109.4	113.1	115.3	120.3	123.5
Manchester-Nashua, NH	79.0	82.3	89.1	92.4	94.8	95.5	96.9	96.4	95.4	96.6	99.1	100.0	101.0	102.5	106.6	109.5	111.0	114.5	115.7
Manhattan, KS	67.8	68.0	70.7	73.8	75.8	81.9	88.3	93.4	93.0	97.8	101.4	100.0	96.2	93.2	94.8	91.8	90.6	89.8	87.6
Mankato, MN	75.4	79.1	78.9	84.3	87.7	95.2	93.0	94.1	90.3	94.0	96.9	100.0	102.4	106.5	106.7	105.2	106.4	108.7	110.7
Mansfield, OH	103.6	108.2	109.0	113.1	115.0	114.9	109.4	105.8	91.2	95.9	99.5	100.0	99.7	101.4	99.0	98.7	99.4	101.4	101.8
McAllen-Edinburg-Mission, TX	80.8	85.9	87.8	88.8	91.1	95.9	100.7	98.6	98.2	97.9	99.3	100.0	103.9	105.1	106.1	106.8	108.2	110.3	112.3
Medford, OR	90.0	94.2	97.1	101.4	103.0	108.3	110.9	109.4	105.1	102.0	101.9	100.0	103.4	106.0	111.2	116.1	121.7	125.3	128.8
Memphis, TN-MS-AR	97.0	98.6	99.8	101.9	103.3	103.3	101.1	100.3	96.3	96.5	97.3	100.0	100.5	99.6	101.7	103.0	104.3	106.4	106.5
Merced, CA	77.3	82.3	90.1	98.9	103.5	106.5	117.5	104.2	98.3	98.7	102.9	100.0	104.7	117.1	119.4	120.2	129.0	128.7	134.8
Miami-Fort Lauderdale-Pompano Beach, FL	88.4	91.5	94.7	99.8	106.3	108.0	107.3	102.9	97.0	99.9	100.0	100.0	102.9	106.5	111.4	115.4	120.1	125.0	127.1
Michigan City-La Porte, IN	100.0	99.9	99.8	103.6	101.5	104.0	105.6	106.3	97.2	101.2	99.8	100.0	100.7	103.8	99.9	99.7	99.7	100.6	101.3
Midland, MI	108.7	112.1	106.7	112.1	100.1	101.6	102.5	98.6	92.4	96.7	98.1	100.0	98.3	112.5	122.6	114.3	113.6	117.7	117.1
Midland, TX	36.6	37.6	36.0	37.9	40.3	47.3	52.6	58.1	62.5	68.0	79.3	100.0	103.3	112.1	124.3	128.1	149.8	188.0	223.1
Milwaukee-Waukesha, WI	89.9	90.2	92.8	94.7	97.6	99.0	99.5	98.3	95.2	97.5	99.6	100.0	99.8	100.2	101.7	102.4	103.2	106.2	107.1
Minneapolis-St. Paul-Bloomington, MN-WI	85.2	86.3	90.6	94.4	97.3	95.9	96.8	96.8	93.2	96.0	98.4	100.0	102.4	106.6	108.5	110.3	112.6	116.1	117.0
Missoula, MT	83.4	87.1	89.8	92.1	94.0	95.9	99.0	101.9	101.4	99.6	101.1	100.0	99.9	100.8	104.7	107.6	113.7	116.5	116.8
Mobile, AL	83.7	84.2	85.1	87.8	91.1	96.6	97.4	98.1	97.8	99.1	101.1	100.0	100.6	100.8	100.2	101.8	101.3	103.1	104.8
Modesto, CA	86.3	89.9	94.0	99.8	103.5	108.7	106.9	103.6	101.1	100.7	101.2	100.0	101.6	109.1	113.7	116.3	121.9	125.3	130.0
Monroe, LA	91.0	97.6	100.0	105.2	109.7	110.4	97.2	94.2	100.4	101.8	98.5	100.0	105.4	107.2	110.4	110.8	108.6	111.2	109.5
Monroe, MI	101.2	106.5	108.9	106.9	107.0	110.4	110.0	104.2	96.5	102.0	102.9	100.0	103.4	102.7	103.0	103.7	103.1	101.4	102.9
Montgomery, AL	86.8	88.6	90.9	95.0	98.1	100.8	100.2	99.1	95.9	98.5	99.8	100.0	100.1	98.8	100.8	102.7	102.2	102.8	103.8
Morgantown, WV	73.5	75.6	76.9	80.8	85.3	85.9	86.1	88.8	93.2	99.3	99.6	100.0	106.1	105.9	109.1	108.5	109.1	108.7	109.0
Morristown, TN	89.3	89.5	89.6	93.3	93.0	97.6	98.6	96.0	88.2	95.8	96.8	100.0	101.0	102.8	104.7	105.1	105.6	107.2	109.8
Mount Vernon-Anacortes, WA	92.9	111.6	106.7	100.0	122.0	115.5	118.5	120.4	123.7	124.0	102.5	100.0	106.2	111.2	129.4	127.9	129.3	135.6	139.6
Muncie, IN	117.0	116.3	119.5	116.3	114.5	116.4	111.1	108.8	104.3	112.4	119.9	100.0	101.3	101.4	101.3	100.5	102.3	102.6	104.7
Muskegon, MI	97.0	98.5	98.3	99.2	100.5	101.3	100.5	97.8	92.9	96.0	97.3	100.0	102.8	104.3	106.3	105.3	105.5	106.7	106.4
Myrtle Beach-Conway-North Myrtle Beach, SC-NC	88.9	90.6	94.8	101.0	108.8	107.0	108.1	103.8	98.0	98.9	100.6	100.0	103.2	107.7	110.6	114.9	120.7	123.8	127.9
Napa, CA	89.3	93.5	94.4	93.0	97.7	100.3	102.5	100.9	97.2	95.2	95.4	100.0	104.4	111.2	117.6	119.5	122.2	123.2	126.0
Naples-Marco Island, FL	95.8	100.3	104.9	109.5	121.1	122.6	119.9	108.4	99.0	101.1	100.1	100.0	102.1	108.1	114.9	119.8	121.8	126.6	131.4
Nashville-Davidson--Murfreesboro--Franklin, TN	71.3	74.1	77.7	82.6	85.3	88.7	88.3	92.0	90.0	91.4	94.7	100.0	102.2	107.1	114.3	117.8	121.7	125.8	128.7
New Bern, NC	87.1	85.7	89.4	93.1	99.6	101.4	104.9	103.2	100.4	103.0	101.1	100.0	104.1	107.3	107.0	99.7	99.1	100.1	103.9
New Haven-Milford, CT	91.6	94.3	94.4	100.9	102.1	105.6	106.1	106.8	102.5	103.6	102.4	100.0	100.3	99.4	100.6	102.0	102.7	104.9	106.5
New Orleans-Metairie, LA	102.6	104.9	110.1	113.3	117.1	110.1	115.5	120.9	120.1	129.8	99.0	100.0	96.3	97.9	98.5	98.7	103.4	104.8	108.1
New York-Newark-Jersey City, NY-NJ-PA	85.9	85.5	85.8	87.6	90.4	92.2	92.8	90.8	92.8	95.9	96.0	100.0	100.6	102.0	104.1	106.2	107.9	111.0	112.3
Niles, MI	97.9	100.2	101.6	104.5	101.8	106.0	110.5	103.2	90.2	99.8	100.5	100.0	101.4	102.0	104.1	108.6	113.7	112.2	110.7
North Port-Sarasota-Bradenton, FL	89.1	96.2	101.3	111.0	121.9	126.6	121.6	111.2	103.6	101.2	101.1	100.0	102.7	107.5	114.9	118.5	122.2	128.8	133.2
Norwich-New London, CT	86.1	90.5	95.6	106.0	109.9	116.9	124.9	115.5	102.7	101.8	100.7	100.0	102.5	96.4	99.0	98.9	103.3	102.9	103.7
Ocala, FL	83.0	86.4	92.0	97.3	105.9	118.8	120.2	116.9	105.5	103.7	101.3	100.0	100.6	101.6	104.3	110.6	111.4	115.0	119.7
Ocean City, NJ	90.9	95.3	100.0	104.1	107.3	108.7	107.0	103.3	99.7	101.0	100.5	100.0	100.1	101.0	100.7	100.5	99.4	98.0	104.9
Odessa, TX	43.9	47.1	44.9	46.6	47.8	56.0	61.9	67.1	68.9	72.8	84.9	100.0	101.4	102.2	90.6	79.6	86.3	101.0	104.6
Ogden-Clearfield, UT	78.6	80.7	82.4	84.3	88.8	97.5	100.7	99.7	99.9	100.9	101.4	100.0	104.0	105.2	108.2	113.2	120.1	124.3	129.2
Oklahoma City, OK	67.8	69.1	71.5	74.4	77.9	83.1	83.4	89.2	91.1	90.8	94.2	100.0	103.8	108.2	115.5	113.9	114.2	117.7	119.0
Olympia-Lacey-Tumwater, WA	83.6	84.7	86.0	86.8	90.4	95.1	100.6	103.6	100.4	100.7	99.1	100.0	101.7	104.3	104.1	109.6	114.3	122.2	125.2
Omaha-Council Bluffs, NE-IA	75.8	77.9	81.0	84.7	86.9	88.8	91.1	91.0	91.3	94.0	98.7	100.0	97.7	102.9	106.1	105.7	110.7	111.2	114.1
Orlando-Kissimmee-Sanford, FL	83.0	86.2	90.5	95.9	103.3	105.2	106.6	103.7	96.8	97.6	97.6	100.0	102.8	106.5	111.9	116.4	121.4	126.8	129.9
Oshkosh-Neenah, WI	86.9	95.1	95.8	97.0	97.9	99.4	99.3	97.3	95.1	97.5	98.8	100.0	98.9	100.1	100.2	103.3	103.2	105.7	108.4
Owensboro, KY	82.3	87.3	91.7	91.5	91.4	95.8	92.7	97.0	94.8	99.2	100.2	100.0	105.3	103.9	104.0	103.6	103.5	104.9	106.0
Oxnard-Thousand Oaks-Ventura, CA	80.0	82.2	87.6	96.7	101.6	114.4	122.0	111.1	109.5	108.3	101.8	100.0	101.7	101.8	103.0	102.8	102.1	103.2	106.1
Palm Bay-Melbourne-Titusville, FL	77.6	80.1	85.1	93.1	99.8	106.5	112.1	112.8	106.6	106.6	103.1	100.0	101.2	103.2	107.4	111.1	116.2	121.2	128.0
Panama City, FL	81.4	86.4	90.4	98.3	105.5	110.4	109.2	108.4	104.9	103.4	101.2	100.0	100.9	103.2	105.5	107.0	108.4	110.8	111.6
Parkersburg-Vienna, WV	97.2	100.8	100.7	100.6	99.6	104.7	99.9	108.4	104.4	102.3	101.8	100.0	95.8	95.2	93.9	91.4	90.1	90.8	91.8
Pensacola-Ferry Pass-Brent, FL	86.8	88.1	91.0	94.9	98.4	104.8	104.5	101.6	98.5	99.1	99.9	100.0	100.9	101.3	105.4	107.0	108.7	111.9	117.2
Peoria, IL	59.1	58.8	60.0	62.3	65.4	70.7	74.3	75.6	73.7	79.9	90.2	100.0	85.7	83.6	76.7	72.5	69.7	71.6	70.2

Quantity Indexes for Real GDP by Metropolitan Area—*Continued*

(2012 = 100.0)

Metropolitan Statistical Area	2001	2002	2003	2004	2005	2006	2007	2008	2009	2010	2011	2012	2013	2014	2015	2016	2017	2018	2019
Philadelphia-Camden-Wilmington, PA-NJ-DE-MD	84.2	84.8	88.5	92.0	92.8	93.4	96.5	98.5	95.3	97.0	97.7	100.0	100.6	103.0	105.0	106.2	105.6	107.3	109.8
Phoenix-Mesa-Chandler, AZ	77.8	80.6	86.1	90.6	98.6	103.8	106.1	102.8	93.6	94.1	96.9	100.0	100.8	102.9	106.8	110.4	114.3	119.4	123.3
Pine Bluff, AR	96.8	96.1	99.6	103.9	103.6	104.9	99.7	100.5	98.3	101.0	99.2	100.0	102.6	96.8	92.7	91.7	89.8	89.2	87.8
Pittsburgh, PA	84.8	85.8	87.7	89.3	90.0	89.7	91.7	94.1	92.6	96.4	98.7	100.0	101.5	104.0	107.4	107.3	109.7	113.7	116.2
Pittsfield, MA	87.7	90.3	89.0	91.0	93.4	95.1	94.0	94.3	92.8	94.2	95.9	100.0	100.3	102.3	102.2	100.5	98.4	100.6	102.5
Pocatello, ID	92.1	87.4	88.0	94.1	99.6	102.2	103.2	106.0	101.8	100.8	100.3	100.0	99.2	97.4	99.2	99.7	102.6	106.3	109.3
Portland-South Portland, ME	90.4	91.4	95.1	99.2	99.5	99.4	99.0	99.7	98.7	100.1	99.7	100.0	99.0	101.9	103.5	106.5	109.5	113.0	114.8
Portland-Vancouver-Hillsboro, OR-WA	73.2	74.0	78.6	83.5	87.2	91.4	93.8	97.6	93.0	95.0	98.5	100.0	100.7	104.4	110.1	115.5	121.1	127.7	131.3
Port St. Lucie, FL	78.8	82.7	85.4	94.1	104.0	111.4	112.3	106.4	101.7	101.0	98.9	100.0	100.5	100.2	104.2	106.4	109.0	112.3	115.9
Poughkeepsie-Newburgh-Middletown, NY	80.0	81.2	85.7	88.7	90.6	91.9	92.9	96.5	97.0	99.3	98.8	100.0	99.9	99.5	101.9	102.7	104.8	108.4	112.0
Prescott Valley-Prescott, AZ	81.9	86.3	92.2	99.1	109.4	118.6	118.4	114.8	106.0	102.7	100.0	100.0	101.9	105.6	107.8	111.4	117.3	119.1	121.9
Providence-Warwick, RI-MA	89.6	92.4	95.4	98.2	99.2	102.3	99.9	98.5	97.0	99.3	99.6	100.0	100.4	101.8	104.6	104.7	105.4	106.6	107.9
Provo-Orem, UT	63.8	64.9	67.4	71.7	77.0	84.6	92.0	92.3	93.0	95.3	98.1	100.0	104.0	109.0	117.4	125.1	131.8	143.8	152.1
Pueblo, CO	79.4	80.8	83.0	87.2	81.9	86.8	87.5	92.9	92.1	94.4	97.3	100.0	98.1	97.0	100.3	102.7	105.3	107.6	111.3
Punta Gorda, FL	86.5	90.8	94.3	99.7	110.0	117.1	113.6	108.1	102.2	100.2	99.5	100.0	101.5	102.3	107.8	111.8	114.8	119.1	127.4
Racine, WI	98.3	98.5	100.5	103.8	102.7	106.0	102.6	99.2	95.6	101.2	100.4	100.0	96.8	97.6	96.0	94.9	93.4	96.1	96.8
Raleigh-Cary, NC	73.6	75.5	77.5	81.0	85.7	90.2	93.9	96.1	91.5	97.2	97.6	100.0	105.9	112.2	120.8	127.9	135.2	143.4	147.6
Rapid City, SD	83.2	93.8	94.5	91.3	94.4	91.1	93.1	95.4	93.5	96.4	98.5	100.0	99.2	102.4	104.2	104.5	106.5	108.0	109.4
Reading, PA	88.3	89.4	90.9	92.2	93.9	99.0	98.9	98.9	95.4	97.9	99.7	100.0	100.8	104.2	108.9	109.7	108.4	111.2	113.0
Redding, CA	91.5	102.4	106.1	105.0	103.5	112.4	109.9	103.6	98.5	101.3	103.8	100.0	101.6	103.3	106.6	111.3	117.3	117.0	125.7
Reno, NV	92.5	93.3	96.1	103.8	108.8	110.6	108.8	102.6	95.8	100.5	98.8	100.0	98.7	100.1	108.0	112.2	118.8	117.3	120.8
Richmond, VA	89.5	87.2	88.7	89.7	94.5	95.7	96.4	95.5	93.4	95.8	98.2	100.0	102.7	103.3	107.9	109.1	111.9	113.7	116.0
Riverside-San Bernardino-Ontario, CA	76.3	80.6	86.7	93.5	99.6	105.9	106.9	103.1	96.1	96.7	99.3	100.0	103.6	108.0	113.9	117.2	120.9	124.0	129.6
Roanoke, VA	91.4	91.0	92.3	92.4	96.6	101.0	103.5	102.9	99.4	100.2	100.6	100.0	101.3	101.9	105.0	103.1	102.6	103.9	106.0
Rochester, MN	72.1	77.0	82.9	87.1	88.7	91.6	91.9	94.2	92.5	97.9	98.2	100.0	103.1	102.9	106.2	108.2	112.1	117.1	118.6
Rochester, NY	92.1	93.6	94.5	94.5	95.3	97.7	97.9	98.6	98.9	101.3	99.4	100.0	98.8	97.6	99.6	99.9	100.6	102.0	104.5
Rockford, IL	90.6	92.2	94.2	96.5	98.5	104.3	105.6	104.0	95.3	96.8	100.0	100.0	98.0	99.5	100.2	100.1	101.8	105.1	104.5
Rocky Mount, NC	107.8	106.0	107.3	107.6	109.0	114.5	115.1	114.3	134.9	124.4	114.8	100.0	100.9	125.5	149.7	155.4	147.0	145.7	118.1
Rome, GA	111.5	99.2	100.1	104.4	101.5	104.4	105.5	105.0	101.5	101.9	102.0	100.0	97.8	101.2	105.0	107.9	105.4	105.4	107.6
Sacramento-Roseville-Folsom, CA	83.6	86.9	92.2	96.1	101.2	104.3	104.8	104.0	99.5	97.3	99.0	100.0	103.2	106.5	111.5	114.0	117.5	121.2	126.4
Saginaw, MI	103.8	106.3	110.9	108.9	110.1	109.0	106.2	99.1	92.7	99.1	100.5	100.0	101.1	99.4	100.1	102.4	100.9	103.3	103.6
St. Cloud, MN	86.4	89.0	89.8	93.8	94.9	97.4	97.4	99.4	96.4	97.3	100.1	100.0	102.8	107.6	109.8	113.1	115.3	116.5	116.6
St. George, UT	70.2	73.8	79.1	86.2	95.7	107.1	110.7	106.0	96.3	95.4	96.2	100.0	106.7	112.1	118.8	128.4	142.0	151.8	153.8
St. Joseph, MO-KS	79.3	81.4	82.8	87.3	87.0	90.1	91.4	94.4	92.6	93.1	93.3	100.0	102.2	98.3	95.4	95.8	98.9	100.5	102.6
St. Louis, MO-IL	90.5	91.8	94.6	96.1	97.6	97.2	97.6	100.3	97.9	99.4	99.2	100.0	99.1	99.0	100.4	100.2	101.5	103.5	104.6
Salem, OR	89.1	90.1	92.8	93.9	97.9	106.8	105.4	106.1	101.4	101.6	100.4	100.0	101.3	104.1	110.6	116.5	122.0	128.6	132.2
Salinas, CA	97.9	103.8	104.3	94.3	96.8	106.5	102.1	99.6	105.6	102.5	97.1	100.0	106.4	109.2	118.9	122.0	122.8	125.7	129.2
Salisbury, MD-DE	87.8	85.8	88.2	93.2	99.4	103.7	104.5	103.6	101.7	99.1	98.2	100.0	100.4	110.8	120.7	118.3	116.2	118.7	122.7
Salt Lake City, UT	73.6	75.1	75.8	80.3	84.9	91.1	95.5	94.0	91.2	93.5	97.7	100.0	101.6	104.6	108.7	112.9	116.3	123.0	127.2
San Angelo, TX	70.8	70.0	68.0	68.1	69.3	72.3	74.4	77.3	80.4	84.9	89.6	100.0	111.2	121.2	124.3	118.3	119.1	124.3	129.6
San Antonio-New Braunfels, TX	72.8	75.2	78.3	81.0	83.6	87.9	90.8	91.9	90.1	93.5	97.5	100.0	103.9	109.4	116.0	117.7	118.5	123.8	126.1
San Diego-Chula Vista-Carlsbad, CA	80.2	83.8	88.6	93.8	98.8	100.9	102.2	100.8	95.8	96.7	98.7	100.0	103.9	107.5	111.6	113.5	117.1	120.6	123.3
San Francisco-Oakland-Berkeley, CA	84.4	83.1	84.6	86.1	90.0	92.3	92.6	96.7	92.3	92.1	92.7	100.0	104.0	111.0	117.8	124.9	134.1	139.8	145.0
San Jose-Sunnyvale-Santa Clara, CA	60.7	58.1	61.5	64.1	68.1	73.3	80.0	84.1	82.4	89.7	96.6	100.0	109.3	117.6	129.1	137.6	147.3	158.4	165.8
San Luis Obispo-Paso Robles, CA	79.8	88.6	91.1	91.9	95.1	99.8	99.6	92.9	90.9	95.1	97.3	100.0	103.6	105.5	111.7	113.7	115.2	118.9	121.2
Santa Cruz-Watsonville, CA	91.9	91.9	93.5	92.4	92.5	96.3	96.0	94.9	95.9	102.8	101.5	100.0	103.2	106.7	108.9	110.6	112.1	115.9	120.6
Santa Fe, NM	93.4	104.9	95.5	96.7	100.2	103.2	107.9	111.9	103.2	103.0	101.1	100.0	99.6	98.3	98.9	98.4	97.7	99.3	101.2
Santa Maria-Santa Barbara, CA	77.9	81.3	85.0	88.2	92.2	95.6	96.9	96.9	98.1	97.1	98.1	100.0	101.9	105.1	111.4	112.1	115.7	119.5	122.6
Santa Rosa-Petaluma, CA	90.7	94.8	94.8	95.0	96.7	100.7	101.9	99.6	95.2	97.0	99.0	100.0	103.1	107.9	113.4	115.9	119.4	123.9	127.1
Savannah, GA	76.4	77.8	80.0	84.4	89.5	95.0	96.3	94.9	93.5	95.3	97.1	100.0	101.3	105.9	109.9	112.7	115.7	119.4	120.5
Scranton--Wilkes-Barre, PA	86.6	86.2	87.9	90.0	91.0	93.6	95.7	97.5	96.8	99.2	100.0	100.0	100.8	103.0	105.9	107.4	108.3	110.0	112.8
Seattle-Tacoma-Bellevue, WA	74.3	74.5	75.6	77.1	82.4	85.5	91.7	93.0	90.0	92.2	95.2	100.0	103.6	108.2	113.8	118.4	125.6	135.4	142.2
Sebastian-Vero Beach, FL	85.2	89.7	95.4	100.9	109.6	114.7	114.1	110.3	102.9	98.9	98.7	100.0	101.9	106.8	112.9	119.3	123.2	126.9	132.0
Sebring-Avon Park, FL	79.4	85.7	88.4	93.8	100.7	116.0	114.5	107.8	105.7	102.4	99.0	100.0	95.8	96.1	98.4	100.7	102.8	103.1	110.2
Sheboygan, WI	92.5	94.3	96.6	102.8	100.0	101.1	102.2	100.9	95.7	98.0	97.6	100.0	99.8	101.2	103.9	107.2	109.1	110.9	111.6
Sherman-Denison, TX	73.4	75.0	76.7	81.6	81.7	88.4	88.9	90.5	90.7	92.1	97.3	100.0	100.7	102.3	105.4	106.4	109.6	114.7	116.3
Shreveport-Bossier City, LA	73.9	74.4	77.3	81.1	85.6	88.4	81.6	82.4	95.8	100.8	105.8	100.0	92.8	92.3	95.5	94.8	98.6	100.7	103.6
Sierra Vista-Douglas, AZ	75.3	76.5	82.1	84.9	90.5	95.6	101.5	101.9	102.2	105.4	104.9	100.0	97.3	95.0	96.7	99.2	97.8	98.8	102.6
Sioux City, IA-NE-SD	106.0	95.7	93.8	99.4	103.2	105.8	108.0	113.7	106.6	109.1	104.5	100.0	98.6	97.7	102.4	103.3	101.6	105.4	106.7
Sioux Falls, SD	52.8	61.6	61.3	71.7	76.7	83.4	85.2	86.9	89.2	87.1	92.8	100.0	96.5	100.3	101.9	102.7	103.0	105.9	107.7
South Bend-Mishawaka, IN-MI	94.1	96.9	101.4	104.1	104.1	106.6	107.2	103.6	93.6	98.5	99.1	100.0	100.7	104.9	106.5	106.4	107.4	111.2	114.0
Spartanburg, SC	87.3	90.1	94.2	99.8	102.9	108.9	107.8	105.9	96.5	100.9	102.4	100.0	101.7	103.1	107.3	113.7	121.4	125.3	130.0
Spokane-Spokane Valley, WA	82.6	82.5	84.5	87.4	91.6	96.5	100.8	102.3	98.9	98.9	99.3	100.0	102.0	104.3	106.2	109.5	114.6	122.1	127.4
Springfield, IL	96.9	98.8	96.6	97.0	96.5	99.2	99.6	99.2	99.5	101.7	102.1	100.0	99.9	101.6	101.7	101.5	102.9	106.9	107.7
Springfield, MA	91.1	92.3	94.4	95.3	95.3	95.9	95.6	96.3	94.3	96.7	98.8	100.0	99.9	101.0	103.6	104.3	105.6	106.9	108.5
Springfield, MO	85.7	88.0	91.9	96.1	100.4	101.3	101.8	103.4	100.6	99.9	99.2	100.0	99.4	102.4	105.7	106.0	107.5	110.6	111.4

Quantity Indexes for Real GDP by Metropolitan Area—*Continued*

(2012 = 100.0)

Metropolitan Statistical Area	2001	2002	2003	2004	2005	2006	2007	2008	2009	2010	2011	2012	2013	2014	2015	2016	2017	2018	2019
Springfield, OH	104.1	105.4	104.1	108.0	107.6	111.7	105.3	102.4	97.3	98.6	101.0	100.0	100.7	101.7	101.8	101.3	101.9	103.8	104.7
State College, PA	75.3	77.4	79.2	82.9	87.6	87.4	88.8	91.4	91.7	95.2	98.1	100.0	101.6	102.7	104.2	107.0	109.5	109.4	110.5
Staunton, VA	96.1	91.1	89.5	95.4	99.4	101.6	103.5	103.7	105.9	107.6	104.5	100.0	100.7	100.9	100.7	99.9	100.5	101.9	103.7
Stockton, CA	88.5	92.8	97.4	102.2	107.4	109.3	108.1	104.5	101.5	99.2	98.6	100.0	103.6	107.8	114.5	116.8	121.2	125.8	129.8
Sumter, SC	84.9	86.0	89.1	91.3	92.2	96.8	98.1	95.5	92.7	95.3	96.2	100.0	100.9	97.3	97.7	97.6	102.2	104.4	107.7
Syracuse, NY	85.6	86.4	88.8	90.6	92.4	94.1	95.8	95.1	95.5	98.6	97.3	100.0	101.4	102.3	104.5	103.6	105.2	107.1	110.0
Tallahassee, FL	92.9	95.0	96.5	99.3	99.5	103.7	107.0	104.7	102.0	100.8	99.9	100.0	98.4	99.9	101.2	103.4	106.5	109.0	111.5
Tampa-St. Petersburg-Clearwater, FL	82.8	86.3	90.2	95.5	100.8	104.3	104.6	101.5	98.0	98.6	98.7	100.0	101.6	103.4	108.0	111.3	113.9	118.3	122.6
Terre Haute, IN	89.3	92.0	96.0	97.8	97.4	99.8	101.5	102.2	97.5	101.9	102.3	100.0	110.7	110.2	104.2	102.6	100.8	100.3	101.6
Texarkana, TX-AR	85.6	87.7	88.1	91.3	93.6	99.0	99.8	101.9	99.3	100.0	100.5	100.0	95.3	93.7	94.9	95.2	94.9	95.7	96.5
The Villages, FL	46.6	50.9	59.0	61.4	71.3	84.0	90.7	89.1	86.4	89.2	94.4	100.0	105.8	107.2	110.0	111.7	117.6	125.6	133.9
Toledo, OH	99.4	100.8	101.7	102.5	105.0	106.3	104.8	100.1	96.7	99.7	103.0	100.0	102.5	109.2	104.1	104.2	104.5	108.1	109.9
Topeka, KS	92.1	92.9	93.1	94.8	93.7	91.2	95.1	97.1	95.9	95.9	98.8	100.0	98.0	99.8	101.2	103.0	104.0	106.2	105.9
Trenton-Princeton, NJ	86.6	89.2	91.1	92.1	93.3	94.4	93.1	97.0	93.4	94.1	94.5	100.0	100.5	99.3	101.2	104.8	104.6	106.2	111.0
Tucson, AZ	86.6	86.5	91.8	91.0	96.0	99.7	103.7	103.6	97.0	99.0	98.8	100.0	99.1	99.6	99.6	103.4	108.5	112.1	115.3
Tulsa, OK	80.2	80.2	78.9	81.1	85.7	94.2	94.3	97.2	91.8	90.2	95.2	100.0	101.6	108.6	111.3	104.7	106.7	110.9	114.3
Tuscaloosa, AL	80.8	85.4	90.0	96.3	100.7	101.6	106.2	101.3	93.3	96.5	104.5	100.0	102.8	99.8	97.4	98.8	102.0	104.7	108.4
Twin Falls, ID	80.0	81.2	81.7	86.1	90.7	96.6	101.7	100.5	91.1	96.6	95.7	100.0	104.8	110.7	114.0	120.1	122.2	126.8	131.2
Tyler, TX	76.4	76.6	78.1	87.2	91.3	97.0	97.1	96.4	95.0	97.4	97.9	100.0	100.9	100.6	102.6	103.4	102.5	106.4	107.6
Urban Honolulu, HI	77.6	79.7	83.0	88.0	91.8	93.3	94.5	96.3	94.4	96.9	98.3	100.0	101.1	101.4	106.4	107.9	110.5	111.5	111.1
Utica-Rome, NY	86.3	88.4	89.3	90.2	90.7	96.4	98.1	97.4	97.9	100.1	99.4	100.0	99.2	98.0	97.4	98.8	100.4	102.9	107.9
Valdosta, GA	84.8	88.4	91.8	92.5	96.2	99.5	100.1	101.7	100.3	100.7	99.5	100.0	99.6	99.7	101.2	102.5	104.9	108.1	110.2
Vallejo, CA	76.4	78.8	86.0	87.1	89.6	90.5	92.9	100.3	95.3	95.3	92.4	100.0	105.8	107.7	109.4	111.9	111.7	113.9	118.0
Victoria, TX	88.3	86.8	87.6	92.2	97.4	105.4	100.6	97.6	90.0	91.4	93.7	100.0	102.5	103.3	95.7	88.1	87.8	92.4	92.2
Vineland-Bridgeton, NJ	91.7	93.2	98.7	102.8	104.7	106.2	103.8	105.3	103.1	101.8	99.6	100.0	100.1	99.8	101.5	103.1	100.6	100.5	102.2
Virginia Beach-Norfolk-Newport News, VA-NC	86.7	88.2	92.2	96.6	100.8	101.6	102.5	102.1	101.1	101.2	101.0	100.0	100.5	99.7	102.6	102.3	102.9	104.5	106.4
Visalia, CA	81.4	76.7	81.6	90.4	100.1	99.2	109.1	103.0	93.7	101.4	105.4	100.0	103.2	116.1	117.2	124.2	130.3	130.7	138.4
Waco, TX	80.2	81.6	84.8	87.5	88.5	92.5	93.3	92.9	92.2	93.8	95.5	100.0	108.8	113.1	110.8	112.9	116.9	120.6	120.4
Walla Walla, WA	88.2	82.4	85.6	83.1	85.9	97.9	93.5	96.0	98.6	97.0	101.5	100.0	98.8	101.1	109.1	116.5	120.6	123.8	127.0
Warner Robins, GA	81.4	84.6	87.3	89.9	92.7	97.6	98.5	98.3	97.8	98.9	100.2	100.0	98.7	98.8	99.7	101.0	103.6	106.9	110.8
Washington-Arlington-Alexandria, DC-VA-MD-WV	74.7	77.5	80.5	85.7	90.0	90.2	91.2	93.3	93.4	97.3	99.3	100.0	99.5	100.6	102.7	105.3	107.1	108.9	110.6
Waterloo-Cedar Falls, IA	64.7	67.8	67.5	76.4	79.1	78.5	80.8	78.7	79.3	84.4	83.6	100.0	88.2	98.2	92.3	83.4	82.8	86.0	85.1
Watertown-Fort Drum, NY	67.2	67.6	70.3	74.0	81.5	89.8	90.8	94.9	97.0	101.5	103.4	100.0	97.6	95.3	91.8	88.7	87.4	87.8	88.1
Wausau-Weston, WI	83.5	85.7	89.3	93.1	96.3	98.5	98.7	97.0	93.0	94.8	98.5	100.0	100.8	105.3	107.8	110.9	111.9	116.3	118.4
Weirton-Steubenville, WV-OH	107.9	113.2	110.0	105.3	105.5	100.5	104.0	112.2	102.6	102.5	99.5	100.0	112.6	125.9	136.8	109.3	117.8	123.8	140.1
Wenatchee, WA	74.9	82.8	82.2	82.5	77.6	87.6	88.2	86.1	86.4	90.5	100.0	100.0	98.4	98.5	105.2	108.3	112.9	114.3	114.8
Wheeling, WV-OH	93.5	94.2	95.2	95.2	97.0	97.8	99.1	101.4	99.0	99.9	100.4	100.0	110.8	128.4	151.7	168.4	188.0	189.5	190.0
Wichita, KS	91.5	90.5	89.1	88.9	89.3	98.5	105.0	104.8	93.6	97.8	100.2	100.0	94.1	99.8	105.4	114.3	116.3	118.2	119.9
Wichita Falls, TX	91.3	92.7	91.4	90.5	89.8	96.4	96.5	97.5	97.0	96.8	96.1	100.0	99.3	98.4	96.8	98.1	98.8	100.7	104.1
Williamsport, PA	71.0	69.6	71.7	73.7	75.1	76.2	76.3	76.2	76.6	82.3	91.6	100.0	104.4	113.9	113.1	111.0	111.8	110.2	111.7
Wilmington, NC	82.8	84.8	87.3	90.1	97.0	102.4	107.4	108.7	103.8	105.9	106.5	100.0	105.7	110.3	112.0	116.3	116.9	122.0	126.3
Winchester, VA-WV	83.6	85.0	86.9	89.9	96.2	99.9	98.7	94.9	97.0	99.9	100.2	100.0	101.7	102.3	104.4	104.5	106.0	108.4	110.9
Winston-Salem, NC	95.0	94.7	97.3	101.2	102.8	106.8	105.0	108.2	104.4	104.2	99.7	100.0	101.3	103.4	103.9	104.4	106.0	106.8	109.1
Worcester, MA-CT	82.5	85.0	88.3	89.4	90.0	94.1	94.9	95.1	92.1	95.9	99.4	100.0	100.7	101.0	103.3	104.3	105.7	107.3	109.4
Yakima, WA	78.5	82.1	85.2	88.5	90.7	94.1	100.6	98.1	96.0	99.7	99.7	100.0	99.6	106.7	107.1	112.5	116.1	122.3	126.2
York-Hanover, PA	83.6	85.1	88.6	94.2	99.2	98.1	102.7	106.7	100.6	102.2	102.2	100.0	100.8	101.0	102.8	104.2	105.9	107.1	108.5
Youngstown-Warren-Boardman, OH-PA	102.0	105.4	106.2	108.6	110.3	111.1	108.6	105.5	95.1	98.4	102.0	100.0	100.0	99.5	99.1	98.2	96.1	97.6	99.3
Yuba City, CA	78.6	90.3	92.9	94.5	93.4	101.9	102.0	107.7	111.7	106.5	103.9	100.0	104.2	101.1	104.6	107.7	111.0	114.6	121.4
Yuma, AZ	80.4	92.6	90.3	99.1	106.3	113.5	119.8	110.7	105.8	110.3	107.7	100.0	105.1	103.6	111.6	118.6	123.1	125.8	131.8

PART C

INCOME AND POVERTY BY STATE

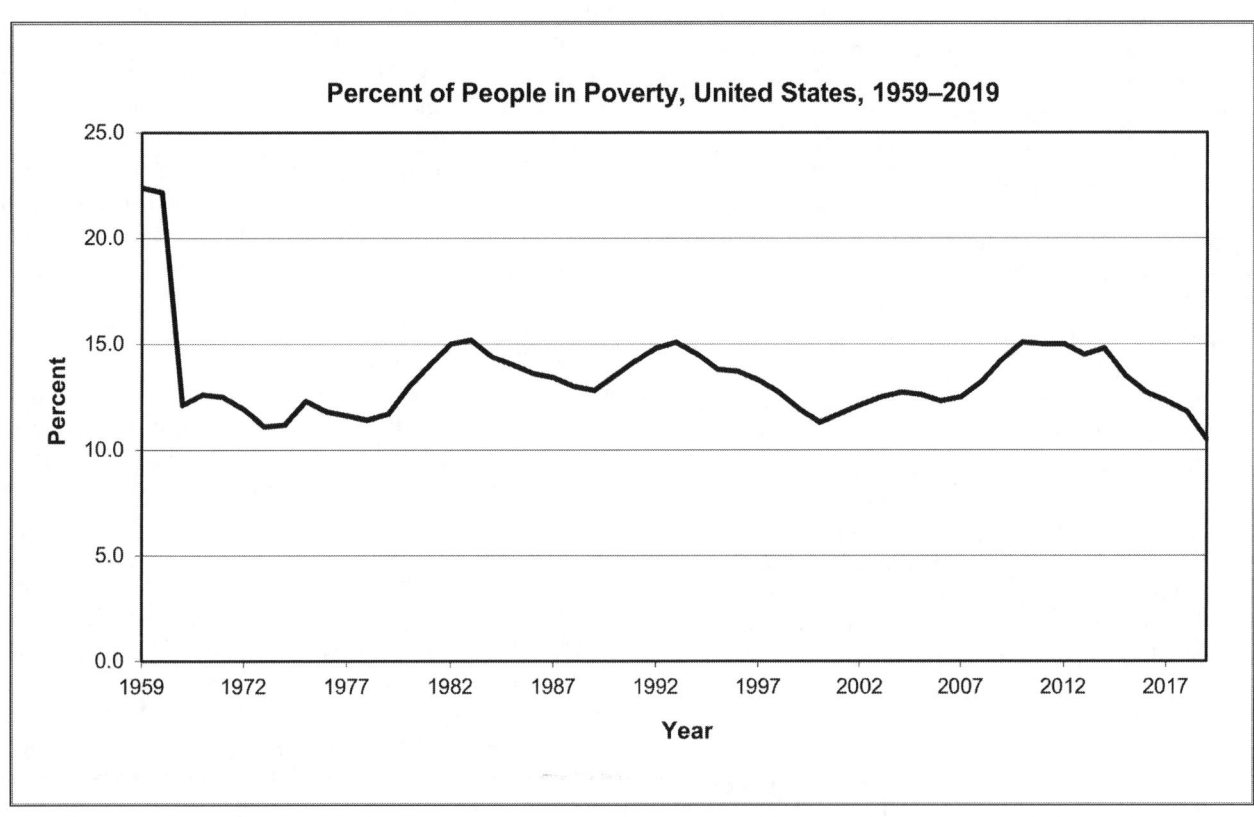

Percent of People in Poverty, United States, 1959–2019

HIGHLIGHTS:

- The percent of people in poverty in the United States fell from 11.8 percent in 2018 to 10.5 percent in 2019.

- The median household income in the United States increased 6.8 percent to $68,703 in 2019. The median income rose for the seventh year in a row, after declining for five consecutive years from 2008 through 2012.

- The South was the region with the highest poverty rate among U.S., with 12.0 percent of the population living in poverty in 2019, followed by the Midwest at 9.7 percent, the West at 9.5 percent, and the Northeast at 9.4 percent.

- In 2019, Maryland had the highest median household income at $95,572 (in 2019 dollars), followed by the District of Columbia ($93,111), Hawaii ($88,006), New Jersey ($87,726), and Massachusetts ($87,707). Mississippi and Louisiana had the lowest median household incomes at $43,787 and $51,707 respectively.

PART C NOTES AND DEFINITIONS: MEDIAN HOUSEHOLD INCOME AND POVERTY

Source: U.S. Department of Commerce, Bureau of the Census, <http://www.census.gov>

These data are derived from the Current Population Survey (CPS), which is also the source of the widely followed monthly report on the civilian labor force, employment, and unemployment. In March of each year (with some data also collected in February and April), the households in this survey are asked additional questions concerning earnings and other income in the previous year. This additional information, informally known as the "March Supplement," is now formally known as the Current Population Survey Annual Social and Economic Supplement (CPS-ASEC). It was previously called the Annual Demographic Supplement.

The population represented by the income and poverty survey is the civilian noninstitutional population of the United States and members of the armed forces in the United States living off post or with their families on post, but excluding all other members of the armed forces. This is slightly different from the population base for the civilian employment and unemployment data, which excludes those armed forces households. As it is a survey of households, homeless persons are not included.

Definitions

A *household* consists of all persons who occupy a housing unit. A household includes the related family members and all the unrelated persons, if any (such as lodgers, foster children, wards, or employees), who share the housing unit. A person living alone in a housing unit or a group of unrelated persons sharing a housing unit as partners is also counted as a household. The count of households excludes group quarters.

Earnings includes all income from work, including wages, salaries, armed forces pay, commissions, tips, piece-rate payments, and cash bonuses, before deductions such as taxes, bonds, pensions, and union dues. This category also includes net income from farm and nonfarm self-employment. Wage and salary supplements that are paid directly by the employer, such as the employer share of Social Security taxes and the cost of employer-provided health insurance, are not included.

Income, in the official definition used in the survey, is money income, including *earnings* from work as defined above; unemployment compensation; workers' compensation; Social Security; Supplemental Security Income; cash public assistance (welfare payments); veterans' payments; survivor benefits; disability benefits; pension or retirement income; interest income; dividends (but not capital gains); rents, royalties, and payments from estates or trusts; educational assistance, such as scholarships or grants; child support; alimony; financial assistance from outside of the household; and other cash income regularly received, such as foster child payments, military family allotments, and foreign government pensions. Receipts not counted as income include capital gains or losses, withdrawals of bank deposits, money borrowed, tax refunds, gifts, and lump-sum inheritances or insurance payments.

Median income is the amount of income that divides a ranked income distribution into two equal groups, with half of the households having incomes above the median, and half having incomes below the median.

Historical income figures are shown in constant *2019 dollars*. All constant-dollar figures are converted from current-dollar values using the *CPI-U-RS* (the Consumer Price Index, All Urban, Research Series), compiled by the Bureau of Labor Statistics, which measures changes in prices for past periods using the methodologies of the current CPI-U.

The *number of people below poverty level*, or the number of poor people, is the number of people with family or individual incomes below a specified level representing the estimated cost of a minimum standard of living. These minimum levels vary by size and composition of family and are known as *poverty thresholds*. These poverty thresholds have been adjusted each year for price increases, using the percent change in the Consumer Price Index for All Urban Consumers (CPI-U).

The *poverty rate* for a demographic group is the number of poor people in that group expressed as a percentage of the total number of people in the group.

The data in this chapter were derived from the "Historical Income Tables" and "Historical Poverty Tables," which are available on the Census Web site.

A different set of estimates of median household income and poverty for states and smaller geographic units is also available. It is based on a different, more comprehensive Census survey, the American Community Survey (ACS); it is more precise but less timely, and it does not provide the historical record that is available in the CPS-ASEC data presented here. (The median household income data by state are available even farther back than shown here; they begin in 1984.) Further information on ACS and small-area statistics and on other research in measuring poverty can be found in the report referenced above and other reports posted on the Census website, under the subjects "Income" and "Poverty."

Median Household Income by State

(2019 CPI-U-RS adjusted dollars)

State	1990	1991	1992	1993	1994	1995	1996	1997	1998	1999	2000	2001	2002	2003	2004	2005	2006
United States	56,966	55,302	54,874	54,581	55,215	56,945	57,772	58,961	61,128	62,641	62,512	61,126	60,435	60,360	60,150	60,794	61,268
Alabama	44,436	44,692	46,226	43,821	46,542	43,434	49,324	50,889	57,011	55,799	52,737	50,895	53,586	51,912	49,697	48,752	48,241
Alaska	74,764	74,551	74,874	75,005	77,639	80,136	85,911	76,469	79,689	79,111	78,675	83,034	75,206	72,230	74,707	73,346	71,713
Arizona	55,598	56,424	52,585	53,304	53,554	51,575	51,497	52,165	58,306	56,944	59,226	61,815	56,623	57,361	59,488	59,375	59,306
Arkansas	43,350	43,019	42,776	40,251	43,751	43,138	44,150	41,684	43,490	45,688	44,211	48,259	46,153	44,592	47,465	48,106	47,103
California	63,333	61,797	62,517	59,529	60,464	61,846	63,176	63,245	64,349	67,156	69,696	68,413	67,600	68,695	66,782	67,918	70,316
Colorado	58,469	57,822	58,184	60,254	64,746	68,024	66,657	68,884	73,255	74,156	71,816	71,503	68,822	69,587	69,040	66,204	70,796
Connecticut	73,949	77,382	73,152	69,038	70,332	67,250	68,559	70,082	73,112	77,875	74,693	77,221	76,080	76,589	74,757	74,585	79,322
Delaware	58,604	59,816	63,905	63,007	61,392	58,368	63,985	68,565	65,173	71,772	74,980	71,800	70,754	68,304	65,191	67,236	66,654
District of Columbia	52,113	54,860	54,177	47,703	51,539	51,383	52,033	50,763	52,558	59,523	61,368	59,593	55,677	62,765	58,952	59,044	61,619
Florida	50,768	50,026	48,986	49,880	50,133	49,707	49,876	51,711	54,878	55,153	57,846	52,720	54,186	54,304	54,996	56,416	58,059
Georgia	52,434	49,953	51,580	55,318	53,851	56,983	52,896	58,416	60,782	60,685	62,379	61,630	61,191	59,134	55,605	60,269	62,721
Hawaii	74,046	68,372	75,431	74,535	72,314	71,609	67,995	65,221	64,181	68,503	76,738	68,669	67,409	72,226	76,307	78,195	76,863
Idaho	48,142	47,941	49,622	54,178	53,970	54,605	56,498	53,223	57,662	55,105	55,993	55,355	53,746	59,042	60,183	57,972	58,741
Illinois	61,910	58,529	56,513	57,404	60,036	63,621	64,384	65,777	67,877	71,313	68,577	66,833	60,864	62,917	62,515	63,513	61,866
Indiana	51,230	49,727	51,102	51,496	47,675	55,790	57,211	61,962	62,458	62,860	60,837	58,449	58,494	59,116	57,430	55,690	57,717
Iowa	51,915	52,414	51,483	50,077	56,610	59,356	54,056	53,827	58,195	63,260	61,025	59,314	58,497	57,665	58,871	61,022	61,173
Kansas	56,916	53,777	54,354	52,011	48,469	50,703	53,040	58,110	57,711	57,488	61,126	59,949	60,734	61,633	55,717	55,152	57,901
Kentucky	47,143	43,623	42,065	42,587	45,514	49,816	52,760	53,300	56,989	51,931	53,989	55,638	52,388	51,467	48,314	48,160	50,189
Louisiana	42,625	46,441	45,565	45,970	43,941	46,706	49,259	52,994	49,888	50,263	45,731	48,234	48,463	46,689	49,425	48,865	46,380
Maine	52,250	51,157	53,049	47,937	51,882	56,580	56,477	52,216	56,027	59,818	55,479	52,997	52,518	51,714	56,073	57,640	58,016
Maryland	73,925	67,832	66,636	69,777	67,082	68,584	71,610	74,384	78,626	80,356	81,188	77,486	80,383	72,895	77,475	79,410	80,928
Massachusetts	68,959	65,560	65,124	64,755	69,310	64,461	64,287	66,956	66,567	67,735	69,603	75,637	71,046	71,001	70,577	73,511	70,330
Michigan	56,954	58,957	57,795	57,064	60,384	60,872	63,849	61,728	65,744	70,942	67,755	65,206	60,871	62,734	57,331	60,278	61,835
Minnesota	59,861	54,114	55,492	58,846	57,577	63,390	66,723	67,818	75,341	72,403	80,765	76,257	77,839	73,604	76,119	71,147	71,450
Mississippi	38,388	35,750	36,844	38,770	43,469	44,348	43,424	45,408	45,777	49,992	51,062	43,659	44,009	45,604	47,154	43,142	44,149
Missouri	51,998	51,263	49,008	50,110	51,666	58,196	55,775	58,240	63,197	63,699	67,137	59,839	60,958	60,979	57,170	56,411	56,664
Montana	44,470	45,575	47,510	46,246	47,287	46,385	46,691	46,544	49,640	47,775	48,796	46,503	49,642	47,527	46,070	48,966	52,249
Nebraska	52,284	54,243	53,821	54,174	54,411	55,028	55,366	55,275	57,242	59,455	62,155	63,128	60,987	61,274	59,407	62,890	61,197
Nevada	60,923	60,462	57,152	62,571	61,388	60,300	62,734	61,907	62,497	63,819	68,121	65,722	64,068	62,960	64,044	63,265	66,456
New Hampshire	77,631	66,144	70,636	66,327	60,317	65,459	64,145	65,323	70,675	70,890	75,815	74,303	78,836	77,428	77,084	74,780	78,770
New Jersey	73,691	73,518	69,855	70,758	72,356	73,402	77,266	76,513	78,328	76,553	75,039	74,940	77,762	78,094	74,995	83,158	86,510
New Mexico	47,636	48,719	46,319	46,749	46,044	43,434	40,834	47,936	49,586	50,139	52,244	47,948	50,528	48,916	53,676	51,110	50,880
New York	60,101	58,364	55,617	55,378	54,591	55,193	57,639	57,037	58,784	61,553	60,657	60,961	59,804	59,621	60,578	61,909	61,295
North Carolina	50,090	49,294	49,742	50,351	51,536	53,440	57,950	57,104	56,338	57,343	57,044	55,240	52,036	51,945	54,593	55,190	50,586
North Dakota	48,064	47,530	48,288	49,125	48,394	48,611	51,225	50,446	47,639	50,276	53,588	51,811	51,587	56,308	53,212	55,369	52,175
Ohio	57,099	54,685	56,249	54,658	54,515	58,390	55,458	57,573	61,191	60,783	63,959	60,485	60,827	60,641	58,415	58,008	58,344
Oklahoma	46,390	46,740	45,287	45,879	46,191	43,968	44,661	49,952	53,020	50,307	48,283	51,545	51,955	50,026	53,747	49,402	49,367
Oregon	55,706	55,419	57,186	57,895	53,833	60,785	57,772	59,346	61,414	62,523	63,270	59,744	59,570	58,019	55,619	57,950	59,857
Pennsylvania	55,181	55,744	53,523	54,151	54,877	57,693	56,807	59,776	61,333	58,119	62,789	62,966	60,562	59,823	59,841	60,760	61,619
Rhode Island	60,818	56,605	54,508	58,544	54,640	59,089	60,204	55,443	63,959	65,755	62,820	66,185	60,447	62,301	65,036	64,938	68,304
South Carolina	54,668	50,414	49,396	45,517	51,077	48,581	56,426	54,590	52,297	56,124	55,932	54,624	53,884	53,617	52,494	52,794	50,357
South Dakota	46,746	45,230	47,034	48,459	50,884	49,428	48,061	47,312	51,540	55,148	54,301	57,425	53,971	55,070	55,772	56,627	57,742
Tennessee	42,981	44,888	43,557	43,856	49,012	48,487	50,119	48,813	53,592	56,216	50,760	51,797	52,770	52,285	51,654	51,713	51,725
Texas	53,703	50,909	50,068	50,189	52,633	53,541	53,833	55,885	56,252	59,550	57,478	59,146	57,215	54,721	56,166	54,358	55,048
Utah	57,344	51,429	61,349	62,522	61,123	60,962	60,289	68,154	69,639	70,882	70,789	68,529	68,205	68,660	69,020	71,931	69,438
Vermont	59,163	53,520	58,669	54,274	61,270	56,523	52,671	55,850	61,894	64,008	58,945	59,050	61,276	60,280	64,214	66,539	66,073
Virginia	66,726	66,336	68,418	63,652	64,428	60,531	63,826	68,444	68,154	70,333	70,213	72,725	70,727	76,335	69,386	68,127	72,604
Washington	61,092	62,358	60,720	62,293	57,387	59,438	59,700	71,001	74,547	69,994	63,308	61,505	64,388	66,198	67,732	66,463	69,558
West Virginia	42,115	42,491	36,308	39,172	40,327	41,577	41,096	43,797	41,979	45,095	43,785	42,952	41,838	45,652	45,279	47,827	48,834
Wisconsin	58,427	57,151	59,660	55,498	60,562	68,440	65,112	63,087	64,967	70,293	67,124	65,639	65,414	64,472	62,047	58,594	65,706
Wyoming	56,047	53,327	54,109	51,438	56,715	52,688	50,384	53,253	55,414	57,334	58,997	57,494	56,665	59,297	61,593	58,684	59,794

Median Household Income by State—*Continued*

(2019 CPI-U-RS adjusted dollars)

State	2007	2008	2009	2010	2011	2012	2013[1]	2013[2]	2014	2015	2016	2017	2017[3]	2018	2019
United States	62,090	59,877	59,458	57,904	57,021	56,912	57,095	58,904	58,001	60,987	62,898	64,007	63,761	64,324	68,703
Alabama	52,176	52,941	47,755	48,100	48,518	48,487	45,489	52,017	45,701	48,030	50,308	53,308	53,049	50,841	56,200
Alaska	77,862	76,168	73,585	67,977	65,424	71,003	67,206	79,666	73,105	81,054	80,673	75,332	81,335	69,979	78,394
Arizona	58,360	55,843	54,634	55,107	55,388	52,480	55,625	57,834	53,242	56,381	60,832	63,749	62,263	63,411	70,674
Arkansas	50,425	47,120	43,644	45,343	47,051	43,527	43,882	43,285	48,559	46,184	48,908	50,926	51,887	50,683	54,539
California	68,890	67,865	67,051	63,788	60,795	63,609	63,239	66,829	65,384	68,670	70,993	72,754	73,045	71,766	78,105
Colorado	75,573	72,542	66,807	70,779	66,789	63,871	69,662	74,654	65,874	71,864	75,179	77,357	78,204	74,357	72,499
Connecticut	79,281	76,993	77,463	77,554	74,520	71,671	74,510	76,170	75,842	78,655	80,886	75,905	77,494	74,131	87,291
Delaware	67,475	60,352	62,249	64,882	62,268	54,631	57,403	59,461	62,179	62,325	61,840	64,994	67,750	66,190	74,194
District of Columbia	62,770	66,170	63,476	66,896	62,941	72,786	66,698	66,019	73,805	75,614	75,622	86,962	84,772	87,304	93,111
Florida	56,604	53,394	54,505	51,782	51,383	51,395	52,640	53,350	49,876	52,687	54,521	55,986	55,365	55,634	58,368
Georgia	60,123	55,025	51,769	51,842	52,372	53,682	52,148	51,657	53,567	54,784	57,026	59,464	60,475	56,832	56,628
Hawaii	79,134	73,230	66,472	69,964	67,265	62,765	67,504	70,612	76,990	69,617	76,848	76,734	76,759	81,559	88,006
Idaho	60,794	56,445	55,875	55,288	54,064	53,460	56,906	53,278	57,765	55,708	60,261	62,793	62,052	59,792	65,988
Illinois	64,900	63,390	63,152	59,610	57,685	57,717	62,874	59,291	59,362	65,192	65,398	67,383	68,801	71,416	74,399
Indiana	58,654	55,374	52,921	54,218	50,631	51,492	55,571	54,364	51,951	56,095	59,761	61,401	61,290	60,977	66,693
Iowa	60,453	59,685	60,585	57,598	57,209	59,618	60,300	66,128	62,491	65,669	62,957	66,207	66,192	69,963	66,054
Kansas	59,945	56,989	53,414	54,118	52,570	55,781	56,596	52,567	57,771	59,205	60,523	60,357	59,343	65,096	73,151
Kentucky	48,765	48,980	50,961	48,301	45,403	45,834	46,343	49,334	46,250	45,740	48,335	53,553	51,805	55,543	55,662
Louisiana	51,065	47,093	54,269	46,181	46,317	43,601	43,555	51,034	45,839	49,555	44,954	45,788	45,436	50,878	51,707
Maine	59,199	56,217	56,740	56,323	56,609	54,838	55,097	60,413	55,897	54,771	54,180	53,882	55,605	59,726	66,546
Maryland	81,122	75,837	76,669	75,442	78,462	80,137	71,741	76,238	82,332	79,416	78,581	84,565	85,618	87,785	95,572
Massachusetts	72,263	71,800	70,920	71,603	72,125	71,012	69,213	68,736	68,264	73,229	76,990	76,371	79,517	87,909	87,707
Michigan	61,024	59,264	54,939	54,379	55,682	55,795	53,645	62,182	56,216	58,491	60,823	60,177	58,827	61,544	64,119
Minnesota	71,762	65,379	66,998	61,482	65,868	68,936	66,953	70,709	72,688	74,167	74,808	75,008	72,979	73,118	81,426
Mississippi	46,079	43,383	41,900	44,842	46,809	40,875	44,905	35,548	38,397	43,204	43,785	45,306	45,139	43,556	44,787
Missouri	56,864	54,800	58,254	53,839	52,145	55,515	55,305	50,900	61,215	63,879	58,612	59,327	58,957	62,844	60,597
Montana	53,960	51,065	48,301	48,508	45,883	50,298	48,513	47,490	55,239	55,461	60,806	61,624	59,872	58,724	60,195
Nebraska	60,781	60,383	59,240	61,697	63,357	58,228	59,112	63,343	61,474	65,258	63,255	62,179	62,141	68,799	73,071
Nevada	66,818	65,163	61,437	60,165	53,591	52,803	49,873	56,993	53,913	56,122	59,054	58,978	60,533	62,985	70,906
New Hampshire	83,527	78,771	76,603	78,300	75,049	75,656	78,402	75,958	79,340	81,661	81,245	78,013	78,877	82,820	86,900
New Jersey	74,791	77,735	77,375	73,993	71,014	74,399	67,915	70,083	70,525	73,764	72,943	76,131	74,299	75,520	87,726
New Mexico	54,826	50,115	52,010	53,037	47,825	48,442	46,309	44,153	50,466	48,688	51,618	49,910	47,559	49,158	53,113
New York	60,497	60,065	59,982	58,497	57,684	53,190	59,188	54,926	58,707	62,594	65,453	65,128	64,185	68,493	71,855
North Carolina	53,784	51,101	50,056	51,504	51,498	46,355	45,299	50,937	50,572	54,815	57,278	52,505	51,674	54,336	61,159
North Dakota	58,348	59,077	59,814	59,937	64,205	62,210	58,138	65,024	65,647	61,957	64,118	62,457	62,750	67,710	70,031
Ohio	60,689	55,867	54,802	53,920	50,862	49,503	51,004	55,786	53,663	57,517	57,514	62,334	63,294	62,750	64,663
Oklahoma	53,417	54,887	54,800	50,650	55,199	54,001	48,123	50,745	51,020	50,801	54,273	57,368	54,110	55,420	59,397
Oregon	62,094	61,572	58,647	59,462	58,698	57,758	61,897	53,863	63,642	65,646	63,000	67,384	65,181	70,418	74,413
Pennsylvania	59,870	61,185	57,540	56,773	56,857	57,902	59,308	60,631	59,640	65,166	64,965	65,885	63,916	65,693	70,582
Rhode Island	67,006	63,374	61,676	60,662	55,858	62,544	63,551	61,914	63,380	60,107	65,550	69,241	68,209	63,394	70,151
South Carolina	54,649	50,178	49,094	48,999	45,663	49,532	48,092	47,888	48,567	50,027	57,888	57,331	56,879	58,485	62,028
South Dakota	57,375	61,421	54,738	53,293	53,796	55,125	59,859	58,715	57,348	59,421	61,205	59,337	59,358	60,540	64,255
Tennessee	50,919	47,258	48,397	45,348	48,164	47,963	46,718	47,665	47,255	51,074	54,700	57,612	57,681	57,076	56,627
Texas	56,924	55,338	56,708	55,542	55,874	57,926	58,291	56,509	58,237	60,940	61,947	61,841	62,672	60,868	67,444
Utah	66,164	74,439	69,866	66,629	63,217	65,083	69,218	67,107	68,515	71,499	71,892	74,381	72,785	78,463	84,523
Vermont	58,576	60,357	62,493	65,721	59,080	62,005	60,286	72,016	65,623	64,200	64,814	66,545	66,416	71,335	74,305
Virginia	73,126	73,782	72,267	70,937	71,331	72,101	74,333	72,450	71,511	66,350	70,795	74,354	73,851	78,549	81,313
Washington	71,790	67,409	72,137	65,997	64,763	69,373	66,073	70,268	63,850	72,562	74,906	78,656	74,612	81,170	82,454
West Virginia	52,026	45,225	48,364	50,267	47,642	48,586	44,236	47,344	42,754	46,212	47,253	47,341	48,973	51,489	53,706
Wisconsin	63,381	60,945	61,202	59,167	59,304	59,213	60,743	56,861	62,782	59,809	63,727	66,175	66,208	63,764	67,355
Wyoming	60,250	63,488	62,674	61,341	62,096	64,158	61,229	74,136	60,199	65,745	61,609	60,320	62,092	63,672	65,134

[1]The 2014 CPS ASEC included redesigned questions for income and health insurance coverage. All of the approximately 98,000 addresses were eligible to receive the redesigned set of health insurance coverage questions. The redesigned income questions were implemented to a subsample of the 98,000 addresses using a probability split panel design. Approximately 68,000 addresses were eligible to receive a set of income questions similar to those used in the 2013 CPS ASEC and the remaining 30,000 addresses were eligible to receive the redesigned income questions. The source of these 2013 estimates is the portion of the CPS ASEC sample which received the income questions consistent with the 2013 CPS ASEC, approximately 68,000 addresses.
[2]The source of these 2013 estimates is the portion of the CPS ASEC sample which received the redesigned income questions, approximately 30,000 addresses.
[3]Estimates reflect the implementation of an updated data processing system, allowing users to evaluate the impact, and should be used to make comparisons to 2018 and subsequent years.

Poverty Rate by State

(Percent of population.)

State	2000	2001	2002	2003	2004	2005	2006	2007	2008	2009	2010	2011	2012	2013	2014	2015	2016	2017	2018	2019
United States............	11.3	11.7	12.1	12.5	12.7	12.6	12.3	12.5	13.2	14.3	15.1	15.0	15.0	14.5	14.8	13.5	12.7	12.3	11.8	10.5
Alabama..................	13.3	15.9	14.5	15.0	16.9	16.7	14.3	14.5	14.3	16.6	17.2	15.4	16.2	16.7	17.8	16.3	16.2	15.3	16.0	12.9
Alaska....................	7.6	8.5	8.8	9.6	9.1	10.0	8.9	7.6	8.2	11.7	12.5	11.7	10.0	10.9	11.9	9.2	12.6	12.1	13.1	10.2
Arizona..................	11.7	14.6	13.5	13.5	14.4	15.2	14.4	14.3	18.0	21.2	18.8	17.2	19.0	20.2	21.2	17.2	16.1	13.6	12.8	9.9
Arkansas................	16.5	17.8	19.8	17.8	15.1	13.8	17.7	13.8	15.3	18.9	15.3	18.7	20.1	17.1	18.4	16.1	16.0	14.9	15.9	14.1
California................	12.7	12.6	13.1	13.1	13.2	13.2	12.2	12.7	14.6	15.3	16.3	16.9	15.9	14.9	15.8	13.9	13.9	12.1	11.9	10.1
Colorado	9.8	8.7	9.8	9.7	10.0	11.4	9.7	9.8	11.0	12.3	12.3	13.2	11.9	10.6	12.3	9.9	8.5	8.9	9.1	9.3
Connecticut.............	7.7	7.3	8.3	8.1	10.1	9.3	8.0	8.9	8.1	8.4	8.6	10.1	10.3	11.3	8.6	9.1	9.8	10.6	10.2	8.3
Delaware	8.4	6.7	9.1	7.3	9.0	9.2	9.3	9.3	9.6	12.3	12.2	13.7	13.5	14.0	11.0	11.1	11.6	8.8	7.4	6.5
D.C......................	15.2	18.2	17.0	16.8	17.0	21.3	18.3	18.0	16.5	17.9	19.5	19.9	18.4	21.3	19.0	16.6	16.3	13.9	14.7	12.5
Florida..................	11.0	12.7	12.6	12.7	11.6	11.1	11.5	12.5	13.1	14.6	16.0	14.9	15.3	14.9	16.7	16.2	13.0	13.4	13.7	11.5
Georgia	12.1	12.9	11.2	11.9	13.0	14.4	12.6	13.6	15.5	18.4	18.8	18.4	18.1	16.3	16.8	18.1	15.4	13.1	14.8	12.1
Hawaii..................	8.9	11.4	11.3	9.3	8.6	8.6	9.2	7.5	9.9	12.5	12.4	12.1	13.8	11.1	10.8	10.9	9.3	10.6	9.2	8.4
Idaho....................	12.5	11.5	11.3	10.2	9.9	9.9	9.5	9.9	12.2	13.7	13.8	15.7	14.4	12.9	12.4	12.3	11.1	11.5	11.5	7.1
Illinois	10.7	10.1	12.8	12.6	12.3	11.5	10.6	10.0	12.3	13.2	14.1	14.2	12.6	13.3	13.7	10.9	12.1	11.5	10.3	9.3
Indiana..................	8.5	8.5	9.1	9.9	11.6	12.6	10.6	11.8	14.3	16.1	16.3	15.6	15.2	11.6	14.6	13.5	11.8	11.7	11.6	10.1
Iowa......................	8.3	7.4	9.2	8.9	10.9	11.3	10.3	8.9	9.5	10.7	10.3	10.4	10.3	10.8	10.3	10.4	9.8	7.5	8.9	9.5
Kansas	8.0	10.1	10.1	10.8	11.4	12.5	12.8	11.7	12.7	13.7	14.5	14.3	14.0	13.2	12.1	14.2	11.2	14.3	7.5	9.5
Kentucky................	12.6	12.6	14.2	14.4	17.8	14.8	16.8	15.5	17.1	17.0	17.7	16.0	17.9	20.0	20.0	19.5	15.2	13.5	15.7	13.6
Louisiana	17.2	16.2	17.5	17.0	16.8	18.3	17.0	16.1	18.2	14.3	21.5	21.1	21.1	19.2	23.1	18.6	20.2	20.5	19.0	17.9
Maine....................	10.1	10.3	13.4	11.6	11.6	12.6	10.2	10.9	12.0	11.4	12.6	13.4	12.8	12.3	14.6	12.3	12.7	12.4	11.6	10.4
Maryland................	7.4	7.2	7.4	8.6	9.9	9.7	8.4	8.8	8.7	9.6	10.9	9.3	9.9	10.3	9.9	9.6	7.1	7.6	8.0	7.0
Massachusetts.........	9.8	8.9	10.0	10.3	9.3	10.1	12.0	11.2	11.3	10.8	10.9	10.6	11.3	11.9	13.6	11.5	9.6	11.2	8.7	7.5
Michigan	9.9	9.4	11.6	11.4	13.3	12.0	13.3	10.8	13.0	14.0	15.7	15.0	13.7	14.5	14.8	12.8	11.1	11.5	10.5	10.2
Minnesota..............	5.7	7.4	6.5	7.4	7.0	8.1	8.2	9.3	9.9	11.1	10.8	10.0	10.0	12.0	8.3	7.8	8.7	8.5	7.9	5.7
Mississippi..............	14.9	19.3	18.4	16.0	18.7	20.1	20.6	22.6	18.1	23.1	22.5	17.4	22.0	22.5	22.1	19.1	21.1	18.5	19.6	19.2
Missouri.................	9.2	9.7	9.9	10.7	12.2	11.6	11.4	12.8	13.3	15.5	15.0	15.4	15.2	13.7	10.4	9.8	13.0	11.4	12.4	9.4
Montana.................	14.1	13.3	13.5	15.1	14.2	13.8	13.5	13.0	12.9	13.5	14.5	16.5	13.4	14.5	12.0	11.9	11.7	10.3	10.3	9.7
Nebraska................	8.6	9.4	10.6	9.8	9.5	9.5	10.2	9.9	10.6	9.9	10.2	10.2	12.2	11.0	11.8	10.3	9.6	11.5	10.5	8.7
Nevada..................	8.8	7.1	8.9	10.9	10.9	10.6	9.5	9.7	10.8	13.0	16.6	15.5	15.8	17.4	17.0	13.0	10.1	13.2	13.0	10.4
New Hampshire........	4.5	6.5	5.8	5.8	5.5	5.6	5.4	5.8	7.0	7.8	6.5	7.6	8.1	9.0	7.2	7.3	6.4	7.2	6.1	3.7
New Jersey	7.3	8.1	7.9	8.6	8.0	6.8	8.8	8.7	9.2	9.3	11.1	11.4	9.3	11.1	11.3	11.2	9.4	9.9	8.2	6.3
New Mexico	17.5	18.0	17.9	18.1	16.5	17.9	16.9	14.0	19.3	19.3	18.3	22.2	20.4	21.7	20.0	19.7	17.8	19.7	16.6	15.3
New York................	13.9	14.2	14.0	14.3	15.0	14.5	14.0	14.5	14.2	15.8	16.0	16.0	17.2	14.5	14.0	14.2	11.9	12.7	11.1	12.5
North Carolina..........	12.5	12.5	14.3	15.7	14.6	13.1	13.8	15.5	13.9	16.9	17.4	15.4	17.2	18.6	17.1	15.3	13.6	15.2	13.1	12.7
North Dakota............	10.4	13.8	11.6	9.7	9.7	11.2	11.4	9.3	11.8	10.9	12.6	9.9	11.4	9.9	9.7	10.7	11.1	12.4	9.7	8.1
Ohio	10.0	10.5	9.8	10.9	11.6	12.3	12.1	12.8	13.7	13.3	15.4	15.1	15.4	13.7	15.6	13.6	13.7	12.9	11.9	12.4
Oklahoma...............	14.9	15.1	14.1	12.8	10.8	15.6	15.2	13.4	13.6	12.9	16.3	13.9	18.0	14.0	17.3	14.2	14.6	12.8	13.4	10.8
Oregon..................	10.9	11.8	10.9	12.5	11.8	12.0	11.8	12.8	10.6	13.4	14.3	14.4	13.5	15.1	14.4	11.9	11.8	11.5	9.7	8.1
Pennsylvania............	8.6	9.6	9.5	10.5	11.4	11.2	11.3	10.4	11.0	11.1	12.2	12.6	13.9	12.4	12.5	12.3	11.1	10.9	11.8	8.7
Rhode Island............	10.2	9.6	11.0	11.5	11.5	12.1	10.5	9.5	12.7	13.0	14.0	13.4	13.6	13.5	11.3	11.8	11.4	11.3	8.9	9.2
South Carolina	11.1	15.1	14.3	12.7	14.9	15.0	11.2	14.1	14.0	13.7	16.9	19.0	16.7	15.9	16.5	14.3	14.1	15.2	12.8	15.1
South Dakota	10.7	8.4	11.5	12.7	13.5	11.8	10.7	9.4	13.1	14.1	13.6	14.5	12.8	10.3	12.8	13.9	14.5	10.7	10.6	10.6
Tennessee	13.5	14.1	14.8	14.0	15.9	14.9	14.9	14.8	15.0	16.5	16.7	16.3	18.6	18.1	17.3	14.7	14.9	11.3	12.0	13.1
Texas....................	15.5	14.9	15.6	17.0	16.5	16.2	16.4	16.5	15.9	17.3	18.4	17.4	17.0	16.8	16.4	14.7	13.8	13.2	13.7	11.1
Utah	7.6	10.5	9.9	9.1	10.1	9.2	9.3	9.6	7.6	9.7	10.0	11.0	11.0	8.3	10.2	9.3	8.6	8.7	6.9	7.3
Vermont..................	10.0	9.7	9.9	8.5	7.8	7.6	7.8	9.9	9.0	9.4	10.8	11.6	11.2	8.7	9.3	10.7	9.6	8.6	9.7	8.6
Virginia..................	8.3	8.0	9.9	10.0	9.4	9.2	8.6	8.6	10.3	10.7	10.7	11.4	10.6	10.4	10.2	10.9	11.4	10.5	9.8	8.8
Washington..............	10.8	10.7	11.0	12.6	11.4	10.2	8.0	10.2	10.4	11.7	11.6	12.5	11.6	12.0	12.0	11.4	11.0	10.9	8.6	7.0
West Virginia............	14.7	16.4	16.8	17.4	14.2	15.4	15.3	14.8	14.5	15.8	16.8	17.5	16.7	17.3	20.6	14.5	18.0	17.1	15.9	13.9
Wisconsin	9.3	7.9	8.6	9.8	12.4	10.2	10.1	11.0	9.8	10.8	10.1	13.1	11.4	11.0	10.9	11.4	10.7	9.2	8.6	8.4
Wyoming	10.8	8.7	9.0	9.8	10.0	10.6	10.0	10.9	10.1	9.2	9.6	10.7	9.6	11.8	9.7	9.8	10.9	13.0	9.5	9.2

Number and Percent of People in Poverty by Region

(Numbers in thousands, percent.)

Year	All Regions Below Poverty		Northeast Below Poverty		Midwest Below Poverty		South Below Poverty		West Below Poverty	
	Number	Percent	Number	Percent	Number	Percent	Number	Percent	Number	Percent
1959.................	39,490	22.4					19,116	35.4		
1960.................	39,851	22.2								
1969.................	24,147	12.1	4,108	8.6	5,424	9.6	11,090	17.9	3,525	10.4
1970.................	25,420	12.6					11,480	18.5		
1971.................	25,559	12.5	4,512	9.3	5,764	10.3	11,182	17.5	4,101	11.4
1972.................	24,460	11.9	4,266	8.7	5,258	9.3	10,928	16.9	4,008	11.1
1973.................	22,973	11.1	4,207	8.6	4,864	8.6	10,061	15.3	3,841	10.5
1974.................	23,370	11.2	4,473	9.3	4,990	8.8	10,761	16.1	4,036	10.7
1975.................	25,877	12.3	4,904	10.2	5,459	9.7	11,059	16.2	4,454	11.7
1976.................	24,975	11.8	4,949	10.2	5,657	9.9	10,354	15.2	4,015	10.5
1977.................	24,720	11.6	4,956	10.2	5,589	9.8	10,249	14.8	3,927	10.1
1978.................	24,497	11.4	5,050	10.4	5,192	9.1	10,255	14.7	4,000	10.0
1979.................	26,072	11.7	5,029	10.4	5,594	9.7	10,627	15.0	4,095	10.0
1980.................	29,272	13.0	5,369	11.1	6,592	11.4	12,363	16.5	4,958	11.4
1981.................	31,822	14.0	5,815	11.9	7,142	12.3	13,256	17.4	5,609	12.7
1982.................	34,398	15.0	6,364	13.0	7,772	13.3	13,967	18.1	6,296	14.1
1983.................	35,303	15.2	6,561	13.4	8,536	14.6	13,484	17.2	6,684	14.7
1984.................	33,700	14.4	6,531	13.2	8,303	14.1	12,792	16.2	6,074	13.1
1985.................	33,064	14.0	5,751	11.6	8,191	13.9	12,921	16.0	6,201	13.0
1986.................	32,370	13.6	5,211	10.5	7,641	13.0	13,106	16.1	6,412	13.2
1987.................	32,221	13.4	5,476	11.0	7,499	12.7	13,287	16.1	6,285	12.6
1988.................	31,745	13.0	5,089	10.1	6,804	11.4	13,530	16.1	6,322	12.7
1989.................	31,528	12.8	5,061	10.0	7,043	11.9	12,943	15.4	6,481	12.5
1990.................	33,585	13.5	5,794	11.4	7,458	12.4	13,456	15.8	6,877	13.0
1991.................	35,708	14.2	6,177	12.2	7,989	13.2	13,783	16.0	7,759	14.3
1992	38,014	14.8	6,414	12.6	8,060	13.3	15,198	17.1	8,343	14.8
1993.................	39,265	15.1	6,839	13.3	8,172	13.4	15,375	17.1	8,879	15.6
1994.................	38,059	14.5	6,597	12.9	7,965	13.0	14,729	16.1	8,768	15.3
1995.................	36,425	13.8	6,445	12.5	6,785	11.0	14,458	15.7	8,736	14.9
1996.................	36,529	13.7	6,558	12.7	6,654	10.7	14,098	15.1	9,219	15.4
1997.................	35,574	13.3	6,474	12.6	6,493	10.4	13,748	14.6	8,858	14.6
1998.................	34,476	12.7	6,357	12.3	6,501	10.3	12,992	13.7	8,625	14.0
1999.................	32,791	11.9	5,814	11.0	6,250	9.8	12,744	13.2	7,982	12.7
2000.................	31,581	11.3	5,474	10.3	5,916	9.3	12,705	12.8	7,485	11.8
2001.................	32,907	11.7	5,687	10.7	5,966	9.4	13,515	13.5	7,739	12.1
2002.................	34,570	12.1	5,871	10.9	6,616	10.3	14,019	13.8	8,064	12.4
2003.................	35,861	12.5	6,052	11.3	6,932	10.7	14,548	14.1	8,329	12.6
2004.................	37,040	12.7	6,260	11.6	7,545	11.7	14,817	14.1	8,419	12.5
2005.................	36,950	12.6	6,103	11.3	7,419	11.4	14,854	14.0	8,573	12.6
2006.................	36,460	12.3	6,222	11.5	7,324	11.2	14,882	13.8	8,032	11.6
2007.................	37,276	12.5	6,166	11.4	7,237	11.1	15,501	14.2	8,372	12.0
2008.................	39,829	13.2	6,295	11.6	8,120	12.4	15,862	14.3	9,552	13.5
2009.................	43,569	14.3	6,650	12.2	8,768	13.3	17,609	15.7	10,542	14.8
2010.................	46,343	15.1	7,038	12.9	9,216	14.0	19,123	16.8	10,966	15.3
2011.................	46,247	15.0	7,208	13.1	9,221	14.0	18,380	16.0	11,437	15.8
2012.................	46,496	15.0	7,490	13.6	8,851	13.3	19,106	16.5	11,049	15.1
2013.................	45,318	14.5	7,046	12.7	8,590	12.9	18,870	16.1	10,812	14.7
2014.................	46,657	14.8	7,020	12.6	8,714	13.0	19,531	16.5	11,391	15.2
2015.................	43,123	13.5	6,891	12.4	7,849	11.7	18,305	15.3	10,079	13.3
2016.................	40,616	12.7	5,969	10.8	7,809	11.7	17,028	14.1	9,810	12.8
2017.................	39,564	12.3	6,347	11.3	7,571	11.2	16,474	13.5	9,172	11.9
2018.................	38,146	11.8	5,682	10.3	7,005	10.4	16,757	13.6	8,701	11.2
2019.................	33,984	10.5	5,177	9.4	6,518	9.7	14,845	12.0	7,443	9.5

APPENDIX

Metropolitan Statistical Areas, Metropolitan Divisions, and Components

Core based statistical area (CBSA)	State/County FIPS code	Title and Geographic Components
10180		Abilene, TX
10180	48059	Callahan County
10180	48253	Jones County
10180	48441	Taylor County
10420		Akron, OH
10420	39133	Portage County
10420	39153	Summit County
10500		Albany, GA
10500	13095	Dougherty County
10500	13177	Lee County
10500	13273	Terrell County
10500	13321	Worth County
10540		Albany-Lebanon, OR
10540	41043	Linn County
10580		Albany-Schenectady-Troy, NY
10580	36001	Albany County
10580	36083	Rensselaer County
10580	36091	Saratoga County
10580	36093	Schenectady County
10580	36095	Schoharie County
10740		Albuquerque, NM
10740	35001	Bernalillo County
10740	35043	Sandoval County
10740	35057	Torrance County
10740	35061	Valencia County
10780		Alexandria, LA
10780	22043	Grant Parish
10780	22079	Rapides Parish
10900		Allentown-Bethlehem-Easton, PA-NJ
10900	34041	Warren County, NJ
10900	42025	Carbon County, PA
10900	42077	Lehigh County, PA
10900	42095	Northampton County, PA
11020		Altoona, PA
11020	42013	Blair County
11100		Amarillo, TX
11100	48011	Armstrong County
11100	48065	Carson County
11100	48359	Oldham County
11100	48375	Potter County
11100	48381	Randall County
11180		Ames, IA
11180	19015	Boone County
11180	19169	Story County
11260		Anchorage, AK
11260	02020	Anchorage Municipality
11260	02170	Matanuska-Susitna Borough
11460		Ann Arbor, MI
11460	26161	Washtenaw County
11500		Anniston-Oxford, AL
11500	01015	Calhoun County
11540		Appleton, WI
11540	55015	Calumet County
11540	55087	Outagamie County
11700		Asheville, NC
11700	37021	Buncombe County
11700	37087	Haywood County
11700	37089	Henderson County
11700	37115	Madison County
12020		Athens-Clarke County, GA
12020	13059	Clarke County
12020	13195	Madison County
12020	13219	Oconee County
12020	13221	Oglethorpe County
12060		Atlanta-Sandy Springs-Alpharetta, GA
12060	13013	Barrow County
12060	13015	Bartow County
12060	13035	Butts County
12060	13045	Carroll County
12060	13057	Cherokee County
12060	13063	Clayton County
12060	13067	Cobb County
12060	13077	Coweta County
12060	13085	Dawson County
12060	13089	DeKalb County
12060	13097	Douglas County
12060	13113	Fayette County
12060	13117	Forsyth County
12060	13121	Fulton County
12060	13135	Gwinnett County
12060	13143	Haralson County
12060	13149	Heard County
12060	13151	Henry County
12060	13159	Jasper County
12060	13171	Lamar County
12060	13199	Meriwether County
12060	13211	Morgan County
12060	13217	Newton County
12060	13223	Paulding County
12060	13227	Pickens County
12060	13231	Pike County
12060	13247	Rockdale County
12060	13255	Spalding County
12060	13297	Walton County
12100		Atlantic City-Hammonton, NJ
12100	34001	Atlantic County
12220		Auburn-Opelika, AL
12220	01081	Lee County
12260		Augusta-Richmond County, GA-SC
12260	13033	Burke County
12260	13073	Columbia County
12260	13181	Lincoln County
12260	13189	McDuffie County
12260	13245	Richmond County
12260	45003	Aiken County
12260	45037	Edgefield County
12420		Austin-Round Rock-Georgetown, TX
12420	48021	Bastrop County
12420	48055	Caldwell County
12420	48209	Hays County
12420	48453	Travis County
12420	48491	Williamson County
12540		Bakersfield, CA
12540	06029	Kern County
12580		Baltimore-Columbia-Towson, MD
12580	24003	Anne Arundel County
12580	24005	Baltimore County
12580	24013	Carroll County
12580	24025	Harford County
12580	24027	Howard County
12580	24035	Queen Anne's County
12580	24510	Baltimore city
12620		Bangor, ME
12620	23019	Penobscot County
12700		Barnstable Town, MA
12700	25001	Barnstable County
12940		Baton Rouge, LA
12940	22005	Ascension Parish
12940	22007	Assumption Parish
12940	22033	East Baton Rouge Parish
12940	22037	East Feliciana Parish
12940	22047	Iberville Parish
12940	22063	Livingston Parish
12940	22077	Pointe Coupee Parish
12940	22091	St. Helena Parish
12940	22121	West Baton Rouge Parish
12940	22125	West Feliciana Parish
12980		Battle Creek, MI
12980	26025	Calhoun County
13020		Bay City, MI
13020	26017	Bay County
13140		Beaumont-Port Arthur, TX
13140	48199	Hardin County

Metropolitan Statistical Areas, Metropolitan Divisions, and Components—*Continued*

Core based statistical area (CBSA)	State/ County FIPS code	Title and Geographic Components	Core based statistical area (CBSA)	State/ County FIPS code	Title and Geographic Components
13140	48245	Jefferson County	15940	39019	Carroll County
13140	48361	Orange County	15940	39151	Stark County
13220		Beckley, WV	15980		Cape Coral-Fort Myers, FL
13220	54019	Fayette County	15980	12071	Lee County
13220	54081	Raleigh County	16020		Cape Girardeau, MO-IL
13380		Bellingham, WA	16020	17003	Alexander County, IL
13380	53073	Whatcom County	16020	29017	Bollinger County, MO
13460		Bend, OR	16020	29031	Cape Girardeau County, MO
13460	41017	Deschutes County	16060		Carbondale-Marion, IL
13740		Billings, MT	16060	17077	Jackson County
13740	30009	Carbon County	16060	17087	Johnson County
13740	30095	Stillwater County	16060	17199	Williamson County
13740	30111	Yellowstone County	16180		Carson City, NV
13780		Binghamton, NY	16180	32510	Carson City
13780	36007	Broome County	16220		Casper, WY
13780	36107	Tioga County	16220	56025	Natrona County
13820		Birmingham-Hoover, AL	16300		Cedar Rapids, IA
13820	01007	Bibb County	16300	19011	Benton County
13820	01009	Blount County	16300	19105	Jones County
13820	01021	Chilton County	16300	19113	Linn County
13820	01073	Jefferson County	16540		Chambersburg-Waynesboro, PA
13820	01115	St. Clair County	16540	42055	Franklin County
13820	01117	Shelby County	16580		Champaign-Urbana, IL
13900		Bismarck, ND	16580	17019	Champaign County
13900	38015	Burleigh County	16580	17147	Piatt County
13900	38059	Morton County	16620		Charleston, WV
13900	38065	Oliver County	16620	54005	Boone County
13980		Blacksburg-Christiansburg, VA	16620	54015	Clay County
13980	51071	Giles County	16620	54035	Jackson County
13980	51155	Pulaski County	16620	54039	Kanawha County
13980	51933	Montgomery + Radford	16620	54043	Lincoln County
14010		Bloomington, IL	16700		Charleston-North Charleston, SC
14010	17113	McLean County	16700	45015	Berkeley County
14020		Bloomington, IN	16700	45019	Charleston County
14020	18105	Monroe County	16700	45035	Dorchester County
14020	18119	Owen County	16740		Charlotte-Concord-Gastonia, NC-SC
14100		Bloomsburg-Berwick, PA	16740	37007	Anson County, NC
14100	42037	Columbia County	16740	37025	Cabarrus County, NC
14100	42093	Montour County	16740	37071	Gaston County, NC
14260		Boise City, ID	16740	37097	Iredell County, NC
14260	16001	Ada County	16740	37109	Lincoln County, NC
14260	16015	Boise County	16740	37119	Mecklenburg County, NC
14260	16027	Canyon County	16740	37159	Rowan County, NC
14260	16045	Gem County	16740	37179	Union County, NC
14260	16073	Owyhee County	16740	45023	Chester County, SC
14460		Boston-Cambridge-Newton, MA-NH	16740	45057	Lancaster County, SC
14460		Boston, MA Div 14454	16740	45091	York County, SC
14460	25021	Norfolk County	16820		Charlottesville, VA
14460	25023	Plymouth County	16820	51065	Fluvanna County
14460	25025	Suffolk County	16820	51079	Greene County
14460		Cambridge-Newton-Framingham, MA Div 15764	16820	51125	Nelson County
14460	25009	Essex County	16820	51901	Albemarle + Charlottesville
14460	25017	Middlesex County	16860		Chattanooga, TN-GA
14460		Rockingham County-Strafford County, NH Div 40484	16860	13047	Catoosa County, GA
14460	33015	Rockingham County	16860	13083	Dade County, GA
14460	33017	Strafford County	16860	13295	Walker County, GA
14500		Boulder, CO	16860	47065	Hamilton County, TN
14500	08013	Boulder County	16860	47115	Marion County, TN
14540		Bowling Green, KY	16860	47153	Sequatchie County, TN
14540	21003	Allen County	16940		Cheyenne, WY
14540	21031	Butler County	16940	56021	Laramie County
14540	21061	Edmonson County	16980		Chicago-Naperville-Elgin, IL-IN-WI
14540	21227	Warren County	16980		Chicago-Naperville-Evanston, IL Div 16984
14740		Bremerton-Silverdale-Port Orchard, WA	16980	17031	Cook County
14740	53035	Kitsap County	16980	17043	DuPage County
14860		Bridgeport-Stamford-Norwalk, CT	16980	17063	Grundy County
14860	09001	Fairfield County	16980	17111	McHenry County
15180		Brownsville-Harlingen, TX	16980	17197	Will County
15180	48061	Cameron County	16980		Elgin, IL Div 20994
15260		Brunswick, GA	16980	17037	DeKalb County
15260	13025	Brantley County	16980	17089	Kane County
15260	13127	Glynn County	16980	17093	Kendall County
15260	13191	McIntosh County	16980		Gary, IN Div 23844
15380		Buffalo-Cheektowaga, NY	16980	18073	Jasper County
15380	36029	Erie County	16980	18089	Lake County
15380	36063	Niagara County	16980	18111	Newton County
15500		Burlington, NC	16980	18127	Porter County
15500	37001	Alamance County	16980		Lake County-Kenosha County, IL-WI Div 29404
15540		Burlington-South Burlington, VT	16980	17097	Lake County, IL
15540	50007	Chittenden County	16980	55059	Kenosha County, WI
15540	50011	Franklin County	17020		Chico, CA
15540	50013	Grand Isle County	17020	06007	Butte County
15680		California-Lexington Park, MD	17140		Cincinnati, OH-KY-IN
15680	24037	St. Mary's County	17140	18029	Dearborn County, IN
15940		Canton-Massillon, OH	17140	18047	Franklin County, IN

Metropolitan Statistical Areas, Metropolitan Divisions, and Components—*Continued*

Core based statistical area (CBSA)	State/ County FIPS code	Title and Geographic Components	Core based statistical area (CBSA)	State/ County FIPS code	Title and Geographic Components
17140	18115	Ohio County, IN	19100	48113	Dallas County
17140	18161	Union County, IN	19100	48121	Denton County
17140	21015	Boone County, KY	19100	48139	Ellis County
17140	21023	Bracken County, KY	19100	48231	Hunt County
17140	21037	Campbell County, KY	19100	48257	Kaufman County
17140	21077	Gallatin County, KY	19100	48397	Rockwall County
17140	21081	Grant County, KY	19100		Fort Worth-Arlington-Grapevine, TX Div 23104
17140	21117	Kenton County, KY	19100	48251	Johnson County
17140	21191	Pendleton County, KY	19100	48367	Parker County
17140	39015	Brown County, OH	19100	48439	Tarrant County
17140	39017	Butler County, OH	19100	48497	Wise County
17140	39025	Clermont County, OH	19140		Dalton, GA
17140	39061	Hamilton County, OH	19140	13213	Murray County
17140	39165	Warren County, OH	19140	13313	Whitfield County
17300		Clarksville, TN-KY	19180		Danville, IL
17300	21047	Christian County, KY	19180	17183	Vermilion County
17300	21221	Trigg County, KY	19300		Daphne-Fairhope-Foley, AL
17300	47125	Montgomery County, TN	19300	01003	Baldwin County
17300	47161	Stewart County, TN	19340		Davenport-Moline-Rock Island, IA-IL
17420		Cleveland, TN	19340	17073	Henry County, IL
17420	47011	Bradley County	19340	17131	Mercer County, IL
17420	47139	Polk County	19340	17161	Rock Island County, IL
17460		Cleveland-Elyria, OH	19340	19163	Scott County, IA
17460	39035	Cuyahoga County	19380		Dayton-Kettering, OH
17460	39055	Geauga County	19380	39057	Greene County
17460	39085	Lake County	19380	39109	Miami County
17460	39093	Lorain County	19380	39113	Montgomery County
17460	39103	Medina County	19460		Decatur, AL
17660		Coeur d'Alene, ID	19460	01079	Lawrence County
17660	16055	Kootenai County	19460	01103	Morgan County
17780		College Station-Bryan, TX	19500		Decatur, IL
17780	48041	Brazos County	19500	17115	Macon County
17780	48051	Burleson County	19660		Deltona-Daytona Beach-Ormond Beach, FL
17780	48395	Robertson County	19660	12035	Flagler County
17820		Colorado Springs, CO	19660	12127	Volusia County
17820	08041	El Paso County	19740		Denver-Aurora-Lakewood, CO
17820	08119	Teller County	19740	08001	Adams County
17860		Columbia, MO	19740	08005	Arapahoe County
17860	29019	Boone County	19740	08014	Broomfield County
17860	29053	Cooper County	19740	08019	Clear Creek County
17860	29089	Howard County	19740	08031	Denver County
17900		Columbia, SC	19740	08035	Douglas County
17900	45017	Calhoun County	19740	08039	Elbert County
17900	45039	Fairfield County	19740	08047	Gilpin County
17900	45055	Kershaw County	19740	08059	Jefferson County
17900	45063	Lexington County	19740	08093	Park County
17900	45079	Richland County	19780		Des Moines-West Des Moines, IA
17900	45081	Saluda County	19780	19049	Dallas County
17980		Columbus, GA-AL	19780	19077	Guthrie County
17980	01113	Russell County, AL	19780	19099	Jasper County
17980	13053	Chattahoochee County, GA	19780	19121	Madison County
17980	13145	Harris County, GA	19780	19153	Polk County
17980	13197	Marion County, GA	19780	19181	Warren County
17980	13215	Muscogee County, GA	19820		Detroit-Warren-Dearborn, MI
17980	13259	Stewart County, GA	19820		Detroit-Dearborn-Livonia, MI Div 19804
17980	13263	Talbot County, GA	19820	26163	Wayne County
18020		Columbus, IN	19820		Warren-Troy-Farmington Hills, MI 47664
18020	18005	Bartholomew County	19820	26087	Lapeer County
18140		Columbus, OH	19820	26093	Livingston County
18140	39041	Delaware County	19820	26099	Macomb County
18140	39045	Fairfield County	19820	26125	Oakland County
18140	39049	Franklin County	19820	26147	St. Clair County
18140	39073	Hocking County	20020		Dothan, AL
18140	39089	Licking County	20020	01061	Geneva County
18140	39097	Madison County	20020	01067	Henry County
18140	39117	Morrow County	20020	01069	Houston County
18140	39127	Perry County	20100		Dover, DE
18140	39129	Pickaway County	20100	10001	Kent County
18140	39159	Union County	20220		Dubuque, IA
18580		Corpus Christi, TX	20220	19061	Dubuque County
18580	48355	Nueces County	20260		Duluth, MN-WI
18580	48409	San Patricio County	20260	27017	Carlton County, MN
18700		Corvallis, OR	20260	27075	Lake County, MN
18700	41003	Benton County	20260	27137	St. Louis County, MN
18880		Crestview-Fort Walton Beach-Destin, FL	20260	55031	Douglas County, WI
18880	12091	Okaloosa County	20500		Durham-Chapel Hill, NC
18880	12131	Walton County	20500	37037	Chatham County
19060		Cumberland, MD-WV	20500	37063	Durham County
19060	24001	Allegany County, MD	20500	37077	Granville County
19060	54057	Mineral County, WV	20500	37135	Orange County
19100		Dallas-Fort Worth-Arlington, TX	20500	37145	Person County
19100		Dallas-Plano-Irving, TX Div 19124	20700		East Stroudsburg, PA
19100	48085	Collin County	20700	42089	Monroe County

Metropolitan Statistical Areas, Metropolitan Divisions, and Components—*Continued*

Core based statistical area (CBSA)	State/County FIPS code	Title and Geographic Components	Core based statistical area (CBSA)	State/County FIPS code	Title and Geographic Components
20740		Eau Claire, WI	24220	38035	Grand Forks County, ND
20740	55017	Chippewa County	24260		Grand Island, NE
20740	55035	Eau Claire County	24260	31079	Hall County
20940		El Centro, CA	24260	31093	Howard County
20940	06025	Imperial County	24260	31121	Merrick County
21060		Elizabethtown-Fort Knox, KY	24300		Grand Junction, CO
21060	21093	Hardin County	24300	08077	Mesa County
21060	21123	Larue County	24340		Grand Rapids-Kentwood, MI
21060	21163	Meade County	24340	26067	Ionia County
21140		Elkhart-Goshen, IN	24340	26081	Kent County
21140	18039	Elkhart County	24340	26117	Montcalm County
21300		Elmira, NY	24340	26139	Ottawa County
21300	36015	Chemung County	24420		Grants Pass, OR
21340		El Paso, TX	24420	41033	Josephine County
21340	48141	El Paso County	24500		Great Falls, MT
21340	48229	Hudspeth County	24500	30013	Cascade County
21420		Enid, OK	24540		Greeley, CO
21420	40047	Garfield County	24540	08123	Weld County
21500		Erie, PA	24580		Green Bay, WI
21500	42049	Erie County	24580	55009	Brown County
21660		Eugene-Springfield, OR	24580	55061	Kewaunee County
21660	41039	Lane County	24580	55083	Oconto County
21780		Evansville, IN-KY	24660		Greensboro-High Point, NC
21780	18129	Posey County, IN	24660	37081	Guilford County
21780	18163	Vanderburgh County, IN	24660	37151	Randolph County
21780	18173	Warrick County, IN	24660	37157	Rockingham County
21780	21101	Henderson County, KY	24780		Greenville, NC
21820		Fairbanks, AK	24780	37147	Pitt County
21820	02090	Fairbanks North Star Borough	24860		Greenville-Anderson, SC
22020		Fargo, ND-MN	24860	45007	Anderson County
22020	27027	Clay County, MN	24860	45045	Greenville County
22020	38017	Cass County, ND	24860	45059	Laurens County
22140		Farmington, NM	24860	45077	Pickens County
22140	35045	San Juan County	25060		Gulfport-Biloxi, MS
22180		Fayetteville, NC	25060	28045	Hancock County
22180	37051	Cumberland County	25060	28047	Harrison County
22180	37085	Harnett County	25060	28059	Jackson County
22180	37093	Hoke County	25060	28131	Stone County
22220		Fayetteville-Springdale-Rogers, AR-MO	25180		Hagerstown-Martinsburg, MD-WV
22220	05007	Benton County, AR	25180	24043	Washington County, MD
22220	05087	Madison County, AR	25180	54003	Berkeley County, WV
22220	05143	Washington County, AR	25180	54065	Morgan County, WV
22380		Flagstaff, AZ	25220		Hammond, LA
22380	04005	Coconino County	25220	22105	Tangipahoa Parish
22420		Flint, MI	25260		Hanford-Corcoran, CA
22420	26049	Genesee County	25260	06031	Kings County
22500		Florence, SC	25420		Harrisburg-Carlisle, PA
22500	45031	Darlington County	25420	42041	Cumberland County
22500	45041	Florence County	25420	42043	Dauphin County
22520		Florence-Muscle Shoals, AL	25420	42099	Perry County
22520	01033	Colbert County	25500		Harrisonburg, VA
22520	01077	Lauderdale County	25500	51947	Rockingham + Harrisonburg, VA
22540		Fond du Lac, WI	25540		Hartford-East Hartford-Middletown, CT
22540	55039	Fond du Lac County	25540	09003	Hartford County
22660		Fort Collins, CO	25540	09007	Middlesex County
22660	08069	Larimer County	25540	09013	Tolland County
22900		Fort Smith, AR-OK	25620		Hattiesburg, MS
22900	05033	Crawford County, AR	25620	28031	Covington County
22900	05047	Franklin County, AR	25620	28035	Forrest County
22900	05131	Sebastian County, AR	25620	28073	Lamar County
22900	40135	Sequoyah County, OK	25620	28111	Perry County
23060		Fort Wayne, IN	25860		Hickory-Lenoir-Morganton, NC
23060	18003	Allen County	25860	37003	Alexander County
23060	18183	Whitley County	25860	37023	Burke County
23420		Fresno, CA	25860	37027	Caldwell County
23420	06019	Fresno County	25860	37035	Catawba County
23460		Gadsden, AL	25940		Hilton Head Island-Bluffton, SC
23460	01055	Etowah County	25940	45013	Beaufort County
23540		Gainesville, FL	25940	45053	Jasper County
23540	12001	Alachua County	25980		Hinesville, GA
23540	12041	Gilchrist County	25980	13179	Liberty County
23540	12075	Levy County	25980	13183	Long County
23580		Gainesville, GA	26140		Homosassa Springs, FL
23580	13139	Hall County	26140	12017	Citrus County
23900		Gettysburg, PA	26300		Hot Springs, AR
23900	42001	Adams County	26300	05051	Garland County
24020		Glens Falls, NY	26380		Houma-Thibodaux, LA
24020	36113	Warren County	26380	22057	Lafourche Parish
24020	36115	Washington County	26380	22109	Terrebonne Parish
24140		Goldsboro, NC	26420		Houston-The Woodlands-Sugar Land, TX
24140	37191	Wayne County	26420	48015	Austin County
24220		Grand Forks, ND-MN	26420	48039	Brazoria County
24220	27119	Polk County, MN	26420	48071	Chambers County

Metropolitan Statistical Areas, Metropolitan Divisions, and Components—*Continued*

Core based statistical area (CBSA)	State/ County FIPS code	Title and Geographic Components	Core based statistical area (CBSA)	State/ County FIPS code	Title and Geographic Components
26420	48157	Fort Bend County	28020	26077	Kalamazoo County
26420	48167	Galveston County	28100		Kankakee, IL
26420	48201	Harris County	28100	17091	Kankakee County
26420	48291	Liberty County	28140		Kansas City, MO-KS
26420	48339	Montgomery County	28140	20091	Johnson County, KS
26420	48473	Waller County	28140	20103	Leavenworth County, KS
26580		Huntington-Ashland, WV-KY-OH	28140	20107	Linn County, KS
26580	21019	Boyd County, KY	28140	20121	Miami County, KS
26580	21043	Carter County, KY	28140	20209	Wyandotte County, KS
26580	21089	Greenup County, KY	28140	29013	Bates County, MO
26580	39087	Lawrence County, OH	28140	29025	Caldwell County, MO
26580	54011	Cabell County, WV	28140	29037	Cass County, MO
26580	54079	Putnam County, WV	28140	29047	Clay County, MO
26580	54099	Wayne County, WV	28140	29049	Clinton County, MO
26620		Huntsville, AL	28140	29095	Jackson County, MO
26620	01083	Limestone County	28140	29107	Lafayette County, MO
26620	01089	Madison County	28140	29165	Platte County, MO
26820		Idaho Falls, ID	28140	29177	Ray County, MO
26820	16019	Bonneville County	28420		Kennewick-Richland, WA
26820	16023	Butte County	28420	53005	Benton County
26820	16051	Jefferson County	28420	53021	Franklin County
26900		Indianapolis-Carmel-Anderson, IN	28660		Killeen-Temple, TX
26900	18011	Boone County	28660	48027	Bell County
26900	18013	Brown County	28660	48099	Coryell County
26900	18057	Hamilton County	28660	48281	Lampasas County
26900	18059	Hancock County	28700		Kingsport-Bristol, TN-VA
26900	18063	Hendricks County	28700	47073	Hawkins County, TN
26900	18081	Johnson County	28700	47163	Sullivan County, TN
26900	18095	Madison County	28700	51169	Scott County, VA
26900	18097	Marion County	28700	51953	Washington + Bristol, VA
26900	18109	Morgan County	28740		Kingston, NY
26900	18133	Putnam County	28740	36111	Ulster County
26900	18145	Shelby County	28940		Knoxville, TN
26980		Iowa City, IA	28940	47001	Anderson County
26980	19103	Johnson County	28940	47009	Blount County
26980	19183	Washington County	28940	47013	Campbell County
27060		Ithaca, NY	28940	47093	Knox County
27060	36109	Tompkins County	28940	47105	Loudon County
27100		Jackson, MI	28940	47129	Morgan County
27100	26075	Jackson County	28940	47145	Roane County
27140		Jackson, MS	28940	47173	Union County
27140	28029	Copiah County	29020		Kokomo, IN
27140	28049	Hinds County	29020	18067	Howard County
27140	28051	Holmes County	29100		La Crosse-Onalaska, WI-MN
27140	28089	Madison County	29100	27055	Houston County, MN
27140	28121	Rankin County	29100	55063	La Crosse County, WI
27140	28127	Simpson County	29180		Lafayette, LA
27140	28163	Yazoo County	29180	22001	Acadia Parish
27180		Jackson, TN	29180	22045	Iberia Parish
27180	47023	Chester County	29180	22055	Lafayette Parish
27180	47033	Crockett County	29180	22099	St. Martin Parish
27180	47053	Gibson County	29180	22113	Vermilion Parish
27180	47113	Madison County	29200		Lafayette-West Lafayette, IN
27260		Jacksonville, FL	29200	18007	Benton County
27260	12003	Baker County	29200	18015	Carroll County
27260	12019	Clay County	29200	18157	Tippecanoe County
27260	12031	Duval County	29200	18171	Warren County
27260	12089	Nassau County	29340		Lake Charles, LA
27260	12109	St. Johns County	29340	22019	Calcasieu Parish
27340		Jacksonville, NC	29340	22023	Cameron Parish
27340	37133	Onslow County	29420		Lake Havasu City-Kingman, AZ
27500		Janesville-Beloit, WI	29420	04015	Mohave County
27500	55105	Rock County	29460		Lakeland-Winter Haven, FL
27620		Jefferson City, MO	29460	12105	Polk County
27620	29027	Callaway County	29540		Lancaster, PA
27620	29051	Cole County	29540	42071	Lancaster County
27620	29135	Moniteau County	29620		Lansing-East Lansing, MI
27620	29151	Osage County	29620	26037	Clinton County
27740		Johnson City, TN	29620	26045	Eaton County
27740	47019	Carter County	29620	26065	Ingham County
27740	47171	Unicoi County	29620	26155	Shiawassee County
27740	47179	Washington County	29700		Laredo, TX
27780		Johnstown, PA	29700	48479	Webb County
27780	42021	Cambria County	29740		Las Cruces, NM
27860		Jonesboro, AR	29740	35013	Doña Ana County
27860	05031	Craighead County	29820		Las Vegas-Henderson-Paradise, NV
27860	05111	Poinsett County	29820	32003	Clark County
27900		Joplin, MO	29940		Lawrence, KS
27900	29097	Jasper County	29940	20045	Douglas County
27900	29145	Newton County	30020		Lawton, OK
27980		Kahului-Wailuku-Lahaina, HI	30020	40031	Comanche County
27980	15009	Maui County	30020	40033	Cotton County
28020		Kalamazoo-Portage, MI	30140		Lebanon, PA

Metropolitan Statistical Areas, Metropolitan Divisions, and Components—*Continued*

Core based statistical area (CBSA)	State/ County FIPS code	Title and Geographic Components	Core based statistical area (CBSA)	State/ County FIPS code	Title and Geographic Components
30140	42075	Lebanon County	32580		McAllen-Edinburg-Mission, TX
30300		Lewiston, ID-WA	32580	48215	Hidalgo County
30300	16069	Nez Perce County, ID	32780		Medford, OR
30300	53003	Asotin County, WA	32780	41029	Jackson County
30340		Lewiston-Auburn, ME	32820		Memphis, TN-MS-AR
30340	23001	Androscoggin County	32820	05035	Crittenden County, AR
30460		Lexington-Fayette, KY	32820	28033	DeSoto County, MS
30460	21017	Bourbon County	32820	28093	Marshall County, MS
30460	21049	Clark County	32820	28137	Tate County, MS
30460	21067	Fayette County	32820	28143	Tunica County, MS
30460	21113	Jessamine County	32820	47047	Fayette County, TN
30460	21209	Scott County	32820	47157	Shelby County, TN
30460	21239	Woodford County	32820	47167	Tipton County, TN
30620		Lima, OH	32900		Merced, CA
30620	39003	Allen County	32900	06047	Merced County
30700		Lincoln, NE	33100		Miami-Fort Lauderdale-Pompano Beach, FL
30700	31109	Lancaster County	33100		Fort Lauderdale-Pompano Beach-Sunrise, FL Div 22744
30700	31159	Seward County	33100	12011	Broward County
30780		Little Rock-North Little Rock-Conway, AR	33100		Miami-Miami Beach-Kendall, FL Div 33124
30780	05045	Faulkner County	33100	12086	Miami-Dade County
30780	05053	Grant County	33100		West Palm Beach-Boca Raton-Boynton Beach, FL Div 48424
30780	05085	Lonoke County	33100	12099	Palm Beach County
30780	05105	Perry County	33140		Michigan City-La Porte, IN
30780	05119	Pulaski County	33140	18091	LaPorte County
30780	05125	Saline County	33220		Midland, MI
30860		Logan, UT-ID	33220	26111	Midland County
30860	16041	Franklin County, ID	33260		Midland, TX
30860	49005	Cache County, UT	33260	48317	Martin County
30980		Longview, TX	33260	48329	Midland County
30980	48183	Gregg County	33340		Milwaukee-Waukesha, WI
30980	48203	Harrison County	33340	55079	Milwaukee County
30980	48401	Rusk County	33340	55089	Ozaukee County
30980	48459	Upshur County	33340	55131	Washington County
31020		Longview, WA	33340	55133	Waukesha County
31020	53015	Cowlitz County	33460		Minneapolis-St. Paul-Bloomington, MN-WI
31080		Los Angeles-Long Beach-Anaheim, CA	33460	27003	Anoka County, MN
31080		Anaheim-Santa Ana-Irvine, CA Div 11244	33460	27019	Carver County, MN
31080	06059	Orange County	33460	27025	Chisago County, MN
31080		Los Angeles-Long Beach-Glendale, CA Div 31084	33460	27037	Dakota County, MN
31080	06037	Los Angeles County	33460	27053	Hennepin County, MN
31140		Louisville/Jefferson County, KY-IN	33460	27059	Isanti County, MN
31140	18019	Clark County, IN	33460	27079	Le Sueur County, MN
31140	18043	Floyd County, IN	33460	27095	Mille Lacs County, MN
31140	18061	Harrison County, IN	33460	27123	Ramsey County, MN
31140	18175	Washington County, IN	33460	27139	Scott County, MN
31140	21029	Bullitt County, KY	33460	27141	Sherburne County, MN
31140	21103	Henry County, KY	33460	27163	Washington County, MN
31140	21111	Jefferson County, KY	33460	27171	Wright County, MN
31140	21185	Oldham County, KY	33460	55093	Pierce County, WI
31140	21211	Shelby County, KY	33460	55109	St. Croix County, WI
31140	21215	Spencer County, KY	33540		Missoula, MT
31180		Lubbock, TX	33540	30063	Missoula County
31180	48107	Crosby County	33660		Mobile, AL
31180	48303	Lubbock County	33660	01097	Mobile County
31180	48305	Lynn County	33660	01129	Washington County
31340		Lynchburg, VA	33700		Modesto, CA
31340	51009	Amherst County	33700	06099	Stanislaus County
31340	51011	Appomattox County	33740		Monroe, LA
31340	51909	Bedford County	33740	22067	Morehouse Parish
31340	51911	Campbell + Lynchburg, VA	33740	22073	Ouachita Parish
31420		Macon-Bibb County, GA	33740	22111	Union Parish
31420	13021	Bibb County	33780		Monroe, MI
31420	13079	Crawford County	33780	26115	Monroe County
31420	13169	Jones County	33860		Montgomery, AL
31420	13207	Monroe County	33860	01001	Autauga County
31420	13289	Twiggs County	33860	01051	Elmore County
31460		Madera, CA	33860	01085	Lowndes County
31460	06039	Madera County	33860	01101	Montgomery County
31540		Madison, WI	34060		Morgantown, WV
31540	55021	Columbia County	34060	54061	Monongalia County
31540	55025	Dane County	34060	54077	Preston County
31540	55045	Green County	34100		Morristown, TN
31540	55049	Iowa County	34100	47057	Grainger County
31700		Manchester-Nashua, NH	34100	47063	Hamblen County
31700	33011	Hillsborough County	34100	47089	Jefferson County
31740		Manhattan, KS	34580		Mount Vernon-Anacortes, WA
31740	20061	Geary County	34580	53057	Skagit County
31740	20149	Pottawatomie County	34620		Muncie, IN
31740	20161	Riley County	34620	18035	Delaware County
31860		Mankato, MN	34740		Muskegon, MI
31860	27013	Blue Earth County	34740	26121	Muskegon County
31860	27103	Nicollet County	34820		Myrtle Beach-Conway-North Myrtle Beach, SC-NC
31900		Mansfield, OH	34820	37019	Brunswick County, NC
31900	39139	Richland County	34820	45051	Horry County, SC

Metropolitan Statistical Areas, Metropolitan Divisions, and Components—*Continued*

Core based statistical area (CBSA)	State/ County FIPS code	Title and Geographic Components	Core based statistical area (CBSA)	State/ County FIPS code	Title and Geographic Components
34900		Napa, CA	36420	40081	Lincoln County
34900	06055	Napa County	36420	40083	Logan County
34940		Naples-Marco Island, FL	36420	40087	McClain County
34940	12021	Collier County	36420	40109	Oklahoma County
34980		Nashville-Davidson—Murfreesboro—Franklin, TN	36500		Olympia-Lacey-Tumwater, WA
34980	47015	Cannon County	36500	53067	Thurston County
34980	47021	Cheatham County	36540		Omaha-Council Bluffs, NE-IA
34980	47037	Davidson County	36540	19085	Harrison County, IA
34980	47043	Dickson County	36540	19129	Mills County, IA
34980	47111	Macon County	36540	19155	Pottawattamie County, IA
34980	47119	Maury County	36540	31025	Cass County, NE
34980	47147	Robertson County	36540	31055	Douglas County, NE
34980	47149	Rutherford County	36540	31153	Sarpy County, NE
34980	47159	Smith County	36540	31155	Saunders County, NE
34980	47165	Sumner County	36540	31177	Washington County, NE
34980	47169	Trousdale County	36740		Orlando-Kissimmee-Sanford, FL
34980	47187	Williamson County	36740	12069	Lake County
34980	47189	Wilson County	36740	12095	Orange County
35100		New Bern, NC	36740	12097	Osceola County
35100	37049	Craven County	36740	12117	Seminole County
35100	37103	Jones County	36780		Oshkosh-Neenah, WI
35100	37137	Pamlico County	36780	55139	Winnebago County
35300		New Haven-Milford, CT	36980		Owensboro, KY
35300	09009	New Haven County	36980	21059	Daviess County
35380		New Orleans-Metairie, LA	36980	21091	Hancock County
35380	22051	Jefferson Parish	36980	21149	McLean County
35380	22071	Orleans Parish	37100		Oxnard-Thousand Oaks-Ventura, CA
35380	22075	Plaquemines Parish	37100	06111	Ventura County
35380	22087	St. Bernard Parish	37340		Palm Bay-Melbourne-Titusville, FL
35380	22089	St. Charles Parish	37340	12009	Brevard County
35380	22093	St. James Parish	37460		Panama City, FL
35380	22095	St. John the Baptist Parish	37460	12005	Bay County
35380	22103	St. Tammany Parish	37620		Parkersburg-Vienna, WV
35620		New York-Newark-Jersey City, NY-NJ-PA	37620	54105	Wirt County
35620		Nassau County-Suffolk County, NY Div 35004	37620	54107	Wood County
35620	36059	Nassau County	37860		Pensacola-Ferry Pass-Brent, FL
35620	36103	Suffolk County	37860	12033	Escambia County
35620		Newark, NJ-PA Div 35084	37860	12113	Santa Rosa County
35620	34013	Essex County, NJ	37900		Peoria, IL
35620	34019	Hunterdon County, NJ	37900	17057	Fulton County
35620	34027	Morris County, NJ	37900	17123	Marshall County
35620	34037	Sussex County, NJ	37900	17143	Peoria County
35620	34039	Union County, NJ	37900	17175	Stark County
35620	42103	Pike County, PA	37900	17179	Tazewell County
35620		New Brunswick-Lakewood, NJ Div 35154	37900	17203	Woodford County
35620	34023	Middlesex County	37980		Philadelphia-Camden-Wilmington, PA-NJ-DE-MD
35620	34025	Monmouth County	37980		Camden, NJ Div 15804
35620	34029	Ocean County	37980	34005	Burlington County, NJ
35620	34035	Somerset County	37980	34007	Camden County, NJ
35620		New York-Jersey City-White Plains, NY-NJ Div 35614	37980	34015	Gloucester County, NJ
35620	34003	Bergen County, NJ	37980		Montgomery County-Bucks County-Chester County, PA Div 33874
35620	34017	Hudson County, NJ	37980	42017	Bucks County, PA
35620	34031	Passaic County, NJ	37980	42029	Chester County, PA
35620	36005	Bronx County, NY	37980	42091	Montgomery County, PA
35620	36047	Kings County, NY	37980		Philadelphia, PA Div 37964
35620	36061	New York County, NY	37980	42045	Delaware County, PA
35620	36079	Putnam County, NY	37980	42101	Philadelphia County, PA
35620	36081	Queens County, NY	37980		Wilmington, DE-MD-NJ Div 48864
35620	36085	Richmond County, NY	37980	10003	New Castle County, DE
35620	36087	Rockland County, NY	37980	24015	Cecil County, MD
35620	36119	Westchester County, NY	37980	34033	Salem County, NJ
35660		Niles-Benton Harbor, MI	38060		Phoenix-Mesa-Chandler, AZ
35660	26021	Berrien County	38060	04013	Maricopa County
35840		North Port-Sarasota-Bradenton, FL	38060	04021	Pinal County
35840	12081	Manatee County	38220		Pine Bluff, AR
35840	12115	Sarasota County	38220	05025	Cleveland County
35980		Norwich-New London, CT	38220	05069	Jefferson County
35980	09011	New London County	38220	05079	Lincoln County
36100		Ocala, FL	38300		Pittsburgh, PA
36100	12083	Marion County	38300	42003	Allegheny County
36140		Ocean City, NJ	38300	42005	Armstrong County
36140	34009	Cape May County	38300	42007	Beaver County
36220		Odessa, TX	38300	42019	Butler County
36220	48135	Ector County	38300	42051	Fayette County
36260		Ogden-Clearfield, UT	38300	42125	Washington County
36260	49003	Box Elder County	38300	42129	Westmoreland County
36260	49011	Davis County	38340		Pittsfield, MA
36260	49029	Morgan County	38340	25003	Berkshire County
36260	49057	Weber County	38540		Pocatello, ID
36420		Oklahoma City, OK	38540	16005	Bannock County
36420	40017	Canadian County	38540	16077	Power County
36420	40027	Cleveland County	38860		Portland-South Portland, ME
36420	40051	Grady County	38860	23005	Cumberland County

Metropolitan Statistical Areas, Metropolitan Divisions, and Components—*Continued*

Core based statistical area (CBSA)	State/ County FIPS code	Title and Geographic Components	Core based statistical area (CBSA)	State/ County FIPS code	Title and Geographic Components
38860	23023	Sagadahoc County	40420		Rockford, IL
38860	23031	York County	40420	17007	Boone County
38900		Portland-Vancouver-Hillsboro, OR-WA	40420	17201	Winnebago County
38900	41005	Clackamas County, OR	40580		Rocky Mount, NC
38900	41009	Columbia County, OR	40580	37065	Edgecombe County
38900	41051	Multnomah County, OR	40580	37127	Nash County
38900	41067	Washington County, OR	40660		Rome, GA
38900	41071	Yamhill County, OR	40660	13115	Floyd County
38900	53011	Clark County, WA	40900		Sacramento—Roseville—Folsom, CA
38900	53059	Skamania County, WA	40900	06017	El Dorado County
38940		Port St. Lucie, FL	40900	06061	Placer County
38940	12085	Martin County	40900	06067	Sacramento County
38940	12111	St. Lucie County	40900	06113	Yolo County
39100		Poughkeepsie-Newburgh-Middletown, NY	40980		Saginaw, MI
39100	36027	Dutchess County	40980	26145	Saginaw County
39100	36071	Orange County	41060		St. Cloud, MN
39140		Prescott Valley-Prescott, AZ	41060	27009	Benton County
39140	04025	Yavapai County	41060	27145	Stearns County
39300		Providence-Warwick, RI-MA	41100		St. George, UT
39300	25005	Bristol County, MA	41100	49053	Washington County
39300	44001	Bristol County, RI	41140		St. Joseph, MO-KS
39300	44003	Kent County, RI	41140	20043	Doniphan County, KS
39300	44005	Newport County, RI	41140	29003	Andrew County, MO
39300	44007	Providence County, RI	41140	29021	Buchanan County, MO
39300	44009	Washington County, RI	41140	29063	DeKalb County, MO
39340		Provo-Orem, UT	41180		St. Louis, MO-IL
39340	49023	Juab County	41180	17005	Bond County, IL
39340	49049	Utah County	41180	17013	Calhoun County, IL
39380		Pueblo, CO	41180	17027	Clinton County, IL
39380	08101	Pueblo County	41180	17083	Jersey County, IL
39460		Punta Gorda, FL	41180	17117	Macoupin County, IL
39460	12015	Charlotte County	41180	17119	Madison County, IL
39540		Racine, WI	41180	17133	Monroe County, IL
39540	55101	Racine County	41180	17163	St. Clair County, IL
39580		Raleigh-Cary, NC	41180	29055	Crawford County + Sullivan, MO
39580	37069	Franklin County	41180	29071	Franklin County, MO
39580	37101	Johnston County	41180	29099	Jefferson County, MO
39580	37183	Wake County	41180	29113	Lincoln County, MO
39660		Rapid City, SD	41180	29183	St. Charles County, MO
39660	46093	Meade County	41180	29189	St. Louis County, MO
39660	46103	Pennington County	41180	29219	Warren County, MO
39740		Reading, PA	41180	29510	St. Louis city, MO
39740	42011	Berks County	41420		Salem, OR
39820		Redding, CA	41420	41047	Marion County
39820	06089	Shasta County	41420	41053	Polk County
39900		Reno, NV	41500		Salinas, CA
39900	32029	Storey County	41500	06053	Monterey County
39900	32031	Washoe County	41540		Salisbury, MD-DE
40060		Richmond, VA	41540	10005	Sussex County, DE
40060	51007	Amelia County	41540	24039	Somerset County, MD
40060	51036	Charles City County	41540	24045	Wicomico County, MD
40060	51041	Chesterfield County	41540	24047	Worcester County, MD
40060	51075	Goochland County	41620		Salt Lake City, UT
40060	51085	Hanover County	41620	49035	Salt Lake County
40060	51087	Henrico County	41620	49045	Tooele County
40060	51097	King and Queen County	41660		San Angelo, TX
40060	51101	King William County	41660	48235	Irion County
40060	51127	New Kent County	41660	48431	Sterling County
40060	51145	Powhatan County	41660	48451	Tom Green County
40060	51183	Sussex County	41700		San Antonio-New Braunfels, TX
40060	51760	Richmond city	41700	48013	Atascosa County
40060	51918	Dinwiddie, Colonial Heights + Petersburg, VA	41700	48019	Bandera County
40060	51941	Prince George + Hopewell, VA	41700	48029	Bexar County
40140		Riverside-San Bernardino-Ontario, CA	41700	48091	Comal County
40140	06065	Riverside County	41700	48187	Guadalupe County
40140	06071	San Bernardino County	41700	48259	Kendall County
40220		Roanoke, VA	41700	48325	Medina County
40220	51023	Botetourt County	41700	48493	Wilson County
40220	51045	Craig County	41740		San Diego-Chula Vista-Carlsbad, CA
40220	51067	Franklin County	41740	06073	San Diego County
40220	51770	Roanoke city	41860		San Francisco-Oakland-Berkeley, CA
40220	51944	Roanoke + Salem, VA	41860		Oakland-Berkeley-Livermore, CA Div 36084
40340		Rochester, MN	41860	06001	Alameda County
40340	27039	Dodge County	41860	06013	Contra Costa County
40340	27045	Fillmore County	41860		San Francisco-San Mateo-Redwood City, CA Div 41884
40340	27109	Olmsted County	41860	06075	San Francisco County
40340	27157	Wabasha County	41860	06081	San Mateo County
40380		Rochester, NY	41860		San Rafael, CA Div 42034
40380	36051	Livingston County	41860	06041	Marin County
40380	36055	Monroe County	41940		San Jose-Sunnyvale-Santa Clara, CA
40380	36069	Ontario County	41940	06069	San Benito County
40380	36073	Orleans County	41940	06085	Santa Clara County
40380	36117	Wayne County	42020		San Luis Obispo-Paso Robles, CA
40380	36123	Yates County	42020	06079	San Luis Obispo County

Metropolitan Statistical Areas, Metropolitan Divisions, and Components—*Continued*

Core based statistical area (CBSA)	State/ County FIPS code	Title and Geographic Components
42100		Santa Cruz-Watsonville, CA
42100	06087	Santa Cruz County
42140		Santa Fe, NM
42140	35049	Santa Fe County
42200		Santa Maria-Santa Barbara, CA
42200	06083	Santa Barbara County
42220		Santa Rosa-Petaluma, CA
42220	06097	Sonoma County
42340		Savannah, GA
42340	13029	Bryan County
42340	13051	Chatham County
42340	13103	Effingham County
42540		Scranton—Wilkes-Barre, PA
42540	42069	Lackawanna County
42540	42079	Luzerne County
42540	42131	Wyoming County
42660		Seattle-Tacoma-Bellevue, WA
42660		Seattle-Bellevue-Kent, WA Div 42644
42660	53033	King County
42660	53061	Snohomish County
42660		Tacoma-Lakewood, WA Div 45104
42660	53053	Pierce County
42680		Sebastian-Vero Beach, FL
42680	12061	Indian River County
42700		Sebring-Avon Park, FL
42700	12055	Highlands County
43100		Sheboygan, WI
43100	55117	Sheboygan County
43300		Sherman-Denison, TX
43300	48181	Grayson County
43340		Shreveport-Bossier City, LA
43340	22015	Bossier Parish
43340	22017	Caddo Parish
43340	22031	De Soto Parish
43420		Sierra Vista-Douglas, AZ
43420	04003	Cochise County
43580		Sioux City, IA-NE-SD
43580	19193	Woodbury County, IA
43580	31043	Dakota County, NE
43580	31051	Dixon County, NE
43580	46127	Union County, SD
43620		Sioux Falls, SD
43620	46083	Lincoln County
43620	46087	McCook County
43620	46099	Minnehaha County
43620	46125	Turner County
43780		South Bend-Mishawaka, IN-MI
43780	18141	St. Joseph County, IN
43780	26027	Cass County, MI
43900		Spartanburg, SC
43900	45083	Spartanburg County
44060		Spokane-Spokane Valley, WA
44060	53063	Spokane County
44060	53065	Stevens County
44100		Springfield, IL
44100	17129	Menard County
44100	17167	Sangamon County
44140		Springfield, MA
44140	25011	Franklin County
44140	25013	Hampden County
44140	25015	Hampshire County
44180		Springfield, MO
44180	29043	Christian County
44180	29059	Dallas County
44180	29077	Greene County
44180	29167	Polk County
44180	29225	Webster County
44220		Springfield, OH
44220	39023	Clark County
44300		State College, PA
44300	42027	Centre County
44420		Staunton, VA
44420	51907	Augusta County + Staunton + Waynesboro, VA
44700		Stockton, CA
44700	06077	San Joaquin County
44940		Sumter, SC
44940	45027	Clarendon County
44940	45085	Sumter County
45060		Syracuse, NY
45060	36053	Madison County
45060	36067	Onondaga County
45060	36075	Oswego County

Core based statistical area (CBSA)	State/ County FIPS code	Title and Geographic Components
45220		Tallahassee, FL
45220	12039	Gadsden County
45220	12065	Jefferson County
45220	12073	Leon County
45220	12129	Wakulla County
45300		Tampa-St. Petersburg-Clearwater, FL
45300	12053	Hernando County
45300	12057	Hillsborough County
45300	12101	Pasco County
45300	12103	Pinellas County
45460		Terre Haute, IN
45460	18021	Clay County
45460	18121	Parke County
45460	18153	Sullivan County
45460	18165	Vermillion County
45460	18167	Vigo County
45500		Texarkana, TX-AR
45500	05081	Little River County, AR
45500	05091	Miller County, AR
45500	48037	Bowie County, TX
45540		The Villages, FL
45540	12119	Sumter County
45780		Toledo, OH
45780	39051	Fulton County
45780	39095	Lucas County
45780	39123	Ottawa County
45780	39173	Wood County
45820		Topeka, KS
45820	20085	Jackson County
45820	20087	Jefferson County
45820	20139	Osage County
45820	20177	Shawnee County
45820	20197	Wabaunsee County
45940		Trenton-Princeton, NJ
45940	34021	Mercer County
46060		Tucson, AZ
46060	04019	Pima County
46140		Tulsa, OK
46140	40037	Creek County
46140	40111	Okmulgee County
46140	40113	Osage County
46140	40117	Pawnee County
46140	40131	Rogers County
46140	40143	Tulsa County
46140	40145	Wagoner County
46220		Tuscaloosa, AL
46220	01063	Greene County
46220	01065	Hale County
46220	01107	Pickens County
46220	01125	Tuscaloosa County
46300		Twin Falls, ID
46300	16053	Jerome County
46300	16083	Twin Falls County
46340		Tyler, TX
46340	48423	Smith County
46520		Urban Honolulu, HI
46520	15003	Honolulu County
46540		Utica-Rome, NY
46540	36043	Herkimer County
46540	36065	Oneida County
46660		Valdosta, GA
46660	13027	Brooks County
46660	13101	Echols County
46660	13173	Lanier County
46660	13185	Lowndes County
46700		Vallejo, CA
46700	06095	Solano County
47020		Victoria, TX
47020	48175	Goliad County
47020	48469	Victoria County
47220		Vineland-Bridgeton, NJ
47220	34011	Cumberland County
47260		Virginia Beach-Norfolk-Newport News, VA-NC
47260	37029	Camden County, NC
47260	37053	Currituck County, NC
47260	37073	Gates County, NC
47260	51073	Gloucester County, VA
47260	51093	Isle of Wight County, VA
47260	51115	Mathews County, VA
47260	51175	Southampton County, VA
47260	51550	Chesapeake city, VA
47260	51650	Hampton city, VA

Metropolitan Statistical Areas, Metropolitan Divisions, and Components—*Continued*

Core based statistical area (CBSA)	State/ County FIPS code	Title and Geographic Components	Core based statistical area (CBSA)	State/ County FIPS code	Title and Geographic Components
47260	51700	Newport News city, VA	48260	39081	Jefferson County, OH
47260	51710	Norfolk city, VA	48260	54009	Brooke County, WV
47260	51735	Poquoson city, VA	48260	54029	Hancock County, WV
47260	51740	Portsmouth city, VA	48300		Wenatchee, WA
47260	51800	Suffolk city, VA	48300	53007	Chelan County
47260	51810	Virginia Beach city, VA	48300	53017	Douglas County
47260	51931	James City County + Williamsburg, VA	48540		Wheeling, WV-OH
47300		Visalia, CA	48540	39013	Belmont County, OH
47300	06107	Tulare County	48540	54051	Marshall County, WV
47380		Waco, TX	48540	54069	Ohio County, WV
47380	48145	Falls County	48620		Wichita, KS
47380	48309	McLennan County	48620	20015	Butler County
47460		Walla Walla, WA	48620	20079	Harvey County
47460	53071	Walla Walla County	48620	20173	Sedgwick County
47580		Warner Robins, GA	48620	20191	Sumner County
47580	13153	Houston County	48660		Wichita Falls, TX
47580	13225	Peach County	48660	48009	Archer County
47900		Washington-Arlington-Alexandria, DC-VA-MD-WV	48660	48077	Clay County
47900		Frederick-Gaithersburg-Rockville, MD Div 23224	48660	48485	Wichita County
47900	24021	Frederick County, MD	48700		Williamsport, PA
47900	24031	Montgomery County, MD	48700	42081	Lycoming County
47900		Washington-Arlington-Alexandria, DC-VA-MD-WV Div 47894	48900		Wilmington, NC
47900	11001	District of Columbia, DC	48900	37129	New Hanover County
47900	24009	Calvert County, MD	48900	37141	Pender County
47900	24017	Charles County, MD	49020		Winchester, VA-WV
47900	24033	Prince George's County, MD	49020	51921	Frederick County + Winchester, VA
47900	51013	Arlington County, VA	49020	54027	Hampshire County, WV
47900	51043	Clarke County, VA	49180		Winston-Salem, NC
47900	51047	Culpeper County, VA	49180	37057	Davidson County
47900	51061	Fauquier County, VA	49180	37059	Davie County
47900	51107	Loudoun County, VA	49180	37067	Forsyth County
47900	51113	Madison County, VA	49180	37169	Stokes County
47900	51157	Rappahannock County, VA	49180	37197	Yadkin County
47900	51179	Stafford County, VA	49340		Worcester, MA-CT
47900	51187	Warren County, VA	49340	09015	Windham County, CT
47900	51510	Alexandria city, VA	49340	25027	Worcester County, MA
47900	51919	Fairfax County + Fairfax + Falls Church, VA	49420		Yakima, WA
47900	51942	Prince William County + Manassas + Manassas Park, VA	49420	53077	Yakima County
47900	51951	Spotsylvania County + Fredericksburg, VA	49620		York-Hanover, PA
47900	54037	Jefferson County, WV	49620	42133	York County
47940		Waterloo-Cedar Falls, IA	49660		Youngstown-Warren-Boardman, OH-PA
47940	19013	Black Hawk County	49660	39099	Mahoning County, OH
47940	19017	Bremer County	49660	39155	Trumbull County, OH
47940	19075	Grundy County	49660	42085	Mercer County, PA
48060		Watertown-Fort Drum, NY	49700		Yuba City, CA
48060	36045	Jefferson County	49700	06101	Sutter County
48140		Wausau-Weston, WI	49700	06115	Yuba County
48140	55069	Lincoln County	49740		Yuma, AZ
48140	55073	Marathon County	49740	04027	Yuma County
48260		Weirton-Steubenville, WV-OH			